FP Markets

Canadian Demographics

2001

74th Edition

DISTRIBUTED BY
SEND ORDERS TO:

**INTERNATIONAL PRESS PUBLICATIONS INC.,
90 NOLAN COURT # 21,
MARKHAM, ONT., CANADA L3R 4L9
TEL: 905 946 9588 FAX: 905 946 9590**

DIRECTORIES, SERIALS, DICTIONARIES, BOOKS.

Annual.
Continues: Canadian Markets, ISSN 0832-2503
ISSN 1481-4900
ISBN 1-55251-049-2 (74th ed.)

1. Market surveys - Canada - Periodicals.
2. Canada - Economic conditions - 1991 - Statistics Periodicals. I. Financial Post (Firm).
    II. Title: Financial Post Markets, Canadian Demographics

HCIII.B823   330.971'0648   C99-390000-3

Printed in Canada

Table of Contents

Preface

We are pleased to present the 74th edition of FP Markets - Canadian Demographics, an easy-to-use reference guide on Canada's cities, towns, census divisions, provinces and territories.

Much has changed with this year's publication.

The estimates and projections in the book, and in the companion CD product, have been provided by Compusearch Inc., (a division of Equifax, Inc.), under the guidance of Dr. Tony Lea, V-P, development and custom research. Additional expertise was provided by Tom McCormack, President of Strategic Projections Inc., and Dr. Tom Exter, Sr. Director of data development at Compusearch.

In addition to supplying the data for population, households, income, retail sales, labour force, occupations, schooling, average household expenditures, families, housing, marital status, and home language, Compusearch has supplied PSYTE cluster information. This is their national market segmentation system, which divides Canada into 60 target groups. They have also supplied Finan¢ial P$YTE data, a 19-cluster system that groups neighbourhoods with similar banking and credit histories.

Other valuable data, new to the book, and again supplied by Compusearch, are: disposable and discretionary income and liquid assets.

As well, Equifax Canada, has supplied, for each area, some credit variables, such as the average credit limit per person and the number of instalment loans outstanding in each area.

New vehicle data from Polk Canada Inc. shows the total number of vehicles for several model years.

All of the above combined with shopping centre information, newspaper circulation figures, radio and tv data, industrial development contacts, plus much more, gives you an up-to-date look at the demographic profiles of Canada's urban areas.

Altogether, this publication has extensive demographic data on 74 economic regions, 112 census agglomerations, 271 census subdivisions, 289 census divisions, 25 metropolitan areas, plus Canada, the provinces and territories.

We trust you will find this updated version more useful than ever for making your marketing decisions.

The Editors
October 2000

Methodology/Sources

Estimates & Projections

Compusearch annually produces a set of estimates and projections for population (by age and sex), households, and aggregate and average household income. Although the lowest level for which the data are presented here is the CSD level, the estimating methodology involves a combination of top-down methods, using traditional demographic estimation and projection techniques, and bottom-up methods using demographic techniques along with proprietary spatial modeling techniques.

Control totals for total population were provided by SPI (Strategic Projections Inc.) for the development by Compusearch of population and household characteristics at the CSD level and higher. These demographic characteristics include: population by age and sex, households by age of maintainer, educational attainment, marital status, labour force characteristics, household income, consumer spending, retail sales and daytime population.

Using the Statistics Canada post-censal estimates of net undercoverage at the CD level, both Compusearch and SPI made undercount adjustments to the base population that conform to the most likely distribution of the population missed in the 1996 Census.

Compusearch produced all current and projected variables for this publication at the EA level and aggregated results to all higher levels of geography. The bottom-up variables were made consistent with the top-down control totals through a process of iterative proportional fitting which ensures both horizontal and vertical consistency across all geographic layers. Differential growth trends across all geographies are captured by taking into account patterns of historical growth, local population density, and recent housing start development trends.

The components of the demographic estimates and projections are as follows:

Population & Households

Compusearch implemented a small-area demographic estimation model for all enumeration areas (EA's) using Census Division (CD) level control totals for population (by age and sex), and households. Total population at the Census Subdivision (CSD) level (provided by SPI) informed the allocation of demographic components below the CD level.

The total population in each CD was determined through a demographic cohort-component model. The process begins with base year data from the 1996 census, which provides the population by single years of age by sex. The population in each age group is then aged to the year 2001. For example, the total population in year 2001 in each CD is equal to the population in 1996, plus births, minus deaths, plus net migration (in or out) that is estimated for the period 1996 to 2001.

CSD level data are derived from the CD results in a manner consistent with differential growth patterns among CSD populations. Households are generated by applying maintainer rates by age to the population by age.

Income

Compusearch developed income estimates and projections for households, families and working men and women. The model used inflation-controlled growth factors after modeling income averages and distributions for Enumeration Areas including those where the census data are suppressed by Statistics Canada. The estimates were matched to SPI's CD level income estimates and projections. SPI's estimates and projections take into account the impact of the following phenomena: (a) expected future gains in Canadian real incomes per household; (b) projected shifts over time at the CD level in the age distribution of household maintainers and (c) growth in provincial and national aggregate household income. Provincial household income growth rates are constrained to SPI's national and provincial economic forecast totals. The Compusearch models guarantee that all the EA-level data sum to the published CSD totals as well as to the higher-level Census Division projections.

Retail Sales

Compusearch applied a small area retail sales allocation model to provincial projections of retail sales by category of business. The projections are drawn from SPI's national and provincial economic models. The Compusearch model involved spatially aggregated estimates of employees and retail sales by detailed kind of business.

Census Variables and Estimates

Every 5 years, a national census is conducted by Statistics Canada. The most recent census was in 1996. The following methodology was used to derive current year estimates for a select number of census variables - Labour Force, Occupation, Level of Schooling, Families, Housing, Marital Status, and Home Language:

Compusearch derived base rates from the 1996 Census data at the EA level. The base rates were applied to the appropriate 2001 population estimates. Adjustments were made to the labour force and occupation estimates to account for the impact of economic factors. The EA numbers were rolled up to all higher levels of geography and mathematical techniques were used to smooth out any inconsistencies created by rounding of numbers during the aggregation processes.

Daytime Population

Compusearch produces estimates of daytime population for all levels of Canadian geography (including EA's and FSA's) on an annual basis. A component method was employed which used the following EA-level components: at-home population by age group (<15, 15 to 64, and 65+ years), daytime employees from business data geocoded to the EA, and a population at-work estimate of employees who work outside the EA but live in the EA. Constraints include the reconciling of daytime population with total population within major labor markets and within provinces for areas outside major labour markets.

Average Household Expenditures

The estimate of average household expenditures by category for 2001 was based upon: a) Compusearch's Consumer Spending Potential (CSP) database which is based on Statistics Canada Family Expenditure survey (FAMEX), and b) Estimates of Household Income and Total Expenditure.

The estimates are modeled for small areas based on Compusearch's CSP proportional expenditure rates matrix by PSYTE cluster which is applied to Compusearch's 2001 Household, Income and Expenditure Estimates.

PSYTE

PSYTE is Compusearch's advanced geodemographic market segmentation system that places every Canadian Enumeration Area and postal code into one of 60 pre-defined clusters or categories. A description of each of these clusters can be found in the glossary.

PSYTE was developed using a rigorous set of multivariate statistical research techniques which included use of principal components analysis, factor analysis, non-heirarchical cluster analysis (both neural net and k-means) and linear programming. The variables used in the construction of PSYTE were as follows: a) Socio-economic and demographic data from the 1996 Census data; b) New measures of settlement context, density, access to urban amenities, etc.; c) New vehicle registrations; d) Behavioural purchase data from Prospects Unlimited; and e) Behavioural purchase data from selected clients.

Finan¢ial P$YTE

Finan¢ial P$YTE was developed using variables from Equifax aggregated credit data and the following Compusearch data: PSYTE (and all of its ingredients), Disposable and Discretionary Income data, Liquid Assets. This cluster system groups together neighbourhoods with similar demographic and financial characteristics into 19 clusters.

The number and percent of 2001 households that fall into a particular Finan¢ial P$YTE cluster are also presented, along with the index. A description of each of these clusters can be found in the glossary.

Disposable and Discretionary Income

Compusearch created estimates of average household disposable incomes and various discretionary incomes at the EA level. By linking income, taxes, and expenditures in the one data set, this product estimates the amount of income available to households for purchasing products depending on where they live, how much they eat, etc. This data set includes disposable income and several types of available discretionary income after basic necessities (e.g., food, shelter, health care, child care, transportation, etc.) and after statutory deductions (CPP/QPP & EI). Taxation rates (by province) are assumed static at the 1999 rates.

Liquid Assets

Liquid Assets provides a picture of household assets at an EA level for 1999. Within Liquid Assets, estimates are provided for interest-bearing and equity investments separately (definitions of each are provided in the glossary).

Vehicle Data

Polk Canada Inc. has supplied a selection of vehicle data for this publication. These data were extracted from the Total Vehicles in Operation file, which is a census of all vehicles on the road as of July 1998, and from the 1999 New Vehicles Registration file. The data provided here are retail and fleet vehicle registrations for 1981 to 1999 combined. This information has been grouped by model year into three segments: a new car buyer segment for model year 1999, a segment for dealer-pay service representing model years 1997 and 1998, and a segment covering the do-it-yourself group for model years between 1981 and 1996.

Note: The Total Vehicles in Operation file includes data from all 10 provinces. New vehicle registrations include data from all 10 provinces plus Yukon Territory, the Northwest Territories and Nunavut. Previous tracking for the Northwest Territories included Nunavut counts before Nunavut became a separate reporting entity. For comparisons over time on New Vehicle counts, the Northwest Territories and Nunavut should be combined, so that the areas covered match.

Credit Data

Equifax, a leading international provider of consumer and commercial credit information, provided 7 credit variables from their national consumer credit database. This credit database contains information collected from banks, retailers, finance companies and other financial institutions. For confidentiality purposes data were suppressed for EA's where the data were comprised of fewer than 15 individuals. The data were then provided to Compusearch where the data was further aggregated to a high spatial scale for the purposes of this publication. These data refer to the Equifax credit information as of July 2000.

Sources for all Data Shown in the Book

Compusearch Inc. 330 Front St. West, Suite 1100, Toronto Ontario M5V 3B7. (416) 348-9180 www.compusearch.ca. Offices in Montreal (514) 879-1912 and Vancouver (604) 688-5355. Buying Power, Retail Sales, Population, Income, Daytime Population, Labour Force, Occupations, Level of Schooling, Average Household Expenditures, Private Households, Families, Housing, Marital Status, Home Language, PSYTE, Financial P$YTE, Liquid Assets, Disposable & Discretionary Income. (Alex Antoniuk/Max Stiles)

Equifax Canada 110 Sheppard Avenue East, Toronto, Ontario M2N 6S1. (416) 227-8500. Credit Information. (Harriet Sidler)

Polk Canada Marketing Services Inc. 703 Evans Ave., Suite 501, Toronto Ontario M9C 5E9 (416) 626-5222. Vehicle Information. (Michele Sexsmith)

Strategic Projections Inc. 125 Lakeshore Road East, Suite #302 Oakville, Ontario L6J 1H3. 1-888-SPI-9009 or (905) 338-7148. spinc@globalserve.net www.s-p-inc.com. Control totals (CD level and higher) for Population by age and sex , Households, Income, and Retail Sales. CSD estimates and projections for population (Tom McCormack).

Statistics Canada. Average weekly earnings, number of employees, building permits, capital expenditures, manufacturing, travel, retail trade and vital statistics. Offices throughout Canada are:

Halifax: (902-426-5331) Regina: (306-780-5405)

Montreal: (514-283-5725) Edmonton: (780-495-3027)

Ottawa: (613-951-8116) Calgary: (403-292-6717)

Toronto: (416-973-6586) Vancouver: (604-666-3691)

Winnipeg: (204-983-4020)

Revenue Canada. 875 Heron Rd., Ottawa Ontario K1A 0L8. Taxation Statistics.

CARD. 777 Bay St., Toronto, Ontario M5W 1A7. Newspaper circulation and radio and TV power (July 2000 edition)

Canada Mortgage and Housing Corporation. 700 Montreal Rd., Ottawa, Ontario K1A 0P7. Homes built.

Monday Report on Retailers. 777 Bay St., Toronto, Ontario M5W 1A7. Shopping Centre Data.

Bureau of Broadcast Measurement. 305 -1500 Don Mills Rd., Toronto, Ontario M3B 3L7. Radio and TV weekly reach and average hours tuned.

1 – Estimates by Province, Economic Region and Census Division

	'96 to '01 Hhld. Change %	Total No. (000s)	% Canadian Total	Avg. Annual Rate of Growth %	Total Pop. (000s)	Total Millions $	% Canadian Total	Per Hhld. $	Per Capita $	Income Rating Index	Total Millions $	% Canadian Total	Per Hhld. $	Per Capita $	Market Rating Index
		Households July 1, 2001				Income 2001					Retail Sales 2001				
CANADA	7.82	12,084.9	100.00	1.52	31,134.5	656,440.2	100.00	54,300	21,100	100	278,705.8	100.00	23,100	9,000	100
NEWFOUNDLAND	2.68	195.4	1.62	0.53	533.2	9,074.4	1.38	46,400	17,000	81	4,628.5	1.66	23,700	8,700	97
Avalon Peninsula	4.33	92.1	0.76	0.85	248.6	4,608.8	0.70	50,000	18,500	88	2,244.0	0.81	24,400	9,000	101
Division No. 1	4.33	92.1	0.76	0.85	248.6	4,608.8	0.70	50,000	18,500	88	2,244.0	0.81	24,400	9,000	101
South Coast - Burin Peninsula	0.63	16.7	0.14	0.13	46.5	653.0	0.10	39,000	14,000	67	299.1	0.11	17,900	6,400	72
Division No. 2	0.94	9.3	0.08	0.19	25.7	373.3	0.06	40,000	14,500	69	165.8	0.06	17,800	6,400	72
Division No. 3	0.24	7.4	0.06	0.05	20.8	279.7	0.04	37,700	13,400	64	133.4	0.05	18,000	6,400	72
West Coast - Northern Peninsula - Labrador	2.64	42.0	0.35	0.52	116.4	1,930.9	0.29	45,900	16,600	79	1,086.8	0.39	25,900	9,300	104
Division No. 4	1.03	8.9	0.07	0.21	23.8	317.0	0.05	35,700	13,300	63	172.0	0.06	19,400	7,200	81
Division No. 5	2.75	15.9	0.13	0.55	43.1	722.1	0.11	45,400	16,800	80	519.3	0.19	32,700	12,100	135
Division No. 9	-0.79	7.4	0.06	-0.16	20.6	301.4	0.05	40,600	14,600	69	160.2	0.06	21,600	7,800	87
Division No. 10	6.75	9.8	0.08	1.32	28.9	590.3	0.09	60,000	20,400	97	235.2	0.08	23,900	8,100	91
Notre Dame - Central Bonavista Bay	0.18	44.5	0.37	0.04	121.6	1,881.8	0.29	42,300	15,500	73	998.6	0.36	22,400	8,200	92
Division No. 6	0.98	13.9	0.12	0.19	37.5	676.9	0.10	48,600	18,000	86	521.7	0.19	37,400	13,900	155
Division No. 7	1.48	14.6	0.12	0.30	39.7	595.0	0.09	40,900	15,000	71	267.8	0.10	18,400	6,800	75
Division No. 8	-1.65	16.0	0.13	-0.33	44.4	609.9	0.09	38,100	13,700	65	209.1	0.08	13,100	4,700	53
PRINCE EDWARD ISLAND	5.58	52.0	0.43	1.09	138.2	2,331.7	0.36	44,900	16,900	80	1,205.9	0.43	23,200	8,700	97
Prince Edward Island	5.58	52.0	0.43	1.09	138.2	2,331.7	0.36	44,900	16,900	80	1,205.9	0.43	23,200	8,700	97
Kings County	3.90	7.3	0.06	0.77	19.7	313.0	0.05	43,000	15,900	76	105.8	0.04	14,500	5,400	60
Queens County	7.21	27.8	0.23	1.40	73.6	1,292.7	0.20	46,400	17,600	83	716.8	0.26	25,700	9,700	109
Prince County	3.70	16.8	0.14	0.73	44.9	726.0	0.11	43,100	16,200	77	383.2	0.14	22,800	8,500	95
NOVA SCOTIA	5.23	371.6	3.07	1.03	947.6	17,180.6	2.62	46,200	18,100	86	8,693.8	3.12	23,400	9,200	102
Cape Breton	0.40	58.6	0.48	0.08	155.6	2,361.7	0.36	40,300	15,200	72	1,310.0	0.47	22,400	8,400	94
Inverness County	0.87	7.6	0.06	0.17	20.7	339.1	0.05	44,300	16,400	78	226.0	0.08	29,600	10,900	122
Richmond County	0.49	4.1	0.03	0.10	10.9	164.2	0.03	40,100	15,000	71	45.2	0.02	11,000	4,100	46
Cape Breton County	0.22	43.7	0.36	0.04	115.5	1,725.7	0.26	39,500	14,900	71	999.2	0.36	22,900	8,600	97
Victoria County	1.67	3.2	0.03	0.33	8.5	132.7	0.02	41,900	15,700	74	39.6	0.01	12,500	4,700	52
North Shore	2.92	64.6	0.53	0.58	165.1	2,674.0	0.41	41,400	16,200	77	1,615.3	0.58	25,000	9,800	109
Colchester County	5.64	20.5	0.17	1.10	51.8	866.1	0.13	42,300	16,700	79	585.8	0.21	28,600	11,300	126
Cumberland County	0.32	13.7	0.11	0.06	33.9	508.0	0.08	37,100	15,000	71	342.3	0.12	25,000	10,100	113
Pictou County	1.73	19.1	0.16	0.34	48.9	803.7	0.12	42,200	16,400	78	440.3	0.16	23,100	9,000	101
Guysborough County	-2.71	4.1	0.03	-0.55	10.3	139.9	0.02	34,500	13,500	64	43.4	0.02	10,700	4,200	47
Antigonish County	7.08	7.3	0.06	1.38	20.1	356.2	0.05	49,100	17,700	84	203.4	0.07	28,000	10,100	113
Annapolis Valley	6.95	49.4	0.41	1.35	128.7	2,144.2	0.33	43,400	16,700	79	1,017.5	0.37	20,600	7,900	88
Annapolis County	2.36	9.2	0.08	0.47	22.5	346.3	0.05	37,600	15,400	73	115.8	0.04	12,600	5,100	57
Kings County	7.48	24.5	0.20	1.45	63.3	1,079.2	0.16	44,100	17,100	81	610.8	0.22	25,000	9,700	108
Hants County	8.97	15.7	0.13	1.73	42.9	718.8	0.11	45,600	16,800	79	290.9	0.10	18,500	6,800	76
Southern	1.92	50.5	0.42	0.38	126.0	2,113.4	0.32	41,800	16,800	80	1,178.2	0.42	23,300	9,400	104
Shelburne County	2.82	6.9	0.06	0.56	16.9	297.2	0.05	43,100	17,500	83	172.1	0.06	25,000	10,200	113
Yarmouth County	1.15	10.7	0.09	0.23	27.5	448.4	0.07	41,800	16,300	77	197.4	0.07	18,400	7,200	80
Digby County	-0.17	8.2	0.07	-0.03	20.4	310.5	0.05	37,700	15,200	72	209.1	0.08	25,400	10,200	114
Queens County	-1.33	4.9	0.04	-0.27	12.1	225.6	0.03	46,000	18,600	88	97.7	0.04	19,900	8,100	90
Lunenburg County	3.77	19.8	0.16	0.74	49.0	831.6	0.13	42,000	17,000	81	501.9	0.18	25,300	10,300	115
Halifax	9.00	148.5	1.23	1.74	372.2	7,887.3	1.20	53,100	21,200	101	3,572.8	1.28	24,100	9,600	107
Halifax County	9.00	148.5	1.23	1.74	372.2	7,887.3	1.20	53,100	21,200	101	3,572.8	1.28	24,100	9,600	107
NEW BRUNSWICK	5.29	293.2	2.43	1.04	759.1	13,511.2	2.06	46,100	17,800	84	7,095.9	2.55	24,200	9,300	104
Campbellton - Miramichi	4.13	67.8	0.56	0.81	178.8	2,872.9	0.44	42,400	16,100	76	1,791.9	0.64	26,400	10,000	112
Northumberland County	3.57	19.5	0.16	0.70	52.3	844.9	0.13	43,400	16,200	77	502.4	0.18	25,800	9,600	107
Restigouche County	2.44	14.9	0.12	0.48	38.4	623.0	0.09	41,900	16,200	77	363.3	0.13	24,400	9,500	106
Gloucester County	5.23	33.4	0.28	1.02	88.1	1,405.0	0.21	42,000	15,900	76	926.2	0.33	27,700	10,500	117

	'96 to '01 Hhld. Change %	Total No. (000s)	% Canadian Total	Avg. Annual Rate of Growth %	Total Pop. (000s)	Total Millions $	% Canadian Totall	Per Hhld. $	Per Capita $	Income Rating Index	Total Millions $	% Canadian Total	Per Hhld. $	Per Capita $	Market Rating Index
Moncton - Richibucto	7.08	73.1	0.61	1.38	187.6	3,540.2	0.54	48,400	18,900	90	1,750.2	0.63	23,900	9,300	104
Albert County	7.06	10.2	0.08	1.37	27.4	558.1	0.09	54,600	20,400	97	78.2	0.03	7,700	2,900	32
Westmorland County	7.44	50.5	0.42	1.44	127.2	2,490.5	0.38	49,300	19,600	93	1,409.2	0.51	27,900	11,100	124
Kent County	5.65	12.4	0.10	1.10	33.0	491.7	0.07	39,600	14,900	71	262.7	0.09	21,200	8,000	89
Saint John - St. Stephen	3.76	68.2	0.56	0.74	175.5	3,246.7	0.49	47,600	18,500	88	1,338.5	0.48	19,600	7,600	85
Saint John County	0.60	32.6	0.27	0.12	78.8	1,373.4	0.21	42,100	17,400	83	880.2	0.32	27,000	11,200	125
Charlotte County	3.72	11.2	0.09	0.73	28.3	479.4	0.07	42,800	16,900	80	143.2	0.05	12,800	5,100	56
Kings County	8.33	24.3	0.20	1.61	68.3	1,393.9	0.21	57,200	20,400	97	315.1	0.11	12,900	4,600	52
Fredericton - Oromocto	6.78	50.7	0.42	1.32	129.3	2,535.9	0.39	50,000	19,600	93	1,311.5	0.47	25,900	10,100	113
Sunbury County	10.87	9.9	0.08	2.09	27.8	471.3	0.07	47,800	17,000	80	174.4	0.06	17,700	6,300	70
Queens County	0.26	5.0	0.04	0.05	12.4	182.1	0.03	36,700	14,700	70	64.6	0.02	13,000	5,200	58
York County	6.66	35.9	0.30	1.30	89.1	1,882.5	0.29	52,400	21,100	100	1,072.5	0.38	29,900	12,000	134
Edmundston - Woodstock	4.78	33.3	0.28	0.94	87.9	1,315.5	0.20	39,500	15,000	71	903.7	0.32	27,100	10,300	115
Carleton County	5.09	10.3	0.09	1.00	28.3	416.4	0.06	40,300	14,700	70	341.7	0.12	33,100	12,100	135
Victoria County	3.91	8.4	0.07	0.77	22.5	304.9	0.05	36,400	13,600	64	265.8	0.10	31,700	11,800	132
Madawaska County	5.07	14.6	0.12	0.99	37.2	594.2	0.09	40,600	16,000	76	296.3	0.11	20,300	8,000	89
QUÉBEC	5.55	3,063.9	25.35	1.09	7,445.1	143,773.8	21.90	46,900	19,300	92	64,688.8	23.21	21,100	8,700	97
Gaspésie - Îles-de-la-Madeleine	1.25	39.4	0.33	0.25	102.9	1,621.6	0.25	41,100	15,800	75	879.9	0.32	22,300	8,500	95
Les Îles-de-la-Madeleine	-0.40	4.9	0.04	-0.08	13.3	238.4	0.04	48,200	17,900	85	168.4	0.06	34,000	12,600	141
Pabok	1.23	8.1	0.07	0.25	20.8	315.6	0.05	39,200	15,200	72	155.3	0.06	19,300	7,500	84
La Côte-de-Gaspé	1.04	7.5	0.06	0.21	20.2	337.0	0.05	44,900	16,700	79	174.8	0.06	23,300	8,600	97
Denis-Riverin	-0.73	5.3	0.04	-0.15	13.3	178.0	0.03	33,700	13,400	63	85.2	0.03	16,100	6,400	71
Bonaventure	1.66	7.5	0.06	0.33	19.1	302.3	0.05	40,500	15,800	75	192.1	0.07	25,700	10,000	112
Avignon	4.17	6.2	0.05	0.82	16.1	250.3	0.04	40,600	15,500	74	104.0	0.04	16,900	6,400	72
Bas-Saint-Laurent	3.46	83.8	0.69	0.68	205.8	3,405.9	0.52	40,700	16,500	78	1,909.7	0.69	22,800	9,300	104
La Matapédia	2.44	7.9	0.07	0.48	20.6	295.6	0.04	37,400	14,400	68	113.4	0.04	14,300	5,500	62
Matane	1.53	9.8	0.08	0.30	23.1	379.3	0.06	38,600	16,400	78	239.9	0.09	24,400	10,400	116
La Mitis	1.14	7.9	0.07	0.23	20.0	290.2	0.04	36,600	14,500	69	131.1	0.05	16,600	6,600	73
Rimouski-Neigette	5.55	22.8	0.19	1.09	53.5	1,078.8	0.16	47,300	20,200	96	518.5	0.19	22,700	9,700	108
Les Basques	17.43	4.0	0.03	3.27	8.8	136.8	0.02	33,800	15,500	74	84.4	0.03	20,800	9,600	107
Rivière-du-Loup	1.24	13.5	0.11	0.25	33.9	550.5	0.08	40,900	16,200	77	423.3	0.15	31,400	12,400	139
Témiscouata	2.37	8.8	0.07	0.47	22.9	322.8	0.05	36,600	14,100	67	157.7	0.06	17,900	6,900	77
Kamouraska	2.33	8.9	0.07	0.46	23.0	351.8	0.05	39,300	15,300	72	242.4	0.09	27,100	10,500	118
Québec	4.50	282.5	2.34	0.88	647.5	13,470.4	2.05	47,700	20,800	99	7,099.3	2.55	25,100	11,000	122
Charlevoix-Est	1.93	6.5	0.05	0.38	16.7	265.1	0.04	40,800	15,900	75	151.8	0.05	23,400	9,100	101
Charlevoix	1.91	5.0	0.04	0.38	13.4	196.9	0.03	39,700	14,700	70	106.5	0.04	21,400	7,900	89
L'Île-d'Orléans	4.68	2.7	0.02	0.92	6.9	151.9	0.02	56,600	21,900	104	25.3	0.01	9,400	3,600	41
La Côte-de-Beaupré	4.82	8.8	0.07	0.95	22.3	424.7	0.06	48,200	19,100	90	272.0	0.10	30,900	12,200	136
La Jacques-Cartier	12.56	9.9	0.08	2.40	27.1	568.6	0.09	57,500	21,000	100	75.4	0.03	7,600	2,800	31
Communauté urbaine de Québec	4.24	230.9	1.91	0.83	514.3	11,061.7	1.69	47,900	21,500	102	5,985.7	2.15	25,900	11,600	130
Portneuf	5.15	18.8	0.16	1.01	46.7	801.5	0.12	42,700	17,200	81	482.5	0.17	25,700	10,300	115
Chaudière - Appalaches	6.06	152.0	1.26	1.18	393.5	6,863.4	1.05	45,200	17,400	83	3,849.5	1.38	25,300	9,800	109
L'Islet	2.24	7.7	0.06	0.44	19.8	292.6	0.04	38,100	14,800	70	148.6	0.05	19,300	7,500	84
Montmagny	2.08	9.6	0.08	0.41	23.8	373.5	0.06	39,100	15,700	74	258.1	0.09	27,000	10,900	121
Bellechasse	2.16	11.1	0.09	0.43	29.9	466.0	0.07	42,100	15,600	74	222.3	0.08	20,100	7,400	83
Desjardins	5.81	21.9	0.18	1.14	52.9	1,032.6	0.16	47,100	19,500	93	869.0	0.31	39,600	16,400	183
Les Chutes-de-la-Chaudière	13.01	31.0	0.26	2.48	82.9	1,770.1	0.27	57,100	21,300	101	512.3	0.18	16,500	6,200	69
La Nouvelle-Beauce	5.82	9.5	0.08	1.14	25.9	429.3	0.07	45,400	16,600	79	283.4	0.10	29,900	10,900	122
Robert-Cliche	5.16	7.0	0.06	1.01	19.0	286.6	0.04	40,700	15,100	71	134.6	0.05	19,100	7,100	79
Les Etchemins	1.57	6.8	0.06	0.31	18.1	256.4	0.04	37,500	14,200	67	150.7	0.05	22,000	8,300	93
Beauce-Sartigan	9.16	18.9	0.16	1.77	49.1	813.5	0.12	43,100	16,600	79	578.2	0.21	30,700	11,800	131
L'Amiante	1.66	18.1	0.15	0.33	44.3	716.7	0.11	39,500	16,200	77	423.5	0.15	23,300	9,600	107
Lotbinière	4.71	10.3	0.09	0.92	27.6	426.0	0.06	41,200	15,500	73	268.9	0.10	26,000	9,800	109
Estrie	6.85	123.4	1.02	1.33	292.5	5,149.4	0.78	41,700	17,600	84	2,366.3	0.85	19,200	8,100	90
Le Granit	5.33	8.6	0.07	1.04	21.9	347.9	0.05	40,300	15,900	75	257.3	0.09	29,800	11,800	131
Asbestos	1.63	6.2	0.05	0.32	14.9	234.6	0.04	37,700	15,700	75	107.2	0.04	17,200	7,200	80
Le Haut-Saint-François	5.67	8.8	0.07	1.11	22.9	332.5	0.05	37,700	14,500	69	120.3	0.04	13,600	5,200	59
Le Val-Saint-François	8.15	13.8	0.11	1.58	34.9	615.7	0.09	44,700	17,600	84	192.3	0.07	14,000	5,500	61
Sherbrooke	6.96	62.2	0.51	1.36	139.7	2,605.5	0.40	41,900	18,600	88	1,271.9	0.46	20,500	9,100	102
Coaticook	3.78	6.0	0.05	0.74	16.1	249.4	0.04	41,400	15,500	74	112.2	0.04	18,600	7,000	78
Memphrémagog	9.84	17.8	0.15	1.89	42.0	763.9	0.12	43,000	18,200	86	305.3	0.11	17,200	7,300	81
Montérégie	7.53	524.6	4.34	1.46	1,338.8	27,401.4	4.17	52,200	20,500	97	11,855.8	4.25	22,600	8,900	99
Brome-Missisquoi	5.04	19.7	0.16	0.99	47.3	825.5	0.13	42,000	17,500	83	437.7	0.16	22,300	9,300	103
La Haute-Yamaska	8.90	34.1	0.28	1.72	82.1	1,523.3	0.23	44,700	18,600	88	868.1	0.31	25,500	10,600	118
Acton	6.45	6.2	0.05	1.26	16.0	247.8	0.04	40,000	15,500	73	95.3	0.03	15,400	6,000	67
Le Bas-Richelieu	0.71	21.7	0.18	0.14	51.2	928.7	0.14	42,700	18,200	86	478.4	0.17	22,000	9,400	104
Les Maskoutains	4.61	33.0	0.27	0.91	80.4	1,419.5	0.22	43,100	17,700	84	866.2	0.31	26,300	10,800	120
Rouville	7.27	13.1	0.11	1.41	34.8	615.2	0.09	47,000	17,700	84	236.3	0.08	18,000	6,800	76
Le Haut-Richelieu	7.69	41.8	0.35	1.49	103.6	1,868.6	0.28	44,700	18,000	86	1,114.3	0.40	26,700	10,800	120
La Vallée-du-Richelieu	10.61	45.5	0.38	2.04	123.7	2,904.3	0.44	63,800	23,500	111	1,318.6	0.47	28,900	10,700	119
Champlain	5.29	131.5	1.09	1.04	321.1	6,982.0	1.06	53,100	21,700	103	2,721.5	0.98	20,700	8,500	95
Lajemmerais	14.86	39.0	0.32	2.81	107.7	2,670.8	0.41	68,500	24,800	118	1,108.3	0.40	28,400	10,300	115
Roussillon	11.06	55.3	0.46	2.12	155.2	3,187.1	0.49	57,600	20,500	97	935.1	0.34	16,900	6,000	67

	'96 to '01 Hhld. Change %	Total No. (000s)	% Canadian Total	Avg. Annual Rate of Growth %	Total Pop. (000s)	Total Millions $	% Canadian Total	Per Hhld. $	Per Capita $	Income Rating Index	Total Millions $	% Canadian Total	Per Hhld. $	Per Capita $	Market Rating Index
Les Jardins-de-Napierville	6.28	9.0	0.07	1.23	23.8	401.5	0.06	44,600	16,900	80	270.4	0.10	30,000	11,400	127
Le Haut-Saint-Laurent	0.40	9.6	0.08	0.08	24.9	401.2	0.06	41,900	16,100	76	145.1	0.05	15,100	5,800	65
Beauharnois-Salaberry	2.39	25.1	0.21	0.47	60.0	1,046.3	0.16	41,700	17,400	83	597.1	0.21	23,800	10,000	111
Vaudreuil-Soulanges	12.63	40.0	0.33	2.41	107.2	2,379.7	0.36	59,500	22,200	105	663.5	0.24	16,600	6,200	69
Montréal	1.30	806.1	6.67	0.26	1,798.7	35,866.4	5.46	44,500	19,900	95	14,008.7	5.03	17,400	7,800	87
Communauté urbaine de Montréal	1.30	806.1	6.67	0.26	1,798.7	35,866.4	5.46	44,500	19,900	95	14,008.7	5.03	17,400	7,800	87
Laval	8.48	136.9	1.13	1.64	353.3	7,336.9	1.12	53,600	20,800	98	3,360.1	1.21	24,600	9,500	106
Laval	8.48	136.9	1.13	1.64	353.3	7,336.9	1.12	53,600	20,800	98	3,360.1	1.21	24,600	9,500	106
Lanaudière	12.37	157.2	1.30	2.36	416.6	7,681.0	1.17	48,800	18,400	87	3,598.0	1.29	22,900	8,600	96
D'Autray	11.68	16.0	0.13	2.23	42.1	662.1	0.10	41,400	15,700	75	212.1	0.08	13,200	5,000	56
L'Assomption	12.09	41.0	0.34	2.31	111.9	2,374.4	0.36	57,900	21,200	101	949.6	0.34	23,200	8,500	95
Joliette	6.39	22.7	0.19	1.25	55.1	978.4	0.15	43,200	17,800	84	788.2	0.28	34,800	14,300	160
Matawinie	12.75	20.0	0.17	2.43	46.6	734.4	0.11	36,700	15,800	75	263.2	0.09	13,100	5,700	63
Montcalm	11.45	16.3	0.14	2.19	42.8	644.1	0.10	39,500	15,100	71	251.4	0.09	15,400	5,900	66
Les Moulins	16.73	41.2	0.34	3.14	118.1	2,287.6	0.35	55,500	19,400	92	1,133.6	0.41	27,500	9,600	107
Laurentides	13.84	193.6	1.60	2.63	490.2	9,422.4	1.44	48,700	19,200	91	3,908.6	1.40	20,200	8,000	89
Deux-Montagnes	11.02	32.6	0.27	2.11	88.0	1,699.9	0.26	52,100	19,300	92	647.7	0.23	19,900	7,400	82
Thérèse-De Blainville	16.53	49.8	0.41	3.11	137.4	2,970.7	0.45	59,600	21,600	103	1,091.4	0.39	21,900	7,900	89
Mirabel	24.88	10.2	0.08	4.54	28.5	521.4	0.08	51,400	18,300	87	171.8	0.06	16,900	6,000	67
La Rivière-du-Nord	16.47	39.2	0.32	3.10	93.5	1,708.6	0.26	43,500	18,300	87	812.1	0.29	20,700	8,700	97
Argenteuil	-0.95	12.3	0.10	-0.19	31.1	480.3	0.07	38,900	15,500	73	178.1	0.06	14,400	5,700	64
Les Pays-d'en-Haut	18.98	16.3	0.13	3.54	34.5	792.5	0.12	48,700	23,000	109	241.4	0.09	14,800	7,000	78
Les Laurentides	13.19	18.3	0.15	2.51	41.2	704.9	0.11	38,600	17,100	81	404.7	0.15	22,200	9,800	110
Antoine-Labelle	7.57	14.9	0.12	1.47	36.0	544.1	0.08	36,500	15,100	72	361.3	0.13	24,200	10,000	112
Outaouais	8.13	131.9	1.09	1.58	326.9	6,694.4	1.02	50,800	20,500	97	2,573.0	0.92	19,500	7,900	88
Papineau	7.24	9.5	0.08	1.41	21.4	354.9	0.05	37,500	16,600	79	123.4	0.04	13,000	5,800	65
Communauté urbaine de l'Outaouais	7.09	92.5	0.77	1.38	229.3	4,897.1	0.75	52,900	21,400	101	2,010.0	0.72	21,700	8,800	98
Les Collines-de-l'Outaouais	15.84	14.3	0.12	2.98	38.7	876.2	0.13	61,400	22,600	107	115.4	0.04	8,100	3,000	33
La Vallée-de-la-Gatineau	13.46	9.5	0.08	2.56	21.9	337.1	0.05	35,400	15,400	73	221.6	0.08	23,200	10,100	113
Pontiac	1.26	6.1	0.05	0.25	15.7	229.1	0.03	37,400	14,600	69	102.6	0.04	16,700	6,500	73
Abitibi - Témiscamingue	4.64	63.0	0.52	0.91	156.2	2,872.0	0.44	45,600	18,400	87	1,541.9	0.55	24,500	9,900	110
Témiscamingue	5.92	7.3	0.06	1.16	18.7	328.6	0.05	45,000	17,500	83	134.2	0.05	18,400	7,200	80
Rouyn-Noranda	5.24	18.4	0.15	1.03	43.3	867.1	0.13	47,100	20,000	95	429.2	0.15	23,300	9,900	111
Abitibi-Ouest	0.52	8.9	0.07	0.10	23.0	378.9	0.06	42,700	16,400	78	215.1	0.08	24,200	9,300	104
Abitibi	5.38	10.0	0.08	1.05	25.6	437.3	0.07	43,800	17,100	81	271.7	0.10	27,200	10,600	119
Vallée-de-l'Or	5.22	18.5	0.15	1.02	45.5	860.1	0.13	46,600	18,900	90	491.7	0.18	26,600	10,800	121
Mauricie - Bois-Francs	4.90	204.5	1.69	0.96	488.4	8,364.8	1.27	40,900	17,100	81	4,120.3	1.48	20,100	8,400	94
L'Érable	2.03	9.2	0.08	0.40	24.6	360.6	0.05	39,000	14,700	70	169.9	0.06	18,400	6,900	77
Mékinac	2.08	5.6	0.05	0.41	13.3	198.4	0.03	35,200	14,900	71	72.8	0.03	12,900	5,500	61
Le Centre-de-la-Mauricie	1.85	29.2	0.24	0.37	67.1	1,108.6	0.17	38,000	16,500	78	505.6	0.18	17,300	7,500	84
Francheville	4.38	62.9	0.52	0.86	143.0	2,708.7	0.41	43,000	18,900	90	1,143.7	0.41	18,200	8,000	89
Bécancour	4.68	7.8	0.06	0.92	20.0	335.2	0.05	42,800	16,800	79	128.7	0.05	16,400	6,400	72
Arthabaska	7.58	26.4	0.22	1.47	66.1	1,102.0	0.17	41,700	16,700	79	654.5	0.23	24,800	9,900	111
Drummond	8.97	37.0	0.31	1.73	89.5	1,541.2	0.23	41,600	17,200	82	975.2	0.35	26,300	10,900	122
Nicolet-Yamaska	3.26	9.4	0.08	0.64	24.1	371.0	0.06	39,600	15,400	73	185.4	0.07	19,800	7,700	86
Maskinongé	2.41	10.0	0.08	0.48	24.1	354.2	0.05	35,400	14,700	70	146.2	0.05	14,600	6,100	68
Le Haut-Saint-Maurice	4.43	6.8	0.06	0.87	16.6	284.9	0.04	41,900	17,100	81	138.4	0.05	20,300	8,300	93
Saguenay - Lac-Saint-Jean	5.24	112.1	0.93	1.03	289.7	4,859.5	0.74	43,400	16,800	80	2,552.7	0.92	22,800	8,800	98
Le Domaine-du-Roy	4.36	12.6	0.10	0.86	34.1	573.9	0.09	45,500	16,800	80	299.2	0.11	23,700	8,800	98
Maria-Chapdelaine	4.09	10.3	0.09	0.80	27.9	420.5	0.06	40,800	15,100	72	275.6	0.10	26,700	9,900	110
Lac-Saint-Jean-Est	5.81	20.1	0.17	1.14	53.2	866.8	0.13	43,100	16,300	77	448.3	0.16	22,300	8,400	94
Le Fjord-du-Saguenay	5.40	69.0	0.57	1.06	174.5	2,998.2	0.46	43,400	17,200	81	1,529.6	0.55	22,200	8,800	98
Côte-Nord	4.06	40.3	0.33	0.80	103.3	2,049.2	0.31	50,900	19,800	94	809.6	0.29	20,100	7,800	88
La Haute-Côte-Nord	3.03	5.2	0.04	0.60	13.4	202.2	0.03	38,600	15,100	72	119.1	0.04	22,700	8,900	100
Manicouagan	3.27	14.1	0.12	0.65	35.8	741.0	0.11	52,600	20,700	98	252.7	0.09	17,900	7,100	79
Sept-Rivières - Caniapiscau	4.98	16.6	0.14	0.98	41.5	908.4	0.14	54,700	21,900	104	356.3	0.13	21,400	8,600	96
Minganie - Basse-Côte-Nord	4.44	4.3	0.04	0.87	12.7	197.6	0.03	45,900	15,600	74	81.5	0.03	18,900	6,400	72
Nord-du-Québec	9.31	12.7	0.11	1.80	40.7	715.2	0.11	56,300	17,600	83	255.3	0.09	20,100	6,300	70
Nord-du-Québec	9.31	12.7	0.11	1.80	40.7	715.2	0.11	56,300	17,600	83	255.3	0.09	20,100	6,300	70
ONTARIO	8.76	4,436.2	36.71	1.69	11,817.0	269,996.8	41.13	60,900	22,800	108	106,349.4	38.16	24,000	9,000	101
Ottawa	6.93	449.3	3.72	1.35	1,138.2	27,429.5	4.18	61,100	24,100	114	10,813.1	3.88	24,100	9,500	106
Stormont, Dundas and Glengarry United Counties	2.59	45.2	0.37	0.51	116.1	2,159.1	0.33	47,700	18,600	88	1,104.1	0.40	24,400	9,500	106
Prescott and Russell United Counties	8.37	29.0	0.24	1.62	80.5	1,570.1	0.24	54,100	19,500	92	569.7	0.20	19,600	7,100	79
Ottawa-Carleton Regional Municipality	7.87	310.7	2.57	1.53	775.3	20,425.9	3.11	65,700	26,300	125	7,636.9	2.74	24,600	9,900	110
Leeds and Grenville United Counties	4.30	39.8	0.33	0.85	101.6	1,983.7	0.30	49,900	19,500	93	966.2	0.35	24,300	9,500	106
Lanark County	6.03	24.5	0.20	1.18	64.6	1,290.6	0.20	52,700	20,000	95	536.2	0.19	21,900	8,300	93
Kingston - Pembroke	3.81	172.1	1.42	0.75	433.8	8,593.2	1.31	49,900	19,800	94	3,973.2	1.43	23,100	9,200	102
Frontenac County	4.30	58.1	0.48	0.85	140.7	3,155.4	0.48	54,300	22,400	106	1,352.5	0.49	23,300	9,600	107

	'96 to '01 Hhld. Change %	Total No. (000s)	% Canadian Total	Avg. Annual Rate of Growth %	Total Pop. (000s)	Total Millions $	% Canadian Totall	Per Hhld. $	Per Capita $	Income Rating Index	Total Millions $	% Canadian Total	Per Hhld. $	Per Capita $	Market Rating Index
		Households July 1, 2001				Income 2001					Retail Sales 2001				
Lennox and Addington County	4.01	15.0	0.12	0.79	41.0	744.7	0.11	49,600	18,200	86	215.6	0.08	14,300	5,300	59
Hastings County	2.50	49.1	0.41	0.49	124.2	2,320.2	0.35	47,200	18,700	89	1,418.3	0.51	28,900	11,400	128
Prince Edward County	4.21	10.5	0.09	0.83	26.4	530.2	0.08	50,600	20,100	95	94.1	0.03	9,000	3,600	40
Renfrew County	4.57	39.3	0.33	0.90	101.6	1,842.6	0.28	46,900	18,100	86	892.7	0.32	22,700	8,800	98
Muskoka - Kawarthas	6.09	143.1	1.18	1.19	361.2	7,088.3	1.08	49,500	19,600	93	3,311.1	1.19	23,100	9,200	102
Northumberland County	6.11	33.3	0.28	1.19	86.7	1,757.3	0.27	52,700	20,300	96	635.3	0.23	19,100	7,300	82
Peterborough County	5.77	51.9	0.43	1.13	130.8	2,600.3	0.40	50,100	19,900	94	1,182.7	0.42	22,800	9,000	101
Victoria County	7.56	29.0	0.24	1.47	73.4	1,417.7	0.22	48,900	19,300	92	585.3	0.21	20,200	8,000	89
Muskoka District Municipality	5.08	21.6	0.18	1.00	54.0	1,024.4	0.16	47,400	19,000	90	733.9	0.26	33,900	13,600	152
Haliburton County	5.53	7.3	0.06	1.08	16.3	288.6	0.04	39,600	17,700	84	173.9	0.06	23,900	10,700	119
Toronto	12.56	1,830.7	15.15	2.40	5,120.4	124,810.0	19.01	68,200	24,400	116	43,006.0	15.43	23,500	8,400	94
Durham Regional Municipality	14.00	181.3	1.50	2.66	524.1	12,712.3	1.94	70,100	24,300	115	4,154.8	1.49	22,900	7,900	89
York Regional Municipality	25.70	231.2	1.91	4.68	740.2	19,932.3	3.04	86,200	26,900	128	6,232.2	2.24	27,000	8,400	94
Toronto Metropolitan Municipality	6.66	1,000.0	8.27	1.30	2,579.5	59,739.1	9.10	59,700	23,200	110	22,393.4	8.03	22,400	8,700	97
Peel Regional Municipality	21.99	336.3	2.78	4.06	1,039.2	25,244.3	3.85	75,100	24,300	115	8,090.5	2.90	24,100	7,800	87
Halton Regional Municipality*	13.17	138.1	1.14	2.50	386.6	11,470.8	1.75	83,100	29,700	141	3,707.1	1.33	26,900	9,600	107
Kitchener - Waterloo - Barrie	12.84	403.0	3.33	2.44	1,081.3	23,499.3	3.58	58,300	21,700	103	10,126.4	3.63	25,100	9,400	105
Dufferin County	12.02	17.7	0.15	2.30	51.9	1,135.1	0.17	64,000	21,900	104	391.6	0.14	22,100	7,500	84
Wellington County	11.22	71.0	0.59	2.15	191.4	4,359.4	0.66	61,400	22,800	108	1,775.3	0.64	25,000	9,300	104
Waterloo Regional Municipality	11.49	171.3	1.42	2.20	452.8	10,287.5	1.57	60,100	22,700	108	4,731.2	1.70	27,600	10,400	117
Simcoe County	15.44	143.0	1.18	2.91	385.1	7,717.4	1.18	54,000	20,000	95	3,228.3	1.16	22,600	8,400	94
Hamilton - Niagara Peninsula	6.06	509.7	4.22	1.18	1,318.7	28,515.9	4.34	56,000	21,600	103	11,416.8	4.10	22,400	8,700	97
Halton Regional Municipality*	13.17	138.1	1.14	2.50	386.6	11,470.8	1.75	83,100	29,700	141	3,707.1	1.33	26,900	9,600	107
Hamilton-Wentworth Regional Municipality	6.22	195.8	1.62	1.21	503.1	10,697.6	1.63	54,600	21,300	101	3,705.9	1.33	18,900	7,400	82
Niagara Regional Municipality	5.73	169.7	1.40	1.12	429.1	8,838.5	1.35	52,100	20,600	98	4,320.8	1.55	25,500	10,100	112
Haldimand-Norfolk Regional Municipality	5.68	40.3	0.33	1.11	109.6	2,177.3	0.33	54,000	19,900	94	839.3	0.30	20,800	7,700	86
Brant County	4.38	47.6	0.39	0.86	127.7	2,513.8	0.38	52,800	19,700	93	978.7	0.35	20,600	7,700	86
London	5.62	237.4	1.96	1.10	603.9	13,112.0	2.00	55,200	21,700	103	5,632.8	2.02	23,700	9,300	104
Oxford County	4.84	38.5	0.32	0.95	102.6	2,102.7	0.32	54,600	20,500	97	704.4	0.25	18,300	6,900	77
Elgin County	5.73	31.2	0.26	1.12	84.9	1,647.8	0.25	52,800	19,400	92	649.9	0.23	20,800	7,700	85
Middlesex County	5.77	167.7	1.39	1.13	416.3	9,361.5	1.43	55,800	22,500	107	4,278.6	1.54	25,500	10,300	115
Windsor - Sarnia	6.35	244.1	2.02	1.24	629.8	14,259.9	2.17	58,400	22,600	107	6,343.3	2.28	26,000	10,100	113
Kent County	1.35	43.2	0.36	0.27	111.6	2,262.1	0.34	52,400	20,300	96	1,299.3	0.47	30,100	11,600	130
Essex County	9.71	149.5	1.24	1.87	387.4	9,106.3	1.39	60,900	23,500	111	3,850.4	1.38	25,800	9,900	111
Lambton County	1.53	51.5	0.43	0.30	130.8	2,891.5	0.44	56,200	22,100	105	1,193.6	0.43	23,200	9,100	102
Stratford - Bruce Peninsula	2.55	114.1	0.94	0.50	294.5	5,679.9	0.87	49,800	19,300	91	3,083.6	1.11	27,000	10,500	117
Perth County	3.83	28.2	0.23	0.75	75.0	1,542.9	0.24	54,700	20,600	98	936.7	0.34	33,200	12,500	140
Huron County	1.55	23.3	0.19	0.31	61.4	1,126.6	0.17	48,400	18,400	87	539.9	0.19	23,200	8,800	98
Bruce County	0.11	25.9	0.21	0.02	66.7	1,295.6	0.20	50,100	19,400	92	674.3	0.24	26,100	10,100	113
Grey County	3.98	36.7	0.30	0.78	91.4	1,714.8	0.26	46,700	18,800	89	932.7	0.33	25,400	10,200	114
Northeast	1.07	235.7	1.95	0.21	583.9	11,620.7	1.77	49,300	19,900	94	6,197.2	2.22	26,300	10,600	119
Nipissing District	0.91	34.2	0.28	0.18	84.2	1,598.8	0.24	46,800	19,000	90	952.3	0.34	27,900	11,300	126
Parry Sound District	4.45	17.8	0.15	0.88	41.9	730.8	0.11	41,000	17,400	83	433.4	0.16	24,300	10,300	116
Manitoulin District	4.45	5.1	0.04	0.88	13.3	213.2	0.03	42,100	16,100	76	111.2	0.04	22,000	8,400	94
Sudbury District	2.19	10.2	0.08	0.43	25.4	489.3	0.07	47,800	19,300	91	191.1	0.07	18,700	7,500	84
Sudbury Regional Municipality	1.50	66.3	0.55	0.30	163.0	3,565.4	0.54	53,800	21,900	104	1,791.4	0.64	27,000	11,000	123
Timiskaming District	-3.30	14.9	0.12	-0.67	36.6	664.1	0.10	44,600	18,100	86	442.8	0.16	29,700	12,100	135
Cochrane District	1.60	36.1	0.30	0.32	93.0	1,879.7	0.29	52,000	20,200	96	906.6	0.33	25,100	9,700	109
Algoma District	-0.10	51.1	0.42	-0.02	126.5	2,479.4	0.38	48,500	19,600	93	1,368.5	0.49	26,800	10,800	121
Northwest	2.09	97.0	0.80	0.42	251.1	5,388.1	0.82	55,500	21,500	102	2,445.9	0.88	25,200	9,700	109
Thunder Bay District	1.26	63.6	0.53	0.25	159.1	3,606.4	0.55	56,700	22,700	108	1,495.0	0.54	23,500	9,400	105
Rainy River District	1.70	9.2	0.08	0.34	23.6	474.5	0.07	51,600	20,100	95	243.3	0.09	26,400	10,300	115
Kenora District	4.49	24.2	0.20	0.88	68.4	1,307.2	0.20	54,000	19,100	91	707.5	0.25	29,200	10,300	116
MANITOBA	4.00	445.9	3.69	0.79	1,155.4	22,747.3	3.47	51,000	19,700	93	9,652.6	3.46	21,600	8,400	93
Southeast	8.78	31.5	0.26	1.70	89.3	1,644.9	0.25	52,300	18,400	87	673.5	0.24	21,400	7,500	84
Division No. 1	6.15	7.0	0.06	1.20	16.9	321.2	0.05	45,700	19,000	90	116.9	0.04	16,600	6,900	77
Division No. 2	9.84	17.1	0.14	1.89	52.4	895.6	0.14	52,200	17,100	81	441.3	0.16	25,700	8,400	94
Division No. 12	8.93	7.3	0.06	1.72	20.0	428.1	0.07	58,800	21,400	101	115.3	0.04	15,800	5,800	64
South Central	3.87	18.4	0.15	0.76	53.3	852.0	0.13	46,200	16,000	76	416.6	0.15	22,600	7,800	87
Division No. 3	5.29	14.8	0.12	1.04	43.0	697.2	0.11	47,100	16,200	77	373.8	0.13	25,300	8,700	97
Division No. 4	-1.48	3.7	0.03	-0.30	10.3	154.8	0.02	42,400	15,000	71	42.8	0.02	11,700	4,100	46
Southwest	1.75	42.7	0.35	0.35	106.6	1,885.4	0.29	44,200	17,700	84	1,144.1	0.41	26,800	10,700	120
Division No. 5	-0.58	5.8	0.05	-0.12	14.6	250.6	0.04	43,100	17,200	81	151.4	0.05	26,100	10,400	116
Division No. 6	0.63	4.0	0.03	0.13	10.7	153.3	0.02	38,300	14,300	68	87.5	0.03	21,800	8,100	91
Division No. 7	2.97	23.7	0.20	0.59	58.5	1,111.1	0.17	46,900	19,000	90	749.3	0.27	31,600	12,800	143
Division No. 15	0.66	9.2	0.08	0.13	22.8	370.4	0.06	40,400	16,300	77	155.9	0.06	17,000	6,800	77
North Central	3.53	16.5	0.14	0.70	49.0	776.9	0.12	47,100	15,800	75	450.8	0.16	27,300	9,200	103
Division No. 8	3.52	5.1	0.04	0.69	15.5	193.3	0.03	38,200	12,500	59	76.0	0.03	15,000	4,900	55
Division No. 9	-0.37	8.4	0.07	-0.07	23.5	380.4	0.06	45,100	16,200	77	317.8	0.11	37,600	13,500	151
Division No. 10	16.34	3.0	0.02	3.07	10.1	203.2	0.03	67,600	20,100	95	57.0	0.02	19,000	5,600	63

*Halton Regional Municipality is split between two economic regions. Data are for both parts.

	'96 to '01 Hhld. Change %	Total No. (000s)	% Canadian Total	Avg. Annual Rate of Growth %	Total Pop. (000s)	Total Millions $	% Canadian Total	Per Hhld. $	Per Capita $	Income Rating Index	Total Millions $	% Canadian Total	Per Hhld. $	Per Capita $	Market Rating Index
Winnipeg	2.83	259.0	2.14	0.56	633.0	13,715.7	2.09	52,900	21,700	103	5,422.1	1.95	20,900	8,600	96
Division No. 11	2.83	259.0	2.14	0.56	633.0	13,715.7	2.09	52,900	21,700	103	5,422.1	1.95	20,900	8,600	96
Interlake	9.52	31.0	0.26	1.84	85.9	1,724.6	0.26	55,600	20,100	95	546.4	0.20	17,600	6,400	71
Division No. 13	10.35	15.4	0.13	1.99	43.6	1,006.3	0.15	65,200	23,100	109	282.5	0.10	18,300	6,500	72
Division No. 14	11.90	6.4	0.05	2.27	18.7	356.8	0.05	55,400	19,100	90	66.5	0.02	10,300	3,600	40
Division No. 18	6.57	9.2	0.08	1.28	23.6	361.5	0.06	39,500	15,300	73	197.5	0.07	21,600	8,400	94
Parklands	-0.82	18.7	0.15	-0.16	46.1	720.3	0.11	38,500	15,600	74	442.1	0.16	23,600	9,600	107
Division No. 16	1.09	4.3	0.04	0.22	10.9	162.0	0.02	38,100	14,800	70	105.8	0.04	24,800	9,700	108
Division No. 17	-1.39	9.8	0.08	-0.28	23.6	378.0	0.06	38,400	16,000	76	199.9	0.07	20,300	8,500	95
Division No. 20	-1.30	4.6	0.04	-0.26	11.6	180.2	0.03	39,000	15,600	74	136.4	0.05	29,500	11,800	132
North	11.67	28.0	0.23	2.23	92.1	1,427.5	0.22	51,000	15,500	74	557.0	0.20	19,900	6,000	68
Division No. 19	19.80	5.1	0.04	3.68	17.9	148.8	0.02	29,000	8,300	39	41.1	0.01	8,000	2,300	26
Division No. 21	4.36	8.6	0.07	0.86	23.9	475.6	0.07	55,200	19,900	94	209.8	0.08	24,400	8,800	98
Division No. 22	15.29	11.4	0.09	2.89	40.1	629.9	0.10	55,500	15,700	74	261.4	0.09	23,000	6,500	73
Division No. 23	7.88	2.9	0.02	1.53	10.1	173.2	0.03	59,100	17,100	81	44.8	0.02	15,300	4,400	49
SASKATCHEWAN	4.13	402.7	3.33	0.81	1,034.3	19,435.7	2.96	48,300	18,800	89	8,157.3	2.93	20,300	7,900	88
Regina - Moose Mountain	3.96	114.0	0.94	0.78	285.5	6,089.4	0.93	53,400	21,300	101	2,429.8	0.87	21,300	8,500	95
Division No. 1	3.31	13.0	0.11	0.65	33.6	693.6	0.11	53,200	20,600	98	231.4	0.08	17,700	6,900	77
Division No. 2	0.51	9.4	0.08	0.10	23.1	458.2	0.07	49,000	19,900	94	130.6	0.05	14,000	5,700	63
Division No. 6	4.42	91.6	0.76	0.87	228.8	4,937.6	0.75	53,900	21,600	102	2,067.8	0.74	22,600	9,000	101
Swift Current - Moose Jaw	0.87	44.2	0.37	0.17	110.0	2,098.6	0.32	47,500	19,100	90	851.3	0.31	19,300	7,700	86
Division No. 3	-2.05	6.3	0.05	-0.41	15.9	294.0	0.04	46,600	18,500	88	136.0	0.05	21,500	8,600	96
Division No. 4	0.06	4.6	0.04	0.01	12.2	209.2	0.03	45,000	17,100	81	62.1	0.02	13,400	5,100	57
Division No. 7	1.64	20.2	0.17	0.33	49.8	946.4	0.14	46,900	19,000	90	373.8	0.13	18,500	7,500	84
Division No. 8	1.43	13.1	0.11	0.28	32.1	649.0	0.10	49,700	20,200	96	279.5	0.10	21,400	8,700	97
Saskatoon - Biggar	6.38	119.2	0.99	1.24	298.6	5,980.3	0.91	50,200	20,000	95	2,343.4	0.84	19,700	7,800	88
Division No. 11	7.03	100.2	0.83	1.37	247.8	5,060.3	0.77	50,500	20,400	97	2,021.7	0.73	20,200	8,200	91
Division No. 12	3.18	9.2	0.08	0.63	25.2	441.5	0.07	47,700	17,500	83	121.5	0.04	13,100	4,800	54
Division No. 13	2.96	9.7	0.08	0.58	25.6	478.5	0.07	49,400	18,700	89	200.2	0.07	20,700	7,800	87
Yorkton - Melville	-2.17	37.9	0.31	-0.44	93.5	1,456.8	0.22	38,500	15,600	74	680.7	0.24	18,000	7,300	81
Division No. 5	-1.79	13.9	0.12	-0.36	34.7	577.2	0.09	41,500	16,600	79	256.9	0.09	18,500	7,400	83
Division No. 9	-2.82	15.8	0.13	-0.57	38.1	589.5	0.09	37,300	15,500	73	282.8	0.10	17,900	7,400	83
Division No. 10	-1.55	8.2	0.07	-0.31	20.7	290.2	0.04	35,400	14,000	67	141.0	0.05	17,200	6,800	76
Prince Albert	4.69	77.6	0.64	0.92	210.0	3,392.1	0.52	43,700	16,200	77	1,718.4	0.62	22,100	8,200	91
Division No. 14	-0.56	16.2	0.13	-0.11	41.1	661.5	0.10	40,800	16,100	76	301.8	0.11	18,600	7,300	82
Division No. 15	4.78	31.5	0.26	0.94	85.1	1,467.0	0.22	46,600	17,200	82	772.0	0.28	24,500	9,100	101
Division No. 16	3.72	14.8	0.12	0.73	39.5	602.0	0.09	40,700	15,200	72	303.0	0.11	20,500	7,700	86
Division No. 17	11.78	15.2	0.13	2.25	44.3	661.6	0.10	43,500	14,900	71	341.7	0.12	22,500	7,700	86
Northern	17.72	9.8	0.08	3.32	36.7	418.6	0.06	42,600	11,400	54	133.7	0.05	13,600	3,600	41
Division No. 18	17.72	9.8	0.08	3.32	36.7	418.6	0.06	42,600	11,400	54	133.7	0.05	13,600	3,600	41
ALBERTA	13.67	1,153.3	9.54	2.60	3,065.6	68,436.5	10.43	59,300	22,300	106	31,754.6	11.39	27,500	10,400	116
Lethbridge - Medicine Hat	9.22	90.1	0.75	1.78	246.7	4,481.9	0.68	49,800	18,200	86	3,457.2	1.24	38,400	14,000	157
Division No. 1	10.37	26.8	0.22	1.99	69.0	1,362.5	0.21	50,800	19,700	94	876.6	0.31	32,700	12,700	142
Division No. 2	9.93	50.6	0.42	1.91	137.8	2,557.2	0.39	50,500	18,600	88	2,334.7	0.84	46,100	16,900	189
Division No. 3	4.23	12.7	0.10	0.83	39.9	562.2	0.09	44,400	14,100	67	245.9	0.09	19,400	6,200	69
Drumheller - Stettler - Wainwright	6.70	37.0	0.31	1.31	104.1	1,866.9	0.28	50,400	17,900	85	838.8	0.30	22,700	8,100	90
Division No. 4	-1.70	4.3	0.04	-0.34	11.8	223.5	0.03	51,400	18,900	90	107.9	0.04	24,800	9,100	102
Division No. 5	10.82	16.6	0.14	2.08	48.7	827.4	0.13	49,900	17,000	81	338.9	0.12	20,400	7,000	78
Division No. 7	5.10	16.1	0.13	1.00	43.6	816.0	0.12	50,800	18,700	89	392.1	0.14	24,400	9,000	100
Calgary	19.14	401.1	3.32	3.56	1,049.5	26,909.3	4.10	67,100	25,600	122	10,863.6	3.90	27,100	10,400	116
Division No. 6	19.14	401.1	3.32	3.56	1,049.5	26,909.3	4.10	67,100	25,600	122	10,863.6	3.90	27,100	10,400	116
Athabasca - Jasper - Banff	11.71	49.8	0.41	2.24	133.0	2,694.6	0.41	54,100	20,300	96	1,390.6	0.50	27,900	10,500	117
Division No. 13	8.21	24.9	0.21	1.59	67.6	1,250.8	0.19	50,200	18,500	88	605.3	0.22	24,300	9,000	100
Division No. 14	11.24	11.2	0.09	2.15	30.1	636.8	0.10	57,100	21,200	100	304.1	0.11	27,300	10,100	113
Division No. 15	19.13	13.7	0.11	3.56	35.4	807.0	0.12	58,800	22,800	108	481.1	0.17	35,000	13,600	152
Red Deer - Rocky Mountain House	12.74	65.3	0.54	2.43	177.7	3,561.3	0.54	54,600	20,000	95	2,180.2	0.78	33,400	12,300	137
Division No. 8	12.60	57.9	0.48	2.40	157.4	3,189.0	0.49	55,100	20,300	96	1,974.5	0.71	34,100	12,500	140
Division No. 9	13.80	7.4	0.06	2.62	20.3	372.3	0.06	50,500	18,300	87	205.7	0.07	27,900	10,100	113
Edmonton	11.51	383.3	3.17	2.20	996.0	21,808.5	3.32	56,900	21,900	104	9,396.8	3.37	24,500	9,400	105
Division No. 11	11.51	383.3	3.17	2.20	996.0	21,808.5	3.32	56,900	21,900	104	9,396.8	3.37	24,500	9,400	105
Grande Prairie - Peace River	13.94	57.8	0.48	2.65	169.0	3,298.6	0.50	57,100	19,500	93	1,639.9	0.59	28,400	9,700	108
Division No. 17	15.23	20.0	0.17	2.87	63.5	1,067.2	0.16	53,300	16,800	80	476.1	0.17	23,800	7,500	84
Division No. 18	12.21	5.6	0.05	2.33	16.2	331.6	0.05	59,300	20,400	97	94.6	0.03	16,900	5,800	65
Division No. 19	13.46	32.2	0.27	2.56	89.3	1,899.8	0.29	59,100	21,300	101	1,069.2	0.38	33,200	12,000	134
Wood Buffalo - Camrose	7.95	69.0	0.57	1.54	189.5	3,815.6	0.58	55,300	20,100	95	1,987.7	0.71	28,800	10,500	117
Division No. 10	4.48	32.1	0.27	0.88	83.7	1,520.6	0.23	47,400	18,200	86	899.5	0.32	28,000	10,700	120
Division No. 12	8.08	22.1	0.18	1.57	65.3	1,108.5	0.17	50,100	17,000	80	605.2	0.22	27,300	9,300	103
Division No. 16	16.12	14.8	0.12	3.03	40.5	1,186.4	0.18	80,200	29,300	139	483.0	0.17	32,700	11,900	133

1 – By Province, Economic Region and Census Division	'96 to '01 Hhld. Change %	Total No. (000s)	% Canadian Total	Avg. Annual Rate of Growth %	Total Pop. (000s)	Total Millions $	% Canadian Totall	Per Hhld. $	Per Capita $	Income Rating Index	Total Millions $	% Canadian Total	Per Hhld. $	Per Capita $	Market Rating Index
BRITISH COLUMBIA	9.54	1,636.6	13.54	1.84	4,137.4	87,782.5	13.37	53,600	21,200	101	36,141.4	12.97	22,100	8,700	98
Vancouver Island and Coast	5.59	306.2	2.53	1.09	726.2	15,032.8	2.29	49,100	20,700	98	5,874.5	2.11	19,200	8,100	90
Capital Regional District	3.44	146.8	1.21	0.68	335.7	7,522.5	1.15	51,200	22,400	106	2,818.6	1.01	19,200	8,400	94
Cowichan Valley Regional District	7.73	30.5	0.25	1.50	77.9	1,418.2	0.22	46,500	18,200	86	488.9	0.18	16,000	6,300	70
Nanaimo Regional District	10.48	57.1	0.47	2.01	136.1	2,665.2	0.41	46,700	19,600	93	1,057.5	0.38	18,500	7,800	87
Alberni-Clayoquot Regional District	-0.71	12.7	0.10	-0.14	31.1	568.6	0.09	44,900	18,300	87	243.0	0.09	19,200	7,800	87
Comox-Strathcona Regional District	9.16	43.4	0.36	1.77	107.1	2,099.2	0.32	48,400	19,600	93	938.2	0.34	21,600	8,800	98
Powell River Regional District	1.98	8.7	0.07	0.39	20.4	394.7	0.06	45,600	19,300	92	189.9	0.07	21,900	9,300	104
Mount Waddington Regional District	0.34	5.7	0.05	0.07	14.2	308.9	0.05	54,600	21,800	103	110.8	0.04	19,600	7,800	87
Central Coast Regional District	-0.07	1.4	0.01	-0.01	3.8	55.4	0.01	39,800	14,400	68	27.5	0.01	19,800	7,200	80
Lower Mainland - Southwest	12.09	934.5	7.73	2.31	2,407.9	53,624.6	8.17	57,400	22,300	106	20,127.6	7.22	21,500	8,400	93
Fraser Valley Regional District	10.41	91.0	0.75	2.00	251.0	4,479.5	0.68	49,200	17,800	85	2,199.0	0.79	24,200	8,800	98
Greater Vancouver Regional District	12.19	816.8	6.76	2.33	2,092.7	47,738.1	7.27	58,400	22,800	108	17,323.8	6.22	21,200	8,300	92
Sunshine Coast Regional District	9.58	12.0	0.10	1.85	27.9	559.6	0.09	46,800	20,100	95	255.9	0.09	21,400	9,200	102
Squamish-Lillooet Regional District	19.60	14.7	0.12	3.64	36.2	847.5	0.13	57,700	23,400	111	348.8	0.13	23,800	9,600	108
Thompson - Okanagan	8.70	200.9	1.66	1.68	495.8	9,184.0	1.40	45,700	18,500	88	5,068.0	1.82	25,200	10,200	114
Okanagan-Similkameen Regional District	4.15	35.0	0.29	0.82	81.2	1,427.3	0.22	40,800	17,600	83	690.8	0.25	19,800	8,500	95
Thompson-Nicola Regional District	8.76	50.8	0.42	1.69	128.2	2,494.0	0.38	49,100	19,500	92	1,296.4	0.47	25,500	10,100	113
Central Okanagan Regional District	12.45	63.0	0.52	2.38	156.7	3,029.4	0.46	48,100	19,300	92	1,845.9	0.66	29,300	11,800	132
North Okanagan Regional District	7.81	31.1	0.26	1.51	78.0	1,334.8	0.20	43,000	17,100	81	692.7	0.25	22,300	8,900	99
Columbia-Shuswap Regional District	6.97	21.1	0.17	1.36	51.8	898.6	0.14	42,600	17,300	82	542.3	0.19	25,700	10,500	117
Kootenay	4.69	64.0	0.53	0.92	154.3	2,823.8	0.43	44,100	18,300	87	1,860.7	0.67	29,100	12,100	135
East Kootenay Regional District	6.64	24.4	0.20	1.29	59.5	1,181.8	0.18	48,500	19,900	94	826.5	0.30	33,900	13,900	155
Central Kootenay Regional District	5.03	25.6	0.21	0.99	61.5	1,026.1	0.16	40,100	16,700	79	694.8	0.25	27,200	11,300	126
Kootenay Boundary Regional District	0.90	14.1	0.12	0.18	33.3	615.9	0.09	43,700	18,500	88	339.4	0.12	24,100	10,200	114
Cariboo	6.50	65.9	0.55	1.27	174.4	3,588.4	0.55	54,500	20,600	98	1,619.0	0.58	24,600	9,300	104
Cariboo Regional District	6.58	27.1	0.22	1.28	71.0	1,307.6	0.20	48,200	18,400	87	618.9	0.22	22,800	8,700	97
Fraser-Fort George Regional District	6.45	38.8	0.32	1.26	103.4	2,280.8	0.35	58,800	22,100	105	1,000.1	0.36	25,800	9,700	108
North Coast	1.37	24.8	0.21	0.27	68.1	1,358.8	0.21	54,800	19,900	95	501.4	0.18	20,200	7,400	82
Skeena-Queen Charlotte Regional District	-4.02	8.8	0.07	-0.82	23.7	461.0	0.07	52,500	19,400	92	169.0	0.06	19,300	7,100	80
Kitimat-Stikine Regional District	4.60	16.0	0.13	0.90	44.4	897.8	0.14	56,100	20,200	96	332.4	0.12	20,800	7,500	84
Nechako	7.13	16.6	0.14	1.39	45.5	890.8	0.14	53,700	19,600	93	402.4	0.14	24,300	8,800	99
Bulkley-Nechako Regional District	7.62	16.0	0.13	1.48	44.4	868.3	0.13	54,200	19,600	93	391.5	0.14	24,400	8,800	99
Stikine Region	-5.22	0.6	0.00	-1.07	1.2	22.5	0.00	40,000	19,100	91	10.9	0.00	19,300	9,200	103
Northeast	5.12	23.8	0.20	1.00	65.0	1,279.2	0.19	53,800	19,700	93	687.8	0.25	28,900	10,600	118
Peace River Regional District	4.79	21.6	0.18	0.94	58.7	1,148.8	0.18	53,100	19,600	93	641.7	0.23	29,700	10,900	122
Fort Nelson-Liard Regional District	8.48	2.2	0.02	1.64	6.4	130.5	0.02	60,000	20,500	97	46.0	0.02	21,200	7,200	81
NORTHWEST TERRITORIES	7.07	14.4	0.12	1.38	42.2	1,029.0	0.16	71,700	24,400	116	128.7	0.05	9,000	3,000	34
Fort Smith Region	8.53	11.2	0.09	1.65	32.5	845.9	0.13	75,700	26,000	123	111.8	0.04	10,000	3,400	38
Inuvik Region	2.22	3.2	0.03	0.44	9.7	183.1	0.03	57,700	19,000	90	16.9	0.01	5,300	1,700	20
NUNAVUT	12.31	7.4	0.06	2.35	28.2	409.3	0.06	55,500	14,500	69	42.3	0.02	5,700	1,500	17
Baffin Region	10.63	4.0	0.03	2.04	15.4	232.0	0.04	58,000	15,100	72	25.6	0.01	6,400	1,700	19
Keewatin Region	18.90	2.0	0.02	3.52	7.6	110.8	0.02	54,400	14,500	69	11.2	0.00	5,500	1,500	16
Kitikmeot Region	8.11	1.3	0.01	1.57	5.2	66.5	0.01	49,400	12,900	61	5.5	0.00	4,100	1,100	12
YUKON TERRITORY	3.00	12.4	0.10	0.59	31.4	731.2	0.11	59,100	23,300	111	166.9	0.06	13,500	5,300	59

2 – Estimates by Province and Urban Market

	Households July 1, 2001				Income 2001					Retail Sales 2001				
	'96 to '01 Hhld. Change %	Total No. (000s)	% Canadian Total	Avg. Annual Rate of Growth %	Total Pop. (000s)	Total Millions $	% Canadian Total	Per Hhld. $	Per Capita $	Income Rating Index	Total Millions $	% Canadian Total	Per Hhld. $	Per Capita $	Market Rating Index
CANADA	7.82	12,084.9	100.00	1.52	31,134.5	656,440.2	100.00	54,300	21,100	100	278,705.8	100.00	23,100	9,000	100
NEWFOUNDLAND	2.68	195.4	1.62	0.53	533.2	9,074.4	1.38	46,400	17,000	81	4,628.5	1.66	23,700	8,700	97
Corner Brook, CA	2.78	10.3	0.09	0.55	27.2	490.4	0.07	47,700	18,100	86	338.1	0.12	32,900	12,500	139
Gander, CA	2.51	4.5	0.04	0.50	11.8	240.0	0.04	53,900	20,400	97	197.1	0.07	44,200	16,800	187
Grand Falls-Windsor, CA	1.22	7.2	0.06	0.24	19.5	345.6	0.05	47,900	17,700	84	302.2	0.11	41,900	15,500	173
Labrador City, CA	3.66	3.6	0.03	0.72	10.0	258.8	0.04	70,900	25,900	123	98.5	0.04	27,000	9,900	110
St. John's, CMA	5.27	65.4	0.54	1.03	173.8	3,521.0	0.54	53,800	20,300	96	1,904.7	0.68	29,100	11,000	122
PRINCE EDWARD ISLAND	5.58	52.0	0.43	1.09	138.2	2,331.7	0.36	44,900	16,900	80	1,205.9	0.43	23,200	8,700	97
Charlottetown, CA	7.18	22.9	0.19	1.40	59.6	1,066.9	0.16	46,500	17,900	85	666.1	0.24	29,000	11,200	125
Summerside, CA	6.56	6.6	0.05	1.28	16.4	287.5	0.04	43,500	17,500	83	263.8	0.09	39,900	16,000	179
NOVA SCOTIA	5.23	371.6	3.07	1.03	947.6	17,180.6	2.62	46,200	18,100	86	8,693.8	3.12	23,400	9,200	102
Cape Breton, CA	0.22	43.7	0.36	0.04	115.5	1,725.7	0.26	39,500	14,900	71	999.2	0.36	22,900	8,600	97
Halifax, CMA	9.14	144.1	1.19	1.77	361.4	7,707.8	1.17	53,500	21,300	101	3,529.7	1.27	24,500	9,800	109
Kentville, CA	7.12	10.5	0.09	1.39	26.6	468.4	0.07	44,700	17,600	83	312.6	0.11	29,800	11,700	131
New Glasgow, CA	2.20	15.0	0.12	0.44	38.3	632.1	0.10	42,300	16,500	78	400.1	0.14	26,800	10,400	117
Truro, CA	5.66	18.4	0.15	1.11	46.3	786.4	0.12	42,800	17,000	81	555.3	0.20	30,300	12,000	134
NEW BRUNSWICK	5.29	293.2	2.43	1.04	759.1	13,511.2	2.06	46,100	17,800	84	7,095.9	2.55	24,200	9,300	104
Bathurst, CA	3.34	10.1	0.08	0.66	25.4	454.8	0.07	45,000	17,900	85	487.0	0.17	48,200	19,200	214
Campbellton, CA	2.27	6.5	0.05	0.45	16.6	261.5	0.04	40,200	15,700	75	213.2	0.08	32,800	12,800	143
Edmundston, CA	5.75	9.4	0.08	1.12	23.0	405.2	0.06	42,900	17,600	83	240.5	0.09	25,500	10,400	117
Fredericton, CA	7.66	33.4	0.28	1.49	83.2	1,796.6	0.27	53,800	21,600	102	1,046.3	0.38	31,300	12,600	140
Moncton, CA	8.14	47.4	0.39	1.58	120.1	2,431.7	0.37	51,300	20,300	96	1,259.2	0.45	26,600	10,500	117
Saint John, CMA	3.23	49.7	0.41	0.64	128.1	2,461.0	0.37	49,500	19,200	91	1,057.5	0.38	21,300	8,300	92
QUÉBEC	5.55	3,063.9	25.35	1.09	7,445.1	143,773.8	21.90	46,900	19,300	92	64,688.8	23.21	21,100	8,700	97
Alma, CA	5.23	12.0	0.10	1.02	30.8	541.8	0.08	45,000	17,600	84	356.0	0.13	29,600	11,600	129
Baie-Comeau, CA	2.29	12.4	0.10	0.45	31.0	673.4	0.10	54,100	21,700	103	228.3	0.08	18,400	7,400	82
Chicoutimi-Jonquière, CMA	5.44	64.7	0.54	1.07	162.5	2,829.1	0.43	43,700	17,400	83	1,474.9	0.53	22,800	9,100	101
Cowansville, CA	10.03	5.3	0.04	1.93	12.3	208.0	0.03	39,300	17,000	80	183.8	0.07	34,800	15,000	167
Dolbeau, CA	5.59	5.9	0.05	1.09	15.3	246.2	0.04	41,500	16,100	76	165.2	0.06	27,900	10,800	121
Drummondville, CA	9.49	29.6	0.24	1.83	69.5	1,227.4	0.19	41,500	17,700	84	895.8	0.32	30,300	12,900	144
Granby, CA	8.12	26.6	0.22	1.57	62.0	1,175.9	0.18	44,300	19,000	90	792.2	0.28	29,800	12,800	143
Joliette, CA	5.89	15.4	0.13	1.15	35.6	638.2	0.10	41,400	17,900	85	686.7	0.25	44,600	19,300	216
La Tuque, CA	4.00	5.8	0.05	0.79	13.0	249.6	0.04	42,900	19,300	91	127.7	0.05	21,900	9,900	110
Lachute, CA	-5.29	5.3	0.04	-1.08	12.8	191.6	0.03	36,200	15,000	71	118.4	0.04	22,400	9,300	104
Magog, CA	9.22	9.8	0.08	1.78	22.8	406.4	0.06	41,500	17,800	84	241.8	0.09	24,700	10,600	118
Matane, CA	1.64	7.2	0.06	0.33	16.6	291.0	0.04	40,200	17,500	83	217.7	0.08	30,100	13,100	146
Montréal, CMA	5.37	1,451.5	12.01	1.05	3,500.8	72,022.9	10.97	49,600	20,600	98	28,737.3	10.31	19,800	8,200	92
Québec, CMA	5.45	299.9	2.48	1.07	693.2	14,766.7	2.25	49,200	21,300	101	7,599.5	2.73	25,300	11,000	122
Rimouski, CA	5.49	21.0	0.17	1.07	48.9	1,010.7	0.15	48,000	20,600	98	500.7	0.18	23,800	10,200	114
Rivière-du-Loup, CA	1.92	9.9	0.08	0.38	24.3	420.2	0.06	42,500	17,300	82	393.4	0.14	39,800	16,200	181
Rouyn-Noranda, CA	5.03	17.0	0.14	0.99	39.6	800.3	0.12	47,100	20,200	96	417.0	0.15	24,600	10,500	118
Saint-Georges, CA	9.71	11.3	0.09	1.87	28.3	499.9	0.08	44,100	17,600	84	432.3	0.16	38,200	15,300	170
Saint-Hyacinthe, CA	4.01	22.1	0.18	0.79	50.6	920.2	0.14	41,700	18,200	86	694.9	0.25	31,500	13,700	153
Saint-Jean-sur-Richelieu, CA	7.01	33.2	0.27	1.36	80.7	1,490.3	0.23	44,900	18,500	88	942.8	0.34	28,400	11,700	130
Salaberry-de-Valleyfield, CA	1.23	16.9	0.14	0.24	39.2	673.0	0.10	39,800	17,200	81	510.8	0.18	30,200	13,000	145
Sept-Îles, CA	6.17	11.7	0.10	1.20	28.9	607.8	0.09	51,900	21,000	100	277.2	0.10	23,700	9,600	107
Shawinigan, CA	1.57	26.3	0.22	0.31	59.6	990.1	0.15	37,600	16,600	79	492.5	0.18	18,700	8,300	92
Sherbrooke, CMA	7.23	68.2	0.56	1.41	155.8	2,898.6	0.44	42,500	18,600	88	1,311.3	0.47	19,200	8,400	94
Sorel, CA	0.63	18.1	0.15	0.13	41.9	781.7	0.12	43,300	18,600	88	439.7	0.16	24,300	10,500	117
Thetford Mines, CA	1.26	11.6	0.10	0.25	27.1	464.7	0.07	40,100	17,100	81	352.8	0.13	30,500	13,000	145
Trois-Rivières, CMA	4.56	62.6	0.52	0.90	142.8	2,720.0	0.41	43,500	19,100	90	1,146.7	0.41	18,300	8,000	90
Val-d'Or, CA	5.88	13.9	0.11	1.15	33.6	679.4	0.10	49,000	20,200	96	432.2	0.16	31,200	12,900	144
Victoriaville, CA	8.16	17.7	0.15	1.58	42.6	729.9	0.11	41,200	17,100	81	560.2	0.20	31,600	13,100	147

	'96 to '01 Hhld. Change %	Total No. (000s)	% Canadian Total	Avg. Annual Rate of Growth %	Total Pop. (000s)	Total Millions $	% Canadian Total	Per Hhld. $	Per Capita $	Income Rating Index	Total Millions $	% Canadian Total	Per Hhld. $	Per Capita $	Market Rating Index
		Households July 1, 2001				Income 2001					Retail Sales 2001				
ONTARIO	8.76	4,436.2	36.71	1.69	11,817.0	269,996.8	41.13	60,900	22,800	108	106,349.4	38.16	24,000	9,000	101
Barrie, CA	21.92	53.1	0.44	4.04	146.0	2,967.8	0.45	55,900	20,300	96	1,575.5	0.57	29,700	10,800	121
Belleville, CA	1.24	38.1	0.32	0.25	96.4	1,934.9	0.29	50,800	20,100	95	1,170.9	0.42	30,700	12,200	136
Brantford, CA	4.38	42.3	0.35	0.86	111.5	2,159.1	0.33	51,100	19,400	92	922.6	0.33	21,800	8,300	92
Brockville, CA	1.64	17.3	0.14	0.33	43.6	855.4	0.13	49,300	19,600	93	426.0	0.15	24,600	9,800	109
Chatham, CA	1.35	26.8	0.22	0.27	67.7	1,371.7	0.21	51,200	20,300	96	880.5	0.32	32,900	13,000	145
Cobourg, CA	8.02	7.1	0.06	1.55	17.2	366.7	0.06	51,900	21,300	101	199.4	0.07	28,200	11,600	129
Collingwood, CA	6.54	7.1	0.06	1.28	17.2	321.8	0.05	45,400	18,700	89	220.2	0.08	31,100	12,800	143
Cornwall, CA	1.63	25.8	0.21	0.32	64.0	1,159.5	0.18	45,000	18,100	86	758.0	0.27	29,400	11,800	132
Elliot Lake, CA	-2.27	5.8	0.05	-0.46	13.5	248.2	0.04	43,000	18,400	87	104.9	0.04	18,200	7,800	87
Guelph, CA	11.27	45.2	0.37	2.16	118.2	2,726.3	0.42	60,300	23,100	109	1,341.6	0.48	29,700	11,400	127
Haileybury, CA	-3.48	5.2	0.04	-0.71	13.3	255.3	0.04	48,700	19,300	91	261.7	0.09	49,900	19,800	221
Hamilton, CMA	6.71	259.6	2.15	1.31	673.7	15,500.5	2.36	59,700	23,000	109	5,465.9	1.96	21,100	8,100	91
Hawkesbury, CA	4.57	5.1	0.04	0.90	12.1	193.7	0.03	37,800	16,000	76	234.9	0.08	45,800	19,400	217
Kenora, CA	5.71	7.1	0.06	1.12	17.6	402.6	0.06	56,800	22,900	108	256.6	0.09	36,200	14,600	163
Kingston, CA	4.35	60.1	0.50	0.86	147.5	3,314.4	0.50	55,100	22,500	107	1,369.2	0.49	22,800	9,300	104
Kitchener, CMA	11.75	163.4	1.35	2.25	428.9	9,742.3	1.48	59,600	22,700	108	4,550.0	1.63	27,800	10,600	118
Leamington, CA	9.55	16.1	0.13	1.84	44.4	938.1	0.14	58,100	21,100	100	406.3	0.15	25,200	9,200	102
Lindsay, CA	9.12	9.7	0.08	1.76	23.5	445.1	0.07	45,900	19,000	90	392.5	0.14	40,500	16,700	187
London, CMA	5.77	172.7	1.43	1.13	426.3	9,556.4	1.46	55,300	22,400	106	4,355.1	1.56	25,200	10,200	114
Midland, CA	8.15	14.2	0.12	1.58	35.7	661.7	0.10	46,400	18,500	88	331.7	0.12	23,300	9,300	104
North Bay, CA	0.97	26.0	0.22	0.19	64.0	1,277.1	0.19	49,100	19,900	95	807.7	0.29	31,000	12,600	141
Orillia, CA	13.17	17.2	0.14	2.51	42.9	799.5	0.12	46,400	18,600	88	419.0	0.15	24,300	9,800	109
Oshawa, CMA	13.15	109.5	0.91	2.50	304.8	7,151.3	1.09	65,300	23,500	111	2,433.5	0.87	22,200	8,000	89
Ottawa-Hull, CMA	8.07	431.9	3.57	1.56	1,085.9	27,101.5	4.13	62,800	25,000	118	10,000.2	3.59	23,200	9,200	103
Owen Sound, CA	2.32	12.7	0.10	0.46	30.5	575.8	0.09	45,400	18,900	89	439.4	0.16	34,700	14,400	161
Pembroke, CA	3.57	9.9	0.08	0.70	24.8	453.3	0.07	45,600	18,300	87	316.5	0.11	31,800	12,800	143
Peterborough, CA	6.43	42.4	0.35	1.25	106.3	2,145.6	0.33	50,600	20,200	96	1,085.9	0.39	25,600	10,200	114
Port Hope, CA	4.10	4.8	0.04	0.81	12.1	250.3	0.04	52,500	20,700	98	104.5	0.04	21,900	8,600	96
Sarnia, CA	0.73	35.0	0.29	0.15	86.5	1,966.3	0.30	56,200	22,700	108	818.3	0.29	23,400	9,500	106
Sault Ste. Marie, CA	0.41	34.1	0.28	0.08	84.2	1,707.9	0.26	50,100	20,300	96	1,001.0	0.36	29,400	11,900	133
Simcoe, CA	3.67	6.5	0.05	0.72	15.8	332.4	0.05	51,000	21,100	100	315.3	0.11	48,400	20,000	223
Smiths Falls, CA	3.39	6.6	0.05	0.67	16.9	319.6	0.05	48,100	19,000	90	190.3	0.07	28,700	11,300	126
St. Catharines-Niagara, CMA	5.63	158.1	1.31	1.10	395.6	8,083.0	1.23	51,100	20,400	97	4,003.5	1.44	25,300	10,100	113
Stratford, CA	3.89	12.6	0.10	0.77	30.5	652.6	0.10	51,600	21,400	101	515.9	0.19	40,800	16,900	189
Strathroy, CA	12.23	4.9	0.04	2.34	13.2	258.8	0.04	52,800	19,600	93	217.8	0.08	44,500	16,500	184
Sudbury, CMA	1.48	64.9	0.54	0.29	159.5	3,493.5	0.53	53,800	21,900	104	1,763.4	0.63	27,200	11,100	124
Thunder Bay, CMA	2.26	51.9	0.43	0.45	127.5	2,887.4	0.44	55,600	22,600	107	1,264.7	0.45	24,400	9,900	111
Tillsonburg, CA	9.21	6.0	0.05	1.78	14.5	303.5	0.05	50,200	20,900	99	118.9	0.04	19,700	8,200	91
Timmins, CA	2.32	18.7	0.15	0.46	47.3	987.8	0.15	52,900	20,900	99	452.9	0.16	24,300	9,600	107
Toronto, CMA	12.65	1,738.3	14.38	2.41	4,867.6	118,824.7	18.10	68,400	24,400	116	40,759.1	14.62	23,400	8,400	94
Windsor, CMA	10.03	121.1	1.00	1.93	308.8	7,368.2	1.12	60,900	23,900	113	3,246.5	1.16	26,800	10,500	117
Woodstock, CA	6.57	13.9	0.11	1.28	34.4	693.6	0.11	50,100	20,100	96	355.3	0.13	25,600	10,300	115
MANITOBA	4.00	445.9	3.69	0.79	1,155.4	22,747.3	3.47	51,000	19,700	93	9,652.6	3.46	21,600	8,400	93
Brandon, CA	3.82	17.5	0.14	0.75	41.5	811.0	0.12	46,300	19,500	93	666.5	0.24	38,000	16,000	179
Portage la Prairie, CA	-0.53	7.5	0.06	-0.11	20.5	329.9	0.05	44,300	16,100	76	306.5	0.11	41,100	15,000	167
Thompson, CA	3.27	5.3	0.04	0.65	14.2	369.9	0.06	70,100	26,100	124	158.5	0.06	30,100	11,200	125
Winnipeg, CMA	3.22	276.1	2.28	0.64	684.5	14,884.9	2.27	53,900	21,700	103	5,625.1	2.02	20,400	8,200	92
SASKATCHEWAN	4.13	402.7	3.33	0.81	1,034.3	19,435.7	2.96	48,300	18,800	89	8,157.3	2.93	20,300	7,900	88
Estevan, CA	6.38	5.2	0.04	1.24	13.5	323.0	0.05	61,700	23,900	113	113.7	0.04	21,700	8,400	94
Moose Jaw, CA	2.98	15.0	0.12	0.59	35.4	716.8	0.11	47,800	20,300	96	313.3	0.11	20,900	8,900	99
North Battleford, CA	3.54	7.5	0.06	0.70	18.4	331.7	0.05	44,500	18,100	86	143.7	0.05	19,300	7,800	87
Prince Albert, CA	5.84	16.4	0.14	1.14	43.9	834.2	0.13	50,900	19,000	90	574.1	0.21	35,000	13,100	146
Regina, CMA	4.49	80.8	0.67	0.88	200.6	4,486.1	0.68	55,500	22,400	106	1,912.1	0.69	23,700	9,500	106
Saskatoon, CMA	7.46	94.9	0.79	1.46	235.0	4,823.9	0.73	50,800	20,500	97	1,905.3	0.68	20,100	8,100	91
Swift Current, CA	4.61	7.3	0.06	0.91	17.0	357.1	0.05	48,700	21,000	99	172.7	0.06	23,600	10,100	113
Yorkton, CA	0.46	7.4	0.06	0.09	17.9	312.9	0.05	42,200	17,500	83	188.7	0.07	25,400	10,600	118
ALBERTA	13.67	1,153.3	9.54	2.60	3,065.6	68,436.5	10.43	59,300	22,300	106	31,754.6	11.39	27,500	10,400	116
Calgary, CMA	19.04	375.5	3.11	3.55	978.0	25,120.0	3.83	66,900	25,700	122	10,340.7	3.71	27,500	10,600	118
Camrose, CA	6.07	5.9	0.05	1.19	14.4	275.7	0.04	46,400	19,200	91	253.0	0.09	42,600	17,600	197
Edmonton, CMA	11.57	368.6	3.05	2.21	956.5	21,039.9	3.21	57,100	22,000	104	8,837.3	3.17	24,000	9,200	103
Grand Centre, CA	8.07	13.7	0.11	1.56	40.7	742.1	0.11	54,200	18,200	87	395.8	0.14	28,900	9,700	109
Grande Prairie, CA	16.56	13.0	0.11	3.11	35.8	808.6	0.12	62,000	22,600	107	664.3	0.24	50,900	18,600	208
Lethbridge, CA	8.38	27.5	0.23	1.62	68.3	1,341.3	0.20	48,700	19,600	93	1,809.3	0.65	65,700	26,500	296
Lloydminster, CA	13.37	8.2	0.07	2.54	21.4	433.6	0.07	53,100	20,300	96	430.3	0.15	52,700	20,100	225
Medicine Hat, CA	10.40	24.9	0.21	2.00	62.7	1,257.5	0.19	50,600	20,000	95	843.8	0.30	33,900	13,500	150
Red Deer, CA	9.16	26.1	0.22	1.77	68.4	1,400.5	0.21	53,700	20,500	97	1,320.2	0.47	50,600	19,300	216
Wetaskiwin, CA	9.24	4.7	0.04	1.78	11.8	223.1	0.03	47,200	18,900	90	340.7	0.12	72,100	28,900	323
Wood Buffalo, CA	16.02	14.7	0.12	3.02	39.9	1,182.4	0.18	80,400	29,600	140	483.0	0.17	32,900	12,100	135
BRITISH COLUMBIA	9.54	1,636.6	13.54	1.84	4,137.4	87,782.5	13.37	53,600	21,200	101	36,141.4	12.97	22,100	8,700	98
Abbotsford, CA	11.37	54.2	0.45	2.18	155.0	2,828.4	0.43	52,200	18,200	87	1,263.0	0.45	23,300	8,100	91

2 – By Province and Urban Market	Households July 1, 2001					Income 2001					Retail Sales 2001				
	'96 to '01 Hhld. Change %	Total No. (000s)	% Canadian Total	Avg. Annual Rate of Growth %	Total Pop. (000s)	Total Millions $	% Canadian Total	Per Hhld. $	Per Capita $	Income Rating Index	Total Millions $	% Canadian Total	Per Hhld. $	Per Capita $	Market Rating Index
Campbell River, CA	3.54	14.4	0.12	0.70	36.6	757.9	0.12	52,700	20,700	98	365.9	0.13	25,400	10,000	112
Chilliwack, CA	10.92	28.9	0.24	2.09	75.5	1,318.5	0.20	45,600	17,500	83	752.2	0.27	26,000	10,000	111
Courtenay, CA	14.77	26.1	0.22	2.79	63.1	1,204.6	0.18	46,200	19,100	91	525.1	0.19	20,100	8,300	93
Cranbrook, CA	10.05	8.0	0.07	1.93	19.4	361.3	0.06	45,200	18,600	88	414.2	0.15	51,800	21,300	238
Dawson Creek, CA	0.99	4.6	0.04	0.20	11.0	198.3	0.03	43,400	18,000	85	162.7	0.06	35,600	14,700	165
Duncan, CA	6.53	15.2	0.13	1.27	38.7	676.5	0.10	44,500	17,500	83	370.8	0.13	24,400	9,600	107
Fort St. John, CA	4.90	6.0	0.05	0.96	15.5	344.5	0.05	57,300	22,200	105	299.2	0.11	49,700	19,300	216
Kamloops, CA	9.45	36.6	0.30	1.82	92.0	1,884.4	0.29	51,600	20,500	97	1,013.6	0.36	27,700	11,000	123
Kelowna, CA	12.45	63.0	0.52	2.38	156.7	3,029.4	0.46	48,100	19,300	92	1,845.9	0.66	29,300	11,800	132
Kitimat, CA	-2.03	4.0	0.03	-0.41	10.6	262.8	0.04	65,600	24,900	118	77.7	0.03	19,400	7,300	82
Nanaimo, CA	7.39	38.2	0.32	1.44	92.9	1,788.3	0.27	46,800	19,200	91	788.9	0.28	20,700	8,500	95
Penticton, CA	5.47	19.5	0.16	1.07	44.5	793.6	0.12	40,700	17,800	85	481.1	0.17	24,700	10,800	121
Port Alberni, CA	-0.67	10.9	0.09	-0.14	26.3	491.5	0.07	45,100	18,700	89	198.2	0.07	18,200	7,500	84
Powell River, CA	1.98	8.7	0.07	0.39	20.4	394.7	0.06	45,600	19,300	92	189.9	0.07	21,900	9,300	104
Prince George, CA	5.44	29.5	0.24	1.07	77.7	1,704.5	0.26	57,800	21,900	104	907.8	0.33	30,800	11,700	130
Prince Rupert, CA	-5.09	6.1	0.05	-1.04	16.4	334.8	0.05	55,200	20,400	97	131.8	0.05	21,700	8,000	90
Quesnel, CA	5.54	10.3	0.08	1.08	26.8	500.3	0.08	48,700	18,700	89	163.4	0.06	15,900	6,100	68
Terrace, CA	8.47	8.2	0.07	1.64	22.0	475.0	0.07	58,100	21,600	103	216.8	0.08	26,500	9,900	110
Vancouver, CMA	12.19	816.8	6.76	2.33	2,092.7	47,738.1	7.27	58,400	22,800	108	17,323.8	6.22	21,200	8,300	92
Vernon, CA	7.11	24.1	0.20	1.38	59.8	1,051.1	0.16	43,600	17,600	83	622.0	0.22	25,800	10,400	116
Victoria, CMA	3.27	139.9	1.16	0.65	320.5	7,206.6	1.10	51,500	22,500	107	2,722.3	0.98	19,500	8,500	95
Williams Lake, CA	8.27	16.0	0.13	1.60	41.7	780.5	0.12	48,800	18,700	89	432.2	0.16	27,000	10,400	116
NORTHWEST TERRITORIES	7.07	14.4	0.12	1.38	42.2	1,029.0	0.16	71,700	24,400	116	128.7	0.05	9,000	3,000	34
Yellowknife, CA	10.05	6.7	0.06	1.93	18.9	597.5	0.09	88,700	31,600	150	69.8	0.03	10,400	3,700	41
NUNAVUT	12.31	7.4	0.06	2.35	28.2	409.3	0.06	55,500	14,500	69	42.3	0.02	5,700	1,500	17
YUKON TERRITORY	3.00	12.4	0.10	0.59	31.4	731.2	0.11	59,100	23,300	111	166.9	0.06	13,500	5,300	59
Whitehorse, CA	1.69	8.6	0.07	0.34	21.8	553.8	0.08	64,300	25,400	121	150.6	0.05	17,500	6,900	77

Buying Power Indices, 2001

3 – Estimates by Metropolitan Areas, Cities and Towns
(arranged in order of population)

	'96 to '01 Hhld. Change %	Total No. (000s)	% Canadian Total	Avg. Annual Rate of Growth %	Total Pop. (000s)	Total Millions $	% Canadian Total	Per Hhld. $	Per Capita $	Income Rating Index	Total Millions $	% Canadian Total	Per Hhld. $	Per Capita $	Market Rating Index
		Households July 1, 2001				**Income 2001**					**Retail Sales 2001**				
Population 100,000+															
Toronto, CMA	12.65	1,738.3	14.38	2.41	4,867.6	118,824.7	18.10	68,400	24,400	116	40,759.1	14.62	23,400	8,400	94
Montréal, CMA	5.37	1,451.5	12.01	1.05	3,500.8	72,022.9	10.97	49,600	20,600	98	28,737.3	10.31	19,800	8,200	92
Vancouver, CMA	12.19	816.8	6.76	2.33	2,092.7	47,738.1	7.27	58,400	22,800	108	17,323.8	6.22	21,200	8,300	92
Ottawa-Hull, CMA	8.07	431.9	3.57	1.56	1,085.9	27,101.5	4.13	62,800	25,000	118	10,000.2	3.59	23,200	9,200	103
Calgary, CMA	19.04	375.5	3.11	3.55	978.0	25,120.0	3.83	66,900	25,700	122	10,340.7	3.71	27,500	10,600	118
Edmonton, CMA	11.57	368.6	3.05	2.21	956.5	21,039.9	3.21	57,100	22,000	104	8,837.3	3.17	24,000	9,200	103
Québec, CMA	5.45	299.9	2.48	1.07	693.2	14,766.7	2.25	49,200	21,300	101	7,599.5	2.73	25,300	11,000	122
Winnipeg, CMA	3.22	276.1	2.28	0.64	684.5	14,884.9	2.27	53,900	21,700	103	5,625.1	2.02	20,400	8,200	92
Hamilton, CMA	6.71	259.6	2.15	1.31	673.7	15,500.5	2.36	59,700	23,000	109	5,465.9	1.96	21,100	8,100	91
Kitchener, CMA	11.75	163.4	1.35	2.25	428.9	9,742.3	1.48	59,600	22,700	108	4,550.0	1.63	27,800	10,600	118
London, CMA	5.77	172.7	1.43	1.13	426.3	9,556.4	1.46	55,300	22,400	106	4,355.1	1.56	25,200	10,200	114
St. Catharines-Niagara, CMA	5.63	158.1	1.31	1.10	395.6	8,083.0	1.23	51,100	20,400	97	4,003.5	1.44	25,300	10,100	113
Halifax, CMA	9.14	144.1	1.19	1.77	361.4	7,707.8	1.17	53,500	21,300	101	3,529.7	1.27	24,500	9,800	109
Victoria, CMA	3.27	139.9	1.16	0.65	320.5	7,206.6	1.10	51,500	22,500	107	2,722.3	0.98	19,500	8,500	95
Windsor, CMA	10.03	121.1	1.00	1.93	308.8	7,368.2	1.12	60,900	23,900	113	3,246.5	1.16	26,800	10,500	117
Oshawa, CMA	13.15	109.5	0.91	2.50	304.8	7,151.3	1.09	65,300	23,500	111	2,433.5	0.87	22,200	8,000	89
Saskatoon, CMA	7.46	94.9	0.79	1.45	235.0	4,823.9	0.73	50,800	20,500	97	1,905.3	0.68	20,100	8,100	91
Regina, CMA	4.49	80.8	0.67	0.88	200.6	4,486.1	0.68	55,500	22,400	106	1,912.1	0.69	23,700	9,500	106
St. John's, CMA	5.27	65.4	0.54	1.03	173.8	3,521.0	0.54	53,800	20,300	96	1,904.7	0.68	29,100	11,000	122
Chicoutimi-Jonquière, CMA	5.44	64.7	0.54	1.07	162.5	2,829.1	0.43	43,700	17,400	83	1,474.9	0.53	22,800	9,100	101
Sudbury, CMA	1.48	64.9	0.54	0.29	159.5	3,493.5	0.53	53,800	21,900	104	1,763.4	0.63	27,200	11,100	124
Kelowna, CA	12.45	63.0	0.52	2.38	156.7	3,029.4	0.46	48,100	19,300	92	1,845.9	0.66	29,300	11,800	132
Sherbrooke, CMA	7.23	68.2	0.56	1.41	155.8	2,898.6	0.44	42,500	18,600	88	1,311.3	0.47	19,200	8,400	94
Abbotsford, CA	11.37	54.2	0.45	2.18	155.0	2,828.4	0.43	52,200	18,200	87	1,263.0	0.45	23,300	8,100	91
Kingston, CA	4.35	60.1	0.50	0.86	147.5	3,314.4	0.50	55,100	22,500	107	1,369.2	0.49	22,800	9,300	104
Barrie, CA	21.92	53.1	0.44	4.04	146.0	2,967.8	0.45	55,900	20,300	96	1,575.5	0.57	29,700	10,800	121
Trois-Rivières, CMA	4.56	62.6	0.52	0.90	142.8	2,720.0	0.41	43,500	19,100	90	1,146.7	0.41	18,300	8,000	90
Saint John, CMA	3.23	49.8	0.41	0.64	128.1	2,461.0	0.37	49,500	19,200	91	1,057.5	0.38	21,300	8,300	92
Thunder Bay, CMA	2.26	51.9	0.43	0.45	127.5	2,887.4	0.44	55,600	22,600	107	1,264.7	0.45	24,400	9,900	111
Moncton, CA	8.14	47.4	0.39	1.58	120.1	2,431.7	0.37	51,300	20,300	96	1,259.2	0.45	26,600	10,500	117
Guelph, CA	11.27	45.2	0.37	2.16	118.2	2,726.3	0.42	60,300	23,100	109	1,341.6	0.48	29,700	11,400	127
Cape Breton, CA	0.22	43.7	0.36	0.04	115.5	1,725.7	0.26	39,500	14,900	71	999.2	0.36	22,900	8,600	97
Brantford, CA	4.38	42.3	0.35	0.86	111.5	2,159.1	0.33	51,100	19,400	92	922.6	0.33	21,800	8,300	92
Peterborough, CA	6.43	42.4	0.35	1.25	106.3	2,145.6	0.33	50,600	20,200	96	1,085.9	0.39	25,600	10,200	114
Population 30,000 To 100,000															
Belleville, CA	1.24	38.1	0.32	0.25	96.4	1,934.9	0.29	50,800	20,100	95	1,170.9	0.42	30,700	12,200	136
Nanaimo, CA	7.39	38.2	0.32	1.44	92.9	1,788.3	0.27	46,800	19,200	91	788.9	0.28	20,700	8,500	95
Kamloops, CA	9.45	36.6	0.30	1.82	92.0	1,884.4	0.29	51,600	20,500	97	1,013.6	0.36	27,700	11,000	123
Sarnia, CA	0.73	35.0	0.29	0.15	86.5	1,966.3	0.30	56,200	22,700	108	818.3	0.29	23,400	9,500	106
Sault Ste. Marie, CA	0.41	34.1	0.28	0.08	84.2	1,707.9	0.26	50,100	20,300	96	1,001.0	0.36	29,400	11,900	133
Fredericton, CA	7.66	33.4	0.28	1.49	83.2	1,796.6	0.27	53,800	21,600	102	1,046.3	0.38	31,300	12,600	140
Saint-Jean-sur-Richelieu, CA	7.01	33.2	0.27	1.36	80.7	1,490.3	0.23	44,900	18,500	88	942.8	0.34	28,400	11,700	130
Prince George, CA	5.44	29.5	0.24	1.07	77.7	1,704.5	0.26	57,800	21,900	104	907.8	0.33	30,800	11,700	130
Chilliwack, CA	10.92	28.9	0.24	2.09	75.5	1,318.5	0.20	45,600	17,500	83	752.2	0.27	26,000	10,000	111
Drummondville, CA	9.49	29.6	0.24	1.83	69.5	1,227.4	0.19	41,500	17,700	84	895.8	0.32	30,300	12,900	144
Red Deer, CA	9.16	26.1	0.22	1.77	68.4	1,400.5	0.21	53,700	20,500	97	1,320.2	0.47	50,600	19,300	216
Lethbridge, CA	8.38	27.6	0.23	1.62	68.3	1,341.3	0.20	48,700	19,600	93	1,809.3	0.65	65,700	26,500	296
Chatham, CA	1.35	26.8	0.22	0.27	67.7	1,371.7	0.21	51,200	20,300	96	880.5	0.32	32,900	13,000	145
North Bay, CA	0.97	26.0	0.22	0.19	64.0	1,277.1	0.19	49,100	19,900	95	807.7	0.29	31,000	12,600	141
Cornwall, CA	1.63	25.8	0.21	0.32	64.0	1,159.5	0.18	45,000	18,100	86	758.0	0.27	29,400	11,800	132
Courtenay, CA	14.77	26.1	0.22	2.79	63.1	1,204.6	0.18	46,200	19,100	91	525.1	0.19	20,100	8,300	93
Medicine Hat, CA	10.40	24.9	0.21	2.00	62.7	1,257.5	0.19	50,600	20,000	95	843.8	0.30	33,900	13,500	150
Granby, CA	8.12	26.6	0.22	1.57	62.0	1,175.9	0.18	44,300	19,000	90	792.2	0.28	29,800	12,800	143
Vernon, CA	7.11	24.1	0.20	1.38	59.8	1,051.1	0.16	43,600	17,600	83	622.0	0.22	25,800	10,400	116
Charlottetown, CA	7.18	22.9	0.19	1.40	59.6	1,066.9	0.16	46,500	17,900	85	666.1	0.24	29,000	11,200	125
Shawinigan, CA	1.57	26.3	0.22	0.31	59.6	990.1	0.15	37,600	16,600	79	492.5	0.18	18,700	8,300	92

	'96 to '01 Hhld. Change %	Total No. (000s)	% Canadian Total	Avg. Annual Rate of Growth %	Total Pop. (000s)	Total Millions $	% Canadian Total	Per Hhld. $	Per Capita $	Income Rating Index	Total Millions $	% Canadian Total	Per Hhld. $	Per Capita $	Market Rating Index
Saint-Hyacinthe, CA	4.01	22.1	0.18	0.79	50.6	920.2	0.14	41,700	18,200	86	694.9	0.25	31,500	13,700	153
Rimouski, CA	5.49	21.0	0.17	1.07	48.9	1,010.7	0.15	48,000	20,600	98	500.7	0.18	23,800	10,200	114
Timmins, CA	2.32	18.7	0.15	0.46	47.3	987.8	0.15	52,900	20,900	99	452.9	0.16	24,300	9,600	107
Truro, CA	5.66	18.4	0.15	1.11	46.3	786.4	0.12	42,800	17,000	81	555.3	0.20	30,300	12,000	134
Penticton, CA	5.47	19.5	0.16	1.07	44.5	793.6	0.12	40,700	17,800	85	481.1	0.17	24,700	10,800	121
Leamington, CA	9.55	16.1	0.13	1.84	44.4	938.1	0.14	58,100	21,100	100	406.3	0.15	25,200	9,200	102
Prince Albert, CA	5.84	16.4	0.14	1.14	43.9	834.2	0.13	50,900	19,000	90	574.1	0.21	35,000	13,100	146
Brockville, CA	1.64	17.3	0.14	0.33	43.6	855.4	0.13	49,300	19,600	93	426.0	0.15	24,600	9,800	109
Orillia, CA	13.17	17.2	0.14	2.51	42.9	799.5	0.12	46,400	18,600	88	419.0	0.15	24,300	9,800	109
Victoriaville, CA	8.16	17.7	0.15	1.58	42.6	729.9	0.11	41,200	17,100	81	560.2	0.20	31,600	13,100	147
Sorel, CA	0.63	18.1	0.15	0.13	41.9	781.7	0.12	43,300	18,600	88	439.7	0.16	24,300	10,500	117
Williams Lake, CA	8.27	16.0	0.13	1.60	41.7	780.5	0.12	48,800	18,700	89	432.2	0.16	27,000	10,400	116
Brandon, CA	3.82	17.5	0.14	0.75	41.5	811.0	0.12	46,300	19,500	93	666.5	0.24	38,000	16,000	179
Grand Centre, CA	8.07	13.7	0.11	1.56	40.7	742.1	0.11	54,200	18,200	87	395.8	0.14	28,900	9,700	109
Wood Buffalo, CA	16.02	14.7	0.12	3.02	39.9	1,182.4	0.18	80,400	29,600	140	483.0	0.17	32,900	12,100	135
Rouyn-Noranda, CA	5.03	17.0	0.14	0.99	39.6	800.3	0.12	47,100	20,200	96	417.0	0.15	24,600	10,500	118
Salaberry-de-Valleyfield, CA	1.23	16.9	0.14	0.24	39.2	673.0	0.10	39,800	17,200	81	510.8	0.18	30,200	13,000	145
Duncan, CA	6.53	15.2	0.13	1.27	38.7	676.5	0.10	44,500	17,500	83	370.8	0.13	24,400	9,600	107
New Glasgow, CA	2.20	15.0	0.12	0.44	38.3	632.1	0.10	42,300	16,500	78	400.1	0.14	26,800	10,400	117
Campbell River, CA	3.54	14.4	0.12	0.70	36.6	757.9	0.12	52,700	20,700	98	365.9	0.13	25,400	10,000	112
Grande Prairie, CA	16.56	13.1	0.11	3.11	35.8	808.6	0.12	62,000	22,600	107	664.3	0.24	50,900	18,600	208
Midland, CA	8.15	14.3	0.12	1.58	35.7	661.7	0.10	46,400	18,500	88	331.7	0.12	23,300	9,300	104
Joliette, CA	5.89	15.4	0.13	1.15	35.6	638.2	0.10	41,400	17,900	85	686.7	0.25	44,600	19,300	216
Moose Jaw, CA	2.98	15.0	0.12	0.59	35.4	716.8	0.11	47,800	20,300	96	313.3	0.11	20,900	8,900	99
Woodstock, CA	6.57	13.9	0.11	1.28	34.4	693.6	0.11	50,100	20,100	96	355.3	0.13	25,600	10,300	115
Val-d'Or, CA	5.88	13.9	0.11	1.15	33.6	679.4	0.10	49,000	20,200	96	432.2	0.16	31,200	12,900	144
Baie-Comeau, CA	2.29	12.4	0.10	0.45	31.0	673.4	0.10	54,100	21,700	103	228.3	0.08	18,400	7,400	82
Alma, CA	5.23	12.0	0.10	1.02	30.8	541.8	0.08	45,000	17,600	84	356.0	0.13	29,600	11,600	129
Stratford, CA	3.89	12.6	0.10	0.77	30.5	652.6	0.10	51,600	21,400	101	515.9	0.19	40,800	16,900	189
Owen Sound, CA	2.32	12.7	0.10	0.46	30.5	575.8	0.09	45,400	18,900	89	439.4	0.16	34,700	14,400	161

Population 10,000 To 30,000

	'96 to '01 Hhld. Change %	Total No. (000s)	% Canadian Total	Avg. Annual Rate of Growth %	Total Pop. (000s)	Total Millions $	% Canadian Total	Per Hhld. $	Per Capita $	Income Rating Index	Total Millions $	% Canadian Total	Per Hhld. $	Per Capita $	Market Rating Index
Sept-Îles, CA	6.17	11.7	0.10	1.20	28.9	607.8	0.09	51,900	21,000	100	277.2	0.10	23,700	9,600	107
Saint-Georges, CA	9.71	11.3	0.09	1.87	28.3	499.9	0.08	44,100	17,600	84	432.3	0.16	38,200	15,300	170
Corner Brook, CA	2.78	10.3	0.09	0.55	27.2	490.4	0.07	47,700	18,100	86	338.1	0.12	32,900	12,500	139
Thetford Mines, CA	1.26	11.6	0.10	0.25	27.1	464.7	0.07	40,100	17,100	81	352.8	0.13	30,500	13,000	145
Lunenburg, MD	4.03	10.4	0.09	0.79	26.9	436.8	0.07	42,000	16,200	77	134.3	0.05	12,900	5,000	56
Quesnel, CA	5.54	10.3	0.08	1.08	26.8	500.3	0.08	48,700	18,700	89	163.4	0.06	15,900	6,100	68
Kentville, CA	7.12	10.5	0.09	1.39	26.6	468.4	0.07	44,700	17,600	83	312.6	0.11	29,800	11,700	131
Port Alberni, CA	-0.67	10.9	0.09	-0.14	26.3	491.5	0.07	45,100	18,700	89	198.2	0.07	18,200	7,500	84
Bathurst, CA	3.34	10.1	0.08	0.66	25.4	454.8	0.07	45,000	17,900	85	487.0	0.17	48,200	19,200	214
Nanticoke, C	3.82	9.1	0.08	0.75	24.9	492.2	0.07	53,900	19,700	94	94.4	0.03	10,300	3,800	42
Pembroke, CA	3.57	9.9	0.08	0.70	24.8	453.3	0.07	45,600	18,300	87	316.5	0.11	31,800	12,800	143
Kings, Subd. A, SCM	9.46	9.0	0.07	1.83	24.6	402.7	0.06	44,600	16,400	78	250.1	0.09	27,700	10,200	114
Haldimand, T	8.52	8.5	0.07	1.65	24.3	510.5	0.08	60,300	21,000	100	202.4	0.07	23,900	8,300	93
Rivière-du-Loup, CA	1.92	9.9	0.08	0.38	24.3	420.2	0.06	42,500	17,300	82	393.4	0.14	39,800	16,200	181
Nanaimo, Subd. B, SRD	15.98	9.9	0.08	3.01	23.6	474.0	0.07	48,000	20,100	95	91.1	0.03	9,200	3,900	43
Lindsay, CA	9.12	9.7	0.08	1.76	23.5	445.1	0.07	45,900	19,000	90	392.5	0.14	40,500	16,700	187
Edmundston, CA	5.75	9.4	0.08	1.12	23.0	405.2	0.06	42,900	17,600	83	240.5	0.09	25,500	10,400	117
Magog, CA	9.22	9.8	0.08	1.78	22.8	406.4	0.06	41,500	17,800	84	241.8	0.09	24,700	10,600	118
Terrace, CA	8.47	8.2	0.07	1.64	22.0	475.0	0.07	58,100	21,600	103	216.8	0.08	26,500	9,900	110
East Hants, MD	10.10	7.8	0.06	1.94	21.8	382.7	0.06	49,200	17,500	83	158.2	0.06	20,300	7,200	81
Whitehorse, CA	1.69	8.6	0.07	0.34	21.8	553.8	0.08	64,300	25,400	121	150.6	0.05	17,500	6,900	77
Lloydminster, CA	13.37	8.2	0.07	2.54	21.4	433.6	0.07	53,100	20,300	96	430.3	0.15	52,700	20,100	225
Red Deer County No. 23, CM	20.29	7.3	0.06	3.76	21.2	481.5	0.07	66,000	22,700	108	74.8	0.03	10,200	3,500	39
Portage la Prairie, CA	-0.53	7.5	0.06	-0.11	20.5	329.9	0.05	44,300	16,100	76	306.5	0.11	41,100	15,000	167
Powell River, CA	1.98	8.7	0.07	0.39	20.4	394.7	0.06	45,600	19,300	92	189.9	0.07	21,900	9,300	104
Scugog, TP	6.48	7.1	0.06	1.26	20.0	494.5	0.08	69,700	24,700	117	211.6	0.08	29,800	10,600	118
Grand Falls-Windsor, CA	1.22	7.2	0.06	0.24	19.5	345.6	0.05	47,900	17,700	84	302.2	0.11	41,900	15,500	173
Cranbrook, CA	10.05	8.0	0.07	1.93	19.4	361.3	0.06	45,200	18,600	88	414.2	0.15	51,800	21,300	238
Yellowknife, CA	10.05	6.7	0.06	1.93	18.9	597.5	0.09	88,700	31,600	150	69.8	0.03	10,400	3,700	41
Essa, TP	13.19	6.3	0.05	2.51	18.5	343.6	0.05	54,800	18,600	88	80.9	0.03	12,900	4,400	49
North Battleford, CA	3.54	7.5	0.06	0.70	18.4	331.7	0.05	44,500	18,100	86	143.7	0.05	19,300	7,800	87
Miramichi, C	-1.66	7.1	0.06	-0.33	18.3	343.8	0.05	48,600	18,800	89	400.2	0.14	56,600	21,800	244
Oro-Medonte, TP	6.87	6.6	0.05	1.34	18.1	393.4	0.06	59,400	21,700	103	139.0	0.05	21,000	7,700	86
Yorkton, CA	0.46	7.4	0.06	0.09	17.9	312.9	0.05	42,200	17,500	83	188.7	0.07	25,400	10,600	118
Delhi, TP	5.68	6.5	0.05	1.11	17.7	342.4	0.05	52,600	19,400	92	89.0	0.03	13,700	5,000	56
Foothills No. 31, MD	28.60	6.1	0.05	5.16	17.6	620.8	0.09	101,500	35,200	167	184.9	0.07	30,200	10,500	117
Kenora, CA	5.71	7.1	0.06	1.12	17.6	402.6	0.06	56,800	22,900	108	256.6	0.09	36,200	14,600	163
Collingwood, CA	6.54	7.1	0.06	1.28	17.2	321.8	0.05	45,400	18,700	89	220.2	0.08	31,100	12,800	143
Cobourg, CA	8.02	7.1	0.06	1.55	17.2	366.7	0.06	51,900	21,300	101	199.4	0.07	28,200	11,600	129
Huntsville, T	7.00	6.8	0.06	1.36	17.1	325.2	0.05	48,100	19,000	90	235.7	0.08	34,900	13,800	154
Swift Current, CA	4.61	7.3	0.06	0.91	17.0	357.1	0.05	48,700	21,000	99	172.7	0.06	23,600	10,100	113
Smiths Falls, CA	3.39	6.6	0.05	0.67	16.9	319.6	0.05	48,100	19,000	90	190.3	0.07	28,700	11,300	126
Central Kootenay, Subd. B, SRD	7.50	6.9	0.06	1.46	16.7	281.1	0.04	40,800	16,800	80	60.5	0.02	8,800	3,600	41

(arranged in order of population)	'96 to '01 Hhld. Change %	Total No. (000s)	% Canadian Total	Avg. Annual Rate of Growth %	Total Pop. (000s)	Total Millions $	% Canadian Total	Per Hhld. $	Per Capita $	Income Rating Index	Total Millions $	% Canadian Total	Per Hhld. $	Per Capita $	Market Rating Index
Matane, CA	1.64	7.2	0.06	0.33	16.6	291.0	0.04	40,200	17,500	83	217.7	0.08	30,100	13,100	146
Campbellton, CA	2.27	6.5	0.05	0.45	16.6	261.5	0.04	40,200	15,700	75	213.2	0.08	32,800	12,800	143
Summerside, CA	6.56	6.6	0.05	1.28	16.4	287.5	0.04	43,500	17,500	83	263.8	0.09	39,900	16,000	179
Prince Rupert, CA	-5.09	6.1	0.05	-1.04	16.4	334.8	0.05	55,200	20,400	97	131.8	0.05	21,700	8,000	90
Salmon Arm, DM	13.05	6.7	0.06	2.48	16.4	300.4	0.05	44,800	18,400	87	218.0	0.08	32,500	13,300	149
Squamish, DM	13.81	6.2	0.05	2.62	16.1	362.8	0.06	59,000	22,500	107	107.2	0.04	17,400	6,600	74
Gaspé, V	2.09	6.0	0.05	0.41	16.1	275.8	0.04	45,900	17,100	81	153.7	0.06	25,600	9,500	106
Cowichan Valley, Subd. C, SRD	11.25	6.2	0.05	2.16	16.0	329.8	0.05	53,500	20,600	98	39.7	0.01	6,500	2,500	28
Columbia-Shuswap, Subd. C, SRD	13.32	6.6	0.05	2.53	16.0	256.4	0.04	38,600	16,000	76	63.9	0.02	9,600	4,000	45
Grande Prairie County No. 1, CM	17.38	5.4	0.04	3.26	16.0	347.0	0.05	64,800	21,800	103	49.7	0.02	9,300	3,100	35
Simcoe, CA	3.67	6.5	0.05	0.72	15.8	332.4	0.05	51,000	21,100	100	315.3	0.11	48,400	20,000	223
Fort St. John, CA	4.90	6.0	0.05	0.96	15.5	344.5	0.05	57,300	22,200	105	299.2	0.11	49,700	19,300	216
Dolbeau, CA	5.59	5.9	0.05	1.09	15.3	246.2	0.04	41,500	16,100	76	165.2	0.06	27,900	10,800	121
Fraser-Fort George, Subd. A, SRD	13.86	5.5	0.05	2.63	15.2	346.3	0.05	63,500	22,700	108	16.7	0.01	3,100	1,100	12
Capital, Subd. A, SRD	7.22	6.8	0.06	1.40	14.9	314.6	0.05	46,200	21,100	100	95.0	0.03	13,900	6,400	71
Sunshine Coast, Subd. A, SRD	8.61	6.1	0.05	1.67	14.7	301.5	0.05	49,700	20,500	97	25.9	0.01	4,300	1,800	20
Wilmot, TP	6.69	5.2	0.04	1.30	14.7	353.9	0.05	68,300	24,100	114	168.9	0.06	32,600	11,500	128
West Hants, MD	5.45	5.4	0.04	1.07	14.6	236.6	0.04	44,000	16,200	77	123.0	0.04	22,900	8,400	94
Tillsonburg, CA	9.21	6.0	0.05	1.78	14.5	303.5	0.05	50,200	20,900	99	118.9	0.04	19,700	8,200	91
Bracebridge, T	8.24	5.6	0.05	1.60	14.4	288.6	0.04	51,300	20,100	95	228.1	0.08	40,600	15,900	177
Camrose, CA	6.07	5.9	0.05	1.19	14.4	275.7	0.04	46,400	19,200	91	253.0	0.09	42,600	17,600	197
Thompson, CA	3.27	5.3	0.04	0.65	14.2	369.9	0.06	70,100	26,100	124	158.5	0.06	30,100	11,200	125
Norfolk, TP	6.87	4.8	0.04	1.34	13.7	247.8	0.04	51,900	18,100	86	63.9	0.02	13,400	4,700	52
Amos, V	5.08	5.7	0.05	1.00	13.7	247.4	0.04	43,800	18,100	86	228.4	0.08	40,400	16,700	187
Clearview, TP	7.11	4.9	0.04	1.38	13.5	240.2	0.04	49,400	17,700	84	76.8	0.03	15,800	5,700	63
Estevan, CA	6.38	5.2	0.04	1.24	13.5	323.0	0.05	61,700	23,900	113	113.7	0.04	21,700	8,400	94
Elliot Lake, CA	-2.27	5.8	0.05	-0.46	13.5	248.2	0.04	43,000	18,400	87	104.9	0.04	18,200	7,800	87
Haileybury, CA	-3.48	5.2	0.04	-0.71	13.3	255.3	0.04	48,700	19,300	91	261.7	0.09	49,900	19,800	221
Strathroy, CA	12.23	4.9	0.04	2.34	13.2	258.8	0.04	52,800	19,600	93	217.8	0.08	44,500	16,500	184
Dunnville, T	5.98	5.0	0.04	1.17	13.2	251.9	0.04	50,900	19,100	91	74.3	0.03	15,000	5,600	63
Mountain View County, CM	16.74	4.7	0.04	3.14	13.2	274.0	0.04	58,300	20,800	99	4.0	0.00	800	300	3
La Tuque, CA	4.00	5.8	0.05	0.79	13.0	249.6	0.04	42,900	19,300	91	127.7	0.05	21,900	9,900	110
Lachute, CA	-5.29	5.3	0.04	-1.08	12.8	191.6	0.03	36,200	15,000	71	118.4	0.04	22,400	9,300	104
Brock, TP	7.40	4.6	0.04	1.44	12.5	240.5	0.04	52,100	19,300	92	63.9	0.02	13,800	5,100	57
Cowansville, CA	10.03	5.3	0.04	1.93	12.3	208.0	0.03	39,300	17,000	80	183.8	0.07	34,800	15,000	167
West Lincoln, TP	5.21	3.9	0.03	1.02	12.2	241.4	0.04	62,000	19,800	94	129.4	0.05	33,200	10,600	119
Port Hope, CA	4.10	4.8	0.04	0.81	12.1	250.3	0.04	52,500	20,700	98	104.5	0.04	21,900	8,600	96
Hawkesbury, CA	4.57	5.1	0.04	0.90	12.1	193.7	0.03	37,800	16,000	76	234.9	0.08	45,800	19,400	217
Clearwater No. 99, MD	12.52	4.4	0.04	2.39	12.0	217.6	0.03	49,200	18,100	86	201.0	0.07	45,500	16,700	187
Lacombe County, CM	12.15	3.9	0.03	2.32	12.0	225.0	0.03	57,800	18,800	89	21.5	0.01	5,500	1,800	20
Montmagny, V	2.04	4.9	0.04	0.40	11.8	199.7	0.03	40,700	16,900	80	228.0	0.08	46,400	19,300	215
Wetaskiwin, CA	9.24	4.7	0.04	1.78	11.8	223.1	0.03	47,200	18,900	90	340.7	0.12	72,100	28,900	323
Gander, CA	2.51	4.5	0.04	0.50	11.8	240.0	0.04	53,900	20,400	97	197.1	0.07	44,200	16,800	187
Saint-Lin, M	26.32	4.2	0.03	4.78	11.8	169.0	0.03	40,300	14,400	68		0.00			0
Amherstburg, T	14.91	4.3	0.04	2.82	11.7	260.4	0.04	60,300	22,300	106	111.6	0.04	25,900	9,600	107
Wasaga Beach, T	21.28	5.1	0.04	3.93	11.7	223.0	0.03	43,800	19,100	91	43.5	0.02	8,500	3,700	42
Wetaskiwin County No. 10, CM	12.01	4.2	0.03	2.29	11.6	230.6	0.04	55,600	19,800	94	55.1	0.02	13,300	4,700	53
Roberval, V	3.92	4.4	0.04	0.77	11.5	213.3	0.03	48,200	18,500	88	82.8	0.03	18,700	7,200	80
Peace River, Subd. B, SRD	12.53	3.8	0.03	2.39	11.5	226.5	0.03	59,900	19,700	94	53.7	0.02	14,200	4,700	52
Sainte-Marie, V	7.14	4.4	0.04	1.39	11.5	201.5	0.03	46,300	17,600	83	174.2	0.06	40,000	15,200	170
St. Andrews, RM	9.85	3.9	0.04	1.90	11.4	269.0	0.04	69,700	23,700	112	22.3	0.01	5,800	2,000	22
Summerland, DM	3.92	4.6	0.04	0.77	11.3	209.8	0.03	45,300	18,500	88	49.2	0.02	10,600	4,300	48
Parksville, C	17.94	5.2	0.04	3.36	11.3	208.7	0.03	40,100	18,500	88	146.8	0.05	28,200	13,000	145
Canmore, T	34.96	4.4	0.04	6.18	11.3	285.0	0.04	65,100	25,300	120	147.8	0.05	33,800	13,100	146
Brooks, T	11.16	4.2	0.03	2.14	11.3	247.1	0.04	58,700	21,900	104	34.8	0.01	8,300	3,100	35
Hinton, T	14.09	4.1	0.03	2.67	11.2	270.2	0.04	66,100	24,000	114	127.6	0.05	31,200	11,400	127
Kenora, Unorganized, UNO	2.26	4.1	0.03	0.45	11.2	244.6	0.04	59,400	21,800	103	36.9	0.01	9,000	3,300	37
Norwich, TP	2.69	3.6	0.03	0.53	11.2	211.1	0.03	58,900	18,800	89	63.7	0.02	17,800	5,700	64
Dawson Creek, CA	0.99	4.6	0.04	0.20	11.0	198.3	0.03	43,400	18,000	85	162.7	0.06	35,600	14,700	165
Hanover, RM	13.44	3.2	0.03	2.55	11.0	163.7	0.02	50,800	14,900	70	25.3	0.01	7,800	2,300	26
Okotoks, T	28.87	3.4	0.03	5.20	11.0	276.6	0.04	80,600	25,100	119	43.1	0.02	12,500	3,900	44
Yarmouth, MD	1.84	4.1	0.03	0.37	10.9	176.5	0.03	42,600	16,200	77	51.1	0.02	12,300	4,700	52
Hamilton, TP	6.27	3.9	0.03	1.22	10.8	255.7	0.04	65,100	23,600	112	49.2	0.02	12,500	4,600	51
Chester, MD	2.97	4.4	0.04	0.59	10.8	184.0	0.03	41,400	17,100	81	69.9	0.03	15,700	6,500	72
Whistler, DM	37.11	4.7	0.04	6.52	10.7	309.4	0.05	65,200	28,900	137	162.6	0.06	34,300	15,200	169
Lethbridge County No. 26, CM	14.50	3.1	0.03	2.75	10.6	177.2	0.03	56,500	16,700	79	139.1	0.05	44,400	13,100	147
Kitimat, CA	-2.03	4.0	0.03	-0.41	10.6	262.8	0.04	65,600	24,900	118	77.7	0.03	19,400	7,300	82
Selkirk, T	9.41	4.1	0.03	1.82	10.5	200.9	0.03	48,500	19,100	91	170.6	0.06	41,200	16,200	181
Ingersoll, T	4.76	4.0	0.03	0.93	10.4	215.9	0.03	53,900	20,700	98	67.8	0.02	16,900	6,500	73
Adjala-Tosorontio, TP	9.27	3.4	0.03	1.79	10.3	247.9	0.04	73,300	24,000	114	17.4	0.01	5,200	1,700	19
Gravenhurst, T	4.35	4.3	0.04	0.86	10.3	186.5	0.03	43,700	18,100	86	120.3	0.04	28,200	11,700	130
Fergus, T	15.46	3.9	0.03	2.92	10.3	226.0	0.03	58,400	22,000	104	135.5	0.05	35,000	13,200	147
Yellowhead No. 94, MD	11.70	3.8	0.03	2.24	10.3	201.9	0.03	53,700	19,700	93	72.1	0.03	19,200	7,000	78
Weyburn, C	6.51	4.4	0.04	1.27	10.0	203.0	0.03	46,600	20,200	96	90.5	0.03	20,800	9,000	101
Lacombe, T	18.53	3.6	0.03	3.46	10.0	209.0	0.03	57,500	20,800	99	136.2	0.05	37,500	13,600	152

Retail Sales Estimates, 2001

By Class of Business (Sales in $ millions)
1 – By Province, Economic Region and Census Division

	Total Sales		Supermarkets & Groceries		All Other Food		Women's Clothing		Men's Clothing		Other Clothing		Shoes		Motor Vehicles & Recreation Vehicles		Gas Service Stations	
	$mill. Sales	% of Cdn Total	$mill. Sales	% of Cdn Total	$mill. Sales	% of Cdn Total	$mill. Sales	% of Cdn Total	$mill. Sales	% of Cdn Total	$mill. Sales	% of Cdn Total	$mill. Sales	% of Cdn Total	$mill. Sales	% of Cdn Total	$mill. Sales	% of Cdn Total
CANADA	278,705.8	100.00	55,982.1	100.00	4,504.3	100.00	4,847.4	100.00	1,638.6	100.00	7,148.5	100.00	1,707.9	100.0	76,689.3	100.00	18,935.4	100.00
NEWFOUNDLAND	4,628.5	1.66	1,183.6	2.11	55.2	1.23	64.6	1.33	19.3	1.18	74.2	1.04	15.9	0.9	1,177.3	1.54	340.1	1.80
Avalon Peninsula	2,244.0	0.81	572.6	1.02	26.7	0.59	41.2	0.85	14.7	0.90	40.4	0.56	11.7	0.7	550.9	0.72	126.7	0.70
Division No. 1	2,244.0	0.81	572.6	1.02	26.7	0.59	41.2	0.85	14.7	0.90	40.4	0.56	11.7	0.7	550.9	0.72	126.7	0.70
South Coast - Burin Peninsula	299.1	0.11	103.9	0.19	4.8	0.11	2.9	0.06	0.1	0.01	5.9	0.08	0.2	0.0	43.0	0.06	26.4	0.10
Division No. 2	165.8	0.06	56.6	0.10	2.6	0.06	1.4	0.03	0.1	0.01	1.2	0.02	0.2	0.0	33.8	0.04	14.4	0.10
Division No. 3	133.4	0.05	47.3	0.08	2.2	0.05	1.5	0.03	0.0	0.00	4.7	0.07	0.0	0.0	9.2	0.01	12.0	0.10
West Coast - Northern Peninsula - Labrador	1,086.8	0.39	281.8	0.50	13.2	0.29	11.6	0.24	1.8	0.11	15.1	0.21	1.8	0.1	283.4	0.37	78.8	0.40
Division No. 4	172.0	0.06	48.5	0.09	2.3	0.05	1.7	0.04	0.0	0.00	0.7	0.01	0.2	0.0	28.9	0.04	10.7	0.10
Division No. 5	519.3	0.19	133.1	0.24	6.2	0.14	7.2	0.15	1.8	0.11	9.1	0.13	0.4	0.0	166.0	0.22	35.3	0.20
Division No. 9	160.2	0.06	34.8	0.06	1.6	0.04	0.4	0.01	0.0	0.00	1.9	0.03	0.0	0.0	41.8	0.05	20.0	0.10
Division No. 10	235.2	0.08	65.5	0.12	3.1	0.07	2.2	0.05	0.0	0.00	3.4	0.05	1.2	0.1	46.7	0.06	12.9	0.10
Notre Dame - Central Bonavista Bay	998.6	0.36	225.3	0.40	10.5	0.23	9.0	0.18	2.6	0.16	12.8	0.18	2.2	0.1	300.0	0.39	108.1	0.60
Division No. 6	521.7	0.19	90.9	0.16	4.2	0.09	5.6	0.12	2.6	0.16	8.2	0.11	1.8	0.1	209.0	0.27	40.6	0.20
Division No. 7	267.8	0.10	69.1	0.12	3.2	0.07	2.0	0.04	0.0	0.00	2.8	0.04	0.0	0.0	65.2	0.08	36.6	0.20
Division No. 8	209.1	0.08	65.3	0.12	3.0	0.07	1.4	0.03	0.0	0.00	1.8	0.02	0.4	0.0	25.8	0.03	30.9	0.20
PRINCE EDWARD ISLAND	1,205.9	0.43	295.1	0.53	16.6	0.37	21.3	0.44	6.7	0.41	31.8	0.45	6.0	0.4	259.3	0.34	126.0	0.70
Prince Edward Island	1,205.9	0.43	295.1	0.53	16.6	0.37	21.3	0.44	6.7	0.41	31.8	0.45	6.0	0.4	259.3	0.34	126.0	0.70
Kings County	105.8	0.04	32.9	0.06	1.9	0.04	0.6	0.01	0.9	0.05	1.9	0.03	0.2	0.0	17.5	0.02	18.0	0.10
Queens County	716.8	0.26	167.6	0.30	9.4	0.21	14.0	0.29	3.4	0.21	23.9	0.33	4.3	0.3	150.9	0.20	66.2	0.30
Prince County	383.2	0.14	94.6	0.17	5.3	0.12	6.7	0.14	2.4	0.15	6.1	0.08	1.6	0.1	90.9	0.12	41.8	0.20
NOVA SCOTIA	8,693.8	3.12	2,065.5	3.69	94.3	2.09	137.0	2.83	22.3	1.36	170.7	2.39	27.6	1.6	2,191.6	2.86	676.5	3.60
Cape Breton	1,310.0	0.47	369.6	0.66	16.9	0.37	19.8	0.41	4.1	0.25	23.1	0.32	2.5	0.2	286.9	0.37	98.8	0.50
Inverness County	226.0	0.08	76.5	0.14	3.5	0.08	1.5	0.03	0.9	0.05	0.7	0.01	0.3	0.0	40.6	0.05	19.5	0.10
Richmond County	45.2	0.02	15.7	0.03	0.7	0.02	0.4	0.01	0.0	0.00	0.2	0.00	0.0	0.0	3.3	0.00	6.5	0.00
Cape Breton County	999.2	0.36	266.1	0.48	12.1	0.27	17.6	0.36	3.3	0.20	22.2	0.31	2.2	0.1	238.0	0.31	66.3	0.40
Victoria County	39.6	0.01	11.4	0.02	0.5	0.01	0.4	0.01	0.0	0.00	0.0	0.00	0.0	0.0	5.0	0.01	6.5	0.00
North Shore	1,615.3	0.58	412.6	0.74	18.8	0.42	20.9	0.43	5.0	0.31	26.0	0.36	4.2	0.1	444.3	0.58	131.9	0.70
Colchester County	585.8	0.21	159.1	0.28	7.3	0.16	8.3	0.17	1.9	0.11	8.3	0.12	1.5	0.1	162.9	0.21	34.8	0.20
Cumberland County	342.3	0.12	78.2	0.14	3.6	0.08	2.4	0.05	0.6	0.04	9.1	0.13	0.3	0.0	102.3	0.13	29.7	0.20
Pictou County	440.3	0.16	110.9	0.20	5.1	0.11	7.2	0.15	0.9	0.05	2.9	0.04	0.8	0.1	113.4	0.15	39.4	0.20
Guysborough County	43.4	0.02	12.4	0.02	0.6	0.01	0.0	0.00	0.8	0.05	0.0	0.00	0.0	0.0	5.0	0.01	5.3	0.00
Antigonish County	203.4	0.07	52.0	0.09	2.4	0.05	3.1	0.06	0.9	0.05	5.7	0.08	1.6	0.1	60.6	0.08	22.7	0.10
Annapolis Valley	1,017.5	0.37	259.0	0.46	11.8	0.26	8.5	0.17	2.4	0.14	16.4	0.23	0.9	0.1	257.5	0.34	107.8	0.60
Annapolis County	115.8	0.04	26.2	0.05	1.2	0.03	1.3	0.03	0.0	0.00	0.5	0.01	0.1	0.0	36.7	0.05	13.4	0.10
Kings County	610.8	0.22	128.1	0.23	5.9	0.13	5.5	0.11	1.1	0.07	13.1	0.18	0.9	0.1	170.7	0.22	46.4	0.20
Hants County	290.9	0.10	104.7	0.19	4.8	0.11	1.7	0.03	1.3	0.08	2.8	0.04	0.0	0.0	50.0	0.07	48.0	0.30
Southern	1,178.2	0.42	280.4	0.50	12.8	0.28	10.5	0.22	1.9	0.11	16.5	0.23	3.0	0.2	312.0	0.41	86.7	0.50
Shelburne County	172.1	0.06	63.0	0.11	2.9	0.06	1.8	0.04	0.0	0.00	0.9	0.01	0.3	0.0	24.5	0.03	20.6	0.10
Yarmouth County	197.4	0.07	32.9	0.06	1.5	0.03	2.6	0.05	0.3	0.02	4.5	0.06	0.3	0.0	28.9	0.04	15.1	0.10
Digby County	209.1	0.08	50.3	0.09	2.3	0.05	1.7	0.03	0.0	0.00	0.9	0.01	0.0	0.0	79.5	0.10	18.5	0.10
Queens County	97.7	0.04	14.5	0.03	0.7	0.01	0.0	0.00	0.0	0.00	3.3	0.05	0.5	0.0	39.5	0.05	3.9	0.00
Lunenburg County	501.9	0.18	119.7	0.21	5.5	0.12	4.4	0.09	1.6	0.10	7.1	0.10	1.8	0.1	139.6	0.18	28.5	0.20
Halifax	3,572.8	1.28	743.8	1.33	34.0	0.75	77.3	1.60	8.9	0.54	88.8	1.24	17.1	1.0	890.9	1.16	251.3	1.30
Halifax County	3,572.8	1.28	743.8	1.33	34.0	0.75	77.3	1.60	8.9	0.54	88.8	1.24	17.1	1.0	890.9	1.16	251.3	1.30
NEW BRUNSWICK	7,095.9	2.55	1,697.9	3.03	65.0	1.44	95.6	1.97	29.9	1.83	142.9	2.00	27.1	1.6	1,974.2	2.57	526.5	2.80
Campbellton - Miramichi	1,791.9	0.64	413.3	0.74	15.8	0.35	21.4	0.44	5.4	0.33	35.8	0.50	7.0	0.4	535.8	0.70	170.2	0.90
Northumberland County	502.4	0.18	89.1	0.16	3.4	0.08	4.4	0.09	1.1	0.07	8.6	0.12	3.7	0.2	185.9	0.24	41.7	0.20
Restigouche County	363.3	0.13	90.1	0.16	3.4	0.08	2.5	0.05	1.5	0.09	5.4	0.08	0.3	0.0	99.0	0.13	30.3	0.20
Gloucester County	926.2	0.33	234.2	0.42	9.0	0.20	14.6	0.30	2.7	0.17	21.9	0.31	3.0	0.2	250.9	0.33	98.1	0.50
Moncton - Richibucto	1,750.2	0.63	434.0	0.78	16.6	0.37	22.9	0.47	2.5	0.15	36.5	0.51	5.7	0.3	501.8	0.65	145.9	0.80
Albert County	78.2	0.03	13.3	0.02	0.5	0.01	1.3	0.03	0.0	0.00	1.5	0.02	0.0	0.0	6.8	0.01	7.8	0.00
Westmorland County	1,409.2	0.51	289.0	0.52	11.1	0.25	21.4	0.44	2.5	0.15	29.6	0.41	5.7	0.3	440.6	0.57	121.1	0.60
Kent County	262.7	0.09	131.7	0.24	5.0	0.11	0.1	0.00	0.0	0.00	5.4	0.08	0.0	0.0	54.4	0.07	16.9	0.10
Saint John - St. Stephen	1,338.5	0.48	371.7	0.66	14.2	0.32	16.4	0.34	10.6	0.65	23.2	0.32	7.2	0.4	311.1	0.41	61.2	0.30
Saint John County	880.2	0.32	200.9	0.36	7.7	0.17	12.7	0.26	9.4	0.57	17.6	0.25	6.4	0.4	214.5	0.28	35.2	0.20
Charlotte County	143.2	0.05	40.6	0.07	1.6	0.03	0.9	0.02	0.1	0.01	3.6	0.05	0.3	0.0	41.7	0.05	10.9	0.10
Kings County	315.1	0.11	130.2	0.23	5.0	0.11	2.9	0.06	1.1	0.07	1.9	0.03	0.5	0.0	54.8	0.07	15.2	0.10
Fredericton - Oromocto	1,311.5	0.47	277.7	0.50	10.6	0.24	24.7	0.51	6.7	0.41	30.3	0.42	5.2	0.3	322.7	0.42	83.2	0.40
Sunbury County	174.4	0.06	55.7	0.10	2.1	0.05	1.3	0.03	0.0	0.00	0.0	0.00	0.0	0.0	58.7	0.08	7.6	0.00
Queens County	64.6	0.02	22.9	0.04	0.9	0.02	0.3	0.01	0.0	0.00	0.0	0.00	0.0	0.0	5.3	0.01	15.4	0.10
York County	1,072.5	0.38	199.1	0.36	7.6	0.17	23.1	0.48	6.7	0.41	29.8	0.42	5.2	0.3	258.7	0.34	60.2	0.30

Retail Sales Estimates, 2001

By Class of Business (Sales in $ millions)
1 – By Province, Economic Region and Census Division

	Auto Parts Accessories & Services		Household Furniture & Appliances		Household Furnishings		Other Durable Goods		Other Semi-Durable Goods		General Merchandise		Drugs and Patent Medicine		All Other Retail	
	$mill. Sales	% of Cdn Total	$mill. Sales	% of Cdn Total	$mill. Sales	% of Cdn Total	$mill. Sales	% of Cdn Total	$mill. Sales	% of Cdn Total	$mill. Sales	% of Cdn Total	$mill. Sales	% of Cdn Total	$mill. Sales	% of Cdn Total
CANADA	16,210.0	100.00	12,009.0	100.00	2,750.8	100.00	7,732.4	100.00	9,056.8	100.00	32,232.2	100.00	14,024.8	100.0	13,236.4	100.00
NEWFOUNDLAND	241.9	1.49	151.1	1.26	9.6	0.35	59.5	0.77	102.7	1.13	701.8	2.18	263.4	1.9	168.2	1.27
Avalon Peninsula	116.9	0.72	86.8	0.72	6.4	0.23	36.2	0.47	60.7	0.67	296.8	0.92	142.7	1.0	112.5	0.85
Division No. 1	116.9	0.72	86.8	0.72	6.4	0.23	36.2	0.47	60.7	0.67	296.8	0.92	142.7	1.0	112.5	0.85
South Coast - Burin Peninsula	12.4	0.08	10.3	0.09	0.5	0.02	2.8	0.04	7.3	0.08	55.9	0.17	17.3	0.1	5.4	0.04
Division No. 2	5.5	0.03	8.1	0.07	0.2	0.01	1.7	0.02	3.8	0.04	23.1	0.07	11.0	0.1	2.0	0.02
Division No. 3	6.9	0.04	2.1	0.02	0.2	0.01	1.1	0.01	3.5	0.04	32.8	0.10	6.3	0.0	3.4	0.03
West Coast - Northern Peninsula - Labrador	57.6	0.36	26.3	0.22	1.7	0.06	10.6	0.14	19.2	0.21	204.1	0.63	53.3	0.4	26.5	0.20
Division No. 4	8.3	0.05	3.5	0.03	0.5	0.02	1.0	0.01	3.9	0.04	42.3	0.13	13.1	0.1	6.4	0.05
Division No. 5	33.0	0.20	8.4	0.07	0.7	0.03	5.0	0.07	8.6	0.09	69.3	0.21	20.0	0.1	15.3	0.12
Division No. 9	5.8	0.04	2.6	0.02	0.0	0.00	2.6	0.03	2.3	0.02	37.7	0.12	7.3	0.1	1.4	0.01
Division No. 10	10.5	0.06	11.7	0.10	0.4	0.02	2.0	0.03	4.5	0.05	54.8	0.17	12.8	0.1	3.4	0.03
Notre Dame - Central Bonavista Bay	55.0	0.34	27.8	0.23	1.0	0.04	9.8	0.13	15.5	0.17	145.1	0.45	50.1	0.4	23.8	0.18
Division No. 6	35.4	0.22	15.2	0.13	0.5	0.02	5.5	0.07	6.8	0.08	54.6	0.17	24.3	0.2	16.5	0.12
Division No. 7	11.7	0.07	5.0	0.04	0.4	0.02	1.3	0.02	4.7	0.05	48.4	0.15	12.1	0.1	5.3	0.04
Division No. 8	8.0	0.05	7.6	0.06	0.1	0.00	3.0	0.04	4.0	0.04	42.0	0.13	13.8	0.1	2.0	0.02
PRINCE EDWARD ISLAND	75.8	0.47	32.3	0.27	18.1	0.66	24.7	0.32	52.3	0.58	111.7	0.35	73.5	0.5	54.6	0.41
Prince Edward Island	75.8	0.47	32.3	0.27	18.1	0.66	24.7	0.32	52.3	0.58	111.7	0.35	73.5	0.5	54.6	0.41
Kings County	5.8	0.04	3.2	0.03	1.1	0.04	2.1	0.03	7.0	0.08	8.0	0.02	1.8	0.0	3.1	0.02
Queens County	49.6	0.31	20.6	0.17	11.5	0.42	15.7	0.20	34.3	0.38	59.1	0.18	49.1	0.4	37.4	0.28
Prince County	20.4	0.13	8.5	0.07	5.5	0.20	6.9	0.09	11.0	0.12	44.7	0.14	22.6	0.2	14.1	0.11
NOVA SCOTIA	486.9	3.00	264.6	2.20	63.7	2.32	193.4	2.50	277.8	3.07	1,004.3	3.12	561.9	4.0	455.6	3.44
Cape Breton	82.0	0.51	23.1	0.19	11.9	0.43	21.2	0.27	41.8	0.46	143.7	0.45	106.3	0.8	58.3	0.44
Inverness County	10.6	0.07	1.5	0.01	1.6	0.06	2.3	0.03	11.3	0.12	30.8	0.10	14.4	0.1	10.2	0.08
Richmond County	4.3	0.03	0.7	0.01	0.3	0.01	0.0	0.00	1.7	0.02	1.7	0.01	8.7	0.1	1.0	0.01
Cape Breton County	65.4	0.40	20.0	0.17	9.9	0.36	18.9	0.24	22.7	0.25	109.7	0.34	78.9	0.6	45.8	0.35
Victoria County	1.6	0.01	1.0	0.01	0.1	0.00	0.0	0.00	6.1	0.07	1.4	0.00	4.3	0.0	1.3	0.01
North Shore	119.7	0.74	38.6	0.32	11.0	0.40	28.6	0.37	47.9	0.53	151.7	0.47	81.5	0.6	72.4	0.55
Colchester County	50.7	0.31	13.4	0.11	2.0	0.07	16.3	0.21	26.5	0.29	48.9	0.15	17.0	0.1	27.1	0.20
Cumberland County	21.6	0.13	5.7	0.05	2.1	0.08	5.0	0.07	7.9	0.09	43.6	0.14	15.7	0.1	14.6	0.11
Pictou County	30.3	0.19	15.7	0.13	5.9	0.21	4.7	0.06	8.1	0.09	43.9	0.14	31.5	0.2	19.5	0.15
Guysborough County	0.5	0.00	0.1	0.00	0.0	0.00	0.3	0.00	1.3	0.01	8.8	0.03	5.0	0.0	3.3	0.02
Antigonish County	16.6	0.10	3.6	0.03	0.9	0.03	2.3	0.03	4.1	0.05	6.6	0.02	12.4	0.1	7.9	0.06
Annapolis Valley	56.3	0.35	25.0	0.21	6.6	0.24	20.3	0.26	37.8	0.42	78.9	0.24	67.8	0.5	60.6	0.46
Annapolis County	4.6	0.03	4.0	0.03	0.5	0.02	2.6	0.03	7.5	0.08	6.9	0.02	3.9	0.0	6.4	0.05
Kings County	36.3	0.22	14.8	0.12	4.7	0.17	13.6	0.18	23.2	0.26	61.9	0.19	46.5	0.3	38.3	0.29
Hants County	15.5	0.10	6.3	0.05	1.3	0.05	4.1	0.05	7.0	0.08	10.1	0.03	17.4	0.1	15.9	0.12
Southern	84.5	0.52	42.9	0.36	4.4	0.16	24.1	0.31	36.1	0.40	107.1	0.33	99.4	0.7	56.0	0.42
Shelburne County	7.8	0.05	11.5	0.10	0.0	0.00	4.7	0.06	5.0	0.05	6.3	0.02	18.9	0.1	3.9	0.03
Yarmouth County	22.1	0.14	5.3	0.04	0.7	0.02	5.6	0.07	5.0	0.05	34.6	0.11	25.2	0.2	12.8	0.10
Digby County	14.8	0.09	4.4	0.04	0.9	0.03	2.1	0.03	2.8	0.03	7.2	0.02	15.9	0.1	7.7	0.06
Queens County	5.4	0.03	0.3	0.00	0.7	0.02	0.5	0.01	3.8	0.04	9.9	0.03	8.3	0.1	6.6	0.05
Lunenburg County	34.4	0.21	21.5	0.18	2.1	0.08	11.1	0.14	19.5	0.22	49.1	0.15	31.1	0.2	25.0	0.19
Halifax	144.4	0.89	135.0	1.12	29.9	1.09	99.2	1.28	114.2	1.26	522.9	1.62	206.8	1.5	208.3	1.57
Halifax County	144.4	0.89	135.0	1.12	29.9	1.09	99.2	1.28	114.2	1.26	522.9	1.62	206.8	1.5	208.3	1.57
NEW BRUNSWICK	434.8	2.68	211.9	1.76	59.1	2.15	129.1	1.67	214.8	2.37	817.4	2.54	376.7	2.7	293.0	2.21
Campbellton - Miramichi	94.2	0.58	50.9	0.42	16.0	0.58	35.7	0.46	42.5	0.47	215.6	0.67	94.9	0.7	37.3	0.28
Northumberland County	25.4	0.16	12.2	0.10	2.7	0.10	13.4	0.17	7.9	0.09	67.4	0.21	22.2	0.2	13.3	0.10
Restigouche County	20.1	0.12	9.1	0.08	2.1	0.08	6.9	0.09	8.2	0.09	49.5	0.15	29.7	0.2	5.1	0.04
Gloucester County	48.7	0.30	29.6	0.25	11.2	0.41	15.4	0.20	26.4	0.29	98.7	0.31	43.0	0.3	18.9	0.14
Moncton - Richibucto	96.1	0.59	51.5	0.43	13.6	0.49	35.6	0.46	60.9	0.67	128.3	0.40	117.0	0.8	81.5	0.62
Albert County	6.7	0.04	5.5	0.05	2.0	0.07	1.1	0.01	5.1	0.06	7.6	0.02	15.0	0.1	4.0	0.03
Westmorland County	81.7	0.50	41.9	0.35	10.3	0.38	32.8	0.42	49.7	0.55	105.9	0.33	96.5	0.7	69.3	0.52
Kent County	7.7	0.05	4.1	0.03	1.3	0.05	1.6	0.02	6.0	0.07	14.8	0.05	5.5	0.0	8.1	0.06
Saint John - St. Stephen	76.5	0.47	43.2	0.36	8.3	0.30	28.1	0.36	46.5	0.51	209.1	0.65	60.8	0.4	50.3	0.38
Saint John County	41.9	0.26	29.1	0.24	7.4	0.27	17.9	0.23	24.4	0.27	182.8	0.57	37.6	0.3	34.8	0.26
Charlotte County	12.1	0.07	4.0	0.03	0.3	0.01	1.4	0.02	9.3	0.10	8.2	0.03	3.1	0.0	5.1	0.04
Kings County	22.5	0.14	10.2	0.08	0.7	0.03	8.8	0.11	12.8	0.14	18.1	0.06	20.1	0.1	10.4	0.08
Fredericton - Oromocto	93.7	0.58	31.3	0.26	15.4	0.56	17.5	0.23	32.6	0.36	191.0	0.59	73.9	0.5	95.0	0.72
Sunbury County	9.7	0.06	1.6	0.01	0.4	0.02	1.1	0.01	3.8	0.04	15.2	0.05	10.2	0.1	6.6	0.05
Queens County	6.8	0.04	1.2	0.01	0.3	0.01	0.3	0.00	1.4	0.02	7.6	0.02	0.3	0.0	1.7	0.01
York County	77.2	0.48	28.4	0.24	14.7	0.53	16.2	0.21	27.3	0.30	168.2	0.52	63.4	0.5	86.7	0.66

Retail Sales, 2001 1 – By Province, Economic Region and Census Division	Total Sales		Supermarkets & Groceries		All Other Food		Women's Clothing		Men's Clothing		Other Clothing		Shoes		Motor Vehicles & Recreation Vehicles		Gas Service Stations	
	$mill. Sales	% of Cdn Total	$mill. Sales	% of Cdn Total	$mill. Sales	% of Cdn Total	$mill. Sales	% of Cdn Total	$mill. Sales	% of Cdn Total	$mill. Sales	% of Cdn Total	$mill. Sales	% of Cdn Total	$mill. Sales	% of Cdn Total	$mill. Sales	% of Cdn Total
Edmundston - Woodstock	903.7	0.32	201.1	0.36	7.7	0.17	10.2	0.21	4.7	0.29	17.2	0.24	2.0	0.1	302.8	0.39	66.0	0.30
Carleton County	341.7	0.12	62.6	0.11	2.4	0.05	2.0	0.04	1.9	0.12	2.6	0.04	0.7	0.0	161.1	0.21	14.4	0.10
Victoria County	265.8	0.10	39.5	0.07	1.5	0.03	3.3	0.07	1.1	0.07	7.9	0.11	0.8	0.0	102.4	0.13	20.0	0.10
Madawaska County	296.3	0.11	99.1	0.18	3.8	0.08	4.8	0.10	1.7	0.10	6.7	0.09	0.6	0.0	39.3	0.05	31.6	0.20
QUÉBEC	64,688.8	23.21	14,656.9	26.18	1,342.7	29.81	1,299.1	26.80	352.5	21.51	1,810.5	25.33	576.7	33.8	18,575.2	24.22	3,777.6	19.90
Gaspésie - Îles-de-la-Madeleine	879.9	0.32	335.5	0.60	30.7	0.68	5.8	0.12	2.7	0.16	17.4	0.24	4.6	0.3	197.4	0.26	70.8	0.40
Les Îles-de-la-Madeleine	168.4	0.06	66.1	0.12	6.1	0.13	1.6	0.03	0.7	0.04	6.3	0.09	0.7	0.0	27.9	0.04	18.1	0.10
Pabok	155.3	0.06	67.4	0.12	6.2	0.14	0.9	0.02	0.4	0.02	3.3	0.05	1.3	0.1	27.9	0.04	7.1	0.00
La Côte-de-Gaspé	174.8	0.06	63.2	0.11	5.8	0.13	0.4	0.01	0.6	0.04	3.1	0.04	0.5	0.0	41.1	0.05	16.5	0.10
Denis-Riverin	85.2	0.03	37.7	0.07	3.5	0.08	0.7	0.01	0.2	0.01	1.2	0.02	0.0	0.0	11.8	0.02	5.2	0.00
Bonaventure	192.1	0.07	53.3	0.10	4.9	0.11	1.3	0.03	0.5	0.03	0.5	0.01	2.1	0.1	77.9	0.10	10.0	0.10
Avignon	104.0	0.04	47.7	0.09	4.4	0.10	0.9	0.02	0.4	0.02	3.0	0.04	0.0	0.0	10.8	0.01	13.9	0.10
Bas-Saint-Laurent	1,909.7	0.69	488.1	0.87	44.7	0.99	16.8	0.35	8.8	0.53	47.2	0.66	11.4	0.7	612.3	0.80	189.8	1.00
La Matapédia	113.4	0.04	36.3	0.06	3.3	0.07	0.5	0.01	1.2	0.07	1.5	0.02	1.1	0.1	27.4	0.04	11.0	0.10
Matane	239.9	0.09	69.6	0.12	6.4	0.14	2.0	0.04	1.2	0.07	4.4	0.06	0.8	0.1	73.5	0.10	25.2	0.10
La Mitis	131.1	0.05	42.1	0.08	3.9	0.09	0.4	0.01	0.2	0.01	2.4	0.03	0.4	0.0	35.3	0.05	14.6	0.10
Rimouski-Neigette	518.5	0.19	157.9	0.28	14.5	0.32	5.9	0.12	3.0	0.18	11.6	0.16	3.8	0.2	141.1	0.18	17.5	0.10
Les Basques	84.4	0.03	26.3	0.05	2.4	0.05	0.4	0.01	0.2	0.01	0.9	0.01	0.7	0.0	28.9	0.04	3.9	0.00
Rivière-du-Loup	422.3	0.15	46.8	0.08	4.3	0.10	5.3	0.11	2.1	0.13	20.0	0.28	1.9	0.1	180.8	0.24	61.4	0.30
Témiscouata	157.7	0.06	35.9	0.06	3.3	0.07	1.0	0.02	0.4	0.02	4.4	0.06	0.6	0.0	36.7	0.05	30.1	0.20
Kamouraska	242.4	0.09	73.2	0.13	6.7	0.15	1.2	0.02	0.6	0.04	1.9	0.03	2.2	0.1	88.7	0.12	26.2	0.10
Québec	7,099.3	2.55	1,540.6	2.75	141.1	3.13	155.4	3.21	40.5	2.47	327.8	4.59	80.1	4.7	1,883.0	2.46	439.1	2.30
Charlevoix-Est	151.8	0.05	28.6	0.05	2.6	0.06	4.8	0.10	1.1	0.06	4.9	0.07	2.0	0.1	41.1	0.05	16.2	0.10
Charlevoix	106.5	0.04	41.4	0.07	3.8	0.08	1.9	0.04	0.3	0.02	1.7	0.02	0.7	0.0	20.6	0.03	5.2	0.00
L'Île-d'Orléans	25.3	0.01	9.7	0.02	0.9	0.02	0.0	0.00	0.0	0.00	0.0	0.00	0.0	0.0	1.5	0.00	5.5	0.00
La Côte-de-Beaupré	272.0	0.10	52.8	0.09	4.8	0.11	0.7	0.01	0.0	0.00	3.7	0.05	1.9	0.1	142.6	0.19	13.3	0.10
La Jacques-Cartier	75.4	0.03	22.0	0.04	2.0	0.04	0.0	0.00	0.0	0.00	0.5	0.01	0.0	0.0	16.7	0.02	14.2	0.10
Communauté urbaine de Québec	5,985.7	2.15	1,302.9	2.33	119.4	2.65	145.3	3.00	37.7	2.30	312.2	4.37	74.5	4.4	1,435.8	1.87	347.9	1.80
Portneuf	482.5	0.17	83.3	0.15	7.6	0.17	2.7	0.06	1.4	0.09	4.8	0.07	1.1	0.1	224.8	0.29	36.9	0.20
Chaudière - Appalaches	3,849.5	1.38	938.8	1.68	86.0	1.91	41.9	0.86	11.9	0.73	71.1	0.99	14.9	0.9	1,253.1	1.63	261.9	1.40
L'Islet	148.6	0.05	67.8	0.12	6.2	0.14	0.5	0.01	0.8	0.05	0.9	0.01	0.1	0.0	22.5	0.03	13.9	0.10
Montmagny	258.1	0.09	47.2	0.08	4.3	0.10	4.4	0.09	1.1	0.06	4.9	0.07	1.3	0.1	86.7	0.11	20.4	0.10
Bellechasse	222.3	0.08	71.5	0.13	6.6	0.15	0.4	0.01	0.6	0.04	3.0	0.04	0.5	0.0	66.1	0.09	22.6	0.10
Desjardins	869.0	0.31	115.2	0.21	10.6	0.23	9.9	0.20	2.2	0.14	21.8	0.30	4.2	0.3	355.6	0.46	42.4	0.20
Les Chutes-de-la-Chaudière	512.3	0.18	181.1	0.32	16.6	0.37	1.0	0.02	0.2	0.01	8.2	0.12	1.8	0.1	98.0	0.13	43.0	0.20
La Nouvelle-Beauce	283.4	0.10	67.3	0.12	6.2	0.14	5.7	0.12	0.8	0.05	3.3	0.05	1.3	0.1	82.8	0.11	11.3	0.10
Robert-Cliche	134.6	0.05	33.2	0.06	3.0	0.07	1.8	0.04	0.5	0.03	1.8	0.03	0.2	0.0	38.7	0.05	9.1	0.00
Les Etchemins	150.7	0.05	25.1	0.04	2.3	0.05	1.3	0.03	0.2	0.01	3.5	0.05	0.7	0.0	71.5	0.09	10.3	0.10
Beauce-Sartigan	578.2	0.21	180.7	0.32	16.6	0.37	10.3	0.21	3.9	0.24	11.0	0.15	2.0	0.1	160.7	0.21	25.9	0.10
L'Amiante	423.5	0.15	76.7	0.14	7.0	0.16	5.5	0.11	1.6	0.10	9.7	0.14	2.4	0.1	160.7	0.21	36.5	0.20
Lotbinière	268.9	0.10	73.0	0.13	6.7	0.15	1.0	0.02	0.2	0.01	3.1	0.04	0.5	0.0	109.7	0.14	26.5	0.10
Estrie	2,366.3	0.85	569.9	1.02	52.2	1.16	52.6	1.09	10.0	0.61	98.2	1.37	18.2	1.1	632.4	0.82	138.1	0.70
Le Granit	257.3	0.09	47.9	0.09	4.4	0.10	26.4	0.54	0.5	0.03	60.6	0.85	1.1	0.1	40.2	0.05	17.5	0.10
Asbestos	107.2	0.04	57.2	0.10	5.2	0.12	4.1	0.08	1.3	0.08	1.9	0.03	0.5	0.0	2.9	0.00	7.4	0.00
Le Haut-Saint-François	120.3	0.04	32.9	0.06	3.0	0.07	0.0	0.00	0.0	0.00	1.5	0.02	0.1	0.0	32.3	0.04	17.8	0.10
Le Val-Saint-François	192.3	0.07	56.4	0.10	5.2	0.11	0.5	0.01	0.8	0.05	4.4	0.06	1.6	0.1	66.6	0.09	10.3	0.10
Sherbrooke	1,271.9	0.46	240.2	0.43	22.0	0.49	17.8	0.37	6.0	0.36	25.9	0.36	12.2	0.7	373.3	0.49	63.4	0.30
Coaticook	112.2	0.04	32.9	0.06	3.0	0.07	0.5	0.01	0.6	0.04	0.5	0.01	0.0	0.0	36.3	0.05	2.3	0.00
Memphrémagog	305.3	0.11	102.4	0.18	9.4	0.21	3.3	0.07	1.0	0.06	3.3	0.05	2.7	0.2	80.8	0.11	19.4	0.10
Montérégie	11,855.8	4.25	2,638.1	4.71	241.7	5.37	205.2	4.23	62.7	3.83	260.5	3.64	102.6	6.0	3,924.3	5.12	718.8	3.80
Brome-Missisquoi	437.7	0.16	143.2	0.26	13.1	0.29	6.6	0.14	0.8	0.05	12.5	0.17	1.9	0.1	91.6	0.12	26.2	0.10
La Haute-Yamaska	868.1	0.31	186.3	0.33	17.1	0.38	21.6	0.45	5.3	0.32	18.6	0.26	7.2	0.4	288.5	0.38	44.9	0.20
Acton	95.3	0.03	23.6	0.04	2.2	0.05	1.2	0.02	0.9	0.05	2.7	0.04	0.5	0.0	33.3	0.04	5.8	0.00
Le Bas-Richelieu	478.4	0.17	98.8	0.18	9.0	0.20	6.9	0.14	2.7	0.16	16.9	0.24	4.0	0.2	170.0	0.22	29.4	0.20
Les Maskoutains	866.2	0.31	181.5	0.32	16.6	0.37	6.9	0.14	6.2	0.38	26.4	0.37	4.0	0.2	338.5	0.44	42.7	0.20
Rouville	236.3	0.08	70.1	0.13	6.4	0.14	0.3	0.01	0.0	0.00	0.5	0.01	0.6	0.0	64.2	0.08	28.8	0.20
Le Haut-Richelieu	1,114.3	0.40	266.1	0.48	24.4	0.54	13.6	0.28	1.9	0.12	16.1	0.23	9.4	0.6	388.0	0.51	44.3	0.20
La Vallée-du-Richelieu	1,318.6	0.47	203.9	0.36	18.7	0.41	61.1	1.26	14.9	0.91	40.3	0.56	26.7	1.6	408.5	0.53	60.8	0.30
Champlain	2,721.5	0.98	600.6	1.07	55.0	1.22	46.8	0.97	14.2	0.86	81.2	1.14	26.9	1.6	813.2	1.06	147.4	0.80
Lajemmerais	1,108.3	0.40	261.7	0.47	24.0	0.53	7.9	0.16	5.5	0.34	11.5	0.16	4.0	0.2	463.4	0.60	55.0	0.30
Roussillon	935.1	0.34	210.1	0.38	19.2	0.43	9.9	0.20	2.1	0.13	11.5	0.16	1.6	0.1	315.5	0.41	96.4	0.50
Les Jardins-de-Napierville	270.4	0.10	45.4	0.08	4.2	0.09	1.6	0.03	0.4	0.02	1.7	0.02	1.2	0.1	126.9	0.17	25.9	0.10
Le Haut-Saint-Laurent	145.1	0.05	38.8	0.07	3.6	0.08	0.2	0.00	0.0	0.00	1.4	0.02	0.5	0.0	39.7	0.05	10.7	0.10
Beauharnois-Salaberry	597.1	0.21	147.6	0.26	13.5	0.30	10.8	0.22	6.2	0.38	12.5	0.17	9.5	0.6	178.3	0.23	32.3	0.20
Vaudreuil-Soulanges	663.5	0.24	160.4	0.29	14.7	0.33	9.7	0.20	1.7	0.11	6.8	0.10	4.6	0.3	204.8	0.27	68.2	0.40
Montréal	14,008.7	5.03	2,717.1	4.85	248.9	5.53	500.6	10.33	115.7	7.06	493.9	6.91	165.6	9.7	3,175.8	4.14	551.9	2.90
Communauté urbaine de Montréal	14,008.7	5.03	2,717.1	4.85	248.9	5.53	500.6	10.33	115.7	7.06	493.9	6.91	165.6	9.7	3,175.8	4.14	551.9	2.90
Laval	3,360.1	1.21	593.1	1.06	54.3	1.21	69.2	1.43	29.5	1.80	110.9	1.55	42.4	2.5	1,085.5	1.42	176.5	0.90
Laval	3,360.1	1.21	593.1	1.06	54.3	1.21	69.2	1.43	29.5	1.80	110.9	1.55	42.4	2.5	1,085.5	1.42	176.5	0.90
Lanaudière	3,598.0	1.29	933.4	1.67	85.5	1.90	41.6	0.86	12.1	0.74	68.4	0.96	25.9	1.5	1,107.1	1.44	222.1	1.20
D'Autray	212.1	0.08	74.0	0.13	6.8	0.15	1.9	0.04	0.7	0.04	3.0	0.04	1.8	0.1	53.4	0.07	21.0	0.10
L'Assomption	949.6	0.34	232.1	0.41	21.3	0.47	9.1	0.19	2.7	0.16	11.0	0.15	7.2	0.4	285.6	0.37	42.7	0.20
Joliette	788.2	0.28	158.5	0.28	14.5	0.32	17.7	0.36	4.2	0.26	20.1	0.28	7.1	0.4	336.5	0.44	23.3	0.10
Matawinie	263.2	0.09	112.9	0.20	10.3	0.23	0.5	0.01	0.0	0.00	1.8	0.03	1.5	0.1	19.6	0.03	51.7	0.30
Montcalm	251.4	0.09	91.2	0.16	8.4	0.19	3.2	0.07	1.7	0.11	1.2	0.02	0.6	0.0	41.1	0.05	42.7	0.20
Les Moulins	1,133.6	0.41	264.8	0.47	24.3	0.54	9.2	0.19	2.8	0.17	31.4	0.44	7.8	0.5	370.8	0.48	40.7	0.20
Laurentides	3,908.6	1.40	909.2	1.62	83.3	1.85	57.7	1.19	14.3	0.87	82.6	1.16	25.8	1.5	1,324.6	1.73	248.6	1.30
Deux-Montagnes	647.7	0.23	178.2	0.32	16.3	0.36	6.2	0.13	2.0	0.12	9.9	0.14	4.4	0.3	217.5	0.28	26.5	0.10
Thérèse-De Blainville	1,091.4	0.39	249.7	0.45	22.9	0.51	21.0	0.43	5.6	0.34	23.3	0.33	6.9	0.4	401.2	0.52	56.9	0.30
Mirabel	171.8	0.06	8.9	0.02	0.8	0.02	0.4	0.01	0.0	0.00	3.6	0.05	0.0	0.0	85.2	0.11	16.2	0.10
La Rivière-du-Nord	812.1	0.29	185.1	0.33	17.0	0.38	14.8	0.31	2.6	0.16	17.5	0.25	7.4	0.4	211.1	0.28	51.7	0.30
Argenteuil	178.1	0.06	37.9	0.07	3.5	0.08	1.0	0.02	1.3	0.08	0.9	0.01	0.9	0.1	66.6	0.09	12.9	0.10
Les Pays-d'en-Haut	241.4	0.09	84.5	0.15	7.7	0.17	6.0	0.12	0.9	0.05	8.8	0.12	1.6	0.1	50.0	0.07	33.3	0.20

Retail Sales, 2001
1 – By Province, Economic Region and Census Division

	Auto Parts Accessories & Services		Household Furniture & Appliances		Household Furnishings		Other Durable Goods		Other Semi-Durable Goods		General Merchandise		Drugs and Patent Medicine		All Other Retail	
	$mill. Sales	% of Cdn Total	$mill. Sales	% of Cdn Total	$mill. Sales	% of Cdn Total	$mill. Sales	% of Cdn Total	$mill. Sales	% of Cdn Total	$mill. Sales	% of Cdn Total	$mill. Sales	% of Cdn Total	$mill. Sales	% of Cdn Total
Edmundston - Woodstock	74.4	0.46	35.0	0.29	5.8	0.21	12.2	0.16	32.3	0.36	73.4	0.23	30.0	0.2	29.0	0.22
Carleton County	22.5	0.14	6.9	0.06	1.0	0.04	1.9	0.02	15.3	0.17	30.2	0.09	8.8	0.1	7.5	0.06
Victoria County	24.7	0.15	8.6	0.07	3.0	0.11	3.0	0.04	6.9	0.08	21.0	0.07	13.4	0.1	8.6	0.06
Madawaska County	27.1	0.17	19.5	0.16	1.8	0.07	7.3	0.09	10.0	0.11	22.2	0.07	7.8	0.1	13.0	0.10
QUÉBEC	3,994.5	24.64	3,137.9	26.13	505.5	18.38	1,590.0	20.56	1,765.2	19.49	6,277.0	19.47	2,963.4	21.1	2,064.1	15.59
Gaspésie - Îles-de-la-Madeleine	40.2	0.25	49.3	0.41	5.6	0.20	19.9	0.26	22.9	0.25	34.5	0.11	29.6	0.2	12.9	0.10
Les Îles-de-la-Madeleine	5.4	0.03	7.4	0.06	0.8	0.03	5.4	0.07	5.0	0.06	5.5	0.02	7.5	0.1	3.8	0.03
Pabok	9.4	0.06	6.0	0.05	2.0	0.07	4.4	0.06	4.6	0.05	6.1	0.02	7.3	0.1	1.1	0.01
La Côte-de-Gaspé	6.3	0.04	7.4	0.06	1.0	0.04	2.9	0.04	4.9	0.05	12.3	0.04	5.9	0.0	2.8	0.02
Denis-Riverin	5.0	0.03	5.1	0.04	0.2	0.01	1.6	0.02	2.6	0.03	4.8	0.01	5.4	0.0	0.5	0.00
Bonaventure	8.9	0.06	18.1	0.15	0.9	0.03	3.5	0.05	2.8	0.03	3.3	0.01	1.6	0.0	2.3	0.02
Avignon	5.2	0.03	5.1	0.04	0.7	0.02	2.2	0.03	3.0	0.03	2.6	0.01	1.8	0.0	2.5	0.02
Bas-Saint-Laurent	101.2	0.62	80.7	0.67	13.8	0.50	33.5	0.43	66.9	0.74	100.6	0.31	58.9	0.4	35.1	0.26
La Matapédia	7.2	0.04	7.1	0.06	0.2	0.01	3.3	0.04	5.5	0.06	3.3	0.01	2.6	0.0	1.6	0.01
Matane	8.1	0.05	10.1	0.08	0.8	0.03	1.9	0.02	13.6	0.15	12.1	0.04	6.3	0.0	4.1	0.03
La Mitis	13.1	0.08	4.6	0.04	0.6	0.02	2.5	0.03	3.4	0.04	5.3	0.02	0.5	0.0	1.8	0.01
Rimouski-Neigette	33.5	0.21	22.2	0.18	4.5	0.16	13.5	0.17	15.8	0.17	34.1	0.11	27.4	0.2	12.3	0.09
Les Basques	4.0	0.02	3.4	0.03	0.0	0.00	2.2	0.03	1.8	0.02	3.7	0.01	4.8	0.0	1.0	0.01
Rivière-du-Loup	14.6	0.09	16.8	0.14	4.6	0.17	5.4	0.07	14.2	0.16	25.0	0.08	9.1	0.1	10.2	0.08
Témiscouata	10.6	0.07	11.5	0.10	1.2	0.04	1.3	0.02	3.0	0.03	11.6	0.04	4.8	0.0	1.4	0.01
Kamouraska	10.1	0.06	5.0	0.04	2.0	0.07	3.5	0.05	9.5	0.11	5.5	0.02	3.4	0.0	2.7	0.02
Québec	446.0	2.75	370.5	3.09	51.4	1.87	229.5	2.97	221.2	2.44	538.8	1.67	387.8	2.8	246.3	1.86
Charlevoix-Est	13.8	0.09	8.5	0.07	0.7	0.02	4.9	0.06	8.3	0.09	2.9	0.01	7.4	0.1	4.0	0.03
Charlevoix	5.5	0.03	5.3	0.04	0.4	0.02	1.0	0.01	6.8	0.07	4.6	0.01	4.5	0.0	2.9	0.02
L'Île-d'Orléans	3.0	0.02	1.2	0.01	0.1	0.00	0.0	0.00	1.3	0.01	0.0	0.00	2.0	0.0	0.1	0.00
La Côte-de-Beaupré	12.3	0.08	2.8	0.02	0.3	0.01	10.9	0.14	8.1	0.09	2.9	0.01	13.2	0.1	1.8	0.01
La Jacques-Cartier	5.2	0.03	2.7	0.02	0.7	0.02	2.6	0.03	1.2	0.01	0.2	0.00	6.0	0.0	1.4	0.01
Communauté urbaine de Québec	381.4	2.35	338.8	2.82	47.9	1.74	204.2	2.64	188.5	2.08	487.7	1.51	332.6	2.4	229.0	1.73
Portneuf	24.7	0.15	11.2	0.09	1.4	0.05	5.9	0.08	7.0	0.08	40.4	0.13	22.0	0.2	7.1	0.05
Chaudière - Appalaches	299.8	1.85	150.0	1.25	25.5	0.93	59.3	0.77	117.8	1.30	248.4	0.77	137.2	1.0	131.7	1.00
L'Islet	13.0	0.08	2.5	0.02	0.6	0.02	2.2	0.03	8.5	0.09	5.0	0.02	3.6	0.0	0.4	0.00
Montmagny	13.6	0.08	18.6	0.16	2.2	0.08	6.1	0.08	9.2	0.10	12.5	0.04	18.4	0.1	7.4	0.06
Bellechasse	19.8	0.12	6.4	0.05	1.2	0.04	2.5	0.03	7.4	0.08	7.5	0.02	4.2	0.0	2.1	0.02
Desjardins	53.5	0.33	29.3	0.24	6.6	0.24	19.2	0.25	28.6	0.32	86.5	0.27	41.6	0.3	41.9	0.32
Les Chutes-de-la-Chaudière	60.5	0.37	17.2	0.14	2.4	0.09	6.5	0.08	22.5	0.25	10.5	0.03	28.1	0.2	14.8	0.11
La Nouvelle-Beauce	20.0	0.12	21.6	0.18	1.5	0.05	3.6	0.05	12.2	0.14	15.8	0.05	4.7	0.0	25.3	0.19
Robert-Cliche	18.6	0.11	2.3	0.02	0.8	0.03	0.7	0.01	2.8	0.03	11.0	0.03	9.2	0.1	0.9	0.01
Les Etchemins	13.0	0.08	2.8	0.02	0.3	0.01	1.3	0.02	5.5	0.06	8.8	0.03	3.6	0.0	0.4	0.00
Beauce-Sartigan	39.2	0.24	25.0	0.21	5.3	0.19	6.8	0.09	9.7	0.11	51.6	0.16	8.4	0.1	21.2	0.16
L'Amiante	33.0	0.20	17.0	0.14	3.5	0.13	7.7	0.10	7.2	0.08	33.8	0.10	12.5	0.1	8.8	0.07
Lotbinière	15.6	0.10	7.3	0.06	1.3	0.05	2.8	0.04	4.2	0.05	5.5	0.02	3.0	0.0	8.5	0.06
Estrie	156.7	0.97	103.2	0.86	11.9	0.43	45.3	0.59	65.7	0.73	238.8	0.74	113.1	0.8	59.9	0.45
Le Granit	11.2	0.07	4.1	0.03	0.5	0.02	2.2	0.03	5.5	0.06	26.6	0.08	6.4	0.1	2.4	0.02
Asbestos	6.7	0.04	3.2	0.03	1.1	0.04	1.2	0.02	2.2	0.02	4.4	0.01	4.5	0.0	3.4	0.03
Le Haut-Saint-François	8.6	0.05	3.9	0.03	0.2	0.01	0.0	0.00	4.3	0.05	10.8	0.03	3.6	0.0	1.2	0.01
Le Val-Saint-François	13.8	0.09	5.1	0.04	2.4	0.09	2.0	0.03	5.6	0.06	9.2	0.03	6.2	0.0	2.0	0.02
Sherbrooke	98.2	0.61	65.3	0.54	6.4	0.23	32.9	0.43	38.0	0.42	159.3	0.49	69.6	0.5	41.4	0.31
Coaticook	7.0	0.04	4.8	0.04	0.0	0.00	0.3	0.00	1.3	0.01	13.4	0.04	9.2	0.1	0.2	0.00
Memphrémagog	11.3	0.07	16.8	0.14	1.3	0.05	6.7	0.09	8.8	0.10	15.1	0.05	13.6	0.1	9.3	0.07
Montérégie	824.4	5.09	602.1	5.01	76.9	2.79	274.5	3.55	286.2	3.16	778.1	2.41	524.1	3.7	335.5	2.54
Brome-Missisquoi	28.9	0.18	23.4	0.19	1.4	0.05	10.3	0.13	12.4	0.14	34.5	0.11	20.6	0.2	10.2	0.08
La Haute-Yamaska	52.0	0.32	41.3	0.34	6.2	0.22	29.2	0.38	30.9	0.34	39.7	0.12	36.2	0.3	43.2	0.33
Acton	7.0	0.04	7.1	0.06	0.7	0.02	1.9	0.02	2.0	0.02	4.4	0.01	0.6	0.0	1.5	0.01
Le Bas-Richelieu	27.6	0.17	20.8	0.17	3.3	0.12	14.8	0.19	7.2	0.08	28.1	0.09	24.9	0.2	14.0	0.11
Les Maskoutains	77.4	0.48	65.1	0.54	2.9	0.11	18.6	0.24	20.1	0.22	31.8	0.10	13.2	0.1	14.5	0.11
Rouville	35.7	0.22	6.2	0.05	0.5	0.02	3.9	0.05	3.9	0.04	2.9	0.01	9.7	0.1	2.5	0.02
Le Haut-Richelieu	79.0	0.49	60.8	0.51	6.9	0.25	29.5	0.38	22.3	0.25	76.7	0.24	49.8	0.4	25.5	0.19
La Vallée-du-Richelieu	50.2	0.31	35.5	0.30	2.7	0.10	40.6	0.53	46.3	0.51	217.2	0.67	60.3	0.4	31.0	0.23
Champlain	203.8	1.26	164.4	1.37	28.8	1.05	71.0	0.92	52.4	0.58	185.4	0.58	123.2	0.9	107.3	0.81
Lajemmerais	72.6	0.45	41.7	0.35	11.4	0.41	11.2	0.14	24.9	0.27	36.7	0.11	58.0	0.4	19.0	0.14
Roussillon	74.1	0.46	40.4	0.34	5.5	0.20	17.4	0.23	28.1	0.31	31.2	0.10	46.5	0.3	25.5	0.19
Les Jardins-de-Napierville	17.4	0.11	4.4	0.04	0.7	0.02	1.5	0.02	4.4	0.05	17.1	0.05	6.3	0.0	11.5	0.09
Le Haut-Saint-Laurent	5.5	0.03	25.9	0.22	0.2	0.01	1.0	0.01	3.7	0.04	6.2	0.02	4.7	0.0	3.0	0.02
Beauharnois-Salaberry	42.4	0.26	39.7	0.33	4.1	0.15	16.8	0.22	12.3	0.14	22.8	0.07	33.0	0.2	15.3	0.12
Vaudreuil-Soulanges	51.1	0.31	25.4	0.21	1.7	0.06	7.0	0.09	15.4	0.17	43.5	0.13	37.1	0.3	11.5	0.09
Montréal	658.6	4.06	785.0	6.54	141.9	5.16	355.1	4.59	422.7	4.67	2,266.3	7.03	759.1	5.4	650.6	4.92
Communauté urbaine de Montréal	658.6	4.06	785.0	6.54	141.9	5.16	355.1	4.59	422.7	4.67	2,266.3	7.03	759.1	5.4	650.6	4.92
Laval	217.9	1.34	211.1	1.76	66.9	2.43	113.0	1.46	63.0	0.70	279.8	0.87	147.3	1.1	99.8	0.75
Laval	217.9	1.34	211.1	1.76	66.9	2.43	113.0	1.46	63.0	0.70	279.8	0.87	147.3	1.1	99.8	0.75
Lanaudière	224.7	1.39	115.5	0.96	18.0	0.66	80.2	1.04	100.9	1.11	357.0	1.11	125.7	0.9	79.8	0.60
D'Autray	19.5	0.12	3.9	0.03	0.9	0.03	3.6	0.05	3.9	0.04	10.1	0.03	3.9	0.0	3.8	0.03
L'Assomption	45.5	0.28	27.5	0.23	3.3	0.12	37.7	0.49	32.0	0.35	121.2	0.38	42.4	0.3	28.5	0.22
Joliette	44.8	0.28	35.3	0.29	7.1	0.26	19.4	0.25	15.3	0.17	37.8	0.12	27.7	0.2	18.8	0.14
Matawinie	15.8	0.10	12.6	0.10	0.2	0.01	3.5	0.05	8.4	0.09	4.2	0.01	17.7	0.1	2.3	0.02
Montcalm	17.6	0.11	17.0	0.14	0.5	0.02	1.5	0.02	9.0	0.10	4.4	0.01	7.0	0.0	4.2	0.03
Les Moulins	81.3	0.50	19.2	0.16	6.1	0.22	14.5	0.19	32.4	0.36	179.3	0.56	26.9	0.2	22.1	0.17
Laurentides	249.3	1.54	163.0	1.36	26.0	0.94	103.7	1.34	94.8	1.05	246.3	0.76	184.9	1.3	94.5	0.71
Deux-Montagnes	55.5	0.34	21.8	0.18	4.9	0.18	18.1	0.23	9.7	0.11	29.4	0.09	27.0	0.2	20.3	0.15
Thérèse-De Blainville	42.6	0.26	52.7	0.44	8.2	0.30	23.1	0.30	31.7	0.35	59.1	0.18	65.9	0.5	20.6	0.16
Mirabel	25.4	0.16	9.4	0.08	0.5	0.02	0.4	0.01	3.0	0.03	8.3	0.03	4.7	0.0	5.0	0.04
La Rivière-du-Nord	63.8	0.39	34.2	0.29	5.3	0.19	29.9	0.39	22.2	0.25	90.1	0.28	35.3	0.3	23.8	0.18
Argenteuil	5.9	0.04	3.2	0.03	1.2	0.04	3.9	0.05	3.2	0.04	24.2	0.08	7.4	0.1	4.1	0.03
Les Pays-d'en-Haut	7.5	0.05	7.6	0.06	1.1	0.04	4.8	0.06	6.3	0.07	3.3	0.01	10.8	0.1	7.2	0.05

Retail Sales, 2001
1 - By Province, Economic Region and Census Division

	Total Sales		Supermarkets & Groceries		All Other Food		Women's Clothing		Men's Clothing		Other Clothing		Shoes		Motor Vehicles & Recreation Vehicles		Gas Service Stations	
	$mill. Sales	% of Cdn Total	$mill. Sales	% of Cdn Total	$mill. Sales	% of Cdn Total	$mill. Sales	% of Cdn Total	$mill. Sales	% of Cdn Total	$mill. Sales	% of Cdn Total	$mill. Sales	% of Cdn Total	$mill. Sales	% of Cdn Total	$mill. Sales	% of Cdn Total
Les Laurentides	404.7	0.15	84.8	0.15	7.8	0.17	4.8	0.10	0.7	0.04	14.2	0.20	2.9	0.2	159.7	0.21	27.5	0.10
Antoine-Labelle	361.3	0.13	80.2	0.14	7.3	0.16	3.4	0.07	1.3	0.08	4.4	0.06	1.5	0.1	133.2	0.17	23.6	0.10
Outaouais	2,573.0	0.92	729.3	1.30	66.8	1.48	13.7	0.28	5.1	0.31	29.6	0.41	14.5	0.9	816.6	1.06	111.9	0.60
Papineau	123.4	0.04	59.7	0.11	5.5	0.12	0.2	0.00	0.0	0.00	0.4	0.01	0.7	0.0	19.6	0.03	14.2	0.10
Communauté urbaine de l'Outaouais	2,010.0	0.72	545.2	0.97	49.9	1.11	12.4	0.26	4.4	0.27	28.0	0.39	12.4	0.7	657.4	0.86	59.8	0.30
Les Collines-de-l'Outaouais	115.4	0.04	50.2	0.09	4.6	0.10	0.3	0.01	0.0	0.00	0.0	0.00	0.0	0.0	19.6	0.03	9.4	0.00
La Vallée-de-la-Gatineau	221.6	0.08	41.5	0.07	3.8	0.08	0.7	0.01	0.2	0.01	1.2	0.02	1.3	0.1	98.5	0.13	13.6	0.10
Pontiac	102.6	0.04	32.7	0.06	3.0	0.07	0.1	0.00	0.5	0.03	0.1	0.00	0.1	0.0	21.6	0.03	14.9	0.10
Abitibi - Témiscamingue	1,541.9	0.55	372.8	0.67	34.2	0.76	23.4	0.48	6.2	0.38	27.6	0.39	8.0	0.5	457.0	0.60	146.5	0.80
Témiscamingue	134.2	0.05	41.9	0.07	3.8	0.09	1.1	0.02	1.0	0.06	1.5	0.02	0.8	0.1	35.8	0.05	10.0	0.10
Rouyn-Noranda	429.2	0.15	88.5	0.16	8.1	0.18	8.5	0.17	2.1	0.13	9.4	0.13	2.1	0.1	110.2	0.14	37.2	0.20
Abitibi-Ouest	215.1	0.08	53.5	0.10	4.9	0.11	1.9	0.04	1.1	0.06	5.5	0.08	0.8	0.1	73.5	0.10	14.6	0.10
Abitibi	271.7	0.10	66.1	0.12	6.1	0.13	3.5	0.07	0.3	0.02	2.8	0.04	0.9	0.1	97.5	0.13	27.5	0.10
Vallée-de-l'Or	491.7	0.18	122.7	0.22	11.2	0.25	8.5	0.17	1.7	0.11	8.2	0.12	3.3	0.2	140.1	0.18	57.2	0.30
Mauricie - Bois-Francs	4,120.3	1.48	954.5	1.70	87.4	1.94	65.9	1.36	18.7	1.14	116.0	1.62	36.2	2.1	1,076.7	1.40	285.2	1.50
L'Érable	169.9	0.06	47.9	0.09	4.4	0.10	1.4	0.03	1.2	0.07	1.4	0.02	0.1	0.0	31.4	0.04	26.8	0.10
Mékinac	72.8	0.03	34.6	0.06	3.2	0.07	0.9	0.02	0.6	0.04	0.9	0.01	0.1	0.0	5.9	0.01	9.1	0.00
Le Centre-de-la-Mauricie	505.6	0.18	136.4	0.24	12.5	0.28	6.4	0.13	1.9	0.12	18.3	0.26	4.5	0.3	104.8	0.14	38.2	0.20
Francheville	1,143.7	0.41	236.9	0.42	21.7	0.48	23.7	0.49	7.4	0.45	31.8	0.45	13.1	0.8	320.4	0.42	44.6	0.20
Bécancour	128.7	0.05	47.7	0.09	4.4	0.10	0.3	0.01	0.0	0.00	0.8	0.01	0.9	0.1	30.4	0.04	21.7	0.10
Arthabaska	654.5	0.23	115.0	0.21	10.5	0.23	10.9	0.22	2.5	0.15	29.5	0.41	8.4	0.5	165.1	0.22	29.7	0.20
Drummond	975.2	0.35	191.1	0.34	17.5	0.39	18.9	0.39	4.5	0.28	24.9	0.35	6.2	0.4	299.8	0.39	78.9	0.40
Nicolet-Yamaska	185.4	0.07	52.0	0.09	4.8	0.11	1.0	0.02	0.0	0.00	1.7	0.02	0.6	0.0	58.3	0.08	17.5	0.10
Maskinongé	146.2	0.05	41.2	0.07	3.8	0.08	0.8	0.02	0.4	0.02	4.0	0.06	0.7	0.0	37.2	0.05	9.4	0.00
Le Haut-Saint-Maurice	138.4	0.05	51.6	0.09	4.7	0.10	1.6	0.03	0.2	0.01	2.7	0.04	1.6	0.1	23.5	0.03	9.4	0.00
Saguenay - Lac-Saint-Jean	2,552.7	0.92	665.2	1.19	60.9	1.35	40.6	0.84	10.1	0.62	45.6	0.64	22.0	1.3	774.0	1.01	135.2	0.70
Le Domaine-du-Roy	299.2	0.11	72.9	0.13	6.7	0.15	4.6	0.10	1.6	0.10	3.1	0.04	1.8	0.1	119.5	0.16	15.8	0.10
Maria-Chapdelaine	275.6	0.10	84.5	0.15	7.7	0.17	5.1	0.10	2.3	0.14	12.5	0.17	2.5	0.1	64.2	0.08	6.8	0.00
Lac-Saint-Jean-Est	448.3	0.16	117.5	0.21	10.8	0.24	3.8	0.08	1.2	0.07	5.2	0.07	4.1	0.2	114.6	0.15	31.4	0.20
Le Fjord-du-Saguenay	1,529.6	0.55	390.4	0.70	35.8	0.79	27.1	0.56	5.0	0.31	24.9	0.35	13.7	0.8	475.7	0.62	81.2	0.40
Côte-Nord	809.6	0.29	198.1	0.35	18.1	0.40	6.5	0.13	3.0	0.18	8.0	0.11	2.6	0.2	220.4	0.29	54.6	0.30
La Haute-Côte-Nord	119.1	0.04	29.2	0.05	2.7	0.06	0.3	0.01	0.0	0.00	1.3	0.02	0.9	0.1	27.4	0.04	16.5	0.10
Manicouagan	252.7	0.09	47.0	0.08	4.3	0.10	2.9	0.06	0.5	0.03	1.5	0.02	0.5	0.0	81.8	0.11	23.3	0.10
Sept-Rivières - Caniapiscau	356.3	0.13	97.8	0.17	9.0	0.20	2.9	0.06	2.5	0.15	5.2	0.07	1.2	0.1	110.2	0.14	11.3	0.10
Minganie - Basse-Côte-Nord	81.5	0.03	24.2	0.04	2.2	0.05	0.4	0.01	0.0	0.00	0.0	0.00	0.0	0.0	1.0	0.00	3.6	0.00
Nord-du-Québec	255.3	0.09	73.2	0.13	6.7	0.15	2.1	0.04	1.3	0.08	5.8	0.08	1.8	0.1	34.8	0.05	26.5	0.10
Nord-du-Québec	255.3	0.09	73.2	0.13	6.7	0.15	2.1	0.04	1.3	0.08	5.8	0.08	1.8	0.1	34.8	0.05	26.5	0.10
ONTARIO	106,349.4	38.16	17,440.9	31.15	2,003.3	44.48	1,953.4	40.30	716.1	43.70	2,791.7	39.05	642.5	37.6	29,840.8	38.91	7,299.9	38.60
Ottawa	10,813.1	3.88	1,996.6	3.57	229.3	5.09	194.1	4.00	79.7	4.86	219.0	3.06	52.7	3.1	3,305.2	4.31	801.0	4.20
Stormont, Dundas and Glengarry United Counties	1,104.1	0.40	182.9	0.33	21.0	0.47	11.6	0.24	5.1	0.31	12.7	0.18	13.9	0.8	341.1	0.44	107.7	0.60
Prescott and Russell United Counties	569.7	0.20	81.7	0.15	9.4	0.21	4.5	0.09	1.8	0.11	8.0	0.11	2.5	0.2	190.9	0.25	86.4	0.50
Ottawa-Carleton Regional Municipality	7,636.9	2.74	1,485.4	2.65	170.6	3.79	158.0	3.26	63.5	3.88	164.4	2.30	30.1	1.8	2,278.5	2.97	451.1	2.40
Leeds and Grenville United Counties	966.2	0.35	147.6	0.26	17.0	0.38	10.5	0.22	5.0	0.30	23.5	0.33	4.1	0.2	323.4	0.42	108.1	0.60
Lanark County	536.2	0.19	99.0	0.18	11.4	0.25	9.5	0.20	4.2	0.26	10.4	0.14	2.1	0.1	171.4	0.22	47.8	0.30
Kingston - Pembroke	3,973.2	1.43	625.4	1.12	71.8	1.59	62.6	1.29	24.0	1.46	84.7	1.19	32.5	1.9	1,156.3	1.51	413.4	2.20
Frontenac County	1,352.5	0.49	214.1	0.38	24.6	0.55	28.5	0.59	13.3	0.81	37.5	0.52	14.6	0.9	394.7	0.51	109.7	0.60
Lennox and Addington County	215.6	0.08	51.5	0.09	5.9	0.13	2.9	0.06	0.3	0.02	3.9	0.05	0.5	0.0	52.4	0.07	21.7	0.10
Hastings County	1,418.3	0.51	154.4	0.28	17.7	0.39	16.5	0.34	6.9	0.42	20.1	0.28	11.9	0.7	474.8	0.62	176.4	0.90
Prince Edward County	94.1	0.03	10.1	0.02	1.2	0.03	0.0	0.00	0.0	0.00	1.4	0.02	0.7	0.0	13.0	0.02	23.7	0.10
Renfrew County	892.7	0.32	195.3	0.35	22.4	0.50	14.8	0.31	3.5	0.21	21.8	0.31	4.8	0.3	221.5	0.29	81.9	0.40
Muskoka - Kawarthas	3,311.1	1.19	475.8	0.85	54.7	1.21	43.6	0.90	16.3	0.99	49.9	0.70	9.5	0.6	1,138.7	1.48	292.8	1.50
Northumberland County	635.3	0.23	87.2	0.16	10.0	0.22	10.3	0.21	3.0	0.18	8.0	0.11	2.4	0.1	184.4	0.24	95.6	0.50
Peterborough County	1,182.7	0.42	153.9	0.27	17.7	0.39	16.1	0.33	8.3	0.51	19.6	0.27	4.2	0.3	391.7	0.51	60.7	0.30
Victoria County	585.3	0.21	104.4	0.19	12.0	0.27	8.3	0.17	1.7	0.10	7.4	0.10	2.3	0.1	200.3	0.26	42.6	0.20
Muskoka District Municipality	733.9	0.26	108.5	0.19	12.5	0.28	6.8	0.14	3.3	0.20	14.4	0.20	0.6	0.0	277.4	0.36	82.8	0.40
Haliburton County	173.9	0.06	21.8	0.04	2.5	0.06	2.1	0.04	0.0	0.00	0.5	0.01	0.0	0.0	84.8	0.11	11.2	0.10
Toronto	43,006.0	15.43	6,693.8	11.96	768.9	17.07	929.2	19.17	325.9	19.89	1,381.8	19.33	319.0	18.7	11,755.3	15.33	2,283.3	12.10
Durham Regional Municipality	4,154.8	1.49	714.6	1.28	82.1	1.82	49.9	1.03	19.9	1.22	81.0	1.13	17.3	1.0	1,186.4	1.55	359.5	1.90
York Regional Municipality	6,232.2	2.24	828.0	1.48	95.1	2.11	98.2	2.03	37.3	2.28	170.4	2.38	31.2	1.8	2,044.0	2.67	333.8	1.80
Toronto Metropolitan Municipality	22,393.4	8.03	3,446.8	6.16	395.9	8.79	607.6	12.53	211.8	12.92	793.9	11.11	212.9	12.5	5,718.6	7.46	1,070.6	5.70
Peel Regional Municipality	8,090.5	2.90	1,335.1	2.38	153.4	3.40	137.5	2.84	44.2	2.70	277.9	3.89	49.3	2.9	2,117.7	2.76	383.6	2.00
Halton Regional Municipality*	3,707.1	1.33	648.8	1.16	74.5	1.65	65.7	1.35	23.4	1.43	90.7	1.27	22.7	1.3	1,191.7	1.55	218.9	1.20
Kitchener - Waterloo - Barrie	10,126.4	3.63	1,723.8	3.08	198.0	4.40	154.5	3.19	44.2	2.70	275.7	3.86	54.2	3.2	3,150.9	4.11	624.7	3.30
Dufferin County	391.6	0.14	42.5	0.08	4.9	0.11	5.2	0.11	2.1	0.13	4.6	0.06	0.7	0.0	129.6	0.17	30.5	0.20
Wellington County	1,775.3	0.64	244.9	0.44	28.1	0.62	35.3	0.73	14.6	0.89	40.3	0.56	11.3	0.7	668.6	0.87	108.5	0.60
Waterloo Regional Municipality	4,731.2	1.70	935.6	1.67	107.5	2.39	84.4	1.74	16.6	1.01	147.2	2.06	25.4	1.5	1,333.6	1.74	252.7	1.30
Simcoe County	3,228.3	1.16	500.8	0.89	57.5	1.28	29.6	0.61	10.9	0.66	83.6	1.17	16.8	1.0	1,019.1	1.33	233.0	1.20
Hamilton - Niagara Peninsula	11,416.8	4.10	2,145.9	3.83	246.5	5.47	181.1	3.74	74.4	4.54	273.8	3.83	64.6	3.8	2,875.2	3.75	712.6	3.80
Halton Regional Municipality*	3,707.1	1.33	648.8	1.16	74.5	1.65	65.7	1.35	23.4	1.43	90.7	1.27	22.7	1.3	1,191.7	1.55	218.9	1.20
Hamilton-Wentworth Regional Municipality	3,705.9	1.33	773.6	1.38	88.9	1.97	63.1	1.30	29.6	1.81	113.9	1.59	23.1	1.4	741.0	0.97	171.1	0.90
Niagara Regional Municipality	4,320.8	1.55	709.8	1.27	81.5	1.81	71.4	1.47	22.8	1.39	94.5	1.32	17.6	1.0	1,047.9	1.37	359.9	1.90
Haldimand-Norfolk Regional Municipality	839.3	0.30	187.0	0.33	21.5	0.48	7.8	0.16	4.2	0.26	17.9	0.25	3.2	0.2	306.9	0.40	46.2	0.20
Brant County	978.7	0.35	195.9	0.35	22.5	0.50	9.1	0.19	7.1	0.43	15.5	0.22	6.2	0.4	276.3	0.36	52.2	0.30
London	5,632.8	2.02	732.7	1.31	84.2	1.87	121.3	2.50	58.4	3.56	135.4	1.89	35.4	2.1	1,510.4	1.97	398.9	2.10
Oxford County	704.4	0.25	113.9	0.20	13.1	0.29	8.6	0.18	4.1	0.25	8.3	0.12	1.5	0.1	212.7	0.28	32.5	0.20
Elgin County	649.9	0.23	64.5	0.12	7.4	0.16	11.6	0.24	0.0	0.00	8.6	0.12	5.7	0.3	193.8	0.25	59.5	0.30
Middlesex County	4,278.6	1.54	554.3	0.99	63.7	1.41	101.1	2.09	54.3	3.32	118.5	1.66	28.2	1.7	1,103.9	1.44	306.9	1.60
Windsor - Sarnia	6,343.3	2.28	1,049.5	1.87	120.6	2.68	102.7	2.12	41.1	2.51	132.9	1.86	27.7	1.6	1,697.1	2.21	454.7	2.40
Kent County	1,299.3	0.47	162.2	0.29	18.6	0.41	14.9	0.31	7.2	0.44	21.8	0.31	3.2	0.2	424.7	0.55	139.8	0.70
Essex County	3,850.4	1.38	698.0	1.25	80.2	1.78	64.7	1.33	27.0	1.65	86.6	1.21	19.4	1.1	908.9	1.19	244.6	1.30
Lambton County	1,193.6	0.43	189.3	0.34	21.7	0.48	23.1	0.48	6.8	0.41	24.5	0.34	5.1	0.3	363.5	0.47	70.3	0.40
Stratford - Bruce Peninsula	3,083.6	1.11	539.4	0.96	62.0	1.38	51.5	1.06	11.3	0.69	58.4	0.82	9.5	0.6	904.8	1.18	249.1	1.30
Perth County	936.7	0.34	183.9	0.33	21.1	0.47	12.4	0.26	3.0	0.18	12.9	0.18	3.2	0.2	320.5	0.42	51.0	0.30
Huron County	539.9	0.19	58.6	0.10	6.7	0.15	10.2	0.21	3.6	0.22	10.4	0.14	1.6	0.1	165.5	0.22	55.0	0.30

* Halton Regional Municipality is split between two economic regions. Data are for both parts.

Retail Sales, 2001
1 – By Province, Economic Region and Census Division

	Auto Parts Accessories & Services		Household Furniture & Appliances		Household Furnishings		Other Durable Goods		Other Semi-Durable Goods		General Merchandise		Drugs and Patent Medicine		All Other Retail	
	$mill. Sales	% of Cdn Total	$mill. Sales	% of Cdn Total	$mill. Sales	% of Cdn Total	$mill. Sales	% of Cdn Total	$mill. Sales	% of Cdn Total	$mill. Sales	% of Cdn Total	$mill. Sales	% of Cdn Total	$mill. Sales	% of Cdn Total
Les Laurentides	26.1	0.16	20.2	0.17	3.5	0.13	13.1	0.17	7.7	0.09	7.7	0.02	15.3	0.1	8.7	0.07
Antoine-Labelle	22.6	0.14	13.8	0.12	1.3	0.05	10.4	0.14	10.8	0.12	24.2	0.08	18.4	0.1	4.8	0.04
Outaouais	158.0	0.97	102.2	0.85	16.5	0.60	53.4	0.69	57.8	0.64	252.4	0.78	84.3	0.6	60.9	0.46
Papineau	5.5	0.03	6.2	0.05	0.5	0.02	1.7	0.02	2.8	0.03	3.5	0.01	2.0	0.0	0.8	0.01
Communauté urbaine de l'Outaouais	123.7	0.76	81.1	0.67	15.7	0.57	44.3	0.57	42.4	0.47	208.3	0.65	72.6	0.5	52.5	0.40
Les Collines-de-l'Outaouais	8.5	0.05	1.2	0.01	0.0	0.00	2.0	0.03	2.0	0.02	14.3	0.04	1.3	0.0	1.9	0.01
La Vallée-de-la-Gatineau	9.5	0.06	10.6	0.09	0.0	0.00	2.0	0.03	8.2	0.09	19.3	0.06	6.8	0.1	4.5	0.03
Pontiac	10.8	0.07	3.0	0.03	0.3	0.01	3.3	0.04	2.4	0.03	7.0	0.02	1.6	0.0	1.1	0.01
Abitibi - Témiscamingue	95.6	0.59	58.5	0.49	4.3	0.16	41.6	0.54	28.2	0.31	117.8	0.37	65.4	0.5	54.8	0.41
Témiscamingue	8.2	0.05	7.4	0.06	0.2	0.01	2.5	0.03	5.3	0.06	9.5	0.03	2.5	0.0	2.5	0.02
Rouyn-Noranda	30.0	0.19	15.1	0.13	1.7	0.06	12.5	0.16	6.9	0.08	67.4	0.21	20.6	0.2	8.9	0.07
Abitibi-Ouest	9.3	0.06	9.9	0.08	0.6	0.02	7.7	0.10	3.4	0.04	7.2	0.02	17.4	0.1	4.0	0.03
Abitibi	19.3	0.12	10.3	0.09	0.7	0.02	3.3	0.04	4.4	0.05	14.1	0.04	9.2	0.1	5.7	0.04
Vallée-de-l'Or	28.7	0.18	15.8	0.13	1.3	0.05	15.7	0.20	8.2	0.09	19.6	0.06	15.7	0.1	33.7	0.25
Mauricie - Bois-Francs	308.2	1.90	220.5	1.84	27.5	1.00	94.3	1.22	128.2	1.42	382.4	1.19	195.9	1.4	122.7	0.93
L'Érable	13.9	0.09	16.7	0.14	1.3	0.05	1.9	0.02	5.6	0.06	2.2	0.01	8.9	0.1	4.8	0.04
Mékinac	5.6	0.03	1.8	0.01	0.3	0.01	0.7	0.01	3.4	0.04	0.7	0.00	3.4	0.0	1.5	0.01
Le Centre-de-la-Mauricie	32.3	0.20	27.5	0.23	3.8	0.14	13.3	0.17	17.5	0.19	40.6	0.13	33.2	0.2	14.5	0.11
Francheville	98.2	0.61	46.8	0.39	10.4	0.38	33.4	0.43	47.7	0.53	121.9	0.38	43.1	0.3	42.5	0.32
Bécancour	12.3	0.08	3.0	0.03	0.2	0.01	0.4	0.01	2.3	0.03	0.4	0.00	2.6	0.0	1.3	0.01
Arthabaska	44.7	0.28	39.7	0.33	4.8	0.17	20.7	0.27	22.6	0.25	98.9	0.31	32.1	0.2	19.3	0.15
Drummond	65.5	0.40	60.5	0.50	5.1	0.19	15.4	0.20	20.9	0.23	84.3	0.26	50.4	0.4	31.3	0.24
Nicolet-Yamaska	16.0	0.10	7.1	0.06	0.2	0.01	3.5	0.05	3.1	0.03	10.3	0.03	6.4	0.1	3.1	0.02
Maskinongé	10.6	0.07	13.1	0.11	1.0	0.04	2.9	0.04	3.0	0.03	5.0	0.02	10.8	0.1	2.3	0.02
Le Haut-Saint-Maurice	9.0	0.06	4.3	0.04	0.6	0.02	2.0	0.03	2.1	0.02	18.2	0.06	4.8	0.0	2.0	0.02
Saguenay - Lac-Saint-Jean	151.4	0.93	92.9	0.77	12.7	0.46	66.2	0.86	62.7	0.69	238.1	0.74	112.2	0.8	63.0	0.48
Le Domaine-du-Roy	23.6	0.15	13.7	0.11	1.1	0.04	5.7	0.07	7.6	0.08	2.4	0.01	11.8	0.1	7.3	0.06
Maria-Chapdelaine	20.9	0.13	11.2	0.09	1.4	0.05	9.4	0.12	9.1	0.10	15.1	0.05	17.6	0.1	5.5	0.04
Lac-Saint-Jean-Est	30.0	0.19	22.0	0.18	1.7	0.06	9.0	0.12	5.9	0.06	67.4	0.21	13.8	0.1	9.9	0.08
Le Fjord-du-Saguenay	76.8	0.47	46.1	0.38	8.5	0.31	42.1	0.54	40.1	0.44	153.3	0.48	68.9	0.5	40.2	0.30
Côte-Nord	45.7	0.28	25.2	0.21	5.9	0.22	15.1	0.20	22.7	0.25	138.6	0.43	31.8	0.2	13.1	0.10
La Haute-Côte-Nord	6.8	0.04	6.6	0.05	0.5	0.02	1.7	0.02	4.1	0.05	17.1	0.05	3.4	0.0	0.6	0.00
Manicouagan	16.4	0.10	7.6	0.06	3.9	0.14	4.6	0.06	6.8	0.08	24.8	0.08	21.9	0.2	4.9	0.04
Sept-Rivières - Caniapiscau	18.2	0.11	9.8	0.08	1.3	0.05	8.7	0.11	9.1	0.10	57.8	0.18	4.7	0.0	6.8	0.05
Minganie - Basse-Côte-Nord	4.4	0.03	1.2	0.01	0.2	0.01	0.0	0.00	2.6	0.03	38.9	0.12	1.9	0.0	0.9	0.01
Nord-du-Québec	16.7	0.10	8.2	0.07	0.6	0.02	5.2	0.07	3.5	0.04	59.1	0.18	6.2	0.0	3.6	0.03
Nord-du-Québec	16.7	0.10	8.2	0.07	0.6	0.02	5.2	0.07	3.5	0.04	59.1	0.18	6.2	0.0	3.6	0.03
ONTARIO	6,285.3	38.77	4,387.6	36.54	1,185.4	43.09	3,091.0	39.98	4,068.9	44.93	12,854.7	39.88	5,825.7	41.5	5,962.1	45.04
Ottawa	540.2	3.33	428.5	3.57	109.3	3.97	321.5	4.16	424.6	4.69	1,030.9	3.20	392.1	2.8	688.1	5.20
Stormont, Dundas and Glengarry United Counties	67.2	0.41	30.9	0.26	13.9	0.51	23.6	0.31	32.7	0.36	140.6	0.44	50.0	0.4	49.1	0.37
Prescott and Russell United Counties	38.7	0.24	18.7	0.16	2.8	0.10	17.5	0.23	17.6	0.19	27.9	0.09	34.0	0.2	27.5	0.21
Ottawa-Carleton Regional Municipality	354.2	2.19	332.1	2.77	80.2	2.91	254.4	3.29	283.1	3.13	755.9	2.35	246.2	1.8	529.1	4.00
Leeds and Grenville United Counties	46.4	0.29	35.6	0.30	8.9	0.32	17.5	0.23	71.9	0.79	52.7	0.16	39.8	0.3	54.2	0.41
Lanark County	33.7	0.21	11.2	0.09	3.5	0.13	8.6	0.11	19.2	0.21	53.8	0.17	22.1	0.2	28.2	0.21
Kingston - Pembroke	255.9	1.58	173.9	1.45	37.8	1.38	131.3	1.70	143.6	1.59	366.7	1.14	167.8	1.2	225.4	1.70
Frontenac County	95.5	0.59	70.5	0.59	15.5	0.56	56.5	0.73	68.7	0.76	71.1	0.22	62.6	0.5	75.2	0.57
Lennox and Addington County	14.3	0.09	8.3	0.07	1.3	0.05	4.9	0.06	6.4	0.07	23.2	0.07	5.4	0.0	12.5	0.09
Hastings County	62.9	0.39	56.7	0.47	15.1	0.55	43.7	0.57	41.0	0.45	194.6	0.60	62.6	0.5	63.0	0.48
Prince Edward County	13.3	0.08	5.2	0.04	0.8	0.03	3.8	0.05	3.7	0.04	1.8	0.01	6.1	0.0	9.4	0.07
Renfrew County	69.9	0.43	33.2	0.28	5.1	0.19	22.4	0.29	23.8	0.26	75.9	0.24	31.1	0.2	65.3	0.49
Muskoka - Kawarthas	204.0	1.26	112.0	0.93	30.2	1.10	73.1	0.95	110.6	1.22	385.3	1.20	147.1	1.1	167.6	1.27
Northumberland County	36.4	0.22	22.3	0.19	10.4	0.38	9.6	0.12	19.9	0.22	58.0	0.18	28.2	0.2	49.5	0.37
Peterborough County	95.8	0.59	50.6	0.42	9.6	0.35	30.8	0.40	41.1	0.45	163.6	0.51	62.4	0.4	56.6	0.43
Victoria County	32.9	0.20	14.3	0.12	3.0	0.11	10.1	0.13	16.9	0.19	76.8	0.24	24.8	0.2	27.5	0.21
Muskoka District Municipality	34.9	0.22	16.2	0.14	5.9	0.21	20.1	0.26	27.3	0.30	68.0	0.21	25.3	0.2	29.7	0.22
Haliburton County	4.0	0.02	8.5	0.07	1.3	0.05	2.4	0.03	5.4	0.06	18.8	0.06	6.3	0.0	4.4	0.03
Toronto	2,503.0	15.44	1,831.9	15.25	503.3	18.30	1,368.6	17.70	1,688.2	18.64	5,151.3	15.98	2,803.3	20.0	2,699.0	20.39
Durham Regional Municipality	215.3	1.33	143.3	1.19	49.4	1.80	142.1	1.84	115.4	1.27	471.0	1.46	296.6	2.1	211.1	1.59
York Regional Municipality	405.6	2.50	301.1	2.51	82.9	3.01	186.4	2.41	241.2	2.66	719.4	2.23	284.3	2.0	373.2	2.82
Toronto Metropolitan Municipality	1,169.3	7.21	915.4	7.62	248.8	9.04	772.3	9.99	798.6	8.82	2,799.2	8.68	1,739.4	12.4	1,492.2	11.27
Peel Regional Municipality	554.9	3.42	397.7	3.31	100.8	3.66	201.2	2.60	443.3	4.89	987.7	3.06	404.5	2.9	501.7	3.79
Halton Regional Municipality*	227.1	1.40	170.8	1.42	42.6	1.55	106.5	1.38	150.5	1.66	321.5	1.00	146.9	1.1	204.8	1.55
Kitchener - Waterloo - Barrie	576.3	3.56	423.8	3.53	114.5	4.16	287.2	3.71	412.9	4.56	1,172.4	3.64	402.5	2.9	510.8	3.86
Dufferin County	19.6	0.12	8.8	0.07	5.5	0.20	6.8	0.09	20.5	0.23	71.7	0.22	15.0	0.1	23.6	0.18
Wellington County	97.7	0.60	65.7	0.55	21.4	0.78	48.6	0.63	95.8	1.06	171.6	0.53	54.1	0.4	68.8	0.52
Waterloo Regional Municipality	260.8	1.61	218.0	1.82	48.5	1.76	140.7	1.82	181.7	2.01	555.5	1.72	161.0	1.2	261.9	1.98
Simcoe County	198.2	1.22	131.4	1.09	39.0	1.42	91.1	1.18	114.9	1.27	373.5	1.16	172.4	1.2	156.5	1.18
Hamilton - Niagara Peninsula	666.6	4.11	456.9	3.80	133.3	4.84	274.8	3.55	438.8	4.85	1,625.0	5.04	658.1	4.7	589.3	4.45
Halton Regional Municipality*	227.1	1.40	170.8	1.42	42.6	1.55	106.5	1.38	150.5	1.66	321.5	1.00	146.9	1.1	204.8	1.55
Hamilton-Wentworth Regional Municipality	222.4	1.37	145.0	1.21	39.4	1.43	103.3	1.34	108.7	1.20	657.2	2.04	230.1	1.6	195.4	1.48
Niagara Regional Municipality	248.6	1.53	141.0	1.17	55.6	2.02	91.6	1.18	198.8	2.20	681.7	2.12	270.7	1.9	227.2	1.72
Haldimand-Norfolk Regional Municipality	44.8	0.28	28.0	0.23	6.7	0.24	16.1	0.21	29.4	0.32	51.8	0.16	36.2	0.3	31.8	0.24
Brant County	81.6	0.50	46.3	0.39	10.4	0.38	23.9	0.31	41.3	0.46	86.8	0.27	52.5	0.4	51.0	0.39
London	460.1	2.84	265.3	2.21	69.1	2.51	156.6	2.03	240.0	2.65	722.0	2.24	314.1	2.2	328.9	2.48
Oxford County	57.4	0.35	27.0	0.22	10.0	0.36	13.8	0.18	27.8	0.31	91.9	0.29	49.7	0.4	32.3	0.24
Elgin County	38.0	0.23	15.7	0.13	5.7	0.21	17.1	0.22	29.3	0.32	133.7	0.41	35.0	0.3	24.1	0.18
Middlesex County	364.7	2.25	222.6	1.85	53.5	1.94	125.7	1.63	183.0	2.02	496.4	1.54	229.4	1.6	272.4	2.06
Windsor - Sarnia	454.0	2.80	283.1	2.36	77.3	2.81	173.1	2.24	225.4	2.49	766.1	2.38	430.7	3.1	307.3	2.32
Kent County	89.5	0.55	44.8	0.37	11.2	0.41	22.7	0.29	30.8	0.34	178.9	0.56	64.8	0.5	64.1	0.48
Essex County	278.7	1.72	188.9	1.57	53.0	1.93	116.4	1.51	147.8	1.63	447.5	1.39	304.9	2.2	183.6	1.39
Lambton County	85.8	0.53	49.4	0.41	13.1	0.48	33.9	0.44	46.8	0.52	139.7	0.43	61.0	0.4	59.7	0.45
Stratford - Bruce Peninsula	152.9	0.94	99.9	0.83	29.3	1.07	75.2	0.97	123.6	1.37	452.1	1.40	145.7	1.0	119.0	0.90
Perth County	42.4	0.26	28.3	0.24	8.9	0.32	17.5	0.23	31.8	0.35	124.9	0.39	47.6	0.3	27.3	0.21
Huron County	29.2	0.18	14.5	0.12	4.9	0.18	16.1	0.21	26.6	0.29	86.4	0.27	22.4	0.2	28.2	0.21

* Halton Regional Municipality is split between two economic regions. Data are for both parts.

Retail Sales, 2001
1 – By Province, Economic Region and Census Division

	Total Sales		Supermarkets & Groceries		All Other Food		Women's Clothing		Men's Clothing		Other Clothing		Shoes		Motor Vehicles & Recreation Vehicles		Gas Service Stations	
	$mill. Sales	% of Cdn Total	$mill. Sales	% of Cdn Total	$mill. Sales	% of Cdn Total	$mill. Sales	% of Cdn Total	$mill. Sales	% of Cdn Total	$mill. Sales	% of Cdn Total	$mill. Sales	% of Cdn Total	$mill. Sales	% of Cdn Total	$mill. Sales	% of Cdn Total
Bruce County	674.3	0.24	154.8	0.28	17.8	0.39	11.0	0.23	2.0	0.12	14.0	0.20	1.5	0.1	198.5	0.26	55.8	0.30
Grey County	932.7	0.33	142.1	0.25	16.3	0.36	18.0	0.37	2.7	0.17	21.2	0.30	3.2	0.2	220.3	0.29	87.2	0.50
Northeast	6,197.2	2.22	1,101.3	1.97	126.5	2.81	80.0	1.65	23.5	1.44	122.1	1.71	32.2	1.9	1,699.4	2.22	682.5	3.60
Nipissing District	952.3	0.34	148.8	0.27	17.1	0.38	13.7	0.28	4.1	0.25	25.4	0.36	6.2	0.4	285.7	0.37	79.1	0.40
Parry Sound District	433.4	0.16	69.1	0.12	7.9	0.18	3.3	0.07	0.5	0.03	11.9	0.17	0.4	0.0	128.4	0.17	74.3	0.40
Manitoulin District	111.2	0.04	11.2	0.02	1.3	0.03	1.7	0.04	0.0	0.00	2.5	0.04	0.0	0.0	40.6	0.05	27.3	0.10
Sudbury District	191.1	0.07	34.0	0.06	3.9	0.09	1.6	0.03	0.3	0.02	3.6	0.05	0.0	0.0	8.8	0.01	63.9	0.30
Sudbury Regional Municipality	1,791.4	0.64	333.1	0.59	38.3	0.85	23.8	0.49	6.3	0.39	33.6	0.47	9.8	0.6	481.9	0.63	158.3	0.80
Timiskaming District	442.8	0.16	74.0	0.13	8.5	0.19	6.2	0.13	1.4	0.08	6.9	0.10	1.6	0.1	110.7	0.14	71.9	0.40
Cochrane District	906.6	0.33	128.8	0.23	14.8	0.33	9.2	0.19	4.8	0.29	15.1	0.21	4.4	0.3	264.5	0.34	92.4	0.50
Algoma District	1,368.5	0.49	302.3	0.54	34.7	0.77	20.3	0.42	6.2	0.38	23.1	0.32	9.7	0.6	378.8	0.49	115.3	0.60
Northwest	2,445.9	0.88	356.7	0.64	41.0	0.91	32.7	0.68	17.2	1.05	58.1	0.81	5.3	0.3	647.4	0.84	386.8	2.00
Thunder Bay District	1,495.0	0.54	197.9	0.35	22.7	0.50	25.4	0.52	12.8	0.78	33.1	0.46	3.4	0.2	401.2	0.52	235.4	1.20
Rainy River District	243.3	0.09	48.1	0.09	5.5	0.12	2.4	0.05	1.1	0.06	7.2	0.10	0.4	0.0	83.6	0.11	31.7	0.20
Kenora District	707.5	0.25	110.7	0.20	12.7	0.28	4.9	0.10	3.3	0.20	17.7	0.25	1.5	0.1	162.6	0.21	119.7	0.60
MANITOBA	9,652.6	3.46	2,170.5	3.88	77.4	1.72	126.9	2.62	50.4	3.08	212.5	2.97	47.9	2.8	2,889.7	3.77	722.5	3.80
Southeast	673.5	0.24	121.7	0.22	4.3	0.10	0.4	0.01	1.4	0.08	7.7	0.11	0.6	0.0	283.3	0.37	88.1	0.50
Division No. 1	116.9	0.04	26.9	0.05	1.0	0.02	0.1	0.00	0.0	0.00	1.5	0.02	0.0	0.0	25.8	0.03	26.7	0.10
Division No. 2	441.3	0.16	62.7	0.11	2.2	0.05	0.4	0.01	1.4	0.08	4.2	0.06	0.6	0.0	221.2	0.29	46.1	0.20
Division No. 12	115.3	0.04	32.1	0.06	1.1	0.03	0.0	0.00	0.0	0.00	2.0	0.03	0.0	0.0	36.3	0.05	15.3	0.10
South Central	416.6	0.15	95.7	0.17	3.4	0.08	1.1	0.02	1.2	0.07	11.1	0.16	1.0	0.1	109.5	0.14	29.4	0.20
Division No. 3	373.8	0.13	81.1	0.14	2.9	0.06	1.1	0.02	0.9	0.05	10.6	0.15	1.0	0.1	106.9	0.14	23.1	0.10
Division No. 4	42.8	0.02	14.6	0.03	0.5	0.01	0.0	0.00	0.3	0.02	0.5	0.01	0.0	0.0	2.6	0.00	6.4	0.00
Southwest	1,144.1	0.41	234.4	0.42	8.4	0.19	4.0	0.08	6.9	0.42	24.5	0.34	6.0	0.4	452.8	0.59	84.5	0.40
Division No. 5	151.4	0.05	20.9	0.04	0.7	0.02	0.5	0.01	1.0	0.06	1.4	0.02	0.7	0.0	84.8	0.11	3.7	0.00
Division No. 6	87.5	0.03	20.2	0.04	0.7	0.02	0.0	0.00	1.0	0.06	2.5	0.03	1.4	0.1	27.9	0.04	15.7	0.10
Division No. 7	749.3	0.27	154.9	0.28	5.5	0.12	3.2	0.07	4.8	0.29	18.4	0.26	2.7	0.2	295.4	0.39	49.0	0.30
Division No. 15	155.9	0.06	38.5	0.07	1.4	0.03	0.3	0.01	0.0	0.00	2.2	0.03	1.1	0.1	44.8	0.06	16.1	0.10
North Central	450.8	0.16	100.1	0.18	3.6	0.08	0.6	0.01	0.7	0.04	5.9	0.08	1.0	0.1	148.0	0.19	34.1	0.20
Division No. 8	76.0	0.03	10.5	0.02	0.4	0.01	0.0	0.00	0.0	0.00	0.0	0.00	0.0	0.0	33.2	0.04	13.9	0.10
Division No. 9	317.8	0.11	79.5	0.14	2.8	0.06	0.6	0.01	0.7	0.04	5.6	0.08	1.0	0.1	86.9	0.11	15.9	0.10
Division No. 10	57.0	0.02	10.0	0.02	0.4	0.01	0.0	0.00	0.0	0.00	0.2	0.00	0.0	0.0	27.9	0.04	4.3	0.00
Winnipeg	5,422.1	1.95	1,220.9	2.18	43.5	0.97	119.1	2.46	35.7	2.18	141.4	1.98	37.1	2.2	1,415.4	1.85	334.9	1.80
Division No. 11	5,422.1	1.95	1,220.9	2.18	43.5	0.97	119.1	2.46	35.7	2.18	141.4	1.98	37.1	2.2	1,415.4	1.85	334.9	1.80
Interlake	546.4	0.20	150.1	0.27	5.4	0.12	0.5	0.01	0.2	0.01	4.1	0.06	0.3	0.0	199.0	0.26	59.3	0.30
Division No. 13	282.5	0.10	59.5	0.11	2.1	0.05	0.3	0.01	0.0	0.00	0.6	0.01	0.3	0.0	139.0	0.18	26.5	0.10
Division No. 14	66.5	0.02	31.4	0.06	1.1	0.02	0.2	0.00	0.2	0.01	0.9	0.01	0.0	0.0	2.6	0.00	5.6	0.00
Division No. 18	197.5	0.07	59.2	0.11	2.1	0.05	0.0	0.00	0.0	0.00	2.6	0.04	0.0	0.0	57.4	0.07	27.1	0.10
Parklands	442.1	0.16	87.6	0.16	3.1	0.07	0.6	0.01	1.6	0.09	6.1	0.09	1.6	0.1	170.1	0.22	50.4	0.30
Division No. 16	105.8	0.04	32.3	0.06	1.2	0.03	0.0	0.00	0.7	0.04	2.2	0.03	0.7	0.0	42.1	0.05	7.0	0.00
Division No. 17	199.9	0.07	34.2	0.06	1.2	0.03	0.4	0.01	0.5	0.03	1.4	0.02	0.9	0.1	61.1	0.08	29.8	0.20
Division No. 20	136.4	0.05	21.1	0.04	0.8	0.02	0.2	0.00	0.3	0.02	2.5	0.03	0.0	0.0	66.9	0.09	13.6	0.10
North	557.0	0.20	160.0	0.29	5.7	0.13	0.6	0.01	2.8	0.17	11.7	0.16	0.4	0.0	111.6	0.15	41.8	0.20
Division No. 19	41.1	0.01	22.3	0.04	0.8	0.02	0.0	0.00	0.0	0.00	0.0	0.00	0.0	0.0	1.1	0.00	2.5	0.00
Division No. 21	209.8	0.08	84.5	0.15	3.0	0.07	0.3	0.01	1.9	0.12	7.7	0.11	0.4	0.0	45.8	0.06	15.1	0.10
Division No. 22	261.4	0.09	35.5	0.06	1.3	0.03	0.2	0.00	0.9	0.05	4.0	0.06	0.0	0.0	60.6	0.08	19.2	0.10
Division No. 23	44.8	0.02	17.7	0.03	0.6	0.01	0.0	0.00	0.0	0.00	0.0	0.00	0.0	0.0	4.2	0.01	5.0	0.00
SASKATCHEWAN	8,157.3	2.93	1,856.6	3.32	62.1	1.38	105.9	2.18	35.8	2.18	182.3	2.55	23.0	1.4	2,094.7	2.73	683.2	3.60
Regina - Moose Mountain	2,429.8	0.87	438.7	0.78	14.7	0.33	38.0	0.78	11.4	0.69	40.4	0.57	8.1	0.5	552.5	0.72	182.6	1.00
Division No. 1	231.4	0.08	52.4	0.09	1.8	0.04	2.5	0.05	1.1	0.06	2.4	0.03	0.3	0.0	71.1	0.09	24.8	0.10
Division No. 2	130.6	0.05	26.3	0.05	0.9	0.02	2.3	0.05	0.7	0.04	0.9	0.01	1.1	0.1	44.7	0.06	12.5	0.10
Division No. 6	2,067.8	0.74	360.0	0.64	12.0	0.27	33.2	0.69	9.6	0.59	37.1	0.52	6.6	0.4	436.7	0.57	145.3	0.80
Swift Current - Moose Jaw	851.3	0.31	273.0	0.49	9.1	0.20	8.8	0.18	3.5	0.21	26.6	0.37	1.7	0.1	171.7	0.22	78.1	0.40
Division No. 3	136.0	0.05	63.9	0.11	2.1	0.05	1.4	0.03	0.9	0.06	3.5	0.05	0.3	0.0	24.8	0.03	6.2	0.00
Division No. 4	62.1	0.02	16.5	0.03	0.6	0.01	1.6	0.03	0.4	0.02	1.5	0.02	0.0	0.0	18.0	0.02	3.0	0.00
Division No. 7	373.8	0.13	122.7	0.22	4.1	0.09	1.8	0.04	0.9	0.06	15.1	0.21	0.3	0.0	55.9	0.07	41.4	0.20
Division No. 8	279.5	0.10	69.9	0.12	2.3	0.05	3.9	0.08	1.3	0.08	6.5	0.09	1.0	0.1	73.1	0.10	27.5	0.10
Saskatoon - Biggar	2,343.4	0.84	464.8	0.83	15.5	0.34	41.2	0.85	12.0	0.73	67.7	0.95	9.2	0.5	604.8	0.79	184.6	1.00
Division No. 11	2,021.7	0.73	363.4	0.65	12.2	0.27	36.3	0.75	10.8	0.66	61.9	0.87	9.0	0.5	538.1	0.70	145.0	0.80
Division No. 12	121.5	0.04	32.3	0.06	1.1	0.02	3.1	0.06	0.1	0.01	1.1	0.02	0.0	0.0	23.2	0.03	20.0	0.10
Division No. 13	200.2	0.07	69.1	0.12	2.3	0.05	1.8	0.04	1.1	0.06	4.7	0.07	0.3	0.0	43.5	0.06	19.6	0.10
Yorkton - Melville	680.7	0.24	165.9	0.30	5.5	0.12	9.4	0.19	2.6	0.16	13.1	0.18	1.2	0.1	170.5	0.22	87.7	0.50
Division No. 5	256.9	0.09	64.7	0.12	2.2	0.05	2.5	0.05	0.2	0.01	5.5	0.08	0.0	0.0	73.9	0.10	31.2	0.20
Division No. 9	282.8	0.10	57.7	0.10	1.9	0.04	4.9	0.10	2.1	0.13	5.8	0.08	1.2	0.1	71.1	0.09	29.6	0.20
Division No. 10	141.0	0.05	43.4	0.08	1.5	0.03	2.1	0.04	0.2	0.01	1.8	0.02	0.0	0.0	25.5	0.03	26.9	0.10
Prince Albert	1,718.4	0.62	468.3	0.84	15.7	0.35	8.4	0.17	6.3	0.39	32.2	0.45	2.8	0.2	588.8	0.77	131.2	0.70
Division No. 14	301.8	0.11	82.4	0.15	2.8	0.06	3.3	0.07	1.1	0.06	8.1	0.11	0.0	0.0	88.2	0.12	27.1	0.10
Division No. 15	772.0	0.28	257.3	0.46	8.6	0.19	3.3	0.07	2.9	0.18	9.0	0.13	2.1	0.1	245.5	0.32	41.4	0.20
Division No. 16	303.0	0.11	72.1	0.13	2.4	0.05	1.0	0.02	0.8	0.05	7.3	0.10	0.4	0.0	89.4	0.12	35.5	0.20
Division No. 17	341.7	0.12	56.6	0.10	1.9	0.04	0.8	0.02	1.5	0.09	7.8	0.11	0.3	0.0	165.7	0.22	27.3	0.10
Northern	133.7	0.05	46.0	0.08	1.5	0.03	0.0	0.00	0.0	0.00	2.3	0.03	0.0	0.0	6.4	0.01	18.9	0.10
Division No. 18	133.7	0.05	46.0	0.08	1.5	0.03	0.0	0.00	0.0	0.00	2.3	0.03	0.0	0.0	6.4	0.01	18.9	0.10
ALBERTA	31,754.6	11.39	6,577.4	11.75	193.3	4.29	458.8	9.46	209.0	12.75	818.2	11.45	138.1	8.1	8,872.1	11.57	2,203.2	11.60
Lethbridge - Medicine Hat	3,457.2	1.24	992.9	1.77	29.2	0.65	46.3	0.95	33.2	2.03	63.1	0.88	7.0	0.4	833.6	1.09	159.5	0.80
Division No. 1	876.6	0.31	160.9	0.29	4.7	0.10	25.0	0.51	26.3	1.60	15.5	0.22	2.4	0.1	260.7	0.34	41.9	0.20
Division No. 2	2,334.7	0.84	786.5	1.40	23.1	0.51	15.7	0.32	5.6	0.34	38.3	0.54	4.6	0.3	509.2	0.66	72.4	0.40
Division No. 3	245.9	0.09	45.5	0.08	1.3	0.03	5.7	0.12	1.4	0.08	9.3	0.13	0.0	0.0	63.7	0.08	45.1	0.20
Drumheller - Stettler - Wainwright	838.8	0.30	198.4	0.35	5.8	0.13	9.8	0.20	4.2	0.26	16.9	0.24	1.8	0.1	228.3	0.30	92.9	0.50
Division No. 4	107.9	0.04	21.7	0.04	0.6	0.01	1.4	0.03	0.4	0.02	1.2	0.02	0.0	0.0	21.4	0.03	14.9	0.10
Division No. 5	338.9	0.12	112.6	0.20	3.3	0.07	3.9	0.08	0.6	0.04	7.9	0.11	0.4	0.0	92.4	0.12	32.2	0.20
Division No. 7	392.1	0.14	64.1	0.11	1.9	0.04	4.5	0.09	3.3	0.20	7.8	0.11	1.4	0.1	114.5	0.15	45.8	0.20

Retail Sales, 2001 1 - By Province, Economic Region and Census Division	Auto Parts Accessories & Services		Household Furniture & Appliances		Household Furnishings		Other Durable Goods		Other Semi-Durable Goods		General Merchandise		Drugs and Patent Medicine		All Other Retail	
	$mill. Sales	% of Cdn Total	$mill. Sales	% of Cdn Total	$mill. Sales	% of Cdn Total	$mill. Sales	% of Cdn Total	$mill. Sales	% of Cdn Total	$mill. Sales	% of Cdn Total	$mill. Sales	% of Cdn Total	$mill. Sales	% of Cdn Total
Bruce County	30.7	0.19	17.8	0.15	5.4	0.20	15.6	0.20	29.0	0.32	60.0	0.19	35.2	0.3	25.2	0.19
Grey County	50.5	0.31	39.2	0.33	10.1	0.37	26.0	0.34	36.2	0.40	180.9	0.56	40.5	0.3	38.3	0.29
Northeast	338.0	2.09	214.2	1.78	55.3	2.01	148.4	1.92	184.3	2.03	860.9	2.67	288.2	2.1	240.3	1.82
Nipissing District	41.7	0.26	34.9	0.29	10.1	0.37	32.3	0.42	28.1	0.31	137.1	0.43	48.3	0.3	39.7	0.30
Parry Sound District	16.9	0.10	12.1	0.10	4.3	0.16	11.5	0.15	20.3	0.22	28.3	0.09	22.4	0.2	21.5	0.16
Manitoulin District	2.9	0.02	1.7	0.01	0.4	0.01	0.2	0.00	4.3	0.05	10.0	0.03	3.2	0.0	3.8	0.03
Sudbury District	21.4	0.13	2.1	0.02	0.7	0.02	5.2	0.07	5.4	0.06	24.6	0.08	9.0	0.1	6.5	0.05
Sudbury Regional Municipality	114.8	0.71	72.6	0.60	18.0	0.65	42.0	0.54	44.1	0.49	249.5	0.77	92.5	0.7	72.8	0.55
Timiskaming District	21.7	0.13	12.3	0.10	1.4	0.05	7.2	0.09	12.8	0.14	65.8	0.20	21.1	0.2	19.2	0.15
Cochrane District	37.8	0.23	34.4	0.29	7.4	0.27	22.7	0.29	28.8	0.32	176.2	0.55	41.0	0.3	24.4	0.18
Algoma District	80.8	0.50	44.1	0.37	13.0	0.47	27.3	0.35	40.5	0.45	169.4	0.53	50.7	0.4	52.3	0.40
Northwest	134.3	0.83	98.0	0.82	25.9	0.94	81.3	1.05	76.8	0.85	321.9	1.00	76.0	0.5	86.4	0.65
Thunder Bay District	93.5	0.58	64.5	0.54	18.7	0.68	50.5	0.65	49.4	0.55	172.5	0.54	50.5	0.4	63.5	0.48
Rainy River District	5.5	0.03	11.2	0.09	1.8	0.07	9.4	0.12	7.8	0.09	8.9	0.03	13.6	0.1	5.0	0.04
Kenora District	35.3	0.22	22.3	0.19	5.4	0.20	21.3	0.28	19.7	0.22	140.6	0.44	11.9	0.1	17.9	0.13
MANITOBA	492.0	3.04	366.3	3.05	62.7	2.28	238.7	3.09	240.7	2.66	1,261.5	3.91	301.3	2.2	391.4	2.96
Southeast	48.0	0.30	20.9	0.17	5.2	0.19	6.9	0.09	19.3	0.21	30.4	0.09	15.8	0.1	19.4	0.15
Division No. 1	6.8	0.04	2.3	0.02	0.2	0.01	0.3	0.00	3.9	0.04	16.3	0.05	2.8	0.0	2.4	0.02
Division No. 2	36.1	0.22	17.3	0.14	4.1	0.15	5.4	0.07	9.7	0.11	9.2	0.03	9.1	0.1	11.5	0.09
Division No. 12	5.1	0.03	1.3	0.01	0.9	0.03	1.2	0.02	5.6	0.06	4.9	0.02	3.8	0.0	5.5	0.04
South Central	26.7	0.16	36.1	0.30	3.8	0.14	9.3	0.12	14.6	0.16	29.1	0.09	21.4	0.2	23.1	0.17
Division No. 3	22.7	0.14	33.8	0.28	3.4	0.12	7.8	0.10	12.6	0.14	24.9	0.08	18.4	0.1	22.6	0.17
Division No. 4	4.0	0.02	2.3	0.02	0.4	0.01	1.5	0.02	2.0	0.02	4.2	0.01	3.0	0.0	0.5	0.00
Southwest	48.9	0.30	43.7	0.36	5.5	0.20	25.1	0.33	29.7	0.33	94.0	0.29	29.4	0.2	46.3	0.35
Division No. 5	4.9	0.03	4.9	0.04	0.9	0.03	1.7	0.02	5.3	0.06	16.1	0.05	2.7	0.0	1.2	0.01
Division No. 6	5.4	0.03	1.6	0.01	0.2	0.01	0.5	0.01	2.6	0.03	3.3	0.01	3.0	0.0	1.5	0.01
Division No. 7	28.0	0.17	29.6	0.25	3.6	0.13	21.8	0.28	14.1	0.16	62.7	0.19	16.5	0.1	39.0	0.29
Division No. 15	10.6	0.07	7.6	0.06	0.8	0.03	1.2	0.02	7.7	0.09	11.9	0.04	7.2	0.1	4.5	0.03
North Central	23.9	0.15	14.5	0.12	1.0	0.04	8.9	0.11	7.1	0.08	79.2	0.25	12.5	0.1	9.9	0.07
Division No. 8	4.3	0.03	2.3	0.02	0.3	0.01	0.3	0.00	1.9	0.02	4.8	0.01	2.6	0.0	1.5	0.01
Division No. 9	17.7	0.11	9.7	0.08	0.7	0.02	5.3	0.07	2.7	0.03	73.5	0.23	8.4	0.1	6.8	0.05
Division No. 10	1.9	0.01	2.5	0.02	0.0	0.00	3.3	0.04	2.5	0.03	0.9	0.00	1.5	0.0	1.5	0.01
Winnipeg	277.0	1.71	211.8	1.76	42.7	1.55	156.7	2.03	130.0	1.44	812.8	2.52	181.8	1.3	261.3	1.97
Division No. 11	277.0	1.71	211.8	1.76	42.7	1.55	156.7	2.03	130.0	1.44	812.8	2.52	181.8	1.3	261.3	1.97
Interlake	34.2	0.21	14.6	0.12	2.1	0.07	7.2	0.09	13.9	0.15	31.0	0.10	13.5	0.1	11.1	0.08
Division No. 13	13.9	0.09	7.7	0.06	1.5	0.05	3.5	0.04	8.6	0.10	5.9	0.02	6.8	0.1	6.2	0.05
Division No. 14	7.6	0.05	4.4	0.04	0.2	0.01	2.1	0.03	2.9	0.03	5.3	0.02	0.9	0.0	1.1	0.01
Division No. 18	12.7	0.08	2.5	0.02	0.4	0.01	1.7	0.02	2.5	0.03	19.8	0.06	5.8	0.0	3.8	0.03
Parklands	20.1	0.12	13.3	0.11	1.5	0.05	8.7	0.11	14.6	0.16	37.6	0.12	15.4	0.1	9.8	0.07
Division No. 16	4.0	0.02	1.3	0.01	0.7	0.02	0.8	0.01	3.2	0.04	4.4	0.01	2.5	0.0	2.7	0.02
Division No. 17	9.6	0.06	9.1	0.08	0.7	0.03	5.1	0.07	7.0	0.08	26.9	0.08	8.1	0.1	3.8	0.03
Division No. 20	6.5	0.04	2.9	0.02	0.1	0.00	2.9	0.04	4.5	0.05	6.2	0.02	4.8	0.0	3.2	0.02
North	13.2	0.08	11.4	0.10	1.0	0.04	15.8	0.20	11.5	0.13	147.4	0.46	11.6	0.1	10.6	0.08
Division No. 19	1.0	0.01	0.1	0.00	0.0	0.00	1.1	0.01	0.2	0.00	11.0	0.03	0.4	0.0	0.7	0.01
Division No. 21	3.6	0.02	4.4	0.04	1.0	0.04	7.8	0.10	5.7	0.06	14.5	0.04	9.4	0.1	4.6	0.04
Division No. 22	8.3	0.05	5.6	0.05	0.0	0.00	5.3	0.07	3.9	0.04	110.4	0.34	1.5	0.0	5.0	0.04
Division No. 23	0.3	0.00	1.3	0.01	0.0	0.00	1.7	0.02	1.8	0.02	11.5	0.04	0.4	0.0	0.2	0.00
SASKATCHEWAN	539.1	3.33	279.6	2.33	81.4	2.96	211.2	2.73	193.1	2.13	1,129.2	3.50	400.1	2.9	280.0	2.12
Regina - Moose Mountain	167.5	1.03	85.2	0.71	24.0	0.87	45.1	0.58	53.4	0.59	564.8	1.75	98.3	0.7	105.1	0.79
Division No. 1	20.4	0.13	2.5	0.02	2.1	0.08	2.4	0.03	3.9	0.04	28.6	0.09	8.8	0.1	6.4	0.05
Division No. 2	11.9	0.07	5.8	0.05	1.6	0.06	2.4	0.03	2.9	0.03	8.9	0.03	5.2	0.0	2.4	0.02
Division No. 6	135.2	0.83	76.9	0.64	20.3	0.74	40.3	0.52	46.5	0.51	527.3	1.64	84.3	0.6	96.3	0.73
Swift Current - Moose Jaw	48.9	0.30	28.7	0.24	7.8	0.28	20.7	0.27	18.9	0.21	92.2	0.29	37.9	0.3	23.9	0.18
Division No. 3	6.8	0.04	3.4	0.03	0.9	0.03	0.3	0.00	3.3	0.04	9.8	0.03	6.2	0.0	1.9	0.01
Division No. 4	8.3	0.05	1.5	0.01	0.4	0.01	1.0	0.01	1.0	0.01	3.3	0.01	3.8	0.0	1.2	0.01
Division No. 7	17.3	0.11	13.0	0.11	3.8	0.14	16.1	0.21	6.3	0.07	39.7	0.12	18.1	0.1	17.3	0.13
Division No. 8	16.4	0.10	10.9	0.09	2.7	0.10	3.3	0.04	8.3	0.09	39.4	0.12	9.7	0.1	3.4	0.03
Saskatoon - Biggar	183.5	1.13	86.3	0.72	32.1	1.17	90.9	1.18	79.6	0.88	209.5	0.65	170.2	1.2	91.6	0.69
Division No. 11	157.0	0.97	78.3	0.65	30.0	1.09	80.7	1.04	67.3	0.74	196.9	0.61	149.7	1.1	85.1	0.64
Division No. 12	11.5	0.07	3.6	0.03	0.4	0.01	5.1	0.07	7.0	0.08	2.6	0.01	6.7	0.1	3.7	0.03
Division No. 13	14.9	0.09	4.4	0.04	1.6	0.06	5.1	0.07	5.3	0.06	10.0	0.03	13.8	0.1	2.8	0.02
Yorkton - Melville	44.4	0.27	20.4	0.17	6.7	0.24	12.3	0.16	13.2	0.15	73.0	0.23	38.5	0.3	16.3	0.12
Division No. 5	16.7	0.10	7.3	0.06	3.9	0.14	3.8	0.05	4.7	0.05	18.6	0.06	14.9	0.1	6.9	0.05
Division No. 9	21.0	0.13	10.1	0.08	2.1	0.08	7.5	0.10	6.3	0.07	38.6	0.12	15.6	0.1	7.1	0.05
Division No. 10	6.7	0.04	3.1	0.03	0.7	0.02	1.0	0.01	2.1	0.02	15.7	0.05	8.1	0.1	2.3	0.02
Prince Albert	93.1	0.57	56.0	0.47	10.9	0.40	41.6	0.54	27.8	0.31	140.8	0.44	53.1	0.4	41.3	0.31
Division No. 14	18.4	0.11	11.7	0.10	3.5	0.13	5.6	0.07	8.1	0.09	17.7	0.05	16.2	0.1	7.6	0.06
Division No. 15	32.8	0.20	23.3	0.19	2.7	0.10	19.8	0.26	9.0	0.10	79.2	0.25	20.6	0.2	14.6	0.11
Division No. 16	16.5	0.10	8.3	0.07	3.2	0.12	11.6	0.15	5.3	0.06	31.0	0.10	6.4	0.1	11.7	0.09
Division No. 17	25.4	0.16	12.7	0.11	1.5	0.05	4.6	0.06	5.4	0.06	12.9	0.04	9.9	0.1	7.5	0.06
Northern	1.8	0.01	2.9	0.02	0.0	0.00	0.6	0.01	0.3	0.00	48.9	0.15	2.1	0.0	1.9	0.01
Division No. 18	1.8	0.01	2.9	0.02	0.0	0.00	0.6	0.01	0.3	0.00	48.9	0.15	2.1	0.0	1.9	0.01
ALBERTA	1,777.0	10.96	1,536.8	12.80	321.1	11.67	924.6	11.96	914.0	10.09	3,722.5	11.55	1,362.5	9.7	1,726.3	13.04
Lethbridge - Medicine Hat	112.6	0.69	140.1	1.17	30.7	1.12	74.7	0.97	72.6	0.80	307.4	0.95	143.7	1.0	410.7	3.10
Division No. 1	33.6	0.21	46.0	0.38	11.6	0.42	26.9	0.35	26.9	0.30	106.4	0.33	25.9	0.2	61.8	0.47
Division No. 2	66.0	0.41	84.6	0.70	16.5	0.60	43.3	0.56	38.3	0.42	190.5	0.59	97.5	0.7	342.6	2.59
Division No. 3	13.0	0.08	9.4	0.08	2.6	0.09	4.5	0.06	7.4	0.08	10.5	0.03	20.2	0.1	6.3	0.05
Drumheller - Stettler - Wainwright	49.9	0.31	31.8	0.26	6.8	0.25	19.1	0.25	23.5	0.26	69.9	0.22	55.3	0.4	24.3	0.18
Division No. 4	7.1	0.04	7.0	0.06	1.6	0.06	1.5	0.02	4.6	0.05	8.5	0.03	12.9	0.1	3.0	0.02
Division No. 5	16.1	0.10	15.1	0.13	1.2	0.04	5.0	0.06	8.1	0.09	13.1	0.04	18.6	0.1	8.3	0.06
Division No. 7	26.7	0.16	9.6	0.08	4.0	0.14	12.6	0.16	10.9	0.12	48.3	0.15	23.8	0.2	13.0	0.10

Retail Sales, 2001
1 – By Province, Economic Region and Census Division

Region	Total Sales $mill.	Total Sales % of Cdn Total	Supermarkets & Groceries $mill.	Supermarkets & Groceries % of Cdn Total	All Other Food $mill.	All Other Food % of Cdn Total	Women's Clothing $mill.	Women's Clothing % of Cdn Total	Men's Clothing $mill.	Men's Clothing % of Cdn Total	Other Clothing $mill.	Other Clothing % of Cdn Total	Shoes $mill.	Shoes % of Cdn Total	Motor Vehicles & Recreation Vehicles $mill.	Motor Vehicles & Recreation Vehicles % of Cdn Total	Gas Service Stations $mill.	Gas Service Stations % of Cdn Total
Calgary	10,863.6	3.90	2,132.2	3.81	62.7	1.39	200.6	4.14	91.7	5.60	263.4	3.68	52.5	3.1	2,773.9	3.62	715.1	3.80
Division No. 6	10,863.6	3.90	2,132.2	3.81	62.7	1.39	200.6	4.14	91.7	5.60	263.4	3.68	52.5	3.1	2,773.9	3.62	715.1	3.80
Athabasca - Jasper - Banff	1,390.6	0.50	254.5	0.45	7.5	0.17	21.8	0.45	10.4	0.64	69.5	0.97	3.4	0.2	352.6	0.46	211.4	1.10
Division No. 13	605.3	0.22	95.4	0.17	2.8	0.06	2.9	0.06	4.4	0.27	12.2	0.17	1.3	0.1	197.7	0.26	80.9	0.40
Division No. 14	304.1	0.11	68.4	0.12	2.0	0.04	6.6	0.14	1.0	0.06	6.9	0.10	1.9	0.1	83.9	0.11	45.1	0.20
Division No. 15	481.1	0.17	90.7	0.16	2.7	0.06	12.3	0.25	5.0	0.31	50.5	0.71	0.3	0.0	71.0	0.09	85.4	0.50
Red Deer - Rocky Mountain House	2,180.2	0.78	315.5	0.56	9.3	0.21	20.4	0.42	11.2	0.68	44.8	0.63	10.7	0.6	779.2	1.02	206.5	1.10
Division No. 8	1,974.5	0.71	288.6	0.52	8.5	0.19	20.2	0.42	10.4	0.64	43.1	0.60	10.7	0.6	732.0	0.95	153.0	0.80
Division No. 9	205.7	0.07	27.0	0.05	0.8	0.02	0.2	0.00	0.8	0.05	1.7	0.02	0.0	0.0	47.1	0.06	53.6	0.30
Edmonton	9,396.8	3.37	1,975.1	3.53	58.0	1.29	126.6	2.61	42.1	2.57	276.0	3.86	48.1	2.8	2,808.2	3.66	458.6	2.40
Division No. 11	9,396.8	3.37	1,975.1	3.53	58.0	1.29	126.6	2.61	42.1	2.57	276.0	3.86	48.1	2.8	2,808.2	3.66	458.6	2.40
Grande Prairie - Peace River	1,639.9	0.59	258.7	0.46	7.6	0.17	14.1	0.29	7.7	0.47	40.4	0.57	4.1	0.2	562.5	0.73	171.1	0.90
Division No. 17	476.1	0.17	62.1	0.11	1.8	0.04	3.2	0.07	3.9	0.24	9.8	0.14	0.0	0.0	181.2	0.24	61.4	0.30
Division No. 18	94.6	0.03	23.6	0.04	0.7	0.02	1.1	0.02	1.0	0.06	3.2	0.04	0.0	0.0	7.3	0.01	20.8	0.10
Division No. 19	1,069.2	0.38	173.0	0.31	5.1	0.11	9.8	0.20	2.9	0.18	27.4	0.38	4.1	0.2	374.0	0.49	89.0	0.50
Wood Buffalo - Camrose	1,987.7	0.71	450.0	0.80	13.2	0.29	19.3	0.40	8.3	0.51	44.1	0.62	10.7	0.6	533.7	0.70	188.0	1.00
Division No. 10	899.5	0.32	216.8	0.39	6.4	0.14	10.4	0.21	3.3	0.20	21.8	0.30	6.6	0.4	230.1	0.30	78.6	0.40
Division No. 12	605.2	0.22	130.0	0.23	3.8	0.08	1.8	0.04	2.5	0.15	13.0	0.18	2.5	0.2	184.2	0.24	59.1	0.30
Division No. 16	483.0	0.17	103.2	0.18	3.0	0.07	7.0	0.15	2.5	0.15	9.3	0.13	1.5	0.1	119.4	0.16	50.3	0.30
BRITISH COLUMBIA	36,141.4	12.97	7,967.6	14.23	592.4	13.15	579.9	11.96	194.5	11.87	904.9	12.66	201.6	11.8	8,720.0	11.37	2,556.4	13.50
Vancouver Island and Coast	5,874.5	2.11	1,433.7	2.56	106.6	2.37	82.7	1.71	32.4	1.98	128.9	1.80	31.1	1.8	1,422.2	1.85	388.8	2.10
Capital Regional District	2,818.6	1.01	764.2	1.37	56.8	1.26	44.7	0.92	16.6	1.02	73.3	1.03	16.0	0.9	504.6	0.66	166.5	0.90
Cowichan Valley Regional District	488.9	0.18	131.8	0.24	9.8	0.22	7.2	0.15	2.6	0.16	7.7	0.11	1.5	0.1	124.2	0.16	46.4	0.20
Nanaimo Regional District	1,057.5	0.38	190.9	0.34	14.2	0.32	9.6	0.20	3.3	0.20	21.4	0.30	7.3	0.4	371.5	0.48	69.2	0.40
Alberni-Clayoquot Regional District	243.0	0.09	51.5	0.09	3.8	0.09	2.6	0.05	2.8	0.17	3.1	0.04	0.3	0.0	73.3	0.10	27.1	0.10
Comox-Strathcona Regional District	938.2	0.34	231.2	0.41	17.2	0.38	14.6	0.30	4.6	0.28	15.3	0.21	3.6	0.2	289.2	0.38	56.1	0.30
Powell River Regional District	189.9	0.07	39.6	0.07	2.9	0.07	3.6	0.07	1.3	0.08	5.9	0.08	1.0	0.1	34.9	0.05	13.1	0.10
Mount Waddington Regional District	110.8	0.04	23.0	0.04	1.7	0.04	0.1	0.00	1.3	0.08	2.1	0.03	1.4	0.1	23.4	0.03	4.9	0.00
Central Coast Regional District	27.5	0.01	1.5	0.00	0.1	0.00	0.1	0.00	0.0	0.00	0.0	0.00	0.0	0.0	1.0	0.00	5.5	0.00
Lower Mainland - Southwest	20,127.6	7.22	4,302.5	7.69	319.9	7.10	385.6	7.96	127.9	7.81	533.9	7.47	127.6	7.5	4,732.8	6.17	1,233.8	6.50
Fraser Valley Regional District	2,199.0	0.79	597.3	1.07	44.4	0.99	26.7	0.55	6.1	0.37	35.2	0.49	7.1	0.4	567.5	0.74	189.4	1.00
Greater Vancouver Regional District	17,323.8	6.22	3,550.1	6.34	264.0	5.86	351.0	7.24	116.7	7.12	453.5	6.34	118.7	7.0	4,081.0	5.32	977.4	5.20
Sunshine Coast Regional District	255.9	0.09	77.2	0.14	5.7	0.13	2.7	0.06	1.0	0.06	6.4	0.09	1.1	0.1	53.4	0.07	19.2	0.10
Squamish-Lillooet Regional District	348.8	0.13	78.0	0.14	5.8	0.13	5.2	0.11	4.1	0.25	38.7	0.54	0.7	0.0	30.9	0.04	47.9	0.30
Thompson - Okanagan	5,068.0	1.82	1,061.1	1.90	78.9	1.75	62.7	1.29	17.1	1.05	113.9	1.59	22.3	1.3	1,320.9	1.72	434.3	2.30
Okanagan-Similkameen Regional District	690.8	0.25	139.7	0.25	10.4	0.23	6.7	0.14	3.3	0.20	12.1	0.17	4.2	0.2	144.1	0.19	64.0	0.30
Thompson-Nicola Regional District	1,296.4	0.47	322.2	0.58	24.0	0.53	17.1	0.35	4.9	0.30	29.9	0.42	5.5	0.3	317.1	0.41	140.6	0.70
Central Okanagan Regional District	1,845.9	0.66	343.4	0.61	25.5	0.57	27.2	0.56	6.1	0.37	44.8	0.63	9.3	0.5	516.1	0.67	118.0	0.60
North Okanagan Regional District	692.7	0.25	125.0	0.22	9.3	0.21	8.6	0.18	1.6	0.10	14.2	0.20	1.9	0.1	212.4	0.28	44.2	0.20
Columbia-Shuswap Regional District	542.3	0.19	130.8	0.23	9.7	0.22	3.2	0.07	1.3	0.08	12.9	0.18	1.4	0.1	131.1	0.17	67.4	0.40
Kootenay	1,860.7	0.67	503.5	0.90	37.4	0.83	17.8	0.37	4.5	0.27	33.6	0.47	4.7	0.3	420.9	0.55	207.1	1.10
East Kootenay Regional District	826.5	0.30	273.9	0.49	20.4	0.45	7.7	0.16	1.8	0.11	18.0	0.25	1.5	0.1	198.0	0.26	84.8	0.40
Central Kootenay Regional District	694.8	0.25	168.8	0.30	12.5	0.28	6.6	0.14	2.0	0.12	12.4	0.17	2.0	0.1	134.1	0.17	70.7	0.40
Kootenay Boundary Regional District	339.4	0.12	60.8	0.11	4.5	0.10	3.5	0.07	0.8	0.05	3.2	0.05	1.2	0.1	88.8	0.12	51.5	0.30
Cariboo	1,619.0	0.58	320.5	0.57	23.8	0.53	20.5	0.42	5.6	0.34	53.9	0.75	7.0	0.4	392.4	0.51	115.9	0.60
Cariboo Regional District	618.9	0.22	120.1	0.21	8.9	0.20	4.4	0.09	0.9	0.05	14.7	0.21	2.9	0.2	179.0	0.23	31.7	0.20
Fraser-Fort George Regional District	1,000.1	0.36	200.5	0.36	14.9	0.33	16.1	0.33	4.8	0.29	39.2	0.55	4.2	0.2	213.4	0.28	84.2	0.40
North Coast	501.4	0.18	123.1	0.22	9.2	0.20	6.0	0.12	2.5	0.15	14.0	0.20	3.8	0.2	117.2	0.15	47.9	0.30
Skeena-Queen Charlotte Regional District	169.0	0.06	59.5	0.11	4.4	0.10	0.8	0.02	1.1	0.07	5.4	0.08	1.3	0.1	24.9	0.03	13.4	0.10
Kitimat-Stikine Regional District	332.4	0.12	63.6	0.11	4.7	0.11	5.2	0.11	1.4	0.08	8.6	0.12	2.5	0.2	92.3	0.12	34.5	0.20
Nechako	402.4	0.14	91.0	0.16	6.8	0.15	0.7	0.01	2.5	0.15	11.6	0.16	1.0	0.1	107.7	0.14	50.9	0.30
Bulkley-Nechako Regional District	391.5	0.14	85.9	0.15	6.4	0.14	0.7	0.01	2.5	0.15	11.6	0.16	1.0	0.1	107.7	0.14	47.9	0.30
Stikine Region	10.9	0.00	5.1	0.01	0.4	0.01	0.0	0.00	0.0	0.00	0.0	0.00	0.0	0.0	0.0	0.00	3.0	0.00
Northeast	687.8	0.25	132.1	0.24	9.8	0.22	4.0	0.08	1.9	0.11	15.1	0.21	4.1	0.2	205.9	0.27	77.8	0.40
Peace River Regional District	641.7	0.23	113.3	0.20	8.4	0.19	3.8	0.08	1.6	0.10	12.8	0.18	4.1	0.2	205.9	0.27	70.1	0.40
Fort Nelson-Liard Regional District	46.0	0.02	18.9	0.03	1.4	0.03	0.1	0.00	0.3	0.02	2.3	0.03	0.0	0.0	0.0	0.00	7.6	0.00
NORTHWEST TERRITORIES	128.7	0.05	25.8	0.05	0.7	0.02	1.5	0.03	0.5	0.03	2.7	0.04	0.3	0.0	31.7	0.04	6.9	0.00
Fort Smith Region	111.8	0.04	23.7	0.04	0.6	0.01	1.4	0.03	0.5	0.03	2.3	0.03	0.3	0.0	30.9	0.04	5.8	0.00
Inuvik Region	16.9	0.01	2.1	0.00	0.1	0.00	0.1	0.00	0.0	0.00	0.4	0.01	0.0	0.0	0.8	0.00	1.1	0.00
NUNAVUT	42.3	0.02	14.4	0.03	0.4	0.01	0.0	0.00	0.0	0.00	1.5	0.02	0.0	0.0	3.1	0.00	0.4	0.00
Baffin Region	25.6	0.01	8.9	0.02	0.2	0.01	0.0	0.00	0.0	0.00	1.4	0.02	0.0	0.0	0.8	0.00	0.4	0.00
Keewatin Region	11.2	0.00	4.2	0.01	0.1	0.00	0.0	0.00	0.0	0.00	0.1	0.00	0.0	0.0	1.7	0.00	0.0	0.00
Kitikmeot Region	5.5	0.00	1.4	0.00	0.0	0.00	0.0	0.00	0.0	0.00	0.0	0.00	0.0	0.0	0.6	0.00	0.0	0.00
YUKON TERRITORY	166.9	0.06	30.0	0.05	0.8	0.02	3.3	0.07	1.7	0.11	4.5	0.06	1.2	0.1	59.5	0.08	16.2	0.10

Retail Sales, 2001 1 – By Province, Economic Region and Census Division	Auto Parts Accessories & Services		Household Furniture & Appliances		Household Furnishings		Other Durable Goods		Other Semi-Durable Goods		General Merchandise		Drugs and Patent Medicine		All Other Retail	
	$mill. Sales	% of Cdn Total	$mill. Sales	% of Cdn Total	$mill. Sales	% of Cdn Total	$mill. Sales	% of Cdn Total	$mill. Sales	% of Cdn Total	$mill. Sales	% of Cdn Total	$mill. Sales	% of Cdn Total	$mill. Sales	% of Cdn Total
Calgary	598.1	3.69	622.5	5.18	111.2	4.04	336.0	4.35	320.8	3.54	1,517.0	4.71	445.1	3.2	620.7	4.69
Division No. 6	598.1	3.69	622.5	5.18	111.2	4.04	336.0	4.35	320.8	3.54	1,517.0	4.71	445.1	3.2	620.7	4.69
Athabasca - Jasper - Banff	64.3	0.40	46.0	0.38	14.2	0.52	46.8	0.61	65.8	0.73	92.5	0.29	70.7	0.5	59.1	0.45
Division No. 13	34.7	0.21	22.4	0.19	4.0	0.14	5.6	0.07	22.7	0.25	51.9	0.16	39.5	0.3	26.9	0.20
Division No. 14	16.7	0.10	13.6	0.11	4.8	0.17	5.4	0.07	5.8	0.06	17.8	0.06	12.7	0.1	11.6	0.09
Division No. 15	12.9	0.08	10.1	0.08	5.5	0.20	35.7	0.46	37.3	0.41	22.8	0.07	18.4	0.1	20.6	0.16
Red Deer - Rocky Mountain House	119.8	0.74	94.7	0.79	18.7	0.68	58.1	0.75	50.7	0.56	258.3	0.80	92.0	0.7	90.3	0.68
Division No. 8	110.0	0.68	88.1	0.73	18.6	0.67	53.7	0.69	46.6	0.51	222.4	0.69	84.4	0.6	84.2	0.64
Division No. 9	9.8	0.06	6.6	0.05	0.1	0.00	4.3	0.06	4.1	0.05	36.0	0.11	7.5	0.1	6.2	0.05
Edmonton	609.2	3.76	476.1	3.96	97.4	3.54	313.7	4.06	282.8	3.12	1,059.3	3.29	406.5	2.9	359.0	2.71
Division No. 11	609.2	3.76	476.1	3.96	97.4	3.54	313.7	4.06	282.8	3.12	1,059.3	3.29	406.5	2.9	359.0	2.71
Grande Prairie - Peace River	107.3	0.66	60.7	0.51	20.5	0.74	25.3	0.33	39.3	0.43	170.3	0.53	61.5	0.4	88.8	0.67
Division No. 17	29.6	0.18	11.6	0.10	1.4	0.05	8.9	0.11	13.1	0.15	45.4	0.14	22.9	0.2	19.9	0.15
Division No. 18	7.7	0.05	0.2	0.00	0.4	0.01	2.2	0.03	3.9	0.04	6.7	0.02	7.3	0.1	8.4	0.06
Division No. 19	70.1	0.43	48.9	0.41	18.7	0.68	14.3	0.18	22.2	0.24	118.2	0.37	31.3	0.2	60.4	0.46
Wood Buffalo - Camrose	115.6	0.71	64.9	0.54	21.6	0.78	50.9	0.66	58.4	0.64	247.8	0.77	87.8	0.6	73.3	0.55
Division No. 10	64.1	0.40	23.9	0.20	9.0	0.33	23.4	0.30	34.9	0.38	96.5	0.30	34.3	0.2	39.4	0.30
Division No. 12	33.1	0.20	21.9	0.18	7.4	0.27	13.2	0.17	12.7	0.14	70.7	0.22	34.9	0.3	14.3	0.11
Division No. 16	18.4	0.11	19.1	0.16	5.2	0.19	14.3	0.18	10.9	0.12	80.6	0.25	18.6	0.1	19.6	0.15
BRITISH COLUMBIA	1,863.8	11.50	1,624.6	13.53	440.7	16.02	1,260.3	16.30	1,217.6	13.44	4,312.5	13.38	1,881.7	13.4	1,822.7	13.77
Vancouver Island and Coast	277.8	1.71	277.0	2.31	86.7	3.15	205.9	2.66	233.1	2.57	634.7	1.97	309.3	2.2	223.6	1.69
Capital Regional District	141.3	0.87	154.4	1.29	33.2	1.21	107.6	1.39	121.2	1.34	332.6	1.03	169.4	1.2	116.1	0.88
Cowichan Valley Regional District	32.4	0.20	15.1	0.13	7.8	0.28	11.6	0.15	18.5	0.20	13.6	0.04	37.5	0.3	21.3	0.16
Nanaimo Regional District	40.5	0.25	56.7	0.47	24.9	0.90	34.9	0.45	40.1	0.44	91.3	0.28	41.4	0.3	40.4	0.31
Alberni-Clayoquot Regional District	14.9	0.09	12.1	0.10	2.7	0.10	8.3	0.11	9.5	0.10	8.3	0.03	14.9	0.1	7.7	0.06
Comox-Strathcona Regional District	33.6	0.21	31.8	0.26	14.1	0.51	37.9	0.49	33.6	0.37	95.2	0.30	32.5	0.2	27.6	0.21
Powell River Regional District	10.6	0.07	3.5	0.03	3.5	0.13	3.8	0.05	6.0	0.07	52.7	0.16	1.5	0.0	6.0	0.05
Mount Waddington Regional District	3.8	0.02	3.4	0.03	0.4	0.02	1.8	0.02	4.1	0.05	24.4	0.08	11.2	0.1	3.9	0.03
Central Coast Regional District	0.9	0.01	0.0	0.00	0.2	0.01	0.0	0.00	0.1	0.00	16.7	0.05	1.0	0.0	0.5	0.00
Lower Mainland - Southwest	1,033.9	6.38	942.9	7.85	250.6	9.11	733.3	9.48	664.9	7.34	2,501.7	7.76	1,027.5	7.3	1,208.6	9.13
Fraser Valley Regional District	111.9	0.69	72.2	0.60	17.8	0.65	51.6	0.67	49.3	0.54	225.1	0.70	113.1	0.8	84.4	0.64
Greater Vancouver Regional District	902.7	5.57	852.3	7.10	226.0	8.22	629.1	8.14	592.4	6.54	2,247.2	6.97	867.6	6.2	1,094.4	8.27
Sunshine Coast Regional District	8.1	0.05	9.1	0.08	3.7	0.13	7.5	0.10	8.6	0.09	13.4	0.04	25.5	0.2	13.1	0.10
Squamish-Lillooet Regional District	11.3	0.07	9.4	0.08	3.1	0.11	45.1	0.58	14.6	0.16	16.0	0.05	21.3	0.2	16.7	0.13
Thompson - Okanagan	253.1	1.56	220.7	1.84	55.9	2.03	167.1	2.16	170.5	1.88	635.8	1.97	248.8	1.8	205.1	1.55
Okanagan-Similkameen Regional District	28.2	0.17	26.9	0.22	5.8	0.21	17.8	0.23	24.4	0.27	141.1	0.44	39.4	0.3	22.7	0.17
Thompson-Nicola Regional District	60.2	0.37	55.5	0.46	11.8	0.43	39.2	0.51	37.0	0.41	122.0	0.38	57.5	0.4	51.8	0.39
Central Okanagan Regional District	91.0	0.56	84.9	0.71	26.3	0.96	72.5	0.94	66.2	0.73	258.7	0.80	74.9	0.5	80.8	0.61
North Okanagan Regional District	39.3	0.24	35.5	0.30	5.7	0.21	21.6	0.28	19.7	0.22	67.4	0.21	51.6	0.4	34.8	0.26
Columbia-Shuswap Regional District	34.4	0.21	17.8	0.15	6.2	0.22	16.0	0.21	23.2	0.26	46.7	0.14	25.3	0.2	14.9	0.11
Kootenay	94.5	0.58	64.3	0.54	13.6	0.49	51.0	0.66	57.8	0.64	170.7	0.53	110.6	0.8	68.8	0.52
East Kootenay Regional District	40.1	0.25	30.8	0.26	7.1	0.26	24.7	0.32	26.6	0.29	39.9	0.12	19.3	0.1	31.9	0.24
Central Kootenay Regional District	39.5	0.24	24.7	0.21	5.4	0.20	16.8	0.22	21.4	0.24	89.9	0.28	68.7	0.5	19.2	0.15
Kootenay Boundary Regional District	14.9	0.09	8.7	0.07	1.1	0.04	9.5	0.12	9.8	0.11	40.8	0.13	22.6	0.2	17.7	0.13
Cariboo	105.7	0.65	68.5	0.57	20.0	0.73	53.7	0.69	50.5	0.56	246.4	0.76	66.0	0.5	68.5	0.52
Cariboo Regional District	37.5	0.23	25.6	0.21	8.4	0.31	23.7	0.31	13.1	0.14	108.6	0.34	14.6	0.1	24.7	0.19
Fraser-Fort George Regional District	68.1	0.42	42.9	0.36	11.6	0.42	30.1	0.39	37.4	0.41	137.8	0.43	51.3	0.4	43.8	0.33
North Coast	22.6	0.14	19.0	0.16	6.0	0.22	20.7	0.27	11.5	0.13	49.6	0.15	31.0	0.2	17.4	0.13
Skeena-Queen Charlotte Regional District	5.1	0.03	5.0	0.04	3.5	0.13	10.3	0.13	5.5	0.06	19.3	0.06	5.0	0.0	4.5	0.03
Kitimat-Stikine Regional District	17.5	0.11	14.0	0.12	2.5	0.09	10.5	0.14	6.0	0.07	30.3	0.09	26.0	0.2	12.9	0.10
Nechako	23.8	0.15	9.9	0.08	1.9	0.07	9.0	0.12	12.0	0.13	24.6	0.08	37.9	0.3	11.1	0.08
Bulkley-Nechako Regional District	23.3	0.14	9.9	0.08	1.9	0.07	8.8	0.11	11.7	0.13	23.9	0.07	37.9	0.3	10.4	0.08
Stikine Region	0.5	0.00	0.0	0.00	0.0	0.00	0.2	0.00	0.3	0.00	0.7	0.00	0.0	0.0	0.7	0.01
Northeast	52.5	0.32	22.4	0.19	6.0	0.22	19.6	0.25	17.3	0.19	49.1	0.15	50.6	0.4	19.6	0.15
Peace River Regional District	49.0	0.30	20.4	0.17	5.4	0.20	18.0	0.23	16.1	0.18	46.3	0.14	48.1	0.3	18.5	0.14
Fort Nelson-Liard Regional District	3.5	0.02	2.0	0.02	0.6	0.02	1.6	0.02	1.3	0.01	2.9	0.01	2.5	0.0	1.1	0.01
NORTHWEST TERRITORIES	4.4	0.03	7.6	0.06	2.1	0.07	4.5	0.06	3.6	0.04	20.5	0.06	8.9	0.1	6.9	0.05
Fort Smith Region	4.0	0.02	6.4	0.05	2.1	0.07	3.0	0.04	3.4	0.04	12.8	0.04	8.2	0.1	6.4	0.05
Inuvik Region	0.4	0.00	1.2	0.01	0.0	0.00	1.5	0.02	0.3	0.00	7.7	0.02	0.7	0.0	0.5	0.00
NUNAVUT	0.5	0.00	0.5	0.00	0.0	0.00	0.8	0.01	0.9	0.01	16.2	0.05	0.8	0.0	2.9	0.02
Baffin Region	0.5	0.00	0.5	0.00	0.0	0.00	0.6	0.01	0.8	0.01	8.8	0.03	0.8	0.0	2.0	0.01
Keewatin Region	0.0	0.00	0.0	0.00	0.0	0.00	0.2	0.00	0.1	0.00	3.9	0.01	0.0	0.0	0.9	0.01
Kitikmeot Region	0.0	0.00	0.0	0.00	0.0	0.00	0.0	0.00	0.0	0.00	3.6	0.01	0.0	0.0	0.0	0.00
YUKON TERRITORY	14.1	0.09	8.3	0.07	1.3	0.05	4.6	0.06	5.2	0.06	2.8	0.01	4.8	0.0	8.7	0.07

Retail Sales Estimates, 2001

By Class of Business (Sales in $ millions)
2 – By Province and Urban Market

	Total Sales		Supermarkets & Groceries		All Other Food		Women's Clothing		Men's Clothing		Other Clothing		Shoes		Motor Vehicles & Recreation Vehicles		Gas Service Stations	
	$mill. Sales	% of Cdn Total	$mill. Sales	% of Cdn Total	$mill. Sales	% of Cdn Total	$mill. Sales	% of Cdn Total	$mill. Sales	% of Cdn Total	$mill. Sales	% of Cdn Total	$mill. Sales	% of Cdn Total	$mill. Sales	% of Cdn Total	$mill. Sales	% of Cdn Total
CANADA	278,705.8	100.00	55,982.1	100.00	4,504.3	100.00	4,847.4	100.00	1,638.6	100.00	7,148.5	100.00	1,707.9	100.00	76,689.3	100.00	18,935.4	100.00
NEWFOUNDLAND	4,628.5	1.66	1,183.6	2.11	55.2	1.23	64.6	1.33	19.3	1.18	74.2	1.04	15.9	0.9	1,177.3	1.54	340.1	1.80
Corner Brook, CA	338.1	0.12	120.1	0.21	5.6	0.12	7.2	0.15	1.8	0.11	8.6	0.12	0.4	0.0	46.1	0.06	21.5	0.10
Gander, CA	197.1	0.07	30.2	0.05	1.4	0.03	3.9	0.08	1.8	0.11	5.5	0.08	0.9	0.1	78.7	0.10	11.3	0.10
Grand Falls-Windsor, CA	302.2	0.11	51.8	0.09	2.4	0.05	1.7	0.04	0.8	0.05	2.1	0.03	0.9	0.1	127.9	0.17	27.5	0.10
Labrador City, CA	98.5	0.04	28.2	0.05	1.3	0.03	1.2	0.03	0.0	0.00	3.0	0.04	1.1	0.1	35.0	0.05	4.7	0.00
St. John's, CMA	1,904.7	0.68	452.5	0.81	21.1	0.47	38.9	0.80	14.4	0.88	35.0	0.49	10.5	0.6	515.2	0.67	78.6	0.40
PRINCE EDWARD ISLAND	1,205.9	0.43	295.1	0.53	16.6	0.37	21.3	0.44	6.7	0.41	31.8	0.45	6.0	0.4	259.3	0.34	126.0	0.70
Charlottetown, CA	666.1	0.24	151.3	0.27	8.5	0.19	12.8	0.26	3.4	0.21	23.3	0.33	4.3	0.3	149.9	0.20	53.5	0.30
Summerside, CA	263.8	0.09	74.9	0.13	4.2	0.09	6.5	0.13	2.4	0.15	4.7	0.07	1.6	0.1	72.5	0.09	16.8	0.10
NOVA SCOTIA	8,693.8	3.12	2,065.5	3.69	94.3	2.09	137.0	2.83	22.3	1.36	170.7	2.39	27.6	1.6	2,191.6	2.86	676.5	3.60
Cape Breton, CA	999.2	0.36	266.1	0.48	12.1	0.27	17.6	0.36	3.3	0.20	22.2	0.31	2.2	0.1	238.0	0.31	66.3	0.40
Halifax, CMA	3,529.7	1.27	730.9	1.31	33.4	0.74	77.3	1.60	8.9	0.54	88.6	1.24	17.0	1.0	886.4	1.16	242.3	1.30
Kentville, CA	312.6	0.11	50.1	0.09	2.3	0.05	3.5	0.07	1.1	0.07	5.9	0.08	0.5	0.0	108.4	0.14	34.5	0.20
New Glasgow, CA	400.1	0.14	101.4	0.18	4.6	0.10	7.0	0.14	0.9	0.05	1.4	0.02	0.8	0.1	110.7	0.14	27.6	0.10
Truro, CA	555.3	0.20	146.7	0.26	6.7	0.15	8.3	0.17	1.9	0.11	8.3	0.12	1.5	0.1	160.2	0.21	31.8	0.20
NEW BRUNSWICK	7,095.9	2.55	1,697.9	3.03	65.0	1.44	95.6	1.97	29.9	1.83	142.9	2.00	27.1	1.6	1,974.2	2.57	526.5	2.80
Bathurst, CA	487.0	0.17	98.7	0.18	3.8	0.08	6.4	0.13	1.0	0.06	6.7	0.09	1.3	0.1	183.0	0.24	43.5	0.20
Campbellton, CA	213.2	0.08	37.7	0.07	2.0	0.05	1.2	0.02	0.9	0.06	3.2	0.05	0.0	0.0	61.2	0.08	18.3	0.10
Edmundston, CA	240.5	0.09	83.4	0.15	3.2	0.07	4.4	0.09	1.7	0.10	6.4	0.09	0.4	0.0	35.4	0.05	15.9	0.10
Fredericton, CA	1,046.3	0.38	205.7	0.37	7.9	0.17	22.9	0.47	6.7	0.41	29.8	0.42	5.1	0.3	265.0	0.35	36.9	0.20
Moncton, CA	1,259.2	0.45	229.9	0.41	8.8	0.20	21.8	0.45	2.5	0.15	29.6	0.41	5.5	0.3	425.6	0.55	80.9	0.40
Saint John, CMA	1,057.5	0.38	302.1	0.54	11.6	0.26	12.7	0.26	9.9	0.60	18.0	0.25	6.5	0.4	226.1	0.29	42.5	0.20
QUÉBEC	64,688.8	23.21	14,656.9	26.18	1,342.7	29.81	1,299.1	26.80	352.5	21.51	1,810.5	25.33	576.7	33.8	18,575.2	24.22	3,777.6	19.90
Alma, CA	356.0	0.13	81.0	0.14	7.4	0.16	3.5	0.07	1.2	0.07	3.9	0.05	3.4	0.2	103.4	0.13	15.8	0.10
Baie-Comeau, CA	228.3	0.08	41.7	0.07	3.8	0.08	2.7	0.06	0.5	0.03	1.4	0.02	0.5	0.0	64.7	0.08	22.6	0.10
Chicoutimi-Jonquière, CMA	1,474.9	0.53	363.7	0.65	33.3	0.74	27.0	0.56	5.0	0.31	24.2	0.34	13.3	0.8	466.8	0.61	75.3	0.40
Cowansville, CA	183.8	0.07	37.3	0.07	3.4	0.08	2.4	0.05	0.2	0.01	8.5	0.12	1.2	0.1	65.6	0.09	6.5	0.00
Dolbeau, CA	165.2	0.06	39.4	0.07	3.6	0.08	4.1	0.08	2.3	0.09	11.3	0.16	2.1	0.1	43.6	0.06	2.3	0.00
Drummondville, CA	895.8	0.32	161.9	0.29	14.8	0.33	18.9	0.39	4.5	0.28	24.4	0.34	6.2	0.4	292.9	0.38	69.5	0.40
Granby, CA	792.2	0.28	165.6	0.30	15.2	0.34	21.4	0.44	4.5	0.28	18.3	0.26	7.2	0.4	262.6	0.34	34.9	0.20
Joliette, CA	686.7	0.25	124.5	0.22	11.4	0.25	17.6	0.36	3.7	0.22	19.6	0.27	6.7	0.4	314.0	0.41	6.8	0.00
La Tuque, CA	127.7	0.05	46.4	0.08	4.2	0.09	1.6	0.03	0.2	0.01	2.7	0.04	1.6	0.1	23.5	0.03	7.8	0.00
Lachute, CA	118.4	0.04	14.5	0.03	1.3	0.03	1.0	0.02	1.3	0.08	0.6	0.01	0.9	0.1	50.5	0.07	4.2	0.00
Magog, CA	241.8	0.09	75.9	0.14	7.0	0.15	3.3	0.07	1.0	0.06	3.2	0.05	2.7	0.2	71.0	0.09	9.1	0.00
Matane, CA	217.7	0.08	60.1	0.11	5.5	0.12	2.0	0.04	1.2	0.07	4.4	0.06	0.7	0.1	68.6	0.09	22.6	0.10
Montréal, CMA	28,737.3	10.31	5,829.2	10.41	534.0	11.86	766.2	15.81	199.3	12.16	852.6	11.93	306.2	17.9	8,005.4	10.44	1,351.2	7.10
Québec, CMA	7,599.5	2.73	1,634.3	2.92	149.7	3.32	156.1	3.22	40.1	2.45	341.7	4.78	80.5	4.7	2,024.6	2.64	455.6	2.40
Rimouski, CA	500.7	0.18	148.2	0.26	13.6	0.30	5.9	0.12	3.0	0.18	11.3	0.16	3.8	0.2	140.1	0.18	14.6	0.10
Rivière-du-Loup, CA	393.4	0.14	39.0	0.07	3.6	0.08	5.3	0.11	2.1	0.13	18.8	0.26	1.8	0.1	180.8	0.24	54.0	0.30
Rouyn-Noranda, CA	417.0	0.15	81.6	0.15	7.5	0.17	8.5	0.17	2.1	0.13	9.4	0.13	2.1	0.1	110.2	0.14	36.2	0.20
Saint-Georges, CA	432.3	0.16	123.1	0.22	11.3	0.25	8.6	0.18	3.9	0.24	8.5	0.12	1.8	0.1	130.3	0.17	15.5	0.10
Saint-Hyacinthe, CA	694.9	0.25	139.3	0.25	12.8	0.28	6.7	0.14	6.2	0.38	26.4	0.37	4.0	0.2	306.7	0.40	22.3	0.10
Saint-Jean-sur-Richelieu, CA	942.8	0.34	217.2	0.39	19.9	0.44	13.5	0.28	1.9	0.12	15.3	0.21	9.4	0.6	313.5	0.41	33.6	0.20
Salaberry-de-Valleyfield, CA	510.8	0.18	121.7	0.22	11.2	0.25	9.7	0.20	5.9	0.36	11.5	0.16	9.1	0.5	162.6	0.21	25.9	0.10
Sept-Îles, CA	277.2	0.10	60.7	0.11	5.6	0.12	2.6	0.05	2.4	0.15	3.1	0.04	0.7	0.0	109.7	0.14	4.9	0.00
Shawinigan, CA	492.5	0.18	129.7	0.23	11.9	0.26	6.3	0.13	1.9	0.12	18.3	0.26	4.5	0.3	103.4	0.13	38.2	0.20
Sherbrooke, CMA	1,311.3	0.47	257.8	0.46	23.6	0.52	17.8	0.37	6.0	0.36	25.9	0.36	12.2	0.7	382.1	0.50	63.4	0.30
Sorel, CA	439.7	0.16	84.5	0.15	7.7	0.17	6.9	0.14	2.7	0.16	16.9	0.24	4.0	0.2	155.8	0.20	27.2	0.10
Thetford Mines, CA	352.8	0.13	44.4	0.08	4.1	0.09	5.1	0.10	1.3	0.08	8.6	0.12	1.9	0.1	155.3	0.20	25.5	0.10
Trois-Rivières, CMA	1,146.7	0.41	239.2	0.43	21.9	0.49	24.1	0.50	7.1	0.43	31.4	0.44	14.0	0.8	312.0	0.41	53.4	0.30
Val-d'Or, CA	432.2	0.16	97.0	0.17	8.9	0.20	7.9	0.16	1.2	0.07	7.3	0.10	2.9	0.2	137.2	0.18	44.3	0.20
Victoriaville, CA	560.2	0.20	84.5	0.15	7.7	0.17	10.7	0.22	2.4	0.15	19.3	0.27	8.0	0.5	157.7	0.21	14.2	0.10
ONTARIO	106,349.4	38.16	17,440.9	31.15	2,003.3	44.48	1,953.4	40.30	716.1	43.70	2,791.7	39.05	642.5	37.6	29,840.8	38.91	7,299.9	38.60
Barrie, CA	1,575.5	0.57	176.4	0.32	20.3	0.45	11.3	0.23	6.0	0.37	51.9	0.73	11.2	0.7	556.7	0.73	99.2	0.50
Belleville, CA	1,170.9	0.42	107.6	0.19	12.4	0.27	16.1	0.33	5.7	0.35	18.2	0.25	11.5	0.7	421.2	0.55	128.5	0.70
Brantford, CA	922.6	0.33	186.7	0.33	21.4	0.48	9.1	0.19	6.9	0.42	14.0	0.20	6.0	0.4	274.5	0.36	42.2	0.20
Brockville, CA	426.0	0.15	62.5	0.11	7.2	0.16	7.6	0.16	4.5	0.28	17.6	0.25	2.0	0.1	121.3	0.16	37.8	0.20
Chatham, CA	880.5	0.32	117.1	0.21	13.5	0.30	11.6	0.24	6.5	0.40	14.0	0.20	2.5	0.2	263.9	0.34	63.5	0.30
Cobourg, CA	199.4	0.07	21.6	0.04	2.5	0.06	7.8	0.16	2.4	0.15	5.5	0.08	1.6	0.1	37.7	0.05	27.7	0.10
Collingwood, CA	220.2	0.08	55.8	0.10	6.4	0.14	3.5	0.07	0.9	0.06	4.4	0.06	0.3	0.0	60.1	0.08	12.1	0.10

Retail Sales Estimates, 2001

By Class of Business (Sales in $ millions)
2- By Province and Urban Market

	Auto Parts Accessories & Services		Household Furniture & Appliances		Household Furnishings		Other Durable Goods		Other Semi-Durable Goods		General Merchandise		Drugs and Patent Medicine		All Other Retail	
	$mill. Sales	% of Cdn Total	$mill. Sales	% of Cdn Total	$mill. Sales	% of Cdn Total	$mill. Sales	% of Cdn Total	$mill. Sales	% of Cdn Total	$mill. Sales	% of Cdn Total	$mill. Sales	% of Cdn Total	$mill. Sales	% of Cdn Total
CANADA	16,210.0	100.00	12,009.0	100.00	2,750.8	100.00	7,732.4	100.00	9,056.8	100.00	32,232.2	100.00	14,024.8	100.0	13,236.4	100.00
NEWFOUNDLAND	241.9	1.49	151.1	1.26	9.6	0.35	59.5	0.77	102.7	1.13	701.8	2.18	263.4	1.9	168.2	1.27
Corner Brook, CA	23.4	0.14	5.1	0.04	0.5	0.02	3.6	0.05	6.8	0.07	62.7	0.19	13.6	0.1	11.1	0.08
Gander, CA	7.4	0.05	5.5	0.05	0.3	0.01	2.8	0.04	3.0	0.03	33.2	0.10	3.4	0.0	7.8	0.06
Grand Falls-Windsor, CA	26.1	0.16	9.4	0.08	0.2	0.01	2.5	0.03	3.6	0.04	19.6	0.06	18.0	0.1	7.8	0.06
Labrador City, CA	5.1	0.03	1.8	0.02	0.2	0.01	0.6	0.01	1.4	0.01	12.0	0.04	2.4	0.0	0.6	0.00
St. John's, CMA	93.5	0.58	75.1	0.63	5.5	0.20	32.8	0.42	51.1	0.56	257.4	0.80	116.7	0.8	106.3	0.80
PRINCE EDWARD ISLAND	75.8	0.47	32.3	0.27	18.1	0.66	24.7	0.32	52.3	0.58	111.7	0.35	73.5	0.5	54.6	0.41
Charlottetown, CA	46.7	0.29	20.4	0.17	11.0	0.40	15.5	0.20	31.8	0.35	56.2	0.17	41.6	0.3	35.9	0.27
Summerside, CA	15.2	0.09	7.0	0.06	3.2	0.12	6.4	0.08	6.5	0.07	21.1	0.07	11.3	0.1	9.5	0.07
NOVA SCOTIA	486.9	3.00	264.6	2.20	63.7	2.32	193.4	2.50	277.8	3.07	1,004.3	3.12	561.9	4.0	455.6	3.44
Cape Breton, CA	65.4	0.40	20.0	0.17	9.9	0.36	18.9	0.24	22.7	0.25	109.7	0.34	78.9	0.6	45.8	0.35
Halifax, CMA	143.4	0.88	133.5	1.11	29.5	1.07	99.2	1.28	112.7	1.24	517.7	1.61	202.4	1.4	206.4	1.56
Kentville, CA	17.1	0.11	8.1	0.07	1.7	0.06	9.1	0.12	12.2	0.13	23.7	0.07	14.8	0.1	19.5	0.15
New Glasgow, CA	28.6	0.18	13.8	0.12	5.9	0.21	4.3	0.06	7.2	0.08	42.6	0.13	25.9	0.2	17.6	0.13
Truro, CA	48.9	0.30	13.0	0.11	2.0	0.07	15.5	0.20	22.4	0.25	48.1	0.15	16.3	0.1	23.8	0.18
NEW BRUNSWICK	434.8	2.68	211.9	1.76	59.1	2.15	129.1	1.67	214.8	2.37	817.4	2.54	376.7	2.7	293.0	2.21
Bathurst, CA	19.2	0.12	14.1	0.12	8.5	0.31	7.9	0.10	13.5	0.15	50.6	0.16	18.3	0.1	10.6	0.08
Campbellton, CA	9.7	0.06	7.3	0.06	1.8	0.07	4.6	0.06	5.4	0.06	41.5	0.13	13.7	0.1	4.7	0.04
Edmundston, CA	22.5	0.14	17.7	0.15	1.7	0.06	5.0	0.06	6.6	0.07	20.1	0.06	4.1	0.0	11.9	0.09
Fredericton, CA	76.8	0.47	28.4	0.24	14.7	0.53	15.4	0.20	27.2	0.30	158.3	0.49	59.9	0.4	85.8	0.65
Moncton, CA	74.6	0.46	40.9	0.34	11.3	0.41	33.0	0.43	48.3	0.53	95.6	0.30	87.4	0.6	63.4	0.48
Saint John, CMA	52.2	0.32	34.3	0.29	7.9	0.29	24.3	0.31	31.2	0.34	186.7	0.58	49.8	0.4	41.7	0.32
QUÉBEC	3,994.5	24.64	3,137.9	26.13	505.5	18.38	1,590.0	20.56	1,765.2	19.49	6,277.0	19.47	2,963.4	21.1	2,064.1	15.59
Alma, CA	18.0	0.11	19.9	0.17	1.5	0.05	8.1	0.11	4.8	0.05	66.1	0.21	10.1	0.1	8.0	0.06
Baie-Comeau, CA	16.3	0.10	7.4	0.06	3.9	0.14	4.6	0.06	6.5	0.07	24.8	0.08	21.9	0.2	4.9	0.04
Chicoutimi-Jonquière, CMA	72.9	0.45	45.1	0.38	8.5	0.31	41.8	0.54	36.7	0.41	153.3	0.48	67.9	0.5	40.0	0.30
Cowansville, CA	6.9	0.04	12.2	0.10	0.5	0.02	2.0	0.03	3.0	0.03	13.2	0.04	18.4	0.1	2.5	0.02
Dolbeau, CA	8.9	0.06	7.4	0.06	1.4	0.05	6.8	0.09	8.3	0.09	9.4	0.03	10.6	0.1	3.7	0.03
Drummondville, CA	53.1	0.33	54.6	0.45	4.3	0.15	15.4	0.20	19.0	0.21	82.8	0.26	47.9	0.3	25.4	0.19
Granby, CA	47.0	0.29	39.6	0.33	6.2	0.22	28.9	0.37	27.9	0.31	39.7	0.12	31.1	0.2	42.3	0.32
Joliette, CA	35.1	0.22	31.6	0.26	6.1	0.22	17.8	0.23	13.1	0.14	36.0	0.11	27.2	0.2	15.6	0.12
La Tuque, CA	7.8	0.05	4.1	0.03	0.6	0.02	2.0	0.03	2.0	0.02	16.3	0.05	4.8	0.0	2.0	0.02
Lachute, CA	4.4	0.03	2.3	0.02	1.1	0.04	2.6	0.03	1.5	0.02	22.4	0.07	7.0	0.1	2.8	0.02
Magog, CA	9.4	0.06	15.4	0.13	1.3	0.05	6.7	0.09	7.5	0.08	7.9	0.02	13.6	0.1	7.0	0.05
Matane, CA	7.0	0.04	8.5	0.07	0.8	0.03	1.9	0.02	12.2	0.13	11.9	0.04	6.3	0.0	4.0	0.03
Montréal, CMA	1,604.4	9.90	1,463.1	12.18	286.9	10.43	735.5	9.51	779.2	8.60	3,535.1	10.97	1,426.2	10.2	1,063.0	8.03
Québec, CMA	504.0	3.11	390.2	3.25	57.7	2.10	236.4	3.06	242.9	2.68	584.8	1.81	412.6	2.9	288.3	2.18
Rimouski, CA	32.5	0.20	21.6	0.18	4.5	0.16	13.5	0.17	15.3	0.17	33.0	0.10	27.4	0.2	12.3	0.09
Rivière-du-Loup, CA	10.3	0.06	14.4	0.12	4.3	0.16	5.1	0.07	13.4	0.15	23.5	0.07	8.3	0.1	8.8	0.07
Rouyn-Noranda, CA	28.8	0.18	15.1	0.13	1.7	0.06	12.5	0.16	6.2	0.07	65.9	0.20	20.6	0.2	8.7	0.07
Saint-Georges, CA	27.4	0.17	22.7	0.19	4.1	0.15	6.7	0.09	6.0	0.07	47.0	0.15	4.4	0.0	11.1	0.08
Saint-Hyacinthe, CA	43.4	0.27	42.7	0.36	2.8	0.10	11.2	0.14	15.7	0.17	30.5	0.09	11.4	0.1	12.8	0.10
Saint-Jean-sur-Richelieu, CA	67.7	0.42	55.2	0.46	6.4	0.23	29.5	0.38	17.4	0.19	74.0	0.23	47.4	0.3	20.9	0.16
Salaberry-de-Valleyfield, CA	36.0	0.22	27.7	0.23	4.1	0.15	16.8	0.22	8.6	0.10	21.1	0.07	26.9	0.2	12.0	0.09
Sept-Îles, CA	14.9	0.09	9.4	0.08	1.3	0.05	7.1	0.09	7.2	0.08	37.6	0.12	4.7	0.0	5.3	0.04
Shawinigan, CA	30.4	0.19	27.1	0.23	3.8	0.14	13.3	0.17	15.9	0.18	40.6	0.13	32.8	0.2	14.5	0.11
Sherbrooke, CMA	102.8	0.63	66.9	0.56	6.6	0.24	33.1	0.43	38.8	0.43	159.3	0.49	71.7	0.5	43.3	0.33
Sorel, CA	22.4	0.14	20.4	0.17	3.3	0.12	14.5	0.19	6.7	0.07	28.1	0.09	24.9	0.2	13.9	0.11
Thetford Mines, CA	26.5	0.16	15.1	0.13	3.5	0.13	5.2	0.07	5.1	0.06	31.8	0.10	10.8	0.1	8.5	0.06
Trois-Rivières, CMA	99.6	0.61	46.5	0.39	10.1	0.37	32.9	0.43	48.2	0.53	121.2	0.38	41.4	0.3	43.7	0.33
Val-d'Or, CA	24.6	0.15	14.2	0.12	1.3	0.05	15.2	0.20	6.8	0.08	18.2	0.06	12.8	0.1	32.4	0.24
Victoriaville, CA	35.1	0.22	34.4	0.29	4.4	0.16	19.9	0.26	16.8	0.19	97.5	0.30	30.4	0.2	17.1	0.13
ONTARIO	6,285.3	38.77	4,387.6	36.54	1,185.4	43.09	3,091.0	39.98	4,068.9	44.93	12,854.7	39.88	5,825.7	41.5	5,962.1	45.04
Barrie, CA	117.8	0.73	67.9	0.57	18.0	0.65	41.4	0.54	47.8	0.53	200.6	0.62	70.7	0.5	78.2	0.59
Belleville, CA	51.1	0.32	41.5	0.35	13.9	0.51	38.6	0.50	26.8	0.30	174.3	0.54	51.4	0.4	52.2	0.39
Brantford, CA	72.5	0.45	41.0	0.34	8.1	0.30	22.9	0.30	36.1	0.40	83.9	0.26	49.3	0.4	48.0	0.36
Brockville, CA	13.1	0.08	20.7	0.17	4.9	0.18	9.3	0.12	54.3	0.60	9.7	0.03	20.6	0.2	32.8	0.25
Chatham, CA	47.5	0.29	36.3	0.30	9.6	0.35	15.4	0.20	21.4	0.24	158.1	0.49	45.1	0.3	54.7	0.41
Cobourg, CA	11.7	0.07	14.3	0.12	1.6	0.06	4.0	0.05	5.7	0.06	27.2	0.08	11.2	0.1	16.8	0.13
Collingwood, CA	11.0	0.07	7.3	0.06	3.4	0.12	10.3	0.13	9.9	0.11	9.3	0.03	13.1	0.1	12.5	0.09

Retail Sales, 2001
2 - By Province and City

	Total Sales		Supermarkets & Groceries		All Other Food		Women's Clothing		Men's Clothing		Other Clothing		Shoes		Motor Vehicles & Recreation Vehicles		Gas Service Stations	
	$mill. Sales	% of Cdn Total	$mill. Sales	% of Cdn Total	$mill. Sales	% of Cdn Total	$mill. Sales	% of Cdn Total	$mill. Sales	% of Cdn Total	$mill. Sales	% of Cdn Total	$mill. Sales	% of Cdn Total	$mill. Sales	% of Cdn Total	$mill. Sales	% of Cdn Total
Cornwall, CA	758.0	0.27	151.3	0.27	17.4	0.39	8.1	0.17	4.2	0.26	7.5	0.11	5.6	0.3	226.2	0.29	42.6	0.20
Elliot Lake, CA	104.9	0.04	37.9	0.07	4.3	0.10	1.4	0.03	0.5	0.03	0.0	0.00	0.0	0.0	21.2	0.03	8.4	0.00
Guelph, CA	1,341.6	0.48	152.7	0.27	17.5	0.39	30.4	0.63	13.3	0.81	36.4	0.51	10.2	0.6	531.9	0.69	60.7	0.30
Haileybury, CA	261.7	0.09	42.0	0.08	4.8	0.11	4.3	0.09	0.8	0.05	3.8	0.05	1.4	0.1	58.9	0.08	47.8	0.30
Hamilton, CMA	5,465.9	1.96	1,077.1	1.92	123.7	2.75	93.0	1.92	41.1	2.51	146.1	2.04	37.7	2.2	1,308.9	1.71	265.5	1.40
Hawkesbury, CA	234.9	0.08	48.4	0.09	5.2	0.12	1.3	0.03	1.4	0.08	4.4	0.06	1.5	0.1	96.3	0.13	12.5	0.10
Kenora, CA	256.6	0.09	34.0	0.06	3.9	0.09	2.7	0.06	2.3	0.14	4.7	0.07	1.1	0.1	81.9	0.11	23.7	0.10
Kingston, CA	1,369.2	0.49	230.7	0.41	26.5	0.59	28.5	0.59	13.3	0.81	37.5	0.52	14.3	0.8	390.0	0.51	109.3	0.60
Kitchener, CMA	4,550.0	1.63	905.7	1.62	104.0	2.31	83.5	1.72	14.5	0.88	147.2	2.06	25.4	1.5	1,228.8	1.60	235.8	1.20
Leamington, CA	406.3	0.15	73.9	0.13	8.5	0.19	6.5	0.13	3.0	0.18	5.8	0.08	0.9	0.1	93.1	0.12	29.3	0.20
Lindsay, CA	392.5	0.14	76.0	0.14	8.7	0.19	6.5	0.13	1.1	0.06	4.1	0.06	1.7	0.1	151.4	0.20	7.2	0.00
London, CMA	4,355.1	1.56	484.1	0.86	55.6	1.23	108.4	2.24	53.7	3.28	122.7	1.72	29.1	1.7	1,159.3	1.51	308.5	1.60
Midland, CA	331.7	0.12	80.3	0.14	9.2	0.20	3.2	0.07	0.6	0.04	5.6	0.08	1.4	0.1	134.9	0.18	22.9	0.10
North Bay, CA	807.7	0.29	122.8	0.22	14.1	0.31	12.9	0.27	2.6	0.16	22.8	0.32	5.8	0.3	247.4	0.32	53.4	0.30
Orillia, CA	419.0	0.15	71.0	0.13	8.2	0.18	5.4	0.11	1.2	0.07	9.1	0.13	2.7	0.2	87.2	0.11	16.9	0.10
Oshawa, CMA	2,433.5	0.87	489.6	0.87	56.2	1.25	23.8	0.49	7.4	0.45	46.8	0.65	8.8	0.5	615.0	0.80	259.1	1.40
Ottawa-Hull, CMA	10,000.2	3.59	2,113.3	3.78	229.0	5.08	172.5	3.56	68.0	4.15	194.7	2.72	42.8	2.5	3,049.3	3.98	537.6	2.80
Owen Sound, CA	439.4	0.16	49.7	0.09	5.7	0.13	8.1	0.17	1.2	0.07	12.7	0.18	2.3	0.1	111.9	0.15	50.2	0.30
Pembroke, CA	316.5	0.11	69.6	0.12	8.0	0.18	10.5	0.22	2.9	0.18	7.7	0.11	2.9	0.2	101.9	0.13	31.3	0.20
Peterborough, CA	1,085.9	0.39	134.1	0.24	15.4	0.34	15.7	0.32	8.3	0.51	18.5	0.26	4.2	0.3	357.0	0.47	54.6	0.30
Port Hope, CA	104.5	0.04	9.8	0.02	1.1	0.03	0.8	0.02	0.6	0.04	0.6	0.01	0.4	0.0	28.9	0.04	23.7	0.10
Sarnia, CA	818.3	0.29	126.3	0.23	14.5	0.32	19.7	0.41	5.4	0.33	17.4	0.24	4.6	0.3	186.1	0.24	34.1	0.20
Sault Ste. Marie, CA	1,001.0	0.36	217.4	0.39	25.0	0.55	18.1	0.37	5.3	0.32	20.6	0.29	9.6	0.6	277.4	0.36	61.9	0.30
Simcoe, CA	315.3	0.11	95.2	0.17	10.9	0.24	5.6	0.11	3.0	0.18	9.1	0.13	2.6	0.2	109.6	0.14	3.6	0.00
Smiths Falls, CA	190.3	0.07	14.4	0.03	1.7	0.04	1.0	0.02	3.0	0.18	0.9	0.01	0.9	0.1	68.9	0.09	20.5	0.10
St. Catharines-Niagara Falls, CMA	4,003.5	1.44	663.4	1.19	76.2	1.69	71.2	1.47	22.0	1.34	94.3	1.32	17.5	1.0	930.7	1.21	338.6	1.80
Stratford, CA	515.9	0.19	112.5	0.20	12.9	0.29	9.5	0.20	2.4	0.15	9.3	0.13	1.8	0.1	134.3	0.18	33.7	0.20
Strathroy, CA	217.8	0.08	87.1	0.16	10.0	0.22	1.9	0.04	0.5	0.03	2.0	0.03	0.5	0.0	30.0	0.04	14.9	0.10
Sudbury, CMA	1,763.4	0.63	324.6	0.58	37.3	0.83	23.5	0.49	6.2	0.38	33.6	0.47	9.8	0.6	470.1	0.61	156.7	0.80
Thunder Bay, CMA	1,264.7	0.45	147.5	0.26	16.9	0.38	24.0	0.50	11.8	0.72	31.7	0.44	3.2	0.2	390.5	0.51	142.6	0.80
Tillsonburg, CA	118.9	0.04	26.8	0.05	3.1	0.07	3.0	0.06	1.2	0.07	0.9	0.01	0.3	0.0	21.8	0.03	3.6	0.00
Timmins, CA	452.9	0.16	38.3	0.07	4.4	0.10	5.2	0.11	1.7	0.10	11.1	0.16	3.2	0.2	150.2	0.20	30.1	0.20
Toronto, CMA	40,759.1	14.62	6,208.0	11.09	713.1	15.83	909.4	18.76	320.3	19.55	1,339.1	18.73	311.0	18.2	11,154.5	14.55	2,044.3	10.80
Windsor, CMA	3,246.5	1.16	580.2	1.04	66.6	1.48	56.6	1.17	23.5	1.44	77.8	1.09	18.1	1.1	745.2	0.97	206.5	1.10
Woodstock, CA	355.3	0.13	39.5	0.07	4.5	0.10	3.7	0.08	2.9	0.18	2.7	0.04	1.0	0.1	108.4	0.14	16.1	0.10
MANITOBA	9,652.6	3.46	2,170.5	3.88	77.4	1.72	126.9	2.62	50.4	3.08	212.5	2.97	47.9	2.8	2,889.7	3.77	722.5	3.80
Brandon, CA	666.5	0.24	134.5	0.24	4.8	0.11	3.0	0.06	4.8	0.29	17.7	0.25	2.7	0.2	282.8	0.37	24.4	0.10
Portage la Prairie, CA	306.5	0.11	76.9	0.14	2.7	0.06	0.6	0.01	0.7	0.04	5.6	0.08	1.0	0.1	84.2	0.11	11.6	0.10
Thompson, CA	158.5	0.06	12.6	0.02	0.5	0.01	0.2	0.00	0.9	0.05	4.0	0.06	0.0	0.0	45.3	0.06	12.4	0.10
Winnipeg, CMA	5,625.1	2.02	1,275.5	2.28	45.5	1.01	119.1	2.46	35.7	2.18	142.6	2.00	37.1	2.2	1,476.5	1.93	362.0	1.90
SASKATCHEWAN	8,157.3	2.93	1,856.6	3.32	62.1	1.38	105.9	2.18	35.8	2.18	182.3	2.55	23.0	1.4	2,094.7	2.73	683.2	3.60
Estevan, CA	113.7	0.04	8.2	0.01	0.3	0.01	1.4	0.03	1.1	0.06	0.1	0.00	0.0	0.0	36.3	0.05	13.7	0.10
Moose Jaw, CA	313.3	0.11	100.8	0.18	3.4	0.07	1.8	0.04	0.9	0.06	14.8	0.21	0.3	0.0	53.5	0.07	20.9	0.10
North Battleford, CA	143.7	0.05	37.8	0.07	1.3	0.03	1.0	0.02	0.8	0.05	4.7	0.07	0.4	0.0	16.4	0.02	20.2	0.10
Prince Albert, CA	574.1	0.21	176.6	0.32	5.9	0.13	2.7	0.06	2.3	0.14	8.2	0.12	1.8	0.1	202.0	0.26	19.3	0.10
Regina, CMA	1,912.1	0.69	317.2	0.57	10.6	0.24	31.4	0.65	9.4	0.57	36.0	0.50	6.6	0.4	392.8	0.51	120.2	0.60
Saskatoon, CMA	1,905.3	0.68	338.3	0.60	11.3	0.25	36.9	0.76	10.4	0.64	60.8	0.85	9.0	0.5	479.1	0.62	134.6	0.70
Swift Current, CA	172.7	0.06	24.1	0.04	0.8	0.02	2.5	0.05	1.2	0.07	5.4	0.08	1.0	0.1	45.9	0.06	20.5	0.10
Yorkton, CA	188.7	0.07	31.3	0.06	1.0	0.02	3.5	0.07	1.5	0.09	3.8	0.05	0.8	0.1	54.7	0.07	4.8	0.00
ALBERTA	31,754.6	11.39	6,577.4	11.75	193.3	4.29	458.8	9.46	209.0	12.75	818.2	11.45	138.1	8.1	8,872.1	11.57	2,203.2	11.60
Calgary, CMA	10,340.7	3.71	2,024.5	3.62	59.5	1.32	198.1	4.09	89.0	5.43	255.5	3.57	52.4	3.1	2,532.8	3.30	668.0	3.50
Camrose, CA	253.0	0.09	68.9	0.12	2.0	0.04	4.3	0.09	1.5	0.09	6.2	0.09	0.3	0.0	47.1	0.06	12.3	0.10
Edmonton, CMA	8,837.3	3.17	1,887.2	3.37	55.5	1.23	121.6	2.51	39.6	2.42	269.5	3.77	47.3	2.8	2,536.5	3.31	424.5	2.20
Grand Centre, CA	395.8	0.14	96.0	0.17	2.8	0.06	0.9	0.02	1.5	0.09	9.1	0.13	1.8	0.1	98.5	0.13	41.9	0.20
Grande Prairie, CA	664.3	0.24	38.7	0.07	1.1	0.03	9.5	0.20	2.3	0.14	24.5	0.34	3.6	0.2	271.2	0.35	37.3	0.20
Lethbridge, CA	1,809.3	0.65	692.1	1.24	20.3	0.45	13.4	0.28	4.2	0.26	24.5	0.34	4.1	0.2	273.0	0.36	40.3	0.20
Lloydminster, CA	430.3	0.15	85.0	0.15	2.5	0.06	6.1	0.13	2.3	0.14	12.4	0.17	6.1	0.4	129.0	0.17	48.1	0.30
Medicine Hat, CA	843.8	0.30	154.8	0.28	4.6	0.10	25.0	0.51	26.3	1.60	15.5	0.22	2.4	0.1	253.4	0.33	37.7	0.20
Red Deer, CA	1,320.2	0.47	155.3	0.28	4.6	0.10	15.7	0.32	7.5	0.46	32.2	0.45	10.1	0.6	530.1	0.69	56.5	0.30
Wetaskiwin, CA	340.7	0.12	46.1	0.08	1.4	0.03	3.4	0.07	1.4	0.08	2.9	0.04	0.4	0.0	192.2	0.25	15.9	0.10
Wood Buffalo, CA	483.0	0.17	103.2	0.18	3.0	0.07	7.0	0.15	2.5	0.15	9.3	0.13	1.5	0.1	119.4	0.16	50.3	0.30
BRITISH COLUMBIA	36,141.4	12.97	7,967.6	14.23	592.4	13.15	579.9	11.96	194.5	11.87	904.9	12.66	201.6	11.8	8,720.0	11.37	2,556.4	13.50
Abbotsford, CA	1,263.0	0.45	370.6	0.66	27.6	0.61	15.1	0.31	3.6	0.22	20.2	0.28	3.6	0.2	348.1	0.45	63.1	0.30
Campbell River, CA	365.9	0.13	44.0	0.08	3.3	0.07	7.6	0.16	2.0	0.12	8.4	0.12	2.5	0.2	140.1	0.18	18.6	0.10
Chilliwack, CA	752.2	0.27	177.1	0.32	13.2	0.29	9.9	0.20	2.5	0.15	13.4	0.19	3.6	0.2	192.0	0.25	64.0	0.30
Courtenay, CA	525.1	0.19	162.0	0.29	12.0	0.27	7.0	0.14	2.6	0.16	6.6	0.09	1.1	0.1	149.1	0.19	29.3	0.20
Cranbrook, CA	414.2	0.15	153.1	0.27	11.4	0.25	6.9	0.14	1.4	0.08	9.5	0.13	0.8	0.1	103.7	0.14	24.4	0.10
Dawson Creek, CA	162.7	0.06	18.9	0.03	1.4	0.03	0.0	0.00	0.1	0.01	0.6	0.01	0.0	0.0	98.2	0.13	10.4	0.10
Duncan, CA	370.8	0.13	95.7	0.17	7.1	0.16	5.7	0.12	1.9	0.11	7.2	0.10	1.0	0.1	112.7	0.15	32.9	0.20
Fort St. John, CA	299.2	0.11	50.2	0.09	3.7	0.08	2.0	0.04	1.5	0.09	8.0	0.11	3.1	0.2	96.7	0.13	18.3	0.10
Kamloops, CA	1,013.6	0.36	238.4	0.43	17.7	0.39	17.1	0.35	4.3	0.26	25.6	0.36	5.5	0.3	297.2	0.39	81.4	0.40
Kelowna, CA	1,845.9	0.66	343.4	0.61	25.5	0.57	27.2	0.56	6.1	0.37	44.8	0.63	9.3	0.5	516.1	0.67	118.0	0.60
Kitimat, CA	77.7	0.03	20.8	0.04	1.5	0.03	1.1	0.02	0.0	0.00	2.6	0.04	0.0	0.0	10.5	0.01	13.4	0.10
Nanaimo, CA	788.9	0.28	113.3	0.20	8.4	0.19	6.0	0.12	3.0	0.18	16.8	0.23	6.5	0.4	302.2	0.39	44.2	0.20
Penticton, CA	481.1	0.17	84.2	0.15	6.3	0.14	5.5	0.11	3.3	0.20	8.4	0.12	3.6	0.2	108.2	0.14	25.3	0.10
Port Alberni, CA	198.2	0.07	41.0	0.07	3.0	0.07	2.2	0.04	2.8	0.17	2.2	0.03	0.3	0.0	66.8	0.09	17.4	0.10
Powell River, CA	189.9	0.07	39.6	0.07	2.9	0.07	3.6	0.07	1.3	0.08	5.9	0.08	1.0	0.1	34.9	0.05	13.1	0.10
Prince George, CA	907.8	0.33	165.6	0.30	12.3	0.27	15.1	0.31	4.4	0.27	37.4	0.52	4.2	0.2	210.9	0.28	65.6	0.30
Prince Rupert, CA	131.8	0.05	52.5	0.09	3.9	0.09	0.5	0.01	1.1	0.07	3.6	0.05	1.1	0.1	22.9	0.03	3.4	0.00
Quesnel, CA	163.4	0.06	19.1	0.03	1.4	0.03	0.8	0.02	0.3	0.02	4.1	0.06	0.3	0.0	52.9	0.07	8.8	0.00

	Auto Parts Accessories & Services		Household Furniture & Appliances		Household Furnishings		Other Durable Goods		Other Semi-Durable Goods		General Merchandise		Drugs and Patent Medicine		All Other Retail	
	$mill. Sales	% of Cdn Total	$mill. Sales	% of Cdn Total	$mill. Sales	% of Cdn Total	$mill. Sales	% of Cdn Total	$mill. Sales	% of Cdn Total	$mill. Sales	% of Cdn Total	$mill. Sales	% of Cdn Total	$mill. Sales	% of Cdn Total
Cornwall, CA	48.9	0.30	17.1	0.14	6.7	0.24	19.1	0.25	19.7	0.22	108.3	0.34	34.2	0.2	41.0	0.31
Elliot Lake, CA	4.5	0.03	4.5	0.04	2.9	0.11	2.6	0.03	1.4	0.01	6.2	0.02	6.3	0.0	2.9	0.02
Guelph, CA	72.0	0.44	51.0	0.42	15.8	0.57	42.1	0.54	81.0	0.89	129.1	0.40	43.5	0.3	54.1	0.41
Haileybury, CA	14.2	0.09	5.9	0.05	1.2	0.04	4.4	0.06	4.6	0.05	46.3	0.14	13.6	0.1	7.8	0.06
Hamilton, CMA	303.9	1.87	243.0	2.02	62.4	2.27	146.1	1.89	176.4	1.95	842.5	2.61	312.0	2.2	286.3	2.16
Hawkesbury, CA	12.3	0.08	6.9	0.06	0.9	0.03	10.8	0.14	4.5	0.05	11.3	0.03	10.7	0.1	6.6	0.05
Kenora, CA	10.0	0.06	12.6	0.11	1.6	0.06	4.4	0.06	10.8	0.12	52.9	0.16	4.3	0.0	5.9	0.04
Kingston, CA	95.1	0.59	73.1	0.61	15.8	0.57	55.8	0.72	70.0	0.77	64.9	0.20	64.1	0.5	80.4	0.61
Kitchener, CMA	255.2	1.57	215.7	1.80	48.2	1.75	140.4	1.82	177.6	1.96	548.9	1.70	159.8	1.1	259.2	1.96
Leamington, CA	21.0	0.13	25.9	0.22	9.9	0.36	9.6	0.12	15.3	0.17	51.6	0.16	32.3	0.2	19.8	0.15
Lindsay, CA	20.3	0.13	9.7	0.08	2.0	0.07	6.8	0.09	7.6	0.08	54.9	0.17	18.4	0.1	16.1	0.12
London, CMA	361.2	2.23	199.3	1.66	53.2	1.93	136.9	1.77	195.9	2.16	580.8	1.80	239.1	1.7	267.4	2.02
Midland, CA	8.4	0.05	9.3	0.08	2.6	0.10	9.1	0.12	9.7	0.11	5.5	0.02	18.2	0.1	10.6	0.08
North Bay, CA	38.7	0.24	29.6	0.25	10.1	0.37	29.2	0.38	24.2	0.27	119.1	0.37	42.3	0.3	32.7	0.25
Orillia, CA	27.8	0.17	16.2	0.14	5.8	0.21	13.5	0.17	15.9	0.18	82.8	0.26	27.4	0.2	27.9	0.21
Oshawa, CMA	131.5	0.81	71.2	0.59	33.8	1.23	86.4	1.12	64.5	0.71	279.0	0.87	151.9	1.1	108.6	0.82
Ottawa-Hull, CMA	504.4	3.11	419.3	3.49	97.6	3.55	306.2	3.96	338.3	3.73	993.6	3.08	341.2	2.4	592.4	4.48
Owen Sound, CA	24.8	0.15	19.7	0.16	5.3	0.19	14.5	0.19	16.1	0.18	75.7	0.23	19.4	0.1	22.1	0.17
Pembroke, CA	16.8	0.10	7.4	0.06	1.8	0.07	12.2	0.16	6.8	0.08	14.4	0.04	4.6	0.0	17.7	0.13
Peterborough, CA	90.4	0.56	47.5	0.40	8.0	0.29	30.4	0.39	36.1	0.40	157.9	0.49	56.5	0.4	51.2	0.39
Port Hope, CA	10.3	0.06	2.1	0.02	0.7	0.02	1.2	0.02	5.2	0.06	2.7	0.01	8.3	0.1	8.2	0.06
Sarnia, CA	72.1	0.44	41.7	0.35	11.7	0.43	28.7	0.37	32.6	0.36	125.8	0.39	49.7	0.4	48.0	0.36
Sault Ste. Marie, CA	62.0	0.38	34.7	0.29	9.9	0.36	22.4	0.29	32.2	0.36	130.6	0.41	39.1	0.3	34.8	0.26
Simcoe, CA	11.7	0.07	7.8	0.06	2.9	0.11	5.6	0.07	8.9	0.10	20.4	0.06	8.0	0.1	10.5	0.08
Smiths Falls, CA	12.6	0.08	4.5	0.04	1.2	0.04	3.3	0.04	3.5	0.04	34.5	0.11	8.3	0.1	11.0	0.08
St. Catharines-Niagara Falls, CMA	229.3	1.41	131.5	1.10	51.3	1.86	87.4	1.13	190.8	2.11	640.6	1.99	249.6	1.8	209.1	1.58
Stratford, CA	24.7	0.15	10.5	0.09	4.3	0.16	12.1	0.16	17.6	0.19	75.1	0.23	37.2	0.3	17.9	0.13
Strathroy, CA	16.7	0.10	16.2	0.14	2.0	0.07	3.7	0.05	4.7	0.05	12.6	0.04	9.5	0.1	5.5	0.04
Sudbury, CMA	114.5	0.71	71.9	0.60	18.0	0.65	41.8	0.54	43.6	0.48	248.9	0.77	91.0	0.7	72.0	0.54
Thunder Bay, CMA	81.1	0.50	62.2	0.52	18.5	0.67	43.4	0.56	41.1	0.45	151.0	0.47	43.4	0.3	55.9	0.42
Tillsonburg, CA	10.5	0.06	5.7	0.05	2.2	0.08	4.9	0.06	5.3	0.06	7.1	0.02	14.5	0.1	7.9	0.06
Timmins, CA	15.3	0.09	19.9	0.17	5.8	0.21	13.1	0.17	15.8	0.17	103.8	0.32	19.2	0.1	15.7	0.12
Toronto, CMA	2,385.7	14.72	1,765.0	14.70	476.3	17.31	1,286.3	16.63	1,638.1	18.09	4,930.1	15.30	2,666.0	19.0	2,611.8	19.73
Windsor, CMA	249.2	1.54	158.5	1.32	41.9	1.52	104.5	1.35	123.4	1.36	386.6	1.20	261.5	1.9	146.4	1.11
Woodstock, CA	24.9	0.15	10.9	0.09	5.8	0.21	7.0	0.09	11.4	0.13	73.7	0.23	27.7	0.2	15.1	0.11
MANITOBA	492.0	3.04	366.3	3.05	62.7	2.28	238.7	3.09	240.7	2.66	1,261.5	3.91	301.3	2.2	391.4	2.96
Brandon, CA	24.1	0.15	27.3	0.23	3.6	0.13	20.9	0.27	11.2	0.12	56.3	0.17	14.6	0.1	33.8	0.26
Portage la Prairie, CA	17.5	0.11	9.5	0.08	0.7	0.02	5.3	0.07	2.5	0.03	72.8	0.23	8.4	0.1	6.5	0.05
Thompson, CA	5.4	0.03	5.6	0.05	0.0	0.00	5.1	0.07	3.9	0.04	56.6	0.18	1.0	0.0	5.0	0.04
Winnipeg, CMA	288.0	1.78	220.2	1.83	47.4	1.72	160.9	2.08	139.9	1.54	818.5	2.54	184.0	1.3	272.1	2.06
SASKATCHEWAN	539.1	3.33	279.6	2.33	81.4	2.96	211.2	2.73	193.1	2.13	1,129.2	3.50	400.1	2.9	280.0	2.12
Estevan, CA	12.0	0.07	1.5	0.01	1.9	0.07	1.9	0.02	2.3	0.03	23.9	0.07	4.7	0.0	4.5	0.03
Moose Jaw, CA	12.3	0.08	12.7	0.11	3.8	0.14	15.5	0.20	4.3	0.05	37.8	0.12	16.2	0.1	14.3	0.11
North Battleford, CA	12.8	0.08	5.8	0.05	2.5	0.09	12.0	0.15	1.2	0.01	13.9	0.04	4.0	0.0	8.8	0.07
Prince Albert, CA	22.0	0.14	17.5	0.15	1.3	0.05	16.1	0.21	3.6	0.04	69.5	0.22	14.7	0.1	10.5	0.08
Regina, CMA	126.0	0.78	73.5	0.61	18.5	0.67	39.9	0.52	43.7	0.48	517.4	1.61	75.0	0.5	93.9	0.71
Saskatoon, CMA	151.6	0.94	78.2	0.65	29.5	1.07	78.9	1.02	67.2	0.74	192.1	0.60	144.3	1.0	83.0	0.63
Swift Current, CA	11.4	0.07	9.3	0.08	2.7	0.10	2.7	0.04	6.8	0.07	31.3	0.10	5.5	0.0	1.6	0.01
Yorkton, CA	16.0	0.10	8.6	0.07	2.1	0.08	6.7	0.09	3.8	0.04	35.6	0.11	8.5	0.1	6.0	0.05
ALBERTA	1,777.0	10.96	1,536.8	12.80	321.1	11.67	924.6	11.96	914.0	10.09	3,722.5	11.55	1,362.5	9.7	1,726.3	13.04
Calgary, CMA	581.0	3.58	612.9	5.10	108.5	3.94	324.9	4.20	304.1	3.36	1,507.7	4.68	414.0	3.0	607.8	4.59
Camrose, CA	15.8	0.10	11.8	0.10	3.7	0.13	7.8	0.10	12.2	0.13	35.3	0.11	5.0	0.0	18.6	0.14
Edmonton, CMA	582.6	3.59	462.5	3.85	95.3	3.46	298.9	3.87	263.2	2.91	1,026.4	3.18	387.8	2.8	339.0	2.56
Grand Centre, CA	20.4	0.13	17.8	0.15	3.8	0.14	10.2	0.13	8.7	0.10	50.9	0.16	22.9	0.2	8.6	0.06
Grande Prairie, CA	39.8	0.25	33.8	0.28	11.3	0.41	9.1	0.12	13.9	0.15	100.6	0.31	20.8	0.2	46.8	0.35
Lethbridge, CA	32.6	0.20	63.8	0.53	12.8	0.47	34.9	0.45	22.2	0.25	173.5	0.54	70.1	0.5	327.4	2.47
Lloydminster, CA	32.0	0.20	15.4	0.13	5.5	0.20	10.1	0.13	11.6	0.13	39.6	0.12	12.8	0.1	11.8	0.09
Medicine Hat, CA	30.8	0.19	44.7	0.37	11.6	0.42	24.9	0.32	25.3	0.28	103.4	0.32	22.4	0.2	61.1	0.46
Red Deer, CA	82.8	0.51	69.7	0.58	12.8	0.47	41.2	0.53	23.4	0.26	179.3	0.56	39.0	0.3	60.0	0.45
Wetaskiwin, CA	10.6	0.07	6.4	0.05	0.7	0.02	4.5	0.06	7.6	0.08	27.1	0.08	10.2	0.1	8.2	0.06
Wood Buffalo, CA	18.4	0.11	19.1	0.16	5.2	0.19	14.3	0.18	10.9	0.12	80.6	0.25	18.6	0.1	19.6	0.15
BRITISH COLUMBIA	1,863.8	11.50	1,624.6	13.53	440.7	16.02	1,260.3	16.30	1,217.6	13.44	4,312.5	13.38	1,881.7	13.4	1,822.7	13.77
Abbotsford, CA	70.5	0.43	44.6	0.37	8.5	0.31	26.8	0.35	30.0	0.33	117.4	0.36	74.7	0.5	38.8	0.29
Campbell River, CA	16.4	0.10	14.1	0.12	5.7	0.21	14.9	0.19	17.0	0.19	46.1	0.14	15.9	0.1	9.3	0.07
Chilliwack, CA	35.6	0.22	27.1	0.23	7.9	0.29	21.6	0.28	15.9	0.18	103.8	0.32	26.3	0.2	38.6	0.29
Courtenay, CA	15.6	0.10	17.7	0.15	8.3	0.30	21.6	0.28	15.6	0.17	43.2	0.13	15.1	0.1	18.2	0.14
Cranbrook, CA	22.9	0.14	15.3	0.13	3.7	0.13	10.8	0.14	9.2	0.10	10.1	0.03	10.7	0.1	20.3	0.15
Dawson Creek, CA	9.7	0.06	4.4	0.04	2.2	0.08	5.2	0.07	4.1	0.04	1.3	0.00	1.7	0.0	4.4	0.03
Duncan, CA	27.7	0.17	11.4	0.10	7.3	0.27	8.3	0.11	14.1	0.16	4.2	0.01	18.6	0.1	14.9	0.11
Fort St. John, CA	21.7	0.13	14.1	0.12	3.1	0.11	8.0	0.10	9.3	0.10	29.8	0.09	22.3	0.2	7.2	0.05
Kamloops, CA	44.7	0.28	50.1	0.42	11.6	0.42	34.9	0.45	24.6	0.27	84.7	0.26	35.2	0.3	40.4	0.31
Kelowna, CA	91.0	0.56	84.9	0.71	26.3	0.96	72.5	0.94	66.2	0.73	258.7	0.80	74.9	0.5	80.8	0.61
Kitimat, CA	3.1	0.02	3.2	0.03	0.6	0.02	3.9	0.05	1.5	0.02	2.9	0.01	11.2	0.1	1.5	0.01
Nanaimo, CA	30.3	0.19	49.1	0.41	9.1	0.33	28.4	0.37	30.6	0.34	85.3	0.26	21.8	0.2	33.8	0.26
Penticton, CA	15.8	0.10	22.7	0.19	3.9	0.14	14.2	0.18	15.5	0.17	130.8	0.41	17.9	0.1	15.6	0.12
Port Alberni, CA	14.4	0.09	9.6	0.08	2.6	0.09	7.7	0.10	7.7	0.08	2.4	0.01	11.9	0.1	6.3	0.05
Powell River, CA	10.6	0.07	3.5	0.03	3.5	0.13	3.8	0.05	6.0	0.07	52.7	0.16	1.5	0.0	6.0	0.05
Prince George, CA	65.0	0.40	41.7	0.35	11.0	0.40	30.1	0.39	33.2	0.37	130.5	0.40	43.9	0.3	37.0	0.28
Prince Rupert, CA	2.5	0.02	3.4	0.03	2.6	0.09	8.8	0.11	3.8	0.04	12.7	0.04	5.0	0.0	4.0	0.03
Quesnel, CA	12.9	0.08	8.2	0.07	3.4	0.12	10.0	0.13	4.4	0.05	21.7	0.07	8.2	0.1	7.0	0.05

	Total Sales		Supermarkets & Groceries		All Other Food		Women's Clothing		Men's Clothing		Other Clothing		Shoes		Motor Vehicles & Recreation Vehicles		Gas Service Stations	
	$mill. Sales	% of Cdn Total	$mill. Sales	% of Cdn Total	$mill. Sales	% of Cdn Total	$mill. Sales	% of Cdn Total	$mill. Sales	% of Cdn Total	$mill. Sales	% of Cdn Total	$mill. Sales	% of Cdn Total	$mill. Sales	% of Cdn Total	$mill. Sales	% of Cdn Total
Terrace, CA	216.8	0.08	29.3	0.05	2.2	0.05	4.1	0.08	1.4	0.08	5.7	0.08	2.5	0.2	79.3	0.10	14.6	0.10
Vancouver, CMA	17,323.8	6.22	3,550.1	6.34	264.0	5.86	351.0	7.24	116.7	7.12	453.5	6.34	118.7	7.0	4,081.0	5.32	977.4	5.20
Vernon, CA	622.0	0.22	92.3	0.16	6.9	0.15	8.0	0.17	1.3	0.08	13.9	0.19	1.9	0.1	209.4	0.27	37.8	0.20
Victoria, CMA	2,722.3	0.98	722.4	1.29	53.7	1.19	43.7	0.90	15.9	0.97	71.5	1.00	15.8	0.9	504.6	0.66	157.4	0.80
Williams Lake, CA	432.2	0.16	100.8	0.18	7.5	0.17	3.6	0.07	0.6	0.04	10.6	0.15	2.5	0.2	126.2	0.16	16.8	0.10
NORTHWEST TERRITORIES	128.7	0.05	25.8	0.05	0.7	0.02	1.5	0.03	0.5	0.03	2.7	0.04	0.3	0.0	31.7	0.04	6.9	0.00
Yellowknife, CA	69.8	0.03	10.7	0.02	0.3	0.01	1.2	0.02	0.5	0.03	1.9	0.03	0.3	0.0	20.5	0.03	2.5	0.00
NUNAVUT	42.3	0.02	14.4	0.03	0.4	0.01	0.0	0.00	0.0	0.00	1.5	0.02	0.0	0.0	3.1	0.00	0.4	0.00
YUKON TERRITORY	166.9	0.06	30.0	0.05	0.8	0.02	3.3	0.07	1.7	0.11	4.5	0.06	1.2	0.1	59.5	0.08	16.2	0.10
Whitehorse, CA	150.6	0.05	27.2	0.05	0.7	0.02	3.0	0.06	1.7	0.11	3.9	0.05	1.2	0.1	59.3	0.08	10.7	0.10

	Auto Parts Accessories & Services		Household Furniture & Appliances		Household Furnishings		Other Durable Goods		Other Semi-Durable Goods		General Merchandise		Drugs and Patent Medicine		All Other Retail	
	$mill. Sales	% of Cdn Total	$mill. Sales	% of Cdn Total	$mill. Sales	% of Cdn Total	$mill. Sales	% of Cdn Total	$mill. Sales	% of Cdn Total	$mill. Sales	% of Cdn Total	$mill. Sales	% of Cdn Total	$mill. Sales	% of Cdn Total
Terrace, CA	12.5	0.08	9.1	0.08	1.3	0.05	6.5	0.08	4.1	0.05	20.4	0.06	12.4	0.1	11.4	0.09
Vancouver, CMA	902.7	5.57	852.3	7.10	226.0	8.22	629.1	8.14	592.4	6.54	2,247.2	6.97	867.6	6.2	1,094.4	8.27
Vernon, CA	36.8	0.23	31.5	0.26	5.7	0.21	19.6	0.25	17.6	0.19	63.4	0.20	45.4	0.3	30.5	0.23
Victoria, CMA	139.7	0.86	152.9	1.27	29.7	1.08	106.0	1.37	116.8	1.29	320.3	0.99	159.0	1.1	112.8	0.85
Williams Lake, CA	24.4	0.15	17.3	0.14	5.1	0.18	13.7	0.18	8.8	0.10	70.2	0.22	6.4	0.1	17.7	0.13
NORTHWEST TERRITORIES	4.4	0.03	7.6	0.06	2.1	0.07	4.5	0.06	3.6	0.04	20.5	0.06	8.9	0.1	6.9	0.05
Yellowknife, CA	2.4	0.01	5.5	0.05	1.9	0.07	2.8	0.04	2.0	0.02	6.5	0.02	4.6	0.0	6.2	0.05
NUNAVUT	0.5	0.00	0.5	0.00	0.0	0.00	0.8	0.01	0.9	0.01	16.2	0.05	0.8	0.0	2.9	0.02
YUKON TERRITORY	14.1	0.09	8.3	0.07	1.3	0.05	4.6	0.06	5.2	0.06	2.8	0.01	4.8	0.0	8.7	0.07
Whitehorse, CA	12.1	0.07	8.3	0.07	1.3	0.05	4.3	0.06	4.1	0.05	0.8	0.00	3.5	0.0	8.3	0.06

Ranking of Income 2001

Estimates by Metropolitan Areas, Cities and Towns

Expressed as Per Capita Income Dollars.

POPULATION 100,000+

Calgary, CMA	25,700
Ottawa-Hull, CMA	25,000
Toronto, CMA	24,400
Windsor, CMA	23,900
Oshawa, CMA	23,500
Guelph, CA	23,100
Hamilton, CMA	23,000
Vancouver, CMA	22,800
Kitchener, CMA	22,700
Thunder Bay, CMA	22,600
Kingston, CA	22,500
Victoria, CMA	22,500
London, CMA	22,400
Regina, CMA	22,400
Edmonton, CMA	22,000
Sudbury, CMA	21,900
Winnipeg, CMA	21,700
Halifax, CMA	21,300
Québec, CMA	21,300
Montréal, CMA	20,600
Saskatoon, CMA	20,500
St. Catharines-Niagara Falls, CMA	20,400
Barrie, CA	20,300
Moncton, CA	20,300
St. John's, CMA	20,300
Peterborough, CA	20,200
Brantford, CA	19,400
Kelowna, CA	19,300
Saint John, CMA	19,200
Trois-Rivières, CMA	19,100
Sherbrooke, CMA	18,600
Abbotsford, CA	18,200
Chicoutimi-Jonquière, CMA	17,400
Cape Breton, CA	14,900

POPULATION 30,000 TO 100,000

Wood Buffalo, CA	29,600
Sarnia, CA	22,700
Grande Prairie, CA	22,600
Prince George, CA	21,900
Baie-Comeau, CA	21,700
Fredericton, CA	21,600
Stratford, CA	21,400
Leamington, CA	21,100
Timmins, CA	20,900
Campbell River, CA	20,700
Rimouski, CA	20,600
Kamloops, CA	20,500
Red Deer, CA	20,500
Chatham, CA	20,300
Moose Jaw, CA	20,300
Sault Ste. Marie, CA	20,300
Rouyn-Noranda, CA	20,200
Val-d'Or, CA	20,200
Belleville, CA	20,100
Woodstock, CA	20,100
Medicine Hat, CA	20,000
North Bay, CA	19,900
Brockville, CA	19,600
Lethbridge, CA	19,600
Brandon, CA	19,500
Nanaimo, CA	19,200
Courtenay, CA	19,100
Granby, CA	19,000
Prince Albert, CA	19,000
Owen Sound, CA	18,900
Williams Lake, CA	18,700
Orillia, CA	18,600
Sorel, CA	18,600
Midland, CA	18,500
Saint-Jean-sur-Richelieu, CA	18,500
Grand Centre, CA	18,200
Saint-Hyacinthe, CA	18,200
Cornwall, CA	18,100
Charlottetown, CA	17,900
Joliette, CA	17,900
Penticton, CA	17,800
Drummondville, CA	17,700
Alma, CA	17,600
Vernon, CA	17,600
Chilliwack, CA	17,500
Duncan, CA	17,500

Salaberry-de-Valleyfield, CA	17,200
Victoriaville, CA	17,100
Truro, CA	17,000
Shawinigan, CA	16,600
New Glasgow, CA	16,500

POPULATION 10,000 TO 30,000

Foothills No. 31, MD	35,200
Yellowknife, CA	31,600
Whistler, DM	28,900
Thompson, CA	26,100
Whitehorse, CA	25,400
Canmore, T	25,300
Okotoks, T	25,100
Kitimat, CA	24,900
Scugog, TP	24,700
Wilmot, TP	24,100
Adjala-Tosorontio, TP	24,000
Hinton, T	24,000
Estevan, CA	23,900
St. Andrews, RM	23,700
Hamilton, TP	23,600
Kenora, CA	22,900
Fraser-Fort George, Subd. A, SRD	22,700
Red Deer County No. 23, CM	22,700
Squamish, DM	22,500
Amherstburg, T	22,300
Fort St. John, CA	22,200
Fergus, T	22,000
Brooks, T	21,900
Grande Prairie County No. 1, CM	21,800
Kenora, Unorganized, UNO	21,800
Oro-Medonte, TP	21,700
Terrace, CA	21,600
Cobourg, CA	21,300
Capital, Subd. A, SRD	21,100
Simcoe, CA	21,100
Haldimand, T	21,000
Sept-Îles, CA	21,000
Swift Current, CA	21,000
Tillsonburg, CA	20,900
Lacombe, T	20,800
Mountain View County No. 17, CM	20,800
Ingersoll, T	20,700
Port Hope, CA	20,700
Cowichan Valley, Subd. C, SRD	20,600
Sunshine Coast, Subd. A, SRD	20,500
Gander, CA	20,400
Prince Rupert, CA	20,400
Lloydminster, CA	20,300
Weyburn, C	20,200
Bracebridge, T	20,100
Nanaimo, Subd. B, SRD	20,100
West Lincoln, TP	19,800
Wetaskiwin County No. 10, CM	19,800
Nanticoke, C	19,700
Peace River, Subd. B, SRD	19,700
Yellowhead No. 94, MD	19,700
Strathroy, CA	19,600
Delhi, TP	19,400
Brock, TP	19,300
Haileybury, CA	19,300
La Tuque, CA	19,300
Powell River, CA	19,300
Camrose, CA	19,200
Dunnville, T	19,100
Selkirk, T	19,100
Wasaga Beach, T	19,100
Huntsville, T	19,000
Lindsay, CA	19,000
Smiths Falls, CA	19,000
Wetaskiwin, CA	18,900
Lacombe County, CM	18,800
Miramichi, C	18,800
Norwich, TP	18,800
Collingwood, CA	18,700
Port Alberni, CA	18,700
Quesnel, CA	18,700
Cranbrook, CA	18,600
Essa, TP	18,600
Parksville, C	18,500
Roberval, V	18,500
Summerland, DM	18,500
Elliot Lake, CA	18,400
Salmon Arm, DM	18,400
Pembroke, CA	18,300

Amos, V	18,100
Clearwater No. 99, MD	18,100
Corner Brook, CA	18,100
Gravenhurst, T	18,100
Norfolk, TP	18,100
North Battleford, CA	18,100
Dawson Creek, CA	18,000
Bathurst, CA	17,900
Magog, CA	17,800
Clearview, TP	17,700
Grand Falls-Windsor, CA	17,700
Edmundston, CA	17,600
Kentville, CA	17,600
Saint-Georges, CA	17,600
Sainte-Marie, V	17,600
East Hants, MD	17,500
Matane, CA	17,500
Summerside, CA	17,500
Yorkton, CA	17,500
Rivière-du-Loup, CA	17,300
Chester, MD	17,100
Gaspé, V	17,100
Thetford Mines, CA	17,100
Cowansville, CA	17,000
Montmagny, V	16,900
Central Kootenay, Subd. B, SRD	16,800
Lethbridge County No. 26, CM	16,700
Kings, Subd. A, SCM	16,400
Lunenburg, MD	16,200
West Hants, MD	16,200
Yarmouth, MD	16,200
Dolbeau, CA	16,100
Portage la Prairie, CA	16,100
Columbia-Shuswap, Subd. C, SRD	16,000
Hawkesbury, CA	16,000
Campbellton, CA	15,700
Lachute, CA	15,000
Hanover, RM	14,900
Saint-Lin, M	14,400

Ranking of Retail Sales, 2001

Estimates by Metropolitan Areas, Cities and Towns

Expressed as Per Capita Retail Sales Dollars.

POPULATION 100,000+

Kelowna, CA	11,800
Guelph, CA	11,400
Sudbury, CMA	11,100
Québec, CMA	11,000
St. John's, CMA	11,000
Barrie, CA	10,800
Calgary, CMA	10,600
Kitchener, CMA	10,600
Moncton, CA	10,500
Windsor, CMA	10,500
London, CMA	10,200
Peterborough, CA	10,200
St. Catharines-Niagara Falls, CMA	10,100
Thunder Bay, CMA	9,900
Halifax, CMA	9,800
Regina, CMA	9,500
Kingston, CMA	9,300
Edmonton, CMA	9,200
Ottawa-Hull, CMA	9,200
Chicoutimi-Jonquière, CMA	9,100
Cape Breton, CA	8,600
Victoria, CMA	8,500
Sherbrooke, CMA	8,400
Toronto, CMA	8,400
Brantford, CA	8,300
Saint John, CMA	8,300
Vancouver, CMA	8,300
Montréal, CMA	8,200
Winnipeg, CMA	8,200
Abbotsford, CA	8,100
Hamilton, CMA	8,100
Saskatoon, CMA	8,100
Oshawa, CMA	8,000
Trois-Rivières, CMA	8,000

POPULATION 30,000 TO 100,000

Lethbridge, CA	26,500
Joliette, CA	19,300
Red Deer, CA	19,300
Grande Prairie, CA	18,600
Stratford, CA	16,900
Brandon, CA	16,000
Owen Sound, CA	14,400
Saint-Hyacinthe, CA	13,700
Medicine Hat, CA	13,500
Prince Albert, CA	13,100
Victoriaville, CA	13,100
Chatham, CA	13,000
Salaberry-de-Valleyfield, CA	13,000
Drummondville, CA	12,900
Val-d'Or, CA	12,900
Granby, CA	12,800
Fredericton, CA	12,600
North Bay, CA	12,600
Belleville, CA	12,200
Wood Buffalo, CA	12,100
Truro, CA	12,000
Sault Ste. Marie, CA	11,900
Cornwall, CA	11,800
Prince George, CA	11,700
Saint-Jean-sur-Richelieu, CA	11,700
Alma, CA	11,600
Charlottetown, CA	11,200
Kamloops, CA	11,000
Penticton, CA	10,800
Rouyn-Noranda, CA	10,500
Sorel, CA	10,500
New Glasgow, CA	10,400
Vernon, CA	10,400
Williams Lake, CA	10,400
Woodstock, CA	10,300
Rimouski, CA	10,200
Campbell River, CA	10,000
Chilliwack, CA	10,000
Brockville, CA	9,800
Orillia, CA	9,800
Grand Centre, CA	9,700
Duncan, CA	9,600
Timmins, CA	9,600
Sarnia, CA	9,500
Midland, CA	9,300
Leamington, CA	9,200
Moose Jaw, CA	8,900
Nanaimo, CA	8,500

Courtenay, CA	8,300
Shawinigan, CA	8,300
Baie-Comeau, CA	7,400

POPULATION 10,000 TO 30,000

Wetaskiwin, CA	28,900
Miramichi, C	21,800
Cranbrook, CA	21,300
Lloydminster, CA	20,100
Simcoe, CA	20,000
Haileybury, CA	19,800
Hawkesbury, CA	19,400
Fort St. John, CA	19,300
Montmagny, V	19,300
Bathurst, CA	19,200
Camrose, CA	17,600
Gander, CA	16,800
Amos, V	16,700
Clearwater No. 99, MD	16,700
Lindsay, CA	16,700
Strathroy, CA	16,500
Rivière-du-Loup, CA	16,200
Selkirk, T	16,200
Summerside, CA	16,000
Bracebridge, T	15,900
Grand Falls-Windsor, CA	15,500
Saint-Georges, CA	15,300
Sainte-Marie, V	15,200
Whistler, DM	15,200
Cowansville, CA	15,000
Portage la Prairie, CA	15,000
Dawson Creek, CA	14,700
Kenora, CA	14,600
Huntsville, T	13,800
Lacombe, T	13,600
Salmon Arm, DM	13,300
Fergus, T	13,200
Canmore, T	13,100
Lethbridge County No. 26, CM	13,100
Matane, CA	13,100
Parksville, C	13,000
Thetford Mines, CA	13,000
Campbellton, CA	12,800
Collingwood, CA	12,800
Pembroke, CA	12,800
Corner Brook, CA	12,500
Gravenhurst, T	11,700
Kentville, CA	11,700
Cobourg, CA	11,600
Wilmot, TP	11,500
Hinton, T	11,400
Smiths Falls, CA	11,300
Thompson, CA	11,200
Dolbeau, CA	10,800
Magog, CA	10,600
Scugog, TP	10,600
West Lincoln, TP	10,600
Yorkton, CA	10,600
Foothills No. 31, MD	10,500
Edmundston, CA	10,400
Kings, Subd. A, SCM	10,200
Swift Current, CA	10,100
La Tuque, CA	9,900
Terrace, CA	9,900
Amherstburg, T	9,600
Sept-Îles, CA	9,600
Gaspé, V	9,500
Lachute, CA	9,300
Powell River, CA	9,300
Weyburn, C	9,000
Port Hope, CA	8,600
Estevan, CA	8,400
West Hants, MD	8,400
Haldimand, T	8,300
Tillsonburg, CA	8,200
Prince Rupert, CA	8,000
Elliot Lake, CA	7,800
North Battleford, CA	7,800
Oro-Medonte, TP	7,700
Port Alberni, CA	7,500
Kitimat, CA	7,300
East Hants, MD	7,200
Roberval, V	7,200
Yellowhead No. 94, MD	7,000
Whitehorse, CA	6,900

Squamish, DM	6,600
Chester, MD	6,500
Ingersoll, T	6,500
Capital, Subd. A, SRD	6,400
Quesnel, CA	6,100
Clearview, TP	5,700
Norwich, TP	5,700
Dunnville, T	5,600
Brock, TP	5,100
Delhi, TP	5,000
Lunenburg, MD	5,000
Norfolk, TP	4,700
Peace River, Subd. B, SRD	4,700
Wetaskiwin County No. 10, CM	4,700
Yarmouth, MD	4,700
Hamilton, TP	4,600
Essa, TP	4,400
Summerland, DM	4,300
Columbia-Shuswap, Subd. C, SRD	4,000
Nanaimo, Subd. B, SRD	3,900
Okotoks, T	3,900
Nanticoke, C	3,800
Wasaga Beach, T	3,700
Yellowknife, CA	3,700
Central Kootenay, Subd. B, SRD	3,600
Red Deer County No. 23, CM	3,500
Kenora, Unorganized, UNO	3,300
Brooks, T	3,100
Grande Prairie County No. 1, CM	3,100
Cowichan Valley, Subd. C, SRD	2,500
Hanover, RM	2,300
St. Andrews, RM	2,000
Lacombe County, CM	1,800
Sunshine Coast, Subd. A, SRD	1,800
Adjala-Tosorontio, TP	1,700
Fraser-Fort George, Subd. A, SRD	1,100
Mountain View County, CM	300

Population and Household Projections

	Population in 000's			Households in 000's		
	Estimated	Projections		Estimated	Projections	
	2001	2003	2006	2001	2003	2006
Canada	31,135	31,892	33,046	12,085	12,466	13,069
Newfoundland	533	536	541	195	200	207
Prince Edward Island	138	138	138	52	53	54
Nova Scotia	948	962	987	372	381	396
New Brunswick	759	769	783	293	300	311
Québec	7,445	7,605	7,871	3,064	3,154	3,298
Ontario	11,817	12,118	12,556	4,436	4,576	4,794
Manitoba	1,155	1,182	1,230	446	458	481
Saskatchewan	1,034	1,045	1,056	403	410	421
Alberta	3,066	3,164	3,281	1,153	1,201	1,268
British Columbia	4,137	4,267	4,490	1,637	1,698	1,803
Northwest Territories	42	44	46	14	15	16
Nunavut	28	30	32	7	8	9
Yukon Territory	31	32	34	12	13	14

Census Metropolitan Areas

	Population in 000's			Households in 000's		
	Estimated	Projections		Estimated	Projections	
	2001	2003	2006	2001	2003	2006
St. John's	174	174	175	65	67	69
Halifax	361	372	391	144	149	159
Saint John	128	131	136	50	51	53
Chicoutimi-Jonquière	163	164	166	65	67	69
Québec	693	702	722	300	307	320
Sherbrooke	156	159	164	68	70	72
Trois-Rivières	143	144	145	63	64	65
Montréal	3,501	3,608	3,796	1,451	1,501	1,584
Ottawa-Hull	1,086	1,113	1,159	432	446	471
Oshawa	305	314	327	109	114	120
Toronto	4,868	5,064	5,364	1,738	1,815	1,937
Hamilton	674	678	682	260	263	269
St. Catharines-Niagara Falls	396	402	411	158	162	167
Kitchener	429	442	459	163	170	179
London	426	433	445	173	177	184
Windsor	309	317	326	121	125	130
Sudbury	159	160	160	65	66	68
Thunder Bay	128	130	133	52	53	56
Winnipeg	685	702	738	276	284	300
Regina	201	203	207	81	83	86
Saskatoon	235	238	241	95	97	100
Calgary	978	1,019	1,079	375	394	423
Edmonton	957	979	1,006	369	382	400
Vancouver	2,093	2,182	2,349	817	856	925
Victoria	320	331	352	140	144	153

Income Projections

	Estimated 2001		Projections 2003		2006	
	Millions $	Per Capita $	Millions $	Per Capita $	Millions $	Per Capita $
Canada	656,440	21,100	712,779	22,400	808,883	24,500
Newfoundland	9,074	17,000	9,633	18,000	10,630	19,600
Prince Edward Island	2,332	16,900	2,478	17,900	2,712	19,700
Nova Scotia	17,181	18,100	18,503	19,200	20,821	21,100
New Brunswick	13,511	17,800	14,495	18,900	16,180	20,700
Québec	143,774	19,300	155,618	20,500	176,229	22,400
Ontario	269,997	22,800	293,569	24,200	333,278	26,500
Manitoba	22,747	19,700	24,611	20,800	27,922	22,700
Saskatchewan	19,436	18,800	20,757	19,900	22,989	21,800
Alberta	68,437	22,300	74,663	23,600	84,556	25,800
British Columbia	87,783	21,200	96,061	22,500	110,768	24,700
Northwest Territories	1,029	24,400	1,132	26,000	1,320	29,000
Nunavut	409	14,500	464	15,600	563	17,500
Yukon Territory	731	23,300	794	24,600	915	27,200

Census Metropolitan Areas

	Estimated 2001		Projections 2003		2006	
	Millions $	Per Capita $	Millions $	Per Capita $	Millions $	Per Capita $
St. John's	3,521	20,300	3,717	21,300	4,058	23,200
Halifax	7,708	21,300	8,397	22,600	9,645	24,700
Saint John	2,461	19,200	2,663	20,300	3,028	22,300
Chicoutimi-Jonquière	2,829	17,400	3,007	18,300	3,277	19,700
Québec	14,767	21,300	15,947	22,700	18,035	25,000
Sherbrooke	2,899	18,600	3,113	19,600	3,443	21,000
Trois-Rivières	2,720	19,100	2,906	20,200	3,201	22,100
Montréal	72,023	20,600	78,488	21,800	90,122	23,700
Ottawa-Hull	27,102	25,000	29,295	26,300	33,077	28,500
Oshawa	7,151	23,500	7,838	25,000	8,989	27,500
Toronto	118,825	24,400	131,348	25,900	152,984	28,500
Hamilton	15,500	23,000	16,493	24,300	18,111	26,600
St. Catharines-Niagara Falls	8,083	20,400	8,567	21,300	9,349	22,800
Kitchener	9,742	22,700	10,653	24,100	12,059	26,300
London	9,556	22,400	10,291	23,700	11,536	25,900
Windsor	7,368	23,900	8,047	25,400	9,126	28,000
Sudbury	3,493	21,900	3,730	23,300	4,104	25,600
Thunder Bay	2,887	22,600	3,118	24,100	3,512	26,500
Winnipeg	14,885	21,700	16,149	23,000	18,471	25,000
Regina	4,486	22,400	4,831	23,800	5,431	26,300
Saskatoon	4,824	20,500	5,174	21,700	5,713	23,700
Calgary	25,120	25,700	27,682	27,200	32,021	29,700
Edmonton	21,040	22,000	22,778	23,300	25,527	25,400
Vancouver	47,738	22,800	53,039	24,300	62,744	26,700
Victoria	7,207	22,500	7,787	23,500	8,882	25,200

Total Retail Sales Projections

	Estimated 2001		Projections 2003		2006	
	Millions $	Per Capita $	Millions $	Per Capita $	Millions $	Per Capita $
Canada	278,706	9,000	306,192	9,600	347,863	10,500
Newfoundland	4,628	8,700	4,978	9,300	5,500	10,200
Prince Edward Island	1,206	8,700	1,291	9,300	1,409	10,200
Nova Scotia	8,694	9,200	9,464	9,800	10,655	10,800
New Brunswick	7,096	9,300	7,685	10,000	8,571	11,000
Québec	64,689	8,700	70,840	9,300	80,354	10,200
Ontario	106,349	9,000	117,224	9,700	133,486	10,600
Manitoba	9,653	8,400	10,593	9,000	12,066	9,800
Saskatchewan	8,157	7,900	8,814	8,400	9,733	9,200
Alberta	31,755	10,400	34,969	11,100	39,584	12,100
British Columbia	36,141	8,700	39,980	9,400	46,125	10,300
Northwest Territories	129	3,000	136	3,100	147	3,200
Nunavut	42	1,500	45	1,500	49	1,500
Yukon Territory	167	5,300	174	5,400	184	5,500

Census Metropolitan Areas

	Estimated 2001		Projections 2003		2006	
	Millions $	Per Capita $	Millions $	Per Capita $	Millions $	Per Capita $
St. John's	1,905	11,000	2,015	11,600	2,169	12,400
Halifax	3,530	9,800	3,861	10,400	4,395	11,200
Saint John	1,058	8,300	1,148	8,800	1,291	9,500
Chicoutimi-Jonquière	1,475	9,100	1,606	9,800	1,800	10,800
Québec	7,600	11,000	8,221	11,700	9,219	12,800
Sherbrooke	1,311	8,400	1,446	9,100	1,647	10,100
Trois-Rivières	1,147	8,000	1,244	8,700	1,384	9,600
Montréal	28,737	8,200	31,840	8,800	36,850	9,700
Ottawa-Hull	10,000	9,200	10,926	9,800	12,363	10,700
Oshawa	2,433	8,000	2,689	8,600	3,067	9,400
Toronto	40,759	8,400	45,724	9,000	53,423	10,000
Hamilton	5,466	8,100	5,894	8,700	6,506	9,500
St. Catharines-Niagara Falls	4,004	10,100	4,374	10,900	4,916	12,000
Kitchener	4,550	10,600	5,053	11,400	5,773	12,600
London	4,355	10,200	4,789	11,000	5,438	12,200
Windsor	3,246	10,500	3,563	11,300	4,009	12,300
Sudbury	1,763	11,100	1,894	11,800	2,081	13,000
Thunder Bay	1,265	9,900	1,386	10,700	1,566	11,800
Winnipeg	5,625	8,200	6,198	8,800	7,147	9,700
Regina	1,912	9,500	2,067	10,200	2,293	11,100
Saskatoon	1,905	8,100	2,071	8,700	2,301	9,500
Calgary	10,341	10,600	11,508	11,300	13,301	12,300
Edmonton	8,837	9,200	9,660	9,900	10,845	10,800
Vancouver	17,324	8,300	19,450	8,900	23,039	9,800
Victoria	2,722	8,500	3,003	9,100	3,484	9,900

By Province and City

	Total		Lease Area (000's Sq. Ft.)								Store Distribution					
	Centres	Stores	40.0-99.9	100.0-199.9	200.0-299.9	300.0-399.9	400.0-499.9	500.0-699.9	700.0+	Unknown	1-25	26-50	51-100	101-250	251-350+	Unknown
CANADA	2,241	77,132	879	576	236	124	63	68	64	231	1,166	516	250	140	8	161
NEWFOUNDLAND	31	892	12	15	2	0	1	1	0	0	17	9	2	1	0	2
Bay Roberts	1	17	1	0	0	0	0	0	0	0	1	0	0	0	0	0
Carbonear	1	37	0	1	0	0	0	0	0	0	0	1	0	0	0	0
Channel-Port aux Basques	1	28	1	0	0	0	0	0	0	0	1	0	0	0	0	0
Clarenville	1	20	1	0	0	0	0	0	0	0	1	0	0	0	0	0
Conception Bay	1	7	1	0	0	0	0	0	0	0	1	0	0	0	0	0
Corner Brook	3	148	0	2	1	0	0	0	0	0	0	2	1	0	0	0
Gander	2	49	0	2	0	0	0	0	0	0	0	1	1	0	0	0
Grand Falls	2	81	0	2	0	0	0	0	0	0	0	2	0	0	0	0
Labrador City	2	40	0	1	1	0	0	0	0	0	0	1	0	0	0	1
Lewisporte	1	19	1	0	0	0	0	0	0	0	1	0	0	0	0	0
Marystown	2	56	1	1	0	0	0	0	0	0	1	1	0	0	0	0
Mount Pearl	3	54	1	2	0	0	0	0	0	0	2	1	0	0	0	0
St. Anthony	1	14	1	0	0	0	0	0	0	0	1	0	0	0	0	0
St. John's	10	338	4	4	0	0	1	1	0	0	7	0	1	1	0	1
Stephenville	1	24	0	1	0	0	0	0	0	0	1	0	0	0	0	0
PRINCE EDWARD ISLAND	10	334	2	5	1	1	1	0	0	0	5	2	2	0	0	1
Charlottetown	6	200	2	1	1	1	1	0	0	0	3	0	2	0	0	1
Sherwood	1	45	0	1	0	0	0	0	0	0	0	1	0	0	0	0
Summerside	3	89	0	3	0	0	0	0	0	0	2	1	0	0	0	0
NOVA SCOTIA	70	2,555	19	21	17	6	2	3	1	1	34	20	13	3	0	0
Amherst	1	47	0	0	1	0	0	0	0	0	0	1	0	0	0	0
Antigonish	1	36	0	0	1	0	0	0	0	0	0	1	0	0	0	0
Bedford	3	138	0	1	1	1	0	0	0	0	1	0	2	0	0	0
Bridgewater	4	123	3	0	1	0	0	0	0	0	3	0	1	0	0	0
Dartmouth	12	492	2	6	2	0	1	1	0	0	6	4	1	1	0	0
Digby	1	8	1	0	0	0	0	0	0	0	1	0	0	0	0	0
Fall River	1	9	1	0	0	0	0	0	0	0	1	0	0	0	0	0
Glace Bay	1	11	1	0	0	0	0	0	0	0	1	0	0	0	0	0
Greenwood	2	80	0	1	0	1	0	0	0	0	1	0	1	0	0	0
Halifax	17	776	5	4	3	0	1	2	1	1	4	8	3	2	0	0
Hants County	1	20	1	0	0	0	0	0	0	0	1	0	0	0	0	0
Lower Sackville	4	95	0	2	1	1	0	0	0	0	3	1	0	0	0	0
New Glasgow	3	141	1	0	1	1	0	0	0	0	1	0	2	0	0	0
New Minas	3	98	1	0	1	1	0	0	0	0	1	1	1	0	0	0
North Sydney	1	26	0	1	0	0	0	0	0	0	1	0	0	0	0	0
Port Hawkesbury	2	55	0	2	0	0	0	0	0	0	1	1	0	0	0	0
Shelburne	1	13	1	0	0	0	0	0	0	0	1	0	0	0	0	0
Sydney	5	175	1	1	2	1	0	0	0	0	3	1	1	0	0	0
Truro	3	103	1	1	1	0	0	0	0	0	2	0	1	0	0	0
Upper Tantallon	1	25	0	1	0	0	0	0	0	0	1	0	0	0	0	0
Yarmouth	2	64	0	0	2	0	0	0	0	0	1	1	0	0	0	0
NEW BRUNSWICK	51	1,740	17	19	10	0	2	1	1	1	23	21	3	3	0	1
Bathurst	2	80	0	0	2	0	0	0	0	0	0	2	0	0	0	0
Big River	1	44	0	0	1	0	0	0	0	0	0	1	0	0	0	0
Bouctouche	1	14	1	0	0	0	0	0	0	0	1	0	0	0	0	0
Campbellton	2	61	1	1	0	0	0	0	0	0	1	1	0	0	0	0
Caraquet	2	58	2	0	0	0	0	0	0	0	0	2	0	0	0	0
Dalhousie	1	25	1	0	0	0	0	0	0	0	1	0	0	0	0	0
Dieppe	1	194	0	0	0	0	0	0	1	0	0	0	0	1	0	0
Edmundston	3	78	2	1	0	0	0	0	0	0	1	2	0	0	0	0
Fredericton	6	306	2	2	1	0	1	0	0	0	2	2	1	1	0	0
Miramichi	3	78	1	2	0	0	0	0	0	0	2	1	0	0	0	0
Moncton	6	128	0	3	2	0	0	1	0	0	4	0	1	0	0	1
Oromocto	1	29	0	1	0	0	0	0	0	0	0	1	0	0	0	0
Quispamsis	1	16	1	0	0	0	0	0	0	0	1	0	0	0	0	0
Riverview	1	38	0	1	0	0	0	0	0	0	0	1	0	0	0	0
Rothesay	1	11	1	0	0	0	0	0	0	0	1	0	0	0	0	0
Saint John	11	376	2	4	3	0	1	0	0	1	5	4	1	1	0	0
Shippagan	1	14	1	0	0	0	0	0	0	0	1	0	0	0	0	0
St. Basile	1	50	0	0	0	0	0	0	0	0	0	1	0	0	0	0
St. Stephen	1	11	1	0	0	0	0	0	0	0	1	0	0	0	0	0
Sussex	2	47	0	2	0	0	0	0	0	0	1	1	0	0	0	0
Tracadie	1	30	0	1	0	0	0	0	0	0	0	1	0	0	0	0
QUÉBEC	488	17,159	119	88	53	32	11	14	12	159	271	89	65	34	2	27
Alma	3	232	0	2	1	0	0	0	0	0	2	0	1	0	0	0
Amos	1	35	0	1	0	0	0	0	0	0	0	1	0	0	0	0
Amqui	1	18	1	0	0	0	0	0	0	0	1	0	0	0	0	0

	Centres	Total Stores	Lease Area (000's Sq. Ft.) 40.0-99.9	100.0-199.9	200.0-299.9	300.0-399.9	400.0-499.9	500.0-699.9	700.0+	Unknown	Store Distribution 1-25	26-50	51-100	101-250	251-350+	Unknown
Ancienne-Lorette	1	15	1	0	0	0	0	0	0	0	1	0	0	0	0	0
Anjou	3	250	1	1	0	0	0	0	1	0	1	1	0	1	0	0
Auteuil	1	16	0	0	0	0	0	0	0	1	1	0	0	0	0	0
Aylmer	2	75	1	0	1	0	0	0	0	0	1	0	1	0	0	0
Baie-Comeau	2	95	0	1	1	0	0	0	0	0	0	1	1	0	0	0
Baie-d'Urfé	1	15	1	0	0	0	0	0	0	0	1	0	0	0	0	0
Baie-Saint-Paul	1	30	1	0	0	0	0	0	0	0	0	1	0	0	0	0
Beaconsfield	2	48	0	0	0	0	0	0	0	1	1	1	0	0	0	0
Beauport	3	74	2	0	1	0	0	0	0	0	2	0	1	0	0	0
Beloeil	3	133	0	0	0	1	0	0	0	2	2	0	0	1	0	0
Blainville	1	12	1	0	0	0	0	0	0	0	1	0	0	0	0	0
Boisbriand	1	11	0	0	0	0	0	0	0	1	1	0	0	0	0	0
Boucherville	4	104	3	1	0	0	0	0	0	0	2	1	1	0	0	0
Bromont	1	14	1	0	0	0	0	0	0	0	1	0	0	0	0	0
Brossard	15	464	5	1	1	0	1	1	0	6	11	2	1	1	0	0
Buckingham	1	20	1	0	0	0	0	0	0	0	1	0	0	0	0	0
Cabano	1	17	1	0	0	0	0	0	0	0	1	0	0	0	0	0
Cap-de-la-Madeleine	1	60	0	0	0	1	0	0	0	0	0	0	1	0	0	0
Cap-Rouge	1	40	1	0	0	0	0	0	0	0	0	1	0	0	0	0
Chambly	1	28	1	0	0	0	0	0	0	0	0	1	0	0	0	0
Chandler	1	27	1	0	0	0	0	0	0	0	0	1	0	0	0	0
Charlesbourg	7	170	2	0	2	0	0	0	0	3	5	1	1	0	0	0
Châteauguay	7	125	1	2	1	0	0	0	0	3	5	0	1	0	0	1
Chicoutimi	4	255	1	0	1	0	0	1	0	1	1	0	1	1	0	1
Côte-Saint-Luc	2	115	0	1	0	1	0	0	0	0	0	1	1	0	0	0
Cowansville	1	39	0	1	0	0	0	0	0	0	0	1	0	0	0	0
Delson	1	19	0	1	0	0	0	0	0	0	1	0	0	0	0	0
Dollard-des-Ormeaux	11	256	1	1	0	1	0	0	0	8	7	2	2	0	0	0
Dorval	3	83	1	0	0	1	0	0	0	1	2	0	1	0	0	0
Drummondville	4	213	1	1	1	0	0	0	0	0	2	1	0	1	0	0
East Angus	1	13	1	0	0	0	0	0	0	0	1	0	0	0	0	0
Forestville	1	20	1	0	0	0	0	0	0	0	1	0	0	0	0	0
Gaspé	2	55	1	1	0	0	0	0	0	0	1	1	0	0	0	0
Gatineau	5	316	1	2	0	1	0	0	1	0	2	1	0	1	0	1
Granby	2	133	0	1	0	1	0	0	0	0	0	1	0	1	0	0
Greenfield Park	5	74	2	1	1	1	0	0	0	0	2	2	0	0	0	1
Hull	6	217	3	0	3	0	0	0	0	0	1	2	2	0	0	1
Île-Perrot	1	21	0	0	0	0	0	0	0	1	1	0	0	0	0	0
Joliette	1	150	0	0	0	0	0	1	0	0	0	0	1	0	0	0
Jonquière	3	124	0	2	1	0	0	0	0	0	0	0	2	0	0	1
Kirkland	4	58	1	0	1	0	0	0	0	2	4	0	0	0	0	0
La Baie	1	34	1	0	0	0	0	0	0	0	0	1	0	0	0	0
La Pocatière	1	25	0	1	0	0	0	0	0	0	1	0	0	0	0	0
La Prairie	3	69	1	1	0	0	0	0	0	1	0	2	0	0	0	1
La Sarre	2	59	0	2	0	0	0	0	0	0	1	1	0	0	0	0
La Tuque	1	21	0	1	0	0	0	0	0	0	0	1	0	0	0	0
Lac-Mégantic	1	19	1	0	0	0	0	0	0	0	1	0	0	0	0	0
Lachine	2	46	0	1	0	0	0	0	0	1	1	1	0	0	0	0
Lachute	2	40	0	2	0	0	0	0	0	0	0	1	0	0	0	1
LaSalle	14	438	2	5	0	1	0	0	1	5	9	3	0	1	0	1
Laval	52	1,233	6	5	1	1	2	2	1	34	41	4	4	2	0	1
Laval-Pont-Viau	2	17	0	0	0	0	0	0	0	2	2	0	0	0	0	0
Lévis	6	229	2	2	1	0	0	1	0	0	3	2	0	1	0	0
Longueuil	7	304	1	2	3	1	0	0	0	0	4	2	0	1	0	0
Magog	1	55	1	0	0	0	0	0	0	0	0	0	1	0	0	0
Maniwaki	1	30	0	1	0	0	0	0	0	0	0	1	0	0	0	0
Mascouche	1	0	0	0	0	1	0	0	0	0	0	0	0	0	0	1
Matane	2	91	1	1	0	0	0	0	0	0	0	1	1	0	0	0
Mont-Joli	1	37	1	0	0	0	0	0	0	0	0	1	0	0	0	0
Mont-Royal	2	214	0	1	0	0	0	1	0	0	0	1	0	1	0	0
Montmagny	1	45	0	1	0	0	0	0	0	0	0	1	0	0	0	0
Montréal	55	2,406	11	8	8	9	1	1	1	16	21	8	16	5	0	5
Montréal-Nord	5	142	0	1	0	0	0	0	0	2	3	1	1	0	0	0
Neufchâtel	1	54	0	1	0	0	0	0	0	0	0	0	1	0	0	0
New Richmond	1	31	1	0	0	0	0	0	0	0	0	1	0	0	0	0
Nicolet	1	21	1	0	0	0	0	0	0	0	1	0	0	0	0	0
Paspébiac	1	12	0	0	0	0	0	0	0	0	1	0	0	0	0	0
Pierrefonds	7	81	1	0	0	0	0	0	0	6	7	0	0	0	0	0
Pincourt	1	70	0	1	0	0	0	0	0	0	0	0	1	0	0	0
Plessisville	1	25	0	0	0	0	0	0	0	0	1	0	0	0	0	0
Pointe-aux-Trembles	5	85	0	1	0	0	0	0	0	4	4	1	0	0	0	0
Pointe-Claire	8	369	1	1	2	0	0	0	1	3	3	2	1	1	0	1
Port-Cartier	2	42	2	0	0	0	0	0	0	0	0	1	0	0	0	1
Québec	10	726	2	3	1	2	0	0	2	0	3	2	2	2	0	1
Repentigny	8	238	1	1	1	0	0	1	0	3	5	1	0	1	0	1
Rimouski	4	157	2	1	0	1	0	0	0	0	2	0	2	0	0	0
Rivière-du-Loup	3	106	2	0	1	0	0	0	0	0	2	0	1	0	0	0
Roberval	1	55	0	1	0	0	0	0	0	0	0	1	0	0	0	0
Rock Forest	1	50	0	1	0	0	0	0	0	0	0	1	0	0	0	0
Rosemère	5	238	1	0	1	0	0	1	0	2	3	1	0	1	0	0

	Centres	Stores	40.0-99.9	100.0-199.9	200.0-299.9	300.0-399.9	400.0-499.9	500.0-699.9	700.0+	Unknown	1-25	26-50	51-100	101-250	251-350+	Unknown
			Lease Area (000's Sq. Ft.)								Store Distribution					
Rouyn-Noranda	3	103	0	1	2	0	0	0	0	0	0	1	1	0	0	1
Roxboro	1	12	0	0	0	0	0	0	0	1	1	0	0	0	0	0
Salaberry-de-Valleyfield	3	92	1	1	1	0	0	0	0	0	2	1	0	0	0	0
Sept-Îles	3	114	1	0	2	0	0	0	0	0	1	1	1	0	0	0
Shawinigan	1	80	0	0	1	0	0	0	0	0	0	0	1	0	0	0
Sherbrooke	5	368	1	2	1	0	0	0	1	0	2	1	1	1	0	0
Sorel	2	118	1	0	0	1	0	0	0	0	1	0	0	1	0	0
Saint-Antoine-des-Laurentides	1	90	0	0	0	0	1	0	0	0	0	0	1	0	0	0
Saint-Basile-le-Grand	1	11	0	0	0	0	0	0	0	1	1	0	0	0	0	0
Saint-Bruno	3	43	0	0	0	0	0	0	0	3	3	0	0	0	0	0
Saint-Bruno-de-Montarville	1	272	0	0	0	0	0	0	1	0	0	0	0	0	1	0
Saint-Constant	1	20	1	0	0	0	0	0	0	0	1	0	0	0	0	0
Saint-Eustache	10	151	2	0	0	1	0	0	0	7	8	0	1	0	0	1
Saint-Félicien	1	36	1	0	0	0	0	0	0	0	0	1	0	0	0	0
Saint-Georges	1	50	0	1	0	0	0	0	0	0	0	1	0	0	0	0
Saint-Georges-de-Beauce	1	86	0	0	1	0	0	0	0	0	0	1	0	0	0	0
Saint-Hubert	5	101	0	2	1	0	0	0	0	2	3	0	1	0	0	1
Saint-Hyacinthe	3	135	1	0	1	0	1	0	0	0	1	0	0	1	0	1
Saint-Jean	1	120	0	0	0	0	1	0	0	0	0	0	0	1	0	0
Saint-Jean-sur-Richelieu	3	79	1	1	1	0	0	0	0	0	1	2	0	0	0	0
Saint-Jérôme	3	137	2	0	0	0	0	1	0	0	2	0	0	1	0	0
Saint-Lambert	4	36	1	0	0	0	0	0	0	3	4	0	0	0	0	0
Saint-Laurent	12	450	2	1	1	0	1	0	1	6	7	2	2	1	0	0
Saint-Léonard	16	240	1	4	0	0	1	0	0	10	14	1	1	0	0	0
Saint-Nicolas	1	50	1	0	0	0	0	0	0	0	0	1	0	0	0	0
Saint-Raymond	1	23	1	0	0	0	0	0	0	0	1	0	0	0	0	0
Saint-Romuald	1	33	0	1	0	0	0	0	0	0	0	1	0	0	0	0
Saint-Vincent-de-Paul	1	9	0	0	0	0	0	0	0	1	1	0	0	0	0	0
Saint-Eustache	1	2	1	0	0	0	0	0	0	0	1	0	0	0	0	0
Sainte-Adèle	1	17	1	0	0	0	0	0	0	0	1	0	0	0	0	0
Sainte-Agathe-des-Monts	1	11	1	0	0	0	0	0	0	0	1	0	0	0	0	0
Sainte-Anne-de-Beaupré	1	28	1	0	0	0	0	0	0	0	0	1	0	0	0	0
Sainte-Foy	4	513	1	0	1	0	1	1	0	0	1	1	0	1	1	0
Sainte-Julie	7	87	1	0	0	0	0	0	0	6	7	0	0	0	0	0
Sainte-Julie-de-Verchères	1	17	0	0	0	0	0	0	0	1	1	0	0	0	0	0
Sainte-Marie-de-Beauce	1	54	0	1	0	0	0	0	0	0	0	1	0	0	0	0
Sainte-Marthe-sur-le-Lac	1	78	0	0	1	0	0	0	0	0	0	1	0	0	0	0
Sainte-Thérèse-de-Blainville	1	24	0	1	0	0	0	0	0	0	1	0	0	0	0	0
Terrebonne	7	162	1	0	1	0	0	0	0	5	6	0	1	0	0	0
Thetford-Mines	3	92	1	2	0	0	0	0	0	0	1	2	0	0	0	0
Tracy	1	46	0	0	1	0	0	0	0	0	0	1	0	0	0	0
Trois-Pistoles	1	30	0	1	0	0	0	0	0	0	0	1	0	0	0	0
Trois-Rivières	4	155	1	2	0	0	0	1	0	0	3	0	0	1	0	0
Trois-Rivières-Ouest	2	104	1	0	0	1	0	0	0	0	1	0	1	0	0	0
Val-Bélair	1	18	1	0	0	0	0	0	0	0	1	0	0	0	0	0
Val-d'Or	3	63	1	0	2	0	0	0	0	0	1	1	0	0	0	1
Vanier	5	91	3	2	0	0	0	0	0	0	3	1	0	0	0	1
Varennes	1	35	1	0	0	0	0	0	0	0	1	0	0	0	0	0
Vaudreuil	1	12	0	0	0	0	0	0	0	1	1	0	0	0	0	0
Vaudreuil-Dorion	4	49	3	0	0	0	0	0	0	1	3	0	0	0	0	1
Verdun	1	15	1	0	0	0	0	0	0	0	1	0	0	0	0	0
Victoriaville	2	215	0	0	0	1	1	0	0	0	0	0	1	1	0	0
Ville Mont-Royal	1	21	0	0	0	0	0	0	0	1	1	0	0	0	0	0
Westmount	2	45	1	0	0	0	0	0	0	1	0	1	0	0	0	1
ONTARIO	888	29,456	402	238	98	51	23	27	33	16	462	178	95	53	4	96
Ajax	12	199	5	3	2	0	1	0	0	1	6	3	0	0	0	3
Alliston	1	20	1	0	0	0	0	0	0	0	1	0	0	0	0	0
Amherstburg	1	35	0	1	0	0	0	0	0	0	0	1	0	0	0	0
Ancaster	6	73	3	1	0	1	0	0	0	1	4	0	0	0	0	2
Arnprior	2	40	1	1	0	0	0	0	0	0	1	1	0	0	0	0
Aurora	5	79	3	1	1	0	0	0	0	0	3	1	0	0	0	1
Barrie	10	526	2	2	2	2	1	1	0	0	4	0	2	2	0	2
Beamsville	1	14	1	0	0	0	0	0	0	0	1	0	0	0	0	0
Belleville	8	280	4	1	2	0	0	1	0	0	5	1	1	1	0	0
Bolton	2	55	2	0	0	0	0	0	0	0	1	1	0	0	0	0
Bowmanville	2	39	0	2	0	0	0	0	0	0	0	1	0	0	0	1
Bracebridge	1	18	0	1	0	0	0	0	0	0	0	1	0	0	0	0
Bradford	1	13	1	0	0	0	0	0	0	0	1	0	0	0	0	0
Brampton	27	939	9	9	2	1	1	2	3	0	12	7	1	1	1	5
Brantford	11	260	7	2	0	2	0	0	0	0	9	1	1	0	0	0
Brockville	2	87	0	0	2	0	0	0	0	0	0	1	1	0	0	0
Burlington	23	680	12	7	1	2	0	1	0	0	13	6	0	2	0	2
Cambridge	13	236	6	5	0	0	0	1	1	0	11	1	0	0	0	1
Chatham	5	137	2	0	3	0	0	0	0	0	3	1	1	0	0	0
Chelmsford	1	35	0	1	0	0	0	0	0	0	0	1	0	0	0	0
Cobourg	2	80	0	1	0	0	0	0	0	0	0	0	1	0	0	0
Collingwood	2	23	0	2	0	0	0	0	0	0	0	0	0	0	0	0
Concord	1	0	1	0	0	0	0	0	0	0	0	0	0	0	0	1
Cornwall	6	186	1	2	3	0	0	0	0	0	3	2	1	0	0	0

Shopping Centre Data, 2000

	Total		Lease Area (000's Sq. Ft.)								Store Distribution					
	Centres	Stores	40.0-99.9	100.0-199.9	200.0-299.9	300.0-399.9	400.0-499.9	500.0-699.9	700.0+	Unknown	1-25	26-50	51-100	101-250	251-350+	Unknown
Courtice	1	0	1	0	0	0	0	0	0	0	0	0	0	0	0	1
Downsview	7	143	3	2	1	1	0	0	0	0	2	1	1	0	0	3
Dundas	2	70	1	1	0	0	0	0	0	0	0	2	0	0	0	0
East York	2	0	0	1	0	1	0	0	0	0	0	0	0	0	0	2
Elliot Lake	1	36	1	0	0	0	0	0	0	0	0	1	0	0	0	0
Espanola	1	30	0	1	0	0	0	0	0	0	0	1	0	0	0	0
Etobicoke	19	1,127	8	4	3	1	1	1	1	0	7	6	1	4	0	1
Fergus	2	27	2	0	0	0	0	0	0	0	2	0	0	0	0	0
Flamborough	1	0	0	0	0	1	0	0	0	0	0	0	0	0	0	1
Fort Erie	2	39	1	1	0	0	0	0	0	0	1	1	0	0	0	0
Garson	1	20	1	0	0	0	0	0	0	0	1	0	0	0	0	0
Georgetown	3	78	2	0	0	1	0	0	0	0	2	0	1	0	0	0
Gloucester	12	266	4	6	1	1	0	0	0	0	10	1	1	0	0	0
Goderich	3	19	0	2	1	0	0	0	0	0	2	0	0	0	0	1
Guelph	8	328	3	2	1	1	0	1	0	0	3	2	1	1	0	1
Hamilton	27	1,105	14	7	1	2	1	0	2	0	15	5	2	3	0	2
Hanover	1	13	1	0	0	0	0	0	0	0	1	0	0	0	0	0
Hawkesbury	2	53	2	0	0	0	0	0	0	0	1	1	0	0	0	0
Huntsville	2	39	1	0	0	0	0	0	0	0	2	0	0	0	0	0
Kanata	7	118	4	1	0	0	0	1	0	1	4	1	0	0	0	2
Kapuskasing	1	61	0	0	1	0	0	0	0	0	0	0	1	0	0	0
Kenora	1	23	0	1	0	0	0	0	0	0	0	1	0	0	0	0
Keswick	2	36	1	0	0	0	0	0	0	0	0	1	0	0	0	1
Kincardine	1	10	1	0	0	0	0	0	0	0	1	0	0	0	0	0
Kingston	11	343	4	3*	1	1	0	2	0	0	7	0	2	1	0	1
Kirkland Lake	1	13	1	0	0	0	0	0	0	0	1	0	0	0	0	0
Kitchener	22	569	12	6	2	1	0	0	1	0	14	4	2	1	0	1
Leamington	4	35	2	1	1	0	0	0	0	0	3	0	0	0	0	0
Lindsay	2	48	0	2	0	0	0	0	0	0	1	1	0	0	0	0
Listowel	1	0	1	0	0	0	0	0	0	0	0	0	0	0	0	1
London	42	1,530	22	11	5	0	0	3	1	0	29	7	2	4	0	0
Maple	1	25	0	1	0	0	0	0	0	0	1	0	0	0	0	0
Markham	11	527	2	4	2	1	0	0	2	0	2	3	0	2	0	4
Midland	2	78	0	0	0	1	0	0	0	0	1	1	0	0	0	0
Milton	2	69	1	0	0	0	0	0	0	0	1	0	1	0	0	0
Mississauga	59	2,068	32	13	5	4	0	1	4	0	33	10	6	4	1	5
Morrisburg	1	70	0	1	0	0	0	0	0	0	0	0	1	0	0	0
Napanee	1	20	0	0	0	0	0	0	0	0	1	0	0	0	0	0
Nepean	12	384	6	3	1	0	0	1	1	0	7	2	1	1	0	1
New Liskeard	3	36	0	3	0	0	0	0	0	0	1	1	0	0	0	1
Newmarket	7	365	2	2	2	0	0	0	1	0	3	0	1	0	0	2
Niagara Falls	8	245	2	4	0	2	0	0	0	0	3	2	2	0	0	1
North Bay	6	196	2	2	2	0	0	0	0	0	4	0	2	0	0	0
North York	27	1,211	13	6	4	2	1	0	1	0	8	9	4	3	0	3
Oakville	15	423	2	3	6	1	1	1	0	1	2	6	1	1	0	5
Orangeville	5	57	2	2	0	1	0	0	0	0	2	1	0	0	0	2
Orillia	3	66	1	1	0	1	0	0	0	0	2	0	1	0	0	0
Orleans	4	258	1	1	0	1	0	0	1	0	1	1	0	1	0	1
Oshawa	13	413	3	3	1	0	0	1	1	1	9	1	1	1	0	1
Ottawa	31	1,300	15	8	3	0	1	3	1	0	14	7	3	4	0	3
Owen Sound	3	107	1	1	0	1	0	0	0	0	2	0	1	0	0	0
Parry Sound	1	32	0	1	0	0	0	0	0	0	0	1	0	0	0	0
Pelham	1	19	1	0	0	0	0	0	0	0	1	0	0	0	0	0
Pembroke	2	83	0	1	1	0	0	0	0	0	0	1	0	0	0	0
Petawawa	1	16	1	0	0	0	0	0	0	0	1	0	0	0	0	0
Peterborough	7	243	3	1	3	0	0	0	0	0	3	1	3	0	0	0
Pickering	10	409	6	2	1	0	0	0	1	0	6	3	0	1	0	0
Port Colborne	2	38	1	1	0	0	0	0	0	0	1	1	0	0	0	0
Port Elgin	1	7	1	0	0	0	0	0	0	0	1	0	0	0	0	0
Port Hope	2	40	2	0	0	0	0	0	0	0	2	0	0	0	0	0
Renfrew	1	26	0	1	0	0	0	0	0	0	0	1	0	0	0	0
Rexdale	3	95	2	0	1	0	0	0	0	0	2	0	1	0	0	0
Richmond Hill	14	461	9	3	1	0	0	1	0	0	6	4	1	1	0	2
Sarnia	6	241	3	1	1	1	0	0	0	0	3	1	2	0	0	0
Sault Ste. Marie	8	263	1	5	0	1	1	0	0	0	4	2	0	1	0	1
Scarborough	45	1429	25	7	4	5	1	1	1	1	24	7	8	1	0	5
Simcoe	3	74	0	3	0	0	0	0	0	0	2	1	0	0	0	0
Smiths Falls	1	30	0	1	0	0	0	0	0	0	0	1	0	0	0	0
South Porcupine	1	19	1	0	0	0	0	0	0	0	1	0	0	0	0	0
St. Catharines	13	377	6	4	0	0	2	0	1	0	9	1	1	1	0	1
St. Thomas	1	67	0	0	1	0	0	0	0	0	0	1	0	0	0	0
Stittsville	2	43	2	0	0	0	0	0	0	0	2	0	0	0	0	0
Stoney Creek	5	192	1	3	0	0	0	1	0	0	1	2	0	1	0	1
Stratford	4	88	1	1	2	0	0	0	0	0	1	2	0	0	0	1
Strathroy	2	27	2	0	0	0	0	0	0	0	2	0	0	0	0	0
Sudbury	15	434	8	3	1	1	1	0	1	0	9	3	1	1	0	0
Thornhill	9	429	5	1	2	0	0	1	0	0	5	2	1	1	0	0
Thunder Bay	10	328	4	2	1	2	1	0	0	0	5	3	0	1	0	1
Tilbury	1	6	1	0	0	0	0	0	0	0	1	0	0	0	0	0
Tillsonburg	2	70	0	1	1	0	0	0	0	0	1	1	0	0	0	0

	Total		Lease Area (000's Sq. Ft.)								Store Distribution					
	Centres	Stores	40.0-99.9	100.0-199.9	200.0-299.9	300.0-399.9	400.0-499.9	500.0-699.9	700.0+	Un-known	1-25	26-50	51-100	101-250	251-350+	Un-known
Timmins	4	114	3	0	0	1	0	0	0	0	2	0	1	0	0	1
Toronto	66	3,095	25	15	6	5	2	1	3	9	24	15	20	3	1	3
Tottenham	1	18	1	0	0	0	0	0	0	0	1	0	0	0	0	0
Trenton	2	19	0	1	1	0	0	0	0	0	1	0	0	0	0	1
Uxbridge	1	3	1	0	0	0	0	0	0	0	1	0	0	0	0	0
Val Caron	1	33	0	1	0	0	0	0	0	0	0	1	0	0	0	0
Vaughan	10	145	4	1	1	2	0	0	2	0	5	2	0	0	0	3
Wallaceburg	1	16	0	1	0	0	0	0	0	0	1	0	0	0	0	0
Waterdown	2	44	2	0	0	0	0	0	0	0	1	1	0	0	0	0
Waterloo	13	361	7	1	3	0	2	0	0	0	7	2	2	0	0	2
Welland	7	228	4	2	0	0	0	1	0	0	6	0	0	1	0	0
Weston	1	49	0	1	0	0	0	0	0	0	1	0	0	0	0	0
Whitby	9	195	2	3	2	0	1	0	0	1	4	2	1	0	0	2
Willowdale	7	578	3	2	0	0	0	1	1	0	1	3	1	1	1	0
Windsor	25	535	12	10	1	0	0	0	2	0	20	3	0	1	0	1
Woodbridge	6	153	3	2	0	0	1	0	0	0	3	1	1	0	0	1
Woodstock	4	55	3	0	1	0	0	0	0	0	3	1	0	0	0	0
York	1	23	0	0	1	0	0	0	0	0	1	0	0	0	0	0
MANITOBA	67	1,988	27	22	7	2	4	2	2	1	35	14	6	3	0	9
Brandon	2	128	0	0	1	1	0	0	0	0	1	1	0	0	0	0
Dauphin	1	30	0	1	0	0	0	0	0	0	0	1	0	0	0	0
Portage La Prairie	2	45	0	2	0	0	0	0	0	0	1	1	0	0	0	0
Selkirk	1	20	0	1	0	0	0	0	0	0	1	0	0	0	0	0
Steinbach	1	40	0	0	1	0	0	0	0	0	0	1	0	0	0	0
The Pas	1	23	0	1	0	0	0	0	0	0	1	0	0	0	0	0
Thompson	2	61	1	1	0	0	0	0	0	0	0	2	0	0	0	0
Winkler	1	42	0	1	0	0	0	0	0	0	0	1	0	0	0	0
Winnipeg	56	1,599	26	15	5	1	4	2	2	1	32	7	5	3	0	9
SASKATCHEWAN	45	1,782	14	14	7	5	1	2	1	1	20	12	10	2	0	1
Estevan	1	26	0	1	0	0	0	0	0	0	0	1	0	0	0	0
Humboldt	1	21	0	1	0	0	0	0	0	0	1	0	0	0	0	0
Kindersley	1	24	0	1	0	0	0	0	0	0	1	0	0	0	0	0
Meadow Lake	1	15	1	0	0	0	0	0	0	0	1	0	0	0	0	0
Melfort	1	7	1	0	0	0	0	0	0	0	1	0	0	0	0	0
Moose Jaw	2	59	1	0	0	1	0	0	0	0	1	0	1	0	0	0
North Battleford	2	50	0	1	1	0	0	0	0	0	1	1	0	0	0	0
Prince Albert	2	124	0	0	1	1	0	0	0	0	1	1	0	0	0	0
Regina	14	556	3	4	3	1	1	1	0	1	5	4	3	1	0	1
Saskatoon	14	705	5	4	1	2	0	1	1	0	5	4	4	1	0	0
Swift Current	3	112	1	1	1	0	0	0	0	0	1	2	0	0	0	0
Tisdale	1	25	1	0	0	0	0	0	0	0	1	0	0	0	0	0
Weyburn	1	21	1	0	0	0	0	0	0	0	1	0	0	0	0	0
Yorkton	2	77	0	1	1	0	0	0	0	0	1	0	1	0	0	0
ALBERTA	306	10,478	144	64	20	12	11	9	7	39	170	83	23	18	2	10
Airdrie	2	57	1	1	0	0	0	0	0	0	1	1	0	0	0	0
Banff	1	60	0	1	0	0	0	0	0	0	0	0	1	0	0	0
Blairmore	1	17	1	0	0	0	0	0	0	0	1	0	0	0	0	0
Brooks	1	25	1	0	0	0	0	0	0	0	1	0	0	0	0	0
Calgary	133	4,429	55	30	5	4	1	5	3	30	68	46	10	6	1	2
Camrose	2	61	1	0	1	0	0	0	0	0	1	0	1	0	0	0
Drayton Valley	1	16	1	0	0	0	0	0	0	0	1	0	0	0	0	0
Edmonton	92	3,757	51	15	8	3	7	3	4	1	57	19	5	8	1	2
Fort McMurray	3	115	1	1	1	0	0	0	0	0	1	0	2	0	0	0
Fort Saskatchewan	3	57	1	1	0	0	0	0	0	1	2	1	0	0	0	0
Grande Prairie	5	104	2	0	2	1	0	0	0	0	1	0	1	0	0	3
Hinton	1	28	0	1	0	0	0	0	0	0	0	1	0	0	0	0
Innisfail	1	11	1	0	0	0	0	0	0	0	1	0	0	0	0	0
Lacombe	1	28	0	0	0	0	0	0	0	1	0	1	0	0	0	0
Lake Louise	1	16	1	0	0	0	0	0	0	0	1	0	0	0	0	0
Leduc	2	28	2	0	0	0	0	0	0	0	2	0	0	0	0	0
Lethbridge	9	326	3	1	0	1	2	1	0	1	4	2	1	1	0	0
Lloydminster	3	65	1	0	1	0	0	0	0	1	2	1	0	0	0	0
Medicine Hat	5	189	3	1	0	0	0	1	0	0	3	1	0	1	0	0
Olds	1	19	1	0	0	0	0	0	0	0	1	0	0	0	0	0
Peace River	1	17	1	0	0	0	0	0	0	0	1	0	0	0	0	0
Pincher Creek	1	15	1	0	0	0	0	0	0	0	1	0	0	0	0	0
Red Deer	7	313	3	2	0	0	2	0	0	0	3	1	0	2	0	1
Sherwood Park	8	224	1	4	0	1	0	0	0	2	3	3	1	0	0	0
Spruce Grove	3	81	2	1	0	0	0	0	0	0	2	1	0	0	0	0
St. Albert	12	286	4	4	0	1	0	0	0	3	8	3	1	0	0	0
Stettler	1	15	1	0	0	0	0	0	0	0	1	0	0	0	0	0
Stony Plain	1	25	1	0	0	0	0	0	0	0	1	0	0	0	0	0
Strathmore	1	3	1	0	0	0	0	0	0	0	1	0	0	0	0	0
Vermilion	1	16	1	0	0	0	0	0	0	0	1	0	0	0	0	0
Wetaskiwin	1	35	0	1	0	0	0	0	0	0	0	1	0	0	0	0

	Centres	Stores	Lease Area (000's Sq. Ft.)								Store Distribution					
			40.0-99.9	100.0-199.9	200.0-299.9	300.0-399.9	400.0-499.9	500.0-699.9	700.0+	Unknown	1-25	26-50	51-100	101-250	251-350+	Unknown
BRITISH COLUMBIA	283	10,710	123	88	21	15	7	9	7	13	128	87	31	23	0	14
100 Mile House	2	39	2	0	0	0	0	0	0	0	2	0	0	0	0	0
Abbotsford	9	224	3	2	2	0	0	1	0	1	2	2	0	1	0	4
Aldergrove	2	56	2	0	0	0	0	0	0	0	1	1	0	0	0	0
Burnaby	15	994	6	4	0	1	0	2	2	0	6	4	0	4	0	1
Campbell River	4	121	1	2	0	1	0	0	0	0	2	2	0	0	0	0
Castlegar	1	17	1	0	0	0	0	0	0	0	1	0	0	0	0	0
Chilliwack	6	178	4	1	0	1	0	0	0	0	4	1	1	0	0	0
Coquitlam	12	507	7	1	3	0	0	0	1	0	6	4	1	1	0	0
Courtenay	4	81	1	2	1	0	0	0	0	0	3	1	0	0	0	0
Cranbrook	3	67	1	1	1	0	0	0	0	0	1	1	0	0	0	1
Dawson Creek	2	44	1	1	0	0	0	0	0	0	1	1	0	0	0	0
Delta	10	310	4	3	1	0	0	0	0	2	4	3	2	0	0	1
Duncan	1	23	0	1	0	0	0	0	0	0	1	0	0	0	0	0
Fernie	1	14	1	0	0	0	0	0	0	0	1	0	0	0	0	0
Fort St. James	1	13	1	0	0	0	0	0	0	0	1	0	0	0	0	0
Fort St. John	2	40	1	1	0	0	0	0	0	0	1	1	0	0	0	0
Gibsons	2	18	2	0	0	0	0	0	0	0	1	0	0	0	0	1
Kamloops	11	350	1	7	2	0	1	0	0	0	5	2	2	1	0	1
Kelowna	7	310	2	3	1	0	0	1	0	0	2	4	0	1	0	0
Kitimat	1	33	0	1	0	0	0	0	0	0	0	1	0	0	0	0
Ladner	1	37	0	1	0	0	0	0	0	0	0	1	0	0	0	0
Ladysmith	1	30	1	0	0	0	0	0	0	0	0	1	0	0	0	0
Langley	11	391	3	5	0	2	0	1	0	0	5	3	1	1	0	1
Lillooet	1	12	1	0	0	0	0	0	0	0	1	0	0	0	0	0
Maple Ridge	6	193	3	2	1	0	0	0	0	0	3	2	1	0	0	0
Mission	2	71	0	1	0	1	0	0	0	0	1	1	0	0	0	0
Nanaimo	8	401	2	2	1	1	1	0	1	0	2	3	2	1	0	0
Nelson	1	33	0	1	0	0	0	0	0	0	0	1	0	0	0	0
New Westminster	6	308	2	2	0	2	0	0	0	0	1	2	3	0	0	0
North Vancouver	8	365	4	3	0	0	1	0	0	0	2	3	3	0	0	0
Oliver	1	16	1	0	0	0	0	0	0	0	1	0	0	0	0	0
Parksville	1	31	1	0	0	0	0	0	0	0	0	1	0	0	0	0
Penticton	2	96	0	0	2	0	0	0	0	0	0	1	1	0	0	0
Pitt Meadows	1	52	0	1	0	0	0	0	0	0	0	0	1	0	0	0
Port Alberni	2	55	1	1	0	0	0	0	0	0	1	1	0	0	0	0
Port Coquitlam	4	99	1	3	0	0	0	0	0	0	2	2	0	0	0	0
Port Hardy	1	25	1	0	0	0	0	0	0	0	1	0	0	0	0	0
Port Moody	1	5	1	0	0	0	0	0	0	0	1	0	0	0	0	0
Powell River	2	91	0	2	0	0	0	0	0	0	0	1	1	0	0	0
Prince George	5	241	1	2	0	1	0	1	0	0	2	1	1	1	0	0
Prince Rupert	2	51	1	0	1	0	0	0	0	0	1	1	0	0	0	0
Quesnel	2	59	0	2	0	0	0	0	0	0	1	1	0	0	0	0
Richmond	26	1,136	11	7	0	0	1	1	0	6	14	3	4	4	0	1
Salmon Arm	1	36	0	1	0	0	0	0	0	0	0	1	0	0	0	0
Smithers	1	10	1	0	0	0	0	0	0	0	1	0	0	0	0	0
Sooke	1	17	1	0	0	0	0	0	0	0	1	0	0	0	0	0
Sparwood	1	23	1	0	0	0	0	0	0	0	1	0	0	0	0	0
Squamish	1	16	1	0	0	0	0	0	0	0	1	0	0	0	0	0
Surrey	32	989	18	7	1	1	1	1	1	2	19	9	1	2	0	1
Terrace	2	47	1	1	0	0	0	0	0	0	1	1	0	0	0	0
Trail	1	40	0	1	0	0	0	0	0	0	0	1	0	0	0	0
Vancouver	26	1,055	17	6	0	0	0	1	1	1	9	10	4	2	0	1
Vernon	4	118	0	2	1	1	0	0	0	0	1	1	0	0	0	1
Victoria	15	717	5	3	2	3	2	0	0	0	7	4	1	3	0	0
West Vancouver	2	253	1	0	0	0	0	0	1	0	0	1	0	1	0	0
Westbank	1	21	0	1	0	0	0	0	0	0	1	0	0	0	0	0
White Rock	3	86	1	1	0	0	0	0	0	1	2	1	0	0	0	0
Williams Lake	1	45	0	0	1	0	0	0	0	0	0	1	0	0	0	0
NORTHWEST TERRITORIES	1	28	0	1	0	0	0	0	0	0	0	1	0	0	0	0
Yellowknife	1	28	0	1	0	0	0	0	0	0	0	1	0	0	0	0
YUKON TERRITORY	1	10	0	1	0	0	0	0	0	0	1	0	0	0	0	0
Whitehorse	1	10	0	1	0	0	0	0	0	0	1	0	0	0	0	0

	Area Type	Total Population	Population Male	Population Female	Total Private Households	Dwellings Owned	Dwellings Rented	Total Families	Lone Parent Families
Newfoundland									
Bay Roberts	T	5,470	2,685	2,785	1,997	1,645	352	1,622	129
Carbonear	T	5,095	2,449	2,646	1,899	1,517	382	1,602	224
Channel-Port aux Basques	T	4,806	2,340	2,466	1,915	1,471	444	1,606	208
Clarenville	T	6,054	2,966	3,088	2,288	1,531	757	1,922	229
Corner Brook	C	21,208	10,184	11,024	8,177	5,583	2,594	6,691	982
Deer Lake	T	5,205	2,462	2,743	1,851	1,340	511	1,629	220
Gander	T	10,160	5,003	5,157	3,859	2,411	1,448	3,116	354
Grand Falls-Windsor	T	13,457	6,502	6,955	4,996	3,604	1,392	4,209	494
Happy Valley-Goose Bay	T	8,834	4,415	4,419	3,130	1,528	1,602	2,716	314
Labrador City	T	8,141	4,230	3,911	2,973	2,326	647	2,592	262
Marystown	T	6,512	3,241	3,271	2,279	1,613	666	2,015	271
Paradise	T	8,376	4,138	4,238	2,899	2,554	345	2,600	216
Placentia	T	4,655	2,284	2,371	1,711	1,340	371	1,379	235
Portugal Cove-St. Philip's	T	5,958	2,972	2,986	2,065	1,871	194	1,862	195
Stephenville	T	7,742	3,709	4,033	3,015	1,503	1,512	2,435	541
Torbay	T	5,635	2,781	2,854	1,922	1,596	326	1,642	162
Prince Edward Island									
Charlottetown	C	33,440	15,473	17,967	14,034	6,968	7,066	8,927	1,935
Stratford	T	6,279	3,055	3,224	2,133	1,706	427	1,829	208
Summerside	C	14,980	7,198	7,782	6,053	3,540	2,513	4,433	823
Nova Scotia									
Amherst	T	9,752	4,513	5,239	4,169	2,507	1,662	2,765	639
Annapolis, Subd. A	SCM	5,834	2,896	2,938	2,352	2,036	316	1,747	169
Annapolis, Subd. C	SCM	5,765	2,832	2,933	2,250	1,925	325	1,795	211
Antigonish, Subd. A	SCM	7,952	4,004	3,948	2,751	2,334	417	2,171	266
Antigonish, Subd. B	SCM	6,950	3,524	3,426	2,350	2,110	240	1,872	224
Argyle	MD	8,942	4,461	4,481	3,284	3,033	251	2,735	260
Barrington	MD	8,061	4,024	4,037	3,201	2,888	313	2,522	223
Bridgewater	T	7,658	3,552	4,106	3,337	2,020	1,317	2,271	431
Cape Breton	RGM	112,010	53,594	58,416	42,717	31,232	11,485	32,305	7,224
Clare	MD	9,259	4,590	4,669	3,676	3,172	504	2,772	256
Colchester, Subd. B	SCM	19,353	9,596	9,757	7,286	5,857	1,429	5,875	834
Colchester, Subd. C	SCM	13,604	6,664	6,940	4,978	4,199	779	4,029	432
Cumberland, Subd. C	SCM	5,672	2,808	2,864	2,077	1,874	203	1,721	134
Digby	MD	8,912	4,405	4,507	3,534	3,018	516	2,711	331
Guysborough	MD	5,624	2,816	2,808	2,216	2,001	215	1,675	266
Halifax, Subd. F	SCM	6,531	3,287	3,244	2,596	2,286	310	2,061	228
Inverness, Subd. A	SCM	6,409	3,213	3,196	2,479	2,045	434	1,861	189
Inverness, Subd. B	SCM	6,036	2,996	3,040	2,166	1,716	450	1,592	308
Kentville	T	5,731	2,711	3,020	2,455	1,469	986	1,688	293
Kings, Subd. B	SCM	12,141	5,938	6,203	4,561	3,482	1,079	3,697	544
Kings, Subd. C	SCM	8,749	4,263	4,486	3,464	2,481	983	2,640	351
Kings, Subd. D	SCM	5,366	2,692	2,674	2,018	1,760	258	1,617	138
New Glasgow	T	9,924	4,552	5,372	4,253	2,531	1,722	2,817	649
Pictou, Subd. A	SCM	6,607	3,335	3,272	2,495	2,167	328	1,978	216
Pictou, Subd. B	SCM	6,730	3,365	3,365	2,457	2,105	352	1,938	178
Pictou, Subd. C	SCM	9,547	4,777	4,770	3,501	3,018	483	2,864	375
Queens, Subd. B	SCM	6,103	3,010	3,093	2,419	2,176	243	1,855	158
Shelburne	MD	5,268	2,627	2,641	2,110	1,890	220	1,625	160
Truro	T	12,419	5,790	6,629	5,759	2,829	2,930	3,433	727
Yarmouth	T	7,576	3,363	4,213	3,257	1,500	1,757	2,157	560
New Brunswick									
Alnwick	PAR	6,973	3,521	3,452	2,391	2,111	280	1,999	339
Bathurst	C	13,417	6,519	6,898	5,667	3,565	2,102	4,007	679
Bathurst	PAR	5,696	2,857	2,839	2,077	1,880	197	1,800	148
Beaubassin East	RC	6,818	3,454	3,364	2,467	2,227	240	2,173	276
Beresford	PAR	6,912	3,497	3,415	2,480	2,187	293	2,200	259
Campbellton	C	8,182	3,729	4,453	3,426	1,996	1,430	2,330	540
Dieppe	T	14,434	7,036	7,398	5,352	3,897	1,455	4,265	481
Douglas	PAR	6,085	3,094	2,991	2,120	1,943	177	1,837	177
Dundas	PAR	6,436	3,220	3,216	2,431	2,150	281	2,002	170
Edmundston	C	11,198	5,194	6,004	5,064	2,842	2,222	3,333	517
Fredericton	C	46,819	22,136	24,683	20,582	12,254	8,328	13,833	2,558
Grand Falls (Grand-Sault)	C	6,269	2,986	3,283	2,403	1,560	843	1,785	251
Kingsclear	PAR	6,652	3,376	3,276	2,339	2,162	177	2,048	165
Lincoln	PAR	6,342	3,165	3,177	2,276	2,148	128	1,942	262
Moncton	C	62,042	29,323	32,719	26,110	15,156	10,954	17,544	2,765
Moncton	PAR	9,101	4,596	4,505	3,203	2,968	235	2,797	269
Oromocto	T	9,304	4,879	4,425	3,206	875	2,331	2,742	240
Quispamsis	T	9,357	4,609	4,748	3,036	2,787	249	2,663	221
Riverview	T	17,052	8,241	8,811	6,296	5,265	1,031	5,162	500
Sackville	T	5,367	2,506	2,861	2,225	1,735	490	1,582	165
Saumarez	PAR	7,384	3,770	3,614	2,528	2,176	352	2,204	406
Shippagan	PAR	5,844	2,935	2,909	2,202	1,977	225	1,787	319
Woodstock	T	5,468	2,512	2,956	2,251	1,494	757	1,507	271

Municipal Summary Profiles - 2001 Estimates

	Area Type	Total Population	Population Male	Population Female	Total Private Households	Dwellings Owned	Dwellings Rented	Total Families	Lone Parent Families
Québec									
Alma	V	26,501	13,107	13,394	10,608	6,614	3,994	7,964	1,257
Amqui	V	6,931	3,413	3,518	2,679	1,701	978	1,993	284
Asbestos	V	6,195	2,885	3,310	2,850	1,678	1,172	1,892	284
Ascot	M	8,970	4,402	4,568	3,975	1,645	2,330	2,599	464
Baie-Comeau	V	24,743	12,620	12,123	10,039	6,708	3,331	7,714	983
Beauharnois	V	6,484	3,173	3,311	2,756	1,506	1,250	1,962	388
Bois-des-Filion	V	8,014	3,976	4,038	2,949	2,229	720	2,402	413
Cantley	M	6,482	3,331	3,151	2,293	2,032	261	1,979	150
Carignan	V	5,860	2,982	2,878	2,062	1,874	188	1,763	149
Charlemagne	V	5,822	2,899	2,923	2,345	1,298	1,047	1,775	307
Chelsea	M	6,744	3,423	3,321	2,491	2,213	278	2,069	218
Chibougamau	V	8,360	4,379	3,981	3,390	2,252	1,138	2,576	261
Coaticook	V	6,658	3,158	3,500	2,813	1,647	1,166	1,946	254
Contrecoeur	M	5,253	2,655	2,598	2,136	1,517	619	1,585	180
Cowansville	V	12,264	6,212	6,052	5,287	2,669	2,618	3,430	542
Delson	V	7,723	3,918	3,805	2,681	2,030	651	2,314	298
Des Ruisseaux	M	5,852	2,991	2,861	2,127	1,786	341	1,741	133
Dolbeau	V	8,384	4,135	4,249	3,363	1,907	1,456	2,472	385
Donnacona	V	5,768	2,924	2,844	2,512	1,558	954	1,691	227
Drummondville	V	46,889	22,506	24,383	21,421	9,769	11,652	13,460	2,492
Farnham	V	6,042	2,910	3,132	2,677	1,421	1,256	1,723	287
Granby	V	44,582	21,330	23,252	20,283	8,599	11,684	13,042	2,467
Granby	CT	12,051	6,115	5,936	3,998	3,763	235	3,662	273
Grand-Mère	V	14,197	6,794	7,403	6,534	3,525	3,009	4,153	753
Hampstead	V	6,889	3,242	3,647	2,537	1,636	901	1,938	175
Iberville	V	9,984	4,831	5,153	4,196	2,217	1,979	2,883	479
Joliette	V	17,877	8,157	9,720	8,266	3,196	5,070	4,801	1,181
L'Acadie	M	5,895	3,031	2,864	2,068	1,946	122	1,748	129
L'Île-Perrot	V	10,310	5,078	5,232	4,220	2,520	1,700	3,046	540
La Pêche	M	6,423	3,196	3,227	2,462	1,962	500	1,944	270
La Sarre	V	8,153	4,011	4,142	3,403	2,028	1,375	2,419	386
La Tuque	V	11,810	5,910	5,900	5,335	3,117	2,218	3,671	567
Lac-Beauport	M	5,655	2,912	2,743	2,072	1,881	191	1,688	122
Lac-Brome	V	5,358	2,663	2,695	2,299	1,840	459	1,564	191
Lac-Mégantic	V	5,953	2,900	3,053	2,675	1,560	1,115	1,760	264
Lac-Saint-Charles	M	9,421	4,771	4,650	3,351	2,892	459	2,934	302
Lachute	V	12,752	6,086	6,666	5,286	2,880	2,406	3,540	632
Lafontaine	VL	10,804	5,233	5,571	4,512	2,188	2,324	3,256	541
Lavaltrie	VL	7,488	3,757	3,731	2,574	2,073	501	2,183	249
LeMoyne	V	4,868	2,403	2,465	2,532	568	1,964	1,304	294
Lorraine	V	9,456	4,746	4,710	3,020	2,898	122	2,772	266
Louiseville	V	7,923	3,814	4,109	3,491	1,914	1,577	2,260	361
Magog	V	14,467	6,890	7,577	6,487	2,953	3,534	4,202	807
Magog	CT	6,036	3,042	2,994	2,486	2,001	485	1,897	150
Marieville	V	5,870	2,908	2,962	2,409	1,377	1,032	1,725	311
Masson-Angers	V	10,633	5,356	5,277	3,959	3,055	904	3,258	357
Matane	V	11,959	5,594	6,365	5,439	3,116	2,323	3,565	668
Mercier	V	10,402	5,124	5,278	3,562	2,878	684	3,089	332
Mistassini	V	6,929	3,467	3,462	2,565	1,669	896	2,040	273
Mont-Joli	V	6,207	2,898	3,309	2,680	1,391	1,289	1,720	312
Mont-Laurier	V	8,188	3,959	4,229	3,532	1,609	1,923	2,253	410
Montréal-Ouest	V	5,377	2,609	2,768	1,914	1,446	468	1,521	152
Notre-Dame-de-l'Île-Perrot	P	9,265	4,675	4,590	3,245	2,944	301	2,758	166
Notre-Dame-des-Prairies	M	7,248	3,498	3,750	2,982	2,161	821	2,178	285
Otterburn Park	V	8,714	4,341	4,373	3,192	2,684	508	2,593	295
Pintendre	M	7,023	3,523	3,500	2,439	1,769	670	2,076	226
Plessisville	V	6,664	3,151	3,513	2,838	1,693	1,145	1,919	265
Pointe-Calumet	VL	6,549	3,290	3,259	2,450	1,976	474	1,904	254
Pointe-du-Lac	M	6,590	3,294	3,296	2,472	2,169	303	2,008	243
Port-Cartier	V	6,871	3,595	3,276	2,739	1,871	868	2,144	259
Prévost	M	8,622	4,399	4,223	3,278	2,655	623	2,582	296
Rigaud	M	6,288	3,040	3,248	2,437	1,748	689	1,785	230
Rimouski	V	32,285	15,069	17,216	14,508	7,879	6,629	9,601	1,840
Rivière-du-Loup	V	16,600	7,707	8,893	7,082	3,712	3,370	4,595	794
Rouyn-Noranda	V	28,746	14,038	14,708	13,090	6,276	6,814	8,609	1,581
Roxboro	V	6,081	2,972	3,109	2,142	1,737	405	1,755	231
Saint-Amable	M	8,636	4,446	4,190	2,968	2,388	580	2,595	291
Saint-Athanase	P	6,736	3,486	3,250	2,420	1,964	456	2,006	195
Saint-Charles-Borromée	M	10,438	4,963	5,475	4,165	2,395	1,770	3,055	527
Saint-Charles-de-Drummond	M	5,887	2,966	2,921	2,197	1,799	398	1,731	150
Saint-Colomban	P	8,404	4,299	4,105	3,302	2,841	461	2,532	225
Saint-Élie-d'Orford	M	7,657	3,874	3,783	2,747	2,451	296	2,366	183
Saint-Émile	V	13,648	6,742	6,906	4,974	4,172	802	4,179	404
Saint-Étienne-de-Lauzon	M	9,031	4,636	4,395	3,111	2,569	542	2,654	315
Saint-Félicien	V	9,716	4,823	4,893	3,667	2,589	1,078	2,804	367
Saint-Georges	V	20,823	10,122	10,701	8,829	5,028	3,801	5,836	980
Saint-Hippolyte	P	6,664	3,399	3,265	2,892	2,380	512	2,070	181
Saint-Hyacinthe	V	38,634	17,867	20,767	17,699	7,409	10,290	10,858	2,082

	Area Type	Total Population	Population Male	Population Female	Total Private Households	Dwellings Owned	Dwellings Rented	Total Families	Lone Parent Families
Saint-Jean-sur-Richelieu	V	35,949	17,216	18,733	16,754	7,028	9,726	10,317	2,084
Saint-Lin	M	11,764	6,024	5,740	4,199	3,598	601	3,444	431
Saint-Louis-de-France	V	7,807	3,994	3,813	2,773	2,291	482	2,368	193
Saint-Luc	V	22,152	11,054	11,098	7,760	6,208	1,552	6,626	798
Saint-Nicéphore	M	10,484	5,418	5,066	3,690	2,975	715	3,159	395
Saint-Raymond	V	9,209	4,612	4,597	3,647	2,739	908	2,691	360
Saint-Rédempteur	V	6,742	3,302	3,440	2,328	1,733	595	2,002	297
Saint-Rémi	V	5,641	2,843	2,798	2,200	1,478	722	1,656	182
Saint-Timothée	V	8,661	4,290	4,371	3,257	2,554	703	2,608	290
Sainte-Adèle	V	6,712	3,219	3,493	3,256	2,051	1,205	2,118	420
Sainte-Agathe-des-Monts	V	5,833	2,680	3,153	2,714	1,160	1,554	1,667	376
Sainte-Anne-des-Monts	V	5,500	2,660	2,840	2,259	1,435	824	1,581	265
Sainte-Julienne	P	7,561	3,835	3,726	3,025	2,526	499	2,254	321
Sainte-Marthe-du-Cap	M	6,423	3,264	3,159	2,379	2,031	348	1,931	217
Sainte-Marthe-sur-le-Lac	V	9,273	4,647	4,626	3,362	2,928	434	2,773	254
Sainte-Sophie	M	9,640	4,892	4,748	3,612	2,831	781	2,896	327
Salaberry-de-Valleyfield	V	25,836	12,181	13,655	11,791	5,549	6,242	7,487	1,496
Sept-Îles	V	25,679	12,714	12,965	10,681	6,358	4,323	7,868	1,372
Shawinigan	V	17,780	8,255	9,525	8,694	3,382	5,312	4,941	1,080
Shawinigan-Sud	V	12,007	5,635	6,372	5,087	3,291	1,796	3,576	585
Sorel	V	22,514	10,821	11,693	9,736	5,966	3,770	6,758	1,128
Thetford Mines	V	17,131	8,103	9,028	7,641	5,054	2,587	5,215	705
Tracy	V	12,473	5,996	6,477	5,392	3,591	1,801	3,874	559
Val-d'Or	V	24,627	12,417	12,210	10,637	5,373	5,264	7,163	1,198
Val-des-Monts	M	9,159	4,747	4,412	3,487	2,953	534	2,819	308
Victoriaville	V	40,203	19,265	20,938	16,908	10,258	6,650	11,743	1,814
Ontario									
Adjala-Tosorontio	TP	10,340	5,199	5,141	3,382	2,809	573	2,983	188
Algoma, Unorganized, North Part	UNO	7,484	3,851	3,633	2,804	2,473	331	2,285	206
Ameliasburgh	TP	5,789	2,871	2,918	2,160	1,921	239	1,819	159
Anderdon	TP	6,209	3,139	3,070	2,053	1,909	144	1,805	116
Arnprior	T	7,587	3,535	4,052	3,177	1,760	1,417	2,132	391
Augusta	TP	7,977	3,999	3,978	2,787	2,522	265	2,423	140
Aylmer	T	7,876	3,789	4,087	2,897	1,888	1,009	2,105	266
Barrie	C	100,144	48,756	51,388	36,930	24,022	12,908	28,631	4,664
Beckwith	TP	6,430	3,211	3,219	2,265	2,141	124	1,926	118
Belleville	C	37,957	17,961	19,996	16,390	8,515	7,875	10,641	1,924
Blandford-Blenheim	TP	7,750	3,937	3,813	2,658	2,207	451	2,254	145
Bosanquet	TP	5,634	2,834	2,800	2,252	1,989	263	1,788	132
Brantford	C	94,334	45,349	48,985	36,227	23,470	12,757	26,374	4,606
Brantford	TP	7,179	3,650	3,529	2,435	2,163	272	2,147	220
Brockville	C	21,786	10,345	11,441	9,608	5,231	4,377	6,273	1,017
Burford	TP	6,281	3,154	3,127	2,135	1,825	310	1,771	151
Cambridge	TP	6,810	3,473	3,337	2,203	1,829	374	1,915	167
Caradoc	TP	6,412	3,184	3,228	2,277	1,923	354	1,888	126
Carleton Place	T	9,389	4,560	4,829	3,500	2,448	1,052	2,625	388
Cavan	TP	5,817	3,043	2,774	1,936	1,765	171	1,760	112
Charlottenburgh	TP	8,392	4,211	4,181	3,016	2,642	374	2,501	203
Chatham	C	44,045	21,086	22,959	17,730	10,956	6,774	12,239	2,193
Chatham	TP	6,227	3,197	3,030	2,398	1,856	542	1,822	130
Cobourg	T	17,215	8,025	9,190	7,059	4,386	2,673	5,130	832
Colchester South	TP	6,440	3,282	3,158	2,330	2,024	306	1,924	187
Collingwood	T	17,218	8,137	9,081	7,084	4,696	2,388	4,968	900
Cornwall	C	48,347	23,127	25,220	20,170	11,132	9,038	13,894	2,815
Cornwall	TP	7,243	3,615	3,628	2,574	2,230	344	2,180	177
Dryden	T	7,235	3,522	3,713	2,963	2,018	945	2,045	227
Dysart and Others	TP	5,925	2,877	3,048	2,582	2,091	491	1,866	140
East Zorra-Tavistock	TP	7,562	3,748	3,814	2,672	2,113	559	2,214	182
Elizabethtown	TP	7,996	3,949	4,047	2,821	2,570	251	2,429	146
Elliot Lake	C	13,476	6,655	6,821	5,768	3,236	2,532	4,147	480
Emily	TP	7,223	3,699	3,524	2,562	2,309	253	2,218	191
Eramosa	TP	6,982	3,574	3,408	2,433	1,984	449	2,076	147
Erin	TP	8,863	4,420	4,443	2,960	2,667	293	2,609	119
Ernestown	TP	13,246	6,930	6,316	4,621	3,546	1,075	3,944	549
Espanola	T	5,496	2,702	2,794	2,282	1,570	712	1,674	263
Essex	T	7,136	3,431	3,705	2,798	2,087	711	2,071	294
Fenelon	TP	6,237	3,121	3,116	2,483	2,243	240	1,953	104
Fergus	T	10,270	4,999	5,271	3,868	2,769	1,099	2,895	310
Fort Frances	T	8,784	4,235	4,549	3,710	2,583	1,127	2,502	405
Gananoque	T	5,200	2,488	2,712	2,310	1,438	872	1,515	178
Goderich	T	7,651	3,678	3,973	3,321	2,274	1,047	2,206	274
Gosfield South	TP	7,988	4,021	3,967	2,837	2,426	411	2,420	233
Guelph	C	107,731	52,710	55,021	41,659	25,166	16,493	30,200	4,205
Hanover	T	6,988	3,234	3,754	3,054	1,872	1,182	2,020	292
Harwich	TP	6,870	3,526	3,344	2,463	2,055	408	2,018	165
Hawkesbury	T	10,583	5,017	5,566	4,525	2,257	2,268	3,115	639
Hearst	T	5,990	2,998	2,992	2,437	1,389	1,048	1,779	232
Ingersoll	T	10,437	5,091	5,346	4,006	2,964	1,042	3,000	436

	Area Type	Total Population	Population Male	Female	Total Private Households	Dwellings Owned	Dwellings Rented	Total Families	Lone Parent Families
Innisfil	T	29,031	14,384	14,647	10,452	9,221	1,231	8,578	789
Iroquois Falls	T	5,471	2,742	2,729	2,150	1,606	544	1,629	186
Kenora	T	10,823	5,250	5,573	4,588	2,930	1,658	3,119	601
Kincardine	T	6,664	3,149	3,515	2,649	1,812	837	1,912	210
Kingston	TP	46,505	23,127	23,378	16,991	13,812	3,179	14,113	1,660
Kingston	C	54,457	25,296	29,161	26,598	10,420	16,178	14,328	3,156
Kingsville	T	6,314	3,001	3,313	2,419	1,716	703	1,781	229
Kirkland Lake	T	9,431	4,593	4,838	4,336	2,535	1,801	2,711	519
Leamington	T	18,405	8,754	9,651	6,913	4,383	2,530	5,120	605
Lindsay	T	18,812	8,837	9,975	8,044	4,934	3,110	5,445	872
Listowel	T	5,598	2,641	2,957	2,289	1,412	877	1,564	188
Lobo	TP	5,744	2,921	2,823	1,922	1,736	186	1,650	72
Loughborough	TP	5,467	2,704	2,763	1,948	1,702	246	1,675	142
Malahide	TP	6,582	3,346	3,236	1,920	1,491	429	1,647	65
Manvers	TP	6,151	3,152	2,999	2,106	1,946	160	1,812	93
Mariposa	TP	8,099	4,142	3,957	2,791	2,463	328	2,416	196
McNab	TP	6,097	3,068	3,029	2,194	1,964	230	1,841	114
Mersea	TP	9,905	5,065	4,840	3,305	2,702	603	2,820	218
Midland	T	16,010	7,606	8,404	6,536	4,179	2,357	4,600	861
Mono	TP	7,464	3,752	3,712	2,456	2,213	243	2,173	154
Moore	TP	10,989	5,544	5,445	3,920	3,314	606	3,301	334
Murray	TP	7,898	4,019	3,879	2,758	2,413	345	2,355	166
Muskoka Lakes	TP	6,734	3,437	3,297	2,683	2,352	331	2,125	178
Napanee	T	5,695	2,664	3,031	2,506	1,151	1,355	1,564	303
New Liskeard	T	4,835	2,351	2,484	2,051	1,354	697	1,380	191
North Bay	C	52,858	25,331	27,527	21,853	12,481	9,372	15,455	2,863
North Dorchester	TP	9,629	4,871	4,758	3,337	2,961	376	2,859	198
North Dumfries	TP	9,258	4,725	4,533	3,105	2,724	381	2,705	136
Onaping Falls	T	5,063	2,501	2,562	1,924	1,587	337	1,582	110
Orillia	C	30,515	14,569	15,946	12,576	7,645	4,931	8,681	1,593
Otonabee	TP	5,741	2,888	2,853	1,976	1,770	206	1,704	152
Owen Sound	C	21,274	9,941	11,333	9,344	5,466	3,878	6,018	1,037
Oxford-on-Rideau	TP	8,303	4,157	4,146	2,883	2,637	246	2,444	165
Paris	T	10,012	4,875	5,137	3,610	2,882	728	2,754	327
Parry Sound	T	6,569	3,084	3,485	3,033	1,791	1,242	1,963	388
Pembroke	C	14,504	6,746	7,758	6,316	3,670	2,646	4,013	782
Penetanguishene	T	7,916	3,857	4,059	3,151	2,109	1,042	2,251	375
Perth	T	6,134	2,804	3,330	2,841	1,616	1,225	1,662	236
Petawawa	TP	9,346	5,115	4,231	3,144	1,837	1,307	2,797	141
Petawawa	VL	7,334	3,731	3,603	2,650	1,391	1,259	2,176	282
Peterborough	C	73,436	34,352	39,084	30,520	18,890	11,630	20,855	3,521
Pittsburgh	TP	14,013	7,668	6,345	4,834	3,533	1,301	4,209	294
Plympton	TP	5,292	2,654	2,638	1,839	1,592	247	1,540	52
Port Elgin	T	7,223	3,506	3,717	2,793	1,995	798	2,074	297
Port Hope	T	12,111	5,893	6,218	4,770	3,429	1,341	3,484	454
Portland	TP	5,300	2,681	2,619	1,936	1,700	236	1,609	142
Puslinch	TP	6,148	3,122	3,026	2,211	1,869	342	1,871	112
Raleigh	TP	5,528	2,852	2,676	2,028	1,674	354	1,607	159
Ramara	TP	9,051	4,499	4,552	3,608	3,088	520	2,923	300
Renfrew	T	8,217	3,795	4,422	3,617	2,207	1,410	2,297	460
Rockland	T	9,349	4,598	4,751	3,313	2,279	1,034	2,768	388
Sandwich South	TP	8,346	4,161	4,185	2,661	2,398	263	2,401	163
Sarnia	C	72,519	35,081	37,438	29,833	20,570	9,263	21,171	3,031
Sault Ste. Marie	C	80,574	38,886	41,688	32,762	21,788	10,974	23,746	4,206
Severn	TP	12,417	6,073	6,344	4,668	4,036	632	3,781	383
Sidney	TP	16,192	8,176	8,016	5,743	4,403	1,340	4,874	369
Simcoe	T	15,776	7,519	8,257	6,518	4,299	2,219	4,577	638
Smith	TP	9,759	4,904	4,855	3,581	3,214	367	3,035	273
Smiths Falls	T	8,868	4,075	4,793	3,779	2,130	1,649	2,358	468
South Dumfries	TP	6,589	3,274	3,315	2,133	1,934	199	1,881	127
South-West Oxford	TP	8,533	4,339	4,194	2,863	2,373	490	2,397	162
Springwater	TP	16,845	8,441	8,404	5,677	4,749	928	4,890	373
St. Marys	T	6,449	3,085	3,364	2,528	1,809	719	1,778	142
Stratford	C	30,537	14,717	15,820	12,642	7,885	4,757	8,645	1,362
Strathroy	T	13,225	6,413	6,812	4,899	3,624	1,275	3,821	484
Sturgeon Falls	T	6,365	3,004	3,361	2,796	1,495	1,301	1,876	369
Sudbury, Unorganized, North Part	UNO	7,036	3,641	3,395	2,822	2,393	429	2,254	162
Tay	TP	11,819	5,877	5,942	4,561	3,946	615	3,576	446
Thunder Bay, Unorganized	UNO	8,793	4,601	4,192	3,201	2,796	405	2,531	231
Thurlow	TP	8,528	4,266	4,262	2,907	2,592	315	2,557	169
Tillsonburg	T	14,525	6,925	7,600	6,045	3,895	2,150	4,319	569
Timmins	C	47,262	23,597	23,665	18,662	12,039	6,623	13,930	2,028
Tiny	TP	9,353	4,697	4,656	3,598	3,189	409	2,874	272
Trenton	C	17,872	8,606	9,266	7,293	4,080	3,213	5,254	960
Wainfleet	TP	6,567	3,327	3,240	2,305	2,008	297	1,948	135
Walkerton	T	5,139	2,463	2,676	2,112	1,432	680	1,470	217
Wallaceburg	T	11,934	5,732	6,202	4,648	3,279	1,369	3,312	506
Wasaga Beach	T	11,652	5,760	5,892	5,095	4,311	784	3,914	412
Wellesley	TP	9,183	4,677	4,506	2,679	2,327	352	2,318	143

	Area Type	Total Population	Population Male	Population Female	Total Private Households	Dwellings Owned	Dwellings Rented	Total Families	Lone Parent Families
Woodstock	C	34,426	16,627	17,799	13,858	8,733	5,125	9,827	1,424
Yarmouth	TP	6,903	3,558	3,345	2,358	2,072	286	2,050	111
Zorra	TP	8,211	4,153	4,058	2,835	2,339	496	2,349	183
Manitoba									
Brandon	C	40,051	19,004	21,047	17,025	10,359	6,666	11,088	1,771
Dauphin	T	8,169	3,783	4,386	3,789	2,572	1,217	2,204	287
East St. Paul	RM	7,317	3,733	3,584	2,326	2,229	97	2,094	91
Flin Flon (Part)	C	6,174	3,104	3,070	2,603	1,867	736	1,764	239
Hanover	RM	11,023	5,633	5,390	3,224	2,802	422	2,887	150
Morden	T	6,193	2,937	3,256	2,469	1,858	611	1,743	131
Portage la Prairie	C	13,298	6,305	6,993	5,296	3,479	1,817	3,452	664
Portage la Prairie	RM	6,392	3,281	3,111	1,931	1,544	387	1,593	128
Ritchot	RM	5,643	2,895	2,748	1,844	1,650	194	1,580	77
Rockwood	RM	8,113	4,521	3,592	2,677	2,455	222	2,262	225
Selkirk	T	10,520	5,111	5,409	4,138	2,680	1,458	2,975	689
St. Clements	RM	9,551	4,935	4,616	3,389	3,225	164	2,818	246
Steinbach	T	8,963	4,250	4,713	3,493	2,185	1,308	2,540	241
Taché	RM	9,050	4,637	4,413	2,771	2,556	215	2,497	188
The Pas	T	5,772	2,891	2,881	2,315	1,318	997	1,667	357
Thompson	C	14,195	7,227	6,968	5,274	3,008	2,266	4,070	808
Winkler	T	8,180	3,980	4,200	2,905	2,011	894	2,113	116
Saskatchewan									
Corman Park No. 344	RM	7,756	4,024	3,732	2,499	2,291	208	2,209	150
Estevan	C	11,567	5,773	5,794	4,541	3,198	1,343	3,183	382
Humboldt	T	5,363	2,550	2,813	2,300	1,717	583	1,487	153
Lloydminster (Part)	C	8,655	4,354	4,301	3,176	1,609	1,567	2,355	453
Melfort	C	6,108	2,855	3,253	2,566	1,619	947	1,630	213
Moose Jaw	C	33,528	16,180	17,348	14,405	9,388	5,017	9,314	1,479
North Battleford	C	14,404	6,788	7,616	5,944	3,610	2,334	3,863	732
Prince Albert	C	36,778	17,458	19,320	13,997	7,956	6,041	10,014	2,233
Swift Current	C	15,485	7,319	8,166	6,802	4,522	2,280	4,488	503
Weyburn	C	10,047	4,755	5,292	4,353	2,844	1,509	2,796	329
Yorkton	C	15,370	7,122	8,248	6,521	4,371	2,150	4,223	579
Alberta									
Athabasca County No. 12	CM	8,241	4,294	3,947	2,912	2,568	344	2,379	191
Banff	T	6,415	3,173	3,242	2,626	905	1,721	1,342	122
Barrhead County No. 11	CM	6,174	3,201	2,973	2,077	1,880	197	1,705	54
Beaumont	T	7,099	3,537	3,562	2,102	1,885	217	1,925	190
Beaver County No. 9	CM	6,010	3,183	2,827	2,009	1,776	233	1,612	55
Big Lakes	MD	7,009	3,567	3,442	2,398	1,982	416	1,847	288
Bonnyville	T	5,797	2,957	2,840	2,099	1,227	872	1,487	233
Bonnyville No. 87	MD	19,599	10,388	9,211	6,280	4,425	1,855	5,352	408
Brazeau No. 77	MD	7,146	3,748	3,398	2,506	2,222	284	2,103	147
Camrose	C	14,355	6,802	7,553	5,942	4,046	1,896	3,939	484
Camrose County No. 22	CM	7,934	4,083	3,851	2,672	2,389	283	2,209	109
Canmore	T	11,272	5,615	5,657	4,378	3,257	1,121	3,320	316
Coaldale	T	6,444	3,255	3,189	2,215	1,846	369	1,778	187
Cochrane	T	11,084	5,470	5,614	3,752	3,041	711	3,150	293
Crowsnest Pass	T	6,075	3,048	3,027	2,704	2,189	515	1,901	236
Cypress No. 1	MD	5,972	3,091	2,881	1,961	1,652	309	1,701	76
Drayton Valley	T	6,103	3,083	3,020	2,257	1,606	651	1,665	186
Drumheller	C	7,022	3,658	3,364	2,846	1,936	910	1,845	249
Edson	T	7,771	3,899	3,872	2,973	1,870	1,103	2,226	341
Grande Prairie	C	35,751	18,102	17,649	13,047	8,230	4,817	9,808	1,286
Greenview No. 16	MD	5,732	2,927	2,805	1,969	1,828	141	1,605	102
High River	T	8,879	4,377	4,502	3,450	2,704	746	2,591	250
Hinton	T	11,240	5,743	5,497	4,088	2,885	1,203	3,301	331
Innisfail	T	7,181	3,465	3,716	2,723	1,947	776	1,970	219
Lac Ste. Anne County	MD	9,443	4,983	4,460	3,542	3,175	367	2,746	155
Lacombe	T	10,045	4,782	5,263	3,633	2,758	875	2,744	287
Lethbridge	C	68,314	32,945	35,369	27,546	18,964	8,582	19,332	2,690
Lethbridge County No. 26	CM	10,606	5,426	5,180	3,134	2,219	915	2,674	187
Lloydminster (Part)	C	12,748	6,381	6,367	4,988	2,885	2,103	3,583	472
Mackenzie No. 23	MD	8,965	4,544	4,421	2,363	2,023	340	2,032	109
Medicine Hat	C	51,795	25,294	26,501	21,134	15,164	5,970	15,064	1,874
Morinville	T	6,817	3,405	3,412	2,136	1,832	304	1,864	162
Newell County No. 4	CM	7,141	3,747	3,394	2,201	1,778	423	1,882	88
Okotoks	T	11,010	5,480	5,530	3,433	2,874	559	3,035	345
Olds	T	6,358	3,038	3,320	2,551	1,817	734	1,774	162
Peace River	T	6,780	3,437	3,343	2,516	1,507	1,009	1,840	254
Ponoka	T	7,089	3,349	3,740	2,812	2,013	799	1,907	306
Ponoka County No. 3	CM	9,608	4,993	4,615	3,201	2,910	291	2,714	168
Red Deer	C	68,368	33,585	34,783	26,075	15,516	10,559	18,266	3,094
Rocky Mountain House	T	6,365	3,065	3,300	2,413	1,580	833	1,720	238
Slave Lake	T	7,880	4,015	3,865	2,629	1,813	816	2,155	334
St. Paul County No. 19	CM	7,095	3,635	3,460	2,417	2,108	309	2,008	173

	Area Type	Total Population	Population Male	Female	Total Private Households	Dwellings Owned	Dwellings Rented	Total Families	Lone Parent Families
Stettler	T	5,601	2,638	2,963	2,276	1,613	663	1,517	122
Stettler County No. 6	CM	5,443	2,832	2,611	1,729	1,473	256	1,410	65
Stony Plain	T	10,008	4,839	5,169	3,579	2,679	900	2,773	317
Strathmore	T	6,662	3,255	3,407	2,344	1,851	493	1,845	243
Sylvan Lake	T	6,862	3,431	3,431	2,531	1,808	723	1,909	279
Taber	T	8,132	4,075	4,057	3,059	2,230	829	2,250	244
Taber No. 14	MD	6,260	3,299	2,961	1,791	1,381	410	1,571	62
Vegreville	T	5,653	2,690	2,963	2,421	1,804	617	1,537	172
Vermilion River County No. 24	CM	7,623	3,894	3,729	2,558	2,226	332	2,087	102
Wainwright	T	5,529	2,686	2,843	2,195	1,551	644	1,503	190
Westlock No. 92	MD	7,006	3,708	3,298	2,453	2,081	372	1,982	105
Wetaskiwin	C	11,784	5,613	6,171	4,727	2,972	1,755	3,224	430
Wheatland County No. 16	CM	7,666	3,942	3,724	2,277	1,833	444	1,990	124
Whitecourt	T	8,661	4,579	4,082	2,942	2,011	931	2,311	278
Willow Creek No. 26	MD	5,508	2,892	2,616	1,580	1,195	385	1,373	77
Wood Buffalo	SM	38,679	20,199	18,480	14,290	9,286	4,945	11,419	1,542
Yellowhead No. 94	MD	10,268	5,427	4,841	3,761	3,376	385	2,983	240

British Columbia

	Area Type	Total Population	Population Male	Female	Total Private Households	Dwellings Owned	Dwellings Rented	Total Families	Lone Parent Families
Abbotsford	C	120,623	59,524	61,099	42,530	29,969	12,561	33,798	4,094
Alberni-Clayoquot, Subd. A	SRD	7,921	4,022	3,899	3,208	2,705	503	2,521	199
Bulkley-Nechako, Subd. A	SRD	7,269	3,806	3,463	2,617	2,263	354	2,089	152
Bulkley-Nechako, Subd. B	SRD	6,848	3,573	3,275	2,370	2,017	353	1,916	111
Campbell River	DM	30,261	15,212	15,049	11,991	8,462	3,529	8,914	1,365
Capital, Subd. B	SRD	764	392	372	270	258	12	228	12
Cariboo, Subd. A	SRD	18,035	9,316	8,719	6,634	5,741	893	5,400	550
Cariboo, Subd. B	SRD	28,369	14,494	13,875	10,789	9,251	1,538	8,852	753
Castlegar	C	7,025	3,432	3,593	2,904	2,178	726	2,057	254
Central Kootenay, Subd. A	SRD	8,689	4,389	4,300	3,437	2,968	469	2,668	272
Central Kootenay, Subd. C	SRD	8,850	4,402	4,448	3,461	2,944	517	2,728	236
Central Okanagan, Subd. A	SRD	4,417	2,259	2,158	1,616	1,446	170	1,388	89
Central Okanagan, Subd. B	SRD	27,389	13,543	13,846	9,895	8,394	1,501	8,420	780
Chilliwack	DM	69,025	33,754	35,271	26,299	18,603	7,696	19,435	2,722
Coldstream	DM	9,443	4,756	4,687	3,327	2,887	440	2,800	186
Comox	T	11,849	5,720	6,129	4,808	3,445	1,363	3,675	398
Comox-Strathcona, Subd. B	SRD	5,469	2,847	2,622	2,073	1,743	330	1,700	172
Comox-Strathcona, Subd. C	SRD	24,772	12,466	12,306	9,971	8,372	1,599	7,680	764
Courtenay	C	23,576	11,370	12,206	10,102	6,232	3,870	6,812	1,233
Cowichan Valley, Subd. B	SRD	7,315	3,689	3,626	2,986	2,561	425	2,272	206
Cranbrook	C	19,424	9,461	9,963	7,994	5,378	2,616	5,735	964
Dawson Creek	C	11,044	5,379	5,665	4,572	2,902	1,670	3,158	650
East Kootenay, Subd. B	SRD	8,856	4,565	4,291	3,430	3,025	405	2,837	228
Fort St. John	C	15,503	7,920	7,583	6,015	3,605	2,410	4,263	640
Hope	DM	6,494	3,177	3,317	2,659	1,891	768	1,895	270
Kamloops	C	82,501	40,653	41,848	32,770	23,048	9,722	23,951	3,949
Kelowna	C	98,618	47,424	51,194	41,020	27,442	13,578	28,312	4,127
Kimberley	C	6,820	3,355	3,465	3,079	2,444	635	2,052	235
Kitimat	DM	10,573	5,436	5,137	4,005	3,058	947	3,141	392
Kitimat-Stikine, Subd. C	SRD	8,078	4,199	3,879	3,089	2,420	641	2,321	249
Kootenay Boundary, Subd. B	SRD	7,589	3,913	3,676	3,063	2,629	434	2,357	223
Ladysmith	T	7,935	3,883	4,052	3,186	2,402	784	2,368	302
Lake Country	DM	9,962	5,027	4,935	3,701	2,928	773	2,939	253
Mackenzie	DM	5,985	3,223	2,762	2,071	1,671	400	1,689	139
Merritt	C	8,029	3,963	4,066	3,084	2,054	1,030	2,320	403
Mission	DM	33,643	16,960	16,683	11,408	8,690	2,718	9,242	1,338
Nanaimo	C	76,278	37,214	39,064	31,503	21,038	10,465	22,120	3,878
Nanaimo, Subd. A	SRD	15,977	7,921	8,056	6,482	5,464	1,018	4,890	515
Nelson	C	9,700	4,599	5,101	4,182	2,736	1,446	2,669	597
North Cowichan	DM	27,908	13,643	14,265	10,966	8,025	2,941	8,317	1,093
North Okanagan, Subd. B	SRD	11,530	5,895	5,635	4,058	3,500	558	3,418	367
Okanagan-Similkameen, Subd. A	SRD	10,346	5,105	5,241	4,061	3,422	639	3,294	267
Okanagan-Similkameen, Subd. B	SRD	9,500	4,720	4,780	3,814	2,980	834	2,895	203
Parksville	C	11,300	5,254	6,046	5,206	3,711	1,495	3,491	422
Peace River, Subd. C	SRD	9,938	5,112	4,826	3,489	3,116	373	2,909	227
Penticton	C	32,998	15,677	17,321	14,847	9,167	5,680	9,621	1,549
Port Alberni	C	17,843	8,956	8,887	7,514	5,204	2,310	5,263	916
Port Hardy	DM	5,080	2,583	2,497	2,059	1,281	778	1,546	266
Powell River	DM	13,005	6,530	6,475	5,477	4,164	1,313	3,811	450
Powell River, Subd. A	SRD	6,800	3,473	3,327	2,925	2,308	617	2,111	263
Prince George	C	77,703	38,999	38,704	29,493	20,284	9,209	22,306	3,879
Prince Rupert	C	15,744	8,026	7,718	5,836	3,471	2,365	4,343	745
Qualicum Beach	T	8,190	3,859	4,331	3,750	3,107	643	2,843	207
Quesnel	C	8,554	4,184	4,370	3,571	1,904	1,667	2,464	539
Revelstoke	C	7,854	3,993	3,861	3,198	2,332	866	2,228	293
Sechelt	DM	8,257	3,969	4,288	3,660	2,761	899	2,560	405
Smithers	T	6,088	3,062	3,026	2,350	1,551	799	1,685	287
Spallumcheen	DM	5,627	2,848	2,779	2,005	1,699	306	1,689	173
Terrace	C	13,501	6,790	6,711	4,963	3,202	1,761	3,907	621
Thompson-Nicola, Subd. A	SRD	9,169	4,734	4,435	3,518	2,762	756	2,745	328

	Area Type	Total Population	Population Male	Population Female	Total Private Households	Dwellings Owned	Dwellings Rented	Total Families	Lone Parent Families
Trail	C	7,237	3,406	3,831	3,519	2,377	1,142	2,108	301
University Endowment Area	SRD	10,241	4,957	5,284	4,212	1,265	2,947	2,706	304
Vernon	C	34,160	16,191	17,969	14,810	9,525	5,285	9,867	1,804
View Royal	T	6,873	3,378	3,495	2,808	1,833	975	1,965	291
Whistler	DM	10,722	5,888	4,834	4,744	2,040	2,704	2,460	264
Williams Lake	C	10,371	5,202	5,169	4,061	2,359	1,702	2,903	496
Northwest Territories									
Yellowknife	C	18,920	9,661	9,259	6,735	3,398	3,337	5,186	712
Yukon Territory									
Whitehorse	C	18,842	9,505	9,337	7,384	4,629	2,567	5,321	939

Provincial Markets

Comparative Market Data

Region	Population (at July 1)				Households (at July1)		Income				Retail Sales				Taxation Statistics, 1997					
	*1996 Census (000)	2001 Estimate (000)	% of Cdn. Total	% Chg. 96-'01	2001 Estimate (000)	% of Cdn. Total	2001 Estimate $millions	% of Cdn. Total	Per Hhld. $	Income Rating Index	2001 Estimate $millions	% of Cdn. Total	Per Hhld. $	Market Rating Index	Total No. of Returns	Total Income $millions	Total No. Taxable Returns	Total Tax $millions	Avg. Income $	Avg. Tax $
Canada	29,671.7	31,134.5	100.00	4.93	12,084.9	100.00	656,440.2	100.00	54,300	100	278,705.8	100.00	23,100	100	21,084,180	579,104.4	14,430,980	104,218.0	27,466	7,222
Newfoundland	560.6	533.2	1.71	-4.88	195.4	1.62	9,074.4	1.38	46,400	81	4,628.5	1.66	23,700	97	386,380	7,677.0	227,580	1,332.7	19,869	5,856
Prince Edward Island	136.2	138.2	0.44	1.45	52.0	0.43	2,331.7	0.36	44,900	80	1,205.9	0.43	23,200	97	96,250	2,096.1	65,750	337.0	21,778	5,126
Nova Scotia	931.2	947.6	3.04	1.76	371.6	3.07	17,180.6	2.62	46,200	86	8,693.8	3.12	23,400	102	653,010	15,219.0	426,290	2,674.0	23,306	6,273
New Brunswick	753.0	759.1	2.44	0.81	293.2	2.43	13,511.2	2.06	46,100	84	7,095.9	2.55	24,200	104	538,100	11,835.7	344,780	2,071.6	21,995	6,009
Québec	7,274.0	7,445.1	23.91	2.35	3,063.9	25.35	143,773.8	21.90	46,900	92	64,688.8	23.21	21,100	97	5,237,640	129,461.9	3,498,070	15,372.1	24,718	4,394
Ontario	11,100.9	11,817.0	37.95	6.45	4,436.2	36.71	269,996.8	41.13	60,900	108	106,349.4	38.16	24,000	101	7,890,620	236,829.6	5,488,640	48,038.0	30,014	8,752
Manitoba	1,134.3	1,155.4	3.71	1.85	445.9	3.69	22,747.3	3.47	51,000	93	9,652.6	3.46	21,600	93	800,990	19,508.6	542,150	3,702.0	24,356	6,828
Saskatchewan	1,019.4	1,034.3	3.32	1.46	402.7	3.33	19,435.7	2.96	48,300	89	8,157.3	2.93	20,300	88	696,830	17,143.0	475,880	3,242.1	24,601	6,813
Alberta	2,780.6	3,065.6	9.85	10.25	1,153.3	9.54	68,436.5	10.43	59,300	106	31,754.6	11.39	27,500	116	1,986,460	60,305.4	1,424,320	12,024.1	30,358	8,442
British Columbia	3,882.0	4,137.4	13.29	6.58	1,636.6	13.54	87,782.5	13.37	53,600	101	36,141.4	12.97	22,100	98	2,740,780	77,255.6	1,898,700	15,115.8	28,187	7,961
Northwest Territories	41.8	42.2	0.14	0.88	14.4	0.12	1,029.0	0.16	71,700	116	128.7	0.05	9,000	34	24,180	815.5	17,140	149.7	33,726	8,733
Nunavut	25.7	28.2	0.09	9.4	7.4	0.06	409.3	0.06	55,500	69	42.3	0.02	5,700	17	12,790	341.6	7,240	58.2	26,710	8,040
Yukon	31.9	31.4	0.10	-1.78	12.4	0.10	731.2	0.11	59,100	111	166.9	0.06	13,500	59	20,160	615.3	14,460	100.6	30,521	6,957

*Adjusted

Canada in 2000 and 2001

Canada in 2000 and 2001

	1999	Forecast 2000	Forecast 2001	Percentage Changes 1999	Percentage Changes Forecast 2000	Percentage Changes Forecast 2001
Gross domestic product ($billion)	957.9	1035.0	1093.0	+6.2%	+8.0%	+5.6%
GDP in 1992$ ($ billion)	880.3	922.0	954.0	+4.5%	+4.7%	+3.5%
Domestic demand ($ billion)	852.9	895.5	927.0	+4.4%	+5.0%	+3.5%
GDP price index (1992 = 100)	108.8	112.3	114.5	+1.6%	+3.2%	+2.0%
Consumer price index 1992 = 100	110.5	113.5	116.3	+1.7%	+2.7%	+2.5%
Labor force (million)	15.72	15.99	16.25	+2.0%	+1.7%	+1.6%
Employment (million)	14.53	14.90	15.17	+2.8%	+2.5%	+1.8%
Unemployment ('000)	1,190	1,090	1,080	–7%	–8%	–1%
Unemployment rate (%)	7.6%	6.8%	6.6%			
Misery index *	9.3%	9.5%	9.1%			
Housing starts ('000)	145	155	160	–3%	+7%	+3%
Goods trade balance ($ billion)	+33.8	+48	+44			
Services & investment income ($ billion)	–37.2	–34	–36			
Current account balance ($ billion)	–3.4	+14	+8			
Wages and salaries per employee($)	34,329	35,880	37,050	+2.3%	+4.5%	+3.3%
After-tax corporate profits ($ billion)	56.4	70.5	74.0	+25%	+25%	+5%
Banks prime lending rate (%), annual average	6.4	7.3	8.0			
C$ (in US¢), annual average	67.3	68.0	70.0			

* Sum of unemployment rate and increase in consumer price index

Canada

POPULATION

July 1, 2001 Estimate	31,134,505
% Cdn. Total	100.00
% Change, '96 -'01	4.93
Avg. Annual Growth Rate, %	0.97
2003 Projected Population	31,891,636
2006 Projected Population	33,045,549
2001 Households Estimate	12,084,891
2003 Projected Households	12,466,157
2006 Projected Households	13,069,125

INCOME

2001 Total Income Estimate	$656,440,220,000
% Cdn. Total	100.00
2001 Average Hhld. Income	$54,300
2001 Per Capita	$21,100
2003 Projected Total Income	$712,778,650,000
2006 Projected Total Income	$808,882,820,000

RETAIL SALES

2001 Retail Sales Estimate	$278,705,820,000
% Cdn. Total	100.00
2001 per Household	$23,100
2001 per Capita	$9,000
2001 No. of Establishments	243,487
2003 Projected Retail Sales	$306,192,170,000
2006 Projected Retail Sales	$347,863,260,000

POPULATION

2001 Estimates:

Total	31,134,505
Male	15,287,679
Female	15,846,826

Age Groups	Male	Female
0-4	979,883	932,277
5-9	1,036,947	986,834
10-14	1,067,443	1,014,106
15-19	1,067,097	1,015,735
20-24	1,039,763	1,010,913
25-29	1,041,990	1,042,509
30-34	1,150,114	1,169,690
35-39	1,258,715	1,287,218
40-44	1,256,587	1,288,462
45-49	1,170,986	1,198,107
50-54	1,003,681	1,023,243
55-59	808,876	828,630
60-64	662,757	694,872
65-69	563,407	622,852
70+	1,179,433	1,731,378

DAYTIME POPULATION

2001 Estimates:

Working Population	15,268,025
At Home Population	15,883,912
Total	31,151,937

INCOME

2001 Estimates:

Avg. Household Income	$54,319
Avg. Family Income	$60,945
Per Capita Income	$21,084
Male:	
Avg. Employment Income	$35,883
Avg. Employment Income (Full Time)	$47,575
Female:	
Avg. Employment Income	$22,533
Avg. Employment Income (Full Time)	$33,582

DISPOSABLE & DISCRETIONARY INCOME

2001 Estimates:	*Per Hhld.*
Disposable Income	$41,957
Discretionary Income 1 (minus Food & Shelter)	$28,753
Discretionary Income 2 (minus Food, Shelter, & Other Expenditures)	$20,336

LIQUID ASSETS

1999 Estimates:	*Per Hhld.*
Equity Investments	$76,485
Interest Bearing Investments	$66,458
Total Liquid Assets	$142,943

CREDIT DATA

July 2000:

Pool of Credit	$286,807,042,949
Revolving Credit, No.	55,676,806
Fixed Loans, No.	17,202,485
Avg. Credit Limit, per Person	$11,189
Avg. Spent, per Person	$5,051
Satisfactory Ratings, No. per Person	2.72
Avg. No. of Cards, per Person	1.03

LABOUR FORCE

2001 Estimates:

Male:	
In the Labour Force	8,880,243
Participation Rate	72.8
Employed	8,250,689
Unemployed	629,554
Unemployment Rate	7.1
Not in Labour Force	3,323,163
Female:	
In the Labour Force	7,521,116
Participation Rate	58.2
Employed	6,999,114
Unemployed	522,002
Unemployment Rate	6.9
Not in Labour Force	5,392,493

AVERAGE WEEKLY EARNINGS

(Including overtime, industrial aggregate)

Apr 2000	$622.92
Apr 1999	$608.07
Apr 1998	$608.06
Apr 1997	$597.26
Apr 1996	$575.79

NUMBER OF EMPLOYEES

(Industrial aggregate)

Apr 2000	12,019,452
Apr 1999	11,702,471
Apr 1998	11,514,443
Apr 1997	11,131,076
Apr 1996	10,902,158

MANUFACTURING INDUSTRIES

	1997	1992
Plants	34,935	34,511
Employees	1,840,923	1,674,444
	$000	
Salaries, Wages	71,058,681	58,211,524
Mfg. Materials, Cost	251,038,171	162,426,958
Mfg. Shipments, Value	434,082,931	286,043,310
Total Value Added	182,668,107	124,412,071

Note: Latest available data.

OCCUPATIONS BY MAJOR GROUPS

2001 Estimates:	*Male*	*Female*
Management	991,156	448,587
Business, Finance & Admin.	853,247	2,200,844
Natural & Applied Sciences & Related	651,125	136,416
Health	160,812	619,332
Social Sciences, Gov't Services & Religion	182,420	235,166
Education	234,427	384,603
Arts, Culture, Recreation & Sport	189,992	218,174
Sales & Service	1,794,997	2,364,005
Trades, Transport & Equipment Operators & Related	2,132,557	129,245
Primary Industries	581,425	161,574
Processing, Mfg. & Utilities	853,930	351,125

LEVEL OF SCHOOLING

2001 Estimates:

Population 15 years +	25,117,015
Less than Grade 9	2,980,766
Grades 9-13 w/o Certif.	5,732,601
Grade 9-13 with Certif.	3,602,574
Trade Certif. /Dip.	918,809
Non-Univ. w/o Certif./Dip.	1,635,272
Non-Univ. with Certif./Dip.	4,492,775
Univ. w/o Degree	2,420,373
Univ. w/o Degree/Certif.	1,066,833
Univ. with Certif.	1,353,540
Univ. with Degree	3,333,845

RETAIL SALES

	1999 $000,000	1998 $000,000
Supermarkets & Groceries	54,500	53,346
All Other Food	4,389	4,318
Drugs & Patent Medicine	13,335	12,944
Shoes	1,626	1,670
Men's Clothing	1,536	1,582
Women's Clothing	4,505	4,406
Other Clothing	6,667	6,259
Hhld. Furniture & Appliances	11,082	10,107
Hhld. Furnishings	2,572	2,429
Motor & Recreation Vehicles	69,376	64,458
Gas Service Stations	18,000	16,187
Auto Parts, Accessories & Services	14,938	14,336
General Merchandise	29,990	27,956
Other Semi-Durable Goods	8,493	8,217
Other Durable Goods	7,060	6,750
Other Retail	12,621	11,675
Total	260,691	246,641

AVERAGE HOUSEHOLD EXPENDITURES

2001 Estimates:

Food	$6,332
Shelter	$9,015
Clothing	$2,245
Transportation	$6,412
Health & Personal Care	$1,963
Recr'n, Read'g & Education	$3,650
Taxes & Securities	$14,092
Other	$8,325
Total Expenditures	$52,034

PRIVATE HOUSEHOLDS

2001 Estimates:

Private Households, Total	12,084,891
Pop. in Private Households	30,490,245
Avg. No. per Household	2.5

FAMILIES

2001 Estimates:

Families in Private Households	8,784,083
Husband-Wife Families	7,532,134
Lone-Parent Families	1,251,949
Avg. No. Persons per Family	3.0
Avg. No. Sons/Daughters at Home	1.2

HOUSING

2001 Estimates:

Occupied Private Dwellings	12,084,891
Owned	7,732,158
Rented	4,305,990
Band Housing	46,743
Single-Detached House	6,899,081
Semi-Detached House	554,662
Row Houses	609,503
Apartment, 5+ Storeys	1,099,904
Owned Apartment, 5+ Storeys	177,166
Apartment, 5 or Fewer Storeys	2,211,177
Apartment, Detached Duplex	490,534
Other Single-Attached	40,836
Movable Dwellings	179,194

VEHICLES

2001 Estimates:

Model Yrs. '81-'96, No.	13,999,187
% Total	78.65
Model Yrs. '97-'98, No.	2,296,081
% Total	12.90
'99 Vehicles registered in Model Yr. '99, No.	1,503,751
% Total	8.45
Total No. '81-'99	17,799,019

LEGAL MARITAL STATUS

2001 Estimates: (Age 15+)

Single (Never Married)	8,019,788
Legally Married (Not Separated)	12,980,461
Legally Married (Separated)	753,127
Widowed	1,575,321
Divorced	1,788,318

PSYTE CATEGORIES

2001 Estimates	*No. of House-holds*	*% of Total Hhds.*	*Index*
Canadian Establishment	20,112	0.17	100
The Affluentials	77,266	0.64	100
Urban Gentry	217,170	1.80	100
Suburban Executives	173,215	1.43	100
Mortgaged in Suburbia	167,982	1.39	100
Technocrafts & Bureaucrats	340,037	2.81	100
Asian Heights	76,585	0.63	100
Boomers & Teens	216,646	1.79	100
Stable Suburban Families	157,543	1.30	100
Small City Elite	207,096	1.71	100
Old Bungalow Burbs	200,293	1.66	100
Suburban Nesters	193,692	1.60	100
Brie & Chablis	108,268	0.90	100
Aging Erudites	182,307	1.51	100
Satellite Suburbs	346,685	2.87	100
Kindergarten Boom	316,862	2.62	100
Blue Collar Winners	304,255	2.52	100
Town Boomers	122,491	1.01	100
Old Towns' New Fringe	473,003	3.91	100
Participation Quebec	348,243	2.88	100
New Quebec Rows	132,436	1.10	100
Quebec Melange	320,243	2.65	100
Traditional French Cdn. Families	324,527	2.69	100
Northern Lights	59,816	0.49	100
The New Frontier	182,274	1.51	100
Rustic Prosperity	218,062	1.80	100
Pick-ups & Dirt Bikes	100,909	0.84	100
Quebec's Heartland	118,635	0.98	100
The Grain Belt	71,595	0.59	100
Europa	150,239	1.24	100

(2001 Estimates)

2001 Estimates	No. of House-holds	% of Total Hhds.	Index
Asian Mosaic	165,664	1.37	100
High Rise Melting Pot	181,154	1.50	100
Conservative Homebodies	435,722	3.61	100
High Rise Sunsets	172,815	1.43	100
Young Urban Professionals	229,316	1.90	100
Young Urban Mix	256,105	2.12	100
Young Urban Intelligentsia	183,878	1.52	100
University Enclaves	246,652	2.04	100
Young City Singles	277,145	2.29	100
Urban Bohemia	141,430	1.17	100
Old Leafy Towns	308,870	2.56	100
Town Renters	104,447	0.86	100
Nesters & Young Homesteaders	282,073	2.33	100
Young Grey Collar	101,097	0.84	100
Quiet Towns	257,140	2.13	100
Agrarian Blues	25,874	0.21	100
Rod & Rifle	279,523	2.31	100
Down, Down East	84,737	0.70	100
Big Country Families	172,388	1.43	100
Quebec Rural Blues	294,439	2.44	100
Old Cdn. Rustics	118,522	0.98	100
Euro Quebec	105,992	0.88	100
Old Quebec Walkups	221,432	1.83	100
Quebec Town Elders	341,498	2.83	100
Aging Quebec Urbanites	34,875	0.29	100
Quebec's New Urban Mosaic	291,119	2.41	100
Struggling Downtowns	380,550	3.15	100
Aged Pensioners	160,779	1.33	100
Big City Stress	136,462	1.13	100
Old Grey Towers	66,931	0.55	100

FINANCIAL P$YTE

2001 Estimates	No. of House-holds	% of Total Hhds.	Index
Platinum Estates	97,378	0.81	100
Four Star Investors	607,031	5.02	100
Successful Suburbanites	801,963	6.64	100
Canadian Comfort	1,174,219	9.72	100
Urban Heights	519,891	4.30	100
Miners & Credit-Liners	382,567	3.17	100
Mortgages & Minivans	797,541	6.60	100
Dollars & Sense	315,903	2.61	100
Tractors & Tradelines	691,065	5.72	100
Bills & Wills	1,000,697	8.28	100
Country Credit	817,274	6.76	100
Revolving Renters	555,985	4.60	100
Young Urban Struggle	571,960	4.73	100
Rural Family Blues	975,596	8.07	100
Limited Budgets	375,662	3.11	100
Loan Parent Stress	703,797	5.82	100
Towering Debt	943,296	7.81	100
NSF	427,581	3.54	100
Senior Survivors	227,710	1.88	100

HOME LANGUAGE

2001 Estimates:		% Total
English	20,953,517	67.30
French	6,736,596	21.64
Arabic	97,871	0.31
Armenian	20,726	0.07
Bengali	12,545	0.04
Blackfoot	2,028	0.01
Bulgarian	4,390	0.01
Chinese	662,448	2.13
Chipewyan	699	0.00
Cree	61,036	0.20
Creoles	17,724	0.06
Croatian	26,798	0.09
Czech	8,946	0.03
Dakota/Sioux	2,850	0.01
Danish	1,305	0.00
Dogrib	1,430	0.00
Dutch	14,140	0.05
Estonian	4,483	0.01
Finnish	6,813	0.02
Flemish	705	0.00
Gaelic Languages	175	0.00
German	122,196	0.39
Greek	73,235	0.24
Gujarati	29,297	0.09
Hebrew	7,560	0.02
Hindi	26,024	0.08
Hungarian	26,399	0.08
Inuktitut (Eskimo)	25,147	0.08
Italian	232,343	0.75
Japanese	19,375	0.06
Khmer (Cambodian)	11,902	0.04
Korean	47,057	0.15
Kurdish	3,282	0.01
Kutchin-Gwich'in (Loucheux)	86	0.00
Lao	10,321	0.03
Latvian (Lettish)	3,599	0.01
Lithuanian	3,661	0.01
Macedonian	11,639	0.04
Malayalam	2,122	0.01
Malay-Bahasa	2,160	0.01
Maltese	1,622	0.01
Micmac	5,114	0.02
Montagnais-Naskapi	8,952	0.03
Norwegian	630	0.00
Ojibway	12,688	0.04
Pashto	1,978	0.01
Persian (Farsi)	48,686	0.16
Polish	131,486	0.42
Portuguese	133,119	0.43
Punjabi	178,550	0.57
Romanian	22,178	0.07
Russian	36,706	0.12
Serbian	21,787	0.07
Serbo-Croatian	15,084	0.05
Slovak	6,211	0.02
Slovenian	4,495	0.01
South Slave	1,369	0.00
Spanish	152,216	0.49
Swedish	1,271	0.00
Tagalog (Pilipino)	79,463	0.26
Tamil	60,731	0.20
Thai	1,147	0.00
Turkish	7,841	0.03
Ukrainian	33,767	0.11
Urdu	30,058	0.10
Vietnamese	100,728	0.32
Yiddish	7,232	0.02
Other Languages	104,724	0.34
Multiple Responses	630,042	2.02
Total	31,134,505	100.00

BUILDING PERMITS

	1999	1998	1997
		$000	
Value	35,770,367	33,199,192	31,248,908

HOMES BUILT

	1999	1998	1997
No.	140,986	133,941	143,386

CAPITAL EXPENDITURES

(Public & Private)	2000	1999	1998
		$000,000	
Total Expends.	n.a.	n.a.	208,600.3
Capital Expends.	183,848.1	174,544.1	167,376.9
Construction	108,117.4	99,985.0	95,445.7
Machinery & Equip.	75,730.7	74,559.1	71,931.2
Repair Expends.	n.a.	n.a.	41,223.4
Construction	n.a.	n.a.	16,125.6
Machinery & Equip.	n.a.	n.a.	25,097.8

TAXATION

Income Class:	1997	% Total
Under $5,000	2,860,760	13.57
$5,000-$10,000	2,794,290	13.25
$10,000-$15,000	3,115,450	14.78
$15,000-$20,000	2,078,530	9.86
$20,000-$25,000	1,728,850	8.20
$25,000-$30,000	1,598,460	7.58
$30,000-$40,000	2,504,630	11.88
$40,000-$50,000	1,628,910	7.73
$50,000 +	2,774,320	13.16
Total Returns, No.	21,084,180	
Total Income, $000	579,104,439	
Total Taxable Returns	14,430,980	
Total Tax, $000	104,217,998	
Avg. Income, $	27,466	
Avg. Tax, $	7,222	

VITAL STATISTICS

	1997	1996	1995	1994
Births	348,598	366,200	378,016	385,114
Deaths	215,669	212,860	210,733	207,077
Natural Increase	132,929	153,340	167,283	178,037
Marriages	159,350	156,691	160,251	159,959

Note: Latest available data.

TRAVEL STATISTICS

Tourists in Canada	1999	1998
From the U.S. entering by:		
Automobile	36,926,395	36,464,026
Bus	1,807,487	1,752,999
Rail	115,545	103,990
Air	4,285,224	4,086,421
Marine	750,498	679,372
Other Methods	745,054	770,384
Total	44,630,203	43,857,192
Other Countries:		
Land (via U.S.)	762,591	829,217
Air	3,590,715	3,318,889
Marine	71,974	58,431
Total	4,425,280	4,206,537
Residents of Canada Returning from the U.S. by:		
Automobile	34,975,433	35,995,936
Bus	1,393,378	1,351,619
Rail	35,492	31,565
Air	5,111,816	4,736,250
Marine	122,238	131,867
Other Methods	558,071	520,494
Total	42,196,428	42,767,731
From Other Countries:		
Land (via U.S.)	29	32
Air	4,244,365	4,210,265
Marine	7,263	7,339
Total	4,251,657	4,217,636

Newfoundland

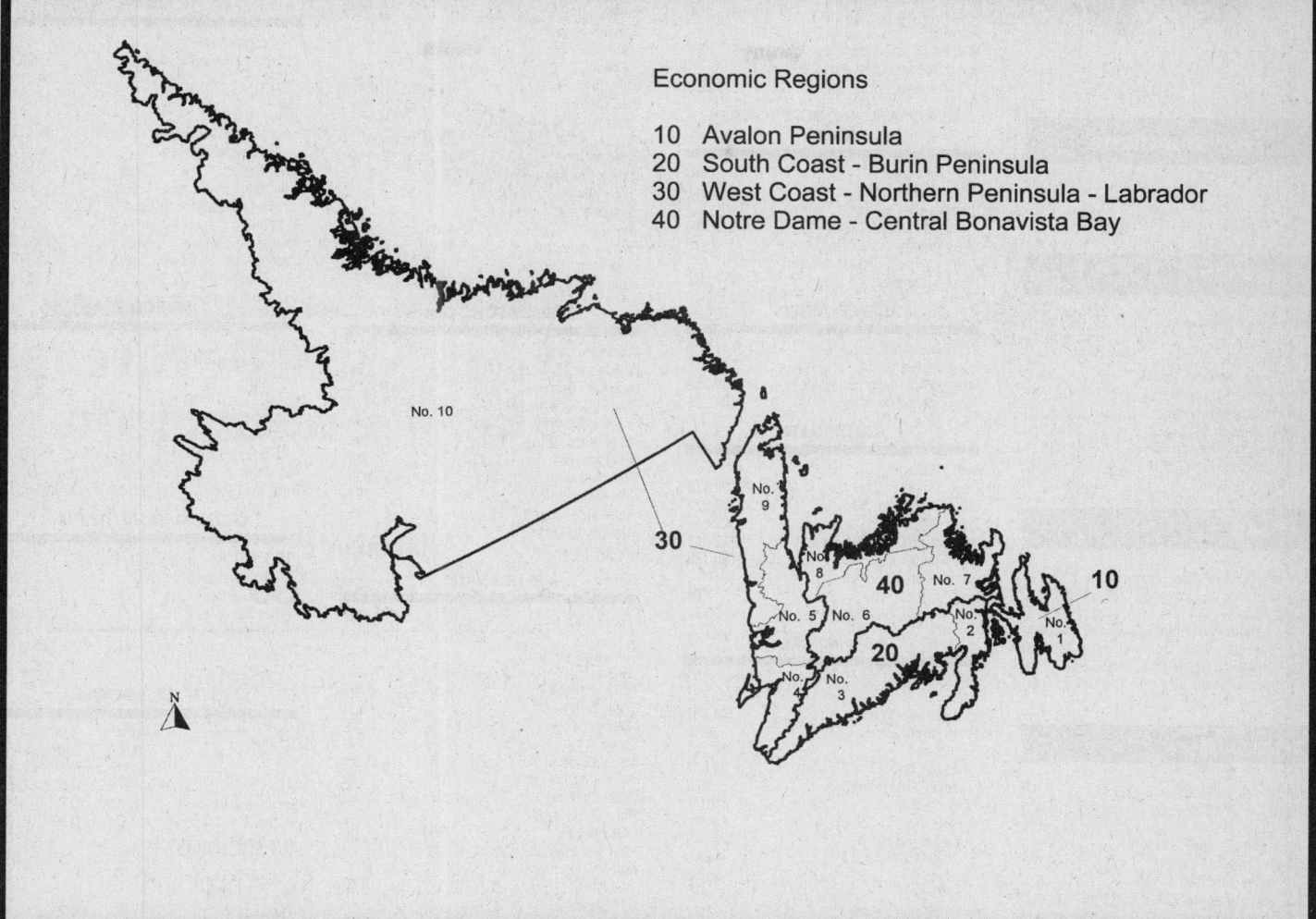

Economic Regions

10 Avalon Peninsula
20 South Coast - Burin Peninsula
30 West Coast - Northern Peninsula - Labrador
40 Notre Dame - Central Bonavista Bay

Region	Population (at July 1)				Households (at July1)		Income				Retail Sales				Taxation Statistics, 1997					
	*1996 Census (000)	2001 Estimate (000)	% of Cdn. Total	% Chg. '96-'01	2001 Estimate (000)	% of Cdn. Total	2001 Estimate $millions	% of Cdn. Total	Per Hhld. $	Income Rating Index	2001 Estimate $millions	% of Cdn. Total	Per Hhld. $	Market Rating Index	Total No. of Returns	Total Income $millions	Total No. Taxable Returns	Total Tax $millions	Avg. Income $	Avg. Tax $
Newfoundland	560.6	533.2	1.71	-4.88	195.4	1.62	9,074.4	1.38	46,400	81	4,628.5	1.66	23,700	97	386,380	7,677.0	227,580	1,332.7	19,869	5,856
Avalon Peninsula (10)	255.7	248.6	0.80	-2.77	92.1	0.76	4,608.8	0.70	50,000	88	2,244.0	0.81	24,400	101	177,950	3,908.0	109,240	738.5	21,961	6,761
Division No. 1	255.7	248.6	0.80	-2.77	92.1	0.76	4,608.8	0.70	50,000	88	2,244.0	0.81	24,400	101	177,950	3,908.0	109,240	738.5	21,961	6,761
South Coast - Burin Peninsula (20)	50.9	46.5	0.15	-8.59	16.7	0.14	653.0	0.10	39,000	67	299.1	0.11	17,900	72	34,770	566.7	19,010	82.1	16,299	4,319
Division No. 2	28.1	25.7	0.08	-8.54	9.3	0.08	373.3	0.06	40,000	69	165.8	0.06	17,800	72	19,120	322.8	10,510	48.2	16,885	4,583
Division No. 3	22.8	20.8	0.07	-8.66	7.4	0.06	279.7	0.04	37,700	64	133.4	0.05	18,000	72	15,650	243.9	8,500	33.9	15,582	3,993
West Coast - Northern Peninsula - Labrador (30)	123.2	116.4	0.37	-5.48	42.0	0.35	1,930.9	0.29	45,900	79	1,086.8	0.39	25,900	104	83,490	1,642.8	48,880	274.2	19,677	5,610
Division No. 4	25.2	23.8	0.08	-5.43	8.9	0.07	317.0	0.05	35,700	63	172.0	0.06	19,400	81	17,240	280.9	8,360	42.7	16,293	5,109
Division No. 5	45.0	43.1	0.14	-4.35	15.9	0.13	722.1	0.11	45,400	80	519.3	0.19	32,700	135	30,910	613.2	18,280	105.2	19,838	5,752
Division No. 9	23.2	20.6	0.07	-10.88	7.4	0.06	301.4	0.05	40,600	69	160.2	0.06	21,600	87	15,780	252.5	9,560	36.3	16,002	3,795
Division No. 10	29.8	28.9	0.09	-3.03	9.8	0.08	590.3	0.09	60,000	97	235.2	0.08	23,900	91	19,560	496.2	12,680	90.0	25,369	7,102
Notre Dame - Central Bonavista Bay (40)	130.8	121.6	0.39	-7	44.5	0.37	1,881.8	0.29	42,300	73	998.6	0.36	22,400	92	90,170	1,559.5	50,440	237.9	17,295	4,716
Division No. 6	39.7	37.5	0.12	-5.48	13.9	0.12	676.9	0.10	48,600	86	521.7	0.19	37,400	155	27,470	578.6	16,800	103.2	21,063	6,143
Division No. 7	42.1	39.7	0.13	-5.86	14.6	0.12	595.0	0.09	40,900	71	267.8	0.10	18,400	75	29,550	473.8	16,050	67.6	16,034	4,212
Division No. 8	48.9	44.4	0.14	-9.23	16.0	0.13	609.9	0.09	38,100	65	209.1	0.08	13,100	53	33,150	507.1	17,590	67.1	15,297	3,814

*Adjusted.

Newfoundland

POPULATION

July 1, 2001 Estimate	533,216
% Cdn. Total	1.71
% Change, '96 -'01	-4.88
Avg. Annual Growth Rate, %	-1.00
2003 Projected Population	535,682
2006 Projected Population	541,132
2001 Households Estimate	195,368
2003 Projected Households	199,625
2006 Projected Households	206,877

INCOME

% Above/Below National Average	-19
2001 Total Income Estimate	$9,074,450,000
% Cdn. Total	1.38
2001 Average Hhld. Income	$46,400
2001 Per Capita	$17,000
2003 Projected Total Income	$9,633,190,000
2006 Projected Total Income	$10,629,840,000

RETAIL SALES

% Above/Below National Average	-3
2001 Retail Sales Estimate	$4,628,470,000
% Cdn. Total	1.66
2001 per Household	$23,700
2001 per Capita	$8,700
2001 No. of Establishments	4,528
2003 Projected Retail Sales	$4,977,730,000
2006 Projected Retail Sales	$5,500,470,000

POPULATION

2001 Estimates:

Total	533,216
Male	262,842
Female	270,374

Age Groups	Male	Female
0-4	13,384	12,637
5-9	15,276	14,640
10-14	18,027	17,456
15-19	20,691	19,925
20-24	21,334	20,189
25-29	19,506	19,245
30-34	19,049	19,930
35-39	19,973	21,219
40-44	20,945	22,213
45-49	21,070	21,663
50-54	18,641	18,739
55-59	14,747	14,649
60-64	11,553	11,593
65-69	9,384	9,947
70+	19,262	26,329

DAYTIME POPULATION

2001 Estimates:

Working Population	224,644
At Home Population	308,567
Total	533,211

INCOME

2001 Estimates:

Avg. Household Income	$46,448
Avg. Family Income	$48,576
Per Capita Income	$17,018
Male:	
Avg. Employment Income	$29,561
Avg. Employment Income (Full Time)	$45,317
Female:	
Avg. Employment Income	$17,864
Avg. Employment Income (Full Time)	$29,711

DISPOSABLE & DISCRETIONARY INCOME

2001 Estimates:	*Per Hhld.*
Disposable Income	$36,933
Discretionary Income 1 (minus Food & Shelter)	$25,531
Discretionary Income 2 (minus Food, Shelter, & Other Expenditures)	$17,168

LIQUID ASSETS

1999 Estimates:	*Per Hhld.*
Equity Investments	$43,881
Interest Bearing Investments	$49,350
Total Liquid Assets	$93,231

CREDIT DATA

July 2000:

Pool of Credit	$5,148,190,175
Revolving Credit, No.	703,079
Fixed Loans, No.	522,547
Avg. Credit Limit, per Person	$12,018
Avg. Spent, per Person	$6,788
Satisfactory Ratings, No. per Person	2.64
Avg. No. of Cards, per Person	0.70

LABOUR FORCE

2001 Estimates:

Male:	
In the Labour Force	144,807
Participation Rate	67.0
Employed	114,745
Unemployed	30,062
Unemployment Rate	20.8
Not in Labour Force	71,348
Female:	
In the Labour Force	122,589
Participation Rate	54.3
Employed	102,093
Unemployed	20,496
Unemployment Rate	16.7
Not in Labour Force	103,052

AVERAGE WEEKLY EARNINGS

(Including overtime, industrial aggregate)

	Newfoundland	Canada
Apr 2000	$554.60	$622.92
Apr 1999	$554.65	$608.07
Apr 1998	$528.20	$608.06
Apr 1997	$527.63	$597.26
Apr 1996	$528.80	$575.79

NUMBER OF EMPLOYEES

(Industrial aggregate)

Apr 2000	148,261
Apr 1999	146,357
Apr 1998	141,630
Apr 1997	134,531
Apr 1996	138,135

MANUFACTURING INDUSTRIES

	1997	1992
Plants	314	288
Employees	11,230	12,323
	$000	
Salaries, Wages	358,101	346,189
Mfg. Materials, Cost	780,757	577,514
Mfg. Shipments, Value	1,658,205	1,279,612
Total Value Added	851,730	668,785

Note: Latest available data.

OCCUPATIONS BY MAJOR GROUPS

2001 Estimates:	*Male*	*Female*
Management	11,870	5,961
Business, Finance & Admin.	9,970	27,691
Natural & Applied Sciences & Related	9,063	1,151
Health	2,573	11,042
Social Sciences, Gov't Services & Religion	3,049	3,616
Education	5,308	7,645
Arts, Culture, Recreation & Sport	2,065	2,401
Sales & Service	24,882	45,120
Trades, Transport & Equipment Operators & Related	41,410	1,402
Primary Industries	15,424	2,109
Processing, Mfg. & Utilities	10,228	5,236

LEVEL OF SCHOOLING

2001 Estimates:

Population 15 years +	441,796
Less than Grade 9	76,159
Grades 9-13 w/o Certif.	123,415
Grade 9-13 with Certif.	43,549
Trade Certif. /Dip.	12,898
Non-Univ. w/o Certif./Dip.	17,353
Non-Univ. with Certif./Dip.	85,098
Univ. w/o Degree	47,284
Univ. w/o Degree/Certif.	23,223
Univ. with Certif.	24,061
Univ. with Degree	36,040

RETAIL SALES

	1999 $000,000	1998 $000,000
Supermarkets & Groceries	1,097	1,089
All Other Food	n.a.	n.a.
Drugs & Patent Medicine	242	236
Shoes	15	14
Men's Clothing	18	20
Women's Clothing	58	56
Other Clothing	67	62
Hhld. Furniture & Appliances	135	116
Hhld. Furnishings	8	9
Motor & Recreation Vehicles	1,025	886
Gas Service Stations	370	358
Auto Parts, Accessories & Services	220	199
General Merchandise	620	576
Other Semi-Durable Goods	90	84
Other Durable Goods	52	46
Other Retail	155	147
Total	4,223	3,939

AVERAGE HOUSEHOLD EXPENDITURES

2001 Estimates:

Food	$6,167
Shelter	$7,043
Clothing	$2,037
Transportation	$6,307
Health & Personal Care	$1,833
Recr'n, Read'g & Education	$3,280
Taxes & Securities	$11,298
Other	$8,169
Total Expenditures	$46,134

PRIVATE HOUSEHOLDS

2001 Estimates:

Private Households, Total	195,368
Pop. in Private Households	523,557
Average no. per Household	2.7

FAMILIES

2001 Estimates:

Families in Private Households	163,585
Husband-Wife Families	142,356
Lone-Parent Families	21,229
Aver. No. Persons per Family	3.1
Aver. No. Sons/Daughters at Home	1.3

HOUSING

2001 Estimates:

Occupied Private Dwellings	195,368
Owned	150,318
Rented	44,954
Band Housing	96
Single-Detached House	144,512
Semi-Detached House	7,372
Row Houses	10,550
Apartment, 5+ Storeys	821
Owned Apartment, 5+ Storeys	31
Apartment, 5 or Fewer Storeys	9,877
Apartment, Detached Duplex	19,735
Other Single-Attached	874
Movable Dwellings	1,627

VEHICLES

2001 Estimates:

Model Yrs. '81-'96, No.	232,816
% Total	80.32
Model Yrs. '97-'98, No.	32,996
% Total	11.38
'99 Vehicles registered in Model Yr. '99, No.	24,040
% Total	8.29
Total No. '81-'99	289,852

LEGAL MARITAL STATUS

2001 Estimates: (Age 15+)

Single (Never Married)	142,749
Legally Married (Not Separated)	246,293
Legally Married (Separated)	7,879
Widowed	27,313
Divorced	17,562

PSYTE CATEGORIES

2001 Estimates	*No. of House-holds*	*% of Total Hhds.*	*Index*
Urban Gentry	1,704	0.87	49
Suburban Executives	1,359	0.70	49
Mortgaged in Suburbia	174	0.09	6
Technocrafts & Bureaucrats	5,150	2.64	94
Boomers & Teens	277	0.14	8
Stable Suburban Families	561	0.29	22
Small City Elite	5,310	2.72	159
Old Bungalow Burbs	1,712	0.88	53
Aging Erudites	4,306	2.20	146
Satellite Suburbs	2,208	1.13	39
Kindergarten Boom	5,292	2.71	103
Blue Collar Winners	65	0.03	1
Town Boomers	7,744	3.96	391
Old Towns' New Fringe	16,317	8.35	213
Northern Lights	7,141	3.66	738
The New Frontier	5,183	2.65	176
Rustic Prosperity	46	0.02	1
Pick-ups & Dirt Bikes	2,257	1.16	138
Conservative Homebodies	3,450	1.77	49
High Rise Sunsets	820	0.42	29
Young Urban Professionals	527	0.27	14
Young Urban Mix	757	0.39	18
University Enclaves	5,119	2.62	128
Young City Singles	288	0.15	6
Old Leafy Towns	1,600	0.82	32
Town Renters	1,729	0.88	102
Nesters & Young Homesteaders	1,310	0.67	29
Young Grey Collar	1,038	0.53	64
Quiet Towns	9,699	4.96	233
Agrarian Blues	1,208	0.62	289
Rod & Rifle	18,772	9.61	415
Down, Down East	68,956	35.30	5,034
Big Country Families	3,936	2.01	141
Old Cdn. Rustics	865	0.44	45
Struggling Downtowns	6,214	3.18	101
Aged Pensioners	490	0.25	19
Old Grey Towers	234	0.12	22

FINANCIAL P$YTE

2001 Estimates	No. of House-holds	% of Total Hhds.	Index
Four Star Investors	3,340	1.71	34
Successful Suburbanites	13,026	6.67	100
Canadian Comfort	15,327	7.85	81
Urban Heights	4,833	2.47	58
Miners & Credit-Liners	6,895	3.53	111
Mortgages & Minivans	5,292	2.71	41
Tractors & Tradelines	16,363	8.38	146
Bills & Wills	5,807	2.97	36
Country Credit	2,257	1.16	17
Revolving Renters	3,168	1.62	35
Young Urban Struggle	5,119	2.62	55
Rural Family Blues	92,872	47.54	589
Limited Budgets	10,564	5.41	174
Towering Debt	8,231	4.21	54
Senior Survivors	724	0.37	20

HOME LANGUAGE

2001 Estimates:		% Total
English	528,331	99.08
French	860	0.16
Chinese	509	0.10
Montagnais-Naskapi	1,274	0.24
Other Languages	1,536	0.29
Multiple Responses	706	0.13
Total	533,216	100.00

BUILDING PERMITS

	1999	1998 $000	1997
Value	303,051	252,703	213,585

HOMES BUILT

	1999	1998	1997
No.	1,754	1,974	1,988

CAPITAL EXPENDITURES

(Public & Private)	2000	1999 $000,000	1998
Total Expends.	n.a.	n.a.	3,369.2
Capital Expends.	3,229.8	3,338.2	2,774.2
Construction	2,436.4	2,574.6	2,012.8
Machinery & Equip.	793.4	763.6	761.4
Repair Expends.	n.a.	n.a.	595.0
Construction	n.a.	n.a.	176.0
Machinery & Equip.	n.a.	n.a.	419.0

TAXATION

Income Class:	1997	% Total
Under $5,000	73,230	18.95
$5,000-$10,000	59,000	15.27
$10,000-$15,000	75,650	19.58
$15,000-$20,000	40,760	10.55
$20,000-$25,000	32,630	8.45
$25,000-$30,000	25,730	6.66
$30,000-$40,000	33,120	8.57
$40,000-$50,000	20,780	5.38
$50,000 +	25,470	6.59
Total Returns, No.	386,380	
Total Income, $000	7,677,025	
Total Taxable Returns	227,580	
Total Tax, $000	1,332,745	
Average Income, $	19,869	
Average Tax, $	5,856	

VITAL STATISTICS

	1997	1996	1995	1994
Births	5,416	5,747	5,859	6,339
Deaths	4,318	3,928	3,935	4,050
Natural Increase	1,098	1,819	1,924	2,289
Marriages	3,235	3,194	3,404	3,318

Note: Latest available data.

TRAVEL STATISTICS

Tourists in Canada	1999	1998
From the U.S. entering by:		
Air	18,601	18,850
Marine	3,689	3,245
Total	22,290	22,095
Other Countries:		
Air	21,780	19,704
Marine	6,579	6,312
Total	28,359	26,016
Residents of Canada Returning from the U.S. by:		
Air	3,180	3,180
Marine	127	229
Total	3,307	3,409
From Other Countries:		
Air	7,754	8,472
Marine	7,246	7,299
Total	15,000	15,771

Newfoundland

Newfoundland

Corner Brook
(Census Agglomeration)

The Census Agglomeration of Corner Brook includes: Corner Brook, C; Humber Arm South, T; Irishtown-Summerside, T; plus several smaller areas. All are in census division No. 5.

POPULATION

July 1, 2001 Estimate	27,152
% Cdn. Total	0.09
% Change, '96 -'01	-4.35
Avg. Annual Growth Rate, %	-0.89
2003 Projected Population	27,525
2006 Projected Population	28,187
2001 Households Estimate	10,279
2003 Projected Households	10,585
2006 Projected Households	11,052

INCOME

% Above/Below National Average	-14
2001 Total Income Estimate	$490,390,000
% Cdn. Total	0.07
2001 Average Hhld. Income	$47,700
2001 Per Capita	$18,100
2003 Projected Total Income	$526,650,000
2006 Projected Total Income	$588,520,000

RETAIL SALES

% Above/Below National Average	+39
2001 Retail Sales Estimate	$338,050,000
% Cdn. Total	0.12
2001 per Household	$32,900
2001 per Capita	$12,500
2001 No. of Establishments	246
2003 Projected Retail Sales	$361,860,000
2006 Projected Retail Sales	$398,460,000

POPULATION

2001 Estimates:

Total		27,152
Male		13,172
Female		13,980

Age Groups	Male	Female
0-4	681	647
5-9	753	732
10-14	860	828
15-19	986	949
20-24	1,025	1,031
25-29	934	1,009
30-34	904	999
35-39	971	1,060
40-44	1,045	1,125
45-49	1,059	1,125
50-54	945	965
55-59	769	775
60-64	642	678
65-69	540	618
70+	1,058	1,439

DAYTIME POPULATION

2001 Estimates:

Working Population	12,621
At Home Population	14,531
Total	27,152

INCOME

2001 Estimates:

Avg. Household Income	$47,708
Avg. Family Income	$50,253
Per Capita Income	$18,061
Male:	
Avg. Employment Income	$31,130
Avg. Employment Income (Full Time)	$43,683
Female:	
Avg. Employment Income	$17,834
Avg. Employment Income (Full Time)	$27,707

DISPOSABLE & DISCRETIONARY INCOME

2001 Estimates: Per Hhld.

Disposable Income	$37,876
Discretionary Income 1 (minus Food & Shelter)	$26,079
Discretionary Income 2 (minus Food, Shelter, & Other Expenditures)	$17,509

LIQUID ASSETS

1999 Estimates: Per Hhld.

Equity Investments	$45,092
Interest Bearing Investments	$51,070
Total Liquid Assets	$96,162

CREDIT DATA

July 2000:

Pool of Credit	$295,882,594
Revolving Credit, No.	41,948
Fixed Loans, No.	27,281
Avg. Credit Limit, per Person	$12,567
Avg. Spent, per Person	$6,941
Satisfactory Ratings, No. per Person	2.74
Avg. No. of Cards, per Person	0.75

LABOUR FORCE

2001 Estimates:

Male:

In the Labour Force	7,507
Participation Rate	69.0
Employed	6,403
Unemployed	1,104
Unemployment Rate	14.7
Not in Labour Force	3,371

Female:

In the Labour Force	6,472
Participation Rate	55.0
Employed	5,891
Unemployed	581
Unemployment Rate	9.0
Not in Labour Force	5,301

OCCUPATIONS BY MAJOR GROUPS

2001 Estimates:	Male	Female
Management	700	281
Business, Finance & Admin.	581	1,513
Natural & Applied Sciences & Related	294	21
Health	157	802
Social Sciences, Gov't Services & Religion	147	193
Education	251	363
Arts, Culture, Recreation & Sport	113	158
Sales & Service	1,522	2,643
Trades, Transport & Equipment Operators & Related	2,250	35
Primary Industries	289	29
Processing, Mfg. & Utilities	773	195

LEVEL OF SCHOOLING

2001 Estimates:

Population 15 years +	22,651
Less than Grade 9	3,282
Grades 9-13 w/o Certif.	6,074
Grade 9-13 with Certif.	2,512
Trade Certif. /Dip.	813
Non-Univ. w/o Certif./Dip.	933
Non-Univ. with Certif./Dip.	4,524
Univ. w/o Degree	2,719
Univ. w/o Degree/Certif.	1,218
Univ. with Certif.	1,501
Univ. with Degree	1,794

AVERAGE HOUSEHOLD EXPENDITURES

2001 Estimates:

Food	$6,072
Shelter	$7,709
Clothing	$2,113
Transportation	$6,466
Health & Personal Care	$1,968
Recr'n, Read'g & Education	$3,215
Taxes & Securities	$11,469
Other	$8,271
Total Expenditures	$47,283

PRIVATE HOUSEHOLDS

2001 Estimates:

Private Households, Total	10,279
Pop. in Private Households	26,740
Average no. per Household	2.6

FAMILIES

2001 Estimates:

Families in Private Households	8,529
Husband-Wife Families	7,402
Lone-Parent Families	1,127
Aver. No. Persons per Family	3.0
Aver. No. Sons/Daughters at Home	1.2

HOUSING

2001 Estimates:

Occupied Private Dwellings	10,279
Owned	7,420
Rented	2,859
Single-Detached House	7,245
Semi-Detached House	462
Row Houses	403
Apartment, 5 or Fewer Storeys	838
Apartment, Detached Duplex	1,192
Other Single-Attached	40
Movable Dwellings	99

VEHICLES

2001 Estimates:

Model Yrs. '81-'96, No.	11,741
% Total	76.43
Model Yrs. '97-'98, No.	2,163
% Total	14.08
'99 Vehicles registered in Model Yr. '99, No.	1,458
% Total	9.49
Total No. '81-'99	15,362

LEGAL MARITAL STATUS

2001 Estimates: (Age 15+)

Single (Never Married)	6,858
Legally Married (Not Separated)	12,805
Legally Married (Separated)	410
Widowed	1,438
Divorced	1,140

PSYTE CATEGORIES

2001 Estimates	No. of House-holds	% of Total Hhds.	Index
Town Boomers	3,049	29.66	2,926
Pick-ups & Dirt Bikes	585	5.69	682
Nesters & Young Homesteaders	156	1.52	65
Young Grey Collar	580	5.64	674
Quiet Towns	3,722	36.21	1,702
Rod & Rifle	112	1.09	47
Down, Down East	1,961	19.08	2,721
Big Country Families	31	0.30	21

FINANCIAL P$YTE

2001 Estimates	No. of House-holds	% of Total Hhds.	Index
Canadian Comfort	3,049	29.66	305
Country Credit	585	5.69	84
Revolving Renters	736	7.16	156
Rural Family Blues	2,104	20.47	254
Limited Budgets	3,722	36.21	1,165

HOME LANGUAGE

2001 Estimates:		% Total
English	27,122	99.89
Other Languages	30	0.11
Total	27,152	100.00

BUILDING PERMITS

	1999	1998	1997
		$000	
Value	17,960	24,544	22,039

HOMES BUILT

	1999	1998	1997
No.	122	97	101

TAXATION

Income Class:	1997	% Total
Under $5,000	3,730	17.72
$5,000-$10,000	3,110	14.77
$10,000-$15,000	3,700	17.58
$15,000-$20,000	2,050	9.74
$20,000-$25,000	1,910	9.07
$25,000-$30,000	1,580	7.51
$30,000-$40,000	2,050	9.74
$40,000-$50,000	1,290	6.13
$50,000 +	1,630	7.74
Total Returns, No.	21,050	
Total Income, $000	443,987	
Total Taxable Returns	12,960	
Total Tax, $000	80,025	
Average Income, $	21,092	
Average Tax, $	6,175	

VITAL STATISTICS

	1997	1996	1995	1994
Births	296	306	302	288
Deaths	238	219	197	225
Natural Increase	58	87	105	63
Marriages	208	178	195	236

Note: Latest available data.

DAILY NEWSPAPER(S)

	Circulation Average Paid
The Western Star	8,820

COMMUNITY NEWSPAPER(S)

	Total Circulation
Corner Brook: Humber Log	3,267

RADIO STATION(S)

	Power
CBY	10,000w
CFCB	1,000w
CKOZ-FM	50,000w
CKXX-FM	n.a.

TELEVISION STATION(S)

CBYT-TV
CJWN-TV

Gander
(Census Agglomeration)

The Census Agglomeration of Gander includes: Gander, T; plus several smaller areas. All are in census division No. 6.

POPULATION

July 1, 2001 Estimate	11,764
% Cdn. Total	0.04
% Change, '96 -'01	-3.62
Avg. Annual Growth Rate, %	-0.73
2003 Projected Population	12,014
2006 Projected Population	12,443
2001 Households Estimate	4,454
2003 Projected Households	4,612
2006 Projected Households	4,877

INCOME

% Above/Below National Average	-3
2001 Total Income Estimate	$240,000,000
% Cdn. Total	0.04
2001 Average Hhld. Income	$53,900
2001 Per Capita	$20,400
2003 Projected Total Income	$259,270,000
2006 Projected Total Income	$293,450,000

RETAIL SALES

% Above/Below National Average	+87
2001 Retail Sales Estimate	$197,070,000
% Cdn. Total	0.07
2001 per Household	$44,200
2001 per Capita	$16,800
2001 No. of Establishments	140
2003 Projected Retail Sales	$215,370,000
2006 Projected Retail Sales	$242,990,000

POPULATION

2001 Estimates:

Total	11,764
Male	5,814
Female	5,950

Age Groups	Male	Female
0-4	317	292
5-9	365	318
10-14	421	369
15-19	440	413
20-24	424	441
25-29	420	477
30-34	473	492
35-39	523	534
40-44	513	531
45-49	475	482
50-54	387	380
55-59	287	290
60-64	236	231
65-69	183	208
70+	350	492

DAYTIME POPULATION

2001 Estimates:

Working Population	6,378
At Home Population	5,391
Total	11,769

INCOME

2001 Estimates:

Avg. Household Income	$53,885
Avg. Family Income	$55,938
Per Capita Income	$20,402
Male:	
Avg. Employment Income	$32,087
Avg. Employment Income (Full Time)	$45,062
Female:	
Avg. Employment Income	$19,039
Avg. Employment Income (Full Time)	$29,687

DISPOSABLE & DISCRETIONARY INCOME

2001 Estimates:	Per Hhld.
Disposable Income	$42,340
Discretionary Income 1 (minus Food & Shelter)	$29,808
Discretionary Income 2 (minus Food, Shelter, & Other Expenditures)	$20,468

LIQUID ASSETS

1999 Estimates:	Per Hhld.
Equity Investments	$47,124
Interest Bearing Investments	$56,112
Total Liquid Assets	$103,236

CREDIT DATA

July 2000:	
Pool of Credit	$140,059,118
Revolving Credit, No.	19,521
Fixed Loans, No.	12,055
Avg. Credit Limit, per Person	$14,743
Avg. Spent, per Person	$7,952
Satisfactory Ratings, No. per Person	3.02
Avg. No. of Cards, per Person	0.95

LABOUR FORCE

2001 Estimates:

Male:	
In the Labour Force	3,513
Participation Rate	74.6
Employed	3,216
Unemployed	297
Unemployment Rate	8.5
Not in Labour Force	1,198
Female:	
In the Labour Force	3,205
Participation Rate	64.5
Employed	3,035
Unemployed	170
Unemployment Rate	5.3
Not in Labour Force	1,766

OCCUPATIONS BY MAJOR GROUPS

2001 Estimates:	Male	Female
Management	417	252
Business, Finance & Admin.	279	716
Natural & Applied Sciences & Related	407	31
Health	82	401
Social Sciences, Gov't Services & Religion	105	191
Education	104	130
Arts, Culture, Recreation & Sport	48	76
Sales & Service	1,032	1,284
Trades, Transport & Equipment Operators & Related	686	20
Primary Industries	148	n.a.
Processing, Mfg. & Utilities	115	9

LEVEL OF SCHOOLING

2001 Estimates:

Population 15 years +	9,682
Less than Grade 9	715
Grades 9-13 w/o Certif.	2,206
Grade 9-13 with Certif.	1,168
Trade Certif./Dip.	251
Non-Univ. w/o Certif./Dip.	437
Non-Univ. with Certif./Dip.	2,643
Univ. w/o Degree	1,342
Univ. w/o Degree/Certif.	612
Univ. with Certif.	730
Univ. with Degree	920

AVERAGE HOUSEHOLD EXPENDITURES

2001 Estimates:

Food	$6,262
Shelter	$8,461
Clothing	$2,361
Transportation	$7,126
Health & Personal Care	$2,183
Recr'n, Read'g & Education	$3,985
Taxes & Securities	$13,400
Other	$8,747
Total Expenditures	$52,525

PRIVATE HOUSEHOLDS

2001 Estimates:

Private Households, Total	4,454
Pop. in Private Households	11,561
Average no. per Household	2.6

FAMILIES

2001 Estimates:

Families in Private Households	3,638
Husband-Wife Families	3,244
Lone-Parent Families	394
Aver. No. Persons per Family	3.0
Aver. No. Sons/Daughters at Home	1.1

HOUSING

2001 Estimates:

Occupied Private Dwellings	4,454
Owned	2,901
Rented	1,553
Single-Detached House	2,747
Semi-Detached House	234
Row Houses	192
Apartment, 5+ Storeys	21
Apartment, 5 or Fewer Storeys	509
Apartment, Detached Duplex	741
Movable Dwellings	10

VEHICLES

2001 Estimates:

Model Yrs. '81-'96, No.	5,763
% Total	75.74
Model Yrs. '97-'98, No.	1,017
% Total	13.37
'99 Vehicles registered in Model Yr. '99, No.	829
% Total	10.89
Total No. '81-'99	7,609

LEGAL MARITAL STATUS

2001 Estimates: (Age 15+)

Single (Never Married)	2,912
Legally Married (Not Separated)	5,614
Legally Married (Separated)	172
Widowed	506
Divorced	478

PSYTE CATEGORIES

2001 Estimates	No. of House -holds	% of Total Hhds.	Index
Town Boomers	1,553	34.87	3,440
Old Towns' New Fringe	218	4.89	125
The New Frontier	1,103	24.76	1,642
Old Leafy Towns	83	1.86	73
Nesters & Young Homesteaders	94	2.11	90
Quiet Towns	971	21.80	1,025
Rod & Rifle	310	6.96	301
Down, Down East	64	1.44	205

FINANÇIAL P$YTE

2001 Estimates	No. of House -holds	% of Total Hhds.	Index
Canadian Comfort	1,553	34.87	359
Miners & Credit-Liners	1,103	24.76	782
Tractors & Tradelines	218	4.89	86
Bills & Wills	83	1.86	23
Revolving Renters	94	2.11	46
Rural Family Blues	374	8.40	104
Limited Budgets	971	21.80	701

Newfoundland

HOME LANGUAGE

2001 Estimates:		% Total
English	11,726.	99.68
French	10.	0.09
Arabic	14.	0.12
Tagalog (Pilipino)	14.	0.12
Total	11,764.	100.00

BUILDING PERMITS

	1999	1998	1997
		$000	
Value	29,380.	8,062.	7,507

HOMES BUILT

	1999	1998	1997
No	37.	48.	32

TAXATION

Income Class:	1997	% Total
Under $5,000	1,270.	15.51
$5,000-$10,000	1,000.	12.21
$10,000-$15,000	1,170.	14.29
$15,000-$20,000	800.	9.77
$20,000-$25,000	750.	9.16
$25,000-$30,000	700.	8.55
$30,000-$40,000	1,040.	12.70
$40,000-$50,000	660.	8.06
$50,000 +	820.	10.01
Total Returns, No.	8,190	
Total Income, $000	199,428	
Total Taxable Returns	5,690	
Total Tax, $000	38,805	
Average Income, $	24,350	
Average Tax, $	6,820	

VITAL STATISTICS

	1997	1996	1995	1994
Births	111	138	124	136
Deaths	84	65	74	84
Natural Increase	27	73	50	52
Marriages	89	89	108	83

Note: Latest available data.

COMMUNITY NEWSPAPER(S)

	Total Circulation
Gander: Beacon	5,434

RADIO STATION(S)

	Power
CBG	4,000w
CHOS-FM	50,000w
CKGA	5,000w
CKXD	1,000w

Newfoundland

Grand Falls-Windsor
(Census Agglomeration)

The Census Agglomeration of Grand Falls-Windsor includes: Grand Falls-Windsor, T; Badger, T, Botwood, T; Peterview, T; plus several smaller areas. All are in census division No. 6.

POPULATION

July 1, 2001 Estimate	19,514
% Cdn. Total	0.06
% Change, '96 -'01	-5.71
Avg. Annual Growth Rate, %	-1.17
2003 Projected Population	19,747
2006 Projected Population	20,192
2001 Households Estimate	7,218
2003 Projected Households	7,413
2006 Projected Households	7,742

INCOME

% Above/Below National Average	-16
2001 Total Income Estimate	$345,600,000
% Cdn. Total	0.05
2001 Average Hhld. Income	$47,900
2001 Per Capita	$17,700
2003 Projected Total Income	$370,660,000
2006 Projected Total Income	$415,080,000

RETAIL SALES

% Above/Below National Average	+73
2001 Retail Sales Estimate	$302,210,000
% Cdn. Total	0.11
2001 per Household	$41,900
2001 per Capita	$15,500
2001 No. of Establishments	199
2003 Projected Retail Sales	$347,390,000
2006 Projected Retail Sales	$418,890,000

POPULATION

2001 Estimates:

Total		19,514
Male		9,519
Female		9,995

Age Groups	Male	Female
0-4	447	440
5-9	499	515
10-14	625	611
15-19	745	696
20-24	743	704
25-29	657	670
30-34	624	690
35-39	689	752
40-44	779	799
45-49	770	798
50-54	679	730
55-59	571	604
60-64	498	494
65-69	414	412
70+	779	1,080

DAYTIME POPULATION

2001 Estimates:

Working Population	8,368
At Home Population	11,146
Total	19,514

INCOME

2001 Estimates:

Avg. Household Income	$47,880
Avg. Family Income	$50,114
Per Capita Income	$17,710
Male:	
Avg. Employment Income	$32,152
Avg. Employment Income (Full Time)	$48,180
Female:	
Avg. Employment Income	$16,890
Avg. Employment Income (Full Time)	$28,826

DISPOSABLE & DISCRETIONARY INCOME

2001 Estimates:	Per Hhld.
Disposable Income	$38,300
Discretionary Income 1 (minus Food & Shelter)	$26,378
Discretionary Income 2 (minus Food, Shelter, & Other Expenditures)	$17,709

LIQUID ASSETS

1999 Estimates:	Per Hhld.
Equity Investments	$43,291
Interest Bearing Investments	$50,005
Total Liquid Assets	$93,296

CREDIT DATA

July 2000:

Pool of Credit	$203,473,817
Revolving Credit, No.	29,564
Fixed Loans, No.	23,155
Avg. Credit Limit, per Person	$12,164
Avg. Spent, per Person	$6,904
Satisfactory Ratings, No. per Person	2.92
Avg. No. of Cards, per Person	0.72

LABOUR FORCE

2001 Estimates:

Male:	
In the Labour Force	5,291
Participation Rate	66.6
Employed	4,334
Unemployed	957
Unemployment Rate	18.1
Not in Labour Force	2,657
Female:	
In the Labour Force	4,254
Participation Rate	50.5
Employed	3,758
Unemployed	496
Unemployment Rate	11.7
Not in Labour Force	4,175

OCCUPATIONS BY MAJOR GROUPS

2001 Estimates:	Male	Female
Management	571	165
Business, Finance & Admin.	449	932
Natural & Applied Sciences & Related	220	18
Health	158	523
Social Sciences, Gov't Services & Religion	89	119
Education	225	221
Arts, Culture, Recreation & Sport	73	160
Sales & Service	868	1,707
Trades, Transport & Equipment Operators & Related	1,632	72
Primary Industries	306	32
Processing, Mfg. & Utilities	489	41

LEVEL OF SCHOOLING

2001 Estimates:

Population 15 years +	16,377
Less than Grade 9	2,501
Grades 9-13 w/o Certif.	5,223
Grade 9-13 with Certif.	1,520
Trade Certif. /Dip.	520
Non-Univ. w/o Certif./Dip.	411
Non-Univ. with Certif./Dip.	3,409
Univ. w/o Degree	1,587
Univ. w/o Degree/Certif.	688
Univ. with Certif.	899
Univ. with Degree	1,206

AVERAGE HOUSEHOLD EXPENDITURES

2001 Estimates:

Food	$6,297
Shelter	$7,504
Clothing	$2,101
Transportation	$6,505
Health & Personal Care	$1,945
Recr'n, Read'g & Education	$3,350
Taxes & Securities	$11,394
Other	$8,402
Total Expenditures	$47,498

PRIVATE HOUSEHOLDS

2001 Estimates:

Private Households, Total	7,218
Pop. in Private Households	19,249
Average no. per Household	2.7

FAMILIES

2001 Estimates:

Families in Private Households	6,142
Husband-Wife Families	5,513
Lone-Parent Families	629
Aver. No. Persons per Family	3.0
Aver. No. Sons/Daughters at Home	1.2

HOUSING

2001 Estimates:

Occupied Private Dwellings	7,218
Owned	5,397
Rented	1,821
Single-Detached House	5,370
Semi-Detached House	290
Row Houses	452
Apartment, 5 or Fewer Storeys	445
Apartment, Detached Duplex	612
Other Single-Attached	22
Movable Dwellings	27

VEHICLES

2001 Estimates:

Model Yrs. '81-'96, No.	9,551
% Total	84.59
Model Yrs. '97-'98, No.	1,011
% Total	8.95
'99 Vehicles registered in Model Yr. '99, No.	729
% Total	6.46
Total No. '81-'99	11,291

LEGAL MARITAL STATUS

2001 Estimates: (Age 15+)

Single (Never Married)	4,742
Legally Married (Not Separated)	9,618
Legally Married (Separated)	334
Widowed	1,046
Divorced	637

PSYTE CATEGORIES

2001 Estimates	No. of House-holds	% of Total Hhds.	Index
Old Bungalow Burbs	22	0.30	18
Town Boomers	1,534	21.25	2,097
The New Frontier	46	0.64	42
Quiet Towns	1,637	22.68	1,066
Rod & Rifle	1,516	21.00	908
Down, Down East	1,643	22.76	3,246
Big Country Families	756	10.47	734

FINANCIAL P$YTE

2001 Estimates	No. of House-holds	% of Total Hhds.	Index
Canadian Comfort	1,534	21.25	219
Miners & Credit-Liners	68	0.94	30
Rural Family Blues	3,915	54.24	672
Limited Budgets	1,637	22.68	730

HOME LANGUAGE

2001 Estimates:		% Total
English	19,414	99.49
Chinese	24	0.12
Punjabi	42	0.22
Spanish	24	0.12
Other Languages	10	0.05
Total	19,514	100.00

BUILDING PERMITS

	1999	1998	1997
		$000	
Value	9,439	6,711	7,286

HOMES BUILT

	1999	1998	1997
No.	49	59	87

TAXATION

Income Class:	1997	% Total
Under $5,000	2,920	19.96
$5,000-$10,000	2,140	14.63
$10,000-$15,000	2,540	17.36
$15,000-$20,000	1,360	9.30
$20,000-$25,000	1,200	8.20
$25,000-$30,000	1,050	7.18
$30,000-$40,000	1,420	9.71
$40,000-$50,000	890	6.08
$50,000 +	1,110	7.59
Total Returns, No.	14,630	
Total Income, $000	300,275	
Total Taxable Returns	8,610	
Total Tax, $000	52,906	
Average Income, $	20,525	
Average Tax, $	6,145	

VITAL STATISTICS

	1997	1996	1995	1994
Births	189	202	198	228
Deaths	186	182	168	136
Natural Increase	3	20	30	92
Marriages	148	116	174	129

Note: Latest available data.

COMMUNITY NEWSPAPER(S)

	Total Circulation
Grand Falls-Windsor: Advertiser	
Mon	3,464
Thu	4,133

RADIO STATION(S)

	Power
CBT	10,000w
CHOS-FM	n.a.
CKCM	10,000w
CKXG	10,000w

TELEVISION STATION(S)

CBAFT-TV
CBNAT-TV
CJCN-TV

Labrador City
(Census Agglomeration)

The Census Agglomeration of Labrador City includes: Labrador City, T; and Wabush, T; in census division No. 10.

POPULATION

July 1, 2001 Estimate 9,978
% Cdn. Total 0.03
% Change, '96 -'01 . . . . -6.67
Avg. Annual Growth Rate, % . . . . -1.37
2003 Projected Population 9,866
2006 Projected Population 9,746
2001 Households Estimate 3,649
2003 Projected Households 3,719
2006 Projected Households 3,825

INCOME

% Above/Below National Average . . . . +23
2001 Total Income Estimate $258,760,000
% Cdn. Total 0.04
2001 Average Hhld. Income $70,900
2001 Per Capita $25,900
2003 Projected Total Income . . . $273,990,000
2006 Projected Total Income $299,060,000

RETAIL SALES

% Above/Below National Average . . . . +10
2001 Retail Sales Estimate $98,480,000
% Cdn. Total 0.04
2001 per Household $27,000
2001 per Capita $9,900
2001 No. of Establishments 80
2003 Projected Retail Sales $104,000,000
2006 Projected Retail Sales $110,230,000

POPULATION

2001 Estimates:
Total 9,978
Male 5,198
Female 4,780

Age Groups	Male	Female
0-4	239	218
5-9	255	214
10-14	314	289
15-19	463	444
20-24	544	476
25-29	428	376
30-34	311	298
35-39	294	324
40-44	429	476
45-49	572	567
50-54	550	491
55-59	389	307
60-64	225	151
65-69	112	77
70+	73	72

DAYTIME POPULATION

2001 Estimates:
Working Population 5,393
At Home Population 4,585
Total 9,978

INCOME

2001 Estimates:
Avg. Household Income $70,913
Avg. Family Income $73,806
Per Capita Income $25,933
Male:
Avg. Employment Income $51,626
Avg. Employment Income
 (Full Time) $66,364
Female:
Avg. Employment Income $17,819
Avg. Employment Income
 (Full Time) $32,494

DISPOSABLE & DISCRETIONARY INCOME

2001 Estimates: Per Hhld.
Disposable Income $55,063
Discretionary Income 1
 (minus Food & Shelter) $41,524
Discretionary Income 2
 (minus Food, Shelter, & Other
 Expenditures) $30,167

LIQUID ASSETS

1999 Estimates: Per Hhld.
Equity Investments $69,438
Interest Bearing Investments $72,519
Total Liquid Assets $141,957

CREDIT DATA

July 2000:
Pool of Credit $171,832,768
Revolving Credit, No. 17,975
Fixed Loans, No. 15,809
Avg. Credit Limit, per Person $20,232
Avg. Spent, per Person $11,095
Satisfactory Ratings,
 No. per Person 3.58
Avg. No. of Cards, per Person 1.01

LABOUR FORCE

2001 Estimates:
Male:
In the Labour Force 3,627
Participation Rate 82.6
Employed 3,362
Unemployed 265
Unemployment Rate 7.3
Not in Labour Force 763
Female:
In the Labour Force 2,314
Participation Rate 57.0
Employed 1,888
Unemployed 426
Unemployment Rate 18.4
Not in Labour Force 1,745

OCCUPATIONS BY MAJOR GROUPS

2001 Estimates:	Male	Female
Management	205	141
Business, Finance & Admin.	105	429
Natural & Applied Sciences & Related	200	22
Health	10	128
Social Sciences, Gov't Services & Religion	50	53
Education	73	156
Arts, Culture, Recreation & Sport	73	35
Sales & Service	401	1,135
Trades, Transport & Equipment Operators & Related	1,716	39
Primary Industries	334	37
Processing, Mfg. & Utilities	351	n.a.

LEVEL OF SCHOOLING

2001 Estimates:
Population 15 years + ... 8,449
Less than Grade 9 460
Grades 9-13 w/o Certif. 2,095
Grade 9-13 with Certif. 1,247
Trade Certif. /Dip. 307
Non-Univ. w/o Certif./Dip. 305
Non-Univ. with Certif./Dip. 2,306
Univ. w/o Degree 1,199
 Univ. w/o Degree/Certif. 617
 Univ. with Certif. 582
Univ. with Degree 530

AVERAGE HOUSEHOLD EXPENDITURES

2001 Estimates:
Food $7,129
Shelter $8,951
Clothing $2,813
Transportation $9,390
Health & Personal Care $2,136
Recr'n, Read'g & Education $5,486
Taxes & Securities $19,069
Other $11,656
Total Expenditures $66,630

PRIVATE HOUSEHOLDS

2001 Estimates:
Private Households, Total 3,649
Pop. in Private Households 9,925
Average no. per Household 2.7

FAMILIES

2001 Estimates:
Families in Private Households 3,238
Husband-Wife Families 2,894
Lone-Parent Families 344
Aver. No. Persons per Family 3.2
Aver. No. Sons/Daughters
 at Home 1.3

HOUSING

2001 Estimates:
Occupied Private Dwellings 3,649
 Owned 2,874
 Rented 775
Single-Detached House 1,680
Semi-Detached House 553
Row Houses 622
Apartment, 5+ Storeys 48
Apartment, 5 or Fewer Storeys 297
Apartment, Detached Duplex 22
Other Single-Attached 11
Movable Dwellings 416

VEHICLES

2001 Estimates:
Model Yrs. '81-'96, No. 5,395
 % Total 83.73
Model Yrs. '97-'98, No. 616
 % Total 9.56
'99 Vehicles registered in
 Model Yr. '99, No. 432
 % Total 6.70
Total No. '81-'99 6,443

LEGAL MARITAL STATUS

2001 Estimates: (Age 15+)
Single (Never Married) 2,994
Legally Married
 (Not Separated) 4,839
Legally Married (Separated) 158
Widowed 144
Divorced 314

PSYTE CATEGORIES

2001 Estimates	No. of House-holds	% of Total Hhds.	Index
Northern Lights	3,592	98.44	19,888
The New Frontier	56	1.53	102

FINANCIAL P$YTE

2001 Estimates	No. of House-holds	% of Total Hhds.	Index
Successful Suburbanites	3,592	98.44	1,483
Miners & Credit-Liners	56	1.53	48

HOME LANGUAGE

2001 Estimates		% Total
English	9,671	96.92
French	216	2.16
Italian	10	0.10
Portuguese	14	0.14
Multiple Responses	67	0.67
Total	9,978	100.00

Newfoundland

BUILDING PERMITS

	1999	1998 $000	1997
Value	5,236	5,523	3,083

HOMES BUILT

	1999	1998	1997
No.	5	13	2

TAXATION

Income Class:	1997	% Total
Under $5,000	1,700	23.55
$5,000-$10,000	790	10.94
$10,000-$15,000	580	8.03
$15,000-$20,000	370	5.12
$20,000-$25,000	280	3.88
$25,000-$30,000	300	4.16
$30,000-$40,000	440	6.09
$40,000-$50,000	380	5.26
$50,000 +	2,380	32.96

Total Returns, No. 7,220
Total Income, $000 . . . 235,313
Total Taxable
 Returns 4,790
Total Tax, $000 49,236
Average Income, $. . . . 32,592
Average Tax, $ 10,279

VITAL STATISTICS

	1997	1996	1995	1994
Births	108	106	117	104
Deaths	23	27	24	20
Natural Increase	85	79	93	84
Marriages	64	59	46	45

Note: Latest available data.

COMMUNITY NEWSPAPER(S)

	Total Circulation
Labrador City: The Aurora	3,203

RADIO STATION(S)

	Power
CBDO-FM	1,000w
CBDQ-FM	n.a.
CBSI	1,000w
CBSI-FM	n.a.
CFLW	n.a.
CJRM-FM	500w

TELEVISION STATION(S)

CBNLT-TV

Newfoundland

St. John's
(Census Metropolitan Area)

POPULATION

July 1, 2001 Estimate	173,833
% Cdn. Total	0.56
% Change, '96 -'01	-1.77
Avg. Annual Growth Rate, %	-0.36
2003 Projected Population	174,324
2006 Projected Population	175,204
2001 Households Estimate	65,442
2003 Projected Households	66,716
2006 Projected Households	68,694

INCOME

% Above/Below National Average	-4
2001 Total Income Estimate	$3,521,000,000
% Cdn. Total	0.54
2001 Average Hhld. Income	$53,800
2001 Per Capita	$20,300
2003 Projected Total Income	$3,717,050,000
2006 Projected Total Income	$4,057,700,000

RETAIL SALES

% Above/Below National Average	+22
2001 Retail Sales Estimate	$1,904,660,000
% Cdn. Total	0.68
2001 per Household	$29,100
2001 per Capita	$11,000
2001 No. of Establishments	1,225
2003 Projected Retail Sales	$2,014,820,000
2006 Projected Retail Sales	$2,168,730,000

POPULATION

2001 Estimates:

Total		173,833
Male		83,691
Female		90,142

Age Groups	Male	Female
0-4	4,698	4,507
5-9	5,162	5,022
10-14	5,757	5,564
15-19	6,260	6,036
20-24	6,728	6,696
25-29	6,784	7,048
30-34	6,844	7,433
35-39	6,922	7,622
40-44	6,882	7,527
45-49	6,541	6,981
50-54	5,653	5,979
55-59	4,446	4,619
60-64	3,357	3,567
65-69	2,580	2,999
70+	5,077	8,542

DAYTIME POPULATION

2001 Estimates:

Working Population	90,171
At Home Population	83,662
Total	173,833

INCOME

2001 Estimates:

Avg. Household Income	$53,803
Avg. Family Income	$58,144
Per Capita Income	$20,255
Male:	
Avg. Employment Income	$33,284
Avg. Employment Income (Full Time)	$46,585
Female:	
Avg. Employment Income	$21,487
Avg. Employment Income (Full Time)	$31,659

DISPOSABLE & DISCRETIONARY INCOME

2001 Estimates:	Per Hhld.
Disposable Income	$42,005
Discretionary Income 1 (minus Food & Shelter)	$28,962
Discretionary Income 2 (minus Food, Shelter, & Other Expenditures)	$20,524

LIQUID ASSETS

1999 Estimates:	Per Hhld.
Equity Investments	$54,783
Interest Bearing Investments	$57,550
Total Liquid Assets	$112,333

CREDIT DATA

July 2000:

Pool of Credit	$1,873,740,713
Revolving Credit, No.	252,742
Fixed Loans, No.	134,710
Avg. Credit Limit, per Person	$13,698
Avg. Spent, per Person	$7,637
Satisfactory Ratings, No. per Person	2.70
Avg. No. of Cards, per Person	0.87

LABOUR FORCE

2001 Estimates:

Male:	
In the Labour Force	49,739
Participation Rate	73.1
Employed	44,940
Unemployed	4,799
Unemployment Rate	9.6
Not in Labour Force	18,335
Female:	
In the Labour Force	46,766
Participation Rate	62.3
Employed	43,487
Unemployed	3,279
Unemployment Rate	7.0
Not in Labour Force	28,283

OCCUPATIONS BY MAJOR GROUPS

2001 Estimates:	Male	Female
Management	5,986	2,558
Business, Finance & Admin.	5,704	14,317
Natural & Applied Sciences & Related	4,567	791
Health	1,392	5,314
Social Sciences, Gov't Services & Religion	1,456	1,528
Education	2,022	3,091
Arts, Culture, Recreation & Sport	1,170	1,195
Sales & Service	11,154	14,976
Trades, Transport & Equipment Operators & Related	10,756	363
Primary Industries	1,266	149
Processing, Mfg. & Utilities	1,736	420

LEVEL OF SCHOOLING

2001 Estimates:

Population 15 years +	143,123
Less than Grade 9	12,677
Grades 9-13 w/o Certif.	33,755
Grade 9-13 with Certif.	14,203
Trade Certif. /Dip.	3,585
Non-Univ. w/o Certif./Dip.	6,562
Non-Univ. with Certif./Dip.	29,307
Univ. w/o Degree	22,825
Univ. w/o Degree/Certif.	11,154
Univ. with Certif.	11,671
Univ. with Degree	20,209

AVERAGE HOUSEHOLD EXPENDITURES

2001 Estimates:

Food	$6,184
Shelter	$9,045
Clothing	$2,193
Transportation	$6,452
Health & Personal Care	$1,931
Recr'n, Read'g & Education	$3,857
Taxes & Securities	$14,112
Other	$8,535
Total Expenditures	$52,309

PRIVATE HOUSEHOLDS

2001 Estimates:

Private Households, Total	65,442
Pop. in Private Households	170,554
Average no. per Household	2.6

FAMILIES

2001 Estimates:

Families in Private Households	51,633
Husband-Wife Families	43,095
Lone-Parent Families	8,538
Aver. No. Persons per Family	3.1
Aver. No. Sons/Daughters at Home	1.3

HOUSING

2001 Estimates:

Occupied Private Dwellings	65,442
Owned	44,305
Rented	21,137
Single-Detached House	35,603
Semi-Detached House	3,049
Row Houses	6,331
Apartment, 5+ Storeys	624
Owned Apartment, 5+ Storeys	31
Apartment, 5 or Fewer Storeys	5,324
Apartment, Detached Duplex	13,919
Other Single-Attached	269
Movable Dwellings	323

VEHICLES

2001 Estimates:

Model Yrs. '81-'96, No.	78,488
% Total	76.15
Model Yrs. '97-'98, No.	14,565
% Total	14.13
'99 Vehicles registered in Model Yr. '99, No.	10,022
% Total	9.72
Total No. '81-'99	103,075

RADIO STATION DATA

Station	Market	Format	Wkly. Reach%*	Aver. Hrs. Tuned
All Stations			97	22.3
CBN	St. John's	News, Talk	25	11.1
CBN-FM	St. John's	Multi-format	5	11.8
CHOZ-FM	St. John's	AOR	42	10.1
CJYQ	St. John's	Oldies	10	4.7
CKIX-FM	St. John's	Country	31	8.4
CKVO	St. John's	News	n.a.	n.a.
VOAR	Mt. Pearl	Gospel	n.a.	n.a.
VOCM	St. John's	Adult Contemp.	52	11.2
VOCM-FM	St. John's	Adult Contemp.	35	8.7
VOWR	St. John's	Multi-format	n.a.	n.a.

BBM Spring 2000 Radio Reach Survey; area coverage.
*Mon-Sun 5a.m - 1a.m , All Persons 12+

TV STATION DATA

Station	Market	Network Affiliation	Wkly. Reach%*	Aver. Hrs. Tuned
All Stations			92	24.0
A & E	n.a.	Ind.	24	2.7
ASN	Maritimes	CTV	34	3.0
CBNT	St. John's	CBC	65	4.6
CHCH	Toronto/Hamilton	Ind.	12	1.4
CITV	Edmonton	Ind.	18	2.1
CJON	St. John's	CTV	79	7.0
DSCVRY	n.a.	Ind.	10	1.9
FAMILY	n.a.	Ind.	12	2.6
HDLSP	n.a.	Ind.	4	2.6
HISTTV	n.a.	Ind.	5	2.2
MMM	n.a.	Ind.	6	2.4
MMUSIC	n.a.	Ind.	8	1.9
NEWSWD	n.a.	CBC	7	2.4
OTHERS	n.a.	n.a.	7	2.4
PRIME	n.a.	Ind.	16	2.6
SHWCSE	n.a.	Ind.	8	2.5
SNET	n.a.	CTV	8	2.4
SPACE	n.a.	Ind.	7	3.0
STAR	n.a.	Ind.	8	1.6
TLC	n.a.	Ind.	13	2.4
TMN	Toronto	Ind.	7	3.2
TNN	Nashville TN	Ind.	11	1.8
TOON	n.a.	Ind.	6	2.8
TREE	n.a.	Ind.	9	5.1
TSN	n.a.	Ind.	21	4.0
VCR	n.a.	n.a.	22	3.5
VISION	n.a.	Ind.	10	1.8
WBZ	Boston MA	CBS	24	2.5
WCVB	Boston MA	ABC	40	2.0
WHDH	Boston MA	NBC	37	2.3
WTBS	Atlanta GA	Ind.	24	3.8
WTN	n.a.	Ind.	9	2.0
WTVS	Detroit MI	PBS	13	1.3
WUHF	Rochester NY	FOX	27	2.4
YTV	n.a.	Ind.	12	2.3

BBM Spring 2000 TV Reach Survey;, CMA coverage.
*Mon-Sun 6a.m - 2a.m , All Persons 2 +

St. John's
(Census Metropolitan Area)
(Cont'd)

LEGAL MARITAL STATUS

2001 Estimates: (Age 15+)

Single (Never Married)	49,838
Legally Married (Not Separated)	74,073
Legally Married (Separated)	3,296
Widowed	8,396
Divorced	7,520

PSYTE CATEGORIES

2001 Estimates	No. of House-holds	% of Total Hhds.	Index
Urban Gentry	1,704	2.60	145
Suburban Executives	1,359	2.08	145
Mortgaged in Suburbia	174	0.27	19
Technocrafts & Bureaucrats	5,150	7.87	280
Boomers & Teens	213	0.33	18
Stable Suburban Families	561	0.86	66
Small City Elite	5,310	8.11	473
Old Bungalow Burbs	1,690	2.58	156
Aging Erudites	4,306	6.58	436
Satellite Suburbs	2,208	3.37	118
Kindergarten Boom	5,276	8.06	307
Blue Collar Winners	65	0.10	4
Old Towns' New Fringe	14,697	22.46	574
Conservative Homebodies	3,450	5.27	146
High Rise Sunsets	820	1.25	88
Young Urban Professionals	527	0.81	42
Young Urban Mix	757	1.16	55
University Enclaves	5,119	7.82	383
Young City Singles	288	0.44	19
Town Renters	1,729	2.64	306
Nesters & Young Homesteaders	1,060	1.62	69
Rod & Rifle	1,512	2.31	100
Struggling Downtowns	6,214	9.50	302
Aged Pensioners	490	0.75	56
Old Grey Towers	234	0.36	65

FINANCIAL PSYTE

2001 Estimates	No. of House-holds	% of Total Hhds.	Index
Four Star Investors	3,276	5.01	100
Successful Suburbanites	5,885	8.99	136
Canadian Comfort	7,583	11.59	119
Urban Heights	4,833	7.39	172
Miners & Credit-Liners	1,690	2.58	82
Mortgages & Minivans	5,276	8.06	122
Tractors & Tradelines	14,697	22.46	393
Bills & Wills	4,207	6.43	78
Revolving Renters	1,880	2.87	62
Young Urban Struggle	5,119	7.82	165
Rural Family Blues	1,512	2.31	29
Towering Debt	8,231	12.58	161
Senior Survivors	724	1.11	59

HOME LANGUAGE

2001 Estimates:		% Total
English	172,061	98.98
French	197	0.11
Chinese	391	0.22
Vietnamese	91	0.05
Other Languages	737	0.42
Multiple Responses	356	0.20
Total	173,833	100.00

BUILDING PERMITS

	1999	1998	1997
		$000	
Value	173,807	150,885	123,026

HOMES BUILT

	1999	1998	1997
No	725	791	1,036

TAXATION

Income Class:	1997	% Total
Under $5,000	18,810	15.48
$5,000-$10,000	16,910	13.91
$10,000-$15,000	19,200	15.80
$15,000-$20,000	11,430	9.40
$20,000-$25,000	11,260	9.26
$25,000-$30,000	9,800	8.06
$30,000-$40,000	13,630	11.21
$40,000-$50,000	8,830	7.27
$50,000 +	11,720	9.64
Total Returns, No.	121,540	
Total Income, $000	2,995,061	
Total Taxable Returns	79,270	
Total Tax, $000	605,268	
Average Income, $	24,643	
Average Tax, $	7,636	

VITAL STATISTICS

	1997	1996	1995	1994
Births	1,925	1,981	1,933	2,070
Deaths	1,254	1,149	1,172	1,217
Natural Increase	671	832	761	853
Marriages	1,103	1,102	1,099	1,075

Note: Latest available data.

DAILY NEWSPAPER(S)

	Circulation Average Paid
The Telegram	
Sat	57,811
Sun	33,543
Mon-Fri	33,007

COMMUNITY NEWSPAPER(S)

	Total Circulation
Paradise: The Shoreline News	13,800
Placentia: The Charter	1,404
St. John's: The Express	45,978

Newfoundland

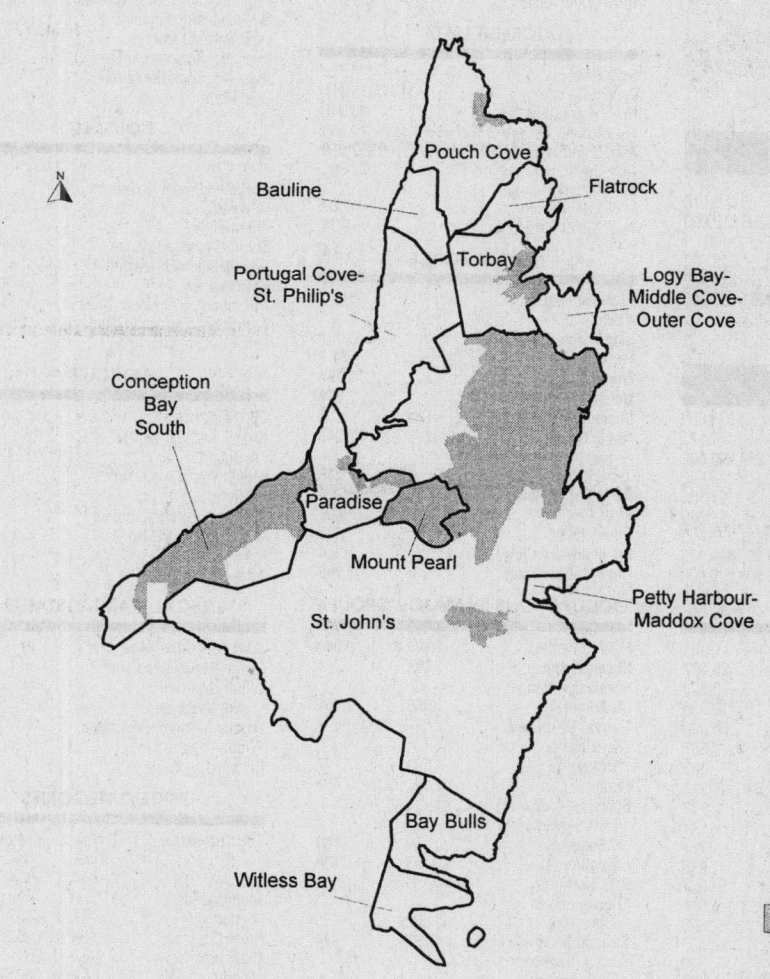

Pouch Cove
Bauline
Flatrock
Portugal Cove-St. Philip's
Torbay
Logy Bay-Middle Cove-Outer Cove
Conception Bay South
Paradise
Mount Pearl
Petty Harbour-Maddox Cove
St. John's
Bay Bulls
Witless Bay

Urban Areas

Newfoundland

Conception Bay South

(Town)
St. John's , CMA

In census division 1.

POPULATION

July 1, 2001 Estimate	20,492
% Cdn. Total	0.07
% Change, '96 -'01	4.63
Avg. Annual Growth Rate, %	0.91
2003 Projected Population	21,198
2006 Projected Population	22,272
2001 Households Estimate	7,186
2003 Projected Households	7,562
2006 Projected Households	8,155

INCOME

% Above/Below National Average	-18
2001 Total Income Estimate	$356,010,000
% Cdn. Total	0.05
2001 Average Hhld. Income	$49,500
2001 Per Capita	$17,400
2003 Projected Total Income	$391,290,000
2006 Projected Total Income	$452,960,000

RETAIL SALES

% Above/Below National Average	-71
2001 Retail Sales Estimate	$53,850,000
% Cdn. Total	0.02
2001 per Household	$7,500
2001 per Capita	$2,600
2001 No. of Establishments	103
2003 Projected Retail Sales	$58,680,000
2006 Projected Retail Sales	$66,220,000

POPULATION

2001 Estimates:

Total		20,492
Male		10,102
Female		10,390

Age Groups	Male	Female
0-4	577	587
5-9	665	666
10-14	762	733
15-19	817	748
20-24	773	744
25-29	747	781
30-34	819	888
35-39	876	937
40-44	881	911
45-49	800	825
50-54	674	693
55-59	526	520
60-64	389	381
65-69	287	304
70+	509	672

DAYTIME POPULATION

2001 Estimates:

Working Population	1,601
At Home Population	9,910
Total	11,511

INCOME

2001 Estimates:

Avg. Household Income	$49,542
Avg. Family Income	$52,197
Per Capita Income	$17,373
Male:	
Avg. Employment Income	$28,813
Avg. Employment Income (Full Time)	$39,931
Female:	
Avg. Employment Income	$19,075
Avg. Employment Income (Full Time)	$29,013

DISPOSABLE & DISCRETIONARY INCOME

2001 Estimates:	Per Hhld.
Disposable Income	$39,442
Discretionary Income 1 (minus Food & Shelter)	$27,384
Discretionary Income 2 (minus Food, Shelter, & Other Expenditures)	$18,863

LIQUID ASSETS

1999 Estimates:	Per Hhld.
Equity Investments	$42,329
Interest Bearing Investments	$51,206
Total Liquid Assets	$93,535

CREDIT DATA

July 2000:

Pool of Credit	$171,675,811
Revolving Credit, No.	23,340
Fixed Loans, No.	14,253
Avg. Credit Limit, per Person	$12,969
Avg. Spent, per Person	$7,305
Satisfactory Ratings, No. per Person	2.67
Avg. No. of Cards, per Person	0.76

LABOUR FORCE

2001 Estimates:

Male:	
In the Labour Force	6,051
Participation Rate	74.7
Employed	5,407
Unemployed	644
Unemployment Rate	10.6
Not in Labour Force	2,047
Female:	
In the Labour Force	5,245
Participation Rate	62.4
Employed	4,807
Unemployed	438
Unemployment Rate	8.4
Not in Labour Force	3,159

OCCUPATIONS BY MAJOR GROUPS

2001 Estimates:	Male	Female
Management	588	244
Business, Finance & Admin.	566	1,751
Natural & Applied Sciences & Related	603	72
Health	181	488
Social Sciences, Gov't Services & Religion	58	130
Education	153	256
Arts, Culture, Recreation & Sport	52	73
Sales & Service	1,092	1,774
Trades, Transport & Equipment Operators & Related	2,044	65
Primary Industries	232	47
Processing, Mfg. & Utilities	256	59

LEVEL OF SCHOOLING

2001 Estimates:

Population 15 years +	16,502
Less than Grade 9	1,620
Grades 9-13 w/o Certif.	4,290
Grade 9-13 with Certif.	1,873
Trade Certif. /Dip.	398
Non-Univ. w/o Certif./Dip.	849
Non-Univ. with Certif./Dip.	4,055
Univ. w/o Degree	2,111
Univ. w/o Degree/Certif.	814
Univ. with Certif.	1,297
Univ. with Degree	1,306

AVERAGE HOUSEHOLD EXPENDITURES

2001 Estimates:

Food	$5,942
Shelter	$8,117
Clothing	$1,982
Transportation	$6,559
Health & Personal Care	$1,882
Recr'n, Read'g & Education	$3,744
Taxes & Securities	$12,450
Other	$8,328
Total Expenditures	$49,004

PRIVATE HOUSEHOLDS

2001 Estimates:

Private Households, Total	7,186
Pop. in Private Households	20,029
Average no. per Household	2.8

FAMILIES

2001 Estimates:

Families in Private Households	6,216
Husband-Wife Families	5,548
Lone-Parent Families	668
Aver. No. Persons per Family	3.2
Aver. No. Sons/Daughters at Home	1.3

HOUSING

2001 Estimates:

Occupied Private Dwellings	7,186
Owned	5,815
Rented	1,371
Single-Detached House	5,746
Semi-Detached House	103
Row Houses	28
Apartment, 5 or Fewer Storeys	102
Apartment, Detached Duplex	1,162
Other Single-Attached	45

VEHICLES

2001 Estimates:

Model Yrs. '81-'96, No.	9,817
% Total	83.93
Model Yrs. '97-'98, No.	1,121
% Total	9.58
'99 Vehicles registered in Model Yr. '99, No.	759
% Total	6.49
Total No. '81-'99	11,697

LEGAL MARITAL STATUS

2001 Estimates: (Age 15+)

Single (Never Married)	4,914
Legally Married (Not Separated)	9,727
Legally Married (Separated)	361
Widowed	762
Divorced	738

PSYTE CATEGORIES

2001 Estimates	No. of House-holds	% of Total Hhds.	Index
Mortgaged in Suburbia	174	2.42	174
Small City Elite	1,454	20.23	1,181
Old Towns' New Fringe	4,493	62.52	1,597
Rod & Rifle	1,065	14.82	641

FINANCIAL P$YTE

2001 Estimates	No. of House-holds	% of Total Hhds.	Index
Successful Suburbanites	174	2.42	36
Canadian Comfort	1,454	20.23	208
Tractors & Tradelines	4,493	62.52	1,093
Rural Family Blues	1,065	14.82	184

HOME LANGUAGE

2001 Estimates:		% Total
English	20,438	99.74
Chinese	26	0.13
Other Languages	11	0.05
Multiple Responses	17	0.08
Total	20,492	100.00

BUILDING PERMITS

	1999	1998	1997
		$000	
Value	13,135	8,689	7,769

HOMES BUILT

	1999	1998	1997
No.	91	68	129

TAXATION

Income Class:	1997	% Total
Under $5,000	2,400	17.24
$5,000-$10,000	1,930	13.86
$10,000-$15,000	2,290	16.45
$15,000-$20,000	1,390	9.99
$20,000-$25,000	1,300	9.34
$25,000-$30,000	1,190	8.55
$30,000-$40,000	1,600	11.49
$40,000-$50,000	890	6.39
$50,000 +	950	6.82
Total Returns, No.	13,920	
Total Income, $000	294,294	
Total Taxable Returns	8,880	
Total Tax, $000	52,200	
Average Income, $	21,142	
Average Tax, $	5,878	

VITAL STATISTICS

	1997	1996	1995	1994
Births	235	282	252	263
Deaths	104	118	99	119
Natural Increase	131	164	153	144
Marriages	109	94	92	99

Note: Latest available data.

MEDIA INFO
see St. John's, , CMA

Mount Pearl
(City)
St. John's , CMA
In census division 1.

POPULATION

July 1, 2001 Estimate	26,772
% Cdn. Total	0.09
% Change, '96 -'01	3.19
Avg. Annual Growth Rate, %	0.63
2003 Projected Population	27,496
2006 Projected Population	28,603
2001 Households Estimate	9,528
2003 Projected Households	9,970
2006 Projected Households	10,658

INCOME

% Above/Below National Average	+2
2001 Total Income Estimate	$573,920,000
% Cdn. Total	0.09
2001 Average Hhld. Income	$60,200
2001 Per Capita	$21,400
2003 Projected Total Income	$619,930,000
2006 Projected Total Income	$699,330,000

RETAIL SALES

% Above/Below National Average	+2
2001 Retail Sales Estimate	$244,800,000
% Cdn. Total	0.09
2001 per Household	$25,700
2001 per Capita	$9,100
2001 No. of Establishments	131
2003 Projected Retail Sales	$265,890,000
2006 Projected Retail Sales	$299,370,000

POPULATION

2001 Estimates:

Total		26,772
Male		13,079
Female		13,693

Age Groups	Male	Female
0-4	730	709
5-9	851	811
10-14	1,024	963
15-19	1,136	1,082
20-24	1,161	1,105
25-29	1,061	1,084
30-34	1,015	1,130
35-39	1,065	1,204
40-44	1,147	1,285
45-49	1,149	1,226
50-54	958	974
55-59	661	662
60-64	412	435
65-69	266	321
70+	443	702

DAYTIME POPULATION

2001 Estimates:

Working Population	5,929
At Home Population	11,560
Total	17,489

INCOME

2001 Estimates:

Avg. Household Income	$60,235
Avg. Family Income	$62,943
Per Capita Income	$21,437
Male:	
Avg. Employment Income	$35,150
Avg. Employment Income (Full Time)	$46,874
Female:	
Avg. Employment Income	$22,121
Avg. Employment Income (Full Time)	$31,739

DISPOSABLE & DISCRETIONARY INCOME

2001 Estimates:	*Per Hhld.*
Disposable Income	$47,017
Discretionary Income 1 (minus Food & Shelter)	$32,458
Discretionary Income 2 (minus Food, Shelter, & Other Expenditures)	$22,980

LIQUID ASSETS

1999 Estimates:	*Per Hhld.*
Equity Investments	$60,982
Interest Bearing Investments	$62,734
Total Liquid Assets	$123,716

CREDIT DATA

July 2000:

Pool of Credit	$299,793,360
Revolving Credit, No.	40,634
Fixed Loans, No.	23,364
Avg. Credit Limit, per Person	$14,628
Avg. Spent, per Person	$8,203
Satisfactory Ratings, No. per Person	2.96
Avg. No. of Cards, per Person	0.93

LABOUR FORCE

2001 Estimates:
Male:

In the Labour Force	8,146
Participation Rate	77.8
Employed	7,582
Unemployed	564
Unemployment Rate	6.9
Not in Labour Force	2,328
Female:	
In the Labour Force	7,717
Participation Rate	68.8
Employed	7,245
Unemployed	472
Unemployment Rate	6.1
Not in Labour Force	3,493

OCCUPATIONS BY MAJOR GROUPS

2001 Estimates:	Male	Female
Management	1,124	458
Business, Finance & Admin.	1,101	2,557
Natural & Applied Sciences & Related	690	134
Health	205	967
Social Sciences, Gov't Services & Religion	210	253
Education	190	371
Arts, Culture, Recreation & Sport	261	149
Sales & Service	1,928	2,405
Trades, Transport & Equipment Operators & Related	1,676	58
Primary Industries	90	n.a.
Processing, Mfg. & Utilities	293	25

LEVEL OF SCHOOLING

2001 Estimates:

Population 15 years +	21,684
Less than Grade 9	1,262
Grades 9-13 w/o Certif.	4,817
Grade 9-13 with Certif.	2,312
Trade Certif. /Dip.	603
Non-Univ. w/o Certif./Dip.	1,183
Non-Univ. with Certif./Dip.	5,434
Univ. w/o Degree	3,842
Univ. w/o Degree/Certif.	1,885
Univ. with Certif.	1,957
Univ. with Degree	2,231

AVERAGE HOUSEHOLD EXPENDITURES

2001 Estimates:

Food	$6,875
Shelter	$9,985
Clothing	$2,469
Transportation	$7,327
Health & Personal Care	$2,084
Recr'n, Read'g & Education	$4,286
Taxes & Securities	$15,877
Other	$9,000
Total Expenditures	$57,903

PRIVATE HOUSEHOLDS

2001 Estimates:

Private Households, Total	9,528
Pop. in Private Households	26,604
Average no. per Household	2.8

FAMILIES

2001 Estimates:

Families in Private Households	8,245
Husband-Wife Families	7,079
Lone-Parent Families	1,166
Aver. No. Persons per Family	3.2
Aver. No. Sons/Daughters at Home	1.3

HOUSING

2001 Estimates:

Occupied Private Dwellings	9,528
Owned	6,571
Rented	2,957
Single-Detached House	4,283
Semi-Detached House	530
Row Houses	879
Apartment, 5 or Fewer Storeys	228
Apartment, Detached Duplex	3,608

VEHICLES

2001 Estimates:

Model Yrs. '81-'96, No.	10,775
% Total	73.70
Model Yrs. '97-'98, No.	2,315
% Total	15.83
'99 Vehicles registered in Model Yr. '99, No.	1,531
% Total	10.47
Total No. '81-'99	14,621

LEGAL MARITAL STATUS

2001 Estimates: (Age 15+)

Single (Never Married)	6,916
Legally Married (Not Separated)	12,411
Legally Married (Separated)	463
Widowed	850
Divorced	1,044

PSYTE CATEGORIES

2001 Estimates	No. of House-holds	% of Total Hhds.	Index
Technocrafts & Bureaucrats	1,784	18.72	665
Old Bungalow Burbs	666	6.99	422
Satellite Suburbs	1,803	18.92	660
Kindergarten Boom	3,109	32.63	1,244
Old Towns' New Fringe	1,103	11.58	296
Conservative Homebodies	724	7.60	211
Struggling Downtowns	101	1.06	34
Old Grey Towers	234	2.46	443

Newfoundland

FINANCIAL P$YTE

2001 Estimates	No. of House-holds	% of Total Hhds.	Index
Successful Suburbanites	1,784	18.72	282
Canadian Comfort	1,803	18.92	195
Miners & Credit-Liners	666	6.99	221
Mortgages & Minivans	3,109	32.63	494
Tractors & Tradelines	1,103	11.58	202
Bills & Wills	724	7.60	92
Towering Debt	101	1.06	14
Senior Survivors	234	2.46	130

HOME LANGUAGE

2001 Estimates:		% Total
English	26,606	99.38
Greek	31	0.12
Norwegian	16	0.06
Other Languages	68	0.25
Multiple Responses	51	0.19
Total	26,772	100.00

BUILDING PERMITS

	1999	1998	1997
		$000	
Value	19,988	16,919	17,797

HOMES BUILT

	1999	1998	1997
No.	63	122	84

TAXATION

Income Class:	1997	% Total
Under $5,000	2,600	14.71
$5,000-$10,000	2,190	12.39
$10,000-$15,000	2,480	14.04
$15,000-$20,000	1,630	9.22
$20,000-$25,000	1,760	9.96
$25,000-$30,000	1,570	8.89
$30,000-$40,000	2,290	12.96
$40,000-$50,000	1,510	8.55
$50,000+	1,650	9.34
Total Returns, No.	17,670	
Total Income, $000	438,730	
Total Taxable Returns	12,390	
Total Tax, $000	86,628	
Average Income, $	24,829	
Average Tax, $	6,992	

VITAL STATISTICS

	1997	1996	1995	1994
Births	269	299	300	298
Deaths	109	91	96	82
Natural Increase	160	208	204	216
Marriages	74	102	104	89

Note: Latest available data.

MEDIA INFO
see St. John's , CMA

Newfoundland

St. John's
(City)
St. John's , CMA

In census division 1.

POPULATION

July 1, 2001 Estimate	98,367
% Cdn. Total	0.32
% Change, '96 -'01	-5.09
Avg. Annual Growth Rate, %	-1.04
2003 Projected Population	96,889
2006 Projected Population	94,751
2001 Households Estimate	39,053
2003 Projected Households	39,155
2006 Projected Households	39,290

INCOME

% Above/Below National Average	-2
2001 Total Income Estimate	$2,024,170,000
% Cdn. Total	0.31
2001 Average Hhld. Income	$51,800
2001 Per Capita	$20,600
2003 Projected Total Income	$2,093,630,000
2006 Projected Total Income	$2,213,830,000

RETAIL SALES

% Above/Below National Average	+68
2001 Retail Sales Estimate	$1,477,390,000
% Cdn. Total	0.53
2001 per Household	$37,800
2001 per Capita	$15,000
2001 No. of Establishments	841
2003 Projected Retail Sales	$1,551,050,000
2006 Projected Retail Sales	$1,647,250,000

POPULATION

2001 Estimates:

Total		98,367
Male		46,502
Female		51,865

Age Groups	Male	Female
0-4	2,596	2,425
5-9	2,693	2,604
10-14	2,901	2,814
15-19	3,199	3,116
20-24	3,751	3,839
25-29	3,966	4,157
30-34	3,848	4,165
35-39	3,660	4,105
40-44	3,540	3,791
45-49	3,451	3,791
50-54	3,121	3,421
55-59	2,582	2,794
60-64	2,044	2,270
65-69	1,646	2,001
70+	3,504	6,346

DAYTIME POPULATION

2001 Estimates:

Working Population	79,909
At Home Population	49,405
Total	129,314

INCOME

2001 Estimates:

Avg. Household Income	$51,831
Avg. Family Income	$57,539
Per Capita Income	$20,578
Male:	
Avg. Employment Income	$33,919
Avg. Employment Income (Full Time)	$48,333
Female:	
Avg. Employment Income	$21,804
Avg. Employment Income (Full Time)	$32,452

DISPOSABLE & DISCRETIONARY INCOME

2001 Estimates:	Per Hhld.
Disposable Income	$40,279
Discretionary Income 1 (minus Food & Shelter)	$27,594
Discretionary Income 2 (minus Food, Shelter, & Other Expenditures)	$19,751

LIQUID ASSETS

1999 Estimates:	Per Hhld.
Equity Investments	$54,451
Interest Bearing Investments	$56,308
Total Liquid Assets	$110,759

CREDIT DATA

July 2000:

Pool of Credit	$1,151,081,707
Revolving Credit, No.	154,864
Fixed Loans, No.	75,399
Avg. Credit Limit, per Person	$13,686
Avg. Spent, per Person	$7,572
Satisfactory Ratings, No. per Person	2.63
Avg. No. of Cards, per Person	0.89

LABOUR FORCE

2001 Estimates:

Male:	
In the Labour Force	26,800
Participation Rate	70.0
Employed	24,251
Unemployed	2,549
Unemployment Rate	9.5
Not in Labour Force	11,512
Female:	
In the Labour Force	26,025
Participation Rate	59.1
Employed	24,211
Unemployed	1,814
Unemployment Rate	7.0
Not in Labour Force	17,997

OCCUPATIONS BY MAJOR GROUPS

2001 Estimates:	Male	Female
Management	3,278	1,454
Business, Finance & Admin.	3,120	7,284
Natural & Applied Sciences & Related	2,461	458
Health	884	2,962
Social Sciences, Gov't Services & Religion	1,009	1,011
Education	1,406	2,043
Arts, Culture, Recreation & Sport	731	788
Sales & Service	6,524	8,419
Trades, Transport & Equipment Operators & Related	4,506	170
Primary Industries	586	72
Processing, Mfg. & Utilities	793	208

LEVEL OF SCHOOLING

2001 Estimates:

Population 15 years +	82,334
Less than Grade 9	7,626
Grades 9-13 w/o Certif.	19,013
Grade 9-13 with Certif.	7,647
Trade Certif. /Dip.	2,008
Non-Univ. w/o Certif./Dip.	3,604
Non-Univ. with Certif./Dip.	14,640
Univ. w/o Degree	13,561
Univ. w/o Degree/Certif.	6,971
Univ. with Certif.	6,590
Univ. with Degree	14,235

AVERAGE HOUSEHOLD EXPENDITURES

2001 Estimates:

Food	$5,921
Shelter	$8,908
Clothing	$2,139
Transportation	$5,947
Health & Personal Care	$1,851
Recr'n, Read'g & Education	$3,654
Taxes & Securities	$13,852
Other	$8,220
Total Expenditures	$50,492

PRIVATE HOUSEHOLDS

2001 Estimates:

Private Households, Total	39,053
Pop. in Private Households	96,170
Average no. per Household	2.5

FAMILIES

2001 Estimates:

Families in Private Households	28,585
Husband-Wife Families	22,787
Lone-Parent Families	5,798
Aver. No. Persons per Family	3.0
Aver. No. Sons/Daughters at Home	1.2

HOUSING

2001 Estimates:

Occupied Private Dwellings	39,053
Owned	23,347
Rented	15,706
Single-Detached House	17,194
Semi-Detached House	2,184
Row Houses	5,413
Apartment, 5+ Storeys	624
Owned Apartment, 5+ Storeys	31
Apartment, 5 or Fewer Storeys	4,847
Apartment, Detached Duplex	8,288
Other Single-Attached	213
Movable Dwellings	290

VEHICLES

2001 Estimates:

Model Yrs. '81-'96, No.	44,984
% Total	73.57
Model Yrs. '97-'98, No.	9,554
% Total	15.63
'99 Vehicles registered in Model Yr. '99, No.	6,606
% Total	10.80
Total No. '81-'99	61,144

LEGAL MARITAL STATUS

2001 Estimates: (Age 15+)

Single (Never Married)	31,131
Legally Married (Not Separated)	38,409
Legally Married (Separated)	2,058
Widowed	5,824
Divorced	4,912

PSYTE CATEGORIES

2001 Estimates	No. of House-holds	% of Total Hhds.	Index
Urban Gentry	1,704	4.36	243
Suburban Executives	1,359	3.48	243
Technocrafts & Bureaucrats	3,337	8.54	304
Stable Suburban Families	486	1.24	95
Small City Elite	1,231	3.15	184
Old Bungalow Burbs	957	2.45	148
Aging Erudites	4,271	10.94	725
Kindergarten Boom	2,167	5.55	212
Blue Collar Winners	37	0.09	4
Old Towns' New Fringe	3,384	8.67	221
Conservative Homebodies	2,726	6.98	194
High Rise Sunsets	820	2.10	147
Young Urban Professionals	527	1.35	71
Young Urban Mix	757	1.94	91
University Enclaves	5,119	13.11	642
Young City Singles	288	0.74	32
Town Renters	1,729	4.43	512
Nesters & Young Homesteaders	1,060	2.71	116
Struggling Downtowns	6,113	15.65	497
Aged Pensioners	490	1.25	94

FINANCIAL P$YTE

2001 Estimates	No. of House-holds	% of Total Hhds.	Index
Four Star Investors	3,063	7.84	156
Successful Suburbanites	3,823	9.79	148
Canadian Comfort	1,268	3.25	33
Urban Heights	4,798	12.29	286
Miners & Credit-Liners	957	2.45	77
Mortgages & Minivans	2,167	5.55	84
Tractors & Tradelines	3,384	8.67	152
Bills & Wills	3,483	8.92	108
Revolving Renters	1,880	4.81	105
Young Urban Struggle	5,119	13.11	277
Towering Debt	8,130	20.82	267
Senior Survivors	490	1.25	67

HOME LANGUAGE

2001 Estimates:		% Total
English	96,903	98.51
French	161	0.16
Arabic	60	0.06
Chinese	354	0.36
Norwegian	65	0.07
Polish	69	0.07
Russian	59	0.06
Vietnamese	91	0.09
Other Languages	348	0.35
Multiple Responses	257	0.26
Total	98,367	100.00

BUILDING PERMITS

	1999	1998	1997
		$000	
Value	107,856	95,197	70,270

HOMES BUILT

	1999	1998	1997
No.	384	380	533

TAXATION

Income Class:	1997	% Total
Under $5,000	11,180	15.48
$5,000-$10,000	10,600	14.67
$10,000-$15,000	11,570	16.02
$15,000-$20,000	6,530	9.04
$20,000-$25,000	6,280	8.69
$25,000-$30,000	5,400	7.48
$30,000-$40,000	7,640	10.58
$40,000-$50,000	5,200	7.20
$50,000 +	7,830	10.84
Total Returns, No.	72,240	
Total Income, $000	1,860,476	
Total Taxable Returns	45,850	
Total Tax, $000	390,979	
Average Income, $	25,754	
Average Tax, $	8,527	

VITAL STATISTICS

	1997	1996	1995	1994
Births	1,106	1,096	1,075	1,221
Deaths	913	813	876	890
Natural Increase	193	283	199	331
Marriages	806	828	805	780

Note: Latest available data.

MEDIA INFO

see St. John's, , CMA

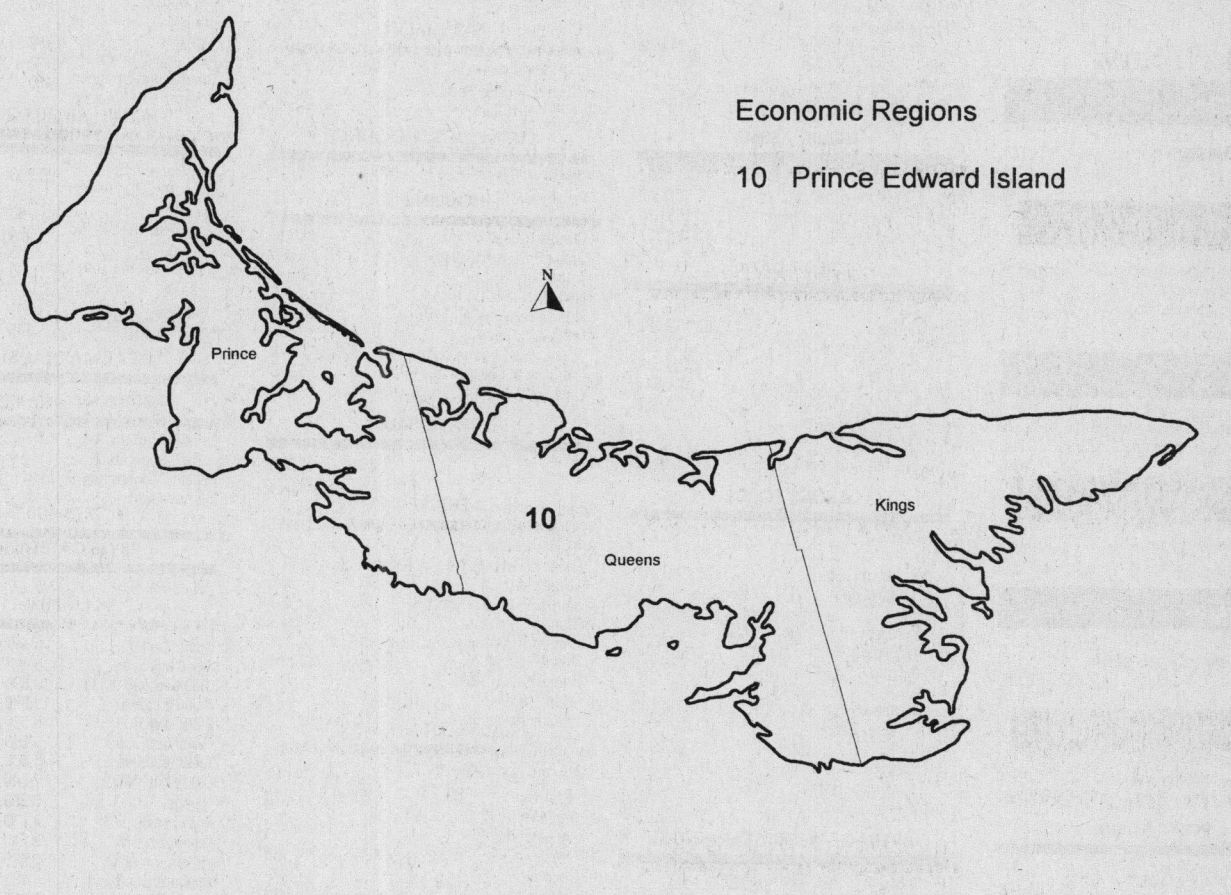

Economic Regions

10   Prince Edward Island

Prince

N

10

Queens

Kings

Region	Population (at July 1)				Households (at July1)		Income				Retail Sales				Taxation Statistics, 1997					
	*1996 Census (000)	2001 Estimate (000)	% of Cdn. Total	% Chg. '96-'01	2001 Estimate (000)	% of Cdn. Total	2001 Estimate $millions	% of Cdn. Total	Per Hhld. $	Income Rating Index	2001 Estimate $millions	% of Cdn. Total	Per Hhld. $	Market Rating Index	Total No. of Returns	Total Income $millions	Total No. Taxable Returns	Total Tax $millions	Avg. Income $	Avg. Tax $
Prince Edward Island	136.2	138.2	0.44	1.45	52.0	0.43	2,331.7	0.36	44,900	80	1,205.9	0.43	23,200	97	96,250	2,096.1	65,750	337.0	21,778	5,126
Prince Edward Island (10)	136.2	138.2	0.44	1.45	52.0	0.43	2,331.7	0.36	44,900	80	1,205.9	0.43	23,200	97	96,240	2,096.1	65,750	337.0	21,780	5,126
Kings County	19.8	19.7	0.06	-0.54	7.3	0.06	313.0	0.05	43,000	76	105.8	0.04	14,500	60	13,460	258.3	9,030	37.6	19,194	4,168
Queens County	71.4	73.6	0.24	3.13	27.8	0.23	1,292.7	0.20	46,400	83	716.8	0.26	25,700	109	50,120	1,174.9	34,450	201.2	23,442	5,839
Prince County	45.1	44.9	0.14	-0.34	16.8	0.14	726.0	0.11	43,100	77	383.2	0.14	22,800	95	32,660	662.9	22,270	98.2	20,296	4,411

*Adjusted.

Prince Edward Island

POPULATION

July 1, 2001 Estimate	138,166
% Cdn. Total	0.44
% Change, '96 -'01	1.45
Avg. Annual Growth Rate, %	0.29
2003 Projected Population	138,337
2006 Projected Population	137,891
2001 Households Estimate	51,966
2003 Projected Households	52,774
2006 Projected Households	53,764

INCOME

% Above/Below National Average	-20
2001 Total Income Estimate	$2,331,720,000
% Cdn. Total	0.36
2001 Average Hhld. Income	$44,900
2001 Per Capita	$16,900
2003 Projected Total Income	$2,477,660,000
2006 Projected Total Income	$2,711,920,000

RETAIL SALES

% Above/Below National Average	-3
2001 Retail Sales Estimate	$1,205,860,000
% Cdn. Total	0.43
2001 per Household	$23,200
2001 per Capita	$8,700
2001 No. of Establishments	1,344
2003 Projected Retail Sales	$1,290,950,000
2006 Projected Retail Sales	$1,408,660,000

POPULATION

2001 Estimates:

Total		138,166
Male		67,591
Female		70,575

Age Groups	Male	Female
0-4	4,446	4,206
5-9	4,764	4,592
10-14	5,027	4,904
15-19	5,137	4,981
20-24	5,010	4,868
25-29	4,688	4,722
30-34	4,803	4,926
35-39	5,108	5,278
40-44	5,132	5,253
45-49	4,985	5,089
50-54	4,328	4,368
55-59	3,522	3,526
60-64	2,864	2,972
65-69	2,430	2,639
70+	5,347	8,251

DAYTIME POPULATION

2001 Estimates:

Working Population	66,810
At Home Population	71,499
Total	138,309

INCOME

2001 Estimates:

Avg. Household Income	$44,870
Avg. Family Income	$50,298
Per Capita Income	$16,876
Male:	
Avg. Employment Income	$24,307
Avg. Employment Income (Full Time)	$35,994
Female:	
Avg. Employment Income	$15,978
Avg. Employment Income (Full Time)	$26,886

DISPOSABLE & DISCRETIONARY INCOME

2001 Estimates:	*Per Hhld.*
Disposable Income	$35,298
Discretionary Income 1 (minus Food & Shelter)	$24,039
Discretionary Income 2 (minus Food, Shelter, & Other Expenditures)	$16,106

LIQUID ASSETS

1999 Estimates:	*Per Hhld.*
Equity Investments	$51,209
Interest Bearing Investments	$53,518
Total Liquid Assets	$104,727

CREDIT DATA

July 2000:

Pool of Credit	$1,361,173,182
Revolving Credit, No.	192,287
Fixed Loans, No.	157,014
Avg. Credit Limit, per Person	$11,541
Avg. Spent, per Person	$6,182
Satisfactory Ratings, No. per Person	2.81
Avg. No. of Cards, per Person	0.72

LABOUR FORCE

2001 Estimates:

Male:	
In the Labour Force	39,912
Participation Rate	74.8
Employed	34,662
Unemployed	5,250
Unemployment Rate	13.2
Not in Labour Force	13,442
Female:	
In the Labour Force	34,706
Participation Rate	61.0
Employed	29,958
Unemployed	4,748
Unemployment Rate	13.7
Not in Labour Force	22,167

AVERAGE WEEKLY EARNINGS

(Including overtime, industrial aggregate)

	Prince Edward Island	Canada
Apr 2000	$490.17	$622.92
Apr 1999	$488.93	$608.07
Apr 1998	$493.32	$608.06
Apr 1997	$487.81	$597.26
Apr 1996	$484.51	$575.79

NUMBER OF EMPLOYEES

(Industrial aggregate)

Apr 2000	49,858
Apr 1999	46,694
Apr 1998	43,794
Apr 1997	42,888
Apr 1996	44,401

MANUFACTURING INDUSTRIES

	1997	1992
Plants	154	135
Employees	4,810	3,910
	$000	
Salaries, Wages	113,604	84,863
Mfg. Materials, Cost	530,921	280,167
Mfg. Shipments, Value	802,257	501,386
Total Value Added	270,960	218,235

Note: Latest available data.

OCCUPATIONS BY MAJOR GROUPS

2001 Estimates:	Male	Female
Management	3,432	1,669
Business, Finance & Admin.	2,727	7,701
Natural & Applied Sciences & Related	1,956	361
Health	514	3,418
Social Sciences, Gov't Services & Religion	781	971
Education	927	1,552
Arts, Culture, Recreation & Sport	573	955
Sales & Service	6,830	11,880
Trades, Transport & Equipment Operators & Related	10,573	675
Primary Industries	8,188	2,124
Processing, Mfg. & Utilities	2,888	2,545

LEVEL OF SCHOOLING

2001 Estimates:

Population 15 years +	110,227
Less than Grade 9	14,462
Grades 9-13 w/o Certif.	31,236
Grade 9-13 with Certif.	11,565
Trade Certif. /Dip.	3,679
Non-Univ. w/o Certif./Dip.	4,749
Non-Univ. with Certif./Dip.	20,192
Univ. w/o Degree	12,494
Univ. w/o Degree/Certif.	5,978
Univ. with Certif.	6,516
Univ. with Degree	11,850

RETAIL SALES

	1999	1998
	$000,000	*$000,000*
Supermarkets & Groceries	293	256
All Other Food	n.a.	n.a.
Drugs & Patent Medicine	72	73
Shoes	n.a.	n.a.
Men's Clothing	n.a.	n.a.
Women's Clothing	n.a.	n.a.
Other Clothing	31	28
Hhld. Furniture & Appliances	32	27
Hhld. Furnishings	17	16
Motor & Recreation Vehicles	228	213
Gas Service Stations	130	118
Auto Parts, Accessories & Services	74	68
General Merchandise	105	93
Other Semi-Durable Goods	51	49
Other Durable Goods	22	18
Other Retail	54	50
Total	1,157	1,054

AVERAGE HOUSEHOLD EXPENDITURES

2001 Estimates:

Food	$5,646
Shelter	$7,425
Clothing	$1,859
Transportation	$6,090
Health & Personal Care	$1,792
Recr'n, Read'g & Education	$3,142
Taxes & Securities	$10,506
Other	$7,822
Total Expenditures	$44,282

PRIVATE HOUSEHOLDS

2001 Estimates:

Private Households, Total	51,966
Pop. in Private Households	134,578
Average no. per Household	2.6

FAMILIES

2001 Estimates:

Families in Private Households	38,762
Husband-Wife Families	33,223
Lone-Parent Families	5,539
Aver. No. Persons per Family	3.2
Aver. No. Sons/Daughters at Home	1.3

HOUSING

2001 Estimates:

Occupied Private Dwellings	51,966
Owned	37,573
Rented	14,333
Band Housing	60
Single-Detached House	37,637
Semi-Detached House	2,253
Row Houses	1,188
Apartment, 5+ Storeys	94
Apartment, 5 or Fewer Storeys	7,087
Apartment, Detached Duplex	1,131
Other Single-Attached	226
Movable Dwellings	2,350

VEHICLES

2001 Estimates:

Model Yrs. '81-'96, No.	73,160
% Total	87.99
Model Yrs. '97-'98, No.	5,264
% Total	6.33
'99 Vehicles registered in Model Yr. '99, No.	4,722
% Total	5.68
Total No. '81-'99	83,146

LEGAL MARITAL STATUS

2001 Estimates: (Age 15+)

Single (Never Married)	33,960
Legally Married (Not Separated)	59,519
Legally Married (Separated)	3,605
Widowed	7,851
Divorced	5,292

PSYTE CATEGORIES

2001 Estimates	No. of House-holds	% of Total Hhds.	Index
Urban Gentry	449	0.86	48
Small City Elite	6,802	13.09	764
Old Bungalow Burbs	139	0.27	16
Aging Erudites	213	0.41	27
Blue Collar Winners	158	0.30	12
Town Boomers	1,473	2.83	280
Old Towns' New Fringe	6,973	13.42	343
Rustic Prosperity	4,176	8.04	445
Pick-ups & Dirt Bikes	2,081	4.00	480
Quebec's Heartland	185	0.36	36
Young City Singles	183	0.35	15
Old Leafy Towns	817	1.57	62
Town Renters	237	0.46	53
Nesters & Young Homesteaders	7,114	13.69	587
Young Grey Collar	438	0.84	101
Quiet Towns	5,050	9.72	457
Agrarian Blues	730	1.40	656
Rod & Rifle	9,852	18.96	820
Down, Down East	2,797	5.38	768
Big Country Families	112	0.22	15
Quebec Rural Blues	590	1.14	47
Aged Pensioners	1,124	2.16	163

2001 Estimates	No. of House -holds	% of Total Hhds.	Index
Four Star Investors	449	0.86	17
Canadian Comfort	8,433	16.23	167
Urban Heights	213	0.41	10
Miners & Credit-Liners	139	0.27	8
Tractors & Tradelines	11,149	21.45	375
Bills & Wills	817	1.57	19
Country Credit	2,081	4.00	59
Revolving Renters	7,552	14.53	316
Rural Family Blues	14,266	27.45	340
Limited Budgets	5,050	9.72	313
Towering Debt	420	0.81	10
Senior Survivors	1,124	2.16	115

HOME LANGUAGE

2001 Estimates:		% Total
English	134,286	97.19
French	2,939	2.13
Arabic	110	0.08
Chinese	176	0.13
Other Languages	258	0.19
Multiple Responses	397	0.29
Total	138,166	100.00

BUILDING PERMITS

	1999	1998 $000	1997
Value	140,925	116,075	110,004

HOMES BUILT

	1999	1998	1997
No	626	400	548

CAPITAL EXPENDITURES

(Public & Private)	2000	1999 $000,000	1998
Total Expends.	n.a.	n.a.	616.5
Capital Expends.	484.1	454.5	462.3
Construction	301.8	271.7	262.9
Machinery & Equip.	182.3	182.9	199.4
Repair Expends.	n.a.	n.a.	154.3
Construction	n.a.	n.a.	64.0
Machinery & Equip.	n.a.	n.a.	90.3

TAXATION

Income Class:	1997	% Total
Under $5,000	11,220	11.66
$5,000-$10,000	13,780	14.32
$10,000-$15,000	19,190	19.94
$15,000-$20,000	12,240	12.72
$20,000-$25,000	9,920	10.31
$25,000-$30,000	8,420	8.75
$30,000-$40,000	10,070	10.46
$40,000-$50,000	5,210	5.41
$50,000 +	6,200	6.44
Total Returns, No.	96,250	
Total Income, $000	2,096,135	
Total Taxable Returns	65,750	
Total Tax, $000	337,021	
Average Income, $	21,778	
Average Tax, $	5,126	

VITAL STATISTICS

	1997	1996	1995	1994
Births	1,591	1,694	1,754	1,716
Deaths	1,030	1,268	1,153	1,114
Natural Increase	561	426	601	602
Marriages	960	924	877	850

Note: Latest available data.

TRAVEL STATISTICS

Tourists in Canada	1999	1998
From the U.S. entering by:		
Air	345	428
Marine	6	12
Total	351	440
Other Countries:		
Air	1	18
Marine	15	n.a.
Total	16	18
Residents of Canada Returning from the U.S. by:		
Air	103	86
Marine	4	3
Total	107	89
From Other Countries:		
Air	n.a.	2
Marine	n.a.	6
Total	n.a.	8

Prince Edward Island

Prince Edward Island

Charlottetown
(Census Agglomeration)

The Census Agglomeration of Charlottetown includes: Charlottetown, C; Cornwall, T; Lots 31, 33, 34, 35, 36, 48, 49, and 65; Miltonvale Park, COM; Stratford, T; plus several smaller areas. All are in Queens County.

POPULATION

July 1, 2001 Estimate	59,610
% Cdn. Total	0.19
% Change, '96 -'01	2.81
Avg. Annual Growth Rate, %	0.56
2003 Projected Population	59,806
2006 Projected Population	59,765
2001 Households Estimate	22,932
2003 Projected Households	23,288
2006 Projected Households	23,733

INCOME

% Above/Below National Average	-15
2001 Total Income Estimate	$1,066,910,000
% Cdn. Total	0.16
2001 Average Hhld. Income	$46,500
2001 Per Capita	$17,900
2003 Projected Total Income	$1,133,140,000
2006 Projected Total Income	$1,239,480,000

RETAIL SALES

% Above/Below National Average	+25
2001 Retail Sales Estimate	$666,130,000
% Cdn. Total	0.24
2001 per Household	$29,000
2001 per Capita	$11,200
2001 No. of Establishments	580
2003 Projected Retail Sales	$713,600,000*
2006 Projected Retail Sales	$779,500,000

POPULATION

2001 Estimates:

Total		59,610
Male		28,491
Female		31,119

Age Groups	Male	Female
0-4	1,950	1,842
5-9	2,010	1,944
10-14	2,080	2,030
15-19	2,125	2,087
20-24	2,150	2,179
25-29	2,063	2,183
30-34	2,073	2,230
35-39	2,154	2,346
40-44	2,178	2,395
45-49	2,163	2,355
50-54	1,876	1,994
55-59	1,488	1,555
60-64	1,166	1,251
65-69	934	1,097
70+	2,081	3,631

DAYTIME POPULATION

2001 Estimates:

Working Population	29,740
At Home Population	30,010
Total	59,750

INCOME

2001 Estimates:

Avg. Household Income	$46,525
Avg. Family Income	$53,143
Per Capita Income	$17,898
Male:	
Avg. Employment Income	$26,612
Avg. Employment Income (Full Time)	$38,725
Female:	
Avg. Employment Income	$18,042
Avg. Employment Income (Full Time)	$28,440

DISPOSABLE & DISCRETIONARY INCOME

2001 Estimates:	Per Hhld.
Disposable Income	$36,373
Discretionary Income 1 (minus Food & Shelter)	$24,788
Discretionary Income 2 (minus Food, Shelter, & Other Expenditures)	$17,043

LIQUID ASSETS

1999 Estimates:	Per Hhld.
Equity Investments	$51,750
Interest Bearing Investments	$54,946
Total Liquid Assets	$106,696

CREDIT DATA

July 2000:

Pool of Credit	$612,034,875
Revolving Credit, No.	92,814
Fixed Loans, No.	50,679
Avg. Credit Limit, per Person	$12,265
Avg. Spent, per Person	$6,356
Satisfactory Ratings, No. per Person	2.72
Avg. No. of Cards, per Person	0.82

LABOUR FORCE

2001 Estimates:

Male:	
In the Labour Force	16,943
Participation Rate	75.5
Employed	14,893
Unemployed	2,050
Unemployment Rate	12.1
Not in Labour Force	5,508
Female:	
In the Labour Force	15,620
Participation Rate	61.7
Employed	13,916
Unemployed	1,704
Unemployment Rate	10.9
Not in Labour Force	9,683

OCCUPATIONS BY MAJOR GROUPS

2001 Estimates:	Male	Female
Management	2,160	1,009
Business, Finance & Admin.	1,549	4,162
Natural & Applied Sciences & Related	1,047	233
Health	254	1,621
Social Sciences, Gov't Services & Religion	506	576
Education	552	864
Arts, Culture, Recreation & Sport	367	537
Sales & Service	3,821	5,276
Trades, Transport & Equipment Operators & Related	4,328	230
Primary Industries	1,327	361
Processing, Mfg. & Utilities	758	247

LEVEL OF SCHOOLING

2001 Estimates:

Population 15 years +	47,754
Less than Grade 9	3,777
Grades 9-13 w/o Certif.	11,340
Grade 9-13 with Certif.	4,583
Trade Certif. /Dip.	1,669
Non-Univ. w/o Certif./Dip.	2,238
Non-Univ. with Certif./Dip.	9,527
Univ. w/o Degree	7,146
Univ. w/o Degree/Certif.	3,570
Univ. with Certif.	3,576
Univ. with Degree	7,474

AVERAGE HOUSEHOLD EXPENDITURES

2001 Estimates:

Food	$5,548
Shelter	$8,046
Clothing	$1,897
Transportation	$5,956
Health & Personal Care	$1,817
Recr'n, Read'g & Education	$3,423
Taxes & Securities	$11,137
Other	$7,848
Total Expenditures	$45,672

PRIVATE HOUSEHOLDS

2001 Estimates:

Private Households, Total	22,932
Pop. in Private Households	57,774
Average no. per Household	2.5

FAMILIES

2001 Estimates:

Families in Private Households	16,396
Husband-Wife Families	13,647
Lone-Parent Families	2,749
Aver. No. Persons per Family	3.1
Aver. No. Sons/Daughters at Home	1.3

HOUSING

2001 Estimates:

Occupied Private Dwellings	22,932
Owned	14,452
Rented	8,480
Single-Detached House	14,098
Semi-Detached House	1,446
Row Houses	454
Apartment, 5+ Storeys	38
Apartment, 5 or Fewer Storeys	5,078
Apartment, Detached Duplex	696
Other Single-Attached	134
Movable Dwellings	988

VEHICLES

2001 Estimates:

Model Yrs. '81-'96, No.	29,630
% Total	83.68
Model Yrs. '97-'98, No.	3,144
% Total	8.88
'99 Vehicles registered in Model Yr. '99, No.	2,633
% Total	7.44
Total No. '81-'99	35,407

LEGAL MARITAL STATUS

2001 Estimates: (Age 15+)

Single (Never Married)	15,674
Legally Married (Not Separated)	24,605
Legally Married (Separated)	1,629
Widowed	3,216
Divorced	2,630

PSYTE CATEGORIES

2001 Estimates	No. of House -holds	% of Total Hhds.	Index
Urban Gentry	449	1.96	109
Small City Elite	6,802	29.66	1,731
Old Bungalow Burbs	139	0.61	37
Aging Erudites	213	0.93	62
Old Towns' New Fringe	5,945	25.92	662
Rustic Prosperity	256	1.12	62
Young City Singles	183	0.80	35
Old Leafy Towns	146	0.64	25
Town Renters	237	1.03	120
Nesters & Young Homesteaders	7,114	31.02	1,329
Young Grey Collar	438	1.91	228
Rod & Rifle	151	0.66	28
Aged Pensioners	680	2.97	223

FINANCIAL P$YTE

2001 Estimates	No. of House -holds	% of Total Hhds.	Index
Four Star Investors	449	1.96	39
Canadian Comfort	6,802	29.66	305
Urban Heights	213	0.93	22
Miners & Credit-Liners	139	0.61	19
Tractors & Tradelines	6,201	27.04	473
Bills & Wills	146	0.64	8
Revolving Renters	7,552	32.93	716
Rural Family Blues	151	0.66	8
Towering Debt	420	1.83	23
Senior Survivors	680	2.97	157

HOME LANGUAGE

2001 Estimates:		% Total
English	58,599	98.30
French	446	0.75
Arabic	110	0.18
Chinese	120	0.20
Dutch	39	0.07
Serbo-Croatian	47	0.08
Other Languages	76	0.13
Multiple Responses	173	0.29
Total	59,610	100.00

BUILDING PERMITS

	1999	1998	1997
		$000	
Value	44,177	40,585	43,364

HOMES BUILT

	1999	1998	1997
No	288	232	245

TAXATION

Income Class:	1997	% Total
Under $5,000	4,730	11.44
$5,000-$10,000	5,760	13.93
$10,000-$15,000	7,130	17.24
$15,000-$20,000	4,820	11.66
$20,000-$25,000	3,990	9.65
$25,000-$30,000	3,630	8.78
$30,000-$40,000	4,930	11.92
$40,000-$50,000	2,770	6.70
$50,000 +	3,570	8.63
Total Returns, No.	41,350	
Total Income, $000	997,658	
Total Taxable Returns	28,640	
Total Tax, $000	174,897	
Average Income, $	24,127	
Average Tax, $	6,107	

VITAL STATISTICS

	1997	1996	1995	1994
Births	681	709	756	739
Deaths	443	543	509	500
Natural Increase	238	166	247	239
Marriages	374	378	369	370

Note: Latest available data.

Charlottetown
(Census Agglomeration)
(Cont'd)

DAILY NEWSPAPER(S)

	Circulation Average Paid
The Guardian	21,267

RADIO STATION(S)

	Power
CBAF-FM	n.a.
CBCT-FM	100,000w
CFCY	10,000w
CHLQ-FM	75,000w
CHTN	10,000w

TELEVISION STATION(S)

CBAFT-TV
CBCT-TV
CKCW-TV
GLOBAL-TV

Summerside
(Census Agglomeration)

The Census Agglomeration of Summerside includes: Summerside, C; plus several smaller areas. All are in Prince County.

POPULATION

July 1, 2001 Estimate	16,444
% Cdn. Total	0.05
% Change, '96 -'01	1.61
Avg. Annual Growth Rate, %	0.32
2003 Projected Population	16,571
2006 Projected Population	16,691
2001 Households Estimate	6,608
2003 Projected Households	6,757
2006 Projected Households	6,952

INCOME

% Above/Below National Average	-17
2001 Total Income Estimate	$287,490,000
% Cdn. Total	0.04
2001 Average Hhld. Income	$43,500
2001 Per Capita	$17,500
2003 Projected Total Income	$307,530,000
2006 Projected Total Income	$339,530,000

RETAIL SALES

% Above/Below National Average	+79
2001 Retail Sales Estimate	$263,780,000
% Cdn. Total	0.09
2001 per Household	$39,900
2001 per Capita	$16,000
2001 No. of Establishments	257
2003 Projected Retail Sales	$284,590,000
2006 Projected Retail Sales	$314,140,000

POPULATION

2001 Estimates:

Total		16,444
Male		7,925
Female		8,519

Age Groups	Male	Female
0-4	541	516
5-9	562	534
10-14	578	543
15-19	579	538
20-24	569	571
25-29	577	604
30-34	620	633
35-39	621	647
40-44	603	625
45-49	575	601
50-54	491	507
55-59	410	400
60-64	349	359
65-69	274	333
70+	576	1,108

DAYTIME POPULATION

2001 Estimates:

Working Population	8,050
At Home Population	8,394
Total	16,444

INCOME

2001 Estimates:

Avg. Household Income	$43,506
Avg. Family Income	$48,085
Per Capita Income	$17,483

Male:

Avg. Employment Income	$25,310
Avg. Employment Income (Full Time)	$35,696

Female:

Avg. Employment Income	$16,014
Avg. Employment Income (Full Time)	$25,093

DISPOSABLE & DISCRETIONARY INCOME

2001 Estimates:	Per Hhld.
Disposable Income	$34,303
Discretionary Income 1 (minus Food & Shelter)	$23,066
Discretionary Income 2 (minus Food, Shelter, & Other Expenditures)	$15,299

LIQUID ASSETS

1999 Estimates:	Per Hhld.
Equity Investments	$51,561
Interest Bearing Investments	$53,148
Total Liquid Assets	$104,709

CREDIT DATA

July 2000:

Pool of Credit	$164,772,812
Revolving Credit, No.	24,099
Fixed Loans, No.	20,720
Avg. Credit Limit, per Person	$11,703
Avg. Spent, per Person	$6,194
Satisfactory Ratings, No. per Person	3.00
Avg. No. of Cards, per Person	0.77

LABOUR FORCE

2001 Estimates:

Male:

In the Labour Force	4,613
Participation Rate	73.9
Employed	4,132
Unemployed	481
Unemployment Rate	10.4
Not in Labour Force	1,631

Female:

In the Labour Force	4,155
Participation Rate	60.0
Employed	3,702
Unemployed	453
Unemployment Rate	10.9
Not in Labour Force	2,771

OCCUPATIONS BY MAJOR GROUPS

2001 Estimates:	Male	Female
Management	525	167
Business, Finance & Admin.	393	917
Natural & Applied Sciences & Related	216	36
Health	83	414
Social Sciences, Gov't Services & Religion	119	99
Education	108	160
Arts, Culture, Recreation & Sport	44	63
Sales & Service	1,027	1,699
Trades, Transport & Equipment Operators & Related	1,290	83
Primary Industries	289	74
Processing, Mfg. & Utilities	419	327

LEVEL OF SCHOOLING

2001 Estimates:

Population 15 years +	13,170
Less than Grade 9	1,747
Grades 9-13 w/o Certif.	3,777
Grade 9-13 with Certif.	1,439
Trade Certif. /Dip.	426
Non-Univ. w/o Certif./Dip.	606
Non-Univ. with Certif./Dip.	2,687
Univ. w/o Degree	1,248
Univ. w/o Degree/Certif.	542
Univ. with Certif.	706
Univ. with Degree	1,240

Prince Edward Island

AVERAGE HOUSEHOLD EXPENDITURES

2001 Estimates:

Food	$5,350
Shelter	$7,755
Clothing	$1,827
Transportation	$5,953
Health & Personal Care	$1,794
Recr'n, Read'g & Education	$2,861
Taxes & Securities	$10,242
Other	$7,378
Total Expenditures	$43,160

PRIVATE HOUSEHOLDS

2001 Estimates:

Private Households, Total	6,608
Pop. in Private Households	16,113
Average no. per Household	2.4

FAMILIES

2001 Estimates:

Families in Private Households	4,872
Husband-Wife Families	3,998
Lone-Parent Families	874
Aver. No. Persons per Family	3.0
Aver. No. Sons/Daughters at Home	1.2

HOUSING

2001 Estimates:

Occupied Private Dwellings	6,608
Owned	3,964
Rented	2,644
Single-Detached House	4,049
Semi-Detached House	443
Row Houses	347
Apartment, 5 or Fewer Storeys	1,147
Apartment, Detached Duplex	273
Other Single-Attached	22
Movable Dwellings	327

VEHICLES

2001 Estimates:

Model Yrs. '81-'96, No.	7,845
% Total	87.70
Model Yrs. '97-'98, No.	593
% Total	6.63
'99 Vehicles registered in Model Yr. '99, No.	507
% Total	5.67
Total No. '81-'99	8,945

LEGAL MARITAL STATUS

2001 Estimates: (Age 15+)

Single (Never Married)	4,053
Legally Married (Not Separated)	6,655
Legally Married (Separated)	607
Widowed	1,040
Divorced	815

Prince Edward Island

Summerside
(Census Agglomeration)
(Cont'd)

PSYTE CATEGORIES

2001 Estimates	No. of House -holds	% of Total Hhds.	Index
Town Boomers	1,473	22.29	2,199
Old Towns' New Fringe	455	6.89	176
Pick-ups & Dirt Bikes	166	2.51	301
Old Leafy Towns	124	1.88	73
Quiet Towns	3,608	54.60	2,566
Rod & Rifle	262	3.96	171
Aged Pensioners	444	6.72	505

FINANÇIAL P$YTE

2001 Estimates	No. of House -holds	% of Total Hhds.	Index
Canadian Comfort	1,473	22.29	229
Tractors & Tradelines	455	6.89	120
Bills & Wills	124	1.88	23
Country Credit	166	2.51	37
Rural Family Blues	262	3.96	49
Limited Budgets	3,608	54.60	1,756
Senior Survivors	444	6.72	357

HOME LANGUAGE

2001 Estimates:		% Total
English	15,882	96.58
French	391	2.38
Chinese	56	0.34
Hindi	10	0.06
Multiple Responses	105	0.64
Total	16,444	100.00

BUILDING PERMITS

	1999	1998	1997
		$000	
Value	17,036	23,774	24,250

HOMES BUILT

	1999	1998	1997
No	59	44	71

TAXATION

Income Class:	1997	% Total
Under $5,000	1,500	11.54
$5,000-$10,000	1,800	13.85
$10,000-$15,000	2,550	19.62
$15,000-$20,000	1,640	12.62
$20,000-$25,000	1,420	10.92
$25,000-$30,000	1,270	9.77
$30,000-$40,000	1,370	10.54
$40,000-$50,000	680	5.23
$50,000 +	770	5.92
Total Returns, No.	13,000	
Total Income, $000	279,993	
Total Taxable Returns	8,970	
Total Tax, $000	43,999	
Average Income, $	21,538	
Average Tax, $	4,905	

VITAL STATISTICS

	1997	1996	1995	1994
Births	193	197	212	193
Deaths	145	171	124	147
Natural Increase	48	26	88	46
Marriages	105	132	101	105

Note: Latest available data.

DAILY NEWSPAPER(S)

	Circulation Average Paid
Journal Pioneer	10,251

COMMUNITY NEWSPAPER(S)

	Total Circulation
Summerside: La Voix Acadienne	602

RADIO STATION(S)

	Power
CJRW	n.a.
CJRW-FM	n.a.

Economic Regions & Census Divisions

Nova Scotia

Economic Regions

10 Cape Breton
20 North Shore
30 Annapolis Valley
40 Southern
50 Halifax

Region	Population (at July 1)				Households (at July 1)		Personal Income				Retail Sales				Taxation Statistics, 1997					
	*1996 Census (000)	2001 Estimate (000)	% of Cdn. Total	% Chg. '96-'01	2001 Estimate (000)	% of Cdn. Total	2001 Estimate $millions	% of Cdn. Total	Per Capita $	Income Rating Index	2001 Estimate $millions	% of Cdn. Total	Per Capita $	Market Rating Index	Total No. of Returns	Total Income $millions	Total No. Taxable Returns	Total Tax $millions	Avg. Income $	Avg. Tax $
Nova Scotia	931.2	947.6	3.04	1.76	371.6	3.07	17,180.6	2.62	46,200	86	8,693.8	3.12	23,400	102	653,010	15,219.0	426,290	2,674.0	23,306	6,273
Cape Breton (10)	161.7	155.6	0.50	-3.72	58.6	0.48	2,361.7	0.36	40,300	72	1,310.0	0.47	22,400	94	110,840	2,201.1	65,320	335.8	19,858	5,141
Inverness County	21.4	20.7	0.07	-3.14	7.6	0.06	339.1	0.05	44,300	78	226.0	0.08	29,600	122	14,880	312.9	9,240	51.4	21,028	5,566
Richmond County	11.3	10.9	0.04	-2.75	4.1	0.03	164.2	0.03	40,100	71	45.2	0.02	11,000	46	7,510	139.6	4,230	20.3	18,595	4,797
Cape Breton County	120.4	115.5	0.37	-4.02	43.7	0.36	1,725.7	0.26	39,500	71	999.2	0.36	22,900	97	83,210	1,649.6	48,540	249.5	19,824	5,140
Victoria County	8.7	8.5	0.03	-2.28	3.2	0.02	132.7	0.02	41,900	74	39.6	0.01	12,500	52	5,240	99.0	3,310	14.6	18,887	4,415
North Shore (20)	165.9	165.1	0.53	-0.52	64.6	0.53	2,674.0	0.41	41,400	77	1,615.3	0.58	25,000	109	115,780	2,443.8	72,310	393.8	21,107	5,447
Colchester County	50.4	51.8	0.17	2.62	20.5	0.17	866.1	0.13	42,300	79	585.8	0.21	28,600	126	35,270	762.8	22,780	125.3	21,627	5,501
Cumberland County	34.6	33.9	0.11	-1.81	13.7	0.11	508.0	0.08	37,100	71	342.3	0.12	25,000	113	24,580	479.4	14,980	69.2	19,505	4,617
Pictou County	49.8	48.9	0.16	-1.77	19.1	0.16	803.7	0.12	42,200	78	440.3	0.16	23,100	101	34,880	768.3	21,630	131.5	22,026	6,079
Guysborough County	11.1	10.3	0.03	-7.16	4.1	0.03	139.9	0.02	34,500	64	43.4	0.02	10,700	47	7,480	131.5	4,380	18.3	17,582	4,168
Antigonish County	20.0	20.1	0.06	0.63	7.3	0.06	356.2	0.05	49,100	84	203.4	0.07	28,000	113	13,570	301.8	8,540	49.6	22,239	5,810
Annapolis Valley (30)	123.9	128.7	0.41	3.86	49.4	0.41	2,144.2	0.33	43,400	79	1,017.5	0.37	20,600	88	88,500	1,887.8	56,690	304.9	21,331	5,378
Annapolis County	22.8	22.5	0.07	-1.21	9.2	0.08	346.3	0.05	37,600	73	115.8	0.04	12,600	57	14,110	268.5	8,440	38.4	19,030	4,553
Kings County	60.7	63.3	0.20	4.28	24.5	0.20	1,079.2	0.16	44,100	81	610.8	0.22	25,000	108	42,670	938.3	27,630	155.6	21,991	5,632
Hants County	40.4	42.9	0.14	6.1	15.7	0.13	718.8	0.11	45,600	79	290.9	0.10	18,500	76	31,720	680.9	20,620	110.9	21,467	5,376
Southern (40)	127.5	126.0	0.40	-1.25	50.5	0.42	2,113.4	0.32	41,800	80	1,178.2	0.42	23,300	104	89,410	1,879.0	55,500	306.8	21,016	5,527
Shelburne County	17.4	16.9	0.05	-2.56	6.9	0.06	297.2	0.05	43,100	83	172.1	0.06	25,000	113	12,120	243.9	7,770	39.0	20,122	5,026
Yarmouth County	27.9	27.5	0.09	-1.54	10.7	0.09	448.4	0.07	41,800	77	197.4	0.07	18,400	80	20,250	437.2	12,660	70.5	21,589	5,566
Digby County	21.0	20.4	0.07	-2.44	8.2	0.07	310.5	0.05	37,700	72	209.1	0.08	25,400	114	14,650	272.2	8,910	39.2	18,577	4,403
Queens County	12.7	12.1	0.04	-4.51	4.9	0.04	225.6	0.03	46,000	88	97.7	0.04	19,900	90	9,260	201.8	5,480	35.7	21,795	6,523
Lunenburg County	48.6	49.0	0.16	0.76	19.8	0.16	831.6	0.13	42,000	81	501.9	0.18	25,300	115	33,130	724.0	20,680	122.3	21,854	5,913
Halifax (50)	352.1	372.2	1.20	5.7	148.5	1.23	7,887.3	1.20	53,100	101	3,572.8	1.28	24,100	107	248,510	6,807.3	176,480	1,332.6	27,392	7,551
Halifax County	352.1	372.2	1.20	5.7	148.5	1.23	7,887.3	1.20	53,100	101	3,572.8	1.28	24,100	107	248,510	6,807.3	176,480	1,332.6	27,392	7,551

*Adjusted.

Nova Scotia

POPULATION

July 1, 2001 Estimate 947,599
% Cdn. Total 3.04
% Change, '96 -'01 . . . . 1.76
Avg. Annual Growth Rate, % 0.35
2003 Projected Population 962,469
2006 Projected Population 987,439
2001 Households Estimate 371,610
2003 Projected Households 380,774
2006 Projected Households 396,161

INCOME

% Above/Below National Average . . . . -14
2001 Total Income Estimate . . $17,180,580,000
% Cdn. Total 2.62
2001 Average Hhld. Income $46,200
2001 Per Capita $18,100
2003 Projected Total Income $18,503,050,000
2006 Projected Total Income . $20,820,810,000

RETAIL SALES

% Above/Below National Average . . . . +2
2001 Retail Sales Estimate . . . $8,693,770,000
% Cdn. Total 3.12
2001 per Household $23,400
2001 per Capita $9,200
2001 No. of Establishments 7,062
2003 Projected Retail Sales . . $9,464,010,000
2006 Projected Retail Sales . $10,654,950,000

POPULATION

2001 Estimates:
Total 947,599
Male 460,828
Female 486,771

Age Groups	Male	Female
0-4	27,343	25,994
5-9	30,014	28,692
10-14	31,990	30,511
15-19	32,502	31,094
20-24	32,021	31,580
25-29	31,460	32,045
30-34	33,985	35,302
35-39	37,026	38,789
40-44	37,141	39,151
45-49	35,605	37,019
50-54	31,205	31,979
55-59	25,426	25,958
60-64	20,725	21,601
65-69	17,172	19,202
70+	37,213	57,854

DAYTIME POPULATION

2001 Estimates:
Working Population 427,872
At Home Population 520,450
Total 948,322

INCOME

2001 Estimates:
Avg. Household Income $46,233
Avg. Family Income $51,391
Per Capita Income $18,131
Male:
Avg. Employment Income $30,015
Avg. Employment Income
(Full Time) $41,759
Female:
Avg. Employment Income $18,278
Avg. Employment Income
(Full Time) $28,987

DISPOSABLE & DISCRETIONARY INCOME

2001 Estimates:	Per Hhld.
Disposable Income	$36,197
Discretionary Income 1 (minus Food & Shelter)	$24,531
Discretionary Income 2 (minus Food, Shelter, & Other Expenditures)	$16,802

LIQUID ASSETS

1999 Estimates:	Per Hhld.
Equity Investments	$52,898
Interest Bearing Investments	$53,608
Total Liquid Assets	$106,506

CREDIT DATA

July 2000:
Pool of Credit $9,910,392,940
Revolving Credit, No. 1,531,503
Fixed Loans, No. 730,049
Avg. Credit Limit, per Person $11,956
Avg. Spent, per Person $6,245
Satisfactory Ratings,
No. per Person 2.57
Avg. No. of Cards, per Person 0.78

LABOUR FORCE

2001 Estimates:
Male:
In the Labour Force 242,301
Participation Rate 65.2
Employed 220,059
Unemployed 22,242
Unemployment Rate 9.2
Not in Labour Force 129,180
Female:
In the Labour Force 222,270
Participation Rate 55.3
Employed 203,146
Unemployed 19,124
Unemployment Rate 8.6
Not in Labour Force 179,304

AVERAGE WEEKLY EARNINGS

(Including overtime, industrial aggregate)

	Nova Scotia	Canada
Apr 2000	$524.17	$622.92
Apr 1999	$522.58	$608.07
Apr 1998	$510.60	$608.06
Apr 1997	$501.21	$597.26
Apr 1996	$486.50	$575.79

NUMBER OF EMPLOYEES

(Industrial aggregate)

Apr 2000	332,518
Apr 1999	323,772
Apr 1998	313,070
Apr 1997	302,788
Apr 1996	298,670

MANUFACTURING INDUSTRIES

	1997	1992
Plants	727	708
Employees	35,799	37,168
	$000	
Salaries, Wages	1,160,586	1,103,668
Mfg. Materials, Cost	3,867,092	2,997,505
Mfg. Shipments, Value	6,464,560	5,119,723
Total Value Added	2,482,839	2,040,635

Note: Latest available data.

OCCUPATIONS BY MAJOR GROUPS

2001 Estimates:	Male	Female
Management	24,993	12,196
Business, Finance & Admin.	19,048	58,670
Natural & Applied Sciences & Related	14,093	2,754
Health	4,049	22,453
Social Sciences, Gov't Services & Religion	4,720	6,702
Education	7,031	11,071
Arts, Culture, Recreation & Sport	4,800	5,871
Sales & Service	53,086	79,234
Trades, Transport & Equipment Operators & Related	62,313	2,822
Primary Industries	23,760	4,049
Processing, Mfg. & Utilities	18,322	8,187

LEVEL OF SCHOOLING

2001 Estimates:
Population 15 years + ... 773,055
Less than Grade 9 84,539
Grades 9-13 w/o Certif. 215,870
Grade 9-13 with Certif. 76,218
Trade Certif. /Dip. 29,871
Non-Univ. w/o Certif./Dip. 30,119
Non-Univ. with Certif./Dip. 154,774
Univ. w/o Degree 86,614
Univ. w/o Degree/Certif. 42,423
Univ. with Certif. 44,191
Univ. with Degree 95,050

RETAIL SALES

	1999 $000,000	1998 $000,000
Supermarkets & Groceries	1,993	1,896
All Other Food	n.a.	n.a.
Drugs & Patent Medicine	530	523
Shoes	26	27
Men's Clothing	21	21
Women's Clothing	126	126
Other Clothing	159	146
Hhld. Furniture & Appliances	244	204
Hhld. Furnishings	57	42
Motor & Recreation Vehicles	1,973	1,947
Gas Service Stations	711	592
Auto Parts, Accessories & Services	437	427
General Merchandise	924	850
Other Semi-Durable Goods	261	256
Other Durable Goods	176	164
Other Retail	431	401
Total	8,160	7,711

AVERAGE HOUSEHOLD EXPENDITURES

2001 Estimates:
Food $5,684
Shelter $7,851
Clothing $1,898
Transportation $5,830
Health & Personal Care $1,793
Recr'n, Read'g & Education $3,233
Taxes & Securities $11,525
Other $7,782
Total Expenditures $45,596

PRIVATE HOUSEHOLDS

2001 Estimates:
Private Households, Total 371,610
Pop. in Private Households 930,299
Average no. per Household 2.5

FAMILIES

2001 Estimates:
Families in Private Households 275,501
Husband-Wife Families 233,086
Lone-Parent Families 42,415
Aver. No. Persons per Family 3.0
Aver. No. Sons/Daughters
at Home 1.1

HOUSING

2001 Estimates:
Occupied Private Dwellings 371,610
Owned 261,924
Rented 107,706
Band Housing 1,980
Single-Detached House 253,058
Semi-Detached House 18,012
Row Houses 8,476
Apartment, 5+ Storeys 12,570
Owned Apartment, 5+ Storeys 1,355
Apartment, 5 or Fewer Storeys 50,004
Apartment, Detached Duplex 13,632
Other Single-Attached 1,277
Movable Dwellings 14,581

VEHICLES

2001 Estimates:
Model Yrs. '81-'96, No. 375,102
% Total 80.64
Model Yrs. '97-'98, No. 44,004
% Total 9.46
'99 Vehicles registered in
Model Yr. '99, No. 46,024
% Total 9.89
Total No. '81-'99 465,130

LEGAL MARITAL STATUS

2001 Estimates: (Age 15+)
Single (Never Married) 234,897
Legally Married
(Not Separated) 409,259
Legally Married (Separated) 23,605
Widowed 55,389
Divorced 49,905

PSYTE CATEGORIES

2001 Estimates	No. of House-holds	% of Total Hhds.	Index
Canadian Establishment	134	0.04	22
Urban Gentry	5,057	1.36	76
Suburban Executives	1,689	0.45	32
Mortgaged in Suburbia	3,060	0.82	59
Technocrafts & Bureaucrats	6,865	1.85	66
Stable Suburban Families	1,876	0.50	39
Small City Elite	22,437	6.04	352
Old Bungalow Burbs	6,645	1.79	108
Suburban Nesters	118	0.03	2
Aging Erudites	11,474	3.09	205
Satellite Suburbs	4,161	1.12	39
Kindergarten Boom	3,869	1.04	40
Blue Collar Winners	858	0.23	9
Town Boomers	2,270	0.61	60
Old Towns' New Fringe	51,693	13.91	355
The New Frontier	33	0.01	1
Rustic Prosperity	2,100	0.57	31
Pick-ups & Dirt Bikes	2,814	0.76	91
High Rise Melting Pot	471	0.13	8
Conservative Homebodies	4,672	1.26	35
High Rise Sunsets	1,808	0.49	34
Young Urban Professionals	6,215	1.67	88
Young Urban Mix	803	0.22	10
Young Urban Intelligentsia	6,981	1.88	123
University Enclaves	14,288	3.84	188
Young City Singles	10,931	2.94	128

2001 Estimates	No. of House-holds	% of Total Hhds.	Index
Urban Bohemia	1,292	0.35	30
Old Leafy Towns	12,235	3.29	129
Town Renters	1,739	0.47	54
Nesters & Young Homesteaders	18,402	4.95	212
Young Grey Collar	2,831	0.76	91
Quiet Towns	27,912	7.51	353
Agrarian Blues	4,077	1.10	512
Rod & Rifle	93,520	25.17	1,088
Down, Down East	3,945	1.06	151
Big Country Families	3,792	1.02	72
Quebec Rural Blues	6,758	1.82	75
Quebec Town Elders	447	0.12	4
Struggling Downtowns	12,615	3.39	108
Aged Pensioners	1,956	0.53	40
Big City Stress	3,543	0.95	84
Old Grey Towers	477	0.13	23

FINAN¢IAL P$YTE

2001 Estimates	No. of House-holds	% of Total Hhds.	Index
Platinum Estates	134	0.04	4
Four Star Investors	6,746	1.82	36
Successful Suburbanites	11,801	3.18	48
Canadian Comfort	29,844	8.03	83
Urban Heights	17,689	4.76	111
Miners & Credit-Liners	6,678	1.80	57
Mortgages & Minivans	3,869	1.04	16
Tractors & Tradelines	53,793	14.48	253
Bills & Wills	17,710	4.77	58
Country Credit	2,814	0.76	11
Revolving Renters	23,041	6.20	135
Young Urban Struggle	22,561	6.07	128
Rural Family Blues	112,092	30.16	374
Limited Budgets	27,912	7.51	242
Loan Parent Stress	447	0.12	2
Towering Debt	25,756	6.93	89
NSF	3,543	0.95	27
Senior Survivors	2,433	0.65	35

HOME LANGUAGE

2001 Estimates:		% Total
English	910,520	96.09
French	20,374	2.15
Arabic	1,793	0.19
Chinese	1,534	0.16
German	1,019	0.11
Greek	483	0.05
Micmac	3,377	0.36
Other Languages	4,218	0.45
Multiple Responses	4,281	0.45
Total	947,599	100.00

BUILDING PERMITS

	1999	1998 $000	1997
Value	907,206	637,115	630,684

HOMES BUILT

	1999	1998	1997
No	4,237	3,416	3,756

CAPITAL EXPENDITURES

(Public & Private)	2000	1999 $000,000	1998
Total Expends.	n.a.	n.a.	5,464.0
Capital Expends.	4,086.2	5,086.1	4,304.7
Construction	2,353.4	3,335.6	2,807.6
Machinery & Equip.	1,732.8	1,750.5	1,497.1
Repair Expends.	n.a.	n.a.	1,159.3
Construction	n.a.	n.a.	510.4
Machinery & Equip.	n.a.	n.a.	648.9

TAXATION

Income Class:	1997	% Total
Under $5,000	98,590	15.10
$5,000-$10,000	90,280	13.83
$10,000-$15,000	112,890	17.29
$15,000-$20,000	69,940	10.71
$20,000-$25,000	56,970	8.72
$25,000-$30,000	49,180	7.53
$30,000-$40,000	72,020	11.03
$40,000-$50,000	46,170	7.07
$50,000 +	56,990	8.73
Total Returns, No.	653,010	
Total Income, $000	15,218,969	
Total Taxable Returns	426,290	
Total Tax, $000	2,673,961	
Average Income, $	23,306	
Average Tax, $	6,273	

VITAL STATISTICS

	1997	1996	1995	1994
Births	9,952	10,573	10,726	11,099
Deaths	8,044	7,751	7,687	7,770
Natural Increase	1,908	2,822	3,039	3,329
Marriages	5,525	5,392	5,329	5,374

Note: Latest available data.

TRAVEL STATISTICS

Tourists in Canada	1999	1998
From the U.S. entering by:		
Automobile	80,935	74,404
Bus	15,824	15,623
Air	70,778	69,639
Marine	69,821	30,210
Other Methods	46,284	48,981
Total	283,642	238,857
Other Countries:		
Land (via U.S.)	2,654	2,258
Air	63,066	62,810
Marine	5,328	4,384
Total	71,048	69,452
Residents of Canada Returning from the U.S. by:		
Automobile	14,455	13,381
Bus	750	1,089
Air	55,998	56,410
Marine	1,393	977
Other Methods	2,139	2,883
Total	74,735	74,740
From Other Countries:		
Air	74,503	60,386
Marine	13	30
Total	74,516	60,416

Nova Scotia

Nova Scotia

Cape Breton
(Census Agglomeration)

The Census Agglomeration of Cape Breton includes: Cape Breton, RGM; Eskasoni 3, R; plus one other area. All are in Cape Breton County.

POPULATION

July 1, 2001 Estimate	115,521
% Cdn. Total	0.37
% Change, '96 -'01	-4.02
Avg. Annual Growth Rate, %	-0.82
2003 Projected Population	115,563
2006 Projected Population	115,493
2001 Households Estimate	43,689
2003 Projected Households	44,252
2006 Projected Households	45,008

INCOME

% Above/Below National Average	-29
2001 Total Income Estimate	$1,725,670,000
% Cdn. Total	0.26
2001 Average Hhld. Income	$39,500
2001 Per Capita	$14,900
2003 Projected Total Income	$1,827,570,000
2006 Projected Total Income	$1,992,010,000

RETAIL SALES

% Above/Below National Average	-3
2001 Retail Sales Estimate	$999,190,000
% Cdn. Total	0.36
2001 per Household	$22,900
2001 per Capita	$8,600
2001 No. of Establishments	751
2003 Projected Retail Sales	$1,073,990,000
2006 Projected Retail Sales	$1,182,440,000

POPULATION

2001 Estimates:

Total		115,521
Male		55,345
Female		60,176

Age Groups	Male	Female
0-4	3,122	2,974
5-9	3,532	3,367
10-14	3,965	3,763
15-19	4,276	4,117
20-24	4,190	4,059
25-29	3,596	3,612
30-34	3,389	3,702
35-39	3,750	4,232
40-44	4,143	4,549
45-49	4,291	4,491
50-54	3,855	4,001
55-59	3,249	3,381
60-64	2,762	2,964
65-69	2,343	2,698
70+	4,882	8,266

DAYTIME POPULATION

2001 Estimates:

Working Population	39,958
At Home Population	75,563
Total	115,521

INCOME

2001 Estimates:

Avg. Household Income	$39,499
Avg. Family Income	$43,472
Per Capita Income	$14,938
Male:	
Avg. Employment Income	$25,682
Avg. Employment Income (Full Time)	$38,886
Female:	
Avg. Employment Income	$16,424
Avg. Employment Income (Full Time)	$27,683

DISPOSABLE & DISCRETIONARY INCOME

2001 Estimates:	Per Hhld.
Disposable Income	$31,458
Discretionary Income 1 (minus Food & Shelter)	$21,131
Discretionary Income 2 (minus Food, Shelter, & Other Expenditures)	$14,246

LIQUID ASSETS

1999 Estimates:	Per Hhld.
Equity Investments	$40,568
Interest Bearing Investments	$45,107
Total Liquid Assets	$85,675

CREDIT DATA

July 2000:

Pool of Credit	$1,018,930,213
Revolving Credit, No.	157,788
Fixed Loans, No.	83,400
Avg. Credit Limit, per Person	$10,420
Avg. Spent, per Person	$5,737
Satisfactory Ratings, No. per Person	2.28
Avg. No. of Cards, per Person	0.65

LABOUR FORCE

2001 Estimates:

Male:	
In the Labour Force	24,915
Participation Rate	55.7
Employed	19,895
Unemployed	5,020
Unemployment Rate	20.1
Not in Labour Force	19,811
Female:	
In the Labour Force	22,817
Participation Rate	45.6
Employed	19,128
Unemployed	3,689
Unemployment Rate	16.2
Not in Labour Force	27,255

OCCUPATIONS BY MAJOR GROUPS

2001 Estimates:	Male	Female
Management	1,401	1,058
Business, Finance & Admin.	1,780	4,533
Natural & Applied Sciences & Related	865	145
Health	515	2,740
Social Sciences, Gov't Services & Religion	495	743
Education	906	1,466
Arts, Culture, Recreation & Sport	401	448
Sales & Service	5,546	9,219
Trades, Transport & Equipment Operators & Related	7,585	191
Primary Industries	2,568	237
Processing, Mfg. & Utilities	1,392	383

LEVEL OF SCHOOLING

2001 Estimates:

Population 15 years +	94,798
Less than Grade 9	12,630
Grades 9-13 w/o Certif.	30,673
Grade 9-13 with Certif.	9,299
Trade Certif. /Dip.	4,163
Non-Univ. w/o Certif./Dip.	2,892
Non-Univ. with Certif./Dip.	15,645
Univ. w/o Degree	11,571
Univ. w/o Degree/Certif.	5,522
Univ. with Certif.	6,049
Univ. with Degree	7,925

AVERAGE HOUSEHOLD EXPENDITURES

2001 Estimates:

Food	$5,106
Shelter	$6,792
Clothing	$1,630
Transportation	$5,169
Health & Personal Care	$1,600
Recr'n, Read'g & Education	$2,822
Taxes & Securities	$9,642
Other	$7,139
Total Expenditures	$39,900

PRIVATE HOUSEHOLDS

2001 Estimates:

Private Households, Total	43,689
Pop. in Private Households	113,514
Average no. per Household	2.6

FAMILIES

2001 Estimates:

Families in Private Households	33,065
Husband-Wife Families	25,539
Lone-Parent Families	7,526
Aver. No. Persons per Family	3.1
Aver. No. Sons/Daughters at Home	1.3

HOUSING

2001 Estimates:

Occupied Private Dwellings	43,689
Owned	31,392
Rented	11,641
Band Housing	656
Single-Detached House	32,872
Semi-Detached House	2,779
Row Houses	628
Apartment, 5+ Storeys	267
Apartment, 5 or Fewer Storeys	4,062
Apartment, Detached Duplex	2,088
Other Single-Attached	69
Movable Dwellings	924

VEHICLES

2001 Estimates:

Model Yrs. '81-'96, No.	43,285
% Total	86.37
Model Yrs. '97-'98, No.	3,468
% Total	6.92
'99 Vehicles registered in Model Yr. '99, No.	3,362
% Total	6.71
Total No. '81-'99	50,115

LEGAL MARITAL STATUS

2001 Estimates: (Age 15+)

Single (Never Married)	30,657
Legally Married (Not Separated)	46,974
Legally Married (Separated)	2,909
Widowed	8,579
Divorced	5,679

PSYTE CATEGORIES

2001 Estimates	No. of House-holds	% of Total Hhds.	Index
Small City Elite	4,150	9.50	554
Old Bungalow Burbs	1,031	2.36	142
Aging Erudites	355	0.81	54
Old Towns' New Fringe	7,072	16.19	414
University Enclaves	351	0.80	39
Old Leafy Towns	391	0.89	35
Nesters & Young Homesteaders	5,802	13.28	569
Rod & Rifle	16,702	38.23	1,653
Down, Down East	478	1.09	156
Big Country Families	972	2.22	156
Struggling Downtowns	5,705	13.06	415
Aged Pensioners	346	0.79	60

FINANCIAL P$YTE

2001 Estimates	No. of House-holds	% of Total Hhds.	Index
Canadian Comfort	4,150	9.50	98
Urban Heights	355	0.81	19
Miners & Credit-Liners	1,031	2.36	75
Tractors & Tradelines	7,072	16.19	283
Bills & Wills	391	0.89	11
Revolving Renters	5,802	13.28	289
Young Urban Struggle	351	0.80	17
Rural Family Blues	18,152	41.55	515
Towering Debt	5,705	13.06	167
Senior Survivors	346	0.79	42

HOME LANGUAGE

2001 Estimates:		% Total
English	112,678	97.54
French	188	0.16
Chinese	90	0.08
Micmac	2,175	1.88
Other Languages	146	0.13
Multiple Responses	244	0.21
Total	115,521	100.00

BUILDING PERMITS

	1999	1998	1997
		$000	
Value	46,964	59,233	44,174

HOMES BUILT

	1999	1998	1997
No.	178	199	278

TAXATION

Income Class:	1997	% Total
Under $5,000	13,870	16.67
$5,000-$10,000	13,170	15.83
$10,000-$15,000	15,860	19.06
$15,000-$20,000	9,620	11.56
$20,000-$25,000	7,300	8.77
$25,000-$30,000	5,940	7.14
$30,000-$40,000	8,020	9.64
$40,000-$50,000	4,650	5.59
$50,000+	4,770	5.73
Total Returns, No.	83,210	
Total Income, $000	1,649,553	
Total Taxable Returns	48,540	
Total Tax, $000	249,502	
Average Income, $	19,824	
Average Tax, $	5,140	

Cape Breton
(Census Agglomeration)
(Cont'd)

VITAL STATISTICS

	1997	1996	1995	1994
Births	1,176	1,276	1,350	1,401
Deaths	1,158	1,201	1,236	1,241
Natural Increase	18	75	114	160
Marriages	599	648	622	685

Note: Latest available data.

DAILY NEWSPAPER(S)

	Circulation Average Paid
Cape Breton Post	27,231

RADIO STATION(S)

	Power
CBI	n.a.
CBI-FM	10,000w
CHER	n.a.
CJCB	10,000w
CKPE-FM	61,000w

TELEVISION STATION(S)

CBAFT-TV
CBIT-TV
CJCB-TV
GLOBAL-TV

Chester
(Municipal District)
In Lunenburg County.

POPULATION

July 1, 2001 Estimate	10,790
% Cdn. Total	0.03
% Change, '96 -'01	-0.38
Avg. Annual Growth Rate, %	-0.08
2003 Projected Population	10,803
2006 Projected Population	10,805
2001 Households Estimate	4,445
2003 Projected Households	4,487
2006 Projected Households	4,553

INCOME

% Above/Below National Average	-19
2001 Total Income Estimate	$184,000,000
% Cdn. Total	0.03
2001 Average Hhld. Income	$41,400
2001 Per Capita	$17,100
2003 Projected Total Income	$194,200,000
2006 Projected Total Income	$211,000,000

RETAIL SALES

% Above/Below National Average	-28
2001 Retail Sales Estimate	$69,930,000
% Cdn. Total	0.03
2001 per Household	$15,700
2001 per Capita	$6,500
2001 No. of Establishments	87
2003 Projected Retail Sales	$75,450,000
2006 Projected Retail Sales	$83,630,000

POPULATION

2001 Estimates:

Total	10,790
Male	5,442
Female	5,348

Age Groups	Male	Female
0-4	263	230
5-9	293	259
10-14	338	276
15-19	361	299
20-24	335	297
25-29	310	268
30-34	346	320
35-39	407	419
40-44	425	447
45-49	433	445
50-54	411	402
55-59	348	346
60-64	301	299
65-69	274	272
70+	597	769

DAYTIME POPULATION

2001 Estimates:

Working Population	3,272
At Home Population	6,220
Total	9,492

INCOME

2001 Estimates:

Avg. Household Income	$41,395
Avg. Family Income	$45,595
Per Capita Income	$17,053
Male:	
Avg. Employment Income	$28,005
Avg. Employment Income (Full Time)	$38,768
Female:	
Avg. Employment Income	$16,474
Avg. Employment Income (Full Time)	$25,787

DISPOSABLE & DISCRETIONARY INCOME

2001 Estimates: Per Hhld.

Disposable Income	$32,577
Discretionary Income 1 (minus Food & Shelter)	$21,802
Discretionary Income 2 (minus Food, Shelter, & Other Expenditures)	$14,411

LIQUID ASSETS

1999 Estimates: Per Hhld.

Equity Investments	$42,628
Interest Bearing Investments	$47,700
Total Liquid Assets	$90,328

CREDIT DATA

July 2000:

Pool of Credit	$131,416,363
Revolving Credit, No.	18,814
Fixed Loans, No.	9,478
Avg. Credit Limit, per Person	$12,139
Avg. Spent, per Person	$6,169
Satisfactory Ratings, No. per Person	2.50
Avg. No. of Cards, per Person	0.76

LABOUR FORCE

2001 Estimates:

Male:	
In the Labour Force	2,734
Participation Rate	60.1
Employed	2,503
Unemployed	231
Unemployment Rate	8.4
Not in Labour Force	1,814
Female:	
In the Labour Force	2,250
Participation Rate	49.1
Employed	1,978
Unemployed	272
Unemployment Rate	12.1
Not in Labour Force	2,333

OCCUPATIONS BY MAJOR GROUPS

2001 Estimates:	Male	Female
Management	266	107
Business, Finance & Admin.	165	529
Natural & Applied Sciences & Related	156	22
Health	19	173
Social Sciences, Gov't Services & Religion	76	54
Education	58	83
Arts, Culture, Recreation & Sport	34	68
Sales & Service	300	783
Trades, Transport & Equipment Operators & Related	861	79
Primary Industries	347	38
Processing, Mfg. & Utilities	389	189

LEVEL OF SCHOOLING

2001 Estimates:

Population 15 years +	9,131
Less than Grade 9	1,255
Grades 9-13 w/o Certif.	2,873
Grade 9-13 with Certif.	808
Trade Certif. /Dip.	365
Non-Univ. w/o Certif./Dip.	410
Non-Univ. with Certif./Dip.	1,937
Univ. w/o Degree	695
Univ. w/o Degree/Certif.	281
Univ. with Certif.	414
Univ. with Degree	788

Nova Scotia

AVERAGE HOUSEHOLD EXPENDITURES

2001 Estimates:

Food	$5,349
Shelter	$6,972
Clothing	$1,572
Transportation	$5,640
Health & Personal Care	$1,669
Recr'n, Read'g & Education	$2,893
Taxes & Securities	$10,348
Other	$7,065
Total Expenditures	$41,508

PRIVATE HOUSEHOLDS

2001 Estimates:

Private Households, Total	4,445
Pop. in Private Households	10,591
Average no. per Household	2.4

FAMILIES

2001 Estimates:

Families in Private Households	3,330
Husband-Wife Families	2,980
Lone-Parent Families	350
Aver. No. Persons per Family	2.8
Aver. No. Sons/Daughters at Home	1.0

HOUSING

2001 Estimates:

Occupied Private Dwellings	4,445
Owned	3,806
Rented	639
Single-Detached House	4,082
Semi-Detached House	41
Apartment, 5 or Fewer Storeys	131
Apartment, Detached Duplex	64
Other Single-Attached	31
Movable Dwellings	96

VEHICLES

2001 Estimates:

Model Yrs. '81-'96, No.	4,795
% Total	86.41
Model Yrs. '97-'98, No.	372
% Total	6.70
'99 Vehicles registered in Model Yr. '99, No.	382
% Total	6.88
Total No. '81-'99	5,549

LEGAL MARITAL STATUS

2001 Estimates: (Age 15+)

Single (Never Married)	2,369
Legally Married (Not Separated)	5,133
Legally Married (Separated)	244
Widowed	753
Divorced	632

PSYTE CATEGORIES

2001 Estimates	No. of Households	% of Total 'Hhds.	Index
Old Towns' New Fringe	436	9.81	251
Old Leafy Towns	1,504	33.84	1,324
Rod & Rifle	2,454	55.21	2,387

Chester
(Municipal District)
(Cont'd)

FINAN¢IAL P$YTE

2001 Estimates	No. of House-holds	% of Total Hhds.	Index
Tractors & Tradelines	436	9.81	172
Bills & Wills	1,504	33.84	409
Rural Family Blues	2,454	55.21	684

HOME LANGUAGE

2001 Estimates:		% Total
English	10,760	99.72
French	20	0.19
Other Languages	10	0.09
Total	10,790	100.00

BUILDING PERMITS

	1999	1998	1997
		$000	
Value	13,767	15,695	11,067

TAXATION

Income Class:	1997	% Total
Under $5,000	1,000	17.15
$5,000-$10,000	860	14.75
$10,000-$15,000	1,100	18.87
$15,000-$20,000	660	11.32
$20,000-$25,000	500	8.58
$25,000-$30,000	410	7.03
$30,000-$40,000	550	9.43
$40,000-$50,000	350	6.00
$50,000 +	410	7.03
Total Returns, No.	5,830	
Total Income, $000	124,371	
Total Taxable Returns	3,580	
Total Tax, $000	20,536	
Average Income, $	21,333	
Average Tax, $	5,736	

VITAL STATISTICS

	1997	1996	1995	1994
Births	78	95	88	88
Deaths	96	101	98	111
Natural Increase	-18	-6	-10	-23
Marriages	57	83	63	48

Note: Latest available data.

East Hants
(Municipal District)

In Hants County.

POPULATION

July 1, 2001 Estimate	21,824
% Cdn. Total	0.07
% Change, '96 -'01	7.79
Avg. Annual Growth Rate, %	1.51
2003 Projected Population	22,560
2006 Projected Population	23,661
2001 Households Estimate	7,773
2003 Projected Households	8,111
2006 Projected Households	8,666

INCOME

% Above/Below National Average	-17
2001 Total Income Estimate	$382,660,000
% Cdn. Total	0.06
2001 Average Hhld. Income	$49,200
2001 Per Capita	$17,500
2003 Projected Total Income	$422,410,000
2006 Projected Total Income	$492,230,000

RETAIL SALES

% Above/Below National Average	-19
2001 Retail Sales Estimate	$158,170,000
% Cdn. Total	0.06
2001 per Household	$20,300
2001 per Capita	$7,200
2001 No. of Establishments	142
2003 Projected Retail Sales	$173,480,000
2006 Projected Retail Sales	$198,210,000

POPULATION

2001 Estimates:		
Total		21,824
Male		10,997
Female		10,827
Age Groups	Male	Female
0-4	699	641
5-9	796	716
10-14	836	751
15-19	832	748
20-24	753	713
25-29	713	743
30-34	815	874
35-39	937	968
40-44	965	954
45-49	891	851
50-54	724	695
55-59	571	537
60-64	449	425
65-69	360	360
70+	656	851

DAYTIME POPULATION

2001 Estimates:	
Working Population	7,695
At Home Population	11,360
Total	19,055

INCOME

2001 Estimates:	
Avg. Household Income	$49,229
Avg. Family Income	$51,998
Per Capita Income	$17,534
Male:	
Avg. Employment Income	$29,739
Avg. Employment Income (Full Time)	$40,165
Female:	
Avg. Employment Income	$18,804
Avg. Employment Income (Full Time)	$28,299

DISPOSABLE & DISCRETIONARY INCOME

2001 Estimates:	Per Hhld.
Disposable Income	$38,772
Discretionary Income 1 (minus Food & Shelter)	$26,521
Discretionary Income 2 (minus Food, Shelter, & Other Expenditures)	$17,990

LIQUID ASSETS

1999 Estimates:	Per Hhld.
Equity Investments	$54,501
Interest Bearing Investments	$56,253
Total Liquid Assets	$110,754

CREDIT DATA

July 2000:	
Pool of Credit	$269,951,083
Revolving Credit, No.	40,912
Fixed Loans, No.	21,044
Avg. Credit Limit, per Person	$12,064
Avg. Spent, per Person	$6,678
Satisfactory Ratings, No. per Person	2.57
Avg. No. of Cards, per Person	0.72

LABOUR FORCE

2001 Estimates:	
Male:	
In the Labour Force	6,047
Participation Rate	69.8
Employed	5,610
Unemployed	437
Unemployment Rate	7.2
Not in Labour Force	2,619
Female:	
In the Labour Force	5,129
Participation Rate	58.8
Employed	4,703
Unemployed	426
Unemployment Rate	8.3
Not in Labour Force	3,590

OCCUPATIONS BY MAJOR GROUPS

2001 Estimates:	Male	Female
Management	587	267
Business, Finance & Admin.	359	1,450
Natural & Applied Sciences & Related	412	80
Health	52	417
Social Sciences, Gov't Services & Religion	34	110
Education	35	251
Arts, Culture, Recreation & Sport	50	48
Sales & Service	1,004	1,854
Trades, Transport & Equipment Operators & Related	2,195	100
Primary Industries	679	230
Processing, Mfg. & Utilities	587	106

LEVEL OF SCHOOLING

2001 Estimates:	
Population 15 years +	17,385
Less than Grade 9	1,995
Grades 9-13 w/o Certif.	5,419
Grade 9-13 with Certif.	1,842
Trade Certif. /Dip.	912
Non-Univ. w/o Certif./Dip.	634
Non-Univ. with Certif./Dip.	3,883
Univ. w/o Degree	1,467
Univ. w/o Degree/Certif.	655
Univ. with Certif.	812
Univ. with Degree	1,233

AVERAGE HOUSEHOLD EXPENDITURES

2001 Estimates:	
Food	$5,989
Shelter	$8,111
Clothing	$1,893
Transportation	$6,520
Health & Personal Care	$1,857
Recr'n, Read'g & Education	$3,588
Taxes & Securities	$11,882
Other	$8,448
Total Expenditures	$48,288

PRIVATE HOUSEHOLDS

2001 Estimates:	
Private Households, Total	7,773
Pop. in Private Households	21,733
Average no. per Household	2.8

FAMILIES

2001 Estimates:	
Families in Private Households	6,565
Husband-Wife Families	5,911
Lone-Parent Families	654
Aver. No. Persons per Family	3.1
Aver. No. Sons/Daughters at Home	1.2

HOUSING

2001 Estimates:	
Occupied Private Dwellings	7,773
Owned	6,765
Rented	1,008
Single-Detached House	6,729
Semi-Detached House	140
Apartment, 5 or Fewer Storeys	345
Apartment, Detached Duplex	110
Other Single-Attached	191
Movable Dwellings	258

VEHICLES

2001 Estimates:	
Model Yrs. '81-'96, No.	9,356
% Total	86.62
Model Yrs. '97-'98, No.	741
% Total	6.86
'99 Vehicles registered in Model Yr. '99, No.	704
% Total	6.52
Total No. '81-'99	10,801

LEGAL MARITAL STATUS

2001 Estimates: (Age 15+)	
Single (Never Married)	4,670
Legally Married (Not Separated)	10,533
Legally Married (Separated)	486
Widowed	861
Divorced	835

PSYTE CATEGORIES

2001 Estimates	No. of House-holds	% of Total Hhds.	Index
Small City Elite	125	1.61	94
Old Towns' New Fringe	5,162	66.41	1,697
Rustic Prosperity	236	3.04	168
Agrarian Blues	266	3.42	1,598
Rod & Rifle	1,984	25.52	1,104

FINAN¢IAL P$YTE

2001 Estimates	No. of House-holds	% of Total Hhds.	Index
Canadian Comfort	125	1.61	17
Tractors & Tradelines	5,398	69.45	1,214
Rural Family Blues	2,250	28.95	359

HOME LANGUAGE

2001 Estimates:		% Total
English	21,429	98.19
French	32	0.15
Gaelic Languages	12	0.05
German	318	1.46
Other Languages	11	0.05
Multiple Responses	22	0.10
Total	21,824	100.00

East Hants
(Municipal District)
(Cont'd)

BUILDING PERMITS

	1999	1998	1997
		$000	
Value	20,940	21,122	n.a.

TAXATION

Income Class:	1997	% Total
Under $5,000	3,030	17.24
$5,000-$10,000	2,250	12.80
$10,000-$15,000	2,660	15.13
$15,000-$20,000	1,710	9.73
$20,000-$25,000	1,510	8.59
$25,000-$30,000	1,520	8.65
$30,000-$40,000	2,300	13.08
$40,000-$50,000	1,440	8.19
$50,000 +	1,150	6.54
Total Returns, No.	17,580	
Total Income, $000	383,229	
Total Taxable Returns	11,640	
Total Tax, $000	63,527	
Average Income, $	21,799	
Average Tax, $	5,458	

VITAL STATISTICS

	1997	1996	1995	1994
Births	246	282	246	263
Deaths	111	107	114	119
Natural Increase	135	175	132	144
Marriages	94	82	94	94

Note: Latest available data.

Halifax
(Census Metropolitan Area)

On Apr. 1, 1996, Halifax, C, Halifax Subdivisions A, B, C, D & E, Dartmouth, C & Bedford, T, amalgamated to form Halifax, RGM.

POPULATION

July 1, 2001 Estimate	361,378
% Cdn. Total	1.16
% Change, '96 -'01	5.85
Avg. Annual Growth Rate, %	1.14
2003 Projected Population	371,934
2006 Projected Population	390,731
2001 Households Estimate	144,144
2003 Projected Households	149,346
2006 Projected Households	158,514

INCOME

% Above/Below National Average	+1
2001 Total Income Estimate	$7,707,790,000
% Cdn. Total	1.17
2001 Average Hhld. Income	$53,500
2001 Per Capita	$21,300
2003 Projected Total Income	$8,396,680,000
2006 Projected Total Income	$9,645,070,000

RETAIL SALES

% Above/Below National Average	+9
2001 Retail Sales Estimate	$3,529,680,000
% Cdn. Total	1.27
2001 per Household	$24,500
2001 per Capita	$9,800
2001 No. of Establishments	2,261
2003 Projected Retail Sales	$3,860,970,000
2006 Projected Retail Sales	$4,395,410,000

POPULATION

2001 Estimates:

Total	361,378
Male	174,748
Female	186,630

Age Groups	Male	Female
0-4	11,381	10,864
5-9	11,950	11,461
10-14	12,051	11,468
15-19	11,529	11,088
20-24	11,844	12,170
25-29	13,089	13,849
30-34	14,941	15,760
35-39	15,839	16,750
40-44	15,050	16,160
45-49	13,670	14,651
50-54	11,539	12,164
55-59	8,957	9,361
60-64	6,936	7,281
65-69	5,458	6,170
70+	10,514	17,433

DAYTIME POPULATION

2001 Estimates:

Working Population	186,333
At Home Population	175,046
Total	361,379

INCOME

2001 Estimates:

Avg. Household Income	$53,473
Avg. Family Income	$60,441
Per Capita Income	$21,329

Male:

Avg. Employment Income	$34,535
Avg. Employment Income (Full Time)	$45,337

Female:

Avg. Employment Income	$21,460
Avg. Employment Income (Full Time)	$31,411

DISPOSABLE & DISCRETIONARY INCOME

2001 Estimates:	Per Hhld.
Disposable Income	$41,334
Discretionary Income 1 (minus Food & Shelter)	$28,375
Discretionary Income 2 (minus Food, Shelter, & Other Expenditures)	$20,267

LIQUID ASSETS

1999 Estimates:	Per Hhld.
Equity Investments	$66,412
Interest Bearing Investments	$63,153
Total Liquid Assets	$129,565

CREDIT DATA

July 2000:

Pool of Credit	$4,152,643,931
Revolving Credit, No.	688,667
Fixed Loans, No.	257,828
Avg. Credit Limit, per Person	$13,176
Avg. Spent, per Person	$6,646
Satisfactory Ratings, No. per Person	2.83
Avg. No. of Cards, per Person	0.92

LABOUR FORCE

2001 Estimates:

Male:

In the Labour Force	98,476
Participation Rate	70.7
Employed	93,719
Unemployed	4,757
Unemployment Rate	4.8
Not in Labour Force	40,890

Female:

In the Labour Force	95,966
Participation Rate	62.8
Employed	91,927
Unemployed	4,039
Unemployment Rate	4.2
Not in Labour Force	56,871

OCCUPATIONS BY MAJOR GROUPS

2001 Estimates:	Male	Female
Management	13,154	6,150
Business, Finance & Admin.	11,006	30,795
Natural & Applied Sciences & Related	8,099	1,673
Health	2,160	9,915
Social Sciences, Gov't Services & Religion	2,193	3,280
Education	3,061	4,655
Arts, Culture, Recreation & Sport	2,859	3,031
Sales & Service	27,067	31,404
Trades, Transport & Equipment Operators & Related	21,204	1,050
Primary Industries	1,925	345
Processing, Mfg. & Utilities	3,444	1,152

LEVEL OF SCHOOLING

2001 Estimates:

Population 15 years +	292,203
Less than Grade 9	18,631
Grades 9-13 w/o Certif.	65,360
Grade 9-13 with Certif.	28,938
Trade Certif. /Dip.	9,317
Non-Univ. w/o Certif./Dip.	12,822
Non-Univ. with Certif./Dip.	60,156
Univ. w/o Degree	41,803
Univ. w/o Degree/Certif.	21,210
Univ. with Certif.	20,593
Univ. with Degree	55,176

Nova Scotia

AVERAGE HOUSEHOLD EXPENDITURES

2001 Estimates:

Food	$6,107
Shelter	$9,104
Clothing	$2,196
Transportation	$6,109
Health & Personal Care	$1,916
Recr'n, Read'g & Education	$3,813
Taxes & Securities	$14,019
Other	$8,391
Total Expenditures	$51,655

PRIVATE HOUSEHOLDS

2001 Estimates:

Private Households, Total	144,144
Pop. in Private Households	355,268
Average no. per Household	2.5

FAMILIES

2001 Estimates:

Families in Private Households	103,350
Husband-Wife Families	87,289
Lone-Parent Families	16,061
Aver. No. Persons per Family	3.0
Aver. No. Sons/Daughters at Home	1.1

HOUSING

2001 Estimates:

Occupied Private Dwellings	144,144
Owned	87,654
Rented	56,479
Band Housing	11
Single-Detached House	73,194
Semi-Detached House	10,996
Row Houses	5,563
Apartment, 5+ Storeys	12,193
Owned Apartment, 5+ Storeys	1,355
Apartment, 5 or Fewer Storeys	30,779
Apartment, Detached Duplex	6,601
Other Single-Attached	417
Movable Dwellings	4,401

VEHICLES

2001 Estimates:

Model Yrs. '81-'96, No.	129,825
% Total	73.43
Model Yrs. '97-'98, No.	21,990
% Total	12.44
'99 Vehicles registered in Model Yr. '99, No.	24,988
% Total	14.13
Total No. '81-'99	176,803

LEGAL MARITAL STATUS

2001 Estimates: (Age 15+)

Single (Never Married)	95,705
Legally Married (Not Separated)	151,178
Legally Married (Separated)	9,180
Widowed	15,986
Divorced	20,154

Nova Scotia

Halifax
(Census Metropolitan Area)
(Cont'd)

PSYTE CATEGORIES

2001 Estimates	No. of House-holds	% of Total Hhds.	Index
Urban Gentry	5,057	3.51	195
Suburban Executives	1,689	1.17	82
Mortgaged in Suburbia	3,060	2.12	153
Technocrafts & Bureaucrats	6,865	4.76	169
Stable Suburban Families	1,876	1.30	100
Small City Elite	14,558	10.10	589
Old Bungalow Burbs	5,614	3.89	235
Suburban Nesters	118	0.08	5
Aging Erudites	10,810	7.50	497
Satellite Suburbs	4,161	2.89	101
Kindergarten Boom	3,869	2.68	102
Blue Collar Winners	858	0.60	24
Old Towns' New Fringe	20,752	14.40	368
High Rise Melting Pot	471	0.33	22
Conservative Homebodies	4,672	3.24	90
High Rise Sunsets	1,808	1.25	88
Young Urban Professionals	5,824	4.04	213
Young Urban Mix	803	0.56	26
Young Urban Intelligentsia	6,981	4.84	318
University Enclaves	13,540	9.39	460
Young City Singles	10,579	7.34	320
Urban Bohemia	1,292	0.90	77
Old Leafy Towns	1,097	0.76	30
Town Renters	1,739	1.21	140
Nesters & Young Homesteaders	406	0.28	12
Rod & Rifle	2,027	1.41	61
Struggling Downtowns	6,910	4.79	152
Aged Pensioners	1,610	1.12	84
Big City Stress	3,543	2.46	218
Old Grey Towers	385	0.27	48

FINANCIAL P$YTE

2001 Estimates	No. of House-holds	% of Total Hhds.	Index
Four Star Investors	6,746	4.68	93
Successful Suburbanites	11,801	8.19	123
Canadian Comfort	19,695	13.66	141
Urban Heights	16,634	11.54	268
Miners & Credit-Liners	5,614	3.89	123
Mortgages & Minivans	3,869	2.68	41
Tractors & Tradelines	20,752	14.40	252
Bills & Wills	6,572	4.56	55
Revolving Renters	2,214	1.54	33
Young Urban Struggle	21,813	15.13	320
Rural Family Blues	2,027	1.41	17
Towering Debt	19,699	13.67	175
NSF	3,543	2.46	69
Senior Survivors	1,995	1.38	73

HOME LANGUAGE

2001 Estimates:		% Total
English	348,569	96.46
French	3,679	1.02
Arabic	1,735	0.48
Chinese	1,231	0.34
Greek	463	0.13
Hindi	193	0.05
Italian	252	0.07
Polish	282	0.08
Punjabi	185	0.05
Serbo-Croatian	208	0.06
Spanish	215	0.06
Urdu	250	0.07
Other Languages	1,839	0.51
Multiple Responses	2,277	0.63
Total	361,378	100.00

BUILDING PERMITS

	1999	1998	1997
		$000	
Value	388,081	239,514	262,799

HOMES BUILT

	1999	1998	1997
No	2,257	1,816	1,849

RADIO STATION DATA

Station	Market	Format	Wkly. Reach%*	Aver. Hrs. Tuned
All Stations			96	20.1
CBH-FM	Halifax	Multi-format	7	9.1
CBHA-FM	Halifax	Multi-format	24	12.7
CFDR	Halifax	Country	7	12.2
CFRQ-FM	Halifax	Classic Rock	29	9.1
CHFX-FM	Halifax	Country	23	13.6
CHNS	Halifax	Oldies	13	9.3
CIEZ-FM	Halifax	Adult Contemp.	19	8.8
CIOO-FM	Halifax	Contemp. Hit Radio	44	11.3
CJCH	Halifax	News, Talk	9	7.3
KIXX	Halifax	Country	n.a.	n.a.

BBM Spring 2000 Radio Reach Survey; area coverage.
*Mon-Sun 5a.m - 1a.m , All Persons 12+

TV STATION DATA

Station	Market	Network Affiliation	Wkly. Reach%*	Aver. Hrs. Tuned
All Stations			96	23.7
A & E	n.a.	Ind.	28	3.0
ASN	Maritimes	CTV	44	3.7
CBHT	Halifax	CBC	52	3.4
CIHF	Halifax/Dartmouth	Global	n.a.	n.a.
CIHFNS	Halifax	n.a.	62	3.3
CJCH	Halifax	CTV	78	6.4
CNN	n.a.	Ind.	6	2.7
DSCVRY	n.a.	Ind.	7	1.7
FAMILY	n.a.	Ind.	6	2.5
HISTTV	n.a.	Ind.	5	2.7
MMUSIC	n.a.	Ind.	8	1.5
NEWSWD	n.a.	CBC	9	1.6
OTHERS	n.a.	n.a.	10	4.0
PRIME	n.a.	Ind.	13	2.4
SPACE	n.a.	Ind.	9	2.5
TLC	n.a.	Ind.	18	1.9
TNN	Nashville TN	Ind.	9	2.4
TOON	n.a.	Ind.	8	3.2
TREE	n.a.	Ind.	7	3.6
TSN	n.a.	Ind.	20	4.5
VCR	n.a.	n.a.	32	4.3
VISION	n.a.	Ind.	6	2.1
WBZ	Boston MA	CBS	32	2.7
WCVB	Boston MA	ABC	28	1.9
WFXT	Boston MA	FOX	-	1.2
WGBH	Boston MA	PBS	18	2.1
WHDH	Boston MA	NBC	32	1.9
WSBK	Boston MA	UPN	1	4.2
WTBS	Atlanta GA	Ind.	16	4.2
WTN	n.a.	Ind.	9	1.4
WUHF	Rochester NY	FOX	27	3.0
YTV	n.a.	Ind.	14	3.2

BBM Spring 2000 TV Reach Survey; CMA coverage.
*Mon-Sun 6a.m.-2a.m., All Persons 2+

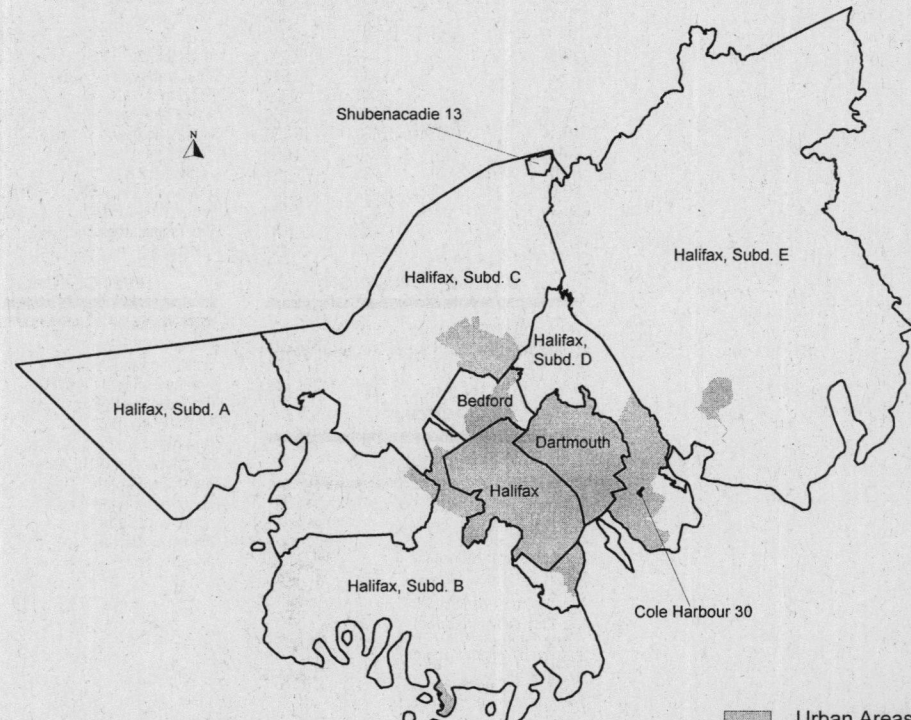

Shubenacadie 13

Halifax, Subd. E

Halifax, Subd. C

Halifax, Subd. D

Bedford

Halifax, Subd. A

Dartmouth

Halifax

Halifax, Subd. B

Cole Harbour 30

Urban Areas

Halifax
(Census Metropolitan Area)
(Cont'd)
TAXATION

Income Class:	1997	% Total
Under $5,000	31,910	13.18
$5,000-$10,000	29,850	12.33
$10,000-$15,000	33,020	13.64
$15,000-$20,000	22,860	9.45
$20,000-$25,000	21,140	8.73
$25,000-$30,000	20,010	8.27
$30,000-$40,000	31,560	13.04
$40,000-$50,000	21,520	8.89
$50,000 +	30,170	12.47
Total Returns, No.	242,030	
Total Income, $000	6,679,986	
Total Taxable Returns	172,670	
Total Tax, $000	1,313,364	
Average Income, $	27,600	
Average Tax, $	7,606	

VITAL STATISTICS

	1997	1996	1995	1994
Births	4,102	4,249	4,313	4,524
Deaths	2,250	2,213	2,143	2,174
Natural Increase	1,852	2,036	2,170	2,350
Marriages	1,838	1,983	1,923	1,966

Note: Latest available data.

DAILY NEWSPAPER(S)

	Circulation Average Paid
The Chronicle-Herald, The Mail-Star, The Sunday Herald	
Sun	42,257
Morn	89,691
Eve	24,163
Comb.	113,854
The Daily News, The Sunday Daily News	
Sun	33,977
Mon-Sat	24,349

COMMUNITY NEWSPAPER(S)

	Total Circulation
Halifax: Trident (biwkly)	n.a.

Bedford
(Town)
Halifax CMA

On Apr. 1, 1996, Halifax, C, Halifax Subdivisions A, B, C, D & E, Dartmouth, C & Bedford, T, amalgamated to form Halifax, RGM.

POPULATION

July 1, 2001 Estimate	16,429
% Cdn. Total	0.05
% Change, '96 -'01	17.33
Avg. Annual Growth Rate, %	3.25
2003 Projected Population	17,835
2006 Projected Population	20,089
2001 Households Estimate	6,142
2003 Projected Households	6,735
2006 Projected Households	7,698

INCOME

% Above/Below National Average	+32
2001 Total Income Estimate	$458,050,000
% Cdn. Total	0.07
2001 Average Hhld. Income	$74,600
2001 Per Capita	$27,900
2003 Projected Total Income	$533,720,000
2006 Projected Total Income	$670,420,000

RETAIL SALES

% Above/Below National Average	-24
2001 Retail Sales Estimate	$112,290,000
% Cdn. Total	0.04
2001 per Household	$18,300
2001 per Capita	$6,800
2001 No. of Establishments	168
2003 Projected Retail Sales	$130,120,000
2006 Projected Retail Sales	$159,880,000

POPULATION

2001 Estimates:

Total		16,429
Male		7,972
Female		8,457
Age Groups	Male	Female
0-4	530	507
5-9	608	562
10-14	628	591
15-19	582	580
20-24	528	575
25-29	552	609
30-34	633	703
35-39	702	779
40-44	697	771
45-49	657	710
50-54	555	592
55-59	423	430
60-64	308	308
65-69	217	228
70+	352	512

DAYTIME POPULATION

2001 Estimates:

Working Population	7,535
At Home Population	7,347
Total	14,882

INCOME

2001 Estimates:

Avg. Household Income	$74,576
Avg. Family Income	$81,881
Per Capita Income	$27,880
Male:	
Avg. Employment Income	$49,285
Avg. Employment Income (Full Time)	$62,277
Female:	
Avg. Employment Income	$26,586
Avg. Employment Income (Full Time)	$38,205

DISPOSABLE & DISCRETIONARY INCOME

2001 Estimates:	Per Hhld.
Disposable Income	$56,740
Discretionary Income 1 (minus Food & Shelter)	$40,856
Discretionary Income 2 (minus Food, Shelter, & Other Expenditures)	$30,480

LIQUID ASSETS

1999 Estimates:	Per Hhld.
Equity Investments	$114,571
Interest Bearing Investments	$92,324
Total Liquid Assets	$206,895

CREDIT DATA

July 2000:

Pool of Credit	$241,467,976
Revolving Credit, No.	36,155
Fixed Loans, No.	12,167
Avg. Credit Limit, per Person	$16,953
Avg. Spent, per Person	$8,034
Satisfactory Ratings, No. per Person	3.23
Avg. No. of Cards, per Person	1.12

LABOUR FORCE

2001 Estimates:

Male:	
In the Labour Force	4,694
Participation Rate	75.6
Employed	4,617
Unemployed	77
Unemployment Rate	1.6
Not in Labour Force	1,512
Female:	
In the Labour Force	4,501
Participation Rate	66.2
Employed	4,410
Unemployed	91
Unemployment Rate	2.0
Not in Labour Force	2,296

OCCUPATIONS BY MAJOR GROUPS

2001 Estimates:	Male	Female
Management	1,047	391
Business, Finance & Admin.	597	1,175
Natural & Applied Sciences & Related	451	115
Health	161	554
Social Sciences, Gov't Services & Religion	114	193
Education	108	381
Arts, Culture, Recreation & Sport	91	123
Sales & Service	1,151	1,403
Trades, Transport & Equipment Operators & Related	663	46
Primary Industries	59	n.a.
Processing, Mfg. & Utilities	137	40

LEVEL OF SCHOOLING

2001 Estimates:

Population 15 years +	13,003
Less than Grade 9	361
Grades 9-13 w/o Certif.	2,331
Grade 9-13 with Certif.	1,093
Trade Certif. /Dip.	313
Non-Univ. w/o Certif./Dip.	408
Non-Univ. with Certif./Dip.	2,583
Univ. w/o Degree	2,252
Univ. w/o Degree/Certif.	1,024
Univ. with Certif.	1,228
Univ. with Degree	3,662

Nova Scotia

AVERAGE HOUSEHOLD EXPENDITURES

2001 Estimates:

Food	$7,561
Shelter	$11,276
Clothing	$2,959
Transportation	$8,079
Health & Personal Care	$2,368
Recr'n, Read'g & Education	$5,115
Taxes & Securities	$21,461
Other	$10,096
Total Expenditures	$68,915

PRIVATE HOUSEHOLDS

2001 Estimates:

Private Households, Total	6,142
Pop. in Private Households	16,372
Average no. per Household	2.7

FAMILIES

2001 Estimates:

Families in Private Households	4,890
Husband-Wife Families	4,377
Lone-Parent Families	513
Aver. No. Persons per Family	3.1
Aver. No. Sons/Daughters at Home	1.2

HOUSING

2001 Estimates:

Occupied Private Dwellings	6,142
Owned	4,366
Rented	1,776
Single-Detached House	3,759
Semi-Detached House	431
Row Houses	202
Apartment, 5+ Storeys	70
Owned Apartment, 5+ Storeys	32
Apartment, 5 or Fewer Storeys	1,530
Apartment, Detached Duplex	150

VEHICLES

2001 Estimates:

Model Yrs. '81-'96, No.	6,499
% Total	66.26
Model Yrs. '97-'98, No.	1,998
% Total	20.37
'99 Vehicles registered in Model Yr. '99, No.	1,312
% Total	13.38
Total No. '81-'99	9,809

LEGAL MARITAL STATUS

2001 Estimates: (Age 15+)

Single (Never Married)	3,502
Legally Married (Not Separated)	7,824
Legally Married (Separated)	391
Widowed	506
Divorced	780

Nova Scotia

Bedford
(Town)
Halifax CMA
(Cont'd)

PSYTE CATEGORIES

2001 Estimates	No. of House -holds	% of Total Hhds.	Index
Suburban Executives	878	14.30	997
Mortgaged in Suburbia	641	10.44	751
Technocrafts & Bureaucrats	1,386	22.57	802
Small City Elite	516	8.40	490
Aging Erudites	1,818	29.60	1,962
Old Towns' New Fringe	347	5.65	144
University Enclaves	556	9.05	444

FINANÇIAL P$YTE

2001 Estimates	No. of House -holds	% of Total Hhds.	Index
Four Star Investors	878	14.30	285
Successful Suburbanites	2,027	33.00	497
Canadian Comfort	516	8.40	86
Urban Heights	1,818	29.60	688
Tractors & Tradelines	347	5.65	99
Young Urban Struggle	556	9.05	191

HOME LANGUAGE

2001 Estimates:		% Total
English	15,768	95.98
French	89	0.54
Arabic	140	0.85
Chinese	162	0.99
Dutch	24	0.15
German	18	0.11
Hindi	12	0.07
Malayalam	12	0.07
Polish	18	0.11
Portuguese	12	0.07
Other Languages	30	0.18
Multiple Responses	144	0.88
Total	16,429	100.00

HOMES BUILT

	1999	1998	1997
No.	n.a.	285	294

TAXATION

Income Class:	1997	% Total
Under $5,000	1,380	12.57
$5,000-$10,000	1,110	10.11
$10,000-$15,000	1,140	10.38
$15,000-$20,000	810	7.38
$20,000-$25,000	770	7.01
$25,000-$30,000	820	7.47
$30,000-$40,000	1,430	13.02
$40,000-$50,000	1,060	9.65
$50,000 +	2,470	22.50
Total Returns, No.	10,980	
Total Income, $000	403,804	
Total Taxable Returns	8,340	
Total Tax, $000	94,102	
Average Income, $	36,776	
Average Tax, $	11,283	

VITAL STATISTICS

	1997	1996	1995	1994
Births	202	179	215	208
Deaths	57	44	45	54
Natural Increase	145	135	170	154
Marriages	59	56	61	49

Note: Latest available data.

MEDIA INFO
see Halifax, CMA

Dartmouth
(City)
Halifax CMA

On Apr. 1, 1996, Halifax, C, Halifax Subdivisions A, B, C, D & E, Dartmouth, C & Bedford, T, amalgamated to form Halifax, RGM.

POPULATION

July 1, 2001 Estimate	67,234
% Cdn. Total	0.22
% Change, '96 -'01	-0.23
Avg. Annual Growth Rate, %	-0.05
2003 Projected Population	67,009
2006 Projected Population	67,209
2001 Households Estimate	28,174
2003 Projected Households	28,347
2006 Projected Households	28,840

INCOME

% Above/Below National Average	-9
2001 Total Income Estimate	$1,291,400,000
% Cdn. Total	0.20
2001 Average Hhld. Income	$45,800
2001 Per Capita	$19,200
2003 Projected Total Income	$1,345,710,000
2006 Projected Total Income	$1,446,380,000

RETAIL SALES

% Above/Below National Average	+93
2001 Retail Sales Estimate	$1,162,820,000
% Cdn. Total	0.42
2001 per Household	$41,300
2001 per Capita	$17,300
2001 No. of Establishments	541
2003 Projected Retail Sales	$1,252,580,000
2006 Projected Retail Sales	$1,395,170,000

POPULATION

2001 Estimates:		
Total		67,234
Male		32,178
Female		35,056

Age Groups	Male	Female
0-4	2,076	1,967
5-9	2,173	2,132
10-14	2,111	2,071
15-19	1,986	1,938
20-24	2,051	2,151
25-29	2,195	2,393
30-34	2,525	2,696
35-39	2,811	2,966
40-44	2,756	2,994
45-49	2,585	2,761
50-54	2,176	2,335
55-59	1,706	1,914
60-64	1,457	1,619
65-69	1,262	1,440
70+	2,308	3,679

DAYTIME POPULATION

2001 Estimates:	
Working Population	42,154
At Home Population	34,457
Total	76,611

INCOME

2001 Estimates:	
Avg. Household Income	$45,837
Avg. Family Income	$52,236
Per Capita Income	$19,208
Male:	
Avg. Employment Income	$31,197
Avg. Employment Income (Full Time)	$40,429
Female:	
Avg. Employment Income	$19,542
Avg. Employment Income (Full Time)	$29,453

DISPOSABLE & DISCRETIONARY INCOME

2001 Estimates:	Per Hhld.
Disposable Income	$35,617
Discretionary Income 1 (minus Food & Shelter)	$23,942
Discretionary Income 2 (minus Food, Shelter, & Other Expenditures)	$17,038

LIQUID ASSETS

1999 Estimates:	Per Hhld.
Equity Investments	$48,054
Interest Bearing Investments	$53,714
Total Liquid Assets	$101,768

CREDIT DATA

July 2000:	
Pool of Credit	$731,405,632
Revolving Credit, No.	129,116
Fixed Loans, No.	46,561
Avg. Credit Limit, per Person	$11,857
Avg. Spent, per Person	$5,781
Satisfactory Ratings, No. per Person	2.69
Avg. No. of Cards, per Person	0.86

LABOUR FORCE

2001 Estimates:	
Male:	
In the Labour Force	17,463
Participation Rate	67.6
Employed	16,529
Unemployed	934
Unemployment Rate	5.3
Not in Labour Force	8,355
Female:	
In the Labour Force	17,089
Participation Rate	59.2
Employed	16,193
Unemployed	896
Unemployment Rate	5.2
Not in Labour Force	11,797

OCCUPATIONS BY MAJOR GROUPS

2001 Estimates:	Male	Female
Management	2,227	1,034
Business, Finance & Admin.	2,044	5,381
Natural & Applied Sciences & Related	1,491	259
Health	353	1,489
Social Sciences, Gov't Services & Religion	287	550
Education	477	639
Arts, Culture, Recreation & Sport	552	484
Sales & Service	5,374	6,158
Trades, Transport & Equipment Operators & Related	3,438	166
Primary Industries	217	42
Processing, Mfg. & Utilities	567	280

LEVEL OF SCHOOLING

2001 Estimates:	
Population 15 years +	54,704
Less than Grade 9	3,652
Grades 9-13 w/o Certif.	12,815
Grade 9-13 with Certif.	5,914
Trade Certif. /Dip.	1,868
Non-Univ. w/o Certif./Dip.	2,599
Non-Univ. with Certif./Dip.	11,907
Univ. w/o Degree	7,389
Univ. w/o Degree/Certif.	3,567
Univ. with Certif.	3,822
Univ. with Degree	8,560

Dartmouth
(City)
Halifax CMA
(Cont'd)

AVERAGE HOUSEHOLD EXPENDITURES

2001 Estimates:
Food	$5,469
Shelter	$8,137
Clothing	$1,944
Transportation	$5,132
Health & Personal Care	$1,669
Recr'n, Read'g & Education	$3,224
Taxes & Securities	$12,079
Other	$7,496
Total Expenditures	$45,150

PRIVATE HOUSEHOLDS

2001 Estimates:
Private Households, Total	28,174
Pop. in Private Households	66,306
Average no. per Household	2.4

FAMILIES

2001 Estimates:
Families in Private Households	19,611
Husband-Wife Families	15,606
Lone-Parent Families	4,005
Aver. No. Persons per Family	2.9
Aver. No. Sons/Daughters at Home	1.1

HOUSING

2001 Estimates:
Occupied Private Dwellings	28,174
Owned	14,522
Rented	13,652
Single-Detached House	12,196
Semi-Detached House	2,773
Row Houses	1,048
Apartment, 5+ Storeys	2,302
Owned Apartment, 5+ Storeys	329
Apartment, 5 or Fewer Storeys	8,360
Apartment, Detached Duplex	1,147
Other Single-Attached	32
Movable Dwellings	316

VEHICLES

2001 Estimates:
Model Yrs. '81-'96, No.	24,864
% Total	73.13
Model Yrs. '97-'98, No.	4,487
% Total	13.20
'99 Vehicles registered in Model Yr. '99, No.	4,648
% Total	13.67
Total No. '81-'99	33,999

LEGAL MARITAL STATUS

2001 Estimates: (Age 15+)
Single (Never Married)	17,917
Legally Married (Not Separated)	26,694
Legally Married (Separated)	2,144
Widowed	3,230
Divorced	4,719

PSYTE CATEGORIES

2001 Estimates	No. of House-holds	% of Total Hhds.	Index
Urban Gentry	384	1.36	76
Suburban Executives	234	0.83	58
Mortgaged in Suburbia	394	1.40	101
Technocrafts & Bureaucrats	1,806	6.41	228
Stable Suburban Families	426	1.51	116
Small City Elite	1,299	4.61	269
Old Bungalow Burbs	3,235	11.48	693
Aging Erudites	2,249	7.98	529
Satellite Suburbs	399	1.42	49
Old Towns' New Fringe	282	1.00	26
Conservative Homebodies	2,707	9.61	266
Young Urban Mix	362	1.28	61

2001 Estimates	No. of House-holds	% of Total Hhds.	Index
University Enclaves	4,368	15.50	760
Young City Singles	4,374	15.52	677
Town Renters	939	3.33	386
Struggling Downtowns	2,583	9.17	291
Aged Pensioners	767	2.72	205
Big City Stress	1,272	4.51	400

FINANÇIAL P$YTE

2001 Estimates	No. of House-holds	% of Total Hhds.	Index
Four Star Investors	618	2.19	44
Successful Suburbanites	2,626	9.32	140
Canadian Comfort	1,698	6.03	62
Urban Heights	2,249	7.98	186
Miners & Credit-Liners	3,235	11.48	363
Tractors & Tradelines	282	1.00	18
Bills & Wills	3,069	10.89	132
Young Urban Struggle	4,368	15.50	328
Towering Debt	7,896	28.03	359
NSF	1,272	4.51	128
Senior Survivors	767	2.72	144

HOME LANGUAGE

2001 Estimates:		% Total
English	64,950	96.60
French	938	1.40
Arabic	211	0.31
Chinese	185	0.28
Greek	67	0.10
Portuguese	97	0.14
Punjabi	88	0.13
Spanish	61	0.09
Other Languages	263	0.39
Multiple Responses	374	0.56
Total	67,234	100.00

HOMES BUILT

	1999	1998	1997
No	n.a.	149	111

TAXATION

Income Class:	1997	% Total
Under $5,000	8,880	13.63
$5,000-$10,000	8,290	12.72
$10,000-$15,000	8,890	13.65
$15,000-$20,000	6,210	9.53
$20,000-$25,000	5,530	8.49
$25,000-$30,000	5,160	7.92
$30,000-$40,000	8,330	12.79
$40,000-$50,000	6,060	9.30
$50,000 +	7,800	11.97
Total Returns, No.	65,150	
Total Income, $000	1,712,523	
Total Taxable Returns	45,960	
Total Tax, $000	324,306	
Average Income, $	26,286	
Average Tax, $	7,056	

VITAL STATISTICS

	1997	1996	1995	1994
Births	1,078	1,185	1,205	1,309
Deaths	474	479	453	425
Natural Increase	604	706	752	884
Marriages	536	601	556	500

Note: Latest available data.

MEDIA INFO
see Halifax, CMA

Halifax
(City)
Halifax CMA

On Apr. 1, 1996, Halifax, C, Halifax Subdivisions A, B, C, D & E, Dartmouth, C & Bedford, T, amalgamated to form Halifax, RGM.

POPULATION

July 1, 2001 Estimate	119,264
% Cdn. Total	0.38
% Change, '96 -'01	1.98
Avg. Annual Growth Rate, %	0.39
2003 Projected Population	120,175
2006 Projected Population	122,489
2001 Households Estimate	55,580
2003 Projected Households	56,538
2006 Projected Households	58,465

INCOME

% Above/Below National Average	+6
2001 Total Income Estimate	$2,653,570,000
% Cdn. Total	0.40
2001 Average Hhld. Income	$47,700
2001 Per Capita	$22,300
2003 Projected Total Income	$2,792,990,000
2006 Projected Total Income	$3,047,680,000

RETAIL SALES

% Above/Below National Average	+61
2001 Retail Sales Estimate	$1,722,500,000
% Cdn. Total	0.62
2001 per Household	$31,000
2001 per Capita	$14,400
2001 No. of Establishments	951
2003 Projected Retail Sales	$1,878,320,000
2006 Projected Retail Sales	$2,122,460,000

POPULATION

2001 Estimates:
Total		119,264
Male		55,877
Female		63,387

Age Groups	Male	Female
0-4	3,528	3,372
5-9	3,065	2,972
10-14	2,879	2,760
15-19	2,866	2,772
20-24	3,900	4,094
25-29	5,093	5,354
30-34	5,405	5,540
35-39	4,926	5,189
40-44	4,348	4,897
45-49	4,003	4,622
50-54	3,574	4,008
55-59	2,909	3,229
60-64	2,371	2,716
65-69	2,036	2,547
70+	4,974	9,315

DAYTIME POPULATION

2001 Estimates:
Working Population	117,048
At Home Population	59,983
Total	177,031

INCOME

2001 Estimates:
Avg. Household Income	$47,743
Avg. Family Income	$59,011
Per Capita Income	$22,250
Male:	
Avg. Employment Income	$31,947
Avg. Employment Income (Full Time)	$45,008
Female:	
Avg. Employment Income	$21,554
Avg. Employment Income (Full Time)	$31,724

Nova Scotia

DISPOSABLE & DISCRETIONARY INCOME

2001 Estimates:	Per Hhld.
Disposable Income	$36,621
Discretionary Income 1 (minus Food & Shelter)	$24,447
Discretionary Income 2 (minus Food, Shelter, & Other Expenditures)	$17,589

LIQUID ASSETS

1999 Estimates:	Per Hhld.
Equity Investments	$61,538
Interest Bearing Investments	$57,750
Total Liquid Assets	$119,288

CREDIT DATA

July 2000:	
Pool of Credit	$1,458,594,997
Revolving Credit, No.	251,401
Fixed Loans, No.	74,441
Avg. Credit Limit, per Person	$12,034
Avg. Spent, per Person	$5,945
Satisfactory Ratings, No. per Person	2.57
Avg. No. of Cards, per Person	0.92

LABOUR FORCE

2001 Estimates:	
Male:	
In the Labour Force	30,871
Participation Rate	66.5
Employed	29,041
Unemployed	1,830
Unemployment Rate	5.9
Not in Labour Force	15,534
Female:	
In the Labour Force	32,535
Participation Rate	59.9
Employed	31,109
Unemployed	1,426
Unemployment Rate	4.4
Not in Labour Force	21,748

OCCUPATIONS BY MAJOR GROUPS

2001 Estimates:	Male	Female
Management	3,985	2,414
Business, Finance & Admin.	3,910	9,885
Natural & Applied Sciences & Related	2,558	685
Health	1,167	3,623
Social Sciences, Gov't Services & Religion	1,125	1,434
Education	1,468	1,853
Arts, Culture, Recreation & Sport	1,372	1,472
Sales & Service	8,870	9,887
Trades, Transport & Equipment Operators & Related	4,460	273
Primary Industries	358	71
Processing, Mfg. & Utilities	767	181

Nova Scotia

Halifax
(City)
Halifax CMA
(Cont'd)

LEVEL OF SCHOOLING

2001 Estimates:
Population 15 years +	100,688
Less than Grade 9	6,738
Grades 9-13 w/o Certif.	19,217
Grade 9-13 with Certif.	8,159
Trade Certif./Dip.	2,434
Non-Univ. w/o Certif./Dip.	3,974
Non-Univ. with Certif./Dip.	16,200
Univ. w/o Degree	16,605
Univ. w/o Degree/Certif.	8,941
Univ. with Certif.	7,664
Univ. with Degree	27,361

AVERAGE HOUSEHOLD EXPENDITURES

2001 Estimates:
Food	$5,524
Shelter	$8,824
Clothing	$2,019
Transportation	$4,949
Health & Personal Care	$1,764
Recr'n, Read'g & Education	$3,370
Taxes & Securities	$12,680
Other	$7,671
Total Expenditures	$46,801

PRIVATE HOUSEHOLDS

2001 Estimates:
Private Households, Total	55,580
Pop. in Private Households	115,791
Average no. per Household	2.1

FAMILIES

2001 Estimates:
Families in Private Households	31,266
Husband-Wife Families	25,009
Lone-Parent Families	6,257
Aver. No. Persons per Family	2.7
Aver. No. Sons/Daughters at Home	1.0

HOUSING

2001 Estimates:
Occupied Private Dwellings	55,580
Owned	22,032
Rented	33,548
Single-Detached House	16,920
Semi-Detached House	2,264
Row Houses	3,638
Apartment, 5+ Storeys	9,821
Owned Apartment, 5+ Storeys	994
Apartment, 5 or Fewer Storeys	18,384
Apartment, Detached Duplex	4,043
Other Single-Attached	258
Movable Dwellings	252

VEHICLES

2001 Estimates:
Model Yrs. '81-'96, No.	40,170
% Total	71.12
Model Yrs. '97-'98, No.	8,070
% Total	14.29
'99 Vehicles registered in Model Yr. '99, No.	8,239
% Total	14.59
Total No. '81-'99	56,479

LEGAL MARITAL STATUS

2001 Estimates: (Age 15+)
Single (Never Married)	41,071
Legally Married (Not Separated)	40,736
Legally Married (Separated)	3,362
Widowed	7,575
Divorced	7,944

PSYTE CATEGORIES

2001 Estimates	No. of House-holds	% of Total Hhds.	Index
Urban Gentry	4,673	8.41	468
Technocrafts & Bureaucrats	275	0.49	18
Stable Suburban Families	1,450	2.61	200
Old Bungalow Burbs	796	1.43	86
Suburban Nesters	118	0.21	13
Aging Erudites	6,743	12.13	804
Satellite Suburbs	98	0.18	6
Old Towns' New Fringe	405	0.73	19
High Rise Melting Pot	471	0.85	57
Conservative Homebodies	1,821	3.28	91
High Rise Sunsets	1,808	3.25	227
Young Urban Professionals	5,824	10.48	552
Young Urban Mix	441	0.79	37
Young Urban Intelligentsia	6,981	12.56	825
University Enclaves	8,469	15.24	747
Young City Singles	6,167	11.10	484
Urban Bohemia	1,292	2.32	199
Struggling Downtowns	3,450	6.21	197
Aged Pensioners	843	1.52	114
Big City Stress	2,271	4.09	362
Old Grey Towers	385	0.69	125

FINAN¢IAL P$YTE

2001 Estimates	No. of House-holds	% of Total Hhds.	Index
Four Star Investors	4,673	8.41	167
Successful Suburbanites	1,725	3.10	47
Canadian Comfort	216	0.39	4
Urban Heights	12,567	22.61	526
Miners & Credit-Liners	796	1.43	45
Tractors & Tradelines	405	0.73	13
Bills & Wills	2,262	4.07	49
Revolving Renters	1,808	3.25	71
Young Urban Struggle	16,742	30.12	636
Towering Debt	10,088	18.15	233
NSF	2,271	4.09	115
Senior Survivors	1,228	2.21	117

HOME LANGUAGE

2001 Estimates:		% Total
English	112,405	94.25
French	825	0.69
Arabic	1,220	1.02
Chinese	775	0.65
Greek	362	0.30
Hindi	144	0.12
Italian	214	0.18
Korean	149	0.12
Persian (Farsi)	80	0.07
Polish	217	0.18
Punjabi	85	0.07
Russian	69	0.06
Serbo-Croatian	178	0.15
Spanish	138	0.12
Tagalog (Pilipino)	83	0.07
Urdu	250	0.21
Vietnamese	176	0.15
Other Languages	660	0.55
Multiple Responses	1,234	1.03
Total	119,264	100.00

BUILDING PERMITS

	1999	1998	1997
		$000	
Value	388,081	239,514	97,748

HOMES BUILT

	1999	1998	1997
No.	n.a.	532	273

TAXATION

Income Class:	1997	% Total
Under $5,000	10,530	12.34
$5,000-$10,000	11,240	13.17
$10,000-$15,000	12,790	14.99
$15,000-$20,000	8,550	10.02
$20,000-$25,000	7,630	8.94
$25,000-$30,000	6,890	8.07
$30,000-$40,000	10,130	11.87
$40,000-$50,000	6,450	7.56
$50,000 +	11,130	13.04
Total Returns, No.	85,340	
Total Income, $000	2,469,651	
Total Taxable Returns	59,500	
Total Tax, $000	506,113	
Average Income, $	28,939	
Average Tax, $	8,506	

VITAL STATISTICS

	1997	1996	1995	1994
Births	1,240	1,272	1,266	1,349
Deaths	1,149	1,178	1,121	1,178
Natural Increase	91	94	145	171
Marriages	787	843	854	976

Note: Latest available data.

MEDIA INFO
see Halifax, CMA

Halifax, Subd. A
(Subd. County Municipality)
Halifax CMA

On Apr. 1, 1996, Halifax, C, Halifax Subdivisions A, B, C, D & E, Dartmouth, C & Bedford, T, amalgamated to form Halifax, RGM.

POPULATION

July 1, 2001 Estimate	14,014
% Cdn. Total	0.05
% Change, '96 -'01	15.33
Avg. Annual Growth Rate, %	2.89
2003 Projected Population	15,069
2006 Projected Population	16,774
2001 Households Estimate	5,102
2003 Projected Households	5,541
2006 Projected Households	6,256

INCOME

% Above/Below National Average	+10
2001 Total Income Estimate	$324,440,000
% Cdn. Total	0.05
2001 Average Hhld. Income	$63,600
2001 Per Capita	$23,200
2003 Projected Total Income	$373,750,000
2006 Projected Total Income	$462,230,000

RETAIL SALES

% Above/Below National Average	-84
2001 Retail Sales Estimate	$20,680,000
% Cdn. Total	0.01
2001 per Household	$4,100
2001 per Capita	$1,500
2001 No. of Establishments	47
2003 Projected Retail Sales	$23,610,000
2006 Projected Retail Sales	$29,000,000

POPULATION

2001 Estimates:

Total		14,014
Male		6,959
Female		7,055

Age Groups	Male	Female
0-4	454	436
5-9	527	493
10-14	538	501
15-19	494	481
20-24	423	448
25-29	446	474
30-34	563	606
35-39	654	700
40-44	643	661
45-49	567	584
50-54	490	465
55-59	379	340
60-64	272	245
65-69	196	190
70+	313	431

DAYTIME POPULATION

2001 Estimates:

Working Population	860
At Home Population	6,285
Total	7,145

INCOME

2001 Estimates:

Avg. Household Income	$63,592
Avg. Family Income	$66,593
Per Capita Income	$23,151

Male:

Avg. Employment Income	$38,161
Avg. Employment Income (Full Time)	$46,814

Female:

Avg. Employment Income	$23,222
Avg. Employment Income (Full Time)	$35,395

DISPOSABLE & DISCRETIONARY INCOME

2001 Estimates: Per Hhld.

Disposable Income	$49,164
Discretionary Income 1 (minus Food & Shelter)	$35,196
Discretionary Income 2 (minus Food, Shelter, & Other Expenditures)	$24,765

LIQUID ASSETS

1999 Estimates: Per Hhld.

Equity Investments	$93,881
Interest Bearing Investments	$76,028
Total Liquid Assets	$169,909

CREDIT DATA

July 2000:

Pool of Credit	$179,351,852
Revolving Credit, No.	28,120
Fixed Loans, No.	11,852
Avg. Credit Limit, per Person	$14,854
Avg. Spent, per Person	$7,596
Satisfactory Ratings, No. per Person	3.11
Avg. No. of Cards, per Person	0.95

LABOUR FORCE

2001 Estimates:

Male:

In the Labour Force	4,064
Participation Rate	74.7
Employed	3,922
Unemployed	142
Unemployment Rate	3.5
Not in Labour Force	1,376

Female:

In the Labour Force	3,790
Participation Rate	67.4
Employed	3,674
Unemployed	116
Unemployment Rate	3.1
Not in Labour Force	1,835

OCCUPATIONS BY MAJOR GROUPS

2001 Estimates:

	Male	Female
Management	640	250
Business, Finance & Admin.	448	1,306
Natural & Applied Sciences & Related	425	45
Health	73	352
Social Sciences, Gov't Services & Religion	95	197
Education	165	239
Arts, Culture, Recreation & Sport	100	145
Sales & Service	707	1,107
Trades, Transport & Equipment Operators & Related	1,087	55
Primary Industries	40	n.a.
Processing, Mfg. & Utilities	193	43

LEVEL OF SCHOOLING

2001 Estimates:

Population 15 years +	11,065
Less than Grade 9	632
Grades 9-13 w/o Certif.	2,215
Grade 9-13 with Certif.	1,193
Trade Certif. /Dip.	436
Non-Univ. w/o Certif./Dip.	512
Non-Univ. with Certif./Dip.	2,287
Univ. w/o Degree	1,583
Univ. w/o Degree/Certif.	710
Univ. with Certif.	873
Univ. with Degree	2,207

AVERAGE HOUSEHOLD EXPENDITURES

2001 Estimates:

Food	$7,145
Shelter	$9,641
Clothing	$2,551
Transportation	$8,227
Health & Personal Care	$2,348
Recr'n, Read'g & Education	$4,710
Taxes & Securities	$15,876
Other	$9,768
Total Expenditures	$60,266

PRIVATE HOUSEHOLDS

2001 Estimates:

Private Households, Total	5,102
Pop. in Private Households	13,922
Average no. per Household	2.7

FAMILIES

2001 Estimates:

Families in Private Households	4,329
Husband-Wife Families	3,951
Lone-Parent Families	378
Aver. No. Persons per Family	3.1
Aver. No. Sons/Daughters at Home	1.1

HOUSING

2001 Estimates:

Occupied Private Dwellings	5,102
Owned	4,499
Rented	603
Single-Detached House	4,213
Semi-Detached House	681
Row Houses	31
Apartment, 5 or Fewer Storeys	12
Apartment, Detached Duplex	142
Movable Dwellings	23

VEHICLES

2001 Estimates:

Model Yrs. '81-'96, No.	5,624
% Total	82.07
Model Yrs. '97-'98, No.	632
% Total	9.22
'99 Vehicles registered in Model Yr. '99, No.	597
% Total	8.71
Total No. '81-'99	6,853

LEGAL MARITAL STATUS

2001 Estimates: (Age 15+)

Single (Never Married)	2,656
Legally Married (Not Separated)	7,082
Legally Married (Separated)	271
Widowed	460
Divorced	596

PSYTE CATEGORIES

2001 Estimates

	No. of House-holds	% of Total Hhds.	Index
Small City Elite	3,655	71.64	4,180
Satellite Suburbs	414	8.11	283
Old Towns' New Fringe	258	5.06	129
Old Leafy Towns	775	15.19	594

FINANCIAL P$YTE

2001 Estimates

	No. of House-holds	% of Total Hhds.	Index
Canadian Comfort	4,069	79.75	821
Tractors & Tradelines	258	5.06	88
Bills & Wills	775	15.19	183

HOME LANGUAGE

2001 Estimates: % Total

English	13,837	98.74
French	45	0.32
Arabic	24	0.17
German	18	0.13
Norwegian	18	0.13
Multiple Responses	72	0.51
Total	14,014	100.00

HOMES BUILT

	1999	1998	1997
No	n.a.	191	287

TAXATION

Income Class:	1997	% Total
Under $5,000	1,640	12.37
$5,000-$10,000	1,400	10.56
$10,000-$15,000	1,600	12.07
$15,000-$20,000	1,200	9.05
$20,000-$25,000	1,160	8.75
$25,000-$30,000	1,160	8.75
$30,000-$40,000	2,020	15.23
$40,000-$50,000	1,350	10.18
$50,000 +	1,720	12.97
Total Returns, No.	13,260	
Total Income, $000	375,683	
Total Taxable Returns	9,930	
Total Tax, $000	73,150	
Average Income, $	28,332	
Average Tax, $	7,367	

VITAL STATISTICS

	1997	1996	1995	1994
Births	73	129	108	102
Deaths	44	36	46	36
Natural Increase	29	93	62	66
Marriages	25	36	22	24

Note: Latest available data.

MEDIA INFO
see Halifax, CMA

Nova Scotia

Halifax, Subd. B
(Subd. County Municipality)
Halifax CMA

On Apr. 1, 1996, Halifax, C, Halifax Subdivisions A, B, C, D & E, Dartmouth, C & Bedford, T, amalgamated to form Halifax, RGM.

POPULATION

July 1, 2001 Estimate	17,301
% Cdn. Total	0.06
% Change, '96 - '01	8.01
Avg. Annual Growth Rate, %	1.55
2003 Projected Population	17,955
2006 Projected Population	19,081
2001 Households Estimate	6,199
2003 Projected Households	6,493
2006 Projected Households	6,996

INCOME

% Above/Below National Average	-6
2001 Total Income Estimate	$344,480,000
% Cdn. Total	0.05
2001 Average Hhld. Income	$55,600
2001 Per Capita	$19,900
2003 Projected Total Income	$380,280,000
2006 Projected Total Income	$444,540,000

RETAIL SALES

% Above/Below National Average	-65
2001 Retail Sales Estimate	$53,780,000
% Cdn. Total	0.02
2001 per Household	$8,700
2001 per Capita	$3,100
2001 No. of Establishments	69
2003 Projected Retail Sales	$59,980,000
2006 Projected Retail Sales	$71,290,000

POPULATION

2001 Estimates:

Total		17,301
Male		8,620
Female		8,681

Age Groups	Male	Female
0-4	548	526
5-9	619	590
10-14	641	612
15-19	603	573
20-24	536	537
25-29	547	598
30-34	703	743
35-39	828	854
40-44	815	832
45-49	724	725
50-54	581	558
55-59	440	429
60-64	337	334
65-69	259	261
70+	439	509

DAYTIME POPULATION

2001 Estimates:

Working Population	1,278
At Home Population	8,048
Total	9,326

INCOME

2001 Estimates:

Avg. Household Income	$55,570
Avg. Family Income	$58,356
Per Capita Income	$19,911
Male:	
Avg. Employment Income	$31,940
Avg. Employment Income (Full Time)	$42,451
Female:	
Avg. Employment Income	$21,950
Avg. Employment Income (Full Time)	$31,097

DISPOSABLE & DISCRETIONARY INCOME

2001 Estimates:	Per Hhld.
Disposable Income	$43,298
Discretionary Income 1 (minus Food & Shelter)	$30,141
Discretionary Income 2 (minus Food, Shelter, & Other Expenditures)	$20,809

LIQUID ASSETS

1999 Estimates:	Per Hhld.
Equity Investments	$64,236
Interest Bearing Investments	$63,535
Total Liquid Assets	$127,771

CREDIT DATA

July 2000:

Pool of Credit	$161,573,884
Revolving Credit, No.	24,892
Fixed Loans, No.	11,564
Avg. Credit Limit, per Person	$14,315
Avg. Spent, per Person	$7,736
Satisfactory Ratings, No. per Person	3.02
Avg. No. of Cards, per Person	0.89

LABOUR FORCE

2001 Estimates:

Male:

In the Labour Force	4,968
Participation Rate	72.9
Employed	4,667
Unemployed	301
Unemployment Rate	6.1
Not in Labour Force	1,844

Female:

In the Labour Force	4,547
Participation Rate	65.4
Employed	4,416
Unemployed	131
Unemployment Rate	2.9
Not in Labour Force	2,406

OCCUPATIONS BY MAJOR GROUPS

2001 Estimates:	Male	Female
Management	497	237
Business, Finance & Admin.	467	1,658
Natural & Applied Sciences & Related	305	37
Health	44	546
Social Sciences, Gov't Services & Religion	87	100
Education	135	220
Arts, Culture, Recreation & Sport	117	83
Sales & Service	971	1,443
Trades, Transport & Equipment Operators & Related	1,625	58
Primary Industries	359	43
Processing, Mfg. & Utilities	277	84

LEVEL OF SCHOOLING

2001 Estimates:

Population 15 years +	13,765
Less than Grade 9	1,443
Grades 9-13 w/o Certif.	3,805
Grade 9-13 with Certif.	1,434
Trade Certif. /Dip.	462
Non-Univ. w/o Certif./Dip.	505
Non-Univ. with Certif./Dip.	3,101
Univ. w/o Degree	1,478
Univ. w/o Degree/Certif.	649
Univ. with Certif.	829
Univ. with Degree	1,537

AVERAGE HOUSEHOLD EXPENDITURES

2001 Estimates:

Food	$6,525
Shelter	$8,895
Clothing	$2,184
Transportation	$7,205
Health & Personal Care	$2,075
Recr'n, Read'g & Education	$4,086
Taxes & Securities	$13,539
Other	$9,135
Total Expenditures	$53,644

PRIVATE HOUSEHOLDS

2001 Estimates:

Private Households, Total	6,199
Pop. in Private Households	17,234
Average no. per Household	2.8

FAMILIES

2001 Estimates:

Families in Private Households	5,282
Husband-Wife Families	4,779
Lone-Parent Families	503
Aver. No. Persons per Family	3.1
Aver. No. Sons/Daughters at Home	1.2

HOUSING

2001 Estimates:

Occupied Private Dwellings	6,199
Owned	5,451
Rented	748
Single-Detached House	5,044
Semi-Detached House	182
Apartment, 5 or Fewer Storeys	303
Apartment, Detached Duplex	205
Other Single-Attached	52
Movable Dwellings	413

VEHICLES

2001 Estimates:

Model Yrs. '81-'96, No.	6,584
% Total	82.30
Model Yrs. '97-'98, No.	757
% Total	9.46
'99 Vehicles registered in Model Yr. '99, No.	659
% Total	8.24
Total No. '81-'99	8,000

LEGAL MARITAL STATUS

2001 Estimates: (Age 15+)

Single (Never Married)	3,738
Legally Married (Not Separated)	8,306
Legally Married (Separated)	326
Widowed	588
Divorced	807

PSYTE CATEGORIES

2001 Estimates	No. of House -holds	% of Total Hhds.	Index
Small City Elite	1,859	29.99	1,750
Old Towns' New Fringe	2,970	47.91	1,224
Old Leafy Towns	250	4.03	158
Rod & Rifle	699	11.28	488
Struggling Downtowns	415	6.69	213

FINANCIAL P$YTE

2001 Estimates	No. of House -holds	% of Total Hhds.	Index
Canadian Comfort	1,859	29.99	309
Tractors & Tradelines	2,970	47.91	838
Bills & Wills	250	4.03	49
Rural Family Blues	699	11.28	140
Towering Debt	415	6.69	86

HOME LANGUAGE

2001 Estimates:		% Total
English	17,162	99.20
French	57	0.33
Greek	34	0.20
Japanese	11	0.06
Polish	37	0.21
Total	17,301	100.00

HOMES BUILT

	1999	1998	1997
No	n.a.	77	79

TAXATION

Income Class:	1997	% Total
Under $5,000	1,160	13.70
$5,000-$10,000	980	11.57
$10,000-$15,000	1,100	12.99
$15,000-$20,000	820	9.68
$20,000-$25,000	820	9.68
$25,000-$30,000	790	9.33
$30,000-$40,000	1,230	14.52
$40,000-$50,000	770	9.09
$50,000 +	790	9.33
Total Returns, No.	8,470	
Total Income, $000	211,578	
Total Taxable Returns	6,140	
Total Tax, $000	38,071	
Average Income, $	24,980	
Average Tax, $	6,200	

VITAL STATISTICS

	1997	1996	1995	1994
Births	297	266	289	270
Deaths	74	69	73	75
Natural Increase	223	197	216	195
Marriages	69	72	71	61

Note: Latest available data.

MEDIA INFO
see Halifax, CMA

Halifax, Subd. C
(Subd. County Municipality)
Halifax CMA

On Apr. 1, 1996, Halifax, C, Halifax Subdivisions A, B, C, D & E, Dartmouth, C & Bedford, T, amalgamated to form Halifax, RGM.

POPULATION

July 1, 2001 Estimate	59,804
% Cdn. Total	0.19
% Change, '96 -'01	12.52
Avg. Annual Growth Rate, %	2.39
2003 Projected Population	63,459
2006 Projected Population	69,455
2001 Households Estimate	20,167
2003 Projected Households	21,624
2006 Projected Households	24,012

INCOME

% Above/Below National Average	-1
2001 Total Income Estimate	$1,249,020,000
% Cdn. Total	0.19
2001 Average Hhld. Income	$61,900
2001 Per Capita	$20,900
2003 Projected Total Income	$1,423,190,000
2006 Projected Total Income	$1,737,360,000

RETAIL SALES

% Above/Below National Average	-61
2001 Retail Sales Estimate	$210,820,000
% Cdn. Total	0.08
2001 per Household	$10,500
2001 per Capita	$3,500
2001 No. of Establishments	257
2003 Projected Retail Sales	$239,380,000
2006 Projected Retail Sales	$288,370,000

POPULATION

2001 Estimates:

Total	59,804
Male	29,636
Female	30,168

Age Groups	Male	Female
0-4	2,045	1,970
5-9	2,324	2,233
10-14	2,402	2,284
15-19	2,296	2,214
20-24	2,089	2,127
25-29	2,084	2,187
30-34	2,481	2,660
35-39	2,788	2,963
40-44	2,668	2,789
45-49	2,384	2,457
50-54	1,969	1,979
55-59	1,490	1,431
60-64	1,042	956
65-69	675	672
70+	899	1,246

DAYTIME POPULATION

2001 Estimates:

Working Population	5,196
At Home Population	27,054
Total	32,250

INCOME

2001 Estimates:

Avg. Household Income	$61,934
Avg. Family Income	$62,845
Per Capita Income	$20,885

Male:

Avg. Employment Income	$36,012
Avg. Employment Income (Full Time)	$45,508

Female:

Avg. Employment Income	$21,008
Avg. Employment Income (Full Time)	$30,195

DISPOSABLE & DISCRETIONARY INCOME

2001 Estimates:	Per Hhld.
Disposable Income	$48,168
Discretionary Income 1 (minus Food & Shelter)	$34,008
Discretionary Income 2 (minus Food, Shelter, & Other Expenditures)	$24,211

LIQUID ASSETS

1999 Estimates:	Per Hhld.
Equity Investments	$76,362
Interest Bearing Investments	$70,873
Total Liquid Assets	$147,235

CREDIT DATA

July 2000:

Pool of Credit	$678,472,475
Revolving Credit, No.	106,312
Fixed Loans, No.	50,298
Avg. Credit Limit, per Person	$15,034
Avg. Spent, per Person	$7,875
Satisfactory Ratings, No. per Person	3.20
Avg. No. of Cards, per Person	0.96

LABOUR FORCE

2001 Estimates:

Male:

In the Labour Force	17,490
Participation Rate	76.5
Employed	16,768
Unemployed	722
Unemployment Rate	4.1
Not in Labour Force	5,375

Female:

In the Labour Force	16,002
Participation Rate	67.6
Employed	15,427
Unemployed	575
Unemployment Rate	3.6
Not in Labour Force	7,679

OCCUPATIONS BY MAJOR GROUPS

2001 Estimates:	Male	Female
Management	2,416	829
Business, Finance & Admin.	1,789	5,539
Natural & Applied Sciences & Related	1,376	290
Health	154	1,628
Social Sciences, Gov't Services & Religion	168	387
Education	366	557
Arts, Culture, Recreation & Sport	294	356
Sales & Service	4,640	5,598
Trades, Transport & Equipment Operators & Related	4,805	140
Primary Industries	386	78
Processing, Mfg. & Utilities	694	167

LEVEL OF SCHOOLING

2001 Estimates:

Population 15 years +	46,546
Less than Grade 9	2,466
Grades 9-13 w/o Certif.	11,322
Grade 9-13 with Certif.	5,615
Trade Certif./Dip.	1,808
Non-Univ. w/o Certif./Dip.	2,260
Non-Univ. with Certif./Dip.	11,542
Univ. w/o Degree	5,963
Univ. w/o Degree/Certif.	3,055
Univ. with Certif.	2,908
Univ. with Degree	5,570

AVERAGE HOUSEHOLD EXPENDITURES

2001 Estimates:

Food	$6,913
Shelter	$9,710
Clothing	$2,486
Transportation	$7,628
Health & Personal Care	$2,166
Recr'n, Read'g & Education	$4,546
Taxes & Securities	$15,966
Other	$9,456
Total Expenditures	$58,871

PRIVATE HOUSEHOLDS

2001 Estimates:

Private Households, Total	20,167
Pop. in Private Households	59,092
Average no. per Household	2.9

FAMILIES

2001 Estimates:

Families in Private Households	17,953
Husband-Wife Families	15,864
Lone-Parent Families	2,089
Aver. No. Persons per Family	3.2
Aver. No. Sons/Daughters at Home	1.3

HOUSING

2001 Estimates:

Occupied Private Dwellings	20,167
Owned	17,140
Rented	3,027
Single-Detached House	13,933
Semi-Detached House	2,020
Row Houses	178
Apartment, 5 or Fewer Storeys	1,241
Apartment, Detached Duplex	572
Other Single-Attached	45
Movable Dwellings	2,178

VEHICLES

2001 Estimates:

Model Yrs. '81-'96, No.	21,850
% Total	81.46
Model Yrs. '97-'98, No.	2,574
% Total	9.60
'99 Vehicles registered in Model Yr. '99, No.	2,399
% Total	8.94
Total No. '81-'99	26,823

LEGAL MARITAL STATUS

2001 Estimates: (Age 15+)

Single (Never Married)	12,603
Legally Married (Not Separated)	28,563
Legally Married (Separated)	1,275
Widowed	1,555
Divorced	2,550

PSYTE CATEGORIES

2001 Estimates	No. of House-holds	% of Total Hhds.	Index
Mortgaged in Suburbia	2,025	10.04	722
Technocrafts & Bureaucrats	1,068	5.30	188
Small City Elite	5,267	26.12	1,524
Old Bungalow Burbs	944	4.68	282
Satellite Suburbs	903	4.48	156
Kindergarten Boom	1,823	9.04	345
Blue Collar Winners	28	0.14	6
Old Towns' New Fringe	6,925	34.34	877
Young City Singles	38	0.19	8
Old Leafy Towns	72	0.36	14

Nova Scotia

2001 Estimates	No. of House-holds	% of Total Hhds.	Index
Town Renters	472	2.34	271
Nesters & Young Homesteaders	365	1.81	78
Rod & Rifle	140	0.69	30

FINANCIAL P$YTE

2001 Estimates	No. of House-holds	% of Total Hhds.	Index
Successful Suburbanites	3,093	15.34	231
Canadian Comfort	6,198	30.73	316
Miners & Credit-Liners	944	4.68	148
Mortgages & Minivans	1,823	9.04	137
Tractors & Tradelines	6,925	34.34	600
Bills & Wills	72	0.36	4
Revolving Renters	365	1.81	39
Rural Family Blues	140	0.69	9
Towering Debt	510	2.53	32

HOME LANGUAGE

2001 Estimates		% Total
English	58,807	98.33
French	577	0.96
Arabic	90	0.15
Chinese	49	0.08
Persian (Farsi)	49	0.08
Other Languages	89	0.15
Multiple Responses	143	0.24
Total	59,804	100.00

HOMES BUILT

	1999	1998	1997
No	n.a.	313	424

TAXATION

Income Class:	1997	% Total
Under $5,000	5,010	14.21
$5,000-$10,000	4,150	11.77
$10,000-$15,000	4,270	12.11
$15,000-$20,000	3,080	8.74
$20,000-$25,000	3,060	8.68
$25,000-$30,000	3,080	8.74
$30,000-$40,000	5,040	14.30
$40,000-$50,000	3,440	9.76
$50,000 +	4,130	11.72
Total Returns, No.	35,250	
Total Income, $000	920,992	
Total Taxable Returns	25,820	
Total Tax, $000	172,458	
Average Income, $	26,127	
Average Tax, $	6,679	

VITAL STATISTICS

	1997	1996	1995	1994
Births	743	709	751	759
Deaths	183	159	177	166
Natural Increase	560	550	574	593
Marriages	203	223	206	198

Note: Latest available data.

MEDIA INFO
see Halifax, CMA

Nova Scotia

Halifax, Subd. D
(Subd. County Municipality)
Halifax CMA

On Apr. 1, 1996, Halifax, C, Halifax Subdivisions A, B, C, D & E, Dartmouth, C & Bedford, T, amalgamated to form Halifax, RGM.

POPULATION

July 1, 2001 Estimate	44,489
% Cdn. Total	0.14
% Change, '96 -'01	8.33
Avg. Annual Growth Rate, %	1.61
2003 Projected Population	46,296
2006 Projected Population	49,370
2001 Households Estimate	14,868
2003 Projected Households	15,622
2006 Projected Households	16,915

INCOME

% Above/Below National Average	+1
2001 Total Income Estimate	$952,060,000
% Cdn. Total	0.15
2001 Average Hhld. Income	$64,000
2001 Per Capita	$21,400
2003 Projected Total Income	$1,055,310,000
2006 Projected Total Income	$1,242,210,000

RETAIL SALES

% Above/Below National Average	-52
2001 Retail Sales Estimate	$189,380,000
% Cdn. Total	0.07
2001 per Household	$12,700
2001 per Capita	$4,300
2001 No. of Establishments	150
2003 Projected Retail Sales	$211,630,000
2006 Projected Retail Sales	$249,450,000

POPULATION

2001 Estimates:

Total		44,489
Male		22,068
Female		22,421

Age Groups	Male	Female
0-4	1,478	1,387
5-9	1,761	1,658
10-14	1,873	1,754
15-19	1,770	1,690
20-24	1,545	1,516
25-29	1,459	1,490
30-34	1,760	1,865
35-39	2,079	2,191
40-44	2,060	2,148
45-49	1,822	1,879
50-54	1,450	1,495
55-59	1,056	1,044
60-64	747	713
65-69	511	513
70+	697	1,078

DAYTIME POPULATION

2001 Estimates:

Working Population	6,677
At Home Population	20,331
Total	27,008

INCOME

2001 Estimates:

Avg. Household Income	$64,034
Avg. Family Income	$65,054
Per Capita Income	$21,400
Male:	
Avg. Employment Income	$38,144
Avg. Employment Income (Full Time)	$47,335
Female:	
Avg. Employment Income	$21,677
Avg. Employment Income (Full Time)	$31,815

DISPOSABLE & DISCRETIONARY INCOME

2001 Estimates:	*Per Hhld.*
Disposable Income	$49,631
Discretionary Income 1 (minus Food & Shelter)	$34,800
Discretionary Income 2 (minus Food, Shelter, & Other Expenditures)	$24,869

LIQUID ASSETS

1999 Estimates:	*Per Hhld.*
Equity Investments	$76,763
Interest Bearing Investments	$73,208
Total Liquid Assets	$149,971

CREDIT DATA

July 2000:

Pool of Credit	$504,862,695
Revolving Credit, No.	82,041
Fixed Loans, No.	36,014
Avg. Credit Limit, per Person	$14,558
Avg. Spent, per Person	$7,532
Satisfactory Ratings, No. per Person	3.17
Avg. No. of Cards, per Person	0.95

LABOUR FORCE

2001 Estimates:

Male:	
In the Labour Force	12,695
Participation Rate	74.9
Employed	12,260
Unemployed	435
Unemployment Rate	3.4
Not in Labour Force	4,261
Female:	
In the Labour Force	12,001
Participation Rate	68.1
Employed	11,505
Unemployed	496
Unemployment Rate	4.1
Not in Labour Force	5,621

OCCUPATIONS BY MAJOR GROUPS

2001 Estimates:	Male	Female
Management	1,784	698
Business, Finance & Admin.	1,299	3,979
Natural & Applied Sciences & Related	1,096	187
Health	109	1,259
Social Sciences, Gov't Services & Religion	220	303
Education	206	555
Arts, Culture, Recreation & Sport	220	224
Sales & Service	4,002	4,070
Trades, Transport & Equipment Operators & Related	2,860	149
Primary Industries	222	26
Processing, Mfg. & Utilities	462	177

LEVEL OF SCHOOLING

2001 Estimates:

Population 15 years +	34,578
Less than Grade 9	1,622
Grades 9-13 w/o Certif.	8,461
Grade 9-13 with Certif.	3,854
Trade Certif. /Dip.	1,267
Non-Univ. w/o Certif./Dip.	1,600
Non-Univ. with Certif./Dip.	8,130
Univ. w/o Degree	4,736
Univ. w/o Degree/Certif.	2,337
Univ. with Certif.	2,399
Univ. with Degree	4,908

AVERAGE HOUSEHOLD EXPENDITURES

2001 Estimates:

Food	$7,115
Shelter	$10,201
Clothing	$2,557
Transportation	$7,689
Health & Personal Care	$2,183
Recr'n, Read'g & Education	$4,551
Taxes & Securities	$16,626
Other	$9,569
Total Expenditures	$60,491

PRIVATE HOUSEHOLDS

2001 Estimates:

Private Households, Total	14,868
Pop. in Private Households	43,821
Average no. per Household	2.9

FAMILIES

2001 Estimates:

Families in Private Households	13,226
Husband-Wife Families	11,637
Lone-Parent Families	1,589
Aver. No. Persons per Family	3.2
Aver. No. Sons/Daughters at Home	1.3

HOUSING

2001 Estimates:

Occupied Private Dwellings	14,868
Owned	12,555
Rented	2,313
Single-Detached House	10,186
Semi-Detached House	2,621
Row Houses	443
Apartment, 5 or Fewer Storeys	872
Apartment, Detached Duplex	210
Other Single-Attached	18
Movable Dwellings	518

VEHICLES

2001 Estimates:

Model Yrs. '81-'96, No.	14,011
% Total	79.22
Model Yrs. '97-'98, No.	1,867
% Total	10.56
'99 Vehicles registered in Model Yr. '99, No.	1,808
% Total	10.22
Total No. '81-'99	17,686

LEGAL MARITAL STATUS

2001 Estimates: (Age 15+)

Single (Never Married)	9,436
Legally Married (Not Separated)	21,148
Legally Married (Separated)	958
Widowed	1,264
Divorced	1,772

PSYTE CATEGORIES

2001 Estimates	No. of House-holds	% of Total Hhds.	Index
Suburban Executives	577	3.88	271
Technocrafts & Bureaucrats	2,219	14.92	530
Small City Elite	1,475	9.92	579
Old Bungalow Burbs	639	4.30	259
Satellite Suburbs	1,964	13.21	460
Kindergarten Boom	2,025	13.62	519
Old Towns' New Fringe	4,516	30.37	776
Conservative Homebodies	144	0.97	27
University Enclaves	147	0.99	48
Town Renters	328	2.21	255
Rod & Rifle	216	1.45	63
Struggling Downtowns	462	3.11	99

FINANCIAL P$YTE

2001 Estimates	No. of House-holds	% of Total Hhds.	Index
Four Star Investors	577	3.88	77
Successful Suburbanites	2,219	14.92	225
Canadian Comfort	3,439	23.13	238
Miners & Credit-Liners	639	4.30	136
Mortgages & Minivans	2,025	13.62	206
Tractors & Tradelines	4,516	30.37	531
Bills & Wills	144	0.97	12
Young Urban Struggle	147	0.99	21
Rural Family Blues	216	1.45	18
Towering Debt	790	5.31	68

HOME LANGUAGE

2001 Estimates:		% Total
English	43,096	96.87
French	960	2.16
Arabic	23	0.05
Chinese	60	0.13
Other Languages	101	0.23
Multiple Responses	249	0.56
Total	44,489	100.00

HOMES BUILT

	1999	1998	1997
No	n.a.	139	240

TAXATION

Income Class:	1997	% Total
Under $5,000	1,460	13.63
$5,000-$10,000	1,190	11.11
$10,000-$15,000	1,270	11.86
$15,000-$20,000	950	8.87
$20,000-$25,000	960	8.96
$25,000-$30,000	990	9.24
$30,000-$40,000	1,640	15.31
$40,000-$50,000	1,220	11.39
$50,000 +	1,050	9.80
Total Returns, No.	10,710	
Total Income, $000	278,580	
Total Taxable Returns	7,900	
Total Tax, $000	51,194	
Average Income, $	26,011	
Average Tax, $	6,480	

VITAL STATISTICS

	1997	1996	1995	1994
Births	200	236	226	235
Deaths	150	143	128	134
Natural Increase	50	93	98	101
Marriages	74	84	85	90

Note: Latest available data.

MEDIA INFO
see Halifax, CMA

Halifax, Subd. E
(Subd. County Municipality)
Halifax CMA

On Apr. 1, 1996, Halifax, C, Halifax Subdivisions A, B, C, D & E, Dartmouth, C & Bedford, T, amalgamated to form Halifax, RGM.

POPULATION

July 1, 2001 Estimate	22,775
% Cdn. Total	0.07
% Change, '96 -'01	10.40
Avg. Annual Growth Rate, %	2.00
2003 Projected Population	24,057
2006 Projected Population	26,169
2001 Households Estimate	7,890
2003 Projected Households	8,420
2006 Projected Households	9,301

INCOME

% Above/Below National Average	-10
2001 Total Income Estimate	$434,410,000
% Cdn. Total	0.07
2001 Average Hhld. Income	$55,100
2001 Per Capita	$19,100
2003 Projected Total Income	$491,310,000
2006 Projected Total Income	$593,760,000

RETAIL SALES

% Above/Below National Average	-72
2001 Retail Sales Estimate	$57,420,000
% Cdn. Total	0.02
2001 per Household	$7,300
2001 per Capita	$2,500
2001 No. of Establishments	77
2003 Projected Retail Sales	$65,340,000
2006 Projected Retail Sales	$79,780,000

POPULATION

2001 Estimates:

Total	22,775
Male	11,402
Female	11,373

Age Groups	Male	Female
0-4	720	696
5-9	870	818
10-14	976	893
15-19	929	839
20-24	767	719
25-29	708	741
30-34	868	941
35-39	1,048	1,105
40-44	1,060	1,066
45-49	925	912
50-54	742	730
55-59	553	542
60-64	402	389
65-69	302	319
70+	532	663

DAYTIME POPULATION

2001 Estimates:

Working Population	5,585
At Home Population	11,492
Total	17,077

INCOME

2001 Estimates:

Avg. Household Income	$55,058
Avg. Family Income	$57,762
Per Capita Income	$19,074
Male:	
Avg. Employment Income	$33,082
Avg. Employment Income (Full Time)	$42,027
Female:	
Avg. Employment Income	$21,723
Avg. Employment Income (Full Time)	$30,215

DISPOSABLE & DISCRETIONARY INCOME

2001 Estimates:	Per Hhld.
Disposable Income	$43,025
Discretionary Income 1 (minus Food & Shelter)	$29,660
Discretionary Income 2 (minus Food, Shelter, & Other Expenditures)	$20,493

LIQUID ASSETS

1999 Estimates:	Per Hhld.
Equity Investments	$66,102
Interest Bearing Investments	$63,210
Total Liquid Assets	$129,312

CREDIT DATA

July 2000:

Pool of Credit	$196,212,567
Revolving Credit, No.	30,494
Fixed Loans, No.	14,839
Avg. Credit Limit, per Person	$13,250
Avg. Spent, per Person	$7,216
Satisfactory Ratings, No. per Person	2.84
Avg. No. of Cards, per Person	0.81

LABOUR FORCE

2001 Estimates:

Male:	
In the Labour Force	6,216
Participation Rate	70.3
Employed	5,900
Unemployed	316
Unemployment Rate	5.1
Not in Labour Force	2,620
Female:	
In the Labour Force	5,485
Participation Rate	61.2
Employed	5,192
Unemployed	293
Unemployment Rate	5.3
Not in Labour Force	3,481

OCCUPATIONS BY MAJOR GROUPS

2001 Estimates:	Male	Female
Management	558	297
Business, Finance & Admin.	452	1,872
Natural & Applied Sciences & Related	397	55
Health	99	464
Social Sciences, Gov't Services & Religion	97	116
Education	136	211
Arts, Culture, Recreation & Sport	113	144
Sales & Service	1,337	1,738
Trades, Transport & Equipment Operators & Related	2,266	163
Primary Industries	284	85
Processing, Mfg. & Utilities	347	180

LEVEL OF SCHOOLING

2001 Estimates:

Population 15 years +	17,802
Less than Grade 9	1,717
Grades 9-13 w/o Certif.	5,176
Grade 9-13 with Certif.	1,676
Trade Certif. /Dip.	729
Non-Univ. w/o Certif./Dip.	947
Non-Univ. with Certif./Dip.	4,389
Univ. w/o Degree	1,797
Univ. w/o Degree/Certif.	927
Univ. with Certif.	870
Univ. with Degree	1,371

AVERAGE HOUSEHOLD EXPENDITURES

2001 Estimates:

Food	$6,369
Shelter	$9,053
Clothing	$2,103
Transportation	$7,085
Health & Personal Care	$1,970
Recr'n, Read'g & Education	$3,934
Taxes & Securities	$13,805
Other	$8,896
Total Expenditures	$53,215

PRIVATE HOUSEHOLDS

2001 Estimates:

Private Households, Total	7,890
Pop. in Private Households	22,662
Average no. per Household	2.9

FAMILIES

2001 Estimates:

Families in Private Households	6,771
Husband-Wife Families	6,044
Lone-Parent Families	727
Aver. No. Persons per Family	3.1
Aver. No. Sons/Daughters at Home	1.2

HOUSING

2001 Estimates:

Occupied Private Dwellings	7,890
Owned	7,078
Rented	812
Single-Detached House	6,921
Semi-Detached House	24
Row Houses	23
Apartment, 5 or Fewer Storeys	77
Apartment, Detached Duplex	132
Other Single-Attached	12
Movable Dwellings	701

VEHICLES

2001 Estimates:

Model Yrs. '81-'96, No.	10,206
% Total	59.57
Model Yrs. '97-'98, No.	1,604
% Total	9.36
'99 Vehicles registered in Model Yr. '99, No.	5,323
% Total	31.07
Total No. '81-'99	17,133

LEGAL MARITAL STATUS

2001 Estimates: (Age 15+)

Single (Never Married)	4,762
Legally Married (Not Separated)	10,805
Legally Married (Separated)	447
Widowed	808
Divorced	980

PSYTE CATEGORIES

2001 Estimates	No. of House-holds	% of Total Hhds.	Index
Technocrafts & Bureaucrats	111	1.41	50
Small City Elite	487	6.17	360
Satellite Suburbs	383	4.85	169
Blue Collar Winners	830	10.52	418
Old Towns' New Fringe	5,049	63.99	1,635
Nesters & Young Homesteaders	41	0.52	22
Rod & Rifle	972	12.32	533

FINAN¢IAL P$YTE

2001 Estimates	No. of House-holds	% of Total Hhds.	Index
Successful Suburbanites	111	1.41	21
Canadian Comfort	1,700	21.55	222
Tractors & Tradelines	5,049	63.99	1,119
Revolving Renters	41	0.52	11
Rural Family Blues	972	12.32	153

HOME LANGUAGE

2001 Estimates:		% Total
English	22,488	98.74
French	188	0.83
Arabic	27	0.12
Norwegian	12	0.05
Other Languages	11	0.05
Multiple Responses	49	0.22
Total	22,775	100.00

HOMES BUILT

	1999	1998	1997
No.	n.a.	130	141

TAXATION

Income Class:	1997	% Total
Under $5,000	1,850	14.37
$5,000-$10,000	1,490	11.58
$10,000-$15,000	1,960	15.23
$15,000-$20,000	1,240	9.63
$20,000-$25,000	1,210	9.40
$25,000-$30,000	1,120	8.70
$30,000-$40,000	1,740	13.52
$40,000-$50,000	1,170	9.09
$50,000 +	1,080	8.39
Total Returns, No.	12,870	
Total Income, $000	307,175	
Total Taxable Returns	9,080	
Total Tax, $000	53,970	
Average Income, $	23,868	
Average Tax, $	5,944	

VITAL STATISTICS

	1997	1996	1995	1994
Births	269	273	253	292
Deaths	119	105	100	106
Natural Increase	150	168	153	186
Marriages	85	68	68	68

Note: Latest available data.

MEDIA INFO
See Halifax, CMA

Nova Scotia

Kentville
(Census Agglomeration)

The Census Agglomeration of Kentville includes: Kentville, T; King's Subd. B, SCM; King's Subd. C; SCM. All are in Kings County.

POPULATION

July 1, 2001 Estimate	26,621
% Cdn. Total	0.09
% Change, '96 -'01	3.54
Avg. Annual Growth Rate, %	0.70
2003 Projected Population	27,269
2006 Projected Population	28,249
2001 Households Estimate	10,480
2003 Projected Households	10,812
2006 Projected Households	11,329

INCOME

% Above/Below National Average	-17
2001 Total Income Estimate	$468,360,000
% Cdn. Total	0.07
2001 Average Hhld. Income	$44,700
2001 Per Capita	$17,600
2003 Projected Total Income	$510,060,000
2006 Projected Total Income	$581,270,000

RETAIL SALES

% Above/Below National Average	+31
2001 Retail Sales Estimate	$312,580,000
% Cdn. Total	0.11
2001 per Household	$29,800
2001 per Capita	$11,700
2001 No. of Establishments	270
2003 Projected Retail Sales	$347,590,000
2006 Projected Retail Sales	$401,110,000

POPULATION

2001 Estimates:

Total	26,621
Male	12,912
Female	13,709

Age Groups	Male	Female
0-4	792	766
5-9	886	851
10-14	918	892
15-19	926	882
20-24	906	896
25-29	891	940
30-34	978	1,020
35-39	1,058	1,111
40-44	1,063	1,108
45-49	991	1,018
50-54	829	874
55-59	670	714
60-64	560	606
65-69	469	529
70+	975	1,502

DAYTIME POPULATION

2001 Estimates:

Working Population	12,486
At Home Population	14,134
Total	26,620

INCOME

2001 Estimates:

Avg. Household Income	$44,691
Avg. Family Income	$49,089
Per Capita Income	$17,594
Male:	
Avg. Employment Income	$26,957
Avg. Employment Income (Full Time)	$38,252
Female:	
Avg. Employment Income	$17,578
Avg. Employment Income (Full Time)	$28,550

DISPOSABLE & DISCRETIONARY INCOME

2001 Estimates:	Per Hhld.
Disposable Income	$35,170
Discretionary Income 1 (minus Food & Shelter)	$23,615
Discretionary Income 2 (minus Food, Shelter, & Other Expenditures)	$15,745

LIQUID ASSETS

1999 Estimates:	Per Hhld.
Equity Investments	$48,976
Interest Bearing Investments	$50,833
Total Liquid Assets	$99,809

CREDIT DATA

July 2000:

Pool of Credit	$265,446,305
Revolving Credit, No.	42,193
Fixed Loans, No.	21,724
Avg. Credit Limit, per Person	$11,719
Avg. Spent, per Person	$6,155
Satisfactory Ratings, No. per Person	2.61
Avg. No. of Cards, per Person	0.79

LABOUR FORCE

2001 Estimates:

Male:	
In the Labour Force	6,916
Participation Rate	67.0
Employed	6,417
Unemployed	499
Unemployment Rate	7.2
Not in Labour Force	3,400
Female:	
In the Labour Force	6,527
Participation Rate	58.3
Employed	5,959
Unemployed	568
Unemployment Rate	8.7
Not in Labour Force	4,673

OCCUPATIONS BY MAJOR GROUPS

2001 Estimates:	Male	Female
Management	643	310
Business, Finance & Admin.	456	1,596
Natural & Applied Sciences & Related	294	122
Health	158	546
Social Sciences, Gov't Services & Religion	122	260
Education	281	244
Arts, Culture, Recreation & Sport	67	91
Sales & Service	1,414	2,465
Trades, Transport & Equipment Operators & Related	1,704	85
Primary Industries	901	291
Processing, Mfg. & Utilities	764	355

LEVEL OF SCHOOLING

2001 Estimates:

Population 15 years +	21,516
Less than Grade 9	2,156
Grades 9-13 w/o Certif.	6,260
Grade 9-13 with Certif.	1,972
Trade Certif./Dip.	891
Non-Univ. w/o Certif./Dip.	775
Non-Univ. with Certif./Dip.	4,902
Univ. w/o Degree	1,979
Univ. w/o Degree/Certif.	976
Univ. with Certif.	1,003
Univ. with Degree	2,581

AVERAGE HOUSEHOLD EXPENDITURES

2001 Estimates:

Food	$5,571
Shelter	$7,796
Clothing	$1,783
Transportation	$6,060
Health & Personal Care	$1,791
Recr'n, Read'g & Education	$3,155
Taxes & Securities	$10,459
Other	$7,786
Total Expenditures	$44,401

PRIVATE HOUSEHOLDS

2001 Estimates:

Private Households, Total	10,480
Pop. in Private Households	26,308
Average no. per Household	2.5

FAMILIES

2001 Estimates:

Families in Private Households	8,025
Husband-Wife Families	6,837
Lone-Parent Families	1,188
Aver. No. Persons per Family	3.0
Aver. No. Sons/Daughters at Home	1.1

HOUSING

2001 Estimates:

Occupied Private Dwellings	10,480
Owned	7,432
Rented	3,048
Single-Detached House	7,551
Semi-Detached House	508
Row Houses	11
Apartment, 5+ Storeys	21
Apartment, 5 or Fewer Storeys	1,399
Apartment, Detached Duplex	408
Other Single-Attached	22
Movable Dwellings	560

VEHICLES

2001 Estimates:

Model Yrs. '81-'96, No.	11,130
% Total	86.11
Model Yrs. '97-'98, No.	908
% Total	7.02
'99 Vehicles registered in Model Yr. '99, No.	888
% Total	6.87
Total No. '81-'99	12,926

LEGAL MARITAL STATUS

2001 Estimates: (Age 15+)

Single (Never Married)	5,951
Legally Married (Not Separated)	11,790
Legally Married (Separated)	753
Widowed	1,376
Divorced	1,646

PSYTE CATEGORIES

2001 Estimates	No. of House-holds	% of Total Hhds.	Index
Small City Elite	988	9.43	550
Old Towns' New Fringe	2,116	20.19	516
Rustic Prosperity	843	8.04	446
Old Leafy Towns	360	3.44	134
Nesters & Young Homesteaders	2,461	23.48	1,006
Quiet Towns	1,198	11.43	537
Rod & Rifle	2,511	23.96	1,036

FINANCIAL P$YTE

2001 Estimates	No. of House-holds	% of Total Hhds.	Index
Canadian Comfort	988	9.43	97
Tractors & Tradelines	2,959	28.23	494
Bills & Wills	360	3.44	41
Revolving Renters	2,461	23.48	510
Rural Family Blues	2,511	23.96	297
Limited Budgets	1,198	11.43	368

HOME LANGUAGE

2001 Estimates:		% Total
English	26,399	99.17
French	53	0.20
Chinese	22	0.08
Dutch	22	0.08
Japanese	37	0.14
Other Languages	45	0.17
Multiple Responses	43	0.16
Total	26,621	100.00

BUILDING PERMITS

	1999	1998	1997
		$000	
Value	6,048	5,513	6,287

HOMES BUILT

	1999	1998	1997
No.	68	113	172

TAXATION

Income Class:	1997	% Total
Under $5,000	2,760	15.45
$5,000-$10,000	2,680	15.01
$10,000-$15,000	3,310	18.53
$15,000-$20,000	1,940	10.86
$20,000-$25,000	1,670	9.35
$25,000-$30,000	1,350	7.56
$30,000-$40,000	1,800	10.08
$40,000-$50,000	1,140	6.38
$50,000 +	1,230	6.89
Total Returns, No.	17,860	
Total Income, $000	386,843	
Total Taxable Returns	11,550	
Total Tax, $000	63,577	
Average Income, $	21,660	
Average Tax, $	5,505	

VITAL STATISTICS

	1997	1996	1995	1994
Births	297	282	296	295
Deaths	171	162	163	172
Natural Increase	126	120	133	123
Marriages	147	132	157	160

Note: Latest available data.

COMMUNITY NEWSPAPER(S)

	Total Circulation
Kentville: The Advertiser	
Tue.	6,631
Fri.	5,350
Kentville: Teleguide	n.a.

RADIO STATION(S)

	Power
CKEN	1,000w
CKWM-FM	18,000w

Kings, Subd. A
(Subd. County Municipality)
In Kings County.

POPULATION

July 1, 2001 Estimate	24,584
% Cdn. Total	0.08
% Change, '96 -'01	5.67
Avg. Annual Growth Rate, %	1.11
2003 Projected Population	25,446
2006 Projected Population	26,743
2001 Households Estimate	9,033
2003 Projected Households	9,423
2006 Projected Households	10,027

INCOME

% Above/Below National Average	-22
2001 Total Income Estimate	$402,660,000
% Cdn. Total	0.06
2001 Average Hhld. Income	$44,600
2001 Per Capita	$16,400
2003 Projected Total Income	$445,290,000
2006 Projected Total Income	$518,590,000

RETAIL SALES

% Above/Below National Average	+14
2001 Retail Sales Estimate	$250,110,000
% Cdn. Total	0.09
2001 per Household	$27,700
2001 per Capita	$10,200
2001 No. of Establishments	150
2003 Projected Retail Sales	$279,280,000
2006 Projected Retail Sales	$323,570,000

POPULATION

2001 Estimates:

Total		24,584
Male		12,327
Female		12,257

Age Groups	Male	Female
0-4	807	740
5-9	968	901
10-14	1,003	959
15-19	901	874
20-24	744	771
25-29	763	812
30-34	1,059	1,040
35-39	1,229	1,158
40-44	1,084	1,014
45-49	866	839
50-54	675	695
55-59	572	578
60-64	500	489
65-69	395	404
70+	761	983

DAYTIME POPULATION

2001 Estimates:

Working Population	12,412
At Home Population	13,410
Total	25,822

INCOME

2001 Estimates:

Avg. Household Income	$44,577
Avg. Family Income	$47,058
Per Capita Income	$16,379
Male:	
Avg. Employment Income	$29,800
Avg. Employment Income (Full Time)	$38,551
Female:	
Avg. Employment Income	$15,096
Avg. Employment Income (Full Time)	$25,003

DISPOSABLE & DISCRETIONARY INCOME

2001 Estimates:	Per Hhld.
Disposable Income	$35,281
Discretionary Income 1 (minus Food & Shelter)	$24,003
Discretionary Income 2 (minus Food, Shelter, & Other Expenditures)	$15,985

LIQUID ASSETS

1999 Estimates:	Per Hhld.
Equity Investments	$42,163
Interest Bearing Investments	$48,896
Total Liquid Assets	$91,059

CREDIT DATA

July 2000:

Pool of Credit	$266,593,953
Revolving Credit, No.	42,405
Fixed Loans, No.	23,127
Avg. Credit Limit, per Person	$11,526
Avg. Spent, per Person	$6,011
Satisfactory Ratings, No. per Person	2.65
Avg. No. of Cards, per Person	0.78

LABOUR FORCE

2001 Estimates:

Male:	
In the Labour Force	6,513
Participation Rate	68.2
Employed	6,214
Unemployed	299
Unemployment Rate	4.6
Not in Labour Force	3,036
Female:	
In the Labour Force	5,248
Participation Rate	54.3
Employed	4,857
Unemployed	391
Unemployment Rate	7.5
Not in Labour Force	4,409

OCCUPATIONS BY MAJOR GROUPS

2001 Estimates:	Male	Female
Management	824	256
Business, Finance & Admin.	254	1,029
Natural & Applied Sciences & Related	339	33
Health	64	455
Social Sciences, Gov't Services & Religion	62	123
Education	21	206
Arts, Culture, Recreation & Sport	84	120
Sales & Service	1,966	2,074
Trades, Transport & Equipment Operators & Related	1,447	88
Primary Industries	835	369
Processing, Mfg. & Utilities	558	244

LEVEL OF SCHOOLING

2001 Estimates:

Population 15 years +	19,206
Less than Grade 9	2,074
Grades 9-13 w/o Certif.	5,496
Grade 9-13 with Certif.	2,184
Trade Certif. /Dip.	774
Non-Univ. w/o Certif./Dip.	879
Non-Univ. with Certif./Dip.	4,662
Univ. w/o Degree	1,631
Univ. w/o Degree/Certif.	726
Univ. with Certif.	905
Univ. with Degree	1,506

AVERAGE HOUSEHOLD EXPENDITURES

2001 Estimates:

Food	$5,595
Shelter	$7,438
Clothing	$1,779
Transportation	$6,171
Health & Personal Care	$1,774
Recr'n, Read'g & Education	$3,152
Taxes & Securities	$10,652
Other	$7,751
Total Expenditures	$44,312

PRIVATE HOUSEHOLDS

2001 Estimates:

Private Households, Total	9,033
Pop. in Private Households	24,062
Average no. per Household	2.7

FAMILIES

2001 Estimates:

Families in Private Households	7,266
Husband-Wife Families	6,511
Lone-Parent Families	755
Aver. No. Persons per Family	3.1
Aver. No. Sons/Daughters at Home	1.2

HOUSING

2001 Estimates:

Occupied Private Dwellings	9,033
Owned	6,775
Rented	2,258
Single-Detached House	7,223
Semi-Detached House	512
Row Houses	511
Apartment, 5 or Fewer Storeys	262
Apartment, Detached Duplex	134
Other Single-Attached	57
Movable Dwellings	334

VEHICLES

2001 Estimates:

Model Yrs. '81-'96, No.	10,953
% Total	88.37
Model Yrs. '97-'98, No.	717
% Total	5.78
'99 Vehicles registered in Model Yr. '99, No.	725
% Total	5.85
Total No. '81-'99	12,395

LEGAL MARITAL STATUS

2001 Estimates: (Age 15+)

Single (Never Married)	4,720
Legally Married (Not Separated)	11,572
Legally Married (Separated)	594
Widowed	1,044
Divorced	1,276

PSYTE CATEGORIES

2001 Estimates	No. of House-holds	% of Total Hhds.	Index
Small City Elite	463	5.13	299
Old Towns' New Fringe	2,646	29.29	748
Rustic Prosperity	747	8.27	458
Pick-ups & Dirt Bikes	404	4.47	536
Old Leafy Towns	430	4.76	186
Quiet Towns	1,387	15.35	722
Rod & Rifle	2,915	32.27	1,395

FINANCIAL P$YTE

2001 Estimates	No. of House-holds	% of Total Hhds.	Index
Canadian Comfort	463	5.13	53
Tractors & Tradelines	3,393	37.56	657
Bills & Wills	430	4.76	57
Country Credit	404	4.47	66
Rural Family Blues	2,915	32.27	400
Limited Budgets	1,387	15.35	494

Nova Scotia

HOME LANGUAGE

2001 Estimates:		% Total
English	23,836	96.96
French	438	1.78
German	189	0.77
Spanish	27	0.11
Other Languages	33	0.13
Multiple Responses	61	0.25
Total	24,584	100.00

BUILDING PERMITS

	1999	1998	1997
		$000	
Value	39,438	25,664	n.a.

TAXATION

Income Class:	1997	% Total
Under $5,000	2,770	18.20
$5,000-$10,000	2,050	13.47
$10,000-$15,000	2,290	15.05
$15,000-$20,000	1,460	9.59
$20,000-$25,000	1,190	7.82
$25,000-$30,000	1,020	6.70
$30,000-$40,000	1,750	11.50
$40,000-$50,000	1,540	10.12
$50,000 +	1,170	7.69
Total Returns, No.	15,220	
Total Income, $000	336,009	
Total Taxable Returns	9,970	
Total Tax, $000	56,490	
Average Income, $	22,077	
Average Tax, $	5,666	

VITAL STATISTICS

	1997	1996	1995	1994
Births	285	322	323	307
Deaths	140	142	108	125
Natural Increase	145	180	215	182
Marriages	96	85	76	80

Note: Latest available data.

Nova Scotia

Lunenburg
(Municipal District)

In Lunenburg County.

POPULATION

July 1, 2001 Estimate	26,913
% Cdn. Total	0.09
% Change, '96 -'01	1.52
Avg. Annual Growth Rate, %	0.30
2003 Projected Population	27,204
2006 Projected Population	27,606
2001 Households Estimate	10,405
2003 Projected Households	10,599
2006 Projected Households	10,910

INCOME

% Above/Below National Average	-23
2001 Total Income Estimate	$436,780,000
% Cdn. Total	0.07
2001 Average Hhld. Income	$42,000
2001 Per Capita	$16,200
2003 Projected Total Income	$470,410,000
2006 Projected Total Income	$527,150,000

RETAIL SALES

% Above/Below National Average	-44
2001 Retail Sales Estimate	$134,310,000
% Cdn. Total	0.05
2001 per Household	$12,900
2001 per Capita	$5,000
2001 No. of Establishments	190
2003 Projected Retail Sales	$146,020,000
2006 Projected Retail Sales	$164,870,000

POPULATION

2001 Estimates:

Total		26,913
Male		13,518
Female		13,395
Age Groups	Male	Female
0-4	688	642
5-9	812	712
10-14	920	796
15-19	927	867
20-24	846	789
25-29	781	743
30-34	868	882
35-39	1,030	1,044
40-44	1,113	1,101
45-49	1,097	1,082
50-54	992	965
55-59	836	805
60-64	682	689
65-69	579	615
70+	1,347	1,663

DAYTIME POPULATION

2001 Estimates:

Working Population	5,038
At Home Population	14,959
Total	19,997

INCOME

2001 Estimates:

Avg. Household Income	$41,977
Avg. Family Income	$44,708
Per Capita Income	$16,229
Male:	
Avg. Employment Income	$28,168
Avg. Employment Income (Full Time)	$36,500
Female:	
Avg. Employment Income	$14,612
Avg. Employment Income (Full Time)	$23,907

DISPOSABLE & DISCRETIONARY INCOME

2001 Estimates:	Per Hhld.
Disposable Income	$33,277
Discretionary Income 1 (minus Food & Shelter)	$22,397
Discretionary Income 2 (minus Food, Shelter, & Other Expenditures)	$14,797

LIQUID ASSETS

1999 Estimates:	Per Hhld.
Equity Investments	$45,527
Interest Bearing Investments	$48,506
Total Liquid Assets	$94,033

CREDIT DATA

July 2000:

Pool of Credit	$233,310,880
Revolving Credit, No.	34,985
Fixed Loans, No.	16,759
Avg. Credit Limit, per Person	$11,396
Avg. Spent, per Person	$5,743
Satisfactory Ratings, No. per Person	2.44
Avg. No. of Cards, per Person	0.76

LABOUR FORCE

2001 Estimates:

Male:	
In the Labour Force	6,949
Participation Rate	62.6
Employed	6,442
Unemployed	507
Unemployment Rate	7.3
Not in Labour Force	4,149
Female:	
In the Labour Force	5,737
Participation Rate	51.0
Employed	5,247
Unemployed	490
Unemployment Rate	8.5
Not in Labour Force	5,508

OCCUPATIONS BY MAJOR GROUPS

2001 Estimates:	Male	Female
Management	558	287
Business, Finance & Admin.	288	1,249
Natural & Applied Sciences & Related	358	44
Health	21	482
Social Sciences, Gov't Services & Religion	95	145
Education	144	180
Arts, Culture, Recreation & Sport	141	206
Sales & Service	925	2,210
Trades, Transport & Equipment Operators & Related	2,078	135
Primary Industries	1,177	171
Processing, Mfg. & Utilities	1,079	444

LEVEL OF SCHOOLING

2001 Estimates:

Population 15 years +	22,343
Less than Grade 9	3,866
Grades 9-13 w/o Certif.	6,704
Grade 9-13 with Certif.	2,179
Trade Certif. /Dip.	858
Non-Univ. w/o Certif./Dip.	841
Non-Univ. with Certif./Dip.	4,956
Univ. w/o Degree.	1,524
Univ. w/o Degree/Certif.	731
Univ. with Certif.	793
Univ. with Degree	1,415

AVERAGE HOUSEHOLD EXPENDITURES

2001 Estimates:

Food	$5,566
Shelter	$6,827
Clothing	$1,672
Transportation	$5,680
Health & Personal Care	$1,747
Recr'n, Read'g & Education	$2,892
Taxes & Securities	$10,206
Other	$7,508
Total Expenditures	$42,098

PRIVATE HOUSEHOLDS

2001 Estimates:

Private Households, Total	10,405
Pop. in Private Households	26,618
Average no. per Household	2.6

FAMILIES

2001 Estimates:

Families in Private Households	8,405
Husband-Wife Families	7,670
Lone-Parent Families	735
Aver. No. Persons per Family	2.9
Aver. No. Sons/Daughters at Home	1.0

HOUSING

2001 Estimates:

Occupied Private Dwellings	10,405
Owned	9,161
Rented	1,244
Single-Detached House	9,438
Semi-Detached House	91
Row Houses	11
Apartment, 5 or Fewer Storeys	215
Apartment, Detached Duplex	113
Other Single-Attached	17
Movable Dwellings	520

VEHICLES

2001 Estimates:

Model Yrs. '81-'96, No.	12,502
% Total	87.24
Model Yrs. '97-'98, No.	962
% Total	6.71
'99 Vehicles registered in Model Yr. '99, No.	867
% Total	6.05
Total No. '81-'99	14,331

LEGAL MARITAL STATUS

2001 Estimates: (Age 15+)

Single (Never Married)	5,554
Legally Married (Not Separated)	13,356
Legally Married (Separated)	537
Widowed	1,604
Divorced	1,292

PSYTE CATEGORIES

2001 Estimates	No. of House-holds	% of Total Hhds.	Index
Old Towns' New Fringe	531	5.10	130
Pick-ups & Dirt Bikes	362	3.48	417
Old Leafy Towns	1,288	12.38	484
Quiet Towns	166	1.60	75
Rod & Rifle	7,670	73.71	3,187
Big Country Families	381	3.66	257

FINANCIAL P$YTE

2001 Estimates	No. of House-holds	% of Total Hhds.	Index
Tractors & Tradelines	531	5.10	89
Bills & Wills	1,288	12.38	149
Country Credit	362	3.48	51
Rural Family Blues	8,051	77.38	958
Limited Budgets	166	1.60	51

HOME LANGUAGE

2001 Estimates:		% Total
English	26,721	99.29
French	47	0.17
German	36	0.13
Other Languages	30	0.11
Multiple Responses	79	0.29
Total	26,913	100.00

BUILDING PERMITS

	1999	1998	1997
		$000	
Value	15,786	18,642	25,173

TAXATION

Income Class:	1997	% Total
Under $5,000	1,480	19.32
$5,000-$10,000	1,070	13.97
$10,000-$15,000	1,520	19.84
$15,000-$20,000	840	10.97
$20,000-$25,000	660	8.62
$25,000-$30,000	440	5.74
$30,000-$40,000	670	8.75
$40,000-$50,000	490	6.40
$50,000 +	490	6.40
Total Returns, No.	7,660	
Total Income, $000	153,706	
Total Taxable Returns	4,520	
Total Tax, $000	24,650	
Average Income, $	20,066	
Average Tax, $	5,454	

VITAL STATISTICS

	1997	1996	1995	1994
Births	218	227	207	242
Deaths	214	228	304	232
Natural Increase	4	-1	-97	10
Marriages	97	85	85	84

Note: Latest available data.

COMMUNITY NEWSPAPER(S)

	Total Circulation
Lunenburg: Progress/Bulletin	4,056

New Glasgow
(Census Agglomeration)

The Census Agglomeration of New Glasgow includes: New Glasgow, T; Pictou, Subd. B, SCM; Pictou, Subd. C, SCM; Stellarton, T; Trenton, T; Westville, T; plus two smaller areas. All are in Pictou County.

POPULATION

July 1, 2001 Estimate	38,321
% Cdn. Total	0.12
% Change, '96 -'01	-1.53
Avg. Annual Growth Rate, %	-0.31
2003 Projected Population	38,384
2006 Projected Population	38,431
2001 Households Estimate	14,953
2003 Projected Households	15,145
2006 Projected Households	15,414

INCOME

% Above/Below National Average	-22
2001 Total Income Estimate	$632,140,000
% Cdn. Total	0.10
2001 Average Hhld. Income	$42,300
2001 Per Capita	$16,500
2003 Projected Total Income	$667,890,000
2006 Projected Total Income	$725,100,000

RETAIL SALES

% Above/Below National Average	+17
2001 Retail Sales Estimate	$400,150,000
% Cdn. Total	0.14
2001 per Household	$26,800
2001 per Capita	$10,400
2001 No. of Establishments	343
2003 Projected Retail Sales	$429,940,000
2006 Projected Retail Sales	$475,140,000

POPULATION

2001 Estimates:

Total		38,321
Male		18,480
Female		19,841

Age Groups	Male	Female
0-4	1,007	982
5-9	1,108	1,107
10-14	1,266	1,252
15-19	1,426	1,381
20-24	1,388	1,330
25-29	1,198	1,192
30-34	1,159	1,215
35-39	1,302	1,374
40-44	1,435	1,505
45-49	1,466	1,525
50-54	1,337	1,320
55-59	1,062	1,038
60-64	843	872
65-69	714	842
70+	1,769	2,906

DAYTIME POPULATION

2001 Estimates:

Working Population	16,576
At Home Population	22,469
Total	39,045

INCOME

2001 Estimates:

Avg. Household Income	$42,275
Avg. Family Income	$46,982
Per Capita Income	$16,496
Male:	
Avg. Employment Income	$29,412
Avg. Employment Income (Full Time)	$42,119
Female:	
Avg. Employment Income	$16,588
Avg. Employment Income (Full Time)	$26,784

DISPOSABLE & DISCRETIONARY INCOME

2001 Estimates: Per Hhld.

Disposable Income	$33,346
Discretionary Income 1 (minus Food & Shelter)	$22,244
Discretionary Income 2 (minus Food, Shelter, & Other Expenditures)	$14,647

LIQUID ASSETS

1999 Estimates: Per Hhld.

Equity Investments	$46,935
Interest Bearing Investments	$49,210
Total Liquid Assets	$96,145

CREDIT DATA

July 2000:

Pool of Credit	$396,389,091
Revolving Credit, No.	57,747
Fixed Loans, No.	31,722
Avg. Credit Limit, per Person	$11,609
Avg. Spent, per Person	$6,099
Satisfactory Ratings, No. per Person	2.45
Avg. No. of Cards, per Person	0.72

LABOUR FORCE

2001 Estimates:

Male:	
In the Labour Force	9,459
Participation Rate	62.6
Employed	8,500
Unemployed	959
Unemployment Rate	10.1
Not in Labour Force	5,640
Female:	
In the Labour Force	8,254
Participation Rate	50.0
Employed	7,323
Unemployed	931
Unemployment Rate	11.3
Not in Labour Force	8,246

OCCUPATIONS BY MAJOR GROUPS

2001 Estimates:	Male	Female
Management	782	357
Business, Finance & Admin.	601	2,001
Natural & Applied Sciences & Related	376	43
Health	79	839
Social Sciences, Gov't Services & Religion	157	190
Education	201	537
Arts, Culture, Recreation & Sport	141	64
Sales & Service	1,776	3,175
Trades, Transport & Equipment Operators & Related	2,723	141
Primary Industries	634	144
Processing, Mfg. & Utilities	1,662	305

LEVEL OF SCHOOLING

2001 Estimates:

Population 15 years +	31,599
Less than Grade 9	3,566
Grades 9-13 w/o Certif.	10,265
Grade 9-13 with Certif.	3,243
Trade Certif. /Dip.	1,615
Non-Univ. w/o Certif./Dip.	1,377
Non-Univ. with Certif./Dip.	6,368
Univ. w/o Degree	2,759
Univ. w/o Degree/Certif.	1,354
Univ. with Certif.	1,405
Univ. with Degree.	2,406

AVERAGE HOUSEHOLD EXPENDITURES

2001 Estimates:

Food	$5,415
Shelter	$7,422
Clothing	$1,712
Transportation	$5,712
Health & Personal Care	$1,793
Recr'n, Read'g & Education	$2,900
Taxes & Securities	$9,942
Other	$7,415
Total Expenditures	$42,311

PRIVATE HOUSEHOLDS

2001 Estimates:

Private Households, Total	14,953
Pop. in Private Households	37,657
Average no. per Household	2.5

FAMILIES

2001 Estimates:

Families in Private Households	11,090
Husband-Wife Families	9,141
Lone-Parent Families	1,949
Aver. No. Persons per Family	3.0
Aver. No. Sons/Daughters at Home	1.2

HOUSING

2001 Estimates:

Occupied Private Dwellings	14,953
Owned	10,925
Rented	3,905
Band Housing	123
Single-Detached House	11,204
Semi-Detached House	555
Row Houses	276
Apartment, 5 or Fewer Storeys	1,356
Apartment, Detached Duplex	729
Other Single-Attached	25
Movable Dwellings	808

VEHICLES

2001 Estimates:

Model Yrs. '81-'96, No.	15,832
% Total	83.10
Model Yrs. '97-'98, No.	1,706
% Total	8.95
'99 Vehicles registered in Model Yr. '99, No.	1,513
% Total	7.94
Total No. '81-'99	19,051

LEGAL MARITAL STATUS

2001 Estimates: (Age 15+)

Single (Never Married)	9,452
Legally Married (Not Separated)	16,332
Legally Married (Separated)	947
Widowed	2,711
Divorced	2,157

PSYTE CATEGORIES

2001 Estimates	No. of House-holds	% of Total Hhds.	Index
Small City Elite	881	5.89	344
Old Towns' New Fringe	1,600	10.70	273
Old Leafy Towns	698	4.67	183
Nesters & Young Homesteaders	1,505	10.06	431
Young Grey Collar	1,165	7.79	931
Quiet Towns	4,355	29.12	1,369
Rod & Rifle	4,461	29.83	1,290
Big Country Families	123	0.82	58

FINANCIAL P$YTE

2001 Estimates	No. of House-holds	% of Total Hhds.	Index
Canadian Comfort	881	5.89	61
Tractors & Tradelines	1,600	10.70	187
Bills & Wills	698	4.67	56
Revolving Renters	2,670	17.86	388
Rural Family Blues	4,584	30.66	380
Limited Budgets	4,355	29.12	937

Nova Scotia

HOME LANGUAGE

2001 Estimates:		% Total
English	37,963	99.07
French	41	0.11
German	32	0.08
Micmac	157	0.41
Other Languages	30	0.08
Multiple Responses	98	0.26
Total	38,321	100.00

BUILDING PERMITS

	1999	1998	1997
		$000	
Value	36,899	35,066	19,398

HOMES BUILT

	1999	1998	1997
No	74	68	74

TAXATION

Income Class:	1997	% Total
Under $5,000	4,430	16.45
$5,000-$10,000	3,820	14.18
$10,000-$15,000	5,040	18.72
$15,000-$20,000	2,940	10.92
$20,000-$25,000	2,150	7.98
$25,000-$30,000	1,850	6.87
$30,000-$40,000	2,650	9.84
$40,000-$50,000	1,880	6.98
$50,000 +	2,220	8.24
Total Returns, No.	26,930	
Total Income, $000	599,345	
Total Taxable Returns	16,620	
Total Tax, $000	103,521	
Average Income, $	22,256	
Average Tax, $	6,229	

VITAL STATISTICS

	1997	1996	1995	1994
Births	408	405	458	430
Deaths	387	380	358	360
Natural Increase	21	25	100	70
Marriages	228	232	248	250

Note: Latest available data.

DAILY NEWSPAPER(S)

	Circulation Average Paid
The Evening News	8,362

COMMUNITY NEWSPAPER(S)

	Total Circulation
Pictou: Pictou Advocate	4,021

RADIO STATION(S)

	Power
CBAF-FM	n.a.
CBH-FM	n.a.
CBHN-FM	n.a.
CKEC	25,000w

TELEVISION STATION(S)

CBAFT-TV
CBHT-TV
CJCB-TV
GLOBAL-TV

Nova Scotia

Truro
(Census Agglomeration)

The Census Agglomeration of Truro includes: Colchester, Subd. B, SCM; Colchester, Subd. C, SCM; Truro, T; plus one smaller area. All are in Colchester County.

POPULATION

July 1, 2001 Estimate	46,328
% Cdn. Total	0.15
% Change, '96 -'01	2.61
Avg. Annual Growth Rate, %	0.52
2003 Projected Population	47,314
2006 Projected Population	48,758
2001 Households Estimate	18,355
2003 Projected Households	18,849
2006 Projected Households	19,677

INCOME

% Above/Below National Average	-19
2001 Total Income Estimate	$786,360,000
% Cdn. Total	0.12
2001 Average Hhld. Income	$42,800
2001 Per Capita	$17,000
2003 Projected Total Income	$844,920,000
2006 Projected Total Income	$948,500,000

RETAIL SALES

% Above/Below National Average	+34
2001 Retail Sales Estimate	$555,340,000
% Cdn. Total	0.20
2001 per Household	$30,300
2001 per Capita	$12,000
2001 No. of Establishments	436
2003 Projected Retail Sales	$610,550,000
2006 Projected Retail Sales	$694,820,000

POPULATION

2001 Estimates:

Total		46,328
Male		22,517
Female		23,811

Age Groups	Male	Female
0-4	1,363	1,309
5-9	1,523	1,458
10-14	1,629	1,541
15-19	1,629	1,552
20-24	1,554	1,579
25-29	1,502	1,593
30-34	1,599	1,716
35-39	1,762	1,873
40-44	1,799	1,876
45-49	1,703	1,743
50-54	1,503	1,502
55-59	1,237	1,267
60-64	1,013	1,060
65-69	830	941
70+	1,871	2,801

DAYTIME POPULATION

2001 Estimates:

Working Population	21,376
At Home Population	24,953
Total	46,329

INCOME

2001 Estimates:

Avg. Household Income	$42,842
Avg. Family Income	$48,012
Per Capita Income	$16,974

Male:

Avg. Employment Income	$28,155
Avg. Employment Income (Full Time)	$38,298

Female:

Avg. Employment Income	$15,952
Avg. Employment Income (Full Time)	$25,314

DISPOSABLE & DISCRETIONARY INCOME

2001 Estimates:	Per Hhld.
Disposable Income	$33,765
Discretionary Income 1 (minus Food & Shelter)	$22,469
Discretionary Income 2 (minus Food, Shelter, & Other Expenditures)	$15,148

LIQUID ASSETS

1999 Estimates:	Per Hhld.
Equity Investments	$45,044
Interest Bearing Investments	$48,873
Total Liquid Assets	$93,917

CREDIT DATA

July 2000:

Pool of Credit	$403,206,912
Revolving Credit, No.	61,772
Fixed Loans, No.	29,092
Avg. Credit Limit, per Person	$11,831
Avg. Spent, per Person	$6,058
Satisfactory Ratings, No. per Person	2.50
Avg. No. of Cards, per Person	0.77

LABOUR FORCE

2001 Estimates:

Male:

In the Labour Force	11,851
Participation Rate	65.8
Employed	11,090
Unemployed	761
Unemployment Rate	6.4
Not in Labour Force	6,151

Female:

In the Labour Force	10,999
Participation Rate	56.4
Employed	10,131
Unemployed	868
Unemployment Rate	7.9
Not in Labour Force	8,504

OCCUPATIONS BY MAJOR GROUPS

2001 Estimates:	Male	Female
Management	1,267	615
Business, Finance & Admin.	906	2,492
Natural & Applied Sciences & Related	588	158
Health	133	1,077
Social Sciences, Gov't Services & Religion	262	346
Education	447	504
Arts, Culture, Recreation & Sport	109	196
Sales & Service	2,193	4,043
Trades, Transport & Equipment Operators & Related	3,594	124
Primary Industries	1,008	187
Processing, Mfg. & Utilities	1,117	907

LEVEL OF SCHOOLING

2001 Estimates:

Population 15 years +	37,505
Less than Grade 9	3,462
Grades 9-13 w/o Certif.	11,799
Grade 9-13 with Certif.	4,090
Trade Certif. /Dip.	1,466
Non-Univ. w/o Certif./Dip.	1,527
Non-Univ. with Certif./Dip.	7,451
Univ. w/o Degree	3,919
Univ. w/o Degree/Certif.	1,757
Univ. with Certif.	2,162
Univ. with Degree	3,791

AVERAGE HOUSEHOLD EXPENDITURES

2001 Estimates:

Food	$5,367
Shelter	$7,670
Clothing	$1,746
Transportation	$5,538
Health & Personal Care	$1,722
Recr'n, Read'g & Education	$3,083
Taxes & Securities	$10,116
Other	$7,592
Total Expenditures	$42,834

PRIVATE HOUSEHOLDS

2001 Estimates:

Private Households, Total	18,355
Pop. in Private Households	45,433
Average no. per Household	2.5

FAMILIES

2001 Estimates:

Families in Private Households	13,588
Husband-Wife Families	11,508
Lone-Parent Families	2,080
Aver. No. Persons per Family	3.0
Aver. No. Sons/Daughters at Home	1.1

HOUSING

2001 Estimates:

Occupied Private Dwellings	18,355
Owned	12,989
Rented	5,182
Band Housing	184
Single-Detached House	12,885
Semi-Detached House	306
Row Houses	184
Apartment, 5+ Storeys	53
Apartment, 5 or Fewer Storeys	2,747
Apartment, Detached Duplex	875
Other Single-Attached	93
Movable Dwellings	1,212

VEHICLES

2001 Estimates:

Model Yrs. '81-'96, No.	19,907
% Total	83.92
Model Yrs. '97-'98, No.	1,928
% Total	8.13
'99 Vehicles registered in Model Yr. '99, No.	1,887
% Total	7.95
Total No. '81-'99	23,722

LEGAL MARITAL STATUS

2001 Estimates: (Age 15+)

Single (Never Married)	10,585
Legally Married (Not Separated)	20,235
Legally Married (Separated)	1,290
Widowed	2,755
Divorced	2,640

PSYTE CATEGORIES

2001 Estimates	No. of House-holds	% of Total Hhds.	Index
Small City Elite	610	3.32	194
Town Boomers	937	5.10	504
Old Towns' New Fringe	5,171	28.17	720
Pick-ups & Dirt Bikes	300	1.63	196
Old Leafy Towns	449	2.45	96
Nesters & Young Homesteaders	6,145	33.48	1,434
Young Grey Collar	869	4.73	566
Quiet Towns	320	1.74	82
Rod & Rifle	2,971	16.19	700
Down, Down East	97	0.53	75
Big Country Families	373	2.03	142

FINANCIAL P$YTE

2001 Estimates	No. of House-holds	% of Total Hhds.	Index
Canadian Comfort	1,547	8.43	87
Tractors & Tradelines	5,171	28.17	493
Bills & Wills	449	2.45	30
Country Credit	300	1.63	24
Revolving Renters	7,014	38.21	831
Rural Family Blues	3,441	18.75	232
Limited Budgets	320	1.74	56

HOME LANGUAGE

2001 Estimates:

		% Total
English	45,961	99.21
French	68	0.15
German	33	0.07
Micmac	40	0.09
Other Languages	108	0.23
Multiple Responses	118	0.25
Total	46,328	100.00

BUILDING PERMITS

	1999	1998	1997
		$000	
Value	40,934	35,608	41,945

HOMES BUILT

	1999	1998	1997
No.	99	188	241

TAXATION

Income Class:	1997	% Total
Under $5,000	4,500	15.45
$5,000-$10,000	3,950	13.56
$10,000-$15,000	5,240	17.99
$15,000-$20,000	3,310	11.36
$20,000-$25,000	2,710	9.30
$25,000-$30,000	2,310	7.93
$30,000-$40,000	3,280	11.26
$40,000-$50,000	1,720	5.90
$50,000 +	2,140	7.35
Total Returns, No.	29,130	
Total Income, $000	645,533	
Total Taxable Returns	18,890	
Total Tax, $000	108,201	
Average Income, $	22,160	
Average Tax, $	5,728	

VITAL STATISTICS

	1997	1996	1995	1994
Births	463	511	535	547
Deaths	420	368	391	347
Natural Increase	43	143	144	200
Marriages	268	271	242	270

Note: Latest available data.

Truro
(Census Agglomeration)
(Cont'd)

DAILY NEWSPAPER(S)

	Circulation Average Paid
The Daily News	
Sat.	8,572
Mon-Fri	6,776

COMMUNITY NEWSPAPER(S)

	Total Circulation
Truro/Parsboro: The Shoreline Journal	1,350

RADIO STATION(S)

	Power
CBH-FM	n.a.
CBHC-FM	n.a.
CKCL	n.a.
CKTO-FM	50,000w

TELEVISION STATION(S)

CBHT-TV
CJCH-TV
GLOBAL-TV

West Hants
(Municipal District)
In Hants County.

POPULATION

July 1, 2001 Estimate	14,609
% Cdn. Total	0.05
% Change, '96 -'01	3.41
Avg. Annual Growth Rate, %	0.67
2003 Projected Population	14,787
2006 Projected Population	15,052
2001 Households Estimate	5,375
2003 Projected Households	5,495
2006 Projected Households	5,702

INCOME

% Above/Below National Average	-23
2001 Total Income Estimate	$236,580,000
% Cdn. Total	0.04
2001 Average Hhld. Income	$44,000
2001 Per Capita	$16,200
2003 Projected Total Income	$254,530,000
2006 Projected Total Income	$285,760,000

RETAIL SALES

% Above/Below National Average	-6
2001 Retail Sales Estimate	$122,990,000
% Cdn. Total	0.04
2001 per Household	$22,900
2001 per Capita	$8,400
2001 No. of Establishments	125
2003 Projected Retail Sales	$134,640,000
2006 Projected Retail Sales	$151,780,000

POPULATION

2001 Estimates:

Total	14,609
Male	7,347
Female	7,262

Age Groups	Male	Female
0-4	388	370
5-9	460	428
10-14	525	465
15-19	561	484
20-24	537	477
25-29	454	445
30-34	484	502
35-39	565	584
40-44	582	613
45-49	564	579
50-54	508	513
55-59	433	428
60-64	362	357
65-69	309	299
70+	615	718

DAYTIME POPULATION

2001 Estimates:

Working Population	3,975
At Home Population	8,035
Total	12,010

INCOME

2001 Estimates:

Avg. Household Income	$44,015
Avg. Family Income	$47,080
Per Capita Income	$16,194
Male:	
Avg. Employment Income	$26,472
Avg. Employment Income (Full Time)	$36,691
Female:	
Avg. Employment Income	$15,974
Avg. Employment Income (Full Time)	$24,648

DISPOSABLE & DISCRETIONARY INCOME

2001 Estimates: | Per Hhld.

Disposable Income	$35,001
Discretionary Income 1 (minus Food & Shelter)	$23,669
Discretionary Income 2 (minus Food, Shelter, & Other Expenditures)	$15,825

LIQUID ASSETS

1999 Estimates: | Per Hhld.

Equity Investments	$46,982
Interest Bearing Investments	$50,497
Total Liquid Assets	$97,479

CREDIT DATA

July 2000:

Pool of Credit	$176,138,641
Revolving Credit, No.	26,043
Fixed Loans, No.	15,515
Avg. Credit Limit, per Person	$11,140
Avg. Spent, per Person	$5,957
Satisfactory Ratings, No. per Person	2.45
Avg. No. of Cards, per Person	0.69

LABOUR FORCE

2001 Estimates:
Male:

In the Labour Force	3,936
Participation Rate	65.9
Employed	3,502
Unemployed	434
Unemployment Rate	11.0
Not in Labour Force	2,038
Female:	
In the Labour Force	3,183
Participation Rate	53.1
Employed	2,948
Unemployed	235
Unemployment Rate	7.4
Not in Labour Force	2,816

OCCUPATIONS BY MAJOR GROUPS

2001 Estimates:	Male	Female
Management	334	171
Business, Finance & Admin.	236	875
Natural & Applied Sciences & Related	160	23
Health	20	334
Social Sciences, Gov't Services & Religion	68	44
Education	10	98
Arts, Culture, Recreation & Sport	45	78
Sales & Service	620	1,037
Trades, Transport & Equipment Operators & Related	1,664	24
Primary Industries	441	270
Processing, Mfg. & Utilities	246	95

LEVEL OF SCHOOLING

2001 Estimates:

Population 15 years +	11,973
Less than Grade 9	1,773
Grades 9-13 w/o Certif.	3,745
Grade 9-13 with Certif.	1,077
Trade Certif. /Dip.	728
Non-Univ. w/o Certif./Dip.	451
Non-Univ. with Certif./Dip.	2,494
Univ. w/o Degree	969
Univ. w/o Degree/Certif.	338
Univ. with Certif.	631
Univ. with Degree	736

Nova Scotia

AVERAGE HOUSEHOLD EXPENDITURES

2001 Estimates:

Food	$5,594
Shelter	$7,392
Clothing	$1,710
Transportation	$5,935
Health & Personal Care	$1,766
Recr'n, Read'g & Education	$3,099
Taxes & Securities	$10,724
Other	$7,645
Total Expenditures	$43,865

PRIVATE HOUSEHOLDS

2001 Estimates:

Private Households, Total	5,375
Pop. in Private Households	14,536
Average no. per Household	2.7

FAMILIES

2001 Estimates:

Families in Private Households	4,450
Husband-Wife Families	3,962
Lone-Parent Families	488
Aver. No. Persons per Family	3.0
Aver. No. Sons/Daughters at Home	1.1

HOUSING

2001 Estimates:

Occupied Private Dwellings	5,375
Owned	4,775
Rented	600
Single-Detached House	4,846
Semi-Detached House	50
Row Houses	10
Apartment, 5 or Fewer Storeys	134
Apartment, Detached Duplex	44
Other Single-Attached	33
Movable Dwellings	258

VEHICLES

2001 Estimates:

Model Yrs. '81-'96, No.	7,033
% Total	86.35
Model Yrs. '97-'98, No.	489
% Total	6.00
'99 Vehicles registered in Model Yr. '99, No.	623
% Total	7.65
Total No. '81-'99	8,145

LEGAL MARITAL STATUS

2001 Estimates: (Age 15+)

Single (Never Married)	3,208
Legally Married (Not Separated)	6,908
Legally Married (Separated)	343
Widowed	771
Divorced	743

PSYTE CATEGORIES

2001 Estimates	No. of House -holds	% of Total Hhds.	Index
Old Towns' New Fringe	1,988	36.99	945
Old Leafy Towns	460	8.56	335
Quiet Towns	420	7.81	367
Rod & Rifle	2,507	46.64	2,017

Nova Scotia

West Hants
(Municipal District)
(Cont'd)

FINANCIAL P$YTE

2001 Estimates	No. of House-holds	% of Total Hhds.	Index
Tractors &			
Tradelines	1,988	36.99	647
Bills & Wills	460	8.56	103
Rural Family Blues	2,507	46.64	578
Limited Budgets	420	7.81	251

HOME LANGUAGE

2001 Estimates:		% Total
English	14,549	99.59
French	27	0.18
Dutch	11	0.08
Other Languages	11	0.08
Multiple Responses	11	0.08
Total	14,609	100.00

BUILDING PERMITS

	1999	1998	1997
		$000	
Value	8,847	10,938	6,423

TAXATION

Income Class:	1997	% Total
Under $5,000	1,080	16.77
$5,000-$10,000	900	13.98
$10,000-$15,000	1,080	16.77
$15,000-$20,000	710	11.02
$20,000-$25,000	590	9.16
$25,000-$30,000	490	7.61
$30,000-$40,000	760	11.80
$40,000-$50,000	430	6.68
$50,000 +	410	6.37
Total Returns, No.	6,440	
Total Income, $000	135,491	
Total Taxable Returns	4,200	
Total Tax, $000	21,881	
Average Income, $	21,039	
Average Tax, $	5,210	

VITAL STATISTICS

	1997	1996	1995	1994
Births	119	124	119	140
Deaths	88	87	89	80
Natural Increase	31	37	30	60
Marriages	49	62	53	44

Note: Latest available data.

Yarmouth
(Municipal District)
In Yarmouth County.

POPULATION

July 1, 2001 Estimate	10,885
% Cdn. Total	0.03
% Change, '96 -'01	-0.66
Avg. Annual Growth Rate, %	-0.13
2003 Projected Population	10,920
2006 Projected Population	10,957
2001 Households Estimate	4,143
2003 Projected Households	4,201
2006 Projected Households	4,288

INCOME

% Above/Below National Average	-23
2001 Total Income Estimate	$176,520,000
% Cdn. Total	0.03
2001 Average Hhld. Income	$42,600
2001 Per Capita	$16,200
2003 Projected Total Income	$188,830,000
2006 Projected Total Income	$209,350,000

RETAIL SALES

% Above/Below National Average	-48
2001 Retail Sales Estimate	$51,140,000
% Cdn. Total	0.02
2001 per Household	$12,300
2001 per Capita	$4,700
2001 No. of Establishments	59
2003 Projected Retail Sales	$55,360,000
2006 Projected Retail Sales	$61,430,000

POPULATION

2001 Estimates:		
Total		10,885
Male		5,294
Female		5,591
Age Groups	Male	Female
0-4	292	273
5-9	333	300
10-14	374	359
15-19	403	388
20-24	369	352
25-29	332	326
30-34	349	364
35-39	366	417
40-44	395	443
45-49	410	435
50-54	394	389
55-59	334	313
60-64	250	265
65-69	197	231
70+	496	736

DAYTIME POPULATION

2001 Estimates:	
Working Population	1,964
At Home Population	5,996
Total	7,960

INCOME

2001 Estimates:	
Avg. Household Income	$42,608
Avg. Family Income	$45,438
Per Capita Income	$16,217
Male:	
Avg. Employment Income	$25,632
Avg. Employment Income (Full Time)	$35,034
Female:	
Avg. Employment Income	$14,805
Avg. Employment Income (Full Time)	$26,142

DISPOSABLE & DISCRETIONARY INCOME

2001 Estimates:	Per Hhld.
Disposable Income	$33,752
Discretionary Income 1 (minus Food & Shelter)	$22,754
Discretionary Income 2 (minus Food, Shelter, & Other Expenditures)	$14,877

LIQUID ASSETS

1999 Estimates:	Per Hhld.
Equity Investments	$41,401
Interest Bearing Investments	$47,176
Total Liquid Assets	$88,577

CREDIT DATA

July 2000:	
Pool of Credit	$98,632,105
Revolving Credit, No.	13,984
Fixed Loans, No.	9,091
Avg. Credit Limit, per Person	$10,668
Avg. Spent, per Person	$5,536
Satisfactory Ratings, No. per Person	2.34
Avg. No. of Cards, per Person	0.67

LABOUR FORCE

2001 Estimates:	
Male:	
In the Labour Force	2,868
Participation Rate	66.8
Employed	2,598
Unemployed	270
Unemployment Rate	9.4
Not in Labour Force	1,427
Female:	
In the Labour Force	2,445
Participation Rate	52.5
Employed	2,197
Unemployed	248
Unemployment Rate	10.1
Not in Labour Force	2,214

OCCUPATIONS BY MAJOR GROUPS

2001 Estimates:	Male	Female
Management	193	134
Business, Finance & Admin.	190	556
Natural & Applied Sciences & Related	115	n.a.
Health	40	336
Social Sciences, Gov't Services & Religion	80	36
Education	81	119
Arts, Culture, Recreation & Sport	46	55
Sales & Service	537	915
Trades, Transport & Equipment Operators & Related	684	33
Primary Industries	634	53
Processing, Mfg. & Utilities	212	158

LEVEL OF SCHOOLING

2001 Estimates:	
Population 15 years +	8,954
Less than Grade 9	1,285
Grades 9-13 w/o Certif.	2,892
Grade 9-13 with Certif.	739
Trade Certif. /Dip.	314
Non-Univ. w/o Certif./Dip.	319
Non-Univ. with Certif./Dip.	2,218
Univ. w/o Degree	671
Univ. w/o Degree/Certif.	349
Univ. with Certif.	322
Univ. with Degree	516

AVERAGE HOUSEHOLD EXPENDITURES

2001 Estimates:	
Food	$5,633
Shelter	$6,964
Clothing	$1,747
Transportation	$5,905
Health & Personal Care	$1,809
Recr'n, Read'g & Education	$2,766
Taxes & Securities	$10,101
Other	$7,811
Total Expenditures	$42,735

PRIVATE HOUSEHOLDS

2001 Estimates:	
Private Households, Total	4,143
Pop. in Private Households	10,707
Average no. per Household	2.6

FAMILIES

2001 Estimates:	
Families in Private Households	3,316
Husband-Wife Families	2,911
Lone-Parent Families	405
Aver. No. Persons per Family	2.9
Aver. No. Sons/Daughters at Home	1.0

HOUSING

2001 Estimates:	
Occupied Private Dwellings	4,143
Owned	3,578
Rented	565
Single-Detached House	3,828
Semi-Detached House	57
Row Houses	47
Apartment, 5 or Fewer Storeys	90
Apartment, Detached Duplex	64
Other Single-Attached	10
Movable Dwellings	47

VEHICLES

2001 Estimates:	
Model Yrs. '81-'96, No.	4,784
% Total	85.14
Model Yrs. '97-'98, No.	382
% Total	6.80
'99 Vehicles registered in Model Yr. '99, No.	453
% Total	8.06
Total No. '81-'99	5,619

LEGAL MARITAL STATUS

2001 Estimates: (Age 15+)	
Single (Never Married)	2,292
Legally Married (Not Separated)	5,215
Legally Married (Separated)	203
Widowed	634
Divorced	610

PSYTE CATEGORIES

2001 Estimates	No. of House-holds	% of Total Hhds.	Index
Town Boomers	88	2.12	210
Pick-ups & Dirt Bikes	322	7.77	931
Quiet Towns	861	20.78	977
Agrarian Blues	223	5.38	2,514
Rod & Rifle	2,611	63.02	2,725

FINANCIAL P$YTE

2001 Estimates	No. of House-holds	% of Total Hhds.	Index
Canadian Comfort	88	2.12	22
Country Credit	322	7.77	115
Rural Family Blues	2,834	68.40	847
Limited Budgets	861	20.78	669

Yarmouth
(Municipal District)
(Cont'd)

HOME LANGUAGE

2001 Estimates:		% Total
English	10,607	97.45
French	243	2.23
Multiple Responses	35	0.32
Total	10,885	100.00

BUILDING PERMITS

	1999	1998	1997
		$000	
Value	9,574	12,428	6,460

TAXATION

Income Class:	1997	% Total
Under $5,000	660	15.31
$5,000-$10,000	670	15.55
$10,000-$15,000	860	19.95
$15,000-$20,000	540	12.53
$20,000-$25,000	430	9.98
$25,000-$30,000	310	7.19
$30,000-$40,000	390	9.05
$40,000-$50,000	240	5.57
$50,000 +	220	5.10
Total Returns, No.	4,310	
Total Income, $000	84,588	
Total Taxable Returns	2,730	
Total Tax, $000	12,441	
Average Income, $	19,626	
Average Tax, $	4,557	

VITAL STATISTICS

	1997	1996	1995	1994
Births	94	115	110	106
Deaths	92	76	190	109
Natural Increase	2	39	-80	-3
Marriages	29	26	34	51

Note: Latest available data.

COMMUNITY NEWSPAPER(S)

	Total Circulation
Yarmouth: Le Courrier de la Nouvelle-Écosse	1,473
Yarmouth: The Vanguard	
Tue.	6,326
Fri	4,595

RADIO STATION(S)

	Power
CBAF-FM	n.a.
CBH-FM	n.a.
CBHY-FM	n.a.
CJLS	5,000w

TELEVISION STATION(S)

CBAFT-TV
CBHT-TV
CJCH-TV
GLOBAL-TV

Economic Regions & Census Divisions

New Brunswick

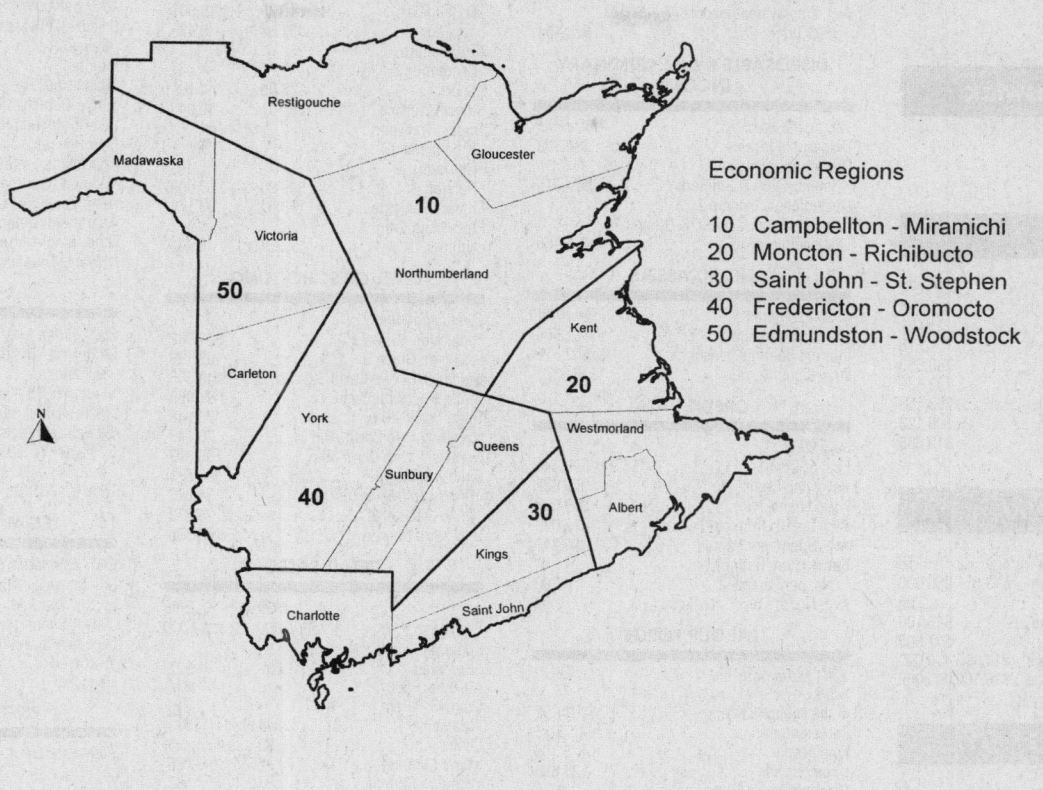

Economic Regions

10 Campbellton - Miramichi
20 Moncton - Richibucto
30 Saint John - St. Stephen
40 Fredericton - Oromocto
50 Edmundston - Woodstock

Region	Population (at July 1)				Households (at July1)		Income				Retail Sales				Taxation Statistics, 1997					
	*1996 Census (000)	2001 Estimate (000)	% of Cdn. Total	% Chg. '96-'01	2001 Estimate (000)	% of Cdn. Total	2001 Estimate $millions	% of Cdn. Total	Per Hhld. $	Income Rating Index	2001 Estimate $millions	% of Cdn. Total	Per Hhld. $	Market Rating Index	Total No. of Returns	Total Income $millions	Total No. Taxable Returns	Total Tax $millions	Avg. Income $	Avg. Tax $
New Brunswick	753.0	759.1	2.44	0.81	293.2	2.43	13,511.2	2.06	46,100	84	7,095.9	2.55	24,200	104	538,100	11,835.7	344,780	2,071.6	21,995	6,009
Campbellton - Miramichi (10)	182.2	178.8	0.57	-1.86	67.8	0.56	2,872.9	0.44	42,400	76	1,791.9	0.64	26,400	112	132,900	2,551.2	78,080	417.4	19,196	5,346
Northumberland County	53.5	52.3	0.17	-2.26	19.5	0.16	844.9	0.13	43,400	77	502.4	0.18	25,800	107	38,980	762.8	22,840	125.8	19,570	5,510
Restigouche County	39.4	38.4	0.12	-2.64	14.9	0.12	623.0	0.09	41,900	77	363.3	0.13	24,400	106	28,050	548.7	16,640	86.7	19,562	5,210
Gloucester County	89.3	88.1	0.28	-1.27	33.4	0.28	1,405.0	0.21	42,000	76	926.2	0.33	27,700	117	65,870	1,239.6	38,600	204.8	18,820	5,307
Moncton - Richibucto (20)	182.8	187.6	0.60	2.58	73.1	0.61	3,540.2	0.54	48,400	90	1,750.2	0.63	23,900	104	133,790	2,996.7	89,710	528.1	22,399	5,887
Albert County	27.0	27.4	0.09	1.35	10.2	0.08	558.1	0.09	54,600	97	78.2	0.03	7,700	32	17,870	448.8	12,650	84.1	25,115	6,652
Westmorland County	123.1	127.2	0.41	3.35	50.5	0.42	2,490.5	0.38	49,300	93	1,409.2	0.51	27,900	124	91,850	2,137.5	62,570	386.3	23,272	6,173
Kent County	32.8	33.0	0.11	0.73	12.4	0.10	491.7	0.07	39,600	71	262.7	0.09	21,200	89	24,070	410.4	14,490	57.7	17,050	3,984
Saint John - St. Stephen (30)	174.6	175.5	0.56	0.51	68.2	0.56	3,246.7	0.49	47,600	88	1,338.5	0.48	19,600	85	121,370	2,891.4	79,740	529.7	23,823	6,642
Saint John County	80.8	78.8	0.25	-2.44	32.6	0.27	1,373.4	0.21	42,100	83	880.2	0.32	27,000	125	56,550	1,284.2	36,200	225.5	22,709	6,230
Charlotte County	27.9	28.3	0.09	1.65	11.2	0.09	479.4	0.07	42,800	80	143.2	0.05	12,800	56	20,880	444.1	13,860	72.6	21,271	5,235
Kings County	65.9	68.3	0.22	3.64	24.3	0.20	1,393.9	0.21	57,200	97	315.1	0.11	12,900	52	43,940	1,163.1	29,680	231.6	26,470	7,802
Fredericton - Oromocto (40)	126.1	129.3	0.42	2.52	50.7	0.42	2,535.9	0.39	50,000	93	1,311.5	0.47	25,900	113	87,630	2,162.4	59,570	403.9	24,677	6,781
Sunbury County	25.9	27.8	0.09	7.19	9.9	0.08	471.3	0.07	47,800	80	174.4	0.06	17,700	70	16,390	375.9	11,640	65.1	22,934	5,597
Queens County	12.7	12.4	0.04	-2.49	5.0	0.04	182.1	0.03	36,700	70	64.6	0.02	13,000	58	9,030	169.8	5,390	24.7	18,805	4,574
York County	87.5	89.1	0.29	1.86	35.9	0.30	1,882.5	0.29	52,400	100	1,072.5	0.38	29,900	134	62,210	1,616.7	42,540	314.1	25,988	7,384
Edmundston - Woodstock (50)	87.3	87.9	0.28	0.78	33.3	0.28	1,315.5	0.20	39,500	71	903.7	0.32	27,100	115	62,400	1,234.0	37,660	192.5	19,775	5,112
Carleton County	27.4	28.3	0.09	2.98	10.3	0.09	416.4	0.06	40,300	70	341.7	0.12	33,100	135	19,140	401.5	11,910	65.2	20,979	5,473
Victoria County	22.3	22.5	0.07	0.69	8.4	0.07	304.9	0.05	36,400	64	265.8	0.10	31,700	132	16,730	304.8	9,530	43.1	18,218	4,520
Madawaska County	37.5	37.2	0.12	-0.78	14.6	0.12	594.2	0.09	40,600	76	296.3	0.11	20,300	89	26,530	527.6	16,220	84.3	19,888	5,195

*Adjusted.

New Brunswick

POPULATION

July 1, 2001 Estimate	759,072
% Cdn. Total	2.44
% Change, '96 -'01	0.81
Avg. Annual Growth Rate, %	0.16
2003 Projected Population	768,658
2006 Projected Population	782,536
2001 Households Estimate	293,158
2003 Projected Households	300,123
2006 Projected Households	310,656

INCOME

% Above/Below National Average	-16
2001 Total Income Estimate	$13,511,250,000
% Cdn. Total	2.06
2001 Average Hhld. Income	$46,100
2001 Per Capita	$17,800
2003 Projected Total Income	$14,495,410,000
2006 Projected Total Income	$16,180,090,000

RETAIL SALES

% Above/Below National Average	+4
2001 Retail Sales Estimate	$7,095,860,000
% Cdn. Total	2.55
2001 per Household	$24,200
2001 per Capita	$9,300
2001 No. of Establishments	6,178
2003 Projected Retail Sales	$7,684,700,000
2006 Projected Retail Sales	$8,570,550,000

POPULATION

2001 Estimates:

Total		759,072
Male		372,724
Female		386,348
Age Groups	Male	Female
0-4	21,564	20,427
5-9	23,561	22,134
10-14	25,340	23,984
15-19	26,573	25,435
20-24	26,904	26,273
25-29	26,264	26,300
30-34	27,910	28,347
35-39	30,085	30,699
40-44	30,519	31,192
45-49	29,327	29,782
50-54	25,468	25,422
55-59	20,222	20,216
60-64	16,067	16,791
65-69	13,324	15,074
70+	29,596	44,272

DAYTIME POPULATION

2001 Estimates:

Working Population	333,306
At Home Population	426,240
Total	759,546

INCOME

2001 Estimates:

Avg. Household Income	$46,089
Avg. Family Income	$50,370
Per Capita Income	$17,800
Male:	
Avg. Employment Income	$29,659
Avg. Employment Income (Full Time)	$42,352
Female:	
Avg. Employment Income	$17,428
Avg. Employment Income (Full Time)	$28,464

DISPOSABLE & DISCRETIONARY INCOME

2001 Estimates:	*Per Hhld.*
Disposable Income	$36,163
Discretionary Income 1 (minus Food & Shelter)	$24,415
Discretionary Income 2 (minus Food, Shelter, & Other Expenditures)	$16,466

LIQUID ASSETS

1999 Estimates:	*Per Hhld.*
Equity Investments	$51,506
Interest Bearing Investments	$52,815
Total Liquid Assets	$104,321

CREDIT DATA

July 2000:

Pool of Credit	$5,927,593,648
Revolving Credit, No.	977,527
Fixed Loans, No.	509,595
Avg. Credit Limit, per Person	$12,075
Avg. Spent, per Person	$6,242
Satisfactory Ratings, No. per Person	2.80
Avg. No. of Cards, per Person	0.85

LABOUR FORCE

2001 Estimates:

Male:	
In the Labour Force	201,192
Participation Rate	66.6
Employed	175,306
Unemployed	25,886
Unemployment Rate	12.9
Not in Labour Force	101,067
Female:	
In the Labour Force	172,296
Participation Rate	53.9
Employed	154,443
Unemployed	17,853
Unemployment Rate	10.4
Not in Labour Force	147,507

AVERAGE WEEKLY EARNINGS

(Including overtime, industrial aggregate)

	New Brunswick	Canada
Apr 2000	$549.56	$622.92
Apr 1999	$525.74	$608.07
Apr 1998	$530.31	$608.06
Apr 1997	$520.34	$597.26
Apr 1996	$511.72	$575.79

NUMBER OF EMPLOYEES

(Industrial aggregate)

Apr 2000	258,922
Apr 1999	255,777
Apr 1998	248,930
Apr 1997	235,314
Apr 1996	236,411

MANUFACTURING INDUSTRIES

	1997	1992
Plants	696	643
Employees	33,456	31,550
	$000	
Salaries, Wages	1,088,366	1,019,144
Mfg. Materials, Cost	5,336,831	3,645,167
Mfg. Shipments, Value	8,434,620	5,786,273
Total Value Added	2,770,644	1,879,496

Note: Latest available data.

OCCUPATIONS BY MAJOR GROUPS

2001 Estimates:	Male	Female
Management	18,379	8,314
Business, Finance & Admin.	14,864	45,983
Natural & Applied Sciences & Related	11,453	1,895
Health	3,183	16,318
Social Sciences, Gov't Services & Religion	4,135	5,009
Education	5,357	9,435
Arts, Culture, Recreation & Sport	2,995	4,105
Sales & Service	38,791	60,340
Trades, Transport & Equipment Operators & Related	59,590	3,003
Primary Industries	18,987	3,174
Processing, Mfg. & Utilities	17,956	8,684

LEVEL OF SCHOOLING

2001 Estimates:

Population 15 years +	622,062
Less than Grade 9	102,139
Grades 9-13 w/o Certif.	149,506
Grade 9-13 with Certif.	91,456
Trade Certif. /Dip.	20,243
Non-Univ. w/o Certif./Dip.	26,149
Non-Univ. with Certif./Dip.	108,303
Univ. w/o Degree	60,871
Univ. w/o Degree/Certif.	31,996
Univ. with Certif.	28,875
Univ. with Degree	63,395

RETAIL SALES

	1999	1998
	$000,000	*$000,000*
Supermarkets & Groceries	1,607	1,502
All Other Food	n.a.	n.a.
Drugs & Patent Medicine	344	333
Shoes	25	23
Men's Clothing	27	28
Women's Clothing	87	82
Other Clothing	131	122
Hhld. Furniture & Appliances	190	171
Hhld. Furnishings	54	48
Motor & Recreation Vehicles	1,791	1,519
Gas Service Stations	590	547
Auto Parts, Accessories & Services	375	376
General Merchandise	738	694
Other Semi-Durable Goods	197	178
Other Durable Goods	115	106
Other Retail	275	253
Total	6,608	6,043

AVERAGE HOUSEHOLD EXPENDITURES

2001 Estimates:

Food	$5,944
Shelter	$7,615
Clothing	$2,019
Transportation	$6,048
Health & Personal Care	$1,831
Recr'n, Read'g & Education	$3,139
Taxes & Securities	$11,244
Other	$7,673
Total Expenditures	$45,513

PRIVATE HOUSEHOLDS

2001 Estimates:

Private Households, Total	293,158
Pop. in Private Households	743,442
Average no. per Household	2.5

FAMILIES

2001 Estimates:

Families in Private Households	224,248
Husband-Wife Families	192,838
Lone-Parent Families	31,410
Aver. No. Persons per Family	3.0
Aver. No. Sons/Daughters at Home	1.2

HOUSING

2001 Estimates:

Occupied Private Dwellings	293,158
Owned	217,319
Rented	74,762
Band Housing	1,077
Single-Detached House	211,034
Semi-Detached House	8,306
Row Houses	6,662
Apartment, 5+ Storeys	3,902
Owned Apartment, 5+ Storeys	212
Apartment, 5 or Fewer Storeys	35,888
Apartment, Detached Duplex	12,987
Other Single-Attached	1,218
Movable Dwellings	13,161

VEHICLES

2001 Estimates:

Model Yrs. '81-'96, No.	421,440
% Total	80.85
Model Yrs. '97-'98, No.	63,728
% Total	12.23
'99 Vehicles registered in Model Yr. '99, No.	36,078
% Total	6.92
Total No. '81-'99	521,246

LEGAL MARITAL STATUS

2001 Estimates: (Age 15+)

Single (Never Married)	193,733
Legally Married (Not Separated)	330,417
Legally Married (Separated)	21,518
Widowed	42,240
Divorced	34,154

PSYTE CATEGORIES

2001 Estimates	No. of House -holds	% of Total Hhds.	Index
Urban Gentry	1,273	0.43	24
Suburban Executives	1,284	0.44	31
Mortgaged in Suburbia	751	0.26	18
Technocrafts & Bureaucrats	3,377	1.15	41
Boomers & Teens	124	0.04	2
Stable Suburban Families	896	0.31	23
Small City Elite	18,142	6.19	361
Old Bungalow Burbs	1,877	0.64	39
Suburban Nesters	407	0.14	9
Aging Erudites	4,787	1.63	108
Satellite Suburbs	1,327	0.45	16
Kindergarten Boom	893	0.30	12
Blue Collar Winners	1,048	0.36	14
Town Boomers	5,428	1.85	183
Old Towns' New Fringe	33,732	11.51	294
Participation Quebec	3,567	1.22	42
New Quebec Rows	373	0.13	12
Quebec Melange	4,168	1.42	54
Traditional French Cdn. Families	13,476	4.60	171
Rustic Prosperity	723	0.25	14
Pick-ups & Dirt Bikes	6,524	2.23	267
Quebec's Heartland	734	0.25	26
The Grain Belt	17	0.01	1
Conservative Homebodies	3,143	1.07	30
High Rise Sunsets	316	0.11	8
Young Urban Professionals	1,484	0.51	27
Young Urban Mix	438	0.15	7
Young Urban Intelligentsia	388	0.13	9

2001 Estimates	No. of House -holds	% of Total Hhds.	Index
University Enclaves	10,024	3.42	168
Young City Singles	4,207	1.44	63
Old Leafy Towns	5,616	1.92	75
Town Renters	304	0.10	12
Nesters & Young Homesteaders	11,221	3.83	164
Young Grey Collar	1,176	0.40	48
Quiet Towns	11,794	4.02	189
Agrarian Blues	454	0.15	72
Rod & Rifle	44,789	15.28	661
Down, Down East	4,943	1.69	240
Big Country Families	7,066	2.41	169
Quebec Rural Blues	47,388	16.16	663
Old Cdn. Rustics	363	0.12	13
Old Quebec Walkups	308	0.11	6
Quebec Town Elders	10,814	3.69	131
Struggling Downtowns	14,873	5.07	161
Aged Pensioners	4,173	1.42	107
Big City Stress	520	0.18	16
Old Grey Towers	653	0.22	40

FINANCIAL P$YTE

2001 Estimates	No. of House -holds	% of Total Hhds.	Index
Four Star Investors	2,681	0.91	18
Successful Suburbanites	5,024	1.71	26
Canadian Comfort	26,352	8.99	93
Urban Heights	6,271	2.14	50
Miners & Credit-Liners	1,877	0.64	20
Mortgages & Minivans	4,833	1.65	25
Tractors & Tradelines	34,455	11.75	206
Bills & Wills	9,197	3.14	38
Country Credit	24,185	8.25	122
Revolving Renters	12,713	4.34	94
Young Urban Struggle	10,412	3.55	75
Rural Family Blues	105,374	35.94	445
Limited Budgets	12,157	4.15	133
Loan Parent Stress	11,122	3.79	65
Towering Debt	19,384	6.61	85
NSF	520	0.18	5
Senior Survivors	4,826	1.65	87

HOME LANGUAGE

2001 Estimates:		% Total
English	520,120	68.52
French	227,361	29.95
Chinese	722	0.10
German	381	0.05
Micmac	1,251	0.16
Other Languages	1,858	0.24
Multiple Responses	7,379	0.97
Total	759,072	100.00

BUILDING PERMITS

	1999	1998 $000	1997
Value	481,233	481,016	459,016

HOMES BUILT

	1999	1998	1997
No	2,366	2,371	3,084

CAPITAL EXPENDITURES

(Public & Private)	2000	1999 $000,000	1998
Total Expends	n.a.	n.a.	4,107.5
Capital Expends	3,639.0	3,677.1	3,046.1
Construction	2,366.3	2,303.2	1,750.7
Machinery & Equip.	1,272.7	1,373.9	1,295.4
Repair Expends	n.a.	n.a.	1,061.4
Construction	n.a.	n.a.	294.5
Machinery & Equip.	n.a.	n.a.	766.5

TAXATION

Income Class:	1997	% Total
Under $5,000	77,320	14.37
$5,000-$10,000	85,430	15.88
$10,000-$15,000	97,600	18.14
$15,000-$20,000	56,690	10.54
$20,000-$25,000	48,860	9.08
$25,000-$30,000	41,180	7.65
$30,000-$40,000	55,550	10.32
$40,000-$50,000	34,290	6.37
$50,000 +	41,180	7.65
Total Returns, No.	538,100	
Total Income, $000	11,835,708	
Total Taxable Returns	344,780	
Total Tax, $000	2,071,621	
Average Income, $	21,995	
Average Tax, $	6,009	

VITAL STATISTICS

	1997	1996	1995	1994
Births	7,922	8,176	8,563	8,978
Deaths	5,944	5,896	5,938	5,917
Natural Increase	1,978	2,280	2,625	3,061
Marriages	4,340	4,366	4,252	4,219

Note: Latest available data.

TRAVEL STATISTICS

Tourists in Canada	1999	1998
From the U.S. entering by:		
Automobile	2,050,901	1,934,710
Bus	35,394	39,019
Air	3,999	5,465
Marine	27,264	20,459
Other Methods	35,434	33,226
Total	2,152,992	2,032,879
Other Countries:		
Land (via U.S.)	6,151	6,646
Air	1,577	313
Marine	885	1,229
Total	8,613	8,188
Residents of Canada Returning from the U.S. by:		
Automobile	4,479,344	4,855,589
Bus	15,010	14,668
Air	6,094	5,031
Marine	1,041	1,038
Other Methods	55,448	61,767
Total	4,556,937	4,938,093
From Other Countries:		
Land (via U.S.)	5	n.a.
Air	1,528	156
Marine	n.a.	1
Total	1,533	157

New Brunswick

Bathurst

(Census Agglomeration)

The Census Agglomeration of Bathurst includes: Bathurst, C; Bathurst, PAR; Beresford, T; plus two smaller areas. All are Gloucester County.

POPULATION

July 1, 2001 Estimate	25,367
% Cdn. Total	0.08
% Change, '96 -'01	-2.06
Avg. Annual Growth Rate, %	-0.42
2003 Projected Population	25,322
2006 Projected Population	25,203
2001 Households Estimate	10,105
2003 Projected Households	10,291
2006 Projected Households	10,507

INCOME

% Above/Below National Average	-15
2001 Total Income Estimate	$454,800,000
% Cdn. Total	0.07
2001 Average Hhld. Income	$45,000
2001 Per Capita	$17,900
2003 Projected Total Income	$482,240,000
2006 Projected Total Income	$524,710,000

RETAIL SALES

% Above/Below National Average	+114
2001 Retail Sales Estimate	$486,950,000
% Cdn. Total	0.17
2001 per Household	$48,200
2001 per Capita	$19,200
2001 No. of Establishments	280
2003 Projected Retail Sales	$521,270,000
2006 Projected Retail Sales	$568,660,000

POPULATION

2001 Estimates:

Total		25,367
Male		12,426
Female		12,941

Age Groups	Male	Female
0-4	684	645
5-9	719	692
10-14	786	744
15-19	866	827
20-24	902	863
25-29	861	854
30-34	882	917
35-39	956	999
40-44	988	1,051
45-49	998	1,070
50-54	932	961
55-59	797	790
60-64	644	617
65-69	490	514
70+	921	1,397

DAYTIME POPULATION

2001 Estimates:

Working Population	11,027
At Home Population	14,347
Total	25,374

INCOME

2001 Estimates:

Avg. Household Income	$45,008
Avg. Family Income	$49,481
Per Capita Income	$17,929
Male:	
Avg. Employment Income	$30,323
Avg. Employment Income (Full Time)	$44,347
Female:	
Avg. Employment Income	$18,040
Avg. Employment Income (Full Time)	$28,552

DISPOSABLE & DISCRETIONARY INCOME

2001 Estimates:	Per Hhld.
Disposable Income	$35,317
Discretionary Income 1 (minus Food & Shelter)	$24,023
Discretionary Income 2 (minus Food, Shelter, & Other Expenditures)	$16,087

LIQUID ASSETS

1999 Estimates:	Per Hhld.
Equity Investments	$47,578
Interest Bearing Investments	$51,047
Total Liquid Assets	$98,625

CREDIT DATA

July 2000:

Pool of Credit	$214,042,945
Revolving Credit, No.	37,443
Fixed Loans, No.	17,883
Avg. Credit Limit, per Person	$11,704
Avg. Spent, per Person	$5,798
Satisfactory Ratings, No. per Person	2.77
Avg. No. of Cards, per Person	0.86

LABOUR FORCE

2001 Estimates:

Male:

In the Labour Force	6,662
Participation Rate	65.1
Employed	5,796
Unemployed	866
Unemployment Rate	13.0
Not in Labour Force	3,575

Female:

In the Labour Force	5,635
Participation Rate	51.9
Employed	5,104
Unemployed	531
Unemployment Rate	9.4
Not in Labour Force	5,225

OCCUPATIONS BY MAJOR GROUPS

2001 Estimates:	Male	Female
Management	820	277
Business, Finance & Admin.	534	1,514
Natural & Applied Sciences & Related	468	44
Health	130	681
Social Sciences, Gov't Services & Religion	61	153
Education	138	374
Arts, Culture, Recreation & Sport	113	63
Sales & Service	1,534	2,074
Trades, Transport & Equipment Operators & Related	1,653	70
Primary Industries	660	49
Processing, Mfg. & Utilities	387	93

LEVEL OF SCHOOLING

2001 Estimates:

Population 15 years +	21,097
Less than Grade 9	3,704
Grades 9-13 w/o Certif.	4,789
Grade 9-13 with Certif.	3,334
Trade Certif. /Dip.	859
Non-Univ. w/o Certif./Dip.	1,062
Non-Univ. with Certif./Dip.	3,549
Univ. w/o Degree	1,725
Univ. w/o Degree/Certif.	829
Univ. with Certif.	896
Univ. with Degree	2,075

AVERAGE HOUSEHOLD EXPENDITURES

2001 Estimates:

Food	$5,872
Shelter	$7,185
Clothing	$2,100
Transportation	$6,131
Health & Personal Care	$1,787
Recr'n, Read'g & Education	$3,192
Taxes & Securities	$11,015
Other	$7,326
Total Expenditures	$44,608

PRIVATE HOUSEHOLDS

2001 Estimates:

Private Households, Total	10,105
Pop. in Private Households	24,971
Average no. per Household	2.5

FAMILIES

2001 Estimates:

Families in Private Households	7,750
Husband-Wife Families	6,675
Lone-Parent Families	1,075
Aver. No. Persons per Family	3.0
Aver. No. Sons/Daughters at Home	1.1

HOUSING

2001 Estimates:

Occupied Private Dwellings	10,105
Owned	7,260
Rented	2,830
Band Housing	15
Single-Detached House	6,896
Semi-Detached House	253
Row Houses	342
Apartment, 5+ Storeys	36
Apartment, 5 or Fewer Storeys	1,269
Apartment, Detached Duplex	764
Other Single-Attached	43
Movable Dwellings	502

VEHICLES

2001 Estimates:

Model Yrs. '81-'96, No.	13,115
% Total	79.56
Model Yrs. '97-'98, No.	2,279
% Total	13.83
'99 Vehicles registered in Model Yr. '99, No.	1,090
% Total	6.61
Total No. '81-'99	16,484

LEGAL MARITAL STATUS

2001 Estimates: (Age 15+)

Single (Never Married)	6,831
Legally Married (Not Separated)	10,917
Legally Married (Separated)	839
Widowed	1,347
Divorced	1,163

PSYTE CATEGORIES

2001 Estimates	No. of House -holds	% of Total Hhds.	Index
Small City Elite	73	0.72	42
Town Boomers	2,056	20.35	2,007
Participation Quebec	346	3.42	119
Traditional French Cdn. Families	1,339	13.25	493
Pick-ups & Dirt Bikes	121	1.20	143
Young City Singles	42	0.42	18
Old Leafy Towns	327	3.24	127
Quiet Towns	1,484	14.69	690

2001 Estimates	No. of House -holds	% of Total Hhds.	Index
Rod & Rifle	168	1.66	72
Big Country Families	1,388	13.74	963
Quebec Rural Blues	2,053	20.32	834
Old Cdn. Rustics	301	2.98	304
Quebec Town Elders	407	4.03	143

FINANCIAL P$YTE

2001 Estimates	No. of House -holds	% of Total Hhds.	Index
Canadian Comfort	2,129	21.07	217
Mortgages & Minivans	346	3.42	52
Bills & Wills	327	3.24	39
Country Credit	1,460	14.45	214
Rural Family Blues	3,609	35.71	442
Limited Budgets	1,785	17.66	568
Loan Parent Stress	407	4.03	69
Towering Debt	42	0.42	5

HOME LANGUAGE

2001 Estimates:		% Total
English	12,465	49.14
French	12,239	48.25
Vietnamese	31	0.12
Other Languages	30	0.12
Multiple Responses	602	2.37
Total	25,367	100.00

BUILDING PERMITS

	1999	1998	1997
		$000	
Value	10,172	18,254	16,075

HOMES BUILT

	1999	1998	1997
No	55	49	118

TAXATION

Income Class	1997	% Total
Under $5,000	3,060	15.12
$5,000-$10,000	3,490	17.24
$10,000-$15,000	3,640	17.98
$15,000-$20,000	1,960	9.68
$20,000-$25,000	1,530	7.56
$25,000-$30,000	1,310	6.47
$30,000-$40,000	1,810	8.94
$40,000-$50,000	1,340	6.62
$50,000 +	2,120	10.47
Total Returns, No.	20,240	
Total Income, $000	455,998	
Total Taxable Returns	12,580	
Total Tax, $000	85,101	
Average Income, $	22,530	
Average Tax, $	6,765	

VITAL STATISTICS

	1997	1996	1995	1994
Births	280	259	285	298
Deaths	192	179	160	191
Natural Increase	88	80	125	107
Marriages	134	149	133	164

Note: Latest available data.

COMMUNITY NEWSPAPER(S)

	Total Circulation
Bathurst: Northern Light	6,907
Bathurst: Northern Light (suppl.), Marketplace	6,427

Radio Station(s)

	Power
CBA-FM	n.a.
CJVA	
CKBC	10,000w
CKLE-FM	n.a.

TELEVISION STATION(S)

CKAM-TV

Campbellton
(Census Agglomeration)

The Census Agglomeration of Campbellton includes: Campbellton, C; Addington, PAR; Atholville, VL; and Tide Head, VL. All are in Restigouche County, N.B. It also includes Listuguj, R and Pointe-a-la-Croix, M. Both are in census division Avignon, Que.

POPULATION

July 1, 2001 Estimate	16,618
% Cdn. Total	0.05
% Change, '96 -'01	-3.19
Avg. Annual Growth Rate, %	-0.65
2003 Projected Population	16,518
2006 Projected Population	16,319
2001 Households Estimate	6,501
2003 Projected Households	6,567
2006 Projected Households	6,644

INCOME

% Above/Below National Average	-25
2001 Total Income Estimate	$261,490,000
% Cdn. Total	0.04
2001 Average Hhld. Income	$40,200
2001 Per Capita	$15,700
2003 Projected Total Income	$275,540,000
2006 Projected Total Income	$298,320,000

RETAIL SALES

% Above/Below National Average	+43
2001 Retail Sales Estimate	$213,240,000
% Cdn. Total	0.08
2001 per Household	$32,800
2001 per Capita	$12,800
2001 No. of Establishments	175
2003 Projected Retail Sales	$226,660,000
2006 Projected Retail Sales	$244,550,000

POPULATION

2001 Estimates:
Total		16,618
Male		7,932
Female		8,686

Age Groups	Male	Female
0-4	463	446
5-9	494	520
10-14	527	558
15-19	546	564
20-24	530	550
25-29	498	529
30-34	565	593
35-39	657	665
40-44	674	686
45-49	631	647
50-54	532	545
55-59	435	451
60-64	376	416
65-69	320	399
70+	684	1,117

DAYTIME POPULATION

2001 Estimates:
Working Population	5,721
At Home Population	10,897
Total	16,618

INCOME

2001 Estimates:
Avg. Household Income	$40,223
Avg. Family Income	$43,083
Per Capita Income	$15,735

Male:
Avg. Employment Income	$25,830
Avg. Employment Income (Full Time)	$39,847

Female:
Avg. Employment Income	$17,872
Avg. Employment Income (Full Time)	$29,032

DISPOSABLE & DISCRETIONARY INCOME

2001 Estimates:	Per Hhld.
Disposable Income	$31,728
Discretionary Income 1 (minus Food & Shelter)	$21,031
Discretionary Income 2 (minus Food, Shelter, & Other Expenditures)	$14,219

LIQUID ASSETS

1999 Estimates:	Per Hhld.
Equity Investments	$42,724
Interest Bearing Investments	$46,119
Total Liquid Assets	$88,843

CREDIT DATA

July 2000:
Pool of Credit	$134,882,401
Revolving Credit, No.	26,143
Fixed Loans, No.	15,338
Avg. Credit Limit, per Person	$10,284
Avg. Spent, per Person	$5,256
Satisfactory Ratings, No. per Person	2.78
Avg. No. of Cards, per Person	0.76

LABOUR FORCE

2001 Estimates:

Male:
In the Labour Force	3,759
Participation Rate	58.3
Employed	2,773
Unemployed	986
Unemployment Rate	26.2
Not in Labour Force	2,689

Female:
In the Labour Force	3,312
Participation Rate	46.2
Employed	2,856
Unemployed	456
Unemployment Rate	13.8
Not in Labour Force	3,850

OCCUPATIONS BY MAJOR GROUPS

2001 Estimates:	Male	Female
Management	342	240
Business, Finance & Admin.	223	665
Natural & Applied Sciences & Related	180	10
Health	165	438
Social Sciences, Gov't Services & Religion	48	155
Education	129	232
Arts, Culture, Recreation & Sport	73	51
Sales & Service	716	1,202
Trades, Transport & Equipment Operators & Related	1,101	n.a.
Primary Industries	291	19
Processing, Mfg. & Utilities	236	61

LEVEL OF SCHOOLING

2001 Estimates:
Population 15 years +	13,610
Less than Grade 9	3,174
Grades 9-13 w/o Certif.	3,320
Grade 9-13 with Certif.	1,739
Trade Certif. /Dip.	457
Non-Univ. w/o Certif./Dip.	567
Non-Univ. with Certif./Dip.	2,174
Univ. w/o Degree	1,060
Univ. w/o Degree/Certif.	508
Univ. with Certif.	552
Univ. with Degree	1,119

AVERAGE HOUSEHOLD EXPENDITURES

2001 Estimates:
Food	$5,633
Shelter	$6,611
Clothing	$1,891
Transportation	$5,007
Health & Personal Care	$1,647
Recr'n, Read'g & Education	$2,923
Taxes & Securities	$10,095
Other	$6,701
Total Expenditures	$40,508

PRIVATE HOUSEHOLDS

2001 Estimates:
Private Households, Total	6,501
Pop. in Private Households	16,075
Average no. per Household	2.5

FAMILIES

2001 Estimates:
Families in Private Households	4,790
Husband-Wife Families	3,739
Lone-Parent Families	1,051
Aver. No. Persons per Family	2.9
Aver. No. Sons/Daughters at Home	1.2

HOUSING

2001 Estimates:
Occupied Private Dwellings	6,501
Owned	4,455
Rented	2,046
Single-Detached House	4,400
Semi-Detached House	169
Row Houses	220
Apartment, 5+ Storeys	84
Apartment, 5 or Fewer Storeys	1,145
Apartment, Detached Duplex	327
Other Single-Attached	51
Movable Dwellings	105

VEHICLES

2001 Estimates:
Model Yrs. '81-'96, No.	8,563
% Total	80.84
Model Yrs. '97-'98, No.	1,150
% Total	10.86
'99 Vehicles registered in Model Yr. '99, No.	879
% Total	8.30
Total No. '81-'99	10,592

LEGAL MARITAL STATUS

2001 Estimates: (Age 15+)
Single (Never Married)	4,852
Legally Married (Not Separated)	6,213
Legally Married (Separated)	568
Widowed	1,091
Divorced	886

PSYTE CATEGORIES

2001 Estimates	No. of House-holds	% of Total Hhds.	Index
Town Boomers	744	11.44	1,129
Quebec Melange	43	0.66	25
Traditional French Cdn. Families	323	4.97	185
Pick-ups & Dirt Bikes	59	0.91	109
Young City Singles	66	1.02	44
Young Grey Collar	332	5.11	610
Quiet Towns	254	3.91	184
Down, Down East	222	3.41	487
Big Country Families	1,123	17.27	1,211
Quebec Rural Blues	1,328	20.43	838
Quebec Town Elders	1,887	29.03	1,027

FINANCIAL P$YTE

2001 Estimates	No. of House-holds	% of Total Hhds.	Index
Canadian Comfort	744	11.44	118
Country Credit	425	6.54	97
Revolving Renters	332	5.11	111
Rural Family Blues	2,673	41.12	509
Limited Budgets	254	3.91	126
Loan Parent Stress	1,887	29.03	498
Towering Debt	66	1.02	13

HOME LANGUAGE

2001 Estimates:		% Total
English	7,562	45.50
French	8,222	49.48
Chinese	10	0.06
Croatian	10	0.06
Micmac	351	2.11
Persian (Farsi)	16	0.10
Other Languages	21	0.13
Multiple Responses	426	2.56
Total	16,618	100.00

BUILDING PERMITS

	1999	1998	1997
		$000	
Value	13,311	9,500	10,409

Note: Data for New Brunswick part only in 1997.

HOMES BUILT

	1999	1998	1997
No	18	31	36

New Brunswick

Campbellton
(Census Agglomeration)
(Cont'd)

TAXATION

Income Class:	1997	% Total
Under $5,000	1,660	14.29
$5,000-$10,000	2,050	17.64
$10,000-$15,000	2,240	19.28
$15,000-$20,000	1,290	11.10
$20,000-$25,000	1,130	9.72
$25,000-$30,000	910	7.83
$30,000-$40,000	1,110	9.55
$40,000-$50,000	690	5.94
$50,000 +	550	4.73
Total Returns, No.	11,620	
Total Income, $000	227,196	
Total Taxable Returns	7,030	
Total Tax, $000	35,027	
Average Income, $	19,552	
Average Tax, $	4,983	

VITAL STATISTICS

	1997	1996	1995	1994
Births	199	160	193	230
Deaths	127	146	165	160
Natural Increase	72	14	28	70
Marriages	84	75	76	82

Note: Latest available data.

COMMUNITY NEWSPAPER(S)

	Total Circulation
Campbellton: L'Aviron	7,564
Campbellton: The Tribune	4,490

RADIO STATION(S)

	Power
CBA-FM	n.a.
CBAE-FM	n.a.
CBAF-FM	2,400w
CIMS-FM	n.a.
CKNB	10,000w

TELEVISION STATION(S)

CKCD-TV
CKCO-TV

Edmundston
(Census Agglomeration)

The Census Agglomeration of Edmundston includes: Edmundston, C; Saint-Basile, T; Saint-Jacques, PAR; Saint-Jacques, VL; Saint-Joseph, PAR; plus several smaller areas. All are in Madawaska County.

POPULATION

July 1, 2001 Estimate	23,036
% Cdn. Total	0.07
% Change, '96 -'01	-0.01
Avg. Annual Growth Rate, %	0.00
2003 Projected Population	23,237
2006 Projected Population	23,502
2001 Households Estimate	9,439
2003 Projected Households	9,689
2006 Projected Households	10,023

INCOME

% Above/Below National Average	-17
2001 Total Income Estimate	$405,160,000
% Cdn. Total	0.06
2001 Average Hhld. Income	$42,900
2001 Per Capita	$17,600
2003 Projected Total Income	$433,200,000
2006 Projected Total Income	$478,140,000

RETAIL SALES

% Above/Below National Average	+17
2001 Retail Sales Estimate	$240,510,000
% Cdn. Total	0.09
2001 per Household	$25,500
2001 per Capita	$10,400
2001 No. of Establishments	219
2003 Projected Retail Sales	$258,140,000
2006 Projected Retail Sales	$285,530,000

POPULATION

2001 Estimates:

Total		23,036
Male		11,008
Female		12,028
Age Groups	Male	Female
0-4	570	563
5-9	590	584
10-14	704	655
15-19	794	760
20-24	807	780
25-29	739	734
30-34	760	810
35-39	884	965
40-44	982	1,042
45-49	991	1,020
50-54	830	838
55-59	622	659
60-64	473	584
65-69	408	536
70+	854	1,498

DAYTIME POPULATION

2001 Estimates:

Working Population	10,552
At Home Population	12,482
Total	23,034

INCOME

2001 Estimates:

Avg. Household Income	$42,925
Avg. Family Income	$49,434
Per Capita Income	$17,588
Male:	
Avg. Employment Income	$29,701
Avg. Employment Income (Full Time)	$40,109
Female:	
Avg. Employment Income	$16,246
Avg. Employment Income (Full Time)	$25,391

DISPOSABLE & DISCRETIONARY INCOME

2001 Estimates:	Per Hhld.
Disposable Income	$33,797
Discretionary Income 1 (minus Food & Shelter)	$22,589
Discretionary Income 2 (minus Food, Shelter, & Other Expenditures)	$15,572

LIQUID ASSETS

1999 Estimates:	Per Hhld.
Equity Investments	$48,970
Interest Bearing Investments	$50,487
Total Liquid Assets	$99,457

CREDIT DATA

July 2000:

Pool of Credit	$172,466,716
Revolving Credit, No.	39,230
Fixed Loans, No.	15,544
Avg. Credit Limit, per Person	$9,821
Avg. Spent, per Person	$4,526
Satisfactory Ratings, No. per Person	2.85
Avg. No. of Cards, per Person	0.88

LABOUR FORCE

2001 Estimates:

Male:	
In the Labour Force	6,021
Participation Rate	65.8
Employed	5,426
Unemployed	595
Unemployment Rate	9.9
Not in Labour Force	3,123
Female:	
In the Labour Force	5,531
Participation Rate	54.1
Employed	5,002
Unemployed	529
Unemployment Rate	9.6
Not in Labour Force	4,695

OCCUPATIONS BY MAJOR GROUPS

2001 Estimates:	Male	Female
Management	479	211
Business, Finance & Admin.	428	1,411
Natural & Applied Sciences & Related	364	66
Health	161	533
Social Sciences, Gov't Services & Religion	128	195
Education	187	354
Arts, Culture, Recreation & Sport	94	101
Sales & Service	1,276	2,004
Trades, Transport & Equipment Operators & Related	1,723	135
Primary Industries	378	63
Processing, Mfg. & Utilities	656	281

LEVEL OF SCHOOLING

2001 Estimates:

Population 15 years +	19,370
Less than Grade 9	3,548
Grades 9-13 w/o Certif.	3,745
Grade 9-13 with Certif.	3,402
Trade Certif./Dip.	471
Non-Univ. w/o Certif./Dip.	776
Non-Univ. with Certif./Dip.	2,864
Univ. w/o Degree:	2,375
Univ. w/o Degree/Certif.	939
Univ. with Certif.	1,436
Univ. with Degree	2,189

AVERAGE HOUSEHOLD EXPENDITURES

2001 Estimates:

Food	$5,933
Shelter	$6,811
Clothing	$1,919
Transportation	$5,345
Health & Personal Care	$1,749
Recr'n, Read'g & Education	$2,780
Taxes & Securities	$11,744
Other	$6,546
Total Expenditures	$42,827

PRIVATE HOUSEHOLDS

2001 Estimates:

Private Households, Total	9,439
Pop. in Private Households	22,410
Average no. per Household	2.4

FAMILIES

2001 Estimates:

Families in Private Households	6,948
Husband-Wife Families	6,081
Lone-Parent Families	867
Aver. No. Persons per Family	3.0
Aver. No. Sons/Daughters at Home	1.1

HOUSING

2001 Estimates:

Occupied Private Dwellings	9,439
Owned	6,472
Rented	2,967
Single-Detached House	6,044
Semi-Detached House	417
Row Houses	137
Apartment, 5+ Storeys	114
Owned Apartment, 5+ Storeys	11
Apartment, 5 or Fewer Storeys	1,648
Apartment, Detached Duplex	748
Other Single-Attached	71
Movable Dwellings	260

VEHICLES

2001 Estimates:

Model Yrs. '81-'96, No.	12,994
% Total	79.72
Model Yrs. '97-'98, No.	2,065
% Total	12.67
'99 Vehicles registered in Model Yr. '99, No.	1,240
% Total	7.61
Total No. '81-'99	16,299

LEGAL MARITAL STATUS

2001 Estimates: (Age 15+)

Single (Never Married)	6,338
Legally Married (Not Separated)	9,764
Legally Married (Separated)	811
Widowed	1,536
Divorced	921

PSYTE CATEGORIES

2001 Estimates	No. of House-holds	% of Total Hhds.	Index
Small City Elite	140	1.48	87
Participation Quebec	732	7.76	269
Quebec Melange	1,600	16.95	640
Traditional French Cdn. Families	2,240	23.73	884
Quebec Rural Blues	1,371	14.52	596
Quebec Town Elders	3,292	34.88	1,234
Old Grey Towers	27	0.29	52

Edmundston
(Census Agglomeration)
(Cont'd)

FINANCIAL P$YTE

2001 Estimates	No. of House -holds	% of Total Hhds.	Index
Canadian Comfort	140	1.48	15
Mortgages & Minivans	732	7.76	118
Country Credit	3,840	40.68	602
Rural Family Blues	1,371	14.52	180
Loan Parent Stress	3,292	34.88	599
Senior Survivors	27	0.29	15

HOME LANGUAGE

2001 Estimates		% Total
English	1,090	4.73
French	21,531	93.47
Arabic	20	0.09
Chinese	20	0.09
Urdu	16	0.07
Other Languages	10	0.04
Multiple Responses	349	1.52
Total	23,036	100.00

BUILDING PERMITS

	1999	1998 $000	1997
Value	11,755	9,440	16,362

HOMES BUILT

	1999	1998	1997
No	89	72	71

TAXATION

Income Class:	1997	% Total
Under $5,000	2,370	13.88
$5,000-$10,000	2,830	16.57
$10,000-$15,000	3,150	18.44
$15,000-$20,000	1,920	11.24
$20,000-$25,000	1,540	9.02
$25,000-$30,000	1,260	7.38
$30,000-$40,000	1,640	9.60
$40,000-$50,000	1,030	6.03
$50,000 +	1,370	8.02
Total Returns, No.	17,080	
Total Income, $000	367,010	
Total Taxable Returns	10,840	
Total Tax, $000	62,383	
Average Income, $	21,488	
Average Tax, $	5,755	

VITAL STATISTICS

	1997	1996	1995	1994
Births	186	172	195	214
Deaths	200	203	209	201
Natural Increase	-14	-31	-14	13
Marriages	94	101	86	119

Note: Latest available data.

COMMUNITY NEWSPAPER(S)

	Total Circulation
Edmundston: Le Madawaska	7,317
Edmundston: Info Week-End	13,712

RADIO STATION(S)

	Power
CBAF-FM	20,400w
CBAM	n.a.
CFAI-FM	1,000w
CJEM-FM	n.a.
CKMV	1,000w

TELEVISION STATION(S)

CBAFT-TV
CIMT-TV

Fredericton
(Census Agglomeration)

The Census Agglomeration of Fredericton includes: Fredericton, C; Bright, PAR; Douglas, PAR; Kingsclear, PAR; New Maryland, PAR; Mew Maryland, VL; St. Marys, PAR; & several smaller areas. All are in York County. It also includes Lincoln, PAR and Maugerville, PAR in Sunbury County.

POPULATION

July 1, 2001 Estimate	83,248
% Cdn. Total	0.27
% Change, '96 -'01	3.30
Avg. Annual Growth Rate, %	0.65
2003 Projected Population	85,333
2006 Projected Population	88,315
2001 Households Estimate	33,412
2003 Projected Households	34,535
2006 Projected Households	36,242

INCOME

% Above/Below National Average	+2
2001 Total Income Estimate	$1,796,610,000
% Cdn. Total	0.27
2001 Average Hhld. Income	$53,800
2001 Per Capita	$21,600
2003 Projected Total Income	$1,934,380,000
2006 Projected Total Income	$2,170,520,000

RETAIL SALES

% Above/Below National Average	+40
2001 Retail Sales Estimate	$1,046,310,000
% Cdn. Total	0.38
2001 per Household	$31,300
2001 per Capita	$12,600
2001 No. of Establishments	699
2003 Projected Retail Sales	$1,134,560,000
2006 Projected Retail Sales	$1,263,240,000

POPULATION

2001 Estimates:		
Total		83,248
Male		40,605
Female		42,643
Age Groups	Male	Female
0-4	2,518	2,419
5-9	2,585	2,463
10-14	2,676	2,537
15-19	2,783	2,653
20-24	3,048	3,098
25-29	3,191	3,358
30-34	3,340	3,479
35-39	3,354	3,478
40-44	3,227	3,442
45-49	3,109	3,326
50-54	2,758	2,856
55-59	2,204	2,236
60-64	1,721	1,763
65-69	1,339	1,451
70+	2,752	4,084

DAYTIME POPULATION

2001 Estimates:	
Working Population	42,872
At Home Population	40,415
Total	83,287

INCOME

2001 Estimates:	
Avg. Household Income	$53,772
Avg. Family Income	$59,153
Per Capita Income	$21,581
Male:	
Avg. Employment Income	$32,627
Avg. Employment Income (Full Time)	$45,031
Female:	
Avg. Employment Income	$20,780
Avg. Employment Income (Full Time)	$31,369

DISPOSABLE & DISCRETIONARY INCOME

2001 Estimates:	Per Hhld.
Disposable Income	$41,733
Discretionary Income 1 (minus Food & Shelter)	$28,744
Discretionary Income 2 (minus Food, Shelter, & Other Expenditures)	$20,360

LIQUID ASSETS

1999 Estimates:	Per Hhld.
Equity Investments	$68,439
Interest Bearing Investments	$63,852
Total Liquid Assets	$132,291

CREDIT DATA

July 2000:	
Pool of Credit	$960,037,442
Revolving Credit, No.	145,540
Fixed Loans, No.	66,818
Avg. Credit Limit, per Person	$13,671
Avg. Spent, per Person	$7,051
Satisfactory Ratings, No. per Person	2.83
Avg. No. of Cards, per Person	0.99

LABOUR FORCE

2001 Estimates:	
Male:	
In the Labour Force	23,962
Participation Rate	73.0
Employed	22,347
Unemployed	1,615
Unemployment Rate	6.7
Not in Labour Force	8,864
Female:	
In the Labour Force	21,701
Participation Rate	61.6
Employed	20,491
Unemployed	1,210
Unemployment Rate	5.6
Not in Labour Force	13,523

OCCUPATIONS BY MAJOR GROUPS

2001 Estimates:	Male	Female
Management	2,673	1,381
Business, Finance & Admin.	2,403	6,483
Natural & Applied Sciences & Related	2,632	540
Health	329	1,612
Social Sciences, Gov't Services & Religion	1,072	904
Education	957	1,460
Arts, Culture, Recreation & Sport	590	870
Sales & Service	5,484	7,165
Trades, Transport & Equipment Operators & Related	5,482	294
Primary Industries	1,033	244
Processing, Mfg. & Utilities	808	186

New Brunswick

LEVEL OF SCHOOLING

2001 Estimates:	
Population 15 years +	68,050
Less than Grade 9	5,741
Grades 9-13 w/o Certif.	12,863
Grade 9-13 with Certif.	9,041
Trade Certif. /Dip.	1,762
Non-Univ. w/o Certif./Dip.	2,716
Non-Univ. with Certif./Dip.	12,018
Univ. w/o Degree	9,850
Univ. w/o Degree/Certif.	5,791
Univ. with Certif.	4,059
Univ. with Degree	14,059

AVERAGE HOUSEHOLD EXPENDITURES

2001 Estimates:	
Food	$6,195
Shelter	$9,092
Clothing	$2,186
Transportation	$6,385
Health & Personal Care	$1,990
Recr'n, Read'g & Education	$3,830
Taxes & Securities	$13,415
Other	$8,724
Total Expenditures	$51,817

PRIVATE HOUSEHOLDS

2001 Estimates:	
Private Households, Total	33,412
Pop. in Private Households	82,121
Average no. per Household	2.5

FAMILIES

2001 Estimates:	
Families in Private Households	24,891
Husband-Wife Families	21,246
Lone-Parent Families	3,645
Aver. No. Persons per Family	3.0
Aver. No. Sons/Daughters at Home	1.1

HOUSING

2001 Estimates:	
Occupied Private Dwellings	33,412
Owned	23,837
Rented	9,341
Band Housing	234
Single-Detached House	21,988
Semi-Detached House	725
Row Houses	283
Apartment, 5+ Storeys	402
Owned Apartment, 5+ Storeys	11
Apartment, 5 or Fewer Storeys	5,537
Apartment, Detached Duplex	1,862
Other Single-Attached	22
Movable Dwellings	2,593

VEHICLES

2001 Estimates:	
Model Yrs. '81-'96, No.	45,558
% Total	75.69
Model Yrs. '97-'98, No.	9,013
% Total	14.97
'99 Vehicles registered in Model Yr. '99, No.	5,619
% Total	9.34
Total No. '81-'99	60,190

New Brunswick

Fredericton
(Census Agglomeration)
(Cont'd)

LEGAL MARITAL STATUS

2001 Estimates: (Age 15+)
Single (Never Married)	21,124
Legally Married (Not Separated)	36,617
Legally Married (Separated)	2,126
Widowed	3,902
Divorced	4,281

PSYTE CATEGORIES

2001 Estimates	No. of House-holds	% of Total Hhds.	Index
Urban Gentry	759	2.27	126
Technocrafts & Bureaucrats	1,772	5.30	188
Stable Suburban Families	408	1.22	94
Small City Elite	7,390	22.12	1,291
Old Bungalow Burbs	323	0.97	58
Aging Erudites	1,512	4.53	300
Old Towns' New Fringe	5,845	17.49	447
Rustic Prosperity	48	0.14	8
Young Urban Professionals	1,484	4.44	234
Young Urban Intelligentsia	204	0.61	40
University Enclaves	2,313	6.92	339
Young City Singles	1,415	4.24	185
Old Leafy Towns	239	0.72	28
Nesters & Young Homesteaders	6,572	19.67	843
Rod & Rifle	1,695	5.07	219
Big Country Families	359	1.07	75
Struggling Downtowns	607	1.82	58
Aged Pensioners	285	0.85	64
Old Grey Towers	53	0.16	29

FINANCIAL P$YTE

2001 Estimates	No. of House-holds	% of Total Hhds.	Index
Four Star Investors	759	2.27	45
Successful Suburbanites	2,180	6.52	98
Canadian Comfort	7,390	22.12	228
Urban Heights	2,996	8.97	208
Miners & Credit-Liners	323	0.97	31
Tractors & Tradelines	5,893	17.64	308
Bills & Wills	239	0.72	9
Revolving Renters	6,572	19.67	428
Young Urban Struggle	2,517	7.53	159
Rural Family Blues	2,054	6.15	76
Towering Debt	2,022	6.05	78
Senior Survivors	338	1.01	54

HOME LANGUAGE

2001 Estimates:		% Total
English	78,279	94.03
French	3,240	3.89
Arabic	62	0.07
Bengali	62	0.07
Chinese	417	0.50
German	57	0.07
Hindi	50	0.06
Other Languages	396	0.48
Multiple Responses	685	0.82
Total	83,248	100.00

BUILDING PERMITS

	1999	1998 $000	1997
Value	55,067	66,466	45,183

HOMES BUILT

	1999	1998	1997
No	559	529	424

TAXATION

Income Class:	1997	% Total
Under $5,000	7,780	13.57
$5,000-$10,000	7,650	13.34
$10,000-$15,000	8,010	13.97
$15,000-$20,000	5,550	9.68
$20,000-$25,000	4,720	8.23
$25,000-$30,000	4,680	8.16
$30,000-$40,000	7,450	12.99
$40,000-$50,000	4,590	8.01
$50,000 +	6,980	12.18
Total Returns, No.	57,330	
Total Income, $000	1,519,410	
Total Taxable Returns	40,080	
Total Tax, $000	297,612	
Average Income, $	26,503	
Average Tax, $	7,425	

VITAL STATISTICS

	1997	1996	1995	1994
Births	911	988	976	1,060
Deaths	544	555	554	558
Natural Increase	367	433	422	502
Marriages	562	612	552	515

Note: Latest available data.

DAILY NEWSPAPER(S)

	Circulation Average Paid
Daily Gleaner	
Fri	29,104
Mon-Thu, Sat	25,546

COMMUNITY NEWSPAPER(S)

	Total Circulation
Fredericton: Northside News	9,570

RADIO STATION(S)

	Power
CBAF-FM	10,000w
CBD-FM	n.a.
CBZ	10,000w
CBZ-FM	10,000w
CHSR-FM	n.a.
CIBX-FM	100,000w
CIHI	10,000w
CJCJ	n.a.
CJPN-FM	1,000w
CKHJ-FM	100,000w

TELEVISION STATION(S)

CBAFT-TV
CBAT-TV
CKLT-TV
GLOBAL-TV

Miramichi
(City)
In Northumberland County.

POPULATION

July 1, 2001 Estimate	18,318
% Cdn. Total	0.06
% Change, '96 -'01	-7.24
Avg. Annual Growth Rate, %.	-1.49
2003 Projected Population	17,655
2006 Projected Population	16,632
2001 Households Estimate	7,069
2003 Projected Households	6,964
2006 Projected Households	6,753

INCOME

% Above/Below National Average	-11
2001 Total Income Estimate	$343,830,000
% Cdn. Total	0.05
2001 Average Hhld. Income	$48,600
2001 Per Capita	$18,800
2003 Projected Total Income	$351,720,000
2006 Projected Total Income	$361,940,000

RETAIL SALES

% Above/Below National Average	+144
2001 Retail Sales Estimate	$400,160,000
% Cdn. Total	0.14
2001 per Household	$56,600
2001 per Capita	$21,800
2001 No. of Establishments	225
2003 Projected Retail Sales	$418,760,000
2006 Projected Retail Sales	$439,150,000

POPULATION

2001 Estimates:
Total		18,318
Male		8,924
Female		9,394
Age Groups	Male	Female
0-4	498	451
5-9	542	483
10-14	584	560
15-19	658	615
20-24	702	648
25-29	612	631
30-34	584	643
35-39	627	680
40-44	706	746
45-49	735	745
50-54	645	634
55-59	499	513
60-64	401	435
65-69	356	385
70+	775	1,225

DAYTIME POPULATION

2001 Estimates:
Working Population	11,628
At Home Population	10,549
Total	22,177

INCOME

2001 Estimates:
Avg. Household Income	$48,639
Avg. Family Income	$52,741
Per Capita Income	$18,770
Male:	
Avg. Employment Income	$31,492
Avg. Employment Income (Full Time)	$46,396
Female:	
Avg. Employment Income	$17,042
Avg. Employment Income (Full Time)	$27,498

DISPOSABLE & DISCRETIONARY INCOME

2001 Estimates:	Per Hhld.
Disposable Income	$37,807
Discretionary Income 1 (minus Food & Shelter)	$26,075
Discretionary Income 2 (minus Food, Shelter, & Other Expenditures).	$17,830

LIQUID ASSETS

1999 Estimates:	Per Hhld.
Equity Investments	$56,679
Interest Bearing Investments	$56,824
Total Liquid Assets	$113,503

CREDIT DATA

July 2000:
Pool of Credit	$221,647,224
Revolving Credit, No.	31,724
Fixed Loans, No.	19,547
Avg. Credit Limit, per Person.	$13,818
Avg. Spent, per Person	$7,281
Satisfactory Ratings, No. per Person.	2.99
Avg. No. of Cards, per Person	0.83

LABOUR FORCE

2001 Estimates:
Male:	
In the Labour Force	4,849
Participation Rate	66.4
Employed	4,144
Unemployed	705
Unemployment Rate	14.5
Not in Labour Force	2,451
Female:	
In the Labour Force	4,059
Participation Rate	51.4
Employed	3,592
Unemployed	467
Unemployment Rate	11.5
Not in Labour Force	3,841

OCCUPATIONS BY MAJOR GROUPS

2001 Estimates:	Male	Female
Management	531	162
Business, Finance & Admin.	407	1,012
Natural & Applied Sciences & Related	211	20
Health	86	517
Social Sciences, Gov't Services & Religion	79	155
Education	147	287
Arts, Culture, Recreation & Sport	55	55
Sales & Service	954	1,530
Trades, Transport & Equipment Operators & Related	1,365	37
Primary Industries	191	49
Processing, Mfg. & Utilities	630	43

LEVEL OF SCHOOLING

2001 Estimates:
Population 15 years +	15,200
Less than Grade 9	1,579
Grades 9-13 w/o Certif.	3,527
Grade 9-13 with Certif.	2,460
Trade Certif. /Dip.	546
Non-Univ. w/o Certif./Dip.	719
Non-Univ. with Certif./Dip.	3,296
Univ. w/o Degree.	1,604
Univ. w/o Degree/Certif.	795
Univ. with Certif.	809
Univ. with Degree	1,469

Miramichi
(City)
(Cont'd)

AVERAGE HOUSEHOLD EXPENDITURES

2001 Estimates:

Food	$5,905
Shelter	$7,796
Clothing	$2,104
Transportation	$6,198
Health & Personal Care	$1,945
Recr'n, Read'g & Education	$3,380
Taxes & Securities	$11,886
Other	$8,343
Total Expenditures	$47,557

PRIVATE HOUSEHOLDS

2001 Estimates:

Private Households, Total	7,069
Pop. in Private Households	17,864
Average no. per Household	2.5

FAMILIES

2001 Estimates:

Families in Private Households	5,404
Husband-Wife Families	4,441
Lone-Parent Families	963
Aver. No. Persons per Family	3.0
Aver. No. Sons/Daughters at Home	1.2

HOUSING

2001 Estimates:

Occupied Private Dwellings	7,069
Owned	5,415
Rented	1,654
Single-Detached House	5,304
Semi-Detached House	196
Row Houses	41
Apartment, 5 or Fewer Storeys	856
Apartment, Detached Duplex	216
Other Single-Attached	32
Movable Dwellings	424

VEHICLES

2001 Estimates:

Model Yrs. '81-'96, No.	10,018
% Total	76.91
Model Yrs. '97-'98, No.	1,846
% Total	14.17
'99 Vehicles registered in Model Yr. '99, No.	1,161
% Total	8.91
Total No. '81-'99	13,025

LEGAL MARITAL STATUS

2001 Estimates: (Age 15+)

Single (Never Married)	4,809
Legally Married (Not Separated)	7,919
Legally Married (Separated)	492
Widowed	1,194
Divorced	786

PSYTE CATEGORIES

2001 Estimates	No. of House -holds	% of Total Hhds.	Index
Town Boomers	2,068	29.25	2,886
Old Towns' New Fringe	384	5.43	139
Pick-ups & Dirt Bikes	934	13.21	1,582
Old Leafy Towns	459	6.49	254
Nesters & Young Homesteaders	353	4.99	214
Young Grey Collar	844	11.94	1,427
Quiet Towns	1,120	15.84	745
Rod & Rifle	591	8.36	361
Down, Down East	197	2.79	397

FINANCIAL P$YTE

2001 Estimates	No. of House -holds	% of Total Hhds.	Index
Canadian Comfort	2,068	29.25	301
Tractors & Tradelines	384	5.43	95
Bills & Wills	459	6.49	78
Country Credit	934	13.21	195
Revolving Renters	1,197	16.93	368
Rural Family Blues	788	11.15	138
Limited Budgets	1,120	15.84	510

HOME LANGUAGE

2001 Estimates:

		% Total
English	17,362	94.78
French	736	4.02
Chinese	29	0.16
Czech	10	0.05
Malayalam	24	0.13
Multiple Responses	157	0.86
Total	18,318	100.00

BUILDING PERMITS

	1999	1998	1997
		$000	
Value	n.a.	7,813	28,415

HOMES BUILT

	1999	1998	1997
No	71	45	n.a.

TAXATION

Income Class:	1997	% Total
Under $5,000	2,210	15.04
$5,000-$10,000	2,360	16.07
$10,000-$15,000	2,500	17.02
$15,000-$20,000	1,360	9.26
$20,000-$25,000	1,240	8.44
$25,000-$30,000	1,040	7.08
$30,000-$40,000	1,410	9.60
$40,000-$50,000	1,020	6.94
$50,000 +	1,560	10.62
Total Returns, No.	14,690	
Total Income, $000	337,916	
Total Taxable Returns	9,240	
Total Tax, $000	61,839	
Average Income, $	23,003	
Average Tax, $	6,693	

VITAL STATISTICS

	1997	1996	1995	1994
Births	225	214	243	251
Deaths	191	175	194	182
Natural Increase	34	39	49	69
Marriages	156	167	163	158

Note: Latest available data.

COMMUNITY NEWSPAPER(S)

	Total Circulation
Miramichi: Miramichi Leader	7,501
Miramichi: Miramichi Weekend	7,916

RADIO STATION(S)

	Power
CBA-FM	50w
CFAN	5,000w

Moncton
(Census Agglomeration)

The Census Agglomeration of Moncton includes: Dieppe, T; Memramcook, VL; Moncton, C; Moncton, PAR; plus several smaller areas, all in Westmorland County. It also includes: Coverdale, PAR; Hillsborough, PAR; Hillsborough, VL; & Riverview, T, & one small area, all in Albert County.

POPULATION

July 1, 2001 Estimate	120,062
% Cdn. Total	0.39
% Change, '96 -'01	3.64
Avg. Annual Growth Rate, %	0.72
2003 Projected Population	123,028
2006 Projected Population	127,226
2001 Households Estimate	47,411
2003 Projected Households	48,933
2006 Projected Households	51,299

INCOME

% Above/Below National Average	-4
2001 Total Income Estimate	$2,431,660,000
% Cdn. Total	0.37
2001 Average Hhld. Income	$51,300
2001 Per Capita	$20,300
2003 Projected Total Income	$2,638,400,000
2006 Projected Total Income	$2,997,630,000

RETAIL SALES

% Above/Below National Average	+17
2001 Retail Sales Estimate	$1,259,240,000
% Cdn. Total	0.45
2001 per Household	$26,600
2001 per Capita	$10,500
2001 No. of Establishments	960
2003 Projected Retail Sales	$1,391,750,000
2006 Projected Retail Sales	$1,595,210,000

POPULATION

2001 Estimates:

Total	120,062
Male	58,276
Female	61,786

Age Groups	Male	Female
0-4	3,405	3,262
5-9	3,541	3,399
10-14	3,728	3,616
15-19	3,842	3,808
20-24	4,152	4,205
25-29	4,381	4,376
30-34	4,666	4,702
35-39	4,881	4,978
40-44	4,852	5,007
45-49	4,674	4,810
50-54	4,086	4,139
55-59	3,177	3,207
60-64	2,441	2,605
65-69	1,988	2,386
70+	4,462	7,286

DAYTIME POPULATION

2001 Estimates:

Working Population	59,380
At Home Population	60,682
Total	120,062

New Brunswick

INCOME

2001 Estimates:

Avg. Household Income	$51,289
Avg. Family Income	$56,751
Per Capita Income	$20,253
Male:	
Avg. Employment Income	$32,541
Avg. Employment Income (Full Time)	$43,911
Female:	
Avg. Employment Income	$19,605
Avg. Employment Income (Full Time)	$29,476

DISPOSABLE & DISCRETIONARY INCOME

2001 Estimates:	Per Hhld.
Disposable Income	$40,040
Discretionary Income 1 (minus Food & Shelter)	$27,299
Discretionary Income 2 (minus Food, Shelter, & Other Expenditures)	$19,209

LIQUID ASSETS

1999 Estimates:	Per Hhld.
Equity Investments	$60,437
Interest Bearing Investments	$59,204
Total Liquid Assets	$119,641

CREDIT DATA

July 2000:	
Pool of Credit	$1,138,686,615
Revolving Credit, No.	198,969
Fixed Loans, No.	85,777
Avg. Credit Limit, per Person	$12,301
Avg. Spent, per Person	$6,113
Satisfactory Ratings, No. per Person	2.89
Avg. No. of Cards, per Person	0.93

LABOUR FORCE

2001 Estimates:

Male:	
In the Labour Force	32,854
Participation Rate	69.0
Employed	30,826
Unemployed	2,028
Unemployment Rate	6.2
Not in Labour Force	14,748
Female:	
In the Labour Force	29,932
Participation Rate	58.1
Employed	28,221
Unemployed	1,711
Unemployment Rate	5.7
Not in Labour Force	21,577

New Brunswick

Moncton
(Census Agglomeration)
(Cont'd)

OCCUPATIONS BY MAJOR GROUPS

2001 Estimates:	Male	Female
Management	3,817	1,518
Business, Finance & Admin.	3,831	9,673
Natural & Applied Sciences & Related	2,049	293
Health	772	3,137
Social Sciences, Gov't Services & Religion	758	979
Education	1,086	1,539
Arts, Culture, Recreation & Sport	621	875
Sales & Service	7,924	9,958
Trades, Transport & Equipment Operators & Related	8,635	462
Primary Industries	748	140
Processing, Mfg. & Utilities	1,957	513

LEVEL OF SCHOOLING

2001 Estimates:
Population 15 years +	99,111
Less than Grade 9	10,918
Grades 9-13 w/o Certif.	21,936
Grade 9-13 with Certif.	14,441
Trade Certif. /Dip.	2,911
Non-Univ. w/o Certif./Dip.	5,375
Non-Univ. with Certif./Dip.	19,735
Univ. w/o Degree	11,185
Univ. w/o Degree/Certif.	5,842
Univ. with Certif.	5,343
Univ. with Degree	12,610

AVERAGE HOUSEHOLD EXPENDITURES

2001 Estimates:
Food	$6,172
Shelter	$8,585
Clothing	$2,119
Transportation	$6,148
Health & Personal Care	$1,892
Recr'n, Read'g & Education	$3,554
Taxes & Securities	$13,281
Other	$8,255
Total Expenditures	$50,006

PRIVATE HOUSEHOLDS

2001 Estimates:
Private Households, Total	47,411
Pop. in Private Households	117,307
Average no. per Household	2.5

FAMILIES

2001 Estimates:
Families in Private Households	35,011
Husband-Wife Families	30,450
Lone-Parent Families	4,561
Aver. No. Persons per Family	2.9
Aver. No. Sons/Daughters at Home	1.1

HOUSING

2001 Estimates:
Occupied Private Dwellings	47,411
Owned	32,929
Rented	14,482
Single-Detached House	29,820
Semi-Detached House	2,649
Row Houses	1,224
Apartment, 5+ Storeys	1,351
Owned Apartment, 5+ Storeys	33
Apartment, 5 or Fewer Storeys	7,505
Apartment, Detached Duplex	2,459
Other Single-Attached	112
Movable Dwellings	2,291

VEHICLES

2001 Estimates:
Model Yrs. '81-'96, No.	62,463
% Total	74.24
Model Yrs. '97-'98, No.	12,919
% Total	15.36
'99 Vehicles registered in Model Yr. '99, No.	8,752
% Total	10.40
Total No. '81-'99	84,134

LEGAL MARITAL STATUS

2001 Estimates: (Age 15+)
Single (Never Married)	31,445
Legally Married (Not Separated)	51,978
Legally Married (Separated)	3,338
Widowed	6,173
Divorced	6,177

PSYTE CATEGORIES

2001 Estimates	No. of House-holds	% of Total Hhds.	Index
Suburban Executives	455	0.96	67
Mortgaged in Suburbia	751	1.58	114
Technocrafts & Bureaucrats	1,192	2.51	89
Stable Suburban Families	429	0.90	69
Small City Elite	2,555	5.39	314
Old Bungalow Burbs	1,008	2.13	128
Suburban Nesters	407	0.86	54
Aging Erudites	2,398	5.06	335
Satellite Suburbs	1,327	2.80	98
Kindergarten Boom	856	1.81	69
Old Towns' New Fringe	9,506	20.05	512
Participation Quebec	2,424	5.11	177
New Quebec Rows	373	0.79	72
Quebec Melange	923	1.95	73
Traditional French Cdn. Families	2,141	4.52	168
Quebec's Heartland	38	0.08	8
Conservative Homebodies	2,740	5.78	160
University Enclaves	3,723	7.85	385
Young City Singles	1,447	3.05	133
Town Renters	304	0.64	74
Rod & Rifle	1,632	3.44	149
Quebec Rural Blues	625	1.32	54
Old Quebec Walkups	308	0.65	35
Quebec Town Elders	1,463	3.09	109
Struggling Downtowns	5,391	11.37	361
Aged Pensioners	2,063	4.35	327
Old Grey Towers	573	1.21	218

FINANCIAL P$YTE

2001 Estimates	No. of House-holds	% of Total Hhds.	Index
Four Star Investors	455	0.96	19
Successful Suburbanites	2,372	5.00	75
Canadian Comfort	4,289	9.05	93
Urban Heights	2,398	5.06	118
Miners & Credit-Liners	1,008	2.13	67
Mortgages & Minivans	3,653	7.70	117
Tractors & Tradelines	9,506	20.05	351
Bills & Wills	2,740	5.78	70
Country Credit	3,064	6.46	96
Young Urban Struggle	3,723	7.85	166
Rural Family Blues	2,295	4.84	60
Loan Parent Stress	1,771	3.74	64
Towering Debt	7,142	15.06	193
Senior Survivors	2,636	5.56	295

HOME LANGUAGE

2001 Estimates:		% Total
English	86,176	71.78
French	31,839	26.52
Other Languages	337	0.28
Multiple Responses	1,710	1.42
Total	120,062	100.00

BUILDING PERMITS

	1999	1998 $000	1997
Value	110,415	110,069	108,578

HOMES BUILT

	1999	1998	1997
No.	499	599	718

TAXATION

Income Class:	1997	% Total
Under $5,000	10,750	12.68
$5,000-$10,000	12,020	14.17
$10,000-$15,000	13,280	15.66
$15,000-$20,000	8,940	10.54
$20,000-$25,000	8,300	9.79
$25,000-$30,000	7,220	8.51
$30,000-$40,000	10,250	12.09
$40,000-$50,000	6,490	7.65
$50,000 +	7,630	9.00
Total Returns, No.	84,810	
Total Income, $000	2,066,470	
Total Taxable Returns	58,690	
Total Tax, $000	385,120	
Average Income, $	24,366	
Average Tax, $	6,562	

VITAL STATISTICS

	1997	1996	1995	1994
Births	1,169	1,247	1,317	1,293
Deaths	777	794	811	746
Natural Increase	392	453	506	547
Marriages	700	719	703	738

Note: Latest available data.

DAILY NEWSPAPER(S)

	Circulation Average Paid
L'Acadie Nouvelle	16,593
Times & Transcript	
Sat	44,920
Mon-Fri	38,332

Saint John
(Census Metropolitan Area)

POPULATION

July 1, 2001 Estimate	128,061
% Cdn. Total	0.41
% Change, '96 -'01	0.01
Avg. Annual Growth Rate, %	0.00
2003 Projected Population	130,872
2006 Projected Population	135,707
2001 Households Estimate	49,747
2003 Projected Households	51,094
2006 Projected Households	53,468

INCOME

% Above/Below National Average	-9
2001 Total Income Estimate	$2,460,960,000
% Cdn. Total	0.37
2001 Average Hhld. Income	$49,500
2001 Per Capita	$19,200
2003 Projected Total Income	$2,662,700,000
2006 Projected Total Income	$3,027,990,000

RETAIL SALES

% Above/Below National Average	-8
2001 Retail Sales Estimate	$1,057,500,000
% Cdn. Total	0.38
2001 per Household	$21,300
2001 per Capita	$8,300
2001 No. of Establishments	871
2003 Projected Retail Sales	$1,147,720,000
2006 Projected Retail Sales	$1,291,200,000

POPULATION

2001 Estimates:

Total		128,061
Male		61,798
Female		66,263

Age Groups	Male	Female
0-4	3,796	3,571
5-9	4,256	3,938
10-14	4,408	4,169
15-19	4,488	4,326
20-24	4,434	4,397
25-29	4,224	4,397
30-34	4,516	4,805
35-39	4,899	5,291
40-44	5,003	5,392
45-49	4,811	5,108
50-54	4,179	4,342
55-59	3,319	3,407
60-64	2,609	2,785
65-69	2,143	2,525
70+	4,713	7,810

DAYTIME POPULATION

2001 Estimates:

Working Population	57,076
At Home Population	70,986
Total	128,062

INCOME

2001 Estimates:

Avg. Household Income	$49,469
Avg. Family Income	$55,216
Per Capita Income	$19,217
Male:	
Avg. Employment Income	$34,577
Avg. Employment Income (Full Time)	$46,591
Female:	
Avg. Employment Income	$18,975
Avg. Employment Income (Full Time)	$28,998

DISPOSABLE & DISCRETIONARY INCOME

2001 Estimates:	Per Hhld.
Disposable Income	$38,364
Discretionary Income 1 (minus Food & Shelter)	$26,096
Discretionary Income 2 (minus Food, Shelter, & Other Expenditures)	$18,105

LIQUID ASSETS

1999 Estimates:	Per Hhld.
Equity Investments	$58,634
Interest Bearing Investments	$57,364
Total Liquid Assets	$115,998

CREDIT DATA

July 2000:

Pool of Credit	$1,209,389,636
Revolving Credit, No.	201,117
Fixed Loans, No.	92,894
Avg. Credit Limit, per Person	$12,240
Avg. Spent, per Person	$6,253
Satisfactory Ratings, No. per Person	2.75
Avg. No. of Cards, per Person	0.88

LABOUR FORCE

2001 Estimates:

Male:

In the Labour Force	33,316
Participation Rate	67.5
Employed	29,356
Unemployed	3,960
Unemployment Rate	11.9
Not in Labour Force	16,022

Female:

In the Labour Force	29,296
Participation Rate	53.7
Employed	27,286
Unemployed	2,010
Unemployment Rate	6.9
Not in Labour Force	25,289

OCCUPATIONS BY MAJOR GROUPS

2001 Estimates:	Male	Female
Management	3,110	1,515
Business, Finance & Admin.	3,136	8,715
Natural & Applied Sciences & Related	2,123	338
Health	622	3,073
Social Sciences, Gov't Services & Religion	846	776
Education	826	1,462
Arts, Culture, Recreation & Sport	627	748
Sales & Service	7,012	10,372
Trades, Transport & Equipment Operators & Related	10,071	421
Primary Industries	1,216	217
Processing, Mfg. & Utilities	2,455	414

LEVEL OF SCHOOLING

2001 Estimates:

Population 15 years +	103,923
Less than Grade 9	10,804
Grades 9-13 w/o Certif.	25,633
Grade 9-13 with Certif.	16,659
Trade Certif. /Dip.	4,212
Non-Univ. w/o Certif./Dip.	4,551
Non-Univ. with Certif./Dip.	19,133
Univ. w/o Degree	11,298
Univ. w/o Degree/Certif.	6,244
Univ. with Certif.	5,054
Univ. with Degree	11,633

AVERAGE HOUSEHOLD EXPENDITURES

2001 Estimates:

Food	$5,859
Shelter	$8,434
Clothing	$2,007
Transportation	$6,088
Health & Personal Care	$1,836
Recr'n, Read'g & Education	$3,522
Taxes & Securities	$12,244
Other	$8,305
Total Expenditures	$48,295

PRIVATE HOUSEHOLDS

2001 Estimates:

Private Households, Total	49,747
Pop. in Private Households	125,627
Average no. per Household	2.5

FAMILIES

2001 Estimates:

Families in Private Households	36,616
Husband-Wife Families	30,611
Lone-Parent Families	6,005
Aver. No. Persons per Family	3.0
Aver. No. Sons/Daughters at Home	1.2

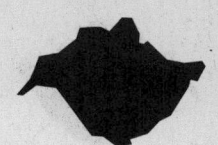

New Brunswick

HOUSING

2001 Estimates:

Occupied Private Dwellings	49,747
Owned	32,975
Rented	16,772
Single-Detached House	29,092
Semi-Detached House	1,004
Row Houses	1,982
Apartment, 5+ Storeys	1,771
Owned Apartment, 5+ Storeys	146
Apartment, 5 or Fewer Storeys	10,566
Apartment, Detached Duplex	3,454
Other Single-Attached	222
Movable Dwellings	1,656

RADIO STATION DATA

Station	Market	Format	Wkly. Reach%	Aver. Hrs. Tuned
All Stations			94	21.3
CBAF-FM	Moncton	Multi-format	8	11.3
CBD-FM	Saint John	News, Info.	21	13.8
CFBC	Saint John	Oldies	n.a.	n.a.
CHSJ-FM	Saint John	Country	32	13.0
CIOK-FM	Saint John	Adult Contemp.	n.a.	n.a.
CJYC-FM	Saint John	Rock	n.a.	n.a.

BBM Spring 2000 Radio Reach Survey;area coverage.
*Mon-Sun 5a.m - 1a.m , All Persons 12+

TV STATION DATA

Station	Market	Network Affiliation	Wkly. Reach%*	Aver. Hrs. Tuned
All Stations			96	23.1
A & E	n.a.	Ind.	22	3.2
ASN	Maritimes	CTV	38	3.4
CBAT	Saint John	CBC	55	3.7
CHSJ	Saint John	CBC	n.a.	n.a.
CIHFNB	Saint John	Global	63	3.3
CJCH	Halifax	CTV	4	4.5
CKCW	Moncton	CTV	70	6.0
CKLT	Saint John	CTV	n.a.	n.a.
CMT	n.a.	Ind.	5	3.0
CNN	n.a.	Ind.	5	3.1
FAMILY	n.a.	Ind.	6	2.9
HGTV	n.a.	Ind.	8	1.8
NEWSWD	n.a.	CBC	9	2.2
OTHERS	n.a.	n.a.	10	2.9
PRIME	n.a.	Ind.	22	2.5
SHWCSE	n.a.	Ind.	9	2.0
SPACE	n.a.	Ind.	5	5.0
TLC	n.a.	Ind.	15	2.2
TMN	Toronto	Ind.	8	4.9
TNN	Nashville TN	Ind.	11	2.1
TSN	n.a.	Ind.	22	4.9
VCR	n.a.	n.a.	19	4.7
VISION	n.a.	Ind.	8	2.2
WBZ	Boston MA	CBS	39	3.3
WLBZ	Bangor ME	NBC	31	2.2
WMED	Calais ME	PBS	14	1.2
WTBS	Atlanta GA	Ind.	14	3.4
WUHF	Rochester NY	FOX	30	3.2
WXYZ	Detroit MI	ABC	29	2.2
YTV	n.a.	Ind.	20	3.1

BBM Spring 2000 TV Reach Survey;CMA coverage.
*Mon-Sun 6a.m - 2a.m , All Persons 2 +

New Brunswick

Saint John
(Census Metropolitan Area)
(Cont'd)

VEHICLES

2001 Estimates:
Model Yrs. '81-'96, No. 66,380
  % Total .79.84
Model Yrs. '97-'98, No. 10,608
  % Total .12.76
'99 Vehicles registered in
  Model Yr. '99, No. 6,154
  % Total 7.40
Total No. '81-'99 83,142

LEGAL MARITAL STATUS

2001 Estimates: (Age 15+)
Single (Never Married) 31,528
Legally Married
  (Not Separated) 54,945
Legally Married (Separated) 3,525
Widowed .7,292
Divorced .6,633

PSYTE CATEGORIES

2001 Estimates	No. of House-holds	% of Total Hhds.	Index
Urban Gentry	514	1.03	57
Suburban Executives	829	1.67	116
Technocrafts & Bureaucrats	413	0.83	30
Boomers & Teens	104	0.21	12
Small City Elite	7,419	14.91	870
Old Bungalow Burbs	546	1.10	66
Aging Erudites	877	1.76	117
Kindergarten Boom	37	0.07	3
Blue Collar Winners	964	1.94	77
Old Towns' New Fringe	13,654	27.45	701
Rustic Prosperity	162	0.33	18
Conservative Homebodies	403	0.81	22
High Rise Sunsets	316	0.64	44
Young Urban Mix	438	0.88	42
Young Urban Intelligentsia	184	0.37	24
University Enclaves	3,988	8.02	393
Young City Singles	489	0.98	43
Nesters & Young Homesteaders	3,652	7.34	315
Rod & Rifle	3,285	6.60	285
Struggling Downtowns	8,875	17.84	567
Aged Pensioners	1,825	3.67	276
Big City Stress	520	1.05	93

FINANCIAL P$YTE

2001 Estimates	No. of House-holds	% of Total Hhds.	Index
Four Star Investors	1,447	2.91	58
Successful Suburbanites	413	0.83	13
Canadian Comfort	8,383	16.85	173
Urban Heights	877	1.76	41
Miners & Credit-Liners	546	1.10	35
Mortgages & Minivans	37	0.07	1
Tractors & Tradelines	13,816	27.77	486
Bills & Wills	841	1.69	20
Revolving Renters	3,968	7.98	173
Young Urban Struggle	4,172	8.39	177
Rural Family Blues	3,285	6.60	82
Towering Debt	9,364	18.82	241
NSF	520	1.05	30
Senior Survivors	1,825	3.67	195

HOME LANGUAGE

2001 Estimates:		% Total
English	124,862	97.50
French	2,144	1.67
Chinese	109	0.09
Greek	78	0.06
Other Languages	383	0.30
Multiple Responses	485	0.38
Total	128,061	100.00

BUILDING PERMITS

	1999	1998 $000	1997
Value	84,581	67,605	71,360

HOMES BUILT

	1999	1998	1997
No.	246	240	303

TAXATION

Income Class:	1997	% Total
Under $5,000	12,150	13.71
$5,000-$10,000	13,290	14.99
$10,000-$15,000	14,230	16.05
$15,000-$20,000	8,830	9.96
$20,000-$25,000	7,840	8.84
$25,000-$30,000	6,800	7.67
$30,000-$40,000	9,740	10.99
$40,000-$50,000	6,590	7.43
$50,000 +	9,280	10.47
Total Returns, No.	88,650	
Total Income, $000	2,209,490	
Total Taxable Returns	58,800	
Total Tax, $000	419,509	
Average Income, $	24,924	
Average Tax, $	7,135	

VITAL STATISTICS

	1997	1996	1995	1994
Births	1,478	1,536	1,598	1,675
Deaths	1,033	1,034	1,106	1,075
Natural Increase	445	502	492	600
Marriages	741	752	795	755

Note: Latest available data.

DAILY NEWSPAPER(S)

	Circulation Average Paid
Telegraph Journal / Times Globe	
Sat	48,214
Morn	22,398
Eve	23,410
Comb	45,808

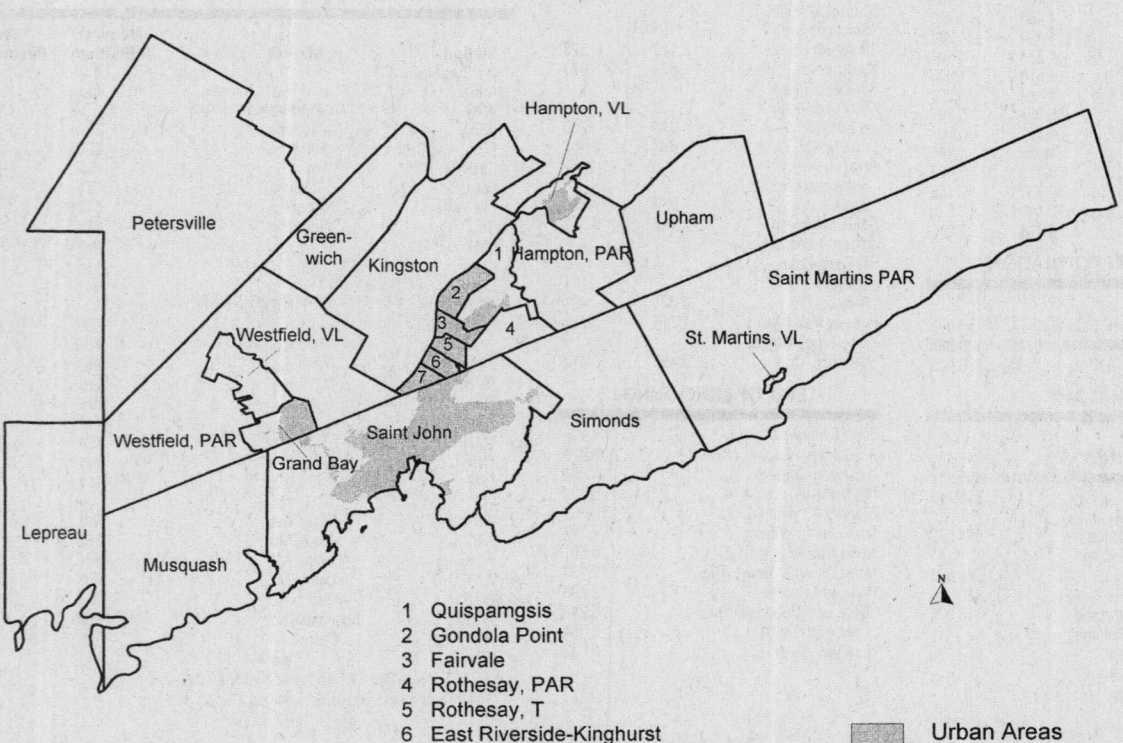

1 Quispamgsis
2 Gondola Point
3 Fairvale
4 Rothesay, PAR
5 Rothesay, T
6 East Riverside-Kinghurst
7 Renforth

Urban Areas

Saint John
(City)
Saint John CMA
In Saint John County.

POPULATION

July 1, 2001 Estimate	71,645
% Cdn. Total	0.23
% Change, '96 -'01	-3.01
Avg. Annual Growth Rate, %	-0.61
2003 Projected Population	72,089
2006 Projected Population	73,088
2001 Households Estimate	30,129
2003 Projected Households	30,451
2006 Projected Households	31,135

INCOME

% Above/Below National Average	-17
2001 Total Income Estimate	$1,254,680,000
% Cdn. Total	0.19
2001 Average Hhld. Income	$41,600
2001 Per Capita	$17,500
2003 Projected Total Income	$1,328,060,000
2006 Projected Total Income	$1,462,260,000

RETAIL SALES

% Above/Below National Average	+29
2001 Retail Sales Estimate	$829,960,000
% Cdn. Total	0.30
2001 per Household	$27,500
2001 per Capita	$11,600
2001 No. of Establishments	603
2003 Projected Retail Sales	$898,470,000
2006 Projected Retail Sales	$1,004,530,000

POPULATION

2001 Estimates:

Total		71,645
Male		33,582
Female		38,063

Age Groups	Male	Female
0-4	2,097	2,022
5-9	2,195	2,092
10-14	2,155	2,068
15-19	2,177	2,159
20-24	2,335	2,436
25-29	2,431	2,645
30-34	2,650	2,835
35-39	2,708	2,948
40-44	2,603	2,868
45-49	2,447	2,689
50-54	2,145	2,340
55-59	1,755	1,925
60-64	1,474	1,672
65-69	1,294	1,621
70+	3,116	5,743

DAYTIME POPULATION

2001 Estimates:

Working Population	49,994
At Home Population	41,671
Total	91,665

INCOME

2001 Estimates:

Avg. Household Income	$41,643
Avg. Family Income	$47,603
Per Capita Income	$17,512
Male:	
Avg. Employment Income	$29,855
Avg. Employment Income (Full Time)	$40,572
Female:	
Avg. Employment Income	$18,194
Avg. Employment Income (Full Time)	$27,432

DISPOSABLE & DISCRETIONARY INCOME

2001 Estimates:	Per Hhld.
Disposable Income	$32,711
Discretionary Income 1 (minus Food & Shelter)	$21,560
Discretionary Income 2 (minus Food, Shelter, & Other Expenditures)	$14,829

LIQUID ASSETS

1999 Estimates:	Per Hhld.
Equity Investments	$42,799
Interest Bearing Investments	$47,695
Total Liquid Assets	$90,494

CREDIT DATA

July 2000:

Pool of Credit	$670,377,302
Revolving Credit, No.	122,001
Fixed Loans, No.	55,032
Avg. Credit Limit, per Person	$10,583
Avg. Spent, per Person	$5,391
Satisfactory Ratings, No. per Person	2.58
Avg. No. of Cards, per Person	0.82

LABOUR FORCE

2001 Estimates:

Male:	
In the Labour Force	17,420
Participation Rate	64.2
Employed	15,099
Unemployed	2,321
Unemployment Rate	13.3
Not in Labour Force	9,715
Female:	
In the Labour Force	16,240
Participation Rate	50.9
Employed	14,946
Unemployed	1,294
Unemployment Rate	8.0
Not in Labour Force	15,641

OCCUPATIONS BY MAJOR GROUPS

2001 Estimates:	Male	Female
Management	1,311	812
Business, Finance & Admin.	1,570	4,676
Natural & Applied Sciences & Related	977	209
Health	327	1,504
Social Sciences, Gov't Services & Religion	523	474
Education	343	630
Arts, Culture, Recreation & Sport	351	426
Sales & Service	4,485	6,139
Trades, Transport & Equipment Operators & Related	4,899	212
Primary Industries	435	47
Processing, Mfg. & Utilities	1,348	251

LEVEL OF SCHOOLING

2001 Estimates:

Population 15 years +	59,016
Less than Grade 9	7,326
Grades 9-13 w/o Certif.	15,290
Grade 9-13 with Certif.	9,307
Trade Certif. /Dip.	2,331
Non-Univ. w/o Certif./Dip.	2,659
Non-Univ. with Certif./Dip.	10,335
Univ. w/o Degree	6,052
Univ. w/o Degree/Certif.	3,494
Univ. with Certif.	2,558
Univ. with Degree	5,716

AVERAGE HOUSEHOLD EXPENDITURES

2001 Estimates:

Food	$5,222
Shelter	$7,688
Clothing	$1,747
Transportation	$5,035
Health & Personal Care	$1,599
Recr'n, Read'g & Education	$2,960
Taxes & Securities	$9,991
Other	$7,529
Total Expenditures	$41,771

PRIVATE HOUSEHOLDS

2001 Estimates:

Private Households, Total	30,129
Pop. in Private Households	69,751
Average no. per Household	2.3

FAMILIES

2001 Estimates:

Families in Private Households	19,925
Husband-Wife Families	15,558
Lone-Parent Families	4,367
Aver. No. Persons per Family	2.9
Aver. No. Sons/Daughters at Home	1.1

HOUSING

2001 Estimates:

Occupied Private Dwellings	30,129
Owned	15,816
Rented	14,313
Single-Detached House	12,292
Semi-Detached House	889
Row Houses	1,824
Apartment, 5+ Storeys	1,771
Owned Apartment, 5+ Storeys	146
Apartment, 5 or Fewer Storeys	9,653
Apartment, Detached Duplex	2,889
Other Single-Attached	153
Movable Dwellings	658

VEHICLES

2001 Estimates:

Model Yrs. '81-'96, No.	37,243
% Total	77.91
Model Yrs. '97-'98, No.	6,458
% Total	13.51
'99 Vehicles registered in Model Yr. '99, No.	4,104
% Total	8.58
Total No. '81-'99	47,805

LEGAL MARITAL STATUS

2001 Estimates: (Age 15+)

Single (Never Married)	19,891
Legally Married (Not Separated)	26,901
Legally Married (Separated)	2,460
Widowed	5,241
Divorced	4,523

PSYTE CATEGORIES

2001 Estimates	No. of House -holds	% of Total Hhds.	Index
Small City Elite	2,035	6.75	394
Old Bungalow Burbs	546	1.81	109
Aging Erudites	877	2.91	193
Old Towns' New Fringe	5,754	19.10	488
Conservative Homebodies	403	1.34	37
High Rise Sunsets	316	1.05	73
Young Urban Intelligentsia	184	0.61	40
University Enclaves	3,988	13.24	649
Young City Singles	489	1.62	71
Nesters & Young Homesteaders	3,652	12.12	519
Rod & Rifle	581	1.93	83
Struggling Downtowns	8,711	28.91	918
Aged Pensioners	1,825	6.06	455
Big City Stress	520	1.73	153

New Brunswick

FINANCIAL P$YTE

2001 Estimates	No. of House -holds	% of Total Hhds.	Index
Canadian Comfort	2,035	6.75	70
Urban Heights	877	2.91	68
Miners & Credit-Liners	546	1.81	57
Tractors & Tradelines	5,754	19.10	334
Bills & Wills	403	1.34	16
Revolving Renters	3,968	13.17	286
Young Urban Struggle	4,172	13.85	293
Rural Family Blues	581	1.93	24
Towering Debt	9,200	30.54	391
NSF	520	1.73	49
Senior Survivors	1,825	6.06	321

HOME LANGUAGE

2001 Estimates:		% Total
English	69,412	96.88
French	1,432	2.00
Chinese	89	0.12
Greek	67	0.09
Italian	40	0.06
Portuguese	39	0.05
Spanish	45	0.06
Other Languages	142	0.20
Multiple Responses	379	0.53
Total	71,645	100.00

BUILDING PERMITS

	1999	1998	1997
	$000		
Value	62,962	47,496	50,610

HOMES BUILT

	1999	1998	1997
No.	95	127	139

TAXATION

Income Class:	1997	% Total
Under $5,000	6,940	12.93
$5,000-$10,000	8,770	16.34
$10,000-$15,000	9,610	17.91
$15,000-$20,000	5,690	10.60
$20,000-$25,000	4,930	9.19
$25,000-$30,000	4,100	7.64
$30,000-$40,000	5,640	10.51
$40,000-$50,000	3,560	6.63
$50,000 +	4,440	8.27
Total Returns, No.	53,660	
Total Income, $000	1,226,756	
Total Taxable Returns	34,420	
Total Tax, $000	216,079	
Average Income, $	22,862	
Average Tax, $	6,278	

VITAL STATISTICS

	1997	1996	1995	1994
Births	884	913	995	1,041
Deaths	764	764	841	820
Natural Increase	120	149	154	221
Marriages	508	533	563	543

Note: Latest available data.

MEDIA INFO
see Saint John, CMA

Québec

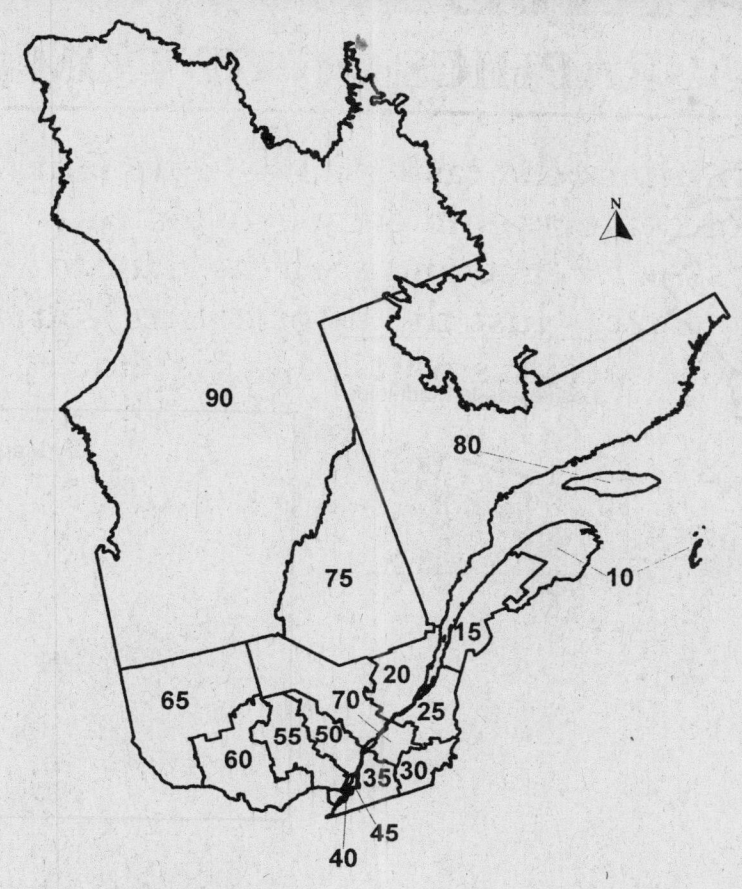

Economic Regions

10 Gaspésie - Îles-de-la-Madeleine
15 Bas-Saint-Laurent
20 Québec
25 Chaudière - Appalaches
30 Estrie
35 Montérégie
40 Montréal
45 Laval
50 Lanaudière
55 Laurentides
60 Outaouais
65 Abitibi - Témiscamingue
70 Mauricie - Bois-Francs
75 Saguenay - Lac-Saint-Jean
80 Côte-Nord
90 Nord-du-Québec

Region	Population (at July 1)				Households (at July1)		Income				Retail Sales				Taxation Statistics, 1997					
	*1996 Census (000)	2001 Estimate (000)	% of Cdn. Total	% Chg. '96-'01	2001 Estimate (000)	% of Cdn. Total	2001 Estimate $millions	% of Cdn. Total	Per Hhld. $	Income Rating Index	2001 Estimate $millions	% of Cdn. Total	Per Hhld. $	Market Rating Index	Total No. of Returns	Total Income $millions	Total No. Taxable Returns	Total Tax $millions	Avg. Income $	Avg. Tax $
Québec	7,274.0	7,445.1	23.91	2.35	3,063.9	25.35	143,773.8	21.90	46,900	92	64,688.8	23.21	21,100	97	5,237,640	129,461.9	3,498,070	15,372.1	24,718	4,394
Gaspésie - Îles-de-la-Madeleine (10)	106.8	102.9	0.33	-3.6	39.4	0.33	1,621.6	0.25	41,100	75	879.9	0.32	22,300	95	76,430	1,452.8	43,920	141.1	19,009	3,212
Bas-Saint-Laurent (15)	209.2	205.8	0.66	-1.62	83.8	0.69	3,405.9	0.52	40,700	78	1,909.7	0.69	22,800	104	148,810	3,032.5	89,610	302.8	20,378	3,379
Québec (20)	644.5	647.5	2.08	0.46	282.5	2.34	13,470.4	2.05	47,700	99	7,099.3	2.55	25,100	122	476,450	12,169.4	327,620	1,438.9	25,542	4,392
Chaudière - Appalaches (25)	386.8	393.5	1.26	1.71	152.0	1.26	6,863.4	1.05	45,200	83	3,849.5	1.38	25,300	109	278,020	6,204.8	186,200	647.5	22,318	3,477
Estrie (30)	283.3	292.5	0.94	3.24	123.4	1.02	5,149.4	0.78	41,700	84	2,366.3	0.85	19,200	90	206,970	4,690.0	138,070	505.5	22,660	3,661
Montérégie (35)	1,287.1	1,338.8	4.30	4.02	524.6	4.34	27,401.4	4.17	52,200	97	11,855.8	4.25	22,600	99	917,780	24,025.6	647,310	2,944.0	26,178	4,548
Montréal (40)	1,808.2	1,798.7	5.78	-0.52	806.1	6.67	35,866.4	5.46	44,500	95	14,008.7	5.03	17,400	87	1,322,420	34,315.6	851,250	4,375.4	25,949	5,140
Laval (45)	336.2	353.3	1.13	5.09	136.9	1.13	7,336.9	1.12	53,600	98	3,360.1	1.21	24,600	106	246,210	6,495.4	176,790	793.6	26,381	4,489
Lanaudière (50)	381.9	416.6	1.34	9.08	157.2	1.30	7,681.0	1.17	48,800	87	3,598.0	1.29	22,900	96	272,560	6,487.5	186,530	737.8	23,802	3,955
Laurentides (55)	440.9	490.2	1.57	11.17	193.6	1.60	9,422.4	1.44	48,700	91	3,908.6	1.40	20,200	89	318,880	7,886.3	219,830	932.5	24,731	4,242
Outaouais (60)	313.0	326.9	1.05	4.44	131.9	1.09	6,694.4	1.02	50,800	97	2,573.0	0.92	19,500	88	217,110	5,494.6	149,770	647.3	25,308	4,322
Abitibi - Témiscamingue (65)	156.5	156.2	0.50	-0.19	63.0	0.52	2,872.0	0.44	45,600	87	1,541.9	0.55	24,500	110	107,530	2,588.9	69,530	303.2	24,076	4,360
Mauricie - Bois-Francs (70)	484.1	488.4	1.57	0.89	204.5	1.69	8,364.8	1.27	40,900	81	4,120.3	1.48	20,100	94	350,290	7,544.9	223,430	790.2	21,539	3,537
Saguenay - Lac-Saint-Jean (75)	291.1	289.7	0.93	-0.46	112.1	0.93	4,859.5	0.74	43,400	80	2,552.7	0.92	22,800	98	202,710	4,661.9	129,290	530.4	22,998	4,102
Côte-Nord (80)	105.1	103.3	0.33	-1.69	40.3	0.33	2,049.2	0.31	50,900	94	809.6	0.29	20,100	88	73,240	1,867.8	47,460	225.9	25,502	4,761
Nord-du-Québec (90)	39.2	40.7	0.13	3.85	12.7	0.11	715.2	0.11	56,300	83	255.3	0.09	20,100	70	22,220	543.9	11,480	56.0	24,478	4,878

*Adjusted.

Gaspésie – Îles-de-la-Madeleine

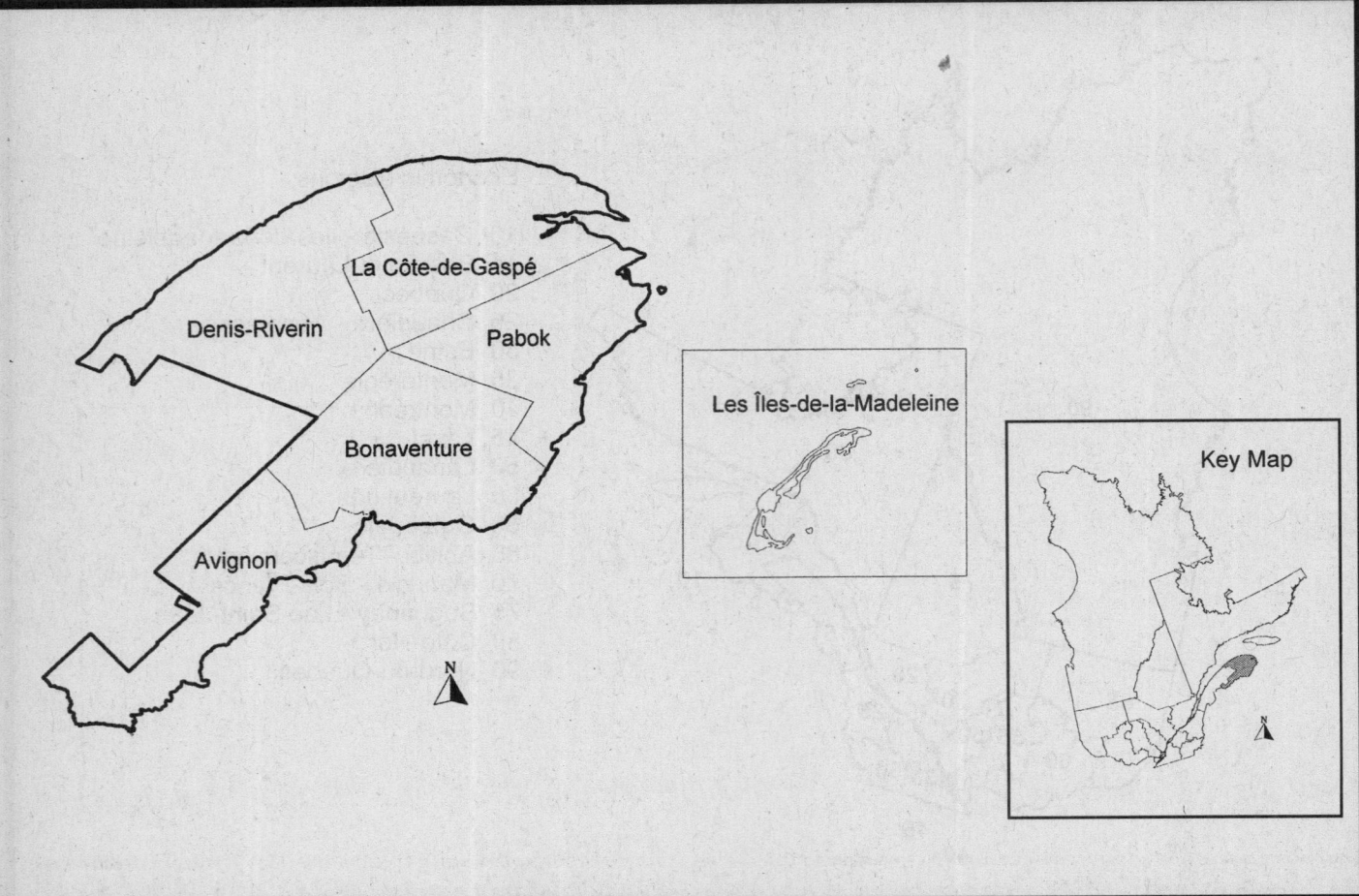

Region	Population (at July 1)				Households (at July1)		Income				Retail Sales				Taxation Statistics, 1997					
	*1996 Census (000)	2001 Estimate (000)	% of Cdn. Total	% Chg. 96-'01	2001 Estimate (000)	% of Cdn. Total	2001 Estimate $millions	% of Cdn. Total	Per Hhld. $	Income Rating Index	2001 Estimate $millions	% of Cdn. Total	Per Hhld. $	Market Rating Index	Total No. of Returns	Total Income $millions	Total No. Taxable Returns	Total Tax $millions	Avg. Income $	Avg. Tax $
Gaspésie - Îles-de-la-Madeleine (10)	106.8	102.9	0.33	-3.6	39.4	0.33	1,621.6	0.25	41,100	75	879.9	0.32	22,300	95	76,430	1,452.8	43,920	141.1	19,009	3,212
Les Îles-de-la-Madeleine	14.0	13.3	0.04	-4.91	4.9	0.04	238.4	0.04	48,200	85	168.4	0.06	34,000	141	10,190	207.0	6,690	19.1	20,318	2,858
Pabok	21.7	20.8	0.07	-4.25	8.1	0.07	315.6	0.05	39,200	72	155.3	0.06	19,300	84	15,700	286.6	8,780	28.1	18,254	3,197
La Côte-de-Gaspé	21.2	20.2	0.06	-4.4	7.5	0.06	337.0	0.05	44,900	79	174.8	0.06	23,300	97	15,010	312.6	9,040	33.5	20,824	3,704
Denis-Riverin	13.9	13.3	0.04	-4.51	5.3	0.04	178.0	0.03	33,700	63	85.2	0.03	16,100	71	10,120	169.7	5,070	14.9	16,770	2,936
Bonaventure	19.8	19.1	0.06	-3.5	7.5	0.06	302.3	0.05	40,500	75	192.1	0.07	25,700	112	14,220	271.1	8,270	26.4	19,067	3,192
Avignon	16.1	16.1	0.05	0.11	6.2	0.05	250.3	0.04	40,600	74	104.0	0.04	16,900	72	11,190	205.8	6,070	19.1	18,390	3,151

*Adjusted.

Economic Region & Census Divisions

Bas-Saint-Laurent

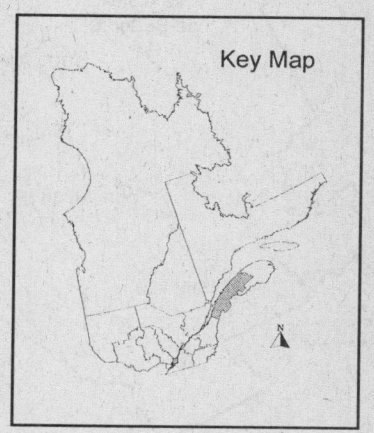

Key Map

Region	Population (at July 1)				Households (at July1)		Income				Retail Sales				Taxation Statistics, 1997					
	*1996 Census (000)	2001 Estimate (000)	% of Cdn. Total	% Chg. '96-'01	2001 Estimate (000)	% of Cdn. Total	2001 Estimate $millions	% of Cdn. Total	Per Hhld. $	Income Rating Index	2001 Estimate $millions	% of Cdn. Total	Per Hhld. $	Market Rating Index	Total No. of Returns	Total Income $millions	Total No. Taxable Returns	Total Tax $millions	Avg. Income $	Avg. Tax $
Bas-Saint-Laurent (15)	209.2	205.8	0.66	-1.62	83.8	0.69	3,405.9	0.52	40,700	78	1,909.7	0.69	22,800	104	148,810	3,032.5	89,610	302.8	20,378	3,379
La Matapédia	21.2	20.6	0.07	-3.03	7.9	0.07	295.6	0.05	37,400	68	113.4	0.04	14,300	62	14,740	264.1	8,100	23.7	17,920	2,927
Matane	24.1	23.1	0.07	-4.13	9.8	0.08	379.3	0.06	38,600	78	239.9	0.09	24,400	116	17,410	338.0	10,180	32.9	19,416	3,237
La Mitis	20.5	20.0	0.06	-2.29	7.9	0.07	290.2	0.04	36,600	69	131.1	0.05	16,600	73	14,230	264.0	7,970	24.6	18,555	3,083
Rimouski-Neigette	53.5	53.5	0.17	-0.07	22.8	0.19	1,078.8	0.16	47,300	96	518.5	0.19	22,700	108	38,930	918.2	25,480	102.3	23,586	4,017
Les Basques	9.1	8.8	0.03	-2.72	4.0	0.03	136.8	0.02	33,800	74	84.4	0.03	20,800	107	7,460	131.6	4,020	11.1	17,635	2,768
Rivière-du-Loup	33.9	33.9	0.11	0.08	13.5	0.11	550.5	0.08	40,900	77	422.3	0.15	31,400	139	23,440	503.4	15,070	52.6	21,476	3,487
Témiscouata	23.4	22.9	0.07	-2.19	8.8	0.07	322.8	0.05	36,600	67	157.7	0.06	17,900	77	16,530	300.6	9,220	26.3	18,188	2,854
Kamouraska	23.5	23.0	0.07	-2.14	8.9	0.07	351.8	0.05	39,300	72	242.4	0.09	27,100	118	16,070	312.5	9,570	29.2	19,444	3,056

*Adjusted.

Economic Region & Census Divisions

Québec

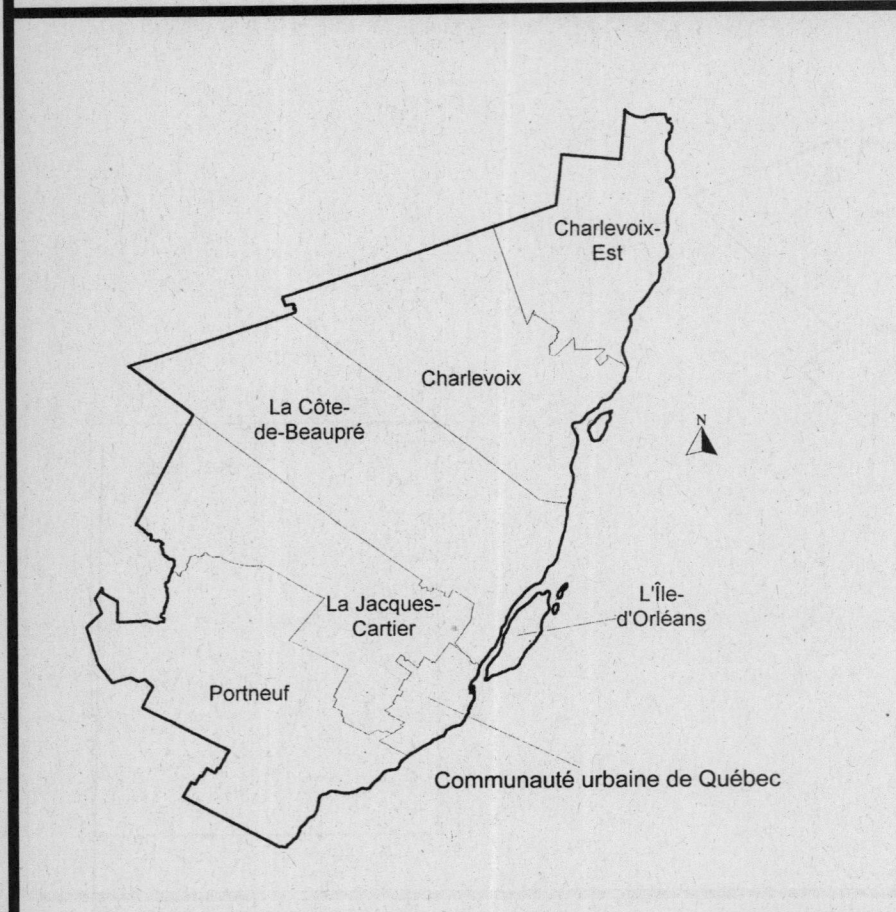

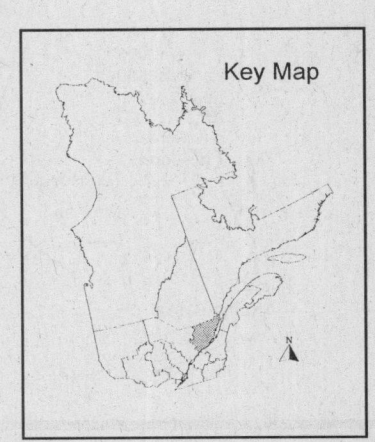

Key Map

Region	Population (at July 1)				Households (at July1)		Income				Retail Sales				Taxation Statistics, 1997					
	*1996 Census (000)	2001 Estimate (000)	% of Cdn. Total	% Chg. '96-'01	2001 Estimate (000)	% of Cdn. Total	2001 Estimate $millions	% of Cdn. Total	Per Hhld. $	Income Rating Index	2001 Estimate $millions	% of Cdn. Total	Per Hhld. $	Market Rating Index	Total No. of Returns	Total Income $millions	Total No. Taxable Returns	Total Tax $millions	Avg. Income $	Avg. Tax $
Québec (20)	644.5	647.5	2.08	0.46	282.5	2.34	13,470.4	2.05	47,700	99	7,099.3	2.55	25,100	122	476,450	12,169.4	327,620	1,438.9	25,542	4,392
Charlevoix-Est	17.2	16.7	0.05	-2.85	6.5	0.05	265.1	0.04	40,800	75	151.8	0.05	23,400	101	12,310	249.4	7,660	25.4	20,260	3,310
Charlevoix	13.6	13.4	0.04	-1.78	5.0	0.04	196.9	0.03	39,700	70	106.5	0.04	21,400	89	10,180	194.1	6,190	18.0	19,069	2,914
L'Île-d'Orléans	7.0	6.9	0.02	-0.67	2.7	0.02	151.9	0.02	56,600	104[1]	25.3	0.01	9,400	41	5,180	140.1	3,640	17.1	27,053	4,707
La Côte-de-Beaupré	22.0	22.3	0.07	1.27	8.8	0.07	424.7	0.06	48,200	90	272.0	0.10	30,900	136	16,510	397.2	11,360	44.6	24,055	3,922
La Jacques-Cartier	25.3	27.1	0.09	6.94	9.9	0.08	568.6	0.09	57,500	100	75.4	0.03	7,600	31	18,010	487.4	13,330	60.2	27,064	4,515
Communauté urbaine de Québec	513.4	514.3	1.65	0.17	230.9	1.91	11,061.7	1.69	47,900	102	5,985.7	2.15	25,900	130	381,320	9,980.1	264,080	1,199.4	26,172	4,542
Portneuf	45.9	46.7	0.15	1.74	18.8	0.16	801.5	0.12	42,700	81	482.5	0.17	25,700	115	32,940	721.1	21,360	74.3	21,892	3,477

*Adjusted.

Economic Region & Census Divisions

Chaudière – Appalaches

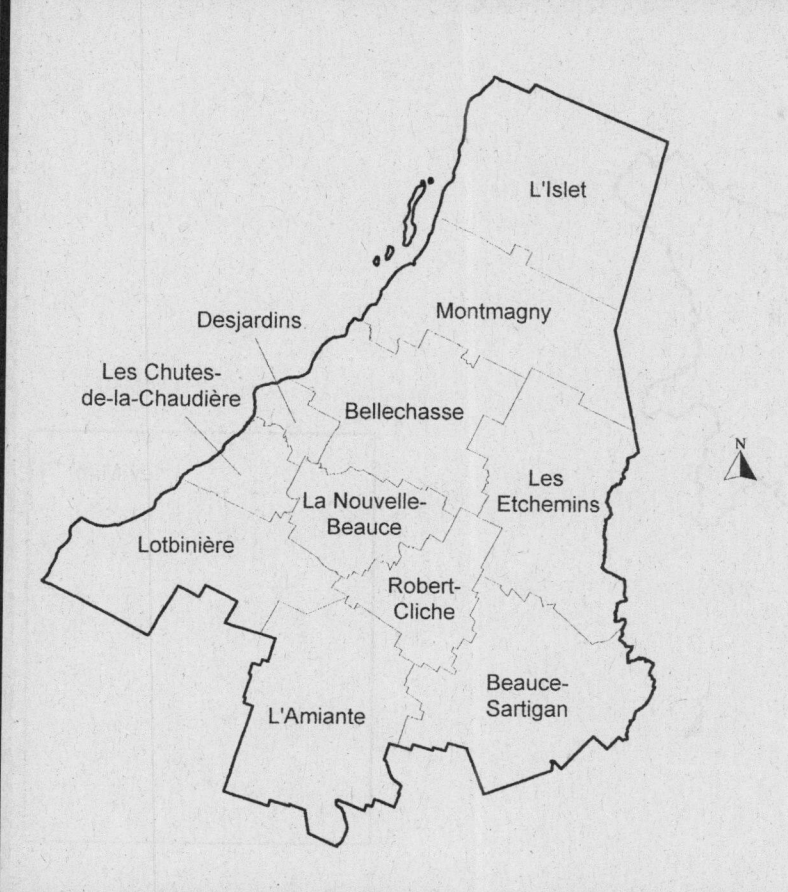

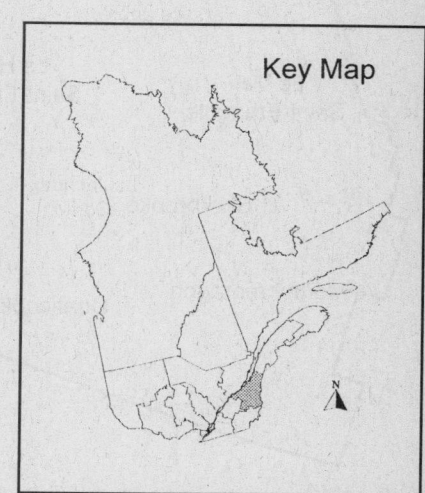

Key Map

Region	Population (at July 1)				Households (at July1)		Income				Retail Sales				Taxation Statistics, 1997					
	*1996 Census (000)	2001 Estimate (000)	% of Cdn. Total	% Chg. '96-01	2001 Estimate (000)	% of Cdn. Total	2001 Estimate $millions	% of Cdn. Total	Per Hhld. $	Income Rating Index	2001 Estimate $millions	% of Cdn. Total	Per Hhld. $	Market Rating Index	Total No. of Returns	Total Income $millions	Total No. Taxable Returns	Total Tax $millions	Avg. Income $	Avg. Tax $
Chaudière - Appalaches (25)	386.8	393.5	1.26	1.71	152.0	1.26	6,863.4	1.05	45,200	83	3,849.5	1.38	25,300	109	278,020	6,204.8	186,200	647.5	22,318	3,477
L'Islet	20.1	19.8	0.06	-1.55	7.7	0.06	292.6	0.04	38,100	70	148.6	0.05	19,300	84	14,180	266.6	8,500	24.1	18,803	2,831
Montmagny	24.2	23.8	0.08	-1.59	9.6	0.08	373.5	0.06	39,100	74	258.1	0.09	27,000	121	17,750	354.1	11,020	33.7	19,951	3,062
Bellechasse	30.1	29.9	0.10	-0.77	11.1	0.09	466.0	0.07	42,100	74	222.3	0.08	20,100	83	21,630	450.3	13,750	43.7	20,817	3,176
Desjardins	52.1	52.9	0.17	1.63	21.9	0.18	1,032.6	0.16	47,100	93	869.0	0.31	39,600	183	38,430	934.8	26,570	105.6	24,325	3,976
Les Chutes-de-la-Chaudière	77.0	82.9	0.27	7.71	31.0	0.26	1,770.1	0.27	57,100	101	512.3	0.18	16,500	69	54,300	1,463.9	40,440	175.2	26,960	4,333
La Nouvelle-Beauce	25.5	25.9	0.08	1.77	9.5	0.08	429.3	0.07	45,400	79	283.4	0.10	29,900	122	18,430	411.6	12,730	41.7	22,334	3,278
Robert-Cliche	19.0	19.0	0.06	0.04	7.0	0.06	286.6	0.04	40,700	71	134.6	0.05	.19,100	79	13,630	275.3	8,780	26.1	20,198	2,971
Les Etchemins	18.6	18.1	0.06	-2.93	6.8	0.06	256.4	0.04	37,500	67	150.7	0.05	22,000	93	13,120	244.5	7,860	20.5	18,636	2,609
Beauce-Sartigan	47.1	49.1	0.16	4.2	18.9	0.16	813.5	0.12	43,100	79	578.2	0.21	30,700	131	34,090	733.4	22,770	73.9	21,513	3,247
L'Amiante	45.7	44.3	0.14	-2.97	18.1	0.15	716.7	0.11	39,500	77	423.5	0.15	23,300	107	33,360	685.8	21,260	66.8	20,556	3,140
Lotbinière	27.4	27.6	0.09	0.8	10.3	0.09	426.0	0.06	41,200	73	268.9	0.10	26,000	109	19,100	384.5	12,520	36.1	20,131	2,887

*Adjusted.

Estrie

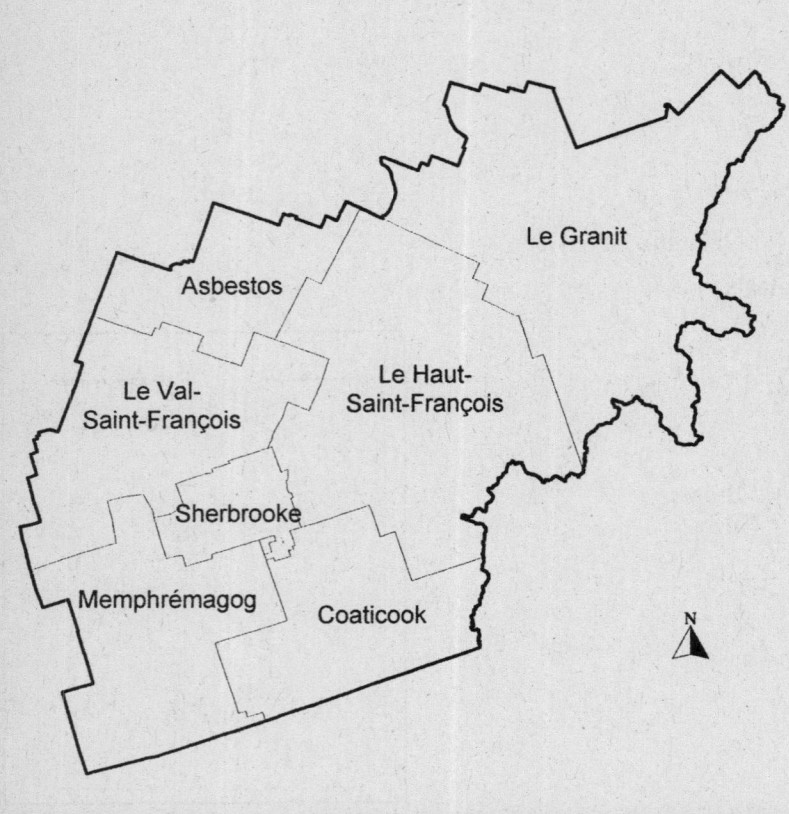

Le Granit

Asbestos

Le Val-Saint-François

Le Haut-Saint-François

Sherbrooke

Memphrémagog

Coaticook

N

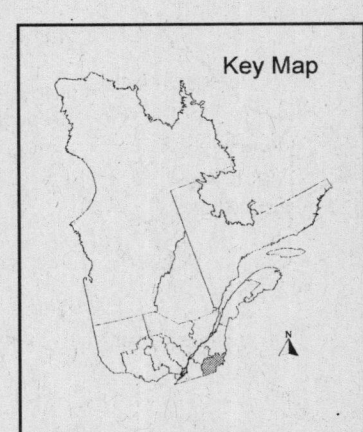

Key Map

N

Region	Population (at July 1)				Households (at July 1)		Personal Income				Retail Sales				Taxation Statistics, 1997					
	*1996 Census (000)	2001 Estimate (000)	% of Cdn. Total	% Chg. '96-'01	2001 Estimate (000)	% of Cdn. Total	2001 Estimate $millions	% of Cdn. Total	Per Capita $	Income Rating Index	2001 Estimate $millions	% of Cdn. Total	Per Capita $	Market Rating Index	Total No. of Returns	Total Income $millions	Total No. Taxable Returns	Total Tax $millions	Avg. Income $	Avg. Tax $
Estrie (30)	283.3	292.5	0.94	3.24	123.4	1.02	5,149.4	0.78	41,700	84	2,366.3	0.85	19,200	90	206,970	4,690.0	138,070	505.5	22,660	3,661
Le Granit	21.6	21.9	0.07	1.1	8.6	0.07	347.9	0.05	40,300	75	257.3	0.09	29,800	131	15,890	320.9	10,540	30.6	20,192	2,903
Asbestos	15.2	14.9	0.05	-1.81	6.2	0.05	234.6	0.04	37,700	75	107.2	0.04	17,200	80	11,150	230.5	7,160	23.0	20,670	3,211
Le Haut-Saint-François	22.3	22.9	0.07	2.96	8.8	0.07	332.5	0.05	37,700	69	120.3	0.04	13,600	59	15,440	296.3	9,590	27.6	19,191	2,874
Le Val-Saint-François	34.0	34.9	0.11	2.84	13.8	0.11	615.7	0.09	44,700	84	192.3	0.07	14,000	61	24,710	573.4	17,240	63.4	23,206	3,680
Sherbrooke	134.9	139.7	0.45	3.57	62.2	0.51	2,605.5	0.40	41,900	88	1,271.9	0.46	20,500	102	98,730	2,341.4	65,830	261.3	23,715	3,970
Coaticook	16.2	16.1	0.05	-0.61	6.0	0.05	249.4	0.04	41,400	74	112.2	0.04	18,600	78	10,650	219.2	7,200	20.5	20,579	2,843
Memphrémagog	39.1	42.0	0.13	7.31	17.8	0.15	763.9	0.12	43,000	86	305.3	0.11	17,200	81	30,400	708.4	20,510	79.2	23,303	3,860

*Adjusted.

Montérégie

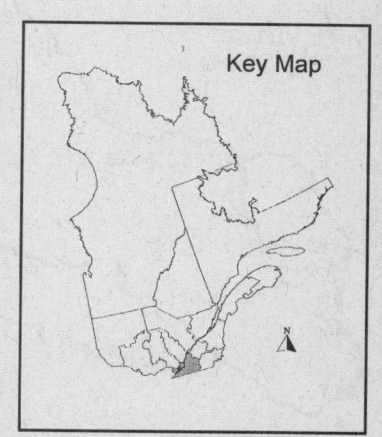

Key Map

Region	Population (at July 1)				Households (at July1)		Income				Retail Sales				Taxation Statistics, 1997					
	*1996 Census (000)	2001 Estimate (000)	% of Cdn. Total	% Chg. '96-'01	2001 Estimate (000)	% of Cdn. Total	2001 Estimate $millions	% of Cdn. Total	Per Hhld. $	Income Rating Index	2001 Estimate $millions	% of Cdn. Total	Per Hhld. $	Market Rating Index	Total No. of Returns	Total Income $millions	Total No. Taxable Returns	Total Tax $millions	Avg. Income $	Avg. Tax $
Montérégie (35)	1,287.1	1,338.8	4.30	4.02	524.6	4.34	27,401.4	4.17	52,200	97	11,855.8	4.25	22,600	99	917,780	24,025.6	647,310	2,944.0	26,178	4,548
Brome-Missisquoi	46.7	47.3	0.15	1.26	19.7	0.16	825.5	0.13	42,000	83	437.7	0.16	22,300	103	33,320	776.0	22,350	87.4	23,290	3,911
La Haute-Yamaska	78.3	82.1	0.26	4.8	34.1	0.28	1,523.3	0.23	44,700	88	868.1	0.31	25,500	118	57,330	1,334.6	39,910	150.4	23,279	3,769
Acton	15.6	16.0	0.05	2.8	6.2	0.05	247.8	0.04	40,000	73	95.3	0.03	15,400	67	11,000	214.6	7,360	20.2	19,507	2,740
Le Bas-Richelieu	53.1	51.2	0.16	-3.57	21.7	0.18	928.7	0.14	42,700	86	478.4	0.17	22,000	104	38,710	896.2	24,660	100.7	23,151	4,084
Les Maskoutains	80.1	80.4	0.26	0.38	33.0	0.27	1,419.5	0.22	43,100	84	866.2	0.31	26,300	120	58,810	1,334.6	40,310	141.5	22,693	3,509
Rouville	33.6	34.8	0.11	3.57	13.1	0.11	615.2	0.09	47,000	84	236.3	0.08	18,000	76	23,490	545.1	16,540	59.9	23,206	3,620
Le Haut-Richelieu	99.2	103.6	0.33	4.42	41.8	0.35	1,868.6	0.28	44,700	86	1,114.3	0.40	26,700	120	71,570	1,650.7	48,800	181.3	23,065	3,715
La Vallée-du-Richelieu	115.8	123.7	0.40	6.8	45.5	0.38	2,904.3	0.44	63,800	111	1,318.6	0.47	28,900	119	82,260	2,511.0	61,890	335.4	30,525	5,419
Champlain	319.5	321.1	1.03	0.5	131.5	1.09	6,982.0	1.06	53,100	103	2,721.5	0.98	20,700	95	228,230	6,159.7	158,610	782.1	26,989	4,931
Lajemmerais	97.4	107.7	0.35	10.63	39.0	0.32	2,670.8	0.41	68,500	118	1,108.3	0.40	28,400	115	70,420	2,281.5	54,730	313.7	32,398	5,732
Roussillon	142.0	155.2	0.50	9.27	55.3	0.46	3,187.1	0.49	57,600	97	935.1	0.34	16,900	67	97,110	2,628.0	70,760	327.0	27,062	4,622
Les Jardins-de-Napierville	23.3	23.8	0.08	1.95	9.0	0.07	401.5	0.06	44,600	80	270.4	0.10	30,000	127	16,610	374.1	11,360	41.0	22,522	3,607
Le Haut-Saint-Laurent	24.7	24.9	0.08	0.59	9.6	0.08	401.2	0.06	41,900	76	145.1	0.05	15,100	65	16,700	337.5	9,880	34.2	20,207	3,459
Beauharnois-Salaberry	60.7	60.0	0.19	-1.26	25.1	0.21	1,046.3	0.16	41,700	83	597.1	0.21	23,800	111	43,890	1,014.2	29,050	112.2	23,107	3,863
Vaudreuil-Soulanges	97.1	107.2	0.34	10.45	40.0	0.33	2,379.7	0.36	59,500	105	663.5	0.24	16,600	69	68,330	1,968.0	51,100	257.1	28,801	5,031

*Adjusted.

Montréal

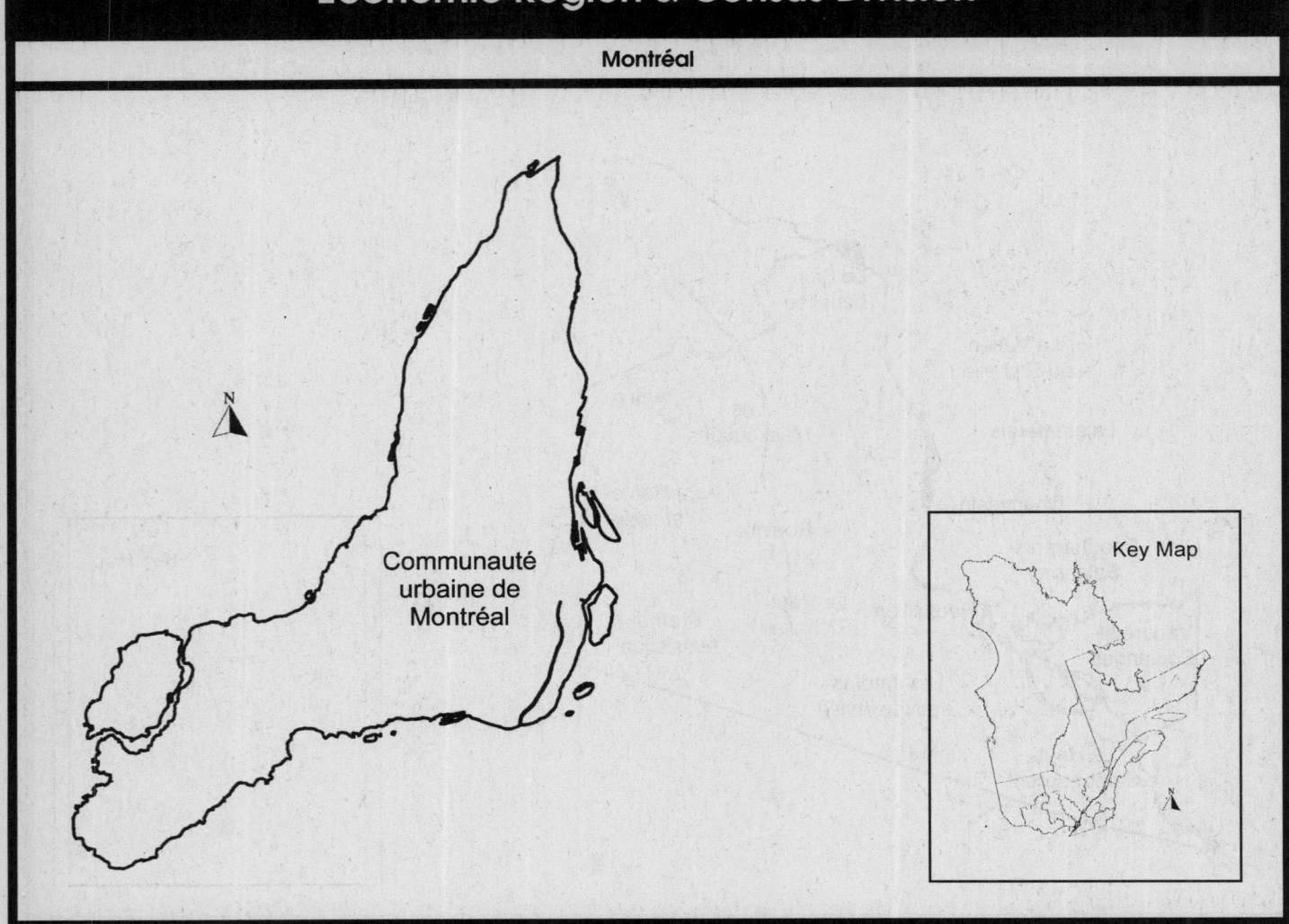

Communauté urbaine de Montréal

Key Map

Region	Population (at July 1)				Households (at July1)		Personal Income				Retail Sales				Taxation Statistics, 1997					
	*1996 Census (000)	2001 Estimate (000)	% of Cdn. Total	% Chg. '96-'01	2001 Estimate (000)	% of Cdn. Total	2001 Estimate $millions	% of Cdn. Total	Per Capita $	Income Rating Index	2001 Estimate $millions	% of Cdn. Total	Per Capita $	Market Rating Index	Total No. of Returns	Total Income $millions	Total No. Taxable Returns	Total Tax $millions	Avg. Income $	Avg. Tax $
Montréal (40)	1,808.2	1,798.7	5.78	-0.52	806.1	6.67	35,866.4	5.46	44,500	95	14,008.7	5.03	17,400	87	1,322,420	34,315.6	851,250	4,375.4	25,949	5,140
Communauté urbaine de Montréal	1,808.2	1,798.7	5.78	-0.52	806.1	6.67	35,866.4	5.46	44,500	95	14,008.7	5.03	17,400	87	1,322,420	34,315.6	851,250	4,375.4	25,949	5,140

*Adjusted.

Laval

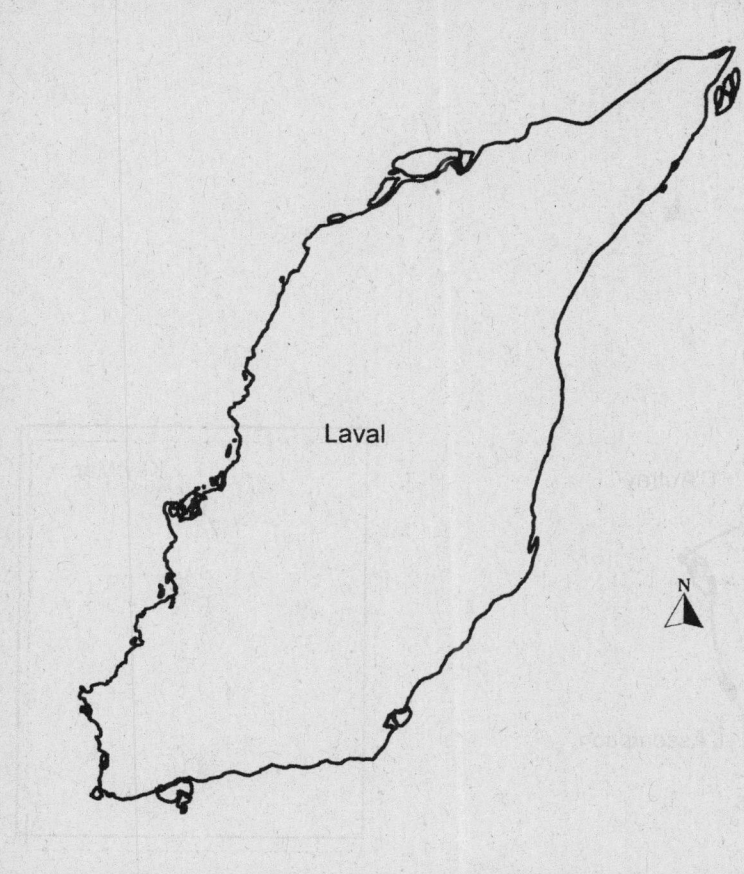

Laval

N

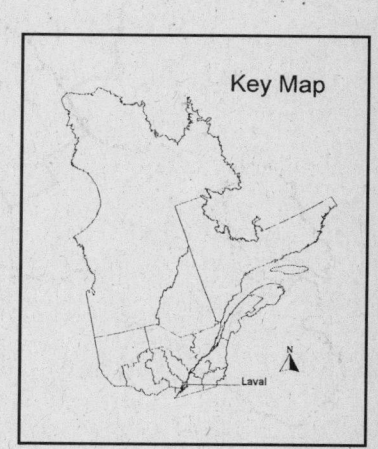

Key Map

Laval

Region	Population (at July 1)				Households (at July1)		Income				Retail Sales				Taxation Statistics, 1997					
	*1996 Census (000)	2001 Estimate (000)	% of Cdn. Total	% Chg. '96-'01	2001 Estimate (000)	% of Cdn. Total	2001 Estimate $millions	% of Cdn. Total	Per Hhld. $	Income Rating Index	2001 Estimate $millions	% of Cdn. Total	Per Hhld. $	Market Rating Index	Total No. of Returns	Total Income $millions	Total No. Taxable Returns	Total Tax $millions	Avg. Income $	Avg. Tax $
Laval (45)	336.2	353.3	1.13	5.09	136.9	1.13	7,336.9	1.12	53,600	98	3,360.1	1.21	24,600	106	246,210	6,495.4	176,790	793.6	26,381	4,489
Laval	336.2	353.3	1.13	5.09	136.9	1.13	7,336.9	1.12	53,600	98	3,360.1	1.21	24,600	106	246,210	6,495.4	176,790	793.6	26,381	4,489

*Adjusted.

Lanaudière

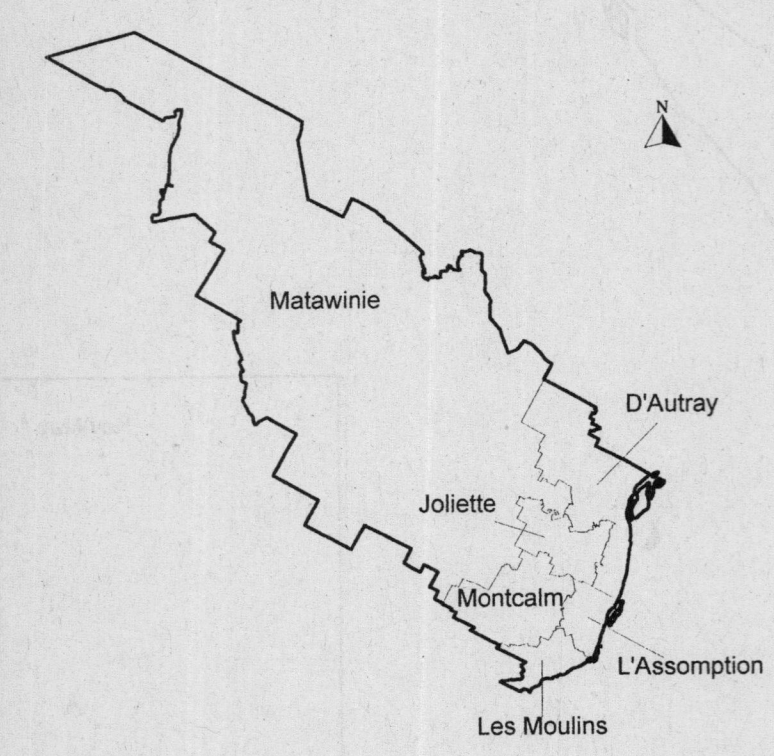

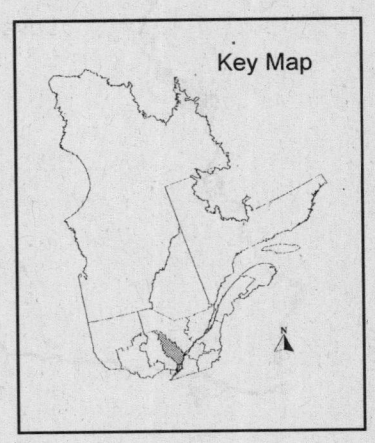

Key Map

Region	Population (at July 1)				Households (at July 1)		Income				Retail Sales				Taxation Statistics, 1997					
	*1996 Census (000)	2001 Estimate (000)	% of Cdn. Total	% Chg. '96-'01	2001 Estimate (000)	% of Cdn. Total	2001 Estimate $millions	% of Cdn. Total	Per Hhld. $	Income Rating Index	2001 Estimate $millions	% of Cdn. Total	Per Hhld. $	Market Rating Index	Total No. of Returns	Total Income $millions	Total No. Taxable Returns	Total Tax $millions	Avg. Income $	Avg. Tax $
Lanaudière (50)	381.9	416.6	1.34	9.08	157.2	1.30	7,681.0	1.17	48,800	87	3,598.0	1.29	22,900	96	272,560	6,487.5	186,530	737.8	23,802	3,955
D'Autray	38.2	42.1	0.14	10.25	16.0	0.13	662.1	0.10	41,400	75	212.1	0.08	13,200	56	27,780	559.7	17,350	55.7	20,147	3,212
L'Assomption	104.0	111.9	0.36	7.64	41.0	0.34	2,374.4	0.36	57,900	101	949.6	0.34	23,200	95	72,720	2,007.6	54,050	250.2	27,608	4,629
Joliette	53.7	55.1	0.18	2.55	22.7	0.19	978.4	0.15	43,200	84	788.2	0.28	34,800	160	39,670	910.2	26,070	99.1	22,943	3,803
Matawinie	42.0	46.6	0.15	10.83	20.0	0.17	734.4	0.11	36,700	75	263.2	0.09	13,100	63	31,470	611.4	18,890	58.4	19,428	3,093
Montcalm	38.8	42.8	0.14	10.3	16.3	0.14	644.1	0.10	39,500	71	251.4	0.09	15,400	66	27,340	534.0	16,640	52.2	19,531	3,134
Les Moulins	105.2	118.1	0.38	12.28	41.2	0.34	2,287.6	0.35	55,500	92	1,133.6	0.41	27,500	107	73,580	1,864.6	53,530	222.1	25,342	4,149

*Adjusted.

Laurentides

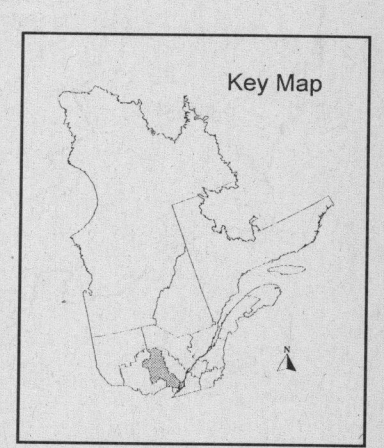

Key Map

Region	Population (at July 1)				Households (at July1)		Income					Retail Sales				Taxation Statistics, 1997					
	*1996 Census (000)	2001 Estimate (000)	% of Cdn. Total	% Chg. '96-'01	2001 Estimate (000)	% of Cdn. Total	2001 Estimate $millions	% of Cdn. Total	Per Hhld. $	Income Rating Index	2001 Estimate $millions	% of Cdn. Total	Per Hhld. $	Market Rating Index	Total No. of Returns	Total Income $millions	Total No. Taxable Returns	Total Tax $millions	Avg. Income $	Avg. Tax $
Laurentides (55)	440.9	490.2	1.57	11.17	193.6	1.60	9,422.4	1.44	48,700	91	3,908.6	1.40	20,200	89	318,880	7,886.3	219,830	932.5	24,731	4,242
Deux-Montagnes	81.6	88.0	0.28	7.93	32.6	0.27	1,699.9	0.26	52,100	92	647.7	0.23	19,900	82	57,050	1,411.1	40,220	165.5	24,734	4,115
Thérèse-De Blainville	121.6	137.4	0.44	13.02	49.8	0.41	2,970.7	0.45	59,600	103	1,091.4	0.39	21,900	89	85,410	2,506.6	63,280	328.9	29,348	5,198
Mirabel	23.2	28.5	0.09	22.84	10.2	0.08	521.4	0.08	51,400	87	171.8	0.06	16,900	67	15,920	381.7	11,430	43.9	23,979	3,842
La Rivière-du-Nord	83.9	93.5	0.30	11.45	39.2	0.32	1,708.6	0.26	43,500	87	812.1	0.29	20,700	97	63,640	1,442.2	42,640	159.4	22,663	3,737
Argenteuil	30.5	31.1	0.10	1.96	12.3	0.10	480.3	0.07	38,900	73	178.1	0.06	14,400	64	21,040	442.8	13,330	46.1	21,045	3,459
Les Pays-d'en-Haut	28.8	34.5	0.11	19.97	16.3	0.13	792.5	0.12	48,700	109	241.4	0.09	14,800	78	23,220	644.3	16,190	82.2	27,747	5,074
Les Laurentides	37.0	41.2	0.13	11.33	18.3	0.15	704.9	0.11	38,600	81	404.7	0.15	22,200	110	28,090	587.1	18,260	62.0	20,899	3,395
Antoine-Labelle	34.5	36.0	0.12	4.37	14.9	0.12	544.1	0.08	36,500	72	361.3	0.13	24,200	112	24,510	470.4	14,480	44.5	19,193	3,075

*Adjusted.

Outaouais

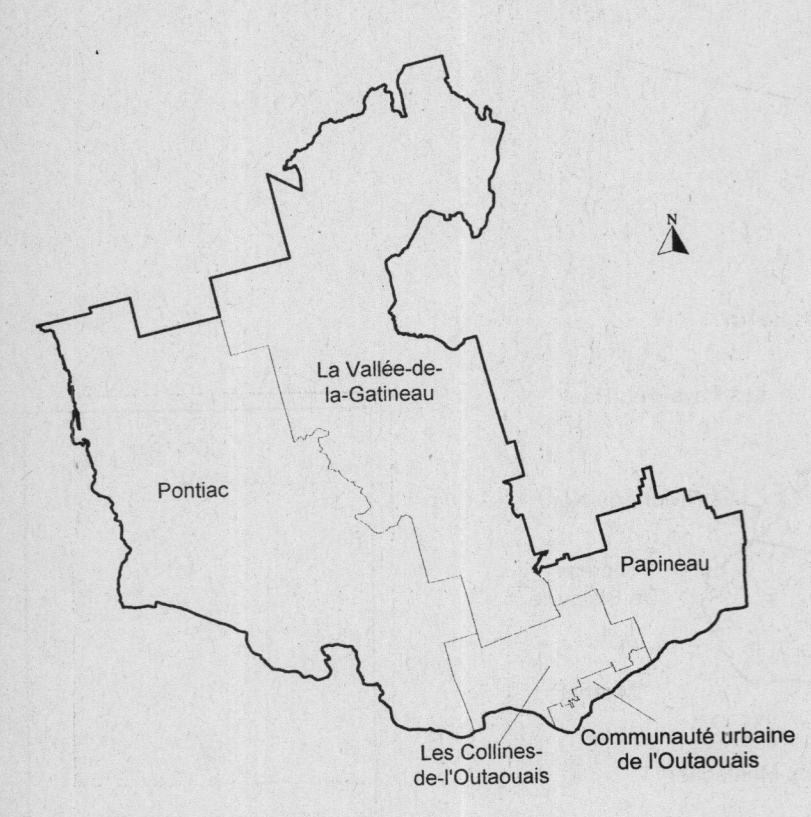

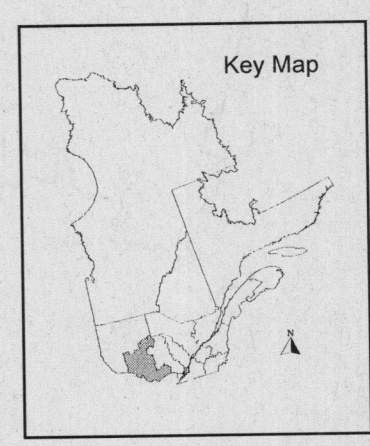

Key Map

Region	Population (at July 1)				Households (at July 1)		Income				Retail Sales				Taxation Statistics, 1997					
	*1996 Census (000)	2001 Estimate (000)	% of Cdn. Total	% Chg. '96-'01	2001 Estimate (000)	% of Cdn. Total	2001 Estimate $millions	% of Cdn. Total	Per Hhld. $	Income Rating Index	2001 Estimate $millions	% of Cdn. Total	Per Hhld. $	Market Rating Index	Total No. of Returns	Total Income $millions	Total No. Taxable Returns	Total Tax $millions	Avg. Income $	Avg. Tax $
Outaouais (60)	313.0	326.9	1.05	4.44	131.9	1.09	6,694.4	1.02	50,800	97	2,573.0	0.92	19,500	88	217,110	5,494.6	149,770	647.3	25,308	4,322
Papineau	20.7	21.4	0.07	3.37	9.5	0.08	354.9	0.05	37,500	79	123.4	0.04	13,000	65	14,560	282.8	8,660	27.5	19,426	3,171
Communauté urbaine de l'Outaouais	221.6	229.3	0.74	3.44	92.5	0.77	4,897.1	0.75	52,900	101	2,010.0	0.72	21,700	98	155,190	4,142.4	111,330	501.0	26,693	4,500
Les Collines-de-l'Outaouais	34.3	38.7	0.12	12.89	14.3	0.12	876.2	0.13	61,400	107	115.4	0.04	8,100	33	22,120	599.0	15,710	74.8	27,080	4,759
La Vallée-de-la-Gatineau	20.6	21.9	0.07	6.15	9.5	0.08	337.1	0.05	35,400	73	221.6	0.08	23,200	113	14,910	268.1	8,140	23.8	17,981	2,918
Pontiac	15.8	15.7	0.05	-0.79	6.1	0.05	229.1	0.03	37,400	69	102.6	0.04	16,700	73	10,330	202.2	5,930	20.3	19,574	3,426

*Adjusted.

Economic Region & Census Divisions

Abitibi – Témiscamingue

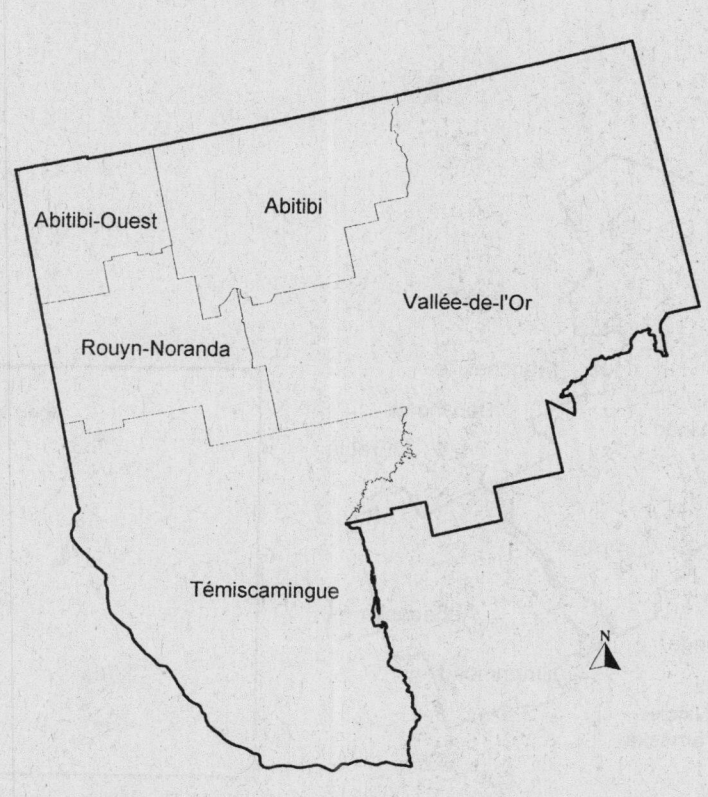

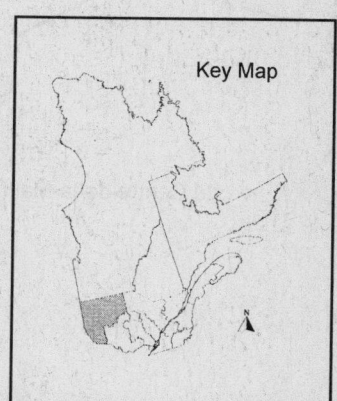

Key Map

Region	Population (at July 1)				Households (at July1)		Income				Retail Sales				Taxation Statistics, 1997					
	*1996 Census (000)	2001 Estimate (000)	% of Cdn. Total	% Chg. '96-'01	2001 Estimate (000)	% of Cdn. Total	2001 Estimate $millions	% of Cdn. Total	Per Hhld. $	Income Rating Index	2001 Estimate $millions	% of Cdn. Total	Per Hhld. $	Market Rating Index	Total No. of Returns	Total Income $millions	Total No. Taxable Returns	Total Tax $millions	Avg. Income $	Avg. Tax $
Abitibi - Témiscamingue (65)	156.5	156.2	0.50	-0.19	63.0	0.52	2,872.0	0.44	45,600	87	1,541.9	0.55	24,500	110	107,530	2,588.9	69,530	303.2	24,076	4,360
Témiscamingue	18.3	18.7	0.06	2.27	7.3	0.06	328.6	0.05	45,000	83	134.2	0.05	18,400	80	12,360	281.7	7,620	31.3	22,791	4,111
Rouyn-Noranda	43.4	43.3	0.14	-0.14	18.4	0.15	867.1	0.13	47,100	95	429.2	0.15	23,300	111	30,280	774.6	20,260	94.7	25,580	4,673
Abitibi-Ouest	23.9	23.0	0.07	-3.75	8.9	0.07	378.9	0.06	42,700	78	215.1	0.08	24,200	104	16,160	350.2	9,810	37.3	21,671	3,797
Abitibi	25.7	25.6	0.08	-0.55	10.0	0.08	437.3	0.07	43,800	81	271.7	0.10	27,200	119	17,490	412.1	11,400	46.7	23,560	4,094
Vallée-de-l'Or	45.2	45.5	0.15	0.85	18.5	0.15	860.1	0.13	46,600	90	491.7	0.18	26,600	121	31,240	770.4	20,440	93.2	24,661	4,562

*Adjusted.

Mauricie – Bois-Francs

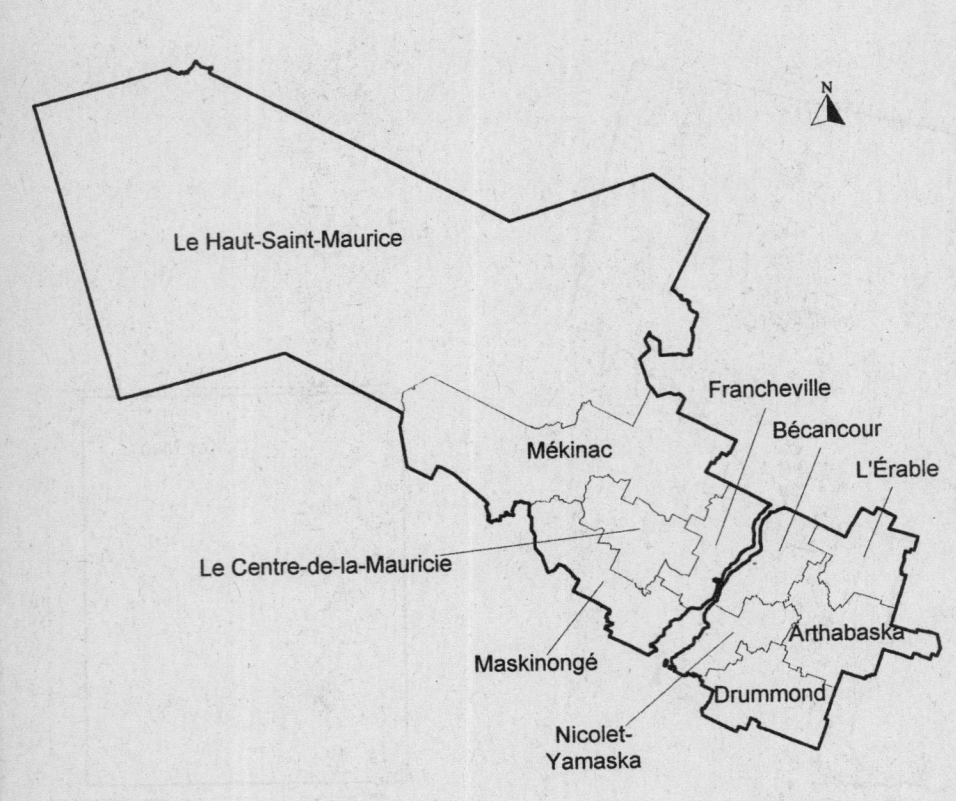

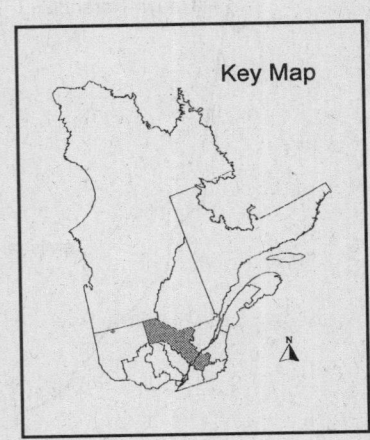

Key Map

Region	Population (at July 1)				Households (at July1)		Income				Retail Sales				Taxation Statistics, 1997					
	*1996 Census (000)	2001 Estimate (000)	% of Cdn. Total	% Chg. '96-'01	2001 Estimate (000)	% of Cdn. Total	2001 Estimate $millions	% of Cdn. Total	Per Hhld. $	Income Rating Index	2001 Estimate $millions	% of Cdn. Total	Per Hhld. $	Market Rating Index	Total No. of Returns	Total Income $millions	Total No. Taxable Returns	Total Tax $millions	Avg. Income $	Avg. Tax $
Mauricie - Bois-Francs (70)	484.1	488.4	1.57	0.89	204.5	1.69	8,364.8	1.27	40,900	81	4,120.3	1.48	20,100	94	350,290	7,544.9	223,430	790.2	21,539	3,537
L'Érable	25.1	24.6	0.08	-1.97	9.2	0.08	360.6	0.05	39,000	70	169.9	0.06	18,400	77	17,630	348.6	11,720	31.9	18,644	2,855
Mékinac	13.7	13.3	0.04	-2.71	5.6	0.05	198.4	0.03	35,200	71	72.8	0.03	12,900	61	9,770	182.2	5,760	16.4	20,994	3,577
Le Centre-de-la-Mauricie	68.1	67.1	0.22	-1.45	29.2	0.24	1,108.6	0.17	38,000	78	505.6	0.18	17,300	84	102,740	2,392.0	65,750	269.4	23,282	4,097
Francheville	142.8	143.0	0.46	0.12	62.9	0.52	2,708.7	0.41	43,000	90	1,143.7	0.41	18,200	89	14,030	298.4	8,640	30.9	21,266	3,575
Bécancour	20.0	20.0	0.06	0.16	7.8	0.06	335.2	0.05	42,800	79	128.7	0.05	16,400	72	46,270	994.4	30,860	102.6	21,491	3,323
Arthabaska	64.0	66.1	0.21	3.25	26.4	0.22	1,102.0	0.17	41,700	79	654.5	0.23	24,800	111	62,720	1,346.1	41,720	139.5	21,462	3,343
Drummond	85.7	89.5	0.29	4.46	37.0	0.31	1,541.2	0.23	41,600	82	975.2	0.35	26,300	122	17,660	345.0	10,570	31.9	19,538	3,022
Nicolet-Yamaska	24.0	24.1	0.08	0.23	9.4	0.08	371.0	0.06	39,600	73	185.4	0.07	19,800	86	17,800	334.6	10,870	30.7	18,797	2,826
Maskinongé	24.2	24.1	0.08	-0.44	10.0	0.08	354.2	0.05	35,400	70	146.2	0.05	14,600	68	11,320	246.6	6,750	26.7	21,782	3,958
Le Haut-Saint-Maurice	16.5	16.6	0.05	0.54	6.8	0.06	284.9	0.04	41,900	81	138.4	0.05	20,300	93						

*Adjusted.

Economic Region & Census Divisions

Saguenay – Lac-Saint-Jean

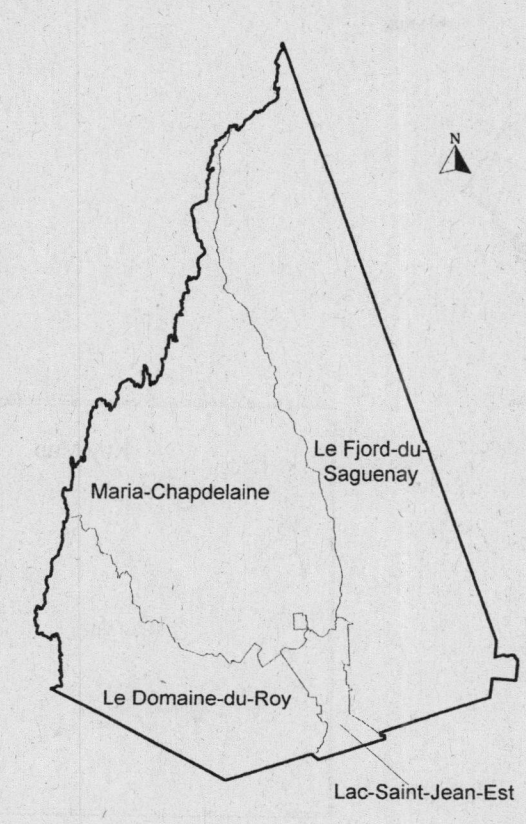

Le Fjord-du-Saguenay

Maria-Chapdelaine

Le Domaine-du-Roy

Lac-Saint-Jean-Est

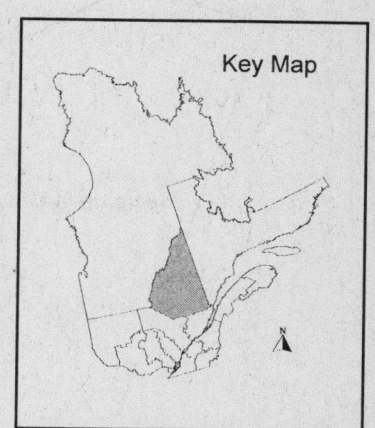

Key Map

Region	Population (at July 1)				Households (at July1)		Income				Retail Sales				Taxation Statistics, 1997					
	*1996 Census (000)	2001 Estimate (000)	% of Cdn. Total	% Chg. '96-'01	2001 Estimate (000)	% of Cdn. Total	2001 Estimate $millions	% of Cdn. Total	Per Hhld. $	Income Rating Index	2001 Estimate $millions	% of Cdn. Total	Per Hhld. $	Market Rating Index	Total No. of Returns	Total Income $millions	Total No. Taxable Returns	Total Tax $millions	Avg. Income $	Avg. Tax $
Saguenay - Lac-Saint-Jean (75)	291.1	289.7	0.93	-0.46	112.1	0.93	4,859.5	0.74	43,400	80	2,552.7	0.92	22,800	98	202,710	4,661.9	129,290	530.4	22,998	4,102
Le Domaine-du-Roy	34.4	34.1	0.11	-0.77	12.6	0.10	573.9	0.09	45,500	80	299.2	0.11	23,700	98	23,660	508.3	14,360	53.8	21,483	3,747
Maria-Chapdelaine	28.5	27.9	0.09	-2.1	10.3	0.09	420.5	0.06	40,800	72	275.6	0.10	26,700	110	19,650	413.1	11,870	43.5	21,025	3,665
Lac-Saint-Jean-Est	53.2	53.2	0.17	-0.01	20.1	0.17	866.8	0.13	43,100	77	448.3	0.16	22,300	94	36,860	811.4	23,310	89.2	22,014	3,827
Le Fjord-du-Saguenay	175.0	174.5	0.56	-0.27	69.0	0.57	2,998.2	0.46	43,400	81	1,529.6	0.55	22,200	98	122,540	2,929.0	79,750	343.9	23,903	4,312

*Adjusted.

Economic Region & Census Divisions

Côte-Nord

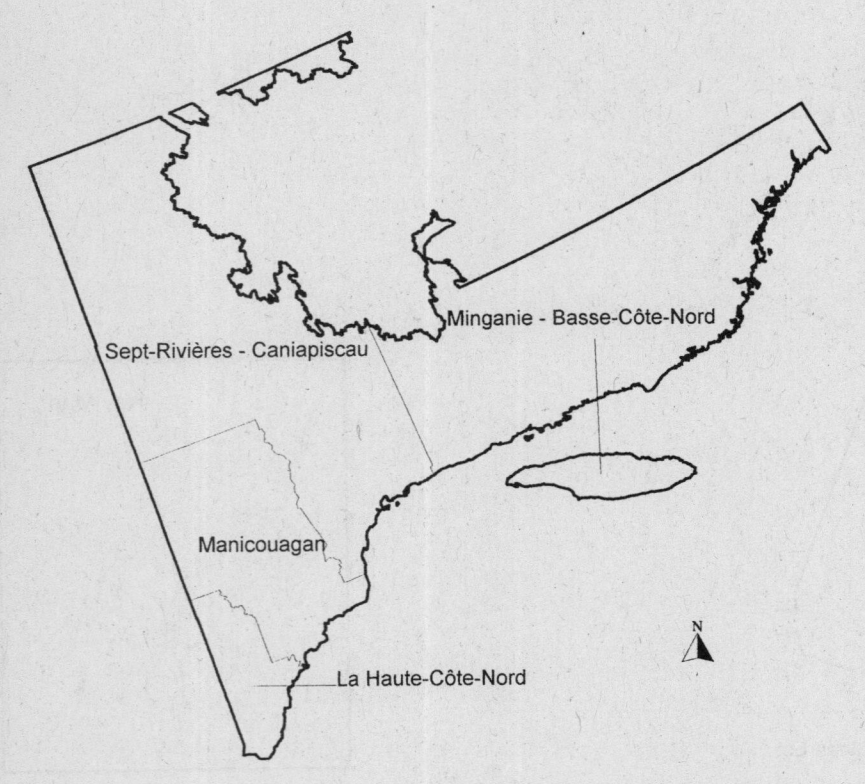

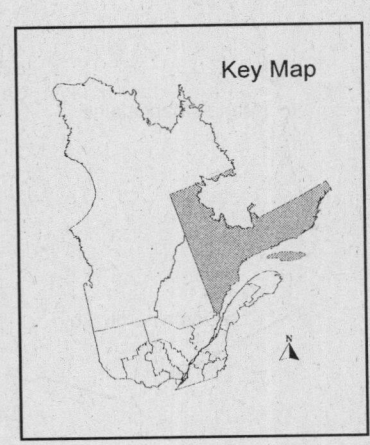

Key Map

Region	Population (at July 1)				Households (at July 1)		Income				Retail Sales				Taxation Statistics, 1997					
	*1996 Census (000)	2001 Estimate (000)	% of Cdn. Total	% Chg. '96-'01	2001 Estimate (000)	% of Cdn. Total	2001 Estimate $millions	% of Cdn. Total	Per Hhld. $	Income Rating Index	2001 Estimate $millions	% of Cdn. Total	Per Hhld. $	Market Rating Index	Total No. of Returns	Total Income $millions	Total No. Taxable Returns	Total Tax $millions	Avg. Income $	Avg. Tax $
Côte-Nord (80)	105.1	103.3	0.33	-1.69	40.3	0.33	2,049.2	0.31	50,900	94	809.6	0.29	20,100	88	73,240	1,867.8	47,460	225.9	25,502	4,761
La Haute-Côte-Nord	13.7	13.4	0.04	-2.28	5.2	0.04	202.2	0.03	38,600	72	119.1	0.04	22,700	100	9,670	192.8	5,900	19.4	19,941	3,293
Manicouagan	36.9	35.8	0.12	-2.9	14.1	0.12	741.0	0.11	52,600	98	252.7	0.09	17,900	79	25,570	695.0	17,360	87.2	27,180	5,026
Sept-Rivières - Caniapiscau	41.6	41.5	0.13	-0.44	16.6	0.14	908.4	0.14	54,700	104	356.3	0.13	21,400	96	28,940	807.2	19,000	103.5	27,892	5,448
Minganie - Basse-Côte-Nord	12.9	12.7	0.04	-1.67	4.3	0.04	197.6	0.03	45,900	74	81.5	0.03	18,900	72	9,060	172.8	5,200	15.8	19,068	3,031

*Adjusted.

Nord-du-Québec

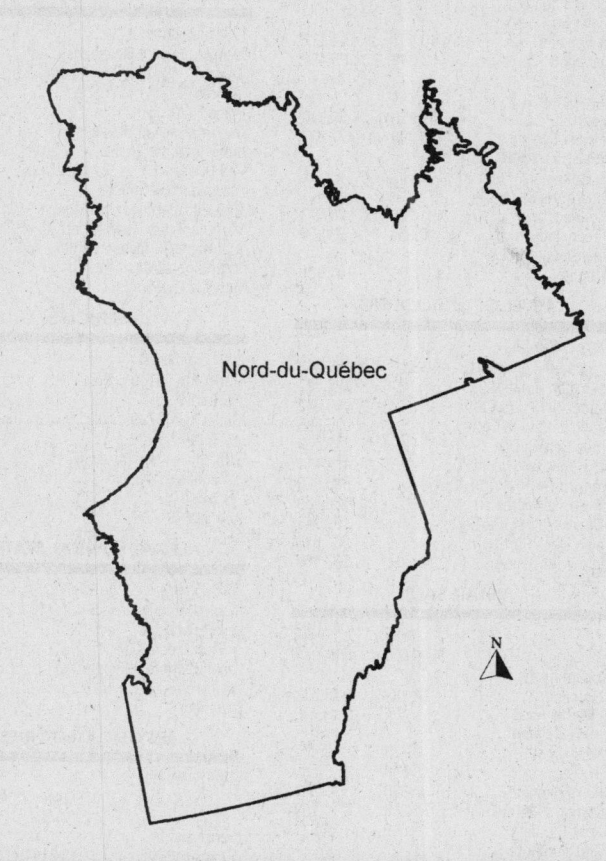

Nord-du-Québec

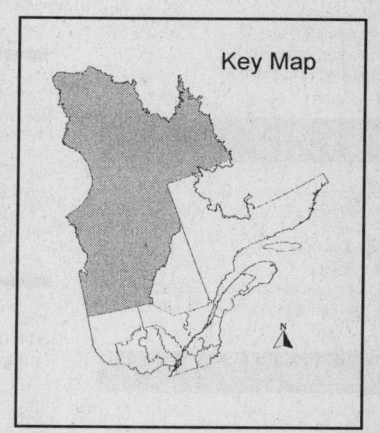

Key Map

Region	Population (at July 1)				Households (at July1)		Income				Retail Sales				Taxation Statistics, 1997					
	*1996 Census (000)	2001 Estimate (000)	% of Cdn. Total	% Chg. '96-'01	2001 Estimate (000)	% of Cdn. Total	2001 Estimate $millions	% of Cdn. Total	Per Hhld. $	Income Rating Index	2001 Estimate $millions	% of Cdn. Total	Per Hhld. $	Market Rating Index	Total No. of Returns	Total Income $millions	Total No. Taxable Returns	Total Tax $millions	Avg. Income $	Avg. Tax $
Nord-du-Québec (90)	39.2	40.7	0.13	3.85	12.7	0.11	715.2	0.11	56,300	83	255.3	0.09	20,100	70	22,220	543.9	11,480	56.0	24,478	4,878
Nord-du-Québec	39.2	40.7	0.13	3.85	12.7	0.11	715.2	0.11	56,300	83	255.3	0.09	20,100	70	22,220	543.9	11,480	56.0	24,478	4,878

*Adjusted.

Québec

POPULATION

July 1, 2001 Estimate	7,445,060
% Cdn. Total	23.91
% Change, '96 -'01	2.35
Avg. Annual Growth Rate, %	0.47
2003 Projected Population	7,604,909
2006 Projected Population	7,871,052
2001 Households Estimate	3,063,893
2003 Projected Households	3,153,915
2006 Projected Households	3,298,015

INCOME

% Above/Below National Average	-8
2001 Total Income Estimate	$143,773,820,000
% Cdn. Total	21.90
2001 Average Hhld. Income	$46,900
2001 Per Capita	$19,300
2003 Projected Total Income	$155,618,250,000
2006 Projected Total Income	$176,229,120,000

RETAIL SALES

% Above/Below National Average	-3
2001 Retail Sales Estimate	$64,688,750,000
% Cdn. Total	23.21
2001 per Household	$21,100
2001 per Capita	$8,700
2001 No. of Establishments	66,973
2003 Projected Retail Sales	$70,840,240,000
2006 Projected Retail Sales	$80,354,220,000

POPULATION

2001 Estimates:

Total		7,445,060
Male		3,641,156
Female		3,803,904
Age Groups	Male	Female
0-4	219,236	209,387
5-9	231,282	221,930
10-14	236,873	226,503
15-19	247,074	235,235
20-24	245,187	235,647
25-29	241,016	236,522
30-34	268,196	266,729
35-39	303,353	304,959
40-44	309,759	314,482
45-49	291,504	297,873
50-54	256,798	263,418
55-59	209,171	217,307
60-64	169,098	182,474
65-69	140,394	162,821
70+	272,215	428,617

DAYTIME POPULATION

2001 Estimates:

Working Population	3,431,568
At Home Population	3,981,712
Total	7,413,280

INCOME

2001 Estimates:

Avg. Household Income	$46,925
Avg. Family Income	$54,686
Per Capita Income	$19,311
Male:	
Avg. Employment Income	$33,323
Avg. Employment Income (Full Time)	$43,757
Female:	
Avg. Employment Income	$21,612
Avg. Employment Income (Full Time)	$31,472

DISPOSABLE & DISCRETIONARY INCOME

2001 Estimates:	Per Hhld.
Disposable Income	$32,243
Discretionary Income 1 (minus Food & Shelter)	$20,143
Discretionary Income 2 (minus Food, Shelter, & Other Expenditures)	$12,863

LIQUID ASSETS

1999 Estimates:	Per Hhld.
Equity Investments	$55,811
Interest Bearing Investments	$54,973
Total Liquid Assets	$110,784

CREDIT DATA

July 2000:

Pool of Credit	$45,956,981,088
Revolving Credit, No.	12,618,172
Fixed Loans, No.	4,023,803
Avg. Credit Limit, per Person	$7,880
Avg. Spent, per Person	$3,477
Satisfactory Ratings, No. per Person	2.70
Avg. No. of Cards, per Person	1.06

LABOUR FORCE

2001 Estimates:

Male:	
In the Labour Force	2,106,942
Participation Rate	71.3
Employed	1,927,111
Unemployed	179,831
Unemployment Rate	8.5
Not in Labour Force	846,823
Female:	
In the Labour Force	1,679,031
Participation Rate	53.4
Employed	1,552,062
Unemployed	126,969
Unemployment Rate	7.6
Not in Labour Force	1,467,053

AVERAGE WEEKLY EARNINGS

(Including overtime, industrial aggregate)

	Québec	Canada
Apr 2000	$581.00	$622.92
Apr 1999	$570.32	$608.07
Apr 1998	$576.10	$608.06
Apr 1997	$562.41	$597.26
Apr 1996	$549.94	$575.79

NUMBER OF EMPLOYEES

(Industrial aggregate)

Apr 2000	2,852,093
Apr 1999	2,778,757
Apr 1998	2,753,024
Apr 1997	2,662,872
Apr 1996	2,655,063

MANUFACTURING INDUSTRIES

	1997	1992
Plants	10,176	11,129
Employees	500,906	454,767
	$000	
Salaries, Wages	17,768,654	14,982,393
Mfg. Materials, Cost	54,583,930	36,399,357
Mfg. Shipments, Value	102,825,558	69,220,354
Total Value Added	46,859,109	31,966,054

Note: Latest available data.

OCCUPATIONS BY MAJOR GROUPS

2001 Estimates:	Male	Female
Management	225,782	93,401
Business, Finance & Admin.	208,386	505,458
Natural & Applied Sciences & Related	158,513	34,403
Health	46,489	150,831
Social Sciences, Gov't Services & Religion	40,637	49,922
Education	59,549	88,481
Arts, Culture, Recreation & Sport	49,768	50,540
Sales & Service	425,403	477,939
Trades, Transport & Equipment Operators & Related	481,999	28,973
Primary Industries	90,855	21,985
Processing, Mfg. & Utilities	232,171	101,369

LEVEL OF SCHOOLING

2001 Estimates:

Population 15 years +	6,099,849
Less than Grade 9	1,098,372
Grades 9-13 w/o Certif.	1,069,342
Grade 9-13 with Certif.	1,075,666
Trade Certif. /Dip.	272,865
Non-Univ. w/o Certif./Dip.	437,411
Non-Univ. with Certif./Dip.	928,826
Univ. w/o Degree	480,260
Univ. w/o Degree/Certif.	93,743
Univ. with Certif.	386,517
Univ. with Degree	737,107

RETAIL SALES

	1999 $000,000	1998 $000,000
Supermarkets & Groceries	14,233	13,632
All Other Food	n.a.	n.a.
Drugs & Patent Medicine	2,779	2,875
Shoes	548	565
Men's Clothing	330	353
Women's Clothing	1,206	1,226
Other Clothing	1,689	1,615
Hhld. Furniture & Appliances	2,907	2,628
Hhld. Furnishings	481	473
Motor & Recreation Vehicles	16,881	15,278
Gas Service Stations	3,775	3,237
Auto Parts, Accessories & Services	3,707	3,567
General Merchandise	5,816	5,471
Other Semi-Durable Goods	1,654	1,780
Other Durable Goods	1,452	1,364
Other Retail	1,992	1,763
Total	60,766	57,158

AVERAGE HOUSEHOLD EXPENDITURES

2001 Estimates:

Food	$6,127
Shelter	$7,832
Clothing	$2,100
Transportation	$5,377
Health & Personal Care	$1,853
Recr'n, Read'g & Education	$3,067
Taxes & Securities	$12,648
Other	$7,053
Total Expenditures	$46,057

PRIVATE HOUSEHOLDS

2001 Estimates:

Private Households, Total	3,063,893
Pop. in Private Households	7,279,892
Average no. per Household	2.4

FAMILIES

2001 Estimates:

Families in Private Households	2,124,883
Husband-Wife Families	1,793,643
Lone-Parent Families	331,240
Aver. No. Persons per Family	3.0
Aver. No. Sons/Daughters at Home	1.1

HOUSING

2001 Estimates:

Occupied Private Dwellings	3,063,893
Owned	1,752,109
Rented	1,307,907
Band Housing	3,877
Single-Detached House	1,414,600
Semi-Detached House	141,009
Row Houses	77,353
Apartment, 5+ Storeys	152,309
Owned Apartment, 5+ Storeys	23,351
Apartment, 5 or Fewer Storeys	1,058,300
Apartment, Detached Duplex	182,550
Other Single-Attached	16,650
Movable Dwellings	21,122

VEHICLES

2001 Estimates:

Model Yrs. '81-'96, No.	3,288,491
% Total	77.16
Model Yrs. '97-'98, No.	599,447
% Total	14.07
'99 Vehicles registered in Model Yr. '99, No.	373,707
% Total	8.77
Total No. '81-'99	4,261,645

LEGAL MARITAL STATUS

2001 Estimates: (Age 15+)

Single (Never Married)	2,321,174
Legally Married (Not Separated)	2,687,624
Legally Married (Separated)	148,912
Widowed	393,190
Divorced	548,949

PSYTE CATEGORIES

2001 Estimates	No. of House -holds	% of Total Hhds.	Index
Canadian Establishment	3,644	0.12	71
The Affluentials	5,594	0.18	29
Urban Gentry	39,124	1.28	71
Suburban Executives	19,368	0.63	44
Mortgaged in Suburbia	2,328	0.08	5
Technocrafts & Bureaucrats	39,997	1.31	46
Asian Heights	1,325	0.04	7
Boomers & Teens	460	0.02	1
Stable Suburban Families	27,458	0.90	69
Small City Elite	8,043	0.26	15
Old Bungalow Burbs	24,186	0.79	48
Suburban Nesters	12,120	0.40	25
Brie & Chablis	11,379	0.37	41
Aging Erudites	19,567	0.64	42
Satellite Suburbs	709	0.02	1
Kindergarten Boom	3,161	0.10	4
Blue Collar Winners	841	0.03	1
Old Towns' New Fringe	1,066	0.03	1
Participation Quebec	331,889	10.83	376
New Quebec Rows	132,063	4.31	393
Quebec Melange	311,528	10.17	384
Traditional French Cdn. Families	304,217	9.93	370
Northern Lights	3,612	0.12	24
The New Frontier	2,268	0.07	5
Rustic Prosperity	1,907	0.06	3
Quebec's Heartland	113,524	3.71	377
The Grain Belt	40	0.00	
Europa	25,602	0.84	67
Asian Mosaic	268	0.01	1
High Rise Melting Pot	4,572	0.15	10
Conservative Homebodies	1,864	0.06	2

PSYTE CATEGORIES

2001 Estimates	No. of House-holds	% of Total Hhds.	Index
High Rise Sunsets	22,633	0.74	52
Young Urban Professionals	51,532	1.68	89
Young Urban Mix	8,960	0.29	14
Young Urban Intelligentsia	31,388	1.02	67
University Enclaves	6,702	0.22	11
Young City Singles	8,216	0.27	12
Urban Bohemia	103,155	3.37	288
Old Leafy Towns	7,763	0.25	10
Town Renters	2,691	0.09	10
Young Grey Collar	3,180	0.10	12
Quiet Towns	772	0.03	1
Agrarian Blues	3,666	0.12	56
Rod & Rifle	9,899	0.32	14
Down, Down East	1,576	0.05	7
Big Country Families	40,324	1.32	92
Quebec Rural Blues	231,875	7.57	311
Old Cdn. Rustics	565	0.02	2
Euro Quebec	105,992	3.46	394
Old Quebec Walkups	217,667	7.10	388
Quebec Town Elders	320,086	10.45	370
Aging Quebec Urbanites	33,280	1.09	376
Quebec's New Urban Mosaic	287,516	9.38	390
Struggling Downtowns	383	0.01	.
Aged Pensioners	25,156	0.82	62
Big City Stress	46,587	1.52	135
Old Grey Towers	16,114	0.53	95

FINANCIAL PSYTE

2001 Estimates	No. of House-holds	% of Total Hhds.	Index
Platinum Estates	9,238	0.30	37
Four Star Investors	58,952	1.92	38
Successful Suburbanites	74,720	2.44	37
Canadian Comfort	21,713	0.71	7
Urban Heights	82,478	2.69	63
Miners & Credit-Liners	26,454	0.86	27
Mortgages & Minivans	467,113	15.25	231
Dollars & Sense	25,870	0.84	32
Tractors & Tradelines	2,973	0.10	2
Bills & Wills	18,587	0.61	7
Country Credit	615,785	20.10	297
Revolving Renters	25,813	0.84	18
Young Urban Struggle	141,245	4.61	97
Rural Family Blues	400,864	13.08	162
Limited Budgets	1,337	0.04	1
Loan Parent Stress	677,025	22.10	379
Towering Debt	15,862	0.52	7
NSF	334,103	10.90	308
Senior Survivors	41,270	1.35	71

HOME LANGUAGE

2001 Estimates:		% Total
English	744,889	10.01
French	6,119,515	82.20
Arabic	36,339	0.49
Armenian	12,204	0.16
Bengali	5,128	0.07
Chinese	34,549	0.46
Cree	12,346	0.17
Creoles	15,673	0.21
German	4,238	0.06
Greek	29,096	0.39
Inuktitut (Eskimo)	8,002	0.11
Italian	63,892	0.86
Khmer (Cambodian)	5,345	0.07
Montagnais-Naskapi	7,678	0.10
Persian (Farsi)	6,517	0.09
Polish	10,471	0.14
Portuguese	18,911	0.25
Punjabi	5,421	0.07
Romanian	6,767	0.09
Russian	7,607	0.10
Spanish	47,705	0.64
Tagalog (Pilipino)	4,740	0.06
Tamil	7,289	0.10
Vietnamese	20,314	0.27
Yiddish	5,159	0.07
Other Languages	48,047	0.65
Multiple Responses	157,218	2.11
Total	7,445,060	100.00

BUILDING PERMITS

	1999	1998	1997
		$000	
Value	5,939,609	5,588,153	5,133,178

HOMES BUILT

	1999	1998	1997
No.	24,141	22,944	26,308

CAPITAL EXPENDITURES

(Public & Private)	2000	1999	1998
		$000,000	
Total Expends.	n.a.	n.a.	39,820.6
Capital Expends.	34,246.3	32,506.0	31,285.3
Construction	18,422.1	17,325.9	16,986.9
Machinery & Equip.	15,824.2	15,180.2	14,298.4
Repair Expends.	n.a.	n.a.	8,535.3
Construction	n.a.	n.a.	3,617.9
Machinery & Equip.	n.a.	n.a.	4,917.4

TAXATION

Income Class:	1997	% Total
Under $5,000	694,970	13.27
$5,000-$10,000	794,850	15.18
$10,000-$15,000	845,810	16.15
$15,000-$20,000	530,260	10.12
$20,000-$25,000	439,410	8.39
$25,000-$30,000	411,400	7.85
$30,000-$40,000	598,400	11.42
$40,000-$50,000	375,090	7.16
$50,000 +	547,460	10.45
Total Returns, No.	5,237,640	
Total Income, $000	129,461,928	
Total Taxable Returns	3,498,070	
Total Tax, $000	15,372,131	
Average Income, $	24,718	
Average Tax, $	4,394	

VITAL STATISTICS

	1997	1996	1995	1994
Births	79,774	85,226	87,417	90,578
Deaths	54,399	52,336	52,734	51,366
Natural Increase	25,375	32,890	34,683	39,212
Marriages	23,875	23,968	24,238	24,985

Note: Latest available data.

TRAVEL STATISTICS

Tourists in Canada	1999	1998
From the U.S. entering by:		
Automobile	2,400,179	2,191,387
Bus	229,941	217,774
Rail	17,846	12,102
Air	663,481	607,038
Marine	8,901	7,285
Other Methods	28,264	27,196
Total	3,348,612	3,062,782
Other Countries:		
Land (via U.S.)	129,709	130,810
Air	633,865	571,625
Marine	492	478
Total	764,066	702,913
Residents of Canada		
Returning from the U.S. by:		
Automobile	4,080,756	3,909,932
Bus	212,189	214,063
Rail	7,475	5,592
Air	720,039	648,386
Marine	26,544	26,052
Other Methods	54,638	48,229
Total	5,101,641	4,852,254
From Other Countries:		
Land (via U.S.)	2	2
Air	886,153	865,770
Marine	3	2
Total	886,158	865,774

Québec

Québec

Alma
(Census Agglomeration)

The Census Agglomeration of Alma includes: Alma, V; and Delisle, M. Both are in census division Lac-Saint-Jean-Est.

POPULATION

July 1, 2001 Estimate	30,769
% Cdn. Total	0.10
% Change, '96 -'01	-0.25
Avg. Annual Growth Rate, %	-0.05
2003 Projected Population	30,716
2006 Projected Population	30,406
2001 Households Estimate	12,042
2003 Projected Households	12,304
2006 Projected Households	12,619

INCOME

% Above/Below National Average	-16
2001 Total Income Estimate	$541,830,000
% Cdn. Total	0.08
2001 Average Hhld. Income	$45,000
2001 Per Capita	$17,600
2003 Projected Total Income	$573,000,000
2006 Projected Total Income	$618,720,000

RETAIL SALES

% Above/Below National Average	+29
2001 Retail Sales Estimate	$355,960,000
% Cdn. Total	0.13
2001 per Household	$29,600
2001 per Capita	$11,600
2001 No. of Establishments	363
2003 Projected Retail Sales	$384,400,000
2006 Projected Retail Sales	$420,740,000

POPULATION

2001 Estimates:

Total		30,769
Male		15,235
Female		15,534
Age Groups	Male	Female
0-4	812	769
5-9	903	848
10-14	1,038	1,020
15-19	1,234	1,228
20-24	1,209	1,131
25-29	983	879
30-34	985	901
35-39	1,204	1,187
40-44	1,351	1,362
45-49	1,245	1,268
50-54	1,039	1,088
55-59	846	902
60-64	715	796
65-69	616	714
70+	1,055	1,441

DAYTIME POPULATION

2001 Estimates:

Working Population	13,425
At Home Population	17,344
Total	30,769

INCOME

2001 Estimates:

Avg. Household Income	$44,995
Avg. Family Income	$51,060
Per Capita Income	$17,610
Male:	
Avg. Employment Income	$33,015
Avg. Employment Income (Full Time)	$44,812
Female:	
Avg. Employment Income	$17,835
Avg. Employment Income (Full Time)	$29,122

DISPOSABLE & DISCRETIONARY INCOME

2001 Estimates:	Per Hhld.
Disposable Income	$31,449
Discretionary Income 1 (minus Food & Shelter)	$20,003
Discretionary Income 2 (minus Food, Shelter, & Other Expenditures)	$13,024

LIQUID ASSETS

1999 Estimates:	Per Hhld.
Equity Investments	$53,948
Interest Bearing Investments	$54,540
Total Liquid Assets	$108,488

CREDIT DATA

July 2000:

Pool of Credit	$185,124,469
Revolving Credit, No.	58,725
Fixed Loans, No.	20,218
Avg. Credit Limit, per Person	$7,823
Avg. Spent, per Person	$3,232
Satisfactory Ratings, No. per Person	3.05
Avg. No. of Cards, per Person	0.97

LABOUR FORCE

2001 Estimates:

Male:	
In the Labour Force	8,773
Participation Rate	70.3
Employed	7,737
Unemployed	1,036
Unemployment Rate	11.8
Not in Labour Force	3,709
Female:	
In the Labour Force	6,300
Participation Rate	48.8
Employed	5,657
Unemployed	643
Unemployment Rate	10.2
Not in Labour Force	6,597

OCCUPATIONS BY MAJOR GROUPS

2001 Estimates:	Male	Female
Management	685	189
Business, Finance & Admin.	704	1,747
Natural & Applied Sciences & Related	487	72
Health	244	632
Social Sciences, Gov't Services & Religion	172	110
Education	345	478
Arts, Culture, Recreation & Sport	114	162
Sales & Service	1,710	2,318
Trades, Transport & Equipment Operators & Related	2,426	43
Primary Industries	386	43
Processing, Mfg. & Utilities	1,104	74

LEVEL OF SCHOOLING

2001 Estimates:

Population 15 years +	25,379
Less than Grade 9	4,245
Grades 9-13 w/o Certif.	4,629
Grade 9-13 with Certif.	5,197
Trade Certif./Dip.	2,059
Non-Univ. w/o Certif./Dip.	1,683
Non-Univ. with Certif./Dip.	4,073
Univ. w/o Degree	1,366
Univ. w/o Degree/Certif.	160
Univ. with Certif.	1,206
Univ. with Degree	2,127

AVERAGE HOUSEHOLD EXPENDITURES

2001 Estimates:

Food	$6,027
Shelter	$7,003
Clothing	$1,927
Transportation	$5,322
Health & Personal Care	$1,770
Recr'n, Read'g & Education	$2,939
Taxes & Securities	$12,684
Other	$6,751
Total Expenditures	$44,423

PRIVATE HOUSEHOLDS

2001 Estimates:

Private Households, Total	12,042
Pop. in Private Households	30,313
Average no. per Household	2.5

FAMILIES

2001 Estimates:

Families in Private Households	9,208
Husband-Wife Families	7,840
Lone-Parent Families	1,368
Aver. No. Persons per Family	3.1
Aver. No. Sons/Daughters at Home	1.3

HOUSING

2001 Estimates:

Occupied Private Dwellings	12,042
Owned	7,707
Rented	4,335
Single-Detached House	6,236
Semi-Detached House	474
Row Houses	175
Apartment, 5+ Storeys	11
Apartment, 5 or Fewer Storeys	3,068
Apartment, Detached Duplex	1,971
Other Single-Attached	21
Movable Dwellings	86

VEHICLES

2001 Estimates:

Model Yrs. '81-'96, No.	15,126
% Total	81.33
Model Yrs. '97-'98, No.	2,130
% Total	11.45
'99 Vehicles registered in Model Yr. '99, No.	1,342
% Total	7.22
Total No. '81-'99	18,598

LEGAL MARITAL STATUS

2001 Estimates: (Age 15+)

Single (Never Married)	9,139
Legally Married (Not Separated)	11,982
Legally Married (Separated)	501
Widowed	1,500
Divorced	2,257

PSYTE CATEGORIES

2001 Estimates	No. of House -holds	% of Total Hhds.	Index
Participation Quebec	1,369	11.37	395
Quebec Melange	2,551	21.18	799
Traditional French Cdn. Families	3,533	29.34	1,093
Quebec's Heartland	150	1.25	127
Quebec Town Elders	4,037	33.52	1,186
Quebec's New Urban Mosaic	402	3.34	139

FINANCIAL P$YTE

2001 Estimates	No. of House -holds	% of Total Hhds.	Index
Mortgages & Minivans	1,369	11.37	172
Country Credit	6,084	50.52	747
Rural Family Blues	150	1.25	15
Loan Parent Stress	4,037	33.52	576
NSF	402	3.34	94

HOME LANGUAGE

2001 Estimates:		% Total
English	91	0.30
French	30,571	99.36
Other Languages	10	0.03
Multiple Responses	97	0.32
Total	30,769	100.00

BUILDING PERMITS

	1999	1998	1997
		$000	
Value	24,093	39,405	22,439

HOMES BUILT

	1999	1998	1997
No.	94	125	114

TAXATION

Income Class:	1997	% Total
Under $5,000	3,410	15.62
$5,000-$10,000	3,550	16.26
$10,000-$15,000	3,170	14.52
$15,000-$20,000	2,000	9.16
$20,000-$25,000	1,680	7.70
$25,000-$30,000	1,680	7.70
$30,000-$40,000	2,350	10.77
$40,000-$50,000	1,600	7.33
$50,000 +	2,410	11.04
Total Returns, No.	21,830	
Total Income, $000	512,555	
Total Taxable Returns	14,230	
Total Tax, $000	59,321	
Average Income, $	23,479	
Average Tax, $	4,169	

VITAL STATISTICS

	1997	1996	1995	1994
Births	291	322	306	333
Deaths	154	178	166	192
Natural Increase	137	144	140	141
Marriages	101	119	124	113

Note: Latest available data.

COMMUNITY NEWSPAPER(S)

	Total Circulation
Alma: Le Lac-St-Jean	20,933

RADIO STATION(S)

	Power
CFGT	10,000w
CKYK-FM	50,000w

TELEVISION STATION(S)

CBMT
CIVV

Amos
(Ville)

In census division Abitibi.

POPULATION

July 1, 2001 Estimate	13,657
% Cdn. Total	0.04
% Change, '96 -'01	-1.45
Avg. Annual Growth Rate, %	-0.29
2003 Projected Population	13,536
2006 Projected Population	13,263
2001 Households Estimate	5,650
2003 Projected Households	5,724
2006 Projected Households	5,781

INCOME

% Above/Below National Average	-14
2001 Total Income Estimate	$247,370,000
% Cdn. Total	0.04
2001 Average Hhld. Income	$43,800
2001 Per Capita	$18,100
2003 Projected Total Income	$258,640,000
2006 Projected Total Income	$273,280,000

RETAIL SALES

% Above/Below National Average	+87
2001 Retail Sales Estimate	$228,400,000
% Cdn. Total	0.08
2001 per Household	$40,400
2001 per Capita	$16,700
2001 No. of Establishments	154
2003 Projected Retail Sales	$244,820,000
2006 Projected Retail Sales	$265,410,000

POPULATION

2001 Estimates:

Total		13,657
Male		6,780
Female		6,877

Age Groups	Male	Female
0-4	406	401
5-9	446	430
10-14	485	453
15-19	549	506
20-24	527	494
25-29	462	447
30-34	474	473
35-39	555	544
40-44	587	584
45-49	561	562
50-54	478	474
55-59	364	360
60-64	269	263
65-69	202	231
70+	415	655

DAYTIME POPULATION

2001 Estimates:

Working Population	10,404
At Home Population	7,381
Total	17,785

INCOME

2001 Estimates:

Avg. Household Income	$43,782
Avg. Family Income	$50,784
Per Capita Income	$18,113
Male:	
Avg. Employment Income	$30,582
Avg. Employment Income (Full Time)	$40,204
Female:	
Avg. Employment Income	$20,375
Avg. Employment Income (Full Time)	$29,210

DISPOSABLE & DISCRETIONARY INCOME

2001 Estimates: Per Hhld.

Disposable Income	$30,176
Discretionary Income 1 (minus Food & Shelter)	$18,968
Discretionary Income 2 (minus Food, Shelter, & Other Expenditures)	$12,084

LIQUID ASSETS

1999 Estimates: Per Hhld.

Equity Investments	$54,197
Interest Bearing Investments	$54,049
Total Liquid Assets	$108,246

CREDIT DATA

July 2000:

Pool of Credit	$72,370,514
Revolving Credit, No.	18,884
Fixed Loans, No.	7,184
Avg. Credit Limit, per Person	$7,692
Avg. Spent, per Person	$3,542
Satisfactory Ratings, No. per Person	2.53
Avg. No. of Cards, per Person	0.91

LABOUR FORCE

2001 Estimates:

Male:

In the Labour Force	3,802
Participation Rate	69.9
Employed	3,489
Unemployed	313
Unemployment Rate	8.2
Not in Labour Force	1,641

Female:

In the Labour Force	3,048
Participation Rate	54.5
Employed	2,839
Unemployed	209
Unemployment Rate	6.9
Not in Labour Force	2,545

OCCUPATIONS BY MAJOR GROUPS

2001 Estimates:

	Male	Female
Management	458	136
Business, Finance & Admin.	388	804
Natural & Applied Sciences & Related	214	40
Health	113	418
Social Sciences, Gov't Services & Religion	43	98
Education	103	233
Arts, Culture, Recreation & Sport	26	62
Sales & Service	750	1,029
Trades, Transport & Equipment Operators & Related	946	n.a.
Primary Industries	372	86
Processing, Mfg. & Utilities	365	20

LEVEL OF SCHOOLING

2001 Estimates:

Population 15 years +	11,036
Less than Grade 9	2,209
Grades 9-13 w/o Certif.	2,279
Grade 9-13 with Certif.	2,232
Trade Certif./Dip.	562
Non-Univ. w/o Certif./Dip.	701
Non-Univ. with Certif./Dip.	1,485
Univ. w/o Degree	622
Univ. w/o Degree/Certif.	53
Univ. with Certif.	569
Univ. with Degree	946

AVERAGE HOUSEHOLD EXPENDITURES

2001 Estimates:

Food	$5,885
Shelter	$6,866
Clothing	$1,879
Transportation	$5,253
Health & Personal Care	$1,711
Recr'n, Read'g & Education	$2,980
Taxes & Securities	$12,135
Other	$6,715
Total Expenditures	$43,424

PRIVATE HOUSEHOLDS

2001 Estimates:

Private Households, Total	5,650
Pop. in Private Households	13,372
Average no. per Household	2.4

FAMILIES

2001 Estimates:

Families in Private Households	3,997
Husband-Wife Families	3,348
Lone-Parent Families	649
Aver. No. Persons per Family	3.0
Aver. No. Sons/Daughters at Home	1.2

HOUSING

2001 Estimates:

Occupied Private Dwellings	5,650
Owned	3,133
Rented	2,517
Single-Detached House	2,986
Semi-Detached House	150
Row Houses	175
Apartment, 5 or Fewer Storeys	1,465
Apartment, Detached Duplex	804
Other Single-Attached	48
Movable Dwellings	22

VEHICLES

2001 Estimates:

Model Yrs. '81-'96, No.	7,124
% Total	80.23
Model Yrs. '97-'98, No.	1,132
% Total	12.75
'99 Vehicles registered in Model Yr. '99, No.	624
% Total	7.03
Total No. '81-'99	8,880

LEGAL MARITAL STATUS

2001 Estimates: (Age 15+)

Single (Never Married)	4,758
Legally Married (Not Separated)	4,316
Legally Married (Separated)	334
Widowed	678
Divorced	950

PSYTE CATEGORIES

2001 Estimates	No. of House-holds	% of Total Hhds.	Index
Participation Quebec	422	7.47	259
Quebec Melange	1,612	28.53	1,077
Traditional French Cdn. Families	1,334	23.61	879
Big Country Families	432	7.65	536
Quebec Rural Blues	37	0.65	27
Quebec Town Elders	1,766	31.26	1,106

FINANÇIAL P$YTE

2001 Estimates	No. of House-holds	% of Total Hhds.	Index
Mortgages & Minivans	422	7.47	113
Country Credit	2,946	52.14	771
Rural Family Blues	469	8.30	103
Loan Parent Stress	1,766	31.26	537

Québec

HOME LANGUAGE

2001 Estimates:		% Total
English	86	0.63
French	13,510	98.92
Multiple Responses	61	0.45
Total	13,657	100.00

BUILDING PERMITS

	1999	1998	1997
		$000	
Value	8,680	11,895	9,680

HOMES BUILT

	1999	1998	1997
No	34	34	49

TAXATION

Income Class:	1997	% Total
Under $5,000	1,320	12.75
$5,000-$10,000	1,560	15.07
$10,000-$15,000	1,650	15.94
$15,000-$20,000	980	9.47
$20,000-$25,000	780	7.54
$25,000-$30,000	860	8.31
$30,000-$40,000	1,310	12.66
$40,000-$50,000	800	7.73
$50,000 +	1,100	10.63
Total Returns, No.	10,350	
Total Income, $000	255,263	
Total Taxable Returns	6,890	
Total Tax, $000	29,259	
Average Income, $	24,663	
Average Tax, $	4,247	

VITAL STATISTICS

	1997	1996	1995	1994
Births	182	196	179	204
Deaths	95	91	112	98
Natural Increase	87	105	67	106
Marriages	42	62	60	40

Note: Latest available data.

COMMUNITY NEWSPAPER(S)

	Total Circulation
Amos, La Sarre, Malartic, Matagami, Val-d'Or: Échos Abitibiens	8,355

RADIO STATION(S)

	Power
CHAD	1,000w

TELEVISION STATION(S)

CFEM-TV
CKRN-TV

Québec

Baie-Comeau
(Census Agglomeration)

The Census Agglomeration of Baie-Comeau includes: Baie-Comeau, V; Chute-aux-Outardes, VL; Franquelin, M; Pointe-Lebel, VL; and Ragueneau, P. All are in census division Manicouagan.

POPULATION

July 1, 2001 Estimate	31,033
% Cdn. Total	0.10
% Change, '96-'01	-4.08
Avg. Annual Growth Rate, %	-0.83
2003 Projected Population	30,820
2006 Projected Population	30,277
2001 Households Estimate	12,440
2003 Projected Households	12,657
2006 Projected Households	12,865

INCOME

% Above/Below National Average	+3
2001 Total Income Estimate	$673,360,000
% Cdn. Total	0.10
2001 Average Hhld. Income	$54,100
2001 Per Capita	$21,700
2003 Projected Total Income	$707,530,000
2006 Projected Total Income	$754,660,000

RETAIL SALES

% Above/Below National Average	-18
2001 Retail Sales Estimate	$228,340,000
% Cdn. Total	0.08
2001 per Household	$18,400
2001 per Capita	$7,400
2001 No. of Establishments	267
2003 Projected Retail Sales	$244,000,000
2006 Projected Retail Sales	$263,540,000

POPULATION

2001 Estimates:

Total	31,033
Male	15,893
Female	15,140

Age Groups	Male	Female
0-4	909	867
5-9	977	894
10-14	1,076	943
15-19	1,201	1,050
20-24	1,180	1,064
25-29	1,048	981
30-34	1,131	1,104
35-39	1,350	1,361
40-44	1,434	1,407
45-49	1,346	1,263
50-54	1,173	1,083
55-59	963	888
60-64	752	702
65-69	551	540
70+	802	993

DAYTIME POPULATION

2001 Estimates:

Working Population	15,413
At Home Population	15,620
Total	31,033

INCOME

2001 Estimates:

Avg. Household Income	$54,129
Avg. Family Income	$59,505
Per Capita Income	$21,698
Male:	
Avg. Employment Income	$39,757
Avg. Employment Income (Full Time)	$49,250
Female:	
Avg. Employment Income	$19,704
Avg. Employment Income (Full Time)	$29,248

DISPOSABLE & DISCRETIONARY INCOME

2001 Estimates:	Per Hhld.
Disposable Income	$36,880
Discretionary Income 1 (minus Food & Shelter)	$23,953
Discretionary Income 2 (minus Food, Shelter, & Other Expenditures)	$15,508

LIQUID ASSETS

1999 Estimates:	Per Hhld.
Equity Investments	$66,677
Interest Bearing Investments	$66,174
Total Liquid Assets	$132,851

CREDIT DATA

July 2000:

Pool of Credit	$215,338,696
Revolving Credit, No.	49,936
Fixed Loans, No.	24,685
Avg. Credit Limit, per Person	$9,476
Avg. Spent, per Person	$4,615
Satisfactory Ratings, No. per Person	2.98
Avg. No. of Cards, per Person	1.06

LABOUR FORCE

2001 Estimates:

Male:	
In the Labour Force	9,853
Participation Rate	76.2
Employed	9,111
Unemployed	742
Unemployment Rate	7.5
Not in Labour Force	3,078
Female:	
In the Labour Force	6,810
Participation Rate	54.8
Employed	6,318
Unemployed	492
Unemployment Rate	7.2
Not in Labour Force	5,626

OCCUPATIONS BY MAJOR GROUPS

2001 Estimates:	Male	Female
Management	686	451
Business, Finance & Admin.	607	1,874
Natural & Applied Sciences & Related	812	90
Health	139	789
Social Sciences, Gov't Services & Religion	128	257
Education	235	458
Arts, Culture, Recreation & Sport	57	61
Sales & Service	1,473	2,355
Trades, Transport & Equipment Operators & Related	3,131	106
Primary Industries	206	19
Processing, Mfg. & Utilities	2,111	71

LEVEL OF SCHOOLING

2001 Estimates:

Population 15 years +	25,367
Less than Grade 9	3,993
Grades 9-13 w/o Certif.	4,592
Grade 9-13 with Certif.	5,119
Trade Certif./Dip.	1,469
Non-Univ. w/o Certif./Dip.	1,944
Non-Univ. with Certif./Dip.	5,267
Univ. w/o Degree	1,159
Univ. w/o Degree/Certif.	81
Univ. with Certif.	1,078
Univ. with Degree	1,824

AVERAGE HOUSEHOLD EXPENDITURES

2001 Estimates:

Food	$6,778
Shelter	$7,999
Clothing	$2,287
Transportation	$6,536
Health & Personal Care	$2,080
Recr'n, Read'g & Education	$3,444
Taxes & Securities	$15,072
Other	$7,751
Total Expenditures	$51,947

PRIVATE HOUSEHOLDS

2001 Estimates:

Private Households, Total	12,440
Pop. in Private Households	30,543
Average no. per Household	2.5

FAMILIES

2001 Estimates:

Families in Private Households	9,596
Husband-Wife Families	8,334
Lone-Parent Families	1,262
Aver. No. Persons per Family	3.0
Aver. No. Sons/Daughters at Home	1.2

HOUSING

2001 Estimates:

Occupied Private Dwellings	12,440
Owned	8,616
Rented	3,824
Single-Detached House	6,123
Semi-Detached House	650
Row Houses	260
Apartment, 5+ Storeys	130
Apartment, 5 or Fewer Storeys	2,767
Apartment, Detached Duplex	908
Other Single-Attached	26
Movable Dwellings	1,576

VEHICLES

2001 Estimates:

Model Yrs. '81-'96, No.	16,469
% Total	78.13
Model Yrs. '97-'98, No.	2,849
% Total	13.52
'99 Vehicles registered in Model Yr. '99, No.	1,761
% Total	8.35
Total No. '81-'99	21,079

LEGAL MARITAL STATUS

2001 Estimates: (Age 15+)

Single (Never Married)	10,694
Legally Married (Not Separated)	11,060
Legally Married (Separated)	446
Widowed	1,100
Divorced	2,067

PSYTE CATEGORIES

2001 Estimates	No. of House-holds	% of Total Hhds.	Index
Participation Quebec	3,060	24.60	854
Quebec Melange	5,056	40.64	1,534
Traditional French Cdn. Families	1,613	12.97	483
Big Country Families	385	3.09	217
Quebec Rural Blues	361	2.90	119
Quebec Town Elders	1,947	15.65	554

FINANCIAL P$YTE

2001 Estimates	No. of House-holds	% of Total Hhds.	Index
Mortgages & Minivans	3,060	24.60	373
Country Credit	6,669	53.61	793
Rural Family Blues	746	6.00	74
Loan Parent Stress	1,947	15.65	269

HOME LANGUAGE

2001 Estimates:		% Total
English	138	0.44
French	30,763	99.13
Montagnais-Naskapi	26	0.08
Multiple Responses	106	0.34
Total	31,033	100.00

BUILDING PERMITS

	1999	1998	1997
		$000	
Value	10,654	20,005	24,472

HOMES BUILT

	1999	1998	1997
No.	28	53	68

TAXATION

Income Class:	1997	% Total
Under $5,000	3,070	13.63
$5,000-$10,000	2,920	12.97
$10,000-$15,000	2,820	12.52
$15,000-$20,000	1,760	7.82
$20,000-$25,000	1,470	6.53
$25,000-$30,000	1,500	6.66
$30,000-$40,000	2,380	10.57
$40,000-$50,000	2,180	9.68
$50,000 +	4,450	19.76
Total Returns, No.	22,520	
Total Income, $000	645,240	
Total Taxable Returns	16,130	
Total Tax, $000	82,362	
Average Income, $	28,652	
Average Tax, $	5,106	

VITAL STATISTICS

	1997	1996	1995	1994
Births	319	363	385	358
Deaths	151	150	162	139
Natural Increase	168	213	223	219
Marriages	78	67	70	84

Note: Latest available data.

COMMUNITY NEWSPAPER(S)

	Total Circulation
Baie-Comeau: Baie-Comeau-Objectif Plein Jour	15,853
Baie-Comeau: Baie-Comeau-Plein Jour sur la Manicouagan	15,273

RADIO STATION(S)

	Power
CBMI-FM	n.a.
CBSI-FM	n.a.
CFRP	1,000w
CHLC-FM	10,000w

TELEVISION STATION(S)

CBMT-TV
CBST-TV
CFER-TV

Chicoutimi-Jonquière
(Census Metropolitan Area)

POPULATION

July 1, 2001 Estimate	162,509
% Cdn. Total	0.52
% Change, '96 -'01	-0.27
Avg. Annual Growth Rate, %	-0.05
2003 Projected Population	164,041
2006 Projected Population	166,235
2001 Households Estimate	64,706
2003 Projected Households	66,605
2006 Projected Households	69,243

INCOME

% Above/Below National Average	-17
2001 Total Income Estimate	$2,829,080,000
% Cdn. Total	0.43
2001 Average Hhld. Income	$43,700
2001 Per Capita	$17,400
2003 Projected Total Income	$3,006,560,000
2006 Projected Total Income	$3,276,680,000

RETAIL SALES

% Above/Below National Average	+1
2001 Retail Sales Estimate	$1,474,900,000
% Cdn. Total	0.53
2001 per Household	$22,800
2001 per Capita	$9,100
2001 No. of Establishments	1,357
2003 Projected Retail Sales	$1,605,700,000
2006 Projected Retail Sales	$1,800,160,000

POPULATION

2001 Estimates:

Total		162,509
Male		80,070
Female		82,439

Age Groups	Male	Female
0-4	4,424	4,233
5-9	4,781	4,565
10-14	5,408	5,060
15-19	6,377	5,866
20-24	6,190	5,661
25-29	5,127	4,807
30-34	5,203	5,176
35-39	6,345	6,475
40-44	7,032	7,148
45-49	6,792	6,721
50-54	5,885	5,832
55-59	4,594	4,731
60-64	3,614	4,009
65-69	2,938	3,640
70+	5,360	8,515

DAYTIME POPULATION

2001 Estimates:

Working Population	70,303
At Home Population	92,206
Total	162,509

INCOME

2001 Estimates:

Avg. Household Income	$43,722
Avg. Family Income	$49,698
Per Capita Income	$17,409
Male:	
Avg. Employment Income	$33,041
Avg. Employment Income (Full Time)	$44,256
Female:	
Avg. Employment Income	$18,285
Avg. Employment Income (Full Time)	$29,347

DISPOSABLE & DISCRETIONARY INCOME

2001 Estimates:	Per Hhld.
Disposable Income	$30,103
Discretionary Income 1 (minus Food & Shelter)	$19,074
Discretionary Income 2 (minus Food, Shelter, & Other Expenditures)	$12,262

LIQUID ASSETS

1999 Estimates:	Per Hhld.
Equity Investments	$48,879
Interest Bearing Investments	$52,230
Total Liquid Assets	$101,109

CREDIT DATA

July 2000:

Pool of Credit	$1,001,581,724
Revolving Credit, No.	309,831
Fixed Loans, No.	110,280
Avg. Credit Limit, per Person	$8,213
Avg. Spent, per Person	$3,629
Satisfactory Ratings, No. per Person	3.23
Avg. No. of Cards, per Person	1.14

LABOUR FORCE

2001 Estimates:

Male:	
In the Labour Force	45,497
Participation Rate	69.5
Employed	41,219
Unemployed	4,278
Unemployment Rate	9.4
Not in Labour Force	19,960
Female:	
In the Labour Force	32,078
Participation Rate	46.8
Employed	28,999
Unemployed	3,079
Unemployment Rate	9.6
Not in Labour Force	36,503

OCCUPATIONS BY MAJOR GROUPS

2001 Estimates:	Male	Female
Management	3,965	1,541
Business, Finance & Admin.	3,477	9,056
Natural & Applied Sciences & Related	3,469	424
Health	1,134	3,033
Social Sciences, Gov't Services & Religion	798	806
Education	2,070	2,178
Arts, Culture, Recreation & Sport	888	781
Sales & Service	9,814	11,347
Trades, Transport & Equipment Operators & Related	11,284	333
Primary Industries	1,290	158
Processing, Mfg. & Utilities	5,116	488

LEVEL OF SCHOOLING

2001 Estimates:

Population 15 years +	134,038
Less than Grade 9	19,797
Grades 9-13 w/o Certif.	22,618
Grade 9-13 with Certif.	25,171
Trade Certif. /Dip.	10,773
Non-Univ. w/o Certif./Dip.	9,610
Non-Univ. with Certif./Dip.	23,696
Univ. w/o Degree	9,450
Univ. w/o Degree/Certif.	1,119
Univ. with Certif.	8,331
Univ. with Degree	12,923

AVERAGE HOUSEHOLD EXPENDITURES

2001 Estimates:

Food	$5,755
Shelter	$6,848
Clothing	$1,886
Transportation	$5,194
Health & Personal Care	$1,723
Recr'n, Read'g & Education	$2,861
Taxes & Securities	$12,448
Other	$6,535
Total Expenditures	$43,250

PRIVATE HOUSEHOLDS

2001 Estimates:

Private Households, Total	64,706
Pop. in Private Households	159,395
Average no. per Household	2.5

FAMILIES

2001 Estimates:

Families in Private Households	48,638
Husband-Wife Families	41,409
Lone-Parent Families	7,229
Aver. No. Persons per Family	3.0
Aver. No. Sons/Daughters at Home	1.2

HOUSING

2001 Estimates:

Occupied Private Dwellings	64,706
Owned	39,393
Rented	25,313
Single-Detached House	31,477
Semi-Detached House	3,617
Row Houses	1,714
Apartment, 5+ Storeys	1,026
Owned Apartment, 5+ Storeys	22
Apartment, 5 or Fewer Storeys	15,898
Apartment, Detached Duplex	10,268
Other Single-Attached	312
Movable Dwellings	394

VEHICLES

2001 Estimates:

Model Yrs. '81-'96, No.	74,338
% Total	78.76
Model Yrs. '97-'98, No.	12,602
% Total	13.35
'99 Vehicles registered in Model Yr. '99, No.	7,445
% Total	7.89
Total No. '81-'99	94,385

LEGAL MARITAL STATUS

2001 Estimates: (Age 15+)

Single (Never Married)	48,188
Legally Married (Not Separated)	63,571
Legally Married (Separated)	2,771
Widowed	8,454
Divorced	11,054

PSYTE CATEGORIES

2001 Estimates	No. of House-holds	% of Total Hhds.	Index
Urban Gentry	569	0.88	49
Stable Suburban Families	523	0.81	62
Old Towns' New Fringe	383	0.59	15
Participation Quebec	10,970	16.95	588
New Quebec Rows	249	0.38	35
Quebec Melange	14,279	22.07	833
Traditional French Cdn. Families	13,712	21.19	789
Quebec Rural Blues	1,030	1.59	65
Old Quebec Walkups	1,490	2.30	126
Quebec Town Elders	16,425	25.38	898
Aging Quebec Urbanites	406	0.63	217
Quebec's New Urban Mosaic	3,917	6.05	251
Aged Pensioners	414	0.64	48

Québec

FINANCIAL P$YTE

2001 Estimates	No. of House-holds	% of Total Hhds.	Index
Four Star Investors	569	0.88	18
Successful Suburbanites	523	0.81	12
Mortgages & Minivans	11,219	17.34	263
Tractors & Tradelines	383	0.59	10
Country Credit	27,991	43.26	640
Rural Family Blues	1,030	1.59	20
Loan Parent Stress	18,321	28.31	486
NSF	3,917	6.05	171
Senior Survivors	414	0.64	34

HOME LANGUAGE

2001 Estimates:		% Total
English	883	0.54
French	160,946	99.04
Other Languages	137	0.08
Multiple Responses	543	0.33
Total	162,509	100.00

BUILDING PERMITS

	1999	1998	1997
		$000	
Value	155,679	155,074	151,068

HOMES BUILT

	1999	1998	1997
No.	351	508	476

TAXATION

Income Class:	1997	% Total
Under $5,000	18,320	16.04
$5,000-$10,000	17,130	15.00
$10,000-$15,000	16,640	14.57
$15,000-$20,000	10,240	8.97
$20,000-$25,000	8,360	7.32
$25,000-$30,000	8,250	7.22
$30,000-$40,000	12,060	10.56
$40,000-$50,000	8,890	7.78
$50,000 +	14,330	12.55
Total Returns, No.	114,210	
Total Income, $000	2,764,420	
Total Taxable Returns	74,730	
Total Tax, $000	327,022	
Average Income, $	24,205	
Average Tax, $	4,376	

VITAL STATISTICS

	1997	1996	1995	1994
Births	1,576	1,689	1,755	1,801
Deaths	1,149	1,155	1,088	1,139
Natural Increase	427	534	667	662
Marriages	516	553	574	514

Note: Latest available data.

Chicoutimi-Jonquière
(Census Metropolitan Area)
(Cont'd)

DAILY NEWSPAPER(S)

	Circulation Average Paid
Le Quotidien	29,111

COMMUNITY NEWSPAPER(S)

	Total Circulation
Chicoutimi, Jonquière, La Baie: Le Réveil	69,092
Chicoutimi, Jonquière, La Baie, Lac-Saint-Jean area: Le Progrès Dimanche	45,440

RADIO STATION DATA

Station	Market	Format	Wkly. Reach%*	Aver. Hrs. Tuned
All Stations			92	21.6
CBJ-FM	Chicoutimi-Jonquière	News, Talk	9	11.9
CBJX-FM	Chicoutimi-Jonquière	Classical, Jazz,	3	10.9
CFIX-FM	Chicoutimi-Jonquière	Adult Contemp.	41	11.0
CFQR-FM	Montréal	Adult Contemp.	n.a.	n.a.
CIKI-FM	Rimouski	Pop, Rock	n.a.	n.a.
CJAB-FM	Chicoutimi-Jonquière	Contemp. Hits	51	11.9
CKAC	Montréal	Multi-format	1	21.6
CKAJ-FM	Chicoutimi-Jonquière		11	11.2
CKMN-FM	Rimouski	Multi-format	-	32.5
CKOI-FM	Montréal	Contemp. Hit Radio	1	10.1
CKRS	Chicoutimi-Jonquière	News, Talk, Sports	33	15.1

BBM Spring 2000 Radio Reach Survey; area coverage
*Mon-Sun 5a.m - 1a.m , All Persons 12+

TV STATION DATA

Station	Market	Network Affiliation	Wkly. Reach%*	Aver. Hrs. Tuned
All Stations			98	32.3
CANALD	n.a.	n.a.	19	3.2
CBFT	Montréal	SRC	4	6.5
CBMT	Montréal	CBC	n.a.	n.a.
CFER	Rimouski	TVA	1	30.0
CFJP	Montréal-Rimouski	TQS	5	4.8
CFRS	Chicoutimi	TQS	75	6.2
CIVM	Montréal	Télé-Qué.	24	2.7
CIVV	Jonquière	Télé-Qué.	n.a.	n.a.
CJPM	Chicoutimi	TVA	83	11.9
CKTV	Jonquière	SRC	83	8.4
CPTM	Montréal	n.a.	3	17.9
ECRAN	n.a.	n.a.	9	4.8
FAMILE	n.a.	n.a.	23	3.9
HIST(FR)	n.a.	Ind.	6	3.1
LCN	n.a.	n.a.	9	2.0
OTHERS	n.a.	n.a.	12	2.0
RDI	n.a.	n.a.	13	2.4
RDS	n.a.	Ind.	14	4.1
SERIES	n.a.	Ind.	11	3.2
TOON(FR)	n.a.	Ind.	25	3.7
VCR	n.a.	n.a.	17	4.6
VIE	n.a.	n.a.	18	2.7
WCAX	Burlington VT	CBS	7	2.6

BBM Spring 2000 TV Reach Survey; CMA coverage.
*Mon-Sun 6a.m - 2a.m , All Persons 2 +

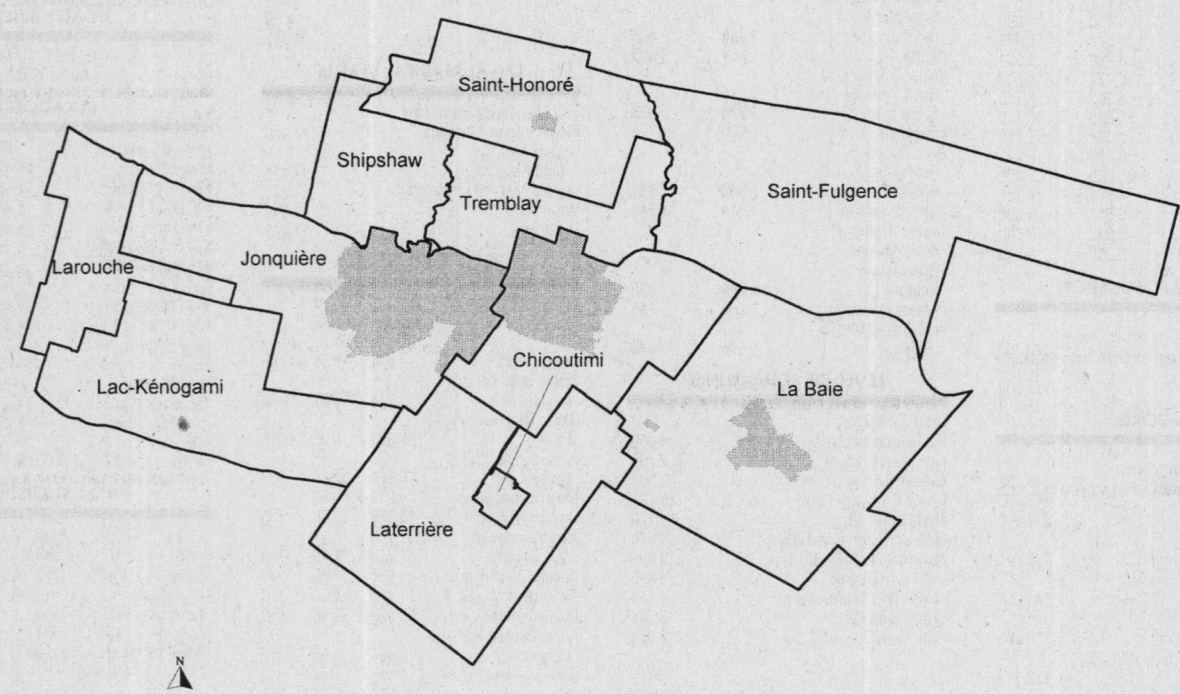

Urban Areas

Chicoutimi

(Ville)

Chicoutimi-Jonquière CMA

In census division Le Fjord-du-Saguenay.

POPULATION

July 1, 2001 Estimate	64,313
% Cdn. Total	0.21
% Change, '96 -'01	0.43
Avg. Annual Growth Rate, %	0.09
2003 Projected Population	65,134
2006 Projected Population	66,328
2001 Households Estimate	26,243
2003 Projected Households	27,107
2006 Projected Households	28,318

INCOME

% Above/Below National Average	-14
2001 Total Income Estimate	$1,166,280,000
% Cdn. Total	0.18
2001 Average Hhld. Income	$44,400
2001 Per Capita	$18,100
2003 Projected Total Income	$1,245,150,000
2006 Projected Total Income	$1,365,620,000

RETAIL SALES

% Above/Below National Average	+65
2001 Retail Sales Estimate	$951,180,000
% Cdn. Total	0.34
2001 per Household	$36,200
2001 per Capita	$14,800
2001 No. of Establishments	703
2003 Projected Retail Sales	$1,043,560,000
2006 Projected Retail Sales	$1,180,690,000

POPULATION

2001 Estimates:

Total		64,313
Male		31,334
Female		32,979
Age Groups	Male	Female
0-4	1,762	1,668
5-9	1,849	1,762
10-14	2,099	1,949
15-19	2,478	2,261
20-24	2,461	2,275
25-29	2,161	2,007
30-34	2,159	2,111
35-39	2,466	2,535
40-44	2,685	2,803
45-49	2,606	2,699
50-54	2,285	2,362
55-59	1,778	1,912
60-64	1,395	1,610
65-69	1,119	1,479
70+	2,031	3,546

DAYTIME POPULATION

2001 Estimates:

Working Population	31,774
At Home Population	35,552
Total	67,326

INCOME

2001 Estimates:

Avg. Household Income	$44,441
Avg. Family Income	$51,967
Per Capita Income	$18,134
Male:	
Avg. Employment Income	$33,979
Avg. Employment Income (Full Time)	$45,444
Female:	
Avg. Employment Income	$19,391
Avg. Employment Income (Full Time)	$30,025

DISPOSABLE & DISCRETIONARY INCOME

2001 Estimates: *Per Hhld.*

Disposable Income	$30,273
Discretionary Income 1 (minus Food & Shelter)	$19,075
Discretionary Income 2 (minus Food, Shelter, & Other Expenditures)	$12,299

LIQUID ASSETS

1999 Estimates: *Per Hhld.*

Equity Investments	$52,834
Interest Bearing Investments	$53,881
Total Liquid Assets	$106,715

CREDIT DATA

July 2000:

Pool of Credit	$442,534,247
Revolving Credit, No.	130,256
Fixed Loans, No.	46,346
Avg. Credit Limit, per Person	$8,604
Avg. Spent, per Person	$3,794
Satisfactory Ratings, No. per Person	3.24
Avg. No. of Cards, per Person	1.15

LABOUR FORCE

2001 Estimates:

Male:

In the Labour Force	17,966
Participation Rate	70.1
Employed	16,354
Unemployed	1,612
Unemployment Rate	9.0
Not in Labour Force	7,658

Female:

In the Labour Force	13,595
Participation Rate	49.3
Employed	12,459
Unemployed	1,136
Unemployment Rate	8.4
Not in Labour Force	14,005

OCCUPATIONS BY MAJOR GROUPS

2001 Estimates:

	Male	Female
Management	1,867	686
Business, Finance & Admin.	1,629	3,735
Natural & Applied Sciences & Related	1,203	168
Health	672	1,428
Social Sciences, Gov't Services & Religion	473	400
Education	892	1,055
Arts, Culture, Recreation & Sport	439	298
Sales & Service	4,248	4,695
Trades, Transport & Equipment Operators & Related	3,838	129
Primary Industries	404	51
Processing, Mfg. & Utilities	1,423	164

LEVEL OF SCHOOLING

2001 Estimates:

Population 15 years +	53,224
Less than Grade 9	7,258
Grades 9-13 w/o Certif.	8,675
Grade 9-13 with Certif.	10,523
Trade Certif. /Dip.	3,760
Non-Univ. w/o Certif./Dip.	3,755
Non-Univ. with Certif./Dip.	8,229
Univ. w/o Degree	4,288
Univ. w/o Degree/Certif.	432
Univ. with Certif.	3,856
Univ. with Degree	6,736

AVERAGE HOUSEHOLD EXPENDITURES

2001 Estimates:

Food	$5,750
Shelter	$7,099
Clothing	$1,905
Transportation	$5,088
Health & Personal Care	$1,754
Recr'n, Read'g & Education	$2,897
Taxes & Securities	$12,725
Other	$6,654
Total Expenditures	$43,872

PRIVATE HOUSEHOLDS

2001 Estimates:

Private Households, Total	26,243
Pop. in Private Households	62,569
Average no. per Household	2.4

FAMILIES

2001 Estimates:

Families in Private Households	19,011
Husband-Wife Families	15,896
Lone-Parent Families	3,115
Aver. No. Persons per Family	3.0
Aver. No. Sons/Daughters at Home	1.2

HOUSING

2001 Estimates:

Occupied Private Dwellings	26,243
Owned	14,466
Rented	11,777
Single-Detached House	11,511
Semi-Detached House	1,263
Row Houses	829
Apartment, 5+ Storeys	747
Owned Apartment, 5+ Storeys	11
Apartment, 5 or Fewer Storeys	7,634
Apartment, Detached Duplex	4,048
Other Single-Attached	138
Movable Dwellings	73

VEHICLES

2001 Estimates:

Model Yrs. '81-'96, No.	28,236
% Total	74.75
Model Yrs. '97-'98, No.	5,844
% Total	15.47
'99 Vehicles registered in Model Yr. '99, No.	3,693
% Total	9.78
Total No. '81-'99	37,773

LEGAL MARITAL STATUS

2001 Estimates: (Age 15+)

Single (Never Married)	19,975
Legally Married (Not Separated)	23,929
Legally Married (Separated)	1,241
Widowed	3,512
Divorced	4,567

PSYTE CATEGORIES

2001 Estimates	No. of House-holds	% of Total Hhds.	Index
Urban Gentry	569	2.17	121
Stable Suburban Families	465	1.77	136
Participation Quebec	4,989	19.01	660
New Quebec Rows	201	0.77	70
Quebec Melange	5,771	21.99	830
Traditional French Cdn. Families	2,887	11.00	410
Quebec Rural Blues	124	0.47	19
Old Quebec Walkups	1,490	5.68	310
Quebec Town Elders	5,497	20.95	741
Aging Quebec Urbanites	406	1.55	536
Quebec's New Urban Mosaic	3,341	12.73	528
Aged Pensioners	298	1.14	85

Québec

FINANCIAL P$YTE

2001 Estimates	No. of House-holds	% of Total Hhds.	Index
Four Star Investors	569	2.17	43
Successful Suburbanites	465	1.77	27
Mortgages & Minivans	5,190	19.78	300
Country Credit	8,658	32.99	488
Rural Family Blues	124	0.47	6
Loan Parent Stress	7,393	28.17	484
NSF	3,341	12.73	360
Senior Survivors	298	1.14	60

HOME LANGUAGE

2001 Estimates:		% Total
English	213.	0.33
French	63,884.	99.33
Other Languages	77.	0.12
Multiple Responses	139.	0.22
Total	64,313.	100.00

BUILDING PERMITS

	1999	1998	1997
		$000	
Value	34,257	72,191	55,089

HOMES BUILT

	1999	1998	1997
No.	119	135	107

TAXATION

Income Class:	1997	% Total
Under $5,000	7,210	15.14
$5,000-$10,000	7,280	15.29
$10,000-$15,000	7,340	15.41
$15,000-$20,000	4,370	9.18
$20,000-$25,000	3,580	7.52
$25,000-$30,000	3,490	7.33
$30,000-$40,000	5,110	10.73
$40,000-$50,000	3,630	7.62
$50,000 +	5,610	11.78
Total Returns, No.	47,620	
Total Income, $000	1,170,489	
Total Taxable Returns	31,070	
Total Tax, $000	140,119	
Average Income, $.	24,580	
Average Tax, $.	4,510	

VITAL STATISTICS

	1997	1996	1995	1994
Births	599	631	689	678
Deaths	503	500	448	479
Natural Increase	96	131	241	199
Marriages	286	295	300	256

Note: Latest available data.

MEDIA INFO

see Chicoutimi-Jonquière, CMA

Québec

Jonquière
(Ville)
Chicoutimi-Jonquière CMA

In census division Le Fjord-du-Saguenay.

POPULATION

July 1, 2001 Estimate	56,211
% Cdn. Total	0.18
% Change, '96 -'01	-2.04
Avg. Annual Growth Rate, %	-0.41
2003 Projected Population	56,219
2006 Projected Population	56,211
2001 Households Estimate	22,964
2003 Projected Households	23,432
2006 Projected Households	24,043

INCOME

% Above/Below National Average	-19
2001 Total Income Estimate	$956,990,000
% Cdn. Total	0.15
2001 Average Hhld. Income	$41,700
2001 Per Capita	$17,000
2003 Projected Total Income	$1,002,790,000
2006 Projected Total Income	$1,069,960,000

RETAIL SALES

% Above/Below National Average	-22
2001 Retail Sales Estimate	$393,300,000
% Cdn. Total	0.14
2001 per Household	$17,100
2001 per Capita	$7,000
2001 No. of Establishments	409
2003 Projected Retail Sales	$421,800,000
2006 Projected Retail Sales	$463,500,000

POPULATION

2001 Estimates:

Total	56,211
Male	27,427
Female	28,784

Age Groups	Male	Female
0-4	1,424	1,351
5-9	1,535	1,437
10-14	1,756	1,623
15-19	2,152	1,992
20-24	2,124	1,925
25-29	1,652	1,553
30-34	1,581	1,623
35-39	2,029	2,134
40-44	2,393	2,453
45-49	2,361	2,343
50-54	2,066	2,098
55-59	1,656	1,761
60-64	1,351	1,550
65-69	1,142	1,451
70+	2,205	3,490

DAYTIME POPULATION

2001 Estimates:

Working Population	26,337
At Home Population	32,744
Total	59,081

INCOME

2001 Estimates:

Avg. Household Income	$41,674
Avg. Family Income	$47,784
Per Capita Income	$17,025
Male:	
Avg. Employment Income	$32,471
Avg. Employment Income (Full Time)	$44,040
Female:	
Avg. Employment Income	$17,909
Avg. Employment Income (Full Time)	$29,164

DISPOSABLE & DISCRETIONARY INCOME

2001 Estimates:	Per Hhld.
Disposable Income	$28,684
Discretionary Income 1 (minus Food & Shelter)	$18,120
Discretionary Income 2 (minus Food, Shelter, & Other Expenditures)	$11,701

LIQUID ASSETS

1999 Estimates:	Per Hhld.
Equity Investments	$44,223
Interest Bearing Investments	$49,945
Total Liquid Assets	$94,168

CREDIT DATA

July 2000:

Pool of Credit	$356,200,867
Revolving Credit, No.	116,639
Fixed Loans, No.	39,294
Avg. Credit Limit, per Person	$7,892
Avg. Spent, per Person	$3,449
Satisfactory Ratings, No. per Person	3.25
Avg. No. of Cards, per Person	1.13

LABOUR FORCE

2001 Estimates:

Male:	
In the Labour Force	15,319
Participation Rate	67.4
Employed	13,793
Unemployed	1,526
Unemployment Rate	10.0
Not in Labour Force	7,393
Female:	
In the Labour Force	10,852
Participation Rate	44.5
Employed	9,690
Unemployed	1,162
Unemployment Rate	10.7
Not in Labour Force	13,521

OCCUPATIONS BY MAJOR GROUPS

2001 Estimates:	Male	Female
Management	1,206	549
Business, Finance & Admin.	1,224	3,125
Natural & Applied Sciences & Related	1,379	161
Health	290	980
Social Sciences, Gov't Services & Religion	170	258
Education	798	715
Arts, Culture, Recreation & Sport	266	293
Sales & Service	3,067	3,732
Trades, Transport & Equipment Operators & Related	3,766	144
Primary Industries	330	28
Processing, Mfg. & Utilities	1,967	120

LEVEL OF SCHOOLING

2001 Estimates:

Population 15 years +	47,085
Less than Grade 9	7,223
Grades 9-13 w/o Certif.	7,507
Grade 9-13 with Certif.	7,943
Trade Certif. /Dip.	4,014
Non-Univ. w/o Certif./Dip.	3,436
Non-Univ. with Certif./Dip.	9,659
Univ. w/o Degree	3,258
Univ. w/o Degree/Certif.	397
Univ. with Certif.	2,861
Univ. with Degree	4,045

AVERAGE HOUSEHOLD EXPENDITURES

2001 Estimates:

Food	$5,478
Shelter	$6,561
Clothing	$1,774
Transportation	$4,815
Health & Personal Care	$1,676
Recr'n, Read'g & Education	$2,692
Taxes & Securities	$12,219
Other	$6,198
Total Expenditures	$41,413

PRIVATE HOUSEHOLDS

2001 Estimates:

Private Households, Total	22,964
Pop. in Private Households	55,350
Average no. per Household	2.4

FAMILIES

2001 Estimates:

Families in Private Households	16,980
Husband-Wife Families	14,272
Lone-Parent Families	2,708
Aver. No. Persons per Family	3.0
Aver. No. Sons/Daughters at Home	1.2

HOUSING

2001 Estimates:

Occupied Private Dwellings	22,964
Owned	13,907
Rented	9,057
Single-Detached House	10,749
Semi-Detached House	1,396
Row Houses	628
Apartment, 5+ Storeys	228
Owned Apartment, 5+ Storeys	11
Apartment, 5 or Fewer Storeys	5,782
Apartment, Detached Duplex	4,030
Other Single-Attached	130
Movable Dwellings	21

VEHICLES

2001 Estimates:

Model Yrs. '81-'96, No.	27,625
% Total	82.32
Model Yrs. '97-'98, No.	3,758
% Total	11.20
'99 Vehicles registered in Model Yr. '99, No.	2,175
% Total	6.48
Total No. '81-'99	33,558

LEGAL MARITAL STATUS

2001 Estimates: (Age 15+)

Single (Never Married)	16,589
Legally Married (Not Separated)	22,181
Legally Married (Separated)	917
Widowed	3,332
Divorced	4,066

PSYTE CATEGORIES

2001 Estimates	No. of House-holds	% of Total Hhds.	Index
Stable Suburban Families	58	0.25	19
Participation Quebec	4,776	20.80	722
New Quebec Rows	48	0.21	19
Quebec Melange	6,865	29.89	1,128
Traditional French Cdn. Families	1,537	6.69	249
Quebec Rural Blues	360	1.57	64
Quebec Town Elders	8,529	37.14	1,314
Quebec's New Urban Mosaic	576	2.51	104
Aged Pensioners	116	0.51	38

FINANCIAL PSYTE

2001 Estimates	No. of House-holds	% of Total Hhds.	Index
Successful Suburbanites	58	0.25	4
Mortgages & Minivans	4,824	21.01	318
Country Credit	8,402	36.59	541
Rural Family Blues	360	1.57	19
Loan Parent Stress	8,529	37.14	638
NSF	576	2.51	71
Senior Survivors	116	0.51	27

HOME LANGUAGE

2001 Estimates:		% Total
English	333	0.59
French	55,664	99.03
Other Languages	20	0.04
Multiple Responses	194	0.35
Total	56,211	100.00

BUILDING PERMITS

	1999	1998	1997
		$000	
Value	82,398	48,592	50,593

HOMES BUILT

	1999	1998	1997
No	108	194	92

TAXATION

Income Class:	1997	% Total
Under $5,000	6,510	15.61
$5,000-$10,000	6,520	15.64
$10,000-$15,000	5,960	14.29
$15,000-$20,000	3,700	8.87
$20,000-$25,000	3,000	7.19
$25,000-$30,000	2,960	7.10
$30,000-$40,000	4,290	10.29
$40,000-$50,000	3,200	7.67
$50,000 +	5,560	13.33
Total Returns, No.	41,700	
Total Income, $000	1,005,185	
Total Taxable Returns	27,350	
Total Tax, $000	118,014	
Average Income, $.	24,105	
Average Tax, $	4,315	

VITAL STATISTICS

	1997	1996	1995	1994
Births	548	597	560	603
Deaths	439	431	424	448
Natural Increase	109	166	136	155
Marriages	154	161	183	182

Note: Latest available data.

MEDIA INFO
see Chicoutimi-Jonquière, CMA

La Baie
(Ville)
Chicoutimi-Jonquière CMA

In census division Le Fjord-du-Saguenay.

POPULATION

July 1, 2001 Estimate	21,416
% Cdn. Total	0.07
% Change, '96 -'01	0.14
Avg. Annual Growth Rate, %	0.03
2003 Projected Population	21,663
2006 Projected Population	22,016
2001 Households Estimate	8,151
2003 Projected Households	8,406
2006 Projected Households	8,768

INCOME

% Above/Below National Average	-20
2001 Total Income Estimate	$361,670,000
% Cdn. Total	0.06
2001 Average Hhld. Income	$44,400
2001 Per Capita	$16,900
2003 Projected Total Income	$386,400,000
2006 Projected Total Income	$424,680,000

RETAIL SALES

% Above/Below National Average	-46
2001 Retail Sales Estimate	$103,230,000
% Cdn. Total	0.04
2001 per Household	$12,700
2001 per Capita	$4,800
2001 No. of Establishments	137
2003 Projected Retail Sales	$111,350,000
2006 Projected Retail Sales	$123,980,000

POPULATION

2001 Estimates:

Total	21,416
Male	10,684
Female	10,732

Age Groups	Male	Female
0-4	639	633
5-9	725	722
10-14	774	770
15-19	836	785
20-24	760	698
25-29	639	622
30-34	778	758
35-39	1,010	965
40-44	1,031	970
45-49	870	816
50-54	691	650
55-59	518	524
60-64	407	456
65-69	344	410
70+	662	953

DAYTIME POPULATION

2001 Estimates:

Working Population	8,791
At Home Population	12,430
Total	21,221

INCOME

2001 Estimates:

Avg. Household Income	$44,372
Avg. Family Income	$48,910
Per Capita Income	$16,888
Male:	
Avg. Employment Income	$34,108
Avg. Employment Income (Full Time)	$43,347
Female:	
Avg. Employment Income	$16,688
Avg. Employment Income (Full Time)	$27,443

DISPOSABLE & DISCRETIONARY INCOME

2001 Estimates:	Per Hhld.
Disposable Income	$31,001
Discretionary Income 1 (minus Food & Shelter)	$19,691
Discretionary Income 2 (minus Food, Shelter, & Other Expenditures)	$12,656

LIQUID ASSETS

1999 Estimates:	Per Hhld.
Equity Investments	$45,061
Interest Bearing Investments	$51,121
Total Liquid Assets	$96,182

CREDIT DATA

July 2000:

Pool of Credit	$109,952,551
Revolving Credit, No.	33,862
Fixed Loans, No.	13,249
Avg. Credit Limit, per Person	$7,953
Avg. Spent, per Person	$3,524
Satisfactory Ratings, No. per Person	3.15
Avg. No. of Cards, per Person	1.12

LABOUR FORCE

2001 Estimates:

Male:

In the Labour Force	6,006
Participation Rate	70.3
Employed	5,556
Unemployed	450
Unemployment Rate	7.5
Not in Labour Force	2,540

Female:

In the Labour Force	3,764
Participation Rate	43.7
Employed	3,404
Unemployed	360
Unemployment Rate	9.6
Not in Labour Force	4,843

OCCUPATIONS BY MAJOR GROUPS

2001 Estimates:	Male	Female
Management	584	114
Business, Finance & Admin.	331	994
Natural & Applied Sciences & Related	466	27
Health	81	380
Social Sciences, Gov't Services & Religion	97	50
Education	153	228
Arts, Culture, Recreation & Sport	129	99
Sales & Service	1,389	1,507
Trades, Transport & Equipment Operators & Related	1,578	21
Primary Industries	156	22
Processing, Mfg. & Utilities	864	106

LEVEL OF SCHOOLING

2001 Estimates:

Population 15 years +	17,153
Less than Grade 9	2,821
Grades 9-13 w/o Certif.	3,263
Grade 9-13 with Certif.	3,483
Trade Certif. /Dip.	1,419
Non-Univ. w/o Certif./Dip.	1,191
Non-Univ. with Certif./Dip.	2,789
Univ. w/o Degree	1,072
Univ. w/o Degree/Certif.	186
Univ. with Certif.	886
Univ. with Degree	1,115

AVERAGE HOUSEHOLD EXPENDITURES

2001 Estimates:

Food	$5,966
Shelter	$6,898
Clothing	$1,898
Transportation	$5,449
Health & Personal Care	$1,725
Recr'n, Read'g & Education	$2,954
Taxes & Securities	$12,304
Other	$6,733
Total Expenditures	$43,927

PRIVATE HOUSEHOLDS

2001 Estimates:

Private Households, Total	8,151
Pop. in Private Households	21,033
Average no. per Household	2.6

FAMILIES

2001 Estimates:

Families in Private Households	6,429
Husband-Wife Families	5,687
Lone-Parent Families	742
Aver. No. Persons per Family	3.1
Aver. No. Sons/Daughters at Home	1.2

HOUSING

2001 Estimates:

Occupied Private Dwellings	8,151
Owned	4,914
Rented	3,237
Single-Detached House	3,636
Semi-Detached House	483
Row Houses	246
Apartment, 5+ Storeys	33
Apartment, 5 or Fewer Storeys	2,055
Apartment, Detached Duplex	1,489
Other Single-Attached	22
Movable Dwellings	187

VEHICLES

2001 Estimates:

Model Yrs. '81-'96, No.	8,913
% Total	78.69
Model Yrs. '97-'98, No.	1,561
% Total	13.78
'99 Vehicles registered in Model Yr. '99, No.	853
% Total	7.53
Total No. '81-'99	11,327

LEGAL MARITAL STATUS

2001 Estimates: (Age 15+)

Single (Never Married)	5,630
Legally Married (Not Separated)	9,005
Legally Married (Separated)	332
Widowed	1,016
Divorced	1,170

PSYTE CATEGORIES

2001 Estimates	No. of House-holds	% of Total Hhds.	Index
Old Towns' New Fringe	383	4.70	120
Participation Quebec	593	7.28	252
Quebec Melange	1,643	20.16	761
Traditional French Cdn. Families	3,065	37.60	1,400
Quebec Rural Blues	33	0.40	17
Quebec Town Elders	2,399	29.43	1,042

FINANCIAL P$YTE

2001 Estimates	No. of House-holds	% of Total Hhds.	Index
Mortgages & Minivans	593	7.28	110
Tractors & Tradelines	383	4.70	82
Country Credit	4,708	57.76	854
Rural Family Blues	33	0.40	5
Loan Parent Stress	2,399	29.43	505

Québec

HOME LANGUAGE

2001 Estimates:		% Total
English	316	1.48
French	20,925	97.71
Romanian	20	0.09
Other Languages	20	0.09
Multiple Responses	135	0.63
Total	21,416	100.00

BUILDING PERMITS

	1999	1998	1997
		$000	
Value	19,115	17,526	26,166

HOMES BUILT

	1999	1998	1997
No.	35	70	140

TAXATION

Income Class:	1997	% Total
Under $5,000	2,540	17.73
$5,000-$10,000	1,960	13.68
$10,000-$15,000	1,960	13.68
$15,000-$20,000	1,230	8.58
$20,000-$25,000	990	6.91
$25,000-$30,000	1,010	7.05
$30,000-$40,000	1,520	10.61
$40,000-$50,000	1,250	8.72
$50,000 +	1,870	13.05
Total Returns, No.	14,330	
Total Income, $000	344,309	
Total Taxable Returns	9,390	
Total Tax, $000	40,918	
Average Income, $	24,027	
Average Tax, $	4,358	

VITAL STATISTICS

	1997	1996	1995	1994
Births	201	243	280	275
Deaths	138	162	145	144
Natural Increase	63	81	135	131
Marriages	42	65	49	50

Note: Latest available data.

MEDIA INFO

see Chicoutimi-Jonquière, CMA

Québec

Cowansville
(Census Agglomeration)

The Census Agglomeration of Cowansville consists solely of Cowansville, V. It is in census division Brome-Missisquoi.

POPULATION

July 1, 2001 Estimate	12,264
% Cdn. Total	0.04
% Change, '96 -'01	0.25
Avg. Annual Growth Rate, %	0.05
2003 Projected Population	12,238
2006 Projected Population	12,109
2001 Households Estimate	5,287
2003 Projected Households	5,339
2006 Projected Households	5,393

INCOME

% Above/Below National Average	-20
2001 Total Income Estimate	$208,000,000
% Cdn. Total	0.03
2001 Average Hhld. Income	$39,300
2001 Per Capita	$17,000
2003 Projected Total Income	$217,660,000
2006 Projected Total Income	$232,100,000

RETAIL SALES

% Above/Below National Average	+67
2001 Retail Sales Estimate	$183,840,000
% Cdn. Total	0.07
2001 per Household	$34,800
2001 per Capita	$15,000
2001 No. of Establishments	139
2003 Projected Retail Sales	$198,920,000
2006 Projected Retail Sales	$218,000,000

POPULATION

2001 Estimates:

Total		12,264
Male		6,212
Female		6,052

Age Groups	Male	Female
0-4	347	314
5-9	378	348
10-14	391	370
15-19	419	396
20-24	435	376
25-29	439	342
30-34	484	392
35-39	546	459
40-44	529	458
45-49	489	448
50-54	442	407
55-59	353	350
60-64	262	292
65-69	204	247
70+	494	853

DAYTIME POPULATION

2001 Estimates:

Working Population	5,685
At Home Population	6,579
Total	12,264

INCOME

2001 Estimates:

Avg. Household Income	$39,342
Avg. Family Income	$48,311
Per Capita Income	$16,960
Male:	
Avg. Employment Income	$28,302
Avg. Employment Income (Full Time)	$36,321
Female:	
Avg. Employment Income	$19,227
Avg. Employment Income (Full Time)	$26,841

DISPOSABLE & DISCRETIONARY INCOME

2001 Estimates:	Per Hhld.
Disposable Income	$26,988
Discretionary Income 1 (minus Food & Shelter)	$16,380
Discretionary Income 2 (minus Food, Shelter, & Other Expenditures)	$10,401

LIQUID ASSETS

1999 Estimates:	Per Hhld.
Equity Investments	$43,353
Interest Bearing Investments	$47,107
Total Liquid Assets	$90,460

CREDIT DATA

July 2000:

Pool of Credit	$71,546,171
Revolving Credit, No.	18,412
Fixed Loans, No.	6,859
Avg. Credit Limit, per Person	$7,946
Avg. Spent, per Person	$3,592
Satisfactory Ratings, No. per Person	2.64
Avg. No. of Cards, per Person	0.95

LABOUR FORCE

2001 Estimates:

Male:	
In the Labour Force	3,308
Participation Rate	64.9
Employed	3,136
Unemployed	172
Unemployment Rate	5.2
Not in Labour Force	1,788
Female:	
In the Labour Force	2,704
Participation Rate	53.9
Employed	2,576
Unemployed	128
Unemployment Rate	4.7
Not in Labour Force	2,316

OCCUPATIONS BY MAJOR GROUPS

2001 Estimates:	Male	Female
Management	254	94
Business, Finance & Admin.	364	613
Natural & Applied Sciences & Related	178	50
Health	59	309
Social Sciences, Gov't Services & Religion	53	43
Education	73	156
Arts, Culture, Recreation & Sport	52	54
Sales & Service	614	885
Trades, Transport & Equipment Operators & Related	648	40
Primary Industries	100	20
Processing, Mfg. & Utilities	793	314

LEVEL OF SCHOOLING

2001 Estimates:

Population 15 years +	10,116
Less than Grade 9	2,167
Grades 9-13 w/o Certif.	2,185
Grade 9-13 with Certif.	2,014
Trade Certif. /Dip.	385
Non-Univ. w/o Certif./Dip.	767
Non-Univ. with Certif./Dip.	1,337
Univ. w/o Degree	526
Univ. w/o Degree/Certif.	58
Univ. with Certif.	468
Univ. with Degree	735

AVERAGE HOUSEHOLD EXPENDITURES

2001 Estimates:

Food	$5,467
Shelter	$6,557
Clothing	$1,672
Transportation	$4,359
Health & Personal Care	$1,611
Recr'n, Read'g & Education	$2,552
Taxes & Securities	$10,999
Other	$6,165
Total Expenditures	$39,382

PRIVATE HOUSEHOLDS

2001 Estimates:

Private Households, Total	5,287
Pop. in Private Households	11,416
Average no. per Household	2.2

FAMILIES

2001 Estimates:

Families in Private Households	3,430
Husband-Wife Families	2,888
Lone-Parent Families	542
Aver. No. Persons per Family	2.9
Aver. No. Sons/Daughters at Home	1.1

HOUSING

2001 Estimates:

Occupied Private Dwellings	5,287
Owned	2,669
Rented	2,618
Single-Detached House	2,220
Semi-Detached House	174
Row Houses	34
Apartment, 5+ Storeys	23
Owned Apartment, 5+ Storeys	11
Apartment, 5 or Fewer Storeys	2,159
Apartment, Detached Duplex	627
Other Single-Attached	40
Movable Dwellings	10

VEHICLES

2001 Estimates:

Model Yrs. '81-'96, No.	5,726
% Total	79.15
Model Yrs. '97-'98, No.	976
% Total	13.49
'99 Vehicles registered in Model Yr. '99, No.	532
% Total	7.35
Total No. '81-'99	7,234

LEGAL MARITAL STATUS

2001 Estimates: (Age 15+)

Single (Never Married)	3,892
Legally Married (Not Separated)	4,059
Legally Married (Separated)	247
Widowed	886
Divorced	1,032

PSYTE CATEGORIES

2001 Estimates	No. of House-holds	% of Total Hhds.	Index
Participation Quebec	173	3.27	114
New Quebec Rows	43	0.81	74
Quebec Melange	889	16.81	635
Traditional French Cdn. Families	715	13.52	504
Quebec Rural Blues	119	2.25	92
Quebec Town Elders	2,530	47.85	1,693
Quebec's New Urban Mosaic	328	6.20	258
Aged Pensioners	286	5.41	407

FINANCIAL PSYTE

2001 Estimates	No. of House-holds	% of Total Hhds.	Index
Mortgages & Minivans	216	4.09	62
Country Credit	1,604	30.34	449
Rural Family Blues	119	2.25	28
Loan Parent Stress	2,530	47.85	822
NSF	328	6.20	175
Senior Survivors	286	5.41	287

HOME LANGUAGE

2001 Estimates:		% Total
English	2,040	16.63
French	9,932	80.98
Greek	12	0.10
Italian	22	0.18
Polish	10	0.08
Multiple Responses	248	2.02
Total	12,264	100.00

BUILDING PERMITS

	1999	1998 $000	1997
Value	9,919	12,084	5,851

HOMES BUILT

	1999	1998	1997
No	62	22	34

TAXATION

Income Class:	1997	% Total
Under $5,000	1,010	11.66
$5,000-$10,000	1,300	15.01
$10,000-$15,000	1,640	18.94
$15,000-$20,000	950	10.97
$20,000-$25,000	750	8.66
$25,000-$30,000	730	8.43
$30,000-$40,000	1,080	12.47
$40,000-$50,000	600	6.93
$50,000 +	610	7.04
Total Returns, No.	8,660	
Total Income, $000	196,150	
Total Taxable Returns	5,850	
Total Tax, $000	21,528	
Average Income, $.	22,650	
Average Tax, $	3,680	

VITAL STATISTICS

	1997	1996	1995	1994
Births	122	136	130	174
Deaths	102	138	133	139
Natural Increase	20	-2	-3	35
Marriages	90	100	107	89

Note: Latest available data.

COMMUNITY NEWSPAPER(S)

	Total Circulation
Cowansville: Le Guide	17,329

Dolbeau
(Census Agglomeration)

The Census Agglomeration of Dolbeau consists of: Dolbeau, V and Mistassini, V. Both are in census division Maria-Chapdelaine.

POPULATION

July 1, 2001 Estimate	15,313
% Cdn. Total	0.05
% Change, '96 -'01	-0.87
Avg. Annual Growth Rate, %	-0.17
2003 Projected Population	15,323
2006 Projected Population	15,228
2001 Households Estimate	5,928
2003 Projected Households	6,086
2006 Projected Households	6,280

INCOME

% Above/Below National Average	-24
2001 Total Income Estimate	$246,200,000
% Cdn. Total	0.04
2001 Average Hhld. Income	$41,500
2001 Per Capita	$16,100
2003 Projected Total Income	$261,610,000
2006 Projected Total Income	$283,690,000

RETAIL SALES

% Above/Below National Average	+21
2001 Retail Sales Estimate	$165,250,000
% Cdn. Total	0.06
2001 per Household	$27,900
2001 per Capita	$10,800
2001 No. of Establishments	202
2003 Projected Retail Sales	$178,320,000
2006 Projected Retail Sales	$196,220,000

POPULATION

2001 Estimates:

Total		15,313
Male		7,602
Female		7,711

Age Groups	Male	Female
0-4	426	384
5-9	446	426
10-14	524	504
15-19	647	612
20-24	610	571
25-29	493	458
30-34	500	480
35-39	580	600
40-44	640	657
45-49	616	620
50-54	540	528
55-59	437	418
60-64	345	349
65-69	280	320
70+	518	784

DAYTIME POPULATION

2001 Estimates:

Working Population	6,136
At Home Population	9,177
Total	15,313

INCOME

2001 Estimates:

Avg. Household Income	$41,531
Avg. Family Income	$47,502
Per Capita Income	$16,078
Male:	
Avg. Employment Income	$29,596
Avg. Employment Income (Full Time)	$43,362
Female:	
Avg. Employment Income	$16,189
Avg. Employment Income (Full Time)	$25,091

DISPOSABLE & DISCRETIONARY INCOME

2001 Estimates:	Per Hhld.
Disposable Income	$29,058
Discretionary Income 1 (minus Food & Shelter)	$18,095
Discretionary Income 2 (minus Food, Shelter, & Other Expenditures)	$11,335

LIQUID ASSETS

1999 Estimates:	Per Hhld.
Equity Investments	$48,779
Interest Bearing Investments	$50,045
Total Liquid Assets	$98,824

CREDIT DATA

July 2000:	
Pool of Credit	$82,153,569
Revolving Credit, No.	21,154
Fixed Loans, No.	10,145
Avg. Credit Limit, per Person	$8,998
Avg. Spent, per Person	$4,144
Satisfactory Ratings, No. per Person	3.11
Avg. No. of Cards, per Person	1.02

LABOUR FORCE

2001 Estimates:

Male:	
In the Labour Force	4,171
Participation Rate	67.2
Employed	3,555
Unemployed	616
Unemployment Rate	14.8
Not in Labour Force	2,035
Female:	
In the Labour Force	2,902
Participation Rate	45.4
Employed	2,558
Unemployed	344
Unemployment Rate	11.9
Not in Labour Force	3,495

OCCUPATIONS BY MAJOR GROUPS

2001 Estimates:	Male	Female
Management	310	168
Business, Finance & Admin.	266	678
Natural & Applied Sciences & Related	124	44
Health	82	346
Social Sciences, Gov't Services & Religion	66	86
Education	105	124
Arts, Culture, Recreation & Sport	28	20
Sales & Service	772	1,119
Trades, Transport & Equipment Operators & Related	1,373	35
Primary Industries	386	52
Processing, Mfg. & Utilities	505	30

LEVEL OF SCHOOLING

2001 Estimates:

Population 15 years +	12,603
Less than Grade 9	2,622
Grades 9-13 w/o Certif.	2,694
Grade 9-13 with Certif.	2,360
Trade Certif. /Dip.	809
Non-Univ. w/o Certif./Dip.	810
Non-Univ. with Certif./Dip.	1,982
Univ. w/o Degree	567
Univ. w/o Degree/Certif.	93
Univ. with Certif.	474
Univ. with Degree	759

AVERAGE HOUSEHOLD EXPENDITURES

2001 Estimates:

Food	$5,879
Shelter	$6,561
Clothing	$1,865
Transportation	$5,202
Health & Personal Care	$1,633
Recr'n, Read'g & Education	$2,845
Taxes & Securities	$11,012
Other	$6,476
Total Expenditures	$41,473

PRIVATE HOUSEHOLDS

2001 Estimates:

Private Households, Total	5,928
Pop. in Private Households	14,929
Average no. per Household	2.5

FAMILIES

2001 Estimates:

Families in Private Households	4,512
Husband-Wife Families	3,854
Lone-Parent Families	658
Aver. No. Persons per Family	3.1
Aver. No. Sons/Daughters at Home	1.3

HOUSING

2001 Estimates:

Occupied Private Dwellings	5,928
Owned	3,576
Rented	2,352
Single-Detached House	3,236
Semi-Detached House	267
Row Houses	33
Apartment, 5 or Fewer Storeys	1,554
Apartment, Detached Duplex	669
Other Single-Attached	60
Movable Dwellings	109

VEHICLES

2001 Estimates:

Model Yrs. '81-'96, No.	8,442
% Total	84.86
Model Yrs. '97-'98, No.	898
% Total	9.03
'99 Vehicles registered in Model Yr. '99, No.	608
% Total	6.11
Total No. '81-'99	9,948

LEGAL MARITAL STATUS

2001 Estimates: (Age 15+)

Single (Never Married)	4,541
Legally Married (Not Separated)	5,902
Legally Married (Separated)	254
Widowed	852
Divorced	1,054

PSYTE CATEGORIES

2001 Estimates	No. of House-holds	% of Total Hhds.	Index
Quebec Melange	408	6.88	260
Traditional French Cdn. Families	2,391	40.33	1,502
Big Country Families	381	6.43	451
Quebec Rural Blues	635	10.71	440
Quebec Town Elders	2,102	35.46	1,255

FINANCIAL P$YTE

2001 Estimates	No. of House-holds	% of Total Hhds.	Index
Country Credit	2,799	47.22	698
Rural Family Blues	1,016	17.14	212
Loan Parent Stress	2,102	35.46	609

HOME LANGUAGE

2001 Estimates:		% Total
English	25	0.16
French	15,232	99.47
Lao	15	0.10
Other Languages	10	0.07
Multiple Responses	31	0.20
Total	15,313	100.00

Québec

BUILDING PERMITS

	1999	1998 $000	1997
Value	10,784	11,503	10,839

HOMES BUILT

	1999	1998	1997
No.	51	45	50

TAXATION

Income Class:	1997	% Total
Under $5,000	1,810	16.47
$5,000-$10,000	1,720	15.65
$10,000-$15,000	2,010	18.29
$15,000-$20,000	960	8.74
$20,000-$25,000	860	7.83
$25,000-$30,000	730	6.64
$30,000-$40,000	1,090	9.92
$40,000-$50,000	790	7.19
$50,000 +	1,030	9.37
Total Returns, No.	10,990	
Total Income, $000	241,185	
Total Taxable Returns	6,750	
Total Tax, $000	26,302	
Average Income, $.	21,946	
Average Tax, $.	3,897	

VITAL STATISTICS

	1997	1996	1995	1994
Births	169	148	169	175
Deaths	129	100	113	97
Natural Increase	40	48	56	78
Marriages	48	48	49	71

Note: Latest available data.

COMMUNITY NEWSPAPER(S)

	Total Circulation
Dolbeau: Le Point	11,474
Dolbeau, Chicoutimi, Jonquière, La Baie, Lac-Saint-Jean area: Le Progrès Dimanche	45,440
Dolbeau, Mistassini: Nouvelles Hebdo.	11,779

RADIO STATION(S)

	Power
CBJ-FM	n.a.
CHVD	10,000w

Québec

Drummondville
(Census Agglomeration)

The Census Agglomeration of Drummondville includes: Drummondville, V; Saint-Charles-de-Drummond, M; Saint-Cyrille-de-Wendover, M; Saint-Lucien, P; Saint-Majorique-de-Grantham, P; and Saint-Nicephore, M. All are in census division Drummond.

POPULATION

July 1, 2001 Estimate	69,481
% Cdn. Total	0.22
% Change, '96 -'01	4.89
Avg. Annual Growth Rate, %	0.96
2003 Projected Population	71,093
2006 Projected Population	73,034
2001 Households Estimate	29,584
2003 Projected Households	30,589
2006 Projected Households	31,826

INCOME

% Above/Below National Average	-16
2001 Total Income Estimate	$1,227,360,000
% Cdn. Total	0.19
2001 Average Hhld. Income	$41,500
2001 Per Capita	$17,700
2003 Projected Total Income	$1,337,880,000
2006 Projected Total Income	$1,509,750,000

RETAIL SALES

% Above/Below National Average	+44
2001 Retail Sales Estimate	$895,770,000
% Cdn. Total	0.32
2001 per Household	$30,300
2001 per Capita	$12,900
2001 No. of Establishments	718
2003 Projected Retail Sales	$985,510,000
2006 Projected Retail Sales	$1,113,850,000

POPULATION

2001 Estimates:

Total	69,481
Male	34,090
Female	35,391

Age Groups	Male	Female
0-4	1,971	1,863
5-9	2,107	1,945
10-14	2,230	2,068
15-19	2,503	2,390
20-24	2,537	2,418
25-29	2,375	2,196
30-34	2,446	2,298
35-39	2,656	2,643
40-44	2,801	2,844
45-49	2,716	2,763
50-54	2,435	2,445
55-59	1,927	1,987
60-64	1,493	1,609
65-69	1,225	1,440
70+	2,668	4,482

DAYTIME POPULATION

2001 Estimates:

Working Population	33,203
At Home Population	36,287
Total	69,490

INCOME

2001 Estimates:

Avg. Household Income	$41,487
Avg. Family Income	$49,587
Per Capita Income	$17,665
Male:	
Avg. Employment Income	$29,492
Avg. Employment Income (Full Time)	$38,057
Female:	
Avg. Employment Income	$18,283
Avg. Employment Income (Full Time)	$26,580

DISPOSABLE & DISCRETIONARY INCOME

2001 Estimates:	Per Hhld.
Disposable Income	$29,195
Discretionary Income 1 (minus Food & Shelter)	$18,216
Discretionary Income 2 (minus Food, Shelter, & Other Expenditures)	$11,698

LIQUID ASSETS

1999 Estimates:	Per Hhld.
Equity Investments	$42,192
Interest Bearing Investments	$47,030
Total Liquid Assets	$89,222

CREDIT DATA

July 2000:

Pool of Credit	$322,090,774
Revolving Credit, No.	103,415
Fixed Loans, No.	32,925
Avg. Credit Limit, per Person	$6,453
Avg. Spent, per Person	$2,838
Satisfactory Ratings, No. per Person	2.58
Avg. No. of Cards, per Person	0.94

LABOUR FORCE

2001 Estimates:

Male:	
In the Labour Force	19,833
Participation Rate	71.4
Employed	18,602
Unemployed	1,231
Unemployment Rate	6.2
Not in Labour Force	7,949
Female:	
In the Labour Force	15,677
Participation Rate	53.1
Employed	14,744
Unemployed	933
Unemployment Rate	6.0
Not in Labour Force	13,838

OCCUPATIONS BY MAJOR GROUPS

2001 Estimates:	Male	Female
Management	1,959	805
Business, Finance & Admin.	1,555	4,035
Natural & Applied Sciences & Related	960	210
Health	337	1,359
Social Sciences, Gov't Services & Religion	355	413
Education	540	826
Arts, Culture, Recreation & Sport	346	327
Sales & Service	3,560	4,812
Trades, Transport & Equipment Operators & Related	4,873	481
Primary Industries	613	170
Processing, Mfg. & Utilities	4,108	1,710

LEVEL OF SCHOOLING

2001 Estimates:

Population 15 years +	57,297
Less than Grade 9	11,116
Grades 9-13 w/o Certif.	10,245
Grade 9-13 with Certif.	11,143
Trade Certif. /Dip.	3,671
Non-Univ. w/o Certif./Dip.	4,743
Non-Univ. with Certif./Dip.	8,942
Univ. w/o Degree	3,012
Univ. w/o Degree/Certif.	349
Univ. with Certif.	2,663
Univ. with Degree	4,425

AVERAGE HOUSEHOLD EXPENDITURES

2001 Estimates:

Food	$5,712
Shelter	$6,825
Clothing	$1,847
Transportation	$4,869
Health & Personal Care	$1,691
Recr'n, Read'g & Education	$2,739
Taxes & Securities	$11,656
Other	$6,451
Total Expenditures	$41,790

PRIVATE HOUSEHOLDS

2001 Estimates:

Private Households, Total	29,584
Pop. in Private Households	67,354
Average no. per Household	2.3

FAMILIES

2001 Estimates:

Families in Private Households	20,218
Husband-Wife Families	16,986
Lone-Parent Families	3,232
Aver. No. Persons per Family	2.9
Aver. No. Sons/Daughters at Home	1.1

HOUSING

2001 Estimates:

Occupied Private Dwellings	29,584
Owned	16,416
Rented	13,168
Single-Detached House	13,946
Semi-Detached House	1,077
Row Houses	661
Apartment, 5+ Storeys	333
Apartment, 5 or Fewer Storeys	9,583
Apartment, Detached Duplex	3,472
Other Single-Attached	253
Movable Dwellings	259

VEHICLES

2001 Estimates:

Model Yrs. '81-'96, No.	36,109
% Total	83.07
Model Yrs. '97-'98, No.	4,544
% Total	10.45
'99 Vehicles registered in Model Yr. '99, No.	2,813
% Total	6.47
Total No. '81-'99	43,466

LEGAL MARITAL STATUS

2001 Estimates: (Age 15+)

Single (Never Married)	21,397
Legally Married (Not Separated)	24,555
Legally Married (Separated)	1,114
Widowed	4,116
Divorced	6,115

PSYTE CATEGORIES

2001 Estimates	No. of House-holds	% of Total Hhds.	Index
Participation			
Quebec	3,074	10.39	361
New Quebec Rows	923	3.12	285
Quebec Melange	4,674	15.80	596
Traditional French Cdn. Families	6,577	22.23	828
Quebec's Heartland	842	2.85	290
Quebec Rural Blues	318	1.07	44
Old Quebec Walkups	880	2.97	162
Quebec Town Elders	7,524	25.43	900
Quebec's New Urban Mosaic	3,410	11.53	478
Aged Pensioners	635	2.15	161
Old Grey Towers	227	0.77	139

FINANCIAL P$YTE

2001 Estimates	No. of House-holds	% of Total Hhds.	Index
Mortgages & Minivans	3,997	13.51	205
Country Credit	11,251	38.03	562
Rural Family Blues	1,160	3.92	49
Loan Parent Stress	8,404	28.41	488
NSF	3,410	11.53	326
Senior Survivors	862	2.91	155

HOME LANGUAGE

2001 Estimates:		% Total
English	521	0.75
French	68,437	98.50
Khmer (Cambodian)	38	0.05
Lao	64	0.09
Other Languages	55	0.08
Multiple Responses	366	0.53
Total	69,481	100.00

BUILDING PERMITS

	1999	1998	1997
		$000	
Value	94,929	86,863	74,341

HOMES BUILT

	1999	1998	1997
No	384	455	528

TAXATION

Income Class:	1997	% Total
Under $5,000	5,920	12.09
$5,000-$10,000	7,750	15.82
$10,000-$15,000	8,910	18.19
$15,000-$20,000	5,640	11.51
$20,000-$25,000	4,370	8.92
$25,000-$30,000	4,330	8.84
$30,000-$40,000	5,910	12.07
$40,000-$50,000	3,010	6.15
$50,000 +	3,160	6.45
Total Returns, No.	48,980	
Total Income, $000	1,074,451	
Total Taxable Returns	32,810	
Total Tax, $000	113,563	
Average Income, $	21,937	
Average Tax, $	3,461	

Drummondville
(Census Agglomeration)
(Cont'd)
VITAL STATISTICS

	1997	1996	1995	1994
Births	728	704	764	772
Deaths	543	551	525	490
Natural Increase	185	153	239	282
Marriages	211	220	233	197

Note: Latest available data.

COMMUNITY NEWSPAPER(S)

	Total Circulation
Drummondville: La Parole	39,555
Drummondville: L'Express	43,102

RADIO STATION(S)

	Power
CHRD-FM	3,000w
CJDM-FM	3,000w

Gaspé
(Ville)
In census division La Côte-de-Gaspé.

POPULATION

July 1, 2001 Estimate	16,133
% Cdn. Total	0.05
% Change, '96 -'01	-3.72
Avg. Annual Growth Rate, %	-0.76
2003 Projected Population	16,110
2006 Projected Population	15,955
2001 Households Estimate	6,008
2003 Projected Households	6,117
2006 Projected Households	6,255

INCOME

% Above/Below National Average	-19
2001 Total Income Estimate	$275,830,000
% Cdn. Total	0.04
2001 Average Hhld. Income	$45,900
2001 Per Capita	$17,100
2003 Projected Total Income	$294,790,000
2006 Projected Total Income	$324,310,000

RETAIL SALES

% Above/Below National Average	+6
2001 Retail Sales Estimate	$153,660,000
% Cdn. Total	0.06
2001 per Household	$25,600
2001 per Capita	$9,500
2001 No. of Establishments	184
2003 Projected Retail Sales	$164,880,000
2006 Projected Retail Sales	$179,580,000

POPULATION

2001 Estimates:

Total		16,133
Male		7,885
Female		8,248

Age Groups	Male	Female
0-4	433	414
5-9	440	443
10-14	511	489
15-19	591	549
20-24	544	533
25-29	473	493
30-34	524	563
35-39	636	686
40-44	719	730
45-49	687	667
50-54	563	573
55-59	434	478
60-64	352	398
65-69	313	357
70+	665	875

DAYTIME POPULATION

2001 Estimates:

Working Population	7,169
At Home Population	9,765
Total	16,934

INCOME

2001 Estimates:

Avg. Household Income	$45,910
Avg. Family Income	$49,119
Per Capita Income	$17,097

Male:

Avg. Employment Income	$25,889
Avg. Employment Income (Full Time)	$40,031

Female:

Avg. Employment Income	$20,525
Avg. Employment Income (Full Time)	$31,636

DISPOSABLE & DISCRETIONARY INCOME

2001 Estimates: — Per Hhld.

Disposable Income	$32,834
Discretionary Income 1 (minus Food & Shelter)	$20,809
Discretionary Income 2 (minus Food, Shelter, & Other Expenditures)	$12,239

LIQUID ASSETS

1999 Estimates: — Per Hhld.

Equity Investments	$47,502
Interest Bearing Investments	$52,223
Total Liquid Assets	$99,725

CREDIT DATA

July 2000:

Pool of Credit	$80,901,926
Revolving Credit, No.	18,060
Fixed Loans, No.	8,817
Avg. Credit Limit, per Person	$9,447
Avg. Spent, per Person	$4,625
Satisfactory Ratings, No. per Person	2.97
Avg. No. of Cards, per Person	0.95

LABOUR FORCE

2001 Estimates:

Male:

In the Labour Force	4,176
Participation Rate	64.2
Employed	3,327
Unemployed	849
Unemployment Rate	20.3
Not in Labour Force	2,325

Female:

In the Labour Force	3,497
Participation Rate	50.7
Employed	3,020
Unemployed	477
Unemployment Rate	13.6
Not in Labour Force	3,405

OCCUPATIONS BY MAJOR GROUPS

2001 Estimates:

	Male	Female
Management	350	134
Business, Finance & Admin.	254	870
Natural & Applied Sciences & Related	255	51
Health	156	398
Social Sciences, Gov't Services & Religion	102	128
Education	212	347
Arts, Culture, Recreation & Sport	45	93
Sales & Service	930	1,116
Trades, Transport & Equipment Operators & Related	977	26
Primary Industries	407	11
Processing, Mfg. & Utilities	233	80

LEVEL OF SCHOOLING

2001 Estimates:

Population 15 years +	13,403
Less than Grade 9	3,523
Grades 9-13 w/o Certif.	2,422
Grade 9-13 with Certif.	2,184
Trade Certif. /Dip.	555
Non-Univ. w/o Certif./Dip.	786
Non-Univ. with Certif./Dip.	2,048
Univ. w/o Degree	684
Univ. w/o Degree/Certif.	66
Univ. with Certif.	618
Univ. with Degree	1,201

Québec

AVERAGE HOUSEHOLD EXPENDITURES

2001 Estimates:

Food	$6,538
Shelter	$7,155
Clothing	$2,301
Transportation	$6,666
Health & Personal Care	$1,917
Recr'n, Read'g & Education	$2,947
Taxes & Securities	$10,567
Other	$7,169
Total Expenditures	$45,260

PRIVATE HOUSEHOLDS

2001 Estimates:

Private Households, Total	6,008
Pop. in Private Households	15,674
Average no. per Household	2.6

FAMILIES

2001 Estimates:

Families in Private Households	4,886
Husband-Wife Families	4,300
Lone-Parent Families	586
Aver. No. Persons per Family	3.0
Aver. No. Sons/Daughters at Home	1.1

HOUSING

2001 Estimates:

Occupied Private Dwellings	6,008
Owned	4,458
Rented	1,550
Single-Detached House	4,538
Semi-Detached House	214
Row Houses	104
Apartment, 5+ Storeys	10
Apartment, 5 or Fewer Storeys	858
Apartment, Detached Duplex	176
Other Single-Attached	25
Movable Dwellings	83

VEHICLES

2001 Estimates:

Model Yrs. '81-'96, No.	8,030
% Total	84.10
Model Yrs. '97-'98, No.	1,224
% Total	12.82
'99 Vehicles registered in Model Yr. '99, No.	294
% Total	3.08
Total No. '81-'99	9,548

LEGAL MARITAL STATUS

2001 Estimates: (Age 15+)

Single (Never Married)	5,430
Legally Married (Not Separated)	6,210
Legally Married (Separated)	194
Widowed	881
Divorced	688

Québec

Gaspé
(Ville)
(Cont'd)

PSYTE CATEGORIES

2001 Estimates	No. of House-holds	% of Total Hhds.	Index
Quebec Melange	1,100	18.31	691
Traditional French Cdn. Families	831	13.83	515
Big Country Families	645	10.74	753
Quebec Rural Blues	3,100	51.60	2,118
Quebec Town Elders	236	3.93	139

FINANCIAL P$YTE

2001 Estimates	No. of House-holds	% of Total Hhds.	Index
Country Credit	1,931	32.14	475
Rural Family Blues	3,745	62.33	772
Loan Parent Stress	236	3.93	67

HOME LANGUAGE

2001 Estimates:		% Total
English	2,186	13.55
French	13,721	85.05
Multiple Responses	226	1.40
Total	16,133	100.00

BUILDING PERMITS

	1999	1998 $000	1997
Value	6,031	19,705	8,851

HOMES BUILT

	1999	1998	1997
No.	21	21	31

TAXATION

Income Class:	1997	% Total
Under $5,000	1,790	15.02
$5,000-$10,000	1,920	16.11
$10,000-$15,000	2,280	19.13
$15,000-$20,000	1,250	10.49
$20,000-$25,000	1,070	8.98
$25,000-$30,000	990	8.31
$30,000-$40,000	1,160	9.73
$40,000-$50,000	660	5.54
$50,000 +	800	6.71
Total Returns, No.	11,920	
Total Income, $000	245,260	
Total Taxable Returns	7,260	
Total Tax, $000	25,556	
Average Income, $	20,576	
Average Tax, $	3,520	

VITAL STATISTICS

	1997	1996	1995	1994
Births	128	167	147	166
Deaths	135	148	156	124
Natural Increase	-7	19	-9	42
Marriages	35	34	46	24

Note: Latest available data.

COMMUNITY NEWSPAPER(S)

	Total Circulation
Gaspé: Le Pharillon	8,918
Gaspé: Spec	2,704

RADIO STATION(S)

	Power
CBGA-FM	n.a.
CBVG-FM	n.a.
CHGM	5,000w
CJMC-FM	1,000w
CJRG-FM	n.a.

TELEVISION STATION(S)

CBGAT-TV
CFER-TV
CHAU-TV
CIVK-TV

Granby
(Census Agglomeration)

The Census Agglomeration of Granby includes: Granby, V; Granby, CT; and Bromont, V. All are in census division La Haute-Yamaska.

POPULATION

July 1, 2001 Estimate	61,987
% Cdn. Total	0.20
% Change, '96 -'01	3.50
Avg. Annual Growth Rate, %	0.69
2003 Projected Population	62,800
2006 Projected Population	63,644
2001 Households Estimate	26,565
2003 Projected Households	27,257
2006 Projected Households	28,139

INCOME

% Above/Below National Average	-10
2001 Total Income Estimate	$1,175,920,000
% Cdn. Total	0.18
2001 Average Hhld. Income	$44,300
2001 Per Capita	$19,000
2003 Projected Total Income	$1,264,960,000
2006 Projected Total Income	$1,405,130,000

RETAIL SALES

% Above/Below National Average	+43
2001 Retail Sales Estimate	$792,220,000
% Cdn. Total	0.28
2001 per Household	$29,800
2001 per Capita	$12,800
2001 No. of Establishments	666
2003 Projected Retail Sales	$866,700,000
2006 Projected Retail Sales	$972,510,000

POPULATION

2001 Estimates:		
Total		61,987
Male		30,120
Female		31,867

Age Groups	Male	Female
0-4	1,743	1,673
5-9	1,867	1,858
10-14	2,036	1,986
15-19	2,182	2,105
20-24	2,097	1,986
25-29	1,952	1,847
30-34	2,142	2,089
35-39	2,496	2,548
40-44	2,633	2,727
45-49	2,486	2,541
50-54	2,119	2,186
55-59	1,682	1,771
60-64	1,332	1,479
65-69	1,096	1,368
70+	2,257	3,703

DAYTIME POPULATION

2001 Estimates:	
Working Population	30,872
At Home Population	31,116
Total	61,988

INCOME

2001 Estimates:	
Avg. Household Income	$44,266
Avg. Family Income	$51,795
Per Capita Income	$18,970
Male:	
Avg. Employment Income	$32,166
Avg. Employment Income (Full Time)	$41,252
Female:	
Avg. Employment Income	$19,557
Avg. Employment Income (Full Time)	$28,727

DISPOSABLE & DISCRETIONARY INCOME

2001 Estimates:	Per Hhld.
Disposable Income	$31,147
Discretionary Income 1 (minus Food & Shelter)	$19,840
Discretionary Income 2 (minus Food, Shelter, & Other Expenditures)	$13,059

LIQUID ASSETS

1999 Estimates:	Per Hhld.
Equity Investments	$48,622
Interest Bearing Investments	$51,143
Total Liquid Assets	$99,765

CREDIT DATA

July 2000:	
Pool of Credit	$328,956,375
Revolving Credit, No.	99,823
Fixed Loans, No.	32,243
Avg. Credit Limit, per Person	$6,931
Avg. Spent, per Person	$2,942
Satisfactory Ratings, No. per Person	2.58
Avg. No. of Cards, per Person	0.92

LABOUR FORCE

2001 Estimates:	
Male:	
In the Labour Force	18,051
Participation Rate	73.8
Employed	17,097
Unemployed	954
Unemployment Rate	5.3
Not in Labour Force	6,423
Female:	
In the Labour Force	14,873
Participation Rate	56.4
Employed	13,951
Unemployed	922
Unemployment Rate	6.2
Not in Labour Force	11,477

OCCUPATIONS BY MAJOR GROUPS

2001 Estimates:	Male	Female
Management	1,889	844
Business, Finance & Admin.	1,606	3,675
Natural & Applied Sciences & Related	1,448	355
Health	261	1,107
Social Sciences, Gov't Services & Religion	236	304
Education	438	627
Arts, Culture, Recreation & Sport	321	292
Sales & Service	3,377	4,379
Trades, Transport & Equipment Operators & Related	4,025	354
Primary Industries	437	104
Processing, Mfg. & Utilities	3,464	2,331

LEVEL OF SCHOOLING

2001 Estimates:	
Population 15 years +	50,824
Less than Grade 9	10,089
Grades 9-13 w/o Certif.	9,978
Grade 9-13 with Certif.	10,572
Trade Certif. /Dip.	2,315
Non-Univ. w/o Certif./Dip.	3,788
Non-Univ. with Certif./Dip.	7,051
Univ. w/o Degree	2,940
Univ. w/o Degree/Certif.	294
Univ. with Certif.	2,646
Univ. with Degree	4,091

Granby
(Census Agglomeration)
(Cont'd)

AVERAGE HOUSEHOLD EXPENDITURES

2001 Estimates:
Food	$5,854
Shelter	$7,109
Clothing	$1,926
Transportation	$5,086
Health & Personal Care	$1,746
Recr'n, Read'g & Education	$2,847
Taxes & Securities	$12,793
Other	$6,578
Total Expenditures	$43,939

PRIVATE HOUSEHOLDS

2001 Estimates:
Private Households, Total	26,565
Pop. in Private Households	60,418
Average no. per Household	2.3

FAMILIES

2001 Estimates:
Families in Private Households	18,316
Husband-Wife Families	15,342
Lone-Parent Families	2,974
Aver. No. Persons per Family	2.9
Aver. No. Sons/Daughters at Home	1.1

HOUSING

2001 Estimates:
Occupied Private Dwellings	26,565
Owned	13,704
Rented	12,861
Single-Detached House	11,590
Semi-Detached House	965
Row Houses	52
Apartment, 5+ Storeys	330
Apartment, 5 or Fewer Storeys	10,356
Apartment, Detached Duplex	2,486
Other Single-Attached	97
Movable Dwellings	689

VEHICLES

2001 Estimates:
Model Yrs. '81-'96, No.	31,402
% Total	79.96
Model Yrs. '97-'98, No.	4,837
% Total	12.32
'99 Vehicles registered in Model Yr. '99, No.	3,034
% Total	7.73
Total No. '81-'99	39,273

LEGAL MARITAL STATUS

2001 Estimates: (Age 15+)
Single (Never Married)	18,379
Legally Married (Not Separated)	21,630
Legally Married (Separated)	1,023
Widowed	3,414
Divorced	6,378

PSYTE CATEGORIES

2001 Estimates	No. of House-holds	% of Total Hhds.	Index
Urban Gentry	142	0.53	30
Small City Elite	431	1.62	95
Participation Quebec	2,761	10.39	361
New Quebec Rows	3,864	14.55	1,327
Quebec Melange	3,709	13.96	527
Traditional French Cdn. Families	3,768	14.18	528
Quebec's Heartland	192	0.72	74
Agrarian Blues	485	1.83	853
Quebec Rural Blues	110	0.41	17
Old Quebec Walkups	1,281	4.82	263
Quebec Town Elders	7,381	27.78	983
Quebec's New Urban Mosaic	2,026	7.63	317
Aged Pensioners	134	0.50	38
Old Grey Towers	38	0.14	26

FINANCIAL P$YTE

2001 Estimates	No. of House-holds	% of Total Hhds.	Index
Four Star Investors	142	0.53	11
Canadian Comfort	431	1.62	17
Mortgages & Minivans	6,625	24.94	378
Country Credit	7,477	28.15	416
Rural Family Blues	787	2.96	37
Loan Parent Stress	8,662	32.61	560
NSF	2,026	7.63	216
Senior Survivors	172	0.65	34

HOME LANGUAGE

2001 Estimates:		% Total
English	1,335	2.15
French	59,516	96.01
Arabic	32	0.05
Chinese	43	0.07
German	45	0.07
Spanish	37	0.06
Vietnamese	32	0.05
Other Languages	67	0.11
Multiple Responses	880	1.42
Total	61,987	100.00

BUILDING PERMITS

	1999	1998	1997
		$000	
Value	79,874	44,797	57,464

HOMES BUILT

	1999	1998	1997
No	247	303	356

TAXATION

Income Class:	1997	% Total
Under $5,000	5,160	11.25
$5,000-$10,000	7,060	15.40
$10,000-$15,000	7,860	17.14
$15,000-$20,000	5,170	11.28
$20,000-$25,000	4,230	9.23
$25,000-$30,000	3,760	8.20
$30,000-$40,000	5,400	11.78
$40,000-$50,000	3,260	7.11
$50,000 +	3,980	8.68
Total Returns, No.	45,850	
Total Income, $000	1,084,957	
Total Taxable Returns	31,900	
Total Tax, $000	123,756	
Average Income, $	23,663	
Average Tax, $	3,879	

VITAL STATISTICS

	1997	1996	1995	1994
Births	667	667	788	704
Deaths	483	393	456	421
Natural Increase	184	274	332	283
Marriages	237	258	237	236

Note: Latest available data.

DAILY NEWSPAPER(S)

	Circulation Average Paid
La Voix de L'Est	
Sat	18,655
Mon-Fri	15,176

COMMUNITY NEWSPAPER(S)

	Total Circulation
Granby: Samedi Express	44,000
Granby, Bromont, Cowansville: La Voix de L'Est Plus	44,587

RADIO STATION(S)

	Power
CFXM-FM	3,000w

Joliette
(Census Agglomeration)

The Census Agglomeration of Joliette includes: Joliette, V; Notre-Dame-des-Prairies, M; and Saint-Charles-Borromée, M. All are in census division Joliette.

POPULATION

July 1, 2001 Estimate	35,563
% Cdn. Total	0.11
% Change, '96 -'01	1.75
Avg. Annual Growth Rate, %	0.35
2003 Projected Population	35,792
2006 Projected Population	35,874
2001 Households Estimate	15,413
2003 Projected Households	15,719
2006 Projected Households	16,061

INCOME

% Above/Below National Average	-15
2001 Total Income Estimate	$638,170,000
% Cdn. Total	0.10
2001 Average Hhld. Income	$41,400
2001 Per Capita	$17,900
2003 Projected Total Income	$683,420,000
2006 Projected Total Income	$753,710,000

RETAIL SALES

% Above/Below National Average	+116
2001 Retail Sales Estimate	$686,720,000
% Cdn. Total	0.25
2001 per Household	$44,600
2001 per Capita	$19,300
2001 No. of Establishments	502
2003 Projected Retail Sales	$750,650,000
2006 Projected Retail Sales	$837,840,000

POPULATION

2001 Estimates:
Total	35,563
Male	16,618
Female	18,945

Age Groups	Male	Female
0-4	915	855
5-9	972	888
10-14	1,051	988
15-19	1,190	1,130
20-24	1,193	1,140
25-29	1,047	1,047
30-34	1,027	1,092
35-39	1,196	1,347
40-44	1,326	1,532
45-49	1,350	1,536
50-54	1,255	1,415
55-59	1,030	1,203
60-64	831	1,009
65-69	721	925
70+	1,514	2,838

DAYTIME POPULATION

2001 Estimates:
Working Population	16,308
At Home Population	19,255
Total	35,563

INCOME

2001 Estimates:
Avg. Household Income	$41,405
Avg. Family Income	$50,574
Per Capita Income	$17,945
Male:	
Avg. Employment Income	$31,644
Avg. Employment Income (Full Time)	$41,165
Female:	
Avg. Employment Income	$19,436
Avg. Employment Income (Full Time)	$28,360

Québec

DISPOSABLE & DISCRETIONARY INCOME

2001 Estimates:	Per Hhld.
Disposable Income	$28,697
Discretionary Income 1 (minus Food & Shelter)	$17,920
Discretionary Income 2 (minus Food, Shelter, & Other Expenditures)	$11,532

LIQUID ASSETS

1999 Estimates:	Per Hhld.
Equity Investments	$45,191
Interest Bearing Investments	$48,194
Total Liquid Assets	$93,385

CREDIT DATA

July 2000:	
Pool of Credit	$152,174,741
Revolving Credit, No.	46,730
Fixed Loans, No.	12,824
Avg. Credit Limit, per Person	$6,220
Avg. Spent, per Person	$2,685
Satisfactory Ratings, No. per Person	2.31
Avg. No. of Cards, per Person	0.94

LABOUR FORCE

2001 Estimates:	
Male:	
In the Labour Force	9,405
Participation Rate	68.8
Employed	8,601
Unemployed	804
Unemployment Rate	8.5
Not in Labour Force	4,275
Female:	
In the Labour Force	8,463
Participation Rate	52.2
Employed	7,813
Unemployed	650
Unemployment Rate	7.7
Not in Labour Force	7,751

OCCUPATIONS BY MAJOR GROUPS

2001 Estimates:	Male	Female
Management	1,116	359
Business, Finance & Admin.	903	2,241
Natural & Applied Sciences & Related	453	83
Health	327	1,021
Social Sciences, Gov't Services & Religion	252	311
Education	388	557
Arts, Culture, Recreation & Sport	169	175
Sales & Service	2,138	2,730
Trades, Transport & Equipment Operators & Related	1,810	93
Primary Industries	250	154
Processing, Mfg. & Utilities	1,207	307

Québec

Joliette
(Census Agglomeration)
(Cont'd)

LEVEL OF SCHOOLING

2001 Estimates:
Population 15 years +	29,894
Less than Grade 9	5,692
Grades 9-13 w/o Certif.	5,303
Grade 9-13 with Certif.	6,054
Trade Certif. /Dip.	1,221
Non-Univ. w/o Certif./Dip.	2,283
Non-Univ. with Certif./Dip.	4,562
Univ. w/o Degree	1,906
Univ. w/o Degree/Certif.	179
Univ. with Certif.	1,727
Univ. with Degree	2,873

AVERAGE HOUSEHOLD EXPENDITURES

2001 Estimates:
Food	$5,539
Shelter	$6,785
Clothing	$1,807
Transportation	$4,715
Health & Personal Care	$1,692
Recr'n, Read'g & Education	$2,685
Taxes & Securities	$12,022
Other	$6,365
Total Expenditures	$41,610

PRIVATE HOUSEHOLDS

2001 Estimates:
Private Households, Total	15,413
Pop. in Private Households	34,111
Average no. per Household	2.2

FAMILIES

2001 Estimates:
Families in Private Households	10,034
Husband-Wife Families	8,041
Lone-Parent Families	1,993
Aver. No. Persons per Family	2.8
Aver. No. Sons/Daughters at Home	1.1

HOUSING

2001 Estimates:
Occupied Private Dwellings	15,413
Owned	7,752
Rented	7,661
Single-Detached House	6,755
Semi-Detached House	327
Row Houses	173
Apartment, 5+ Storeys	178
Apartment, 5 or Fewer Storeys	5,781
Apartment, Detached Duplex	1,947
Other Single-Attached	241
Movable Dwellings	11

VEHICLES

2001 Estimates:
Model Yrs. '81-'96, No.	17,144
% Total	78.74
Model Yrs. '97-'98, No.	2,866
% Total	13.16
'99 Vehicles registered in Model Yr. '99, No.	1,763
% Total	8.10
Total No. '81-'99	21,773

LEGAL MARITAL STATUS

2001 Estimates: (Age 15+)
Single (Never Married)	11,340
Legally Married (Not Separated)	12,015
Legally Married (Separated)	688
Widowed	2,455
Divorced	3,396

PSYTE CATEGORIES

2001 Estimates	No. of House-holds	% of Total Hhds.	Index
Participation Quebec	2,395	15.54	539
New Quebec Rows	800	5.19	474
Quebec Melange	4,018	26.07	984
Traditional French Cdn. Families	936	6.07	226
Quebec's Heartland	142	0.92	94
Quebec Town Elders	4,292	27.85	985
Quebec's New Urban Mosaic	2,204	14.30	594
Aged Pensioners	428	2.78	209

FINANÇIAL P$YTE

2001 Estimates	No. of House-holds	% of Total Hhds.	Index
Mortgages & Minivans	3,195	20.73	314
Country Credit	4,954	32.14	475
Rural Family Blues	142	0.92	11
Loan Parent Stress	4,292	27.85	478
NSF	2,204	14.30	404
Senior Survivors	428	2.78	147

HOME LANGUAGE

2001 Estimates:		% Total
English	137	0.39
French	35,040	98.53
Spanish	21	0.06
Other Languages	159	0.45
Multiple Responses	206	0.58
Total	35,563	100.00

BUILDING PERMITS

	1999	1998 $000	1997
Value	40,563	45,843	49,715

HOMES BUILT

	1999	1998	1997
No	194	231	236

TAXATION

Income Class:	1997	% Total
Under $5,000	3,080	11.54
$5,000-$10,000	4,640	17.39
$10,000-$15,000	4,810	18.03
$15,000-$20,000	2,720	10.19
$20,000-$25,000	2,230	8.36
$25,000-$30,000	2,020	7.57
$30,000-$40,000	2,910	10.91
$40,000-$50,000	1,900	7.12
$50,000 +	2,410	9.03
Total Returns, No.	26,680	
Total Income, $000	621,885	
Total Taxable Returns	17,240	
Total Tax, $000	68,516	
Average Income, $	23,309	
Average Tax, $	3,974	

VITAL STATISTICS

	1997	1996	1995	1994
Births	298	313	299	351
Deaths	357	340	364	370
Natural Increase	-59	-27	-65	-19
Marriages	307	311	295	324

Note: Latest available data.

COMMUNITY NEWSPAPER(S)

	Total Circulation
Joliette: L'Action	46,775
Joliette: L'Expression de Lanaudière	47,545

RADIO STATION(S)

	Power
CJLM-FM	3,000w

La Tuque
(Census Agglomeration)

The Census Agglomeration of La Tuque consists of: La Tuque, V and two smaller areas. All are in census division Le Haut-Saint-Maurice.

POPULATION

July 1, 2001 Estimate	12,963
% Cdn. Total	0.04
% Change, '96 -'01	-3.07
Avg. Annual Growth Rate, %	-0.62
2003 Projected Population	12,751
2006 Projected Population	12,412
2001 Households Estimate	5,823
2003 Projected Households	5,834
2006 Projected Households	5,865

INCOME

% Above/Below National Average	-9
2001 Total Income Estimate	$249,630,000
% Cdn. Total	0.04
2001 Average Hhld. Income	$42,900
2001 Per Capita	$19,300
2003 Projected Total Income	$261,560,000
2006 Projected Total Income	$281,470,000

RETAIL SALES

% Above/Below National Average	+10
2001 Retail Sales Estimate	$127,690,000
% Cdn. Total	0.05
2001 per Household	$21,900
2001 per Capita	$9,900
2001 No. of Establishments	134
2003 Projected Retail Sales	$134,270,000
2006 Projected Retail Sales	$141,410,000

POPULATION

2001 Estimates:

Total		12,963
Male		6,480
Female		6,483

Age Groups	Male	Female
0-4	321	304
5-9	365	330
10-14	421	381
15-19	446	402
20-24	399	374
25-29	345	335
30-34	381	384
35-39	517	498
40-44	570	542
45-49	521	524
50-54	473	476
55-59	431	414
60-64	370	360
65-69	317	333
70+	603	826

DAYTIME POPULATION

2001 Estimates:

Working Population	5,649
At Home Population	7,314
Total	12,963

INCOME

2001 Estimates:

Avg. Household Income	$42,870
Avg. Family Income	$50,275
Per Capita Income	$19,257
Male:	
Avg. Employment Income	$33,986
Avg. Employment Income (Full Time)	$43,687
Female:	
Avg. Employment Income	$17,239
Avg. Employment Income (Full Time)	$25,733

DISPOSABLE & DISCRETIONARY INCOME

2001 Estimates:	Per Hhld.
Disposable Income	$29,792
Discretionary Income 1 (minus Food & Shelter)	$18,206
Discretionary Income 2 (minus Food, Shelter, & Other Expenditures)	$11,145

LIQUID ASSETS

1999 Estimates:	Per Hhld.
Equity Investments	$43,657
Interest Bearing Investments	$48,520
Total Liquid Assets	$92,177

CREDIT DATA

July 2000:

Pool of Credit	$76,366,892
Revolving Credit, No.	19,776
Fixed Loans, No.	6,447
Avg. Credit Limit, per Person	$8,007
Avg. Spent, per Person	$3,781
Satisfactory Ratings, No. per Person	2.66
Avg. No. of Cards, per Person	1.00

LABOUR FORCE

2001 Estimates:

Male:	
In the Labour Force	3,573
Participation Rate	66.5
Employed	3,243
Unemployed	330
Unemployment Rate	9.2
Not in Labour Force	1,800
Female:	
In the Labour Force	2,686
Participation Rate	49.1
Employed	2,450
Unemployed	236
Unemployment Rate	8.8
Not in Labour Force	2,782

OCCUPATIONS BY MAJOR GROUPS

2001 Estimates:	Male	Female
Management	245	77
Business, Finance & Admin.	117	617
Natural & Applied Sciences & Related	275	57
Health	40	253
Social Sciences, Gov't Services & Religion	31	106
Education	72	123
Arts, Culture, Recreation & Sport	33	44
Sales & Service	573	1,188
Trades, Transport & Equipment Operators & Related	1,256	46
Primary Industries	124	10
Processing, Mfg. & Utilities	713	56

LEVEL OF SCHOOLING

2001 Estimates:

Population 15 years +	10,841
Less than Grade 9	2,120
Grades 9-13 w/o Certif.	2,384
Grade 9-13 with Certif.	2,482
Trade Certif./Dip.	596
Non-Univ. w/o Certif./Dip.	544
Non-Univ. with Certif./Dip.	1,808
Univ. w/o Degree	411
Univ. w/o Degree/Certif.	70
Univ. with Certif.	341
Univ. with Degree	496

AVERAGE HOUSEHOLD EXPENDITURES

2001 Estimates:

Food	$6,167
Shelter	$7,012
Clothing	$1,998
Transportation	$5,213
Health & Personal Care	$1,655
Recr'n, Read'g & Education	$3,337
Taxes & Securities	$10,292
Other	$7,108
Total Expenditures	$42,782

PRIVATE HOUSEHOLDS

2001 Estimates:

Private Households, Total	5,823
Pop. in Private Households	12,759
Average no. per Household	2.2

FAMILIES

2001 Estimates:

Families in Private Households	4,058
Husband-Wife Families	3,443
Lone-Parent Families	615
Aver. No. Persons per Family	2.9
Aver. No. Sons/Daughters at Home	1.0

HOUSING

2001 Estimates:

Occupied Private Dwellings	5,823
Owned	3,558
Rented	2,265
Single-Detached House	3,151
Semi-Detached House	82
Row Houses	80
Apartment, 5 or Fewer Storeys	1,464
Apartment, Detached Duplex	1,046

VEHICLES

2001 Estimates:

Model Yrs. '81-'96, No.	6,335
% Total	78.65
Model Yrs. '97-'98, No.	1,057
% Total	13.12
'99 Vehicles registered in Model Yr. '99, No.	663
% Total	8.23
Total No. '81-'99	8,055

LEGAL MARITAL STATUS

2001 Estimates: (Age 15+)

Single (Never Married)	3,988
Legally Married (Not Separated)	4,659
Legally Married (Separated)	257
Widowed	851
Divorced	1,086

PSYTE CATEGORIES

2001 Estimates	No. of House-holds	% of Total Hhds.	Index
Traditional French Cdn. Families	433	7.44	277
Big Country Families	2,048	35.17	2,466
Quebec Rural Blues	1,147	19.70	808
Quebec Town Elders	2,176	37.37	1,322

FINANCIAL PSYTE

2001 Estimates	No. of House-holds	% of Total Hhds.	Index
Country Credit	433	7.44	110
Rural Family Blues	3,195	54.87	680
Loan Parent Stress	2,176	37.37	642

HOME LANGUAGE

2001 Estimates:		% Total
English	211	1.63
French	12,584	97.08
Other Languages	61	0.47
Multiple Responses	107	0.83
Total	12,963	100.00

Québec

BUILDING PERMITS

	1999	1998	1997
		$000	
Value	13,746	11,922	6,961

HOMES BUILT

	1999	1998	1997
No.	11	17	14

TAXATION

Income Class:	1997	% Total
Under $5,000	1,330	13.70
$5,000-$10,000	1,500	15.45
$10,000-$15,000	1,600	16.48
$15,000-$20,000	910	9.37
$20,000-$25,000	730	7.52
$25,000-$30,000	780	8.03
$30,000-$40,000	1,130	11.64
$40,000-$50,000	750	7.72
$50,000 +	990	10.20
Total Returns, No.	9,710	
Total Income, $000	225,354	
Total Taxable Returns	6,400	
Total Tax, $000	25,452	
Average Income, $	23,208	
Average Tax, $	3,977	

VITAL STATISTICS

	1997	1996	1995	1994
Births	112	135	145	124
Deaths	115	113	124	126
Natural Increase	-3	22	21	-2
Marriages	28	36	20	34

Note: Latest available data.

COMMUNITY NEWSPAPER(S)

	Total Circulation
La Tuque: L'Écho	6,801

RADIO STATION(S)

	Power
CBME	n.a.
CBVE	n.a.
CFLM	1,000w

TELEVISION STATION(S)

CBMT-TV
CBVT-TV

Québec

Lachute
(Census Agglomeration)

The Census Agglomeration of Lachute consists solely of Lachute, V, in census division Argenteuil.

POPULATION

July 1, 2001 Estimate	12,752
% Cdn. Total	0.04
% Change, '96 -'01	-3.21
Avg. Annual Growth Rate, %	-0.65
2003 Projected Population	12,007
2006 Projected Population	12,411
2001 Households Estimate	5,286
2003 Projected Households	5,270
2006 Projected Households	5,222

INCOME

% Above/Below National Average	-29
2001 Total Income Estimate	$191,610,000
% Cdn. Total	0.03
2001 Average Hhld. Income	$36,200
2001 Per Capita	$15,000
2003 Projected Total Income	$198,870,000
2006 Projected Total Income	$209,730,000

RETAIL SALES

% Above/Below National Average	+4
2001 Retail Sales Estimate	$118,440,000
% Cdn. Total	0.04
2001 per Household	$22,400
2001 per Capita	$9,300
2001 No. of Establishments	131
2003 Projected Retail Sales	$121,350,000
2006 Projected Retail Sales	$140,180,000

POPULATION

2001 Estimates:

Total		12,752
Male		6,086
Female		6,666

Age Groups	Male	Female
0-4	337	296
5-9	367	336
10-14	377	374
15-19	397	390
20-24	381	357
25-29	337	325
30-34	365	379
35-39	451	484
40-44	495	543
45-49	491	525
50-54	443	481
55-59	389	413
60-64	334	371
65-69	299	363
70+	623	1,029

DAYTIME POPULATION

2001 Estimates:

Working Population	5,147
At Home Population	7,605
Total	12,752

INCOME

2001 Estimates:

Avg. Household Income	$36,249
Avg. Family Income	$42,893
Per Capita Income	$15,026
Male:	
Avg. Employment Income	$27,479
Avg. Employment Income (Full Time)	$37,111
Female:	
Avg. Employment Income	$19,092
Avg. Employment Income (Full Time)	$28,004

DISPOSABLE & DISCRETIONARY INCOME

2001 Estimates:	Per Hhld.
Disposable Income	$26,007
Discretionary Income 1 (minus Food & Shelter)	$15,685
Discretionary Income 2 (minus Food, Shelter, & Other Expenditures)	$10,071

LIQUID ASSETS

1999 Estimates:	Per Hhld.
Equity Investments	$36,555
Interest Bearing Investments	$42,051
Total Liquid Assets	$78,606

CREDIT DATA

July 2000:

Pool of Credit	$66,455,763
Revolving Credit, No.	17,576
Fixed Loans, No.	5,833
Avg. Credit Limit, per Person	$7,448
Avg. Spent, per Person	$3,561
Satisfactory Ratings, No. per Person	2.53
Avg. No. of Cards, per Person	0.91

LABOUR FORCE

2001 Estimates:

Male:

In the Labour Force	3,159
Participation Rate	63.1
Employed	2,804
Unemployed	355
Unemployment Rate	11.2
Not in Labour Force	1,846

Female:

In the Labour Force	2,562
Participation Rate	45.3
Employed	2,346
Unemployed	216
Unemployment Rate	8.4
Not in Labour Force	3,098

OCCUPATIONS BY MAJOR GROUPS

2001 Estimates:	Male	Female
Management	321	131
Business, Finance & Admin.	252	616
Natural & Applied Sciences & Related	155	11
Health	101	270
Social Sciences, Gov't Services & Religion	64	80
Education	72	147
Arts, Culture, Recreation & Sport	12	10
Sales & Service	746	783
Trades, Transport & Equipment Operators & Related	614	51
Primary Industries	99	10
Processing, Mfg. & Utilities	518	301

LEVEL OF SCHOOLING

2001 Estimates:

Population 15 years +	10,665
Less than Grade 9	2,695
Grades 9-13 w/o Certif.	2,477
Grade 9-13 with Certif.	2,055
Trade Certif. /Dip.	398
Non-Univ. w/o Certif./Dip.	562
Non-Univ. with Certif./Dip.	1,265
Univ. w/o Degree	558
Univ. w/o Degree/Certif.	121
Univ. with Certif.	437
Univ. with Degree	655

AVERAGE HOUSEHOLD EXPENDITURES

2001 Estimates:

Food	$5,212
Shelter	$6,437
Clothing	$1,532
Transportation	$3,976
Health & Personal Care	$1,563
Recr'n, Read'g & Education	$2,327
Taxes & Securities	$10,152
Other	$5,781
Total Expenditures	$36,980

PRIVATE HOUSEHOLDS

2001 Estimates:

Private Households, Total	5,286
Pop. in Private Households	12,478
Average no. per Household	2.4

FAMILIES

2001 Estimates:

Families in Private Households	3,540
Husband-Wife Families	2,908
Lone-Parent Families	632
Aver. No. Persons per Family	2.8
Aver. No. Sons/Daughters at Home	1.0

HOUSING

2001 Estimates:

Occupied Private Dwellings	5,286
Owned	2,880
Rented	2,406
Single-Detached House	2,817
Semi-Detached House	215
Row Houses	76
Apartment, 5+ Storeys	27
Apartment, 5 or Fewer Storeys	1,572
Apartment, Detached Duplex	547
Other Single-Attached	32

VEHICLES

2001 Estimates:

Model Yrs. '81-'96, No.	5,579
% Total	80.04
Model Yrs. '97-'98, No.	865
% Total	12.41
'99 Vehicles registered in Model Yr. '99, No.	526
% Total	7.55
Total No. '81-'99	6,970

LEGAL MARITAL STATUS

2001 Estimates: (Age 15+)

Single (Never Married)	3,436
Legally Married (Not Separated)	4,825
Legally Married (Separated)	261
Widowed	1,056
Divorced	1,087

PSYTE CATEGORIES

2001 Estimates	No. of House-holds	% of Total Hhds.	Index
Quebec Melange	804	15.21	574
Old Leafy Towns	265	5.01	196
Quebec Rural Blues	470	8.89	365
Quebec Town Elders	3,525	66.69	2,360
Old Grey Towers	184	3.48	629

FINANCIAL P$YTE

2001 Estimates	No. of House-holds	% of Total Hhds.	Index
Bills & Wills	265	5.01	61
Country Credit	804	15.21	225
Rural Family Blues	470	8.89	110
Loan Parent Stress	3,525	66.69	1,145
Senior Survivors	184	3.48	185

HOME LANGUAGE

2001 Estimates:		% Total
English	1,969	15.44
French	10,602	83.14
Chinese	22	0.17
Portuguese	11	0.09
Spanish	11	0.09
Multiple Responses	137	1.07
Total	12,752	100.00

BUILDING PERMITS

	1999	1998 $000	1997
Value	5,570	6,908	13,249

HOMES BUILT

	1999	1998	1997
No.	4	13	19

TAXATION

Income Class:	1997	% Total
Under $5,000	1,210	12.36
$5,000-$10,000	1,770	18.08
$10,000-$15,000	2,000	20.43
$15,000-$20,000	1,070	10.93
$20,000-$25,000	790	8.07
$25,000-$30,000	730	7.46
$30,000-$40,000	1,020	10.42
$40,000-$50,000	610	6.23
$50,000 +	600	6.13
Total Returns, No.	9,790	
Total Income, $000	204,160	
Total Taxable Returns	6,030	
Total Tax, $000	20,865	
Average Income, $	20,854	
Average Tax, $	3,460	

VITAL STATISTICS

	1997	1996	1995	1994
Births	110	122	100	118
Deaths	161	143	165	173
Natural Increase	-51	-21	-65	-55
Marriages	37	46	46	40

Note: Latest available data.

COMMUNITY NEWSPAPER(S)

	Total Circulation
Lachute: L'Argenteuil	12,718
Lachute: La/The Tribune/Express/Le Progrès/	12,784

RADIO STATION(S)

	Power
CJLA-FM	3,000w

Magog
(Census Agglomeration)

The Census Agglomeration of Magog includes: Magog, V; Magog, CT; and Omerville, VL. All are in census division Memphrémagog.

POPULATION

July 1, 2001 Estimate	22,837
% Cdn. Total	0.07
% Change, '96 -'01	5.19
Avg. Annual Growth Rate, %	1.02
2003 Projected Population	23,190
2006 Projected Population	23,656
2001 Households Estimate	9,783
2003 Projected Households	9,948
2006 Projected Households	10,179

INCOME

% Above/Below National Average	-16
2001 Total Income Estimate	$406,380,000
% Cdn. Total	0.06
2001 Average Hhld. Income	$41,500
2001 Per Capita	$17,800
2003 Projected Total Income	$431,720,000
2006 Projected Total Income	$473,570,000

RETAIL SALES

% Above/Below National Average	+18
2001 Retail Sales Estimate	$241,840,000
% Cdn. Total	0.09
2001 per Household	$24,700
2001 per Capita	$10,600
2001 No. of Establishments	249
2003 Projected Retail Sales	$261,200,000
2006 Projected Retail Sales	$288,720,000

POPULATION

2001 Estimates:

Total		22,837
Male		11,096
Female		11,741

Age Groups	Male	Female
0-4	650	646
5-9	707	735
10-14	750	746
15-19	767	744
20-24	726	708
25-29	717	696
30-34	758	784
35-39	845	873
40-44	886	871
45-49	858	869
50-54	778	815
55-59	665	686
60-64	576	597
65-69	492	537
70+	921	1,434

DAYTIME POPULATION

2001 Estimates:

Working Population	10,605
At Home Population	12,232
Total	22,837

INCOME

2001 Estimates:

Avg. Household Income	$41,539
Avg. Family Income	$48,239
Per Capita Income	$17,795
Male:	
Avg. Employment Income	$28,894
Avg. Employment Income (Full Time)	$36,654
Female:	
Avg. Employment Income	$18,256
Avg. Employment Income (Full Time)	$27,341

DISPOSABLE & DISCRETIONARY INCOME

2001 Estimates:	Per Hhld.
Disposable Income	$29,156
Discretionary Income 1 (minus Food & Shelter)	$18,277
Discretionary Income 2 (minus Food, Shelter, & Other Expenditures)	$11,567

LIQUID ASSETS

1999 Estimates:	Per Hhld.
Equity Investments	$43,888
Interest Bearing Investments	$47,851
Total Liquid Assets	$91,739

CREDIT DATA

July 2000:

Pool of Credit	$126,170,679
Revolving Credit, No.	35,460
Fixed Loans, No.	12,418
Avg. Credit Limit, per Person	$7,649
Avg. Spent, per Person	$3,430
Satisfactory Ratings, No. per Person	2.71
Avg. No. of Cards, per Person	1.02

LABOUR FORCE

2001 Estimates:

Male:	
In the Labour Force	6,343
Participation Rate	70.6
Employed	5,882
Unemployed	461
Unemployment Rate	7.3
Not in Labour Force	2,646
Female:	
In the Labour Force	5,208
Participation Rate	54.2
Employed	4,795
Unemployed	413
Unemployment Rate	7.9
Not in Labour Force	4,406

OCCUPATIONS BY MAJOR GROUPS

2001 Estimates:	Male	Female
Management	580	243
Business, Finance & Admin.	346	1,336
Natural & Applied Sciences & Related	316	37
Health	65	288
Social Sciences, Gov't Services & Religion	102	106
Education	158	239
Arts, Culture, Recreation & Sport	100	66
Sales & Service	1,169	1,655
Trades, Transport & Equipment Operators & Related	1,684	64
Primary Industries	98	11
Processing, Mfg. & Utilities	1,513	935

LEVEL OF SCHOOLING

2001 Estimates:

Population 15 years +	18,603
Less than Grade 9	4,231
Grades 9-13 w/o Certif.	3,802
Grade 9-13 with Certif.	3,482
Trade Certif. /Dip.	877
Non-Univ. w/o Certif./Dip.	1,199
Non-Univ. with Certif./Dip.	2,559
Univ. w/o Degree	847
Univ. w/o Degree/Certif.	119
Univ. with Certif.	728
Univ. with Degree	1,606

AVERAGE HOUSEHOLD EXPENDITURES

2001 Estimates:

Food	$5,714
Shelter	$6,700
Clothing	$1,832
Transportation	$5,079
Health & Personal Care	$1,683
Recr'n, Read'g & Education	$2,756
Taxes & Securities	$11,270
Other	$6,565
Total Expenditures	$41,599

PRIVATE HOUSEHOLDS

2001 Estimates:

Private Households, Total	9,783
Pop. in Private Households	22,359
Average no. per Household	2.3

FAMILIES

2001 Estimates:

Families in Private Households	6,774
Husband-Wife Families	5,722
Lone-Parent Families	1,052
Aver. No. Persons per Family	2.9
Aver. No. Sons/Daughters at Home	1.1

HOUSING

2001 Estimates:

Occupied Private Dwellings	9,783
Owned	5,613
Rented	4,170
Single-Detached House	5,319
Semi-Detached House	205
Row Houses	134
Apartment, 5+ Storeys	12
Apartment, 5 or Fewer Storeys	3,102
Apartment, Detached Duplex	926
Other Single-Attached	49
Movable Dwellings	36

VEHICLES

2001 Estimates:

Model Yrs. '81-'96, No.	11,329
% Total	77.44
Model Yrs. '97-'98, No.	2,048
% Total	14.00
'99 Vehicles registered in Model Yr. '99, No.	1,252
% Total	8.56
Total No. '81-'99	14,629

LEGAL MARITAL STATUS

2001 Estimates: (Age 15+)

Single (Never Married)	6,452
Legally Married (Not Separated)	8,315
Legally Married (Separated)	419
Widowed	1,357
Divorced	2,060

PSYTE CATEGORIES

2001 Estimates	No. of House-holds	% of Total Hhds.	Index
Stable Suburban Families	143	1.46	112
Small City Elite	156	1.59	93
Quebec Melange	2,345	23.97	905
Traditional French Cdn. Families	2,381	24.34	906
Quebec's Heartland	314	3.21	327
Big Country Families	237	2.42	170
Quebec Rural Blues	503	5.14	211
Old Quebec Walkups	63	0.64	35
Quebec Town Elders	2,888	29.52	1,045
Quebec's New Urban Mosaic	712	7.28	302

Québec

FINANCIAL P$YTE

2001 Estimates	No. of House-holds	% of Total Hhds.	Index
Successful Suburbanites	143	1.46	22
Canadian Comfort	156	1.59	16
Country Credit	4,726	48.31	714
Rural Family Blues	1,054	10.77	133
Loan Parent Stress	2,951	30.16	518
NSF	712	7.28	206

HOME LANGUAGE

2001 Estimates:		% Total
English	1,321	5.78
French	21,118	92.47
Other Languages	22	0.10
Multiple Responses	376	1.65
Total	22,837	100.00

BUILDING PERMITS

	1999	1998	1997
		$000	
Value	36,870	26,740	17,046

HOMES BUILT

	1999	1998	1997
No.	118	105	132

TAXATION

Income Class:	1997	% Total
Under $5,000	1,860	10.80
$5,000-$10,000	2,630	15.27
$10,000-$15,000	3,090	17.94
$15,000-$20,000	2,090	12.14
$20,000-$25,000	1,540	8.94
$25,000-$30,000	1,500	8.71
$30,000-$40,000	2,170	12.60
$40,000-$50,000	1,050	6.10
$50,000 +	1,300	7.55
Total Returns, No.	17,220	
Total Income, $000	404,138	
Total Taxable Returns	11,910	
Total Tax, $000	45,573	
Average Income, $	23,469	
Average Tax, $	3,826	

VITAL STATISTICS

	1997	1996	1995	1994
Births	223	277	283	275
Deaths	191	168	192	174
Natural Increase	32	109	91	101
Marriages	71	65	82	79

Note: Latest available data.

COMMUNITY NEWSPAPER(S)

	Total Circulation
Magog: Le Reflet du Lac	21,154

RADIO STATION(S)

	Power
CIMO-FM	50,000w

TELEVISION STATION(S)

CBMT-TV

Québec

Matane
(Census Agglomeration)

The Census Agglomeration of Matane consists of Matane, V; Petit-Matane, M; Saint-Jérôme-de-Matane, P; and three smaller areas. All are in census division Matane.

POPULATION

July 1, 2001 Estimate	16,638
% Cdn. Total	0.05
% Change, '96 - '01	-4.22
Avg. Annual Growth Rate, %	-0.86
2003 Projected Population	16,405
2006 Projected Population	15,953
2001 Households Estimate	7,241
2003 Projected Households	7,294
2006 Projected Households	7,326

INCOME

% Above/Below National Average	-17
2001 Total Income Estimate	$291,040,000
% Cdn. Total	0.04
2001 Average Hhld. Income	$40,200
2001 Per Capita	$17,500
2003 Projected Total Income	$306,690,000
2006 Projected Total Income	$330,010,000

RETAIL SALES

% Above/Below National Average	+46
2001 Retail Sales Estimate	$217,650,000
% Cdn. Total	0.08
2001 per Household	$30,100
2001 per Capita	$13,100
2001 No. of Establishments	230
2003 Projected Retail Sales	$230,720,000
2006 Projected Retail Sales	$247,050,000

POPULATION

2001 Estimates:

Total		16,638
Male		8,024
Female		8,614

Age Groups	Male	Female
0-4	410	367
5-9	449	406
10-14	483	474
15-19	553	545
20-24	554	520
25-29	466	449
30-34	460	518
35-39	597	661
40-44	690	749
45-49	691	743
50-54	643	663
55-59	519	521
60-64	398	424
65-69	339	394
70+	772	1,180

DAYTIME POPULATION

2001 Estimates:

Working Population	6,959
At Home Population	9,687
Total	16,646

INCOME

2001 Estimates:

Avg. Household Income	$40,193
Avg. Family Income	$46,868
Per Capita Income	$17,492
Male:	
Avg. Employment Income	$30,303
Avg. Employment Income (Full Time)	$41,664
Female:	
Avg. Employment Income	$17,696
Avg. Employment Income (Full Time)	$28,184

DISPOSABLE & DISCRETIONARY INCOME

2001 Estimates:	*Per Hhld.*
Disposable Income	$28,476
Discretionary Income 1 (minus Food & Shelter)	$17,701
Discretionary Income 2 (minus Food, Shelter, & Other Expenditures)	$11,027

LIQUID ASSETS

1999 Estimates:	*Per Hhld.*
Equity Investments	$42,983
Interest Bearing Investments	$46,149
Total Liquid Assets	$89,132

CREDIT DATA

July 2000:

Pool of Credit	$74,925,888
Revolving Credit, No.	22,243
Fixed Loans, No.	8,530
Avg. Credit Limit, per Person	$6,356
Avg. Spent, per Person	$2,920
Satisfactory Ratings, No. per Person	2.42
Avg. No. of Cards, per Person	0.94

LABOUR FORCE

2001 Estimates:

Male:	
In the Labour Force	4,365
Participation Rate	65.3
Employed	3,717
Unemployed	648
Unemployment Rate	14.8
Not in Labour Force	2,317
Female:	
In the Labour Force	3,639
Participation Rate	49.4
Employed	3,235
Unemployed	404
Unemployment Rate	11.1
Not in Labour Force	3,728

OCCUPATIONS BY MAJOR GROUPS

2001 Estimates:	Male	Female
Management	502	221
Business, Finance & Admin.	359	967
Natural & Applied Sciences & Related	190	39
Health	78	225
Social Sciences, Gov't Services & Religion	113	93
Education	136	271
Arts, Culture, Recreation & Sport	48	21
Sales & Service	846	1,302
Trades, Transport & Equipment Operators & Related	1,145	34
Primary Industries	285	51
Processing, Mfg. & Utilities	465	224

LEVEL OF SCHOOLING

2001 Estimates:

Population 15 years +	14,049
Less than Grade 9	3,419
Grades 9-13 w/o Certif.	2,416
Grade 9-13 with Certif.	2,684
Trade Certif. /Dip.	821
Non-Univ. w/o Certif./Dip.	850
Non-Univ. with Certif./Dip.	2,003
Univ. w/o Degree	645
Univ. w/o Degree/Certif.	54
Univ. with Certif.	591
Univ. with Degree	1,211

AVERAGE HOUSEHOLD EXPENDITURES

2001 Estimates:

Food	$5,678
Shelter	$6,550
Clothing	$1,832
Transportation	$4,994
Health & Personal Care	$1,673
Recr'n, Read'g & Education	$2,647
Taxes & Securities	$10,824
Other	$6,288
Total Expenditures	$40,486

PRIVATE HOUSEHOLDS

2001 Estimates:

Private Households, Total	7,241
Pop. in Private Households	16,223
Average no. per Household	2.2

FAMILIES

2001 Estimates:

Families in Private Households	5,047
Husband-Wife Families	4,228
Lone-Parent Families	819
Aver. No. Persons per Family	2.9
Aver. No. Sons/Daughters at Home	1.0

HOUSING

2001 Estimates:

Occupied Private Dwellings	7,241
Owned	4,615
Rented	2,626
Single-Detached House	4,176
Semi-Detached House	370
Row Houses	67
Apartment, 5 or Fewer Storeys	1,596
Apartment, Detached Duplex	801
Other Single-Attached	46
Movable Dwellings	185

VEHICLES

2001 Estimates:

Model Yrs. '81-'96, No.	8,723
% Total	81.58
Model Yrs. '97-'98, No.	1,181
% Total	11.04
'99 Vehicles registered in Model Yr. '99, No.	789
% Total	7.38
Total No. '81-'99	10,693

LEGAL MARITAL STATUS

2001 Estimates: (Age 15+)

Single (Never Married)	5,349
Legally Married (Not Separated)	6,034
Legally Married (Separated)	233
Widowed	1,125
Divorced	1,308

PSYTE CATEGORIES

2001 Estimates	No. of House -holds	% of Total Hhds.	Index
Participation Quebec	375	5.18	180
Quebec Melange	1,479	20.43	771
Traditional French Cdn. Families	716	9.89	368
Big Country Families	395	5.46	382
Quebec Rural Blues	1,421	19.62	805
Quebec Town Elders	2,797	38.63	1,367

FINANCIAL P$YTE

2001 Estimates	No. of House -holds	% of Total Hhds.	Index
Mortgages & Minivans	375	5.18	78
Country Credit	2,195	30.31	448
Rural Family Blues	1,816	25.08	311
Loan Parent Stress	2,797	38.63	663

HOME LANGUAGE

2001 Estimates:		% Total
English	53	0.32
French	16,561	99.54
Italian	14	0.08
Multiple Responses	10	0.06
Total	16,638	100.00

BUILDING PERMITS

	1999	1998	1997
		$000	
Value	6,900	10,535	19,216

HOMES BUILT

	1999	1998	1997
No	10	15	21

TAXATION

Income Class:	1997	% Total
Under $5,000	1,740	13.75
$5,000-$10,000	2,180	17.23
$10,000-$15,000	2,570	20.32
$15,000-$20,000	1,340	10.59
$20,000-$25,000	1,050	8.30
$25,000-$30,000	1,000	7.91
$30,000-$40,000	1,160	9.17
$40,000-$50,000	780	6.17
$50,000 +	830	6.56
Total Returns, No.	12,650	
Total Income, $000	258,177	
Total Taxable Returns	7,680	
Total Tax, $000	26,087	
Average Income, $.	20,409	
Average Tax, $.	3,397	

VITAL STATISTICS

	1997	1996	1995	1994
Births	126	145	123	171
Deaths	154	159	166	166
Natural Increase	-28	-14	-43	5
Marriages	33	35	42	36

Note: Latest available data.

COMMUNITY NEWSPAPER(S)

	Total Circulation
Matane: La Voix du Dimanche	10,125
Matane: La Voix Gaspésienne	4,979

RADIO STATION(S)

	Power
CBGA	10,000w
CHOE-FM	12,730w
CHRM	10,000w

TELEVISION STATION(S)

CBGAT-TV
CFER-TV
CIVF-TV

Montmagny
(Ville)

In census division Montmagny.

POPULATION

July 1, 2001 Estimate	11,830
% Cdn. Total	0.04
% Change, '96 -'01	-2.00
Avg. Annual Growth Rate, %	-0.40
2003 Projected Population	11,788
2006 Projected Population	11,643
2001 Households Estimate	4,912
2003 Projected Households	4,941
2006 Projected Households	4,961

INCOME

% Above/Below National Average	-20
2001 Total Income Estimate	$199,690,000
% Cdn. Total	0.03
2001 Average Hhld. Income	$40,700
2001 Per Capita	$16,900
2003 Projected Total Income	$209,860,000
2006 Projected Total Income	$225,310,000

RETAIL SALES

% Above/Below National Average	+115
2001 Retail Sales Estimate	$227,960,000
% Cdn. Total	0.08
2001 per Household	$46,400
2001 per Capita	$19,300
2001 No. of Establishments	162
2003 Projected Retail Sales	$246,310,000
2006 Projected Retail Sales	$270,380,000

POPULATION

2001 Estimates:

Total		11,830
Male		5,677
Female		6,153

Age Groups	Male	Female
0-4	306	281
5-9	311	289
10-14	328	314
15-19	371	358
20-24	385	382
25-29	370	356
30-34	415	365
35-39	448	419
40-44	453	465
45-49	455	478
50-54	426	450
55-59	369	376
60-64	281	324
65-69	228	298
70+	531	998

DAYTIME POPULATION

2001 Estimates:

Working Population	8,702
At Home Population	6,459
Total	15,161

INCOME

2001 Estimates:

Avg. Household Income	$40,654
Avg. Family Income	$47,122
Per Capita Income	$16,880
Male:	
Avg. Employment Income	$28,148
Avg. Employment Income (Full Time)	$34,704
Female:	
Avg. Employment Income	$18,911
Avg. Employment Income (Full Time)	$26,498

DISPOSABLE & DISCRETIONARY INCOME

2001 Estimates:	Per Hhld.
Disposable Income	$28,514
Discretionary Income 1 (minus Food & Shelter)	$17,310
Discretionary Income 2 (minus Food, Shelter, & Other Expenditures)	$11,131

LIQUID ASSETS

1999 Estimates:	Per Hhld.
Equity Investments	$45,977
Interest Bearing Investments	$47,750
Total Liquid Assets	$93,727

CREDIT DATA

July 2000:

Pool of Credit	$48,507,288
Revolving Credit, No.	18,149
Fixed Loans, No.	4,595
Avg. Credit Limit, per Person	$5,948
Avg. Spent, per Person	$2,331
Satisfactory Ratings, No. per Person	2.67
Avg. No. of Cards, per Person	1.14

LABOUR FORCE

2001 Estimates:

Male:	
In the Labour Force	3,510
Participation Rate	74.2
Employed	3,189
Unemployed	321
Unemployment Rate	9.1
Not in Labour Force	1,222
Female:	
In the Labour Force	2,409
Participation Rate	45.7
Employed	2,252
Unemployed	157
Unemployment Rate	6.5
Not in Labour Force	2,860

OCCUPATIONS BY MAJOR GROUPS

2001 Estimates:	Male	Female
Management	235	93
Business, Finance & Admin.	265	606
Natural & Applied Sciences & Related	135	10
Health	126	293
Social Sciences, Gov't Services & Religion	78	68
Education	121	114
Arts, Culture, Recreation & Sport	65	89
Sales & Service	610	847
Trades, Transport & Equipment Operators & Related	771	31
Primary Industries	129	32
Processing, Mfg. & Utilities	829	162

LEVEL OF SCHOOLING

2001 Estimates:

Population 15 years +	10,001
Less than Grade 9	2,562
Grades 9-13 w/o Certif.	1,940
Grade 9-13 with Certif.	1,935
Trade Certif. /Dip.	534
Non-Univ. w/o Certif./Dip.	475
Non-Univ. with Certif./Dip.	1,507
Univ. w/o Degree	428
Univ. w/o Degree/Certif.	38
Univ. with Certif.	390
Univ. with Degree	620

AVERAGE HOUSEHOLD EXPENDITURES

2001 Estimates:

Food	$5,885
Shelter	$6,760
Clothing	$1,750
Transportation	$4,490
Health & Personal Care	$1,664
Recr'n, Read'g & Education	$2,665
Taxes & Securities	$11,391
Other	$6,331
Total Expenditures	$40,936

PRIVATE HOUSEHOLDS

2001 Estimates:

Private Households, Total	4,912
Pop. in Private Households	11,381
Average no. per Household	2.3

FAMILIES

2001 Estimates:

Families in Private Households	3,415
Husband-Wife Families	2,923
Lone-Parent Families	492
Aver. No. Persons per Family	2.9
Aver. No. Sons/Daughters at Home	1.1

HOUSING

2001 Estimates:

Occupied Private Dwellings	4,912
Owned	2,940
Rented	1,972
Single-Detached House	2,598
Semi-Detached House	136
Row Houses	79
Apartment, 5 or Fewer Storeys	1,307
Apartment, Detached Duplex	692
Other Single-Attached	16
Movable Dwellings	84

VEHICLES

2001 Estimates:

Model Yrs. '81-'96, No.	6,079
% Total	81.13
Model Yrs. '97-'98, No.	877
% Total	11.70
'99 Vehicles registered in Model Yr. '99, No.	537
% Total	7.17
Total No. '81-'99	7,493

LEGAL MARITAL STATUS

2001 Estimates: (Age 15+)

Single (Never Married)	3,921
Legally Married (Not Separated)	4,327
Legally Married (Separated)	153
Widowed	931
Divorced	669

PSYTE CATEGORIES

2001 Estimates	No. of House-holds	% of Total Hhds.	Index
Traditional French Cdn. Families	1,168	23.78	885
Quebec Rural Blues	494	10.06	413
Quebec Town Elders	3,174	64.62	2,287

FINANCIAL PSYTE

2001 Estimates	No. of House-holds	% of Total Hhds.	Index
Country Credit	1,168	23.78	352
Rural Family Blues	494	10.06	125
Loan Parent Stress	3,174	64.62	1,110

HOME LANGUAGE

2001 Estimates:		% Total
English	31	0.26
French	11,773	99.52
Other Languages	11	0.09
Multiple Responses	15	0.13
Total	11,830	100.00

Québec

BUILDING PERMITS

	1999	1998	1997
		$000	
Value	8,027	5,386	10,945

HOMES BUILT

	1999	1998	1997
No.	17	15	16

TAXATION

Income Class:	1997	% Total
Under $5,000	1,110	12.35
$5,000-$10,000	1,370	15.24
$10,000-$15,000	1,810	20.13
$15,000-$20,000	970	10.79
$20,000-$25,000	830	9.23
$25,000-$30,000	700	7.79
$30,000-$40,000	1,160	12.90
$40,000-$50,000	520	5.78
$50,000 +	520	5.78
Total Returns, No.	8,990	
Total Income, $000	192,036	
Total Taxable Returns	5,830	
Total Tax, $000	19,311	
Average Income, $.	21,361	
Average Tax, $.	3,312	

VITAL STATISTICS

	1997	1996	1995	1994
Births	112	115	130	118
Deaths	130	118	138	123
Natural Increase	-18	-3	-8	-5
Marriages	48	46	60	72

Note: Latest available data.

COMMUNITY NEWSPAPER(S)

	Total Circulation
Montmagny: Le Peuple de la Côte-du-Sud	19,620
Montmagny: L'Oie Blanche	20,124

RADIO STATION(S)

	Power
CFEL-FM	8,740w

Québec

Montréal
(Census Metropolitan Area)

POPULATION

July 1, 2001 Estimate	3,500,756
% Cdn. Total	11.24
% Change, '96 -'01	3.15
Avg. Annual Growth Rate, %	0.62
2003 Projected Population	3,607,948
2006 Projected Population	3,796,046
2001 Households Estimate	1,451,466
2003 Projected Households	1,500,618
2006 Projected Households	1,584,277

INCOME

% Above/Below National Average	-2
2001 Total Income Estimate	$72,022,910,000
% Cdn. Total	10.97
2001 Average Hhld. Income	$49,600
2001 Per Capita	$20,600
2003 Projected Total Income	$78,487,830,000
2006 Projected Total Income	$90,121,810,000

RETAIL SALES

% Above/Below National Average	-8
2001 Retail Sales Estimate	$28,737,340,000
% Cdn. Total	10.31
2001 per Household	$19,800
2001 per Capita	$8,200
2001 No. of Establishments	28,988
2003 Projected Retail Sales	$31,840,340,000
2006 Projected Retail Sales	$36,849,560,000

POPULATION

2001 Estimates:

Total	3,500,756
Male	1,696,089
Female	1,804,667

Age Groups	Male	Female
0-4	106,937	102,089
5-9	109,882	105,515
10-14	106,850	102,505
15-19	107,534	102,737
20-24	110,125	107,178
25-29	115,881	115,786
30-34	132,625	132,700
35-39	147,076	148,070
40-44	144,748	149,226
45-49	133,205	140,583
50-54	117,054	124,577
55-59	96,032	103,358
60-64	78,454	87,067
65-69	65,305	77,579
70+	124,381	205,697

DAYTIME POPULATION

2001 Estimates:

Working Population	1,670,377
At Home Population	1,830,389
Total	3,500,766

INCOME

2001 Estimates:

Avg. Household Income	$49,621
Avg. Family Income	$58,648
Per Capita Income	$20,574

Male:

Avg. Employment Income	$35,647
Avg. Employment Income (Full Time)	$46,411

Female:

Avg. Employment Income	$23,409
Avg. Employment Income (Full Time)	$33,086

DISPOSABLE & DISCRETIONARY INCOME

2001 Estimates:	Per Hhld.
Disposable Income	$33,552
Discretionary Income 1 (minus Food & Shelter)	$20,866
Discretionary Income 2 (minus Food, Shelter, & Other Expenditures)	$13,507

LIQUID ASSETS

1999 Estimates:	Per Hhld.
Equity Investments	$64,033
Interest Bearing Investments	$59,099
Total Liquid Assets	$123,132

CREDIT DATA

July 2000:

Pool of Credit	$24,657,430,359
Revolving Credit, No.	6,456,043
Fixed Loans, No.	1,859,640
Avg. Credit Limit, per Person	$8,435
Avg. Spent, per Person	$3,685
Satisfactory Ratings, No. per Person	2.71
Avg. No. of Cards, per Person	1.11

LABOUR FORCE

2001 Estimates:

Male:

In the Labour Force	994,970
Participation Rate	72.5
Employed	916,946
Unemployed	78,024
Unemployment Rate	7.8
Not in Labour Force	377,450

Female:

In the Labour Force	820,834
Participation Rate	54.9
Employed	762,842
Unemployed	57,992
Unemployment Rate	7.1
Not in Labour Force	673,724

OCCUPATIONS BY MAJOR GROUPS

2001 Estimates:	Male	Female
Management	119,779	49,617
Business, Finance & Admin.	119,692	264,382
Natural & Applied Sciences & Related	87,259	19,763
Health	22,691	70,326
Social Sciences, Gov't Services & Religion	19,824	25,198
Education	27,134	41,342
Arts, Culture, Recreation & Sport	30,429	30,610
Sales & Service	218,913	212,667
Trades, Transport & Equipment Operators & Related	198,266	13,212
Primary Industries	11,854	2,708
Processing, Mfg. & Utilities	92,398	52,605

LEVEL OF SCHOOLING

2001 Estimates:

Population 15 years +	2,866,978
Less than Grade 9	457,188
Grades 9-13 w/o Certif.	457,247
Grade 9-13 with Certif.	486,548
Trade Certif. /Dip.	101,771
Non-Univ. w/o Certif./Dip.	218,891
Non-Univ. with Certif./Dip.	426,497
Univ. w/o Degree	283,843
Univ. w/o Degree/Certif.	63,513
Univ. with Certif.	220,330
Univ. with Degree	434,993

AVERAGE HOUSEHOLD EXPENDITURES

2001 Estimates:

Food	$6,203
Shelter	$8,513
Clothing	$2,170
Transportation	$5,368
Health & Personal Care	$1,903
Recr'n, Read'g & Education	$3,260
Taxes & Securities	$13,488
Other	$7,313
Total Expenditures	$48,218

PRIVATE HOUSEHOLDS

2001 Estimates:

Private Households, Total	1,451,466
Pop. in Private Households	3,433,488
Average no. per Household	2.4

FAMILIES

2001 Estimates:

Families in Private Households	972,279
Husband-Wife Families	806,480
Lone-Parent Families	165,799
Aver. No. Persons per Family	3.0
Aver. No. Sons/Daughters at Home	1.1

HOUSING

2001 Estimates:

Occupied Private Dwellings	1,451,466
Owned	719,164
Rented	732,302
Single-Detached House	470,618
Semi-Detached House	71,030
Row Houses	47,695
Apartment, 5+ Storeys	120,944
Owned Apartment, 5+ Storeys	19,489
Apartment, 5 or Fewer Storeys	672,488
Apartment, Detached Duplex	57,918
Other Single-Attached	6,509
Movable Dwellings	4,264

VEHICLES

2001 Estimates:

Model Yrs. '81-'96, No.	1,343,605
% Total	72.80
Model Yrs. '97-'98, No.	305,101
% Total	16.53
'99 Vehicles registered in Model Yr. '99, No.	196,890
% Total	10.67
Total No. '81-'99	1,845,596

LEGAL MARITAL STATUS

2001 Estimates: (Age 15+)

Single (Never Married)	1,095,411
Legally Married (Not Separated)	1,242,400
Legally Married (Separated)	79,030
Widowed	183,491
Divorced	266,646

PSYTE CATEGORIES

2001 Estimates	No. of House-holds	% of Total Hhds.	Index
Canadian Establishment	3,553	0.24	147
The Affluentials	5,464	0.38	59
Urban Gentry	28,952	1.99	111
Suburban Executives	16,880	1.16	81
Mortgaged in Suburbia	2,302	0.16	11
Technocrafts & Bureaucrats	26,085	1.80	64
Asian Heights	1,325	0.09	14
Boomers & Teens	460	0.03	2
Stable Suburban Families	19,229	1.32	102
Small City Elite	1,572	0.11	6
Old Bungalow Burbs	19,279	1.33	80
Suburban Nesters	10,946	0.75	47
Brie & Chablis	9,655	0.67	74
Aging Erudites	17,349	1.20	79
Satellite Suburbs	709	0.05	2
Kindergarten Boom	2,459	0.17	6
Blue Collar Winners	308	0.02	1
Participation Quebec	182,579	12.58	437
New Quebec Rows	77,593	5.35	488
Quebec Melange	122,578	8.45	319
Traditional French Cdn. Families	72,728	5.01	187
Rustic Prosperity	268	0.02	1
Quebec's Heartland	4,354	0.30	15
Europa	25,556	1.76	142
Asian Mosaic	268	0.02	1
High Rise Melting Pot	4,572	0.31	21
Conservative Homebodies	1,580	0.11	3
High Rise Sunsets	20,529	1.41	99
Young Urban Professionals	38,883	2.68	141
Young Urban Mix	8,960	0.62	29
Young Urban Intelligentsia	27,499	1.89	125
University Enclaves	4,564	0.31	15
Young City Singles	4,232	0.29	13
Urban Bohemia	82,207	5.66	484
Old Leafy Towns	296	0.02	1
Town Renters	1,711	0.12	14
Agrarian Blues	473	0.03	15
Big Country Families	479	0.03	2
Quebec Rural Blues	1,324	0.09	4
Euro Quebec	105,820	7.29	831
Old Quebec Walkups	180,530	12.44	679
Quebec Town Elders	40,141	2.77	98
Aging Quebec Urbanites	22,108	1.52	528
Quebec's New Urban Mosaic	170,904	11.77	489
Struggling Downtowns	325	0.02	1
Aged Pensioners	13,218	0.91	68
Big City Stress	44,989	3.10	274
Old Grey Towers	12,299	0.85	153

FINANCIAL P$YTE

2001 Estimates	No. of House-holds	% of Total Hhds.	Index
Platinum Estates	9,017	0.62	77
Four Star Investors	46,292	3.19	63
Successful Suburbanites	48,941	3.37	51
Canadian Comfort	13,535	0.93	10
Urban Heights	65,887	4.54	106
Miners & Credit-Liners	19,279	1.33	42
Mortgages & Minivans	262,631	18.09	274
Dollars & Sense	25,824	1.78	68
Tractors & Tradelines	268	0.02	
Bills & Wills	10,836	0.75	9
Country Credit	195,306	13.46	199
Revolving Renters	20,529	1.41	31
Young Urban Struggle	114,270	7.87	166
Rural Family Blues	6,630	0.46	1
Loan Parent Stress	348,599	24.02	412
Towering Debt	10,840	0.75	10
NSF	215,893	14.87	420
Senior Survivors	25,517	1.76	93

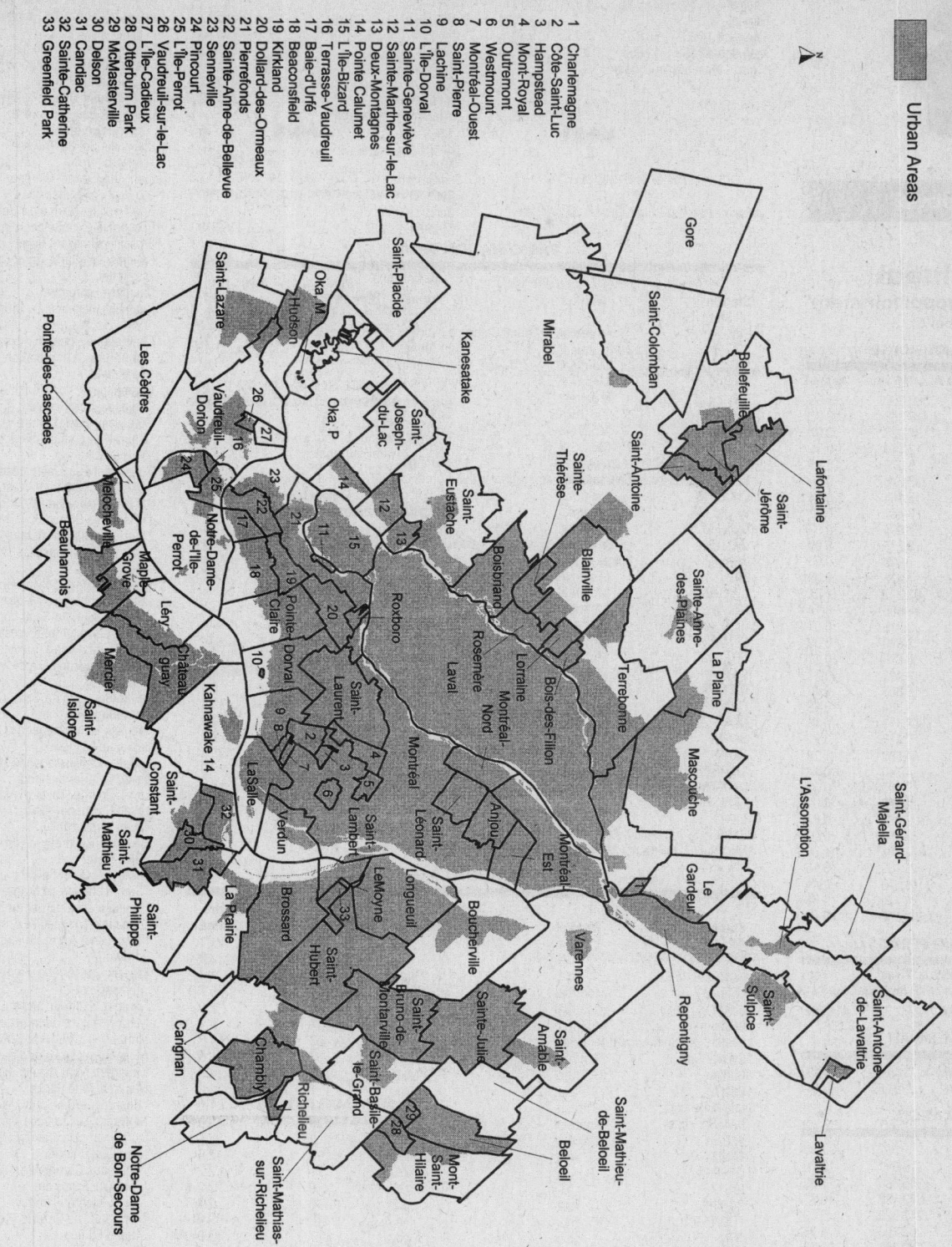

Québec

Montréal
(Census Metropolitan Area)
(Cont'd)

HOME LANGUAGE

2001 Estimates:		% Total
English	580,860	16.59
French	2,426,398	69.31
Arabic	34,028	0.97
Armenian	12,144	0.35
Bengali	5,078	0.15
Chinese	33,245	0.95
Creoles	15,464	0.44
German	2,469	0.07
Greek	28,694	0.82
Gujarati	3,215	0.09
Hebrew	2,025	0.06
Hungarian	3,025	0.09
Italian	63,272	1.81
Khmer (Cambodian)	4,856	0.14
Korean	2,319	0.07
Lao	2,990	0.09
Persian (Farsi)	6,070	0.17
Polish	9,493	0.27
Portuguese	16,868	0.48
Punjabi	5,384	0.15
Romanian	6,373	0.18
Russian	7,416	0.21
Spanish	44,652	1.28
Tagalog (Pilipino)	4,740	0.14
Tamil	7,289	0.21
Turkish	2,556	0.07
Ukrainian	2,294	0.07
Urdu	3,080	0.09
Vietnamese	19,208	0.55
Yiddish	5,159	0.15
Other Languages	15,313	0.44
Multiple Responses	124,779	3.56
Total	3,500,756	100.00

BUILDING PERMITS

	1999	1998	1997
		$000	
Value	2,935,143	2,781,920	2,414,381

HOMES BUILT

	1999	1998	1997
No	11,276	9,862	10,097

TAXATION

Income Class:	1997	% Total
Under $5,000	318,640	12.98
$5,000-$10,000	365,370	14.89
$10,000-$15,000	373,130	15.20
$15,000-$20,000	242,820	9.89
$20,000-$25,000	202,190	8.24
$25,000-$30,000	190,720	7.77
$30,000-$40,000	282,930	11.53
$40,000-$50,000	184,600	7.52
$50,000 +	294,570	12.00
Total Returns, No.	2,454,520	
Total Income, $000	65,257,939	
Total Taxable Returns	1,670,300	
Total Tax, $000	8,269,009	
Average Income, $	26,587	
Average Tax, $	4,951	

VITAL STATISTICS

	1997	1996	1995	1994
Births	39,778	42,612	43,385	45,041
Deaths	24,846	23,938	24,154	23,626
Natural Increase	14,932	18,674	19,231	21,415
Marriages	12,559	12,057	12,141	12,761

Note: Latest available data.

DAILY NEWSPAPER(S)

	Circulation Average Paid
La Presse	
Sat	265,973
Sun	178,730
Mon-Fri	168,203
Le Devoir	
Sat	41,892
Mon-Fri	26,799
Le Journal de Montréal	
Sat	334,726
Sun	277,833
Mon-Fri	267,374
The Gazette	
Sat	188,350
Sun	132,597
Mon-Fri	138,813

RADIO STATION DATA

Station	Market	Format	Wkly. Reach%*	Aver. Hrs. Tuned
All Stations			94	23.8
CBF	Montréal	Adult Contemp., Variety	n.a.	n.a.
CBF-FM	Montréal	Multi-format	8	11.4
CBFX-FM	Montréal	Music, Culture, Info.	3	8.0
CBM-FM	Montréal	Multi-format	3	11.8
CBME-FM	Montréal	n.a.	3	12.3
CFGL-FM	Laval	Soft Rock	12	10.5
CFMB	Montréal	Ethnic, Multicult.	n.a.	n.a.
CFQR-FM	Montréal	Adult Contemp.	15	9.4
CHAA	Loungueuil	Multi-format	n.a.	n.a.
CHAI-FM	Châteauguay	Adult Contemp.	n.a.	n.a.
CHCR-FM	Montréal	Ethnic, Multiling.	n.a.	n.a.
CHOM-FM	Montréal	AOR	14	7.1
CIBL-FM	Montréal	Community	n.a.	n.a.
CIEL-FM	Montréal	Adult Contemp.	9	7.8
CIME-FM	Saint-Jérôme	Top 40	n.a.	n.a.
CINF	Montréal	News	4	6.2
CINQ-FM	Montréal	Ethnic, Multiling.	n.a.	n.a.
CINW	Montréal	News	3	5.1
CIQC	Montréal	News, Talk	n.a.	n.a.
CIRA-FM	Montréal	Christian	n.a.	n.a.
CITE-FM	Montréal	Adult Contemp.	19	13.0
CJAD	Montréal	News, Talk	10	14.2
CJFM-FM	Montréal	Contemp. Hits	18	9.0
CJPX-FM	Montréal	Classical	13	9.6
CKAC	Montréal	Multi-format	18	13.8
CKGM	Montréal	Oldies	4	9.7
CKHQ	Kanesatake	Native, Country	n.a.	n.a.
CKMF-FM	Montréal	Contemp. Hit Radio	21	10.0
CKOI-FM	Montréal	Contemp. Hit Radio	27	8.6
CKRK-FM	Kahnawake	Multi-format	n.a.	n.a.
CKVL	Montréal	Multi-format	n.a.	n.a.

BBM Spring 2000 Radio Reach Survey; area coverage
*Mon-Sun 5a.m - 1a.m , All Persons 12+

TV STATION DATA

Station	Market	Network Affiliation	Wkly. Reach%*	Aver. Hrs. Tuned
All Stations			97	24.1
A & E	n.a.	Ind.	6	3.8
CANALD	n.a.	n.a.	11	2.2
CBFT	Montréal	SRC	62	6.0
CBMT	Montréal	CBC	16	2.6
CFCF	Montréal	CTV	37	4.7
CFJP	Montréal-Rimouski	TQS	53	4.6
CFTM	Montréal	TVA	62	9.5
CIVM	Montréal	Télé-Qué.	22	2.3
CJNT	n.a.		1	2.8
CJOH	Ottawa	CTV	14	1.9
CKMI	Montréal	Global	25	2.6
ECRAN	n.a.	n.a.	3	5.6
FAMILE	n.a.	n.a.	10	2.6
OTHERS	n.a.	n.a.	9	2.2
RDI	n.a.	n.a.	9	2.2
RDS	n.a.	Ind.	10	2.4
TOON(FR)	n.a.	Ind.	13	3.9
TSN	n.a.	Ind.	7	3.0
TV5	n.a.	n.a.	7	2.2
VCR	n.a.	n.a.	25	4.2
VIE	n.a.	n.a.	8	1.8
WCAX	Burlington VT	CBS	21	2.9
WCFE	Plattsburg NY	PBS	7	2.1
WETK	Burlington VT	PBS	7	1.7
WFFF	Burlington VT	FOX, WB	12	2.6
WPIX	New York NY	WB	-	2.1
WPTZ	Plattsburg NY	NBC	15	2.6
WVNY	Burlington VT	ABC	18	2.5
WWBI	Plattsburg NY	PAX, WB	-	2.0
YTV	n.a.	Ind.	6	2.6

BBM Spring 2000 TV Reach Survey; CMA coverage.
*Mon-Sun 6a.m - 2a.m , All Persons 2 +

COMMUNITY NEWSPAPER(S)

	Total Circulation
Anjou: La Plume Communautaire	1,000
Anjou, Montréal: Le Flambeau de l'Est	49,861
Beauharnois, Châteauguay, Saint-Rémi: L'Information Régionale	28,399
Beloeil: L'Oeil Régional	27,100
Beloeil/Saint-Hilaire: Le Riverain	21,000
Blainville, Sainte-Thérèse: Courrier De Groulx	44,091
Blainville, Sainte-Thérèse: Le Nord Info.	48,364
Blainville, Sainte-Thérèse: La Voix des Milles-Îles	47,719
Boucherville: Journal La Relève	40,225
Boucherville: La Seigneurie	23,848
Brossard: Brossard-Éclair	23,753
Candiac, La Prairie, Saint-Constant: Le Reflet	31,566
Chambly: Le Journal	21,492
Chambly, Richelieu: Le Messager du Fort	19,000
Châteauguay, Beauharnois, Saint-Rémi: L'Information Régionale	28,399
Châteauguay, Valleyfield: Le Soleil du Saint-Laurent	27,940
Côte-Saint-Paul, Montréal, Saint-Henri, Ville-Émard: La Voix Populaire	23,129
Côte-Saint-Luc, Hampstead, Montréal, Montréal West, N.D.G., Snowdon: The Monitor	28,149
Dollard-des-Ormeaux, Pierrefonds,Pointe-Claire, West Island: Cités Nouvelles/City News	54,670
Greenfield Park, LeMoyne, Saint-Lambert: Le Magazine	21,000
Hampstead, Côte-Saint-Luc, Montréal, Montréal West, N.G.D., Snowdon: The Monitor	28,149
Hudson: Hudson Lake of Two Mountains Gazette	8,000
La Prairie, Candiac, Saint-Constant: Le Reflet	31,566
Lachine: Le Messager de Lachine	24,600
Laplaine: Le Plus	22,411
LaSalle: Le Messager de LaSalle	31,615
Laval: Courrier du Jeudi	42,031
Laval: Courrier-Laval	103,470
Laval: Chomedey News	25,000
Laval: Vivre (mthly)	3,000
Lavaltrie, Repentigny: Hebdo Rive-Nord	43,533
LeMoyne, Greenfield Park, Saint-Lambert: Le Magazine	21,000
Longueuil: Le Courrier du Sud	120,000
Longueuil: Longueuil Extra	50,000
Mascouche, Terrebonne: Le Trait d'Union	40,191
Mascouche,Terrebonne: La Revue de Terrebonne	40,191
Mirabel, Saint-Eustache: L'Éveil	40,651
Mont-Royal: Le Journal de Mont-Royal (mthly)	10,000
Mont-Royal: Le Point d'Outremont	16,000
Montréal: Nuns' Island Journal	n.a.
Montréal: Vue Sur La Bourgogne/Burgundy Vision	5,500
Montréal: Les Hebdos Métropolitains: (combined circulation)	254,677
Montréal: Courrier Bordeaux/Cartierville	16,055
Montréal: Échos du Vieux-Montréal (mthly)	16,000
Montréal: The Gazette West Island Edition	41,867
Montréal: L'Itinéraire (mthly)	16,000
Montréal: Le Journal de la rue (bimthly)	n.a.
Montréal: Le Soi-Distant (4/yr)	n.a.
Montréal: Nouvelles Parc-Extension News	9,000
Montréal: Nuns' Island Magazine	7,922
Montréal: Place Publique (bimthly)	16,000
Montréal: Vision Voisins (bimthly)	4,000
Montréal: The Gazette	n.a.
Montréal: The Suburban	105,000

Montréal
(Census Metropolitan Area)
(Cont'd)

	Total Circulation
Montréal: The Suburban, West End	64,000
Montréal: The West Island Suburban	41,000
Montréal (Centre-Sud): Les Faubourgs (bimthly)	n.a.
Montréal (Côte-des-Neiges): Actualités CDN (bimthly)	20,000
Montréal (Hochelaga-Maisonneuve): Nouvelles de l'Est	22,612
Montréal (Plateau Mont-Royal): Le Plateau	24,588
Montréal (Rosemont): Le Journal de Rosemont/Petit Patri	56,704
Montréal (Saint-Michel): Journal de St-Michel	23,500
Montréal (Villeray): Le Progrès de Villeray	21,651
Montréal West, Côte-Saint-Luc, Hampstead, Montréal, N.D.G., Snowdon: The Monitor	28,149
Montréal, Ahuntsic: Courrier Ahuntsic	33,426
Montréal, Côte-Saint-Luc, Hampstead, Montréal West, N.D.G., Snowdon: The Monitor	28,149
Montréal, Côte-Saint-Paul, Saint-Henri, Ville-Émard: La Voix Populaire	23,129
Montréal, Saint-Michel, Villeray: Journal Le Monde (mthly)	44,500
Montréal-Est, Pointe-aux-Trembles, Repentigny: L'Avenir de l'Est	42,516
Montréal-Nord: Le Guide de Montréal-Nord	32,053
Mount Royal: Weekly Post/L'Hebdo de Ville Mont-Royal	8,500
N.D.G., Côte-Saint-Luc, Hampstead, Montréal, Montréal West, Snowdon: The Monitor	28,149
Outremont: L'Express d'Outremont	15,975
Pierrefonds, Dollard-des-Ormeaux, Pointe-Claire, West Island: Cités Nouvelles/City News	54,670
Pointe-aux-Trembles, Mtl. Est, Repentigny: L'Avenir de l'Est	42,516
Pointe-aux-Trembles, Repentigny: L'Artisan	45,877
Pointe-Claire, Dollard-des-Ormeaux, Pierrefonds, West Island: Cités Nouvelles/City News	54,670
Pointe-Claire, West Island: The Chronicle	15,681
Repentigny, Lavaltrie: Hebdo Rive-Nord	43,533
Repentigny, Montréal-Est, Pointe-aux-Trembles: L'Avenir de l'Est	42,516
Repentigny, Pointe-aux-Trembles: L'Artisan	45,877
Richelieu, Chambly: Le Messager du Fort	19,000
Rivière-des-Prairies: L'Informateur	17,474
Saint-Amable, Saint-Bruno, Sainte-Julie: Le Montagnard	21,000
Saint-Bruno: Le Journal de St-Bruno	14,515
Saint-Bruno, Saint-Amable, Sainte-Julie: Le Montagnard	21,000
Saint-Constant, Candiac, La Prairie: Le Reflet	31,566
Saint-Eustache: La Concorde	39,048
Saint-Eustache, Mirabel: L'Éveil	40,651
Saint-Henri, Côte-Saint-Paul, Montréal, Ville-Émard: La Voix Populaire	23,129
Saint-Hubert: Le Journal de St-Hubert	28,050
Saint-Jérôme: Journal Le Mirabel	36,629
Saint-Jérôme: L'Écho du Nord	7,652
Saint-Jérôme, Saint-Sauveur: Journal le Nord	34,828
Saint-Lambert: St-Lambert Journal	n.a.
Saint-Lambert: Journal	n.a.
Saint-Lambert, Greenfield Park, LeMoyne: Le Magazine	21,000
Saint-Laurent: L'Interligne	28,000
Saint-Laurent: Nouvelles St-Laurent	26,250
Saint-Laurent: Aujourd'hui Demain	n.a.
Saint-Léonard, Nouveau Rosemont: Le Progrès de St-Léonard	29,760
Saint-Michel, Montréal, Villeray: Journal Le Monde (mthly)	44,500
Saint-Remi, Beauharnois, Châteauguay: L'Information Régionale	28,399
Sainte-Anne-des-Plaines: Le point d'impact	6,000
Sainte-Julie: L'Information	19,708
Sainte-Julie, Saint-Amable, Saint-Bruno: Le Montagnard	21,000
Sainte-Thérèse, Blainville: Courrier De Groulx	44,091
Sainte-Thérèse, Blainville: La Voix des Milles-Îles	47,719
Sainte-Thérèse, Blainville: Le Nord Info	48,364
Snowdon, Côte-Saint-Luc, Hampstead, Montréal, Montréal West, N.D.G.: The Monitor	28,149
Terrebonne, Mascouche: La Revue de Terrebonne	40,191
Terrebonne, Mascouche: Le Trait d'Union	40,191
Vaudreuil-Dorion: L'Étoile de L'Outaouais Saint-Laurent	38,503
Vaudreuil-Dorion: 1ère Edition du Sud-Ouest	38,634
Verdun: Le Messager de Verdun	24,400
Ville-Émard, Côte-Saint-Paul, Montréal, Saint-Henri: La Voix Populaire	23,129
Villeray, Montréal, Saint-Michel: Journal Le Monde (mthly)	44,500
West Island, Dollard-des-Ormeaux, Pierrefonds, Pointe-Claire: Cités Nouvelles/City News	54,670
West Island, Pointe-Claire: The Chronicle	15,681
Westmount: Westmount Examiner	9,271

Anjou
(Ville)
Montréal CMA

In census division Communauté urbaine de Montréal.

POPULATION

July 1, 2001 Estimate	37,840
% Cdn. Total	0.12
% Change, '96 -'01	-0.38
Avg. Annual Growth Rate, %	-0.08
2003 Projected Population	38,262
2006 Projected Population	39,093
2001 Households Estimate	16,945
2003 Projected Households	17,076
2006 Projected Households	17,315

INCOME

% Above/Below National Average	same
2001 Total Income Estimate	$794,740,000
% Cdn. Total	0.12
2001 Average Hhld. Income	$46,900
2001 Per Capita	$21,000
2003 Projected Total Income	$838,920,000
2006 Projected Total Income	$914,850,000

RETAIL SALES

% Above/Below National Average	+59
2001 Retail Sales Estimate	$537,510,000
% Cdn. Total	0.19
2001 per Household	$31,700
2001 per Capita	$14,200
2001 No. of Establishments	293
2003 Projected Retail Sales	$588,840,000
2006 Projected Retail Sales	$665,640,000

POPULATION

2001 Estimates:

Total		37,840
Male		17,631
Female		20,209
Age Groups	Male	Female
0-4	1,064	989
5-9	1,019	919
10-14	934	882
15-19	965	961
20-24	1,078	1,100
25-29	1,192	1,220
30-34	1,333	1,371
35-39	1,395	1,516
40-44	1,349	1,560
45-49	1,305	1,562
50-54	1,280	1,539
55-59	1,179	1,428
60-64	1,054	1,319
65-69	923	1,212
70+	1,561	2,631

DAYTIME POPULATION

2001 Estimates:

Working Population	27,696
At Home Population	19,820
Total	47,516

INCOME

2001 Estimates:

Avg. Household Income	$46,901
Avg. Family Income	$55,312
Per Capita Income	$21,003
Male:	
Avg. Employment Income	$33,072
Avg. Employment Income (Full Time)	$42,470
Female:	
Avg. Employment Income	$23,446
Avg. Employment Income (Full Time)	$32,312

Québec

DISPOSABLE & DISCRETIONARY INCOME

2001 Estimates:	Per Hhld.
Disposable Income	$31,434
Discretionary Income 1 (minus Food & Shelter)	$18,301
Discretionary Income 2 (minus Food, Shelter, & Other Expenditures)	$11,259

LIQUID ASSETS

1999 Estimates:	Per Hhld.
Equity Investments	$51,433
Interest Bearing Investments	$54,677
Total Liquid Assets	$106,110

CREDIT DATA

July 2000:	
Pool of Credit	$273,462,939
Revolving Credit, No.	82,441
Fixed Loans, No.	21,039
Avg. Credit Limit, per Person	$7,717
Avg. Spent, per Person	$3,186
Satisfactory Ratings, No. per Person	2.79
Avg. No. of Cards, per Person	1.11

LABOUR FORCE

2001 Estimates:	
Male:	
In the Labour Force	10,272
Participation Rate	70.3
Employed	9,612
Unemployed	660
Unemployment Rate	6.4
Not in Labour Force	4,342
Female:	
In the Labour Force	9,421
Participation Rate	54.1
Employed	8,723
Unemployed	698
Unemployment Rate	7.4
Not in Labour Force	7,998

OCCUPATIONS BY MAJOR GROUPS

2001 Estimates:	Male	Female
Management	1,166	451
Business, Finance & Admin.	1,396	3,503
Natural & Applied Sciences & Related	813	176
Health	274	831
Social Sciences, Gov't Services & Religion	170	348
Education	300	419
Arts, Culture, Recreation & Sport	262	212
Sales & Service	2,379	2,256
Trades, Transport & Equipment Operators & Related	2,103	155
Primary Industries	71	21
Processing, Mfg. & Utilities	881	619

Québec

Anjou
(Ville)
Montréal CMA
(Cont'd)

LEVEL OF SCHOOLING

2001 Estimates:
Population 15 years +	32,033
Less than Grade 9	6,032
Grades 9-13 w/o Certif.	4,793
Grade 9-13 with Certif.	5,965
Trade Certif. /Dip.	1,093
Non-Univ. w/o Certif./Dip.	2,434
Non-Univ. with Certif./Dip.	4,485
Univ. w/o Degree	3,101
Univ. w/o Degree/Certif.	562
Univ. with Certif.	2,539
Univ. with Degree	4,130

AVERAGE HOUSEHOLD EXPENDITURES

2001 Estimates:
Food	$6,222
Shelter	$8,820
Clothing	$2,112
Transportation	$5,025
Health & Personal Care	$1,820
Recr'n, Read'g & Education	$3,070
Taxes & Securities	$12,036
Other	$7,060
Total Expenditures	$46,165

PRIVATE HOUSEHOLDS

2001 Estimates:
Private Households, Total	16,945
Pop. in Private Households	37,342
Average no. per Household	2.2

FAMILIES

2001 Estimates:*
Families in Private Households	11,015
Husband-Wife Families	8,855
Lone-Parent Families	2,160
Aver. No. Persons per Family	2.8
Aver. No. Sons/Daughters at Home	1.0

HOUSING

2001 Estimates:
Occupied Private Dwellings	16,945
Owned	6,893
Rented	10,052
Single-Detached House	1,541
Semi-Detached House	637
Row Houses	760
Apartment, 5+ Storeys	1,897
Owned Apartment, 5+ Storeys	691
Apartment, 5 or Fewer Storeys	11,595
Apartment, Detached Duplex	505
Other Single-Attached	10

VEHICLES

2001 Estimates:
Model Yrs. '81-'96, No.	17,386
% Total	70.28
Model Yrs. '97-'98, No.	4,512
% Total	18.24
'99 Vehicles registered in Model Yr. '99, No.	2,839
% Total	11.48
Total No. '81-'99.	24,737

LEGAL MARITAL STATUS

2001 Estimates: (Age 15+)
Single (Never Married)	11,739
Legally Married (Not Separated)	13,377
Legally Married (Separated)	1,045
Widowed	2,392
Divorced	3,480

PSYTE CATEGORIES

2001 Estimates	No. of House -holds	% of Total Hhds.	Index
Urban Gentry	264	1.56	87
Suburban Nesters	368	2.17	135
Brie & Chablis	564	3.33	372
New Quebec Rows	1,325	7.82	714
Quebec Melange	1,035	6.11	230
Europa	378	2.23	179
High Rise Sunsets	325	1.92	134
Euro Quebec	4,263	25.16	2,868
Old Quebec Walkups	5,255	31.01	1,693
Quebec Town Elders	342	2.02	71
Aging Quebec Urbanites	637	3.76	1,303
Quebec's New Urban Mosaic	1,403	8.28	344
Aged Pensioners	690	4.07	306

FINANÇIAL P$YTE

2001 Estimates	No. of House -holds	% of Total Hhds.	Index
Four Star Investors	264	1.56	31
Canadian Comfort	368	2.17	22
Urban Heights	564	3.33	77
Mortgages & Minivans	1,325	7.82	118
Dollars & Sense	378	2.23	85
Country Credit	1,035	6.11	90
Revolving Renters	325	1.92	42
Loan Parent Stress	10,497	61.95	1,064
NSF	1,403	8.28	234
Senior Survivors	690	4.07	216

HOME LANGUAGE

2001 Estimates:		% Total
English	2,731	7.22
French	29,986	79.24
Arabic	283	0.75
Chinese	257	0.68
Creoles	276	0.73
Greek	65	0.17
Hungarian	20	0.05
Italian	782	2.07
Khmer (Cambodian)	92	0.24
Persian (Farsi)	99	0.26
Polish	147	0.39
Portuguese	406	1.07
Romanian	20	0.05
Spanish	736	1.95
Vietnamese	404	1.07
Other Languages	60	0.16
Multiple Responses	1,476	3.90
Total	37,840	100.00

BUILDING PERMITS

	1999	1998 $000	1997
Value	60,796	37,857	37,771

HOMES BUILT

	1999	1998	1997
No	124	108	119

TAXATION

Income Class:	1997	% Total
Under $5,000	3,000	10.49
$5,000-$10,000	3,930	13.74
$10,000-$15,000	4,450	15.56
$15,000-$20,000	3,030	10.59
$20,000-$25,000	2,550	8.92
$25,000-$30,000	2,510	8.78
$30,000-$40,000	3,760	13.15
$40,000-$50,000	2,280	7.97
$50,000 +	3,090	10.80
Total Returns, No.	28,600	
Total Income, $000	730,518	
Total Taxable Returns	20,620	
Total Tax, $000	86,012	
Average Income, $	25,543	
Average Tax, $	4,171	

VITAL STATISTICS

	1997	1996	1995	1994
Births	393	415	402	434
Deaths	299	231	234	213
Natural Increase	94	184	168	221
Marriages	26	30	39	33

Note: Latest available data.

MEDIA INFO
see Montréal, CMA

Beaconsfield
(Ville)
Montréal CMA

In census division Communauté urbaine de Montréal.

POPULATION

July 1, 2001 Estimate	19,486
% Cdn. Total	0.06
% Change, '96 -'01	-1.42
Avg. Annual Growth Rate, %	-0.29
2003 Projected Population	19,601
2006 Projected Population	19,871
2001 Households Estimate	6,568
2003 Projected Households	6,586
2006 Projected Households	6,624

INCOME

% Above/Below National Average	+64
2001 Total Income Estimate	$673,670,000
% Cdn. Total	0.10
2001 Average Hhld. Income	$102,600
2001 Per Capita	$34,600
2003 Projected Total Income	$714,380,000
2006 Projected Total Income	$783,790,000

RETAIL SALES

% Above/Below National Average	-51
2001 Retail Sales Estimate	$85,700,000
% Cdn. Total	0.03
2001 per Household	$13,000
2001 per Capita	$4,400
2001 No. of Establishments	88
2003 Projected Retail Sales	$92,830,000
2006 Projected Retail Sales	$104,070,000

POPULATION

2001 Estimates:

Total		19,486
Male		9,468
Female		10,018

Age Groups	Male	Female
0-4	508	488
5-9	643	612
10-14	720	692
15-19	739	742
20-24	664	687
25-29	501	515
30-34	454	487
35-39	552	651
40-44	681	835
45-49	800	922
50-54	818	871
55-59	698	699
60-64	549	525
65-69	424	423
70+	717	869

DAYTIME POPULATION

2001 Estimates:

Working Population	3,048
At Home Population	9,043
Total	12,091

INCOME

2001 Estimates:

Avg. Household Income	$102,568
Avg. Family Income	$108,474
Per Capita Income	$34,572
Male:	
Avg. Employment Income	$68,216
Avg. Employment Income (Full Time)	$83,952
Female:	
Avg. Employment Income	$29,005
Avg. Employment Income (Full Time)	$45,902

DISPOSABLE & DISCRETIONARY INCOME

2001 Estimates:	Per Hhld.
Disposable Income	$66,063
Discretionary Income 1 (minus Food & Shelter)	$46,439
Discretionary Income 2 (minus Food, Shelter, & Other Expenditures)	$33,328

LIQUID ASSETS

1999 Estimates:	Per Hhld.
Equity Investments	$212,049
Interest Bearing Investments	$137,939
Total Liquid Assets	$349,988

CREDIT DATA

July 2000:

Pool of Credit	$246,402,627
Revolving Credit, No.	46,227
Fixed Loans, No.	9,987
Avg. Credit Limit, per Person	$14,342
Avg. Spent, per Person	$5,604
Satisfactory Ratings, No. per Person	3.18
Avg. No. of Cards, per Person	1.32

LABOUR FORCE

2001 Estimates:

Male:	
In the Labour Force	5,964
Participation Rate	78.5
Employed	5,830
Unemployed	134
Unemployment Rate	2.2
Not in Labour Force	1,633
Female:	
In the Labour Force	4,718
Participation Rate	57.4
Employed	4,579
Unemployed	139
Unemployment Rate	2.9
Not in Labour Force	3,508

OCCUPATIONS BY MAJOR GROUPS

2001 Estimates:	Male	Female
Management	2,027	520
Business, Finance & Admin.	895	1,414
Natural & Applied Sciences & Related	810	203
Health	150	432
Social Sciences, Gov't Services & Religion	147	122
Education	268	461
Arts, Culture, Recreation & Sport	191	323
Sales & Service	895	1,106
Trades, Transport & Equipment Operators & Related	313	11
Primary Industries	32	11
Processing, Mfg. & Utilities	117	47

LEVEL OF SCHOOLING

2001 Estimates:

Population 15 years +	15,823
Less than Grade 9	427
Grades 9-13 w/o Certif.	1,539
Grade 9-13 with Certif.	1,454
Trade Certif./Dip.	357
Non-Univ. w/o Certif./Dip.	1,157
Non-Univ. with Certif./Dip.	2,170
Univ. w/o Degree	2,792
Univ. w/o Degree/Certif.	853
Univ. with Certif.	1,939
Univ. with Degree	5,927

AVERAGE HOUSEHOLD EXPENDITURES

2001 Estimates:

Food	$8,988
Shelter	$14,516
Clothing	$3,750
Transportation	$10,291
Health & Personal Care	$3,043
Recr'n, Read'g & Education	$6,731
Taxes & Securities	$30,737
Other	$12,308
Total Expenditures	$90,364

PRIVATE HOUSEHOLDS

2001 Estimates:

Private Households, Total	6,568
Pop. in Private Households	19,310
Average no. per Household	2.9

FAMILIES

2001 Estimates:

Families in Private Households	5,669
Husband-Wife Families	5,171
Lone-Parent Families	498
Aver. No. Persons per Family	3.2
Aver. No. Sons/Daughters at Home	1.3

HOUSING

2001 Estimates:

Occupied Private Dwellings	6,568
Owned	5,739
Rented	829
Single-Detached House	5,714
Semi-Detached House	102
Row Houses	450
Apartment, 5 or Fewer Storeys	292
Apartment, Detached Duplex	10

VEHICLES

2001 Estimates:

Model Yrs. '81-'96, No.	8,245
% Total	69.99
Model Yrs. '97-'98, No.	2,212
% Total	18.78
'99 Vehicles registered in Model Yr. '99, No.	1,323
% Total	11.23
Total No. '81-'99	11,780

LEGAL MARITAL STATUS

2001 Estimates: (Age 15+)

Single (Never Married)	4,265
Legally Married (Not Separated)	9,779
Legally Married (Separated)	272
Widowed	685
Divorced	822

PSYTE CATEGORIES

2001 Estimates	No. of House-holds	% of Total Hhds.	Index
Urban Gentry	2,910	44.31	2,465
Suburban Executives	2,941	44.78	3,124
Stable Suburban Families	369	5.62	431
Aging Erudites	348	5.30	351

FINANCIAL P$YTE

2001 Estimates	No. of House-holds	% of Total Hhds.	Index
Four Star Investors	5,851	89.08	1,773
Successful Suburbanites	369	5.62	85
Urban Heights	348	5.30	123

Québec

HOME LANGUAGE

2001 Estimates:		% Total
English	13,903	71.35
French	4,013	20.59
Arabic	116	0.60
Bengali	10	0.05
Chinese	197	1.01
Croatian	10	0.05
Czech	10	0.05
Danish	10	0.05
Dutch	25	0.13
Estonian	10	0.05
German	116	0.60
Greek	15	0.08
Hungarian	10	0.05
Italian	30	0.15
Japanese	15	0.08
Korean	41	0.21
Persian (Farsi)	194	1.00
Polish	21	0.11
Portuguese	35	0.18
Punjabi	11	0.06
Romanian	40	0.21
Spanish	105	0.54
Swedish	10	0.05
Ukrainian	10	0.05
Urdu	10	0.05
Vietnamese	20	0.10
Other Languages	10	0.05
Multiple Responses	489	2.51
Total	19,486	100.00

BUILDING PERMITS

	1999	1998 $000	1997
Value	6,125	5,676	3,648

HOMES BUILT

	1999	1998	1997
No.	29	12	8

TAXATION

Income Class:	1997	% Total
Under $5,000	1,630	12.57
$5,000-$10,000	1,160	8.94
$10,000-$15,000	1,050	8.10
$15,000-$20,000	900	6.94
$20,000-$25,000	750	5.78
$25,000-$30,000	760	5.86
$30,000-$40,000	1,290	9.95
$40,000-$50,000	1,150	8.87
$50,000 +	4,290	33.08
Total Returns, No.	12,970	
Total Income, $000	683,908	
Total Taxable Returns	10,010	
Total Tax, $000	123,072	
Average Income, $	52,730	
Average Tax, $	12,295	

VITAL STATISTICS

	1997	1996	1995	1994
Births	193	192	210	204
Deaths	82	85	88	81
Natural Increase	111	107	122	123
Marriages	58	54	65	51

Note: Latest available data.

MEDIA INFO
see Montréal, CMA

Québec

Bellefeuille
(Paroisse)
Montréal CMA

In census division La
Rivière-du-Nord.

POPULATION

July 1, 2001 Estimate	14,817
% Cdn. Total	0.05
% Change, '96 -'01	13.58
Avg. Annual Growth Rate, %	2.58
2003 Projected Population	16,289
2006 Projected Population	18,135
2001 Households Estimate	5,622
2003 Projected Households	6,100
2006 Projected Households	6,917

INCOME

% Above/Below National Average	-4
2001 Total Income Estimate	$300,040,000
% Cdn. Total	0.05
2001 Average Hhld. Income	$53,400
2001 Per Capita	$20,300
2003 Projected Total Income	$344,070,000
2006 Projected Total Income	$426,670,000

RETAIL SALES

% Above/Below National Average	-60
2001 Retail Sales Estimate	$53,200,000
% Cdn. Total	0.02
2001 per Household	$9,500
2001 per Capita	$3,600
2001 No. of Establishments	90
2003 Projected Retail Sales	$62,260,000
2006 Projected Retail Sales	$76,600,000

POPULATION

2001 Estimates:

Total		14,817
Male		7,456
Female		7,361

Age Groups	Male	Female
0-4	493	455
5-9	582	539
10-14	614	607
15-19	596	588
20-24	494	472
25-29	428	438
30-34	517	568
35-39	692	736
40-44	750	741
45-49	659	642
50-54	536	505
55-59	396	359
60-64	280	253
65-69	185	179
70+	234	279

DAYTIME POPULATION

2001 Estimates:

Working Population	937
At Home Population	6,976
Total	7,913

INCOME

2001 Estimates:

Avg. Household Income	$53,370
Avg. Family Income	$58,299
Per Capita Income	$20,250
Male:	
Avg. Employment Income	$34,534
Avg. Employment Income (Full Time)	$44,611
Female:	
Avg. Employment Income	$21,489
Avg. Employment Income (Full Time)	$31,396

DISPOSABLE & DISCRETIONARY INCOME

2001 Estimates:	Per Hhld.
Disposable Income	$36,975
Discretionary Income 1 (minus Food & Shelter)	$24,599
Discretionary Income 2 (minus Food, Shelter, & Other Expenditures)	$16,314

LIQUID ASSETS

1999 Estimates:	Per Hhld.
Equity Investments	$59,342
Interest Bearing Investments	$60,669
Total Liquid Assets	$120,011

CREDIT DATA

July 2000:

Pool of Credit	$118,397,701
Revolving Credit, No.	28,318
Fixed Loans, No.	10,828
Avg. Credit Limit, per Person	$9,705
Avg. Spent, per Person	$4,690
Satisfactory Ratings, No. per Person	3.04
Avg. No. of Cards, per Person	1.07

LABOUR FORCE

2001 Estimates:

Male:	
In the Labour Force	4,636
Participation Rate	80.4
Employed	4,364
Unemployed	272
Unemployment Rate	5.9
Not in Labour Force	1,131
Female:	
In the Labour Force	3,602
Participation Rate	62.5
Employed	3,390
Unemployed	212
Unemployment Rate	5.9
Not in Labour Force	2,158

OCCUPATIONS BY MAJOR GROUPS

2001 Estimates:	Male	Female
Management	561	234
Business, Finance & Admin.	327	1,147
Natural & Applied Sciences & Related	367	57
Health	108	348
Social Sciences, Gov't Services & Religion	87	141
Education	105	181
Arts, Culture, Recreation & Sport	89	65
Sales & Service	1,007	1,020
Trades, Transport & Equipment Operators & Related	1,231	80
Primary Industries	67	25
Processing, Mfg. & Utilities	556	221

LEVEL OF SCHOOLING

2001 Estimates:

Population 15 years +	11,527
Less than Grade 9	1,573
Grades 9-13 w/o Certif.	2,012
Grade 9-13 with Certif.	2,338
Trade Certif. /Dip.	807
Non-Univ. w/o Certif./Dip.	836
Non-Univ. with Certif./Dip.	2,053
Univ. w/o Degree	1,023
Univ. w/o Degree/Certif.	116
Univ. with Certif.	907
Univ. with Degree	885

AVERAGE HOUSEHOLD EXPENDITURES

2001 Estimates:

Food	$6,603
Shelter	$7,673
Clothing	$2,374
Transportation	$6,498
Health & Personal Care	$2,006
Recr'n, Read'g & Education	$3,421
Taxes & Securities	$15,850
Other	$7,255
Total Expenditures	$51,680

PRIVATE HOUSEHOLDS

2001 Estimates:

Private Households, Total	5,622
Pop. in Private Households	14,626
Average no. per Household	2.6

FAMILIES

2001 Estimates:

Families in Private Households	4,496
Husband-Wife Families	3,965
Lone-Parent Families	531
Aver. No. Persons per Family	3.1
Aver. No. Sons/Daughters at Home	1.2

HOUSING

2001 Estimates:

Occupied Private Dwellings	5,622
Owned	4,262
Rented	1,360
Single-Detached House	3,938
Semi-Detached House	302
Row Houses	99
Apartment, 5 or Fewer Storeys	726
Apartment, Detached Duplex	433
Other Single-Attached	62
Movable Dwellings	62

VEHICLES

2001 Estimates:

Model Yrs. '81-'96, No.	6,543
% Total	77.61
Model Yrs. '97-'98, No.	1,214
% Total	14.40
'99 Vehicles registered in Model Yr. '99, No.	674
% Total	7.99
Total No. '81-'99	8,431

LEGAL MARITAL STATUS

2001 Estimates: (Age 15+)

Single (Never Married)	4,198
Legally Married (Not Separated)	5,459
Legally Married (Separated)	272
Widowed	364
Divorced	1,234

PSYTE CATEGORIES

2001 Estimates	No. of House-holds	% of Total Hhds.	Index
Participation Quebec	2,920	51.94	1,802
New Quebec Rows	583	10.37	946
Quebec Melange	349	6.21	234
Traditional French Cdn. Families	1,480	26.33	980
Quebec's New Urban Mosaic	264	4.70	195

FINANCIAL P$YTE

2001 Estimates	No. of House-holds	% of Total Hhds.	Index
Mortgages & Minivans	3,503	62.31	944
Country Credit	1,829	32.53	481
NSF	264	4.70	133

HOME LANGUAGE

2001 Estimates:		% Total
English	198	1.34
French	14,330	96.71
Lao	11	0.07
Multiple Responses	278	1.88
Total	14,817	100.00

BUILDING PERMITS

	1999	1998	1997
		$000	
Value	21,289	9,862	9,419

HOMES BUILT

	1999	1998	1997
No	77	80	94

TAXATION

Income Class:	1997	% Total
Under $5,000	1,240	12.88
$5,000-$10,000	1,220	12.67
$10,000-$15,000	1,230	12.77
$15,000-$20,000	960	9.97
$20,000-$25,000	800	8.31
$25,000-$30,000	870	9.03
$30,000-$40,000	1,300	13.50
$40,000-$50,000	850	8.83
$50,000 +	1,170	12.15
Total Returns, No.	9,630	
Total Income, $000	251,541	
Total Taxable Returns	7,080	
Total Tax, $000	30,785	
Average Income, $	26,121	
Average Tax, $	4,348	

VITAL STATISTICS

	1997	1996	1995	1994
Births	153	191	186	177
Deaths	51	38	39	47
Natural Increase	102	153	147	130
Marriages	4	7	8	9

Note: Latest available data.

MEDIA INFO
see Montréal, CMA

Beloeil
(Ville)
Montréal CMA

In census division La Vallée-du-Richelieu.

POPULATION

July 1, 2001 Estimate	20,131
% Cdn. Total	0.06
% Change, '96 -'01	2.51
Avg. Annual Growth Rate, %	0.50
2003 Projected Population	20,635
2006 Projected Population	21,618
2001 Households Estimate	7,517
2003 Projected Households	7,774
2006 Projected Households	8,257

INCOME

% Above/Below National Average	+5
2001 Total Income Estimate	$445,520,000
% Cdn. Total	0.07
2001 Average Hhld. Income	$59,300
2001 Per Capita	$22,100
2003 Projected Total Income	$488,170,000
2006 Projected Total Income	$567,330,000

RETAIL SALES

% Above/Below National Average	+6
2001 Retail Sales Estimate	$190,660,000
% Cdn. Total	0.07
2001 per Household	$25,400
2001 per Capita	$9,500
2001 No. of Establishments	193
2003 Projected Retail Sales	$210,310,000
2006 Projected Retail Sales	$242,450,000

POPULATION

2001 Estimates:

Total	20,131
Male	9,773
Female	10,358

Age Groups	Male	Female
0-4	547	532
5-9	608	605
10-14	672	673
15-19	787	748
20-24	743	692
25-29	592	574
30-34	583	603
35-39	713	764
40-44	814	868
45-49	836	898
50-54	783	842
55-59	641	668
60-64	478	501
65-69	364	408
70+	612	982

DAYTIME POPULATION

2001 Estimates:

Working Population	4,244
At Home Population	9,582
Total	13,826

INCOME

2001 Estimates:

Avg. Household Income	$59,269
Avg. Family Income	$64,740
Per Capita Income	$22,131
Male:	
Avg. Employment Income	$39,599
Avg. Employment Income (Full Time)	$49,180
Female:	
Avg. Employment Income	$22,189
Avg. Employment Income (Full Time)	$33,716

DISPOSABLE & DISCRETIONARY INCOME

2001 Estimates:	Per Hhld.
Disposable Income	$40,513
Discretionary Income 1 (minus Food & Shelter)	$26,798
Discretionary Income 2 (minus Food, Shelter, & Other Expenditures)	$17,906

LIQUID ASSETS

1999 Estimates:	Per Hhld.
Equity Investments	$74,307
Interest Bearing Investments	$69,662
Total Liquid Assets	$143,969

CREDIT DATA

July 2000:	
Pool of Credit	$142,623,073
Revolving Credit, No.	38,512
Fixed Loans, No.	11,643
Avg. Credit Limit, per Person	$9,244
Avg. Spent, per Person	$4,112
Satisfactory Ratings, No. per Person	3.08
Avg. No. of Cards, per Person	1.21

LABOUR FORCE

2001 Estimates:

Male:	
In the Labour Force	6,041
Participation Rate	76.0
Employed	5,806
Unemployed	235
Unemployment Rate	3.9
Not in Labour Force	1,905
Female:	
In the Labour Force	4,878
Participation Rate	57.1
Employed	4,704
Unemployed	174
Unemployment Rate	3.6
Not in Labour Force	3,670

OCCUPATIONS BY MAJOR GROUPS

2001 Estimates:	Male	Female
Management	771	319
Business, Finance & Admin.	634	1,688
Natural & Applied Sciences & Related	580	27
Health	139	439
Social Sciences, Gov't Services & Religion	124	79
Education	176	342
Arts, Culture, Recreation & Sport	182	126
Sales & Service	1,288	1,529
Trades, Transport & Equipment Operators & Related	1,407	33
Primary Industries	147	22
Processing, Mfg. & Utilities	472	138

LEVEL OF SCHOOLING

2001 Estimates:

Population 15 years +	16,494
Less than Grade 9	1,938
Grades 9-13 w/o Certif.	2,590
Grade 9-13 with Certif.	3,482
Trade Certif./Dip.	681
Non-Univ. w/o Certif./Dip.	1,421
Non-Univ. with Certif./Dip.	2,844
Univ. w/o Degree	1,447
Univ. w/o Degree/Certif.	169
Univ. with Certif.	1,278
Univ. with Degree	2,091

AVERAGE HOUSEHOLD EXPENDITURES

2001 Estimates:

Food	$7,166
Shelter	$8,587
Clothing	$2,501
Transportation	$6,812
Health & Personal Care	$2,256
Recr'n, Read'g & Education	$3,682
Taxes & Securities	$17,604
Other	$8,001
Total Expenditures	$56,609

PRIVATE HOUSEHOLDS

2001 Estimates:

Private Households, Total	7,517
Pop. in Private Households	19,788
Average no. per Household	2.6

FAMILIES

2001 Estimates:

Families in Private Households	6,053
Husband-Wife Families	5,153
Lone-Parent Families	900
Aver. No. Persons per Family	3.1
Aver. No. Sons/Daughters at Home	1.2

HOUSING

2001 Estimates:

Occupied Private Dwellings	7,517
Owned	5,551
Rented	1,966
Single-Detached House	5,274
Semi-Detached House	143
Row Houses	109
Apartment, 5 or Fewer Storeys	1,740
Apartment, Detached Duplex	229
Other Single-Attached	22

VEHICLES

2001 Estimates:

Model Yrs. '81-'96, No.	10,130
% Total	76.30
Model Yrs. '97-'98, No.	2,068
% Total	15.58
'99 Vehicles registered in Model Yr. '99, No.	1,078
% Total	8.12
Total No. '81-'99	13,276

LEGAL MARITAL STATUS

2001 Estimates: (Age 15+)

Single (Never Married)	5,637
Legally Married (Not Separated)	8,019
Legally Married (Separated)	388
Widowed	923
Divorced	1,527

PSYTE CATEGORIES

2001 Estimates	No. of House-holds	% of Total Hhds.	Index
Participation			
Quebec	3,626	48.24	1,674
New Quebec Rows	466	6.20	566
Quebec Melange	2,180	29.00	1,094
Quebec Town Elders	1,245	16.56	586

FINANCIAL P$YTE

2001 Estimates	No. of House-holds	% of Total Hhds.	Index
Mortgages & Minivans	4,092	54.44	825
Country Credit	2,180	29.00	429
Loan Parent Stress	1,245	16.56	284

HOME LANGUAGE

2001 Estimates		% Total
English	560	2.78
French	19,276	95.75
Dutch	20	0.10
Greek	47	0.23
Spanish	11	0.05
Multiple Responses	217	1.08
Total	20,131	100.00

Québec

BUILDING PERMITS

	1999	1998	1997
		$000	
Value	9,988.	6,933	9,571

HOMES BUILT

	1999	1998	1997
No.	34	37	41

TAXATION

Income Class:	1997	% Total
Under $5,000	1,820	12.84
$5,000-$10,000	1,810	12.77
$10,000-$15,000	1,930	13.62
$15,000-$20,000	1,340	9.46
$20,000-$25,000	1,090	7.69
$25,000-$30,000	1,080	7.62
$30,000-$40,000	1,720	12.14
$40,000-$50,000	1,270	8.96
$50,000 +	2,100	14.82
Total Returns, No.	14,170	
Total Income, $000	388,475	
Total Taxable Returns	10,370	
Total Tax, $000	49,076	
Average Income, $.	27,415	
Average Tax, $.	4,732	

VITAL STATISTICS

	1997	1996	1995	1994
Births	189	201	220	209
Deaths	142	92	99	132
Natural Increase	47	109	121	77
Marriages	55	36	65	54

Note: Latest available data.

MEDIA INFO
see Montréal, CMA

Québec

Blainville
(Ville)
Montréal CMA

In census division Thérèse-De Blainville.

POPULATION

July 1, 2001 Estimate	38,266
% Cdn. Total	0.12
% Change, '96 -'01	26.74
Avg. Annual Growth Rate, %	4.85
2003 Projected Population	43,784
2006 Projected Population	52,911
2001 Households Estimate	13,473
2003 Projected Households	15,549
2006 Projected Households	19,021

INCOME

% Above/Below National Average	+4
2001 Total Income Estimate	$836,900,000
% Cdn. Total	0.13
2001 Average Hhld. Income	$62,100
2001 Per Capita	$21,900
2003 Projected Total Income	$1,022,390,000
2006 Projected Total Income	$1,363,050,000

RETAIL SALES

% Above/Below National Average	same
2001 Retail Sales Estimate	$342,920,000
% Cdn. Total	0.12
2001 per Household	$25,500
2001 per Capita	$9,000
2001 No. of Establishments	219
2003 Projected Retail Sales	$429,160,000
2006 Projected Retail Sales	$581,720,000

POPULATION

2001 Estimates:

Total	38,266
Male	18,955
Female	19,311

Age Groups	Male	Female
0-4	1,475	1,441
5-9	1,628	1,605
10-14	1,529	1,491
15-19	1,371	1,337
20-24	1,177	1,172
25-29	1,226	1,279
30-34	1,681	1,803
35-39	1,984	2,066
40-44	1,814	1,851
45-49	1,444	1,443
50-54	1,147	1,130
55-59	886	865
60-64	629	637
65-69	421	462
70+	543	729

DAYTIME POPULATION

2001 Estimates:

Working Population	6,568
At Home Population	17,352
Total	23,920

INCOME

2001 Estimates:

Avg. Household Income	$62,117
Avg. Family Income	$65,206
Per Capita Income	$21,870
Male:	
Avg. Employment Income	$40,347
Avg. Employment Income (Full Time)	$48,366
Female:	
Avg. Employment Income	$24,389
Avg. Employment Income (Full Time)	$33,299

DISPOSABLE & DISCRETIONARY INCOME

2001 Estimates:	Per Hhld.
Disposable Income	$42,794
Discretionary Income 1 (minus Food & Shelter)	$28,508
Discretionary Income 2 (minus Food, Shelter, & Other Expenditures)	$19,262

LIQUID ASSETS

1999 Estimates:	Per Hhld.
Equity Investments	$81,664
Interest Bearing Investments	$73,678
Total Liquid Assets	$155,342

CREDIT DATA

July 2000:

Pool of Credit	$288,548,006
Revolving Credit, No.	65,802
Fixed Loans, No.	28,039
Avg. Credit Limit, per Person	$11,380
Avg. Spent, per Person	$5,562
Satisfactory Ratings, No. per Person	3.46
Avg. No. of Cards, per Person	1.33

LABOUR FORCE

2001 Estimates:

Male:

In the Labour Force	12,130
Participation Rate	84.7
Employed	11,648
Unemployed	482
Unemployment Rate	4.0
Not in Labour Force	2,193

Female:

In the Labour Force	9,686
Participation Rate	65.6
Employed	9,180
Unemployed	506
Unemployment Rate	5.2
Not in Labour Force	5,088

OCCUPATIONS BY MAJOR GROUPS

2001 Estimates:	Male	Female
Management	1,645	531
Business, Finance & Admin.	1,196	3,387
Natural & Applied Sciences & Related	1,202	196
Health	101	838
Social Sciences, Gov't Services & Religion	189	222
Education	131	401
Arts, Culture, Recreation & Sport	146	200
Sales & Service	2,521	2,781
Trades, Transport & Equipment Operators & Related	2,947	162
Primary Industries	236	59
Processing, Mfg. & Utilities	1,537	544

LEVEL OF SCHOOLING

2001 Estimates:

Population 15 years +	29,097
Less than Grade 9	3,584
Grades 9-13 w/o Certif.	5,843
Grade 9-13 with Certif.	5,606
Trade Certif. /Dip.	1,187
Non-Univ. w/o Certif./Dip.	2,389
Non-Univ. with Certif./Dip.	5,178
Univ. w/o Degree	2,213
Univ. w/o Degree/Certif.	373
Univ. with Certif.	1,840
Univ. with Degree	3,097

AVERAGE HOUSEHOLD EXPENDITURES

2001 Estimates:

Food	$7,441
Shelter	$9,072
Clothing	$2,709
Transportation	$7,131
Health & Personal Care	$2,258
Recr'n, Read'g & Education	$3,804
Taxes & Securities	$18,128
Other	$8,222
Total Expenditures	$58,765

PRIVATE HOUSEHOLDS

2001 Estimates:

Private Households, Total	13,473
Pop. in Private Households	38,165
Average no. per Household	2.8

FAMILIES

2001 Estimates:

Families in Private Households	11,431
Husband-Wife Families	10,231
Lone-Parent Families	1,200
Aver. No. Persons per Family	3.2
Aver. No. Sons/Daughters at Home	1.3

HOUSING

2001 Estimates:

Occupied Private Dwellings	13,473
Owned	10,582
Rented	2,891
Single-Detached House	10,024
Semi-Detached House	725
Row Houses	213
Apartment, 5 or Fewer Storeys	1,643
Apartment, Detached Duplex	832
Other Single-Attached	36

VEHICLES

2001 Estimates:

Model Yrs. '81-'96, No.	15,088
% Total	70.04
Model Yrs. '97-'98, No.	3,852
% Total	17.88
'99 Vehicles registered in Model Yr. '99, No.	2,602
% Total	12.08
Total No. '81-'99	21,542

LEGAL MARITAL STATUS

2001 Estimates: (Age 15+)

Single (Never Married)	10,881
Legally Married (Not Separated)	13,827
Legally Married (Separated)	627
Widowed	869
Divorced	2,893

PSYTE CATEGORIES

2001 Estimates	No. of House-holds	% of Total Hhds.	Index
Technocrafts & Bureaucrats	611	4.53	161
Participation Quebec	5,566	41.31	1,434
New Quebec Rows	2,773	20.58	1,878
Quebec Melange	1,380	10.24	387
Traditional French Cdn. Families	2,072	15.38	573
Euro Quebec	424	3.15	359
Quebec's New Urban Mosaic	647	4.80	199

FINANCIAL P$YTE

2001 Estimates	No. of House-holds	% of Total Hhds.	Index
Successful Suburbanites	611	4.53	68
Mortgages & Minivans	8,339	61.89	938
Country Credit	3,452	25.62	379
Loan Parent Stress	424	3.15	54
NSF	647	4.80	136

HOME LANGUAGE

2001 Estimates:		% Total
English	787	2.06
French	36,322	94.92
Arabic	44	0.11
Armenian	30	0.08
Italian	121	0.32
Portuguese	334	0.87
Spanish	35	0.09
Vietnamese	25	0.07
Other Languages	55	0.14
Multiple Responses	513	1.34
Total	38,266	100.00

BUILDING PERMITS

	1999	1998	1997
		$000	
Value	98,597	91,756	78,652

HOMES BUILT

	1999	1998	1997
No.	549	434	388

TAXATION

Income Class:	1997	% Total
Under $5,000	2,680	12.15
$5,000-$10,000	2,400	10.88
$10,000-$15,000	2,470	11.20
$15,000-$20,000	1,940	8.80
$20,000-$25,000	1,890	8.57
$25,000-$30,000	1,820	8.25
$30,000-$40,000	3,220	14.60
$40,000-$50,000	2,280	10.34
$50,000 +	3,360	15.24
Total Returns, No.	22,050	
Total Income, $000	641,444	
Total Taxable Returns	16,860	
Total Tax, $000	83,000	
Average Income, $	29,090	
Average Tax, $	4,923	

VITAL STATISTICS

	1997	1996	1995	1994
Births	529	531	747	657
Deaths	86	99	87	104
Natural Increase	443	432	660	553
Marriages	37	70	39	50

Note: Latest available data.

MEDIA INFO
see Montréal, CMA

Boisbriand
(Ville)
Montréal CMA

In census division Thérèse-De Blainville.

POPULATION

July 1, 2001 Estimate	29,959
% Cdn. Total	0.10
% Change, '96 -'01	16.44
Avg. Annual Growth Rate, %	3.09
2003 Projected Population	32,640
2006 Projected Population	37,294
2001 Households Estimate	10,514
2003 Projected Households	11,531
2006 Projected Households	13,308

INCOME

% Above/Below National Average	-2
2001 Total Income Estimate	$618,040,000
% Cdn. Total	0.09
2001 Average Hhld. Income	$58,800
2001 Per Capita	$20,600
2003 Projected Total Income	$708,040,000
2006 Projected Total Income	$875,390,000

RETAIL SALES

% Above/Below National Average	-76
2001 Retail Sales Estimate	$65,300,000
% Cdn. Total	0.02
2001 per Household	$6,200
2001 per Capita	$2,200
2001 No. of Establishments	157
2003 Projected Retail Sales	$75,490,000
2006 Projected Retail Sales	$94,300,000

POPULATION

2001 Estimates:

Total		29,959
Male		14,875
Female		15,084

Age Groups	Male	Female
0-4	1,212	1,161
5-9	1,373	1,326
10-14	1,294	1,238
15-19	1,119	1,070
20-24	961	956
25-29	949	1,013
30-34	1,230	1,344
35-39	1,494	1,570
40-44	1,408	1,420
45-49	1,138	1,148
50-54	883	894
55-59	659	645
60-64	456	439
65-69	312	303
70+	387	557

DAYTIME POPULATION

2001 Estimates:

Working Population	8,671
At Home Population	14,345
Total	23,016

INCOME

2001 Estimates:

Avg. Household Income	$58,782
Avg. Family Income	$62,950
Per Capita Income	$20,629
Male:	
Avg. Employment Income	$38,566
Avg. Employment Income (Full Time)	$47,186
Female:	
Avg. Employment Income	$25,010
Avg. Employment Income (Full Time)	$32,971

DISPOSABLE & DISCRETIONARY INCOME

2001 Estimates:	Per Hhld.
Disposable Income	$40,738
Discretionary Income 1 (minus Food & Shelter)	$27,127
Discretionary Income 2 (minus Food, Shelter, & Other Expenditures)	$18,350

LIQUID ASSETS

1999 Estimates:	Per Hhld.
Equity Investments	$71,068
Interest Bearing Investments	$69,567
Total Liquid Assets	$140,635

CREDIT DATA

July 2000:	
Pool of Credit	$207,760,290
Revolving Credit, No.	47,324
Fixed Loans, No.	20,141
Avg. Credit Limit, per Person	$11,097
Avg. Spent, per Person	$5,313
Satisfactory Ratings, No. per Person	3.37
Avg. No. of Cards, per Person	1.28

LABOUR FORCE

2001 Estimates:

Male:	
In the Labour Force	9,253
Participation Rate	84.1
Employed	8,721
Unemployed	532
Unemployment Rate	5.7
Not in Labour Force	1,743
Female:	
In the Labour Force	7,211
Participation Rate	63.5
Employed	6,843
Unemployed	368
Unemployment Rate	5.1
Not in Labour Force	4,148

OCCUPATIONS BY MAJOR GROUPS

2001 Estimates:	Male	Female
Management	1,242	452
Business, Finance & Admin.	1,008	2,503
Natural & Applied Sciences & Related	839	215
Health	239	533
Social Sciences, Gov't Services & Religion	161	235
Education	326	404
Arts, Culture, Recreation & Sport	112	184
Sales & Service	1,693	1,794
Trades, Transport & Equipment Operators & Related	2,223	162
Primary Industries	72	46
Processing, Mfg. & Utilities	1,049	402

LEVEL OF SCHOOLING

2001 Estimates:

Population 15 years +	22,355
Less than Grade 9	2,337
Grades 9-13 w/o Certif.	3,917
Grade 9-13 with Certif.	4,544
Trade Certif. /Dip.	1,125
Non-Univ. w/o Certif./Dip.	1,750
Non-Univ. with Certif./Dip.	4,335
Univ. w/o Degree	2,044
Univ. w/o Degree/Certif.	374
Univ. with Certif.	1,670
Univ. with Degree	2,303

AVERAGE HOUSEHOLD EXPENDITURES

2001 Estimates:

Food	$7,028
Shelter	$8,726
Clothing	$2,579
Transportation	$6,710
Health & Personal Care	$2,152
Recr'n, Read'g & Education	$3,707
Taxes & Securities	$17,196
Other	$7,925
Total Expenditures	$56,023

PRIVATE HOUSEHOLDS

2001 Estimates:

Private Households, Total	10,514
Pop. in Private Households	29,831
Average no. per Household	2.8

FAMILIES

2001 Estimates:

Families in Private Households	8,687
Husband-Wife Families	7,500
Lone-Parent Families	1,187
Aver. No. Persons per Family	3.2
Aver. No. Sons/Daughters at Home	1.4

HOUSING

2001 Estimates:

Occupied Private Dwellings	10,514
Owned	6,884
Rented	3,630
Single-Detached House	5,843
Semi-Detached House	584
Row Houses	362
Apartment, 5 or Fewer Storeys	3,547
Apartment, Detached Duplex	135
Other Single-Attached	43

VEHICLES

2001 Estimates:

Model Yrs. '81-'96, No.	11,929
% Total	72.36
Model Yrs. '97-'98, No.	2,892
% Total	17.54
'99 Vehicles registered in Model Yr. '99, No.	1,665
% Total	10.10
Total No. '81-'99	16,486

LEGAL MARITAL STATUS

2001 Estimates: (Age 15+)

Single (Never Married)	8,253
Legally Married (Not Separated)	10,639
Legally Married (Separated)	554
Widowed	674
Divorced	2,235

PSYTE CATEGORIES

2001 Estimates	No. of House-holds	% of Total Hhds.	Index
Technocrafts & Bureaucrats	682	6.49	231
Participation Quebec	4,263	40.55	1,407
New Quebec Rows	2,117	20.14	1,837
Quebec Melange	1,386	13.18	497
Traditional French Cdn. Families	409	3.89	145
Big Country Families	463	4.40	309
Euro Quebec	387	3.68	420
Quebec's New Urban Mosaic	807	7.68	319

FINANCIAL P$YTE

2001 Estimates	No. of House-holds	% of Total Hhds.	Index
Successful Suburbanites	682	6.49	98
Mortgages & Minivans	6,380	60.68	919
Country Credit	1,795	17.07	252
Rural Family Blues	463	4.40	55
Loan Parent Stress	387	3.68	63
NSF	807	7.68	217

Québec

HOME LANGUAGE

2001 Estimates:		% Total
English	837	2.79
French	26,744	89.27
Armenian	29	0.10
Creoles	18	0.06
Dutch	17	0.06
Greek	34	0.11
Khmer (Cambodian)	256	0.85
Lao	143	0.48
Polish	23	0.08
Portuguese	39	0.13
Spanish	24	0.08
Yiddish	1,174	3.92
Other Languages	124	0.41
Multiple Responses	497	1.66
Total	29,959	100.00

BUILDING PERMITS

	1999	1998	1997
		$000	
Value	29,554	22,103	30,501

HOMES BUILT

	1999	1998	1997
No.	154	120	132

TAXATION

Income Class:	1997	% Total
Under $5,000	2,130	12.26
$5,000-$10,000	2,020	11.62
$10,000-$15,000	2,070	11.91
$15,000-$20,000	1,550	8.92
$20,000-$25,000	1,390	8.00
$25,000-$30,000	1,440	8.29
$30,000-$40,000	2,430	13.98
$40,000-$50,000	1,750	10.07
$50,000 +	2,590	14.90
Total Returns, No.	17,380	
Total Income, $000	492,745	
Total Taxable Returns	13,000	
Total Tax, $000	62,238	
Average Income, $	28,351	
Average Tax, $	4,788	

VITAL STATISTICS

	1997	1996	1995	1994
Births	435	494	476	508
Deaths	78	50	66	64
Natural Increase	357	444	410	444
Marriages	49	32	34	27

Note: Latest available data.

MEDIA INFO
see Montréal, CMA

Québec

Boucherville
(Ville)
Montréal CMA

In census division Lajemmerais.

POPULATION

July 1, 2001 Estimate	36,637
% Cdn. Total	0.12
% Change, '96 -'01	2.83
Avg. Annual Growth Rate, %	0.56
2003 Projected Population	37,441
2006 Projected Population	39,151
2001 Households Estimate	13,472
2003 Projected Households	13,859
2006 Projected Households	14,637

INCOME

% Above/Below National Average	+34
2001 Total Income Estimate	$1,035,170,000
% Cdn. Total	0.16
2001 Average Hhld. Income	$76,800
2001 Per Capita	$28,300
2003 Projected Total Income	$1,123,960,000
2006 Projected Total Income	$1,291,330,000

RETAIL SALES

% Above/Below National Average	+97
2001 Retail Sales Estimate	$644,680,000
% Cdn. Total	0.23
2001 per Household	$47,900
2001 per Capita	$17,600
2001 No. of Establishments	301
2003 Projected Retail Sales	$712,780,000
2006 Projected Retail Sales	$828,090,000

POPULATION

2001 Estimates:

Total	36,637
Male	17,888
Female	18,749

Age Groups	Male	Female
0-4	925	904
5-9	1,050	973
10-14	1,154	1,073
15-19	1,330	1,239
20-24	1,343	1,212
25-29	1,111	1,008
30-34	1,026	1,039
35-39	1,185	1,341
40-44	1,385	1,607
45-49	1,504	1,728
50-54	1,545	1,706
55-59	1,377	1,447
60-64	1,079	1,106
65-69	796	827
70+	1,078	1,539

DAYTIME POPULATION

2001 Estimates:

Working Population	25,453
At Home Population	15,907
Total	41,360

INCOME

2001 Estimates:

Avg. Household Income	$76,839
Avg. Family Income	$82,992
Per Capita Income	$28,255
Male:	
Avg. Employment Income	$47,845
Avg. Employment Income (Full Time)	$61,338
Female:	
Avg. Employment Income	$28,340
Avg. Employment Income (Full Time)	$39,792

DISPOSABLE & DISCRETIONARY INCOME

2001 Estimates:	Per Hhld.
Disposable Income	$52,133
Discretionary Income 1 (minus Food & Shelter)	$35,648
Discretionary Income 2 (minus Food, Shelter, & Other Expenditures)	$24,945

LIQUID ASSETS

1999 Estimates:	Per Hhld.
Equity Investments	$112,377
Interest Bearing Investments	$93,140
Total Liquid Assets	$205,517

CREDIT DATA

July 2000:

Pool of Credit	$338,855,475
Revolving Credit, No.	78,954
Fixed Loans, No.	20,389
Avg. Credit Limit, per Person	$11,362
Avg. Spent, per Person	$4,508
Satisfactory Ratings, No. per Person	3.21
Avg. No. of Cards, per Person	1.34

LABOUR FORCE

2001 Estimates:

Male:	
In the Labour Force	11,629
Participation Rate	78.8
Employed	11,325
Unemployed	304
Unemployment Rate	2.6
Not in Labour Force	3,130
Female:	
In the Labour Force	9,924
Participation Rate	62.8
Employed	9,603
Unemployed	321
Unemployment Rate	3.2
Not in Labour Force	5,875

OCCUPATIONS BY MAJOR GROUPS

2001 Estimates:	Male	Female
Management	2,406	809
Business, Finance & Admin.	1,515	3,528
Natural & Applied Sciences & Related	1,466	267
Health	243	1,043
Social Sciences, Gov't Services & Religion	281	392
Education	362	608
Arts, Culture, Recreation & Sport	313	410
Sales & Service	2,353	2,245
Trades, Transport & Equipment Operators & Related	1,739	133
Primary Industries	168	17
Processing, Mfg. & Utilities	555	228

LEVEL OF SCHOOLING

2001 Estimates:

Population 15 years +	30,558
Less than Grade 9	2,013
Grades 9-13 w/o Certif.	3,489
Grade 9-13 with Certif.	5,508
Trade Certif. /Dip.	1,112
Non-Univ. w/o Certif./Dip.	2,832
Non-Univ. with Certif./Dip.	5,574
Univ. w/o Degree.	3,641
Univ. w/o Degree/Certif.	459
Univ. with Certif.	3,182
Univ. with Degree	6,389

AVERAGE HOUSEHOLD EXPENDITURES

2001 Estimates:

Food	$8,337
Shelter	$10,982
Clothing	$3,026
Transportation	$8,220
Health & Personal Care	$2,582
Recr'n, Read'g & Education	$4,707
Taxes & Securities	$22,192
Other	$10,537
Total Expenditures	$70,583

PRIVATE HOUSEHOLDS

2001 Estimates:

Private Households, Total	13,472
Pop. in Private Households	35,903
Average no. per Household	2.7

FAMILIES

2001 Estimates:

Families in Private Households	11,264
Husband-Wife Families	9,903
Lone-Parent Families	1,361
Aver. No. Persons per Family	3.1
Aver. No. Sons/Daughters at Home	1.2

HOUSING

2001 Estimates:

Occupied Private Dwellings	13,472
Owned	10,998
Rented	2,474
Single-Detached House	9,235
Semi-Detached House	1,110
Row Houses	530
Apartment, 5+ Storeys	101
Apartment, 5 or Fewer Storeys	2,166
Apartment, Detached Duplex	330

VEHICLES

2001 Estimates:

Model Yrs. '81-'96, No.	17,847
% Total	67.46
Model Yrs. '97-'98, No.	5,239
% Total	19.80
'99 Vehicles registered in Model Yr. '99, No.	3,371
% Total	12.74
Total No. '81-'99	26,457

LEGAL MARITAL STATUS

2001 Estimates: (Age 15+)

Single (Never Married)	10,287
Legally Married (Not Separated)	15,645
Legally Married (Separated)	598
Widowed	1,417
Divorced	2,611

PSYTE CATEGORIES

2001 Estimates	No. of House-holds	% of Total Hhds.	Index
Suburban Executives	768	5.70	398
Technocrafts & Bureaucrats	1,789	13.28	472
Stable Suburban Families	2,864	21.26	1,631
Old Bungalow Burbs	1,464	10.87	656
Participation Quebec	2,391	17.75	616
New Quebec Rows	947	7.03	641
Quebec Melange	1,906	14.15	534
Quebec's Heartland	136	1.01	103
Old Quebec Walkups	762	5.66	309
Quebec Town Elders	432	3.21	113

FINANCIAL P$YTE

2001 Estimates	No. of House-holds	% of Total Hhds.	Index
Four Star Investors	768	5.70	113
Successful Suburbanites	4,653	34.54	520
Miners & Credit-Liners	1,464	10.87	343
Mortgages & Minivans	3,338	24.78	375
Country Credit	1,906	14.15	209
Rural Family Blues	136	1.01	13
Loan Parent Stress	1,194	8.86	152

HOME LANGUAGE

2001 Estimates:		% Total
English	1,073	2.93
French	35,039	95.64
Arabic	43	0.12
Chinese	26	0.07
Greek	38	0.10
Italian	41	0.11
Portuguese	90	0.25
Spanish	21	0.06
Other Languages	36	0.10
Multiple Responses	230	0.63
Total	36,637	100.00

BUILDING PERMITS

	1999	1998 $000	1997
Value	50,783	64,407	56,545

HOMES BUILT

	1999	1998	1997
No	254	243	256

TAXATION

Income Class:	1997	% Total
Under $5,000	2,780	10.34
$5,000-$10,000	2,730	10.15
$10,000-$15,000	2,660	9.89
$15,000-$20,000	2,040	7.59
$20,000-$25,000	1,810	6.73
$25,000-$30,000	1,990	7.40
$30,000-$40,000	3,530	13.13
$40,000-$50,000	2,760	10.26
$50,000 +	6,590	24.51
Total Returns, No.	26,890	
Total Income, $000	988,136	
Total Taxable Returns	21,210	
Total Tax, $000	144,845	
Average Income, $	36,747	
Average Tax, $	6,829	

VITAL STATISTICS

	1997	1996	1995	1994
Births	309	318	354	332
Deaths	181	160	160	142
Natural Increase	128	158	194	190
Marriages	61	75	68	60

Note: Latest available data.

MEDIA INFO
see Montréal, CMA

Brossard
(Ville)
Montréal CMA
In census division Champlain.

POPULATION

July 1, 2001 Estimate	67,983
% Cdn. Total	0.22
% Change, '96 -'01	1.45
Avg. Annual Growth Rate, %	0.29
2003 Projected Population	69,150
2006 Projected Population	71,271
2001 Households Estimate	24,147
2003 Projected Households	24,816
2006 Projected Households	25,862

INCOME

% Above/Below National Average	+16
2001 Total Income Estimate	$1,655,630,000
% Cdn. Total	0.25
2001 Average Hhld. Income	$68,600
2001 Per Capita	$24,400
2003 Projected Total Income	$1,803,060,000
2006 Projected Total Income	$2,054,870,000

RETAIL SALES

% Above/Below National Average	+16
2001 Retail Sales Estimate	$703,130,000
% Cdn. Total	0.25
2001 per Household	$29,100
2001 per Capita	$10,300
2001 No. of Establishments	548
2003 Projected Retail Sales	$774,760,000
2006 Projected Retail Sales	$885,380,000

POPULATION

2001 Estimates:

Total		67,983
Male		33,297
Female		34,686

Age Groups	Male	Female
0-4	1,813	1,695
5-9	1,932	1,793
10-14	2,209	2,051
15-19	2,684	2,437
20-24	2,803	2,553
25-29	2,380	2,213
30-34	2,035	2,068
35-39	2,056	2,327
40-44	2,376	2,813
45-49	2,779	3,208
50-54	2,889	3,143
55-59	2,464	2,594
60-64	1,852	1,923
65-69	1,304	1,367
70+	1,721	2,501

DAYTIME POPULATION

2001 Estimates:

Working Population	18,327
At Home Population	32,254
Total	50,581

INCOME

2001 Estimates:

Avg. Household Income	$68,565
Avg. Family Income	$72,723
Per Capita Income	$24,354
Male:	
Avg. Employment Income	$41,633
Avg. Employment Income (Full Time)	$55,823
Female:	
Avg. Employment Income	$26,373
Avg. Employment Income (Full Time)	$37,949

DISPOSABLE & DISCRETIONARY INCOME

2001 Estimates:	*Per Hhld.*
Disposable Income	$46,473
Discretionary Income 1 (minus Food & Shelter)	$31,423
Discretionary Income 2 (minus Food, Shelter, & Other Expenditures)	$21,585

LIQUID ASSETS

1999 Estimates:	*Per Hhld.*
Equity Investments	$106,166
Interest Bearing Investments	$85,027
Total Liquid Assets	$191,193

CREDIT DATA

July 2000:

Pool of Credit	$617,813,813
Revolving Credit, No.	151,366
Fixed Loans, No.	39,863
Avg. Credit Limit, per Person	$10,293
Avg. Spent, per Person	$4,226
Satisfactory Ratings, No. per Person	3.04
Avg. No. of Cards, per Person	1.26

LABOUR FORCE

2001 Estimates:
Male:

In the Labour Force	20,526
Participation Rate	75.1
Employed	19,380
Unemployed	1,146
Unemployment Rate	5.6
Not in Labour Force	6,817
Female:	
In the Labour Force	17,265
Participation Rate	59.2
Employed	16,244
Unemployed	1,021
Unemployment Rate	5.9
Not in Labour Force	11,882

OCCUPATIONS BY MAJOR GROUPS

2001 Estimates:	*Male*	*Female*
Management	3,337	1,174
Business, Finance & Admin.	2,754	5,992
Natural & Applied Sciences & Related	2,395	527
Health	455	1,629
Social Sciences, Gov't Services & Religion	445	406
Education	492	703
Arts, Culture, Recreation & Sport	493	675
Sales & Service	5,368	4,304
Trades, Transport & Equipment Operators & Related	2,940	315
Primary Industries	82	n.a.
Processing, Mfg. & Utilities	1,005	816

LEVEL OF SCHOOLING

2001 Estimates:

Population 15 years +	56,490
Less than Grade 9	5,670
Grades 9-13 w/o Certif.	7,580
Grade 9-13 with Certif.	9,898
Trade Certif./Dip.	1,563
Non-Univ. w/o Certif./Dip.	4,762
Non-Univ. with Certif./Dip.	8,156
Univ. w/o Degree	7,507
Univ. w/o Degree/Certif.	1,571
Univ. with Certif.	5,936
Univ. with Degree	11,354

AVERAGE HOUSEHOLD EXPENDITURES

2001 Estimates:

Food	$7,523
Shelter	$10,083
Clothing	$2,821
Transportation	$7,624
Health & Personal Care	$2,337
Recr'n, Read'g & Education	$4,269
Taxes & Securities	$20,079
Other	$9,088
Total Expenditures	$63,824

PRIVATE HOUSEHOLDS

2001 Estimates:

Private Households, Total	24,147
Pop. in Private Households	67,374
Average no. per Household	2.8

FAMILIES

2001 Estimates:

Families in Private Households	19,988
Husband-Wife Families	17,244
Lone-Parent Families	2,744
Aver. No. Persons per Family	3.2
Aver. No. Sons/Daughters at Home	1.3

HOUSING

2001 Estimates:

Occupied Private Dwellings	24,147
Owned	17,915
Rented	6,232
Single-Detached House	12,766
Semi-Detached House	2,735
Row Houses	1,466
Apartment, 5+ Storeys	1,087
Owned Apartment, 5+ Storeys	659
Apartment, 5 or Fewer Storeys	5,408
Apartment, Detached Duplex	599
Other Single-Attached	86

VEHICLES

2001 Estimates:

Model Yrs. '81-'96, No.	26,526
% Total	72.96
Model Yrs. '97-'98, No.	6,208
% Total	17.08
'99 Vehicles registered in Model Yr. '99, No.	3,623
% Total	9.97
Total No. '81-'99	36,357

LEGAL MARITAL STATUS

2001 Estimates: (Age 15+)

Single (Never Married)	19,344
Legally Married (Not Separated)	28,982
Legally Married (Separated)	1,188
Widowed	2,584
Divorced	4,392

PSYTE CATEGORIES

2001 Estimates	No. of House-holds	% of Total Hhds.	Index
Suburban Executives	2,393	9.91	691
Technocrafts & Bureaucrats	2,218	9.19	326
Asian Heights	677	2.80	442
Stable Suburban Families	2,296	9.51	729
Old Bungalow Burbs	817	3.38	204
Brie & Chablis	413	1.71	191
Participation Quebec	5,057	20.94	727
New Quebec Rows	2,723	11.28	1,029
Quebec Melange	4,651	19.26	727
Town Renters	319	1.32	153
Euro Quebec	759	3.14	358
Old Quebec Walkups	1,184	4.90	268
Quebec's New Urban Mosaic	381	1.58	65
Aged Pensioners	155	0.64	48

Québec

FINANCIAL P$YTE

2001 Estimates	No. of House-holds	% of Total Hhds.	Index
Four Star Investors	2,393	9.91	197
Successful Suburbanites	5,191	21.50	324
Urban Heights	413	1.71	40
Miners & Credit-Liners	817	3.38	107
Mortgages & Minivans	7,780	32.22	488
Country Credit	4,651	19.26	285
Loan Parent Stress	1,943	8.05	138
Towering Debt	319	1.32	17
NSF	381	1.58	45
Senior Survivors	155	0.64	34

HOME LANGUAGE

2001 Estimates:		% Total
English	12,977	19.09
French	38,762	57.02
Arabic	915	1.35
Armenian	289	0.43
Bengali	111	0.16
Chinese	5,580	8.21
Creoles	309	0.45
German	134	0.20
Greek	772	1.14
Hebrew	57	0.08
Hindi	105	0.15
Hungarian	102	0.15
Italian	206	0.30
Khmer (Cambodian)	52	0.08
Korean	67	0.10
Persian (Farsi)	105	0.15
Polish	268	0.39
Portuguese	399	0.59
Punjabi	310	0.46
Romanian	336	0.49
Russian	61	0.09
Spanish	1,161	1.71
Tagalog (Pilipino)	144	0.21
Turkish	45	0.07
Urdu	302	0.44
Vietnamese	1,162	1.71
Other Languages	189	0.28
Multiple Responses	3,063	4.51
Total	67,983	100.00

BUILDING PERMITS

	1999	1998	1997
		$000	
Value	81,027	29,131	30,139

HOMES BUILT

	1999	1998	1997
No	174	97	163

Québec

Brossard
(Ville)
Montréal CMA
(Cont'd)

TAXATION

Income Class:	1997	% Total
Under $5,000	7,830	16.56
$5,000-$10,000	6,470	13.68
$10,000-$15,000	5,950	12.58
$15,000-$20,000	3,930	8.31
$20,000-$25,000	3,230	6.83
$25,000-$30,000	3,180	6.72
$30,000-$40,000	5,120	10.83
$40,000-$50,000	3,700	7.82
$50,000 +	7,890	16.68
Total Returns, No.	47,290	
Total Income, $000	1,392,666	
Total Taxable Returns	32,370	
Total Tax, $000	192,778	
Average Income, $	29,449	
Average Tax, $	5,955	

VITAL STATISTICS

	1997	1996	1995	1994
Births	565	576	641	702
Deaths	272	289	279	288
Natural Increase	293	287	362	414
Marriages	39	42	18	46

Note: Latest available data.

MEDIA INFO
see Montréal, CMA

Candiac
(Ville)
Montréal CMA

In census division Roussillon.

POPULATION

July 1, 2001 Estimate	13,508
% Cdn. Total	0.04
% Change, '96 -'01	6.51
Avg. Annual Growth Rate, %	1.27
2003 Projected Population	14,134
2006 Projected Population	15,304
2001 Households Estimate	4,788
2003 Projected Households	5,046
2006 Projected Households	5,529

INCOME

% Above/Below National Average	+31
2001 Total Income Estimate	$373,380,000
% Cdn. Total	0.06
2001 Average Hhld. Income	$78,000
2001 Per Capita	$27,600
2003 Projected Total Income	$417,520,000
2006 Projected Total Income	$502,370,000

RETAIL SALES

% Above/Below National Average	-52
2001 Retail Sales Estimate	$58,560,000
% Cdn. Total	0.02
2001 per Household	$12,200
2001 per Capita	$4,300
2001 No. of Establishments	56
2003 Projected Retail Sales	$65,630,000
2006 Projected Retail Sales	$79,140,000

POPULATION

2001 Estimates:		
Total		13,508
Male		6,700
Female		6,808

Age Groups	Male	Female
0-4	434	403
5-9	483	445
10-14	499	461
15-19	515	495
20-24	480	473
25-29	438	434
30-34	476	504
35-39	530	601
40-44	558	633
45-49	560	621
50-54	541	559
55-59	439	416
60-64	308	284
65-69	190	198
70+	249	281

DAYTIME POPULATION

2001 Estimates:	
Working Population	3,659
At Home Population	5,692
Total	9,351

INCOME

2001 Estimates:	
Avg. Household Income	$77,982
Avg. Family Income	$83,495
Per Capita Income	$27,641
Male:	
Avg. Employment Income	$47,496
Avg. Employment Income (Full Time)	$60,652
Female:	
Avg. Employment Income	$29,465
Avg. Employment Income (Full Time)	$39,940

DISPOSABLE & DISCRETIONARY INCOME

2001 Estimates:	Per Hhld.
Disposable Income	$52,465
Discretionary Income 1 (minus Food & Shelter)	$35,930
Discretionary Income 2 (minus Food, Shelter, & Other Expenditures)	$25,022

LIQUID ASSETS

1999 Estimates:	Per Hhld.
Equity Investments	$118,034
Interest Bearing Investments	$95,344
Total Liquid Assets	$213,378

CREDIT DATA

July 2000:	
Pool of Credit	$128,848,923
Revolving Credit, No.	28,157
Fixed Loans, No.	9,084
Avg. Credit Limit, per Person	$12,803
Avg. Spent, per Person	$5,626
Satisfactory Ratings, No. per Person	3.51
Avg. No. of Cards, per Person	1.41

LABOUR FORCE

2001 Estimates:	
Male:	
In the Labour Force	4,361
Participation Rate	82.5
Employed	4,242
Unemployed	119
Unemployment Rate	2.7
Not in Labour Force	923
Female:	
In the Labour Force	3,646
Participation Rate	66.3
Employed	3,555
Unemployed	91
Unemployment Rate	2.5
Not in Labour Force	1,853

OCCUPATIONS BY MAJOR GROUPS

2001 Estimates:	Male	Female
Management	923	233
Business, Finance & Admin.	578	1,466
Natural & Applied Sciences & Related	496	112
Health	96	324
Social Sciences, Gov't Services & Religion	86	124
Education	179	298
Arts, Culture, Recreation & Sport	48	138
Sales & Service	952	670
Trades, Transport & Equipment Operators & Related	660	86
Primary Industries	38	n.a.
Processing, Mfg. & Utilities	268	86

LEVEL OF SCHOOLING

2001 Estimates:	
Population 15 years +	10,783
Less than Grade 9	536
Grades 9-13 w/o Certif.	1,467
Grade 9-13 with Certif.	1,787
Trade Certif. /Dip.	262
Non-Univ. w/o Certif./Dip.	796
Non-Univ. with Certif./Dip.	2,073
Univ. w/o Degree	1,426
Univ. w/o Degree/Certif.	246
Univ. with Certif.	1,180
Univ. with Degree	2,436

AVERAGE HOUSEHOLD EXPENDITURES

2001 Estimates:	
Food	$8,280
Shelter	$11,125
Clothing	$3,196
Transportation	$8,504
Health & Personal Care	$2,578
Recr'n, Read'g & Education	$4,935
Taxes & Securities	$22,899
Other	$9,913
Total Expenditures	$71,430

PRIVATE HOUSEHOLDS

2001 Estimates:	
Private Households, Total	4,788
Pop. in Private Households	13,461
Average no. per Household	2.8

FAMILIES

2001 Estimates:	
Families in Private Households	4,063
Husband-Wife Families	3,552
Lone-Parent Families	511
Aver. No. Persons per Family	3.1
Aver. No. Sons/Daughters at Home	1.3

HOUSING

2001 Estimates:	
Occupied Private Dwellings	4,788
Owned	3,927
Rented	861
Single-Detached House	3,194
Semi-Detached House	405
Row Houses	195
Apartment, 5+ Storeys	53
Apartment, 5 or Fewer Storeys	941

VEHICLES

2001 Estimates:	
Model Yrs. '81-'96, No.	6,913
% Total	73.15
Model Yrs. '97-'98, No.	1,578
% Total	16.70
'99 Vehicles registered in Model Yr. '99, No.	960
% Total	10.16
Total No. '81-'99	9,451

LEGAL MARITAL STATUS

2001 Estimates: (Age 15+)	
Single (Never Married)	3,709
Legally Married (Not Separated)	5,508
Legally Married (Separated)	263
Widowed	335
Divorced	968

PSYTE CATEGORIES

2001 Estimates	No. of House-holds	% of Total Hhds.	Index
Suburban Executives	658	13.74	959
Technocrafts & Bureaucrats	833	17.40	618
Old Bungalow Burbs	544	11.36	686
Participation Quebec	1,583	33.06	1,147
New Quebec Rows	274	5.72	522
Quebec Melange	756	15.79	596
University Enclaves	140	2.92	143

FINANCIAL P$YTE

2001 Estimates	No. of House-holds	% of Total Hhds.	Index
Four Star Investors	658	13.74	274
Successful Suburbanites	833	17.40	262
Miners & Credit-Liners	544	11.36	359
Mortgages & Minivans	1,857	38.78	588
Country Credit	756	15.79	233
Young Urban Struggle	140	2.92	62

Candiac
(Ville)
Montréal CMA
(Cont'd)

HOME LANGUAGE

2001 Estimates:		% Total
English	1,883	13.94
French	11,062	81.89
Creoles	22	0.16
Greek	97	0.72
Hungarian	40	0.30
Portuguese	28	0.21
Romanian	17	0.13
Spanish	67	0.50
Multiple Responses	292	2.16
Total	13,508	100.00

BUILDING PERMITS

	1999	1998	1997
		$000	
Value	24,923	19,113	13,548

HOMES BUILT

	1999	1998	1997
No	81	54	75

TAXATION

Income Class:	1997	% Total
Under $5,000	920	10.72
$5,000-$10,000	780	9.09
$10,000-$15,000	800	9.32
$15,000-$20,000	650	7.58
$20,000-$25,000	660	7.69
$25,000-$30,000	710	8.28
$30,000-$40,000	1,200	13.99
$40,000-$50,000	910	10.61
$50,000 +	1,960	22.84
Total Returns, No.	8,580	
Total Income, $000	321,154	
Total Taxable Returns	6,820	
Total Tax, $000	48,334	
Average Income, $	37,431	
Average Tax, $	7,087	

VITAL STATISTICS

	1997	1996	1995	1994
Births	150	143	146	160
Deaths	40	24	24	32
Natural Increase	110	119	122	128
Marriages	11	12	6	17

Note: Latest available data.

MEDIA INFO
see Montréal, CMA

Chambly
(Ville)
Montréal CMA

In census division La Vallée-du-Richelieu.

POPULATION

July 1, 2001 Estimate	24,017
% Cdn. Total	0.08
% Change, '96 -'01	19.72
Avg. Annual Growth Rate, %	3.67
2003 Projected Population	26,789
2006 Projected Population	31,242
2001 Households Estimate	8,971
2003 Projected Households	10,094
2006 Projected Households	11,937

INCOME

% Above/Below National Average	-2
2001 Total Income Estimate	$494,460,000
% Cdn. Total	0.08
2001 Average Hhld. Income	$55,100
2001 Per Capita	$20,600
2003 Projected Total Income	$594,470,000
2006 Projected Total Income	$778,980,000

RETAIL SALES

% Above/Below National Average	+24
2001 Retail Sales Estimate	$267,200,000
% Cdn. Total	0.10
2001 per Household	$29,800
2001 per Capita	$11,100
2001 No. of Establishments	179
2003 Projected Retail Sales	$320,900,000
2006 Projected Retail Sales	$414,030,000

POPULATION

2001 Estimates:		
Total		24,017
Male		11,771
Female		12,246

Age Groups	Male	Female
0-4	925	876
5-9	1,008	971
10-14	953	914
15-19	835	799
20-24	701	675
25-29	728	803
30-34	1,004	1,122
35-39	1,171	1,261
40-44	1,088	1,103
45-49	883	878
50-54	690	676
55-59	521	503
60-64	391	395
65-69	296	337
70+	577	933

DAYTIME POPULATION

2001 Estimates:	
Working Population	6,464
At Home Population	11,788
Total	18,252

INCOME

2001 Estimates:	
Avg. Household Income	$55,118
Avg. Family Income	$59,937
Per Capita Income	$20,588
Male:	
Avg. Employment Income	$36,348
Avg. Employment Income (Full Time)	$45,806
Female:	
Avg. Employment Income	$23,812
Avg. Employment Income (Full Time)	$31,843

DISPOSABLE & DISCRETIONARY INCOME

2001 Estimates:	Per Hhld.
Disposable Income	$38,036
Discretionary Income 1 (minus Food & Shelter)	$24,937
Discretionary Income 2 (minus Food, Shelter, & Other Expenditures)	$16,573

LIQUID ASSETS

1999 Estimates:	Per Hhld.
Equity Investments	$66,719
Interest Bearing Investments	$64,363
Total Liquid Assets	$131,082

CREDIT DATA

July 2000:	
Pool of Credit	$154,166,485
Revolving Credit, No.	39,210
Fixed Loans, No.	14,206
Avg. Credit Limit, per Person	$9,862
Avg. Spent, per Person	$4,713
Satisfactory Ratings, No. per Person	3.22
Avg. No. of Cards, per Person	1.21

LABOUR FORCE

2001 Estimates:	
Male:	
In the Labour Force	6,949
Participation Rate	78.2
Employed	6,640
Unemployed	309
Unemployment Rate	4.4
Not in Labour Force	1,936
Female:	
In the Labour Force	5,831
Participation Rate	61.5
Employed	5,591
Unemployed	240
Unemployment Rate	4.1
Not in Labour Force	3,654

OCCUPATIONS BY MAJOR GROUPS

2001 Estimates:	Male	Female
Management	865	376
Business, Finance & Admin.	722	1,990
Natural & Applied Sciences & Related	680	136
Health	115	525
Social Sciences, Gov't Services & Religion	158	197
Education	70	298
Arts, Culture, Recreation & Sport	120	104
Sales & Service	1,585	1,610
Trades, Transport & Equipment Operators & Related	1,650	100
Primary Industries	80	12
Processing, Mfg. & Utilities	727	259

LEVEL OF SCHOOLING

2001 Estimates:	
Population 15 years +	18,370
Less than Grade 9	2,056
Grades 9-13 w/o Certif.	3,268
Grade 9-13 with Certif.	3,153
Trade Certif. /Dip.	895
Non-Univ. w/o Certif./Dip.	1,568
Non-Univ. with Certif./Dip.	3,649
Univ. w/o Degree	1,567
Univ. w/o Degree/Certif.	246
Univ. with Certif.	1,321
Univ. with Degree	2,214

Québec

AVERAGE HOUSEHOLD EXPENDITURES

2001 Estimates:	
Food	$6,764
Shelter	$8,302
Clothing	$2,365
Transportation	$6,367
Health & Personal Care	$2,121
Recr'n, Read'g & Education	$3,359
Taxes & Securities	$16,360
Other	$7,608
Total Expenditures	$53,246

PRIVATE HOUSEHOLDS

2001 Estimates:	
Private Households, Total	8,971
Pop. in Private Households	23,687
Average no. per Household	2.6

FAMILIES

2001 Estimates:	
Families in Private Households	7,053
Husband-Wife Families	6,094
Lone-Parent Families	959
Aver. No. Persons per Family	3.1
Aver. No. Sons/Daughters at Home	1.2

HOUSING

2001 Estimates:	
Occupied Private Dwellings	8,971
Owned	6,124
Rented	2,847
Single-Detached House	5,181
Semi-Detached House	374
Row Houses	389
Apartment, 5 or Fewer Storeys	2,641
Apartment, Detached Duplex	349
Other Single-Attached	37

VEHICLES

2001 Estimates:	
Model Yrs. '81-'96, No.	10,374
% Total	73.81
Model Yrs. '97-'98, No.	2,360
% Total	16.79
'99 Vehicles registered in Model Yr. '99, No.	1,321
% Total	9.40
Total No. '81-'99	14,055

LEGAL MARITAL STATUS

2001 Estimates: (Age 15+)	
Single (Never Married)	6,819
Legally Married (Not Separated)	8,363
Legally Married (Separated)	465
Widowed	932
Divorced	1,791

PSYTE CATEGORIES

2001 Estimates	No. of Households	% of Total Hhds.	Index
Participation			
Quebec	3,049	33.99	1,179
New Quebec Rows	1,522	16.97	1,548
Quebec Melange	3,021	33.68	1,271
Quebec Town Elders	1,021	11.38	403
Quebec's New Urban Mosaic	221	2.46	102
Aged Pensioners	130	1.45	109

Québec

Chambly
(Ville)
Montréal CMA
(Cont'd)

FINANCIAL P$YTE

2001 Estimates	No. of House -holds	% of Total Hhds.	Index
Mortgages & Minivans	4,571	50.95	772
Country Credit	3,021	33.68	498
Loan Parent Stress	1,021	11.38	195
NSF	221	2.46	70
Senior Survivors	130	1.45	77

HOME LANGUAGE

2001 Estimates:		% Total
English	1,410	5.87
French	22,101	92.02
Greek	91	0.38
Korean	23	0.10
Spanish	59	0.25
Other Languages	12	0.05
Multiple Responses	321	1.34
Total	24,017	100.00

BUILDING PERMITS

	1999	1998 $000	1997
Value	16,371	13,312	11,766

HOMES BUILT

	1999	1998	1997
No.	38	38	80

TAXATION

Income Class:	1997	% Total
Under $5,000	1,620	11.91
$5,000-$10,000	1,560	11.47
$10,000-$15,000	1,640	12.06
$15,000-$20,000	1,230	9.04
$20,000-$25,000	1,170	8.60
$25,000-$30,000	1,200	8.82
$30,000-$40,000	1,970	14.49
$40,000-$50,000	1,360	10.00
$50,000 +	1,840	13.53
Total Returns, No.	13,600	
Total Income, $000	371,145	
Total Taxable Returns	10,140	
Total Tax, $000	45,587	
Average Income, $	27,290	
Average Tax, $	4,496	

VITAL STATISTICS

	1997	1996	1995	1994
Births	319	320	364	366
Deaths	105	90	103	99
Natural Increase	214	230	261	267
Marriages	45	47	45	50

Note: Latest available data.

MEDIA INFO
see Montréal, CMA

Châteauguay
(Ville)
Montréal CMA

In census division Roussillon.

POPULATION

July 1, 2001 Estimate	45,322
% Cdn. Total	0.15
% Change, '96 -'01	1.84
Avg. Annual Growth Rate, %	0.36
2003 Projected Population	46,313
2006 Projected Population	48,576
2001 Households Estimate	16,533
2003 Projected Households	17,015
2006 Projected Households	18,041

INCOME

% Above/Below National Average	-9
2001 Total Income Estimate	$873,700,000
% Cdn. Total	0.13
2001 Average Hhld. Income	$52,800
2001 Per Capita	$19,300
2003 Projected Total Income	$952,010,000
2006 Projected Total Income	$1,105,270,000

RETAIL SALES

% Above/Below National Average	-34
2001 Retail Sales Estimate	$268,880,000
% Cdn. Total	0.10
2001 per Household	$16,300
2001 per Capita	$5,900
2001 No. of Establishments	293
2003 Projected Retail Sales	$299,860,000
2006 Projected Retail Sales	$351,860,000

POPULATION

2001 Estimates:		
Total		45,322
Male		22,197
Female		23,125

Age Groups	Male	Female
0-4	1,348	1,271
5-9	1,564	1,459
10-14	1,649	1,538
15-19	1,664	1,560
20-24	1,511	1,443
25-29	1,336	1,317
30-34	1,438	1,514
35-39	1,720	1,855
40-44	1,828	1,933
45-49	1,734	1,797
50-54	1,506	1,606
55-59	1,258	1,391
60-64	1,107	1,213
65-69	958	1,029
70+	1,576	2,199

DAYTIME POPULATION

2001 Estimates:	
Working Population	9,915
At Home Population	23,976
Total	33,891

INCOME

2001 Estimates:	
Avg. Household Income	$52,846
Avg. Family Income	$57,136
Per Capita Income	$19,278
Male:	
Avg. Employment Income	$35,115
Avg. Employment Income (Full Time)	$43,505
Female:	
Avg. Employment Income	$22,657
Avg. Employment Income (Full Time)	$32,334

DISPOSABLE & DISCRETIONARY INCOME

2001 Estimates:	Per Hhld.
Disposable Income	$36,709
Discretionary Income 1 (minus Food & Shelter)	$24,003
Discretionary Income 2 (minus Food, Shelter, & Other Expenditures)	$15,758

LIQUID ASSETS

1999 Estimates:	Per Hhld.
Equity Investments	$60,846
Interest Bearing Investments	$61,241
Total Liquid Assets	$122,087

CREDIT DATA

July 2000:	
Pool of Credit	$323,898,336
Revolving Credit, No.	83,422
Fixed Loans, No.	29,060
Avg. Credit Limit, per Person	$9,468
Avg. Spent, per Person	$4,492
Satisfactory Ratings, No. per Person	3.11
Avg. No. of Cards, per Person	1.12

LABOUR FORCE

2001 Estimates:	
Male:	
In the Labour Force	12,549
Participation Rate	71.2
Employed	11,862
Unemployed	687
Unemployment Rate	5.5
Not in Labour Force	5,087
Female:	
In the Labour Force	10,110
Participation Rate	53.6
Employed	9,434
Unemployed	676
Unemployment Rate	6.7
Not in Labour Force	8,747

OCCUPATIONS BY MAJOR GROUPS

2001 Estimates:	Male	Female
Management	1,379	514
Business, Finance & Admin.	1,478	3,588
Natural & Applied Sciences & Related	785	171
Health	196	944
Social Sciences, Gov't Services & Religion	181	182
Education	282	489
Arts, Culture, Recreation & Sport	237	208
Sales & Service	2,858	2,889
Trades, Transport & Equipment Operators & Related	3,059	214
Primary Industries	150	28
Processing, Mfg. & Utilities	1,485	420

LEVEL OF SCHOOLING

2001 Estimates:	
Population 15 years +	36,493
Less than Grade 9	5,104
Grades 9-13 w/o Certif.	6,717
Grade 9-13 with Certif.	8,146
Trade Certif. /Dip.	1,569
Non-Univ. w/o Certif./Dip.	3,160
Non-Univ. with Certif./Dip.	6,169
Univ. w/o Degree	2,845
Univ. w/o Degree/Certif.	777
Univ. with Certif.	2,068
Univ. with Degree	2,783

AVERAGE HOUSEHOLD EXPENDITURES

2001 Estimates:	
Food	$6,512
Shelter	$8,086
Clothing	$2,178
Transportation	$6,339
Health & Personal Care	$2,051
Recr'n, Read'g & Education	$3,344
Taxes & Securities	$15,063
Other	$7,781
Total Expenditures	$51,354

PRIVATE HOUSEHOLDS

2001 Estimates:	
Private Households, Total	16,533
Pop. in Private Households	44,667
Average no. per Household	2.7

FAMILIES

2001 Estimates:	
Families in Private Households	13,209
Husband-Wife Families	11,434
Lone-Parent Families	1,775
Aver. No. Persons per Family	3.1
Aver. No. Sons/Daughters at Home	1.2

HOUSING

2001 Estimates:	
Occupied Private Dwellings	16,533
Owned	12,411
Rented	4,122
Single-Detached House	11,702
Semi-Detached House	877
Row Houses	211
Apartment, 5+ Storeys	76
Apartment, 5 or Fewer Storeys	2,946
Apartment, Detached Duplex	676
Other Single-Attached	45

VEHICLES

2001 Estimates:	
Model Yrs. '81-'96, No.	19,055
% Total	77.29
Model Yrs. '97-'98, No.	3,459
% Total	14.03
'99 Vehicles registered in Model Yr. '99, No.	2,139
% Total	8.68
Total No. '81-'99	24,653

LEGAL MARITAL STATUS

2001 Estimates: (Age 15+)	
Single (Never Married)	11,554
Legally Married (Not Separated)	18,809
Legally Married (Separated)	885
Widowed	2,234
Divorced	3,011

PSYTE CATEGORIES

2001 Estimates	No. of House -holds	% of Total Hhds.	Index
Old Bungalow Burbs	1,768	10.69	645
Participation Quebec	2,865	17.33	601
Quebec Melange	9,737	58.89	2,222
Conservative Homebodies	475	2.87	80
Quebec Town Elders	1,613	9.76	345

FINANCIAL P$YTE

2001 Estimates	No. of House -holds	% of Total Hhds.	Index
Miners & Credit-Liners	1,768	10.69	338
Mortgages & Minivans	2,865	17.33	263
Bills & Wills	475	2.87	35
Country Credit	9,737	58.89	871
Loan Parent Stress	1,613	9.76	168

Châteauguay
(Ville)
Montréal CMA
(Cont'd)

HOME LANGUAGE

2001 Estimates:		% Total
English	14,599	32.21
French	28,671	63.26
Arabic	67	0.15
Armenian	33	0.07
Chinese	55	0.12
German	138	0.30
Greek	100	0.22
Italian	159	0.35
Korean	29	0.06
Persian (Farsi)	55	0.12
Polish	76	0.17
Spanish	121	0.27
Other Languages	98	0.22
Multiple Responses	1,121	2.47
Total	45,322	100.00

BUILDING PERMITS

	1999	1998	1997
		$000	
Value	19,896	26,412	24,422

HOMES BUILT

	1999	1998	1997
No.	56	176	92

TAXATION

Income Class:	1997	% Total
Under $5,000	3,780	12.97
$5,000-$10,000	3,700	12.70
$10,000-$15,000	3,860	13.25
$15,000-$20,000	2,750	9.44
$20,000-$25,000	2,560	8.79
$25,000-$30,000	2,580	8.85
$30,000-$40,000	4,020	13.80
$40,000-$50,000	2,580	8.85
$50,000 +	3,320	11.39
Total Returns, No.	29,140	
Total Income, $000	740,204	
Total Taxable Returns	20,930	
Total Tax, $000	88,154	
Average Income, $	25,402	
Average Tax, $	4,212	

VITAL STATISTICS

	1997	1996	1995	1994
Births	402	443	482	563
Deaths	277	291	304	246
Natural Increase	125	152	178	317
Marriages	102	111	109	116

Note: Latest available data.

MEDIA INFO
see Montréal, CMA

Côte-Saint-Luc
(Cité)
Montréal CMA

In census division Communauté urbaine de Montréal.

POPULATION

July 1, 2001 Estimate	29,728
% Cdn. Total	0.10
% Change, '96 -'01	-1.70
Avg. Annual Growth Rate, %	-0.34
2003 Projected Population	29,859
2006 Projected Population	30,204
2001 Households Estimate	13,618
2003 Projected Households	13,618
2006 Projected Households	13,688

INCOME

% Above/Below National Average	+29
2001 Total Income Estimate	$809,080,000
% Cdn. Total	0.12
2001 Average Hhld. Income	$59,400
2001 Per Capita	$27,200
2003 Projected Total Income	$848,440,000
2006 Projected Total Income	$918,620,000

RETAIL SALES

% Above/Below National Average	-62
2001 Retail Sales Estimate	$100,570,000
% Cdn. Total	0.04
2001 per Household	$7,400
2001 per Capita	$3,400
2001 No. of Establishments	285
2003 Projected Retail Sales	$107,170,000
2006 Projected Retail Sales	$118,030,000

POPULATION

2001 Estimates:		
Total		29,728
Male		13,406
Female		16,322

Age Groups	Male	Female
0-4	655	607
5-9	701	654
10-14	737	694
15-19	771	740
20-24	794	786
25-29	769	797
30-34	723	772
35-39	735	795
40-44	765	857
45-49	831	981
50-54	826	1,001
55-59	750	931
60-64	699	918
65-69	694	974
70+	2,956	4,815

DAYTIME POPULATION

2001 Estimates:	
Working Population	3,986
At Home Population	17,651
Total	21,637

INCOME

2001 Estimates:	
Avg. Household Income	$59,412
Avg. Family Income	$75,169
Per Capita Income	$27,216
Male:	
Avg. Employment Income	$41,797
Avg. Employment Income (Full Time)	$54,529
Female:	
Avg. Employment Income	$24,685
Avg. Employment Income (Full Time)	$34,725

DISPOSABLE & DISCRETIONARY INCOME

2001 Estimates:	Per Hhld.
Disposable Income	$38,279
Discretionary Income 1 (minus Food & Shelter)	$23,537
Discretionary Income 2 (minus Food, Shelter, & Other Expenditures)	$15,320

LIQUID ASSETS

1999 Estimates:	Per Hhld.
Equity Investments	$105,891
Interest Bearing Investments	$77,078
Total Liquid Assets	$182,969

CREDIT DATA

July 2000:	
Pool of Credit	$293,102,752
Revolving Credit, No.	68,763
Fixed Loans, No.	10,528
Avg. Credit Limit, per Person	$10,486
Avg. Spent, per Person	$3,606
Satisfactory Ratings, No. per Person	2.77
Avg. No. of Cards, per Person	1.34

LABOUR FORCE

2001 Estimates:	
Male:	
In the Labour Force	7,041
Participation Rate	62.2
Employed	6,601
Unemployed	440
Unemployment Rate	6.2
Not in Labour Force	4,272
Female:	
In the Labour Force	6,086
Participation Rate	42.4
Employed	5,606
Unemployed	480
Unemployment Rate	7.9
Not in Labour Force	8,281

OCCUPATIONS BY MAJOR GROUPS

2001 Estimates:	Male	Female
Management	1,553	611
Business, Finance & Admin.	1,071	1,988
Natural & Applied Sciences & Related	482	181
Health	333	570
Social Sciences, Gov't Services & Religion	298	192
Education	196	473
Arts, Culture, Recreation & Sport	211	191
Sales & Service	1,861	1,468
Trades, Transport & Equipment Operators & Related	458	39
Primary Industries	20	n.a.
Processing, Mfg. & Utilities	229	110

LEVEL OF SCHOOLING

2001 Estimates:	
Population 15 years +	25,680
Less than Grade 9	3,102
Grades 9-13 w/o Certif.	4,242
Grade 9-13 with Certif.	3,748
Trade Certif. /Dip.	553
Non-Univ. w/o Certif./Dip.	1,430
Non-Univ. with Certif./Dip.	2,500
Univ. w/o Degree	3,666
Univ. w/o Degree/Certif.	1,345
Univ. with Certif.	2,321
Univ. with Degree	6,439

Québec

AVERAGE HOUSEHOLD EXPENDITURES

2001 Estimates:	
Food	$6,318
Shelter	$11,011
Clothing	$2,265
Transportation	$5,973
Health & Personal Care	$2,226
Recr'n, Read'g & Education	$3,797
Taxes & Securities	$15,428
Other	$9,094
Total Expenditures	$56,112

PRIVATE HOUSEHOLDS

2001 Estimates:	
Private Households, Total	13,618
Pop. in Private Households	28,915
Average no. per Household	2.1

FAMILIES

2001 Estimates:	
Families in Private Households	8,432
Husband-Wife Families	7,522
Lone-Parent Families	910
Aver. No. Persons per Family	2.8
Aver. No. Sons/Daughters at Home	0.9

HOUSING

2001 Estimates:	
Occupied Private Dwellings	13,618
Owned	6,003
Rented	7,615
Single-Detached House	2,045
Semi-Detached House	1,438
Row Houses	564
Apartment, 5+ Storeys	7,499
Owned Apartment, 5+ Storeys	1,685
Apartment, 5 or Fewer Storeys	1,943
Apartment, Detached Duplex	109
Other Single-Attached	10
Movable Dwellings	10

VEHICLES

2001 Estimates:	
Model Yrs. '81-'96, No.	10,845
% Total	71.63
Model Yrs. '97-'98, No.	2,737
% Total	18.08
'99 Vehicles registered in Model Yr. '99, No.	1,558
% Total	10.29
Total No. '81-'99	15,140

LEGAL MARITAL STATUS

2001 Estimates: (Age 15+)	
Single (Never Married)	5,968
Legally Married (Not Separated)	14,207
Legally Married (Separated)	435
Widowed	3,648
Divorced	1,422

Québec

Côte-Saint-Luc
(Cité)
Montréal CMA
(Cont'd)

PSYTE CATEGORIES

2001 Estimates	No. of House-holds	% of Total Hhds.	Index
Urban Gentry	3,139	23.05	1,283
Suburban Executives	557	4.09	285
Suburban Nesters	669	4.91	307
Brie & Chablis	113	0.83	93
Aging Erudites	378	2.78	184
High Rise Melting Pot	398	2.92	195
High Rise Sunsets	7,581	55.67	3,893
Aged Pensioners	383	2.81	211
Old Grey Towers	77	0.57	102

FINANÇIAL P$YTE

2001 Estimates	No. of House-holds	% of Total Hhds.	Index
Four Star Investors	3,696	27.14	540
Canadian Comfort	669	4.91	51
Urban Heights	491	3.61	84
Revolving Renters	7,581	55.67	1,210
Towering Debt	398	2.92	37
Senior Survivors	460	3.38	179

HOME LANGUAGE

2001 Estimates:		% Total
English	20,788	69.93
French	2,999	10.09
Arabic	222	0.75
Armenian	30	0.10
Bulgarian	46	0.15
Chinese	292	0.98
Creoles	15	0.05
Czech	20	0.07
German	15	0.05
Greek	72	0.24
Gujarati	36	0.12
Hebrew	466	1.57
Hungarian	266	0.89
Italian	346	1.16
Korean	147	0.49
Persian (Farsi)	356	1.20
Polish	123	0.41
Portuguese	46	0.15
Romanian	299	1.01
Russian	818	2.75
Serbian	26	0.09
Spanish	189	0.64
Tagalog (Pilipino)	82	0.28
Turkish	22	0.07
Vietnamese	82	0.28
Yiddish	476	1.60
Other Languages	111	0.37
Multiple Responses	1,338	4.50
Total	29,728	100.00

BUILDING PERMITS

	1999	1998	1997
		$000	
Value	23,780	9,291	3,508

HOMES BUILT

	1999	1998	1997
No.	33	7	4

TAXATION

Income Class:	1997	% Total
Under $5,000	2,170	11.60
$5,000-$10,000	2,080	11.12
$10,000-$15,000	2,760	14.75
$15,000-$20,000	2,000	10.69
$20,000-$25,000	1,630	8.71
$25,000-$30,000	1,370	7.32
$30,000-$40,000	2,080	11.12
$40,000-$50,000	1,320	7.06
$50,000 +	3,300	17.64
Total Returns, No.	18,710	
Total Income, $000	662,831	
Total Taxable Returns	13,290	
Total Tax, $000	93,721	
Average Income, $	35,427	
Average Tax, $	7,052	

VITAL STATISTICS

	1997	1996	1995	1994
Births	220	242	229	236
Deaths	484	462	483	496
Natural Increase	-264	-220	-254	-260
Marriages	107	75	111	123

Note: Latest available data.

MEDIA INFO
see Montréal, CMA

Deux-Montagnes
(Ville)
Montréal CMA

In census division
Deux-Montagnes.

POPULATION

July 1, 2001 Estimate	19,342
% Cdn. Total	0.06
% Change, '96 -'01	17.39
Avg. Annual Growth Rate, %	3.26
2003 Projected Population	21,404
2006 Projected Population	24,762
2001 Households Estimate	7,203
2003 Projected Households	8,037
2006 Projected Households	9,409

INCOME

% Above/Below National Average	-4
2001 Total Income Estimate	$391,100,000
% Cdn. Total	0.06
2001 Average Hhld. Income	$54,300
2001 Per Capita	$20,200
2003 Projected Total Income	$465,860,000
2006 Projected Total Income	$603,830,000

RETAIL SALES

% Above/Below National Average	-57
2001 Retail Sales Estimate	$73,780,000
% Cdn. Total	0.03
2001 per Household	$10,200
2001 per Capita	$3,800
2001 No. of Establishments	74
2003 Projected Retail Sales	$85,530,000
2006 Projected Retail Sales	$106,140,000

POPULATION

2001 Estimates:		
Total		19,342
Male		9,230
Female		10,112

Age Groups	Male	Female
0-4	721	668
5-9	800	758
10-14	752	733
15-19	692	685
20-24	584	617
25-29	570	659
30-34	715	851
35-39	862	970
40-44	864	907
45-49	726	766
50-54	566	607
55-59	413	430
60-64	286	309
65-69	222	272
70+	457	880

DAYTIME POPULATION

2001 Estimates:	
Working Population	1,813
At Home Population	10,006
Total	11,819

INCOME

2001 Estimates:	
Avg. Household Income	$54,297
Avg. Family Income	$59,112
Per Capita Income	$20,220
Male:	
Avg. Employment Income	$38,358
Avg. Employment Income (Full Time)	$47,098
Female:	
Avg. Employment Income	$23,423
Avg. Employment Income (Full Time)	$33,508

DISPOSABLE & DISCRETIONARY INCOME

2001 Estimates:	Per Hhld.
Disposable Income	$37,474
Discretionary Income 1 (minus Food & Shelter)	$24,505
Discretionary Income 2 (minus Food, Shelter, & Other Expenditures)	$16,100

LIQUID ASSETS

1999 Estimates:	Per Hhld.
Equity Investments	$65,408
Interest Bearing Investments	$62,672
Total Liquid Assets	$128,080

CREDIT DATA

July 2000:	
Pool of Credit	$119,649,404
Revolving Credit, No.	30,682
Fixed Loans, No.	11,031
Avg. Credit Limit, per Person	$9,367
Avg. Spent, per Person	$4,506
Satisfactory Ratings, No. per Person	3.09
Avg. No. of Cards, per Person	1.15

LABOUR FORCE

2001 Estimates:	
Male:	
In the Labour Force	5,320
Participation Rate	76.5
Employed	5,055
Unemployed	265
Unemployment Rate	5.0
Not in Labour Force	1,637
Female:	
In the Labour Force	4,506
Participation Rate	56.7
Employed	4,216
Unemployed	290
Unemployment Rate	6.4
Not in Labour Force	3,447

OCCUPATIONS BY MAJOR GROUPS

2001 Estimates:	Male	Female
Management	623	283
Business, Finance & Admin.	715	1,464
Natural & Applied Sciences & Related	547	167
Health	51	355
Social Sciences, Gov't Services & Religion	50	101
Education	83	219
Arts, Culture, Recreation & Sport	86	127
Sales & Service	1,100	1,363
Trades, Transport & Equipment Operators & Related	1,377	64
Primary Industries	31	12
Processing, Mfg. & Utilities	473	170

LEVEL OF SCHOOLING

2001 Estimates:	
Population 15 years +	14,910
Less than Grade 9	1,589
Grades 9-13 w/o Certif.	3,049
Grade 9-13 with Certif.	3,133
Trade Certif. /Dip.	689
Non-Univ. w/o Certif./Dip.	1,307
Non-Univ. with Certif./Dip.	2,502
Univ. w/o Degree	1,270
Univ. w/o Degree/Certif.	220
Univ. with Certif.	1,050
Univ. with Degree	1,371

Deux-Montagnes
(Ville)
Montréal CMA
(Cont'd)

AVERAGE HOUSEHOLD EXPENDITURES

2001 Estimates:
Food	$6,665
Shelter	$8,230
Clothing	$2,329
Transportation	$6,442
Health & Personal Care	$2,103
Recr'n, Read'g & Education	$3,321
Taxes & Securities	$15,995
Other	$7,578
Total Expenditures	$52,663

PRIVATE HOUSEHOLDS

2001 Estimates:
Private Households, Total	7,203
Pop. in Private Households	19,178
Average no. per Household	2.7

FAMILIES

2001 Estimates:
Families in Private Households	5,652
Husband-Wife Families	4,707
Lone-Parent Families	945
Aver. No. Persons per Family	3.1
Aver. No. Sons/Daughters at Home	1.3

HOUSING

2001 Estimates:
Occupied Private Dwellings	7,203
Owned	5,172
Rented	2,031
Single-Detached House	4,658
Semi-Detached House	540
Row Houses	381
Apartment, 5+ Storeys	20
Apartment, 5 or Fewer Storeys	1,266
Apartment, Detached Duplex	326
Other Single-Attached	12

VEHICLES

2001 Estimates:
Model Yrs. '81-'96, No.	7,152
% Total	77.70
Model Yrs. '97-'98, No.	1,297
% Total	14.09
'99 Vehicles registered in Model Yr. '99, No.	756
% Total	8.21
Total No. '81-'99	9,205

LEGAL MARITAL STATUS

2001 Estimates: (Age 15+)
Single (Never Married)	5,395
Legally Married (Not Separated)	6,703
Legally Married (Separated)	405
Widowed	869
Divorced	1,538

PSYTE CATEGORIES

2001 Estimates	No. of House-holds	% of Total Hhds.	Index
Participation Quebec	1,941	26.95	935
New Quebec Rows	1,168	16.22	1,480
Quebec Melange	3,413	47.38	1,788
Town Renters	132	1.83	212
Euro Quebec	103	1.43	163
Quebec Town Elders	446	6.19	219

FINAN¢IAL P$YTE

2001 Estimates	No. of House-holds	% of Total Hhds.	Index
Mortgages & Minivans	3,109	43.16	654
Country Credit	3,413	47.38	701
Loan Parent Stress	549	7.62	131
Towering Debt	132	1.83	23

HOME LANGUAGE

2001 Estimates:		% Total
English	4,630	23.94
French	14,202	73.43
Arabic	12	0.06
German	12	0.06
Khmer (Cambodian)	18	0.09
Lao	60	0.31
Spanish	24	0.12
Other Languages	12	0.06
Multiple Responses	372	1.92
Total	19,342	100.00

BUILDING PERMITS

	1999	1998 $000	1997
Value	13,780	8,919	19,303

HOMES BUILT

	1999	1998	1997
No	114	92	168

TAXATION

Income Class:	1997	% Total
Under $5,000	1,430	12.77
$5,000-$10,000	1,330	11.88
$10,000-$15,000	1,460	13.04
$15,000-$20,000	1,010	9.02
$20,000-$25,000	1,010	9.02
$25,000-$30,000	1,020	9.11
$30,000-$40,000	1,610	14.38
$40,000-$50,000	1,040	9.29
$50,000 +	1,290	11.52
Total Returns, No.	11,200	
Total Income, $000	289,690	
Total Taxable Returns	8,130	
Total Tax, $000	34,814	
Average Income, $	25,865	
Average Tax, $	4,282	

VITAL STATISTICS

	1997	1996	1995	1994
Births	229	256	248	261
Deaths	116	90	94	113
Natural Increase	113	166	154	148
Marriages	38	41	45	43

Note: Latest available data.

MEDIA INFO

see Montréal, CMA

Dollard-des-Ormeaux
(Ville)
Montréal CMA

In census division Communauté urbaine de Montréal.

POPULATION

July 1, 2001 Estimate	49,157
% Cdn. Total	0.16
% Change, '96 -'01	0.94
Avg. Annual Growth Rate, %	0.19
2003 Projected Population	50,039
2006 Projected Population	51,615
2001 Households Estimate	15,807
2003 Projected Households	16,031
2006 Projected Households	16,413

INCOME

% Above/Below National Average	+7
2001 Total Income Estimate	$1,110,240,000
% Cdn. Total	0.17
2001 Average Hhld. Income	$70,200
2001 Per Capita	$22,600
2003 Projected Total Income	$1,193,360,000
2006 Projected Total Income	$1,337,290,000

RETAIL SALES

% Above/Below National Average	-26
2001 Retail Sales Estimate	$326,970,000
% Cdn. Total	0.12
2001 per Household	$20,700
2001 per Capita	$6,700
2001 No. of Establishments	330
2003 Projected Retail Sales	$362,570,000
2006 Projected Retail Sales	$418,060,000

POPULATION

2001 Estimates:
Total	49,157
Male	24,144
Female	25,013

Age Groups	Male	Female
0-4	1,424	1,353
5-9	1,644	1,614
10-14	1,904	1,796
15-19	2,038	1,901
20-24	1,946	1,805
25-29	1,615	1,518
30-34	1,482	1,532
35-39	1,632	1,836
40-44	1,828	2,131
45-49	1,979	2,209
50-54	1,890	1,994
55-59	1,531	1,578
60-64	1,159	1,155
65-69	849	877
70+	1,223	1,714

DAYTIME POPULATION

2001 Estimates:
Working Population	7,450
At Home Population	23,391
Total	30,841

INCOME

2001 Estimates:
Avg. Household Income	$70,237
Avg. Family Income	$74,243
Per Capita Income	$22,586
Male:	
Avg. Employment Income	$41,999
Avg. Employment Income (Full Time)	$54,758
Female:	
Avg. Employment Income	$24,309
Avg. Employment Income (Full Time)	$35,539

Québec

DISPOSABLE & DISCRETIONARY INCOME

2001 Estimates:	Per Hhld.
Disposable Income	$47,461
Discretionary Income 1 (minus Food & Shelter)	$32,371
Discretionary Income 2 (minus Food, Shelter, & Other Expenditures)	$22,427

LIQUID ASSETS

1999 Estimates:	Per Hhld.
Equity Investments	$108,994
Interest Bearing Investments	$87,379
Total Liquid Assets	$196,373

CREDIT DATA

July 2000:	
Pool of Credit	$519,703,541
Revolving Credit, No.	118,267
Fixed Loans, No.	30,312
Avg. Credit Limit, per Person	$11,861
Avg. Spent, per Person	$4,978
Satisfactory Ratings, No. per Person	3.25
Avg. No. of Cards, per Person	1.31

LABOUR FORCE

2001 Estimates:	
Male:	
In the Labour Force	14,762
Participation Rate	77.0
Employed	14,005
Unemployed	757
Unemployment Rate	5.1
Not in Labour Force	4,410
Female:	
In the Labour Force	12,109
Participation Rate	59.8
Employed	11,598
Unemployed	511
Unemployment Rate	4.2
Not in Labour Force	8,141

OCCUPATIONS BY MAJOR GROUPS

2001 Estimates:	Male	Female
Management	2,722	905
Business, Finance & Admin.	2,292	4,176
Natural & Applied Sciences & Related	1,640	422
Health	319	1,067
Social Sciences, Gov't Services & Religion	303	231
Education	464	694
Arts, Culture, Recreation & Sport	206	386
Sales & Service	3,667	3,158
Trades, Transport & Equipment Operators & Related	1,702	99
Primary Industries	78	n.a.
Processing, Mfg. & Utilities	906	541

Québec

Dollard-des-Ormeaux
(Ville)
Montréal CMA
(Cont'd)

LEVEL OF SCHOOLING

2001 Estimates:
Population 15 years +	39,422
Less than Grade 9	2,476
Grades 9-13 w/o Certif.	5,074
Grade 9-13 with Certif.	5,903
Trade Certif./Dip.	951
Non-Univ. w/o Certif./Dip.	3,229
Non-Univ. with Certif./Dip.	5,952
Univ. w/o Degree	6,491
Univ. w/o Degree/Certif.	1,905
Univ. with Certif.	4,586
Univ. with Degree	9,346

AVERAGE HOUSEHOLD EXPENDITURES

2001 Estimates:
Food	$7,312
Shelter	$10,447
Clothing	$2,759
Transportation	$7,671
Health & Personal Care	$2,298
Recr'n, Read'g & Education	$4,468
Taxes & Securities	$20,320
Other	$9,895
Total Expenditures	$65,170

PRIVATE HOUSEHOLDS

2001 Estimates:
Private Households, Total	15,807
Pop. in Private Households	48,865
Average no. per Household	3.1

FAMILIES

2001 Estimates:
Families in Private Households	13,318
Husband-Wife Families	11,814
Lone-Parent Families	1,504
Aver. No. Persons per Family	3.4
Aver. No. Sons/Daughters at Home	1.5

HOUSING

2001 Estimates:
Occupied Private Dwellings	15,807
Owned	11,779
Rented	4,028
Single-Detached House	9,696
Semi-Detached House	284
Row Houses	2,899
Apartment, 5+ Storeys	521
Owned Apartment, 5+ Storeys	37
Apartment, 5 or Fewer Storeys	2,397
Other Single-Attached	10

VEHICLES

2001 Estimates:
Model Yrs. '81-'96, No.	18,886
% Total	71.02
Model Yrs. '97-'98, No.	4,785
% Total	17.99
'99 Vehicles registered in Model Yr. '99, No.	2,923
% Total	10.99
Total No. '81-'99	26,594

LEGAL MARITAL STATUS

2001 Estimates: (Age 15+)
Single (Never Married)	12,045
Legally Married (Not Separated)	22,703
Legally Married (Separated)	736
Widowed	1,741
Divorced	2,197

PSYTE CATEGORIES

2001 Estimates	No. of House-holds	% of Total Hhds.	Index
Suburban Executives	2,034	12.87	898
Technocrafts & Bureaucrats	2,521	15.95	567
Stable Suburban Families	4,117	26.05	1,998
Old Bungalow Burbs	393	2.49	150
Aging Erudites	1,530	9.68	642
Kindergarten Boom	1,560	9.87	376
Participation Quebec	315	1.99	69
New Quebec Rows	797	5.04	460
Quebec Melange	266	1.68	64
Young Urban Mix	1,557	9.85	465
Young City Singles	646	4.09	178

FINANCIAL P$YTE

2001 Estimates	No. of House-holds	% of Total Hhds.	Index
Four Star Investors	2,034	12.87	256
Successful Suburbanites	6,638	41.99	633
Urban Heights	1,530	9.68	225
Miners & Credit-Liners	393	2.49	79
Mortgages & Minivans	2,672	16.90	256
Bills & Wills	1,557	9.85	119
Country Credit	266	1.68	25
Towering Debt	646	4.09	52

HOME LANGUAGE

2001 Estimates:		% Total
English	29,651	60.32
French	8,514	17.32
Arabic	1,487	3.03
Armenian	482	0.98
Chinese	800	1.63
Creoles	145	0.29
Croatian	119	0.24
Dutch	31	0.06
Estonian	36	0.07
German	65	0.13
Greek	697	1.42
Gujarati	102	0.21
Hebrew	196	0.40
Hindi	99	0.20
Hungarian	51	0.10
Italian	439	0.89
Khmer (Cambodian)	76	0.15
Korean	25	0.05
Malayalam	35	0.07
Persian (Farsi)	311	0.63
Polish	170	0.35
Portuguese	246	0.50
Punjabi	523	1.06
Romanian	112	0.23
Russian	66	0.13
Serbo-Croatian	97	0.20
Slovak	31	0.06
Spanish	544	1.11
Swedish	61	0.12
Tagalog (Pilipino)	149	0.30
Tamil	51	0.10
Ukrainian	56	0.11
Urdu	80	0.16
Vietnamese	305	0.62
Other Languages	282	0.57
Multiple Responses	3,023	6.15
Total	49,157	100.00

BUILDING PERMITS

	1999	1998	1997
		$000	
Value	30,171	26,242	13,773

HOMES BUILT

	1999	1998	1997
No.	138	89	38

TAXATION

Income Class:	1997	% Total
Under $5,000	5,360	16.32
$5,000-$10,000	4,110	12.52
$10,000-$15,000	4,070	12.39
$15,000-$20,000	2,850	8.68
$20,000-$25,000	2,440	7.43
$25,000-$30,000	2,270	6.91
$30,000-$40,000	3,670	11.18
$40,000-$50,000	2,590	7.89
$50,000 +	5,490	16.72
Total Returns, No.	32,840	
Total Income, $000	973,821	
Total Taxable Returns	22,690	
Total Tax, $000	131,035	
Average Income, $	29,654	
Average Tax, $	5,775	

VITAL STATISTICS

	1997	1996	1995	1994
Births	469	512	582	585
Deaths	182	188	173	155
Natural Increase	287	324	409	430
Marriages	86	101	81	82

Note: Latest available data.

MEDIA INFO
see Montréal, CMA

Dorval
(Cité)
Montréal CMA

In census division Communauté urbaine de Montréal.

POPULATION

July 1, 2001 Estimate	18,054
% Cdn. Total	0.06
% Change, '96 -'01	0.90
Avg. Annual Growth Rate, %	0.18
2003 Projected Population	18,376
2006 Projected Population	18,951
2001 Households Estimate	7,756
2003 Projected Households	7,873
2006 Projected Households	8,068

INCOME

% Above/Below National Average	+22
2001 Total Income Estimate	$464,960,000
% Cdn. Total	0.07
2001 Average Hhld. Income	$59,900
2001 Per Capita	$25,800
2003 Projected Total Income	$494,690,000
2006 Projected Total Income	$545,830,000

RETAIL SALES

% Above/Below National Average	+139
2001 Retail Sales Estimate	$386,530,000
% Cdn. Total	0.14
2001 per Household	$49,800
2001 per Capita	$21,400
2001 No. of Establishments	185
2003 Projected Retail Sales	$428,080,000
2006 Projected Retail Sales	$492,230,000

POPULATION

2001 Estimates:

Total		18,054
Male		8,558
Female		9,496

Age Groups	Male	Female
0-4	463	471
5-9	464	469
10-14	482	476
15-19	511	497
20-24	510	516
25-29	530	548
30-34	607	620
35-39	686	699
40-44	709	717
45-49	692	723
50-54	639	687
55-59	536	591
60-64	440	510
65-69	377	477
70+	912	1,495

DAYTIME POPULATION

2001 Estimates:

Working Population	49,974
At Home Population	10,421
Total	60,395

INCOME

2001 Estimates:

Avg. Household Income	$59,948
Avg. Family Income	$74,968
Per Capita Income	$25,754
Male:	
Avg. Employment Income	$43,380
Avg. Employment Income (Full Time)	$49,699
Female:	
Avg. Employment Income	$27,660
Avg. Employment Income (Full Time)	$36,338

DISPOSABLE & DISCRETIONARY INCOME

2001 Estimates:	Per Hhld.
Disposable Income	$38,270
Discretionary Income 1 (minus Food & Shelter)	$24,036
Discretionary Income 2 (minus Food, Shelter, & Other Expenditures)	$15,375

LIQUID ASSETS

1999 Estimates:	Per Hhld.
Equity Investments	$94,186
Interest Bearing Investments	$75,298
Total Liquid Assets	$169,484

CREDIT DATA

July 2000:

Pool of Credit	$174,056,007
Revolving Credit, No.	43,289
Fixed Loans, No.	9,975
Avg. Credit Limit, per Person	$10,008
Avg. Spent, per Person	$4,058
Satisfactory Ratings, No. per Person	2.96
Avg. No. of Cards, per Person	1.18

LABOUR FORCE

2001 Estimates:

Male:	
In the Labour Force	4,707
Participation Rate	65.8
Employed	4,433
Unemployed	274
Unemployment Rate	5.8
Not in Labour Force	2,442
Female:	
In the Labour Force	3,986
Participation Rate	49.3
Employed	3,815
Unemployed	171
Unemployment Rate	4.3
Not in Labour Force	4,094

OCCUPATIONS BY MAJOR GROUPS

2001 Estimates:	Male	Female
Management	705	398
Business, Finance & Admin.	824	1,524
Natural & Applied Sciences & Related	630	140
Health	100	281
Social Sciences, Gov't Services & Religion	21	87
Education	147	158
Arts, Culture, Recreation & Sport	123	114
Sales & Service	1,064	1,112
Trades, Transport & Equipment Operators & Related	749	26
Primary Industries	20	n.a.
Processing, Mfg. & Utilities	193	58

LEVEL OF SCHOOLING

2001 Estimates:

Population 15 years +	15,229
Less than Grade 9	1,157
Grades 9-13 w/o Certif.	2,064
Grade 9-13 with Certif.	2,715
Trade Certif. /Dip.	397
Non-Univ. w/o Certif./Dip.	1,339
Non-Univ. with Certif./Dip.	2,297
Univ. w/o Degree	2,145
Univ. w/o Degree/Certif.	705
Univ. with Certif.	1,440
Univ. with Degree	3,115

AVERAGE HOUSEHOLD EXPENDITURES

2001 Estimates:

Food	$6,617
Shelter	$10,055
Clothing	$2,289
Transportation	$6,521
Health & Personal Care	$2,106
Recr'n, Read'g & Education	$4,037
Taxes & Securities	$16,667
Other	$8,944
Total Expenditures	$57,236

PRIVATE HOUSEHOLDS

2001 Estimates:

Private Households, Total	7,756
Pop. in Private Households	16,899
Average no. per Household	2.2

FAMILIES

2001 Estimates:

Families in Private Households	5,004
Husband-Wife Families	4,337
Lone-Parent Families	667
Aver. No. Persons per Family	2.7
Aver. No. Sons/Daughters at Home	1.0

HOUSING

2001 Estimates:

Occupied Private Dwellings	7,756
Owned	4,411
Rented	3,345
Single-Detached House	4,242
Semi-Detached House	212
Row Houses	211
Apartment, 5+ Storeys	590
Owned Apartment, 5+ Storeys	20
Apartment, 5 or Fewer Storeys	2,400
Apartment, Detached Duplex	101

VEHICLES

2001 Estimates:

Model Yrs. '81-'96, No.	8,910
% Total	30.74
Model Yrs. '97-'98, No.	9,934
% Total	34.28
'99 Vehicles registered in Model Yr. '99, No.	10,138
% Total	34.98
Total No. '81-'99	28,982

LEGAL MARITAL STATUS

2001 Estimates: (Age 15+)

Single (Never Married)	4,949
Legally Married (Not Separated)	7,259
Legally Married (Separated)	427
Widowed	1,176
Divorced	1,418

PSYTE CATEGORIES

2001 Estimates	No. of House-holds	% of Total Hhds.	Index
Urban Gentry	839	10.82	602
Stable Suburban Families	315	4.06	312
Old Bungalow Burbs	439	5.66	342
Suburban Nesters	418	5.39	336
Aging Erudites	2,713	34.98	2,319
Conservative Homebodies	407	5.25	146
High Rise Sunsets	250	3.22	225
Young Urban Mix	614	7.92	374
Young City Singles	992	12.79	558
Aging Quebec Urbanites	387	4.99	1,729

Québec

FINANCIAL P$YTE

2001 Estimates	No. of House-holds	% of Total Hhds.	Index
Four Star Investors	839	10.82	215
Successful Suburbanites	315	4.06	61
Canadian Comfort	418	5.39	55
Urban Heights	2,713	34.98	813
Miners & Credit-Liners	439	5.66	179
Bills & Wills	1,021	13.16	159
Revolving Renters	250	3.22	70
Loan Parent Stress	387	4.99	86
Towering Debt	992	12.79	164

HOME LANGUAGE

2001 Estimates:		% Total
English	10,544	58.40
French	5,247	29.06
Arabic	114	0.63
Chinese	352	1.95
Croatian	11	0.06
Dutch	12	0.07
German	11	0.06
Greek	21	0.12
Hindi	11	0.06
Hungarian	11	0.06
Inuktitut (Eskimo)	28	0.16
Italian	93	0.52
Khmer (Cambodian)	11	0.06
Korean	104	0.58
Latvian (Lettish)	11	0.06
Persian (Farsi)	58	0.32
Polish	110	0.61
Portuguese	33	0.18
Punjabi	11	0.06
Romanian	110	0.61
Russian	33	0.18
Serbian	22	0.12
Slovak	16	0.09
Spanish	83	0.46
Tagalog (Pilipino)	28	0.16
Tamil	16	0.09
Urdu	50	0.28
Vietnamese	44	0.24
Other Languages	103	0.57
Multiple Responses	756	4.19
Total	18,054	100.00

BUILDING PERMITS

	1999	1998 $000	1997
Value	32,577	36,210	72,060

HOMES BUILT

	1999	1998	1997
No	36	9	22

Québec

Dorval
(Cité)
Montréal CMA
(Cont'd)

TAXATION

Income Class:	1997	% Total
Under $5,000	1,440	10.98
$5,000-$10,000	1,460	11.14
$10,000-$15,000	1,680	12.81
$15,000-$20,000	1,270	9.69
$20,000-$25,000	1,080	8.24
$25,000-$30,000	1,080	8.24
$30,000-$40,000	1,750	13.35
$40,000-$50,000	1,220	9.31
$50,000 +	2,140	16.32
Total Returns, No.	13,110	
Total Income, $000	410,074	
Total Taxable Returns	9,800	
Total Tax, $000	55,919	
Average Income, $	31,279	
Average Tax, $	5,706	

VITAL STATISTICS

	1997	1996	1995	1994
Births	172	181	189	182
Deaths	190	136	173	172
Natural Increase	-18	.45	15	10
Marriages	37	54	42	52

Note: Latest available data.

MEDIA INFO
see Montréal, CMA

Greenfield Park
(Ville)
Montréal CMA

In census division Champlain.

POPULATION

July 1, 2001 Estimate	17,376
% Cdn. Total	0.06
% Change, '96 -'01	-1.40
Avg. Annual Growth Rate, %	-0.28
2003 Projected Population	17,425
2006 Projected Population	17,590
2001 Households Estimate	7,028
2003 Projected Households	7,126
2006 Projected Households	7,283

INCOME

% Above/Below National Average	-4
2001 Total Income Estimate	$351,030,000
% Cdn. Total	0.05
2001 Average Hhld. Income	$49,900
2001 Per Capita	$20,200
2003 Projected Total Income	$373,480,000
2006 Projected Total Income	$411,300,000

RETAIL SALES

% Above/Below National Average	+112
2001 Retail Sales Estimate	$329,080,000
% Cdn. Total	0.12
2001 per Household	$46,800
2001 per Capita	$18,900
2001 No. of Establishments	145
2003 Projected Retail Sales	$359,270,000
2006 Projected Retail Sales	$404,620,000

POPULATION

2001 Estimates:

Total		17,376
Male		8,360
Female		9,016

Age Groups	Male	Female
0-4	493	478
5-9	543	508
10-14	561	532
15-19	589	552
20-24	591	547
25-29	541	529
30-34	560	583
35-39	628	671
40-44	659	728
45-49	643	735
50-54	605	691
55-59	521	574
60-64	437	480
65-69	357	422
70+	632	986

DAYTIME POPULATION

2001 Estimates:

Working Population	8,427
At Home Population	9,022
Total	17,449

INCOME

2001 Estimates:

Avg. Household Income	$49,947
Avg. Family Income	$56,889
Per Capita Income	$20,202
Male:	
Avg. Employment Income	$32,839
Avg. Employment Income (Full Time)	$43,214
Female:	
Avg. Employment Income	$23,275
Avg. Employment Income (Full Time)	$33,630

DISPOSABLE & DISCRETIONARY INCOME

2001 Estimates:	Per Hhld.
Disposable Income	$34,237
Discretionary Income 1 (minus Food & Shelter)	$21,720
Discretionary Income 2 (minus Food, Shelter, & Other Expenditures)	$14,227

LIQUID ASSETS

1999 Estimates:	Per Hhld.
Equity Investments	$51,371
Interest Bearing Investments	$56,400
Total Liquid Assets	$107,771

CREDIT DATA

July 2000:

Pool of Credit	$131,356,433
Revolving Credit, No.	36,196
Fixed Loans, No.	10,077
Avg. Credit Limit, per Person	$8,844
Avg. Spent, per Person	$3,824
Satisfactory Ratings, No. per Person	2.95
Avg. No. of Cards, per Person	1.12

LABOUR FORCE

2001 Estimates:

Male:	
In the Labour Force	4,875
Participation Rate	72.1
Employed	4,540
Unemployed	335
Unemployment Rate	6.9
Not in Labour Force	1,888
Female:	
In the Labour Force	4,156
Participation Rate	55.4
Employed	3,868
Unemployed	288
Unemployment Rate	6.9
Not in Labour Force	3,342

OCCUPATIONS BY MAJOR GROUPS

2001 Estimates:	Male	Female
Management	635	248
Business, Finance & Admin.	683	1,548
Natural & Applied Sciences & Related	507	76
Health	91	353
Social Sciences, Gov't Services & Religion	59	154
Education	107	150
Arts, Culture, Recreation & Sport	145	89
Sales & Service	1,034	1,146
Trades, Transport & Equipment Operators & Related	1,034	47
Primary Industries	32	n.a.
Processing, Mfg. & Utilities	325	116

LEVEL OF SCHOOLING

2001 Estimates:

Population 15 years +	14,261
Less than Grade 9	1,698
Grades 9-13 w/o Certif.	2,351
Grade 9-13 with Certif.	2,723
Trade Certif./Dip.	578
Non-Univ. w/o Certif./Dip.	1,273
Non-Univ. with Certif./Dip.	2,184
Univ. w/o Degree	1,632
Univ. w/o Degree/Certif.	390
Univ. with Certif.	1,242
Univ. with Degree	1,822

AVERAGE HOUSEHOLD EXPENDITURES

2001 Estimates:

Food	$6,278
Shelter	$8,207
Clothing	$2,130
Transportation	$5,630
Health & Personal Care	$1,906
Recr'n, Read'g & Education	$3,207
Taxes & Securities	$14,243
Other	$7,334
Total Expenditures	$48,935

PRIVATE HOUSEHOLDS

2001 Estimates:

Private Households, Total	7,028
Pop. in Private Households	17,183
Average no. per Household	2.4

FAMILIES

2001 Estimates:

Families in Private Households	5,078
Husband-Wife Families	4,180
Lone-Parent Families	898
Aver. No. Persons per Family	3.0
Aver. No. Sons/Daughters at Home	1.2

HOUSING

2001 Estimates:

Occupied Private Dwellings	7,028
Owned	4,208
Rented	2,820
Single-Detached House	3,013
Semi-Detached House	499
Row Houses	946
Apartment, 5+ Storeys	135
Apartment, 5 or Fewer Storeys	2,241
Apartment, Detached Duplex	167
Other Single-Attached	27

VEHICLES

2001 Estimates:

Model Yrs. '81-'96, No.	7,019
% Total	78.87
Model Yrs. '97-'98, No.	1,160
% Total	13.04
'99 Vehicles registered in Model Yr. '99, No.	720
% Total	8.09
Total No. '81-'99	8,899

LEGAL MARITAL STATUS

2001 Estimates: (Age 15+)

Single (Never Married)	4,950
Legally Married (Not Separated)	6,676
Legally Married (Separated)	373
Widowed	943
Divorced	1,319

PSYTE CATEGORIES

2001 Estimates	No. of House -holds	% of Total Hhds.	Index
Old Bungalow Burbs	868	12.35	745
Participation Quebec	1,475	20.99	728
New Quebec Rows	400	5.69	519
Quebec Melange	1,216	17.30	653
Conservative Homebodies	416	5.92	164
University Enclaves	311	4.43	217
Old Quebec Walkups	801	11.40	622
Quebec Town Elders	384	5.46	193
Aging Quebec Urbanites	379	5.39	1,869
Quebec's New Urban Mosaic	774	11.01	457

Greenfield Park
(Ville)
Montréal CMA
(Cont'd)

FINANCIAL P$YTE

2001 Estimates	No. of House-holds	% of Total Hhds.	Index
Miners & Credit-Liners	868	12.35	390
Mortgages & Minivans	1,875	26.68	404
Bills & Wills	416	5.92	71
Country Credit	1,216	17.30	256
Young Urban Struggle	311	4.43	93
Loan Parent Stress	1,564	22.25	382
NSF	774	11.01	311

HOME LANGUAGE

2001 Estimates:		% Total
English	7,406	42.62
French	8,301	47.77
Arabic	174	1.00
Chinese	85	0.49
Creoles	15	0.09
Croatian	10	0.06
German	20	0.12
Greek	96	0.55
Gujarati	20	0.12
Hindi	10	0.06
Hungarian	11	0.06
Italian	70	0.40
Japanese	20	0.12
Khmer (Cambodian)	10	0.06
Latvian (Lettish)	10	0.06
Polish	56	0.32
Portuguese	30	0.17
Romanian	25	0.14
Serbian	25	0.14
Slovenian	42	0.24
Spanish	207	1.19
Tagalog (Pilipino)	15	0.09
Tamil	10	0.06
Turkish	11	0.06
Vietnamese	35	0.20
Other Languages	20	0.12
Multiple Responses	642	3.69
Total	17,376	100.00

BUILDING PERMITS

	1999	1998 $000	1997
Value	3,042	21,901	10,705

HOMES BUILT

	1999	1998	1997
No.	44	72	73

TAXATION

Income Class:	1997	% Total
Under $5,000	1,640	13.27
$5,000-$10,000	1,750	14.16
$10,000-$15,000	1,750	14.16
$15,000-$20,000	1,210	9.79
$20,000-$25,000	1,010	8.17
$25,000-$30,000	1,050	8.50
$30,000-$40,000	1,510	12.22
$40,000-$50,000	1,040	8.41
$50,000 +	1,400	11.33
Total Returns, No.	12,360	
Total Income, $000	309,619	
Total Taxable Returns	8,610	
Total Tax, $000	36,261	
Average Income, $	25,050	
Average Tax, $	4,211	

VITAL STATISTICS

	1997	1996	1995	1994
Births	164	197	212	196
Deaths	132	113	120	120
Natural Increase	32	84	92	76
Marriages	71	82	61	85

Note: Latest available data.

MEDIA INFO
see Montréal, CMA

Kirkland
(Ville)
Montréal CMA

In census division Communauté urbaine de Montréal.

POPULATION

July 1, 2001 Estimate	19,950
% Cdn. Total	0.06
% Change, '96 -'01	4.90
Avg. Annual Growth Rate, %	0.96
2003 Projected Population	20,718
2006 Projected Population	21,967
2001 Households Estimate	6,166
2003 Projected Households	6,373
2006 Projected Households	6,694

INCOME

% Above/Below National Average	+37
2001 Total Income Estimate	$578,070,000
% Cdn. Total	0.09
2001 Average Hhld. Income	$93,800
2001 Per Capita	$29,000
2003 Projected Total Income	$637,930,000
2006 Projected Total Income	$741,660,000

RETAIL SALES

% Above/Below National Average	-54
2001 Retail Sales Estimate	$82,340,000
% Cdn. Total	0.03
2001 per Household	$13,400
2001 per Capita	$4,100
2001 No. of Establishments	127
2003 Projected Retail Sales	$91,040,000
2006 Projected Retail Sales	$106,550,000

POPULATION

2001 Estimates:		
Total		19,950
Male		9,769
Female		10,181

Age Groups	Male	Female
0-4	565	508
5-9	720	677
10-14	856	824
15-19	904	862
20-24	769	730
25-29	532	528
30-34	439	528
35-39	608	773
40-44	804	985
45-49	950	1,040
50-54	888	859
55-59	660	593
60-64	437	386
65-69	265	268
70+	372	620

DAYTIME POPULATION

2001 Estimates:	
Working Population	5,475
At Home Population	8,981
Total	14,456

INCOME

2001 Estimates:	
Avg. Household Income	$93,752
Avg. Family Income	$97,452
Per Capita Income	$28,976
Male:	
Avg. Employment Income	$58,078
Avg. Employment Income (Full Time)	$72,913
Female:	
Avg. Employment Income	$29,662
Avg. Employment Income (Full Time)	$44,136

DISPOSABLE & DISCRETIONARY INCOME

2001 Estimates:	Per Hhld.
Disposable Income	$61,304
Discretionary Income 1 (minus Food & Shelter)	$42,803
Discretionary Income 2 (minus Food, Shelter, & Other Expenditures)	$30,462

LIQUID ASSETS

1999 Estimates:	Per Hhld.
Equity Investments	$160,884
Interest Bearing Investments	$118,529
Total Liquid Assets	$279,413

CREDIT DATA

July 2000:	
Pool of Credit	$254,355,317
Revolving Credit, No.	50,016
Fixed Loans, No.	12,667
Avg. Credit Limit, per Person	$14,863
Avg. Spent, per Person	$6,123
Satisfactory Ratings, No. per Person	3.51
Avg. No. of Cards, per Person	1.43

LABOUR FORCE

2001 Estimates:	
Male:	
In the Labour Force	6,200
Participation Rate	81.3
Employed	6,031
Unemployed	169
Unemployment Rate	2.7
Not in Labour Force	1,428
Female:	
In the Labour Force	5,063
Participation Rate	62.0
Employed	4,871
Unemployed	192
Unemployment Rate	3.8
Not in Labour Force	3,109

OCCUPATIONS BY MAJOR GROUPS

2001 Estimates:	Male	Female
Management	1,885	549
Business, Finance & Admin.	900	1,899
Natural & Applied Sciences & Related	828	190
Health	150	455
Social Sciences, Gov't Services & Religion	97	132
Education	194	314
Arts, Culture, Recreation & Sport	116	162
Sales & Service	1,253	1,119
Trades, Transport & Equipment Operators & Related	369	12
Primary Industries	35	12
Processing, Mfg. & Utilities	189	110

LEVEL OF SCHOOLING

2001 Estimates:	
Population 15 years +	15,800
Less than Grade 9	706
Grades 9-13 w/o Certif.	1,721
Grade 9-13 with Certif.	2,166
Trade Certif. /Dip.	417
Non-Univ. w/o Certif./Dip.	1,271
Non-Univ. with Certif./Dip.	2,357
Univ. w/o Degree	2,460
Univ. w/o Degree/Certif.	711
Univ. with Certif.	1,749
Univ. with Degree	4,702

Québec

AVERAGE HOUSEHOLD EXPENDITURES

2001 Estimates:	
Food	$8,673
Shelter	$13,449
Clothing	$3,676
Transportation	$9,737
Health & Personal Care	$2,773
Recr'n, Read'g & Education	$5,992
Taxes & Securities	$28,094
Other	$11,356
Total Expenditures	$83,750

PRIVATE HOUSEHOLDS

2001 Estimates:	
Private Households, Total	6,166
Pop. in Private Households	19,853
Average no. per Household	3.2

FAMILIES

2001 Estimates:	
Families in Private Households	5,561
Husband-Wife Families	5,105
Lone-Parent Families	456
Aver. No. Persons per Family	3.4
Aver. No. Sons/Daughters at Home	1.5

HOUSING

2001 Estimates:	
Occupied Private Dwellings	6,166
Owned	5,654
Rented	512
Single-Detached House	5,331
Semi-Detached House	61
Row Houses	404
Apartment, 5+ Storeys	337
Apartment, 5 or Fewer Storeys	22
Apartment, Detached Duplex	11

VEHICLES

2001 Estimates:	
Model Yrs. '81-'96, No.	8,029
% Total	64.32
Model Yrs. '97-'98, No.	2,743
% Total	21.98
'99 Vehicles registered in Model Yr. '99, No.	1,710
% Total	13.70
Total No. '81-'99	12,482

LEGAL MARITAL STATUS

2001 Estimates: (Age 15+)	
Single (Never Married)	4,146
Legally Married (Not Separated)	10,012
Legally Married (Separated)	209
Widowed	627
Divorced	806

Québec

Kirkland
(Ville)
Montréal CMA
(Cont'd)

PSYTE CATEGORIES

2001 Estimates	No. of House -holds	% of Total Hhds.	Index
Suburban Executives	3,046	49.40	3,447
Technocrafts & Bureaucrats	1,909	30.96	1,100
Stable Suburban Families	423	6.86	526
Aging Erudites	391	6.34	420
High Rise Sunsets	397	6.44	450

FINAN¢IAL P$YTE

2001 Estimates	No. of House -holds	% of Total Hhds.	Index
Four Star Investors	3,046	49.40	983
Successful Suburbanites	2,332	37.82	570
Urban Heights	391	6.34	147
Revolving Renters	397	6.44	140

HOME LANGUAGE

2001 Estimates:		% Total
English	13,099	65.66
French	4,476	22.44
Arabic	124	0.62
Armenian	10	0.05
Chinese	298	1.49
Creoles	10	0.05
Croatian	11	0.06
Finnish	11	0.06
German	48	0.24
Greek	165	0.83
Gujarati	10	0.05
Hindi	31	0.16
Italian	299	1.50
Korean	32	0.16
Lao	23	0.12
Persian (Farsi)	90	0.45
Polish	16	0.08
Punjabi	59	0.30
Romanian	11	0.06
Russian	11	0.06
Spanish	88	0.44
Thai	11	0.06
Ukrainian	37	0.19
Urdu	83	0.42
Other Languages	33	0.17
Multiple Responses	864	4.33
Total	19,950	100.00

BUILDING PERMITS

	1999	1998 $000	1997
Value	66,415	38,806	40,776

HOMES BUILT

	1999	1998	1997
No	203	106	47

TAXATION

Income Class:	1997	% Total
Under $5,000	1,760	13.71
$5,000-$10,000	1,300	10.12
$10,000-$15,000	1,130	8.80
$15,000-$20,000	880	6.85
$20,000-$25,000	760	5.92
$25,000-$30,000	790	6.15
$30,000-$40,000	1,350	10.51
$40,000-$50,000	1,180	9.19
$50,000 +	3,690	28.74
Total Returns, No.	12,840	
Total Income, $000	538,838	
Total Taxable Returns	9,700	
Total Tax, $000	88,622	
Average Income, $	41,966	
Average Tax, $	9,136	

VITAL STATISTICS

	1997	1996	1995	1994
Births	207	205	195	198
Deaths	48	48	60	57
Natural Increase	159	157	135	141
Marriages	6	5	6	12

Note: Latest available data.

MEDIA INFO
see Montréal, CMA

L'Assomption
(Ville)
Montréal CMA

In census division L'Assomption.

POPULATION

July 1, 2001 Estimate	11,767
% Cdn. Total	0.04
% Change, '96 -'01	1.76
Avg. Annual Growth Rate, %	0.35
2003 Projected Population	12,098
2006 Projected Population	12,747
2001 Households Estimate	4,413
2003 Projected Households	4,578
2006 Projected Households	4,887

INCOME

% Above/Below National Average	-13
2001 Total Income Estimate	$215,090,000
% Cdn. Total	0.03
2001 Average Hhld. Income	$48,700
2001 Per Capita	$18,300
2003 Projected Total Income	$235,380,000
2006 Projected Total Income	$273,840,000

RETAIL SALES

% Above/Below National Average	-2
2001 Retail Sales Estimate	$103,220,000
% Cdn. Total	0.04
2001 per Household	$23,400
2001 per Capita	$8,800
2001 No. of Establishments	132
2003 Projected Retail Sales	$112,350,000
2006 Projected Retail Sales	$128,230,000

POPULATION

2001 Estimates:		
Total		11,767
Male		5,930
Female		5,837
Age Groups	Male	Female
0-4	360	340
5-9	419	385
10-14	436	398
15-19	442	376
20-24	393	328
25-29	335	323
30-34	403	406
35-39	508	513
40-44	527	537
45-49	497	481
50-54	426	395
55-59	333	300
60-64	255	249
65-69	206	216
70+	390	590

DAYTIME POPULATION

2001 Estimates:	
Working Population	3,883
At Home Population	6,077
Total	9,960

INCOME

2001 Estimates:	
Avg. Household Income	$48,740
Avg. Family Income	$54,455
Per Capita Income	$18,279
Male:	
Avg. Employment Income	$31,953
Avg. Employment Income (Full Time)	$39,722
Female:	
Avg. Employment Income	$21,554
Avg. Employment Income (Full Time)	$31,456

DISPOSABLE & DISCRETIONARY INCOME

2001 Estimates:	Per Hhld.
Disposable Income	$34,313
Discretionary Income 1 (minus Food & Shelter)	$22,200
Discretionary Income 2 (minus Food, Shelter, & Other Expenditures)	$14,653

LIQUID ASSETS

1999 Estimates:	Per Hhld.
Equity Investments	$51,577
Interest Bearing Investments	$56,289
Total Liquid Assets	$107,866

CREDIT DATA

July 2000:	
Pool of Credit	$65,610,687
Revolving Credit, No.	16,400
Fixed Loans, No.	6,324
Avg. Credit Limit, per Person	$8,935
Avg. Spent, per Person	$4,242
Satisfactory Ratings, No. per Person	2.90
Avg. No. of Cards, per Person	1.14

LABOUR FORCE

2001 Estimates:	
Male:	
In the Labour Force	3,542
Participation Rate	75.1
Employed	3,342
Unemployed	200
Unemployment Rate	5.6
Not in Labour Force	1,173
Female:	
In the Labour Force	2,489
Participation Rate	52.8
Employed	2,343
Unemployed	146
Unemployment Rate	5.9
Not in Labour Force	2,225

OCCUPATIONS BY MAJOR GROUPS

2001 Estimates:	Male	Female
Management	285	101
Business, Finance & Admin.	222	744
Natural & Applied Sciences & Related	225	21
Health	91	298
Social Sciences, Gov't Services & Religion	55	110
Education	102	138
Arts, Culture, Recreation & Sport	54	27
Sales & Service	582	711
Trades, Transport & Equipment Operators & Related	1,178	43
Primary Industries	131	34
Processing, Mfg. & Utilities	538	191

LEVEL OF SCHOOLING

2001 Estimates:	
Population 15 years +	9,429
Less than Grade 9	1,852
Grades 9-13 w/o Certif.	2,017
Grade 9-13 with Certif.	1,748
Trade Certif. /Dip.	572
Non-Univ. w/o Certif./Dip.	647
Non-Univ. with Certif./Dip.	1,430
Univ. w/o Degree	515
Univ. w/o Degree/Certif.	62
Univ. with Certif.	453
Univ. with Degree	648

L'Assomption
(Ville)
Montréal CMA
(Cont'd)

AVERAGE HOUSEHOLD EXPENDITURES

2001 Estimates:
Food	$6,422
Shelter	$7,412
Clothing	$2,122
Transportation	$5,749
Health & Personal Care	$1,915
Recr'n, Read'g & Education	$3,168
Taxes & Securities	$14,049
Other	$7,078
Total Expenditures	$47,915

PRIVATE HOUSEHOLDS

2001 Estimates:
Private Households, Total	4,413
Pop. in Private Households	11,379
Average no. per Household	2.6

FAMILIES

2001 Estimates:
Families in Private Households	3,455
Husband-Wife Families	2,994
Lone-Parent Families	461
Aver. No. Persons per Family	3.0
Aver. No. Sons/Daughters at Home	1.2

HOUSING

2001 Estimates:
Occupied Private Dwellings	4,413
Owned	2,872
Rented	1,541
Single-Detached House	2,641
Semi-Detached House	210
Row Houses	43
Apartment, 5+ Storeys	10
Apartment, 5 or Fewer Storeys	1,070
Apartment, Detached Duplex	298
Other Single-Attached	10
Movable Dwellings	131

VEHICLES

2001 Estimates:
Model Yrs. '81-'96, No.	5,677
% Total	79.81
Model Yrs. '97-'98, No.	870
% Total	12.23
'99 Vehicles registered in Model Yr. '99, No.	566
% Total	7.96
Total No. '81-'99	7,113

LEGAL MARITAL STATUS

2001 Estimates: (Age 15+)
Single (Never Married)	3,391
Legally Married (Not Separated)	4,420
Legally Married (Separated)	232
Widowed	576
Divorced	810

PSYTE CATEGORIES

2001 Estimates	No. of House -holds	% of Total Hhds.	Index
Participation Quebec	1,209	27.40	951
Quebec Melange	775	17.56	663
Traditional French Cdn. Families	1,019	23.09	860
Quebec's Heartland	195	4.42	450
Quebec Town Elders	1,172	26.56	940

FINANCIAL P$YTE

2001 Estimates	No. of House -holds	% of Total Hhds.	Index
Mortgages & Minivans	1,209	27.40	415
Country Credit	1,794	40.65	601
Rural Family Blues	195	4.42	55
Loan Parent Stress	1,172	26.56	456

HOME LANGUAGE

2001 Estimates:		% Total
English	26	0.22
French	11,662	99.11
Greek	11	0.09
Italian	10	0.08
Multiple Responses	58	0.49
Total	11,767	100.00

BUILDING PERMITS

	1999	1998	1997
		$000	
Value	10,310	14,717	3,850

HOMES BUILT

	1999	1998	1997
No	19	14	n.a.

TAXATION

Income Class:	1997	% Total
Under $5,000	1,070	13.38
$5,000-$10,000	1,030	12.88
$10,000-$15,000	1,140	14.25
$15,000-$20,000	810	10.13
$20,000-$25,000	680	8.50
$25,000-$30,000	720	9.00
$30,000-$40,000	1,090	13.63
$40,000-$50,000	670	8.38
$50,000 +	800	10.00
Total Returns, No.	8,000	
Total Income, $000	198,112	
Total Taxable Returns	5,630	
Total Tax, $000	23,120	
Average Income, $	24,764	
Average Tax, $	4,107	

VITAL STATISTICS

	1997	1996	1995	1994
Births	127	145	144	155
Deaths	94	84	86	82
Natural Increase	33	61	58	73
Marriages	23	22	18	18

Note: Latest available data.

MEDIA INFO
see Montréal, CMA

L'Île-Bizard
(Ville)
Montréal CMA

In census division Communauté urbaine de Montréal.

POPULATION

July 1, 2001 Estimate	14,836
% Cdn. Total	0.05
% Change, '96-'01	11.77
Avg. Annual Growth Rate, %	2.25
2003 Projected Population	15,941
2006 Projected Population	17,677
2001 Households Estimate	5,051
2003 Projected Households	5,411
2006 Projected Households	5,955

INCOME

% Above/Below National Average	+33
2001 Total Income Estimate	$416,560,000
% Cdn. Total	0.06
2001 Average Hhld. Income	$82,500
2001 Per Capita	$28,100
2003 Projected Total Income	$476,180,000
2006 Projected Total Income	$579,220,000

RETAIL SALES

% Above/Below National Average	-80
2001 Retail Sales Estimate	$26,340,000
% Cdn. Total	0.01
2001 per Household	$5,200
2001 per Capita	$1,800
2001 No. of Establishments	96
2003 Projected Retail Sales	$29,740,000
2006 Projected Retail Sales	$35,940,000

POPULATION

2001 Estimates:
Total	14,836
Male	7,314
Female	7,522

Age Groups	Male	Female
0-4	470	459
5-9	590	564
10-14	631	599
15-19	589	552
20-24	472	438
25-29	398	397
30-34	451	493
35-39	612	689
40-44	710	787
45-49	690	725
50-54	567	543
55-59	398	362
60-64	261	247
65-69	180	180
70+	295	487

DAYTIME POPULATION

2001 Estimates:
Working Population	1,049
At Home Population	6,475
Total	7,524

INCOME

2001 Estimates:
Avg. Household Income	$82,471
Avg. Family Income	$86,804
Per Capita Income	$28,078
Male:	
Avg. Employment Income	$55,370
Avg. Employment Income (Full Time)	$62,267
Female:	
Avg. Employment Income	$28,806
Avg. Employment Income (Full Time)	$40,455

Québec

DISPOSABLE & DISCRETIONARY INCOME

2001 Estimates:	Per Hhld.
Disposable Income	$56,983
Discretionary Income 1 (minus Food & Shelter)	$39,579
Discretionary Income 2 (minus Food, Shelter, & Other Expenditures)	$27,897

LIQUID ASSETS

1999 Estimates:	Per Hhld.
Equity Investments	$142,688
Interest Bearing Investments	$102,421
Total Liquid Assets	$245,109

CREDIT DATA

July 2000:	
Pool of Credit	$142,635,028
Revolving Credit, No.	29,809
Fixed Loans, No.	9,646
Avg. Credit Limit, per Person	$13,306
Avg. Spent, per Person	$5,825
Satisfactory Ratings, No. per Person	3.50
Avg. No. of Cards, per Person	1.43

LABOUR FORCE

2001 Estimates:
Male:	
In the Labour Force	4,643
Participation Rate	82.6
Employed	4,556
Unemployed	87
Unemployment Rate	1.9
Not in Labour Force	980
Female:	
In the Labour Force	3,840
Participation Rate	65.1
Employed	3,729
Unemployed	111
Unemployment Rate	2.9
Not in Labour Force	2,060

OCCUPATIONS BY MAJOR GROUPS

2001 Estimates:	Male	Female
Management	1,146	389
Business, Finance & Admin.	564	1,412
Natural & Applied Sciences & Related	585	58
Health	73	268
Social Sciences, Gov't Services & Religion	74	111
Education	149	303
Arts, Culture, Recreation & Sport	87	110
Sales & Service	966	856
Trades, Transport & Equipment Operators & Related	695	82
Primary Industries	61	13
Processing, Mfg. & Utilities	168	110

Québec

L'Île-Bizard
(Ville)
Montréal CMA
(Cont'd)

LEVEL OF SCHOOLING

2001 Estimates:
Population 15 years + ...11,523
Less than Grade 9 1,101
Grades 9-13 w/o Certif. 1,465
Grade 9-13 with Certif. 1,939
Trade Certif. /Dip. 374
Non-Univ. w/o Certif./Dip. 919
Non-Univ. with Certif./Dip. 2,030
Univ. w/o Degree 1,479
 Univ. w/o Degree/Certif. 302
 Univ. with Certif. 1,177
Univ. with Degree 2,216

AVERAGE HOUSEHOLD EXPENDITURES

2001 Estimates:
Food $8,986
Shelter $11,286
Clothing $3,480
Transportation $9,121
Health & Personal Care $2,811
Recr'n, Read'g & Education $5,166
Taxes & Securities $24,119
Other $10,147
Total Expenditures $75,116

PRIVATE HOUSEHOLDS

2001 Estimates:
Private Households, Total 5,051
Pop. in Private Households 14,554
Average no. per Household 2.9

FAMILIES

2001 Estimates:
Families in Private Households 4,286
Husband-Wife Families 3,865
Lone-Parent Families 421
Aver. No. Persons per Family 3.2
Aver. No. Sons/Daughters
 at Home 1.3

HOUSING

2001 Estimates:
Occupied Private Dwellings 5,051
 Owned 4,242
 Rented 809
Single-Detached House 3,903
Semi-Detached House 151
Row Houses 182
Apartment, 5 or Fewer Storeys 542
Apartment, Detached Duplex 161
Movable Dwellings 112

VEHICLES

2001 Estimates:
Model Yrs. '81-'96, No. 5,840
 % Total 69.88
Model Yrs. '97-'98, No. 1,620
 % Total 19.38
'99 Vehicles registered in
 Model Yr. '99, No. 897
 % Total 10.73
Total No. '81-'99 8,357

LEGAL MARITAL STATUS

2001 Estimates: (Age 15+)
Single (Never Married) 3,366
Legally Married
 (Not Separated) 6,455
Legally Married (Separated) 238
Widowed 536
Divorced 928

PSYTE CATEGORIES

2001 Estimates	No. of House -holds	% of Total Hhds.	Index
Technocrafts & Bureaucrats	1,381	27.34	972
Participation Quebec	3,138	62.13	2,156
New Quebec Rows	485	9.60	876

FINANCIAL P$YTE

2001 Estimates	No. of House -holds	% of Total Hhds.	Index
Successful Suburbanites	1,381	27.34	412
Mortgages & Minivans	3,623	71.73	1,087

HOME LANGUAGE

2001 Estimates:		% Total
English	3,654	24.63
French	10,309	69.49
Arabic	34	0.23
Chinese	76	0.51
Creoles	23	0.16
German	33	0.22
Greek	58	0.39
Gujarati	12	0.08
Hungarian	17	0.11
Italian	41	0.28
Portuguese	45	0.30
Romanian	50	0.34
Other Languages	12	0.08
Multiple Responses	472	3.18
Total	14,836	100.00

BUILDING PERMITS

	1999	1998 $000	1997
Value	15,407	11,203	11,026

HOMES BUILT

	1999	1998	1997
No.	66	50	n.a.

TAXATION

Income Class:	1997	% Total
Under $5,000	1,020	11.27
$5,000-$10,000	870	9.61
$10,000-$15,000	900	9.94
$15,000-$20,000	750	8.29
$20,000-$25,000	680	7.51
$25,000-$30,000	620	6.85
$30,000-$40,000	1,190	13.15
$40,000-$50,000	900	9.94
$50,000 +	2,120	23.43
Total Returns, No.	9,050	
Total Income, $000	331,000	
Total Taxable Returns	7,120	
Total Tax, $000	49,518	
Average Income, $	36,575	
Average Tax, $	6,955	

VITAL STATISTICS

	1997	1996	1995	1994
Births	174	159	179	192
Deaths	75	73	67	72
Natural Increase	99	86	112	120
Marriages	32	24	25	19

Note: Latest available data.

MEDIA INFO
 see Montréal, CMA

La Plaine
(Ville)
Montréal CMA

In census division Les Moulins.

POPULATION

July 1, 2001 Estimate 19,478
% Cdn. Total 0.06
% Change, '96 -'01 . . . . .32.58
Avg. Annual Growth Rate, % 5.80
2003 Projected Population 22,889
2006 Projected Population 28,412
2001 Households Estimate 6,438
2003 Projected Households 7,653
2006 Projected Households 9,666

INCOME

% Above/Below National Average . . . .-22
2001 Total Income Estimate $318,620,000
% Cdn. Total 0.05
2001 Average Hhld. Income $49,500
2001 Per Capita $16,400
2003 Projected Total Income . . $404,570,000
2006 Projected Total Income . . . $566,620,000

RETAIL SALES

% Above/Below National Average . . . .-64
2001 Retail Sales Estimate $62,420,000
% Cdn. Total 0.02
2001 per Household $9,700
2001 per Capita $3,200
2001 No. of Establishments 106
2003 Projected Retail Sales $77,400,000
2006 Projected Retail Sales . . . $103,670,000

POPULATION

2001 Estimates:

Total		19,478
Male		9,870
Female		9,608

Age Groups	Male	Female
0-4	794	769
5-9	954	931
10-14	918	869
15-19	759	721
20-24	592	575
25-29	619	669
30-34	865	930
35-39	1,020	1,021
40-44	936	897
45-49	740	685
50-54	552	478
55-59	386	330
60-64	263	249
65-69	203	199
70+	269	285

DAYTIME POPULATION

2001 Estimates:
Working Population 861
At Home Population 10,162
Total 11,023

INCOME

2001 Estimates:
Avg. Household Income $49,490
Avg. Family Income $49,982
Per Capita Income $16,358
Male:
Avg. Employment Income $32,322
Avg. Employment Income
 (Full Time) $38,453
Female:
Avg. Employment Income $17,742
Avg. Employment Income
 (Full Time) $26,745

DISPOSABLE & DISCRETIONARY INCOME

2001 Estimates:	Per Hhld.
Disposable Income	$36,030
Discretionary Income 1 (minus Food & Shelter)	$23,999
Discretionary Income 2 (minus Food, Shelter, & Other Expenditures)	$15,890

LIQUID ASSETS

1999 Estimates:	Per Hhld.
Equity Investments	$48,187
Interest Bearing Investments	$54,005
Total Liquid Assets	$102,192

CREDIT DATA

July 2000:
Pool of Credit $95,568,381
Revolving Credit, No. 22,821
Fixed Loans, No. 12,088
Avg. Credit Limit, per Person $10,000
Avg. Spent, per Person $5,571
Satisfactory Ratings,
 No. per Person 3.37
Avg. No. of Cards, per Person 1.18

LABOUR FORCE

2001 Estimates:
Male:
In the Labour Force 5,884
Participation Rate 81.7
Employed 5,457
Unemployed 427
Unemployment Rate 7.3
Not in Labour Force 1,320
Female:
In the Labour Force 4,049
Participation Rate 57.5
Employed 3,752
Unemployed 297
Unemployment Rate 7.3
Not in Labour Force 2,990

OCCUPATIONS BY MAJOR GROUPS

2001 Estimates:	Male	Female
Management	429	185
Business, Finance & Admin.	493	1,229
Natural & Applied Sciences & Related	350	46
Health	58	274
Social Sciences, Gov't Services & Religion	55	81
Education	56	65
Arts, Culture, Recreation & Sport	52	85
Sales & Service	915	1,210
Trades, Transport & Equipment Operators & Related	2,375	281
Primary Industries	97	23
Processing, Mfg. & Utilities	812	374

LEVEL OF SCHOOLING

2001 Estimates:
Population 15 years + ...14,243
Less than Grade 9 2,249
Grades 9-13 w/o Certif. 3,799
Grade 9-13 with Certif. 3,436
Trade Certif. /Dip. 761
Non-Univ. w/o Certif./Dip. 995
Non-Univ. with Certif./Dip. 2,188
Univ. w/o Degree 505
 Univ. w/o Degree/Certif. 104
 Univ. with Certif. 401
Univ. with Degree 310

La Plaine
(Ville)
Montréal CMA
(Cont'd)

AVERAGE HOUSEHOLD EXPENDITURES

2001 Estimates:

Food	$6,570
Shelter	$7,210
Clothing	$2,262
Transportation	$6,538
Health & Personal Care	$1,850
Recr'n, Read'g & Education	$3,268
Taxes & Securities	$13,825
Other	$7,096
Total Expenditures	$48,619

PRIVATE HOUSEHOLDS

2001 Estimates:

Private Households, Total	6,438
Pop. in Private Households	19,384
Average no. per Household	3.0

FAMILIES

2001 Estimates:

Families in Private Households	5,731
Husband-Wife Families	5,088
Lone-Parent Families	643
Aver. No. Persons per Family	3.3
Aver. No. Sons/Daughters at Home	1.4

HOUSING

2001 Estimates:

Occupied Private Dwellings	6,438
Owned	5,577
Rented	861
Single-Detached House	4,876
Semi-Detached House	442
Row Houses	96
Apartment, 5 or Fewer Storeys	329
Apartment, Detached Duplex	137
Movable Dwellings	558

VEHICLES

2001 Estimates:

Model Yrs. '81-'96, No.	7,249
% Total	80.75
Model Yrs. '97-'98, No.	1,092
% Total	12.16
'99 Vehicles registered in Model Yr. '99, No.	636
% Total	7.08
Total No. '81-'99	8,977

LEGAL MARITAL STATUS

2001 Estimates: (Age 15+)

Single (Never Married)	5,542
Legally Married (Not Separated)	6,602
Legally Married (Separated)	332
Widowed	407
Divorced	1,360

PSYTE CATEGORIES

2001 Estimates	No. of House-holds	% of Total Hhds.	Index
Participation Quebec	1,501	23.31	809
New Quebec Rows	527	8.19	747
Traditional French Cdn. Families	4,171	64.79	2,413
Quebec Rural Blues	239	3.71	152

FINAN¢IAL P$YTE

2001 Estimates	No. of House-holds	% of Total Hhds.	Index
Mortgages & Minivans	2,028	31.50	477
Country Credit	4,171	64.79	958
Rural Family Blues	239	3.71	46

HOME LANGUAGE

2001 Estimates:

		% Total
English	419	2.15
French	18,838	96.71
Greek	16	0.08
Italian	20	0.10
Portuguese	38	0.20
Multiple Responses	147	0.75
Total	19,478	100.00

BUILDING PERMITS

	1999	1998 $000	1997
Value	8,249	11,664	14,901

HOMES BUILT

	1999	1998	1997
No.	50	56	86

TAXATION

Income Class:	1997	% Total
Under $5,000	1,650	16.80
$5,000-$10,000	1,350	13.75
$10,000-$15,000	1,310	13.34
$15,000-$20,000	930	9.47
$20,000-$25,000	900	9.16
$25,000-$30,000	870	8.86
$30,000-$40,000	1,370	13.95
$40,000-$50,000	780	7.94
$50,000 +	660	6.72
Total Returns, No.	9,820	
Total Income, $000	211,694	
Total Taxable Returns	6,710	
Total Tax, $000	22,934	
Average Income, $	21,557	
Average Tax, $	3,418	

VITAL STATISTICS

	1997	1996	1995	1994
Births	235	258	275	261
Deaths	48	51	31	36
Natural Increase	187	207	244	225
Marriages	14	22	24	9

Note: Latest available data.

MEDIA INFO
see Montréal, CMA

La Prairie
(Ville)
Montréal CMA

In census division Roussillon.

POPULATION

July 1, 2001 Estimate	20,027
% Cdn. Total	0.06
% Change, '96 -'01	8.84
Avg. Annual Growth Rate, %	1.71
2003 Projected Population	21,197
2006 Projected Population	23,305
2001 Households Estimate	7,570
2003 Projected Households	8,051
2006 Projected Households	8,930

INCOME

% Above/Below National Average	+2
2001 Total Income Estimate	$429,640,000
% Cdn. Total	0.07
2001 Average Hhld. Income	$56,800
2001 Per Capita	$21,500
2003 Projected Total Income	$485,150,000
2006 Projected Total Income	$591,670,000

RETAIL SALES

% Above/Below National Average	-20
2001 Retail Sales Estimate	$144,300,000
% Cdn. Total	0.05
2001 per Household	$19,100
2001 per Capita	$7,200
2001 No. of Establishments	152
2003 Projected Retail Sales	$162,820,000
2006 Projected Retail Sales	$196,450,000

POPULATION

2001 Estimates:

Total		20,027
Male		9,844
Female		10,183

Age Groups	Male	Female
0-4	669	642
5-9	711	671
10-14	657	652
15-19	622	617
20-24	596	595
25-29	641	662
30-34	797	831
35-39	952	945
40-44	908	899
45-49	787	801
50-54	666	677
55-59	522	528
60-64	405	412
65-69	307	347
70+	604	904

DAYTIME POPULATION

2001 Estimates:

Working Population	4,981
At Home Population	9,491
Total	14,472

INCOME

2001 Estimates:

Avg. Household Income	$56,756
Avg. Family Income	$62,207
Per Capita Income	$21,453
Male:	
Avg. Employment Income	$37,160
Avg. Employment Income (Full Time)	$47,404
Female:	
Avg. Employment Income	$25,169
Avg. Employment Income (Full Time)	$33,773

Québec

DISPOSABLE & DISCRETIONARY INCOME

2001 Estimates:	Per Hhld.
Disposable Income	$39,576
Discretionary Income 1 (minus Food & Shelter)	$25,953
Discretionary Income 2 (minus Food, Shelter, & Other Expenditures)	$17,885

LIQUID ASSETS

1999 Estimates:	Per Hhld.
Equity Investments	$64,109
Interest Bearing Investments	$66,455
Total Liquid Assets	$130,564

CREDIT DATA

July 2000:	
Pool of Credit	$154,842,736
Revolving Credit, No.	38,103
Fixed Loans, No.	12,886
Avg. Credit Limit, per Person	$10,573
Avg. Spent, per Person	$4,813
Satisfactory Ratings, No. per Person	3.29
Avg. No. of Cards, per Person	1.31

LABOUR FORCE

2001 Estimates:

Male:	
In the Labour Force	6,022
Participation Rate	77.1
Employed	5,736
Unemployed	286
Unemployment Rate	4.7
Not in Labour Force	1,785
Female:	
In the Labour Force	5,084
Participation Rate	61.9
Employed	4,798
Unemployed	286
Unemployment Rate	5.6
Not in Labour Force	3,134

OCCUPATIONS BY MAJOR GROUPS

2001 Estimates:	Male	Female
Management	999	362
Business, Finance & Admin.	750	1,707
Natural & Applied Sciences & Related	570	188
Health	166	476
Social Sciences, Gov't Services & Religion	109	145
Education	122	264
Arts, Culture, Recreation & Sport	157	128
Sales & Service	1,145	1,330
Trades, Transport & Equipment Operators & Related	1,256	93
Primary Industries	72	17
Processing, Mfg. & Utilities	582	147

Québec

La Prairie
(Ville)
Montréal CMA
(Cont'd)

LEVEL OF SCHOOLING

2001 Estimates:
Population 15 years +	16,025
Less than Grade 9	2,268
Grades 9-13 w/o Certif.	2,321
Grade 9-13 with Certif.	3,136
Trade Certif./Dip.	565
Non-Univ. w/o Certif./Dip.	1,218
Non-Univ. with Certif./Dip.	2,597
Univ. w/o Degree	1,418
Univ. w/o Degree/Certif.	153
Univ. with Certif.	1,265
Univ. with Degree	2,502

AVERAGE HOUSEHOLD EXPENDITURES

2001 Estimates:
Food	$6,984
Shelter	$8,751
Clothing	$2,406
Transportation	$5,971
Health & Personal Care	$2,111
Recr'n, Read'g & Education	$3,533
Taxes & Securities	$16,675
Other	$7,899
Total Expenditures	$54,330

PRIVATE HOUSEHOLDS

2001 Estimates:
Private Households, Total	7,570
Pop. in Private Households	19,551
Average no. per Household	2.6

FAMILIES

2001 Estimates:
Families in Private Households	5,725
Husband-Wife Families	4,969
Lone-Parent Families	756
Aver. No. Persons per Family	3.0
Aver. No. Sons/Daughters at Home	1.1

HOUSING

2001 Estimates:
Occupied Private Dwellings	7,570
Owned	4,951
Rented	2,619
Single-Detached House	4,127
Semi-Detached House	247
Row Houses	249
Apartment, 5+ Storeys	109
Owned Apartment, 5+ Storeys	68
Apartment, 5 or Fewer Storeys	2,383
Apartment, Detached Duplex	437
Other Single-Attached	18

VEHICLES

2001 Estimates:
Model Yrs. '81-'96, No.	8,586
% Total	73.66
Model Yrs. '97-'98, No.	1,915
% Total	16.43
'99 Vehicles registered in Model Yr. '99, No.	1,155
% Total	9.91
Total No. '81-'99	11,656

LEGAL MARITAL STATUS

2001 Estimates: (Age 15+)
Single (Never Married)	5,979
Legally Married (Not Separated)	7,189
Legally Married (Separated)	404
Widowed	924
Divorced	1,529

PSYTE CATEGORIES

2001 Estimates	No. of House-holds	% of Total Hhds.	Index
Technocrafts & Bureaucrats	463	6.12	217
Stable Suburban Families	362	4.78	367
Participation Quebec	1,862	24.60	854
New Quebec Rows	1,041	13.75	1,255
Traditional French Cdn. Families	361	4.77	178
Old Quebec Walkups	458	6.05	330
Quebec Town Elders	2,205	29.13	1,031
Quebec's New Urban Mosaic	759	10.03	416

FINANCIAL P$YTE

2001 Estimates	No. of House-holds	% of Total Hhds.	Index
Successful Suburbanites	825	10.90	164
Mortgages & Minivans	2,903	38.35	581
Country Credit	361	4.77	71
Loan Parent Stress	2,663	35.18	604
NSF	759	10.03	283

HOME LANGUAGE

2001 Estimates:		% Total
English	755	3.77
French	18,062	90.19
Arabic	17	0.08
Chinese	250	1.25
Creoles	23	0.11
Dutch	23	0.11
Greek	106	0.53
Hungarian	12	0.06
Italian	23	0.11
Khmer (Cambodian)	11	0.05
Korean	49	0.24
Polish	68	0.34
Portuguese	125	0.62
Spanish	34	0.17
Vietnamese	23	0.11
Multiple Responses	446	2.23
Total	20,027	100.00

BUILDING PERMITS

	1999	1998 $000	1997
Value	24,389	18,500	24,416

HOMES BUILT

	1999	1998	1997
No.	153	208	188

TAXATION

Income Class:	1997	% Total
Under $5,000	1,460	11.20
$5,000-$10,000	1,540	11.81
$10,000-$15,000	1,750	13.42
$15,000-$20,000	1,160	8.90
$20,000-$25,000	1,040	7.98
$25,000-$30,000	1,030	7.90
$30,000-$40,000	1,690	12.96
$40,000-$50,000	1,290	9.89
$50,000 +	2,090	16.03
Total Returns, No.	13,040	
Total Income, $000	380,999	
Total Taxable Returns	9,640	
Total Tax, $000	49,554	
Average Income, $	29,218	
Average Tax, $	5,140	

VITAL STATISTICS

	1997	1996	1995	1994
Births	252	247	276	235
Deaths	136	133	113	95
Natural Increase	116	114	163	140
Marriages	44	47	48	37

Note: Latest available data.

MEDIA INFO
see Montréal, CMA

Lachenaie
(Ville)
Montréal CMA
In census division Les Moulins.

POPULATION

July 1, 2001 Estimate	22,571
% Cdn. Total	0.07
% Change, '96 -'01	19.78
Avg. Annual Growth Rate, %	3.68
2003 Projected Population	24,976
2006 Projected Population	29,023
2001 Households Estimate	7,721
2003 Projected Households	8,646
2006 Projected Households	10,231

INCOME

% Above/Below National Average	+7
2001 Total Income Estimate	$510,290,000
% Cdn. Total	0.08
2001 Average Hhld. Income	$66,100
2001 Per Capita	$22,600
2003 Projected Total Income	$609,520,000
2006 Projected Total Income	$798,150,000

RETAIL SALES

% Above/Below National Average	-53
2001 Retail Sales Estimate	$95,700,000
% Cdn. Total	0.03
2001 per Household	$12,400
2001 per Capita	$4,200
2001 No. of Establishments	130
2003 Projected Retail Sales	$112,140,000
2006 Projected Retail Sales	$141,590,000

POPULATION

2001 Estimates:

Total		22,571
Male		11,384
Female		11,187

Age Groups	Male	Female
0-4	821	764
5-9	930	872
10-14	949	880
15-19	900	807
20-24	742	687
25-29	682	712
30-34	875	970
35-39	1,116	1,202
40-44	1,131	1,165
45-49	975	951
50-54	787	737
55-59	581	527
60-64	390	348
65-69	242	226
70+	263	339

DAYTIME POPULATION

2001 Estimates:

Working Population	2,494
At Home Population	10,020
Total	12,514

INCOME

2001 Estimates:

Avg. Household Income	$66,091
Avg. Family Income	$68,647
Per Capita Income	$22,608
Male:	
Avg. Employment Income	$40,781
Avg. Employment Income (Full Time)	$49,597
Female:	
Avg. Employment Income	$25,787
Avg. Employment Income (Full Time)	$34,750

DISPOSABLE & DISCRETIONARY INCOME

2001 Estimates:	*Per Hhld.*
Disposable Income	$45,513
Discretionary Income 1 (minus Food & Shelter)	$30,892
Discretionary Income 2 (minus Food, Shelter, & Other Expenditures)	$21,020

LIQUID ASSETS

1999 Estimates:	*Per Hhld.*
Equity Investments	$89,335
Interest Bearing Investments	$78,507
Total Liquid Assets	$167,842

CREDIT DATA

July 2000:

Pool of Credit	$166,766,780
Revolving Credit, No.	38,574
Fixed Loans, No.	16,074
Avg. Credit Limit, per Person	$10,971
Avg. Spent, per Person	$5,375
Satisfactory Ratings, No. per Person	3.36
Avg. No. of Cards, per Person	1.29

LABOUR FORCE

2001 Estimates:
Male:

In the Labour Force	7,224
Participation Rate	83.2
Employed	6,977
Unemployed	247
Unemployment Rate	3.4
Not in Labour Force	1,460
Female:	
In the Labour Force	5,681
Participation Rate	65.5
Employed	5,469
Unemployed	212
Unemployment Rate	3.7
Not in Labour Force	2,990

OCCUPATIONS BY MAJOR GROUPS

2001 Estimates:	*Male*	*Female*
Management	793	405
Business, Finance & Admin.	733	2,225
Natural & Applied Sciences & Related	514	74
Health	117	528
Social Sciences, Gov't Services & Religion	55	156
Education	139	317
Arts, Culture, Recreation & Sport	168	136
Sales & Service	1,412	1,245
Trades, Transport & Equipment Operators & Related	2,521	106
Primary Industries	77	n.a.
Processing, Mfg. & Utilities	600	372

LEVEL OF SCHOOLING

2001 Estimates:

Population 15 years +	17,355
Less than Grade 9	2,160
Grades 9-13 w/o Certif.	3,312
Grade 9-13 with Certif.	3,633
Trade Certif. /Dip.	1,062
Non-Univ. w/o Certif./Dip.	1,458
Non-Univ. with Certif./Dip.	3,065
Univ. w/o Degree	1,214
Univ. w/o Degree/Certif.	115
Univ. with Certif.	1,099
Univ. with Degree	1,451

AVERAGE HOUSEHOLD EXPENDITURES

2001 Estimates:

Food	$7,754
Shelter	$9,168
Clothing	$2,871
Transportation	$7,771
Health & Personal Care	$2,368
Recr'n, Read'g & Education	$4,183
Taxes & Securities	$19,524
Other	$8,505
Total Expenditures	$62,144

PRIVATE HOUSEHOLDS

2001 Estimates:

Private Households, Total	7,721
Pop. in Private Households	22,461
Average no. per Household	2.9

FAMILIES

2001 Estimates:

Families in Private Households	6,896
Husband-Wife Families	6,240
Lone-Parent Families	656
Aver. No. Persons per Family	3.2
Aver. No. Sons/Daughters at Home	1.3

HOUSING

2001 Estimates:

Occupied Private Dwellings	7,721
Owned	6,786
Rented	935
Single-Detached House	6,438
Semi-Detached House	338
Row Houses	41
Apartment, 5 or Fewer Storeys	425
Apartment, Detached Duplex	327
Other Single-Attached	44
Movable Dwellings	108

VEHICLES

2001 Estimates:

Model Yrs. '81-'96, No.	9,683
% Total	72.53
Model Yrs. '97-'98, No.	2,269
% Total	17.00
'99 Vehicles registered in Model Yr. '99, No.	1,398
% Total	10.47
Total No. '81-'99	13,350

LEGAL MARITAL STATUS

2001 Estimates: (Age 15+)

Single (Never Married)	6,197
Legally Married (Not Separated)	8,855
Legally Married (Separated)	353
Widowed	425
Divorced	1,525

PSYTE CATEGORIES

2001 Estimates	*No. of House-holds*	*% of Total Hhds.*	*Index*
Technocrats & Bureaucrats	506	6.55	233
Participation Quebec	4,953	64.15	2,226
New Quebec Rows	783	10.14	925
Traditional French Cdn. Families	1,479	19.16	713

FINANCIAL P$YTE

2001 Estimates	*No. of House-holds*	*% of Total Hhds.*	*Index*
Successful Suburbanites	506	6.55	99
Mortgages & Minivans	5,736	74.29	1,126
Country Credit	1,479	19.16	283

Québec

HOME LANGUAGE

2001 Estimates:		*% Total*
English	339	1.50
French	21,935	97.18
Greek	12	0.05
Italian	28	0.12
Lao	18	0.08
Portuguese	18	0.08
Other Languages	12	0.05
Multiple Responses	209	0.93
Total	22,571	100.00

BUILDING PERMITS

	1999	*1998 $000*	*1997*
Value	28,858	32,527	24,116

HOMES BUILT

	1999	*1998*	*1997*
No.	304	235	298

TAXATION

Income Class:	*1997*	*% Total*
Under $5,000	1,600	11.72
$5,000-$10,000	1,280	9.38
$10,000-$15,000	1,450	10.62
$15,000-$20,000	1,280	9.38
$20,000-$25,000	1,140	8.35
$25,000-$30,000	1,260	9.23
$30,000-$40,000	2,050	15.02
$40,000-$50,000	1,510	11.06
$50,000 +	2,080	15.24
Total Returns, No.	13,650	
Total Income, $000	402,627	
Total Taxable Returns	10,740	
Total Tax, $000	52,213	
Total Taxable, $	29,496	
Average Tax, $	4,862	

VITAL STATISTICS

	1997	*1996*	*1995*	*1994*
Births	265	274	269	289
Deaths	49	37	44	45
Natural Increase	216	237	225	244
Marriages	12	12	13	6

Note: Latest available data.

MEDIA INFO
see Montréal, CMA

Québec

Lachine
(Ville)
Montréal CMA

In census division Communauté urbaine de Montréal.

POPULATION

July 1, 2001 Estimate	35,518
% Cdn. Total	0.11
% Change, '96 -'01	-0.83
Avg. Annual Growth Rate, %	-0.17
2003 Projected Population	35,840
2006 Projected Population	36,498
2001 Households Estimate	16,038
2003 Projected Households	16,126
2006 Projected Households	16,303

INCOME

% Above/Below National Average	-10
2001 Total Income Estimate	$675,940,000
% Cdn. Total	0.10
2001 Average Hhld. Income	$42,100
2001 Per Capita	$19,000
2003 Projected Total Income	$710,720,000
2006 Projected Total Income	$770,700,000

RETAIL SALES

% Above/Below National Average	-6
2001 Retail Sales Estimate	$297,360,000
% Cdn. Total	0.11
2001 per Household	$18,500
2001 per Capita	$8,400
2001 No. of Establishments	232
2003 Projected Retail Sales	$322,420,000
2006 Projected Retail Sales	$360,880,000

POPULATION

2001 Estimates:

Total		35,518
Male		16,636
Female		18,882

Age Groups	Male	Female
0-4	1,013	958
5-9	1,040	1,020
10-14	979	965
15-19	942	931
20-24	958	946
25-29	1,004	1,037
30-34	1,225	1,260
35-39	1,453	1,468
40-44	1,474	1,499
45-49	1,351	1,420
50-54	1,160	1,257
55-59	929	1,060
60-64	784	930
65-69	700	914
70+	1,624	3,217

DAYTIME POPULATION

2001 Estimates:

Working Population	27,371
At Home Population	19,680
Total	47,051

INCOME

2001 Estimates:

Avg. Household Income	$42,146
Avg. Family Income	$51,691
Per Capita Income	$19,031
Male:	
Avg. Employment Income	$31,104
Avg. Employment Income (Full Time)	$39,969
Female:	
Avg. Employment Income	$23,871
Avg. Employment Income (Full Time)	$31,751

DISPOSABLE & DISCRETIONARY INCOME

2001 Estimates:	Per Hhld.
Disposable Income	$28,581
Discretionary Income 1 (minus Food & Shelter)	$17,243
Discretionary Income 2 (minus Food, Shelter, & Other Expenditures)	$11,091

LIQUID ASSETS

1999 Estimates:	Per Hhld.
Equity Investments	$43,534
Interest Bearing Investments	$49,273
Total Liquid Assets	$92,807

CREDIT DATA

July 2000:

Pool of Credit	$238,321,661
Revolving Credit, No.	65,987
Fixed Loans, No.	17,797
Avg. Credit Limit, per Person	$7,646
Avg. Spent, per Person	$3,326
Satisfactory Ratings, No. per Person	2.61
Avg. No. of Cards, per Person	1.01

LABOUR FORCE

2001 Estimates:

Male:	
In the Labour Force	9,452
Participation Rate	69.5
Employed	8,706
Unemployed	746
Unemployment Rate	7.9
Not in Labour Force	4,152
Female:	
In the Labour Force	7,925
Participation Rate	49.7
Employed	7,412
Unemployed	513
Unemployment Rate	6.5
Not in Labour Force	8,014

OCCUPATIONS BY MAJOR GROUPS

2001 Estimates:	Male	Female
Management	913	426
Business, Finance & Admin.	1,285	2,586
Natural & Applied Sciences & Related	1,059	259
Health	145	793
Social Sciences, Gov't Services & Religion	125	148
Education	242	338
Arts, Culture, Recreation & Sport	202	231
Sales & Service	2,056	2,242
Trades, Transport & Equipment Operators & Related	1,867	110
Primary Industries	72	11
Processing, Mfg. & Utilities	1,005	434

LEVEL OF SCHOOLING

2001 Estimates:

Population 15 years +	29,543
Less than Grade 9	5,697
Grades 9-13 w/o Certif.	5,141
Grade 9-13 with Certif.	5,146
Trade Certif./Dip.	911
Non-Univ. w/o Certif./Dip.	2,272
Non-Univ. with Certif./Dip.	4,114
Univ. w/o Degree	2,564
Univ. w/o Degree/Certif.	595
Univ. with Certif.	1,969
Univ. with Degree	3,698

AVERAGE HOUSEHOLD EXPENDITURES

2001 Estimates:

Food	$5,484
Shelter	$7,740
Clothing	$1,857
Transportation	$4,397
Health & Personal Care	$1,660
Recr'n, Read'g & Education	$2,871
Taxes & Securities	$11,663
Other	$6,404
Total Expenditures	$42,076

PRIVATE HOUSEHOLDS

2001 Estimates:

Private Households, Total	16,038
Pop. in Private Households	34,238
Average no. per Household	2.1

FAMILIES

2001 Estimates:

Families in Private Households	9,672
Husband-Wife Families	7,728
Lone-Parent Families	1,944
Aver. No. Persons per Family	2.8
Aver. No. Sons/Daughters at Home	1.0

HOUSING

2001 Estimates:

Occupied Private Dwellings	16,038
Owned	6,128
Rented	9,910
Single-Detached House	2,785
Semi-Detached House	593
Row Houses	890
Apartment, 5+ Storeys	471
Owned Apartment, 5+ Storeys	42
Apartment, 5 or Fewer Storeys	9,986
Apartment, Detached Duplex	1,245
Other Single-Attached	68

VEHICLES

2001 Estimates:

Model Yrs. '81-'96, No.	13,720
% Total	71.69
Model Yrs. '97-'98, No.	3,256
% Total	17.01
'99 Vehicles registered in Model Yr. '99, No.	2,161
% Total	11.29
Total No. '81-'99	19,137

LEGAL MARITAL STATUS

2001 Estimates: (Age 15+)

Single (Never Married)	11,287
Legally Married (Not Separated)	11,410
Legally Married (Separated)	940
Widowed	2,755
Divorced	3,151

PSYTE CATEGORIES

2001 Estimates	No. of House -holds	% of Total Hhds.	Index
Urban Gentry	387	2.41	134
Aging Erudites	2,144	13.37	886
New Quebec Rows	1,381	8.61	786
Young Urban Professionals	196	1.22	64
University Enclaves	340	2.12	104
Old Quebec Walkups	5,362	33.43	1,825
Quebec Town Elders	371	2.31	82
Aging Quebec Urbanites	335	2.09	724
Quebec's New Urban Mosaic	3,680	22.95	953
Aged Pensioners	299	1.86	140
Big City Stress	1,129	7.04	623
Old Grey Towers	155	0.97	175

FINANCIAL P$YTE

2001 Estimates	No. of House -holds	% of Total Hhds.	Index
Four Star Investors	387	2.41	48
Urban Heights	2,340	14.59	339
Mortgages & Minivans	1,381	8.61	130
Young Urban Struggle	340	2.12	45
Loan Parent Stress	6,068	37.84	650
NSF	4,809	29.99	847
Senior Survivors	454	2.83	150

HOME LANGUAGE

2001 Estimates:		% Total
English	10,108	28.46
French	22,281	62.73
Chinese	46	0.13
Greek	20	0.06
Gujarati	61	0.17
Hungarian	20	0.06
Italian	361	1.02
Lao	47	0.13
Polish	103	0.29
Punjabi	84	0.24
Romanian	57	0.16
Russian	56	0.16
Spanish	468	1.32
Tagalog (Pilipino)	25	0.07
Ukrainian	144	0.41
Urdu	111	0.31
Vietnamese	51	0.14
Other Languages	227	0.64
Multiple Responses	1,248	3.51
Total	35,518	100.00

BUILDING PERMITS

	1999	1998	1997
		$000	
Value	45,035	12,234	16,083

HOMES BUILT

	1999	1998	1997
No.	66	74	71

TAXATION

Income Class:	1997	% Total
Under $5,000	2,680	10.23
$5,000-$10,000	3,840	14.66
$10,000-$15,000	4,470	17.07
$15,000-$20,000	2,800	10.69
$20,000-$25,000	2,330	8.90
$25,000-$30,000	2,180	8.32
$30,000-$40,000	3,170	12.10
$40,000-$50,000	2,000	7.64
$50,000 +	2,720	10.39
Total Returns, No.	26,190	
Total Income, $000	649,247	
Total Taxable Returns	17,820	
Total Tax, $000	75,500	
Average Income, $	24,790	
Average Tax, $	4,237	

VITAL STATISTICS

	1997	1996	1995	1994
Births	400	417	421	481
Deaths	403	397	413	407
Natural Increase	-3	20	8	74
Marriages	146	130	132	145

Note: Latest available data.

MEDIA INFO
see Montréal, CMA

LaSalle
(Ville)
Montréal CMA

In census division Communauté urbaine de Montréal.

POPULATION

July 1, 2001 Estimate	71,498
% Cdn. Total	0.23
% Change, '96 -'01	-2.51
Avg. Annual Growth Rate, %	-0.51
2003 Projected Population	71,498
2006 Projected Population	71,929
2001 Households Estimate	30,805
2003 Projected Households	30,718
2006 Projected Households	30,642

INCOME

% Above/Below National Average	-10
2001 Total Income Estimate	$1,352,030,000
% Cdn. Total	0.21
2001 Average Hhld. Income	$43,900
2001 Per Capita	$18,900
2003 Projected Total Income	$1,414,180,000
2006 Projected Total Income	$1,519,920,000

RETAIL SALES

% Above/Below National Average	-19
2001 Retail Sales Estimate	$515,570,000
% Cdn. Total	0.18
2001 per Household	$16,700
2001 per Capita	$7,200
2001 No. of Establishments	476
2003 Projected Retail Sales	$557,020,000
2006 Projected Retail Sales	$620,560,000

POPULATION

2001 Estimates:

Total	71,498
Male	33,620
Female	37,878

Age Groups	Male	Female
0-4	2,099	2,032
5-9	1,985	1,953
10-14	1,817	1,822
15-19	1,870	1,832
20-24	2,014	2,039
25-29	2,301	2,416
30-34	2,640	2,745
35-39	2,747	2,846
40-44	2,596	2,818
45-49	2,473	2,819
50-54	2,321	2,743
55-59	2,068	2,484
60-64	1,895	2,208
65-69	1,686	2,039
70+	3,108	5,082

DAYTIME POPULATION

2001 Estimates:

Working Population	22,074
At Home Population	38,496
Total	60,570

INCOME

2001 Estimates:

Avg. Household Income	$43,890
Avg. Family Income	$50,603
Per Capita Income	$18,910

Male:
Avg. Employment Income	$29,764
Avg. Employment Income (Full Time)	$38,316

Female:
Avg. Employment Income	$22,490
Avg. Employment Income (Full Time)	$31,089

DISPOSABLE & DISCRETIONARY INCOME

2001 Estimates: Per Hhld.

Disposable Income	$29,937
Discretionary Income 1 (minus Food & Shelter)	$17,005
Discretionary Income 2 (minus Food, Shelter, & Other Expenditures)	$10,321

LIQUID ASSETS

1999 Estimates: Per Hhld.

Equity Investments	$47,597
Interest Bearing Investments	$50,542
Total Liquid Assets	$98,139

CREDIT DATA

July 2000:

Pool of Credit	$505,500,001
Revolving Credit, No.	146,616
Fixed Loans, No.	39,739
Avg. Credit Limit, per Person	$7,587
Avg. Spent, per Person	$3,294
Satisfactory Ratings, No. per Person	2.68
Avg. No. of Cards, per Person	1.11

LABOUR FORCE

2001 Estimates:

Male:
In the Labour Force	18,964
Participation Rate	68.4
Employed	17,336
Unemployed	1,628
Unemployment Rate	8.6
Not in Labour Force	8,755

Female:
In the Labour Force	17,170
Participation Rate	53.5
Employed	15,852
Unemployed	1,318
Unemployment Rate	7.7
Not in Labour Force	14,901

OCCUPATIONS BY MAJOR GROUPS

2001 Estimates:	Male	Female
Management	1,460	929
Business, Finance & Admin.	2,817	6,419
Natural & Applied Sciences & Related	1,462	302
Health	443	1,508
Social Sciences, Gov't Services & Religion	257	390
Education	219	544
Arts, Culture, Recreation & Sport	293	361
Sales & Service	4,699	4,536
Trades, Transport & Equipment Operators & Related	4,085	223
Primary Industries	164	9
Processing, Mfg. & Utilities	2,190	1,220

LEVEL OF SCHOOLING

2001 Estimates:

Population 15 years +	59,790
Less than Grade 9	10,904
Grades 9-13 w/o Certif.	10,351
Grade 9-13 with Certif.	11,116
Trade Certif./Dip.	1,970
Non-Univ. w/o Certif./Dip.	5,165
Non-Univ. with Certif./Dip.	8,985
Univ. w/o Degree	5,762
Univ. w/o Degree/Certif.	1,368
Univ. with Certif.	4,394
Univ. with Degree	5,537

AVERAGE HOUSEHOLD EXPENDITURES

2001 Estimates:

Food	$6,082
Shelter	$8,622
Clothing	$2,056
Transportation	$4,613
Health & Personal Care	$1,729
Recr'n, Read'g & Education	$3,054
Taxes & Securities	$10,869
Other	$6,709
Total Expenditures	$43,734

PRIVATE HOUSEHOLDS

2001 Estimates:

Private Households, Total	30,805
Pop. in Private Households	70,537
Average no. per Household	2.3

FAMILIES

2001 Estimates:

Families in Private Households	20,383
Husband-Wife Families	16,439
Lone-Parent Families	3,944
Aver. No. Persons per Family	2.9
Aver. No. Sons/Daughters at Home	1.1

HOUSING

2001 Estimates:

Occupied Private Dwellings	30,805
Owned	10,876
Rented	19,929
Single-Detached House	1,283
Semi-Detached House	1,409
Row Houses	749
Apartment, 5+ Storeys	683
Apartment, 5 or Fewer Storeys	24,636
Apartment, Detached Duplex	1,958
Other Single-Attached	87

VEHICLES

2001 Estimates:

Model Yrs. '81-'96, No.	26,929
% Total	75.38
Model Yrs. '97-'98, No.	5,435
% Total	15.21
'99 Vehicles registered in Model Yr. '99, No.	3,360
% Total	9.41
Total No. '81-'99	35,724

LEGAL MARITAL STATUS

2001 Estimates: (Age 15+)

Single (Never Married)	21,065
Legally Married (Not Separated)	26,836
Legally Married (Separated)	1,758
Widowed	4,546
Divorced	5,585

PSYTE CATEGORIES

2001 Estimates	No. of House-holds	% of Total Hhds.	Index
Suburban Nesters	127	0.41	26
Brie & Chablis	101	0.33	37
Satellite Suburbs	304	0.99	34
New Quebec Rows	1,971	6.40	584
Quebec Melange	233	0.76	29
Europa	323	1.05	84
High Rise Sunsets	395	1.28	90
Euro Quebec	12,328	40.02	4,563
Old Quebec Walkups	11,177	36.28	1,980
Aging Quebec Urbanites	491	1.59	552
Quebec's New Urban Mosaic	1,130	3.67	152
Aged Pensioners	776	2.52	189
Big City Stress	1,187	3.85	341
Old Grey Towers	137	0.44	80

FINANCIAL PSYTE

2001 Estimates	No. of House-holds	% of Total Hhds.	Index
Canadian Comfort	431	1.40	14
Urban Heights	101	0.33	8
Mortgages & Minivans	1,971	6.40	97
Dollars & Sense	323	1.05	40
Country Credit	233	0.76	11
Revolving Renters	395	1.28	28
Loan Parent Stress	23,996	77.90	1,338
NSF	2,317	7.52	213
Senior Survivors	913	2.96	157

Québec

HOME LANGUAGE

2001 Estimates:		% Total
English	25,745	36.01
French	32,663	45.68
Arabic	361	0.50
Chinese	1,053	1.47
Creoles	65	0.09
Croatian	64	0.09
Czech	36	0.05
Greek	460	0.64
Gujarati	166	0.23
Italian	2,942	4.11
Korean	91	0.13
Lithuanian	115	0.16
Persian (Farsi)	89	0.12
Polish	938	1.31
Portuguese	402	0.56
Punjabi	846	1.18
Romanian	74	0.10
Russian	200	0.28
Spanish	972	1.36
Tagalog (Pilipino)	105	0.15
Ukrainian	289	0.40
Vietnamese	80	0.11
Other Languages	514	0.72
Multiple Responses	3,228	4.51
Total	71,498	100.00

BUILDING PERMITS

	1999	1998 $000	1997
Value	44,159	51,027	33,750

HOMES BUILT

	1999	1998	1997
No	233	223	264

TAXATION

Income Class:	1997	% Total
Under $5,000	6,560	12.12
$5,000-$10,000	7,920	14.64
$10,000-$15,000	8,340	15.41
$15,000-$20,000	6,020	11.13
$20,000-$25,000	5,260	9.72
$25,000-$30,000	4,950	9.15
$30,000-$40,000	6,620	12.23
$40,000-$50,000	4,020	7.43
$50,000 +	4,420	8.17
Total Returns, No.	54,110	
Total Income, $000	1,249,576	
Total Taxable Returns	37,700	
Total Tax, $000	138,502	
Average Income, $.	23,093	
Average Tax, $.	3,674	

VITAL STATISTICS

	1997	1996	1995	1994
Births	811	961	903	967
Deaths	636	629	549	548
Natural Increase	175	332	354	419
Marriages	117	106	115	156

Note: Latest available data.

MEDIA INFO
see Montréal, CMA

Québec

Laval
(Ville)
Montréal CMA

In census division Laval.

POPULATION

July 1, 2001 Estimate	353,333
% Cdn. Total	1.13
% Change, '96 -'01	5.09
Avg. Annual Growth Rate, %	1.00
2003 Projected Population	364,176
2006 Projected Population	382,779
2001 Households Estimate	136,865
2003 Projected Households	142,024
2006 Projected Households	150,545

INCOME

% Above/Below National Average	-2
2001 Total Income Estimate	$7,336,920,000
% Cdn. Total	1.12
2001 Average Hhld. Income	$53,600
2001 Per Capita	$20,800
2003 Projected Total Income	$8,019,870,000
2006 Projected Total Income	$9,234,040,000

RETAIL SALES

% Above/Below National Average	+6
2001 Retail Sales Estimate	$3,360,120,000
% Cdn. Total	1.21
2001 per Household	$24,600
2001 per Capita	$9,500
2001 No. of Establishments	2,890
2003 Projected Retail Sales	$3,750,800,000
2006 Projected Retail Sales	$4,374,830,000

POPULATION

2001 Estimates:

Total		353,333
Male		172,538
Female		180,795

Age Groups	Male	Female
0-4	10,330	9,932
5-9	11,006	10,659
10-14	11,059	10,665
15-19	11,361	10,825
20-24	11,344	10,577
25-29	11,194	10,687
30-34	12,523	12,390
35-39	14,293	14,530
40-44	14,294	15,098
45-49	13,273	14,241
50-54	12,047	12,956
55-59	10,375	11,172
60-64	8,953	9,650
65-69	7,623	8,500
70+	12,863	18,913

DAYTIME POPULATION

2001 Estimates:

Working Population	120,219
At Home Population	176,193
Total	296,412

INCOME

2001 Estimates:

Avg. Household Income	$53,607
Avg. Family Income	$59,300
Per Capita Income	$20,765
Male:	
Avg. Employment Income	$34,543
Avg. Employment Income (Full Time)	$43,966
Female:	
Avg. Employment Income	$23,658
Avg. Employment Income (Full Time)	$32,780

DISPOSABLE & DISCRETIONARY INCOME

2001 Estimates:	Per Hhld.
Disposable Income	$36,906
Discretionary Income 1 (minus Food & Shelter)	$23,718
Discretionary Income 2 (minus Food, Shelter, & Other Expenditures)	$15,631

LIQUID ASSETS

1999 Estimates:	Per Hhld.
Equity Investments	$64,435
Interest Bearing Investments	$63,068
Total Liquid Assets	$127,503

CREDIT DATA

July 2000:

Pool of Credit	$2,681,814,092
Revolving Credit, No.	700,512
Fixed Loans, No.	218,621
Avg. Credit Limit, per Person	$9,397
Avg. Spent, per Person	$4,139
Satisfactory Ratings, No. per Person	3.05
Avg. No. of Cards, per Person	1.20

LABOUR FORCE

2001 Estimates:

Male:
In the Labour Force	103,146
Participation Rate	73.6
Employed	97,322
Unemployed	5,824
Unemployment Rate	5.6
Not in Labour Force	36,997

Female:
In the Labour Force	85,010
Participation Rate	56.8
Employed	80,310
Unemployed	4,700
Unemployment Rate	5.5
Not in Labour Force	64,529

OCCUPATIONS BY MAJOR GROUPS

2001 Estimates:	Male	Female
Management	12,881	5,064
Business, Finance & Admin.	12,647	29,369
Natural & Applied Sciences & Related	9,129	1,988
Health	2,308	8,030
Social Sciences, Gov't Services & Religion	1,809	2,325
Education	2,254	3,821
Arts, Culture, Recreation & Sport	1,950	2,255
Sales & Service	24,146	22,250
Trades, Transport & Equipment Operators & Related	23,219	1,480
Primary Industries	1,164	182
Processing, Mfg. & Utilities	8,537	4,987

LEVEL OF SCHOOLING

2001 Estimates:

Population 15 years +	289,682
Less than Grade 9	44,544
Grades 9-13 w/o Certif.	46,660
Grade 9-13 with Certif.	53,909
Trade Certif. /Dip.	12,188
Non-Univ. w/o Certif./Dip.	23,106
Non-Univ. with Certif./Dip.	47,897
Univ. w/o Degree	26,887
Univ. w/o Degree/Certif.	4,970
Univ. with Certif.	21,917
Univ. with Degree	34,491

AVERAGE HOUSEHOLD EXPENDITURES

2001 Estimates:

Food	$6,634
Shelter	$8,571
Clothing	$2,304
Transportation	$6,113
Health & Personal Care	$2,026
Recr'n, Read'g & Education	$3,370
Taxes & Securities	$15,215
Other	$7,641
Total Expenditures	$51,874

PRIVATE HOUSEHOLDS

2001 Estimates:

Private Households, Total	136,865
Pop. in Private Households	347,635
Average no. per Household	2.5

FAMILIES

2001 Estimates:

Families in Private Households	103,939
Husband-Wife Families	89,014
Lone-Parent Families	14,925
Aver. No. Persons per Family	3.0
Aver. No. Sons/Daughters at Home	1.1

HOUSING

2001 Estimates:

Occupied Private Dwellings	136,865
Owned	89,134
Rented	47,731
Single-Detached House	66,106
Semi-Detached House	13,703
Row Houses	3,199
Apartment, 5+ Storeys	8,621
Owned Apartment, 5+ Storeys	1,856
Apartment, 5 or Fewer Storeys	39,699
Apartment, Detached Duplex	4,710
Other Single-Attached	241
Movable Dwellings	586

VEHICLES

2001 Estimates:

Model Yrs. '81-'96, No.	152,823
% Total	73.12
Model Yrs. '97-'98, No.	34,573
% Total	16.54
'99 Vehicles registered in Model Yr. '99, No.	21,597
% Total	10.33
Total No. '81-'99	208,993

LEGAL MARITAL STATUS

2001 Estimates: (Age 15+)

Single (Never Married)	99,544
Legally Married (Not Separated)	139,960
Legally Married (Separated)	7,051
Widowed	17,257
Divorced	25,870

PSYTE CATEGORIES

2001 Estimates	No. of House-holds	% of Total Hhds.	Index
Suburban Executives	756	0.55	39
Mortgaged in Suburbia	997	0.73	52
Technocrafts & Bureaucrats	2,218	1.62	58
Stable Suburban Families	2,150	1.57	121
Old Bungalow Burbs	6,091	4.45	269
Suburban Nesters	2,903	2.12	132
Brie & Chablis	1,170	0.85	95
Participation Quebec	29,609	21.63	751
New Quebec Rows	14,191	10.37	946
Quebec Melange	29,826	21.79	822
Traditional French Cdn. Families	5,495	4.01	150
High Rise Sunsets	803	0.59	41
University Enclaves	361	0.26	13
Euro Quebec	7,164	5.23	597
Old Quebec Walkups	11,796	8.62	470
Quebec Town Elders	4,651	3.40	120
Aging Quebec Urbanites	3,601	2.63	912
Quebec's New Urban Mosaic	6,955	5.08	211
Aged Pensioners	1,603	1.17	88
Big City Stress	1,105	0.81	71
Old Grey Towers	2,541	1.86	335

FINANCIAL P$YTE

2001 Estimates	No. of House-holds	% of Total Hhds.	Index
Four Star Investors	756	0.55	11
Successful Suburbanites	5,365	3.92	59
Canadian Comfort	2,903	2.12	22
Urban Heights	1,170	0.85	20
Miners & Credit-Liners	6,091	4.45	141
Mortgages & Minivans	43,800	32.00	485
Country Credit	35,321	25.81	382
Revolving Renters	803	0.59	13
Young Urban Struggle	361	0.26	6
Loan Parent Stress	27,212	19.88	341
NSF	8,060	5.89	166
Senior Survivors	4,144	3.03	161

HOME LANGUAGE

2001 Estimates:		% Total
English	35,461	10.04
French	273,257	77.34
Arabic	3,644	1.03
Armenian	4,388	1.24
Chinese	670	0.19
Creoles	895	0.25
Croatian	231	0.07
German	447	0.13
Greek	8,493	2.40
Hungarian	198	0.06
Italian	4,019	1.14
Khmer (Cambodian)	663	0.19
Lao	413	0.12
Persian (Farsi)	270	0.08
Polish	354	0.10
Portuguese	2,064	0.58
Punjabi	303	0.09
Romanian	402	0.11
Spanish	2,644	0.75
Vietnamese	542	0.15
Other Languages	1,150	0.33
Multiple Responses	12,825	3.63
Total	353,333	100.00

Laval
(Ville)
Montréal CMA
(Cont'd)

BUILDING PERMITS

	1999	1998	1997
		$000	
Value	270,333	261,482	317,024

HOMES BUILT

	1999	1998	1997
No	1,600	1,245	1,358

TAXATION

Income Class:	1997	% Total
Under $5,000	29,880	12.14
$5,000-$10,000	32,660	13.27
$10,000-$15,000	35,060	14.24
$15,000-$20,000	24,700	10.03
$20,000-$25,000	21,130	8.58
$25,000-$30,000	20,880	8.48
$30,000-$40,000	31,600	12.83
$40,000-$50,000	20,900	8.49
$50,000 +	29,410	11.95
Total Returns, No.	246,210	
Total Income, $000	6,495,351	
Total Taxable Returns	176,790	
Total Tax, $000	793,604	
Average Income, $	26,381	
Average Tax, $	4,489	

VITAL STATISTICS

	1997	1996	1995	1994
Births	3,694	3,983	4,073	4,371
Deaths	2,170	2,133	2,011	1,916
Natural Increase	1,524	1,850	2,062	2,455
Marriages	1,058	1,094	973	1,104

Note: Latest available data.

MEDIA INFO
see Montréal, CMA

Le Gardeur
(Ville)
Montréal CMA

In census division L'Assomption.

POPULATION

July 1, 2001 Estimate	19,911
% Cdn. Total	0.06
% Change, '96 -'01	16.09
Avg. Annual Growth Rate, %	3.03
2003 Projected Population	22,000
2006 Projected Population	25,405
2001 Households Estimate	6,925
2003 Projected Households	7,739
2006 Projected Households	9,078

INCOME

% Above/Below National Average	-3
2001 Total Income Estimate	$405,690,000
% Cdn. Total	0.06
2001 Average Hhld. Income	$58,600
2001 Per Capita	$20,400
2003 Projected Total Income	$482,970,000
2006 Projected Total Income	$626,410,000

RETAIL SALES

% Above/Below National Average	-71
2001 Retail Sales Estimate	$51,280,000
% Cdn. Total	0.02
2001 per Household	$7,400
2001 per Capita	$2,600
2001 No. of Establishments	110
2003 Projected Retail Sales	$60,510,000
2006 Projected Retail Sales	$75,340,000

POPULATION

2001 Estimates:

Total	19,911
Male	9,919
Female	9,992

Age Groups	Male	Female
0-4	715	685
5-9	844	812
10-14	853	808
15-19	770	721
20-24	634	586
25-29	573	595
30-34	745	850
35-39	1,008	1,089
40-44	1,028	1,039
45-49	846	832
50-54	653	634
55-59	467	442
60-64	297	299
65-69	197	207
70+	289	393

DAYTIME POPULATION

2001 Estimates:

Working Population	2,395
At Home Population	8,989
Total	11,384

INCOME

2001 Estimates:

Avg. Household Income	$58,583
Avg. Family Income	$60,815
Per Capita Income	$20,375

Male:
Avg. Employment Income	$37,805
Avg. Employment Income (Full Time)	$44,544

Female:
Avg. Employment Income	$23,455
Avg. Employment Income (Full Time)	$32,939

DISPOSABLE & DISCRETIONARY INCOME

2001 Estimates:	Per Hhld.
Disposable Income	$41,337
Discretionary Income 1 (minus Food & Shelter)	$27,949
Discretionary Income 2 (minus Food, Shelter, & Other Expenditures)	$18,865

LIQUID ASSETS

1999 Estimates:	Per Hhld.
Equity Investments	$64,037
Interest Bearing Investments	$64,990
Total Liquid Assets	$129,027

CREDIT DATA

July 2000:

Pool of Credit	$120,454,666
Revolving Credit, No.	29,360
Fixed Loans, No.	12,237
Avg. Credit Limit, per Person	$9,876
Avg. Spent, per Person	$4,921
Satisfactory Ratings, No. per Person	3.20
Avg. No. of Cards, per Person	1.22

LABOUR FORCE

2001 Estimates:

Male:
In the Labour Force	6,201
Participation Rate	82.6
Employed	5,887
Unemployed	314
Unemployment Rate	5.1
Not in Labour Force	1,306

Female:
In the Labour Force	5,256
Participation Rate	68.4
Employed	4,946
Unemployed	310
Unemployment Rate	5.9
Not in Labour Force	2,431

OCCUPATIONS BY MAJOR GROUPS

2001 Estimates:	Male	Female
Management	564	333
Business, Finance & Admin.	704	1,962
Natural & Applied Sciences & Related	487	78
Health	67	453
Social Sciences, Gov't Services & Religion	73	36
Education	86	137
Arts, Culture, Recreation & Sport	123	65
Sales & Service	1,251	1,505
Trades, Transport & Equipment Operators & Related	1,948	82
Primary Industries	58	45
Processing, Mfg. & Utilities	670	356

LEVEL OF SCHOOLING

2001 Estimates:

Population 15 years +	15,194
Less than Grade 9	1,979
Grades 9-13 w/o Certif.	2,722
Grade 9-13 with Certif.	3,621
Trade Certif. /Dip.	796
Non-Univ. w/o Certif./Dip.	1,122
Non-Univ. with Certif./Dip.	2,915
Univ. w/o Degree	1,063
Univ. w/o Degree/Certif.	164
Univ. with Certif.	899
Univ. with Degree	976

Québec

AVERAGE HOUSEHOLD EXPENDITURES

2001 Estimates:

Food	$7,144
Shelter	$8,271
Clothing	$2,556
Transportation	$7,172
Health & Personal Care	$2,184
Recr'n, Read'g & Education	$3,715
Taxes & Securities	$17,196
Other	$7,874
Total Expenditures	$56,112

PRIVATE HOUSEHOLDS

2001 Estimates:

Private Households, Total	6,925
Pop. in Private Households	19,612
Average no. per Household	2.8

FAMILIES

2001 Estimates:

Families in Private Households	6,024
Husband-Wife Families	5,322
Lone-Parent Families	702
Aver. No. Persons per Family	3.2
Aver. No. Sons/Daughters at Home	1.3

HOUSING

2001 Estimates:

Occupied Private Dwellings	6,925
Owned	5,804
Rented	1,121
Single-Detached House	4,406
Semi-Detached House	736
Row Houses	442
Apartment, 5+ Storeys	12
Apartment, 5 or Fewer Storeys	978
Apartment, Detached Duplex	351

VEHICLES

2001 Estimates:

Model Yrs. '81-'96, No.	8,145
% Total	75.76
Model Yrs. '97-'98, No.	1,686
% Total	15.68
'99 Vehicles registered in Model Yr. '99, No.	920
% Total	8.56
Total No. '81-'99	10,751

LEGAL MARITAL STATUS

2001 Estimates: (Age 15+)

Single (Never Married)	5,372
Legally Married (Not Separated)	7,654
Legally Married (Separated)	315
Widowed	470
Divorced	1,383

PSYTE CATEGORIES

2001 Estimates	No. of House -holds	% of Total Hhds.	Index
Participation Quebec	3,628	52.39	1,818
New Quebec Rows	503	7.26	663
Quebec Melange	1,181	17.05	644
Traditional French Cdn. Families	1,613	23.29	867

Québec

Le Gardeur
(Ville)
Montréal CMA
(Cont'd)

FINANCIAL P$YTE

2001 Estimates	No. of House-holds	% of Total Hhds.	Index
Mortgages & Minivans	4,131	59.65	904
Country Credit	2,794	40.35	597

HOME LANGUAGE

2001 Estimates:		% Total
English	259	1.30
French	19,426	97.56
Arabic	12	0.06
Italian	12	0.06
Portuguese	12	0.06
Spanish	29	0.15
Other Languages	10	0.05
Multiple Responses	151	0.76
Total	19,911	100.00

BUILDING PERMITS

	1999	1998	1997
		$000	
Value	8,461	12,697	13,776

HOMES BUILT

	1999	1998	1997
No	55	70	89

TAXATION

Income Class:	1997	% Total
Under $5,000	1,400	11.99
$5,000-$10,000	1,220	10.45
$10,000-$15,000	1,300	11.13
$15,000-$20,000	1,000	8.56
$20,000-$25,000	1,010	8.65
$25,000-$30,000	1,180	10.10
$30,000-$40,000	1,870	16.01
$40,000-$50,000	1,290	11.04
$50,000 +	1,420	12.16
Total Returns, No.	11,680	
Total Income, $000	314,335	
Total Taxable Returns	9,070	
Total Tax, $000	38,258	
Average Income, $	26,912	
Average Tax, $	4,218	

VITAL STATISTICS

	1997	1996	1995	1994
Births	209	252	251	297
Deaths	66	55	58	52
Natural Increase	143	197	193	245
Marriages	27	28	23	27

Note: Latest available data.

MEDIA INFO
see Montréal, CMA

Longueuil
(Ville)
Montréal CMA
In census division Champlain.

POPULATION

July 1, 2001 Estimate	128,678
% Cdn. Total	0.41
% Change, '96 -'01	-1.08
Avg. Annual Growth Rate, %	-0.22
2003 Projected Population	129,224
2006 Projected Population	130,730
2001 Households Estimate	57,844
2003 Projected Households	59,202
2006 Projected Households	61,309

INCOME

% Above/Below National Average	-7
2001 Total Income Estimate	$2,534,270,000
% Cdn. Total	0.39
2001 Average Hhld. Income	$43,800
2001 Per Capita	$19,700
2003 Projected Total Income	$2,690,510,000
2006 Projected Total Income	$2,953,100,000

RETAIL SALES

% Above/Below National Average	-26
2001 Retail Sales Estimate	$849,270,000
% Cdn. Total	0.30
2001 per Household	$14,700
2001 per Capita	$6,600
2001 No. of Establishments	883
2003 Projected Retail Sales	$917,170,000
2006 Projected Retail Sales	$1,022,720,000

POPULATION

2001 Estimates:

Total		128,678
Male		62,071
Female		66,607

Age Groups	Male	Female
0-4	3,893	3,678
5-9	3,851	3,632
10-14	3,624	3,453
15-19	3,823	3,660
20-24	4,339	4,150
25-29	4,611	4,434
30-34	4,897	4,697
35-39	5,174	5,177
40-44	5,147	5,474
45-49	4,851	5,503
50-54	4,482	5,176
55-59	3,772	4,280
60-64	3,012	3,414
65-69	2,418	2,876
70+	4,177	7,003

DAYTIME POPULATION

2001 Estimates:

Working Population	54,428
At Home Population	67,075
Total	121,503

INCOME

2001 Estimates:

Avg. Household Income	$43,812
Avg. Family Income	$51,732
Per Capita Income	$19,695
Male:	
Avg. Employment Income	$32,351
Avg. Employment Income (Full Time)	$42,486
Female:	
Avg. Employment Income	$22,646
Avg. Employment Income (Full Time)	$31,615

DISPOSABLE & DISCRETIONARY INCOME

2001 Estimates:	Per Hhld.
Disposable Income	$29,861
Discretionary Income 1 (minus Food & Shelter)	$18,054
Discretionary Income 2 (minus Food, Shelter, & Other Expenditures)	$11,595

LIQUID ASSETS

1999 Estimates:	Per Hhld.
Equity Investments	$45,735
Interest Bearing Investments	$50,772
Total Liquid Assets	$96,507

CREDIT DATA

July 2000:	
Pool of Credit	$849,849,361
Revolving Credit, No.	235,633
Fixed Loans, No.	75,013
Avg. Credit Limit, per Person	$7,574
Avg. Spent, per Person	$3,415
Satisfactory Ratings, No. per Person	2.61
Avg. No. of Cards, per Person	1.05

LABOUR FORCE

2001 Estimates:

Male:	
In the Labour Force	36,801
Participation Rate	72.6
Employed	33,498
Unemployed	3,303
Unemployment Rate	9.0
Not in Labour Force	13,902
Female:	
In the Labour Force	30,533
Participation Rate	54.7
Employed	28,286
Unemployed	2,247
Unemployment Rate	7.4
Not in Labour Force	25,311

OCCUPATIONS BY MAJOR GROUPS

2001 Estimates:	Male	Female
Management	3,470	1,448
Business, Finance & Admin.	4,422	9,950
Natural & Applied Sciences & Related	3,307	734
Health	861	2,922
Social Sciences, Gov't Services & Religion	717	963
Education	870	1,336
Arts, Culture, Recreation & Sport	1,255	1,016
Sales & Service	7,551	8,129
Trades, Transport & Equipment Operators & Related	8,371	542
Primary Industries	333	88
Processing, Mfg. & Utilities	3,810	1,757

LEVEL OF SCHOOLING

2001 Estimates:

Population 15 years +	106,547
Less than Grade 9	18,609
Grades 9-13 w/o Certif.	18,997
Grade 9-13 with Certif.	17,958
Trade Certif. /Dip.	4,215
Non-Univ. w/o Certif./Dip.	8,225
Non-Univ. with Certif./Dip.	16,192
Univ. w/o Degree.	8,728
Univ. w/o Degree/Certif.	1,511
Univ. with Certif.	7,217
Univ. with Degree	13,623

AVERAGE HOUSEHOLD EXPENDITURES

2001 Estimates:

Food	$5,746
Shelter	$7,933
Clothing	$1,979
Transportation	$4,605
Health & Personal Care	$1,732
Recr'n, Read'g & Education	$2,897
Taxes & Securities	$11,932
Other	$6,630
Total Expenditures	$43,454

PRIVATE HOUSEHOLDS

2001 Estimates:

Private Households, Total	57,844
Pop. in Private Households	126,768
Average no. per Household	2.2

FAMILIES

2001 Estimates:

Families in Private Households	37,501
Husband-Wife Families	28,669
Lone-Parent Families	8,832
Aver. No. Persons per Family	2.8
Aver. No. Sons/Daughters at Home	1.1

HOUSING

2001 Estimates:

Occupied Private Dwellings	57,844
Owned	22,978
Rented	34,866
Single-Detached House	13,325
Semi-Detached House	2,532
Row Houses	2,117
Apartment, 5+ Storeys	4,250
Owned Apartment, 5+ Storeys	640
Apartment, 5 or Fewer Storeys	31,229
Apartment, Detached Duplex	4,236
Other Single-Attached	155

VEHICLES

2001 Estimates:

Model Yrs. '81-'96, No.	53,109
% Total	75.05
Model Yrs. '97-'98, No.	10,997
% Total	15.54
'99 Vehicles registered in Model Yr. '99, No.	6,660
% Total	9.41
Total No. '81-'99	70,766

LEGAL MARITAL STATUS

2001 Estimates: (Age 15+)

Single (Never Married)	45,212
Legally Married (Not Separated)	38,365
Legally Married (Separated)	3,466
Widowed	6,616
Divorced	12,888

PSYTE CATEGORIES

2001 Estimates	No. of House-holds	% of Total Hhds.	Index
Mortgaged in Suburbia	127	0.22	16
Technocrafts & Bureaucrats	2,239	3.87	138
Stable Suburban Families	818	1.41	108
Old Bungalow Burbs	68	0.12	7
Suburban Nesters	248	0.43	27
Brie & Chablis	423	0.73	82
Participation Quebec	2,784	4.81	167
New Quebec Rows	4,973	8.60	785
Quebec Melange	3,536	6.11	231
High Rise Sunsets	433	0.75	52
Young Urban Professionals	787	1.36	72
University Enclaves	433	0.75	37
Urban Bohemia	1,220	2.11	180
Town Renters	396	0.68	79
Euro Quebec	5,167	8.93	1,018
Old Quebec Walkups	15,567	26.91	1,469
Quebec Town Elders	2,233	3.86	137
Aging Quebec Urbanites	1,952	3.37	1,169
Quebec's New Urban Mosaic	13,119	22.68	941
Aged Pensioners	401	0.69	52
Big City Stress	364	0.63	56
Old Grey Towers	306	0.53	96

Longueuil
(Ville)
Montréal CMA
(Cont'd)

FINANCIAL PSYTE

2001 Estimates	No. of House -holds	% of Total Hhds.	Index
Successful Suburbanites	3,184	5.50	83
Canadian Comfort	248	0.43	4
Urban Heights	1,210	2.09	49
Miners & Credit-Liners	68	0.12	4
Mortgages & Minivans	7,757	13.41	203
Country Credit	3,536	6.11	90
Revolving Renters	433	0.75	16
Young Urban Struggle	1,653	2.86	60
Loan Parent Stress	24,919	43.08	740
Towering Debt	396	0.68	9
NSF	13,483	23.31	659
Senior Survivors	707	1.22	65

HOME LANGUAGE

2001 Estimates:		% Total
English	3,659	2.84
French	115,955	90.11
Arabic	552	0.43
Chinese	958	0.74
Creoles	314	0.24
Greek	101	0.08
Italian	429	0.33
Khmer (Cambodian)	147	0.11
Lao	195	0.15
Persian (Farsi)	212	0.16
Polish	157	0.12
Portuguese	334	0.26
Spanish	1,290	1.00
Vietnamese	737	0.57
Other Languages	481	0.37
Multiple Responses	3,157	2.45
Total	128,678	100.00

BUILDING PERMITS

	1999	1998 $000	1997
Value	73,935	65,098	69,181

HOMES BUILT

	1999	1998	1997
No	210	235	323

TAXATION

Income Class:	1997	% Total
Under $5,000	11,550	12.27
$5,000-$10,000	15,820	16.81
$10,000-$15,000	14,310	15.21
$15,000-$20,000	9,250	9.83
$20,000-$25,000	7,730	8.21
$25,000-$30,000	7,440	7.91
$30,000-$40,000	10,870	11.55
$40,000-$50,000	7,060	7.50
$50,000 +	10,080	10.71
Total Returns, No.	94,100	
Total Income, $000	2,310,352	
Total Taxable Returns	63,000	
Total Tax, $000	272,319	
Average Income, $	24,552	
Average Tax, $	4,323	

VITAL STATISTICS

	1997	1996	1995	1994
Births	1,428	1,676	1,641	1,784
Deaths	899	882	844	846
Natural Increase	529	794	797	938
Marriages	872	714	752	735

Note: Latest available data.

MEDIA INFO

see Montréal, CMA

Mascouche
(Ville)
Montréal CMA

In census division Les Moulins.

POPULATION

July 1, 2001 Estimate	30,751
% Cdn. Total	0.10
% Change, '96 -'01	7.37
Avg. Annual Growth Rate, %	1.43
2003 Projected Population	32,036
2006 Projected Population	34,547
2001 Households Estimate	10,359
2003 Projected Households	10,912
2006 Projected Households	11,963

INCOME

% Above/Below National Average	-11
2001 Total Income Estimate	$579,960,000
% Cdn. Total	0.09
2001 Average Hhld. Income	$56,000
2001 Per Capita	$18,900
2003 Projected Total Income	$649,200,000
2006 Projected Total Income	$782,210,000

RETAIL SALES

% Above/Below National Average	-9
2001 Retail Sales Estimate	$250,840,000
% Cdn. Total	0.09
2001 per Household	$24,200
2001 per Capita	$8,200
2001 No. of Establishments	223
2003 Projected Retail Sales	$283,880,000
2006 Projected Retail Sales	$341,250,000

POPULATION

2001 Estimates:		
Total		30,751
Male		15,564
Female		15,187
Age Groups	Male	Female
0-4	1,026	968
5-9	1,207	1,147
10-14	1,250	1,210
15-19	1,238	1,157
20-24	1,097	984
25-29	958	907
30-34	1,100	1,149
35-39	1,350	1,413
40-44	1,429	1,482
45-49	1,353	1,356
50-54	1,161	1,059
55-59	877	746
60-64	579	520
65-69	377	381
70+	562	708

DAYTIME POPULATION

2001 Estimates:	
Working Population	4,592
At Home Population	14,885
Total	19,477

INCOME

2001 Estimates:	
Avg. Household Income	$55,986
Avg. Family Income	$57,823
Per Capita Income	$18,860
Male:	
Avg. Employment Income	$34,469
Avg. Employment Income (Full Time)	$43,037
Female:	
Avg. Employment Income	$21,499
Avg. Employment Income (Full Time)	$30,463

DISPOSABLE & DISCRETIONARY INCOME

2001 Estimates:	Per Hhld.
Disposable Income	$39,328
Discretionary Income 1 (minus Food & Shelter)	$26,223
Discretionary Income 2 (minus Food, Shelter, & Other Expenditures)	$17,400

LIQUID ASSETS

1999 Estimates:	Per Hhld.
Equity Investments	$69,170
Interest Bearing Investments	$65,514
Total Liquid Assets	$134,684

CREDIT DATA

July 2000:	
Pool of Credit	$211,411,306
Revolving Credit, No.	49,328
Fixed Loans, No.	21,662
Avg. Credit Limit, per Person	$10,056
Avg. Spent, per Person	$5,139
Satisfactory Ratings, No. per Person	3.16
Avg. No. of Cards, per Person	1.16

LABOUR FORCE

2001 Estimates:	
Male:	
In the Labour Force	9,593
Participation Rate	79.4
Employed	9,118
Unemployed	475
Unemployment Rate	5.0
Not in Labour Force	2,488
Female:	
In the Labour Force	7,085
Participation Rate	59.7
Employed	6,610
Unemployed	475
Unemployment Rate	6.7
Not in Labour Force	4,777

OCCUPATIONS BY MAJOR GROUPS

2001 Estimates:	Male	Female
Management	1,018	323
Business, Finance & Admin.	880	2,519
Natural & Applied Sciences & Related	420	93
Health	142	637
Social Sciences, Gov't Services & Religion	45	102
Education	170	262
Arts, Culture, Recreation & Sport	174	151
Sales & Service	1,809	1,922
Trades, Transport & Equipment Operators & Related	3,539	240
Primary Industries	123	12
Processing, Mfg. & Utilities	966	528

LEVEL OF SCHOOLING

2001 Estimates:	
Population 15 years +	23,943
Less than Grade 9	3,546
Grades 9-13 w/o Certif.	4,915
Grade 9-13 with Certif.	5,139
Trade Certif. /Dip.	1,188
Non-Univ. w/o Certif./Dip.	2,139
Non-Univ. with Certif./Dip.	4,292
Univ. w/o Degree	1,520
Univ. w/o Degree/Certif.	353
Univ. with Certif.	1,167
Univ. with Degree	1,204

Québec

AVERAGE HOUSEHOLD EXPENDITURES

2001 Estimates:	
Food	$7,061
Shelter	$7,978
Clothing	$2,461
Transportation	$7,029
Health & Personal Care	$2,082
Recr'n, Read'g & Education	$3,620
Taxes & Securities	$15,969
Other	$7,753
Total Expenditures	$53,953

PRIVATE HOUSEHOLDS

2001 Estimates:	
Private Households, Total	10,359
Pop. in Private Households	30,537
Average no. per Household	2.9

FAMILIES

2001 Estimates:	
Families in Private Households	9,030
Husband-Wife Families	8,004
Lone-Parent Families	1,026
Aver. No. Persons per Family	3.2
Aver. No. Sons/Daughters at Home	1.3

HOUSING

2001 Estimates:	
Occupied Private Dwellings	10,359
Owned	8,844
Rented	1,515
Single-Detached House	8,517
Semi-Detached House	396
Row Houses	105
Apartment, 5 or Fewer Storeys	846
Apartment, Detached Duplex	386
Other Single-Attached	109

VEHICLES

2001 Estimates:	
Model Yrs. '81-'96, No.	14,664
% Total	76.16
Model Yrs. '97-'98, No.	2,782
% Total	14.45
'99 Vehicles registered in Model Yr. '99, No.	1,809
% Total	9.39
Total No. '81-'99	19,255

LEGAL MARITAL STATUS

2001 Estimates: (Age 15+)	
Single (Never Married)	8,750
Legally Married (Not Separated)	11,681
Legally Married (Separated)	530
Widowed	901
Divorced	2,081

PSYTE CATEGORIES

2001 Estimates	No. of House -holds	% of Total Hhds.	Index
Participation Quebec	3,892	37.57	1,304
New Quebec Rows	525	5.07	462
Quebec Melange	1,137	10.98	414
Traditional French Cdn. Families	4,492	43.36	1,615
Quebec's Heartland	33	0.32	32
Old Quebec Walkups	22	0.21	12
Quebec Town Elders	258	2.49	88

Québec

Mascouche
(Ville)
Montréal CMA
(Cont'd)

FINANCIAL P$YTE

2001 Estimates	No. of House -holds	% of Total Hhds.	Index
Mortgages & Minivans	4,417	42.64	646
Country Credit	5,629	54.34	804
Rural Family Blues	33	0.32	4
Loan Parent Stress	280	2.70	46

HOME LANGUAGE

2001 Estimates:		% Total
English	986	3.21
French	29,236	95.07
Italian	22	0.07
Slovak	23	0.07
Spanish	66	0.21
Other Languages	33	0.11
Multiple Responses	385	1.25
Total	30,751	100.00

BUILDING PERMITS

	1999	1998 $000	1997
Value	26,724	34,629	34,588

HOMES BUILT

	1999	1998	1997
No.	151	135	186

TAXATION

Income Class:	1997	% Total
Under $5,000	2,910	14.70
$5,000-$10,000	2,450	12.37
$10,000-$15,000	2,640	13.33
$15,000-$20,000	1,780	8.99
$20,000-$25,000	1,740	8.79
$25,000-$30,000	1,660	8.38
$30,000-$40,000	2,850	14.39
$40,000-$50,000	1,800	9.09
$50,000 +	2,000	10.10
Total Returns, No.	19,800	
Total Income, $000	480,236	
Total Taxable Returns	14,170	
Total Tax, $000	55,776	
Average Income, $	24,254	
Average Tax, $	3,936	

VITAL STATISTICS

	1997	1996	1995	1994
Births	315	388	382	407
Deaths	120	84	101	95
Natural Increase	195	304	281	312
Marriages	56	54	56	59

Note: Latest available data.

MEDIA INFO
see Montréal, CMA

Mirabel
(Ville)
Montréal CMA
In census division Mirabel.

POPULATION

July 1, 2001 Estimate	28,518
% Cdn. Total	0.09
% Change, '96 -'01	22.84
Avg. Annual Growth Rate, %	4.20
2003 Projected Population	31,897
2006 Projected Population	37,881
2001 Households Estimate	10,154
2003 Projected Households	11,339
2006 Projected Households	13,475

INCOME

% Above/Below National Average	-13
2001 Total Income Estimate	$521,440,000
% Cdn. Total	0.08
2001 Average Hhld. Income	$51,400
2001 Per Capita	$18,300
2003 Projected Total Income	$627,210,000
2006 Projected Total Income	$838,860,000

RETAIL SALES

% Above/Below National Average	-33
2001 Retail Sales Estimate	$171,820,000
% Cdn. Total	0.06
2001 per Household	$16,900
2001 per Capita	$6,000
2001 No. of Establishments	206
2003 Projected Retail Sales	$209,870,000
2006 Projected Retail Sales	$279,310,000

POPULATION

2001 Estimates:		
Total		28,518
Male		14,295
Female		14,223
Age Groups	Male	Female
0-4	1,118	1,078
5-9	1,226	1,196
10-14	1,101	1,097
15-19	947	932
20-24	813	847
25-29	932	1,031
30-34	1,278	1,370
35-39	1,465	1,440
40-44	1,323	1,203
45-49	1,081	950
50-54	857	783
55-59	648	621
60-64	499	471
65-69	395	365
70+	612	839

DAYTIME POPULATION

2001 Estimates:	
Working Population	11,737
At Home Population	14,314
Total	26,051

INCOME

2001 Estimates:	
Avg. Household Income	$51,353
Avg. Family Income	$54,635
Per Capita Income	$18,285
Male:	
Avg. Employment Income	$33,931
Avg. Employment Income (Full Time)	$41,165
Female:	
Avg. Employment Income	$20,773
Avg. Employment Income (Full Time)	$29,921

DISPOSABLE & DISCRETIONARY INCOME

2001 Estimates:	Per Hhld.
Disposable Income	$36,873
Discretionary Income 1 (minus Food & Shelter)	$23,811
Discretionary Income 2 (minus Food, Shelter, & Other Expenditures)	$15,501

LIQUID ASSETS

1999 Estimates:	Per Hhld.
Equity Investments	$49,811
Interest Bearing Investments	$54,974
Total Liquid Assets	$104,785

CREDIT DATA

July 2000:	
Pool of Credit	$137,429,775
Revolving Credit, No.	34,141
Fixed Loans, No.	14,977
Avg. Credit Limit, per Person	$9,243
Avg. Spent, per Person	$4,735
Satisfactory Ratings, No. per Person	3.08
Avg. No. of Cards, per Person	1.12

LABOUR FORCE

2001 Estimates:	
Male:	
In the Labour Force	8,712
Participation Rate	80.3
Employed	8,288
Unemployed	424
Unemployment Rate	4.9
Not in Labour Force	2,138
Female:	
In the Labour Force	6,468
Participation Rate	59.6
Employed	5,958
Unemployed	510
Unemployment Rate	7.9
Not in Labour Force	4,384

OCCUPATIONS BY MAJOR GROUPS

2001 Estimates:	Male	Female
Management	617	209
Business, Finance & Admin.	720	1,955
Natural & Applied Sciences & Related	499	183
Health	107	437
Social Sciences, Gov't Services & Religion	63	158
Education	117	298
Arts, Culture, Recreation & Sport	90	76
Sales & Service	1,366	1,841
Trades, Transport & Equipment Operators & Related	2,845	160
Primary Industries	882	291
Processing, Mfg. & Utilities	1,209	533

LEVEL OF SCHOOLING

2001 Estimates:	
Population 15 years +	21,702
Less than Grade 9	4,077
Grades 9-13 w/o Certif.	4,281
Grade 9-13 with Certif.	4,462
Trade Certif. /Dip.	1,375
Non-Univ. w/o Certif./Dip.	1,377
Non-Univ. with Certif./Dip.	3,658
Univ. w/o Degree	1,254
Univ. w/o Degree/Certif.	182
Univ. with Certif.	1,072
Univ. with Degree	1,218

AVERAGE HOUSEHOLD EXPENDITURES

2001 Estimates:	
Food	$7,047
Shelter	$7,917
Clothing	$2,357
Transportation	$6,327
Health & Personal Care	$2,052
Recr'n, Read'g & Education	$3,275
Taxes & Securities	$13,676
Other	$7,725
Total Expenditures	$50,376

PRIVATE HOUSEHOLDS

2001 Estimates:	
Private Households, Total	10,154
Pop. in Private Households	28,028
Average no. per Household	2.8

FAMILIES

2001 Estimates:	
Families in Private Households	8,207
Husband-Wife Families	7,375
Lone-Parent Families	832
Aver. No. Persons per Family	3.1
Aver. No. Sons/Daughters at Home	1.2

HOUSING

2001 Estimates:	
Occupied Private Dwellings	10,154
Owned	7,329
Rented	2,825
Single-Detached House	7,581
Semi-Detached House	372
Row Houses	44
Apartment, 5 or Fewer Storeys	1,263
Apartment, Detached Duplex	793
Other Single-Attached	39
Movable Dwellings	62

VEHICLES

2001 Estimates:	
Model Yrs. '81-'96, No.	13,616
% Total	78.86
Model Yrs. '97-'98, No.	2,243
% Total	12.99
'99 Vehicles registered in Model Yr. '99, No.	1,406
% Total	8.14
Total No. '81-'99	17,265

LEGAL MARITAL STATUS

2001 Estimates: (Age 15+)	
Single (Never Married)	8,399
Legally Married (Not Separated)	10,061
Legally Married (Separated)	493
Widowed	874
Divorced	1,875

PSYTE CATEGORIES

2001 Estimates	No. of House -holds	% of Total Hhds.	Index
Participation			
Quebec	1,018	10.03	348
New Quebec Rows	410	4.04	368
Quebec Melange	1,898	18.69	705
Traditional French Cdn. Families	4,010	39.49	1,471
Quebec's Heartland	2,275	22.40	2,282
Quebec Town Elders	339	3.34	118
Quebec's New Urban Mosaic	177	1.74	72

FINANCIAL P$YTE

2001 Estimates	No. of House -holds	% of Total Hhds.	Index
Mortgages & Minivans	1,428	14.06	213
Country Credit	5,908	58.18	860
Rural Family Blues	2,275	22.40	278
Loan Parent Stress	339	3.34	57
NSF	177	1.74	49

Mirabel
(Ville)
Montréal CMA
(Cont'd)

HOME LANGUAGE

2001 Estimates:		% Total
* English	445	1.56
French	27,628	96.88
Greek	25	0.09
Japanese	44	0.15
Portuguese	35	0.12
Thai	19	0.07
Ukrainian	16	0.06
Other Languages	43	0.15
Multiple Responses	263	0.92
Total	28,518	100.00

BUILDING PERMITS

	1999	1998	1997
		$000	
Value	29,036	41,534	44,799

HOMES BUILT

	1999	1998	1997
No	367	296	328

TAXATION

Income Class:	1997	% Total
Under $5,000	2,230	14.01
$5,000-$10,000	1,960	12.31
$10,000-$15,000	2,250	14.13
$15,000-$20,000	1,680	10.55
$20,000-$25,000	1,520	9.55
$25,000-$30,000	1,370	8.61
$30,000-$40,000	2,080	13.07
$40,000-$50,000	1,360	8.54
$50,000 +	1,500	9.42
Total Returns, No.	15,920	
Total Income, $000	381,745	
Total Taxable		
Returns	11,430	
Total Tax, $000	43,915	
Average Income, $	23,979	
Average Tax, $	3,842	

VITAL STATISTICS

	1997	1996	1995	1994
Births	377	414	409	391
Deaths	122	120	102	102
Natural				
Increase	255	294	307	289
Marriages	60	68	52	47

Note: Latest available data.

MEDIA INFO
see Montréal, CMA

Mont-Royal
(Ville)
Montréal CMA

In census division Communauté urbaine de Montréal.

POPULATION

July 1, 2001 Estimate	18,561
% Cdn. Total	0.06
% Change, '96 -'01	-0.30
Avg. Annual Growth Rate, %	-0.06
2003 Projected Population	18,777
2006 Projected Population	19,195
2001 Households Estimate	7,204
2003 Projected Households	7,265
2006 Projected Households	7,371

INCOME

% Above/Below National Average	+100
2001 Total Income Estimate	$781,890,000
% Cdn. Total	0.12
2001 Average Hhld. Income	$108,500
2001 Per Capita	$42,100
2003 Projected Total Income	$832,230,000
2006 Projected Total Income	$918,460,000

RETAIL SALES

% Above/Below National Average	+125
2001 Retail Sales Estimate	$373,470,000
% Cdn. Total	0.13
2001 per Household	$51,800
2001 per Capita	$20,100
2001 No. of Establishments	302
2003 Projected Retail Sales	$405,820,000
2006 Projected Retail Sales	$455,020,000

POPULATION

2001 Estimates:		
Total		18,561
Male		8,763
Female		9,798
Age Groups	Male	Female
0-4	457	437
5-9	515	493
10-14	581	524
15-19	613	557
20-24	593	552
25-29	534	526
30-34	504	514
35-39	525	582
40-44	574	669
45-49	641	744
50-54	643	734
55-59	580	677
60-64	522	578
65-69	466	523
70+	1,015	1,688

DAYTIME POPULATION

2001 Estimates:	
Working Population	23,464
At Home Population	9,414
Total	32,878

INCOME

2001 Estimates:	
Avg. Household Income	$108,536
Avg. Family Income	$130,449
Per Capita Income	$42,126
Male:	
Avg. Employment Income	$75,065
Avg. Employment Income	
(Full Time)	$91,973
Female:	
Avg. Employment Income	$38,213
Avg. Employment Income	
(Full Time)	$52,372

DISPOSABLE & DISCRETIONARY INCOME

2001 Estimates:	Per Hhld.
Disposable Income	$64,239
Discretionary Income 1	
(minus Food & Shelter)	$43,578
Discretionary Income 2	
(minus Food, Shelter, & Other	
Expenditures)	$31,218

LIQUID ASSETS

1999 Estimates:	Per Hhld.
Equity Investments	$314,853
Interest Bearing Investments	$163,293
Total Liquid Assets	$478,146

CREDIT DATA

July 2000:	
Pool of Credit	$226,480,272
Revolving Credit, No.	43,395
Fixed Loans, No.	7,349
Avg. Credit Limit, per Person	$12,663
Avg. Spent, per Person	$4,400
Satisfactory Ratings,	
No. per Person	2.77
Avg. No. of Cards, per Person	1.31

LABOUR FORCE

2001 Estimates:	
Male:	
In the Labour Force	5,245
Participation Rate	72.7
Employed	5,063
Unemployed	182
Unemployment Rate	3.5
Not in Labour Force	1,965
Female:	
In the Labour Force	4,512
Participation Rate	54.1
Employed	4,386
Unemployed	126
Unemployment Rate	2.8
Not in Labour Force	3,832

OCCUPATIONS BY MAJOR GROUPS

2001 Estimates:	Male	Female
Management	1,555	608
Business, Finance		
& Admin.	645	1,189
Natural & Applied		
Sciences &		
Related	607	196
Health	530	561
Social Sciences,		
Gov't Services		
& Religion	353	200
Education	260	322
Arts, Culture,		
Recreation &		
Sport	211	277
Sales & Service	695	954
Trades, Transport		
& Equipment		
Operators &		
Related	139	29
Primary Industries	22	n.a.
Processing, Mfg. &		
Utilities	95	57

LEVEL OF SCHOOLING

2001 Estimates:	
Population 15 years +	15,554
Less than Grade 9	742
Grades 9-13 w/o Certif.	1,317
Grade 9-13 with Certif.	1,634
Trade Certif. /Dip.	223
Non-Univ. w/o Certif./Dip.	755
Non-Univ. with Certif./Dip.	1,545
Univ. w/o Degree	2,347
Univ. w/o Degree/Certif.	585
Univ. with Certif.	1,762
Univ. with Degree	6,991

Québec

AVERAGE HOUSEHOLD EXPENDITURES

2001 Estimates:	
Food	$8,780
Shelter	$16,277
Clothing	$3,748
Transportation	$9,336
Health & Personal Care	$3,048
Recr'n, Read'g & Education	$6,688
Taxes & Securities	$30,752
Other	$15,776
Total Expenditures	$94,405

PRIVATE HOUSEHOLDS

2001 Estimates:	
Private Households, Total	7,204
Pop. in Private Households	18,215
Average no. per Household	2.5

FAMILIES

2001 Estimates:	
Families in Private Households	5,277
Husband-Wife Families	4,674
Lone-Parent Families	603
Aver. No. Persons per Family	3.0
Aver. No. Sons/Daughters	
at Home	1.2

HOUSING

2001 Estimates:	
Occupied Private Dwellings	7,204
Owned	4,479
Rented	2,725
Single-Detached House	2,584
Semi-Detached House	1,436
Row Houses	220
Apartment, 5+ Storeys	837
Owned Apartment, 5+ Storeys	63
Apartment, 5 or Fewer Storeys	1,943
Apartment, Detached Duplex	96
Other Single-Attached	88

VEHICLES

2001 Estimates:	
Model Yrs. '81-'96, No.	8,194
% Total	49.36
Model Yrs. '97-'98, No.	4,808
% Total	28.97
'99 Vehicles registered in	
Model Yr. '99, No.	3,597
% Total	21.67
Total No. '81-'99	16,599

LEGAL MARITAL STATUS

2001 Estimates: (Age 15+)	
Single (Never Married)	4,612
Legally Married	
(Not Separated)	8,497
Legally Married (Separated)	273
Widowed	1,283
Divorced	889

Québec

Mont-Royal
(Ville)
Montréal CMA
(Cont'd)

PSYTE CATEGORIES

2001 Estimates	No. of House-holds	% of Total Hhds.	Index
Canadian Establishment	327	4.54	2,727
The Affluentials	2,156	29.93	4,681
Urban Gentry	2,598	36.06	2,007
Aging Erudites	317	4.40	292
High Rise Sunsets	741	10.29	719
Young Urban Professionals	352	4.89	258
Young Urban Mix	362	5.02	237
Urban Bohemia	223	3.10	265

FINANCIAL P$YTE

2001 Estimates	No. of House-holds	% of Total Hhds.	Index
Platinum Estates	2,483	34.47	4,277
Four Star Investors	2,598	36.06	718
Urban Heights	669	9.29	216
Bills & Wills	362	5.02	61
Revolving Renters	741	10.29	224
Young Urban Struggle	223	3.10	65

HOME LANGUAGE

2001 Estimates:		% Total
English	7,437	40.07
French	7,649	41.21
Arabic	684	3.69
Armenian	215	1.16
Bulgarian	11	0.06
Chinese	111	0.60
Czech	15	0.08
German	11	0.06
Greek	464	2.50
Hebrew	15	0.08
Hindi	26	0.14
Hungarian	111	0.60
Italian	129	0.70
Korean	10	0.05
Latvian (Lettish)	15	0.08
Persian (Farsi)	93	0.50
Polish	15	0.08
Portuguese	62	0.33
Romanian	20	0.11
Russian	48	0.26
Serbian	36	0.19
Spanish	52	0.28
Tamil	31	0.17
Ukrainian	10	0.05
Vietnamese	442	2.38
Other Languages	26	0.14
Multiple Responses	823	4.43
Total	18,561	100.00

BUILDING PERMITS

	1999	1998	1997
		$000	
Value	11,340	24,288	16,284

HOMES BUILT

	1999	1998	1997
No	43	57	39

TAXATION

Income Class:	1997	% Total
Under $5,000	1,600	11.87
$5,000-$10,000	1,220	9.05
$10,000-$15,000	1,340	9.94
$15,000-$20,000	970	7.20
$20,000-$25,000	800	5.93
$25,000-$30,000	810	6.01
$30,000-$40,000	1,300	9.64
$40,000-$50,000	1,030	7.64
$50,000 +	4,410	32.72
Total Returns, No.	13,480	
Total Income, $000	812,747	
Total Taxable Returns	10,140	
Total Tax, $000	151,941	
Average Income, $	60,293	
Average Tax, $	14,984	

VITAL STATISTICS

	1997	1996	1995	1994
Births	157	138	162	168
Deaths	190	141	177	157
Natural Increase	-33	-3	-15	11
Marriages	89	87	78	77

Note: Latest available data.

MEDIA INFO
see Montréal, CMA

Mont-Saint-Hilaire
(Ville)
Montréal CMA

In census division La Vallée-du-Richelieu.

POPULATION

July 1, 2001 Estimate	13,880
% Cdn. Total	0.04
% Change, '96 -'01	4.37
Avg. Annual Growth Rate, %	0.86
2003 Projected Population	14,362
2006 Projected Population	15,249
2001 Households Estimate	5,367
2003 Projected Households	5,605
2006 Projected Households	6,041

INCOME

% Above/Below National Average	+26
2001 Total Income Estimate	$369,760,000
% Cdn. Total	0.06
2001 Average Hhld. Income	$68,900
2001 Per Capita	$26,600
2003 Projected Total Income	$409,680,000
2006 Projected Total Income	$484,080,000

RETAIL SALES

% Above/Below National Average	-59
2001 Retail Sales Estimate	$50,600,000
% Cdn. Total	0.02
2001 per Household	$9,400
2001 per Capita	$3,600
2001 No. of Establishments	114
2003 Projected Retail Sales	$55,730,000
2006 Projected Retail Sales	$64,660,000

POPULATION

2001 Estimates:		
Total		13,880
Male		6,820
Female		7,060
Age Groups	Male	Female
0-4	351	338
5-9	405	380
10-14	462	424
15-19	546	497
20-24	522	453
25-29	422	356
30-34	393	387
35-39	469	529
40-44	568	648
45-49	624	691
50-54	585	628
55-59	469	472
60-64	336	348
65-69	250	266
70+	418	643

DAYTIME POPULATION

2001 Estimates:	
Working Population	2,465
At Home Population	6,207
Total	8,672

INCOME

2001 Estimates:	
Avg. Household Income	$68,895
Avg. Family Income	$78,107
Per Capita Income	$26,640
Male:	
Avg. Employment Income	$46,311
Avg. Employment Income (Full Time)	$57,419
Female:	
Avg. Employment Income	$27,050
Avg. Employment Income (Full Time)	$36,822

DISPOSABLE & DISCRETIONARY INCOME

2001 Estimates:	Per Hhld.
Disposable Income	$45,129
Discretionary Income 1 (minus Food & Shelter)	$29,687
Discretionary Income 2 (minus Food, Shelter, & Other Expenditures)	$19,641

LIQUID ASSETS

1999 Estimates:	Per Hhld.
Equity Investments	$105,556
Interest Bearing Investments	$84,668
Total Liquid Assets	$190,224

CREDIT DATA

July 2000:	
Pool of Credit	$123,291,713
Revolving Credit, No.	28,311
Fixed Loans, No.	8,254
Avg. Credit Limit, per Person	$11,379
Avg. Spent, per Person	$4,962
Satisfactory Ratings, No. per Person	3.21
Avg. No. of Cards, per Person	1.31

LABOUR FORCE

2001 Estimates:	
Male:	
In the Labour Force	4,263
Participation Rate	76.1
Employed	4,122
Unemployed	141
Unemployment Rate	3.3
Not in Labour Force	1,339
Female:	
In the Labour Force	3,642
Participation Rate	61.5
Employed	3,512
Unemployed	130
Unemployment Rate	3.6
Not in Labour Force	2,276

OCCUPATIONS BY MAJOR GROUPS

2001 Estimates:	Male	Female
Management	799	253
Business, Finance & Admin.	418	1,204
Natural & Applied Sciences & Related	478	119
Health	156	355
Social Sciences, Gov't Services & Religion	108	131
Education	181	355
Arts, Culture, Recreation & Sport	126	178
Sales & Service	794	805
Trades, Transport & Equipment Operators & Related	723	11
Primary Industries	122	70
Processing, Mfg. & Utilities	269	89

LEVEL OF SCHOOLING

2001 Estimates:	
Population 15 years +	11,520
Less than Grade 9	947
Grades 9-13 w/o Certif.	1,574
Grade 9-13 with Certif.	2,088
Trade Certif./Dip.	358
Non-Univ. w/o Certif./Dip.	910
Non-Univ. with Certif./Dip.	2,084
Univ. w/o Degree	1,221
Univ. w/o Degree/Certif.	176
Univ. with Certif.	1,045
Univ. with Degree	2,338

Mont-Saint-Hilaire
(Ville)
Montréal CMA
(Cont'd)

AVERAGE HOUSEHOLD EXPENDITURES

2001 Estimates:
Food	$7,906
Shelter	$9,963
Clothing	$2,854
Transportation	$7,795
Health & Personal Care	$2,457
Recr'n, Read'g & Education	$4,213
Taxes & Securities	$19,944
Other	$9,083
Total Expenditures	$64,215

PRIVATE HOUSEHOLDS

2001 Estimates:
Private Households, Total	5,367
Pop. in Private Households	13,687
Average no. per Household	2.6

FAMILIES

2001 Estimates:
Families in Private Households	4,108
Husband-Wife Families	3,594
Lone-Parent Families	514
Aver. No. Persons per Family	3.0
Aver. No. Sons/Daughters at Home	1.2

HOUSING

2001 Estimates:
Occupied Private Dwellings	5,367
Owned	4,012
Rented	1,355
Single-Detached House	3,692
Semi-Detached House	255
Row Houses	54
Apartment, 5+ Storeys	119
Apartment, 5 or Fewer Storeys	1,090
Apartment, Detached Duplex	102
Other Single-Attached	17
Movable Dwellings	38

VEHICLES

2001 Estimates:
Model Yrs. '81-'96, No.	6,993
% Total	73.98
Model Yrs. '97-'98, No.	1,604
% Total	16.97
'99 Vehicles registered in Model Yr. '99, No.	856
% Total	9.06
Total No. '81-'99	9,453

LEGAL MARITAL STATUS

2001 Estimates: (Age 15+)
Single (Never Married)	4,044
Legally Married (Not Separated)	5,385
Legally Married (Separated)	273
Widowed	652
Divorced	1,166

PSYTE CATEGORIES

2001 Estimates	No. of House-holds	% of Total Hhds.	Index
Technocrafts & Bureaucrats	502	9.35	332
Stable Suburban Families	381	7.10	545
Participation Quebec	2,261	42.13	1,462
New Quebec Rows	425	7.92	723
Quebec Melange	893	16.64	628
Old Quebec Walkups	470	8.76	478
Aging Quebec Urbanites	435	8.11	2,809

FINANCIAL P$YTE

2001 Estimates	No. of House-holds	% of Total Hhds.	Index
Successful Suburbanites	883	16.45	248
Mortgages & Minivans	2,686	50.05	758
Country Credit	893	16.64	246
Loan Parent Stress	905	16.86	290

HOME LANGUAGE

2001 Estimates:		% Total
English	689	4.96
French	12,959	93.36
Dutch	11	0.08
Italian	11	0.08
Russian	26	0.19
Serbian	31	0.22
Vietnamese	21	0.15
Multiple Responses	132	0.95
Total	13,880	100.00

BUILDING PERMITS

	1999	1998	1997
		$000	
Value	20,480	20,204	18,580

HOMES BUILT

	1999	1998	1997
No	144	161	250

TAXATION

Income Class:	1997	% Total
Under $5,000	1,080	10.82
$5,000-$10,000	1,160	11.62
$10,000-$15,000	1,240	12.42
$15,000-$20,000	840	8.42
$20,000-$25,000	760	7.62
$25,000-$30,000	760	7.62
$30,000-$40,000	1,240	12.42
$40,000-$50,000	910	9.12
$50,000 +	2,000	20.04
Total Returns, No.	9,980	
Total Income, $000	344,694	
Total Taxable Returns	7,520	
Total Tax, $000	48,167	
Average Income, $	34,538	
Average Tax, $	6,405	

VITAL STATISTICS

	1997	1996	1995	1994
Births	132	122	120	137
Deaths	56	60	67	82
Natural Increase	76	62	53	55
Marriages	69	56	48	55

Note: Latest available data.

MEDIA INFO
see Montréal, CMA

Montréal
(Ville)
Montréal CMA

In census division Communauté urbaine de Montréal.

POPULATION

July 1, 2001 Estimate	1,027,655
% Cdn. Total	3.30
% Change, '96 -'01	-0.70
Avg. Annual Growth Rate, %	-0.14
2003 Projected Population	1,037,438
2006 Projected Population	1,057,438
2001 Households Estimate	489,281
2003 Projected Households	498,440
2006 Projected Households	513,438

INCOME

% Above/Below National Average	-16
2001 Total Income Estimate	$18,126,170,000
% Cdn. Total	2.76
2001 Average Hhld. Income	$37,000
2001 Per Capita	$17,600
2003 Projected Total Income	$19,200,040,000
2006 Projected Total Income	$21,039,880,000

RETAIL SALES

% Above/Below National Average	-24
2001 Retail Sales Estimate	$6,981,840,000
% Cdn. Total	2.51
2001 per Household	$14,300
2001 per Capita	$6,800
2001 No. of Establishments	9,615
2003 Projected Retail Sales	$7,591,600,000
2006 Projected Retail Sales	$8,536,210,000

POPULATION

2001 Estimates:
Total	1,027,655
Male	494,634
Female	533,021

Age Groups	Male	Female
0-4	31,201	29,754
5-9	27,733	26,646
10-14	24,245	23,464
15-19	24,453	23,803
20-24	30,324	30,862
25-29	38,841	38,850
30-34	46,029	43,079
35-39	47,666	43,783
40-44	43,681	41,750
45-49	37,964	38,414
50-54	31,722	33,704
55-59	25,806	28,806
60-64	22,178	26,247
65-69	19,932	25,617
70+	42,859	78,242

DAYTIME POPULATION

2001 Estimates:
Working Population	711,291
At Home Population	585,831
Total	1,297,122

INCOME

2001 Estimates:
Avg. Household Income	$37,047
Avg. Family Income	$46,301
Per Capita Income	$17,638

Male:
Avg. Employment Income	$28,223
Avg. Employment Income (Full Time)	$38,597

Female:
Avg. Employment Income	$21,836
Avg. Employment Income (Full Time)	$31,391

Québec

DISPOSABLE & DISCRETIONARY INCOME

2001 Estimates:	Per Hhld.
Disposable Income	$24,937
Discretionary Income 1 (minus Food & Shelter)	$13,950
Discretionary Income 2 (minus Food, Shelter, & Other Expenditures)	$8,334

LIQUID ASSETS

1999 Estimates:	Per Hhld.
Equity Investments	$40,385
Interest Bearing Investments	$43,138
Total Liquid Assets	$83,523

CREDIT DATA

July 2000:
Pool of Credit	$5,833,936,076
Revolving Credit, No.	1,742,299
Fixed Loans, No.	408,737
Avg. Credit Limit, per Person	$6,234
Avg. Spent, per Person	$2,644
Satisfactory Ratings, No. per Person	2.20
Avg. No. of Cards, per Person	0.98

LABOUR FORCE

2001 Estimates:
Male:
In the Labour Force	275,406
Participation Rate	66.9
Employed	240,152
Unemployed	35,254
Unemployment Rate	12.8
Not in Labour Force	136,049

Female:
In the Labour Force	229,688
Participation Rate	50.7
Employed	207,667
Unemployed	22,021
Unemployment Rate	9.6
Not in Labour Force	223,469

OCCUPATIONS BY MAJOR GROUPS

2001 Estimates:	Male	Female
Management	23,556	12,121
Business, Finance & Admin.	33,776	63,528
Natural & Applied Sciences & Related	22,684	5,858
Health	7,032	18,033
Social Sciences, Gov't Services & Religion	7,069	8,931
Education	9,445	12,127
Arts, Culture, Recreation & Sport	14,309	13,011
Sales & Service	64,522	57,161
Trades, Transport & Equipment Operators & Related	41,612	3,297
Primary Industries	1,628	356
Processing, Mfg. & Utilities	27,741	20,726

Québec

Montréal
(Ville)
Montréal CMA
(Cont'd)

LEVEL OF SCHOOLING

2001 Estimates:
Population 15 years + ...864,612
Less than Grade 9. 171,135
Grades 9-13 w/o Certif. 127,467
Grade 9-13 with Certif. 122,537
Trade Certif. /Dip. 23,290
Non-Univ. w/o Certif./Dip. 60,672
Non-Univ. with Certif./Dip. 110,556
Univ. w/o Degree 93,585
  Univ. w/o Degree/Certif. 23,200
  Univ. with Certif. 70,385
Univ. with Degree 155,370

AVERAGE HOUSEHOLD EXPENDITURES

2001 Estimates:
Food $5,204
Shelter $7,612
Clothing. $1,730
Transportation. $3,724
Health & Personal Care $1,613
Recr'n, Read'g & Education $2,610
Taxes & Securities $9,179
Other $5,951
Total Expenditures $37,623

PRIVATE HOUSEHOLDS

2001 Estimates:
Private Households, Total 489,281
Pop. in Private Households 996,713
Average no. per Household 2.0

FAMILIES

2001 Estimates:
Families in Private Households 253,396
Husband-Wife Families 195,768
Lone-Parent Families 57,628
Aver. No. Persons per Family 2.8
Aver. No. Sons/Daughters
  at Home 1.0

HOUSING

2001 Estimates:
Occupied Private Dwellings 489,281
  Owned. 132,550
  Rented. 356,731
Single-Detached House 24,839
Semi-Detached House 14,803
Row Houses 16,055
Apartment, 5+ Storeys 60,429
  Owned Apartment, 5+ Storeys 6,426
Apartment, 5 or Fewer Storeys 351,950
Apartment, Detached Duplex 17,468
Other Single-Attached 3,674
Movable Dwellings. 63

VEHICLES

2001 Estimates:
Model Yrs. '81-'96, No. 302,660
  % Total 73.87
Model Yrs. '97-'98, No. 64,480
  % Total 15.74
'99 Vehicles registered in
  Model Yr. '99, No. 42,592
  % Total 10.40
Total No. '81-'99. 409,732

LEGAL MARITAL STATUS

2001 Estimates: (Age 15+)
Single (Never Married). 390,089
Legally Married
  (Not Separated) 297,484
Legally Married (Separated) 28,412
Widowed 65,678
Divorced 82,949

PSYTE CATEGORIES

2001 Estimates	No. of House -holds	% of Total Hhds.	Index
The Affluentials	857	0.18.	27
Urban Gentry.	4,025	0.82.	46
Stable Suburban Families.	743	0.15.	12
Old Bungalow Burbs. . .	304	0.06.	4
Suburban Nesters	4,356	0.89.	56
Brie & Chablis.	2,935	0.60.	67
Aging Erudites	160	0.03.	2
Participation Quebec	3,581	0.73.	25
New Quebec Rows . . .	11,195	2.29.	209
Quebec Melange	5,104	1.04.	39
Traditional French Cdn. Families	103	0.02.	1
Europa	13,210	2.70.	217
High Rise Melting Pot.	1,495	0.31.	20
Conservative Homebodies	88	0.02.	
High Rise Sunsets . . .	4,497	0.92.	64
Young Urban Professionals	23,159	4.73.	249
Young Urban Mix . . .	2,378	0.49.	23
Young Urban Intelligentsia. . . .	25,550	5.22.	343
University Enclaves	1,494	0.31.	15
Young City Singles . . .	1,645	0.34.	15
Urban Bohemia.	78,371	16.02.	1,369
Town Renters	124	0.03.	3
Euro Quebec	35,527	7.26.	828
Old Quebec Walkups . . .	99,419	20.32.	1,109
Quebec Town Elders. . .	1,285	0.26.	9
Aging Quebec Urbanites.	9,531	1.95.	675
Quebec's New Urban Mosaic	106,579	21.78.	904
Aged Pensioners. . .	5,937	1.21.	91
Big City Stress	35,377	7.23.	640
Old Grey Towers . . .	4,447	0.91.	164

FINANCIAL P$YTE

2001 Estimates	No. of House -holds	% of Total Hhds.	Index
Platinum Estates.	857	0.18.	22
Four Star Investors	4,025	0.82.	16
Successful Suburbanites. . . .	743	0.15.	2
Canadian Comfort . . .	4,356	0.89.	9
Urban Heights.	26,254	5.37.	125
Miners & Credit-Liners	304	0.06.	2
Mortgages & Minivans. . . .	14,776	3.02.	46
Dollars & Sense . . .	13,210	2.70.	103
Bills & Wills	2,466	0.50.	6
Country Credit. . . .	5,207	1.06.	16
Revolving Renters. . .	4,497	0.92.	20
Young Urban Struggle. . . .	105,415	21.54.	455
Loan Parent Stress . . .	145,762	29.79.	512
Towering Debt	3,264	0.67.	9
NSF	141,956	29.01.	820
Senior Survivors . . .	10,384	2.12.	113

HOME LANGUAGE

2001 Estimates:		% Total
English	157,327	15.31
French	626,533	60.97
Arabic.	13,267	1.29
Armenian	4,506	0.44
Bengali	4,564	0.44
Bulgarian	679	0.07
Chinese	15,353	1.49
Creoles	9,264	0.90
Greek	12,332	1.20
Gujarati	2,360	0.23
Hebrew.	539	0.05
Hungarian	1,402	0.14
Italian	31,686	3.08
Khmer (Cambodian)	2,462	0.24
Korean	1,159	0.11
Lao	1,406	0.14
Persian (Farsi).	2,631	0.26
Polish	4,263	0.41
Portuguese	10,260	1.00
Punjabi	2,243	0.22
Romanian	3,539	0.34
Russian	5,315	0.52
Spanish	27,212	2.65
Tagalog (Pilipino) . . .	3,689	0.36
Tamil.	6,240	0.61
Turkish	1,818	0.18
Ukrainian	1,135	0.11
Urdu	1,636	0.16
Vietnamese	12,852	1.25
Yiddish	1,586	0.15
Other Languages	7,311	0.71
Multiple Responses . . .	51,086	4.97
Total	1,027,655	100.00

BUILDING PERMITS

	1999	1998 $000	1997
Value	686,471	697,025	533,377

HOMES BUILT

	1999	1998	1997
No.	1,355	1,474	1,355

TAXATION

Income Class:	1997	% Total
Under $5,000	106,200	13.64
$5,000-$10,000	144,840	18.61
$10,000-$15,000	141,570	18.19
$15,000-$20,000	82,040	10.54
$20,000-$25,000	62,950	8.09
$25,000-$30,000	55,320	7.11
$30,000-$40,000	74,870	9.62
$40,000-$50,000	44,610	5.73
$50,000 + ...	66,100	8.49

Total Returns, No. 778,480
Total Income, $000. . .17,886,251
Total Taxable
  Returns. 476,350
Total Tax, $000 2,091,974
Average Income, $ 22,976
Average Tax, $ 4,392

VITAL STATISTICS

	1997	1996	1995	1994
Births . . .	12,302	13,442	13,405.	13,791
Deaths . . .	9,666	9,825	10,023.	9,759
Natural Increase .	2,636	3,617	3,382	4,032
Marriages.	5,953	5,576	5,881	6,075

Note: Latest available data.

MEDIA INFO
  see Montréal, CMA

Montréal-Nord
(Ville)
Montréal CMA

In census division Communauté urbaine de Montréal.

POPULATION

July 1, 2001 Estimate	79,557
% Cdn. Total	0.26
% Change, '96 -'01	-4.23
Avg. Annual Growth Rate, %	-0.86
2003 Projected Population	78,893
2006 Projected Population	78,301
2001 Households Estimate	34,959
2003 Projected Households	34,549
2006 Projected Households	34,037

INCOME

% Above/Below National Average	-28
2001 Total Income Estimate	$1,208,290,000
% Cdn. Total	0.18
2001 Average Hhld. Income	$34,600
2001 Per Capita	$15,200
2003 Projected Total Income	$1,245,590,000
2006 Projected Total Income	$1,311,320,000

RETAIL SALES

% Above/Below National Average	-27
2001 Retail Sales Estimate	$516,960,000
% Cdn. Total	0.19
2001 per Household	$14,800
2001 per Capita	$6,500
2001 No. of Establishments	644
2003 Projected Retail Sales	$555,840,000
2006 Projected Retail Sales	$612,530,000

POPULATION

2001 Estimates:

Total		79,557
Male		36,106
Female		43,451

Age Groups	Male	Female
0-4	2,308	2,217
5-9	2,236	2,305
10-14	1,995	2,072
15-19	2,107	2,121
20-24	2,300	2,272
25-29	2,315	2,434
30-34	2,516	2,609
35-39	2,653	2,791
40-44	2,521	2,915
45-49	2,475	3,005
50-54	2,408	2,910
55-59	2,245	2,736
60-64	2,106	2,612
65-69	1,891	2,514
70+	4,030	7,938

DAYTIME POPULATION

2001 Estimates:

Working Population	19,940
At Home Population	48,757
Total	68,697

INCOME

2001 Estimates:

Avg. Household Income	$34,563
Avg. Family Income	$40,869
Per Capita Income	$15,188
Male:	
Avg. Employment Income	$25,163
Avg. Employment Income (Full Time)	$33,576
Female:	
Avg. Employment Income	$18,722
Avg. Employment Income (Full Time)	$26,786

DISPOSABLE & DISCRETIONARY INCOME

2001 Estimates:	Per Hhld.
Disposable Income	$24,714
Discretionary Income 1 (minus Food & Shelter)	$13,345
Discretionary Income 2 (minus Food, Shelter, & Other Expenditures)	$7,696

LIQUID ASSETS

1999 Estimates:	Per Hhld.
Equity Investments	$32,307
Interest Bearing Investments	$38,788
Total Liquid Assets	$71,095

CREDIT DATA

July 2000:

Pool of Credit	$394,060,192
Revolving Credit, No.	140,004
Fixed Loans, No.	35,408
Avg. Credit Limit, per Person	$5,346
Avg. Spent, per Person	$2,310
Satisfactory Ratings, No. per Person	2.25
Avg. No. of Cards, per Person	0.87

LABOUR FORCE

2001 Estimates:

Male:	
In the Labour Force	19,079
Participation Rate	64.5
Employed	16,569
Unemployed	2,510
Unemployment Rate	13.2
Not in Labour Force	10,488
Female:	
In the Labour Force	16,396
Participation Rate	44.5
Employed	14,379
Unemployed	2,017
Unemployment Rate	12.3
Not in Labour Force	20,461

OCCUPATIONS BY MAJOR GROUPS

2001 Estimates:	Male	Female
Management	1,269	600
Business, Finance & Admin.	2,130	5,016
Natural & Applied Sciences & Related	930	167
Health	276	1,318
Social Sciences, Gov't Services & Religion	250	343
Education	298	479
Arts, Culture, Recreation & Sport	281	327
Sales & Service	4,385	4,219
Trades, Transport & Equipment Operators & Related	5,029	347
Primary Industries	98	39
Processing, Mfg. & Utilities	2,728	2,233

LEVEL OF SCHOOLING

2001 Estimates:

Population 15 years +	66,424
Less than Grade 9	17,648
Grades 9-13 w/o Certif.	12,916
Grade 9-13 with Certif.	11,763
Trade Certif. /Dip.	2,335
Non-Univ. w/o Certif./Dip.	5,446
Non-Univ. with Certif./Dip.	8,342
Univ. w/o Degree	4,211
Univ. w/o Degree/Certif.	947
Univ. with Certif.	3,264
Univ. with Degree	3,763

AVERAGE HOUSEHOLD EXPENDITURES

2001 Estimates:

Food	$5,200
Shelter	$7,545
Clothing	$1,694
Transportation	$3,727
Health & Personal Care	$1,452
Recr'n, Read'g & Education	$2,484
Taxes & Securities	$7,635
Other	$5,957
Total Expenditures	$35,694

PRIVATE HOUSEHOLDS

2001 Estimates:

Private Households, Total	34,959
Pop. in Private Households	77,959
Average no. per Household	2.2

FAMILIES

2001 Estimates:

Families in Private Households	21,966
Husband-Wife Families	16,129
Lone-Parent Families	5,837
Aver. No. Persons per Family	2.8
Aver. No. Sons/Daughters at Home	1.1

HOUSING

2001 Estimates:

Occupied Private Dwellings	34,959
Owned	9,779
Rented	25,180
Single-Detached House	2,636
Semi-Detached House	1,681
Row Houses	757
Apartment, 5+ Storeys	4,086
Owned Apartment, 5+ Storeys	445
Apartment, 5 or Fewer Storeys	24,453
Apartment, Detached Duplex	1,224
Other Single-Attached	122

VEHICLES

2001 Estimates:

Model Yrs. '81-'96, No.	26,312
% Total	80.34
Model Yrs. '97-'98, No.	3,984
% Total	12.16
'99 Vehicles registered in Model Yr. '99, No.	2,456
% Total	7.50
Total No. '81-'99	32,752

LEGAL MARITAL STATUS

2001 Estimates: (Age 15+)

Single (Never Married)	24,364
Legally Married (Not Separated)	25,850
Legally Married (Separated)	2,508
Widowed	6,659
Divorced	7,043

PSYTE CATEGORIES

2001 Estimates	No. of House -holds	% of Total Hhds.	Index
Europa	1,677	4.80	386
High Rise Sunsets	502	1.44	100
Euro Quebec	17,840	51.03	5,818
Old Quebec Walkups	4,607	13.18	719
Aging Quebec Urbanites	418	1.20	414
Quebec's New Urban Mosaic	3,966	11.34	471
Aged Pensioners	691	1.98	149
Big City Stress	2,317	6.63	587
Old Grey Towers	2,599	7.43	1,342

FINANCIAL PSYTE

2001 Estimates	No. of House -holds	% of Total Hhds.	Index
Dollars & Sense	1,677	4.80	184
Revolving Renters	502	1.44	31
Loan Parent Stress	22,865	65.41	1,123
NSF	6,283	17.97	508
Senior Survivors	3,290	9.41	499

Québec

HOME LANGUAGE

2001 Estimates:		% Total
English	5,744	7.22
French	56,611	71.16
Arabic	1,619	2.04
Chinese	273	0.34
Creoles	2,054	2.58
Greek	182	0.23
Hungarian	40	0.05
Italian	5,341	6.71
Khmer (Cambodian)	90	0.11
Persian (Farsi)	56	0.07
Polish	96	0.12
Portuguese	295	0.37
Punjabi	86	0.11
Romanian	190	0.24
Russian	104	0.13
Spanish	1,773	2.23
Turkish	109	0.14
Vietnamese	146	0.18
Other Languages	331	0.42
Multiple Responses	4,417	5.55
Total	79,557	100.00

BUILDING PERMITS

	1999	1998	1997
		$000	
Value	25,286	15,726	10,334

HOMES BUILT

	1999	1998	1997
No	9	3	7

TAXATION

Income Class:	1997	% Total
Under $5,000	7,530	13.05
$5,000-$10,000	10,560	18.30
$10,000-$15,000	11,810	20.47
$15,000-$20,000	7,200	12.48
$20,000-$25,000	5,340	9.25
$25,000-$30,000	4,260	7.38
$30,000-$40,000	5,430	9.41
$40,000-$50,000	2,880	4.99
$50,000+	2,680	4.64
Total Returns, No.	57,700	
Total Income, $000	1,106,500	
Total Taxable Returns	35,140	
Total Tax, $000	105,454	
Average Income, $	19,177	
Average Tax, $	3,001	

VITAL STATISTICS

	1997	1996	1995	1994
Births	1,048	1,019	1,056	1,011
Deaths	914	796	772	827
Natural Increase	134	223	284	184
Marriages	99	134	156	139

Note: Latest available data.

MEDIA INFO
see Montréal, CMA

Québec

Outremont
(Ville)
Montréal CMA

In census division Communauté urbaine de Montréal.

POPULATION

July 1, 2001 Estimate	22,556
% Cdn. Total	0.07
% Change, '96 -'01	-1.84
Avg. Annual Growth Rate, %	-0.37
2003 Projected Population	22,635
2006 Projected Population	22,877
2001 Households Estimate	9,437
2003 Projected Households	9,437
2006 Projected Households	9,464

INCOME

% Above/Below National Average	+58
2001 Total Income Estimate	$749,170,000
% Cdn. Total	0.11
2001 Average Hhld. Income	$79,400
2001 Per Capita	$33,200
2003 Projected Total Income	$786,340,000
2006 Projected Total Income	$850,710,000

RETAIL SALES

% Above/Below National Average	-59
2001 Retail Sales Estimate	$81,790,000
% Cdn. Total	0.03
2001 per Household	$8,700
2001 per Capita	$3,600
2001 No. of Establishments	163
2003 Projected Retail Sales	$87,190,000
2006 Projected Retail Sales	$95,690,000

POPULATION

2001 Estimates:

Total		22,556
Male		10,146
Female		12,410
Age Groups	Male	Female
0-4	621	596
5-9	663	634
10-14	675	653
15-19	714	688
20-24	751	724
25-29	720	731
30-34	696	749
35-39	706	794
40-44	750	899
45-49	799	990
50-54	756	931
55-59	615	752
60-64	479	594
65-69	361	527
70+	840	2,148

DAYTIME POPULATION

2001 Estimates:

Working Population	4,042
At Home Population	10,998
Total	15,040

INCOME

2001 Estimates:

Avg. Household Income	$79,387
Avg. Family Income	$98,489
Per Capita Income	$33,214
Male:	
Avg. Employment Income	$57,397
Avg. Employment Income (Full Time)	$78,388
Female:	
Avg. Employment Income	$31,967
Avg. Employment Income (Full Time)	$46,058

DISPOSABLE & DISCRETIONARY INCOME

2001 Estimates:	Per Hhld.
Disposable Income	$46,173
Discretionary Income 1 (minus Food & Shelter)	$29,498
Discretionary Income 2 (minus Food, Shelter, & Other Expenditures)	$20,223

LIQUID ASSETS

1999 Estimates:	Per Hhld.
Equity Investments	$176,144
Interest Bearing Investments	$109,485
Total Liquid Assets	$285,629

CREDIT DATA

July 2000:

Pool of Credit	$202,815,037
Revolving Credit, No.	41,014
Fixed Loans, No.	7,931
Avg. Credit Limit, per Person	$10,523
Avg. Spent, per Person	$4,007
Satisfactory Ratings, No. per Person	2.48
Avg. No. of Cards, per Person	1.26

LABOUR FORCE

2001 Estimates:

Male:	
In the Labour Force	6,125
Participation Rate	74.8
Employed	5,908
Unemployed	217
Unemployment Rate	3.5
Not in Labour Force	2,062
Female:	
In the Labour Force	5,899
Participation Rate	56.0
Employed	5,665
Unemployed	234
Unemployment Rate	4.0
Not in Labour Force	4,628

OCCUPATIONS BY MAJOR GROUPS

2001 Estimates:	Male	Female
Management	1,011	681
Business, Finance & Admin.	731	1,291
Natural & Applied Sciences & Related	618	233
Health	439	513
Social Sciences, Gov't Services & Religion	455	405
Education	734	736
Arts, Culture, Recreation & Sport	578	802
Sales & Service	1,007	1,003
Trades, Transport & Equipment Operators & Related	274	10
Primary Industries	20	n.a.
Processing, Mfg. & Utilities	142	20

LEVEL OF SCHOOLING

2001 Estimates:

Population 15 years +	18,714
Less than Grade 9	1,173
Grades 9-13 w/o Certif.	1,507
Grade 9-13 with Certif.	1,809
Trade Certif. /Dip.	399
Non-Univ. w/o Certif./Dip.	1,097
Non-Univ. with Certif./Dip.	1,797
Univ. w/o Degree	2,525
Univ. w/o Degree/Certif.	594
Univ. with Certif.	1,931
Univ. with Degree	8,407

AVERAGE HOUSEHOLD EXPENDITURES

2001 Estimates:

Food	$7,269
Shelter	$12,825
Clothing	$3,152
Transportation	$6,656
Health & Personal Care	$2,396
Recr'n, Read'g & Education	$5,056
Taxes & Securities	$22,094
Other	$11,774
Total Expenditures	$71,222

PRIVATE HOUSEHOLDS

2001 Estimates:

Private Households, Total	9,437
Pop. in Private Households	21,800
Average no. per Household	2.3

FAMILIES

2001 Estimates:

Families in Private Households	5,696
Husband-Wife Families	4,572
Lone-Parent Families	1,124
Aver. No. Persons per Family	3.0
Aver. No. Sons/Daughters at Home	1.3

HOUSING

2001 Estimates:

Occupied Private Dwellings	9,437
Owned	4,187
Rented	5,250
Single-Detached House	708
Semi-Detached House	884
Row Houses	586
Apartment, 5+ Storeys	2,040
Owned Apartment, 5+ Storeys	267
Apartment, 5 or Fewer Storeys	4,874
Apartment, Detached Duplex	314
Other Single-Attached	31

VEHICLES

2001 Estimates:

Model Yrs. '81-'96, No.	6,792
% Total	69.73
Model Yrs. '97-'98, No.	1,786
% Total	18.33
'99 Vehicles registered in Model Yr. '99, No.	1,163
% Total	11.94
Total No. '81-'99	9,741

LEGAL MARITAL STATUS

2001 Estimates: (Age 15+)

Single (Never Married)	8,262
Legally Married (Not Separated)	6,896
Legally Married (Separated)	503
Widowed	1,268
Divorced	1,785

PSYTE CATEGORIES

2001 Estimates	No. of House-holds	% of Total Hhds.	Index
Canadian Establishment	541	5.73	3,445
The Affluentials	593	6.28	983
Urban Gentry	2,216	23.48	1,307
High Rise Sunsets	352	3.73	261
Young Urban Professionals	4,639	49.16	2,591
Young Urban Mix	429	4.55	215
Young Urban Intelligentsia	128	1.36	89
Old Grey Towers	368	3.90	704

FINANCIAL P$YTE

2001 Estimates	No. of House-holds	% of Total Hhds.	Index
Platinum Estates	1,134	12.02	1,491
Four Star Investors	2,216	23.48	467
Urban Heights	4,639	49.16	1,143
Bills & Wills	429	4.55	55
Revolving Renters	352	3.73	81
Young Urban Struggle	128	1.36	29
Senior Survivors	368	3.90	207

HOME LANGUAGE

2001 Estimates:		% Total
English	3,139	13.92
French	15,546	68.92
Arabic	192	0.85
Armenian	45	0.20
Bulgarian	40	0.18
Chinese	80	0.35
Creoles	30	0.13
Greek	313	1.39
Hebrew	30	0.13
Hungarian	30	0.13
Italian	100	0.44
Polish	78	0.35
Portuguese	31	0.14
Russian	20	0.09
Serbo-Croatian	35	0.16
Spanish	85	0.38
Ukrainian	20	0.09
Vietnamese	25	0.11
Yiddish	1,779	7.89
Other Languages	50	0.22
Multiple Responses	888	3.94
Total	22,556	100.00

BUILDING PERMITS

	1999	1998 $000	1997
Value	14,223	14,582	8,440

HOMES BUILT

	1999	1998	1997
No.	61	54	n.a.

TAXATION

Income Class:	1997	% Total
Under $5,000	1,550	11.36
$5,000-$10,000	1,420	10.40
$10,000-$15,000	1,490	10.92
$15,000-$20,000	940	6.89
$20,000-$25,000	840	6.15
$25,000-$30,000	780	5.71
$30,000-$40,000	1,410	10.33
$40,000-$50,000	1,200	8.79
$50,000 +	4,020	29.45
Total Returns, No.	13,650	
Total Income, $000	707,400	
Total Taxable Returns	10,140	
Total Tax, $000	125,127	
Average Income, $	51,824	
Average Tax, $	12,340	

VITAL STATISTICS

	1997	1996	1995	1994
Births	274	267	229	232
Deaths	170	117	132	104
Natural Increase	104	150	97	128
Marriages	113	105	82	88

Note: Latest available data.

MEDIA INFO
see Montréal, CMA

Pierrefonds
(Ville)
Montréal CMA

In census division Communauté urbaine de Montréal.

POPULATION

July 1, 2001 Estimate	57,474
% Cdn. Total	0.18
% Change, '96 -'01	6.53
Avg. Annual Growth Rate, %	1.27
2003 Projected Population	60,169
2006 Projected Population	64,516
2001 Households Estimate	21,104
2003 Projected Households	22,032
2006 Projected Households	23,461

INCOME

% Above/Below National Average	same
2001 Total Income Estimate	$1,213,870,000
% Cdn. Total	0.18
2001 Average Hhld. Income	$57,500
2001 Per Capita	$21,100
2003 Projected Total Income	$1,339,640,000
2006 Projected Total Income	$1,555,430,000

RETAIL SALES

% Above/Below National Average	-78
2001 Retail Sales Estimate	$115,390,000
% Cdn. Total	0.04
2001 per Household	$5,500
2001 per Capita	$2,000
2001 No. of Establishments	276
2003 Projected Retail Sales	$128,160,000
2006 Projected Retail Sales	$149,040,000

POPULATION

2001 Estimates:

Total		57,474
Male		27,777
Female		29,697
Age Groups	Male	Female
0-4	1,952	1,911
5-9	2,140	2,075
10-14	2,068	1,977
15-19	1,946	1,864
20-24	1,815	1,761
25-29	1,813	1,847
30-34	2,183	2,282
35-39	2,521	2,655
40-44	2,446	2,590
45-49	2,146	2,253
50-54	1,801	1,877
55-59	1,412	1,550
60-64	1,131	1,332
65-69	926	1,172
70+	1,477	2,551

DAYTIME POPULATION

2001 Estimates:

Working Population	4,895
At Home Population	28,153
Total	33,048

INCOME

2001 Estimates:

Avg. Household Income	$57,519
Avg. Family Income	$62,701
Per Capita Income	$21,120
Male:	
Avg. Employment Income	$38,159
Avg. Employment Income (Full Time)	$48,563
Female:	
Avg. Employment Income	$24,956
Avg. Employment Income (Full Time)	$34,733

DISPOSABLE & DISCRETIONARY INCOME

2001 Estimates:	Per Hhld.
Disposable Income	$39,487
Discretionary Income 1 (minus Food & Shelter)	$25,803
Discretionary Income 2 (minus Food, Shelter, & Other Expenditures)	$17,394

LIQUID ASSETS

1999 Estimates:	Per Hhld.
Equity Investments	$68,886
Interest Bearing Investments	$67,253
Total Liquid Assets	$136,139

CREDIT DATA

July 2000:

Pool of Credit	$495,992,159
Revolving Credit, No.	121,732
Fixed Loans, No.	35,014
Avg. Credit Limit, per Person	$10,482
Avg. Spent, per Person	$4,572
Satisfactory Ratings, No. per Person	3.16
Avg. No. of Cards, per Person	1.26

LABOUR FORCE

2001 Estimates:

Male:	
In the Labour Force	17,025
Participation Rate	78.8
Employed	15,966
Unemployed	1,059
Unemployment Rate	6.2
Not in Labour Force	4,592
Female:	
In the Labour Force	14,075
Participation Rate	59.3
Employed	13,218
Unemployed	857
Unemployment Rate	6.1
Not in Labour Force	9,659

OCCUPATIONS BY MAJOR GROUPS

2001 Estimates:	Male	Female
Management	2,434	1,002
Business, Finance & Admin.	2,243	4,861
Natural & Applied Sciences & Related	2,474	481
Health	197	1,312
Social Sciences, Gov't Services & Religion	239	438
Education	345	580
Arts, Culture, Recreation & Sport	427	529
Sales & Service	3,999	3,556
Trades, Transport & Equipment Operators & Related	2,586	83
Primary Industries	230	10
Processing, Mfg. & Utilities	1,189	614

LEVEL OF SCHOOLING

2001 Estimates:

Population 15 years +	45,351
Less than Grade 9	3,958
Grades 9-13 w/o Certif.	6,509
Grade 9-13 with Certif.	7,430
Trade Certif. /Dip.	1,572
Non-Univ. w/o Certif./Dip.	3,761
Non-Univ. with Certif./Dip.	7,666
Univ. w/o Degree	5,990
Univ. w/o Degree/Certif.	1,447
Univ. with Certif.	4,543
Univ. with Degree	8,465

AVERAGE HOUSEHOLD EXPENDITURES

2001 Estimates:

Food	$6,751
Shelter	$9,174
Clothing	$2,394
Transportation	$6,335
Health & Personal Care	$2,046
Recr'n, Read'g & Education	$3,701
Taxes & Securities	$16,322
Other	$8,322
Total Expenditures	$55,045

PRIVATE HOUSEHOLDS

2001 Estimates:

Private Households, Total	21,104
Pop. in Private Households	56,724
Average no. per Household	2.7

FAMILIES

2001 Estimates:

Families in Private Households	16,080
Husband-Wife Families	13,687
Lone-Parent Families	2,393
Aver. No. Persons per Family	3.1
Aver. No. Sons/Daughters at Home	1.3

HOUSING

2001 Estimates:

Occupied Private Dwellings	21,104
Owned	13,616
Rented	7,488
Single-Detached House	10,528
Semi-Detached House	1,070
Row Houses	1,432
Apartment, 5+ Storeys	905
Owned Apartment, 5+ Storeys	124
Apartment, 5 or Fewer Storeys	6,950
Apartment, Detached Duplex	122
Other Single-Attached	97

VEHICLES

2001 Estimates:

Model Yrs. '81-'96, No.	22,163
% Total	76.20
Model Yrs. '97-'98, No.	4,389
% Total	15.09
'99 Vehicles registered in Model Yr. '99, No.	2,535
% Total	8.72
Total No. '81-'99	29,087

LEGAL MARITAL STATUS

2001 Estimates: (Age 15+)

Single (Never Married)	14,406
Legally Married (Not Separated)	23,722
Legally Married (Separated)	1,152
Widowed	2,292
Divorced	3,779

PSYTE CATEGORIES

2001 Estimates	No. of House -holds	% of Total Hhds.	Index
Mortgaged in Suburbia	407	1.93	139
Technocrafts & Bureaucrats	1,221	5.79	206
Stable Suburban Families	1,026	4.86	373
Old Bungalow Burbs	4,140	19.62	1,184
Aging Erudites	408	1.93	128
Satellite Suburbs	405	1.92	67
Kindergarten Boom	899	4.26	162
Participation Quebec	2,355	11.16	387
New Quebec Rows	2,846	13.49	1,231
Quebec Melange	2,206	10.45	394
High Rise Sunsets	344	1.63	114
Young Urban Mix	1,185	5.62	265
University Enclaves	613	2.90	142
Young City Singles	949	4.50	196
Town Renters	592	2.81	325
Old Quebec Walkups	646	3.06	167
Quebec's New Urban Mosaic	332	1.57	65
Aged Pensioners	162	0.77	58
Big City Stress	339	1.61	142

FINANCIAL P$YTE

2001 Estimates	No. of House -holds	% of Total Hhds.	Index
Successful Suburbanites	2,654	12.58	190
Canadian Comfort	405	1.92	20
Urban Heights	408	1.93	45
Miners & Credit-Liners	4,140	19.62	620
Mortgages & Minivans	6,100	28.90	438
Bills & Wills	1,185	5.62	68
Country Credit	2,206	10.45	155
Revolving Renters	344	1.63	35
Young Urban Struggle	613	2.90	61
Loan Parent Stress	646	3.06	53
Towering Debt	1,541	7.30	94
NSF	671	3.18	90
Senior Survivors	162	0.77	41

HOME LANGUAGE

2001 Estimates:		% Total
English	27,463	47.78
French	20,982	36.51
Arabic	905	1.57
Armenian	207	0.36
Chinese	350	0.61
Creoles	383	0.67
Czech	55	0.10
Dutch	36	0.06
German	75	0.13
Greek	387	0.67
Hindi	33	0.06
Hungarian	70	0.12
Italian	225	0.39
Japanese	32	0.06
Lao	92	0.16
Latvian (Lettish)	38	0.07
Persian (Farsi)	368	0.64
Polish	642	1.12
Portuguese	123	0.21
Punjabi	389	0.68
Romanian	159	0.28
Russian	37	0.06
Slovak	39	0.07
Spanish	345	0.60
Tagalog (Pilipino)	106	0.18
Tamil	121	0.21
Urdu	210	0.37
Vietnamese	155	0.27
Other Languages	604	1.05
Multiple Responses	2,843	4.95
Total	57,474	100.00

BUILDING PERMITS

	1999	1998	1997
		$000	
Value	27,344	27,918	28,837

HOMES BUILT

	1999	1998	1997
No	143	114	108

Québec

Pierrefonds
(Ville)
Montréal CMA
(Cont'd)

TAXATION

Income Class:	1997	% Total
Under $5,000	5,090	13.81
$5,000-$10,000	4,490	12.18
$10,000-$15,000	4,730	12.84
$15,000-$20,000	3,300	8.96
$20,000-$25,000	2,900	7.87
$25,000-$30,000	2,820	7.65
$30,000-$40,000	4,750	12.89
$40,000-$50,000	3,220	8.74
$50,000 +	5,560	15.09

Total Returns, No. ... 36,850
Total Income, $000 ... 1,023,515
Total Taxable
  Returns ... 26,310
Total Tax, $000 ... 131,364
Average Income, $ ... 27,775
Average Tax, $ ... 4,993

VITAL STATISTICS

	1997	1996	1995	1994
Births	790	860	895	893
Deaths	239	244	285	269
Natural Increase	551	616	610	624
Marriages	151	129	142	189

Note: Latest available data.

MEDIA INFO
see Montréal, CMA

Pincourt
(Ville)
Montréal CMA

In census division Vaudreuil-Soulanges.

POPULATION

July 1, 2001 Estimate ... 10,325
% Cdn. Total ... 0.03
% Change, '96 -'01 ... 1.17
Avg. Annual Growth Rate, % ... 0.23
2003 Projected Population ... 10,513
2006 Projected Population ... 10,939
2001 Households Estimate ... 3,560
2003 Projected Households ... 3,628
2006 Projected Households ... 3,787

INCOME

% Above/Below National Average ... +1
2001 Total Income Estimate ... $219,010,000
% Cdn. Total ... 0.03
2001 Average Hhld. Income ... $61,500
2001 Per Capita ... $21,200
2003 Projected Total Income ... $236,280,000
2006 Projected Total Income ... $270,100,000

RETAIL SALES

% Above/Below National Average ... -37
2001 Retail Sales Estimate ... $58,360,000
% Cdn. Total ... 0.02
2001 per Household ... $16,400
2001 per Capita ... $5,700
2001 No. of Establishments ... 58
2003 Projected Retail Sales ... $64,040,000
2006 Projected Retail Sales ... $73,180,000

POPULATION

2001 Estimates:
Total ... 10,325
Male ... 5,149
Female ... 5,176

Age Groups	Male	Female
0-4	325	301
5-9	389	369
10-14	416	398
15-19	413	392
20-24	339	310
25-29	269	260
30-34	317	347
35-39	428	462
40-44	495	506
45-49	461	445
50-54	385	353
55-59	288	259
60-64	215	194
65-69	153	168
70+	256	412

DAYTIME POPULATION

2001 Estimates:
Working Population ... 1,124
At Home Population ... 4,906
Total ... 6,030

INCOME

2001 Estimates:
Avg. Household Income ... $61,518
Avg. Family Income ... $65,454
Per Capita Income ... $21,211
Male:
Avg. Employment Income ... $38,968
Avg. Employment Income
  (Full Time) ... $46,931
Female:
Avg. Employment Income ... $24,285
Avg. Employment Income
  (Full Time) ... $34,464

DISPOSABLE & DISCRETIONARY INCOME

2001 Estimates:	Per Hhld.
Disposable Income	$42,582
Discretionary Income 1 (minus Food & Shelter)	$28,725
Discretionary Income 2 (minus Food, Shelter, & Other Expenditures)	$19,550

LIQUID ASSETS

1999 Estimates:	Per Hhld.
Equity Investments	$70,554
Interest Bearing Investments	$70,542
Total Liquid Assets	$141,096

CREDIT DATA

July 2000:
Pool of Credit ... $85,466,434
Revolving Credit, No. ... 20,492
Fixed Loans, No. ... 7,180
Avg. Credit Limit, per Person ... $10,858
Avg. Spent, per Person ... $5,261
Satisfactory Ratings,
  No. per Person ... 3.35
Avg. No. of Cards, per Person ... 1.20

LABOUR FORCE

2001 Estimates:
Male:
In the Labour Force ... 3,182
Participation Rate ... 79.2
Employed ... 3,083
Unemployed ... 99
Unemployment Rate ... 3.1
Not in Labour Force ... 837
Female:
In the Labour Force ... 2,411
Participation Rate ... 58.7
Employed ... 2,292
Unemployed ... 119
Unemployment Rate ... 4.9
Not in Labour Force ... 1,697

OCCUPATIONS BY MAJOR GROUPS

2001 Estimates:	Male	Female
Management	431	147
Business, Finance & Admin.	388	974
Natural & Applied Sciences & Related	373	55
Health	37	116
Social Sciences, Gov't Services & Religion	32	27
Education	13	124
Arts, Culture, Recreation & Sport	70	60
Sales & Service	700	621
Trades, Transport & Equipment Operators & Related	633	28
Primary Industries	78	n.a.
Processing, Mfg. & Utilities	357	109

LEVEL OF SCHOOLING

2001 Estimates:
Population 15 years + ... 8,127
Less than Grade 9 ... 820
Grades 9-13 w/o Certif. ... 1,581
Grade 9-13 with Certif. ... 1,630
Trade Certif. /Dip. ... 302
Non-Univ. w/o Certif./Dip. ... 793
Non-Univ. with Certif./Dip. ... 1,380
Univ. w/o Degree ... 860
  Univ. w/o Degree/Certif. ... 261
  Univ. with Certif. ... 599
Univ. with Degree ... 761

AVERAGE HOUSEHOLD EXPENDITURES

2001 Estimates:
Food ... $7,345
Shelter ... $8,734
Clothing ... $2,641
Transportation ... $7,161
Health & Personal Care ... $2,245
Recr'n, Read'g & Education ... $3,986
Taxes & Securities ... $18,256
Other ... $8,114
Total Expenditures ... $58,482

PRIVATE HOUSEHOLDS

2001 Estimates:
Private Households, Total ... 3,560
Pop. in Private Households ... 10,214
Average no. per Household ... 2.9

FAMILIES

2001 Estimates:
Families in Private Households ... 3,003
Husband-Wife Families ... 2,690
Lone-Parent Families ... 313
Aver. No. Persons per Family ... 3.2
Aver. No. Sons/Daughters
  at Home ... 1.3

HOUSING

2001 Estimates:
Occupied Private Dwellings ... 3,560
  Owned ... 3,015
  Rented ... 545
Single-Detached House ... 2,913
Semi-Detached House ... 191
Row Houses ... 31
Apartment, 5 or Fewer Storeys ... 351
Apartment, Detached Duplex ... 63
Movable Dwellings ... 11

VEHICLES

2001 Estimates:
Model Yrs. '81-'96, No. ... 4,948
  % Total ... 79.28
Model Yrs. '97-'98, No. ... 807
  % Total ... 12.93
'99 Vehicles registered in
  Model Yr. '99, No. ... 486
  % Total ... 7.79
Total No. '81-'99 ... 6,241

LEGAL MARITAL STATUS

2001 Estimates: (Age 15+)
Single (Never Married) ... 2,391
Legally Married
  (Not Separated) ... 4,525
Legally Married (Separated) ... 164
Widowed ... 422
Divorced ... 625

PSYTE CATEGORIES

2001 Estimates	No. of House -holds	% of Total Hhds.	Index
Old Bungalow Burbs	405	11.38	686
Participation Quebec	2,256	63.37	2,199
Traditional French Cdn. Families	456	12.81	477
Old Quebec Walkups	443	12.44	679

FINANCIAL P$YTE

2001 Estimates	No. of House -holds	% of Total Hhds.	Index
Miners & Credit-Liners	405	11.38	359
Mortgages & Minivans	2,256	63.37	960
Country Credit	456	12.81	189
Loan Parent Stress	443	12.44	214

Pincourt
(Ville)
Montréal CMA
(Cont'd)

HOME LANGUAGE

2001 Estimates:

		% Total
English	4,278	41.43
French	5,743	55.62
Arabic	26	0.25
Czech	10	0.10
German	15	0.15
Gujarati	16	0.15
Polish	31	0.30
Multiple Responses	206	2.00
Total	10,325	100.00

BUILDING PERMITS

	1999	1998 $000	1997
Value	3,922	3,500	4,214

HOMES BUILT

	1999	1998	1997
No.	26	18	27

TAXATION

Income Class:	1997	% Total
Under $5,000	850	12.32
$5,000-$10,000	690	10.00
$10,000-$15,000	810	11.74
$15,000-$20,000	610	8.84
$20,000-$25,000	580	8.41
$25,000-$30,000	620	8.99
$30,000-$40,000	1,060	15.36
$40,000-$50,000	730	10.58
$50,000 +	960	13.91
Total Returns, No.	6,900	
Total Income, $000	192,704	
Total Taxable Returns	5,270	
Total Tax, $000	24,176	
Average Income, $	27,928	
Average Tax, $	4,587	

VITAL STATISTICS

	1997	1996	1995	1994
Births	111	111	124	133
Deaths	37	46	43	37
Natural Increase	74	65	81	96
Marriages	18	15	15	9

Note: Latest available data.

MEDIA INFO

see Montréal, CMA

Pointe-Claire
(Ville)
Montréal CMA

In census division Communauté urbaine de Montréal.

POPULATION

July 1, 2001 Estimate	29,442
% Cdn. Total	0.09
% Change, '96 -'01	1.69
Avg. Annual Growth Rate, %	0.34
2003 Projected Population	30,084
2006 Projected Population	31,200
2001 Households Estimate	11,609
2003 Projected Households	11,833
2006 Projected Households	12,201

INCOME

% Above/Below National Average	+27
2001 Total Income Estimate	$786,620,000
% Cdn. Total	0.12
2001 Average Hhld. Income	$67,800
2001 Per Capita	$26,700
2003 Projected Total Income	$843,580,000
2006 Projected Total Income	$941,960,000

RETAIL SALES

% Above/Below National Average	+46
2001 Retail Sales Estimate	$383,900,000
% Cdn. Total	0.14
2001 per Household	$33,100
2001 per Capita	$13,000
2001 No. of Establishments	301
2003 Projected Retail Sales	$426,000,000
2006 Projected Retail Sales	$490,400,000

POPULATION

2001 Estimates:

Total		29,442
Male		14,023
Female		15,419

Age Groups	Male	Female
0-4	827	803
5-9	960	921
10-14	987	956
15-19	975	919
20-24	877	805
25-29	760	749
30-34	850	918
35-39	1,054	1,180
40-44	1,169	1,325
45-49	1,166	1,309
50-54	1,055	1,128
55-59	847	875
60-64	667	712
65-69	539	657
70+	1,290	2,162

DAYTIME POPULATION

2001 Estimates:

Working Population	39,381
At Home Population	14,836
Total	54,217

INCOME

2001 Estimates:

Avg. Household Income	$67,759
Avg. Family Income	$75,997
Per Capita Income	$26,718

Male:

Avg. Employment Income	$43,884
Avg. Employment Income (Full Time)	$56,020

Female:

Avg. Employment Income	$27,902
Avg. Employment Income (Full Time)	$38,824

DISPOSABLE & DISCRETIONARY INCOME

2001 Estimates: | Per Hhld.

Disposable Income	$44,470
Discretionary Income 1 (minus Food & Shelter)	$29,062
Discretionary Income 2 (minus Food, Shelter, & Other Expenditures)	$19,661

LIQUID ASSETS

1999 Estimates: | Per Hhld.

Equity Investments	$94,334
Interest Bearing Investments	$81,334
Total Liquid Assets	$175,668

CREDIT DATA

July 2000:

Pool of Credit	$309,716,088
Revolving Credit, No.	70,214
Fixed Loans, No.	16,286
Avg. Credit Limit, per Person	$11,630
Avg. Spent, per Person	$4,743
Satisfactory Ratings, No. per Person	3.14
Avg. No. of Cards, per Person	1.24

LABOUR FORCE

2001 Estimates:

Male:

In the Labour Force	8,427
Participation Rate	74.9
Employed	8,134
Unemployed	293
Unemployment Rate	3.5
Not in Labour Force	2,822

Female:

In the Labour Force	7,110
Participation Rate	55.8
Employed	6,912
Unemployed	198
Unemployment Rate	2.8
Not in Labour Force	5,629

OCCUPATIONS BY MAJOR GROUPS

2001 Estimates:

	Male	Female
Management	1,435	692
Business, Finance & Admin.	1,156	2,255
Natural & Applied Sciences & Related	1,289	287
Health	171	659
Social Sciences, Gov't Services & Religion	218	227
Education	360	529
Arts, Culture, Recreation & Sport	392	372
Sales & Service	1,736	1,676
Trades, Transport & Equipment Operators & Related	1,053	48
Primary Industries	106	11
Processing, Mfg. & Utilities	394	153

LEVEL OF SCHOOLING

2001 Estimates:

Population 15 years +	23,988
Less than Grade 9	1,346
Grades 9-13 w/o Certif.	2,873
Grade 9-13 with Certif.	3,526
Trade Certif. /Dip.	504
Non-Univ. w/o Certif./Dip.	1,886
Non-Univ. with Certif./Dip.	3,790
Univ. w/o Degree	3,634
Univ. w/o Degree/Certif.	1,169
Univ. with Certif.	2,465
Univ. with Degree	6,429

Québec

AVERAGE HOUSEHOLD EXPENDITURES

2001 Estimates:

Food	$7,209
Shelter	$10,979
Clothing	$2,576
Transportation	$7,064
Health & Personal Care	$2,343
Recr'n, Read'g & Education	$4,577
Taxes & Securities	$18,926
Other	$9,802
Total Expenditures	$63,476

PRIVATE HOUSEHOLDS

2001 Estimates:

Private Households, Total	11,609
Pop. in Private Households	29,106
Average no. per Household	2.5

FAMILIES

2001 Estimates:

Families in Private Households	8,401
Husband-Wife Families	7,424
Lone-Parent Families	977
Aver. No. Persons per Family	3.0
Aver. No. Sons/Daughters at Home	1.1

HOUSING

2001 Estimates:

Occupied Private Dwellings	11,609
Owned	8,148
Rented	3,461
Single-Detached House	6,649
Semi-Detached House	965
Row Houses	1,068
Apartment, 5+ Storeys	1,494
Owned Apartment, 5+ Storeys	189
Apartment, 5 or Fewer Storeys	1,233
Apartment, Detached Duplex	179
Other Single-Attached	21

VEHICLES

2001 Estimates:

Model Yrs. '81-'96, No.	12,896
% Total	64.88
Model Yrs. '97-'98, No.	3,983
% Total	20.04
'99 Vehicles registered in Model Yr. '99, No.	2,998
% Total	15.08
Total No. '81-'99	19,877

LEGAL MARITAL STATUS

2001 Estimates: (Age 15+)

Single (Never Married)	6,614
Legally Married (Not Separated)	13,308
Legally Married (Separated)	496
Widowed	1,798
Divorced	1,772

Québec

Pointe-Claire
(Ville)
Montréal CMA
(Cont'd)

PSYTE CATEGORIES

2001 Estimates	No. of House -holds	% of Total Hhds.	Index
Urban Gentry	1,516	13.06	727
Technocrafts & Bureaucrats	990	8.53	303
Stable Suburban Families	405	3.49	268
Brie & Chablis	48	0.41	46
Aging Erudites	5,117	44.08	2,922
Participation Quebec	429	3.70	128
High Rise Sunsets	1,202	10.35	724
Young Urban Professionals	289	2.49	131
Young Urban Mix	332	2.86	135
University Enclaves	697	6.00	294
Old Quebec Walkups	442	3.81	208
Quebec Town Elders	79	0.68	24

FINAN¢IAL P$YTE

2001 Estimates	No. of House -holds	% of Total Hhds.	Index
Four Star Investors	1,516	13.06	260
Successful Suburbanites	1,395	12.02	181
Urban Heights	5,454	46.98	1,092
Mortgages & Minivans	429	3.70	56
Bills & Wills	332	2.86	35
Revolving Renters	1,202	10.35	225
Young Urban Struggle	697	6.00	127
Loan Parent Stress	521	4.49	77

HOME LANGUAGE

2001 Estimates:		% Total
English	20,303	68.96
French	5,717	19.42
Arabic	105	0.36
Armenian	119	0.40
Bengali	82	0.28
Chinese	357	1.21
Creoles	17	0.06
Czech	25	0.08
Dutch	20	0.07
Estonian	16	0.05
German	82	0.28
Greek	66	0.22
Gujarati	17	0.06
Hebrew	39	0.13
Hungarian	78	0.26
Italian	85	0.29
Japanese	45	0.15
Korean	56	0.19
Lao	65	0.22
Persian (Farsi)	121	0.41
Polish	199	0.68
Portuguese	82	0.28
Punjabi	78	0.26
Romanian	25	0.08
Russian	15	0.05
Serbo-Croatian	42	0.14
Spanish	129	0.44
Tagalog (Pilipino)	31	0.11
Turkish	100	0.34
Ukrainian	46	0.16
Vietnamese	26	0.09
Other Languages	113	0.38
Multiple Responses	1,141	3.88
Total	29,442	100.00

BUILDING PERMITS

	1999	1998 $000	1997
Value	29,412	38,510	32,061

HOMES BUILT

	1999	1998	1997
No	40	44	56

TAXATION

Income Class:	1997	% Total
Under $5,000	2,420	11.73
$5,000-$10,000	1,910	9.26
$10,000-$15,000	2,140	10.37
$15,000-$20,000	1,690	8.19
$20,000-$25,000	1,470	7.13
$25,000-$30,000	1,530	7.42
$30,000-$40,000	2,700	13.09
$40,000-$50,000	2,110	10.23
$50,000 +	4,670	22.64
Total Returns, No.	20,630	
Total Income, $000	745,846	
Total Taxable Returns	15,890	
Total Tax, $000	110,297	
Average Income, $	36,153	
Average Tax, $	6,941	

VITAL STATISTICS

	1997	1996	1995	1994
Births	336	344	391	360
Deaths	219	247	206	220
Natural Increase	117	97	185	140
Marriages	156	154	145	134

Note: Latest available data.

MEDIA INFO
see Montréal, CMA

Repentigny
(Ville)
Montréal CMA

In census division L'Assomption.

POPULATION

July 1, 2001 Estimate	57,236
% Cdn. Total	0.18
% Change, '96 -'01	4.50
Avg. Annual Growth Rate, %	0.88
2003 Projected Population	59,681
2006 Projected Population	64,078
2001 Households Estimate	21,206
2003 Projected Households	22,345
2006 Projected Households	24,353

INCOME

% Above/Below National Average	+12
2001 Total Income Estimate	$1,347,390,000
% Cdn. Total	0.21
2001 Average Hhld. Income	$63,500
2001 Per Capita	$23,500
2003 Projected Total Income	$1,496,240,000
2006 Projected Total Income	$1,775,570,000

RETAIL SALES

% Above/Below National Average	+37
2001 Retail Sales Estimate	$703,970,000
% Cdn. Total	0.25
2001 per Household	$33,200
2001 per Capita	$12,300
2001 No. of Establishments	491
2003 Projected Retail Sales	$796,350,000
2006 Projected Retail Sales	$950,600,000

POPULATION

2001 Estimates:		
Total		57,236
Male		28,148
Female		29,088
Age Groups	Male	Female
0-4	1,619	1,544
5-9	1,881	1,774
10-14	2,056	1,967
15-19	2,188	2,095
20-24	1,995	1,906
25-29	1,631	1,622
30-34	1,688	1,795
35-39	2,189	2,363
40-44	2,552	2,762
45-49	2,525	2,709
50-54	2,241	2,356
55-59	1,794	1,810
60-64	1,322	1,380
65-69	996	1,085
70+	1,471	1,920

DAYTIME POPULATION

2001 Estimates:	
Working Population	11,278
At Home Population	25,842
Total	37,120

INCOME

2001 Estimates:	
Avg. Household Income	$63,538
Avg. Family Income	$68,192
Per Capita Income	$23,541
Male:	
Avg. Employment Income	$40,963
Avg. Employment Income (Full Time)	$49,758
Female:	
Avg. Employment Income	$25,264
Avg. Employment Income (Full Time)	$34,510

DISPOSABLE & DISCRETIONARY INCOME

2001 Estimates:	Per Hhld.
Disposable Income	$43,470
Discretionary Income 1 (minus Food & Shelter)	$29,232
Discretionary Income 2 (minus Food, Shelter, & Other Expenditures)	$19,873

LIQUID ASSETS

1999 Estimates:	Per Hhld.
Equity Investments	$82,191
Interest Bearing Investments	$75,538
Total Liquid Assets	$157,729

CREDIT DATA

July 2000:	
Pool of Credit	$468,768,235
Revolving Credit, No.	109,011
Fixed Loans, No.	37,778
Avg. Credit Limit, per Person.	$10,618
Avg. Spent, per Person	$4,798
Satisfactory Ratings, No. per Person.	3.16
Avg. No. of Cards, per Person	1.28

LABOUR FORCE

2001 Estimates:	
Male:	
In the Labour Force	17,861
Participation Rate	79.1
Employed	17,181
Unemployed	680
Unemployment Rate	3.8
Not in Labour Force	4,731
Female:	
In the Labour Force	14,720
Participation Rate	61.8
Employed	14,066
Unemployed	654
Unemployment Rate	4.4
Not in Labour Force	9,083

OCCUPATIONS BY MAJOR GROUPS

2001 Estimates:	Male	Female
Management	2,718	820
Business, Finance & Admin.	1,983	5,512
Natural & Applied Sciences & Related	1,364	196
Health	438	1,698
Social Sciences, Gov't Services & Religion	277	417
Education	418	1,005
Arts, Culture, Recreation & Sport	272	341
Sales & Service	4,468	3,721
Trades, Transport & Equipment Operators & Related	4,173	159
Primary Industries	128	33
Processing, Mfg. & Utilities	1,222	315

LEVEL OF SCHOOLING

2001 Estimates:	
Population 15 years +	46,395
Less than Grade 9	4,991
Grades 9-13 w/o Certif.	7,276
Grade 9-13 with Certif.	10,066
Trade Certif. /Dip.	1,950
Non-Univ. w/o Certif./Dip.	3,840
Non-Univ. with Certif./Dip.	8,631
Univ. w/o Degree	4,066
Univ. w/o Degree/Certif.	591
Univ. with Certif.	3,475
Univ. with Degree	5,575

Repentigny
(Ville)
Montréal CMA
(Cont'd)

AVERAGE HOUSEHOLD EXPENDITURES

2001 Estimates:

Food	$7,425
Shelter	$9,091
Clothing	$2,714
Transportation	$7,185
Health & Personal Care	$2,332
Recr'n, Read'g & Education	$3,900
Taxes & Securities	$18,866
Other	$8,380
Total Expenditures	$59,893

PRIVATE HOUSEHOLDS

2001 Estimates:

Private Households, Total	21,206
Pop. in Private Households	56,691
Average no. per Household	2.7

FAMILIES

2001 Estimates:

Families in Private Households	17,543
Husband-Wife Families	15,435
Lone-Parent Families	2,108
Aver. No. Persons per Family	3.1
Aver. No. Sons/Daughters at Home	1.2

HOUSING

2001 Estimates:

Occupied Private Dwellings	21,206
Owned	16,436
Rented	4,770
Single-Detached House	14,327
Semi-Detached House	762
Row Houses	743
Apartment, 5+ Storeys	1,099
Owned Apartment, 5+ Storeys	628
Apartment, 5 or Fewer Storeys	3,975
Apartment, Detached Duplex	212
Other Single-Attached	44
Movable Dwellings	44

VEHICLES

2001 Estimates:

Model Yrs. '81-'96, No.	25,743
% Total	70.93
Model Yrs. '97-'98, No.	6,539
% Total	18.02
'99 Vehicles registered in Model Yr. '99, No.	4,013
% Total	11.06
Total No. '81-'99	36,295

LEGAL MARITAL STATUS

2001 Estimates: (Age 15+)

Single (Never Married)	15,358
Legally Married (Not Separated)	23,693
Legally Married (Separated)	1,148
Widowed	1,919
Divorced	4,277

PSYTE CATEGORIES

2001 Estimates	No. of House-holds	% of Total Hhds.	Index
Urban Gentry	39	0.18	10
Technocrafts & Bureaucrats	396	1.87	66
Stable Suburban Families	408	1.92	148
Old Bungalow Burbs	801	3.78	228
Participation Quebec	11,402	53.77	1,866
New Quebec Rows	3,551	16.75	1,528
Quebec Melange	2,737	12.91	487
Old Quebec Walkups	229	1.08	59
Quebec's New Urban Mosaic	1,609	7.59	315

FINANCIAL P$YTE

2001 Estimates	No. of House-holds	% of Total Hhds.	Index
Four Star Investors	39	0.18	4
Successful Suburbanites	804	3.79	57
Miners & Credit-Liners	801	3.78	119
Mortgages & Minivans	14,953	70.51	1,068
Country Credit	2,737	12.91	191
Loan Parent Stress	229	1.08	19
NSF	1,609	7.59	214

HOME LANGUAGE

2001 Estimates:		% Total
English	830	1.45
French	55,811	97.51
Italian	79	0.14
Khmer (Cambodian)	52	0.09
Vietnamese	31	0.05
Other Languages	86	0.15
Multiple Responses	347	0.61
Total	57,236	100.00

BUILDING PERMITS

	1999	1998	1997
		$000	
Value	32,704	25,567	33,709

HOMES BUILT

	1999	1998	1997
No.	164	135	278

TAXATION

Income Class:	1997	% Total
Under $5,000	4,440	11.30
$5,000-$10,000	4,390	11.17
$10,000-$15,000	4,480	11.40
$15,000-$20,000	3,390	8.63
$20,000-$25,000	3,200	8.14
$25,000-$30,000	3,240	8.25
$30,000-$40,000	5,500	14.00
$40,000-$50,000	3,980	10.13
$50,000 +	6,680	17.00
Total Returns, No.	39,290	
Total Income, $000	1,183,702	
Total Taxable Returns	29,940	
Total Tax, $000	154,492	
Average Income, $	30,127	
Average Tax, $	5,160	

VITAL STATISTICS

	1997	1996	1995	1994
Births	477	563	632	700
Deaths	233	232	228	221
Natural Increase	244	331	404	479
Marriages	81	65	60	62

Note: Latest available data.

MEDIA INFO
see Montréal, CMA

Rosemère
(Ville)
Montréal CMA

In census division Thérèse-De Blainville.

POPULATION

July 1, 2001 Estimate	12,998
% Cdn. Total	0.04
% Change, '96 -'01	5.98
Avg. Annual Growth Rate, %.	1.17
2003 Projected Population	13,456
2006 Projected Population	14,404
2001 Households Estimate	4,476
2003 Projected Households	4,674
2006 Projected Households	5,066

INCOME

% Above/Below National Average	+27
2001 Total Income Estimate	$349,130,000
% Cdn. Total	0.05
2001 Average Hhld. Income	$78,000
2001 Per Capita	$26,900
2003 Projected Total Income	$381,710,000
2006 Projected Total Income	$444,630,000

RETAIL SALES

% Above/Below National Average	+44
2001 Retail Sales Estimate	$167,570,000
% Cdn. Total	0.06
2001 per Household	$37,400
2001 per Capita	$12,900
2001 No. of Establishments	177
2003 Projected Retail Sales	$185,900,000
2006 Projected Retail Sales	$218,140,000

POPULATION

2001 Estimates:

Total		12,998
Male		6,461
Female		6,537
Age Groups	Male	Female
0-4	356	315
5-9	471	422
10-14	543	519
15-19	525	527
20-24	444	417
25-29	335	310
30-34	330	357
35-39	454	521
40-44	580	642
45-49	628	622
50-54	565	530
55-59	409	385
60-64	274	268
65-69	197	210
70+	350	492

DAYTIME POPULATION

2001 Estimates:

Working Population	3,429
At Home Population	5,933
Total	9,362

INCOME

2001 Estimates:

Avg. Household Income	$77,999
Avg. Family Income	$83,723
Per Capita Income	$26,860
Male:	
Avg. Employment Income	$49,795
Avg. Employment Income (Full Time)	$59,302
Female:	
Avg. Employment Income	$27,941
Avg. Employment Income (Full Time)	$38,083

Québec

DISPOSABLE & DISCRETIONARY INCOME

2001 Estimates:	Per Hhld.
Disposable Income	$51,418
Discretionary Income 1 (minus Food & Shelter)	$35,024
Discretionary Income 2 (minus Food, Shelter, & Other Expenditures)	$23,741

LIQUID ASSETS

1999 Estimates:	Per Hhld.
Equity Investments	$133,270
Interest Bearing Investments	$98,179
Total Liquid Assets	$231,449

CREDIT DATA

July 2000:

Pool of Credit	$141,362,629
Revolving Credit, No.	29,147
Fixed Loans, No.	8,891
Avg. Credit Limit, per Person	$13,237
Avg. Spent, per Person	$5,619
Satisfactory Ratings, No. per Person	3.40
Avg. No. of Cards, per Person	1.38

LABOUR FORCE

2001 Estimates:

Male:	
In the Labour Force	4,001
Participation Rate	78.6
Employed	3,882
Unemployed	119
Unemployment Rate	3.0
Not in Labour Force	1,090
Female:	
In the Labour Force	3,261
Participation Rate	61.7
Employed	3,148
Unemployed	113
Unemployment Rate	3.5
Not in Labour Force	2,020

OCCUPATIONS BY MAJOR GROUPS

2001 Estimates:	Male	Female
Management	1,029	294
Business, Finance & Admin.	357	1,175
Natural & Applied Sciences & Related	396	45
Health	157	304
Social Sciences, Gov't Services & Religion	60	135
Education	187	278
Arts, Culture, Recreation & Sport	59	152
Sales & Service	712	697
Trades, Transport & Equipment Operators & Related	718	50
Primary Industries	57	n.a.
Processing, Mfg. & Utilities	205	85

Québec

Rosemère
(Ville)
Montréal CMA
(Cont'd)

LEVEL OF SCHOOLING

2001 Estimates:
Population 15 years + ...10,372
Less than Grade 9. 667
Grades 9-13 w/o Certif. 1,344
Grade 9-13 with Certif. 1,962
Trade Certif. /Dip. 445
Non-Univ. w/o Certif./Dip. 990
Non-Univ. with Certif./Dip. 1,755
Univ. w/o Degree 1,360
  Univ. w/o Degree/Certif. 202
  Univ. with Certif. 1,158
Univ. with Degree 1,849

AVERAGE HOUSEHOLD EXPENDITURES

2001 Estimates:
Food $8,671
Shelter $10,354
Clothing. $3,296
Transportation. $8,839
Health & Personal Care $2,752
Recr'n, Read'g & Education $4,876
Taxes & Securities $23,138
Other. $9,573
Total Expenditures $71,499

PRIVATE HOUSEHOLDS

2001 Estimates:
Private Households, Total. 4,476
Pop. in Private Households. 12,818
Average no. per Household 2.9

FAMILIES

2001 Estimates:
Families in Private Households 3,783
Husband-Wife Families 3,416
Lone-Parent Families 367
Aver. No. Persons per Family 3.2
Aver. No. Sons/Daughters
  at Home 1.3

HOUSING

2001 Estimates:
Occupied Private Dwellings 4,476
  Owned. 3,918
  Rented. 558
Single-Detached House 3,787
Semi-Detached House 22
Row Houses 158
Apartment, 5 or Fewer Storeys 419
Apartment, Detached Duplex 90

VEHICLES

2001 Estimates:
Model Yrs. '81-'96, No. 6,080
  % Total 69.43
Model Yrs. '97-'98, No. 1,691
  % Total 19.31
'99 Vehicles registered in
  Model Yr. '99, No. 986
  % Total 11.26
Total No. '81-'99 8,757

LEGAL MARITAL STATUS

2001 Estimates: (Age 15+)
Single (Never Married). 3,173
Legally Married
  (Not Separated) 5,568
Legally Married (Separated) 217
Widowed 502
Divorced 912

PSYTE CATEGORIES

2001 Estimates	No. of House -holds	% of Total Hhds.	Index
Technocrafts & Bureaucrats.	417	9.32	331
Participation Quebec	4,059	90.68	3,147

FINANÇIAL P$YTE

2001 Estimates	No. of House -holds	% of Total Hhds.	Index
Successful Suburbanites.	417	9.32	140
Mortgages & Minivans	4,059	90.68	1,374

HOME LANGUAGE

2001 Estimates:		% Total
English	2,902	22.33
French	9,601	73.87
Arabic	64	0.49
Dutch	11	0.08
German	22	0.17
Greek	39	0.30
Italian	64	0.49
Portuguese	22	0.17
Russian	16	0.12
Ukrainian	10	0.08
Multiple Responses	247	1.90
Total	12,998	100.00

BUILDING PERMITS

	1999	1998 $000	1997
Value	19,931	40,462	30,287

HOMES BUILT

	1999	1998	1997
No	123	87	119

TAXATION

Income Class:	1997	% Total
Under $5,000	980	11.16
$5,000-$10,000	880	10.02
$10,000-$15,000	930	10.59
$15,000-$20,000	730	8.31
$20,000-$25,000	630	7.18
$25,000-$30,000	660	7.52
$30,000-$40,000	1,070	12.19
$40,000-$50,000	820	9.34
$50,000 +	2,080	23.69
Total Returns, No.	8,780	
Total Income, $000	327,088	
Total Taxable Returns	6,780	
Total Tax, $000	48,140	
Average Income, $	37,254	
Average Tax, $	7,100	

VITAL STATISTICS

	1997	1996	1995	1994
Births	119	108	112	123
Deaths	67	56	60	60
Natural Increase	52	52	52	63
Marriages	62	32	38	37

Note: Latest available data.

MEDIA INFO
see Montréal, CMA

Saint-Antoine
(Ville)
Montréal CMA

In census division La Rivière-du-Nord.

POPULATION

July 1, 2001 Estimate 11,384
% Cdn. Total. 0.04
% Change, '96 -'01 . . . . .3.37
Avg. Annual Growth Rate, %. 0.66
2003 Projected Population. 11,893
2006 Projected Population. 12,394
2001 Households Estimate 4,568
2003 Projected Households 4,711
2006 Projected Households 4,999

INCOME

% Above/Below National Average . . . . -12
2001 Total Income Estimate $212,340,000
% Cdn. Total. 0.03
2001 Average Hhld. Income. $46,500
2001 Per Capita $18,700
2003 Projected Total Income $229,820,000
2006 Projected Total Income $264,040,000

RETAIL SALES

% Above/Below National Average . . . . +17
2001 Retail Sales Estimate $119,570,000
% Cdn. Total. 0.04
2001 per Household. $26,200
2001 per Capita $10,500
2001 No. of Establishments 88
2003 Projected Retail Sales $135,630,000
2006 Projected Retail Sales $157,080,000

POPULATION

2001 Estimates:		
Total		11,384
Male.		5,590
Female		5,794
Age Groups	*Male*	*Female*
0-4	365	333
5-9	417	368
10-14	436	379
15-19	422	375
20-24	393	372
25-29	380	384
30-34	424	444
35-39	477	528
40-44	482	516
45-49	436	468
50-54	372	399
55-59	294	314
60-64	227	247
65-69	170	207
70+	295	460

DAYTIME POPULATION

2001 Estimates:
Working Population 2,274
At Home Population. 5,668
Total 7,942

INCOME

2001 Estimates:
Avg. Household Income $46,484
Avg. Family Income $51,195
Per Capita Income $18,652
Male:
Avg. Employment Income $33,367
Avg. Employment Income
  (Full Time). $41,569
Female:
Avg. Employment Income $19,685
Avg. Employment Income
  (Full Time). $30,345

DISPOSABLE & DISCRETIONARY INCOME

2001 Estimates:	Per Hhld.
Disposable Income	$32,919
Discretionary Income 1 (minus Food & Shelter)	$21,331
Discretionary Income 2 (minus Food, Shelter, & Other Expenditures).	$13,984

LIQUID ASSETS

1999 Estimates:	Per Hhld.
Equity Investments	$49,216
Interest Bearing Investments	$52,580
Total Liquid Assets	$101,796

CREDIT DATA

July 2000:
Pool of Credit. $67,319,293
Revolving Credit, No. 17,998
Fixed Loans, No. 6,484
Avg. Credit Limit, per Person $8,204
Avg. Spent, per Person $3,898
Satisfactory Ratings,
  No. per Person. 2.82
Avg. No. of Cards, per Person 0.99

LABOUR FORCE

2001 Estimates:
Male:
In the Labour Force 3,398
Participation Rate 77.7
Employed. 3,135
Unemployed. 263
Unemployment Rate 7.7
Not in Labour Force. 974
Female:
In the Labour Force 2,807
Participation Rate 59.5
Employed. 2,553
Unemployed. 254
Unemployment Rate 9.0
Not in Labour Force. 1,907

OCCUPATIONS BY MAJOR GROUPS

2001 Estimates:	Male	Female
Management	303	117
Business, Finance & Admin.	331	779
Natural & Applied Sciences & Related	241	10
Health	65	309
Social Sciences, Gov't Services & Religion	86	45
Education	70	121
Arts, Culture, Recreation & Sport	45	36
Sales & Service	773	925
Trades, Transport & Equipment Operators & Related	796	77
Primary Industries	34	10
Processing, Mfg. & Utilities	581	214

LEVEL OF SCHOOLING

2001 Estimates:
Population 15 years + ...9,086
Less than Grade 9 1,507
Grades 9-13 w/o Certif. 1,729
Grade 9-13 with Certif. 1,835
Trade Certif. /Dip. 599
Non-Univ. w/o Certif./Dip. 691
Non-Univ. with Certif./Dip. 1,584
Univ. w/o Degree 556
  Univ. w/o Degree/Certif. 69
  Univ. with Certif. 487
Univ. with Degree 585

Saint-Antoine
(Ville)
Montréal CMA
(Cont'd)

AVERAGE HOUSEHOLD EXPENDITURES

2001 Estimates:
Food	$6,069
Shelter	$7,188
Clothing	$2,031
Transportation	$5,681
Health & Personal Care	$1,814
Recr'n, Read'g & Education	$2,959
Taxes & Securities	$13,422
Other	$6,818
Total Expenditures	$45,982

PRIVATE HOUSEHOLDS

2001 Estimates:
Private Households, Total	4,568
Pop. in Private Households	11,165
Average no. per Household	2.4

FAMILIES

2001 Estimates:
Families in Private Households	3,424
Husband-Wife Families	2,930
Lone-Parent Families	494
Aver. No. Persons per Family	3.0
Aver. No. Sons/Daughters at Home	1.2

HOUSING

2001 Estimates:
Occupied Private Dwellings	4,568
Owned	2,701
Rented	1,867
Single-Detached House	2,463
Semi-Detached House	217
Row Houses	38
Apartment, 5 or Fewer Storeys	1,363
Apartment, Detached Duplex	464
Other Single-Attached	23

VEHICLES

2001 Estimates:
Model Yrs. '81-'96, No.	6,588
% Total	77.64
Model Yrs. '97-'98, No.	1,103
% Total	13.00
'99 Vehicles registered in Model Yr. '99, No.	794
% Total	9.36
Total No. '81-'99	8,485

LEGAL MARITAL STATUS

2001 Estimates: (Age 15+)
Single (Never Married)	3,402
Legally Married (Not Separated)	4,030
Legally Married (Separated)	224
Widowed	495
Divorced	935

PSYTE CATEGORIES

2001 Estimates	No. of House-holds	% of Total Hhds.	Index
Participation Quebec	567	12.41	431
New Quebec Rows	674	14.75	1,346
Quebec Melange	1,455	31.85	1,202
Traditional French Cdn. Families	1,079	23.62	880
Quebec Town Elders	675	14.78	523
Quebec's New Urban Mosaic	72	1.58	65

FINANCIAL PSYTE

2001 Estimates	No. of House-holds	% of Total Hhds.	Index
Mortgages & Minivans	1,241	27.17	412
Country Credit	2,534	55.47	820
Loan Parent Stress	675	14.78	254
NSF	72	1.58	45

HOME LANGUAGE

2001 Estimates:		% Total
English	69	0.61
French	11,213	98.50
Arabic	11	0.10
Khmer (Cambodian)	10	0.09
Spanish	22	0.19
Multiple Responses	59	0.52
Total	11,384	100.00

BUILDING PERMITS

	1999	1998 $000	1997
Value	7,951	6,913	8,502

HOMES BUILT

	1999	1998	1997
No	57	74	90

TAXATION

Income Class:	1997	% Total
Under $5,000	1,050	12.27
$5,000-$10,000	1,320	15.42
$10,000-$15,000	1,300	15.19
$15,000-$20,000	910	10.63
$20,000-$25,000	790	9.23
$25,000-$30,000	800	9.35
$30,000-$40,000	1,020	11.92
$40,000-$50,000	670	7.83
$50,000 +	700	8.18
Total Returns, No.	8,560	
Total Income, $000	196,081	
Total Taxable Returns	5,980	
Total Tax, $000	21,582	
Average Income, $	22,907	
Average Tax, $	3,609	

VITAL STATISTICS

	1997	1996	1995	1994
Births	144	142	149	141
Deaths	68	57	58	61
Natural Increase	76	85	91	80
Marriages	21	11	11	14

Note: Latest available data.

MEDIA INFO
see Montréal, CMA

Saint-Basile-le-Grand
(Ville)
Montréal CMA

In census division La Vallée-du-Richelieu.

POPULATION

July 1, 2001 Estimate	13,498
% Cdn. Total	0.04
% Change, '96 -'01	12.69
Avg. Annual Growth Rate, %	2.42
2003 Projected Population	14,553
2006 Projected Population	16,297
2001 Households Estimate	4,693
2003 Projected Households	5,118
2006 Projected Households	5,831

INCOME

% Above/Below National Average	+6
2001 Total Income Estimate	$302,490,000
% Cdn. Total	0.05
2001 Average Hhld. Income	$64,500
2001 Per Capita	$22,400
2003 Projected Total Income	$351,870,000
2006 Projected Total Income	$443,070,000

RETAIL SALES

% Above/Below National Average	-12
2001 Retail Sales Estimate	$106,160,000
% Cdn. Total	0.04
2001 per Household	$22,600
2001 per Capita	$7,900
2001 No. of Establishments	81
2003 Projected Retail Sales	$125,110,000
2006 Projected Retail Sales	$158,120,000

POPULATION

2001 Estimates:
Total		13,498
Male		6,816
Female		6,682

Age Groups	Male	Female
0-4	454	447
5-9	538	505
10-14	564	507
15-19	559	496
20-24	466	421
25-29	409	403
30-34	503	532
35-39	627	664
40-44	670	672
45-49	577	593
50-54	463	467
55-59	347	318
60-64	245	224
65-69	167	165
70+	227	268

DAYTIME POPULATION

2001 Estimates:
Working Population	1,744
At Home Population	6,077
Total	7,821

INCOME

2001 Estimates:
Avg. Household Income	$64,456
Avg. Family Income	$67,169
Per Capita Income	$22,410
Male:	
Avg. Employment Income	$38,659
Avg. Employment Income (Full Time)	$47,899
Female:	
Avg. Employment Income	$24,956
Avg. Employment Income (Full Time)	$35,168

Québec

DISPOSABLE & DISCRETIONARY INCOME

2001 Estimates:	Per Hhld.
Disposable Income	$44,602
Discretionary Income 1 (minus Food & Shelter)	$30,138
Discretionary Income 2 (minus Food, Shelter, & Other Expenditures)	$20,443

LIQUID ASSETS

1999 Estimates:	Per Hhld.
Equity Investments	$80,548
Interest Bearing Investments	$74,632
Total Liquid Assets	$155,180

CREDIT DATA

July 2000:
Pool of Credit	$99,409,803
Revolving Credit, No.	24,880
Fixed Loans, No.	8,828
Avg. Credit Limit, per Person	$10,959
Avg. Spent, per Person	$5,186
Satisfactory Ratings, No. per Person	3.50
Avg. No. of Cards, per Person	1.30

LABOUR FORCE

2001 Estimates:
Male:	
In the Labour Force	4,204
Participation Rate	79.9
Employed	4,053
Unemployed	151
Unemployment Rate	3.6
Not in Labour Force	1,056
Female:	
In the Labour Force	3,408
Participation Rate	65.2
Employed	3,308
Unemployed	100
Unemployment Rate	2.9
Not in Labour Force	1,815

OCCUPATIONS BY MAJOR GROUPS

2001 Estimates:	Male	Female
Management	549	151
Business, Finance & Admin.	626	1,310
Natural & Applied Sciences & Related	443	85
Health	111	341
Social Sciences, Gov't Services & Religion	36	130
Education	79	171
Arts, Culture, Recreation & Sport	129	104
Sales & Service	774	819
Trades, Transport & Equipment Operators & Related	998	92
Primary Industries	68	36
Processing, Mfg. & Utilities	325	76

Québec

Saint-Basile-le-Grand
(Ville)
Montréal CMA
(Cont'd)

LEVEL OF SCHOOLING

2001 Estimates:
Population 15 years +	10,483
Less than Grade 9	896
Grades 9-13 w/o Certif.	1,818
Grade 9-13 with Certif.	1,979
Trade Certif. /Dip.	481
Non-Univ. w/o Certif./Dip.	1,001
Non-Univ. with Certif./Dip.	2,091
Univ. w/o Degree	985
Univ. w/o Degree/Certif.	191
Univ. with Certif.	794
Univ. with Degree	1,232

AVERAGE HOUSEHOLD EXPENDITURES

2001 Estimates:
Food	$7,692
Shelter	$8,991
Clothing	$2,781
Transportation	$7,580
Health & Personal Care	$2,369
Recr'n, Read'g & Education	$4,003
Taxes & Securities	$19,113
Other	$8,383
Total Expenditures	$60,912

PRIVATE HOUSEHOLDS

2001 Estimates:
Private Households, Total	4,693
Pop. in Private Households	13,473
Average no. per Household	2.9

FAMILIES

2001 Estimates:
Families in Private Households	4,031
Husband-Wife Families	3,600
Lone-Parent Families	431
Aver. No. Persons per Family	3.2
Aver. No. Sons/Daughters at Home	1.3

HOUSING

2001 Estimates:
Occupied Private Dwellings	4,693
Owned	4,052
Rented	641
Single-Detached House	3,587
Semi-Detached House	225
Row Houses	36
Apartment, 5 or Fewer Storeys	391
Apartment, Detached Duplex	136
Other Single-Attached	11
Movable Dwellings	307

VEHICLES

2001 Estimates:
Model Yrs. '81-'96, No.	5,802
% Total	75.80
Model Yrs. '97-'98, No.	1,179
% Total	15.40
'99 Vehicles registered in Model Yr. '99, No.	673
% Total	8.79
Total No. '81-'99	7,654

LEGAL MARITAL STATUS

2001 Estimates: (Age 15+)
Single (Never Married)	3,790
Legally Married (Not Separated)	5,210
Legally Married (Separated)	229
Widowed	314
Divorced	940

PSYTE CATEGORIES

2001 Estimates	No. of House -holds	% of Total Hhds.	Index
Participation Quebec	2,833	60.37	2,095
New Quebec Rows	473	10.08	920
Quebec Melange	435	9.27	350
Traditional French Cdn. Families	767	16.34	609
Quebec Town Elders	185	3.94	140

FINANCIAL PSYTE

2001 Estimates	No. of House -holds	% of Total Hhds.	Index
Mortgages & Minivans	3,306	70.45	1,067
Country Credit	1,202	25.61	379
Loan Parent Stress	185	3.94	68

HOME LANGUAGE

2001 Estimates:		% Total
English	522	3.87
French	12,882	95.44
Greek	11	0.08
Portuguese	22	0.16
Multiple Responses	61	0.45
Total	13,498	100.00

BUILDING PERMITS

	1999	1998 $000	1997
Value	6,195	8,873	11,076

HOMES BUILT

	1999	1998	1997
No	66	81	74

TAXATION

Income Class:	1997	% Total
Under $5,000	1,000	12.08
$5,000-$10,000	850	10.27
$10,000-$15,000	840	10.14
$15,000-$20,000	680	8.21
$20,000-$25,000	700	8.45
$25,000-$30,000	740	8.94
$30,000-$40,000	1,250	15.10
$40,000-$50,000	900	10.87
$50,000 +	1,330	16.06
Total Returns, No.	8,280	
Total Income, $000	240,714	
Total Taxable Returns	6,460	
Total Tax, $000	30,849	
Average Income, $	29,072	
Average Tax, $	4,775	

VITAL STATISTICS

	1997	1996	1995	1994
Births	160	169	159	184
Deaths	32	39	27	19
Natural Increase	128	130	132	165
Marriages	26	14	23	23

Note: Latest available data.

MEDIA INFO
see Montréal, CMA

Saint-Bruno-de-Montarville
(Ville)
Montréal CMA

In census division La Vallée-du-Richelieu.

POPULATION

2001 Estimates:
July 1, 2001 Estimate	23,816
% Cdn. Total	0.08
% Change, '96 -'01	-1.31
Avg. Annual Growth Rate, %.	-0.26
2003 Projected Population	23,942
2006 Projected Population	24,398
2001 Households Estimate	8,667
2003 Projected Households	8,794
2006 Projected Households	9,093

INCOME

2001 Estimates:
% Above/Below National Average	+34
2001 Total Income Estimate	$674,410,000
% Cdn. Total	0.10
2001 Average Hhld. Income	$77,800
2001 Per Capita	$28,300
2003 Projected Total Income	$722,540,000
2006 Projected Total Income	$813,080,000

RETAIL SALES

2001 Estimates:
% Above/Below National Average	+110
2001 Retail Sales Estimate	$447,760,000
% Cdn. Total	0.16
2001 per Household	$51,700
2001 per Capita	$18,800
2001 No. of Establishments	264
2003 Projected Retail Sales	$486,620,000
2006 Projected Retail Sales	$548,620,000

POPULATION

2001 Estimates:
Total		23,816
Male		11,742
Female		12,074
Age Groups	Male	Female
0-4	600	593
5-9	690	672
10-14	785	746
15-19	938	872
20-24	956	855
25-29	742	665
30-34	627	613
35-39	718	788
40-44	863	974
45-49	990	1,129
50-54	1,082	1,152
55-59	932	961
60-64	688	702
65-69	487	493
70+	644	859

DAYTIME POPULATION

2001 Estimates:
Working Population	11,417
At Home Population	10,415
Total	21,832

INCOME

2001 Estimates:
Avg. Household Income	$77,814
Avg. Family Income	$84,939
Per Capita Income	$28,318
Male:	
Avg. Employment Income	$48,561
Avg. Employment Income (Full Time)	$63,795
Female:	
Avg. Employment Income	$27,854
Avg. Employment Income (Full Time)	$40,040

DISPOSABLE & DISCRETIONARY INCOME

2001 Estimates:	Per Hhld.
Disposable Income	$51,668
Discretionary Income 1 (minus Food & Shelter)	$35,311
Discretionary Income 2 (minus Food, Shelter, & Other Expenditures)	$24,530

LIQUID ASSETS

1999 Estimates:	Per Hhld.
Equity Investments	$120,158
Interest Bearing Investments	$96,531
Total Liquid Assets	$216,689

CREDIT DATA

July 2000:
Pool of Credit	$239,084,560
Revolving Credit, No.	53,524
Fixed Loans, No.	13,851
Avg. Credit Limit, per Person.	$12,290
Avg. Spent, per Person	$5,017
Satisfactory Ratings, No. per Person.	3.33
Avg. No. of Cards, per Person	1.33

LABOUR FORCE

2001 Estimates:
Male:	
In the Labour Force	7,608
Participation Rate	78.7
Employed	7,422
Unemployed	186
Unemployment Rate	2.4
Not in Labour Force	2,059
Female:	
In the Labour Force	6,222
Participation Rate	61.8
Employed	6,023
Unemployed	199
Unemployment Rate	3.2
Not in Labour Force	3,841

OCCUPATIONS BY MAJOR GROUPS

2001 Estimates:	Male	Female
Management	1,629	456
Business, Finance & Admin.	1,100	2,217
Natural & Applied Sciences & Related	1,032	208
Health	187	521
Social Sciences, Gov't Services & Religion	138	239
Education	232	530
Arts, Culture, Recreation & Sport	297	288
Sales & Service	1,583	1,504
Trades, Transport & Equipment Operators & Related	908	86
Primary Industries	80	10
Processing, Mfg. & Utilities	307	44

LEVEL OF SCHOOLING

2001 Estimates:
Population 15 years +	19,730
Less than Grade 9	1,145
Grades 9-13 w/o Certif.	2,293
Grade 9-13 with Certif.	2,959
Trade Certif. /Dip.	704
Non-Univ. w/o Certif./Dip.	1,622
Non-Univ. with Certif./Dip.	3,563
Univ. w/o Degree	2,586
Univ. w/o Degree/Certif.	363
Univ. with Certif.	2,223
Univ. with Degree	4,858

Saint-Bruno-de-Montarville
(Ville)
Montréal CMA
(Cont'd)

AVERAGE HOUSEHOLD EXPENDITURES

2001 Estimates:

Food	$8,188
Shelter	$11,055
Clothing	$3,119
Transportation	$8,378
Health & Personal Care	$2,589
Recr'n, Read'g & Education	$4,888
Taxes & Securities	$23,117
Other	$10,001
Total Expenditures	$71,335

PRIVATE HOUSEHOLDS

2001 Estimates:

Private Households, Total	8,667
Pop. in Private Households	23,654
Average no. per Household	2.7

FAMILIES

2001 Estimates:

Families in Private Households	7,239
Husband-Wife Families	6,370
Lone-Parent Families	869
Aver. No. Persons per Family	3.1
Aver. No. Sons/Daughters at Home	1.3

HOUSING

2001 Estimates:

Occupied Private Dwellings	8,667
Owned	7,056
Rented	1,611
Single-Detached House	6,511
Semi-Detached House	438
Row Houses	21
Apartment, 5+ Storeys	42
Owned Apartment, 5+ Storeys	32
Apartment, 5 or Fewer Storeys	1,546
Apartment, Detached Duplex	109

VEHICLES

2001 Estimates:

Model Yrs. '81-'96, No.	11,491
% Total	72.04
Model Yrs. '97-'98, No.	2,778
% Total	17.42
'99 Vehicles registered in Model Yr. '99, No.	1,682
% Total	10.54
Total No. '81-'99	15,951

LEGAL MARITAL STATUS

2001 Estimates: (Age 15+)

Single (Never Married)	6,504
Legally Married (Not Separated)	10,451
Legally Married (Separated)	404
Widowed	773
Divorced	1,598

PSYTE CATEGORIES

2001 Estimates	No. of House-holds	% of Total Hhds.	Index
Urban Gentry	354	4.08	227
Suburban Executives	1,215	14.02	978
Technocrafts & Bureaucrats	777	8.97	319
Stable Suburban Families	1,189	13.72	1,052
Old Bungalow Burbs	407	4.70	283
Participation Quebec	2,754	31.78	1,103
New Quebec Rows	417	4.81	439
Quebec Melange	391	4.51	170
Old Quebec Walkups	1,131	13.05	712

FINANCIAL PSYTE

2001 Estimates	No. of House-holds	% of Total Hhds.	Index
Four Star Investors	1,569	18.10	360
Successful Suburbanites	1,966	22.68	342
Miners & Credit-Liners	407	4.70	148
Mortgages & Minivans	3,171	36.59	554
Country Credit	391	4.51	67
Loan Parent Stress	1,131	13.05	224

HOME LANGUAGE

2001 Estimates		% Total
English	3,059	12.84
French	19,963	83.82
Arabic	30	0.13
German	15	0.06
Italian	30	0.13
Korean	20	0.08
Polish	20	0.08
Portuguese	55	0.23
Spanish	45	0.19
Ukrainian	20	0.08
Other Languages	30	0.13
Multiple Responses	529	2.22
Total	23,816	100.00

BUILDING PERMITS

	1999	1998	1997
		$000	
Value	35,919	25,635	32,271

HOMES BUILT

	1999	1998	1997
No	160	137	97

TAXATION

Income Class:	1997	% Total
Under $5,000	2,080	11.92
$5,000-$10,000	1,790	10.26
$10,000-$15,000	1,830	10.49
$15,000-$20,000	1,270	7.28
$20,000-$25,000	1,170	6.70
$25,000-$30,000	1,250	7.16
$30,000-$40,000	2,160	12.38
$40,000-$50,000	1,730	9.91
$50,000 +	4,170	23.90
Total Returns, No.	17,450	
Total Income, $000	642,901	
Total Taxable Returns	13,480	
Total Tax, $000	95,988	
Average Income, $	36,842	
Average Tax, $	7,121	

VITAL STATISTICS

	1997	1996	1995	1994
Births	203	216	221	228
Deaths	122	116	101	102
Natural Increase	81	100	120	126
Marriages	55	63	62	61

Note: Latest available data.

MEDIA INFO
see Montréal, CMA

Saint-Constant
(Ville)
Montréal CMA

In census division Roussillon.

POPULATION

July 1, 2001 Estimate	27,000
% Cdn. Total	0.09
% Change, '96 -'01	14.59
Avg. Annual Growth Rate, %	2.76
2003 Projected Population	29,401
2006 Projected Population	33,491
2001 Households Estimate	8,961
2003 Projected Households	9,820
2006 Projected Households	11,303

INCOME

% Above/Below National Average	-5
2001 Total Income Estimate	$538,030,000
% Cdn. Total	0.08
2001 Average Hhld. Income	$60,000
2001 Per Capita	$19,900
2003 Projected Total Income	$627,470,000
2006 Projected Total Income	$797,250,000

RETAIL SALES

% Above/Below National Average	-56
2001 Retail Sales Estimate	$106,040,000
% Cdn. Total	0.04
2001 per Household	$11,800
2001 per Capita	$3,900
2001 No. of Establishments	142
2003 Projected Retail Sales	$123,740,000
2006 Projected Retail Sales	$155,540,000

POPULATION

2001 Estimates:

Total	27,000
Male	13,621
Female	13,379

Age Groups	Male	Female
0-4	1,017	947
5-9	1,166	1,102
10-14	1,130	1,077
15-19	1,041	971
20-24	895	818
25-29	827	831
30-34	1,037	1,158
35-39	1,324	1,410
40-44	1,328	1,335
45-49	1,150	1,085
50-54	915	833
55-59	651	598
60-64	431	417
65-69	302	301
70+	407	496

DAYTIME POPULATION

2001 Estimates:

Working Population	2,528
At Home Population	12,583
Total	15,111

INCOME

2001 Estimates:

Avg. Household Income	$60,042
Avg. Family Income	$61,401
Per Capita Income	$19,927
Male:	
Avg. Employment Income	$38,165
Avg. Employment Income (Full Time)	$45,668
Female:	
Avg. Employment Income	$23,061
Avg. Employment Income (Full Time)	$31,773

Québec

DISPOSABLE & DISCRETIONARY INCOME

2001 Estimates:	Per Hhld.
Disposable Income	$42,014
Discretionary Income 1 (minus Food & Shelter)	$28,220
Discretionary Income 2 (minus Food, Shelter, & Other Expenditures)	$19,034

LIQUID ASSETS

1999 Estimates:	Per Hhld.
Equity Investments	$71,689
Interest Bearing Investments	$69,598
Total Liquid Assets	$141,287

CREDIT DATA

July 2000:

Pool of Credit	$171,593,336
Revolving Credit, No.	40,912
Fixed Loans, No.	17,981
Avg. Credit Limit, per Person.	$10,470
Avg. Spent, per Person	$5,249
Satisfactory Ratings, No. per Person	3.34
Avg. No. of Cards, per Person	1.22

LABOUR FORCE

2001 Estimates:

Male:	
In the Labour Force	8,480
Participation Rate	82.3
Employed	8,129
Unemployed	351
Unemployment Rate	4.1
Not in Labour Force	1,828
Female:	
In the Labour Force	6,490
Participation Rate	63.3
Employed	6,158
Unemployed	332
Unemployment Rate	5.1
Not in Labour Force	3,763

OCCUPATIONS BY MAJOR GROUPS

2001 Estimates:	Male	Female
Management	827	271
Business, Finance & Admin.	885	2,522
Natural & Applied Sciences & Related	708	166
Health	86	540
Social Sciences, Gov't Services & Religion	40	113
Education	125	134
Arts, Culture, Recreation & Sport	107	118
Sales & Service	1,611	1,726
Trades, Transport & Equipment Operators & Related	2,704	124
Primary Industries	142	31
Processing, Mfg. & Utilities	1,059	553

Québec

Saint-Constant

(Ville)
Montréal CMA
(Cont'd)

LEVEL OF SCHOOLING

2001 Estimates:
Population 15 years +	20,561
Less than Grade 9	2,805
Grades 9-13 w/o Certif.	3,847
Grade 9-13 with Certif.	4,396
Trade Certif. /Dip.	820
Non-Univ. w/o Certif./Dip.	1,883
Non-Univ. with Certif./Dip.	3,919
Univ. w/o Degree	1,380
Univ. w/o Degree/Certif.	194
Univ. with Certif.	1,186
Univ. with Degree	1,511

AVERAGE HOUSEHOLD EXPENDITURES

2001 Estimates:
Food	$7,351
Shelter	$8,530
Clothing	$2,615
Transportation	$7,225
Health & Personal Care	$2,210
Recr'n, Read'g & Education	$3,743
Taxes & Securities	$17,519
Other	$8,015
Total Expenditures	$57,208

PRIVATE HOUSEHOLDS

2001 Estimates:
Private Households, Total	8,961
Pop. in Private Households	26,874
Average no. per Household	3.0

FAMILIES

2001 Estimates:
Families in Private Households	7,977
Husband-Wife Families	7,108
Lone-Parent Families	869
Aver. No. Persons per Family	3.2
Aver. No. Sons/Daughters at Home	1.3

HOUSING

2001 Estimates:
Occupied Private Dwellings	8,961
Owned	7,317
Rented	1,644
Single-Detached House	6,864
Semi-Detached House	412
Row Houses	179
Apartment, 5 or Fewer Storeys	1,196
Apartment, Detached Duplex	269
Movable Dwellings	41

VEHICLES

2001 Estimates:
Model Yrs. '81-'96, No.	11,007
% Total	75.99
Model Yrs. '97-'98, No.	2,193
% Total	15.14
'99 Vehicles registered in Model Yr. '99, No.	1,284
% Total	8.86
Total No. '81-'99	14,484

LEGAL MARITAL STATUS

2001 Estimates: (Age 15+)
Single (Never Married)	7,372
Legally Married (Not Separated)	10,409
Legally Married (Separated)	402
Widowed	620
Divorced	1,758

PSYTE CATEGORIES

2001 Estimates	No. of House-holds	% of Total Hhds.	Index
Participation Quebec	3,815	42.57	1,477
New Quebec Rows	1,355	15.12	1,380
Quebec Melange	964	10.76	406
Traditional French Cdn. Families	2,602	29.04	1,081
Quebec Town Elders	225	2.51	89

FINANCIAL P$YTE

2001 Estimates	No. of House-holds	% of Total Hhds.	Index
Mortgages & Minivans	5,170	57.69	874
Country Credit	3,566	39.79	588
Loan Parent Stress	225	2.51	43

HOME LANGUAGE

2001 Estimates:		% Total
English	1,514	5.61
French	24,526	90.84
Greek	26	0.10
Italian	61	0.23
Lao	18	0.07
Polish	81	0.30
Portuguese	32	0.12
Punjabi	47	0.17
Romanian	32	0.12
Spanish	155	0.57
Thai	35	0.13
Other Languages	24	0.09
Multiple Responses	449	1.66
Total	27,000	100.00

BUILDING PERMITS

	1999	1998 $000	1997
Value	12,023	19,748	13,102

HOMES BUILT

	1999	1998	1997
No	90	52	78

TAXATION

Income Class:	1997	% Total
Under $5,000	1,860	12.34
$5,000-$10,000	1,640	10.88
$10,000-$15,000	1,690	11.21
$15,000-$20,000	1,360	9.02
$20,000-$25,000	1,290	8.56
$25,000-$30,000	1,360	9.02
$30,000-$40,000	2,270	15.06
$40,000-$50,000	1,570	10.42
$50,000 +	2,030	13.47
Total Returns, No.	15,070	
Total Income, $000	409,448	
Total Taxable Returns	11,520	
Total Tax, $000	50,655	
Average Income, $	27,170	
Average Tax, $	4,397	

VITAL STATISTICS

	1997	1996	1995	1994
Births	340	338	373	357
Deaths	67	76	78	60
Natural Increase	273	262	295	297
Marriages	33	37	28	36

Note: Latest available data.

MEDIA INFO
see Montréal, CMA

Saint-Eustache

(Ville)
Montréal CMA

**In census division
Deux-Montagnes.**

POPULATION

July 1, 2001 Estimate	42,814
% Cdn. Total	0.14
% Change, '96 -'01	4.02
Avg. Annual Growth Rate, %	0.79
2003 Projected Population	44,352
2006 Projected Population	47,221
2001 Households Estimate	15,950
2003 Projected Households	16,652
2006 Projected Households	17,920

INCOME

% Above/Below National Average	-8
2001 Total Income Estimate	$828,380,000
% Cdn. Total	0.13
2001 Average Hhld. Income	$51,900
2001 Per Capita	$19,300
2003 Projected Total Income	$917,440,000
2006 Projected Total Income	$1,083,750,000

RETAIL SALES

% Above/Below National Average	+13
2001 Retail Sales Estimate	$434,320,000
% Cdn. Total	0.16
2001 per Household	$27,200
2001 per Capita	$10,100
2001 No. of Establishments	425
2003 Projected Retail Sales	$489,770,000
2006 Projected Retail Sales	$581,920,000

POPULATION

2001 Estimates:		
Total		42,814
Male		21,057
Female		21,757

Age Groups	Male	Female
0-4	1,275	1,234
5-9	1,425	1,413
10-14	1,556	1,519
15-19	1,680	1,591
20-24	1,564	1,468
25-29	1,373	1,295
30-34	1,437	1,465
35-39	1,683	1,844
40-44	1,847	1,993
45-49	1,817	1,881
50-54	1,614	1,586
55-59	1,212	1,190
60-64	862	897
65-69	624	721
70+	1,088	1,660

DAYTIME POPULATION

2001 Estimates:
Working Population	16,971
At Home Population	20,532
Total	37,503

INCOME

2001 Estimates:
Avg. Household Income	$51,936
Avg. Family Income	$57,601
Per Capita Income	$19,348
Male:	
Avg. Employment Income	$35,009
Avg. Employment Income (Full Time)	$44,272
Female:	
Avg. Employment Income	$20,567
Avg. Employment Income (Full Time)	$29,728

DISPOSABLE & DISCRETIONARY INCOME

2001 Estimates:	Per Hhld.
Disposable Income	$36,042
Discretionary Income 1 (minus Food & Shelter)	$23,491
Discretionary Income 2 (minus Food, Shelter, & Other Expenditures)	$15,542

LIQUID ASSETS

1999 Estimates:	Per Hhld.
Equity Investments	$56,497
Interest Bearing Investments	$59,194
Total Liquid Assets	$115,691

CREDIT DATA

July 2000:
Pool of Credit	$281,970,542
Revolving Credit, No.	70,985
Fixed Loans, No.	26,831
Avg. Credit Limit, per Person	$9,245
Avg. Spent, per Person	$4,363
Satisfactory Ratings, No. per Person	3.02
Avg. No. of Cards, per Person	1.15

LABOUR FORCE

2001 Estimates:
Male:	
In the Labour Force	13,244
Participation Rate	78.8
Employed	12,457
Unemployed	787
Unemployment Rate	5.9
Not in Labour Force	3,557
Female:	
In the Labour Force	10,533
Participation Rate	59.9
Employed	9,815
Unemployed	718
Unemployment Rate	6.8
Not in Labour Force	7,058

OCCUPATIONS BY MAJOR GROUPS

2001 Estimates:	Male	Female
Management	1,358	459
Business, Finance & Admin.	1,394	3,818
Natural & Applied Sciences & Related	1,172	235
Health	122	809
Social Sciences, Gov't-Services & Religion	133	259
Education	343	485
Arts, Culture, Recreation & Sport	281	228
Sales & Service	2,718	3,090
Trades, Transport & Equipment Operators & Related	3,567	267
Primary Industries	339	51
Processing, Mfg. & Utilities	1,483	463

LEVEL OF SCHOOLING

2001 Estimates:
Population 15 years +	34,392
Less than Grade 9	5,008
Grades 9-13 w/o Certif.	7,057
Grade 9-13 with Certif.	7,385
Trade Certif. /Dip.	1,680
Non-Univ. w/o Certif./Dip.	2,833
Non-Univ. with Certif./Dip.	5,642
Univ. w/o Degree	2,468
Univ. w/o Degree/Certif.	474
Univ. with Certif.	1,994
Univ. with Degree	2,319

Saint-Eustache
(Ville)
Montréal CMA
(Cont'd)

AVERAGE HOUSEHOLD EXPENDITURES

2001 Estimates:
Food	$6,551
Shelter	$7,839
Clothing	$2,235
Transportation	$6,045
Health & Personal Care	$2,028
Recr'n, Read'g & Education	$3,314
Taxes & Securities	$15,110
Other	$7,407
Total Expenditures	$50,529

PRIVATE HOUSEHOLDS

2001 Estimates:
Private Households, Total	15,950
Pop. in Private Households	42,343
Average no. per Household	2.7

FAMILIES

2001 Estimates:
Families in Private Households	12,522
Husband-Wife Families	10,651
Lone-Parent Families	1,871
Aver. No. Persons per Family	3.1
Aver. No. Sons/Daughters at Home	1.3

HOUSING

2001 Estimates:
Occupied Private Dwellings	15,950
Owned	10,562
Rented	5,388
Single-Detached House	9,415
Semi-Detached House	1,161
Row Houses	188
Apartment, 5+ Storeys	11
Apartment, 5 or Fewer Storeys	4,670
Apartment, Detached Duplex	478
Other Single-Attached	27

VEHICLES

2001 Estimates:
Model Yrs. '81-'96, No.	20,541
% Total	74.27
Model Yrs. '97-'98, No.	4,426
% Total	16.00
'99 Vehicles registered in Model Yr. '99, No.	2,692
% Total	9.73
Total No. '81-'99	27,659

LEGAL MARITAL STATUS

2001 Estimates: (Age 15+)
Single (Never Married)	12,228
Legally Married (Not Separated)	16,080
Legally Married (Separated)	864
Widowed	1,722
Divorced	3,498

PSYTE CATEGORIES

2001 Estimates	No. of House-holds	% of Total Hhds.	Index
Participation Quebec	5,971	37.44	1,299
New Quebec Rows	320	2.01	183
Quebec Melange	4,038	25.32	955
Traditional French Cdn. Families	1,194	7.49	279
Quebec's Heartland	164	1.03	105
Quebec Town Elders	3,012	18.88	668
Quebec's New Urban Mosaic	868	5.44	226
Aged Pensioners	381	2.39	180

FINANCIAL P$YTE

2001 Estimates	No. of House-holds	% of Total Hhds.	Index
Mortgages & Minivans	6,291	39.44	598
Country Credit	5,232	32.80	485
Rural Family Blues	164	1.03	13
Loan Parent,Stress	3,012	18.88	324
NSF	868	5.44	154
Senior Survivors	381	2.39	127

HOME LANGUAGE

2001 Estimates:		% Total
English	1,488	3.48
French	40,460	94.50
Arabic	54	0.13
German	44	0.10
Spanish	27	0.06
Other Languages	149	0.35
Multiple Responses	592	1.38
Total	42,814	100.00

BUILDING PERMITS

	1999	1998	1997
		$000	
Value	26,161	32,262	28,217

HOMES BUILT

	1999	1998	1997
No	106	113	217

TAXATION

Income Class:	1997	% Total
Under $5,000	3,700	12.88
$5,000-$10,000	3,740	13.02
$10,000-$15,000	4,070	14.17
$15,000-$20,000	2,860	9.95
$20,000-$25,000	2,390	8.32
$25,000-$30,000	2,330	8.11
$30,000-$40,000	3,760	13.09
$40,000-$50,000	2,490	8.67
$50,000 +	3,390	11.80
Total Returns, No.	28,730	
Total Income, $000	729,533	
Total Taxable Returns	20,690	
Total Tax, $000	86,922	
Average Income, $	25,393	
Average Tax, $	4,201	

VITAL STATISTICS

	1997	1996	1995	1994
Births	472	444	495	557
Deaths	216	220	241	224
Natural Increase	256	224	254	333
Marriages	84	86	74	85

Note: Latest available data.

MEDIA INFO
see Montréal, CMA

Saint-Hubert
(Ville)
Montréal CMA

In census division Champlain.

POPULATION

July 1, 2001 Estimate	80,872
% Cdn. Total	0.26
% Change, '96 -'01	3.27
Avg. Annual Growth Rate, %	0.65
2003 Projected Population	83,019
2006 Projected Population	86,660
2001 Households Estimate	29,469
2003 Projected Households	30,594
2006 Projected Households	32,334

INCOME

% Above/Below National Average	-6
2001 Total Income Estimate	$1,610,590,000
% Cdn. Total	0.25
2001 Average Hhld. Income	$54,700
2001 Per Capita	$19,900
2003 Projected Total Income	$1,769,790,000
2006 Projected Total Income	$2,042,100,000

RETAIL SALES

% Above/Below National Average	-4
2001 Retail Sales Estimate	$692,020,000
% Cdn. Total	0.25
2001 per Household	$23,500
2001 per Capita	$8,600
2001 No. of Establishments	544
2003 Projected Retail Sales	$769,320,000
2006 Projected Retail Sales	$891,050,000

POPULATION

2001 Estimates:
Total		80,872
Male		39,823
Female		41,049
Age Groups	Male	Female
0-4	2,492	2,410
5-9	2,776	2,751
10-14	2,945	2,857
15-19	3,005	2,859
20-24	2,831	2,676
25-29	2,573	2,509
30-34	2,800	2,884
35-39	3,367	3,533
40-44	3,546	3,698
45-49	3,407	3,599
50-54	3,049	3,132
55-59	2,394	2,402
60-64	1,712	1,748
65-69	1,211	1,309
70+	1,715	2,682

DAYTIME POPULATION

2001 Estimates:
Working Population	20,129
At Home Population	38,610
Total	58,739

INCOME

2001 Estimates:
Avg. Household Income	$54,654
Avg. Family Income	$58,558
Per Capita Income	$19,915
Male:	
Avg. Employment Income	$35,022
Avg. Employment Income (Full Time)	$44,026
Female:	
Avg. Employment Income	$22,228
Avg. Employment Income (Full Time)	$31,151

Québec

DISPOSABLE & DISCRETIONARY INCOME

2001 Estimates:	Per Hhld.
Disposable Income	$37,915
Discretionary Income 1 (minus Food & Shelter)	$24,913
Discretionary Income 2 (minus Food, Shelter, & Other Expenditures)	$16,430

LIQUID ASSETS

1999 Estimates:	Per Hhld.
Equity Investments	$58,307
Interest Bearing Investments	$61,702
Total Liquid Assets	$120,009

CREDIT DATA

July 2000:	
Pool of Credit	$570,914,697
Revolving Credit, No.	153,119
Fixed Loans, No.	53,783
Avg. Credit Limit, per Person	$9,355
Avg. Spent, per Person	$4,391
Satisfactory Ratings, No. per Person	3.18
Avg. No. of Cards, per Person	1.18

LABOUR FORCE

2001 Estimates:
Male:	
In the Labour Force	25,022
Participation Rate	79.2
Employed	23,469
Unemployed	1,553
Unemployment Rate	6.2
Not in Labour Force	6,588
Female:	
In the Labour Force	19,755
Participation Rate	59.8
Employed	18,594
Unemployed	1,161
Unemployment Rate	5.9
Not in Labour Force	13,276

OCCUPATIONS BY MAJOR GROUPS

2001 Estimates:	Male	Female
Management	2,364	956
Business, Finance & Admin.	3,090	7,204
Natural & Applied Sciences & Related	2,182	457
Health	331	1,904
Social Sciences, Gov't Services & Religion	297	363
Education	392	680
Arts, Culture, Recreation & Sport	500	397
Sales & Service	5,579	5,634
Trades, Transport & Equipment Operators & Related	6,666	373
Primary Industries	142	46
Processing, Mfg. & Utilities	2,402	1,039

Saint-Hubert
(Ville)
Montréal CMA
(Cont'd)

LEVEL OF SCHOOLING

2001 Estimates:
Population 15 years +	64,641
Less than Grade 9	10,010
Grades 9-13 w/o Certif.	11,811
Grade 9-13 with Certif.	12,497
Trade Certif./Dip.	3,136
Non-Univ. w/o Certif./Dip.	5,335
Non-Univ. with Certif./Dip.	11,382
Univ. w/o Degree	5,172
Univ. w/o Degree/Certif.	958
Univ. with Certif.	4,214
Univ. with Degree	5,298

AVERAGE HOUSEHOLD EXPENDITURES

2001 Estimates:
Food	$6,760
Shelter	$8,201
Clothing	$2,396
Transportation	$6,556
Health & Personal Care	$2,082
Recr'n, Read'g & Education	$3,497
Taxes & Securities	$15,710
Other	$7,644
Total Expenditures	$52,846

PRIVATE HOUSEHOLDS

2001 Estimates:
Private Households, Total	29,469
Pop. in Private Households	80,040
Average no. per Household	2.7

FAMILIES

2001 Estimates:
Families in Private Households	23,918
Husband-Wife Families	20,461
Lone-Parent Families	3,457
Aver. No. Persons per Family	3.1
Aver. No. Sons/Daughters at Home	1.3

HOUSING

2001 Estimates:
Occupied Private Dwellings	29,469
Owned	21,407
Rented	8,062
Single-Detached House	17,539
Semi-Detached House	2,206
Row Houses	412
Apartment, 5+ Storeys	32
Owned Apartment, 5+ Storeys	11
Apartment, 5 or Fewer Storeys	6,880
Apartment, Detached Duplex	1,746
Other Single-Attached	78
Movable Dwellings	576

VEHICLES

2001 Estimates:
Model Yrs. '81-'96, No.	34,422
% Total	77.70
Model Yrs. '97-'98, No.	6,250
% Total	14.11
'99 Vehicles registered in Model Yr. '99, No.	3,627
% Total	8.19
Total No. '81-'99	44,299

LEGAL MARITAL STATUS

2001 Estimates: (Age 15+)
Single (Never Married)	23,368
Legally Married (Not Separated)	30,960
Legally Married (Separated)	1,538
Widowed	3,033
Divorced	5,742

PSYTE CATEGORIES

2001 Estimates	No. of House-holds	% of Total Hhds.	Index
Technocrafts & Bureaucrats	459	1.56	55
Participation Quebec	9,997	33.92	1,177
New Quebec Rows	2,171	7.37	672
Quebec Melange	8,447	28.66	1,082
Traditional French Cdn. Families	3,672	12.46	464
Euro Quebec	1,710	5.80	662
Old Quebec Walkups	1,352	4.59	250
Quebec's New Urban Mosaic	1,588	5.39	224

FINANCIAL P$YTE

2001 Estimates	No. of House-holds	% of Total Hhds.	Index
Successful Suburbanites	459	1.56	23
Mortgages & Minivans	12,168	41.29	626
Country Credit	12,119	41.12	608
Loan Parent Stress	3,062	10.39	178
NSF	1,588	5.39	152

HOME LANGUAGE

2001 Estimates:		% Total
English	7,939	9.82
French	68,018	84.11
Arabic	211	0.26
Chinese	179	0.22
Creoles	251	0.31
German	52	0.06
Greek	222	0.27
Hungarian	47	0.06
Italian	133	0.16
Lao	153	0.19
Polish	61	0.08
Portuguese	238	0.29
Punjabi	62	0.08
Slovenian	115	0.14
Spanish	659	0.81
Tagalog (Pilipino)	68	0.08
Vietnamese	172	0.21
Other Languages	259	0.32
Multiple Responses	2,033	2.51
Total	80,872	100.00

BUILDING PERMITS

	1999	1998	1997
		$000	
Value	50,696	39,432	39,625

HOMES BUILT

	1999	1998	1997
No	289	209	275

TAXATION

Income Class:	1997	% Total
Under $5,000	7,070	12.99
$5,000-$10,000	7,120	13.08
$10,000-$15,000	7,160	13.15
$15,000-$20,000	5,140	9.44
$20,000-$25,000	4,610	8.47
$25,000-$30,000	4,860	8.93
$30,000-$40,000	7,480	13.74
$40,000-$50,000	4,960	9.11
$50,000 +	6,020	11.06
Total Returns, No.	54,440	
Total Income, $000	1,368,368	
Total Taxable Returns	39,320	
Total Tax, $000	160,778	
Average Income, $	25,135	
Average Tax, $	4,089	

VITAL STATISTICS

	1997	1996	1995	1994
Births	859	959	953	1,001
Deaths	403	344	376	363
Natural Increase	456	615	577	638
Marriages	171	114	143	139

Note: Latest available data.

MEDIA INFO
see Montréal, CMA ·

Saint-Jérôme
(Ville)
Montréal CMA

In census division La Rivière-du-Nord.

POPULATION

July 1, 2001 Estimate	22,982
% Cdn. Total	0.07
% Change, '96 -'01	0.49
Avg. Annual Growth Rate, %	0.10
2003 Projected Population	23,687
2006 Projected Population	24,214
2001 Households Estimate	11,394
2003 Projected Households	11,587
2006 Projected Households	12,048

INCOME

% Above/Below National Average	-26
2001 Total Income Estimate	$360,490,000
% Cdn. Total	0.05
2001 Average Hhld. Income	$31,600
2001 Per Capita	$15,700
2003 Projected Total Income	$382,020,000
2006 Projected Total Income	$425,340,000

RETAIL SALES

% Above/Below National Average	+88
2001 Retail Sales Estimate	$387,730,000
% Cdn. Total	0.14
2001 per Household	$34,000
2001 per Capita	$16,900
2001 No. of Establishments	296
2003 Projected Retail Sales	$429,310,000
2006 Projected Retail Sales	$481,850,000

POPULATION

2001 Estimates:

Total	22,982
Male	10,722
Female	12,260

Age Groups	Male	Female
0-4	603	596
5-9	590	601
10-14	601	604
15-19	669	676
20-24	746	760
25-29	762	735
30-34	823	754
35-39	866	840
40-44	847	902
45-49	789	896
50-54	717	839
55-59	634	757
60-64	540	677
65-69	478	680
70+	1,057	1,943

DAYTIME POPULATION

2001 Estimates:

Working Population	17,442
At Home Population	14,184
Total	31,626

INCOME

2001 Estimates:

Avg. Household Income	$31,639
Avg. Family Income	$39,687
Per Capita Income	$15,686
Male:	
Avg. Employment Income	$25,728
Avg. Employment Income (Full Time)	$34,997
Female:	
Avg. Employment Income	$17,867
Avg. Employment Income (Full Time)	$26,542

DISPOSABLE & DISCRETIONARY INCOME

2001 Estimates:	Per Hhld.
Disposable Income	$22,370
Discretionary Income 1 (minus Food & Shelter)	$13,079
Discretionary Income 2 (minus Food, Shelter, & Other Expenditures)	$8,390

LIQUID ASSETS

1999 Estimates:	Per Hhld.
Equity Investments	$30,418
Interest Bearing Investments	$36,090
Total Liquid Assets	$66,508

CREDIT DATA

July 2000:

Pool of Credit	$121,863,305
Revolving Credit, No.	37,675
Fixed Loans, No.	11,085
Avg. Credit Limit, per Person	$6,191
Avg. Spent, per Person	$2,820
Satisfactory Ratings, No. per Person	2.36
Avg. No. of Cards, per Person	0.81

LABOUR FORCE

2001 Estimates:

Male:	
In the Labour Force	5,620
Participation Rate	62.9
Employed	4,751
Unemployed	869
Unemployment Rate	15.5
Not in Labour Force	3,308
Female:	
In the Labour Force	4,722
Participation Rate	45.1
Employed	4,191
Unemployed	531
Unemployment Rate	11.2
Not in Labour Force	5,737

OCCUPATIONS BY MAJOR GROUPS

2001 Estimates:	Male	Female
Management	330	168
Business, Finance & Admin.	458	1,170
Natural & Applied Sciences & Related	223	20
Health	85	425
Social Sciences, Gov't Services & Religion	105	149
Education	148	205
Arts, Culture, Recreation & Sport	158	117
Sales & Service	1,286	1,682
Trades, Transport & Equipment Operators & Related	1,302	79
Primary Industries	111	31
Processing, Mfg. & Utilities	993	370

LEVEL OF SCHOOLING

2001 Estimates:

Population 15 years +	19,387
Less than Grade 9	5,116
Grades 9-13 w/o Certif.	4,378
Grade 9-13 with Certif.	3,253
Trade Certif. /Dip.	911
Non-Univ. w/o Certif./Dip.	1,574
Non-Univ. with Certif./Dip.	2,202
Univ. w/o Degree	888
Univ. w/o Degree/Certif.	55
Univ. with Certif.	833
Univ. with Degree	1,065

AVERAGE HOUSEHOLD EXPENDITURES

2001 Estimates:

Food	$4,602
Shelter	$6,038
Clothing	$1,418
Transportation	$3,145
Health & Personal Care	$1,390
Recr'n, Read'g & Education	$2,109
Taxes & Securities	$8,800
Other	$5,417
Total Expenditures	$32,919

PRIVATE HOUSEHOLDS

2001 Estimates:

Private Households, Total	11,394
Pop. in Private Households	22,413
Average no. per Household	2.0

FAMILIES

2001 Estimates:

Families in Private Households	6,639
Husband-Wife Families	4,986
Lone-Parent Families	1,653
Aver. No. Persons per Family	2.7
Aver. No. Sons/Daughters at Home	0.9

HOUSING

2001 Estimates:

Occupied Private Dwellings	11,394
Owned	3,558
Rented	7,836
Single-Detached House	2,120
Semi-Detached House	309
Row Houses	205
Apartment, 5+ Storeys	787
Owned Apartment, 5+ Storeys	71
Apartment, 5 or Fewer Storeys	5,437
Apartment, Detached Duplex	2,344
Other Single-Attached	182
Movable Dwellings	10

VEHICLES

2001 Estimates:

Model Yrs. '81-'96, No.	11,166
% Total	77.50
Model Yrs. '97-'98, No.	1,979
% Total	13.74
'99 Vehicles registered in Model Yr. '99, No.	1,263
% Total	8.77
Total No. '81-'99	14,408

LEGAL MARITAL STATUS

2001 Estimates: (Age 15+)

Single (Never Married)	7,833
Legally Married (Not Separated)	6,414
Legally Married (Separated)	657
Widowed	1,845
Divorced	2,638

PSYTE CATEGORIES

2001 Estimates	No. of House -holds	% of Total Hhds.	Index
New Quebec Rows	531	4.66	425
Quebec Melange	970	8.51	321
Big Country Families	16	0.14	10
Old Quebec Walkups	765	6.71	366
Quebec Town Elders	4,274	37.51	1,327
Quebec's New Urban Mosaic	4,203	36.89	1,531
Aged Pensioners	273	2.40	180
Old Grey Towers	313	2.75	496

FINANCIAL P$YTE

2001 Estimates	No. of House -holds	% of Total Hhds.	Index
Mortgages & Minivans	531	4.66	71
Country Credit	970	8.51	126
Rural Family Blues	16	0.14	2
Loan Parent Stress	5,039	44.23	759
NSF	4,203	36.89	1,043
Senior Survivors	586	5.14	273

Québec

HOME LANGUAGE

2001 Estimates:		% Total
English	188	0.82
French	22,569	98.20
Chinese	15	0.07
Croatian	43	0.19
Italian	20	0.09
Romanian	14	0.06
Multiple Responses	133	0.58
Total	22,982	100.00

BUILDING PERMITS

	1999	1998 $000	1997
Value	23,972	26,990	17,062

HOMES BUILT

	1999	1998	1997
No.	25	21	29

TAXATION

Income Class:	1997	% Total
Under $5,000	2,140	11.13
$5,000-$10,000	4,050	21.07
$10,000-$15,000	4,050	21.07
$15,000-$20,000	2,150	11.19
$20,000-$25,000	1,620	8.43
$25,000-$30,000	1,420	7.39
$30,000-$40,000	1,730	9.00
$40,000-$50,000	980	5.10
$50,000 +	1,090	5.67
Total Returns, No.	19,220	
Total Income, $000	382,789	
Total Taxable Returns	11,450	
Total Tax, $000	37,854	
Average Income, $	19,916	
Average Tax, $	3,306	

VITAL STATISTICS

	1997	1996	1995	1994
Births	241	267	281	307
Deaths	314	271	258	273
Natural Increase	-73	-4	23	34
Marriages	374	451	407	411

Note: Latest available data.

MEDIA INFO
see Montréal, CMA

Québec

Saint-Lambert
(Ville)
Montréal CMA

In census division Champlain.

POPULATION

July 1, 2001 Estimate	21,318
% Cdn. Total	0.07
% Change, '96 -'01	0.00
Avg. Annual Growth Rate, %	0.00
2003 Projected Population	21,532
2006 Projected Population	21,961
2001 Households Estimate	10,508
2003 Projected Households	10,736
2006 Projected Households	11,083

INCOME

% Above/Below National Average	+67
2001 Total Income Estimate	$751,540,000
% Cdn. Total	0.11
2001 Average Hhld. Income	$71,500
2001 Per Capita	$35,300
2003 Projected Total Income	$803,220,000
2006 Projected Total Income	$889,480,000

RETAIL SALES

% Above/Below National Average	-41
2001 Retail Sales Estimate	$112,900,000
% Cdn. Total	0.04
2001 per Household	$10,700
2001 per Capita	$5,300
2001 No. of Establishments	166
2003 Projected Retail Sales	$120,230,000
2006 Projected Retail Sales	$132,480,000

POPULATION

2001 Estimates:

Total		21,318
Male		9,572
Female		11,746

Age Groups	Male	Female
0-4	450	447
5-9	473	474
10-14	485	477
15-19	528	517
20-24	537	523
25-29	520	503
30-34	534	582
35-39	630	699
40-44	710	833
45-49	758	952
50-54	777	966
55-59	718	882
60-64	618	767
65-69	532	725
70+	1,302	2,399

DAYTIME POPULATION

2001 Estimates:

Working Population	5,573
At Home Population	10,557
Total	16,130

INCOME

2001 Estimates:

Avg. Household Income	$71,521
Avg. Family Income	$94,198
Per Capita Income	$35,254
Male:	
Avg. Employment Income	$56,738
Avg. Employment Income (Full Time)	$70,257
Female:	
Avg. Employment Income	$32,975
Avg. Employment Income (Full Time)	$43,131

DISPOSABLE & DISCRETIONARY INCOME

2001 Estimates:	*Per Hhld.*
Disposable Income	$43,576
Discretionary Income 1 (minus Food & Shelter)	$27,020
Discretionary Income 2 (minus Food, Shelter, & Other Expenditures)	$17,557

LIQUID ASSETS

1999 Estimates:	*Per Hhld.*
Equity Investments	$131,881
Interest Bearing Investments	$92,429
Total Liquid Assets	$224,310

CREDIT DATA

July 2000:

Pool of Credit	$222,239,187
Revolving Credit, No.	52,026
Fixed Loans, No.	10,671
Avg. Credit Limit, per Person	$11,182
Avg. Spent, per Person	$4,134
Satisfactory Ratings, No. per Person	3.05
Avg. No. of Cards, per Person	1.32

LABOUR FORCE

2001 Estimates:

Male:	
In the Labour Force	5,730
Participation Rate	70.2
Employed	5,543
Unemployed	187
Unemployment Rate	3.3
Not in Labour Force	2,434
Female:	
In the Labour Force	5,472
Participation Rate	52.9
Employed	5,310
Unemployed	162
Unemployment Rate	3.0
Not in Labour Force	4,876

OCCUPATIONS BY MAJOR GROUPS

2001 Estimates:	Male	Female
Management	1,218	581
Business, Finance & Admin.	842	1,482
Natural & Applied Sciences & Related	693	174
Health	362	599
Social Sciences, Gov't Services & Religion	300	431
Education	242	518
Arts, Culture, Recreation & Sport	348	459
Sales & Service	1,048	976
Trades, Transport & Equipment Operators & Related	389	30
Primary Industries	33	20
Processing, Mfg. & Utilities	134	41

LEVEL OF SCHOOLING

2001 Estimates:

Population 15 years +	18,512
Less than Grade 9	1,341
Grades 9-13 w/o Certif.	1,804
Grade 9-13 with Certif.	2,249
Trade Certif. /Dip.	586
Non-Univ. w/o Certif./Dip.	1,098
Non-Univ. with Certif./Dip.	2,353
Univ. w/o Degree	2,465
Univ. w/o Degree/Certif.	361
Univ. with Certif.	2,104
Univ. with Degree	6,616

AVERAGE HOUSEHOLD EXPENDITURES

2001 Estimates:

Food	$7,493
Shelter	$12,124
Clothing	$2,813
Transportation	$6,997
Health & Personal Care	$2,437
Recr'n, Read'g & Education	$4,727
Taxes & Securities	$19,701
Other	$10,013
Total Expenditures	$66,305

PRIVATE HOUSEHOLDS

2001 Estimates:

Private Households, Total	10,508
Pop. in Private Households	20,896
Average no. per Household	2.0

FAMILIES

2001 Estimates:

Families in Private Households	6,213
Husband-Wife Families	5,382
Lone-Parent Families	831
Aver. No. Persons per Family	2.7
Aver. No. Sons/Daughters at Home	0.9

HOUSING

2001 Estimates:

Occupied Private Dwellings	10,508
Owned	5,838
Rented	4,670
Single-Detached House	3,183
Semi-Detached House	576
Row Houses	511
Apartment, 5+ Storeys	2,631
Owned Apartment, 5+ Storeys	782
Apartment, 5 or Fewer Storeys	3,104
Apartment, Detached Duplex	454
Other Single-Attached	49

VEHICLES

2001 Estimates:

Model Yrs. '81-'96, No.	9,220
% Total	72.60
Model Yrs. '97-'98, No.	2,214
% Total	17.43
'99 Vehicles registered in Model Yr. '99, No.	1,265
% Total	9.96
Total No. '81-'99	12,699

LEGAL MARITAL STATUS

2001 Estimates: (Age 15+)

Single (Never Married)	6,003
Legally Married (Not Separated)	8,172
Legally Married (Separated)	457
Widowed	1,953
Divorced	1,927

PSYTE CATEGORIES

2001 Estimates	No. of House-holds	% of Total Hhds.	Index
Urban Gentry	3,127	29.76	1,656
Suburban Executives	400	3.81	266
Brie & Chablis	491	4.67	522
New Quebec Rows	614	5.84	533
High Rise Sunsets	400	3.81	266
Young Urban Professionals	2,846	27.08	1,427
Old Quebec Walkups	674	6.41	350
Aging Quebec Urbanites	711	6.77	2,345
Old Grey Towers	1,122	10.68	1,928

FINANCIAL P$YTE

2001 Estimates	No. of House-holds	% of Total Hhds.	Index
Four Star Investors	3,527	33.56	668
Urban Heights	3,337	31.76	738
Mortgages & Minivans	614	5.84	89
Revolving Renters	400	3.81	83
Loan Parent Stress	1,385	13.18	226
Senior Survivors	1,122	10.68	567

HOME LANGUAGE

2001 Estimates:		% Total
English	4,576	21.47
French	15,439	72.42
Arabic	61	0.29
Bulgarian	28	0.13
Chinese	139	0.65
Czech	20	0.09
Estonian	16	0.08
Hungarian	72	0.34
Italian	20	0.09
Korean	47	0.22
Persian (Farsi)	41	0.19
Romanian	26	0.12
Slovak	15	0.07
Spanish	41	0.19
Vietnamese	25	0.12
Other Languages	70	0.33
Multiple Responses	682	3.20
Total	21,318	100.00

BUILDING PERMITS

	1999	1998	1997
		$000	
Value	26,303	19,244	18,592

HOMES BUILT

	1999	1998	1997
No.	165	43	45

TAXATION

Income Class:	1997	% Total
Under $5,000	1,320	8.07
$5,000-$10,000	1,390	8.50
$10,000-$15,000	1,850	11.31
$15,000-$20,000	1,380	8.44
$20,000-$25,000	1,210	7.40
$25,000-$30,000	1,170	7.15
$30,000-$40,000	2,070	12.65
$40,000-$50,000	1,610	9.84
$50,000 +	4,360	26.65
Total Returns, No.	16,360	
Total Income, $000	707,227	
Total Taxable Returns	13,000	
Total Tax, $000	113,163	
Average Income, $	43,229	
Average Tax, $	8,705	

VITAL STATISTICS

	1997	1996	1995	1994
Births	184	159	151	170
Deaths	254	237	220	226
Natural Increase	-70	-78	-69	-56
Marriages	49	78	62	78

Note: Latest available data.

MEDIA INFO

see Montréal, CMA

Saint-Laurent
(Ville)
Montréal CMA

In census division Communauté urbaine de Montréal.

POPULATION

July 1, 2001 Estimate	76,678
% Cdn. Total	0.25
% Change, '96 -'01	1.44
Avg. Annual Growth Rate, %	0.29
2003 Projected Population	78,245
2006 Projected Population	81,032
2001 Households Estimate	30,926
2003 Projected Households	31,475
2006 Projected Households	32,385

INCOME

% Above/Below National Average	-14
2001 Total Income Estimate	$1,385,540,000
% Cdn. Total	0.21
2001 Average Hhld. Income	$44,800
2001 Per Capita	$18,100
2003 Projected Total Income	$1,495,620,000
2006 Projected Total Income	$1,685,880,000

RETAIL SALES

% Above/Below National Average	+148
2001 Retail Sales Estimate	$1,699,950,000
% Cdn. Total	0.61
2001 per Household	$55,000
2001 per Capita	$22,200
2001 No. of Establishments	883
2003 Projected Retail Sales	$1,882,770,000
2006 Projected Retail Sales	$2,160,340,000

POPULATION

2001 Estimates:

Total		76,678
Male		36,260
Female		40,418

Age Groups	Male	Female
0-4	2,232	2,091
5-9	2,162	2,043
10-14	2,091	1,974
15-19	2,218	2,063
20-24	2,423	2,255
25-29	2,558	2,512
30-34	2,768	2,729
35-39	2,830	2,782
40-44	2,645	2,795
45-49	2,478	2,840
50-54	2,282	2,716
55-59	2,039	2,401
60-64	1,841	2,220
65-69	1,710	2,179
70+	3,983	6,818

DAYTIME POPULATION

2001 Estimates:

Working Population	123,237
At Home Population	45,411
Total	168,648

INCOME

2001 Estimates:

Avg. Household Income	$44,802
Avg. Family Income	$50,505
Per Capita Income	$18,070
Male:	
Avg. Employment Income	$29,794
Avg. Employment Income (Full Time)	$41,365
Female:	
Avg. Employment Income	$21,422
Avg. Employment Income (Full Time)	$30,712

DISPOSABLE & DISCRETIONARY INCOME

2001 Estimates:	*Per Hhld.*
Disposable Income	$31,057
Discretionary Income 1 (minus Food & Shelter)	$18,547
Discretionary Income 2 (minus Food, Shelter, & Other Expenditures)	$11,673

LIQUID ASSETS

1999 Estimates:	*Per Hhld.*
Equity Investments	$54,922
Interest Bearing Investments	$54,992
Total Liquid Assets	$109,914

CREDIT DATA

July 2000:

Pool of Credit	$605,081,049
Revolving Credit, No.	172,486
Fixed Loans, No.	33,317
Avg. Credit Limit, per Person	$7,897
Avg. Spent, per Person	$3,031
Satisfactory Ratings, No. per Person	2.59
Avg. No. of Cards, per Person	1.12

LABOUR FORCE

2001 Estimates:
Male:

In the Labour Force	19,823
Participation Rate	66.6
Employed	17,867
Unemployed	1,956
Unemployment Rate	9.9
Not in Labour Force	9,952
Female:	
In the Labour Force	16,587
Participation Rate	48.3
Employed	14,913
Unemployed	1,674
Unemployment Rate	10.1
Not in Labour Force	17,723

OCCUPATIONS BY MAJOR GROUPS

2001 Estimates:	Male	Female
Management	2,758	1,121
Business, Finance & Admin.	2,721	5,139
Natural & Applied Sciences & Related	2,075	480
Health	567	1,028
Social Sciences, Gov't Services & Religion	269	410
Education	527	852
Arts, Culture, Recreation & Sport	503	494
Sales & Service	4,751	4,080
Trades, Transport & Equipment Operators & Related	2,222	289
Primary Industries	67	21
Processing, Mfg. & Utilities	1,974	1,593

LEVEL OF SCHOOLING

2001 Estimates:

Population 15 years +	64,085
Less than Grade 9	9,732
Grades 9-13 w/o Certif.	9,008
Grade 9-13 with Certif.	10,034
Trade Certif. /Dip.	1,762
Non-Univ. w/o Certif./Dip.	4,913
Non-Univ. with Certif./Dip.	8,063
Univ. w/o Degree	8,096
Univ. w/o Degree/Certif.	2,112
Univ. with Certif.	5,984
Univ. with Degree	12,477

AVERAGE HOUSEHOLD EXPENDITURES

2001 Estimates:

Food	$5,762
Shelter	$8,673
Clothing	$1,970
Transportation	$4,999
Health & Personal Care	$1,701
Recr'n, Read'g & Education	$3,000
Taxes & Securities	$11,374
Other	$6,708
Total Expenditures	$44,187

PRIVATE HOUSEHOLDS

2001 Estimates:

Private Households, Total	30,926
Pop. in Private Households	75,749
Average no. per Household	2.4

FAMILIES

2001 Estimates:

Families in Private Households	20,843
Husband-Wife Families	17,223
Lone-Parent Families	3,620
Aver. No. Persons per Family	3.0
Aver. No. Sons/Daughters at Home	1.2

HOUSING

2001 Estimates:

Occupied Private Dwellings	30,926
Owned	12,056
Rented	18,870
Single-Detached House	3,819
Semi-Detached House	2,109
Row Houses	1,192
Apartment, 5+ Storeys	9,871
Owned Apartment, 5+ Storeys	2,334
Apartment, 5 or Fewer Storeys	12,237
Apartment, Detached Duplex	1,579
Other Single-Attached	45
Movable Dwellings	74

VEHICLES

2001 Estimates:

Model Yrs. '81-'96, No.	31,936
% Total	62.70
Model Yrs. '97-'98, No.	10,437
% Total	20.49
'99 Vehicles registered in Model Yr. '99, No.	8,564
% Total	16.81
Total No. '81-'99	50,937

LEGAL MARITAL STATUS

2001 Estimates: (Age 15+)

Single (Never Married)	21,528
Legally Married (Not Separated)	31,129
Legally Married (Separated)	1,520
Widowed	5,326
Divorced	4,582

Québec

PSYTE CATEGORIES

2001 Estimates	No. of House-holds	% of Total Hhds.	Index
Urban Gentry	750	2.43	135
Mortgaged in Suburbia	70	0.23	16
Asian Heights	648	2.10	331
Suburban Nesters	1,122	3.63	226
Brie & Chablis	2,172	7.02	784
Aging Erudites	2,248	7.27	482
New Quebec Rows	525	1.70	155
Quebec Melange	801	2.59	98
Asian Mosaic	222	0.72	52
High Rise Melting Pot	2,679	8.66	578
Conservative Homebodies	116	0.38	10
High Rise Sunsets	1,838	5.94	416
Young Urban Professionals	499	1.61	85
Young Urban Mix	2,103	6.80	321
Young Urban Intelligentsia	75	0.24	16
University Enclaves	79	0.26	13
Urban Bohemia	1,932	6.25	534
Euro Quebec	3,139	10.15	1,157
Old Quebec Walkups	4,240	13.71	748
Aging Quebec Urbanites	2,194	7.09	2,458
Struggling Downtowns	325	1.05	33
Aged Pensioners	363	1.17	88
Big City Stress	2,614	8.45	749

FINANCIAL PSYTE

2001 Estimates	No. of House-holds	% of Total Hhds.	Index
Four Star Investors	750	2.43	48
Successful Suburbanites	718	2.32	35
Canadian Comfort	1,122	3.63	37
Urban Heights	4,919	15.91	370
Mortgages & Minivans	525	1.70	26
Dollars & Sense	222	0.72	27
Bills & Wills	2,219	7.18	87
Country Credit	801	2.59	38
Revolving Renters	1,838	5.94	129
Young Urban Struggle	2,086	6.75	143
Loan Parent Stress	9,573	30.95	532
Towering Debt	3,004	9.71	124
NSF	2,614	8.45	239
Senior Survivors	363	1.17	62

Québec

Saint-Laurent
(Ville)
Montréal CMA
(Cont'd)

HOME LANGUAGE

2001 Estimates:		% Total
English	19,650	25.63
French	27,464	35.82
Arabic	6,200	8.09
Armenian	1,592	2.08
Bengali	103	0.13
Bulgarian	52	0.07
Chinese	3,776	4.92
Creoles	441	0.58
Croatian	120	0.16
Czech	40	0.05
German	130	0.17
Greek	2,361	3.08
Gujarati	304	0.40
Hebrew	492	0.64
Hindi	143	0.19
Hungarian	117	0.15
Italian	504	0.66
Japanese	77	0.10
Khmer (Cambodian)	713	0.93
Lao	250	0.33
Pashto	41	0.05
Persian (Farsi)	475	0.62
Polish	464	0.61
Portuguese	159	0.21
Punjabi	267	0.35
Romanian	318	0.41
Russian	288	0.38
Serbo-Croatian	109	0.14
Spanish	877	1.14
Tagalog (Pilipino)	119	0.16
Tamil	530	0.69
Turkish	90	0.12
Urdu	256	0.33
Vietnamese	1,243	1.62
Yiddish	76	0.10
Other Languages	529	0.69
Multiple Responses	6,308	8.23
Total	76,678	100.00

BUILDING PERMITS

	1999	1998	1997
		$000	
Value	181,039	167,328	100,891

HOMES BUILT

	1999	1998	1997
No.	285	259	142

TAXATION

Income Class:	1997	% Total
Under $5,000	10,140	17.85
$5,000-$10,000	8,710	15.33
$10,000-$15,000	9,310	16.39
$15,000-$20,000	5,710	10.05
$20,000-$25,000	4,510	7.94
$25,000-$30,000	3,820	6.72
$30,000-$40,000	5,370	9.45
$40,000-$50,000	3,410	6.00
$50,000 +	5,820	10.24
Total Returns, No.	56,810	
Total Income, $000	1,334,690	
Total Taxable Returns	35,190	
Total Tax, $000	159,320	
Average Income, $	23,494	
Average Tax, $	4,527	

VITAL STATISTICS

	1997	1996	1995	1994
Births	1,013	980	1,020	1,041
Deaths	614	539	601	594
Natural Increase	399	441	419	447
Marriages	290	269	277	302

Note: Latest available data.

MEDIA INFO

see Montréal, CMA

Saint-Lazare
(Paroisse)
Montréal CMA

**In census division
Vaudreuil-Soulanges.**

POPULATION

July 1, 2001 Estimate	13,563
% Cdn. Total	0.04
% Change, '96 -'01	18.99
Avg. Annual Growth Rate, %	3.54
2003 Projected Population	15,082
2006 Projected Population	17,571
2001 Households Estimate	4,554
2003 Projected Households	5,073
2006 Projected Households	5,937

INCOME

% Above/Below National Average	+26
2001 Total Income Estimate	$360,750,000
% Cdn. Total	0.05
2001 Average Hhld. Income	$79,200
2001 Per Capita	$26,600
2003 Projected Total Income	$428,980,000
2006 Projected Total Income	$556,590,000

RETAIL SALES

% Above/Below National Average	-48
2001 Retail Sales Estimate	$62,760,000
% Cdn. Total	0.02
2001 per Household	$13,800
2001 per Capita	$4,600
2001 No. of Establishments	81
2003 Projected Retail Sales	$73,870,000
2006 Projected Retail Sales	$91,750,000

POPULATION

2001 Estimates:		
Total		13,563
Male		6,820
Female		6,743
Age Groups	Male	Female
0-4	470	438
5-9	578	570
10-14	602	578
15-19	536	496
20-24	394	367
25-29	324	342
30-34	450	525
35-39	642	725
40-44	709	744
45-49	665	607
50-54	518	439
55-59	348	294
60-64	233	204
65-69	155	151
70+	196	263

DAYTIME POPULATION

2001 Estimates:	
Working Population	1,093
At Home Population	6,121
Total	7,214

INCOME

2001 Estimates:	
Avg. Household Income	$79,216
Avg. Family Income	$80,376
Per Capita Income	$26,598
Male:	
Avg. Employment Income	$51,562
Avg. Employment Income (Full Time)	$62,991
Female:	
Avg. Employment Income	$28,818
Avg. Employment Income (Full Time)	$40,241

DISPOSABLE & DISCRETIONARY INCOME

2001 Estimates:	Per Hhld.
Disposable Income	$54,360
Discretionary Income 1 (minus Food & Shelter)	$37,783
Discretionary Income 2 (minus Food, Shelter, & Other Expenditures)	$26,125

LIQUID ASSETS

1999 Estimates:	Per Hhld.
Equity Investments	$140,209
Interest Bearing Investments	$99,584
Total Liquid Assets	$239,793

CREDIT DATA

July 2000:	
Pool of Credit	$112,170,674
Revolving Credit, No.	21,135
Fixed Loans, No.	7,903
Avg. Credit Limit, per Person	$14,401
Avg. Spent, per Person	$6,952
Satisfactory Ratings, No. per Person	3.53
Avg. No. of Cards, per Person	1.37

LABOUR FORCE

2001 Estimates:	
Male:	
In the Labour Force	4,441
Participation Rate	85.9
Employed	4,313
Unemployed	128
Unemployment Rate	2.9
Not in Labour Force	729
Female:	
In the Labour Force	3,207
Participation Rate	62.2
Employed	3,050
Unemployed	157
Unemployment Rate	4.9
Not in Labour Force	1,950

OCCUPATIONS BY MAJOR GROUPS

2001 Estimates:	Male	Female
Management	1,096	325
Business, Finance & Admin.	461	1,083
Natural & Applied Sciences & Related	512	112
Health	17	184
Social Sciences, Gov't Services & Religion	81	74
Education	92	203
Arts, Culture, Recreation & Sport	97	88
Sales & Service	912	923
Trades, Transport & Equipment Operators & Related	812	51
Primary Industries	135	36
Processing, Mfg. & Utilities	199	71

LEVEL OF SCHOOLING

2001 Estimates:	
Population 15 years +	10,327
Less than Grade 9	864
Grades 9-13 w/o Certif.	1,492
Grade 9-13 with Certif.	1,726
Trade Certif. /Dip.	360
Non-Univ. w/o Certif./Dip.	845
Non-Univ. with Certif./Dip.	1,975
Univ. w/o Degree	1,353
Univ. w/o Degree/Certif.	399
Univ. with Certif.	954
Univ. with Degree	1,712

Saint-Lazare
(Paroisse)
Montréal CMA
(Cont'd)

AVERAGE HOUSEHOLD EXPENDITURES

2001 Estimates:
Food	$8,463
Shelter	$11,030
Clothing	$3,212
Transportation	$9,261
Health & Personal Care	$2,662
Recr'n, Read'g & Education	$5,188
Taxes & Securities	$22,064
Other	$10,622
Total Expenditures	$72,502

PRIVATE HOUSEHOLDS

2001 Estimates:
Private Households, Total	4,554
Pop. in Private Households	13,528
Average no. per Household	3.0

FAMILIES

2001 Estimates:
Families in Private Households	4,059
Husband-Wife Families	3,738
Lone-Parent Families	321
Aver. No. Persons per Family	3.2
Aver. No. Sons/Daughters at Home	1.3

HOUSING

2001 Estimates:
Occupied Private Dwellings	4,554
Owned	4,103
Rented	451
Single-Detached House	4,309
Apartment, 5 or Fewer Storeys	160
Apartment, Detached Duplex	60
Other Single-Attached	25

VEHICLES

2001 Estimates:
Model Yrs. '81-'96, No.	5,768
% Total	73.73
Model Yrs. '97-'98, No.	1,298
% Total	16.59
'99 Vehicles registered in Model Yr. '99, No.	757
% Total	9.68
Total No. '81-'99	7,823

LEGAL MARITAL STATUS

2001 Estimates: (Age 15+)
Single (Never Married)	2,861
Legally Married (Not Separated)	6,237
Legally Married (Separated)	188
Widowed	244
Divorced	797

PSYTE CATEGORIES

2001 Estimates	No. of House-holds	% of Total Hhds.	Index
Suburban Executives	217	4.77	332
Technocrafts & Bureaucrats	497	10.91	388
Boomers & Teens	460	10.10	563
Small City Elite	993	21.81	1,272
Participation Quebec	1,246	27.36	949
Quebec Melange	248	5.45	206
Traditional French Cdn. Families	893	19.61	730

FINANCIAL P$YTE

2001 Estimates	No. of House-holds	% of Total Hhds.	Index
Four Star Investors	677	14.87	296
Successful Suburbanites	497	10.91	164
Canadian Comfort	993	21.81	224
Mortgages & Minivans	1,246	27.36	415
Country Credit	1,141	25.05	370

HOME LANGUAGE

2001 Estimates:		% Total
English	6,112	45.06
French	7,038	51.89
German	43	0.32
Polish	39	0.29
Spanish	24	0.18
Tagalog (Pilipino)	12	0.09
Multiple Responses	295	2.18
Total	13,563	100.00

BUILDING PERMITS

	1999	1998 $000	1997
Value	18,507	15,123	16,099

HOMES BUILT

	1999	1998	1997
No	141	80	92

TAXATION

Income Class:	1997	% Total
Under $5,000	920	12.12
$5,000-$10,000	680	8.96
$10,000-$15,000	740	9.75
$15,000-$20,000	560	7.38
$20,000-$25,000	580	7.64
$25,000-$30,000	540	7.11
$30,000-$40,000	1,030	13.57
$40,000-$50,000	770	10.14
$50,000 +	1,760	23.19
Total Returns, No.	7,590	
Total Income, $000	276,108	
Total Taxable Returns	5,960	
Total Tax, $000	41,697	
Average Income, $	36,378	
Average Tax, $	6,996	

VITAL STATISTICS

	1997	1996	1995	1994
Births	166	162	197	177
Deaths	28	29	32	28
Natural Increase	138	133	165	149
Marriages	15	29	15	24

Note: Latest available data.

MEDIA INFO
see Montréal, CMA

Saint-Léonard
(Ville)
Montréal CMA

In census division Communauté urbaine de Montréal.

POPULATION

July 1, 2001 Estimate	70,780
% Cdn. Total	0.23
% Change, '96 -'01	-2.54
Avg. Annual Growth Rate, %	-0.51
2003 Projected Population	70,780
2006 Projected Population	71,167
2001 Households Estimate	28,490
2003 Projected Households	28,407
2006 Projected Households	28,332

INCOME

% Above/Below National Average	-16
2001 Total Income Estimate	$1,247,980,000
% Cdn. Total	0.19
2001 Average Hhld. Income	$43,800
2001 Per Capita	$17,600
2003 Projected Total Income	$1,303,330,000
2006 Projected Total Income	$1,397,700,000

RETAIL SALES

% Above/Below National Average	+15
2001 Retail Sales Estimate	$731,380,000
% Cdn. Total	0.26
2001 per Household	$25,700
2001 per Capita	$10,300
2001 No. of Establishments	708
2003 Projected Retail Sales	$790,590,000
2006 Projected Retail Sales	$881,090,000

POPULATION

2001 Estimates:
Total		70,780
Male		33,181
Female		37,599
Age Groups	Male	Female
0-4	2,239	2,150
5-9	2,034	1,972
10-14	1,741	1,699
15-19	1,751	1,715
20-24	2,036	2,082
25-29	2,518	2,661
30-34	2,881	2,967
35-39	2,722	2,873
40-44	2,272	2,626
45-49	2,043	2,591
50-54	1,949	2,564
55-59	1,924	2,465
60-64	1,946	2,380
65-69	1,829	2,179
70+	3,296	4,675

DAYTIME POPULATION

2001 Estimates:
Working Population	32,332
At Home Population	39,875
Total	72,207

INCOME

2001 Estimates:
Avg. Household Income	$43,804
Avg. Family Income	$48,115
Per Capita Income	$17,632
Male:	
Avg. Employment Income	$28,216
Avg. Employment Income (Full Time)	$36,307
Female:	
Avg. Employment Income	$20,673
Avg. Employment Income (Full Time)	$28,247

Québec

DISPOSABLE & DISCRETIONARY INCOME

2001 Estimates:	Per Hhld.
Disposable Income	$30,929
Discretionary Income 1 (minus Food & Shelter)	$17,020
Discretionary Income 2 (minus Food, Shelter, & Other Expenditures)	$9,456

LIQUID ASSETS

1999 Estimates:	Per Hhld.
Equity Investments	$48,057
Interest Bearing Investments	$50,241
Total Liquid Assets	$98,298

CREDIT DATA

July 2000:	
Pool of Credit	$450,013,415
Revolving Credit, No.	139,263
Fixed Loans, No.	35,441
Avg. Credit Limit, per Person	$6,806
Avg. Spent, per Person	$2,822
Satisfactory Ratings, No. per Person	2.51
Avg. No. of Cards, per Person	1.05

LABOUR FORCE

2001 Estimates:
Male:	
In the Labour Force	18,318
Participation Rate	67.4
Employed	16,313
Unemployed	2,005
Unemployment Rate	10.9
Not in Labour Force	8,849
Female:	
In the Labour Force	16,646
Participation Rate	52.4
Employed	14,981
Unemployed	1,665
Unemployment Rate	10.0
Not in Labour Force	15,132

OCCUPATIONS BY MAJOR GROUPS

2001 Estimates:	Male	Female
Management	1,762	760
Business, Finance & Admin.	2,410	5,917
Natural & Applied Sciences & Related	1,167	222
Health	298	1,105
Social Sciences, Gov't Services & Religion	135	223
Education	287	564
Arts, Culture, Recreation & Sport	311	208
Sales & Service	4,623	4,229
Trades, Transport & Equipment Operators & Related	3,776	334
Primary Industries	199	n.a.
Processing, Mfg. & Utilities	2,218	2,046

Québec

Saint-Léonard
(Ville)
Montréal CMA
(Cont'd)

LEVEL OF SCHOOLING

2001 Estimates:
Population 15 years +	58,945
Less than Grade 9	16,354
Grades 9-13 w/o Certif.	7,773
Grade 9-13 with Certif.	9,887
Trade Certif. /Dip.	2,103
Non-Univ. w/o Certif./Dip.	4,644
Non-Univ. with Certif./Dip.	7,966
Univ. w/o Degree	4,680
Univ. w/o Degree/Certif.	1,017
Univ. with Certif.	3,663
Univ. with Degree	5,538

AVERAGE HOUSEHOLD EXPENDITURES

2001 Estimates:
Food	$6,282
Shelter	$9,091
Clothing	$2,038
Transportation	$5,396
Health & Personal Care	$1,647
Recr'n, Read'g & Education	$2,867
Taxes & Securities	$9,228
Other	$7,128
Total Expenditures	$43,677

PRIVATE HOUSEHOLDS

2001 Estimates:
Private Households, Total	28,490
Pop. in Private Households	70,020
Average no. per Household	2.5

FAMILIES

2001 Estimates:
Families in Private Households	20,883
Husband-Wife Families	16,926
Lone-Parent Families	3,957
Aver. No. Persons per Family	2.9
Aver. No. Sons/Daughters at Home	1.1

HOUSING

2001 Estimates:
Occupied Private Dwellings	28,490
Owned	9,462
Rented	19,028
Single-Detached House	1,740
Semi-Detached House	608
Row Houses	20
Apartment, 5+ Storeys	887
Owned Apartment, 5+ Storeys	91
Apartment, 5 or Fewer Storeys	23,847
Apartment, Detached Duplex	1,343
Other Single-Attached	45

VEHICLES

2001 Estimates:
Model Yrs. '81-'96, No.	27,229
% Total	75.95
Model Yrs. '97-'98, No.	5,189
% Total	14.47
'99 Vehicles registered in Model Yr. '99, No.	3,432
% Total	9.57
Total No. '81-'99.	35,850

LEGAL MARITAL STATUS

2001 Estimates: (Age 15+)
Single (Never Married)	19,341
Legally Married (Not Separated)	28,941
Legally Married (Separated)	1,700
Widowed	4,097
Divorced	4,866

PSYTE CATEGORIES

2001 Estimates	No. of House -holds	% of Total Hhds.	Index
Old Bungalow Burbs.	385	1.35.	82
Europa	9,968	34.99.	2,814
Euro Quebec	15,939	55.95.	6,379
Old Quebec Walkups	547	1.92.	105
Aging Quebec Urbanites.	689	2.42.	838
Aged Pensioners.	375	1.32.	99
Big City Stress	441	1.55.	137

FINANCIAL PSYTE

2001 Estimates	No. of House -holds	% of Total Hhds.	Index
Miners & Credit-Liners	385	1.35.	43
Dollars & Sense	9,968	34.99.	1,338
Loan Parent Stress	17,175	60.28.	1,035
NSF	441	1.55.	44
Senior Survivors	375	1.32.	70

HOME LANGUAGE

2001 Estimates:		% Total
English	14,367	20.30
French	30,565	43.18
Arabic	1,371	1.94
Chinese	233	0.33
Creoles	782	1.10
Greek	232	0.33
Italian	13,312	18.81
Khmer (Cambodian)	69	0.10
Polish	475	0.67
Portuguese	308	0.44
Romanian	111	0.16
Russian	65	0.09
Slovenian	40	0.06
Spanish	3,022	4.27
Ukrainian	299	0.42
Urdu	50	0.07
Vietnamese	282	0.40
Other Languages	216	0.31
Multiple Responses	4,981	7.04
Total	70,780	100.00

BUILDING PERMITS

	1999	1998 $000	1997
Value	32,425	29,580.	15,473

HOMES BUILT

	1999	1998	1997
No	144	117	15

TAXATION

Income Class:	1997	% Total
Under $5,000	6,820	12.91
$5,000-$10,000	8,140	15.40
$10,000-$15,000	9,350	17.69
$15,000-$20,000	6,500	12.30
$20,000-$25,000	5,320	10.07
$25,000-$30,000	4,660	8.82
$30,000-$40,000	5,690	10.77
$40,000-$50,000	3,090	5.85
$50,000 +	3,270	6.19
Total Returns, No.	52,840	
Total Income, $000	1,120,447	
Total Taxable Returns.	35,440	
Total Tax, $000	115,842	
Average Income, $	21,205	
Average Tax, $	3,269	

VITAL STATISTICS

	1997	1996	1995	1994
Births	1,001	1,016	1,083	1,058
Deaths	501	463	434	451
Natural Increase	500	553	649	607
Marriages	178	174	162	217

Note: Latest available data.

MEDIA INFO
see Montréal, CMA

Sainte-Anne-des-Plaines
(Ville)
Montréal CMA

In census division Thérèse-De Blainville.

POPULATION

July 1, 2001 Estimate	15,359
% Cdn. Total	0.05
% Change, '96 -'01	16.67
Avg. Annual Growth Rate, %	3.13
2003 Projected Population	16,752
2006 Projected Population	19,160
2001 Households Estimate	5,209
2003 Projected Households	5,740
2006 Projected Households	6,658

INCOME

% Above/Below National Average	-19
2001 Total Income Estimate	$263,750,000
% Cdn. Total	0.04
2001 Average Hhld. Income	$50,600
2001 Per Capita	$17,200
2003 Projected Total Income	$305,370,000
2006 Projected Total Income	$383,110,000

RETAIL SALES

% Above/Below National Average	-59
2001 Retail Sales Estimate	$56,330,000
% Cdn. Total	0.02
2001 per Household	$10,800
2001 per Capita	$3,700
2001 No. of Establishments	86
2003 Projected Retail Sales	$64,760,000
2006 Projected Retail Sales	$80,190,000

POPULATION

2001 Estimates:

Total		15,359
Male		8,126
Female		7,233

Age Groups	Male	Female
0-4	502	513
5-9	626	616
10-14	672	615
15-19	632	559
20-24	531	457
25-29	524	453
30-34	713	613
35-39	865	728
40-44	842	666
45-49	686	536
50-54	511	397
55-59	360	290
60-64	245	228
65-69	166	190
70+	251	372

DAYTIME POPULATION

2001 Estimates:

Working Population	2,313
At Home Population	8,012
Total	10,325

INCOME

2001 Estimates:

Avg. Household Income	$50,633
Avg. Family Income	$53,156
Per Capita Income	$17,172
Male:	
Avg. Employment Income	$32,842
Avg. Employment Income (Full Time)	$40,483
Female:	
Avg. Employment Income	$19,830
Avg. Employment Income (Full Time)	$29,572

DISPOSABLE & DISCRETIONARY INCOME

2001 Estimates:	Per Hhld.
Disposable Income	$35,695
Discretionary Income 1 (minus Food & Shelter)	$23,864
Discretionary Income 2 (minus Food, Shelter, & Other Expenditures)	$16,058

LIQUID ASSETS

1999 Estimates:	Per Hhld.
Equity Investments	$50,177
Interest Bearing Investments	$55,912
Total Liquid Assets	$106,089

CREDIT DATA

July 2000:

Pool of Credit	$76,130,240
Revolving Credit, No.	18,841
Fixed Loans, No.	8,748
Avg. Credit Limit, per Person	$8,323
Avg. Spent, per Person	$4,342
Satisfactory Ratings, No. per Person	2.83
Avg. No. of Cards, per Person	1.01

LABOUR FORCE

2001 Estimates:

Male:	
In the Labour Force	4,403
Participation Rate	69.6
Employed	4,222
Unemployed	181
Unemployment Rate	4.1
Not in Labour Force	1,923
Female:	
In the Labour Force	3,215
Participation Rate	58.6
Employed	3,032
Unemployed	183
Unemployment Rate	5.7
Not in Labour Force	2,274

OCCUPATIONS BY MAJOR GROUPS

2001 Estimates:	Male	Female
Management	357	98
Business, Finance & Admin.	374	1,042
Natural & Applied Sciences & Related	269	n.a.
Health	63	291
Social Sciences, Gov't Services & Religion	37	38
Education	46	193
Arts, Culture, Recreation & Sport	109	25
Sales & Service	883	947
Trades, Transport & Equipment Operators & Related	1,452	79
Primary Industries	153	66
Processing, Mfg. & Utilities	553	285

LEVEL OF SCHOOLING

2001 Estimates:

Population 15 years +	11,815
Less than Grade 9	1,811
Grades 9-13 w/o Certif.	2,836
Grade 9-13 with Certif.	2,420
Trade Certif. /Dip.	600
Non-Univ. w/o Certif./Dip.	930
Non-Univ. with Certif./Dip.	2,012
Univ. w/o Degree	665
Univ. w/o Degree/Certif.	110
Univ. with Certif.	555
Univ. with Degree	541

AVERAGE HOUSEHOLD EXPENDITURES

2001 Estimates:

Food	$6,285
Shelter	$7,329
Clothing	$2,219
Transportation	$6,056
Health & Personal Care	$1,939
Recr'n, Read'g & Education	$3,294
Taxes & Securities	$15,128
Other	$6,969
Total Expenditures	$49,219

PRIVATE HOUSEHOLDS

2001 Estimates:

Private Households, Total	5,209
Pop. in Private Households	14,447
Average no. per Household	2.8

FAMILIES

2001 Estimates:

Families in Private Households	4,450
Husband-Wife Families	3,896
Lone-Parent Families	554
Aver. No. Persons per Family	3.1
Aver. No. Sons/Daughters at Home	1.3

HOUSING

2001 Estimates:

Occupied Private Dwellings	5,209
Owned	3,940
Rented	1,269
Single-Detached House	3,779
Semi-Detached House	291
Apartment, 5+ Storeys	19
Apartment, 5 or Fewer Storeys	891
Apartment, Detached Duplex	201
Other Single-Attached	13
Movable Dwellings	15

VEHICLES

2001 Estimates:

Model Yrs. '81-'96, No.	5,884
% Total	78.75
Model Yrs. '97-'98, No.	995
% Total	13.32
'99 Vehicles registered in Model Yr. '99, No.	593
% Total	7.94
Total No. '81-'99	7,472

LEGAL MARITAL STATUS

2001 Estimates: (Age 15+)

Single (Never Married)	4,662
Legally Married (Not Separated)	5,397
Legally Married (Separated)	295
Widowed	422
Divorced	1,039

PSYTE CATEGORIES

2001 Estimates	No. of House-holds	% of Total Hhds.	Index
Participation Quebec	3,024	58.05	2,015
Quebec Melange	528	10.14	383
Traditional French Cdn. Families	691	13.27	494
Quebec Town Elders	508	9.75	345
Quebec's New Urban Mosaic	197	3.78	157

FINANCIAL PSYTE

2001 Estimates	No. of House-holds	% of Total Hhds.	Index
Mortgages & Minivans	3,024	58.05	880
Country Credit	1,219	23.40	346
Loan Parent Stress	508	9.75	167
NSF	197	3.78	107

Québec

HOME LANGUAGE

2001 Estimates:		% Total
English	99	0.64
French	15,150	98.64
Hungarian	13	0.08
Italian	25	0.16
Multiple Responses	72	0.47
Total	15,359	100.00

BUILDING PERMITS

	1999	1998	1997
		$000	
Value	8,659	3,984	7,774

HOMES BUILT

	1999	1998	1997
No.	21	8	30

TAXATION

Income Class:	1997	% Total
Under $5,000	1,310	16.03
$5,000-$10,000	1,080	13.22
$10,000-$15,000	1,150	14.08
$15,000-$20,000	780	9.55
$20,000-$25,000	680	8.32
$25,000-$30,000	710	8.69
$30,000-$40,000	1,040	12.73
$40,000-$50,000	710	8.69
$50,000 +	720	8.81
Total Returns, No.	8,170	
Total Income, $000	185,616	
Total Taxable Returns	5,670	
Total Tax, $000	20,833	
Average Income, $.	22,719	
Average Tax, $.	3,674	

VITAL STATISTICS

	1997	1996	1995	1994
Births	153	180	178	214
Deaths	59	45	33	44
Natural Increase	94	135	145	170
Marriages	15	16	28	20

Note: Latest available data.

MEDIA INFO
see Montréal, CMA

Québec

Sainte-Catherine
(Ville)
Montréal CMA

In census division Roussillon.

POPULATION

July 1, 2001 Estimate	19,795
% Cdn. Total	0.06
% Change, '96 -'01	34.28
Avg. Annual Growth Rate, %	6.07
2003 Projected Population	23,671
2006 Projected Population	29,875
2001 Households Estimate	7,141
2003 Projected Households	8,608
2006 Projected Households	11,002

INCOME

% Above/Below National Average	-5
2001 Total Income Estimate	$395,320,000
% Cdn. Total	0.06
2001 Average Hhld. Income	$55,400
2001 Per Capita	$20,000
2003 Projected Total Income	$508,390,000
2006 Projected Total Income	$719,860,000

RETAIL SALES

% Above/Below National Average	-57
2001 Retail Sales Estimate	$77,060,000
% Cdn. Total	0.03
2001 per Household	$10,800
2001 per Capita	$3,900
2001 No. of Establishments	81
2003 Projected Retail Sales	$100,040,000
2006 Projected Retail Sales	$139,800,000

POPULATION

2001 Estimates:

Total		19,795
Male		9,974
Female		9,821

Age Groups	Male	Female
0-4	769	722
5-9	862	778
10-14	824	744
15-19	729	670
20-24	605	609
25-29	671	705
30-34	903	959
35-39	1,048	1,072
40-44	954	952
45-49	761	763
50-54	586	563
55-59	419	403
60-64	306	291
65-69	233	222
70+	304	368

DAYTIME POPULATION

2001 Estimates:

Working Population	3,260
At Home Population	9,038
Total	12,298

INCOME

2001 Estimates:

Avg. Household Income	$55,359
Avg. Family Income	$59,452
Per Capita Income	$19,971
Male:	
Avg. Employment Income	$36,650
Avg. Employment Income (Full Time)	$42,999
Female:	
Avg. Employment Income	$22,262
Avg. Employment Income (Full Time)	$31,099

DISPOSABLE & DISCRETIONARY INCOME

2001 Estimates:	*Per Hhld.*
Disposable Income	$38,444
Discretionary Income 1 (minus Food & Shelter)	$25,490
Discretionary Income 2 (minus Food, Shelter, & Other Expenditures)	$16,809

LIQUID ASSETS

1999 Estimates:	*Per Hhld.*
Equity Investments	$60,824
Interest Bearing Investments	$62,744
Total Liquid Assets	$123,568

CREDIT DATA

July 2000:

Pool of Credit	$124,185,162
Revolving Credit, No.	30,593
Fixed Loans, No.	14,441
Avg. Credit Limit, per Person	$10,187
Avg. Spent, per Person	$5,272
Satisfactory Ratings, No. per Person	3.43
Avg. No. of Cards, per Person	1.21

LABOUR FORCE

2001 Estimates:

Male:	
In the Labour Force	6,241
Participation Rate	83.0
Employed	5,976
Unemployed	265
Unemployment Rate	4.2
Not in Labour Force	1,278
Female:	
In the Labour Force	5,036
Participation Rate	66.5
Employed	4,736
Unemployed	300
Unemployment Rate	6.0
Not in Labour Force	2,541

OCCUPATIONS BY MAJOR GROUPS

2001 Estimates:	Male	Female
Management	674	274
Business, Finance & Admin.	779	1,811
Natural & Applied Sciences & Related	553	87
Health	53	459
Social Sciences, Gov't Services & Religion	22	125
Education	83	119
Arts, Culture, Recreation & Sport	91	92
Sales & Service	1,094	1,551
Trades, Transport & Equipment Operators & Related	1,773	114
Primary Industries	44	n.a.
Processing, Mfg. & Utilities	909	272

LEVEL OF SCHOOLING

2001 Estimates:

Population 15 years +	15,096
Less than Grade 9	2,248
Grades 9-13 w/o Certif.	2,687
Grade 9-13 with Certif.	3,321
Trade Certif./Dip.	925
Non-Univ. w/o Certif./Dip.	1,140
Non-Univ. with Certif./Dip.	2,529
Univ. w/o Degree	1,189
Univ. w/o Degree/Certif.	249
Univ. with Certif.	940
Univ. with Degree	1,057

AVERAGE HOUSEHOLD EXPENDITURES

2001 Estimates:

Food	$6,860
Shelter	$8,035
Clothing	$2,419
Transportation	$6,836
Health & Personal Care	$2,085
Recr'n, Read'g & Education	$3,477
Taxes & Securities	$16,117
Other	$7,626
Total Expenditures	$53,455

PRIVATE HOUSEHOLDS

2001 Estimates:

Private Households, Total	7,141
Pop. in Private Households	19,650
Average no. per Household	2.8

FAMILIES

2001 Estimates:

Families in Private Households	5,867
Husband-Wife Families	5,167
Lone-Parent Families	700
Aver. No. Persons per Family	3.1
Aver. No. Sons/Daughters at Home	1.2

HOUSING

2001 Estimates:

Occupied Private Dwellings	7,141
Owned	5,384
Rented	1,757
Single-Detached House	4,248
Semi-Detached House	344
Row Houses	287
Apartment, 5 or Fewer Storeys	2,068
Apartment, Detached Duplex	194

VEHICLES

2001 Estimates:

Model Yrs. '81-'96, No.	6,202
% Total	75.22
Model Yrs. '97-'98, No.	1,276
% Total	15.48
'99 Vehicles registered in Model Yr. '99, No.	767
% Total	9.30
Total No. '81-'99	8,245

LEGAL MARITAL STATUS

2001 Estimates: (Age 15+)

Single (Never Married)	5,896
Legally Married (Not Separated)	6,722
Legally Married (Separated)	371
Widowed	557
Divorced	1,550

PSYTE CATEGORIES

2001 Estimates	No. of House-holds	% of Total Hhds.	Index
Participation Quebec	2,376	33.27	1,155
New Quebec Rows	903	12.65	1,154
Quebec Melange	2,019	28.27	1,067
Traditional French Cdn. Families	1,843	25.81	961

FINANCIAL P$YTE

2001 Estimates	No. of House-holds	% of Total Hhds.	Index
Mortgages & Minivans	3,279	45.92	696
Country Credit	3,862	54.08	800

HOME LANGUAGE

2001 Estimates:		% Total
English	640	3.23
French	18,875	95.35
Polish	21	0.11
Romanian	27	0.14
Slovenian	16	0.08
Spanish	19	0.10
Other Languages	14	0.07
Multiple Responses	183	0.92
Total	19,795	100.00

BUILDING PERMITS

	1999	1998 $000	1997
Value	16,677	26,030	20,130

HOMES BUILT

	1999	1998	1997
No.	159	178	198

TAXATION

Income Class:	1997	% Total
Under $5,000	1,180	11.49
$5,000-$10,000	1,110	10.81
$10,000-$15,000	1,100	10.71
$15,000-$20,000	1,000	9.74
$20,000-$25,000	960	9.35
$25,000-$30,000	1,040	10.13
$30,000-$40,000	1,570	15.29
$40,000-$50,000	1,130	11.00
$50,000 +	1,190	11.59
Total Returns, No.	10,270	
Total Income, $000	272,878	
Total Taxable Returns	7,960	
Total Tax, $000	32,925	
Average Income, $.	26,570	
Average Tax, $	4,136	

VITAL STATISTICS

	1997	1996	1995	1994
Births	241	260	258	242
Deaths	49	50	43	35
Natural Increase	192	210	215	207
Marriages	11	10	13	15

Note: Latest available data.

MEDIA INFO
see Montréal, CMA

Sainte-Julie
(Ville).
Montréal CMA
In census division Lajemmerais.

POPULATION

July 1, 2001 Estimate	27,903
% Cdn. Total	0.09
% Change, '96 -'01	14.04
Avg. Annual Growth Rate, %	2.66
2003 Projected Population	30,085
2006 Projected Population	33,764
2001 Households Estimate	9,796
2003 Projected Households	10,632
2006 Projected Households	12,066

INCOME

% Above/Below National Average	+19
2001 Total Income Estimate	$701,090,000
% Cdn. Total	0.11
2001 Average Hhld. Income	$71,600
2001 Per Capita	$25,100
2003 Projected Total Income	$810,700,000
2006 Projected Total Income	$1,015,260,000

RETAIL SALES

% Above/Below National Average	-23
2001 Retail Sales Estimate	$191,180,000
% Cdn. Total	0.07
2001 per Household	$19,500
2001 per Capita	$6,900
2001 No. of Establishments	184
2003 Projected Retail Sales	$223,450,000
2006 Projected Retail Sales	$279,280,000

POPULATION

2001 Estimates:

Total		27,903
Male		14,048
Female		13,855

Age Groups	Male	Female
0-4	1,006	977
5-9	1,102	1,064
10-14	1,085	1,023
15-19	1,053	1,000
20-24	985	947
25-29	940	955
30-34	1,141	1,186
35-39	1,343	1,381
40-44	1,294	1,323
45-49	1,173	1,201
50-54	1,043	1,024
55-59	790	721
60-64	494	427
65-69	283	242
70+	316	384

DAYTIME POPULATION

2001 Estimates:

Working Population	5,463
At Home Population	11,600
Total	17,063

INCOME

2001 Estimates:

Avg. Household Income	$71,569
Avg. Family Income	$74,658
Per Capita Income	$25,126
Male:	
Avg. Employment Income	$45,211
Avg. Employment Income (Full Time)	$54,605
Female:	
Avg. Employment Income	$24,579
Avg. Employment Income (Full Time)	$35,208

DISPOSABLE & DISCRETIONARY INCOME

2001 Estimates:	Per Hhld.
Disposable Income	$48,890
Discretionary Income 1 (minus Food & Shelter)	$33,172
Discretionary Income 2 (minus Food, Shelter, & Other Expenditures)	$22,794

LIQUID ASSETS

1999 Estimates:	Per Hhld.
Equity Investments	$98,226
Interest Bearing Investments	$84,837
Total Liquid Assets	$183,063

CREDIT DATA

July 2000:	
Pool of Credit	$219,742,010
Revolving Credit, No.	50,245
Fixed Loans, No.	18,754
Avg. Credit Limit, per Person	$11,427
Avg. Spent, per Person	$5,297
Satisfactory Ratings, No. per Person	3.38
Avg. No. of Cards, per Person	1.31

LABOUR FORCE

2001 Estimates:

Male:	
In the Labour Force	9,362
Participation Rate	86.2
Employed	9,175
Unemployed	187
Unemployment Rate	2.0
Not in Labour Force	1,493
Female:	
In the Labour Force	7,304
Participation Rate	67.7
Employed	7,045
Unemployed	259
Unemployment Rate	3.5
Not in Labour Force	3,487

OCCUPATIONS BY MAJOR GROUPS

2001 Estimates:	Male	Female
Management	1,468	557
Business, Finance & Admin.	937	2,557
Natural & Applied Sciences & Related	1,167	235
Health	134	698
Social Sciences, Gov't Services & Religion	147	186
Education	266	342
Arts, Culture, Recreation & Sport	175	139
Sales & Service	1,976	2,033
Trades, Transport & Equipment Operators & Related	2,266	127
Primary Industries	86	n.a.
Processing, Mfg. & Utilities	676	273

LEVEL OF SCHOOLING

2001 Estimates:

Population 15 years +	21,646
Less than Grade 9	1,883
Grades 9-13 w/o Certif.	3,097
Grade 9-13 with Certif.	4,245
Trade Certif. /Dip.	912
Non-Univ. w/o Certif./Dip.	1,721
Non-Univ. with Certif./Dip.	4,613
Univ. w/o Degree	1,981
Univ. w/o Degree/Certif.	311
Univ. with Certif.	1,670
Univ. with Degree	3,194

AVERAGE HOUSEHOLD EXPENDITURES

2001 Estimates:

Food	$8,216
Shelter	$10,030
Clothing	$3,073
Transportation	$8,055
Health & Personal Care	$2,525
Recr'n, Read'g & Education	$4,337
Taxes & Securities	$21,349
Other	$9,031
Total Expenditures	$66,616

PRIVATE HOUSEHOLDS

2001 Estimates:

Private Households, Total	9,796
Pop. in Private Households	27,742
Average no. per Household	2.8

FAMILIES

2001 Estimates:

Families in Private Households	8,408
Husband-Wife Families	7,504
Lone-Parent Families	904
Aver. No. Persons per Family	3.2
Aver. No. Sons/Daughters at Home	1.3

HOUSING

2001 Estimates:

Occupied Private Dwellings	9,796
Owned	7,806
Rented	1,990
Single-Detached House	7,211
Semi-Detached House	322
Row Houses	153
Apartment, 5 or Fewer Storeys	1,854
Apartment, Detached Duplex	171
Other Single-Attached	85

VEHICLES

2001 Estimates:

Model Yrs. '81-'96, No.	12,332
% Total	73.10
Model Yrs. '97-'98, No.	2,900
% Total	17.19
'99 Vehicles registered in Model Yr. '99, No.	1,637
% Total	9.70
Total No. '81-'99	16,869

LEGAL MARITAL STATUS

2001 Estimates: (Age 15+)

Single (Never Married)	8,059
Legally Married (Not Separated)	10,692
Legally Married (Separated)	503
Widowed	526
Divorced	1,866

PSYTE CATEGORIES

2001 Estimates	No. of House-holds	% of Total Hhds.	Index
Technocrafts & Bureaucrats	752	7.68	273
Stable Suburban Families	203	2.07	159
Participation Quebec	5,452	55.66	1,931
New Quebec Rows	2,489	25.41	2,319
Traditional French Cdn. Families	900	9.19	342

FINANCIAL P$YTE

2001 Estimates	No. of House-holds	% of Total Hhds.	Index
Successful Suburbanites	955	9.75	147
Mortgages & Minivans	7,941	81.06	1,228
Country Credit	900	9.19	136

Québec

HOME LANGUAGE

2001 Estimates:		% Total
English	622.	2.23
French	26,990.	96.73
Chinese	25.	0.09
Italian.	62.	0.22
Khmer (Cambodian)	25.	0.09
Spanish	29.	0.10
Multiple Responses.	150.	0.54
Total	27,903.	100.00

BUILDING PERMITS

	1999	1998	1997
		$000	
Value	31,745.	42,291	41,303

HOMES BUILT

	1999	1998	1997
No	242	207	245

TAXATION

Income Class:	1997	% Total
Under $5,000	2,040.	11.62
$5,000-$10,000	1,670.	9.51
$10,000-$15,000	1,730.	9.85
$15,000-$20,000	1,380.	7.86
$20,000-$25,000	1,330.	7.57
$25,000-$30,000	1,500.	8.54
$30,000-$40,000	2,600.	14.81
$40,000-$50,000	1,930.	10.99
$50,000 +	3,380.	19.25
Total Returns, No.	17,560	
Total Income, $000	555,099	
Total Taxable Returns	13,990	
Total Tax, $000	74,097	
Average Income, $	31,612	
Average Tax, $	5,296	

VITAL STATISTICS

	1997	1996	1995	1994
Births	345	394	401	388
Deaths	48	57	76	50
Natural Increase	297	337	325	338
Marriages	44	35	31	35

Note: Latest available data.

MEDIA INFO
see Montréal, CMA

Québec

Sainte-Thérèse

(Ville)
Montréal CMA

In census division Thérèse-De Blainville.

POPULATION

July 1, 2001 Estimate	23,394
% Cdn. Total	0.08
% Change, '96 -'01	-2.28
Avg. Annual Growth Rate, %	-0.46
2003 Projected Population	23,229
2006 Projected Population	23,434
2001 Households Estimate	10,175
2003 Projected Households	10,201
2006 Projected Households	10,421

INCOME

% Above/Below National Average	-6
2001 Total Income Estimate	$464,210,000
% Cdn. Total	0.07
2001 Average Hhld. Income	$45,600
2001 Per Capita	$19,800
2003 Projected Total Income	$478,190,000
2006 Projected Total Income	$510,220,000

RETAIL SALES

% Above/Below National Average	+79
2001 Retail Sales Estimate	$375,530,000
% Cdn. Total	0.13
2001 per Household	$36,900
2001 per Capita	$16,100
2001 No. of Establishments	202
2003 Projected Retail Sales	$405,170,000
2006 Projected Retail Sales	$456,350,000

POPULATION

2001 Estimates:

Total		23,394
Male		11,234
Female		12,160

Age Groups	Male	Female
0-4	693	652
5-9	679	659
10-14	674	661
15-19	729	726
20-24	796	819
25-29	850	855
30-34	873	869
35-39	916	919
40-44	900	982
45-49	872	1,002
50-54	832	935
55-59	690	754
60-64	531	588
65-69	440	495
70+	759	1,244

DAYTIME POPULATION

2001 Estimates:

Working Population	10,837
At Home Population	11,695
Total	22,532

INCOME

2001 Estimates:

Avg. Household Income	$45,623
Avg. Family Income	$54,407
Per Capita Income	$19,843
Male:	
Avg. Employment Income	$33,892
Avg. Employment Income (Full Time)	$43,788
Female:	
Avg. Employment Income	$21,121
Avg. Employment Income (Full Time)	$30,397

DISPOSABLE & DISCRETIONARY INCOME

2001 Estimates:	*Per Hhld.*
Disposable Income	$31,371
Discretionary Income 1 (minus Food & Shelter)	$19,873
Discretionary Income 2 (minus Food, Shelter, & Other Expenditures)	$13,208

LIQUID ASSETS

1999 Estimates:	*Per Hhld.*
Equity Investments	$50,681
Interest Bearing Investments	$54,432
Total Liquid Assets	$105,113

CREDIT DATA

July 2000:

Pool of Credit	$172,543,948
Revolving Credit, No.	43,874
Fixed Loans, No.	16,158
Avg. Credit Limit, per Person	$8,889
Avg. Spent, per Person	$4,114
Satisfactory Ratings, No. per Person	2.92
Avg. No. of Cards, per Person	1.13

LABOUR FORCE

2001 Estimates:

Male:	
In the Labour Force	6,855
Participation Rate	74.6
Employed	6,358
Unemployed	497
Unemployment Rate	7.3
Not in Labour Force	2,333
Female:	
In the Labour Force	5,728
Participation Rate	56.2
Employed	5,395
Unemployed	333
Unemployment Rate	5.8
Not in Labour Force	4,460

OCCUPATIONS BY MAJOR GROUPS

2001 Estimates:	Male	Female
Management	971	371
Business, Finance & Admin.	670	1,579
Natural & Applied Sciences & Related	511	106
Health	124	445
Social Sciences, Gov't Services & Religion	160	181
Education	191	436
Arts, Culture, Recreation & Sport	138	168
Sales & Service	1,542	1,813
Trades, Transport & Equipment Operators & Related	1,434	105
Primary Industries	82	21
Processing, Mfg. & Utilities	803	272

LEVEL OF SCHOOLING

2001 Estimates:

Population 15 years +	19,376
Less than Grade 9	3,468
Grades 9-13 w/o Certif.	3,338
Grade 9-13 with Certif.	3,333
Trade Certif. /Dip.	922
Non-Univ. w/o Certif./Dip.	1,703
Non-Univ. with Certif./Dip.	2,798
Univ. w/o Degree	1,298
Univ. w/o Degree/Certif.	237
Univ. with Certif.	1,061
Univ. with Degree	2,516

AVERAGE HOUSEHOLD EXPENDITURES

2001 Estimates:

Food	$5,742
Shelter	$7,573
Clothing	$1,978
Transportation	$4,901
Health & Personal Care	$1,754
Recr'n, Read'g & Education	$2,994
Taxes & Securities	$13,212
Other	$6,753
Total Expenditures	$44,907

PRIVATE HOUSEHOLDS

2001 Estimates:

Private Households, Total	10,175
Pop. in Private Households	22,979
Average no. per Household	2.3

FAMILIES

2001 Estimates:

Families in Private Households	6,828
Husband-Wife Families	5,504
Lone-Parent Families	1,324
Aver. No. Persons per Family	2.8
Aver. No. Sons/Daughters at Home	1.0

HOUSING

2001 Estimates:

Occupied Private Dwellings	10,175
Owned	4,659
Rented	5,516
Single-Detached House	3,647
Semi-Detached House	350
Row Houses	67
Apartment, 5+ Storeys	10
Apartment, 5 or Fewer Storeys	5,013
Apartment, Detached Duplex	1,032
Other Single-Attached	56

VEHICLES

2001 Estimates:

Model Yrs. '81-'96, No.	11,253
% Total	71.93
Model Yrs. '97-'98, No.	2,641
% Total	16.88
'99 Vehicles registered in Model Yr. '99, No.	1,751
% Total	11.19
Total No. '81-'99	15,645

LEGAL MARITAL STATUS

2001 Estimates: (Age 15+)

Single (Never Married)	7,719
Legally Married (Not Separated)	7,575
Legally Married (Separated)	567
Widowed	1,195
Divorced	2,320

PSYTE CATEGORIES

2001 Estimates	No. of House-holds	% of Total Hhds.	Index
Technocrafts & Bureaucrats	1,150	11.30	402
Stable Suburban Families	387	3.80	292
Participation Quebec	654	6.43	223
New Quebec Rows	834	8.20	748
Quebec Melange	1,499	14.73	556
Old Quebec Walkups	1,647	16.19	883
Quebec Town Elders	2,355	23.14	819
Quebec's New Urban Mosaic	1,566	15.39	639

FINANCIAL P$YTE

2001 Estimates	No. of House-holds	% of Total Hhds.	Index
Successful Suburbanites	1,537	15.11	228
Mortgages & Minivans	1,488	14.62	222
Country Credit	1,499	14.73	218
Loan Parent Stress	4,002	39.33	675
NSF	1,566	15.39	435

HOME LANGUAGE

2001 Estimates:		% Total
English	919	3.93
French	21,805	93.21
Arabic	20	0.09
Hungarian	20	0.09
Italian	112	0.48
Portuguese	143	0.61
Other Languages	30	0.13
Multiple Responses	345	1.47
Total	23,394	100.00

BUILDING PERMITS

	1999	1998	1997
		$000	
Value	14,924	45,252	20,940

HOMES BUILT

	1999	1998	1997
No.	106	138	89

TAXATION

Income Class:	1997	% Total
Under $5,000	1,880	10.74
$5,000-$10,000	2,720	15.53
$10,000-$15,000	2,730	15.59
$15,000-$20,000	1,860	10.62
$20,000-$25,000	1,560	8.91
$25,000-$30,000	1,380	7.88
$30,000-$40,000	2,040	11.65
$40,000-$50,000	1,250	7.14
$50,000 +	2,100	11.99
Total Returns, No.	17,510	
Total Income, $000	461,155	
Total Taxable Returns	12,270	
Total Tax, $000	56,815	
Average Income, $.	26,337	
Average Tax, $.	4,630	

VITAL STATISTICS

	1997	1996	1995	1994
Births	290	256	51	176
Deaths	186	185	179	154
Natural Increase	104	71	-128	22
Marriages	55	31	69	81

Note: Latest available data.

MEDIA INFO

see Montréal, CMA

Terrebonne
(Ville)
Montréal CMA

In census division Les Moulins.

POPULATION

July 1, 2001 Estimate	45,316
% Cdn. Total	0.15
% Change, '96 -'01	5.32
Avg. Annual Growth Rate, %	1.04
2003 Projected Population	46,737
2006 Projected Population	49,700
2001 Households Estimate	16,698
2003 Projected Households	17,423
2006 Projected Households	18,865

INCOME

% Above/Below National Average	-8
2001 Total Income Estimate	$878,700,000
% Cdn. Total	0.13
2001 Average Hhld. Income	$52,600
2001 Per Capita	$19,400
2003 Projected Total Income	$966,430,000
2006 Projected Total Income	$1,137,040,000

RETAIL SALES

% Above/Below National Average	+79
2001 Retail Sales Estimate	$724,660,000
% Cdn. Total	0.26
2001 per Household	$43,400
2001 per Capita	$16,000
2001 No. of Establishments	413
2003 Projected Retail Sales	$810,060,000
2006 Projected Retail Sales	$955,760,000

POPULATION

2001 Estimates:

Total		45,316
Male		22,398
Female		22,918

Age Groups	Male	Female
0-4	1,420	1,363
5-9	1,681	1,618
10-14	1,786	1,665
15-19	1,779	1,641
20-24	1,578	1,511
25-29	1,304	1,350
30-34	1,451	1,608
35-39	1,897	2,081
40-44	2,094	2,217
45-49	1,966	2,023
50-54	1,680	1,652
55-59	1,239	1,228
60-64	893	887
65-69	677	671
70+	953	1,403

DAYTIME POPULATION

2001 Estimates:

Working Population	15,291
At Home Population	21,746
Total	37,037

INCOME

2001 Estimates:

Avg. Household Income	$52,623
Avg. Family Income	$56,191
Per Capita Income	$19,391

Male:

Avg. Employment Income	$34,971
Avg. Employment Income (Full Time)	$43,361

Female:

Avg. Employment Income	$22,212
Avg. Employment Income (Full Time)	$31,327

DISPOSABLE & DISCRETIONARY INCOME

2001 Estimates:

Disposable Income	$37,080
Discretionary Income 1 (minus Food & Shelter)	$24,668
Discretionary Income 2 (minus Food, Shelter, & Other Expenditures)	$16,562

LIQUID ASSETS

1999 Estimates:	Per Hhld.
Equity Investments	$57,694
Interest Bearing Investments	$60,353
Total Liquid Assets	$118,047

CREDIT DATA

July 2000:

Pool of Credit	$323,473,564
Revolving Credit, No.	78,203
Fixed Loans, No.	32,492
Avg. Credit Limit, per Person	$9,593
Avg. Spent, per Person	$4,756
Satisfactory Ratings, No. per Person	3.07
Avg. No. of Cards, per Person	1.16

LABOUR FORCE

2001 Estimates:

Male:

In the Labour Force	13,922
Participation Rate	79.5
Employed	13,156
Unemployed	766
Unemployment Rate	5.5
Not in Labour Force	3,589

Female:

In the Labour Force	11,084
Participation Rate	60.7
Employed	10,332
Unemployed	752
Unemployment Rate	6.8
Not in Labour Force	7,188

OCCUPATIONS BY MAJOR GROUPS

2001 Estimates:	Male	Female
Management	1,735	653
Business, Finance & Admin.	1,396	3,746
Natural & Applied Sciences & Related	926	164
Health	153	838
Social Sciences, Gov't Services & Religion	200	242
Education	315	581
Arts, Culture, Recreation & Sport	272	260
Sales & Service	2,818	3,323
Trades, Transport & Equipment Operators & Related	4,245	168
Primary Industries	174	n.a.
Processing, Mfg. & Utilities	1,300	593

LEVEL OF SCHOOLING

2001 Estimates:

Population 15 years +	35,783
Less than Grade 9	5,653
Grades 9-13 w/o Certif.	6,476
Grade 9-13 with Certif.	7,870
Trade Certif./Dip.	1,616
Non-Univ. w/o Certif./Dip.	2,935
Non-Univ. with Certif./Dip.	6,300
Univ. w/o Degree	2,485
Univ. w/o Degree/Certif.	347
Univ. with Certif.	2,138
Univ. with Degree	2,448

AVERAGE HOUSEHOLD EXPENDITURES

2001 Estimates:

Food	$6,543
Shelter	$7,719
Clothing	$2,283
Transportation	$6,282
Health & Personal Care	$2,014
Recr'n, Read'g & Education	$3,362
Taxes & Securities	$15,556
Other	$7,269
Total Expenditures	$51,028

PRIVATE HOUSEHOLDS

2001 Estimates:

Private Households, Total	16,698
Pop. in Private Households	44,819
Average no. per Household	2.7

FAMILIES

2001 Estimates:

Families in Private Households	13,679
Husband-Wife Families	11,524
Lone-Parent Families	2,155
Aver. No. Persons per Family	3.1
Aver. No. Sons/Daughters at Home	1.2

HOUSING

2001 Estimates:

Occupied Private Dwellings	16,698
Owned	11,697
Rented	5,001
Single-Detached House	10,099
Semi-Detached House	1,009
Row Houses	101
Apartment, 5+ Storeys	12
Apartment, 5 or Fewer Storeys	4,076
Apartment, Detached Duplex	1,059
Other Single-Attached	55
Movable Dwellings	287

VEHICLES

2001 Estimates:

Model Yrs. '81-'96, No.	20,400
% Total	72.61
Model Yrs. '97-'98, No.	4,832
% Total	17.20
'99 Vehicles registered in Model Yr. '99, No.	2,862
% Total	10.19
Total No. '81-'99	28,094

LEGAL MARITAL STATUS

2001 Estimates: (Age 15+)

Single (Never Married)	12,954
Legally Married (Not Separated)	16,567
Legally Married (Separated)	978
Widowed	1,601
Divorced	3,683

PSYTE CATEGORIES

2001 Estimates	No. of House-holds	% of Total Hhds.	Index
Participation Quebec	7,084	42.42	1,472
New Quebec Rows	940	5.63	514
Quebec Melange	3,576	21.42	808
Traditional French Cdn. Families	2,449	14.67	546
Old Quebec Walkups	323	1.93	106
Quebec Town Elders	2,004	12.00	425
Quebec's New Urban Mosaic	322	1.93	80

FINANÇIAL PSYTE

2001 Estimates	No. of House-holds	% of Total Hhds.	Index
Mortgages & Minivans	8,024	48.05	728
Country Credit	6,025	36.08	534
Loan Parent Stress	2,327	13.94	239
NSF	322	1.93	55

Québec

HOME LANGUAGE

2001 Estimates:		% Total
English	825	1.82
French	43,760	96.57
Arabic	39	0.09
Italian	71	0.16
Portuguese	32	0.07
Spanish	34	0.08
Other Languages	57	0.13
Multiple Responses	498	1.10
Total	45,316	100.00

BUILDING PERMITS

	1999	1998	1997
		$000	
Value	51,616	33,531	51,900

HOMES BUILT

	1999	1998	1997
No	232	144	184

TAXATION

Income Class:	1997	% Total
Under $5,000	3,780	12.47
$5,000-$10,000	3,980	13.13
$10,000-$15,000	4,210	13.89
$15,000-$20,000	2,850	9.40
$20,000-$25,000	2,630	8.68
$25,000-$30,000	2,610	8.61
$30,000-$40,000	3,940	13.00
$40,000-$50,000	2,790	9.20
$50,000 +	3,530	11.65
Total Returns, No.	30,310	
Total Income, $000	770,082	
Total Taxable Returns	21,910	
Total Tax, $000	91,177	
Average Income, $	25,407	
Average Tax, $	4,161	

VITAL STATISTICS

	1997	1996	1995	1994
Births	475	525	559	622
Deaths	235	190	198	193
Natural Increase	240	335	361	429
Marriages	80	65	65	59

Note: Latest available data.

MEDIA INFO
see Montréal, CMA

Québec

Varennes
(Ville)
Montréal CMA

In census division Lajemmerais.

POPULATION

July 1, 2001 Estimate	23,843
% Cdn. Total	0.08
% Change, '96 -'01	24.25
Avg. Annual Growth Rate, %	4.44
2003 Projected Population	26,997
2006 Projected Population	32,094
2001 Households Estimate	8,546
2003 Projected Households	9,762
2006 Projected Households	11,753

INCOME

% Above/Below National Average	+13
2001 Total Income Estimate	$566,450,000
% Cdn. Total	0.09
2001 Average Hhld. Income	$66,300
2001 Per Capita	$23,800
2003 Projected Total Income	$685,210,000
2006 Projected Total Income	$904,960,000

RETAIL SALES

% Above/Below National Average	-11
2001 Retail Sales Estimate	$189,990,000
% Cdn. Total	0.07
2001 per Household	$22,200
2001 per Capita	$8,000
2001 No. of Establishments	161
2003 Projected Retail Sales	$234,010,000
2006 Projected Retail Sales	$309,820,000

POPULATION

2001 Estimates:

Total		23,843
Male		11,902
Female		11,941
Age Groups	Male	Female
0-4	902	850
5-9	1,027	990
10-14	1,021	986
15-19	899	869
20-24	713	713
25-29	719	768
30-34	972	1,071
35-39	1,223	1,296
40-44	1,201	1,217
45-49	991	943
50-54	741	662
55-59	505	442
60-64	338	322
65-69	239	250
70+	411	562

DAYTIME POPULATION

2001 Estimates:

Working Population	6,233
At Home Population	10,600
Total	16,833

INCOME

2001 Estimates:

Avg. Household Income	$66,282
Avg. Family Income	$69,729
Per Capita Income	$23,757
Male:	
Avg. Employment Income	$42,481
Avg. Employment Income (Full Time)	$51,797
Female:	
Avg. Employment Income	$26,051
Avg. Employment Income (Full Time)	$35,470

DISPOSABLE & DISCRETIONARY INCOME

2001 Estimates:	Per Hhld.
Disposable Income	$45,605
Discretionary Income 1 (minus Food & Shelter)	$30,476
Discretionary Income 2 (minus Food, Shelter, & Other Expenditures)	$20,776

LIQUID ASSETS

1999 Estimates:	Per Hhld.
Equity Investments	$81,070
Interest Bearing Investments	$77,323
Total Liquid Assets	$158,393

CREDIT DATA

July 2000:

Pool of Credit	$160,531,365
Revolving Credit, No.	36,649
Fixed Loans, No.	13,618
Avg. Credit Limit, per Person	$11,584
Avg. Spent, per Person	$5,390
Satisfactory Ratings, No. per Person	3.43
Avg. No. of Cards, per Person	1.34

LABOUR FORCE

2001 Estimates:

Male:	
In the Labour Force	7,649
Participation Rate	85.4
Employed	7,412
Unemployed	237
Unemployment Rate	3.1
Not in Labour Force	1,303
Female:	
In the Labour Force	6,151
Participation Rate	67.5
Employed	5,798
Unemployed	353
Unemployment Rate	5.7
Not in Labour Force	2,964

OCCUPATIONS BY MAJOR GROUPS

2001 Estimates:	Male	Female
Management	958	401
Business, Finance & Admin.	801	2,428
Natural & Applied Sciences & Related	802	199
Health	162	601
Social Sciences, Gov't Services & Religion	127	110
Education	215	241
Arts, Culture, Recreation & Sport	163	126
Sales & Service	1,458	1,532
Trades, Transport & Equipment Operators & Related	1,786	60
Primary Industries	162	32
Processing, Mfg. & Utilities	863	229

LEVEL OF SCHOOLING

2001 Estimates:

Population 15 years +	18,067
Less than Grade 9	1,739
Grades 9-13 w/o Certif.	2,671
Grade 9-13 with Certif.	3,573
Trade Certif./Dip.	834
Non-Univ. w/o Certif./Dip.	1,510
Non-Univ. with Certif./Dip.	3,846
Univ. w/o Degree	1,664
Univ. w/o Degree/Certif.	245
Univ. with Certif.	1,419
Univ. with Degree	2,230

AVERAGE HOUSEHOLD EXPENDITURES

2001 Estimates:

Food	$7,857
Shelter	$9,640
Clothing	$2,848
Transportation	$7,473
Health & Personal Care	$2,400
Recr'n, Read'g & Education	$4,007
Taxes & Securities	$19,561
Other	$8,562
Total Expenditures	$62,348

PRIVATE HOUSEHOLDS

2001 Estimates:

Private Households, Total	8,546
Pop. in Private Households	23,600
Average no. per Household	2.8

FAMILIES

2001 Estimates:

Families in Private Households	7,156
Husband-Wife Families	6,435
Lone-Parent Families	721
Aver. No. Persons per Family	3.2
Aver. No. Sons/Daughters at Home	1.3

HOUSING

2001 Estimates:

Occupied Private Dwellings	8,546
Owned	6,865
Rented	1,681
Single-Detached House	6,033
Semi-Detached House	473
Row Houses	126
Apartment, 5+ Storeys	24
Owned Apartment, 5+ Storeys	16
Apartment, 5 or Fewer Storeys	1,647
Apartment, Detached Duplex	231
Other Single-Attached	12

VEHICLES

2001 Estimates:

Model Yrs. '81-'96, No.	9,371
% Total	73.10
Model Yrs. '97-'98, No.	2,072
% Total	16.16
'99 Vehicles registered in Model Yr. '99, No.	1,376
% Total	10.73
Total No. '81-'99	12,819

LEGAL MARITAL STATUS

2001 Estimates: (Age 15+)

Single (Never Married)	6,580
Legally Married (Not Separated)	9,010
Legally Married (Separated)	355
Widowed	589
Divorced	1,533

PSYTE CATEGORIES

2001 Estimates	No. of House-holds	% of Total Hhds.	Index
Technocrafts & Bureaucrats	472	5.52	196
Participation Quebec	3,103	36.31	1,260
New Quebec Rows	2,054	24.03	2,193
Quebec Melange	957	11.20	423
Traditional French Cdn. Families	974	11.40	424
Old Quebec Walkups	504	5.90	322
Quebec Town Elders	449	5.25	186

FINANCIAL P$YTE

2001 Estimates	No. of House-holds	% of Total Hhds.	Index
Successful Suburbanites	472	5.52	83
Mortgages & Minivans	5,157	60.34	914
Country Credit	1,931	22.60	334
Loan Parent Stress	953	11.15	191

HOME LANGUAGE

2001 Estimates:		% Total
English	118	0.49
French	23,525	98.67
Multiple Responses	200	0.84
Total	23,843	100.00

BUILDING PERMITS

	1999	1998	1997
		$000	
Value	28,730	15,982	26,449

HOMES BUILT

	1999	1998	1997
No.	101	87	110

TAXATION

Income Class:	1997	% Total
Under $5,000	1,400	10.61
$5,000-$10,000	1,220	9.24
$10,000-$15,000	1,300	9.85
$15,000-$20,000	1,010	7.65
$20,000-$25,000	980	7.42
$25,000-$30,000	1,180	8.94
$30,000-$40,000	2,010	15.23
$40,000-$50,000	1,480	11.21
$50,000 +	2,630	19.92
Total Returns, No.	13,200	
Total Income, $000	424,091	
Total Taxable Returns	10,600	
Total Tax, $000	57,263	
Average Income, $	32,128	
Average Tax, $	5,402	

VITAL STATISTICS

	1997	1996	1995	1994
Births	300	280	311	316
Deaths	86	64	69	57
Natural Increase	214	216	242	259
Marriages	36	32	33	35

Note: Latest available data.

MEDIA INFO
see Montréal, CMA

Vaudreuil-Dorion
(Ville)
Montréal CMA

In census division
Vaudreuil-Soulanges.

POPULATION

July 1, 2001 Estimate	19,813
% Cdn. Total	0.06
% Change, '96 -'01	5.37
Avg. Annual Growth Rate, %	1.05
2003 Projected Population	20,600
2006 Projected Population	22,069
2001 Households Estimate	7,708
2003 Projected Households	8,025
2006 Projected Households	8,616

INCOME

% Above/Below National Average	+5
2001 Total Income Estimate	$439,960,000
% Cdn. Total	0.07
2001 Average Hhld. Income	$57,100
2001 Per Capita	$22,200
2003 Projected Total Income	$485,190,000
2006 Projected Total Income	$570,830,000

RETAIL SALES

% Above/Below National Average	+30
2001 Retail Sales Estimate	$229,890,000
% Cdn. Total	0.08
2001 per Household	$29,800
2001 per Capita	$11,600
2001 No. of Establishments	198
2003 Projected Retail Sales	$258,260,000
2006 Projected Retail Sales	$306,430,000

POPULATION

2001 Estimates:

Total		19,813
Male		9,679
Female		10,134

Age Groups	Male	Female
0-4	634	604
5-9	688	654
10-14	682	634
15-19	661	633
20-24	622	624
25-29	613	640
30-34	743	772
35-39	859	892
40-44	860	905
45-49	788	841
50-54	661	709
55-59	527	540
60-64	418	408
65-69	326	351
70+	597	927

DAYTIME POPULATION

2001 Estimates:

Working Population	8,257
At Home Population	9,099
Total	17,356

INCOME

2001 Estimates:

Avg. Household Income	$57,078
Avg. Family Income	$62,604
Per Capita Income	$22,205
Male:	
Avg. Employment Income	$39,208
Avg. Employment Income (Full Time)	$48,698
Female:	
Avg. Employment Income	$22,881
Avg. Employment Income (Full Time)	$32,492

DISPOSABLE & DISCRETIONARY INCOME

2001 Estimates:	Per Hhld.
Disposable Income	$38,412
Discretionary Income 1 (minus Food & Shelter)	$24,924
Discretionary Income 2 (minus Food, Shelter, & Other Expenditures)	$16,105

LIQUID ASSETS

1999 Estimates:	Per Hhld.
Equity Investments	$72,846
Interest Bearing Investments	$67,424
Total Liquid Assets	$140,270

CREDIT DATA

July 2000:

Pool of Credit	$197,351,002
Revolving Credit, No.	45,269
Fixed Loans, No.	16,341
Avg. Credit Limit, per Person	$10,661
Avg. Spent, per Person	$4,986
Satisfactory Ratings, No. per Person	3.16
Avg. No. of Cards, per Person	1.19

LABOUR FORCE

2001 Estimates:

Male:	
In the Labour Force	6,081
Participation Rate	79.2
Employed	5,879
Unemployed	202
Unemployment Rate	3.3
Not in Labour Force	1,594
Female:	
In the Labour Force	5,118
Participation Rate	62.1
Employed	4,880
Unemployed	238
Unemployment Rate	4.7
Not in Labour Force	3,124

OCCUPATIONS BY MAJOR GROUPS

2001 Estimates:	Male	Female
Management	819	352
Business, Finance & Admin.	832	1,759
Natural & Applied Sciences & Related	565	164
Health	153	341
Social Sciences, Gov't Services & Religion	35	77
Education	163	356
Arts, Culture, Recreation & Sport	69	138
Sales & Service	1,285	1,436
Trades, Transport & Equipment Operators & Related	1,364	122
Primary Industries	186	27
Processing, Mfg. & Utilities	439	222

LEVEL OF SCHOOLING

2001 Estimates:

Population 15 years +	15,917
Less than Grade 9	1,807
Grades 9-13 w/o Certif.	3,028
Grade 9-13 with Certif.	3,053
Trade Certif. /Dip.	527
Non-Univ. w/o Certif./Dip.	1,464
Non-Univ. with Certif./Dip.	2,917
Univ. w/o Degree	1,434
Univ. w/o Degree/Certif.	322
Univ. with Certif.	1,112
Univ. with Degree	1,687

AVERAGE HOUSEHOLD EXPENDITURES

2001 Estimates:

Food	$6,874
Shelter	$8,633
Clothing	$2,369
Transportation	$6,840
Health & Personal Care	$2,148
Recr'n, Read'g & Education	$3,677
Taxes & Securities	$16,113
Other	$8,072
Total Expenditures	$54,726

PRIVATE HOUSEHOLDS

2001 Estimates:

Private Households, Total	7,708
Pop. in Private Households	19,451
Average no. per Household	2.5

FAMILIES

2001 Estimates:

Families in Private Households	5,877
Husband-Wife Families	5,044
Lone-Parent Families	833
Aver. No. Persons per Family	3.0
Aver. No. Sons/Daughters at Home	1.1

HOUSING

2001 Estimates:

Occupied Private Dwellings	7,708
Owned	5,165
Rented	2,543
Single-Detached House	4,540
Semi-Detached House	311
Row Houses	291
Apartment, 5 or Fewer Storeys	2,162
Apartment, Detached Duplex	345
Other Single-Attached	21
Movable Dwellings	38

VEHICLES

2001 Estimates:

Model Yrs. '81-'96, No.	9,925
% Total	74.87
Model Yrs. '97-'98, No.	2,046
% Total	15.43
'99 Vehicles registered in Model Yr. '99, No.	1,285
% Total	9.69
Total No. '81-'99	13,256

LEGAL MARITAL STATUS

2001 Estimates: (Age 15+)

Single (Never Married)	5,558
Legally Married (Not Separated)	7,562
Legally Married (Separated)	383
Widowed	868
Divorced	1,546

PSYTE CATEGORIES

2001 Estimates	No. of House-holds	% of Total Hhds.	Index
Technocrafts & Bureaucrats	133	1.73	61
Small City Elite	364	4.72	276
Blue Collar Winners	308	4.00	159
Participation Quebec	1,990	25.82	896
Quebec Melange	2,495	32.37	1,221
Traditional French Cdn. Families	405	5.25	196
Rustic Prosperity	268	3.48	193
Town Renters	148	1.92	222
Old Quebec Walkups	375	4.87	266
Quebec Town Elders	1,184	15.36	544

Québec

FINANCIAL P$YTE

2001 Estimates	No. of House-holds	% of Total Hhds.	Index
Successful Suburbanites	133	1.73	26
Canadian Comfort	672	8.72	90
Mortgages & Minivans	1,990	25.82	391
Tractors & Tradelines	268	3.48	61
Country Credit	2,900	37.62	556
Loan Parent Stress	1,559	20.23	347
Towering Debt	148	1.92	25

HOME LANGUAGE

2001 Estimates:		% Total
English	3,458	17.45
French	15,702	79.25
Chinese	21	0.11
German	11	0.06
Greek	14	0.07
Hungarian	10	0.05
Italian	45	0.23
Portuguese	10	0.05
Spanish	42	0.21
Multiple Responses	500	2.52
Total	19,813	100.00

BUILDING PERMITS

	1999	1998	1997
		$000	
Value	32,776	22,120	22,207

HOMES BUILT

	1999	1998	1997
No	179	119	85

TAXATION

Income Class:	1997	% Total
Under $5,000	1,320	10.42
$5,000-$10,000	1,520	12.00
$10,000-$15,000	1,630	12.87
$15,000-$20,000	1,260	9.94
$20,000-$25,000	1,140	9.00
$25,000-$30,000	1,160	9.16
$30,000-$40,000	1,780	14.05
$40,000-$50,000	1,280	10.10
$50,000 +	1,610	12.71
Total Returns, No.	12,670	
Total Income, $000	350,295	
Total Taxable Returns	9,630	
Total Tax, $000	43,459	
Average Income, $	27,648	
Average Tax, $	4,513	

VITAL STATISTICS

	1997	1996	1995	1994
Births	218	286	282	270
Deaths	133	121	125	110
Natural Increase	85	165	157	160
Marriages	80	73	71	53

Note: Latest available data.

MEDIA INFO
see Montréal, CMA

Québec

Verdun
(Ville)
Montréal CMA

In census division Communauté urbaine de Montréal.

POPULATION

July 1, 2001 Estimate	59,189
% Cdn. Total	0.19
% Change, '96 -'01	-2.65
Avg. Annual Growth Rate, %	-0.54
2003 Projected Population	59,189
2006 Projected Population	59,422
2001 Households Estimate	29,467
2003 Projected Households	29,371
2006 Projected Households	29,273

INCOME

% Above/Below National Average	-6
2001 Total Income Estimate	$1,176,640,000
% Cdn. Total	0.18
2001 Average Hhld. Income	$39,900
2001 Per Capita	$19,900
2003 Projected Total Income	$1,223,580,000
2006 Projected Total Income	$1,303,600,000

RETAIL SALES

% Above/Below National Average	-44
2001 Retail Sales Estimate	$294,350,000
% Cdn. Total	0.11
2001 per Household	$10,000
2001 per Capita	$5,000
2001 No. of Establishments	369
2003 Projected Retail Sales	$317,090,000
2006 Projected Retail Sales	$351,750,000

POPULATION

2001 Estimates:

Total		59,189
Male		27,499
Female		31,690

Age Groups	Male	Female
0-4	1,757	1,665
5-9	1,666	1,628
10-14	1,391	1,362
15-19	1,283	1,237
20-24	1,408	1,432
25-29	1,705	1,834
30-34	2,159	2,280
35-39	2,498	2,619
40-44	2,480	2,660
45-49	2,239	2,434
50-54	1,916	2,166
55-59	1,604	1,895
60-64	1,434	1,787
65-69	1,296	1,734
70+	2,663	4,957

DAYTIME POPULATION

2001 Estimates:

Working Population	13,390
At Home Population	33,294
Total	46,684

INCOME

2001 Estimates:

Avg. Household Income	$39,931
Avg. Family Income	$49,347
Per Capita Income	$19,879
Male:	
Avg. Employment Income	$34,020
Avg. Employment Income (Full Time)	$43,887
Female:	
Avg. Employment Income	$24,892
Avg. Employment Income (Full Time)	$33,410

DISPOSABLE & DISCRETIONARY INCOME

2001 Estimates:	Per Hhld.
Disposable Income	$26,224
Discretionary Income 1 (minus Food & Shelter)	$15,595
Discretionary Income 2 (minus Food, Shelter, & Other Expenditures)	$9,920

LIQUID ASSETS

1999 Estimates:	Per Hhld.
Equity Investments	$50,687
Interest Bearing Investments	$49,976
Total Liquid Assets	$100,663

CREDIT DATA

July 2000:

Pool of Credit	$435,772,802
Revolving Credit, No.	110,485
Fixed Loans, No.	28,802
Avg. Credit Limit, per Person	$7,836
Avg. Spent, per Person	$3,351
Satisfactory Ratings, No. per Person	2.41
Avg. No. of Cards, per Person	1.02

LABOUR FORCE

2001 Estimates:

Male:	
In the Labour Force	14,920
Participation Rate	65.8
Employed	13,444
Unemployed	1,476
Unemployment Rate	9.9
Not in Labour Force	7,765
Female:	
In the Labour Force	13,718
Participation Rate	50.7
Employed	12,494
Unemployed	1,224
Unemployment Rate	8.9
Not in Labour Force	13,317

OCCUPATIONS BY MAJOR GROUPS

2001 Estimates:	Male	Female
Management	1,943	1,147
Business, Finance & Admin.	2,145	4,887
Natural & Applied Sciences & Related	1,233	342
Health	474	1,027
Social Sciences, Gov't Services & Religion	451	500
Education	417	413
Arts, Culture, Recreation & Sport	461	564
Sales & Service	3,304	3,358
Trades, Transport & Equipment Operators & Related	2,261	184
Primary Industries	91	22
Processing, Mfg. & Utilities	1,191	478

LEVEL OF SCHOOLING

2001 Estimates:

Population 15 years +	49,720
Less than Grade 9	9,454
Grades 9-13 w/o Certif.	8,811
Grade 9-13 with Certif.	8,063
Trade Certif. /Dip.	1,587
Non-Univ. w/o Certif./Dip.	3,482
Non-Univ. with Certif./Dip.	5,864
Univ. w/o Degree	4,265
Univ. w/o Degree/Certif.	959
Univ. with Certif.	3,306
Univ. with Degree	8,194

AVERAGE HOUSEHOLD EXPENDITURES

2001 Estimates:

Food	$5,064
Shelter	$7,548
Clothing	$1,818
Transportation	$3,939
Health & Personal Care	$1,582
Recr'n, Read'g & Education	$2,767
Taxes & Securities	$10,441
Other	$6,557
Total Expenditures	$39,716

PRIVATE HOUSEHOLDS

2001 Estimates:

Private Households, Total	29,467
Pop. in Private Households	57,920
Average no. per Household	2.0

FAMILIES

2001 Estimates:

Families in Private Households	16,086
Husband-Wife Families	12,096
Lone-Parent Families	3,990
Aver. No. Persons per Family	2.6
Aver. No. Sons/Daughters at Home	0.9

HOUSING

2001 Estimates:

Occupied Private Dwellings	29,467
Owned	7,678
Rented	21,789
Single-Detached House	892
Semi-Detached House	242
Row Houses	1,588
Apartment, 5+ Storeys	4,696
Owned Apartment, 5+ Storeys	1,871
Apartment, 5 or Fewer Storeys	21,678
Apartment, Detached Duplex	250
Other Single-Attached	121

VEHICLES

2001 Estimates:

Model Yrs. '81-'96, No.	17,281
% Total	71.49
Model Yrs. '97-'98, No.	4,400
% Total	18.20
'99 Vehicles registered in Model Yr. '99, No.	2,493
% Total	10.31
Total No. '81-'99	24,174

LEGAL MARITAL STATUS

2001 Estimates: (Age 15+)

Single (Never Married)	21,032
Legally Married (Not Separated)	16,518
Legally Married (Separated)	1,888
Widowed	4,360
Divorced	5,922

PSYTE CATEGORIES

2001 Estimates	No. of House-holds	% of Total Hhds.	Index
The Affluentials	182	0.62	97
Urban Gentry	1,189	4.04	225
Technocrafts & Bureaucrats	56	0.19	7
Brie & Chablis	1,153	3.91	437
Aging Erudites	820	2.78	184
Asian Mosaic	46	0.16	11
Young Urban Professionals	2,161	7.33	386
Young Urban Intelligentsia	1,163	3.95	259
University Enclaves	96	0.33	16
Urban Bohemia	461	1.56	134
Old Quebec Walkups	6,072	20.61	1,125
Quebec's New Urban Mosaic	14,924	50.65	2,102
Aged Pensioners	525	1.78	134
Big City Stress	116	0.39	35
Old Grey Towers	142	0.48	87

FINANCIAL P$YTE

2001 Estimates	No. of House-holds	% of Total Hhds.	Index
Platinum Estates	182	0.62	77
Four Star Investors	1,189	4.04	80
Successful Suburbanites	56	0.19	3
Urban Heights	4,134	14.03	326
Dollars & Sense	46	0.16	6
Young Urban Struggle	1,720	5.84	123
Loan Parent Stress	6,072	20.61	354
NSF	15,040	51.04	1,443
Senior Survivors	667	2.26	120

HOME LANGUAGE

2001 Estimates:		% Total
English	13,963	23.59
French	40,408	68.27
Arabic	469	0.79
Bengali	106	0.18
Bulgarian	50	0.08
Chinese	713	1.20
Greek	76	0.13
Hungarian	44	0.07
Italian	88	0.15
Korean	137	0.23
Lithuanian	30	0.05
Persian (Farsi)	197	0.33
Polish	159	0.27
Portuguese	41	0.07
Romanian	70	0.12
Russian	46	0.08
Spanish	495	0.84
Swedish	36	0.06
Urdu	30	0.05
Vietnamese	222	0.38
Other Languages	270	0.46
Multiple Responses	1,539	2.60
Total	59,189	100.00

BUILDING PERMITS

	1999	1998 $000	1997
Value	45,395	29,684	19,935

HOMES BUILT

	1999	1998	1997
No	220	199	105

Verdun
(Ville)
Montréal CMA
(Cont'd)

TAXATION

Income Class:	1997	% Total
Under $5,000	5,040	11.36
$5,000-$10,000	7,750	17.47
$10,000-$15,000	7,170	16.16
$15,000-$20,000	4,350	9.81
$20,000-$25,000	3,670	8.27
$25,000-$30,000	3,230	7.28
$30,000-$40,000	4,690	10.57
$40,000-$50,000	2,830	6.38
$50,000 +	5,630	12.69
Total Returns, No.	44,360	
Total Income, $000	1,268,869	
Total Taxable		
Returns	28,920	
Total Tax, $000	174,029	
Average Income, $	28,604	
Average Tax, $	6,018	

VITAL STATISTICS

	1997	1996	1995	1994
Births	740	750	790	841
Deaths	606	536	604	629
Natural Increase	134	214	186	212
Marriages	112	117	126	143

Note: Latest available data.

MEDIA INFO
see Montréal, CMA

Westmount
(Ville)
Montréal CMA

In census division Communauté urbaine de Montréal.

POPULATION

July 1, 2001 Estimate	20,818
% Cdn. Total	0.07
% Change, '96 -'01	0.11
Avg. Annual Growth Rate, %	0.02
2003 Projected Population	21,102
2006 Projected Population	21,645
2001 Households Estimate	9,280
2003 Projected Households	9,388
2006 Projected Households	9,571

INCOME

% Above/Below National Average	+172
2001 Total Income Estimate	$1,195,400,000
% Cdn. Total	0.18
2001 Average Hhld. Income	$128,800
2001 Per Capita	$57,400
2003 Projected Total Income	$1,267,890,000
2006 Projected Total Income	$1,392,320,000

RETAIL SALES

% Above/Below National Average	+7
2001 Retail Sales Estimate	$198,480,000
% Cdn. Total	0.07
2001 per Household	$21,400
2001 per Capita	$9,500
2001 No. of Establishments	333
2003 Projected Retail Sales	$215,250,000
2006 Projected Retail Sales	$240,960,000

POPULATION

2001 Estimates:

Total	20,818
Male	9,385
Female	11,433

Age Groups	Male	Female
0-4	485	467
5-9	510	493
10-14	575	538
15-19	626	596
20-24	611	620
25-29	565	620
30-34	547	626
35-39	556	672
40-44	578	750
45-49	668	912
50-54	737	965
55-59	704	850
60-64	596	693
65-69	507	590
70+	1,120	2,041

DAYTIME POPULATION

2001 Estimates:

Working Population	13,533
At Home Population	10,273
Total	23,806

INCOME

2001 Estimates:

Avg. Household Income	$128,814
Avg. Family Income	$176,456
Per Capita Income	$57,421
Male:	
Avg. Employment Income	$105,182
Avg. Employment Income (Full Time)	$141,559
Female:	
Avg. Employment Income	$36,381
Avg. Employment Income (Full Time)	$53,566

DISPOSABLE & DISCRETIONARY INCOME

2001 Estimates:	*Per Hhld.*
Disposable Income	$62,292
Discretionary Income 1 (minus Food & Shelter)	$36,982
Discretionary Income 2 (minus Food, Shelter, & Other Expenditures)	$24,498

LIQUID ASSETS

1999 Estimates:	*Per Hhld.*
Equity Investments	$407,785
Interest Bearing Investments	$199,785
Total Liquid Assets	$607,570

CREDIT DATA

July 2000:

Pool of Credit	$268,443,784
Revolving Credit, No.	46,048
Fixed Loans, No.	7,088
Avg. Credit Limit, per Person	$12,946
Avg. Spent, per Person	$4,602
Satisfactory Ratings, No. per Person	2.52
Avg. No. of Cards, per Person	1.29

LABOUR FORCE

2001 Estimates:

Male:	
In the Labour Force	5,828
Participation Rate	74.6
Employed	5,696
Unemployed	132
Unemployment Rate	2.3
Not in Labour Force	1,987
Female:	
In the Labour Force	5,197
Participation Rate	52.3
Employed	5,031
Unemployed	166
Unemployment Rate	3.2
Not in Labour Force	4,738

OCCUPATIONS BY MAJOR GROUPS

2001 Estimates:	*Male*	*Female*
Management	1,706	781
Business, Finance & Admin.	824	1,238
Natural & Applied Sciences & Related	525	182
Health	527	388
Social Sciences, Gov't Services & Religion	434	348
Education	391	456
Arts, Culture, Recreation & Sport	320	636
Sales & Service	798	1,022
Trades, Transport & Equipment Operators & Related	105	50
Primary Industries	36	n.a.
Processing, Mfg. & Utilities	32	37

LEVEL OF SCHOOLING

2001 Estimates:

Population 15 years +	17,750
Less than Grade 9	386
Grades 9-13 w/o Certif.	1,338
Grade 9-13 with Certif.	1,421
Trade Certif. /Dip.	298
Non-Univ. w/o Certif./Dip.	746
Non-Univ. with Certif./Dip.	1,471
Univ. w/o Degree	2,835
Univ. w/o Degree/Certif.	1,075
Univ. with Certif.	1,760
Univ. with Degree	9,255

Québec

AVERAGE HOUSEHOLD EXPENDITURES

2001 Estimates:

Food	$10,194
Shelter	$19,944
Clothing	$5,478
Transportation	$8,307
Health & Personal Care	$3,405
Recr'n, Read'g & Education	$7,000
Taxes & Securities	$34,936
Other	$19,277
Total Expenditures	$108,541

PRIVATE HOUSEHOLDS

2001 Estimates:

Private Households, Total	9,280
Pop. in Private Households	20,137
Average no. per Household	2.2

FAMILIES

2001 Estimates:

Families in Private Households	5,567
Husband-Wife Families	4,828
Lone-Parent Families	739
Aver. No. Persons per Family	2.8
Aver. No. Sons/Daughters at Home	1.0

HOUSING

2001 Estimates:

Occupied Private Dwellings	9,280
Owned	4,262
Rented	5,018
Single-Detached House	1,104
Semi-Detached House	1,447
Row Houses	1,206
Apartment, 5+ Storeys	3,825
Owned Apartment, 5+ Storeys	414
Apartment, 5 or Fewer Storeys	1,571
Apartment, Detached Duplex	42
Other Single-Attached	85

VEHICLES

2001 Estimates:

Model Yrs. '81-'96, No.	7,360
% Total	65.43
Model Yrs. '97-'98, No.	2,515
% Total	22.36
'99 Vehicles registered in Model Yr. '99, No.	1,374
% Total	12.21
Total No. '81-'99	11,249

LEGAL MARITAL STATUS

2001 Estimates: (Age 15+)

Single (Never Married)	5,971
Legally Married (Not Separated)	8,592
Legally Married (Separated)	338
Widowed	1,525
Divorced	1,324

Québec

Westmount
(Ville)
Montréal CMA
(Cont'd)

PSYTE CATEGORIES

2001 Estimates	No. of House-holds	% of Total Hhds.	Index
Canadian Establishment	2,307	24.86	14,938
The Affluentials	541	5.83	912
Urban Gentry	2,308	24.87	1,384
Brie & Chablis	72	0.78	87
High Rise Sunsets	469	5.05	353
Young Urban Professionals	2,795	30.12	1,587
Young Urban Intelligentsia	583	6.28	413

FINANCIAL P$YTE

2001 Estimates	No. of House-holds	% of Total Hhds.	Index
Platinum Estates	2,848	30.69	3,809
Four Star Investors	2,308	24.87	495
Urban Heights	2,867	30.89	718
Revolving Renters	469	5.05	110
Young Urban Struggle	583	6.28	133

HOME LANGUAGE

2001 Estimates:		% Total
English	14,812	71.15
French	3,886	18.67
Arabic	213	1.02
Armenian	43	0.21
Bulgarian	33	0.16
Chinese	251	1.21
Czech	30	0.14
German	81	0.39
Greek	53	0.25
Hungarian	56	0.27
Italian	20	0.10
Japanese	41	0.20
Korean	66	0.32
Persian (Farsi)	66	0.32
Romanian	100	0.48
Russian	99	0.48
Serbian	32	0.15
Serbo-Croatian	27	0.13
Spanish	76	0.37
Tagalog (Pilipino)	89	0.43
Turkish	27	0.13
Other Languages	70	0.34
Multiple Responses	647	3.11
Total	20,818	100.00

BUILDING PERMITS

	1999	1998 $000	1997
Value	24,038	19,403	14,664

HOMES BUILT

	1999	1998	1997
No	17	n.a.	n.a.

TAXATION

Income Class:	1997	% Total
Under $5,000	1,380	10.72
$5,000-$10,000	1,070	8.31
$10,000-$15,000	1,120	8.70
$15,000-$20,000	870	6.76
$20,000-$25,000	720	5.59
$25,000-$30,000	710	5.52
$30,000-$40,000	1,220	9.48
$40,000-$50,000	920	7.15
$50,000 +	4,880	37.92
Total Returns, No.	12,870	
Total Income, $000	1,046,104	
Total Taxable Returns	9,860	
Total Tax, $000	208,409	
Average Income, $	81,282	
Average Tax, $	21,137	

VITAL STATISTICS

	1997	1996	1995	1994
Births	166	130	122	151
Deaths	218	159	173	160
Natural Increase	-52	-29	-51	-9
Marriages	215	216	180	192

Note: Latest available data.

MEDIA INFO

see Montréal, CMA

Ottawa-Hull
(Census Metropolitan Area)

Note: Ottawa-Hull straddles the Ontario-Quebec border. Refer to Ottawa-Hull, CMA, in Ontario section for statistics on cities located in Ontario.

POPULATION

July 1, 2001 Estimate	1,085,918
% Cdn. Total	3.49
% Change, '96 -'01	4.60
Avg. Annual Growth Rate, %	0.90
2003 Projected Population	1,112,736
2006 Projected Population	1,158,862
2001 Households Estimate	431,851
2003 Projected Households	446,292
2006 Projected Households	470,840

INCOME

% Above/Below National Average	+18
2001 Total Income Estimate	$27,101,540,000
% Cdn. Total	4.13
2001 Average Hhld. Income	$62,800
2001 Per Capita	$25,000
2003 Projected Total Income	$29,294,630,000
2006 Projected Total Income	$33,077,460,000

RETAIL SALES

% Above/Below National Average	+3
2001 Retail Sales Estimate	$10,000,190,000
% Cdn. Total	3.59
2001 per Household	$23,200
2001 per Capita	$9,200
2001 No. of Establishments	6,626
2003 Projected Retail Sales	$10,925,820,000
2006 Projected Retail Sales	$12,362,680,000

POPULATION

2001 Estimates:		
Total		1,085,918
Male		531,076
Female		554,842

Age Groups	Male	Female
0-4	35,278	33,674
5-9	36,842	35,185
10-14	36,979	35,051
15-19	35,481	33,765
20-24	35,255	34,573
25-29	37,587	37,799
30-34	42,912	43,634
35-39	46,467	48,243
40-44	45,608	47,958
45-49	42,442	44,417
50-54	36,144	37,355
55-59	28,127	28,947
60-64	21,542	22,696
65-69	17,068	19,292
70+	33,344	52,253

DAYTIME POPULATION

2001 Estimates:	
Working Population	583,065
At Home Population	502,852
Total	1,085,917

INCOME

2001 Estimates:	
Avg. Household Income	$62,757
Avg. Family Income	$71,040
Per Capita Income	$24,957
Male:	
Avg. Employment Income	$39,755
Avg. Employment Income (minus Food)	$52,042
Female:	
Avg. Employment Income	$27,409
Avg. Employment Income (minus Food)	$38,913

DISPOSABLE & DISCRETIONARY INCOME

2001 Estimates:	Per Hhld.
Disposable Income	$49,174
Discretionary Income 1 (minus Food & Shelter)	$34,707
Discretionary Income 2 (minus Food, Shelter, & Other Expenditures)	$25,772

LIQUID ASSETS

1999 Estimates:	Per Hhld.
Equity Investments	$89,085
Interest Bearing Investments	$76,857
Total Liquid Assets	$165,942

CREDIT DATA

July 2000:	
Pool of Credit	$11,702,079,877
Revolving Credit, No.	2,225,399
Fixed Loans, No.	629,979
Avg. Credit Limit, per Person	$12,184
Avg. Spent, per Person	$5,255
Satisfactory Ratings, No. per Person	2.84
Avg. No. of Cards, per Person	1.10

LABOUR FORCE

2001 Estimates:	
Male:	
In the Labour Force	325,786
Participation Rate	77.2
Employed	307,673
Unemployed	18,113
Unemployment Rate	5.6
Not in Labour Force	96,191
Female:	
In the Labour Force	288,182
Participation Rate	63.9
Employed	273,668
Unemployed	14,514
Unemployment Rate	5.0
Not in Labour Force	162,750

OCCUPATIONS BY MAJOR GROUPS

2001 Estimates:	Male	Female
Management	48,210	24,489
Business, Finance & Admin.	44,275	94,213
Natural & Applied Sciences & Related	44,848	11,465
Health	6,430	22,603
Social Sciences, Gov't Services & Religion	11,812	12,275
Education	9,716	16,767
Arts, Culture, Recreation & Sport	10,488	12,494
Sales & Service	72,092	75,160
Trades, Transport & Equipment Operators & Related	52,737	3,434
Primary Industries	6,345	1,728
Processing, Mfg. & Utilities	8,313	3,333

Ottawa-Hull
(Census Metropolitan Area)
(Cont'd)

LEVEL OF SCHOOLING

2001 Estimates:

Population 15 years +	872,909
Less than Grade 9	69,558
Grades 9-13 w/o Certif.	152,691
Grade 9-13 with Certif.	126,011
Trade Certif./Dip.	23,682
Non-Univ. w/o Certif./Dip.	56,499
Non-Univ. with Certif./Dip.	145,686
Univ. w/o Degree	101,485
Univ. w/o Degree/Certif.	48,313
Univ. with Certif.	53,172
Univ. with Degree	197,297

AVERAGE HOUSEHOLD EXPENDITURES

2001 Estimates:

Food	$6,831
Shelter	$10,140
Clothing	$2,570
Transportation	$6,778
Health & Personal Care	$2,149
Recr'n, Read'g & Education	$4,156
Taxes & Securities	$17,387
Other	$8,858
Total Expenditures	$58,869

PRIVATE HOUSEHOLDS

2001 Estimates:

Private Households, Total	431,851
Pop. in Private Households	1,065,437
Average no. per Household	2.5

FAMILIES

2001 Estimates:

Families in Private Households	305,984
Husband-Wife Families	259,196
Lone-Parent Families	46,788
Aver. No. Persons per Family	3.0
Aver. No. Sons/Daughters at Home	1.2

HOUSING

2001 Estimates:

Occupied Private Dwellings	431,851
Owned	258,348
Rented	173,503
Single-Detached House	196,365
Semi-Detached House	29,321
Row Houses	58,607
Apartment, 5+ Storeys	69,297
Owned Apartment, 5+ Storeys	9,668
Apartment, 5 or Fewer Storeys	60,372
Apartment, Detached Duplex	15,045
Other Single-Attached	1,002
Movable Dwellings	1,842

VEHICLES

2001 Estimates:

Model Yrs. '81-'96, No.	459,125
% Total	76.45
Model Yrs. '97-'98, No.	82,167
% Total	13.68
'99 Vehicles registered in Model Yr. '99, No.	59,279
% Total	9.87
Total No. '81-'99	600,571

LEGAL MARITAL STATUS

2001 Estimates: (Age 15+)

Single (Never Married)	291,776
Legally Married (Not Separated)	440,839
Legally Married (Separated)	29,378
Widowed	46,910
Divorced	64,006

PSYTE CATEGORIES

2001 Estimates	No. of House-holds	% of Total Hhds.	Index
Canadian Establishment	284	0.07	40
The Affluentials	1,783	0.41	65
Urban Gentry	21,861	5.06	282
Suburban Executives	18,274	4.23	295
Mortgaged in Suburbia	10,487	2.43	175
Technocrafts & Bureaucrats	51,647	11.96	425
Boomers & Teens	4,978	1.15	64
Stable Suburban Families	8,878	2.06	158
Small City Elite	8,720	2.02	118
Old Bungalow Burbs	7,335	1.70	102
Suburban Nesters	11,668	2.70	169
Brie & Chablis	3,702	0.86	96
Aging Erudites	14,500	3.36	223
Satellite Suburbs	3,070	0.71	25
Kindergarten Boom	13,133	3.04	116
Blue Collar Winners	12,784	2.96	118
Old Towns' New Fringe	3,610	0.84	21
Participation Quebec	27,243	6.31	219
New Quebec Rows	16,535	3.83	349
Quebec Melange	16,537	3.83	145
Traditional French Cdn. Families	7,943	1.84	68
Rustic Prosperity	325	0.08	4
Quebec's Heartland	91	0.02	2
High Rise Melting Pot	2,924	0.68	45
Conservative Homebodies	6,830	1.58	44
High Rise Sunsets	11,927	2.76	193
Young Urban Professionals	19,496	4.51	238
Young Urban Mix	8,370	1.94	91
Young Urban Intelligentsia	13,817	3.20	210
University Enclaves	14,846	3.44	168
Young City Singles	18,336	4.25	185
Urban Bohemia	8,999	2.08	178
Old Leafy Towns	565	0.13	5
Town Renters	7,217	1.67	193
Rod & Rifle	753	0.17	8
Quebec Rural Blues	1,021	0.24	10
Old Quebec Walkups	9,857	2.28	125
Quebec Town Elders	6,736	1.56	55
Aging Quebec Urbanites	2,012	0.47	161
Quebec's New Urban Mosaic	12,993	3.01	125
Struggling Downtowns	2,520	0.58	19
Aged Pensioners	4,268	0.99	74
Big City Stress	6,449	1.49	132
Old Grey Towers	3,884	0.90	162

FINAN¢IAL P$YTE

2001 Estimates	No. of House-holds	% of Total Hhds.	Index
Platinum Estates	2,067	0.48	59
Four Star Investors	45,113	10.45	208
Successful Suburbanites	71,012	16.44	248
Canadian Comfort	36,242	8.39	86
Urban Heights	37,698	8.73	203
Miners & Credit-Liners	7,335	1.70	54
Mortgages & Minivans	56,911	13.18	200
Tractors & Tradelines	3,935	0.91	16
Bills & Wills	15,765	3.65	44
Country Credit	24,480	5.67	84
Revolving Renters	11,927	2.76	60
Young Urban Struggle	37,662	8.72	184
Rural Family Blues	1,865	0.43	5
Loan Parent Stress	18,605	4.31	74
Towering Debt	30,997	7.18	92
NSF	19,442	4.50	127
Senior Survivors	8,152	1.89	100

Québec

RADIO STATION DATA

Station	Market	Format	Wkly. Reach%*	Aver. Hrs. Tuned
All Stations			95	22.4
CBO-FM	Ottawa-Hull	News, Info.	17	12.0
CBOF-FM	Ottawa-Hull	News, Info.	4	12.1
CBOQ-FM	Ottawa-Hull	Music, Arts	8	9.5
CBOX-FM	Ottawa-Hull	Classical, Jazz	3	4.6
CFGO	Ottawa-Hull	Sports	9	8.3
CFMO-FM	Ottawa	New Rock Alternative	13	6.7
CFRA	Ottawa-Hull	News, Talk	14	10.4
CHEZ-FM	Ottawa-Hull	Classic Rock	16	8.1
CHRI-FM	Ottawa-Hull	Contemp. Christian	n.a.	n.a.
CIMF-FM	Ottawa-Hull	Adult Contemp.	14	13.5
CIWW	Ottawa-Hull	Oldies	7	7.6
CIZN-FM	Cambridge	Adult Top 40	n.a.	n.a.
CJMJ-FM	Ottawa-Hull	Adult Contemp.	21	11.6
CJRC	Gatineau	Classic Rock	7	12.3
CKBY-FM	Ottawa-Hull	Country	13	12.9
CKKL-FM	Ottawa-Hull	Adult Contemp. Hits	28	8.5
CKQB-FM	Ottawa-Hull	AOR	17	7.6
CKTF-FM	Gatineau	Top 40	14	12.5

BBM Spring 2000 Radio Reach Surveys; area coverage.
* Mon-Sun 5a.m.-1a.m., All Persons 12+

TV STATION DATA

Station	Market	Network Affiliation	Wkly. Reach%*	Aver. Hrs. Tuned
All Stations			96	21.2
A & E	n.a.	Ind.	15	3.1
CBOFT	Ottawa	SRC	23	6.0
CBOT	Ottawa	CBC	37	3.0
CFGS	Hull	TQS	16	3.8
CFMT	Toronto	Ind.	20	1.9
CHCH	Toronto/Hamilton	Ind.	30	2.3
CHOT	Hull	TVA	20	7.2
CHRO	Ottawa	Ind.	22	2.4
CICO-E	n.a.	n.a.	18	2.8
CIII	n.a.	Global	52	2.9
CITY	Toronto	Ind.	27	2.1
CIVM	Montréal	Télé-Qué.	6	2.0
CIVO	Hull	Télé-Qué.	n.a.	n.a.
CJOH	Ottawa	CTV	61	5.0
DSCVRY	n.a.	Ind.	6	1.8
NEWSWD	n.a.	CBC	8	1.4
OTHERS	n.a.	n.a.	11	2.2
PRIME	n.a.	Ind.	6	2.8
RDI	n.a.	n.a.	5	2.8
RDS	n.a.	Ind.	5	2.4
SNET	n.a.	CTV	15	2.8
SPACE	n.a.	Ind.	7	2.8
TLC	n.a.	Ind.	10	1.8
TMN	Toronto	Ind.	5	4.6
TOON(FR)	n.a.	Ind.	4	4.6
TOON-E	n.a.	Ind.	7	1.9
TSN	n.a.	Ind.	12	3.7
VCR	n.a.	n.a.	32	4.2
WHEC	Rochester NY	NBC	12	1.3
WOKR	Rochester NY	ABC	18	1.8
WPBS	Watertown NY	PBS	12	1.9
WROC	Rochester NY	CBS	14	1.8
WTBS	Atlanta GA	Ind.	12	2.7
WUTV	Buffalo NY	FOX	20	1.9
YTV	n.a.	Ind.	12	2.5

BBM Spring 2000 TV Reach Surveys; CMA coverage.
*Mon-Sun 6a.m.-2a.m., All Persons 2+

Québec

Ottawa-Hull
(Census Metropolitan Area)
(Cont'd)

HOME LANGUAGE

2001 Estimates:		% Total
English	659,173	60.70
French	318,600	29.34
Arabic	12,661	1.17
Bengali	874	0.08
Chinese	12,463	1.15
Creoles	742	0.07
German	1,028	0.09
Greek	1,092	0.10
Hindi	869	0.08
Hungarian	905	0.08
Italian	4,780	0.44
Khmer (Cambodian)	612	0.06
Persian (Farsi)	2,446	0.23
Polish	3,809	0.35
Portuguese	3,510	0.32
Punjabi	1,621	0.15
Romanian	647	0.06
Russian	1,421	0.13
Serbian	783	0.07
Serbo-Croatian	1,221	0.11
Spanish	5,400	0.50
Tagalog (Pilipino)	1,155	0.11
Tamil	716	0.07
Urdu	1,043	0.10
Vietnamese	4,730	0.44
Other Languages	13,934	1.28
Multiple Responses	29,683	2.73
Total	1,085,918	100.00

BUILDING PERMITS

	1999	1998	1997
		$000	
Value	1,282,551	1,149,908	913,151

HOMES BUILT

	1999	1998	1997
No	5,265	4,621	4,771

TAXATION

Income Class:	1997	% Total
Under $5,000	65,690	11.85
$5,000-$10,000	62,320	11.24
$10,000-$15,000	65,150	11.75
$15,000-$20,000	45,350	8.18
$20,000-$25,000	39,440	7.12
$25,000-$30,000	38,430	6.93
$30,000-$40,000	71,690	12.93
$40,000-$50,000	52,710	9.51
$50,000 +	113,590	20.49
Total Returns, No.	554,250	
Total Income, $000	18,315,723	
Total Taxable Returns	400,160	
Total Tax, $000	3,815,649	
Average Income, $	33,046	
Average Tax, $	9,535	

VITAL STATISTICS

	1997	1996	1995	1994
Births	12,096	12,562	12,831	13,087
Deaths	6,063	6,120	6,111	6,052
Natural Increase	6,063	6,442	6,720	7,035
Marriages	4,963	5,312	5,362	5,395

Note: Latest available data.

DAILY NEWSPAPER(S)

	Circulation Average Paid
Le Droit	
Sat	40,645
Mon-Fri.	34,335
Ottawa Citizen	
Sat	181,568
Sun	133,810
Mon-Fri.	137,146
Ottawa Sun / Sunday Sun	
Sat	48,265
Sun	57,348
Mon-Fri.	52,124

COMMUNITY NEWSPAPER(S)

	Total Circulation
Aylmer: Bulletin d'Aylmer	13,791
Aylmer, Gatineau, Hull: Week-end Outaouais	64,831
Aylmer, Gatineau, Hull: Bonjour Dimanche	74,348
Aylmer, Gatineau, Hull: Le Régional Combiné Outaouais (suppl.)	74,421
Aylmer, Hull: Le Régional Aylmer-Hull	37,810
Buckingham: The West-Québec Post	n.a.
Buckingham: Le Bulletin	11,525
Gatineau: Outaouais Affaires	17,500
Gatineau: La Revue de Gatineau	39,490
Gatineau, Aylmer, Hull: Bonjour Dimanche	74,348
Gatineau, Aylmer, Hull: L'Hebdo de l'Avenir Outaouais	74,597
Gatineau, Aylmer, Hull: Week-end Outaouais	64,831
Gatineau, Hull, Aylmer: Le Régional Combiné Outaouais	74,421
Hull, Aylmer, Gatineau: Bonjour Dimanche	74,348
Hull, Aylmer, Gatineau: Week-end Outaouais	64,831
Hull, Aylmer, Gatineau: Le Régional Combiné Outaouais (suppl.)	74,421
Kanata: Kanata Kourier-Standard	19,468
Nepean: Nepean Clarion	n.a.
Nepean: Nepean This Week	43,699
Nepean: Ottawa Pennysaver	n.a.
Ottawa: Hunt Club Riverside News	35,930
Ottawa: Ottawa-Carleton This Month (mthly)	n.a.
Ottawa: The Alta Vista News	35,930
Ottawa: Greenboro Hunt Club Park News	35,930
Ottawa: Ottawa Centretown News (biwkly)	n.a.
Rockland: Vision	20,000
Russell: Russell Villager	1,097

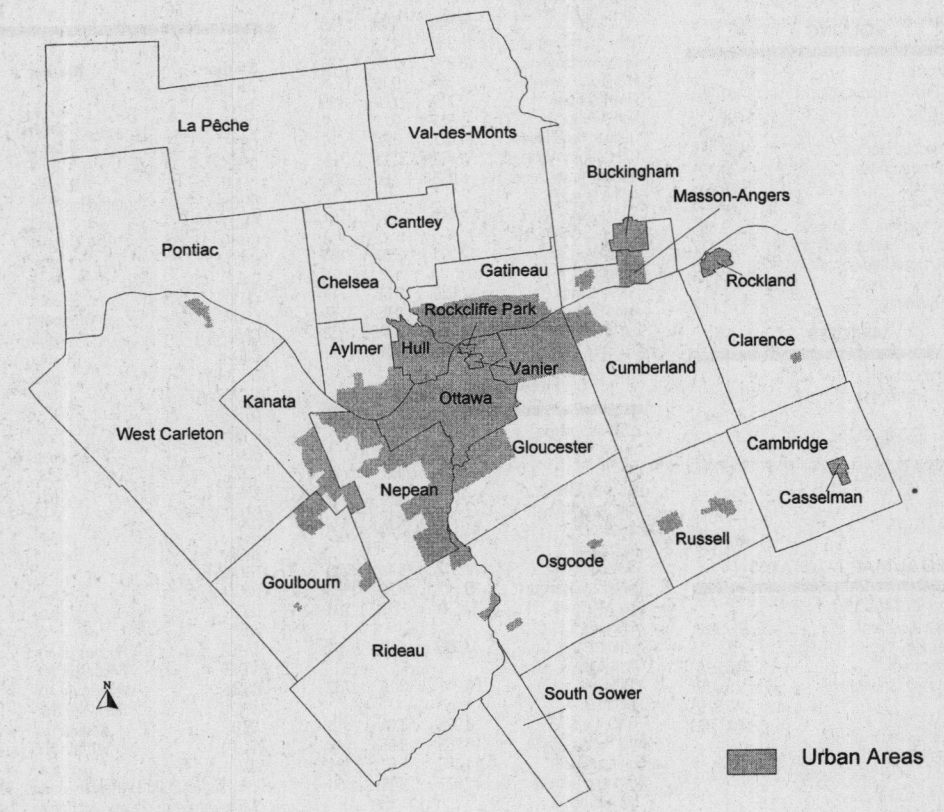

Urban Areas

Aylmer
(Ville)
Ottawa-Hull CMA

In census division Communauté urbaine de l'Outaouais.

POPULATION

July 1, 2001 Estimate	36,712
% Cdn. Total	0.12
% Change, '96 -'01	3.27
Avg. Annual Growth Rate, %	0.65
2003 Projected Population	37,557
2006 Projected Population	39,047
2001 Households Estimate	13,181
2003 Projected Households	13,656
2006 Projected Households	14,448

INCOME

% Above/Below National Average	+12
2001 Total Income Estimate	$864,790,000
% Cdn. Total	0.13
2001 Average Hhld. Income	$65,600
2001 Per Capita	$23,600
2003 Projected Total Income	$934,550,000
2006 Projected Total Income	$1,056,020,000

RETAIL SALES

% Above/Below National Average	-44
2001 Retail Sales Estimate	$183,210,000
% Cdn. Total	0.07
2001 per Household	$13,900
2001 per Capita	$5,000
2001 No. of Establishments	138
2003 Projected Retail Sales	$200,120,000
2006 Projected Retail Sales	$227,330,000

POPULATION

2001 Estimates:

Total		36,712
Male		17,886
Female		18,826

Age Groups	Male	Female
0-4	1,158	1,114
5-9	1,352	1,331
10-14	1,488	1,473
15-19	1,473	1,450
20-24	1,251	1,248
25-29	1,069	1,117
30-34	1,190	1,315
35-39	1,465	1,644
40-44	1,644	1,813
45-49	1,585	1,673
50-54	1,334	1,326
55-59	979	935
60-64	682	660
65-69	473	517
70+	743	1,210

DAYTIME POPULATION

2001 Estimates:

Working Population	9,506
At Home Population	17,377
Total	26,883

INCOME

2001 Estimates:

Avg. Household Income	$65,609
Avg. Family Income	$70,306
Per Capita Income	$23,556
Male:	
Avg. Employment Income	$40,661
Avg. Employment Income (minus Food)	$51,741
Female:	
Avg. Employment Income	$28,658
Avg. Employment Income (minus Food)	$39,123

DISPOSABLE & DISCRETIONARY INCOME

2001 Estimates: | Per Hhld.

Disposable Income	$44,502
Discretionary Income 1 (minus Food & Shelter)	$29,783
Discretionary Income 2 (minus Food, Shelter, & Other Expenditures)	$20,369

LIQUID ASSETS

1999 Estimates: | Per Hhld.

Equity Investments	$86,595
Interest Bearing Investments	$77,816
Total Liquid Assets	$164,411

CREDIT DATA

July 2000:

Pool of Credit	$326,211,015
Revolving Credit, No.	66,701
Fixed Loans, No.	23,727
Avg. Credit Limit, per Person	$11,110
Avg. Spent, per Person	$5,363
Satisfactory Ratings, No. per Person	2.93
Avg. No. of Cards, per Person	1.03

LABOUR FORCE

2001 Estimates:

Male:	
In the Labour Force	10,738
Participation Rate	77.3
Employed	10,197
Unemployed	541
Unemployment Rate	5.0
Not in Labour Force	3,150
Female:	
In the Labour Force	9,441
Participation Rate	63.3
Employed	9,019
Unemployed	422
Unemployment Rate	4.5
Not in Labour Force	5,467

OCCUPATIONS BY MAJOR GROUPS

2001 Estimates:	Male	Female
Management	1,483	790
Business, Finance & Admin.	1,445	3,472
Natural & Applied Sciences & Related	1,365	232
Health	179	546
Social Sciences, Gov't Services & Religion	428	462
Education	503	704
Arts, Culture, Recreation & Sport	380	379
Sales & Service	2,462	2,327
Trades, Transport & Equipment Operators & Related	1,702	91
Primary Industries	194	20
Processing, Mfg. & Utilities	264	112

LEVEL OF SCHOOLING

2001 Estimates:

Population 15 years +	28,796
Less than Grade 9	2,324
Grades 9-13 w/o Certif.	5,609
Grade 9-13 with Certif.	4,242
Trade Certif. /Dip.	860
Non-Univ. w/o Certif./Dip.	2,323
Non-Univ. with Certif./Dip.	4,525
Univ. w/o Degree	3,147
Univ. w/o Degree/Certif.	994
Univ. with Certif.	2,153
Univ. with Degree	5,766

AVERAGE HOUSEHOLD EXPENDITURES

2001 Estimates:

Food	$7,243
Shelter	$9,996
Clothing	$2,718
Transportation	$7,234
Health & Personal Care	$2,249
Recr'n, Read'g & Education	$4,307
Taxes & Securities	$18,911
Other	$8,855
Total Expenditures	$61,513

PRIVATE HOUSEHOLDS

2001 Estimates:

Private Households, Total	13,181
Pop. in Private Households	36,236
Average no. per Household	2.7

FAMILIES

2001 Estimates:

Families in Private Households	10,684
Husband-Wife Families	9,088
Lone-Parent Families	1,596
Aver. No. Persons per Family	3.2
Aver. No. Sons/Daughters at Home	1.3

HOUSING

2001 Estimates:

Occupied Private Dwellings	13,181
Owned	9,930
Rented	3,251
Single-Detached House	7,989
Semi-Detached House	1,585
Row Houses	1,306
Apartment, 5+ Storeys	419
Apartment, 5 or Fewer Storeys	1,394
Apartment, Detached Duplex	488

VEHICLES

2001 Estimates:

Model Yrs. '81-'96, No.	15,156
% Total	79.13
Model Yrs. '97-'98, No.	2,426
% Total	12.67
'99 Vehicles registered in Model Yr. '99, No.	1,571
% Total	8.20
Total No. '81-'99	19,153

LEGAL MARITAL STATUS

2001 Estimates: (Age 15+)

Single (Never Married)	9,199
Legally Married (Not Separated)	15,133
Legally Married (Separated)	851
Widowed	1,253
Divorced	2,360

PSYTE CATEGORIES

2001 Estimates	No. of House -holds	% of Total Hhds.	Index
Urban Gentry	506	3.84	214
Suburban Executives	769	5.83	407
Technocrafts & Bureaucrats	2,501	18.97	674
Small City Elite	395	3.00	175
Old Bungalow Burbs	1,619	12.28	741
Aging Erudites	106	0.80	53
Kindergarten Boom	702	5.33	203
Participation Quebec	1,873	14.21	493
New Quebec Rows	1,295	9.82	897
Quebec Melange	1,688	12.81	483
Conservative Homebodies	284	2.15	60
Young City Singles	457	3.47	151
Town Renters	270	2.05	237
Old Quebec Walkups	276	2.09	114
Quebec Town Elders	408	3.10	110

Québec

FINAN¢IAL P$YTE

2001 Estimates	No. of House -holds	% of Total Hhds.	Index
Four Star Investors	1,275	9.67	193
Successful Suburbanites	2,501	18.97	286
Canadian Comfort	395	3.00	31
Urban Heights	106	0.80	19
Miners & Credit-Liners	1,619	12.28	388
Mortgages & Minivans	3,870	29.36	445
Bills & Wills	284	2.15	26
Country Credit	1,688	12.81	189
Loan Parent Stress	684	5.19	89
Towering Debt	727	5.52	71

HOME LANGUAGE

2001 Estimates:		% Total
English	13,818	37.64
French	20,494	55.82
Arabic	306	0.83
Czech	26	0.07
German	36	0.10
Italian	26	0.07
Persian (Farsi)	36	0.10
Polish	114	0.31
Portuguese	193	0.53
Punjabi	27	0.07
Spanish	89	0.24
Other Languages	53	0.14
Multiple Responses	1,494	4.07
Total	36,712	100.00

BUILDING PERMITS

	1999	1998	1997
		$000	
Value	27,570	21,583	23,261

HOMES BUILT

	1999	1998	1997
No	147	121	134

TAXATION

Income Class:	1997	% Total
Under $5,000	2,800	11.95
$5,000-$10,000	2,630	11.22
$10,000-$15,000	2,530	10.79
$15,000-$20,000	1,860	7.94
$20,000-$25,000	1,630	6.95
$25,000-$30,000	1,830	7.81
$30,000-$40,000	3,530	15.06
$40,000-$50,000	2,500	10.67
$50,000 +	4,130	17.62
Total Returns, No.	23,440	
Total Income, $000	712,637	
Total Taxable Returns	17,590	
Total Tax, $000	93,748	
Average Income, $	30,403	
Average Tax, $	5,330	

VITAL STATISTICS

	1997	1996	1995	1994
Births	430	450	259	277
Deaths	169	173	159	148
Natural Increase	261	277	100	129
Marriages	63	67	66	80

Note: Latest available data.

MEDIA INFO
see Ottawa-Hull, CMA

Québec

Buckingham

(Ville)

Ottawa-Hull CMA

In census division Communauté urbaine de l'Outaouais.

POPULATION

July 1, 2001 Estimate	12,526
% Cdn. Total	0.04
% Change, '96 -'01	5.32
Avg. Annual Growth Rate, %	1.04
2003 Projected Population	12,945
2006 Projected Population	13,653
2001 Households Estimate	5,014
2003 Projected Households	5,245
2006 Projected Households	5,622

INCOME

% Above/Below National Average	-7
2001 Total Income Estimate	$245,810,000
% Cdn. Total	0.04
2001 Average Hhld. Income	$49,000
2001 Per Capita	$19,600
2003 Projected Total Income	$266,670,000
2006 Projected Total Income	$302,690,000

RETAIL SALES

% Above/Below National Average	+28
2001 Retail Sales Estimate	$144,070,000
% Cdn. Total	0.05
2001 per Household	$28,700
2001 per Capita	$11,500
2001 No. of Establishments	88
2003 Projected Retail Sales	$161,010,000
2006 Projected Retail Sales	$188,070,000

POPULATION

2001 Estimates:

Total		12,526
Male		6,072
Female		6,454

Age Groups	Male	Female
0-4	414	398
5-9	446	442
10-14	451	445
15-19	417	401
20-24	381	379
25-29	381	419
30-34	482	528
35-39	567	584
40-44	544	555
45-49	466	481
50-54	376	374
55-59	281	277
60-64	211	236
65-69	190	224
70+	465	711

DAYTIME POPULATION

2001 Estimates:

Working Population	4,413
At Home Population	6,972
Total	11,385

INCOME

2001 Estimates:

Avg. Household Income	$49,024
Avg. Family Income	$54,975
Per Capita Income	$19,624
Male:	
Avg. Employment Income	$37,004
Avg. Employment Income (minus Food)	$46,077
Female:	
Avg. Employment Income	$23,816
Avg. Employment Income (minus Food)	$32,378

DISPOSABLE & DISCRETIONARY INCOME

2001 Estimates:	Per Hhld.
Disposable Income	$33,931
Discretionary Income 1 (minus Food & Shelter)	$21,839
Discretionary Income 2 (minus Food, Shelter, & Other Expenditures)	$14,407

LIQUID ASSETS

1999 Estimates:	Per Hhld.
Equity Investments	$53,172
Interest Bearing Investments	$56,871
Total Liquid Assets	$110,043

CREDIT DATA

July 2000:

Pool of Credit	$92,004,816
Revolving Credit, No.	20,983
Fixed Loans, No.	9,737
Avg. Credit Limit, per Person	$9,148
Avg. Spent, per Person	$4,648
Satisfactory Ratings, No. per Person	2.75
Avg. No. of Cards, per Person	0.86

LABOUR FORCE

2001 Estimates:

Male:	
In the Labour Force	3,268
Participation Rate	68.6
Employed	2,962
Unemployed	306
Unemployment Rate	9.4
Not in Labour Force	1,493
Female:	
In the Labour Force	2,756
Participation Rate	53.3
Employed	2,586
Unemployed	170
Unemployment Rate	6.2
Not in Labour Force	2,413

OCCUPATIONS BY MAJOR GROUPS

2001 Estimates:	Male	Female
Management	333	154
Business, Finance & Admin.	397	1,077
Natural & Applied Sciences & Related	252	27
Health	83	292
Social Sciences, Gov't Services & Religion	67	78
Education	99	135
Arts, Culture, Recreation & Sport	57	44
Sales & Service	660	790
Trades, Transport & Equipment Operators & Related	728	11
Primary Industries	44	11
Processing, Mfg. & Utilities	389	n.a.

LEVEL OF SCHOOLING

2001 Estimates:

Population 15 years +	9,930
Less than Grade 9	1,627
Grades 9-13 w/o Certif.	2,103
Grade 9-13 with Certif.	1,897
Trade Certif. /Dip.	388
Non-Univ. w/o Certif./Dip.	693
Non-Univ. with Certif./Dip.	1,676
Univ. w/o Degree	680
Univ. w/o Degree/Certif.	124
Univ. with Certif.	556
Univ. with Degree	866

AVERAGE HOUSEHOLD EXPENDITURES

2001 Estimates:

Food	$6,202
Shelter	$7,624
Clothing	$2,061
Transportation	$5,591
Health & Personal Care	$1,927
Recr'n, Read'g & Education	$3,072
Taxes & Securities	$14,455
Other	$7,058
Total Expenditures	$47,990

PRIVATE HOUSEHOLDS

2001 Estimates:

Private Households, Total	5,014
Pop. in Private Households	12,246
Average no. per Household	2.4

FAMILIES

2001 Estimates:

Families in Private Households	3,755
Husband-Wife Families	3,149
Lone-Parent Families	606
Aver. No. Persons per Family	2.9
Aver. No. Sons/Daughters at Home	1.1

HOUSING

2001 Estimates:

Occupied Private Dwellings	5,014
Owned	3,175
Rented	1,839
Single-Detached House	2,609
Semi-Detached House	1,029
Row Houses	313
Apartment, 5 or Fewer Storeys	670
Apartment, Detached Duplex	325
Other Single-Attached	11
Movable Dwellings	57

VEHICLES

2001 Estimates:

Model Yrs. '81-'96, No.	6,185
% Total	79.77
Model Yrs. '97-'98, No.	1,014
% Total	13.08
'99 Vehicles registered in Model Yr. '99, No.	555
% Total	7.16
Total No. '81-'99	7,754

LEGAL MARITAL STATUS

2001 Estimates: (Age 15+)

Single (Never Married)	3,525
Legally Married (Not Separated)	4,581
Legally Married (Separated)	248
Widowed	691
Divorced	885

PSYTE CATEGORIES

2001 Estimates	No. of House -holds	% of Total Hhds.	Index
Technocrafts & Bureaucrats	107	2.13	76
Participation Quebec	887	17.69	614
New Quebec Rows	458	9.13	834
Quebec Melange	1,860	37.10	1,400
Quebec Town Elders	1,623	32.37	1,145

FINANCIAL P$YTE

2001 Estimates	No. of House -holds	% of Total Hhds.	Index
Successful Suburbanites	107	2.13	32
Mortgages & Minivans	1,345	26.82	406
Country Credit	1,860	37.10	549
Loan Parent Stress	1,623	32.37	556

HOME LANGUAGE

2001 Estimates:		% Total
English	1,190	9.50
French	11,045	88.18
Spanish	11	0.09
Multiple Responses	280	2.24
Total	12,526	100.00

BUILDING PERMITS

	1999	1998 $000	1997
Value	3,136	2,924	2,920

HOMES BUILT

	1999	1998	1997
No.	12	17	20

TAXATION

Income Class:	1997	% Total
Under $5,000	1,290	13.16
$5,000-$10,000	1,450	14.80
$10,000-$15,000	1,420	14.49
$15,000-$20,000	850	8.67
$20,000-$25,000	800	8.16
$25,000-$30,000	850	8.67
$30,000-$40,000	1,270	12.96
$40,000-$50,000	840	8.57
$50,000 +	1,040	10.61
Total Returns, No.	9,800	
Total Income, $000	242,005	
Total Taxable Returns	6,530	
Total Tax, $000	28,247	
Average Income, $.	24,694	
Average Tax, $.	4,326	

VITAL STATISTICS

	1997	1996	1995	1994
Births	140	158	162	181
Deaths	125	110	104	105
Natural Increase	15	48	58	76
Marriages	29	26	36	40

Note: Latest available data.

MEDIA INFO
see Ottawa-Hull, CMA

Gatineau
(Ville)
Ottawa-Hull CMA

In census division Communauté urbaine de l'Outaouais.

POPULATION

July 1, 2001 Estimate	106,667
% Cdn. Total	0.34
% Change, '96 -'01	3.99
Avg. Annual Growth Rate, %	0.79
2003 Projected Population	109,521
2006 Projected Population	114,452
2001 Households Estimate	40,356
2003 Projected Households	41,924
2006 Projected Households	44,553

INCOME

% Above/Below National Average	same
2001 Total Income Estimate	$2,242,590,000
% Cdn. Total	0.34
2001 Average Hhld. Income	$55,600
2001 Per Capita	$21,000
2003 Projected Total Income	$2,415,200,000
2006 Projected Total Income	$2,715,980,000

RETAIL SALES

% Above/Below National Average	-9
2001 Retail Sales Estimate	$872,710,000
% Cdn. Total	0.31
2001 per Household	$21,600
2001 per Capita	$8,200
2001 No. of Establishments	616
2003 Projected Retail Sales	$963,840,000
2006 Projected Retail Sales	$1,109,480,000

POPULATION

2001 Estimates:

Total	106,667
Male	52,382
Female	54,285

Age Groups	Male	Female
0-4	3,613	3,481
5-9	3,897	3,790
10-14	3,908	3,730
15-19	3,749	3,630
20-24	3,608	3,540
25-29	3,639	3,677
30-34	4,162	4,384
35-39	4,687	5,049
40-44	4,677	5,020
45-49	4,300	4,513
50-54	3,678	3,773
55-59	2,800	2,845
60-64	2,043	2,140
65-69	1,505	1,662
70+	2,116	3,051

DAYTIME POPULATION

2001 Estimates:

Working Population	21,980
At Home Population	49,677
Total	71,657

INCOME

2001 Estimates:

Avg. Household Income	$55,570
Avg. Family Income	$60,153
Per Capita Income	$21,024

Male:
Avg. Employment Income	$34,834
Avg. Employment Income (minus Food)	$44,501

Female:
Avg. Employment Income	$25,547
Avg. Employment Income (minus Food)	$34,285

DISPOSABLE & DISCRETIONARY INCOME

2001 Estimates: Per Hhld.
Disposable Income	$38,331
Discretionary Income 1 (minus Food & Shelter)	$25,177
Discretionary Income 2 (minus Food, Shelter, & Other Expenditures)	$16,967

LIQUID ASSETS

1999 Estimates: Per Hhld.
Equity Investments	$62,757
Interest Bearing Investments	$64,730
Total Liquid Assets	$127,487

CREDIT DATA

July 2000:
Pool of Credit	$833,626,217
Revolving Credit, No.	194,001
Fixed Loans, No.	78,296
Avg. Credit Limit, per Person	$9,994
Avg. Spent, per Person	$4,924
Satisfactory Ratings, No. per Person	3.04
Avg. No. of Cards, per Person	1.02

LABOUR FORCE

2001 Estimates:

Male:
In the Labour Force	32,338
Participation Rate	78.9
Employed	30,318
Unemployed	2,020
Unemployment Rate	6.2
Not in Labour Force	8,626

Female:
In the Labour Force	27,740
Participation Rate	64.1
Employed	26,387
Unemployed	1,353
Unemployment Rate	4.9
Not in Labour Force	15,544

OCCUPATIONS BY MAJOR GROUPS

2001 Estimates:	Male	Female
Management	3,408	1,629
Business, Finance & Admin.	5,030	10,930
Natural & Applied Sciences & Related	2,710	653
Health	601	2,088
Social Sciences, Gov't Services & Religion	710	1,022
Education	722	1,191
Arts, Culture, Recreation & Sport	815	752
Sales & Service	7,833	7,772
Trades, Transport & Equipment Operators & Related	7,786	360
Primary Industries	379	42
Processing, Mfg. & Utilities	1,257	231

LEVEL OF SCHOOLING

2001 Estimates:
Population 15 years +	84,248
Less than Grade 9	11,091
Grades 9-13 w/o Certif.	16,972
Grade 9-13 with Certif.	15,109
Trade Certif. /Dip.	3,521
Non-Univ. w/o Certif./Dip.	6,641
Non-Univ. with Certif./Dip.	14,072
Univ. w/o Degree	7,062
Univ. w/o Degree/Certif.	1,636
Univ. with Certif.	5,426
Univ. with Degree	9,780

AVERAGE HOUSEHOLD EXPENDITURES

2001 Estimates:
Food	$6,695
Shelter	$8,529
Clothing	$2,386
Transportation	$6,212
Health & Personal Care	$2,067
Recr'n, Read'g & Education	$3,428
Taxes & Securities	$16,420
Other	$7,639
Total Expenditures	$53,376

PRIVATE HOUSEHOLDS

2001 Estimates:
Private Households, Total	40,356
Pop. in Private Households	105,633
Average no. per Household	2.6

FAMILIES

2001 Estimates:
Families in Private Households	32,184
Husband-Wife Families	26,647
Lone-Parent Families	5,537
Aver. No. Persons per Family	3.0
Aver. No. Sons/Daughters at Home	1.2

HOUSING

2001 Estimates:
Occupied Private Dwellings	40,356
Owned	26,441
Rented	13,915
Single-Detached House	19,089
Semi-Detached House	5,172
Row Houses	2,666
Apartment, 5+ Storeys	331
Apartment, 5 or Fewer Storeys	9,931
Apartment, Detached Duplex	2,503
Other Single-Attached	118
Movable Dwellings	546

VEHICLES

2001 Estimates:
Model Yrs. '81-'96, No.	44,695
% Total	76.79
Model Yrs. '97-'98, No.	8,350
% Total	14.35
'99 Vehicles registered in Model Yr. '99, No.	5,161
% Total	8.87
Total No. '81-'99	58,206

LEGAL MARITAL STATUS

2001 Estimates: (Age 15+)
Single (Never Married)	30,529
Legally Married (Not Separated)	40,145
Legally Married (Separated)	2,537
Widowed	3,526
Divorced	7,511

PSYTE CATEGORIES

2001 Estimates	No. of House -holds	% of Total Hhds.	Index
Suburban Executives	688	1.70	119
Technocrafts & Bureaucrats	2,012	4.99	177
Stable Suburban Families	471	1.17	90
Old Bungalow Burbs	1,027	2.54	154
Participation Quebec	9,259	22.94	796
New Quebec Rows	8,544	21.17	1,932
Quebec Melange	8,944	22.16	836
Traditional French Cdn. Families	830	2.06	77
Town Renters	710	1.76	204
Old Quebec Walkups	1,019	2.53	138
Quebec Town Elders	3,820	9.47	335
Quebec's New Urban Mosaic	2,579	6.39	265
Aged Pensioners	390	0.97	73

Québec

FINANCIAL P$YTE

2001 Estimates	No. of House -holds	% of Total Hhds.	Index
Four Star Investors	688	1.70	34
Successful Suburbanites	2,483	6.15	93
Miners & Credit-Liners	1,027	2.54	80
Mortgages & Minivans	17,803	44.11	668
Country Credit	9,774	24.22	358
Loan Parent Stress	4,839	11.99	206
Towering Debt	710	1.76	23
NSF	2,579	6.39	181
Senior Survivors	390	0.97	51

HOME LANGUAGE

2001 Estimates:		% Total
English	7,164	6.72
French	95,418	89.45
Arabic	892	0.84
Chinese	97	0.09
Creoles	58	0.05
Greek	58	0.05
Hungarian	116	0.11
Portuguese	602	0.56
Spanish	157	0.15
Other Languages	224	0.21
Multiple Responses	1,881	1.76
Total	106,667	100.00

BUILDING PERMITS

	1999	1998 $000	1997
Value	76,413	81,107	73,630

HOMES BUILT

	1999	1998	1997
No.	428	455	484

TAXATION

Income Class:	1997	% Total
Under $5,000	8,120	11.55
$5,000-$10,000	9,660	13.74
$10,000-$15,000	8,790	12.50
$15,000-$20,000	6,040	8.59
$20,000-$25,000	5,510	7.83
$25,000-$30,000	6,010	8.55
$30,000-$40,000	10,760	15.30
$40,000-$50,000	6,910	9.83
$50,000 +	8,550	12.16
Total Returns, No.	70,330	
Total Income, $000	1,860,250	
Total Taxable Returns	51,070	
Total Tax, $000	222,300	
Average Income, $.	26,450	
Average Tax, $	4,353	

VITAL STATISTICS

	1997	1996	1995	1994
Births	1,208	1,298	1,179	1,354
Deaths	403	437	428	404
Natural Increase	805	861	751	950
Marriages	161	198	194	212

Note: Latest available data.

MEDIA INFO
see Ottawa-Hull, CMA

Québec

Hull
(Ville)
Ottawa-Hull CMA

In census division Communauté urbaine de l'Outaouais.

POPULATION

July 1, 2001 Estimate	62,737
% Cdn. Total	0.20
% Change, '96 -'01	-1.20
Avg. Annual Growth Rate, %	-0.24
2003 Projected Population	62,737
2006 Projected Population	63,169
2001 Households Estimate	29,981
2003 Projected Households	30,360
2006 Projected Households	31,108

INCOME

% Above/Below National Average	same
2001 Total Income Estimate	$1,325,640,000
% Cdn. Total	0.20
2001 Average Hhld. Income	$44,200
2001 Per Capita	$21,100
2003 Projected Total Income	$1,387,600,000
2006 Projected Total Income	$1,497,620,000

RETAIL SALES

% Above/Below National Average	+37
2001 Retail Sales Estimate	$771,360,000
% Cdn. Total	0.28
2001 per Household	$25,700
2001 per Capita	$12,300
2001 No. of Establishments	451
2003 Projected Retail Sales	$837,810,000
2006 Projected Retail Sales	$939,320,000

POPULATION

2001 Estimates:

Total		62,737
Male		30,030
Female		32,707
Age Groups	Male	Female
0-4	1,960	1,899
5-9	1,773	1,747
10-14	1,586	1,559
15-19	1,567	1,509
20-24	1,907	1,959
25-29	2,363	2,463
30-34	2,732	2,784
35-39	2,899	2,904
40-44	2,713	2,790
45-49	2,421	2,507
50-54	1,997	2,094
55-59	1,555	1,694
60-64	1,254	1,452
65-69	1,097	1,399
70+	2,206	3,947

DAYTIME POPULATION

2001 Estimates:

Working Population	58,378
At Home Population	31,928
Total	90,306

INCOME

2001 Estimates:

Avg. Household Income	$44,216
Avg. Family Income	$54,429
Per Capita Income	$21,130
Male:	
Avg. Employment Income	$31,601
Avg. Employment Income (minus Food)	$41,380
Female:	
Avg. Employment Income	$26,459
Avg. Employment Income (minus Food)	$35,975

DISPOSABLE & DISCRETIONARY INCOME

2001 Estimates:	Per Hhld.
Disposable Income	$29,567
Discretionary Income 1 (minus Food & Shelter)	$17,800
Discretionary Income 2 (minus Food, Shelter, & Other Expenditures)	$11,358

LIQUID ASSETS

1999 Estimates:	Per Hhld.
Equity Investments	$48,290
Interest Bearing Investments	$52,544
Total Liquid Assets	$100,834

CREDIT DATA

July 2000:

Pool of Credit	$452,574,260
Revolving Credit, No.	116,754
Fixed Loans, No.	36,680
Avg. Credit Limit, per Person	$8,003
Avg. Spent, per Person	$3,713
Satisfactory Ratings, No. per Person	2.57
Avg. No. of Cards, per Person	0.95

LABOUR FORCE

2001 Estimates:

Male:	
In the Labour Force	17,610
Participation Rate	71.3
Employed	16,197
Unemployed	1,413
Unemployment Rate	8.0
Not in Labour Force	7,101
Female:	
In the Labour Force	15,990
Participation Rate	58.1
Employed	15,115
Unemployed	875
Unemployment Rate	5.5
Not in Labour Force	11,512

OCCUPATIONS BY MAJOR GROUPS

2001 Estimates:	Male	Female
Management	1,738	972
Business, Finance & Admin.	2,440	5,278
Natural & Applied Sciences & Related	1,863	554
Health	389	1,239
Social Sciences, Gov't Services & Religion	901	892
Education	681	1,177
Arts, Culture, Recreation & Sport	820	966
Sales & Service	4,588	4,047
Trades, Transport & Equipment Operators & Related	2,584	121
Primary Industries	219	n.a.
Processing, Mfg. & Utilities	377	118

LEVEL OF SCHOOLING

2001 Estimates:

Population 15 years +	52,213
Less than Grade 9	8,359
Grades 9-13 w/o Certif.	8,501
Grade 9-13 with Certif.	6,952
Trade Certif. /Dip.	1,473
Non-Univ. w/o Certif./Dip.	3,629
Non-Univ. with Certif./Dip.	7,103
Univ. w/o Degree	5,366
Univ. w/o Degree/Certif.	1,412
Univ. with Certif.	3,954
Univ. with Degree	10,830

AVERAGE HOUSEHOLD EXPENDITURES

2001 Estimates:

Food	$5,727
Shelter	$8,045
Clothing	$1,969
Transportation	$4,490
Health & Personal Care	$1,804
Recr'n, Read'g & Education	$2,853
Taxes & Securities	$12,137
Other	$6,662
Total Expenditures	$43,687

PRIVATE HOUSEHOLDS

2001 Estimates:

Private Households, Total	29,981
Pop. in Private Households	61,242
Average no. per Household	2.0

FAMILIES

2001 Estimates:

Families in Private Households	17,188
Husband-Wife Families	13,508
Lone-Parent Families	3,680
Aver. No. Persons per Family	2.7
Aver. No. Sons/Daughters at Home	1.0

HOUSING

2001 Estimates:

Occupied Private Dwellings	29,981
Owned	12,191
Rented	17,790
Single-Detached House	6,632
Semi-Detached House	3,229
Row Houses	1,419
Apartment, 5+ Storeys	4,892
Owned Apartment, 5+ Storeys	459
Apartment, 5 or Fewer Storeys	10,233
Apartment, Detached Duplex	3,501
Other Single-Attached	75

VEHICLES

2001 Estimates:

Model Yrs. '81-'96, No.	25,227
% Total	76.05
Model Yrs. '97-'98, No.	4,838
% Total	14.59
'99 Vehicles registered in Model Yr. '99, No.	3,105
% Total	9.36
Total No. '81-'99	33,170

LEGAL MARITAL STATUS

2001 Estimates: (Age 15+)

Single (Never Married)	22,355
Legally Married (Not Separated)	18,877
Legally Married (Separated)	1,773
Widowed	3,716
Divorced	5,492

PSYTE CATEGORIES

2001 Estimates	No. of House-holds	% of Total Hhds.	Index
The Affluentials	57	0.19	30
Urban Gentry	384	1.28	71
Technocrafts & Bureaucrats	905	3.02	107
Stable Suburban Families	721	2.40	184
Suburban Nesters	809	2.70	168
Aging Erudites	295	0.98	65
Participation Quebec	1,157	3.86	134
New Quebec Rows	4,980	16.61	1,516
Quebec Melange	1,009	3.37	127
High Rise Sunsets	194	0.65	45
Young Urban Professionals	458	1.53	81
Young Urban Intelligentsia	215	0.72	47
University Enclaves	132	0.44	22
Young City Singles	448	1.49	65
Urban Bohemia	3,208	10.70	914
Old Quebec Walkups	5,165	17.23	940
Quebec Town Elders	389	1.30	46
Aging Quebec Urbanites	642	2.14	742
Quebec's New Urban Mosaic	7,539	25.15	1,044
Aged Pensioners	546	1.82	137
Big City Stress	132	0.44	39
Old Grey Towers	399	1.33	240

FINANCIAL PSYTE

2001 Estimates	No. of House-holds	% of Total Hhds.	Index
Platinum Estates	57	0.19	24
Four Star Investors	384	1.28	25
Successful Suburbanites	1,626	5.42	82
Canadian Comfort	809	2.70	28
Urban Heights	753	2.51	58
Mortgages & Minivans	6,137	20.47	310
Country Credit	1,009	3.37	50
Revolving Renters	194	0.65	14
Young Urban Struggle	3,555	11.86	251
Loan Parent Stress	6,196	20.67	355
Towering Debt	448	1.49	19
NSF	7,671	25.59	723
Senior Survivors	945	3.15	167

HOME LANGUAGE

2001 Estimates:		% Total
English	6,099	9.72
French	51,176	81.57
Arabic	380	0.61
Chinese	184	0.29
Croatian	137	0.22
Dutch	40	0.06
Hungarian	35	0.06
Khmer (Cambodian)	103	0.16
Lao	57	0.09
Persian (Farsi)	91	0.15
Polish	35	0.06
Portuguese	869	1.39
Romanian	116	0.18
Serbian	116	0.18
Serbo-Croatian	465	0.74
Spanish	507	0.81
Vietnamese	365	0.58
Other Languages	265	0.42
Multiple Responses	1,697	2.70
Total	62,737	100.00

BUILDING PERMITS

	1999	1998	1997
		$000	
Value	82,182	58,981	60,493

Hull
(Ville)
Ottawa-Hull CMA
(Cont'd)

HOMES BUILT

No.	1999	1998	1997
No.	324	296	220

TAXATION

Income Class:	1997	% Total
Under $5,000	4,660	10.25
$5,000-$10,000	7,130	15.69
$10,000-$15,000	6,580	14.48
$15,000-$20,000	4,210	9.26
$20,000-$25,000	3,500	7.70
$25,000-$30,000	3,680	8.10
$30,000-$40,000	6,190	13.62
$40,000-$50,000	4,080	8.98
$50,000 +	5,420	11.93
Total Returns, No.	45,450	
Total Income, $000	1,179,870	
Total Taxable Returns	31,680	
Total Tax, $000	140,379	
Average Income, $	25,960	
Average Tax, $	4,431	

VITAL STATISTICS

	1997	1996	1995	1994
Births	784	752	623	637
Deaths	532	524	517	466
Natural Increase	252	228	106	171
Marriages	431	512	486	458

Note: Latest available data.

MEDIA INFO
see Ottawa-Hull, CMA

Québec
(Census Metropolitan Area)

POPULATION

July 1, 2001 Estimate	693,228
% Cdn. Total	2.23
% Change, '96 -'01	1.39
Avg. Annual Growth Rate, %	0.28
2003 Projected Population	702,097
2006 Projected Population	721,678
2001 Households Estimate	299,854
2003 Projected Households	307,251
2006 Projected Households	319,607

INCOME

% Above/Below National Average	+1
2001 Total Income Estimate	$14,766,740,000
% Cdn. Total	2.25
2001 Average Hhld. Income	$49,200
2001 Per Capita	$21,300
2003 Projected Total Income	$15,947,110,000
2006 Projected Total Income	$18,035,490,000

RETAIL SALES

% Above/Below National Average	+22
2001 Retail Sales Estimate	$7,599,530,000
% Cdn. Total	2.73
2001 per Household	$25,300
2001 per Capita	$11,000
2001 No. of Establishments	5,825
2003 Projected Retail Sales	$8,220,950,000
2006 Projected Retail Sales	$9,218,880,000

POPULATION

2001 Estimates:

Total		693,228
Male		334,154
Female		359,074

Age Groups	Male	Female
0-4	19,791	19,012
5-9	19,537	19,012
10-14	19,914	19,055
15-19	21,683	20,812
20-24	23,301	22,845
25-29	23,760	23,340
30-34	25,580	25,045
35-39	28,053	28,128
40-44	28,756	30,017
45-49	27,901	29,712
50-54	25,162	26,805
55-59	20,135	21,573
60-64	15,455	17,353
65-69	12,263	15,188
70+	22,863	41,177

DAYTIME POPULATION

2001 Estimates:

Working Population	343,479
At Home Population	352,252
Total	695,731

INCOME

2001 Estimates:

Avg. Household Income	$49,246
Avg. Family Income	$59,322
Per Capita Income	$21,301
Male:	
Avg. Employment Income	$34,998
Avg. Employment Income (Full Time)	$45,947
Female:	
Avg. Employment Income	$22,913
Avg. Employment Income (Full Time)	$33,277

DISPOSABLE & DISCRETIONARY INCOME

2001 Estimates:	Per Hhld.
Disposable Income	$33,411
Discretionary Income 1 (minus Food & Shelter)	$21,110
Discretionary Income 2 (minus Food, Shelter, & Other Expenditures)	$13,695

LIQUID ASSETS

1999 Estimates:	Per Hhld.
Equity Investments	$54,913
Interest Bearing Investments	$56,258
Total Liquid Assets	$111,171

CREDIT DATA

July 2000:

Pool of Credit	$4,450,802,823
Revolving Credit, No.	1,319,170
Fixed Loans, No.	472,702
Avg. Credit Limit, per Person	$8,173
Avg. Spent, per Person	$3,417
Satisfactory Ratings, No. per Person	3.09
Avg. No. of Cards, per Person	1.23

LABOUR FORCE

2001 Estimates:

Male:	
In the Labour Force	201,282
Participation Rate	73.2
Employed	187,777
Unemployed	13,505
Unemployment Rate	6.7
Not in Labour Force	73,630
Female:	
In the Labour Force	169,207
Participation Rate	56.0
Employed	157,714
Unemployed	11,493
Unemployment Rate	6.8
Not in Labour Force	132,788

OCCUPATIONS BY MAJOR GROUPS

2001 Estimates:	Male	Female
Management	23,658	9,793
Business, Finance & Admin.	23,292	54,962
Natural & Applied Sciences & Related	20,355	4,443
Health	6,017	17,342
Social Sciences, Gov't Services & Religion	5,923	5,483
Education	7,454	8,702
Arts, Culture, Recreation & Sport	5,239	5,308
Sales & Service	48,040	49,692
Trades, Transport & Equipment Operators & Related	40,496	2,149
Primary Industries	3,133	759
Processing, Mfg. & Utilities	10,548	3,462

LEVEL OF SCHOOLING

2001 Estimates:

Population 15 years +	576,907
Less than Grade 9	74,286
Grades 9-13 w/o Certif.	81,413
Grade 9-13 with Certif.	111,762
Trade Certif. /Dip.	26,988
Non-Univ. w/o Certif./Dip.	41,039
Non-Univ. with Certif./Dip.	102,763
Univ. w/o Degree	47,629
Univ. w/o Degree/Certif.	6,320
Univ. with Certif.	41,309
Univ. with Degree	91,027

Québec

AVERAGE HOUSEHOLD EXPENDITURES

2001 Estimates:

Food	$6,205
Shelter	$8,062
Clothing	$2,145
Transportation	$5,503
Health & Personal Care	$1,926
Recr'n, Read'g & Education	$3,203
Taxes & Securities	$13,853
Other	$7,261
Total Expenditures	$48,158

PRIVATE HOUSEHOLDS

2001 Estimates:

Private Households, Total	299,854
Pop. in Private Households	676,893
Average no. per Household	2.3

FAMILIES

2001 Estimates:

Families in Private Households	199,671
Husband-Wife Families	168,076
Lone-Parent Families	31,595
Aver. No. Persons per Family	2.9
Aver. No. Sons/Daughters at Home	1.1

HOUSING

2001 Estimates:

Occupied Private Dwellings	299,854
Owned	166,462
Rented	133,392
Single-Detached House	127,305
Semi-Detached House	14,137
Row Houses	7,410
Apartment, 5+ Storeys	17,650
Owned Apartment, 5+ Storeys	2,918
Apartment, 5 or Fewer Storeys	109,814
Apartment, Detached Duplex	20,030
Other Single-Attached	1,801
Movable Dwellings	1,707

VEHICLES

2001 Estimates:

Model Yrs. '81-'96, No.	306,598
% Total	75.02
Model Yrs. '97-'98, No.	63,350
% Total	15.50
'99 Vehicles registered in Model Yr. '99, No.	38,726
% Total	9.48
Total No. '81-'99	408,674

LEGAL MARITAL STATUS

2001 Estimates: (Age 15+)

Single (Never Married)	239,005
Legally Married (Not Separated)	238,142
Legally Married (Separated)	14,050
Widowed	34,256
Divorced	51,454

Québec

Québec
(Census Metropolitan Area)
(Cont'd)

PSYTE CATEGORIES

2001 Estimates	No. of House-holds	% of Total Hhds.	Index
Urban Gentry	6,466	2.16	120
Suburban Executives	871	0.29	20
Mortgaged in Suburbia	26	0.01	1
Technocrafts & Bureaucrats	5,429	1.81	64
Stable Suburban Families	5,364	1.79	137
Old Bungalow Burbs	1,821	0.61	37
Suburban Nesters	365	0.12	8
Brie & Chablis	1,724	0.57	64
Aging Erudites	765	0.26	17
Old Towns' New Fringe	500	0.17	4
Participation Quebec	58,320	19.45	675
New Quebec Rows	20,810	6.94	633
Quebec Melange	42,887	14.30	540
Traditional French Cdn. Families	25,870	8.63	321
Quebec's Heartland	302	0.10	10
High Rise Sunsets	1,884	0.63	44
Young Urban Professionals	9,040	3.01	159
Young Urban Intelligentsia	3,304	1.10	72
University Enclaves	926	0.31	15
Young City Singles	1,517	0.51	22
Urban Bohemia	15,334	5.11	437
Big Country Families	880	0.29	21
Quebec Rural Blues	958	0.32	13
Euro Quebec	172	0.06	7
Old Quebec Walkups	13,822	4.61	252
Quebec Town Elders	20,006	6.67	236
Aging Quebec Urbanites	7,439	2.48	860
Quebec's New Urban Mosaic	44,545	14.86	617
Aged Pensioners	3,461	1.15	87
Big City Stress	1,125	0.38	33
Old Grey Towers	2,111	0.70	127

FINANCIAL P$YTE

2001 Estimates	No. of House-holds	% of Total Hhds.	Index
Four Star Investors	7,337	2.45	49
Successful Suburbanites	10,819	3.61	54
Canadian Comfort	365	0.12	1
Urban Heights	11,529	3.84	89
Miners & Credit-Liners	1,821	0.61	19
Mortgages & Minivans	79,130	26.39	400
Tractors & Tradelines	500	0.17	3
Country Credit	68,757	22.93	339
Revolving Renters	1,884	0.63	14
Young Urban Struggle	19,564	6.52	138
Rural Family Blues	2,140	0.71	9
Loan Parent Stress	41,439	13.82	237
Towering Debt	1,517	0.51	6
NSF	45,670	15.23	430
Senior Survivors	5,572	1.86	99

HOME LANGUAGE

2001 Estimates:		% Total
English	8,218	1.19
French	674,872	97.35
Chinese	567	0.08
Serbo-Croatian	795	0.11
Spanish	842	0.12
Vietnamese	389	0.06
Other Languages	2,887	0.42
Multiple Responses	4,658	0.67
Total	693,228	100.00

BUILDING PERMITS

	1999	1998 $000	1997
Value	513,416	448,506	515,071

HOMES BUILT

	1999	1998	1997
No.	1,771	1,838	2,524

TAXATION

Income Class:	1997	% Total
Under $5,000	61,340	12.17
$5,000–$10,000	70,660	14.02
$10,000–$15,000	73,340	14.55
$15,000–$20,000	48,380	9.60
$20,000–$25,000	42,480	8.43
$25,000–$30,000	43,200	8.57
$30,000–$40,000	64,050	12.71
$40,000–$50,000	40,370	8.01
$50,000 +	60,250	11.96
Total Returns, No.	503,930	
Total Income, $000	13,181,557	
Total Taxable Returns	352,920	
Total Tax, $000	1,578,207	
Average Income, $	26,158	
Average Tax, $	4,472	

VITAL STATISTICS

	1997	1996	1995	1994
Births	6,888	7,260	7,639	7,717
Deaths	4,849	4,773	4,623	4,551
Natural Increase	2,039	2,437	3,016	3,166
Marriages	1,968	1,925	1,975	2,161

Note: Latest available data.

DAILY NEWSPAPER(S)

	Circulation Average Paid
Le Journal de Québec	
Sat	121,020
Sun	98,128
Mon-Fri.	94,253
Le Soleil	
Sat	126,771
Sun	89,134
Mon-Fri.	80,640

COMMUNITY NEWSPAPER(S)

	Total Circulation
Beauport: Beauport Express	37,963
Charlesbourg, Lac Saint-Charles: Charlesbourg Express	30,101
Lévis: Le Peuple Tribune	26,239
Loretteville, Neufchâtel, Saint-Émile, Val-Bélair, Vanier: L'Actuel	41,012

	Total Circulation
Québec: Québec Chronicle Telegraph	1,640
Québec: Droit de Parole (mthly)	15,000
Québec: La Quête (mthly)	n.a.
Québec, Basse-ville, Des Rivières, Haute-ville, Limoilou: Journal Le Carrefour	72,500
Saint-François: L'Écho de St-François (mthly)	650
Saint-Jean, Port-Joli: L'Attisée (mthly)	2,100
Saint-Jean-Chrysostome-de-Lévis, Saint-Romuald, Charny, Saint-Jean: Le Peuple Chaudière	29,339
Sainte-Foy, Sillery, Cap Rouge: L'Appel	45,104

RADIO STATION DATA

Station	Market	Format	Wkly. Reach%*	Aver. Hrs. Tuned
All Stations			96	22.6
CBV-FM	Sainte-Foy	Multi-format	12	11.7
CBVE-FM	Québec	News, Info.	1	4.9
CBVX-FM	Sainte-Foy	Multi-format	7	9.7
CFOM-FM	Lévis	Adult Contemp.	23	12.5
CFZZ-FM	Saint-Jean	Adult Contemp.	n.a.	n.a.
CHIK-FM	Québec	Contemp. Hit Radio	37	9.4
CHOI-FM	Québec	AOR	24	10.9
CHRC	Québec	News, Talk, Sports	19	12.9
CITF-FM	Québec	Adult Contemp.	33	11.0
CJAS-FM	Saint-Augustin	Community	n.a.	n.a.
CJMF-FM	Québec	Classic Rock	31	11.0
CJPX-FM	Montréal	Classical	2	12.6
CKIA-FM	Québec	Multi-format	n.a.	n.a.
CKRL-FM	Québec	Multi-format	n.a.	n.a.

BBM Spring 2000 Radio Reach Surveys; area coverage.
* Mon-Sun 5a.m.-1a.m., All Persons 12+

TV STATION DATA

Station	Market	Network Affiliation	Wkly. Reach%*	Aver. Hrs. Tuned
All Stations			97	24.8
CABLE	n.a.	n.a.	6	2.6
CANALD	n.a.	n.a.	14	2.1
CBMT	Montréal	CBC	6	2.9
CBVT	Québec	SRC	82	5.9
CFAP	Québec	TQS	72	4.7
CFCF	Montréal	CTV	8	2.1
CFCM	Québec	TVA	79	11.0
CIVM	Montréal	Télé-Qué.	25	2.0
CIVQ	Québec	Télé-Qué.	n.a.	n.a.
CKMI	Montréal	Global	10	2.0
ECRAN	n.a.	n.a.	5	5.1
FAMILE	n.a.	n.a.	11	3.1
HIST(FR)	n.a.	Ind.	8	1.8
OTHERS	n.a.	n.a.	7	3.1
RDI	n.a.	n.a.	13	3.8
RDS	n.a.	Ind.	11	2.4
SERIES	n.a.	Ind.	6	3.1
TOON(FR)	n.a.	Ind.	15	4.8
TV5	n.a.	n.a.	9	2.2
VCR	n.a.	n.a.	26	3.8
VIE	n.a.	n.a.	10	1.8
WCAX	Burlington VT	CBS	10	2.1
WWNY	Burlington VT	ABC	8	2.5

BBM Spring 2000 TV Reach Surveys; CMA coverage.
*Mon-Sun 6a.m.-2a.m., All Persons 2+

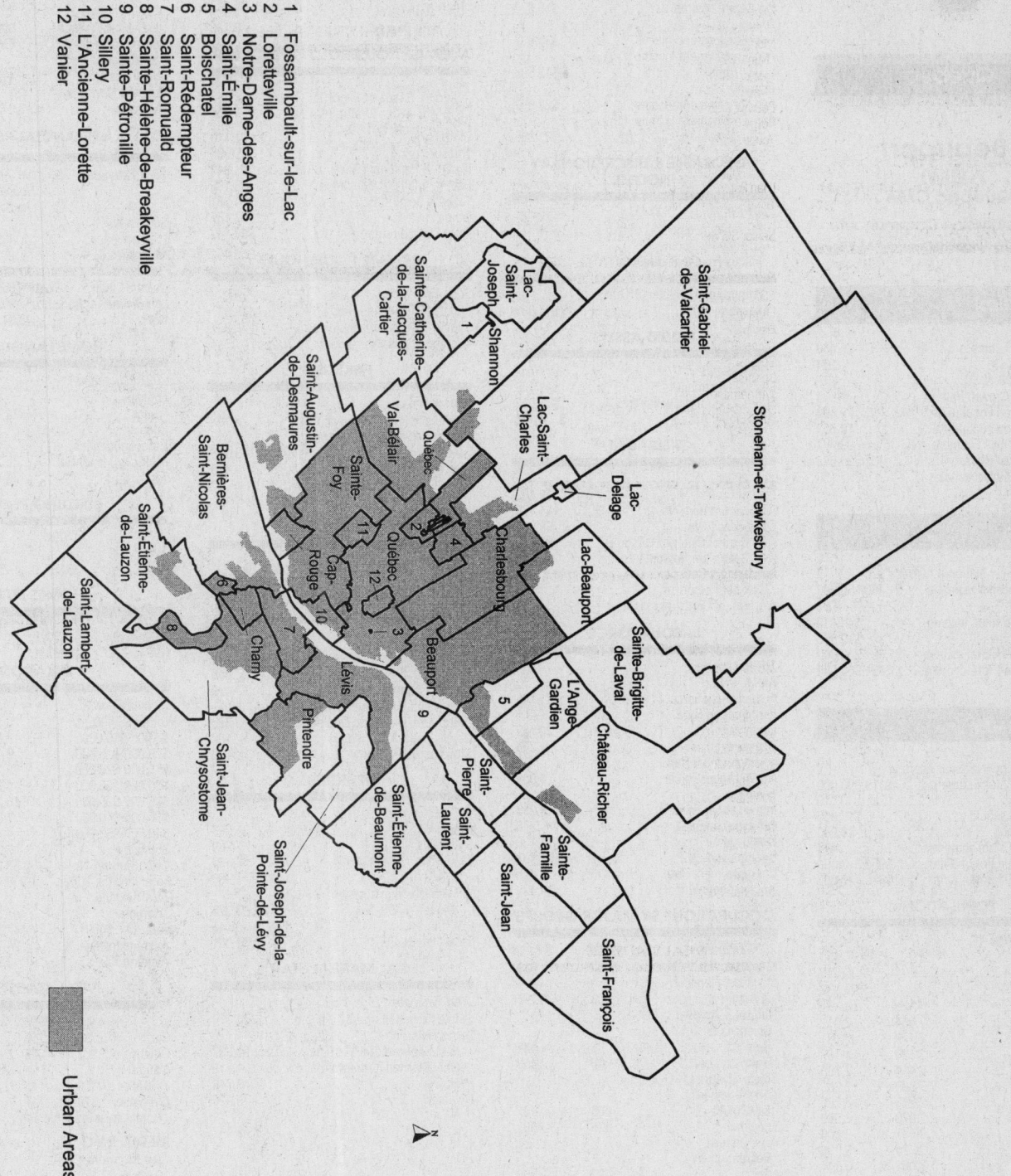

1 Fossambault-sur-le-Lac
2 Loretteville
3 Notre-Dame-des-Anges
4 Saint-Émile
5 Boischatel
6 Saint-Rédempteur
7 Saint-Romuald
8 Sainte-Hélène-de-Breakeyville
9 Sainte-Pétronille
10 Sillery
11 L'Ancienne-Lorette
12 Vanier

Urban Areas

Québec

Beauport

(Ville)
Québec CMA

In census division Communauté urbaine de Québec.

POPULATION

July 1, 2001 Estimate	75,458
% Cdn. Total	0.24
% Change, '96 -'01	1.70
Avg. Annual Growth Rate, %	0.34
2003 Projected Population	76,432
2006 Projected Population	78,553
2001 Households Estimate	29,987
2003 Projected Households	30,809
2006 Projected Households	32,156

INCOME

% Above/Below National Average	-7
2001 Total Income Estimate	$1,480,450,000
% Cdn. Total	0.23
2001 Average Hhld. Income	$49,400
2001 Per Capita	$19,600
2003 Projected Total Income	$1,604,230,000
2006 Projected Total Income	$1,821,350,000

RETAIL SALES

% Above/Below National Average	-23
2001 Retail Sales Estimate	$519,880,000
% Cdn. Total	0.19
2001 per Household	$17,300
2001 per Capita	$6,900
2001 No. of Establishments	444
2003 Projected Retail Sales	$564,310,000
2006 Projected Retail Sales	$636,720,000

POPULATION

2001 Estimates:

Total		75,458
Male		36,325
Female		39,133
Age Groups	Male	Female
0-4	2,064	2,011
5-9	2,179	2,161
10-14	2,328	2,187
15-19	2,464	2,288
20-24	2,388	2,253
25-29	2,272	2,206
30-34	2,570	2,596
35-39	3,037	3,108
40-44	3,224	3,336
45-49	3,052	3,241
50-54	2,721	2,911
55-59	2,220	2,360
60-64	1,727	1,935
65-69	1,390	1,709
70+	2,689	4,831

DAYTIME POPULATION

2001 Estimates:

Working Population	8,852
At Home Population	37,905
Total	46,757

INCOME

2001 Estimates:

Avg. Household Income	$49,370
Avg. Family Income	$56,790
Per Capita Income	$19,620
Male:	
Avg. Employment Income	$33,837
Avg. Employment Income (Full Time)	$42,698
Female:	
Avg. Employment Income	$23,092
Avg. Employment Income (Full Time)	$31,835

DISPOSABLE & DISCRETIONARY INCOME

2001 Estimates:	Per Hhld.
Disposable Income	$34,311
Discretionary Income 1 (minus Food & Shelter)	$22,145
Discretionary Income 2 (minus Food, Shelter, & Other Expenditures)	$14,682

LIQUID ASSETS

1999 Estimates:	Per Hhld.
Equity Investments	$49,100
Interest Bearing Investments	$55,013
Total Liquid Assets	$104,113

CREDIT DATA

July 2000:

Pool of Credit	$472,229,480
Revolving Credit, No.	144,170
Fixed Loans, No.	58,327
Avg. Credit Limit, per Person	$8,433
Avg. Spent, per Person	$3,662
Satisfactory Ratings, No. per Person	3.38
Avg. No. of Cards, per Person	1.33

LABOUR FORCE

2001 Estimates:

Male:	
In the Labour Force	21,745
Participation Rate	73.1
Employed	20,459
Unemployed	1,286
Unemployment Rate	5.9
Not in Labour Force	8,009
Female:	
In the Labour Force	18,296
Participation Rate	55.8
Employed	17,108
Unemployed	1,188
Unemployment Rate	6.5
Not in Labour Force	14,478

OCCUPATIONS BY MAJOR GROUPS

2001 Estimates:	Male	Female
Management	2,050	810
Business, Finance & Admin.	2,953	6,297
Natural & Applied Sciences & Related	2,185	441
Health	806	2,453
Social Sciences, Gov't Services & Religion	458	442
Education	425	682
Arts, Culture, Recreation & Sport	427	262
Sales & Service	5,365	5,569
Trades, Transport & Equipment Operators & Related	5,084	205
Primary Industries	181	42
Processing, Mfg. & Utilities	1,105	285

LEVEL OF SCHOOLING

2001 Estimates:

Population 15 years +	62,528
Less than Grade 9	8,837
Grades 9-13 w/o Certif.	9,320
Grade 9-13 with Certif.	13,915
Trade Certif. /Dip.	3,550
Non-Univ. w/o Certif./Dip.	4,477
Non-Univ. with Certif./Dip.	11,768
Univ. w/o Degree	4,271
Univ. w/o Degree/Certif.	436
Univ. with Certif.	3,835
Univ. with Degree	6,390

AVERAGE HOUSEHOLD EXPENDITURES

2001 Estimates:

Food	$6,312
Shelter	$7,669
Clothing	$2,140
Transportation	$5,595
Health & Personal Care	$1,942
Recr'n, Read'g & Education	$3,186
Taxes & Securities	$14,531
Other	$7,167
Total Expenditures	$48,542

PRIVATE HOUSEHOLDS

2001 Estimates:

Private Households, Total	29,987
Pop. in Private Households	71,827
Average no. per Household	2.4

FAMILIES

2001 Estimates:

Families in Private Households	22,198
Husband-Wife Families	18,810
Lone-Parent Families	3,388
Aver. No. Persons per Family	3.0
Aver. No. Sons/Daughters at Home	1.1

HOUSING

2001 Estimates:

Occupied Private Dwellings	29,987
Owned	18,689
Rented	11,298
Single-Detached House	14,924
Semi-Detached House	1,370
Row Houses	243
Apartment, 5+ Storeys	808
Owned Apartment, 5+ Storeys	88
Apartment, 5 or Fewer Storeys	9,051
Apartment, Detached Duplex	3,393
Other Single-Attached	100
Movable Dwellings	98

VEHICLES

2001 Estimates:

Model Yrs. '81-'96, No.	31,393
% Total	74.69
Model Yrs. '97-'98, No.	6,663
% Total	15.85
'99 Vehicles registered in Model Yr. '99, No.	3,975
% Total	9.46
Total No. '81-'99	42,031

LEGAL MARITAL STATUS

2001 Estimates: (Age 15+)

Single (Never Married)	24,716
Legally Married (Not Separated)	27,337
Legally Married (Separated)	1,419
Widowed	3,746
Divorced	5,310

PSYTE CATEGORIES

2001 Estimates	No. of House-holds	% of Total Hhds.	Index
Stable Suburban Families	409	1.36	105
Participation Quebec	10,723	35.76	1,241
New Quebec Rows	748	2.49	228
Quebec Melange	4,252	14.18	535
Traditional French Cdn. Families	1,703	5.68	211
Old Quebec Walkups	839	2.80	153
Quebec Town Elders	6,651	22.18	785
Aging Quebec Urbanites	412	1.37	476
Quebec's New Urban Mosaic	3,841	12.81	532

FINANÇIAL P$YTE

2001 Estimates	No. of House-holds	% of Total Hhds.	Index
Successful Suburbanites	409	1.36	21
Mortgages & Minivans	11,471	38.25	580
Country Credit	5,955	19.86	294
Loan Parent Stress	7,902	26.35	452
NSF	3,841	12.81	362

HOME LANGUAGE

2001 Estimates:		% Total
English	290	0.38
French	74,724	99.03
Spanish	79	0.10
Other Languages	149	0.20
Multiple Responses	216	0.29
Total	75,458	100.00

BUILDING PERMITS

	1999	1998 $000	1997
Value	35,863	25,591	42,689

HOMES BUILT

	1999	1998	1997
No.	156	143	169

TAXATION

Income Class:	1997	% Total
Under $5,000	6,130	11.51
$5,000-$10,000	7,100	13.33
$10,000-$15,000	8,080	15.17
$15,000-$20,000	5,170	9.70
$20,000-$25,000	4,780	8.97
$25,000-$30,000	5,210	9.78
$30,000-$40,000	7,030	13.19
$40,000-$50,000	4,430	8.31
$50,000 +	5,350	10.04
Total Returns, No.	53,280	
Total Income, $000	1,318,185	
Total Taxable Returns	37,650	
Total Tax, $000	147,074	
Average Income, $.	24,741	
Average Tax, $	3,906	

VITAL STATISTICS

	1997	1996	1995	1994
Births	767	766	844	879
Deaths	667	623	561	629
Natural Increase	100	143	283	250
Marriages	128	117	107	129

Note: Latest available data.

MEDIA INFO
see Montréal, CMA

Cap-Rouge
(Ville)
Québec CMA

In census division Communauté urbaine de Québec.

POPULATION

July 1, 2001 Estimate	14,079
% Cdn. Total	0.05
% Change, '96 -'01	-2.30
Avg. Annual Growth Rate, %	-0.47
2003 Projected Population	13,973
2006 Projected Population	13,942
2001 Households Estimate	5,031
2003 Projected Households	5,065
2006 Projected Households	5,129

INCOME

% Above/Below National Average	+51
2001 Total Income Estimate	$447,050,000
% Cdn. Total	0.07
2001 Average Hhld. Income	$88,900
2001 Per Capita	$31,800
2003 Projected Total Income	$473,150,000
2006 Projected Total Income	$518,400,000

RETAIL SALES

% Above/Below National Average	-63
2001 Retail Sales Estimate	$46,580,000
% Cdn. Total	0.02
2001 per Household	$9,300
2001 per Capita	$3,300
2001 No. of Establishments	82
2003 Projected Retail Sales	$49,400,000
2006 Projected Retail Sales	$53,730,000

POPULATION

2001 Estimates:

Total		14,079
Male		6,939
Female		7,140

Age Groups	Male	Female
0-4	355	330
5-9	426	403
10-14	528	489
15-19	635	561
20-24	601	527
25-29	413	381
30-34	306	323
35-39	395	477
40-44	581	707
45-49	701	828
50-54	693	764
55-59	549	534
60-64	356	312
65-69	202	196
70+	198	308

DAYTIME POPULATION

2001 Estimates:

Working Population	n.a.
At Home Population	5,617
Total	5,617

INCOME

2001 Estimates:

Avg. Household Income	$88,859
Avg. Family Income	$95,819
Per Capita Income	$31,753
Male:	
Avg. Employment Income	$54,117
Avg. Employment Income (Full Time)	$68,432
Female:	
Avg. Employment Income	$31,750
Avg. Employment Income (Full Time)	$46,307

DISPOSABLE & DISCRETIONARY INCOME

2001 Estimates:	*Per Hhld.*
Disposable Income	$58,466
Discretionary Income 1 (minus Food & Shelter)	$40,165
Discretionary Income 2 (minus Food, Shelter, & Other Expenditures)	$27,977

LIQUID ASSETS

1999 Estimates:	*Per Hhld.*
Equity Investments	$132,564
Interest Bearing Investments	$105,331
Total Liquid Assets	$237,895

CREDIT DATA

July 2000:

Pool of Credit	$132,353,183
Revolving Credit, No.	30,088
Fixed Loans, No.	9,203
Avg. Credit Limit, per Person	$12,623
Avg. Spent, per Person	$4,960
Satisfactory Ratings, No. per Person	3.55
Avg. No. of Cards, per Person	1.56

LABOUR FORCE

2001 Estimates:

Male:	
In the Labour Force	4,599
Participation Rate	81.7
Employed	4,478
Unemployed	121
Unemployment Rate	2.6
Not in Labour Force	1,031
Female:	
In the Labour Force	4,081
Participation Rate	69.0
Employed	3,901
Unemployed	180
Unemployment Rate	4.4
Not in Labour Force	1,837

OCCUPATIONS BY MAJOR GROUPS

2001 Estimates:	*Male*	*Female*
Management	1,015	368
Business, Finance & Admin.	553	1,111
Natural & Applied Sciences & Related	728	166
Health	183	603
Social Sciences, Gov't Services & Religion	268	270
Education	418	375
Arts, Culture, Recreation & Sport	192	214
Sales & Service	686	836
Trades, Transport & Equipment Operators & Related	359	15
Primary Industries	59	n.a.
Processing, Mfg. & Utilities	62	20

LEVEL OF SCHOOLING

2001 Estimates:

Population 15 years +	11,548
Less than Grade 9	371
Grades 9-13 w/o Certif.	851
Grade 9-13 with Certif.	1,465
Trade Certif. /Dip.	398
Non-Univ. w/o Certif./Dip.	710
Non-Univ. with Certif./Dip.	1,820
Univ. w/o Degree	1,544
Univ. w/o Degree/Certif.	142
Univ. with Certif.	1,402
Univ. with Degree	4,389

AVERAGE HOUSEHOLD EXPENDITURES

2001 Estimates:

Food	$9,144
Shelter	$12,377
Clothing	$3,574
Transportation	$9,498
Health & Personal Care	$2,867
Recr'n, Read'g & Education	$5,575
Taxes & Securities	$25,902
Other	$11,444
Total Expenditures	$80,381

PRIVATE HOUSEHOLDS

2001 Estimates:

Private Households, Total	5,031
Pop. in Private Households	13,937
Average no. per Household	2.8

FAMILIES

2001 Estimates:

Families in Private Households	4,181
Husband-Wife Families	3,677
Lone-Parent Families	504
Aver. No. Persons per Family	3.2
Aver. No. Sons/Daughters at Home	1.4

HOUSING

2001 Estimates:

Occupied Private Dwellings	5,031
Owned	4,145
Rented	886
Single-Detached House	3,366
Semi-Detached House	631
Row Houses	205
Apartment, 5 or Fewer Storeys	745
Apartment, Detached Duplex	73
Other Single-Attached	11

VEHICLES

2001 Estimates:

Model Yrs. '81-'96, No.	6,097
% Total	69.44
Model Yrs. '97-'98, No.	1,688
% Total	19.23
'99 Vehicles registered in Model Yr. '99, No.	995
% Total	11.33
Total No. '81-'99	8,780

LEGAL MARITAL STATUS

2001 Estimates: (Age 15+)

Single (Never Married)	4,175
Legally Married (Not Separated)	5,795
Legally Married (Separated)	320
Widowed	284
Divorced	974

PSYTE CATEGORIES

2001 Estimates	No. of House-holds	% of Total Hhds.	Index
Urban Gentry	178	3.54	197
Suburban Executives	408	8.11	566
Technocrafts & Bureaucrats	1,684	33.47	1,190
Stable Suburban Families	858	17.05	1,308
Participation Quebec	1,512	30.05	1,043
New Quebec Rows	387	7.69	702

FINANÇIAL P$YTE

2001 Estimates	No. of House-holds	% of Total Hhds.	Index
Four Star Investors	586	11.65	232
Successful Suburbanites	2,542	50.53	761
Mortgages & Minivans	1,899	37.75	572

Québec

HOME LANGUAGE

2001 Estimates:		% Total
English	289	2.05
French	13,632	96.83
Japanese	15	0.11
Multiple Responses	143	1.02
Total	14,079	100.00

BUILDING PERMITS

	1999	1998 $000	1997
Value	4,868	3,112	3,765

HOMES BUILT

	1999	1998	1997
No.	9	13	13

TAXATION

Income Class:	1997	% Total
Under $5,000	1,190	11.88
$5,000-$10,000	930	9.28
$10,000-$15,000	820	8.18
$15,000-$20,000	570	5.69
$20,000-$25,000	530	5.29
$25,000-$30,000	660	6.59
$30,000-$40,000	1,160	11.58
$40,000-$50,000	1,030	10.28
$50,000 +	3,120	31.14
Total Returns, No.	10,020	
Total Income, $000	401,698	
Total Taxable Returns	7,870	
Total Tax, $000	60,396	
Average Income, $	40,090	
Average Tax, $	7,674	

VITAL STATISTICS

	1997	1996	1995	1994
Births	106	118	132	127
Deaths	39	36	39	29
Natural Increase	67	82	93	98
Marriages	46	46	35	34

Note: Latest available data.

MEDIA INFO
see Québec, CMA

Québec

Charlesbourg
(Ville)
Québec CMA

In census division Communauté urbaine de Québec.

POPULATION

July 1, 2001 Estimate	70,396
% Cdn. Total	0.23
% Change, '96 -'01	-2.47
Avg. Annual Growth Rate, %	-0.50
2003 Projected Population	69,822
2006 Projected Population	69,570
2001 Households Estimate	30,133
2003 Projected Households	30,312
2006 Projected Households	30,666

INCOME

% Above/Below National Average	+5
2001 Total Income Estimate	$1,551,180,000
% Cdn. Total	0.24
2001 Average Hhld. Income	$51,500
2001 Per Capita	$22,000
2003 Projected Total Income	$1,638,560,000
2006 Projected Total Income	$1,790,950,000

RETAIL SALES

% Above/Below National Average	-15
2001 Retail Sales Estimate	$537,930,000
% Cdn. Total	0.19
2001 per Household	$17,900
2001 per Capita	$7,600
2001 No. of Establishments	462
2003 Projected Retail Sales	$574,920,000
2006 Projected Retail Sales	$633,440,000

POPULATION

2001 Estimates:

Total		70,396
Male		33,664
Female		36,732

Age Groups	Male	Female
0-4	1,807	1,763
5-9	1,667	1,657
10-14	1,763	1,743
15-19	2,182	2,096
20-24	2,506	2,381
25-29	2,421	2,329
30-34	2,387	2,300
35-39	2,499	2,579
40-44	2,593	2,916
45-49	2,670	3,158
50-54	2,717	3,145
55-59	2,404	2,722
60-64	1,981	2,232
65-69	1,592	1,862
70+	2,475	3,849

DAYTIME POPULATION

2001 Estimates:

Working Population	5,352
At Home Population	34,217
Total	39,569

INCOME

2001 Estimates:

Avg. Household Income	$51,478
Avg. Family Income	$59,218
Per Capita Income	$22,035

Male:

Avg. Employment Income	$34,705
Avg. Employment Income (Full Time)	$46,929

Female:

Avg. Employment Income	$22,849
Avg. Employment Income (Full Time)	$33,072

DISPOSABLE & DISCRETIONARY INCOME

2001 Estimates: Per Hhld.

Disposable Income	$35,417
Discretionary Income 1 (minus Food & Shelter)	$22,770
Discretionary Income 2 (minus Food, Shelter, & Other Expenditures)	$14,967

LIQUID ASSETS

1999 Estimates: Per Hhld.

Equity Investments	$54,029
Interest Bearing Investments	$57,791
Total Liquid Assets	$111,820

CREDIT DATA

July 2000:

Pool of Credit	$491,596,864
Revolving Credit, No.	145,486
Fixed Loans, No.	53,027
Avg. Credit Limit, per Person	$8,556
Avg. Spent, per Person	$3,601
Satisfactory Ratings, No. per Person	3.23
Avg. No. of Cards, per Person	1.26

LABOUR FORCE

2001 Estimates:

Male:

In the Labour Force	20,381
Participation Rate	71.7
Employed	19,034
Unemployed	1,347
Unemployment Rate	6.6
Not in Labour Force	8,046

Female:

In the Labour Force	18,170
Participation Rate	57.6
Employed	17,141
Unemployed	1,029
Unemployment Rate	5.7
Not in Labour Force	13,399

OCCUPATIONS BY MAJOR GROUPS

2001 Estimates:

	Male	Female
Management	2,466	834
Business, Finance & Admin.	2,577	6,644
Natural & Applied Sciences & Related	2,078	445
Health	558	1,952
Social Sciences, Gov't Services & Religion	565	477
Education	685	770
Arts, Culture, Recreation & Sport	513	439
Sales & Service	5,061	5,276
Trades, Transport & Equipment Operators & Related	4,217	270
Primary Industries	173	20
Processing, Mfg. & Utilities	819	361

LEVEL OF SCHOOLING

2001 Estimates:

Population 15 years +	59,996
Less than Grade 9	7,151
Grades 9-13 w/o Certif.	8,604
Grade 9-13 with Certif.	13,731
Trade Certif./Dip.	2,723
Non-Univ. w/o Certif./Dip.	4,250
Non-Univ. with Certif./Dip.	10,813
Univ. w/o Degree	5,035
Univ. w/o Degree/Certif.	563
Univ. with Certif.	4,472
Univ. with Degree	7,689

AVERAGE HOUSEHOLD EXPENDITURES

2001 Estimates:

Food	$6,416
Shelter	$8,188
Clothing	$2,175
Transportation	$5,924
Health & Personal Care	$1,970
Recr'n, Read'g & Education	$3,198
Taxes & Securities	$14,894
Other	$7,507
Total Expenditures	$50,272

PRIVATE HOUSEHOLDS

2001 Estimates:

Private Households, Total	30,133
Pop. in Private Households	69,577
Average no. per Household	2.3

FAMILIES

2001 Estimates:

Families in Private Households	21,521
Husband-Wife Families	17,881
Lone-Parent Families	3,640
Aver. No. Persons per Family	2.9
Aver. No. Sons/Daughters at Home	1.1

HOUSING

2001 Estimates:

Occupied Private Dwellings	30,133
Owned	18,202
Rented	11,931
Single-Detached House	14,393
Semi-Detached House	1,283
Row Houses	735
Apartment, 5+ Storeys	1,346
Owned Apartment, 5+ Storeys	147
Apartment, 5 or Fewer Storeys	9,905
Apartment, Detached Duplex	2,393
Other Single-Attached	62
Movable Dwellings	16

VEHICLES

2001 Estimates:

Model Yrs. '81-'96, No.	33,769
% Total	75.54
Model Yrs. '97-'98, No.	6,766
% Total	15.14
'99 Vehicles registered in Model Yr. '99, No.	4,166
% Total	9.32
Total No. '81-'99	44,701

LEGAL MARITAL STATUS

2001 Estimates: (Age 15+)

Single (Never Married)	23,487
Legally Married (Not Separated)	25,991
Legally Married (Separated)	1,486
Widowed	3,419
Divorced	5,613

PSYTE CATEGORIES

2001 Estimates	No. of House-holds	% of Total Hhds.	Index
Stable Suburban Families	1,900	6.31	484
Old Bungalow Burbs	1,044	3.46	209
Suburban Nesters	365	1.21	76
Participation Quebec	4,323	14.35	498
New Quebec Rows	3,618	12.01	1,096
Quebec Melange	8,838	29.33	1,107

	No. of House-holds	% of Total Hhds.	Index
2001 Estimates			
Traditional French Cdn. Families	898	2.98	111
Old Quebec Walkups	3,898	12.94	706
Quebec Town Elders	1,258	4.17	148
Aging Quebec Urbanites	1,608	5.34	1,849
Quebec's New Urban Mosaic	2,287	7.59	315

FINANCIAL P$YTE

2001 Estimates	No. of House-holds	% of Total Hhds.	Index
Successful Suburbanites	1,900	6.31	95
Canadian Comfort	365	1.21	12
Miners & Credit-Liners	1,044	3.46	109
Mortgages & Minivans	7,941	26.35	399
Country Credit	9,736	32.31	478
Loan Parent Stress	6,764	22.45	385
NSF	2,287	7.59	215

HOME LANGUAGE

2001 Estimates:		% Total
English	485	0.69
French	69,118	98.18
Chinese	120	0.17
Portuguese	65	0.09
Serbo-Croatian	64	0.09
Other Languages	134	0.19
Multiple Responses	410	0.58
Total	70,396	100.00

BUILDING PERMITS

	1999	1998	1997
		$000	
Value	32,677	22,036	25,038

HOMES BUILT

	1999	1998	1997
No.	145	183	228

TAXATION

Income Class:	1997	% Total
Under $5,000	6,560	12.01
$5,000-$10,000	7,670	14.04
$10,000-$15,000	7,720	14.13
$15,000-$20,000	5,420	9.92
$20,000-$25,000	4,750	8.70
$25,000-$30,000	4,920	9.01
$30,000-$40,000	7,000	12.82
$40,000-$50,000	4,450	8.15
$50,000 +	6,150	11.26
Total Returns, No.	54,620	
Total Income, $000	1,389,219	
Total Taxable Returns	38,850	
Total Tax, $000	159,648	
Average Income, $	25,434	
Average Tax, $	4,109	

VITAL STATISTICS

	1997	1996	1995	1994
Births	645	678	668	685
Deaths	415	435	406	420
Natural Increase	230	243	262	265
Marriages	117	133	143	137

Note: Latest available data.

MEDIA INFO
see Québec, CMA

Charny
(Ville)
Québec CMA

In census division Les
Chutes-de-la-Chaudière.

POPULATION

July 1, 2001 Estimate	10,926
% Cdn. Total	0.04
% Change, '96 -'01	0.61
Avg. Annual Growth Rate, %	0.12
2003 Projected Population	10,995
2006 Projected Population	11,230
2001 Households Estimate	4,629
2003 Projected Households	4,734
2006 Projected Households	4,938

INCOME

% Above/Below National Average	-3
2001 Total Income Estimate	$223,160,000
% Cdn. Total	0.03
2001 Average Hhld. Income	$48,200
2001 Per Capita	$20,400
2003 Projected Total Income	$240,090,000
2006 Projected Total Income	$271,300,000

RETAIL SALES

% Above/Below National Average	-51
2001 Retail Sales Estimate	$48,410,000
% Cdn. Total	0.02
2001 per Household	$10,500
2001 per Capita	$4,400
2001 No. of Establishments	75
2003 Projected Retail Sales	$51,270,000
2006 Projected Retail Sales	$56,380,000

POPULATION

2001 Estimates:

Total		10,926
Male		5,209
Female		5,717

Age Groups	Male	Female
0-4	312	301
5-9	316	300
10-14	333	319
15-19	372	364
20-24	391	410
25-29	392	401
30-34	389	402
35-39	423	449
40-44	461	505
45-49	454	513
50-54	398	440
55-59	309	329
60-64	211	247
65-69	148	202
70+	300	535

DAYTIME POPULATION

2001 Estimates:

Working Population	1,715
At Home Population	4,987
Total	6,702

INCOME

2001 Estimates:

Avg. Household Income	$48,209
Avg. Family Income	$54,822
Per Capita Income	$20,425
Male:	
Avg. Employment Income	$32,695
Avg. Employment Income (Full Time)	$42,618
Female:	
Avg. Employment Income	$21,661
Avg. Employment Income (Full Time)	$32,201

DISPOSABLE & DISCRETIONARY INCOME

2001 Estimates:	Per Hhld.
Disposable Income	$33,402
Discretionary Income 1 (minus Food & Shelter)	$21,474
Discretionary Income 2 (minus Food, Shelter, & Other Expenditures)	$14,292

LIQUID ASSETS

1999 Estimates:	Per Hhld.
Equity Investments	$50,742
Interest Bearing Investments	$55,470
Total Liquid Assets	$106,212

CREDIT DATA

July 2000:

Pool of Credit	$69,958,117
Revolving Credit, No.	20,813
Fixed Loans, No.	8,198
Avg. Credit Limit, per Person	$8,425
Avg. Spent, per Person	$3,603
Satisfactory Ratings, No. per Person	3.29
Avg. No. of Cards, per Person	1.27

LABOUR FORCE

2001 Estimates:

Male:	
In the Labour Force	3,319
Participation Rate	78.1
Employed	3,177
Unemployed	142
Unemployment Rate	4.3
Not in Labour Force	929
Female:	
In the Labour Force	2,919
Participation Rate	60.9
Employed	2,763
Unemployed	156
Unemployment Rate	5.3
Not in Labour Force	1,878

OCCUPATIONS BY MAJOR GROUPS

2001 Estimates:	Male	Female
Management	334	158
Business, Finance & Admin.	299	989
Natural & Applied Sciences & Related	478	76
Health	11	333
Social Sciences, Gov't Services & Religion	55	46
Education	136	163
Arts, Culture, Recreation & Sport	112	86
Sales & Service	862	906
Trades, Transport & Equipment Operators & Related	702	11
Primary Industries	32	11
Processing, Mfg. & Utilities	251	58

LEVEL OF SCHOOLING

2001 Estimates:

Population 15 years +	9,045
Less than Grade 9	868
Grades 9-13 w/o Certif.	1,402
Grade 9-13 with Certif.	1,667
Trade Certif. /Dip.	402
Non-Univ. w/o Certif./Dip.	655
Non-Univ. with Certif./Dip.	1,860
Univ. w/o Degree	827
Univ. w/o Degree/Certif.	139
Univ. with Certif.	688
Univ. with Degree	1,364

AVERAGE HOUSEHOLD EXPENDITURES

2001 Estimates:

Food	$6,143
Shelter	$7,552
Clothing	$2,082
Transportation	$5,361
Health & Personal Care	$1,888
Recr'n, Read'g & Education	$3,023
Taxes & Securities	$14,728
Other	$6,700
Total Expenditures	$47,477

PRIVATE HOUSEHOLDS

2001 Estimates:

Private Households, Total	4,629
Pop. in Private Households	10,758
Average no. per Household	2.3

FAMILIES

2001 Estimates:

Families in Private Households	3,339
Husband-Wife Families	2,739
Lone-Parent Families	600
Aver. No. Persons per Family	2.9
Aver. No. Sons/Daughters at Home	1.1

HOUSING

2001 Estimates:

Occupied Private Dwellings	4,629
Owned	2,562
Rented	2,067
Single-Detached House	1,838
Semi-Detached House	490
Row Houses	38
Apartment, 5 or Fewer Storeys	1,865
Apartment, Detached Duplex	349
Other Single-Attached	38
Movable Dwellings	11

VEHICLES

2001 Estimates:

Model Yrs. '81-'96, No.	4,978
% Total	76.55
Model Yrs. '97-'98, No.	961
% Total	14.78
'99 Vehicles registered in Model Yr. '99, No.	564
% Total	8.67
Total No. '81-'99	6,503

LEGAL MARITAL STATUS

2001 Estimates: (Age 15+)

Single (Never Married)	3,782
Legally Married (Not Separated)	3,633
Legally Married (Separated)	235
Widowed	476
Divorced	919

PSYTE CATEGORIES

2001 Estimates	No. of House-holds	% of Total Hhds.	Index
Participation Quebec	1,436	31.02	1,077
New Quebec Rows	869	18.77	1,713
Quebec Melange	755	16.31	615
Old Quebec Walkups	356	7.69	420
Quebec Town Elders	1,192	25.75	911

FINANCIAL P$YTE

2001 Estimates	No. of House-holds	% of Total Hhds.	Index
Mortgages & Minivans	2,305	49.79	755
Country Credit	755	16.31	241
Loan Parent Stress	1,548	33.44	574

Québec

HOME LANGUAGE

2001 Estimates:		% Total
English	47	0.43
French	10,772	98.59
Arabic	10	0.09
Vietnamese	10	0.09
Multiple Responses	87	0.80
Total	10,926	100.00

BUILDING PERMITS

	1999	1998	1997
		$000	
Value	3,323	3,930	8,459

HOMES BUILT

	1999	1998	1997
No.	8	7	8

TAXATION

Income Class:	1997	% Total
Under $5,000	900	11.69
$5,000-$10,000	940	12.21
$10,000-$15,000	1,070	13.90
$15,000-$20,000	780	10.13
$20,000-$25,000	730	9.48
$25,000-$30,000	690	8.96
$30,000-$40,000	1,070	13.90
$40,000-$50,000	670	8.70
$50,000 +	850	11.04
Total Returns, No.	7,700	
Total Income, $000	197,333	
Total Taxable Returns	5,710	
Total Tax, $000	22,387	
Average Income, $.	25,628	
Average Tax, $.	3,921	

VITAL STATISTICS

	1997	1996	1995	1994
Births	126	86	127	119
Deaths	66	63	57	54
Natural Increase	60	23	70	65
Marriages	15	13	16	19

Note: Latest available data.

MEDIA INFO
see Québec, CMA

Québec

L'Ancienne-Lorette
(Ville)
Québec CMA

In census division Communauté urbaine de Québec.

POPULATION

July 1, 2001 Estimate	16,298
% Cdn. Total	0.05
% Change, '96 -'01	0.78
Avg. Annual Growth Rate, %	0.16
2003 Projected Population	16,428
2006 Projected Population	16,775
2001 Households Estimate	6,279
2003 Projected Households	6,416
2006 Projected Households	6,647

INCOME

% Above/Below National Average	+5
2001 Total Income Estimate	$360,930,000
% Cdn. Total	0.05
2001 Average Hhld. Income	$57,500
2001 Per Capita	$22,100
2003 Projected Total Income	$387,810,000
2006 Projected Total Income	$435,090,000

RETAIL SALES

% Above/Below National Average	-25
2001 Retail Sales Estimate	$109,920,000
% Cdn. Total	0.04
2001 per Household	$17,500
2001 per Capita	$6,700
2001 No. of Establishments	143
2003 Projected Retail Sales	$118,000,000
2006 Projected Retail Sales	$131,660,000

POPULATION

2001 Estimates:

Total		16,298
Male		8,017
Female		8,281

Age Groups	Male	Female
0-4	453	430
5-9	457	449
10-14	502	464
15-19	599	549
20-24	647	589
25-29	581	526
30-34	544	542
35-39	612	641
40-44	655	705
45-49	676	739
50-54	667	727
55-59	550	592
60-64	407	432
65-69	280	300
70+	387	596

DAYTIME POPULATION

2001 Estimates:

Working Population	2,745
At Home Population	7,382
Total	10,127

INCOME

2001 Estimates:

Avg. Household Income	$57,483
Avg. Family Income	$63,843
Per Capita Income	$22,146
Male:	
Avg. Employment Income	$36,437
Avg. Employment Income (Full Time)	$45,875
Female:	
Avg. Employment Income	$21,848
Avg. Employment Income (Full Time)	$32,851

DISPOSABLE & DISCRETIONARY INCOME

2001 Estimates:	*Per Hhld.*
Disposable Income	$39,546
Discretionary Income 1 (minus Food & Shelter)	$26,071
Discretionary Income 2 (minus Food, Shelter, & Other Expenditures)	$17,306

LIQUID ASSETS

1999 Estimates:	*Per Hhld.*
Equity Investments	$61,800
Interest Bearing Investments	$64,817
Total Liquid Assets	$126,617

CREDIT DATA

July 2000:

Pool of Credit	$119,313,797
Revolving Credit, No.	34,267
Fixed Loans, No.	12,080
Avg. Credit Limit, per Person	$9,251
Avg. Spent, per Person	$3,849
Satisfactory Ratings, No. per Person	3.40
Avg. No. of Cards, per Person	1.39

LABOUR FORCE

2001 Estimates:

Male:	
In the Labour Force	5,016
Participation Rate	75.9
Employed	4,825
Unemployed	191
Unemployment Rate	3.8
Not in Labour Force	1,589
Female:	
In the Labour Force	4,404
Participation Rate	63.5
Employed	4,084
Unemployed	320
Unemployment Rate	7.3
Not in Labour Force	2,534

OCCUPATIONS BY MAJOR GROUPS

2001 Estimates:	Male	Female
Management	653	255
Business, Finance & Admin.	663	1,503
Natural & Applied Sciences & Related	580	97
Health	118	428
Social Sciences, Gov't Services & Religion	90	48
Education	237	272
Arts, Culture, Recreation & Sport	98	67
Sales & Service	1,128	1,421
Trades, Transport & Equipment Operators & Related	1,072	77
Primary Industries	54	n.a.
Processing, Mfg. & Utilities	230	63

LEVEL OF SCHOOLING

2001 Estimates:

Population 15 years +	13,543
Less than Grade 9	1,413
Grades 9-13 w/o Certif.	1,739
Grade 9-13 with Certif.	2,915
Trade Certif. /Dip.	713
Non-Univ. w/o Certif./Dip.	974
Non-Univ. with Certif./Dip.	2,734
Univ. w/o Degree.	1,121
Univ. w/o Degree/Certif.	110
Univ. with Certif.	1,011
Univ. with Degree	1,934

AVERAGE HOUSEHOLD EXPENDITURES

2001 Estimates:

Food	$6,981
Shelter	$8,536
Clothing	$2,456
Transportation	$6,719
Health & Personal Care	$2,210
Recr'n, Read'g & Education	$3,555
Taxes & Securities	$16,833
Other	$7,933
Total Expenditures	$55,223

PRIVATE HOUSEHOLDS

2001 Estimates:

Private Households, Total	6,279
Pop. in Private Households	16,189
Average no. per Household	2.6

FAMILIES

2001 Estimates:

Families in Private Households	4,933
Husband-Wife Families	4,249
Lone-Parent Families	684
Aver. No. Persons per Family	3.1
Aver. No. Sons/Daughters at Home	1.2

HOUSING

2001 Estimates:

Occupied Private Dwellings	6,279
Owned	4,588
Rented	1,691
Single-Detached House	4,019
Semi-Detached House	401
Row Houses	11
Apartment, 5 or Fewer Storeys	1,313
Apartment, Detached Duplex	508
Other Single-Attached	16
Movable Dwellings	11

VEHICLES

2001 Estimates:

Model Yrs. '81-'96, No.	8,181
% Total	74.62
Model Yrs. '97-'98, No.	1,810
% Total	16.51
'99 Vehicles registered in Model Yr. '99, No.	973
% Total	8.87
Total No. '81-'99	10,964

LEGAL MARITAL STATUS

2001 Estimates: (Age 15+)

Single (Never Married)	5,079
Legally Married (Not Separated)	6,525
Legally Married (Separated)	251
Widowed	598
Divorced	1,090

PSYTE CATEGORIES

2001 Estimates	No. of House -holds	% of Total Hhds.	Index
Participation Quebec	2,360	37.59	1,304
New Quebec Rows	454	7.23	660
Quebec Melange	2,405	38.30	1,445
Old Quebec Walkups	204	3.25	177
Quebec Town Elders	512	8.15	289
Quebec's New Urban Mosaic	344	5.48	227

FINANCIAL P$YTE

2001 Estimates	No. of House -holds	% of Total Hhds.	Index
Mortgages & Minivans	2,814	44.82	679
Country Credit	2,405	38.30	566
Loan Parent Stress	716	11.40	196
NSF	344	5.48	155

HOME LANGUAGE

2001 Estimates:		% Total
English	158	0.97
French	16,001	98.18
Chinese	10	0.06
Spanish	62	0.38
Vietnamese	10	0.06
Multiple Responses	57	0.35
Total	16,298	100.00

BUILDING PERMITS

	1999	1998 *$000*	1997
Value	9,185	8,466	8,745

HOMES BUILT

	1999	1998	1997
No	56	70	75

TAXATION

Income Class:	1997	% Total
Under $5,000	1,560	12.52
$5,000-$10,000	1,440	11.56
$10,000-$15,000	1,610	12.92
$15,000-$20,000	1,110	8.91
$20,000-$25,000	1,010	8.11
$25,000-$30,000	1,140	9.15
$30,000-$40,000	1,780	14.29
$40,000-$50,000	1,220	9.79
$50,000 +	1,620	13.00
Total Returns, No.	12,460	
Total Income, $000	333,946	
Total Taxable Returns	9,290	
Total Tax, $000	38,888	
Average Income, $	26,801	
Average Tax, $	4,186	

VITAL STATISTICS

	1997	1996	1995	1994
Births	150	169	163	164
Deaths	66	71	71	74
Natural Increase	84	98	92	90
Marriages	61	60	62	61

Note: Latest available data.

MEDIA INFO

see Québec, CMA

Lévis
(Ville)
Québec CMA

In census division Desjardins.

POPULATION

July 1, 2001 Estimate	40,975
% Cdn. Total	0.13
% Change, '96 -'01	-0.28
Avg. Annual Growth Rate, %	-0.06
2003 Projected Population	41,048
2006 Projected Population	41,436
2001 Households Estimate	17,722
2003 Projected Households	18,027
2006 Projected Households	18,491

INCOME

% Above/Below National Average	-6
2001 Total Income Estimate	$807,880,000
% Cdn. Total	0.12
2001 Average Hhld. Income	$45,600
2001 Per Capita	$19,700
2003 Projected Total Income	$859,650,000
2006 Projected Total Income	$946,930,000

RETAIL SALES

% Above/Below National Average	+110
2001 Retail Sales Estimate	$769,190,000
% Cdn. Total	0.28
2001 per Household	$43,400
2001 per Capita	$18,800
2001 No. of Establishments	396
2003 Projected Retail Sales	$837,650,000
2006 Projected Retail Sales	$943,090,000

POPULATION

2001 Estimates:

Total		40,975
Male		19,309
Female		21,666
Age Groups	Male	Female
0-4	1,056	1,025
5-9	1,021	1,043
10-14	1,083	1,074
15-19	1,292	1,241
20-24	1,396	1,391
25-29	1,343	1,313
30-34	1,371	1,334
35-39	1,513	1,545
40-44	1,590	1,717
45-49	1,590	1,759
50-54	1,486	1,619
55-59	1,188	1,360
60-64	946	1,123
65-69	795	1,028
70+	1,639	3,094

DAYTIME POPULATION

2001 Estimates:

Working Population	15,790
At Home Population	21,601
Total	37,391

INCOME

2001 Estimates:

Avg. Household Income	$45,586
Avg. Family Income	$54,793
Per Capita Income	$19,716
Male:	
Avg. Employment Income	$32,050
Avg. Employment Income (Full Time)	$43,722
Female:	
Avg. Employment Income	$21,344
Avg. Employment Income (Full Time)	$30,128

DISPOSABLE & DISCRETIONARY INCOME

2001 Estimates:	Per Hhld.
Disposable Income	$30,781
Discretionary Income 1 (minus Food & Shelter)	$18,956
Discretionary Income 2 (minus Food, Shelter, & Other Expenditures)	$12,091

LIQUID ASSETS

1999 Estimates:	Per Hhld.
Equity Investments	$48,771
Interest Bearing Investments	$52,286
Total Liquid Assets	$101,057

CREDIT DATA

July 2000:

Pool of Credit	$223,924,835
Revolving Credit, No.	75,068
Fixed Loans, No.	26,676
Avg. Credit Limit, per Person	$6,926
Avg. Spent, per Person	$2,751
Satisfactory Ratings, No. per Person	2.99
Avg. No. of Cards, per Person	1.17

LABOUR FORCE

2001 Estimates:

Male:	
In the Labour Force	11,526
Participation Rate	71.4
Employed	10,499
Unemployed	1,027
Unemployment Rate	8.9
Not in Labour Force	4,623
Female:	
In the Labour Force	9,759
Participation Rate	52.7
Employed	9,093
Unemployed	666
Unemployment Rate	6.8
Not in Labour Force	8,765

OCCUPATIONS BY MAJOR GROUPS

2001 Estimates:	Male	Female
Management	1,078	540
Business, Finance & Admin.	1,337	3,200
Natural & Applied Sciences & Related	757	298
Health	341	1,071
Social Sciences, Gov't Services & Religion	289	264
Education	425	377
Arts, Culture, Recreation & Sport	249	276
Sales & Service	2,617	2,931
Trades, Transport & Equipment Operators & Related	2,499	89
Primary Industries	182	10
Processing, Mfg. & Utilities	1,258	231

LEVEL OF SCHOOLING

2001 Estimates:

Population 15 years +	34,673
Less than Grade 9	5,375
Grades 9-13 w/o Certif.	5,238
Grade 9-13 with Certif.	7,078
Trade Certif./Dip.	1,814
Non-Univ. w/o Certif./Dip.	2,601
Non-Univ. with Certif./Dip.	6,009
Univ. w/o Degree	2,609
Univ. w/o Degree/Certif.	382
Univ. with Certif.	2,227
Univ. with Degree	3,949

AVERAGE HOUSEHOLD EXPENDITURES

2001 Estimates:

Food	$6,024
Shelter	$7,532
Clothing	$1,963
Transportation	$5,029
Health & Personal Care	$1,822
Recr'n, Read'g & Education	$2,968
Taxes & Securities	$12,937
Other	$6,917
Total Expenditures	$45,192

PRIVATE HOUSEHOLDS

2001 Estimates:

Private Households, Total	17,722
Pop. in Private Households	39,848
Average no. per Household	2.2

FAMILIES

2001 Estimates:

Families in Private Households	11,976
Husband-Wife Families	10,011
Lone-Parent Families	1,965
Aver. No. Persons per Family	2.9
Aver. No. Sons/Daughters at Home	1.1

HOUSING

2001 Estimates:

Occupied Private Dwellings	17,722
Owned	9,672
Rented	8,050
Single-Detached House	7,741
Semi-Detached House	797
Row Houses	531
Apartment, 5+ Storeys	750
Owned Apartment, 5+ Storeys	111
Apartment, 5 or Fewer Storeys	5,821
Apartment, Detached Duplex	1,969
Other Single-Attached	97
Movable Dwellings	16

VEHICLES

2001 Estimates:

Model Yrs. '81-'96, No.	19,312
% Total	76.68
Model Yrs. '97-'98, No.	3,680
% Total	14.61
'99 Vehicles registered in Model Yr. '99, No.	2,192
% Total	8.70
Total No. '81-'99	25,184

LEGAL MARITAL STATUS

2001 Estimates: (Age 15+)

Single (Never Married)	14,068
Legally Married (Not Separated)	14,465
Legally Married (Separated)	772
Widowed	2,497
Divorced	2,871

PSYTE CATEGORIES

2001 Estimates	No. of House-holds	% of Total Hhds.	Index
Stable Suburban Families	272	1.53	118
Participation Quebec	2,052	11.58	402
New Quebec Rows	1,381	7.79	711
Quebec Melange	3,798	21.43	809
Traditional French Cdn. Families	811	4.58	170
Urban Bohemia	96	0.54	46
Big Country Families	880	4.97	348
Old Quebec Walkups	1,155	6.52	356
Quebec Town Elders	4,529	25.56	904
Aging Quebec Urbanites	277	1.56	542
Quebec's New Urban Mosaic	2,154	12.15	505
Old Grey Towers	229	1.29	233

FINANCIAL PSYTE

2001 Estimates	No. of House-holds	% of Total Hhds.	Index
Successful Suburbanites	272	1.53	23
Mortgages & Minivans	3,433	19.37	294
Country Credit	4,609	26.01	385
Young Urban Struggle	96	0.54	11
Rural Family Blues	880	4.97	62
Loan Parent Stress	5,961	33.64	578
NSF	2,154	12.15	344
Senior Survivors	229	1.29	69

HOME LANGUAGE

2001 Estimates:		% Total
English	194	0.47
French	40,656	99.22
Other Languages	32	0.08
Multiple Responses	93	0.23
Total	40,975	100.00

BUILDING PERMITS

	1999	1998	1997
		$000	
Value	30,262	32,660	37,412

HOMES BUILT

	1999	1998	1997
No.	146	152	172

TAXATION

Income Class:	1997	% Total
Under $5,000	3,790	12.27
$5,000-$10,000	4,400	14.24
$10,000-$15,000	4,830	15.64
$15,000-$20,000	3,250	10.52
$20,000-$25,000	2,760	8.93
$25,000-$30,000	2,640	8.55
$30,000-$40,000	3,980	12.88
$40,000-$50,000	2,290	7.41
$50,000 +	2,950	9.55
Total Returns, No.	30,890	
Total Income, $000	756,274	
Total Taxable Returns	21,160	
Total Tax, $000	86,262	
Average Income, $	24,483	
Average Tax, $	4,077	

VITAL STATISTICS

	1997	1996	1995	1994
Births	391	370	401	375
Deaths	351	365	328	309
Natural Increase	40	5	73	66
Marriages	64	71	68	98

Note: Latest available data.

MEDIA INFO
see Québec, CMA

Québec

Loretteville
(Ville)
Québec CMA

In census division Communauté urbaine de Québec.

POPULATION

July 1, 2001 Estimate	13,998
% Cdn. Total	0.04
% Change, '96 -'01	-2.89
Avg. Annual Growth Rate, %	-0.58
2003 Projected Population	13,851
2006 Projected Population	13,756
2001 Households Estimate	5,799
2003 Projected Households	5,819
2006 Projected Households	5,870

INCOME

% Above/Below National Average	-1
2001 Total Income Estimate	$292,410,000
% Cdn. Total	0.04
2001 Average Hhld. Income	$50,400
2001 Per Capita	$20,900
2003 Projected Total Income	$309,220,000
2006 Projected Total Income	$338,750,000

RETAIL SALES

% Above/Below National Average	-8
2001 Retail Sales Estimate	$115,730,000
% Cdn. Total	0.04
2001 per Household	$20,000
2001 per Capita	$8,300
2001 No. of Establishments	.105
2003 Projected Retail Sales	$122,520,000
2006 Projected Retail Sales	$133,280,000

POPULATION

2001 Estimates:

Total		13,998
Male		6,712
Female		7,286

Age Groups	Male	Female
0-4	381	362
5-9	374	357
10-14	391	347
15-19	455	429
20-24	530	494
25-29	516	452
30-34	496	449
35-39	489	488
40-44	473	544
45-49	496	599
50-54	532	601
55-59	465	515
60-64	364	414
65-69	275	342
70+	475	893

DAYTIME POPULATION

2001 Estimates:

Working Population	1,796
At Home Population	7,090
Total	8,886

INCOME

2001 Estimates:

Avg. Household Income	$50,424
Avg. Family Income	$57,437
Per Capita Income	$20,889
Male:	
Avg. Employment Income	$33,405
Avg. Employment Income (Full Time)	$45,177
Female:	
Avg. Employment Income	$20,972
Avg. Employment Income (Full Time)	$30,989

DISPOSABLE & DISCRETIONARY INCOME

2001 Estimates:	Per Hhld.
Disposable Income	$34,868
Discretionary Income 1 (minus Food & Shelter)	$22,242
Discretionary Income 2 (minus Food, Shelter, & Other Expenditures)	$14,555

LIQUID ASSETS

1999 Estimates:	Per Hhld.
Equity Investments	$49,593
Interest Bearing Investments	$55,755
Total Liquid Assets	$105,348

CREDIT DATA

July 2000:

Pool of Credit	$91,612,327
Revolving Credit, No.	27,687
Fixed Loans, No.	10,035
Avg. Credit Limit, per Person	$7,935
Avg. Spent, per Person	$3,367
Satisfactory Ratings, No. per Person	3.09
Avg. No. of Cards, per Person	1.24

LABOUR FORCE

2001 Estimates:

Male:	
In the Labour Force	4,006
Participation Rate	72.0
Employed	3,741
Unemployed	265
Unemployment Rate	6.6
Not in Labour Force	1,560
Female:	
In the Labour Force	3,384
Participation Rate	54.4
Employed	3,182
Unemployed	202
Unemployment Rate	6.0
Not in Labour Force	2,836

OCCUPATIONS BY MAJOR GROUPS

2001 Estimates:	Male	Female
Management	450	114
Business, Finance & Admin.	511	1,151
Natural & Applied Sciences & Related	390	49
Health	98	347
Social Sciences, Gov't Services & Religion	61	112
Education	131	225
Arts, Culture, Recreation & Sport	126	91
Sales & Service	1,029	1,033
Trades, Transport & Equipment Operators & Related	797	50
Primary Industries	32	n.a.
Processing, Mfg. & Utilities	242	99

LEVEL OF SCHOOLING

2001 Estimates:

Population 15 years +	11,786
Less than Grade 9	1,774
Grades 9-13 w/o Certif.	1,613
Grade 9-13 with Certif.	2,415
Trade Certif./Dip.	507
Non-Univ. w/o Certif./Dip.	946
Non-Univ. with Certif./Dip.	2,218
Univ. w/o Degree	962
Univ. w/o Degree/Certif.	194
Univ. with Certif.	768
Univ. with Degree	1,351

AVERAGE HOUSEHOLD EXPENDITURES

2001 Estimates:

Food	$6,424
Shelter	$8,005
Clothing	$2,064
Transportation	$5,722
Health & Personal Care	$2,020
Recr'n, Read'g & Education	$3,146
Taxes & Securities	$14,328
Other	$7,739
Total Expenditures	$49,448

PRIVATE HOUSEHOLDS

2001 Estimates:

Private Households, Total	5,799
Pop. in Private Households	13,751
Average no. per Household	2.4

FAMILIES

2001 Estimates:

Families in Private Households	4,287
Husband-Wife Families	3,552
Lone-Parent Families	735
Aver. No. Persons per Family	2.9
Aver. No. Sons/Daughters at Home	1.1

HOUSING

2001 Estimates:

Occupied Private Dwellings	5,799
Owned	3,508
Rented	2,291
Single-Detached House	2,993
Semi-Detached House	237
Row Houses	20
Apartment, 5+ Storeys	10
Apartment, 5 or Fewer Storeys	1,839
Apartment, Detached Duplex	680
Other Single-Attached	20

VEHICLES

2001 Estimates:

Model Yrs. '81-'96, No.	7,296
% Total	78.40
Model Yrs. '97-'98, No.	1,225
% Total	13.16
'99 Vehicles registered in Model Yr. '99, No.	785
% Total	8.44
Total No. '81-'99	9,306

LEGAL MARITAL STATUS

2001 Estimates: (Age 15+)

Single (Never Married)	4,479
Legally Married (Not Separated)	5,266
Legally Married (Separated)	266
Widowed	767
Divorced	1,008

PSYTE CATEGORIES

2001 Estimates	No. of House-holds	% of Total Hhds.	Index
Stable Suburban Families	426	7.35	564
Participation Quebec	660	11.38	395
Quebec Melange	2,573	44.37	1,674
Quebec Town Elders	1,513	26.09	923
Quebec's New Urban Mosaic	400	6.90	286
Old Grey Towers	197	3.40	613

FINANCIAL P$YTE

2001 Estimates	No. of House-holds	% of Total Hhds.	Index
Successful Suburbanites	426	7.35	111
Mortgages & Minivans	660	11.38	172
Country Credit	2,573	44.37	656
Loan Parent Stress	1,513	26.09	448
NSF	400	6.90	195
Senior Survivors	197	3.40	180

HOME LANGUAGE

2001 Estimates		% Total
English	122	0.87
French	13,685	97.76
Montagnais-Naskapi	25	0.18
Portuguese	30	0.21
Spanish	20	0.14
Multiple Responses	116	0.83
Total	13,998	100.00

BUILDING PERMITS

	1999	1998 $000	1997
Value	3,644	4,556	2,575

HOMES BUILT

	1999	1998	1997
No.	12	9	15

TAXATION

Income Class:	1997	% Total
Under $5,000	1,370	12.80
$5,000-$10,000	1,570	14.67
$10,000-$15,000	1,610	15.05
$15,000-$20,000	1,090	10.19
$20,000-$25,000	960	8.97
$25,000-$30,000	900	8.41
$30,000-$40,000	1,330	12.43
$40,000-$50,000	810	7.57
$50,000 +	1,050	9.81
Total Returns, No.	10,700	
Total Income, $000	255,583	
Total Taxable Returns	7,400	
Total Tax, $000	28,414	
Average Income, $	23,886	
Average Tax, $	3,840	

VITAL STATISTICS

	1997	1996	1995	1994
Births	139	147	149	163
Deaths	123	124	102	95
Natural Increase	16	23	47	68
Marriages	20	25	34	43

Note: Latest available data.

MEDIA INFO
see Québec, CMA

Québec
(Ville)
Québec CMA

In census division Communauté urbaine de Québec.

Québec

POPULATION

July 1, 2001 Estimate	165,495
% Cdn. Total	0.53
% Change, '96 -'01	-2.76
Avg. Annual Growth Rate, %	-0.56
2003 Projected Population	163,903
2006 Projected Population	162,977
2001 Households Estimate	85,886
2003 Projected Households	86,300
2006 Projected Households	87,088

INCOME

% Above/Below National Average	-8
2001 Total Income Estimate	$3,217,350,000
% Cdn. Total	0.49
2001 Average Hhld. Income	$37,500
2001 Per Capita	$19,400
2003 Projected Total Income	$3,382,920,000
2006 Projected Total Income	$3,669,540,000

RETAIL SALES

% Above/Below National Average	+53
2001 Retail Sales Estimate	$2,271,460,000
% Cdn. Total	0.82
2001 per Household	$26,400
2001 per Capita	$13,700
2001 No. of Establishments	1,793
2003 Projected Retail Sales	$2,420,740,000
2006 Projected Retail Sales	$2,651,210,000

POPULATION

2001 Estimates:

Total		165,495
Male		78,042
Female		87,453

Age Groups	Male	Female
0-4	4,466	4,250
5-9	3,796	3,672
10-14	3,512	3,352
15-19	3,808	3,736
20-24	4,891	4,961
25-29	6,006	5,955
30-34	6,781	6,340
35-39	7,146	6,690
40-44	6,946	6,843
45-49	6,517	6,712
50-54	5,713	6,160
55-59	4,657	5,199
60-64	3,776	4,557
65-69	3,219	4,411
70+	6,808	14,615

DAYTIME POPULATION

2001 Estimates:

Working Population	244,971
At Home Population	94,374
Total	339,345

INCOME

2001 Estimates:

Avg. Household Income	$37,461
Avg. Family Income	$48,947
Per Capita Income	$19,441
Male:	
Avg. Employment Income	$29,482
Avg. Employment Income (Full Time)	$40,188
Female:	
Avg. Employment Income	$21,480
Avg. Employment Income (Full Time)	$31,453

DISPOSABLE & DISCRETIONARY INCOME

2001 Estimates:	Per Hhld.
Disposable Income	$25,027
Discretionary Income 1 (minus Food & Shelter)	$14,479
Discretionary Income 2 (minus Food, Shelter, & Other Expenditures)	$8,838

LIQUID ASSETS

1999 Estimates:	Per Hhld.
Equity Investments	$36,311
Interest Bearing Investments	$42,939
Total Liquid Assets	$79,250

CREDIT DATA

July 2000:

Pool of Credit	$972,482,853
Revolving Credit, No.	311,415
Fixed Loans, No.	104,659
Avg. Credit Limit, per Person	$6,852
Avg. Spent, per Person	$2,846
Satisfactory Ratings, No. per Person	2.76
Avg. No. of Cards, per Person	1.10

LABOUR FORCE

2001 Estimates:

Male:	
In the Labour Force	44,798
Participation Rate	67.6
Employed	40,350
Unemployed	4,448
Unemployment Rate	9.9
Not in Labour Force	21,470
Female:	
In the Labour Force	38,164
Participation Rate	50.1
Employed	34,876
Unemployed	3,288
Unemployment Rate	8.6
Not in Labour Force	38,015

OCCUPATIONS BY MAJOR GROUPS

2001 Estimates:	Male	Female
Management	4,619	2,258
Business, Finance & Admin.	5,321	11,472
Natural & Applied Sciences & Related	4,181	1,055
Health	1,355	3,412
Social Sciences, Gov't Services & Religion	1,618	1,536
Education	1,649	1,918
Arts, Culture, Recreation & Sport	1,781	1,757
Sales & Service	11,907	11,572
Trades, Transport & Equipment Operators & Related	7,233	420
Primary Industries	446	61
Processing, Mfg. & Utilities	1,849	723

LEVEL OF SCHOOLING

2001 Estimates:

Population 15 years +	142,447
Less than Grade 9	23,950
Grades 9-13 w/o Certif.	20,780
Grade 9-13 with Certif.	25,096
Trade Certif. /Dip.	5,365
Non-Univ. w/o Certif./Dip.	10,360
Non-Univ. with Certif./Dip.	22,339
Univ. w/o Degree	11,321
Univ. w/o Degree/Certif.	1,744
Univ. with Certif.	9,577
Univ. with Degree	23,236

AVERAGE HOUSEHOLD EXPENDITURES

2001 Estimates:

Food	$5,139
Shelter	$7,218
Clothing	$1,733
Transportation	$3,797
Health & Personal Care	$1,633
Recr'n, Read'g & Education	$2,545
Taxes & Securities	$9,826
Other	$6,195
Total Expenditures	$38,086

PRIVATE HOUSEHOLDS

2001 Estimates:

Private Households, Total	85,886
Pop. in Private Households	160,816
Average no. per Household	1.9

FAMILIES

2001 Estimates:

Families in Private Households	43,560
Husband-Wife Families	34,162
Lone-Parent Families	9,398
Aver. No. Persons per Family	2.7
Aver. No. Sons/Daughters at Home	0.9

HOUSING

2001 Estimates:

Occupied Private Dwellings	85,886
Owned	28,482
Rented	57,404
Single-Detached House	13,202
Semi-Detached House	2,817
Row Houses	2,666
Apartment, 5+ Storeys	9,371
Owned Apartment, 5+ Storeys	1,623
Apartment, 5 or Fewer Storeys	51,093
Apartment, Detached Duplex	5,579
Other Single-Attached	1,158

VEHICLES

2001 Estimates:

Model Yrs. '81-'96, No.	67,012
% Total	74.26
Model Yrs. '97-'98, No.	14,275
% Total	15.82
'99 Vehicles registered in Model Yr. '99, No.	8,952
% Total	9.92
Total No. '81-'99	90,239

LEGAL MARITAL STATUS

2001 Estimates: (Age 15+)

Single (Never Married)	67,479
Legally Married (Not Separated)	44,877
Legally Married (Separated)	3,952
Widowed	11,426
Divorced	14,713

PSYTE CATEGORIES

2001 Estimates	No. of House -holds	% of Total Hhds.	Index
Technocrafts & Bureaucrats	1,166	1.36	48
Old Bungalow Burbs	777	0.90	55
Brie & Chablis	963	1.12	125
Participation Quebec	6,841	7.97	276
New Quebec Rows	4,568	5.32	485
Quebec Melange	6,107	7.11	268
Traditional French Cdn. Families	873	1.02	38
High Rise Sunsets	1,223	1.42	100
Young Urban Professionals	6,251	7.28	384
Young Urban Intelligentsia	704	0.82	54
Young City Singles	131	0.15	7
Urban Bohemia	11,441	13.32	1,138
Euro Quebec	172	0.20	23
Old Quebec Walkups	2,793	3.25	177
Quebec Town Elders	2,650	3.09	109
Aging Quebec Urbanites	2,433	2.83	982
Quebec's New Urban Mosaic	31,403	36.56	1,518
Aged Pensioners	2,000	2.33	175
Big City Stress	1,125	1.31	116
Old Grey Towers	1,563	1.82	329

FINANÇIAL P$YTE

2001 Estimates	No. of House -holds	% of Total Hhds.	Index
Successful Suburbanites	1,166	1.36	20
Urban Heights	7,214	8.40	195
Miners & Credit-Liners	777	0.90	29
Mortgages & Minivans	11,409	13.28	201
Country Credit	6,980	8.13	120
Revolving Renters	1,223	1.42	31
Young Urban Struggle	12,145	14.14	299
Loan Parent Stress	8,048	9.37	161
Towering Debt	131	0.15	2
NSF	32,528	37.87	1,070
Senior Survivors	3,563	4.15	220

HOME LANGUAGE

2001 Estimates		% Total
English	1,870	1.13
French	160,275	96.85
Khmer (Cambodian)	165	0.10
Serbo-Croatian	277	0.17
Spanish	373	0.23
Vietnamese	264	0.16
Other Languages	762	0.46
Multiple Responses	1,509	0.91
Total	165,495	100.00

BUILDING PERMITS

	1999	1998 $000	1997
Value	130,729	137,202	157,329

HOMES BUILT

	1999	1998	1997
No	199	201	431

TAXATION

Income Class:	1997	% Total
Under $5,000	14,610	11.34
$5,000-$10,000	23,420	18.18
$10,000-$15,000	22,170	17.21
$15,000-$20,000	12,820	9.95
$20,000-$25,000	10,690	8.30
$25,000-$30,000	10,340	8.03
$30,000-$40,000	14,190	11.01
$40,000-$50,000	8,350	6.48
$50,000 +	12,240	9.50
Total Returns, No.	128,830	
Total Income, $000	3,017,112	
Total Taxable Returns	83,100	
Total Tax, $000	337,045	
Average Income, $.	23,419	
Average Tax, $	4,056	

VITAL STATISTICS

	1997	1996	1995	1994
Births	1,563	1,662	1,714	1,681
Deaths	1,696	1,675	1,715	1,645
Natural Increase	-133	-13	-1	36
Marriages	1,154	1,094	1,116	1,218

Note: Latest available data.

MEDIA INFO
see Québec, CMA

Québec

Saint-Augustin-de-Desmaures

(Municipalité)
Québec CMA

In census division Communauté urbaine de Québec.

POPULATION

July 1, 2001 Estimate	16,671
% Cdn. Total	0.05
% Change, '96 -'01	10.91
Avg. Annual Growth Rate, %	2.09
2003 Projected Population	17,677
2006 Projected Population	19,344
2001 Households Estimate	5,690
2003 Projected Households	6,122
2006 Projected Households	6,803

INCOME

% Above/Below National Average	+29
2001 Total Income Estimate	$455,050,000
% Cdn. Total	0.07
2001 Average Hhld. Income	$80,000
2001 Per Capita	$27,300
2003 Projected Total Income	$516,770,000
2006 Projected Total Income	$625,510,000

RETAIL SALES

% Above/Below National Average	-80
2001 Retail Sales Estimate	$29,190,000
% Cdn. Total	0.01
2001 per Household	$5,100
2001 per Capita	$1,800
2001 No. of Establishments	94
2003 Projected Retail Sales	$33,240,000
2006 Projected Retail Sales	$40,510,000

POPULATION

2001 Estimates:

Total		16,671
Male		8,372
Female		8,299
Age Groups	Male	Female
0-4	537	513
5-9	670	635
10-14	754	720
15-19	738	694
20-24	570	536
25-29	419	409
30-34	476	538
35-39	735	785
40-44	900	937
45-49	865	836
50-54	650	585
55-59	404	344
60-64	236	211
65-69	162	155
70+	256	401

DAYTIME POPULATION

2001 Estimates:

Working Population	2,041
At Home Population	7,500
Total	9,541

INCOME

2001 Estimates:

Avg. Household Income	$79,974
Avg. Family Income	$85,827
Per Capita Income	$27,296
Male:	
Avg. Employment Income	$51,570
Avg. Employment Income (Full Time)	$60,915
Female:	
Avg. Employment Income	$28,575
Avg. Employment Income (Full Time)	$41,611

DISPOSABLE & DISCRETIONARY INCOME

2001 Estimates:	Per Hhld.
Disposable Income	$53,916
Discretionary Income 1 (minus Food & Shelter)	$37,025
Discretionary Income 2 (minus Food, Shelter, & Other Expenditures)	$25,595

LIQUID ASSETS

1999 Estimates:	Per Hhld.
Equity Investments	$119,904
Interest Bearing Investments	$93,127
Total Liquid Assets	$213,031

CREDIT DATA

July 2000:

Pool of Credit	$105,026,826
Revolving Credit, No.	25,113
Fixed Loans, No.	8,669
Avg. Credit Limit, per Person	$11,440
Avg. Spent, per Person	$4,727
Satisfactory Ratings, No. per Person	3.47
Avg. No. of Cards, per Person	1.49

LABOUR FORCE

2001 Estimates:

Male:	
In the Labour Force	5,204
Participation Rate	81.2
Employed	5,044
Unemployed	160
Unemployment Rate	3.1
Not in Labour Force	1,207
Female:	
In the Labour Force	4,256
Participation Rate	66.2
Employed	4,068
Unemployed	188
Unemployment Rate	4.4
Not in Labour Force	2,175

OCCUPATIONS BY MAJOR GROUPS

2001 Estimates:	Male	Female
Management	1,044	298
Business, Finance & Admin.	643	1,512
Natural & Applied Sciences & Related	753	100
Health	167	548
Social Sciences, Gov't Services & Religion	172	176
Education	197	323
Arts, Culture, Recreation & Sport	115	108
Sales & Service	889	942
Trades, Transport & Equipment Operators & Related	826	42
Primary Industries	58	26
Processing, Mfg. & Utilities	264	65

LEVEL OF SCHOOLING

2001 Estimates:

Population 15 years +	12,842
Less than Grade 9	903
Grades 9-13 w/o Certif.	1,548
Grade 9-13 with Certif.	2,075
Trade Certif. /Dip.	488
Non-Univ. w/o Certif./Dip.	720
Non-Univ. with Certif./Dip.	2,387
Univ. w/o Degree	1,387
Univ. w/o Degree/Certif.	192
Univ. with Certif.	1,195
Univ. with Degree	3,334

AVERAGE HOUSEHOLD EXPENDITURES

2001 Estimates:

Food	$8,692
Shelter	$10,998
Clothing	$3,344
Transportation	$8,993
Health & Personal Care	$2,710
Recr'n, Read'g & Education	$5,016
Taxes & Securities	$23,432
Other	$9,930
Total Expenditures	$73,115

PRIVATE HOUSEHOLDS

2001 Estimates:

Private Households, Total	5,690
Pop. in Private Households	16,352
Average no. per Household	2.9

FAMILIES

2001 Estimates:

Families in Private Households	4,918
Husband-Wife Families	4,451
Lone-Parent Families	467
Aver. No. Persons per Family	3.3
Aver. No. Sons/Daughters at Home	1.4

HOUSING

2001 Estimates:

Occupied Private Dwellings	5,690
Owned	4,843
Rented	847
Single-Detached House	4,646
Semi-Detached House	252
Row Houses	13
Apartment, 5 or Fewer Storeys	578
Apartment, Detached Duplex	171
Other Single-Attached	12
Movable Dwellings	18

VEHICLES

2001 Estimates:

Model Yrs. '81-'96, No.	7,198
% Total	72.26
Model Yrs. '97-'98, No.	1,654
% Total	16.60
'99 Vehicles registered in Model Yr. '99, No.	1,109
% Total	11.13
Total No. '81-'99	9,961

LEGAL MARITAL STATUS

2001 Estimates: (Age 15+)

Single (Never Married)	4,619
Legally Married (Not Separated)	6,672
Legally Married (Separated)	232
Widowed	425
Divorced	894

PSYTE CATEGORIES

2001 Estimates	No. of House-holds	% of Total Hhds.	Index
Suburban Executives	463	8.14	568
Technocrafts & Bureaucrats	848	14.90	530
Participation Quebec	3,062	53.81	1,867
New Quebec Rows	301	5.29	483
Quebec Melange	464	8.15	308
Traditional French Cdn. Families	492	8.65	322

FINANCIAL P$YTE

2001 Estimates	No. of House-holds	% of Total Hhds.	Index
Four Star Investors	463	8.14	162
Successful Suburbanites	848	14.90	225
Mortgages & Minivans	3,363	59.10	896
Country Credit	956	16.80	248

HOME LANGUAGE

2001 Estimates:		% Total
English	186	1.12
French	16,441	98.62
Dutch	11	0.07
Multiple Responses	33	0.20
Total	16,671	100.00

BUILDING PERMITS

	1999	1998	1997
		$000	
Value	20,138	16,376	19,915

HOMES BUILT

	1999	1998	1997
No	60	73	103

TAXATION

Income Class:	1997	% Total
Under $5,000	1,260	12.52
$5,000-$10,000	890	8.85
$10,000-$15,000	900	8.95
$15,000-$20,000	730	7.26
$20,000-$25,000	690	6.86
$25,000-$30,000	810	8.05
$30,000-$40,000	1,350	13.42
$40,000-$50,000	1,060	10.54
$50,000 +	2,370	23.56
Total Returns, No.	10,060	
Total Income, $000	357,751	
Total Taxable Returns	7,810	
Total Tax, $000	51,242	
Average Income, $	35,562	
Average Tax, $	6,561	

VITAL STATISTICS

	1997	1996	1995	1994
Births	176	190	212	221
Deaths	66	65	67	58
Natural Increase	110	125	145	263
Marriages	12	8	15	15

Note: Latest available data.

MEDIA INFO
see Québec, CMA

Saint-Jean-Chrysostome

(Ville)

Québec CMA

In census division Les
Chutes-de-la-Chaudière.

POPULATION

July 1, 2001 Estimate	19,808
% Cdn. Total	0.06
% Change, '96 -'01	20.34
Avg. Annual Growth Rate, %	3.77
2003 Projected Population	21,954
2006 Projected Population	25,438
2001 Households Estimate	6,935
2003 Projected Households	7,814
2006 Projected Households	9,247

INCOME

% Above/Below National Average	+3
2001 Total Income Estimate	$429,380,000
% Cdn. Total	0.07
2001 Average Hhld. Income	$61,900
2001 Per Capita	$21,700
2003 Projected Total Income	$516,110,000
2006 Projected Total Income	$675,450,000

RETAIL SALES

% Above/Below National Average	-27
2001 Retail Sales Estimate	$129,200,000
% Cdn. Total	0.05
2001 per Household	$18,600
2001 per Capita	$6,500
2001 No. of Establishments	117
2003 Projected Retail Sales	$151,220,000
2006 Projected Retail Sales	$189,530,000

POPULATION

2001 Estimates:

Total		19,808
Male		9,941
Female		9,867

Age Groups	Male	Female
0-4	752	722
5-9	853	796
10-14	875	778
15-19	845	791
20-24	686	713
25-29	632	713
30-34	787	881
35-39	953	1,038
40-44	986	1,024
45-49	913	869
50-54	688	618
55-59	427	363
60-64	236	207
65-69	134	135
70+	174	219

DAYTIME POPULATION

2001 Estimates:

Working Population	310
At Home Population	8,604
Total	8,914

INCOME

2001 Estimates:

Avg. Household Income	$61,915
Avg. Family Income	$65,756
Per Capita Income	$21,677
Male:	
Avg. Employment Income	$39,248
Avg. Employment Income (Full Time)	$49,200
Female:	
Avg. Employment Income	$22,239
Avg. Employment Income (Full Time)	$31,166

DISPOSABLE & DISCRETIONARY INCOME

2001 Estimates:	Per Hhld.
Disposable Income	$43,222
Discretionary Income 1 (minus Food & Shelter)	$29,543
Discretionary Income 2 (minus Food, Shelter, & Other Expenditures)	$20,234

LIQUID ASSETS

1999 Estimates:	Per Hhld.
Equity Investments	$73,227
Interest Bearing Investments	$69,992
Total Liquid Assets	$143,219

CREDIT DATA

July 2000:

Pool of Credit	$104,600,266
Revolving Credit, No.	30,262
Fixed Loans, No.	12,504
Avg. Credit Limit, per Person	$9,200
Avg. Spent, per Person	$4,004
Satisfactory Ratings, No. per Person	3.54
Avg. No. of Cards, per Person	1.43

LABOUR FORCE

2001 Estimates:

Male:	
In the Labour Force	6,256
Participation Rate	83.8
Employed	6,046
Unemployed	210
Unemployment Rate	3.4
Not in Labour Force	1,205
Female:	
In the Labour Force	5,293
Participation Rate	69.9
Employed	5,074
Unemployed	219
Unemployment Rate	4.1
Not in Labour Force	2,278

OCCUPATIONS BY MAJOR GROUPS

2001 Estimates:	Male	Female
Management	1,017	322
Business, Finance & Admin.	720	1,784
Natural & Applied Sciences & Related	760	120
Health	143	515
Social Sciences, Gov't Services & Religion	95	186
Education	214	143
Arts, Culture, Recreation & Sport	86	150
Sales & Service	1,114	1,673
Trades, Transport & Equipment Operators & Related	1,434	47
Primary Industries	149	123
Processing, Mfg. & Utilities	471	77

LEVEL OF SCHOOLING

2001 Estimates:

Population 15 years +	15,032
Less than Grade 9	972
Grades 9-13 w/o Certif.	1,966
Grade 9-13 with Certif.	2,714
Trade Certif. /Dip.	1,013
Non-Univ. w/o Certif./Dip.	1,198
Non-Univ. with Certif./Dip.	3,577
Univ. w/o Degree	1,236
Univ. w/o Degree/Certif.	86
Univ. with Certif.	1,150
Univ. with Degree	2,356

AVERAGE HOUSEHOLD EXPENDITURES

2001 Estimates:

Food	$7,290
Shelter	$8,546
Clothing	$2,715
Transportation	$7,269
Health & Personal Care	$2,287
Recr'n, Read'g & Education	$3,884
Taxes & Securities	$19,037
Other	$7,869
Total Expenditures	$58,897

PRIVATE HOUSEHOLDS

2001 Estimates:

Private Households, Total	6,935
Pop. in Private Households	19,618
Average no. per Household	2.8

FAMILIES

2001 Estimates:

Families in Private Households	5,977
Husband-Wife Families	5,409
Lone-Parent Families	568
Aver. No. Persons per Family	3.3
Aver. No. Sons/Daughters at Home	1.4

HOUSING

2001 Estimates:

Occupied Private Dwellings	6,935
Owned	5,541
Rented	1,394
Single-Detached House	5,198
Semi-Detached House	243
Row Houses	45
Apartment, 5 or Fewer Storeys	1,175
Apartment, Detached Duplex	188
Other Single-Attached	24
Movable Dwellings	62

VEHICLES

2001 Estimates:

Model Yrs. '81-'96, No.	7,962
% Total	77.60
Model Yrs. '97-'98, No.	1,492
% Total	14.54
'99 Vehicles registered in Model Yr. '99, No.	806
% Total	7.86
Total No. '81-'99	10,260

LEGAL MARITAL STATUS

2001 Estimates: (Age 15+)

Single (Never Married)	5,772
Legally Married (Not Separated)	7,514
Legally Married (Separated)	324
Widowed	274
Divorced	1,148

PSYTE CATEGORIES

2001 Estimates	No. of House -holds	% of Total Hhds.	Index
Participation Quebec	5,610	80.89	2,807
New Quebec Rows	953	13.74	1,254
Traditional French Cdn. Families	372	5.36	200

FINANÇIAL PŜYTE

2001 Estimates	No. of House -holds	% of Total Hhds.	Index
Mortgages & Minivans	6,563	94.64	1,434
Country Credit	372	5.36	79

HOME LANGUAGE

2001 Estimates:		% Total
English	124	0.63
French	19,618	99.04
Spanish	12	0.06
Multiple Responses	54	0.27
Total	19,808	100.00

Québec

BUILDING PERMITS

	1999	1998 $000	1997
Value	12,768	13,639	15,100

HOMES BUILT

	1999	1998	1997
No.	83	93	113

TAXATION

Income Class:	1997	% Total
Under $5,000	1,440	12.75
$5,000-$10,000	1,090	9.65
$10,000-$15,000	1,080	9.57
$15,000-$20,000	1,010	8.95
$20,000-$25,000	1,000	8.86
$25,000-$30,000	1,130	10.01
$30,000-$40,000	1,820	16.12
$40,000-$50,000	1,230	10.89
$50,000 +	1,510	13.37
Total Returns, No.	11,290	
Total Income, $000	317,870	
Total Taxable Returns	8,770	
Total Tax, $000	38,692	
Average Income, $.	28,155	
Average Tax, $.	4,412	

VITAL STATISTICS

	1997	1996	1995	1994
Births	253	291	288	291
Deaths	33	21	24	33
Natural Increase	220	270	265	258
Marriages	13	15	13	17

Note: Latest available data.

MEDIA INFO

see Québec, CMA

Québec

Saint-Nicolas
(Ville)
Québec CMA

In census division Les Chutes-de-la-Chaudière. Name changed from Bernières-Saint-Nicolas Jan. 1, 1999.

POPULATION

July 1, 2001 Estimate	16,487
% Cdn. Total	0.05
% Change, '96 -'01	3.78
Avg. Annual Growth Rate, %	0.75
2003 Projected Population	16,859
2006 Projected Population	17,617
2001 Households Estimate	5,911
2003 Projected Households	6,147
2006 Projected Households	6,566

INCOME

% Above/Below National Average	+14
2001 Total Income Estimate	$395,800,000
% Cdn. Total	0.06
2001 Average Hhld. Income	$67,000
2001 Per Capita	$24,000
2003 Projected Total Income	$436,490,000
2006 Projected Total Income	$511,350,000

RETAIL SALES

% Above/Below National Average	-4
2001 Retail Sales Estimate	$141,150,000
% Cdn. Total	0.05
2001 per Household	$23,900
2001 per Capita	$8,600
2001 No. of Establishments	152
2003 Projected Retail Sales	$156,130,000
2006 Projected Retail Sales	$180,750,000

POPULATION

2001 Estimates:

Total		16,487
Male		8,246
Female		8,241

Age Groups	Male	Female
0-4	522	515
5-9	589	573
10-14	654	601
15-19	699	650
20-24	607	579
25-29	497	518
30-34	543	606
35-39	674	722
40-44	741	789
45-49	762	787
50-54	698	688
55-59	502	465
60-64	306	272
65-69	189	168
70+	263	308

DAYTIME POPULATION

2001 Estimates:

Working Population	3,148
At Home Population	7,266
Total	10,414

INCOME

2001 Estimates:

Avg. Household Income	$66,960
Avg. Family Income	$70,551
Per Capita Income	$24,007

Male:

Avg. Employment Income	$39,091
Avg. Employment Income (Full Time)	$50,421

Female:

Avg. Employment Income	$26,084
Avg. Employment Income (Full Time)	$37,105

DISPOSABLE & DISCRETIONARY INCOME

2001 Estimates: Per Hhld.

Disposable Income	$46,213
Discretionary Income 1 (minus Food & Shelter)	$31,456
Discretionary Income 2 (minus Food, Shelter, & Other Expenditures)	$21,411

LIQUID ASSETS

1999 Estimates: Per Hhld.

Equity Investments	$100,036
Interest Bearing Investments	$80,802
Total Liquid Assets	$180,838

CREDIT DATA

July 2000:

Pool of Credit	$121,529,387
Revolving Credit, No.	31,815
Fixed Loans, No.	11,936
Avg. Credit Limit, per Person	$10,659
Avg. Spent, per Person	$4,459
Satisfactory Ratings, No. per Person	3.62
Avg. No. of Cards, per Person	1.48

LABOUR FORCE

2001 Estimates:

Male:

In the Labour Force	5,163
Participation Rate	79.7
Employed	4,968
Unemployed	195
Unemployment Rate	3.8
Not in Labour Force	1,318

Female:

In the Labour Force	4,459
Participation Rate	68.1
Employed	4,234
Unemployed	225
Unemployment Rate	5.0
Not in Labour Force	2,093

OCCUPATIONS BY MAJOR GROUPS

2001 Estimates:	Male	Female
Management	744	323
Business, Finance & Admin.	548	1,416
Natural & Applied Sciences & Related	690	210
Health	142	512
Social Sciences, Gov't Services & Religion	117	155
Education	240	295
Arts, Culture, Recreation & Sport	76	91
Sales & Service	1,085	1,130
Trades, Transport & Equipment Operators & Related	1,071	55
Primary Industries	185	79
Processing, Mfg. & Utilities	188	34

LEVEL OF SCHOOLING

2001 Estimates:

Population 15 years +	13,033
Less than Grade 9	1,001
Grades 9-13 w/o Certif.	1,695
Grade 9-13 with Certif.	2,197
Trade Certif./Dip.	620
Non-Univ. w/o Certif./Dip.	937
Non-Univ. with Certif./Dip.	2,766
Univ. w/o Degree	1,140
Univ. w/o Degree/Certif.	181
Univ. with Certif.	959
Univ. with Degree	2,677

AVERAGE HOUSEHOLD EXPENDITURES

2001 Estimates:

Food	$7,836
Shelter	$9,208
Clothing	$2,870
Transportation	$7,862
Health & Personal Care	$2,458
Recr'n, Read'g & Education	$4,140
Taxes & Securities	$19,905
Other	$8,598
Total Expenditures	$62,877

PRIVATE HOUSEHOLDS

2001 Estimates:

Private Households, Total	5,911
Pop. in Private Households	16,306
Average no. per Household	2.8

FAMILIES

2001 Estimates:

Families in Private Households	4,949
Husband-Wife Families	4,390
Lone-Parent Families	559
Aver. No. Persons per Family	3.2
Aver. No. Sons/Daughters at Home	1.3

HOUSING

2001 Estimates:

Occupied Private Dwellings	5,911
Owned	4,946
Rented	965
Single-Detached House	4,721
Semi-Detached House	344
Apartment, 5 or Fewer Storeys	660
Apartment, Detached Duplex	186

VEHICLES

2001 Estimates:

Model Yrs. '81-'96, No.	8,934
% Total	75.19
Model Yrs. '97-'98, No.	1,837
% Total	15.46
'99 Vehicles registered in Model Yr. '99, No.	1,111
% Total	9.35
Total No. '81-'99	11,882

LEGAL MARITAL STATUS

2001 Estimates: (Age 15+)

Single (Never Married)	4,984
Legally Married (Not Separated)	6,291
Legally Married (Separated)	327
Widowed	361
Divorced	1,070

PSYTE CATEGORIES

2001 Estimates	No. of House-holds	% of Total Hhds.	Index
Participation Quebec	3,957	66.94	2,323
New Quebec Rows	592	10.02	914
Quebec Melange	784	13.26	501
Traditional French Cdn. Families	578	9.78	364

FINANCIAL P$YTE

2001 Estimates	No. of House-holds	% of Total Hhds.	Index
Mortgages & Minivans	4,549	76.96	1,166
Country Credit	1,362	23.04	341

HOME LANGUAGE

2001 Estimates:		% Total
English	215	1.30
French	16,207	98.30
German	11	0.07
Lao	11	0.07
Slovak	16	0.10
Multiple Responses	27	0.16
Total	16,487	100.00

BUILDING PERMITS

	1999	1998	1997
		$000	
Value	23,374	20,964	19,058

HOMES BUILT

	1999	1998	1997
No	138	128	143

TAXATION

Income Class:	1997	% Total
Under $5,000	1,510	13.34
$5,000-$10,000	1,150	10.16
$10,000-$15,000	1,230	10.87
$15,000-$20,000	940	8.30
$20,000-$25,000	920	8.13
$25,000-$30,000	1,010	8.92
$30,000-$40,000	1,600	14.13
$40,000-$50,000	1,070	9.45
$50,000 +	1,900	16.78
Total Returns, No.	11,320	
Total Income, $000	342,903	
Total Taxable Returns	8,660	
Total Tax, $000	44,435	
Average Income, $	30,292	
Average Tax, $	5,131	

VITAL STATISTICS

	1997	1996	1995	1994
Births	194	236	218	191
Deaths	39	38	44	36
Natural Increase	155	198	174	255
Marriages	17	9	15	4

Note: Latest available data.

MEDIA INFO
see Québec, CMA

Saint-Romuald
(Ville)
Québec CMA

In census division Les Chutes-de-la-Chaudière.

POPULATION

July 1, 2001 Estimate	11,198
% Cdn. Total	0.04
% Change, '96 -'01	3.67
Avg. Annual Growth Rate, %	0.72
2003 Projected Population	11,437
2006 Projected Population	11,941
2001 Households Estimate	4,898
2003 Projected Households	5,092
2006 Projected Households	5,440

INCOME

% Above/Below National Average	+1
2001 Total Income Estimate	$237,350,000
% Cdn. Total	0.04
2001 Average Hhld. Income	$48,500
2001 Per Capita	$21,200
2003 Projected Total Income	$259,760,000
2006 Projected Total Income	$301,070,000

RETAIL SALES

% Above/Below National Average	+2
2001 Retail Sales Estimate	$102,710,000
% Cdn. Total	0.04
2001 per Household	$21,000
2001 per Capita	$9,200
2001 No. of Establishments	105
2003 Projected Retail Sales	$113,380,000
2006 Projected Retail Sales	$130,510,000

POPULATION

2001 Estimates:

Total		11,198
Male		5,325
Female		5,873

Age Groups	Male	Female
0-4	312	321
5-9	283	319
10-14	275	297
15-19	315	325
20-24	373	376
25-29	416	399
30-34	445	418
35-39	438	447
40-44	430	480
45-49	421	472
50-54	402	448
55-59	333	363
60-64	271	286
65-69	214	253
70+	397	669

DAYTIME POPULATION

2001 Estimates:

Working Population	3,496
At Home Population	5,573
Total	9,069

INCOME

2001 Estimates:

Avg. Household Income	$48,458
Avg. Family Income	$56,364
Per Capita Income	$21,195
Male:	
Avg. Employment Income	$33,456
Avg. Employment Income (Full Time)	$43,453
Female:	
Avg. Employment Income	$22,916
Avg. Employment Income (Full Time)	$31,499

DISPOSABLE & DISCRETIONARY INCOME

2001 Estimates: Per Hhld.

Disposable Income	$33,031
Discretionary Income 1 (minus Food & Shelter)	$20,944
Discretionary Income 2 (minus Food, Shelter, & Other Expenditures)	$13,635

LIQUID ASSETS

1999 Estimates: Per Hhld.

Equity Investments	$62,567
Interest Bearing Investments	$58,233
Total Liquid Assets	$120,800

CREDIT DATA

July 2000:

Pool of Credit	$71,313,358
Revolving Credit, No.	20,936
Fixed Loans, No.	7,720
Avg. Credit Limit, per Person	$8,324
Avg. Spent, per Person	$3,451
Satisfactory Ratings, No. per Person	3.17
Avg. No. of Cards, per Person	1.25

LABOUR FORCE

2001 Estimates:

Male:	
In the Labour Force	3,269
Participation Rate	73.4
Employed	3,118
Unemployed	151
Unemployment Rate	4.6
Not in Labour Force	1,186
Female:	
In the Labour Force	2,695
Participation Rate	54.6
Employed	2,552
Unemployed	143
Unemployment Rate	5.3
Not in Labour Force	2,241

OCCUPATIONS BY MAJOR GROUPS

2001 Estimates:	Male	Female
Management	408	171
Business, Finance & Admin.	333	785
Natural & Applied Sciences & Related	329	91
Health	76	226
Social Sciences, Gov't Services & Religion	120	77
Education	124	216
Arts, Culture, Recreation & Sport	57	n.a.
Sales & Service	704	906
Trades, Transport & Equipment Operators & Related	711	47
Primary Industries	51	n.a.
Processing, Mfg. & Utilities	312	74

LEVEL OF SCHOOLING

2001 Estimates:

Population 15 years +	9,391
Less than Grade 9	1,323
Grades 9-13 w/o Certif.	1,449
Grade 9-13 with Certif.	1,656
Trade Certif. /Dip.	482
Non-Univ. w/o Certif./Dip.	721
Non-Univ. with Certif./Dip.	1,576
Univ. w/o Degree	745
Univ. w/o Degree/Certif.	92
Univ. with Certif.	653
Univ. with Degree	1,439

AVERAGE HOUSEHOLD EXPENDITURES

2001 Estimates:

Food	$6,109
Shelter	$7,815
Clothing	$2,034
Transportation	$5,486
Health & Personal Care	$1,906
Recr'n, Read'g & Education	$3,123
Taxes & Securities	$14,194
Other	$6,943
Total Expenditures	$47,610

PRIVATE HOUSEHOLDS

2001 Estimates:

Private Households, Total	4,898
Pop. in Private Households	10,904
Average no. per Household	2.2

FAMILIES

2001 Estimates:

Families in Private Households	3,314
Husband-Wife Families	2,835
Lone-Parent Families	479
Aver. No. Persons per Family	2.9
Aver. No. Sons/Daughters at Home	1.0

HOUSING

2001 Estimates:

Occupied Private Dwellings	4,898
Owned	2,891
Rented	2,007
Single-Detached House	2,121
Semi-Detached House	370
Row Houses	50
Apartment, 5 or Fewer Storeys	1,921
Apartment, Detached Duplex	263
Movable Dwellings	173

VEHICLES

2001 Estimates:

Model Yrs. '81-'96, No.	5,761
% Total	76.95
Model Yrs. '97-'98, No.	1,070
% Total	14.29
'99 Vehicles registered in Model Yr. '99, No.	656
% Total	8.76
Total No. '81-'99	7,487

LEGAL MARITAL STATUS

2001 Estimates: (Age 15+)

Single (Never Married)	3,916
Legally Married (Not Separated)	3,820
Legally Married (Separated)	233
Widowed	546
Divorced	876

PSYTE CATEGORIES

2001 Estimates	No. of House-holds	% of Total Hhds.	Index
Aging Erudites	432	8.82	585
Participation Quebec	683	13.94	484
New Quebec Rows	321	6.55	598
Quebec Melange	1,529	31.22	1,178
Urban Bohemia	33	0.67	58
Old Quebec Walkups	972	19.84	1,083
Quebec Town Elders	928	18.95	670

FINANCIAL PSYTE

2001 Estimates	No. of House-holds	% of Total Hhds.	Index
Urban Heights	432	8.82	205
Mortgages & Minivans	1,004	20.50	311
Country Credit	1,529	31.22	462
Young Urban Struggle	33	0.67	14
Loan Parent Stress	1,900	38.79	666

Québec

HOME LANGUAGE

2001 Estimates:		% Total
English	59	0.53
French	11,024	98.45
Chinese	22	0.20
Multiple Responses	93	0.83
Total	11,198	100.00

BUILDING PERMITS

	1999	1998 $000	1997
Value	12,159	8,215	7,647

HOMES BUILT

	1999	1998	1997
No.	26	46	107

TAXATION

Income Class:	1997	% Total
Under $5,000	950	11.54
$5,000-$10,000	1,160	14.09
$10,000-$15,000	1,330	16.16
$15,000-$20,000	880	10.69
$20,000-$25,000	700	8.51
$25,000-$30,000	670	8.14
$30,000-$40,000	1,010	12.27
$40,000-$50,000	640	7.78
$50,000 +	880	10.69
Total Returns, No.	8,230	
Total Income, $000	206,732	
Total Taxable Returns	5,750	
Total Tax, $000	23,864	
Average Income, $	25,119	
Average Tax, $	4,150	

VITAL STATISTICS

	1997	1996	1995	1994
Births	88	130	128	137
Deaths	91	90	65	64
Natural Increase	-3	40	63	73
Marriages	19	20	27	16

Note: Latest available data.

MEDIA INFO
see Québec, CMA

Québec

Sainte-Foy
(Ville)
Québec CMA

In census division Communauté urbaine de Québec.

POPULATION

July 1, 2001 Estimate	72,675
% Cdn. Total	0.23
% Change, '96 -'01	-1.24
Avg. Annual Growth Rate, %	-0.25
2003 Projected Population	72,484
2006 Projected Population	72,854
2001 Households Estimate	34,986
2003 Projected Households	35,439
2006 Projected Households	36,223

INCOME

% Above/Below National Average	+16
2001 Total Income Estimate	$1,777,630,000
% Cdn. Total	0.27
2001 Average Hhld. Income	$50,800
2001 Per Capita	$24,500
2003 Projected Total Income	$1,876,320,000
2006 Projected Total Income	$2,048,170,000

RETAIL SALES

% Above/Below National Average	+160
2001 Retail Sales Estimate	$1,688,410,000
% Cdn. Total	0.61
2001 per Household	$48,300
2001 per Capita	$23,200
2001 No. of Establishments	756
2003 Projected Retail Sales	$1,826,820,000
2006 Projected Retail Sales	$2,041,520,000

POPULATION

2001 Estimates:

Total		72,675
Male		33,848
Female		38,827
Age Groups	Male	Female
0-4	1,947	1,886
5-9	1,578	1,591
10-14	1,538	1,507
15-19	1,927	1,965
20-24	2,717	2,963
25-29	2,999	3,067
30-34	2,765	2,609
35-39	2,520	2,492
40-44	2,481	2,767
45-49	2,508	2,989
50-54	2,379	2,928
55-59	2,037	2,599
60-64	1,767	2,293
65-69	1,569	2,112
70+	3,116	5,059

DAYTIME POPULATION

2001 Estimates:

Working Population	33,552
At Home Population	36,989
Total	70,541

INCOME

2001 Estimates:

Avg. Household Income	$50,810
Avg. Family Income	$66,185
Per Capita Income	$24,460
Male:	
Avg. Employment Income	$37,730
Avg. Employment Income (Full Time)	$52,185
Female:	
Avg. Employment Income	$24,131
Avg. Employment Income (Full Time)	$36,700

DISPOSABLE & DISCRETIONARY INCOME

2001 Estimates:	Per Hhld.
Disposable Income	$33,134
Discretionary Income 1 (minus Food & Shelter)	$20,264
Discretionary Income 2 (minus Food, Shelter, & Other Expenditures)	$12,817

LIQUID ASSETS

1999 Estimates:	Per Hhld.
Equity Investments	$55,692
Interest Bearing Investments	$58,025
Total Liquid Assets	$113,717

CREDIT DATA

July 2000:

Pool of Credit	$560,122,692
Revolving Credit, No.	161,082
Fixed Loans, No.	45,248
Avg. Credit Limit, per Person	$8,511
Avg. Spent, per Person	$3,237
Satisfactory Ratings, No. per Person	2.98
Avg. No. of Cards, per Person	1.23

LABOUR FORCE

2001 Estimates:

Male:

In the Labour Force	20,421
Participation Rate	70.9
Employed	18,972
Unemployed	1,449
Unemployment Rate	7.1
Not in Labour Force	8,364

Female:

In the Labour Force	18,781
Participation Rate	55.5
Employed	17,284
Unemployed	1,497
Unemployment Rate	8.0
Not in Labour Force	15,062

OCCUPATIONS BY MAJOR GROUPS

2001 Estimates:	Male	Female
Management	2,838	1,248
Business, Finance & Admin.	2,457	5,571
Natural & Applied Sciences & Related	2,660	618
Health	853	1,959
Social Sciences, Gov't Services & Religion	895	776
Education	1,335	1,486
Arts, Culture, Recreation & Sport	674	725
Sales & Service	4,783	5,154
Trades, Transport & Equipment Operators & Related	2,344	189
Primary Industries	307	69
Processing, Mfg. & Utilities	512	153

LEVEL OF SCHOOLING

2001 Estimates:

Population 15 years +	62,628
Less than Grade 9	4,097
Grades 9-13 w/o Certif.	6,607
Grade 9-13 with Certif.	9,610
Trade Certif./Dip.	2,327
Non-Univ. w/o Certif./Dip.	4,542
Non-Univ. with Certif./Dip.	10,700
Univ. w/o Degree	7,791
Univ. w/o Degree/Certif.	918
Univ. with Certif.	6,873
Univ. with Degree	16,954

AVERAGE HOUSEHOLD EXPENDITURES

2001 Estimates:

Food	$6,168
Shelter	$8,877
Clothing	$2,167
Transportation	$5,452
Health & Personal Care	$1,962
Recr'n, Read'g & Education	$3,329
Taxes & Securities	$14,165
Other	$7,381
Total Expenditures	$49,501

PRIVATE HOUSEHOLDS

2001 Estimates:

Private Households, Total	34,986
Pop. in Private Households	71,701
Average no. per Household	2.0

FAMILIES

2001 Estimates:

Families in Private Households	20,404
Husband-Wife Families	17,008
Lone-Parent Families	3,396
Aver. No. Persons per Family	2.8
Aver. No. Sons/Daughters at Home	1.0

HOUSING

2001 Estimates:

Occupied Private Dwellings	34,986
Owned	17,050
Rented	17,936
Single-Detached House	11,354
Semi-Detached House	1,697
Row Houses	1,018
Apartment, 5+ Storeys	4,606
Owned Apartment, 5+ Storeys	740
Apartment, 5 or Fewer Storeys	14,983
Apartment, Detached Duplex	961
Other Single-Attached	42
Movable Dwellings	325

VEHICLES

2001 Estimates:

Model Yrs. '81-'96, No.	32,449
% Total	70.42
Model Yrs. '97-'98, No.	8,384
% Total	18.19
'99 Vehicles registered in Model Yr. '99, No.	5,249
% Total	11.39
Total No. '81-'99	46,082

LEGAL MARITAL STATUS

2001 Estimates: (Age 15+)

Single (Never Married)	26,576
Legally Married (Not Separated)	24,571
Legally Married (Separated)	1,716
Widowed	3,945
Divorced	5,820

PSYTE CATEGORIES

2001 Estimates	No. of House-holds	% of Total Hhds.	Index
Urban Gentry	3,415	9.76	543
Technocrafts & Bureaucrats	491	1.40	50
Stable Suburban Families	1,158	3.31	254
Brie & Chablis	761	2.18	243
Aging Erudites	333	0.95	63
Participation Quebec	3,167	9.05	314
New Quebec Rows	3,863	11.04	1,008
Quebec Melange	3,879	11.09	418
Traditional French Cdn. Families	729	2.08	78
High Rise Sunsets	343	0.98	69
Young Urban Professionals	1,507	4.31	227
Young Urban Intelligentsia	2,600	7.43	488
University Enclaves	926	2.65	130
Young City Singles	1,386	3.96	173
Urban Bohemia	3,764	10.76	919
Old Quebec Walkups	3,124	8.93	487
Aging Quebec Urbanites	2,634	7.53	2,609
Quebec's New Urban Mosaic	397	1.13	47
Aged Pensioners	306	0.87	66
Old Grey Towers	122	0.35	63

FINANCIAL P$YTE

2001 Estimates	No. of House-holds	% of Total Hhds.	Index
Four Star Investors	3,415	9.76	194
Successful Suburbanites	1,649	4.71	71
Urban Heights	2,601	7.43	173
Mortgages & Minivans	7,030	20.09	304
Country Credit	4,608	13.17	195
Revolving Renters	343	0.98	21
Young Urban Struggle	7,290	20.84	440
Loan Parent Stress	5,758	16.46	283
Towering Debt	1,386	3.96	51
NSF	397	1.13	32
Senior Survivors	428	1.22	65

HOME LANGUAGE

2001 Estimates:		% Total
English	1,349	1.86
French	68,438	94.17
Arabic	228	0.31
Chinese	268	0.37
Croatian	55	0.08
Czech	40	0.06
German	40	0.06
Khmer (Cambodian)	60	0.08
Persian (Farsi)	187	0.26
Polish	165	0.23
Portuguese	71	0.10
Romanian	91	0.13
Serbo-Croatian	393	0.54
Spanish	106	0.15
Vietnamese	80	0.11
Other Languages	286	0.39
Multiple Responses	818	1.13
Total	72,675	100.00

BUILDING PERMITS

	1999	1998	1997
		$000	
Value	91,730	53,236	63,123

Sainte-Foy
(Ville)
Québec CMA
(Cont'd)

HOMES BUILT

	1999	1998	1997
No.	226	154	282

TAXATION

Income Class:	1997	% Total
Under $5,000	6,440	11.61
$5,000-$10,000	7,020	12.66
$10,000-$15,000	7,480	13.48
$15,000-$20,000	5,000	9.01
$20,000-$25,000	4,280	7.72
$25,000-$30,000	4,250	7.66
$30,000-$40,000	6,680	12.04
$40,000-$50,000	4,710	8.49
$50,000 +	9,610	17.32
Total Returns, No.	55,470	
Total Income, $000	1,682,344	
Total Taxable		
Returns	39,980	
Total Tax, $000	222,913	
Average Income, $	30,329	
Average Tax, $	5,576	

VITAL STATISTICS

	1997	1996	1995	1994
Births	577	617	666	678
Deaths	480	475	469	429
Natural				
Increase	97	142	197	249
Marriages	42	59	65	89

Note: Latest available data.

MEDIA INFO
see Québec, CMA

Sillery
(Ville)
Québec CMA

In census division Communauté urbaine de Québec.

POPULATION

July 1, 2001 Estimate	11,502
% Cdn. Total	0.04
% Change, '96 -'01	-5.81
Avg. Annual Growth Rate, %	-1.19
2003 Projected Population	11,213
2006 Projected Population	10,881
2001 Households Estimate	4,833
2003 Projected Households	4,778
2006 Projected Households	4,708

INCOME

% Above/Below National Average	+76
2001 Total Income Estimate	$425,720,000
% Cdn. Total	0.06
2001 Average Hhld. Income	$88,100
2001 Per Capita	$37,000
2003 Projected Total Income	$441,510,000
2006 Projected Total Income	$469,360,000

RETAIL SALES

% Above/Below National Average	-10
2001 Retail Sales Estimate	$92,750,000
% Cdn. Total	0.03
2001 per Household	$19,200
2001 per Capita	$8,100
2001 No. of Establishments	123
2003 Projected Retail Sales	$95,930,000
2006 Projected Retail Sales	$100,520,000

POPULATION

2001 Estimates:

Total	11,502
Male	5,286
Female	6,216

Age Groups	Male	Female
0-4	220	198
5-9	223	204
10-14	267	254
15-19	343	323
20-24	399	356
25-29	389	310
30-34	327	268
35-39	305	311
40-44	362	433
45-49	422	518
50-54	448	503
55-59	378	414
60-64	291	361
65-69	245	360
70+	667	1,403

DAYTIME POPULATION

2001 Estimates:

Working Population	7,145
At Home Population	5,925
Total	13,070

INCOME

2001 Estimates:

Avg. Household Income	$88,085
Avg. Family Income	$112,276
Per Capita Income	$37,012
Male:	
Avg. Employment Income	$58,733
Avg. Employment Income	
(Full Time)	$75,399
Female:	
Avg. Employment Income	$32,877
Avg. Employment Income	
(Full Time)	$51,987

DISPOSABLE & DISCRETIONARY INCOME

2001 Estimates:	*Per Hhld.*
Disposable Income	$51,809
Discretionary Income 1	
(minus Food & Shelter)	$33,134
Discretionary Income 2	
(minus Food, Shelter, & Other	
Expenditures)	$21,878

LIQUID ASSETS

1999 Estimates:	*Per Hhld.*
Equity Investments	$180,873
Interest Bearing Investments	$118,062
Total Liquid Assets	$298,935

CREDIT DATA

July 2000:

Pool of Credit	$109,576,252
Revolving Credit, No.	26,501
Fixed Loans, No.	5,498
Avg. Credit Limit, per Person	$9,883
Avg. Spent, per Person	$3,440
Satisfactory Ratings,	
No. per Person	2.78
Avg. No. of Cards, per Person	1.24

LABOUR FORCE

2001 Estimates:

Male:	
In the Labour Force	3,091
Participation Rate	67.5
Employed	2,979
Unemployed	112
Unemployment Rate	3.6
Not in Labour Force	1,485
Female:	
In the Labour Force	2,891
Participation Rate	52.0
Employed	2,729
Unemployed	162
Unemployment Rate	5.6
Not in Labour Force	2,669

OCCUPATIONS BY MAJOR GROUPS

2001 Estimates:	*Male*	*Female*
Management	575	216
Business, Finance		
& Admin.	292	785
Natural & Applied		
Sciences & Related	349	54
Health	296	434
Social Sciences,		
Gov't Services & Religion	327	225
Education	315	399
Arts, Culture,		
Recreation & Sport	116	216
Sales & Service	561	449
Trades, Transport		
& Equipment		
Operators & Related	145	10
Primary Industries	21	10
Processing, Mfg. &		
Utilities	20	20

LEVEL OF SCHOOLING

2001 Estimates:

Population 15 years +	10,136
Less than Grade 9	649
Grades 9-13 w/o Certif.	924
Grade 9-13 with Certif.	1,263
Trade Certif. /Dip.	205
Non-Univ. w/o Certif./Dip.	445
Non-Univ. with Certif./Dip.	1,135
Univ. w/o Degree	1,180
Univ. w/o Degree/Certif.	178
Univ. with Certif.	1,002
Univ. with Degree	4,335

AVERAGE HOUSEHOLD EXPENDITURES

2001 Estimates:

Food	$8,347
Shelter	$13,945
Clothing	$3,238
Transportation	$8,428
Health & Personal Care	$2,867
Recr'n, Read'g & Education	$6,193
Taxes & Securities	$24,624
Other	$12,065
Total Expenditures	$79,707

Québec

PRIVATE HOUSEHOLDS

2001 Estimates:

Private Households, Total	4,833
Pop. in Private Households	10,388
Average no. per Household	2.1

FAMILIES

2001 Estimates:

Families in Private Households	3,207
Husband-Wife Families	2,736
Lone-Parent Families	471
Aver. No. Persons per Family	2.8
Aver. No. Sons/Daughters	
at Home	1.0

HOUSING

2001 Estimates:

Occupied Private Dwellings	4,833
Owned	3,281
Rented	1,552
Single-Detached House	2,630
Semi-Detached House	211
Row Houses	222
Apartment, 5+ Storeys	598
Owned Apartment, 5+ Storeys	209
Apartment, 5 or Fewer Storeys	808
Apartment, Detached Duplex	300
Other Single-Attached	48
Movable Dwellings	16

VEHICLES

2001 Estimates:

Model Yrs. '81-'96, No.	5,063
% Total	72.80
Model Yrs. '97-'98, No.	1,197
% Total	17.21
'99 Vehicles registered in	
Model Yr. '99, No.	695
% Total	9.99
Total No. '81-'99	6,955

LEGAL MARITAL STATUS

2001 Estimates: (Age 15+)

Single (Never Married)	4,282
Legally Married	
(Not Separated)	4,070
Legally Married (Separated)	239
Widowed	816
Divorced	729

PSYTE CATEGORIES

2001 Estimates	*No. of House-holds*	*% of Total Hhds.*	*Index*
Urban Gentry	2,839	58.74	3,269
High Rise Sunsets	318	6.58	460
Young Urban Professionals	1,282	26.53	1,398
Aging Quebec Urbanites	75	1.55	538
Quebec's New Urban Mosaic	116	2.40	100

Québec

Sillery
(Ville)
Québec CMA
(Cont'd)

FINANCIAL P$YTE

2001 Estimates	No. of House-holds	% of Total Hhds.	Index
Four Star Investors	2,839	58.74	1,169
Urban Heights	1,282	26.53	617
Revolving Renters	318	6.58	143
Loan Parent Stress	75	1.55	27
NSF	116	2.40	68

HOME LANGUAGE

2001 Estimates:		% Total
English	591	5.14
French	10,560	91.81
Arabic	15	0.13
Bulgarian	20	0.17
Chinese	30	0.26
Dutch	10	0.09
Khmer (Cambodian)	10	0.09
Polish	25	0.22
Spanish	40	0.35
Multiple Responses	201	1.75
Total	11,502	100.00

BUILDING PERMITS

	1999	1998 $000	1997
Value	8,410	11,872	8,734

HOMES BUILT

	1999	1998	1997
No.	5	12	16

TAXATION

Income Class:	1997	% Total
Under $5,000	880	9.99
$5,000-$10,000	870	9.88
$10,000-$15,000	1,260	14.30
$15,000-$20,000	660	7.49
$20,000-$25,000	520	5.90
$25,000-$30,000	540	6.13
$30,000-$40,000	810	9.19
$40,000-$50,000	610	6.92
$50,000 +	2,650	30.08
Total Returns, No.	8,810	
Total Income, $000	402,852	
Total Taxable Returns	6,390	
Total Tax, $000	67,814	
Average Income, $	45,727	
Average Tax, $	10,613	

VITAL STATISTICS

	1997	1996	1995	1994
Births	56	66	90	77
Deaths	129	138	161	139
Natural Increase	-73	-72	-71	-62
Marriages	43	43	48	38

Note: Latest available data.

MEDIA INFO
see Québec, CMA

Val-Bélair
(Ville)
Québec CMA

In census division Communauté urbaine de Québec.

POPULATION

July 1, 2001 Estimate	22,942
% Cdn. Total	0.07
% Change, '96 -'01	11.77
Avg. Annual Growth Rate, %	2.25
2003 Projected Population	24,425
2006 Projected Population	26,858
2001 Households Estimate	8,385
2003 Projected Households	9,059
2006 Projected Households	10,118

INCOME

% Above/Below National Average	-13
2001 Total Income Estimate	$421,780,000
% Cdn. Total	0.06
2001 Average Hhld. Income	$50,300
2001 Per Capita	$18,400
2003 Projected Total Income	$482,040,000
2006 Projected Total Income	$588,270,000

RETAIL SALES

% Above/Below National Average	-40
2001 Retail Sales Estimate	$122,270,000
% Cdn. Total	0.04
2001 per Household	$14,600
2001 per Capita	$5,300
2001 No. of Establishments	111
2003 Projected Retail Sales	$139,030,000
2006 Projected Retail Sales	$166,340,000

POPULATION

2001 Estimates:		
Total		22,942
Male		11,528
Female		11,414
Age Groups	Male	Female
0-4	886	833
5-9	946	853
10-14	896	847
15-19	845	811
20-24	809	773
25-29	870	867
30-34	1,056	1,077
35-39	1,156	1,160
40-44	1,052	1,043
45-49	905	904
50-54	731	724
55-59	523	503
60-64	347	347
65-69	219	246
70+	287	426

DAYTIME POPULATION

2001 Estimates:	
Working Population	n.a.
At Home Population	11,213
Total	11,213

INCOME

2001 Estimates:	
Avg. Household Income	$50,302
Avg. Family Income	$53,337
Per Capita Income	$18,385
Male:	
Avg. Employment Income	$33,015
Avg. Employment Income (Full Time)	$41,161
Female:	
Avg. Employment Income	$19,414
Avg. Employment Income (Full Time)	$28,299

DISPOSABLE & DISCRETIONARY INCOME

2001 Estimates:	Per Hhld.
Disposable Income	$35,815
Discretionary Income 1 (minus Food & Shelter)	$23,694
Discretionary Income 2 (minus Food, Shelter, & Other Expenditures)	$15,579

LIQUID ASSETS

1999 Estimates:	Per Hhld.
Equity Investments	$46,114
Interest Bearing Investments	$54,056
Total Liquid Assets	$100,170

CREDIT DATA

July 2000:	
Pool of Credit	$134,220,789
Revolving Credit, No.	37,837
Fixed Loans, No.	18,501
Avg. Credit Limit, per Person	$8,947
Avg. Spent, per Person	$4,327
Satisfactory Ratings, No. per Person	3.48
Avg. No. of Cards, per Person	1.31

LABOUR FORCE

2001 Estimates:	
Male:	
In the Labour Force	7,074
Participation Rate	80.4
Employed	6,693
Unemployed	381
Unemployment Rate	5.4
Not in Labour Force	1,726
Female:	
In the Labour Force	5,446
Participation Rate	61.3
Employed	4,935
Unemployed	511
Unemployment Rate	9.4
Not in Labour Force	3,435

OCCUPATIONS BY MAJOR GROUPS

2001 Estimates:	Male	Female
Management	704	267
Business, Finance & Admin.	648	1,943
Natural & Applied Sciences & Related	575	92
Health	135	287
Social Sciences, Gov't Services & Religion	85	108
Education	140	141
Arts, Culture, Recreation & Sport	70	147
Sales & Service	2,170	1,835
Trades, Transport & Equipment Operators & Related	1,949	183
Primary Industries	58	n.a.
Processing, Mfg. & Utilities	371	220

LEVEL OF SCHOOLING

2001 Estimates:	
Population 15 years +	17,681
Less than Grade 9	2,160
Grades 9-13 w/o Certif.	3,121
Grade 9-13 with Certif.	4,363
Trade Certif. /Dip.	1,080
Non-Univ. w/o Certif./Dip.	1,340
Non-Univ. with Certif./Dip.	3,444
Univ. w/o Degree	1,059
Univ. w/o Degree/Certif.	200
Univ. with Certif.	859
Univ. with Degree	1,114

AVERAGE HOUSEHOLD EXPENDITURES

2001 Estimates:	
Food	$6,452
Shelter	$7,460
Clothing	$2,236
Transportation	$6,419
Health & Personal Care	$1,934
Recr'n, Read'g & Education	$3,277
Taxes & Securities	$14,427
Other	$7,263
Total Expenditures	$49,468

PRIVATE HOUSEHOLDS

2001 Estimates:	
Private Households, Total	8,385
Pop. in Private Households	22,736
Average no. per Household	2.7

FAMILIES

2001 Estimates:	
Families in Private Households	6,938
Husband-Wife Families	6,014
Lone-Parent Families	924
Aver. No. Persons per Family	3.1
Aver. No. Sons/Daughters at Home	1.3

HOUSING

2001 Estimates:	
Occupied Private Dwellings	8,385
Owned	6,168
Rented	2,217
Single-Detached House	5,425
Semi-Detached House	575
Row Houses	318
Apartment, 5 or Fewer Storeys	1,707
Apartment, Detached Duplex	343
Other Single-Attached	17

VEHICLES

2001 Estimates:	
Model Yrs. '81-'96, No.	9,610
% Total	79.52
Model Yrs. '97-'98, No.	1,573
% Total	13.02
'99 Vehicles registered in Model Yr. '99, No.	902
% Total	7.46
Total No. '81-'99	12,085

LEGAL MARITAL STATUS

2001 Estimates: (Age 15+)	
Single (Never Married)	7,179
Legally Married (Not Separated)	8,073
Legally Married (Separated)	416
Widowed	587
Divorced	1,426

PSYTE CATEGORIES

2001 Estimates	No. of House-holds	% of Total Hhds.	Index
Participation Quebec	2,366	28.22	979
New Quebec Rows	522	6.23	568
Quebec Melange	2,261	26.96	1,018
Traditional French Cdn. Families	2,883	34.38	1,280
Quebec's New Urban Mosaic	353	4.21	175

FINANCIAL P$YTE

2001 Estimates	No. of House-holds	% of Total Hhds.	Index
Mortgages & Minivans	2,888	34.44	522
Country Credit	5,144	61.35	907
NSF	353	4.21	119

Val-Bélair
(Ville)
Québec CMA
(Cont'd)

HOME LANGUAGE

2001 Estimates:		% Total
English	297	1.29
French	22,388	97.59
German	22	0.10
Other Languages	22	0.10
Multiple Responses	213	0.93
Total	22,942	100.00

BUILDING PERMITS

	1999	1998	1997
		$000	
Value	8,933	12,442	16,793

HOMES BUILT

	1999	1998	1997
No	57	93	105

TAXATION

Income Class:	1997	% Total
Under $5,000	2,110	14.69
$5,000-$10,000	1,770	12.33
$10,000-$15,000	1,800	12.53
$15,000-$20,000	1,400	9.75
$20,000-$25,000	1,200	8.36
$25,000-$30,000	1,310	9.12
$30,000-$40,000	2,410	16.78
$40,000-$50,000	1,400	9.75
$50,000 +	950	6.62
Total Returns, No.	14,360	
Total Income, $000	332,435	
Total Taxable Returns	10,320	
Total Tax, $000	36,273	
Average Income, $	23,150	
Average Tax, $	3,515	

VITAL STATISTICS

	1997	1996	1995	1994
Births	336	357	380	353
Deaths	62	74	80	55
Natural Increase	274	283	300	298
Marriages	27	18	16	18

Note: Latest available data.

MEDIA INFO
see Québec, CMA

Vanier
(Ville)
Québec CMA

In census division Communauté urbaine de Québec.

POPULATION

July 1, 2001 Estimate	11,352
% Cdn. Total	0.04
% Change, '96 -'01	-0.16
Avg. Annual Growth Rate, %	-0.03
2003 Projected Population	11,391
2006 Projected Population	11,555
2001 Households Estimate	5,566
2003 Projected Households	5,665
2006 Projected Households	5,835

INCOME

% Above/Below National Average	-28
2001 Total Income Estimate	$172,340,000
% Cdn. Total	0.03
2001 Average Hhld. Income	$31,000
2001 Per Capita	$15,200
2003 Projected Total Income	$182,950,000
2006 Projected Total Income	$201,500,000

RETAIL SALES

% Above/Below National Average	+251
2001 Retail Sales Estimate	$356,500,000
% Cdn. Total	0.13
2001 per Household	$64,100
2001 per Capita	$31,400
2001 No. of Establishments	160
2003 Projected Retail Sales	$391,630,000
2006 Projected Retail Sales	$446,550,000

POPULATION

2001 Estimates:		
Total		11,352
Male		5,400
Female		5,952

Age Groups	Male	Female
0-4	300	290
5-9	287	261
10-14	293	255
15-19	308	276
20-24	347	325
25-29	396	387
30-34	448	425
35-39	454	446
40-44	432	433
45-49	399	432
50-54	377	425
55-59	333	396
60-64	280	349
65-69	249	330
70+	497	922

DAYTIME POPULATION

2001 Estimates:	
Working Population	7,335
At Home Population	6,791
Total	14,126

INCOME

2001 Estimates:	
Avg. Household Income	$30,964
Avg. Family Income	$37,343
Per Capita Income	$15,182
Male:	
Avg. Employment Income	$26,195
Avg. Employment Income (Full Time)	$32,932
Female:	
Avg. Employment Income	$17,774
Avg. Employment Income (Full Time)	$24,235

DISPOSABLE & DISCRETIONARY INCOME

2001 Estimates:	Per Hhld.
Disposable Income	$22,845
Discretionary Income 1 (minus Food & Shelter)	$13,402
Discretionary Income 2 (minus Food, Shelter, & Other Expenditures)	$8,537

LIQUID ASSETS

1999 Estimates:	Per Hhld.
Equity Investments	$24,963
Interest Bearing Investments	$34,234
Total Liquid Assets	$59,197

CREDIT DATA

July 2000:	
Pool of Credit	$53,474,821
Revolving Credit, No.	19,279
Fixed Loans, No.	7,928
Avg. Credit Limit, per Person	$5,819
Avg. Spent, per Person	$2,643
Satisfactory Ratings, No. per Person	2.73
Avg. No. of Cards, per Person	0.92

LABOUR FORCE

2001 Estimates:	
Male:	
In the Labour Force	3,023
Participation Rate	66.9
Employed	2,657
Unemployed	366
Unemployment Rate	12.1
Not in Labour Force	1,497
Female:	
In the Labour Force	2,266
Participation Rate	44.0
Employed	2,025
Unemployed	241
Unemployment Rate	10.6
Not in Labour Force	2,880

OCCUPATIONS BY MAJOR GROUPS

2001 Estimates:	Male	Female
Management	176	49
Business, Finance & Admin.	302	729
Natural & Applied Sciences & Related	189	14
Health	49	182
Social Sciences, Gov't Services & Religion	22	30
Education	21	n.a.
Arts, Culture, Recreation & Sport	96	44
Sales & Service	868	878
Trades, Transport & Equipment Operators & Related	798	69
Primary Industries	31	n.a.
Processing, Mfg. & Utilities	263	98

LEVEL OF SCHOOLING

2001 Estimates:	
Population 15 years +	9,666
Less than Grade 9	2,814
Grades 9-13 w/o Certif.	1,981
Grade 9-13 with Certif.	1,610
Trade Certif. /Dip.	507
Non-Univ. w/o Certif./Dip.	679
Non-Univ. with Certif./Dip.	1,400
Univ. w/o Degree	326
Univ. w/o Degree/Certif.	62
Univ. with Certif.	264
Univ. with Degree	349

AVERAGE HOUSEHOLD EXPENDITURES

2001 Estimates:	
Food	$4,562
Shelter	$6,364
Clothing	$1,514
Transportation	$3,246
Health & Personal Care	$1,407
Recr'n, Read'g & Education	$2,113
Taxes & Securities	$7,481
Other	$5,858
Total Expenditures	$32,545

Québec

PRIVATE HOUSEHOLDS

2001 Estimates:	
Private Households, Total	5,566
Pop. in Private Households	11,089
Average no. per Household	2.0

FAMILIES

2001 Estimates:	
Families in Private Households	3,216
Husband-Wife Families	2,569
Lone-Parent Families	647
Aver. No. Persons per Family	2.7
Aver. No. Sons/Daughters at Home	0.9

HOUSING

2001 Estimates:	
Occupied Private Dwellings	5,566
Owned	1,464
Rented	4,102
Single-Detached House	487
Semi-Detached House	184
Row Houses	182
Apartment, 5+ Storeys	145
Apartment, 5 or Fewer Storeys	3,867
Apartment, Detached Duplex	669
Other Single-Attached	32

VEHICLES

2001 Estimates:	
Model Yrs. '81-'96, No.	4,955
% Total	63.64
Model Yrs. '97-'98, No.	1,721
% Total	22.10
'99 Vehicles registered in Model Yr. '99, No.	1,110
% Total	14.26
Total No. '81-'99	7,786

LEGAL MARITAL STATUS

2001 Estimates: (Age 15+)	
Single (Never Married)	3,926
Legally Married (Not Separated)	3,473
Legally Married (Separated)	297
Widowed	1,011
Divorced	959

PSYTE CATEGORIES

2001 Estimates	No. of House -holds	% of Total Hhds.	Index
New Quebec Rows	241	4.33	395
Quebec Melange	375	6.74	254
Old Quebec Walkups	481	8.64	472
Quebec Town Elders	59	1.06	38
Quebec's New Urban Mosaic	3,246	58.32	2,421
Aged Pensioners	1,155	20.75	1,560

Rimouski
(Census Agglomeration)

The Census Agglomeration of Rimouski includes: Rimouski, V; Le Bic, M; Pointe-au-Père, V; Rimouski-Est, VL: Saint-Anaclet-de-Lessard, P; plus several smaller areas. All are in census division Rimouski-Neigette.

Québec

Vanier
(Ville)
Québec CMA
(Cont'd)

FINANÇIAL P$YTE

2001 Estimates	No. of House-holds	% of Total Hhds.	Index
Mortgages & Minivans	241	4.33	66
Country Credit	375	6.74	100
Loan Parent Stress	540	9.70	167
NSF	3,246	58.32	1,648
Senior Survivors	1,155	20.75	1,101

HOME LANGUAGE

2001 Estimates		% Total
English	52	0.46
French	10,924	96.23
Chinese	26	0.23
Czech	27	0.24
Khmer (Cambodian)	10	0.09
Kurdish	20	0.18
Polish	10	0.09
Romanian	15	0.13
Serbo-Croatian	61	0.54
Spanish	41	0.36
Other Languages	88	0.78
Multiple Responses	78	0.69
Total	11,352	100.00

BUILDING PERMITS

	1999	1998 $000	1997
Value	10,044	7,119	7,642

TAXATION

Income Class:	1997	% Total
Under $5,000	1,060	12.82
$5,000-$10,000	1,550	18.74
$10,000-$15,000	1,780	21.52
$15,000-$20,000	1,030	12.45
$20,000-$25,000	760	9.19
$25,000-$30,000	690	8.34
$30,000-$40,000	770	9.31
$40,000-$50,000	390	4.72
$50,000 +	250	3.02
Total Returns, No.	8,270	
Total Income, $000	149,430	
Total Taxable Returns	4,970	
Total Tax, $000	12,915	
Average Income, $	18,069	
Average Tax, $	2,599	

VITAL STATISTICS

	1997	1996	1995	1994
Births	108	96	109	144
Deaths	159	97	92	123
Natural Increase	-51	-1	17	21
Marriages	15	10	17	15

Note: Latest available data.

MEDIA INFO
see Québec, CMA

POPULATION

July 1, 2001 Estimate	48,945
% Cdn. Total	0.16
% Change, '96 -'01	0.13
Avg. Annual Growth Rate, %	0.03
2003 Projected Population	49,356
2006 Projected Population	49,608
2001 Households Estimate	21,041
2003 Projected Households	21,551
2006 Projected Households	22,098

INCOME

% Above/Below National Average	-2
2001 Total Income Estimate	$1,010,690,000
% Cdn. Total	0.15
2001 Average Hhld. Income	$48,000
2001 Per Capita	$20,600
2003 Projected Total Income	$1,087,460,000
2006 Projected Total Income	$1,200,350,000

RETAIL SALES

% Above/Below National Average	+14
2001 Retail Sales Estimate	$500,710,000
% Cdn. Total	0.18
2001 per Household	$23,800
2001 per Capita	$10,200
2001 No. of Establishments	528
2003 Projected Retail Sales	$542,430,000
2006 Projected Retail Sales	$599,160,000

POPULATION

2001 Estimates:

Total		48,945
Male		23,456
Female		25,489

Age Groups	Male	Female
0-4	1,311	1,284
5-9	1,335	1,305
10-14	1,476	1,442
15-19	1,745	1,709
20-24	1,798	1,768
25-29	1,597	1,564
30-34	1,548	1,602
35-39	1,819	1,974
40-44	2,103	2,259
45-49	2,096	2,208
50-54	1,819	1,899
55-59	1,374	1,451
60-64	994	1,143
65-69	798	1,024
70+	1,643	2,857

DAYTIME POPULATION

2001 Estimates:

Working Population	23,297
At Home Population	25,647
Total	48,944

INCOME

2001 Estimates:

Avg. Household Income	$48,034
Avg. Family Income	$57,110
Per Capita Income	$20,649
Male:	
Avg. Employment Income	$33,425
Avg. Employment Income (Full Time)	$45,728
Female:	
Avg. Employment Income	$22,061
Avg. Employment Income (Full Time)	$33,194

DISPOSABLE & DISCRETIONARY INCOME

2001 Estimates:	Per Hhld.
Disposable Income	$32,966
Discretionary Income 1 (minus Food & Shelter)	$20,899
Discretionary Income 2 (minus Food, Shelter, & Other Expenditures)	$13,364

LIQUID ASSETS

1999 Estimates:	Per Hhld.
Equity Investments	$53,312
Interest Bearing Investments	$54,891
Total Liquid Assets	$108,203

CREDIT DATA

July 2000:

Pool of Credit	$254,942,389
Revolving Credit, No.	82,981
Fixed Loans, No.	32,780
Avg. Credit Limit, per Person	$7,096
Avg. Spent, per Person	$3,129
Satisfactory Ratings, No. per Person	3.06
Avg. No. of Cards, per Person	1.21

LABOUR FORCE

2001 Estimates:

Male:	
In the Labour Force	13,596
Participation Rate	70.3
Employed	12,119
Unemployed	1,477
Unemployment Rate	10.9
Not in Labour Force	5,738
Female:	
In the Labour Force	12,128
Participation Rate	56.5
Employed	11,269
Unemployed	859
Unemployment Rate	7.1
Not in Labour Force	9,330

OCCUPATIONS BY MAJOR GROUPS

2001 Estimates:	Male	Female
Management	1,696	590
Business, Finance & Admin.	1,342	3,750
Natural & Applied Sciences & Related	1,344	206
Health	432	1,473
Social Sciences, Gov't Services & Religion	368	428
Education	663	858
Arts, Culture, Recreation & Sport	372	200
Sales & Service	2,821	3,826
Trades, Transport & Equipment Operators & Related	2,948	117
Primary Industries	574	113
Processing, Mfg. & Utilities	400	69

INCOME

2001 Estimates:

(See INCOME above.)

LEVEL OF SCHOOLING

2001 Estimates:

Population 15 years +	40,792
Less than Grade 9	5,950
Grades 9-13 w/o Certif.	5,933
Grade 9-13 with Certif.	6,999
Trade Certif. /Dip.	2,073
Non-Univ. w/o Certif./Dip.	3,426
Non-Univ. with Certif./Dip.	7,253
Univ. w/o Degree	3,789
Univ. w/o Degree/Certif.	432
Univ. with Certif.	3,357
Univ. with Degree	5,369

AVERAGE HOUSEHOLD EXPENDITURES

2001 Estimates:

Food	$6,317
Shelter	$7,456
Clothing	$2,085
Transportation	$5,770
Health & Personal Care	$1,894
Recr'n, Read'g & Education	$3,118
Taxes & Securities	$13,502
Other	$7,146
Total Expenditures	$47,288

PRIVATE HOUSEHOLDS

2001 Estimates:

Private Households, Total	21,041
Pop. in Private Households	47,492
Average no. per Household	2.3

FAMILIES

2001 Estimates:

Families in Private Households	14,736
Husband-Wife Families	12,402
Lone-Parent Families	2,334
Aver. No. Persons per Family	2.9
Aver. No. Sons/Daughters at Home	1.1

HOUSING

2001 Estimates:

Occupied Private Dwellings	21,041
Owned	13,088
Rented	7,953
Single-Detached House	11,290
Semi-Detached House	1,284
Row Houses	337
Apartment, 5+ Storeys	521
Owned Apartment, 5+ Storeys	12
Apartment, 5 or Fewer Storeys	5,847
Apartment, Detached Duplex	1,522
Other Single-Attached	55
Movable Dwellings	185

VEHICLES

2001 Estimates:

Model Yrs. '81-'96, No.	24,745
% Total	80.71
Model Yrs. '97-'98, No.	3,469
% Total	11.31
'99 Vehicles registered in Model Yr. '99, No.	2,445
% Total	7.97
Total No. '81-'99	30,659

LEGAL MARITAL STATUS

2001 Estimates: (Age 15+)

Single (Never Married)	17,348
Legally Married (Not Separated)	16,809
Legally Married (Separated)	838
Widowed	2,381
Divorced	3,416

Rimouski
(Census Agglomeration)
(Cont'd)
PSYTE CATEGORIES

2001 Estimates	No. of House -holds	% of Total Hhds.	Index
Participation Quebec	3,909	18.58	645
New Quebec Rows	154	0.73	67
Quebec Melange	4,777	22.70	857
Traditional French Cdn. Families	4,679	22.24	828
Quebec Rural Blues	357	1.70	70
Old Quebec Walkups	215	1.02	56
Quebec Town Elders	4,761	22.63	801
Quebec's New Urban Mosaic	1,020	4.85	201
Aged Pensioners	926	4.40	331

FINANCIAL P$YTE

2001 Estimates	No. of House -holds	% of Total Hhds.	Index
Mortgages & Minivans	4,063	19.31	293
Country Credit	9,456	44.94	665
Rural Family Blues	357	1.70	21
Loan Parent Stress	4,976	23.65	406
NSF	1,020	4.85	137
Senior Survivors	926	4.40	234

HOME LANGUAGE

2001 Estimates:		% Total
English	239	0.49
French	48,536	99.16
Other Languages	43	0.09
Multiple Responses	127	0.26
Total	48,945	100.00

BUILDING PERMITS

	1999	1998 $000	1997
Value	41,354	33,900	36,136

HOMES BUILT

	1999	1998	1997
No.	109	233	274

TAXATION

Income Class:	1997	% Total
Under $5,000	4,640	12.92
$5,000-$10,000	5,160	14.37
$10,000-$15,000	6,190	17.24
$15,000-$20,000	3,580	9.97
$20,000-$25,000	2,940	8.19
$25,000-$30,000	3,030	8.44
$30,000-$40,000	4,290	11.95
$40,000-$50,000	2,620	7.30
$50,000 +	3,490	9.72
Total Returns, No.	35,900	
Total Income, $000	867,327	
Total Taxable Returns	23,810	
Total Tax, $000	97,996	
Average Income, $	24,160	
Average Tax, $	4,116	

VITAL STATISTICS

	1997	1996	1995	1994
Births	440	482	453	490
Deaths	371	322	354	327
Natural Increase	69	160	99	163
Marriages	117	119	169	186

Note: Latest available data.

COMMUNITY NEWSPAPER(S)

	Total Circulation
Rimouski: L'Avantage votre journal	35,295
Rimouski: Le Progrès-Écho Dimanche	29,238
Rimouski: Le Rimouskois	25,257

RADIO STATION(S)

	Power
CFLP	n.a.
CIKI-FM	100,000w
CJBR	10,000w
CJBR-FM	20,000w
CKMN-FM	6,400w

TELEVISION STATION(S)

CFER-TV
CIVB-TV
CJBR-TV
CJBRT-TV
CJPC-TV

Rivière-du-Loup
(Census Agglomeration)

The Census Agglomeration of Rivière-du-Loup includes: Rivière-du-Loup, V; Notre-Dame-du-Portage, P; Saint-Antonin, P; and Saint-Patrice-de-la-Rivière-du-Loup, P. All are in census division Rivière-du-Loup.

POPULATION

July 1, 2001 Estimate	24,280
% Cdn. Total	0.08
% Change, '96 -'01	1.10
Avg. Annual Growth Rate, %	0.22
2003 Projected Population	23,584
2006 Projected Population	24,705
2001 Households Estimate	9,884
2003 Projected Households	10,139
2006 Projected Households	10,471

INCOME

% Above/Below National Average	-18
2001 Total Income Estimate	$420,240,000
% Cdn. Total	0.06
2001 Average Hhld. Income	$42,500
2001 Per Capita	$17,300
2003 Projected Total Income	$450,250,000
2006 Projected Total Income	$497,340,000

RETAIL SALES

% Above/Below National Average	+81
2001 Retail Sales Estimate	$393,370,000
% Cdn. Total	0.14
2001 per Household	$39,800
2001 per Capita	$16,200
2001 No. of Establishments	278
2003 Projected Retail Sales	$416,270,000
2006 Projected Retail Sales	$488,370,000

POPULATION

2001 Estimates:		
Total		24,280
Male		11,553
Female		12,727
Age Groups	Male	Female
0-4	644	606
5-9	656	649
10-14	721	729
15-19	885	883
20-24	897	881
25-29	762	750
30-34	762	787
35-39	883	931
40-44	992	1,067
45-49	990	1,066
50-54	846	895
55-59	655	679
60-64	488	552
65-69	393	526
70+	979	1,726

DAYTIME POPULATION

2001 Estimates:	
Working Population	11,386
At Home Population	12,894
Total	24,280

Québec

INCOME

2001 Estimates:	
Avg. Household Income	$42,517
Avg. Family Income	$50,006
Per Capita Income	$17,308
Male:	
Avg. Employment Income	$29,090
Avg. Employment Income (Full Time)	$40,824
Female:	
Avg. Employment Income	$18,777
Avg. Employment Income (Full Time)	$27,647

DISPOSABLE & DISCRETIONARY INCOME

2001 Estimates:	Per Hhld.
Disposable Income	$29,547
Discretionary Income 1 (minus Food & Shelter)	$18,429
Discretionary Income 2 (minus Food, Shelter, & Other Expenditures)	$11,741

LIQUID ASSETS

1999 Estimates:	Per Hhld.
Equity Investments	$44,829
Interest Bearing Investments	$48,916
Total Liquid Assets	$93,745

CREDIT DATA

July 2000:	
Pool of Credit	$99,356,173
Revolving Credit, No.	39,007
Fixed Loans, No.	11,016
Avg. Credit Limit, per Person	$6,060
Avg. Spent, per Person	$2,352
Satisfactory Ratings, No. per Person	2.91
Avg. No. of Cards, per Person	1.12

LABOUR FORCE

2001 Estimates:	
Male:	
In the Labour Force	6,746
Participation Rate	70.8
Employed	6,231
Unemployed	515
Unemployment Rate	7.6
Not in Labour Force	2,786
Female:	
In the Labour Force	5,594
Participation Rate	52.1
Employed	5,206
Unemployed	388
Unemployment Rate	6.9
Not in Labour Force	5,149

Rivière-du-Loup
(Census Agglomeration)
(Cont'd)

OCCUPATIONS BY MAJOR GROUPS

2001 Estimates:	Male	Female
Management	794	215
Business, Finance & Admin.	579	1,531
Natural & Applied Sciences & Related	301	50
Health	197	663
Social Sciences, Gov't Services & Religion	141	178
Education	332	341
Arts, Culture, Recreation & Sport	127	91
Sales & Service	1,586	2,165
Trades, Transport & Equipment Operators & Related	1,751	42
Primary Industries	248	42
Processing, Mfg. & Utilities	473	133

LEVEL OF SCHOOLING

2001 Estimates:	
Population 15 years +	20,275
Less than Grade 9	3,671
Grades 9-13 w/o Certif.	3,291
Grade 9-13 with Certif.	3,903
Trade Certif./Dip.	1,195
Non-Univ. w/o Certif./Dip.	1,483
Non-Univ. with Certif./Dip.	3,677
Univ. w/o Degree	1,447
Univ. w/o Degree/Certif.	101
Univ. with Certif.	1,346
Univ. with Degree	1,608

AVERAGE HOUSEHOLD EXPENDITURES

2001 Estimates:	
Food	$5,860
Shelter	$6,770
Clothing	$1,851
Transportation	$5,054
Health & Personal Care	$1,680
Recr'n, Read'g & Education	$2,914
Taxes & Securities	$11,794
Other	$6,574
Total Expenditures	$42,497

PRIVATE HOUSEHOLDS

2001 Estimates:	
Private Households, Total	9,884
Pop. in Private Households	23,314
Average no. per Household	2.4

FAMILIES

2001 Estimates:	
Families in Private Households	6,838
Husband-Wife Families	5,856
Lone-Parent Families	982
Aver. No. Persons per Family	3.0
Aver. No. Sons/Daughters at Home	1.1

HOUSING

2001 Estimates:	
Occupied Private Dwellings	9,884
Owned	6,048
Rented	3,836
Single-Detached House	5,345
Semi-Detached House	552
Row Houses	233
Apartment, 5+ Storeys	46
Owned Apartment, 5+ Storeys	28
Apartment, 5 or Fewer Storeys	3,042
Apartment, Detached Duplex	630
Movable Dwellings	36

VEHICLES

2001 Estimates:	
Model Yrs. '81-'96, No.	11,663
% Total	81.93
Model Yrs. '97-'98, No.	1,653
% Total	11.61
'99 Vehicles registered in Model Yr. '99, No.	920
% Total	6.46
Total No. '81-'99	14,236

LEGAL MARITAL STATUS

2001 Estimates: (Age 15+)	
Single (Never Married)	8,163
Legally Married (Not Separated)	8,754
Legally Married (Separated)	402
Widowed	1,409
Divorced	1,547

PSYTE CATEGORIES

2001 Estimates	No. of Households	% of Total Hhds.	Index
Participation Quebec	825	8.35	290
Quebec Melange	1,426	14.43	544
Traditional French Cdn. Families	2,296	23.23	865
Big Country Families	822	8.32	583
Quebec Rural Blues	400	4.05	166
Quebec Town Elders	3,984	40.31	1,426

FINANCIAL PSYTE

2001 Estimates	No. of Households	% of Total Hhds.	Index
Mortgages & Minivans	825	8.35	126
Country Credit	3,722	37.66	557
Rural Family Blues	1,222	12.36	153
Loan Parent Stress	3,984	40.31	692

HOME LANGUAGE

2001 Estimates:		% Total
English	24	0.10
French	24,188	99.62
Other Languages	34	0.14
Multiple Responses	34	0.14
Total	24,280	100.00

BUILDING PERMITS

	1999	1998 $000	1997
Value	19,601	29,288	27,603

HOMES BUILT

	1999	1998	1997
No	132	143	133

TAXATION

Income Class:	1997	% Total
Under $5,000	2,100	12.67
$5,000-$10,000	2,390	14.42
$10,000-$15,000	3,060	18.47
$15,000-$20,000	1,750	10.56
$20,000-$25,000	1,550	9.35
$25,000-$30,000	1,450	8.75
$30,000-$40,000	1,850	11.16
$40,000-$50,000	1,040	6.28
$50,000 +	1,400	8.45
Total Returns, No.	16,570	
Total Income, $000	379,691	
Total Taxable Returns	11,130	
Total Tax, $000	41,606	
Average Income, $	22,914	
Average Tax, $	3,738	

VITAL STATISTICS

	1997	1996	1995	1994
Births	181	193	220	225
Deaths	158	196	177	189
Natural Increase	23	-3	43	36
Marriages	91	87	75	78

Note: Latest available data.

COMMUNITY NEWSPAPER(S)

	Total Circulation
Rivière-du-Loup, Cabano, Trois-Pistoles: Info Dimanche	28,968
Rivière-du-Loup, Trois-Pistoles, La Pocatière, Saint-Pascal, Cabano: St-Laurent Portage	37,059

RADIO STATION(S)

	Power
CIBM-FM	100,000w
CJFP-FM	60,000w

TELEVISION STATION(S)

CFTF-TV
CIMT-TV
CKRT-TV

252   Financial Post

Roberval
(Ville)

In census division Le Domaine-du-Roy.

POPULATION

July 1, 2001 Estimate	11,533
% Cdn. Total	0.04
% Change, '96 -'01	-2.42
Avg. Annual Growth Rate, %	-0.49
2003 Projected Population	11,487
2006 Projected Population	11,340
2001 Households Estimate	4,422
2003 Projected Households	4,483
2006 Projected Households	4,564

INCOME

% Above/Below National Average	-12
2001 Total Income Estimate	$213,260,000
% Cdn. Total	0.03
2001 Average Hhld. Income	$48,200
2001 Per Capita	$18,500
2003 Projected Total Income	$226,910,000
2006 Projected Total Income	$248,490,000

RETAIL SALES

% Above/Below National Average	-20
2001 Retail Sales Estimate	$82,750,000
% Cdn. Total	0.03
2001 per Household	$18,700
2001 per Capita	$7,200
2001 No. of Establishments	135
2003 Projected Retail Sales	$89,600,000
2006 Projected Retail Sales	$98,010,000

POPULATION

2001 Estimates:

Total		11,533
Male		5,614
Female		5,919

Age Groups	Male	Female
0-4	311	292
5-9	329	329
10-14	392	381
15-19	464	422
20-24	434	379
25-29	336	315
30-34	354	362
35-39	446	453
40-44	487	496
45-49	484	469
50-54	414	423
55-59	325	361
60-64	257	316
65-69	202	274
70+	379	647

DAYTIME POPULATION

2001 Estimates:

Working Population	5,680
At Home Population	6,196
Total	11,876

INCOME

2001 Estimates:

Avg. Household Income	$48,228
Avg. Family Income	$54,910
Per Capita Income	$18,492

Male:

Avg. Employment Income	$33,504
Avg. Employment Income (Full Time)	$46,113

Female:

Avg. Employment Income	$20,656
Avg. Employment Income (Full Time)	$28,996

DISPOSABLE & DISCRETIONARY INCOME

2001 Estimates:	Per Hhld.
Disposable Income	$33,475
Discretionary Income 1 (minus Food & Shelter)	$21,541
Discretionary Income 2 (minus Food, Shelter, & Other Expenditures)	$14,038

LIQUID ASSETS

1999 Estimates:	Per Hhld.
Equity Investments	$60,160
Interest Bearing Investments	$57,089
Total Liquid Assets	$117,249

CREDIT DATA

July 2000:

Pool of Credit	$64,411,959
Revolving Credit, No.	18,779
Fixed Loans, No.	7,782
Avg. Credit Limit, per Person	$7,821
Avg. Spent, per Person	$3,478
Satisfactory Ratings, No. per Person	2.92
Avg. No. of Cards, per Person	1.02

LABOUR FORCE

2001 Estimates:

Male:

In the Labour Force	3,132
Participation Rate	68.4
Employed	2,833
Unemployed	299
Unemployment Rate	9.5
Not in Labour Force	1,450

Female:

In the Labour Force	2,649
Participation Rate	53.9
Employed	2,514
Unemployed	135
Unemployment Rate	5.1
Not in Labour Force	2,268

OCCUPATIONS BY MAJOR GROUPS

2001 Estimates:	Male	Female
Management	346	110
Business, Finance & Admin.	216	701
Natural & Applied Sciences & Related	132	37
Health	170	502
Social Sciences, Gov't Services & Religion.	146	110
Education	124	138
Arts, Culture, Recreation & Sport	26	30
Sales & Service	702	893
Trades, Transport & Equipment Operators & Related	741	33
Primary Industries	164	18
Processing, Mfg. & Utilities	338	10

LEVEL OF SCHOOLING

2001 Estimates:

Population 15 years +	9,499
Less than Grade 9	1,664
Grades 9-13 w/o Certif.	1,861
Grade 9-13 with Certif.	1,822
Trade Certif. /Dip.	682
Non-Univ. w/o Certif./Dip.	727
Non-Univ. with Certif./Dip.	1,326
Univ. w/o Degree	603
Univ. w/o Degree/Certif.	46
Univ. with Certif.	557
Univ. with Degree	814

AVERAGE HOUSEHOLD EXPENDITURES

2001 Estimates:

Food	$6,313
Shelter	$7,294
Clothing	$2,074
Transportation	$5,780
Health & Personal Care	$1,876
Recr'n, Read'g & Education	$3,132
Taxes & Securities	$13,798
Other	$7,007
Total Expenditures	$47,274

PRIVATE HOUSEHOLDS

2001 Estimates:

Private Households, Total	4,422
Pop. in Private Households	11,071
Average no. per Household	2.5

FAMILIES

2001 Estimates:

Families in Private Households	3,312
Husband-Wife Families	2,830
Lone-Parent Families	482
Aver. No. Persons per Family	3.1
Aver. No. Sons/Daughters at Home	1.2

HOUSING

2001 Estimates:

Occupied Private Dwellings	4,422
Owned	2,815
Rented	1,607
Single-Detached House	2,381
Semi-Detached House	268
Row Houses	58
Apartment, 5+ Storeys	10
Owned Apartment, 5+ Storeys	10
Apartment, 5 or Fewer Storeys	1,113
Apartment, Detached Duplex	529
Movable Dwellings	63

VEHICLES

2001 Estimates:

Model Yrs. '81-'96, No.	5,543
% Total	81.61
Model Yrs. '97-'98, No.	754
% Total	11.10
'99 Vehicles registered in Model Yr. '99, No.	495
% Total	7.29
Total No. '81-'99	6,792

LEGAL MARITAL STATUS

2001 Estimates: (Age 15+)

Single (Never Married)	3,696
Legally Married (Not Separated)	4,278
Legally Married (Separated)	216
Widowed	554
Divorced	755

PSYTE CATEGORIES

2001 Estimates	No. of House -holds	% of Total Hhds.	Index
Participation Quebec	1,069	24.17	839
Quebec Melange	872	19.72	744
Traditional French Cdn. Families	1,064	24.06	896
Quebec Rural Blues	94	2.13	87
Quebec Town Elders	1,263	28.56	1,011

FINANCIAL PSYTE

2001 Estimates	No. of House -holds	% of Total Hhds.	Index
Mortgages & Minivans	1,069	24.17	366
Country Credit	1,936	43.78	647
Rural Family Blues	94	2.13	26
Loan Parent Stress	1,263	28.56	490

Québec

HOME LANGUAGE

2001 Estimates:		% Total
English	10	0.09
French	11,503	99.74
Chinese	10	0.09
Multiple Responses	10	0.09
Total	11,533	100.00

BUILDING PERMITS

	1999	1998 $000	1997
Value	7,250	13,629	6,216

HOMES BUILT

	1999	1998	1997
No	18	21	17

TAXATION

Income Class:	1997	% Total
Under $5,000	1,270	15.01
$5,000-$10,000	1,330	15.72
$10,000-$15,000	1,380	16.31
$15,000-$20,000	760	8.98
$20,000-$25,000	660	7.80
$25,000-$30,000	680	8.04
$30,000-$40,000	1,100	13.00
$40,000-$50,000	660	7.80
$50,000 +	620	7.33
Total Returns, No.	8,460	
Total Income, $000	190,279	
Total Taxable Returns	5,420	
Total Tax, $000	20,678	
Average Income, $.	22,492	
Average Tax, $.	3,815	

VITAL STATISTICS

	1997	1996	1995	1994
Births	94	117	104	121
Deaths	81	99	88	82
Natural Increase	13	18	16	39
Marriages	52	45	54	47

Note: Latest available data.

COMMUNITY NEWSPAPER(S)

	Total Circulation
Roberval, St-Félicien: L'Étoile du Lac	13,295

RADIO STATION(S)

	Power
CHRL	10,000w
CJMD	1,000w

Québec

Rouyn-Noranda
(Census Agglomeration)

The Census Agglomeration of Rouyn-Noranda includes: Rouyn-Noranda, V; Beaudry, M; Evain, M; McWatters, M; plus several smaller areas. All are in census division Rouyn-Noranda.

POPULATION

July 1, 2001 Estimate	39,642
% Cdn. Total	0.13
% Change, '96 -'01	-0.31
Avg. Annual Growth Rate, %	-0.06
2003 Projected Population	39,782
2006 Projected Population	39,699
2001 Households Estimate	16,984
2003 Projected Households	17,325
2006 Projected Households	17,705

INCOME

% Above/Below National Average	-4
2001 Total Income Estimate	$800,340,000
% Cdn. Total	0.12
2001 Average Hhld. Income	$47,100
2001 Per Capita	$20,200
2003 Projected Total Income	$852,000,000
2006 Projected Total Income	$928,210,000

RETAIL SALES

% Above/Below National Average	+18
2001 Retail Sales Estimate	$417,020,000
% Cdn. Total	0.15
2001 per Household	$24,600
2001 per Capita	$10,500
2001 No. of Establishments	343
2003 Projected Retail Sales	$448,850,000
2006 Projected Retail Sales	$491,450,000

POPULATION

2001 Estimates:

Total		39,642
Male		19,642
Female		20,000

Age Groups	Male	Female
0-4	1,224	1,221
5-9	1,292	1,310
10-14	1,361	1,347
15-19	1,453	1,416
20-24	1,423	1,393
25-29	1,362	1,362
30-34	1,482	1,510
35-39	1,701	1,695
40-44	1,747	1,720
45-49	1,594	1,565
50-54	1,355	1,284
55-59	1,029	996
60-64	771	808
65-69	637	715
70+	1,211	1,658

DAYTIME POPULATION

2001 Estimates:

Working Population	18,424
At Home Population	21,237
Total	39,661

INCOME

2001 Estimates:

Avg. Household Income	$47,123
Avg. Family Income	$55,609
Per Capita Income	$20,189

Male:

Avg. Employment Income	$35,672
Avg. Employment Income (Full Time)	$47,491

Female:

Avg. Employment Income	$20,044
Avg. Employment Income (Full Time)	$30,659

DISPOSABLE & DISCRETIONARY INCOME

2001 Estimates:	Per Hhld.
Disposable Income	$32,390
Discretionary Income 1 (minus Food & Shelter)	$20,525
Discretionary Income 2 (minus Food, Shelter, & Other Expenditures)	$13,211

LIQUID ASSETS

1999 Estimates:	Per Hhld.
Equity Investments	$51,446
Interest Bearing Investments	$54,365
Total Liquid Assets	$105,811

CREDIT DATA

July 2000:

Pool of Credit	$216,134,378
Revolving Credit, No.	56,647
Fixed Loans, No.	22,102
Avg. Credit Limit, per Person	$8,023
Avg. Spent, per Person	$3,672
Satisfactory Ratings, No. per Person	2.72
Avg. No. of Cards, per Person	0.97

LABOUR FORCE

2001 Estimates:

Male:

In the Labour Force	11,478
Participation Rate	72.8
Employed	10,442
Unemployed	1,036
Unemployment Rate	9.0
Not in Labour Force	4,287

Female:

In the Labour Force	8,725
Participation Rate	54.1
Employed	8,000
Unemployed	725
Unemployment Rate	8.3
Not in Labour Force	7,397

OCCUPATIONS BY MAJOR GROUPS

2001 Estimates:	Male	Female
Management	997	432
Business, Finance & Admin.	1,057	2,690
Natural & Applied Sciences & Related	988	227
Health	186	833
Social Sciences, Gov't Services & Religion	193	268
Education	390	608
Arts, Culture, Recreation & Sport	164	190
Sales & Service	2,155	2,845
Trades, Transport & Equipment Operators & Related	2,952	129
Primary Industries	961	47
Processing, Mfg. & Utilities	1,031	72

LEVEL OF SCHOOLING

2001 Estimates:

Population 15 years +	31,887
Less than Grade 9	5,968
Grades 9-13 w/o Certif.	6,184
Grade 9-13 with Certif.	5,018
Trade Certif./Dip.	1,743
Non-Univ. w/o Certif./Dip.	2,599
Non-Univ. with Certif./Dip.	4,948
Univ. w/o Degree	2,292
Univ. w/o Degree/Certif.	444
Univ. with Certif.	1,848
Univ. with Degree	3,135

AVERAGE HOUSEHOLD EXPENDITURES

2001 Estimates:

Food	$6,235
Shelter	$7,302
Clothing	$2,025
Transportation	$5,557
Health & Personal Care	$1,859
Recr'n, Read'g & Education	$3,078
Taxes & Securities	$13,188
Other	$7,068
Total Expenditures	$46,312

PRIVATE HOUSEHOLDS

2001 Estimates:

Private Households, Total	16,984
Pop. in Private Households	38,895
Average no. per Household	2.3

FAMILIES

2001 Estimates:

Families in Private Households	11,932
Husband-Wife Families	10,063
Lone-Parent Families	1,869
Aver. No. Persons per Family	3.0
Aver. No. Sons/Daughters at Home	1.1

HOUSING

2001 Estimates:

Occupied Private Dwellings	16,984
Owned	9,635
Rented	7,349
Single-Detached House	7,827
Semi-Detached House	1,222
Row Houses	228
Apartment, 5+ Storeys	33
Apartment, 5 or Fewer Storeys	5,522
Apartment, Detached Duplex	1,780
Other Single-Attached	142
Movable Dwellings	230

VEHICLES

2001 Estimates:

Model Yrs. '81-'96, No.	20,989
% Total	81.51
Model Yrs. '97-'98, No.	2,991
% Total	11.62
'99 Vehicles registered in Model Yr. '99, No.	1,769
% Total	6.87
Total No. '81-'99	25,749

LEGAL MARITAL STATUS

2001 Estimates: (Age 15+)

Single (Never Married)	13,401
Legally Married (Not Separated)	12,933
Legally Married (Separated)	934
Widowed	1,785
Divorced	2,834

PSYTE CATEGORIES

2001 Estimates	No. of House -holds	% of Total Hhds.	Index
Participation Quebec	2,500	14.72	511
Quebec Melange	3,398	20.01	755
Traditional French Cdn. Families	4,116	24.23	902
Young Grey Collar	407	2.40	286
Quebec Rural Blues	175	1.03	42
Quebec Town Elders	4,848	28.54	1,010
Quebec's New Urban Mosaic	1,487	8.76	363

FINANCIAL P$YTE

2001 Estimates	No. of House -holds	% of Total Hhds.	Index
Mortgages & Minivans	2,500	14.72	223
Country Credit	7,514	44.24	654
Revolving Renters	407	2.40	52
Rural Family Blues	175	1.03	13
Loan Parent Stress	4,848	28.54	490
NSF	1,487	8.76	247

HOME LANGUAGE

2001 Estimates:		% Total
English	1,046	2.64
French	38,041	95.96
Italian	30	0.08
Polish	40	0.10
Spanish	20	0.05
Other Languages	70	0.18
Multiple Responses	395	1.00
Total	39,642	100.00

BUILDING PERMITS

	1999	1998 $000	1997
Value	22,293	28,398	27,702

HOMES BUILT

	1999	1998	1997
No	48	139	121

TAXATION

Income Class:	1997	% Total
Under $5,000	3,620	12.97
$5,000-$10,000	4,170	14.94
$10,000-$15,000	4,290	15.37
$15,000-$20,000	2,500	8.95
$20,000-$25,000	2,150	7.70
$25,000-$30,000	2,030	7.27
$30,000-$40,000	3,340	11.96
$40,000-$50,000	2,200	7.88
$50,000 +	3,670	13.14
Total Returns, No.	27,920	
Total Income, $000	720,244	
Total Taxable Returns	18,860	
Total Tax, $000	88,084	
Average Income, $.	25,797	
Average Tax, $.	4,670	

VITAL STATISTICS

	1997	1996	1995	1994
Births	109	523	516	547
Deaths	30	302	251	272
Natural Increase	79	221	265	275
Marriages	179	119	132	161

Note: Latest available data.

COMMUNITY NEWSPAPER(S)

	Total Circulation
Rouyn-Noranda: Le Citoyen Rouyn-Noranda	19,165
Rouyn-Noranda: La Frontière	5,614

RADIO STATION(S)

	Power
CBMA	n.a.
CHOA-FM	n.a.
CJMM-FM	3,800w
CKRN	50,000w

TELEVISION STATION(S)

CFEM-TV
CFVS-TV
CIVA-TV
CKRN-TV

Saint-Georges
(Census Agglomeration)

The Census Agglomeration of Saint-Georges includes: Aubert-Gallion, M; Saint-Georges, V; Saint-Georges-Est, P; and Saint-Jean-de-la-Lande, P. All are in census division Beauce-Sartigan.

POPULATION

July 1, 2001 Estimate	28,346
% Cdn. Total	0.09
% Change, '96 -'01	4.76
Avg. Annual Growth Rate, %	0.93
2003 Projected Population	28,917
2006 Projected Population	29,589
2001 Households Estimate	11,332
2003 Projected Households	11,732
2006 Projected Households	12,310

INCOME

% Above/Below National Average	-16
2001 Total Income Estimate	$499,890,000
% Cdn. Total	0.08
2001 Average Hhld. Income	$44,100
2001 Per Capita	$17,600
2003 Projected Total Income	$547,360,000
2006 Projected Total Income	$626,210,000

RETAIL SALES

% Above/Below National Average	+70
2001 Retail Sales Estimate	$432,320,000
% Cdn. Total	0.16
2001 per Household	$38,200
2001 per Capita	$15,300
2001 No. of Establishments	381
2003 Projected Retail Sales	$468,660,000
2006 Projected Retail Sales	$520,990,000

POPULATION

2001 Estimates:

Total		28,346
Male		13,952
Female		14,394

Age Groups	Male	Female
0-4	834	813
5-9	874	831
10-14	968	929
15-19	1,080	1,054
20-24	1,072	1,044
25-29	1,009	940
30-34	1,060	1,025
35-39	1,186	1,175
40-44	1,209	1,228
45-49	1,147	1,193
50-54	979	1,014
55-59	745	762
60-64	556	583
65-69	419	494
70+	814	1,309

DAYTIME POPULATION

2001 Estimates:

Working Population	14,213
At Home Population	14,133
Total	28,346

INCOME

2001 Estimates:

Avg. Household Income	$44,113
Avg. Family Income	$51,223
Per Capita Income	$17,635
Male:	
Avg. Employment Income	$29,570
Avg. Employment Income (Full Time)	$38,036
Female:	
Avg. Employment Income	$18,921
Avg. Employment Income (Full Time)	$26,965

DISPOSABLE & DISCRETIONARY INCOME

2001 Estimates:	Per Hhld.
Disposable Income	$30,839
Discretionary Income 1 (minus Food & Shelter)	$19,598
Discretionary Income 2 (minus Food, Shelter, & Other Expenditures)	$12,666

LIQUID ASSETS

1999 Estimates:	Per Hhld.
Equity Investments	$46,763
Interest Bearing Investments	$50,578
Total Liquid Assets	$97,341

CREDIT DATA

July 2000:	
Pool of Credit	$121,361,375
Revolving Credit, No.	37,645
Fixed Loans, No.	12,555
Avg. Credit Limit, per Person	$6,768
Avg. Spent, per Person	$2,805
Satisfactory Ratings, No. per Person	2.69
Avg. No. of Cards, per Person	1.04

LABOUR FORCE

2001 Estimates:

Male:	
In the Labour Force	8,280
Participation Rate	73.4
Employed	7,876
Unemployed	404
Unemployment Rate	4.9
Not in Labour Force	2,996
Female:	
In the Labour Force	6,760
Participation Rate	57.2
Employed	6,368
Unemployed	392
Unemployment Rate	5.8
Not in Labour Force	5,061

OCCUPATIONS BY MAJOR GROUPS

2001 Estimates:	Male	Female
Management	883	327
Business, Finance & Admin.	663	1,617
Natural & Applied Sciences & Related	423	50
Health	238	680
Social Sciences, Gov't Services & Religion	114	276
Education	327	396
Arts, Culture, Recreation & Sport	89	120
Sales & Service	1,569	2,202
Trades, Transport & Equipment Operators & Related	2,197	161
Primary Industries	276	52
Processing, Mfg. & Utilities	1,371	665

LEVEL OF SCHOOLING

2001 Estimates:

Population 15 years +	23,097
Less than Grade 9	4,445
Grades 9-13 w/o Certif.	4,308
Grade 9-13 with Certif.	4,577
Trade Certif./Dip.	1,422
Non-Univ. w/o Certif./Dip.	1,576
Non-Univ. with Certif./Dip.	3,555
Univ. w/o Degree	1,194
Univ. w/o Degree/Certif.	100
Univ. with Certif.	1,094
Univ. with Degree	2,020

AVERAGE HOUSEHOLD EXPENDITURES

2001 Estimates:

Food	$5,876
Shelter	$6,981
Clothing	$1,937
Transportation	$5,250
Health & Personal Care	$1,750
Recr'n, Read'g & Education	$2,923
Taxes & Securities	$12,512
Other	$6,709
Total Expenditures	$43,938

PRIVATE HOUSEHOLDS

2001 Estimates:

Private Households, Total	11,332
Pop. in Private Households	27,560
Average no. per Household	2.4

FAMILIES

2001 Estimates:

Families in Private Households	7,983
Husband-Wife Families	6,821
Lone-Parent Families	1,162
Aver. No. Persons per Family	3.1
Aver. No. Sons/Daughters at Home	1.3

HOUSING

2001 Estimates:

Occupied Private Dwellings	11,332
Owned	7,252
Rented	4,080
Single-Detached House	6,925
Semi-Detached House	541
Row Houses	110
Apartment, 5+ Storeys	77
Owned Apartment, 5+ Storeys	22
Apartment, 5 or Fewer Storeys	2,868
Apartment, Detached Duplex	757
Other Single-Attached	37
Movable Dwellings	17

VEHICLES

2001 Estimates:

Model Yrs. '81-'96, No.	14,968
% Total	80.54
Model Yrs. '97-'98, No.	2,297
% Total	12.36
'99 Vehicles registered in Model Yr. '99, No.	1,319
% Total	7.10
Total No. '81-'99	18,584

LEGAL MARITAL STATUS

2001 Estimates: (Age 15+)

Single (Never Married)	9,039
Legally Married (Not Separated)	10,387
Legally Married (Separated)	370
Widowed	1,290
Divorced	2,011

PSYTE CATEGORIES

2001 Estimates	No. of House-holds	% of Total Hhds.	Index
Participation Quebec.	1,588	14.01	486
New Quebec Rows	587	5.18	473
Quebec Melange.	2,965	26.16	987
Traditional French Cdn. Families	2,018	17.81	663
Quebec's Heartland	171	1.51	154
Big Country Families	450	3.97	278
Quebec Town Elders	2,475	21.84	773
Quebec's New Urban Mosaic	964	8.51	353

FINANCIAL P$YTE

2001 Estimates	No. of House-holds	% of Total Hhds.	Index
Mortgages & Minivans	2,175	19.19	291
Country Credit	4,983	43.97	650
Rural Family Blues	621	5.48	68
Loan Parent Stress	2,475	21.84	375
NSF	964	8.51	240

HOME LANGUAGE

2001 Estimates:	% Total
English	157 ... 0.55
French	28,141 ... 99.28
Other Languages	11 ... 0.04
Multiple Responses	37 ... 0.13
Total	28,346 ... 100.00

BUILDING PERMITS

	1999	1998 $000	1997
Value	34,527	35,697	49,558

HOMES BUILT

	1999	1998	1997
No.	129	230	180

TAXATION

Income Class:	1997	% Total
Under $5,000	2,490	12.28
$5,000-$10,000	3,230	15.93
$10,000-$15,000	3,440	16.97
$15,000-$20,000	2,260	11.15
$20,000-$25,000	2,010	9.92
$25,000-$30,000	1,860	9.18
$30,000-$40,000	2,350	11.59
$40,000-$50,000	1,260	6.22
$50,000 +	1,420	7.01
Total Returns, No.	20,270	
Total Income, $000	457,885	
Total Taxable Returns	13,560	
Total Tax, $000	48,284	
Average Income, $.	22,589	
Average Tax, $	3,561	

VITAL STATISTICS

	1997	1996	1995	1994
Births	289	336	305	320
Deaths	225	189	173	157
Natural Increase	64	147	132	163
Marriages	76	67	65	67

Note: Latest available data.

COMMUNITY NEWSPAPER(S)

	Total Circulation
Saint-Georges de Beauce: L'Impact	27,044
Saint-Georges, Beauceville: L'Eclaireur Progrès-Beauce Nouvelle	28,685

RADIO STATION(S)

	Power
CBV	n.a.
CHJM-FM	100,000w
CKRB-FM	n.a.

Québec

Saint-Hyacinthe
(Census Agglomeration)

The Census Agglomeration of Saint-Hyacinthe includes: Saint-Hyacinthe, V; Saint-Hyacinthe-le-Confesseur, P; Saint-Thomas-d'Aquin, P; Sainte-Rosalie, P; and Sainte-Rosalie, VL. All are in census division Les Maskoutains.

POPULATION

July 1, 2001 Estimate	50,623
% Cdn. Total	0.16
% Change, '96 -'01	-0.45
Avg. Annual Growth Rate, %	-0.09
2003 Projected Population	50,825
2006 Projected Population	50,778
2001 Households Estimate	22,084
2003 Projected Households	22,459
2006 Projected Households	22,818

INCOME

% Above/Below National Average	-14
2001 Total Income Estimate	$920,200,000
% Cdn. Total	0.14
2001 Average Hhld. Income	$41,700
2001 Per Capita	$18,200
2003 Projected Total Income	$980,500,000
2006 Projected Total Income	$1,072,520,000

RETAIL SALES

% Above/Below National Average	+53
2001 Retail Sales Estimate	$694,910,000
% Cdn. Total	0.25
2001 per Household	$31,500
2001 per Capita	$13,700
2001 No. of Establishments	551
2003 Projected Retail Sales	$751,820,000
2006 Projected Retail Sales	$828,410,000

POPULATION

2001 Estimates:

Total		50,623
Male		23,840
Female		26,783

Age Groups	Male	Female
0-4	1,353	1,328
5-9	1,382	1,334
10-14	1,445	1,396
15-19	1,657	1,585
20-24	1,722	1,687
25-29	1,605	1,617
30-34	1,654	1,691
35-39	1,820	1,901
40-44	1,920	2,034
45-49	1,908	2,018
50-54	1,728	1,863
55-59	1,394	1,568
60-64	1,125	1,301
65-69	941	1,221
70+	2,186	4,239

DAYTIME POPULATION

2001 Estimates:

Working Population	24,124
At Home Population	26,511
Total	50,635

INCOME

2001 Estimates:

Avg. Household Income	$41,668
Avg. Family Income	$50,140
Per Capita Income	$18,177
Male:	
Avg. Employment Income	$29,562
Avg. Employment Income (Full Time)	$37,406
Female:	
Avg. Employment Income	$19,395
Avg. Employment Income (Full Time)	$27,399

DISPOSABLE & DISCRETIONARY INCOME

2001 Estimates:	*Per Hhld.*
Disposable Income	$29,377
Discretionary Income 1 (minus Food & Shelter)	$18,425
Discretionary Income 2 (minus Food, Shelter, & Other Expenditures)	$11,945

LIQUID ASSETS

1999 Estimates:	*Per Hhld.*
Equity Investments	$42,412
Interest Bearing Investments	$48,327
Total Liquid Assets	$90,739

CREDIT DATA

July 2000:

Pool of Credit	$244,396,978
Revolving Credit, No.	77,550
Fixed Loans, No.	22,097
Avg. Credit Limit, per Person	$6,332
Avg. Spent, per Person	$2,647
Satisfactory Ratings, No. per Person	2.42
Avg. No. of Cards, per Person	0.97

LABOUR FORCE

2001 Estimates:

Male:	
In the Labour Force	13,905
Participation Rate	70.7
Employed	13,181
Unemployed	724
Unemployment Rate	5.2
Not in Labour Force	5,755
Female:	
In the Labour Force	11,820
Participation Rate	52.0
Employed	11,110
Unemployed	710
Unemployment Rate	6.0
Not in Labour Force	10,905

OCCUPATIONS BY MAJOR GROUPS

2001 Estimates:	*Male*	*Female*
Management	1,322	504
Business, Finance & Admin.	1,221	3,277
Natural & Applied Sciences & Related	732	307
Health	500	1,340
Social Sciences, Gov't Services & Religion	262	311
Education	380	493
Arts, Culture, Recreation & Sport	204	211
Sales & Service	3,007	3,603
Trades, Transport & Equipment Operators & Related	3,279	164
Primary Industries	422	155
Processing, Mfg. & Utilities	2,109	1,012

LEVEL OF SCHOOLING

2001 Estimates:

Population 15 years +	42,385
Less than Grade 9	9,153
Grades 9-13 w/o Certif.	7,715
Grade 9-13 with Certif.	7,688
Trade Certif./Dip.	2,194
Non-Univ. w/o Certif./Dip.	3,238
Non-Univ. with Certif./Dip.	6,309
Univ. w/o Degree	2,251
Univ. w/o Degree/Certif.	271
Univ. with Certif.	1,980
Univ. with Degree	3,837

AVERAGE HOUSEHOLD EXPENDITURES

2001 Estimates:

Food	$5,636
Shelter	$6,900
Clothing	$1,828
Transportation	$4,795
Health & Personal Care	$1,710
Recr'n, Read'g & Education	$2,741
Taxes & Securities	$11,773
Other	$6,526
Total Expenditures	$41,909

PRIVATE HOUSEHOLDS

2001 Estimates:

Private Households, Total	22,084
Pop. in Private Households	48,301
Average no. per Household	2.2

FAMILIES

2001 Estimates:

Families in Private Households	14,532
Husband-Wife Families	12,021
Lone-Parent Families	2,511
Aver. No. Persons per Family	2.8
Aver. No. Sons/Daughters at Home	1.0

HOUSING

2001 Estimates:

Occupied Private Dwellings	22,084
Owned	10,757
Rented	11,327
Single-Detached House	8,292
Semi-Detached House	925
Row Houses	498
Apartment, 5+ Storeys	218
Apartment, 5 or Fewer Storeys	9,484
Apartment, Detached Duplex	2,471
Other Single-Attached	163
Movable Dwellings	33

VEHICLES

2001 Estimates:

Model Yrs. '81-'96, No.	25,597
% Total	78.35
Model Yrs. '97-'98, No.	4,410
% Total	13.50
'99 Vehicles registered in Model Yr. '99, No.	2,663
% Total	8.15
Total No. '81-'99	32,670

LEGAL MARITAL STATUS

2001 Estimates: (Age 15+)

Single (Never Married)	16,566
Legally Married (Not Separated)	17,133
Legally Married (Separated)	950
Widowed	3,237
Divorced	4,499

PSYTE CATEGORIES

2001 Estimates	*No. of House-holds*	*% of Total Hhds.*	*Index*
Participation			
Quebec	2,340	10.60	368
New Quebec Rows	216	0.98	89
Quebec Melange	5,429	24.58	928
Traditional French Cdn. Families	2,376	10.76	401
Quebec's Heartland	151	0.68	70
Quebec Rural Blues	111	0.50	21
Old Quebec Walkups	880	3.98	217
Quebec Town Elders	5,294	23.97	848
Quebec's New Urban Mosaic	4,512	20.43	848
Aged Pensioners	310	1.40	106

FINANCIAL P$YTE

2001 Estimates	*No. of House-holds*	*% of Total Hhds.*	*Index*
Mortgages & Minivans	2,556	11.57	175
Country Credit	7,805	35.34	523
Rural Family Blues	262	1.19	15
Loan Parent Stress	6,174	27.96	480
NSF	4,512	20.43	577
Senior Survivors	310	1.40	74

HOME LANGUAGE

2001 Estimates:		*% Total*
English	261	0.52
French	49,876	98.52
Italian	46	0.09
Spanish	34	0.07
Vietnamese	76	0.15
Other Languages	65	0.13
Multiple Responses	265	0.52
Total	50,623	100.00

BUILDING PERMITS

	1999	*1998*	*1997*
		$000	
Value	41,910	37,047	46,968

HOMES BUILT

	1999	*1998*	*1997*
No	91	120	136

TAXATION

Income Class:	*1997*	*% Total*
Under $5,000	4,170	10.70
$5,000-$10,000	5,990	15.37
$10,000-$15,000	7,200	18.48
$15,000-$20,000	4,120	10.57
$20,000-$25,000	3,610	9.27
$25,000-$30,000	3,430	8.80
$30,000-$40,000	4,680	12.01
$40,000-$50,000	2,770	7.11
$50,000 +	2,980	7.65
Total Returns, No.	38,960	
Total Income, $000	902,631	
Total Taxable Returns	26,390	
Total Tax, $000	97,930	
Average Income, $	23,168	
Average Tax, $	3,711	

VITAL STATISTICS

	1997	*1996*	*1995*	*1994*
Births	465	504	531	540
Deaths	502	513	504	513
Natural Increase	-37	-9	27	27
Marriages	206	195	210	226

Note: Latest available data.

COMMUNITY NEWSPAPER(S)

	Total Circulation
Saint-Hyacinthe: L'Impact	27,700
Saint-Hyacinthe: Le Clairon Régional	33,447
Saint-Hyacinthe: Le Courrier	11,915

RADIO STATION(S)

	Power
CFEI-FM	n.a.

Saint-Jean-sur-Richelieu
(Census Agglomeration)

The Census Agglomeration of Saint-Jean-sur-Richelieu includes:
Saint-Jean-sur-Richelieu, V; Iberville, V; L'Acadie, M; Saint-Athanase, P; and Saint-Luc, V. All are in census division Le Haut-Richelieu.

POPULATION

July 1, 2001 Estimate	80,716
% Cdn. Total	0.26
% Change, '96 -'01	3.77
Avg. Annual Growth Rate, %	0.74
2003 Projected Population	82,339
2006 Projected Population	84,437
2001 Households Estimate	33,198
2003 Projected Households	34,208
2006 Projected Households	35,583

INCOME

% Above/Below National Average	-12
2001 Total Income Estimate	$1,490,320,000
% Cdn. Total	0.23
2001 Average Hhld. Income	$44,900
2001 Per Capita	$18,500
2003 Projected Total Income	$1,620,890,000
2006 Projected Total Income	$1,833,630,000

RETAIL SALES

% Above/Below National Average	+30
2001 Retail Sales Estimate	$942,830,000
% Cdn. Total	0.34
2001 per Household	$28,400
2001 per Capita	$11,700
2001 No. of Establishments	749
2003 Projected Retail Sales	$1,025,250,000
2006 Projected Retail Sales	$1,142,440,000

POPULATION

2001 Estimates:

Total		80,716
Male		39,618
Female		41,098

Age Groups	Male	Female
0-4	2,437	2,293
5-9	2,716	2,546
10-14	2,790	2,630
15-19	2,854	2,649
20-24	2,655	2,490
25-29	2,472	2,442
30-34	2,822	2,828
35-39	3,290	3,358
40-44	3,402	3,475
45-49	3,186	3,279
50-54	2,782	2,834
55-59	2,225	2,262
60-64	1,731	1,852
65-69	1,409	1,636
70+	2,847	4,524

DAYTIME POPULATION

2001 Estimates:

Working Population	38,801
At Home Population	41,915
Total	80,716

INCOME

2001 Estimates:

Avg. Household Income	$44,892
Avg. Family Income	$52,181
Per Capita Income	$18,464
Male:	
Avg. Employment Income	$31,396
Avg. Employment Income (Full Time)	$40,010
Female:	
Avg. Employment Income	$20,540
Avg. Employment Income (Full Time)	$29,191

DISPOSABLE & DISCRETIONARY INCOME

2001 Estimates:	Per Hhld.
Disposable Income	$31,555
Discretionary Income 1 (minus Food & Shelter)	$19,989
Discretionary Income 2 (minus Food, Shelter, & Other Expenditures)	$12,960

LIQUID ASSETS

1999 Estimates:	Per Hhld.
Equity Investments	$47,415
Interest Bearing Investments	$51,060
Total Liquid Assets	$98,475

CREDIT DATA

July 2000:

Pool of Credit	$495,010,722
Revolving Credit, No.	132,244
Fixed Loans, No.	44,439
Avg. Credit Limit, per Person	$8,301
Avg. Spent, per Person	$3,746
Satisfactory Ratings, No. per Person	2.79
Avg. No. of Cards, per Person	1.01

LABOUR FORCE

2001 Estimates:

Male:	
In the Labour Force	23,214
Participation Rate	73.3
Employed	21,578
Unemployed	1,636
Unemployment Rate	7.0
Not in Labour Force	8,461
Female:	
In the Labour Force	18,613
Participation Rate	55.3
Employed	17,337
Unemployed	1,276
Unemployment Rate	6.9
Not in Labour Force	15,016

OCCUPATIONS BY MAJOR GROUPS

2001 Estimates:	Male	Female
Management	2,780	1,292
Business, Finance & Admin.	2,269	5,219
Natural & Applied Sciences & Related	1,483	285
Health	287	1,834
Social Sciences, Gov't Services & Religion	353	441
Education	629	910
Arts, Culture, Recreation & Sport	338	447
Sales & Service	5,020	5,494
Trades, Transport & Equipment Operators & Related	5,477	379
Primary Industries	638	98
Processing, Mfg. & Utilities	3,036	1,484

LEVEL OF SCHOOLING

2001 Estimates:

Population 15 years +	65,304
Less than Grade 9	11,489
Grades 9-13 w/o Certif.	12,347
Grade 9-13 with Certif.	12,118
Trade Certif. /Dip.	3,113
Non-Univ. w/o Certif./Dip.	5,450
Non-Univ. with Certif./Dip.	10,835
Univ. w/o Degree	4,492
Univ. w/o Degree/Certif.	746
Univ. with Certif.	3,746
Univ. with Degree	5,460

AVERAGE HOUSEHOLD EXPENDITURES

2001 Estimates:

Food	$6,010
Shelter	$7,240
Clothing	$1,991
Transportation	$5,306
Health & Personal Care	$1,778
Recr'n, Read'g & Education	$2,922
Taxes & Securities	$12,396
Other	$6,861
Total Expenditures	$44,504

PRIVATE HOUSEHOLDS

2001 Estimates:

Private Households, Total	33,198
Pop. in Private Households	79,097
Average no. per Household	2.4

FAMILIES

2001 Estimates:

Families in Private Households	23,580
Husband-Wife Families	19,895
Lone-Parent Families	3,685
Aver. No. Persons per Family	3.0
Aver. No. Sons/Daughters at Home	1.1

HOUSING

2001 Estimates:

Occupied Private Dwellings	33,198
Owned	19,363
Rented	13,835
Single-Detached House	16,666
Semi-Detached House	1,106
Row Houses	896
Apartment, 5+ Storeys	106
Apartment, 5 or Fewer Storeys	11,442
Apartment, Detached Duplex	1,974
Other Single-Attached	133
Movable Dwellings	875

VEHICLES

2001 Estimates:

Model Yrs. '81-'96, No.	39,132
% Total	80.68
Model Yrs. '97-'98, No.	5,814
% Total	11.99
'99 Vehicles registered in Model Yr. '99, No.	3,558
% Total	7.34
Total No. '81-'99	48,504

LEGAL MARITAL STATUS

2001 Estimates: (Age 15+)

Single (Never Married)	24,180
Legally Married (Not Separated)	28,294
Legally Married (Separated)	1,688
Widowed	4,250
Divorced	6,892

Québec

PSYTE CATEGORIES

2001 Estimates	No. of House-holds	% of Total Hhds.	Index
Stable Suburban Families	108	0.33	25
Participation Quebec	3,930	11.84	411
New Quebec Rows	1,855	5.59	510
Quebec Melange	5,646	17.01	642
Traditional French Cdn. Families	6,965	20.98	781
Quebec's Heartland	211	0.64	65
Europa	46	0.14	11
Big Country Families	480	1.45	101
Quebec Rural Blues	715	2.15	88
Old Quebec Walkups	717	2.16	118
Quebec Town Elders	4,986	15.02	531
Aging Quebec Urbanites	651	1.96	680
Quebec's New Urban Mosaic	6,132	18.47	767
Aged Pensioners	279	0.84	63
Old Grey Towers	220	0.66	120

FINANCIAL PSYTE

2001 Estimates	No. of House-holds	% of Total Hhds.	Index
Successful Suburbanites	108	0.33	5
Mortgages & Minivans	5,785	17.43	264
Dollars & Sense	46	0.14	5
Country Credit	12,611	37.99	562
Rural Family Blues	1,406	4.24	52
Loan Parent Stress	6,354	19.14	329
NSF	6,132	18.47	522
Senior Survivors	499	1.50	80

HOME LANGUAGE

2001 Estimates		% Total
English	2,029	2.51
French	77,720	96.29
Italian	86	0.11
Other Languages	139	0.17
Multiple Responses	742	0.92
Total	80,716	100.00

BUILDING PERMITS

	1999	1998	1997
		$000	
Value	64,292	54,398	55,678

HOMES BUILT

	1999	1998	1997
No	396	373	304

Québec

Saint-Jean-sur-Richelieu
(Census Agglomeration)
(Cont'd)

TAXATION

Income Class:	1997	% Total
Under $5,000	6,750	.11.98
$5,000-$10,000	8,480	.15.05
$10,000-$15,000	8,990	.15.96
$15,000-$20,000	5,780	.10.26
$20,000-$25,000	5,390	.9.57
$25,000-$30,000	4,730	.8.40
$30,000-$40,000	6,990	.12.41
$40,000-$50,000	4,270	.7.58
$50,000 +	4,930	.8.75
Total Returns, No.	56,340	
Total Income, $000	1,328,643	
Total Taxable Returns	38,770	
Total Tax, $000	149,340	
Average Income, $	23,583	
Average Tax, $	3,852	

VITAL STATISTICS

	1997	1996	1995	1994
Births	853	893	982	972
Deaths	594	565	603	566
Natural Increase	259	328	379	406
Marriages	268	259	270	316

Note: Latest available data.

COMMUNITY NEWSPAPER(S)

	Total Circulation
Saint-Jean-sur-Richelieu: Le Richelieu Dimanche	35,584
Saint-Jean-sur-Richelieu: Le Canada Français	14,081
Saint-Jean-sur-Richelieu: Servir (mthly)	n.a.

RADIO STATION(S)

	Power
CFZZ-FM	n.a.

Sainte-Marie
(Ville)

In census division La Nouvelle-Beauce.

POPULATION

July 1, 2001 Estimate	11,467
% Cdn. Total	0.04
% Change, '96 -'01	2.82
Avg. Annual Growth Rate, %	0.56
2003 Projected Population	11,616
2006 Projected Population	11,756
2001 Households Estimate	4,354
2003 Projected Households	4,469
2006 Projected Households	4,631

INCOME

% Above/Below National Average	-17
2001 Total Income Estimate	$201,520,000
% Cdn. Total	0.03
2001 Average Hhld. Income	$46,300
2001 Per Capita	$17,600
2003 Projected Total Income	$217,380,000
2006 Projected Total Income	$243,030,000

RETAIL SALES

% Above/Below National Average	+70
2001 Retail Sales Estimate	$174,200,000
% Cdn. Total	0.06
2001 per Household	$40,000
2001 per Capita	$15,200
2001 No. of Establishments	170
2003 Projected Retail Sales	$189,570,000
2006 Projected Retail Sales	$211,540,000

POPULATION

2001 Estimates:		
Total		11,467
Male		5,732
Female		5,735
Age Groups	Male	Female
0-4	321	332
5-9	345	350
10-14	385	380
15-19	437	415
20-24	432	411
25-29	399	366
30-34	431	388
35-39	462	441
40-44	487	477
45-49	478	459
50-54	414	411
55-59	323	318
60-64	255	256
65-69	199	218
70+	364	513

DAYTIME POPULATION

2001 Estimates:	
Working Population	9,373
At Home Population	5,521
Total	14,894

INCOME

2001 Estimates:	
Avg. Household Income	$46,285
Avg. Family Income	$52,160
Per Capita Income	$17,574
Male:	
Avg. Employment Income	$29,219
Avg. Employment Income (Full Time)	$36,798
Female:	
Avg. Employment Income	$18,144
Avg. Employment Income (Full Time)	$25,798

DISPOSABLE & DISCRETIONARY INCOME

2001 Estimates:	Per Hhld.
Disposable Income	$32,642
Discretionary Income 1 (minus Food & Shelter)	$20,697
Discretionary Income 2 (minus Food, Shelter, & Other Expenditures)	$13,351

LIQUID ASSETS

1999 Estimates:	Per Hhld.
Equity Investments	$44,891
Interest Bearing Investments	$52,826
Total Liquid Assets	$97,717

CREDIT DATA

July 2000:	
Pool of Credit	$48,987,498
Revolving Credit, No.	16,952
Fixed Loans, No.	5,456
Avg. Credit Limit, per Person	$6,464
Avg. Spent, per Person	$2,423
Satisfactory Ratings, No. per Person	2.79
Avg. No. of Cards, per Person	1.09

LABOUR FORCE

2001 Estimates:	
Male:	
In the Labour Force	3,584
Participation Rate	76.6
Employed	3,440
Unemployed	144
Unemployment Rate	4.0
Not in Labour Force	1,097
Female:	
In the Labour Force	2,752
Participation Rate	58.9
Employed	2,578
Unemployed	174
Unemployment Rate	6.3
Not in Labour Force	1,921

OCCUPATIONS BY MAJOR GROUPS

2001 Estimates:	Male	Female
Management	265	135
Business, Finance & Admin.	238	713
Natural & Applied Sciences & Related	189	87
Health	56	170
Social Sciences, Gov't Services & Religion	21	76
Education	75	86
Arts, Culture, Recreation & Sport	51	52
Sales & Service	592	829
Trades, Transport & Equipment Operators & Related	963	80
Primary Industries	229	56
Processing, Mfg. & Utilities	857	336

LEVEL OF SCHOOLING

2001 Estimates:	
Population 15 years +	9,354
Less than Grade 9	1,757
Grades 9-13 w/o Certif.	1,792
Grade 9-13 with Certif.	2,033
Trade Certif. /Dip.	514
Non-Univ. w/o Certif./Dip.	485
Non-Univ. with Certif./Dip.	1,528
Univ. w/o Degree	509
Univ. w/o Degree/Certif.	87
Univ. with Certif.	422
Univ. with Degree	736

AVERAGE HOUSEHOLD EXPENDITURES

2001 Estimates:	
Food	$6,419
Shelter	$7,203
Clothing	$2,095
Transportation	$5,535
Health & Personal Care	$1,859
Recr'n, Read'g & Education	$3,003
Taxes & Securities	$12,723
Other	$6,923
Total Expenditures	$45,760

PRIVATE HOUSEHOLDS

2001 Estimates:	
Private Households, Total	4,354
Pop. in Private Households	11,261
Average no. per Household	2.6

FAMILIES

2001 Estimates:	
Families in Private Households	3,362
Husband-Wife Families	2,937
Lone-Parent Families	425
Aver. No. Persons per Family	3.1
Aver. No. Sons/Daughters at Home	1.3

HOUSING

2001 Estimates:	
Occupied Private Dwellings	4,354
Owned	2,968
Rented	1,386
Single-Detached House	2,894
Semi-Detached House	214
Row Houses	38
Apartment, 5 or Fewer Storeys	810
Apartment, Detached Duplex	354
Other Single-Attached	44

VEHICLES

2001 Estimates:	
Model Yrs. '81-'96, No.	6,443
% Total	79.67
Model Yrs. '97-'98, No.	1,142
% Total	14.12
'99 Vehicles registered in Model Yr. '99, No.	502
% Total	6.21
Total No. '81-'99	8,087

LEGAL MARITAL STATUS

2001 Estimates: (Age 15+)	
Single (Never Married)	3,502
Legally Married (Not Separated)	4,726
Legally Married (Separated)	140
Widowed	461
Divorced	525

PSYTE CATEGORIES

2001 Estimates	No. of House-holds	% of Total Hhds.	Index
Participation Quebec	763	17.52	608
Quebec Melange	142	3.26	123
Traditional French Cdn. Families	1,371	31.49	1,173
Quebec's Heartland	571	13.11	1,336
Quebec Rural Blues	230	5.28	217
Quebec Town Elders	1,268	29.12	1,031

FINANCIAL P$YTE

2001 Estimates	No. of House-holds	% of Total Hhds.	Index
Mortgages & Minivans	763	17.52	266
Country Credit	1,513	34.75	514
Rural Family Blues	801	18.40	228
Loan Parent Stress	1,268	29.12	500

Sainte-Marie
(Ville)
(Cont'd)

HOME LANGUAGE

2001 Estimates:
		% Total
English	27	0.24
French	11,440	99.76
Total	11,467	100.00

BUILDING PERMITS

	1999	1998	1997
		$000	
Value	17,230	11,444	11,527

HOMES BUILT

	1999	1998	1997
No	41	60	62

TAXATION

Income Class:	1997	% Total
Under $5,000	1,010	12.23
$5,000-$10,000	1,110	13.44
$10,000-$15,000	1,320	15.98
$15,000-$20,000	870	10.53
$20,000-$25,000	720	8.72
$25,000-$30,000	710	8.60
$30,000-$40,000	1,270	15.38
$40,000-$50,000	610	7.38
$50,000 +	650	7.87
Total Returns, No.	8,260	
Total Income, $000	199,514	
Total Taxable Returns	5,880	
Total Tax, $000	21,730	
Average Income, $	24,154	
Average Tax, $	3,696	

VITAL STATISTICS

	1997	1996	1995	1994
Births	128	119	139	131
Deaths	68	58	65	61
Natural Increase	60	61	74	70
Marriages	37	40	32	25

Note: Latest available data.

COMMUNITY NEWSPAPER(S)

	Total Circulation
Sainte-Marie de Beauce: Beauce Week-End	16,657
Sainte-Marie, Saint-Joseph: Beauce Media	17,648

RADIO STATION(S)

	Power
CHEQ-FM	n.a.

Salaberry-de-Valleyfield
(Census Agglomeration)

The Census Agglomeration of Salaberry-de-Valleyfield includes:
Salaberry-de-Valleyfield, V; Grande-Ile, M; and Saint-Timothée, V. All are in census division Beauharnois-Salaberry.

POPULATION

July 1, 2001 Estimate	39,225
% Cdn. Total	0.13
% Change, '96-'01	-2.43
Avg. Annual Growth Rate, %	-0.49
2003 Projected Population	38,864
2006 Projected Population	38,166
2001 Households Estimate	16,926
2003 Projected Households	16,952
2006 Projected Households	16,933

INCOME

% Above/Below National Average	-19
2001 Total Income Estimate	$672,980,000
% Cdn. Total	0.10
2001 Average Hhld. Income	$39,800
2001 Per Capita	$17,200
2003 Projected Total Income	$701,870,000
2006 Projected Total Income	$748,540,000

RETAIL SALES

% Above/Below National Average	+45
2001 Retail Sales Estimate	$510,750,000
% Cdn. Total	0.18
2001 per Household	$30,200
2001 per Capita	$13,000
2001 No. of Establishments	434
2003 Projected Retail Sales	$544,220,000
2006 Projected Retail Sales	$589,560,000

POPULATION

2001 Estimates:
Total		39,225
Male		18,809
Female		20,416

Age Groups	Male	Female
0-4	1,080	1,011
5-9	1,151	1,078
10-14	1,170	1,125
15-19	1,243	1,252
20-24	1,250	1,220
25-29	1,181	1,133
30-34	1,266	1,260
35-39	1,487	1,517
40-44	1,542	1,617
45-49	1,506	1,581
50-54	1,403	1,484
55-59	1,161	1,244
60-64	939	1,058
65-69	788	968
70+	1,642	2,868

DAYTIME POPULATION

2001 Estimates:
Working Population	17,215
At Home Population	22,010
Total	39,225

INCOME

2001 Estimates:
Avg. Household Income	$39,760
Avg. Family Income	$47,903
Per Capita Income	$17,157
Male:	
Avg. Employment Income	$31,592
Avg. Employment Income (Full Time)	$41,777
Female:	
Avg. Employment Income	$18,673
Avg. Employment Income (Full Time)	$28,224

DISPOSABLE & DISCRETIONARY INCOME

2001 Estimates:
	Per Hhld.
Disposable Income	$27,890
Discretionary Income 1 (minus Food & Shelter)	$17,196
Discretionary Income 2 (minus Food, Shelter, & Other Expenditures)	$11,028

LIQUID ASSETS

1999 Estimates:
	Per Hhld.
Equity Investments	$40,818
Interest Bearing Investments	$46,178
Total Liquid Assets	$86,996

CREDIT DATA

July 2000:
Pool of Credit	$186,712,116
Revolving Credit, No.	56,206
Fixed Loans, No.	18,039
Avg. Credit Limit, per Person	$6,410
Avg. Spent, per Person	$2,896
Satisfactory Ratings, No. per Person	2.41
Avg. No. of Cards, per Person	0.92

LABOUR FORCE

2001 Estimates:
Male:	
In the Labour Force	10,678
Participation Rate	69.3
Employed	9,604
Unemployed	1,074
Unemployment Rate	10.1
Not in Labour Force	4,730
Female:	
In the Labour Force	8,499
Participation Rate	49.4
Employed	7,687
Unemployed	812
Unemployment Rate	9.6
Not in Labour Force	8,703

OCCUPATIONS BY MAJOR GROUPS

2001 Estimates:
	Male	Female
Management	771	304
Business, Finance & Admin.	712	2,402
Natural & Applied Sciences & Related	552	92
Health	177	910
Social Sciences, Gov't Services & Religion	179	154
Education	151	340
Arts, Culture, Recreation & Sport	252	110
Sales & Service	2,082	2,998
Trades, Transport & Equipment Operators & Related	2,773	116
Primary Industries	180	67
Processing, Mfg. & Utilities	2,250	578

Québec

LEVEL OF SCHOOLING

2001 Estimates:
Population 15 years +	32,610
Less than Grade 9	7,509
Grades 9-13 w/o Certif.	6,804
Grade 9-13 with Certif.	6,503
Trade Certif./Dip.	1,455
Non-Univ. w/o Certif./Dip.	2,315
Non-Univ. with Certif./Dip.	4,530
Univ. w/o Degree	1,693
Univ. w/o Degree/Certif.	215
Univ. with Certif.	1,478
Univ. with Degree	1,801

AVERAGE HOUSEHOLD EXPENDITURES

2001 Estimates:
Food	$5,579
Shelter	$6,578
Clothing	$1,739
Transportation	$4,581
Health & Personal Care	$1,614
Recr'n, Read'g & Education	$2,647
Taxes & Securities	$10,969
Other	$6,308
Total Expenditures	$40,015

PRIVATE HOUSEHOLDS

2001 Estimates:
Private Households, Total	16,926
Pop. in Private Households	38,204
Average no. per Household	2.3

FAMILIES

2001 Estimates:
Families in Private Households	11,533
Husband-Wife Families	9,567
Lone-Parent Families	1,966
Aver. No. Persons per Family	2.9
Aver. No. Sons/Daughters at Home	1.1

HOUSING

2001 Estimates:
Occupied Private Dwellings	16,926
Owned	9,500
Rented	7,426
Single-Detached House	7,982
Semi-Detached House	961
Row Houses	391
Apartment, 5+ Storeys	211
Apartment, 5 or Fewer Storeys	4,207
Apartment, Detached Duplex	2,968
Other Single-Attached	179
Movable Dwellings	27

VEHICLES

2001 Estimates:
Model Yrs. '81-'96, No.	19,276
% Total	80.57
Model Yrs. '97-'98, No.	2,948
% Total	12.32
'99 Vehicles registered in Model Yr. '99, No.	1,700
% Total	7.11
Total No. '81-'99	23,924

Québec

Salaberry-de-Valleyfield
(Census Agglomeration)
(Cont'd)

LEGAL MARITAL STATUS

2001 Estimates: (Age 15+)
Single (Never Married) 11,497
Legally Married
 (Not Separated) 13,956
Legally Married (Separated) 895
Widowed 2,836
Divorced 3,426

PSYTE CATEGORIES

2001 Estimates	No. of House-holds	% of Total Hhds.	Index
Participation Quebec	811	4.79	166
Quebec Melange	1,884	11.13	420
Traditional French Cdn. Families	4,567	26.98	1,005
Quebec's Heartland	260	1.54	156
Quebec Rural Blues	84	0.50	20
Quebec Town Elders	6,483	38.30	1,355
Quebec's New Urban Mosaic	1,985	11.73	487
Aged Pensioners	786	4.64	349

FINANCIAL P$YTE

2001 Estimates	No. of House-holds	% of Total Hhds.	Index
Mortgages & Minivans	811	4.79	73
Country Credit	6,451	38.11	564
Rural Family Blues	344	2.03	25
Loan Parent Stress	6,483	38.30	658
NSF	1,985	11.73	331
Senior Survivors	786	4.64	246

HOME LANGUAGE

2001 Estimates:		% Total
English	773	1.97
French	37,912	96.65
Chinese	59	0.15
Spanish	20	0.05
Vietnamese	39	0.10
Other Languages	11	0.03
Multiple Responses	411	1.05
Total	39,225	100.00

BUILDING PERMITS

	1999	1998	1997
		$000	
Value	38,584	26,163	25,181

HOMES BUILT

	1999	1998	1997
No.	38	26	40

TAXATION

Income Class:	1997	% Total
Under $5,000	3,540	12.03
$5,000-$10,000	5,010	17.02
$10,000-$15,000	5,160	17.53
$15,000-$20,000	3,030	10.30
$20,000-$25,000	2,370	8.05
$25,000-$30,000	2,110	7.17
$30,000-$40,000	3,080	10.47
$40,000-$50,000	2,370	8.05
$50,000 +	2,790	9.48
Total Returns, No.	29,430	
Total Income, $000	676,787	
Total Taxable Returns	19,100	
Total Tax, $000	75,177	
Average Income, $	22,997	
Average Tax, $	3,936	

VITAL STATISTICS

	1997	1996	1995	1994
Births	377	401	443	463
Deaths	341	355	329	355
Natural Increase	36	46	114	108
Marriages	240	240	252	239

Note: Latest available data.

COMMUNITY NEWSPAPER(S)

	Total Circulation
Valleyfield: Journal Le Suroît Régional et Agricol (bimthly)	30,000
Valleyfield: L'Impact Jeunesse (mthly)	n.a.
Valleyfield: Le Saint-François Journal	29,714
Valleyfield, Châteauguay: Le Soleil du Saint-Laurent	28,440

RADIO STATION(S)

	Power
CKOD-FM	3,000w

Sept-Îles
(Census Agglomeration)

The Census Agglomeration of Sept-Iles includes: Sept-Iles, V; and several smaller areas. All are in census division Sept-Rivières-Caniapiscau.

POPULATION

July 1, 2001 Estimate 28,927
% Cdn. Total 0.09
% Change, '96 -'01 . . . . 1.46
Avg. Annual Growth Rate, % 0.29
2003 Projected Population 29,197
2006 Projected Population 29,454
2001 Households Estimate 11,720
2003 Projected Households 12,089
2006 Projected Households 12,543

INCOME

% Above/Below National Average . . . . . . same
2001 Total Income Estimate $607,840,000
% Cdn. Total 0.09
2001 Average Hhld. Income $51,900
2001 Per Capita $21,000
2003 Projected Total Income $658,820,000
2006 Projected Total Income $738,390,000

RETAIL SALES

% Above/Below National Average . . . . +7
2001 Retail Sales Estimate $277,240,000
% Cdn. Total 0.10
2001 per Household $23,700
2001 per Capita $9,600
2001 No. of Establishments 313
2003 Projected Retail Sales $304,930,000
2006 Projected Retail Sales $344,770,000

POPULATION

2001 Estimates:
Total 28,927
Male 14,374
Female 14,553

Age Groups	Male	Female
0-4	936	872
5-9	945	931
10-14	932	973
15-19	1,032	1,025
20-24	1,053	997
25-29	1,011	985
30-34	1,050	1,122
35-39	1,163	1,229
40-44	1,209	1,239
45-49	1,196	1,182
50-54	1,049	1,047
55-59	873	861
60-64	706	684
65-69	519	519
70+	700	887

DAYTIME POPULATION

2001 Estimates:
Working Population 13,481
At Home Population 15,445
Total 28,926

INCOME

2001 Estimates:
Avg. Household Income $51,863
Avg. Family Income $58,355
Per Capita Income $21,013
Male:
Avg. Employment Income $37,281
Avg. Employment Income
 (Full Time) $50,162
Female:
Avg. Employment Income $20,099
Avg. Employment Income
 (Full Time) $31,455

DISPOSABLE & DISCRETIONARY INCOME

2001 Estimates:	Per Hhld.
Disposable Income	$35,841
Discretionary Income 1 (minus Food & Shelter)	$23,162
Discretionary Income 2 (minus Food, Shelter, & Other Expenditures)	$14,913

LIQUID ASSETS

1999 Estimates:	Per Hhld.
Equity Investments	$57,779
Interest Bearing Investments	$60,181
Total Liquid Assets	$117,960

CREDIT DATA

July 2000:
Pool of Credit $202,394,537
Revolving Credit, No. 43,105
Fixed Loans, No. 19,956
Avg. Credit Limit, per Person $9,992
Avg. Spent, per Person $4,962
Satisfactory Ratings,
 No. per Person 2.88
Avg. No. of Cards, per Person 1.01

LABOUR FORCE

2001 Estimates:
Male:
In the Labour Force 8,748
Participation Rate 75.7
Employed 7,531
Unemployed 1,217
Unemployment Rate 13.9
Not in Labour Force 2,813
Female:
In the Labour Force 6,642
Participation Rate 56.4
Employed 5,944
Unemployed 698
Unemployment Rate 10.5
Not in Labour Force 5,135

OCCUPATIONS BY MAJOR GROUPS

2001 Estimates:	Male	Female
Management	754	426
Business, Finance & Admin.	568	1,873
Natural & Applied Sciences & Related	659	120
Health	166	542
Social Sciences, Gov't Services & Religion	160	204
Education	227	441
Arts, Culture, Recreation & Sport	158	201
Sales & Service	1,744	2,309
Trades, Transport & Equipment Operators & Related	2,848	74
Primary Industries	263	58
Processing, Mfg. & Utilities	870	86

LEVEL OF SCHOOLING

2001 Estimates:
Population 15 years + ... 23,338
Less than Grade 9 4,442
Grades 9-13 w/o Certif. 4,744
Grade 9-13 with Certif. 4,170
Trade Certif. /Dip. 1,326
Non-Univ. w/o Certif./Dip. 1,824
Non-Univ. with Certif./Dip. 3,782
Univ. w/o Degree. 1,292
 Univ. w/o Degree/Certif. 214
Univ. with Certif. 1,078
Univ. with Degree 1,758

Sept-Îles
(Census Agglomeration)
(Cont'd)

AVERAGE HOUSEHOLD EXPENDITURES

2001 Estimates:
Food	$6,582
Shelter	$7,959
Clothing	$2,248
Transportation	$6,147
Health & Personal Care	$2,084
Recr'n, Read'g & Education	$3,543
Taxes & Securities	$13,868
Other	$7,915
Total Expenditures	$50,346

PRIVATE HOUSEHOLDS

2001 Estimates:
Private Households, Total	11,720
Pop. in Private Households	28,622
Average no. per Household	2.4

FAMILIES

2001 Estimates:
Families in Private Households	8,735
Husband-Wife Families	7,110
Lone-Parent Families	1,625
Aver. No. Persons per Family	3.0
Aver. No. Sons/Daughters at Home	1.2

HOUSING

2001 Estimates:
Occupied Private Dwellings	11,720
Owned	6,825
Rented	4,478
Band Housing	417
Single-Detached House	6,702
Semi-Detached House	565
Row Houses	508
Apartment, 5+ Storeys	309
Apartment, 5 or Fewer Storeys	3,049
Apartment, Detached Duplex	517
Other Single-Attached	43
Movable Dwellings	27

VEHICLES

2001 Estimates:
Model Yrs. '81-'96, No.	13,574
% Total	81.29
Model Yrs. '97-'98, No.	2,014
% Total	12.06
'99 Vehicles registered in Model Yr. '99, No.	1,110
% Total	6.65
Total No. '81-'99	16,698

LEGAL MARITAL STATUS

2001 Estimates: (Age 15+)
Single (Never Married)	10,431
Legally Married (Not Separated)	9,254
Legally Married (Separated)	528
Widowed	1,042
Divorced	2,083

PSYTE CATEGORIES

2001 Estimates	No. of House -holds	% of Total Hhds.	Index
Participation Quebec	2,494	21.28	738
Quebec Melange	3,574	30.49	1,151
Traditional French Cdn. Families	157	1.34	50
Young Grey Collar	2,016	17.20	2,056
Big Country Families	1,368	11.67	818
Quebec Rural Blues	393	3.35	138
Quebec Town Elders	1,311	11.19	396
Aged Pensioners	394	3.36	253

FINANCIAL PSYTE

2001 Estimates	No. of House -holds	% of Total Hhds.	Index
Mortgages & Minivans	2,494	21.28	322
Country Credit	3,731	31.83	471
Revolving Renters	2,016	17.20	374
Rural Family Blues	1,761	15.03	186
Loan Parent Stress	1,311	11.19	192
Senior Survivors	394	3.36	178

HOME LANGUAGE

2001 Estimates:		% Total
English	874	3.02
French	25,740	88.98
Montagnais-Naskapi	1,959	6.77
Portuguese	25	0.09
Other Languages	20	0.07
Multiple Responses	309	1.07
Total	28,927	100.00

BUILDING PERMITS

	1999	1998 $000	1997
Value	15,340	17,215	12,845

HOMES BUILT

	1999	1998	1997
No	15	83	46

TAXATION

Income Class:	1997	% Total
Under $5,000	2,840	14.13
$5,000-$10,000	3,000	14.93
$10,000-$15,000	2,760	13.73
$15,000-$20,000	1,720	8.56
$20,000-$25,000	1,360	6.77
$25,000-$30,000	1,470	7.31
$30,000-$40,000	2,260	11.24
$40,000-$50,000	1,600	7.96
$50,000 +	3,100	15.42
Total Returns, No.	20,100	
Total Income, $000	527,536	
Total Taxable Returns	13,250	
Total Tax, $000	65,663	
Average Income, $	26,246	
Average Tax, $	4,956	

VITAL STATISTICS

	1997	1996	1995	1994
Births	369	379	412	379
Deaths	156	158	145	116
Natural Increase	213	221	267	263
Marriages	80	95	79	82

Note: Latest available data.

COMMUNITY NEWSPAPER(S)

	Total Circulation
Sept-Îles: Le Nord-Est	12,756
Sept-Îles, Havre-Saint-Pierre, Blanc-Sablon: Le Nord-Est Plus	14,109

RADIO STATION(S)

	Power
CBSE-FM	n.a.
CBSI-FM	n.a.
CIPC-FM	n.a.
CKCN	n.a.
CKCN-FM	n.a.

TELEVISION STATION(S)

CBGAT-TV
CBMT-TV
CBST-TV
CFER-TV
CIVG-TV

Shawinigan
(Census Agglomeration)

The Census Agglomeration of Shawinigan includes:
Shawinigan, V; Grand-Mère, V; Lac-à-la-Tortue, M; Saint-Boniface-de-Shawinigan, VL; Saint-Georges, VL; Saint-Gérard-des-Laurentides, P; Shawinigan-Sud, V; & three smaller areas. All are in census division Le Centre-de-la-Mauricie.

POPULATION

July 1, 2001 Estimate	59,606
% Cdn. Total	0.19
% Change, '96 -'01	-1.88
Avg. Annual Growth Rate, %	-0.38
2003 Projected Population	59,222
2006 Projected Population	58,222
2001 Households Estimate	26,300
2003 Projected Households	26,463
2006 Projected Households	26,563

INCOME

% Above/Below National Average	-21
2001 Total Income Estimate	$990,060,000
% Cdn. Total	0.15
2001 Average Hhld. Income	$37,600
2001 Per Capita	$16,600
2003 Projected Total Income	$1,044,920,000
2006 Projected Total Income	$1,129,650,000

RETAIL SALES

% Above/Below National Average	-8
2001 Retail Sales Estimate	$492,480,000
% Cdn. Total	0.18
2001 per Household	$18,700
2001 per Capita	$8,300
2001 No. of Establishments	624
2003 Projected Retail Sales	$521,740,000
2006 Projected Retail Sales	$557,630,000

POPULATION

2001 Estimates:
Total		59,606
Male		28,553
Female		31,053
Age Groups	Male	Female
0-4	1,429	1,312
5-9	1,541	1,421
10-14	1,704	1,635
15-19	1,931	1,864
20-24	1,874	1,794
25-29	1,579	1,513
30-34	1,682	1,633
35-39	2,122	2,162
40-44	2,429	2,487
45-49	2,391	2,442
50-54	2,127	2,218
55-59	1,764	1,882
60-64	1,498	1,726
65-69	1,392	1,762
70+	3,090	5,202

DAYTIME POPULATION

2001 Estimates:
Working Population	23,330
At Home Population	36,277
Total	59,607

Québec

INCOME

2001 Estimates:
Avg. Household Income	$37,645
Avg. Family Income	$45,696
Per Capita Income	$16,610
Male:	
Avg. Employment Income	$30,400
Avg. Employment Income (Full Time)	$42,552
Female:	
Avg. Employment Income	$17,195
Avg. Employment Income (Full Time)	$27,495

DISPOSABLE & DISCRETIONARY INCOME

2001 Estimates:	Per Hhld.
Disposable Income	$26,808
Discretionary Income 1 (minus Food & Shelter)	$16,576
Discretionary Income 2 (minus Food, Shelter, & Other Expenditures)	$10,623

LIQUID ASSETS

1999 Estimates:	Per Hhld.
Equity Investments	$37,862
Interest Bearing Investments	$42,943
Total Liquid Assets	$80,805

CREDIT DATA

July 2000:
Pool of Credit	$222,263,732
Revolving Credit, No.	85,798
Fixed Loans, No.	25,632
Avg. Credit Limit, per Person	$5,239
Avg. Spent, per Person	$2,167
Satisfactory Ratings, No. per Person	2.47
Avg. No. of Cards, per Person	0.93

LABOUR FORCE

2001 Estimates:
Male:	
In the Labour Force	15,122
Participation Rate	63.3
Employed	13,334
Unemployed	1,788
Unemployment Rate	11.8
Not in Labour Force	8,757
Female:	
In the Labour Force	11,324
Participation Rate	42.4
Employed	9,992
Unemployed	1,332
Unemployment Rate	11.8
Not in Labour Force	15,361

Québec

Shawinigan
(Census Agglomeration)
(Cont'd)

OCCUPATIONS BY MAJOR GROUPS

2001 Estimates:	Male	Female
Management	1,259	465
Business, Finance & Admin.	1,259	3,811
Natural & Applied Sciences & Related	890	105
Health	381	1,375
Social Sciences, Gov't Services & Religion	220	196
Education	489	500
Arts, Culture, Recreation & Sport	197	177
Sales & Service	2,681	3,204
Trades, Transport & Equipment Operators & Related	3,836	193
Primary Industries	478	171
Processing, Mfg. & Utilities	2,614	360

LEVEL OF SCHOOLING

2001 Estimates:	
Population 15 years +	50,564
Less than Grade 9	9,703
Grades 9-13 w/o Certif.	9,349
Grade 9-13 with Certif.	10,280
Trade Certif. /Dip.	3,076
Non-Univ. w/o Certif./Dip.	3,569
Non-Univ. with Certif./Dip.	8,269
Univ. w/o Degree	2,970
Univ. w/o Degree/Certif.	349
Univ. with Certif.	2,621
Univ. with Degree	3,348

AVERAGE HOUSEHOLD EXPENDITURES

2001 Estimates:	
Food	$5,350
Shelter	$6,298
Clothing	$1,685
Transportation	$4,418
Health & Personal Care	$1,551
Recr'n, Read'g & Education	$2,520
Taxes & Securities	$10,489
Other	$5,981
Total Expenditures	$38,292

PRIVATE HOUSEHOLDS

2001 Estimates:	
Private Households, Total	26,300
Pop. in Private Households	58,125
Average no. per Household	2.2

FAMILIES

2001 Estimates:	
Families in Private Households	17,351
Husband-Wife Families	14,425
Lone-Parent Families	2,926
Aver. No. Persons per Family	2.8
Aver. No. Sons/Daughters at Home	1.0

HOUSING

2001 Estimates:	
Occupied Private Dwellings	26,300
Owned	15,151
Rented	11,149
Single-Detached House	13,397
Semi-Detached House	869
Row Houses	380
Apartment, 5+ Storeys	364
Owned Apartment, 5+ Storeys	10
Apartment, 5 or Fewer Storeys	8,140
Apartment, Detached Duplex	3,029
Other Single-Attached	94
Movable Dwellings	27

VEHICLES

2001 Estimates:	
Model Yrs. '81-'96, No.	30,696
% Total	86.39
Model Yrs. '97-'98, No.	2,995
% Total	8.43
'99 Vehicles registered in Model Yr. '99, No.	1,842
% Total	5.18
Total No. '81-'99	35,533

LEGAL MARITAL STATUS

2001 Estimates: (Age 15+)	
Single (Never Married)	17,506
Legally Married (Not Separated)	22,107
Legally Married (Separated)	1,122
Widowed	4,610
Divorced	5,219

PSYTE CATEGORIES

2001 Estimates	No. of House-holds	% of Total Hhds.	Index
Suburban Executives	63	0.24	17
Participation Quebec	982	3.73	130
Quebec Melange	2,063	7.84	296
Traditional French Cdn. Families	6,219	23.65	881
Quebec Rural Blues	1,733	6.59	270
Old Quebec Walkups	765	2.91	159
Quebec Town Elders	10,333	39.29	1,390
Quebec's New Urban Mosaic	3,655	13.90	577
Aged Pensioners	321	1.22	92

FINANCIAL P$YTE

2001 Estimates	No. of House-holds	% of Total Hhds.	Index
Four Star Investors	63	0.24	5
Mortgages & Minivans	982	3.73	57
Country Credit	8,282	31.49	466
Rural Family Blues	1,733	6.59	82
Loan Parent Stress	11,098	42.20	725
NSF	3,655	13.90	393
Senior Survivors	321	1.22	65

HOME LANGUAGE

2001 Estimates:		% Total
English	441	0.74
French	58,912	98.84
Greek	51	0.09
Other Languages	30	0.05
Multiple Responses	172	0.29
Total	59,606	100.00

BUILDING PERMITS

	1999	1998	1997
		$000	
Value	51,542	39,142	47,773

HOMES BUILT

	1999	1998	1997
No.	108	100	121

TAXATION

Income Class:	1997	% Total
Under $5,000	6,180	13.74
$5,000-$10,000	8,000	17.78
$10,000-$15,000	8,650	19.23
$15,000-$20,000	4,810	10.69
$20,000-$25,000	3,720	8.27
$25,000-$30,000	3,060	6.80
$30,000-$40,000	4,070	9.05
$40,000-$50,000	2,790	6.20
$50,000 +	3,710	8.25
Total Returns, No.	44,990	
Total Income, $000	949,121	
Total Taxable Returns	27,460	
Total Tax, $000	99,173	
Average Income, $	21,096	
Average Tax, $	3,612	

VITAL STATISTICS

	1997	1996	1995	1994
Births	489	491	535	566
Deaths	617	579	619	596
Natural Increase	-128	-88	-84	-30
Marriages	159	167	161	184

Note: Latest available data.

COMMUNITY NEWSPAPER(S)

	Total Circulation
Shawinigan, Grand-Mère: Hebdo du Saint-Maurice	29,501

Sherbrooke
(Census Metropolitan Area)

POPULATION

July 1, 2001 Estimate	155,790
% Cdn. Total	0.50
% Change, '96 -'01	3.80
Avg. Annual Growth Rate, %	0.75
2003 Projected Population	159,133
2006 Projected Population	163,646
2001 Households Estimate	68,163
2003 Projected Households	70,005
2006 Projected Households	72,432

INCOME

% Above/Below National Average	-12
2001 Total Income Estimate	$2,898,570,000
% Cdn. Total	0.44
2001 Average Hhld. Income	$42,500
2001 Per Capita	$18,600
2003 Projected Total Income	$3,113,050,000
2006 Projected Total Income	$3,443,290,000

RETAIL SALES

% Above/Below National Average	-6
2001 Retail Sales Estimate	$1,311,270,000
% Cdn. Total	0.47
2001 per Household	$19,200
2001 per Capita	$8,400
2001 No. of Establishments	1,470
2003 Projected Retail Sales	$1,446,260,000
2006 Projected Retail Sales	$1,646,600,000

POPULATION

2001 Estimates:

Total		155,790
Male		75,161
Female		80,629

Age Groups	Male	Female
0-4	4,669	4,457
5-9	4,736	4,520
10-14	4,907	4,630
15-19	5,269	5,093
20-24	5,661	5,649
25-29	5,641	5,592
30-34	5,751	5,684
35-39	6,083	6,148
40-44	6,187	6,443
45-49	5,914	6,290
50-54	5,240	5,579
55-59	4,161	4,436
60-64	3,182	3,554
65-69	2,532	3,121
70+	5,228	9,433

DAYTIME POPULATION

2001 Estimates:

Working Population	75,196
At Home Population	80,595
Total	155,791

INCOME

2001 Estimates:

Avg. Household Income	$42,524
Avg. Family Income	$51,908
Per Capita Income	$18,606

Male:

Avg. Employment Income	$31,054
Avg. Employment Income (Full Time)	$41,395

Female:

Avg. Employment Income	$19,916
Avg. Employment Income (Full Time)	$29,633

DISPOSABLE & DISCRETIONARY INCOME

2001 Estimates:	Per Hhld.
Disposable Income	$29,425
Discretionary Income 1 (minus Food & Shelter)	$18,439
Discretionary Income 2 (minus Food, Shelter, & Other Expenditures)	$11,920

LIQUID ASSETS

1999 Estimates:	Per Hhld.
Equity Investments	$45,647
Interest Bearing Investments	$49,282
Total Liquid Assets	$94,929

CREDIT DATA

July 2000:

Pool of Credit	$896,805,215
Revolving Credit, No.	257,568
Fixed Loans, No.	84,989
Avg. Credit Limit, per Person	$7,437
Avg. Spent, per Person	$3,255
Satisfactory Ratings, No. per Person	2.66
Avg. No. of Cards, per Person	1.02

LABOUR FORCE

2001 Estimates:

Male:

In the Labour Force	43,119
Participation Rate	70.9
Employed	40,325
Unemployed	2,794
Unemployment Rate	6.5
Not in Labour Force	17,730

Female:

In the Labour Force	37,752
Participation Rate	56.3
Employed	35,107
Unemployed	2,645
Unemployment Rate	7.0
Not in Labour Force	29,270

OCCUPATIONS BY MAJOR GROUPS

2001 Estimates:	Male	Female
Management	4,230	1,558
Business, Finance & Admin.	3,780	9,888
Natural & Applied Sciences & Related	3,275	570
Health	1,504	4,777
Social Sciences, Gov't Services & Religion	1,105	1,357
Education	2,367	2,591
Arts, Culture, Recreation & Sport	1,033	893
Sales & Service	8,696	11,304
Trades, Transport & Equipment Operators & Related	9,034	576
Primary Industries	994	223
Processing, Mfg. & Utilities	5,518	2,463

LEVEL OF SCHOOLING

2001 Estimates:

Population 15 years +	127,871
Less than Grade 9	19,448
Grades 9-13 w/o Certif.	20,589
Grade 9-13 with Certif.	20,826
Trade Certif. /Dip.	6,257
Non-Univ. w/o Certif./Dip.	9,701
Non-Univ. with Certif./Dip.	22,276
Univ. w/o Degree	10,279
Univ. w/o Degree/Certif.	1,417
Univ. with Certif.	8,862
Univ. with Degree	18,495

AVERAGE HOUSEHOLD EXPENDITURES

2001 Estimates:

Food	$5,573
Shelter	$7,159
Clothing	$1,900
Transportation	$4,844
Health & Personal Care	$1,692
Recr'n, Read'g & Education	$2,843
Taxes & Securities	$11,923
Other	$6,475
Total Expenditures	$42,409

PRIVATE HOUSEHOLDS

2001 Estimates:

Private Households, Total	68,163
Pop. in Private Households	150,519
Average no. per Household	2.2

FAMILIES

2001 Estimates:

Families in Private Households	44,265
Husband-Wife Families	36,887
Lone-Parent Families	7,378
Aver. No. Persons per Family	2.9
Aver. No. Sons/Daughters at Home	1.1

Québec

HOUSING

2001 Estimates:

Occupied Private Dwellings	68,163
Owned	34,774
Rented	33,389
Single-Detached House	29,271
Semi-Detached House	1,828
Row Houses	1,142
Apartment, 5+ Storeys	2,158
Owned Apartment, 5+ Storeys	319
Apartment, 5 or Fewer Storeys	28,157
Apartment, Detached Duplex	4,935
Other Single-Attached	409
Movable Dwellings	263

RADIO STATION DATA

Station	Market	Format	Wkly. Reach%*	Aver. Hrs. Tuned
All Stations			93	21.3
CBF-FM	Montréal	Multi-format	13	13.2
CBFX-FM	Montréal	Music, Culture, Info.	5	6.8
CBME-FM	Montréal		2	7.6
CFGL-FM	Laval	Soft Rock	n.a.	n.a.
CFLX-FM	Sherbrooke	Multi-format	n.a.	n.a.
CFQR-FM	Montréal	Adult Contemp.	n.a.	n.a.
CHLT	Sherbrooke	News, Talk, Sports	27	9.9
CHOM-FM	Montréal	AOR	n.a.	n.a.
CIMO-FM	Sherbrooke	Top 40	49	11.7
CITE-F3	Montréal	Adult Contemp.	1	19.1
CITE-F4	Sherbrooke	Adult Contemp.	43	12.6
CJAD	Montréal	News, Talk	4	17.9
CJPX-FM	Montréal	Classical	2	9.0
CKAC	Montréal	Multi-format	3	8.3
CKOI-FM	Montréal	Contemp. Hit Radio	5	7.4

BBM Spring 2000 Radio Reach Surveys; area coverage.
* Mon-Sun 5a.m.-1a.m. , All Persons 12+

TV STATION DATA

Station	Market	Network Affiliation	Wkly. Reach%*	Aver. Hrs. Tuned
All Stations			97	29.4
CANALD	n.a.	n.a.	13	2.2
CBFT	Montréal	SRC	6	2.9
CBMT	Montréal	CBC	10	1.8
CFCF	Montréal	CTV	18	3.5
CFKS	Sherbrooke	TQS	60	6.5
CFTM	Montréal	TVA	5	6.8
CHLT	Sherbrooke	TVA	76	13.4
CIVM	Montréal	Télé-Qué.	21	2.7
CIVS	Sherbrooke	Télé-Qué.	n.a.	n.a.
CKMI	Montréal	Global	18	2.9
CKSH	Sherbrooke	SRC	71	5.4
ECRAN	n.a.	n.a.	7	6.3
FAMILE	n.a.	n.a.	12	1.9
MUSIQUE	n.a.	Ind.	7	1.9
OTHERS	n.a.	n.a.	9	2.2
RDI	n.a.	n.a.	7	2.9
RDS	n.a.	Ind.	15	4.0
TOON(FR)	n.a.	Ind.	16	4.7
TSN	n.a.	Ind.	4	4.3
TV5	n.a.	n.a.	4	4.0
VCR	n.a.	n.a.	24	3.4
VIE	n.a.	n.a.	9	1.9
WCAX	Burlington VT	CBS	21	5.1
WETK	Burlington VT	PBS	9	2.4
WFFF	Burlington VT	FOX, WB	8	2.0
WPTZ	Plattsburg NY	NBC	14	2.6
WVNY	Burlington VT	ABC	14	4.0

BBM Spring 2000 TV Reach Surveys; CMA coverage.
*Mon-Sun 6a.m.-2a.m. , All Persons 2+

Québec

Sherbrooke
(Census Metropolitan Area)
(Cont'd)

VEHICLES

2001 Estimates:

Model Yrs. '81-'96, No. 67,396
  % Total 77.05
Model Yrs. '97-'98, No. 12,839
  % Total 14.68
'99 Vehicles registered in
  Model Yr. '99, No. 7,241
  % Total 8.28
Total No. '81-'99 87,476

LEGAL MARITAL STATUS

2001 Estimates: (Age 15+)

Single (Never Married) 51,388
Legally Married
  (Not Separated) 51,488
Legally Married (Separated) 2,788
Widowed 8,187
Divorced 14,020

PSYTE CATEGORIES

2001 Estimates	No. of House-holds	% of Total Hhds.	Index
Urban Gentry	984	1.44	80
Suburban Executives	97	0.14	10
Stable Suburban Families	455	0.67	51
Small City Elite	647	0.95	55
Aging Erudites	999	1.47	97
Participation Quebec	8,483	12.45	432
New Quebec Rows	3,897	5.72	522
Quebec Melange	6,413	9.41	355
Traditional French Cdn. Families	10,117	14.84	553
Quebec's Heartland	845	1.24	126
Young Urban Professionals	2,584	3.79	200
Young Urban Intelligentsia	240	0.35	23
University Enclaves	1,013	1.49	73
Young City Singles	524	0.77	34
Urban Bohemia	1,777	2.61	223
Old Leafy Towns	250	0.37	14
Old Quebec Walkups	7,432	10.90	595
Quebec Town Elders	4,758	6.98	247
Aging Quebec Urbanites	1,145	1.68	582
Quebec's New Urban Mosaic	13,353	19.59	813
Aged Pensioners	630	0.92	69
Big City Stress	325	0.48	42
Old Grey Towers	386	0.57	102

FINANCIAL P$YTE

2001 Estimates	No. of House-holds	% of Total Hhds.	Index
Four Star Investors	1,081	1.59	32
Successful Suburbanites	455	0.67	10
Canadian Comfort	647	0.95	10
Urban Heights	3,583	5.26	122
Mortgages & Minivans	12,380	18.16	275
Bills & Wills	250	0.37	4
Country Credit	16,530	24.25	359
Young Urban Struggle	3,030	4.45	94
Rural Family Blues	845	1.24	15
Loan Parent Stress	13,335	19.56	336
Towering Debt	524	0.77	10
NSF	13,678	20.07	567
Senior Survivors	1,016	1.49	79

HOME LANGUAGE

2001 Estimates:		% Total
English	8,493	5.45
French	142,786	91.65
Arabic	237	0.15
Chinese	89	0.06
Hungarian	101	0.06
Polish	104	0.07
Serbian	140	0.09
Serbo-Croatian	654	0.42
Spanish	698	0.45
Other Languages	591	0.38
Multiple Responses	1,897	1.22
Total	155,790	100.00

BUILDING PERMITS

	1999	1998 $000	1997
Value	114,895	129,871	120,261

HOMES BUILT

	1999	1998	1997
No	534	665	755

TAXATION

Income Class:	1997	% Total
Under $5,000	12,870	11.75
$5,000-$10,000	17,230	15.73
$10,000-$15,000	18,440	16.83
$15,000-$20,000	11,860	10.83
$20,000-$25,000	9,600	8.76
$25,000-$30,000	8,900	8.12
$30,000-$40,000	12,840	11.72
$40,000-$50,000	7,800	7.12
$50,000 +	10,120	9.24

Total Returns, No. 109,550
Total Income, $000 2,612,854
Total Taxable
  Returns 73,560
Total Tax, $000 292,901
Average Income, $ 23,851
Average Tax, $ 3,982

VITAL STATISTICS

	1997	1996	1995	1994
Births	1,752	1,812	1,759	1,787
Deaths	1,187	1,061	1,141	1,001
Natural Increase	565	751	618	786
Marriages	586	575	618	629

Note: Latest available data.

DAILY NEWSPAPER(S)

	Circulation Average Paid
La Tribune	
Sat	39,538
Mon-Fri	31,227
Record	5,121

COMMUNITY NEWSPAPER(S)

	Total Circulation
Lennoxville: The Townships Sun (mthly)	796
Sherbrooke: Entrée Libre (bimthly)	9,000
Sherbrooke: La Nouvelle de Sherbrooke	43,410

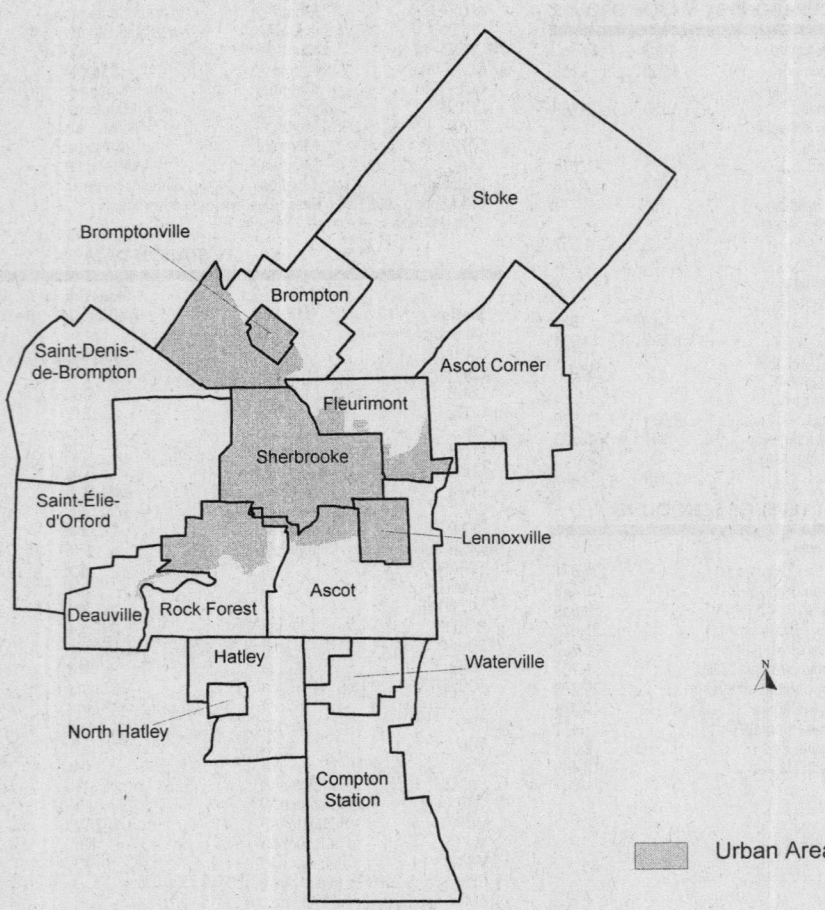

Urban Areas

Fleurimont
(Ville)
Sherbrooke CMA
In census division Sherbrooke.

POPULATION

July 1, 2001 Estimate	17,865
% Cdn. Total	0.06
% Change, '96 -'01	7.85
Avg. Annual Growth Rate, %	1.52
2003 Projected Population	18,595
2006 Projected Population	19,651
2001 Households Estimate	6,448
2003 Projected Households	6,769
2006 Projected Households	7,222

INCOME

% Above/Below National Average	-7
2001 Total Income Estimate	$351,560,000
% Cdn. Total	0.05
2001 Average Hhld. Income	$54,500
2001 Per Capita	$19,700
2003 Projected Total Income	$385,500,000
2006 Projected Total Income	$438,980,000

RETAIL SALES

% Above/Below National Average	-61
2001 Retail Sales Estimate	$62,460,000
% Cdn. Total	0.02
2001 per Household	$9,700
2001 per Capita	$3,500
2001 No. of Establishments	129
2003 Projected Retail Sales	$68,950,000
2006 Projected Retail Sales	$79,200,000

POPULATION

2001 Estimates:

Total		17,865
Male		8,773
Female		9,092

Age Groups	Male	Female
0-4	553	521
5-9	637	590
10-14	722	687
15-19	783	755
20-24	695	684
25-29	563	592
30-34	599	615
35-39	701	744
40-44	791	852
45-49	770	841
50-54	652	693
55-59	465	467
60-64	312	307
65-69	210	221
70+	320	523

DAYTIME POPULATION

2001 Estimates:

Working Population	2,272
At Home Population	7,822
Total	10,094

INCOME

2001 Estimates:

Avg. Household Income	$54,522
Avg. Family Income	$59,440
Per Capita Income	$19,679
Male:	
Avg. Employment Income	$34,207
Avg. Employment Income (Full Time)	$44,355
Female:	
Avg. Employment Income	$21,905
Avg. Employment Income (Full Time)	$31,596

DISPOSABLE & DISCRETIONARY INCOME

2001 Estimates:	Per Hhld.
Disposable Income	$38,025
Discretionary Income 1 (minus Food & Shelter)	$25,175
Discretionary Income 2 (minus Food, Shelter, & Other Expenditures)	$16,742

LIQUID ASSETS

1999 Estimates:	Per Hhld.
Equity Investments	$63,672
Interest Bearing Investments	$63,680
Total Liquid Assets	$127,352

CREDIT DATA

July 2000:

Pool of Credit	$104,686,259
Revolving Credit, No.	29,438
Fixed Loans, No.	10,567
Avg. Credit Limit, per Person	$8,547
Avg. Spent, per Person	$3,827
Satisfactory Ratings, No. per Person	3.04
Avg. No. of Cards, per Person	1.15

LABOUR FORCE

2001 Estimates:

Male:	
In the Labour Force	5,441
Participation Rate	79.3
Employed	5,349
Unemployed	92
Unemployment Rate	1.7
Not in Labour Force	1,420
Female:	
In the Labour Force	4,814
Participation Rate	66.0
Employed	4,611
Unemployed	203
Unemployment Rate	4.2
Not in Labour Force	2,480

OCCUPATIONS BY MAJOR GROUPS

2001 Estimates:	Male	Female
Management	567	236
Business, Finance & Admin.	549	1,293
Natural & Applied Sciences & Related	312	93
Health	341	965
Social Sciences, Gov't Services & Religion	107	166
Education	173	208
Arts, Culture, Recreation & Sport	81	43
Sales & Service	1,249	1,299
Trades, Transport & Equipment Operators & Related	1,327	74
Primary Industries	95	12
Processing, Mfg. & Utilities	572	252

LEVEL OF SCHOOLING

2001 Estimates:

Population 15 years +	14,155
Less than Grade 9	1,592
Grades 9-13 w/o Certif.	2,471
Grade 9-13 with Certif.	2,631
Trade Certif. /Dip.	759
Non-Univ. w/o Certif./Dip.	1,128
Non-Univ. with Certif./Dip.	2,950
Univ. w/o Degree	872
Univ. w/o Degree/Certif.	49
Univ. with Certif.	823
Univ. with Degree	1,752

AVERAGE HOUSEHOLD EXPENDITURES

2001 Estimates:

Food	$6,867
Shelter	$7,939
Clothing	$2,428
Transportation	$6,635
Health & Personal Care	$2,031
Recr'n, Read'g & Education	$3,514
Taxes & Securities	$15,890
Other	$7,430
Total Expenditures	$52,734

PRIVATE HOUSEHOLDS

2001 Estimates:

Private Households, Total	6,448
Pop. in Private Households	17,452
Average no. per Household	2.7

FAMILIES

2001 Estimates:

Families in Private Households	5,271
Husband-Wife Families	4,578
Lone-Parent Families	693
Aver. No. Persons per Family	3.2
Aver. No. Sons/Daughters at Home	1.3

HOUSING

2001 Estimates:

Occupied Private Dwellings	6,448
Owned	4,863
Rented	1,585
Single-Detached House	4,394
Semi-Detached House	281
Row Houses	145
Apartment, 5+ Storeys	12
Apartment, 5 or Fewer Storeys	1,322
Apartment, Detached Duplex	275
Movable Dwellings	19

VEHICLES

2001 Estimates:

Model Yrs. '81-'96, No.	7,733
% Total	73.58
Model Yrs. '97-'98, No.	1,762
% Total	16.76
'99 Vehicles registered in Model Yr. '99, No.	1,015
% Total	9.66
Total No. '81-'99	10,510

LEGAL MARITAL STATUS

2001 Estimates: (Age 15+)

Single (Never Married)	5,098
Legally Married (Not Separated)	6,808
Legally Married (Separated)	308
Widowed	563
Divorced	1,378

PSYTE CATEGORIES

2001 Estimates	No. of House-holds	% of Total Hhds.	Index
Participation Quebec	2,560	39.70	1,378
New Quebec Rows	768	11.91	1,087
Traditional French Cdn. Families	2,258	35.02	1,304
Old Quebec Walkups	439	6.81	372
Quebec Town Elders	147	2.28	81
Quebec's New Urban Mosaic	220	3.41	142

FINANÇIAL P$YTE

2001 Estimates	No. of House-holds	% of Total Hhds.	Index
Mortgages & Minivans	3,328	51.61	782
Country Credit	2,258	35.02	518
Loan Parent Stress	586	9.09	156
NSF	220	3.41	96

Québec

HOME LANGUAGE

2001 Estimates:		% Total
English	226	1.27
French	17,423	97.53
Persian (Farsi)	13	0.07
Portuguese	10	0.06
Russian	16	0.09
Spanish	44	0.25
Vietnamese	48	0.27
Multiple Responses	85	0.48
Total	17,865	100.00

BUILDING PERMITS

	1999	1998 $000	1997
Value	9,591	16,297	12,076

HOMES BUILT

	1999	1998	1997
No.	54	59	109

TAXATION

Income Class:	1997	% Total
Under $5,000	1,270	11.43
$5,000-$10,000	1,250	11.25
$10,000-$15,000	1,470	13.23
$15,000-$20,000	1,110	9.99
$20,000-$25,000	1,050	9.45
$25,000-$30,000	1,120	10.08
$30,000-$40,000	1,590	14.31
$40,000-$50,000	1,070	9.63
$50,000 +	1,180	10.62
Total Returns, No.	11,110	
Total Income, $000	290,333	
Total Taxable Returns	8,380	
Total Tax, $000	33,838	
Average Income, $	26,133	
Average Tax, $	4,038	

VITAL STATISTICS

	1997	1996	1995	1994
Births	200	197	197	222
Deaths	67	81	82	63
Natural Increase	133	116	115	159
Marriages	7	6	9	7

Note: Latest available data.

MEDIA INFO
see Sherbrooke, CMA

Québec

Rock Forest
(Ville)
Sherbrooke CMA

In census division Sherbrooke.

POPULATION

July 1, 2001 Estimate	18,774
% Cdn. Total	0.06
% Change, '96 -'01	11.01
Avg. Annual Growth Rate, %	2.11
2003 Projected Population	19,847
2006 Projected Population	21,405
2001 Households Estimate	6,936
2003 Projected Households	7,395
2006 Projected Households	8,053

INCOME

% Above/Below National Average	-3
2001 Total Income Estimate	$382,680,000
% Cdn. Total	0.06
2001 Average Hhld. Income	$55,200
2001 Per Capita	$20,400
2003 Projected Total Income	$426,680,000
2006 Projected Total Income	$496,620,000

RETAIL SALES

% Above/Below National Average	+38
2001 Retail Sales Estimate	$232,090,000
% Cdn. Total	0.08
2001 per Household	$33,500
2001 per Capita	$12,400
2001 No. of Establishments	176
2003 Projected Retail Sales	$268,290,000
2006 Projected Retail Sales	$325,550,000

POPULATION

2001 Estimates:

Total		18,774
Male		9,438
Female		9,336

Age Groups	Male	Female
0-4	610	562
5-9	699	641
10-14	762	686
15-19	791	703
20-24	693	627
25-29	572	577
30-34	662	710
35-39	789	841
40-44	835	886
45-49	817	845
50-54	715	693
55-59	545	503
60-64	362	338
65-69	233	233
70+	353	491

DAYTIME POPULATION

2001 Estimates:

Working Population	4,125
At Home Population	8,310
Total	12,435

INCOME

2001 Estimates:

Avg. Household Income	$55,174
Avg. Family Income	$59,127
Per Capita Income	$20,384
Male:	
Avg. Employment Income	$34,115
Avg. Employment Income (Full Time)	$42,194
Female:	
Avg. Employment Income	$21,225
Avg. Employment Income (Full Time)	$31,367

DISPOSABLE & DISCRETIONARY INCOME

2001 Estimates:	Per Hhld.
Disposable Income	$38,643
Discretionary Income 1 (minus Food & Shelter)	$25,722
Discretionary Income 2 (minus Food, Shelter, & Other Expenditures)	$17,137

LIQUID ASSETS

1999 Estimates:	Per Hhld.
Equity Investments	$62,874
Interest Bearing Investments	$63,155
Total Liquid Assets	$126,029

CREDIT DATA

July 2000:

Pool of Credit	$122,379,423
Revolving Credit, No.	31,990
Fixed Loans, No.	12,732
Avg. Credit Limit, per Person	$9,297
Avg. Spent, per Person	$4,231
Satisfactory Ratings, No. per Person	3.16
Avg. No. of Cards, per Person	1.22

LABOUR FORCE

2001 Estimates:

Male:	
In the Labour Force	5,982
Participation Rate	81.2
Employed	5,798
Unemployed	184
Unemployment Rate	3.1
Not in Labour Force	1,385
Female:	
In the Labour Force	4,910
Participation Rate	65.9
Employed	4,609
Unemployed	301
Unemployment Rate	6.1
Not in Labour Force	2,537

OCCUPATIONS BY MAJOR GROUPS

2001 Estimates:	Male	Female
Management	707	253
Business, Finance & Admin.	589	1,452
Natural & Applied Sciences & Related	482	101
Health	143	430
Social Sciences, Gov't Services & Religion	151	163
Education	179	305
Arts, Culture, Recreation & Sport	93	100
Sales & Service	1,166	1,430
Trades, Transport & Equipment Operators & Related	1,460	85
Primary Industries	129	11
Processing, Mfg. & Utilities	751	344

LEVEL OF SCHOOLING

2001 Estimates:

Population 15 years +	14,814
Less than Grade 9	1,524
Grades 9-13 w/o Certif.	2,450
Grade 9-13 with Certif.	2,844
Trade Certif. /Dip.	1,018
Non-Univ. w/o Certif./Dip.	1,298
Non-Univ. with Certif./Dip.	2,813
Univ. w/o Degree	851
Univ. w/o Degree/Certif.	134
Univ. with Certif.	717
Univ. with Degree	2,016

AVERAGE HOUSEHOLD EXPENDITURES

2001 Estimates:

Food	$6,865
Shelter	$8,016
Clothing	$2,438
Transportation	$6,744
Health & Personal Care	$2,065
Recr'n, Read'g & Education	$3,473
Taxes & Securities	$16,172
Other	$7,546
Total Expenditures	$53,319

PRIVATE HOUSEHOLDS

2001 Estimates:

Private Households, Total	6,936
Pop. in Private Households	18,559
Average no. per Household	2.7

FAMILIES

2001 Estimates:

Families in Private Households	5,688
Husband-Wife Families	4,968
Lone-Parent Families	720
Aver. No. Persons per Family	3.2
Aver. No. Sons/Daughters at Home	1.3

HOUSING

2001 Estimates:

Occupied Private Dwellings	6,936
Owned	5,143
Rented	1,793
Single-Detached House	4,759
Semi-Detached House	366
Row Houses	173
Apartment, 5 or Fewer Storeys	1,364
Apartment, Detached Duplex	262
Other Single-Attached	12

VEHICLES

2001 Estimates:

Model Yrs. '81-'96, No.	8,742
% Total	74.58
Model Yrs. '97-'98, No.	1,801
% Total	15.36
'99 Vehicles registered in Model Yr. '99, No.	1,179
% Total	10.06
Total No. '81-'99	11,722

LEGAL MARITAL STATUS

2001 Estimates: (Age 15+)

Single (Never Married)	5,332
Legally Married (Not Separated)	7,148
Legally Married (Separated)	290
Widowed	507
Divorced	1,537

PSYTE CATEGORIES

2001 Estimates	No. of House -holds	% of Total Hhds.	Index
Participation Quebec	2,596	37.43	1,299
New Quebec Rows	1,197	17.26	1,575
Quebec Melange	1,019	14.69	554
Traditional French Cdn. Families	1,945	28.04	1,044
Quebec's New Urban Mosaic	179	2.58	107

FINANCIAL PSYTE

2001 Estimates	No. of House -holds	% of Total Hhds.	Index
Mortgages & Minivans	3,793	54.69	829
Country Credit	2,964	42.73	632
NSF	179	2.58	73

HOME LANGUAGE

2001 Estimates:		% Total
English	352	1.87
French	18,145	96.65
Arabic	67	0.36
Armenian	11	0.06
Chinese	11	0.06
Polish	12	0.06
Spanish	54	0.29
Multiple Responses	122	0.65
Total	18,774	100.00

BUILDING PERMITS

	1999	1998 $000	1997
Value	22,060	16,311	18,354

HOMES BUILT

	1999	1998	1997
No	172	162	186

TAXATION

Income Class:	1997	% Total
Under $5,000	1,510	12.09
$5,000-$10,000	1,450	11.61
$10,000-$15,000	1,620	12.97
$15,000-$20,000	1,260	10.09
$20,000-$25,000	1,150	9.21
$25,000-$30,000	1,160	9.29
$30,000-$40,000	1,800	14.41
$40,000-$50,000	1,110	8.89
$50,000 +	1,450	11.61
Total Returns, No.	12,490	
Total Income, $000	327,465	
Total Taxable Returns	9,420	
Total Tax, $000	39,020	
Average Income, $	26,218	
Average Tax, $	4,142	

VITAL STATISTICS

	1997	1996	1995	1994
Births	219	227	203	216
Deaths	66	47	79	59
Natural Increase	153	180	124	157
Marriages	20	24	24	21

Note: Latest available data.

MEDIA INFO
see Sherbrooke, CMA

Sherbrooke

(Ville)
Sherbrooke CMA
In census division Sherbrooke.

POPULATION

July 1, 2001 Estimate	77,983
% Cdn. Total	0.25
% Change, '96 -'01	-0.30
Avg. Annual Growth Rate, %	-0.06
2003 Projected Population	77,975
2006 Projected Population	77,710
2001 Households Estimate	38,481
2003 Projected Households	38,785
2006 Projected Households	39,044

INCOME

% Above/Below National Average	-14
2001 Total Income Estimate	$1,411,580,000
% Cdn. Total	0.22
2001 Average Hhld. Income	$36,700
2001 Per Capita	$18,100
2003 Projected Total Income	$1,473,350,000
2006 Projected Total Income	$1,561,520,000

RETAIL SALES

% Above/Below National Average	+18
2001 Retail Sales Estimate	$826,490,000
% Cdn. Total	0.30
2001 per Household	$21,500
2001 per Capita	$10,600
2001 No. of Establishments	819
2003 Projected Retail Sales	$892,320,000
2006 Projected Retail Sales	$982,830,000

POPULATION

2001 Estimates:

Total		77,983
Male		36,451
Female		41,532

Age Groups	Male	Female
0-4	2,188	2,096
5-9	1,963	1,906
10-14	1,904	1,841
15-19	2,160	2,218
20-24	2,846	2,949
25-29	3,145	3,021
30-34	2,981	2,809
35-39	2,863	2,846
40-44	2,808	2,953
45-49	2,690	2,951
50-54	2,425	2,778
55-59	1,989	2,371
60-64	1,643	2,075
65-69	1,440	1,986
70+	3,406	6,732

DAYTIME POPULATION

2001 Estimates:

Working Population	55,083
At Home Population	43,553
Total	98,636

INCOME

2001 Estimates:

Avg. Household Income	$36,682
Avg. Family Income	$47,619
Per Capita Income	$18,101
Male:	
Avg. Employment Income	$28,953
Avg. Employment Income (Full Time)	$40,818
Female:	
Avg. Employment Income	$19,123
Avg. Employment Income (Full Time)	$28,776

DISPOSABLE & DISCRETIONARY INCOME

2001 Estimates:	*Per Hhld.*
Disposable Income	$25,095
Discretionary Income 1 (minus Food & Shelter)	$15,005
Discretionary Income 2 (minus Food, Shelter, & Other Expenditures)	$9,557

LIQUID ASSETS

1999 Estimates:	*Per Hhld.*
Equity Investments	$37,584
Interest Bearing Investments	$43,012
Total Liquid Assets	$80,596

CREDIT DATA

July 2000:

Pool of Credit	$425,510,244
Revolving Credit, No.	128,416
Fixed Loans, No.	37,441
Avg. Credit Limit, per Person	$6,680
Avg. Spent, per Person	$2,795
Satisfactory Ratings, No. per Person	2.45
Avg. No. of Cards, per Person	0.96

LABOUR FORCE

2001 Estimates:

Male:

In the Labour Force	19,762
Participation Rate	65.0
Employed	17,967
Unemployed	1,795
Unemployment Rate	9.1
Not in Labour Force	10,634

Female:

In the Labour Force	18,391
Participation Rate	51.5
Employed	16,885
Unemployed	1,506
Unemployment Rate	8.2
Not in Labour Force	17,298

OCCUPATIONS BY MAJOR GROUPS

2001 Estimates:	Male	Female
Management	1,856	745
Business, Finance & Admin.	1,840	4,763
Natural & Applied Sciences & Related	1,621	300
Health	771	2,245
Social Sciences, Gov't Services & Religion	596	772
Education	1,397	1,273
Arts, Culture, Recreation & Sport	568	520
Sales & Service	4,308	5,713
Trades, Transport & Equipment Operators & Related	3,109	250
Primary Industries	208	41
Processing, Mfg. & Utilities	2,418	962

LEVEL OF SCHOOLING

2001 Estimates:

Population 15 years +	66,085
Less than Grade 9	11,457
Grades 9-13 w/o Certif.	9,603
Grade 9-13 with Certif.	9,787
Trade Certif. /Dip.	2,621
Non-Univ. w/o Certif./Dip.	4,913
Non-Univ. with Certif./Dip.	10,834
Univ. w/o Degree	6,247
Univ. w/o Degree/Certif.	823
Univ. with Certif.	5,424
Univ. with Degree	10,623

AVERAGE HOUSEHOLD EXPENDITURES

2001 Estimates:

Food	$4,911
Shelter	$6,841
Clothing	$1,644
Transportation	$3,813
Health & Personal Care	$1,528
Recr'n, Read'g & Education	$2,495
Taxes & Securities	$10,145
Other	$5,920
Total Expenditures	$37,297

PRIVATE HOUSEHOLDS

2001 Estimates:

Private Households, Total	38,481
Pop. in Private Households	74,308
Average no. per Household	1.9

FAMILIES

2001 Estimates:

Families in Private Households	21,296
Husband-Wife Families	16,682
Lone-Parent Families	4,614
Aver. No. Persons per Family	2.7
Aver. No. Sons/Daughters at Home	1.0

HOUSING

2001 Estimates:

Occupied Private Dwellings	38,481
Owned	13,689
Rented	24,792
Single-Detached House	9,311
Semi-Detached House	908
Row Houses	718
Apartment, 5+ Storeys	2,111
Owned Apartment, 5+ Storeys	319
Apartment, 5 or Fewer Storeys	21,581
Apartment, Detached Duplex	3,538
Other Single-Attached	304
Movable Dwellings	10

VEHICLES

2001 Estimates:

Model Yrs. '81-'96, No.	31,670
% Total	76.73
Model Yrs. '97-'98, No.	6,188
% Total	14.99
'99 Vehicles registered in Model Yr. '99, No.	3,419
% Total	8.28
Total No. '81-'99	41,277

LEGAL MARITAL STATUS

2001 Estimates: (Age 15+)

Single (Never Married)	28,832
Legally Married (Not Separated)	22,336
Legally Married (Separated)	1,652
Widowed	5,473
Divorced	7,792

PSYTE CATEGORIES

2001 Estimates	No. of House-holds	% of Total Hhds.	Index
Urban Gentry	984	2.56	142
Stable Suburban Families	455	1.18	91
Participation Quebec	868	2.26	78
New Quebec Rows	1,567	4.07	372
Quebec Melange	4,230	10.99	415
Young Urban Professionals	2,563	6.66	351
Young Urban Intelligentsia	240	0.62	41
University Enclaves	374	0.97	48
Young City Singles	524	1.36	59
Urban Bohemia	1,777	4.62	395
Old Quebec Walkups	6,332	16.45	898
Quebec Town Elders	4,143	10.77	381
Aging Quebec Urbanites	1,145	2.98	1,031
Quebec's New Urban Mosaic	11,817	30.71	1,275
Aged Pensioners	385	1.00	75
Old Grey Towers	386	1.00	181

Québec

FINANCIAL P$YTE

2001 Estimates	No. of House-holds	% of Total Hhds.	Index
Four Star Investors	984	2.56	51
Successful Suburbanites	455	1.18	18
Urban Heights	2,563	6.66	155
Mortgages & Minivans	2,435	6.33	96
Country Credit	4,230	10.99	163
Young Urban Struggle	2,391	6.21	131
Loan Parent Stress	11,620	30.20	519
Towering Debt	524	1.36	17
NSF	11,817	30.71	868
Senior Survivors	771	2.00	106

HOME LANGUAGE

2001 Estimates:		% Total
English	2,150	2.76
French	73,057	93.68
Arabic	140	0.18
Chinese	78	0.10
Hungarian	101	0.13
Lao	47	0.06
Serbian	130	0.17
Serbo-Croatian	448	0.57
Spanish	479	0.61
Other Languages	366	0.47
Multiple Responses	987	1.27
Total	77,983	100.00

BUILDING PERMITS

	1999	1998 *$000*	1997
Value	45,701	57,260	51,569

HOMES BUILT

	1999	1998	1997
No.	113	181	126

TAXATION

Income Class:	1997	% Total
Under $5,000	6,530	11.16
$5,000-$10,000	10,700	18.28
$10,000-$15,000	11,150	19.05
$15,000-$20,000	6,590	11.26
$20,000-$25,000	4,890	8.35
$25,000-$30,000	4,260	7.28
$30,000-$40,000	5,930	10.13
$40,000-$50,000	3,570	6.10
$50,000 +	4,910	8.39
Total Returns, No.	58,530	
Total Income, $000	1,330,434	
Total Taxable Returns	36,660	
Total Tax, $000	145,061	
Average Income, $	22,731	
Average Tax, $	3,957	

VITAL STATISTICS

	1997	1996	1995	1994
Births	794	853	822	837
Deaths	811	720	751	672
Natural Increase	-17	133	71	165
Marriages	421	412	443	466

Note: Latest available data.

MEDIA INFO
see Sherbrooke, CMA

Québec

Sorel
(Census Agglomeration)

The Census Agglomeration of Sorel includes: Sorel, V; Saint-Joseph-de-Sorel, V; Sainte-Anne-de-Sorel, P; Sainte-Victoire-de-Sorel, P; and Tracy, V. All are in census division Le Bas-Richelieu.

POPULATION

July 1, 2001 Estimate	41,942
% Cdn. Total	0.13
% Change, '96 - '01	-3.89
Avg. Annual Growth Rate, %	-0.79
2003 Projected Population	41,237
2006 Projected Population	39,899
2001 Households Estimate	18,060
2003 Projected Households	18,080
2006 Projected Households	17,978

INCOME

% Above/Below National Average	-12
2001 Total Income Estimate	$781,660,000
% Cdn. Total	0.12
2001 Average Hhld. Income	$43,300
2001 Per Capita	$18,600
2003 Projected Total Income	$817,760,000
2006 Projected Total Income	$870,860,000

RETAIL SALES

% Above/Below National Average	+17
2001 Retail Sales Estimate	$439,740,000
% Cdn. Total	0.16
2001 per Household	$24,300
2001 per Capita	$10,500
2001 No. of Establishments	477
2003 Projected Retail Sales	$466,910,000
2006 Projected Retail Sales	$499,400,000

POPULATION

2001 Estimates:

Total		41,942
Male		20,284
Female		21,658

Age Groups	Male	Female
0-4	940	927
5-9	958	979
10-14	1,115	1,108
15-19	1,380	1,350
20-24	1,380	1,325
25-29	1,160	1,119
30-34	1,140	1,160
35-39	1,445	1,486
40-44	1,736	1,784
45-49	1,835	1,891
50-54	1,768	1,775
55-59	1,467	1,485
60-64	1,147	1,249
65-69	946	1,157
70+	1,867	2,863

DAYTIME POPULATION

2001 Estimates:

Working Population	18,161
At Home Population	23,781
Total	41,942

INCOME

2001 Estimates:

Avg. Household Income	$43,281
Avg. Family Income	$50,509
Per Capita Income	$18,637
Male:	
Avg. Employment Income	$36,549
Avg. Employment Income (Full Time)	$46,593
Female:	
Avg. Employment Income	$18,242
Avg. Employment Income (Full Time)	$28,225

DISPOSABLE & DISCRETIONARY INCOME

2001 Estimates:	Per Hhld.
Disposable Income	$30,479
Discretionary Income 1 (minus Food & Shelter)	$19,217
Discretionary Income 2 (minus Food, Shelter, & Other Expenditures)	$12,374

LIQUID ASSETS

1999 Estimates:	Per Hhld.
Equity Investments	$44,959
Interest Bearing Investments	$49,483
Total Liquid Assets	$94,442

CREDIT DATA

July 2000:

Pool of Credit	$211,199,803
Revolving Credit, No.	71,504
Fixed Loans, No.	18,026
Avg. Credit Limit, per Person	$6,317
Avg. Spent, per Person	$2,509
Satisfactory Ratings, No. per Person	2.57
Avg. No. of Cards, per Person	0.89

LABOUR FORCE

2001 Estimates:

Male:

In the Labour Force	11,643
Participation Rate	67.4
Employed	10,545
Unemployed	1,098
Unemployment Rate	9.4
Not in Labour Force	5,628

Female:

In the Labour Force	8,446
Participation Rate	45.3
Employed	7,601
Unemployed	845
Unemployment Rate	10.0
Not in Labour Force	10,198

OCCUPATIONS BY MAJOR GROUPS

2001 Estimates:	Male	Female
Management	1,044	287
Business, Finance & Admin.	840	2,214
Natural & Applied Sciences & Related	837	76
Health	278	1,122
Social Sciences, Gov't Services & Religion	133	136
Education	291	335
Arts, Culture, Recreation & Sport	127	151
Sales & Service	1,685	2,982
Trades, Transport & Equipment Operators & Related	3,396	157
Primary Industries	194	36
Processing, Mfg. & Utilities	2,211	307

LEVEL OF SCHOOLING

2001 Estimates:

Population 15 years +	35,915
Less than Grade 9	7,182
Grades 9-13 w/o Certif.	6,090
Grade 9-13 with Certif.	6,812
Trade Certif. /Dip.	2,181
Non-Univ. w/o Certif./Dip.	2,730
Non-Univ. with Certif./Dip.	6,744
Univ. w/o Degree	1,903
Univ. w/o Degree/Certif.	169
Univ. with Certif.	1,734
Univ. with Degree	2,273

AVERAGE HOUSEHOLD EXPENDITURES

2001 Estimates:

Food	$5,871
Shelter	$6,930
Clothing	$1,874
Transportation	$5,169
Health & Personal Care	$1,752
Recr'n, Read'g & Education	$2,813
Taxes & Securities	$12,149
Other	$6,630
Total Expenditures	$43,188

PRIVATE HOUSEHOLDS

2001 Estimates:

Private Households, Total	18,060
Pop. in Private Households	41,035
Average no. per Household	2.3

FAMILIES

2001 Estimates:

Families in Private Households	12,731
Husband-Wife Families	10,823
Lone-Parent Families	1,908
Aver. No. Persons per Family	2.8
Aver. No. Sons/Daughters at Home	1.0

HOUSING

2001 Estimates:

Occupied Private Dwellings	18,060
Owned	11,769
Rented	6,291
Single-Detached House	10,250
Semi-Detached House	1,013
Row Houses	215
Apartment, 5+ Storeys	372
Owned Apartment, 5+ Storeys	20
Apartment, 5 or Fewer Storeys	4,084
Apartment, Detached Duplex	1,969
Other Single-Attached	116
Movable Dwellings	41

VEHICLES

2001 Estimates:

Model Yrs. '81-'96, No.	21,416
% Total	83.33
Model Yrs. '97-'98, No.	2,727
% Total	10.61
'99 Vehicles registered in Model Yr. '99, No.	1,556
% Total	6.05
Total No. '81-'99	25,699

LEGAL MARITAL STATUS

2001 Estimates: (Age 15+)

Single (Never Married)	12,501
Legally Married (Not Separated)	16,547
Legally Married (Separated)	703
Widowed	2,711
Divorced	3,453

PSYTE CATEGORIES

2001 Estimates	No. of House-holds	% of Total Hhds.	Index
Participation Quebec	1,624	8.99	312
Quebec Melange	4,872	26.98	1,018
Traditional French Cdn. Families	3,268	18.10	674
Quebec's Heartland	122	0.68	69
Quebec Rural Blues	658	3.64	150
Quebec Town Elders	6,411	35.50	1,256
Quebec's New Urban Mosaic	310	1.72	71
Aged Pensioners	690	3.82	287

FINANCIAL P$YTE

2001 Estimates	No. of House-holds	% of Total Hhds.	Index
Mortgages & Minivans	1,624	8.99	136
Country Credit	8,140	45.07	666
Rural Family Blues	780	4.32	53
Loan Parent Stress	6,411	35.50	610
NSF	310	1.72	49
Senior Survivors	690	3.82	203

HOME LANGUAGE

2001 Estimates:		% Total
English	129	0.31
French	41,582	99.14
Other Languages	50	0.12
Multiple Responses	181	0.43
Total	41,942	100.00

BUILDING PERMITS

	1999	1998	1997
		$000	
Value	29,731	27,990	16,099

HOMES BUILT

	1999	1998	1997
No	59	50	48

TAXATION

Income Class:	1997	% Total
Under $5,000	4,660	14.49
$5,000-$10,000	5,290	16.45
$10,000-$15,000	5,350	16.64
$15,000-$20,000	3,070	9.55
$20,000-$25,000	2,450	7.62
$25,000-$30,000	2,130	6.62
$30,000-$40,000	2,920	9.08
$40,000-$50,000	2,300	7.15
$50,000 +	4,060	12.62
Total Returns, No.	32,160	
Total Income, $000	759,717	
Total Taxable Returns	20,540	
Total Tax, $000	86,906	
Average Income, $	23,623	
Average Tax, $	4,231	

VITAL STATISTICS

	1997	1996	1995	1994
Births	344	361	358	368
Deaths	407	377	359	351
Natural Increase	-63	-16	-1	17
Marriages	139	133	129	139

Note: Latest available data.

COMMUNITY NEWSPAPER(S)

	Total Circulation
Sorel, Tracy: Journal la Voix	27,800
Sorel, Tracy: Les 2 Rives	27,923

RADIO STATION(S)

	Power
CJSO-FM	n.a.

Thetford Mines
(Census Agglomeration)

The Census Agglomeration of Thetford Mines includes: Black Lake, V; Thetford Mines, V; Thetford-Partie-Sud, CT; plus two smaller areas. All are in census division L'Amiante.

POPULATION

July 1, 2001 Estimate	27,133
% Cdn. Total	0.09
% Change, '96 -'01	-3.66
Avg. Annual Growth Rate, %	-0.74
2003 Projected Population	26,740
2006 Projected Population	25,966
2001 Households Estimate	11,580
2003 Projected Households	11,646
2006 Projected Households	11,662

INCOME

% Above/Below National Average	-19
2001 Total Income Estimate	$464,730,000
% Cdn. Total	0.07
2001 Average Hhld. Income	$40,100
2001 Per Capita	$17,100
2003 Projected Total Income	$486,910,000
2006 Projected Total Income	$519,630,000

RETAIL SALES

% Above/Below National Average	+45
2001 Retail Sales Estimate	$352,830,000
% Cdn. Total	0.13
2001 per Household	$30,500
2001 per Capita	$13,000
2001 No. of Establishments	376
2003 Projected Retail Sales	$378,520,000
2006 Projected Retail Sales	$411,370,000

POPULATION

2001 Estimates:

Total		27,133
Male		12,976
Female		14,157
Age Groups	Male	Female
0-4	624	596
5-9	628	600
10-14	718	674
15-19	941	858
20-24	959	895
25-29	796	759
30-34	722	724
35-39	845	872
40-44	995	1,035
45-49	1,068	1,129
50-54	1,025	1,094
55-59	861	955
60-64	733	887
65-69	668	853
70+	1,393	2,226

DAYTIME POPULATION

2001 Estimates:

Working Population	14,224
At Home Population	15,348
Total	29,572

INCOME

2001 Estimates:

Avg. Household Income	$40,132
Avg. Family Income	$47,804
Per Capita Income	$17,128
Male:	
Avg. Employment Income	$28,670
Avg. Employment Income (Full Time)	$38,399
Female:	
Avg. Employment Income	$17,242
Avg. Employment Income (Full Time)	$28,721

DISPOSABLE & DISCRETIONARY INCOME

2001 Estimates:	Per Hhld.
Disposable Income	$28,181
Discretionary Income 1 (minus Food & Shelter)	$17,395
Discretionary Income 2 (minus Food, Shelter, & Other Expenditures)	$11,129

LIQUID ASSETS

1999 Estimates:	Per Hhld.
Equity Investments	$43,773
Interest Bearing Investments	$47,158
Total Liquid Assets	$90,931

CREDIT DATA

July 2000:

Pool of Credit	$119,116,321
Revolving Credit, No.	44,617
Fixed Loans, No.	10,452
Avg. Credit Limit, per Person	$5,650
Avg. Spent, per Person	$2,009
Satisfactory Ratings, No. per Person	2.52
Avg. No. of Cards, per Person	1.03

LABOUR FORCE

2001 Estimates:

Male:	
In the Labour Force	7,195
Participation Rate	65.4
Employed	6,708
Unemployed	487
Unemployment Rate	6.8
Not in Labour Force	3,811
Female:	
In the Labour Force	5,981
Participation Rate	48.7
Employed	5,628
Unemployed	353
Unemployment Rate	5.9
Not in Labour Force	6,306

OCCUPATIONS BY MAJOR GROUPS

2001 Estimates:	Male	Female
Management	767	378
Business, Finance & Admin.	524	1,399
Natural & Applied Sciences & Related	346	49
Health	152	754
Social Sciences, Gov't Services & Religion	88	189
Education	296	355
Arts, Culture, Recreation & Sport	63	91
Sales & Service	1,208	1,969
Trades, Transport & Equipment Operators & Related	1,971	162
Primary Industries	478	58
Processing, Mfg. & Utilities	1,095	338

LEVEL OF SCHOOLING

2001 Estimates:

Population 15 years +	23,293
Less than Grade 9	4,941
Grades 9-13 w/o Certif.	3,951
Grade 9-13 with Certif.	4,110
Trade Certif. /Dip.	1,689
Non-Univ. w/o Certif./Dip.	1,582
Non-Univ. with Certif./Dip.	4,258
Univ. w/o Degree	1,155
Univ. w/o Degree/Certif.	146
Univ. with Certif.	1,009
Univ. with Degree	1,607

AVERAGE HOUSEHOLD EXPENDITURES

2001 Estimates:

Food	$5,634
Shelter	$6,593
Clothing	$1,745
Transportation	$4,617
Health & Personal Care	$1,652
Recr'n, Read'g & Education	$2,599
Taxes & Securities	$11,194
Other	$6,234
Total Expenditures	$40,268

PRIVATE HOUSEHOLDS

2001 Estimates:

Private Households, Total	11,580
Pop. in Private Households	26,380
Average no. per Household	2.3

FAMILIES

2001 Estimates:

Families in Private Households	8,189
Husband-Wife Families	7,105
Lone-Parent Families	1,084
Aver. No. Persons per Family	2.9
Aver. No. Sons/Daughters at Home	1.0

HOUSING

2001 Estimates:

Occupied Private Dwellings	11,580
Owned	8,021
Rented	3,559
Single-Detached House	7,220
Semi-Detached House	202
Row Houses	61
Apartment, 5 or Fewer Storeys	2,226
Apartment, Detached Duplex	1,608
Other Single-Attached	110
Movable Dwellings	153

VEHICLES

2001 Estimates:

Model Yrs. '81-'96, No.	15,813
% Total	85.76
Model Yrs. '97-'98, No.	1,643
% Total	8.91
'99 Vehicles registered in Model Yr. '99, No.	982
% Total	5.33
Total No. '81-'99	18,438

LEGAL MARITAL STATUS

2001 Estimates: (Age 15+)

Single (Never Married)	7,550
Legally Married (Not Separated)	11,497
Legally Married (Separated)	419
Widowed	2,005
Divorced	1,822

PSYTE CATEGORIES

2001 Estimates	No. of House-holds	% of Total Hhds.	Index
Participation Quebec	385	3.32	115
Quebec Melange	1,756	15.16	572
Traditional French Cdn. Families	1,907	16.47	613
Quebec Rural Blues	1,153	9.96	409
Quebec Town Elders	5,829	50.34	1,781
Quebec's New Urban Mosaic	483	4.17	173

FINANCIAL PSYTE

2001 Estimates	No. of House-holds	% of Total Hhds.	Index
Mortgages & Minivans	385	3.32	50
Country Credit	3,663	31.63	468
Rural Family Blues	1,153	9.96	123
Loan Parent Stress	5,829	50.34	864
NSF	483	4.17	118

Québec

HOME LANGUAGE

2001 Estimates:		% Total
English	185	0.68
French	26,820	98.85
Italian	20	0.07
Spanish	29	0.11
Other Languages	10	0.04
Multiple Responses	69	0.25
Total	27,133	100.00

BUILDING PERMITS

	1999	1998 $000	1997
Value	18,174	13,587	23,131

HOMES BUILT

	1999	1998	1997
No.	9	18	48

TAXATION

Income Class:	1997	% Total
Under $5,000	2,880	13.07
$5,000-$10,000	3,360	15.25
$10,000-$15,000	3,980	18.06
$15,000-$20,000	2,660	12.07
$20,000-$25,000	2,120	9.62
$25,000-$30,000	1,710	7.76
$30,000-$40,000	2,330	10.57
$40,000-$50,000	1,480	6.72
$50,000 +	1,550	7.03
Total Returns, No.	22,040	
Total Income, $000	478,798	
Total Taxable Returns	14,440	
Total Tax, $000	48,406	
Average Income, $.	21,724	
Average Tax, $	3,352	

VITAL STATISTICS

	1997	1996	1995	1994
Births	219	249	218	253
Deaths	267	247	275	285
Natural Increase	-48	2	-57	-32
Marriages	88	81	106	81

Note: Latest available data.

COMMUNITY NEWSPAPER(S)

	Total Circulation
Thetford Mines: Le Courrier Frontenac	20,248
Thetford Mines: Le P'tit Journal (mthly)	n.a.

RADIO STATION(S)

	Power
CBMC-FM	n.a.
CBV-FM	n.a.
CFJO-FM	100,000w
CKLD-FM	n.a.

TELEVISION STATION(S)

CBMT-TV
CBVT-TV

Québec

Trois-Rivières
(Census Metropolitan Area)

POPULATION

July 1, 2001 Estimate 142,783
% Cdn. Total 0.46
% Change, '96 -'01 . . . . 0.40
Avg. Annual Growth Rate, % 0.08
2003 Projected Population 143,846
2006 Projected Population 144,911
2001 Households Estimate 62,594
2003 Projected Households 63,654
2006 Projected Households 64,987

INCOME

% Above/Below National Average . . . . -10
2001 Total Income Estimate . . . $2,720,020,000
% Cdn. Total 0.41
2001 Average Hhld. Income $43,500
2001 Per Capita $19,100
2003 Projected Total Income . $2,905,550,000
2006 Projected Total Income . . $3,201,060,000

RETAIL SALES

% Above/Below National Average . . . . -10
2001 Retail Sales Estimate . . . $1,146,680,000
% Cdn. Total 0.41
2001 per Household $18,300
2001 per Capita $8,000
2001 No. of Establishments 1,291
2003 Projected Retail Sales . . . $1,244,390,000
2006 Projected Retail Sales . . . $1,384,290,000

POPULATION

2001 Estimates:
Total 142,783
Male 68,806
Female 73,977

Age Groups	Male	Female
0-4	3,938	3,700
5-9	4,033	3,788
10-14	4,195	4,030
15-19	4,668	4,560
20-24	4,777	4,738
25-29	4,471	4,446
30-34	4,715	4,760
35-39	5,377	5,556
40-44	5,765	5,988
45-49	5,680	5,832
50-54	5,134	5,262
55-59	4,214	4,466
60-64	3,420	3,866
65-69	2,895	3,532
70+	5,524	9,453

DAYTIME POPULATION

2001 Estimates:
Working Population 64,395
At Home Population 78,388
Total 142,783

INCOME

2001 Estimates:
Avg. Household Income $43,455
Avg. Family Income $52,499
Per Capita Income $19,050
Male:
Avg. Employment Income $34,361
Avg. Employment Income
(Full Time) $45,054
Female:
Avg. Employment Income $19,388
Avg. Employment Income
(Full Time) $29,720

DISPOSABLE & DISCRETIONARY INCOME

2001 Estimates: / Per Hhld.
Disposable Income $29,965
Discretionary Income 1
(minus Food & Shelter) $18,676
Discretionary Income 2
(minus Food, Shelter, & Other
Expenditures) $11,916

LIQUID ASSETS

1999 Estimates: / Per Hhld.
Equity Investments $44,514
Interest Bearing Investments $49,292
Total Liquid Assets $93,806

CREDIT DATA

July 2000:
Pool of Credit $684,332,493
Revolving Credit, No. 223,873
Fixed Loans, No. 68,859
Avg. Credit Limit, per Person $6,469
Avg. Spent, per Person $2,717
Satisfactory Ratings,
No. per Person 2.63
Avg. No. of Cards, per Person 1.11

LABOUR FORCE

2001 Estimates:
Male:
In the Labour Force 39,459
Participation Rate 69.7
Employed 35,994
Unemployed 3,465
Unemployment Rate 8.8
Not in Labour Force 17,181
Female:
In the Labour Force 30,845
Participation Rate 49.4
Employed 28,524
Unemployed 2,321
Unemployment Rate 7.5
Not in Labour Force 31,614

OCCUPATIONS BY MAJOR GROUPS

2001 Estimates:	Male	Female
Management	3,944	1,560
Business, Finance & Admin.	3,415	8,584
Natural & Applied Sciences & Related	3,026	523
Health	1,043	3,169
Social Sciences, Gov't Services & Religion	769	1,133
Education	1,580	2,118
Arts, Culture, Recreation & Sport	568	701
Sales & Service	7,568	9,480
Trades, Transport & Equipment Operators & Related	10,021	540
Primary Industries	903	307
Processing, Mfg. & Utilities	4,738	1,221

LEVEL OF SCHOOLING

2001 Estimates:
Population 15 years + ... 119,099
Less than Grade 9 19,906
Grades 9-13 w/o Certif. 17,496
Grade 9-13 with Certif. 21,881
Trade Certif. /Dip. 5,733
Non-Univ. w/o Certif./Dip. 9,579
Non-Univ. with Certif./Dip. 21,667
Univ. w/o Degree 9,159
Univ. w/o Degree/Certif. 1,084
Univ. with Certif. 8,075
Univ. with Degree 13,678

AVERAGE HOUSEHOLD EXPENDITURES

2001 Estimates:
Food $5,813
Shelter $7,176
Clothing $1,953
Transportation $5,036
Health & Personal Care $1,738
Recr'n, Read'g & Education $2,856
Taxes & Securities $12,084
Other $6,671
Total Expenditures $43,327

PRIVATE HOUSEHOLDS

2001 Estimates:
Private Households, Total 62,594
Pop. in Private Households 138,839
Average no. per Household 2.2

FAMILIES

2001 Estimates:
Families in Private Households 41,628
Husband-Wife Families 35,004
Lone-Parent Families 6,624
Aver. No. Persons per Family 2.9
Aver. No. Sons/Daughters at Home 1.1

HOUSING

2001 Estimates:
Occupied Private Dwellings 62,594
Owned 34,903
Rented 27,691
Single-Detached House 28,929
Semi-Detached House 2,461
Row Houses 1,034
Apartment, 5+ Storeys 1,213
Owned Apartment, 5+ Storeys 11
Apartment, 5 or Fewer Storeys 22,726
Apartment, Detached Duplex 5,750
Other Single-Attached 239
Movable Dwellings 242

VEHICLES

2001 Estimates:
Model Yrs. '81-'96, No. 70,959
% Total 81.40
Model Yrs. '97-'98, No. 9,928
% Total 11.39
'99 Vehicles registered in
Model Yr. '99, No. 6,283
% Total 7.21
Total No. '81-'99 87,170

RADIO STATION DATA

Station	Market	Format	Wkly. Reach%*	Aver. Hrs. Tuned
All Stations			94	23.3
CBF-FM	Montréal	Multi-format	8	13.1
CBFX-FM	Montréal	Music, Culture, Info.	4	9.5
CBM-FM	Montréal	Multi-format	n.a.	n.a.
CFOM-FM	Lévis	Adult Contemp.	2	11.4
CHEY-FM	Trois-Rivières	Adult Contemp.	39	14.5
CHIK-FM	Québec	Contemp. Hit Radio	7	6.0
CHLN	Trois-Rivières	News, Talk, Sports	27	13.1
CHOI-FM	Québec	AOR	12	7.4
CHOM-FM	Montréal	AOR	3	5.6
CIGB-FM	Trois-Rivières	Contemp. Hits	48	12.9
CITE-F4	Sherbrooke	Adult Contemp.	n.a.	n.a.
CITF-FM	Québec	Adult Contemp.	n.a.	n.a.
CJFM-FM	Montréal	Contemp. Hits	n.a.	n.a.
CJMF-FM	Québec	Classic Rock	4	4.9
CJPX-FM	Montréal	Classical	4	15.5
CKAC	Montréal	Multi-format	6	13.2
CKOI-FM	Montréal	Contemp. Hit Radio	12	5.7
CKVL	Montréal	Multi-format	n.a.	n.a.

BBM Spring 2000 Radio Reach Surveys; area coverage.
* Mon-Sun 5a.m.-1a.m., All Persons 12+

TV STATION DATA

Station	Market	Network Affiliation	Wkly. Reach%*	Aver. Hrs. Tuned
All Stations			99	26.8
CANALD	n.a.	n.a.	15	2.0
CBFT	Montréal	SRC	10	1.9
CBMT	Montréal	CBC	n.a.	n.a.
CFCF	Montréal	CTV	11	1.6
CFKM	Trois-Rivières	TQS	63	5.3
CFTM	Montréal	TVA	7	2.8
CHEM	Trois-Rivières	TVA	85	11.4
CIVC	Trois-Rivières	Télé-Qué.	n.a.	n.a.
CIVM	Montréal	Télé-Qué.	24	2.1
CKTM	Trois-Rivières	SRC	81	7.1
ECRAN	n.a.	n.a.	4	3.5
FAMILE	n.a.	n.a.	20	2.3
HIST(FR)	n.a.	Ind.	8	2.5
LCN	n.a.	n.a.	9	2.1
MUSMAX	n.a.	Ind.	6	2.2
RDI	n.a.	n.a.	15	3.7
RDS	n.a.	Ind.	18	3.5
SERIES	n.a.	Ind.	5	3.8
TOON(FR)	n.a.	Ind.	19	3.3
TSN	n.a.	Ind.	5	3.5
TV5	n.a.	n.a.	9	1.9
VCR	n.a.	n.a.	21	4.1
VIE	n.a.	n.a.	16	1.9
WCAX	Burlington VT	CBS	10	2.9
WVNY	Burlington VT	ABC	7	2.4

BBM Spring 2000 TV Reach Surveys; CMA coverage.
*Mon-Sun 6a.m.-2a.m., All Persons 2+

Trois-Rivières
(Census Metropolitan Area)
(Cont'd)

LEGAL MARITAL STATUS

2001 Estimates: (Age 15+)
Single (Never Married) 46,197
Legally Married
 (Not Separated) 49,965
Legally Married (Separated) 2,515
Widowed 8,210
Divorced 12,212

PSYTE CATEGORIES

2001 Estimates	No. of House -holds	% of Total Hhds.	Index
Urban Gentry	415	0.66	37
Technocrafts & Bureaucrats	1,414	2.26	80
Stable Suburban Families	388	0.62	48
Old Bungalow Burbs	440	0.70	42
Participation Quebec	7,017	11.21	389
New Quebec Rows	3,002	4.80	438
Quebec Melange	7,774	12.42	469
Traditional French Cdn. Families	10,422	16.65	620
Quebec's Heartland	2,128	3.40	346
Young Urban Professionals	364	0.58	31
Young City Singles	1,038	1.66	72
Urban Bohemia	629	1.00	86
Quebec Rural Blues	1,294	2.07	85
Old Quebec Walkups	2,842	4.54	248
Quebec Town Elders	9,144	14.61	517
Aging Quebec Urbanites	889	1.42	492
Quebec's New Urban Mosaic	12,016	19.20	797
Aged Pensioners	619	0.99	74
Old Grey Towers	250	0.40	72

FINANCIAL P$YTE

2001 Estimates	No. of House -holds	% of Total Hhds.	Index
Four Star Investors	415	0.66	13
Successful Suburbanites	1,802	2.88	43
Urban Heights	364	0.58	14
Miners & Credit-Liners	440	0.70	22
Mortgages & Minivans	10,019	16.01	243
Country Credit	18,196	29.07	430
Young Urban Struggle	629	1.00	21
Rural Family Blues	3,422	5.47	68
Loan Parent Stress	12,875	20.57	353
Towering Debt	1,038	1.66	21
NSF	12,016	19.20	543
Senior Survivors	869	1.39	74

HOME LANGUAGE

2001 Estimates:		% Total
English	1,123	0.79
French	140,685	98.53
Other Languages	403	0.28
Multiple Responses	572	0.40
Total	142,783	100.00

BUILDING PERMITS

	1999	1998	1997
		$000	
Value	109,335	106,215	102,155

HOMES BUILT

	1999	1998	1997
No.	526	529	498

TAXATION

Income Class:	1997	% Total
Under $5,000	13,360	13.10
$5,000-$10,000	17,060	16.72
$10,000-$15,000	17,780	17.43
$15,000-$20,000	10,230	10.03
$20,000-$25,000	8,220	8.06
$25,000-$30,000	7,160	7.02
$30,000-$40,000	10,140	9.94
$40,000-$50,000	7,020	6.88
$50,000 +	11,090	10.87
Total Returns, No.	102,020	
Total Income, $000.	2,407,258	
Total Taxable Returns.	65,640	
Total Tax, $000.	273,661	
Average Income, $	23,596	
Average Tax, $	4,169	

VITAL STATISTICS

	1997	1996	1995	1994
Births	1,373	1,442	1,551	1,587
Deaths	1,137	1,033	1,086	1,057
Natural Increase	236	409	465	530
Marriages	311	374	401	427

Note: Latest available data.

Québec

DAILY NEWSPAPER(S)

	Circulation Average Paid
Le Nouvelliste	
Sat	46,134
Mon-Fri	41,644

COMMUNITY NEWSPAPER(S)

	Total Circulation
Bécancour, Nicolet: Le Courrier du Sud	21,966
Trois-Rivières: La Gazette Populaire (11/yr)	71,000
Trois-Rivières, Cap-de-la-Madeleine: L'Hebdo-Journal	47,032

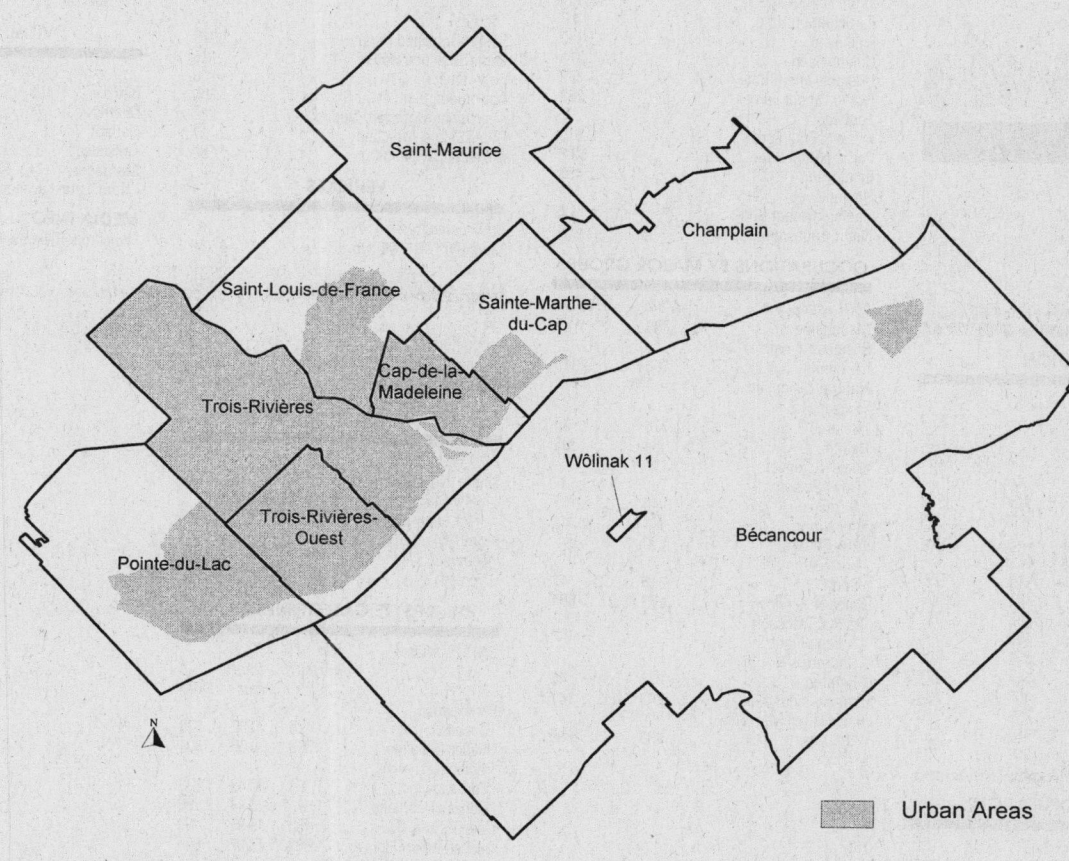

Urban Areas

Québec

Bécancour
(Ville)
Trois-Rivières CMA

In census division Bécancour.

POPULATION

July 1, 2001 Estimate	11,873
% Cdn. Total	0.04
% Change, '96 -'01	1.81
Avg. Annual Growth Rate, %	0.36
2003 Projected Population	12,060
2006 Projected Population	12,273
2001 Households Estimate	4,581
2003 Projected Households	4,678
2006 Projected Households	4,859

INCOME

% Above/Below National Average	-14
2001 Total Income Estimate	$215,300,000
% Cdn. Total	0.03
2001 Average Hhld. Income	$47,000
2001 Per Capita	$18,100
2003 Projected Total Income	$231,120,000
2006 Projected Total Income	$259,270,000

RETAIL SALES

% Above/Below National Average	-18
2001 Retail Sales Estimate	$87,040,000
% Cdn. Total	0.03
2001 per Household	$19,000
2001 per Capita	$7,300
2001 No. of Establishments	100
2003 Projected Retail Sales	$94,630,000
2006 Projected Retail Sales	$105,020,000

POPULATION

2001 Estimates:

Total		11,873
Male		6,012
Female		5,861

Age Groups	Male	Female
0-4	335	319
5-9	399	366
10-14	439	401
15-19	468	431
20-24	414	393
25-29	351	335
30-34	386	374
35-39	468	457
40-44	521	502
45-49	514	471
50-54	460	394
55-59	338	320
60-64	257	257
65-69	207	224
70+	455	617

DAYTIME POPULATION

2001 Estimates:

Working Population	11,295
At Home Population	6,121
Total	17,416

INCOME

2001 Estimates:

Avg. Household Income	$46,998
Avg. Family Income	$51,747
Per Capita Income	$18,134
Male:	
Avg. Employment Income	$31,958
Avg. Employment Income (Full Time)	$41,100
Female:	
Avg. Employment Income	$18,867
Avg. Employment Income (Full Time)	$26,396

DISPOSABLE & DISCRETIONARY INCOME

2001 Estimates:	Per Hhld.
Disposable Income	$32,484
Discretionary Income 1 (minus Food & Shelter)	$20,166
Discretionary Income 2 (minus Food, Shelter, & Other Expenditures)	$12,516

LIQUID ASSETS

1999 Estimates:	Per Hhld.
Equity Investments	$48,436
Interest Bearing Investments	$53,138
Total Liquid Assets	$101,574

CREDIT DATA

July 2000:

Pool of Credit	$46,400,847
Revolving Credit, No.	15,919
Fixed Loans, No.	4,897
Avg. Credit Limit, per Person	$5,521
Avg. Spent, per Person	$2,254
Satisfactory Ratings, No. per Person	2.35
Avg. No. of Cards, per Person	0.99

LABOUR FORCE

2001 Estimates:

Male:	
In the Labour Force	3,581
Participation Rate	74.0
Employed	3,370
Unemployed	211
Unemployment Rate	5.9
Not in Labour Force	1,258
Female:	
In the Labour Force	2,570
Participation Rate	53.8
Employed	2,458
Unemployed	112
Unemployment Rate	4.4
Not in Labour Force	2,205

OCCUPATIONS BY MAJOR GROUPS

2001 Estimates:	Male	Female
Management	269	125
Business, Finance & Admin.	166	640
Natural & Applied Sciences & Related	318	35
Health	64	305
Social Sciences, Gov't Services & Religion	45	101
Education	81	241
Arts, Culture, Recreation & Sport	16	47
Sales & Service	477	694
Trades, Transport & Equipment Operators & Related	1,273	46
Primary Industries	293	147
Processing, Mfg. & Utilities	493	99

LEVEL OF SCHOOLING

2001 Estimates:

Population 15 years +	9,614
Less than Grade 9	1,932
Grades 9-13 w/o Certif.	1,469
Grade 9-13 with Certif.	1,718
Trade Certif./Dip.	576
Non-Univ. w/o Certif./Dip.	665
Non-Univ. with Certif./Dip.	1,815
Univ. w/o Degree	606
Univ. w/o Degree/Certif.	45
Univ. with Certif.	561
Univ. with Degree	833

AVERAGE HOUSEHOLD EXPENDITURES

2001 Estimates:

Food	$6,658
Shelter	$7,398
Clothing	$2,185
Transportation	$5,710
Health & Personal Care	$1,930
Recr'n, Read'g & Education	$2,985
Taxes & Securities	$12,280
Other	$7,158
Total Expenditures	$46,304

PRIVATE HOUSEHOLDS

2001 Estimates:

Private Households, Total	4,581
Pop. in Private Households	11,488
Average no. per Household	2.5

FAMILIES

2001 Estimates:

Families in Private Households	3,458
Husband-Wife Families	3,013
Lone-Parent Families	445
Aver. No. Persons per Family	3.1
Aver. No. Sons/Daughters at Home	1.2

HOUSING

2001 Estimates:

Occupied Private Dwellings	4,581
Owned	3,344
Rented	1,237
Single-Detached House	3,319
Semi-Detached House	126
Row Houses	108
Apartment, 5 or Fewer Storeys	700
Apartment, Detached Duplex	231
Other Single-Attached	37
Movable Dwellings	60

VEHICLES

2001 Estimates:

Model Yrs. '81-'96, No.	6,756
% Total	83.70
Model Yrs. '97-'98, No.	842
% Total	10.43
'99 Vehicles registered in Model Yr. '99, No.	474
% Total	5.87
Total No. '81-'99	8,072

LEGAL MARITAL STATUS

2001 Estimates: (Age 15+)

Single (Never Married)	3,703
Legally Married (Not Separated)	4,377
Legally Married (Separated)	172
Widowed	599
Divorced	763

PSYTE CATEGORIES

2001 Estimates	No. of House-holds	% of Total Hhds.	Index
Participation Quebec	427	9.32	323
Quebec Melange	369	8.06	304
Traditional French Cdn. Families	1,394	30.43	1,133
Quebec's Heartland	1,074	23.44	2,388
Quebec Rural Blues	455	9.93	408
Quebec Town Elders	862	18.82	666

FINANCIAL P$YTE

2001 Estimates	No. of House-holds	% of Total Hhds.	Index
Mortgages & Minivans	427	9.32	141
Country Credit	1,763	38.49	569
Rural Family Blues	1,529	33.38	413
Loan Parent Stress	862	18.82	323

HOME LANGUAGE

2001 Estimates:		% Total
English	21	0.18
French	11,780	99.22
German	51	0.43
Multiple Responses	21	0.18
Total	11,873	100.00

BUILDING PERMITS

	1999	1998	1997
		$000	
Value	11,629	9,305	9,849

HOMES BUILT

	1999	1998	1997
No.	27	25	16

TAXATION

Income Class:	1997	% Total
Under $5,000	1,170	14.16
$5,000-$10,000	1,180	14.29
$10,000-$15,000	1,520	18.40
$15,000-$20,000	830	10.05
$20,000-$25,000	670	8.11
$25,000-$30,000	580	7.02
$30,000-$40,000	820	9.93
$40,000-$50,000	550	6.66
$50,000 +	950	11.50
Total Returns, No.	8,260	
Total Income, $000	194,849	
Total Taxable Returns	5,420	
Total Tax, $000	21,937	
Average Income, $	23,589	
Average Tax, $	4,047	

VITAL STATISTICS

	1997	1996	1995	1994
Births	103	111	147	144
Deaths	71	63	68	69
Natural Increase	32	48	79	75
Marriages	14	20	21	20

Note: Latest available data.

MEDIA INFO
see Trois-Rivières, CMA

Cap-de-la-Madeleine
(Ville)
Trois-Rivières CMA
In census division Francheville.

POPULATION

July 1, 2001 Estimate	33,055
% Cdn. Total	0.11
% Change, '96 -'01	-2.73
Avg. Annual Growth Rate, %	-0.55
2003 Projected Population	32,736
2006 Projected Population	32,137
2001 Households Estimate	14,822
2003 Projected Households	14,860
2006 Projected Households	14,822

INCOME

% Above/Below National Average	-16
2001 Total Income Estimate	$587,630,000
% Cdn. Total	0.09
2001 Average Hhld. Income	$39,600
2001 Per Capita	$17,800
2003 Projected Total Income	$617,640,000
2006 Projected Total Income	$662,410,000

RETAIL SALES

% Above/Below National Average	-13
2001 Retail Sales Estimate	$258,590,000
% Cdn. Total	0.09
2001 per Household	$17,400
2001 per Capita	$7,800
2001 No. of Establishments	273
2003 Projected Retail Sales	$275,290,000
2006 Projected Retail Sales	$296,750,000

POPULATION

2001 Estimates:

Total		33,055
Male		15,670
Female		17,385

Age Groups	Male	Female
0-4	859	810
5-9	896	825
10-14	930	874
15-19	1,026	978
20-24	1,043	986
25-29	944	917
30-34	984	1,019
35-39	1,178	1,263
40-44	1,293	1,397
45-49	1,270	1,370
50-54	1,176	1,277
55-59	1,015	1,150
60-64	887	1,032
65-69	770	964
70+	1,399	2,523

DAYTIME POPULATION

2001 Estimates:

Working Population	11,564
At Home Population	19,016
Total	30,580

INCOME

2001 Estimates:

Avg. Household Income	$39,646
Avg. Family Income	$48,191
Per Capita Income	$17,777
Male:	
Avg. Employment Income	$32,642
Avg. Employment Income (Full Time)	$43,546
Female:	
Avg. Employment Income	$17,902
Avg. Employment Income (Full Time)	$27,635

DISPOSABLE & DISCRETIONARY INCOME

2001 Estimates:	Per Hhld.
Disposable Income	$27,343
Discretionary Income 1 (minus Food & Shelter)	$16,923
Discretionary Income 2 (minus Food, Shelter, & Other Expenditures)	$10,967

LIQUID ASSETS

1999 Estimates:	Per Hhld.
Equity Investments	$36,204
Interest Bearing Investments	$44,347
Total Liquid Assets	$80,551

CREDIT DATA

July 2000:

Pool of Credit	$150,045,157
Revolving Credit, No.	51,975
Fixed Loans, No.	15,606
Avg. Credit Limit, per Person	$6,117
Avg. Spent, per Person	$2,543
Satisfactory Ratings, No. per Person	2.62
Avg. No. of Cards, per Person	1.13

LABOUR FORCE

2001 Estimates:

Male:	
In the Labour Force	8,807
Participation Rate	67.8
Employed	7,964
Unemployed	843
Unemployment Rate	9.6
Not in Labour Force	4,178
Female:	
In the Labour Force	6,714
Participation Rate	45.1
Employed	6,075
Unemployed	639
Unemployment Rate	9.5
Not in Labour Force	8,162

OCCUPATIONS BY MAJOR GROUPS

2001 Estimates:	Male	Female
Management	859	383
Business, Finance & Admin.	891	1,842
Natural & Applied Sciences & Related	563	72
Health	192	652
Social Sciences, Gov't Services & Religion	162	144
Education	232	362
Arts, Culture, Recreation & Sport	102	146
Sales & Service	1,821	2,280
Trades, Transport & Equipment Operators & Related	2,147	111
Primary Industries	88	n.a.
Processing, Mfg. & Utilities	1,254	314

LEVEL OF SCHOOLING

2001 Estimates:

Population 15 years +	27,861
Less than Grade 9	5,172
Grades 9-13 w/o Certif.	4,324
Grade 9-13 with Certif.	5,616
Trade Certif. /Dip.	1,379
Non-Univ. w/o Certif./Dip.	2,403
Non-Univ. with Certif./Dip.	4,971
Univ. w/o Degree	1,876
Univ. w/o Degree/Certif.	206
Univ. with Certif.	1,670
Univ. with Degree	2,120

AVERAGE HOUSEHOLD EXPENDITURES

2001 Estimates:

Food	$5,327
Shelter	$6,609
Clothing	$1,715
Transportation	$4,319
Health & Personal Care	$1,626
Recr'n, Read'g & Education	$2,615
Taxes & Securities	$11,810
Other	$6,058
Total Expenditures	$40,079

PRIVATE HOUSEHOLDS

2001 Estimates:

Private Households, Total	14,822
Pop. in Private Households	32,269
Average no. per Household	2.2

FAMILIES

2001 Estimates:

Families in Private Households	9,891
Husband-Wife Families	8,138
Lone-Parent Families	1,753
Aver. No. Persons per Family	2.8
Aver. No. Sons/Daughters at Home	1.0

HOUSING

2001 Estimates:

Occupied Private Dwellings	14,822
Owned	7,752
Rented	7,070
Single-Detached House	6,059
Semi-Detached House	548
Row Houses	32
Apartment, 5+ Storeys	345
Owned Apartment, 5+ Storeys	11
Apartment, 5 or Fewer Storeys	5,796
Apartment, Detached Duplex	2,020
Other Single-Attached	22

VEHICLES

2001 Estimates:

Model Yrs. '81-'96, No.	16,278
% Total	84.47
Model Yrs. '97-'98, No.	1,919
% Total	9.96
'99 Vehicles registered in Model Yr. '99, No.	1,073
% Total	5.57
Total No. '81-'99	19,270

LEGAL MARITAL STATUS

2001 Estimates: (Age 15+)

Single (Never Married)	10,014
Legally Married (Not Separated)	11,973
Legally Married (Separated)	544
Widowed	2,199
Divorced	3,131

PSYTE CATEGORIES

2001 Estimates	No. of House-holds	% of Total Hhds.	Index
Old Bungalow Burbs	325	2.19	132
Participation Quebec	2,581	17.41	604
New Quebec Rows	394	2.66	243
Quebec Melange	2,746	18.53	699
Old Quebec Walkups	787	5.31	290
Quebec Town Elders	6,022	40.63	1,438
Quebec's New Urban Mosaic	1,890	12.75	529

FINANCIAL P$YTE

2001 Estimates	No. of House-holds	% of Total Hhds.	Index
Miners & Credit-Liners	325	2.19	69
Mortgages & Minivans	2,975	20.07	304
Country Credit	2,746	18.53	274
Loan Parent Stress	6,809	45.94	789
NSF	1,890	12.75	360

Québec

HOME LANGUAGE

2001 Estimates:		% Total
English	256	0.77
French	32,673	98.84
Arabic	20	0.06
Bulgarian	25	0.08
Other Languages	25	0.08
Multiple Responses	56	0.17
Total	33,055	100.00

BUILDING PERMITS

	1999	1998	1997
		$000	
Value	15,279	24,936	16,829

HOMES BUILT

	1999	1998	1997
No.	173	94	78

TAXATION

Income Class:	1997	% Total
Under $5,000	3,200	12.93
$5,000-$10,000	4,310	17.42
$10,000-$15,000	4,490	18.15
$15,000-$20,000	2,590	10.47
$20,000-$25,000	2,140	8.65
$25,000-$30,000	1,740	7.03
$30,000-$40,000	2,370	9.58
$40,000-$50,000	1,660	6.71
$50,000 +	2,270	9.18
Total Returns, No.	24,740	
Total Income, $000	551,577	
Total Taxable Returns	15,510	
Total Tax, $000	59,432	
Average Income, $	22,295	
Average Tax, $	3,832	

VITAL STATISTICS

	1997	1996	1995	1994
Births	330	325	382	370
Deaths	289	287	266	282
Natural Increase	41	38	116	88
Marriages	38	52	57	67

Note: Latest available data.

MEDIA INFO
see Trois-Rivières, CMA

Québec

Trois-Rivières
(Ville)
Trois-Rivières CMA

In census division Francheville.

POPULATION

July 1, 2001 Estimate	47,425
% Cdn. Total	0.15
% Change, '96 -'01	-3.61
Avg. Annual Growth Rate, %	-0.73
2003 Projected Population	46,728
2006 Projected Population	45,523
2001 Households Estimate	23,581
2003 Projected Households	23,513
2006 Projected Households	23,286

INCOME

% Above/Below National Average	-14
2001 Total Income Estimate	$857,030,000
% Cdn. Total	0.13
2001 Average Hhld. Income	$36,300
2001 Per Capita	$18,100
2003 Projected Total Income	$886,510,000
2006 Projected Total Income	$929,190,000

RETAIL SALES

% Above/Below National Average	+17
2001 Retail Sales Estimate	$497,570,000
% Cdn. Total	0.18
2001 per Household	$21,100
2001 per Capita	$10,500
2001 No. of Establishments	502
2003 Projected Retail Sales	$528,220,000
2006 Projected Retail Sales	$568,110,000

POPULATION

2001 Estimates:

Total		47,425
Male		22,142
Female		25,283

Age Groups	Male	Female
0-4	1,198	1,102
5-9	1,041	966
10-14	1,017	1,007
15-19	1,246	1,294
20-24	1,579	1,653
25-29	1,647	1,632
30-34	1,619	1,531
35-39	1,649	1,602
40-44	1,683	1,725
45-49	1,685	1,795
50-54	1,588	1,751
55-59	1,389	1,586
60-64	1,212	1,516
65-69	1,133	1,523
70+	2,456	4,600

DAYTIME POPULATION

2001 Estimates:

Working Population	32,168
At Home Population	28,147
Total	60,315

INCOME

2001 Estimates:

Avg. Household Income	$36,344
Avg. Family Income	$48,353
Per Capita Income	$18,071

Male:

Avg. Employment Income	$30,612
Avg. Employment Income (Full Time)	$42,536

Female:

Avg. Employment Income	$18,954
Avg. Employment Income (Full Time)	$29,723

DISPOSABLE & DISCRETIONARY INCOME

2001 Estimates:	Per Hhld.
Disposable Income	$24,578
Discretionary Income 1 (minus Food & Shelter)	$14,523
Discretionary Income 2 (minus Food, Shelter, & Other Expenditures)	$8,923

LIQUID ASSETS

1999 Estimates:	Per Hhld.
Equity Investments	$34,247
Interest Bearing Investments	$41,815
Total Liquid Assets	$76,062

CREDIT DATA

July 2000:

Pool of Credit	$226,830,828
Revolving Credit, No.	77,503
Fixed Loans, No.	21,109
Avg. Credit Limit, per Person	$5,926
Avg. Spent, per Person	$2,394
Satisfactory Ratings, No. per Person	2.46
Avg. No. of Cards, per Person	1.02

LABOUR FORCE

2001 Estimates:

Male:

In the Labour Force	11,883
Participation Rate	62.9
Employed	10,449
Unemployed	1,434
Unemployment Rate	12.1
Not in Labour Force	7,003

Female:

In the Labour Force	9,942
Participation Rate	44.8
Employed	9,081
Unemployed	861
Unemployment Rate	8.7
Not in Labour Force	12,266

OCCUPATIONS BY MAJOR GROUPS

2001 Estimates:	Male	Female
Management	1,077	404
Business, Finance & Admin.	1,176	2,677
Natural & Applied Sciences & Related	878	148
Health	369	1,031
Social Sciences, Gov't Services & Religion	300	516
Education	772	743
Arts, Culture, Recreation & Sport	275	275
Sales & Service	2,712	3,036
Trades, Transport & Equipment Operators & Related	2,226	161
Primary Industries	150	48
Processing, Mfg. & Utilities	1,138	342

LEVEL OF SCHOOLING

2001 Estimates:

Population 15 years +	41,094
Less than Grade 9	7,855
Grades 9-13 w/o Certif.	5,811
Grade 9-13 with Certif.	6,426
Trade Certif. /Dip.	1,563
Non-Univ. w/o Certif./Dip.	3,104
Non-Univ. with Certif./Dip.	6,960
Univ. w/o Degree	3,580
Univ. w/o Degree/Certif.	495
Univ. with Certif.	3,085
Univ. with Degree	5,795

AVERAGE HOUSEHOLD EXPENDITURES

2001 Estimates:

Food	$4,971
Shelter	$6,653
Clothing	$1,662
Transportation	$3,995
Health & Personal Care	$1,528
Recr'n, Read'g & Education	$2,457
Taxes & Securities	$9,935
Other	$5,956
Total Expenditures	$37,157

PRIVATE HOUSEHOLDS

2001 Estimates:

Private Households, Total	23,581
Pop. in Private Households	45,399
Average no. per Household	1.9

FAMILIES

2001 Estimates:

Families in Private Households	13,036
Husband-Wife Families	10,511
Lone-Parent Families	2,525
Aver. No. Persons per Family	2.7
Aver. No. Sons/Daughters at Home	1.0

HOUSING

2001 Estimates:

Occupied Private Dwellings	23,581
Owned	9,532
Rented	14,049
Single-Detached House	6,471
Semi-Detached House	855
Row Houses	605
Apartment, 5+ Storeys	868
Apartment, 5 or Fewer Storeys	11,925
Apartment, Detached Duplex	2,746
Other Single-Attached	63
Movable Dwellings	48

VEHICLES

2001 Estimates:

Model Yrs. '81-'96, No.	22,470
% Total	77.24
Model Yrs. '97-'98, No.	3,849
% Total	13.23
'99 Vehicles registered in Model Yr. '99, No.	2,774
% Total	9.53
Total No. '81-'99	29,093

LEGAL MARITAL STATUS

2001 Estimates: (Age 15+)

Single (Never Married)	17,369
Legally Married (Not Separated)	14,704
Legally Married (Separated)	984
Widowed	3,537
Divorced	4,500

PSYTE CATEGORIES

2001 Estimates	No. of House-holds	% of Total Hhds.	Index
Urban Gentry	415	1.76	98
Old Bungalow Burbs	115	0.49	29
Participation Quebec	2,036	8.63	300
New Quebec Rows	608	2.58	235
Quebec Melange	2,635	11.17	422
Traditional French Cdn. Families	1,185	5.03	187

2001 Estimates	No. of House-holds	% of Total Hhds.	Index
Young Urban Professionals	364	1.54	81
Young City Singles	1,038	4.40	192
Urban Bohemia	629	2.67	228
Old Quebec Walkups	2,055	8.71	476
Quebec Town Elders	1,565	6.64	235
Aging Quebec Urbanites	889	3.77	1,306
Quebec's New Urban Mosaic	8,811	37.36	1,551
Aged Pensioners	619	2.62	197
Old Grey Towers	250	1.06	191

FINANCIAL P$YTE

2001 Estimates	No. of House-holds	% of Total Hhds.	Index
Four Star Investors	415	1.76	35
Urban Heights	364	1.54	36
Miners & Credit-Liners	115	0.49	15
Mortgages & Minivans	2,644	11.21	170
Country Credit	3,820	16.20	240
Young Urban Struggle	629	2.67	56
Loan Parent Stress	4,509	19.12	328
Towering Debt	1,038	4.40	56
NSF	8,811	37.36	1,056
Senior Survivors	869	3.69	196

HOME LANGUAGE

2001 Estimates:		% Total
English	480	1.01
French	46,531	98.11
Lao	29	0.06
Other Languages	65	0.14
Multiple Responses	320	0.67
Total	47,425	100.00

BUILDING PERMITS

	1999	1998	1997
		$000	
Value	46,367	37,706	34,318

HOMES BUILT

	1999	1998	1997
No	59	127	144

TAXATION

Income Class:	1997	% Total
Under $5,000	4,290	11.89
$5,000-$10,000	7,090	19.65
$10,000-$15,000	6,930	19.21
$15,000-$20,000	3,600	9.98
$20,000-$25,000	2,740	7.59
$25,000-$30,000	2,420	6.71
$30,000-$40,000	3,320	9.20
$40,000-$50,000	2,220	6.15
$50,000 +	3,470	9.62
Total Returns, No.	36,080	
Total Income, $000	816,983	
Total Taxable Returns	21,860	
Total Tax, $000	90,587	
Average Income, $	22,644	
Average Tax, $	4,144	

VITAL STATISTICS

	1997	1996	1995	1994
Births	434	480	470	512
Deaths	536	506	539	499
Natural Increase	-102	-26	-69	13
Marriages	210	241	241	287

Note: Latest available data.

MEDIA INFO
see Trois-Rivières, CMA

Trois-Rivières-Ouest
(Ville)
Trois-Rivières CMA
In census division Francheville.

POPULATION

July 1, 2001 Estimate	25,443
% Cdn. Total	0.08
% Change, '96 -'01	9.38
Avg. Annual Growth Rate, %	1.81
2003 Projected Population	26,760
2006 Projected Population	28,647
2001 Households Estimate	10,337
2003 Projected Households	11,008
2006 Projected Households	11,985

INCOME

% Above/Below National Average	+9
2001 Total Income Estimate	$583,600,000
% Cdn. Total	0.09
2001 Average Hhld. Income	$56,500
2001 Per Capita	$22,900
2003 Projected Total Income	$651,580,000
2006 Projected Total Income	$763,490,000

RETAIL SALES

% Above/Below National Average	+12
2001 Retail Sales Estimate	$255,100,000
% Cdn. Total	0.09
2001 per Household	$24,700
2001 per Capita	$10,000
2001 No. of Establishments	222
2003 Projected Retail Sales	$293,370,000
2006 Projected Retail Sales	$353,630,000

POPULATION

2001 Estimates:

Total		25,443
Male		12,334
Female		13,109

Age Groups	Male	Female
0-4	764	737
5-9	815	793
10-14	897	852
15-19	956	956
20-24	909	950
25-29	829	856
30-34	858	921
35-39	1,001	1,116
40-44	1,105	1,205
45-49	1,091	1,150
50-54	942	961
55-59	728	737
60-64	530	553
65-69	381	439
70+	528	883

DAYTIME POPULATION

2001 Estimates:

Working Population	6,205
At Home Population	12,207
Total	18,412

INCOME

2001 Estimates:

Avg. Household Income	$56,458
Avg. Family Income	$63,026
Per Capita Income	$22,938
Male:	
Avg. Employment Income	$42,382
Avg. Employment Income (Full Time)	$53,201
Female:	
Avg. Employment Income	$21,271
Avg. Employment Income (Full Time)	$33,050

DISPOSABLE & DISCRETIONARY INCOME

2001 Estimates:	Per Hhld.
Disposable Income	$39,097
Discretionary Income 1 (minus Food & Shelter)	$25,679
Discretionary Income 2 (minus Food, Shelter, & Other Expenditures)	$17,218

LIQUID ASSETS

1999 Estimates:	Per Hhld.
Equity Investments	$66,369
Interest Bearing Investments	$64,614
Total Liquid Assets	$130,983

CREDIT DATA

July 2000:

Pool of Credit	$145,784,138
Revolving Credit, No.	41,469
Fixed Loans, No.	14,403
Avg. Credit Limit, per Person	$8,331
Avg. Spent, per Person	$3,627
Satisfactory Ratings, No. per Person	3.03
Avg. No. of Cards, per Person	1.29

LABOUR FORCE

2001 Estimates:

Male:	
In the Labour Force	7,642
Participation Rate	77.5
Employed	7,179
Unemployed	463
Unemployment Rate	6.1
Not in Labour Force	2,216
Female:	
In the Labour Force	6,252
Participation Rate	58.3
Employed	5,977
Unemployed	275
Unemployment Rate	4.4
Not in Labour Force	4,475

OCCUPATIONS BY MAJOR GROUPS

2001 Estimates:	Male	Female
Management	1,012	413
Business, Finance & Admin.	693	1,895
Natural & Applied Sciences & Related	797	169
Health	273	605
Social Sciences, Gov't Services & Religion	173	237
Education	327	453
Arts, Culture, Recreation & Sport	100	116
Sales & Service	1,361	1,942
Trades, Transport & Equipment Operators & Related	1,766	44
Primary Industries	58	n.a.
Processing, Mfg. & Utilities	854	210

LEVEL OF SCHOOLING

2001 Estimates:

Population 15 years +	20,585
Less than Grade 9	2,083
Grades 9-13 w/o Certif.	2,793
Grade 9-13 with Certif.	3,961
Trade Certif. /Dip.	929
Non-Univ. w/o Certif./Dip.	1,764
Non-Univ. with Certif./Dip.	3,970
Univ. w/o Degree	1,908
Univ. w/o Degree/Certif.	224
Univ. with Certif.	1,684
Univ. with Degree	3,177

AVERAGE HOUSEHOLD EXPENDITURES

2001 Estimates:

Food	$6,876
Shelter	$8,663
Clothing	$2,464
Transportation	$6,471
Health & Personal Care	$2,069
Recr'n, Read'g & Education	$3,566
Taxes & Securities	$16,115
Other	$8,016
Total Expenditures	$54,240

PRIVATE HOUSEHOLDS

2001 Estimates:

Private Households, Total	10,337
Pop. in Private Households	25,057
Average no. per Household	2.4

FAMILIES

2001 Estimates:

Families in Private Households	7,699
Husband-Wife Families	6,553
Lone-Parent Families	1,146
Aver. No. Persons per Family	3.0
Aver. No. Sons/Daughters at Home	1.2

HOUSING

2001 Estimates:

Occupied Private Dwellings	10,337
Owned	6,442
Rented	3,895
Single-Detached House	5,222
Semi-Detached House	729
Row Houses	267
Apartment, 5 or Fewer Storeys	3,623
Apartment, Detached Duplex	398
Other Single-Attached	62
Movable Dwellings	36

VEHICLES

2001 Estimates:

Model Yrs. '81-'96, No.	11,512
% Total	78.36
Model Yr. '97-'98, No.	1,989
% Total	13.54
'99 Vehicles registered in Model Yr. '99, No.	1,190
% Total	8.10
Total No. '81-'99	14,691

LEGAL MARITAL STATUS

2001 Estimates: (Age 15+)

Single (Never Married)	7,604
Legally Married (Not Separated)	9,368
Legally Married (Separated)	497
Widowed	982
Divorced	2,134

PSYTE CATEGORIES

2001 Estimates	No. of House-holds	% of Total Hhds.	Index
Technocrafts & Bureaucrats	1,414	13.68	486
Stable Suburban Families	388	3.75	288
Participation Quebec	1,259	12.18	423
New Quebec Rows	2,000	19.35	1,766
Quebec Melange	1,528	14.78	558
Traditional French Cdn. Families	1,538	14.88	554
Quebec Rural Blues	200	1.93	79
Quebec Town Elders	695	6.72	238
Quebec's New Urban Mosaic	1,315	12.72	528

Québec

FINANCIAL P$YTE

2001 Estimates	No. of House-holds	% of Total Hhds.	Index
Successful Suburbanites	1,802	17.43	263
Mortgages & Minivans	3,259	31.53	478
Country Credit	3,066	29.66	439
Rural Family Blues	200	1.93	24
Loan Parent Stress	695	6.72	115
NSF	1,315	12.72	360

HOME LANGUAGE

2001 Estimates:		% Total
English	178	0.70
French	24,961	98.11
Bulgarian	22	0.09
Khmer (Cambodian)	30	0.12
Lao	17	0.07
Polish	35	0.14
Romanian	16	0.06
Other Languages	67	0.26
Multiple Responses	117	0.46
Total	25,443	100.00

BUILDING PERMITS

	1999	1998	1997
		$000	
Value	19,995	17,155	22,303

HOMES BUILT

	1999	1998	1997
No.	167	128	141

TAXATION

Income Class:	1997	% Total
Under $5,000	2,150	13.30
$5,000-$10,000	2,180	13.48
$10,000-$15,000	2,310	14.29
$15,000-$20,000	1,530	9.46
$20,000-$25,000	1,240	7.67
$25,000-$30,000	1,120	6.93
$30,000-$40,000	1,750	10.82
$40,000-$50,000	1,290	7.98
$50,000 +	2,600	16.08
Total Returns, No.	16,170	
Total Income, $000	450,763	
Total Taxable Returns	11,490	
Total Tax, $000	57,537	
Average Income, $	27,876	
Average Tax, $	5,008	

VITAL STATISTICS

	1997	1996	1995	1994
Births	226	247	256	223
Deaths	111	78	93	71
Natural Increase	115	169	163	152
Marriages	15	24	36	23

Note: Latest available data.

MEDIA INFO
see Trois-Rivières, CMA

Québec

Val-d'Or
(Census Agglomeration)

The Census Agglomeration of Val-d'Or includes: Val-d'Or, V; Sullivan, M; plus several smaller areas. All are in census division Vallée-de-l'Or.

POPULATION

July 1, 2001 Estimate	33,612
% Cdn. Total	0.11
% Change, '96 -'01	1.18
Avg. Annual Growth Rate, %	0.23
2003 Projected Population	33,979
2006 Projected Population	34,309
2001 Households Estimate	13,856
2003 Projected Households	14,261
2006 Projected Households	14,816

INCOME

% Above/Below National Average	-4
2001 Total Income Estimate	$679,430,000
% Cdn. Total	0.10
2001 Average Hhld. Income	$49,000
2001 Per Capita	$20,200
2003 Projected Total Income	$732,250,000
2006 Projected Total Income	$816,660,000

RETAIL SALES

% Above/Below National Average	+44
2001 Retail Sales Estimate	$432,190,000
% Cdn. Total	0.16
2001 per Household	$31,200
2001 per Capita	$12,900
2001 No. of Establishments	318
2003 Projected Retail Sales	$468,700,000
2006 Projected Retail Sales	$519,590,000

POPULATION

2001 Estimates:

Total		33,612
Male		17,054
Female		16,558

Age Groups	Male	Female
0-4	1,025	959
5-9	1,157	1,066
10-14	1,286	1,156
15-19	1,309	1,200
20-24	1,184	1,106
25-29	1,097	1,048
30-34	1,230	1,218
35-39	1,496	1,465
40-44	1,572	1,512
45-49	1,423	1,347
50-54	1,186	1,110
55-59	902	851
60-64	673	674
65-69	526	560
70+	988	1,286

DAYTIME POPULATION

2001 Estimates:

Working Population	16,469
At Home Population	17,143
Total	33,612

INCOME

2001 Estimates:

Avg. Household Income	$49,035
Avg. Family Income	$57,411
Per Capita Income	$20,214
Male:	
Avg. Employment Income	$37,486
Avg. Employment Income (Full Time)	$48,517
Female:	
Avg. Employment Income	$18,931
Avg. Employment Income (Full Time)	$28,472

DISPOSABLE & DISCRETIONARY INCOME

2001 Estimates:	Per Hhld.
Disposable Income	$33,411
Discretionary Income 1 (minus Food & Shelter)	$21,247
Discretionary Income 2 (minus Food, Shelter, & Other Expenditures)	$13,607

LIQUID ASSETS

1999 Estimates:	Per Hhld.
Equity Investments	$62,319
Interest Bearing Investments	$58,851
Total Liquid Assets	$121,170

CREDIT DATA

July 2000:

Pool of Credit	$222,369,952
Revolving Credit, No.	53,875
Fixed Loans, No.	24,117
Avg. Credit Limit, per Person	$9,213
Avg. Spent, per Person	$4,520
Satisfactory Ratings, No. per Person	2.98
Avg. No. of Cards, per Person	0.96

LABOUR FORCE

2001 Estimates:

Male:	
In the Labour Force	10,231
Participation Rate	75.3
Employed	9,434
Unemployed	797
Unemployment Rate	7.8
Not in Labour Force	3,355
Female:	
In the Labour Force	7,430
Participation Rate	55.5
Employed	7,061
Unemployed	369
Unemployment Rate	5.0
Not in Labour Force	5,947

OCCUPATIONS BY MAJOR GROUPS

2001 Estimates:	Male	Female
Management	1,009	384
Business, Finance & Admin.	718	2,169
Natural & Applied Sciences & Related	748	111
Health	152	695
Social Sciences, Gov't Services & Religion	140	261
Education	207	518
Arts, Culture, Recreation & Sport	129	106
Sales & Service	1,805	2,889
Trades, Transport & Equipment Operators & Related	2,631	71
Primary Industries	1,454	8
Processing, Mfg. & Utilities	936	34

LEVEL OF SCHOOLING

2001 Estimates:

Population 15 years +	26,963
Less than Grade 9	5,753
Grades 9-13 w/o Certif.	6,395
Grade 9-13 with Certif.	4,807
Trade Certif. /Dip.	1,393
Non-Univ. w/o Certif./Dip.	1,405
Non-Univ. with Certif./Dip.	3,141
Univ. w/o Degree	1,704
Univ. w/o Degree/Certif.	250
Univ. with Certif.	1,454
Univ. with Degree	2,365

AVERAGE HOUSEHOLD EXPENDITURES

2001 Estimates:

Food	$6,358
Shelter	$7,556
Clothing	$2,119
Transportation	$5,755
Health & Personal Care	$1,948
Recr'n, Read'g & Education	$3,187
Taxes & Securities	$13,668
Other	$7,287
Total Expenditures	$47,878

PRIVATE HOUSEHOLDS

2001 Estimates:

Private Households, Total	13,856
Pop. in Private Households	33,018
Average no. per Household	2.4

FAMILIES

2001 Estimates:

Families in Private Households	9,816
Husband-Wife Families	8,369
Lone-Parent Families	1,447
Aver. No. Persons per Family	3.0
Aver. No. Sons/Daughters at Home	1.2

HOUSING

2001 Estimates:

Occupied Private Dwellings	13,856
Owned	7,838
Rented	6,018
Single-Detached House	6,603
Semi-Detached House	751
Row Houses	296
Apartment, 5+ Storeys	11
Apartment, 5 or Fewer Storeys	3,594
Apartment, Detached Duplex	1,872
Other Single-Attached	360
Movable Dwellings	369

VEHICLES

2001 Estimates:

Model Yrs. '81-'96, No.	17,224
% Total	80.88
Model Yrs. '97-'98, No.	2,623
% Total	12.32
'99 Vehicles registered in Model Yr. '99, No.	1,448
% Total	6.80
Total No. '81-'99	21,295

LEGAL MARITAL STATUS

2001 Estimates: (Age 15+)

Single (Never Married)	11,516
Legally Married (Not Separated)	10,476
Legally Married (Separated)	806
Widowed	1,587
Divorced	2,578

PSYTE CATEGORIES

2001 Estimates	No. of House-holds	% of Total Hhds.	Index
Participation Quebec	2,916	21.05	730
Quebec Melange	3,619	26.12	986
Traditional French Cdn. Families	1,360	9.82	366
Young Grey Collar	394	2.84	340
Big Country Families	362	2.61	183
Quebec Rural Blues	602	4.34	178
Quebec Town Elders	3,438	24.81	878
Quebec's New Urban Mosaic	1,082	7.81	324

FINANCIAL P$YTE

2001 Estimates	No. of House-holds	% of Total Hhds.	Index
Mortgages & Minivans	2,916	21.05	319
Country Credit	4,979	35.93	531
Revolving Renters	394	2.84	62
Rural Family Blues	964	6.96	86
Loan Parent Stress	3,438	24.81	426
NSF	1,082	7.81	221

HOME LANGUAGE

2001 Estimates:		% Total
English	926	2.75
French	32,153	95.66
Chinese	61	0.18
Italian	19	0.06
Polish	25	0.07
Ukrainian	21	0.06
Other Languages	15	0.04
Multiple Responses	392	1.17
Total	33,612	100.00

BUILDING PERMITS

	1999	1998	1997
		$000	
Value	21,150	26,641	31,545

HOMES BUILT

	1999	1998	1997
No.	94	142	162

TAXATION

Income Class:	1997	% Total
Under $5,000	2,970	12.68
$5,000-$10,000	3,540	15.12
$10,000-$15,000	3,680	15.71
$15,000-$20,000	2,150	9.18
$20,000-$25,000	1,800	7.69
$25,000-$30,000	1,720	7.34
$30,000-$40,000	2,730	11.66
$40,000-$50,000	1,890	8.07
$50,000 +	2,960	12.64
Total Returns, No.	23,420	
Total Income, $000	602,493	
Total Taxable Returns	15,970	
Total Tax, $000	74,442	
Average Income, $	25,726	
Average Tax, $	4,661	

VITAL STATISTICS

	1997	1996	1995	1994
Births	397	389	429	399
Deaths	210	211	195	202
Natural Increase	187	178	234	197
Marriages	105	100	97	115

Note: Latest available data.

COMMUNITY NEWSPAPER(S)

	Total Circulation
Val-d'Or: Le Citoyen de la Vallée-de-l'Or	19,547
Val-d'Or, Amos, La Sarre, Malartic, Matagami: Échos Abitibiens	8,355

RADIO STATION(S)

	Power
CBML-FM	n.a.
CHGO-FM	10,000w
CJMV-FM	n.a.
CKVD	10,000w

TELEVISION STATION(S)

CFEM-TV
CFVS-TV
CIVA-TV

Victoriaville
(Census Agglomeration)

The Census Agglomeration of Victoriaville consists of Victoriaville, V and Saint-Christophe-d'Arthabaska, P. Both are in census division Arthabaska.

POPULATION

July 1, 2001 Estimate	42,616
% Cdn. Total	0.14
% Change, '96 -'01	3.59
Avg. Annual Growth Rate, %	0.71
2003 Projected Population	43,283
2006 Projected Population	43,982
2001 Households Estimate	17,727
2003 Projected Households	18,252
2006 Projected Households	18,924

INCOME

% Above/Below National Average	-19
2001 Total Income Estimate	$729,890,000
% Cdn. Total	0.11
2001 Average Hhld. Income	$41,200
2001 Per Capita	$17,100
2003 Projected Total Income	$788,740,000
2006 Projected Total Income	$881,360,000

RETAIL SALES

% Above/Below National Average	+47
2001 Retail Sales Estimate	$560,220,000
% Cdn. Total	0.20
2001 per Household	$31,600
2001 per Capita	$13,100
2001 No. of Establishments	546
2003 Projected Retail Sales	$616,440,000
2006 Projected Retail Sales	$694,400,000

POPULATION

2001 Estimates:

Total	42,616
Male	20,570
Female	22,046

Age Groups	Male	Female
0-4	1,214	1,147
5-9	1,300	1,201
10-14	1,379	1,351
15-19	1,570	1,515
20-24	1,561	1,483
25-29	1,394	1,368
30-34	1,422	1,425
35-39	1,540	1,600
40-44	1,648	1,738
45-49	1,602	1,703
50-54	1,430	1,524
55-59	1,170	1,243
60-64	927	1,039
65-69	760	947
70+	1,653	2,762

DAYTIME POPULATION

2001 Estimates:

Working Population	20,533
At Home Population	22,083
Total	42,616

INCOME

2001 Estimates:

Avg. Household Income	$41,174
Avg. Family Income	$49,172
Per Capita Income	$17,127
Male:	
Avg. Employment Income	$28,800
Avg. Employment Income (Full Time)	$37,271
Female:	
Avg. Employment Income	$18,111
Avg. Employment Income (Full Time)	$25,429

DISPOSABLE & DISCRETIONARY INCOME

2001 Estimates:	Per Hhld.
Disposable Income	$29,156
Discretionary Income 1 (minus Food & Shelter)	$18,330
Discretionary Income 2 (minus Food, Shelter, & Other Expenditures)	$11,900

LIQUID ASSETS

1999 Estimates:	Per Hhld.
Equity Investments	$43,293
Interest Bearing Investments	$47,846
Total Liquid Assets	$91,139

CREDIT DATA

July 2000:

Pool of Credit	$185,564,714
Revolving Credit, No.	61,497
Fixed Loans, No.	18,154
Avg. Credit Limit, per Person	$6,309
Avg. Spent, per Person	$2,509
Satisfactory Ratings, No. per Person	2.56
Avg. No. of Cards, per Person	0.99

LABOUR FORCE

2001 Estimates:

Male:	
In the Labour Force	12,020
Participation Rate	72.1
Employed	11,301
Unemployed	719
Unemployment Rate	6.0
Not in Labour Force	4,657
Female:	
In the Labour Force	10,194
Participation Rate	55.6
Employed	9,336
Unemployed	858
Unemployment Rate	8.4
Not in Labour Force	8,153

OCCUPATIONS BY MAJOR GROUPS

2001 Estimates:	Male	Female
Management	1,280	426
Business, Finance & Admin.	1,025	2,551
Natural & Applied Sciences & Related	589	138
Health	286	868
Social Sciences, Gov't Services & Religion	202	298
Education	394	532
Arts, Culture, Recreation & Sport	255	190
Sales & Service	2,230	3,245
Trades, Transport & Equipment Operators & Related	2,905	313
Primary Industries	316	135
Processing, Mfg. & Utilities	2,175	1,027

LEVEL OF SCHOOLING

2001 Estimates:

Population 15 years +	35,024
Less than Grade 9	7,268
Grades 9-13 w/o Certif.	7,100
Grade 9-13 with Certif.	5,926
Trade Certif. /Dip.	1,833
Non-Univ. w/o Certif./Dip.	2,492
Non-Univ. with Certif./Dip.	5,624
Univ. w/o Degree	1,818
Univ. w/o Degree/Certif.	167
Univ. with Certif.	1,651
Univ. with Degree	2,963

AVERAGE HOUSEHOLD EXPENDITURES

2001 Estimates:

Food	$5,642
Shelter	$6,706
Clothing	$1,812
Transportation	$4,831
Health & Personal Care	$1,656
Recr'n, Read'g & Education	$2,708
Taxes & Securities	$11,735
Other	$6,364
Total Expenditures	$41,454

PRIVATE HOUSEHOLDS

2001 Estimates:

Private Households, Total	17,727
Pop. in Private Households	41,340
Average no. per Household	2.3

FAMILIES

2001 Estimates:

Families in Private Households	12,412
Husband-Wife Families	10,543
Lone-Parent Families	1,869
Aver. No. Persons per Family	2.9
Aver. No. Sons/Daughters at Home	1.1

HOUSING

2001 Estimates:

Occupied Private Dwellings	17,727
Owned	10,988
Rented	6,739
Single-Detached House	9,753
Semi-Detached House	756
Row Houses	291
Apartment, 5 or Fewer Storeys	5,394
Apartment, Detached Duplex	1,435
Other Single-Attached	87
Movable Dwellings	11

VEHICLES

2001 Estimates:

Model Yrs. '81-'96, No.	22,321
% Total	84.08
Model Yrs. '97-'98, No.	2,718
% Total	10.24
'99 Vehicles registered in Model Yr. '99, No.	1,509
% Total	5.68
Total No. '81-'99	26,548

LEGAL MARITAL STATUS

2001 Estimates: (Age 15+)

Single (Never Married)	12,942
Legally Married (Not Separated)	15,399
Legally Married (Separated)	696
Widowed	2,456
Divorced	3,531

PSYTE CATEGORIES

2001 Estimates	No. of House-holds	% of Total Hhds.	Index
Participation			
Quebec	1,484	8.37	291
New Quebec Rows	1,199	6.76	617
Quebec Melange	2,705	15.26	576
Traditional French Cdn. Families	4,265	24.06	896
Quebec Rural Blues	70	0.39	16
Quebec Town Elders	5,523	31.16	1,103
Quebec's New Urban Mosaic	1,792	10.11	420
Aged Pensioners	501	2.83	212

FINANCIAL PSYTE

2001 Estimates	No. of House-holds	% of Total Hhds.	Index
Mortgages & Minivans	2,683	15.14	229
Country Credit	6,970	39.32	581
Rural Family Blues	70	0.39	5
Loan Parent Stress	5,523	31.16	535
NSF	1,792	10.11	286
Senior Survivors	501	2.83	150

Québec

HOME LANGUAGE

2001 Estimates:		% Total
English	139	0.33
French	42,224	99.08
German	27	0.06
Serbo-Croatian	32	0.08
Other Languages	80	0.19
Multiple Responses	114	0.27
Total	42,616	100.00

BUILDING PERMITS

	1999	1998	1997
		$000	
Value	33,015	30,869	30,986

HOMES BUILT

	1999	1998	1997
No.	108	198	224

TAXATION

Income Class:	1997	% Total
Under $5,000	3,660	11.95
$5,000-$10,000	4,890	15.97
$10,000-$15,000	5,760	18.81
$15,000-$20,000	3,650	11.92
$20,000-$25,000	2,740	8.95
$25,000-$30,000	2,580	8.43
$30,000-$40,000	3,380	11.04
$40,000-$50,000	1,880	6.14
$50,000 +	2,080	6.79
Total Returns, No.	30,620	
Total Income, $000	672,419	
Total Taxable Returns	20,620	
Total Tax, $000	70,648	
Average Income, $	21,960	
Average Tax, $	3,426	

VITAL STATISTICS

	1997	1996	1995	1994
Births	466	449	473	486
Deaths	334	347	322	309
Natural Increase	132	102	151	177
Marriages	154	147	146	129

Note: Latest available data.

COMMUNITY NEWSPAPER(S)

	Total Circulation
Victoriaville: La Nouvelle	39,442
Victoriaville: L'Union	24,844

RADIO STATION(S)

	Power
CBF-FM	n.a.
CFDA-FM	3,000w
CFJO-FM	100,000w

Economic Regions

Ontario

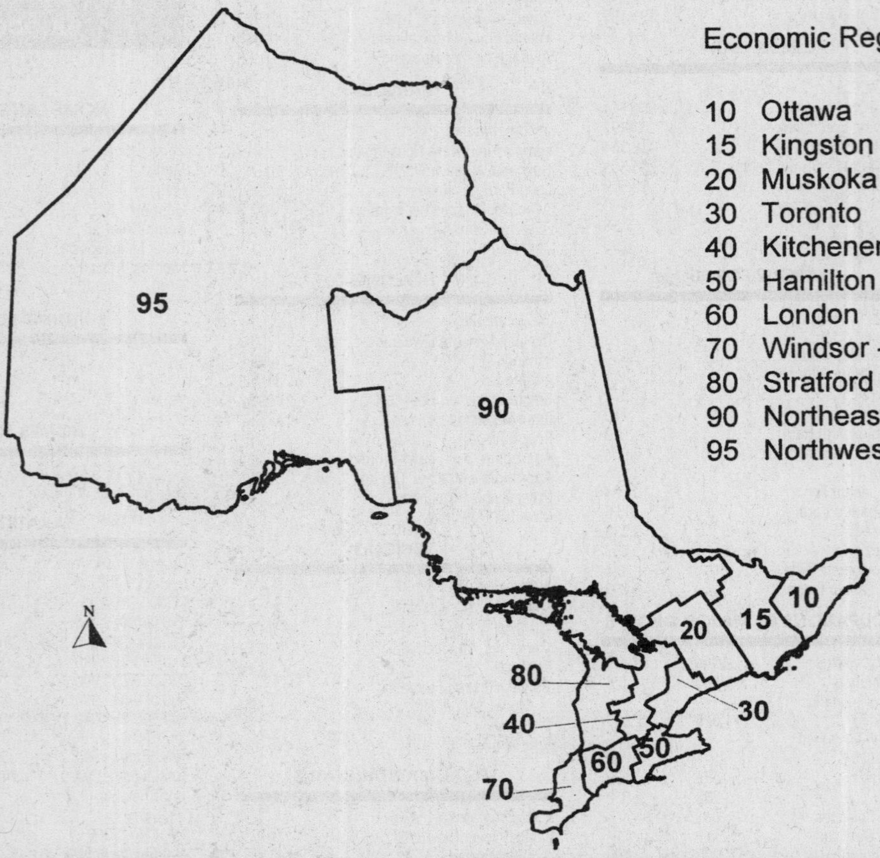

Economic Regions

10 Ottawa
15 Kingston - Pembroke
20 Muskoka - Kawarthas
30 Toronto
40 Kitchener - Waterloo - Barrie
50 Hamilton - Niagara Peninsula
60 London
70 Windsor - Sarnia
80 Stratford - Bruce Peninsula
90 Northeast
95 Northwest

Region	Population (at July 1)				Households (at July 1)		Income				Retail Sales				Taxation Statistics, 1997					
	*1996 Census (000)	2001 Estimate (000)	% of Cdn. Total	% Chg. '96-'01	2001 Estimate (000)	% of Cdn. Total	2001 Estimate $millions	% of Cdn. Total	Per Hhld. $	Income Rating Index	2001 Estimate $millions	% of Cdn. Total	Per Hhld. $	Market Rating Index	Total No. of Returns	Total Income $millions	Total No. Taxable Returns	Total Tax $millions	Avg. Income $	Avg. Tax $
ONTARIO	11,100.9	11,817.0	37.95	6.45	4,436.2	36.71	269,996.8	41.13	60,900	108	106,349.4	38.16	24,000	101	7,890,620	236,829.6	5,488,640	48,038.0	30,014	8,752
Ottawa (10)	1,095.1	1,138.2	3.66	3.93	449.3	3.72	27,429.5	4.18	61,100	114	10,813.1	3.88	24,100	106	774,890	23,893.3	547,910	4,779.2	30,834	8,723
Kingston - Pembroke (15)	429.0	433.8	1.39	1.12	172.1	1.42	8,593.2	1.31	49,900	94	3,973.2	1.43	23,100	102	305,220	7,789.6	204,730	1,351.2	25,521	6,600
Muskoka - Kawarthas (20)	348.1	361.2	1.16	3.78	143.1	1.18	7,088.3	1.08	49,500	93	3,311.1	1.19	23,100	102	241,820	6,172.2	164,300	1,076.2	25,524	6,550
Toronto (30)	4,637.8	5,120.4	16.45	10.41	1,830.7	15.15	124,810.0	19.01	68,200	116	43,006.0	15.43	23,500	94	3,427,750	110,875.9	2,380,960	24,296.2	32,347	10,204
Kitchener - Waterloo - Barrie (40)	982.0	1,081.3	3.47	10.11	403.0	3.33	23,499.3	3.58	58,300	103	10,126.4	3.63	25,100	105	702,460	20,477.5	509,160	3,980.5	29,151	7,818
Hamilton - Niagara Peninsula (50)	1,267.0	1,318.7	4.24	4.08	509.7	4.22	28,515.9	4.34	56,000	103	11,416.8	4.10	22,400	97	794,510	21,882.4	554,440	4,048.4	27,542	7,302
London (60)	584.8	603.9	1.94	3.27	237.4	1.96	13,112.0	2.00	55,200	103	5,632.8	2.02	23,700	104	413,230	11,775.4	291,290	2,211.0	28,496	7,590
Windsor - Sarnia (70)	607.2	629.8	2.02	3.72	244.1	2.02	14,259.9	2.17	58,400	107	6,343.3	2.28	26,000	113	433,660	13,085.0	306,520	2,576.5	30,174	8,406
Stratford - Bruce Peninsula (80)	293.7	294.5	0.95	0.27	114.1	0.94	5,679.9	0.87	49,800	91	3,083.6	1.11	27,000	117	203,610	5,215.9	141,400	884.3	25,617	6,254
Northeast (90)	601.8	583.9	1.88	-2.98	235.7	1.95	11,620.7	1.77	49,300	94	6,197.2	2.22	26,300	119	421,370	10,885.6	272,470	1,947.9	25,834	7,149
Northwest (95)	254.3	251.1	0.81	-1.24	97.0	0.80	5,388.1	0.82	55,500	102	2,445.9	0.88	25,200	109	172,120	4,776.7	115,480	886.6	27,752	7,677

*Adjusted.

Ottawa

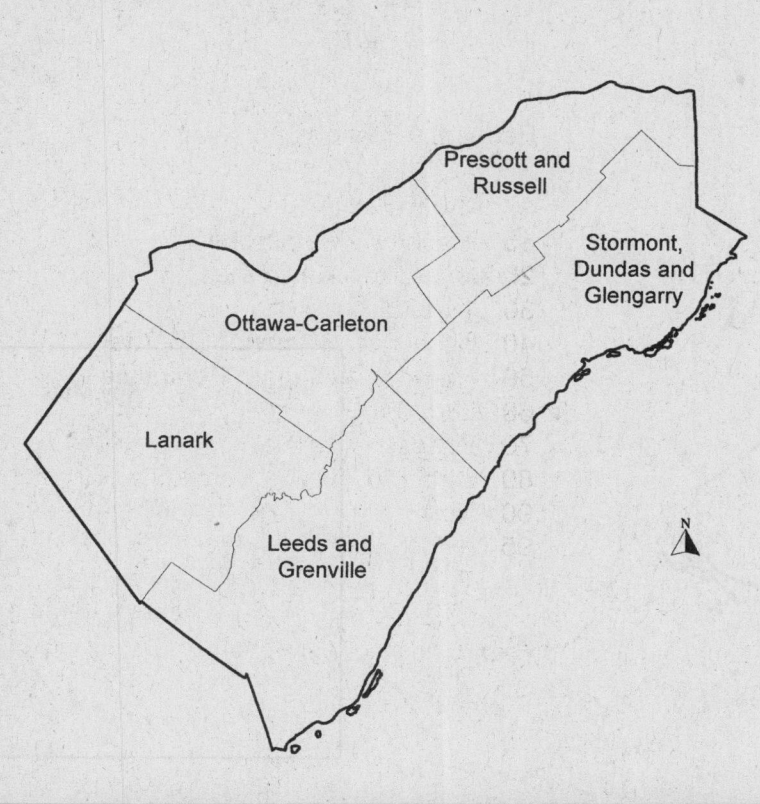

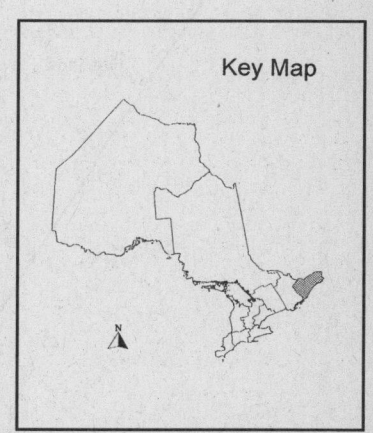

Key Map

Region	Population (at July 1)				Households (at July1)		Income				Retail Sales				Taxation Statistics, 1997					
	*1996 Census (000)	2001 Estimate (000)	% of Cdn. Total	% Chg. '96-'01	2001 Estimate (000)	% of Cdn. Total	2001 Estimate $millions	% of Cdn. Total	Per Hhld. $	Income Rating Index	2001 Estimate $millions	% of Cdn. Total	Per Hhld. $	Market Rating Index	Total No. of Returns	Total Income $millions	Total No. Taxable Returns	Total Tax $millions	Avg. Income $	Avg. Tax $
Ottawa (10)	1,095.1	1,138.2	3.66	3.93	449.3	3.72	27,429.5	4.18	61,100	114	10,813.1	3.88	24,100	106	774,890	23,893.3	547,910	4,779.2	30,834	8,723
Stormont, Dundas and Glengarry United Counties	115.6	116.1	0.37	0.44	45.2	0.37	2,159.1	0.33	47,700	88	1,104.1	0.40	24,400	106	81,390	1,953.7	51,900	324.1	24,004	6,245
Prescott and Russell United Counties	76.1	80.5	0.26	5.8	29.0	0.24	1,570.1	0.24	54,100	92	569.7	0.20	19,600	79	52,430	1,330.5	35,720	228.1	25,377	6,387
Ottawa-Carleton Regional Municipality	743.0	775.3	2.49	4.36	310.7	2.57	20,425.9	3.11	65,700	125	7,636.9	2.74	24,600	110	526,800	17,574.3	380,160	3,685.6	33,360	9,695
Leeds and Grenville United Counties	98.9	101.6	0.33	2.73	39.8	0.33	1,983.7	0.30	49,900	93	966.2	0.35	24,300	106	70,200	1,878.9	49,570	335.0	26,766	6,757
Lanark County	61.5	64.6	0.21	5	24.5	0.20	1,290.6	0.20	52,700	95	536.2	0.19	21,900	93	44,070	1,156.0	30,560	206.5	26,230	6,756

*Adjusted.

Economic Region & Census Divisions

Kingston-Pembroke

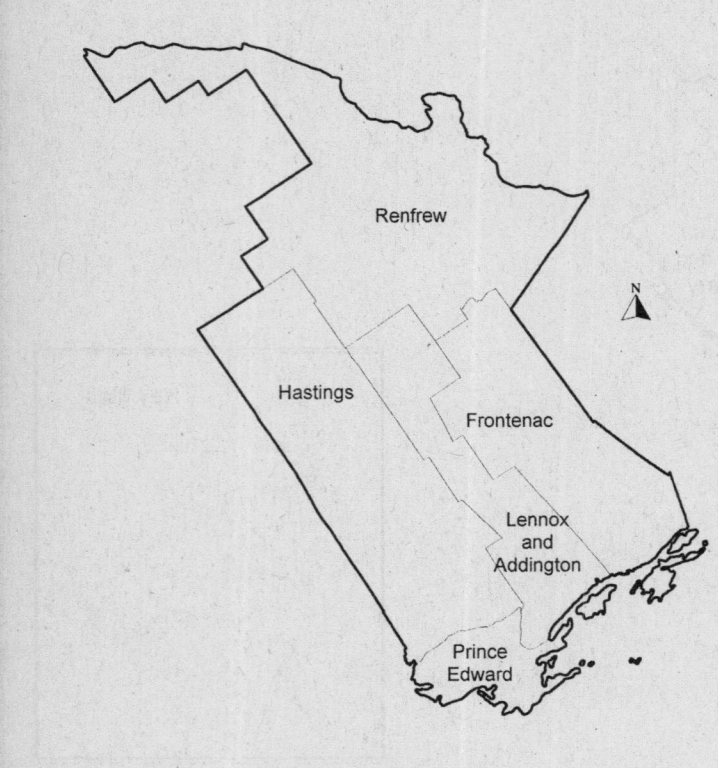

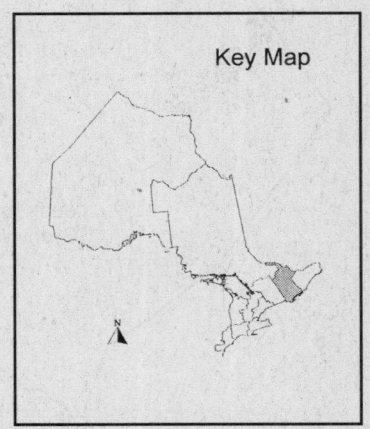

Key Map

Region	Population (at July 1)				Households (at July1)		Income				Retail Sales				Taxation Statistics, 1997					
	*1996 Census (000)	2001 Estimate (000)	% of Cdn. Total	% Chg. '96-'01	2001 Estimate (000)	% of Cdn. Total	2001 Estimate $millions	% of Cdn. Total	Per Hhld. $	Income Rating Index	2001 Estimate $millions	% of Cdn. Total	Per Hhld. $	Market Rating Index	Total No. of Returns	Total Income $millions	Total No. Taxable Returns	Total Tax $millions	Avg. Income $	Avg. Tax $
Kingston - Pembroke (15)	429.0	433.8	1.39	1.12	172.1	1.42	8,593.2	1.31	49,900	94	3,973.2	1.43	23,100	102	305,220	7,789.6	204,730	1,351.2	25,521	6,600
Frontenac County	140.4	140.7	0.45	0.16	58.1	0.48	3,155.4	0.48	54,300	106	1,352.5	0.49	23,300	107	96,470	2,695.5	66,350	500.1	27,941	7,537
Lennox and Addington County	40.3	41.0	0.13	1.8	15.0	0.12	744.7	0.11	49,600	86	215.6	0.08	14,300	59	26,360	644.4	17,520	107.1	24,446	6,111
Hastings County	123.4	124.2	0.40	0.7	49.1	0.41	2,320.2	0.35	47,200	89	1,418.3	0.51	28,900	128	93,680	2,297.5	61,650	388.5	24,525	6,301
Prince Edward County	25.7	26.4	0.08	2.67	10.5	0.09	530.2	0.08	50,600	95	94.1	0.03	9,000	40	17,830	426.5	11,760	68.8	23,918	5,848
Renfrew County	99.2	101.6	0.33	2.33	39.3	0.33	1,842.6	0.28	46,900	86	892.7	0.32	22,700	98	70,880	1,725.7	47,450	286.8	24,347	6,045

*Adjusted.

Economic Region & Census Divisions

Muskoka – Kawarthas

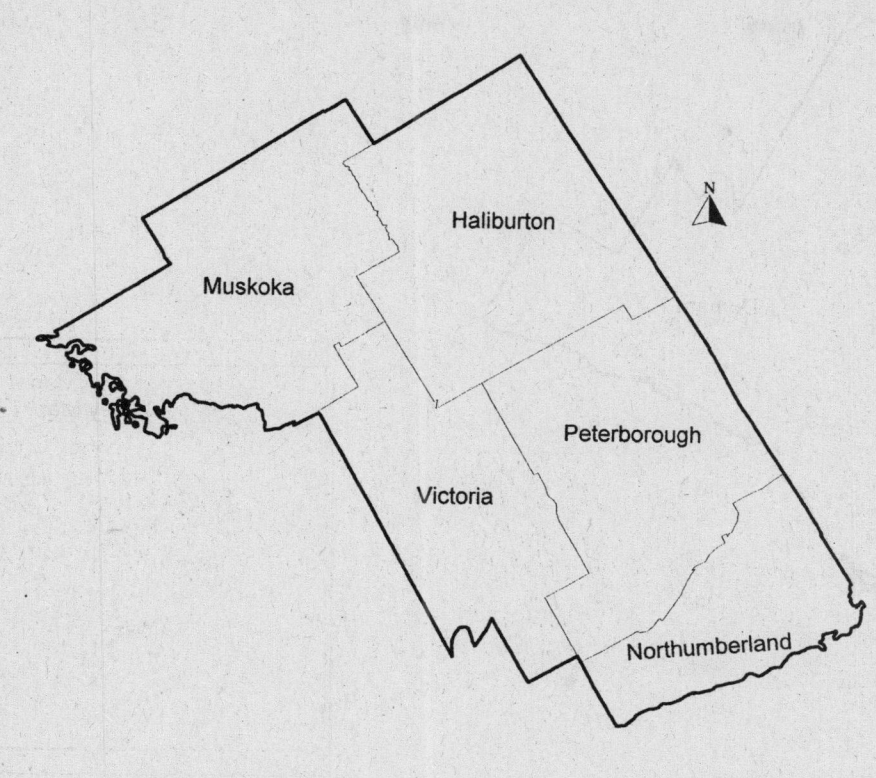

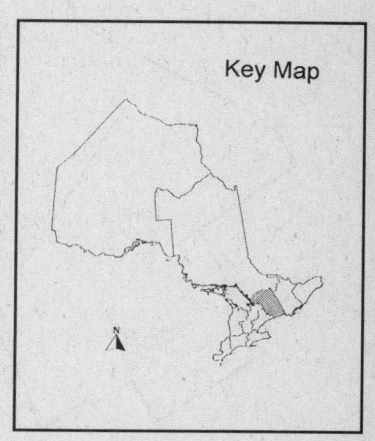

Key Map

Region	Population (at July 1)				Households (at July1)		Income				Retail Sales				Taxation Statistics, 1997					
	*1996 Census (000)	2001 Estimate (000)	% of Cdn. Total	% Chg. '96-'01	2001 Estimate (000)	% of Cdn. Total	2001 Estimate $millions	% of Cdn. Total	Per Hhld. $	Income Rating Index	2001 Estimate $millions	% of Cdn. Total	Per Hhld. $	Market Rating Index	Total No. of Returns	Total Income $millions	Total No. Taxable Returns	Total Tax $millions	Avg. Income $	Avg. Tax $
Muskoka - Kawarthas (20)	348.1	361.2	1.16	3.78	143.1	1.18	7,088.3	1.08	49,500	93	3,311.1	1.19	23,100	102	241,820	6,172.2	164,300	1,076.2	25,524	6,550
Northumberland County	84.0	86.7	0.28	3.29	33.3	0.28	1,757.3	0.27	52,700	96	635.3	0.23	19,100	82	54,850	1,464.9	38,490	262.0	26,707	6,808
Peterborough County	126.7	130.8	0.42	3.18	51.9	0.43	2,600.3	0.40	50,100	94	1,182.7	0.42	22,800	101	90,170	2,337.0	60,850	413.6	25,918	6,797
Victoria County	69.7	73.4	0.24	5.31	29.0	0.24	1,417.7	0.22	48,900	92	585.3	0.21	20,200	89	48,460	1,209.0	32,900	206.8	24,947	6,285
Muskoka District Municipality	52.0	54.0	0.17	3.89	21.6	0.18	1,024.4	0.16	47,400	90	733.9	0.26	33,900	152	37,360	926.5	25,180	158.7	24,799	6,301
Haliburton County	15.7	16.3	0.05	4.01	7.3	0.06	288.6	0.04	39,600	84	173.9	0.06	23,900	119	10,980	234.9	6,880	35.1	21,390	5,098

*Adjusted.

Toronto

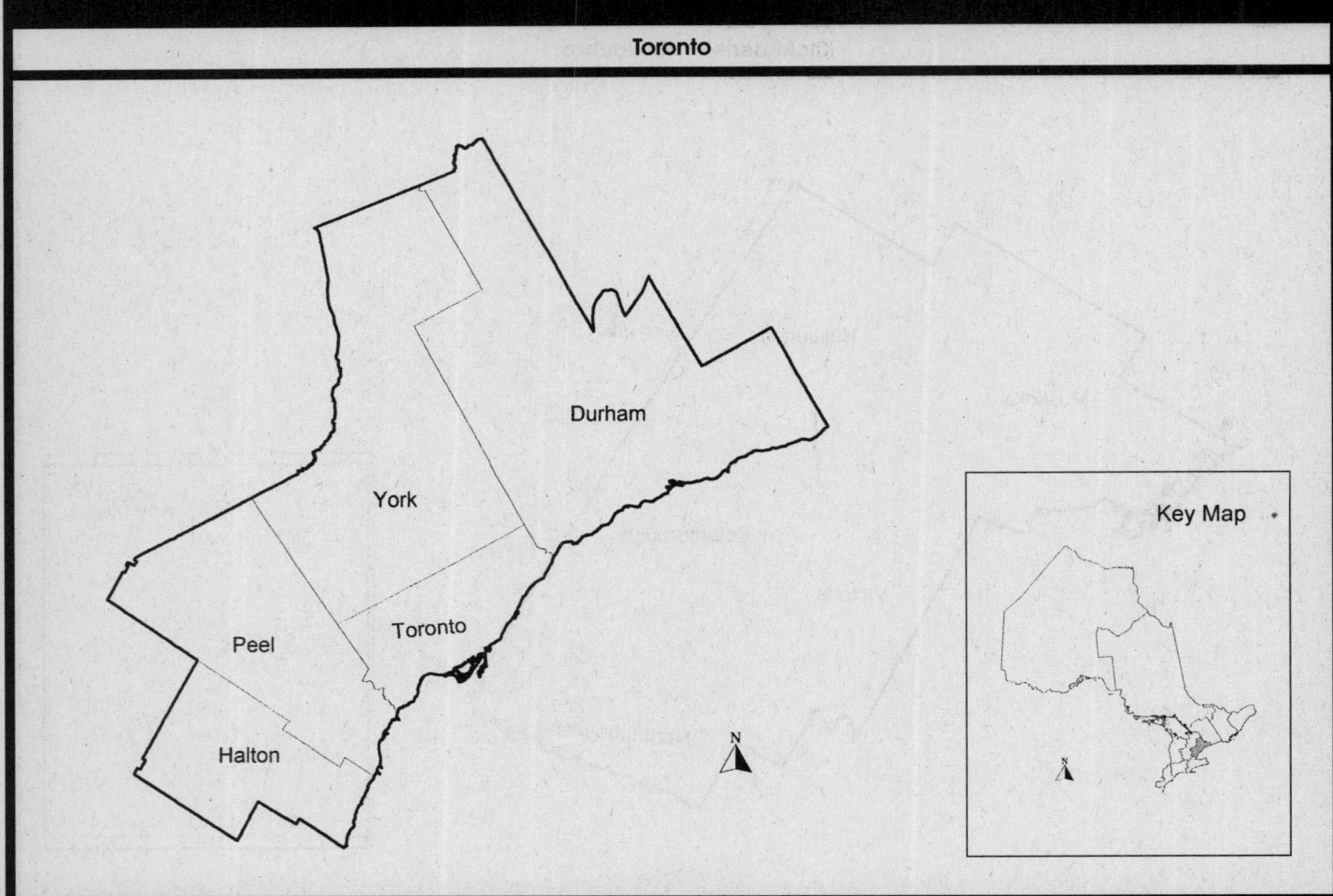

Region	Population (at July 1)				Households (at July1)		Income				Retail Sales				Taxation Statistics, 1997					
	*1996 Census (000)	2001 Estimate (000)	% of Cdn. Total	% Chg. '96-'01	2001 Estimate (000)	% of Cdn. Total	2001 Estimate $millions	% of Cdn. Total	Per Hhld. $	Income Rating Index	2001 Estimate $millions	% of Cdn. Total	Per Hhld. $	Market Rating Index	Total No. of Returns	Total Income $millions	Total No. Taxable Returns	Total Tax $millions	Avg. Income $	Avg. Tax $
Toronto (30)	4,637.8	5,120.4	16.45	10.41	1,830.7	15.15	124,810.0	19.01	68,200	116	43,006.0	15.43	23,500	94	3,427,750	110,875.9	2,380,960	24,296.2	32,347	10,204
Durham Regional Municipality	472.8	524.1	1.68	10.86	181.3	1.50	12,712.3	1.94	70,100	115	4,154.8	1.49	22,900	89	321,340	10,401.5	239,180	2,168.1	32,369	9,065
York Regional Municipality	611.7	740.2	2.38	21.01	231.2	1.91	19,932.3	3.04	86,200	128	6,232.2	2.24	27,000	94	446,740	15,649.4	319,330	3,564.4	35,030	11,162
Toronto Metropolitan Municipality	2,462.5	2,579.5	8.29	4.75	1,000.0	8.27	59,739.1	9.10	59,700	110	22,393.4	8.03	22,400	97	1,782,000	55,110.8	1,173,230	11,989.6	30,926	10,219
Peel Regional Municipality	881.8	1,039.2	3.34	17.85	336.3	2.78	25,244.3	3.85	75,100	115	8,090.5	2.90	24,100	87	626,810	19,381.0	453,550	4,045.5	30,920	8,920
Halton Regional Municipality+	350.2	386.6	1.24	10.4	138.1	1.14	11,470.8	1.75	83,100	141	3,707.1	1.33	26,900	107	250,860	10,333.2	195,670	2,528.7	41,191	12,923

*Adjusted.

+Halton R.M. is split between the economic region of Toronto and the economic region of Hamilton-Niagara Peninsula. Data are for both parts.

Kitchener – Waterloo – Barrie

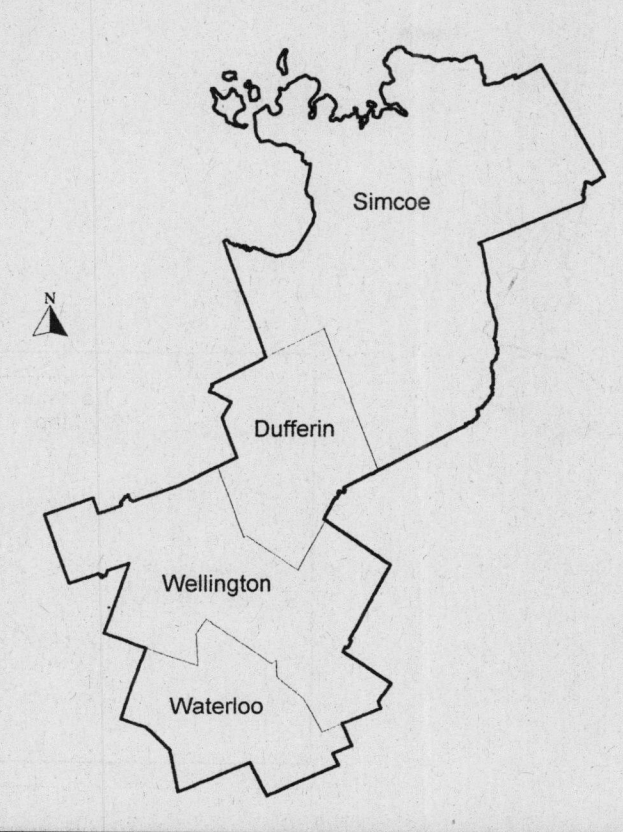

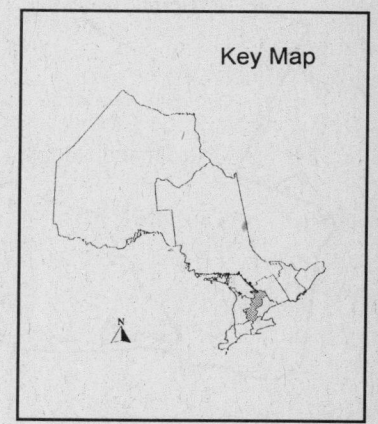

Key Map

Region	Population (at July 1)				Households (at July1)		Income				Retail Sales				Taxation Statistics, 1997					
	*1996 Census (000)	2001 Estimate (000)	% of Cdn. Total	% Chg. '96-'01	2001 Estimate (000)	% of Cdn. Total	2001 Estimate $millions	% of Cdn. Total	Per Hhld. $	Income Rating Index	2001 Estimate $millions	% of Cdn. Total	Per Hhld. $	Market Rating Index	Total No. of Returns	Total Income $millions	Total No. Taxable Returns	Total Tax $millions	Avg. Income $	Avg. Tax $
Kitchener - Waterloo - Barrie (40)	982.0	1,081.3	3.47	10.11	403.0	3.33	23,499.3	3.58	58,300	103	10,126.4	3.63	25,100	105	702,460	20,477.5	509,160	3,980.5	29,151	7,818
Dufferin County	47.0	51.9	0.17	10.38	17.7	0.15	1,135.1	0.17	64,000	104	391.6	0.14	22,100	84	31,450	960.8	23,130	194.8	30,549	8,420
Wellington County	176.7	191.4	0.61	8.3	71.0	0.59	4,359.4	0.66	61,400	108	1,775.3	0.64	25,000	104	125,370	3,829.3	92,970	764.1	30,544	8,219
Waterloo Regional Municipality	418.3	452.8	1.45	8.25	171.3	1.42	10,287.5	1.57	60,100	108	4,731.2	1.70	27,600	117	300,620	8,993.2	220,620	1,775.0	29,916	8,045
Simcoe County	339.9	385.1	1.24	13.3	143.0	1.18	7,717.4	1.18	54,000	95	3,228.3	1.16	22,600	94	245,020	6,694.2	172,440	1,246.6	27,321	7,229

*Adjusted.

Hamilton – Niagara Peninsula

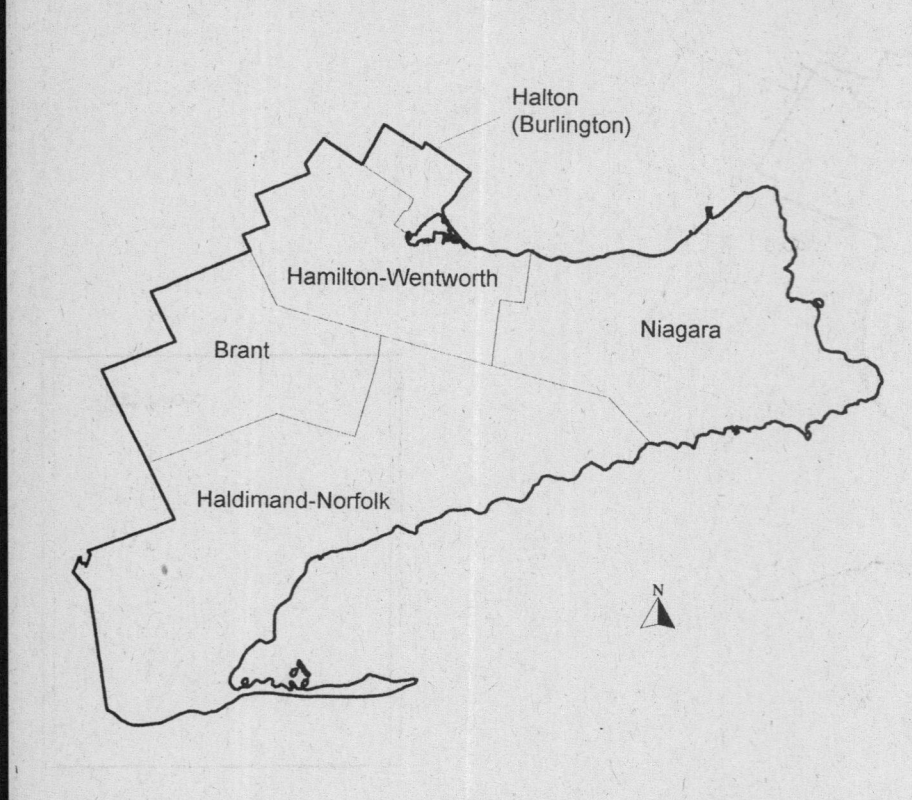

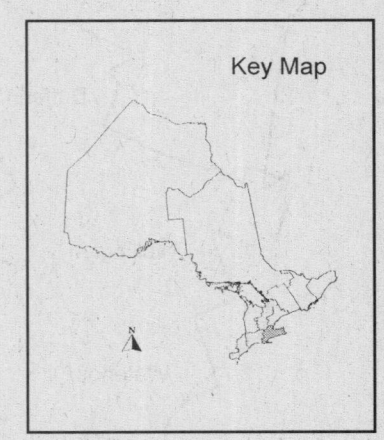

Key Map

Region	Population (at July 1)				Households (at July1)		Income				Retail Sales				Taxation Statistics, 1997					
	*1996 Census (000)	2001 Estimate (000)	% of Cdn. Total	% Chg. '96-'01	2001 Estimate (000)	% of Cdn. Total	2001 Estimate $millions	% of Cdn. Total	Per Hhld. $	Income Rating Index	2001 Estimate $millions	% of Cdn. Total	Per Hhld. $	Market Rating Index	Total No. of Returns	Total Income $millions	Total No. Taxable Returns	Total Tax $millions	Avg. Income $	Avg. Tax $
Hamilton - Niagara Peninsula (50)	1,267.0	1,318.7	4.24	4.08	509.7	4.22	28,515.9	4.34	56,000	103	11,416.8	4.10	22,400	97	794,510	21,882.4	554,440	4,048.4	27,542	7,302
Halton Regional Municipality+	350.2	386.6	1.24	10.4	138.1	1.14	11,470.8	1.75	83,100	141	3,707.1	1.33	26,900	107	250,860	10,333.2	195,670	2,528.7	41,191	12,923
Hamilton-Wentworth Regional Municipality	481.5	503.1	1.62	4.48	195.8	1.62	10,697.6	1.63	54,600	101	3,705.9	1.33	18,900	82	337,000	9,527.0	235,210	1,820.1	28,270	7,738
Niagara Regional Municipality	414.8	429.1	1.38	3.46	169.7	1.40	8,838.5	1.35	52,100	98	4,320.8	1.55	25,500	112	298,520	8,208.3	209,570	1,502.0	27,497	7,167
Haldimand-Norfolk Regional Municipality	106.1	109.6	0.35	3.27	40.3	0.33	2,177.3	0.33	54,000	94	839.3	0.30	20,800	86	74,820	1,910.5	51,480	331.7	25,535	6,444
Brant County	123.5	127.7	0.41	3.43	47.6	0.39	2,513.8	0.38	52,800	93	978.7	0.35	20,600	86	84,170	2,236.7	58,180	394.5	26,573	6,781

*Adjusted.

+Halton R.M. is split between the economic region of Toronto and the economic region of Hamilton-Niagara Peninsula. Data are for both parts.

Economic Region & Census Divisions

London

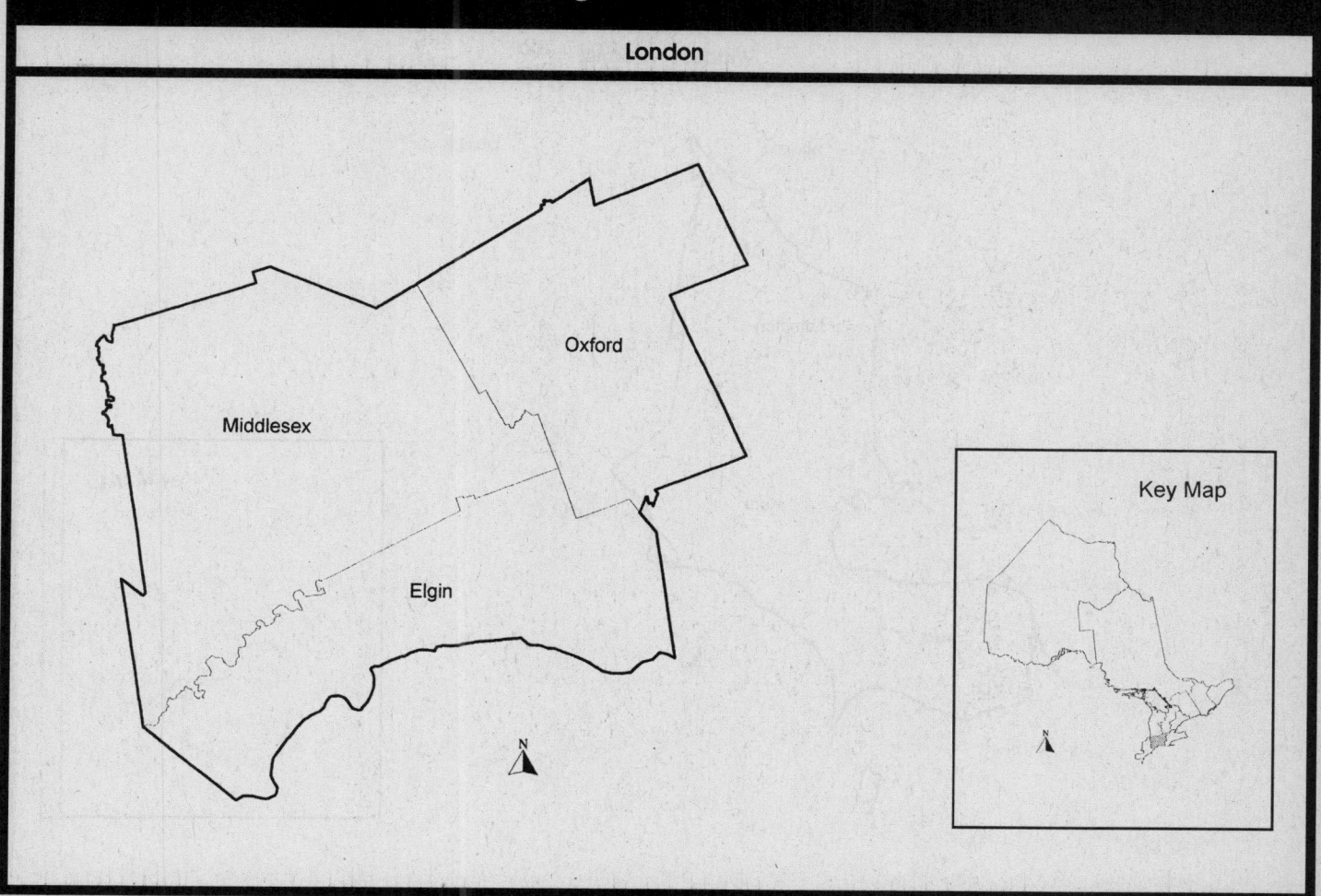

Region	Population (at July 1)				Households (at July1)		Income				Retail Sales				Taxation Statistics, 1997					
	*1996 Census (000)	2001 Estimate (000)	% of Cdn. Total	% Chg. '96-'01	2001 Estimate (000)	% of Cdn. Total	2001 Estimate $millions	% of Cdn. Total	Per Hhld. $	Income Rating Index	2001 Estimate $millions	% of Cdn. Total	Per Hhld. $	Market Rating Index	Total No. of Returns	Total Income $millions	Total No. Taxable Returns	Total Tax $millions	Avg. Income $	Avg. Tax $
London (60)	584.8	603.9	1.94	3.27	237.4	1.96	13,112.0	2.00	55,200	103	5,632.8	2.02	23,700	104	413,230	11,775.4	291,290	2,211.0	28,496	7,590
Oxford County	99.9	102.6	0.33	2.76	38.5	0.32	2,102.7	0.32	54,600	97	704.4	0.25	18,300	77	72,550	1,983.8	52,360	352.8	27,343	6,737
Elgin County	81.4	84.9	0.27	4.37	31.2	0.26	1,647.8	0.25	52,800	92	649.9	0.23	20,800	85	58,050	1,485.1	40,310	251.5	25,583	6,240
Middlesex County	403.5	416.3	1.34	3.17	167.7	1.39	9,361.5	1.43	55,800	107	4,278.6	1.54	25,500	115	282,630	8,306.5	198,620	1,606.7	29,390	8,089

*Adjusted.

Windsor – Sarnia

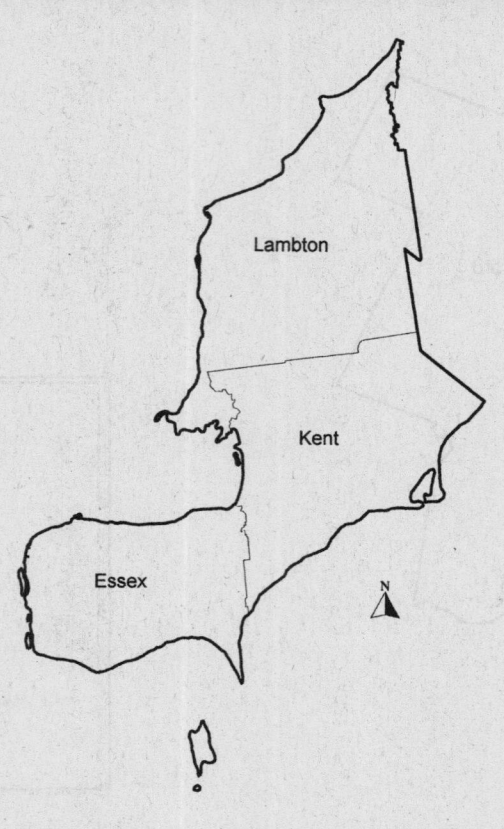

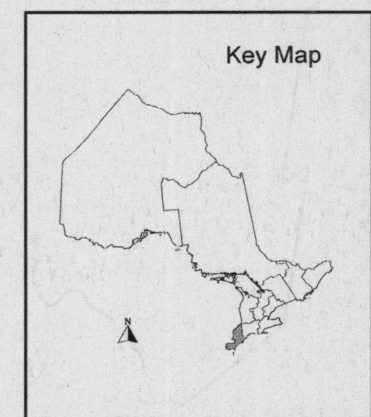

Key Map

Region	Population (at July 1)				Households (at July1)		Income				Retail Sales				Taxation Statistics, 1997					
	*1996 Census (000)	2001 Estimate (000)	% of Cdn. Total	% Chg. '96-'01	2001 Estimate (000)	% of Cdn. Total	2001 Estimate $millions	% of Cdn. Total	Per Hhld. $	Income Rating Index	2001 Estimate $millions	% of Cdn. Total	Per Hhld. $	Market Rating Index	Total No. of Returns	Total Income $millions	Total No. Taxable Returns	Total Tax $millions	Avg. Income $	Avg. Tax $
Windsor - Sarnia (70)	607.2	629.8	2.02	3.72	244.1	2.02	14,259.9	2.17	58,400	107	6,343.3	2.28	26,000	113	433,660	13,085.0	306,520	2,576.5	30,174	8,406
Kent County	112.6	111.6	0.36	-0.94	43.2	0.36	2,262.1	0.34	52,400	96	1,299.3	0.47	30,100	130	83,670	2,263.2	58,130	407.9	27,050	7,016
Essex County	361.3	387.4	1.24	7.22	149.5	1.24	9,106.3	1.39	60,900	111	3,850.4	1.38	25,800	111	258,350	8,138.3	184,100	1,647.6	31,501	8,949
Lambton County	133.3	130.8	0.42	-1.83	51.5	0.43	2,891.5	0.44	56,200	105	1,193.6	0.43	23,200	102	91,640	2,683.5	64,290	521.1	29,283	8,105

*Adjusted.

Economic Region & Census Divisions

Stratford – Bruce Peninsula

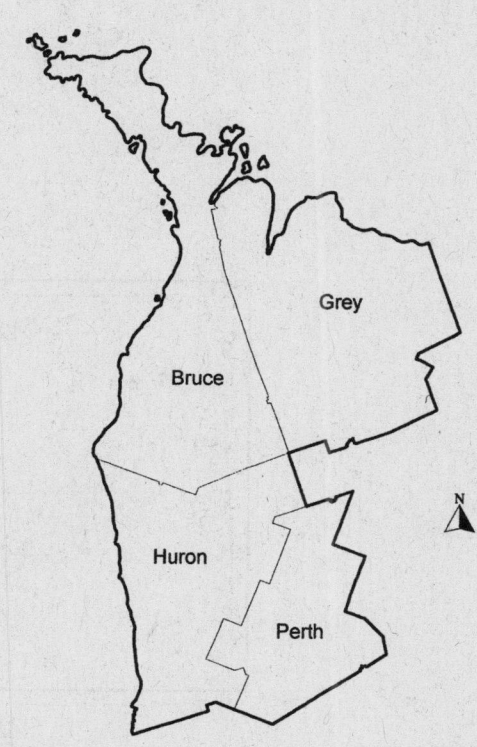

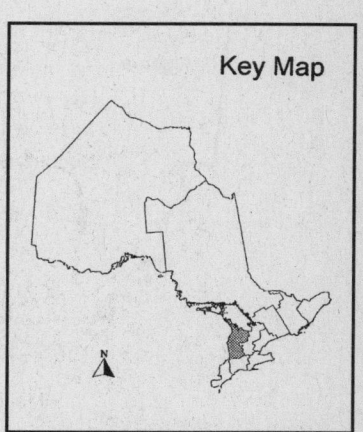

Key Map

Region	Population (at July 1)				Households (at July 1)		Income				Retail Sales				Taxation Statistics, 1997					
	*1996 Census (000)	2001 Estimate (000)	% of Cdn. Total	% Chg. '96-'01	2001 Estimate (000)	% of Cdn. Total	2001 Estimate $millions	% of Cdn. Total	Per Hhld. $	Income Rating Index	2001 Estimate $millions	% of Cdn. Total	Per Hhld. $	Market Rating Index	Total No. of Returns	Total Income $millions	Total No. Taxable Returns	Total Tax $millions	Avg. Income $	Avg. Tax $
Stratford - Bruce Peninsula (80)	293.7	294.5	0.95	0.27	114.1	0.94	5,679.9	0.87	49,800	91	3,083.6	1.11	27,000	117	203,610	5,215.9	141,400	884.3	25,617	6,254
Perth County	74.1	75.0	0.24	1.18	28.2	0.23	1,542.9	0.24	54,700	98	936.7	0.34	33,200	140	53,220	1,462.6	39,440	256.2	27,482	6,496
Huron County	61.7	61.4	0.20	-0.59	23.3	0.19	1,126.6	0.17	48,400	87	539.9	0.19	23,200	98	40,810	1,033.0	28,650	167.8	25,313	5,858
Bruce County	68.0	66.7	0.21	-1.77	25.9	0.21	1,295.6	0.20	50,100	92	674.3	0.24	26,100	113	48,620	1,253.6	32,430	219.9	25,783	6,780
Grey County	89.9	91.4	0.29	1.66	36.7	0.30	1,714.8	0.26	46,700	89	932.7	0.33	25,400	114	60,960	1,466.6	40,880	240.4	24,059	5,881

*Adjusted.

Northeast

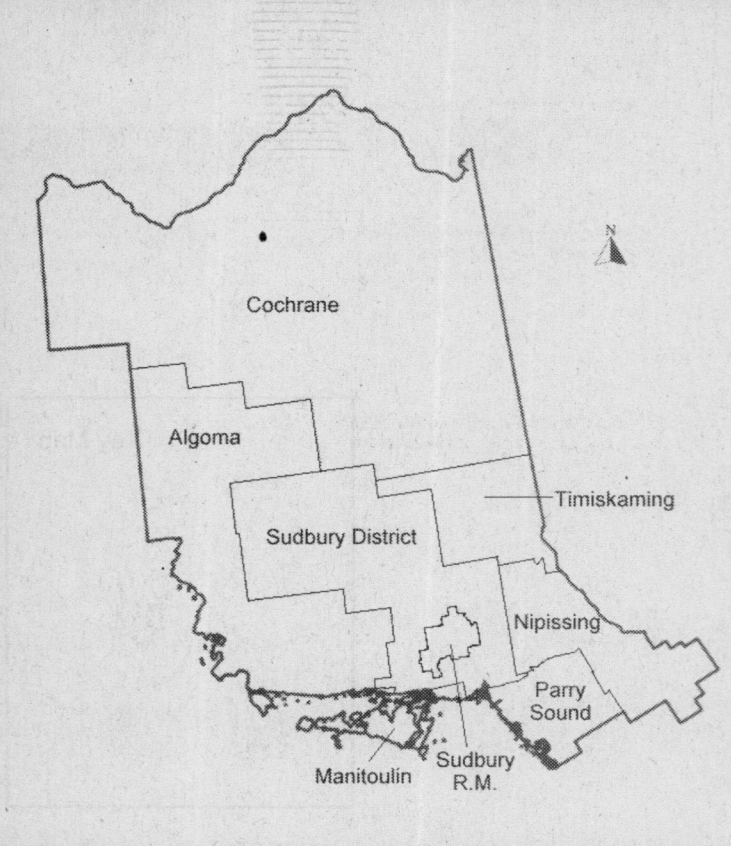

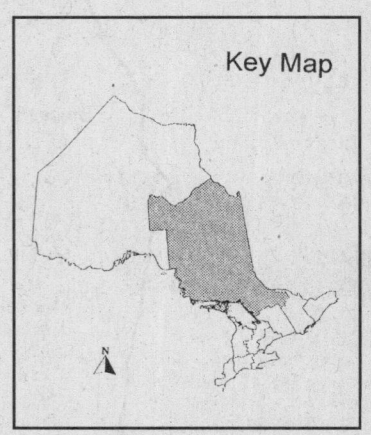

Key Map

Region	Population (at July 1)				Households (at July1)		Income				Retail Sales				Taxation Statistics, 1997					
	*1996 Census (000)	2001 Estimate (000)	% of Cdn. Total	% Chg. '96-'01	2001 Estimate (000)	% of Cdn. Total	2001 Estimate $millions	% of Cdn. Total	Per Hhld. $	Income Rating Index	2001 Estimate $millions	% of Cdn. Total	Per Hhld. $	Market Rating Index	Total No. of Returns	Total Income $millions	Total No. Taxable Returns	Total Tax $millions	Avg. Income $	Avg. Tax $
Northeast (90)	601.8	583.9	1.88	-2.98	235.7	1.95	11,620.7	1.77	49,300	94	6,197.2	2.22	26,300	119	421,370	10,885.6	272,470	1,947.9	25,834	7,149
Nipissing District	87.1	84.2	0.27	-3.3	34.2	0.28	1,598.8	0.24	46,800	90	952.3	0.34	27,900	126	60,610	1,491.9	38,410	254.7	24,615	6,630
Parry Sound District	41.1	41.9	0.13	2.02	17.8	0.15	730.8	0.11	41,000	83	433.4	0.16	24,300	116	30,400	663.2	18,730	100.3	21,816	5,353
Manitoulin District	12.6	13.3	0.04	5.16	5.1	0.04	213.2	0.03	42,100	76	111.2	0.04	22,000	94	8,700	175.1	4,420	25.3	20,132	5,727
Sudbury District	26.3	25.4	0.08	-3.38	10.2	0.08	489.3	0.07	47,800	91	191.1	0.07	18,700	84	16,960	421.1	10,250	74.2	24,831	7,243
Sudbury Regional Municipality	168.7	163.0	0.52	-3.37	66.3	0.55	3,565.4	0.54	53,800	104	1,791.4	0.64	27,000	123	120,030	3,313.6	80,990	627.7	27,607	7,750
Timiskaming District	38.8	36.6	0.12	-5.56	14.9	0.12	664.1	0.10	44,600	86	442.8	0.16	29,700	135	27,130	636.2	16,750	105.4	23,450	6,295
Cochrane District	95.9	93.0	0.30	-2.96	36.1	0.30	1,879.7	0.29	52,000	96	906.6	0.33	25,100	109	65,710	1,823.3	43,180	348.1	27,748	8,062
Algoma District	131.4	126.5	0.41	-3.77	51.1	0.42	2,479.4	0.38	48,500	93	1,368.5	0.49	26,800	121	91,830	2,361.1	59,740	412.2	25,712	6,900

*Adjusted.

Northwest

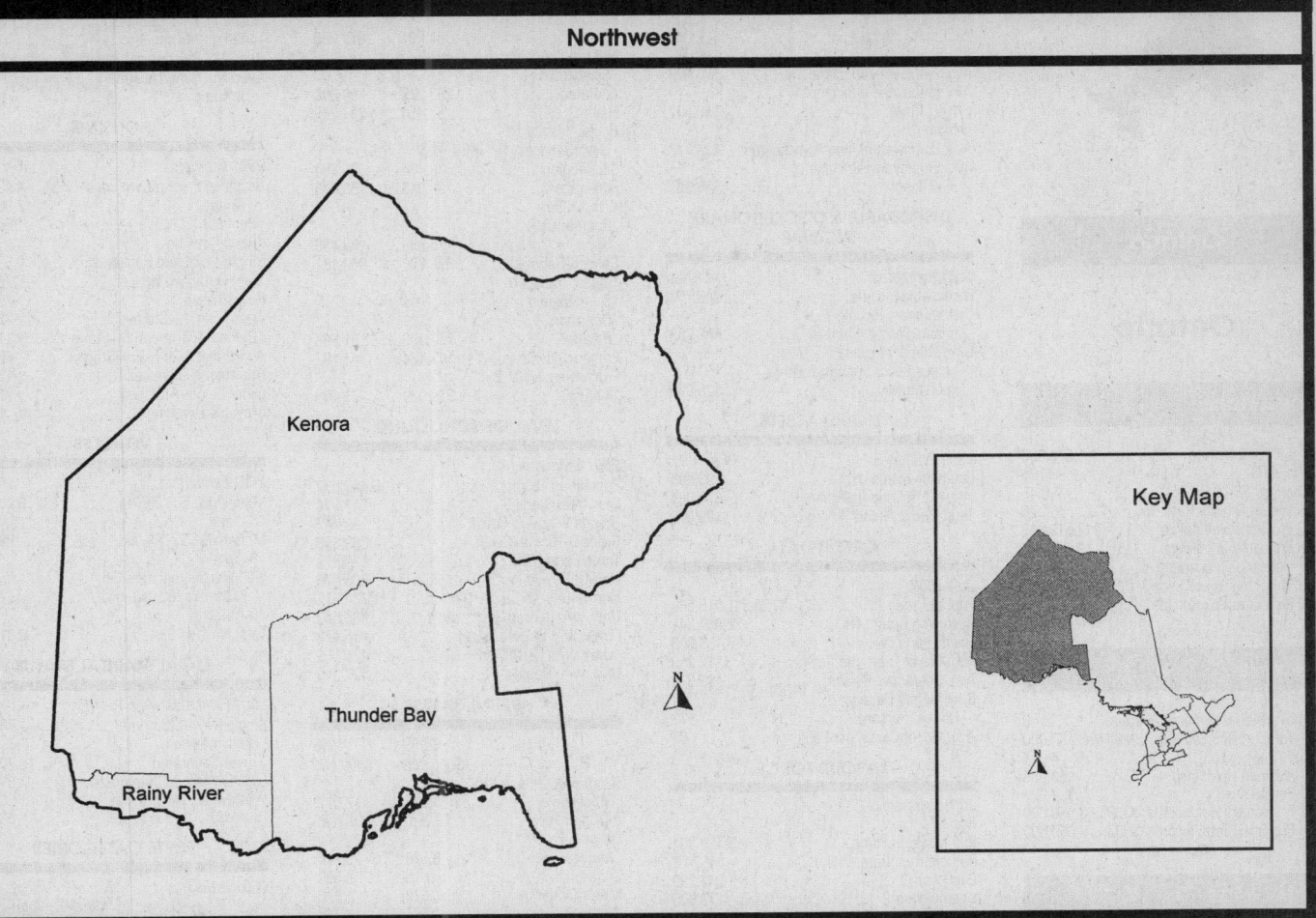

Region	Population (at July 1)				Households (at July 1)		Income				Retail Sales				Taxation Statistics, 1997					
	*1996 Census (000)	2001 Estimate (000)	% of Cdn. Total	% Chg. '96-'01	2001 Estimate (000)	% of Cdn. Total	2001 Estimate $millions	% of Cdn. Total	Per Hhld. $	Income Rating Index	2001 Estimate $millions	% of Cdn. Total	Per Hhld. $	Market Rating Index	Total No. of Returns	Total Income $millions	Total No. Taxable Returns	Total Tax $millions	Avg. Income $	Avg. Tax $
Northwest (95)	254.3	251.1	0.81	-1.24	97.0	0.80	5,388.1	0.82	55,500	102	2,445.9	0.88	25,200	109	172,120	4,776.7	115,480	886.6	27,752	7,677
Thunder Bay District	162.9	159.1	0.51	-2.37	63.6	0.53	3,606.4	0.55	56,700	108	1,495.0	0.54	23,500	105	112,150	3,279.4	79,240	626.2	29,241	7,903
Rainy River District	24.0	23.6	0.08	-1.41	9.2	0.08	474.5	0.07	51,600	95	243.3	0.09	26,400	115	16,100	418.4	10,570	73.6	25,985	6,964
Kenora District	67.4	68.4	0.22	1.55	24.2	0.20	1,307.2	0.20	54,000	91	707.5	0.25	29,200	116	43,870	1,078.9	25,670	186.7	24,594	7,273

*Adjusted.

Ontario

Ontario

POPULATION

July 1, 2001 Estimate	11,816,966
% Cdn. Total	37.95
% Change, '96 -'01	6.45
Avg. Annual Growth Rate, %	1.26
2003 Projected Population	12,117,646
2006 Projected Population	12,555,965
2001 Households Estimate	4,436,202
2003 Projected Households	4,576,218
2006 Projected Households	4,793,781

INCOME

% Above/Below National Average	+8
2001 Total Income Estimate	$269,996,760,000
% Cdn. Total	41.13
2001 Average Hhld. Income	$60,900
2001 Per Capita	$22,800
2003 Projected Total Income	$293,568,550,000
2006 Projected Total Income	$333,278,060,000

RETAIL SALES

% Above/Below National Average	+1
2001 Retail Sales Estimate	$106,349,370,000
% Cdn. Total	38.16
2001 per Household	$24,000
2001 per Capita	$9,000
2001 No. of Establishments	85,539
2003 Projected Retail Sales	$117,223,880,000
2006 Projected Retail Sales	$133,486,310,000

POPULATION

2001 Estimates:

Total		11,816,966
Male		5,779,268
Female		6,037,698

Age Groups	Male	Female
0-4	381,474	362,460
5-9	401,972	381,145
10-14	407,040	385,338
15-19	396,627	377,019
20-24	385,313	376,458
25-29	394,371	399,738
30-34	442,738	456,552
35-39	479,230	496,862
40-44	467,333	488,080
45-49	432,086	451,439
50-54	370,492	384,690
55-59	301,798	313,330
60-64	250,805	265,095
65-69	216,120	239,835
70+	451,869	659,657

DAYTIME POPULATION

2001 Estimates:

Working Population	6,093,714
At Home Population	5,759,828
Total	11,853,542

INCOME

2001 Estimates:

Avg. Household Income	$60,862
Avg. Family Income	$66,908
Per Capita Income	$22,848
Male:	
Avg. Employment Income	$38,878
Avg. Employment Income (Full Time)	$50,832
Female:	
Avg. Employment Income	$24,772
Avg. Employment Income (Full Time)	$36,391

DISPOSABLE & DISCRETIONARY INCOME

2001 Estimates: *Per Hhld.*

Disposable Income	$49,752
Discretionary Income 1 (minus Food & Shelter)	$35,259
Discretionary Income 2 (minus Food, Shelter, & Other Expenditures)	$26,090

LIQUID ASSETS

1999 Estimates: *Per Hhld.*

Equity Investments	$93,595
Interest Bearing Investments	$76,081
Total Liquid Assets	$169,676

CREDIT DATA

July 2000:

Pool of Credit	$125,541,015,586
Revolving Credit, No.	22,687,241
Fixed Loans, No.	6,195,863
Avg. Credit Limit, per Person	$12,250
Avg. Spent, per Person	$5,373
Satisfactory Ratings, No. per Person	2.72
Avg. No. of Cards, per Person	1.07

LABOUR FORCE

2001 Estimates:

Male:

In the Labour Force	3,426,804
Participation Rate	74.7
Employed	3,247,299
Unemployed	179,505
Unemployment Rate	5.2
Not in Labour Force	1,161,978

Female:

In the Labour Force	2,967,109
Participation Rate	60.4
Employed	2,783,515
Unemployed	183,594
Unemployment Rate	6.2
Not in Labour Force	1,941,646

AVERAGE WEEKLY EARNINGS

(Including overtime, industrial aggregate)

	Ontario	Canada
Apr 2000	$664.58	$622.92
Apr 1999	$645.34	$608.07
Apr 1998	$650.21	$608.06
Apr 1997	$636.33	$597.26
Apr 1996	$615.62	$575.79

NUMBER OF EMPLOYEES

(Industrial aggregate)

Apr 2000	4,742,342
Apr 1999	4,612,537
Apr 1998	4,533,005
Apr 1997	4,384,809
Apr 1996	4,290,910

MANUFACTURING INDUSTRIES

	1997	1992
Plants	13,906	13,491
Employees	890,803	829,088
	$000	
Salaries, Wages	36,550,883	29,856,245
Mfg. Materials, Cost	136,050,500	87,558,074
Mfg. Shipments, Value	228,505,241	150,257,077
Total Value Added	94,723,396	65,881,267

Note: Latest available data.

OCCUPATIONS BY MAJOR GROUPS

2001 Estimates:

	Male	Female
Management	412,448	194,014
Business, Finance & Admin.	364,504	879,096
Natural & Applied Sciences & Related	263,276	58,888
Health	57,450	227,769
Social Sciences, Gov't Services & Religion	73,474	95,390
Education	88,946	153,415
Arts, Culture, Recreation & Sport	76,893	89,483
Sales & Service	698,200	890,131
Trades, Transport & Equipment Operators & Related	777,395	51,598
Primary Industries	143,484	44,192
Processing, Mfg. & Utilities	379,029	171,106

LEVEL OF SCHOOLING

2001 Estimates:

Population 15 years +	9,497,537
Less than Grade 9	941,874
Grades 9-13 w/o Certif.	2,189,442
Grade 9-13 with Certif.	1,389,300
Trade Certif. /Dip.	326,375
Non-Univ. w/o Certif./Dip.	606,876
Non-Univ. with Certif./Dip.	1,734,812
Univ. w/o Degree	886,543
Univ. w/o Degree/Certif.	450,478
Univ. with Certif.	436,065
Univ. with Degree	1,422,315

RETAIL SALES

	1999 $000,000	1998 $000,000
Supermarkets & Groceries	17,076	17,077
All Other Food	n.a.	n.a.
Drugs & Patent Medicine	5,578	5,304
Shoes	615	633
Men's Clothing	672	670
Women's Clothing	1,827	1,746
Other Clothing	2,605	2,342
Hhld. Furniture & Appliances	4,035	3,630
Hhld. Furnishings	1,093	1,016
Motor & Recreation Vehicles	27,022	24,435
Gas Service Stations	6,723	5,917
Auto Parts, Accessories & Services	5,758	5,453
General Merchandise	11,947	10,976
Other Semi-Durable Goods	3,815	3,504
Other Durable Goods	2,839	2,690
Other Retail	5,579	5,158
Total	99,150	92,412

AVERAGE HOUSEHOLD EXPENDITURES

2001 Estimates:

Food	$6,675
Shelter	$10,173
Clothing	$2,406
Transportation	$7,082
Health & Personal Care	$2,052
Recr'n, Read'g & Education	$4,014
Taxes & Securities	$15,840
Other	$9,080
Total Expenditures	$57,322

PRIVATE HOUSEHOLDS

2001 Estimates:

Private Households, Total	4,436,202
Pop. in Private Households	11,597,442
Average no. per Household	2.6

FAMILIES

2001 Estimates:

Families in Private Households	3,327,781
Husband-Wife Families	2,857,772
Lone-Parent Families	470,009
Aver. No. Persons per Family	3.1
Aver. No. Sons/Daughters at Home	1.2

HOUSING

2001 Estimates:

Occupied Private Dwellings	4,436,202
Owned	2,868,464
Rented	1,561,999
Band Housing	5,739
Single-Detached House	2,538,157
Semi-Detached House	258,764
Row Houses	294,554
Apartment, 5+ Storeys	727,231
Owned Apartment, 5+ Storeys	111,858
Apartment, 5 or Fewer Storeys	462,571
Apartment, Detached Duplex	124,977
Other Single-Attached	13,391
Movable Dwellings	16,557

VEHICLES

2001 Estimates:

Model Yrs. '81-'96, No.	5,286,397
% Total	77.54
Model Yrs. '97-'98, No.	899,648
% Total	13.20
'99 Vehicles registered in Model Yr. '99, No.	631,598
% Total	9.26
Total No. '81-'99	6,817,643

LEGAL MARITAL STATUS

2001 Estimates: (Age 15+)

Single (Never Married)	2,783,066
Legally Married (Not Separated)	5,203,540
Legally Married (Separated)	318,016
Widowed	601,298
Divorced	591,617

PSYTE CATEGORIES

2001 Estimates	No. of House -holds	% of Total Hhds.	Index
Canadian Establishment	12,547	0.28	170
The Affluentials	41,087	0.93	145
Urban Gentry	109,751	2.47	138
Suburban Executives	101,189	2.28	159
Mortgaged in Suburbia	97,594	2.20	158
Technocrafts & Bureaucrats	163,609	3.69	131
Asian Heights	59,297	1.34	211
Boomers & Teens	146,940	3.31	185
Stable Suburban Families	80,073	1.80	138
Small City Elite	57,055	1.29	75
Old Bungalow Burbs	109,135	2.46	148
Suburban Nesters	147,079	3.32	207
Brie & Chablis	72,427	1.63	182
Aging Erudites	60,190	1.36	90
Satellite Suburbs	215,422	4.86	169
Kindergarten Boom	88,982	2.01	77
Blue Collar Winners	200,241	4.51	179
Town Boomers	25,215	0.57	56
Old Towns' New Fringe	199,304	4.49	115
Participation Quebec	12,787	0.29	10
Quebec Melange	4,379	0.10	4
Traditional French Cdn. Families	6,083	0.14	5
Northern Lights	780	0.02	4
The New Frontier	27,801	0.63	42
Rustic Prosperity	148,088	3.34	185
Pick-ups & Dirt Bikes	10,039	0.23	27
Quebec's Heartland	3,417	0.08	8
The Grain Belt	447	0.01	2
Europa	124,637	2.81	226
Asian Mosaic	40,952	0.92	67
High Rise Melting Pot	175,221	3.95	263

2001 Estimates	No. of House -holds	% of Total Hhds.	Index
Conservative			
Homebodies	300,663	6.78	188
High Rise Sunsets	83,884	1.89	132
Young Urban			
Professionals	99,651	2.25	118
Young Urban Mix	165,778	3.74	176
Young Urban			
Intelligentsia	73,119	1.65	108
University			
Enclaves	83,851	1.89	93
Young City Singles	79,475	1.79	78
Urban Bohemia	20,543	0.46	40
Old Leafy Towns	167,208	3.77	147
Town Renters	56,195	1.27	147
Nesters & Young			
Homesteaders	142,043	3.20	137
Young Grey Collar	22,291	0.50	60
Quiet Towns	76,940	1.73	82
Agrarian Blues	8,322	0.19	88
Rod & Rifle	59,015	1.33	58
Down, Down East	927	0.02	3
Big Country			
Families	20,000	0.45	32
Quebec Rural Blues	6,818	0.15	6
Old Cdn. Rustics	7,559	0.17	17
Old Quebec Walkups	3,397	0.08	4
Quebec Town Elders	10,151	0.23	8
Aging Quebec			
Urbanites	1,595	0.04	12
Quebec's New Urban			
Mosaic	3,603	0.08	3
Struggling			
Downtowns	220,691	4.97	158
Aged Pensioners	55,504	1.25	94
Big City Stress	53,896	1.21	108
Old Grey Towers	33,612	0.76	137

FINAN¢IAL P$YTE

2001 Estimates	No. of House -holds	% of Total Hhds.	Index
Platinum Estates	53,634	1.21	150
Four Star			
Investors	357,880	8.07	161
Successful			
Suburbanites	401,353	9.05	136
Canadian Comfort	645,012	14.54	150
Urban Heights	232,268	5.24	122
Miners &			
Credit-Liners	136,936	3.09	98
Mortgages &			
Minivans	101,769	2.29	35
Dollars & Sense	165,589	3.73	143
Tractors &			
Tradelines	347,392	7.83	137
Bills & Wills	633,649	14.28	172
Country Credit	20,948	0.47	7
Revolving Renters	248,218	5.60	122
Young Urban			
Struggle	177,513	4.00	85
Rural Family Blues	98,499	2.22	28
Limited Budgets	84,499	1.90	61
Loan Parent Stress	15,143	0.34	6
Towering Debt	531,582	11.98	154
NSF	57,499	1.30	37
Senior Survivors	89,116	2.01	107

HOME LANGUAGE

2001 Estimates:		% Total
English	9,757,386	82.57
French	303,551	2.57
Arabic	49,420	0.42
Armenian	8,007	0.07
Bengali	6,310	0.05
Chinese	311,678	2.64
Croatian	19,934	0.17
Dutch	6,877	0.06
German	44,567	0.38
Greek	38,035	0.32
Gujarati	19,682	0.17
Hindi	10,944	0.09
Hungarian	16,989	0.14
Italian	150,958	1.28
Japanese	6,291	0.05
Korean	25,044	0.21
Macedonian	11,399	0.10
Persian (Farsi)	29,153	0.25
Polish	94,094	0.80
Portuguese	100,585	0.85
Punjabi	68,483	0.58
Romanian	12,103	0.10
Russian	21,746	0.18
Serbian	17,381	0.15
Serbo-Croatian	7,286	0.06
Spanish	75,557	0.64
Tagalog (Pilipino)	42,905	0.36
Tamil	52,073	0.44
Ukrainian	18,916	0.16
Urdu	22,967	0.19
Vietnamese	47,934	0.41
Other Languages	133,094	1.13
Multiple Responses	285,617	2.42
Total	11,816,966	100.00

BUILDING PERMITS

	1999	1998 $000	1997
Value	16,760,143	14,007,418	13,299,434

HOMES BUILT

	1999	1998	1997
No	59,835	48,403	51,297

CAPITAL EXPENDITURES

(Public & Private)	2000	1999 $000,000	1998
Total Expends	n.a.	n.a.	74,472.3
Capital Expends	69,361.5	64,496.2	60,386.8
Construction	36,105.4	32,986.4	29,406.7
Machinery			
& Equip	33,256.2	31,509.8	30,980.2
Repair Expends	n.a.	n.a.	14,085.5
Construction	n.a.	n.a.	5,277.4
Machinery			
& Equip	n.a.	n.a.	8,808.1

TAXATION

Income Class:	1997	% Total
Under $5,000	1,057,500	13.40
$5,000-$10,000	940,380	11.92
$10,000-$15,000	1,057,350	13.40
$15,000-$20,000	746,870	9.47
$20,000-$25,000	628,120	7.96
$25,000-$30,000	593,190	7.52
$30,000-$40,000	979,440	12.41
$40,000-$50,000	648,420	8.22
$50,000 +	1,239,360	15.71
Total Returns, No	7,890,620	
Total Income, $000	236,829,568	
Total Taxable		
Returns	5,488,640	
Total Tax, $000	48,038,044	
Average Income, $	30,014	
Average Tax, $	8,752	

VITAL STATISTICS

	1997	1996	1995	1994
Births	133,004	140,012	146,268	147,070
Deaths	79,541	79,099	78,479	77,487
Natural				
Increase	53,463	60,913	67,789	69,583
Marriages	67,540	66,208	67,583	66,694

Note: Latest available data.

TRAVEL STATISTICS

Tourists in Canada	1999	1998
From the U.S. entering by:		
Automobile	26,233,602	26,414,857
Bus	1,256,617	1,188,972
Rail	27,473	27,339
Air	2,053,294	1,955,799
Marine	206,910	218,503
Other Methods	302,263	326,878
Total	30,080,159	30,132,348
Other Countries:		
Land (via U.S.)	317,933	392,623
Air	1,483,381	1,385,367
Marine	2,010	1,799
Total	1,803,324	1,779,789
Residents of Canada		
Returning from the U.S. by:		
Automobile	17,290,358	17,273,260
Bus	806,354	742,589
Rail	24,923	22,480
Air	2,779,777	2,484,515
Marine	33,080	34,751
Other Methods	324,467	289,766
Total	21,258,959	20,847,361
From Other Countries:		
Land (via U.S.)	1	22
Air	2,162,599	2,164,947
Marine	1	n.a.
Total	2,162,601	2,164,969

Ontario

Amherstburg
(Town)

In Essex County. On Jan. 1, 1998, Amherstburg, T, Malden, TP, & Anderdon, TP, amalgamated to form Amherstburg, TP.

POPULATION

July 1, 2001 Estimate	11,681
% Cdn. Total	0.04
% Change, '96 -'01	10.55
Avg. Annual Growth Rate, %	2.03
2003 Projected Population	12,265
2006 Projected Population	13,065
2001 Households Estimate	4,316
2003 Projected Households	4,571
2006 Projected Households	4,939

INCOME

% Above/Below National Average	+6
2001 Total Income Estimate	$260,370,000
% Cdn. Total	0.04
2001 Average Hhld. Income	$60,300
2001 Per Capita	$22,300
2003 Projected Total Income	$290,530,000
2006 Projected Total Income	$339,220,000

RETAIL SALES

% Above/Below National Average	+7
2001 Retail Sales Estimate	$111,580,000
% Cdn. Total	0.04
2001 per Household	$25,900
2001 per Capita	$9,600
2001 No. of Establishments	87
2003 Projected Retail Sales	$125,950,000
2006 Projected Retail Sales	$148,500,000

POPULATION

2001 Estimates:

Total		11,681
Male		5,662
Female		6,019

Age Groups	Male	Female
0-4	393	377
5-9	442	413
10-14	456	430
15-19	442	434
20-24	410	408
25-29	390	402
30-34	427	437
35-39	468	471
40-44	454	477
45-49	415	431
50-54	332	342
55-59	258	259
60-64	198	217
65-69	173	211
70+	404	710

DAYTIME POPULATION

2001 Estimates:

Working Population	5,950
At Home Population	5,845
Total	11,795

INCOME

2001 Estimates:

Avg. Household Income	$60,328
Avg. Family Income	$67,190
Per Capita Income	$22,290
Male:	
Avg. Employment Income	$41,514
Avg. Employment Income (Full Time)	$51,578
Female:	
Avg. Employment Income	$21,292
Avg. Employment Income (Full Time)	$32,783

DISPOSABLE & DISCRETIONARY INCOME

2001 Estimates:	Per Hhld.
Disposable Income	$49,525
Discretionary Income 1 (minus Food & Shelter)	$34,560
Discretionary Income 2 (minus Food, Shelter, & Other Expenditures)	$25,012

LIQUID ASSETS

1999 Estimates:	Per Hhld.
Equity Investments	$72,150
Interest Bearing Investments	$70,639
Total Liquid Assets	$142,789

CREDIT DATA

July 2000:

Pool of Credit	$139,800,436
Revolving Credit, No.	23,518
Fixed Loans, No.	8,476
Avg. Credit Limit, per Person	$14,193
Avg. Spent, per Person	$7,045
Satisfactory Ratings, No. per Person	3.09
Avg. No. of Cards, per Person	1.06

LABOUR FORCE

2001 Estimates:

Male:	
In the Labour Force	3,293
Participation Rate	75.3
Employed	3,193
Unemployed	100
Unemployment Rate	3.0
Not in Labour Force	1,078
Female:	
In the Labour Force	2,631
Participation Rate	54.8
Employed	2,594
Unemployed	37
Unemployment Rate	1.4
Not in Labour Force	2,168

OCCUPATIONS BY MAJOR GROUPS

2001 Estimates:	Male	Female
Management	180	166
Business, Finance & Admin.	221	570
Natural & Applied Sciences & Related	150	39
Health	65	306
Social Sciences, Gov't Services & Religion	76	40
Education	25	105
Arts, Culture, Recreation & Sport	79	85
Sales & Service	744	990
Trades, Transport & Equipment Operators & Related	939	58
Primary Industries	36	n.a.
Processing, Mfg. & Utilities	767	222

LEVEL OF SCHOOLING

2001 Estimates:

Population 15 years +	9,170
Less than Grade 9	892
Grades 9-13 w/o Certif.	2,226
Grade 9-13 with Certif.	1,746
Trade Certif. /Dip.	355
Non-Univ. w/o Certif./Dip.	644
Non-Univ. with Certif./Dip.	1,873
Univ. w/o Degree:	765
Univ. w/o Degree/Certif.	413
Univ. with Certif.	352
Univ. with Degree	669

AVERAGE HOUSEHOLD EXPENDITURES

2001 Estimates:

Food	$6,917
Shelter	$10,276
Clothing	$2,318
Transportation	$7,432
Health & Personal Care	$2,060
Recr'n, Read'g & Education	$3,998
Taxes & Securities	$14,872
Other	$9,585
Total Expenditures	$57,458

PRIVATE HOUSEHOLDS

2001 Estimates:

Private Households, Total	4,316
Pop. in Private Households	11,496
Average no. per Household	2.7

FAMILIES

2001 Estimates:

Families in Private Households	3,343
Husband-Wife Families	2,828
Lone-Parent Families	515
Aver. No. Persons per Family	3.1
Aver. No. Sons/Daughters at Home	1.3

HOUSING

2001 Estimates:

Occupied Private Dwellings	4,316
Owned	3,083
Rented	1,233
Single-Detached House	3,200
Semi-Detached House	47
Row Houses	258
Apartment, 5+ Storeys	313
Apartment, 5 or Fewer Storeys	357
Apartment, Detached Duplex	130
Other Single-Attached	11

VEHICLES

2001 Estimates:

Model Yrs. '81-'96, No.	5,711
% Total	75.28
Model Yrs. '97-'98, No.	1,088
% Total	14.34
'99 Vehicles registered in Model Yr. '99, No.	787
% Total	10.37
Total No. '81-'99	7,586

LEGAL MARITAL STATUS

2001 Estimates: (Age 15+)

Single (Never Married)	2,407
Legally Married (Not Separated)	5,212
Legally Married (Separated)	242
Widowed	683
Divorced	626

PSYTE CATEGORIES

2001 Estimates	No. of House -holds	% of Total Hhds.	Index
Satellite Suburbs	1,171	27.13	946
Blue Collar Winners	280	6.49	258
Conservative Homebodies	1,929	44.69	1,240
Struggling Downtowns	888	20.57	653

FINANCIAL P$YTE

2001 Estimates	No. of House -holds	% of Total Hhds.	Index
Canadian Comfort	1,451	33.62	346
Bills & Wills	1,929	44.69	540
Towering Debt	888	20.57	264

HOME LANGUAGE

2001 Estimates:		% Total
English	11,109	95.10
French	99	0.85
Chinese	27	0.23
Croatian	22	0.19
Italian	320	2.74
Portuguese	33	0.28
Romanian	12	0.10
Ukrainian	12	0.10
Multiple Responses	47	0.40
Total	11,681	100.00

BUILDING PERMITS

	1999	1998 $000	1997
Value	30,173	26,680	23,446

TAXATION

Income Class:	1997	% Total
Under $5,000	1,520	11.69
$5,000-$10,000	1,350	10.38
$10,000-$15,000	1,420	10.92
$15,000-$20,000	1,120	8.62
$20,000-$25,000	890	6.85
$25,000-$30,000	940	7.23
$30,000-$40,000	1,560	12.00
$40,000-$50,000	1,120	8.62
$50,000 +	3,080	23.69
Total Returns, No.	13,000	
Total Income, $000	441,620	
Total Taxable Returns	9,740	
Total Tax, $000	94,040	
Average Income, $.	33,971	
Average Tax, $.	9,655	

VITAL STATISTICS

	1997	1996	1995	1994
Births	203	216	224	239
Deaths	124	118	118	120
Natural Increase	79	98	106	119
Marriages	92	99	68	92

Note: Latest available data.

COMMUNITY NEWSPAPER(S)

	Total Circulation
Amherstburg: Amherstburg Echo Community News	7,843

Barrie
(Census Agglomeration)

The Census Agglomeration of Barrie includes: Barrie, C; Innisfil, T; and Springwater, TP. All are in Simcoe County.

POPULATION

July 1, 2001 Estimate	146,020
% Cdn. Total	0.47
% Change, '96 -'01	19.39
Avg. Annual Growth Rate, %	3.61
2003 Projected Population	158,319
2006 Projected Population	176,691
2001 Households Estimate	53,059
2003 Projected Households	57,347
2006 Projected Households	64,370

INCOME

% Above/Below National Average	-4
2001 Total Income Estimate	$2,967,830,000
% Cdn. Total	0.45
2001 Average Hhld. Income	$55,900
2001 Per Capita	$20,300
2003 Projected Total Income	$3,358,120,000
2006 Projected Total Income	$4,035,880,000

RETAIL SALES

% Above/Below National Average	+21
2001 Retail Sales Estimate	$1,575,500,000
% Cdn. Total	0.57
2001 per Household	$29,700
2001 per Capita	$10,800
2001 No. of Establishments	1,057
2003 Projected Retail Sales	$1,866,900,000
2006 Projected Retail Sales	$2,336,010,000

POPULATION

2001 Estimates:

Total		146,020
Male		71,581
Female		74,439

Age Groups	Male	Female
0-4	5,171	4,922
5-9	5,717	5,487
10-14	5,718	5,490
15-19	5,126	5,041
20-24	4,717	4,746
25-29	4,879	5,054
30-34	5,791	6,108
35-39	6,478	6,726
40-44	6,154	6,190
45-49	5,211	5,180
50-54	4,079	4,147
55-59	3,142	3,280
60-64	2,529	2,689
65-69	2,136	2,438
70+	4,733	6,941

DAYTIME POPULATION

2001 Estimates:

Working Population	77,150
At Home Population	68,870
Total	146,020

INCOME

2001 Estimates:

Avg. Household Income	$55,934
Avg. Family Income	$59,949
Per Capita Income	$20,325
Male:	
Avg. Employment Income	$35,560
Avg. Employment Income (Full Time)	$45,878
Female:	
Avg. Employment Income	$21,132
Avg. Employment Income (Full Time)	$32,154

DISPOSABLE & DISCRETIONARY INCOME

2001 Estimates: Per Hhld.

Disposable Income	$46,028
Discretionary Income 1 (minus Food & Shelter)	$32,585
Discretionary Income 2 (minus Food, Shelter, & Other Expenditures)	$24,000

LIQUID ASSETS

1999 Estimates: Per Hhld.

Equity Investments	$78,452
Interest Bearing Investments	$70,919
Total Liquid Assets	$149,371

CREDIT DATA

July 2000:

Pool of Credit	$1,660,982,478
Revolving Credit, No.	283,145
Fixed Loans, No.	93,372
Avg. Credit Limit, per Person	$13,371
Avg. Spent, per Person	$6,531
Satisfactory Ratings, No. per Person	2.92
Avg. No. of Cards, per Person	1.04

LABOUR FORCE

2001 Estimates:

Male:	
In the Labour Force	43,516
Participation Rate	79.2
Employed	41,490
Unemployed	2,026
Unemployment Rate	4.7
Not in Labour Force	11,459
Female:	
In the Labour Force	37,164
Participation Rate	63.5
Employed	34,927
Unemployed	2,237
Unemployment Rate	6.0
Not in Labour Force	21,376

OCCUPATIONS BY MAJOR GROUPS

2001 Estimates:	Male	Female
Management	5,112	2,247
Business, Finance & Admin.	3,600	11,025
Natural & Applied Sciences & Related	2,610	332
Health	607	2,535
Social Sciences, Gov't Services & Religion	852	1,332
Education	1,035	1,984
Arts, Culture, Recreation & Sport	625	804
Sales & Service	10,489	12,673
Trades, Transport & Equipment Operators & Related	11,798	682
Primary Industries	1,538	275
Processing, Mfg. & Utilities	4,355	1,974

LEVEL OF SCHOOLING

2001 Estimates:

Population 15 years +	113,515
Less than Grade 9	6,496
Grades 9-13 w/o Certif.	29,515
Grade 9-13 with Certif.	18,103
Trade Certif. /Dip.	4,216
Non-Univ. w/o Certif./Dip.	9,399
Non-Univ. with Certif./Dip.	25,533
Univ. w/o Degree	8,791
Univ. w/o Degree/Certif.	4,447
Univ. with Certif.	4,344
Univ. with Degree	11,462

AVERAGE HOUSEHOLD EXPENDITURES

2001 Estimates:

Food	$6,200
Shelter	$9,330
Clothing	$2,182
Transportation	$6,651
Health & Personal Care	$1,873
Recr'n, Read'g & Education	$3,800
Taxes & Securities	$14,681
Other	$8,572
Total Expenditures	$53,289

PRIVATE HOUSEHOLDS

2001 Estimates:

Private Households, Total	53,059
Pop. in Private Households	143,888
Average no. per Household	2.7

FAMILIES

2001 Estimates:

Families in Private Households	42,099
Husband-Wife Families	36,273
Lone-Parent Families	5,826
Aver. No. Persons per Family	3.1
Aver. No. Sons/Daughters at Home	1.2

HOUSING

2001 Estimates:

Occupied Private Dwellings	53,059
Owned	37,992
Rented	15,067
Single-Detached House	37,359
Semi-Detached House	1,524
Row Houses	2,908
Apartment, 5+ Storeys	3,914
Owned Apartment, 5+ Storeys	594
Apartment, 5 or Fewer Storeys	5,259
Apartment, Detached Duplex	1,828
Other Single-Attached	187
Movable Dwellings	80

VEHICLES

2001 Estimates:

Model Yrs. '81-'96, No.	65,024
% Total	77.04
Model Yrs. '97-'98, No.	11,623
% Total	13.77
'99 Vehicles registered in Model Yr. '99, No.	7,757
% Total	9.19
Total No. '81-'99	84,404

LEGAL MARITAL STATUS

2001 Estimates: (Age 15+)

Single (Never Married)	29,427
Legally Married (Not Separated)	64,844
Legally Married (Separated)	4,387
Widowed	6,366
Divorced	8,491

PSYTE CATEGORIES

2001 Estimates	No. of House -holds	% of Total Hhds.	Index
Suburban Executives	592	1.12	78
Mortgaged in Suburbia	2,069	3.90	281
Technocrafts & Bureaucrats	855	1.61	57
Boomers & Teens	1,731	3.26	182
Stable Suburban Families	164	0.31	24
Small City Elite	1,534	2.89	169
Old Bungalow Burbs	1,063	2.00	121
Suburban Nesters	394	0.74	46
Aging Erudites	606	1.14	76
Satellite Suburbs	10,414	19.63	684
Kindergarten Boom	3,647	6.87	262
Blue Collar Winners	4,858	9.16	364
Old Towns' New Fringe	5,728	10.80	276
Rustic Prosperity	690	1.30	72
Conservative Homebodies	4,164	7.85	218
High Rise Sunsets	2,018	3.80	266
Young Urban Mix	849	1.60	76
University Enclaves	2,417	4.56	223
Young City Singles	1,696	3.20	139
Old Leafy Towns	1,180	2.22	87

Ontario

2001 Estimates	No. of House -holds	% of Total Hhds.	Index
Town Renters	394	0.74	86
Rod & Rifle	138	0.26	11
Big Country Families	273	0.51	36
Struggling Downtowns	4,896	9.23	293
Aged Pensioners	181	0.34	26
Old Grey Towers	195	0.37	66

FINANCIAL P$YTE

2001 Estimates	No. of House -holds	% of Total Hhds.	Index
Four Star Investors	2,323	4.38	87
Successful Suburbanites	3,088	5.82	88
Canadian Comfort	17,200	32.42	334
Urban Heights	606	1.14	27
Miners & Credit-Liners	1,063	2.00	63
Mortgages & Minivans	3,647	6.87	104
Tractors & Tradelines	6,418	12.10	212
Bills & Wills	6,193	11.67	141
Revolving Renters	2,018	3.80	83
Young Urban Struggle	2,417	4.56	96
Rural Family Blues	411	0.77	10
Towering Debt	6,986	13.17	169
Senior Survivors	376	0.71	38

HOME LANGUAGE

2001 Estimates		% Total
English	141,674	97.02
French	660	0.45
Chinese	109	0.07
Finnish	85	0.06
German	400	0.27
Greek	146	0.10
Hungarian	118	0.08
Italian	347	0.24
Japanese	170	0.12
Korean	199	0.14
Polish	406	0.28
Portuguese	90	0.06
Spanish	151	0.10
Vietnamese	163	0.11
Other Languages	590	0.40
Multiple Responses	712	0.49
Total	146,020	100.00

BUILDING PERMITS

	1999	1998 $000	1997
Value	428,126	283,531	242,413

HOMES BUILT

	1999	1998	1997
No	2,676	1,822	1,746

Barrie
(Census Agglomeration)
(Cont'd)

TAXATION

Income Class:	1997	% Total
Under $5,000	11,560	12.81
$5,000-$10,000	10,490	11.62
$10,000-$15,000	11,720	12.98
$15,000-$20,000	8,770	9.72
$20,000-$25,000	7,310	8.10
$25,000-$30,000	6,950	7.70
$30,000-$40,000	11,390	12.62
$40,000-$50,000	8,010	8.87
$50,000 +	14,060	15.58
Total Returns, No.	90,260	
Total Income, $000	2,589,390	
Total Taxable Returns	65,110	
Total Tax, $000	503,412	
Average Income, $	28,688	
Average Tax, $	7,732	

VITAL STATISTICS

	1997	1996	1995	1994
Births	1,565	1,768	1,724	1,746
Deaths	781	762	753	720
Natural Increase	784	1,006	971	1,026
Marriages	685	645	669	656

Note: Latest available data.

DAILY NEWSPAPER(S)

	Circulation Average Paid
Barrie Examiner	9,399

COMMUNITY NEWSPAPER(S)

	Total Circulation
Barrie: The Advance Wed/Fri/Sun	45,800
Barrie: The Examiner This Week Tue/Fri	41,667
Innisfil: Innisfil Scope	1,345

RADIO STATION(S)

	Power
CFJB-FM	100,000w
CIQB-FM	n.a.
CJLF-FM	2,000w

TELEVISION STATION(S)

CKVR-TV
CTS-TV
GLOBAL-TV

Belleville
(Census Agglomeration)

The Census Agglomeration of Belleville includes: Belleville, C; Trenton, C; Sidney, TP; Frankford, VL; and Thurlow, TP. All are in Hastings County. It also includes Ameliasburgh, TP, in Prince Edward County, & Murray, TP, in Northumberland County.

POPULATION

July 1, 2001 Estimate	96,372
% Cdn. Total	0.31
% Change, '96 -'01	-0.56
Avg. Annual Growth Rate, %	-0.11
2003 Projected Population	95,552
2006 Projected Population	93,823
2001 Households Estimate	38,100
2003 Projected Households	38,094
2006 Projected Households	38,010

INCOME

% Above/Below National Average	-5
2001 Total Income Estimate	$1,934,890,000
% Cdn. Total	0.29
2001 Average Hhld. Income	$50,800
2001 Per Capita	$20,100
2003 Projected Total Income	$2,025,200,000
2006 Projected Total Income	$2,169,590,000

RETAIL SALES

% Above/Below National Average	+36
2001 Retail Sales Estimate	$1,170,920,000
% Cdn. Total	0.42
2001 per Household	$30,700
2001 per Capita	$12,200
2001 No. of Establishments	845
2003 Projected Retail Sales	$1,254,810,000
2006 Projected Retail Sales	$1,358,510,000

POPULATION

2001 Estimates:

Total		96,372
Male		46,959
Female		49,413
Age Groups	Male	Female
0-4	2,912	2,789
5-9	3,162	3,012
10-14	3,311	3,085
15-19	3,322	3,128
20-24	3,098	3,057
25-29	2,894	2,982
30-34	3,264	3,378
35-39	3,732	3,839
40-44	3,686	3,766
45-49	3,422	3,497
50-54	2,961	3,046
55-59	2,494	2,620
60-64	2,220	2,324
65-69	1,994	2,188
70+	4,487	6,702

DAYTIME POPULATION

2001 Estimates:

Working Population	46,181
At Home Population	50,192
Total	96,373

INCOME

2001 Estimates:

Avg. Household Income	$50,785
Avg. Family Income	$57,105
Per Capita Income	$20,077
Male:	
Avg. Employment Income	$32,843
Avg. Employment Income (Full Time)	$43,187
Female:	
Avg. Employment Income	$20,829
Avg. Employment Income (Full Time)	$31,593

DISPOSABLE & DISCRETIONARY INCOME

2001 Estimates:	Per Hhld.
Disposable Income	$41,902
Discretionary Income 1 (minus Food & Shelter)	$28,804
Discretionary Income 2 (minus Food, Shelter, & Other Expenditures)	$20,531

LIQUID ASSETS

1999 Estimates:	Per Hhld.
Equity Investments	$65,853
Interest Bearing Investments	$61,265
Total Liquid Assets	$127,118

CREDIT DATA

July 2000:

Pool of Credit	$978,651,637
Revolving Credit, No.	176,591
Fixed Loans, No.	57,700
Avg. Credit Limit, per Person	$11,154
Avg. Spent, per Person	$5,070
Satisfactory Ratings, No. per Person	2.53
Avg. No. of Cards, per Person	0.91

LABOUR FORCE

2001 Estimates:

Male:	
In the Labour Force	26,461
Participation Rate	70.4
Employed	24,867
Unemployed	1,594
Unemployment Rate	6.0
Not in Labour Force	11,113
Female:	
In the Labour Force	22,940
Participation Rate	56.6
Employed	21,065
Unemployed	1,875
Unemployment Rate	8.2
Not in Labour Force	17,587

OCCUPATIONS BY MAJOR GROUPS

2001 Estimates:	Male	Female
Management	3,234	1,204
Business, Finance & Admin.	2,039	5,694
Natural & Applied Sciences & Related	1,286	225
Health	530	1,994
Social Sciences, Gov't Services & Religion	426	666
Education	577	1,142
Arts, Culture, Recreation & Sport	320	454
Sales & Service	7,189	7,888
Trades, Transport & Equipment Operators & Related	6,046	441
Primary Industries	1,050	402
Processing, Mfg. & Utilities	3,005	1,854

LEVEL OF SCHOOLING

2001 Estimates:

Population 15 years +	78,101
Less than Grade 9	6,317
Grades 9-13 w/o Certif.	21,328
Grade 9-13 with Certif.	13,067
Trade Certif./Dip.	3,708
Non-Univ. w/o Certif./Dip.	5,531
Non-Univ. with Certif./Dip.	17,185
Univ. w/o Degree.	4,640
Univ. w/o Degree/Certif.	2,305
Univ. with Certif.	2,335
Univ. with Degree	6,325

AVERAGE HOUSEHOLD EXPENDITURES

2001 Estimates:

Food	$5,988
Shelter	$9,132
Clothing	$1,975
Transportation	$6,423
Health & Personal Care	$1,890
Recr'n, Read'g & Education	$3,476
Taxes & Securities	$11,867
Other	$8,462
Total Expenditures	$49,213

PRIVATE HOUSEHOLDS

2001 Estimates:

Private Households, Total	38,100
Pop. in Private Households	94,013
Average no. per Household	2.5

FAMILIES

2001 Estimates:

Families in Private Households	28,111
Husband-Wife Families	24,281
Lone-Parent Families	3,830
Aver. No. Persons per Family	2.9
Aver. No. Sons/Daughters at Home	1.1

HOUSING

2001 Estimates:

Occupied Private Dwellings	38,100
Owned	24,509
Rented	13,591
Single-Detached House	24,927
Semi-Detached House	1,456
Row Houses	1,408
Apartment, 5+ Storeys	2,455
Owned Apartment, 5+ Storeys	99
Apartment, 5 or Fewer Storeys	5,783
Apartment, Detached Duplex	1,063
Other Single-Attached	121
Movable Dwellings	887

VEHICLES

2001 Estimates:

Model Yrs. '81-'96, No.	50,736
% Total	84.56
Model Yrs. '97-'98, No.	5,734
% Total	9.56
'99 Vehicles registered in Model Yr. '99, No.	3,528
% Total	5.88
Total No. '81-'99	59,998

LEGAL MARITAL STATUS

2001 Estimates: (Age 15+)

Single (Never Married)	20,131
Legally Married (Not Separated)	43,558
Legally Married (Separated)	2,676
Widowed	5,942
Divorced	5,794

Belleville
(Census Agglomeration)
(Cont'd)

PSYTE CATEGORIES

2001 Estimates	No. of House -holds	% of Total Hhds.	Index
Urban Gentry	99	0.26	14
Stable Suburban Families	32	0.08	6
Small City Elite	2,615	6.86	401
Old Bungalow Burbs	802	2.10	127
Aging Erudites	377	0.99	66
Kindergarten Boom	36	0.09	4
Blue Collar Winners	3,486	9.15	363
Old Towns' New Fringe	6,615	17.36	444
Rustic Prosperity	2,427	6.37	353
Conservative Homebodies	42	0.11	3
High Rise Sunsets	470	1.23	86
Young City Singles	573	1.50	66
Old Leafy Towns	2,340	6.14	240
Town Renters	365	0.96	111
Nesters & Young Homesteaders	14,381	37.75	1,617
Struggling Downtowns	1,188	3.12	99
Aged Pensioners	1,960	5.14	387

FINANCIAL P$YTE

2001 Estimates	No. of House -holds	% of Total Hhds.	Index
Four Star Investors	99	0.26	5
Successful Suburbanites	32	0.08	1
Canadian Comfort	6,101	16.01	165
Urban Heights	377	0.99	23
Miners & Credit-Liners	802	2.10	66
Mortgages & Minivans	36	0.09	1
Tractors & Tradelines	9,042	23.73	415
Bills & Wills	2,382	6.25	76
Revolving Renters	14,851	38.98	847
Towering Debt	2,126	5.58	71
Senior Survivors	1,960	5.14	273

HOME LANGUAGE

2001 Estimates:		% Total
English	93,053	96.56
French	1,253	1.30
Chinese	224	0.23
German	126	0.13
Greek	143	0.15
Gujarati	50	0.05
Italian	124	0.13
Korean	111	0.12
Polish	104	0.11
Spanish	161	0.17
Vietnamese	135	0.14
Other Languages	415	0.43
Multiple Responses	473	0.49
Total	96,372	100.00

BUILDING PERMITS

	1999	1998	1997
		$000	
Value	93,469	61,482	67,065

HOMES BUILT

	1999	1998	1997
No.	298	289	255

TAXATION

Income Class:	1997	% Total
Under $5,000	8,340	12.42
$5,000-$10,000	8,250	12.28
$10,000-$15,000	10,110	15.05
$15,000-$20,000	7,320	10.90
$20,000-$25,000	5,770	8.59
$25,000-$30,000	5,200	7.74
$30,000-$40,000	8,510	12.67
$40,000-$50,000	5,830	8.68
$50,000 +	7,830	11.66
Total Returns, No.	67,170	
Total Income, $000	1,753,981	
Total Taxable Returns	46,220	
Total Tax, $000	310,167	
Average Income, $	26,113	
Average Tax, $	6,711	

VITAL STATISTICS

	1997	1996	1995	1994
Births	987	1,065	1,114	1,112
Deaths	826	839	798	820
Natural Increase	161	226	316	292
Marriages	606	602	593	592

Note: Latest available data.

DAILY NEWSPAPER(S)

	Circulation Average Paid
The Intelligencer	
Sat	17,629
Sun	15,527
Mon-Fri	15,999

COMMUNITY NEWSPAPER(S)

	Total Circulation
Belleville: Contact	3,200
Belleville: Belleville Shopper's Market	50,000
Belleville, Trenton: The Community Press	38,662
Stirling: Stirling News-Argus	5,060
Stirling, Madoc, Marmora, Tweed: The Community Press	9,833
Trenton: Trentonian Mon/Wed/Fri	n.a.
Trenton: Trentonian (suppl.), Marketplace Today	n.a.

RADIO STATION(S)

	Power
CIGL-FM	50,000w
CJBC-FM	
CJBQ	10,000w
CJOJ-FM	100,000w
CJRT-FM	n.a.

TELEVISION STATION(S)

TFO
TVO

Bracebridge
(Town)
In Muskoka District Municipality.

POPULATION

July 1, 2001 Estimate	14,364
% Cdn. Total	0.05
% Change, '96 -'01	5.46
Avg. Annual Growth Rate, %	1.07
2003 Projected Population	14,622
2006 Projected Population	14,937
2001 Households Estimate	5,624
2003 Projected Households	5,737
2006 Projected Households	5,920

INCOME

% Above/Below National Average	-5
2001 Total Income Estimate	$288,570,000
% Cdn. Total	0.04
2001 Average Hhld. Income	$51,300
2001 Per Capita	$20,100
2003 Projected Total Income	$308,620,000
2006 Projected Total Income	$342,130,000

RETAIL SALES

% Above/Below National Average	+77
2001 Retail Sales Estimate	$228,050,000
% Cdn. Total	0.08
2001 per Household	$40,600
2001 per Capita	$15,900
2001 No. of Establishments	198
2003 Projected Retail Sales	$252,280,000
2006 Projected Retail Sales	$287,950,000

POPULATION

2001 Estimates:

Total		14,364
Male		7,003
Female		7,361
Age Groups	Male	Female
0-4	402	365
5-9	480	397
10-14	532	470
15-19	533	502
20-24	471	438
25-29	421	401
30-34	442	450
35-39	494	527
40-44	534	571
45-49	534	563
50-54	467	503
55-59	387	422
60-64	327	357
65-69	292	322
70+	687	1,073

DAYTIME POPULATION

2001 Estimates:

Working Population	10,244
At Home Population	7,100
Total	17,344

INCOME

2001 Estimates:

Avg. Household Income	$51,310
Avg. Family Income	$56,152
Per Capita Income	$20,090
Male:	
Avg. Employment Income	$30,636
Avg. Employment Income (Full Time)	$40,815
Female:	
Avg. Employment Income	$19,008
Avg. Employment Income (Full Time)	$30,360

Ontario

DISPOSABLE & DISCRETIONARY INCOME

2001 Estimates:	Per Hhld.
Disposable Income	$42,435
Discretionary Income 1 (minus Food & Shelter)	$29,649
Discretionary Income 2 (minus Food, Shelter, & Other Expenditures)	$21,105

LIQUID ASSETS

1999 Estimates:	Per Hhld.
Equity Investments	$69,360
Interest Bearing Investments	$63,189
Total Liquid Assets	$132,549

CREDIT DATA

July 2000:	
Pool of Credit	$154,499,786
Revolving Credit, No.	25,756
Fixed Loans, No.	9,118
Avg. Credit Limit, per Person	$13,082
Avg. Spent, per Person	$5,913
Satisfactory Ratings, No. per Person	2.81
Avg. No. of Cards, per Person	1.07

LABOUR FORCE

2001 Estimates:	
Male:	
In the Labour Force	4,129
Participation Rate	73.9
Employed	3,868
Unemployed	261
Unemployment Rate	6.3
Not in Labour Force	1,460
Female:	
In the Labour Force	3,613
Participation Rate	58.9
Employed	3,398
Unemployed	215
Unemployment Rate	6.0
Not in Labour Force	2,516

OCCUPATIONS BY MAJOR GROUPS

2001 Estimates:	Male	Female
Management	407	221
Business, Finance & Admin.	218	983
Natural & Applied Sciences & Related	228	n.a.
Health	70	259
Social Sciences, Gov't Services & Religion	49	144
Education	105	223
Arts, Culture, Recreation & Sport	33	117
Sales & Service	927	1,297
Trades, Transport & Equipment Operators & Related	1,555	62
Primary Industries	192	11
Processing, Mfg. & Utilities	265	194

Ontario

Bracebridge
(Town)
(Cont'd)

LEVEL OF SCHOOLING

2001 Estimates:
Population 15 years + ... 11,718
Less than Grade 9 829
Grades 9-13 w/o Certif. 3,170
Grade 9-13 with Certif. 2,050
Trade Certif. /Dip. 562
Non-Univ. w/o Certif./Dip. 741
Non-Univ. with Certif./Dip. 2,482
Univ. w/o Degree 745
 Univ. w/o Degree/Certif. 314
 Univ. with Certif. 431
Univ. with Degree 1,139

AVERAGE HOUSEHOLD EXPENDITURES

2001 Estimates:
Food $6,083
Shelter $8,758
Clothing. $1,943
Transportation. $6,723
Health & Personal Care $1,888
Recr'n, Read'g & Education $3,588
Taxes & Securities $12,633
Other $8,140
Total Expenditures $49,756

PRIVATE HOUSEHOLDS

2001 Estimates:
Private Households, Total 5,624
Pop. in Private Households 13,902
Average no. per Household 2.5

FAMILIES

2001 Estimates:
Families in Private Households 4,245
Husband-Wife Families 3,750
Lone-Parent Families 495
Aver. No. Persons per Family 2.9
Aver. No. Sons/Daughters at Home 1.1

HOUSING

2001 Estimates:
Occupied Private Dwellings 5,624
 Owned. 4,278
 Rented. 1,346
Single-Detached House 4,404
Semi-Detached House 111
Row Houses 181
Apartment, 5 or Fewer Storeys 822
Apartment, Detached Duplex. 95
Other Single-Attached 11

VEHICLES

2001 Estimates:
Model Yrs. '81-'96, No. 7,719
 % Total 72.74
Model Yrs. '97-'98, No. 1,690
 % Total 15.93
'99 Vehicles registered in
 Model Yr. '99, No. 1,203
 % Total 11.34
Total No. '81-'99 10,612

LEGAL MARITAL STATUS

2001 Estimates: (Age 15+)
Single (Never Married) 2,896
Legally Married (Not Separated) 6,661
Legally Married (Separated) 382
Widowed 930
Divorced 849

PSYTE CATEGORIES

2001 Estimates	No. of House-holds	% of Total Hhds.	Index
Blue Collar Winners	62	1.10	44
Town Boomers	735	13.07	1,289
Old Towns' New Fringe	1,081	19.22	491
Pick-ups & Dirt Bikes	204	3.63	434
Old Leafy Towns	2,283	40.59	1,588
Nesters & Young Homesteaders	572	10.17	436
Quiet Towns	486	8.64	406
Down, Down East	102	1.81	259

FINAN¢IAL P$YTE

2001 Estimates	No. of House-holds	% of Total Hhds.	Index
Canadian Comfort	797	14.17	146
Tractors & Tradelines	1,081	19.22	336
Bills & Wills	2,283	40.59	490
Country Credit	204	3.63	54
Revolving Renters	572	10.17	221
Rural Family Blues	102	1.81	22
Limited Budgets	486	8.64	278

HOME LANGUAGE

2001 Estimates:		% Total
English	14,197	98.84
Czech	10	0.07
Dutch	11	0.08
German	29	0.20
Hungarian	25	0.17
Latvian (Lettish)	11	0.08
Polish	27	0.19
Other Languages	10	0.07
Multiple Responses	44	0.31
Total	14,364	100.00

BUILDING PERMITS

	1999	1998	1997
		$000	
Value	35,014	16,215	13,805

HOMES BUILT

	1999	1998	1997
No	50	52	60

TAXATION

Income Class:	1997	% Total
Under $5,000	1,370	13.24
$5,000-$10,000	1,300	12.56
$10,000-$15,000	1,590	15.36
$15,000-$20,000	1,090	10.53
$20,000-$25,000	880	8.50
$25,000-$30,000	780	7.54
$30,000-$40,000	1,310	12.66
$40,000-$50,000	850	8.21
$50,000 +	1,200	11.59
Total Returns, No.	10,350	
Total Income, $000	269,575	
Total Taxable Returns	7,150	
Total Tax, $000	47,854	
Average Income, $	26,046	
Average Tax, $	6,693	

VITAL STATISTICS

	1997	1996	1995	1994
Births	136	152	156	164
Deaths	152	134	131	124
Natural Increase	-16	18	25	40
Marriages	140	135	118	126

Note: Latest available data.

COMMUNITY NEWSPAPER(S)

	Total Circulation
Bracebridge: Bracebridge Examiner	5,012
Bracebridge: District Weekender	25,171
Bracebridge: Muskoka Advance	23,487
Bracebridge: The Muskoka Sun (Published May, Oct., Dec., Jan., Mar.)	19,900
Bracebridge: The Muskokan (Published May to Oct.)	n.a.

RADIO STATION(S)

	Power
CFBG-FM	3,000w

Brantford
(Census Agglomeration)

The Census Agglomeration of Brantford includes: Brantford, C; Brantford, TP; and Paris, T. All are in Brant County.

POPULATION

July 1, 2001 Estimate	111,525
% Cdn. Total	0.36
% Change, '96 -'01	3.25
Avg. Annual Growth Rate, %	0.64
2003 Projected Population	113,301
2006 Projected Population	115,323
2001 Households Estimate	42,272
2003 Projected Households	43,348
2006 Projected Households	44,808

INCOME

% Above/Below National Average	-8
2001 Total Income Estimate	$2,159,060,000
% Cdn. Total	0.33
2001 Average Hhld. Income	$51,100
2001 Per Capita	$19,400
2003 Projected Total Income	$2,309,610,000
2006 Projected Total Income	$2,538,170,000

RETAIL SALES

% Above/Below National Average	-8
2001 Retail Sales Estimate	$922,640,000
% Cdn. Total	0.33
2001 per Household	$21,800
2001 per Capita	$8,300
2001 No. of Establishments	741
2003 Projected Retail Sales	$1,009,990,000
2006 Projected Retail Sales	$1,132,990,000

POPULATION

2001 Estimates:

Total		111,525
Male		53,874
Female		57,651

Age Groups	Male	Female
0-4	3,489	3,372
5-9	3,823	3,681
10-14	4,032	3,841
15-19	3,954	3,781
20-24	3,713	3,631
25-29	3,489	3,557
30-34	3,766	3,937
35-39	4,123	4,397
40-44	4,151	4,510
45-49	3,983	4,247
50-54	3,448	3,575
55-59	2,785	2,836
60-64	2,274	2,423
65-69	1,972	2,323
70+	4,872	7,540

DAYTIME POPULATION

2001 Estimates:

Working Population	55,394
At Home Population	56,130
Total	111,524

INCOME

2001 Estimates:

Avg. Household Income	$51,075
Avg. Family Income	$57,506
Per Capita Income	$19,359
Male:	
Avg. Employment Income	$33,649
Avg. Employment Income (Full Time)	$43,838
Female:	
Avg. Employment Income	$20,583
Avg. Employment Income (Full Time)	$31,029

DISPOSABLE & DISCRETIONARY INCOME

2001 Estimates:	Per Hhld.
Disposable Income	$42,126
Discretionary Income 1 (minus Food & Shelter)	$29,340
Discretionary Income 2 (minus Food, Shelter, & Other Expenditures)	$21,384

LIQUID ASSETS

1999 Estimates:	Per Hhld.
Equity Investments	$66,925
Interest Bearing Investments	$62,197
Total Liquid Assets	$129,122

CREDIT DATA

July 2000:

Pool of Credit	$1,010,381,820
Revolving Credit, No.	185,330
Fixed Loans, No.	57,319
Avg. Credit Limit, per Person	$11,742
Avg. Spent, per Person	$5,583
Satisfactory Ratings, No. per Person	2.72
Avg. No. of Cards, per Person	0.95

LABOUR FORCE

2001 Estimates:

Male:	
In the Labour Force	31,156
Participation Rate	73.3
Employed	29,848
Unemployed	1,308
Unemployment Rate	4.2
Not in Labour Force	11,374
Female:	
In the Labour Force	26,977
Participation Rate	57.7
Employed	25,285
Unemployed	1,692
Unemployment Rate	6.3
Not in Labour Force	19,780

OCCUPATIONS BY MAJOR GROUPS

2001 Estimates:	Male	Female
Management	3,073	1,551
Business, Finance & Admin.	2,732	6,607
Natural & Applied Sciences & Related	1,572	246
Health	532	2,284
Social Sciences, Gov't Services & Religion	477	882
Education	601	1,233
Arts, Culture, Recreation & Sport	485	562
Sales & Service	5,745	9,337
Trades, Transport & Equipment Operators & Related	7,809	658
Primary Industries	956	211
Processing, Mfg. & Utilities	6,553	2,339

LEVEL OF SCHOOLING

2001 Estimates:

Population 15 years +	89,287
Less than Grade 9	8,957
Grades 9-13 w/o Certif.	27,029
Grade 9-13 with Certif.	13,288
Trade Certif. /Dip.	3,634
Non-Univ. w/o Certif./Dip.	6,015
Non-Univ. with Certif./Dip.	17,557
Univ. w/o Degree	5,712
Univ. w/o Degree/Certif.	2,886
Univ. with Certif.	2,826
Univ. with Degree	7,095

AVERAGE HOUSEHOLD EXPENDITURES

2001 Estimates:

Food	$5,944
Shelter	$8,788
Clothing	$2,019
Transportation	$6,083
Health & Personal Care	$1,781
Recr'n, Read'g & Education	$3,405
Taxes & Securities	$12,986
Other	$8,395
Total Expenditures	$49,401

PRIVATE HOUSEHOLDS

2001 Estimates:

Private Households, Total	42,272
Pop. in Private Households	109,170
Average no. per Household	2.6

FAMILIES

2001 Estimates:

Families in Private Households	31,275
Husband-Wife Families	26,122
Lone-Parent Families	5,153
Aver. No. Persons per Family	3.0
Aver. No. Sons/Daughters at Home	1.2

HOUSING

2001 Estimates:

Occupied Private Dwellings	42,272
Owned	28,515
Rented	13,757
Single-Detached House	27,269
Semi-Detached House	3,012
Row Houses	2,825
Apartment, 5+ Storeys	3,891
Owned Apartment, 5+ Storeys	229
Apartment, 5 or Fewer Storeys	3,789
Apartment, Detached Duplex	1,408
Other Single-Attached	78

VEHICLES

2001 Estimates:

Model Yrs. '81-'96, No.	52,446
% Total	82.97
Model Yrs. '97-'98, No.	6,538
% Total	10.34
'99 Vehicles registered in Model Yr. '99, No.	4,224
% Total	6.68
Total No. '81-'99	63,208

LEGAL MARITAL STATUS

2001 Estimates: (Age 15+)

Single (Never Married)	23,937
Legally Married (Not Separated)	48,301
Legally Married (Separated)	3,720
Widowed	6,955
Divorced	6,374

PSYTE CATEGORIES

2001 Estimates	No. of House -holds	% of Total Hhds.	Index
Mortgaged in Suburbia	75	0.18	13
Technocrats & Bureaucrats	773	1.83	65
Boomers & Teens	1,443	3.41	190
Stable Suburban Families	522	1.23	95
Old Bungalow Burbs	1,716	4.06	245
Suburban Nesters	464	1.10	68
Aging Erudites	1,224	2.90	192
Satellite Suburbs	3,403	8.05	281
Kindergarten Boom	792	1.87	71
Blue Collar Winners	2,363	5.59	222
Old Towns' New Fringe	2,109	4.99	127
Conservative Homebodies	8,086	19.13	531
High Rise Sunsets	810	1.92	134
Young Urban Mix	368	0.87	41
University Enclaves	308	0.73	36
Old Leafy Towns	86	0.20	8
Town Renters	1,270	3.00	348
Struggling Downtowns	14,565	34.46	1,094
Aged Pensioners	725	1.72	129
Big City Stress	299	0.71	63
Old Grey Towers	407	0.96	174

Ontario

FINANCIAL P$YTE

2001 Estimates	No. of House -holds	% of Total Hhds.	Index
Four Star Investors	1,443	3.41	68
Successful Suburbanites	1,370	3.24	49
Canadian Comfort	6,230	14.74	152
Urban Heights	1,224	2.90	67
Miners & Credit-Liners	1,716	4.06	128
Mortgages & Minivans	792	1.87	28
Tractors & Tradelines	2,109	4.99	87
Bills & Wills	8,540	20.20	244
Revolving Renters	810	1.92	42
Young Urban Struggle	308	0.73	15
Towering Debt	15,835	37.46	480
NSF	299	0.71	20
Senior Survivors	1,132	2.68	142

HOME LANGUAGE

2001 Estimates:		% Total
English	105,105	94.24
French	259	0.23
Arabic	125	0.11
Chinese	209	0.19
Dutch	61	0.05
German	120	0.11
Greek	62	0.06
Hungarian	285	0.26
Italian	658	0.59
Korean	101	0.09
Lao	90	0.08
Polish	1,241	1.11
Portuguese	238	0.21
Punjabi	412	0.37
Spanish	107	0.10
Tagalog (Pilipino)	78	0.07
Ukrainian	128	0.11
Urdu	91	0.08
Vietnamese	352	0.32
Other Languages	473	0.42
Multiple Responses	1,330	1.19
Total	111,525	100.00

BUILDING PERMITS

	1999	1998	1997
		$000	
Value	78,132	71,158	56,215

HOMES BUILT

	1999	1998	1997
No.	338	355	264

Ontario

Brantford
(Census Agglomeration)
(Cont'd)
TAXATION

Income Class:	1997	% Total
Under $5,000	8,660	11.65
$5,000-$10,000	8,480	11.41
$10,000-$15,000	11,600	15.61
$15,000-$20,000	8,640	11.63
$20,000-$25,000	6,660	8.96
$25,000-$30,000	6,010	8.09
$30,000-$40,000	9,410	12.66
$40,000-$50,000	6,090	8.19
$50,000 +	8,790	11.83
Total Returns, No.	74,320	
Total Income, $000	1,962,230	
Total Taxable Returns	51,970	
Total Tax, $000	348,624	
Average Income, $	26,402	
Average Tax, $	6,708	

VITAL STATISTICS

	1997	1996	1995	1994
Births	1,236	1,368	1,378	1,422
Deaths	981	961	931	955
Natural Increase	255	407	447	467
Marriages	571	599	568	604

Note: Latest available data.

DAILY NEWSPAPER(S)

	Circulation Average Paid
The Expositor	23,480

COMMUNITY NEWSPAPER(S)

	Total Circulation
Brantford, Tekawennake-6 Nations:	
New Credit Reporter	n.a.
Paris: The Paris Star	2,111

RADIO STATION(S)

	Power
CKPC	10,000w
CKPC-FM	n.a.

Brock
(Township)
In Durham Regional Municipality.

POPULATION

July 1, 2001 Estimate	12,454
% Cdn. Total	0.04
% Change, '96 -'01	3.21
Avg. Annual Growth Rate, %	0.63
2003 Projected Population	12,593
2006 Projected Population	12,749
2001 Households Estimate	4,618
2003 Projected Households	4,712
2006 Projected Households	4,860

INCOME

% Above/Below National Average	-8
2001 Total Income Estimate	$240,470,000
% Cdn. Total	0.04
2001 Average Hhld. Income	$52,100
2001 Per Capita	$19,300
2003 Projected Total Income	$256,480,000
2006 Projected Total Income	$282,960,000

RETAIL SALES

% Above/Below National Average	-43
2001 Retail Sales Estimate	$63,940,000
% Cdn. Total	0.02
2001 per Household	$13,800
2001 per Capita	$5,100
2001 No. of Establishments	107
2003 Projected Retail Sales	$68,020,000
2006 Projected Retail Sales	$75,420,000

POPULATION

2001 Estimates:

Total	12,454
Male	6,090
Female	6,364

Age Groups	Male	Female
0-4	372	351
5-9	448	417
10-14	487	455
15-19	471	452
20-24	400	389
25-29	324	338
30-34	357	402
35-39	456	488
40-44	494	498
45-49	466	472
50-54	397	379
55-59	312	295
60-64	258	261
65-69	238	253
70+	610	914

DAYTIME POPULATION

2001 Estimates:

Working Population	3,610
At Home Population	6,204
Total	9,814

INCOME

2001 Estimates:

Avg. Household Income	$52,072
Avg. Family Income	$56,489
Per Capita Income	$19,309
Male:	
Avg. Employment Income	$31,606
Avg. Employment Income (Full Time)	$41,076
Female:	
Avg. Employment Income	$21,578
Avg. Employment Income (Full Time)	$33,017

DISPOSABLE & DISCRETIONARY INCOME

2001 Estimates:	Per Hhld.
Disposable Income	$43,200
Discretionary Income 1 (minus Food & Shelter)	$30,248
Discretionary Income 2 (minus Food, Shelter, & Other Expenditures)	$21,386

LIQUID ASSETS

1999 Estimates:	Per Hhld.
Equity Investments	$64,745
Interest Bearing Investments	$61,452
Total Liquid Assets	$126,197

CREDIT DATA

July 2000:

Pool of Credit	$148,244,168
Revolving Credit, No.	22,745
Fixed Loans, No.	7,818
Avg. Credit Limit, per Person	$12,340
Avg. Spent, per Person	$5,832
Satisfactory Ratings, No. per Person	2.47
Avg. No. of Cards, per Person	0.93

LABOUR FORCE

2001 Estimates:

Male:	
In the Labour Force	3,449
Participation Rate	72.1
Employed	3,344
Unemployed	105
Unemployment Rate	3.0
Not in Labour Force	1,334
Female:	
In the Labour Force	2,960
Participation Rate	57.6
Employed	2,842
Unemployed	118
Unemployment Rate	4.0
Not in Labour Force	2,181

OCCUPATIONS BY MAJOR GROUPS

2001 Estimates:	Male	Female
Management	296	233
Business, Finance & Admin.	171	696
Natural & Applied Sciences & Related	126	47
Health	22	255
Social Sciences, Gov't Services & Religion	47	60
Education	114	160
Arts, Culture, Recreation & Sport	58	83
Sales & Service	645	918
Trades, Transport & Equipment Operators & Related	1,194	110
Primary Industries	409	154
Processing, Mfg. & Utilities	274	138

LEVEL OF SCHOOLING

2001 Estimates:

Population 15 years +	9,924
Less than Grade 9	947
Grades 9-13 w/o Certif.	2,764
Grade 9-13 with Certif.	1,786
Trade Certif. /Dip.	417
Non-Univ. w/o Certif./Dip.	691
Non-Univ. with Certif./Dip.	1,875
Univ. w/o Degree	725
Univ. w/o Degree/Certif.	349
Univ. with Certif.	376
Univ. with Degree	719

AVERAGE HOUSEHOLD EXPENDITURES

2001 Estimates:

Food	$6,025
Shelter	$8,904
Clothing	$1,853
Transportation	$7,217
Health & Personal Care	$1,805
Recr'n, Read'g & Education	$3,666
Taxes & Securities	$13,276
Other	$7,917
Total Expenditures	$50,663

PRIVATE HOUSEHOLDS

2001 Estimates:

Private Households, Total	4,618
Pop. in Private Households	12,151
Average no. per Household	2.6

FAMILIES

2001 Estimates:

Families in Private Households	3,637
Husband-Wife Families	3,255
Lone-Parent Families	382
Aver. No. Persons per Family	3.0
Aver. No. Sons/Daughters at Home	1.2

HOUSING

2001 Estimates:

Occupied Private Dwellings	4,618
Owned	3,735
Rented	883
Single-Detached House	3,972
Semi-Detached House	61
Row Houses	111
Apartment, 5 or Fewer Storeys	414
Apartment, Detached Duplex	60

VEHICLES

2001 Estimates:

Model Yrs. '81-'96, No.	5,978
% Total	82.76
Model Yrs. '97-'98, No.	779
% Total	10.78
'99 Vehicles registered in Model Yr. '99, No.	466
% Total	6.45
Total No. '81-'99	7,223

LEGAL MARITAL STATUS

2001 Estimates: (Age 15+)

Single (Never Married)	2,295
Legally Married (Not Separated)	5,907
Legally Married (Separated)	324
Widowed	804
Divorced	594

PSYTE CATEGORIES

2001 Estimates	No. of House-holds	% of Total Hhds.	Index
Blue Collar Winners	654	14.16	563
Old Towns' New Fringe	489	10.59	271
Rustic Prosperity	799	17.30	959
Old Leafy Towns	2,614	56.60	2,215

FINANCIAL P$YTE

2001 Estimates	No. of House-holds	% of Total Hhds.	Index
Canadian Comfort	654	14.16	146
Tractors & Tradelines	1,288	27.89	488
Bills & Wills	2,614	56.60	684

Brock
(Township)
(Cont'd)

HOME LANGUAGE

2001 Estimates:		% Total
English	12,287	98.66
French	16	0.13
German	65	0.52
Greek	26	0.21
Korean	22	0.18
Polish	17	0.14
Multiple Responses	21	0.17
Total	12,454	100.00

BUILDING PERMITS

	1999	1998	1997
		$000	
Value	6,841	7,016	6,709

TAXATION

Income Class:	1997	% Total
Under $5,000	1,250	13.60
$5,000-$10,000	1,140	12.40
$10,000-$15,000	1,390	15.13
$15,000-$20,000	990	10.77
$20,000-$25,000	760	8.27
$25,000-$30,000	720	7.83
$30,000-$40,000	1,090	11.86
$40,000-$50,000	670	7.29
$50,000 +	1,180	12.84
Total Returns, No.	9,190	
Total Income, $000	234,140	
Total Taxable		
Returns	6,290	
Total Tax, $000	41,312	
Average Income, $	25,478	
Average Tax, $	6,568	

VITAL STATISTICS

	1997	1996	1995	1994
Births	152	128	140	160
Deaths	157	144	137	114
Natural				
Increase	-5	-16	3	46
Marriages	53	64	44	52

Note: Latest available data.

COMMUNITY NEWSPAPER(S)

	Total Circulation
Brock: Brock Citizen	1,687

Brockville
(Census Agglomeration)

The Census Agglomeration of Brockville includes: Augusta, TP; Brockville, C; Elizabethtown, TP; Front of Yonge, TP. and two smaller areas. All are in Leeds and Grenville United Counties.

POPULATION

July 1, 2001 Estimate	43,640
% Cdn. Total	0.14
% Change, '96 -'01	-0.54
Avg. Annual Growth Rate, %	-0.11
2003 Projected Population	43,665
2006 Projected Population	43,574
2001 Households Estimate	17,338
2003 Projected Households	17,429
2006 Projected Households	17,558

INCOME

% Above/Below National Average	-7
2001 Total Income Estimate	$855,400,000
% Cdn. Total	0.13
2001 Average Hhld. Income	$49,300
2001 Per Capita	$19,600
2003 Projected Total Income	$886,890,000
2006 Projected Total Income	$934,270,000

RETAIL SALES

% Above/Below National Average	+9
2001 Retail Sales Estimate	$426,010,000
% Cdn. Total	0.15
2001 per Household	$24,600
2001 per Capita	$9,800
2001 No. of Establishments	358
2003 Projected Retail Sales	$456,810,000
2006 Projected Retail Sales	$498,290,000

POPULATION

2001 Estimates:		
Total		43,640
Male		21,225
Female		22,415
Age Groups	Male	Female
0-4	1,251	1,212
5-9	1,366	1,328
10-14	1,448	1,385
15-19	1,447	1,347
20-24	1,400	1,311
25-29	1,355	1,304
30-34	1,414	1,480
35-39	1,570	1,658
40-44	1,622	1,676
45-49	1,574	1,626
50-54	1,429	1,478
55-59	1,219	1,264
60-64	1,035	1,106
65-69	907	1,014
70+	2,188	3,226

DAYTIME POPULATION

2001 Estimates:	
Working Population	22,244
At Home Population	21,395
Total	43,639

INCOME

2001 Estimates:	
Avg. Household Income	$49,337
Avg. Family Income	$55,203
Per Capita Income	$19,601
Male:	
Avg. Employment Income	$31,197
Avg. Employment Income	
(Full Time)	$41,352
Female:	
Avg. Employment Income	$20,199
Avg. Employment Income	
(Full Time)	$30,737

DISPOSABLE & DISCRETIONARY INCOME

2001 Estimates:	Per Hhld.
Disposable Income	$40,602
Discretionary Income 1	
(minus Food & Shelter)	$28,369
Discretionary Income 2	
(minus Food, Shelter, & Other	
Expenditures)	$20,160

LIQUID ASSETS

1999 Estimates:	Per Hhld.
Equity Investments	$66,924
Interest Bearing Investments	$62,186
Total Liquid Assets	$129,110

CREDIT DATA

July 2000:	
Pool of Credit	$415,168,711
Revolving Credit, No.	73,526
Fixed Loans, No.	23,247
Avg. Credit Limit, per Person	$11,743
Avg. Spent, per Person	$5,311
Satisfactory Ratings,	
No. per Person	2.61
Avg. No. of Cards, per Person	0.95

LABOUR FORCE

2001 Estimates:	
Male:	
In the Labour Force	12,593
Participation Rate	73.4
Employed	12,028
Unemployed	565
Unemployment Rate	4.5
Not in Labour Force	4,567
Female:	
In the Labour Force	10,769
Participation Rate	58.2
Employed	10,178
Unemployed	591
Unemployment Rate	5.5
Not in Labour Force	7,721

OCCUPATIONS BY MAJOR GROUPS

2001 Estimates:	Male	Female
Management	1,245	539
Business, Finance		
& Admin.	1,133	2,593
Natural & Applied		
Sciences &		
Related	975	160
Health	255	1,200
Social Sciences,		
Gov't Services		
& Religion	134	282
Education	261	459
Arts, Culture,		
Recreation &		
Sport	177	129
Sales & Service	2,687	3,819
Trades, Transport		
& Equipment		
Operators &		
Related	2,866	197
Primary Industries	738	166
Processing, Mfg. &		
Utilities	1,877	918

LEVEL OF SCHOOLING

2001 Estimates:	
Population 15 years +	35,650
Less than Grade 9	2,652
Grades 9-13 w/o Certif.	8,902
Grade 9-13 with Certif.	5,992
Trade Certif. /Dip.	1,441
Non-Univ. w/o Certif./Dip.	2,478
Non-Univ. with Certif./Dip.	8,725
Univ. w/o Degree	2,278
Univ. w/o Degree/Certif.	1,047
Univ. with Certif.	1,231
Univ. with Degree	3,182

Ontario

AVERAGE HOUSEHOLD EXPENDITURES

2001 Estimates:	
Food	$5,781
Shelter	$8,476
Clothing	$1,966
Transportation	$6,398
Health & Personal Care	$1,870
Recr'n, Read'g & Education	$3,520
Taxes & Securities	$11,427
Other	$8,272
Total Expenditures	$47,710

PRIVATE HOUSEHOLDS

2001 Estimates:	
Private Households, Total	17,338
Pop. in Private Households	42,508
Average no. per Household	2.5

FAMILIES

2001 Estimates:	
Families in Private Households	12,884
Husband-Wife Families	11,473
Lone-Parent Families	1,411
Aver. No. Persons per Family	2.9
Aver. No. Sons/Daughters	
at Home	1.0

HOUSING

2001 Estimates:	
Occupied Private Dwellings	17,338
Owned	12,189
Rented	5,149
Single-Detached House	11,925
Semi-Detached House	859
Row House	556
Apartment, 5+ Storeys	716
Owned Apartment, 5+ Storeys	138
Apartment, 5 or Fewer Storeys	2,835
Apartment, Detached Duplex	289
Other Single-Attached	147
Movable Dwellings	11

VEHICLES

2001 Estimates:	
Model Yrs. '81-'96, No.	22,536
% Total	83.48
Model Yrs. '97-'98, No.	2,707
% Total	10.03
'99 Vehicles registered in	
Model Yr. '99, No.	1,754
% Total	6.50
Total No. '81-'99	26,997

LEGAL MARITAL STATUS

2001 Estimates: (Age 15+)	
Single (Never Married)	8,883
Legally Married	
(Not Separated)	20,586
Legally Married (Separated)	842
Widowed	2,690
Divorced	2,649

Ontario

Brockville
(Census Agglomeration)
(Cont'd)

PSYTE CATEGORIES

2001 Estimates	No. of House -holds	% of Total Hhds.	Index
Small City Elite	2,222	12.82	748
Kindergarten Boom	56	0.32	12
Blue Collar Winners	211	1.22	48
Town Boomers	1,447	8.35	823
Old Towns' New Fringe	2,740	15.80	404
Rustic Prosperity	2,707	15.61	865
High Rise Sunsets	509	2.94	205
Young City Singles	188	1.08	47
Old Leafy Towns	620	3.58	140
Nesters & Young Homesteaders	5,886	33.95	1,454
Young Grey Collar	544	3.14	375

FINANCIAL PSYTE

2001 Estimates	No. of House -holds	% of Total Hhds.	Index
Canadian Comfort	3,880	22.38	230
Mortgages & Minivans	56	0.32	5
Tractors & Tradelines	5,447	31.42	549
Bills & Wills	620	3.58	43
Revolving Renters	6,939	40.02	870
Towering Debt	188	1.08	14

HOME LANGUAGE

2001 Estimates:		% Total
English	42,741	97.94
French	300	0.69
Chinese	84	0.19
Dutch	79	0.18
Greek	81	0.19
Spanish	26	0.06
Vietnamese	76	0.17
Other Languages	80	0.18
Multiple Responses	173	0.40
Total	43,640	100.00

BUILDING PERMITS

	1999	1998 $000	1997
Value	36,483	27,108	19,992

HOMES BUILT

	1999	1998	1997
No	138	94	73

Income Class:	1997	% Total
Under $5,000	3,530	11.75
$5,000-$10,000	3,570	11.89
$10,000-$15,000	4,360	14.52
$15,000-$20,000	3,280	10.92
$20,000-$25,000	2,640	8.79
$25,000-$30,000	2,440	8.13
$30,000-$40,000	4,020	13.39
$40,000-$50,000	2,430	8.09
$50,000 +	3,760	12.52
Total Returns, No.	30,030	
Total Income, $000	821,015	
Total Taxable Returns	21,110	
Total Tax, $000	150,432	
Average Income, $	27,340	
Average Tax, $	7,126	

VITAL STATISTICS

	1997	1996	1995	1994
Births	422	424	465	497
Deaths	451	443	452	466
Natural Increase	-29	-19	13	31
Marriages	268	243	297	261

Note: Latest available data.

DAILY NEWSPAPER(S)

	Circulation Average Paid
The Brockville Recorder and Times	13,761

COMMUNITY NEWSPAPER(S)

	Total Circulation
Brockville: St. Lawrence EMC	23,809

RADIO STATION(S)

	Power
CFJR	5,000w
CHXL-FM	100,000w

Chatham
(Census Agglomeration)

The Census Agglomeration of Chatham consists of Chatham, C; Chatham, TP; Raleigh, TP; and Wallaceburg, T. All are in Kent County. On Jan. 1, 1998, 23 municipalities, including Chatham, C, amalgamated to form Chatham-Kent.

POPULATION

July 1, 2001 Estimate	67,734
% Cdn. Total	0.22
% Change, '96 -'01	-1.68
Avg. Annual Growth Rate, %.	-0.34
2003 Projected Population	66,674
2006 Projected Population	64,716
2001 Households Estimate	26,804
2003 Projected Households	26,748
2006 Projected Households	26,550

INCOME

% Above/Below National Average	-4
2001 Total Income Estimate	$1,371,690,000
% Cdn. Total	0.21
2001 Average Hhld. Income	$51,200
2001 Per Capita	$20,300
2003 Projected Total Income	$1,432,140,000
2006 Projected Total Income	$1,522,650,000

RETAIL SALES

% Above/Below National Average	+45
2001 Retail Sales Estimate	$880,530,000
% Cdn. Total	0.32
2001 per Household	$32,900
2001 per Capita	$13,000
2001 No. of Establishments	525
2003 Projected Retail Sales	$938,220,000
2006 Projected Retail Sales	$1,009,630,000

POPULATION

2001 Estimates:

Total		67,734
Male		32,867
Female		34,867

Age Groups	Male	Female
0-4	2,039	1,925
5-9	2,244	2,086
10-14	2,425	2,302
15-19	2,497	2,404
20-24	2,351	2,295
25-29	2,085	2,110
30-34	2,197	2,297
35-39	2,484	2,588
40-44	2,571	2,640
45-49	2,471	2,515
50-54	2,155	2,185
55-59	1,723	1,808
60-64	1,421	1,539
65-69	1,274	1,442
70+	2,930	4,731

DAYTIME POPULATION

2001 Estimates:

Working Population	33,453
At Home Population	34,281
Total	67,734

INCOME

2001 Estimates:

Avg. Household Income	$51,175
Avg. Family Income	$59,226
Per Capita Income	$20,251
Male:	
Avg. Employment Income	$35,047
Avg. Employment Income (Full Time)	$46,165
Female:	
Avg. Employment Income	$20,237
Avg. Employment Income (Full Time)	$31,285

DISPOSABLE & DISCRETIONARY INCOME

2001 Estimates:	Per Hhld.
Disposable Income	$42,184
Discretionary Income 1 (minus Food & Shelter)	$29,064
Discretionary Income 2 (minus Food, Shelter, & Other Expenditures)	$20,575

LIQUID ASSETS

1999 Estimates:	Per Hhld.
Equity Investments	$64,464
Interest Bearing Investments	$62,108
Total Liquid Assets	$126,572

CREDIT DATA

July 2000:

Pool of Credit	$671,519,214
Revolving Credit, No.	115,738
Fixed Loans, No.	42,797
Avg. Credit Limit, per Person	$12,412
Avg. Spent, per Person	$5,756
Satisfactory Ratings, No. per Person	2.75
Avg. No. of Cards, per Person	0.98

LABOUR FORCE

2001 Estimates:

Male:	
In the Labour Force	19,389
Participation Rate	74.1
Employed	18,277
Unemployed	1,112
Unemployment Rate	5.7
Not in Labour Force	6,770
Female:	
In the Labour Force	16,174
Participation Rate	56.6
Employed	15,159
Unemployed	1,015
Unemployment Rate	6.3
Not in Labour Force	12,380

OCCUPATIONS BY MAJOR GROUPS

2001 Estimates:	Male	Female
Management	1,449	681
Business, Finance & Admin.	1,207	3,912
Natural & Applied Sciences & Related	927	148
Health	267	1,275
Social Sciences, Gov't Services & Religion	332	544
Education	462	707
Arts, Culture, Recreation & Sport	223	339
Sales & Service	3,434	5,630
Trades, Transport & Equipment Operators & Related	5,107	342
Primary Industries	1,482	558
Processing, Mfg. & Utilities	4,160	1,525

Chatham
(Census Agglomeration)
(Cont'd)

LEVEL OF SCHOOLING

2001 Estimates:
Population 15 years + ...54,713
Less than Grade 9 6,460
Grades 9-13 w/o Certif. 15,395
Grade 9-13 with Certif. 8,971
Trade Certif./Dip. 2,089
Non-Univ. w/o Certif./Dip. 3,353
Non-Univ. with Certif./Dip. 10,789
Univ. w/o Degree 3,171
Univ. w/o Degree/Certif. 1,548
Univ. with Certif. 1,623
Univ. with Degree 4,485

AVERAGE HOUSEHOLD EXPENDITURES

2001 Estimates:
Food $6,136
Shelter $9,071
Clothing. $2,044
Transportation $6,538
Health & Personal Care $1,982
Recr'n, Read'g & Education $3,537
Taxes & Securities $11,632
Other $8,698
Total Expenditures $49,638

PRIVATE HOUSEHOLDS

2001 Estimates:
Private Households, Total 26,804
Pop. in Private Households 65,642
Average no. per Household 2.4

FAMILIES

2001 Estimates:
Families in Private Households 18,980
Husband-Wife Families 15,992
Lone-Parent Families 2,988
Aver. No. Persons per Family 3.0
Aver. No. Sons/Daughters
    at Home 1.2

HOUSING

2001 Estimates:
Occupied Private Dwellings 26,804
    Owned 17,765
    Rented 9,039
Single-Detached House 18,768
Semi-Detached House 903
Row Houses 1,291
Apartment, 5+ Storeys 1,520
    Owned Apartment, 5+ Storeys 31
Apartment, 5 or Fewer Storeys 3,509
Apartment, Detached Duplex 610
Other Single-Attached 51
Movable Dwellings 152

VEHICLES

2001 Estimates:
Model Yrs. '81-'96, No. 36,590
    % Total 81.54
Model Yrs. '97-'98, No. 5,159
    % Total 11.50
'99 Vehicles registered in
    Model Yr. '99, No. 3,124
    % Total 6.96
Total No. '81-'99 44,873

LEGAL MARITAL STATUS

2001 Estimates: (Age 15+)
Single (Never Married) 15,478
Legally Married
    (Not Separated) 28,772
Legally Married (Separated) 1,969
Widowed 4,535
Divorced 3,959

PSYTE CATEGORIES

2001 Estimates	No. of House -holds	% of Total Hhds.	Index
Small City Elite	1,681	6.27	366
Old Bungalow Burbs.	549	2.05	124
Blue Collar Winners	361	1.35	53
Town Boomers	1,854	6.92	682
Old Towns' New Fringe	2,413	9.00	230
Rustic Prosperity	2,859	10.67	591
Conservative Homebodies	282	1.05	29
University Enclaves	82	0.31	15
Young City Singles	112	0.42	18
Old Leafy Towns	724	2.70	106
Town Renters	66	0.25	28
Nesters & Young Homesteaders	10,614	39.60	1,697
Young Grey Collar	842	3.14	376
Quiet Towns	1,712	6.39	300
Rod & Rifle	931	3.47	150
Struggling Downtowns	327	1.22	39
Aged Pensioners	513	1.91	144
Big City Stress	108	0.40	36
Old Grey Towers	175	0.65	118

FINANCIAL PSYTE

2001 Estimates	No. of House -holds	% of Total Hhds.	Index
Canadian Comfort	3,896	14.54	150
Miners & Credit-Liners	549	2.05	65
Tractors & Tradelines	5,272	19.67	344
Bills & Wills	1,006	3.75	45
Revolving Renters	11,456	42.74	929
Young Urban Struggle	82	0.31	6
Rural Family Blues	931	3.47	43
Limited Budgets	1,712	6.39	205
Towering Debt	505	1.88	24
NSF	108	0.40	11
Senior Survivors	688	2.57	136

HOME LANGUAGE

2001 Estimates:		% Total
English	64,501	95.23
French	531	0.78
Chinese	128	0.19
Croatian	36	0.05
Czech	62	0.09
Dutch	109	0.16
German	342	0.50
Greek	110	0.16
Italian	190	0.28
Korean	84	0.12
Lao	60	0.09
Polish	257	0.38
Portuguese	381	0.56
Spanish	62	0.09
Vietnamese	254	0.37
Other Languages	220	0.32
Multiple Responses	407	0.60
Total	67,734	100.00

HOMES BUILT

	1999	1998	1997
No	176	172	138

TAXATION

Income Class:	1997	% Total
Under $5,000	6,390	12.51
$5,000-$10,000	5,960	11.67
$10,000-$15,000	7,450	14.59
$15,000-$20,000	5,140	10.07
$20,000-$25,000	4,230	8.28
$25,000-$30,000	3,790	7.42
$30,000-$40,000	6,260	12.26
$40,000-$50,000	4,240	8.30
$50,000 +	7,620	14.92
Total Returns, No.	51,060	
Total Income, $000.	1,401,836	
Total Taxable Returns	35,470	
Total Tax, $000	255,854	
Average Income, $	27,455	
Average Tax, $	7,213	

VITAL STATISTICS

	1997	1996	1995	1994
Births	784	892	892	855
Deaths	701	713	689	688
Natural Increase	83	179	203	167
Marriages	436	522	561	512

Note: Latest available data.

DAILY NEWSPAPER(S)

	Circulation Average Paid
Chatham Daily News	14,803

COMMUNITY NEWSPAPER(S)

	Total Circulation
Chatham: Chatham This Week	18,495
Wallaceburg: Wallaceburg Courier-Press	11,512

RADIO STATION(S)

	Power
CBEE-FM	n.a.
CFCO	10,000w
CKSY-FM	42,000w
CKUE-FM	n.a.

TELEVISION STATION(S)

CBLN-TV
CKCO-TV
TFO
TVO

Ontario

Ontario

Clearview
(Township)
In Simcoe County.

POPULATION

2001 Estimates:
July 1, 2001 Estimate	13,546
% Cdn. Total	0.04
% Change, '96 -'01	5.95
Avg. Annual Growth Rate, %	1.16
2003 Projected Population	13,740
2006 Projected Population	14,028
2001 Households Estimate	4,863
2003 Projected Households	4,919
2006 Projected Households	5,055

INCOME

% Above/Below National Average	-16
2001 Total Income Estimate	$240,190,000
% Cdn. Total	0.04
2001 Average Hhld. Income	$49,400
2001 Per Capita	$17,700
2003 Projected Total Income	$251,750,000
2006 Projected Total Income	$272,620,000

RETAIL SALES

% Above/Below National Average	-37
2001 Retail Sales Estimate	$76,810,000
% Cdn. Total	0.03
2001 per Household	$15,800
2001 per Capita	$5,700
2001 No. of Establishments	125
2003 Projected Retail Sales	$82,990,000
2006 Projected Retail Sales	$93,490,000

POPULATION

2001 Estimates:
Total		13,546
Male		6,704
Female		6,842
Age Groups	Male	Female
0-4	418	409
5-9	496	478
10-14	520	499
15-19	489	462
20-24	417	403
25-29	365	375
30-34	426	455
35-39	499	538
40-44	527	531
45-49	502	496
50-54	442	421
55-59	370	343
60-64	311	290
65-69	275	277
70+	647	865

DAYTIME POPULATION

2001 Estimates:
Working Population	4,660
At Home Population	6,544
Total	11,204

INCOME

2001 Estimates:
Avg. Household Income	$49,391
Avg. Family Income	$52,873
Per Capita Income	$17,731
Male:	
Avg. Employment Income	$29,088
Avg. Employment Income (Full Time)	$36,930
Female:	
Avg. Employment Income	$16,395
Avg. Employment Income (Full Time)	$24,947

DISPOSABLE & DISCRETIONARY INCOME

2001 Estimates:	Per Hhld.
Disposable Income	$40,836
Discretionary Income 1 (minus Food & Shelter)	$28,801
Discretionary Income 2 (minus Food, Shelter, & Other Expenditures)	$20,076

LIQUID ASSETS

1999 Estimates:	Per Hhld.
Equity Investments	$69,709
Interest Bearing Investments	$62,005
Total Liquid Assets	$131,714

CREDIT DATA

July 2000:
Pool of Credit	$137,910,797
Revolving Credit, No.	22,879
Fixed Loans, No.	7,475
Avg. Credit Limit, per Person	$11,755
Avg. Spent, per Person	$5,482
Satisfactory Ratings, No. per Person	2.50
Avg. No. of Cards, per Person	0.88

LABOUR FORCE

2001 Estimates:
Male:	
In the Labour Force	4,048
Participation Rate	76.8
Employed	3,889
Unemployed	159
Unemployment Rate	3.9
Not in Labour Force	1,222
Female:	
In the Labour Force	3,272
Participation Rate	60.0
Employed	3,056
Unemployed	216
Unemployment Rate	6.6
Not in Labour Force	2,184

OCCUPATIONS BY MAJOR GROUPS

2001 Estimates:	Male	Female
Management	427	221
Business, Finance & Admin.	154	742
Natural & Applied Sciences & Related	150	n.a.
Health	70	269
Social Sciences, Gov't Services & Religion	46	43
Education	85	105
Arts, Culture, Recreation & Sport	34	118
Sales & Service	702	1,152
Trades, Transport & Equipment Operators & Related	1,387	74
Primary Industries	540	155
Processing, Mfg. & Utilities	405	282

LEVEL OF SCHOOLING

2001 Estimates:
Population 15 years +	10,726
Less than Grade 9	1,039
Grades 9-13 w/o Certif.	3,195
Grade 9-13 with Certif.	1,696
Trade Certif. /Dip.	598
Non-Univ. w/o Certif./Dip.	682
Non-Univ. with Certif./Dip.	2,205
Univ. w/o Degree	533
Univ. w/o Degree/Certif.	248
Univ. with Certif.	285
Univ. with Degree	778

AVERAGE HOUSEHOLD EXPENDITURES

2001 Estimates:
Food	$5,839
Shelter	$8,134
Clothing	$1,838
Transportation	$7,100
Health & Personal Care	$1,769
Recr'n, Read'g & Education	$3,672
Taxes & Securities	$11,644
Other	$7,981
Total Expenditures	$47,977

PRIVATE HOUSEHOLDS

2001 Estimates:
Private Households, Total	4,863
Pop. in Private Households	13,141
Average no. per Household	2.7

FAMILIES

2001 Estimates:
Families in Private Households	3,894
Husband-Wife Families	3,585
Lone-Parent Families	309
Aver. No. Persons per Family	3.1
Aver. No. Sons/Daughters at Home	1.2

HOUSING

2001 Estimates:
Occupied Private Dwellings	4,863
Owned	4,016
Rented	847
Single-Detached House	4,466
Semi-Detached House	22
Row Houses	97
Apartment, 5 or Fewer Storeys	245
Apartment, Detached Duplex	22
Other Single-Attached	11

VEHICLES

2001 Estimates:
Model Yrs. '81-'96, No.	5,774
% Total	84.19
Model Yrs. '97-'98, No.	663
% Total	9.67
'99 Vehicles registered in Model Yr. '99, No.	421
% Total	6.14
Total No. '81-'99	6,858

LEGAL MARITAL STATUS

2001 Estimates: (Age 15+)
Single (Never Married)	2,406
Legally Married (Not Separated)	6,596
Legally Married (Separated)	299
Widowed	827
Divorced	598

PSYTE CATEGORIES

2001 Estimates	No. of House-holds	% of Total Hhds.	Index
Small City Elite	228	4.69	274
Old Towns' New Fringe	984	20.23	517
Rustic Prosperity	1,874	38.54	2,136
Old Leafy Towns	1,742	35.82	1,402

FINANCIAL P$YTE

2001 Estimates	No. of House-holds	% of Total Hhds.	Index
Canadian Comfort	228	4.69	48
Tractors & Tradelines	2,858	58.77	1,028
Bills & Wills	1,742	35.82	433

HOME LANGUAGE

2001 Estimates:		% Total
English	13,337	98.46
French	11	0.08
Dutch	23	0.17
Flemish	11	0.08
German	22	0.16
Italian	11	0.08
Korean	23	0.17
Lithuanian	28	0.21
Slovak	13	0.10
Multiple Responses	67	0.49
Total	13,546	100.00

BUILDING PERMITS

	1999	1998 $000	1997
Value	17,903	11,254	18,168

TAXATION

Income Class:	1997	% Total
Under $5,000	1,340	14.84
$5,000-$10,000	1,080	11.96
$10,000-$15,000	1,410	15.61
$15,000-$20,000	950	10.52
$20,000-$25,000	780	8.64
$25,000-$30,000	650	7.20
$30,000-$40,000	1,130	12.51
$40,000-$50,000	680	7.53
$50,000 +	1,010	11.18
Total Returns, No.	9,030	
Total Income, $000	225,493	
Total Taxable Returns	6,140	
Total Tax, $000	37,983	
Average Income, $	24,972	
Average Tax, $	6,186	

VITAL STATISTICS

	1997	1996	1995	1994
Births	146	109	149	170
Deaths	137	138	131	145
Natural Increase	9	-29	18	25
Marriages	58	64	58	50

Note: Latest available data.

Cobourg
(Census Agglomeration)

The Census Agglomeration of Cobourg consists solely of Cobourg, T, in Northumberland County.

POPULATION

July 1, 2001 Estimate	17,215
% Cdn. Total	0.06
% Change, '96 -'01	4.66
Avg. Annual Growth Rate, %	0.91
2003 Projected Population	17,447
2006 Projected Population	17,696
2001 Households Estimate	7,059
2003 Projected Households	7,226
2006 Projected Households	7,462

INCOME

% Above/Below National Average	+1
2001 Total Income Estimate	$366,710,000
% Cdn. Total	0.06
2001 Average Hhld. Income	$51,900
2001 Per Capita	$21,300
2003 Projected Total Income	$390,510,000
2006 Projected Total Income	$428,650,000

RETAIL SALES

% Above/Below National Average	+29
2001 Retail Sales Estimate	$199,410,000
% Cdn. Total	0.07
2001 per Household	$28,200
2001 per Capita	$11,600
2001 No. of Establishments	196
2003 Projected Retail Sales	$217,710,000
2006 Projected Retail Sales	$242,960,000

POPULATION

2001 Estimates:

Total		17,215
Male		8,025
Female		9,190

Age Groups	Male	Female
0-4	502	500
5-9	546	544
10-14	585	582
15-19	555	578
20-24	500	530
25-29	481	514
30-34	521	586
35-39	583	670
40-44	624	675
45-49	586	630
50-54	494	537
55-59	405	459
60-64	371	427
65-69	360	439
70+	912	1,519

DAYTIME POPULATION

2001 Estimates:

Working Population	8,099
At Home Population	9,116
Total	17,215

INCOME

2001 Estimates:

Avg. Household Income	$51,949
Avg. Family Income	$60,047
Per Capita Income	$21,302
Male:	
Avg. Employment Income	$36,110
Avg. Employment Income (Full Time)	$48,296
Female:	
Avg. Employment Income	$22,489
Avg. Employment Income (Full Time)	$32,557

DISPOSABLE & DISCRETIONARY INCOME

2001 Estimates: *Per Hhld.*

Disposable Income	$42,667
Discretionary Income 1 (minus Food & Shelter)	$29,564
Discretionary Income 2 (minus Food, Shelter, & Other Expenditures)	$21,114

LIQUID ASSETS

1999 Estimates: *Per Hhld.*

Equity Investments	$65,313
Interest Bearing Investments	$62,849
Total Liquid Assets	$128,162

CREDIT DATA

July 2000:

Pool of Credit	$208,345,071
Revolving Credit, No.	37,274
Fixed Loans, No.	10,234
Avg. Credit Limit, per Person	$12,773
Avg. Spent, per Person	$5,573
Satisfactory Ratings, No. per Person	2.83
Avg. No. of Cards, per Person	0.99

LABOUR FORCE

2001 Estimates:

Male:	
In the Labour Force	4,510
Participation Rate	70.6
Employed	4,242
Unemployed	268
Unemployment Rate	5.9
Not in Labour Force	1,882
Female:	
In the Labour Force	4,120
Participation Rate	54.5
Employed	3,867
Unemployed	253
Unemployment Rate	6.1
Not in Labour Force	3,444

OCCUPATIONS BY MAJOR GROUPS

2001 Estimates:	Male	Female
Management	459	241
Business, Finance & Admin.	374	912
Natural & Applied Sciences & Related	205	80
Health	76	315
Social Sciences, Gov't Services & Religion	44	189
Education	175	265
Arts, Culture, Recreation & Sport	95	113
Sales & Service	987	1,384
Trades, Transport & Equipment Operators & Related	985	34
Primary Industries	118	11
Processing, Mfg. & Utilities	846	427

LEVEL OF SCHOOLING

2001 Estimates:

Population 15 years +	13,956
Less than Grade 9	1,072
Grades 9-13 w/o Certif.	3,890
Grade 9-13 with Certif.	2,260
Trade Certif. /Dip.	498
Non-Univ. w/o Certif./Dip.	831
Non-Univ. with Certif./Dip.	2,812
Univ. w/o Degree	1,013
Univ. w/o Degree/Certif.	534
Univ. with Certif.	479
Univ. with Degree	1,580

AVERAGE HOUSEHOLD EXPENDITURES

2001 Estimates:

Food	$6,136
Shelter	$9,168
Clothing	$2,074
Transportation	$6,523
Health & Personal Care	$1,994
Recr'n, Read'g & Education	$3,666
Taxes & Securities	$11,928
Other	$8,718
Total Expenditures	$50,207

PRIVATE HOUSEHOLDS

2001 Estimates:

Private Households, Total	7,059
Pop. in Private Households	16,646
Average no. per Household	2.4

FAMILIES

2001 Estimates:

Families in Private Households	5,130
Husband-Wife Families	4,298
Lone-Parent Families	832
Aver. No. Persons per Family	2.9
Aver. No. Sons/Daughters at Home	1.1

HOUSING

2001 Estimates:

Occupied Private Dwellings	7,059
Owned	4,386
Rented	2,673
Single-Detached House	4,230
Semi-Detached House	379
Row Houses	682
Apartment, 5+ Storeys	370
Owned Apartment, 5+ Storeys	39
Apartment, 5 or Fewer Storeys	1,245
Apartment, Detached Duplex	115
Other Single-Attached	38

VEHICLES

2001 Estimates:

Model Yrs. '81-'96, No.	8,995
% Total	80.47
Model Yrs. '97-'98, No.	1,288
% Total	11.52
'99 Vehicles registered in Model Yr. '99, No.	895
% Total	8.01
Total No. '81-'99	11,178

LEGAL MARITAL STATUS

2001 Estimates: (Age 15+)

Single (Never Married)	3,405
Legally Married (Not Separated)	7,680
Legally Married (Separated)	543
Widowed	1,386
Divorced	942

PSYTE CATEGORIES

2001 Estimates	No. of House-holds	% of Total Hhds.	Index
Small City Elite	1,741	24.66	1,439
Satellite Suburbs	246	3.48	121
Kindergarten Boom	204	2.89	110
Old Towns' New Fringe	1,187	16.82	430
Nesters & Young Homesteaders	3,599	50.98	2,184

FINANCIAL P$YTE

2001 Estimates	No. of House-holds	% of Total Hhds.	Index
Canadian Comfort	1,987	28.15	290
Mortgages & Minivans	204	2.89	44
Tractors & Tradelines	1,187	16.82	294
Revolving Renters	3,599	50.98	1,108

Ontario

HOME LANGUAGE

2001 Estimates:		% Total
English	16,904	98.19
French	72	0.42
Chinese	48	0.28
German	17	0.10
Italian	21	0.12
Korean	11	0.06
Slovenian	11	0.06
Vietnamese	40	0.23
Multiple Responses	91	0.53
Total	17,215	100.00

BUILDING PERMITS

	1999	1998	1997
		$000	
Value	13,718	15,356	27,644

HOMES BUILT

	1999	1998	1997
No	82	111	152

TAXATION

Income Class:	1997	% Total
Under $5,000	1,720	10.45
$5,000-$10,000	1,830	11.12
$10,000-$15,000	2,230	13.55
$15,000-$20,000	1,640	9.96
$20,000-$25,000	1,430	8.69
$25,000-$30,000	1,400	8.51
$30,000-$40,000	2,230	13.55
$40,000-$50,000	1,450	8.81
$50,000 +	2,540	15.43
Total Returns, No.	16,460	
Total Income, $000	484,629	
Total Taxable Returns	12,090	
Total Tax, $000	92,524	
Average Income, $	29,443	
Average Tax, $	7,653	

VITAL STATISTICS

	1997	1996	1995	1994
Births	198	224	244	252
Deaths	218	235	225	194
Natural Increase	-20	-11	19	58
Marriages	123	125	124	120

Note: Latest available data.

DAILY NEWSPAPER(S)

	Circulation Average Paid
Cobourg Daily Star	4,930

COMMUNITY NEWSPAPER(S)

	Total Circulation
Cobourg: Northumberland News	
Tue	21,515
Fri	21,517

RADIO STATION(S)

	Power
CFMX-FM	86,700w
CHUC	8,000w

Ontario

Collingwood
(Census Agglomeration)

The Census Agglomeration of Collingwood consists solely of Collingwood, T, in Simcoe County.

POPULATION

July 1, 2001 Estimate	17,218
% Cdn. Total	0.06
% Change, '96 -'01	7.12
Avg. Annual Growth Rate, %	1.39
2003 Projected Population	17,572
2006 Projected Population	18,100
2001 Households Estimate	7,084
2003 Projected Households	7,217
2006 Projected Households	7,491

INCOME

% Above/Below National Average	-11
2001 Total Income Estimate	$321,850,000
% Cdn. Total	0.05
2001 Average Hhld. Income	$45,400
2001 Per Capita	$18,700
2003 Projected Total Income	$339,830,000
2006 Projected Total Income	$371,770,000

RETAIL SALES

% Above/Below National Average	+43
2001 Retail Sales Estimate	$220,250,000
% Cdn. Total	0.08
2001 per Household	$31,100
2001 per Capita	$12,800
2001 No. of Establishments	187
2003 Projected Retail Sales	$241,490,000
2006 Projected Retail Sales	$273,090,000

POPULATION

2001 Estimates:

Total		17,218
Male		8,137
Female		9,081

Age Groups	Male	Female
0-4	516	498
5-9	561	545
10-14	618	588
15-19	610	583
20-24	559	559
25-29	526	554
30-34	561	602
35-39	608	668
40-44	623	675
45-49	584	642
50-54	470	535
55-59	391	438
60-64	364	424
65-69	350	414
70+	796	1,356

DAYTIME POPULATION

2001 Estimates:

Working Population	7,918
At Home Population	9,300
Total	17,218

INCOME

2001 Estimates:

Avg. Household Income	$45,433
Avg. Family Income	$50,732
Per Capita Income	$18,692
Male:	
Avg. Employment Income	$29,167
Avg. Employment Income (Full Time)	$38,572
Female:	
Avg. Employment Income	$18,192
Avg. Employment Income (Full Time)	$28,701

DISPOSABLE & DISCRETIONARY INCOME

2001 Estimates:	Per Hhld.
Disposable Income	$37,668
Discretionary Income 1 (minus Food & Shelter)	$25,676
Discretionary Income 2 (minus Food, Shelter, & Other Expenditures)	$18,182

LIQUID ASSETS

1999 Estimates:	Per Hhld.
Equity Investments	$60,879
Interest Bearing Investments	$56,442
Total Liquid Assets	$117;321

CREDIT DATA

July 2000:

Pool of Credit	$179,233,819
Revolving Credit, No.	31,968
Fixed Loans, No.	9,667
Avg. Credit Limit, per Person	$11,681
Avg. Spent, per Person	$5,170
Satisfactory Ratings, No. per Person	2.63
Avg. No. of Cards, per Person	0.99

LABOUR FORCE

2001 Estimates:

Male:	
In the Labour Force	4,479
Participation Rate	69.5
Employed	4,206
Unemployed	273
Unemployment Rate	6.1
Not in Labour Force	1,963
Female:	
In the Labour Force	3,993
Participation Rate	53.6
Employed	3,680
Unemployed	313
Unemployment Rate	7.8
Not in Labour Force	3,457

OCCUPATIONS BY MAJOR GROUPS

2001 Estimates:	Male	Female
Management	467	180
Business, Finance & Admin.	291	868
Natural & Applied Sciences & Related	114	34
Health	96	365
Social Sciences, Gov't Services & Religion	51	155
Education	143	169
Arts, Culture, Recreation & Sport	55	93
Sales & Service	1,115	1,639
Trades, Transport & Equipment Operators & Related	1,042	32
Primary Industries	159	24
Processing, Mfg. & Utilities	834	289

LEVEL OF SCHOOLING

2001 Estimates:

Population 15 years +	13,892
Less than Grade 9	1,400
Grades 9-13 w/o Certif.	4,044
Grade 9-13 with Certif.	2,095
Trade Certif. /Dip.	578
Non-Univ. w/o Certif./Dip.	1,019
Non-Univ. with Certif./Dip.	2,698
Univ. w/o Degree	756
Univ. w/o Degree/Certif.	303
Univ. with Certif.	453
Univ. with Degree	1,302

AVERAGE HOUSEHOLD EXPENDITURES

2001 Estimates:

Food	$5,484
Shelter	$8,425
Clothing	$1,773
Transportation	$5,811
Health & Personal Care	$1,764
Recr'n, Read'g & Education	$3,132
Taxes & Securities	$10,852
Other	$7,558
Total Expenditures	$44,799

PRIVATE HOUSEHOLDS

2001 Estimates:

Private Households, Total	7,084
Pop. in Private Households	16,453
Average no. per Household	2.3

FAMILIES

2001 Estimates:

Families in Private Households	4,968
Husband-Wife Families	4,068
Lone-Parent Families	900
Aver. No. Persons per Family	2.8
Aver. No. Sons/Daughters at Home	1.1

HOUSING

2001 Estimates:

Occupied Private Dwellings	7,084
Owned	4,696
Rented	2,388
Single-Detached House	4,328
Semi-Detached House	414
Row Houses	566
Apartment, 5+ Storeys	291
Owned Apartment, 5+ Storeys	86
Apartment, 5 or Fewer Storeys	1,376
Apartment, Detached Duplex	86
Other Single-Attached	23

VEHICLES

2001 Estimates:

Model Yrs. '81-'96, No.	8,724
% Total	80.57
Model Yrs. '97-'98, No.	1,251
% Total	11.55
'99 Vehicles registered in Model Yr. '99, No.	853
% Total	7.88
Total No. '81-'99	10,828

LEGAL MARITAL STATUS

2001 Estimates: (Age 15+)

Single (Never Married)	3,659
Legally Married (Not Separated)	7,083
Legally Married (Separated)	564
Widowed	1,434
Divorced	1,152

PSYTE CATEGORIES

2001 Estimates	No. of House -holds	% of Total Hhds.	Index
Technocrafts & Bureaucrats	28	0.40	14
Small City Elite	100	1.41	82
Town Boomers	777	10.97	1,082
Old Towns' New Fringe	503	7.10	181
High Rise Sunsets	226	3.19	223
University Enclaves	48	0.68	33
Old Leafy Towns	1,786	25.21	986
Nesters & Young Homesteaders	2,635	37.20	1,594
Quiet Towns	771	10.88	512

FINANCIAL P$YTE

2001 Estimates	No. of House -holds	% of Total Hhds.	Index
Successful Suburbanites	28	0.40	6
Canadian Comfort	877	12.38	127
Tractors & Tradelines	503	7.10	124
Bills & Wills	1,786	25.21	304
Revolving Renters	2,861	40.39	878
Young Urban Struggle	48	0.68	14
Limited Budgets	771	10.88	350

HOME LANGUAGE

2001 Estimates:		% Total
English	16,818	97.68
French	28	0.16
Chinese	42	0.24
German	41	0.24
Italian	11	0.06
Latvian (Lettish)	11	0.06
Serbian	11	0.06
Spanish	23	0.13
Tagalog (Pilipino)	41	0.24
Ukrainian	11	0.06
Vietnamese	109	0.63
Multiple Responses	72	0.42
Total	17,218	100.00

BUILDING PERMITS

	1999	1998	1997
		$000	
Value	25,525	20,491	23,168

HOMES BUILT

	1999	1998	1997
No	122	165	119

TAXATION

Income Class:	1997	% Total
Under $5,000	1,620	12.12
$5,000-$10,000	1,680	12.57
$10,000-$15,000	2,290	17.13
$15,000-$20,000	1,550	11.59
$20,000-$25,000	1,220	9.12
$25,000-$30,000	970	7.26
$30,000-$40,000	1,640	12.27
$40,000-$50,000	940	7.03
$50,000 +	1,480	11.07
Total Returns, No.	13,370	
Total Income, $000	342,852	
Total Taxable Returns	9,090	
Total Tax, $000	59,634	
Average Income, $	25,643	
Average Tax, $	6,560	

VITAL STATISTICS

	1997	1996	1995	1994
Births	175	181	201	198
Deaths	225	190	190	187
Natural Increase	-50	-9	11	11
Marriages	109	115	99	95

Note: Latest available data.

COMMUNITY NEWSPAPER(S)

	Total Circulation
Collingwood: Collingwood Connection	17,900
Collingwood: Collingwood Enterprise Bulletin Tue/Fri	4,214
Collingwood: Collingwood Enterprise-Bulletin This Week Tue/Fri	13,423

RADIO STATION(S)

	Power
CKCB-FM	350w

Cornwall
(Census Agglomeration)

The Census Agglomeration of Cornwall consists mainly of Cornwall, C; and Cornwall, TP; and Charlottenburgh, TP, all of which are in of Stormont, Dundas & Glengarry United Counties.

POPULATION

July 1, 2001 Estimate	63,982
% Cdn. Total	0.21
% Change, '96 -'01	-0.95
Avg. Annual Growth Rate, %	-0.19
2003 Projected Population	63,660
2006 Projected Population	62,849
2001 Households Estimate	25,760
2003 Projected Households	25,938
2006 Projected Households	26,138

INCOME

% Above/Below National Average	-14
2001 Total Income Estimate	$1,159,530,000
% Cdn. Total	0.18
2001 Average Hhld. Income	$45,000
2001 Per Capita	$18,100
2003 Projected Total Income	$1,217,690,000
2006 Projected Total Income	$1,307,940,000

RETAIL SALES

% Above/Below National Average	+32
2001 Retail Sales Estimate	$757,980,000
% Cdn. Total	0.27
2001 per Household	$29,400
2001 per Capita	$11,800
2001 No. of Establishments	523
2003 Projected Retail Sales	$809,760,000
2006 Projected Retail Sales	$876,230,000

POPULATION

2001 Estimates:

Total	63,982
Male	30,953
Female	33,029

Age Groups	Male	Female
0-4	1,920	1,806
5-9	2,102	2,002
10-14	2,201	2,127
15-19	2,227	2,162
20-24	2,137	2,086
25-29	1,906	1,913
30-34	1,970	2,082
35-39	2,266	2,403
40-44	2,404	2,507
45-49	2,360	2,406
50-54	2,096	2,099
55-59	1,733	1,783
60-64	1,471	1,586
65-69	1,297	1,499
70+	2,863	4,568

DAYTIME POPULATION

2001 Estimates:

Working Population	29,134
At Home Population	34,848
Total	63,982

INCOME

2001 Estimates:

Avg. Household Income	$45,013
Avg. Family Income	$52,374
Per Capita Income	$18,123
Male:	
Avg. Employment Income	$31,493
Avg. Employment Income (Full Time)	$41,956
Female:	
Avg. Employment Income	$20,511
Avg. Employment Income (Full Time)	$30,655

DISPOSABLE & DISCRETIONARY INCOME

2001 Estimates:	Per Hhld.
Disposable Income	$37,361
Discretionary Income 1 (minus Food & Shelter)	$25,533
Discretionary Income 2 (minus Food, Shelter, & Other Expenditures)	$18,100

LIQUID ASSETS

1999 Estimates:	Per Hhld.
Equity Investments	$56,892
Interest Bearing Investments	$55,378
Total Liquid Assets	$112,270

CREDIT DATA

July 2000:

Pool of Credit	$566,273,378
Revolving Credit, No.	108,244
Fixed Loans, No.	35,368
Avg. Credit Limit, per Person	$10,495
Avg. Spent, per Person	$4,876
Satisfactory Ratings, No. per Person	2.51
Avg. No. of Cards, per Person	0.85

LABOUR FORCE

2001 Estimates:

Male:	
In the Labour Force	17,423
Participation Rate	70.5
Employed	15,744
Unemployed	1,679
Unemployment Rate	9.6
Not in Labour Force	7,307
Female:	
In the Labour Force	14,420
Participation Rate	53.2
Employed	13,317
Unemployed	1,103
Unemployment Rate	7.6
Not in Labour Force	12,674

OCCUPATIONS BY MAJOR GROUPS

2001 Estimates:	Male	Female
Management	1,679	746
Business, Finance & Admin.	1,253	3,598
Natural & Applied Sciences & Related	887	71
Health	300	1,422
Social Sciences, Gov't Services & Religion	315	362
Education	485	793
Arts, Culture, Recreation & Sport	219	312
Sales & Service	4,005	4,996
Trades, Transport & Equipment Operators & Related	4,145	277
Primary Industries	563	167
Processing, Mfg. & Utilities	2,672	967

LEVEL OF SCHOOLING

2001 Estimates:

Population 15 years +	51,824
Less than Grade 9	6,684
Grades 9-13 w/o Certif.	14,335
Grade 9-13 with Certif.	8,780
Trade Certif. /Dip.	2,028
Non-Univ. w/o Certif./Dip.	3,613
Non-Univ. with Certif./Dip.	9,490
Univ. w/o Degree	3,142
Univ. w/o Degree/Certif.	1,390
Univ. with Certif.	1,752
Univ. with Degree	3,752

AVERAGE HOUSEHOLD EXPENDITURES

2001 Estimates:

Food	$5,395
Shelter	$8,275
Clothing	$1,816
Transportation	$5,739
Health & Personal Care	$1,751
Recr'n, Read'g & Education	$3,107
Taxes & Securities	$10,526
Other	$7,673
Total Expenditures	$44,282

PRIVATE HOUSEHOLDS

2001 Estimates:

Private Households, Total	25,760
Pop. in Private Households	62,384
Average no. per Household	2.4

FAMILIES

2001 Estimates:

Families in Private Households	18,575
Husband-Wife Families	15,380
Lone-Parent Families	3,195
Aver. No. Persons per Family	2.9
Aver. No. Sons/Daughters at Home	1.1

HOUSING

2001 Estimates:

Occupied Private Dwellings	25,760
Owned	16,004
Rented	9,756
Single-Detached House	15,137
Semi-Detached House	1,836
Row Houses	1,106
Apartment, 5+ Storeys	530
Owned Apartment, 5+ Storeys	11
Apartment, 5 or Fewer Storeys	4,909
Apartment, Detached Duplex	2,049
Other Single-Attached	145
Movable Dwellings	48

VEHICLES

2001 Estimates:

Model Yrs. '81-'96, No.	30,243
% Total	82.42
Model Yrs. '97-'98, No.	3,942
% Total	10.74
'99 Vehicles registered in Model Yr. '99, No.	2,509
% Total	6.84
Total No. '81-'99	36,694

LEGAL MARITAL STATUS

2001 Estimates: (Age 15+)

Single (Never Married)	14,092
Legally Married (Not Separated)	27,419
Legally Married (Separated)	2,039
Widowed	4,409
Divorced	3,865

PSYTE CATEGORIES

2001 Estimates	No. of House-holds	% of Total Hhds.	Index
Small City Elite	2,202	8.55	499
Blue Collar Winners	2,039	7.92	314
Town Boomers	1,001	3.89	383
Old Towns' New Fringe	2,294	8.91	228
Quebec Melange	426	1.65	62
Traditional French Cdn. Families	79	0.31	11
Rustic Prosperity	1,186	4.60	255
Old Leafy Towns	311	1.21	47
Town Renters	301	1.17	135
Nesters & Young Homesteaders	13,916	54.02	2,314
Young Grey Collar	686	2.66	318
Aged Pensioners	592	2.30	173
Old Grey Towers	420	1.63	294

Ontario

FINANCIAL P$YTE

2001 Estimates	No. of House-holds	% of Total Hhds.	Index
Canadian Comfort	5,242	20.35	209
Tractors & Tradelines	3,480	13.51	236
Bills & Wills	311	1.21	15
Country Credit	505	1.96	29
Revolving Renters	14,602	56.68	1,232
Towering Debt	301	1.17	15
Senior Survivors	1,012	3.93	208

HOME LANGUAGE

2001 Estimates:		% Total
English	51,632	80.70
French	9,779	15.28
Chinese	181	0.28
German	53	0.08
Greek	68	0.11
Italian	91	0.14
Polish	119	0.19
Punjabi	59	0.09
Tamil	144	0.23
Urdu	38	0.06
Vietnamese	140	0.22
Other Languages	137	0.21
Multiple Responses	1,541	2.41
Total	63,982	100.00

BUILDING PERMITS

	1999	1998	1997
		$000	
Value	48,422	41,014	14,314

HOMES BUILT

	1999	1998	1997
No.	122	76	75

TAXATION

Income Class:	1997	% Total
Under $5,000	6,460	14.10
$5,000-$10,000	6,210	13.55
$10,000-$15,000	8,350	18.22
$15,000-$20,000	5,130	11.19
$20,000-$25,000	3,960	8.64
$25,000-$30,000	3,440	7.51
$30,000-$40,000	4,840	10.56
$40,000-$50,000	3,020	6.59
$50,000 +	4,420	9.64
Total Returns, No.	45,830	
Total Income, $000	1,074,231	
Total Taxable Returns	28,190	
Total Tax, $000	176,740	
Average Income, $	23,439	
Average Tax, $	6,270	

VITAL STATISTICS

	1997	1996	1995	1994
Births	610	710	789	845
Deaths	640	601	595	610
Natural Increase	-30	109	194	235
Marriages	375	371	455	472

Note: Latest available data.

Ontario

Cornwall
(Census Agglomeration)
(Cont'd)

DAILY NEWSPAPER(S)

	Circulation Average Paid
Standard-Freeholder	14,072

COMMUNITY NEWSPAPER(S)

	Total Circulation
Cornwall: Le Journal	2,449
Cornwall: Seaway News	32,913

RADIO STATION(S)

	Power
CBOC-FM	n.a.
CFLG-FM	30,000w
CHOD-FM	19,200w
CJRT-FM	n.a.
CJSS-FM	n.a.

TELEVISION STATION(S)

CJOH-TV

Delhi
(Township)

In Haldimand-Norfolk Regional Municipality.

POPULATION

July 1, 2001 Estimate	17,670
% Cdn. Total	0.06
% Change, '96 -'01	3.37
Avg. Annual Growth Rate, %	0.67
2003 Projected Population	17,759
2006 Projected Population	17,799
2001 Households Estimate	6,510
2003 Projected Households	6,640
2006 Projected Households	6,819

INCOME

% Above/Below National Average	-8
2001 Total Income Estimate	$342,420,000
% Cdn. Total	0.05
2001 Average Hhld. Income	$52,600
2001 Per Capita	$19,400
2003 Projected Total Income	$368,010,000
2006 Projected Total Income	$408,370,000

RETAIL SALES

% Above/Below National Average	-44
2001 Retail Sales Estimate	$88,990,000
% Cdn. Total	0.03
2001 per Household	$13,700
2001 per Capita	$5,000
2001 No. of Establishments	135
2003 Projected Retail Sales	$96,270,000
2006 Projected Retail Sales	$106,810,000

POPULATION

2001 Estimates:

Total		17,670
Male		8,889
Female		8,781
Age Groups	Male	Female
0-4	504	503
5-9	592	563
10-14	652	603
15-19	670	596
20-24	593	537
25-29	513	496
30-34	574	575
35-39	688	666
40-44	737	685
45-49	704	638
50-54	594	555
55-59	489	464
60-64	420	416
65-69	380	401
70+	779	1,083

DAYTIME POPULATION

2001 Estimates:

Working Population	5,674
At Home Population	8,327
Total	14,001

INCOME

2001 Estimates:

Avg. Household Income	$52,598
Avg. Family Income	$58,779
Per Capita Income	$19,378
Male:	
Avg. Employment Income	$29,464
Avg. Employment Income (Full Time)	$39,301
Female:	
Avg. Employment Income	$19,552
Avg. Employment Income (Full Time)	$30,476

DISPOSABLE & DISCRETIONARY INCOME

2001 Estimates:	Per Hhld.
Disposable Income	$43,492
Discretionary Income 1 (minus Food & Shelter)	$30,784
Discretionary Income 2 (minus Food, Shelter, & Other Expenditures)	$21,090

LIQUID ASSETS

1999 Estimates:	Per Hhld.
Equity Investments	$72,241
Interest Bearing Investments	$63,911
Total Liquid Assets	$136,152

CREDIT DATA

July 2000:	
Pool of Credit	$157,358,786
Revolving Credit, No.	26,652
Fixed Loans, No.	9,134
Avg. Credit Limit, per Person	$11,012
Avg. Spent, per Person	$5,147
Satisfactory Ratings, No. per Person	2.41
Avg. No. of Cards, per Person	0.92

LABOUR FORCE

2001 Estimates:

Male:	
In the Labour Force	5,493
Participation Rate	76.9
Employed	5,271
Unemployed	222
Unemployment Rate	4.0
Not in Labour Force	1,648
Female:	
In the Labour Force	4,290
Participation Rate	60.3
Employed	3,984
Unemployed	306
Unemployment Rate	7.1
Not in Labour Force	2,822

OCCUPATIONS BY MAJOR GROUPS

2001 Estimates:	Male	Female
Management	308	190
Business, Finance & Admin.	311	804
Natural & Applied Sciences & Related	144	21
Health	22	476
Social Sciences, Gov't Services & Religion	22	46
Education	58	176
Arts, Culture, Recreation & Sport	99	100
Sales & Service	676	1,063
Trades, Transport & Equipment Operators & Related	1,372	164
Primary Industries	1,491	806
Processing, Mfg. & Utilities	916	379

LEVEL OF SCHOOLING

2001 Estimates:

Population 15 years +	14,253
Less than Grade 9	2,690
Grades 9-13 w/o Certif.	3,805
Grade 9-13 with Certif.	2,368
Trade Certif. /Dip.	563
Non-Univ. w/o Certif./Dip.	702
Non-Univ. with Certif./Dip.	2,824
Univ. w/o Degree	627
Univ. w/o Degree/Certif.	285
Univ. with Certif.	342
Univ. with Degree	674

AVERAGE HOUSEHOLD EXPENDITURES

2001 Estimates:

Food	$6,303
Shelter	$8,352
Clothing	$2,007
Transportation	$7,948
Health & Personal Care	$1,900
Recr'n, Read'g & Education	$3,872
Taxes & Securities	$11,676
Other	$8,900
Total Expenditures	$50,958

PRIVATE HOUSEHOLDS

2001 Estimates:

Private Households, Total	6,510
Pop. in Private Households	17,257
Average no. per Household	2.7

FAMILIES

2001 Estimates:

Families in Private Households	5,102
Husband-Wife Families	4,639
Lone-Parent Families	463
Aver. No. Persons per Family	3.1
Aver. No. Sons/Daughters at Home	1.2

HOUSING

2001 Estimates:

Occupied Private Dwellings	6,510
Owned	5,090
Rented	1,420
Single-Detached House	5,955
Semi-Detached House	60
Row Houses	11
Apartment, 5 or Fewer Storeys	298
Apartment, Detached Duplex	116
Other Single-Attached	43
Movable Dwellings	27

VEHICLES

2001 Estimates:

Model Yrs. '81-'96, No.	10,487
% Total	86.36
Model Yrs. '97-'98, No.	1,069
% Total	8.80
'99 Vehicles registered in Model Yr. '99, No.	587
% Total	4.83
Total No. '81-'99	12,143

LEGAL MARITAL STATUS

2001 Estimates: (Age 15+)

Single (Never Married)	3,375
Legally Married (Not Separated)	8,666
Legally Married (Separated)	319
Widowed	1,051
Divorced	842

PSYTE CATEGORIES

2001 Estimates	No. of House-holds	% of Total Hhds.	Index
Blue Collar Winners	28	0.43	17
Rustic Prosperity	4,364	67.04	3,715
Old Leafy Towns	1,019	15.65	612
Rod & Rifle	937	14.39	622
Struggling Downtowns	162	2.49	79

FINANCIAL P$YTE

2001 Estimates	No. of House-holds	% of Total Hhds.	Index
Canadian Comfort	28	0.43	4
Tractors & Tradelines	4,364	67.04	1,172
Bills & Wills	1,019	15.65	189
Rural Family Blues	937	14.39	178
Towering Debt	162	2.49	32

HOME LANGUAGE

2001 Estimates:		% Total
English	16,406	92.85
French	59	0.33
Croatian	11	0.06
Dutch	34	0.19
Flemish	76	0.43
German	550	3.11
Hungarian	114	0.65
Lithuanian	21	0.12
Polish	22	0.12
Portuguese	95	0.54
Slovenian	16	0.09
Spanish	42	0.24
Multiple Responses	224	1.27
Total	17,670	100.00

Delhi
(Township)
(Cont'd)

BUILDING PERMITS

	1999	1998	1997
		$000	
Value	12,334	9,278	8,101

TAXATION

Income Class:	1997	% Total
Under $5,000	1,130	10.98
$5,000-$10,000	1,310	12.73
$10,000-$15,000	1,760	17.10
$15,000-$20,000	1,260	12.24
$20,000-$25,000	910	8.84
$25,000-$30,000	830	8.07
$30,000-$40,000	1,410	13.70
$40,000-$50,000	740	7.19
$50,000 +	940	9.14
Total Returns, No.	10,290	
Total Income, $000	250,407	
Total Taxable Returns	7,310	
Total Tax, $000	41,240	
Average Income, $	24,335	
Average Tax, $	5,642	

VITAL STATISTICS

	1997	1996	1995	1994
Births	153	161	161	173
Deaths	118	128	100	127
Natural Increase	35	33	61	46
Marriages	64	65	73	57

Note: Latest available data.

COMMUNITY NEWSPAPER(S)

	Total Circulation
Delhi: Delhi News-Record	2,352

Dunnville
(Town)

In Haldimand-Norfolk Regional Municipality.

POPULATION

July 1, 2001 Estimate	13,192
% Cdn. Total	0.04
% Change, '96 -'01	2.24
Avg. Annual Growth Rate, %	0.44
2003 Projected Population	13,186
2006 Projected Population	13,102
2001 Households Estimate	4,947
2003 Projected Households	5,017
2006 Projected Households	5,109

INCOME

% Above/Below National Average	-9
2001 Total Income Estimate	$251,880,000
% Cdn. Total	0.04
2001 Average Hhld. Income	$50,900
2001 Per Capita	$19,100
2003 Projected Total Income	$268,130,000
2006 Projected Total Income	$293,380,000

RETAIL SALES

% Above/Below National Average	-37
2001 Retail Sales Estimate	$74,290,000
% Cdn. Total	0.03
2001 per Household	$15,000
2001 per Capita	$5,600
2001 No. of Establishments	106
2003 Projected Retail Sales	$80,320,000
2006 Projected Retail Sales	$88,600,000

POPULATION

2001 Estimates:		
Total		13,192
Male		6,509
Female		6,683
Age Groups	Male	Female
0-4	388	370
5-9	457	448
10-14	507	493
15-19	513	473
20-24	460	416
25-29	393	372
30-34	404	415
35-39	474	480
40-44	517	494
45-49	483	448
50-54	406	389
55-59	334	335
60-64	290	315
65-69	266	304
70+	617	931

DAYTIME POPULATION

2001 Estimates:	
Working Population	7,063
At Home Population	6,877
Total	13,940

INCOME

2001 Estimates:	
Avg. Household Income	$50,916
Avg. Family Income	$57,784
Per Capita Income	$19,094
Male:	
Avg. Employment Income	$33,968
Avg. Employment Income (Full Time)	$44,144
Female:	
Avg. Employment Income	$18,456
Avg. Employment Income (Full Time)	$29,167

DISPOSABLE & DISCRETIONARY INCOME

2001 Estimates:	Per Hhld.
Disposable Income	$42,098
Discretionary Income 1 (minus Food & Shelter)	$29,506
Discretionary Income 2 (minus Food, Shelter, & Other Expenditures)	$20,551

LIQUID ASSETS

1999 Estimates:	Per Hhld.
Equity Investments	$72,715
Interest Bearing Investments	$63,577
Total Liquid Assets	$136,292

CREDIT DATA

July 2000:	
Pool of Credit	$105,116,073
Revolving Credit, No.	19,068
Fixed Loans, No.	6,221
Avg. Credit Limit, per Person	$10,195
Avg. Spent, per Person	$4,750
Satisfactory Ratings, No. per Person	2.36
Avg. No. of Cards, per Person	0.88

LABOUR FORCE

2001 Estimates:	
Male:	
In the Labour Force	3,820
Participation Rate	74.1
Employed	3,607
Unemployed	213
Unemployment Rate	5.6
Not in Labour Force	1,337
Female:	
In the Labour Force	2,918
Participation Rate	54.3
Employed	2,671
Unemployed	247
Unemployment Rate	8.5
Not in Labour Force	2,454

OCCUPATIONS BY MAJOR GROUPS

2001 Estimates:	Male	Female
Management	197	198
Business, Finance & Admin.	192	641
Natural & Applied Sciences & Related	94	31
Health	11	279
Social Sciences, Gov't Services & Religion	40	9
Education	43	95
Arts, Culture, Recreation & Sport	35	62
Sales & Service	558	1,008
Trades, Transport & Equipment Operators & Related	1,390	68
Primary Industries	477	220
Processing, Mfg. & Utilities	660	167

LEVEL OF SCHOOLING

2001 Estimates:	
Population 15 years +	10,529
Less than Grade 9	1,417
Grades 9-13 w/o Certif.	3,512
Grade 9-13 with Certif.	1,587
Trade Certif. /Dip.	423
Non-Univ. w/o Certif./Dip.	567
Non-Univ. with Certif./Dip.	2,020
Univ. w/o Degree	497
Univ. w/o Degree/Certif.	277
Univ. with Certif.	220
Univ. with Degree	506

Ontario

AVERAGE HOUSEHOLD EXPENDITURES

2001 Estimates:	
Food	$5,971
Shelter	$8,561
Clothing	$1,939
Transportation	$7,185
Health & Personal Care	$1,826
Recr'n, Read'g & Education	$3,599
Taxes & Securities	$12,027
Other	$8,392
Total Expenditures	$49,500

PRIVATE HOUSEHOLDS

2001 Estimates:	
Private Households, Total	4,947
Pop. in Private Households	12,840
Average no. per Household	2.6

FAMILIES

2001 Estimates:	
Families in Private Households	3,764
Husband-Wife Families	3,346
Lone-Parent Families	418
Aver. No. Persons per Family	3.1
Aver. No. Sons/Daughters at Home	1.2

HOUSING

2001 Estimates:	
Occupied Private Dwellings	4,947
Owned	3,724
Rented	1,223
Single-Detached House	3,990
Semi-Detached House	130
Row Houses	137
Apartment, 5+ Storeys	22
Apartment, 5 or Fewer Storeys	453
Apartment, Detached Duplex	187
Movable Dwellings	28

VEHICLES

2001 Estimates:	
Model Yrs. '81-'96, No.	6,617
% Total	88.66
Model Yrs. '97-'98, No.	536
% Total	7.18
'99 Vehicles registered in Model Yr. '99, No.	310
% Total	4.15
Total No. '81-'99	7,463

LEGAL MARITAL STATUS

2001 Estimates: (Age 15+)	
Single (Never Married)	2,608
Legally Married (Not Separated)	6,121
Legally Married (Separated)	296
Widowed	886
Divorced	618

Ontario

Dunnville
(Town)
(Cont'd)

PSYTE CATEGORIES

2001 Estimates	No. of House -holds	% of Total Hhds.	Index
Blue Collar Winners	486	9.82	390
Old Towns' New Fringe	1,292	26.12	667
Rustic Prosperity	1,405	28.40	1,574
Old Leafy Towns	492	9.95	389
Quiet Towns	792	16.01	752
Struggling Downtowns	402	8.13	258

FINAN¢IAL P$YTE

2001 Estimates	No. of House -holds	% of Total Hhds.	Index
Canadian Comfort	486	9.82	101
Tractors & Tradelines	2,697	54.52	953
Bills & Wills	492	9.95	120
Limited Budgets	792	16.01	515
Towering Debt	402	8.13	104

HOME LANGUAGE

2001 Estimates:		% Total
English	12,927	97.99
French	11	0.08
Croatian	26	0.20
Dutch	11	0.08
German	73	0.55
Greek	27	0.20
Polish	20	0.15
Serbo-Croatian	10	0.08
Other Languages	39	0.30
Multiple Responses	48	0.36
Total	13,192	100.00

BUILDING PERMITS

	1999	1998 $000	1997
Value	9,166	6,249	7,208

HOMES BUILT

	1999	1998	1997
No.	16	9	25

TAXATION

Income Class:	1997	% Total
Under $5,000	1,350	14.41
$5,000-$10,000	1,150	12.27
$10,000-$15,000	1,570	16.76
$15,000-$20,000	1,040	11.10
$20,000-$25,000	800	8.54
$25,000-$30,000	720	7.68
$30,000-$40,000	1,010	10.78
$40,000-$50,000	680	7.26
$50,000 +	1,070	11.42
Total Returns, No.	9,370	
Total Income, $000	226,837	
Total Taxable Returns	6,160	
Total Tax, $000	38,133	
Average Income, $	24,209	
Average Tax, $	6,190	

VITAL STATISTICS

	1997	1996	1995	1994
Births	136	147	150	159
Deaths	154	130	160	130
Natural Increase	-18	17	-10	29
Marriages	68	54	53	79

Note: Latest available data.

COMMUNITY NEWSPAPER(S)

	Total Circulation
Dunnville: Dunnville Chronicle	3,210
Dunnville: The Regional News This Week	n.a.

Elliot Lake
(Census Agglomeration)

The Census Agglomeration of Elliot Lake consists solely of Elliot Lake, C in Algoma District.

POPULATION

July 1, 2001 Estimate	13,476
% Cdn. Total	0.04
% Change, '96 -'01	-5.34
Avg. Annual Growth Rate, %	-1.09
2003 Projected Population	13,135
2006 Projected Population	12,555
2001 Households Estimate	5,768
2003 Projected Households	5,723
2006 Projected Households	5,621

INCOME

% Above/Below National Average	-13
2001 Total Income Estimate	$248,160,000
% Cdn. Total	0.04
2001 Average Hhld. Income	$43,000
2001 Per Capita	$18,400
2003 Projected Total Income	$256,790,000
2006 Projected Total Income	$269,330,000

RETAIL SALES

% Above/Below National Average	-13
2001 Retail Sales Estimate	$104,940,000
% Cdn. Total	0.04
2001 per Household	$18,200
2001 per Capita	$7,800
2001 No. of Establishments	101
2003 Projected Retail Sales	$108,780,000
2006 Projected Retail Sales	$114,100,000

POPULATION

2001 Estimates:		
Total		13,476
Male		6,655
Female		6,821
Age Groups	Male	Female
0-4	332	303
5-9	407	369
10-14	466	434
15-19	500	467
20-24	430	403
25-29	304	297
30-34	281	312
35-39	366	451
40-44	443	516
45-49	458	504
50-54	450	487
55-59	467	475
60-64	476	472
65-69	464	461
70+	811	870

DAYTIME POPULATION

2001 Estimates:	
Working Population	4,783
At Home Population	8,693
Total	13,476

INCOME

2001 Estimates:	
Avg. Household Income	$43,024
Avg. Family Income	$49,451
Per Capita Income	$18,415
Male:	
Avg. Employment Income	$35,076
Avg. Employment Income (Full Time)	$53,160
Female:	
Avg. Employment Income	$19,120
Avg. Employment Income (Full Time)	$33,958

DISPOSABLE & DISCRETIONARY INCOME

2001 Estimates:	Per Hhld.
Disposable Income	$35,845
Discretionary Income 1 (minus Food & Shelter)	$24,605
Discretionary Income 2 (minus Food, Shelter, & Other Expenditures)	$16,667

LIQUID ASSETS

1999 Estimates:	Per Hhld.
Equity Investments	$50,934
Interest Bearing Investments	$50,792
Total Liquid Assets	$101,726

CREDIT DATA

July 2000:	
Pool of Credit	$137,453,023
Revolving Credit, No.	22,622
Fixed Loans, No.	7,577
Avg. Credit Limit, per Person	$12,161
Avg. Spent, per Person	$5,558
Satisfactory Ratings, No. per Person	2.56
Avg. No. of Cards, per Person	1.01

LABOUR FORCE

2001 Estimates:	
Male:	
In the Labour Force	2,833
Participation Rate	52.0
Employed	2,472
Unemployed	361
Unemployment Rate	12.7
Not in Labour Force	2,617
Female:	
In the Labour Force	2,507
Participation Rate	43.9
Employed	2,262
Unemployed	245
Unemployment Rate	9.8
Not in Labour Force	3,208

OCCUPATIONS BY MAJOR GROUPS

2001 Estimates:	Male	Female
Management	252	164
Business, Finance & Admin.	186	526
Natural & Applied Sciences & Related	94	10
Health	68	225
Social Sciences, Gov't Services & Religion	52	78
Education	128	185
Arts, Culture, Recreation & Sport	62	142
Sales & Service	552	912
Trades, Transport & Equipment Operators & Related	627	84
Primary Industries	492	21
Processing, Mfg. & Utilities	155	24

LEVEL OF SCHOOLING

2001 Estimates:	
Population 15 years +	11,165
Less than Grade 9	1,458
Grades 9-13 w/o Certif.	3,360
Grade 9-13 with Certif.	1,599
Trade Certif. /Dip.	423
Non-Univ. w/o Certif./Dip.	640
Non-Univ. with Certif./Dip.	2,165
Univ. w/o Degree	745
Univ. w/o Degree/Certif.	341
Univ. with Certif.	404
Univ. with Degree	775

Elliot Lake
(Census Agglomeration)
(Cont'd)

AVERAGE HOUSEHOLD EXPENDITURES

2001 Estimates:
Food	$5,374
Shelter	$7,758
Clothing	$1,823
Transportation	$6,035
Health & Personal Care	$1,893
Recr'n, Read'g & Education	$2,965
Taxes & Securities	$9,706
Other	$7,219
Total Expenditures	$42,773

PRIVATE HOUSEHOLDS

2001 Estimates:
Private Households, Total	5,768
Pop. in Private Households	13,367
Average no. per Household	2.3

FAMILIES

2001 Estimates:
Families in Private Households	4,147
Husband-Wife Families	3,667
Lone-Parent Families	480
Aver. No. Persons per Family	2.9
Aver. No. Sons/Daughters at Home	1.0

HOUSING

2001 Estimates:
Occupied Private Dwellings	5,768
Owned	3,236
Rented	2,532
Single-Detached House	2,715
Semi-Detached House	976
Row Houses	562
Apartment, 5+ Storeys	632
Apartment, 5 or Fewer Storeys	785
Apartment, Detached Duplex	30
Other Single-Attached	10
Movable Dwellings	58

VEHICLES

2001 Estimates:
Model Yrs. '81-'96, No.	6,361
% Total	83.30
Model Yrs. '97-'98, No.	796
% Total	10.42
'99 Vehicles registered in Model Yr. '99, No.	479
% Total	6.27
Total No. '81-'99	7,636

LEGAL MARITAL STATUS

2001 Estimates: (Age 15+)
Single (Never Married)	2,583
Legally Married (Not Separated)	6,428
Legally Married (Separated)	499
Widowed	812
Divorced	843

PSYTE CATEGORIES

2001 Estimates	No. of House -holds	% of Total Hhds.	Index
Town Boomers	221	3.83	378
The New Frontier	1,251	21.69	1,438
High Rise Sunsets	299	5.18	362
Old Leafy Towns	345	5.98	234
Young Grey Collar	155	2.69	321
Quiet Towns	3,120	54.09	2,542
Big Country Families	36	0.62	44
Old Grey Towers	339	5.88	1,061

FINANCIAL P$YTE

2001 Estimates	No. of House -holds	% of Total Hhds.	Index
Canadian Comfort	221	3.83	39
Miners & Credit-Liners	1,251	21.69	685
Bills & Wills	345	5.98	72
Revolving Renters	454	7.87	171
Rural Family Blues	36	0.62	8
Limited Budgets	3,120	54.09	1,740
Senior Survivors	339	5.88	312

HOME LANGUAGE

2001 Estimates		% Total
English	11,328	84.06
French	1,740	12.91
Arabic	17	0.13
Chinese	25	0.19
Estonian	10	0.07
Finnish	10	0.07
Flemish	10	0.07
German	35	0.26
Multiple Responses	301	2.23
Total	13,476	100.00

BUILDING PERMITS

	1999	1998 $000	1997
Value	1,800	6,523	6,982

TAXATION

Income Class:	1997	% Total
Under $5,000	1,380	14.29
$5,000-$10,000	1,280	13.25
$10,000-$15,000	1,650	17.08
$15,000-$20,000	1,130	11.70
$20,000-$25,000	960	9.94
$25,000-$30,000	800	8.28
$30,000-$40,000	980	10.14
$40,000-$50,000	580	6.00
$50,000 +	900	9.32
Total Returns, No.	9,660	
Total Income, $000	219,641	
Total Taxable Returns	6,120	
Total Tax, $000	33,046	
Average Income, $	22,737	
Average Tax, $	5,400	

VITAL STATISTICS

	1997	1996	1995	1994
Births	109	111	137	151
Deaths	134	130	136	113
Natural Increase	-25	-19	.1	38
Marriages	58	60	80	61

Note: Latest available data.

COMMUNITY NEWSPAPER(S)

	Total Circulation
Elliot Lake: North Shore Market Place	9,585
Elliot Lake: The Standard	4,853

RADIO STATION(S)

	Power
CBEC-FM	n.a.
CJRT-FM	n.a.
CKNR-FM	n.a.

TELEVISION STATION(S)

CBEC-TV
CICI-TV

Essa
(Township)

In Simcoe County.

POPULATION

July 1, 2001 Estimate	18,507
% Cdn. Total	0.06
% Change, '96 -'01	9.74
Avg. Annual Growth Rate, %	1.88
2003 Projected Population	19,114
2006 Projected Population	20,021
2001 Households Estimate	6,271
2003 Projected Households	6,461
2006 Projected Households	6,809

INCOME

% Above/Below National Average	-12
2001 Total Income Estimate	$343,580,000
% Cdn. Total	0.05
2001 Average Hhld. Income	$54,800
2001 Per Capita	$18,600
2003 Projected Total Income	$368,890,000
2006 Projected Total Income	$413,340,000

RETAIL SALES

% Above/Below National Average	-51
2001 Retail Sales Estimate	$80,920,000
% Cdn. Total	0.03
2001 per Household	$12,900
2001 per Capita	$4,400
2001 No. of Establishments	73
2003 Projected Retail Sales	$88,750,000
2006 Projected Retail Sales	$102,100,000

POPULATION

2001 Estimates:
Total		18,507
Male		9,365
Female		9,142

Age Groups	Male	Female
0-4	696	657
5-9	819	771
10-14	841	764
15-19	718	646
20-24	553	538
25-29	524	571
30-34	753	795
35-39	969	943
40-44	901	849
45-49	716	681
50-54	537	521
55-59	394	378
60-64	299	290
65-69	239	237
70+	406	501

DAYTIME POPULATION

2001 Estimates:
Working Population	19,785
At Home Population	8,459
Total	28,244

INCOME

2001 Estimates:
Avg. Household Income	$54,789
Avg. Family Income	$56,945
Per Capita Income	$18,565

Male:
Avg. Employment Income	$33,582
Avg. Employment Income (Full Time)	$40,654

Female:
Avg. Employment Income	$19,525
Avg. Employment Income (Full Time)	$30,194

Ontario

DISPOSABLE & DISCRETIONARY INCOME

2001 Estimates:	Per Hhld.
Disposable Income	$45,184
Discretionary Income 1 (minus Food & Shelter)	$31,955
Discretionary Income 2 (minus Food, Shelter, & Other Expenditures)	$23,004

LIQUID ASSETS

1999 Estimates:	Per Hhld.
Equity Investments	$73,027
Interest Bearing Investments	$67,490
Total Liquid Assets	$140,517

CREDIT DATA

July 2000:	
Pool of Credit	$195,307,282
Revolving Credit, No.	31,604
Fixed Loans, No.	12,589
Avg. Credit Limit, per Person.	$12,622
Avg. Spent, per Person	$6,431
Satisfactory Ratings, No. per Person	2.74
Avg. No. of Cards, per Person	0.92

LABOUR FORCE

2001 Estimates:
Male:
In the Labour Force	5,775
Participation Rate	82.4
Employed	5,613
Unemployed	162
Unemployment Rate	2.8
Not in Labour Force	1,234

Female:
In the Labour Force	4,797
Participation Rate	69.0
Employed	4,426
Unemployed	371
Unemployment Rate	7.7
Not in Labour Force	2,153

OCCUPATIONS BY MAJOR GROUPS

2001 Estimates:	Male	Female
Management	654	279
Business, Finance & Admin.	354	1,067
Natural & Applied Sciences & Related	263	67
Health	55	293
Social Sciences, Gov't Services & Religion	n.a.	130
Education	50	100
Arts, Culture, Recreation & Sport	36	85
Sales & Service	1,868	2,056
Trades, Transport & Equipment Operators & Related	1,568	175
Primary Industries	352	85
Processing, Mfg. & Utilities	527	274

Ontario

Essa
(Township)
(Cont'd)

LEVEL OF SCHOOLING

2001 Estimates:
Population 15 years +	13,959
Less than Grade 9	1,008
Grades 9-13 w/o Certif.	3,843
Grade 9-13 with Certif.	2,401
Trade Certif./Dip.	661
Non-Univ. w/o Certif./Dip.	1,104
Non-Univ. with Certif./Dip.	2,841
Univ. w/o Degree	1,103
Univ. w/o Degree/Certif.	478
Univ. with Certif.	625
Univ. with Degree	998

AVERAGE HOUSEHOLD EXPENDITURES

2001 Estimates:
Food	$6,094
Shelter	$9,096
Clothing	$2,035
Transportation	$7,014
Health & Personal Care	$1,851
Recr'n, Read'g & Education	$3,820
Taxes & Securities	$14,027
Other	$8,549
Total Expenditures	$52,486

PRIVATE HOUSEHOLDS

2001 Estimates:
Private Households, Total	6,271
Pop. in Private Households	18,115
Average no. per Household	2.9

FAMILIES

2001 Estimates:
Families in Private Households	5,368
Husband-Wife Families	4,861
Lone-Parent Families	507
Aver. No. Persons per Family	3.2
Aver. No. Sons/Daughters at Home	1.3

HOUSING

2001 Estimates:
Occupied Private Dwellings	6,271
Owned	4,253
Rented	2,018
Single-Detached House	4,952
Semi-Detached House	699
Row Houses	53
Apartment, 5 or Fewer Storeys	315
Apartment, Detached Duplex	113
Movable Dwellings	139

VEHICLES

2001 Estimates:
Model Yrs. '81-'96, No.	8,240
% Total	82.70
Model Yrs. '97-'98, No.	1,055
% Total	10.59
'99 Vehicles registered in Model Yr. '99, No.	669
% Total	6.71
Total No. '81-'99	9,964

LEGAL MARITAL STATUS

2001 Estimates: (Age 15+)
Single (Never Married)	3,292
Legally Married (Not Separated)	8,704
Legally Married (Separated)	525
Widowed	499
Divorced	939

PSYTE CATEGORIES

2001 Estimates	No. of House -holds	% of Total Hhds.	Index
Satellite Suburbs	427	6.81	237
Blue Collar Winners	1,558	24.84	987
Old Towns' New Fringe	4,148	66.15	1,690
Rustic Prosperity	66	1.05	58

FINANCIAL P$YTE

2001 Estimates	No. of House -holds	% of Total Hhds.	Index
Canadian Comfort	1,985	31.65	326
Tractors & Tradelines	4,214	67.20	1,175

HOME LANGUAGE

2001 Estimates:		% Total
English	16,968	91.68
French	1,020	5.51
German	63	0.34
Greek	28	0.15
Hungarian	11	0.06
Italian	23	0.12
Japanese	12	0.06
Korean	17	0.09
Latvian (Lettish)	11	0.06
Polish	46	0.25
Other Languages	23	0.12
Multiple Responses	285	1.54
Total	18,507	100.00

BUILDING PERMITS

	1999	1998 $000	1997
Value	12,000	7,403	7,530

TAXATION

Income Class:	1997	% Total
Under $5,000	1,570	14.59
$5,000-$10,000	1,150	10.69
$10,000-$15,000	1,220	11.34
$15,000-$20,000	910	8.46
$20,000-$25,000	830	7.71
$25,000-$30,000	780	7.25
$30,000-$40,000	1,470	13.66
$40,000-$50,000	1,330	12.36
$50,000 +	1,490	13.85
Total Returns, No.	10,760	
Total Income, $000	293,866	
Total Taxable Returns	7,870	
Total Tax, $000	53,987	
Average Income, $	27,311	
Average Tax, $	6,860	

VITAL STATISTICS

	1997	1996	1995	1994
Births	257	213	280	473
Deaths	59	66	64	229
Natural Increase	198	147	216	244
Marriages	72	56	48	153

Note: Latest available data.

COMMUNITY NEWSPAPER(S)

	Total Circulation
Borden: Borden Citizen	6,000

Gravenhurst
(Town)
In Muskoka District Municipality.

POPULATION

July 1, 2001 Estimate	10,306
% Cdn. Total	0.03
% Change, '96 -'01	-0.27
Avg. Annual Growth Rate, %	-0.05
2003 Projected Population	10,204
2006 Projected Population	9,992
2001 Households Estimate	4,269
2003 Projected Households	4,240
2006 Projected Households	4,188

INCOME

% Above/Below National Average	-14
2001 Total Income Estimate	$186,530,000
% Cdn. Total	0.03
2001 Average Hhld. Income	$43,700
2001 Per Capita	$18,100
2003 Projected Total Income	$193,050,000
2006 Projected Total Income	$203,000,000

RETAIL SALES

% Above/Below National Average	+30
2001 Retail Sales Estimate	$120,330,000
% Cdn. Total	0.04
2001 per Household	$28,200
2001 per Capita	$11,700
2001 No. of Establishments	100
2003 Projected Retail Sales	$128,070,000
2006 Projected Retail Sales	$136,630,000

POPULATION

2001 Estimates:
Total	10,306
Male	5,129
Female	5,177

Age Groups	Male	Female
0-4	249	245
5-9	267	263
10-14	294	301
15-19	328	322
20-24	312	277
25-29	283	241
30-34	316	274
35-39	387	334
40-44	411	383
45-49	397	373
50-54	339	334
55-59	293	301
60-64	287	297
65-69	281	302
70+	685	930

DAYTIME POPULATION

2001 Estimates:
Working Population	4,903
At Home Population	5,743
Total	10,646

INCOME

2001 Estimates:
Avg. Household Income	$43,693
Avg. Family Income	$48,549
Per Capita Income	$18,099
Male:	
Avg. Employment Income	$25,894
Avg. Employment Income (Full Time)	$35,410
Female:	
Avg. Employment Income	$20,207
Avg. Employment Income (Full Time)	$31,773

DISPOSABLE & DISCRETIONARY INCOME

2001 Estimates:	Per Hhld.
Disposable Income	$36,359
Discretionary Income 1 (minus Food & Shelter)	$24,699
Discretionary Income 2 (minus Food, Shelter, & Other Expenditures)	$16,985

LIQUID ASSETS

1999 Estimates:	Per Hhld.
Equity Investments	$49,274
Interest Bearing Investments	$51,769
Total Liquid Assets	$101,043

CREDIT DATA

July 2000:	
Pool of Credit	$94,533,707
Revolving Credit, No.	16,500
Fixed Loans, No.	5,612
Avg. Credit Limit, per Person	$11,381
Avg. Spent, per Person	$5,137
Satisfactory Ratings, No. per Person	2.54
Avg. No. of Cards, per Person	0.96

LABOUR FORCE

2001 Estimates:
Male:	
In the Labour Force	2,752
Participation Rate	63.7
Employed	2,483
Unemployed	269
Unemployment Rate	9.8
Not in Labour Force	1,567
Female:	
In the Labour Force	2,261
Participation Rate	51.8
Employed	2,059
Unemployed	202
Unemployment Rate	8.9
Not in Labour Force	2,107

OCCUPATIONS BY MAJOR GROUPS

2001 Estimates:	Male	Female
Management	268	132
Business, Finance & Admin.	146	509
Natural & Applied Sciences & Related	84	n.a.
Health	106	175
Social Sciences, Gov't Services & Religion	30	88
Education	21	54
Arts, Culture, Recreation & Sport	18	99
Sales & Service	572	964
Trades, Transport & Equipment Operators & Related	1,044	24
Primary Industries	91	32
Processing, Mfg. & Utilities	318	86

LEVEL OF SCHOOLING

2001 Estimates:
Population 15 years +	8,687
Less than Grade 9	1,151
Grades 9-13 w/o Certif.	2,637
Grade 9-13 with Certif.	1,119
Trade Certif./Dip.	440
Non-Univ. w/o Certif./Dip.	635
Non-Univ. with Certif./Dip.	1,750
Univ. w/o Degree	497
Univ. w/o Degree/Certif.	188
Univ. with Certif.	309
Univ. with Degree	458

Gravenhurst
(Town)
(Cont'd)

AVERAGE HOUSEHOLD EXPENDITURES

2001 Estimates:

Food	$5,507
Shelter	$7,942
Clothing	$1,652
Transportation	$6,017
Health & Personal Care	$1,743
Recr'n, Read'g & Education	$2,944
Taxes & Securities	$10,199
Other	$7,242
Total Expenditures	$43,246

PRIVATE HOUSEHOLDS

2001 Estimates:

Private Households, Total	4,269
Pop. in Private Households	9,764
Average no. per Household	2.3

FAMILIES

2001 Estimates:

Families in Private Households	3,191
Husband-Wife Families	2,775
Lone-Parent Families	416
Aver. No. Persons per Family	2.7
Aver. No. Sons/Daughters at Home	0.9

HOUSING

2001 Estimates:

Occupied Private Dwellings	4,269
Owned	3,057
Rented	1,212
Single-Detached House	3,292
Semi-Detached House	83
Row Houses	143
Apartment, 5+ Storeys	11
Apartment, 5 or Fewer Storeys	501
Apartment, Detached Duplex	67
Movable Dwellings	172

VEHICLES

2001 Estimates:

Model Yrs. '81-'96, No.	5,431
% Total	79.75
Model Yrs. '97-'98, No.	876
% Total	12.86
'99 Vehicles registered in Model Yr. '99, No.	503
% Total	7.39
Total No. '81-'99	6,810

LEGAL MARITAL STATUS

2001 Estimates: (Age 15+)

Single (Never Married)	2,137
Legally Married (Not Separated)	4,647
Legally Married (Separated)	327
Widowed	773
Divorced	803

PSYTE CATEGORIES

2001 Estimates	No. of House-holds	% of Total Hhds.	Index
Old Towns' New Fringe	143	3.35	86
Pick-ups & Dirt Bikes	74	1.73	208
Old Leafy Towns	1,767	41.39	1,619
Nesters & Young Homesteaders	106	2.48	106
Quiet Towns	1,037	24.29	1,142
Rod & Rifle	518	12.13	525
Old Cdn. Rustics	116	2.72	277
Aged Pensioners	419	9.81	738

FINANCIAL P$YTE

2001 Estimates	No. of House-holds	% of Total Hhds.	Index
Tractors & Tradelines	143	3.35	59
Bills & Wills	1,767	41.39	500
Country Credit	74	1.73	26
Revolving Renters	106	2.48	54
Rural Family Blues	518	12.13	150
Limited Budgets	1,153	27.01	869
Senior Survivors	419	9.81	521

HOME LANGUAGE

2001 Estimates		% Total
English	10,158	98.56
Chinese	10	0.10
Estonian	15	0.15
Finnish	12	0.12
German	32	0.31
Greek	11	0.11
Hungarian	15	0.15
Polish	10	0.10
Spanish	15	0.15
Multiple Responses	28	0.27
Total	10,306	100.00

BUILDING PERMITS

	1999	1998 $000	1997
Value	21,282	27,363	13,001

HOMES BUILT

	1999	1998	1997
No	66	36	n.a.

TAXATION

Income Class:	1997	% Total
Under $5,000	1,080	13.47
$5,000-$10,000	1,100	13.72
$10,000-$15,000	1,450	18.08
$15,000-$20,000	950	11.85
$20,000-$25,000	750	9.35
$25,000-$30,000	630	7.86
$30,000-$40,000	880	10.97
$40,000-$50,000	520	6.48
$50,000 +	670	8.35
Total Returns, No.	8,020	
Total Income, $000	180,951	
Total Taxable Returns	5,260	
Total Tax, $000	28,326	
Average Income, $	22,562	
Average Tax, $	5,385	

VITAL STATISTICS

	1997	1996	1995	1994
Births	97	94	114	107
Deaths	143	146	130	142
Natural Increase	-46	-52	-16	-35
Marriages	81	76	68	74

Note: Latest available data.

COMMUNITY NEWSPAPER(S)

	Total Circulation
Gravenhurst: District Weekender	25,171
Gravenhurst: Muskoka Advance	23,487
Gravenhurst: Gravenhurst Banner	2,810

Guelph
(Census Agglomeration)

The Census Agglomeration of Guelph consists of: Guelph, C; Guelph, TP; and Eramosa, TP. All are in Wellington County.

POPULATION

July 1, 2001 Estimate	118,174
% Cdn. Total	0.38
% Change, '96 -'01	8.72
Avg. Annual Growth Rate, %	1.69
2003 Projected Population	120,576
2006 Projected Population	123,564
2001 Households Estimate	45,211
2003 Projected Households	46,513
2006 Projected Households	48,361

INCOME

% Above/Below National Average	+9
2001 Total Income Estimate	$2,726,280,000
% Cdn. Total	0.42
2001 Average Hhld. Income	$60,300
2001 Per Capita	$23,100
2003 Projected Total Income	$2,944,030,000
2006 Projected Total Income	$3,299,890,000

RETAIL SALES

% Above/Below National Average	+27
2001 Retail Sales Estimate	$1,341,640,000
% Cdn. Total	0.48
2001 per Household	$29,700
2001 per Capita	$11,400
2001 No. of Establishments	913
2003 Projected Retail Sales	$1,485,110,000
2006 Projected Retail Sales	$1,690,930,000

POPULATION

2001 Estimates:

Total	118,174
Male	58,067
Female	60,107

Age Groups	Male	Female
0-4	3,967	3,709
5-9	4,035	3,703
10-14	4,036	3,710
15-19	3,855	3,613
20-24	3,976	3,973
25-29	4,438	4,447
30-34	4,910	4,875
35-39	5,069	5,053
40-44	4,785	4,818
45-49	4,234	4,321
50-54	3,473	3,612
55-59	2,718	2,881
60-64	2,236	2,418
65-69	1,970	2,212
70+	4,365	6,762

DAYTIME POPULATION

2001 Estimates:

Working Population	65,961
At Home Population	52,213
Total	118,174

INCOME

2001 Estimates:

Avg. Household Income	$60,301
Avg. Family Income	$68,105
Per Capita Income	$23,070
Male:	
Avg. Employment Income	$37,468
Avg. Employment Income (Full Time)	$49,306
Female:	
Avg. Employment Income	$23,159
Avg. Employment Income (Full Time)	$34,094

Ontario

DISPOSABLE & DISCRETIONARY INCOME

2001 Estimates:	Per Hhld.
Disposable Income	$49,393
Discretionary Income 1 (minus Food & Shelter)	$35,021
Discretionary Income 2 (minus Food, Shelter, & Other Expenditures)	$26,124

LIQUID ASSETS

1999 Estimates:	Per Hhld.
Equity Investments	$83,012
Interest Bearing Investments	$73,119
Total Liquid Assets	$156,131

CREDIT DATA

July 2000:

Pool of Credit	$1,471,081,824
Revolving Credit, No.	244,308
Fixed Loans, No.	75,742
Avg. Credit Limit, per Person	$13,266
Avg. Spent, per Person	$6,166
Satisfactory Ratings, No. per Person	2.79
Avg. No. of Cards, per Person	1.06

LABOUR FORCE

2001 Estimates:

Male:	
In the Labour Force	36,069
Participation Rate	78.4
Employed	35,140
Unemployed	929
Unemployment Rate	2.6
Not in Labour Force	9,960
Female:	
In the Labour Force	32,288
Participation Rate	65.9
Employed	30,864
Unemployed	1,424
Unemployment Rate	4.4
Not in Labour Force	16,697

OCCUPATIONS BY MAJOR GROUPS

2001 Estimates:	Male	Female
Management	3,868	1,575
Business, Finance & Admin.	2,800	8,288
Natural & Applied Sciences & Related	3,050	786
Health	661	2,512
Social Sciences, Gov't Services & Religion	696	866
Education	1,713	2,399
Arts, Culture, Recreation & Sport	685	900
Sales & Service	6,968	9,656
Trades, Transport & Equipment Operators & Related	7,325	604
Primary Industries	1,122	468
Processing, Mfg. & Utilities	6,562	3,357

Ontario

Guelph
(Census Agglomeration)
(Cont'd)

LEVEL OF SCHOOLING

2001 Estimates:
Population 15 years +	95,014
Less than Grade 9	7,182
Grades 9-13 w/o Certif.	21,145
Grade 9-13 with Certif.	13,017
Trade Certif. /Dip.	3,140
Non-Univ. w/o Certif./Dip.	5,502
Non-Univ. with Certif./Dip.	16,778
Univ. w/o Degree	9,965
Univ. w/o Degree/Certif.	5,600
Univ. with Certif.	4,365
Univ. with Degree	18,285

AVERAGE HOUSEHOLD EXPENDITURES

2001 Estimates:
Food	$6,585
Shelter	$10,146
Clothing	$2,404
Transportation	$6,813
Health & Personal Care	$2,026
Recr'n, Read'g & Education	$4,042
Taxes & Securities	$16,138
Other	$9,058
Total Expenditures	$57,212

PRIVATE HOUSEHOLDS

2001 Estimates:
Private Households, Total	45,211
Pop. in Private Households	115,792
Average no. per Household	2.6

FAMILIES

2001 Estimates:
Families in Private Households	33,281
Husband-Wife Families	28,858
Lone-Parent Families	4,423
Aver. No. Persons per Family	3.0
Aver. No. Sons/Daughters at Home	1.2

HOUSING

2001 Estimates:
Occupied Private Dwellings	45,211
Owned	28,123
Rented	17,088
Single-Detached House	25,290
Semi-Detached House	1,810
Row Houses	4,416
Apartment, 5+ Storeys	5,854
Owned Apartment, 5+ Storeys	808
Apartment, 5 or Fewer Storeys	5,895
Apartment, Detached Duplex	1,778
Other Single-Attached	112
Movable Dwellings	56

VEHICLES

2001 Estimates:
Model Yrs. '81-'96, No.	57,110
% Total	79.77
Model Yrs. '97-'98, No.	8,884
% Total	12.41
'99 Vehicles registered in Model Yr. '99, No.	5,596
% Total	7.82
Total No. '81-'99	71,590

LEGAL MARITAL STATUS

2001 Estimates: (Age 15+)
Single (Never Married)	29,142
Legally Married (Not Separated)	51,304
Legally Married (Separated)	3,041
Widowed	5,564
Divorced	5,963

PSYTE CATEGORIES

2001 Estimates	No. of House -holds	% of Total Hhds.	Index
The Affluentials	233	0.52	81
Urban Gentry	85	0.19	10
Suburban Executives	1,115	2.47	172
Mortgaged in Suburbia	1,182	2.61	188
Technocrafts & Bureaucrats	3,112	6.88	245
Boomers & Teens	1,363	3.01	168
Stable Suburban Families	797	1.76	135
Old Bungalow Burbs	742	1.64	99
Suburban Nesters	431	0.95	59
Aging Erudites	3,522	7.79	516
Satellite Suburbs	4,746	10.50	366
Kindergarten Boom	2,040	4.51	172
Blue Collar Winners	2,578	5.70	226
Europa	17	0.04	3
High Rise Melting Pot	739	1.63	109
Conservative Homebodies	6,779	14.99	416
High Rise Sunsets	913	2.02	141
Young Urban Professionals	2,458	5.44	287
Young Urban Mix	1,128	2.49	118
Young Urban Intelligentsia	876	1.94	127
University Enclaves	3,489	7.72	378
Young City Singles	1,142	2.53	110
Town Renters	2,136	4.72	547
Struggling Downtowns	2,508	5.55	176
Aged Pensioners	502	1.11	83
Old Grey Towers	188	0.42	75

FINANCIAL P$YTE

2001 Estimates	No. of House -holds	% of Total Hhds.	Index
Platinum Estates	233	0.52	64
Four Star Investors	2,563	5.67	113
Successful Suburbanites	5,091	11.26	170
Canadian Comfort	7,755	17.15	177
Urban Heights	5,980	13.23	307
Miners & Credit-Liners	742	1.64	52
Mortgages & Minivans	2,040	4.51	68
Dollars & Sense	17	0.04	1
Bills & Wills	7,907	17.49	211
Revolving Renters	913	2.02	44
Young Urban Struggle	4,365	9.65	204
Towering Debt	6,525	14.43	185
Senior Survivors	690	1.53	81

HOME LANGUAGE

2001 Estimates:		% Total
English	106,925	90.48
French	398	0.34
Arabic	96	0.08
Chinese	1,260	1.07
Czech	129	0.11
Dutch	98	0.08
German	253	0.21
Greek	187	0.16
Hindi	103	0.09
Hungarian	641	0.54
Italian	1,526	1.29
Korean	88	0.07
Persian (Farsi)	244	0.21
Polish	931	0.79
Punjabi	339	0.29
Romanian	97	0.08
Russian	62	0.05
Serbian	187	0.16
Serbo-Croatian	84	0.07
Spanish	327	0.28
Tagalog (Pilipino)	308	0.26
Ukrainian	120	0.10
Urdu	102	0.09
Vietnamese	999	0.85
Other Languages	953	0.81
Multiple Responses	1,717	1.45
Total	118,174	100.00

BUILDING PERMITS

	1999	1998	1997
		$000	
Value	260,747	182,765	222,007

HOMES BUILT

	1999	1998	1997
No.	992	968	952

TAXATION

Income Class:	1997	% Total
Under $5,000	9,360	11.42
$5,000-$10,000	8,860	10.81
$10,000-$15,000	9,660	11.79
$15,000-$20,000	7,520	9.18
$20,000-$25,000	6,530	7.97
$25,000-$30,000	6,550	7.99
$30,000-$40,000	11,750	14.34
$40,000-$50,000	7,980	9.74
$50,000 +	13,740	16.77
Total Returns, No.	81,950	
Total Income, $000.	2,574,899	
Total Taxable Returns	61,310	
Total Tax, $000.	527,247	
Average Income, $	31,420	
Average Tax, $	8,600	

VITAL STATISTICS

	1997	1996	1995	1994
Births	1,470	1,483	1,487	1,502
Deaths	704	704	748	679
Natural Increase	766	779	739	823
Marriages	703	594	588	635

Note: Latest available data.

DAILY NEWSPAPER(S)

	Circulation Average Paid
The Guelph Mercury	13,478

COMMUNITY NEWSPAPER(S)

	Total Circulation
Guelph: Guelph Tribune Tue/Fri	34,669
Guelph: Guelph Pennysaver	n.a.

RADIO STATION(S)

	Power
CBLA-FM	n.a.
CIMJ-FM	50,000w
CJOY	10,000w

Haileybury
(Census Agglomeration)

The Census Agglomeration of Haileybury includes: Haileybury, T; New Liskeard, T; Cobalt, T; Dymond, TP; plus two smaller areas. All are in Timiskaming District.

POPULATION

July 1, 2001 Estimate	13,252
% Cdn. Total	0.04
% Change, '96 -'01	-5.75
Avg. Annual Growth Rate, %	-1.18
2003 Projected Population	12,934
2006 Projected Population	12,403
2001 Households Estimate	5,242
2003 Projected Households	5,189
2006 Projected Households	5,086

INCOME

% Above/Below National Average	-9
2001 Total Income Estimate	$255,290,000
% Cdn. Total	0.04
2001 Average Hhld. Income	$48,700
2001 Per Capita	$19,300
2003 Projected Total Income	$262,820,000
2006 Projected Total Income	$273,330,000

RETAIL SALES

% Above/Below National Average	+121
2001 Retail Sales Estimate	$261,740,000
% Cdn. Total	0.09
2001 per Household	$49,900
2001 per Capita	$19,800
2001 No. of Establishments	168
2003 Projected Retail Sales	$272,730,000
2006 Projected Retail Sales	$283,320,000

POPULATION

2001 Estimates:

Total	13,252
Male	6,424
Female	6,828

Age Groups	Male	Female
0-4	361	337
5-9	393	363
10-14	435	424
15-19	508	495
20-24	505	476
25-29	401	394
30-34	372	393
35-39	429	464
40-44	480	507
45-49	509	522
50-54	466	468
55-59	378	383
60-64	310	336
65-69	268	312
70+	609	954

DAYTIME POPULATION

2001 Estimates:

Working Population	6,491
At Home Population	6,943
Total	13,434

INCOME

2001 Estimates:

Avg. Household Income	$48,701
Avg. Family Income	$56,189
Per Capita Income	$19,264
Male:	
Avg. Employment Income	$32,924
Avg. Employment Income (Full Time)	$45,480
Female:	
Avg. Employment Income	$19,515
Avg. Employment Income (Full Time)	$31,034

DISPOSABLE & DISCRETIONARY INCOME

2001 Estimates:	*Per Hhld.*
Disposable Income	$40,341
Discretionary Income 1 (minus Food & Shelter)	$28,710
Discretionary Income 2 (minus Food, Shelter, & Other Expenditures)	$20,368

LIQUID ASSETS

1999 Estimates:	*Per Hhld.*
Equity Investments	$74,389
Interest Bearing Investments	$62,498
Total Liquid Assets	$136,887

CREDIT DATA

July 2000:

Pool of Credit	$167,551,881
Revolving Credit, No.	26,686
Fixed Loans, No.	10,323
Avg. Credit Limit, per Person	$12,231
Avg. Spent, per Person	$5,830
Satisfactory Ratings, No. per Person	2.59
Avg. No. of Cards, per Person	0.89

LABOUR FORCE

2001 Estimates:

Male:	
In the Labour Force	3,564
Participation Rate	68.1
Employed	3,213
Unemployed	351
Unemployment Rate	9.8
Not in Labour Force	1,671
Female:	
In the Labour Force	3,294
Participation Rate	57.7
Employed	3,112
Unemployed	182
Unemployment Rate	5.5
Not in Labour Force	2,410

OCCUPATIONS BY MAJOR GROUPS

2001 Estimates:	Male	Female
Management	420	226
Business, Finance & Admin.	213	820
Natural & Applied Sciences & Related	162	29
Health	45	259
Social Sciences, Gov't Services & Religion	50	158
Education	161	192
Arts, Culture, Recreation & Sport	42	49
Sales & Service	820	1,313
Trades, Transport & Equipment Operators & Related	1,111	66
Primary Industries	202	50
Processing, Mfg. & Utilities	252	17

LEVEL OF SCHOOLING

2001 Estimates:

Population 15 years +	10,939
Less than Grade 9	1,477
Grades 9-13 w/o Certif.	3,091
Grade 9-13 with Certif.	1,726
Trade Certif. /Dip.	373
Non-Univ. w/o Certif./Dip.	666
Non-Univ. with Certif./Dip.	2,152
Univ. w/o Degree	675
Univ. w/o Degree/Certif.	332
Univ. with Certif.	343
Univ. with Degree	779

AVERAGE HOUSEHOLD EXPENDITURES

2001 Estimates:

Food	$5,800
Shelter	$7,851
Clothing	$2,124
Transportation	$6,365
Health & Personal Care	$1,936
Recr'n, Read'g & Education	$3,292
Taxes & Securities	$11,755
Other	$8,282
Total Expenditures	$47,405

PRIVATE HOUSEHOLDS

2001 Estimates:

Private Households, Total	5,242
Pop. in Private Households	12,967
Average no. per Household	2.5

FAMILIES

2001 Estimates:

Families in Private Households	3,856
Husband-Wife Families	3,349
Lone-Parent Families	507
Aver. No. Persons per Family	3.0
Aver. No. Sons/Daughters at Home	1:1

HOUSING

2001 Estimates:

Occupied Private Dwellings	5,242
Owned	3,804
Rented	1,438
Single-Detached House	3,948
Semi-Detached House	83
Row Houses	59
Apartment, 5+ Storeys	24
Apartment, 5 or Fewer Storeys	723
Apartment, Detached Duplex	355
Movable Dwellings	50

VEHICLES

2001 Estimates:

Model Yrs. '81-'96, No.	7,063
% Total	80.55
Model Yr. '97-'98, No.	1,073
% Total	12.24
'99 Vehicles registered in Model Yr. '99, No.	632
% Total	7.21
Total No. '81-'99	8,768

LEGAL MARITAL STATUS

2001 Estimates: (Age 15+)

Single (Never Married)	3,088
Legally Married (Not Separated)	5,912
Legally Married (Separated)	394
Widowed	963
Divorced	582

PSYTE CATEGORIES

2001 Estimates	No. of House-holds	% of Total Hhds.	Index
Town Boomers	1,685	32.14	3,171
Rustic Prosperity	178	3.40	188
Pick-ups & Dirt Bikes	940	17.93	2,148
Young Grey Collar	447	8.53	1,019
Quiet Towns	1,898	36.21	1,702
Rod & Rifle	88	1.68	73

FINANCIAL P$YTE

2001 Estimates	No. of House-holds	% of Total Hhds.	Index
Canadian Comfort	1,685	32.14	331
Tractors & Tradelines	178	3.40	59
Country Credit	940	17.93	265
Revolving Renters	447	8.53	185
Rural Family Blues	88	1.68	21
Limited Budgets	1,898	36.21	1,165

Ontario

HOME LANGUAGE

2001 Estimates:		*% Total*
English	9,907	74.76
French	3,062	23.11
Chinese	29	0.22
German	10	0.08
Multiple Responses	244	1.84
Total	13,252	100.00

BUILDING PERMITS

	1999	*1998 $000*	*1997*
Value	6,724	5,425	6,447

HOMES BUILT

	1999	*1998*	*1997*
No.	17	15	23

TAXATION

Income Class:	*1997*	*% Total*
Under $5,000	1,580	14.01
$5,000-$10,000	1,560	13.83
$10,000-$15,000	1,950	17.29
$15,000-$20,000	1,250	11.08
$20,000-$25,000	910	8.07
$25,000-$30,000	840	7.45
$30,000-$40,000	1,270	11.26
$40,000-$50,000	690	6.12
$50,000 +	1,240	10.99
Total Returns, No.	11,280	
Total Income, $000	272,877	
Total Taxable Returns	7,260	
Total Tax, $000	46,575	
Average Income, $	24,191	
Average Tax, $	6,415	

VITAL STATISTICS

	1997	*1996*	*1995*	*1994*
Births	176	175	177	181
Deaths	150	136	152	134
Natural Increase	26	39	25	47
Marriages	120	133	115	128

Note: Latest available data.

COMMUNITY NEWSPAPER(S)

	Total Circulation
New Liskeard: Journal O'Courant (bimthly)	n.a.
New Liskeard: Temiskaming Speaker	6,148

Ontario

Haldimand
(Town)

In Haldimand-Norfolk Regional Municipality.

POPULATION

July 1, 2001 Estimate	24,305
% Cdn. Total	0.08
% Change, '96 -'01	6.15
Avg. Annual Growth Rate, %	1.20
2003 Projected Population	24,760
2006 Projected Population	25,306
2001 Households Estimate	8,468
2003 Projected Households	8,749
2006 Projected Households	9,163

INCOME

% Above/Below National Average	same
2001 Total Income Estimate	$510,480,000
% Cdn. Total	0.08
2001 Average Hhld. Income	$60,300
2001 Per Capita	$21,000
2003 Projected Total Income	$551,870,000
2006 Projected Total Income	$618,170,000

RETAIL SALES

% Above/Below National Average	-7
2001 Retail Sales Estimate	$202,420,000
% Cdn. Total	0.07
2001 per Household	$23,900
2001 per Capita	$8,300
2001 No. of Establishments	234
2003 Projected Retail Sales	$223,790,000
2006 Projected Retail Sales	$255,180,000

POPULATION

2001 Estimates:

Total		24,305
Male		12,069
Female		12,236
Age Groups	Male	Female
0-4	761	724
5-9	892	845
10-14	995	969
15-19	962	965
20-24	824	806
25-29	674	704
30-34	754	819
35-39	937	992
40-44	1,024	1,047
45-49	998	954
50-54	836	791
55-59	650	606
60-64	501	470
65-69	401	413
70+	860	1,131

DAYTIME POPULATION

2001 Estimates:

Working Population	8,516
At Home Population	10,921
Total	19,437

INCOME

2001 Estimates:

Avg. Household Income	$60,283
Avg. Family Income	$64,837
Per Capita Income	$21,003
Male:	
Avg. Employment Income	$37,809
Avg. Employment Income (Full Time)	$49,359
Female:	
Avg. Employment Income	$20,648
Avg. Employment Income (Full Time)	$31,307

DISPOSABLE & DISCRETIONARY INCOME

2001 Estimates:	Per Hhld.
Disposable Income	$50,205
Discretionary Income 1 (minus Food & Shelter)	$35,991
Discretionary Income 2 (minus Food, Shelter, & Other Expenditures)	$26,065

LIQUID ASSETS

1999 Estimates:	Per Hhld.
Equity Investments	$78,671
Interest Bearing Investments	$72,588
Total Liquid Assets	$151,259

CREDIT DATA

July 2000:

Pool of Credit	$270,475,640
Revolving Credit, No.	43,835
Fixed Loans, No.	14,490
Avg. Credit Limit, per Person	$12,647
Avg. Spent, per Person	$6,131
Satisfactory Ratings, No. per Person	2.63
Avg. No. of Cards, per Person	0.95

LABOUR FORCE

2001 Estimates:

Male:	
In the Labour Force	7,589
Participation Rate	80.6
Employed	7,343
Unemployed	246
Unemployment Rate	3.2
Not in Labour Force	1,832
Female:	
In the Labour Force	6,091
Participation Rate	62.8
Employed	5,899
Unemployed	192
Unemployment Rate	3.2
Not in Labour Force	3,607

OCCUPATIONS BY MAJOR GROUPS

2001 Estimates:	Male	Female
Management	924	397
Business, Finance & Admin.	532	1,805
Natural & Applied Sciences & Related	425	73
Health	47	601
Social Sciences, Gov't Services & Religion	121	145
Education	111	328
Arts, Culture, Recreation & Sport	48	154
Sales & Service	919	1,908
Trades, Transport & Equipment Operators & Related	2,540	185
Primary Industries	734	230
Processing, Mfg. & Utilities	1,064	188

LEVEL OF SCHOOLING

2001 Estimates:

Population 15 years +	19,119
Less than Grade 9	1,533
Grades 9-13 w/o Certif.	4,847
Grade 9-13 with Certif.	3,371
Trade Certif. /Dip.	1,042
Non-Univ. w/o Certif./Dip.	1,172
Non-Univ. with Certif./Dip.	4,295
Univ. w/o Degree	1,332
Univ. w/o Degree/Certif.	700
Univ. with Certif.	632
Univ. with Degree	1,527

AVERAGE HOUSEHOLD EXPENDITURES

2001 Estimates:

Food	$6,630
Shelter	$9,766
Clothing	$2,262
Transportation	$7,957
Health & Personal Care	$2,023
Recr'n, Read'g & Education	$4,100
Taxes & Securities	$15,220
Other	$9,188
Total Expenditures	$57,146

PRIVATE HOUSEHOLDS

2001 Estimates:

Private Households, Total	8,468
Pop. in Private Households	24,077
Average no. per Household	2.8

FAMILIES

2001 Estimates:

Families in Private Households	6,982
Husband-Wife Families	6,363
Lone-Parent Families	619
Aver. No. Persons per Family	3.2
Aver. No. Sons/Daughters at Home	1.3

HOUSING

2001 Estimates:

Occupied Private Dwellings	8,468
Owned	7,051
Rented	1,417
Single-Detached House	7,256
Semi-Detached House	220
Row Houses	200
Apartment, 5 or Fewer Storeys	554
Apartment, Detached Duplex	194
Other Single-Attached	44

VEHICLES

2001 Estimates:

Model Yrs. '81-'96, No.	14,821
% Total	84.80
Model Yrs. '97-'98, No.	1,607
% Total	9.19
'99 Vehicles registered in Model Yr. '99, No.	1,050
% Total	6.01
Total No. '81-'99	17,478

LEGAL MARITAL STATUS

2001 Estimates: (Age 15+)

Single (Never Married)	4,521
Legally Married (Not Separated)	12,086
Legally Married (Separated)	498
Widowed	1,127
Divorced	887

PSYTE CATEGORIES

2001 Estimates	No. of House -holds	% of Total Hhds.	Index
Technocrafts & Bureaucrats	430	5.08	180
Small City Elite	407	4.81	280
Satellite Suburbs	310	3.66	128
Blue Collar Winners	2,209	26.09	1,036
Old Towns' New Fringe	1,911	22.57	577
Rustic Prosperity	1,635	19.31	1,070
Old Leafy Towns	750	8.86	347
Quiet Towns	366	4.32	203
Rod & Rifle	186	2.20	95
Struggling Downtowns	264	3.12	99

FINANCIAL P$YTE

2001 Estimates	No. of House -holds	% of Total Hhds.	Index
Successful Suburbanites	430	5.08	77
Canadian Comfort	2,926	34.55	356
Tractors & Tradelines	3,546	41.88	732
Bills & Wills	750	8.86	107
Rural Family Blues	186	2.20	27
Limited Budgets	366	4.32	139
Towering Debt	264	3.12	40

HOME LANGUAGE

2001 Estimates:		% Total
English	24,094	99.13
Dutch	33	0.14
German	22	0.09
Italian	56	0.23
Serbian	22	0.09
Other Languages	45	0.19
Multiple Responses	33	0.14
Total	24,305	100.00

BUILDING PERMITS

	1999	1998 $000	1997
Value	23,019	24,728	22,264

HOMES BUILT

	1999	1998	1997
No	50	63	135

TAXATION

Income Class:	1997	% Total
Under $5,000	2,600	15.28
$5,000-$10,000	1,850	10.87
$10,000-$15,000	2,150	12.63
$15,000-$20,000	1,610	9.46
$20,000-$25,000	1,300	7.64
$25,000-$30,000	1,190	6.99
$30,000-$40,000	1,990	11.69
$40,000-$50,000	1,380	8.11
$50,000 +	2,970	17.45
Total Returns, No.	17,020	
Total Income, $000	470,001	
Total Taxable Returns	11,680	
Total Tax, $000	86,835	
Average Income, $.	27,615	
Average Tax, $.	7,435	

VITAL STATISTICS

	1997	1996	1995	1994
Births	246	256	239	268
Deaths	146	142	163	147
Natural Increase	100	114	76	121
Marriages	106	133	141	123

Note: Latest available data.

COMMUNITY NEWSPAPER(S)

	Total Circulation
Hagersville: The Haldimand Press	4,040

Hamilton
(Census Metropolitan Area)

POPULATION

July 1, 2001 Estimate 673,661
% Cdn. Total 2.16
% Change, '96 -'01 . . . . 4.80
Avg. Annual Growth Rate, % 0.94
2003 Projected Population 677,581
2006 Projected Population 682,126
2001 Households Estimate 259,644
2003 Projected Households 263,238
2006 Projected Households 268,615

INCOME

% Above/Below National Average . . . . +9
2001 Total Income Estimate . $15,500,470,000
% Cdn. Total 2.36
2001 Average Hhld. Income $59,700
2001 Per Capita $23,000
2003 Projected Total Income . $16,492,590,000
2006 Projected Total Income . $18,111,230,000

RETAIL SALES

% Above/Below National Average . . . . -9
2001 Retail Sales Estimate . . . $5,465,860,000
% Cdn. Total 1.96
2001 per Household $21,100
2001 per Capita $8,100
2001 No. of Establishments 4,436
2003 Projected Retail Sales . $5,894,480,000
2006 Projected Retail Sales . $6,506,110,000

POPULATION

2001 Estimates:
Total 673,661
Male 328,186
Female 345,475

Age Groups	Male	Female
0-4	20,929	19,880
5-9	22,116	21,040
10-14	22,413	21,291
15-19	21,769	20,760
20-24	21,285	20,914
25-29	21,916	22,115
30-34	24,312	24,780
35-39	26,431	27,016
40-44	25,897	26,997
45-49	24,119	25,505
50-54	21,171	22,278
55-59	17,816	18,537
60-64	15,159	16,104
65-69	13,410	15,119
70+	29,443	43,139

DAYTIME POPULATION

2001 Estimates:
Working Population 346,076
At Home Population 327,586
Total 673,662

INCOME

2001 Estimates:
Avg. Household Income $59,699
Avg. Family Income $67,748
Per Capita Income $23,009
Male:
Avg. Employment Income $40,437
Avg. Employment Income
(Full Time) $52,088
Female:
Avg. Employment Income $24,099
Avg. Employment Income
(Full Time) $35,690

DISPOSABLE & DISCRETIONARY INCOME

2001 Estimates:	Per Hhld.
Disposable Income	$48,719
Discretionary Income 1	
(minus Food & Shelter)	$34,478
Discretionary Income 2	
(minus Food, Shelter, & Other	
Expenditures)	$25,597

1999 Estimates:	Per Hhld.
Equity Investments	$84,498
Interest Bearing Investments	$73,063
Total Liquid Assets	$157,561

CREDIT DATA

July 2000:
Pool of Credit $7,321,253,091
Revolving Credit, No. 1,357,506
Fixed Loans, No. 360,584
Avg. Credit Limit, per Person $12,755
Avg. Spent, per Person. $5,637
Satisfactory Ratings,
No. per Person 2.89
Avg. No. of Cards, per Person 1.05

LABOUR FORCE

2001 Estimates:
Male:
In the Labour Force 194,075
Participation Rate. 73.9
Employed 185,291
Unemployed 8,784
Unemployment Rate. 4.5
Not in Labour Force 68,653
Female:
In the Labour Force 167,348
Participation Rate. 59.1
Employed 159,171
Unemployed 8,177
Unemployment Rate. 4.9
Not in Labour Force 115,916

OCCUPATIONS BY MAJOR GROUPS

2001 Estimates:	Male	Female
Management	22,718	10,014
Business, Finance		
& Admin.	18,968	49,067
Natural & Applied		
Sciences & Related	13,901	2,730
Health.	3,470	15,606
Social Sciences,		
Gov't Services & Religion.	3,342	4,547
Education	6,313	9,312
Arts, Culture,		
Recreation & Sport. . . .	3,647	4,375
Sales & Service	39,683	53,432
Trades, Transport		
& Equipment		
Operators & Related . . .	46,332	2,899
Primary Industries	5,161	1,894
Processing, Mfg. &		
Utilities.	25,494	7,918

LEVEL OF SCHOOLING

2001 Estimates:
Population 15 years +. 545,992
Less than Grade 9 52,694
Grades 9-13 w/o Certif. 130,083
Grade 9-13 with Certif. 78,669
Trade Certif. /Dip. 21,034
Non-Univ. w/o Certif./Dip. 37,368
Non-Univ. with Certif./Dip. 107,025
Univ. w/o Degree 47,187
Univ. w/o Degree/Certif. 23,773
Univ. with Certif. 23,414
Univ. with Degree. 71,932

AVERAGE HOUSEHOLD EXPENDITURES

2001 Estimates:
Food $6,527
Shelter $9,995
Clothing $2,327
Transportation $6,821
Health & Personal Care $2,010
Recr'n, Read'g & Education $3,892
Taxes & Securities $15,871
Other. $9,059
Total Expenditures $56,502

PRIVATE HOUSEHOLDS

2001 Estimates:
Private Households, Total. 259,644
Pop. in Private Households 663,211
Average no. per Household 2.6

2001 Estimates:
Families in Private Households 191,147
Husband-Wife Families 164,214
Lone-Parent Families 26,933
Aver. No. Persons per Family. 3.0
Aver. No. Sons/Daughters at Home 1.2

HOUSING

2001 Estimates:
Occupied Private Dwellings. 259,644
Owned 170,288
Rented 89,356
Single-Detached House 154,645
Semi-Detached House. 7,919
Row Houses 23,543
Apartment, 5+ Storeys. 44,819
Owned Apartment, 5+ Storeys 4,072
Apartment, 5 or Fewer Storeys 21,693
Apartment, Detached Duplex 6,008
Other Single-Attached 569
Movable Dwellings 448

Ontario

RADIO STATION DATA

Station	Market	Format	Wkly. Reach%*	Aver. Hrs. Tuned
All Stations			95	24.3
CBL-FM	Toronto	All Info.	5	8.1
CBLA-FM	Toronto	News, Info.	7	14.3
CFMX-FM	Toronto	Classical	5	14.1
CFNY-FM	Toronto	Alternative	11	7.6
CFRB	Toronto	News, Talk	9	11.9
CFTR	Toronto	All News	6	4.0
CFYI	Toronto	Talk	3	4.8
CHAM	Hamilton	Country	7	13.8
CHFI-FM	Toronto	Adult Contemp.	5	5.9
CHML	Hamilton	News, Talk	21	12.4
CHOW-FM	Welland	Country	2	7.6
CHTZ-FM	St. Cath.-Niagara	AOR	6	5.8
CHUM	Toronto	All Oldies	3	7.9
CHUM-FM	Toronto	Adult Contemp.	11	8.0
CIDC-FM	Toronto	Dance	3	3.9
CILQ-FM	Toronto	AOR	11	7.2
CING-FM	Burlington	Contemp. Hit Radio	21	8.6
CISS-FM	Toronto	Top 40	10	6.6
CJCL	Toronto	Sports	5	7.1
CJEZ-FM	Toronto	Adult Contemp.	2	9.5
CJRT-FM	Toronto	Classical, Folk, Jazz, Blues	4	6.6
CJXY-FM	Hamilton	AOR	16	10.4
CKFM-FM	Toronto	Adult Contemp.	12	7.3
CKLH-FM	Hamilton	Adult Contemp.	24	12.7
CKOC	Hamilton	Oldies	10	9.4
CKTB	St. Cath.-Niagara	News, Talk, Sports	1	11.2

BBM Spring 2000 Radio Reach Survey;area coverage.
*Mon-Sun 5a.m - 1a.m , All Persons 12+

TV STATION DATA

Station	Market	Network Affiliation	Wkly. Reach%*	Aver. Hrs. Tuned
All Stations			98	22.9
A & E	n.a.	Ind.	26	5.3
CBLT	Toronto	CBC	44	2.1
CFMT	Toronto	Ind.	35	2.0
CFPL	London	Ind.	5	3.0
CFTO	Toronto	CTV	55	3.1
CHCH	Toronto/Hamilton	Ind.	56	3.6
CICO-E	n.a.	n.a.	16	1.9
CIII	n.a.	Global	58	3.5
CITY	Toronto	Ind.	43	2.5
CKCO	Kitchener	CTV	42	2.4
CKVR	Barrie	Ind.	19	1.3
CNN	n.a.	Ind.	13	2.0
COMEDY	n.a.	Ind.	11	3.9
CTS	Toronto/Hamilton	Ind.	11	2.2
HISTTV	n.a.	Ind.	5	3.1
M PIX	n.a.	Ind.	5	2.8
NEWSWD	n.a.	CBC	11	1.7
PRIME	n.a.	Ind.	10	3.0
SNET	n.a.	CTV	8	1.7
TLC	n.a.	Ind.	20	1.3
TMN	Toronto	Ind.	8	3.4
TNN	Nashville TN	Ind.	8	1.8
TSN	n.a.	Ind.	19	6.6
VCR	n.a.	n.a.	37	4.0
WGN	Chicago IL	WB	4	3.2
WGRZ	Buffalo NY	NBC	13	1.6
WIVB	Buffalo NY	CBS	22	2.0
WJET	Erie PA	ABC	2	5.5
WKBW	Buffalo NY	ABC	24	2.0
WNED	Buffalo NY	PBS	22	2.2
WTBS	Atlanta GA	Ind.	24	3.1
WUTV	Buffalo NY	FOX	33	2.9
YTV	n.a.	Ind.	14	2.0

BBM Spring 2000 TV Reach Survey;CMA coverage.
*Mon-Sun 6a.m - 2a.m , All Persons 2 +

Ontario

Hamilton
(Census Metropolitan Area)
(Cont'd)

VEHICLES

2001 Estimates:
Model Yrs. '81-'96, No.	314,469
% Total	79.67
Model Yrs. '97-'98, No.	48,079
% Total	12.18
'99 Vehicles registered in Model Yr. '99, No.	32,179
% Total	8.15
Total No. '81-'99	394,727

LEGAL MARITAL STATUS

2001 Estimates: (Age 15+)
Single (Never Married)	151,028
Legally Married (Not Separated)	303,878
Legally Married (Separated)	16,739
Widowed	37,313
Divorced	37,034

PSYTE CATEGORIES

2001 Estimates	No. of House-holds	% of Total Hhds.	Index
Canadian Establishment	92	0.04	21
The Affluentials	712	0.27	43
Urban Gentry	4,450	1.71	95
Suburban Executives	7,046	2.71	189
Mortgaged in Suburbia	4,539	1.75	126
Technocrafts & Bureaucrats	6,377	2.46	87
Boomers & Teens	13,964	5.38	300
Stable Suburban Families	8,194	3.16	242
Small City Elite	474	0.18	11
Old Bungalow Burbs	12,905	4.97	300
Suburban Nesters	7,932	3.05	191
Brie & Chablis	953	0.37	41
Aging Erudites	7,296	2.81	186
Satellite Suburbs	21,019	8.10	282
Kindergarten Boom	5,523	2.13	81
Blue Collar Winners	16,158	6.22	247
Old Towns' New Fringe	584	0.22	6
Rustic Prosperity	34	0.01	1
Europa	740	0.29	23
High Rise Melting Pot	7,200	2.77	185
Conservative Homebodies	48,654	18.74	520
High Rise Sunsets	9,411	3.62	253
Young Urban Professionals	2,061	0.79	42
Young Urban Mix	4,134	1.59	75
Young Urban Intelligentsia	1,183	0.46	30
University Enclaves	9,962	3.84	188
Young City Singles	7,524	2.90	126
Urban Bohemia	709	0.27	23
Old Leafy Towns	483	0.19	7
Town Renters	4,889	1.88	218
Nesters & Young Homesteaders	394	0.15	7
Struggling Downtowns	31,283	12.05	383
Aged Pensioners	5,388	2.08	156
Big City Stress	3,468	1.34	118
Old Grey Towers	2,166	0.83	151

FINANCIAL P$YTE

2001 Estimates	No. of House-holds	% of Total Hhds.	Index
Platinum Estates	804	0.31	38
Four Star Investors	25,460	9.81	195
Successful Suburbanites	19,110	7.36	111
Canadian Comfort	45,583	17.56	181
Urban Heights	10,310	3.97	92
Miners & Credit-Liners	12,905	4.97	157
Mortgages & Minivans	5,523	2.13	32
Dollars & Sense	740	0.29	11
Tractors & Tradelines	618	0.24	4
Young Urban Bills & Wills	53,271	20.52	248
Revolving Renters	9,805	3.78	82
Struggle	11,854	4.57	96
Towering Debt	50,896	19.60	251
NSF	3,468	1.34	38
Senior Survivors	7,554	2.91	154

HOME LANGUAGE

2001 Estimates:		% Total
English	598,582	88.86
French	2,714	0.40
Arabic	2,414	0.36
Chinese	4,428	0.66
Croatian	3,398	0.50
Dutch	532	0.08
German	1,509	0.22
Greek	1,234	0.18
Hindi	387	0.06
Hungarian	1,444	0.21
Italian	10,272	1.52
Khmer (Cambodian)	881	0.13
Korean	665	0.10
Lao	402	0.06
Lithuanian	457	0.07
Persian (Farsi)	664	0.10
Polish	6,341	0.94
Portuguese	4,934	0.73
Punjabi	2,499	0.37
Romanian	832	0.12
Serbian	2,511	0.37
Serbo-Croatian	380	0.06
Slovenian	453	0.07
Spanish	3,143	0.47
Tagalog (Pilipino)	1,222	0.18
Ukrainian	1,310	0.19
Urdu	682	0.10
Vietnamese	2,066	0.31
Other Languages	4,364	0.65
Multiple Responses	12,941	1.92
Total	673,661	100.00

BUILDING PERMITS

	1999	1998 $000	1997
Value	744,611	768,054	613,775

HOMES BUILT

	1999	1998	1997
No	3,451	3,222	3,409

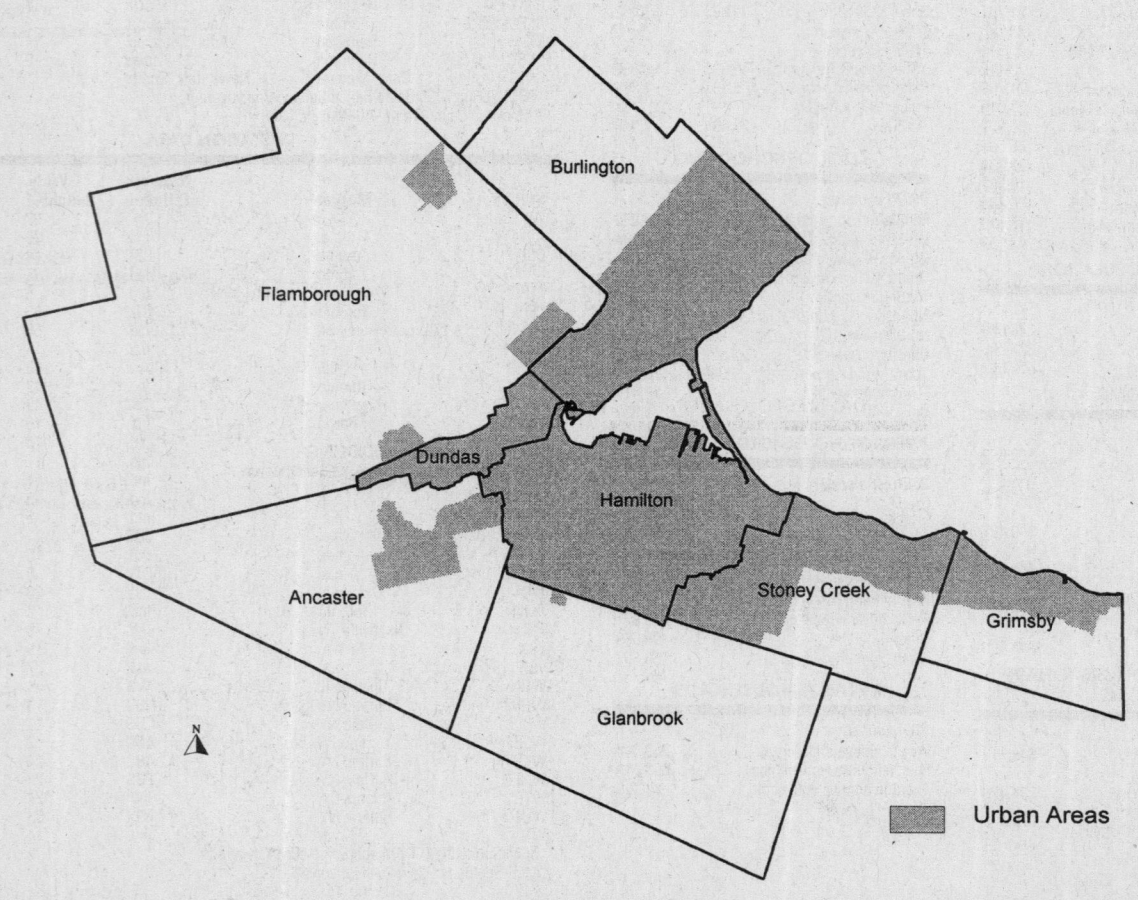

Urban Areas

Hamilton
(Census Metropolitan Area)
(Cont'd)

TAXATION

Income Class:	1997	% Total
Under $5,000	52,650	11.63
$5,000-$10,000	50,060	11.06
$10,000-$15,000	60,920	13.46
$15,000-$20,000	43,940	9.71
$20,000-$25,000	38,000	8.39
$25,000-$30,000	34,820	7.69
$30,000-$40,000	55,780	12.32
$40,000-$50,000	38,570	8.52
$50,000 +	78,040	17.24
Total Returns, No.	452,750	
Total Income, $000	13,897,756	
Total Taxable Returns	325,890	
Total Tax, $000	2,819,881	
Average Income, $	30,696	
Average Tax, $	8,653	

VITAL STATISTICS

	1997	1996	1995	1994
Births	7,528	7,752	7,959	8,217
Deaths	5,064	4,918	4,962	5,088
Natural Increase	2,464	2,834	2,997	3,129
Marriages	3,542	3,697	3,702	3,606

Note: Latest available data.

DAILY NEWSPAPER(S)

	Circulation Average Paid
The Hamilton Spectator	
Sat.	127,539
Mon-Fri	108,437

COMMUNITY NEWSPAPER(S)

	Total Circulation
Ancaster: Ancaster News	9,594
Burlington: Burlington Post	
Wed.	47,613
Fri	45,925
Sun	45,830
Burlington: Burlington News	n.a.
Dundas: Dundas Star	11,263
Dundas, Ancaster: Dundas-Ancaster Recorder	13,000
Grimsby: Grimsby Independent	n.a.
Grimsby: The Grimsby Lincoln News	18,281
Hamilton: The Hamilton Examiner	n.a.
Hamilton: Hamilton News, Mountain Edition	46,316
Hamilton: Hamilton Recorder	20,000
Hamilton, Burlington: L'Information	n.a.
Stoney Creek: Stoney Creek News	23,394
Waterdown: Waterdown Flamborough Review Wed/Fri	10,986
Waterdown: Flamborough Post Wed/Fri	11,000

Ancaster
(Town)
Hamilton CMA

In Hamilton-Wentworth Regional Municipality.

POPULATION

July 1, 2001 Estimate	25,685
% Cdn. Total	0.08
% Change, '96 -'01	6.62
Avg. Annual Growth Rate, %	1.29
2003 Projected Population	26,053
2006 Projected Population	26,550
2001 Households Estimate	8,416
2003 Projected Households	8,628
2006 Projected Households	8,939

INCOME

% Above/Below National Average	+51
2001 Total Income Estimate	$817,880,000
% Cdn. Total	0.12
2001 Average Hhld. Income	$97,200
2001 Per Capita	$31,800
2003 Projected Total Income	$878,250,000
2006 Projected Total Income	$975,770,000

RETAIL SALES

% Above/Below National Average	-26
2001 Retail Sales Estimate	$170,250,000
% Cdn. Total	0.06
2001 per Household	$20,200
2001 per Capita	$6,600
2001 No. of Establishments	154
2003 Projected Retail Sales	$184,400,000
2006 Projected Retail Sales	$205,820,000

POPULATION

2001 Estimates:

Total		25,685
Male		12,727
Female		12,958
Age Groups	Male	Female
0-4	639	628
5-9	852	826
10-14	1,047	1,001
15-19	1,061	1,002
20-24	949	861
25-29	733	671
30-34	626	632
35-39	751	850
40-44	955	1,104
45-49	1,080	1,148
50-54	1,009	1,011
55-59	833	789
60-64	646	614
65-69	508	527
70+	1,038	1,294

DAYTIME POPULATION

2001 Estimates:

Working Population	7,652
At Home Population	11,146
Total	18,798

INCOME

2001 Estimates:

Avg. Household Income	$97,181
Avg. Family Income	$101,630
Per Capita Income	$31,843
Male:	
Avg. Employment Income	$55,886
Avg. Employment Income (Full Time)	$71,230
Female:	
Avg. Employment Income	$30,316
Avg. Employment Income (Full Time)	$45,283

DISPOSABLE & DISCRETIONARY INCOME

2001 Estimates:	Per Hhld.
Disposable Income	$77,284
Discretionary Income 1 (minus Food & Shelter)	$58,524
Discretionary Income 2 (minus Food, Shelter, & Other Expenditures)	$45,654

LIQUID ASSETS

1999 Estimates:	Per Hhld.
Equity Investments	$202,099
Interest Bearing Investments	$129,847
Total Liquid Assets	$331,946

CREDIT DATA

July 2000:	
Pool of Credit	$357,178,998
Revolving Credit, No.	56,869
Fixed Loans, No.	13,117
Avg. Credit Limit, per Person	$17,014
Avg. Spent, per Person	$6,960
Satisfactory Ratings, No. per Person	3.23
Avg. No. of Cards, per Person	1.26

LABOUR FORCE

2001 Estimates:

Male:	
In the Labour Force	7,954
Participation Rate	78.1
Employed	7,817
Unemployed	137
Unemployment Rate	1.7
Not in Labour Force	2,235
Female:	
In the Labour Force	6,747
Participation Rate	64.2
Employed	6,587
Unemployed	160
Unemployment Rate	2.4
Not in Labour Force	3,756

OCCUPATIONS BY MAJOR GROUPS

2001 Estimates:	Male	Female
Management	1,284	457
Business, Finance & Admin.	876	1,949
Natural & Applied Sciences & Related.	579	112
Health.	451	895
Social Sciences, Gov't Services & Religion	243	260
Education	638	764
Arts, Culture, Recreation & Sport.	109	240
Sales & Service	1,568	1,744
Trades, Transport & Equipment Operators & Related.	1,250	90
Primary Industries	415	69
Processing, Mfg. & Utilities.	458	47

LEVEL OF SCHOOLING

2001 Estimates:

Population 15 years +	20,692
Less than Grade 9	753
Grades 9-13 w/o Certif.	3,858
Grade 9-13 with Certif.	2,494
Trade Certif. /Dip.	824
Non-Univ. w/o Certif./Dip.	1,167
Non-Univ. with Certif./Dip.	4,132
Univ. w/o Degree.	2,148
Univ. w/o Degree/Certif.	1,073
Univ. with Certif.	1,075
Univ. with Degree	5,316

Ontario

AVERAGE HOUSEHOLD EXPENDITURES

2001 Estimates:

Food	$8,433
Shelter	$13,755
Clothing	$3,478
Transportation	$10,279
Health & Personal Care.	*$2,755
Recr'n, Read'g & Education.	$6,014
Taxes & Securities.	$29,506
Other	$12,099
Total Expenditures.	$86,319

PRIVATE HOUSEHOLDS

2001 Estimates:

Private Households, Total	8,416
Pop. in Private Households	25,396
Average no. per Household.	3.0

FAMILIES

2001 Estimates:

Families in Private Households	7,384
Husband-Wife Families.	6,864
Lone-Parent Families.	520
Aver. No. Persons per Family	3.3
Aver. No. Sons/Daughters at Home.	1.4

HOUSING

2001 Estimates:

Occupied Private Dwellings	8,416
Owned	7,718
Rented	698
Single-Detached House.	7,564
Semi-Detached House.	90
Row Houses.	419
Apartment, 5 or Fewer Storeys	214
Apartment, Detached Duplex	84
Other Single-Attached.	45

VEHICLES

2001 Estimates:

Model Yrs. '81-'96, No.	13,056
% Total	76.55
Model Yrs. '97-'98, No.	2,412
% Total	14.14
'99 Vehicles registered in Model Yr. '99, No.	1,588
% Total	9.31
Total No. '81-'99	17,056

LEGAL MARITAL STATUS

2001 Estimates: (Age 15+)

Single (Never Married)	4,850
Legally Married (Not Separated).	13,792
Legally Married (Separated)	326
Widowed.	1,037
Divorced.	687

Ontario

Ancaster
(Town)
Hamilton CMA
(Cont'd)

PSYTE CATEGORIES

2001 Estimates	No. of House-holds	% of Total Hhds.	Index
Urban Gentry	524	6.23	346
Suburban Executives	2,595	30.83	2,151
Mortgaged in Suburbia	196	2.33	168
Boomers & Teens	3,057	36.32	2,026
Suburban Nesters	66	0.78	49
Aging Erudites	857	10.18	675
Blue Collar Winners	1,112	13.21	525

FINANCIAL PSYTE

2001 Estimates	No. of House-holds	% of Total Hhds.	Index
Four Star Investors	6,176	73.38	1,461
Successful Suburbanites	196	2.33	35
Canadian Comfort	1,178	14.00	144
Urban Heights	857	10.18	237

HOME LANGUAGE

2001 Estimates:		% Total
English	24,257	94.44
French	30	0.12
Arabic	26	0.10
Armenian	22	0.09
Chinese	212	0.83
Dutch	106	0.41
German	89	0.35
Greek	54	0.21
Hindi	39	0.15
Hungarian	37	0.14
Italian	134	0.52
Latvian (Lettish)	20	0.08
Malayalam	22	0.09
Persian (Farsi)	16	0.06
Polish	23	0.09
Portuguese	27	0.11
Punjabi	64	0.25
Romanian	40	0.16
Russian	17	0.07
Serbian	16	0.06
Tamil	22	0.09
Ukrainian	19	0.07
Urdu	22	0.09
Other Languages	67	0.26
Multiple Responses	304	1.18
Total	25,685	100.00

BUILDING PERMITS

	1999	1998	1997
		$000	
Value	60,256	65,743	49,192

HOMES BUILT

	1999	1998	1997
No	319	350	283

TAXATION

Income Class:	1997	% Total
Under $5,000	1,900	11.30
$5,000-$10,000	1,560	9.28
$10,000-$15,000	1,500	8.92
$15,000-$20,000	1,170	6.96
$20,000-$25,000	1,080	6.42
$25,000-$30,000	1,100	6.54
$30,000-$40,000	1,910	11.36
$40,000-$50,000	1,590	9.46
$50,000 +	5,000	29.74
Total Returns, No.	16,810	
Total Income, $000	756,612	
Total Taxable Returns	13,010	
Total Tax, $000	191,402	
Average Income, $	45,010	
Average Tax, $	14,712	

VITAL STATISTICS

	1997	1996	1995	1994
Births	171	202	188	191
Deaths	119	125	107	121
Natural Increase	52	77	81	70
Marriages	263	250	260	209

Note: Latest available data.

MEDIA INFO
see Hamilton, CMA

Burlington
(City)
Hamilton CMA
In Halton Regional Municipality.

POPULATION

July 1, 2001 Estimate	149,195
% Cdn. Total	0.48
% Change, '96 -'01	5.71
Avg. Annual Growth Rate, %.	1.12
2003 Projected Population	150,826
2006 Projected Population	153,145
2001 Households Estimate	56,247
2003 Projected Households	57,149
2006 Projected Households	58,614

INCOME

% Above/Below National Average	+36
2001 Total Income Estimate	$4,288,770,000
% Cdn. Total	0.65
2001 Average Hhld. Income	$76,200
2001 Per Capita	$28,700
2003 Projected Total Income	$4,570,760,000
2006 Projected Total Income	$5,044,680,000

RETAIL SALES

% Above/Below National Average	+18
2001 Retail Sales Estimate	$1,572,060,000
% Cdn. Total	0.56
2001 per Household	$27,900
2001 per Capita	$10,500
2001 No. of Establishments	1,076
2003 Projected Retail Sales	$1,715,030,000
2006 Projected Retail Sales	$1,925,000,000

POPULATION

2001 Estimates:		
Total		149,195
Male		72,453
Female		76,742
Age Groups	Male	Female
0-4	4,607	4,350
5-9	4,856	4,659
10-14	4,884	4,715
15-19	4,754	4,606
20-24	4,666	4,472
25-29	4,710	4,660
30-34	5,187	5,381
35-39	5,719	6,038
40-44	5,649	6,080
45-49	5,409	5,908
50-54	5,012	5,409
55-59	4,310	4,571
60-64	3,581	3,825
65-69	3,062	3,361
70+	6,047	8,707

DAYTIME POPULATION

2001 Estimates:	
Working Population	101,848
At Home Population	63,635
Total	165,483

INCOME

2001 Estimates:	
Avg. Household Income	$76,249
Avg. Family Income	$83,943
Per Capita Income	$28,746
Male:	
Avg. Employment Income	$48,390
Avg. Employment Income (Full Time)	$60,942
Female:	
Avg. Employment Income	$27,113
Avg. Employment Income (Full Time)	$39,689

DISPOSABLE & DISCRETIONARY INCOME

2001 Estimates:	Per Hhld.
Disposable Income	$61,223
Discretionary Income 1 (minus Food & Shelter)	$44,432
Discretionary Income 2 (minus Food, Shelter, & Other Expenditures)	$33,771

LIQUID ASSETS

1999 Estimates:	Per Hhld.
Equity Investments	$127,431
Interest Bearing Investments	$97,173
Total Liquid Assets	$224,604

CREDIT DATA

July 2000:	
Pool of Credit	$2,063,125,938
Revolving Credit, No.	356,502
Fixed Loans, No.	97,272
Avg. Credit Limit, per Person	$15,741
Avg. Spent, per Person	$6,804
Satisfactory Ratings, No. per Person	3.34
Avg. No. of Cards, per Person	1.22

LABOUR FORCE

2001 Estimates:	
Male:	
In the Labour Force	46,545
Participation Rate	80.1
Employed	45,570
Unemployed	975
Unemployment Rate	2.1
Not in Labour Force	11,561
Female:	
In the Labour Force	41,163
Participation Rate	65.3
Employed	40,117
Unemployed	1,046
Unemployment Rate	2.5
Not in Labour Force	21,855

OCCUPATIONS BY MAJOR GROUPS

2001 Estimates:	Male	Female
Management	9,149	3,196
Business, Finance & Admin.	5,575	13,527
Natural & Applied Sciences & Related	4,255	758
Health	761	3,172
Social Sciences, Gov't Services & Religion	909	1,337
Education	1,300	2,665
Arts, Culture, Recreation & Sport	1,040	1,338
Sales & Service	10,382	12,520
Trades, Transport & Equipment Operators & Related	7,839	576
Primary Industries	655	305
Processing, Mfg. & Utilities	4,168	1,141

LEVEL OF SCHOOLING

2001 Estimates:	
Population 15 years +	121,124
Less than Grade 9	5,212
Grades 9-13 w/o Certif.	24,528
Grade 9-13 with Certif.	17,258
Trade Certif. /Dip.	4,249
Non-Univ. w/o Certif./Dip.	8,053
Non-Univ. with Certif./Dip.	26,408
Univ. w/o Degree	13,384
Univ. w/o Degree/Certif.	6,526
Univ. with Certif.	6,858
Univ. with Degree	22,032

Burlington
(City)
Hamilton CMA
(Cont'd)

AVERAGE HOUSEHOLD EXPENDITURES

2001 Estimates:

Food	$7,750
Shelter	$11,924
Clothing	$2,896
Transportation	$8,231
Health & Personal Care	$2,434
Recr'n, Read'g & Education	$4,812
Taxes & Securities	$20,989
Other	$10,764
Total Expenditures	$69,800

PRIVATE HOUSEHOLDS

2001 Estimates:

Private Households, Total	56,247
Pop. in Private Households	147,540
Average no. per Household	2.6

FAMILIES

2001 Estimates:

Families in Private Households	44,131
Husband-Wife Families	39,097
Lone-Parent Families	5,034
Aver. No. Persons per Family	3.0
Aver. No. Sons/Daughters at Home	1.1

HOUSING

2001 Estimates:

Occupied Private Dwellings	56,247
Owned	40,092
Rented	16,155
Single-Detached House	32,781
Semi-Detached House	1,644
Row Houses	7,814
Apartment, 5+ Storeys	10,012
Owned Apartment, 5+ Storeys	1,889
Apartment, 5 or Fewer Storeys	3,342
Apartment, Detached Duplex	489
Other Single-Attached	154
Movable Dwellings	11

VEHICLES

2001 Estimates:

Model Yrs. '81-'96, No.	75,013
% Total	73.23
Model Yrs. '97-'98, No.	16,576
% Total	16.18
'99 Vehicles registered in Model Yr. '99, No.	10,849
% Total	10.59
Total No. '81-'99	102,438

LEGAL MARITAL STATUS

2001 Estimates: (Age 15+)

Single (Never Married)	30,596
Legally Married (Not Separated)	72,331
Legally Married (Separated)	3,851
Widowed	6,941
Divorced	7,405

PSYTE CATEGORIES

2001 Estimates	No. of House-holds	% of Total Hhds.	Index
Canadian Establishment	92	0.16	98
The Affluentials	391	0.70	109
Urban Gentry	2,168	3.85	214
Suburban Executives	3,724	6.62	462
Mortgaged in Suburbia	1,601	2.85	205
Technocrafts & Bureaucrats	4,995	8.88	316
Boomers & Teens	5,122	9.11	508
Stable Suburban Families	5,577	9.92	761
Old Bungalow Burbs	2,069	3.68	222
Suburban Nesters	4,757	8.46	528
Brie & Chablis	910	1.62	181
Aging Erudites	2,115	3.76	249
Satellite Suburbs	3,792	6.74	235
Kindergarten Boom	476	0.85	32
High Rise Melting Pot	2,580	4.59	306
Conservative Homebodies	6,729	11.96	332

	No. of House-holds	% of Total Hhds.	Index
High Rise Sunsets	2,441	4.34	303
Young Urban Mix	3,012	5.35	253
University Enclaves	1,470	2.61	128
Young City Singles	726	1.29	56
Town Renters	132	0.23	27
Aged Pensioners	669	1.19	89
Old Grey Towers	446	0.79	143

FINANCIAL P$YTE

2001 Estimates	No. of House-holds	% of Total Hhds.	Index
Platinum Estates	483	0.86	107
Four Star Investors	11,014	19.58	390
Successful Suburbanites	12,173	21.64	326
Canadian Comfort	8,549	15.20	156
Urban Heights	3,025	5.38	125
Miners & Credit-Liners	2,069	3.68	116
Mortgages & Minivans	476	0.85	13
Bills & Wills	9,741	17.32	209
Revolving Renters	2,441	4.34	94
Young Urban Struggle	1,470	2.61	55
Towering Debt	3,438	6.11	78
Senior Survivors	1,115	1.98	105

HOME LANGUAGE

2001 Estimates:		% Total
English	141,337	94.73
French	1,029	0.69
Arabic	269	0.18
Chinese	461	0.31
Croatian	218	0.15
Dutch	130	0.09
German	301	0.20
Greek	99	0.07
Hungarian	261	0.17
Italian	236	0.16
Korean	106	0.07
Polish	1,054	0.71
Portuguese	289	0.19
Punjabi	473	0.32
Serbian	106	0.07
Spanish	159	0.11
Tagalog (Pilipino)	89	0.06
Ukrainian	182	0.12
Other Languages	842	0.56
Multiple Responses	1,554	1.04
Total	149,195	100.00

BUILDING PERMITS

	1999	1998 $000	1997
Value	371,126	306,334	233,984

HOMES BUILT

	1999	1998	1997
No	1,425	1,262	1,450

TAXATION

Income Class:	1997	% Total
Under $5,000	10,100	9.92
$5,000-$10,000	9,800	9.62
$10,000-$15,000	10,480	10.29
$15,000-$20,000	8,310	8.16
$20,000-$25,000	7,760	7.62
$25,000-$30,000	7,510	7.37
$30,000-$40,000	13,260	13.02
$40,000-$50,000	9,830	9.65
$50,000 +	24,810	24.36
Total Returns, No.	101,860	
Total Income, $000	3,905,526	
Total Taxable Returns	80,090	
Total Tax, $000	901,991	
Average Income, $	38,342	
Average Tax, $	11,262	

VITAL STATISTICS

	1997	1996	1995	1994
Births	1,605	1,687	1,711	1,749
Deaths	852	859	851	861
Natural Increase	753	828	860	888
Marriages	600	580	597	590

Note: Latest available data.

MEDIA INFO

see Hamilton, CMA

Dundas
(Town)
Hamilton CMA

In Hamilton-Wentworth Regional Municipality.

POPULATION

July 1, 2001 Estimate	25,259
% Cdn. Total	0.08
% Change, '96 -'01	6.12
Avg. Annual Growth Rate, %	1.20
2003 Projected Population	25,546
2006 Projected Population	25,918
2001 Households Estimate	9,710
2003 Projected Households	9,928
2006 Projected Households	10,238

INCOME

% Above/Below National Average	+32
2001 Total Income Estimate	$701,470,000
% Cdn. Total	0.11
2001 Average Hhld. Income	$72,200
2001 Per Capita	$27,800
2003 Projected Total Income	$752,230,000
2006 Projected Total Income	$833,500,000

RETAIL SALES

% Above/Below National Average	-28
2001 Retail Sales Estimate	$162,960,000
% Cdn. Total	0.06
2001 per Household	$16,800
2001 per Capita	$6,500
2001 No. of Establishments	158
2003 Projected Retail Sales	$174,020,000
2006 Projected Retail Sales	$191,840,000

POPULATION

2001 Estimates:

Total	25,259
Male	11,920
Female	13,339

Age Groups	Male	Female
0-4	709	683
5-9	779	752
10-14	839	814
15-19	844	811
20-24	773	754
25-29	746	732
30-34	804	817
35-39	884	959
40-44	925	1,044
45-49	923	1,039
50-54	833	921
55-59	667	734
60-64	545	596
65-69	478	566
70+	1,171	2,117

DAYTIME POPULATION

2001 Estimates:

Working Population	10,356
At Home Population	11,755
Total	22,111

INCOME

2001 Estimates:

Avg. Household Income	$72,242
Avg. Family Income	$81,684
Per Capita Income	$27,771
Male:	
Avg. Employment Income	$48,531
Avg. Employment Income (Full Time)	$61,594
Female:	
Avg. Employment Income	$27,034
Avg. Employment Income (Full Time)	$37,860

Ontario

DISPOSABLE & DISCRETIONARY INCOME

2001 Estimates:	Per Hhld.
Disposable Income	$58,525
Discretionary Income 1 (minus Food & Shelter)	$42,806
Discretionary Income 2 (minus Food, Shelter, & Other Expenditures)	$32,451

LIQUID ASSETS

1999 Estimates:	Per Hhld.
Equity Investments	$117,156
Interest Bearing Investments	$91,168
Total Liquid Assets	$208,324

CREDIT DATA

July 2000:	
Pool of Credit	$312,562,024
Revolving Credit, No.	53,623
Fixed Loans, No.	12,129
Avg. Credit Limit, per Person	$14,825
Avg. Spent, per Person	$6,109
Satisfactory Ratings, No. per Person	3.03
Avg. No. of Cards, per Person	1.19

LABOUR FORCE

2001 Estimates:

Male:	
In the Labour Force	7,358
Participation Rate	76.7
Employed	7,211
Unemployed	147
Unemployment Rate	2.0
Not in Labour Force	2,235
Female:	
In the Labour Force	6,493
Participation Rate	58.5
Employed	6,232
Unemployed	261
Unemployment Rate	4.0
Not in Labour Force	4,597

OCCUPATIONS BY MAJOR GROUPS

2001 Estimates:	Male	Female
Management	869	495
Business, Finance & Admin.	727	1,905
Natural & Applied Sciences & Related	714	201
Health	314	811
Social Sciences, Gov't Services & Religion	182	256
Education	565	477
Arts, Culture, Recreation & Sport	208	233
Sales & Service	1,514	1,693
Trades, Transport & Equipment Operators & Related	1,492	114
Primary Industries	178	72
Processing, Mfg. & Utilities	525	66

Ontario

Dundas
(Town)
Hamilton CMA
(Cont'd)

LEVEL OF SCHOOLING

2001 Estimates:
Population 15 years + ...20,683
Less than Grade 9. 933
Grades 9-13 w/o Certif. 4,047
Grade 9-13 with Certif. 2,355
Trade Certif./Dip. 640
Non-Univ. w/o Certif./Dip. 1,375
Non-Univ. with Certif./Dip. 4,357
Univ. w/o Degree 2,302
 Univ. w/o Degree/Certif. 1,084
 Univ. with Certif. 1,218
Univ. with Degree. 4,674

AVERAGE HOUSEHOLD EXPENDITURES

2001 Estimates:
Food $7,329
Shelter $11,169
Clothing. $2,679
Transportation. $8,048
Health & Personal Care $2,366
Recr'n, Read'g & Education $4,629
Taxes & Securities $20,309
Other $10,562
Total Expenditures $67,091

PRIVATE HOUSEHOLDS

2001 Estimates:
Private Households, Total. 9,710
Pop. in Private Households. . , ...24,290
Average no. per Household 2.5

FAMILIES

2001 Estimates:
Families in Private Households 7,288
Husband-Wife Families 6,405
Lone-Parent Families 883
Aver. No. Persons per Family 2.9
Aver. No. Sons/Daughters
 at Home 1.1

HOUSING

2001 Estimates:
Occupied Private Dwellings 9,710
 Owned. 7,000
 Rented. 2,710
Single-Detached House 6,218
Semi-Detached House 275
Row Houses 837
Apartment, 5+ Storeys 1,244
 Owned Apartment, 5+ Storeys 84
Apartment, 5 or Fewer Storeys 956
Apartment, Detached Duplex. 180

VEHICLES

2001 Estimates:
Model Yrs. '81-'96, No. 11,804
 % Total 80.23
Model Yrs. '97-'98, No. 1,823
 % Total 12.39
'99 Vehicles registered in
 Model Yr. '99, No. 1,085
 % Total 7.37
Total No. '81-'99. 14,712

LEGAL MARITAL STATUS

2001 Estimates: (Age 15+)
Single (Never Married). 5,342
Legally Married
 (Not Separated) 11,691
Legally Married (Separated) 601
Widowed 1,750
Divorced 1,299

PSYTE CATEGORIES

2001 Estimates	No. of House-holds	% of Total Hhds.	Index
Suburban			
Executives.	521	5.37	374
Mortgaged in			
Suburbia	202	2.08	150
Boomers & Teens.	1,820	18.74	1,046
Stable Suburban			
Families.	797	8.21	630
Small City Elite	474	4.88	285
Suburban Nesters	481	4.95	309
Aging Erudites	1,644	16.93	1,122
Blue Collar			
Winners.	183	1.88	75
Conservative			
Homebodies	1,951	20.09	557
High Rise Sunsets	414	4.26	298
University			
Enclaves	764	7.87	386
Town Renters	206	2.12	245

FINANCIAL P$YTE

2001 Estimates	No. of House-holds	% of Total Hhds.	Index
Four Star			
Investors	2,341	24.11	480
Successful			
Suburbanites.	999	10.29	155
Canadian Comfort	1,138	11.72	121
Urban Heights.	1,644	16.93	394
Bills & Wills	1,951	20.09	243
Revolving Renters.	414	4.26	93
Young Urban			
Struggle.	764	7.87	166
Towering Debt	206	2.12	27

HOME LANGUAGE

2001 Estimates:		% Total
English	24,077	95.32
French	.75	0.30
Arabic	.16	0.06
Chinese.	123	0.49
Croatian	.24	0.10
Dutch	.28	0.11
German	.60	0.24
Hebrew	.28	0.11
Hindi	.24	0.10
Hungarian	104	0.41
Korean	.16	0.06
Macedonian	.17	0.07
Malayalam	.24	0.10
Persian (Farsi).	.61	0.24
Polish	.79	0.31
Punjabi	.50	0.20
Russian	.35	0.14
Serbian	.16	0.06
Spanish.	.24	0.10
Other Languages	121	0.48
Multiple Responses	.257	1.02
Total	25,259	100.00

BUILDING PERMITS

	1999	1998 $000	1997
Value	16,824	19,625	20,137

HOMES BUILT

	1999	1998	1997
No.	82	141	179

TAXATION

Income Class:	1997	% Total
Under $5,000	2,210	10.45
$5,000-$10,000	1,940	9.18
$10,000-$15,000	2,400	11.35
$15,000-$20,000	1,810	8.56
$20,000-$25,000	1,670	7.90
$25,000-$30,000	1,600	7.57
$30,000-$40,000	2,810	13.29
$40,000-$50,000	1,950	9.22
$50,000 + ...	4,750	22.47
Total Returns, No.	21,140	
Total Income, $000.	756,762	
Total Taxable		
Returns.	16,190	
Total Tax, $000.	165,660	
Average Income, $	35,798	
Average Tax, $	10,232	

VITAL STATISTICS

	1997	1996	1995	1994
Births	310	306	251	280
Deaths	320	328	312	290
Natural				
Increase	-10	-22	-61	-10
Marriages. . .	96	111	130	133

Note: Latest available data.

MEDIA INFO
see Hamilton, CMA

Flamborough
(Town)
Hamilton CMA

In Hamilton-Wentworth Regional Municipality.

POPULATION

July 1, 2001 Estimate	39,936
% Cdn. Total	0.13
% Change, '96 -'01	13.99
Avg. Annual Growth Rate, %	2.65
2003 Projected Population	41,945
2006 Projected Population	44,851
2001 Households Estimate	13,482
2003 Projected Households	14,305
2006 Projected Households	15,547

INCOME

% Above/Below National Average	+24
2001 Total Income Estimate	$1,044,640,000
% Cdn. Total	0.16
2001 Average Hhld. Income	$77,500
2001 Per Capita	$26,200
2003 Projected Total Income	$1,171,010,000
2006 Projected Total Income	$1,383,420,000

RETAIL SALES

% Above/Below National Average	-55
2001 Retail Sales Estimate	$159,900,000
% Cdn. Total	0.06
2001 per Household	$11,900
2001 per Capita	$4,000
2001 No. of Establishments	286
2003 Projected Retail Sales	$179,300,000
2006 Projected Retail Sales	$208,930,000

POPULATION

2001 Estimates:

Total		39,936
Male		20,138
Female		19,798

Age Groups	Male	Female
0-4	1,285	1,189
5-9	1,512	1,354
10-14	1,614	1,478
15-19	1,511	1,414
20-24	1,300	1,243
25-29	1,205	1,218
30-34	1,374	1,433
35-39	1,613	1,640
40-44	1,662	1,670
45-49	1,566	1,556
50-54	1,384	1,369
55-59	1,146	1,110
60-64	908	884
65-69	734	710
70+	1,324	1,530

DAYTIME POPULATION

2001 Estimates:

Working Population	11,357
At Home Population	16,298
Total	27,655

INCOME

2001 Estimates:

Avg. Household Income	$77,484
Avg. Family Income	$81,692
Per Capita Income	$26,158
Male:	
Avg. Employment Income	$43,767
Avg. Employment Income (Full Time)	$55,250
Female:	
Avg. Employment Income	$26,739
Avg. Employment Income (Full Time)	$39,935

DISPOSABLE & DISCRETIONARY INCOME

2001 Estimates:	Per Hhld.
Disposable Income	$63,236
Discretionary Income 1 (minus Food & Shelter)	$46,202
Discretionary Income 2 (minus Food, Shelter, & Other Expenditures)	$34,850

LIQUID ASSETS

1999 Estimates:	Per Hhld.
Equity Investments	$119,099
Interest Bearing Investments	$95,035
Total Liquid Assets	$214,134

CREDIT DATA

July 2000:

Pool of Credit	$496,427,782
Revolving Credit, No.	77,080
Fixed Loans, No.	22,827
Avg. Credit Limit, per Person	$15,031
Avg. Spent, per Person	$6,723
Satisfactory Ratings, No. per Person	2.92
Avg. No. of Cards, per Person	1.08

LABOUR FORCE

2001 Estimates:

Male:	
In the Labour Force	13,115
Participation Rate	83.4
Employed	12,970
Unemployed	145
Unemployment Rate	1.1
Not in Labour Force	2,612
Female:	
In the Labour Force	10,702
Participation Rate	67.8
Employed	10,446
Unemployed	256
Unemployment Rate	2.4
Not in Labour Force	5,075

OCCUPATIONS BY MAJOR GROUPS

2001 Estimates:	Male	Female
Management	1,883	747
Business, Finance & Admin.	1,074	3,166
Natural & Applied Sciences & Related	988	185
Health	166	1,037
Social Sciences, Gov't Services & Religion	138	330
Education	491	701
Arts, Culture, Recreation & Sport	181	383
Sales & Service	2,353	2,895
Trades, Transport & Equipment Operators & Related	3,315	253
Primary Industries	1,335	529
Processing, Mfg. & Utilities	1,116	288

LEVEL OF SCHOOLING

2001 Estimates:

Population 15 years +	31,504
Less than Grade 9	1,886
Grades 9-13 w/o Certif.	7,190
Grade 9-13 with Certif.	4,409
Trade Certif. /Dip.	1,276
Non-Univ. w/o Certif./Dip.	2,009
Non-Univ. with Certif./Dip.	6,877
Univ. w/o Degree	2,856
Univ. w/o Degree/Certif.	1,470
Univ. with Certif.	1,386
Univ. with Degree	5,001

AVERAGE HOUSEHOLD EXPENDITURES

2001 Estimates:

Food	$7,515
Shelter	$12,013
Clothing	$2,825
Transportation	$9,150
Health & Personal Care	$2,287
Recr'n, Read'g & Education	$4,784
Taxes & Securities	$22,103
Other	$10,493
Total Expenditures	$71,170

PRIVATE HOUSEHOLDS

2001 Estimates:

Private Households, Total	13,482
Pop. in Private Households	39,652
Average no. per Household	2.9

FAMILIES

2001 Estimates:

Families in Private Households	11,672
Husband-Wife Families	10,767
Lone-Parent Families	905
Aver. No. Persons per Family	3.2
Aver. No. Sons/Daughters at Home	1.3

HOUSING

2001 Estimates:

Occupied Private Dwellings	13,482
Owned	11,739
Rented	1,743
Single-Detached House	11,396
Semi-Detached House	415
Row Houses	318
Apartment, 5+ Storeys	461
Apartment, 5 or Fewer Storeys	246
Apartment, Detached Duplex	176
Other Single-Attached	33
Movable Dwellings	437

VEHICLES

2001 Estimates:

Model Yrs. '81-'96, No.	21,282
% Total	78.89
Model Yrs. '97-'98, No.	3,499
% Total	12.97
'99 Vehicles registered in Model Yr. '99, No.	2,197
% Total	8.14
Total No. '81-'99	26,978

LEGAL MARITAL STATUS

2001 Estimates: (Age 15+)

Single (Never Married)	7,353
Legally Married (Not Separated)	20,665
Legally Married (Separated)	678
Widowed	1,319
Divorced	1,489

PSYTE CATEGORIES

2001 Estimates	No. of House-holds	% of Total Hhds.	Index
Suburban Executives	206	1.53	107
Mortgaged in Suburbia	1,950	14.46	1,041
Technocrafts & Bureaucrats	167	1.24	44
Boomers & Teens	1,016	7.54	420
Stable Suburban Families	398	2.95	226
Suburban Nesters	586	4.35	271
Satellite Suburbs	366	2.71	95
Blue Collar Winners	6,885	51.07	2,028
Old Towns' New Fringe	584	4.33	111
Conservative Homebodies	817	6.06	168
Young Urban Mix	507	3.76	177

Ontario

FINANCIAL P$YTE

2001 Estimates	No. of House-holds	% of Total Hhds.	Index
Four Star Investors	1,222	9.06	180
Successful Suburbanites	2,515	18.65	281
Canadian Comfort	7,837	58.13	598
Tractors & Tradelines	584	4.33	76
Bills & Wills	1,324	9.82	119

HOME LANGUAGE

2001 Estimates:		% Total
English	38,840	97.26
French	100	0.25
Arabic	31	0.08
Chinese	29	0.07
Dutch	64	0.16
German	107	0.27
Greek	47	0.12
Italian	89	0.22
Macedonian	34	0.09
Polish	45	0.11
Portuguese	69	0.17
Spanish	93	0.23
Ukrainian	22	0.06
Other Languages	165	0.41
Multiple Responses	201	0.50
Total	39,936	100.00

BUILDING PERMITS

	1999	1998 $000	1997
Value	39,140	36,363	51,869

HOMES BUILT

	1999	1998	1997
No	211	328	384

TAXATION

Income Class:	1997	% Total
Under $5,000	2,000	11.04
$5,000-$10,000	1,720	9.50
$10,000-$15,000	1,820	10.05
$15,000-$20,000	1,390	7.68
$20,000-$25,000	1,280	7.07
$25,000-$30,000	1,370	7.56
$30,000-$40,000	2,340	12.92
$40,000-$50,000	1,760	9.72
$50,000 +	4,430	24.46
Total Returns, No.	18,110	
Total Income, $000	667,945	
Total Taxable Returns	14,150	
Total Tax, $000	148,538	
Average Income, $	36,883	
Average Tax, $	10,497	

VITAL STATISTICS

	1997	1996	1995	1994
Births	435	357	363	346
Deaths	137	128	137	140
Natural Increase	298	229	226	206
Marriages	190	192	187	165

Note: Latest available data.

MEDIA INFO
see Hamilton, CMA

Ontario

Glanbrook

(Township)
Hamilton CMA

In Hamilton-Wentworth Regional Municipality.

POPULATION

July 1, 2001 Estimate	11,803
% Cdn. Total	0.04
% Change, '96 -'01	8.54
Avg. Annual Growth Rate, %	1.65
2003 Projected Population	12,076
2006 Projected Population	12,457
2001 Households Estimate	3,973
2003 Projected Households	4,107
2006 Projected Households	4,311

INCOME

% Above/Below National Average	+15
2001 Total Income Estimate	$286,890,000
% Cdn. Total	0.04
2001 Average Hhld. Income	$72,200
2001 Per Capita	$24,300
2003 Projected Total Income	$312,930,000
2006 Projected Total Income	$356,180,000

RETAIL SALES

% Above/Below National Average	-39
2001 Retail Sales Estimate	$64,120,000
% Cdn. Total	0.02
2001 per Household	$16,100
2001 per Capita	$5,400
2001 No. of Establishments	82
2003 Projected Retail Sales	$70,710,000
2006 Projected Retail Sales	$81,830,000

POPULATION

2001 Estimates:

Total		11,803
Male		5,938
Female		5,865

Age Groups	Male	Female
0-4	332	320
5-9	394	392
10-14	444	445
15-19	439	429
20-24	400	371
25-29	352	331
30-34	357	371
35-39	440	437
40-44	465	465
45-49	468	459
50-54	432	419
55-59	366	355
60-64	307	309
65-69	261	266
70+	481	496

DAYTIME POPULATION

2001 Estimates:

Working Population	4,431
At Home Population	5,486
Total	9,917

INCOME

2001 Estimates:

Avg. Household Income	$72,209
Avg. Family Income	$74,999
Per Capita Income	$24,306

Male:

Avg. Employment Income	$42,326
Avg. Employment Income (Full Time)	$50,846

Female:

Avg. Employment Income	$23,734
Avg. Employment Income (Full Time)	$37,135

DISPOSABLE & DISCRETIONARY INCOME

2001 Estimates:	Per Hhld.
Disposable Income	$58,948
Discretionary Income 1 (minus Food & Shelter)	$42,609
Discretionary Income 2 (minus Food, Shelter, & Other Expenditures)	$31,556

LIQUID ASSETS

1999 Estimates:	Per Hhld.
Equity Investments	$116,803
Interest Bearing Investments	$88,675
Total Liquid Assets	$205,478

CREDIT DATA

July 2000:

Pool of Credit	$137,971,565
Revolving Credit, No.	24,660
Fixed Loans, No.	6,098
Avg. Credit Limit, per Person	$12,861
Avg. Spent, per Person	$5,258
Satisfactory Ratings, No. per Person	2.77
Avg. No. of Cards, per Person	1.01

LABOUR FORCE

2001 Estimates:

Male:

In the Labour Force	3,540
Participation Rate	74.2
Employed	3,471
Unemployed	69
Unemployment Rate	1.9
Not in Labour Force	1,228

Female:

In the Labour Force	2,909
Participation Rate	61.8
Employed	2,791
Unemployed	118
Unemployment Rate	4.1
Not in Labour Force	1,799

OCCUPATIONS BY MAJOR GROUPS

2001 Estimates:	Male	Female
Management	372	107
Business, Finance & Admin.	259	942
Natural & Applied Sciences & Related	188	65
Health	24	232
Social Sciences, Gov't Services & Religion	24	48
Education	105	178
Arts, Culture, Recreation & Sport	24	107
Sales & Service	451	854
Trades, Transport & Equipment Operators & Related	1,319	118
Primary Industries	262	125
Processing, Mfg. & Utilities	424	41

LEVEL OF SCHOOLING

2001 Estimates:

Population 15 years +	9,476
Less than Grade 9	710
Grades 9-13 w/o Certif.	2,415
Grade 9-13 with Certif.	1,488
Trade Certif./Dip.	509
Non-Univ. w/o Certif./Dip.	659
Non-Univ. with Certif./Dip.	2,299
Univ. w/o Degree	654
Univ. w/o Degree/Certif.	337
Univ. with Certif.	317
Univ. with Degree	742

AVERAGE HOUSEHOLD EXPENDITURES

2001 Estimates:

Food	$7,014
Shelter	$11,620
Clothing	$2,540
Transportation	$9,000
Health & Personal Care	$2,165
Recr'n, Read'g & Education	$4,304
Taxes & Securities	$20,489
Other	$9,893
Total Expenditures	$67,025

PRIVATE HOUSEHOLDS

2001 Estimates:

Private Households, Total	3,973
Pop. in Private Households	11,700
Average no. per Household	2.9

FAMILIES

2001 Estimates:

Families in Private Households	3,446
Husband-Wife Families	3,219
Lone-Parent Families	227
Aver. No. Persons per Family	3.2
Aver. No. Sons/Daughters at Home	1.2

HOUSING

2001 Estimates:

Occupied Private Dwellings	3,973
Owned	3,542
Rented	431
Single-Detached House	3,697
Semi-Detached House	12
Row Houses	122
Apartment, 5 or Fewer Storeys	63
Apartment, Detached Duplex	68
Other Single-Attached	11

VEHICLES

2001 Estimates:

Model Yrs. '81-'96, No.	7,447
% Total	82.80
Model Yrs. '97-'98, No.	887
% Total	9.86
'99 Vehicles registered in Model Yr. '99, No.	660
% Total	7.34
Total No. '81-'99	8,994

LEGAL MARITAL STATUS

2001 Estimates: (Age 15+)

Single (Never Married)	2,296
Legally Married (Not Separated)	6,075
Legally Married (Separated)	199
Widowed	443
Divorced	463

PSYTE CATEGORIES

2001 Estimates	No. of House-holds	% of Total Hhds.	Index
Boomers & Teens	397	9.99	557
Blue Collar Winners	2,930	73.75	2,929
Conservative Homebodies	319	8.03	223
Old Leafy Towns	327	8.23	322

FINANCIAL P$YTE

2001 Estimates	No. of House-holds	% of Total Hhds.	Index
Four Star Investors	397	9.99	199
Canadian Comfort	2,930	73.75	759
Bills & Wills	646	16.26	196

HOME LANGUAGE

2001 Estimates:		% Total
English	11,437	96.90
French	11	0.09
Croatian	97	0.82
Dutch	22	0.19
German	17	0.14
Hungarian	58	0.49
Italian	60	0.51
Portuguese	24	0.20
Ukrainian	11	0.09
Other Languages	16	0.14
Multiple Responses	50	0.42
Total	11,803	100.00

BUILDING PERMITS

	1999	1998 $000	1997
Value	26,351	18,161	22,882

HOMES BUILT

	1999	1998	1997
No	216	140	140

TAXATION

Income Class:	1997	% Total
Under $5,000	700	11.82
$5,000-$10,000	570	9.63
$10,000-$15,000	680	11.49
$15,000-$20,000	590	9.97
$20,000-$25,000	480	8.11
$25,000-$30,000	450	7.60
$30,000-$40,000	760	12.84
$40,000-$50,000	580	9.80
$50,000 +	1,110	18.75
Total Returns, No.	5,920	
Total Income, $000	180,986	
Total Taxable Returns	4,440	
Total Tax, $000	34,339	
Average Income, $	30,572	
Average Tax, $	7,734	

VITAL STATISTICS

	1997	1996	1995	1994
Births	66	75	70	83
Deaths	58	38	41	46
Natural Increase	8	37	29	37
Marriages	24	24	28	38

Note: Latest available data.

MEDIA INFO
see Hamilton, CMA

Grimsby
(Town)
Hamilton CMA
In Niagara Regional Municipality.

POPULATION

July 1, 2001 Estimate	21,382
% Cdn. Total	0.07
% Change, '96 -'01	6.21
Avg. Annual Growth Rate, %	1.21
2003 Projected Population	21,621
2006 Projected Population	21,944
2001 Households Estimate	7,614
2003 Projected Households	7,745
2006 Projected Households	7,940

INCOME

% Above/Below National Average	+14
2001 Total Income Estimate	$514,110,000
% Cdn. Total	0.08
2001 Average Hhld. Income	$67,500
2001 Per Capita	$24,000
2003 Projected Total Income	$545,130,000
2006 Projected Total Income	$594,930,000

RETAIL SALES

% Above/Below National Average	-2
2001 Retail Sales Estimate	$187,890,000
% Cdn. Total	0.07
2001 per Household	$24,700
2001 per Capita	$8,800
2001 No. of Establishments	135
2003 Projected Retail Sales	$205,330,000
2006 Projected Retail Sales	$230,830,000

POPULATION

2001 Estimates:

Total	21,382
Male	10,587
Female	10,795

Age Groups	Male	Female
0-4	621	594
5-9	734	725
10-14	822	757
15-19	781	681
20-24	663	603
25-29	593	566
30-34	660	671
35-39	827	842
40-44	896	910
45-49	851	849
50-54	724	733
55-59	599	614
60-64	507	523
65-69	428	465
70+	881	1,262

DAYTIME POPULATION

2001 Estimates:

Working Population	6,948
At Home Population	9,294
Total	16,242

INCOME

2001 Estimates:

Avg. Household Income	$67,522
Avg. Family Income	$73,148
Per Capita Income	$24,044
Male:	
Avg. Employment Income	$43,153
Avg. Employment Income (Full Time)	$53,512
Female:	
Avg. Employment Income	$22,875
Avg. Employment Income (Full Time)	$33,793

DISPOSABLE & DISCRETIONARY INCOME

2001 Estimates: Per Hhld.

Disposable Income	$54,905
Discretionary Income 1 (minus Food & Shelter)	$39,644
Discretionary Income 2 (minus Food, Shelter, & Other Expenditures)	$29,626

LIQUID ASSETS

1999 Estimates: Per Hhld.

Equity Investments	$102,434
Interest Bearing Investments	$84,952
Total Liquid Assets	$187,386

CREDIT DATA

July 2000:

Pool of Credit	$245,830,950
Revolving Credit, No. :	42,999
Fixed Loans, No.	11,746
Avg. Credit Limit, per Person	$14,921
Avg. Spent, per Person	$6,549
Satisfactory Ratings, No. per Person	3.21
Avg. No. of Cards, per Person	1.18

LABOUR FORCE

2001 Estimates:

Male:	
In the Labour Force	6,717
Participation Rate	79.9
Employed	6,596
Unemployed	121
Unemployment Rate	1.8
Not in Labour Force	1,693
Female:	
In the Labour Force	5,597
Participation Rate	64.2
Employed	5,399
Unemployed	198
Unemployment Rate	3.5
Not in Labour Force	3,122

OCCUPATIONS BY MAJOR GROUPS

2001 Estimates:	Male	Female
Management	856	362
Business, Finance & Admin.	629	1,780
Natural & Applied Sciences & Related	539	78
Health	126	595
Social Sciences, Gov't Services & Religion	116	108
Education	142	359
Arts, Culture, Recreation & Sport	83	103
Sales & Service	1,277	1,602
Trades, Transport & Equipment Operators & Related	1,687	104
Primary Industries	327	159
Processing, Mfg. & Utilities	806	191

LEVEL OF SCHOOLING

2001 Estimates:

Population 15 years +	17,129
Less than Grade 9	1,032
Grades 9-13 w/o Certif.	3,556
Grade 9-13 with Certif.	2,843
Trade Certif. /Dip.	667
Non-Univ. w/o Certif./Dip.	1,378
Non-Univ. with Certif./Dip.	3,936
Univ. w/o Degree	1,411
Univ. w/o Degree/Certif.	667
Univ. with Certif.	744
Univ. with Degree	2,306

AVERAGE HOUSEHOLD EXPENDITURES

2001 Estimates:

Food	$6,960
Shelter	$10,667
Clothing	$2,444
Transportation	$7,950
Health & Personal Care	$2,123
Recr'n, Read'g & Education	$4,116
Taxes & Securities	$18,925
Other	$9,722
Total Expenditures	$62,907

PRIVATE HOUSEHOLDS

2001 Estimates:

Private Households, Total	7,614
Pop. in Private Households	20,857
Average no. per Household	2.7

FAMILIES

2001 Estimates:

Families in Private Households	6,275
Husband-Wife Families	5,670
Lone-Parent Families	605
Aver. No. Persons per Family	3.1
Aver. No. Sons/Daughters at Home	1.2

HOUSING

2001 Estimates:

Occupied Private Dwellings	7,614
Owned	6,224
Rented	1,390
Single-Detached House	5,981
Semi-Detached House	176
Row Houses	575
Apartment, 5+ Storeys	169
Apartment, 5 or Fewer Storeys	547
Apartment, Detached Duplex	155
Other Single-Attached	11

VEHICLES

2001 Estimates:

Model Yrs. '81-'96, No.	11,268
% Total	81.04
Model Yrs. '97-'98, No.	1,630
% Total	11.72
'99 Vehicles registered in Model Yr. '99, No.	1,007
% Total	7.24
Total No. '81-'99	13,905

LEGAL MARITAL STATUS

2001 Estimates: (Age 15+)

Single (Never Married)	3,735
Legally Married (Not Separated)	10,933
Legally Married (Separated)	455
Widowed	1,186
Divorced	820

PSYTE CATEGORIES

2001 Estimates	No. of House-holds	% of Total Hhds.	Index
Mortgaged in Suburbia	263	3.45	248
Boomers & Teens	338	4.44	248
Stable Suburban Families	742	9.75	748
Old Bungalow Burbs	780	10.24	618
Suburban Nesters	815	10.70	668
Satellite Suburbs	232	3.05	106
Blue Collar Winners	2,896	38.04	1,511
Conservative Homebodies	781	10.26	284
Old Leafy Towns	156	2.05	80
Nesters & Young Homesteaders	394	5.17	222
Struggling Downtowns	213	2.80	89

Ontario

FINANCIAL P$YTE

2001 Estimates	No. of House -holds	% of Total Hhds.	Index
Four Star Investors	338	4.44	88
Successful Suburbanites	1,005	13.20	199
Canadian Comfort	3,943	51.79	533
Miners & Credit-Liners	780	10.24	324
Bills & Wills	937	12.31	149
Revolving Renters	394	5.17	112
Towering Debt	213	2.80	36

HOME LANGUAGE

2001 Estimates:		% Total
English	20,602	96.35
French	53	0.25
Chinese	42	0.20
Croatian	56	0.26
German	33	0.15
Italian	59	0.28
Polish	147	0.69
Punjabi	22	0.10
Serbian	11	0.05
Serbo-Croatian	21	0.10
Slovenian	16	0.07
Spanish	54	0.25
Ukrainian	58	0.27
Multiple Responses	208	0.97
Total	21,382	100.00

BUILDING PERMITS

	1999	1998	1997
		$000	
Value	31,211	21,508	19,055

HOMES BUILT

	1999	1998	1997
No	148	126	65

TAXATION

Income Class:	1997	% Total
Under $5,000	1,530	11.02
$5,000-$10,000	1,370	9.87
$10,000-$15,000	1,600	11.53
$15,000-$20,000	1,180	8.50
$20,000-$25,000	1,130	8.14
$25,000-$30,000	980	7.06
$30,000-$40,000	1,790	12.90
$40,000-$50,000	1,340	9.65
$50,000 +	2,970	21.40
Total Returns, No.	13,880	
Total Income, $000	465,250	
Total Taxable Returns	10,590	
Total Tax, $000	97,752	
Average Income, $.	33,519	
Average Tax, $.	9,231	

VITAL STATISTICS

	1997	1996	1995	1994
Births	227	210	251	221
Deaths	176	152	156	212
Natural Increase	51	58	95	9
Marriages	80	113	81	89

Note: Latest available data.

MEDIA INFO
see Hamilton, CMA

Ontario

Hamilton
(City)
Hamilton CMA

In Hamilton-Wentworth Regional Municipality.

POPULATION

July 1, 2001 Estimate	339,677
% Cdn. Total	1.09
% Change, '96 -'01	2.37
Avg. Annual Growth Rate, %	0.47
2003 Projected Population	337,360
2006 Projected Population	333,101
2001 Households Estimate	139,447
2003 Projected Households	139,918
2006 Projected Households	140,521

INCOME

% Above/Below National Average	-10
2001 Total Income Estimate	$6,467,710,000
% Cdn. Total	0.99
2001 Average Hhld. Income	$46,400
2001 Per Capita	$19,000
2003 Projected Total Income	$6,760,180,000
2006 Projected Total Income	$7,218,300,000

RETAIL SALES

% Above/Below National Average	-1
2001 Retail Sales Estimate	$3,013,490,000
% Cdn. Total	1.08
2001 per Household	$21,600
2001 per Capita	$8,900
2001 No. of Establishments	2,219
2003 Projected Retail Sales	$3,217,830,000
2006 Projected Retail Sales	$3,493,380,000

POPULATION

2001 Estimates:

Total		339,677
Male		164,633
Female		175,044

Age Groups	Male	Female
0-4	10,895	10,364
5-9	10,978	10,414
10-14	10,595	10,030
15-19	10,191	9,712
20-24	10,482	10,582
25-29	11,644	11,986
30-34	13,283	13,344
35-39	13,944	13,820
40-44	12,980	13,179
45-49	11,482	12,077
50-54	9,693	10,314
55-59	8,161	8,701
60-64	7,270	7,983
65-69	6,812	8,019
70+	16,223	24,519

DAYTIME POPULATION

2001 Estimates:

Working Population	183,979
At Home Population	181,711
Total	365,690

INCOME

2001 Estimates:

Avg. Household Income	$46,381
Avg. Family Income	$53,509
Per Capita Income	$19,041
Male:	
Avg. Employment Income	$33,078
Avg. Employment Income (Full Time)	$43,274
Female:	
Avg. Employment Income	$21,321
Avg. Employment Income (Full Time)	$31,785

DISPOSABLE & DISCRETIONARY INCOME

2001 Estimates: *Per Hhld.*

Disposable Income	$38,375
Discretionary Income 1 (minus Food & Shelter)	$26,127
Discretionary Income 2 (minus Food, Shelter, & Other Expenditures)	$18,818

LIQUID ASSETS

1999 Estimates: *Per Hhld.*

Equity Investments	$52,334
Interest Bearing Investments	$54,778
Total Liquid Assets	$107,112

CREDIT DATA

July 2000:

Pool of Credit	$3,061,696,712
Revolving Credit, No.	623,658
Fixed Loans, No.	165,947
Avg. Credit Limit, per Person	$10,448
Avg. Spent, per Person	$4,793
Satisfactory Ratings, No. per Person	2.60
Avg. No. of Cards, per Person	0.93

LABOUR FORCE

2001 Estimates:

Male:	
In the Labour Force	90,930
Participation Rate	68.8
Employed	84,383
Unemployed	6,547
Unemployment Rate	7.2
Not in Labour Force	41,235
Female:	
In the Labour Force	78,345
Participation Rate	54.3
Employed	72,738
Unemployed	5,607
Unemployment Rate	7.2
Not in Labour Force	65,891

OCCUPATIONS BY MAJOR GROUPS

2001 Estimates:	Male	Female
Management	6,292	3,664
Business, Finance & Admin.	8,367	20,852
Natural & Applied Sciences & Related	5,478	990
Health	1,496	7,632
Social Sciences, Gov't Services & Religion	1,477	1,988
Education	2,649	3,410
Arts, Culture, Recreation & Sport	1,766	1,663
Sales & Service	18,909	27,558
Trades, Transport & Equipment Operators & Related	24,281	1,278
Primary Industries	1,553	525
Processing, Mfg. & Utilities	15,000	4,953

LEVEL OF SCHOOLING

2001 Estimates:

Population 15 years +	276,401
Less than Grade 9	36,993
Grades 9-13 w/o Certif.	72,918
Grade 9-13 with Certif.	39,544
Trade Certif. /Dip.	10,362
Non-Univ. w/o Certif./Dip.	19,573
Non-Univ. with Certif./Dip.	49,111
Univ. w/o Degree	20,593
Univ. w/o Degree/Certif.	10,567
Univ. with Certif.	10,026
Univ. with Degree	27,307

AVERAGE HOUSEHOLD EXPENDITURES

2001 Estimates:

Food	$5,630
Shelter	$8,498
Clothing	$1,916
Transportation	$5,482
Health & Personal Care	$1,711
Recr'n, Read'g & Education	$3,164
Taxes & Securities	$11,479
Other	$7,760
Total Expenditures	$45,640

PRIVATE HOUSEHOLDS

2001 Estimates:

Private Households, Total	139,447
Pop. in Private Households	333,759
Average no. per Household	2.4

FAMILIES

2001 Estimates:

Families in Private Households	93,475
Husband-Wife Families	76,378
Lone-Parent Families	17,097
Aver. No. Persons per Family	2.9
Aver. No. Sons/Daughters at Home	1.1

HOUSING

2001 Estimates:

Occupied Private Dwellings	139,447
Owned	77,586
Rented	61,861
Single-Detached House	72,248
Semi-Detached House	4,811
Row Houses	11,301
Apartment, 5+ Storeys	30,732
Owned Apartment, 5+ Storeys	1,437
Apartment, 5 or Fewer Storeys	15,346
Apartment, Detached Duplex	4,705
Other Single-Attached	304

VEHICLES

2001 Estimates:

Model Yrs. '81-'96, No.	144,356
% Total	83.06
Model Yrs. '97-'98, No.	17,244
% Total	9.92
'99 Vehicles registered in Model Yr. '99, No.	12,199
% Total	7.02
Total No. '81-'99	173,799

LEGAL MARITAL STATUS

2001 Estimates: (Age 15+)

Single (Never Married)	84,493
Legally Married (Not Separated)	138,133
Legally Married (Separated)	9,548
Widowed	21,783
Divorced	22,444

PSYTE CATEGORIES

2001 Estimates	No. of House -holds	% of Total Hhds.	Index
The Affluentials	321	0.23	36
Urban Gentry	1,758	1.26	70
Technocrafts & Bureaucrats	472	0.34	12
Boomers & Teens	463	0.33	19
Stable Suburban Families	680	0.49	37
Old Bungalow Burbs	7,309	5.24	316
Suburban Nesters	1,227	0.88	55
Brie & Chablis	43	0.03	3
Aging Erudites	2,680	1.92	127
Satellite Suburbs	10,807	7.75	270
Kindergarten Boom	5,047	3.62	138
Blue Collar Winners	92	0.07	3
Europa	740	0.53	43
High Rise Melting Pot	4,464	3.20	214
Conservative Homebodies	33,336	23.91	663
High Rise Sunsets	5,359	3.84	269
Young Urban Professionals	2,061	1.48	78
Young Urban Mix	615	0.44	21
Young Urban Intelligentsia	1,183	0.85	56
University Enclaves	7,728	5.54	272
Young City Singles	6,798	4.87	213
Urban Bohemia	709	0.51	43
Town Renters	4,551	3.26	378
Struggling Downtowns	30,056	21.55	684
Aged Pensioners	4,719	3.38	254
Big City Stress	3,468	2.49	220
Old Grey Towers	1,720	1.23	223

FINANCIAL P$YTE

2001 Estimates	No. of House -holds	% of Total Hhds.	Index
Platinum Estates	321	0.23	29
Four Star Investors	2,221	1.59	32
Successful Suburbanites	1,152	0.83	12
Canadian Comfort	12,126	8.70	89
Urban Heights	4,784	3.43	80
Miners & Credit-Liners	7,309	5.24	166
Mortgages & Minivans	5,047	3.62	55
Dollars & Sense	740	0.53	20
Bills & Wills	33,951	24.35	294
Revolving Renters	5,359	3.84	84
Young Urban Struggle	9,620	6.90	146
Towering Debt	45,869	32.89	421
NSF	3,468	2.49	70
Senior Survivors	6,439	4.62	245

HOME LANGUAGE

2001 Estimates:		% Total
English	286,028	84.21
French	1,316	0.39
Arabic	1,993	0.59
Armenian	182	0.05
Chinese	3,484	1.03
Croatian	1,919	0.56
Dutch	171	0.05
German	804	0.24
Greek	965	0.28
Gujarati	180	0.05
Hindi	249	0.07
Hungarian	927	0.27
Italian	7,724	2.27
Khmer (Cambodian)	859	0.25
Korean	488	0.14
Lao	365	0.11
Latvian (Lettish)	177	0.05
Lithuanian	407	0.12
Macedonian	233	0.07
Persian (Farsi)	489	0.14
Polish	4,225	1.24
Portuguese	4,444	1.31
Punjabi	1,226	0.36
Romanian	643	0.19
Russian	179	0.05
Serbian	1,828	0.54
Serbo-Croatian	229	0.07
Slovenian	212	0.06
Spanish	2,673	0.79
Tagalog (Pilipino)	1,117	0.33
Ukrainian	855	0.25
Urdu	544	0.16
Vietnamese	1,996	0.59
Other Languages	2,146	0.63
Multiple Responses	8,400	2.47
Total	339,677	100.00

Hamilton
(City)
Hamilton CMA
(Cont'd)

BUILDING PERMITS

	1999	1998	1997
		$000	
Value	131,740	195,978	174,931

HOMES BUILT

	1999	1998	1997
No.	610	589	661

TAXATION

Income Class:	1997	% Total
Under $5,000	29,490	.12.56
$5,000-$10,000	28,920	.12.31
$10,000-$15,000	37,700	.16.05
$15,000-$20,000	25,700	.10.94
$20,000-$25,000	21,050	.8.96
$25,000-$30,000	18,620	.7.93
$30,000-$40,000	27,780	.11.83
$40,000-$50,000	17,820	.7.59
$50,000 +	27,800	.11.84
Total Returns, No.	234,880	
Total Income, $000	5,967,837	
Total Taxable		
Returns	157,440	
Total Tax, $000	1,049,147	
Average Income, $	25,408	
Average Tax, $	6,664	

VITAL STATISTICS

	1997	1996	1995	1994
Births	4,087	4,347	4,480	4,719
Deaths	3,016	2,940	3,010	3,094
Natural Increase	1,071	1,407	1,470	1,625
Marriages	2,058	.24	2,207	2,177

Note: Latest available data.

MEDIA INFO
see Hamilton, CMA

Stoney Creek
(City)
Hamilton CMA

In Hamilton-Wentworth Regional Municipality.

POPULATION

July 1, 2001 Estimate	60,724
% Cdn. Total	0.20
% Change, '96 -'01	8.61
Avg. Annual Growth Rate, %	1.67
2003 Projected Population	62,154
2006 Projected Population	64,160
2001 Households Estimate	20,755
2003 Projected Households	21,458
2006 Projected Households	22,505

INCOME

% Above/Below National Average	+8
2001 Total Income Estimate	$1,378,990,000
% Cdn. Total	0.21
2001 Average Hhld. Income	$66,400
2001 Per Capita	$22,700
2003 Projected Total Income	$1,502,090,000
2006 Projected Total Income	$1,704,450,000

RETAIL SALES

% Above/Below National Average	-75
2001 Retail Sales Estimate	$135,200,000
% Cdn. Total	0.05
2001 per Household	$6,500
2001 per Capita	$2,200
2001 No. of Establishments	326
2003 Projected Retail Sales	$147,860,000
2006 Projected Retail Sales	$168,490,000

POPULATION

2001 Estimates:

Total	60,724
Male	29,790
Female	30,934

Age Groups	Male	Female
0-4	1,841	1,752
5-9	2,011	1,918
10-14	2,168	2,051
15-19	2,188	2,105
20-24	2,052	2,028
25-29	1,933	1,951
30-34	2,021	2,131
35-39	2,253	2,430
40-44	2,365	2,545
45-49	2,340	2,469
50-54	2,084	2,102
55-59	1,734	1,663
60-64	1,395	1,370
65-69	1,127	1,205
70+	2,278	3,214

DAYTIME POPULATION

2001 Estimates:

Working Population	19,505
At Home Population	28,261
Total	47,766

INCOME

2001 Estimates:

Avg. Household Income	$66,442
Avg. Family Income	$70,207
Per Capita Income	$22,709
Male:	
Avg. Employment Income	$41,114
Avg. Employment Income (Full Time)	$51,539
Female:	
Avg. Employment Income	$24,235
Avg. Employment Income (Full Time)	$35,595

DISPOSABLE & DISCRETIONARY INCOME

2001 Estimates:	*Per Hhld.*
Disposable Income	$54,324
Discretionary Income 1 (minus Food & Shelter)	$38,742
Discretionary Income 2 (minus Food, Shelter, & Other Expenditures)	$28,896

LIQUID ASSETS

1999 Estimates:	*Per Hhld.*
Equity Investments	$88,638
Interest Bearing Investments	$79,019
Total Liquid Assets	$167,657

CREDIT DATA

July 2000:

Pool of Credit	$646,459,122
Revolving Credit, No.	122,115
Fixed Loans, No.	31,448
Avg. Credit Limit, per Person	$13,586
Avg. Spent, per Person	$5,849
Satisfactory Ratings, No. per Person	3.10
Avg. No. of Cards, per Person	1.11

LABOUR FORCE

2001 Estimates:

Male:	
In the Labour Force	17,916
Participation Rate	75.4
Employed	17,273
Unemployed	.643
Unemployment Rate	3.6
Not in Labour Force	5,854
Female:	
In the Labour Force	15,392
Participation Rate	61.0
Employed	14,861
Unemployed	.531
Unemployment Rate	3.4
Not in Labour Force	9,821

OCCUPATIONS BY MAJOR GROUPS

2001 Estimates:	Male	Female
Management	2,013	.986
Business, Finance & Admin.	1,461	4,946
Natural & Applied Sciences & Related	1,160	.341
Health	.132	1,232
Social Sciences, Gov't Services & Religion	.253	.220
Education	.423	.758
Arts, Culture, Recreation & Sport	.236	.308
Sales & Service	3,229	4,566
Trades, Transport & Equipment Operators & Related	5,149	.366
Primary Industries	.436	.110
Processing, Mfg. & Utilities	2,997	1,191

LEVEL OF SCHOOLING

2001 Estimates:

Population 15 years +	48,983
Less than Grade 9	5,175
Grades 9-13 w/o Certif.	11,571
Grade 9-13 with Certif.	8,278
Trade Certif. /Dip.	2,507
Non-Univ. w/o Certif./Dip.	3,154
Non-Univ. with Certif./Dip.	9,905
Univ. w/o Degree	3,839
Univ. w/o Degree/Certif.	2,049
Univ. with Certif.	1,790
Univ. with Degree	4,554

Ontario

AVERAGE HOUSEHOLD EXPENDITURES

2001 Estimates:

Food	$7,184
Shelter	$10,860
Clothing	$2,500
Transportation	$7,645
Health & Personal Care	$2,144
Recr'n, Read'g & Education	$4,338
Taxes & Securities	$17,767
Other	$9,876
Total Expenditures	$62,314

PRIVATE HOUSEHOLDS

2001 Estimates:

Private Households, Total	20,755
Pop. in Private Households	60,017
Average no. per Household	2.9

FAMILIES

2001 Estimates:

Families in Private Households	17,476
Husband-Wife Families	15,814
Lone-Parent Families	1,662
Aver. No. Persons per Family	3.2
Aver. No. Sons/Daughters at Home	1.3

HOUSING

2001 Estimates:

Occupied Private Dwellings	20,755
Owned	16,387
Rented	4,368
Single-Detached House	14,760
Semi-Detached House	496
Row Houses	2,157
Apartment, 5+ Storeys	2,201
Owned Apartment, 5+ Storeys	.662
Apartment, 5 or Fewer Storeys	.979
Apartment, Detached Duplex	151
Other Single-Attached	11

VEHICLES

2001 Estimates:

Model Yrs. '81-'96, No.	30,243
% Total	82.08
Model Yrs. '97-'98, No.	4,008
% Total	10.88
'99 Vehicles registered in Model Yr. '99, No.	2,594
% Total	7.04
Total No. '81-'99	36,845

LEGAL MARITAL STATUS

2001 Estimates: (Age 15+)

Single (Never Married)	12,363
Legally Married (Not Separated)	30,258
Legally Married (Separated)	1,081
Widowed	2,854
Divorced	2,427

Ontario

Stoney Creek
(City)
Hamilton CMA
(Cont'd)

PSYTE CATEGORIES

2001 Estimates	No. of House-holds	% of Total Hhds.	Index
Mortgaged in Suburbia	327	1.58	113
Technocrafts & Bureaucrats	743	3.58	127
Boomers & Teens	1,751	8.44	471
Old Bungalow Burbs	2,747	13.24	799
Satellite Suburbs	5,822	28.05	978
Blue Collar Winners	2,060	9.93	394
Rustic Prosperity	34	0.16	9
High Rise Melting Pot	156	0.75	50
Conservative Homebodies	4,721	22.75	631
High Rise Sunsets	1,197	5.77	403
Struggling Downtowns	1,014	4.89	155

FINANCIAL P$YTE

2001 Estimates	No. of House-holds	% of Total Hhds.	Index
Four Star Investors	1,751	8.44	168
Successful Suburbanites	1,070	5.16	78
Canadian Comfort	7,882	37.98	391
Miners & Credit-Liners	2,747	13.24	418
Tractors & Tradelines	34	0.16	3
Bills & Wills	4,721	22.75	275
Revolving Renters	1,197	5.77	125
Towering Debt	1,170	5.64	72

HOME LANGUAGE

2001 Estimates:		% Total
English	52,004	85.64
French	100	0.16
Arabic	79	0.13
Chinese	77	0.13
Croatian	1,059	1.74
German	98	0.16
Greek	58	0.10
Gujarati	52	0.09
Hungarian	57	0.09
Italian	1,959	3.23
Korean	33	0.05
Persian (Farsi)	39	0.06
Polish	768	1.26
Portuguese	81	0.13
Punjabi	645	1.06
Romanian	97	0.16
Russian	43	0.07
Serbian	517	0.85
Serbo-Croatian	75	0.12
Slovak	49	0.08
Slovenian	192	0.32
Spanish	140	0.23
Ukrainian	163	0.27
Urdu	78	0.13
Other Languages	294	0.48
Multiple Responses	1,967	3.24
Total	60,724	100.00

BUILDING PERMITS

	1999	1998 $000	1997
Value	67,963	104,342	41,725

HOMES BUILT

	1999	1998	1997
No	440	286	247

TAXATION

Income Class:	1997	% Total
Under $5,000	4,720	11.76
$5,000-$10,000	4,180	10.41
$10,000-$15,000	4,740	11.81
$15,000-$20,000	3,790	9.44
$20,000-$25,000	3,550	8.84
$25,000-$30,000	3,190	7.95
$30,000-$40,000	5,130	12.78
$40,000-$50,000	3,700	9.22
$50,000 +	7,170	17.86
Total Returns, No.	40,150	
Total Income, $000	1,196,838	
Total Taxable Returns	29,980	
Total Tax, $000	231,052	
Average Income, $	29,809	
Average Tax, $	7,707	

VITAL STATISTICS

	1997	1996	1995	1994
Births	627	568	645	628
Deaths	386	348	348	324
Natural Increase	241	220	297	304
Marriages	231	199	212	205

Note: Latest available data.

MEDIA INFO
see Hamilton, CMA

Hamilton
(Township)
In Northumberland County.

POPULATION

2001 Estimates:	
July 1, 2001 Estimate	10,820
% Cdn. Total	0.03
% Change, '96 -'01	3.96
Avg. Annual Growth Rate, %	0.78
2003 Projected Population	10,929
2006 Projected Population	11,030
2001 Households Estimate	3,930
2003 Projected Households	4,013
2006 Projected Households	4,125

INCOME

% Above/Below National Average	+12
2001 Total Income Estimate	$255,680,000
% Cdn. Total	0.04
2001 Average Hhld. Income	$65,100
2001 Per Capita	$23,600
2003 Projected Total Income	$275,670,000
2006 Projected Total Income	$308,040,000

RETAIL SALES

% Above/Below National Average	-49
2001 Retail Sales Estimate	$49,240,000
% Cdn. Total	0.02
2001 per Household	$12,500
2001 per Capita	$4,600
2001 No. of Establishments	85
2003 Projected Retail Sales	$54,660,000
2006 Projected Retail Sales	$61,700,000

POPULATION

2001 Estimates:		
Total		10,820
Male		5,383
Female		5,437

Age Groups	Male	Female
0-4	304	282
5-9	361	355
10-14	404	402
15-19	397	381
20-24	335	316
25-29	275	276
30-34	323	336
35-39	409	424
40-44	453	464
45-49	435	444
50-54	383	387
55-59	337	333
60-64	293	279
65-69	242	246
70+	432	512

DAYTIME POPULATION

2001 Estimates:	
Working Population	1,985
At Home Population	4,819
Total	6,804

INCOME

2001 Estimates:	
Avg. Household Income	$65,058
Avg. Family Income	$69,145
Per Capita Income	$23,630
Male:	
Avg. Employment Income	$37,797
Avg. Employment Income (Full Time)	$47,081
Female:	
Avg. Employment Income	$24,338
Avg. Employment Income (Full Time)	$35,285

DISPOSABLE & DISCRETIONARY INCOME

2001 Estimates:	Per Hhld.
Disposable Income	$53,409
Discretionary Income 1 (minus Food & Shelter)	$38,119
Discretionary Income 2 (minus Food, Shelter, & Other Expenditures)	$27,625

LIQUID ASSETS

1999 Estimates:	Per Hhld.
Equity Investments	$102,474
Interest Bearing Investments	$82,695
Total Liquid Assets	$185,169

CREDIT DATA

July 2000:	
Pool of Credit	$97,700,860
Revolving Credit, No.	15,622
Fixed Loans, No.	4,768
Avg. Credit Limit, per Person	$13,134
Avg. Spent, per Person	$6,226
Satisfactory Ratings, No. per Person	2.68
Avg. No. of Cards, per Person	0.93

LABOUR FORCE

2001 Estimates:	
Male:	
In the Labour Force	3,444
Participation Rate	79.8
Employed	3,316
Unemployed	128
Unemployment Rate	3.7
Not in Labour Force	870
Female:	
In the Labour Force	2,810
Participation Rate	63.9
Employed	2,617
Unemployed	193
Unemployment Rate	6.9
Not in Labour Force	1,588

OCCUPATIONS BY MAJOR GROUPS

2001 Estimates:	Male	Female
Management	319	175
Business, Finance & Admin.	226	687
Natural & Applied Sciences & Related	143	41
Health	33	217
Social Sciences, Gov't Services & Religion	31	104
Education	115	117
Arts, Culture, Recreation & Sport	22	49
Sales & Service	578	870
Trades, Transport & Equipment Operators & Related	1,024	73
Primary Industries	248	81
Processing, Mfg. & Utilities	605	276

LEVEL OF SCHOOLING

2001 Estimates:	
Population 15 years +	8,712
Less than Grade 9	682
Grades 9-13 w/o Certif.	2,342
Grade 9-13 with Certif.	1,449
Trade Certif. /Dip.	481
Non-Univ. w/o Certif./Dip.	537
Non-Univ. with Certif./Dip.	1,894
Univ. w/o Degree	524
Univ. w/o Degree/Certif.	250
Univ. with Certif.	274
Univ. with Degree	803

Hamilton
(Township)
(Cont'd)

AVERAGE HOUSEHOLD EXPENDITURES

2001 Estimates:
Food	$6,917
Shelter	$10,609
Clothing	$2,344
Transportation	$8,424
Health & Personal Care	$2,114
Recr'n, Read'g & Education	$4,270
Taxes & Securities	$16,723
Other	$9,640
Total Expenditures	$61,041

PRIVATE HOUSEHOLDS

2001 Estimates:
Private Households, Total	3,930
Pop. in Private Households	10,755
Average no. per Household	2.7

FAMILIES

2001 Estimates:
Families in Private Households	3,299
Husband-Wife Families	3,080
Lone-Parent Families	219
Aver. No. Persons per Family	3.0
Aver. No. Sons/Daughters at Home	1.1

HOUSING

2001 Estimates:
Occupied Private Dwellings	3,930
Owned	3,427
Rented	503
Single-Detached House	3,693
Semi-Detached House	39
Row Houses	11
Apartment, 5 or Fewer Storeys	115
Apartment, Detached Duplex	61
Movable Dwellings	11

VEHICLES

2001 Estimates:
Model Yrs. '81-'96, No.	5,849
% Total	82.38
Model Yrs. '97-'98, No.	758
% Total	10.68
'99 Vehicles registered in Model Yr. '99, No.	493
% Total	6.94
Total No. '81-'99	7,100

LEGAL MARITAL STATUS

2001 Estimates: (Age 15+)
Single (Never Married)	1,934
Legally Married (Not Separated)	5,523
Legally Married (Separated)	260
Widowed	451
Divorced	544

PSYTE CATEGORIES

2001 Estimates	No. of House-holds	% of Total Hhds.	Index
Small City Elite	106	2.70	157
Blue Collar Winners	1,537	39.11	1,553
Old Towns' New Fringe	1,327	33.77	863
Rustic Prosperity	426	10.84	601
Old Leafy Towns	387	9.85	385
Nesters & Young Homesteaders	136	3.46	148

FINANCIAL PSYTE

2001 Estimates	No. of House-holds	% of Total Hhds.	Index
Canadian Comfort	1,643	41.81	430
Tractors & Tradelines	1,753	44.61	780
Bills & Wills	387	9.85	119
Revolving Renters	136	3.46	75

HOME LANGUAGE

2001 Estimates:		% Total
English	10,717	99.05
French	22	0.20
Arabic	11	0.10
German	11	0.10
Polish	16	0.15
Spanish	11	0.10
Multiple Responses	32	0.30
Total	10,820	100.00

BUILDING PERMITS

	1999	1998 $000	1997
Value	9,757	8,830	7,973

TAXATION

Income Class:	1997	% Total
Under $5,000	430	12.01
$5,000-$10,000	400	11.17
$10,000-$15,000	460	12.85
$15,000-$20,000	320	8.94
$20,000-$25,000	310	8.66
$25,000-$30,000	290	8.10
$30,000-$40,000	500	13.97
$40,000-$50,000	310	8.66
$50,000 +	560	15.64
Total Returns, No.	3,580	
Total Income, $000	103,555	
Total Taxable Returns	2,640	
Total Tax, $000	20,024	
Average Income, $	28,926	
Average Tax, $	7,585	

VITAL STATISTICS

	1997	1996	1995	1994
Births	62	65	57	44
Deaths	31	42	30	14
Natural Increase	31	23	27	30
Marriages	17	2,228	29	12

Note: Latest available data.

Hawkesbury
(Census Agglomeration)

The Census Agglomeration of Hawkesbury includes: Hawkesbury, T, in Prescott and Russell United Counties in Ontario; and Grenville, VL, in census division Argenteuil in Quebec.

POPULATION

July 1, 2001 Estimate	12,082
% Cdn. Total	0.04
% Change, '96 -'01	1.39
Avg. Annual Growth Rate, %	0.28
2003 Projected Population	12,072
2006 Projected Population	12,268
2001 Households Estimate	5,123
2003 Projected Households	5,206
2006 Projected Households	5,353

INCOME

% Above/Below National Average	-24
2001 Total Income Estimate	$193,740,000
% Cdn. Total	0.03
2001 Average Hhld. Income	$37,800
2001 Per Capita	$16,000
2003 Projected Total Income	$205,800,000
2006 Projected Total Income	$226,430,000

RETAIL SALES

% Above/Below National Average	+117
2001 Retail Sales Estimate	$234,870,000
% Cdn. Total	0.08
2001 per Household	$45,800
2001 per Capita	$19,400
2001 No. of Establishments	176
2003 Projected Retail Sales	$253,870,000
2006 Projected Retail Sales	$286,010,000

POPULATION

2001 Estimates:
Total	12,082
Male	5,759
Female	6,323

Age Groups	Male	Female
0-4	357	348
5-9	373	367
10-14	397	358
15-19	396	353
20-24	402	377
25-29	390	390
30-34	401	441
35-39	450	483
40-44	464	493
45-49	419	451
50-54	363	415
55-59	305	350
60-64	263	308
65-69	244	296
70+	535	893

DAYTIME POPULATION

2001 Estimates:
Working Population	4,939
At Home Population	7,143
Total	12,082

INCOME

2001 Estimates:
Avg. Household Income	$37,817
Avg. Family Income	$44,275
Per Capita Income	$16,035
Male:	
Avg. Employment Income	$29,633
Avg. Employment Income (Full Time)	$40,146
Female:	
Avg. Employment Income	$17,274
Avg. Employment Income (Full Time)	$26,149

Ontario

DISPOSABLE & DISCRETIONARY INCOME

2001 Estimates:	Per Hhld.
Disposable Income	$31,054
Discretionary Income 1 (minus Food & Shelter)	$20,608
Discretionary Income 2 (minus Food, Shelter, & Other Expenditures)	$15,009

LIQUID ASSETS

1999 Estimates:	Per Hhld.
Equity Investments	$39,813
Interest Bearing Investments	$43,917
Total Liquid Assets	$83,730

CREDIT DATA

July 2000:
Pool of Credit	$91,229,089
Revolving Credit, No.	21,650
Fixed Loans, No.	5,973
Avg. Credit Limit, per Person	$8,495
Avg. Spent, per Person	$3,896
Satisfactory Ratings, No. per Person	2.53
Avg. No. of Cards, per Person	0.84

LABOUR FORCE

2001 Estimates:
Male:	
In the Labour Force	3,010
Participation Rate	65.0
Employed	2,772
Unemployed	238
Unemployment Rate	7.9
Not in Labour Force	1,622
Female:	
In the Labour Force	2,468
Participation Rate	47.0
Employed	2,145
Unemployed	323
Unemployment Rate	13.1
Not in Labour Force	2,782

OCCUPATIONS BY MAJOR GROUPS

2001 Estimates:	Male	Female
Management	263	59
Business, Finance & Admin.	180	433
Natural & Applied Sciences & Related	125	n.a.
Health	51	209
Social Sciences, Gov't Services & Religion	79	90
Education	87	137
Arts, Culture, Recreation & Sport	33	30
Sales & Service	673	944
Trades, Transport & Equipment Operators & Related	617	20
Primary Industries	23	n.a.
Processing, Mfg. & Utilities	715	337

Ontario

Hawkesbury
(Census Agglomeration)
(Cont'd)

LEVEL OF SCHOOLING

2001 Estimates:
Population 15 years +	9,882
Less than Grade 9	2,006
Grades 9-13 w/o Certif.	2,856
Grade 9-13 with Certif.	1,970
Trade Certif. /Dip.	264
Non-Univ. w/o Certif./Dip.	438
Non-Univ. with Certif./Dip.	1,336
Univ. w/o Degree	388
Univ. w/o Degree/Certif.	184
Univ. with Certif.	204
Univ. with Degree	624

AVERAGE HOUSEHOLD EXPENDITURES

2001 Estimates:
Food	$5,357
Shelter	$6,496
Clothing	$1,602
Transportation	$3,924
Health & Personal Care	$1,515
Recr'n, Read'g & Education	$2,769
Taxes & Securities	$10,363
Other	$6,245
Total Expenditures	$38,271

PRIVATE HOUSEHOLDS

2001 Estimates:
Private Households, Total	5,123
Pop. in Private Households	11,731
Average no. per Household	2.3

FAMILIES

2001 Estimates:
Families in Private Households	3,546
Husband-Wife Families	2,821
Lone-Parent Families	725
Aver. No. Persons per Family	2.8
Aver. No. Sons/Daughters at Home	1.1

HOUSING

2001 Estimates:
Occupied Private Dwellings	5,123
Owned	2,613
Rented	2,510
Single-Detached House	2,009
Semi-Detached House	620
Row Houses	154
Apartment, 5+ Storeys	11
Apartment, 5 or Fewer Storeys	1,497
Apartment, Detached Duplex	720
Other Single-Attached	102
Movable Dwellings	10

VEHICLES

2001 Estimates:
Model Yrs. '81-'96, No.	5,432
% Total	78.32
Model Yrs. '97-'98, No.	832
% Total	12.00
'99 Vehicles registered in Model Yr. '99, No.	672
% Total	9.69
Total No. '81-'99	6,936

LEGAL MARITAL STATUS

2001 Estimates: (Age 15+)
Single (Never Married)	3,249
Legally Married (Not Separated)	4,378
Legally Married (Separated)	379
Widowed	1,019
Divorced	857

PSYTE CATEGORIES

2001 Estimates	No. of House-holds	% of Total Hhds.	Index
Quebec Melange	662	12.92	488
Big Country Families	1,007	19.66	1,378
Quebec Town Elders	2,970	57.97	2,052
Quebec's New Urban Mosaic	397	7.75	322

FINAN¢IAL P$YTE

2001 Estimates	No. of House-holds	% of Total Hhds.	Index
Country Credit	662	12.92	191
Rural Family Blues	1,007	19.66	243
Loan Parent Stress	2,970	57.97	995
NSF	397	7.75	219

HOME LANGUAGE

2001 Estimates		% Total
English	1,685	13.95
French	9,978	82.59
Arabic	10	0.08
Bengali	10	0.08
Dutch	20	0.17
German	29	0.24
Gujarati	10	0.08
Multiple Responses	340	2.81
Total	12,082	100.00

BUILDING PERMITS

	1999	1998 $000	1997
Value	11,165	7,326	13,366

HOMES BUILT

	1999	1998	1997
No	76	78	78

TAXATION

Income Class:	1997	% Total
Under $5,000	1,410	12.63
$5,000-$10,000	1,590	14.24
$10,000-$15,000	2,300	20.61
$15,000-$20,000	1,320	11.83
$20,000-$25,000	950	8.51
$25,000-$30,000	730	6.54
$30,000-$40,000	1,010	9.05
$40,000-$50,000	630	5.65
$50,000 +	1,220	10.93
Total Returns, No.	11,160	
Total Income, $000	255,160	
Total Taxable Returns	6,880	
Total Tax, $000	40,140	
Average Income, $	22,864	
Average Tax, $	5,834	

VITAL STATISTICS

	1997	1996	1995	1994
Births	139	120	158	146
Deaths	127	131	149	149
Natural Increase	12	-11	9	-3
Marriages	78	62	71	64

Note: Latest available data.

COMMUNITY NEWSPAPER(S)

	Total Circulation
Hawkesbury: Le Carillon	3,873
Hawkesbury: Hawkesbury/Vankleek Hill Review	4,510
Hawkesbury: Le/The Regional	40,630
Hawkesbury: La/The Tribune/Express	25,457

RADIO STATION(S)

	Power
CHPR-FM	750w

TELEVISION STATION(S)

TFO
TVO

Huntsville
(Town)
In Muskoka District Municipality.

POPULATION

July 1, 2001 Estimate	17,114
% Cdn. Total	0.05
% Change, '96 -'01	4.35
Avg. Annual Growth Rate, %	0.85
2003 Projected Population	17,333
2006 Projected Population	17,574
2001 Households Estimate	6,756
2003 Projected Households	6,860
2006 Projected Households	7,018

INCOME

% Above/Below National Average	-10
2001 Total Income Estimate	$325,200,000
% Cdn. Total	0.05
2001 Average Hhld. Income	$48,100
2001 Per Capita	$19,000
2003 Projected Total Income	$345,020,000
2006 Projected Total Income	$377,240,000

RETAIL SALES

% Above/Below National Average	+54
2001 Retail Sales Estimate	$235,690,000
% Cdn. Total	0.08
2001 per Household	$34,900
2001 per Capita	$13,800
2001 No. of Establishments	210
2003 Projected Retail Sales	$257,860,000
2006 Projected Retail Sales	$288,850,000

POPULATION

2001 Estimates:
Total		17,114
Male		8,312
Female		8,802
Age Groups	Male	Female
0-4	490	486
5-9	555	560
10-14	610	592
15-19	586	575
20-24	515	518
25-29	467	489
30-34	522	570
35-39	617	681
40-44	676	678
45-49	635	608
50-54	524	529
55-59	426	477
60-64	397	439
65-69	393	427
70+	899	1,173

DAYTIME POPULATION

2001 Estimates:
Working Population	15,798
At Home Population	8,877
Total	24,675

INCOME

2001 Estimates:
Avg. Household Income	$48,135
Avg. Family Income	$53,103
Per Capita Income	$19,002
Male:	
Avg. Employment Income	$29,348
Avg. Employment Income (Full Time)	$41,278
Female:	
Avg. Employment Income	$19,400
Avg. Employment Income (Full Time)	$30,486

DISPOSABLE & DISCRETIONARY INCOME

2001 Estimates:	Per Hhld.
Disposable Income	$39,856
Discretionary Income 1 (minus Food & Shelter)	$27,565
Discretionary Income 2 (minus Food, Shelter, & Other Expenditures)	$19,313

LIQUID ASSETS

1999 Estimates:	Per Hhld.
Equity Investments	$63,170
Interest Bearing Investments	$58,638
Total Liquid Assets	$121,808

CREDIT DATA

July 2000:
Pool of Credit	$185,965,067
Revolving Credit, No.	32,051
Fixed Loans, No.	11,079
Avg. Credit Limit, per Person.	$12,273
Avg. Spent, per Person	$5,721
Satisfactory Ratings, No. per Person.	2.72
Avg. No. of Cards, per Person	0.98

LABOUR FORCE

2001 Estimates:
Male:	
In the Labour Force	4,760
Participation Rate	71.5
Employed	4,449
Unemployed	311
Unemployment Rate	6.5
Not in Labour Force	1,897
Female:	
In the Labour Force	4,154
Participation Rate	58.0
Employed	3,833
Unemployed	321
Unemployment Rate	7.7
Not in Labour Force	3,010

OCCUPATIONS BY MAJOR GROUPS

2001 Estimates:	Male	Female
Management	702	306
Business, Finance & Admin.	255	933
Natural & Applied Sciences & Related	274	22
Health	103	297
Social Sciences, Gov't Services & Religion	98	211
Education	68	234
Arts, Culture, Recreation & Sport	40	115
Sales & Service	1,122	1,657
Trades, Transport & Equipment Operators & Related	1,320	47
Primary Industries	163	30
Processing, Mfg. & Utilities	525	192

LEVEL OF SCHOOLING

2001 Estimates:
Population 15 years +	13,821
Less than Grade 9	1,333
Grades 9-13 w/o Certif.	3,939
Grade 9-13 with Certif.	2,138
Trade Certif. /Dip.	702
Non-Univ. w/o Certif./Dip.	725
Non-Univ. with Certif./Dip.	2,620
Univ. w/o Degree	945
Univ. w/o Degree/Certif.	484
Univ. with Certif.	461
Univ. with Degree	1,419

Huntsville
(Town)
(Cont'd)

AVERAGE HOUSEHOLD EXPENDITURES

2001 Estimates:
Food	$5,841
Shelter	$8,432
Clothing	$1,727
Transportation	$6,621
Health & Personal Care	$1,780
Recr'n, Read'g & Education	$3,346
Taxes & Securities	$11,882
Other	$7,438
Total Expenditures	$47,067

PRIVATE HOUSEHOLDS

2001 Estimates:
Private Households, Total	6,756
Pop. in Private Households	16,697
Average no. per Household	2.5

FAMILIES

2001 Estimates:
Families in Private Households	5,029
Husband-Wife Families	4,495
Lone-Parent Families	534
Aver. No. Persons per Family	3.0
Aver. No. Sons/Daughters at Home	1.1

HOUSING

2001 Estimates:
Occupied Private Dwellings	6,756
Owned	5,299
Rented	1,457
Single-Detached House	5,485
Semi-Detached House	44
Row Houses	95
Apartment, 5 or Fewer Storeys	824
Apartment, Detached Duplex	274
Other Single-Attached	11
Movable Dwellings	23

VEHICLES

2001 Estimates:
Model Yrs. '81-'96, No.	9,339
% Total	78.65
Model Yrs. '97-'98, No.	1,537
% Total	12.94
'99 Vehicles registered in Model Yr. '99, No.	998
% Total	8.40
Total No. '81-'99	11,874

LEGAL MARITAL STATUS

2001 Estimates: (Age 15+)
Single (Never Married)	3,273
Legally Married (Not Separated)	8,047
Legally Married (Separated)	472
Widowed	1,033
Divorced	996

PSYTE CATEGORIES

2001 Estimates	No. of House -holds	% of Total Hhds.	Index
Small City Elite	157	2.32	136
Old Towns' New Fringe	423	6.26	160
Pick-ups & Dirt Bikes	360	5.33	638
Old Leafy Towns	4,451	65.88	2,578
Quiet Towns	1,238	18.32	861
Down, Down East	52	0.77	110

FINANCIAL P$YTE

2001 Estimates	No. of House -holds	% of Total Hhds.	Index
Canadian Comfort	157	2.32	24
Tractors & Tradelines	423	6.26	109
Bills & Wills	4,451	65.88	796
Country Credit	360	5.33	79
Rural Family Blues	52	0.77	10
Limited Budgets	1,238	18.32	589

HOME LANGUAGE

2001 Estimates:		% Total
English	16,909	98.80
French	102	0.60
German	11	0.06
Polish	11	0.06
Multiple Responses	81	0.47
Total	17,114	100.00

BUILDING PERMITS

	1999	1998	1997
		$000	
Value	21,078	29,671	17,484

HOMES BUILT

	1999	1998	1997
No	121	104	92

TAXATION

Income Class:	1997	% Total
Under $5,000	1,730	12.95
$5,000-$10,000	1,770	13.25
$10,000-$15,000	2,280	17.07
$15,000-$20,000	1,530	11.45
$20,000-$25,000	1,200	8.98
$25,000-$30,000	1,000	7.49
$30,000-$40,000	1,560	11.68
$40,000-$50,000	930	6.96
$50,000 +	1,360	10.18
Total Returns, No.	13,360	
Total Income, $000	328,235	
Total Taxable Returns	9,050	
Total Tax, $000	56,374	
Average Income, $	24,568	
Average Tax, $	6,229	

VITAL STATISTICS

	1997	1996	1995	1994
Births	196	174	215	215
Deaths	168	152	155	162
Natural Increase	28	22	60	53
Marriages	111	130	109	111

Note: Latest available data.

COMMUNITY NEWSPAPER(S)

	Total Circulation
Huntsville: District Weekender	25,171
Huntsville: Muskoka Advance	23,487
Huntsville: Huntsville Forester	6,620

RADIO STATION(S)

	Power
CBLU-FM	n.a.
CFBK-FM	5,000w
CJRT-FM	n.a.

TELEVISION STATION(S)

TFO
TVO

Kapuskasing
(Town)
In Cochrane District.

POPULATION

2001 Estimates:
July 1, 2001 Estimate	9,744
% Cdn. Total	0.03
% Change, '96 -'01	-5.59
Avg. Annual Growth Rate, %	-1.14
2003 Projected Population	9,503
2006 Projected Population	9,131
2001 Households Estimate	4,029
2003 Projected Households	4,020
2006 Projected Households	3,994

INCOME

% Above/Below National Average	-1
2001 Total Income Estimate	$202,960,000
% Cdn. Total	0.03
2001 Average Hhld. Income	$50,400
2001 Per Capita	$20,800
2003 Projected Total Income	$209,740,000
2006 Projected Total Income	$219,640,000

RETAIL SALES

% Above/Below National Average	+99
2001 Retail Sales Estimate	$173,570,000
% Cdn. Total	0.06
2001 per Household	$43,100
2001 per Capita	$17,800
2001 No. of Establishments	108
2003 Projected Retail Sales	$182,180,000
2006 Projected Retail Sales	$192,170,000

POPULATION

2001 Estimates:
Total		9,744
Male		4,862
Female		4,882

Age Groups	Male	Female
0-4	268	260
5-9	285	273
10-14	347	315
15-19	368	346
20-24	326	321
25-29	266	287
30-34	284	311
35-39	369	380
40-44	407	395
45-49	381	372
50-54	347	312
55-59	280	264
60-64	251	259
65-69	232	253
70+	451	534

DAYTIME POPULATION

2001 Estimates:
Working Population	6,077
At Home Population	5,215
Total	11,292

INCOME

2001 Estimates:
Avg. Household Income	$50,374
Avg. Family Income	$59,426
Per Capita Income	$20,829
Male:	
Avg. Employment Income	$38,015
Avg. Employment Income (Full Time)	$48,380
Female:	
Avg. Employment Income	$19,970
Avg. Employment Income (Full Time)	$30,887

Ontario

DISPOSABLE & DISCRETIONARY INCOME

2001 Estimates:	Per Hhld.
Disposable Income	$41,386
Discretionary Income 1 (minus Food & Shelter)	$28,936
Discretionary Income 2 (minus Food, Shelter, & Other Expenditures)	$20,442

LIQUID ASSETS

1999 Estimates:	Per Hhld.
Equity Investments	$65,885
Interest Bearing Investments	$62,268
Total Liquid Assets	$128,153

CREDIT DATA

July 2000:	
Pool of Credit	$106,623,914
Revolving Credit, No.	16,794
Fixed Loans, No.	7,556
Avg. Credit Limit, per Person.	$12,898
Avg. Spent, per Person	$5,872
Satisfactory Ratings, No. per Person.	2.73
Avg. No. of Cards, per Person	0.97

LABOUR FORCE

2001 Estimates:
Male:	
In the Labour Force	2,769
Participation Rate	69.9
Employed	2,515
Unemployed	254
Unemployment Rate	9.2
Not in Labour Force	1,193
Female:	
In the Labour Force	2,162
Participation Rate	53.6
Employed	1,989
Unemployed	173
Unemployment Rate	8.0
Not in Labour Force	1,872

OCCUPATIONS BY MAJOR GROUPS

2001 Estimates:	Male	Female
Management	234	113
Business, Finance & Admin.	131	516
Natural & Applied Sciences & Related	98	40
Health	20	173
Social Sciences, Gov't Services & Religion	67	39
Education	79	134
Arts, Culture, Recreation & Sport	20	62
Sales & Service	495	855
Trades, Transport & Equipment Operators & Related	840	61
Primary Industries	131	n.a.
Processing, Mfg. & Utilities	600	105

Kapuskasing
(Town)
(Cont'd)

LEVEL OF SCHOOLING

2001 Estimates:
Population 15 years +	7,996
Less than Grade 9	1,486
Grades 9-13 w/o Certif.	2,278
Grade 9-13 with Certif.	1,173
Trade Certif. /Dip.	394
Non-Univ. w/o Certif./Dip.	340
Non-Univ. with Certif./Dip.	1,365
Univ. w/o Degree	539
Univ. w/o Degree/Certif.	211
Univ. with Certif.	328
Univ. with Degree	421

AVERAGE HOUSEHOLD EXPENDITURES

2001 Estimates:
Food	$6,492
Shelter	$7,909
Clothing	$2,190
Transportation	$6,426
Health & Personal Care	$1,932
Recr'n, Read'g & Education	$3,959
Taxes & Securities	$11,569
Other	$8,331
Total Expenditures	$48,808

PRIVATE HOUSEHOLDS

2001 Estimates:
Private Households, Total	4,029
Pop. in Private Households	9,526
Average no. per Household	2.4

FAMILIES

2001 Estimates:
Families in Private Households	2,884
Husband-Wife Families	2,596
Lone-Parent Families	288
Aver. No. Persons per Family	3.0
Aver. No. Sons/Daughters at Home	1.1

HOUSING

2001 Estimates:
Occupied Private Dwellings	4,029
Owned	2,602
Rented	1,427
Single-Detached House	2,503
Semi-Detached House	231
Row Houses	61
Apartment, 5+ Storeys	61
Apartment, 5 or Fewer Storeys	838
Apartment, Detached Duplex	325
Other Single-Attached	10

VEHICLES

2001 Estimates:
Model Yrs. '81-'96, No.	5,149
% Total	78.77
Model Yrs. '97-'98, No.	894
% Total	13.68
'99 Vehicles registered in Model Yr. '99, No.	494
% Total	7.56
Total No. '81-'99	6,537

LEGAL MARITAL STATUS

2001 Estimates: (Age 15+)
Single (Never Married)	2,211
Legally Married (Not Separated)	4,359
Legally Married (Separated)	332
Widowed	660
Divorced	434

PSYTE CATEGORIES

2001 Estimates	No. of House -holds	% of Total Hhds.	Index
Traditional French Cdn. Families	287	7.12	265
The New Frontier	729	18.09	1,200
Quiet Towns	731	18.14	853
Agrarian Blues	334	8.29	3,872
Big Country Families	1,179	29.26	2,051
Quebec Rural Blues	46	1.14	47
Quebec Town Elders	723	17.94	635

FINANCIAL P$YTE

2001 Estimates	No. of House -holds	% of Total Hhds.	Index
Miners & Credit-Liners	729	18.09	572
Country Credit	287	7.12	105
Rural Family Blues	1,559	38.69	479
Limited Budgets	731	18.14	584
Loan Parent Stress	723	17.94	308

HOME LANGUAGE

2001 Estimates:		% Total
English	3,786	38.85
French	5,556	57.02
Chinese	10	0.10
Croatian	34	0.35
Finnish	10	0.10
Polish	10	0.10
Ukrainian	10	0.10
Other Languages	15	0.15
Multiple Responses	313	3.21
Total	9,744	100.00

BUILDING PERMITS

	1999	1998	1997
		$000	
Value	13,356	4,464	11,307

HOMES BUILT

	1999	1998	1997
No.	19	2	5

TAXATION

Income Class:	1997	% Total
Under $5,000	1,020	13.30
$5,000-$10,000	890	11.60
$10,000-$15,000	1,130	14.73
$15,000-$20,000	660	8.60
$20,000-$25,000	540	7.04
$25,000-$30,000	480	6.26
$30,000-$40,000	860	11.21
$40,000-$50,000	600	7.82
$50,000 +	1,500	19.56
Total Returns, No.	7,670	
Total Income, $000	234,251	
Total Taxable Returns	5,260	
Total Tax, $000	48,406	
Average Income, $	30,541	
Average Tax, $	9,203	

VITAL STATISTICS

	1997	1996	1995	1994
Births	99	109	127	118
Deaths	92	88	98	89
Natural Increase	7	21	29	29
Marriages	57	56	44	50

Note: Latest available data.

COMMUNITY NEWSPAPER(S)

	Total Circulation
Kapuskasing: Kapuskasing Northern Times	4,143
Kapuskasing: Le/The Weekender	9,896
Kapuskasing: L'Horizon	n.a.

RADIO STATION(S)

	Power
CBOK-FM	n.a.
CBON-FM	n.a.
CHYK	1,000w
CJRT-FM	n.a.
CKAP	10,000w
CKGN-FM	1,000w

TELEVISION STATION(S)

CFCL-TV
CITO-TV

Kenora
(Census Agglomeration)

The Census Agglomeration of Kenora includes: Kenora, T; Keewatin, T; and Jaffray and Melick, T. All are in Kenora District.

POPULATION

July 1, 2001 Estimate	17,602
% Cdn. Total	0.06
% Change, '96 -'01	1.13
Avg. Annual Growth Rate, %	0.23
2003 Projected Population	17,544
2006 Projected Population	17,498
2001 Households Estimate	7,091
2003 Projected Households	7,106
2006 Projected Households	7,259

INCOME

% Above/Below National Average	+8
2001 Total Income Estimate	$402,560,000
% Cdn. Total	0.06
2001 Average Hhld. Income	$56,800
2001 Per Capita	$22,900
2003 Projected Total Income	$428,040,000
2006 Projected Total Income	$477,340,000

RETAIL SALES

% Above/Below National Average	+63
2001 Retail Sales Estimate	$256,600,000
% Cdn. Total	0.09
2001 per Household	$36,200
2001 per Capita	$14,600
2001 No. of Establishments	187
2003 Projected Retail Sales	$277,260,000
2006 Projected Retail Sales	$305,150,000

POPULATION

2001 Estimates:

Total		17,602
Male		8,623
Female		8,979

Age Groups	Male	Female
0-4	552	517
5-9	615	566
10-14	651	599
15-19	621	609
20-24	563	579
25-29	527	553
30-34	580	640
35-39	691	732
40-44	725	720
45-49	689	639
50-54	566	508
55-59	426	415
60-64	354	372
65-69	322	360
70+	741	1,170

DAYTIME POPULATION

2001 Estimates:

Working Population	9,051
At Home Population	8,598
Total	17,649

INCOME

2001 Estimates:

Avg. Household Income	$56,771
Avg. Family Income	$65,416
Per Capita Income	$22,870
Male:	
Avg. Employment Income	$36,095
Avg. Employment Income (Full Time)	$49,319
Female:	
Avg. Employment Income	$22,343
Avg. Employment Income (Full Time)	$33,473

DISPOSABLE & DISCRETIONARY INCOME

2001 Estimates:	Per Hhld.
Disposable Income	$46,727
Discretionary Income 1 (minus Food & Shelter)	$33,986
Discretionary Income 2 (minus Food, Shelter, & Other Expenditures)	$24,955

LIQUID ASSETS

1999 Estimates:	Per Hhld.
Equity Investments	$92,022
Interest Bearing Investments	$74,218
Total Liquid Assets	$166,240

CREDIT DATA

July 2000:	
Pool of Credit	$170,915,587
Revolving Credit, No.	29,218
Fixed Loans, No.	10,470
Avg. Credit Limit, per Person	$12,531
Avg. Spent, per Person	$5,903
Satisfactory Ratings, No. per Person	2.72
Avg. No. of Cards, per Person	0.99

LABOUR FORCE

2001 Estimates:

Male:	
In the Labour Force	5,169
Participation Rate	76.0
Employed	4,703
Unemployed	466
Unemployment Rate	9.0
Not in Labour Force	1,636
Female:	
In the Labour Force	4,569
Participation Rate	62.6
Employed	4,316
Unemployed	253
Unemployment Rate	5.5
Not in Labour Force	2,728

OCCUPATIONS BY MAJOR GROUPS

2001 Estimates:	Male	Female
Management	596	152
Business, Finance & Admin.	231	1,405
Natural & Applied Sciences & Related	275	23
Health	69	534
Social Sciences, Gov't Services & Religion	114	197
Education	80	249
Arts, Culture, Recreation & Sport	99	47
Sales & Service	1,253	1,687
Trades, Transport & Equipment Operators & Related	1,651	85
Primary Industries	282	17
Processing, Mfg. & Utilities	412	79

LEVEL OF SCHOOLING

2001 Estimates:

Population 15 years +	14,102
Less than Grade 9	1,203
Grades 9-13 w/o Certif.	4,124
Grade 9-13 with Certif.	2,097
Trade Certif. /Dip.	625
Non-Univ. w/o Certif./Dip.	829
Non-Univ. with Certif./Dip.	2,512
Univ. w/o Degree	1,287
Univ. w/o Degree/Certif.	599
Univ. with Certif.	688
Univ. with Degree	1,425

AVERAGE HOUSEHOLD EXPENDITURES

2001 Estimates:

Food	$6,242
Shelter	$8,776
Clothing	$2,456
Transportation	$6,803
Health & Personal Care	$2,151
Recr'n, Read'g & Education	$3,958
Taxes & Securities	$14,723
Other	$8,950
Total Expenditures	$54,059

PRIVATE HOUSEHOLDS

2001 Estimates:	
Private Households, Total	7,091
Pop. in Private Households	17,146
Average no. per Household	2.4

FAMILIES

2001 Estimates:	
Families in Private Households	5,105
Husband-Wife Families	4,285
Lone-Parent Families	820
Aver. No. Persons per Family	3.0
Aver. No. Sons/Daughters at Home	1.2

HOUSING

2001 Estimates:	
Occupied Private Dwellings	7,091
Owned	5,119
Rented	1,972
Single-Detached House	5,232
Semi-Detached House	167
Row Houses	96
Apartment, 5+ Storeys	240
Apartment, 5 or Fewer Storeys	837
Apartment, Detached Duplex	296
Other Single-Attached	11
Movable Dwellings	212

VEHICLES

2001 Estimates:	
Model Yrs. '81-'96, No.	8,291
% Total	80.03
Model Yrs. '97-'98, No.	1,240
% Total	11.97
'99 Vehicles registered in Model Yr. '99, No.	829
% Total	8.00
Total No. '81-'99	10,360

LEGAL MARITAL STATUS

2001 Estimates: (Age 15+)	
Single (Never Married)	4,117
Legally Married (Not Separated)	7,291
Legally Married (Separated)	462
Widowed	1,166
Divorced	1,066

PSYTE CATEGORIES

2001 Estimates	No. of House-holds	% of Total Hhds.	Index
Town Boomers	5,104	71.98	7,101
Young Grey Collar	617	8.70	1,040
Quiet Towns	1,255	17.70	832

FINANÇIAL P$YTE

2001 Estimates	No. of House-holds	% of Total Hhds.	Index
Canadian Comfort	5,104	71.98	741
Revolving Renters	617	8.70	189
Limited Budgets	1,255	17.70	569

HOME LANGUAGE

2001 Estimates:		% Total
English	17,103	97.17
French	44	0.25
Chinese	33	0.19
Czech	11	0.06
German	11	0.06
Ojibway	22	0.12
Slovak	11	0.06
Tagalog (Pilipino)	28	0.16
Ukrainian	84	0.48
Other Languages	11	0.06
Multiple Responses	244	1.39
Total	17,602	100.00

BUILDING PERMITS

	1999	1998 $000	1997
Value	9,696	9,598	16,396

HOMES BUILT

	1999	1998	1997
No	28	30	85

TAXATION

Income Class:	1997	% Total
Under $5,000	1,600	11.78
$5,000-$10,000	1,540	11.34
$10,000-$15,000	1,930	14.21
$15,000-$20,000	1,310	9.65
$20,000-$25,000	1,060	7.81
$25,000-$30,000	1,070	7.88
$30,000-$40,000	1,830	13.48
$40,000-$50,000	1,090	8.03
$50,000 +	2,150	15.83
Total Returns, No.	13,580	
Total Income, $000	380,918	
Total Taxable Returns	9,690	
Total Tax, $000	70,817	
Average Income, $.	28,050	
Average Tax, $.	7,308	

VITAL STATISTICS

	1997	1996	1995	1994
Births	199	234	232	257
Deaths	172	177	178	162
Natural Increase	27	57	54	95
Marriages	124	114	142	118

Note: Latest available data.

DAILY NEWSPAPER(S)

	Circulation Average Paid
Daily Miner & News	4,205

COMMUNITY NEWSPAPER(S)

	Total Circulation
Kenora: Saturday Miner & News	10,600
Kenora: Kenora Enterprise	11,400

RADIO STATION(S)

	Power
CBQX-FM	n.a.
CJRL	5,000w
CJRT-FM	n.a.
CKSB-FM	n.a.

TELEVISION STATION(S)

CBWT-TV
CJBN-TV
TVO

Ontario

Kenora, Unorganized

(Unorganized - Non organisé)

In Kenora District.

POPULATION

July 1, 2001 Estimate	11,240
% Cdn. Total	0.04
% Change, '96 -'01	2.91
Avg. Annual Growth Rate, %	0.58
2003 Projected Population	11,345
2006 Projected Population	11,530
2001 Households Estimate	4,119
2003 Projected Households	4,174
2006 Projected Households	4,343

INCOME

% Above/Below National Average	+3
2001 Total Income Estimate	$244,630,000
% Cdn. Total	0.04
2001 Average Hhld. Income	$59,400
2001 Per Capita	$21,800
2003 Projected Total Income	$261,350,000
2006 Projected Total Income	$293,990,000

RETAIL SALES

% Above/Below National Average	-63
2001 Retail Sales Estimate	$36,870,000
% Cdn. Total	0.01
2001 per Household	$9,000
2001 per Capita	$3,300
2001 No. of Establishments	52
2003 Projected Retail Sales	$40,160,000
2006 Projected Retail Sales	$44,960,000

POPULATION

2001 Estimates:

Total	11,240
Male	5,774
Female	5,466

Age Groups	Male	Female
0-4	324	320
5-9	358	338
10-14	412	393
15-19	417	401
20-24	357	357
25-29	352	334
30-34	413	420
35-39	486	492
40-44	540	495
45-49	501	431
50-54	399	366
55-59	324	298
60-64	283	262
65-69	240	211
70+	368	348

DAYTIME POPULATION

2001 Estimates:

Working Population	4,610
At Home Population	5,229
Total	9,839

INCOME

2001 Estimates:

Avg. Household Income	$59,391
Avg. Family Income	$60,779
Per Capita Income	$21,764
Male:	
Avg. Employment Income	$35,776
Avg. Employment Income (Full Time)	$45,939
Female:	
Avg. Employment Income	$21,367
Avg. Employment Income (Full Time)	$32,251

DISPOSABLE & DISCRETIONARY INCOME

2001 Estimates:	Per Hhld.
Disposable Income	$48,655
Discretionary Income 1 (minus Food & Shelter)	$35,825
Discretionary Income 2 (minus Food, Shelter, & Other Expenditures)	$25,720

LIQUID ASSETS

1999 Estimates:	Per Hhld.
Equity Investments	$86,769
Interest Bearing Investments	$74,462
Total Liquid Assets	$161,231

CREDIT DATA

July 2000:

Pool of Credit	$62,337,003
Revolving Credit, No.	8,854
Fixed Loans, No.	4,840
Avg. Credit Limit, per Person	$12,662
Avg. Spent, per Person	$6,678
Satisfactory Ratings, No. per Person	2.60
Avg. No. of Cards, per Person	0.87

LABOUR FORCE

2001 Estimates:

Male:

In the Labour Force	3,549
Participation Rate	75.8
Employed	3,335
Unemployed	214
Unemployment Rate	6.0
Not in Labour Force	1,131

Female:

In the Labour Force	2,790
Participation Rate	63.2
Employed	2,599
Unemployed	191
Unemployment Rate	6.8
Not in Labour Force	1,625

OCCUPATIONS BY MAJOR GROUPS

2001 Estimates:	Male	Female
Management	505	333
Business, Finance & Admin.	179	697
Natural & Applied Sciences & Related	176	56
Health	34	133
Social Sciences, Gov't Services & Religion	89	132
Education	57	204
Arts, Culture, Recreation & Sport	22	75
Sales & Service	531	971
Trades, Transport & Equipment Operators & Related	1,160	50
Primary Industries	301	92
Processing, Mfg. & Utilities	451	8

LEVEL OF SCHOOLING

2001 Estimates:

Population 15 years +	9,095
Less than Grade 9	875
Grades 9-13 w/o Certif.	2,445
Grade 9-13 with Certif.	1,458
Trade Certif./Dip.	540
Non-Univ. w/o Certif./Dip.	431
Non-Univ. with Certif./Dip.	2,011
Univ. w/o Degree	653
Univ. w/o Degree/Certif.	302
Univ. with Certif.	351
Univ. with Degree	682

AVERAGE HOUSEHOLD EXPENDITURES

2001 Estimates:

Food	$6,750
Shelter	$8,409
Clothing	$2,628
Transportation	$7,763
Health & Personal Care	$2,325
Recr'n, Read'g & Education	$4,709
Taxes & Securities	$14,128
Other	$9,362
Total Expenditures	$56,074

PRIVATE HOUSEHOLDS

2001 Estimates:

Private Households, Total	4,119
Pop. in Private Households	10,688
Average no. per Household	2.6

FAMILIES

2001 Estimates:

Families in Private Households	3,429
Husband-Wife Families	3,138
Lone-Parent Families	291
Aver. No. Persons per Family	2.9
Aver. No. Sons/Daughters at Home	1.1

HOUSING

2001 Estimates:

Occupied Private Dwellings	4,119
Owned	3,567
Rented	552
Single-Detached House	3,602
Semi-Detached House	50
Row Houses	34
Apartment, 5 or Fewer Storeys	33
Apartment, Detached Duplex	11
Other Single-Attached	34
Movable Dwellings	355

VEHICLES

2001 Estimates:

Model Yrs. '81-'96, No.	5,524
% Total	80.88
Model Yrs. '97-'98, No.	834
% Total	12.21
'99 Vehicles registered in Model Yr. '99, No.	472
% Total	6.91
Total No. '81-'99	6,830

LEGAL MARITAL STATUS

2001 Estimates: (Age 15+)

Single (Never Married)	2,349
Legally Married (Not Separated)	5,591
Legally Married (Separated)	247
Widowed	344
Divorced	564

PSYTE CATEGORIES

2001 Estimates	No. of House-holds	% of Total Hhds.	Index
Small City Elite	142	3.45	201
Town Boomers	897	21.78	2,149
Old Towns' New Fringe	23	0.56	14
The New Frontier	1,956	47.49	3,148
Pick-ups & Dirt Bikes	334	8.11	971
Old Leafy Towns	389	9.44	370
Big Country Families	287	6.97	488

FINANCIAL P$YTE

2001 Estimates	No. of House-holds	% of Total Hhds.	Index
Canadian Comfort	1,039	25.22	260
Miners & Credit-Liners	1,956	47.49	1,500
Tractors & Tradelines	23	0.56	10
Bills & Wills	389	9.44	114
Country Credit	334	8.11	120
Rural Family Blues	287	6.97	86

HOME LANGUAGE

2001 Estimates:		% Total
English	10,860	96.62
French	61	0.54
German	144	1.28
Italian	17	0.15
Ojibway	62	0.55
Polish	10	0.09
Other Languages	22	0.20
Multiple Responses	64	0.57
Total	11,240	100.00

TAXATION

Income Class:	1997	% Total
Under $5,000	1,670	35.01
$5,000-$10,000	650	13.63
$10,000-$15,000	640	13.42
$15,000-$20,000	350	7.34
$20,000-$25,000	310	6.50
$25,000-$30,000	260	5.45
$30,000-$40,000	390	8.18
$40,000-$50,000	200	4.19
$50,000 +	310	6.50
Total Returns, No.	4,770	
Total Income, $000	78,108	
Total Taxable Returns	1,620	
Total Tax, $000	9,882	
Average Income, $	16,375	
Average Tax, $	6,100	

VITAL STATISTICS

	1997	1996	1995	1994
Births	527	364	290	322
Deaths	101	85	93	72
Natural Increase	426	279	197	250
Marriages	84	66	83	45

Note: Latest available data.

Kingston
(Census Agglomeration)

The Census Agglomeration of Kingston includes: Kingston, C; Kingston, TP; Loughborough, TP; Pittsburgh, TP; Portland, TP; Storrington, TP, & 2 smaller areas; all in Frontenac County. It also includes: Amherst Island, TP; Bath, VL; and Ernestown, TP in Lennox and Addington County.

POPULATION

July 1, 2001 Estimate	147,539
% Cdn. Total	0.47
% Change, '96 -'01	-0.08
Avg. Annual Growth Rate, %	-0.02
2003 Projected Population	149,187
2006 Projected Population	151,013
2001 Households Estimate	60,134
2003 Projected Households	61,389
2006 Projected Households	63,061

INCOME

% Above/Below National Average	+7
2001 Total Income Estimate	$3,314,380,000
% Cdn. Total	0.50
2001 Average Hhld. Income	$55,100
2001 Per Capita	$22,500
2003 Projected Total Income	$3,557,900,000
2006 Projected Total Income	$3,942,350,000

RETAIL SALES

% Above/Below National Average	+4
2001 Retail Sales Estimate	$1,369,150,000
% Cdn. Total	0.49
2001 per Household	$22,800
2001 per Capita	$9,300
2001 No. of Establishments	1,140
2003 Projected Retail Sales	$1,482,500,000
2006 Projected Retail Sales	$1,642,870,000

POPULATION

2001 Estimates:

Total		147,539
Male		72,651
Female		74,888

Age Groups	Male	Female
0-4	4,531	4,359
5-9	4,623	4,462
10-14	4,665	4,545
15-19	4,724	4,544
20-24	5,296	4,919
25-29	5,632	5,240
30-34	5,951	5,601
35-39	6,021	5,961
40-44	5,733	5,887
45-49	5,346	5,521
50-54	4,649	4,793
55-59	3,815	3,876
60-64	3,159	3,268
65-69	2,676	3,034
70+	5,830	8,878

DAYTIME POPULATION

2001 Estimates:

Working Population	74,302
At Home Population	73,237
Total	147,539

INCOME

2001 Estimates:

Avg. Household Income	$55,117
Avg. Family Income	$63,155
Per Capita Income	$22,464
Male:	
Avg. Employment Income	$34,124
Avg. Employment Income (Full Time)	$45,642
Female:	
Avg. Employment Income	$23,409
Avg. Employment Income (Full Time)	$35,070

DISPOSABLE & DISCRETIONARY INCOME

2001 Estimates:	Per Hhld.
Disposable Income	$45,280
Discretionary Income 1 (minus Food & Shelter)	$31,996
Discretionary Income 2 (minus Food, Shelter, & Other Expenditures)	$23,661

LIQUID ASSETS

1999 Estimates:	Per Hhld.
Equity Investments	$72,490
Interest Bearing Investments	$66,052
Total Liquid Assets	$138,542

CREDIT DATA

July 2000:

Pool of Credit	$1,546,188,653
Revolving Credit, No.	283,153
Fixed Loans, No.	78,281
Avg. Credit Limit, per Person	$11,426
Avg. Spent, per Person	$5,189
Satisfactory Ratings, No. per Person	2.55
Avg. No. of Cards, per Person	0.94

LABOUR FORCE

2001 Estimates:

Male:	
In the Labour Force	41,149
Participation Rate	69.9
Employed	38,646
Unemployed	2,503
Unemployment Rate	6.1
Not in Labour Force	17,683
Female:	
In the Labour Force	37,320
Participation Rate	60.7
Employed	35,155
Unemployed	2,165
Unemployment Rate	5.8
Not in Labour Force	24,202

OCCUPATIONS BY MAJOR GROUPS

2001 Estimates:	Male	Female
Management	5,177	2,342
Business, Finance & Admin.	3,203	9,508
Natural & Applied Sciences & Related	2,724	650
Health	1,221	4,197
Social Sciences, Gov't Services & Religion	906	1,742
Education	2,613	2,584
Arts, Culture, Recreation & Sport	824	1,079
Sales & Service	11,189	12,838
Trades, Transport & Equipment Operators & Related	8,509	413
Primary Industries	1,352	333
Processing, Mfg. & Utilities	2,307	439

LEVEL OF SCHOOLING

2001 Estimates:

Population 15 years +	120,354
Less than Grade 9	7,963
Grades 9-13 w/o Certif.	26,119
Grade 9-13 with Certif.	16,472
Trade Certif. /Dip.	4,224
Non-Univ. w/o Certif./Dip.	8,221
Non-Univ. with Certif./Dip.	24,133
Univ. w/o Degree	12,081
Univ. w/o Degree/Certif.	6,696
Univ. with Certif.	5,385
Univ. with Degree	21,141

AVERAGE HOUSEHOLD EXPENDITURES

2001 Estimates:

Food	$6,179
Shelter	$9,353
Clothing	$2,214
Transportation	$6,327
Health & Personal Care	$1,933
Recr'n, Read'g & Education	$3,832
Taxes & Securities	$14,391
Other	$8,531
Total Expenditures	$52,760

PRIVATE HOUSEHOLDS

2001 Estimates:

Private Households, Total	60,134
Pop. in Private Households	139,658
Average no. per Household	2.3

FAMILIES

2001 Estimates:

Families in Private Households	42,553
Husband-Wife Families	36,444
Lone-Parent Families	6,109
Aver. No. Persons per Family	2.8
Aver. No. Sons/Daughters at Home	1.1

HOUSING

2001 Estimates:

Occupied Private Dwellings	60,134
Owned	37,501
Rented	22,633
Single-Detached House	34,289
Semi-Detached House	4,534
Row Houses	3,611
Apartment, 5+ Storeys	7,016
Owned Apartment, 5+ Storeys	847
Apartment, 5 or Fewer Storeys	9,201
Apartment, Detached Duplex	1,138
Other Single-Attached	229
Movable Dwellings	116

VEHICLES

2001 Estimates:

Model Yrs. '81-'96, No.	69,336
% Total	81.75
Model Yrs. '97-'98, No.	9,109
% Total	10.74
'99 Vehicles registered in Model Yr. '99, No.	6,373
% Total	7.51
Total No. '81-'99	84,818

LEGAL MARITAL STATUS

2001 Estimates: (Age 15+)

Single (Never Married)	37,204
Legally Married (Not Separated)	62,375
Legally Married (Separated)	4,328
Widowed	7,648
Divorced	8,799

PSYTE CATEGORIES

2001 Estimates	No. of House-holds	% of Total Hhds.	Index
Urban Gentry	1,838	3.06	170
Suburban Executives	814	1.35	94
Mortgaged in Suburbia	604	1.00	72
Technocrafts & Bureaucrats	2,685	4.47	159
Boomers & Teens	897	1.49	83
Small City Elite	4,933	8.20	479
Old Bungalow Burbs	1,570	2.61	158
Suburban Nesters	249	0.41	26
Aging Erudites	3,472	5.77	383
Satellite Suburbs	2,507	4.17	145
Kindergarten Boom	1,037	1.72	66
Blue Collar Winners	3,544	5.89	234
Old Towns' New Fringe	8,061	13.41	342
Rustic Prosperity	689	1.15	63
High Rise Melting Pot	92	0.15	10
Conservative Homebodies	737	1.23	34
High Rise Sunsets	2,139	3.56	249

Ontario

2001 Estimates	No. of House-holds	% of Total Hhds.	Index
Young Urban Professionals	2,591	4.31	227
Young Urban Mix	834	1.39	65
Young Urban Intelligentsia	1,025	1.70	112
University Enclaves	4,394	7.31	358
Young City Singles	5,161	8.58	374
Urban Bohemia	497	0.83	71
Old Leafy Towns	1,235	2.05	80
Struggling Downtowns	3,311	5.51	175
Aged Pensioners	1,588	2.64	198
Big City Stress	1,409	2.34	208

FINANCIAL PSYTE

2001 Estimates	No. of House-holds	% of Total Hhds.	Index
Four Star Investors	3,549	5.90	117
Successful Suburbanites	3,289	5.47	82
Canadian Comfort	11,233	18.68	192
Urban Heights	6,063	10.08	234
Miners & Credit-Liners	1,570	2.61	82
Mortgages & Minivans	1,037	1.72	26
Tractors & Tradelines	8,750	14.55	254
Bills & Wills	2,806	4.67	56
Revolving Renters	2,139	3.56	77
Young Urban Struggle	5,916	9.84	208
Towering Debt	8,564	14.24	182
NSF	1,409	2.34	66
Senior Survivors	1,588	2.64	140

HOME LANGUAGE

2001 Estimates:		% Total
English	139,037	94.24
French	2,254	1.53
Arabic	152	0.10
Chinese	629	0.43
German	142	0.10
Greek	296	0.20
Italian	219	0.15
Korean	150	0.10
Persian (Farsi)	98	0.07
Polish	248	0.17
Portuguese	1,145	0.78
Spanish	309	0.21
Tamil	83	0.06
Urdu	75	0.05
Vietnamese	291	0.20
Other Languages	797	0.54
Multiple Responses	1,614	1.09
Total	147,539	100.00

BUILDING PERMITS

	1999	1998 $000	1997
Value	144,315	128,569	119,588

Ontario

Kingston
(Census Agglomeration)
(Cont'd)

HOMES BUILT

	1999	1998	1997
No.	550	508	635

TAXATION

Income Class:	1997	% Total
Under $5,000	12,500	12.45
$5,000-$10,000	12,220	12.17
$10,000-$15,000	14,230	14.17
$15,000-$20,000	9,480	9.44
$20,000-$25,000	7,920	7.89
$25,000-$30,000	7,670	7.64
$30,000-$40,000	12,900	12.85
$40,000-$50,000	9,050	9.01
$50,000 +	14,480	14.42
Total Returns, No.	100,390	
Total Income, $000	2,828,594	
Total Taxable Returns	69,810	
Total Tax, $000	526,800	
Average Income, $	28,176	
Average Tax, $	7,546	

VITAL STATISTICS

	1997	1996	1995	1994
Births	1,360	1,579	1,717	1,752
Deaths	1,189	1,209	1,200	1,113
Natural Increase	171	370	517	639
Marriages	813	936	922	907

Note: Latest available data.

DAILY NEWSPAPER(S)

	Circulation Average Paid
The Kingston Whig-Standard	
Sat.	34,577
Mon-Fri	27,288

COMMUNITY NEWSPAPER(S)

	Total Circulation
Kingston: Kingston This Week	
Tue/Fri	48,287
(Fri. total 53,925)	
Kingston, Amherstview: The Heritage Newspaper	31,413

Kitchener
(Census Metropolitan Area)

POPULATION

July 1, 2001 Estimate	428,936
% Cdn. Total	1.38
% Change, '96 -'01	8.56
Avg. Annual Growth Rate, %	1.66
2003 Projected Population	442,219
2006 Projected Population	458,615
2001 Households Estimate	163,426
2003 Projected Households	169,914
2006 Projected Households	178,915

INCOME

% Above/Below National Average	+8
2001 Total Income Estimate	$9,742,290,000
% Cdn. Total	1.48
2001 Average Hhld. Income	$59,600
2001 Per Capita	$22,700
2003 Projected Total Income	$10,653,100,000
2006 Projected Total Income	$12,059,360,000

RETAIL SALES

% Above/Below National Average	+18
2001 Retail Sales Estimate	$4,549,990,000
% Cdn. Total	1.63
2001 per Household	$27,800
2001 per Capita	$10,600
2001 No. of Establishments	2,823
2003 Projected Retail Sales	$5,052,530,000
2006 Projected Retail Sales	$5,773,040,000

POPULATION

2001 Estimates:

	Total	
Total		428,936
Male		210,723
Female		218,213

Age Groups	Male	Female
0-4	14,506	13,786
5-9	15,150	14,489
10-14	15,216	14,551
15-19	14,745	14,199
20-24	14,851	14,600
25-29	15,789	15,657
30-34	17,440	17,329
35-39	18,128	18,112
40-44	17,063	17,331
45-49	15,388	15,829
50-54	12,920	13,369
55-59	10,397	10,468
60-64	8,343	8,555
65-69	6,868	7,752
70+	13,919	22,186

DAYTIME POPULATION

2001 Estimates:

Working Population	233,913
At Home Population	195,023
Total	428,936

INCOME

2001 Estimates:

Avg. Household Income	$59,613
Avg. Family Income	$66,661
Per Capita Income	$22,713
Male:	
Avg. Employment Income	$38,533
Avg. Employment Income (Full Time)	$49,220
Female:	
Avg. Employment Income	$22,690
Avg. Employment Income (Full Time)	$33,175

DISPOSABLE & DISCRETIONARY INCOME

2001 Estimates:	Per Hhld.
Disposable Income	$48,842
Discretionary Income 1 (minus Food & Shelter)	$34,507
Discretionary Income 2 (minus Food, Shelter, & Other Expenditures)	$25,603

LIQUID ASSETS

1999 Estimates:	Per Hhld.
Equity Investments	$84,670
Interest Bearing Investments	$73,113
Total Liquid Assets	$157,783

CREDIT DATA

July 2000:	
Pool of Credit	$4,605,310,216
Revolving Credit, No.	807,479
Fixed Loans, No.	256,860
Avg. Credit Limit, per Person	$13,018
Avg. Spent, per Person	$6,012
Satisfactory Ratings, No. per Person	2.89
Avg. No. of Cards, per Person	1.05

LABOUR FORCE

2001 Estimates:	
Male:	
In the Labour Force	131,455
Participation Rate	79.3
Employed	126,271
Unemployed	5,184
Unemployment Rate	3.9
Not in Labour Force	34,396
Female:	
In the Labour Force	113,279
Participation Rate	64.6
Employed	106,864
Unemployed	6,415
Unemployment Rate	5.7
Not in Labour Force	62,108

OCCUPATIONS BY MAJOR GROUPS

2001 Estimates:	Male	Female
Management	14,835	6,582
Business, Finance & Admin.	12,758	32,155
Natural & Applied Sciences & Related	10,045	2,050
Health	1,565	7,148
Social Sciences, Gov't Services & Religion	2,283	2,988
Education	4,545	6,342
Arts, Culture, Recreation & Sport	2,378	2,876
Sales & Service	23,884	33,448
Trades, Transport & Equipment Operators & Related	30,267	2,295
Primary Industries	3,127	964
Processing, Mfg. & Utilities	23,107	12,466

LEVEL OF SCHOOLING

2001 Estimates:	
Population 15 years +	341,238
Less than Grade 9	34,177
Grades 9-13 w/o Certif.	83,691
Grade 9-13 with Certif.	50,059
Trade Certif./Dip.	11,271
Non-Univ. w/o Certif./Dip.	21,477
Non-Univ. with Certif./Dip.	64,314
Univ. w/o Degree	29,662
Univ. w/o Degree/Certif.	15,707
Univ. with Certif.	13,955
Univ. with Degree	46,587

Kitchener
(Census Metropolitan Area)
(Cont'd)
AVERAGE HOUSEHOLD EXPENDITURES

2001 Estimates:

Food	$6,599
Shelter	$9,998
Clothing	$2,383
Transportation	$6,828
Health & Personal Care	$2,008
Recr'n, Read'g & Education	$3,952
Taxes & Securities	$15,568
Other	$9,160
Total Expenditures	$56,496

PRIVATE HOUSEHOLDS

2001 Estimates:

Private Households, Total	163,426
Pop. in Private Households	422,461
Average no. per Household	2.6

FAMILIES

2001 Estimates:

Families in Private Households	122,105
Husband-Wife Families	105,622
Lone-Parent Families	16,483
Aver. No. Persons per Family	3.1
Aver. No. Sons/Daughters at Home	1.2

RADIO STATION DATA

Station	Market	Format	Wkly. Reach%*	Aver. Hrs. Tuned
All Stations			94	22.0
CBCL-FM	London	News, Info.	n.a.	n.a.
CBL-FM	Toronto	All Info.	5	6.6
CBLA-FM	Toronto	News, Info.	10	12.4
CFCA-FM	Waterloo	AOR	21	10.4
CFMX-FM	Toronto	Classical	n.a.	n.a.
CFNY-FM	Toronto	Alternative	9	5.1
CFPL-FM	London	Rock	6	4.8
CFRB	Toronto	News, Talk	4	7.6
CFTR	Toronto	All News	n.a.	n.a.
CHAM	Hamilton	Country	5	9.5
CHFI-FM	Toronto	Adult Contemp.	n.a.	n.a.
CHML	Hamilton	News, Talk	5	9.7
CHTZ-FM St.	Cath.-Niagara	AOR	3	7.7
CHUM-FM	Toronto	Adult Contemp.	5	4.6
CHYM-FM	Kitchener	Adult Contemp.	37	13.1
CIDC-FM	Toronto	Dance	15	4.9
CILQ-FM	Toronto	AOR	9	6.6
CING-FM	Burlington	Contemp. Hit Radio	19	6.2
CIZN-FM	Cambridge	Adult Top 40	8	6.5
CJCL	Toronto	Sports	2	5.4
CJXY-FM	Hamilton	AOR	7	7.3
CKDK-FM	London	Classic Rock	4	8.6
CKFM-FM	Toronto	Adult Contemp.	4	3.8
CKGL	Kitchener	All News	10	8.0
CKKW	Waterloo	Oldies	10	9.7
CKLH-FM	Hamilton	Adult Contemp.	2	6.9
CKWR-FM	Waterloo	Light Adult Contemp.	n.a.	n.a.

BBM Spring 2000 Radio Reach Survey; area coverage.
*Mon-Sun 5a.m - 1a.m , All Persons 12+

TV STATION DATA

Station	Market	Network Affiliation	Wkly. Reach%*	Aver. Hrs. Tuned
All Stations			92	20.7
A & E	n.a.	Ind.	18	3.0
CBLN	London	CBC	31	2.2
CFMT	Toronto	Ind.	23	2.0
CFPL	London	Ind.	25	2.1
CHCH	Toronto/Hamilton	Ind.	38	2.3
CICO-E	n.a.	n.a.	17	2.6
CIII	n.a.	Global	59	3.1
CITY	Toronto	Ind.	34	2.4
CKCO	Kitchener	CTV	69	6.0
CNN	n.a.	Ind.	6	2.0
COMEDY	n.a.	Ind.	9	1.5
CTS	Toronto/Hamilton	Ind.	7	1.6
DSCVRY	n.a.	Ind.	8	2.0
FAMILY	n.a.	Ind.	7	1.6
FOOD	n.a.	Ind.	5	2.0
HISTTV	n.a.	Ind.	5	2.3
MMUSIC	n.a.	Ind.	7	2.1
NEWSWD	n.a.	CBC	7	1.8
OTHERS	n.a.	n.a.	10	2.8
PRIME	n.a.	Ind.	10	2.1
SNET	n.a.	CTV	11	2.5
SPACE	n.a.	Ind.	7	2.8
TLC	n.a.	Ind.	13	1.9
TMN	Toronto	Ind.	4	3.8
TNN	Nashville TN	Ind.	8	1.4
TOON	n.a.	Ind.	8	3.2
TREE	n.a.	Ind.	2	5.8
TSN	n.a.	Ind.	17	3.5
VCR	n.a.	n.a.	30	4.9
VISION	n.a.	Ind.	6	2.0
WGRZ	Buffalo NY	NBC	18	1.6
WIVB	Buffalo NY	CBS	14	1.6
WKBW	Buffalo NY	ABC	22	1.4
WNED	Buffalo NY	PBS	16	1.9
WTBS	Atlanta GA	Ind.	13	2.8
WUTV	Buffalo NY	FOX	30	1.8
YTV	n.a.	Ind.	12	2.8

BBM Spring 2000 TV Reach Survey; CMA coverage.
*Mon-Sun 6a.m - 2a.m , All Persons 2 +

HOUSING

2001 Estimates:

Occupied Private Dwellings	163,426
Owned	102,334
Rented	61,092
Single-Detached House	87,744
Semi-Detached House	11,161
Row Houses	15,500
Apartment, 5+ Storeys	18,339
Owned Apartment, 5+ Storeys	2,195
Apartment, 5 or Fewer Storeys	26,068
Apartment, Detached Duplex	3,751
Other Single-Attached	334
Movable Dwellings	529

VEHICLES

2001 Estimates:

Model Yrs. '81-'96, No.	193,070
% Total	78.47
Model Yrs. '97-'98, No.	31,849
% Total	12.94
'99 Vehicles registered in Model Yr. '99, No.	21,131
% Total	8.59
Total No. '81-'99	246,050

LEGAL MARITAL STATUS

2001 Estimates: (Age 15+)

Single (Never Married)	98,971
Legally Married (Not Separated)	189,657
Legally Married (Separated)	11,374
Widowed	19,269
Divorced	21,967

PSYTE CATEGORIES

2001 Estimates	No. of House-holds	% of Total Hhds.	Index
Canadian Establishment	269	0.16	99
Urban Gentry	703	0.43	24
Suburban Executives	4,845	2.96	207
Mortgaged in Suburbia	4,735	2.90	208
Technocrafts & Bureaucrats	8,890	5.44	193
Boomers & Teens	5,095	3.12	174
Stable Suburban Families	4,104	2.51	193
Small City Elite	515	0.32	18
Old Bungalow Burbs	3,927	2.40	145
Suburban Nesters	1,986	1.22	76
Brie & Chablis	384	0.23	26
Aging Erudites	1,894	1.16	77
Satellite Suburbs	17,128	10.48	365
Kindergarten Boom	7,581	4.64	177
Blue Collar Winners	7,695	4.71	187
Old Towns' New Fringe	194	0.12	3
Rustic Prosperity	838	0.51	28
Europa	794	0.49	39
High Rise Melting Pot	362	0.22	15
Conservative Homebodies	25,395	15.54	431
High Rise Sunsets	3,179	1.95	136
Young Urban Professionals	1,110	0.68	36
Young Urban Mix	3,333	2.04	96
Young Urban Intelligentsia	822	0.50	33
University Enclaves	10,628	6.50	319
Young City Singles	7,989	4.89	213
Old Leafy Towns	394	0.24	9
Town Renters	7,230	4.42	512
Nesters & Young Homesteaders	817	0.50	21
Agrarian Blues	365	0.22	104
Struggling Downtowns	25,741	15.75	500
Aged Pensioners	2,223	1.36	102
Big City Stress	1,090	0.67	59
Old Grey Towers	152	0.09	17

Ontario

FINANCIAL P$YTE

2001 Estimates	No. of House-holds	% of Total Hhds.	Index
Platinum Estates	269	0.16	20
Four Star Investors	10,643	6.51	130
Successful Suburbanites	17,729	10.85	163
Canadian Comfort	27,324	16.72	172
Urban Heights	3,388	2.07	48
Miners & Credit-Liners	3,927	2.40	76
Mortgages & Minivans	7,581	4.64	70
Dollars & Sense	794	0.49	19
Tractors & Tradelines	1,032	0.63	11
Bills & Wills	29,122	17.82	215
Revolving Renters	3,996	2.45	53
Young Urban Struggle	11,450	7.01	148
Rural Family Blues	365	0.22	3
Towering Debt	41,322	25.28	324
NSF	1,090	0.67	19
Senior Survivors	2,375	1.45	77

HOME LANGUAGE

2001 Estimates:		% Total
English	376,465	87.77
French	1,662	0.39
Arabic	892	0.21
Armenian	282	0.07
Chinese	2,493	0.58
Croatian	1,057	0.25
Czech	243	0.06
Dutch	241	0.06
German	5,228	1.22
Greek	737	0.17
Gujarati	425	0.10
Hindi	381	0.09
Hungarian	919	0.21
Italian	741	0.17
Japanese	215	0.05
Khmer (Cambodian)	224	0.05
Kurdish	352	0.08
Lao	729	0.17
Persian (Farsi)	431	0.10
Polish	3,786	0.88
Portuguese	7,816	1.82
Punjabi	1,262	0.29
Romanian	2,364	0.55
Serbian	1,078	0.25
Serbo-Croatian	682	0.16
Slovak	333	0.08
Spanish	3,406	0.79
Tagalog (Pilipino)	231	0.05
Turkish	238	0.06
Ukrainian	262	0.06
Urdu	255	0.06
Vietnamese	2,404	0.56
Other Languages	2,850	0.66
Multiple Responses	8,252	1.92
Total	428,936	100.00

Ontario

Kitchener
(Census Metropolitan Area)
(Cont'd)

BUILDING PERMITS

	1999	1998	1997
		$000	
Value	558,780	473,227	422,855

HOMES BUILT

	1999	1998	1997
No	2,690	2,349	2,328

TAXATION

Income Class:	1997	% Total
Under $5,000	32,930	11.62
$5,000-$10,000	31,200	11.00
$10,000-$15,000	35,740	12.61
$15,000-$20,000	27,810	9.81
$20,000-$25,000	24,610	8.68
$25,000-$30,000	23,780	8.39
$30,000-$40,000	39,820	14.05
$40,000-$50,000	25,270	8.91
$50,000 +	42,370	14.94
Total Returns, No.	283,510	
Total Income, $000	8,460,010	
Total Taxable Returns	207,820	
Total Tax, $000	1,671,730	
Average Income, $	29,840	
Average Tax, $	8,044	

VITAL STATISTICS

	1997	1996	1995	1994
Births	5,045	5,408	5,389	5,485
Deaths	2,514	2,566	2,479	2,417
Natural Increase	2,531	2,842	2,910	3,068
Marriages	2,325	2,423	2,446	2,159

Note: Latest available data.

DAILY NEWSPAPER(S)

	Circulation Average Paid
Cambridge Reporter	7,226
The Record	
Sat	85,043
Mon-Fri.	68,187

COMMUNITY NEWSPAPER(S)

	Total Circulation
Cambridge: Cambridge Times	
Tue	34,107
Fri	39,142
Kitchener, Waterloo:	
Kitchener/Waterloo Pennysaver	92,000
Waterloo: Waterloo Chronicle	24,484

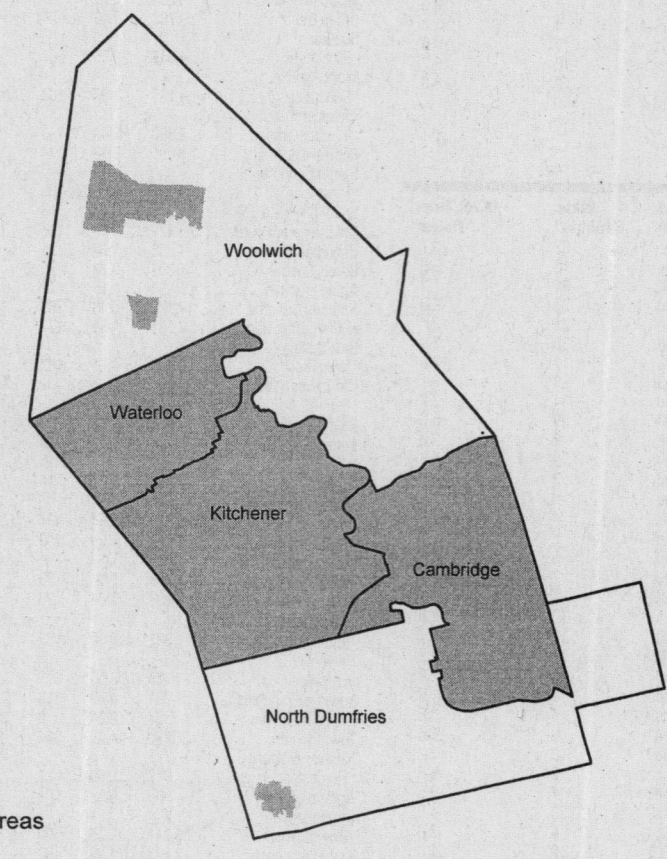

Urban Areas

Cambridge
(City)
Kitchener CMA
In Waterloo Regional Municipality.

POPULATION

July 1, 2001 Estimate	115,278
% Cdn. Total	0.37
% Change, '96 -'01	10.15
Avg. Annual Growth Rate, %	1.95
2003 Projected Population	119,685
2006 Projected Population	125,358
2001 Households Estimate	41,803
2003 Projected Households	43,748
2006 Projected Households	46,488

INCOME

% Above/Below National Average	+2
2001 Total Income Estimate	$2,474,710,000
% Cdn. Total	0.38
2001 Average Hhld. Income	$59,200
2001 Per Capita	$21,500
2003 Projected Total Income	$2,723,480,000
2006 Projected Total Income	$3,111,080,000

RETAIL SALES

% Above/Below National Average	+19
2001 Retail Sales Estimate	$1,227,790,000
% Cdn. Total	0.44
2001 per Household	$29,400
2001 per Capita	$10,700
2001 No. of Establishments	698
2003 Projected Retail Sales	$1,371,380,000
2006 Projected Retail Sales	$1,581,210,000

POPULATION

2001 Estimates:

Total		115,278
Male		56,573
Female		58,705

Age Groups	Male	Female
0-4	3,964	3,736
5-9	4,273	4,139
10-14	4,364	4,205
15-19	4,176	4,010
20-24	3,923	3,807
25-29	3,906	3,924
30-34	4,440	4,552
35-39	4,830	4,927
40-44	4,646	4,702
45-49	4,190	4,223
50-54	3,453	3,498
55-59	2,761	2,732
60-64	2,221	2,228
65-69	1,797	2,009
70+	3,629	6,013

DAYTIME POPULATION

2001 Estimates:

Working Population	62,682
At Home Population	54,021
Total	116,703

INCOME

2001 Estimates:

Avg. Household Income	$59,199
Avg. Family Income	$64,150
Per Capita Income	$21,467
Male:	
Avg. Employment Income	$38,365
Avg. Employment Income (Full Time)	$48,091
Female:	
Avg. Employment Income	$21,835
Avg. Employment Income (Full Time)	$31,583

DISPOSABLE & DISCRETIONARY INCOME

2001 Estimates:	*Per Hhld.*
Disposable Income	$48,924
Discretionary Income 1 (minus Food & Shelter)	$34,318
Discretionary Income 2 (minus Food, Shelter, & Other Expenditures)	$25,208

LIQUID ASSETS

1999 Estimates:	*Per Hhld.*
Equity Investments	$81,208
Interest Bearing Investments	$71,863
Total Liquid Assets	$153,071

CREDIT DATA

July 2000:

Pool of Credit	$1,217,705,704
Revolving Credit, No.	210,054
Fixed Loans, No.	75,559
Avg. Credit Limit, per Person	$13,301
Avg. Spent, per Person	$6,486
Satisfactory Ratings, No. per Person	2.98
Avg. No. of Cards, per Person	1.01

LABOUR FORCE

2001 Estimates:

Male:	
In the Labour Force	34,930
Participation Rate	79.4
Employed	33,400
Unemployed	1,530
Unemployment Rate	4.4
Not in Labour Force	9,042
Female:	
In the Labour Force	29,595
Participation Rate	63.5
Employed	27,591
Unemployed	2,004
Unemployment Rate	6.8
Not in Labour Force	17,030

OCCUPATIONS BY MAJOR GROUPS

2001 Estimates:	Male	Female
Management	3,494	1,466
Business, Finance & Admin.	3,142	8,078
Natural & Applied Sciences & Related	2,517	466
Health	321	1,656
Social Sciences, Gov't Services & Religion	413	637
Education	542	1,140
Arts, Culture, Recreation & Sport	408	608
Sales & Service	6,084	8,851
Trades, Transport & Equipment Operators & Related	8,926	725
Primary Industries	635	170
Processing, Mfg. & Utilities	7,719	4,552

LEVEL OF SCHOOLING

2001 Estimates:

Population 15 years +.	90,597
Less than Grade 9	10,989
Grades 9-13 w/o Certif.	25,111
Grade 9-13 with Certif.	14,486
Trade Certif. /Dip.	3,180
Non-Univ. w/o Certif./Dip.	5,868
Non-Univ. with Certif./Dip.	17,204
Univ. w/o Degree	6,067
Univ. w/o Degree/Certif.	2,884
Univ. with Certif.	3,183
Univ. with Degree	7,692

AVERAGE HOUSEHOLD EXPENDITURES

2001 Estimates:

Food	$6,753
Shelter	$10,044
Clothing	$2,340
Transportation	$7,023
Health & Personal Care	$2,006
Recr'n, Read'g & Education	$3,916
Taxes & Securities	$14,962
Other	$9,264
Total Expenditures	$56,308

PRIVATE HOUSEHOLDS

2001 Estimates:

Private Households, Total	41,803
Pop. in Private Households	113,495
Average no. per Household	2.7

FAMILIES

2001 Estimates:

Families in Private Households	33,008
Husband-Wife Families	28,659
Lone-Parent Families	4,349
Aver. No. Persons per Family	3.1
Aver. No. Sons/Daughters at Home	1.3

HOUSING

2001 Estimates:

Occupied Private Dwellings	41,803
Owned	27,947
Rented	13,856
Single-Detached House	24,009
Semi-Detached House	3,847
Row Houses	4,136
Apartment, 5+ Storeys	2,134
Owned Apartment, 5+ Storeys	305
Apartment, 5 or Fewer Storeys	6,471
Apartment, Detached Duplex	1,006
Other Single-Attached	177
Movable Dwellings	23

VEHICLES

2001 Estimates:

Model Yrs. '81-'96, No.	53,233
% Total	79.53
Model Yrs. '97-'98, No.	8,307
% Total	12.41
'99 Vehicles registered in Model Yr. '99, No.	5,395
% Total	8.06
Total No. '81-'99	66,935

LEGAL MARITAL STATUS

2001 Estimates: (Age 15+)

Single (Never Married)	24,371
Legally Married (Not Separated)	51,818
Legally Married (Separated)	3,117
Widowed	5,452
Divorced	5,839

PSYTE CATEGORIES

2001 Estimates	No. of House -holds	% of Total Hhds.	Index
Suburban Executives	978	2.34	163
Mortgaged in Suburbia	1,113	2.66	192
Technocrafts & Bureaucrats	936	2.24	80
Stable Suburban Families	440	1.05	81
Old Bungalow Burbs	1,064	2.55	154
Suburban Nesters	714	1.71	107
Satellite Suburbs	6,747	16.14	563
Kindergarten Boom	991	2.37	90
Blue Collar Winners	2,772	6.63	263
Europa	794	1.90	153
Conservative Homebodies	8,945	21.40	593
High Rise Sunsets	280	0.67	47
Young City Singles	256	0.61	27
Town Renters	2,812	6.73	778
Nesters & Young Homesteaders	817	1.95	84

Ontario

2001 Estimates	No. of House -holds	% of Total Hhds.	Index
Struggling Downtowns	11,539	27.60	877
Big City Stress	216	0.52	46
Old Grey Towers	152	0.36	66

FINANCIAL P$YTE

2001 Estimates	No. of House -holds	% of Total Hhds.	Index
Four Star Investors	978	2.34	47
Successful Suburbanites	2,489	5.95	90
Canadian Comfort	10,233	24.48	252
Miners & Credit-Liners	1,064	2.55	80
Mortgages & Minivans	991	2.37	36
Dollars & Sense	794	1.90	73
Bills & Wills	8,945	21.40	258
Revolving Renters	1,097	2.62	57
Towering Debt	14,607	34.94	448
NSF	216	0.52	15
Senior Survivors	152	0.36	19

HOME LANGUAGE

2001 Estimates:		% Total
English	102,378	88.81
French	494	0.43
Arabic	172	0.15
Armenian	210	0.18
Chinese	395	0.34
Croatian	113	0.10
German	186	0.16
Greek	119	0.10
Gujarati	176	0.15
Hungarian	239	0.21
Italian	470	0.41
Lao	119	0.10
Persian (Farsi)	59	0.05
Polish	464	0.40
Portuguese	4,921	4.27
Punjabi	350	0.30
Slovak	78	0.07
Spanish	672	0.58
Tagalog (Pilipino)	121	0.10
Urdu	138	0.12
Vietnamese	487	0.42
Other Languages	673	0.58
Multiple Responses	2,244	1.95
Total	115,278	100.00

BUILDING PERMITS

	1999	1998	1997
		$000	
Value	140,351	134,635	121,238

HOMES BUILT

	1999	1998	1997
No.	864	767	471

Cambridge
(City)
Kitchener CMA
(Cont'd)

TAXATION

Income Class:	1997	% Total
Under $5,000	8,890	11.52
$5,000-$10,000	8,530	11.05
$10,000-$15,000	10,140	13.14
$15,000-$20,000	7,780	10.08
$20,000-$25,000	6,880	8.91
$25,000-$30,000	6,320	8.19
$30,000-$40,000	10,720	13.89
$40,000-$50,000	6,910	8.95
$50,000 +	11,020	14.28
Total Returns, No.	77,180	
Total Income, $000	2,211,403	
Total Taxable Returns	56,430	
Total Tax, $000	426,708	
Average Income, $	28,653	
Average Tax, $	7,562	

VITAL STATISTICS

	1997	1996	1995	1994
Births	1,361	1,510	1,493	1,569
Deaths	766	757	724	724
Natural Increase	595	753	769	845
Marriages	520	518	515	518

Note: Latest available data.

MEDIA INFO
see Kitchener, CMA

Kitchener
(City)
Kitchener CMA

In Waterloo Regional Municipality.

POPULATION

July 1, 2001 Estimate	197,530
% Cdn. Total	0.63
% Change, '96 -'01	7.30
Avg. Annual Growth Rate, %	1.42
2003 Projected Population	202,355
2006 Projected Population	207,962
2001 Households Estimate	77,861
2003 Projected Households	80,441
2006 Projected Households	83,954

INCOME

% Above/Below National Average	+1
2001 Total Income Estimate	$4,208,320,000
% Cdn. Total	0.64
2001 Average Hhld. Income	$54,000
2001 Per Capita	$21,300
2003 Projected Total Income	$4,570,560,000
2006 Projected Total Income	$5,123,830,000

RETAIL SALES

% Above/Below National Average	+14
2001 Retail Sales Estimate	$2,014,680,000
% Cdn. Total	0.72
2001 per Household	$25,900
2001 per Capita	$10,200
2001 No. of Establishments	1,186
2003 Projected Retail Sales	$2,223,680,000
2006 Projected Retail Sales	$2,518,000,000

POPULATION

2001 Estimates:

Total		197,530
Male		96,942
Female		100,588

Age Groups	Male	Female
0-4	6,837	6,476
5-9	6,970	6,585
10-14	6,811	6,419
15-19	6,573	6,272
20-24	6,648	6,607
25-29	7,314	7,336
30-34	8,355	8,257
35-39	8,630	8,493
40-44	7,928	7,970
45-49	7,018	7,253
50-54	5,858	6,111
55-59	4,707	4,805
60-64	3,758	3,956
65-69	3,134	3,634
70+	6,401	10,414

DAYTIME POPULATION

2001 Estimates:

Working Population	113,021
At Home Population	91,337
Total	204,358

INCOME

2001 Estimates:

Avg. Household Income	$54,049
Avg. Family Income	$60,531
Per Capita Income	$21,305
Male:	
Avg. Employment Income	$35,253
Avg. Employment Income (Full Time)	$44,922
Female:	
Avg. Employment Income	$22,140
Avg. Employment Income (Full Time)	$32,056

DISPOSABLE & DISCRETIONARY INCOME

2001 Estimates:	Per Hhld.
Disposable Income	$44,507
Discretionary Income 1 (minus Food & Shelter)	$31,045
Discretionary Income 2 (minus Food, Shelter, & Other Expenditures)	$22,788

LIQUID ASSETS

1999 Estimates:	Per Hhld.
Equity Investments	$64,996
Interest Bearing Investments	$64,035
Total Liquid Assets	$129,031

CREDIT DATA

July 2000:

Pool of Credit	$2,008,704,792
Revolving Credit, No.	363,818
Fixed Loans, No.	118,901
Avg. Credit Limit, per Person	$12,468
Avg. Spent, per Person	$5,767
Satisfactory Ratings, No. per Person	2.87
Avg. No. of Cards, per Person	1.03

LABOUR FORCE

2001 Estimates:

Male:

In the Labour Force	59,930
Participation Rate	78.5
Employed	57,320
Unemployed	2,610
Unemployment Rate	4.4
Not in Labour Force	16,394

Female:

In the Labour Force	51,797
Participation Rate	63.9
Employed	48,573
Unemployed	3,224
Unemployment Rate	6.2
Not in Labour Force	29,311

OCCUPATIONS BY MAJOR GROUPS

2001 Estimates:	Male	Female
Management	6,038	2,930
Business, Finance & Admin.	5,744	14,376
Natural & Applied Sciences & Related	4,074	920
Health	455	3,464
Social Sciences, Gov't Services & Religion	940	1,421
Education	1,532	2,465
Arts, Culture, Recreation & Sport	1,132	1,122
Sales & Service	11,558	15,867
Trades, Transport & Equipment Operators & Related	14,564	976
Primary Industries	840	151
Processing, Mfg. & Utilities	11,555	6,045

LEVEL OF SCHOOLING

2001 Estimates:

Population 15 years +	157,432
Less than Grade 9	14,987
Grades 9-13 w/o Certif.	40,322
Grade 9-13 with Certif.	23,222
Trade Certif. /Dip.	5,554
Non-Univ. w/o Certif./Dip.	10,849
Non-Univ. with Certif./Dip.	30,875
Univ. w/o Degree	13,175
Univ. w/o Degree/Certif.	6,765
Univ. with Certif.	6,410
Univ. with Degree	18,448

AVERAGE HOUSEHOLD EXPENDITURES

2001 Estimates:

Food	$6,225
Shelter	$9,332
Clothing	$2,202
Transportation	$6,263
Health & Personal Care	$1,897
Recr'n, Read'g & Education	$3,646
Taxes & Securities	$13,797
Other	$8,642
Total Expenditures	$52,004

PRIVATE HOUSEHOLDS

2001 Estimates:

Private Households, Total	77,861
Pop. in Private Households	194,347
Average no. per Household	2.5

FAMILIES

2001 Estimates:

Families in Private Households	56,263
Husband-Wife Families	47,655
Lone-Parent Families	8,608
Aver. No. Persons per Family	3.0
Aver. No. Sons/Daughters at Home	1.2

HOUSING

2001 Estimates:

Occupied Private Dwellings	77,861
Owned	44,813
Rented	33,048
Single-Detached House	38,041
Semi-Detached House	4,835
Row Houses	7,452
Apartment, 5+ Storeys	11,518
Owned Apartment, 5+ Storeys	724
Apartment, 5 or Fewer Storeys	13,810
Apartment, Detached Duplex	2,073
Other Single-Attached	90
Movable Dwellings	42

VEHICLES

2001 Estimates:

Model Yrs. '81-'96, No.	87,754
% Total	79.60
Model Yrs. '97-'98, No.	13,281
% Total	12.05
'99 Vehicles registered in Model Yr. '99, No.	9,212
% Total	8.36
Total No. '81-'99	110,247

LEGAL MARITAL STATUS

2001 Estimates: (Age 15+)

Single (Never Married)	47,059
Legally Married (Not Separated)	84,016
Legally Married (Separated)	5,801
Widowed	9,218
Divorced	11,338

PSYTE CATEGORIES

2001 Estimates	No. of House-holds	% of Total Hhds.	Index
Suburban Executives	392	0.50	35
Mortgaged in Suburbia	1,229	1.58	114
Technocrafts & Bureaucrats	3,616	4.64	165
Boomers & Teens	3,049	3.92	218
Stable Suburban Families	2,193	2.82	216
Small City Elite	515	0.66	39
Old Bungalow Burbs	2,448	3.14	190
Suburban Nesters	1,272	1.63	102
Aging Erudites	126	0.16	11
Satellite Suburbs	7,668	9.85	343
Kindergarten Boom	5,605	7.20	275
High Rise Melting Pot	362	0.46	31
Conservative Homebodies	13,326	17.12	475
High Rise Sunsets	2,112	2.71	190
Young Urban Professionals	288	0.37	19
Young Urban Mix	2,963	3.81	180
University Enclaves	5,091	6.54	320
Young City Singles	5,220	6.70	292
Town Renters	3,661	4.70	544
Struggling Downtowns	13,796	17.72	563
Aged Pensioners	1,400	1.80	135
Big City Stress	874	1.12	99

Kitchener
(City)
Kitchener CMA
(Cont'd)

FINANCIAL P$YTE

2001 Estimates	No. of Households	% of Total Hhds.	Index
Four Star Investors	3,441	4.42	88
Successful Suburbanites	7,038	9.04	136
Canadian Comfort	9,455	12.14	125
Urban Heights	414	0.53	12
Miners & Credit-Liners	2,448	3.14	99
Mortgages & Minivans	5,605	7.20	109
Bills & Wills	16,289	20.92	253
Revolving Renters	2,112	2.71	59
Young Urban Struggle	5,091	6.54	138
Towering Debt	23,039	29.59	379
NSF	874	1.12	32
Senior Survivors	1,400	1.80	95

HOME LANGUAGE

2001 Estimates:		% Total
English	169,832	85.98
French	798	0.40
Arabic	521	0.26
Chinese	781	0.40
Croatian	866	0.44
Czech	140	0.07
German	1,959	0.99
Greek	462	0.23
Gujarati	230	0.12
Hindi	118	0.06
Hungarian	577	0.29
Italian	164	0.08
Khmer (Cambodian)	224	0.11
Kurdish	135	0.07
Lao	428	0.22
Persian (Farsi)	185	0.09
Polish	2,368	1.20
Portuguese	2,642	1.34
Punjabi	543	0.27
Romanian	2,008	1.02
Russian	113	0.06
Serbian	741	0.38
Serbo-Croatian	655	0.33
Slovak	255	0.13
Spanish	2,335	1.18
Tagalog (Pilipino)	110	0.06
Turkish	185	0.09
Ukrainian	161	0.08
Vietnamese	1,665	0.84
Other Languages	1,986	1.01
Multiple Responses	4,343	2.20
Total	197,530	100.00

BUILDING PERMITS

	1999	1998	1997
		$000	
Value	192,748	158,822	141,742

HOMES BUILT

	1999	1998	1997
No	886	730	986

TAXATION

Income Class:	1997	% Total
Under $5,000	15,330	11.67
$5,000-$10,000	14,860	11.31
$10,000-$15,000	17,430	13.27
$15,000-$20,000	13,420	10.21
$20,000-$25,000	11,670	8.88
$25,000-$30,000	11,390	8.67
$30,000-$40,000	18,910	14.39
$40,000-$50,000	11,470	8.73
$50,000 +	16,900	12.86
Total Returns, No.	131,380	
Total Income, $000	3,627,913	
Total Taxable Returns	94,850	
Total Tax, $000	669,661	
Average Income, $	27,614	
Average Tax, $	7,060	

VITAL STATISTICS

	1997	1996	1995	1994
Births	2,406	2,667	2,692	2,682
Deaths	1,242	1,284	1,240	1,216
Natural Increase	1,164	1,383	1,452	1,466
Marriages	1,238	1,359	1,402	1,145

Note: Latest available data.

MEDIA INFO

see Kitchener, CMA

Waterloo
(City)
Kitchener CMA

In Waterloo Regional Municipality.

POPULATION

July 1, 2001 Estimate	88,612
% Cdn. Total	0.28
% Change, '96 -'01	10.18
Avg. Annual Growth Rate, %	1.96
2003 Projected Population	92,115
2006 Projected Population	96,642
2001 Households Estimate	34,376
2003 Projected Households	36,067
2006 Projected Households	38,457

INCOME

% Above/Below National Average	+25
2001 Total Income Estimate	$2,344,380,000
% Cdn. Total	0.36
2001 Average Hhld. Income	$68,200
2001 Per Capita	$26,500
2003 Projected Total Income	$2,582,540,000
2006 Projected Total Income	$2,953,250,000

RETAIL SALES

% Above/Below National Average	+30
2001 Retail Sales Estimate	$1,029,190,000
% Cdn. Total	0.37
2001 per Household	$29,900
2001 per Capita	$11,600
2001 No. of Establishments	624
2003 Projected Retail Sales	$1,154,880,000
2006 Projected Retail Sales	$1,337,780,000

POPULATION

2001 Estimates:		
Total		88,612
Male		43,519
Female		45,093
Age Groups	Male	Female
0-4	2,918	2,793
5-9	2,984	2,871
10-14	2,995	2,924
15-19	2,917	2,870
20-24	3,284	3,229
25-29	3,689	3,574
30-34	3,766	3,669
35-39	3,684	3,699
40-44	3,440	3,595
45-49	3,136	3,300
50-54	2,651	2,800
55-59	2,125	2,161
60-64	1,712	1,734
65-69	1,407	1,561
70+	2,811	4,313

DAYTIME POPULATION

2001 Estimates:	
Working Population	42,508
At Home Population	38,538
Total	81,046

INCOME

2001 Estimates:	
Avg. Household Income	$68,198
Avg. Family Income	$79,208
Per Capita Income	$26,457
Male:	
Avg. Employment Income	$44,127
Avg. Employment Income (Full Time)	$57,806
Female:	
Avg. Employment Income	$24,452
Avg. Employment Income (Full Time)	$36,900

Ontario

DISPOSABLE & DISCRETIONARY INCOME

2001 Estimates:	Per Hhld.
Disposable Income	$54,896
Discretionary Income 1 (minus Food & Shelter)	$39,624
Discretionary Income 2 (minus Food, Shelter, & Other Expenditures)	$30,250

LIQUID ASSETS

1999 Estimates:	Per Hhld.
Equity Investments	$117,415
Interest Bearing Investments	$88,160
Total Liquid Assets	$205,575

CREDIT DATA

July 2000:	
Pool of Credit	$1,092,533,657
Revolving Credit, No.	188,836
Fixed Loans, No.	49,265
Avg. Credit Limit, per Person	$13,551
Avg. Spent, per Person	$5,944
Satisfactory Ratings, No. per Person	2.86
Avg. No. of Cards, per Person	1.13

LABOUR FORCE

2001 Estimates:	
Male:	
In the Labour Force	27,263
Participation Rate	78.7
Employed	26,342
Unemployed	921
Unemployment Rate	3.4
Not in Labour Force	7,359
Female:	
In the Labour Force	24,502
Participation Rate	67.1
Employed	23,514
Unemployed	988
Unemployment Rate	4.0
Not in Labour Force	12,003

OCCUPATIONS BY MAJOR GROUPS

2001 Estimates:	Male	Female
Management	3,912	1,763
Business, Finance & Admin.	3,012	7,548
Natural & Applied Sciences & Related	2,933	600
Health	659	1,553
Social Sciences, Gov't Services & Religion	834	787
Education	2,228	2,190
Arts, Culture, Recreation & Sport	709	902
Sales & Service	4,948	6,668
Trades, Transport & Equipment Operators & Related	4,295	351
Primary Industries	579	166
Processing, Mfg. & Utilities	2,789	1,386

Ontario

Waterloo
(City)
Kitchener CMA
(Cont'd)

LEVEL OF SCHOOLING

2001 Estimates:

Population 15 years +	71,127
Less than Grade 9	4,360
Grades 9-13 w/o Certif.	13,292
Grade 9-13 with Certif.	9,231
Trade Certif./Dip.	1,690
Non-Univ. w/o Certif./Dip.	3,523
Non-Univ. with Certif./Dip.	12,274
Univ. w/o Degree	8,796
Univ. w/o Degree/Certif.	5,203
Univ. with Certif.	3,593
Univ. with Degree	17,961

AVERAGE HOUSEHOLD EXPENDITURES

2001 Estimates:

Food	$7,006
Shelter	$10,935
Clothing	$2,755
Transportation	$7,159
Health & Personal Care	$2,189
Recr'n, Read'g & Education	$4,494
Taxes & Securities	$18,860
Other	$9,753
Total Expenditures	$63,151

PRIVATE HOUSEHOLDS

2001 Estimates:

Private Households, Total	34,376
Pop. in Private Households	87,520
Average no. per Household	2.5

FAMILIES

2001 Estimates:

Families in Private Households	25,021
Husband-Wife Families	21,993
Lone-Parent Families	3,028
Aver. No. Persons per Family	3.1
Aver. No. Sons/Daughters at Home	1.2

HOUSING

2001 Estimates:

Occupied Private Dwellings	34,376
Owned	21,815
Rented	12,561
Single-Detached House	18,258
Semi-Detached House	1,745
Row Houses	3,781
Apartment, 5+ Storeys	4,687
Owned Apartment, 5+ Storeys	1,166
Apartment, 5 or Fewer Storeys	5,032
Apartment, Detached Duplex	523
Other Single-Attached	35
Movable Dwellings	315

VEHICLES

2001 Estimates:

Model Yrs. '81-'96, No.	38,477
% Total	75.18
Model Yrs. '97-'98, No.	7,833
% Total	15.31
'99 Vehicles registered in Model Yr. '99, No.	4,867
% Total	9.51
Total No. '81-'99	51,177

LEGAL MARITAL STATUS

2001 Estimates: (Age 15+)

Single (Never Married)	21,764
Legally Married (Not Separated)	40,010
Legally Married (Separated)	1,990
Widowed	3,447
Divorced	3,916

PSYTE CATEGORIES

2001 Estimates	No. of House-holds	% of Total Hhds.	Index
Canadian Establishment	269	0.78	470
Urban Gentry	703	2.05	114
Suburban Executives	3,475	10.11	705
Mortgaged in Suburbia	1,960	5.70	410
Technocrafts & Bureaucrats	4,338	12.62	448
Boomers & Teens	1,059	3.08	172
Stable Suburban Families	1,439	4.19	321
Old Bungalow Burbs	415	1.21	73
Brie & Chablis	384	1.12	125
Aging Erudites	1,768	5.14	341
Satellite Suburbs	2,241	6.52	227
Kindergarten Boom	985	2.87	109
Blue Collar Winners	108	0.31	12
Conservative Homebodies	2,714	7.90	219
High Rise Sunsets	787	2.29	160
Young Urban Professionals	822	2.39	126

2001 Estimates	No. of House-holds	% of Total Hhds.	Index
Young Urban Mix	370	1.08	51
Young Urban Intelligentsia	822	2.39	157
University Enclaves	5,537	16.11	789
Young City Singles	2,513	7.31	319
Town Renters	757	2.20	255
Aged Pensioners	823	2.39	180

FINANCIAL P$YTE

2001 Estimates	No. of House-holds	% of Total Hhds.	Index
Platinum Estates	269	0.78	97
Four Star Investors	5,237	15.23	303
Successful Suburbanites	7,737	22.51	339
Canadian Comfort	2,349	6.83	70
Urban Heights	2,974	8.65	201
Miners & Credit-Liners	415	1.21	38
Mortgages & Minivans	985	2.87	43
Bills & Wills	3,084	8.97	108
Revolving Renters	787	2.29	50
Young Urban Struggle	6,359	18.50	391
Towering Debt	3,270	9.51	122
Senior Survivors	823	2.39	127

HOME LANGUAGE

2001 Estimates:		% Total
English	79,522	89.74
French	318	0.36
Arabic	199	0.22
Bengali	51	0.06
Chinese	1,317	1.49
Croatian	78	0.09
Czech	81	0.09
German	953	1.08
Greek	134	0.15
Hindi	209	0.24
Hungarian	103	0.12
Italian	85	0.10
Japanese	123	0.14
Kurdish	217	0.24
Lao	182	0.21
Persian (Farsi)	187	0.21
Polish	954	1.08
Portuguese	180	0.20
Punjabi	369	0.42
Romanian	302	0.34
Serbian	293	0.33
Spanish	399	0.45
Turkish	53	0.06
Ukrainian	72	0.08
Urdu	63	0.07
Vietnamese	252	0.28
Other Languages	528	0.60
Multiple Responses	1,388	1.57
Total	88,612	100.00

BUILDING PERMITS

	1999	1998	1997
		$000	
Value	172,948	130,280	105,728

HOMES BUILT

	1999	1998	1997
No.	805	739	711

TAXATION

Income Class:	1997	% Total
Under $5,000	6,960	11.84
$5,000-$10,000	6,080	10.34
$10,000-$15,000	6,250	10.63
$15,000-$20,000	5,190	8.83
$20,000-$25,000	4,770	8.11
$25,000-$30,000	4,690	7.98
$30,000-$40,000	8,020	13.64
$40,000-$50,000	5,350	9.10
$50,000 +	11,480	19.53
Total Returns, No.	58,790	
Total Income, $000	2,061,269	
Total Taxable Returns	44,190	
Total Tax, $000	454,646	
Average Income, $	35,062	
Average Tax, $	10,288	

VITAL STATISTICS

	1997	1996	1995	1994
Births	986	962	945	971
Deaths	380	389	379	351
Natural Increase	606	573	566	620
Marriages	389	367	350	348

Note: Latest available data.

MEDIA INFO
see Kitchener, CMA

Woolwich
(Township)
Kitchener CMA

In Waterloo Regional Municipality.

POPULATION

July 1, 2001 Estimate 18,258
% Cdn. Total 0.06
% Change, '96 -'01 . . . . 2.15
Avg. Annual Growth Rate, % 0.43
2003 Projected Population 18,238
2006 Projected Population 18,057
2001 Households Estimate 6,281
2003 Projected Households 6,332
2006 Projected Households 6,370

INCOME

% Above/Below National Average . . . . +17
2001 Total Income Estimate $452,070,000
% Cdn. Total 0.07
2001 Average Hhld. Income $72,000
2001 Per Capita $24,800
2003 Projected Total Income . . . $477,760,000
2006 Projected Total Income . . . $513,990,000

RETAIL SALES

% Above/Below National Average . . . . +33
2001 Retail Sales Estimate $217,740,000
% Cdn. Total 0.08
2001 per Household $34,700
2001 per Capita $11,900
2001 No. of Establishments 234
2003 Projected Retail Sales $232,820,000
2006 Projected Retail Sales $251,700,000

POPULATION

2001 Estimates:
Total 18,258
Male 8,964
Female 9,294

Age Groups	Male	Female
0-4	489	502
5-9	567	573
10-14	669	656
15-19	719	705
20-24	685	651
25-29	598	543
30-34	569	529
35-39	607	611
40-44	649	678
45-49	658	694
50-54	622	657
55-59	545	536
60-64	449	445
65-69	372	389
70+	766	1,125

DAYTIME POPULATION

2001 Estimates:
Working Population 11,153
At Home Population 7,300
Total 18,453

INCOME

2001 Estimates:
Avg. Household Income $71,974
Avg. Family Income $78,629
Per Capita Income $24,760
Male:
Avg. Employment Income $42,543
Avg. Employment Income
 (Full Time) $54,742
Female:
Avg. Employment Income $21,611
Avg. Employment Income
 (Full Time) $30,757

DISPOSABLE & DISCRETIONARY INCOME

2001 Estimates:	Per Hhld.
Disposable Income	$58,652
Discretionary Income 1 (minus Food & Shelter)	$42,339
Discretionary Income 2 (minus Food, Shelter, & Other Expenditures)	$31,066

LIQUID ASSETS

1999 Estimates:	Per Hhld.
Equity Investments	$130,852
Interest Bearing Investments	$93,100
Total Liquid Assets	$223,952

CREDIT DATA

July 2000:
Pool of Credit $190,653,827
Revolving Credit, No. 30,911
Fixed Loans, No. 8,338
Avg. Credit Limit, per Person $13,406
Avg. Spent, per Person $5,629
Satisfactory Ratings,
 No. per Person 2.69
Avg. No. of Cards, per Person 1.07

LABOUR FORCE

2001 Estimates:
Male:
In the Labour Force 6,192
Participation Rate 85.5
Employed 6,119
Unemployed 73
Unemployment Rate 1.2
Not in Labour Force 1,047
Female:
In the Labour Force 4,994
Participation Rate 66.0
Employed 4,873
Unemployed 121
Unemployment Rate 2.4
Not in Labour Force 2,569

OCCUPATIONS BY MAJOR GROUPS

2001 Estimates:	Male	Female
Management	844	248
Business, Finance & Admin.	526	1,353
Natural & Applied Sciences & Related	295	51
Health	66	290
Social Sciences, Gov't Services & Religion	58	106
Education	159	368
Arts, Culture, Recreation & Sport	79	144
Sales & Service	849	1,503
Trades, Transport & Equipment Operators & Related	1,674	174
Primary Industries	861	452
Processing, Mfg. & Utilities	736	283

LEVEL OF SCHOOLING

2001 Estimates:
Population 15 years + ... 14,802
Less than Grade 9 3,357
Grades 9-13 w/o Certif. 3,162
Grade 9-13 with Certif. 2,033
Trade Certif. /Dip. 510
Non-Univ. w/o Certif./Dip. 757
Non-Univ. with Certif./Dip. 2,392
Univ. w/o Degree 1,027
 Univ. w/o Degree/Certif. 543
 Univ. with Certif. 484
Univ. with Degree 1,564

AVERAGE HOUSEHOLD EXPENDITURES

2001 Estimates:
Food $7,347
Shelter $11,340
Clothing $2,567
Transportation $9,141
Health & Personal Care $2,198
Recr'n, Read'g & Education $4,433
Taxes & Securities $19,027
Other $10,580
Total Expenditures $66,633

PRIVATE HOUSEHOLDS

2001 Estimates:
Private Households, Total 6,281
Pop. in Private Households 17,934
Average no. per Household 2.9

FAMILIES

2001 Estimates:
Families in Private Households 5,108
Husband-Wife Families 4,746
Lone-Parent Families 362
Aver. No. Persons per Family 3.3
Aver. No. Sons/Daughters
 at Home 1.4

HOUSING

2001 Estimates:
Occupied Private Dwellings 6,281
 Owned 5,035
 Rented 1,246
Single-Detached House 4,685
Semi-Detached House 609
Row Houses 99
Apartment, 5 or Fewer Storeys 645
Apartment, Detached Duplex 104
Other Single-Attached 32
Movable Dwellings 107

VEHICLES

2001 Estimates:
Model Yrs. '81-'96, No. 9,572
 % Total 77.99
Model Yrs. '97-'98, No. 1,610
 % Total 13.12
'99 Vehicles registered in
 Model Yr. '99, No. 1,092
 % Total 8.90
Total No. '81-'99 12,274

LEGAL MARITAL STATUS

2001 Estimates: (Age 15+)
Single (Never Married) 4,070
Legally Married
 (Not Separated) 9,018
Legally Married (Separated) 291
Widowed 875
Divorced 548

PSYTE CATEGORIES

2001 Estimates	No. of House-holds	% of Total Hhds.	Index
Boomers & Teens	473	7.53	420
Stable Suburban Families	32	0.51	39
Satellite Suburbs	472	7.51	262
Blue Collar Winners	2,860	45.53	1,809
Rustic Prosperity	838	13.34	739
Conservative Homebodies	410	6.53	181
Old Leafy Towns	394	6.27	245
Agrarian Blues	365	5.81	2,714
Struggling Downtowns	406	6.46	205

Ontario

FINANCIAL P$YTE

2001 Estimates	No. of House-holds	% of Total Hhds.	Index
Four Star Investors	473	7.53	150
Successful Suburbanites	32	0.51	8
Canadian Comfort	3,332	53.05	546
Tractors & Tradelines	838	13.34	233
Bills & Wills	804	12.80	155
Rural Family Blues	365	5.81	72
Towering Debt	406	6.46	83

HOME LANGUAGE

2001 Estimates:		% Total
English	15,784	86.45
Dutch	108	0.59
German	2,118	11.60
Greek	22	0.12
Italian	11	0.06
Macedonian	11	0.06
Serbo-Croatian	11	0.06
Other Languages	65	0.36
Multiple Responses	128	0.70
Total	18,258	100.00

BUILDING PERMITS

	1999	1998	1997
		$000	
Value	28,637	27,691	27,603

HOMES BUILT

	1999	1998	1997
No	80	76	86

TAXATION

Income Class:	1997	% Total
Under $5,000	1,230	10.59
$5,000-$10,000	1,300	11.20
$10,000-$15,000	1,460	12.58
$15,000-$20,000	1,100	9.47
$20,000-$25,000	940	8.10
$25,000-$30,000	1,030	8.87
$30,000-$40,000	1,570	13.52
$40,000-$50,000	1,080	9.30
$50,000 +	1,910	16.45
Total Returns, No.	11,610	
Total Income, $000	392,149	
Total Taxable Returns	8,790	
Total Tax, $000	83,201	
Average Income, $.	33,777	
Average Tax, $	9,465	

VITAL STATISTICS

	1997	1996	1995	1994
Births	200	197	180	191
Deaths	108	121	113	107
Natural Increase	92	76	67	84
Marriages	157	154	160	126

Note: Latest available data.

MEDIA INFO
 see Kitchener, CMA

Ontario

Leamington
(Census Agglomeration)

The Census Agglomeration of Leamington consists of: Leamington, T; Mersea, TP; Gosfield South, TP; and Kingsville, T in Essex County, plus Wheatley, VL in Kent County.

POPULATION

July 1, 2001 Estimate	44,372
% Cdn. Total	0.14
% Change, '96 -'01	5.77
Avg. Annual Growth Rate, %	1.13
2003 Projected Population	45,548
2006 Projected Population	47,017
2001 Households Estimate	16,135
2003 Projected Households	16,715
2006 Projected Households	17,540

INCOME

% Above/Below National Average	same
2001 Total Income Estimate	$938,080,000
% Cdn. Total	0.14
2001 Average Hhld. Income	$58,100
2001 Per Capita	$21,100
2003 Projected Total Income	$1,019,720,000
2006 Projected Total Income	$1,149,280,000

RETAIL SALES

% Above/Below National Average	+2
2001 Retail Sales Estimate	$406,290,000
% Cdn. Total	0.15
2001 per Household	$25,200
2001 per Capita	$9,200
2001 No. of Establishments	310
2003 Projected Retail Sales	$452,990,000
2006 Projected Retail Sales	$520,700,000

POPULATION

2001 Estimates:

Total		44,372
Male		21,710
Female		22,662

Age Groups	Male	Female
0-4	1,460	1,406
5-9	1,617	1,561
10-14	1,663	1,572
15-19	1,622	1,569
20-24	1,574	1,566
25-29	1,568	1,565
30-34	1,623	1,628
35-39	1,661	1,652
40-44	1,593	1,548
45-49	1,446	1,427
50-54	1,247	1,292
55-59	1,025	1,106
60-64	894	994
65-69	821	948
70+	1,896	2,828

DAYTIME POPULATION

2001 Estimates:

Working Population	22,544
At Home Population	21,828
Total	44,372

INCOME

2001 Estimates:

Avg. Household Income	$58,140
Avg. Family Income	$63,930
Per Capita Income	$21,141
Male:	
Avg. Employment Income	$34,945
Avg. Employment Income (Full Time)	$46,033
Female:	
Avg. Employment Income	$20,595
Avg. Employment Income (Full Time)	$32,370

DISPOSABLE & DISCRETIONARY INCOME

2001 Estimates:	Per Hhld.
Disposable Income	$47,878
Discretionary Income 1 (minus Food & Shelter)	$34,070
Discretionary Income 2 (minus Food, Shelter, & Other Expenditures)	$24,113

LIQUID ASSETS

1999 Estimates:	Per Hhld.
Equity Investments	$82,796
Interest Bearing Investments	$70,586
Total Liquid Assets	$153,382

CREDIT DATA

July 2000:

Pool of Credit	$365,371,182
Revolving Credit, No.	63,817
Fixed Loans, No.	20,912
Avg. Credit Limit, per Person	$12,308
Avg. Spent, per Person	$5,553
Satisfactory Ratings, No. per Person	2.70
Avg. No. of Cards, per Person	0.96

LABOUR FORCE

2001 Estimates:

Male:	
In the Labour Force	12,744
Participation Rate	75.1
Employed	12,418
Unemployed	326
Unemployment Rate	2.6
Not in Labour Force	4,226
Female:	
In the Labour Force	10,475
Participation Rate	57.8
Employed	10,037
Unemployed	438
Unemployment Rate	4.2
Not in Labour Force	7,648

OCCUPATIONS BY MAJOR GROUPS

2001 Estimates:	Male	Female
Management	1,130	443
Business, Finance & Admin.	640	2,334
Natural & Applied Sciences & Related	499	92
Health	133	934
Social Sciences, Gov't Services & Religion	209	123
Education	322	512
Arts, Culture, Recreation & Sport	95	123
Sales & Service	1,822	3,204
Trades, Transport & Equipment Operators & Related	3,346	244
Primary Industries	2,178	1,064
Processing, Mfg. & Utilities	2,261	1,154

LEVEL OF SCHOOLING

2001 Estimates:

Population 15 years +	35,093
Less than Grade 9	7,210
Grades 9-13 w/o Certif.	9,529
Grade 9-13 with Certif.	4,875
Trade Certif. /Dip.	872
Non-Univ. w/o Certif./Dip.	1,871
Non-Univ. with Certif./Dip.	5,954
Univ. w/o Degree	2,241
Univ. w/o Degree/Certif.	1,221
Univ. with Certif.	1,020
Univ. with Degree	2,541

AVERAGE HOUSEHOLD EXPENDITURES

2001 Estimates:

Food	$6,649
Shelter	$9,311
Clothing	$2,165
Transportation	$8,011
Health & Personal Care	$2,000
Recr'n, Read'g & Education	$3,948
Taxes & Securities	$13,757
Other	$9,786
Total Expenditures	$55,627

PRIVATE HOUSEHOLDS

2001 Estimates:

Private Households, Total	16,135
Pop. in Private Households	43,535
Average no. per Household	2.7

FAMILIES

2001 Estimates:

Families in Private Households	12,640
Husband-Wife Families	11,296
Lone-Parent Families	1,344
Aver. No. Persons per Family	3.2
Aver. No. Sons/Daughters at Home	1.3

HOUSING

2001 Estimates:

Occupied Private Dwellings	16,135
Owned	11,728
Rented	4,407
Single-Detached House	12,138
Semi-Detached House	794
Row Houses	460
Apartment, 5+ Storeys	536
Owned Apartment, 5+ Storeys	78
Apartment, 5 or Fewer Storeys	1,645
Apartment, Detached Duplex	392
Other Single-Attached	72
Movable Dwellings	98

VEHICLES

2001 Estimates:

Model Yrs. '81-'96, No.	22,091
% Total	78.06
Model Yrs. '97-'98, No.	3,786
% Total	13.38
'99 Vehicles registered in Model Yr. '99, No.	2,423
% Total	8.56
Total No. '81-'99	28,300

LEGAL MARITAL STATUS

2001 Estimates: (Age 15+)

Single (Never Married)	8,625
Legally Married (Not Separated)	21,273
Legally Married (Separated)	716
Widowed	2,701
Divorced	1,778

PSYTE CATEGORIES

2001 Estimates	No. of House-holds	% of Total Hhds.	Index
Boomers & Teens	239	1.48	83
Stable Suburban Families	407	2.52	193
Old Bungalow Burbs	151	0.94	56
Blue Collar Winners	1,282	7.95	316
Old Towns' New Fringe	2,899	17.97	459
Rustic Prosperity	4,694	29.09	1,612
Conservative Homebodies	340	2.11	58
Old Leafy Towns	689	4.27	167
Nesters & Young Homesteaders	1,751	10.85	465
Quiet Towns	423	2.62	123
Agrarian Blues	2,742	16.99	7,937
Rod & Rifle	362	2.24	97

FINANCIAL P$YTE

2001 Estimates	No. of House-holds	% of Total Hhds.	Index
Four Star Investors	239	1.48	29
Successful Suburbanites	407	2.52	38
Canadian Comfort	1,282	7.95	82
Miners & Credit-Liners	151	0.94	30
Tractors & Tradelines	7,593	47.06	823
Bills & Wills	1,029	6.38	77
Revolving Renters	1,751	10.85	236
Rural Family Blues	3,104	19.24	238
Limited Budgets	423	2.62	84

HOME LANGUAGE

2001 Estimates:		% Total
English	37,516	84.55
French	196	0.44
Arabic	564	1.27
Chinese	69	0.16
Dutch	61	0.14
German	2,914	6.57
Hungarian	53	0.12
Italian	564	1.27
Lao	120	0.27
Persian (Farsi)	27	0.06
Polish	34	0.08
Portuguese	1,071	2.41
Slovak	84	0.19
Spanish	39	0.09
Tagalog (Pilipino)	30	0.07
Vietnamese	38	0.09
Other Languages	38	0.09
Multiple Responses	954	2.15
Total	44,372	100.00

BUILDING PERMITS

	1999	1998	1997
		$000	
Value	112,720	98,020	87,244

HOMES BUILT

	1999	1998	1997
No	123	158	176

TAXATION

Income Class:	1997	% Total
Under $5,000	4,230	13.10
$5,000-$10,000	3,680	11.39
$10,000-$15,000	4,520	13.99
$15,000-$20,000	3,420	10.59
$20,000-$25,000	2,870	8.89
$25,000-$30,000	2,470	7.65
$30,000-$40,000	4,050	12.54
$40,000-$50,000	2,440	7.55
$50,000 +	4,630	14.33
Total Returns, No.	32,300	
Total Income, $000	896,516	
Total Taxable Returns	22,820	
Total Tax, $000	167,928	
Average Income, $	27,756	
Average Tax, $	7,359	

Leamington
(Census Agglomeration)
(Cont'd)

VITAL STATISTICS

	1997	1996	1995	1994
Births	576	621	607	587
Deaths	383	411	382	348
Natural Increase	193	210	225	239
Marriages	270	252	263	246

Note: Latest available data.

COMMUNITY NEWSPAPER(S)

	Total Circulation
Kingsville: Kingsville Reporter	2,209
Leamington: Leamington Post & News	4,588
Wheatley: Wheatley Journal	1,116

RADIO STATION(S)

	Power
CBEF-FM	1,000w
CHYR-FM	n.a.

Lindsay
(Census Agglomeration)

The Census Agglomeration of Lindsay includes: Lindsay, T; and Ops, TP. Both are in Victoria County.

POPULATION

July 1, 2001 Estimate	23,459
% Cdn. Total	0.08
% Change, '96 -'01	4.15
Avg. Annual Growth Rate, %	0.82
2003 Projected Population	23,736
2006 Projected Population	24,031
2001 Households Estimate	9,701
2003 Projected Households	9,869
2006 Projected Households	10,112

INCOME

% Above/Below National Average	-10
2001 Total Income Estimate	$445,070,000
% Cdn. Total	0.07
2001 Average Hhld. Income	$45,900
2001 Per Capita	$19,000
2003 Projected Total Income	$475,100,000
2006 Projected Total Income	$524,990,000

RETAIL SALES

% Above/Below National Average	+87
2001 Retail Sales Estimate	$392,520,000
% Cdn. Total	0.14
2001 per Household	$40,500
2001 per Capita	$16,700
2001 No. of Establishments	239
2003 Projected Retail Sales	$429,500,000
2006 Projected Retail Sales	$481,520,000

POPULATION

2001 Estimates:

Total		23,459
Male		11,172
Female		12,287

Age Groups	Male	Female
0-4	687	665
5-9	764	744
10-14	849	788
15-19	826	789
20-24	740	738
25-29	676	700
30-34	710	777
35-39	833	878
40-44	848	885
45-49	775	808
50-54	651	685
55-59	527	567
60-64	481	545
65-69	479	556
70+	1,326	2,162

DAYTIME POPULATION

2001 Estimates:

Working Population	10,163
At Home Population	13,296
Total	23,459

INCOME

2001 Estimates:

Avg. Household Income	$45,879
Avg. Family Income	$52,695
Per Capita Income	$18,972

Male:

Avg. Employment Income	$33,363
Avg. Employment Income (Full Time)	$45,594

Female:

Avg. Employment Income	$19,069
Avg. Employment Income (Full Time)	$30,383

DISPOSABLE & DISCRETIONARY INCOME

2001 Estimates: Per Hhld.

Disposable Income	$38,125
Discretionary Income 1 (minus Food & Shelter)	$26,197
Discretionary Income 2 (minus Food, Shelter, & Other Expenditures)	$18,256

LIQUID ASSETS

1999 Estimates: Per Hhld.

Equity Investments	$56,237
Interest Bearing Investments	$55,123
Total Liquid Assets	$111,360

CREDIT DATA

July 2000:

Pool of Credit	$189,357,107
Revolving Credit, No.	35,856
Fixed Loans, No.	10,821
Avg. Credit Limit, per Person	$10,740
Avg. Spent, per Person	$4,744
Satisfactory Ratings, No. per Person	2.56
Avg. No. of Cards, per Person	0.92

LABOUR FORCE

2001 Estimates:

Male:

In the Labour Force	5,872
Participation Rate	66.2
Employed	5,358
Unemployed	514
Unemployment Rate	8.8
Not in Labour Force	3,000

Female:

In the Labour Force	5,173
Participation Rate	51.3
Employed	4,744
Unemployed	429
Unemployment Rate	8.3
Not in Labour Force	4,917

OCCUPATIONS BY MAJOR GROUPS

2001 Estimates:

	Male	Female
Management	474	177
Business, Finance & Admin.	393	1,166
Natural & Applied Sciences & Related	199	10
Health	97	487
Social Sciences, Gov't Services & Religion	35	117
Education	217	323
Arts, Culture, Recreation & Sport	93	105
Sales & Service	1,268	2,047
Trades, Transport & Equipment Operators & Related	1,681	68
Primary Industries	327	42
Processing, Mfg. & Utilities	793	373

LEVEL OF SCHOOLING

2001 Estimates:

Population 15 years +	18,962
Less than Grade 9	1,963
Grades 9-13 w/o Certif.	5,975
Grade 9-13 with Certif.	2,860
Trade Certif. /Dip.	970
Non-Univ. w/o Certif./Dip.	1,143
Non-Univ. with Certif./Dip.	3,714
Univ. w/o Degree	909
Univ. w/o Degree/Certif.	382
Univ. with Certif.	527
Univ. with Degree	1,428

Ontario

AVERAGE HOUSEHOLD EXPENDITURES

2001 Estimates:

Food	$5,613
Shelter	$8,245
Clothing	$1,799
Transportation	$6,229
Health & Personal Care	$1,781
Recr'n, Read'g & Education	$3,228
Taxes & Securities	$10,681
Other	$7,678
Total Expenditures	$45,254

PRIVATE HOUSEHOLDS

2001 Estimates:

Private Households, Total	9,701
Pop. in Private Households	22,722
Average no. per Household	2.3

FAMILIES

2001 Estimates:

Families in Private Households	6,878
Husband-Wife Families	5,899
Lone-Parent Families	979
Aver. No. Persons per Family	2.9
Aver. No. Sons/Daughters at Home	1.1

HOUSING

2001 Estimates:

Occupied Private Dwellings	9,701
Owned	6,387
Rented	3,314
Single-Detached House	6,438
Semi-Detached House	368
Row Houses	295
Apartment, 5+ Storeys	659
Apartment, 5 or Fewer Storeys	1,551
Apartment, Detached Duplex	367
Movable Dwellings	23

VEHICLES

2001 Estimates:

Model Yrs. '81-'96, No.	11,502
% Total	81.31
Model Yrs. '97-'98, No.	1,619
% Total	11.45
'99 Vehicles registered in Model Yr. '99, No.	1,024
% Total	7.24
Total No. '81-'99	14,145

LEGAL MARITAL STATUS

2001 Estimates: (Age 15+)

Single (Never Married)	4,656
Legally Married (Not Separated)	10,449
Legally Married (Separated)	686
Widowed	1,907
Divorced	1,264

Ontario

Lindsay
(Census Agglomeration)
(Cont'd)

PSYTE CATEGORIES

2001 Estimates	No. of House-holds	% of Total Hhds.	Index
Small City Elite.	1,049	10.81	631
Blue Collar Winners	107	1.10	44
Old Towns' New Fringe	944	9.73	249
Rustic Prosperity	878	9.05	502
High Rise Sunsets	173	1.78	125
Old Leafy Towns	2,002	20.64	807
Town Renters	191	1.97	228
Nesters & Young Homesteaders	1,510	15.57	667
Quiet Towns	1,676	17.28	812
Struggling Downtowns	460	4.74	151
Aged Pensioners	560	5.77	434

FINAN¢IAL P$YTE

2001 Estimates	No. of House-holds	% of Total Hhds.	Index
Canadian Comfort	1,156	11.92	123
Tractors & Tradelines	1,822	18.78	328
Bills & Wills	2,002	20.64	249
Revolving Renters	1,683	17.35	377
Limited Budgets	1,676	17.28	556
Towering Debt	651	6.71	86
Senior Survivors	560	5.77	306

HOME LANGUAGE

2001 Estimates:		% Total
English	23,162	98.73
French	22	0.09
Chinese	21	0.09
Czech	19	0.08
Dutch	15	0.06
Finnish	15	0.06
German	22	0.09
Hungarian	32	0.14
Maltese	16	0.07
Spanish	35	0.15
Vietnamese	12	0.05
Other Languages	27	0.12
Multiple Responses	61	0.26
Total	23,459	100.00

BUILDING PERMITS

	1999	1998 $000	1997
Value	11,203	15,412	14,829

HOMES BUILT

	1999	1998	1997
No	51	81	59

TAXATION

Income Class:	1997	% Total
Under $5,000	2,170	12.22
$5,000-$10,000	2,190	12.33
$10,000-$15,000	3,070	17.29
$15,000-$20,000	2,010	11.32
$20,000-$25,000	1,700	9.57
$25,000-$30,000	1,460	8.22
$30,000-$40,000	2,060	11.60
$40,000-$50,000	1,130	6.36
$50,000 +	1,970	11.09
Total Returns, No.	17,760	
Total Income, $000	444,066	
Total Taxable Returns	12,010	
Total Tax, $000	74,702	
Average Income, $	25,004	
Average Tax, $	6,220	

VITAL STATISTICS

	1997	1996	1995	1994
Births	225	277	260	169
Deaths	319	280	289	259
Natural Increase	-94	-3	-29	-90
Marriages	97	142	122	146

Note: Latest available data.

DAILY NEWSPAPER(S)

	Circulation Average Paid
The Lindsay Daily Post	
Mon-Sat	4,718
Tue-Sat	4,676

COMMUNITY NEWSPAPER(S)

	Total Circulation
Lindsay: Lindsay This Week	
Tue/Fri	26,724
(Fri. total 27,724)	
Lindsay: Lindsay Weekly Post	n.a.

RADIO STATION(S)

	Power
CKLY	n.a.
CKLY-FM	n.a.

London
(Census Metropolitan Area)

POPULATION

July 1, 2001 Estimate	426,323
% Cdn. Total	1.37
% Change, '96 -'01	3.35
Avg. Annual Growth Rate, %	0.66
2003 Projected Population	433,449
2006 Projected Population	444,794
2001 Households Estimate	172,656
2003 Projected Households	176,867
2006 Projected Households	183,895

INCOME

% Above/Below National Average	+6
2001 Total Income Estimate	$9,556,370,000
% Cdn. Total	1.46
2001 Average Hhld. Income	$55,300
2001 Per Capita	$22,400
2003 Projected Total Income	$10,290,660,000
2006 Projected Total Income	$11,535,790,000

RETAIL SALES

% Above/Below National Average	+14
2001 Retail Sales Estimate	$4,355,150,000
% Cdn. Total	1.56
2001 per Household	$25,200
2001 per Capita	$10,200
2001 No. of Establishments	3,252
2003 Projected Retail Sales	$4,788,830,000
2006 Projected Retail Sales	$5,437,590,000

POPULATION

2001 Estimates:		
Total		426,323
Male		206,694
Female		219,629
Age Groups	Male	Female
0-4	13,996	13,244
5-9	14,544	13,802
10-14	14,562	13,849
15-19	14,088	13,488
20-24	14,209	14,149
25-29	14,991	15,139
30-34	16,397	16,688
35-39	17,107	17,809
40-44	16,451	17,520
45-49	15,184	16,301
50-54	12,962	13,812
55-59	10,409	11,086
60-64	8,424	9,182
65-69	7,168	8,264
70+	16,202	25,296

DAYTIME POPULATION

2001 Estimates:	
Working Population	220,451
At Home Population	205,872
Total	426,323

INCOME

2001 Estimates:	
Avg. Household Income	$55,349
Avg. Family Income	$64,610
Per Capita Income	$22,416
Male:	
Avg. Employment Income	$36,325
Avg. Employment Income (Full Time)	$48,564
Female:	
Avg. Employment Income	$23,278
Avg. Employment Income (Full Time)	$34,406

DISPOSABLE & DISCRETIONARY INCOME

2001 Estimates:	Per Hhld.
Disposable Income	$45,405
Discretionary Income 1 (minus Food & Shelter)	$31,893
Discretionary Income 2 (minus Food, Shelter, & Other Expenditures)	$23,624

LIQUID ASSETS

1999 Estimates:	Per Hhld.
Equity Investments	$74,229
Interest Bearing Investments	$67,649
Total Liquid Assets	$141,878

CREDIT DATA

July 2000:	
Pool of Credit	$4,785,841,569
Revolving Credit, No.	848,609
Fixed Loans, No.	253,990
Avg. Credit Limit, per Person	$12,657
Avg. Spent, per Person	$5,926
Satisfactory Ratings, No. per Person	2.80
Avg. No. of Cards, per Person	1.04

LABOUR FORCE

2001 Estimates:	
Male:	
In the Labour Force	122,576
Participation Rate	74.9
Employed	115,535
Unemployed	7,041
Unemployment Rate	5.7
Not in Labour Force	41,016
Female:	
In the Labour Force	110,572
Participation Rate	61.9
Employed	103,958
Unemployed	6,614
Unemployment Rate	6.0
Not in Labour Force	68,162

OCCUPATIONS BY MAJOR GROUPS

2001 Estimates:	Male	Female
Management	13,896	6,570
Business, Finance & Admin.	12,225	30,904
Natural & Applied Sciences & Related	7,499	1,531
Health	3,284	11,020
Social Sciences, Gov't Services & Religion	2,812	3,340
Education	4,507	6,396
Arts, Culture, Recreation & Sport	2,377	2,957
Sales & Service	26,503	35,233
Trades, Transport & Equipment Operators & Related	27,445	1,799
Primary Industries	4,839	1,320
Processing, Mfg. & Utilities	14,013	5,670

London
(Census Metropolitan Area)
(Cont'd)

LEVEL OF SCHOOLING

2001 Estimates:

Population 15 years +	342,326
Less than Grade 9	23,893
Grades 9-13 w/o Certif.	77,832
Grade 9-13 with Certif.	53,032
Trade Certif. /Dip.	11,703
Non-Univ. w/o Certif./Dip.	23,711
Non-Univ. with Certif./Dip.	66,550
Univ. w/o Degree	32,371
Univ. w/o Degree/Certif.	16,591
Univ. with Certif.	15,780
Univ. with Degree	53,234

AVERAGE HOUSEHOLD EXPENDITURES

2001 Estimates:

Food	$6,154
Shelter	$9,550
Clothing	$2,218
Transportation	$6,286
Health & Personal Care	$1,919
Recr'n, Read'g & Education	$3,706
Taxes & Securities	$14,563
Other	$8,546
Total Expenditures	$52,942

PRIVATE HOUSEHOLDS

2001 Estimates:

Private Households, Total	172,656
Pop. in Private Households	418,617
Average no. per Household	2.4

FAMILIES

2001 Estimates:

Families in Private Households	118,925
Husband-Wife Families	100,707
Lone-Parent Families	18,218
Aver. No. Persons per Family	3.0
Aver. No. Sons/Daughters at Home	1.2

HOUSING

2001 Estimates:

Occupied Private Dwellings	172,656
Owned	103,688
Rented	68,968
Single-Detached House	93,474
Semi-Detached House	6,891
Row Houses	18,080
Apartment, 5+ Storeys	29,863
Owned Apartment, 5+ Storeys	1,392
Apartment, 5 or Fewer Storeys	18,646
Apartment, Detached Duplex	5,021
Other Single-Attached	383
Movable Dwellings	298

VEHICLES

2001 Estimates:

Model Yrs. '81-'96, No.	194,883
% Total	76.38
Model Yrs. '97-'98, No.	35,545
% Total	13.93
'99 Vehicles registered in Model Yr. '99, No.	24,708
% Total	9.68
Total No. '81-'99	255,136

LEGAL MARITAL STATUS

2001 Estimates: (Age 15+)

Single (Never Married)	102,117
Legally Married (Not Separated)	180,415
Legally Married (Separated)	13,073
Widowed	22,057
Divorced	24,664

PSYTE CATEGORIES

2001 Estimates	No. of House-holds	% of Total Hhds.	Index
The Affluentials	982	0.57	89
Urban Gentry	4,064	2.35	131
Suburban Executives	5,451	3.16	220
Mortgaged in Suburbia	677	0.39	28
Technocrafts & Bureaucrats	7,784	4.51	160
Boomers & Teens	4,839	2.80	156
Stable Suburban Families	3,617	2.09	161
Small City Elite	105	0.06	4
Old Bungalow Burbs	5,394	3.12	188
Suburban Nesters	1,139	0.66	41
Brie & Chablis	76	0.04	5
Aging Erudites	6,841	3.96	263
Satellite Suburbs	9,245	5.35	187
Kindergarten Boom	8,947	5.18	198
Blue Collar Winners	10,603	6.14	244
Old Towns' New Fringe	2,853	1.65	42
Rustic Prosperity	1,852	1.07	59
Europa	241	0.14	11
High Rise Melting Pot	1,209	0.70	47
Conservative Homebodies	17,254	9.99	277
High Rise Sunsets	4,147	2.40	168
Young Urban Professionals	4,448	2.58	136
Young Urban Mix	2,394	1.39	65
Young Urban Intelligentsia	4,067	2.36	155
University Enclaves	11,296	6.54	321
Young City Singles	13,782	7.98	348
Urban Bohemia	774	0.45	38
Old Leafy Towns	506	0.29	11
Town Renters	4,967	2.88	333
Nesters & Young Homesteaders	9,106	5.27	226
Struggling Downtowns	15,400	8.92	283
Aged Pensioners	1,799	1.04	78
Big City Stress	2,959	1.71	152
Old Grey Towers	2,209	1.28	231

FINANCIAL P$YTE

2001 Estimates	No. of House-holds	% of Total Hhds.	Index
Platinum Estates	982	0.57	71
Four Star Investors	14,354	8.31	166
Successful Suburbanites	12,078	7.00	105
Canadian Comfort	21,092	12.22	126
Urban Heights	11,365	6.58	153
Miners & Credit-Liners	5,394	3.12	99
Mortgages & Minivans	8,947	5.18	79
Dollars & Sense	241	0.14	5
Tractors & Tradelines	4,705	2.73	48
Bills & Wills	20,154	11.67	141
Revolving Renters	13,253	7.68	167
Young Urban Struggle	16,137	9.35	197
Towering Debt	35,358	20.48	262
NSF	2,959	1.71	48
Senior Survivors	4,008	2.32	123

HOME LANGUAGE

2001 Estimates:		% Total
English	388,136	91.04
French	1,170	0.27
Arabic	2,642	0.62
Chinese	2,383	0.56
Croatian	433	0.10
Dutch	322	0.08
German	772	0.18
Greek	1,298	0.30
Hungarian	517	0.12
Italian	1,605	0.38
Khmer (Cambodian)	506	0.12
Korean	390	0.09
Kurdish	329	0.08
Persian (Farsi)	408	0.10
Polish	5,648	1.32
Portuguese	3,310	0.78
Punjabi	257	0.06
Russian	327	0.08
Serbian	257	0.06
Serbo-Croatian	559	0.13
Spanish	2,777	0.65
Tagalog (Pilipino)	411	0.10
Ukrainian	334	0.08
Vietnamese	1,457	0.34
Other Languages	3,057	0.72
Multiple Responses	7,018	1.65
Total	426,323	100.00

Ontario

RADIO STATION DATA

Station	Market	Format	Wkly. Reach%*	Aver. Hrs. Tuned
All Stations			95	22.2
CBCL-FM	London	News, Info.	n.a.	n.a.
CBL-FM	Toronto	All Info.	10	10.8
CBLA-FM	Toronto	News, Info.	13	12.6
CFCA-FM	Waterloo	AOR	6	4.6
CFHK-FM	London	Top 40	25	8.6
CFPL	London	Talk	12	8.6
CFPL-FM	London	Rock	31	9.5
CIQM-FM	London	Adult Contemp.	28	12.4
CIXX-FM	London	Hit Radio	n.a.	n.a.
CJBK	London	Talk, Sports	11	6.4
CJBX-FM	London	Country	17	13.8
CKDK-FM	London	Classic Rock	20	9.4
CKSL	London	Adult Contemp.	3	9.0

BBM Spring 2000 Radio Reach Survey;area coverage.
*Mon-Sun 5a.m - 1a.m , All Persons 12+

TV STATION DATA

Station	Market	Network Affiliation	Wkly. Reach%*	Aver. Hrs. Tuned
All Stations			96	21.2
A & E	n.a.	Ind.	23	3.1
CBLN	London	CBC	34	2.7
CFMT	Toronto	Ind.	22	2.2
CFPL	London	Ind.	56	4.2
CFTO	Toronto	CTV	5	2.3
CHCH	Toronto/Hamilton	Ind.	38	2.7
CICO-E	n.a.	n.a.	20	2.7
CIII	n.a.	Global	53	3.1
CITY	Toronto	Ind.	37	2.3
CKCO	Kitchener	CTV	57	3.9
CNN	n.a.	Ind.	6	2.5
COMEDY	n.a.	Ind.	7	1.8
HGTV	n.a.	Ind.	6	1.8
NEWSWD	n.a.	CBC	7	2.0
OTHERS	n.a.	n.a.	12	2.2
PRIME	n.a.	Ind.	9	2.6
SHWCSE	n.a.	Ind.	6	2.4
SNET	n.a.	CTV	8	2.0
SPACE	n.a.	Ind.	5	2.7
TLC	n.a.	Ind.	14	1.5
TMN	Toronto	Ind.	9	3.8
TNN	Nashville TN	Ind.	10	1.9
TREE	n.a.	Ind.	4	3.3
TSN	n.a.	Ind.	21	3.0
VCR	n.a.	n.a.	27	4.1
WDIV	Detroit MI	NBC	11	2.0
WICU	Erie PA	NBC	15	1.7
WJET	Erie PA	ABC	21	1.7
WJW	Cleveland OH	FOX	-	0.8
WOIO	Shaker Heights OH	CBS	3	2.0
WQLN	Erie PA	PBS	14	2.0
WSEE	Erie PA	CBS	13	1.6
WTBS	Atlanta GA	Ind.	16	3.2
WUAB	Lorain OH	UPN	20	2.2
WUTV	Buffalo NY	FOX	19	2.0
WXYZ	Detroit MI	ABC	10	1.5
YTV	n.a.	Ind.	12	2.9

BBM Spring 2000 TV Reach Survey;CMA coverage.
*Mon-Sun 6a.m - 2a.m , All Persons 2 +

London
(Census Metropolitan Area)
(Cont'd)

BUILDING PERMITS

	1999	1998	1997
		$000	
Value	394,240	406,400	348,908

HOMES BUILT

	1999	1998	1997
No	1,843	1,620	1,708

TAXATION

Income Class:	1997	% Total
Under $5,000	36,190	12.40
$5,000-$10,000	33,700	11.55
$10,000-$15,000	39,100	13.40
$15,000-$20,000	28,930	9.91
$20,000-$25,000	24,060	8.24
$25,000-$30,000	23,130	7.93
$30,000-$40,000	37,380	12.81
$40,000-$50,000	24,970	8.56
$50,000 +	44,460	15.23
Total Returns, No.	291,860	
Total Income, $000	8,583,763	
Total Taxable Returns	205,150	
Total Tax, $000	1,662,629	
Average Income, $	29,411	
Average Tax, $	8,104	

VITAL STATISTICS

	1997	1996	1995	1994
Births	4,856	5,077	5,555	5,608
Deaths	3,253	3,041	3,112	3,150
Natural Increase	1,603	2,036	2,443	2,458
Marriages	2,438	2,591	2,602	2,561

Note: Latest available data.

DAILY NEWSPAPER(S)

	Circulation Average Paid
The London Free Press	
Sat	124,926
Mon-Fri.	100,395
Times-Journal (St. Thomas)	8,261

COMMUNITY NEWSPAPER(S)

	Total Circulation
London: L'Observateur	n.a.
London: London Pennysaver	n.a.
St. Thomas: Elgin County Market	n.a.

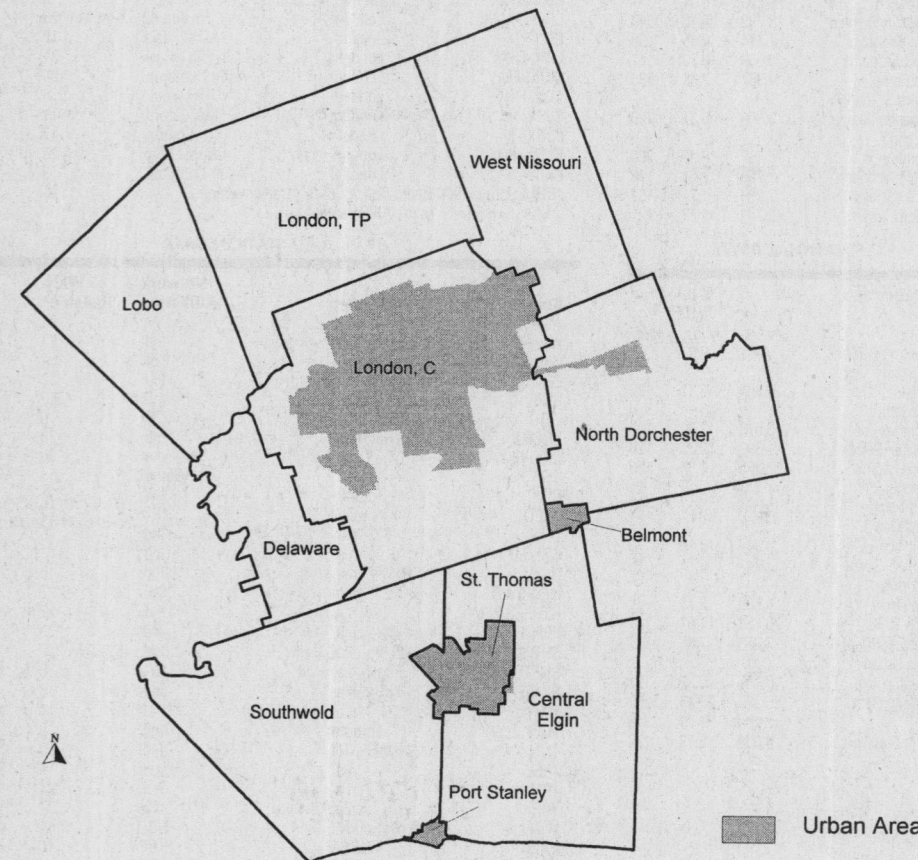

Urban Areas

London
(City)
London CMA

In Middlesex County.

POPULATION

July 1, 2001 Estimate	347,959
% Cdn. Total	1.12
% Change, '96 -'01	3.16
Avg. Annual Growth Rate, %	0.62
2003 Projected Population	353,600
2006 Projected Population	362,675
2001 Households Estimate	143,676
2003 Projected Households	147,110
2006 Projected Households	152,868

INCOME

% Above/Below National Average	+6
2001 Total Income Estimate	$7,770,170,000
% Cdn. Total	1.18
2001 Average Hhld. Income	$54,100
2001 Per Capita	$22,300
2003 Projected Total Income	$8,360,670,000
2006 Projected Total Income	$9,362,860,000

RETAIL SALES

% Above/Below National Average	+20
2001 Retail Sales Estimate	$3,729,830,000
% Cdn. Total	1.34
2001 per Household	$26,000
2001 per Capita	$10,700
2001 No. of Establishments	2,628
2003 Projected Retail Sales	$4,095,610,000
2006 Projected Retail Sales	$4,642,050,000

POPULATION

2001 Estimates:

Total		347,959
Male		167,977
Female		179,982

Age Groups	Male	Female
0-4	11,653	11,021
5-9	11,862	11,259
10-14	11,689	11,167
15-19	11,275	10,826
20-24	11,639	11,677
25-29	12,646	12,834
30-34	13,895	14,106
35-39	14,185	14,783
40-44	13,341	14,392
45-49	12,151	13,266
50-54	10,232	11,145
55-59	8,138	8,883
60-64	6,620	7,380
65-69	5,682	6,699
70+	12,969	20,544

DAYTIME POPULATION

2001 Estimates:

Working Population	185,574
At Home Population	169,703
Total	355,277

INCOME

2001 Estimates:

Avg. Household Income	$54,081
Avg. Family Income	$63,699
Per Capita Income	$22,331
Male:	
Avg. Employment Income	$36,051
Avg. Employment Income (Full Time)	$48,812
Female:	
Avg. Employment Income	$23,312
Avg. Employment Income (Full Time)	$34,567

DISPOSABLE & DISCRETIONARY INCOME

2001 Estimates:	*Per Hhld.*
Disposable Income	$44,357
Discretionary Income 1 (minus Food & Shelter)	$31,116
Discretionary Income 2 (minus Food, Shelter, & Other Expenditures)	$23,105

LIQUID ASSETS

1999 Estimates:	*Per Hhld.*
Equity Investments	$70,616
Interest Bearing Investments	$65,964
Total Liquid Assets	$136,580

CREDIT DATA

July 2000:

Pool of Credit	$3,876,072,769
Revolving Credit, No.	703,914
Fixed Loans, No.	205,402
Avg. Credit Limit, per Person	$12,425
Avg. Spent, per Person	$5,779
Satisfactory Ratings, No. per Person	2.80
Avg. No. of Cards, per Person	1.04

LABOUR FORCE

2001 Estimates:

Male:	
In the Labour Force	98,714
Participation Rate	74.3
Employed	92,654
Unemployed	6,060
Unemployment Rate	6.1
Not in Labour Force	34,059
Female:	
In the Labour Force	90,453
Participation Rate	61.7
Employed	84,843
Unemployed	5,610
Unemployment Rate	6.2
Not in Labour Force	56,082

OCCUPATIONS BY MAJOR GROUPS

2001 Estimates:	*Male*	*Female*
Management	11,295	5,477
Business, Finance & Admin.	10,513	25,078
Natural & Applied Sciences & Related	6,465	1,330
Health	2,750	8,870
Social Sciences, Gov't Services & Religion	2,458	2,893
Education	3,875	5,535
Arts, Culture, Recreation & Sport	2,184	2,545
Sales & Service	22,646	29,549
Trades, Transport & Equipment Operators & Related	21,017	1,254
Primary Industries	2,324	410
Processing, Mfg. & Utilities	10,454	4,252

LEVEL OF SCHOOLING

2001 Estimates:

Population 15 years +	279,308
Less than Grade 9	19,254
Grades 9-13 w/o Certif.	60,895
Grade 9-13 with Certif.	42,363
Trade Certif. /Dip.	9,356
Non-Univ. w/o Certif./Dip.	19,247
Non-Univ. with Certif./Dip.	52,890
Univ. w/o Degree	27,770
Univ. w/o Degree/Certif.	14,461
Univ. with Certif.	13,309
Univ. with Degree	47,533

AVERAGE HOUSEHOLD EXPENDITURES

2001 Estimates:

Food	$6,064
Shelter	$9,367
Clothing	$2,206
Transportation	$6,029
Health & Personal Care	$1,894
Recr'n, Read'g & Education	$3,660
Taxes & Securities	$14,292
Other	$8,373
Total Expenditures	$51,885

PRIVATE HOUSEHOLDS

2001 Estimates:

Private Households, Total	143,676
Pop. in Private Households	342,164
Average no. per Household	2.4

FAMILIES

2001 Estimates:

Families in Private Households	96,390
Husband-Wife Families	80,405
Lone-Parent Families	15,985
Aver. No. Persons per Family	3.0
Aver. No. Sons/Daughters at Home	1.2

HOUSING

2001 Estimates:

Occupied Private Dwellings	143,676
Owned	82,001
Rented	61,675
Single-Detached House	70,982
Semi-Detached House	5,851
Row Houses	17,304
Apartment, 5+ Storeys	29,081
Owned Apartment, 5+ Storeys	1,369
Apartment, 5 or Fewer Storeys	15,894
Apartment, Detached Duplex	4,113
Other Single-Attached	273
Movable Dwellings	178

VEHICLES

2001 Estimates:

Model Yrs. '81-'96, No.	152,974
% Total	75.48
Model Yrs. '97-'98, No.	29,325
% Total	14.47
'99 Vehicles registered in Model Yr. '99, No.	20,369
% Total	10.05
Total No. '81-'99	202,668

LEGAL MARITAL STATUS

2001 Estimates: (Age 15+)

Single (Never Married)	86,588
Legally Married (Not Separated)	143,073
Legally Married (Separated)	11,101
Widowed	17,794
Divorced	20,752

PSYTE CATEGORIES

2001 Estimates	*No. of House-holds*	*% of Total Hhds.*	*Index*
The Affluentials	944	0.66	103
Urban Gentry	4,064	2.83	157
Suburban Executives	5,451	3.79	265
Mortgaged in Suburbia	570	0.40	29
Technocrafts & Bureaucrats	7,784	5.42	193
Boomers & Teens	2,842	1.98	110
Stable Suburban Families	3,617	2.52	193
Small City Elite	25	0.02	1
Old Bungalow Burbs	4,000	2.78	168
Suburban Nesters	1,139	0.79	49
Brie & Chablis	76	0.05	6
Aging Erudites	6,479	4.51	299
Satellite Suburbs	8,665	6.03	210
Kindergarten Boom	8,947	6.23	238
Blue Collar Winners	1,920	1.34	53
Old Towns' New Fringe	460	0.32	8
Europa	241	0.17	13
High Rise Melting Pot	1,209	0.84	56
Conservative Homebodies	16,731	11.64	323
High Rise Sunsets	4,147	2.89	202

Ontario

2001 Estimates	*No. of House-holds*	*% of Total Hhds.*	*Index*
Young Urban Professionals	4,448	3.10	163
Young Urban Mix	2,394	1.67	79
Young Urban Intelligentsia	4,067	2.83	186
University Enclaves	11,296	7.86	385
Young City Singles	13,443	9.36	408
Urban Bohemia	774	0.54	46
Town Renters	4,967	3.46	400
Nesters & Young Homesteaders	562	0.39	17
Struggling Downtowns	14,692	10.23	325
Aged Pensioners	1,799	1.25	94
Big City Stress	2,452	1.71	151
Old Grey Towers	2,209	1.54	278

FINANCIAL P$YTE

2001 Estimates	*No. of House-holds*	*% of Total Hhds.*	*Index*
Platinum Estates	944	0.66	82
Four Star Investors	12,357	8.60	171
Successful Suburbanites	11,971	8.33	126
Canadian Comfort	11,749	8.18	84
Urban Heights	11,003	7.66	178
Miners & Credit-Liners	4,000	2.78	88
Mortgages & Minivans	8,947	6.23	94
Dollars & Sense	241	0.17	6
Tractors & Tradelines	460	0.32	6
Bills & Wills	19,125	13.31	161
Revolving Renters	4,709	3.28	71
Young Urban Struggle	16,137	11.23	237
Towering Debt	34,311	23.88	306
NSF	2,452	1.71	48
Senior Survivors	4,008	2.79	148

HOME LANGUAGE

2001 Estimates:		*% Total*
English	312,187	89.72
French	1,087	0.31
Arabic	2,597	0.75
Chinese	2,242	0.64
Croatian	314	0.09
Dutch	228	0.07
German	409	0.12
Greek	1,274	0.37
Hungarian	485	0.14
Italian	1,524	0.44
Khmer (Cambodian)	361	0.10
Korean	390	0.11
Kurdish	329	0.09
Persian (Farsi)	408	0.12
Polish	5,320	1.53
Portuguese	3,294	0.95
Punjabi	219	0.06
Russian	327	0.09
Serbian	257	0.07
Serbo-Croatian	536	0.15
Spanish	2,754	0.79
Tagalog (Pilipino)	411	0.12
Ukrainian	315	0.09
Vietnamese	1,324	0.38
Other Languages	2,836	0.82
Multiple Responses	6,531	1.88
Total	347,959	100.00

Ontario

London
(City)
London CMA
(Cont'd)

BUILDING PERMITS

	1999	1998	1997
		$000	
Value	298,684	318,190	262,547

HOMES BUILT

	1999	1998	1997
No.	1,333	1,169	1,218

TAXATION

Income Class:	1997	% Total
Under $5,000	29,630	12.43
$5,000-$10,000	27,820	11.67
$10,000-$15,000	32,260	13.53
$15,000-$20,000	23,620	9.91
$20,000-$25,000	19,450	8.16
$25,000-$30,000	18,800	7.89
$30,000-$40,000	30,390	12.75
$40,000-$50,000	20,130	8.45
$50,000 +	36,260	15.21
Total Returns, No.	238,360	
Total Income, $000	7,040,027	
Total Taxable Returns	166,580	
Total Tax, $000	1,378,115	
Average Income, $	29,535	
Average Tax, $	8,273	

VITAL STATISTICS

	1997	1996	1995	1994
Births	4,066	4,216	4,589	4,611
Deaths	2,544	2,373	2,382	2,406
Natural Increase	1,522	1,843	2,207	2,205
Marriages	1,993	2,154	2,104	2,113

Note: Latest available data.

MEDIA INFO
see London, CMA

St. Thomas
(City)
London CMA

In Elgin County.

POPULATION

July 1, 2001 Estimate	35,154
% Cdn. Total	0.11
% Change, '96 -'01	5.97
Avg. Annual Growth Rate, %	1.17
2003 Projected Population	36,024
2006 Projected Population	37,330
2001 Households Estimate	14,014
2003 Projected Households	14,450
2006 Projected Households	15,158

INCOME

% Above/Below National Average	-8
2001 Total Income Estimate	$682,240,000
% Cdn. Total	0.10
2001 Average Hhld. Income	$48,700
2001 Per Capita	$19,400
2003 Projected Total Income	$739,030,000
2006 Projected Total Income	$834,440,000

RETAIL SALES

% Above/Below National Average	+33
2001 Retail Sales Estimate	$417,310,000
% Cdn. Total	0.15
2001 per Household	$29,800
2001 per Capita	$11,900
2001 No. of Establishments	261
2003 Projected Retail Sales	$463,130,000
2006 Projected Retail Sales	$531,890,000

POPULATION

2001 Estimates:

Total	35,154
Male	16,841
Female	18,313

Age Groups	Male	Female
0-4	1,135	1,081
5-9	1,199	1,168
10-14	1,196	1,153
15-19	1,143	1,126
20-24	1,114	1,141
25-29	1,161	1,196
30-34	1,281	1,334
35-39	1,378	1,429
40-44	1,335	1,371
45-49	1,211	1,258
50-54	1,057	1,090
55-59	872	900
60-64	695	763
65-69	596	719
70+	1,468	2,584

DAYTIME POPULATION

2001 Estimates:

Working Population	22,488
At Home Population	18,357
Total	40,845

INCOME

2001 Estimates:

Avg. Household Income	$48,683
Avg. Family Income	$56,024
Per Capita Income	$19,407
Male:	
Avg. Employment Income	$33,604
Avg. Employment Income (Full Time)	$42,384
Female:	
Avg. Employment Income	$20,931
Avg. Employment Income (Full Time)	$31,738

DISPOSABLE & DISCRETIONARY INCOME

2001 Estimates:	*Per Hhld.*
Disposable Income	$40,439
Discretionary Income 1 (minus Food & Shelter)	$27,293
Discretionary Income 2 (minus Food, Shelter, & Other Expenditures)	$19,606

LIQUID ASSETS

1999 Estimates:	*Per Hhld.*
Equity Investments	$59,086
Interest Bearing Investments	$58,437
Total Liquid Assets	$117,523

CREDIT DATA

July 2000:

Pool of Credit	$360,598,935
Revolving Credit, No.	61,799
Fixed Loans, No.	22,218
Avg. Credit Limit, per Person	$12,868
Avg. Spent, per Person	$6,586
Satisfactory Ratings, No. per Person	2.87
Avg. No. of Cards, per Person	1.00

LABOUR FORCE

2001 Estimates:

Male:	
In the Labour Force	9,755
Participation Rate	73.3
Employed	9,150
Unemployed	605
Unemployment Rate	6.2
Not in Labour Force	3,556
Female:	
In the Labour Force	8,256
Participation Rate	55.4
Employed	7,624
Unemployed	632
Unemployment Rate	7.7
Not in Labour Force	6,655

OCCUPATIONS BY MAJOR GROUPS

2001 Estimates:	*Male*	*Female*
Management	765	466
Business, Finance & Admin.	735	1,973
Natural & Applied Sciences & Related	339	44
Health	262	1,117
Social Sciences, Gov't Services & Religion	231	168
Education	255	287
Arts, Culture, Recreation & Sport	47	132
Sales & Service	1,804	2,608
Trades, Transport & Equipment Operators & Related	2,608	207
Primary Industries	229	48
Processing, Mfg. & Utilities	2,219	878

LEVEL OF SCHOOLING

2001 Estimates:

Population 15 years +	28,222
Less than Grade 9	2,274
Grades 9-13 w/o Certif.	8,263
Grade 9-13 with Certif.	4,708
Trade Certif. /Dip.	914
Non-Univ. w/o Certif./Dip.	2,187
Non-Univ. with Certif./Dip.	6,017
Univ. w/o Degree	2,072
Univ. w/o Degree/Certif.	944
Univ. with Certif.	1,128
Univ. with Degree	1,787

AVERAGE HOUSEHOLD EXPENDITURES

2001 Estimates:

Food	$5,965
Shelter	$9,188
Clothing	$1,931
Transportation	$5,829
Health & Personal Care	$1,853
Recr'n, Read'g & Education	$3,317
Taxes & Securities	$11,212
Other	$8,364
Total Expenditures	$47,659

PRIVATE HOUSEHOLDS

2001 Estimates:

Private Households, Total	14,014
Pop. in Private Households	34,251
Average no. per Household	2.4

FAMILIES

2001 Estimates:

Families in Private Households	9,868
Husband-Wife Families	8,420
Lone-Parent Families	1,448
Aver. No. Persons per Family	2.9
Aver. No. Sons/Daughters at Home	1.1

HOUSING

2001 Estimates:

Occupied Private Dwellings	14,014
Owned	8,897
Rented	5,117
Single-Detached House	8,528
Semi-Detached House	825
Row Houses	665
Apartment, 5+ Storeys	782
Owned Apartment, 5+ Storeys	23
Apartment, 5 or Fewer Storeys	2,475
Apartment, Detached Duplex	718
Other Single-Attached	21

VEHICLES

2001 Estimates:

Model Yrs. '81-'96, No.	16,619
% Total	80.38
Model Yrs. '97-'98, No.	2,346
% Total	11.35
'99 Vehicles registered in Model Yr. '99, No.	1,710
% Total	8.27
Total No. '81-'99	20,675

LEGAL MARITAL STATUS

2001 Estimates: (Age 15+)

Single (Never Married)	7,320
Legally Married (Not Separated)	15,096
Legally Married (Separated)	1,144
Widowed	2,345
Divorced	2,317

PSYTE CATEGORIES

2001 Estimates	No. of House -holds	% of Total Hhds.	Index
Mortgaged in Suburbia	107	0.76	55
Small City Elite	80	0.57	33
Old Bungalow Burbs	1,142	8.15	492
Aging Erudites	362	2.58	171
Satellite Suburbs	580	4.14	144
Blue Collar Winners	90	0.64	26
Old Towns' New Fringe	1,637	11.68	298
Conservative Homebodies	460	3.28	91
Young City Singles	339	2.42	105
Nesters & Young Homesteaders	7,854	56.04	2,401
Struggling Downtowns	708	5.05	160
Big City Stress	507	3.62	320

St. Thomas
(City)
London CMA
(Cont'd)

FINANCIAL P$YTE

2001 Estimates	No. of House-holds	% of Total Hhds.	Index
Successful Suburbanites	107	0.76	12
Canadian Comfort	750	5.35	55
Urban Heights	362	2.58	60
Miners & Credit-Liners	1,142	8.15	257
Tractors & Tradelines	1,637	11.68	204
Bills & Wills	460	3.28	40
Revolving Renters	7,854	56.04	1,218
Towering Debt	1,047	7.47	96
NSF	507	3.62	102

HOME LANGUAGE

2001 Estimates:		% Total
English	33,618	95.63
French	61	0.17
Arabic	27	0.08
Chinese	70	0.20
Croatian	98	0.28
Dutch	23	0.07
German	77	0.22
Greek	24	0.07
Hungarian	32	0.09
Italian	36	0.10
Khmer (Cambodian)	145	0.41
Polish	290	0.82
Punjabi	38	0.11
Slovak	18	0.05
Spanish	23	0.07
Urdu	50	0.14
Vietnamese	133	0.38
Other Languages	106	0.30
Multiple Responses	285	0.81
Total	35,154	100.00

BUILDING PERMITS

	1999	1998	1997
		$000	
Value	34,155	31,478	30,845

HOMES BUILT

	1999	1998	1997
No.	208	174	244

TAXATION

Income Class:	1997	% Total
Under $5,000	3,530	12.20
$5,000-$10,000	3,320	11.48
$10,000-$15,000	4,020	13.90
$15,000-$20,000	3,060	10.58
$20,000-$25,000	2,660	9.19
$25,000-$30,000	2,390	8.26
$30,000-$40,000	3,800	13.14
$40,000-$50,000	2,450	8.47
$50,000 +	3,710	12.82
Total Returns, No.	28,930	
Total Income, $000	765,427	
Total Taxable Returns	20,320	
Total Tax, $000	131,875	
Average Income, $	26,458	
Average Tax, $	6,490	

VITAL STATISTICS

	1997	1996	1995	1994
Births	454	486	512	521
Deaths	387	364	361	393
Natural Increase	67	122	151	128
Marriages	246	252	284	267

Note: Latest available data.

MEDIA INFO
see London, CMA

Midland
(Census Agglomeration)

The Census Agglomeration of Midland includes: Midland, T; Penetanguishene, T; and Tay, TP. All are in Simcoe County.

POPULATION

July 1, 2001 Estimate	35,745
% Cdn. Total	0.11
% Change, '96 -'01	4.19
Avg. Annual Growth Rate, %	0.83
2003 Projected Population	35,949
2006 Projected Population	36,238
2001 Households Estimate	14,248
2003 Projected Households	14,287
2006 Projected Households	14,497

INCOME

% Above/Below National Average	-12
2001 Total Income Estimate	$661,660,000
% Cdn. Total	0.10
2001 Average Hhld. Income	$46,400
2001 Per Capita	$18,500
2003 Projected Total Income	$689,560,000
2006 Projected Total Income	$740,610,000

RETAIL SALES

% Above/Below National Average	+4
2001 Retail Sales Estimate	$331,670,000
% Cdn. Total	0.12
2001 per Household	$23,300
2001 per Capita	$9,300
2001 No. of Establishments	310
2003 Projected Retail Sales	$358,040,000
2006 Projected Retail Sales	$398,130,000

POPULATION

2001 Estimates:		
Total		35,745
Male		17,340
Female		18,405

Age Groups	Male	Female
0-4	1,053	1,030
5-9	1,184	1,132
10-14	1,232	1,177
15-19	1,203	1,150
20-24	1,102	1,081
25-29	1,029	1,044
30-34	1,192	1,218
35-39	1,373	1,409
40-44	1,382	1,435
45-49	1,284	1,319
50-54	1,120	1,151
55-59	934	986
60-64	818	884
65-69	736	822
70+	1,698	2,567

DAYTIME POPULATION

2001 Estimates:	
Working Population	16,633
At Home Population	19,113
Total	35,746

INCOME

2001 Estimates:	
Avg. Household Income	$46,438
Avg. Family Income	$52,127
Per Capita Income	$18,510
Male:	
Avg. Employment Income	$30,923
Avg. Employment Income (Full Time)	$41,176
Female:	
Avg. Employment Income	$20,655
Avg. Employment Income (Full Time)	$30,386

DISPOSABLE & DISCRETIONARY INCOME

2001 Estimates:	Per Hhld.
Disposable Income	$38,467
Discretionary Income 1 (minus Food & Shelter)	$26,443
Discretionary Income 2 (minus Food, Shelter, & Other Expenditures)	$18,745

LIQUID ASSETS

1999 Estimates:	Per Hhld.
Equity Investments	$58,720
Interest Bearing Investments	$57,624
Total Liquid Assets	$116,344

CREDIT DATA

July 2000:	
Pool of Credit	$338,469,343
Revolving Credit, No.	60,880
Fixed Loans, No.	20,179
Avg. Credit Limit, per Person	$11,134
Avg. Spent, per Person	$5,104
Satisfactory Ratings, No. per Person	2.59
Avg. No. of Cards, per Person	0.93

LABOUR FORCE

2001 Estimates:	
Male:	
In the Labour Force	9,551
Participation Rate	68.9
Employed	8,869
Unemployed	682
Unemployment Rate	7.1
Not in Labour Force	4,320
Female:	
In the Labour Force	8,322
Participation Rate	55.2
Employed	7,643
Unemployed	679
Unemployment Rate	8.2
Not in Labour Force	6,744

OCCUPATIONS BY MAJOR GROUPS

2001 Estimates:	Male	Female
Management	908	344
Business, Finance & Admin.	479	1,795
Natural & Applied Sciences & Related.	339	10
Health	348	888
Social Sciences, Gov't Services & Religion	136	332
Education	217	383
Arts, Culture, Recreation & Sport.	162	167
Sales & Service	1,698	2,602
Trades, Transport & Equipment Operators & Related.	2,748	174
Primary Industries	273	57
Processing, Mfg. & Utilities.	1,973	1,188

LEVEL OF SCHOOLING

2001 Estimates:	
Population 15 years +	28,937
Less than Grade 9	3,046
Grades 9-13 w/o Certif.	8,906
Grade 9-13 with Certif.	4,311
Trade Certif. /Dip.	1,142
Non-Univ. w/o Certif./Dip.	1,970
Non-Univ. with Certif./Dip.	6,037
Univ. w/o Degree.	1,471
Univ. w/o Degree/Certif.	771
Univ. with Certif.	700
Univ. with Degree	2,054

Ontario

AVERAGE HOUSEHOLD EXPENDITURES

2001 Estimates:	
Food	$5,567
Shelter	$8,341
Clothing	$1,832
Transportation	$5,993
Health & Personal Care	$1,777
Recr'n, Read'g & Education	$3,249
Taxes & Securities	$10,974
Other	$7,799
Total Expenditures	$45,532

PRIVATE HOUSEHOLDS

2001 Estimates:	
Private Households, Total	14,248
Pop. in Private Households	34,718
Average no. per Household	2.4

FAMILIES

2001 Estimates:	
Families in Private Households	10,427
Husband-Wife Families	8,745
Lone-Parent Families	1,682
Aver. No. Persons per Family	2.9
Aver. No. Sons/Daughters at Home	1.1

HOUSING

2001 Estimates:	
Occupied Private Dwellings	14,248
Owned	10,234
Rented	4,014
Single-Detached House	10,644
Semi-Detached House	548
Row Houses	252
Apartment, 5+ Storeys	414
Apartment, 5 or Fewer Storeys	1,577
Apartment, Detached Duplex	734
Other Single-Attached	68
Movable Dwellings	11

VEHICLES

2001 Estimates:	
Model Yrs. '81-'96, No.	17,265
% Total	82.18
Model Yrs. '97-'98, No.	2,252
% Total	10.72
'99 Vehicles registered in Model Yr. '99, No.	1,491
% Total	7.10
Total No. '81-'99	21,008

LEGAL MARITAL STATUS

2001 Estimates: (Age 15+)	
Single (Never Married)	7,750
Legally Married (Not Separated)	15,119
Legally Married (Separated)	1,195
Widowed	2,498
Divorced	2,375

Ontario

Midland
(Census Agglomeration)
(Cont'd)

PSYTE CATEGORIES

2001 Estimates	No. of House -holds	% of Total Hhds.	Index
Small City Elite	445	3.12	182
Satellite Suburbs	95	0.67	23
Blue Collar Winners	269	1.89	75
Town Boomers	1,520	10.67	1,053
Old Towns' New Fringe	1,119	7.85	201
Rustic Prosperity	1,057	7.42	411
Old Leafy Towns	2,329	16.35	640
Town Renters	151	1.06	123
Nesters & Young Homesteaders	6,231	43.73	1,874
Rod & Rifle	783	5.50	238

FINANCIAL P$YTE

2001 Estimates	No. of House -holds	% of Total Hhds.	Index
Canadian Comfort	2,329	16.35	168
Tractors & Tradelines	2,176	15.27	267
Bills & Wills	2,329	16.35	197
Revolving Renters	6,231	43.73	951
Rural Family Blues	783	5.50	68
Towering Debt	151	1.06	14

HOME LANGUAGE

2001 Estimates:		% Total
English	34,464	96.42
French	525	1.47
Chinese	70	0.20
German	226	0.63
Gujarati	40	0.11
Polish	39	0.11
Other Languages	103	0.29
Multiple Responses	278	0.78
Total	35,745	100.00

BUILDING PERMITS

	1999	1998 $000	1997
Value	38,102	23,356	32,603

HOMES BUILT

	1999	1998	1997
No	127	105	133

TAXATION

Income Class:	1997	% Total
Under $5,000	3,620	13.08
$5,000-$10,000	3,560	12.86
$10,000-$15,000	4,650	16.80
$15,000-$20,000	3,020	10.91
$20,000-$25,000	2,400	8.67
$25,000-$30,000	2,300	8.31
$30,000-$40,000	3,460	12.50
$40,000-$50,000	2,070	7.48
$50,000 +	2,610	9.43
Total Returns, No.	27,680	
Total Income, $000	671,332	
Total Taxable Returns	18,360	
Total Tax, $000	112,046	
Average Income, $	24,253	
Average Tax, $	6,103	

VITAL STATISTICS

	1997	1996	1995	1994
Births	398	359	444	429
Deaths	404	382	356	360
Natural Increase	-6	-23	88	69
Marriages	201	223	179	199

Note: Latest available data.

COMMUNITY NEWSPAPER(S)

	Total Circulation
Midland: Midland-Penetanguishene Free Press Tue/Fri	4,908
Midland, Penetanguishene: Mirror Wed	17,247
Fri	17,946
Penetanguishene: Penetanguishene Le Goût de Vivre (biwkly)	n.a.

RADIO STATION(S)

	Power
CBCL-FM	100w
CBCM-FM	n.a.
CFRH-FM	n.a.
CICZ-FM	n.a.
CJBC-FM	n.a.

TELEVISION STATION(S)

CIII-TV

Nanticoke
(City)

In Haldimand-Norfolk Regional Municipality.

POPULATION

July 1, 2001 Estimate	24,943
% Cdn. Total	0.08
% Change, '96 -'01	2.63
Avg. Annual Growth Rate, %	0.52
2003 Projected Population	24,983
2006 Projected Population	24,908
2001 Households Estimate	9,130
2003 Projected Households	9,277
2006 Projected Households	9,478

INCOME

% Above/Below National Average	-6
2001 Total Income Estimate	$492,240,000
% Cdn. Total	0.07
2001 Average Hhld. Income	$53,900
2001 Per Capita	$19,700
2003 Projected Total Income	$525,930,000
2006 Projected Total Income	$578,760,000

RETAIL SALES

% Above/Below National Average	-58
2001 Retail Sales Estimate	$94,390,000
% Cdn. Total	0.03
2001 per Household	$10,300
2001 per Capita	$3,800
2001 No. of Establishments	178
2003 Projected Retail Sales	$102,200,000
2006 Projected Retail Sales	$113,380,000

POPULATION

2001 Estimates:		
Total		24,943
Male		12,503
Female		12,440
Age Groups	Male	Female
0-4	714	687
5-9	834	802
10-14	998	935
15-19	1,025	938
20-24	842	794
25-29	686	679
30-34	727	778
35-39	930	972
40-44	1,044	1,063
45-49	985	935
50-54	818	777
55-59	679	625
60-64	563	559
65-69	506	530
70+	1,152	1,366

DAYTIME POPULATION

2001 Estimates:	
Working Population	17,864
At Home Population	12,138
Total	30,002

INCOME

2001 Estimates:	
Avg. Household Income	$53,915
Avg. Family Income	$58,827
Per Capita Income	$19,735
Male:	
Avg. Employment Income	$33,929
Avg. Employment Income (Full Time)	$45,180
Female:	
Avg. Employment Income	$19,371
Avg. Employment Income (Full Time)	$30,225

DISPOSABLE & DISCRETIONARY INCOME

2001 Estimates:	Per Hhld.
Disposable Income	$44,544
Discretionary Income 1 (minus Food & Shelter)	$31,463
Discretionary Income 2 (minus Food, Shelter, & Other Expenditures)	$21,893

LIQUID ASSETS

1999 Estimates:	Per Hhld.
Equity Investments	$73,293
Interest Bearing Investments	$65,213
Total Liquid Assets	$138,506

CREDIT DATA

July 2000:	
Pool of Credit	$235,525,760
Revolving Credit, No.	38,949
Fixed Loans, No.	12,240
Avg. Credit Limit, per Person	$11,605
Avg. Spent, per Person	$5,432
Satisfactory Ratings, No. per Person	2.44
Avg. No. of Cards, per Person	0.93

LABOUR FORCE

2001 Estimates:	
Male:	
In the Labour Force	7,604
Participation Rate	76.4
Employed	7,318
Unemployed	286
Unemployment Rate	3.8
Not in Labour Force	2,353
Female:	
In the Labour Force	5,968
Participation Rate	59.6
Employed	5,460
Unemployed	508
Unemployment Rate	8.5
Not in Labour Force	4,048

OCCUPATIONS BY MAJOR GROUPS

2001 Estimates:	Male	Female
Management	691	240
Business, Finance & Admin.	385	1,513
Natural & Applied Sciences & Related	271	80
Health	34	452
Social Sciences, Gov't Services & Religion	90	156
Education	152	179
Arts, Culture, Recreation & Sport	29	186
Sales & Service	895	1,915
Trades, Transport & Equipment Operators & Related	2,644	101
Primary Industries	1,277	640
Processing, Mfg. & Utilities	1,062	333

LEVEL OF SCHOOLING

2001 Estimates:	
Population 15 years +	19,973
Less than Grade 9	2,118
Grades 9-13 w/o Certif.	5,317
Grade 9-13 with Certif.	3,555
Trade Certif. /Dip.	1,001
Non-Univ. w/o Certif./Dip.	1,413
Non-Univ. with Certif./Dip.	4,205
Univ. w/o Degree	1,204
Univ. w/o Degree/Certif.	525
Univ. with Certif.	679
Univ. with Degree	1,160

Nanticoke
(City)
(Cont'd)

AVERAGE HOUSEHOLD EXPENDITURES

2001 Estimates:

Food	$6,371
Shelter	$8,760
Clothing	$2,013
Transportation	$7,768
Health & Personal Care	$1,932
Recr'n, Read'g & Education	$3,955
Taxes & Securities	$12,407
Other	$8,830
Total Expenditures	$52,036

PRIVATE HOUSEHOLDS

2001 Estimates:

Private Households, Total	9,130
Pop. in Private Households	24,674
Average no. per Household	2.7

FAMILIES

2001 Estimates:

Families in Private Households	7,275
Husband-Wife Families	6,575
Lone-Parent Families	700
Aver. No. Persons per Family	3.1
Aver. No. Sons/Daughters at Home	1.2

HOUSING

2001 Estimates:

Occupied Private Dwellings	9,130
Owned	7,133
Rented	1,997
Single-Detached House	7,956
Semi-Detached House	220
Row Houses	284
Apartment, 5+ Storeys	11
Owned Apartment, 5+ Storeys	11
Apartment, 5 or Fewer Storeys	420
Apartment, Detached Duplex	152
Other Single-Attached	87

VEHICLES

2001 Estimates:

Model Yrs. '81-'96, No.	14,439
% Total	86.92
Model Yrs. '97-'98, No.	1,390
% Total	8.37
'99 Vehicles registered in Model Yr. '99, No.	782
% Total	4.71
Total No. '81-'99	16,611

LEGAL MARITAL STATUS

2001 Estimates: (Age 15+)

Single (Never Married)	4,684
Legally Married (Not Separated)	12,251
Legally Married (Separated)	536
Widowed	1,279
Divorced	1,223

PSYTE CATEGORIES

2001 Estimates	No. of House -holds	% of Total Hhds.	Index
Small City Elite	229	2.51	146
Blue Collar Winners	82	0.90	36
Old Towns' New Fringe	1,615	17.69	452
Rustic Prosperity	4,002	43.83	2,429
Old Leafy Towns	2,375	26.01	1,018
Nesters & Young Homesteaders	110	1.20	52
Rod & Rifle	717	7.85	340

FINANCIAL PSYTE

2001 Estimates	No. of House -holds	% of Total Hhds.	Index
Canadian Comfort	311	3.41	35
Tractors & Tradelines	5,617	61.52	1,076
Bills & Wills	2,375	26.01	314
Revolving Renters	110	1.20	26
Rural Family Blues	717	7.85	97

HOME LANGUAGE

2001 Estimates:		% Total
English	24,325	97.52
French	54	0.22
Dutch	55	0.22
German	126	0.51
Korean	21	0.08
Polish	54	0.22
Portuguese	32	0.13
Russian	16	0.06
Spanish	22	0.09
Ukrainian	97	0.39
Other Languages	21	0.08
Multiple Responses	120	0.48
Total	24,943	100.00

BUILDING PERMITS

	1999	1998	1997
		$000	
Value	23,579	17,904	24,472

HOMES BUILT

	1999	1998	1997
No	18	38	50

TAXATION

Income Class:	1997	% Total
Under $5,000	1,990	13.41
$5,000-$10,000	1,800	12.13
$10,000-$15,000	2,270	15.30
$15,000-$20,000	1,640	11.05
$20,000-$25,000	1,250	8.42
$25,000-$30,000	1,110	7.48
$30,000-$40,000	1,680	11.32
$40,000-$50,000	1,100	7.41
$50,000 +	2,020	13.61
Total Returns, No.	14,840	
Total Income, $000	381,433	
Total Taxable Returns	10,250	
Total Tax, $000	65,849	
Average Income, $	25,703	
Average Tax, $	6,424	

VITAL STATISTICS

	1997	1996	1995	1994
Births	211	208	215	226
Deaths	163	179	153	170
Natural Increase	48	29	62	56
Marriages	130	129	117	124

Note: Latest available data.

COMMUNITY NEWSPAPER(S)

	Total Circulation
Port Dover: Port Dover Maple Leaf	2,968

Norfolk
(Township)

In Haldimand-Norfolk Regional Municipality.

POPULATION

July 1, 2001 Estimate	13,729
% Cdn. Total	0.04
% Change, '96 -'01	5.36
Avg. Annual Growth Rate, %	1.05
2003 Projected Population	13,936
2006 Projected Population	14,171
2001 Households Estimate	4,773
2003 Projected Households	4,913
2006 Projected Households	5,122

INCOME

% Above/Below National Average	-14
2001 Total Income Estimate	$247,810,000
% Cdn. Total	0.04
2001 Average Hhld. Income	$51,900
2001 Per Capita	$18,100
2003 Projected Total Income	$268,330,000
2006 Projected Total Income	$301,530,000

RETAIL SALES

% Above/Below National Average	-48
2001 Retail Sales Estimate	$63,940,000
% Cdn. Total	0.02
2001 per Household	$13,400
2001 per Capita	$4,700
2001 No. of Establishments	102
2003 Projected Retail Sales	$68,160,000
2006 Projected Retail Sales	$75,060,000

POPULATION

2001 Estimates:

Total		13,729
Male		6,868
Female		6,861

Age Groups	Male	Female
0-4	403	397
5-9	461	479
10-14	546	539
15-19	556	554
20-24	500	512
25-29	467	443
30-34	468	436
35-39	503	472
40-44	503	476
45-49	474	443
50-54	415	399
55-59	361	355
60-64	321	318
65-69	291	307
70+	599	731

DAYTIME POPULATION

2001 Estimates:

Working Population	3,243
At Home Population	6,708
Total	9,951

INCOME

2001 Estimates:

Avg. Household Income	$51,919
Avg. Family Income	$54,897
Per Capita Income	$18,050
Male:	
Avg. Employment Income	$26,875
Avg. Employment Income (Full Time)	$36,418
Female:	
Avg. Employment Income	$17,357
Avg. Employment Income (Full Time)	$28,934

Ontario

DISPOSABLE & DISCRETIONARY INCOME

2001 Estimates:	Per Hhld.
Disposable Income	$42,989
Discretionary Income 1 (minus Food & Shelter)	$30,484
Discretionary Income 2 (minus Food, Shelter, & Other Expenditures)	$20,827

LIQUID ASSETS

1999 Estimates:	Per Hhld.
Equity Investments	$70,355
Interest Bearing Investments	$62,850
Total Liquid Assets	$133,205

CREDIT DATA

July 2000:	
Pool of Credit	$105,326,863
Revolving Credit, No.	16,909
Fixed Loans, No.	6,342
Avg. Credit Limit, per Person	$10,943
Avg. Spent, per Person	$5,239
Satisfactory Ratings, No. per Person	2.32
Avg. No. of Cards, per Person	0.87

LABOUR FORCE

2001 Estimates:	
Male:	
In the Labour Force	4,201
Participation Rate	77.0
Employed	3,932
Unemployed	269
Unemployment Rate	6.4
Not in Labour Force	1,257
Female:	
In the Labour Force	3,377
Participation Rate	62.0
Employed	3,008
Unemployed	369
Unemployment Rate	10.9
Not in Labour Force	2,069

OCCUPATIONS BY MAJOR GROUPS

2001 Estimates:	Male	Female
Management	238	84
Business, Finance & Admin.	168	619
Natural & Applied Sciences & Related	155	18
Health	n.a.	169
Social Sciences, Gov't Services & Religion	23	69
Education	32	99
Arts, Culture, Recreation & Sport	23	34
Sales & Service	335	705
Trades, Transport & Equipment Operators & Related	1,110	93
Primary Industries	1,372	950
Processing, Mfg. & Utilities	713	476

Ontario

Norfolk
(Township)
(Cont'd)

LEVEL OF SCHOOLING

2001 Estimates:
Population 15 years + ... 10,904
Less than Grade 9. 2,485
Grades 9-13 w/o Certif. 3,212
Grade 9-13 with Certif. 1,655
Trade Certif. /Dip. 334
Non-Univ. w/o Certif./Dip. 560
Non-Univ. with Certif./Dip. 1,775
Univ. w/o Degree 466
 Univ. w/o Degree/Certif. 227
 Univ. with Certif. 239
Univ. with Degree. 417

AVERAGE HOUSEHOLD EXPENDITURES

2001 Estimates:
Food $6,183
Shelter $8,258
Clothing. $1,984
Transportation. $7,993
Health & Personal Care $1,857
Recr'n, Read'g & Education $3,875
Taxes & Securities $11,515
Other. $8,763
Total Expenditures $50,428

PRIVATE HOUSEHOLDS

2001 Estimates:
Private Households, Total. 4,773
Pop. in Private Households. 13,467
Average no. per Household 2.8

FAMILIES

2001 Estimates:
Families in Private Households 3,980
Husband-Wife Families 3,618
Lone-Parent Families 362
Aver. No. Persons per Family 3.2
Aver. No. Sons/Daughters
 at Home 1.3

HOUSING

2001 Estimates:
Occupied Private Dwellings 4,773
 Owned. 3,676
 Rented. 1,097
Single-Detached House 4,502
Semi-Detached House 50
Row Houses 44
Apartment, 5 or Fewer Storeys 138
Apartment, Detached Duplex 22
Movable Dwellings. 17

VEHICLES

2001 Estimates:
Model Yrs. '81-'96, No. 8,078
 % Total 86.42
Model Yrs. '97-'98, No. 802
 % Total 8.58
'99 Vehicles registered in
 Model Yr. '99, No. 467
 % Total 5.00
Total No. '81-'99 9,347

LEGAL MARITAL STATUS

2001 Estimates: (Age 15+)
Single (Never Married). 2,713
Legally Married
 (Not Separated) 6,764
Legally Married (Separated) 244
Widowed 632
Divorced 551

PSYTE CATEGORIES

2001 Estimates	No. of House -holds	% of Total Hhds.	Index
Blue Collar Winners.	56	1.17.	.47
Rustic Prosperity.	3,608	75.59.	4,189
Old Leafy Towns	696	14.58.	.571
Rod & Rifle	384	8.05.	.348

FINANCIAL PSYTE

2001 Estimates	No. of House -holds	% of Total Hhds.	Index
Canadian Comfort	56	1.17.	.12
Tractors & Tradelines	3,608	75.59.	1,322
Bills & Wills	696	14.58.	.176
Rural Family Blues	384	8.05.	.100

HOME LANGUAGE

2001 Estimates		% Total
English	11,905	86.71
French	.16	0.12
Dutch	.38	0.28
Flemish	.83	0.60
German	1,469	10.70
Hungarian	.28	0.20
Portuguese	.29	0.21
Ukrainian	.11	0.08
Other Languages	.27	0.20
Multiple Responses	.123	0.90
Total	13,729	100.00

BUILDING PERMITS

	1999	1998 $000	1997
Value	10,855	11,615.	16,449

TAXATION

Income Class:	1997	% Total
Under $5,000	.890	12.92
$5,000-$10,000	1,020	14.80
$10,000-$15,000	1,140	16.55
$15,000-$20,000	.930	13.50
$20,000-$25,000	.610	8.85
$25,000-$30,000	.550	7.98
$30,000-$40,000	.860	12.48
$40,000-$50,000	.420	6.10
$50,000 +	.470	6.82
Total Returns, No.	6,890	
Total Income, $000	152,220	
Total Taxable Returns	4,690	
Total Tax, $000	23,282	
Average Income, $	22,093	
Average Tax, $	4,964	

VITAL STATISTICS

	1997	1996	1995	1994
Births	116	121	125	107
Deaths	65	83	60	63
Natural Increase	51	38	65	44
Marriages	76	68	84	76

Note: Latest available data.

North Bay
(Census Agglomeration)

The Census Agglomeration of North Bay includes: North Bay, C; Bonfield, TP; East Ferris, TP; and Nipissing 10, R. All are in Nipissing District. It also includes North Himsworth, TP in Parry Sound District.

POPULATION

2001 Estimates:
July 1, 2001 Estimate 64,045
% Cdn. Total. 0.21
% Change, '96 -'01 . . . . -3.71
Avg. Annual Growth Rate, %. . . . . -0.75
2003 Projected Population. 63,657
2006 Projected Population. 62,791
2001 Households Estimate 26,036
2003 Projected Households 26,240
2006 Projected Households 26,484

INCOME

% Above/Below National Average . . . . -5
2001 Total Income Estimate . . . $1,277,140,000
% Cdn. Total. 0.19
2001 Average Hhld. Income. $49,100
2001 Per Capita $19,900
2003 Projected Total Income . . $1,343,630,000
2006 Projected Total Income . . $1,446,870,000

RETAIL SALES

% Above/Below National Average . . . . +41
2001 Retail Sales Estimate $807,660,000
% Cdn. Total. 0.29
2001 per Household $31,000
2001 per Capita $12,600
2001 No. of Establishments 639
2003 Projected Retail Sales $856,670,000
2006 Projected Retail Sales $916,980,000

POPULATION

2001 Estimates:
Total 64,045
Male. 30,978
Female 33,067

Age Groups	Male	Female
0-4	1,920	1,820
5-9	2,057	1,963
10-14	2,212	2,113
15-19	2,289	2,162
20-24	2,250	2,146
25-29	2,058	2,041
30-34	2,107	2,258
35-39	2,353	2,570
40-44	2,412	2,604
45-49	2,327	2,448
50-54	2,036	2,151
55-59	1,704	1,845
60-64	1,494	1,598
65-69	1,277	1,437
70+	2,482	3,911

DAYTIME POPULATION

2001 Estimates:
Working Population 30,657
At Home Population. 33,388
Total 64,045

INCOME

2001 Estimates:
Avg. Household Income $49,053
Avg. Family Income $56,242
Per Capita Income $19,941
Male: . . . .
Avg. Employment Income $31,742
Avg. Employment Income
 (Full Time). $43,462
Female: . . . .
Avg. Employment Income $20,670
Avg. Employment Income
 (Full Time). $31,936

DISPOSABLE & DISCRETIONARY INCOME

2001 Estimates:	Per Hhld.
Disposable Income	$40,421
Discretionary Income 1 (minus Food & Shelter)	$27,992
Discretionary Income 2 (minus Food, Shelter, & Other Expenditures).	$20,104

LIQUID ASSETS

1999 Estimates:	Per Hhld.
Equity Investments	$66,186
Interest Bearing Investments	$61,365
Total Liquid Assets	$127,551

CREDIT DATA

July 2000:
Pool of Credit $712,489,569
Revolving Credit, No. 124,224
Fixed Loans, No. 47,773
Avg. Credit Limit, per Person. $12,017
Avg. Spent, per Person $5,797
Satisfactory Ratings,
 No. per Person. 2.68
Avg. No. of Cards, per Person 0.93

LABOUR FORCE

2001 Estimates:
Male:
In the Labour Force 17,442
Participation Rate 70.4
Employed. 16,041
Unemployed. 1,401
Unemployment Rate 8.0
Not in Labour Force 7,347
Female:
In the Labour Force 15,657
Participation Rate 57.6
Employed. 14,443
Unemployed. 1,214
Unemployment Rate 7.8
Not in Labour Force 11,514

OCCUPATIONS BY MAJOR GROUPS

2001 Estimates:	Male	Female
Management.	1,952	1,027
Business, Finance & Admin.	1,777	4,228
Natural & Applied Sciences & Related	1,137	179
Health	420	1,398
Social Sciences, Gov't Services & Religion	405	673
Education	672	871
Arts, Culture, Recreation & Sport	321	324
Sales & Service	4,658	5,755
Trades, Transport & Equipment Operators & Related	4,258	211
Primary Industries	393	55
Processing, Mfg. & Utilities	1,018	320

LEVEL OF SCHOOLING

2001 Estimates:
Population 15 years + ... 51,960
Less than Grade 9 4,626
Grades 9-13 w/o Certif. 12,094
Grade 9-13 with Certif. 7,105
Trade Certif. /Dip. 2,305
Non-Univ. w/o Certif./Dip. 3,923
Non-Univ. with Certif./Dip. 11,728
Univ. w/o Degree. 4,463
 Univ. w/o Degree/Certif. 2,200
 Univ. with Certif. 2,263
Univ. with Degree. 5,716

North Bay
(Census Agglomeration)
(Cont'd)

AVERAGE HOUSEHOLD EXPENDITURES

2001 Estimates:

Food	$5,888
Shelter	$8,579
Clothing	$2,023
Transportation	$5,833
Health & Personal Care	$1,965
Recr'n, Read'g & Education	$3,486
Taxes & Securities	$11,573
Other	$8,261
Total Expenditures	$47,608

PRIVATE HOUSEHOLDS

2001 Estimates:

Private Households, Total	26,036
Pop. in Private Households	62,415
Average no. per Household	2.4

FAMILIES

2001 Estimates:

Families in Private Households	18,812
Husband-Wife Families	15,676
Lone-Parent Families	3,136
Aver. No. Persons per Family	2.9
Aver. No. Sons/Daughters at Home	1.1

HOUSING

2001 Estimates:

Occupied Private Dwellings	26,036
Owned	15,900
Rented	10,107
Band Housing	29
Single-Detached House	14,488
Semi-Detached House	2,445
Row Houses	1,897
Apartment, 5+ Storeys	1,990
Owned Apartment, 5+ Storeys	262
Apartment, 5 or Fewer Storeys	3,539
Apartment, Detached Duplex	1,498
Other Single-Attached	47
Movable Dwellings	132

VEHICLES

2001 Estimates:

Model Yrs. '81-'96, No.	31,135
% Total	76.08
Model Yrs. '97-'98, No.	5,834
% Total	14.26
'99 Vehicles registered in Model Yr. '99, No.	3,954
% Total	9.66
Total No. '81-'99	40,923

LEGAL MARITAL STATUS

2001 Estimates: (Age 15+)

Single (Never Married)	15,104
Legally Married (Not Separated)	26,985
Legally Married (Separated)	2,213
Widowed	3,815
Divorced	3,843

PSYTE CATEGORIES

2001 Estimates	No. of House -holds	% of Total Hhds.	Index
Suburban Executives	405	1.56	109
Small City Elite	2,872	11.03	644
Old Bungalow Burbs	1,141	4.38	264
Kindergarten Boom	375	1.44	55
Blue Collar Winners	462	1.77	70
Town Boomers	1,729	6.64	655
Old Towns' New Fringe	3,039	11.67	298
Old Leafy Towns	346	1.33	52
Town Renters	669	2.57	297
Nesters & Young Homesteaders	8,190	31.46	1,348
Young Grey Collar	4,396	16.88	2,018
Rod & Rifle	313	1.20	52
Big Country Families	261	1.00	70
Aged Pensioners	1,098	4.22	317
Old Grey Towers	394	1.51	273

FINAN¢IAL P$YTE

2001 Estimates	No. of House -holds	% of Total Hhds.	Index
Four Star Investors	405	1.56	31
Canadian Comfort	5,063	19.45	200
Miners & Credit-Liners	1,141	4.38	138
Mortgages & Minivans	375	1.44	22
Tractors & Tradelines	3,039	11.67	204
Bills & Wills	346	1.33	16
Revolving Renters	12,586	48.34	1,051
Rural Family Blues	574	2.20	27
Towering Debt	669	2.57	33
Senior Survivors	1,492	5.73	304

HOME LANGUAGE

2001 Estimates:		% Total
English	57,583	89.91
French	4,781	7.47
Chinese	126	0.20
Cree	58	0.09
Italian	196	0.31
Portuguese	46	0.07
Other Languages	203	0.32
Multiple Responses	1,052	1.64
Total	64,045	100.00

BUILDING PERMITS

	1999	1998	1997
		$000	
Value	34,746	22,231	20,789

HOMES BUILT

	1999	1998	1997
No	127	89	64

TAXATION

Income Class:	1997	% Total
Under $5,000	6,910	14.26
$5,000-$10,000	6,040	12.46
$10,000-$15,000	7,420	15.31
$15,000-$20,000	5,070	10.46
$20,000-$25,000	3,820	7.88
$25,000-$30,000	3,630	7.49
$30,000-$40,000	5,990	12.36
$40,000-$50,000	3,830	7.90
$50,000 +	5,760	11.88
Total Returns, No.	48,470	
Total Income, $000	1,247,523	
Total Taxable Returns	31,720	
Total Tax, $000	221,118	
Average Income, $	25,738	
Average Tax, $	6,971	

VITAL STATISTICS

	1997	1996	1995	1994
Births	644	726	779	854
Deaths	548	589	570	521
Natural Increase	96	137	209	333
Marriages	423	472	473	457

Note: Latest available data.

DAILY NEWSPAPER(S)

	Circulation Average Paid
Nugget	
Fri	21,975
Sat	19,319
Mon-Thu	18,017

RADIO STATION(S)

	Power
CBCN-FM	n.a.
CBON-FM	n.a.
CHIM-FM	50w
CHUR-FM	100,000w
CJRT-FM	n.a.
CKAT	10,000w
CKFX-FM	68,000w
CRFM-FM	n.a.

TELEVISION STATION(S)

CHCH-TV
CHNB-TV
CIII-TV
CKNY-TV
TFO
TVO

Norwich
(Township)

In Oxford County.

POPULATION

July 1, 2001 Estimate	11,205
% Cdn. Total	0.04
% Change, '96 -'01	2.69
Avg. Annual Growth Rate, %	0.53
2003 Projected Population	11,284
2006 Projected Population	11,328
2001 Households Estimate	3,586
2003 Projected Households	3,638
2006 Projected Households	3,706

INCOME

% Above/Below National Average	-11
2001 Total Income Estimate	$211,130,000
% Cdn. Total	0.03
2001 Average Hhld. Income	$58,900
2001 Per Capita	$18,800
2003 Projected Total Income	$225,570,000
2006 Projected Total Income	$248,070,000

RETAIL SALES

% Above/Below National Average	-36
2001 Retail Sales Estimate	$63,700,000
% Cdn. Total	0.02
2001 per Household	$17,800
2001 per Capita	$5,700
2001 No. of Establishments	106
2003 Projected Retail Sales	$69,060,000
2006 Projected Retail Sales	$77,040,000

POPULATION

2001 Estimates:

Total		11,205
Male		5,564
Female		5,641
Age Groups	Male	Female
0-4	367	351
5-9	438	419
10-14	484	477
15-19	491	472
20-24	436	408
25-29	379	352
30-34	371	375
35-39	394	432
40-44	407	412
45-49	378	371
50-54	323	316
55-59	267	271
60-64	228	249
65-69	196	214
70+	405	522

DAYTIME POPULATION

2001 Estimates:

Working Population	5,580
At Home Population	4,906
Total	10,486

INCOME

2001 Estimates:

Avg. Household Income	$58,877
Avg. Family Income	$62,021
Per Capita Income	$18,843
Male:	
Avg. Employment Income	$31,271
Avg. Employment Income (Full Time)	$38,951
Female:	
Avg. Employment Income	$19,478
Avg. Employment Income (Full Time)	$29,056

Ontario

DISPOSABLE & DISCRETIONARY INCOME

2001 Estimates:	Per Hhld.
Disposable Income	$48,529
Discretionary Income 1 (minus Food & Shelter)	$34,779
Discretionary Income 2 (minus Food, Shelter, & Other Expenditures)	$23,826

LIQUID ASSETS

1999 Estimates:	Per Hhld.
Equity Investments	$90,864
Interest Bearing Investments	$72,779
Total Liquid Assets	$163,643

CREDIT DATA

July 2000:	
Pool of Credit	$75,390,984
Revolving Credit, No.	11,730
Fixed Loans, No.	4,238
Avg. Credit Limit, per Person	$10,926
Avg. Spent, per Person	$5,226
Satisfactory Ratings, No. per Person	2.22
Avg. No. of Cards, per Person	0.82

LABOUR FORCE

2001 Estimates:

Male:	
In the Labour Force	3,530
Participation Rate	82.6
Employed	3,440
Unemployed	90
Unemployment Rate	2.5
Not in Labour Force	745
Female:	
In the Labour Force	2,918
Participation Rate	66.4
Employed	2,830
Unemployed	88
Unemployment Rate	3.0
Not in Labour Force	1,476

OCCUPATIONS BY MAJOR GROUPS

2001 Estimates:	Male	Female
Management	248	94
Business, Finance & Admin.	159	736
Natural & Applied Sciences & Related	79	59
Health	11	210
Social Sciences, Gov't Services & Religion	39	33
Education	44	87
Arts, Culture, Recreation & Sport	40	57
Sales & Service	420	730
Trades, Transport & Equipment Operators & Related	1,128	75
Primary Industries	823	561
Processing, Mfg. & Utilities	487	196

Norwich
(Township)
(Cont'd)

LEVEL OF SCHOOLING

2001 Estimates:
Population 15 years +	8,669
Less than Grade 9	1,205
Grades 9-13 w/o Certif.	2,496
Grade 9-13 with Certif.	1,490
Trade Certif. /Dip.	419
Non-Univ. w/o Certif./Dip.	510
Non-Univ. with Certif./Dip.	1,729
Univ. w/o Degree	409
Univ. w/o Degree/Certif.	229
Univ. with Certif.	180
Univ. with Degree	411

AVERAGE HOUSEHOLD EXPENDITURES

2001 Estimates:
Food	$6,838
Shelter	$9,070
Clothing	$2,253
Transportation	$9,152
Health & Personal Care	$2,043
Recr'n, Read'g & Education	$4,424
Taxes & Securities	$12,411
Other	$9,949
Total Expenditures	$56,140

PRIVATE HOUSEHOLDS

2001 Estimates:
Private Households, Total	3,586
Pop. in Private Households	10,975
Average no. per Household	3.1

FAMILIES

2001 Estimates:
Families in Private Households	3,055
Husband-Wife Families	2,818
Lone-Parent Families	237
Aver. No. Persons per Family	3.4
Aver. No. Sons/Daughters at Home	1.5

HOUSING

2001 Estimates:
Occupied Private Dwellings	3,586
Owned	2,897
Rented	689
Single-Detached House	3,217
Semi-Detached House	59
Row Houses	16
Apartment, 5 or Fewer Storeys	175
Apartment, Detached Duplex	68
Other Single-Attached	31
Movable Dwellings	20

VEHICLES

2001 Estimates:
Model Yrs. '81-'96, No.	4,780
% Total	82.44
Model Yrs. '97-'98, No.	646
% Total	11.14
'99 Vehicles registered in Model Yr. '99, No.	372
% Total	6.42
Total No. '81-'99	5,798

LEGAL MARITAL STATUS

2001 Estimates: (Age 15+)
Single (Never Married)	2,174
Legally Married (Not Separated)	5,518
Legally Married (Separated)	189
Widowed	467
Divorced	321

PSYTE CATEGORIES

2001 Estimates	No. of House-holds	% of Total Hhds.	Index
Old Towns' New Fringe	149	4.16	106
Rustic Prosperity	3,413	95.18	5,275
Big Country Families	11	0.31	22

FINANCIAL P$YTE

2001 Estimates	No. of House-holds	% of Total Hhds.	Index
Tractors & Tradelines	3,562	99.33	1,737
Rural Family Blues	11	0.31	4

HOME LANGUAGE

2001 Estimates		% Total
English	10,387	92.70
French	37	0.33
Arabic	10	0.09
Chinese	22	0.20
Dutch	433	3.86
German	179	1.60
Hungarian	69	0.62
Polish	11	0.10
Romanian	10	0.09
Other Languages	10	0.09
Multiple Responses	37	0.33
Total	11,205	100.00

BUILDING PERMITS

	1999	1998 $000	1997
Value	10,862	9,361	12,085

TAXATION

Income Class:	1997	% Total
Under $5,000	700	12.43
$5,000-$10,000	740	13.14
$10,000-$15,000	800	14.21
$15,000-$20,000	600	10.66
$20,000-$25,000	520	9.24
$25,000-$30,000	440	7.82
$30,000-$40,000	850	15.10
$40,000-$50,000	460	8.17
$50,000 +	530	9.41
Total Returns, No.	5,630	
Total Income, $000	138,215	
Total Taxable Returns	3,970	
Total Tax, $000	22,083	
Average Income, $	24,550	
Average Tax, $	5,562	

VITAL STATISTICS

	1997	1996	1995	1994
Births	135	138	146	140
Deaths	71	60	71	66
Natural Increase	64	78	75	74
Marriages	67	56	71	51

Note: Latest available data.

COMMUNITY NEWSPAPER(S)

	Total Circulation
Norwich: Norwich Gazette	1,490

Orillia
(Census Agglomeration)

The Census Agglomeration of Orillia includes: Orillia, C; and Severn, TP. Both are in Simcoe County.

POPULATION

July 1, 2001 Estimate	42,932
% Cdn. Total	0.14
% Change, '96 -'01	9.33
Avg. Annual Growth Rate, %	1.80
2003 Projected Population	44,362
2006 Projected Population	46,494
2001 Households Estimate	17,244
2003 Projected Households	17,749
2006 Projected Households	18,696

INCOME

% Above/Below National Average	-12
2001 Total Income Estimate	$799,530,000
% Cdn. Total	0.12
2001 Average Hhld. Income	$46,400
2001 Per Capita	$18,600
2003 Projected Total Income	$855,150,000
2006 Projected Total Income	$954,080,000

RETAIL SALES

% Above/Below National Average	+9
2001 Retail Sales Estimate	$418,970,000
% Cdn. Total	0.15
2001 per Household	$24,300
2001 per Capita	$9,800
2001 No. of Establishments	407
2003 Projected Retail Sales	$464,670,000
2006 Projected Retail Sales	$533,020,000

POPULATION

2001 Estimates:
Total	42,932
Male	20,642
Female	22,290

Age Groups	Male	Female
0-4	1,313	1,271
5-9	1,447	1,391
10-14	1,496	1,441
15-19	1,418	1,427
20-24	1,307	1,364
25-29	1,259	1,382
30-34	1,409	1,554
35-39	1,578	1,712
40-44	1,602	1,703
45-49	1,523	1,532
50-54	1,303	1,291
55-59	1,064	1,093
60-64	927	984
65-69	862	958
70+	2,134	3,187

DAYTIME POPULATION

2001 Estimates:
Working Population	19,395
At Home Population	23,537
Total	42,932

INCOME

2001 Estimates:
Avg. Household Income	$46,366
Avg. Family Income	$52,793
Per Capita Income	$18,623
Male:	
Avg. Employment Income	$30,063
Avg. Employment Income (Full Time)	$40,803
Female:	
Avg. Employment Income	$20,452
Avg. Employment Income (Full Time)	$31,705

DISPOSABLE & DISCRETIONARY INCOME

2001 Estimates:	Per Hhld.
Disposable Income	$38,445
Discretionary Income 1 (minus Food & Shelter)	$26,139
Discretionary Income 2 (minus Food, Shelter, & Other Expenditures)	$18,498

LIQUID ASSETS

1999 Estimates:	Per Hhld.
Equity Investments	$63,635
Interest Bearing Investments	$57,845
Total Liquid Assets	$121,480

CREDIT DATA

July 2000:
Pool of Credit	$422,204,054
Revolving Credit, No.	75,432
Fixed Loans, No.	26,256
Avg. Credit Limit, per Person	$11,727
Avg. Spent, per Person	$5,488
Satisfactory Ratings, No. per Person	2.69
Avg. No. of Cards, per Person	0.99

LABOUR FORCE

2001 Estimates:
Male:	
In the Labour Force	11,228
Participation Rate	68.5
Employed	10,295
Unemployed	933
Unemployment Rate	8.3
Not in Labour Force	5,158
Female:	
In the Labour Force	9,771
Participation Rate	53.7
Employed	8,961
Unemployed	810
Unemployment Rate	8.3
Not in Labour Force	8,416

OCCUPATIONS BY MAJOR GROUPS

2001 Estimates:	Male	Female
Management	1,195	523
Business, Finance & Admin.	775	2,318
Natural & Applied Sciences & Related	401	46
Health	161	983
Social Sciences, Gov't Services & Religion	435	586
Education	247	424
Arts, Culture, Recreation & Sport	201	204
Sales & Service	2,690	3,484
Trades, Transport & Equipment Operators & Related	2,895	239
Primary Industries	463	58
Processing, Mfg. & Utilities	1,338	382

LEVEL OF SCHOOLING

2001 Estimates:
Population 15 years +	34,573
Less than Grade 9	3,504
Grades 9-13 w/o Certif.	10,133
Grade 9-13 with Certif.	4,900
Trade Certif. /Dip.	1,574
Non-Univ. w/o Certif./Dip.	2,416
Non-Univ. with Certif./Dip.	7,288
Univ. w/o Degree	1,966
Univ. w/o Degree/Certif.	924
Univ. with Certif.	1,042
Univ. with Degree	2,792

Orillia
(Census Agglomeration)
(Cont'd)

AVERAGE HOUSEHOLD EXPENDITURES

2001 Estimates:

Food	$5,640
Shelter	$8,617
Clothing	$1,827
Transportation	$5,899
Health & Personal Care	$1,815
Recr'n, Read'g & Education	$3,234
Taxes & Securities	$10,486
Other	$7,942
Total Expenditures	$45,460

PRIVATE HOUSEHOLDS

2001 Estimates:

Private Households, Total	17,244
Pop. in Private Households	41,536
Average no. per Household	2.4

FAMILIES

2001 Estimates:

Families in Private Households	12,462
Husband-Wife Families	10,486
Lone-Parent Families	1,976
Aver. No. Persons per Family	2.9
Aver. No. Sons/Daughters at Home	1.1

HOUSING

2001 Estimates:

Occupied Private Dwellings	17,244
Owned	11,681
Rented	5,563
Single-Detached House	12,194
Semi-Detached House	326
Row Houses	744
Apartment, 5+ Storeys	967
Owned Apartment, 5+ Storeys	11
Apartment, 5 or Fewer Storeys	2,162
Apartment, Detached Duplex	548
Other Single-Attached	158
Movable Dwellings	145

VEHICLES

2001 Estimates:

Model Yrs. '81-'96, No.	21,581
% Total	77.95
Model Yrs. '97-'98, No.	3,851
% Total	13.91
'99 Vehicles registered in Model Yr. '99, No.	2,255
% Total	8.14
Total No. '81-'99	27,687

LEGAL MARITAL STATUS

2001 Estimates: (Age 15+)

Single (Never Married)	9,243
Legally Married (Not Separated)	18,156
Legally Married (Separated)	1,309
Widowed	3,009
Divorced	2,856

PSYTE CATEGORIES

2001 Estimates	No. of House -holds	% of Total Hhds.	Index
Small City Elite	1,817	10.54	615
Blue Collar Winners	128	0.74	29
Old Towns' New Fringe	2,469	14.32	366
Rustic Prosperity	235	1.36	76
Conservative Homebodies	35	0.20	6
High Rise Sunsets	88	0.51	36
Old Leafy Towns	1,914	11.10	434
Town Renters	283	1.64	190
Nesters & Young Homesteaders	9,138	52.99	2,270
Quiet Towns	150	0.87	41
Rod & Rifle	329	1.91	82
Big Country Families	61	0.35	25
Aged Pensioners	284	1.65	124

FINANCIAL P$YTE

2001 Estimates	No. of House -holds	% of Total Hhds.	Index
Canadian Comfort	1,945	11.28	116
Tractors & Tradelines	2,704	15.68	274
Bills & Wills	1,949	11.30	136
Revolving Renters	9,226	53.50	1,163
Rural Family Blues	390	2.26	28
Limited Budgets	150	0.87	28
Towering Debt	283	1.64	21
Senior Survivors	284	1.65	87

HOME LANGUAGE

2001 Estimates:		% Total
English	42,186	98.26
French	67	0.16
Chinese	24	0.06
German	100	0.23
Italian	127	0.30
Polish	74	0.17
Vietnamese	46	0.11
Other Languages	153	0.36
Multiple Responses	155	0.36
Total	42,932	100.00

BUILDING PERMITS

	1999	1998 $000	1997
Value	48,531	41,965	36,444

HOMES BUILT

	1999	1998	1997
No.	135	216	167

TAXATION

Income Class:	1997	% Total
Under $5,000	5,070	13.82
$5,000-$10,000	4,530	12.35
$10,000-$15,000	5,670	15.45
$15,000-$20,000	4,050	11.04
$20,000-$25,000	3,290	8.97
$25,000-$30,000	2,920	7.96
$30,000-$40,000	4,510	12.29
$40,000-$50,000	2,870	7.82
$50,000 +	3,810	10.38
Total Returns, No.	36,690	
Total Income, $000	916,859	
Total Taxable Returns	24,570	
Total Tax, $000	158,433	
Average Income, $	24,989	
Average Tax, $	6,448	

VITAL STATISTICS

	1997	1996	1995	1994
Births	492	527	556	576
Deaths	483	413	449	471
Natural Increase	9	114	107	105
Marriages	256	294	322	300

Note: Latest available data.

DAILY NEWSPAPER(S)

	Circulation Average Paid
Packet and Times	n.a.

COMMUNITY NEWSPAPER(S)

	Total Circulation
Orillia: Orillia Today	
Tue	18,349
Sat	20,466

RADIO STATION(S)

	Power
CBCO-FM	n.a.
CFJB	n.a.
CICX-FM	50,000w

Oro-Medonte
(Township)
In Simcoe County.

POPULATION

July 1, 2001 Estimate	18,136
% Cdn. Total	0.06
% Change, '96 -'01	5.41
Avg. Annual Growth Rate, %	1.06
2003 Projected Population	18,339
2006 Projected Population	18,646
2001 Households Estimate	6,628
2003 Projected Households	6,684
2006 Projected Households	6,837

INCOME

% Above/Below National Average	+3
2001 Total Income Estimate	$393,400,000
% Cdn. Total	0.06
2001 Average Hhld. Income	$59,400
2001 Per Capita	$21,700
2003 Projected Total Income	$410,930,000
2006 Projected Total Income	$442,660,000

RETAIL SALES

% Above/Below National Average	-14
2001 Retail Sales Estimate	$139,010,000
% Cdn. Total	0.05
2001 per Household	$21,000
2001 per Capita	$7,700
2001 No. of Establishments	131
2003 Projected Retail Sales	$154,270,000
2006 Projected Retail Sales	$176,080,000

POPULATION

2001 Estimates:

Total		18,136
Male		9,133
Female		9,003

Age Groups	Male	Female
0-4	505	477
5-9	604	568
10-14	653	629
15-19	659	616
20-24	590	519
25-29	494	459
30-34	534	554
35-39	661	692
40-44	743	779
45-49	741	760
50-54	664	649
55-59	562	515
60-64	451	434
65-69	385	384
70+	887	968

DAYTIME POPULATION

2001 Estimates:

Working Population	6,879
At Home Population	8,594
Total	15,473

INCOME

2001 Estimates:

Avg. Household Income	$59,354
Avg. Family Income	$61,452
Per Capita Income	$21,691
Male:	
Avg. Employment Income	$34,222
Avg. Employment Income (Full Time)	$43,590
Female:	
Avg. Employment Income	$22,667
Avg. Employment Income (Full Time)	$33,031

Ontario

DISPOSABLE & DISCRETIONARY INCOME

2001 Estimates:	Per Hhld.
Disposable Income	$48,628
Discretionary Income 1 (minus Food & Shelter)	$35,061
Discretionary Income 2 (minus Food, Shelter, & Other Expenditures)	$25,549

LIQUID ASSETS

1999 Estimates:	Per Hhld.
Equity Investments	$82,908
Interest Bearing Investments	$74,429
Total Liquid Assets	$157,337

CREDIT DATA

July 2000:	
Pool of Credit	$128,213,065
Revolving Credit, No.	20,794
Fixed Loans, No.	6,385
Avg. Credit Limit, per Person	$12,803
Avg. Spent, per Person	$5,801
Satisfactory Ratings, No. per Person	2.63
Avg. No. of Cards, per Person	0.99

LABOUR FORCE

2001 Estimates:

Male:	
In the Labour Force	5,388
Participation Rate	73.1
Employed	5,178
Unemployed	210
Unemployment Rate	3.9
Not in Labour Force	1,983
Female:	
In the Labour Force	4,511
Participation Rate	61.6
Employed	4,280
Unemployed	231
Unemployment Rate	5.1
Not in Labour Force	2,818

OCCUPATIONS BY MAJOR GROUPS

2001 Estimates:	Male	Female
Management	607	253
Business, Finance & Admin.	339	1,192
Natural & Applied Sciences & Related	347	60
Health	130	424
Social Sciences, Gov't Services & Religion	163	201
Education	184	310
Arts, Culture, Recreation & Sport	120	95
Sales & Service	1,101	1,264
Trades, Transport & Equipment Operators & Related	1,292	131
Primary Industries	580	206
Processing, Mfg. & Utilities	431	199

Ontario

Oro-Medonte
(Township)
(Cont'd)

LEVEL OF SCHOOLING

2001 Estimates:
Population 15 years +	14,700
Less than Grade 9	840
Grades 9-13 w/o Certif.	3,605
Grade 9-13 with Certif.	2,160
Trade Certif./Dip.	791
Non-Univ. w/o Certif./Dip.	955
Non-Univ. with Certif./Dip.	3,421
Univ. w/o Degree	1,267
Univ. w/o Degree/Certif.	437
Univ. with Certif.	830
Univ. with Degree	1,661

AVERAGE HOUSEHOLD EXPENDITURES

2001 Estimates:
Food	$6,243
Shelter	$9,509
Clothing	$2,214
Transportation	$7,621
Health & Personal Care	$1,974
Recr'n, Read'g & Education	$3,942
Taxes & Securities	$15,866
Other	$8,757
Total Expenditures	$56,126

PRIVATE HOUSEHOLDS

2001 Estimates:
Private Households, Total	6,628
Pop. in Private Households	17,850
Average no. per Household	2.7

FAMILIES

2001 Estimates:
Families in Private Households	5,596
Husband-Wife Families	5,104
Lone-Parent Families	492
Aver. No. Persons per Family	3.0
Aver. No. Sons/Daughters at Home	1.1

HOUSING

2001 Estimates:
Occupied Private Dwellings	6,628
Owned	5,951
Rented	677
Single-Detached House	6,338
Semi-Detached House	87
Row Houses	16
Apartment, 5 or Fewer Storeys	119
Apartment, Detached Duplex	51
Movable Dwellings	17

VEHICLES

2001 Estimates:
Model Yrs. '81-'96, No.	9,979
% Total	79.55
Model Yrs. '97-'98, No.	1,547
% Total	12.33
'99 Vehicles registered in Model Yr. '99, No.	1,019
% Total	8.12
Total No. '81-'99	12,545

LEGAL MARITAL STATUS

2001 Estimates: (Age 15+)
Single (Never Married)	3,362
Legally Married (Not Separated)	9,345
Legally Married (Separated)	412
Widowed	776
Divorced	805

PSYTE CATEGORIES

2001 Estimates
	No. of House-holds	% of Total Hhds.	Index
Boomers & Teens	336	5.07	283
Small City Elite	1,418	21.39	1,248
Blue Collar Winners	2,751	41.51	1,649
Old Towns' New Fringe	952	14.36	367
Rustic Prosperity	298	4.50	249
High Rise Sunsets	242	3.65	255
Old Leafy Towns	555	8.37	328

FINANCIAL P$YTE

2001 Estimates
	No. of House-holds	% of Total Hhds.	Index
Four Star Investors	336	5.07	101
Canadian Comfort	4,169	62.90	647
Tractors & Tradelines	1,250	18.86	330
Bills & Wills	555	8.37	101
Revolving Renters	242	3.65	79

HOME LANGUAGE

2001 Estimates:
		% Total
English	17,845	98.40
French	22	0.12
German	38	0.21
Hungarian	11	0.06
Italian	27	0.15
Polish	22	0.12
Slovenian	45	0.25
Ukrainian	33	0.18
Multiple Responses	93	0.51
Total	18,136	100.00

BUILDING PERMITS

	1999	1998 $000	1997
Value	29,833	18,572	20,716

TAXATION

Income Class:	1997	% Total
Under $5,000	810	12.66
$5,000-$10,000	730	11.41
$10,000-$15,000	790	12.34
$15,000-$20,000	560	8.75
$20,000-$25,000	530	8.28
$25,000-$30,000	510	7.97
$30,000-$40,000	880	13.75
$40,000-$50,000	580	9.06
$50,000 +	1,020	15.94
Total Returns, No.	6,400	
Total Income, $000	189,107	
Total Taxable Returns	4,660	
Total Tax, $000	37,066	
Average Income, $	29,548	
Average Tax, $	7,954	

VITAL STATISTICS

	1997	1996	1995	1994
Births	135	117	121	113
Deaths	71	84	75	63
Natural Increase	64	33	46	50
Marriages	83	72	71	73

Note: Latest available data.

Oshawa
(Census Metropolitan Area)

POPULATION

July 1, 2001 Estimate	304,818
% Cdn. Total	0.98
% Change, '96 -'01	10.02
Avg. Annual Growth Rate, %	1.93
2003 Projected Population	314,081
2006 Projected Population	326,713
2001 Households Estimate	109,458
2003 Projected Households	113,708
2006 Projected Households	120,213

INCOME

% Above/Below National Average	+11
2001 Total Income Estimate	$7,151,320,000
% Cdn. Total	1.09
2001 Average Hhld. Income	$65,300
2001 Per Capita	$23,500
2003 Projected Total Income	$7,838,010,000
2006 Projected Total Income	$8,988,610,000

RETAIL SALES

% Above/Below National Average	-11
2001 Retail Sales Estimate	$2,433,460,000
% Cdn. Total	0.87
2001 per Household	$22,200
2001 per Capita	$8,000
2001 No. of Establishments	1,565
2003 Projected Retail Sales	$2,689,450,000
2006 Projected Retail Sales	$3,067,310,000

POPULATION

2001 Estimates:
	Male	Female
Total		304,818
Male		150,319
Female		154,499
Age Groups		
0-4	10,663	10,155
5-9	11,877	11,274
10-14	11,839	11,232
15-19	10,884	10,434
20-24	9,870	9,747
25-29	9,741	10,085
30-34	11,596	12,211
35-39	13,280	13,632
40-44	12,873	13,022
45-49	11,299	11,485
50-54	9,322	9,400
55-59	7,318	7,347
60-64	5,802	5,932
65-69	4,767	5,199
70+	9,188	13,344

DAYTIME POPULATION

2001 Estimates:
Working Population	159,379
At Home Population	145,440
Total	304,819

INCOME

2001 Estimates:
Avg. Household Income	$65,334
Avg. Family Income	$69,720
Per Capita Income	$23,461
Male:	
Avg. Employment Income	$43,213
Avg. Employment Income (Full Time)	$53,865
Female:	
Avg. Employment Income	$25,637
Avg. Employment Income (Full Time)	$37,270

DISPOSABLE & DISCRETIONARY INCOME

2001 Estimates:	*Per Hhld.*
Disposable Income	$53,000
Discretionary Income 1 (minus Food & Shelter)	$37,731
Discretionary Income 2 (minus Food, Shelter, & Other Expenditures)	$27,988

LIQUID ASSETS

1999 Estimates:	*Per Hhld.*
Equity Investments	$88,648
Interest Bearing Investments	$78,742
Total Liquid Assets	$167,390

CREDIT DATA

July 2000:
Pool of Credit	$3,423,305,284
Revolving Credit, No.	558,749
Fixed Loans, No.	186,800
Avg. Credit Limit, per Person	$14,128
Avg. Spent, per Person	$6,675
Satisfactory Ratings, No. per Person	2.97
Avg. No. of Cards, per Person	1.07

LABOUR FORCE

2001 Estimates:
Male:	
In the Labour Force	90,398
Participation Rate	78.0
Employed	86,290
Unemployed	4,108
Unemployment Rate	4.5
Not in Labour Force	25,542
Female:	
In the Labour Force	76,307
Participation Rate	62.6
Employed	71,483
Unemployed	4,824
Unemployment Rate	6.3
Not in Labour Force	45,531

OCCUPATIONS BY MAJOR GROUPS

2001 Estimates:	Male	Female
Management	9,246	4,486
Business, Finance & Admin.	8,868	23,689
Natural & Applied Sciences & Related	6,723	1,418
Health	965	6,504
Social Sciences, Gov't Services & Religion	1,317	2,027
Education	2,155	3,881
Arts, Culture, Recreation & Sport	1,282	1,595
Sales & Service	16,759	22,963
Trades, Transport & Equipment Operators & Related	23,524	1,487
Primary Industries	2,389	752
Processing, Mfg. & Utilities	14,718	4,285

LEVEL OF SCHOOLING

2001 Estimates:
Population 15 years +	237,778
Less than Grade 9	16,718
Grades 9-13 w/o Certif.	61,430
Grade 9-13 with Certif.	38,283
Trade Certif./Dip.	8,779
Non-Univ. w/o Certif./Dip.	17,595
Non-Univ. with Certif./Dip.	53,138
Univ. w/o Degree	18,653
Univ. w/o Degree/Certif.	8,886
Univ. with Certif.	9,767
Univ. with Degree	23,182

Oshawa
(Census Metropolitan Area)
(Cont'd)

AVERAGE HOUSEHOLD EXPENDITURES

2001 Estimates:
Food	$7,006
Shelter	$10,624
Clothing	$2,512
Transportation	$7,568
Health & Personal Care	$2,117
Recr'n, Read'g & Education	$4,302
Taxes & Securities	$17,427
Other	$9,670
Total Expenditures	$61,226

PRIVATE HOUSEHOLDS

2001 Estimates:
Private Households, Total	109,458
Pop. in Private Households	300,501
Average no. per Household	2.7

FAMILIES

2001 Estimates:
Families in Private Households	87,798
Husband-Wife Families	75,918
Lone-Parent Families	11,880
Aver. No. Persons per Family	3.1
Aver. No. Sons/Daughters at Home	1.3

HOUSING

2001 Estimates:
Occupied Private Dwellings	109,458
Owned	79,072
Rented	30,386
Single-Detached House	70,541
Semi-Detached House	7,786
Row Houses	8,392
Apartment, 5+ Storeys	10,520
Owned Apartment, 5+ Storeys	944
Apartment, 5 or Fewer Storeys	8,882
Apartment, Detached Duplex	3,112
Other Single-Attached	155
Movable Dwellings	70

VEHICLES

2001 Estimates:
Model Yrs. '81-'96, No.	132,342
% Total	75.29
Model Yrs. '97-'98, No.	25,266
% Total	14.37
'99 Vehicles registered in Model Yr. '99, No.	18,172
% Total	10.34
Total No. '81-'99.	175,780

LEGAL MARITAL STATUS

2001 Estimates: (Age 15+)
Single (Never Married)	63,421
Legally Married (Not Separated)	136,655
Legally Married (Separated)	9,188
Widowed	12,407
Divorced	16,107

PSYTE CATEGORIES

2001 Estimates	No. of House-holds	% of Total Hhds.	Index
Urban Gentry	436	0.40	22
Suburban Executives	1,313	1.20	84
Mortgaged in Suburbia	5,406	4.94	355
Technocrafts & Bureaucrats	3,549	3.24	115
Boomers & Teens	9,203	8.41	469
Stable Suburban Families	2,399	2.19	168
Small City Elite	572	0.52	30
Old Bungalow Burbs	4,493	4.10	248
Suburban Nesters	1,087	0.99	62
Brie & Chablis	177	0.16	18
Aging Erudites	340	0.31	21
Satellite Suburbs	19,663	17.96	626
Kindergarten Boom	7,023	6.42	245
Blue Collar Winners	9,493	8.67	344
Old Towns' New Fringe	3,394	3.10	79
High Rise Melting Pot	2,608	2.38	159
Conservative Homebodies	15,424	14.09	391
High Rise Sunsets	2,461	2.25	157
Young Urban Mix	1,063	0.97	46
University Enclaves	638	0.58	29
Young City Singles	1,810	1.65	72
Town Renters	3,026	2.76	320
Struggling Downtowns	10,794	9.86	313
Aged Pensioners	822	0.75	56
Big City Stress	748	0.68	61
Old Grey Towers	654	0.60	108

Ontario

FINANCIAL P$YTE

2001 Estimates	No. of House-holds	% of Total Hhds.	Index
Four Star Investors	10,952	10.01	199
Successful Suburbanites	11,354	10.37	156
Canadian Comfort	30,815	28.15	290
Urban Heights	517	0.47	11
Miners & Credit-Liners	4,493	4.10	130
Mortgages & Minivans	7,023	6.42	97
Tractors & Tradelines	3,394	3.10	54
Bills & Wills	16,487	15.06	182
Revolving Renters	2,461	2.25	49
Young Urban Struggle	638	0.58	12
Towering Debt	18,238	16.66	213
NSF	748	0.68	19
Senior Survivors	1,476	1.35	72

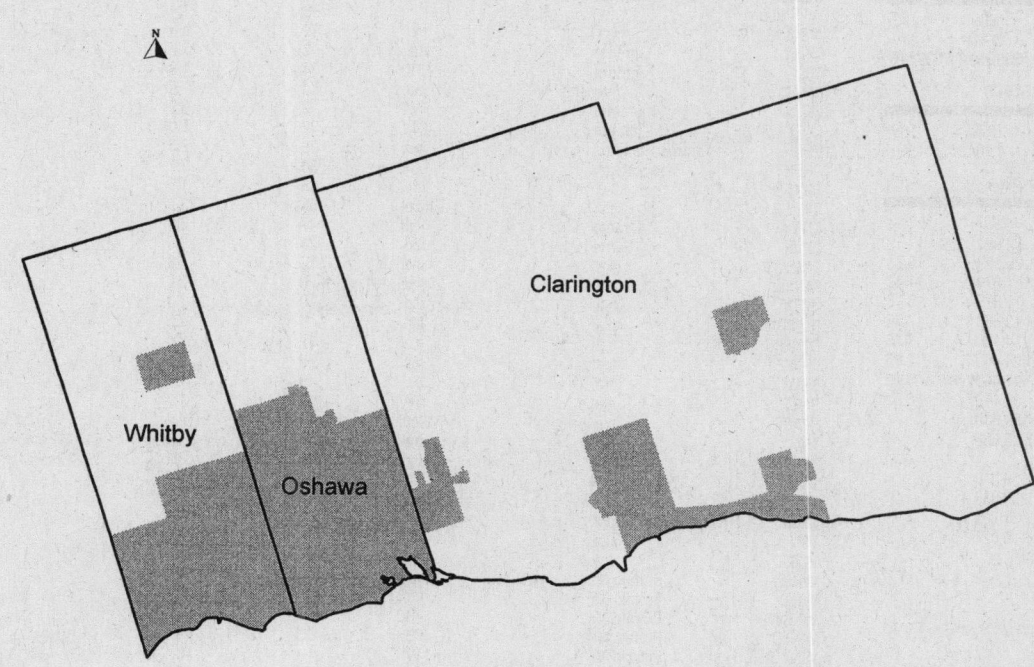

Urban Areas

Ontario

Oshawa
(Census Metropolitan Area)
(Cont'd)

HOME LANGUAGE

2001 Estimates:		% Total
English	288,278	94.57
French	2,292	0.75
Arabic	172	0.06
Chinese	1,008	0.33
German	402	0.13
Greek	450	0.15
Gujarati	207	0.07
Hungarian	309	0.10
Italian	1,487	0.49
Korean	331	0.11
Persian (Farsi)	217	0.07
Polish	2,114	0.69
Portuguese	713	0.23
Punjabi	202	0.07
Spanish	479	0.16
Tagalog (Pilipino)	232	0.08
Ukrainian	931	0.31
Vietnamese	219	0.07
Other Languages	1,694	0.56
Multiple Responses	3,081	1.01
Total	304,818	100.00

BUILDING PERMITS

	1999	1998	1997
		$000	
Value	481,183	336,259	339,515

HOMES BUILT

	1999	1998	1997
No.	2,248	1,764	1,991

TAXATION

Income Class:	1997	% Total
Under $5,000	22,990	12.12
$5,000-$10,000	20,550	10.83
$10,000-$15,000	21,670	11.42
$15,000-$20,000	15,370	8.10
$20,000-$25,000	13,960	7.36
$25,000-$30,000	14,190	7.48
$30,000-$40,000	24,400	12.86
$40,000-$50,000	17,440	9.19
$50,000 +	39,110	20.62
Total Returns, No.	189,680	
Total Income, $000	5,976,608	
Total Taxable Returns	139,310	
Total Tax, $000	1,228,835	
Average Income, $	31,509	
Average Tax, $	8,821	

VITAL STATISTICS

	1997	1996	1995	1994
Births	3,624	3,794	3,940	3,907
Deaths	1,720	1,636	1,667	1,460
Natural Increase	1,904	2,158	2,273	2,447
Marriages	1,267	1,270	1,343	1,202

Note: Latest available data.

COMMUNITY NEWSPAPER(S)

	Total Circulation
Bowmanville:	
Bowmanville Canadian Statesman	n.a.
Clarington, Oshawa, Whitby:	
This Week	
Tue	90,651
Wed	84,887
Fri	90,555
Sun	100,859
Orono: Orono Weekly Times	1,086
Oshawa: Durham Post	
Wed/Fri	n.a.

RADIO STATION DATA

Station	Market	Format	Wkly. Reach%*	Aver. Hrs. Tuned
All Stations			97	24.1
CBL-FM	Toronto	All Info.	3	7.7
CBLA-FM	Toronto	News, Info.	6	8.9
CFMX-FM	Toronto	Classical	5	15.8
CFNY-FM	Toronto	Alternative	10	10.2
CFRB	Toronto	News, Talk	13	11.5
CFTR	Toronto	All News	13	4.6
CFYI	Toronto	Talk	7	3.2
CHAM	Hamilton	Country	n.a.	n.a.
CHFI-FM	Toronto	Adult Contemp.	24	13.3
CHOG	Toronto	News, Talk	n.a.	n.a.
CHTZ-FM	St. Cath.-Niagara	AOR	4	9.1
CHUM	Toronto	All Oldies	10	9.2
CHUM-FM	Toronto	Adult Contemp.	21	8.8
CILQ-FM	Toronto	AOR	15	7.5
CING-FM	Burlington	Contemp. Hit Radio	n.a.	n.a.
CISS-FM	Toronto	Top 40	19	9.1
CJCL	Toronto	Sports	7	7.9
CJEZ-FM	Toronto	Adult Contemp.	7	8.3
CJKX-FM	Oshawa/Ajax	Country	19	12.7
CJRT-FM	Toronto	Classical, Folk, Jazz, Blues	3	7.3
CKFM-FM	Toronto	Adult Contemp.	18	9.0
CKGE-FM	Oshawa/Whitby	Adult Contemp.	16	8.0
CKOC	Hamilton	Oldies	1	10.9

BBM Spring 2000 Radio Reach Survey; area coverage.
*Mon-Sun 5a.m - 1a.m , All Persons 12+

TV STATION DATA

Station	Market	Network Affiliation	Wkly. Reach%*	Aver. Hrs. Tuned
All Stations			98	21.4
A & E	n.a.	Ind.	17	4.6
CBLFT	Toronto	n.a.	2	17.7
CBLT	Toronto	CBC	34	1.8
CFMT	Toronto	Ind.	14	1.9
CFTM	Montréal	TVA	2	9.8
CFTO	Toronto	CTV	72	5.0
CHCH	Toronto/Hamilton	Ind.	39	2.6
CHEX	Peterborough	CBC	30	2.2
CICO-E	n.a.	n.a.	25	1.5
CIII	n.a.	Global	58	3.5
CITY	Toronto	Ind.	47	3.0
CKVR	Barrie	Ind.	27	2.0
DSCVRY	n.a.	Ind.	8	1.6
FAMILY	n.a.	Ind.	8	2.0
HGTV	n.a.	Ind.	10	1.3
HISTTV	n.a.	Ind.	5	2.6
OTHERS	n.a.	n.a.	12	2.4
PRIME	n.a.	Ind.	9	1.9
SHWCSE	n.a.	Ind.	8	1.6
SNET	n.a.	CTV	11	1.4
SPACE	n.a.	Ind.	4	4.4
TLC	n.a.	Ind.	15	1.5
TMN	Toronto	Ind.	8	3.1
TNN	Nashville TN	Ind.	8	2.0
TOON	n.a.	Ind.	12	4.9
TREE	n.a.	Ind.	2	8.6
TSN	n.a.	Ind.	15	2.4
VCR	n.a.	n.a.	31	5.1
WGRZ	Buffalo NY	NBC	12	2.1
WIVB	Buffalo NY	CBS	20	1.1
WKBW	Buffalo NY	ABC	24	1.3
WNED	Buffalo NY	PBS	23	3.1
WNYO	Buffalo NY	WB	4	3.1
WTBS	Atlanta GA	Ind.	17	3.5
WUTV	Buffalo NY	FOX	33	2.4
YTV	n.a.	Ind.	15	1.6

BBM Spring 2000 TV Reach Survey; CMA coverage.
*Mon-Sun 6a.m - 2a.m , All Persons 2 +

Clarington
(Town)
Oshawa CMA
In Durham Regional Municipality.

POPULATION

July 1, 2001 Estimate	77,092
% Cdn. Total	0.25
% Change, '96 -'01	23.38
Avg. Annual Growth Rate, %	4.29
2003 Projected Population	80,308
2006 Projected Population	84,811
2001 Households Estimate	26,378
2003 Projected Households	27,733
2006 Projected Households	29,806

INCOME

% Above/Below National Average	+15
2001 Total Income Estimate	$1,875,550,000
% Cdn. Total	0.29
2001 Average Hhld. Income	$71,100
2001 Per Capita	$24,300
2003 Projected Total Income	$2,077,850,000
2006 Projected Total Income	$2,417,610,000

RETAIL SALES

% Above/Below National Average	-47
2001 Retail Sales Estimate	$366,440,000
% Cdn. Total	0.13
2001 per Household	$13,900
2001 per Capita	$4,800
2001 No. of Establishments	337
2003 Projected Retail Sales	$408,440,000
2006 Projected Retail Sales	$472,700,000

POPULATION

2001 Estimates:

Total		77,092
Male		38,317
Female		38,775

Age Groups	Male	Female
0-4	2,819	2,695
5-9	3,261	3,082
10-14	3,224	3,050
15-19	2,788	2,672
20-24	2,329	2,308
25-29	2,303	2,462
30-34	2,994	3,266
35-39	3,542	3,646
40-44	3,356	3,319
45-49	2,839	2,774
50-54	2,291	2,212
55-59	1,764	1,716
60-64	1,381	1,393
65-69	1,134	1,212
70+	2,292	2,968

DAYTIME POPULATION

2001 Estimates:

Working Population	25,936
At Home Population	35,293
Total	61,229

INCOME

2001 Estimates:

Avg. Household Income	$71,103
Avg. Family Income	$73,593
Per Capita Income	$24,329
Male:	
Avg. Employment Income	$44,816
Avg. Employment Income (Full Time)	$54,777
Female:	
Avg. Employment Income	$26,256
Avg. Employment Income (Full Time)	$37,722

DISPOSABLE & DISCRETIONARY INCOME

2001 Estimates:	*Per Hhld.*
Disposable Income	$57,470
Discretionary Income 1 (minus Food & Shelter)	$41,087
Discretionary Income 2 (minus Food, Shelter, & Other Expenditures)	$30,459

LIQUID ASSETS

1999 Estimates:	*Per Hhld.*
Equity Investments	$102,125
Interest Bearing Investments	$86,079
Total Liquid Assets	$188,204

CREDIT DATA

July 2000:

Pool of Credit	$790,517,671
Revolving Credit, No.	125,535
Fixed Loans, No.	43,507
Avg. Credit Limit, per Person	$14,995
Avg. Spent, per Person	$7,168
Satisfactory Ratings, No. per Person	3.10
Avg. No. of Cards, per Person	1.10

LABOUR FORCE

2001 Estimates:
Male:

In the Labour Force	23,351
Participation Rate	80.5
Employed	22,697
Unemployed	654
Unemployment Rate	2.8
Not in Labour Force	5,662
Female:	
In the Labour Force	19,409
Participation Rate	64.8
Employed	18,529
Unemployed	880
Unemployment Rate	4.5
Not in Labour Force	10,539

OCCUPATIONS BY MAJOR GROUPS

2001 Estimates:	*Male*	*Female*
Management	1,925	1,105
Business, Finance & Admin.	1,907	5,970
Natural & Applied Sciences & Related	1,729	413
Health	285	1,931
Social Sciences, Gov't Services & Religion	298	492
Education	548	1,101
Arts, Culture, Recreation & Sport	281	351
Sales & Service	3,892	5,452
Trades, Transport & Equipment Operators & Related	6,848	506
Primary Industries	1,153	401
Processing, Mfg. & Utilities	4,082	1,100

LEVEL OF SCHOOLING

2001 Estimates:

Population 15 years +	58,961
Less than Grade 9	3,558
Grades 9-13 w/o Certif.	15,082
Grade 9-13 with Certif.	9,318
Trade Certif. /Dip.	2,505
Non-Univ. w/o Certif./Dip.	4,343
Non-Univ. with Certif./Dip.	14,440
Univ. w/o Degree	4,316
Univ. w/o Degree/Certif.	1,827
Univ. with Certif.	2,489
Univ. with Degree	5,399

AVERAGE HOUSEHOLD EXPENDITURES

2001 Estimates:

Food	$7,380
Shelter	$11,416
Clothing	$2,620
Transportation	$8,387
Health & Personal Care	$2,180
Recr'n, Read'g & Education	$4,612
Taxes & Securities	$19,232
Other	$10,240
Total Expenditures	$66,067

PRIVATE HOUSEHOLDS

2001 Estimates:

Private Households, Total	26,378
Pop. in Private Households	76,004
Average no. per Household	2.9

FAMILIES

2001 Estimates:

Families in Private Households	22,585
Husband-Wife Families	20,510
Lone-Parent Families	2,075
Aver. No. Persons per Family	3.2
Aver. No. Sons/Daughters at Home	1.3

HOUSING

2001 Estimates:

Occupied Private Dwellings	26,378
Owned	22,437
Rented	3,941
Single-Detached House	21,200
Semi-Detached House	1,257
Row Houses	1,694
Apartment, 5+ Storeys	278
Owned Apartment, 5+ Storeys	18
Apartment, 5 or Fewer Storeys	1,348
Apartment, Detached Duplex	481
Other Single-Attached	50
Movable Dwellings	70

VEHICLES

2001 Estimates:

Model Yrs. '81-'96, No.	32,181
% Total	77.08
Model Yrs. '97-'98, No.	5,751
% Total	13.78
'99 Vehicles registered in Model Yr. '99, No.	3,816
% Total	9.14
Total No. '81-'99	41,748

LEGAL MARITAL STATUS

2001 Estimates: (Age 15+)

Single (Never Married)	13,610
Legally Married (Not Separated)	37,561
Legally Married (Separated)	1,909
Widowed	2,540
Divorced	3,341

PSYTE CATEGORIES

2001 Estimates	No. of House-holds	% of Total Hhds.	Index
Mortgaged in Suburbia	1,578	5.98	430
Boomers & Teens	1,696	6.43	359
Small City Elite	103	0.39	23
Suburban Nesters	113	0.43	27
Satellite Suburbs	8,444	32.01	1,116
Kindergarten Boom	244	0.93	35
Blue Collar Winners	7,481	28.36	1,126
Old Towns' New Fringe	3,394	12.87	329
Conservative Homebodies	736	2.79	77
High Rise Sunsets	782	2.96	207
Young Urban Mix	226	0.86	40
Struggling Downtowns	1,435	5.44	173

FINANCIAL PSYTE

2001 Estimates	No. of House-holds	% of Total Hhds.	Index
Four Star Investors	1,696	6.43	128
Successful Suburbanites	1,578	5.98	90
Canadian Comfort	16,141	61.19	630
Mortgages & Minivans	244	0.93	14
Tractors & Tradelines	3,394	12.87	225
Bills & Wills	962	3.65	44
Revolving Renters	782	2.96	64
Towering Debt	1,435	5.44	70

HOME LANGUAGE

2001 Estimates:		*% Total*
English	75,207	97.55
French	254	0.33
Dutch	40	0.05
German	102	0.13
Greek	52	0.07
Hungarian	82	0.11
Italian	237	0.31
Korean	61	0.08
Persian (Farsi)	46	0.06
Polish	121	0.16
Portuguese	69	0.09
Spanish	62	0.08
Ukrainian	104	0.13
Other Languages	155	0.20
Multiple Responses	500	0.65
Total	77,092	100.00

BUILDING PERMITS

	1999	1998	1997
		$000	
Value	72,167	85,461	117,396

HOMES BUILT

	1999	1998	1997
No.	585	733	697

TAXATION

Income Class:	1997	% Total
Under $5,000	5,060	11.98
$5,000-$10,000	4,120	9.75
$10,000-$15,000	4,280	10.13
$15,000-$20,000	3,240	7.67
$20,000-$25,000	3,120	7.39
$25,000-$30,000	3,250	7.69
$30,000-$40,000	5,600	13.26
$40,000-$50,000	4,050	9.59
$50,000 +	9,510	22.51

Total Returns, No.	42,240
Total Income, $000	1,369,313
Total Taxable Returns	32,140
Total Tax, $000	282,069
Average Income, $.	32,417
Average Tax, $	8,776

VITAL STATISTICS

	1997	1996	1995	1994
Births	903	950	914	945
Deaths	351	326	331	248
Natural Increase	552	624	583	697
Marriages	219	231	226	146

Note: Latest available data.

MEDIA INFO
see Oshawa, CMA

Ontario

Oshawa
(City)
Oshawa CMA
In Durham Regional Municipality.

POPULATION

July 1, 2001 Estimate	139,052
% Cdn. Total	0.45
% Change, '96 -'01	0.40
Avg. Annual Growth Rate, %	0.08
2003 Projected Population	139,716
2006 Projected Population	140,154
2001 Households Estimate	53,171
2003 Projected Households	53,933
2006 Projected Households	55,093

INCOME

% Above/Below National Average	+2
2001 Total Income Estimate	$3,003,610,000
% Cdn. Total	0.46
2001 Average Hhld. Income	$56,500
2001 Per Capita	$21,600
2003 Projected Total Income	$3,195,060,000
2006 Projected Total Income	$3,507,760,000

RETAIL SALES

% Above/Below National Average	+5
2001 Retail Sales Estimate	$1,305,390,000
% Cdn. Total	0.47
2001 per Household	$24,600
2001 per Capita	$9,400
2001 No. of Establishments	751
2003 Projected Retail Sales	$1,407,180,000
2006 Projected Retail Sales	$1,548,500,000

POPULATION

2001 Estimates:

Total		139,052
Male		68,274
Female		70,778

Age Groups	Male	Female
0-4	4,753	4,516
5-9	5,066	4,834
10-14	4,884	4,691
15-19	4,640	4,470
20-24	4,585	4,455
25-29	4,669	4,683
30-34	5,395	5,456
35-39	5,952	5,901
40-44	5,624	5,657
45-49	4,919	5,097
50-54	4,166	4,368
55-59	3,455	3,609
60-64	2,875	2,998
65-69	2,438	2,701
70+	4,853	7,342

DAYTIME POPULATION

2001 Estimates:

Working Population	91,717
At Home Population	70,374
Total	162,091

INCOME

2001 Estimates:

Avg. Household Income	$56,490
Avg. Family Income	$61,022
Per Capita Income	$21,601
Male:	
Avg. Employment Income	$39,378
Avg. Employment Income (Full Time)	$49,470
Female:	
Avg. Employment Income	$23,637
Avg. Employment Income (Full Time)	$34,498

DISPOSABLE & DISCRETIONARY INCOME

2001 Estimates:	Per Hhld.
Disposable Income	$45,990
Discretionary Income 1 (minus Food & Shelter)	$32,037
Discretionary Income 2 (minus Food, Shelter, & Other Expenditures)	$23,303

LIQUID ASSETS

1999 Estimates:	Per Hhld.
Equity Investments	$68,205
Interest Bearing Investments	$66,980
Total Liquid Assets	$135,185

CREDIT DATA

July 2000:

Pool of Credit	$1,529,066,834
Revolving Credit, No.	259,189
Fixed Loans, No.	88,505
Avg. Credit Limit, per Person	$12,690
Avg. Spent, per Person	$6,082
Satisfactory Ratings, No. per Person	2.79
Avg. No. of Cards, per Person	0.98

LABOUR FORCE

2001 Estimates:

Male:

In the Labour Force	40,322
Participation Rate	75.3
Employed	37,676
Unemployed	2,646
Unemployment Rate	6.6
Not in Labour Force	13,249

Female:

In the Labour Force	33,320
Participation Rate	58.7
Employed	30,565
Unemployed	2,755
Unemployment Rate	8.3
Not in Labour Force	23,417

OCCUPATIONS BY MAJOR GROUPS

2001 Estimates:	Male	Female
Management	3,096	1,556
Business, Finance & Admin.	3,772	9,508
Natural & Applied Sciences & Related	2,370	485
Health	311	2,763
Social Sciences, Gov't Services & Religion	573	780
Education	881	1,518
Arts, Culture, Recreation & Sport	573	629
Sales & Service	7,484	11,066
Trades, Transport & Equipment Operators & Related	11,178	655
Primary Industries	647	175
Processing, Mfg. & Utilities	7,856	2,252

LEVEL OF SCHOOLING

2001 Estimates:

Population 15 years +	110,308
Less than Grade 9	9,769
Grades 9-13 w/o Certif.	31,672
Grade 9-13 with Certif.	17,863
Trade Certif. /Dip.	4,024
Non-Univ. w/o Certif./Dip.	8,404
Non-Univ. with Certif./Dip.	23,427
Univ. w/o Degree	7,194
Univ. w/o Degree/Certif.	3,586
Univ. with Certif.	3,608
Univ. with Degree	7,955

AVERAGE HOUSEHOLD EXPENDITURES

2001 Estimates:

Food	$6,461
Shelter	$9,633
Clothing	$2,225
Transportation	$6,670
Health & Personal Care	$1,969
Recr'n, Read'g & Education	$3,773
Taxes & Securities	$14,346
Other	$8,870
Total Expenditures	$53,947

PRIVATE HOUSEHOLDS

2001 Estimates:

Private Households, Total	53,171
Pop. in Private Households	136,982
Average no. per Household	2.6

FAMILIES

2001 Estimates:

Families in Private Households	39,846
Husband-Wife Families	32,823
Lone-Parent Families	7,023
Aver. No. Persons per Family	3.0
Aver. No. Sons/Daughters at Home	1.2

HOUSING

2001 Estimates:

Occupied Private Dwellings	53,171
Owned	34,022
Rented	19,149
Single-Detached House	28,343
Semi-Detached House	5,632
Row Houses	4,428
Apartment, 5+ Storeys	7,209
Owned Apartment, 5+ Storeys	614
Apartment, 5 or Fewer Storeys	5,418
Apartment, Detached Duplex	2,054
Other Single-Attached	87

VEHICLES

2001 Estimates:

Model Yrs. '81-'96, No.	63,610
% Total	74.77
Model Yrs. '97-'98, No.	11,992
% Total	14.10
'99 Vehicles registered in Model Yr. '99, No.	9,470
% Total	11.13
Total No. '81-'99	85,072

LEGAL MARITAL STATUS

2001 Estimates: (Age 15+)

Single (Never Married)	32,158
Legally Married (Not Separated)	57,069
Legally Married (Separated)	5,060
Widowed	6,812
Divorced	9,209

PSYTE CATEGORIES

2001 Estimates	No. of House -holds	% of Total Hhds.	Index
Urban Gentry	436	0.82	46
Mortgaged in Suburbia	304	0.57	41
Boomers & Teens	2,655	4.99	279
Stable Suburban Families	1,468	2.76	212
Old Bungalow Burbs	3,318	6.24	377
Suburban Nesters	974	1.83	114
Aging Erudites	340	0.64	42
Satellite Suburbs	7,343	13.81	481
Kindergarten Boom	5,653	10.63	405
Blue Collar Winners	362	0.68	27
High Rise Melting Pot	1,780	3.35	223
Conservative Homebodies	11,821	22.23	617
High Rise Sunsets	1,398	2.63	184
Young City Singles	1,810	3.40	148
Town Renters	3,026	5.69	658
Struggling Downtowns	8,220	15.46	491
Aged Pensioners	822	1.55	116
Big City Stress	748	1.41	125
Old Grey Towers	350	0.66	119

FINANCIAL P$YTE

2001 Estimates	No. of House -holds	% of Total Hhds.	Index
Four Star Investors	3,091	5.81	116
Successful Suburbanites	1,772	3.33	50
Canadian Comfort	8,679	16.32	168
Urban Heights	340	0.64	15
Miners & Credit-Liners	3,318	6.24	197
Mortgages & Minivans	5,653	10.63	161
Bills & Wills	11,821	22.23	268
Revolving Renters	1,398	2.63	57
Towering Debt	14,836	27.90	357
NSF	748	1.41	40
Senior Survivors	1,172	2.20	117

HOME LANGUAGE

2001 Estimates:		% Total
English	129,357	93.03
French	1,562	1.12
Chinese	379	0.27
Croatian	77	0.06
German	186	0.13
Greek	229	0.16
Gujarati	107	0.08
Hungarian	181	0.13
Italian	759	0.55
Korean	131	0.09
Persian (Farsi)	115	0.08
Polish	1,655	1.19
Portuguese	479	0.34
Punjabi	109	0.08
Slovak	94	0.07
Spanish	151	0.11
Tamil	79	0.06
Ukrainian	643	0.46
Vietnamese	146	0.10
Other Languages	761	0.55
Multiple Responses	1,852	1.33
Total	139,052	100.00

BUILDING PERMITS

	1999	1998	1997
		$000	
Value	172,465	89,137	79,840

HOMES BUILT

	1999	1998	1997
No	465	332	502

Oshawa
(City)
Oshawa CMA
(Cont'd)

TAXATION

Income Class:	1997	% Total
Under $5,000	11,490	12.08
$5,000-$10,000	11,220	11.80
$10,000-$15,000	12,310	12.95
$15,000-$20,000	8,470	8.91
$20,000-$25,000	7,350	7.73
$25,000-$30,000	7,370	7.75
$30,000-$40,000	12,070	12.69
$40,000-$50,000	8,100	8.52
$50,000 +	16,710	17.57
Total Returns, No.	95,090	
Total Income, $000	2,772,194	
Total Taxable Returns	67,450	
Total Tax, $000	544,264	
Average Income, $	29,153	
Average Tax, $	8,069	

VITAL STATISTICS

	1997	1996	1995	1994
Births	1,753	1,869	2,011	1,968
Deaths	1,003	963	961	880
Natural Increase	750	906	1,050	1,088
Marriages	764	775	842	787

Note: Latest available data.

MEDIA INFO

see Oshawa, CMA

Whitby
(Town)
Oshawa CMA
In Durham Regional Municipality.

POPULATION

July 1, 2001 Estimate	88,674
% Cdn. Total	0.28
% Change, '96 -'01	16.57
Avg. Annual Growth Rate, %	3.11
2003 Projected Population	94,057
2006 Projected Population	101,748
2001 Households Estimate	29,909
2003 Projected Households	32,042
2006 Projected Households	35,314

INCOME

% Above/Below National Average	+22
2001 Total Income Estimate	$2,272,160,000
% Cdn. Total	0.35
2001 Average Hhld. Income	$76,000
2001 Per Capita	$25,600
2003 Projected Total Income	$2,565,100,000
2006 Projected Total Income	$3,063,240,000

RETAIL SALES

% Above/Below National Average	-4
2001 Retail Sales Estimate	$761,630,000
% Cdn. Total	0.27
2001 per Household	$25,500
2001 per Capita	$8,600
2001 No. of Establishments	477
2003 Projected Retail Sales	$873,830,000
2006 Projected Retail Sales	$1,046,110,000

POPULATION

2001 Estimates:

Total		88,674
Male		43,728
Female		44,946
Age Groups	Male	Female
0-4	3,091	2,944
5-9	3,550	3,358
10-14	3,731	3,491
15-19	3,456	3,292
20-24	2,956	2,984
25-29	2,769	2,940
30-34	3,207	3,489
35-39	3,786	4,085
40-44	3,893	4,046
45-49	3,541	3,614
50-54	2,865	2,820
55-59	2,099	2,022
60-64	1,546	1,541
65-69	1,195	1,286
70+	2,043	3,034

DAYTIME POPULATION

2001 Estimates:

Working Population	41,726
At Home Population	39,773
Total	81,499

INCOME

2001 Estimates:

Avg. Household Income	$75,969
Avg. Family Income	$79,933
Per Capita Income	$25,624
Male:	
Avg. Employment Income	$47,384
Avg. Employment Income (Full Time)	$59,095
Female:	
Avg. Employment Income	$27,853
Avg. Employment Income (Full Time)	$40,519

DISPOSABLE & DISCRETIONARY INCOME

2001 Estimates:	Per Hhld.
Disposable Income	$61,566
Discretionary Income 1 (minus Food & Shelter)	$44,934
Discretionary Income 2 (minus Food, Shelter, & Other Expenditures)	$34,172

LIQUID ASSETS

1999 Estimates:	Per Hhld.
Equity Investments	$116,674
Interest Bearing Investments	$95,216
Total Liquid Assets	$211,890

CREDIT DATA

July 2000:

Pool of Credit	$1,103,720,779
Revolving Credit, No.	174,025
Fixed Loans, No.	54,788
Avg. Credit Limit, per Person	$15,977
Avg. Spent, per Person	$7,334
Satisfactory Ratings, No. per Person	3.20
Avg. No. of Cards, per Person	1.19

LABOUR FORCE

2001 Estimates:

Male:	
In the Labour Force	26,725
Participation Rate	80.1
Employed	25,917
Unemployed	808
Unemployment Rate	3.0
Not in Labour Force	6,631
Female:	
In the Labour Force	23,578
Participation Rate	67.1
Employed	22,389
Unemployed	1,189
Unemployment Rate	5.0
Not in Labour Force	11,575

OCCUPATIONS BY MAJOR GROUPS

2001 Estimates:	Male	Female
Management	4,225	1,825
Business, Finance & Admin.	3,189	8,211
Natural & Applied Sciences & Related	2,624	520
Health	369	1,810
Social Sciences, Gov't Services & Religion	446	755
Education	726	1,262
Arts, Culture, Recreation & Sport	428	615
Sales & Service	5,383	6,445
Trades, Transport & Equipment Operators & Related	5,498	326
Primary Industries	589	176
Processing, Mfg. & Utilities	2,780	933

LEVEL OF SCHOOLING

2001 Estimates:

Population 15 years +	68,509
Less than Grade 9	3,391
Grades 9-13 w/o Certif.	14,676
Grade 9-13 with Certif.	11,102
Trade Certif. /Dip.	2,250
Non-Univ. w/o Certif./Dip.	4,848
Non-Univ. with Certif./Dip.	15,271
Univ. w/o Degree	7,143
Univ. w/o Degree/Certif.	3,473
Univ. with Certif.	3,670
Univ. with Degree	9,828

Ontario

AVERAGE HOUSEHOLD EXPENDITURES

2001 Estimates:

Food	$7,650
Shelter	$11,693
Clothing	$2,929
Transportation	$8,446
Health & Personal Care	$2,326
Recr'n, Read'g & Education	$4,971
Taxes & Securities	$21,333
Other	$10,596
Total Expenditures	$69,944

PRIVATE HOUSEHOLDS

2001 Estimates:

Private Households, Total	29,909
Pop. in Private Households	87,515
Average no. per Household	2.9

FAMILIES

2001 Estimates:

Families in Private Households	25,367
Husband-Wife Families	22,585
Lone-Parent Families	2,782
Aver. No. Persons per Family	3.2
Aver. No. Sons/Daughters at Home	1.3

HOUSING

2001 Estimates:

Occupied Private Dwellings	29,909
Owned	22,613
Rented	7,296
Single-Detached House	20,998
Semi-Detached House	897
Row Houses	2,270
Apartment, 5+ Storeys	3,033
Owned Apartment, 5+ Storeys	312
Apartment, 5 or Fewer Storeys	2,116
Apartment, Detached Duplex	577
Other Single-Attached	18

VEHICLES

2001 Estimates:

Model Yrs. '81-'96, No.	36,551
% Total	74.65
Model Yrs. '97-'98, No.	7,523
% Total	15.37
'99 Vehicles registered in Model Yr. '99, No.	4,886
% Total	9.98
Total No. '81-'99	48,960

LEGAL MARITAL STATUS

2001 Estimates: (Age 15+)

Single (Never Married)	17,653
Legally Married (Not Separated)	42,025
Legally Married (Separated)	2,219
Widowed	3,055
Divorced	3,557

Ontario

Whitby
(Town)
Oshawa CMA
(Cont'd)

PSYTE CATEGORIES

2001 Estimates	No. of House-holds	% of Total Hhds.	Index
Suburban Executives	1,313	4.39	306
Mortgaged in Suburbia	3,524	11.78	848
Technocrafts & Bureaucrats	3,549	11.87	422
Boomers & Teens	4,852	16.22	905
Stable Suburban Families	931	3.11	239
Small City Elite	469	1.57	92
Old Bungalow Burbs	1,175	3.93	237
Brie & Chablis	177	0.59	66
Satellite Suburbs	3,876	12.96	452
Kindergarten Boom	1,126	3.76	144
Blue Collar Winners	1,650	5.52	219
High Rise Melting Pot	828	2.77	185
Conservative Homebodies	2,867	9.59	266
High Rise Sunsets	281	0.94	66
Young Urban Mix	837	2.80	132
University Enclaves	638	2.13	105
Struggling Downtowns	1,139	3.81	121
Old Grey Towers	304	1.02	184

FINANCIAL PSYTE

2001 Estimates	No. of House-holds	% of Total Hhds.	Index
Four Star Investors	6,165	20.61	410
Successful Suburbanites	8,004	26.76	403
Canadian Comfort	5,995	20.04	206
Urban Heights	177	0.59	14
Miners & Credit-Liners	1,175	3.93	124
Mortgages & Minivans	1,126	3.76	57
Bills & Wills	3,704	12.38	150
Revolving Renters	281	0.94	20
Young Urban Struggle	638	2.13	45
Towering Debt	1,967	6.58	84
Senior Survivors	304	1.02	54

HOME LANGUAGE

2001 Estimates:		% Total
English	83,714	94.41
French	476	0.54
Arabic	127	0.14
Chinese	629	0.71
Dutch	59	0.07
German	114	0.13
Greek	169	0.19
Gujarati	100	0.11
Hungarian	46	0.05
Italian	491	0.55
Japanese	62	0.07
Korean	139	0.16
Persian (Farsi)	56	0.06
Polish	338	0.38
Portuguese	165	0.19
Punjabi	93	0.10
Slovenian	90	0.10
Spanish	266	0.30
Tagalog (Pilipino)	157	0.18
Ukrainian	184	0.21
Urdu	112	0.13
Vietnamese	61	0.07
Other Languages	297	0.33
Multiple Responses	729	0.82
Total	88,674	100.00

BUILDING PERMITS

	1999	1998	1997
		$000	
Value	236,551	161,661	142,279

HOMES BUILT

	1999	1998	1997
No	1,198	699	792

TAXATION

Income Class:	1997	% Total
Under $5,000	6,440	12.30
$5,000-$10,000	5,210	9.95
$10,000-$15,000	5,080	9.70
$15,000-$20,000	3,660	6.99
$20,000-$25,000	3,490	6.67
$25,000-$30,000	3,570	6.82
$30,000-$40,000	6,730	12.86
$40,000-$50,000	5,290	10.11
$50,000 +	12,890	24.62
Total Returns, No.	52,350	
Total Income, $000	1,835,101	
Total Taxable Returns	39,720	
Total Tax, $000	402,502	
Average Income, $	35,054	
Average Tax, $	10,133	

VITAL STATISTICS

	1997	1996	1995	1994
Births	968	975	1,015	994
Deaths	366	347	375	332
Natural Increase	602	628	640	662
Marriages	284	264	275	269

Note: Latest available data.

MEDIA INFO
see Oshawa, CMA

Ottawa-Hull
(Census Metropolitan Area)

Note: Ottawa-Hull straddles the Ontario-Quebec border. Refer to Ottawa-Hull, CMA, in Quebec section for statistics on Aylmer, Buckingham, Gatineau & Hull. On Jan. 1, 1998 Clarence, TP & Rockland, T amalgamated to form Clarence-Rockland, C.

POPULATION

July 1, 2001 Estimate	1,085,918
% Cdn. Total	3.49
% Change, '96 -'01	4.60
Avg. Annual Growth Rate, %	0.90
2003 Projected Population	1,112,736
2006 Projected Population	1,158,862
2001 Households Estimate	431,851
2003 Projected Households	446,292
2006 Projected Households	470,840

INCOME

% Above/Below National Average	+18
2001 Total Income Estimate	$27,101,540,000
% Cdn. Total	4.13
2001 Average Hhld. Income	$62,800
2001 Per Capita	$25,000
2003 Projected Total Income	$29,294,630,000
2006 Projected Total Income	$33,077,460,000

RETAIL SALES

% Above/Below National Average	+3
2001 Retail Sales Estimate	$10,000,190,000
% Cdn. Total	3.59
2001 per Household	$23,200
2001 per Capita	$9,200
2001 No. of Establishments	6,626
2003 Projected Retail Sales	$10,925,820,000
2006 Projected Retail Sales	$12,362,680,000

POPULATION

2001 Estimates:		
Total		1,085,918
Male		531,076
Female		554,842
Age Groups	Male	Female
0-4	35,278	33,674
5-9	36,842	35,185
10-14	36,979	35,051
15-19	35,481	33,765
20-24	35,255	34,573
25-29	37,587	37,799
30-34	42,912	43,634
35-39	46,467	48,243
40-44	45,608	47,958
45-49	42,442	44,417
50-54	36,144	37,355
55-59	28,127	28,947
60-64	21,542	22,696
65-69	17,068	19,292
70+	33,344	52,253

DAYTIME POPULATION

2001 Estimates:	
Working Population	583,065
At Home Population	502,852
Total	1,085,917

INCOME

2001 Estimates:	
Avg. Household Income	$62,757
Avg. Family Income	$71,040
Per Capita Income	$24,957
Male:	
Avg. Employment Income	$39,755
Avg. Employment Income (Full Time)	$52,042
Female:	
Avg. Employment Income	$27,409
Avg. Employment Income (Full Time)	$38,913

DISPOSABLE & DISCRETIONARY INCOME

2001 Estimates:	Per Hhld.
Disposable Income	$49,174
Discretionary Income 1 (minus Food & Shelter)	$34,707
Discretionary Income 2 (minus Food, Shelter, & Other Expenditures)	$25,772

LIQUID ASSETS

1999 Estimates:	Per Hhld.
Equity Investments	$89,085
Interest Bearing Investments	$76,857
Total Liquid Assets	$165,942

CREDIT DATA

July 2000:	
Pool of Credit	$11,702,079,877
Revolving Credit, No.	2,225,399
Fixed Loans, No.	629,979
Avg. Credit Limit, per Person	$12,184
Avg. Spent, per Person	$5,255
Satisfactory Ratings, No. per Person	2.84
Avg. No. of Cards, per Person	1.10

LABOUR FORCE

2001 Estimates:	
Male:	
In the Labour Force	325,786
Participation Rate	77.2
Employed	307,673
Unemployed	18,113
Unemployment Rate	5.6
Not in Labour Force	96,191
Female:	
In the Labour Force	288,182
Participation Rate	63.9
Employed	273,668
Unemployed	14,514
Unemployment Rate	5.0
Not in Labour Force	162,750

OCCUPATIONS BY MAJOR GROUPS

2001 Estimates:	Male	Female
Management	48,210	24,489
Business, Finance & Admin.	44,275	94,213
Natural & Applied Sciences & Related	44,848	11,465
Health	6,430	22,603
Social Sciences, Gov't Services & Religion	11,812	12,275
Education	9,716	16,767
Arts, Culture, Recreation & Sport	10,488	12,494
Sales & Service	72,092	75,160
Trades, Transport & Equipment Operators & Related	52,737	3,434
Primary Industries	6,345	1,728
Processing, Mfg. & Utilities	8,313	3,333

Ottawa-Hull
(Census Metropolitan Area)
(Cont'd)

LEVEL OF SCHOOLING

2001 Estimates:

Population 15 years +	872,909
Less than Grade 9	69,558
Grades 9-13 w/o Certif.	152,691
Grade 9-13 with Certif.	126,011
Trade Certif./Dip.	23,682
Non-Univ. w/o Certif./Dip.	56,499
Non-Univ. with Certif./Dip.	145,686
Univ. w/o Degree	101,485
Univ. w/o Degree/Certif.	48,313
Univ. with Certif.	53,172
Univ. with Degree	197,297

AVERAGE HOUSEHOLD EXPENDITURES

2001 Estimates:

Food	$6,831
Shelter	$10,140
Clothing	$2,570
Transportation	$6,778
Health & Personal Care	$2,149
Recr'n, Read'g & Education	$4,156
Taxes & Securities	$17,387
Other	$8,858
Total Expenditures	$58,869

PRIVATE HOUSEHOLDS

2001 Estimates:

Private Households, Total	431,851
Pop. in Private Households	1,065,437
Average no. per Household	2.5

FAMILIES

2001 Estimates:

Families in Private Households	305,984
Husband-Wife Families	259,196
Lone-Parent Families	46,788
Aver. No. Persons per Family	3.0
Aver. No. Sons/Daughters at Home	1.2

HOUSING

2001 Estimates:

Occupied Private Dwellings	431,851
Owned	258,348
Rented	173,503
Single-Detached House	196,365
Semi-Detached House	29,321
Row Houses	58,607
Apartment, 5+ Storeys	69,297
Owned Apartment, 5+ Storeys	9,668
Apartment, 5 or Fewer Storeys	60,372
Apartment, Detached Duplex	15,045
Other Single-Attached	1,002
Movable Dwellings	1,842

VEHICLES

2001 Estimates:

Model Yrs. '81-'96, No.	459,125
% Total	76.45
Model Yrs. '97-'98, No.	82,167
% Total	13.68
'99 Vehicles registered in Model Yr. '99, No.	59,279
% Total	9.87
Total No. '81-'99	600,571

LEGAL MARITAL STATUS

2001 Estimates: (Age 15+)

Single (Never Married)	291,776
Legally Married (Not Separated)	440,839
Legally Married (Separated)	29,378
Widowed	46,910
Divorced	64,006

PSYTE CATEGORIES

2001 Estimates	No. of House -holds	% of Total Hhds.	Index
Canadian Establishment	284	0.07	40
The Affluentials	1,783	0.41	65
Urban Gentry	21,861	5.06	282
Suburban Executives	18,274	4.23	295
Mortgaged in Suburbia	10,487	2.43	175
Technocrafts & Bureaucrats	51,647	11.96	425

2001 Estimates	No. of House -holds	% of Total Hhds.	Index
Boomers & Teens	4,978	1.15	64
Stable Suburban Families	8,878	2.06	158
Small City Elite	8,720	2.02	118
Old Bungalow Burbs	7,335	1.70	102
Suburban Nesters	11,668	2.70	169
Brie & Chablis	3,702	0.86	96
Aging Erudites	14,500	3.36	223
Satellite Suburbs	3,070	0.71	25
Kindergarten Boom	13,133	3.04	116
Blue Collar Winners	12,784	2.96	118
Old Towns' New Fringe	3,610	0.84	21
Participation Quebec	27,243	6.31	219
New Quebec Rows	16,535	3.83	349
Quebec Melange	16,537	3.83	145
Traditional French Cdn. Families	7,943	1.84	68
Rustic Prosperity	325	0.08	4
Quebec's Heartland	91	0.02	2
High Rise Melting Pot	2,924	0.68	45
Conservative Homebodies	6,830	1.58	44
High Rise Sunsets	11,927	2.76	193
Young Urban Professionals	19,496	4.51	238
Young Urban Mix	8,370	1.94	91
Young Urban Intelligentsia	13,817	3.20	210
University Enclaves	14,846	3.44	168
Young City Singles	18,336	4.25	185
Urban Bohemia	8,999	2.08	178
Old Leafy Towns	565	0.13	5
Town Renters	7,217	1.67	193
Rod & Rifle	753	0.17	8
Quebec Rural Blues	1,021	0.24	10
Old Quebec Walkups	9,857	2.28	125
Quebec Town Elders	6,736	1.56	55
Aging Quebec Urbanites	2,012	0.47	161
Quebec's New Urban Mosaic	12,993	3.01	125
Struggling Downtowns	2,520	0.58	19
Aged Pensioners	4,268	0.99	74
Big City Stress	6,449	1.49	132
Old Grey Towers	3,884	0.90	162

FINANCIAL P$YTE

2001 Estimates	No. of House -holds	% of Total Hhds.	Index
Platinum Estates	2,067	0.48	59
Four Star Investors	45,113	10.45	208
Successful Suburbanites	71,012	16.44	248
Canadian Comfort	36,242	8.39	86
Urban Heights	37,698	8.73	203
Miners & Credit-Liners	7,335	1.70	54
Mortgages & Minivans	56,911	13.18	200
Tractors & Tradelines	3,935	0.91	16
Bills & Wills	15,765	3.65	44
Country Credit	24,480	5.67	84
Revolving Renters	11,927	2.76	60
Young Urban Struggle	37,662	8.72	184
Rural Family Blues	1,865	0.43	5
Loan Parent Stress	18,605	4.31	74
Towering Debt	30,997	7.18	92
NSF	19,442	4.50	127
Senior Survivors	8,152	1.89	100

HOME LANGUAGE

2001 Estimates:		% Total
English	659,173	60.70
French	318,600	29.34
Arabic	12,661	1.17
Bengali	874	0.08
Chinese	12,463	1.15
Creoles	742	0.07
German	1,028	0.09
Greek	1,092	0.10
Hindi	869	0.08
Hungarian	905	0.08
Italian	4,780	0.44
Khmer (Cambodian)	612	0.06
Persian (Farsi)	2,446	0.23
Polish	3,809	0.35
Portuguese	3,510	0.32
Punjabi	1,621	0.15
Romanian	647	0.06
Russian	1,421	0.13
Serbian	783	0.07
Serbo-Croatian	1,221	0.11
Spanish	5,400	0.50
Tagalog (Pilipino)	1,155	0.11
Tamil	716	0.07
Urdu	1,043	0.10
Vietnamese	4,730	0.44
Other Languages	13,934	1.28
Multiple Responses	29,683	2.73
Total	1,085,918	100.00

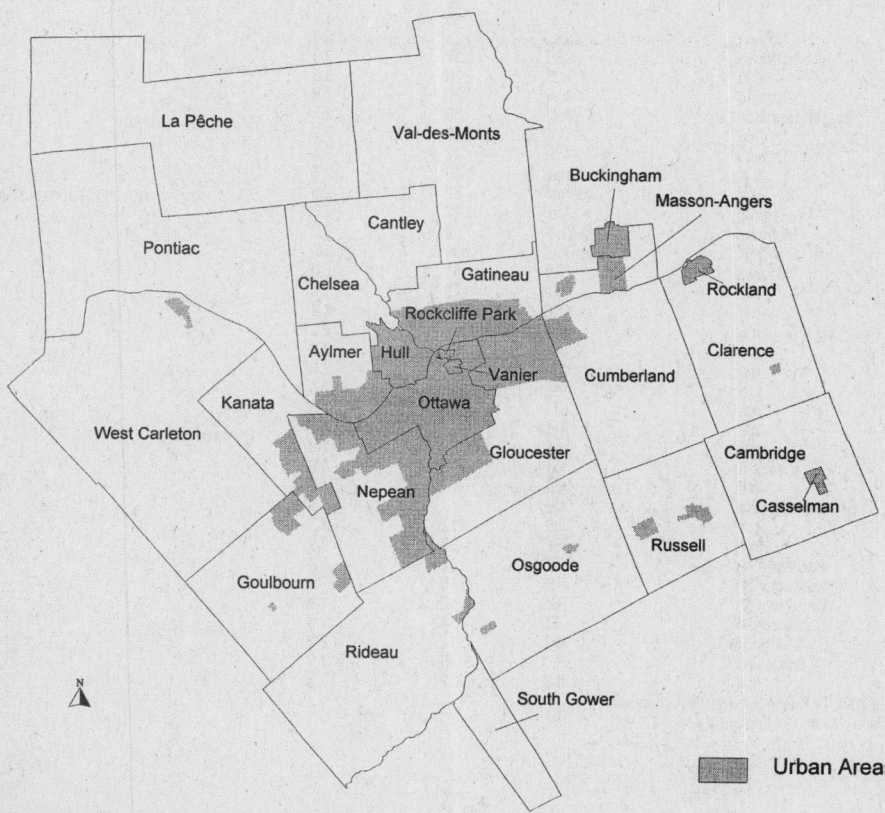

Urban Areas

Ottawa-Hull
(Census Metropolitan Area)
(Cont'd)

BUILDING PERMITS

	1999	1998	1997
		$000	
Value	1,282,551	1,149,908	913,151

HOMES BUILT

	1999	1998	1997
No	5,265	4,621	4,771

TAXATION

Income Class:	1997	% Total
Under $5,000	65,690	11.85
$5,000-$10,000	62,320	11.24
$10,000-$15,000	65,150	11.75
$15,000-$20,000	45,350	8.18
$20,000-$25,000	39,440	7.12
$25,000-$30,000	38,430	6.93
$30,000-$40,000	71,690	12.93
$40,000-$50,000	52,710	9.51
$50,000 +	113,590	20.49
Total Returns, No.	554,250	
Total Income, $000	18,315,723	
Total Taxable Returns	400,160	
Total Tax, $000	3,815,649	
Average Income, $	33,046	
Average Tax, $	9,535	

VITAL STATISTICS

	1997	1996	1995	1994
Births	12,096	12,562	12,831	13,087
Deaths	6,063	6,120	6,111	6,052
Natural Increase	6,063	6,442	6,720	7,035
Marriages	4,963	5,312	5,362	5,395

Note: Latest available data.

DAILY NEWSPAPER(S)

	Circulation Average Paid
Le Droit	
Sat.	40,645
Mon-Fri	34,335
Ottawa Citizen	
Sat.	181,568
Sun	133,810
Mon-Fri	137,146
Ottawa Sun / Sunday Sun	
Sat.	48,265
Sun	57,348
Mon-Fri	52,124

COMMUNITY NEWSPAPER(S)

	Total Circulation
Aylmer: Bulletin d'Aylmer	13,791
Aylmer, Gatineau, Hull: Week-end Outaouais	64,831
Aylmer, Gatineau, Hull: Bonjour Dimanche	74,348
Aylmer, Gatineau, Hull: Le Régional Combiné Outaouais (suppl.)	74,421
Aylmer, Hull: Le Régional Aylmer-Hull	37,810

	Total Circulation
Buckingham: The West-Québec Post	n.a.
Buckingham: Le Bulletin	11,525
Gatineau: Outaouais Affaires	17,500
Gatineau: La Revue de Gatineau	39,490
Gatineau, Aylmer, Hull: Bonjour Dimanche	74,348
Gatineau, Aylmer, Hull: L'Hebdo de l'Avenir Outaouais	74,597
Gatineau, Aylmer, Hull: Week-end Outaouais	64,831
Gatineau, Hull, Aylmer: Le Régional Combiné Outaouais (suppl.)	74,421
Hull, Aylmer, Gatineau: Bonjour Dimanche	74,348
Hull, Aylmer, Gatineau: Week-end Outaouais	64,831

	Total Circulation
Hull, Aylmer, Gatineau: Le Régional Combiné Outaouais (suppl.)	74,421
Kanata: Kanata Kourier-Standard	19,468
Nepean: Nepean Clarion	n.a.
Nepean: Nepean This Week	43,699
Nepean: Ottawa Pennysaver	n.a.
Ottawa: Hunt Club Riverside News	35,930
Ottawa: Ottawa-Carleton This Month (mthly)	n.a.
Ottawa: The Alta Vista News	35,930
Ottawa: Greenboro Hunt Club Park News	35,930
Ottawa: Ottawa Centretown News (biwkly)	n.a.
Rockland: Vision	20,000
Russell: Russell Villager	1,097

RADIO STATION DATA

Station	Market	Format	Wkly. Reach%*	Aver. Hrs. Tuned
All Stations			95	22.4
CBO-FM	Ottawa-Hull	News, Info.	17	12.0
CBOF-FM	Ottawa-Hull	News, Info.	4	12.1
CBOQ-FM	Ottawa-Hull	Music, Arts	8	9.5
CBOX-FM	Ottawa-Hull	Classical, Jazz	3	4.6
CFGO	Ottawa-Hull	Sports	9	8.3
CFMO-FM	Ottawa	New Rock Alternative	13	6.7
CFRA	Ottawa-Hull	News, Talk	14	10.4
CHEZ-FM	Ottawa-Hull	Classic Rock	16	8.1
CHRI-FM	Ottawa-Hull	Contemp. Christian	n.a.	n.a.
CIMF-FM	Ottawa-Hull	Adult Contemp.	14	13.5
CIWW	Ottawa-Hull	Oldies	7	7.6
CIZN-FM	Cambridge	Adult Top 40	n.a.	n.a.
CJMJ-FM	Ottawa-Hull	Adult Contemp.	21	11.6
CJRC	Gatineau	Classic Rock	7	12.3
CKBY-FM	Ottawa-Hull	Country	13	12.9
CKKL-FM	Ottawa-Hull	Adult Contemp. Hits	28	8.5
CKQB-FM	Ottawa-Hull	AOR	17	7.6
CKTF-FM	Gatineau	Top 40	14	12.5

BBM Spring 2000 Radio Reach Survey; area coverage.
*Mon-Sun 5a.m - 1a.m , All Persons 12+

TV STATION DATA

Station	Market	Network Affiliation	Wkly. Reach%*	Aver. Hrs. Tuned
All Stations			96	21.2
A & E	n.a.	Ind.	15	3.1
CBOFT	Ottawa	SRC	23	6.0
CBOT	Ottawa	CBC	37	3.0
CFGS	Hull	TQS	16	3.8
CFMT	Toronto	Ind.	20	1.9
CHCH	Toronto/Hamilton	Ind.	30	2.3
CHOT	Hull	TVA	20	7.2
CHRO	Ottawa	Ind.	22	2.4
CICO-E	n.a.	n.a.	18	2.8
CIII	n.a.	Global	52	2.9
CITY	Toronto	Ind.	27	2.1
CIVM	Montréal	Télé-Qué.	6	2.0
CIVO	Hull	Télé-Qué.	n.a.	n.a.
CJOH	Ottawa	CTV	61	5.0
DSCVRY	n.a.	Ind.	6	1.8
NEWSWD	n.a.	CBC	8	1.4
OTHERS	n.a.	n.a.	11	2.2
PRIME	n.a.	Ind.	6	2.8
RDI	n.a.	n.a.	5	2.8
RDS	n.a.	Ind.	5	2.4
SNET	n.a.	CTV	15	2.8
SPACE	n.a.	Ind.	7	2.8
TLC	n.a.	Ind.	10	1.8
TMN	Toronto	Ind.	5	4.6
TOON(FR)	n.a.	Ind.	4	4.6
TOON-E	n.a.	Ind.	7	1.9
TSN	n.a.	Ind.	12	3.7
VCR	n.a.	n.a.	32	4.2
WHEC	Rochester NY	NBC	12	1.3
WOKR	Rochester NY	ABC	18	1.8
WPBS	Watertown NY	PBS	12	1.9
WROC	Rochester NY	CBS	14	1.8
WTBS	Atlanta GA	Ind.	12	2.7
WUTV	Buffalo NY	FOX	20	1.9
YTV	n.a.	Ind.	12	2.5

BBM Spring 2000 TV Reach Survey; CMA coverage.
*Mon-Sun 6a.m - 2a.m , All Persons 2 +

Clarence
(Township)
Ottawa-Hull CMA

In Prescott and Russell United Counties. On Jan. 1, 1998, Clarence, TP & Rockland, T, amalgamated to form Clarence-Rockland, C.

POPULATION

July 1, 2001 Estimate	12,087
% Cdn. Total	0.04
% Change, '96 -'01	11.27
Avg. Annual Growth Rate, %	2.16
2003 Projected Population	12,875
2006 Projected Population	14,090
2001 Households Estimate	4,072
2003 Projected Households	4,383
2006 Projected Households	4,891

INCOME

% Above/Below National Average	+2
2001 Total Income Estimate	$259,410,000
% Cdn. Total	0.04
2001 Average Hhld. Income	$63,700
2001 Per Capita	$21,500
2003 Projected Total Income	$296,580,000
2006 Projected Total Income	$362,590,000

RETAIL SALES

% Above/Below National Average	-70
2001 Retail Sales Estimate	$32,380,000
% Cdn. Total	0.01
2001 per Household	$8,000
2001 per Capita	$2,700
2001 No. of Establishments	60
2003 Projected Retail Sales	$37,560,000
2006 Projected Retail Sales	$46,160,000

POPULATION

2001 Estimates:

Total		12,087
Male		6,145
Female		5,942
Age Groups	Male	Female
0-4	439	423
5-9	502	452
10-14	514	457
15-19	476	426
20-24	395	373
25-29	398	405
30-34	519	526
35-39	593	581
40-44	556	537
45-49	474	464
50-54	391	360
55-59	297	264
60-64	216	195
65-69	149	147
70+	226	332

DAYTIME POPULATION

2001 Estimates:

Working Population	1,818
At Home Population	5,184
Total	7,002

INCOME

2001 Estimates:

Avg. Household Income	$63,706
Avg. Family Income	$65,518
Per Capita Income	$21,462
Male:	
Avg. Employment Income	$35,164
Avg. Employment Income (Full Time)	$41,503
Female:	
Avg. Employment Income	$26,643
Avg. Employment Income (Full Time)	$35,634

DISPOSABLE & DISCRETIONARY INCOME

2001 Estimates:	Per Hhld.
Disposable Income	$52,363
Discretionary Income 1 (minus Food & Shelter)	$38,309
Discretionary Income 2 (minus Food, Shelter, & Other Expenditures)	$28,621

LIQUID ASSETS

1999 Estimates:	Per Hhld.
Equity Investments	$86,136
Interest Bearing Investments	$78,189
Total Liquid Assets	$164,325

CREDIT DATA

July 2000:

Pool of Credit	$100,504,833
Revolving Credit, No.	16,489
Fixed Loans, No.	7,358
Avg. Credit Limit, per Person	$11,723
Avg. Spent, per Person	$6,027
Satisfactory Ratings, No. per Person	2.61
Avg. No. of Cards, per Person	0.91

LABOUR FORCE

2001 Estimates:

Male:	
In the Labour Force	3,860
Participation Rate	82.3
Employed	3,740
Unemployed	120
Unemployment Rate	3.1
Not in Labour Force	830
Female:	
In the Labour Force	3,092
Participation Rate	67.1
Employed	3,043
Unemployed	49
Unemployment Rate	1.6
Not in Labour Force	1,518

OCCUPATIONS BY MAJOR GROUPS

2001 Estimates:	Male	Female
Management	451	151
Business, Finance & Admin.	433	1,294
Natural & Applied Sciences & Related	283	37
Health	46	196
Social Sciences, Gov't Services & Religion	24	94
Education	35	242
Arts, Culture, Recreation & Sport	57	96
Sales & Service	726	756
Trades, Transport & Equipment Operators & Related	1,359	42
Primary Industries	255	43
Processing, Mfg. & Utilities	107	48

LEVEL OF SCHOOLING

2001 Estimates:

Population 15 years +	9,300
Less than Grade 9	910
Grades 9-13 w/o Certif.	2,020
Grade 9-13 with Certif.	1,964
Trade Certif./Dip.	325
Non-Univ. w/o Certif./Dip.	680
Non-Univ. with Certif./Dip.	2,079
Univ. w/o Degree	586
Univ. w/o Degree/Certif.	222
Univ. with Certif.	364
Univ. with Degree	736

AVERAGE HOUSEHOLD EXPENDITURES

2001 Estimates:

Food	$7,461
Shelter	$8,737
Clothing	$2,732
Transportation	$7,688
Health & Personal Care	$2,299
Recr'n, Read'g & Education	$4,047
Taxes & Securities	$18,864
Other	$8,239
Total Expenditures	$60,067

PRIVATE HOUSEHOLDS

2001 Estimates:

Private Households, Total	4,072
Pop. in Private Households	11,856
Average no. per Household	2.9

FAMILIES

2001 Estimates:

Families in Private Households	3,637
Husband-Wife Families	3,349
Lone-Parent Families	288
Aver. No. Persons per Family	3.2
Aver. No. Sons/Daughters at Home	1.3

HOUSING

2001 Estimates:

Occupied Private Dwellings	4,072
Owned	3,560
Rented	512
Single-Detached House	3,702
Semi-Detached House	54
Row Houses	13
Apartment, 5 or Fewer Storeys	59
Apartment, Detached Duplex	110
Other Single-Attached	12
Movable Dwellings	122

VEHICLES

2001 Estimates:

Model Yrs. '81-'96, No.	5,920
% Total	84.03
Model Yrs. '97-'98, No.	653
% Total	9.27
'99 Vehicles registered in Model Yr. '99, No.	472
% Total	6.70
Total No. '81-'99	7,045

LEGAL MARITAL STATUS

2001 Estimates: (Age 15+)

Single (Never Married)	2,534
Legally Married (Not Separated)	5,688
Legally Married (Separated)	288
Widowed	360
Divorced	430

PSYTE CATEGORIES

2001 Estimates	No. of House-holds	% of Total Hhds.	Index
Blue Collar Winners	238	5.84	232
Participation Quebec	2,984	73.28	2,543
Traditional French Cdn. Families	814	19.99	744

FINANCIAL PSYTE

2001 Estimates	No. of House-holds	% of Total Hhds.	Index
Canadian Comfort	238	5.84	60
Mortgages & Minivans	2,984	73.28	1,110
Country Credit	814	19.99	296

Ontario

HOME LANGUAGE

2001 Estimates:		% Total
English	3,798	31.42
French	7,872	65.13
Chinese	70	0.58
Dutch	11	0.09
German	23	0.19
Greek	23	0.19
Hungarian	12	0.10
Other Languages	35	0.29
Multiple Responses	243	2.01
Total	12,087	100.00

BUILDING PERMITS

	1999	1998	1997
		$000	
Value	11,358	n.a.	5,192

Note: 1999 data for Clarence-Rockland, C.

HOMES BUILT

	1999	1998	1997
No.	67	63	30

Note: 1998 & 1999 data for Clarence-Rockland, C.

TAXATION

Income Class:	1997	% Total
Under $5,000	700	12.48
$5,000-$10,000	600	10.70
$10,000-$15,000	760	13.55
$15,000-$20,000	480	8.56
$20,000-$25,000	480	8.56
$25,000-$30,000	530	9.45
$30,000-$40,000	1,020	18.18
$40,000-$50,000	560	9.98
$50,000 +	500	8.91
Total Returns, No.	5,610	
Total Income, $000	140,868	
Total Taxable Returns	4,090	
Total Tax, $000	23,376	
Average Income, $.	25,110	
Average Tax, $.	5,715	

VITAL STATISTICS

	1997	1996	1995	1994
Births	89	107	108	129
Deaths	39	63	60	75
Natural Increase	50	44	48	54
Marriages	33	33	29	25

Note: Latest available data.

MEDIA INFO
see Ottawa-Hull, CMA

Ontario

Cumberland
(Township)
Ottawa-Hull CMA

In Ottawa-Carleton Regional Municipality.

POPULATION

July 1, 2001 Estimate	54,871
% Cdn. Total	0.18
% Change, '96 -'01	12.44
Avg. Annual Growth Rate, %	2.37
2003 Projected Population	58,092
2006 Projected Population	63,216
2001 Households Estimate	17,598
2003 Projected Households	18,865
2006 Projected Households	20,908

INCOME

% Above/Below National Average	+28
2001 Total Income Estimate	$1,482,600,000
% Cdn. Total	0.23
2001 Average Hhld. Income	$84,200
2001 Per Capita	$27,000
2003 Projected Total Income	$1,676,340,000
2006 Projected Total Income	$2,011,770,000

RETAIL SALES

% Above/Below National Average	-65
2001 Retail Sales Estimate	$173,590,000
% Cdn. Total	0.06
2001 per Household	$9,900
2001 per Capita	$3,200
2001 No. of Establishments	177
2003 Projected Retail Sales	$192,990,000
2006 Projected Retail Sales	$225,900,000

POPULATION

2001 Estimates:

Total		54,871
Male		27,264
Female		27,607

Age Groups	Male	Female
0-4	1,825	1,767
5-9	2,190	2,078
10-14	2,432	2,261
15-19	2,299	2,200
20-24	1,911	1,910
25-29	1,595	1,680
30-34	1,811	2,027
35-39	2,294	2,589
40-44	2,533	2,775
45-49	2,471	2,554
50-54	2,081	1,988
55-59	1,501	1,349
60-64	937	860
65-69	574	559
70+	810	1,010

DAYTIME POPULATION

2001 Estimates:

Working Population	7,180
At Home Population	21,782
Total	28,962

INCOME

2001 Estimates:

Avg. Household Income	$84,248
Avg. Family Income	$84,542
Per Capita Income	$27,020
Male:	
Avg. Employment Income	$46,019
Avg. Employment Income (Full Time)	$56,653
Female:	
Avg. Employment Income	$29,776
Avg. Employment Income (Full Time)	$41,082

DISPOSABLE & DISCRETIONARY INCOME

2001 Estimates:	Per Hhld.
Disposable Income	$68,335
Discretionary Income 1 (minus Food & Shelter)	$50,719
Discretionary Income 2 (minus Food, Shelter, & Other Expenditures)	$39,196

LIQUID ASSETS

1999 Estimates:	Per Hhld.
Equity Investments	$131,344
Interest Bearing Investments	$104,082
Total Liquid Assets	$235,426

CREDIT DATA

July 2000:

Pool of Credit	$675,387,053
Revolving Credit, No.	110,481
Fixed Loans, No.	35,759
Avg. Credit Limit, per Person	$16,466
Avg. Spent, per Person	$7,315
Satisfactory Ratings, No. per Person	3.39
Avg. No. of Cards, per Person	1.25

LABOUR FORCE

2001 Estimates:

Male:

In the Labour Force	17,568
Participation Rate	84.4
Employed	17,111
Unemployed	457
Unemployment Rate	2.6
Not in Labour Force	3,249

Female:

In the Labour Force	15,983
Participation Rate	74.3
Employed	15,392
Unemployed	591
Unemployment Rate	3.7
Not in Labour Force	5,518

OCCUPATIONS BY MAJOR GROUPS

2001 Estimates:	Male	Female
Management	3,348	1,500
Business, Finance & Admin.	2,574	5,720
Natural & Applied Sciences & Related	2,432	551
Health	267	1,435
Social Sciences, Gov't Services & Religion	495	590
Education	473	816
Arts, Culture, Recreation & Sport	285	671
Sales & Service	3,890	3,720
Trades, Transport & Equipment Operators & Related	2,749	210
Primary Industries	485	176
Processing, Mfg. & Utilities	338	76

LEVEL OF SCHOOLING

2001 Estimates:

Population 15 years +	42,318
Less than Grade 9	1,773
Grades 9-13 w/o Certif.	7,673
Grade 9-13 with Certif.	6,870
Trade Certif. /Dip.	1,087
Non-Univ. w/o Certif./Dip.	2,463
Non-Univ. with Certif./Dip.	8,390
Univ. w/o Degree	5,099
Univ. w/o Degree/Certif.	2,702
Univ. with Certif.	2,397
Univ. with Degree	8,963

AVERAGE HOUSEHOLD EXPENDITURES

2001 Estimates:

Food	$8,362
Shelter	$12,315
Clothing	$3,399
Transportation	$9,093
Health & Personal Care	$2,546
Recr'n, Read'g & Education	$5,594
Taxes & Securities	$24,208
Other	$10,818
Total Expenditures	$76,335

PRIVATE HOUSEHOLDS

2001 Estimates:

Private Households, Total	17,598
Pop. in Private Households	54,290
Average no. per Household	3.1

FAMILIES

2001 Estimates:

Families in Private Households	15,986
Husband-Wife Families	14,615
Lone-Parent Families	1,371
Aver. No. Persons per Family	3.3
Aver. No. Sons/Daughters at Home	1.4

HOUSING

2001 Estimates:

Occupied Private Dwellings	17,598
Owned	15,761
Rented	1,837
Single-Detached House	12,735
Semi-Detached House	707
Row Houses	3,149
Apartment, 5+ Storeys	80
Owned Apartment, 5+ Storeys	63
Apartment, 5 or Fewer Storeys	499
Apartment, Detached Duplex	190
Other Single-Attached	12
Movable Dwellings	226

VEHICLES

2001 Estimates:

Model Yrs. '81-'96, No.	21,949
% Total	76.04
Model Yrs. '97-'98, No.	4,101
% Total	14.21
'99 Vehicles registered in Model Yr. '99, No.	2,815
% Total	9.75
Total No. '81-'99	28,865

LEGAL MARITAL STATUS

2001 Estimates: (Age 15+)

Single (Never Married)	10,959
Legally Married (Not Separated)	27,175
Legally Married (Separated)	1,071
Widowed	1,147
Divorced	1,966

PSYTE CATEGORIES

2001 Estimates	No. of House-holds	% of Total Hhds.	Index
Suburban Executives	1,317	7.48	522
Mortgaged in Suburbia	1,717	9.76	702
Technocrafts & Bureaucrats	8,258	46.93	1,668
Boomers & Teens	1,439	8.18	456
Old Bungalow Burbs	845	4.80	290

2001 Estimates	No. of House-holds	% of Total Hhds.	Index
Kindergarten Boom	713	4.05	155
Blue Collar Winners	865	4.92	195
Old Towns' New Fringe	418	2.38	61
Participation Quebec	1,287	7.31	254
Traditional French Cdn. Families	306	1.74	65
Quebec's Heartland	43	0.24	25
Old Quebec Walkups	368	2.09	114

FINANCIAL P$YTE

2001 Estimates	No. of House-holds	% of Total Hhds.	Index
Four Star Investors	2,756	15.66	312
Successful Suburbanites	9,975	56.68	854
Canadian Comfort	865	4.92	51
Miners & Credit-Liners	845	4.80	152
Mortgages & Minivans	2,000	11.36	172
Tractors & Tradelines	418	2.38	42
Country Credit	306	1.74	26
Rural Family Blues	43	0.24	3
Loan Parent Stress	368	2.09	36

HOME LANGUAGE

2001 Estimates:		% Total
English	37,534	68.40
French	14,426	26.29
Arabic	157	0.29
Bengali	60	0.11
Chinese	382	0.70
Greek	37	0.07
Hindi	68	0.12
Persian (Farsi)	80	0.15
Polish	52	0.09
Portuguese	51	0.09
Punjabi	144	0.26
Tagalog (Pilipino)	55	0.10
Urdu	50	0.09
Vietnamese	95	0.17
Other Languages	205	0.37
Multiple Responses	1,475	2.69
Total	54,871	100.00

BUILDING PERMITS

	1999	1998	1997
		$000	
Value	83,086	53,806	39,343

HOMES BUILT

	1999	1998	1997
No.	450	328	360

TAXATION

Income Class:	1997	% Total
Under $5,000	880	10.88
$5,000-$10,000	830	10.26
$10,000-$15,000	910	11.25
$15,000-$20,000	660	8.16
$20,000-$25,000	620	7.66
$25,000-$30,000	660	8.16
$30,000-$40,000	1,190	14.71
$40,000-$50,000	820	10.14
$50,000 +	1,520	18.79
Total Returns, No.	8,090	
Total Income, $000	265,383	
Total Taxable Returns	6,200	
Total Tax, $000	52,986	
Average Income, $	32,804	
Average Tax, $	8,546	

VITAL STATISTICS

	1997	1996	1995	1994
Births	103	117	104	139
Deaths	63	56	51	64
Natural Increase	40	61	53	75
Marriages	112	91	83	76

Note: Latest available data.

MEDIA INFO

see Ottawa-Hull, CMA

Gloucester
(City)
Ottawa-Hull CMA

In Ottawa-Carleton Regional Municipality.

POPULATION

July 1, 2001 Estimate	107,818
% Cdn. Total	0.35
% Change, '96 -'01	0.61
Avg. Annual Growth Rate, %	0.12
2003 Projected Population	107,731
2006 Projected Population	108,138
2001 Households Estimate	37,431
2003 Projected Households	37,826
2006 Projected Households	38,629

INCOME

% Above/Below National Average	+22
2001 Total Income Estimate	$2,768,710,000
% Cdn. Total	0.42
2001 Average Hhld. Income	$74,000
2001 Per Capita	$25,700
2003 Projected Total Income	$2,905,910,000
2006 Projected Total Income	$3,135,920,000

RETAIL SALES

% Above/Below National Average	+42
2001 Retail Sales Estimate	$1,374,460,000
% Cdn. Total	0.49
2001 per Household	$36,700
2001 per Capita	$12,700
2001 No. of Establishments	666
2003 Projected Retail Sales	$1,493,640,000
2006 Projected Retail Sales	$1,671,470,000

POPULATION

2001 Estimates:

Total		107,818
Male		52,996
Female		54,822

Age Groups	Male	Female
0-4	3,369	3,217
5-9	3,715	3,585
10-14	4,080	3,840
15-19	4,211	3,917
20-24	4,050	3,736
25-29	3,632	3,484
30-34	3,667	3,763
35-39	4,001	4,471
40-44	4,240	4,856
45-49	4,332	4,873
50-54	4,010	4,322
55-59	3,187	3,331
60-64	2,354	2,363
65-69	1,685	1,677
70+	2,463	3,387

DAYTIME POPULATION

2001 Estimates:

Working Population	42,092
At Home Population	45,785
Total	87,877

INCOME

2001 Estimates:

Avg. Household Income	$73,968
Avg. Family Income	$76,781
Per Capita Income	$25,679
Male:	
Avg. Employment Income	$40,782
Avg. Employment Income (Full Time)	$52,601
Female:	
Avg. Employment Income	$28,037
Avg. Employment Income (Full Time)	$40,424

DISPOSABLE & DISCRETIONARY INCOME

2001 Estimates:	*Per Hhld.*
Disposable Income	$59,601
Discretionary Income 1 (minus Food & Shelter)	$43,519
Discretionary Income 2 (minus Food, Shelter, & Other Expenditures)	$33,034

LIQUID ASSETS

1999 Estimates:	*Per Hhld.*
Equity Investments	$105,755
Interest Bearing Investments	$90,249
Total Liquid Assets	$196,004

CREDIT DATA

July 2000:	
Pool of Credit	$1,392,644,239
Revolving Credit, No.	247,123
Fixed Loans, No.	70,889
Avg. Credit Limit, per Person	$13,986
Avg. Spent, per Person	$5,934
Satisfactory Ratings, No. per Person	3.05
Avg. No. of Cards, per Person	1.17

LABOUR FORCE

2001 Estimates:

Male:	
In the Labour Force	33,805
Participation Rate	80.8
Employed	32,339
Unemployed	1,466
Unemployment Rate	4.3
Not in Labour Force	8,027
Female:	
In the Labour Force	30,664
Participation Rate	69.4
Employed	29,151
Unemployed	1,513
Unemployment Rate	4.9
Not in Labour Force	13,516

OCCUPATIONS BY MAJOR GROUPS

2001 Estimates:	*Male*	*Female*
Management	6,363	2,798
Business, Finance & Admin.	4,565	10,240
Natural & Applied Sciences & Related	4,321	904
Health	606	2,682
Social Sciences, Gov't Services & Religion	1,194	1,076
Education	794	1,961
Arts, Culture, Recreation & Sport	845	1,177
Sales & Service	8,216	8,084
Trades, Transport & Equipment Operators & Related	4,897	312
Primary Industries	482	60
Processing, Mfg. & Utilities	539	273

LEVEL OF SCHOOLING

2001 Estimates:

Population 15 years +	86,012
Less than Grade 9	4,022
Grades 9-13 w/o Certif.	15,078
Grade 9-13 with Certif.	13,288
Trade Certif./Dip.	2,206
Non-Univ. w/o Certif./Dip.	5,332
Non-Univ. with Certif./Dip.	15,375
Univ. w/o Degree	10,959
Univ. w/o Degree/Certif.	5,542
Univ. with Certif.	5,417
Univ. with Degree	19,752

AVERAGE HOUSEHOLD EXPENDITURES

2001 Estimates:	
Food	$7,578
Shelter	$11,312
Clothing	$2,957
Transportation	$8,151
Health & Personal Care	$2,372
Recr'n, Read'g & Education	$4,926
Taxes & Securities	$20,532
Other	$10,043
Total Expenditures	$67,871

PRIVATE HOUSEHOLDS

2001 Estimates:	
Private Households, Total	37,431
Pop. in Private Households	105,847
Average no. per Household	2.8

FAMILIES

2001 Estimates:	
Families in Private Households	31,273
Husband-Wife Families	26,528
Lone-Parent Families	4,745
Aver. No. Persons per Family	3.2
Aver. No. Sons/Daughters at Home	1.3

HOUSING

2001 Estimates:	
Occupied Private Dwellings	37,431
Owned	26,819
Rented	10,612
Single-Detached House	18,031
Semi-Detached House	2,308
Row Houses	10,881
Apartment, 5+ Storeys	3,207
Owned Apartment, 5+ Storeys	698
Apartment, 5 or Fewer Storeys	2,414
Apartment, Detached Duplex	401
Other Single-Attached	44
Movable Dwellings	145

VEHICLES

2001 Estimates:	
Model Yrs. '81-'96, No.	46,110
% Total	72.77
Model Yrs. '97-'98, No.	9,688
% Total	15.29
'99 Vehicles registered in Model Yr. '99, No.	7,570
% Total	11.95
Total No. '81-'99	63,368

LEGAL MARITAL STATUS

2001 Estimates: (Age 15+)	
Single (Never Married)	26,321
Legally Married (Not Separated)	47,875
Legally Married (Separated)	3,002
Widowed	3,362
Divorced	5,452

PSYTE CATEGORIES

2001 Estimates	No. of House-holds	% Total Hhds.	Index
The Affluentials	459	1.23	192
Urban Gentry	1,234	3.30	183
Suburban Executives	3,436	9.18	640
Technocrafts & Bureaucrats	11,109	29.68	1,055
Boomers & Teens	409	1.09	61
Stable Suburban Families	2,103	5.62	431
Old Bungalow Burbs	1,205	3.22	194
Suburban Nesters	459	1.23	77
Brie & Chablis	399	1.07	119
Aging Erudites	1,297	3.47	230
Satellite Suburbs	368	0.98	34
Kindergarten Boom	6,325	16.90	644
Blue Collar Winners	1,145	3.06	122
Old Towns' New Fringe	1,082	2.89	74
Participation Quebec	702	1.88	65
Quebec Melange	448	1.20	45
High Rise Melting Pot	291	0.78	52
Conservative Homebodies	125	0.33	9
Young Urban Mix	826	2.21	104

Ontario

2001 Estimates	No. of House-holds	% of Total Hhds.	Index
Young Urban Intelligentsia	189	0.50	33
University Enclaves	552	1.47	72
Young City Singles	864	2.31	101
Town Renters	1,372	3.67	424
Old Quebec Walkups	431	1.15	63
Big City Stress	275	0.73	65

FINANÇIAL P$YTE

2001 Estimates	No. of House-holds	% of Total Hhds.	Index
Platinum Estates	459	1.23	152
Four Star Investors	5,079	13.57	270
Successful Suburbanites	13,212	35.30	532
Canadian Comfort	1,972	5.27	54
Urban Heights	1,696	4.53	105
Miners & Credit-Liners	1,205	3.22	102
Mortgages & Minivans	7,027	18.77	284
Tractors & Tradelines	1,082	2.89	51
Bills & Wills	951	2.54	31
Country Credit	448	1.20	18
Young Urban Struggle	741	1.98	42
Loan Parent Stress	431	1.15	20
Towering Debt	2,527	6.75	86
NSF	275	0.73	21

HOME LANGUAGE

2001 Estimates:		% Total
English	74,213	68.83
French	21,800	20.22
Arabic	1,396	1.29
Bengali	233	0.22
Bulgarian	69	0.06
Chinese	1,358	1.26
Creoles	195	0.18
Czech	63	0.06
German	163	0.15
Hindi	131	0.12
Italian	337	0.31
Korean	65	0.06
Persian (Farsi)	342	0.32
Polish	460	0.43
Portuguese	293	0.27
Punjabi	409	0.38
Russian	64	0.06
Spanish	618	0.57
Tagalog (Pilipino)	197	0.18
Turkish	93	0.09
Ukrainian	70	0.06
Urdu	225	0.21
Vietnamese	533	0.49
Other Languages	1,320	1.22
Multiple Responses	3,171	2.94
Total	107,818	100.00

BUILDING PERMITS

	1999	1998	1997
		$000	
Value	152,761	112,303	93,252

Gloucester
(City)
Ottawa-Hull CMA
(Cont'd)

HOMES BUILT

	1999	1998	1997
No.	756	603	730

TAXATION

Income Class:	1997	% Total
Under $5,000	12,170	12.63
$5,000-$10,000	9,850	10.22
$10,000-$15,000	9,350	9.70
$15,000-$20,000	6,910	7.17
$20,000-$25,000	6,320	6.56
$25,000-$30,000	6,530	6.78
$30,000-$40,000	13,360	13.86
$40,000-$50,000	10,390	10.78
$50,000 +	21,490	22.30

Total Returns, No. 96,380
Total Income, $000 . . 3,196,868
Total Taxable
  Returns 71,910
Total Tax, $000 649,967
Average Income, $ 33,169
Average Tax, $ 9,039

VITAL STATISTICS

	1997	1996	1995	1994
Births	1,548	1,635	1,684	1,764
Deaths	518	500	521	473
Natural Increase	1,030	1,135	1,163	1,291
Marriages	374	346	306	355

Note: Latest available data.

MEDIA INFO
see Ottawa-Hull, CMA

Goulbourn
(Township)
Ottawa-Hull CMA

In Ottawa-Carleton Regional Municipality.

POPULATION

July 1, 2001 Estimate 22,827
% Cdn. Total 0.07
% Change, '96 -'01 . . . . 15.00
Avg. Annual Growth Rate, % 2.84
2003 Projected Population 24,468
2006 Projected Population 27,047
2001 Households Estimate 7,853
2003 Projected Households 8,514
2006 Projected Households 9,581

INCOME

% Above/Below National Average . . . . . . +40
2001 Total Income Estimate . . $673,410,000
% Cdn. Total 0.10
2001 Average Hhld. Income $85,800
2001 Per Capita $29,500
2003 Projected Total Income . . $772,180,000
2006 Projected Total Income . . $943,910,000

RETAIL SALES

% Above/Below National Average . . . . . . -36
2001 Retail Sales Estimate $130,160,000
% Cdn. Total 0.05
2001 per Household $16,600
2001 per Capita $5,700
2001 No. of Establishments 153
2003 Projected Retail Sales $147,640,000
2006 Projected Retail Sales $176,870,000

POPULATION

2001 Estimates:

Total		22,827
Male		11,354
Female		11,473

Age Groups	Male	Female
0-4	724	716
5-9	895	883
10-14	969	900
15-19	886	800
20-24	731	658
25-29	649	598
30-34	743	787
35-39	928	1,021
40-44	1,011	1,061
45-49	955	957
50-54	796	784
55-59	609	579
60-64	441	438
65-69	345	376
70+	672	915

DAYTIME POPULATION

2001 Estimates:
Working Population 4,992
At Home Population 9,694
Total 14,686

INCOME

2001 Estimates:
Avg. Household Income $85,752
Avg. Family Income $89,131
Per Capita Income $29,500
Male:
Avg. Employment Income $50,410
Avg. Employment Income
  (Full Time) $62,108
Female:
Avg. Employment Income $27,329
Avg. Employment Income
  (Full Time) $40,494

DISPOSABLE & DISCRETIONARY INCOME

2001 Estimates:	Per Hhld.
Disposable Income	$69,721
Discretionary Income 1 (minus Food & Shelter)	$51,886
Discretionary Income 2 (minus Food, Shelter, & Other Expenditures)	$39,661

LIQUID ASSETS

1999 Estimates:	Per Hhld.
Equity Investments	$138,104
Interest Bearing Investments	$107,356
Total Liquid Assets	$245,460

CREDIT DATA

July 2000:
Pool of Credit $351,628,986
Revolving Credit, No. 54,430
Fixed Loans, No. 15,697
Avg. Credit Limit, per Person . . . $17,078
Avg. Spent, per Person $7,341
Satisfactory Ratings,
  No. per Person 3.27
Avg. No. of Cards, per Person 1.22

LABOUR FORCE

2001 Estimates:
Male:
In the Labour Force 7,091
Participation Rate 80.9
Employed 7,018
Unemployed 73
Unemployment Rate 1.0
Not in Labour Force 1,675
Female:
In the Labour Force 6,089
Participation Rate 67.9
Employed 5,946
Unemployed 143
Unemployment Rate 2.3
Not in Labour Force 2,885

OCCUPATIONS BY MAJOR GROUPS

2001 Estimates:	Male	Female
Management	1,549	737
Business, Finance & Admin.	719	1,898
Natural & Applied Sciences & Related	1,105	186
Health	125	506
Social Sciences, Gov't Services & Religion	162	293
Education	125	278
Arts, Culture, Recreation & Sport	71	136
Sales & Service	1,385	1,557
Trades, Transport & Equipment Operators & Related	1,288	114
Primary Industries	293	136
Processing, Mfg. & Utilities	208	104

LEVEL OF SCHOOLING

2001 Estimates:
Population 15 years + ... 17,740
Less than Grade 9 552
Grades 9-13 w/o Certif. 3,262
Grade 9-13 with Certif. 2,632
Trade Certif. /Dip. 551
Non-Univ. w/o Certif./Dip. 1,177
Non-Univ. with Certif./Dip. 3,789
Univ. w/o Degree 2,151
  Univ. w/o Degree/Certif. 1,081
  Univ. with Certif. 1,070
Univ. with Degree 3,626

AVERAGE HOUSEHOLD EXPENDITURES

2001 Estimates:
Food $8,339
Shelter $12,608
Clothing $3,274
Transportation $9,743
Health & Personal Care $2,620
Recr'n, Read'g & Education $5,635
Taxes & Securities $23,890
Other $11,405
Total Expenditures $77,514

PRIVATE HOUSEHOLDS

2001 Estimates:
Private Households, Total 7,853
Pop. in Private Households 22,651
Average no. per Household 2.9

FAMILIES

2001 Estimates:
Families in Private Households 6,965
Husband-Wife Families 6,450
Lone-Parent Families 515
Aver. No. Persons per Family 3.2
Aver. No. Sons/Daughters
  at Home 1.3

HOUSING

2001 Estimates:
Occupied Private Dwellings 7,853
Owned 7,011
Rented 842
Single-Detached House 6,630
Semi-Detached House 83
Row Houses 694
Apartment, 5 or Fewer Storeys 202
Apartment, Detached Duplex 22
Other Single-Attached 12
Movable Dwellings 210

VEHICLES

2001 Estimates:
Model Yrs. '81-'96, No. 11,134
  % Total 78.56
Model Yrs. '97-'98, No. 1,861
  % Total 13.13
'99 Vehicles registered in
  Model Yr. '99, No. 1,178
  % Total 8.31
Total No. '81-'99 14,173

LEGAL MARITAL STATUS

2001 Estimates: (Age 15+)
Single (Never Married) 3,892
Legally Married
  (Not Separated) 11,964
Legally Married (Separated) 412
Widowed 716
Divorced 756

PSYTE CATEGORIES

2001 Estimates	No. of House -holds	% of Total Hhds.	Index
Suburban Executives	638	8.12	567
Mortgaged in Suburbia	1,031	13.13	945
Technocrafts & Bureaucrats	1,024	13.04	463
Boomers & Teens	350	4.46	249
Small City Elite	2,088	26.59	1,552
Aging Erudites	460	5.86	388
Satellite Suburbs	265	3.37	118
Blue Collar Winners	1,894	24.12	958
High Rise Sunsets	103	1.31	92

FINANCIAL P$YTE

2001 Estimates	No. of House -holds	% of Total Hhds.	Index
Four Star Investors	988	12.58	250
Successful Suburbanites	2,055	26.17	394
Canadian Comfort	4,247	54.08	557
Urban Heights	460	5.86	136
Revolving Renters	103	1.31	29

Goulbourn
(Township)
Ottawa-Hull CMA
(Cont'd)

HOME LANGUAGE

2001 Estimates:		% Total
English	22,216	97.32
French	202	0.88
Chinese	49	0.21
Czech	14	0.06
Dutch	12	0.05
Finnish	22	0.10
German	29	0.13
Italian	13	0.06
Persian (Farsi)	18	0.08
Punjabi	12	0.05
Spanish	19	0.08
Swedish	24	0.11
Thai	12	0.05
Other Languages	11	0.05
Multiple Responses	174	0.76
Total	22,827	100.00

BUILDING PERMITS

	1999	1998	1997
		$000	
Value	57,951	45,026	44,824

HOMES BUILT

	1999	1998	1997
No.	250	279	299

TAXATION

Income Class:	1997	% Total
Under $5,000	1,660	10.57
$5,000-$10,000	1,440	9.17
$10,000-$15,000	1,370	8.72
$15,000-$20,000	1,100	7.00
$20,000-$25,000	1,030	6.56
$25,000-$30,000	1,100	7.00
$30,000-$40,000	2,130	13.56
$40,000-$50,000	1,710	10.88
$50,000 +	4,180	26.61
Total Returns, No.	15,710	
Total Income, $000	604,569	
Total Taxable Returns	12,470	
Total Tax, $000	136,127	
Average Income, $	38,483	
Average Tax, $	10,916	

VITAL STATISTICS

	1997	1996	1995	1994
Births	252	230	242	225
Deaths	66	85	62	51
Natural Increase	186	145	180	174
Marriages	71	74	70	66

Note: Latest available data.

MEDIA INFO
see Ottawa-Hull, CMA

Kanata
(City)
Ottawa-Hull CMA

In Ottawa-Carleton Regional Municipality.

POPULATION

July 1, 2001 Estimate	60,489
% Cdn. Total	0.19
% Change, '96 -'01	22.55
Avg. Annual Growth Rate, %	4.15
2003 Projected Population	67,583
2006 Projected Population	78,547
2001 Households Estimate	20,273
2003 Projected Households	22,918
2006 Projected Households	27,099

INCOME

% Above/Below National Average	+45
2001 Total Income Estimate	$1,846,260,000
% Cdn. Total	0.28
2001 Average Hhld. Income	$91,100
2001 Per Capita	$30,500
2003 Projected Total Income	$2,221,790,000
2006 Projected Total Income	$2,877,970,000

RETAIL SALES

% Above/Below National Average	-55
2001 Retail Sales Estimate	$245,250,000
% Cdn. Total	0.09
2001 per Household	$12,100
2001 per Capita	$4,100
2001 No. of Establishments	190
2003 Projected Retail Sales	$292,260,000
2006 Projected Retail Sales	$370,030,000

POPULATION

2001 Estimates:		
Total		60,489
Male		30,006
Female		30,483

Age Groups	Male	Female
0-4	2,245	2,118
5-9	2,544	2,346
10-14	2,568	2,388
15-19	2,321	2,225
20-24	2,010	2,017
25-29	1,944	2,077
30-34	2,391	2,565
35-39	2,779	3,004
40-44	2,766	2,938
45-49	2,484	2,550
50-54	1,981	1,996
55-59	1,435	1,426
60-64	969	963
65-69	640	668
70+	929	1,202

DAYTIME POPULATION

2001 Estimates:	
Working Population	26,387
At Home Population	24,021
Total	50,408

INCOME

2001 Estimates:	
Avg. Household Income	$91,070
Avg. Family Income	$92,255
Per Capita Income	$30,522
Male:	
Avg. Employment Income	$53,723
Avg. Employment Income (Full Time)	$66,137
Female:	
Avg. Employment Income	$30,235
Avg. Employment Income (Full Time)	$42,201

DISPOSABLE & DISCRETIONARY INCOME

2001 Estimates:	Per Hhld.
Disposable Income	$73,407
Discretionary Income 1 (minus Food & Shelter)	$54,818
Discretionary Income 2 (minus Food, Shelter, & Other Expenditures)	$42,668

LIQUID ASSETS

1999 Estimates:	Per Hhld.
Equity Investments	$153,741
Interest Bearing Investments	$114,392
Total Liquid Assets	$268,133

CREDIT DATA

July 2000:	
Pool of Credit	$771,421,702
Revolving Credit, No.	130,063
Fixed Loans, No.	36,141
Avg. Credit Limit, per Person	$16,574
Avg. Spent, per Person	$6,855
Satisfactory Ratings, No. per Person	3.42
Avg. No. of Cards, per Person	1.31

LABOUR FORCE

2001 Estimates:	
Male:	
In the Labour Force	19,438
Participation Rate	85.8
Employed	19,050
Unemployed	388
Unemployment Rate	2.0
Not in Labour Force	3,211
Female:	
In the Labour Force	17,701
Participation Rate	74.9
Employed	17,048
Unemployed	653
Unemployment Rate	3.7
Not in Labour Force	5,930

OCCUPATIONS BY MAJOR GROUPS

2001 Estimates:	Male	Female
Management	4,026	1,623
Business, Finance & Admin.	2,703	5,593
Natural & Applied Sciences & Related	4,702	1,310
Health	306	1,477
Social Sciences, Gov't Services & Religion	469	582
Education	329	1,193
Arts, Recreation & Sport	585	680
Sales & Service	3,458	4,239
Trades, Transport & Equipment Operators & Related	1,855	220
Primary Industries	257	35
Processing, Mfg. & Utilities	413	333

LEVEL OF SCHOOLING

2001 Estimates:	
Population 15 years +	46,280
Less than Grade 9	1,009
Grades 9-13 w/o Certif.	6,650
Grade 9-13 with Certif.	6,021
Trade Certif. /Dip.	809
Non-Univ. w/o Certif./Dip.	2,818
Non-Univ. with Certif./Dip.	9,354
Univ. w/o Degree	5,884
Univ. w/o Degree/Certif.	2,714
Univ. with Certif.	3,170
Univ. with Degree	13,735

Ontario

AVERAGE HOUSEHOLD EXPENDITURES

2001 Estimates:	
Food	$8,703
Shelter	$13,145
Clothing	$3,610
Transportation	$9,609
Health & Personal Care	$2,651
Recr'n, Read'g & Education	$6,085
Taxes & Securities	$26,224
Other	$11,483
Total Expenditures	$81,510

PRIVATE HOUSEHOLDS

2001 Estimates:	
Private Households, Total	20,273
Pop. in Private Households	60,006
Average no. per Household	3.0

FAMILIES

2001 Estimates:	
Families in Private Households	17,721
Husband-Wife Families	16,006
Lone-Parent Families	1,715
Aver. No. Persons per Family	3.2
Aver. No. Sons/Daughters at Home	1.3

HOUSING

2001 Estimates:	
Occupied Private Dwellings	20,273
Owned	17,124
Rented	3,149
Single-Detached House	11,552
Semi-Detached House	1,526
Row Houses	6,072
Apartment, 5+ Storeys	431
Owned Apartment, 5+ Storeys	50
Apartment, 5 or Fewer Storeys	668
Apartment, Detached Duplex	12
Other Single-Attached	12

VEHICLES

2001 Estimates:	
Model Yrs. '81-'96, No.	23,209
% Total	75.62
Model Yrs. '97-'98, No.	4,560
% Total	14.86
'99 Vehicles registered in Model Yr. '99, No.	2,923
% Total	9.52
Total No. '81-'99	30,692

LEGAL MARITAL STATUS

2001 Estimates: (Age 15+)	
Single (Never Married)	11,793
Legally Married (Not Separated)	29,499
Legally Married (Separated)	1,314
Widowed	1,387
Divorced	2,287

Ontario

Kanata
(City)
Ottawa-Hull CMA
(Cont'd)

PSYTE CATEGORIES

2001 Estimates	No. of House-holds	% of Total Hhds.	Index
Urban Gentry	455	2.24	125
Suburban Executives	2,785	13.74	958
Mortgaged in Suburbia	3,747	18.48	1,330
Technocrafts & Bureaucrats	8,373	41.30	1,468
Boomers & Teens	941	4.64	259
Stable Suburban Families	436	2.15	165
Aging Erudites	367	1.81	120
Satellite Suburbs	1,608	7.93	276
Kindergarten Boom	1,047	5.16	197
Young Urban Mix	492	2.43	115

FINANCIAL P$YTE

2001 Estimates	No. of House-holds	% of Total Hhds.	Index
Four Star Investors	4,181	20.62	411
Successful Suburbanites	12,556	61.93	933
Canadian Comfort	1,608	7.93	82
Urban Heights	367	1.81	42
Mortgages & Minivans	1,047	5.16	78
Bills & Wills	492	2.43	29

HOME LANGUAGE

2001 Estimates:		% Total
English	53,812	88.96
French	1,624	2.68
Arabic	215	0.36
Bengali	38	0.06
Chinese	1,226	2.03
Czech	52	0.09
Dutch	78	0.13
Gujarati	43	0.07
Hindi	114	0.19
Hungarian	71	0.12
Italian	115	0.19
Lao	146	0.24
Persian (Farsi)	125	0.21
Polish	158	0.26
Punjabi	170	0.28
Russian	34	0.06
Serbian	43	0.07
Serbo-Croatian	47	0.08
Slovak	91	0.15
Spanish	119	0.20
Tagalog (Pilipino)	77	0.13
Tamil	54	0.09
Urdu	81	0.13
Vietnamese	145	0.24
Other Languages	422	0.70
Multiple Responses	1,389	2.30
Total	60,489	100.00

BUILDING PERMITS

	1999	1998	1997
			$000
Value	185,835	168,270	111,218

HOMES BUILT

	1999	1998	1997
No	780	702	583

TAXATION

Income Class:	1997	% Total
Under $5,000	4,110	12.17
$5,000-$10,000	3,020	8.94
$10,000-$15,000	2,670	7.91
$15,000-$20,000	2,070	6.13
$20,000-$25,000	1,970	5.83
$25,000-$30,000	2,110	6.25
$30,000-$40,000	4,560	13.50
$40,000-$50,000	3,610	10.69
$50,000 +	9,670	28.63
Total Returns, No.	33,770	
Total Income, $000	1,356,633	
Total Taxable Returns	26,370	
Total Tax, $000	314,452	
Average Income, $	40,173	
Average Tax, $	11,925	

VITAL STATISTICS

	1997	1996	1995	1994
Births	679	715	722	726
Deaths	130	119	131	130
Natural Increase	549	596	591	596
Marriages	126	144	113	113

Note: Latest available data.

MEDIA INFO

see Ottawa-Hull, CMA

Nepean
(City)
Ottawa-Hull CMA

In Ottawa-Carleton Regional Municipality.

POPULATION

July 1, 2001 Estimate	123,659
% Cdn. Total	0.40
% Change, '96 -'01	4.28
Avg. Annual Growth Rate, %	0.84
2003 Projected Population	125,951
2006 Projected Population	130,020
2001 Households Estimate	45,041
2003 Projected Households	46,393
2006 Projected Households	48,699

INCOME

% Above/Below National Average	+30
2001 Total Income Estimate	$3,391,240,000
% Cdn. Total	0.52
2001 Average Hhld. Income	$75,300
2001 Per Capita	$27,400
2003 Projected Total Income	$3,652,390,000
2006 Projected Total Income	$4,095,200,000

RETAIL SALES

% Above/Below National Average	+11
2001 Retail Sales Estimate	$1,223,870,000
% Cdn. Total	0.44
2001 per Household	$27,200
2001 per Capita	$9,900
2001 No. of Establishments	640
2003 Projected Retail Sales	$1,334,700,000
2006 Projected Retail Sales	$1,509,200,000

POPULATION

2001 Estimates:		
Total		123,659
Male		60,605
Female		63,054

Age Groups	Male	Female
0-4	4,068	3,859
5-9	4,348	4,074
10-14	4,321	4,084
15-19	4,064	3,887
20-24	4,032	3,922
25-29	4,285	4,177
30-34	4,871	4,851
35-39	5,208	5,338
40-44	4,932	5,288
45-49	4,545	4,986
50-54	3,945	4,341
55-59	3,275	3,577
60-64	2,698	2,912
65-69	2,211	2,412
70+	3,802	5,346

DAYTIME POPULATION

2001 Estimates:	
Working Population	47,779
At Home Population	54,130
Total	101,909

INCOME

2001 Estimates:	
Avg. Household Income	$75,292
Avg. Family Income	$78,948
Per Capita Income	$27,424
Male:	
Avg. Employment Income	$43,533
Avg. Employment Income (Full Time)	$56,119
Female:	
Avg. Employment Income	$27,673
Avg. Employment Income (Full Time)	$40,117

DISPOSABLE & DISCRETIONARY INCOME

2001 Estimates:	Per Hhld.
Disposable Income	$60,736
Discretionary Income 1 (minus Food & Shelter)	$44,355
Discretionary Income 2 (minus Food, Shelter, & Other Expenditures)	$33,952

LIQUID ASSETS

1999 Estimates:	Per Hhld.
Equity Investments	$119,144
Interest Bearing Investments	$95,004
Total Liquid Assets	$214,148

CREDIT DATA

July 2000:	
Pool of Credit	$1,600,593,036
Revolving Credit, No.	290,148
Fixed Loans, No.	70,965
Avg. Credit Limit, per Person	$14,082
Avg. Spent, per Person	$5,694
Satisfactory Ratings, No. per Person	3.06
Avg. No. of Cards, per Person	1.21

LABOUR FORCE

2001 Estimates:	
Male:	
In the Labour Force	37,995
Participation Rate	79.4
Employed	36,313
Unemployed	1,682
Unemployment Rate	4.4
Not in Labour Force	9,873
Female:	
In the Labour Force	34,281
Participation Rate	67.2
Employed	32,737
Unemployed	1,544
Unemployment Rate	4.5
Not in Labour Force	16,756

OCCUPATIONS BY MAJOR GROUPS

2001 Estimates:	Male	Female
Management	6,344	2,902
Business, Finance & Admin.	4,932	10,823
Natural & Applied Sciences & Related	7,679	2,002
Health	760	2,870
Social Sciences, Gov't Services & Religion	1,307	1,233
Education	1,027	2,066
Arts, Culture, Recreation & Sport	1,059	1,171
Sales & Service	7,956	9,309
Trades, Transport & Equipment Operators & Related	4,694	343
Primary Industries	444	99
Processing, Mfg. & Utilities	885	505

LEVEL OF SCHOOLING

2001 Estimates:	
Population 15 years +	98,905
Less than Grade 9	4,153
Grades 9-13 w/o Certif.	15,313
Grade 9-13 with Certif.	12,671
Trade Certif./Dip.	2,324
Non-Univ. w/o Certif./Dip.	6,244
Non-Univ. with Certif./Dip.	18,211
Univ. w/o Degree	12,888
Univ. w/o Degree/Certif.	6,413
Univ. with Certif.	6,475
Univ. with Degree	27,101

Nepean
(City)
Ottawa-Hull CMA
(Cont'd)

AVERAGE HOUSEHOLD EXPENDITURES

2001 Estimates:

Food	$7,617
Shelter	$11,647
Clothing	$2,989
Transportation	$8,067
Health & Personal Care	$2,379
Recr'n, Read'g & Education	$4,984
Taxes & Securities	$21,187
Other	$10,143
Total Expenditures	$69,013

PRIVATE HOUSEHOLDS

2001 Estimates:

Private Households, Total	45,041
Pop. in Private Households	122,059
Average no. per Household	2.7

FAMILIES

2001 Estimates:

Families in Private Households	36,457
Husband-Wife Families	31,381
Lone-Parent Families	5,076
Aver. No. Persons per Family	3.1
Aver. No. Sons/Daughters at Home	1.2

HOUSING

2001 Estimates:

Occupied Private Dwellings	45,041
Owned	31,690
Rented	13,351
Single-Detached House	22,477
Semi-Detached House	2,905
Row Houses	12,076
Apartment, 5+ Storeys	4,594
Owned Apartment, 5+ Storeys	740
Apartment, 5 or Fewer Storeys	2,617
Apartment, Detached Duplex	55
Other Single-Attached	23
Movable Dwellings	294

VEHICLES

2001 Estimates:

Model Yrs. '81-'96, No.	54,533
% Total	75.41
Model Yrs. '97-'98, No.	10,437
% Total	14.43
'99 Vehicles registered in Model Yr. '99, No.	7,345
% Total	10.16
Total No. '81-'99	72,315

LEGAL MARITAL STATUS

2001 Estimates: (Age 15+)

Single (Never Married)	28,663
Legally Married (Not Separated)	56,764
Legally Married (Separated)	2,884
Widowed	4,696
Divorced	5,898

PSYTE CATEGORIES

2001 Estimates	No. of House-holds	% of Total Hhds.	Index
The Affluentials	297	0.66	103
Urban Gentry	3,398	7.54	420
Suburban Executives	4,992	11.08	773
Mortgaged in Suburbia	2,969	6.59	474
Technocrafts & Bureaucrats	10,720	23.80	846
Stable Suburban Families	2,712	6.02	462
Old Bungalow Burbs	1,909	4.24	256
Suburban Nesters	3,891	8.64	539
Aging Erudites	236	0.52	35
Satellite Suburbs	428	0.95	33
Kindergarten Boom	1,969	4.37	167
Blue Collar Winners	339	0.75	30
High Rise Melting Pot	1,498	3.33	222
Conservative Homebodies	1,940	4.31	119

2001 Estimates	No. of House-holds	% of Total Hhds.	Index
High Rise Sunsets	310	0.69	48
Young Urban Professionals	89	0.20	10
Young Urban Mix	2,667	5.92	279
Young Urban Intelligentsia	367	0.81	54
University Enclaves	2,210	4.91	240
Young City Singles	954	2.12	92
Town Renters	928	2.06	238

FINAN¢IAL P$YTE

2001 Estimates	No. of House-holds	% of Total Hhds.	Index
Platinum Estates	297	0.66	82
Four Star Investors	8,390	18.63	371
Successful Suburbanites	16,401	36.41	549
Canadian Comfort	4,658	10.34	106
Urban Heights	325	0.72	17
Miners & Credit-Liners	1,909	4.24	134
Mortgages & Minivans	1,969	4.37	66
Bills & Wills	4,607	10.23	124
Revolving Renters	310	0.69	15
Young Urban Struggle	2,577	5.72	121
Towering Debt	3,380	7.50	96

HOME LANGUAGE

2001 Estimates:		% Total
English	105,516	85.33
French	2,239	1.81
Arabic	1,623	1.31
Bengali	129	0.10
Chinese	2,458	1.99
Czech	174	0.14
Dutch	79	0.06
German	92	0.07
Greek	167	0.14
Gujarati	157	0.13
Hindi	164	0.13
Hungarian	252	0.20
Italian	1,259	1.02
Korean	114	0.09
Persian (Farsi)	367	0.30
Polish	914	0.74
Portuguese	77	0.06
Punjabi	491	0.40
Romanian	98	0.08
Russian	301	0.24
Serbian	182	0.15
Serbo-Croatian	193	0.16
Slovak	126	0.10
Spanish	362	0.29
Tagalog (Pilipino)	262	0.21
Tamil	219	0.18
Turkish	76	0.06
Urdu	252	0.20
Vietnamese	829	0.67
Other Languages	1,335	1.08
Multiple Responses	3,152	2.55
Total	123,659	100.00

BUILDING PERMITS

	1999	1998 $000	1997
Value	195,094	195,617	165,143

HOMES BUILT

	1999	1998	1997
No	743	567	558

TAXATION

Income Class:	1997	% Total
Under $5,000	9,760	11.85
$5,000-$10,000	8,280	10.05
$10,000-$15,000	8,470	10.29
$15,000-$20,000	6,410	7.78
$20,000-$25,000	5,840	7.09
$25,000-$30,000	5,760	6.99
$30,000-$40,000	10,980	13.33
$40,000-$50,000	8,180	9.93
$50,000 +	18,660	22.66
Total Returns, No.	82,350	
Total Income, $000	2,857,569	
Total Taxable Returns	61,710	
Total Tax, $000	606,469	
Average Income, $	34,700	
Average Tax, $	9,828	

VITAL STATISTICS

	1997	1996	1995	1994
Births	1,448	1,427	1,537	1,591
Deaths	551	626	581	558
Natural Increase	897	801	956	1,033
Marriages	401	429	414	427

Note: Latest available data.

MEDIA INFO
see Ottawa-Hull, CMA

Ontario

Ontario

Osgoode
(Township)
Ottawa-Hull CMA

In Ottawa-Carleton Regional Municipality.

POPULATION

July 1, 2001 Estimate	18,055
% Cdn. Total	0.06
% Change, '96 -'01	10.19
Avg. Annual Growth Rate, %	1.96
2003 Projected Population	18,908
2006 Projected Population	20,282
2001 Households Estimate	6,147
2003 Projected Households	6,509
2006 Projected Households	7,103

INCOME

% Above/Below National Average	+28
2001 Total Income Estimate	$485,790,000
% Cdn. Total	0.07
2001 Average Hhld. Income	$79,000
2001 Per Capita	$26,900
2003 Projected Total Income	$544,620,000
2006 Projected Total Income	$646,430,000

RETAIL SALES

% Above/Below National Average	-69
2001 Retail Sales Estimate	$50,630,000
% Cdn. Total	0.02
2001 per Household	$8,200
2001 per Capita	$2,800
2001 No. of Establishments	95
2003 Projected Retail Sales	$55,830,000
2006 Projected Retail Sales	$64,960,000

POPULATION

2001 Estimates:

Total	18,055
Male	9,116
Female	8,939

Age Groups	Male	Female
0-4	597	566
5-9	708	676
10-14	756	713
15-19	715	661
20-24	573	546
25-29	482	474
30-34	605	645
35-39	772	830
40-44	828	838
45-49	789	759
50-54	661	627
55-59	504	466
60-64	363	326
65-69	265	250
70+	498	562

DAYTIME POPULATION

2001 Estimates:

Working Population	3,346
At Home Population	7,493
Total	10,839

INCOME

2001 Estimates:

Avg. Household Income	$79,028
Avg. Family Income	$82,285
Per Capita Income	$26,906

Male:

Avg. Employment Income	$43,636
Avg. Employment Income (Full Time)	$54,028

Female:

Avg. Employment Income	$29,886
Avg. Employment Income (Full Time)	$41,962

DISPOSABLE & DISCRETIONARY INCOME

2001 Estimates:	Per Hhld.
Disposable Income	$63,806
Discretionary Income 1 (minus Food & Shelter)	$46,832
Discretionary Income 2 (minus Food, Shelter, & Other Expenditures)	$34,907

LIQUID ASSETS

1999 Estimates:	Per Hhld.
Equity Investments	$142,298
Interest Bearing Investments	$101,367
Total Liquid Assets	$243,665

CREDIT DATA

July 2000:

Pool of Credit	$214,631,481
Revolving Credit, No.	32,240
Fixed Loans, No.	10,381
Avg. Credit Limit, per Person	$15,426
Avg. Spent, per Person	$7,037
Satisfactory Ratings, No. per Person	2.94
Avg. No. of Cards, per Person	1.10

LABOUR FORCE

2001 Estimates:

Male:

In the Labour Force	5,744
Participation Rate	81.4
Employed	5,618
Unemployed	126
Unemployment Rate	2.2
Not in Labour Force	1,311

Female:

In the Labour Force	4,908
Participation Rate	70.3
Employed	4,788
Unemployed	120
Unemployment Rate	2.4
Not in Labour Force	2,076

OCCUPATIONS BY MAJOR GROUPS

2001 Estimates:	Male	Female
Management	926	395
Business, Finance & Admin.	627	1,847
Natural & Applied Sciences & Related	606	162
Health	121	372
Social Sciences, Gov't Services & Religion	57	120
Education	105	267
Arts, Culture, Recreation & Sport	129	191
Sales & Service	924	1,130
Trades, Transport & Equipment Operators & Related	1,567	151
Primary Industries	444	141
Processing, Mfg. & Utilities	167	59

LEVEL OF SCHOOLING

2001 Estimates:

Population 15 years +	14,039
Less than Grade 9	836
Grades 9-13 w/o Certif.	2,863
Grade 9-13 with Certif.	2,569
Trade Certif. /Dip.	619
Non-Univ. w/o Certif./Dip.	1,015
Non-Univ. with Certif./Dip.	3,043
Univ. w/o Degree	1,303
Univ. w/o Degree/Certif.	639
Univ. with Certif.	664
Univ. with Degree	1,791

AVERAGE HOUSEHOLD EXPENDITURES

2001 Estimates:

Food	$7,735
Shelter	$12,046
Clothing	$2,912
Transportation	$9,613
Health & Personal Care	$2,451
Recr'n, Read'g & Education	$4,989
Taxes & Securities	$21,842
Other	$10,603
Total Expenditures	$72,191

PRIVATE HOUSEHOLDS

2001 Estimates:

Private Households, Total	6,147
Pop. in Private Households	17,887
Average no. per Household	2.9

FAMILIES

2001 Estimates:

Families in Private Households	5,357
Husband-Wife Families	5,001
Lone-Parent Families	356
Aver. No. Persons per Family	3.2
Aver. No. Sons/Daughters at Home	1.3

HOUSING

2001 Estimates:

Occupied Private Dwellings	6,147
Owned	5,430
Rented	717
Single-Detached House	5,695
Semi-Detached House	86
Row Houses	65
Apartment, 5 or Fewer Storeys	129
Apartment, Detached Duplex	41
Other Single-Attached	47
Movable Dwellings	84

VEHICLES

2001 Estimates:

Model Yrs. '81-'96, No.	9,552
% Total	83.21
Model Yrs. '97-'98, No.	1,119
% Total	9.75
'99 Vehicles registered in Model Yr. '99, No.	808
% Total	7.04
Total No. '81-'99	11,479

LEGAL MARITAL STATUS

2001 Estimates: (Age 15+)

Single (Never Married)	3,280
Legally Married (Not Separated)	9,172
Legally Married (Separated)	365
Widowed	572
Divorced	650

PSYTE CATEGORIES

2001 Estimates	No. of House-holds	% of Total Hhds.	Index
Suburban Executives	738	12.01	838
Small City Elite	1,483	24.13	1,408
Blue Collar Winners	3,214	52.29	2,077
Old Towns' New Fringe	452	7.35	188
Old Leafy Towns	260	4.23	165

FINANCIAL P$YTE

2001 Estimates	No. of House-holds	% of Total Hhds.	Index
Four Star Investors	738	12.01	239
Canadian Comfort	4,697	76.41	786
Tractors & Tradelines	452	7.35	129
Bills & Wills	260	4.23	51

HOME LANGUAGE

2001 Estimates:		% Total
English	17,396	96.35
French	330	1.83
Arabic	11	0.06
Chinese	11	0.06
Creoles	12	0.07
Dutch	18	0.10
Italian	64	0.35
Polish	12	0.07
Portuguese	11	0.06
Multiple Responses	190	1.05
Total	18,055	100.00

BUILDING PERMITS

	1999	1998	1997
		$000	
Value	19,862	25,194	17,266

HOMES BUILT

	1999	1998	1997
No	139	98	100

TAXATION

Income Class:	1997	% Total
Under $5,000	1,080	11.91
$5,000-$10,000	840	9.26
$10,000-$15,000	940	10.36
$15,000-$20,000	720	7.94
$20,000-$25,000	650	7.17
$25,000-$30,000	720	7.94
$30,000-$40,000	1,330	14.66
$40,000-$50,000	960	10.58
$50,000 +	1,840	20.29
Total Returns, No.	9,070	
Total Income, $000	297,515	
Total Taxable Returns	6,980	
Total Tax, $000	61,163	
Average Income, $	32,802	
Average Tax, $	8,763	

VITAL STATISTICS

	1997	1996	1995	1994
Births	219	222	251	244
Deaths	87	85	75	77
Natural Increase	132	137	176	167
Marriages	161	124	120	116

Note: Latest available data.

MEDIA INFO
see Ottawa-Hull, CMA

Ottawa
(City)
Ottawa-Hull CMA

In Ottawa-Carleton Regional Municipality.

POPULATION

July 1, 2001 Estimate	336,934
% Cdn. Total	1.08
% Change, '96 -'01	1.14
Avg. Annual Growth Rate, %	0.23
2003 Projected Population	337,575
2006 Projected Population	340,197
2001 Households Estimate	155,862
2003 Projected Households	157,940
2006 Projected Households	161,913

INCOME

% Above/Below National Average	+18
2001 Total Income Estimate	$8,392,430,000
% Cdn. Total	1.28
2001 Average Hhld. Income	$53,800
2001 Per Capita	$24,900
2003 Projected Total Income	$8,761,180,000
2006 Projected Total Income	$9,376,150,000

RETAIL SALES

% Above/Below National Average	+26
2001 Retail Sales Estimate	$3,802,630,000
% Cdn. Total	1.36
2001 per Household	$24,400
2001 per Capita	$11,300
2001 No. of Establishments	2,510
2003 Projected Retail Sales	$4,110,610,000
2006 Projected Retail Sales	$4,572,040,000

POPULATION

2001 Estimates:

Total		336,934
Male		161,860
Female		175,074

Age Groups	Male	Female
0-4	10,593	10,007
5-9	9,686	9,176
10-14	8,998	8,548
15-19	8,687	8,287
20-24	10,268	10,324
25-29	13,117	13,192
30-34	14,884	14,488
35-39	14,555	14,312
40-44	13,277	13,510
45-49	12,090	12,694
50-54	10,215	10,955
55-59	8,085	8,884
60-64	6,696	7,640
65-69	5,917	7,346
70+	14,792	25,711

DAYTIME POPULATION

2001 Estimates:

Working Population	327,730
At Home Population	169,238
Total	496,968

INCOME

2001 Estimates:

Avg. Household Income	$53,845
Avg. Family Income	$65,406
Per Capita Income	$24,908
Male:	
Avg. Employment Income	$36,181
Avg. Employment Income (Full Time)	$50,061
Female:	
Avg. Employment Income	$26,841
Avg. Employment Income (Full Time)	$39,652

DISPOSABLE & DISCRETIONARY INCOME

2001 Estimates:

	Per Hhld.
Disposable Income	$43,715
Discretionary Income 1 (minus Food & Shelter)	$30,419
Discretionary Income 2 (minus Food, Shelter, & Other Expenditures)	$22,803

LIQUID ASSETS

1999 Estimates:

	Per Hhld.
Equity Investments	$73,192
Interest Bearing Investments	$66,343
Total Liquid Assets	$139,535

CREDIT DATA

July 2000:

Pool of Credit	$3,713,345,328
Revolving Credit, No.	739,316
Fixed Loans, No.	161,910
Avg. Credit Limit, per Person	$10,969
Avg. Spent, per Person	$4,468
Satisfactory Ratings, No. per Person	2.57
Avg. No. of Cards, per Person	1.08

LABOUR FORCE

2001 Estimates:

Male:	
In the Labour Force	96,291
Participation Rate	72.6
Employed	88,867
Unemployed	7,424
Unemployment Rate	7.7
Not in Labour Force	36,292
Female:	
In the Labour Force	85,932
Participation Rate	58.3
Employed	80,215
Unemployed	5,717
Unemployment Rate	6.7
Not in Labour Force	61,411

OCCUPATIONS BY MAJOR GROUPS

2001 Estimates:	Male	Female
Management	12,739	8,013
Business, Finance & Admin.	13,943	23,969
Natural & Applied Sciences & Related	13,339	3,840
Health	2,341	6,249
Social Sciences, Gov't Services & Religion	5,075	4,893
Education	3,648	4,954
Arts, Culture, Recreation & Sport	4,407	5,061
Sales & Service	22,573	23,053
Trades, Transport & Equipment Operators & Related	11,154	783
Primary Industries	917	205
Processing, Mfg. & Utilities	1,886	1,091

LEVEL OF SCHOOLING

2001 Estimates:

Population 15 years +	279,926
Less than Grade 9	21,648
Grades 9-13 w/o Certif.	45,939
Grade 9-13 with Certif.	34,659
Trade Certif./Dip.	5,786
Non-Univ. w/o Certif./Dip.	16,744
Non-Univ. with Certif./Dip.	39,488
Univ. w/o Degree	36,871
Univ. w/o Degree/Certif.	20,772
Univ. with Certif.	16,099
Univ. with Degree	78,791

AVERAGE HOUSEHOLD EXPENDITURES

2001 Estimates:

Food	$6,027
Shelter	$9,671
Clothing	$2,227
Transportation	$5,548
Health & Personal Care	$1,946
Recr'n, Read'g & Education	$3,692
Taxes & Securities	$14,210
Other	$8,191
Total Expenditures	$51,512

PRIVATE HOUSEHOLDS

2001 Estimates:

Private Households, Total	155,862
Pop. in Private Households	327,044
Average no. per Household	2.1

FAMILIES

2001 Estimates:

Families in Private Households	86,443
Husband-Wife Families	69,510
Lone-Parent Families	16,933
Aver. No. Persons per Family	2.8
Aver. No. Sons/Daughters at Home	1.0

HOUSING

2001 Estimates:

Occupied Private Dwellings	155,862
Owned	62,639
Rented	93,223
Single-Detached House	42,817
Semi-Detached House	9,010
Row Houses	19,188
Apartment, 5+ Storeys	53,676
Owned Apartment, 5+ Storeys	6,998
Apartment, 5 or Fewer Storeys	25,521
Apartment, Detached Duplex	5,272
Other Single-Attached	378

VEHICLES

2001 Estimates:

Model Yrs. '81-'96, No.	131,216
% Total	74.74
Model Yrs. '97-'98, No.	24,218
% Total	13.80
'99 Vehicles registered in Model Yr. '99, No.	20,118
% Total	11.46
Total No. '81-'99	175,552

LEGAL MARITAL STATUS

2001 Estimates: (Age 15+)

Single (Never Married)	107,084
Legally Married (Not Separated)	117,817
Legally Married (Separated)	11,376
Widowed	20,505
Divorced	23,144

PSYTE CATEGORIES

2001 Estimates	No. of House-holds	% of Total Hhds.	Index
The Affluentials	583	0.37	59
Urban Gentry	15,178	9.74	542
Suburban Executives	1,267	0.81	57
Mortgaged in Suburbia	1,023	0.66	47
Technocrafts & Bureaucrats	5,119	3.28	117
Stable Suburban Families	2,057	1.32	101
Old Bungalow Burbs	730	0.47	28
Suburban Nesters	6,509	4.18	261
Brie & Chablis	3,303	2.12	237
Aging Erudites	11,486	7.37	489
Satellite Suburbs	401	0.26	9
Kindergarten Boom	2,377	1.53	58
Participation Quebec	20	0.01	
High Rise Melting Pot	1,135	0.73	49
Conservative Homebodies	4,481	2.87	80
High Rise Sunsets	10,662	6.84	478
Young Urban Professionals	18,949	12.16	641
Young Urban Mix	4,385	2.81	133
Young Urban Intelligentsia	13,046	8.37	550

Ontario

2001 Estimates	No. of House-holds	% of Total Hhds.	Index
University Enclaves	10,038	6.44	316
Young City Singles	15,276	9.80	427
Urban Bohemia	5,444	3.49	298
Town Renters	3,861	2.48	287
Old Quebec Walkups	1,537	0.99	54
Aging Quebec Urbanites	1,043	0.67	232
Quebec's New Urban Mosaic	425	0.27	11
Struggling Downtowns	2,453	1.57	50
Aged Pensioners	3,332	2.14	161
Big City Stress	5,021	3.22	285
Old Grey Towers	3,301	2.12	382

FINANCIAL PSYTE

2001 Estimates	No. of House-holds	% of Total Hhds.	Index
Platinum Estates	583	0.37	46
Four Star Investors	16,445	10.55	210
Successful Suburbanites	8,199	5.26	79
Canadian Comfort	6,910	4.43	46
Urban Heights	33,738	21.65	503
Miners & Credit-Liners	730	0.47	15
Mortgages & Minivans	2,397	1.54	23
Bills & Wills	8,866	5.69	69
Revolving Renters	10,662	6.84	149
Young Urban Struggle	28,528	18.30	387
Loan Parent Stress	2,580	1.66	28
Towering Debt	22,725	14.58	187
NSF	5,446	3.49	99
Senior Survivors	6,633	4.26	226

HOME LANGUAGE

2001 Estimates:		% Total
English	248,753	73.83
French	33,888	10.06
Arabic	7,321	2.17
Bengali	374	0.11
Bulgarian	186	0.06
Chinese	6,423	1.91
Creoles	329	0.10
Croatian	312	0.09
German	372	0.11
Greek	706	0.21
Hindi	392	0.12
Hungarian	349	0.10
Italian	2,876	0.85
Khmer (Cambodian)	415	0.12
Kurdish	189	0.06
Persian (Farsi)	1,356	0.40
Polish	1,953	0.58
Portuguese	1,022	0.30
Punjabi	368	0.11
Romanian	384	0.11
Russian	960	0.28
Serbian	399	0.12
Serbo-Croatian	496	0.15
Spanish	3,244	0.96
Tagalog (Pilipino)	482	0.14
Tamil	421	0.12
Turkish	303	0.09
Ukrainian	307	0.09
Urdu	404	0.12
Vietnamese	2,683	0.80
Other Languages	7,307	2.17
Multiple Responses	11,960	3.55
Total	336,934	100.00

Ontario

Ottawa
(City)
Ottawa-Hull CMA
(Cont'd)

BUILDING PERMITS

	1999	1998	1997
		$000	
Value	273,443	288,008	192,715

HOMES BUILT

	1999	1998	1997
No.	754	644	712

TAXATION

Income Class:	1997	% Total
Under $5,000	29,180	11.77
$5,000-$10,000	31,000	12.51
$10,000-$15,000	33,390	13.47
$15,000-$20,000	22,140	8.93
$20,000-$25,000	18,380	7.42
$25,000-$30,000	16,920	6.83
$30,000-$40,000	29,370	11.85
$40,000-$50,000	21,270	8.58
$50,000 +	46,230	18.65
Total Returns, No.	247,870	
Total Income, $000	7,842,922	
Total Taxable Returns	170,660	
Total Tax, $000	1,611,034	
Average Income, $	31,641	
Average Tax, $	9,440	

VITAL STATISTICS

	1997	1996	1995	1994
Births	3,711	3,913	4,327	4,124
Deaths	2,778	2,772	2,776	2,838
Natural Increase	933	1,141	1,551	1,286
Marriages	2,544	2,782	2,980	2,932

Note: Latest available data.

MEDIA INFO
see Ottawa-Hull, CMA

Rideau
(Township)
Ottawa-Hull CMA

In Ottawa-Carleton Regional Municipality.

POPULATION

July 1, 2001 Estimate	13,250
% Cdn. Total	0.04
% Change, '96 -'01	3.35
Avg. Annual Growth Rate, %	0.66
2003 Projected Population	13,419
2006 Projected Population	13,739
2001 Households Estimate	4,568
2003 Projected Households	4,679
2006 Projected Households	4,873

INCOME

% Above/Below National Average	+53
2001 Total Income Estimate	$428,410,000
% Cdn. Total	0.07
2001 Average Hhld. Income	$93,800
2001 Per Capita	$32,300
2003 Projected Total Income	$460,510,000
2006 Projected Total Income	$514,740,000

RETAIL SALES

% Above/Below National Average	+73
2001 Retail Sales Estimate	$204,710,000
% Cdn. Total	0.07
2001 per Household	$44,800
2001 per Capita	$15,400
2001 No. of Establishments	106
2003 Projected Retail Sales	$225,840,000
2006 Projected Retail Sales	$258,800,000

POPULATION

2001 Estimates:

Total		13,250
Male		6,641
Female		6,609

Age Groups	Male	Female
0-4	363	352
5-9	425	449
10-14	490	497
15-19	517	506
20-24	484	429
25-29	407	344
30-34	386	358
35-39	441	461
40-44	510	565
45-49	599	617
50-54	578	562
55-59	451	425
60-64	329	297
65-69	237	221
70+	424	526

DAYTIME POPULATION

2001 Estimates:

Working Population	3,054
At Home Population	5,259
Total	8,313

INCOME

2001 Estimates:

Avg. Household Income	$93,785
Avg. Family Income	$97,331
Per Capita Income	$32,333
Male:	
Avg. Employment Income	$52,688
Avg. Employment Income (Full Time)	$69,314
Female:	
Avg. Employment Income	$30,646
Avg. Employment Income (Full Time)	$43,691

DISPOSABLE & DISCRETIONARY INCOME

2001 Estimates:	Per Hhld.
Disposable Income	$74,871
Discretionary Income 1 (minus Food & Shelter)	$56,428
Discretionary Income 2 (minus Food, Shelter, & Other Expenditures)	$43,403

LIQUID ASSETS

1999 Estimates:	Per Hhld.
Equity Investments	$197,167
Interest Bearing Investments	$124,964
Total Liquid Assets	$322,131

CREDIT DATA

July 2000:

Pool of Credit	$157,780,915
Revolving Credit, No.	23,748
Fixed Loans, No.	6,426
Avg. Credit Limit, per Person	$16,051
Avg. Spent, per Person	$6,810
Satisfactory Ratings, No. per Person	2.97
Avg. No. of Cards, per Person	1.19

LABOUR FORCE

2001 Estimates:

Male:	
In the Labour Force	4,313
Participation Rate	80.4
Employed	4,268
Unemployed	45
Unemployment Rate	1.0
Not in Labour Force	1,050
Female:	
In the Labour Force	3,696
Participation Rate	69.6
Employed	3,646
Unemployed	50
Unemployment Rate	1.4
Not in Labour Force	1,615

OCCUPATIONS BY MAJOR GROUPS

2001 Estimates:	Male	Female
Management	934	400
Business, Finance & Admin.	434	1,100
Natural & Applied Sciences & Related	542	107
Health	69	273
Social Sciences, Gov't Services & Religion	164	96
Education	147	307
Arts, Culture, Recreation & Sport	64	109
Sales & Service	639	992
Trades, Transport & Equipment Operators & Related	801	86
Primary Industries	379	116
Processing, Mfg. & Utilities	107	75

LEVEL OF SCHOOLING

2001 Estimates:

Population 15 years +	10,674
Less than Grade 9	480
Grades 9-13 w/o Certif.	1,814
Grade 9-13 with Certif.	1,419
Trade Certif. /Dip.	335
Non-Univ. w/o Certif./Dip.	670
Non-Univ. with Certif./Dip.	2,314
Univ. w/o Degree	1,317
Univ. w/o Degree/Certif.	654
Univ. with Certif.	663
Univ. with Degree	2,325

AVERAGE HOUSEHOLD EXPENDITURES

2001 Estimates:

Food	$8,538
Shelter	$13,293
Clothing	$3,438
Transportation	$10,444
Health & Personal Care	$2,766
Recr'n, Read'g & Education	$5,776
Taxes & Securities	$27,540
Other	$11,961
Total Expenditures	$83,756

PRIVATE HOUSEHOLDS

2001 Estimates:

Private Households, Total	4,568
Pop. in Private Households	13,045
Average no. per Household	2.9

FAMILIES

2001 Estimates:

Families in Private Households	3,992
Husband-Wife Families	3,680
Lone-Parent Families	312
Aver. No. Persons per Family	3.2
Aver. No. Sons/Daughters at Home	1.2

HOUSING

2001 Estimates:

Occupied Private Dwellings	4,568
Owned	4,077
Rented	491
Single-Detached House	4,390
Semi-Detached House	22
Row Houses	22
Apartment, 5 or Fewer Storeys	101
Apartment, Detached Duplex	22
Other Single-Attached	11

VEHICLES

2001 Estimates:

Model Yrs. '81-'96, No.	8,208
% Total	78.65
Model Yrs. '97-'98, No.	1,371
% Total	13.14
'99 Vehicles registered in Model Yr. '99, No.	857
% Total	8.21
Total No. '81-'99	10,436

LEGAL MARITAL STATUS

2001 Estimates: (Age 15+)

Single (Never Married)	2,714
Legally Married (Not Separated)	6,850
Legally Married (Separated)	249
Widowed	422
Divorced	439

PSYTE CATEGORIES

2001 Estimates	No. of House -holds	% of Total Hhds.	Index
Suburban Executives	1,460	31.96	2,230
Boomers & Teens	574	12.57	701
Stable Suburban Families	378	8.27	635
Small City Elite	809	17.71	1,033
Blue Collar Winners	1,315	28.79	1,143

FINANCIAL P$YTE

2001 Estimates	No. of House -holds	% of Total Hhds.	Index
Four Star Investors	2,034	44.53	886
Successful Suburbanites	378	8.27	125
Canadian Comfort	2,124	46.50	479

Rideau
(Township)
Ottawa-Hull CMA
(Cont'd)

HOME LANGUAGE

2001 Estimates:		% Total
English	12,882	97.22
French	134	1.01
Danish	11	0.08
German	32	0.24
Gujarati	10	0.08
Italian	37	0.28
Latvian (Lettish)	10	0.08
Russian	16	0.12
Tagalog (Pilipino)	32	0.24
Ukrainian	11	0.08
Multiple Responses	75	0.57
Total	13,250	100.00

BUILDING PERMITS

	1999	1998	1997
		$000	
Value	9,325	9,535	15,034

HOMES BUILT

	1999	1998	1997
No	37	47	34

TAXATION

Income Class:	1997	% Total
Under $5,000	1,010	10.52
$5,000-$10,000	900	9.38
$10,000-$15,000	900	9.38
$15,000-$20,000	720	7.50
$20,000-$25,000	620	6.46
$25,000-$30,000	590	6.15
$30,000-$40,000	1,160	12.08
$40,000-$50,000	970	10.10
$50,000 +	2,740	28.54
Total Returns, No.	9,600	
Total Income, $000	397,395	
Total Taxable Returns	7,520	
Total Tax, $000	94,203	
Average Income, $	41,395	
Average Tax, $	12,527	

VITAL STATISTICS

	1997	1996	1995	1994
Births	78	57	92	83
Deaths	25	27	24	23
Natural Increase	53	30	68	60
Marriages	125	125	109	106

Note: Latest available data.

MEDIA INFO
see Ottawa-Hull, CMA

Russell
(Township)
Ottawa-Hull CMA

In Prescott and Russell United Counties.

POPULATION

July 1, 2001 Estimate	12,946
% Cdn. Total	0.04
% Change, '96 -'01	5.98
Avg. Annual Growth Rate, %	1.17
2003 Projected Population	13,439
2006 Projected Population	14,211
2001 Households Estimate	4,269
2003 Projected Households	4,476
2006 Projected Households	4,821

INCOME

% Above/Below National Average	+9
2001 Total Income Estimate	$296,340,000
% Cdn. Total	0.05
2001 Average Hhld. Income	$69,400
2001 Per Capita	$22,900
2003 Projected Total Income	$326,190,000
2006 Projected Total Income	$378,320,000

RETAIL SALES

% Above/Below National Average	-17
2001 Retail Sales Estimate	$95,910,000
% Cdn. Total	0.03
2001 per Household	$22,500
2001 per Capita	$7,400
2001 No. of Establishments	109
2003 Projected Retail Sales	$106,590,000
2006 Projected Retail Sales	$122,860,000

POPULATION

2001 Estimates:		
Total		12,946
Male		6,496
Female		6,450

Age Groups	Male	Female
0-4	445	426
5-9	557	510
10-14	598	572
15-19	544	531
20-24	417	409
25-29	343	368
30-34	454	482
35-39	599	630
40-44	641	657
45-49	574	530
50-54	432	374
55-59	288	253
60-64	196	185
65-69	136	156
70+	272	367

DAYTIME POPULATION

2001 Estimates:	
Working Population	2,601
At Home Population	5,485
Total	8,086

INCOME

2001 Estimates:	
Avg. Household Income	$69,417
Avg. Family Income	$73,821
Per Capita Income	$22,891
Male:	
Avg. Employment Income	$40,562
Avg. Employment Income (Full Time)	$48,255
Female:	
Avg. Employment Income	$28,244
Avg. Employment Income (Full Time)	$36,905

DISPOSABLE & DISCRETIONARY INCOME

2001 Estimates:	Per Hhld.
Disposable Income	$56,476
Discretionary Income 1 (minus Food & Shelter)	$41,713
Discretionary Income 2 (minus Food, Shelter, & Other Expenditures)	$31,040

LIQUID ASSETS

1999 Estimates:	Per Hhld.
Equity Investments	$91,897
Interest Bearing Investments	$83,385
Total Liquid Assets	$175,282

CREDIT DATA

July 2000:	
Pool of Credit	$132,842,009
Revolving Credit, No.	20,669
Fixed Loans, No.	7,431
Avg. Credit Limit, per Person	$14,099
Avg. Spent, per Person	$6,634
Satisfactory Ratings, No. per Person	2.82
Avg. No. of Cards, per Person	1.05

LABOUR FORCE

2001 Estimates:	
Male:	
In the Labour Force	4,020
Participation Rate	82.1
Employed	3,959
Unemployed	61
Unemployment Rate	1.5
Not in Labour Force	876
Female:	
In the Labour Force	3,473
Participation Rate	70.3
Employed	3,369
Unemployed	104
Unemployment Rate	3.0
Not in Labour Force	1,469

OCCUPATIONS BY MAJOR GROUPS

2001 Estimates:	Male	Female
Management	680	245
Business, Finance & Admin.	549	1,220
Natural & Applied Sciences & Related	361	113
Health	41	331
Social Sciences, Gov't Services & Religion	51	88
Education	77	254
Arts, Culture, Recreation & Sport	109	137
Sales & Service	714	780
Trades, Transport & Equipment Operators & Related	1,066	65
Primary Industries	233	92
Processing, Mfg. & Utilities	86	56

LEVEL OF SCHOOLING

2001 Estimates:	
Population 15 years +	9,838
Less than Grade 9	739
Grades 9-13 w/o Certif.	1,996
Grade 9-13 with Certif.	1,859
Trade Certif. /Dip.	220
Non-Univ. w/o Certif./Dip.	770
Non-Univ. with Certif./Dip.	2,085
Univ. w/o Degree:	898
Univ. w/o Degree/Certif.	416
Univ. with Certif.	482
Univ. with Degree	1,271

Ontario

AVERAGE HOUSEHOLD EXPENDITURES

2001 Estimates:	
Food	$7,645
Shelter	$9,728
Clothing	$2,854
Transportation	$8,410
Health & Personal Care	$2,489
Recr'n, Read'g & Education	$4,614
Taxes & Securities	$19,356
Other	$9,457
Total Expenditures	$64,553

PRIVATE HOUSEHOLDS

2001 Estimates:	
Private Households, Total	4,269
Pop. in Private Households	12,684
Average no. per Household	3.0

FAMILIES

2001 Estimates:	
Families in Private Households	3,629
Husband-Wife Families	3,381
Lone-Parent Families	248
Aver. No. Persons per Family	3.3
Aver. No. Sons/Daughters at Home	1.4

HOUSING

2001 Estimates:	
Occupied Private Dwellings	4,269
Owned	3,639
Rented	630
Single-Detached House	3,767
Semi-Detached House	51
Row Houses	89
Apartment, 5 or Fewer Storeys	293
Apartment, Detached Duplex	46
Movable Dwellings	23

VEHICLES

2001 Estimates:	
Model Yrs. '81-'96, No.	6,155
% Total	81.48
Model Yrs. '97-'98, No.	861
% Total	11.40
'99 Vehicles registered in Model Yr. '99, No.	538
% Total	7.12
Total No. '81-'99	7,554

LEGAL MARITAL STATUS

2001 Estimates: (Age 15+)	
Single (Never Married)	2,411
Legally Married (Not Separated)	6,231
Legally Married (Separated)	283
Widowed	433
Divorced	480

PSYTE CATEGORIES

2001 Estimates	No. of House-holds	% of Total Hhds.	Index
Boomers & Teens	74	1.73	97
Small City Elite	1,424	33.36	1,947
Blue Collar Winners	369	8.64	343
Old Towns' New Fringe	138	3.23	83
Participation Quebec	2,217	51.93	1,802

Ontario

Russell
(Township)
Ottawa-Hull CMA
(Cont'd)

FINANCIAL P$YTE

2001 Estimates	No. of House-holds	% of Total Hhds.	Index
Four Star Investors	74	1.73	35
Canadian Comfort	1,793	42.00	432
Mortgages & Minivans	2,217	51.93	787
Tractors & Tradelines	138	3.23	57

HOME LANGUAGE

2001 Estimates:		% Total
English	7,607	58.76
French	5,052	39.02
Arabic	22	0.17
Dutch	22	0.17
German	11	0.08
Multiple Responses	232	1.79
Total	12,946	100.00

BUILDING PERMITS

	1999	1998 $000	1997
Value	13,716	6,350	n.a.

HOMES BUILT

	1999	1998	1997
No.	43	18	n.a.

TAXATION

Income Class:	1997	% Total
Under $5,000	950	11.96
$5,000-$10,000	820	10.33
$10,000-$15,000	880	11.08
$15,000-$20,000	590	7.43
$20,000-$25,000	540	6.80
$25,000-$30,000	620	7.81
$30,000-$40,000	1,250	15.74
$40,000-$50,000	930	11.71
$50,000 +	1,350	17.00
Total Returns, No.	7,940	
Total Income, $000	235,439	
Total Taxable Returns	5,920	
Total Tax, $000	43,877	
Average Income, $	29,652	
Average Tax, $	7,412	

VITAL STATISTICS

	1997	1996	1995	1994
Births	147	143	148	179
Deaths	62	49	57	72
Natural Increase	85	94	91	107
Marriages	27	41	42	52

Note: Latest available data.

MEDIA INFO
see Ottawa-Hull, CMA

Vanier
(City)
Ottawa-Hull CMA

In Ottawa-Carleton Regional Municipality.

POPULATION

July 1, 2001 Estimate	16,855
% Cdn. Total	0.05
% Change, '96 -'01	-5.13
Avg. Annual Growth Rate, %	-1.05
2003 Projected Population	16,365
2006 Projected Population	15,710
2001 Households Estimate	8,683
2003 Projected Households	8,531
2006 Projected Households	8,328

INCOME

% Above/Below National Average	-9
2001 Total Income Estimate	$322,810,000
% Cdn. Total	0.05
2001 Average Hhld. Income	$37,200
2001 Per Capita	$19,200
2003 Projected Total Income	$325,540,000
2006 Projected Total Income	$329,960,000

RETAIL SALES

% Above/Below National Average	+98
2001 Retail Sales Estimate	$299,250,000
% Cdn. Total	0.11
2001 per Household	$34,500
2001 per Capita	$17,800
2001 No. of Establishments	106
2003 Projected Retail Sales	$312,610,000
2006 Projected Retail Sales	$331,660,000

POPULATION

2001 Estimates:

Total		16,855
Male		8,068
Female		8,787

Age Groups	Male	Female
0-4	535	505
5-9	442	429
10-14	345	340
15-19	340	354
20-24	485	515
25-29	645	664
30-34	756	723
35-39	780	739
40-44	705	678
45-49	634	620
50-54	546	564
55-59	469	510
60-64	379	442
65-69	323	421
70+	684	1,283

DAYTIME POPULATION

2001 Estimates:

Working Population	8,068
At Home Population	9,201
Total	17,269

INCOME

2001 Estimates:

Avg. Household Income	$37,177
Avg. Family Income	$43,796
Per Capita Income	$19,152
Male:	
Avg. Employment Income	$26,393
Avg. Employment Income (Full Time)	$36,533
Female:	
Avg. Employment Income	$22,980
Avg. Employment Income (Full Time)	$32,964

DISPOSABLE & DISCRETIONARY INCOME

2001 Estimates:	Per Hhld.
Disposable Income	$30,880
Discretionary Income 1 (minus Food & Shelter)	$19,720
Discretionary Income 2 (minus Food, Shelter, & Other Expenditures)	$14,227

LIQUID ASSETS

1999 Estimates:	Per Hhld.
Equity Investments	$38,357
Interest Bearing Investments	$43,628
Total Liquid Assets	$81,985

CREDIT DATA

July 2000:	
Pool of Credit	$131,374,804
Revolving Credit, No.	29,314
Fixed Loans, No.	8,086
Avg. Credit Limit, per Person	$7,617
Avg. Spent, per Person	$3,455
Satisfactory Ratings, No. per Person	2.07
Avg. No. of Cards, per Person	0.79

LABOUR FORCE

2001 Estimates:

Male:	
In the Labour Force	4,519
Participation Rate	67.0
Employed	3,974
Unemployed	545
Unemployment Rate	12.1
Not in Labour Force	2,227
Female:	
In the Labour Force	4,030
Participation Rate	53.6
Employed	3,634
Unemployed	396
Unemployment Rate	9.8
Not in Labour Force	3,483

OCCUPATIONS BY MAJOR GROUPS

2001 Estimates:	Male	Female
Management	366	340
Business, Finance & Admin.	661	1,330
Natural & Applied Sciences & Related	394	108
Health	63	285
Social Sciences, Gov't Services & Religion	83	145
Education	142	156
Arts, Culture, Recreation & Sport.	150	109
Sales & Service	1,097	1,221
Trades, Transport & Equipment Operators & Related	1,080	21
Primary Industries	50	n.a.
Processing, Mfg. & Utilities	108	30

LEVEL OF SCHOOLING

2001 Estimates:

Population 15 years +	14,259
Less than Grade 9	2,241
Grades 9-13 w/o Certif.	3,136
Grade 9-13 with Certif.	2,224
Trade Certif. /Dip.	320
Non-Univ. w/o Certif./Dip.	1,077
Non-Univ. with Certif./Dip.	2,041
Univ. w/o Degree	1,316
Univ. w/o Degree/Certif.	701
Univ. with Certif.	615
Univ. with Degree	1,904

AVERAGE HOUSEHOLD EXPENDITURES

2001 Estimates:

Food	$5,200
Shelter	$7,731
Clothing	$1,708
Transportation	$3,672
Health & Personal Care	$1,565
Recr'n, Read'g & Education	$2,574
Taxes & Securities	$8,789
Other	$6,532
Total Expenditures	$37,771

PRIVATE HOUSEHOLDS

2001 Estimates:

Private Households, Total	8,683
Pop. in Private Households	16,373
Average no. per Household	1.9

FAMILIES

2001 Estimates:

Families in Private Households	4,455
Husband-Wife Families	3,204
Lone-Parent Families	1,251
Aver. No. Persons per Family	2.5
Aver. No. Sons/Daughters at Home	0.9

HOUSING

2001 Estimates:

Occupied Private Dwellings	8,683
Owned	2,815
Rented	5,868
Single-Detached House	1,311
Semi-Detached House	161
Row Houses	340
Apartment, 5+ Storeys	1,667
Owned Apartment, 5+ Storeys	660
Apartment, 5 or Fewer Storeys	3,979
Apartment, Detached Duplex	1,178
Other Single-Attached	47

VEHICLES

2001 Estimates:

Model Yrs. '81-'96, No.	6,329
% Total	83.27
Model Yrs. '97-'98, No.	752
% Total	9.89
'99 Vehicles registered in Model Yr. '99, No.	520
% Total	6.84
Total No. '81-'99	7,601

LEGAL MARITAL STATUS

2001 Estimates: (Age 15+)

Single (Never Married)	6,132
Legally Married (Not Separated)	4,565
Legally Married (Separated)	776
Widowed	1,170
Divorced	1,616

PSYTE CATEGORIES

2001 Estimates	No. of House-holds	% of Total Hhds.	Index
Aging Erudites	200	2.30	153
High Rise Sunsets	658	7.58	530
University Enclaves	1,914	22.04	1,080
Young City Singles	337	3.88	169
Urban Bohemia	347	4.00	341
Old Quebec Walkups	1,061	12.22	667
Aging Quebec Urbanites	327	3.77	1,305
Quebec's New Urban Mosaic	2,450	28.22	1,171
Struggling Downtowns	67	0.77	25
Big City Stress	1,021	11.76	1,041
Old Grey Towers	184	2.12	383

Vanier
(City)
Ottawa-Hull CMA
(Cont'd)

FINANCIAL P$YTE

2001 Estimates	No. of House-holds	% of Total Hhds.	Index
Urban Heights	200	2.30	54
Revolving Renters	658	7.58	165
Young Urban Struggle	2,261	26.04	550
Loan Parent Stress.	1,388	15.99	274
Towering Debt	404	4.65	60
NSF	3,471	39.97	1,130
Senior Survivors	184	2.12	112

HOME LANGUAGE

2001 Estimates:		% Total
English	7,504	44.52
French	7,347	43.59
Arabic	256	1.52
Bulgarian	51	0.30
Chinese	163	0.97
Creoles	100	0.59
Croatian	10	0.06
Finnish	10	0.06
Inuktitut (Eskimo)	10	0.06
Khmer (Cambodian)	29	0.17
Lao	10	0.06
Macedonian	19	0.11
Persian (Farsi)	10	0.06
Polish	71	0.42
Portuguese	291	1.73
Russian	15	0.09
Serbo-Croatian	20	0.12
Spanish	202	1.20
Tagalog (Pilipino)	50	0.30
Turkish	25	0.15
Vietnamese	26	0.15
Other Languages	20	0.12
Multiple Responses	616	3.65
Total	16,855	100.00

BUILDING PERMITS

	1999	1998 $000	1997
Value	5,152	1,862	1,774

TAXATION

Income Class:	1997	% Total
Under $5,000	1,390	10.99
$5,000-$10,000	2,060	16.28
$10,000-$15,000	2,580	20.40
$15,000-$20,000	1,360	10.75
$20,000-$25,000	1,090	8.62
$25,000-$30,000	910	7.19
$30,000-$40,000	1,570	12.41
$40,000-$50,000	800	6.32
$50,000 +	900	7.11
Total Returns, No.	12,650	
Total Income, $000	277,687	
Total Taxable Returns	7,500	
Total Tax, $000	42,513	
Average Income, $	21,952	
Average Tax, $	5,668	

VITAL STATISTICS

	1997	1996	1995	1994
Births	169	187	237	239
Deaths	133	124	127	169
Natural Increase	36	63	110	70
Marriages	67	56	59	82

Note: Latest available data.

MEDIA INFO
see Ottawa-Hull, CMA

West Carleton
(Township)
Ottawa-Hull CMA

In Ottawa-Carleton Regional Municipality.

POPULATION

July 1, 2001 Estimate	18,648
% Cdn. Total	0.06
% Change, '96 -'01	9.42
Avg. Annual Growth Rate, %	1.82
2003 Projected Population	19,462
2006 Projected Population	20,771
2001 Households Estimate	6,581
2003 Projected Households	6,948
2006 Projected Households	7,543

INCOME

% Above/Below National Average	+29
2001 Total Income Estimate	$505,640,000
% Cdn. Total	0.08
2001 Average Hhld. Income	$76,800
2001 Per Capita	$27,100
2003 Projected Total Income	$563,070,000
2006 Projected Total Income	$660,990,000

RETAIL SALES

% Above/Below National Average	-21
2001 Retail Sales Estimate	$132,010,000
% Cdn. Total	0.05
2001 per Household	$20,100
2001 per Capita	$7,100
2001 No. of Establishments	109
2003 Projected Retail Sales	$147,880,000
2006 Projected Retail Sales	$174,510,000

POPULATION

2001 Estimates:		
Total		18,648
Male		9,442
Female		9,206

Age Groups	Male	Female
0-4	574	564
5-9	695	682
10-14	755	712
15-19	705	657
20-24	590	554
25-29	513	492
30-34	592	635
35-39	761	817
40-44	853	869
45-49	833	841
50-54	734	690
55-59	590	509
60-64	422	374
65-69	311	285
70+	514	525

DAYTIME POPULATION

2001 Estimates:	
Working Population	3,865
At Home Population	7,457
Total	11,322

INCOME

2001 Estimates:	
Avg. Household Income	$76,834
Avg. Family Income	$81,048
Per Capita Income	$27,115
Male:	
Avg. Employment Income	$42,649
Avg. Employment Income (Full Time)	$54,281
Female:	
Avg. Employment Income	$27,500
Avg. Employment Income (Full Time)	$38,181

DISPOSABLE & DISCRETIONARY INCOME

2001 Estimates:	Per Hhld.
Disposable Income	$62,238
Discretionary Income 1 (minus Food & Shelter)	$45,741
Discretionary Income 2 (minus Food, Shelter, & Other Expenditures)	$34,050

LIQUID ASSETS

1999 Estimates:	Per Hhld.
Equity Investments	$117,878
Interest Bearing Investments	$93,715
Total Liquid Assets	$211,593

CREDIT DATA

July 2000:	
Pool of Credit	$243,834,984
Revolving Credit, No.	37,118
Fixed Loans, No.	11,126
Avg. Credit Limit, per Person	$15,245
Avg. Spent, per Person	$6,725
Satisfactory Ratings, No. per Person	2.91
Avg. No. of Cards, per Person	1.10

LABOUR FORCE

2001 Estimates:	
Male:	
In the Labour Force	6,157
Participation Rate	83.0
Employed	6,021
Unemployed	136
Unemployment Rate	2.2
Not in Labour Force	1,261
Female:	
In the Labour Force	5,152
Participation Rate	71.1
Employed	5,025
Unemployed	127
Unemployment Rate	2.5
Not in Labour Force	2,096

OCCUPATIONS BY MAJOR GROUPS

2001 Estimates:	Male	Female
Management	1,029	577
Business, Finance & Admin.	399	1,549
Natural & Applied Sciences & Related	963	247
Health	81	350
Social Sciences, Gov't Services & Religion	83	136
Education	170	193
Arts, Culture, Recreation & Sport	143	196
Sales & Service	1,049	1,287
Trades, Transport & Equipment Operators & Related	1,476	168
Primary Industries	447	222
Processing, Mfg. & Utilities	228	126

LEVEL OF SCHOOLING

2001 Estimates:	
Population 15 years +	14,666
Less than Grade 9	704
Grades 9-13 w/o Certif.	2,913
Grade 9-13 with Certif.	2,208
Trade Certif. /Dip.	608
Non-Univ. w/o Certif./Dip.	873
Non-Univ. with Certif./Dip.	3,177
Univ. w/o Degree	1,462
Univ. w/o Degree/Certif.	698
Univ. with Certif.	764
Univ. with Degree	2,721

AVERAGE HOUSEHOLD EXPENDITURES

2001 Estimates:	
Food	$7,526
Shelter	$11,667
Clothing	$2,799
Transportation	$9,393
Health & Personal Care	$2,399
Recr'n, Read'g & Education	$4,909
Taxes & Securities	$21,084
Other	$10,837
Total Expenditures	$70,614

Ontario

PRIVATE HOUSEHOLDS

2001 Estimates:	
Private Households, Total	6,581
Pop. in Private Households	18,572
Average no. per Household	2.8

FAMILIES

2001 Estimates:	
Families in Private Households	5,679
Husband-Wife Families	5,308
Lone-Parent Families	371
Aver. No. Persons per Family	3.2
Aver. No. Sons/Daughters at Home	1.2

HOUSING

2001 Estimates:	
Occupied Private Dwellings	6,581
Owned	5,840
Rented	741
Single-Detached House	6,299
Semi-Detached House	35
Row Houses	30
Apartment, 5 or Fewer Storeys	87
Apartment, Detached Duplex	70
Movable Dwellings	60

VEHICLES

2001 Estimates:	
Model Yrs. '81-'96, No.	11,058
% Total	83.86
Model Yrs. '97-'98, No.	1,291
% Total	9.79
'99 Vehicles registered in Model Yr. '99, No.	837
% Total	6.35
Total No. '81-'99	13,186

LEGAL MARITAL STATUS

2001 Estimates: (Age 15+)	
Single (Never Married)	3,506
Legally Married (Not Separated)	9,415
Legally Married (Separated)	425
Widowed	502
Divorced	818

PSYTE CATEGORIES

2001 Estimates	No. of House-holds	% of Total Hhds.	Index
Suburban Executives	184	2.80	195
Boomers & Teens	1,191	18.10	1,010
Small City Elite	1,348	20.48	1,195
Blue Collar Winners	2,672	40.60	1,613
Old Towns' New Fringe	861	13.08	334
Rustic Prosperity	325	4.94	274

FINANCIAL P$YTE

2001 Estimates	No. of House-holds	% of Total Hhds.	Index
Four Star Investors	1,375	20.89	416
Canadian Comfort	4,020	61.08	629
Tractors & Tradelines	1,186	18.02	315

Ontario

West Carleton
(Township)
Ottawa-Hull CMA
(Cont'd)

HOME LANGUAGE

2001 Estimates:		% Total
English	18,026	96.66
French	295	1.58
Chinese	11	0.06
Croatian	11	0.06
Czech	11	0.06
German	68	0.36
Greek	11	0.06
Hungarian	11	0.06
Italian	11	0.06
Portuguese	23	0.12
Urdu	11	0.06
Other Languages	11	0.06
Multiple Responses	148	0.79
Total	18,648	100.00

BUILDING PERMITS

	1999	1998	1997
		$000	
Value	22,375	16,038	17,414

HOMES BUILT

	1999	1998	1997
No.	107	64	56

TAXATION

Income Class:	1997	% Total
Under $5,000	1,220	11.42
$5,000-$10,000	1,020	9.55
$10,000-$15,000	950	8.90
$15,000-$20,000	810	7.58
$20,000-$25,000	730	6.84
$25,000-$30,000	730	6.84
$30,000-$40,000	1,520	14.23
$40,000-$50,000	1,090	10.21
$50,000 +	2,630	24.63
Total Returns, No.	10,680	
Total Income, $000	403,234	
Total Taxable Returns	8,320	
Total Tax, $000	89,881	
Average Income, $	37,756	
Average Tax, $	10,803	

VITAL STATISTICS

	1997	1996	1995	1994
Births	292	309	458	424
Deaths	89	82	133	107
Natural Increase	203	227	325	317
Marriages	75	75	76	70

Note: Latest available data.

MEDIA INFO
see Ottawa-Hull, CMA

Owen Sound
(Census Agglomeration)

The Census Agglomeration of Owen Sound includes: Owen Sound, C; Derby, TP; Sarawak, TP; and Sydenham, TP. All are in Grey County.

POPULATION

July 1, 2001 Estimate	30,526
% Cdn. Total	0.10
% Change, '96 -'01	-1.86
Avg. Annual Growth Rate, %	-0.37
2003 Projected Population	30,201
2006 Projected Population	29,563
2001 Households Estimate	12,677
2003 Projected Households	12,648
2006 Projected Households	12,561

INCOME

% Above/Below National Average	-11
2001 Total Income Estimate	$575,850,000
% Cdn. Total	0.09
2001 Average Hhld. Income	$45,400
2001 Per Capita	$18,900
2003 Projected Total Income	$596,240,000
2006 Projected Total Income	$626,340,000

RETAIL SALES

% Above/Below National Average	+61
2001 Retail Sales Estimate	$439,440,000
% Cdn. Total	0.16
2001 per Household	$34,700
2001 per Capita	$14,400
2001 No. of Establishments	334
2003 Projected Retail Sales	$467,770,000
2006 Projected Retail Sales	$503,860,000

POPULATION

2001 Estimates:		
Total		30,526
Male		14,599
Female		15,927

Age Groups	Male	Female
0-4	867	807
5-9	972	908
10-14	1,056	1,019
15-19	1,072	1,057
20-24	987	1,010
25-29	844	903
30-34	860	911
35-39	1,019	1,082
40-44	1,127	1,208
45-49	1,130	1,200
50-54	986	1,044
55-59	791	835
60-64	664	722
65-69	610	728
70+	1,614	2,493

DAYTIME POPULATION

2001 Estimates:	
Working Population	14,793
At Home Population	15,734
Total	30,527

INCOME

2001 Estimates:	
Avg. Household Income	$45,425
Avg. Family Income	$52,928
Per Capita Income	$18,864
Male:	
Avg. Employment Income	$29,198
Avg. Employment Income (Full Time)	$38,616
Female:	
Avg. Employment Income	$19,072
Avg. Employment Income (Full Time)	$28,914

DISPOSABLE & DISCRETIONARY INCOME

2001 Estimates:	Per Hhld.
Disposable Income	$37,556
Discretionary Income 1 (minus Food & Shelter)	$25,629
Discretionary Income 2 (minus Food, Shelter, & Other Expenditures)	$18,081

LIQUID ASSETS

1999 Estimates:	Per Hhld.
Equity Investments	$60,363
Interest Bearing Investments	$57,033
Total Liquid Assets	$117,396

CREDIT DATA

July 2000:	
Pool of Credit	$291,519,108
Revolving Credit, No.	53,695
Fixed Loans, No.	17,276
Avg. Credit Limit, per Person	$11,326
Avg. Spent, per Person	$5,011
Satisfactory Ratings, No. per Person	2.61
Avg. No. of Cards, per Person	0.92

LABOUR FORCE

2001 Estimates:	
Male:	
In the Labour Force	8,225
Participation Rate	70.3
Employed	7,805
Unemployed	420
Unemployment Rate	5.1
Not in Labour Force	3,479
Female:	
In the Labour Force	7,565
Participation Rate	57.3
Employed	6,979
Unemployed	586
Unemployment Rate	7.7
Not in Labour Force	5,628

OCCUPATIONS BY MAJOR GROUPS

2001 Estimates:	Male	Female
Management	943	381
Business, Finance & Admin.	651	1,857
Natural & Applied Sciences & Related	397	61
Health	304	806
Social Sciences, Gov't Services & Religion	134	241
Education	269	453
Arts, Culture, Recreation & Sport	152	171
Sales & Service	1,762	2,717
Trades, Transport & Equipment Operators & Related	2,032	100
Primary Industries	600	110
Processing, Mfg. & Utilities	796	370

LEVEL OF SCHOOLING

2001 Estimates:	
Population 15 years +	24,897
Less than Grade 9	2,754
Grades 9-13 w/o Certif.	6,608
Grade 9-13 with Certif.	3,999
Trade Certif. /Dip.	1,026
Non-Univ. w/o Certif./Dip.	1,521
Non-Univ. with Certif./Dip.	5,059
Univ. w/o Degree	1,632
Univ. w/o Degree/Certif.	763
Univ. with Certif.	869
Univ. with Degree	2,298

AVERAGE HOUSEHOLD EXPENDITURES

2001 Estimates:	
Food	$5,486
Shelter	$8,324
Clothing	$1,797
Transportation	$5,856
Health & Personal Care	$1,756
Recr'n, Read'g & Education	$3,184
Taxes & Securities	$10,485
Other	$7,697
Total Expenditures	$44,585

PRIVATE HOUSEHOLDS

2001 Estimates:	
Private Households, Total	12,677
Pop. in Private Households	29,666
Average no. per Household	2.3

FAMILIES

2001 Estimates:	
Families in Private Households	8,838
Husband-Wife Families	7,644
Lone-Parent Families	1,194
Aver. No. Persons per Family	3.0
Aver. No. Sons/Daughters at Home	1.1

HOUSING

2001 Estimates:	
Occupied Private Dwellings	12,677
Owned	8,523
Rented	4,154
Single-Detached House	8,326
Semi-Detached House	580
Row Houses	381
Apartment, 5+ Storeys	746
Owned Apartment, 5+ Storeys	124
Apartment, 5 or Fewer Storeys	2,068
Apartment, Detached Duplex	451
Other Single-Attached	39
Movable Dwellings	86

VEHICLES

2001 Estimates:	
Model Yrs. '81-'96, No.	15,271
% Total	80.69
Model Yrs. '97-'98, No.	2,285
% Total	12.07
'99 Vehicles registered in Model Yr. '99, No.	1,370
% Total	7.24
Total No. '81-'99	18,926

LEGAL MARITAL STATUS

2001 Estimates: (Age 15+)	
Single (Never Married)	6,413
Legally Married (Not Separated)	13,519
Legally Married (Separated)	868
Widowed	2,217
Divorced	1,880

PSYTE CATEGORIES

2001 Estimates	No. of House-holds	% of Total Hhds.	Index
Small City Elite	954	7.53	439
Blue Collar Winners	226	1.78	71
Town Boomers	454	3.58	353
Old Towns' New Fringe	1,601	12.63	323
Rustic Prosperity	641	5.06	280
Young City Singles	436	3.44	150
Old Leafy Towns	1,628	12.84	502
Town Renters	119	0.94	109
Nesters & Young Homesteaders	5,568	43.92	1,882
Quiet Towns	394	3.11	146
Rod & Rifle	83	0.65	28
Aged Pensioners	389	3.07	231

FINANCIAL PSYTE

2001 Estimates	No. of House-holds	% of Total Hhds.	Index
Canadian Comfort	1,634	12.89	133
Tractors & Tradelines	2,242	17.69	309
Bills & Wills	1,628	12.84	155
Revolving Renters	5,568	43.92	955
Rural Family Blues	83	0.65	8
Limited Budgets	394	3.11	100
Towering Debt	555	4.38	56
Senior Survivors	389	3.07	163

Owen Sound
(Census Agglomeration)
(Cont'd)

HOME LANGUAGE

2001 Estimates:		% Total
English	30,146	98.76
French	26	0.09
Chinese	57	0.19
German	20	0.07
Greek	16	0.05
Gujarati	31	0.10
Spanish	56	0.18
Vietnamese	20	0.07
Other Languages	96	0.31
Multiple Responses	58	0.19
Total	30,526	100.00

BUILDING PERMITS

	1999	1998	1997
		$000	
Value	18,762	13,966	26,394

HOMES BUILT

	1999	1998	1997
No	18	13	27

TAXATION

Income Class:	1997	% Total
Under $5,000	2,700	12.23
$5,000-$10,000	2,770	12.55
$10,000-$15,000	3,600	16.30
$15,000-$20,000	2,590	11.73
$20,000-$25,000	2,050	9.28
$25,000-$30,000	1,710	7.74
$30,000-$40,000	2,730	12.36
$40,000-$50,000	1,600	7.25
$50,000 +	2,350	10.64
Total Returns, No.	22,080	
Total Income, $000	557,483	
Total Taxable Returns	15,000	
Total Tax, $000	94,911	
Average Income, $	25,248	
Average Tax, $	6,327	

VITAL STATISTICS

	1997	1996	1995	1994
Births	339	308	348	366
Deaths	402	333	341	311
Natural Increase	-63	-25	7	55
Marriages	242	228	240	220

Note: Latest available data.

DAILY NEWSPAPER(S)

	Circulation Average Paid
The Sun Times	
Fri	21,951
Mon-Thu, Sat	18,156

COMMUNITY NEWSPAPER(S)

	Total Circulation
Owen Sound: The Owen Sound Tribune	33,513

RADIO STATION(S)

	Power
CBCB-FM	n.a.
CFOS	7,500w
CFPS	n.a.
CIXK-FM	100,000w

TELEVISION STATION(S)

CIII-TV
CKCO-TV
TFO
TVO

Pembroke
(Census Agglomeration)

The Census Agglomeration of Pembroke includes: Pembroke, C; Alice and Fraser, TP; Pembroke, TP; and Stafford, TP. All are in Renfrew County in Ontario. It also includes L'Isle-aux-Allumettes-Partie-Est, CT, in census division Pontiac in Quebec.

POPULATION

2001 Estimates:	
July 1, 2001 Estimate	24,782
% Cdn. Total	0.08
% Change, '96 -'01	1.22
Avg. Annual Growth Rate, %	0.24
2003 Projected Population	24,899
2006 Projected Population	24,927
2001 Households Estimate	9,942
2003 Projected Households	10,065
2006 Projected Households	10,224

INCOME

% Above/Below National Average	-13
2001 Total Income Estimate	$453,330,000
% Cdn. Total	0.07
2001 Average Hhld. Income	$45,600
2001 Per Capita	$18,300
2003 Projected Total Income	$477,430,000
2006 Projected Total Income	$513,990,000

RETAIL SALES

% Above/Below National Average	+43
2001 Retail Sales Estimate	$316,540,000
% Cdn. Total	0.11
2001 per Household	$31,800
2001 per Capita	$12,800
2001 No. of Establishments	288
2003 Projected Retail Sales	$344,120,000
2006 Projected Retail Sales	$381,200,000

POPULATION

2001 Estimates:		
Total		24,782
Male		11,894
Female		12,888
Age Groups	Male	Female
0-4	729	702
5-9	784	756
10-14	829	808
15-19	844	837
20-24	790	809
25-29	749	773
30-34	846	854
35-39	940	943
40-44	937	938
45-49	856	858
50-54	736	780
55-59	638	678
60-64	552	599
65-69	509	580
70+	1,155	1,973

DAYTIME POPULATION

2001 Estimates:	
Working Population	11,271
At Home Population	13,511
Total	24,782

INCOME

2001 Estimates:	
Avg. Household Income	$45,597
Avg. Family Income	$53,022
Per Capita Income	$18,293
Male:	
Avg. Employment Income	$29,803
Avg. Employment Income (Full Time)	$39,794
Female:	
Avg. Employment Income	$19,547
Avg. Employment Income (Full Time)	$30,892

DISPOSABLE & DISCRETIONARY INCOME

2001 Estimates:	Per Hhld.
Disposable Income	$37,578
Discretionary Income 1 (minus Food & Shelter)	$26,078
Discretionary Income 2 (minus Food, Shelter, & Other Expenditures)	$18,369

LIQUID ASSETS

1999 Estimates:	Per Hhld.
Equity Investments	$60,630
Interest Bearing Investments	$56,911
Total Liquid Assets	$117,541

CREDIT DATA

July 2000:	
Pool of Credit	$220,915,379
Revolving Credit, No.	39,315
Fixed Loans, No.	13,161
Avg. Credit Limit, per Person	$11,049
Avg. Spent, per Person	$5,215
Satisfactory Ratings, No. per Person	2.53
Avg. No. of Cards, per Person	0.91

LABOUR FORCE

2001 Estimates:	
Male:	
In the Labour Force	6,715
Participation Rate	70.3
Employed	6,149
Unemployed	566
Unemployment Rate	8.4
Not in Labour Force	2,837
Female:	
In the Labour Force	5,563
Participation Rate	52.4
Employed	5,049
Unemployed	514
Unemployment Rate	9.2
Not in Labour Force	5,059

OCCUPATIONS BY MAJOR GROUPS

2001 Estimates:	Male	Female
Management	719	216
Business, Finance & Admin.	464	1,279
Natural & Applied Sciences & Related	373	48
Health	146	591
Social Sciences, Gov't Services & Religion	117	184
Education	171	275
Arts, Culture, Recreation & Sport	133	136
Sales & Service	1,665	2,252
Trades, Transport & Equipment Operators & Related	1,859	53
Primary Industries	282	56
Processing, Mfg. & Utilities	582	200

Ontario

LEVEL OF SCHOOLING

2001 Estimates:	
Population 15 years +	20,174
Less than Grade 9	2,873
Grades 9-13 w/o Certif.	5,376
Grade 9-13 with Certif.	3,368
Trade Certif. /Dip.	910
Non-Univ. w/o Certif./Dip.	1,111
Non-Univ. with Certif./Dip.	3,775
Univ. w/o Degree	1,088
Univ. w/o Degree/Certif.	483
Univ. with Certif.	605
Univ. with Degree	1,673

AVERAGE HOUSEHOLD EXPENDITURES

2001 Estimates:	
Food	$5,524
Shelter	$7,860
Clothing	$1,861
Transportation	$5,853
Health & Personal Care	$1,800
Recr'n, Read'g & Education	$3,263
Taxes & Securities	$10,731
Other	$7,737
Total Expenditures	$44,629

PRIVATE HOUSEHOLDS

2001 Estimates:	
Private Households, Total	9,942
Pop. in Private Households	24,098
Average no. per Household	2.4

FAMILIES

2001 Estimates:	
Families in Private Households	7,064
Husband-Wife Families	6,003
Lone-Parent Families	1,061
Aver. No. Persons per Family	2.9
Aver. No. Sons/Daughters at Home	1.1

HOUSING

2001 Estimates:	
Occupied Private Dwellings	9,942
Owned	6,836
Rented	3,106
Single-Detached House	6,931
Semi-Detached House	461
Row Houses	250
Apartment, 5+ Storeys	86
Apartment, 5 or Fewer Storeys	1,884
Apartment, Detached Duplex	271
Other Single-Attached	43
Movable Dwellings	16

VEHICLES

2001 Estimates:	
Model Yrs. '81-'96, No.	12,932
% Total	85.29
Model Yrs. '97-'98, No.	1,391
% Total	9.17
'99 Vehicles registered in Model Yr. '99, No.	839
% Total	5.53
Total No. '81-'99	15,162

Ontario

Pembroke
(Census Agglomeration)
(Cont'd)

LEGAL MARITAL STATUS

2001 Estimates: (Age 15+)

Single (Never Married)	5,462
Legally Married (Not Separated)	10,863
Legally Married (Separated)	667
Widowed	1,914
Divorced	1,268

PSYTE CATEGORIES

2001 Estimates	No. of House-holds	% of Total Hhds.	Index
Small City Elite	552	5.55	324
Town Boomers	1,133	11.40	1,124
Old Towns' New Fringe	1,294	13.02	333
Rustic Prosperity	304	3.06	169
Old Leafy Towns	819	8.24	322
Nesters & Young Homesteaders	1,675	16.85	722
Young Grey Collar	1,205	12.12	1,449
Quiet Towns	1,505	15.14	711
Agrarian Blues	229	2.30	1,076
Rod & Rifle	142	1.43	62
Big Country Families	390	3.92	275
Struggling Downtowns	157	1.58	50
Aged Pensioners	396	3.98	299

FINANCIAL PSYTE

2001 Estimates	No. of House-holds	% of Total Hhds.	Index
Canadian Comfort	1,685	16.95	174
Tractors & Tradelines	1,598	16.07	281
Bills & Wills	819	8.24	99
Revolving Renters	2,880	28.97	630
Rural Family Blues	761	7.65	95
Limited Budgets	1,505	15.14	487
Towering Debt	157	1.58	20
Senior Survivors	396	3.98	211

HOME LANGUAGE

2001 Estimates:

		% Total
English	23,855	96.26
French	518	2.09
Chinese	27	0.11
Dutch	26	0.10
German	82	0.33
Hindi	37	0.15
Polish	22	0.09
Other Languages	34	0.14
Multiple Responses	181	0.73
Total	24,782	100.00

BUILDING PERMITS

	1999	1998	1997
		$000	
Value	21,367	14,292	13,049

HOMES BUILT

	1999	1998	1997
No	62	60	67

TAXATION

Income Class:	1997	% Total
Under $5,000	2,400	12.61
$5,000-$10,000	2,430	12.76
$10,000-$15,000	3,310	17.38
$15,000-$20,000	2,020	10.61
$20,000-$25,000	1,660	8.72
$25,000-$30,000	1,610	8.46
$30,000-$40,000	2,530	13.29
$40,000-$50,000	1,370	7.20
$50,000 +	1,720	9.03
Total Returns, No.	19,040	
Total Income, $000	457,722	
Total Taxable Returns	12,470	
Total Tax, $000	74,608	
Average Income, $	24,040	
Average Tax, $	5,983	

VITAL STATISTICS

	1997	1996	1995	1994
Births	289	306	315	348
Deaths	288	291	282	299
Natural Increase	1	15	33	49
Marriages	179	229	242	203

Note: Latest available data.

DAILY NEWSPAPER(S)

	Circulation Average Paid
The Daily Observer	6,430

COMMUNITY NEWSPAPER(S)

	Total Circulation
Pembroke: The Pembroke News	
Tue	18,722
Fri	28,102

RADIO STATION(S)

	Power
CBCD-FM	n.a.
CHVR-FM	100,000w
CJRT-FM	n.a.

TELEVISION STATION(S)

CHRO-TV

Peterborough
(Census Agglomeration)

The Census Agglomeration of Peterborough includes: Peterborough, C; Smith, TP; Douro, TP; Dummer, TP; Ennismore, TP; Lakefield, VL; Otonabee, TP; plus several smaller areas. All are in Peterborough County.

POPULATION

July 1, 2001 Estimate	106,269
% Cdn. Total	0.34
% Change, '96 -'01	3.32
Avg. Annual Growth Rate, %	0.65
2003 Projected Population	108,129
2006 Projected Population	110,366
2001 Households Estimate	42,408
2003 Projected Households	43,398
2006 Projected Households	44,784

INCOME

% Above/Below National Average	-4
2001 Total Income Estimate	$2,145,570,000
% Cdn. Total	0.33
2001 Average Hhld. Income	$50,600
2001 Per Capita	$20,200
2003 Projected Total Income	$2,304,230,000
2006 Projected Total Income	$2,559,630,000

RETAIL SALES

% Above/Below National Average	+14
2001 Retail Sales Estimate	$1,085,920,000
% Cdn. Total	0.39
2001 per Household	$25,600
2001 per Capita	$10,200
2001 No. of Establishments	892
2003 Projected Retail Sales	$1,192,240,000
2006 Projected Retail Sales	$1,342,080,000

POPULATION

2001 Estimates:

Total		106,269
Male		50,712
Female		55,557
Age Groups	Male	Female
0-4	3,072	2,974
5-9	3,401	3,246
10-14	3,629	3,439
15-19	3,585	3,443
20-24	3,471	3,466
25-29	3,266	3,349
30-34	3,325	3,507
35-39	3,594	3,895
40-44	3,797	4,114
45-49	3,715	4,008
50-54	3,281	3,498
55-59	2,673	2,887
60-64	2,274	2,572
65-69	2,146	2,563
70+	5,483	8,596

DAYTIME POPULATION

2001 Estimates:

Working Population	49,717
At Home Population	56,553
Total	106,270

INCOME

2001 Estimates:

Avg. Household Income	$50,593
Avg. Family Income	$57,398
Per Capita Income	$20,190
Male:	
Avg. Employment Income	$33,809
Avg. Employment Income (Full Time)	$46,286
Female:	
Avg. Employment Income	$21,178
Avg. Employment Income (Full Time)	$33,206

DISPOSABLE & DISCRETIONARY INCOME

2001 Estimates:	Per Hhld.
Disposable Income	$41,853
Discretionary Income 1 (minus Food & Shelter)	$29,215
Discretionary Income 2 (minus Food, Shelter, & Other Expenditures)	$21,138

LIQUID ASSETS

1999 Estimates:	Per Hhld.
Equity Investments	$64,116
Interest Bearing Investments	$61,109
Total Liquid Assets	$125,225

CREDIT DATA

July 2000:

Pool of Credit	$1,000,482,067
Revolving Credit, No.	187,838
Fixed Loans, No.	54,934
Avg. Credit Limit, per Person	$11,057
Avg. Spent, per Person	$4,884
Satisfactory Ratings, No. per Person	2.55
Avg. No. of Cards, per Person	0.93

LABOUR FORCE

2001 Estimates:

Male:	
In the Labour Force	28,057
Participation Rate	69.1
Employed	26,090
Unemployed	1,967
Unemployment Rate	7.0
Not in Labour Force	12,553
Female:	
In the Labour Force	25,299
Participation Rate	55.1
Employed	23,457
Unemployed	1,842
Unemployment Rate	7.3
Not in Labour Force	20,599

OCCUPATIONS BY MAJOR GROUPS

2001 Estimates:	Male	Female
Management	2,824	1,407
Business, Finance & Admin.	2,378	6,311
Natural & Applied Sciences & Related	1,832	213
Health	547	2,653
Social Sciences, Gov't Services & Religion	653	937
Education	1,037	1,580
Arts, Culture, Recreation & Sport	544	678
Sales & Service	6,402	8,769
Trades, Transport & Equipment Operators & Related	6,991	367
Primary Industries	1,061	302
Processing, Mfg. & Utilities	2,716	993

LEVEL OF SCHOOLING

2001 Estimates:

Population 15 years +	86,508
Less than Grade 9	6,616
Grades 9-13 w/o Certif.	22,413
Grade 9-13 with Certif.	13,010
Trade Certif./Dip.	3,893
Non-Univ. w/o Certif./Dip.	5,937
Non-Univ. with Certif./Dip.	18,122
Univ. w/o Degree	6,405
Univ. w/o Degree/Certif.	3,280
Univ. with Certif.	3,125
Univ. with Degree	10,112

Peterborough
(Census Agglomeration)
(Cont'd)

AVERAGE HOUSEHOLD EXPENDITURES

2001 Estimates:

Food	$5,848
Shelter	$8,776
Clothing	$1,970
Transportation	$6,254
Health & Personal Care	$1,804
Recr'n, Read'g & Education	$3,466
Taxes & Securities	$12,902
Other	$8,152
Total Expenditures	$49,172

PRIVATE HOUSEHOLDS

2001 Estimates:

Private Households, Total	42,408
Pop. in Private Households	103,814
Average no. per Household	2.4

FAMILIES

2001 Estimates:

Families in Private Households	30,931
Husband-Wife Families	26,513
Lone-Parent Families	4,418
Aver. No. Persons per Family	2.9
Aver. No. Sons/Daughters at Home	1.1

HOUSING

2001 Estimates:

Occupied Private Dwellings	42,408
Owned	29,506
Rented	12,859
Band Housing	43
Single-Detached House	30,129
Semi-Detached House	866
Row Houses	1,998
Apartment, 5+ Storeys	2,701
Owned Apartment, 5+ Storeys	60
Apartment, 5 or Fewer Storeys	4,834
Apartment, Detached Duplex	1,606
Other Single-Attached	72
Movable Dwellings	202

VEHICLES

2001 Estimates:

Model Yrs. '81-'96, No.	53,637
% Total	80.74
Model Yrs. '97-'98, No.	7,177
% Total	10.80
'99 Vehicles registered in Model Yr. '99, No.	5,621
% Total	8.46
Total No. '81-'99	66,435

LEGAL MARITAL STATUS

2001 Estimates: (Age 15+)

Single (Never Married)	22,811
Legally Married (Not Separated)	47,489
Legally Married (Separated)	3,042
Widowed	7,137
Divorced	6,029

PSYTE CATEGORIES

2001 Estimates	No. of House -holds	% of Total Hhds.	Index
Urban Gentry	107	0.25	14
Mortgaged in Suburbia	100	0.24	17
Technocrafts & Bureaucrats	462	1.09	39
Boomers & Teens	1,226	2.89	161
Small City Elite	1,679	3.96	231
Old Bungalow Burbs	1,126	2.66	160
Suburban Nesters	343	0.81	50
Aging Erudites	1,148	2.71	179
Satellite Suburbs	2,065	4.87	170
Blue Collar Winners	3,243	7.65	304
Old Towns' New Fringe	5,575	13.15	336
Rustic Prosperity	451	1.06	59

2001 Estimates	No. of House -holds	% of Total Hhds.	Index
Conservative Homebodies	8,051	18.98	527
High Rise Sunsets	988	2.33	163
University Enclaves	1,887	4.45	218
Young City Singles	2,138	5.04	220
Old Leafy Towns	3,833	9.04	354
Nesters & Young Homesteaders	1,347	3.18	136
Rod & Rifle	63	0.15	6
Big Country Families	274	0.65	45
Struggling Downtowns	4,272	10.07	320
Aged Pensioners	1,353	3.19	240
Old Grey Towers	140	0.33	60

FINANCIAL PSYTE

2001 Estimates	No. of House -holds	% of Total Hhds.	Index
Four Star Investors	1,333	3.14	63
Successful Suburbanites	562	1.33	20
Canadian Comfort	7,330	17.28	178
Urban Heights	1,148	2.71	63
Miners & Credit-Liners	1,126	2.66	84
Tractors & Tradelines	6,026	14.21	248
Bills & Wills	11,884	28.02	338
Revolving Renters	2,335	5.51	120
Young Urban Struggle	1,887	4.45	94
Rural Family Blues	337	0.79	10
Towering Debt	6,410	15.12	194
Senior Survivors	1,493	3.52	187

HOME LANGUAGE

2001 Estimates:		% Total
English	103,768	97.65
French	300	0.28
Chinese	134	0.13
German	130	0.12
Italian	114	0.11
Khmer (Cambodian)	100	0.09
Korean	182	0.17
Ojibway	68	0.06
Polish	360	0.34
Other Languages	544	0.51
Multiple Responses	569	0.54
Total	106,269	100.00

BUILDING PERMITS

	1999	1998 $000	1997
Value	89,858	63,581	75,251

HOMES BUILT

	1999	1998	1997
No	326	307	411

TAXATION

Income Class:	1997	% Total
Under $5,000	9,480	12.45
$5,000-$10,000	9,450	12.41
$10,000-$15,000	11,800	15.49
$15,000-$20,000	8,300	10.90
$20,000-$25,000	6,910	9.07
$25,000-$30,000	5,960	7.82
$30,000-$40,000	9,070	11.91
$40,000-$50,000	5,670	7.44
$50,000 +	9,600	12.60
Total Returns, No.	76,170	
Total Income, $000	2,008,789	
Total Taxable Returns	51,850	
Total Tax, $000	359,107	
Average Income, $	26,372	
Average Tax, $	6,926	

VITAL STATISTICS

	1997	1996	1995	1994
Births	975	1,125	1,162	1,238
Deaths	1,033	1,103	997	1,054
Natural Increase	-58	22	165	184
Marriages	633	685	711	709

Note: Latest available data.

DAILY NEWSPAPER(S)

	Circulation Average Paid
The Examiner	
Sun	20,903
Mon-Sat	22,400

COMMUNITY NEWSPAPER(S)

	Total Circulation
Lakefield: Katchewanooka Herald	1,729
Peterborough: Peterborough This Week	
Wed	45,260
Sat	46,475

RADIO STATION(S)

	Power
CBBL-FM	n.a.
CBCP-FM	100w
CJBC-FM	n.a.
CKPT	10,000w
CKQM-FM	50,000w
CKRU	10,000w
CKWF-FM	n.a.

TELEVISION STATION(S)

CHEX-TV
CIII-TV
TFO
TVO

Ontario

Ontario

Port Hope
(Census Agglomeration)

The Census Agglomeration of Port Hope consists solely of Port Hope, T, in Northumberland County.

POPULATION

July 1, 2001 Estimate	12,111
% Cdn. Total	0.04
% Change, '96 -'01	0.87
Avg. Annual Growth Rate, %	0.17
2003 Projected Population	12,050
2006 Projected Population	11,894
2001 Households Estimate	4,770
2003 Projected Households	4,795
2006 Projected Households	4,823

INCOME

% Above/Below National Average	-2
2001 Total Income Estimate	$250,260,000
% Cdn. Total	0.04
2001 Average Hhld. Income	$52,500
2001 Per Capita	$20,700
2003 Projected Total Income	$263,520,000
2006 Projected Total Income	$284,660,000

RETAIL SALES

% Above/Below National Average	-4
2001 Retail Sales Estimate	$104,540,000
% Cdn. Total	0.04
2001 per Household	$21,900
2001 per Capita	$8,600
2001 No. of Establishments	107
2003 Projected Retail Sales	$112,690,000
2006 Projected Retail Sales	$122,330,000

POPULATION

2001 Estimates:

Total	12,111
Male	5,893
Female	6,218

Age Groups	Male	Female
0-4	361	358
5-9	417	395
10-14	450	409
15-19	466	407
20-24	420	376
25-29	361	353
30-34	381	407
35-39	425	481
40-44	469	477
45-49	466	437
50-54	374	373
55-59	285	301
60-64	239	249
65-69	220	255
70+	559	940

DAYTIME POPULATION

2001 Estimates:

Working Population	6,038
At Home Population	6,073
Total	12,111

INCOME

2001 Estimates:

Avg. Household Income	$52,465
Avg. Family Income	$59,219
Per Capita Income	$20,664
Male:	
Avg. Employment Income	$33,948
Avg. Employment Income (Full Time)	$45,257
Female:	
Avg. Employment Income	$21,276
Avg. Employment Income (Full Time)	$31,669

DISPOSABLE & DISCRETIONARY INCOME

2001 Estimates:	Per Hhld.
Disposable Income	$43,168
Discretionary Income 1 (minus Food & Shelter)	$29,353
Discretionary Income 2 (minus Food, Shelter, & Other Expenditures)	$20,907

LIQUID ASSETS

1999 Estimates:	Per Hhld.
Equity Investments	$66,091
Interest Bearing Investments	$64,188
Total Liquid Assets	$130,279

CREDIT DATA

July 2000:

Pool of Credit	$146,419,232
Revolving Credit, No.	25,604
Fixed Loans, No.	7,018
Avg. Credit Limit, per Person	$12,432
Avg. Spent, per Person	$5,789
Satisfactory Ratings, No. per Person	2.76
Avg. No. of Cards, per Person	0.98

LABOUR FORCE

2001 Estimates:

Male:	
In the Labour Force	3,442
Participation Rate	73.8
Employed	3,351
Unemployed	91
Unemployment Rate	2.6
Not in Labour Force	1,223
Female:	
In the Labour Force	2,889
Participation Rate	57.1
Employed	2,661
Unemployed	228
Unemployment Rate	7.9
Not in Labour Force	2,167

OCCUPATIONS BY MAJOR GROUPS

2001 Estimates:	Male	Female
Management	211	106
Business, Finance & Admin.	273	656
Natural & Applied Sciences & Related	247	10
Health	51	305
Social Sciences, Gov't Services & Religion	79	120
Education	101	168
Arts, Culture, Recreation & Sport	57	50
Sales & Service	739	908
Trades, Transport & Equipment Operators & Related	703	44
Primary Industries	122	42
Processing, Mfg. & Utilities	807	341

LEVEL OF SCHOOLING

2001 Estimates:

Population 15 years +	9,721
Less than Grade 9	675
Grades 9-13 w/o Certif.	2,902
Grade 9-13 with Certif.	1,663
Trade Certif. /Dip.	431
Non-Univ. w/o Certif./Dip.	551
Non-Univ. with Certif./Dip.	2,007
Univ. w/o Degree	533
Univ. w/o Degree/Certif.	268
Univ. with Certif.	265
Univ. with Degree	959

AVERAGE HOUSEHOLD EXPENDITURES

2001 Estimates:

Food	$6,189
Shelter	$9,673
Clothing	$1,974
Transportation	$6,594
Health & Personal Care	$1,923
Recr'n, Read'g & Education	$3,504
Taxes & Securities	$12,405
Other	$8,496
Total Expenditures	$50,758

PRIVATE HOUSEHOLDS

2001 Estimates:

Private Households, Total	4,770
Pop. in Private Households	11,671
Average no. per Household	2.4

FAMILIES

2001 Estimates:

Families in Private Households	3,484
Husband-Wife Families	3,030
Lone-Parent Families	454
Aver. No. Persons per Family	3.0
Aver. No. Sons/Daughters at Home	1.1

HOUSING

2001 Estimates:

Occupied Private Dwellings	4,770
Owned	3,429
Rented	1,341
Single-Detached House	3,214
Semi-Detached House	337
Row Houses	273
Apartment, 5+ Storeys	366
Apartment, 5 or Fewer Storeys	481
Apartment, Detached Duplex	66
Other Single-Attached	33

VEHICLES

2001 Estimates:

Model Yrs. '81-'96, No.	6,393
% Total	81.48
Model Yrs. '97-'98, No.	848
% Total	10.81
'99 Vehicles registered in Model Yr. '99, No.	605
% Total	7.71
Total No. '81-'99	7,846

LEGAL MARITAL STATUS

2001 Estimates: (Age 15+)

Single (Never Married)	2,499
Legally Married (Not Separated)	5,337
Legally Married (Separated)	360
Widowed	842
Divorced	683

PSYTE CATEGORIES

2001 Estimates	No. of House-holds	% of Total Hhds.	Index
Small City Elite	72	1.51	88
Satellite Suburbs	311	6.52	227
Blue Collar Winners	531	11.13	442
Old Towns' New Fringe	429	8.99	230
Young City Singles	27	0.57	25
Old Leafy Towns	1,146	24.03	940
Nesters & Young Homesteaders	1,851	38.81	1,663
Aged Pensioners	329	6.90	518

FINANCIAL P$YTE

2001 Estimates	No. of House-holds	% of Total Hhds.	Index
Canadian Comfort	914	19.16	197
Tractors & Tradelines	429	8.99	157
Bills & Wills	1,146	24.03	290
Revolving Renters	1,851	38.81	843
Towering Debt	27	0.57	7
Senior Survivors	329	6.90	366

HOME LANGUAGE

2001 Estimates:		% Total
English	11,926	98.47
French	20	0.17
Arabic	21	0.17
Chinese	33	0.27
German	16	0.13
Italian	20	0.17
Korean	20	0.17
Malayalam	12	0.10
Polish	10	0.08
Swedish	10	0.08
Multiple Responses	23	0.19
Total	12,111	100.00

BUILDING PERMITS

	1999	1998	1997
		$000	
Value	5,249	4,934	4,119

HOMES BUILT

	1999	1998	1997
No	14	7	10

TAXATION

Income Class:	1997	% Total
Under $5,000	1,220	12.07
$5,000-$10,000	1,110	10.98
$10,000-$15,000	1,420	14.05
$15,000-$20,000	1,030	10.19
$20,000-$25,000	820	8.11
$25,000-$30,000	790	7.81
$30,000-$40,000	1,290	12.76
$40,000-$50,000	860	8.51
$50,000 +	1,560	15.43
Total Returns, No.	10,110	
Total Income, $000	281,525	
Total Taxable Returns	7,320	
Total Tax, $000	51,499	
Average Income, $.	27,846	
Average Tax, $	7,035	

VITAL STATISTICS

	1997	1996	1995	1994
Births	143	157	149	183
Deaths	143	164	138	150
Natural Increase	0	-7	11	33
Marriages	49	77	52	55

Note: Latest available data.

DAILY NEWSPAPER(S)

	Circulation Average Paid
Port Hope Evening Guide	
Fri.	2,910
Mon-Sat.	2,770

COMMUNITY NEWSPAPER(S)

	Total Circulation
Port Hope: Northumberland News	
Tue/Fri	22,371

RADIO STATION(S)

	Power
CHUC	n.a.

Sarnia
(Census Agglomeration)

The Census Agglomeration of Sarnia includes: Moore, TP; Point Edward, VL, Sarnia, C; and one other very small area. All are in Lambton County.

POPULATION

July 1, 2001 Estimate	86,500
% Cdn. Total	0.28
% Change, '96 -'01	-3.19
Avg. Annual Growth Rate, %	-0.65
2003 Projected Population	85,008
2006 Projected Population	82,321
2001 Households Estimate	34,981
2003 Projected Households	34,951
2006 Projected Households	34,748

INCOME

% Above/Below National Average	+8
2001 Total Income Estimate	$1,966,310,000
% Cdn. Total	0.30
2001 Average Hhld. Income	$56,200
2001 Per Capita	$22,700
2003 Projected Total Income	$2,052,800,000
2006 Projected Total Income	$2,177,400,000

RETAIL SALES

% Above/Below National Average	+6
2001 Retail Sales Estimate	$818,300,000
% Cdn. Total	0.29
2001 per Household	$23,400
2001 per Capita	$9,500
2001 No. of Establishments	602
2003 Projected Retail Sales	$866,470,000
2006 Projected Retail Sales	$923,490,000

POPULATION

2001 Estimates:

Total		86,500
Male		42,085
Female		44,415
Age Groups	Male	Female
0-4	2,527	2,404
5-9	2,800	2,724
10-14	3,020	2,955
15-19	3,065	2,999
20-24	2,885	2,834
25-29	2,603	2,568
30-34	2,610	2,699
35-39	2,952	3,167
40-44	3,259	3,471
45-49	3,290	3,383
50-54	2,941	2,932
55-59	2,376	2,390
60-64	1,990	2,125
65-69	1,843	2,034
70+	3,924	5,730

DAYTIME POPULATION

2001 Estimates:

Working Population	41,962
At Home Population	44,537
Total	86,499

INCOME

2001 Estimates:

Avg. Household Income	$56,211
Avg. Family Income	$64,716
Per Capita Income	$22,732
Male:	
Avg. Employment Income	$40,414
Avg. Employment Income (Full Time)	$54,777
Female:	
Avg. Employment Income	$19,833
Avg. Employment Income (Full Time)	$32,063

DISPOSABLE & DISCRETIONARY INCOME

2001 Estimates:	Per Hhld.
Disposable Income	$45,873
Discretionary Income 1 (minus Food & Shelter)	$32,095
Discretionary Income 2 (minus Food, Shelter, & Other Expenditures)	$23,462

LIQUID ASSETS

1999 Estimates:	Per Hhld.
Equity Investments	$77,261
Interest Bearing Investments	$69,593
Total Liquid Assets	$146,854

CREDIT DATA

July 2000:

Pool of Credit	$912,477,452
Revolving Credit, No.	166,774
Fixed Loans, No.	45,867
Avg. Credit Limit, per Person	$12,197
Avg. Spent, per Person	$5,281
Satisfactory Ratings, No. per Person	2.74
Avg. No. of Cards, per Person	1.02

LABOUR FORCE

2001 Estimates:

Male:	
In the Labour Force	24,333
Participation Rate	72.1
Employed	22,423
Unemployed	1,910
Unemployment Rate	7.8
Not in Labour Force	9,405
Female:	
In the Labour Force	20,704
Participation Rate	57.0
Employed	19,388
Unemployed	1,316
Unemployment Rate	6.4
Not in Labour Force	15,628

OCCUPATIONS BY MAJOR GROUPS

2001 Estimates:	Male	Female
Management	2,131	1,004
Business, Finance & Admin.	1,578	5,323
Natural & Applied Sciences & Related	2,533	277
Health	457	2,045
Social Sciences, Gov't Services & Religion	363	583
Education	523	1,049
Arts, Culture, Recreation & Sport	303	491
Sales & Service	4,774	8,180
Trades, Transport & Equipment Operators & Related	7,151	378
Primary Industries	805	283
Processing, Mfg. & Utilities	3,093	213

LEVEL OF SCHOOLING

2001 Estimates:

Population 15 years +	70,070
Less than Grade 9	4,726
Grades 9-13 w/o Certif.	16,052
Grade 9-13 with Certif.	12,115
Trade Certif. /Dip.	3,656
Non-Univ. w/o Certif./Dip.	5,495
Non-Univ. with Certif./Dip.	15,612
Univ. w/o Degree	5,124
Univ. w/o Degree/Certif.	2,394
Univ. with Certif.	2,730
Univ. with Degree	7,290

AVERAGE HOUSEHOLD EXPENDITURES

2001 Estimates:

Food	$6,316
Shelter	$9,666
Clothing	$2,175
Transportation	$6,653
Health & Personal Care	$1,995
Recr'n, Read'g & Education	$3,726
Taxes & Securities	$14,045
Other	$8,946
Total Expenditures	$53,522

PRIVATE HOUSEHOLDS

2001 Estimates:

Private Households, Total	34,981
Pop. in Private Households	85,252
Average no. per Household	2.4

FAMILIES

2001 Estimates:

Families in Private Households	25,395
Husband-Wife Families	21,892
Lone-Parent Families	3,503
Aver. No. Persons per Family	3.0
Aver. No. Sons/Daughters at Home	1.2

HOUSING

2001 Estimates:

Occupied Private Dwellings	34,981
Owned	24,786
Rented	10,137
Band Housing	58
Single-Detached House	24,694
Semi-Detached House	1,311
Row Houses	1,773
Apartment, 5+ Storeys	3,446
Owned Apartment, 5+ Storeys	167
Apartment, 5 or Fewer Storeys	2,541
Apartment, Detached Duplex	913
Other Single-Attached	178
Movable Dwellings	125

VEHICLES

2001 Estimates:

Model Yrs. '81-'96, No.	47,271
% Total	81.00
Model Yrs. '97-'98, No.	6,552
% Total	11.23
'99 Vehicles registered in Model Yr. '99, No.	4,538
% Total	7.78
Total No. '81-'99	58,361

LEGAL MARITAL STATUS

2001 Estimates: (Age 15+)

Single (Never Married)	18,293
Legally Married (Not Separated)	39,595
Legally Married (Separated)	2,317
Widowed	5,132
Divorced	4,733

PSYTE CATEGORIES

2001 Estimates	No. of House-holds	% of Total Hhds.	Index
Urban Gentry	280	0.80	45
Suburban Executives	767	2.19	153
Boomers & Teens	2,419	6.92	386
Small City Elite	1,709	4.89	285
Old Bungalow Burbs	1,797	5.14	310
Suburban Nesters	311	0.89	55
Aging Erudites	1,670	4.77	316
Satellite Suburbs	1,098	3.14	109
Kindergarten Boom	1,861	5.32	203
Blue Collar Winners	1,571	4.49	178
Old Towns' New Fringe	983	2.81	72
Rustic Prosperity	665	1.90	105
Conservative Homebodies	3,165	9.05	251
High Rise Sunsets	855	2.44	171
Young City Singles	420	1.20	52
Old Leafy Towns	352	1.01	39
Nesters & Young Homesteaders	9,217	26.35	1,129
Big Country Families	381	1.09	76
Struggling Downtowns	2,873	8.21	261
Aged Pensioners	2,322	6.64	499

Ontario

FINANCIAL P$YTE

2001 Estimates	No. of House-holds	% of Total Hhds.	Index
Four Star Investors	3,466	9.91	197
Canadian Comfort	4,689	13.40	138
Urban Heights	1,670	4.77	111
Miners & Credit-Liners	1,797	5.14	162
Mortgages & Minivans	1,861	5.32	81
Tractors & Tradelines	1,648	4.71	82
Bills & Wills	3,517	10.05	121
Revolving Renters	10,072	28.79	626
Rural Family Blues	381	1.09	13
Towering Debt	3,293	9.41	121
Senior Survivors	2,322	6.64	352

HOME LANGUAGE

2001 Estimates:		% Total
English	82,617	95.51
French	616	0.71
Chinese	187	0.22
German	96	0.11
Greek	118	0.14
Hungarian	51	0.06
Italian	682	0.79
Polish	204	0.24
Portuguese	273	0.32
Spanish	271	0.31
Ukrainian	50	0.06
Other Languages	436	0.50
Multiple Responses	899	1.04
Total	86,500	100.00

BUILDING PERMITS

	1999	1998	1997
		$000	
Value	62,468	54,756	57,760

HOMES BUILT

	1999	1998	1997
No	210	166	135

TAXATION

Income Class:	1997	% Total
Under $5,000	8,240	13.24
$5,000-$10,000	7,170	11.52
$10,000-$15,000	8,370	13.45
$15,000-$20,000	6,040	9.71
$20,000-$25,000	4,800	7.71
$25,000-$30,000	4,210	6.77
$30,000-$40,000	6,820	10.96
$40,000-$50,000	4,590	7.38
$50,000 +	11,980	19.25
Total Returns, No.	62,220	
Total Income, $000	1,886,190	
Total Taxable Returns	43,680	
Total Tax, $000	379,044	
Average Income, $	30,315	
Average Tax, $	8,678	

Sarnia
(Census Agglomeration)
(Cont'd)

VITAL STATISTICS

	1997	1996	1995	1994
Births	890	975	1,076	1,045
Deaths	712	675	692	680
Natural Increase	178	300	384	365
Marriages	470	558	538	568

Note: Latest available data.

DAILY NEWSPAPER(S)

	Circulation Average Paid
The Observer	21,968

COMMUNITY NEWSPAPER(S)

	Total Circulation
Sarnia: Lambton-Sarnia Shopping News	n.a.
Sarnia: This Week	23,029

RADIO STATION(S)

	Power
CBEG-FM	n.a.
CFGX-FM	26,000w
CHKS-FM	10,000w
CHOK	10,000w
CJRT-FM	n.a.
CKTY	35,000w

TELEVISION STATION(S)

CBLN-TV
CIII-TV
CKCO-TV

Sault Ste. Marie
(Census Agglomeration)

The Census Agglomeration of Sault Ste. Marie includes: Sault Ste. Marie, C; Macdonald, Meredith and Aberdeen Additional, TP; plus several smaller areas, all in Algoma District.

POPULATION

July 1, 2001 Estimate	84,249
% Cdn. Total	0.27
% Change, '96 -'01	-3.84
Avg. Annual Growth Rate, %	-0.78
2003 Projected Population	82,731
2006 Projected Population	80,051
2001 Households Estimate	34,062
2003 Projected Households	34,070
2006 Projected Households	33,851

INCOME

% Above/Below National Average	-4
2001 Total Income Estimate	$1,707,890,000
% Cdn. Total	0.26
2001 Average Hhld. Income	$50,100
2001 Per Capita	$20,300
2003 Projected Total Income	$1,781,860,000
2006 Projected Total Income	$1,891,330,000

RETAIL SALES

% Above/Below National Average	+33
2001 Retail Sales Estimate	$1,000,950,000
% Cdn. Total	0.36
2001 per Household	$29,400
2001 per Capita	$11,900
2001 No. of Establishments	654
2003 Projected Retail Sales	$1,055,270,000
2006 Projected Retail Sales	$1,124,210,000

POPULATION

2001 Estimates:

Total	84,249
Male	40,746
Female	43,503

Age Groups	Male	Female
0-4	2,465	2,305
5-9	2,586	2,466
10-14	2,764	2,653
15-19	2,902	2,801
20-24	2,870	2,797
25-29	2,582	2,610
30-34	2,583	2,790
35-39	2,911	3,277
40-44	3,140	3,442
45-49	3,082	3,274
50-54	2,758	2,910
55-59	2,344	2,504
60-64	2,064	2,202
65-69	1,880	2,065
70+	3,815	5,407

DAYTIME POPULATION

2001 Estimates:

Working Population	38,541
At Home Population	45,707
Total	84,248

INCOME

2001 Estimates:

Avg. Household Income	$50,141
Avg. Family Income	$57,536
Per Capita Income	$20,272
Male:	
Avg. Employment Income	$36,081
Avg. Employment Income (Full Time)	$48,805
Female:	
Avg. Employment Income	$20,526
Avg. Employment Income (Full Time)	$33,811

DISPOSABLE & DISCRETIONARY INCOME

2001 Estimates:	Per Hhld.
Disposable Income	$41,280
Discretionary Income 1 (minus Food & Shelter)	$28,798
Discretionary Income 2 (minus Food, Shelter, & Other Expenditures)	$21,004

LIQUID ASSETS

1999 Estimates:	Per Hhld.
Equity Investments	$66,203
Interest Bearing Investments	$62,150
Total Liquid Assets	$128,353

CREDIT DATA

July 2000:

Pool of Credit	$841,296,440
Revolving Credit, No.	154,015
Fixed Loans, No.	57,485
Avg. Credit Limit, per Person	$12,009
Avg. Spent, per Person	$5,526
Satisfactory Ratings, No. per Person	2.78
Avg. No. of Cards, per Person	0.98

LABOUR FORCE

2001 Estimates:

Male:	
In the Labour Force	22,371
Participation Rate	67.9
Employed	20,346
Unemployed	2,025
Unemployment Rate	9.1
Not in Labour Force	10,560
Female:	
In the Labour Force	19,859
Participation Rate	55.0
Employed	17,989
Unemployed	1,870
Unemployment Rate	9.4
Not in Labour Force	16,220

OCCUPATIONS BY MAJOR GROUPS

2001 Estimates:	Male	Female
Management	1,778	1,025
Business, Finance & Admin.	1,808	4,853
Natural & Applied Sciences & Related	1,615	279
Health	447	1,897
Social Sciences, Gov't Services & Religion	387	666
Education	850	1,220
Arts, Culture, Recreation & Sport	377	471
Sales & Service	4,730	7,833
Trades, Transport & Equipment Operators & Related	6,302	348
Primary Industries	480	120
Processing, Mfg. & Utilities	2,822	180

LEVEL OF SCHOOLING

2001 Estimates:

Population 15 years +	69,010
Less than Grade 9	7,929
Grades 9-13 w/o Certif.	17,465
Grade 9-13 with Certif.	10,195
Trade Certif./Dip.	2,685
Non-Univ. w/o Certif./Dip.	4,271
Non-Univ. with Certif./Dip.	12,700
Univ. w/o Degree	6,424
Univ. w/o Degree/Certif.	3,613
Univ. with Certif.	2,811
Univ. with Degree	7,341

AVERAGE HOUSEHOLD EXPENDITURES

2001 Estimates:

Food	$5,862
Shelter	$8,625
Clothing	$1,988
Transportation	$5,965
Health & Personal Care	$1,790
Recr'n, Read'g & Education	$3,380
Taxes & Securities	$12,724
Other	$8,164
Total Expenditures	$48,498

PRIVATE HOUSEHOLDS

2001 Estimates:

Private Households, Total	34,062
Pop. in Private Households	82,897
Average no. per Household	2.4

FAMILIES

2001 Estimates:

Families in Private Households	24,878
Husband-Wife Families	20,561
Lone-Parent Families	4,317
Aver. No. Persons per Family	2.9
Aver. No. Sons/Daughters at Home	1.1

HOUSING

2001 Estimates:

Occupied Private Dwellings	34,062
Owned	22,950
Rented	11,112
Single-Detached House	22,904
Semi-Detached House	1,659
Row Houses	769
Apartment, 5+ Storeys	1,969
Owned Apartment, 5+ Storeys	122
Apartment, 5 or Fewer Storeys	5,045
Apartment, Detached Duplex	1,596
Other Single-Attached	120

VEHICLES

2001 Estimates:

Model Yrs. '81-'96, No.	44,506
% Total	85.15
Model Yrs. '97-'98, No.	4,710
% Total	9.01
'99 Vehicles registered in Model Yr. '99, No.	3,049
% Total	5.83
Total No. '81-'99	52,265

LEGAL MARITAL STATUS

2001 Estimates: (Age 15+)

Single (Never Married)	19,646
Legally Married (Not Separated)	37,180
Legally Married (Separated)	2,041
Widowed	5,033
Divorced	5,110

Sault Ste. Marie
(Census Agglomeration)
(Cont'd)

PSYTE CATEGORIES

2001 Estimates	No. of House -holds	% of Total Hhds.	Index
Urban Gentry	407	1.19	66
Suburban Executives	831	2.44	170
Technocrafts & Bureaucrats	381	1.12	40
Boomers & Teens	131	0.38	21
Small City Elite	1,083	3.18	186
Old Bungalow Burbs	4,494	13.19	796
Aging Erudites	1,150	3.38	224
Satellite Suburbs	852	2.50	87
Kindergarten Boom	769	2.26	86
Blue Collar Winners	1,354	3.98	158
Old Towns' New Fringe	973	2.86	73
Rustic Prosperity	552	1.62	90
Conservative Homebodies	7,846	23.03	639
High Rise Sunsets	360	1.06	74
University Enclaves	324	0.95	47
Young City Singles	198	0.58	25
Nesters & Young Homesteaders	2,382	6.99	300
Struggling Downtowns	7,911	23.23	738
Aged Pensioners	1,478	4.34	326
Old Grey Towers	246	0.72	130

FINANCIAL PSYTE

2001 Estimates	No. of House -holds	% of Total Hhds.	Index
Four Star Investors	1,369	4.02	80
Successful Suburbanites	381	1.12	17
Canadian Comfort	3,289	9.66	99
Urban Heights	1,150	3.38	78
Miners & Credit-Liners	4,494	13.19	417
Mortgages & Minivans	769	2.26	34
Tractors & Tradelines	1,525	4.48	78
Bills & Wills	7,846	23.03	278
Revolving Renters	2,742	8.05	175
Young Urban Struggle	324	0.95	20
Towering Debt	8,109	23.81	305
Senior Survivors	1,724	5.06	269

HOME LANGUAGE

2001 Estimates:		% Total
English	79,062	93.84
French	831	0.99
Chinese	126	0.15
Croatian	67	0.08
Estonian	71	0.08
Finnish	323	0.38
German	136	0.16
Italian	2,110	2.50
Polish	176	0.21
Portuguese	182	0.22
Ukrainian	58	0.07
Other Languages	286	0.34
Multiple Responses	821	0.97
Total	84,249	100.00

BUILDING PERMITS

	1999	1998 $000	1997
Value	72,992	46,232	39,910

HOMES BUILT

	1999	1998	1997
No	108	162	163

TAXATION

Income Class:	1997	% Total
Under $5,000	8,730	13.82
$5,000-$10,000	7,840	12.41
$10,000-$15,000	9,210	14.58
$15,000-$20,000	6,190	9.80
$20,000-$25,000	5,050	7.99
$25,000-$30,000	4,520	7.15
$30,000-$40,000	7,220	11.43
$40,000-$50,000	5,200	8.23
$50,000 +	9,250	14.64
Total Returns, No.	63,190	
Total Income, $000	1,669,114	
Total Taxable Returns	41,560	
Total Tax, $000	297,609	
Average Income, $	26,414	
Average Tax, $	7,161	

VITAL STATISTICS

	1997	1996	1995	1994
Births	898	922	1,032	992
Deaths	718	758	711	714
Natural Increase	180	164	321	278
Marriages	529	589	546	533

Note: Latest available data.

DAILY NEWSPAPER(S)

	Circulation Average Paid
Star	21,618

COMMUNITY NEWSPAPER(S)

	Total Circulation
Sault Ste. Marie: Sault Ste. Marie This Week	35,077

RADIO STATION(S)

	Power
CBON-FM	n.a.
CBSM-FM	n.a.
CHAS-FM	13,900w
CJQM-FM	100,000w
CJRT-FM	n.a.

TELEVISION STATION(S)

CHBX-TV
CHCH-TV
CIII-TV
CJIC-TV
TFO
TVO

Scugog
(Township)
In Durham Regional Municipality.

POPULATION

July 1, 2001 Estimate	20,023
% Cdn. Total	0.06
% Change, '96 -'01	3.11
Avg. Annual Growth Rate, %	0.61
2003 Projected Population	20,238
2006 Projected Population	20,484
2001 Households Estimate	7,094
2003 Projected Households	7,238
2006 Projected Households	7,456

INCOME

% Above/Below National Average	+17
2001 Total Income Estimate	$494,470,000
% Cdn. Total	0.08
2001 Average Hhld. Income	$69,700
2001 Per Capita	$24,700
2003 Projected Total Income	$527,840,000
2006 Projected Total Income	$582,460,000

RETAIL SALES

% Above/Below National Average	+18
2001 Retail Sales Estimate	$211,570,000
% Cdn. Total	0.08
2001 per Household	$29,800
2001 per Capita	$10,600
2001 No. of Establishments	169
2003 Projected Retail Sales	$229,490,000
2006 Projected Retail Sales	$255,250,000

POPULATION

2001 Estimates:		
Total		20,023
Male		9,954
Female		10,069
Age Groups	Male	Female
0-4	568	553
5-9	676	668
10-14	761	786
15-19	766	783
20-24	685	651
25-29	599	543
30-34	601	610
35-39	741	799
40-44	863	900
45-49	858	849
50-54	726	689
55-59	561	515
60-64	450	414
65-69	362	366
70+	737	943

DAYTIME POPULATION

2001 Estimates:	
Working Population	6,330
At Home Population	8,629
Total	14,959

INCOME

2001 Estimates:	
Avg. Household Income	$69,703
Avg. Family Income	$73,858
Per Capita Income	$24,695
Male:	
Avg. Employment Income	$41,701
Avg. Employment Income (Full Time)	$53,098
Female:	
Avg. Employment Income	$23,813
Avg. Employment Income (Full Time)	$35,043

Ontario

DISPOSABLE & DISCRETIONARY INCOME

2001 Estimates:	Per Hhld.
Disposable Income	$57,024
Discretionary Income 1 (minus Food & Shelter)	$41,163
Discretionary Income 2 (minus Food, Shelter, & Other Expenditures)	$30,402

LIQUID ASSETS

1999 Estimates:	Per Hhld.
Equity Investments	$102,671
Interest Bearing Investments	$85,745
Total Liquid Assets	$188,416

CREDIT DATA

July 2000:	
Pool of Credit	$218,378,518
Revolving Credit, No.	33,458
Fixed Loans, No.	10,181
Avg. Credit Limit, per Person	$14,083
Avg. Spent, per Person	$6,387
Satisfactory Ratings, No. per Person	2.74
Avg. No. of Cards, per Person	1.05

LABOUR FORCE

2001 Estimates:	
Male:	
In the Labour Force	6,440
Participation Rate	81.0
Employed	6,282
Unemployed	158
Unemployment Rate	2.5
Not in Labour Force	1,509
Female:	
In the Labour Force	5,284
Participation Rate	65.5
Employed	4,997
Unemployed	287
Unemployment Rate	5.4
Not in Labour Force	2,778

OCCUPATIONS BY MAJOR GROUPS

2001 Estimates:	Male	Female
Management	723	309
Business, Finance & Admin.	341	1,248
Natural & Applied Sciences & Related	356	58
Health	92	371
Social Sciences, Gov't Services & Religion	57	198
Education	165	265
Arts, Culture, Recreation & Sport	76	200
Sales & Service	1,201	1,801
Trades, Transport & Equipment Operators & Related	1,792	101
Primary Industries	747	263
Processing, Mfg. & Utilities	842	308

Ontario

Scugog
(Township)
(Cont'd)

LEVEL OF SCHOOLING

2001 Estimates:
Population 15 years +	16,011
Less than Grade 9	1,057
Grades 9-13 w/o Certif.	4,226
Grade 9-13 with Certif.	3,181
Trade Certif./Dip.	635
Non-Univ. w/o Certif./Dip.	828
Non-Univ. with Certif./Dip.	3,321
Univ. w/o Degree	1,193
Univ. w/o Degree/Certif.	574
Univ. with Certif.	619
Univ. with Degree	1,570

AVERAGE HOUSEHOLD EXPENDITURES

2001 Estimates:
Food	$6,951
Shelter	$11,182
Clothing	$2,475
Transportation	$8,651
Health & Personal Care	$2,140
Recr'n, Read'g & Education	$4,338
Taxes & Securities	$19,292
Other	$9,899
Total Expenditures	$64,928

PRIVATE HOUSEHOLDS

2001 Estimates:
Private Households, Total	7,094
Pop. in Private Households	19,830
Average no. per Household	2.8

FAMILIES

2001 Estimates:
Families in Private Households	5,930
Husband-Wife Families	5,350
Lone-Parent Families	580
Aver. No. Persons per Family	3.1
Aver. No. Sons/Daughters at Home	1.2

HOUSING

2001 Estimates:
Occupied Private Dwellings	7,094
Owned	5,937
Rented	1,157
Single-Detached House	6,127
Semi-Detached House	221
Row Houses	77
Apartment, 5 or Fewer Storeys	493
Apartment, Detached Duplex	122
Other Single-Attached	43
Movable Dwellings	11

VEHICLES

2001 Estimates:
Model Yrs. '81-'96, No.	11,609
% Total	79.20
Model Yrs. '97-'98, No.	1,848
% Total	12.61
'99 Vehicles registered in Model Yr. '99, No.	1,200
% Total	8.19
Total No. '81-'99	14,657

LEGAL MARITAL STATUS

2001 Estimates: (Age 15+)
Single (Never Married)	3,907
Legally Married (Not Separated)	9,726
Legally Married (Separated)	543
Widowed	894
Divorced	941

PSYTE CATEGORIES

2001 Estimates
	No. of House -holds	% of Total Hhds.	Index
Boomers & Teens	739	10.42	581
Blue Collar Winners	4,032	56.84	2,258
Old Towns' New Fringe	1,863	26.26	671
Old Leafy Towns	308	4.34	170
Struggling Downtowns	109	1.54	49

FINANCIAL P$YTE

2001 Estimates
	No. of House -holds	% of Total Hhds.	Index
Four Star Investors	739	10.42	207
Canadian Comfort	4,032	56.84	585
Tractors & Tradelines	1,863	26.26	459
Bills & Wills	308	4.34	52
Towering Debt	109	1.54	20

HOME LANGUAGE

2001 Estimates:
		% Total
English	19,889	99.33
Dutch	32	0.16
Finnish	11	0.05
German	70	0.35
Other Languages	10	0.05
Multiple Responses	11	0.05
Total	20,023	100.00

BUILDING PERMITS

	1999	1998	1997
		$000	
Value	22,716	20,264	17,487

TAXATION

Income Class:	1997	% Total
Under $5,000	1,590	12.06
$5,000-$10,000	1,480	11.23
$10,000-$15,000	1,550	11.76
$15,000-$20,000	1,140	8.65
$20,000-$25,000	1,040	7.89
$25,000-$30,000	1,020	7.74
$30,000-$40,000	1,570	11.91
$40,000-$50,000	1,050	7.97
$50,000 +	2,730	20.71
Total Returns, No.	13,180	
Total Income, $000	416,631	
Total Taxable Returns	9,770	
Total Tax, $000	85,640	
Average Income, $	31,611	
Average Tax, $	8,766	

VITAL STATISTICS

	1997	1996	1995	1994
Births	208	200	207	181
Deaths	120	137	115	128
Natural Increase	88	63	92	53
Marriages	182	154	156	130

Note: Latest available data.

COMMUNITY NEWSPAPER(S)

	Total Circulation
Port Perry: Port Perry Star Tue/Fri	3,513
(Fri. total 19,054)	
Port Perry: Port Perry Weekend Star	20,297

Simcoe
(Census Agglomeration)

The Census Agglomeration of Simcoe consists solely of Simcoe, T, in Haldimand-Norfolk Regional Municipality.

POPULATION

July 1, 2001 Estimate	15,776
% Cdn. Total	0.05
% Change, '96 -'01	-0.87
Avg. Annual Growth Rate, %	-0.17
2003 Projected Population	15,532
2006 Projected Population	15,075
2001 Households Estimate	6,518
2003 Projected Households	6,515
2006 Projected Households	6,480

INCOME

% Above/Below National Average	same
2001 Total Income Estimate	$332,440,000
% Cdn. Total	0.05
2001 Average Hhld. Income	$51,000
2001 Per Capita	$21,100
2003 Projected Total Income	$348,630,000
2006 Projected Total Income	$372,230,000

RETAIL SALES

% Above/Below National Average	+123
2001 Retail Sales Estimate	$315,300,000
% Cdn. Total	0.11
2001 per Household	$48,400
2001 per Capita	$20,000
2001 No. of Establishments	165
2003 Projected Retail Sales	$333,750,000
2006 Projected Retail Sales	$357,160,000

POPULATION

2001 Estimates:
Total	15,776
Male	7,519
Female	8,257

Age Groups	Male	Female
0-4	421	388
5-9	444	413
10-14	498	451
15-19	558	504
20-24	528	501
25-29	465	463
30-34	457	466
35-39	501	528
40-44	532	604
45-49	551	597
50-54	505	536
55-59	439	456
60-64	384	414
65-69	350	412
70+	886	1,524

DAYTIME POPULATION

2001 Estimates:
Working Population	7,257
At Home Population	8,519
Total	15,776

INCOME

2001 Estimates:
Avg. Household Income	$51,004
Avg. Family Income	$59,597
Per Capita Income	$21,073
Male:	
Avg. Employment Income	$35,199
Avg. Employment Income (Full Time)	$46,450
Female:	
Avg. Employment Income	$19,935
Avg. Employment Income (Full Time)	$31,458

DISPOSABLE & DISCRETIONARY INCOME

2001 Estimates:	*Per Hhld.*
Disposable Income	$42,053
Discretionary Income 1 (minus Food & Shelter)	$28,770
Discretionary Income 2 (minus Food, Shelter, & Other Expenditures)	$20,520

LIQUID ASSETS

1999 Estimates:	*Per Hhld.*
Equity Investments	$64,053
Interest Bearing Investments	$61,892
Total Liquid Assets	$125,945

CREDIT DATA

July 2000:
Pool of Credit	$153,802,874
Revolving Credit, No.	28,738
Fixed Loans, No.	7,546
Avg. Credit Limit, per Person	$11,476
Avg. Spent, per Person	$5,055
Satisfactory Ratings, No. per Person	2.62
Avg. No. of Cards, per Person	1.03

LABOUR FORCE

2001 Estimates:
Male:	
In the Labour Force	4,221
Participation Rate	68.6
Employed	3,908
Unemployed	313
Unemployment Rate	7.4
Not in Labour Force	1,935
Female:	
In the Labour Force	3,693
Participation Rate	52.7
Employed	3,338
Unemployed	355
Unemployment Rate	9.6
Not in Labour Force	3,312

OCCUPATIONS BY MAJOR GROUPS

2001 Estimates:	*Male*	*Female*
Management	522	236
Business, Finance & Admin.	287	810
Natural & Applied Sciences & Related	275	49
Health	80	319
Social Sciences, Gov't Services & Religion	85	103
Education	96	255
Arts, Culture, Recreation & Sport	n.a.	77
Sales & Service	871	1,236
Trades, Transport & Equipment Operators & Related	1,018	12
Primary Industries	251	219
Processing, Mfg. & Utilities	660	229

LEVEL OF SCHOOLING

2001 Estimates:
Population 15 years +	13,161
Less than Grade 9	1,568
Grades 9-13 w/o Certif.	3,752
Grade 9-13 with Certif.	1,915
Trade Certif./Dip.	597
Non-Univ. w/o Certif./Dip.	904
Non-Univ. with Certif./Dip.	2,353
Univ. w/o Degree	900
Univ. w/o Degree/Certif.	397
Univ. with Certif.	503
Univ. with Degree	1,172

Simcoe
(Census Agglomeration)
(Cont'd)

AVERAGE HOUSEHOLD EXPENDITURES

2001 Estimates:
Food	$6,140
Shelter	$9,313
Clothing	$1,985
Transportation	$6,347
Health & Personal Care	$1,968
Recr'n, Read'g & Education	$3,408
Taxes & Securities	$11,839
Other	$8,527
Total Expenditures	$49,527

PRIVATE HOUSEHOLDS

2001 Estimates:
Private Households, Total	6,518
Pop. in Private Households	15,095
Average no. per Household	2.3

FAMILIES

2001 Estimates:
Families in Private Households	4,577
Husband-Wife Families	3,939
Lone-Parent Families	638
Aver. No. Persons per Family	2.8
Aver. No. Sons/Daughters at Home	1.0

HOUSING

2001 Estimates:
Occupied Private Dwellings	6,518
Owned	4,299
Rented	2,219
Single-Detached House	4,200
Semi-Detached House	277
Row Houses	177
Apartment, 5+ Storeys	444
Owned Apartment, 5+ Storeys	122
Apartment, 5 or Fewer Storeys	998
Apartment, Detached Duplex	395
Other Single-Attached	11
Movable Dwellings	16

VEHICLES

2001 Estimates:
Model Yrs. '81-'96, No.	9,073
% Total	83.75
Model Yrs. '97-'98, No.	1,109
% Total	10.24
'99 Vehicles registered in Model Yr. '99, No.	651
% Total	6.01
Total No. '81-'99	10,833

LEGAL MARITAL STATUS

2001 Estimates: (Age 15+)
Single (Never Married)	3,378
Legally Married (Not Separated)	7,054
Legally Married (Separated)	430
Widowed	1,321
Divorced	978

PSYTE CATEGORIES

2001 Estimates	No. of House -holds	% of Total Hhds.	Index
Small City Elite	573	8.79	513
Old Bungalow Burbs	590	9.05	546
Blue Collar Winners	121	1.86	74
Old Towns' New Fringe	346	5.31	136
High Rise Sunsets	79	1.21	85
Old Leafy Towns	527	8.09	316
Nesters & Young Homesteaders	3,115	47.79	2,048
Quiet Towns	820	12.58	591
Rod & Rifle	126	1.93	84
Struggling Downtowns	47	0.72	23

FINANCIAL P$YTE

2001 Estimates	No. of House -holds	% of Total Hhds.	Index
Canadian Comfort	694	10.65	110
Miners & Credit-Liners	590	9.05	286
Tractors & Tradelines	346	5.31	93
Bills & Wills	527	8.09	98
Revolving Renters	3,194	49.00	1,065
Rural Family Blues	126	1.93	24
Limited Budgets	820	12.58	405
Towering Debt	47	0.72	9

HOME LANGUAGE

2001 Estimates:		% Total
English	15,009	95.14
French	71	0.45
Chinese	32	0.20
Czech	10	0.06
German	10	0.06
Hungarian	32	0.20
Persian (Farsi)	27	0.17
Polish	16	0.10
Portuguese	325	2.06
Slovak	16	0.10
Spanish	21	0.13
Swedish	16	0.10
Ukrainian	10	0.06
Other Languages	21	0.13
Multiple Responses	160	1.01
Total	15,776	100.00

BUILDING PERMITS

	1999	1998 $000	1997
Value	9,100	6,847	13,791

HOMES BUILT

	1999	1998	1997
No.	8	9	20

TAXATION

Income Class:	1997	% Total
Under $5,000	1,970	12.00
$5,000-$10,000	1,950	11.88
$10,000-$15,000	2,670	16.26
$15,000-$20,000	1,910	11.63
$20,000-$25,000	1,550	9.44
$25,000-$30,000	1,230	7.49
$30,000-$40,000	1,940	11.81
$40,000-$50,000	1,130	6.88
$50,000 +	2,070	12.61
Total Returns, No.	16,420	
Total Income, $000	429,620	
Total Taxable Returns	11,390	
Total Tax, $000	76,392	
Average Income, $	26,164	
Average Tax, $	6,707	

VITAL STATISTICS

	1997	1996	1995	1994
Births	206	230	270	268
Deaths	274	311	276	291
Natural Increase	-68	-81	-6	-23
Marriages	161	186	215	153

Note: Latest available data.

DAILY NEWSPAPER(S)

	Circulation Average Paid
Reformer	8,625

COMMUNITY NEWSPAPER(S)

	Total Circulation
Simcoe: Tuesday Times-Reformer	19,076

RADIO STATION(S)

	Power
CHCD-FM	10,000w

Smiths Falls
(Census Agglomeration)

The Census Agglomeration of Smiths Falls consists of Montague, TP and Smiths Falls, T in Lanark County; and South Elmsley, TP in Leeds and Grenville United Counties.

POPULATION

July 1, 2001 Estimate	16,865
% Cdn. Total	0.05
% Change, '96 -'01	-0.60
Avg. Annual Growth Rate, %	-0.12
2003 Projected Population	16,899
2006 Projected Population	16,903
2001 Households Estimate	6,640
2003 Projected Households	6,680
2006 Projected Households	6,751

INCOME

% Above/Below National Average	-10
2001 Total Income Estimate	$319,630,000
% Cdn. Total	0.05
2001 Average Hhld. Income	$48,100
2001 Per Capita	$19,000
2003 Projected Total Income	$334,440,000
2006 Projected Total Income	$358,060,000

RETAIL SALES

% Above/Below National Average	+26
2001 Retail Sales Estimate	$190,340,000
% Cdn. Total	0.07
2001 per Household	$28,700
2001 per Capita	$11,300
2001 No. of Establishments	181
2003 Projected Retail Sales	$203,830,000
2006 Projected Retail Sales	$221,520,000

POPULATION

2001 Estimates:
Total	16,865
Male	8,101
Female	8,764

Age Groups	Male	Female
0-4	481	442
5-9	537	512
10-14	557	569
15-19	537	551
20-24	487	505
25-29	458	483
30-34	533	541
35-39	599	625
40-44	660	669
45-49	674	672
50-54	590	607
55-59	473	489
60-64	388	421
65-69	349	410
70+	778	1,268

DAYTIME POPULATION

2001 Estimates:
Working Population	7,656
At Home Population	9,209
Total	16,865

Ontario

INCOME

2001 Estimates:
Avg. Household Income	$48,136
Avg. Family Income	$54,921
Per Capita Income	$18,952
Male:	
Avg. Employment Income	$30,963
Avg. Employment Income (Full Time)	$39,297
Female:	
Avg. Employment Income	$21,174
Avg. Employment Income (Full Time)	$29,131

DISPOSABLE & DISCRETIONARY INCOME

2001 Estimates:	Per Hhld.
Disposable Income	$39,746
Discretionary Income 1 (minus Food & Shelter)	$27,535
Discretionary Income 2 (minus Food, Shelter, & Other Expenditures)	$19,029

LIQUID ASSETS

1999 Estimates:	Per Hhld.
Equity Investments	$64,782
Interest Bearing Investments	$59,288
Total Liquid Assets	$124,070

CREDIT DATA

July 2000:
Pool of Credit	$158,103,016
Revolving Credit, No.	27,231
Fixed Loans, No.	7,887
Avg. Credit Limit, per Person	$11,164
Avg. Spent, per Person	$5,096
Satisfactory Ratings, No. per Person	2.41
Avg. No. of Cards, per Person	0.87

LABOUR FORCE

2001 Estimates:
Male:
In the Labour Force	4,288
Participation Rate	65.7
Employed	3,949
Unemployed	339
Unemployment Rate	7.9
Not in Labour Force	2,238

Female:
In the Labour Force	3,885
Participation Rate	53.7
Employed	3,654
Unemployed	231
Unemployment Rate	5.9
Not in Labour Force	3,356

Ontario

Smiths Falls
(Census Agglomeration)
(Cont'd)

OCCUPATIONS BY MAJOR GROUPS

2001 Estimates:	Male	Female
Management	429	188
Business, Finance & Admin.	326	935
Natural & Applied Sciences & Related	276	33
Health	79	431
Social Sciences, Gov't Services & Religion	103	202
Education	89	173
Arts, Culture, Recreation & Sport	50	100
Sales & Service	936	1,221
Trades, Transport & Equipment Operators & Related	1,070	61
Primary Industries	253	53
Processing, Mfg. & Utilities	500	418

LEVEL OF SCHOOLING

2001 Estimates:
Population 15 years +	13,767
Less than Grade 9	1,436
Grades 9-13 w/o Certif.	3,983
Grade 9-13 with Certif.	2,288
Trade Certif. /Dip.	444
Non-Univ. w/o Certif./Dip.	853
Non-Univ. with Certif./Dip.	3,066
Univ. w/o Degree	870
Univ. w/o Degree/Certif.	465
Univ. with Certif.	405
Univ. with Degree	827

AVERAGE HOUSEHOLD EXPENDITURES

2001 Estimates:
Food	$5,857
Shelter	$8,367
Clothing	$1,844
Transportation	$6,620
Health & Personal Care	$1,902
Recr'n, Read'g & Education	$3,234
Taxes & Securities	$11,275
Other	$7,851
Total Expenditures	$46,950

PRIVATE HOUSEHOLDS

2001 Estimates:
Private Households, Total	6,640
Pop. in Private Households	15,864
Average no. per Household	2.4

FAMILIES

2001 Estimates:
Families in Private Households	4,772
Husband-Wife Families	4,046
Lone-Parent Families	726
Aver. No. Persons per Family	2.8
Aver. No. Sons/Daughters at Home	1.1

HOUSING

2001 Estimates:
Occupied Private Dwellings	6,640
Owned	4,620
Rented	2,020
Single-Detached House	4,590
Semi-Detached House	361
Row Houses	142
Apartment, 5+ Storeys	34
Apartment, 5 or Fewer Storeys	839
Apartment, Detached Duplex	483
Other Single-Attached	30
Movable Dwellings	161

VEHICLES

2001 Estimates:
Model Yrs. '81-'96, No.	8,131
% Total	86.04
Model Yrs. '97-'98, No.	808
% Total	8.55
'99 Vehicles registered in Model Yr. '99, No.	511
% Total	5.41
Total No. '81-'99	9,450

LEGAL MARITAL STATUS

2001 Estimates: (Age 15+)
Single (Never Married)	3,977
Legally Married (Not Separated)	7,030
Legally Married (Separated)	498
Widowed	1,217
Divorced	1,045

PSYTE CATEGORIES

2001 Estimates	No. of House-holds	% of Total Hhds.	Index
Small City Elite	505	7.61	444
Old Towns' New Fringe	1,120	16.87	431
Old Leafy Towns	1,158	17.44	682
Quiet Towns	2,868	43.19	2,030
Rod & Rifle	727	10.95	473

FINAN¢IAL P$YTE

2001 Estimates	No. of House-holds	% of Total Hhds.	Index
Canadian Comfort	505	7.61	78
Tractors & Tradelines	1,120	16.87	295
Bills & Wills	1,158	17.44	211
Rural Family Blues	727	10.95	136
Limited Budgets	2,868	43.19	1,389

HOME LANGUAGE

2001 Estimates:		% Total
English	16,556	98.17
French	136	0.81
Chinese	54	0.32
Greek	31	0.18
Polish	10	0.06
Spanish	15	0.09
Vietnamese	12	0.07
Multiple Responses	51	0.30
Total	16,865	100.00

BUILDING PERMITS

	1999	1998 $000	1997
Value	6,186	6,847	n.a.

HOMES BUILT

	1999	1998	1997
No.	33	2	n.a.

TAXATION

Income Class:	1997	% Total
Under $5,000	2,070	15.59
$5,000-$10,000	1,550	11.67
$10,000-$15,000	1,920	14.46
$15,000-$20,000	1,420	10.69
$20,000-$25,000	1,090	8.21
$25,000-$30,000	1,100	8.28
$30,000-$40,000	1,770	13.33
$40,000-$50,000	1,170	8.81
$50,000 +	1,220	9.19
Total Returns, No.	13,280	
Total Income, $000	318,419	
Total Taxable Returns	8,750	
Total Tax, $000	53,198	
Average Income, $	23,977	
Average Tax, $	6,080	

VITAL STATISTICS

	1997	1996	1995	1994
Births	186	175	216	203
Deaths	182	168	207	183
Natural Increase	4	7	9	20
Marriages	77	148	71	77

Note: Latest available data.

COMMUNITY NEWSPAPER(S)

	Total Circulation
Smiths Falls: Smiths Falls Record News	2,814
Smiths Falls: Smiths Falls Record News EMC	10,428

RADIO STATION(S)

	Power
CFMO-FM	100,000w
CJET	10,000w
CJRT-FM	n.a.

St. Catharines-Niagara Falls
(Census Metropolitan Area)

POPULATION

July 1, 2001 Estimate	395,557
% Cdn. Total	1.27
% Change, '96 -'01	3.33
Avg. Annual Growth Rate, %	0.66
2003 Projected Population	401,835
2006 Projected Population	410,525
2001 Households Estimate	158,145
2003 Projected Households	161,529
2006 Projected Households	166,725

INCOME

% Above/Below National Average	-3
2001 Total Income Estimate	$8,082,950,000
% Cdn. Total	1.23
2001 Average Hhld. Income	$51,100
2001 Per Capita	$20,400
2003 Projected Total Income	$8,566,990,000
2006 Projected Total Income	$9,349,400,000

RETAIL SALES

% Above/Below National Average	+13
2001 Retail Sales Estimate	$4,003,520,000
% Cdn. Total	1.44
2001 per Household	$25,300
2001 per Capita	$10,100
2001 No. of Establishments	2,836
2003 Projected Retail Sales	$4,374,260,000
2006 Projected Retail Sales	$4,916,440,000

POPULATION

2001 Estimates:

Total		395,557
Male		191,771
Female		203,786

Age Groups	Male	Female
0-4	11,626	11,018
5-9	12,551	11,793
10-14	13,079	12,195
15-19	13,072	12,202
20-24	12,723	12,175
25-29	12,302	12,282
30-34	13,058	13,595
35-39	14,113	14,902
40-44	14,354	15,155
45-49	13,840	14,592
50-54	12,500	13,065
55-59	10,658	11,265
60-64	9,223	10,118
65-69	8,519	9,847
70+	20,153	29,582

DAYTIME POPULATION

2001 Estimates:

Working Population	190,941
At Home Population	204,618
Total	395,559

INCOME

2001 Estimates:

Avg. Household Income	$51,111
Avg. Family Income	$58,223
Per Capita Income	$20,434
Male:	
Avg. Employment Income	$35,071
Avg. Employment Income (Full Time)	$46,579
Female:	
Avg. Employment Income	$19,812
Avg. Employment Income (Full Time)	$31,326

DISPOSABLE & DISCRETIONARY INCOME

2001 Estimates:	Per Hhld.
Disposable Income	$42,189
Discretionary Income 1 (minus Food & Shelter)	$29,427
Discretionary Income 2 (minus Food, Shelter, & Other Expenditures)	$21,349

LIQUID ASSETS

1999 Estimates:	Per Hhld.
Equity Investments	$67,697
Interest Bearing Investments	$62,869
Total Liquid Assets	$130,566

CREDIT DATA

July 2000:

Pool of Credit	$3,736,961,578
Revolving Credit, No.	737,845
Fixed Loans, No.	210,694
Avg. Credit Limit, per Person	$11,090
Avg. Spent, per Person	$4,859
Satisfactory Ratings, No. per Person	2.70
Avg. No. of Cards, per Person	0.97

LABOUR FORCE

2001 Estimates:

Male:	
In the Labour Force	109,124
Participation Rate	70.6
Employed	102,656
Unemployed	6,468
Unemployment Rate	5.9
Not in Labour Force	45,391
Female:	
In the Labour Force	94,117
Participation Rate	55.8
Employed	87,615
Unemployed	6,502
Unemployment Rate	6.9
Not in Labour Force	74,663

OCCUPATIONS BY MAJOR GROUPS

2001 Estimates:	Male	Female
Management	10,715	5,225
Business, Finance & Admin.	8,368	24,718
Natural & Applied Sciences & Related	6,279	717
Health	1,370	8,184
Social Sciences, Gov't Services & Religion	1,850	2,527
Education	3,187	4,561
Arts, Culture, Recreation & Sport	1,807	2,393
Sales & Service	22,075	34,554
Trades, Transport & Equipment Operators & Related	28,736	1,503
Primary Industries	5,464	2,268
Processing, Mfg. & Utilities	16,344	3,973

LEVEL OF SCHOOLING

2001 Estimates:

Population 15 years +	323,295
Less than Grade 9	35,102
Grades 9-13 w/o Certif.	83,302
Grade 9-13 with Certif.	51,301
Trade Certif. /Dip.	12,696
Non-Univ. w/o Certif./Dip.	22,285
Non-Univ. with Certif./Dip.	61,249
Univ. w/o Degree	25,625
Univ. w/o Degree/Certif.	13,180
Univ. with Certif.	12,445
Univ. with Degree	31,735

AVERAGE HOUSEHOLD EXPENDITURES

2001 Estimates:

Food	$5,928
Shelter	$8,808
Clothing	$1,999
Transportation	$6,223
Health & Personal Care	$1,808
Recr'n, Read'g & Education	$3,416
Taxes & Securities	$12,946
Other	$8,324
Total Expenditures	$49,452

PRIVATE HOUSEHOLDS

2001 Estimates:

Private Households, Total	158,145
Pop. in Private Households	388,002
Average no. per Household	2.5

FAMILIES

2001 Estimates:

Families in Private Households	114,895
Husband-Wife Families	98,145
Lone-Parent Families	16,750
Aver. No. Persons per Family	2.9
Aver. No. Sons/Daughters at Home	1.1

Ontario

RADIO STATION DATA

Station	Market	Format	Wkly. Reach%*	Aver. Hrs. Tuned
All Stations			94	23.1
CBL-FM	Toronto	All Info.	4	10.8
CBLA-FM	Toronto	News, Info.	6	11.1
CFMX-FM	Toronto	Classical	2	11.7
CFNY-FM	Toronto	Alternative	9	7.3
CFRB	Toronto	News, Talk	5	10.8
CHAM	Hamilton	Country	2	13.4
CHFI-FM	Toronto	Adult Contemp.	6	7.3
CHML	Hamilton	News, Talk	4	9.8
CHOW-FM	Welland	Country	9	10.5
CHRE-FM	St. Cath.-Niagara	Light Rock	17	13.6
CHSC	St. Cath.-Niagara	Adult Contemp.	7	8.3
CHTZ-FM	St. Cath.-Niagara	AOR	16	9.9
CHUM-FM	Toronto	Adult Contemp.	12	8.1
CILQ-FM	Toronto	AOR	9	6.7
CING-FM	Burlington	Contemp. Hit Radio	6	5.1
CISS-FM	Toronto	Top 40	8	5.5
CJCL	Toronto	Sports	3	6.5
CJEZ-FM	Toronto	Adult Contemp.	2	9.1
CJRN	St. Cath.-Niagara	Multi-format	7	6.0
CJRT-FM	Toronto	Classical, Folk, Jazz, Blues	3	4.9
CJXY-FM	Hamilton	AOR	5	11.5
CKEY-FM	Niagara Falls	Modern Adult Contemp.	8	5.3
CKFM-FM	Toronto	Adult Contemp.	10	5.9
CKLH-FM	Hamilton	Adult Contemp.	2	7.4
CKOC	Hamilton	Oldies	n.a.	n.a.
CKTB	St. Cath.-Niagara	News, Talk, Sports	14	12.3

BBM Spring 2000 Radio Reach Survey; area coverage.
*Mon-Sun 5a.m - 1a.m , All Persons 12+

TV STATION DATA

Station	Market	Network Affiliation	Wkly. Reach%*	Aver. Hrs. Tuned
All Stations			93	31.1
A & E	n.a.	Ind.	31	3.3
CBLT	Toronto	CBC	44	2.7
CFMT	Toronto	Ind.	28	2.1
CFTO	Toronto	CTV	63	6.0
CHCH	Toronto/Hamilton	Ind.	48	3.0
CICO-E	n.a.	n.a.	23	4.4
CIII	n.a.	Global	56	3.1
CITY	Toronto	Ind.	26	2.7
CJOH	Ottawa	CTV	4	5.9
CKVR	Barrie	Ind.	14	1.9
COMEDY	n.a.	Ind.	10	1.5
DSCVRY	n.a.	Ind.	10	2.7
FOOD	n.a.	Ind.	8	1.8
HGTV	n.a.	Ind.	10	2.4
HISTTV	n.a.	Ind.	8	3.0
M PIX	n.a.	Ind.	7	2.4
MMUSIC	n.a.	Ind.	11	1.9
PRIME	n.a.	Ind.	15	3.7
SNET	n.a.	CTV	10	1.6
TLC	n.a.	Ind.	16	1.8
TMN	Toronto	Ind.	10	3.3
TOON	n.a.	Ind.	13	2.5
TREE	n.a.	Ind.	11	5.4
TSN	n.a.	Ind.	31	3.5
VCR	n.a.	n.a.	32	4.7
VISION	n.a.	Ind.	9	1.9
WFXT	Boston MA	FOX	9	2.3
WGRZ	Buffalo NY	NBC	38	4.1
WIVB	Buffalo NY	CBS	35	3.1
WKBW	Buffalo NY	ABC	45	5.0
WNED	Buffalo NY	PBS	27	3.2
WTBS	Atlanta GA	Ind.	19	2.4
WUTV	Buffalo NY	FOX	31	3.2
YTV	n.a.	Ind.	12	2.0

BBM Spring 2000 TV Reach Survey; CMA coverage.
*Mon-Sun 6a.m - 2a.m , All Persons 2 +

Ontario

St. Catharines-Niagara Falls
(Census Metropolitan Area)
(Cont'd)

HOUSING

2001 Estimates:
Occupied Private Dwellings	158,145
Owned	112,016
Rented	46,129
Single-Detached House	108,769
Semi-Detached House	8,347
Row Houses	7,167
Apartment, 5+ Storeys	10,181
Owned Apartment, 5+ Storeys	1,146
Apartment, 5 or Fewer Storeys	17,093
Apartment, Detached Duplex	5,309
Other Single-Attached	498
Movable Dwellings	781

VEHICLES

2001 Estimates:
Model Yrs. '81-'96, No.	205,848
% Total	83.07
Model Yrs. '97-'98, No.	25,652
% Total	10.35
'99 Vehicles registered in Model Yr. '99, No.	16,300
% Total	6.58
Total No. '81-'99	247,800

LEGAL MARITAL STATUS

2001 Estimates: (Age 15+)
Single (Never Married)	84,168
Legally Married (Not Separated)	179,350
Legally Married (Separated)	11,386
Widowed	25,736
Divorced	22,655

PSYTE CATEGORIES

2001 Estimates	No. of House-holds	% of Total Hhds.	Index
The Affluentials	436	0.28	43
Urban Gentry	1,649	1.04	58
Mortgaged in Suburbia	215	0.14	10
Technocrafts & Bureaucrats	575	0.36	13
Boomers & Teens	3,117	1.97	110
Stable Suburban Families	2,057	1.30	100
Small City Elite	264	0.17	10
Old Bungalow Burbs	11,446	7.24	437
Suburban Nesters	857	0.54	34
Aging Erudites	4,450	2.81	187
Satellite Suburbs	6,499	4.11	143
Kindergarten Boom	5,243	3.32	126
Blue Collar Winners	11,656	7.37	293
Old Towns' New Fringe	7,835	4.95	127
Rustic Prosperity	2,788	1.76	98
Europa	460	0.29	23
High Rise Melting Pot	300	0.19	13

2001 Estimates	No. of House-holds	% of Total Hhds.	Index
Conservative Homebodies	40,391	25.54	708
High Rise Sunsets	2,179	1.38	96
Young Urban Mix	250	0.16	7
University Enclaves	2,696	1.70	84
Young City Singles	1,725	1.09	48
Old Leafy Towns	2,399	1.52	59
Town Renters	3,649	2.31	267
Nesters & Young Homesteaders	2,121	1.34	57
Quiet Towns	1,754	1.11	52
Agrarian Blues	1,681	1.06	496
Struggling Downtowns	33,052	20.90	664
Aged Pensioners	3,483	2.20	166
Big City Stress	562	0.36	31
Old Grey Towers	929	0.59	106

FINANÇIAL P$YTE

2001 Estimates	No. of House-holds	% of Total Hhds.	Index
Platinum Estates	436	0.28	34
Four Star Investors	4,766	3.01	60
Successful Suburbanites	2,847	1.80	27
Canadian Comfort	19,276	12.19	125
Urban Heights	4,450	2.81	65
Miners & Credit-Liners	11,446	7.24	229
Mortgages & Minivans	5,243	3.32	50
Dollars & Sense	460	0.29	11
Tractors & Tradelines	10,623	6.72	117
Bills & Wills	43,040	27.22	329
Revolving Renters	4,300	2.72	59
Young Urban Struggle	2,696	1.70	36
Rural Family Blues	1,681	1.06	13
Limited Budgets	1,754	1.11	36
Towering Debt	38,726	24.49	314
2NSF	562	0.36	10
Senior Survivors	4,412	2.79	148

HOME LANGUAGE

2001 Estimates:		% Total
English	364,439	92.13
French	5,545	1.40
Arabic	442	0.11
Chinese	1,230	0.31
Croatian	239	0.06
Dutch	321	0.08
German	1,702	0.43
Greek	438	0.11
Hungarian	596	0.15
Italian	6,180	1.56
Korean	354	0.09
Lao	339	0.09
Polish	2,559	0.65
Russian	255	0.06
Serbian	413	0.10
Serbo-Croatian	204	0.05
Spanish	1,145	0.29
Tagalog (Pilipino)	430	0.11
Ukrainian	932	0.24
Vietnamese	417	0.11
Other Languages	2,391	0.60
Multiple Responses	4,986	1.26
Total	395,557	100.00

BUILDING PERMITS

	1999	1998	1997
		$000	
Value	425,417	312,059	341,951

HOMES BUILT

	1999	1998	1997
No	1,234	1,488	1,178

TAXATION

Income Class:	1997	% Total
Under $5,000	32,480	11.74
$5,000-$10,000	33,150	11.99
$10,000-$15,000	42,340	15.31
$15,000-$20,000	30,180	10.91
$20,000-$25,000	24,440	8.84
$25,000-$30,000	22,200	8.03
$30,000-$40,000	33,080	11.96
$40,000-$50,000	20,870	7.55
$50,000 +	37,810	13.67
Total Returns, No.	276,570	
Total Income, $000	7,524,504	
Total Taxable Returns	193,250	
Total Tax, $000	1,365,738	
Average Income, $.	27,207	
Average Tax, $.	7,067	

VITAL STATISTICS

	1997	1996	1995	1994
Births	3,822	4,163	4,370	4,398
Deaths	3,550	3,497	3,484	3,552
Natural Increase	272	666	886	846
Marriages	3,018	2,751	2,695	2,584

Note: Latest available data.

DAILY NEWSPAPER(S)

	Circulation Average Paid
Review (Niagara Falls)	17,206
St. Catharines Standard	
Sat	41,312
Mon-Fri	33,084
Welland-Port Colborne Tribune	15,293

COMMUNITY NEWSPAPER(S)

	Total Circulation
Fort Erie: The Shopping-Times	17,950
Fort Erie: The Times	11,785
Lincoln: Lincoln Post Express	15,656
Niagara Falls: Niagara Shopping News Wed/Sat	29,500
Niagara-on-the-Lake: Niagara Advance	6,186
Port Colborne: In Port	n.a.
Thorold: Thorold News	1,632
Welland: Regional Shopping News	22,000

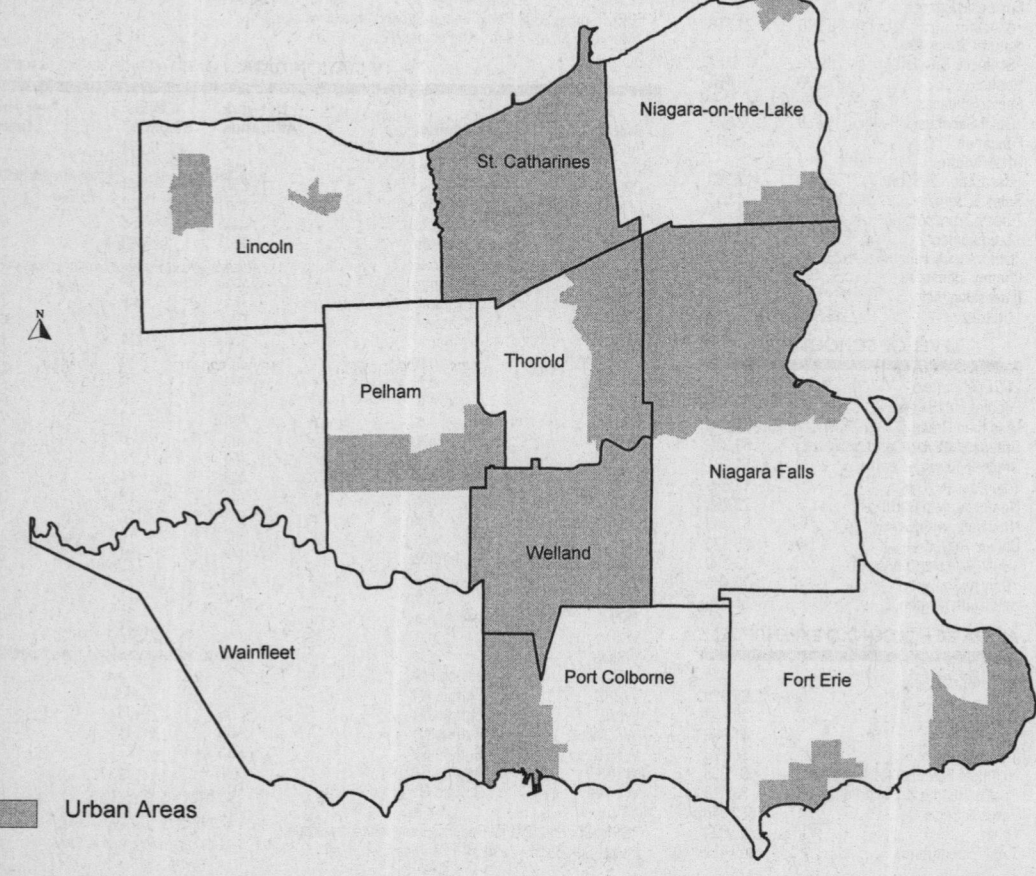

Urban Areas

Fort Erie
(Town)
St. Catharines-Niagara Falls
CMA

In Niagara Regional Municipality.

POPULATION

July 1, 2001 Estimate	29,403
% Cdn. Total	0.09
% Change, '96 -'01	5.22
Avg. Annual Growth Rate, %	1.02
2003 Projected Population	30,145
2006 Projected Population	31,203
2001 Households Estimate	12,027
2003 Projected Households	12,415
2006 Projected Households	13,006

INCOME

% Above/Below National Average	-10
2001 Total Income Estimate	$555,090,000
% Cdn. Total	0.08
2001 Average Hhld. Income	$46,200
2001 Per Capita	$18,900
2003 Projected Total Income	$593,830,000
2006 Projected Total Income	$656,370,000

RETAIL SALES

% Above/Below National Average	same
2001 Retail Sales Estimate	$263,550,000
% Cdn. Total	0.09
2001 per Household	$21,900
2001 per Capita	$9,000
2001 No. of Establishments	192
2003 Projected Retail Sales	$290,770,000
2006 Projected Retail Sales	$330,730,000

POPULATION

2001 Estimates:

Total		29,403
Male		14,213
Female		15,190
Age Groups	Male	Female
0-4	838	817
5-9	926	907
10-14	1,003	954
15-19	1,010	945
20-24	928	877
25-29	835	853
30-34	899	985
35-39	1,059	1,131
40-44	1,090	1,145
45-49	1,030	1,098
50-54	911	971
55-59	783	836
60-64	701	751
65-69	672	743
70+	1,528	2,177

DAYTIME POPULATION

2001 Estimates:

Working Population	12,258
At Home Population	15,530
Total	27,788

INCOME

2001 Estimates:

Avg. Household Income	$46,153
Avg. Family Income	$52,351
Per Capita Income	$18,879
Male:	
Avg. Employment Income	$30,401
Avg. Employment Income (Full Time)	$40,723
Female:	
Avg. Employment Income	$19,031
Avg. Employment Income (Full Time)	$29,673

DISPOSABLE & DISCRETIONARY INCOME

2001 Estimates:	Per Hhld.
Disposable Income	$38,310
Discretionary Income 1 (minus Food & Shelter)	$26,460
Discretionary Income 2 (minus Food, Shelter, & Other Expenditures)	$18,654

LIQUID ASSETS

1999 Estimates:	Per Hhld.
Equity Investments	$49,981
Interest Bearing Investments	$53,589
Total Liquid Assets	$103,570

CREDIT DATA

July 2000:

Pool of Credit	$270,272,004
Revolving Credit, No.	52,452
Fixed Loans, No.	15,480
Avg. Credit Limit, per Person	$10,656
Avg. Spent, per Person	$5,047
Satisfactory Ratings, No. per Person	2.57
Avg. No. of Cards, per Person	0.94

LABOUR FORCE

2001 Estimates:

Male:	
In the Labour Force	7,953
Participation Rate	69.5
Employed	7,455
Unemployed	498
Unemployment Rate	6.3
Not in Labour Force	3,493
Female:	
In the Labour Force	6,833
Participation Rate	54.6
Employed	6,331
Unemployed	502
Unemployment Rate	7.3
Not in Labour Force	5,679

OCCUPATIONS BY MAJOR GROUPS

2001 Estimates:	Male	Female
Management	789	392
Business, Finance & Admin.	743	2,184
Natural & Applied Sciences & Related	420	56
Health	67	481
Social Sciences, Gov't Services & Religion	187	171
Education	171	222
Arts, Culture, Recreation & Sport	133	138
Sales & Service	1,610	2,348
Trades, Transport & Equipment Operators & Related	2,355	109
Primary Industries	367	155
Processing, Mfg. & Utilities	936	338

LEVEL OF SCHOOLING

2001 Estimates:

Population 15 years +	23,958
Less than Grade 9	2,094
Grades 9-13 w/o Certif.	6,954
Grade 9-13 with Certif.	4,249
Trade Certif./Dip.	1,199
Non-Univ. w/o Certif./Dip.	1,630
Non-Univ. with Certif./Dip.	4,126
Univ. w/o Degree	1,831
Univ. w/o Degree/Certif.	951
Univ. with Certif.	880
Univ. with Degree	1,875

AVERAGE HOUSEHOLD EXPENDITURES

2001 Estimates:

Food	$5,537
Shelter	$8,139
Clothing	$1,761
Transportation	$6,080
Health & Personal Care	$1,698
Recr'n, Read'g & Education	$3,224
Taxes & Securities	$11,358
Other	$7,679
Total Expenditures	$45,476

PRIVATE HOUSEHOLDS

2001 Estimates:

Private Households, Total	12,027
Pop. in Private Households	28,852
Average no. per Household	2.4

FAMILIES

2001 Estimates:

Families in Private Households	8,529
Husband-Wife Families	7,332
Lone-Parent Families	1,197
Aver. No. Persons per Family	2.9
Aver. No. Sons/Daughters at Home	1.1

HOUSING

2001 Estimates:

Occupied Private Dwellings	12,027
Owned	9,140
Rented	2,887
Single-Detached House	9,888
Semi-Detached House	151
Row Houses	106
Apartment, 5+ Storeys	327
Apartment, 5 or Fewer Storeys	788
Apartment, Detached Duplex	462
Other Single-Attached	11
Movable Dwellings	294

VEHICLES

2001 Estimates:

Model Yrs. '81-'96, No.	14,507
% Total	85.86
Model Yrs. '97-'98, No.	1,480
% Total	8.76
'99 Vehicles registered in Model Yr. '99, No.	910
% Total	5.39
Total No. '81-'99	16,897

LEGAL MARITAL STATUS

2001 Estimates: (Age 15+)

Single (Never Married)	5,914
Legally Married (Not Separated)	13,151
Legally Married (Separated)	977
Widowed	2,034
Divorced	1,882

PSYTE CATEGORIES

2001 Estimates	No. of House-holds	% of Total Hhds.	Index
Boomers & Teens	150	1.25	70
Blue Collar Winners	585	4.86	193
Old Towns' New Fringe	4,104	34.12	872
Conservative Homebodies	414	3.44	95
Old Leafy Towns	2,399	19.95	780
Nesters & Young Homesteaders	321	2.67	114
Quiet Towns	1,754	14.58	685
Struggling Downtowns	2,270	18.87	599

Ontario

FINANCIAL P$YTE

2001 Estimates	No. of House -holds	% of Total Hhds.	Index
Four Star Investors	150	1.25	25
Canadian Comfort	585	4.86	50
Tractors & Tradelines	4,104	34.12	597
Bills & Wills	2,813	23.39	282
Revolving Renters	321	2.67	58
Limited Budgets	1,754	14.58	469
Towering Debt	2,270	18.87	242

HOME LANGUAGE

2001 Estimates:		% Total
English	28,205	95.93
French	146	0.50
Chinese	189	0.64
German	40	0.14
Greek	34	0.12
Gujarati	16	0.05
Hungarian	47	0.16
Italian	191	0.65
Korean	26	0.09
Russian	43	0.15
Spanish	81	0.28
Ukrainian	23	0.08
Urdu	40	0.14
Other Languages	10	0.03
Multiple Responses	312	1.06
Total	29,403	100.00

BUILDING PERMITS

	1999	1998 $000	1997
Value	47,376	21,506	38,556

HOMES BUILT

	1999	1998	1997
No	126	133	94

TAXATION

Income Class:	1997	% Total
Under $5,000	2,450	12.22
$5,000-$10,000	2,410	12.02
$10,000-$15,000	3,100	15.46
$15,000-$20,000	2,240	11.17
$20,000-$25,000	1,870	9.33
$25,000-$30,000	1,740	8.68
$30,000-$40,000	2,510	12.52
$40,000-$50,000	1,650	8.23
$50,000 +	2,080	10.37
Total Returns, No.	20,050	
Total Income, $000	502,448	
Total Taxable Returns	13,500	
Total Tax, $000	81,143	
Average Income, $	25,060	
Average Tax, $	6,011	

VITAL STATISTICS

	1997	1996	1995	1994
Births	279	267	306	305
Deaths	281	274	240	284
Natural Increase	-2	-7	66	21
Marriages	137	123	148	148

Note: Latest available data.

MEDIA INFO
see St. Catharines-Niagara, CMA

Ontario

Lincoln
(Town)
St. Catharines-Niagara Falls
CMA

In Niagara Regional Municipality.

POPULATION

July 1, 2001 Estimate	21,170
% Cdn. Total	0.07
% Change, '96 -'01	9.55
Avg. Annual Growth Rate, %	1.84
2003 Projected Population	22,166
2006 Projected Population	23,621
2001 Households Estimate	7,561
2003 Projected Households	7,963
2006 Projected Households	8,580

INCOME

% Above/Below National Average	+5
2001 Total Income Estimate	$467,080,000
% Cdn. Total	0.07
2001 Average Hhld. Income	$61,800
2001 Per Capita	$22,100
2003 Projected Total Income	$513,450,000
2006 Projected Total Income	$590,290,000

RETAIL SALES

% Above/Below National Average	-21
2001 Retail Sales Estimate	$149,130,000
% Cdn. Total	0.05
2001 per Household	$19,700
2001 per Capita	$7,000
2001 No. of Establishments	143
2003 Projected Retail Sales	$167,200,000
2006 Projected Retail Sales	$194,910,000

POPULATION

2001 Estimates:

Total		21,170
Male		10,552
Female		10,618

Age Groups	Male	Female
0-4	703	642
5-9	849	742
10-14	871	749
15-19	785	685
20-24	669	624
25-29	633	620
30-34	724	755
35-39	804	834
40-44	820	798
45-49	735	698
50-54	618	605
55-59	512	532
60-64	457	496
65-69	419	465
70+	953	1,373

DAYTIME POPULATION

2001 Estimates:

Working Population	9,878
At Home Population	10,145
Total	20,023

INCOME

2001 Estimates:

Avg. Household Income	$61,775
Avg. Family Income	$66,776
Per Capita Income	$22,063
Male:	
Avg. Employment Income	$37,340
Avg. Employment Income (Full Time)	$47,849
Female:	
Avg. Employment Income	$21,707
Avg. Employment Income (Full Time)	$33,769

DISPOSABLE & DISCRETIONARY INCOME

2001 Estimates:	Per Hhld.
Disposable Income	$50,891
Discretionary Income 1 (minus Food & Shelter)	$36,158
Discretionary Income 2 (minus Food, Shelter, & Other Expenditures)	$26,274

LIQUID ASSETS

1999 Estimates:	Per Hhld.
Equity Investments	$96,180
Interest Bearing Investments	$77,595
Total Liquid Assets	$173,775

CREDIT DATA

July 2000:

Pool of Credit	$197,468,869
Revolving Credit, No.	36,090
Fixed Loans, No.	10,198
Avg. Credit Limit, per Person	$11,496
Avg. Spent, per Person	$4,898
Satisfactory Ratings, No. per Person	2.61
Avg. No. of Cards, per Person	0.93

LABOUR FORCE

2001 Estimates:

Male:	
In the Labour Force	6,235
Participation Rate	76.7
Employed	6,171
Unemployed	64
Unemployment Rate	1.0
Not in Labour Force	1,894
Female:	
In the Labour Force	4,934
Participation Rate	58.1
Employed	4,813
Unemployed	121
Unemployment Rate	2.5
Not in Labour Force	3,551

OCCUPATIONS BY MAJOR GROUPS

2001 Estimates:	Male	Female
Management	688	275
Business, Finance & Admin.	390	1,344
Natural & Applied Sciences & Related	448	37
Health	66	497
Social Sciences, Gov't Services & Religion	57	204
Education	187	233
Arts, Culture, Recreation & Sport	53	95
Sales & Service	987	1,357
Trades, Transport & Equipment Operators & Related	1,653	150
Primary Industries	861	492
Processing, Mfg. & Utilities	762	176

LEVEL OF SCHOOLING

2001 Estimates:

Population 15 years +	16,614
Less than Grade 9	1,576
Grades 9-13 w/o Certif.	3,799
Grade 9-13 with Certif.	2,661
Trade Certif. /Dip.	677
Non-Univ. w/o Certif./Dip.	1,015
Non-Univ. with Certif./Dip.	3,688
Univ. w/o Degree	1,380
Univ. w/o Degree/Certif.	627
Univ. with Certif.	753
Univ. with Degree	1,818

AVERAGE HOUSEHOLD EXPENDITURES

2001 Estimates:

Food	$6,634
Shelter	$10,254
Clothing	$2,285
Transportation	$7,847
Health & Personal Care	$2,035
Recr'n, Read'g & Education	$4,079
Taxes & Securities	$16,041
Other	$9,314
Total Expenditures	$58,489

PRIVATE HOUSEHOLDS

2001 Estimates:

Private Households, Total	7,561
Pop. in Private Households	20,485
Average no. per Household	2.7

FAMILIES

2001 Estimates:

Families in Private Households	6,179
Husband-Wife Families	5,604
Lone-Parent Families	575
Aver. No. Persons per Family	3.1
Aver. No. Sons/Daughters at Home	1.2

HOUSING

2001 Estimates:

Occupied Private Dwellings	7,561
Owned	5,965
Rented	1,596
Single-Detached House	5,446
Semi-Detached House	512
Row Houses	636
Apartment, 5+ Storeys	46
Apartment, 5 or Fewer Storeys	481
Apartment, Detached Duplex	184
Movable Dwellings	256

VEHICLES

2001 Estimates:

Model Yrs. '81-'96, No.	11,608
% Total	83.66
Model Yrs. '97-'98, No.	1,375
% Total	9.91
'99 Vehicles registered in Model Yr. '99, No.	893
% Total	6.44
Total No. '81-'99	13,876

LEGAL MARITAL STATUS

2001 Estimates: (Age 15+)

Single (Never Married)	3,837
Legally Married (Not Separated)	10,452
Legally Married (Separated)	406
Widowed	1,147
Divorced	772

PSYTE CATEGORIES

2001 Estimates	No. of House-holds	% of Total Hhds.	Index
Mortgaged in Suburbia	215	2.84	205
Satellite Suburbs	398	5.26	183
Blue Collar Winners	2,705	35.78	1,421
Old Towns' New Fringe	2,372	31.37	802
Rustic Prosperity	519	6.86	380
Conservative Homebodies	799	10.57	293
High Rise Sunsets	388	5.13	359

FINANCIAL P$YTE

2001 Estimates	No. of House-holds	% of Total Hhds.	Index
Successful Suburbanites	215	2.84	43
Canadian Comfort	3,103	41.04	422
Tractors & Tradelines	2,891	38.24	669
Bills & Wills	799	10.57	128
Revolving Renters	388	5.13	112

HOME LANGUAGE

2001 Estimates:		% Total
English	20,296	95.87
French	64	0.30
Chinese	18	0.09
Dutch	77	0.36
German	193	0.91
Greek	11	0.05
Hungarian	17	0.08
Italian	170	0.80
Polish	17	0.08
Portuguese	29	0.14
Punjabi	18	0.09
Russian	11	0.05
Serbian	17	0.08
Ukrainian	91	0.43
Other Languages	55	0.26
Multiple Responses	86	0.41
Total	21,170	100.00

BUILDING PERMITS

	1999	1998	1997
		$000	
Value	25,780	22,043	34,055

HOMES BUILT

	1999	1998	1997
No	107	154	203

TAXATION

Income Class:	1997	% Total
Under $5,000	1,560	11.60
$5,000-$10,000	1,480	11.00
$10,000-$15,000	1,760	13.09
$15,000-$20,000	1,350	10.04
$20,000-$25,000	1,080	8.03
$25,000-$30,000	1,070	7.96
$30,000-$40,000	1,710	12.71
$40,000-$50,000	1,240	9.22
$50,000 +	2,200	16.36
Total Returns, No.	13,450	
Total Income, $000	398,367	
Total Taxable Returns	9,780	
Total Tax, $000	74,471	
Average Income, $	29,618	
Average Tax, $	7,615	

VITAL STATISTICS

	1997	1996	1995	1994
Births	256	244	251	249
Deaths	196	167	187	188
Natural Increase	60	77	64	61
Marriages	172	137	100	102

Note: Latest available data.

MEDIA INFO

see St. Catharines-Niagara, CMA

Niagara Falls
(City)
St. Catharines-Niagara Falls CMA
In Niagara Regional Municipality.

POPULATION

July 1, 2001 Estimate	81,562
% Cdn. Total	0.26
% Change, '96 -'01	3.15
Avg. Annual Growth Rate, %	0.62
2003 Projected Population	82,770
2006 Projected Population	84,434
2001 Households Estimate	32,770
2003 Projected Households	33,441
2006 Projected Households	34,469

INCOME

% Above/Below National Average	-9
2001 Total Income Estimate	$1,565,130,000
% Cdn. Total	0.24
2001 Average Hhld. Income	$47,800
2001 Per Capita	$19,200
2003 Projected Total Income	$1,647,550,000
2006 Projected Total Income	$1,779,560,000

RETAIL SALES

% Above/Below National Average	+7
2001 Retail Sales Estimate	$778,670,000
% Cdn. Total	0.28
2001 per Household	$23,800
2001 per Capita	$9,500
2001 No. of Establishments	592
2003 Projected Retail Sales	$849,210,000
2006 Projected Retail Sales	$951,510,000

POPULATION

2001 Estimates:

Total		81,562
Male		39,381
Female		42,181

Age Groups	Male	Female
0-4	2,455	2,291
5-9	2,657	2,432
10-14	2,722	2,496
15-19	2,642	2,487
20-24	2,560	2,509
25-29	2,505	2,616
30-34	2,713	2,917
35-39	2,941	3,159
40-44	2,987	3,190
45-49	2,865	3,064
50-54	2,526	2,681
55-59	2,102	2,281
60-64	1,841	2,068
65-69	1,767	2,040
70+	4,098	5,950

DAYTIME POPULATION

2001 Estimates:

Working Population	43,166
At Home Population	42,913
Total	86,079

INCOME

2001 Estimates:

Avg. Household Income	$47,761
Avg. Family Income	$54,205
Per Capita Income	$19,189
Male:	
Avg. Employment Income	$32,938
Avg. Employment Income (Full Time)	$44,248
Female:	
Avg. Employment Income	$18,236
Avg. Employment Income (Full Time)	$29,444

DISPOSABLE & DISCRETIONARY INCOME

2001 Estimates:

	Per Hhld.
Disposable Income	$39,575
Discretionary Income 1 (minus Food & Shelter)	$27,377
Discretionary Income 2 (minus Food, Shelter, & Other Expenditures)	$19,778

LIQUID ASSETS

1999 Estimates:

	Per Hhld.
Equity Investments	$59,752
Interest Bearing Investments	$58,322
Total Liquid Assets	$118,074

CREDIT DATA

July 2000:

Pool of Credit	$778,279,329
Revolving Credit, No.	154,555
Fixed Loans, No.	46,046
Avg. Credit Limit, per Person	$11,392
Avg. Spent, per Person	$5,041
Satisfactory Ratings, No. per Person	2.80
Avg. No. of Cards, per Person	1.01

LABOUR FORCE

2001 Estimates:

Male:	
In the Labour Force	22,112
Participation Rate	70.1
Employed	20,284
Unemployed	1,828
Unemployment Rate	8.3
Not in Labour Force	9,435
Female:	
In the Labour Force	19,826
Participation Rate	56.7
Employed	18,248
Unemployed	1,578
Unemployment Rate	8.0
Not in Labour Force	15,136

OCCUPATIONS BY MAJOR GROUPS

2001 Estimates:

	Male	Female
Management	2,317	1,064
Business, Finance & Admin.	1,778	4,872
Natural & Applied Sciences & Related	1,126	103
Health	200	1,655
Social Sciences, Gov't Services & Religion	264	443
Education	537	666
Arts, Culture, Recreation & Sport	342	435
Sales & Service	5,598	8,884
Trades, Transport & Equipment Operators & Related	5,758	297
Primary Industries	502	113
Processing, Mfg. & Utilities	3,108	540

LEVEL OF SCHOOLING

2001 Estimates:

Population 15 years +	66,509
Less than Grade 9	7,130
Grades 9-13 w/o Certif.	17,734
Grade 9-13 with Certif.	10,779
Trade Certif. /Dip.	2,785
Non-Univ. w/o Certif./Dip.	4,626
Non-Univ. with Certif./Dip.	13,009
Univ. w/o Degree	5,135
Univ. w/o Degree/Certif.	2,623
Univ. with Certif.	2,512
Univ. with Degree	5,311

AVERAGE HOUSEHOLD EXPENDITURES

2001 Estimates:

Food	$5,714
Shelter	$8,352
Clothing	$1,905
Transportation	$5,814
Health & Personal Care	$1,718
Recr'n, Read'g & Education	$3,212
Taxes & Securities	$11,942
Other	$8,014
Total Expenditures	$46,671

PRIVATE HOUSEHOLDS

2001 Estimates:

Private Households, Total	32,770
Pop. in Private Households	80,570
Average no. per Household	2.5

FAMILIES

2001 Estimates:

Families in Private Households	23,874
Husband-Wife Families	20,054
Lone-Parent Families	3,820
Aver. No. Persons per Family	2.9
Aver. No. Sons/Daughters at Home	1.1

HOUSING

2001 Estimates:

Occupied Private Dwellings	32,770
Owned	22,915
Rented	9,855
Single-Detached House	22,245
Semi-Detached House	1,916
Row Houses	1,515
Apartment, 5+ Storeys	1,522
Owned Apartment, 5+ Storeys	153
Apartment, 5 or Fewer Storeys	4,165
Apartment, Detached Duplex	1,160
Other Single-Attached	164
Movable Dwellings	83

VEHICLES

2001 Estimates:

Model Yrs. '81-'96, No.	41,547
% Total	83.40
Model Yrs. '97-'98, No.	5,147
% Total	10.33
'99 Vehicles registered in Model Yr. '99, No.	3,122
% Total	6.27
Total No. '81-'99	49,816

LEGAL MARITAL STATUS

2001 Estimates: (Age 15+)

Single (Never Married)	17,461
Legally Married (Not Separated)	36,191
Legally Married (Separated)	2,366
Widowed	5,266
Divorced	5,225

PSYTE CATEGORIES

2001 Estimates	No. of House -holds	% of Total Hhds.	Index
Boomers & Teens	692	2.11	118
Stable Suburban Families	383	1.17	90
Old Bungalow Burbs	2,940	8.97	541
Suburban Nesters	383	1.17	73
Satellite Suburbs	2,823	8.61	300
Kindergarten Boom	1,329	4.06	155
Blue Collar Winners	664	2.03	80
Old Towns' New Fringe	314	0.96	24
Conservative Homebodies	10,335	31.54	875
Town Renters	534	1.63	189
Nesters & Young Homesteaders	1,075	3.28	141
Struggling Downtowns	9,831	30.00	953
Aged Pensioners	1,017	3.10	233
Old Grey Towers	213	0.65	117

Ontario

FINANCIAL P$YTE

2001 Estimates	No. of House -holds	% of Total Hhds.	Index
Four Star Investors	692	2.11	42
Successful Suburbanites	383	1.17	18
Canadian Comfort	3,870	11.81	122
Miners & Credit-Liners	2,940	8.97	283
Mortgages & Minivans	1,329	4.06	61
Tractors & Tradelines	314	0.96	17
Bills & Wills	10,335	31.54	381
Revolving Renters	1,075	3.28	71
Towering Debt	10,365	31.63	405
Senior Survivors	1,230	3.75	199

HOME LANGUAGE

2001 Estimates		% Total
English	74,939	91.88
French	604	0.74
Bulgarian	71	0.09
Chinese	314	0.38
Croatian	54	0.07
German	80	0.10
Greek	97	0.12
Hungarian	142	0.17
Italian	1,993	2.44
Japanese	79	0.10
Korean	101	0.12
Latvian (Lettish)	52	0.06
Persian (Farsi)	52	0.06
Polish	440	0.54
Serbian	343	0.42
Serbo-Croatian	103	0.13
Spanish	138	0.17
Tagalog (Pilipino)	124	0.15
Ukrainian	118	0.14
Vietnamese	242	0.30
Other Languages	223	0.27
Multiple Responses	1,253	1.54
Total	81,562	100.00

BUILDING PERMITS

	1999	1998 $000	1997
Value	160,081	72,489	79,087

HOMES BUILT

	1999	1998	1997
No	257	298	278

Niagara Falls
(City)
St. Catharines-Niagara Falls CMA
(Cont'd)

TAXATION

Income Class:	1997	% Total
Under $5,000	6,620	11.47
$5,000-$10,000	7,400	12.82
$10,000-$15,000	9,320	16.14
$15,000-$20,000	6,710	11.62
$20,000-$25,000	5,320	9.21
$25,000-$30,000	4,640	8.04
$30,000-$40,000	6,920	11.98
$40,000-$50,000	4,170	7.22
$50,000 +	6,630	11.48
Total Returns, No.	57,740	
Total Income, $000	1,481,549	
Total Taxable Returns	40,180	
Total Tax, $000	258,673	
Average Income, $	25,659	
Average Tax, $	6,438	

VITAL STATISTICS

	1997	1996	1995	1994
Births	814	912	922	897
Deaths	724	667	674	683
Natural Increase	90	245	248	214
Marriages	1,087	843	760	686

Note: Latest available data.

MEDIA INFO
see St. Catharines-Niagara, CMA

Niagara-on-the-Lake
(Town)
St. Catharines-Niagara Falls CMA

In Niagara Regional Municipality.

POPULATION

July 1, 2001 Estimate	14,065
% Cdn. Total	0.05
% Change, '96 -'01	3.38
Avg. Annual Growth Rate, %	0.67
2003 Projected Population	14,288
2006 Projected Population	14,597
2001 Households Estimate	5,222
2003 Projected Households	5,331
2006 Projected Households	5,506

INCOME

% Above/Below National Average	+14
2001 Total Income Estimate	$338,750,000
% Cdn. Total	0.05
2001 Average Hhld. Income	$64,900
2001 Per Capita	$24,100
2003 Projected Total Income	$359,930,000
2006 Projected Total Income	$394,830,000

RETAIL SALES

% Above/Below National Average	+31
2001 Retail Sales Estimate	$165,200,000
% Cdn. Total	0.06
2001 per Household	$31,600
2001 per Capita	$11,700
2001 No. of Establishments	170
2003 Projected Retail Sales	$180,440,000
2006 Projected Retail Sales	$203,050,000

POPULATION

2001 Estimates:

Total		14,065
Male		7,037
Female		7,028

Age Groups	Male	Female
0-4	326	307
5-9	389	354
10-14	465	394
15-19	483	406
20-24	447	394
25-29	379	341
30-34	397	360
35-39	468	446
40-44	538	491
45-49	526	495
50-54	474	473
55-59	431	446
60-64	395	427
65-69	398	411
70+	921	1,283

DAYTIME POPULATION

2001 Estimates:

Working Population	11,810
At Home Population	6,843
Total	18,653

INCOME

2001 Estimates:

Avg. Household Income	$64,869
Avg. Family Income	$70,699
Per Capita Income	$24,084
Male:	
Avg. Employment Income	$35,477
Avg. Employment Income (Full Time)	$51,635
Female:	
Avg. Employment Income	$21,847
Avg. Employment Income (Full Time)	$35,832

DISPOSABLE & DISCRETIONARY INCOME

2001 Estimates:	Per Hhld.
Disposable Income	$52,898
Discretionary Income 1 (minus Food & Shelter)	$38,262
Discretionary Income 2 (minus Food, Shelter, & Other Expenditures)	$28,306

LIQUID ASSETS

1999 Estimates:	Per Hhld.
Equity Investments	$104,910
Interest Bearing Investments	$82,378
Total Liquid Assets	$187,288

CREDIT DATA

July 2000:

Pool of Credit	$155,190,000
Revolving Credit, No.	28,520
Fixed Loans, No.	6,166
Avg. Credit Limit, per Person	$11,462
Avg. Spent, per Person	$4,408
Satisfactory Ratings, No. per Person	2.50
Avg. No. of Cards, per Person	0.96

LABOUR FORCE

2001 Estimates:

Male:	
In the Labour Force	4,271
Participation Rate	72.9
Employed	4,180
Unemployed	91
Unemployment Rate	2.1
Not in Labour Force	1,586
Female:	
In the Labour Force	3,268
Participation Rate	54.7
Employed	3,110
Unemployed	158
Unemployment Rate	4.8
Not in Labour Force	2,705

OCCUPATIONS BY MAJOR GROUPS

2001 Estimates:	Male	Female
Management	496	235
Business, Finance & Admin.	271	798
Natural & Applied Sciences & Related	190	n.a.
Health	21	297
Social Sciences, Gov't Services & Religion	53	106
Education	103	186
Arts, Culture, Recreation & Sport	166	142
Sales & Service	708	936
Trades, Transport & Equipment Operators & Related	925	60
Primary Industries	953	273
Processing, Mfg. & Utilities	314	170

LEVEL OF SCHOOLING

2001 Estimates:

Population 15 years +	11,830
Less than Grade 9	1,403
Grades 9-13 w/o Certif.	2,584
Grade 9-13 with Certif.	1,596
Trade Certif. /Dip.	400
Non-Univ. w/o Certif./Dip.	612
Non-Univ. with Certif./Dip.	2,117
Univ. w/o Degree	1,349
Univ. w/o Degree/Certif.	563
Univ. with Certif.	786
Univ. with Degree	1,769

AVERAGE HOUSEHOLD EXPENDITURES

2001 Estimates:

Food	$6,579
Shelter	$10,329
Clothing	$2,351
Transportation	$7,973
Health & Personal Care	$2,060
Recr'n, Read'g & Education	$4,109
Taxes & Securities	$18,171
Other	$9,224
Total Expenditures	$60,796

PRIVATE HOUSEHOLDS

2001 Estimates:

Private Households, Total	5,222
Pop. in Private Households	13,240
Average no. per Household	2.5

FAMILIES

2001 Estimates:

Families in Private Households	4,160
Husband-Wife Families	3,836
Lone-Parent Families	324
Aver. No. Persons per Family	2.9
Aver. No. Sons/Daughters at Home	1.1

HOUSING

2001 Estimates:

Occupied Private Dwellings	5,222
Owned	4,544
Rented	678
Single-Detached House	4,931
Semi-Detached House	23
Row Houses	62
Apartment, 5 or Fewer Storeys	84
Apartment, Detached Duplex	45
Movable Dwellings	77

VEHICLES

2001 Estimates:

Model Yrs. '81-'96, No.	8,330
% Total	80.58
Model Yrs. '97-'98, No.	1,223
% Total	11.83
'99 Vehicles registered in Model Yr. '99, No.	785
% Total	7.59
Total No. '81-'99	10,338

LEGAL MARITAL STATUS

2001 Estimates: (Age 15+)

Single (Never Married)	2,690
Legally Married (Not Separated)	7,437
Legally Married (Separated)	250
Widowed	966
Divorced	487

PSYTE CATEGORIES

2001 Estimates	No. of House-holds	% of Total Hhds.	Index
Boomers & Teens	313	5.99	334
Small City Elite	264	5.06	295
Aging Erudites	1,300	24.89	1,650
Blue Collar Winners	2,465	47.20	1,875
Rustic Prosperity	363	6.95	385
Conservative Homebodies	369	7.07	196

FINANCIAL PSYTE

2001 Estimates	No. of House-holds	% of Total Hhds.	Index
Four Star Investors	313	5.99	119
Canadian Comfort	2,729	52.26	538
Urban Heights	1,300	24.89	579
Tractors & Tradelines	363	6.95	122
Bills & Wills	369	7.07	85

Niagara-on-the-Lake
(Town)
St. Catharines-Niagara Falls CMA
(Cont'd)

HOME LANGUAGE

2001 Estimates:		% Total
English	12,816	91.12
French	44	0.31
Chinese	27	0.19
Croatian	11	0.08
Estonian	16	0.11
German	610	4.34
Greek	28	0.20
Italian	110	0.78
Korean	10	0.07
Polish	66	0.47
Portuguese	60	0.43
Spanish	135	0.96
Ukrainian	23	0.16
Multiple Responses	109	0.77
Total	14,065	100.00

BUILDING PERMITS

	1999	1998	1997
		$000	
Value	51,461	64,240	55,155

HOMES BUILT

	1999	1998	1997
No.	134	124	53

TAXATION

Income Class:	1997	% Total
Under $5,000	1,050	10.46
$5,000-$10,000	1,130	11.25
$10,000-$15,000	1,360	13.55
$15,000-$20,000	1,030	10.26
$20,000-$25,000	860	8.57
$25,000-$30,000	770	7.67
$30,000-$40,000	1,250	12.45
$40,000-$50,000	810	8.07
$50,000 +	1,770	17.63
Total Returns, No.	10,040	
Total Income, $000	335,947	
Total Taxable Returns	7,420	
Total Tax, $000	68,897	
Average Income, $	33,461	
Average Tax, $	9,285	

VITAL STATISTICS

	1997	1996	1995	1994
Births	91	106	112	121
Deaths	148	151	154	180
Natural Increase	-57	-45	-42	-59
Marriages	262	243	230	186

Note: Latest available data.

MEDIA INFO
see St. Catharines-Niagara, CMA

Pelham
(Town)
St. Catharines-Niagara Falls CMA
In Niagara Regional Municipality.

POPULATION

July 1, 2001 Estimate	15,895
% Cdn. Total	0.05
% Change, '96 -'01	7.82
Avg. Annual Growth Rate, %	1.52
2003 Projected Population	16,505
2006 Projected Population	17,392
2001 Households Estimate	5,746
2003 Projected Households	6,004
2006 Projected Households	6,396

INCOME

% Above/Below National Average	+31
2001 Total Income Estimate	$439,800,000
% Cdn. Total	0.07
2001 Average Hhld. Income	$76,500
2001 Per Capita	$27,700
2003 Projected Total Income	$481,530,000
2006 Projected Total Income	$550,320,000

RETAIL SALES

% Above/Below National Average	+16
2001 Retail Sales Estimate	$165,000,000
% Cdn. Total	0.06
2001 per Household	$28,700
2001 per Capita	$10,400
2001 No. of Establishments	129
2003 Projected Retail Sales	$185,140,000
2006 Projected Retail Sales	$216,390,000

POPULATION

2001 Estimates:

Total		15,895
Male		7,915
Female		7,980

Age Groups	Male	Female
0-4	424	376
5-9	504	441
10-14	604	536
15-19	635	579
20-24	581	521
25-29	474	434
30-34	443	463
35-39	480	559
40-44	562	647
45-49	625	669
50-54	618	606
55-59	517	508
60-64	423	414
65-69	346	348
70+	679	879

DAYTIME POPULATION

2001 Estimates:	
Working Population	3,826
At Home Population	7,222
Total	11,048

INCOME

2001 Estimates:	
Avg. Household Income	$76,541
Avg. Family Income	$82,896
Per Capita Income	$27,669
Male:	
Avg. Employment Income	$45,616
Avg. Employment Income (Full Time)	$61,179
Female:	
Avg. Employment Income	$25,128
Avg. Employment Income (Full Time)	$38,006

DISPOSABLE & DISCRETIONARY INCOME

2001 Estimates:	Per Hhld.
Disposable Income	$61,985
Discretionary Income 1 (minus Food & Shelter)	$45,712
Discretionary Income 2 (minus Food, Shelter, & Other Expenditures)	$34,701

LIQUID ASSETS

1999 Estimates:	Per Hhld.
Equity Investments	$136,158
Interest Bearing Investments	$100,157
Total Liquid Assets	$236,315

CREDIT DATA

July 2000:	
Pool of Credit	$187,840,229
Revolving Credit, No.	32,409
Fixed Loans, No.	8,173
Avg. Credit Limit, per Person	$13,490
Avg. Spent, per Person	$5,325
Satisfactory Ratings, No. per Person	2.80
Avg. No. of Cards, per Person	1.06

LABOUR FORCE

2001 Estimates:	
Male:	
In the Labour Force	4,913
Participation Rate	77.0
Employed	4,756
Unemployed	157
Unemployment Rate	3.2
Not in Labour Force	1,470
Female:	
In the Labour Force	4,018
Participation Rate	60.6
Employed	3,838
Unemployed	180
Unemployment Rate	4.5
Not in Labour Force	2,609

OCCUPATIONS BY MAJOR GROUPS

2001 Estimates:	Male	Female
Management	641	239
Business, Finance & Admin.	375	1,107
Natural & Applied Sciences & Related	413	33
Health	117	486
Social Sciences, Gov't Services & Religion	165	198
Education	359	389
Arts, Culture, Recreation & Sport	47	105
Sales & Service	810	1,029
Trades, Transport & Equipment Operators & Related	1,056	48
Primary Industries	375	157
Processing, Mfg. & Utilities	455	118

LEVEL OF SCHOOLING

2001 Estimates:	
Population 15 years +	13,010
Less than Grade 9	840
Grades 9-13 w/o Certif.	2,581
Grade 9-13 with Certif.	1,763
Trade Certif. /Dip.	435
Non-Univ. w/o Certif./Dip.	756
Non-Univ. with Certif./Dip.	2,559
Univ. w/o Degree	1,307
Univ. w/o Degree/Certif.	795
Univ. with Certif.	512
Univ. with Degree	2,769

Ontario

AVERAGE HOUSEHOLD EXPENDITURES

2001 Estimates:	
Food	$7,330
Shelter	$11,598
Clothing	$2,691
Transportation	$8,733
Health & Personal Care	$2,364
Recr'n, Read'g & Education	$4,764
Taxes & Securities	$21,846
Other	$10,830
Total Expenditures	$70,156

PRIVATE HOUSEHOLDS

2001 Estimates:	
Private Households, Total	5,746
Pop. in Private Households	15,855
Average no. per Household	2.8

FAMILIES

2001 Estimates:	
Families in Private Households	4,692
Husband-Wife Families	4,387
Lone-Parent Families	305
Aver. No. Persons per Family	3.1
Aver. No. Sons/Daughters at Home	1.2

HOUSING

2001 Estimates:	
Occupied Private Dwellings	5,746
Owned	4,881
Rented	865
Single-Detached House	4,837
Semi-Detached House	124
Row Houses	175
Apartment, 5+ Storeys	107
Owned Apartment, 5+ Storeys	101
Apartment, 5 or Fewer Storeys	441
Apartment, Detached Duplex	62

VEHICLES

2001 Estimates:	
Model Yrs. '81-'96, No.	9,104
% Total	80.58
Model Yrs. '97-'98, No.	1,392
% Total	12.32
'99 Vehicles registered in Model Yr. '99, No.	802
% Total	7.10
Total No. '81-'99	11,298

LEGAL MARITAL STATUS

2001 Estimates: (Age 15+)	
Single (Never Married)	3,049
Legally Married (Not Separated)	8,401
Legally Married (Separated)	285
Widowed	699
Divorced	576

Ontario

Pelham
(Town)
St. Catharines-Niagara Falls
CMA
(Cont'd)

PSYTE CATEGORIES

2001 Estimates	No. of House -holds	% of Total Hhds.	Index
Urban Gentry	416	7.24	403
Boomers & Teens.	1,574	27.39	1,528
Stable Suburban Families	434	7.55	579
Aging Erudites	813	14.15	938
Blue Collar Winners	1,533	26.68	1,060
Rustic Prosperity	158	2.75	152
Conservative Homebodies	818	14.24	395

FINANÇIAL P$YTE

2001 Estimates	No. of House -holds	% of Total Hhds.	Index
Four Star Investors	1,990	34.63	689
Successful Suburbanites	434	7.55	114
Canadian Comfort	1,533	26.68	275
Urban Heights	813	14.15	329
Tractors & Tradelines	158	2.75	48
Bills & Wills	818	14.24	172

HOME LANGUAGE

2001 Estimates:		% Total
English	15,274	96.09
French	144	0.91
Armenian	17	0.11
Chinese	11	0.07
Dutch	11	0.07
German	22	0.14
Greek	56	0.35
Hungarian	28	0.18
Italian	60	0.38
Korean	17	0.11
Lithuanian	11	0.07
Persian (Farsi)	33	0.21
Polish	17	0.11
Slovak	22	0.14
Swedish	17	0.11
Ukrainian	33	0.21
Multiple Responses	122	0.77
Total	15,895	100.00

BUILDING PERMITS

	1999	1998 $000	1997
Value	22,429	14,290	17,407

HOMES BUILT

	1999	1998	1997
No	113	114	98

TAXATION

Income Class:	1997	% Total
Under $5,000	1,350	12.20
$5,000-$10,000	1,160	10.48
$10,000-$15,000	1,250	11.29
$15,000-$20,000	850	7.68
$20,000-$25,000	800	7.23
$25,000-$30,000	800	7.23
$30,000-$40,000	1,300	11.74
$40,000-$50,000	950	8.58
$50,000 +	2,590	23.40
Total Returns, No.	11,070	
Total Income, $000	396,493	
Total Taxable Returns	8,230	
Total Tax, $000	87,825	
Average Income, $	35,817	
Average Tax, $	10,671	

VITAL STATISTICS

	1997	1996	1995	1994
Births	118	122	117	142
Deaths	83	63	86	74
Natural Increase	35	59	31	68
Marriages	63	67	76	81

Note: Latest available data.

MEDIA INFO
see St. Catharines-Niagara, CMA

Port Colborne
(City)
St. Catharines-Niagara Falls
CMA

In Niagara Regional Municipality.

POPULATION

July 1, 2001 Estimate	19,003
% Cdn. Total	0.06
% Change, '96 -'01	0.18
Avg. Annual Growth Rate, %	0.04
2003 Projected Population	19,003
2006 Projected Population	18,959
2001 Households Estimate	7,832
2003 Projected Households	7,874
2006 Projected Households	7,947

INCOME

% Above/Below National Average	-10
2001 Total Income Estimate	$358,990,000
% Cdn. Total	0.05
2001 Average Hhld. Income	$45,800
2001 Per Capita	$18,900
2003 Projected Total Income	$372,890,000
2006 Projected Total Income	$395,250,000

RETAIL SALES

% Above/Below National Average	-1
2001 Retail Sales Estimate	$167,770,000
% Cdn. Total	0.06
2001 per Household	$21,400
2001 per Capita	$8,800
2001 No. of Establishments	150
2003 Projected Retail Sales	$179,570,000
2006 Projected Retail Sales	$196,370,000

POPULATION

2001 Estimates:		
Total		19,003
Male		9,175
Female		9,828
Age Groups	Male	Female
0-4	490	479
5-9	539	536
10-14	588	582
15-19	611	580
20-24	585	546
25-29	546	525
30-34	578	577
35-39	646	684
40-44	683	722
45-49	687	709
50-54	617	612
55-59	515	530
60-64	472	507
65-69	479	557
70+	1,139	1,682

DAYTIME POPULATION

2001 Estimates:	
Working Population	6,739
At Home Population	10,534
Total	17,273

INCOME

2001 Estimates:	
Avg. Household Income	$45,836
Avg. Family Income	$52,935
Per Capita Income	$18,891
Male:	
Avg. Employment Income	$32,967
Avg. Employment Income (Full Time)	$41,908
Female:	
Avg. Employment Income	$18,409
Avg. Employment Income (Full Time)	$29,851

DISPOSABLE & DISCRETIONARY INCOME

2001 Estimates:	Per Hhld.
Disposable Income	$38,043
Discretionary Income 1 (minus Food & Shelter)	$26,367
Discretionary Income 2 (minus Food, Shelter, & Other Expenditures)	$18,692

LIQUID ASSETS

1999 Estimates:	Per Hhld.
Equity Investments	$55,140
Interest Bearing Investments	$55,133
Total Liquid Assets	$110,273

CREDIT DATA

July 2000:	
Pool of Credit	$181,654,791
Revolving Credit, No.	35,248
Fixed Loans, No.	11,157
Avg. Credit Limit, per Person	$11,027
Avg. Spent, per Person	$4,949
Satisfactory Ratings, No. per Person	2.68
Avg. No. of Cards, per Person	0.97

LABOUR FORCE

2001 Estimates:	
Male:	
In the Labour Force	4,917
Participation Rate	65.1
Employed	4,634
Unemployed	283
Unemployment Rate	5.8
Not in Labour Force	2,641
Female:	
In the Labour Force	4,148
Participation Rate	50.4
Employed	3,777
Unemployed	371
Unemployment Rate	8.9
Not in Labour Force	4,083

OCCUPATIONS BY MAJOR GROUPS

2001 Estimates:	Male	Female
Management	378	185
Business, Finance & Admin.	305	997
Natural & Applied Sciences & Related	309	24
Health	94	477
Social Sciences, Gov't Services & Religion	65	125
Education	69	156
Arts, Culture, Recreation & Sport	92	83
Sales & Service	816	1,502
Trades, Transport & Equipment Operators & Related	1,508	112
Primary Industries	222	44
Processing, Mfg. & Utilities	928	261

LEVEL OF SCHOOLING

2001 Estimates:	
Population 15 years +	15,789
Less than Grade 9	2,501
Grades 9-13 w/o Certif.	4,206
Grade 9-13 with Certif.	2,523
Trade Certif. /Dip.	527
Non-Univ. w/o Certif./Dip.	1,049
Non-Univ. with Certif./Dip.	3,167
Univ. w/o Degree.	935
Univ. w/o Degree/Certif.	484
Univ. with Certif.	451
Univ. with Degree	881

Port Colborne
(City)
St. Catharines-Niagara Falls CMA
(Cont'd)

AVERAGE HOUSEHOLD EXPENDITURES

2001 Estimates:

Food	$5,543
Shelter	$7,928
Clothing	$1,815
Transportation	$5,998
Health & Personal Care	$1,656
Recr'n, Read'g & Education	$3,087
Taxes & Securities	$11,088
Other	$8,025
Total Expenditures	$45,140

PRIVATE HOUSEHOLDS

2001 Estimates:

Private Households, Total	7,832
Pop. in Private Households	18,599
Average no. per Household	2.4

FAMILIES

2001 Estimates:

Families in Private Households	5,607
Husband-Wife Families	4,841
Lone-Parent Families	766
Aver. No. Persons per Family	2.9
Aver. No. Sons/Daughters at Home	1.0

HOUSING

2001 Estimates:

Occupied Private Dwellings	7,832
Owned	5,637
Rented	2,195
Single-Detached House	5,911
Semi-Detached House	222
Row Houses	42
Apartment, 5+ Storeys	231
Apartment, 5 or Fewer Storeys	895
Apartment, Detached Duplex	451
Other Single-Attached	69
Movable Dwellings	11

VEHICLES

2001 Estimates:

Model Yrs. '81-'96, No.	11,049
% Total	85.62
Model Yrs. '97-'98, No.	1,168
% Total	9.05
'99 Vehicles registered in Model Yr. '99, No.	688
% Total	5.33
Total No. '81-'99	12,905

LEGAL MARITAL STATUS

2001 Estimates: (Age 15+)

Single (Never Married)	3,884
Legally Married (Not Separated)	8,820
Legally Married (Separated)	502
Widowed	1,521
Divorced	1,062

PSYTE CATEGORIES

2001 Estimates	No. of House-holds	% of Total Hhds.	Index
Old Bungalow Burbs	452	5.77	348
Blue Collar Winners	343	4.38	174
Old Towns' New Fringe	154	1.97	50
Rustic Prosperity	602	7.69	426
Conservative Homebodies	2,829	36.12	1,002
Nesters & Young Homesteaders	363	4.63	199
Agrarian Blues	806	10.29	4,807
Struggling Downtowns	2,231	28.49	905

FINANCIAL P$YTE

2001 Estimates	No. of House-holds	% of Total Hhds.	Index
Canadian Comfort	343	4.38	45
Miners & Credit-Liners	452	5.77	182
Tractors & Tradelines	756	9.65	169
Bills & Wills	2,829	36.12	436
Revolving Renters	363	4.63	101
Rural Family Blues	806	10.29	127
Towering Debt	2,231	28.49	365

HOME LANGUAGE

2001 Estimates:		% Total
English	17,579	92.51
French	294	1.55
Arabic	10	0.05
Chinese	48	0.25
Croatian	10	0.05
Dutch	27	0.14
German	36	0.19
Greek	10	0.05
Hungarian	46	0.24
Italian	598	3.15
Korean	52	0.27
Polish	15	0.08
Serbian	10	0.05
Slovak	10	0.05
Other Languages	30	0.16
Multiple Responses	228	1.20
Total	19,003	100.00

BUILDING PERMITS

	1999	1998	1997
		$000	
Value	8,103	14,637	11,872

HOMES BUILT

	1999	1998	1997
No.	25	41	30

TAXATION

Income Class:	1997	% Total
Under $5,000	1,750	11.95
$5,000-$10,000	1,750	11.95
$10,000-$15,000	2,290	15.64
$15,000-$20,000	1,700	11.61
$20,000-$25,000	1,320	9.02
$25,000-$30,000	1,180	8.06
$30,000-$40,000	1,830	12.50
$40,000-$50,000	1,040	7.10
$50,000 +	1,780	12.16
Total Returns, No.	14,640	
Total Income, $000	374,665	
Total Taxable Returns	10,030	
Total Tax, $000	63,549	
Average Income, $	25,592	
Average Tax, $	6,336	

VITAL STATISTICS

	1997	1996	1995	1994
Births	173	182	199	204
Deaths	193	208	221	199
Natural Increase	-20	-26	-22	5
Marriages	100	111	102	109

Note: Latest available data.

MEDIA INFO
see St. Catharines-Niagara, CMA

St. Catharines
(City)
St. Catharines-Niagara Falls CMA
In Niagara Regional Municipality.

POPULATION

July 1, 2001 Estimate	138,004
% Cdn. Total	0.44
% Change, '96 -'01	2.54
Avg. Annual Growth Rate, %	0.50
2003 Projected Population	139,610
2006 Projected Population	141,773
2001 Households Estimate	56,880
2003 Projected Households	57,874
2006 Projected Households	59,398

INCOME

% Above/Below National Average	-2
2001 Total Income Estimate	$2,853,740,000
% Cdn. Total	0.43
2001 Average Hhld. Income	$50,200
2001 Per Capita	$20,700
2003 Projected Total Income	$3,005,750,000
2006 Projected Total Income	$3,249,710,000

RETAIL SALES

% Above/Below National Average	+38
2001 Retail Sales Estimate	$1,698,660,000
% Cdn. Total	0.61
2001 per Household	$29,900
2001 per Capita	$12,300
2001 No. of Establishments	1,002
2003 Projected Retail Sales	$1,852,800,000
2006 Projected Retail Sales	$2,076,130,000

POPULATION

2001 Estimates:

Total	138,004
Male	66,142
Female	71,862

Age Groups	Male	Female
0-4	4,110	3,929
5-9	4,210	4,064
10-14	4,266	4,107
15-19	4,348	4,181
20-24	4,442	4,352
25-29	4,523	4,496
30-34	4,728	4,893
35-39	4,869	5,112
40-44	4,778	5,126
45-49	4,620	5,029
50-54	4,288	4,622
55-59	3,747	4,017
60-64	3,191	3,610
65-69	2,865	3,473
70+	7,157	10,851

DAYTIME POPULATION

2001 Estimates:

Working Population	66,947
At Home Population	71,825
Total	138,772

INCOME

2001 Estimates:

Avg. Household Income	$50,171
Avg. Family Income	$57,912
Per Capita Income	$20,679
Male:	
Avg. Employment Income	$35,671
Avg. Employment Income (Full Time)	$47,225
Female:	
Avg. Employment Income	$19,877
Avg. Employment Income (Full Time)	$31,472

Ontario

DISPOSABLE & DISCRETIONARY INCOME

2001 Estimates:	Per Hhld.
Disposable Income	$41,409
Discretionary Income 1 (minus Food & Shelter)	$28,742
Discretionary Income 2 (minus Food, Shelter, & Other Expenditures)	$21,026

LIQUID ASSETS

1999 Estimates:	Per Hhld.
Equity Investments	$66,915
Interest Bearing Investments	$62,265
Total Liquid Assets	$129,180

CREDIT DATA

July 2000:	
Pool of Credit	$1,291,634,672
Revolving Credit, No.	262,095
Fixed Loans, No.	70,516
Avg. Credit Limit, per Person	$10,890
Avg. Spent, per Person	$4,713
Satisfactory Ratings, No. per Person	2.71
Avg. No. of Cards, per Person	0.98

LABOUR FORCE

2001 Estimates:

Male:	
In the Labour Force	37,564
Participation Rate	70.1
Employed	35,328
Unemployed	2,236
Unemployment Rate	6.0
Not in Labour Force	15,992
Female:	
In the Labour Force	33,091
Participation Rate	55.4
Employed	30,696
Unemployed	2,395
Unemployment Rate	7.2
Not in Labour Force	26,671

OCCUPATIONS BY MAJOR GROUPS

2001 Estimates:	Male	Female
Management	3,625	1,889
Business, Finance & Admin.	2,957	8,534
Natural & Applied Sciences & Related	2,296	273
Health	482	2,595
Social Sciences, Gov't Services & Religion	755	881
Education	1,148	1,953
Arts, Culture, Recreation & Sport	670	911
Sales & Service	7,809	11,959
Trades, Transport & Equipment Operators & Related	9,673	487
Primary Industries	1,396	727
Processing, Mfg. & Utilities	5,589	1,541

Ontario

St. Catharines
(City)
St. Catharines-Niagara Falls CMA
(Cont'd)

LEVEL OF SCHOOLING

2001 Estimates:
Population 15 years +	113,318
Less than Grade 9	11,178
Grades 9-13 w/o Certif.	29,171
Grade 9-13 with Certif.	17,176
Trade Certif. /Dip.	4,159
Non-Univ. w/o Certif./Dip.	7,974
Non-Univ. with Certif./Dip.	21,039
Univ. w/o Degree	9,648
Univ. w/o Degree/Certif.	5,122
Univ. with Certif.	4,526
Univ. with Degree	12,973

AVERAGE HOUSEHOLD EXPENDITURES

2001 Estimates:
Food	$5,888
Shelter	$8,785
Clothing	$2,002
Transportation	$5,831
Health & Personal Care	$1,808
Recr'n, Read'g & Education	$3,366
Taxes & Securities	$12,702
Other	$8,233
Total Expenditures	$48,615

PRIVATE HOUSEHOLDS

2001 Estimates:
Private Households, Total	56,880
Pop. in Private Households	135,129
Average no. per Household	2.4

FAMILIES

2001 Estimates:
Families in Private Households	39,511
Husband-Wife Families	33,066
Lone-Parent Families	6,445
Aver. No. Persons per Family	2.9
Aver. No. Sons/Daughters at Home	1.1

HOUSING

2001 Estimates:
Occupied Private Dwellings	56,880
Owned	37,183
Rented	19,697
Single-Detached House	34,481
Semi-Detached House	3,198
Row Houses	3,786
Apartment, 5+ Storeys	6,446
Owned Apartment, 5+ Storeys	870
Apartment, 5 or Fewer Storeys	7,113
Apartment, Detached Duplex	1,692
Other Single-Attached	142
Movable Dwellings	22

VEHICLES

2001 Estimates:
Model Yrs. '81-'96, No.	70,297
% Total	81.57
Model Yrs. '97-'98, No.	9,462
% Total	10.98
'99 Vehicles registered in Model Yr. '99, No.	6,418
% Total	7.45
Total No. '81-'99	86,177

LEGAL MARITAL STATUS

2001 Estimates: (Age 15+)
Single (Never Married)	30,976
Legally Married (Not Separated)	60,281
Legally Married (Separated)	4,310
Widowed	9,323
Divorced	8,428

PSYTE CATEGORIES

2001 Estimates	No. of House-holds	% of Total Hhds.	Index
The Affluentials	436	0.77	120
Urban Gentry	1,233	2.17	121
Technocrafts & Bureaucrats	575	1.01	36
Boomers & Teens	388	0.68	38
Stable Suburban Families	1,240	2.18	167
Old Bungalow Burbs	5,958	10.47	632
Suburban Nesters	474	0.83	52
Aging Erudites	2,337	4.11	272
Satellite Suburbs	1,124	1.98	69
Kindergarten Boom	3,080	5.41	207
Blue Collar Winners	1,164	2.05	81
Old Towns' New Fringe	94	0.17	4
Europa	71	0.12	10
High Rise Melting Pot	300	0.53	35
Conservative Homebodies	14,275	25.10	696
High Rise Sunsets	1,791	3.15	220
University Enclaves	2,696	4.74	232
Young City Singles	1,404	2.47	108
Town Renters	2,763	4.86	562
Struggling Downtowns	12,075	21.23	674
Aged Pensioners	1,536	2.70	203
Big City Stress	562	0.99	87
Old Grey Towers	716	1.26	227

FINANCIAL P$YTE

2001 Estimates	No. of House-holds	% of Total Hhds.	Index
Platinum Estates	436	0.77	95
Four Star Investors	1,621	2.85	57
Successful Suburbanites	1,815	3.19	48
Canadian Comfort	2,762	4.86	50
Urban Heights	2,337	4.11	96
Miners & Credit-Liners	5,958	10.47	331
Mortgages & Minivans	3,080	5.41	82
Dollars & Sense	71	0.12	5
Tractors & Tradelines	94	0.17	3
Bills & Wills	14,275	25.10	303
Revolving Renters	1,791	3.15	68
Young Urban Struggle	2,696	4.74	100
Towering Debt	16,542	29.08	373
NSF	562	0.99	28
Senior Survivors	2,252	3.96	210

HOME LANGUAGE

2001 Estimates		% Total
English	126,098	91.37
French	1,377	1.00
Arabic	401	0.29
Armenian	90	0.07
Chinese	494	0.36
Czech	82	0.06
Dutch	171	0.12
Estonian	92	0.07
German	664	0.48
Greek	202	0.15
Italian	1,314	0.95
Japanese	101	0.07
Khmer (Cambodian)	85	0.06
Korean	112	0.08
Lao	323	0.23
Lithuanian	96	0.07
Polish	1,724	1.25
Russian	190	0.14
Serbo-Croatian	101	0.07
Slovenian	84	0.06
Spanish	639	0.46
Tagalog (Pilipino)	285	0.21
Ukrainian	520	0.38
Vietnamese	149	0.11
Other Languages	790	0.57
Multiple Responses	1,820	1.32
Total	138,004	100.00

BUILDING PERMITS

	1999	1998 $000	1997
Value	63,334	64,327	61,257

HOMES BUILT

	1999	1998	1997
No.	229	357	200

TAXATION

Income Class:	1997	% Total
Under $5,000	11,350	11.67
$5,000-$10,000	11,600	11.93
$10,000-$15,000	15,190	15.62
$15,000-$20,000	10,660	10.96
$20,000-$25,000	8,430	8.67
$25,000-$30,000	7,660	7.88
$30,000-$40,000	11,240	11.56
$40,000-$50,000	7,080	7.28
$50,000 +	14,060	14.46
Total Returns, No.	97,260	
Total Income, $000	2,696,162	
Total Taxable Returns	67,850	
Total Tax, $000	501,295	
Average Income, $	27,721	
Average Tax, $	7,388	

VITAL STATISTICS

	1997	1996	1995	1994
Births	1,415	1,532	1,611	1,594
Deaths	1,267	1,355	1,305	1,329
Natural Increase	148	177	306	265
Marriages	776	791	868	859

Note: Latest available data.

MEDIA INFO
see St. Catharines-Niagara, CMA

Thorold
(City)
St. Catharines-Niagara Falls CMA
In Niagara Regional Municipality.

POPULATION

July 1, 2001 Estimate	18,953
% Cdn. Total	0.06
% Change, '96 -'01	3.11
Avg. Annual Growth Rate, %	0.61
2003 Projected Population	19,230
2006 Projected Population	19,608
2001 Households Estimate	7,141
2003 Projected Households	7,287
2006 Projected Households	7,505

INCOME

% Above/Below National Average	-4
2001 Total Income Estimate	$382,000,000
% Cdn. Total	0.06
2001 Average Hhld. Income	$53,500
2001 Per Capita	$20,200
2003 Projected Total Income	$405,670,000
2006 Projected Total Income	$443,440,000

RETAIL SALES

% Above/Below National Average	-62
2001 Retail Sales Estimate	$65,260,000
% Cdn. Total	0.02
2001 per Household	$9,100
2001 per Capita	$3,400
2001 No. of Establishments	90
2003 Projected Retail Sales	$70,590,000
2006 Projected Retail Sales	$78,410,000

POPULATION

2001 Estimates:

Total		18,953
Male		9,368
Female		9,585

Age Groups	Male	Female
0-4	570	556
5-9	635	602
10-14	668	642
15-19	627	581
20-24	596	570
25-29	608	579
30-34	685	665
35-39	764	787
40-44	757	789
45-49	680	697
50-54	571	582
55-59	483	493
60-64	435	438
65-69	416	428
70+	873	1,176

DAYTIME POPULATION

2001 Estimates:

Working Population	9,026
At Home Population	9,564
Total	18,590

INCOME

2001 Estimates:

Avg. Household Income	$53,494
Avg. Family Income	$58,962
Per Capita Income	$20,155
Male:	
Avg. Employment Income	$36,835
Avg. Employment Income (Full Time)	$46,894
Female:	
Avg. Employment Income	$19,990
Avg. Employment Income (Full Time)	$29,587

DISPOSABLE & DISCRETIONARY INCOME

2001 Estimates:	Per Hhld.
Disposable Income	$44,194
Discretionary Income 1 (minus Food & Shelter)	$30,504
Discretionary Income 2 (minus Food, Shelter, & Other Expenditures)	$21,781

LIQUID ASSETS

1999 Estimates:	Per Hhld.
Equity Investments	$65,770
Interest Bearing Investments	$64,452
Total Liquid Assets	$130,222

CREDIT DATA

July 2000:	
Pool of Credit	$184,836,559
Revolving Credit, No.	35,479
Fixed Loans, No.	11,021
Avg. Credit Limit, per Person	$11,333
Avg. Spent, per Person	$5,339
Satisfactory Ratings, No. per Person	2.72
Avg. No. of Cards, per Person	0.94

LABOUR FORCE

2001 Estimates:

Male:	
In the Labour Force	5,414
Participation Rate	72.2
Employed	5,075
Unemployed	339
Unemployment Rate	6.3
Not in Labour Force	2,081
Female:	
In the Labour Force	4,553
Participation Rate	58.5
Employed	4,251
Unemployed	302
Unemployment Rate	6.6
Not in Labour Force	3,232

OCCUPATIONS BY MAJOR GROUPS

2001 Estimates:	Male	Female
Management	519	243
Business, Finance & Admin.	380	1,278
Natural & Applied Sciences & Related	338	60
Health	100	470
Social Sciences, Gov't Services & Religion	44	131
Education	177	132
Arts, Culture, Recreation & Sport	97	138
Sales & Service	982	1,719
Trades, Transport & Equipment Operators & Related	1,520	50
Primary Industries	148	69
Processing, Mfg. & Utilities	957	164

LEVEL OF SCHOOLING

2001 Estimates:

Population 15 years +	15,280
Less than Grade 9	2,038
Grades 9-13 w/o Certif.	4,011
Grade 9-13 with Certif.	2,484
Trade Certif./Dip.	568
Non-Univ. w/o Certif./Dip.	1,000
Non-Univ. with Certif./Dip.	2,697
Univ. w/o Degree	1,220
Univ. w/o Degree/Certif.	607
Univ. with Certif.	613
Univ. with Degree	1,262

AVERAGE HOUSEHOLD EXPENDITURES

2001 Estimates:

Food	$6,347
Shelter	$9,335
Clothing	$2,105
Transportation	$6,761
Health & Personal Care	$1,894
Recr'n, Read'g & Education	$3,570
Taxes & Securities	$12,945
Other	$8,625
Total Expenditures	$51,582

PRIVATE HOUSEHOLDS

2001 Estimates:

Private Households, Total	7,141
Pop. in Private Households	18,757
Average no. per Household	2.6

FAMILIES

2001 Estimates:

Families in Private Households	5,545
Husband-Wife Families	4,782
Lone-Parent Families	763
Aver. No. Persons per Family	3.0
Aver. No. Sons/Daughters at Home	1.2

HOUSING

2001 Estimates:

Occupied Private Dwellings	7,141
Owned	5,537
Rented	1,604
Single-Detached House	5,274
Semi-Detached House	661
Row Houses	182
Apartment, 5+ Storeys	114
Apartment, 5 or Fewer Storeys	670
Apartment, Detached Duplex	181
Other Single-Attached	59

VEHICLES

2001 Estimates:

Model Yrs. '81-'96, No.	9,825
% Total	83.50
Model Yrs. '97-'98, No.	1,270
% Total	10.79
'99 Vehicles registered in Model Yr. '99, No.	672
% Total	5.71
Total No. '81-'99	11,767

LEGAL MARITAL STATUS

2001 Estimates: (Age 15+)

Single (Never Married)	4,012
Legally Married (Not Separated)	8,848
Legally Married (Separated)	469
Widowed	1,013
Divorced	938

PSYTE CATEGORIES

2001 Estimates	No. of House-holds	% of Total Hhds.	Index
Old Bungalow Burbs	245	3.43	207
Satellite Suburbs	1,269	17.77	619
Kindergarten Boom	383	5.36	205
Blue Collar Winners	308	4.31	171
Old Towns' New Fringe	461	6.46	165
Europa	389	5.45	438
Conservative Homebodies	2,693	37.71	1,046
Struggling Downtowns	1,051	14.72	467
Aged Pensioners	338	4.73	356

FINANCIAL PSYTE

2001 Estimates	No. of House-holds	% of Total Hhds.	Index
Canadian Comfort	1,577	22.08	227
Miners & Credit-Liners	245	3.43	108
Mortgages & Minivans	383	5.36	81
Dollars & Sense	389	5.45	208
Tractors & Tradelines	461	6.46	113
Bills & Wills	2,693	37.71	455
Towering Debt	1,051	14.72	189
Senior Survivors	338	4.73	251

Ontario

HOME LANGUAGE

2001 Estimates:		% Total
English	17,766	93.74
French	70	0.37
Chinese	11	0.06
Croatian	10	0.05
Estonian	16	0.08
Finnish	12	0.06
German	16	0.08
Hungarian	12	0.06
Italian	726	3.83
Lao	16	0.08
Polish	54	0.28
Spanish	26	0.14
Tagalog (Pilipino)	21	0.11
Ukrainian	21	0.11
Urdu	11	0.06
Other Languages	10	0.05
Multiple Responses	155	0.82
Total	18,953	100.00

BUILDING PERMITS

	1999	1998	1997
		$000	
Value	11,264	10,141	8,750

HOMES BUILT

	1999	1998	1997
No	56	44	53

TAXATION

Income Class:	1997	% Total
Under $5,000	1,410	11.54
$5,000-$10,000	1,320	10.80
$10,000-$15,000	1,740	14.24
$15,000-$20,000	1,320	10.80
$20,000-$25,000	1,140	9.33
$25,000-$30,000	1,040	8.51
$30,000-$40,000	1,520	12.44
$40,000-$50,000	1,040	8.51
$50,000 +	1,690	13.83
Total Returns, No.	12,220	
Total Income, $000	325,042	
Total Taxable Returns	8,880	
Total Tax, $000	57,506	
Average Income, $	26,599	
Average Tax, $	6,476	

VITAL STATISTICS

	1997	1996	1995	1994
Births	166	195	211	232
Deaths	118	134	133	133
Natural Increase	48	61	78	99
Marriages	93	90	70	72

Note: Latest available data.

MEDIA INFO
see St. Catharines-Niagara, CMA

Ontario

Welland
(City)
St. Catharines-Niagara Falls
CMA
In Niagara Regional Municipality.

POPULATION

July 1, 2001 Estimate	50,935
% Cdn. Total	0.16
% Change, '96 -'01	2.35
Avg. Annual Growth Rate, %	0.47
2003 Projected Population	51,486
2006 Projected Population	52,224
2001 Households Estimate	20,661
2003 Projected Households	20,997
2006 Projected Households	21,520

INCOME

% Above/Below National Average	-8
2001 Total Income Estimate	$984,280,000
% Cdn. Total	0.15
2001 Average Hhld. Income	$47,600
2001 Per Capita	$19,300
2003 Projected Total Income	$1,039,940,000
2006 Projected Total Income	$1,129,930,000

RETAIL SALES

% Above/Below National Average	+17
2001 Retail Sales Estimate	$532,630,000
% Cdn. Total	0.19
2001 per Household	$25,800
2001 per Capita	$10,500
2001 No. of Establishments	314
2003 Projected Retail Sales	$579,730,000
2006 Projected Retail Sales	$648,020,000

POPULATION

2001 Estimates:

Total		50,935
Male		24,661
Female		26,274

Age Groups	Male	Female
0-4	1,532	1,453
5-9	1,619	1,516
10-14	1,635	1,491
15-19	1,660	1,511
20-24	1,694	1,574
25-29	1,634	1,646
30-34	1,712	1,787
35-39	1,847	1,946
40-44	1,879	1,979
45-49	1,817	1,887
50-54	1,626	1,685
55-59	1,353	1,427
60-64	1,127	1,237
65-69	998	1,233
70+	2,528	3,902

DAYTIME POPULATION

2001 Estimates:

Working Population	26,094
At Home Population	26,944
Total	53,038

INCOME

2001 Estimates:

Avg. Household Income	$47,639
Avg. Family Income	$54,899
Per Capita Income	$19,324
Male:	
Avg. Employment Income	$34,273
Avg. Employment Income (Full Time)	$45,921
Female:	
Avg. Employment Income	$19,743
Avg. Employment Income (Full Time)	$31,678

DISPOSABLE & DISCRETIONARY INCOME

2001 Estimates:	Per Hhld.
Disposable Income	$39,480
Discretionary Income 1 (minus Food & Shelter)	$27,239
Discretionary Income 2 (minus Food, Shelter, & Other Expenditures)	$19,510

LIQUID ASSETS

1999 Estimates:	Per Hhld.
Equity Investments	$56,783
Interest Bearing Investments	$57,684
Total Liquid Assets	$114,467

CREDIT DATA

July 2000:

Pool of Credit	$436,641,314
Revolving Credit, No.	90,884
Fixed Loans, No.	28,700
Avg. Credit Limit, per Person	$10,455
Avg. Spent, per Person	$4,684
Satisfactory Ratings, No. per Person	2.69
Avg. No. of Cards, per Person	0.94

LABOUR FORCE

2001 Estimates:

Male:	
In the Labour Force	13,708
Participation Rate	69.0
Employed	12,786
Unemployed	922
Unemployment Rate	6.7
Not in Labour Force	6,167
Female:	
In the Labour Force	11,916
Participation Rate	54.6
Employed	11,114
Unemployed	802
Unemployment Rate	6.7
Not in Labour Force	9,898

OCCUPATIONS BY MAJOR GROUPS

2001 Estimates:	Male	Female
Management	1,120	628
Business, Finance & Admin.	1,072	3,138
Natural & Applied Sciences & Related	658	119
Health	180	1,077
Social Sciences, Gov't Services & Religion	237	245
Education	416	560
Arts, Culture, Recreation & Sport	196	306
Sales & Service	2,542	4,403
Trades, Transport & Equipment Operators & Related	3,674	165
Primary Industries	246	79
Processing, Mfg. & Utilities	2,946	604

LEVEL OF SCHOOLING

2001 Estimates:

Population 15 years +	41,689
Less than Grade 9	5,754
Grades 9-13 w/o Certif.	10,744
Grade 9-13 with Certif.	7,175
Trade Certif. /Dip.	1,670
Non-Univ. w/o Certif./Dip.	3,299
Non-Univ. with Certif./Dip.	7,902
Univ. w/o Degree	2,413
Univ. w/o Degree/Certif.	1,224
Univ. with Certif.	1,189
Univ. with Degree	2,732

AVERAGE HOUSEHOLD EXPENDITURES

2001 Estimates:

Food	$5,733
Shelter	$8,368
Clothing	$1,903
Transportation	$5,947
Health & Personal Care	$1,725
Recr'n, Read'g & Education	$3,191
Taxes & Securities	$11,732
Other	$8,061
Total Expenditures	$46,660

PRIVATE HOUSEHOLDS

2001 Estimates:

Private Households, Total	20,661
Pop. in Private Households	49,994
Average no. per Household	2.4

FAMILIES

2001 Estimates:

Families in Private Households	14,850
Husband-Wife Families	12,430
Lone-Parent Families	2,420
Aver. No. Persons per Family	2.9
Aver. No. Sons/Daughters at Home	1.1

HOUSING

2001 Estimates:

Occupied Private Dwellings	20,661
Owned	14,206
Rented	6,455
Single-Detached House	13,604
Semi-Detached House	1,496
Row Houses	663
Apartment, 5+ Storeys	1,388
Owned Apartment, 5+ Storeys	22
Apartment, 5 or Fewer Storeys	2,407
Apartment, Detached Duplex	1,050
Other Single-Attached	53

VEHICLES

2001 Estimates:

Model Yrs. '81-'96, No.	25,861
% Total	84.92
Model Yrs. '97-'98, No.	2,794
% Total	9.17
'99 Vehicles registered in Model Yr. '99, No.	1,798
% Total	5.90
Total No. '81-'99	30,453

LEGAL MARITAL STATUS

2001 Estimates: (Age 15+)

Single (Never Married)	11,158
Legally Married (Not Separated)	22,296
Legally Married (Separated)	1,692
Widowed	3,513
Divorced	3,030

PSYTE CATEGORIES

2001 Estimates	No. of House-holds	% of Total Hhds.	Index
Old Bungalow Burbs	1,851	8.96	541
Satellite Suburbs	885	4.28	149
Kindergarten Boom	451	2.18	83
Blue Collar Winners	986	4.77	190
Old Towns' New Fringe	80	0.39	10
Conservative Homebodies	7,859	38.04	1,055
Young Urban Mix	250	1.21	57
Young City Singles	321	1.55	68
Town Renters	352	1.70	197
Nesters & Young Homesteaders	362	1.75	75
Agrarian Blues	875	4.24	1,978
Struggling Downtowns	5,594	27.08	860
Aged Pensioners	592	2.87	215

FINANCIAL P$YTE

2001 Estimates	No. of House-holds	% of Total Hhds.	Index
Canadian Comfort	1,871	9.06	93
Miners & Credit-Liners	1,851	8.96	283
Mortgages & Minivans	451	2.18	33
Tractors & Tradelines	80	0.39	7
Bills & Wills	8,109	39.25	474
Revolving Renters	362	1.75	38
Rural Family Blues	875	4.24	52
Towering Debt	6,267	30.33	389
Senior Survivors	592	2.87	152

HOME LANGUAGE

2001 Estimates:		% Total
English	45,080	88.50
French	2,734	5.37
Arabic	31	0.06
Chinese	118	0.23
Croatian	101	0.20
German	31	0.06
Hungarian	244	0.48
Italian	1,018	2.00
Korean	36	0.07
Polish	226	0.44
Slovak	48	0.09
Spanish	126	0.25
Ukrainian	103	0.20
Urdu	31	0.06
Vietnamese	26	0.05
Other Languages	132	0.26
Multiple Responses	850	1.67
Total	50,935	100.00

BUILDING PERMITS

	1999	1998	1997
		$000	
Value	31,887	25,427	31,590

HOMES BUILT

	1999	1998	1997
No	160	194	149

TAXATION

Income Class:	1997	% Total
Under $5,000	4,550	12.09
$5,000-$10,000	4,630	12.31
$10,000-$15,000	5,990	15.92
$15,000-$20,000	4,070	10.82
$20,000-$25,000	3,400	9.04
$25,000-$30,000	3,120	8.29
$30,000-$40,000	4,490	11.94
$40,000-$50,000	2,700	7.18
$50,000 +	4,680	12.44
Total Returns, No.	37,620	
Total Income, $000	948,825	
Total Taxable Returns	25,690	
Total Tax, $000	161,378	
Average Income, $	25,221	
Average Tax, $	6,282	

VITAL STATISTICS

	1997	1996	1995	1994
Births	480	569	596	604
Deaths	509	455	463	459
Natural Increase	-29	114	133	145
Marriages	277	310	316	303

Note: Latest available data.

Stratford
(Census Agglomeration)

The Census Agglomeration of Stratford consists solely of Stratford, C, in Perth County.

POPULATION

July 1, 2001 Estimate	30,537
% Cdn. Total	0.10
% Change, '96 -'01	2.48
Avg. Annual Growth Rate, %	0.49
2003 Projected Population	30,763
2006 Projected Population	30,933
2001 Households Estimate	12,642
2003 Projected Households	12,880
2006 Projected Households	13,188

INCOME

% Above/Below National Average	+1
2001 Total Income Estimate	$652,600,000
% Cdn. Total	0.10
2001 Average Hhld. Income	$51,600
2001 Per Capita	$21,400
2003 Projected Total Income	$697,410,000
2006 Projected Total Income	$766,390,000

RETAIL SALES

% Above/Below National Average	+89
2001 Retail Sales Estimate	$515,890,000
% Cdn. Total	0.19
2001 per Household	$40,800
2001 per Capita	$16,900
2001 No. of Establishments	275
2003 Projected Retail Sales	$559,060,000
2006 Projected Retail Sales	$618,120,000

POPULATION

2001 Estimates:

Total		30,537
Male		14,717
Female		15,820

Age Groups	Male	Female
0-4	975	889
5-9	1,007	928
10-14	1,012	963
15-19	995	982
20-24	1,023	1,016
25-29	1,040	1,042
30-34	1,121	1,126
35-39	1,175	1,178
40-44	1,179	1,211
45-49	1,085	1,152
50-54	908	964
55-59	734	775
60-64	600	665
65-69	519	653
70+	1,344	2,276

DAYTIME POPULATION

2001 Estimates:

Working Population	16,437
At Home Population	14,100
Total	30,537

INCOME

2001 Estimates:

Avg. Household Income	$51,622
Avg. Family Income	$59,683
Per Capita Income	$21,371
Male:	
Avg. Employment Income	$33,738
Avg. Employment Income (Full Time)	$41,909
Female:	
Avg. Employment Income	$21,713
Avg. Employment Income (Full Time)	$32,076

DISPOSABLE & DISCRETIONARY INCOME

2001 Estimates:	Per Hhld.
Disposable Income	$42,513
Discretionary Income 1 (minus Food & Shelter)	$28,792
Discretionary Income 2 (minus Food, Shelter, & Other Expenditures)	$20,537

LIQUID ASSETS

1999 Estimates:	Per Hhld.
Equity Investments	$64,412
Interest Bearing Investments	$62,016
Total Liquid Assets	$126,428

CREDIT DATA

July 2000:

Pool of Credit	$330,918,273
Revolving Credit, No.	60,928
Fixed Loans, No.	18,511
Avg. Credit Limit, per Person	$12,217
Avg. Spent, per Person	$5,455
Satisfactory Ratings, No. per Person	2.83
Avg. No. of Cards, per Person	1.02

LABOUR FORCE

2001 Estimates:

Male:	
In the Labour Force	8,871
Participation Rate	75.7
Employed	8,517
Unemployed	354
Unemployment Rate	4.0
Not in Labour Force	2,852
Female:	
In the Labour Force	8,360
Participation Rate	64.1
Employed	7,963
Unemployed	397
Unemployment Rate	4.7
Not in Labour Force	4,680

OCCUPATIONS BY MAJOR GROUPS

2001 Estimates:	Male	Female
Management	952	396
Business, Finance & Admin.	711	1,952
Natural & Applied Sciences & Related	496	121
Health	128	585
Social Sciences, Gov't Services & Religion	115	159
Education	248	263
Arts, Culture, Recreation & Sport	323	315
Sales & Service	1,592	2,578
Trades, Transport & Equipment Operators & Related	1,779	165
Primary Industries	164	22
Processing, Mfg. & Utilities	2,188	1,593

LEVEL OF SCHOOLING

2001 Estimates:

Population 15 years +	24,763
Less than Grade 9	2,163
Grades 9-13 w/o Certif.	7,392
Grade 9-13 with Certif.	3,925
Trade Certif. /Dip.	925
Non-Univ. w/o Certif./Dip.	1,529
Non-Univ. with Certif./Dip.	4,711
Univ. w/o Degree	1,792
Univ. w/o Degree/Certif.	957
Univ. with Certif.	835
Univ. with Degree	2,326

AVERAGE HOUSEHOLD EXPENDITURES

2001 Estimates:

Food	$6,203
Shelter	$9,663
Clothing	$2,036
Transportation	$6,308
Health & Personal Care	$2,009
Recr'n, Read'g & Education	$3,485
Taxes & Securities	$11,472
Other	$8,842
Total Expenditures	$50,018

PRIVATE HOUSEHOLDS

2001 Estimates:

Private Households, Total	12,642
Pop. in Private Households	29,897
Average no. per Household	2.4

FAMILIES

2001 Estimates:

Families in Private Households	8,645
Husband-Wife Families	7,283
Lone-Parent Families	1,362
Aver. No. Persons per Family	2.9
Aver. No. Sons/Daughters at Home	1.1

HOUSING

2001 Estimates:

Occupied Private Dwellings	12,642
Owned	7,885
Rented	4,757
Single-Detached House	7,132
Semi-Detached House	1,214
Row Houses	513
Apartment, 5+ Storeys	377
Owned Apartment, 5+ Storeys	27
Apartment, 5 or Fewer Storeys	2,774
Apartment, Detached Duplex	534
Other Single-Attached	87
Movable Dwellings	11

VEHICLES

2001 Estimates:

Model Yrs. '81-'96, No.	15,270
% Total	80.74
Model Yrs. '97-'98, No.	2,300
% Total	12.16
'99 Vehicles registered in Model Yr. '99, No.	1,343
% Total	7.10
Total No. '81-'99	18,913

LEGAL MARITAL STATUS

2001 Estimates: (Age 15+)

Single (Never Married)	6,940
Legally Married (Not Separated)	12,985
Legally Married (Separated)	933
Widowed	2,121
Divorced	1,784

PSYTE CATEGORIES

2001 Estimates	No. of House-holds	% of Total Hhds.	Index
Small City Elite	1,294	10.24	597
Old Bungalow Burbs	326	2.58	156
Aging Erudites	134	1.06	70
Kindergarten Boom	318	2.52	96
Blue Collar Winners	376	2.97	118
Old Towns' New Fringe	1,536	12.15	310
Nesters & Young Homesteaders	8,147	64.44	2,761
Aged Pensioners	374	2.96	222
Old Grey Towers	129	1.02	184

Ontario

FINANCIAL P$YTE

2001 Estimates	No. of House-holds	% of Total Hhds.	Index
Canadian Comfort	1,670	13.21	136
Urban Heights	134	1.06	25
Miners & Credit-Liners	326	2.58	81
Mortgages & Minivans	318	2.52	38
Tractors & Tradelines	1,536	12.15	212
Revolving Renters	8,147	64.44	1,401
Senior Survivors	503	3.98	211

HOME LANGUAGE

2001 Estimates:		% Total
English	29,426	96.36
French	27	0.09
Arabic	30	0.10
Armenian	26	0.09
Chinese	53	0.17
German	32	0.10
Hindi	27	0.09
Hungarian	23	0.08
Italian	81	0.27
Khmer (Cambodian)	16	0.05
Lao	47	0.15
Malayalam	21	0.07
Polish	70	0.23
Portuguese	16	0.05
Punjabi	150	0.49
Romanian	16	0.05
Russian	32	0.10
Serbian	16	0.05
Spanish	42	0.14
Tagalog (Pilipino)	20	0.07
Vietnamese	51	0.17
Other Languages	65	0.21
Multiple Responses	250	0.82
Total	30,537	100.00

BUILDING PERMITS

	1999	1998 $000	1997
Value	36,317	29,214	34,209

HOMES BUILT

	1999	1998	1997
No	155	55	84

TAXATION

Income Class:	1997	% Total
Under $5,000	2,300	9.54
$5,000-$10,000	2,610	10.83
$10,000-$15,000	3,270	13.57
$15,000-$20,000	2,530	10.50
$20,000-$25,000	2,010	8.34
$25,000-$30,000	1,990	8.26
$30,000-$40,000	4,230	17.55
$40,000-$50,000	2,300	9.54
$50,000 +	2,860	11.87
Total Returns, No.	24,100	
Total Income, $000	680,112	
Total Taxable Returns	18,130	
Total Tax, $000	125,864	
Average Income, $	28,220	
Average Tax, $	6,942	

Ontario

Stratford
(Census Agglomeration)
(Cont'd)

VITAL STATISTICS

	1997	1996	1995	1994
Births	346	382	421	391
Deaths	313	283	300	288
Natural Increase	33	99	121	103
Marriages	238	233	265	263

Note: Latest available data.

DAILY NEWSPAPER(S)

	Circulation Average Paid
The Beacon-Herald	12,262

COMMUNITY NEWSPAPER(S)

	Total Circulation
Stratford: Marketplace	n.a.
Stratford: Inside Stratford/Perth	21,593

RADIO STATION(S)

	Power
CJCS	1,000w

Strathroy
(Census Agglomeration)

The Census Agglomeration of Strathroy consists solely of Strathroy, T in Middlesex County.

POPULATION

July 1, 2001 Estimate	13,225
% Cdn. Total	0.04
% Change, '96 -'01	7.74
Avg. Annual Growth Rate, %	1.50
2003 Projected Population	13,690
2006 Projected Population	14,412
2001 Households Estimate	4,899
2003 Projected Households	5,110
2006 Projected Households	5,450

INCOME

% Above/Below National Average	-7
2001 Total Income Estimate	$258,810,000
% Cdn. Total	0.04
2001 Average Hhld. Income	$52,800
2001 Per Capita	$19,600
2003 Projected Total Income	$286,550,000
2006 Projected Total Income	$334,450,000

RETAIL SALES

% Above/Below National Average	+84
2001 Retail Sales Estimate	$217,760,000
% Cdn. Total	0.08
2001 per Household	$44,500
2001 per Capita	$16,500
2001 No. of Establishments	122
2003 Projected Retail Sales	$239,540,000
2006 Projected Retail Sales	$274,370,000

POPULATION

2001 Estimates:

Total		13,225
Male		6,413
Female		6,812

Age Groups	Male	Female
0-4	467	445
5-9	517	470
10-14	517	483
15-19	466	473
20-24	426	446
25-29	434	471
30-34	499	520
35-39	523	561
40-44	504	513
45-49	440	437
50-54	348	375
55-59	290	317
60-64	249	273
65-69	216	246
70+	517	782

DAYTIME POPULATION

2001 Estimates:

Working Population	6,690
At Home Population	6,535
Total	13,225

INCOME

2001 Estimates:

Avg. Household Income	$52,830
Avg. Family Income	$58,039
Per Capita Income	$19,570
Male:	
Avg. Employment Income	$31,940
Avg. Employment Income (Full Time)	$42,985
Female:	
Avg. Employment Income	$21,026
Avg. Employment Income (Full Time)	$31,062

DISPOSABLE & DISCRETIONARY INCOME

2001 Estimates:	Per Hhld.
Disposable Income	$43,868
Discretionary Income 1 (minus Food & Shelter)	$30,375
Discretionary Income 2 (minus Food, Shelter, & Other Expenditures)	$21,054

LIQUID ASSETS

1999 Estimates:	Per Hhld.
Equity Investments	$66,140
Interest Bearing Investments	$62,258
Total Liquid Assets	$128,398

CREDIT DATA

July 2000:

Pool of Credit	$135,344,332
Revolving Credit, No.	22,901
Fixed Loans, No.	8,745
Avg. Credit Limit, per Person	$12,523
Avg. Spent, per Person	$6,168
Satisfactory Ratings, No. per Person	2.77
Avg. No. of Cards, per Person	0.98

LABOUR FORCE

2001 Estimates:

Male:	
In the Labour Force	3,770
Participation Rate	76.8
Employed	3,605
Unemployed	165
Unemployment Rate	4.4
Not in Labour Force	1,142
Female:	
In the Labour Force	3,160
Participation Rate	58.4
Employed	3,053
Unemployed	107
Unemployment Rate	3.4
Not in Labour Force	2,254

OCCUPATIONS BY MAJOR GROUPS

2001 Estimates:	Male	Female
Management	308	213
Business, Finance & Admin.	240	747
Natural & Applied Sciences & Related	211	59
Health	50	314
Social Sciences, Gov't Services & Religion	84	84
Education	59	92
Arts, Culture, Recreation & Sport	11	54
Sales & Service	699	1,004
Trades, Transport & Equipment Operators & Related	1,001	92
Primary Industries	346	85
Processing, Mfg. & Utilities	714	345

LEVEL OF SCHOOLING

2001 Estimates:

Population 15 years +	10,326
Less than Grade 9	1,606
Grades 9-13 w/o Certif.	2,713
Grade 9-13 with Certif.	1,684
Trade Certif. /Dip.	364
Non-Univ. w/o Certif./Dip.	631
Non-Univ. with Certif./Dip.	2,138
Univ. w/o Degree	516
Univ. w/o Degree/Certif.	241
Univ. with Certif.	275
Univ. with Degree	674

AVERAGE HOUSEHOLD EXPENDITURES

2001 Estimates:

Food	$6,366
Shelter	$9,298
Clothing	$2,031
Transportation	$7,198
Health & Personal Care	$2,059
Recr'n, Read'g & Education	$3,581
Taxes & Securities	$12,101
Other	$8,787
Total Expenditures	$51,421

PRIVATE HOUSEHOLDS

2001 Estimates:

Private Households, Total	4,899
Pop. in Private Households	12,900
Average no. per Household	2.6

FAMILIES

2001 Estimates:

Families in Private Households	3,821
Husband-Wife Families	3,337
Lone-Parent Families	484
Aver. No. Persons per Family	3.1
Aver. No. Sons/Daughters at Home	1.2

HOUSING

2001 Estimates:

Occupied Private Dwellings	4,899
Owned	3,624
Rented	1,275
Single-Detached House	3,289
Semi-Detached House	607
Row Houses	186
Apartment, 5 or Fewer Storeys	714
Apartment, Detached Duplex	91
Other Single-Attached	12

VEHICLES

2001 Estimates:

Model Yrs. '81-'96, No.	6,774
% Total	83.30
Model Yrs. '97-'98, No.	797
% Total	9.80
'99 Vehicles registered in Model Yr. '99, No.	561
% Total	6.90
Total No. '81-'99	8,132

LEGAL MARITAL STATUS

2001 Estimates: (Age 15+)

Single (Never Married)	2,497
Legally Married (Not Separated)	6,091
Legally Married (Separated)	402
Widowed	753
Divorced	583

PSYTE CATEGORIES

2001 Estimates	No. of House-holds	% of Total Hhds.	Index
Old Towns' New Fringe	2,449	49.99	1,277
Quiet Towns	2,339	47.74	2,244
Rod & Rifle	34	0.69	30

FINANCIAL P$YTE

2001 Estimates	No. of House-holds	% of Total Hhds.	Index
Tractors & Tradelines	2,449	49.99	874
Rural Family Blues	34	0.69	9
Limited Budgets	2,339	47.74	1,536

Strathroy
(Census Agglomeration)
(Cont'd)

HOME LANGUAGE

2001 Estimates:		% Total
English	11,984	90.62
French	21	0.16
Chinese	11	0.08
Czech	11	0.08
Dutch	98	0.74
German	11	0.08
Hungarian	22	0.17
Portuguese	883	6.68
Other Languages	11	0.08
Multiple Responses	173	1.31
Total	13,225	100.00

BUILDING PERMITS

	1999	1998	1997
		$000	
Value	15,525	24,048	n.a.

HOMES BUILT

	1999	1998	1997
No	44	74	117

TAXATION

Income Class:	1997	% Total
Under $5,000	1,260	11.38
$5,000–$10,000	1,300	11.74
$10,000–$15,000	1,640	14.81
$15,000–$20,000	1,320	11.92
$20,000–$25,000	1,040	9.39
$25,000–$30,000	960	8.67
$30,000–$40,000	1,480	13.37
$40,000–$50,000	900	8.13
$50,000 +	1,170	10.57
Total Returns, No.	11,070	
Total Income, $000	282,274	
Total Taxable Returns	7,850	
Total Tax, $000	46,747	
Average Income, $	25,499	
Average Tax, $	5,955	

VITAL STATISTICS

	1997	1996	1995	1994
Births	196	205	201	213
Deaths	136	143	147	133
Natural Increase	60	62	54	80
Marriages	67	75	55	74

Note: Latest available data.

COMMUNITY NEWSPAPER(S)

	Total Circulation
Strathroy: Strathroy Age Dispatch	4,957

Sudbury
(Census Metropolitan Area)

POPULATION

July 1, 2001 Estimate	159,453
% Cdn. Total	0.51
% Change, '96 -'01	-3.38
Avg. Annual Growth Rate, %	-0.68
2003 Projected Population	159,884
2006 Projected Population	160,377
2001 Households Estimate	64,914
2003 Projected Households	66,085
2006 Projected Households	67,724

INCOME

% Above/Below National Average	+4
2001 Total Income Estimate	$3,493,450,000
% Cdn. Total	0.53
2001 Average Hhld. Income	$53,800
2001 Per Capita	$21,900
2003 Projected Total Income	$3,729,580,000
2006 Projected Total Income	$4,104,290,000

RETAIL SALES

% Above/Below National Average	+24
2001 Retail Sales Estimate	$1,763,410,000
% Cdn. Total	0.63
2001 per Household	$27,200
2001 per Capita	$11,100
2001 No. of Establishments	1,300
2003 Projected Retail Sales	$1,893,960,000
2006 Projected Retail Sales	$2,080,950,000

POPULATION

2001 Estimates:

Total		159,453
Male		78,070
Female		81,383

Age Groups	Male	Female
0-4	4,951	4,716
5-9	4,985	4,800
10-14	5,095	4,993
15-19	5,460	5,321
20-24	5,860	5,652
25-29	5,671	5,568
30-34	5,788	5,892
35-39	6,043	6,356
40-44	5,955	6,455
45-49	5,836	6,131
50-54	5,291	5,352
55-59	4,381	4,457
60-64	3,600	3,807
65-69	3,119	3,383
70+	6,035	8,500

DAYTIME POPULATION

2001 Estimates:

Working Population	76,164
At Home Population	83,290
Total	159,454

INCOME

2001 Estimates:

Avg. Household Income	$53,817
Avg. Family Income	$62,090
Per Capita Income	$21,909
Male:	
Avg. Employment Income	$38,587
Avg. Employment Income (Full Time)	$51,612
Female:	
Avg. Employment Income	$21,908
Avg. Employment Income (Full Time)	$34,652

DISPOSABLE & DISCRETIONARY INCOME

2001 Estimates:	Per Hhld.
Disposable Income	$44,040
Discretionary Income 1 (minus Food & Shelter)	$30,749
Discretionary Income 2 (minus Food, Shelter, & Other Expenditures)	$22,287

LIQUID ASSETS

1999 Estimates:	Per Hhld.
Equity Investments	$71,563
Interest Bearing Investments	$66,062
Total Liquid Assets	$137,625

CREDIT DATA

July 2000:	
Pool of Credit	$1,580,088,369
Revolving Credit, No.	289,831
Fixed Loans, No.	105,815
Avg. Credit Limit, per Person	$11,432
Avg. Spent, per Person	$5,363
Satisfactory Ratings, No. per Person	2.65
Avg. No. of Cards, per Person	0.92

Ontario

RADIO STATION DATA

Station	Market	Format	Wkly. Reach%*	Aver. Hrs. Tuned
All Stations			95	22.8
CBCS-FM	Sudbury	News, Info.	16	13.8
CBL-FM	Toronto	All Info.	n.a.	n.a.
CBON-FM	Sudbury	Multi-format	3	12.4
CFJB-FM	Barrie	Rock	n.a.	n.a.
CHNO	Sudbury	Oldies	n.a.	n.a.
CHNO-FM	Sudbury	n.a.	34	9.2
CHYC	Sudbury	Adult Contemp.	n.a.	n.a.
CIGM	Sudbury	Country	24	15.6
CJMX-FM	Sudbury	Adult Contemp.	39	13.5
CJRQ-FM	Sudbury	AOR	48	12.0
CJTK-FM	Sudbury	Christian	n.a.	n.a.

BBM Spring 20009 Radio Reach Survey; area coverage.
*Mon-Sun 5a.m - 1a.m , All Persons 12+

TV STATION DATA

Station	Market	Network Affiliation	Wkly. Reach%*	Aver. Hrs. Tuned
All Stations			97	26.4
A & E	n.a.	Ind.	24	3.8
CABLE	n.a.	n.a.	6	3.6
CBLFT	Toronto	n.a.	9	7.6
CFJP	Montréal-Rimouski	TQS	6	6.3
CFTO	Toronto	CTV	3	4.7
CHCH	Toronto/Hamilton	Ind.	53	2.6
CHOT	Hull	TVA	4	9.4
CICI	Sudbury/Tim./NB	CTV	77	7.4
CICO-E	n.a.	n.a.	18	2.4
CIII	n.a.	Global	76	3.7
CKNC	Sudbury/Tim./NB	CBC	44	2.8
CMT	n.a.	Ind.	8	2.5
COMEDY	n.a.	Ind.	13	1.3
DSCVRY	n.a.	Ind.	11	2.8
FAMILY	n.a.	Ind.	8	1.8
HISTTV	n.a.	Ind.	7	2.1
M PIX	n.a.	Ind.	7	2.0
NEWSWD	n.a.	CBC	9	3.0
OTHERS	n.a.	n.a.	6	2.4
SHWCSE	n.a.	Ind.	9	2.4
SNET	n.a.	CTV	10	2.6
SPACE	n.a.	Ind.	10	2.7
TLC	n.a.	Ind.	18	1.7
TMN	Toronto	Ind.	12	2.9
TNN	Nashville TN	Ind.	9	1.8
TOON	n.a.	Ind.	11	1.6
TSN	n.a.	Ind.	24	5.1
VCR	n.a.	n.a.	25	4.2
VISION	n.a.	Ind.	8	2.0
WDIV	Detroit MI	NBC	19	3.0
WEATHR	n.a.	Ind.	13	1.6
WGTQ	S. S. Marie MI	ABC	23	2.1
WSBK	Boston MA	UPN	7	1.8
WTBS	Atlanta GA	Ind.	6	3.5
WTN	n.a.	Ind.	8	1.8
WTVS	Detroit MI	PBS	14	1.7
WUHF	Rochester NY	FOX	21	2.0
WWUP	S. S. Marie MI	CBS	21	2.5
YTV	n.a.	Ind.	16	2.7

BBM Spring 2000 TV Reach Survey; CMA coverage.
*Mon-Sun 6a.m - 2a.m , All Persons 2 +

Ontario

Sudbury
(Census Metropolitan Area)
(Cont'd)

LABOUR FORCE

2001 Estimates:
Male:
In the Labour Force 44,424
Participation Rate 70.5
Employed 40,983
Unemployed 3,441
Unemployment Rate 7.7
Not in Labour Force 18,615
Female:
In the Labour Force 38,006
Participation Rate 56.8
Employed 34,574
Unemployed 3,432
Unemployment Rate 9.0
Not in Labour Force 28,868

OCCUPATIONS BY MAJOR GROUPS

2001 Estimates:	Male	Female
Management	4,117	2,026
Business, Finance & Admin.	3,703	11,486
Natural & Applied Sciences & Related	2,706	421
Health	759	3,395
Social Sciences, Gov't Services & Religion	688	1,257
Education	1,176	2,278
Arts, Culture, Recreation & Sport	520	722
Sales & Service	9,487	13,263
Trades, Transport & Equipment Operators & Related	12,565	800
Primary Industries	4,408	175
Processing, Mfg. & Utilities	2,643	282

LEVEL OF SCHOOLING

2001 Estimates:
Population 15 years + ...129,913
Less than Grade 9......................16,034
Grades 9-13 w/o Certif. 32,078
Grade 9-13 with Certif. 17,814
Trade Certif./Dip. 5,390
Non-Univ. w/o Certif./Dip. 9,217
Non-Univ. with Certif./Dip. 26,284
Univ. w/o Degree 9,925
Univ. w/o Degree/Certif. 5,478
Univ. with Certif. 4,447
Univ. with Degree 13,171

AVERAGE HOUSEHOLD EXPENDITURES

2001 Estimates:
Food $6,239
Shelter $9,119
Clothing $2,111
Transportation $6,472
Health & Personal Care $1,912
Recr'n, Read'g & Education $3,699
Taxes & Securities $13,492
Other $8,692
Total Expenditures $51,736

PRIVATE HOUSEHOLDS

2001 Estimates:
Private Households, Total. 64,914
Pop. in Private Households 156,895
Average no. per Household 2.4

FAMILIES

2001 Estimates:
Families in Private Households 47,310
Husband-Wife Families 40,173
Lone-Parent Families 7,137
Aver. No. Persons per Family 3.0
Aver. No. Sons/Daughters
   at Home 1.2

HOUSING

2001 Estimates:
Occupied Private Dwellings 64,914
Owned 40,770
Rented 24,144
Single-Detached House 38,547
Semi-Detached House 3,410
Row Houses 2,937
Apartment, 5+ Storeys 4,557
   Owned Apartment, 5+ Storeys 155
Apartment, 5 or Fewer Storeys 9,965
Apartment, Detached Duplex 4,560
Other Single-Attached 333
Movable Dwellings 605

VEHICLES

2001 Estimates:
Model Yrs. '81-'96, No. 83,343
   % Total 82.37
Model Yrs. '97-'98, No. 10,967
   % Total 10.84
'99 Vehicles registered in
   Model Yr. '99, No. 6,877
   % Total 6.80
Total No. '81-'99. 101,187

LEGAL MARITAL STATUS

2001 Estimates: (Age 15+)
Single (Never Married) 39,446
Legally Married
   (Not Separated) 68,535
Legally Married (Separated) 4,473
Widowed 8,839
Divorced 8,620

PSYTE CATEGORIES

2001 Estimates	No. of House-holds	% of Total Hhds.	Index
The Affluentials	235	0.36	57
Urban Gentry	1,181	1.82	101
Suburban Executives	357	0.55	38
Technocrafts & Bureaucrats	455	0.70	25
Boomers & Teens	1,605	2.47	138
Stable Suburban Families	606	0.93	72
Small City Elite	1,461	2.25	131
Old Bungalow Burbs	2,260	3.48	210
Aging Erudites	1,155	1.78	118
Satellite Suburbs	1,459	2.25	78
Kindergarten Boom	172	0.26	10
Blue Collar Winners	3,098	4.77	190
Old Towns' New Fringe	14,865	22.90	585
Participation Quebec	1,126	1.73	60
Quebec Melange	977	1.51	57
Traditional French Cdn. Families	498	0.77	29
Rustic Prosperity	198	0.31	17
Conservative Homebodies	8,481	13.06	362
High Rise Sunsets	782	1.20	84
Young Urban Mix	414	0.64	30
University Enclaves	2,195	3.38	166
Young City Singles	1,425	2.20	96
Old Leafy Towns	731	1.13	44
Town Renters	1,900	2.93	339
Nesters & Young Homesteaders	577	0.89	38

2001 Estimates	No. of House-holds	% of Total Hhds.	Index
Agrarian Blues	320	0.49	230
Rod & Rifle	502	0.77	33
Big Country Families	842	1.30	91
Quebec Town Elders	417	0.64	23
Aging Quebec Urbanites	225	0.35	120
Quebec's New Urban Mosaic	331	0.51	21
Struggling Downtowns	9,755	15.03	477
Aged Pensioners	2,261	3.48	262
Big City Stress	1,018	1.57	139
Old Grey Towers	537	0.83	149

FINANCIAL P$YTE

2001 Estimates	No. of House-holds	% of Total Hhds.	Index
Platinum Estates	235	0.36	45
Four Star Investors	3,143	4.84	96
Successful Suburbanites	1,061	1.63	25
Canadian Comfort	6,018	9.27	95
Urban Heights	1,155	1.78	41
Miners & Credit-Liners	2,260	3.48	110
Mortgages & Minivans	1,298	2.00	30
Tractors & Tradelines	15,063	23.20	406
Bills & Wills	9,626	14.83	179
Country Credit	1,475	2.27	34
Revolving Renters	1,359	2.09	46
Young Urban Struggle	2,195	3.38	71
Rural Family Blues	1,664	2.56	32
Loan Parent Stress	642	0.99	17
Towering Debt	13,080	20.15	258
NSF	1,349	2.08	59
Senior Survivors	2,798	4.31	229

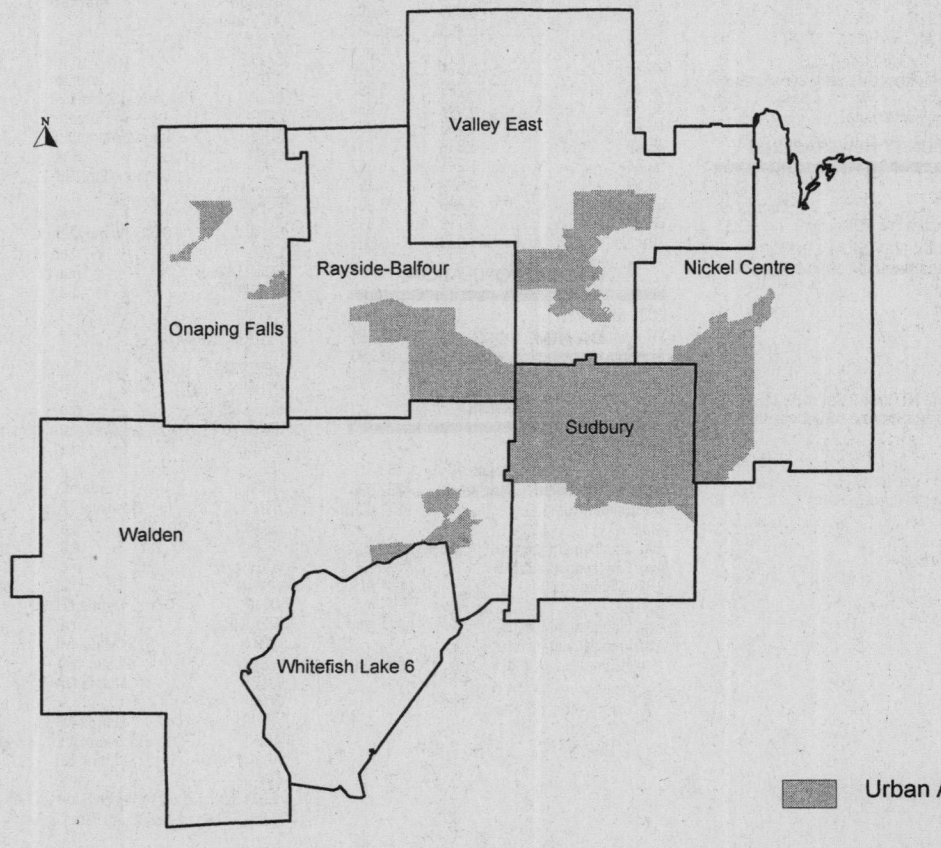

Urban Areas

Sudbury
(Census Metropolitan Area)
(Cont'd)

HOME LANGUAGE

2001 Estimates:		% Total
English	121,626	76.28
French	29,119	18.26
Chinese	274	0.17
Croatian	225	0.14
Finnish	566	0.35
German	165	0.10
Italian	1,574	0.99
Ojibway	140	0.09
Polish	344	0.22
Portuguese	89	0.06
Serbian	136	0.09
Spanish	151	0.09
Ukrainian	264	0.17
Other Languages	616	0.39
Multiple Responses	4,164	2.61
Total	159,453	100.00

BUILDING PERMITS

	1999	1998	1997
		$000	
Value	108,836	66,689	98,366

HOMES BUILT

	1999	1998	1997
No.	135	217	323

TAXATION

Income Class:	1997	% Total
Under $5,000	16,510	14.07
$5,000-$10,000	14,870	12.67
$10,000-$15,000	16,030	13.66
$15,000-$20,000	10,970	9.35
$20,000-$25,000	9,060	7.72
$25,000-$30,000	8,260	7.04
$30,000-$40,000	13,350	11.38
$40,000-$50,000	8,830	7.53
$50,000 +	19,440	16.57
Total Returns, No.	117,330	
Total Income, $000	3,240,974	
Total Taxable Returns	79,200	
Total Tax, $000	614,947	
Average Income, $	27,623	
Average Tax, $	7,764	

VITAL STATISTICS

	1997	1996	1995	1994
Births	1,633	1,746	1,813	1,928
Deaths	1,259	1,228	1,230	1,244
Natural Increase	374	518	583	684
Marriages	927	986	1,036	992

Note: Latest available data.

DAILY NEWSPAPER(S)

	Circulation Average Paid
The Sudbury Star	
Sat.	25,053
Sun-Fri.	21,776

COMMUNITY NEWSPAPER(S)

	Total Circulation
Sudbury: South Side Story	n.a.
Sudbury: Sudbury Northern Life	
Fri	47,617
Sun/Wed.	42,206
Sudbury: Le Voyageur	4,978

Nickel Centre
(Town)
Sudbury CMA
In Sudbury Regional Municipality.

POPULATION

July 1, 2001 Estimate	13,306
% Cdn. Total	0.04
% Change, '96 -'01	-0.58
Avg. Annual Growth Rate, %	-0.12
2003 Projected Population	13,528
2006 Projected Population	13,847
2001 Households Estimate	4,949
2003 Projected Households	5,117
2006 Projected Households	5,363

INCOME

% Above/Below National Average	+4
2001 Total Income Estimate	$291,370,000
% Cdn. Total	0.04
2001 Average Hhld. Income	$58,900
2001 Per Capita	$21,900
2003 Projected Total Income	$316,550,000
2006 Projected Total Income	$357,210,000

RETAIL SALES

% Above/Below National Average	-63
2001 Retail Sales Estimate	$43,840,000
% Cdn. Total	0.02
2001 per Household	$8,900
2001 per Capita	$3,300
2001 No. of Establishments	76
2003 Projected Retail Sales	$46,920,000
2006 Projected Retail Sales	$52,180,000

POPULATION

2001 Estimates:		
Total		13,306
Male		6,661
Female		6,645
Age Groups	Male	Female
0-4	450	420
5-9	477	465
10-14	495	490
15-19	491	486
20-24	458	432
25-29	439	416
30-34	516	525
35-39	578	585
40-44	556	550
45-49	500	482
50-54	415	420
55-59	335	345
60-64	279	280
65-69	244	233
70+	428	516

DAYTIME POPULATION

2001 Estimates:	
Working Population	7,024
At Home Population	6,748
Total	13,772

INCOME

2001 Estimates:	
Avg. Household Income	$58,875
Avg. Family Income	$62,632
Per Capita Income	$21,898
Male:	
Avg. Employment Income	$39,749
Avg. Employment Income (Full Time)	$52,010
Female:	
Avg. Employment Income	$21,147
Avg. Employment Income (Full Time)	$34,113

DISPOSABLE & DISCRETIONARY INCOME

2001 Estimates:	Per Hhld.
Disposable Income	$48,552
Discretionary Income 1 (minus Food & Shelter)	$34,256
Discretionary Income 2 (minus Food, Shelter, & Other Expenditures)	$24,545

LIQUID ASSETS

1999 Estimates:	Per Hhld.
Equity Investments	$79,329
Interest Bearing Investments	$70,583
Total Liquid Assets	$149,912

CREDIT DATA

July 2000:	
Pool of Credit	$140,760,441
Revolving Credit, No.	25,584
Fixed Loans, No.	11,329
Avg. Credit Limit, Per Person	$11,464
Avg. Spent, per Person	$5,735
Satisfactory Ratings, No. per Person	2.74
Avg. No. of Cards, per Person	0.89

LABOUR FORCE

2001 Estimates:	
Male:	
In the Labour Force	3,859
Participation Rate	73.7
Employed	3,572
Unemployed	287
Unemployment Rate	7.4
Not in Labour Force	1,380
Female:	
In the Labour Force	3,247
Participation Rate	61.6
Employed	2,929
Unemployed	318
Unemployment Rate	9.8
Not in Labour Force	2,023

OCCUPATIONS BY MAJOR GROUPS

2001 Estimates:	Male	Female
Management	365	137
Business, Finance & Admin.	339	1,122
Natural & Applied Sciences & Related	202	n.a.
Health	58	306
Social Sciences, Gov't Services & Religion	21	85
Education	42	133
Arts, Culture, Recreation & Sport	31	43
Sales & Service	654	1,126
Trades, Transport & Equipment Operators & Related	1,362	87
Primary Industries	405	n.a.
Processing, Mfg. & Utilities	267	21

LEVEL OF SCHOOLING

2001 Estimates:	
Population 15 years +	10,509
Less than Grade 9	1,034
Grades 9-13 w/o Certif.	2,994
Grade 9-13 with Certif.	1,570
Trade Certif. /Dip.	430
Non-Univ. w/o Certif./Dip.	721
Non-Univ. with Certif./Dip.	2,531
Univ. w/o Degree	672
Univ. w/o Degree/Certif.	363
Univ. with Certif.	309
Univ. with Degree	557

Ontario

AVERAGE HOUSEHOLD EXPENDITURES

2001 Estimates:	
Food	$6,653
Shelter	$9,799
Clothing	$2,195
Transportation	$7,573
Health & Personal Care	$2,060
Recr'n, Read'g & Education	$4,130
Taxes & Securities	$14,444
Other	$9,342
Total Expenditures	$56,196

PRIVATE HOUSEHOLDS

2001 Estimates:	
Private Households, Total	4,949
Pop. in Private Households	13,137
Average no. per Household	2.7

FAMILIES

2001 Estimates:	
Families in Private Households	4,056
Husband-Wife Families	3,569
Lone-Parent Families	487
Aver. No. Persons per Family	3.1
Aver. No. Sons/Daughters at Home	1.2

HOUSING

2001 Estimates:	
Occupied Private Dwellings	4,949
Owned	3,761
Rented	1,188
Single-Detached House	3,642
Semi-Detached House	238
Row Houses	207
Apartment, 5 or Fewer Storeys	278
Apartment, Detached Duplex	425
Movable Dwellings	159

VEHICLES

2001 Estimates:	
Model Yrs. '81-'96, No.	6,985
% Total	86.42
Model Yrs. '97-'98, No.	708
% Total	8.76
'99 Vehicles registered in Model Yr. '99, No.	390
% Total	4.82
Total No. '81-'99	8,083

LEGAL MARITAL STATUS

2001 Estimates: (Age 15+)	
Single (Never Married)	2,740
Legally Married (Not Separated)	6,181
Legally Married (Separated)	346
Widowed	622
Divorced	620

PSYTE CATEGORIES

2001 Estimates	No. of House-holds	% of Total Hhds.	Index
Kindergarten Boom	172	3.48	133
Blue Collar Winners	623	12.59	500
Old Towns' New Fringe	3,263	65.93	1,685
Conservative Homebodies	856	17.30	480

Ontario

Nickel Centre
(Town)
Sudbury CMA
(Cont'd)

FINANCIAL P$YTE

2001 Estimates	No. of House-holds	% of Total Hhds.	Index
Canadian Comfort	623	12.59	130
Mortgages & Minivans	172	3.48	53
Tractors & Tradelines	3,263	65.93	1,153
Bills & Wills	856	17.30	209

HOME LANGUAGE

2001 Estimates:		% Total
English	11,136	83.69
French	1,740	13.08
Italian	41	0.31
Ojibway	36	0.27
Polish	10	0.08
Ukrainian	10	0.08
Multiple Responses	333	2.50
Total	13,306	100.00

BUILDING PERMITS

	1999	1998 $000	1997
Value	2,488	2,144	7,343

HOMES BUILT

	1999	1998	1997
No.	14	14	58

TAXATION

Income Class:	1997	% Total
Under $5,000	1,380	13.94
$5,000-$10,000	1,160	11.72
$10,000-$15,000	1,250	12.63
$15,000-$20,000	970	9.80
$20,000-$25,000	810	8.18
$25,000-$30,000	770	7.78
$30,000-$40,000	1,240	12.53
$40,000-$50,000	820	8.28
$50,000 +	1,490	15.05
Total Returns, No.	9,900	
Total Income, $000	262,803	
Total Taxable Returns	6,930	
Total Tax, $000	47,599	
Average Income, $	26,546	
Average Tax, $	6,869	

VITAL STATISTICS

	1997	1996	1995	1994
Births	151	175	178	150
Deaths	87	84	85	76
Natural Increase	64	91	93	74
Marriages	64	50	55	70

Note: Latest available data.

MEDIA INFO
see Sudbury, CMA

Rayside-Balfour
(Town)
Sudbury CMA
In Sudbury Regional Municipality.

POPULATION

July 1, 2001 Estimate	16,559
% Cdn. Total	0.05
% Change, '96 -'01	0.36
Avg. Annual Growth Rate, %	0.07
2003 Projected Population	16,913
2006 Projected Population	17,435
2001 Households Estimate	6,117
2003 Projected Households	6,348
2006 Projected Households	6,694

INCOME

% Above/Below National Average	-1
2001 Total Income Estimate	$345,470,000
% Cdn. Total	0.05
2001 Average Hhld. Income	$56,500
2001 Per Capita	$20,900
2003 Projected Total Income	$377,330,000
2006 Projected Total Income	$429,450,000

RETAIL SALES

% Above/Below National Average	+45
2001 Retail Sales Estimate	$214,990,000
% Cdn. Total	0.08
2001 per Household	$35,100
2001 per Capita	$13,000
2001 No. of Establishments	121
2003 Projected Retail Sales	$236,950,000
2006 Projected Retail Sales	$272,120,000

POPULATION

2001 Estimates:		
Total		16,559
Male		8,256
Female		8,303
Age Groups	Male	Female
0-4	557	519
5-9	581	557
10-14	583	593
15-19	618	632
20-24	649	624
25-29	612	577
30-34	624	632
35-39	682	708
40-44	679	704
45-49	640	629
50-54	560	531
55-59	440	450
60-64	341	370
65-69	283	288
70+	407	489

DAYTIME POPULATION

2001 Estimates:	
Working Population	2,969
At Home Population	8,689
Total	11,658

INCOME

2001 Estimates:	
Avg. Household Income	$56,478
Avg. Family Income	$61,143
Per Capita Income	$20,863
Male:	
Avg. Employment Income	$40,271
Avg. Employment Income (Full Time)	$52,307
Female:	
Avg. Employment Income	$20,970
Avg. Employment Income (Full Time)	$35,089

DISPOSABLE & DISCRETIONARY INCOME

2001 Estimates:	Per Hhld.
Disposable Income	$46,475
Discretionary Income 1 (minus Food & Shelter)	$32,607
Discretionary Income 2 (minus Food, Shelter, & Other Expenditures)	$23,460

LIQUID ASSETS

1999 Estimates:	Per Hhld.
Equity Investments	$75,937
Interest Bearing Investments	$68,168
Total Liquid Assets	$144,105

CREDIT DATA

July 2000:	
Pool of Credit	$157,978,528
Revolving Credit, No.	28,322
Fixed Loans, No.	11,847
Avg. Credit Limit, per Person	$11,041
Avg. Spent, per Person	$5,393
Satisfactory Ratings, No. per Person	2.56
Avg. No. of Cards, per Person	0.83

LABOUR FORCE

2001 Estimates:	
Male:	
In the Labour Force	4,731
Participation Rate	72.4
Employed	4,451
Unemployed	280
Unemployment Rate	5.9
Not in Labour Force	1,804
Female:	
In the Labour Force	3,666
Participation Rate	55.3
Employed	3,249
Unemployed	417
Unemployment Rate	11.4
Not in Labour Force	2,968

OCCUPATIONS BY MAJOR GROUPS

2001 Estimates:	Male	Female
Management	324	192
Business, Finance & Admin.	215	1,110
Natural & Applied Sciences & Related	183	56
Health	10	306
Social Sciences, Gov't Services & Religion	53	134
Education	59	207
Arts, Culture, Recreation & Sport	52	72
Sales & Service	962	1,282
Trades, Transport & Equipment Operators & Related	1,421	65
Primary Industries	959	54
Processing, Mfg. & Utilities	303	n.a.

LEVEL OF SCHOOLING

2001 Estimates:	
Population 15 years +	13,169
Less than Grade 9	1,881
Grades 9-13 w/o Certif.	3,761
Grade 9-13 with Certif.	1,990
Trade Certif. /Dip.	615
Non-Univ. w/o Certif./Dip.	914
Non-Univ. with Certif./Dip.	2,616
Univ. w/o Degree	626
Univ. w/o Degree/Certif.	343
Univ. with Certif.	283
Univ. with Degree	766

AVERAGE HOUSEHOLD EXPENDITURES

2001 Estimates:	
Food	$6,736
Shelter	$9,169
Clothing	$2,206
Transportation	$7,021
Health & Personal Care	$2,052
Recr'n, Read'g & Education	$3,865
Taxes & Securities	$14,242
Other	$8,959
Total Expenditures	$54,250

PRIVATE HOUSEHOLDS

2001 Estimates:	
Private Households, Total	6,117
Pop. in Private Households	16,415
Average no. per Household	2.7

FAMILIES

2001 Estimates:	
Families in Private Households	5,050
Husband-Wife Families	4,403
Lone-Parent Families	647
Aver. No. Persons per Family	3.1
Aver. No. Sons/Daughters at Home	1.3

HOUSING

2001 Estimates:	
Occupied Private Dwellings	6,117
Owned	4,060
Rented	2,057
Single-Detached House	3,788
Semi-Detached House	400
Row Houses	340
Apartment, 5 or Fewer Storeys	946
Apartment, Detached Duplex	605
Other Single-Attached	38

VEHICLES

2001 Estimates:	
Model Yrs. '81-'96, No.	8,239
% Total	87.07
Model Yrs. '97-'98, No.	778
% Total	8.22
'99 Vehicles registered in Model Yr. '99, No.	446
% Total	4.71
Total No. '81-'99	9,463

LEGAL MARITAL STATUS

2001 Estimates: (Age 15+)	
Single (Never Married)	3,895
Legally Married (Not Separated)	7,487
Legally Married (Separated)	429
Widowed	614
Divorced	744

PSYTE CATEGORIES

2001 Estimates	No. of House-holds	% of Total Hhds.	Index
Blue Collar Winners	402	6.57	261
Old Towns' New Fringe	2,730	44.63	1,140
Participation Quebec	511	8.35	290
Quebec Melange	449	7.34	277
Traditional French Cdn. Families	316	5.17	192
Town Renters	414	6.77	783
Agrarian Blues	320	5.23	2,443
Rod & Rifle	256	4.19	181
Quebec Town Elders	417	6.82	241
Struggling Downtowns	200	3.27	104
Old Grey Towers	98	1.60	289

Rayside-Balfour
(Town)
Sudbury CMA
(Cont'd)

FINANCIAL P$YTE

2001 Estimates	No. of House -holds	% of Total Hhds.	Index
Canadian Comfort	402	6.57	68
Mortgages & Minivans	511	8.35	127
Tractors & Tradelines	2,730	44.63	780
Country Credit	765	12.51	185
Rural Family Blues	576	9.42	117
Loan Parent Stress	417	6.82	117
Towering Debt	614	10.04	129
Senior Survivors	98	1.60	85

HOME LANGUAGE

2001 Estimates:		% Total
English	8,533	51.53
French	7,471	45.12
Finnish	20	0.12
Polish	31	0.19
Spanish	11	0.07
Multiple Responses	493	2.98
Total	16,559	100.00

BUILDING PERMITS

	1999	1998 $000	1997
Value	3,902	4,444	5,794

HOMES BUILT

	1999	1998	1997
No.	14	31	25

TAXATION

Income Class:	1997	% Total
Under $5,000	1,880	16.07
$5,000-$10,000	1,500	12.82
$10,000-$15,000	1,400	11.97
$15,000-$20,000	1,050	8.97
$20,000-$25,000	930	7.95
$25,000-$30,000	740	6.32
$30,000-$40,000	1,330	11.37
$40,000-$50,000	830	7.09
$50,000 +	2,050	17.52
Total Returns, No.	11,700	
Total Income, $000	311,761	
Total Taxable Returns	7,770	
Total Tax, $000	57,878	
Average Income, $	26,646	
Average Tax, $	7,449	

VITAL STATISTICS

	1997	1996	1995	1994
Births	183	187	198	203
Deaths	76	86	70	85
Natural Increase	107	101	128	118
Marriages	72	78	87	71

Note: Latest available data.

MEDIA INFO
see Sudbury, CMA

Sudbury
(City)
Sudbury CMA

In Sudbury Regional Municipality.

POPULATION

July 1, 2001 Estimate	89,360
% Cdn. Total	0.29
% Change, '96 -'01	-5.60
Avg. Annual Growth Rate, %	-1.15
2003 Projected Population	88,530
2006 Projected Population	87,201
2001 Households Estimate	39,726
2003 Projected Households	40,022
2006 Projected Households	40,368

INCOME

% Above/Below National Average	+3
2001 Total Income Estimate	$1,944,770,000
% Cdn. Total	0.30
2001 Average Hhld. Income	$49,000
2001 Per Capita	$21,800
2003 Projected Total Income	$2,043,480,000
2006 Projected Total Income	$2,194,570,000

RETAIL SALES

% Above/Below National Average	+63
2001 Retail Sales Estimate	$1,302,740,000
% Cdn. Total	0.47
2001 per Household	$32,800
2001 per Capita	$14,600
2001 No. of Establishments	867
2003 Projected Retail Sales	$1,391,980,000
2006 Projected Retail Sales	$1,511,840,000

POPULATION

2001 Estimates:		
Total		89,360
Male		42,849
Female		46,511

Age Groups	Male	Female
0-4	2,660	2,565
5-9	2,513	2,467
10-14	2,492	2,469
15-19	2,737	2,663
20-24	3,207	3,201
25-29	3,265	3,320
30-34	3,239	3,276
35-39	3,168	3,354
40-44	3,054	3,436
45-49	3,036	3,383
50-54	2,831	3,028
55-59	2,461	2,589
60-64	2,113	2,307
65-69	1,905	2,178
70+	4,168	6,275

DAYTIME POPULATION

2001 Estimates:	
Working Population	57,387
At Home Population	47,837
Total	105,224

INCOME

2001 Estimates:	
Avg. Household Income	$48,955
Avg. Family Income	$59,765
Per Capita Income	$21,763
Male:	
Avg. Employment Income	$36,336
Avg. Employment Income (Full Time)	$49,373
Female:	
Avg. Employment Income	$22,386
Avg. Employment Income (Full Time)	$34,730

DISPOSABLE & DISCRETIONARY INCOME

2001 Estimates:	Per Hhld.
Disposable Income	$39,989
Discretionary Income 1 (minus Food & Shelter)	$27,615
Discretionary Income 2 (minus Food, Shelter, & Other Expenditures)	$20,108

LIQUID ASSETS

1999 Estimates:	Per Hhld.
Equity Investments	$63,617
Interest Bearing Investments	$60,893
Total Liquid Assets	$124,510

CREDIT DATA

July 2000:	
Pool of Credit	$922,776,362
Revolving Credit, No.	174,687
Fixed Loans, No.	56,567
Avg. Credit Limit, per Person	$10,992
Avg. Spent, per Person	$4,990
Satisfactory Ratings, No. per Person	2.58
Avg. No. of Cards, per Person	0.92

LABOUR FORCE

2001 Estimates:	
Male:	
In the Labour Force	23,990
Participation Rate	68.2
Employed	21,815
Unemployed	2,175
Unemployment Rate	9.1
Not in Labour Force	11,194
Female:	
In the Labour Force	21,518
Participation Rate	55.2
Employed	19,707
Unemployed	1,811
Unemployment Rate	8.4
Not in Labour Force	17,492

OCCUPATIONS BY MAJOR GROUPS

2001 Estimates:	Male	Female
Management	2,406	1,294
Business, Finance & Admin.	2,349	6,274
Natural & Applied Sciences & Related	1,673	248
Health	614	1,966
Social Sciences, Gov't Services & Religion	497	765
Education	802	1,404
Arts, Culture, Recreation & Sport	312	400
Sales & Service	5,845	7,523
Trades, Transport & Equipment Operators & Related	5,606	360
Primary Industries	1,575	70
Processing, Mfg. & Utilities	1,298	154

LEVEL OF SCHOOLING

2001 Estimates:	
Population 15 years +	74,194
Less than Grade 9	9,779
Grades 9-13 w/o Certif.	16,902
Grade 9-13 with Certif.	9,361
Trade Certif. /Dip.	2,791
Non-Univ. w/o Certif./Dip.	5,341
Non-Univ. with Certif./Dip.	14,074
Univ. w/o Degree	6,538
Univ. w/o Degree/Certif.	3,697
Univ. with Certif.	2,841
Univ. with Degree	9,408

Ontario

AVERAGE HOUSEHOLD EXPENDITURES

2001 Estimates:	
Food	$5,718
Shelter	$8,605
Clothing	$1,966
Transportation	$5,665
Health & Personal Care	$1,758
Recr'n, Read'g & Education	$3,309
Taxes & Securities	$12,407
Other	$8,096
Total Expenditures	$47,524

PRIVATE HOUSEHOLDS

2001 Estimates:	
Private Households, Total	39,726
Pop. in Private Households	87,435
Average no. per Household	2.2

FAMILIES

2001 Estimates:	
Families in Private Households	26,003
Husband-Wife Families	21,081
Lone-Parent Families	4,922
Aver. No. Persons per Family	2.9
Aver. No. Sons/Daughters at Home	1.1

HOUSING

2001 Estimates:	
Occupied Private Dwellings	39,726
Owned	21,087
Rented	18,639
Single-Detached House	19,322
Semi-Detached House	2,285
Row Houses	2,137
Apartment, 5+ Storeys	4,427
Owned Apartment, 5+ Storeys	155
Apartment, 5 or Fewer Storeys	8,158
Apartment, Detached Duplex	2,989
Other Single-Attached	284
Movable Dwellings	124

VEHICLES

2001 Estimates:	
Model Yrs. '81-'96, No.	45,013
% Total	79.29
Model Yrs. '97-'98, No.	7,067
% Total	12.45
'99 Vehicles registered in Model Yr. '99, No.	4,693
% Total	8.27
Total No. '81-'99	56,773

LEGAL MARITAL STATUS

2001 Estimates: (Age 15+)	
Single (Never Married)	24,266
Legally Married (Not Separated)	35,167
Legally Married (Separated)	2,841
Widowed	6,263
Divorced	5,657

Ontario

Sudbury
(City)
Sudbury CMA
(Cont'd)

PSYTE CATEGORIES

2001 Estimates	No. of House -holds	% of Total Hhds.	Index
The Affluentials	235	0.59	93
Urban Gentry	1,181	2.97	165
Suburban Executives	357	0.90	63
Technocrafts & Bureaucrats	455	1.15	41
Boomers & Teens	1,605	4.04	225
Stable Suburban Families	552	1.39	107
Small City Elite	628	1.58	92
Old Bungalow Burbs	2,212	5.57	336
Aging Erudites	1,155	2.91	193
Satellite Suburbs	655	1.65	57
Blue Collar Winners	710	1.79	71
Old Towns' New Fringe	1,740	4.38	112
Conservative Homebodies	6,806	17.13	475
High Rise Sunsets	782	1.97	138
Young Urban Mix	414	1.04	49
University Enclaves	2,195	5.53	271
Young City Singles	1,425	3.59	156
Old Leafy Towns	276	0.69	27
Town Renters	1,486	3.74	433
Nesters & Young Homesteaders	577	1.45	62
Aging Quebec Urbanites	225	0.57	196
Quebec's New Urban Mosaic	331	0.83	35
Struggling Downtowns	9,555	24.05	764
Aged Pensioners	2,261	5.69	428
Big City Stress	1,018	2.56	227
Old Grey Towers	439	1.11	200

FINANCIAL PSYTE

2001 Estimates	No. of House -holds	% of Total Hhds.	Index
Platinum Estates	235	0.59	73
Four Star Investors	3,143	7.91	158
Successful Suburbanites	1,007	2.53	38
Canadian Comfort	1,993	5.02	52
Urban Heights	1,155	2.91	68
Miners & Credit-Liners	2,212	5.57	176
Tractors & Tradelines	1,740	4.38	77
Bills & Wills	7,496	18.87	228
Revolving Renters	1,359	3.42	74
Young Urban Struggle	2,195	5.53	117
Loan Parent Stress	225	0.57	10
Towering Debt	12,466	31.38	402
NSF	1,349	3.40	96
Senior Survivors	2,700	6.80	361

HOME LANGUAGE

2001 Estimates:		% Total
English	71,847	80.40
French	11,058	12.37
Arabic	75	0.08
Chinese	274	0.31
Croatian	199	0.22
Finnish	476	0.53
German	134	0.15
Italian	1,508	1.69
Polish	293	0.33
Portuguese	89	0.10
Serbian	136	0.15
Spanish	140	0.16
Ukrainian	233	0.26
Other Languages	472	0.53
Multiple Responses	2,426	2.71
Total	89,360	100.00

BUILDING PERMITS

	1999	1998 $000	1997
Value	86,609	45,720	68,645

HOMES BUILT

	1999	1998	1997
No :	59	89	128

TAXATION

Income Class:	1997	% Total
Under $5,000	8,880	12.96
$5,000-$10,000	9,210	13.44
$10,000-$15,000	10,480	15.29
$15,000-$20,000	6,760	9.87
$20,000-$25,000	5,330	7.78
$25,000-$30,000	4,880	7.12
$30,000-$40,000	7,530	10.99
$40,000-$50,000	4,900	7.15
$50,000 +	10,550	15.40
Total Returns, No.	68,520	
Total Income, $000	1,886,348	
Total Taxable Returns	45,390	
Total Tax, $000	358,174	
Average Income, $	27,530	
Average Tax, $	7,891	

VITAL STATISTICS

	1997	1996	1995	1994
Births	915	966	1,044	1,148
Deaths	936	890	919	929
Natural Increase	-21	76	125	219
Marriages	628	723	718	731

Note: Latest available data.

MEDIA INFO
see Sudbury, CMA

Valley East
(Town)
Sudbury CMA

In Sudbury Regional Municipality.

POPULATION

July 1, 2001 Estimate	24,393
% Cdn. Total	0.08
% Change, '96 -'01	0.79
Avg. Annual Growth Rate, %	0.16
2003 Projected Population	24,979
2006 Projected Population	25,825
2001 Households Estimate	8,202
2003 Projected Households	8,544
2006 Projected Households	9,048

INCOME

% Above/Below National Average	+2
2001 Total Income Estimate	$524,390,000
% Cdn. Total	0.08
2001 Average Hhld. Income	$63,900
2001 Per Capita	$21,500
2003 Projected Total Income	$576,200,000
2006 Projected Total Income	$661,060,000

RETAIL SALES

% Above/Below National Average	-55
2001 Retail Sales Estimate	$98,880,000
% Cdn. Total	0.04
2001 per Household	$12,100
2001 per Capita	$4,100
2001 No. of Establishments	144
2003 Projected Retail Sales	$108,460,000
2006 Projected Retail Sales	$123,570,000

POPULATION

2001 Estimates:		
Total		24,393
Male		12,322
Female		12,071
Age Groups	Male	Female
0-4	828	787
5-9	920	859
10-14	992	926
15-19	1,026	975
20-24	961	882
25-29	854	799
30-34	911	964
35-39	1,047	1,120
40-44	1,036	1,101
45-49	993	977
50-54	857	792
55-59	632	595
60-64	464	456
65-69	349	349
70+	452	489

DAYTIME POPULATION

2001 Estimates:	
Working Population	3,671
At Home Population	11,923
Total	15,594

INCOME

2001 Estimates:	
Avg. Household Income	$63,935
Avg. Family Income	$65,656
Per Capita Income	$21,498
Male:	
Avg. Employment Income	$40,536
Avg. Employment Income (Full Time)	$53,303
Female:	
Avg. Employment Income	$21,067
Avg. Employment Income (Full Time)	$32,838

DISPOSABLE & DISCRETIONARY INCOME

2001 Estimates:	Per Hhld.
Disposable Income	$52,384
Discretionary Income 1 (minus Food & Shelter)	$37,239
Discretionary Income 2 (minus Food, Shelter, & Other Expenditures)	$27,004

LIQUID ASSETS

1999 Estimates:	Per Hhld.
Equity Investments	$86,751
Interest Bearing Investments	$76,536
Total Liquid Assets	$163,287

CREDIT DATA

July 2000:	
Pool of Credit	$228,495,195
Revolving Credit, No.	39,433
Fixed Loans, No.	17,816
Avg. Credit Limit, per Person	$13,035
Avg. Spent, per Person	$6,575
Satisfactory Ratings, No. per Person	2.98
Avg. No. of Cards, per Person	0.98

LABOUR FORCE

2001 Estimates:	
Male:	
In the Labour Force	7,303
Participation Rate	76.2
Employed	6,861
Unemployed	442
Unemployment Rate	6.1
Not in Labour Force	2,279
Female:	
In the Labour Force	5,893
Participation Rate	62.0
Employed	5,331
Unemployed	562
Unemployment Rate	9.5
Not in Labour Force	3,606

OCCUPATIONS BY MAJOR GROUPS

2001 Estimates:	Male	Female
Management	650	240
Business, Finance & Admin.	429	1,892
Natural & Applied Sciences & Related	296	65
Health	44	494
Social Sciences, Gov't Services & Religion	68	157
Education	137	320
Arts, Culture, Recreation & Sport	75	144
Sales & Service	1,408	2,037
Trades, Transport & Equipment Operators & Related	2,661	186
Primary Industries	829	12
Processing, Mfg. & Utilities	502	61

LEVEL OF SCHOOLING

2001 Estimates:	
Population 15 years +	19,081
Less than Grade 9	2,103
Grades 9-13 w/o Certif.	5,111
Grade 9-13 with Certif.	2,838
Trade Certif. /Dip.	901
Non-Univ. w/o Certif./Dip.	1,504
Non-Univ. with Certif./Dip.	4,233
Univ. w/o Degree	1,191
Univ. w/o Degree/Certif.	584
Univ. with Certif.	607
Univ. with Degree	1,200

Valley East
(Town)
Sudbury CMA
(Cont'd)

AVERAGE HOUSEHOLD EXPENDITURES

2001 Estimates:
Food	$7,250
Shelter	$10,202
Clothing	$2,408
Transportation	$7,947
Health & Personal Care	$2,209
Recr'n, Read'g & Education	$4,454
Taxes & Securities	$16,026
Other	$9,843
Total Expenditures	$60,339

PRIVATE HOUSEHOLDS

2001 Estimates:
Private Households, Total	8,202
Pop. in Private Households	24,241
Average no. per Household	3.0

FAMILIES

2001 Estimates:
Families in Private Households	7,320
Husband-Wife Families	6,631
Lone-Parent Families	689
Aver. No. Persons per Family	3.2
Aver. No. Sons/Daughters at Home	1.4

HOUSING

2001 Estimates:
Occupied Private Dwellings	8,202
Owned	6,795
Rented	1,407
Single-Detached House	6,838
Semi-Detached House	212
Row Houses	201
Apartment, 5 or Fewer Storeys	296
Apartment, Detached Duplex	391
Other Single-Attached	11
Movable Dwellings	253

VEHICLES

2001 Estimates:
Model Yrs. '81-'96, No.	13,210
% Total	87.05
Model Yrs. '97-'98, No.	1,211
% Total	7.98
'99 Vehicles registered in Model Yr. '99, No.	755
% Total	4.97
Total No. '81-'99	15,176

LEGAL MARITAL STATUS

2001 Estimates: (Age 15+)
Single (Never Married)	5,330
Legally Married (Not Separated)	11,576
Legally Married (Separated)	539
Widowed	626
Divorced	1,010

PSYTE CATEGORIES

2001 Estimates	No. of House-holds	% of Total Hhds.	Index
Small City Elite	73	0.89	52
Old Bungalow Burbs	22	0.27	16
Satellite Suburbs	804	9.80	342
Blue Collar Winners	597	7.28	289
Old Towns' New Fringe	5,381	65.61	1,676
Participation Quebec	615	7.50	260
Quebec Melange	528	6.44	243
Traditional French Cdn. Families	182	2.22	83

FINAN¢IAL P$YTE

2001 Estimates	No. of House-holds	% of Total Hhds.	Index
Canadian Comfort	1,474	17.97	185
Miners & Credit-Liners	22	0.27	8
Mortgages & Minivans	615	7.50	114
Tractors & Tradelines	5,381	65.61	1,147
Country Credit	710	8.66	128

HOME LANGUAGE

2001 Estimates:		% Total
English	15,432	63.26
French	8,051	33.01
Croatian	16	0.07
German	31	0.13
Italian	25	0.10
Ojibway	57	0.23
Ukrainian	21	0.09
Other Languages	84	0.34
Multiple Responses	676	2.77
Total	24,393	100.00

BUILDING PERMITS

	1999	1998	1997
		$000	
Value	5,127	9,433	8,244

HOMES BUILT

	1999	1998	1997
No	28	45	76

TAXATION

Income Class:	1997	% Total
Under $5,000	2,590	16.09
$5,000-$10,000	1,790	11.12
$10,000-$15,000	1,820	11.30
$15,000-$20,000	1,350	8.39
$20,000-$25,000	1,230	7.64
$25,000-$30,000	1,120	6.96
$30,000-$40,000	2,020	12.55
$40,000-$50,000	1,340	8.32
$50,000 +	2,840	17.64
Total Returns, No.	16,100	
Total Income, $000	440,914	
Total Taxable Returns	11,200	
Total Tax, $000	82,459	
Average Income, $	27,386	
Average Tax, $	7,362	

VITAL STATISTICS

	1997	1996	1995	1994
Births	244	285	278	300
Deaths	79	73	79	78
Natural Increase	165	212	199	222
Marriages	99	82	90	69

Note: Latest available data.

MEDIA INFO
see Sudbury, CMA

Walden
(Town)
Sudbury CMA
In Sudbury Regional Municipality.

POPULATION

2001 Estimates:
July 1, 2001 Estimate	10,472
% Cdn. Total	0.03
% Change, '96 -'01	-1.07
Avg. Annual Growth Rate, %.	-0.21
2003 Projected Population	10,620
2006 Projected Population	10,835
2001 Households Estimate	3,900
2003 Projected Households	4,021
2006 Projected Households	4,201

INCOME

% Above/Below National Average	+20
2001 Total Income Estimate	$265,300,000
% Cdn. Total	0.04
2001 Average Hhld. Income	$68,000
2001 Per Capita	$25,300
2003 Projected Total Income	$287,890,000
2006 Projected Total Income	$324,580,000

RETAIL SALES

% Above/Below National Average	-9
2001 Retail Sales Estimate	$85,780,000
% Cdn. Total	0.03
2001 per Household	$22,000
2001 per Capita	$8,200
2001 No. of Establishments	68
2003 Projected Retail Sales	$91,830,000
2006 Projected Retail Sales	$102,520,000

POPULATION

2001 Estimates:
Total		10,472
Male		5,331
Female		5,141
Age Groups	Male	Female
0-4	315	280
5-9	343	292
10-14	366	333
15-19	394	365
20-24	390	333
25-29	341	297
30-34	337	336
35-39	375	398
40-44	418	446
45-49	447	443
50-54	425	382
55-59	338	297
60-64	248	229
65-69	203	201
70+	391	509

DAYTIME POPULATION

2001 Estimates:
Working Population	3,693
At Home Population	5,167
Total	8,860

INCOME

2001 Estimates:
Avg. Household Income	$68,027
Avg. Family Income	$72,702
Per Capita Income	$25,335
Male:	
Avg. Employment Income	$43,858
Avg. Employment Income (Full Time)	$58,745
Female:	
Avg. Employment Income	$24,151
Avg. Employment Income (Full Time)	$39,382

Ontario

DISPOSABLE & DISCRETIONARY INCOME

2001 Estimates:	Per Hhld.
Disposable Income	$55,001
Discretionary Income 1 (minus Food & Shelter)	$39,310
Discretionary Income 2 (minus Food, Shelter, & Other Expenditures)	$28,309

LIQUID ASSETS

1999 Estimates:	Per Hhld.
Equity Investments	$94,606
Interest Bearing Investments	$82,565
Total Liquid Assets	$177,171

CREDIT DATA

July 2000:	
Pool of Credit	$97,113,704
Revolving Credit, No.	16,425
Fixed Loans, No.	6,204
Avg. Credit Limit, per Person	$12,814
Avg. Spent, per Person	$5,843
Satisfactory Ratings, No. per Person	2.78
Avg. No. of Cards, per Person	0.96

LABOUR FORCE

2001 Estimates:
Male:
In the Labour Force	3,073
Participation Rate	71.3
Employed	2,915
Unemployed	158
Unemployment Rate	5.1
Not in Labour Force	1,234
Female:	
In the Labour Force	2,559
Participation Rate	60.4
Employed	2,329
Unemployed	230
Unemployment Rate	9.0
Not in Labour Force	1,677

OCCUPATIONS BY MAJOR GROUPS

2001 Estimates:	Male	Female
Management	304	121
Business, Finance & Admin.	276	767
Natural & Applied Sciences & Related	292	52
Health	33	270
Social Sciences, Gov't Services & Religion	49	65
Education	79	128
Arts, Culture, Recreation & Sport	41	25
Sales & Service	471	874
Trades, Transport & Equipment Operators & Related	1,027	78
Primary Industries	292	30
Processing, Mfg. & Utilities	140	36

Ontario

Walden
(Town)
Sudbury CMA
(Cont'd)

LEVEL OF SCHOOLING

2001 Estimates:
Population 15 years +	8,543
Less than Grade 9	671
Grades 9-13 w/o Certif.	2,005
Grade 9-13 with Certif.	1,389
Trade Certif./Dip.	340
Non-Univ. w/o Certif./Dip.	522
Non-Univ. with Certif./Dip.	2,040
Univ. w/o Degree	612
Univ. w/o Degree/Certif.	312
Univ. with Certif.	300
Univ. with Degree	964

AVERAGE HOUSEHOLD EXPENDITURES

2001 Estimates:
Food	$7,435
Shelter	$10,826
Clothing	$2,526
Transportation	$8,739
Health & Personal Care	$2,353
Recr'n, Read'g & Education	$4,583
Taxes & Securities	$16,805
Other	$10,278
Total Expenditures	$63,545

PRIVATE HOUSEHOLDS

2001 Estimates:
Private Households, Total	3,900
Pop. in Private Households	10,333
Average no. per Household	2.6

FAMILIES

2001 Estimates:
Families in Private Households	3,203
Husband-Wife Families	2,950
Lone-Parent Families	253
Aver. No. Persons per Family	3.1
Aver. No. Sons/Daughters at Home	1.2

HOUSING

2001 Estimates:
Occupied Private Dwellings	3,900
Owned	3,403
Rented	497
Single-Detached House	3,239
Semi-Detached House	275
Row Houses	22
Apartment, 5+ Storeys	130
Apartment, 5 or Fewer Storeys	128
Apartment, Detached Duplex	48
Movable Dwellings	58

VEHICLES

2001 Estimates:
Model Yrs. '81-'96, No.	6,023
% Total	83.92
Model Yrs. '97-'98, No.	761
% Total	10.60
'99 Vehicles registered in Model Yr. '99, No.	393
% Total	5.48
Total No. '81-'99	7,177

LEGAL MARITAL STATUS

2001 Estimates: (Age 15+)
Single (Never Married)	2,092
Legally Married (Not Separated)	5,401
Legally Married (Separated)	220
Widowed	474
Divorced	356

PSYTE CATEGORIES

2001 Estimates	No. of House-holds	% of Total Hhds.	Index
Stable Suburban Families	54	1.38	106
Small City Elite	760	19.49	1,137
Old Bungalow Burbs.	26	0.67	40
Blue Collar Winners	766	19.64	780
Old Towns' New Fringe	740	18.97	485
Rustic Prosperity	198	5.08	281
Conservative Homebodies	819	21.00	582
Old Leafy Towns	455	11.67	456
Rod & Rifle	80	2.05	89

FINANÇIAL PSYTE

2001 Estimates	No. of House-holds	% of Total Hhds.	Index
Successful Suburbanites	54	1.38	21
Canadian Comfort	1,526	39.13	403
Miners & Credit-Liners	26	0.67	21
Tractors & Tradelines	938	24.05	421
Bills & Wills	1,274	32.67	394
Rural Family Blues	80	2.05	25

HOME LANGUAGE

2001 Estimates:		% Total
English	10,038	95.86
French	208	1.99
Finnish	56	0.53
Other Languages	10	0.10
Multiple Responses	160	1.53
Total	10,472	100.00

BUILDING PERMITS

	1999	1998 $000	1997
Value	9,715	3,946	6,432

HOMES BUILT

	1999	1998	1997
No	17	26	31

TAXATION

Income Class:	1997	% Total
Under $5,000	1,100	14.40
$5,000-$10,000	830	10.86
$10,000-$15,000	770	10.08
$15,000-$20,000	560	7.33
$20,000-$25,000	530	6.94
$25,000-$30,000	550	7.20
$30,000-$40,000	860	11.26
$40,000-$50,000	690	9.03
$50,000 +	1,730	22.64
Total Returns, No.	7,640	
Total Income, $000	237,192	
Total Taxable Returns	5,580	
Total Tax, $000	47,771	
Average Income, $	31,046	
Average Tax, $	8,561	

VITAL STATISTICS

	1997	1996	1995	1994
Births	89	86	83	79
Deaths	58	52	49	44
Natural Increase	31	34	34	35
Marriages	47	34	58	30

Note: Latest available data.

MEDIA INFO
see Sudbury, CMA

Thunder Bay
(Census Metropolitan Area)

POPULATION

July 1, 2001 Estimate	127,546
% Cdn. Total	0.41
% Change, '96 -'01	-1.74
Avg. Annual Growth Rate, %	-0.35
2003 Projected Population	129,574
2006 Projected Population	132,743
2001 Households Estimate	51,910
2003 Projected Households	53,260
2006 Projected Households	55,530

INCOME

% Above/Below National Average	+7
2001 Total Income Estimate	$2,887,400,000
% Cdn. Total	0.44
2001 Average Hhld. Income	$55,600
2001 Per Capita	$22,600
2003 Projected Total Income	$3,117,610,000
2006 Projected Total Income	$3,511,990,000

RETAIL SALES

% Above/Below National Average	+11
2001 Retail Sales Estimate	$1,264,690,000
% Cdn. Total	0.45
2001 per Household	$24,400
2001 per Capita	$9,900
2001 No. of Establishments	960
2003 Projected Retail Sales	$1,385,710,000
2006 Projected Retail Sales	$1,566,110,000

POPULATION

2001 Estimates:

Total	127,546
Male	62,667
Female	64,879

Age Groups	Male	Female
0-4	3,892	3,702
5-9	4,021	3,861
10-14	4,154	3,942
15-19	4,211	3,975
20-24	4,248	4,127
25-29	4,241	4,269
30-34	4,480	4,603
35-39	4,881	5,070
40-44	5,065	5,144
45-49	4,831	4,832
50-54	4,105	4,089
55-59	3,322	3,333
60-64	2,800	2,851
65-69	2,520	2,679
70+	5,896	8,412

DAYTIME POPULATION

2001 Estimates:

Working Population	63,817
At Home Population	63,729
Total	127,546

INCOME

2001 Estimates:

Avg. Household Income	$55,623
Avg. Family Income	$64,308
Per Capita Income	$22,638
Male:	
Avg. Employment Income	$37,297
Avg. Employment Income (Full Time)	$48,907
Female:	
Avg. Employment Income	$22,156
Avg. Employment Income (Full Time)	$33,739

DISPOSABLE & DISCRETIONARY INCOME

2001 Estimates:	Per Hhld.
Disposable Income	$45,685
Discretionary Income 1 (minus Food & Shelter)	$32,075
Discretionary Income 2 (minus Food, Shelter, & Other Expenditures)	$23,476

LIQUID ASSETS

1999 Estimates:	Per Hhld.
Equity Investments	$73,958
Interest Bearing Investments	$68,229
Total Liquid Assets	$142,187

CREDIT DATA

July 2000:

Pool of Credit	$1,307,567,587
Revolving Credit, No.	233,997
Fixed Loans, No.	66,130
Avg. Credit Limit, per Person	$12,834
Avg. Spent, per Person	$5,908
Satisfactory Ratings, No. per Person	2.81
Avg. No. of Cards, per Person	1.06

LABOUR FORCE

2001 Estimates:

Male:

In the Labour Force	36,896
Participation Rate	72.9
Employed	34,077
Unemployed	2,819
Unemployment Rate	7.6
Not in Labour Force	13,704

Female:

In the Labour Force	31,445
Participation Rate	58.9
Employed	29,397
Unemployed	2,048
Unemployment Rate	6.5
Not in Labour Force	21,929

OCCUPATIONS BY MAJOR GROUPS

2001 Estimates:	Male	Female
Management	3,385	1,564
Business, Finance & Admin.	2,964	8,694
Natural & Applied Sciences & Related	2,377	484
Health	727	3,527
Social Sciences, Gov't Services & Religion	920	1,552
Education	1,265	1,524
Arts, Culture, Recreation & Sport	501	697
Sales & Service	7,327	11,207
Trades, Transport & Equipment Operators & Related	11,656	626
Primary Industries	1,369	229
Processing, Mfg. & Utilities	3,549	304

LEVEL OF SCHOOLING

2001 Estimates:

Population 15 years +	103,974
Less than Grade 9	10,992
Grades 9-13 w/o Certif.	25,988
Grade 9-13 with Certif.	13,506
Trade Certif. /Dip.	4,810
Non-Univ. w/o Certif./Dip.	6,761
Non-Univ. with Certif./Dip.	20,189
Univ. w/o Degree	9,585
Univ. w/o Degree/Certif.	4,650
Univ. with Certif.	4,935
Univ. with Degree	12,143

AVERAGE HOUSEHOLD EXPENDITURES

2001 Estimates:

Food	$6,329
Shelter	$9,419
Clothing	$2,166
Transportation	$6,617
Health & Personal Care	$1,942
Recr'n, Read'g & Education	$3,667
Taxes & Securities	$14,301
Other	$8,878
Total Expenditures	$53,319

PRIVATE HOUSEHOLDS

2001 Estimates:

Private Households, Total	51,910
Pop. in Private Households	125,334
Average no. per Household	2.4

FAMILIES

2001 Estimates:

Families in Private Households	36,654
Husband-Wife Families	30,861
Lone-Parent Families	5,793
Aver. No. Persons per Family	3.0
Aver. No. Sons/Daughters at Home	1.1

Ontario

HOUSING

2001 Estimates:

Occupied Private Dwellings	51,910
Owned	36,286
Rented	15,581
Band Housing	43
Single-Detached House	35,540
Semi-Detached House	2,350
Row Houses	1,433
Apartment, 5+ Storeys	2,768
Owned Apartment, 5+ Storeys	403
Apartment, 5 or Fewer Storeys	7,026
Apartment, Detached Duplex	2,214
Other Single-Attached	157
Movable Dwellings	422

RADIO STATION DATA

Station	Market	Format	Wkly. Reach%*	Aver. Hrs. Tuned
All Stations			n.a.	n.a.
CBQ-FM	Thunder Bay	News, Info.	n.a.	n.a.
CJLB-FM	Thunder Bay	Country	n.a.	n.a.
CJSD-FM	Thunder Bay	Rock	n.a.	n.a.
CKPR	Thunder Bay	Multi-format	n.a.	n.a.

*Mon-Sun 5a.m - 1a.m , All Persons 12+

TV STATION DATA

Station	Market	Network Affiliation	Wkly. Reach%*	Aver. Hrs. Tuned
All Stations			95	24.5
A & E	n.a.	Ind.	28	3.4
BRAVO	n.a.	Ind.	8	2.3
CHFD	Thunder Bay	CTV	58	4.6
CICO-E	n.a.	n.a.	18	3.4
CKPR	Thunder Bay	CBC	62	5.3
COMEDY	n.a.	Ind.	8	1.7
CTV NNT	n.a.	CTV	6	2.2
DSCVRY	n.a.	Ind.	11	2.3
FAMILY	n.a.	Ind.	8	1.4
FOOD	n.a.	Ind.	5	2.9
HISTTV	n.a.	Ind.	9	2.4
NEWSWD	n.a.	CBC	10	2.6
OTHERS	n.a.	n.a.	12	2.4
PRIME	n.a.	Ind.	15	2.6
SHWCSE	n.a.	Ind.	9	1.9
SNET	n.a.	CTV	11	2.2
SPACE	n.a.	Ind.	9	2.7
TLC	n.a.	Ind.	17	1.8
TMN	Toronto	Ind.	8	2.6
TNN	Nashville TN	Ind.	10	2.8
TOON	n.a.	Ind.	10	1.6
TREE	n.a.	Ind.	8	3.2
TSN	n.a.	Ind.	23	6.1
VCR	n.a.	n.a.	26	4.7
WDIV	Detroit MI	NBC	34	3.1
WDSE	Duluth MN	PBS	-	1.0
WEATHR	n.a.	Ind.	12	1.8
WTBS	Atlanta GA	Ind.	23	4.0
WTVS	Detroit MI	PBS	12	1.7
WUHF	Rochester NY	FOX	35	3.1
WWJ	Detroit MI	CBS	38	3.9
WXYZ	Detroit MI	ABC	43	3.1
YTV	n.a.	Ind.	13	2.5

BBM Spring 2000 TV Reach Survey; CMA coverage.
*Mon-Sun 6a.m - 2a.m , All Persons 2 +

Ontario

Thunder Bay
(Census Metropolitan Area)
(Cont'd)

VEHICLES

2001 Estimates:
Model Yrs. '81-'96, No. 71,760
  % Total 85.50
Model Yrs. '97-'98, No. 7,257
  % Total 8.65
'99 Vehicles registered in
  Model Yr. '99, No. 4,911
  % Total 5.85
Total No. '81-'99 83,928

LEGAL MARITAL STATUS

2001 Estimates: (Age 15+)
Single (Never Married) 31,791
Legally Married
  (Not Separated) 53,876
Legally Married (Separated) 3,744
Widowed 7,930
Divorced 6,633

PSYTE CATEGORIES

2001 Estimates	No. of House-holds	% of Total Hhds.	Index
The Affluentials	.36	0.07	11
Suburban Executives	.335	0.65	45
Technocrafts & Bureaucrats	1,363	2.63	93
Boomers & Teens	2,182	4.20	234
Stable Suburban Families	1,502	2.89	222
Small City Elite	.170	0.33	19
Old Bungalow Burbs	3,823	7.36	444
Suburban Nesters	1,059	2.04	127
Aging Erudites	2,372	4.57	303
Satellite Suburbs	.881	1.70	59
Kindergarten Boom	.413	0.80	30
Blue Collar Winners	3,848	7.41	294
Old Towns' New Fringe	2,310	4.45	114
Rustic Prosperity	.381	0.73	41
Conservative Homebodies	13,676	26.35	731
High Rise Sunsets	.413	0.80	56
University Enclaves	1,180	2.27	111
Young City Singles	.236	0.45	20
Town Renters	1,869	3.60	417
Nesters & Young Homesteaders . . .	1,236	2.38	102
Big Country Families	.44	0.08	6
Struggling Downtowns	9,357	18.03	572
Aged Pensioners	2,118	4.08	307
Big City Stress	.335	0.65	57
Old Grey Towers	.298	0.57	104

FINANCIAL P$YTE

2001 Estimates	No. of House-holds	% of Total Hhds.	Index
Platinum Estates	.36	0.07	9
Four Star Investors	2,517	4.85	97
Successful Suburbanites	2,865	5.52	83
Canadian Comfort	5,958	11.48	118
Urban Heights	2,372	4.57	106
Miners & Credit-Liners	3,823	7.36	233
Mortgages & Minivans	413	0.80	12
Tractors & Tradelines	2,691	5.18	91
Bills & Wills	13,676	26.35	318
Revolving Renters	1,649	3.18	69
Young Urban Struggle	1,180	2.27	48
Rural Family Blues	44	0.08	1
Towering Debt	11,462	22.08	283
NSF	335	0.65	18
Senior Survivors	2,416	4.65	247

HOME LANGUAGE

2001 Estimates:		% Total
English	119,715	93.86
French	.948	0.74
Chinese	.216	0.17
Cree	.77	0.06
Croatian	.187	0.15
Finnish	1,025	0.80
German	.112	0.09
Greek	.133	0.10
Italian	1,612	1.26
Ojibway	.143	0.11
Persian (Farsi)	.64	0.05
Polish	.695	0.54
Portuguese	.161	0.13
Slovak	.158	0.12
Spanish	.131	0.10
Ukrainian	.214	0.17
Vietnamese	.84	0.07
Other Languages	.389	0.30
Multiple Responses	1,482	1.16
Total	127,546	100.00

BUILDING PERMITS

	1999	1998	1997
		$000	
Value	66,874	78,743	72,651

HOMES BUILT

	1999	1998	1997
No.	282	211	332

TAXATION

Income Class:	1997	% Total
Under $5,000	10,630	11.47
$5,000-$10,000	10,840	11.70
$10,000-$15,000	13,010	14.04
$15,000-$20,000	8,710	9.40
$20,000-$25,000	7,210	7.78
$25,000-$30,000	6,710	7.24
$30,000-$40,000	12,000	12.95
$40,000-$50,000	8,630	9.31
$50,000 + ...	14,920	16.10
Total Returns, No.	92,670	
Total Income, $000. . . .	2,677,828	
Total Taxable Returns	65,900	
Total Tax, $000	501,583	
Average Income, $	28,896	
Average Tax, $	7,611	

VITAL STATISTICS

	1997	1996	1995	1994
Births	1,319	1,557	1,603	1,587
Deaths . . .	1,187	1,209	1,151	1,173
Natural Increase . . .	132	348	452	414
Marriages . .	779	765	842	824

Note: Latest available data.

DAILY NEWSPAPER(S)

	Circulation Average Paid
Chronicle-Journal	
Sat	38,242
Sun	32,085
Mon-Fri	32,259

COMMUNITY NEWSPAPER(S)

	Total Circulation
Thunder Bay: Thunder Bay Post	48,020

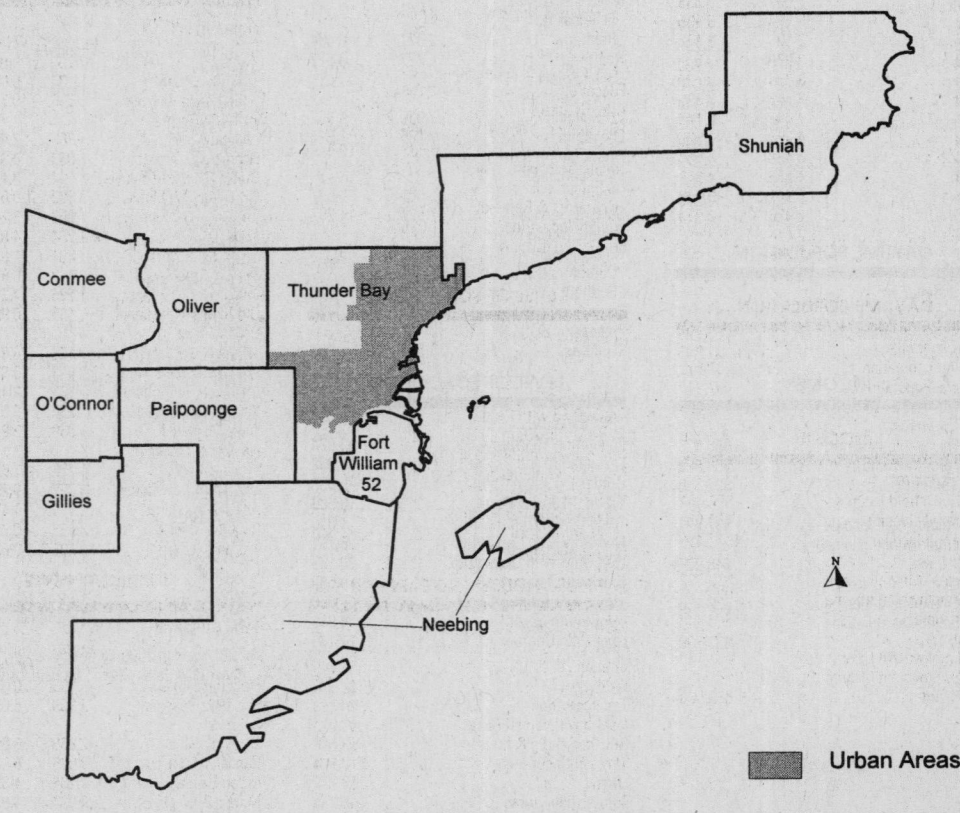

Urban Areas

Thunder Bay

(City)
Thunder Bay CMA
In Thunder Bay District.

POPULATION

July 1, 2001 Estimate	114,675
% Cdn. Total	0.37
% Change, '96 -'01	-2.41
Avg. Annual Growth Rate, %	-0.49
2003 Projected Population	116,066
2006 Projected Population	118,268
2001 Households Estimate	47,380
2003 Projected Households	48,457
2006 Projected Households	50,288

INCOME

% Above/Below National Average	+6
2001 Total Income Estimate	$2,569,930,000
% Cdn. Total	0.39
2001 Average Hhld. Income	$54,200
2001 Per Capita	$22,400
2003 Projected Total Income	$2,758,900,000
2006 Projected Total Income	$3,081,100,000

RETAIL SALES

% Above/Below National Average	+20
2001 Retail Sales Estimate	$1,236,730,000
% Cdn. Total	0.44
2001 per Household	$26,100
2001 per Capita	$10,800
2001 No. of Establishments	909
2003 Projected Retail Sales	$1,354,310,000
2006 Projected Retail Sales	$1,528,260,000

POPULATION

2001 Estimates:

Total		114,675
Male		56,022
Female		58,653

Age Groups	Male	Female
0-4	3,507	3,333
5-9	3,574	3,435
10-14	3,636	3,463
15-19	3,679	3,512
20-24	3,789	3,730
25-29	3,845	3,890
30-34	4,047	4,146
35-39	4,356	4,529
40-44	4,493	4,584
45-49	4,289	4,313
50-54	3,647	3,648
55-59	2,936	2,966
60-64	2,474	2,578
65-69	2,248	2,466
70+	5,502	8,060

DAYTIME POPULATION

2001 Estimates:

Working Population	61,823
At Home Population	57,840
Total	119,663

INCOME

2001 Estimates:

Avg. Household Income	$54,241
Avg. Family Income	$63,232
Per Capita Income	$22,411
Male:	
Avg. Employment Income	$36,602
Avg. Employment Income (Full Time)	$48,463
Female:	
Avg. Employment Income	$22,123
Avg. Employment Income (Full Time)	$33,508

DISPOSABLE & DISCRETIONARY INCOME

2001 Estimates: — Per Hhld.

Disposable Income	$44,560
Discretionary Income 1 (minus Food & Shelter)	$31,192
Discretionary Income 2 (minus Food, Shelter, & Other Expenditures)	$22,840

LIQUID ASSETS

1999 Estimates: — Per Hhld.

Equity Investments	$70,046
Interest Bearing Investments	$66,394
Total Liquid Assets	$136,440

CREDIT DATA

July 2000:

Pool of Credit	$1,249,274,872
Revolving Credit, No.	224,909
Fixed Loans, No.	62,952
Avg. Credit Limit, per Person	$12,795
Avg. Spent, per Person	$5,870
Satisfactory Ratings, No. per Person	2.81
Avg. No. of Cards, per Person	1.07

LABOUR FORCE

2001 Estimates:

Male:

In the Labour Force	32,732
Participation Rate	72.2
Employed	30,226
Unemployed	2,506
Unemployment Rate	7.7
Not in Labour Force	12,573

Female:

In the Labour Force	28,177
Participation Rate	58.2
Employed	26,389
Unemployed	1,788
Unemployment Rate	6.3
Not in Labour Force	20,245

OCCUPATIONS BY MAJOR GROUPS

2001 Estimates:

	Male	Female
Management	3,011	1,410
Business, Finance & Admin.	2,738	7,744
Natural & Applied Sciences & Related	2,064	393
Health	654	3,151
Social Sciences, Gov't Services & Religion	863	1,393
Education	1,158	1,373
Arts, Culture, Recreation & Sport	465	601
Sales & Service	6,833	10,209
Trades, Transport & Equipment Operators & Related	9,853	521
Primary Industries	1,035	174
Processing, Mfg. & Utilities	3,252	259

LEVEL OF SCHOOLING

2001 Estimates:

Population 15 years +	93,727
Less than Grade 9	10,215
Grades 9-13 w/o Certif.	23,276
Grade 9-13 with Certif.	12,183
Trade Certif. /Dip.	4,124
Non-Univ. w/o Certif./Dip.	6,103
Non-Univ. with Certif./Dip.	17,877
Univ. w/o Degree	8,816
Univ. w/o Degree/Certif.	4,271
Univ. with Certif.	4,545
Univ. with Degree	11,133

AVERAGE HOUSEHOLD EXPENDITURES

2001 Estimates:

Food	$6,232
Shelter	$9,249
Clothing	$2,130
Transportation	$6,396
Health & Personal Care	$1,912
Recr'n, Read'g & Education	$3,576
Taxes & Securities	$13,934
Other	$8,735
Total Expenditures	$52,164

PRIVATE HOUSEHOLDS

2001 Estimates:

Private Households, Total	47,380
Pop. in Private Households	112,614
Average no. per Household	2.4

FAMILIES

2001 Estimates:

Families in Private Households	32,808
Husband-Wife Families	27,277
Lone-Parent Families	5,531
Aver. No. Persons per Family	2.9
Aver. No. Sons/Daughters at Home	1.1

HOUSING

2001 Estimates:

Occupied Private Dwellings	47,380
Owned	32,169
Rented	15,211
Single-Detached House	31,408
Semi-Detached House	2,350
Row Houses	1,412
Apartment, 5+ Storeys	2,768
Owned Apartment, 5+ Storeys	403
Apartment, 5 or Fewer Storeys	6,942
Apartment, Detached Duplex	2,204
Other Single-Attached	124
Movable Dwellings	172

VEHICLES

2001 Estimates:

Model Yrs. '81-'96, No.	64,138
% Total	85.22
Model Yrs. '97-'98, No.	6,604
% Total	8.77
'99 Vehicles registered in Model Yr. '99, No.	4,524
% Total	6.01
Total No. '81-'99	75,266

LEGAL MARITAL STATUS

2001 Estimates: (Age 15+)

Single (Never Married)	29,161
Legally Married (Not Separated)	47,439
Legally Married (Separated)	3,476
Widowed	7,521
Divorced	6,130

PSYTE CATEGORIES

2001 Estimates	No. of House -holds	% of Total Hhds.	Index
The Affluentials	36	0.08	12
Suburban Executives	335	0.71	49
Technocrafts & Bureaucrats	1,363	2.88	102
Boomers & Teens	2,063	4.35	243
Stable Suburban Families	1,502	3.17	243
Old Bungalow Burbs	3,823	8.07	487
Suburban Nesters	1,059	2.24	139
Aging Erudites	2,284	4.82	320
Satellite Suburbs	881	1.86	65
Kindergarten Boom	413	0.87	33
Blue Collar Winners	1,995	4.21	167
Old Towns' New Fringe	435	0.92	23
Conservative Homebodies	13,676	28.86	801
High Rise Sunsets	413	0.87	61
University Enclaves	1,180	2.49	122
Young City Singles	236	0.50	22
Town Nesters	1,869	3.94	456
Nesters & Young Homesteaders	1,236	2.61	112
Struggling Downtowns	9,357	19.75	627
Aged Pensioners	2,118	4.47	336
Big City Stress	335	0.71	63
Old Grey Towers	298	0.63	114

FINANCIAL P$YTE

2001 Estimates	No. of House -holds	% of Total Hhds.	Index
Platinum Estates	36	0.08	9
Four Star Investors	2,398	5.06	101
Successful Suburbanites	2,865	6.05	91
Canadian Comfort	3,935	8.31	85
Urban Heights	2,284	4.82	112
Miners & Credit-Liners	3,823	8.07	255

Ontario

2001 Estimates	No. of House -holds	% of Total Hhds.	Index
Mortgages & Minivans	413	0.87	13
Tractors & Tradelines	435	0.92	16
Bills & Wills	13,676	28.86	349
Revolving Renters	1,649	3.48	76
Young Urban Struggle	1,180	2.49	53
Towering Debt	11,462	24.19	310
NSF	335	0.71	20
Senior Survivors	2,416	5.10	271

HOME LANGUAGE

2001 Estimates		% Total
English	107,072	93.37
French	872	0.76
Chinese	216	0.19
Cree	77	0.07
Croatian	187	0.16
Finnish	997	0.87
German	112	0.10
Greek	133	0.12
Italian	1,612	1.41
Ojibway	143	0.12
Persian (Farsi)	64	0.06
Polish	695	0.61
Portuguese	161	0.14
Slovak	158	0.14
Spanish	131	0.11
Ukrainian	214	0.19
Other Languages	408	0.36
Multiple Responses	1,423	1.24
Total	114,675	100.00

BUILDING PERMITS

	1999	1998 $000	1997
Value	49,850	68,445	62,399

HOMES BUILT

	1999	1998	1997
No.	234	170	306

TAXATION

Income Class:	1997	% Total
Under $5,000	10,110	11.38
$5,000-$10,000	10,420	11.73
$10,000-$15,000	12,580	14.16
$15,000-$20,000	8,350	9.40
$20,000-$25,000	6,940	7.81
$25,000-$30,000	6,420	7.23
$30,000-$40,000	11,490	12.93
$40,000-$50,000	8,230	9.26
$50,000 +	14,290	16.09
Total Returns, No.	88,840	
Total Income, $000	2,570,712	
Total Taxable Returns	63,130	
Total Tax, $000	481,919	
Average Income, $.	28,936	
Average Tax, $.	7,634	

VITAL STATISTICS

	1997	1996	1995	1994
Births	1,268	1,472	1,532	1,536
Deaths	1,155	1,169	1,127	1,145
Natural Increase	113	303	405	391
Marriages	743	737	814	782

Note: Latest available data.

MEDIA INFO
see Thunder Bay, CMA

Ontario

Tillsonburg
(Census Agglomeration)

The Census Agglomeration of Tillsonburg consists solely of Tillsonburg, T, in Oxford County.

POPULATION

July 1, 2001 Estimate	14,525
% Cdn. Total	0.05
% Change, '96 -'01	6.90
Avg. Annual Growth Rate, %	1.34
2003 Projected Population	14,954
2006 Projected Population	15,508
2001 Households Estimate	6,045
2003 Projected Households	6,270
2006 Projected Households	6,590

INCOME

% Above/Below National Average	-1
2001 Total Income Estimate	$303,480,000
% Cdn. Total	0.05
2001 Average Hhld. Income	$50,200
2001 Per Capita	$20,900
2003 Projected Total Income	$329,940,000
2006 Projected Total Income	$371,740,000

RETAIL SALES

% Above/Below National Average	-9
2001 Retail Sales Estimate	$118,860,000
% Cdn. Total	0.04
2001 per Household	$19,700
2001 per Capita	$8,200
2001 No. of Establishments	131
2003 Projected Retail Sales	$131,230,000
2006 Projected Retail Sales	$149,600,000

POPULATION

2001 Estimates:

Total	14,525
Male	6,925
Female	7,600

Age Groups	Male	Female
0-4	419	414
5-9	432	427
10-14	454	447
15-19	463	453
20-24	473	470
25-29	498	461
30-34	517	501
35-39	510	543
40-44	490	519
45-49	447	468
50-54	390	409
55-59	344	370
60-64	309	368
65-69	321	392
70+	858	1,358

DAYTIME POPULATION

2001 Estimates:

Working Population	6,791
At Home Population	7,734
Total	14,525

INCOME

2001 Estimates:

Avg. Household Income	$50,203
Avg. Family Income	$59,137
Per Capita Income	$20,894
Male:	
Avg. Employment Income	$32,046
Avg. Employment Income (Full Time)	$42,901
Female:	
Avg. Employment Income	$21,173
Avg. Employment Income (Full Time)	$31,036

DISPOSABLE & DISCRETIONARY INCOME

2001 Estimates:	*Per Hhld.*
Disposable Income	$41,425
Discretionary Income 1 (minus Food & Shelter)	$28,520
Discretionary Income 2 (minus Food, Shelter, & Other Expenditures)	$19,809

LIQUID ASSETS

1999 Estimates:	*Per Hhld.*
Equity Investments	$63,358
Interest Bearing Investments	$60,327
Total Liquid Assets	$123,685

CREDIT DATA

July 2000:

Pool of Credit	$168,349,619
Revolving Credit, No.	28,959
Fixed Loans, No.	9,843
Avg. Credit Limit, per Person	$12,387
Avg. Spent, per Person	$5,554
Satisfactory Ratings, No. per Person	2.74
Avg. No. of Cards, per Person	1.01

LABOUR FORCE

2001 Estimates:

Male:	
In the Labour Force	3,837
Participation Rate	68.3
Employed	3,581
Unemployed	256
Unemployment Rate	6.7
Not in Labour Force	1,783
Female:	
In the Labour Force	3,411
Participation Rate	54.0
Employed	3,244
Unemployed	167
Unemployment Rate	4.9
Not in Labour Force	2,901

OCCUPATIONS BY MAJOR GROUPS

2001 Estimates:	Male	Female
Management	430	183
Business, Finance & Admin.	383	714
Natural & Applied Sciences & Related	88	23
Health	25	292
Social Sciences, Gov't Services & Religion	74	84
Education	99	181
Arts, Culture, Recreation & Sport	24	64
Sales & Service	728	1,113
Trades, Transport & Equipment Operators & Related	962	95
Primary Industries	303	133
Processing, Mfg. & Utilities	680	463

LEVEL OF SCHOOLING

2001 Estimates:

Population 15 years +	11,932
Less than Grade 9	1,714
Grades 9-13 w/o Certif.	3,355
Grade 9-13 with Certif.	1,989
Trade Certif. /Dip.	482
Non-Univ. w/o Certif./Dip.	617
Non-Univ. with Certif./Dip.	2,146
Univ. w/o Degree	609
Univ. w/o Degree/Certif.	333
Univ. with Certif.	276
Univ. with Degree	1,020

AVERAGE HOUSEHOLD EXPENDITURES

2001 Estimates:

Food	$6,052
Shelter	$8,896
Clothing	$1,925
Transportation	$6,736
Health & Personal Care	$1,928
Recr'n, Read'g & Education	$3,498
Taxes & Securities	$11,698
Other	$8,224
Total Expenditures	$48,957

PRIVATE HOUSEHOLDS

2001 Estimates:

Private Households, Total	6,045
Pop. in Private Households	14,114
Average no. per Household	2.3

FAMILIES

2001 Estimates:

Families in Private Households	4,319
Husband-Wife Families	3,750
Lone-Parent Families	569
Aver. No. Persons per Family	2.8
Aver. No. Sons/Daughters at Home	1.0

HOUSING

2001 Estimates:

Occupied Private Dwellings	6,045
Owned	3,895
Rented	2,150
Single-Detached House	3,959
Semi-Detached House	186
Row Houses	263
Apartment, 5+ Storeys	408
Apartment, 5 or Fewer Storeys	885
Apartment, Detached Duplex	311
Other Single-Attached	33

VEHICLES

2001 Estimates:

Model Yrs. '81-'96, No.	7,960
% Total	79.99
Model Yrs. '97-'98, No.	1,223
% Total	12.29
'99 Vehicles registered in Model Yr. '99, No.	768
% Total	7.72
Total No. '81-'99	9,951

LEGAL MARITAL STATUS

2001 Estimates: (Age 15+)

Single (Never Married)	2,879
Legally Married (Not Separated)	6,658
Legally Married (Separated)	418
Widowed	1,144
Divorced	833

PSYTE CATEGORIES

2001 Estimates	No. of House -holds	% of Total Hhds.	Index
Old Towns' New Fringe	2,793	46.20	1,180
Old Leafy Towns	586	9.69	379
Town Renters	407	6.73	779
Nesters & Young Homesteaders	127	2.10	90
Quiet Towns	2,071	34.26	1,610

FINANCIAL P$YTE

2001 Estimates	No. of House -holds	% of Total Hhds.	Index
Tractors & Tradelines	2,793	46.20	808
Bills & Wills	586	9.69	117
Revolving Renters	127	2.10	46
Limited Budgets	2,071	34.26	1,102
Towering Debt	407	6.73	86

HOME LANGUAGE

2001 Estimates:		% Total
English	13,750	94.66
French	23	0.16
Chinese	11	0.08
Dutch	16	0.11
Flemish	51	0.35
German	162	1.12
Gujarati	38	0.26
Hungarian	100	0.69
Japanese	38	0.26
Khmer (Cambodian)	39	0.27
Kurdish	11	0.08
Latvian (Lettish)	11	0.08
Lithuanian	11	0.08
Polish	33	0.23
Portuguese	16	0.11
Vietnamese	90	0.62
Other Languages	11	0.08
Multiple Responses	114	0.78
Total	14,525	100.00

BUILDING PERMITS

	1999	1998	1997
		$000	
Value	16,392	16,922	16,093

HOMES BUILT

	1999	1998	1997
No	89	137	113

TAXATION

Income Class:	1997	% Total
Under $5,000	1,260	9.70
$5,000-$10,000	1,570	12.09
$10,000-$15,000	2,180	16.78
$15,000-$20,000	1,500	11.55
$20,000-$25,000	1,130	8.70
$25,000-$30,000	1,080	8.31
$30,000-$40,000	1,840	14.16
$40,000-$50,000	990	7.62
$50,000 +	1,430	11.01
Total Returns, No.	12,990	
Total Income, $000	350,220	
Total Taxable Returns	9,320	
Total Tax, $000	62,858	
Average Income, $	26,961	
Average Tax, $	6,744	

VITAL STATISTICS

	1997	1996	1995	1994
Births	176	201	198	201
Deaths	166	181	158	155
Natural Increase	10	20	40	46
Marriages	83	96	99	109

Note: Latest available data.

COMMUNITY NEWSPAPER(S)

	Total Circulation
Tillsonburg: Tillsonburg Independent News	10,280
Tillsonburg: Tillsonburg News Wed/Fri	4,838

RADIO STATION(S)

	Power
CKOT	10,000w
CKOT-FM	50,000w

Timmins
(Census Agglomeration)

The Census Agglomeration of Timmins consists solely of Timmins, C, in Cochrane District.

POPULATION

July 1, 2001 Estimate	47,262
% Cdn. Total	0.15
% Change, '96 -'01	-3.24
Avg. Annual Growth Rate, %	-0.66
2003 Projected Population	46,648
2006 Projected Population	45,675
2001 Households Estimate	18,662
2003 Projected Households	18,854
2006 Projected Households	19,088

INCOME

% Above/Below National Average	-1
2001 Total Income Estimate	$987,840,000
% Cdn. Total	0.15
2001 Average Hhld. Income	$52,900
2001 Per Capita	$20,900
2003 Projected Total Income	$1,041,670,000
2006 Projected Total Income	$1,124,650,000

RETAIL SALES

% Above/Below National Average	+7
2001 Retail Sales Estimate	$452,860,000
% Cdn. Total	0.16
2001 per Household	$24,300
2001 per Capita	$9,600
2001 No. of Establishments	359
2003 Projected Retail Sales	$485,400,000
2006 Projected Retail Sales	$526,030,000

POPULATION

2001 Estimates:

Total		47,262
Male		23,597
Female		23,665

Age Groups	Male	Female
0-4	1,509	1,425
5-9	1,639	1,531
10-14	1,704	1,601
15-19	1,754	1,647
20-24	1,717	1,632
25-29	1,608	1,608
30-34	1,755	1,777
35-39	2,013	1,963
40-44	2,014	1,951
45-49	1,824	1,767
50-54	1,527	1,463
55-59	1,189	1,181
60-64	964	973
65-69	792	874
70+	1,588	2,272

DAYTIME POPULATION

2001 Estimates:

Working Population	23,056
At Home Population	24,206
Total	47,262

INCOME

2001 Estimates:

Avg. Household Income	$52,933
Avg. Family Income	$59,946
Per Capita Income	$20,901
Male:	
Avg. Employment Income	$37,717
Avg. Employment Income (Full Time)	$49,029
Female:	
Avg. Employment Income	$20,076
Avg. Employment Income (Full Time)	$31,375

DISPOSABLE & DISCRETIONARY INCOME

2001 Estimates:	Per Hhld.
Disposable Income	$43,531
Discretionary Income 1 (minus Food & Shelter)	$30,991
Discretionary Income 2 (minus Food, Shelter, & Other Expenditures)	$22,554

LIQUID ASSETS

1999 Estimates:	Per Hhld.
Equity Investments	$70,934
Interest Bearing Investments	$65,936
Total Liquid Assets	$136,870

CREDIT DATA

July 2000:

Pool of Credit	$462,004,186
Revolving Credit, No.	75,783
Fixed Loans, No.	33,854
Avg. Credit Limit, per Person	$12,332
Avg. Spent, per Person	$6,133
Satisfactory Ratings, No. per Person	2.73
Avg. No. of Cards, per Person	0.93

LABOUR FORCE

2001 Estimates:

Male:	
In the Labour Force	13,782
Participation Rate	73.5
Employed	12,746
Unemployed	1,036
Unemployment Rate	7.5
Not in Labour Force	4,963
Female:	
In the Labour Force	10,872
Participation Rate	56.9
Employed	10,062
Unemployed	810
Unemployment Rate	7.5
Not in Labour Force	8,236

OCCUPATIONS BY MAJOR GROUPS

2001 Estimates:	Male	Female
Management	1,126	745
Business, Finance & Admin.	824	2,946
Natural & Applied Sciences & Related	1,091	211
Health	177	919
Social Sciences, Gov't Services & Religion	142	438
Education	394	699
Arts, Culture, Recreation & Sport	179	177
Sales & Service	2,309	3,908
Trades, Transport & Equipment Operators & Related	4,249	244
Primary Industries	2,025	107
Processing, Mfg. & Utilities	903	73

LEVEL OF SCHOOLING

2001 Estimates:

Population 15 years +	37,853
Less than Grade 9	4,680
Grades 9-13 w/o Certif.	10,993
Grade 9-13 with Certif.	5,703
Trade Certif. /Dip.	1,885
Non-Univ. w/o Certif./Dip.	2,126
Non-Univ. with Certif./Dip.	7,816
Univ. w/o Degree	1,935
Univ. w/o Degree/Certif.	992
Univ. with Certif.	943
Univ. with Degree.	2,715

AVERAGE HOUSEHOLD EXPENDITURES

2001 Estimates:

Food	$6,369
Shelter	$8,310
Clothing	$2,338
Transportation	$5,673
Health & Personal Care	$2,346
Recr'n, Read'g & Education	$3,931
Taxes & Securities	$12,919
Other	$9,006
Total Expenditures	$50,892

PRIVATE HOUSEHOLDS

2001 Estimates:

Private Households, Total	18,662
Pop. in Private Households	46,360
Average no. per Household	2.5

FAMILIES

2001 Estimates:

Families in Private Households	13,930
Husband-Wife Families	11,902
Lone-Parent Families	2,028
Aver. No. Persons per Family	3.0
Aver. No. Sons/Daughters at Home	1.2

HOUSING

2001 Estimates:

Occupied Private Dwellings	18,662
Owned	12,039
Rented	6,623
Single-Detached House	11,542
Semi-Detached House	1,180
Row Houses	767
Apartment, 5+ Storeys	511
Apartment, 5 or Fewer Storeys	2,671
Apartment, Detached Duplex	1,662
Other Single-Attached	91
Movable Dwellings	238

VEHICLES

2001 Estimates:

Model Yrs. '81-'96, No.	22,540
% Total	82.88
Model Yrs. '97-'98, No.	2,879
% Total	10.59
'99 Vehicles registered in Model Yr. '99, No.	1,776
% Total	6.53
Total No. '81-'99	27,195

LEGAL MARITAL STATUS

2001 Estimates: (Age 15+)

Single (Never Married)	11,444
Legally Married (Not Separated)	19,818
Legally Married (Separated)	1,402
Widowed	2,529
Divorced	2,660

PSYTE CATEGORIES

2001 Estimates	No. of House -holds	% of Total Hhds.	Index
Old Bungalow Burbs	399	2.14	129
Town Boomers	4,683	25.09	2,476
Participation Quebec	467	2.50	87
Pick-ups & Dirt Bikes	226	1.21	145
Young Grey Collar	12,674	67.91	8,118
Big Country Families	53	0.28	20

FINANCIAL P$YTE

2001 Estimates	No. of House -holds	% of Total Hhds.	Index
Canadian Comfort	4,683	25.09	258
Miners & Credit-Liners	399	2.14	68
Mortgages & Minivans	467	2.50	38
Country Credit	226	1.21	18
Revolving Renters	12,674	67.91	1,476
Rural Family Blues	53	0.28	4

Ontario

HOME LANGUAGE

2001 Estimates:		% Total
English	32,431	68.62
French	12,518	26.49
Chinese	76	0.16
Cree	117	0.25
Croatian	40	0.08
Finnish	141	0.30
Italian	156	0.33
Polish	131	0.28
Slovenian	31	0.07
Ukrainian	25	0.05
Other Languages	85	0.18
Multiple Responses	1,511	3.20
Total	47,262	100.00

BUILDING PERMITS

	1999	1998	1997
		$000	
Value	29,977	24,115	34,758

HOMES BUILT

	1999	1998	1997
No.	38	67	111

TAXATION

Income Class:	1997	% Total
Under $5,000	4,540	13.38
$5,000-$10,000	4,250	12.52
$10,000-$15,000	5,090	15.00
$15,000-$20,000	3,080	9.07
$20,000-$25,000	2,390	7.04
$25,000-$30,000	2,190	6.45
$30,000-$40,000	3,700	10.90
$40,000-$50,000	2,790	8.22
$50,000 +	5,910	17.41
Total Returns, No.	33,940	
Total Income, $000	951,381	
Total Taxable Returns	22,870	
Total Tax, $000	184,051	
Average Income, $	28,031	
Average Tax, $	8,048	

VITAL STATISTICS

	1997	1996	1995	1994
Births	513	560	613	605
Deaths	364	398	357	329
Natural Increase	149	162	256	276
Marriages	267	294	319	267

Note: Latest available data.

DAILY NEWSPAPER(S)

	Circulation Average Paid
Daily Press	
Tue.	10,117
Fri.	11,201
Sat.	10,533
Mon-Sat.	10,393

Timmins
(Census Agglomeration)
(Cont'd)

COMMUNITY NEWSPAPER(S)

	Total Circulation
Timmins: Les Nouvelles	n.a.
Timmins: Timmins Times	18,905

RADIO STATION(S)

	Power
CBCJ-FM	n.a.
CBON-FM	n.a.
CHIM-FM	100w
CHYK-FM	33,000w
CJQQ-FM	n.a.
CJRT-FM	n.a.
CKGB	n.a.
CKOY	10,000w

TELEVISION STATION(S)

CFCL-TV
CHCH-TV
CIII-TV
CITO-TV
TFO
TVO

Toronto
(Census Metropolitan Area)

On Jan. 1, 1998, East York, Etobicoke, North York, Scarborough, Toronto & York amalgamated to form the new city of Toronto.

POPULATION

July 1, 2001 Estimate	4,867,645
% Cdn. Total	15.63
% Change, '96 -'01	10.56
Avg. Annual Growth Rate, %	2.03
2003 Projected Population	5,064,056
2006 Projected Population	5,363,509
2001 Households Estimate	1,738,284
2003 Projected Households	1,815,385
2006 Projected Households	1,937,011

INCOME

% Above/Below National Average	+16
2001 Total Income Estimate	$118,824,700,000
% Cdn. Total	18.10
2001 Average Hhld. Income	$68,400
2001 Per Capita	$24,400
2003 Projected Total Income	$131,347,830,000
2006 Projected Total Income	$152,984,400,000

RETAIL SALES

% Above/Below National Average	-6
2001 Retail Sales Estimate	$40,759,060,000
% Cdn. Total	14.62
2001 per Household	$23,400
2001 per Capita	$8,400
2001 No. of Establishments	33,205
2003 Projected Retail Sales	$45,723,680,000
2006 Projected Retail Sales	$53,423,040,000

POPULATION

2001 Estimates:

Total	4,867,645
Male	2,372,414
Female	2,495,231

Age Groups	Male	Female
0-4	164,463	155,839
5-9	166,524	157,307
10-14	161,839	152,742
15-19	156,000	147,737
20-24	155,023	152,476
25-29	168,220	174,199
30-34	195,104	204,158
35-39	207,851	217,867
40-44	196,335	209,171
45-49	178,406	191,450
50-54	151,470	161,189
55-59	122,241	129,400
60-64	100,312	107,330
65-69	84,153	94,205
70+	164,473	240,161

DAYTIME POPULATION

2001 Estimates:

Working Population	2,530,074
At Home Population	2,337,573
Total	4,867,647

INCOME

2001 Estimates:

Avg. Household Income	$68,357
Avg. Family Income	$72,673
Per Capita Income	$24,411
Male:	
Avg. Employment Income	$42,054
Avg. Employment Income (Full Time)	$54,860
Female:	
Avg. Employment Income	$27,908
Avg. Employment Income (Full Time)	$39,281

DISPOSABLE & DISCRETIONARY INCOME

2001 Estimates:	Per Hhld.
Disposable Income	$55,616
Discretionary Income 1 (minus Food & Shelter)	$39,642
Discretionary Income 2 (minus Food, Shelter, & Other Expenditures)	$29,830

LIQUID ASSETS

1999 Estimates:	Per Hhld.
Equity Investments	$120,006
Interest Bearing Investments	$88,025
Total Liquid Assets	$208,031

CREDIT DATA

July 2000:

Pool of Credit	$52,882,004,653
Revolving Credit, No.	9,926,765
Fixed Loans, No.	2,228,800
Avg. Credit Limit, per Person	$12,174
Avg. Spent, per Person	$5,040
Satisfactory Ratings, No. per Person	2.72
Avg. No. of Cards, per Person	1.17

LABOUR FORCE

2001 Estimates:

Male:	
In the Labour Force	1,418,439
Participation Rate	75.5
Employed	1,347,186
Unemployed	71,253
Unemployment Rate	5.0
Not in Labour Force	461,149
Female:	
In the Labour Force	1,253,126
Participation Rate	61.8
Employed	1,173,969
Unemployed	79,157
Unemployment Rate	6.3
Not in Labour Force	776,217

OCCUPATIONS BY MAJOR GROUPS

2001 Estimates:	Male	Female
Management	194,309	90,361
Business, Finance & Admin.	196,790	417,086
Natural & Applied Sciences & Related	120,543	30,003
Health	25,155	77,717
Social Sciences, Gov't Services & Religion	34,116	40,950
Education	32,009	61,632
Arts, Culture, Recreation & Sport	42,919	44,860
Sales & Service	302,507	333,931
Trades, Transport & Equipment Operators & Related	274,850	19,105
Primary Industries	20,257	4,853
Processing, Mfg. & Utilities	131,982	80,414

LEVEL OF SCHOOLING

2001 Estimates:

Population 15 years +	3,908,931
Less than Grade 9	395,105
Grades 9-13 w/o Certif.	800,626
Grade 9-13 with Certif.	539,243
Trade Certif./Dip.	112,311
Non-Univ. w/o Certif./Dip.	245,898
Non-Univ. with Certif./Dip.	648,805
Univ. w/o Degree	428,125
Univ. w/o Degree/Certif.	217,859
Univ. with Certif.	210,266
Univ. with Degree	738,818

AVERAGE HOUSEHOLD EXPENDITURES

2001 Estimates:

Food	$7,224
Shelter	$11,389
Clothing	$2,720
Transportation	$7,567
Health & Personal Care	$2,188
Recr'n, Read'g & Education	$4,351
Taxes & Securities	$18,163
Other	$9,625
Total Expenditures	$63,227

PRIVATE HOUSEHOLDS

2001 Estimates:

Private Households, Total	1,738,284
Pop. in Private Households	4,792,803
Average no. per Household	2.8

FAMILIES

2001 Estimates:

Families in Private Households	1,334,752
Husband-Wife Families	1,132,726
Lone-Parent Families	202,026
Aver. No. Persons per Family	3.1
Aver. No. Sons/Daughters at Home	1.3

HOUSING

2001 Estimates:

Occupied Private Dwellings	1,738,284
Owned	1,029,020
Rented	709,252
Band Housing	12
Single-Detached House	773,930
Semi-Detached House	141,665
Row Houses	116,031
Apartment, 5+ Storeys	483,689
Owned Apartment, 5+ Storeys	86,752
Apartment, 5 or Fewer Storeys	169,583
Apartment, Detached Duplex	48,402
Other Single-Attached	4,243
Movable Dwellings	741

VEHICLES

2001 Estimates:

Model Yrs. '81-'96, No.	1,897,700
% Total	73.45
Model Yrs. '97-'98, No.	392,438
% Total	15.19
'99 Vehicles registered in Model Yr. '99, No.	293,541
% Total	11.36
Total No. '81-'99	2,583,679

LEGAL MARITAL STATUS

2001 Estimates: (Age 15+)

Single (Never Married)	1,231,698
Legally Married (Not Separated)	2,103,519
Legally Married (Separated)	131,478
Widowed	221,333
Divorced	220,903

Toronto
(Census Metropolitan Area)
(Cont'd)
PSYTE CATEGORIES

2001 Estimates	No. of House-holds	% of Total Hhds.	Index
Canadian			
Establishment	11,902	0.68	411
The Affluentials	36,025	2.07	324
Urban Gentry	72,508	4.17	232
Suburban			
Executives	59,248	3.41	238
Mortgaged in			
Suburbia	65,647	3.78	272
Technocrafts &			
Bureaucrats	79,461	4.57	162
Asian Heights	59,297	3.41	538
Boomers & Teens	77,507	4.46	249
Stable Suburban			
Families	45,697	2.63	202
Small City Elite	2,418	0.14	8
Old Bungalow Burbs	37,910	2.18	132
Suburban Nesters	115,522	6.65	415
Brie & Chablis	66,515	3.83	427
Aging Erudites	5,669	0.33	22
Satellite Suburbs	104,609	6.02	210
Kindergarten Boom	26,435	1.52	58
Blue Collar			
Winners	28,185	1.62	64
Old Towns' New			
Fringe	15,921	0.92	23
Rustic Prosperity	441	0.03	1
Europa	121,584	6.99	563
Asian Mosaic	40,952	2.36	172
High Rise			
Melting Pot	159,787	9.19	613
Conservative			
Homebodies	59,386	3.42	95
High Rise Sunsets	36,507	2.10	147
Young Urban			
Professionals	67,172	3.86	204
Young Urban Mix	142,083	8.17	386
Young Urban			
Intelligentsia	51,544	2.97	195
University			
Enclaves	10,806	0.62	30
Young City Singles	11,450	0.66	29
Urban Bohemia	12,365	0.71	61
Old Leafy Towns	2,287	0.13	5
Town Renters	12,860	0.74	86
Nesters & Young			
Homesteaders	4,064	0.23	10
Big Country			
Families	137	0.01	1
Struggling			
Downtowns	15,506	0.89	28
Aged Pensioners	15,942	0.92	69
Big City Stress	32,076	1.85	163
Old Grey Towers	18,872	1.09	196

FINANCIAL P$YTE

2001 Estimates	No. of House-holds	% of Total Hhds.	Index
Platinum Estates	47,927	2.76	342
Four Star			
Investors	209,263	12.04	240
Successful			
Suburbanites	250,102	14.39	217
Canadian Comfort	250,734	14.42	148
Urban Heights	139,356	8.02	186
Miners &			
Credit-Liners	37,910	2.18	69
Mortgages &			
Minivans	26,435	1.52	23
Dollars & Sense	162,536	9.35	358
Tractors &			
Tradelines	16,362	0.94	16
Bills & Wills	203,756	11.72	142
Revolving Renters	40,571	2.33	51
Young Urban			
Struggle	74,715	4.30	91
Rural Family Blues	137	0.01	.
Towering Debt	199,603	11.48	147
NSF	32,076	1.85	52
Senior Survivors	34,814	2.00	106

RADIO STATION DATA

Station	Market	Format	Wkly. Reach%*	Aver. Hrs. Tuned
All Stations			94	21.7
CBL-FM	Toronto	All Info.	6	8.1
CBLA-FM	Toronto	News, Info.	10	11.4
CFMX-FM	Toronto	Classical	7	12.1
CFNY-FM	Toronto	Alternative	10	7.3
CFRB	Toronto	News, Talk	14	10.0
CFTR	Toronto	All News	16	4.8
CFYI	Toronto	Talk	5	5.8
CHAM	Hamilton	Country	2	11.7
CHAY-FM	Barrie	Adult Contemp.	3	9.7
CHFI-FM	Toronto	Adult Contemp.	22	12.1
CHIN	Toronto	Ethnic, Multicult.	n.a.	n.a.
CHIN-FM	Toronto	Ethnic, Multicult.	n.a.	n.a.
CHIR-FM	Toronto	Greek (Hit Mix)	n.a.	n.a.
CHKT	Toronto	Multiling.	n.a.	n.a.
CHOG	Toronto	News, Talk	n.a.	n.a.
CHTZ-FM	St. Cath.-Niagara	AOR	3	5.6
CHUM	Toronto	All Oldies	6	7.9
CHUM-FM	Toronto	Adult Contemp.	21	9.7
CHWO	Oakville	Adult Standards	n.a.	n.a.
CIAO	Brampton	Ethnic, Multicult.	n.a.	n.a.
CIDC-FM	Toronto	Dance	10	4.2
CILQ-FM	Toronto	AOR	13	6.9
CING-FM	Burlington	Contemp. Hit Radio	9	3.3
CIRV-FM	Toronto	Ethnic, Multicult.	n.a.	n.a.
CISS-FM	Toronto	Top 40	21	8.0
CJBC	Toronto	Multi-format	-	3.4
CJCL	Toronto	Sports	5	7.5
CJEZ-FM	Toronto	Adult Contemp.	9	10.8
CJKX-FM	Oshawa/Ajax	Country	n.a.	n.a.
CJMR	Toronto	Ethnic, Religious	n.a.	n.a.
CJRT-FM	Toronto	Classical, Folk, Jazz, Blues	4	5.7
CJXY-FM	Hamilton	AOR	3	8.7
CKDX-FM	Newmarket	Oldies	n.a.	n.a.
CKFM-FM	Toronto	Adult Contemp.	16	7.5
CKOC	Hamilton	Oldies	2	5.2

BBM Spring 2000 Radio Reach Survey; area coverage.
*Mon-Sun 5a.m - 1a.m , All Persons 12+

TV STATION DATA

Station	Market	Network Affiliation	Wkly. Reach%*	Aver. Hrs. Tuned
All Stations			96	21.3
A & E	n.a.	Ind.	18	3.2
BRAVO	n.a.	Ind.	10	1.5
CBLFT	Toronto	n.a.	1	3.4
CBLT	Toronto	CBC	42	2.6
CFMT	Toronto	Ind.	33	1.9
CFTO	Toronto	CTV	74	5.3
CHCH	Toronto/Hamilton	Ind.	38	2.0
CHIN	Toronto	Ind.	n.a.	n.a.
CHLF	Toronto	TVO	n.a.	n.a.
CICA	Toronto	TVO	n.a.	n.a.
CICO-E	n.a.	n.a.	18	2.0
CIII	n.a.	Global	59	3.4
CITY	Toronto	Ind.	47	3.0
CKVR	Barrie	Ind.	19	2.2
CNN	n.a.	Ind.	8	2.1
CP 24	n.a.	Ind.	8	2.1
CTS	Toronto/Hamilton	Ind.	n.a.	n.a.
DSCVRY	n.a.	Ind.	7	1.6
FAIRTV	n.a.	Ind.	1	17.5
FAMILY	n.a.	Ind.	8	1.3
FOOD	n.a.	Ind.	5	3.5
HGTV	n.a.	Ind.	7	2.8
LATINO	Toronto	Ind.	3	6.3
NEWSWD	n.a.	CBC	6	2.2
OTHERS	n.a.	Ind.	10	1.9
PRIME	n.a.	Ind.	7	2.0
SHWCSE	n.a.	Ind.	6	2.1
SNET	n.a.	CTV	14	2.7
SPACE	n.a.	Ind.	8	1.8
TLC	n.a.	Ind.	8	1.6
TMN	Toronto	Ind.	6	3.3
TOON	n.a.	Ind.	9	2.1
TSN	n.a.	Ind.	22	3.0
VCR	n.a.	n.a.	25	4.0
WGRZ	Buffalo NY	NBC	14	1.2
WIVB	Buffalo NY	CBS	15	1.8
WKBW	Buffalo NY	ABC	19	1.9
WNED	Buffalo NY	PBS	18	2.0
WNEQ	Buffalo NY	PBS	-	0.5
WNYO	Buffalo NY	WB	1	1.4
WSBK	Boston MA	UPN	3	3.7
WTBS	Atlanta GA	Ind.	16	3.5
WUTV	Buffalo NY	FOX	32	2.2
YTV	n.a.	Ind.	15	3.6

BBM Spring 2000 TV Reach Survey; CMA coverage.
*Mon-Sun 6a.m - 2a.m , All Persons 2 +

Ontario

HOME LANGUAGE

2001 Estimates:		% Total
English	3,563,964	73.22
French	21,870	0.45
Arabic	25,921	0.53
Armenian	7,007	0.14
Bengali	5,080	0.10
Chinese	279,713	5.75
Croatian	12,375	0.25
Czech	2,665	0.05
Estonian	2,936	0.06
German	8,036	0.17
Greek	30,151	0.62
Gujarati	17,777	0.37
Hebrew	4,857	0.10
Hindi	8,544	0.18
Hungarian	9,464	0.19
Italian	108,518	2.23
Japanese	4,765	0.10
Korean	21,316	0.44
Macedonian	10,178	0.21
Persian (Farsi)	24,136	0.50
Polish	59,880	1.23
Portuguese	75,365	1.55
Punjabi	60,605	1.25
Romanian	7,110	0.15
Russian	18,748	0.39
Serbian	10,327	0.21
Serbo-Croatian	4,192	0.09
Spanish	56,206	1.15
Tagalog (Pilipino)	37,626	0.77
Tamil	50,715	1.04
Turkish	3,331	0.07
Ukrainian	12,738	0.26
Urdu	19,866	0.41
Vietnamese	32,879	0.68
Other Languages	67,598	1.39
Multiple Responses	181,186	3.72
Total	4,867,645	100.00

BUILDING PERMITS

	1999	1998 $000	1997
Value	8,833,418	7,305,393	6,877,279

HOMES BUILT

	1999	1998	1997
No	29,847	21,482	23,342

TAXATION

Income Class:	1997	% Total
Under $5,000	462,190	14.60
$5,000-$10,000	384,850	12.15
$10,000-$15,000	398,360	12.58
$15,000-$20,000	281,160	8.88
$20,000-$25,000	241,340	7.62
$25,000-$30,000	232,340	7.34
$30,000-$40,000	391,400	12.36
$40,000-$50,000	257,470	8.13
$50,000 +	517,720	16.35
Total Returns, No.	3,166,740	
Total Income, $000	101,984,381	
Total Taxable		
Returns	2,185,180	
Total Tax, $000	22,374,002	
Average Income, $	32,205	
Average Tax, $	10,239	

Ontario

Toronto
(Census Metropolitan Area)
(Cont'd)
VITAL STATISTICS

	1997	1996	1995	1994
Births	57,896	60,881	61,916	61,898
Deaths	25,741	25,920	25,599	24,762
Natural Increase	32,155	34,961	36,317	37,136
Marriages	25,464	26,244	27,257	27,549

Note: Latest available data.

DAILY NEWSPAPER(S)

	Circulation Average Paid
National Post	
Mon-Fri	268,747
Sat	314,385
The Globe and Mail-Metro Edition	
Mon-Sat	196,249
Mon-Fri	190,843
Sat	223,281
The Globe and Mail-National Edition	
Mon-Sat	335,090
Mon-Fri	322,834
Sat	396,389
The Toronto Star	
Mon-Fri	467,638
Sat	701,805
Sun	485,373
The Toronto Sun	
Mon-Fri	244,278
Sat	191,839
Sun	413,465

COMMUNITY NEWSPAPER(S)

	Total Circulation
Ajax, Pickering: News Advertiser	
Wed	43,908
Fri	49,294
Sun	43,897
Aurora: Town Crier	n.a.
Aurora: Aurora Weekly	n.a.
Aurora, Georgina, Keswick, Newmarket: Era Banner	
Tue	62,155
Thu	62,754
Sun	63,296
Bolton: Bolton Enterprise	
Wed/Sat	11,869
Bradford West Gwillimbury: Bradford West Gwillimbury Times	10,600
Brampton: Brampton Guardian	
Wed	68,738
Fri	68,065
Sun	68,215
Brampton: Le Métropolitain	10,000
Caledon: Caledon Citizen	9,400
East York: Mirror	34,996
Etobicoke: Etobicoke Guardian	
Wed	68,731
Sun	68,405
Etobicoke: Etobicoke Life	28,735
Etobicoke: Etobicoke Villager	41,930
Georgetown: Georgetown Independent/Acton Free Press	
Wed	17,208
Fri	17,199

	Total Circulation
Keswick, Aurora, Georgina, Newmarket: Era Banner	
Tue	62,155
Thu	62,754
Sun	63,296
Keswick, Sutton, Pefferlaw: Georgina Advocate	14,265
King City: King Weekly	n.a.
Markham: Community Digest	25,000
Markham: Markham Economist & Sun	
Tue	37,356
Sat	37,428
Milton: Milton Canadian Champion	
Tue	11,324
Milton: Milton Shopping News	
Tue/Fri	12,000
Milton: Milton Canadian Champion	
Fri	11,029
Mississauga: Mississauga Booster (biwkly)	n.a.
Mississauga: Mississauga News	
Wed	120,727
Thu	42,753
Fri	117,722
Sun	117,731
Mississauga: The Weekly Voice	30,000
Newmarket, Aurora, Georgina, Keswick: Era Banner	
Tue	62,155
Thu	62,754
Sun	63,296
North York: North York Mirror	
Wed/Fri/Sun	100,029
Oakville: Abbey Oaks News	22,000
Oakville: Oakville Beaver	
Wed	23,000
Fri	39,531
Sun	23,000
Oakville: Oakville North News	23,000
Oakville: Oakville Shopping News	
Tue/Fri	40,688
Orangeville: Orangeville Banner	
Tue/Fri	n.a.
Orangeville: Orangeville Banner (suppl.), The Banner Extra	n.a.
Orangeville: Orangeville Citizen	11,292
Pickering, Ajax: News Advertiser	
Wed	43,908
Fri	49,294
Sun	43,897
Pickering, Ajax: Durham Sun Weekly	n.a.
Richmond Hill: Richmond Hill Weekly	n.a.
Richmond Hill, Thornhill, Vaughan: Liberal	
Tue	78,270
Thu	75,433
Sun	78,248
Scarborough: Scarborough Mirror	
Wed/Fri/Sun	108,301
Stouffville: Stouffville Tribune	
Tue	8,192
Sat	7,968
Stouffville: Stouffville Sun	n.a.
Thornhill, Richmond Hill, Vaughan: Liberal	
Tue	78,270
Thu	75,433
Sun	78,248
Toronto: Beach Metro Community News (biwkly Sept-July)	31,000
Toronto: Bluffs Monitor (mthly)	23,000
Toronto: The Jewish Tribune	n.a.
Toronto: Bayview Post (mthly)	n.a.
Toronto: North Toronto Post (mthly)	n.a.
Toronto: Richmond Hill Post (mthly)	n.a.
Toronto: Thornhill Post (mthly)	n.a.
Toronto: Village Post (mthly)	n.a.
Toronto: Bayview-Mills Town Crier (mthly)	18,072
Toronto: Beach Town Crier (mthly)	25,271
Toronto: Bloor Annex Town Crier	18,208
Toronto: Forest Hill Town Crier (mthly)	25,632
Toronto: Markham Communicator (mthly)	33,878
Toronto: North Toronto Town Crier (mthly)	25,410
Toronto: The Villager (mthly)	43,985
Toronto: East Toronto Advocate (biwkly)	n.a.
Toronto: Leaside Advertiser (biwkly)	n.a.

	Total Circulation
Toronto: Toronto Voice (mthly)	n.a.
Toronto: Lakesider (2 mthly)	n.a.
Toronto: Hi-Rise (in 7 areas) (mthly)	60,000
Toronto: Métro Courrier	n.a.
Toronto: Our Toronto Free Press (biwkly)	80,000
Toronto: East York Times (biwkly)	n.a.
Toronto: North Toronto Herald (biwkly)	n.a.
Toronto: etc... news (every 3 wks.)	n.a.
Toronto: L'Express	n.a.
Toronto: Toronto Jewish Press	n.a.
Toronto: Nouveau Canada	n.a.
Toronto, Leaside: Rosedale Town Crier (mthly)	24,084
Uxbridge: Uxbridge Tribune	
Tue/Wed	8,417
Fri	8,388
Uxbridge: Uxbridge Times-Journal	2,995
Vaughan: Vaughan Weekly	n.a.
Vaughan, Richmond Hill, Thornhill: Liberal	
Tue	78,270
Thu	75,433
Sun	78,248
Woodbridge: Woodbridge Advertiser	n.a.
York: York Guardian	61,076

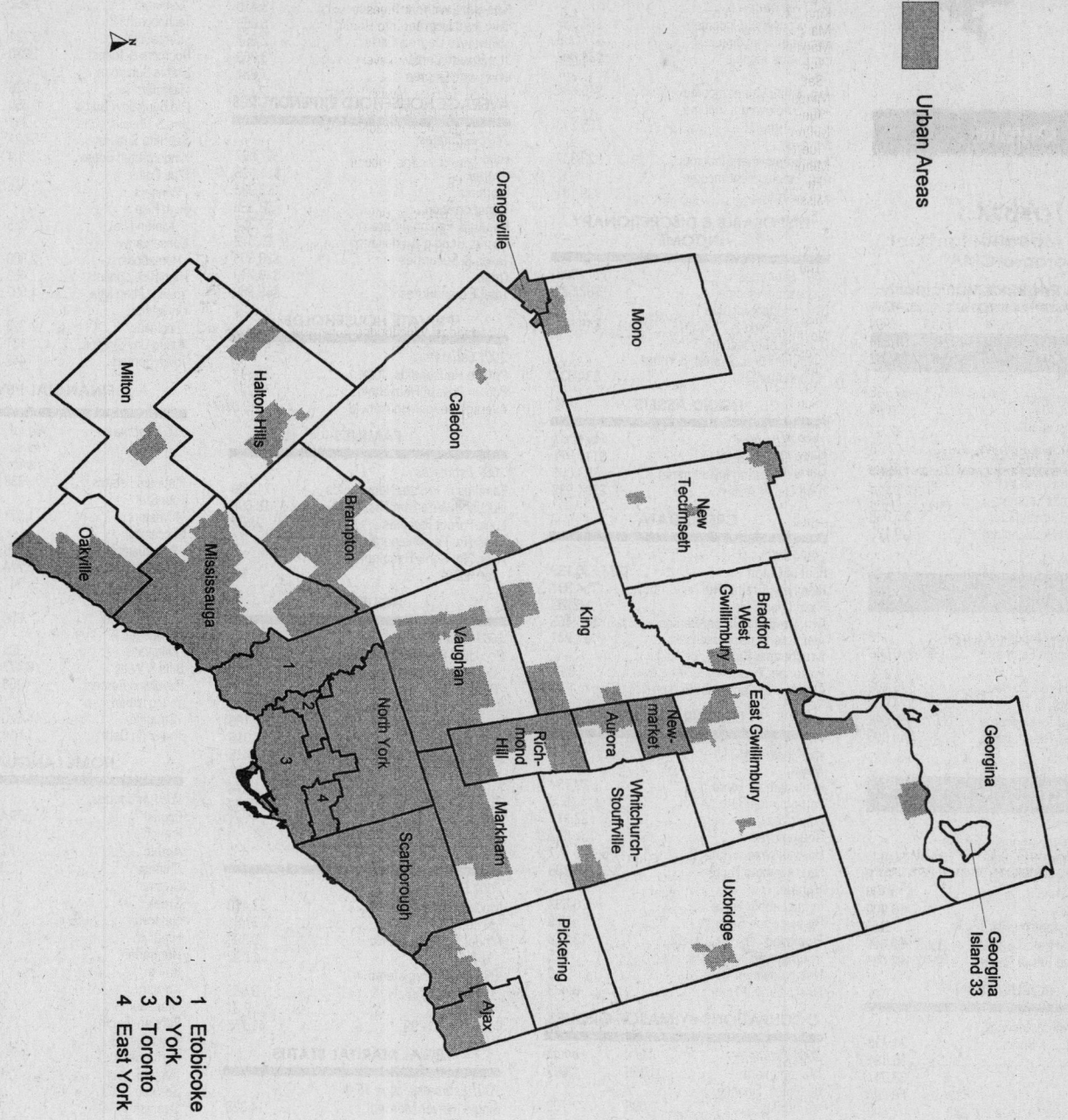

Urban Areas

Orangeville
Mono
Milton
Halton Hills
Caledon
New Tecumseth
Brampton
Bradford West Gwillimbury
Oakville
Mississauga
King
Vaughan
New-market
Aurora
East Gwillimbury
Georgina
North York
Rich-mond Hill
Whitchurch-Stouffville
Markham
Scarborough
Uxbridge
Georgina Island 33
Pickering
Ajax

1 Etobicoke
2 York
3 Toronto
4 East York

Ontario

Ajax
(Town)
Toronto CMA

In Durham Regional Municipality.

POPULATION

July 1, 2001 Estimate	74,738
% Cdn. Total	0.24
% Change, '96 -'01	12.53
Avg. Annual Growth Rate, %	2.39
2003 Projected Population	78,535
2006 Projected Population	83,913
2001 Households Estimate	24,347
2003 Projected Households	25,838
2006 Projected Households	28,123

INCOME

% Above/Below National Average	+18
2001 Total Income Estimate	$1,858,910,000
% Cdn. Total	0.28
2001 Average Hhld. Income	$76,400
2001 Per Capita	$24,900
2003 Projected Total Income	$2,070,850,000
2006 Projected Total Income	$2,426,940,000

RETAIL SALES

% Above/Below National Average	-33
2001 Retail Sales Estimate	$446,330,000
% Cdn. Total	0.16
2001 per Household	$18,300
2001 per Capita	$6,000
2001 No. of Establishments	350
2003 Projected Retail Sales	$505,960,000
2006 Projected Retail Sales	$597,190,000

POPULATION

2001 Estimates:

Total		74,738
Male		36,691
Female		38,047

Age Groups	Male	Female
0-4	2,826	2,698
5-9	3,231	3,103
10-14	3,194	3,090
15-19	2,798	2,713
20-24	2,297	2,250
25-29	2,199	2,276
30-34	2,847	3,090
35-39	3,519	3,872
40-44	3,480	3,722
45-49	2,945	3,016
50-54	2,255	2,221
55-59	1,621	1,579
60-64	1,153	1,183
65-69	851	974
70+	1,475	2,260

DAYTIME POPULATION

2001 Estimates:

Working Population	17,952
At Home Population	32,167
Total	50,119

INCOME

2001 Estimates:

Avg. Household Income	$76,351
Avg. Family Income	$77,068
Per Capita Income	$24,872
Male:	
Avg. Employment Income	$45,684
Avg. Employment Income (Full Time)	$55,243
Female:	
Avg. Employment Income	$28,337
Avg. Employment Income (Full Time)	$39,181

DISPOSABLE & DISCRETIONARY INCOME

2001 Estimates:	Per Hhld.
Disposable Income	$62,529
Discretionary Income 1 (minus Food & Shelter)	$45,569
Discretionary Income 2 (minus Food, Shelter, & Other Expenditures)	$34,832

LIQUID ASSETS

1999 Estimates:	Per Hhld.
Equity Investments	$111,871
Interest Bearing Investments	$93,061
Total Liquid Assets	$204,932

CREDIT DATA

July 2000:

Pool of Credit	$933,236,139
Revolving Credit, No.	154,991
Fixed Loans, No.	50,783
Avg. Credit Limit, per Person	$15,465
Avg. Spent, per Person	$7,247
Satisfactory Ratings, No. per Person	3.27
Avg. No. of Cards, per Person	1.21

LABOUR FORCE

2001 Estimates:

Male:	
In the Labour Force	22,734
Participation Rate	82.8
Employed	22,117
Unemployed	617
Unemployment Rate	2.7
Not in Labour Force	4,706
Female:	
In the Labour Force	20,683
Participation Rate	70.9
Employed	19,858
Unemployed	825
Unemployment Rate	4.0
Not in Labour Force	8,473

OCCUPATIONS BY MAJOR GROUPS

2001 Estimates:	Male	Female
Management	3,055	1,682
Business, Finance & Admin.	3,096	7,700
Natural & Applied Sciences & Related	1,920	495
Health	303	1,652
Social Sciences, Gov't Services & Religion	325	502
Education	427	847
Arts, Culture, Recreation & Sport	388	436
Sales & Service	4,790	5,515
Trades, Transport & Equipment Operators & Related	5,559	439
Primary Industries	319	68
Processing, Mfg. & Utilities	2,108	758

LEVEL OF SCHOOLING

2001 Estimates:

Population 15 years +	56,596
Less than Grade 9	2,450
Grades 9-13 w/o Certif.	12,005
Grade 9-13 with Certif.	9,760
Trade Certif./Dip.	2,015
Non-Univ. w/o Certif./Dip.	4,205
Non-Univ. with Certif./Dip.	13,415
Univ. w/o Degree	5,665
Univ. w/o Degree/Certif.	2,662
Univ. with Certif.	3,003
Univ. with Degree	7,081

AVERAGE HOUSEHOLD EXPENDITURES

2001 Estimates:

Food	$7,867
Shelter	$11,895
Clothing	$2,983
Transportation	$8,355
Health & Personal Care	$2,357
Recr'n, Read'g & Education	$5,012
Taxes & Securities	$20,809
Other	$10,710
Total Expenditures	$69,988

PRIVATE HOUSEHOLDS

2001 Estimates:

Private Households, Total	24,347
Pop. in Private Households	74,227
Average no. per Household	3.0

FAMILIES

2001 Estimates:

Families in Private Households	21,200
Husband-Wife Families	18,608
Lone-Parent Families	2,592
Aver. No. Persons per Family	3.3
Aver. No. Sons/Daughters at Home	1.4

HOUSING

2001 Estimates:

Occupied Private Dwellings	24,347
Owned	19,551
Rented	4,796
Single-Detached House	16,546
Semi-Detached House	1,185
Row Houses	2,316
Apartment, 5+ Storeys	2,415
Owned Apartment, 5+ Storeys	767
Apartment, 5 or Fewer Storeys	1,376
Apartment, Detached Duplex	498
Other Single-Attached	11

VEHICLES

2001 Estimates:

Model Yrs. '81-'96, No.	32,490
% Total	77.81
Model Yrs. '97-'98, No.	5,396
% Total	12.92
'99 Vehicles registered in Model Yr. '99, No.	3,869
% Total	9.27
Total No. '81-'99	41,755

LEGAL MARITAL STATUS

2001 Estimates: (Age 15+)

Single (Never Married)	14,328
Legally Married (Not Separated)	34,791
Legally Married (Separated)	1,978
Widowed	2,351
Divorced	3,148

PSYTE CATEGORIES

2001 Estimates	No. of House-holds	% of Total Hhds.	Index
The Affluentials	338	1.39	217
Suburban Executives	393	1.61	113
Mortgaged in Suburbia	1,962	8.06	580
Technocrafts & Bureaucrats	5,794	23.80	846
Boomers & Teens	1,230	5.05	282
Stable Suburban Families	1,720	7.06	542
Old Bungalow Burbs	650	2.67	161
Brie & Chablis	347	1.43	159
Satellite Suburbs	5,521	22.68	790
Kindergarten Boom	304	1.25	48
Blue Collar Winners	253	1.04	41
High Rise Melting Pot.	955	3.92	262
Conservative Homebodies	2,380	9.78	271
High Rise Sunsets	456	1.87	131
Young Urban Mix	1,097	4.51	213
University Enclaves	323	1.33	65
Young City Singles	121	0.50	22
Town Renters	442	1.82	210

FINANCIAL P$YTE

2001 Estimates	No. of House-holds	% of Total Hhds.	Index
Platinum Estates	338	1.39	172
Four Star Investors	1,623	6.67	133
Successful Suburbanites	9,476	38.92	586
Canadian Comfort	5,774	23.72	244
Urban Heights	347	1.43	33
Miners & Credit-Liners	650	2.67	84
Mortgages & Minivans	304	1.25	19
Bills & Wills	3,477	14.28	172
Revolving Renters	456	1.87	41
Young Urban Struggle	323	1.33	28
Towering Debt	1,518	6.23	80

HOME LANGUAGE

2001 Estimates:		% Total
English	69,464	92.94
French	526	0.70
Arabic	269	0.36
Chinese	813	1.09
German	155	0.21
Greek	152	0.20
Gujarati	72	0.10
Hindi	79	0.11
Hungarian	90	0.12
Italian	156	0.21
Korean	86	0.12
Macedonian	224	0.30
Persian (Farsi)	110	0.15
Polish	172	0.23
Portuguese	134	0.18
Punjabi	148	0.20
Serbian	72	0.10
Spanish	230	0.31
Tagalog (Pilipino)	175	0.23
Tamil	139	0.19
Urdu	246	0.33
Vietnamese	60	0.08
Other Languages	233	0.31
Multiple Responses	933	1.25
Total	74,738	100.00

Ajax
(Town)
Toronto CMA
(Cont'd)

BUILDING PERMITS

	1999	1998	1997
		$000	
Value	131,124	88,544	144,847

HOMES BUILT

	1999	1998	1997
No.	606	387	549

TAXATION

Income Class:	1997	% Total
Under $5,000	5,330	12.05
$5,000-$10,000	4,230	9.57
$10,000-$15,000	4,260	9.63
$15,000-$20,000	3,150	7.12
$20,000-$25,000	2,960	6.69
$25,000-$30,000	3,300	7.46
$30,000-$40,000	6,490	14.68
$40,000-$50,000	5,070	11.47
$50,000 +	9,430	21.33
Total Returns, No.	44,220	
Total Income, $000	1,470,515	
Total Taxable Returns	33,820	
Total Tax, $000	308,715	
Average Income, $	33,255	
Average Tax, $	9,128	

VITAL STATISTICS

	1997	1996	1995	1994
Births	1,016	1,066	1,123	1,162
Deaths	270	235	241	215
Natural Increase	746	831	882	947
Marriages	218	216	182	227

Note: Latest available data.

Aurora
(Town)
Toronto CMA
In York Regional Municipality.

POPULATION

July 1, 2001 Estimate	43,746
% Cdn. Total	0.14
% Change, '96 -'01	21.56
Avg. Annual Growth Rate, %	3.98
2003 Projected Population	46,912
2006 Projected Population	52,055
2001 Households Estimate	14,635
2003 Projected Households	15,745
2006 Projected Households	17,583

INCOME

% Above/Below National Average	+56
2001 Total Income Estimate	$1,436,540,000
% Cdn. Total	0.22
2001 Average Hhld. Income	$98,200
2001 Per Capita	$32,800
2003 Projected Total Income	$1,660,860,000
2006 Projected Total Income	$2,067,900,000

RETAIL SALES

% Above/Below National Average	-2
2001 Retail Sales Estimate	$383,220,000
% Cdn. Total	0.14
2001 per Household	$26,200
2001 per Capita	$8,800
2001 No. of Establishments	214
2003 Projected Retail Sales	$444,700,000
2006 Projected Retail Sales	$546,860,000

POPULATION

2001 Estimates:

Total		43,746
Male		21,564
Female		22,182

Age Groups	Male	Female
0-4	1,574	1,438
5-9	1,853	1,728
10-14	1,890	1,755
15-19	1,665	1,537
20-24	1,380	1,325
25-29	1,292	1,308
30-34	1,544	1,676
35-39	1,937	2,097
40-44	1,994	2,128
45-49	1,756	1,831
50-54	1,372	1,371
55-59	998	997
60-64	746	756
65-69	576	635
70+	987	1,600

DAYTIME POPULATION

2001 Estimates:

Working Population	15,975
At Home Population	18,779
Total	34,754

INCOME

2001 Estimates:

Avg. Household Income	$98,158
Avg. Family Income	$103,101
Per Capita Income	$32,838
Male:	
Avg. Employment Income	$60,307
Avg. Employment Income (Full Time)	$74,893
Female:	
Avg. Employment Income	$32,114
Avg. Employment Income (Full Time)	$47,970

DISPOSABLE & DISCRETIONARY INCOME

2001 Estimates:	Per Hhld.
Disposable Income	$76,950
Discretionary Income 1 (minus Food & Shelter)	$57,293
Discretionary Income 2 (minus Food, Shelter, & Other Expenditures)	$44,959

LIQUID ASSETS

1999 Estimates:	Per Hhld.
Equity Investments	$190,428
Interest Bearing Investments	$127,132
Total Liquid Assets	$317,560

CREDIT DATA

July 2000:	
Pool of Credit	$571,361,153
Revolving Credit, No.	87,781
Fixed Loans, No.	23,378
Avg. Credit Limit, per Person	$17,273
Avg. Spent, per Person	$7,430
Satisfactory Ratings, No. per Person	3.26
Avg. No. of Cards, per Person	1.32

LABOUR FORCE

2001 Estimates:

Male:	
In the Labour Force	13,750
Participation Rate	84.6
Employed	13,544
Unemployed	206
Unemployment Rate	1.5
Not in Labour Force	2,497
Female:	
In the Labour Force	11,701
Participation Rate	67.8
Employed	11,180
Unemployed	521
Unemployment Rate	4.5
Not in Labour Force	5,560

OCCUPATIONS BY MAJOR GROUPS

2001 Estimates:	Male	Female
Management	3,637	1,303
Business, Finance & Admin.	1,572	3,800
Natural & Applied Sciences & Related	1,066	188
Health	112	902
Social Sciences, Gov't Services & Religion	301	566
Education	461	910
Arts, Culture, Recreation & Sport	409	464
Sales & Service	3,007	2,785
Trades, Transport & Equipment Operators & Related	2,236	147
Primary Industries	197	40
Processing, Mfg. & Utilities	610	221

LEVEL OF SCHOOLING

2001 Estimates:

Population 15 years +	33,508
Less than Grade 9	1,203
Grades 9-13 w/o Certif.	6,081
Grade 9-13 with Certif.	4,639
Trade Certif. /Dip.	821
Non-Univ. w/o Certif./Dip.	2,257
Non-Univ. with Certif./Dip.	7,108
Univ. w/o Degree	3,920
Univ. w/o Degree/Certif.	2,035
Univ. with Certif.	1,885
Univ. with Degree	7,479

Ontario

AVERAGE HOUSEHOLD EXPENDITURES

2001 Estimates:

Food	$8,883
Shelter	$14,285
Clothing	$3,875
Transportation	$9,516
Health & Personal Care	$2,789
Recr'n, Read'g & Education	$6,021
Taxes & Securities	$28,291
Other	$12,823
Total Expenditures	$86,483

PRIVATE HOUSEHOLDS

2001 Estimates:

Private Households, Total	14,635
Pop. in Private Households	42,943
Average no. per Household	2.9

FAMILIES

2001 Estimates:

Families in Private Households	12,593
Husband-Wife Families	11,357
Lone-Parent Families	1,236
Aver. No. Persons per Family	3.2
Aver. No. Sons/Daughters at Home	1.3

HOUSING

2001 Estimates:

Occupied Private Dwellings	14,635
Owned	11,699
Rented	2,936
Single-Detached House	10,702
Semi-Detached House	706
Row Houses	1,211
Apartment, 5+ Storeys	920
Owned Apartment, 5+ Storeys	219
Apartment, 5 or Fewer Storeys	814
Apartment, Detached Duplex	282

VEHICLES

2001 Estimates:

Model Yrs. '81-'96, No.	19,299
% Total	72.27
Model Yrs. '97-'98, No.	4,468
% Total	16.73
'99 Vehicles registered in Model Yr. '99, No.	2,937
% Total	11.00
Total No. '81-'99	26,704

LEGAL MARITAL STATUS

2001 Estimates: (Age 15+)

Single (Never Married)	8,076
Legally Married (Not Separated)	21,230
Legally Married (Separated)	987
Widowed	1,513
Divorced	1,702

Ontario

Aurora
(Town)
Toronto CMA
(Cont'd)

PSYTE CATEGORIES

2001 Estimates	No. of House-holds	% of Total Hhds.	Index
Canadian Establishment	728	4.97	2,989
Suburban Executives	3,828	26.16	1,825
Mortgaged in Suburbia	2,087	14.26	1,026
Technocrafts & Bureaucrats	1,111	7.59	270
Boomers & Teens	1,370	9.36	522
Stable Suburban Families	431	2.94	226
Small City Elite	225	1.54	90
Old Bungalow Burbs	631	4.31	260
Suburban Nesters	926	6.33	395
Satellite Suburbs	508	3.47	121
Conservative Homebodies	1,384	9.46	262
High Rise Sunsets	289	1.97	138
Young Urban Professionals	42	0.29	15
Young Urban Mix	523	3.57	169
Town Renters	435	2.97	344

FINANCIAL PSYTE

2001 Estimates	No. of House-holds	% of Total Hhds.	Index
Platinum Estates	728	4.97	617
Four Star Investors	5,198	35.52	707
Successful Suburbanites	3,629	24.80	374
Canadian Comfort	1,659	11.34	117
Urban Heights	42	0.29	7
Miners & Credit-Liners	631	4.31	136
Bills & Wills	1,907	13.03	157
Revolving Renters	289	1.97	43
Towering Debt	435	2.97	38

HOME LANGUAGE

2001 Estimates:		% Total
English	41,847	95.66
French	167	0.38
Arabic	89	0.20
Armenian	52	0.12
Chinese	305	0.70
Croatian	31	0.07
Dutch	41	0.09
German	58	0.13
Hungarian	47	0.11
Italian	180	0.41
Lao	52	0.12
Persian (Farsi)	75	0.17
Polish	163	0.37
Spanish	106	0.24
Tagalog (Pilipino)	35	0.08
Vietnamese	35	0.08
Other Languages	156	0.36
Multiple Responses	307	0.70
Total	43,746	100.00

BUILDING PERMITS

	1999	1998	1997
		$000	
Value	49,568	55,700	57,812

HOMES BUILT

	1999	1998	1997
No	388	261	812

TAXATION

Income Class:	1997	% Total
Under $5,000	2,660	10.54
$5,000-$10,000	2,210	8.76
$10,000-$15,000	2,250	8.92
$15,000-$20,000	1,680	6.66
$20,000-$25,000	1,630	6.46
$25,000-$30,000	1,780	7.06
$30,000-$40,000	3,320	13.16
$40,000-$50,000	2,490	9.87
$50,000 +	7,220	28.62
Total Returns, No.	25,230	
Total Income, $000	1,147,407	
Total Taxable Returns	19,980	
Total Tax, $000	296,308	
Average Income, $	45,478	
Average Tax, $	14,830	

VITAL STATISTICS

	1997	1996	1995	1994
Births	552	501	512	542
Deaths	189	196	191	182
Natural Increase	363	305	321	360
Marriages	126	130	126	125

Note: Latest available data.

MEDIA INFO

see Toronto, CMA

Bradford West Gwillimbury
(Town)
Toronto CMA

In Simcoe County.

POPULATION

July 1, 2001 Estimate	24,190
% Cdn. Total	0.08
% Change, '96 -'01	16.14
Avg. Annual Growth Rate, %	3.04
2003 Projected Population	25,584
2006 Projected Population	27,662
2001 Households Estimate	7,829
2003 Projected Households	8,255
2006 Projected Households	8,972

INCOME

% Above/Below National Average	+3
2001 Total Income Estimate	$523,030,000
% Cdn. Total	0.08
2001 Average Hhld. Income	$66,800
2001 Per Capita	$21,600
2003 Projected Total Income	$575,050,000
2006 Projected Total Income	$665,040,000

RETAIL SALES

% Above/Below National Average	-42
2001 Retail Sales Estimate	$125,500,000
% Cdn. Total	0.05
2001 per Household	$16,000
2001 per Capita	$5,200
2001 No. of Establishments	123
2003 Projected Retail Sales	$141,380,000
2006 Projected Retail Sales	$167,340,000

POPULATION

2001 Estimates:		
Total		24,190
Male		12,114
Female		12,076

Age Groups	Male	Female
0-4	884	869
5-9	1,003	954
10-14	1,045	942
15-19	961	864
20-24	823	814
25-29	810	852
30-34	973	1,047
35-39	1,112	1,149
40-44	1,069	1,063
45-49	911	894
50-54	720	721
55-59	543	522
60-64	401	376
65-69	300	304
70+	559	705

DAYTIME POPULATION

2001 Estimates:	
Working Population	3,655
At Home Population	9,990
Total	13,645

INCOME

2001 Estimates:	
Avg. Household Income	$66,806
Avg. Family Income	$68,076
Per Capita Income	$21,622
Male:	
Avg. Employment Income	$38,334
Avg. Employment Income (Full Time)	$47,628
Female:	
Avg. Employment Income	$23,963
Avg. Employment Income (Full Time)	$33,294

DISPOSABLE & DISCRETIONARY INCOME

2001 Estimates:	Per Hhld.
Disposable Income	$54,970
Discretionary Income 1 (minus Food & Shelter)	$39,668
Discretionary Income 2 (minus Food, Shelter, & Other Expenditures)	$29,711

LIQUID ASSETS

1999 Estimates:	Per Hhld.
Equity Investments	$101,896
Interest Bearing Investments	$85,588
Total Liquid Assets	$187,484

CREDIT DATA

July 2000:	
Pool of Credit	$214,054,050
Revolving Credit, No.	35,420
Fixed Loans, No.	11,298
Avg. Credit Limit, per Person.	$13,611
Avg. Spent, per Person	$6,373
Satisfactory Ratings, No. per Person.	2.86
Avg. No. of Cards, per Person	1.07

LABOUR FORCE

2001 Estimates:	
Male:	
In the Labour Force	7,732
Participation Rate	84.2
Employed	7,546
Unemployed	186
Unemployment Rate	2.4
Not in Labour Force	1,450
Female:	
In the Labour Force	6,609
Participation Rate	71.0
Employed	6,450
Unemployed	159
Unemployment Rate	2.4
Not in Labour Force	2,702

OCCUPATIONS BY MAJOR GROUPS

2001 Estimates:	Male	Female
Management	1,019	478
Business, Finance & Admin.	748	2,052
Natural & Applied Sciences & Related	306	77
Health	68	567
Social Sciences, Gov't Services & Religion	101	194
Education	122	297
Arts, Culture, Recreation & Sport	144	80
Sales & Service	1,338	1,844
Trades, Transport & Equipment Operators & Related	2,409	67
Primary Industries	574	176
Processing, Mfg. & Utilities	812	637

LEVEL OF SCHOOLING

2001 Estimates:	
Population 15 years +	18,493
Less than Grade 9	2,078
Grades 9-13 w/o Certif.	4,524
Grade 9-13 with Certif.	2,895
Trade Certif. /Dip.	719
Non-Univ. w/o Certif./Dip.	1,285
Non-Univ. with Certif./Dip.	3,943
Univ. w/o Degree.	1,461
Univ. w/o Degree/Certif.	702
Univ. with Certif.	759
Univ. with Degree	1,588

Bradford West Gwillimbury
(Town)
Toronto CMA
(Cont'd)

AVERAGE HOUSEHOLD EXPENDITURES

2001 Estimates:
Food	$6,977
Shelter	$10,642
Clothing	$2,522
Transportation	$7,852
Health & Personal Care	$2,072
Recr'n, Read'g & Education	$4,387
Taxes & Securities	$18,084
Other	$9,590
Total Expenditures	$62,126

PRIVATE HOUSEHOLDS

2001 Estimates:
Private Households, Total	7,829
Pop. in Private Households	23,846
Average no. per Household	3.0

FAMILIES

2001 Estimates:
Families in Private Households	6,947
Husband-Wife Families	6,263
Lone-Parent Families	684
Aver. No. Persons per Family	3.3
Aver. No. Sons/Daughters at Home	1.4

HOUSING

2001 Estimates:
Occupied Private Dwellings	7,829
Owned	6,190
Rented	1,639
Single-Detached House	5,765
Semi-Detached House	470
Row Houses	154
Apartment, 5+ Storeys	334
Apartment, 5 or Fewer Storeys	547
Apartment, Detached Duplex	537
Other Single-Attached	22

VEHICLES

2001 Estimates:
Model Yrs. '81-'96, No.	12,923
% Total	81.08
Model Yrs. '97-'98, No.	1,823
% Total	11.44
'99 Vehicles registered in Model Yr. '99, No.	1,193
% Total	7.48
Total No. '81-'99	15,939

LEGAL MARITAL STATUS

2001 Estimates: (Age 15+)
Single (Never Married)	4,675
Legally Married (Not Separated)	11,626
Legally Married (Separated)	552
Widowed	705
Divorced	935

PSYTE CATEGORIES

2001 Estimates	No. of House-holds	% of Total Hhds.	Index
Mortgaged in Suburbia	371	4.74	341
Technocrafts & Bureaucrats	493	6.30	224
Boomers & Teens	782	9.99	557
Satellite Suburbs	2,653	33.89	1,181
Kindergarten Boom	623	7.96	303
Blue Collar Winners	1,294	16.53	656
Conservative Homebodies	1,135	14.50	402
Struggling Downtowns	431	5.51	175

FINANCIAL P$YTE

2001 Estimates	No. of House-holds	% of Total Hhds.	Index
Four Star Investors	782	9.99	199
Successful Suburbanites	864	11.04	166
Canadian Comfort	3,947	50.42	519
Mortgages & Minivans	623	7.96	121
Bills & Wills	1,135	14.50	175
Towering Debt	431	5.51	71

HOME LANGUAGE

2001 Estimates:		% Total
English	21,445	88.65
French	79	0.33
Arabic	23	0.10
Chinese	31	0.13
Croatian	14	0.06
Finnish	28	0.12
German	74	0.31
Hungarian	38	0.16
Italian	211	0.87
Khmer (Cambodian)	49	0.20
Lao	67	0.28
Persian (Farsi)	28	0.12
Polish	147	0.61
Portuguese	1,284	5.31
Slovak	22	0.09
Tagalog (Pilipino)	22	0.09
Vietnamese	24	0.10
Other Languages	81	0.33
Multiple Responses	523	2.16
Total	24,190	100.00

BUILDING PERMITS

	1999	1998 $000	1997
Value	42,481	28,859	34,500

HOMES BUILT

	1999	1998	1997
No	169	77	180

TAXATION

Income Class:	1997	% Total
Under $5,000	1,600	11.70
$5,000-$10,000	1,460	10.68
$10,000-$15,000	1,590	11.63
$15,000-$20,000	1,160	8.49
$20,000-$25,000	1,060	7.75
$25,000-$30,000	1,060	7.75
$30,000-$40,000	2,070	15.14
$40,000-$50,000	1,460	10.68
$50,000 +	2,220	16.24
Total Returns, No.	13,670	
Total Income, $000	407,723	
Total Taxable Returns	10,350	
Total Tax, $000	80,734	
Average Income, $	29,826	
Average Tax, $	7,800	

VITAL STATISTICS

	1997	1996	1995	1994
Births	299	327	321	338
Deaths	101	94	95	101
Natural Increase	198	233	226	237
Marriages	80	69	75	62

Note: Latest available data.

MEDIA INFO
see Toronto, CMA

Brampton
(City)
Toronto CMA

In Peel Regional Municipality.

POPULATION

July 1, 2001 Estimate	324,787
% Cdn. Total	1.04
% Change, '96 -'01	17.06
Avg. Annual Growth Rate, %	3.20
2003 Projected Population	344,001
2006 Projected Population	373,012
2001 Households Estimate	101,874
2003 Projected Households	108,329
2006 Projected Households	118,890

INCOME

% Above/Below National Average	+9
2001 Total Income Estimate	$7,464,820,000
% Cdn. Total	1.14
2001 Average Hhld. Income	$73,300
2001 Per Capita	$23,000
2003 Projected Total Income	$8,401,530,000
2006 Projected Total Income	$10,055,610,000

RETAIL SALES

% Above/Below National Average	-10
2001 Retail Sales Estimate	$2,621,540,000
% Cdn. Total	0.94
2001 per Household	$25,700
2001 per Capita	$8,100
2001 No. of Establishments	1,508
2003 Projected Retail Sales	$2,998,160,000
2006 Projected Retail Sales	$3,589,980,000

POPULATION

2001 Estimates:
Total	324,787
Male	161,330
Female	163,457

Age Groups	Male	Female
0-4	12,126	11,419
5-9	12,666	11,946
10-14	12,329	11,902
15-19	11,780	11,480
20-24	11,528	11,600
25-29	12,357	12,771
30-34	14,088	14,413
35-39	14,479	14,678
40-44	13,140	13,470
45-49	11,744	12,083
50-54	10,098	10,146
55-59	8,058	7,908
60-64	6,076	5,951
65-69	4,384	4,515
70+	6,477	9,175

DAYTIME POPULATION

2001 Estimates:
Working Population	174,533
At Home Population	142,015
Total	316,548

INCOME

2001 Estimates:
Avg. Household Income	$73,275
Avg. Family Income	$70,901
Per Capita Income	$22,984

Male:
Avg. Employment Income	$39,392
Avg. Employment Income (Full Time)	$49,370

Female:
Avg. Employment Income	$25,874
Avg. Employment Income (Full Time)	$36,152

Ontario

DISPOSABLE & DISCRETIONARY INCOME

2001 Estimates:	Per Hhld.
Disposable Income	$60,516
Discretionary Income 1 (minus Food & Shelter)	$43,705
Discretionary Income 2 (minus Food, Shelter, & Other Expenditures)	$33,182

LIQUID ASSETS

1999 Estimates:	Per Hhld.
Equity Investments	$108,443
Interest Bearing Investments	$89,562
Total Liquid Assets	$198,005

CREDIT DATA

July 2000:	
Pool of Credit	$3,554,073,068
Revolving Credit, No.	651,748
Fixed Loans, No.	193,046
Avg. Credit Limit, per Person	$13,141
Avg. Spent, per Person	$5,967
Satisfactory Ratings, No. per Person	3.01
Avg. No. of Cards, per Person	1.13

LABOUR FORCE

2001 Estimates:
Male:
In the Labour Force	102,845
Participation Rate	82.8
Employed	99,677
Unemployed	3,168
Unemployment Rate	3.1
Not in Labour Force	21,364

Female:
In the Labour Force	87,747
Participation Rate	68.5
Employed	82,210
Unemployed	5,537
Unemployment Rate	6.3
Not in Labour Force	40,443

OCCUPATIONS BY MAJOR GROUPS

2001 Estimates:	Male	Female
Management	11,705	4,990
Business, Finance & Admin.	13,785	32,202
Natural & Applied Sciences & Related	7,671	1,649
Health	1,005	4,103
Social Sciences, Gov't Services & Religion	896	1,786
Education	1,575	3,649
Arts, Culture, Recreation & Sport	1,383	1,778
Sales & Service	18,315	23,067
Trades, Transport & Equipment Operators & Related	27,996	1,941
Primary Industries	1,506	443
Processing, Mfg. & Utilities	15,110	9,053

Ontario

Brampton
(City)
Toronto CMA
(Cont'd)

LEVEL OF SCHOOLING

2001 Estimates:
Population 15 years + ... 252,399
Less than Grade 9 21,383
Grades 9-13 w/o Certif. 60,801
Grade 9-13 with Certif. 43,050
Trade Certif. /Dip. 8,484
Non-Univ. w/o Certif./Dip. 18,725
Non-Univ. with Certif./Dip. 48,966
Univ. w/o Degree 22,996
  Univ. w/o Degree/Certif. 11,546
  Univ. with Certif. 11,450
Univ. with Degree 27,994

AVERAGE HOUSEHOLD EXPENDITURES

2001 Estimates:
Food $7,739
Shelter $11,707
Clothing $2,846
Transportation $8,153
Health & Personal Care $2,266
Recr'n, Read'g & Education $4,818
Taxes & Securities $19,808
Other $10,375
Total Expenditures $67,712

PRIVATE HOUSEHOLDS

2001 Estimates:
Private Households, Total 101,874
Pop. in Private Households 321,887
Average no. per Household 3.2

FAMILIES

2001 Estimates:
Families in Private Households 91,414
Husband-Wife Families 79,531
Lone-Parent Families 11,883
Aver. No. Persons per Family 3.3
Aver. No. Sons/Daughters
  at Home 1.4

HOUSING

2001 Estimates:
Occupied Private Dwellings 101,874
  Owned 73,082
  Rented 28,792
Single-Detached House 52,734
Semi-Detached House 11,939
Row Houses 11,242
Apartment, 5+ Storeys 18,758
  Owned Apartment, 5+ Storeys 3,317
Apartment, 5 or Fewer Storeys 4,117
Apartment, Detached Duplex 2,979
Other Single-Attached 46
Movable Dwellings 59

VEHICLES

2001 Estimates:
Model Yrs. '81-'96, No. 135,462
  % Total 77.71
Model Yrs. '97-'98, No. 22,485
  % Total 12.90
'99 Vehicles registered in
  Model Yr. '99, No. 16,373
  % Total 9.39
Total No. '81-'99 174,320

LEGAL MARITAL STATUS

2001 Estimates: (Age 15+)
Single (Never Married) 73,900
Legally Married
  (Not Separated) 146,709
Legally Married (Separated) 8,472
Widowed 10,104
Divorced 13,214

PSYTE CATEGORIES

2001 Estimates	No. of House -holds	% of Total Hhds.	Index
Suburban Executives	2,315	2.27	159
Mortgaged in Suburbia	10,462	10.27	739
Technocrafts & Bureaucrats	4,701	4.61	164
Boomers & Teens	7,027	6.90	385
Stable Suburban Families	3,459	3.40	260
Small City Elite	119	0.12	7
Old Bungalow Burbs	6,772	6.65	401
Suburban Nesters	445	0.44	27
Brie & Chablis	3,146	3.09	345
Satellite Suburbs	34,760	34.12	1,189
Kindergarten Boom	5,070	4.98	190
Blue Collar Winners	1,312	1.29	51
High Rise Melting Pot	6,892	6.77	451
Conservative Homebodies	2,834	2.78	77
High Rise Sunsets	570	0.56	39
Young Urban Mix	6,421	6.30	297
University Enclaves	500	0.49	24
Young City Singles	933	0.92	40
Town Renters	573	0.56	65
Struggling Downtowns	2,259	2.22	70
Aged Pensioners	455	0.45	34
Old Grey Towers	525	0.52	93

FINAN¢IAL P$YTE

2001 Estimates	No. of House -holds	% of Total Hhds.	Index
Four Star Investors	9,342	9.17	183
Successful Suburbanites	18,622	18.28	275
Canadian Comfort	36,636	35.96	370
Urban Heights	3,146	3.09	72
Miners & Credit-Liners	6,772	6.65	210
Mortgages & Minivans	5,070	4.98	75
Bills & Wills	9,255	9.08	110
Revolving Renters	570	0.56	12
Young Urban Struggle	500	0.49	10
Towering Debt	10,657	10.46	134
Senior Survivors	980	0.96	51

HOME LANGUAGE

2001 Estimates:		% Total
English	263,983	81.28
French	1,453	0.45
Arabic	791	0.24
Chinese	3,127	0.96
Croatian	1,052	0.32
Dutch	372	0.11
German	418	0.13
Greek	489	0.15
Gujarati	1,522	0.47
Hindi	1,417	0.44
Hungarian	402	0.12
Italian	3,443	1.06
Korean	224	0.07
Lao	259	0.08
Macedonian	193	0.06
Maltese	212	0.07
Persian (Farsi)	183	0.06
Polish	1,929	0.59
Portuguese	6,441	1.98
Punjabi	15,167	4.67
Serbian	308	0.09
Spanish	2,216	0.68
Tagalog (Pilipino)	1,362	0.42
Tamil	598	0.18
Urdu	1,293	0.40
Vietnamese	1,342	0.41
Other Languages	2,794	0.86
Multiple Responses	11,797	3.63
Total	324,787	100.00

BUILDING PERMITS

	1999	1998 $000	1997
Value	722,953	629,061	498,255

HOMES BUILT

	1999	1998	1997
No.	2,771	2,523	2,810

TAXATION

Income Class:	1997	% Total
Under $5,000	26,610	13.47
$5,000-$10,000	21,940	11.10
$10,000-$15,000	21,540	10.90
$15,000-$20,000	16,630	8.42
$20,000-$25,000	15,890	8.04
$25,000-$30,000	16,890	8.55
$30,000-$40,000	28,930	14.64
$40,000-$50,000	19,200	9.72
$50,000 +	29,940	15.15

Total Returns, No. 197,580
Total Income, $000 5,708,409
Total Taxable
  Returns 145,160
Total Tax, $000 1,108,192
Average Income, $ 28,892
Average Tax, $ 7,634

VITAL STATISTICS

	1997	1996	1995	1994
Births	4,286	4,629	4,539	4,336
Deaths	1,031	1,070	973	949
Natural Increase	3,255	3,559	3,566	3,387
Marriages	1,208	1,163	1,145	1,226

Note: Latest available data.

MEDIA INFO
see Toronto, CMA

Caledon
(Town)
Toronto CMA
In Peel Regional Municipality.

POPULATION

July 1, 2001 Estimate	48,296
% Cdn. Total	0.16
% Change, '96 -'01	17.04
Avg. Annual Growth Rate, %	3.20
2003 Projected Population	51,031
2006 Projected Population	55,159
2001 Households Estimate	15,754
2003 Projected Households	16,710
2006 Projected Households	18,275

INCOME

% Above/Below National Average	+43
2001 Total Income Estimate	$1,455,200,000
% Cdn. Total	0.22
2001 Average Hhld. Income	$92,400
2001 Per Capita	$30,100
2003 Projected Total Income	$1,638,690,000
2006 Projected Total Income	$1,961,090,000

RETAIL SALES

% Above/Below National Average	-15
2001 Retail Sales Estimate	$366,710,000
% Cdn. Total	0.13
2001 per Household	$23,300
2001 per Capita	$7,600
2001 No. of Establishments	350
2003 Projected Retail Sales	$414,600,000
2006 Projected Retail Sales	$489,370,000

POPULATION

2001 Estimates:

Total	48,296
Male	24,232
Female	24,064

Age Groups	Male	Female
0-4	1,518	1,433
5-9	1,755	1,656
10-14	1,905	1,798
15-19	1,813	1,749
20-24	1,606	1,580
25-29	1,512	1,484
30-34	1,726	1,717
35-39	1,966	2,043
40-44	1,991	2,092
45-49	1,919	1,998
50-54	1,760	1,759
55-59	1,501	1,385
60-64	1,161	1,031
65-69	839	766
70+	1,260	1,573

DAYTIME POPULATION

2001 Estimates:

Working Population	12,286
At Home Population	19,778
Total	32,064

INCOME

2001 Estimates:

Avg. Household Income	$92,370
Avg. Family Income	$92,370
Per Capita Income	$30,131

Male:

Avg. Employment Income	$51,422
Avg. Employment Income (Full Time)	$64,321

Female:

Avg. Employment Income	$30,664
Avg. Employment Income (Full Time)	$43,606

DISPOSABLE & DISCRETIONARY INCOME

2001 Estimates:

	Per Hhld.
Disposable Income	$75,096
Discretionary Income 1 (minus Food & Shelter)	$56,646
Discretionary Income 2 (minus Food, Shelter, & Other Expenditures)	$44,154

LIQUID ASSETS

1999 Estimates:

	Per Hhld.
Equity Investments	$174,587
Interest Bearing Investments	$119,113
Total Liquid Assets	$293,700

CREDIT DATA

July 2000:

Pool of Credit	$660,277,531
Revolving Credit, No.	100,726
Fixed Loans, No.	27,629
Avg. Credit Limit, per Person	$15,554
Avg. Spent, per Person	$6,696
Satisfactory Ratings, No. per Person	2.93
Avg. No. of Cards, per Person	1.18

LABOUR FORCE

2001 Estimates:

Male:

In the Labour Force	15,722
Participation Rate	82.5
Employed	15,410
Unemployed	312
Unemployment Rate	2.0
Not in Labour Force	3,332

Female:

In the Labour Force	13,193
Participation Rate	68.8
Employed	12,835
Unemployed	358
Unemployment Rate	2.7
Not in Labour Force	5,984

OCCUPATIONS BY MAJOR GROUPS

2001 Estimates:	Male	Female
Management	3,077	1,069
Business, Finance & Admin.	1,427	4,856
Natural & Applied Sciences & Related	1,198	243
Health	232	786
Social Sciences, Gov't Services & Religion	195	277
Education	427	1,007
Arts, Culture, Recreation & Sport	229	425
Sales & Service	2,821	3,253
Trades, Transport & Equipment Operators & Related	3,873	267
Primary Industries	857	354
Processing, Mfg. & Utilities	1,228	401

LEVEL OF SCHOOLING

2001 Estimates:

Population 15 years +	38,231
Less than Grade 9	2,271
Grades 9-13 w/o Certif.	8,292
Grade 9-13 with Certif.	5,797
Trade Certif. /Dip.	1,463
Non-Univ. w/o Certif./Dip.	2,486
Non-Univ. with Certif./Dip.	8,572
Univ. w/o Degree	3,604
Univ. w/o Degree/Certif.	1,864
Univ. with Certif.	1,740
Univ. with Degree	5,746

AVERAGE HOUSEHOLD EXPENDITURES

2001 Estimates:

Food	$8,163
Shelter	$13,320
Clothing	$3,270
Transportation	$9,982
Health & Personal Care	$2,584
Recr'n, Read'g & Education	$5,613
Taxes & Securities	$27,461
Other	$12,336
Total Expenditures	$82,729

PRIVATE HOUSEHOLDS

2001 Estimates:

Private Households, Total	15,754
Pop. in Private Households	47,825
Average no. per Household	3.0

FAMILIES

2001 Estimates:

Families in Private Households	14,249
Husband-Wife Families	13,172
Lone-Parent Families	1,077
Aver. No. Persons per Family	3.2
Aver. No. Sons/Daughters at Home	1.3

HOUSING

2001 Estimates:

Occupied Private Dwellings	15,754
Owned	13,700
Rented	2,054
Single-Detached House	14,315
Semi-Detached House	168
Row Houses	313
Apartment, 5 or Fewer Storeys	464
Apartment, Detached Duplex	391
Other Single-Attached	44
Movable Dwellings	59

VEHICLES

2001 Estimates:

Model Yrs. '81-'96, No.	26,953
% Total	75.11
Model Yrs. '97-'98, No.	5,260
% Total	14.66
'99 Vehicles registered in Model Yr. '99, No.	3,671
% Total	10.23
Total No. '81-'99	35,884

LEGAL MARITAL STATUS

2001 Estimates: (Age 15+)

Single (Never Married)	9,473
Legally Married (Not Separated)	24,480
Legally Married (Separated)	1,052
Widowed	1,526
Divorced	1,700

PSYTE CATEGORIES

2001 Estimates	No. of House -holds	% of Total Hhds.	Index
Canadian Establishment	111	0.70	423
Suburban Executives	833	5.29	369
Mortgaged in Suburbia	1,407	8.93	643
Technocrafts & Bureaucrats	300	1.90	68
Boomers & Teens	7,947	50.44	2,814
Stable Suburban Families	157	1.00	76
Old Bungalow Burbs	480	3.05	184
Suburban Nesters	59	0.37	23
Satellite Suburbs	483	3.07	107
Blue Collar Winners	3,344	21.23	843
Old Towns' New Fringe	462	2.93	75
Europa	134	0.85	68

Ontario

FINANCIAL P$YTE

2001 Estimates	No. of House -holds	% of Total Hhds.	Index
Platinum Estates	111	0.70	87
Four Star Investors	8,780	55.73	1,110
Successful Suburbanites	1,864	11.83	178
Canadian Comfort	3,886	24.67	254
Miners & Credit-Liners	480	3.05	96
Dollars & Sense	134	0.85	33
Tractors & Tradelines	462	2.93	51

HOME LANGUAGE

2001 Estimates:		% Total
English	45,522	94.26
French	60	0.12
Chinese	34	0.07
Croatian	55	0.11
German	145	0.30
Greek	87	0.18
Italian	1,070	2.22
Korean	37	0.08
Polish	103	0.21
Portuguese	198	0.41
Punjabi	87	0.18
Slovak	35	0.07
Slovenian	47	0.10
Ukrainian	61	0.13
Other Languages	117	0.24
Multiple Responses	638	1.32
Total	48,296	100.00

BUILDING PERMITS

	1999	1998	1997
		$000	
Value	74,196	83,803	126,971

HOMES BUILT

	1999	1998	1997
No.	366	734	646

TAXATION

Income Class:	1997	% Total
Under $5,000	3,340	11.10
$5,000-$10,000	2,870	9.54
$10,000-$15,000	2,860	9.51
$15,000-$20,000	2,300	7.65
$20,000-$25,000	2,070	6.88
$25,000-$30,000	2,290	7.61
$30,000-$40,000	3,980	13.23
$40,000-$50,000	3,040	10.11
$50,000 +	7,340	24.40
Total Returns, No.	30,080	
Total Income, $000	1,199,364	
Total Taxable Returns	23,550	
Total Tax, $000	281,106	
Average Income, $	39,872	
Average Tax, $	11,937	

VITAL STATISTICS

	1997	1996	1995	1994
Births	532	494	500	443
Deaths	201	184	200	159
Natural Increase	331	310	300	284
Marriages	206	239	199	214

Note: Latest available data.

MEDIA INFO
see Toronto, CMA

Ontario

East Gwillimbury
(Town)
Toronto CMA

In York Regional Municipality.

POPULATION

July 1, 2001 Estimate	22,831
% Cdn. Total	0.07
% Change, '96 -'01	11.85
Avg. Annual Growth Rate, %	2.27
2003 Projected Population	23,412
2006 Projected Population	24,478
2001 Households Estimate	7,347
2003 Projected Households	7,560
2006 Projected Households	7,962

INCOME

% Above/Below National Average	+30
2001 Total Income Estimate	$626,860,000
% Cdn. Total	0.10
2001 Average Hhld. Income	$85,300
2001 Per Capita	$27,500
2003 Projected Total Income	$682,850,000
2006 Projected Total Income	$784,790,000

RETAIL SALES

% Above/Below National Average	-77
2001 Retail Sales Estimate	$47,250,000
% Cdn. Total	0.02
2001 per Household	$6,400
2001 per Capita	$2,100
2001 No. of Establishments	154
2003 Projected Retail Sales	$51,920,000
2006 Projected Retail Sales	$58,670,000

POPULATION

2001 Estimates:

Total		22,831
Male		11,565
Female		11,266

Age Groups	Male	Female
0-4	722	692
5-9	879	828
10-14	930	887
15-19	857	826
20-24	742	700
25-29	662	642
30-34	743	759
35-39	934	960
40-44	1,035	1,043
45-49	999	983
50-54	879	820
55-59	690	629
60-64	514	449
65-69	394	358
70+	585	690

DAYTIME POPULATION

2001 Estimates:

Working Population	2,942
At Home Population	8,911
Total	11,853

INCOME

2001 Estimates:

Avg. Household Income	$85,321
Avg. Family Income	$85,887
Per Capita Income	$27,456
Male:	
Avg. Employment Income	$47,308
Avg. Employment Income (Full Time)	$57,986
Female:	
Avg. Employment Income	$28,547
Avg. Employment Income (Full Time)	$39,578

DISPOSABLE & DISCRETIONARY INCOME

2001 Estimates:	Per Hhld.
Disposable Income	$69,579
Discretionary Income 1 (minus Food & Shelter)	$51,722
Discretionary Income 2 (minus Food, Shelter, & Other Expenditures)	$39,535

LIQUID ASSETS

1999 Estimates:	Per Hhld.
Equity Investments	$146,606
Interest Bearing Investments	$107,402
Total Liquid Assets	$254,008

CREDIT DATA

July 2000:

Pool of Credit	$276,878,988
Revolving Credit, No.	41,625
Fixed Loans, No.	11,857
Avg. Credit Limit, per Person	$15,855
Avg. Spent, per Person	$7,020
Satisfactory Ratings, No. per Person	2.98
Avg. No. of Cards, per Person	1.16

LABOUR FORCE

2001 Estimates:

Male:	
In the Labour Force	7,502
Participation Rate	83.0
Employed	7,401
Unemployed	101
Unemployment Rate	1.3
Not in Labour Force	1,532
Female:	
In the Labour Force	6,492
Participation Rate	73.3
Employed	6,343
Unemployed	149
Unemployment Rate	2.3
Not in Labour Force	2,367

OCCUPATIONS BY MAJOR GROUPS

2001 Estimates:	Male	Female
Management	1,331	467
Business, Finance & Admin.	529	2,239
Natural & Applied Sciences & Related	449	116
Health	112	617
Social Sciences, Gov't Services & Religion	187	156
Education	241	329
Arts, Culture, Recreation & Sport	74	198
Sales & Service	1,592	1,795
Trades, Transport & Equipment Operators & Related	1,960	139
Primary Industries	484	132
Processing, Mfg. & Utilities	494	151

LEVEL OF SCHOOLING

2001 Estimates:

Population 15 years +	17,893
Less than Grade 9	946
Grades 9-13 w/o Certif.	3,979
Grade 9-13 with Certif.	2,988

2001 Estimates:	
Trade Certif. /Dip.	801
Non-Univ. w/o Certif./Dip.	1,202
Non-Univ. with Certif./Dip.	4,214
Univ. w/o Degree	1,603
Univ. w/o Degree/Certif.	802
Univ. with Certif.	801
Univ. with Degree	2,160

AVERAGE HOUSEHOLD EXPENDITURES

2001 Estimates:

Food	$7,857
Shelter	$12,785
Clothing	$2,982
Transportation	$9,786
Health & Personal Care	$2,457
Recr'n, Read'g & Education	$5,172
Taxes & Securities	$24,598
Other	$11,629
Total Expenditures	$77,266

PRIVATE HOUSEHOLDS

2001 Estimates:

Private Households, Total	7,347
Pop. in Private Households	22,260
Average no. per Household	3.0

FAMILIES

2001 Estimates:

Families in Private Households	6,653
Husband-Wife Families	6,122
Lone-Parent Families	531
Aver. No. Persons per Family	3.2
Aver. No. Sons/Daughters at Home	1.3

HOUSING

2001 Estimates:

Occupied Private Dwellings	7,347
Owned	6,291
Rented	1,056
Single-Detached House	6,525
Semi-Detached House	90
Row Houses	63
Apartment, 5 or Fewer Storeys	328
Apartment, Detached Duplex	248
Other Single-Attached	67
Movable Dwellings	26

VEHICLES

2001 Estimates:

Model Yrs. '81-'96, No.	11,524
% Total	77.77
Model Yrs. '97-'98, No.	1,952
% Total	13.17
'99 Vehicles registered in Model Yr. '99, No.	1,343
% Total	9.06
Total No. '81-'99	14,819

LEGAL MARITAL STATUS

2001 Estimates: (Age 15+)

Single (Never Married)	4,539
Legally Married (Not Separated)	11,244
Legally Married (Separated)	490
Widowed	674
Divorced	946

PSYTE CATEGORIES

2001 Estimates	No. of House-holds	% of Total Hhds.	Index
Boomers & Teens	2,808	38.22	2,132
Small City Elite	374	5.09	297
Satellite Suburbs	1,223	16.65	580
Blue Collar Winners	2,942	40.04	1,591

FINANCIAL P$YTE

2001 Estimates	No. of House-holds	% of Total Hhds.	Index
Four Star Investors	2,808	38.22	761
Canadian Comfort	4,539	61.78	636

HOME LANGUAGE

2001 Estimates:		% Total
English	22,413	98.17
French	61	0.27
Chinese	19	0.08
Czech	28	0.12
German	27	0.12
Hungarian	38	0.17
Italian	22	0.10
Japanese	13	0.06
Korean	35	0.15
Polish	45	0.20
Other Languages	68	0.30
Multiple Responses	62	0.27
Total	22,831	100.00

BUILDING PERMITS

	1999	1998	1997
		$000	
Value	12,737	23,803	31,961

HOMES BUILT

	1999	1998	1997
No	92	182	109

TAXATION

Income Class:	1997	% Total
Under $5,000	1,440	11.28
$5,000-$10,000	1,320	10.34
$10,000-$15,000	1,370	10.73
$15,000-$20,000	970	7.60
$20,000-$25,000	900	7.05
$25,000-$30,000	920	7.20
$30,000-$40,000	1,780	13.94
$40,000-$50,000	1,210	9.48
$50,000 +	2,870	22.47
Total Returns, No.	12,770	
Total Income, $000	445,732	
Total Taxable Returns	9,850	
Total Tax, $000	97,481	
Average Income, $	34,905	
Average Tax, $	9,897	

VITAL STATISTICS

	1997	1996	1995	1994
Births	203	200	251	241
Deaths	68	87	95	78
Natural Increase	135	113	156	163
Marriages	98	84	72	82

Note: Latest available data.

MEDIA INFO
see Toronto, CMA

East York
(Borough)
Toronto CMA

In Toronto Metropolitan Municipality. On Jan. 1, 1998, East York, Etobicoke, North York, Scarborough, Toronto and York amalgamated to form the new city of Toronto.

POPULATION

July 1, 2001 Estimate	116,749
% Cdn. Total	0.37
% Change, '96 -'01	4.89
Avg. Annual Growth Rate, %	0.96
2003 Projected Population	118,855
2006 Projected Population	121,945
2001 Households Estimate	50,108
2003 Projected Households	51,425
2006 Projected Households	53,383

INCOME

% Above/Below National Average	+11
2001 Total Income Estimate	$2,742,850,000
% Cdn. Total	0.42
2001 Average Hhld. Income	$54,700
2001 Per Capita	$23,500
2003 Projected Total Income	$2,949,400,000
2006 Projected Total Income	$3,289,670,000

RETAIL SALES

% Above/Below National Average	-39
2001 Retail Sales Estimate	$634,530,000
% Cdn. Total	0.23
2001 per Household	$12,700
2001 per Capita	$5,400
2001 No. of Establishments	535
2003 Projected Retail Sales	$685,980,000
2006 Projected Retail Sales	$764,600,000

POPULATION

2001 Estimates:

Total		116,749
Male		54,783
Female		61,966

Age Groups	Male	Female
0-4	3,969	3,705
5-9	3,774	3,554
10-14	3,306	3,126
15-19	2,892	2,833
20-24	2,823	2,992
25-29	3,424	3,854
30-34	4,634	5,114
35-39	5,291	5,768
40-44	5,006	5,485
45-49	4,329	4,706
50-54	3,487	3,783
55-59	2,726	3,094
60-64	2,244	2,734
65-69	1,998	2,595
70+	4,880	8,623

DAYTIME POPULATION

2001 Estimates:

Working Population	28,347
At Home Population	59,093
Total	87,440

INCOME

2001 Estimates:

Avg. Household Income	$54,739
Avg. Family Income	$61,982
Per Capita Income	$23,494
Male:	
Avg. Employment Income	$36,765
Avg. Employment Income (Full Time)	$48,490
Female:	
Avg. Employment Income	$29,756
Avg. Employment Income (Full Time)	$40,653

DISPOSABLE & DISCRETIONARY INCOME

2001 Estimates:

	Per Hhld.
Disposable Income	$44,824
Discretionary Income 1 (minus Food & Shelter)	$30,705
Discretionary Income 2 (minus Food, Shelter, & Other Expenditures)	$22,411

LIQUID ASSETS

1999 Estimates:

	Per Hhld.
Equity Investments	$83,891
Interest Bearing Investments	$69,166
Total Liquid Assets	$153,057

CREDIT DATA

July 2000:

Pool of Credit	$1,158,681,490
Revolving Credit, No.	241,554
Fixed Loans, No.	46,556
Avg. Credit Limit, per Person	$10,668
Avg. Spent, per Person	$4,267
Satisfactory Ratings, No. per Person	2.59
Avg. No. of Cards, per Person	1.14

LABOUR FORCE

2001 Estimates:

Male:

In the Labour Force	31,187
Participation Rate	71.3
Employed	29,101
Unemployed	2,086
Unemployment Rate	6.7
Not in Labour Force	12,547

Female:

In the Labour Force	29,939
Participation Rate	58.0
Employed	27,976
Unemployed	1,963
Unemployment Rate	6.6
Not in Labour Force	21,642

OCCUPATIONS BY MAJOR GROUPS

2001 Estimates:	Male	Female
Management	3,669	2,108
Business, Finance & Admin.	4,847	10,209
Natural & Applied Sciences & Related	2,649	643
Health	509	2,058
Social Sciences, Gov't Services & Religion	883	1,312
Education	830	1,480
Arts, Culture, Recreation & Sport	1,379	1,257
Sales & Service	7,672	7,662
Trades, Transport & Equipment Operators & Related	5,018	325
Primary Industries	344	32
Processing, Mfg. & Utilities	2,150	1,308

LEVEL OF SCHOOLING

2001 Estimates:

Population 15 years +	95,315
Less than Grade 9	10,105
Grades 9-13 w/o Certif.	20,423
Grade 9-13 with Certif.	11,967
Trade Certif. /Dip.	2,254
Non-Univ. w/o Certif./Dip.	5,805
Non-Univ. with Certif./Dip.	14,402
Univ. w/o Degree	11,205
Univ. w/o Degree/Certif.	5,443
Univ. with Certif.	5,762
Univ. with Degree	19,154

AVERAGE HOUSEHOLD EXPENDITURES

2001 Estimates:

Food	$6,276
Shelter	$10,144
Clothing	$2,260
Transportation	$6,297
Health & Personal Care	$1,943
Recr'n, Read'g & Education	$3,532
Taxes & Securities	$13,963
Other	$7,857
Total Expenditures	$52,272

PRIVATE HOUSEHOLDS

2001 Estimates:

Private Households, Total	50,108
Pop. in Private Households	115,134
Average no. per Household	2.3

FAMILIES

2001 Estimates:

Families in Private Households	31,015
Husband-Wife Families	25,314
Lone-Parent Families	5,701
Aver. No. Persons per Family	2.9
Aver. No. Sons/Daughters at Home	1.1

HOUSING

2001 Estimates:

Occupied Private Dwellings	50,108
Owned	22,826
Rented	27,282
Single-Detached House	17,917
Semi-Detached House	4,269
Row Houses	367
Apartment, 5+ Storeys	21,266
Owned Apartment, 5+ Storeys	2,153
Apartment, 5 or Fewer Storeys	4,995
Apartment, Detached Duplex	1,169
Other Single-Attached	125

VEHICLES

2001 Estimates:

Model Yrs. '81-'96, No.	36,630
% Total	78.81
Model Yrs. '97-'98, No.	5,775
% Total	12.43
'99 Vehicles registered in Model Yr. '99, No.	4,073
% Total	8.76
Total No. '81-'99	46,478

LEGAL MARITAL STATUS

2001 Estimates: (Age 15+)

Single (Never Married)	31,497
Legally Married (Not Separated)	45,380
Legally Married (Separated)	3,553
Widowed	7,780
Divorced	7,105

PSYTE CATEGORIES

2001 Estimates	No. of House-holds	% of Total Hhds.	Index
The Affluentials	1,240	2.47	387
Urban Gentry	4,416	8.81	490
Suburban Nesters	8,158	16.28	1,016
Brie & Chablis	2,148	4.29	478
Aging Erudites	851	1.70	113
Asian Mosaic	4,357	8.70	634
High Rise Melting Pot	14,037	28.01	1,869
Conservative Homebodies	3,598	7.18	199
High Rise Sunsets	412	0.82	57
Young Urban Professionals	1,224	2.44	129
Young Urban Mix	4,874	9.73	459
Young Urban Intelligentsia	1,551	3.10	203
University Enclaves	383	0.76	37
Struggling Downtowns	425	0.85	27
Aged Pensioners	1,129	2.25	169
Big City Stress	480	0.96	85
Old Grey Towers	532	1.06	192

Ontario

FINANCIAL P$YTE

2001 Estimates	No. of House-holds	% of Total Hhds.	Index
Platinum Estates	1,240	2.47	307
Four Star Investors	4,416	8.81	175
Canadian Comfort	8,158	16.28	168
Urban Heights	4,223	8.43	196
Dollars & Sense	4,357	8.70	333
Bills & Wills	8,472	16.91	204
Revolving Renters	412	0.82	18
Young Urban Struggle	1,934	3.86	82
Towering Debt	14,462	28.86	370
NSF	480	0.96	27
Senior Survivors	1,661	3.31	176

HOME LANGUAGE

2001 Estimates:		% Total
English	83,759	71.74
French	761	0.65
Arabic	434	0.37
Armenian	66	0.06
Bengali	715	0.61
Bulgarian	461	0.39
Chinese	4,852	4.16
Croatian	121	0.10
Estonian	278	0.24
Finnish	200	0.17
German	204	0.17
Greek	4,603	3.94
Gujarati	1,514	1.30
Hindi	173	0.15
Hungarian	94	0.08
Italian	1,409	1.21
Japanese	103	0.09
Korean	224	0.19
Lao	60	0.05
Latvian (Lettish)	200	0.17
Macedonian	882	0.76
Pashto	113	0.10
Persian (Farsi)	812	0.70
Polish	648	0.56
Portuguese	103	0.09
Punjabi	199	0.17
Romanian	547	0.47
Russian	227	0.19
Serbian	1,066	0.91
Serbo-Croatian	307	0.26
Spanish	388	0.33
Tagalog (Pilipino)	1,907	1.63
Tamil	2,222	1.90
Turkish	66	0.06
Urdu	868	0.74
Vietnamese	205	0.18
Other Languages	1,186	1.02
Multiple Responses	4,772	4.09
Total	116,749	100.00

Ontario

East York
(Borough)
Toronto CMA
(Cont'd)

BUILDING PERMITS

	1999	1998	1997
		$000	
Value	n.a.	n.a.	34,329

HOMES BUILT

	1999	1998	1997
No.	n.a.	n.a.	24

TAXATION

Income Class:	1997	% Total
Under $5,000	1,710	16.54
$5,000-$10,000	1,230	11.90
$10,000-$15,000	1,310	12.67
$15,000-$20,000	920	8.90
$20,000-$25,000	840	8.12
$25,000-$30,000	750	7.25
$30,000-$40,000	1,270	12.28
$40,000-$50,000	870	8.41
$50,000 +	1,440	13.93
Total Returns, No.	10,340	
Total Income, $000	280,463	
Total Taxable Returns	6,930	
Total Tax, $000	54,283	
Average Income, $	27,124	
Average Tax, $	7,833	

VITAL STATISTICS

	1997	1996	1995	1994
Births	671	657	605	505
Deaths	579	583	672	624
Natural Increase	92	74	-67	-119
Marriages	193	190	157	192

Note: Latest available data.

MEDIA INFO
see Toronto, CMA

Etobicoke
(City)
Toronto CMA

In Toronto Metropolitan Municipality. On Jan. 1, 1998, Etobicoke, East York, North York, Scarborough, Toronto and York amalgamated to form the new city of Toronto.

POPULATION

July 1, 2001 Estimate	358,883
% Cdn. Total	1.15
% Change, '96 -'01	5.76
Avg. Annual Growth Rate, %	1.13
2003 Projected Population	366,907
2006 Projected Population	378,768
2001 Households Estimate	134,388
2003 Projected Households	138,407
2006 Projected Households	144,381

INCOME

% Above/Below National Average	+11
2001 Total Income Estimate	$8,405,080,000
% Cdn. Total	1.28
2001 Average Hhld. Income	$62,500
2001 Per Capita	$23,400
2003 Projected Total Income	$9,125,830,000
2006 Projected Total Income	$10,324,080,000

RETAIL SALES

% Above/Below National Average	+31
2001 Retail Sales Estimate	$4,220,250,000
% Cdn. Total	1.51
2001 per Household	$31,400
2001 per Capita	$11,800
2001 No. of Establishments	2,298
2003 Projected Retail Sales	$4,681,800,000
2006 Projected Retail Sales	$5,375,910,000

POPULATION

2001 Estimates:

Total	358,883
Male	173,291
Female	185,592

Age Groups	Male	Female
0-4	11,617	10,991
5-9	11,724	11,043
10-14	10,979	10,371
15-19	10,416	9,792
20-24	10,363	10,159
25-29	11,514	11,925
30-34	13,613	14,114
35-39	14,655	14,998
40-44	13,805	14,373
45-49	12,315	13,239
50-54	10,418	11,456
55-59	8,793	9,858
60-64	8,131	9,179
65-69	7,710	9,005
70+	17,238	25,089

DAYTIME POPULATION

2001 Estimates:

Working Population	187,838
At Home Population	186,367
Total	374,205

INCOME

2001 Estimates:

Avg. Household Income	$62,543
Avg. Family Income	$66,901
Per Capita Income	$23,420
Male:	
Avg. Employment Income	$39,154
Avg. Employment Income (Full Time)	$51,347
Female:	
Avg. Employment Income	$27,296
Avg. Employment Income (Full Time)	$38,655

DISPOSABLE & DISCRETIONARY INCOME

2001 Estimates:	Per Hhld.
Disposable Income	$50,824
Discretionary Income 1 (minus Food & Shelter)	$35,484
Discretionary Income 2 (minus Food, Shelter, & Other Expenditures)	$26,326

LIQUID ASSETS

1999 Estimates:	Per Hhld.
Equity Investments	$110,666
Interest Bearing Investments	$82,423
Total Liquid Assets	$193,089

CREDIT DATA

July 2000:

Pool of Credit	$3,558,677,327
Revolving Credit, No.	705,926
Fixed Loans, No.	139,644
Avg. Credit Limit, per Person	$11,038
Avg. Spent, per Person	$4,309
Satisfactory Ratings, No. per Person	2.55
Avg. No. of Cards, per Person	1.12

LABOUR FORCE

2001 Estimates:

Male:	
In the Labour Force	98,136
Participation Rate	70.6
Employed	91,979
Unemployed	6,157
Unemployment Rate	6.3
Not in Labour Force	40,835
Female:	
In the Labour Force	86,897
Participation Rate	56.7
Employed	80,553
Unemployed	6,344
Unemployment Rate	7.3
Not in Labour Force	66,290

OCCUPATIONS BY MAJOR GROUPS

2001 Estimates:

	Male	Female
Management	11,208	5,451
Business, Finance & Admin.	14,046	29,256
Natural & Applied Sciences & Related	7,729	1,802
Health	1,565	5,111
Social Sciences, Gov't Services & Religion	1,994	2,226
Education	2,172	4,296
Arts, Culture, Recreation & Sport	2,674	2,675
Sales & Service	19,854	23,594
Trades, Transport & Equipment Operators & Related	20,701	1,231
Primary Industries	1,257	152
Processing, Mfg. & Utilities	11,289	6,790

LEVEL OF SCHOOLING

2001 Estimates:

Population 15 years +	292,158
Less than Grade 9	32,964
Grades 9-13 w/o Certif.	62,506
Grade 9-13 with Certif.	41,833
Trade Certif. /Dip.	9,287
Non-Univ. w/o Certif./Dip.	18,780
Non-Univ. with Certif./Dip.	47,116
Univ. w/o Degree	30,181
Univ. w/o Degree/Certif.	14,415
Univ. with Certif.	15,766
Univ. with Degree	49,491

AVERAGE HOUSEHOLD EXPENDITURES

2001 Estimates:

Food	$6,852
Shelter	$10,960
Clothing	$2,529
Transportation	$6,957
Health & Personal Care	$2,095
Recr'n, Read'g & Education	$3,869
Taxes & Securities	$16,079
Other	$9,160
Total Expenditures	$58,501

PRIVATE HOUSEHOLDS

2001 Estimates:

Private Households, Total	134,388
Pop. in Private Households	353,527
Average no. per Household	2.6

FAMILIES

2001 Estimates:

Families in Private Households	100,378
Husband-Wife Families	82,903
Lone-Parent Families	17,475
Aver. No. Persons per Family	3.0
Aver. No. Sons/Daughters at Home	1.2

HOUSING

2001 Estimates:

Occupied Private Dwellings	134,388
Owned	75,156
Rented	59,232
Single-Detached House	60,820
Semi-Detached House	3,897
Row Houses	5,559
Apartment, 5+ Storeys	46,611
Owned Apartment, 5+ Storeys	10,141
Apartment, 5 or Fewer Storeys	14,607
Apartment, Detached Duplex	2,667
Other Single-Attached	227

VEHICLES

2001 Estimates:

Model Yrs. '81-'96, No.	151,341
% Total	70.64
Model Yrs. '97-'98, No.	34,569
% Total	16.14
'99 Vehicles registered in Model Yr. '99, No.	28,337
% Total	13.23
Total No. '81-'99	214,247

LEGAL MARITAL STATUS

2001 Estimates: (Age 15+)

Single (Never Married)	86,151
Legally Married (Not Separated)	154,544
Legally Married (Separated)	11,687
Widowed	21,645
Divorced	18,131

Etobicoke
(City)
Toronto CMA
(Cont'd)

PSYTE CATEGORIES

2001 Estimates	No. of House-holds	% of Total Hhds.	Index
Canadian Establishment	1,219	0.91	545
The Affluentials	3,603	2.68	419
Urban Gentry	5,983	4.45	248
Suburban Executives	660	0.49	34
Mortgaged in Suburbia	628	0.47	34
Technocrafts & Bureaucrats	289	0.22	8
Asian Heights	120	0.09	14
Boomers & Teens	407	0.30	17
Stable Suburban Families	2,737	2.04	156
Old Bungalow Burbs	5,506	4.10	247
Suburban Nesters	23,908	17.79	1,110
Brie & Chablis	8,451	6.29	702
Aging Erudites	678	0.50	33
Satellite Suburbs	5,619	4.18	146
Kindergarten Boom	589	0.44	17
Europa	3,060	2.28	183
High Rise Melting Pot	21,119	15.71	1,048
Conservative Homebodies	11,442	8.51	236
High Rise Sunsets	3,346	2.49	174
Young Urban Professionals	405	0.30	16
Young Urban Mix	22,343	16.63	785
University Enclaves	350	0.26	13
Young City Singles	1,047	0.78	34
Town Renters	1,507	1.12	130
Struggling Downtowns	1,965	1.46	46
Aged Pensioners	1,631	1.21	91
Big City Stress	2,987	2.22	197
Old Grey Towers	1,680	1.25	226

FINAN¢IAL P$YTE

2001 Estimates	No. of House-holds	% of Total Hhds.	Index
Platinum Estates	4,822	3.59	445
Four Star Investors	7,050	5.25	104
Successful Suburbanites	3,774	2.81	42
Canadian Comfort	29,527	21.97	226
Urban Heights	9,534	7.09	165
Miners & Credit-Liners	5,506	4.10	129
Mortgages & Minivans	589	0.44	7
Dollars & Sense	3,060	2.28	87
Bills & Wills	33,785	25.14	304
Revolving Renters	3,346	2.49	54
Young Urban Struggle	350	0.26	6
Towering Debt	25,638	19.08	244
NSF	2,987	2.22	63
Senior Survivors	3,311	2.46	131

HOME LANGUAGE

2001 Estimates:		% Total
English	253,240	70.56
French	1,056	0.29
Arabic	3,453	0.96
Bengali	503	0.14
Chinese	4,226	1.18
Croatian	2,538	0.71
Czech	468	0.13
Estonian	252	0.07
German	852	0.24
Greek	1,091	0.30
Gujarati	1,165	0.32
Hindi	804	0.22
Hungarian	949	0.26
Italian	8,957	2.50
Japanese	314	0.09
Korean	2,888	0.80
Latvian (Lettish)	247	0.07
Lithuanian	446	0.12
Macedonian	385	0.11
Maltese	191	0.05
Persian (Farsi)	1,619	0.45
Polish	13,866	3.86
Portuguese	3,177	0.89
Punjabi	9,312	2.59
Romanian	427	0.12
Russian	628	0.17
Serbian	1,972	0.55
Serbo-Croatian	1,139	0.32
Slovak	244	0.07
Slovenian	669	0.19
Spanish	6,293	1.75
Tagalog (Pilipino)	1,789	0.50
Tamil	2,443	0.68
Turkish	293	0.08
Ukrainian	5,189	1.45
Urdu	1,298	0.36
Vietnamese	1,511	0.42
Other Languages	8,163	2.27
Multiple Responses	14,826	4.13
Total	358,883	100.00

BUILDING PERMITS

	1999	1998	1997
		$000	
Value	n.a.	n.a.	238,588

HOMES BUILT

	1999	1998	1997
No	n.a.	n.a.	474

TAXATION

Income Class:	1997	% Total
Under $5,000	26,430	13.34
$5,000-$10,000	23,430	11.82
$10,000-$15,000	25,510	12.87
$15,000-$20,000	19,270	9.72
$20,000-$25,000	16,570	8.36
$25,000-$30,000	15,610	7.88
$30,000-$40,000	25,820	13.03
$40,000-$50,000	16,030	8.09
$50,000 +	29,550	14.91
Total Returns, No.	198,200	
Total Income, $000	6,166,073	
Total Taxable Returns	138,840	
Total Tax, $000	1,316,166	
Average Income, $	31,110	
Average Tax, $	9,480	

VITAL STATISTICS

	1997	1996	1995	1994
Births	4,100	4,385	4,499	4,326
Deaths	2,408	2,459	2,367	2,310
Natural Increase	1,692	1,926	2,132	2,016
Marriages	1,829	2,208	2,264	2,241

Note: Latest available data.

MEDIA INFO
see Toronto, CMA

Georgina
(Town)
Toronto CMA

In York Regional Municipality.

POPULATION

July 1, 2001 Estimate	43,171
% Cdn. Total	0.14
% Change, '96 -'01	20.23
Avg. Annual Growth Rate, %	3.75
2003 Projected Population	46,016
2006 Projected Population	50,666
2001 Households Estimate	15,516
2003 Projected Households	16,591
2006 Projected Households	18,385

INCOME

% Above/Below National Average	same
2001 Total Income Estimate	$912,140,000
% Cdn. Total	0.14
2001 Average Hhld. Income	$58,800
2001 Per Capita	$21,100
2003 Projected Total Income	$1,032,010,000
2006 Projected Total Income	$1,246,570,000

RETAIL SALES

% Above/Below National Average	-52
2001 Retail Sales Estimate	$185,430,000
% Cdn. Total	0.07
2001 per Household	$12,000
2001 per Capita	$4,300
2001 No. of Establishments	230
2003 Projected Retail Sales	$213,360,000
2006 Projected Retail Sales	$259,900,000

POPULATION

2001 Estimates:		
Total		43,171
Male		21,540
Female		21,631

Age Groups	Male	Female
0-4	1,585	1,503
5-9	1,847	1,709
10-14	1,780	1,658
15-19	1,479	1,431
20-24	1,224	1,213
25-29	1,282	1,302
30-34	1,685	1,799
35-39	2,015	2,127
40-44	1,947	1,928
45-49	1,617	1,533
50-54	1,207	1,181
55-59	903	899
60-64	746	747
65-69	679	691
70+	1,544	1,910

DAYTIME POPULATION

2001 Estimates:	
Working Population	5,152
At Home Population	21,329
Total	26,481

INCOME

2001 Estimates:	
Avg. Household Income	$58,787
Avg. Family Income	$61,888
Per Capita Income	$21,129
Male:	
Avg. Employment Income	$38,279
Avg. Employment Income (Full Time)	$47,711
Female:	
Avg. Employment Income	$24,020
Avg. Employment Income (Full Time)	$34,686

Ontario

DISPOSABLE & DISCRETIONARY INCOME

2001 Estimates:	Per Hhld.
Disposable Income	$48,821
Discretionary Income 1 (minus Food & Shelter)	$34,590
Discretionary Income 2 (minus Food, Shelter, & Other Expenditures)	$25,117

LIQUID ASSETS

1999 Estimates:	Per Hhld.
Equity Investments	$74,757
Interest Bearing Investments	$69,464
Total Liquid Assets	$144,221

CREDIT DATA

July 2000:	
Pool of Credit	$399,299,545
Revolving Credit, No.	63,415
Fixed Loans, No.	23,196
Avg. Credit Limit, per Person	$12,477
Avg. Spent, per Person	$6,185
Satisfactory Ratings, No. per Person	2.61
Avg. No. of Cards, per Person	0.97

LABOUR FORCE

2001 Estimates:	
Male:	
In the Labour Force	12,633
Participation Rate	77.4
Employed	12,124
Unemployed	509
Unemployment Rate	4.0
Not in Labour Force	3,695
Female:	
In the Labour Force	10,010
Participation Rate	59.7
Employed	9,332
Unemployed	678
Unemployment Rate	6.8
Not in Labour Force	6,751

OCCUPATIONS BY MAJOR GROUPS

2001 Estimates:	Male	Female
Management	1,339	735
Business, Finance & Admin.	1,213	3,119
Natural & Applied Sciences & Related	710	181
Health	129	645
Social Sciences, Gov't Services & Religion	218	268
Education	194	286
Arts, Culture, Recreation & Sport	301	165
Sales & Service	2,052	3,010
Trades, Transport & Equipment Operators & Related	4,575	416
Primary Industries	522	137
Processing, Mfg. & Utilities	1,138	665

Ontario

Georgina
(Town)
Toronto CMA
(Cont'd)

LEVEL OF SCHOOLING

2001 Estimates:
Population 15 years +	33,089
Less than Grade 9	2,482
Grades 9-13 w/o Certif.	10,089
Grade 9-13 with Certif.	5,443
Trade Certif./Dip.	1,591
Non-Univ. w/o Certif./Dip.	2,371
Non-Univ. with Certif./Dip.	7,046
Univ. w/o Degree	1,950
Univ. w/o Degree/Certif.	924
Univ. with Certif.	1,026
Univ. with Degree	2,117

AVERAGE HOUSEHOLD EXPENDITURES

2001 Estimates:
Food	$6,616
Shelter	$9,769
Clothing	$2,217
Transportation	$7,409
Health & Personal Care	$1,999
Recr'n, Read'g & Education	$4,137
Taxes & Securities	$14,841
Other	$9,201
Total Expenditures	$56,189

PRIVATE HOUSEHOLDS

2001 Estimates:
Private Households, Total	15,516
Pop. in Private Households	42,508
Average no. per Household	2.7

FAMILIES

2001 Estimates:
Families in Private Households	12,637
Husband-Wife Families	11,064
Lone-Parent Families	1,573
Aver. No. Persons per Family	3.1
Aver. No. Sons/Daughters at Home	1.2

HOUSING

2001 Estimates:
Occupied Private Dwellings	15,516
Owned	12,350
Rented	3,166
Single-Detached House	13,134
Semi-Detached House	222
Row Houses	370
Apartment, 5 or Fewer Storeys	1,179
Apartment, Detached Duplex	493
Other Single-Attached	31
Movable Dwellings	87

VEHICLES

2001 Estimates:
Model Yrs. '81-'96, No.	20,377
% Total	85.47
Model Yrs. '97-'98, No.	2,110
% Total	8.85
'99 Vehicles registered in Model Yr. '99, No.	1,353
% Total	5.68
Total No. '81-'99	23,840

LEGAL MARITAL STATUS

2001 Estimates: (Age 15+)
Single (Never Married)	8,113
Legally Married (Not Separated)	18,934
Legally Married (Separated)	1,530
Widowed	1,988
Divorced	2,524

PSYTE CATEGORIES

2001 Estimates	No. of House-holds	% of Total Hhds.	Index
Mortgaged in Suburbia	571	3.68	265
Small City Elite	426	2.75	160
Satellite Suburbs	1,490	9.60	335
Blue Collar Winners	2,143	13.81	549
Old Towns' New Fringe	7,657	49.35	1,261
Rustic Prosperity	441	2.84	158
Old Leafy Towns	896	5.77	226

2001 Estimates	No. of House-holds	% of Total Hhds.	Index
Town Renters	432	2.78	322
Nesters & Young Homesteaders	688	4.43	190
Struggling Downtowns	690	4.45	141

FINANCIAL PSYTE

2001 Estimates	No. of House-holds	% of Total Hhds.	Index
Successful Suburbanites	571	3.68	55
Canadian Comfort	4,059	26.16	269
Tractors & Tradelines	8,098	52.19	913
Bills & Wills	896	5.77	70
Revolving Renters	688	4.43	96
Towering Debt	1,122	7.23	93

HOME LANGUAGE

2001 Estimates		% Total
English	41,898	97.05
French	132	0.31
Estonian	88	0.20
Finnish	26	0.06
German	91	0.21
Greek	63	0.15
Hungarian	87	0.20
Italian	43	0.10
Polish	84	0.19
Russian	40	0.09
Slovak	24	0.06
Ukrainian	77	0.18
Other Languages	227	0.53
Multiple Responses	291	0.67
Total	43,171	100.00

BUILDING PERMITS

	1999	1998 $000	1997
Value	59,085	35,655	32,183

HOMES BUILT

	1999	1998	1997
No	439	180	94

TAXATION

Income Class:	1997	% Total
Under $5,000	2,850	12.33
$5,000-$10,000	2,610	11.29
$10,000-$15,000	3,290	14.23
$15,000-$20,000	2,310	9.99
$20,000-$25,000	1,860	8.04
$25,000-$30,000	1,790	7.74
$30,000-$40,000	3,240	14.01
$40,000-$50,000	2,030	8.78
$50,000 +	3,150	13.62
Total Returns, No.	23,120	
Total Income, $000	623,536	
Total Taxable Returns	16,350	
Total Tax, $000	114,979	
Average Income, $	26,970	
Average Tax, $	7,032	

VITAL STATISTICS

	1997	1996	1995	1994
Births	494	533	562	612
Deaths	258	253	253	230
Natural Increase	236	280	309	382
Marriages	133	138	139	128

Note: Latest available data.

MEDIA INFO
see Toronto, CMA

Halton Hills
(Town)
Toronto CMA

In Halton Regional Municipality.

POPULATION

July 1, 2001 Estimate	49,908
% Cdn. Total	0.16
% Change, '96 -'01	14.27
Avg. Annual Growth Rate, %	2.70
2003 Projected Population	52,995
2006 Projected Population	57,575
2001 Households Estimate	17,327
2003 Projected Households	18,456
2006 Projected Households	20,209

INCOME

% Above/Below National Average	+25
2001 Total Income Estimate	$1,313,420,000
% Cdn. Total	0.20
2001 Average Hhld. Income	$75,800
2001 Per Capita	$26,300
2003 Projected Total Income	$1,486,180,000
2006 Projected Total Income	$1,784,810,000

RETAIL SALES

% Above/Below National Average	-4
2001 Retail Sales Estimate	$429,520,000
% Cdn. Total	0.15
2001 per Household	$24,800
2001 per Capita	$8,600
2001 No. of Establishments	315
2003 Projected Retail Sales	$489,930,000
2006 Projected Retail Sales	$584,950,000

POPULATION

2001 Estimates:

Total		49,908
Male		25,018
Female		24,890

Age Groups	Male	Female
0-4	1,690	1,600
5-9	1,885	1,722
10-14	1,886	1,743
15-19	1,691	1,612
20-24	1,615	1,515
25-29	1,681	1,621
30-34	2,001	1,998
35-39	2,254	2,274
40-44	2,152	2,147
45-49	1,892	1,874
50-54	1,660	1,624
55-59	1,361	1,335
60-64	1,052	1,039
65-69	824	852
70+	1,374	1,934

DAYTIME POPULATION

2001 Estimates:

Working Population	14,925
At Home Population	20,860
Total	35,785

INCOME

2001 Estimates:

Avg. Household Income	$75,802
Avg. Family Income	$80,478
Per Capita Income	$26,317
Male:	
Avg. Employment Income	$43,789
Avg. Employment Income (Full Time)	$54,238
Female:	
Avg. Employment Income	$27,369
Avg. Employment Income (Full Time)	$39,363

DISPOSABLE & DISCRETIONARY INCOME

2001 Estimates:	*Per Hhld.*
Disposable Income	$61,678
Discretionary Income 1 (minus Food & Shelter)	$45,147
Discretionary Income 2 (minus Food, Shelter, & Other Expenditures)	$34,283

LIQUID ASSETS

1999 Estimates:	*Per Hhld.*
Equity Investments	$118,350
Interest Bearing Investments	$94,643
Total Liquid Assets	$212,993

CREDIT DATA

July 2000:

Pool of Credit	$586,891,265
Revolving Credit, No.	90,688
Fixed Loans, No.	28,711
Avg. Credit Limit, per Person	$15,020
Avg. Spent, per Person	$6,826
Satisfactory Ratings, No. per Person	2.96
Avg. No. of Cards, per Person	1.13

LABOUR FORCE

2001 Estimates:

Male:

In the Labour Force	16,096
Participation Rate	82.3
Employed	15,685
Unemployed	411
Unemployment Rate	2.6
Not in Labour Force	3,461

Female:

In the Labour Force	13,531
Participation Rate	68.3
Employed	13,115
Unemployed	416
Unemployment Rate	3.1
Not in Labour Force	6,294

OCCUPATIONS BY MAJOR GROUPS

2001 Estimates:	Male	Female
Management	2,228	988
Business, Finance & Admin.	1,628	4,210
Natural & Applied Sciences & Related	1,352	289
Health	94	787
Social Sciences, Gov't Services & Religion	265	383
Education	427	799
Arts, Culture, Recreation & Sport	227	284
Sales & Service	2,975	4,127
Trades, Transport & Equipment Operators & Related	4,148	311
Primary Industries	517	191
Processing, Mfg. & Utilities	1,974	887

LEVEL OF SCHOOLING

2001 Estimates:

Population 15 years +	39,382
Less than Grade 9	2,304
Grades 9-13 w/o Certif.	9,368
Grade 9-13 with Certif.	6,221
Trade Certif. /Dip.	1,720
Non-Univ. w/o Certif./Dip.	2,835
Non-Univ. with Certif./Dip.	8,287
Univ. w/o Degree	3,562
Univ. w/o Degree/Certif.	1,669
Univ. with Certif.	1,893
Univ. with Degree	5,085

AVERAGE HOUSEHOLD EXPENDITURES

2001 Estimates:

Food	$7,544
Shelter	$11,568
Clothing	$2,772
Transportation	$8,571
Health & Personal Care	$2,316
Recr'n, Read'g & Education	$4,775
Taxes & Securities	$21,084
Other	$10,826
Total Expenditures	$69,456

PRIVATE HOUSEHOLDS

2001 Estimates:

Private Households, Total	17,327
Pop. in Private Households	48,880
Average no. per Household	2.8

FAMILIES

2001 Estimates:

Families in Private Households	14,563
Husband-Wife Families	13,093
Lone-Parent Families	1,470
Aver. No. Persons per Family	3.1
Aver. No. Sons/Daughters at Home	1.2

HOUSING

2001 Estimates:

Occupied Private Dwellings	17,327
Owned	13,830
Rented	3,497
Single-Detached House	12,730
Semi-Detached House	594
Row Houses	1,180
Apartment, 5+ Storeys	860
Owned Apartment, 5+ Storeys	257
Apartment, 5 or Fewer Storeys	1,338
Apartment, Detached Duplex	525
Other Single-Attached	36
Movable Dwellings	64

VEHICLES

2001 Estimates:

Model Yrs. '81-'96, No.	24,536
% Total	77.55
Model Yrs. '97-'98, No.	4,353
% Total	13.76
'99 Vehicles registered in Model Yr. '99, No.	2,750
% Total	8.69
Total No. '81-'99	31,639

LEGAL MARITAL STATUS

2001 Estimates: (Age 15+)

Single (Never Married)	9,919
Legally Married (Not Separated)	24,176
Legally Married (Separated)	1,121
Widowed	1,940
Divorced	2,226

PSYTE CATEGORIES

2001 Estimates	No. of House-holds	% of Total Hhds.	Index
Mortgaged in Suburbia	1,923	11.10	798
Boomers & Teens	2,968	17.13	956
Stable Suburban Families	1,111	6.41	492
Old Bungalow Burbs	1,355	7.82	472
Brie & Chablis	92	0.53	59
Satellite Suburbs	660	3.81	133
Kindergarten Boom	912	5.26	201
Blue Collar Winners	3,678	21.23	843
Old Towns' New Fringe	646	3.73	95
Conservative Homebodies	1,987	11.47	318
High Rise Sunsets	350	2.02	141
Young Urban Mix	63	0.36	17
Town Renters	399	2.30	266
Struggling Downtowns	1,016	5.86	186

FINANCIAL P$YTE

2001 Estimates	No. of House-holds	% of Total Hhds.	Index
Four Star Investors	2,968	17.13	341
Successful Suburbanites	3,034	17.51	264
Canadian Comfort	4,338	25.04	258
Urban Heights	92	0.53	12
Miners & Credit-Liners	1,355	7.82	247
Mortgages & Minivans	912	5.26	80
Tractors & Tradelines	646	3.73	65
Bills & Wills	2,050	11.83	143
Revolving Renters	350	2.02	44
Towering Debt	1,415	8.17	105

HOME LANGUAGE

2001 Estimates:		% Total
English	48,080	96.34
French	353	0.71
Chinese	41	0.08
Croatian	212	0.42
Dutch	48	0.10
German	114	0.23
Greek	63	0.13
Italian	108	0.22
Korean	41	0.08
Polish	43	0.09
Portuguese	139	0.28
Spanish	53	0.11
Other Languages	251	0.50
Multiple Responses	362	0.73
Total	49,908	100.00

BUILDING PERMITS

	1999	1998	1997
	$000		
Value	102,297	78,229	57,305

HOMES BUILT

	1999	1998	1997
No.	411	289	432

TAXATION

Income Class:	1997	% Total
Under $5,000	3,640	11.05
$5,000-$10,000	3,120	9.47
$10,000-$15,000	3,350	10.17
$15,000-$20,000	2,730	8.29
$20,000-$25,000	2,310	7.01
$25,000-$30,000	2,530	7.68
$30,000-$40,000	4,700	14.27
$40,000-$50,000	3,480	10.57
$50,000 +	7,080	21.50
Total Returns, No.	32,930	
Total Income, $000	1,171,852	
Total Taxable Returns	25,590	
Total Tax, $000	256,485	
Average Income, $.	35,586	
Average Tax, $.	10,023	

VITAL STATISTICS

	1997	1996	1995	1994
Births	630	659	648	642
Deaths	236	217	239	246
Natural Increase	394	442	409	396
Marriages	226	227	227	222

Note: Latest available data.

MEDIA INFO
see Toronto, CMA

King
(Township)
Toronto CMA

In York Regional Municipality.

POPULATION

July 1, 2001 Estimate	19,898
% Cdn. Total	0.06
% Change, '96 -'01	5.74
Avg. Annual Growth Rate, %	1.12
2003 Projected Population	19,829
2006 Projected Population	19,888
2001 Households Estimate	6,683
2003 Projected Households	6,683
2006 Projected Households	6,748

INCOME

% Above/Below National Average	+69
2001 Total Income Estimate	$710,200,000
% Cdn. Total	0.11
2001 Average Hhld. Income	$106,300
2001 Per Capita	$35,700
2003 Projected Total Income	$744,130,000
2006 Projected Total Income	$807,110,000

RETAIL SALES

% Above/Below National Average	-37
2001 Retail Sales Estimate	$112,300,000
% Cdn. Total	0.04
2001 per Household	$16,800
2001 per Capita	$5,600
2001 No. of Establishments	151
2003 Projected Retail Sales	$119,240,000
2006 Projected Retail Sales	$129,910,000

POPULATION

2001 Estimates:

Total	19,898
Male	10,003
Female	9,895

Age Groups	Male	Female
0-4	545	512
5-9	646	603
10-14	737	674
15-19	730	643
20-24	676	605
25-29	602	547
30-34	602	606
35-39	685	764
40-44	747	842
45-49	768	835
50-54	757	756
55-59	686	653
60-64	591	556
65-69	486	453
70+	745	846

DAYTIME POPULATION

2001 Estimates:

Working Population	5,105
At Home Population	7,923
Total	13,028

INCOME

2001 Estimates:

Avg. Household Income	$106,270
Avg. Family Income	$111,109
Per Capita Income	$35,692
Male:	
Avg. Employment Income	$58,449
Avg. Employment Income (Full Time)	$72,697
Female:	
Avg. Employment Income	$33,334
Avg. Employment Income (Full Time)	$46,647

DISPOSABLE & DISCRETIONARY INCOME

2001 Estimates:	Per Hhld.
Disposable Income	$83,191
Discretionary Income 1 (minus Food & Shelter)	$63,384
Discretionary Income 2 (minus Food, Shelter, & Other Expenditures)	$49,767

LIQUID ASSETS

1999 Estimates:	Per Hhld.
Equity Investments	$271,953
Interest Bearing Investments	$151,411
Total Liquid Assets	$423,364

CREDIT DATA

July 2000:

Pool of Credit	$247,696,410
Revolving Credit, No.	37,358
Fixed Loans, No.	8,625
Avg. Credit Limit, per Person	$14,631
Avg. Spent, per Person	$5,813
Satisfactory Ratings, No. per Person	2.65
Avg. No. of Cards, per Person	1.16

LABOUR FORCE

2001 Estimates:

Male:	
In the Labour Force	6,713
Participation Rate	83.1
Employed	6,563
Unemployed	150
Unemployment Rate	2.2
Not in Labour Force	1,362
Female:	
In the Labour Force	5,432
Participation Rate	67.0
Employed	5,352
Unemployed	80
Unemployment Rate	1.5
Not in Labour Force	2,674

OCCUPATIONS BY MAJOR GROUPS

2001 Estimates:	Male	Female
Management	1,516	471
Business, Finance & Admin.	643	1,912
Natural & Applied Sciences & Related	549	166
Health	87	350
Social Sciences, Gov't Services & Religion	183	164
Education	256	317
Arts, Culture, Recreation & Sport	97	185
Sales & Service	1,110	1,312
Trades, Transport & Equipment Operators & Related	1,454	145
Primary Industries	510	241
Processing, Mfg. & Utilities	207	119

LEVEL OF SCHOOLING

2001 Estimates:

Population 15 years +	16,181
Less than Grade 9	1,209
Grades 9-13 w/o Certif.	3,422
Grade 9-13 with Certif.	2,178
Trade Certif. /Dip.	710
Non-Univ. w/o Certif./Dip.	1,002
Non-Univ. with Certif./Dip.	3,232
Univ. w/o Degree	1,390
Univ. w/o Degree/Certif.	737
Univ. with Certif.	653
Univ. with Degree	3,038

AVERAGE HOUSEHOLD EXPENDITURES

2001 Estimates:

Food	$8,624
Shelter	$14,800
Clothing	$3,468
Transportation	$10,915
Health & Personal Care	$2,848
Recr'n, Read'g & Education	$6,146
Taxes & Securities	$31,483
Other	$14,651
Total Expenditures	$92,935

PRIVATE HOUSEHOLDS

2001 Estimates:

Private Households, Total	6,683
Pop. in Private Households	19,770
Average no. per Household	3.0

FAMILIES

2001 Estimates:

Families in Private Households	5,840
Husband-Wife Families	5,389
Lone-Parent Families	451
Aver. No. Persons per Family	3.2
Aver. No. Sons/Daughters at Home	1.3

HOUSING

2001 Estimates:

Occupied Private Dwellings	6,683
Owned	5,499
Rented	1,184
Single-Detached House	6,445
Semi-Detached House	28
Apartment, 5 or Fewer Storeys	160
Apartment, Detached Duplex	39
Movable Dwellings	11

VEHICLES

2001 Estimates:

Model Yrs. '81-'96, No.	10,676
% Total	76.00
Model Yrs. '97-'98, No.	2,076
% Total	14.78
'99 Vehicles registered in Model Yr. '99, No.	1,295
% Total	9.22
Total No. '81-'99	14,047

LEGAL MARITAL STATUS

2001 Estimates: (Age 15+)

Single (Never Married)	4,195
Legally Married (Not Separated)	10,131
Legally Married (Separated)	399
Widowed	725
Divorced	731

PSYTE CATEGORIES

2001 Estimates	No. of House-holds	% of Total Hhds.	Index
The Affluentials	815	12.20	1,907
Urban Gentry	17	0.25	14
Boomers & Teens	4,048	60.57	3,379
Stable Suburban Families	412	6.16	473
Blue Collar Winners	1,201	17.97	714
Conservative Homebodies	190	2.84	79

FINANCIAL P$YTE

2001 Estimates	No. of House-holds	% of Total Hhds.	Index
Platinum Estates	815	12.20	1,513
Four Star Investors	4,065	60.83	1,211
Successful Suburbanites	412	6.16	93
Canadian Comfort	1,201	17.97	185
Bills & Wills	190	2.84	34

HOME LANGUAGE

2001 Estimates:		% Total
English	18,660	93.78
French	70	0.35
Chinese	11	0.06
Croatian	11	0.06
Danish	11	0.06
German	50	0.25
Greek	28	0.14
Hungarian	22	0.11
Italian	487	2.45
Korean	11	0.06
Macedonian	11	0.06
Polish	142	0.71
Serbian	12	0.06
Spanish	22	0.11
Tagalog (Pilipino)	11	0.06
Multiple Responses	339	1.70
Total	19,898	100.00

BUILDING PERMITS

	1999	1998	1997
		$000	
Value	29,387	32,172	18,781

HOMES BUILT

	1999	1998	1997
No	72	46	40

TAXATION

Income Class:	1997	% Total
Under $5,000	1,280	10.22
$5,000-$10,000	1,320	10.53
$10,000-$15,000	1,300	10.38
$15,000-$20,000	990	7.90
$20,000-$25,000	880	7.02
$25,000-$30,000	860	6.86
$30,000-$40,000	1,570	12.53
$40,000-$50,000	1,110	8.86
$50,000 +	3,230	25.78
Total Returns, No.	12,530	
Total Income, $000	594,828	
Total Taxable Returns	9,750	
Total Tax, $000	157,059	
Average Income, $	47,472	
Average Tax, $	16,109	

VITAL STATISTICS

	1997	1996	1995	1994
Births	151	187	143	189
Deaths	91	112	95	110
Natural Increase	60	75	48	79
Marriages	147	147	160	166

Note: Latest available data.

MEDIA INFO
see Toronto, CMA

Markham
(Town)
Toronto CMA
In York Regional Municipality.

POPULATION

July 1, 2001 Estimate	208,059
% Cdn. Total	0.67
% Change, '96 -'01	16.23
Avg. Annual Growth Rate, %	3.05
2003 Projected Population	218,019
2006 Projected Population	234,778
2001 Households Estimate	61,617
2003 Projected Households	64,799
2006 Projected Households	70,298

INCOME

% Above/Below National Average	+30
2001 Total Income Estimate	$5,685,590,000
% Cdn. Total	0.87
2001 Average Hhld. Income	$92,300
2001 Per Capita	$27,300
2003 Projected Total Income	$6,352,060,000
2006 Projected Total Income	$7,565,500,000

RETAIL SALES

% Above/Below National Average	-6
2001 Retail Sales Estimate	$1,744,600,000
% Cdn. Total	0.63
2001 per Household	$28,300
2001 per Capita	$8,400
2001 No. of Establishments	1,997
2003 Projected Retail Sales	$1,979,020,000
2006 Projected Retail Sales	$2,359,480,000

POPULATION

2001 Estimates:

Total	208,059
Male	102,054
Female	106,005

Age Groups	Male	Female
0-4	6,063	5,831
5-9	6,562	6,216
10-14	7,655	7,138
15-19	8,354	7,841
20-24	8,223	7,948
25-29	7,399	7,284
30-34	6,822	7,148
35-39	7,035	7,991
40-44	7,726	9,024
45-49	8,446	9,462
50-54	7,881	8,225
55-59	6,308	6,213
60-64	4,692	4,553
65-69	3,424	3,506
70+	5,464	7,625

DAYTIME POPULATION

2001 Estimates:

Working Population	111,365
At Home Population	95,664
Total	207,029

INCOME

2001 Estimates:

Avg. Household Income	$92,273
Avg. Family Income	$89,017
Per Capita Income	$27,327
Male:	
Avg. Employment Income	$47,998
Avg. Employment Income (Full Time)	$63,898
Female:	
Avg. Employment Income	$30,199
Avg. Employment Income (Full Time)	$43,495

DISPOSABLE & DISCRETIONARY INCOME

2001 Estimates:	*Per Hhld.*
Disposable Income	$74,703
Discretionary Income 1 (minus Food & Shelter)	$56,092
Discretionary Income 2 (minus Food, Shelter, & Other Expenditures)	$43,450

LIQUID ASSETS

1999 Estimates:	*Per Hhld.*
Equity Investments	$188,963
Interest Bearing Investments	$122,841
Total Liquid Assets	$311,804

CREDIT DATA

July 2000:

Pool of Credit	$2,662,417,941
Revolving Credit, No.	490,925
Fixed Loans, No.	95,292
Avg. Credit Limit, per Person	$13,913
Avg. Spent, per Person	$5,319
Satisfactory Ratings, No. per Person	2.99
Avg. No. of Cards, per Person	1.33

LABOUR FORCE

2001 Estimates:

Male:	
In the Labour Force	61,964
Participation Rate	75.8
Employed	59,548
Unemployed	2,416
Unemployment Rate	3.9
Not in Labour Force	19,810
Female:	
In the Labour Force	54,620
Participation Rate	62.9
Employed	52,347
Unemployed	2,273
Unemployment Rate	4.2
Not in Labour Force	32,200

OCCUPATIONS BY MAJOR GROUPS

2001 Estimates:	*Male*	*Female*
Management	11,932	4,725
Business, Finance & Admin.	9,252	19,175
Natural & Applied Sciences & Related	7,266	1,901
Health	1,624	3,853
Social Sciences, Gov't Services & Religion	1,439	1,410
Education	1,493	3,138
Arts, Culture, Recreation & Sport	1,419	1,740
Sales & Service	13,748	13,608
Trades, Transport & Equipment Operators & Related	8,059	593
Primary Industries	1,047	85
Processing, Mfg. & Utilities	3,405	2,823

LEVEL OF SCHOOLING

2001 Estimates:

Population 15 years +	168,594
Less than Grade 9	12,330
Grades 9-13 w/o Certif.	30,328
Grade 9-13 with Certif.	23,239
Trade Certif./Dip.	4,259
Non-Univ. w/o Certif./Dip.	9,241
Non-Univ. with Certif./Dip.	27,381
Univ. w/o Degree	21,759
Univ. w/o Degree/Certif.	11,853
Univ. with Certif.	9,906
Univ. with Degree	40,057

AVERAGE HOUSEHOLD EXPENDITURES

2001 Estimates:

Food	$8,657
Shelter	$13,504
Clothing	$3,417
Transportation	$10,311
Health & Personal Care	$2,581
Recr'n, Read'g & Education	$6,022
Taxes & Securities	$26,560
Other	$11,320
Total Expenditures	$82,372

PRIVATE HOUSEHOLDS

2001 Estimates:

Private Households, Total	61,617
Pop. in Private Households	205,695
Average no. per Household	3.3

FAMILIES

2001 Estimates:

Families in Private Households	58,129
Husband-Wife Families	52,448
Lone-Parent Families	5,681
Aver. No. Persons per Family	3.4
Aver. No. Sons/Daughters at Home	1.5

HOUSING

2001 Estimates:

Occupied Private Dwellings	61,617
Owned	50,834
Rented	10,783
Single-Detached House	47,609
Semi-Detached House	1,246
Row Houses	4,003
Apartment, 5+ Storeys	5,794
Owned Apartment, 5+ Storeys	2,391
Apartment, 5 or Fewer Storeys	1,125
Apartment, Detached Duplex	1,774
Other Single-Attached	66

VEHICLES

2001 Estimates:

Model Yrs. '81-'96, No.	86,166
% Total	65.57
Model Yrs. '97-'98, No.	25,983
% Total	19.77
'99 Vehicles registered in Model Yr. '99, No.	19,263
% Total	14.66
Total No. '81-'99	131,412

LEGAL MARITAL STATUS

2001 Estimates: (Age 15+)

Single (Never Married)	50,518
Legally Married (Not Separated)	101,659
Legally Married (Separated)	3,332
Widowed	7,457
Divorced	5,628

PSYTE CATEGORIES

2001 Estimates	*No. of House-holds*	*% of Total Hhds.*	*Index*
The Affluentials	3,106	5.04	788
Urban Gentry	1,573	2.55	142
Suburban Executives	11,878	19.28	1,345
Mortgaged in Suburbia	540	0.88	63
Technocrafts & Bureaucrats	5,598	9.09	323
Asian Heights	20,424	33.15	5,230
Boomers & Teens	2,645	4.29	239
Stable Suburban Families	4,453	7.23	554
Old Bungalow Burbs	989	1.61	97
Suburban Nesters	2,919	4.74	296
Brie & Chablis	1,051	1.71	190
Aging Erudites	270	0.44	29
Kindergarten Boom	672	1.09	42
Blue Collar Winners	732	1.19	47
Asian Mosaic	491	0.80	58
High Rise Melting Pot	632	1.03	68
Conservative Homebodies	514	0.83	23
High Rise Sunsets	1,964	3.19	223
University Enclaves	438	0.71	35
Old Leafy Towns	90	0.15	6
Big City Stress	129	0.21	19
Old Grey Towers	393	0.64	115

Ontario

FINANCIAL P$YTE

2001 Estimates	*No. of House-holds*	*% of Total Hhds.*	*Index*
Platinum Estates	3,106	5.04	626
Four Star Investors	16,096	26.12	520
Successful Suburbanites	31,015	50.34	759
Canadian Comfort	3,651	5.93	61
Urban Heights	1,321	2.14	50
Miners & Credit-Liners	989	1.61	51
Mortgages & Minivans	672	1.09	17
Dollars & Sense	491	0.80	30
Bills & Wills	604	0.98	12
Revolving Renters	1,964	3.19	69
Young Urban Struggle	438	0.71	15
Towering Debt	632	1.03	13
NSF	129	0.21	6
Senior Survivors	393	0.64	34

HOME LANGUAGE

2001 Estimates:		*% Total*
English	141,295	67.91
French	683	0.33
Arabic	672	0.32
Armenian	902	0.43
Bengali	139	0.07
Chinese	40,067	19.26
Croatian	106	0.05
German	203	0.10
Greek	1,102	0.53
Gujarati	1,287	0.62
Hebrew	210	0.10
Hindi	581	0.28
Hungarian	231	0.11
Italian	2,097	1.01
Japanese	270	0.13
Korean	635	0.31
Lao	118	0.06
Macedonian	1,031	0.50
Persian (Farsi)	1,010	0.49
Polish	295	0.14
Punjabi	1,795	0.86
Russian	497	0.24
Spanish	504	0.24
Tagalog (Pilipino)	1,097	0.53
Tamil	858	0.41
Turkish	178	0.09
Urdu	981	0.47
Vietnamese	222	0.11
Other Languages	1,477	0.71
Multiple Responses	7,516	3.61
Total	208,059	100.00

BUILDING PERMITS

	1999	*1998*	*1997*
		$000	
Value	760,217	541,269	379,406

HOMES BUILT

	1999	*1998*	*1997*
No.	3,346	1,641	1,277

Ontario

Markham
(Town)
Toronto CMA
(Cont'd)

TAXATION

Income Class:	1997	% Total
Under $5,000	30,850	18.06
$5,000-$10,000	20,970	12.28
$10,000-$15,000	17,700	10.36
$15,000-$20,000	12,640	7.40
$20,000-$25,000	10,870	6.36
$25,000-$30,000	10,940	6.41
$30,000-$40,000	19,130	11.20
$40,000-$50,000	13,090	7.66
$50,000 +	34,620	20.27
Total Returns, No.	170,800	
Total Income, $000	5,910,607	
Total Taxable Returns	115,590	
Total Tax, $000	1,353,791	
Average Income, $	34,605	
Average Tax, $	11,712	

VITAL STATISTICS

	1997	1996	1995	1994
Births	2,515	2,567	2,589	2,654
Deaths	807	820	772	747
Natural Increase	1,708	1,747	1,817	1,907
Marriages	1,040	1,023	1,051	961

Note: Latest available data.

MEDIA INFO
see Toronto, CMA

Milton
(Town)
Toronto CMA
In Halton Regional Municipality.

POPULATION

July 1, 2001 Estimate	40,277
% Cdn. Total	0.13
% Change, '96 -'01	21.77
Avg. Annual Growth Rate, %	4.02
2003 Projected Population	44,695
2006 Projected Population	51,293
2001 Households Estimate	13,718
2003 Projected Households	15,356
2006 Projected Households	17,870

INCOME

% Above/Below National Average	+29
2001 Total Income Estimate	$1,097,990,000
% Cdn. Total	0.17
2001 Average Hhld. Income	$80,000
2001 Per Capita	$27,300
2003 Projected Total Income	$1,288,140,000
2006 Projected Total Income	$1,612,430,000

RETAIL SALES

% Above/Below National Average	+15
2001 Retail Sales Estimate	$413,770,000
% Cdn. Total	0.15
2001 per Household	$30,200
2001 per Capita	$10,300
2001 No. of Establishments	313
2003 Projected Retail Sales	$495,780,000
2006 Projected Retail Sales	$627,990,000

POPULATION

2001 Estimates:

Total	40,277
Male	20,114
Female	20,163

Age Groups	Male	Female
0-4	1,174	1,139
5-9	1,293	1,251
10-14	1,468	1,356
15-19	1,566	1,470
20-24	1,494	1,413
25-29	1,310	1,210
30-34	1,339	1,290
35-39	1,508	1,537
40-44	1,606	1,735
45-49	1,729	1,842
50-54	1,612	1,586
55-59	1,241	1,155
60-64	894	824
65-69	658	640
70+	1,222	1,715

DAYTIME POPULATION

2001 Estimates:

Working Population	15,977
At Home Population	16,171
Total	32,148

INCOME

2001 Estimates:

Avg. Household Income	$80,040
Avg. Family Income	$84,465
Per Capita Income	$27,261
Male:	
Avg. Employment Income	$46,225
Avg. Employment Income (Full Time)	$58,198
Female:	
Avg. Employment Income	$26,819
Avg. Employment Income (Full Time)	$38,779

DISPOSABLE & DISCRETIONARY INCOME

2001 Estimates:	Per Hhld.
Disposable Income	$64,961
Discretionary Income 1 (minus Food & Shelter)	$48,102
Discretionary Income 2 (minus Food, Shelter, & Other Expenditures)	$36,866

LIQUID ASSETS

1999 Estimates:	Per Hhld.
Equity Investments	$137,279
Interest Bearing Investments	$102,367
Total Liquid Assets	$239,646

CREDIT DATA

July 2000:

Pool of Credit	$437,892,832
Revolving Credit, No.	68,198
Fixed Loans, No.	20,785
Avg. Credit Limit, per Person	$15,196
Avg. Spent, per Person	$6,810
Satisfactory Ratings, No. per Person	2.99
Avg. No. of Cards, per Person	1.14

LABOUR FORCE

2001 Estimates:

Male:	
In the Labour Force	13,369
Participation Rate	82.6
Employed	13,147
Unemployed	222
Unemployment Rate	1.7
Not in Labour Force	2,810
Female:	
In the Labour Force	11,131
Participation Rate	67.8
Employed	10,824
Unemployed	307
Unemployment Rate	2.8
Not in Labour Force	5,286

OCCUPATIONS BY MAJOR GROUPS

2001 Estimates:	Male	Female
Management	2,111	822
Business, Finance & Admin.	1,404	3,685
Natural & Applied Sciences & Related	1,069	192
Health	154	722
Social Sciences, Gov't Services & Religion	269	275
Education	290	722
Arts, Culture, Recreation & Sport	177	303
Sales & Service	2,707	3,387
Trades, Transport & Equipment Operators & Related	2,989	193
Primary Industries	691	269
Processing, Mfg. & Utilities	1,334	436

LEVEL OF SCHOOLING

2001 Estimates:

Population 15 years +	32,596
Less than Grade 9	1,933
Grades 9-13 w/o Certif.	7,583
Grade 9-13 with Certif.	4,975
Trade Certif. /Dip.	1,119
Non-Univ. w/o Certif./Dip.	2,335
Non-Univ. with Certif./Dip.	6,703
Univ. w/o Degree	3,328
Univ. w/o Degree/Certif.	1,805
Univ. with Certif.	1,523
Univ. with Degree	4,620

AVERAGE HOUSEHOLD EXPENDITURES

2001 Estimates:

Food	$7,522
Shelter	$12,107
Clothing	$2,831
Transportation	$8,869
Health & Personal Care	$2,392
Recr'n, Read'g & Education	$4,890
Taxes & Securities	$23,112
Other	$11,281
Total Expenditures	$73,004

PRIVATE HOUSEHOLDS

2001 Estimates:

Private Households, Total	13,718
Pop. in Private Households	39,291
Average no. per Household	2.9

FAMILIES

2001 Estimates:

Families in Private Households	11,400
Husband-Wife Families	10,305
Lone-Parent Families	1,095
Aver. No. Persons per Family	3.2
Aver. No. Sons/Daughters at Home	1.3

HOUSING

2001 Estimates:

Occupied Private Dwellings	13,718
Owned	10,579
Rented	3,139
Single-Detached House	9,730
Semi-Detached House	576
Row Houses	1,168
Apartment, 5+ Storeys	1,337
Owned Apartment, 5+ Storeys	309
Apartment, 5 or Fewer Storeys	550
Apartment, Detached Duplex	329
Other Single-Attached	14
Movable Dwellings	14

VEHICLES

2001 Estimates:

Model Yrs. '81-'96, No.	17,066
% Total	76.48
Model Yrs. '97-'98, No.	3,152
% Total	14.13
'99 Vehicles registered in Model Yr. '99, No.	2,097
% Total	9.40
Total No. '81-'99	22,315

LEGAL MARITAL STATUS

2001 Estimates: (Age 15+)

Single (Never Married)	9,120
Legally Married (Not Separated)	19,049
Legally Married (Separated)	1,045
Widowed	1,623
Divorced	1,759

PSYTE CATEGORIES

2001 Estimates	No. of House -holds	% of Total Hhds.	Index
Boomers & Teens	6,694	48.80	2,722
Old Bungalow Burbs	934	6.81	411
Suburban Nesters	705	5.14	321
Satellite Suburbs	425	3.10	108
Blue Collar Winners	1,649	12.02	477
Old Towns' New Fringe	474	3.46	88
Europa	50	0.36	29
High Rise Melting Pot	167	1.22	81
Conservative Homebodies	1,083	7.89	219
High Rise Sunsets	416	3.03	212
Young Urban Mix	418	3.05	144
Struggling Downtowns	547	3.99	127

Milton
(Town)
Toronto CMA
(Cont'd)

FINANCIAL PSYTE

2001 Estimates	No. of House-holds	% of Total Hhds.	Index
Four Star Investors	6,694	48.80	971
Canadian Comfort	2,779	20.26	208
Miners & Credit-Liners	934	6.81	215
Dollars & Sense	50	0.36	14
Tractors & Tradelines	474	3.46	60
Bills & Wills	1,501	10.94	132
Revolving Renters	416	3.03	66
Towering Debt	714	5.20	67

HOME LANGUAGE

2001 Estimates:		% Total
English	38,909	96.60
French	111	0.28
Arabic	25	0.06
Chinese	40	0.10
Croatian	95	0.24
Dutch	91	0.23
German	100	0.25
Hindi	52	0.13
Italian	293	0.73
Polish	90	0.22
Portuguese	33	0.08
Slovak	31	0.08
Slovenian	23	0.06
Spanish	56	0.14
Other Languages	153	0.38
Multiple Responses	175	0.43
Total	40,277	100.00

BUILDING PERMITS

	1999	1998 $000	1997
Value	56,627	38,941	26,071

HOMES BUILT

	1999	1998	1997
No	37	22	13

TAXATION

Income Class:	1997	% Total
Under $5,000	2,660	11.25
$5,000-$10,000	2,410	10.19
$10,000-$15,000	2,400	10.15
$15,000-$20,000	1,920	8.12
$20,000-$25,000	1,730	7.32
$25,000-$30,000	1,650	6.98
$30,000-$40,000	3,170	13.40
$40,000-$50,000	2,350	9.94
$50,000 +	5,360	22.66
Total Returns, No.	23,650	
Total Income, $000	873,187	
Total Taxable Returns	18,200	
Total Tax, $000	200,191	
Average Income, $	36,921	
Average Tax, $	11,000	

VITAL STATISTICS

	1997	1996	1995	1994
Births	364	363	376	387
Deaths	222	210	209	212
Natural Increase	142	153	167	175
Marriages	225	215	221	192

Note: Latest available data.

MEDIA INFO
see Toronto, CMA

Mississauga
(City)
Toronto CMA

In Peel Regional Municipality.

POPULATION

July 1, 2001 Estimate	666,152
% Cdn. Total	2.14
% Change, '96 -'01	18.31
Avg. Annual Growth Rate, %	3.42
2003 Projected Population	711,461
2006 Projected Population	779,868
2001 Households Estimate	218,711
2003 Projected Households	234,419
2006 Projected Households	259,938

INCOME

% Above/Below National Average	+16
2001 Total Income Estimate	$16,324,250,000
% Cdn. Total	2.49
2001 Average Hhld. Income	$74,600
2001 Per Capita	$24,500
2003 Projected Total Income	$18,515,470,000
2006 Projected Total Income	$22,387,740,000

RETAIL SALES

% Above/Below National Average	-14
2001 Retail Sales Estimate	$5,102,280,000
% Cdn. Total	1.83
2001 per Household	$23,300
2001 per Capita	$7,700
2001 No. of Establishments	3,712
2003 Projected Retail Sales	$5,873,740,000
2006 Projected Retail Sales	$7,101,310,000

POPULATION

2001 Estimates:		
Total		666,152
Male		327,641
Female		338,511

Age Groups	Male	Female
0-4	24,144	23,114
5-9	24,977	23,657
10-14	24,503	22,986
15-19	23,492	22,312
20-24	22,692	22,718
25-29	24,169	25,505
30-34	27,828	29,573
35-39	29,494	31,096
40-44	27,707	29,105
45-49	24,643	25,948
50-54	20,484	21,367
55-59	16,260	16,540
60-64	12,544	12,795
65-69	9,428	10,104
70+	15,276	21,691

DAYTIME POPULATION

2001 Estimates:	
Working Population	347,351
At Home Population	300,111
Total	647,462

INCOME

2001 Estimates:	
Avg. Household Income	$74,638
Avg. Family Income	$74,621
Per Capita Income	$24,505
Male:	
Avg. Employment Income	$42,291
Avg. Employment Income (Full Time)	$53,953
Female:	
Avg. Employment Income	$27,700
Avg. Employment Income (Full Time)	$38,701

DISPOSABLE & DISCRETIONARY INCOME

2001 Estimates:	Per Hhld.
Disposable Income	$60,780
Discretionary Income 1 (minus Food & Shelter)	$43,963
Discretionary Income 2 (minus Food, Shelter, & Other Expenditures)	$33,438

LIQUID ASSETS

1999 Estimates:	Per Hhld.
Equity Investments	$125,373
Interest Bearing Investments	$94,874
Total Liquid Assets	$220,247

CREDIT DATA

July 2000:	
Pool of Credit	$7,225,132,272
Revolving Credit, No.	1,337,662
Fixed Loans, No.	327,257
Avg. Credit Limit, per Person	$13,170
Avg. Spent, per Person	$5,592
Satisfactory Ratings, No. per Person	2.94
Avg. No. of Cards, per Person	1.21

LABOUR FORCE

2001 Estimates:	
Male:	
In the Labour Force	203,172
Participation Rate	80.0
Employed	195,660
Unemployed	7,512
Unemployment Rate	3.7
Not in Labour Force	50,845
Female:	
In the Labour Force	179,453
Participation Rate	66.8
Employed	168,477
Unemployed	10,976
Unemployment Rate	6.1
Not in Labour Force	89,301

OCCUPATIONS BY MAJOR GROUPS

2001 Estimates:	Male	Female
Management	29,897	14,221
Business, Finance & Admin.	30,065	63,663
Natural & Applied Sciences & Related	18,641	4,757
Health	2,667	10,826
Social Sciences, Gov't Services & Religion	2,820	4,200
Education	3,441	7,331
Arts, Culture, Recreation & Sport	3,630	3,595
Sales & Service	41,080	47,453
Trades, Transport & Equipment Operators & Related	43,513	3,399
Primary Industries	1,773	417
Processing, Mfg. & Utilities	20,724	12,617

LEVEL OF SCHOOLING

2001 Estimates:	
Population 15 years +	522,771
Less than Grade 9	41,329
Grades 9-13 w/o Certif.	104,789
Grade 9-13 with Certif.	77,146
Trade Certif. /Dip.	16,349
Non-Univ. w/o Certif./Dip.	33,732
Non-Univ. with Certif./Dip.	96,014
Univ. w/o Degree	60,155
Univ. w/o Degree/Certif.	29,790
Univ. with Certif.	30,365
Univ. with Degree	93,257

Ontario

AVERAGE HOUSEHOLD EXPENDITURES

2001 Estimates:	
Food	$7,701
Shelter	$11,867
Clothing	$2,982
Transportation	$8,175
Health & Personal Care	$2,315
Recr'n, Read'g & Education	$4,851
Taxes & Securities	$20,350
Other	$10,269
Total Expenditures	$68,510

PRIVATE HOUSEHOLDS

2001 Estimates:	
Private Households, Total	218,711
Pop. in Private Households	660,796
Average no. per Household	3.0

FAMILIES

2001 Estimates:	
Families in Private Households	188,511
Husband-Wife Families	164,062
Lone-Parent Families	24,449
Aver. No. Persons per Family	3.2
Aver. No. Sons/Daughters at Home	1.4

HOUSING

2001 Estimates:	
Occupied Private Dwellings	218,711
Owned	144,900
Rented	73,811
Single-Detached House	96,704
Semi-Detached House	21,617
Row Houses	25,273
Apartment, 5+ Storeys	59,173
Owned Apartment, 5+ Storeys	12,078
Apartment, 5 or Fewer Storeys	12,037
Apartment, Detached Duplex	3,376
Other Single-Attached	215
Movable Dwellings	316

VEHICLES

2001 Estimates:	
Model Yrs. '81-'96, No.	279,146
% Total	66.83
Model Yrs. '97-'98, No.	76,635
% Total	18.35
'99 Vehicles registered in Model Yr. '99, No.	61,903
% Total	14.82
Total No. '81-'99	417,684

LEGAL MARITAL STATUS

2001 Estimates: (Age 15+)	
Single (Never Married)	152,756
Legally Married (Not Separated)	304,101
Legally Married (Separated)	16,362
Widowed	22,700
Divorced	26,852

Ontario

Mississauga
(City)
Toronto CMA
(Cont'd)

PSYTE CATEGORIES

2001 Estimates	No. of House -holds	% of Total Hhds.	Index
The Affluentials	3,919	1.79	280
Urban Gentry	836	0.38	21
Suburban Executives	11,043	5.05	352
Mortgaged in Suburbia	25,250	11.54	831
Technocrafts & Bureaucrats	33,962	15.53	552
Asian Heights	512	0.23	37
Boomers & Teens	7,015	3.21	179
Stable Suburban Families	9,387	4.29	329
Old Bungalow Burbs	7,400	3.38	204
Suburban Nesters	8,024	3.67	229
Brie & Chablis	8,383	3.83	428
Satellite Suburbs	24,893	11.38	397
Kindergarten Boom	9,961	4.55	174
Europa	3,919	1.79	144
Asian Mosaic	376	0.17	13
High Rise Melting Pot	18,363	8.40	560
Conservative Homebodies	4,418	2.02	56
High Rise Sunsets	1,564	0.72	50
Young Urban Mix	28,318	12.95	611
University Enclaves	803	0.37	18
Young City Singles	3,844	1.76	77
Town Renters	3,178	1.45	168
Big Country Families	137	0.06	4
Struggling Downtowns	441	0.20	6
Aged Pensioners	529	0.24	18
Big City Stress	173	0.08	7
Old Grey Towers	1,391	0.64	115

FINANCIAL P$YTE

2001 Estimates	No. of House -holds	% of Total Hhds.	Index
Platinum Estates	3,919	1.79	222
Four Star Investors	18,894	8.64	172
Successful Suburbanites	69,111	31.60	476
Canadian Comfort	32,917	15.05	155
Urban Heights	8,383	3.83	89
Miners & Credit-Liners	7,400	3.38	107
Mortgages & Minivans	9,961	4.55	69
Dollars & Sense	4,295	1.96	75
Bills & Wills	32,736	14.97	181
Revolving Renters	1,564	0.72	16
Young Urban Struggle	803	0.37	8
Rural Family Blues	137	0.06	1
Towering Debt	25,826	11.81	151
NSF	173	0.08	2
Senior Survivors	1,920	0.88	47

HOME LANGUAGE

2001 Estimates:		% Total
English	485,396	72.87
French	3,463	0.52
Arabic	5,739	0.86
Bengali	427	0.06
Chinese	25,117	3.77
Croatian	4,789	0.72
Czech	413	0.06
German	783	0.12
Greek	1,800	0.27
Gujarati	2,151	0.32
Hindi	1,472	0.22
Hungarian	759	0.11
Italian	8,179	1.23
Japanese	806	0.12
Korean	1,977	0.30
Macedonian	767	0.12
Persian (Farsi)	1,849	0.28
Polish	19,572	2.94
Portuguese	10,288	1.54
Punjabi	20,128	3.02
Romanian	435	0.07
Russian	447	0.07
Serbian	1,864	0.28
Serbo-Croatian	817	0.12
Slovak	451	0.07
Slovenian	436	0.07
Spanish	7,188	1.08
Tagalog (Pilipino)	6,492	0.97
Tamil	4,661	0.70
Turkish	484	0.07
Ukrainian	1,875	0.28
Urdu	4,727	0.71
Vietnamese	5,800	0.87
Other Languages	5,739	0.86
Multiple Responses	28,861	4.33
Total	666,152	100.00

BUILDING PERMITS

	1999	1998	1997
		$000	
Value	1,876,846	1,551,280	1,513,880

HOMES BUILT

	1999	1998	1997
No	3,354	3,864	3,853

TAXATION

Income Class:	1997	% Total
Under $5,000	60,110	15.06
$5,000-$10,000	46,310	11.60
$10,000-$15,000	42,910	10.75
$15,000-$20,000	32,900	8.24
$20,000-$25,000	29,820	7.47
$25,000-$30,000	29,810	7.47
$30,000-$40,000	53,440	13.39
$40,000-$50,000	36,300	9.09
$50,000 +	67,550	16.92
Total Returns, No.	399,160	
Total Income, $000	12,473,240	
Total Taxable Returns	284,840	
Total Tax, $000	2,656,215	
Average Income, $	31,249	
Average Tax, $	9,325	

VITAL STATISTICS

	1997	1996	1995	1994
Births	8,146	8,465	8,536	8,740
Deaths	2,381	2,219	2,158	2,173
Natural Increase	5,765	6,246	6,378	6,567
Marriages	2,861	2,944	3,058	3,147

Note: Latest available data.

MEDIA INFO

see Toronto, CMA

New Tecumseth
(Town)
Toronto CMA

In Simcoe County.

POPULATION

July 1, 2001 Estimate	27,080
% Cdn. Total	0.09
% Change, '96 -'01	14.74
Avg. Annual Growth Rate, %	2.79
2003 Projected Population	28,441
2006 Projected Population	30,471
2001 Households Estimate	9,632
2003 Projected Households	10,089
2006 Projected Households	10,884

INCOME

% Above/Below National Average	+10
2001 Total Income Estimate	$629,460,000
% Cdn. Total	0.10
2001 Average Hhld. Income	$65,400
2001 Per Capita	$23,200
2003 Projected Total Income	$689,440,000
2006 Projected Total Income	$794,930,000

RETAIL SALES

% Above/Below National Average	-56
2001 Retail Sales Estimate	$106,010,000
% Cdn. Total	0.04
2001 per Household	$11,000
2001 per Capita	$3,900
2001 No. of Establishments	211
2003 Projected Retail Sales	$118,930,000
2006 Projected Retail Sales	$140,210,000

POPULATION

2001 Estimates:		
Total		27,080
Male		13,277
Female		13,803
Age Groups	Male	Female
0-4	917	871
5-9	1,026	975
10-14	1,054	973
15-19	942	905
20-24	834	848
25-29	834	855
30-34	1,013	1,045
35-39	1,126	1,165
40-44	1,076	1,110
45-49	975	994
50-54	837	848
55-59	649	663
60-64	497	527
65-69	433	506
70+	1,064	1,518

DAYTIME POPULATION

2001 Estimates:	
Working Population	9,202
At Home Population	12,425
Total	21,627

INCOME

2001 Estimates:	
Avg. Household Income	$65,351
Avg. Family Income	$68,583
Per Capita Income	$23,245
Male:	
Avg. Employment Income	$40,659
Avg. Employment Income (Full Time)	$51,343
Female:	
Avg. Employment Income	$22,569
Avg. Employment Income (Full Time)	$34,010

DISPOSABLE & DISCRETIONARY INCOME

2001 Estimates:	Per Hhld.
Disposable Income	$53,624
Discretionary Income 1 (minus Food & Shelter)	$38,396
Discretionary Income 2 (minus Food, Shelter, & Other Expenditures)	$28,251

LIQUID ASSETS

1999 Estimates:	Per Hhld.
Equity Investments	$104,844
Interest Bearing Investments	$84,484
Total Liquid Assets	$189,328

CREDIT DATA

July 2000:	
Pool of Credit	$299,775,338
Revolving Credit, No.	49,289
Fixed Loans, No.	14,865
Avg. Credit Limit, per Person	$13,425
Avg. Spent, per Person	$6,204
Satisfactory Ratings, No. per Person	2.78
Avg. No. of Cards, per Person	1.07

LABOUR FORCE

2001 Estimates:	
Male:	
In the Labour Force	8,142
Participation Rate	79.2
Employed	8,043
Unemployed	99
Unemployment Rate	1.2
Not in Labour Force	2,138
Female:	
In the Labour Force	6,855
Participation Rate	62.4
Employed	6,517
Unemployed	338
Unemployment Rate	4.9
Not in Labour Force	4,129

OCCUPATIONS BY MAJOR GROUPS

2001 Estimates:	Male	Female
Management	1,059	439
Business, Finance & Admin.	590	2,052
Natural & Applied Sciences & Related	500	62
Health	88	510
Social Sciences, Gov't Services & Religion	64	113
Education	175	295
Arts, Culture, Recreation & Sport	124	124
Sales & Service	1,579	2,208
Trades, Transport & Equipment Operators & Related	2,557	173
Primary Industries	408	174
Processing, Mfg. & Utilities	950	567

LEVEL OF SCHOOLING

2001 Estimates:	
Population 15 years +	21,264
Less than Grade 9	1,415
Grades 9-13 w/o Certif.	5,687
Grade 9-13 with Certif.	3,875
Trade Certif. /Dip.	927
Non-Univ. w/o Certif./Dip.	1,400
Non-Univ. with Certif./Dip.	4,490
Univ. w/o Degree	1,696
Univ. w/o Degree/Certif.	862
Univ. with Certif.	834
Univ. with Degree	1,774

New Tecumseth
(Town)
Toronto CMA
(Cont'd)

AVERAGE HOUSEHOLD EXPENDITURES

2001 Estimates:

Food	$6,900
Shelter	$10,604
Clothing	$2,343
Transportation	$8,015
Health & Personal Care	$2,104
Recr'n, Read'g & Education	$4,308
Taxes & Securities	$17,015
Other	$9,691
Total Expenditures	$60,980

PRIVATE HOUSEHOLDS

2001 Estimates:

Private Households, Total	9,632
Pop. in Private Households	26,483
Average no. per Household	2.7

FAMILIES

2001 Estimates:

Families in Private Households	7,977
Husband-Wife Families	7,223
Lone-Parent Families	754
Aver. No. Persons per Family	3.0
Aver. No. Sons/Daughters at Home	1.2

HOUSING

2001 Estimates:

Occupied Private Dwellings	9,632
Owned	7,697
Rented	1,935
Single-Detached House	7,077
Semi-Detached House	635
Row Houses	599
Apartment, 5 or Fewer Storeys	1,003
Apartment, Detached Duplex	254
Other Single-Attached	64

VEHICLES

2001 Estimates:

Model Yrs. '81-'96, No.	12,278
% Total	78.13
Model Yrs. '97-'98, No.	2,082
% Total	13.25
'99 Vehicles registered in Model Yr. '99, No.	1,354
% Total	8.62
Total No. '81-'99	15,714

LEGAL MARITAL STATUS

2001 Estimates: (Age 15+)

Single (Never Married)	5,062
Legally Married (Not Separated)	12,968
Legally Married (Separated)	712
Widowed	1,358
Divorced	1,164

PSYTE CATEGORIES

2001 Estimates	No. of Households	% of Total Hhds.	Index
Boomers & Teens	800	8.31	463
Satellite Suburbs	1,001	10.39	362
Blue Collar Winners	2,473	25.67	1,020
Old Towns' New Fringe	3,878	40.26	1,029
Old Leafy Towns	800	8.31	325
Nesters & Young Homesteaders	606	6.29	270

FINANCIAL P$YTE

2001 Estimates	No. of Households	% of Total Hhds.	Index
Four Star Investors	800	8.31	165
Canadian Comfort	3,474	36.07	371
Tractors & Tradelines	3,878	40.26	704
Bills & Wills	800	8.31	100
Revolving Renters	606	6.29	137

HOME LANGUAGE

2001 Estimates:		% Total
English	26,447	97.66
French	34	0.13
Bengali	19	0.07
Dutch	32	0.12
German	23	0.08
Italian	152	0.56
Japanese	23	0.08
Polish	23	0.08
Vietnamese	58	0.21
Other Languages	110	0.41
Multiple Responses	159	0.59
Total	27,080	100.00

BUILDING PERMITS

	1999	1998 $000	1997
Value	42,926	47,565	65,590

HOMES BUILT

	1999	1998	1997
No	164	205	133

TAXATION

Income Class:	1997	% Total
Under $5,000	2,210	12.35
$5,000-$10,000	1,820	10.17
$10,000-$15,000	2,100	11.74
$15,000-$20,000	1,480	8.27
$20,000-$25,000	1,370	7.66
$25,000-$30,000	1,430	7.99
$30,000-$40,000	2,520	14.09
$40,000-$50,000	1,670	9.33
$50,000 +	3,300	18.45
Total Returns, No.	17,890	
Total Income, $000	556,727	
Total Taxable Returns	13,320	
Total Tax, $000	114,709	
Average Income, $	31,119	
Average Tax, $	8,612	

VITAL STATISTICS

	1997	1996	1995	1994
Births	327	342	369	200
Deaths	193	184	196	55
Natural Increase	134	158	173	145
Marriages	147	132	124	23

Note: Latest available data.

MEDIA INFO

see Toronto, CMA

Newmarket
(Town)
Toronto CMA

In York Regional Municipality.

POPULATION

July 1, 2001 Estimate	75,702
% Cdn. Total	0.24
% Change, '96 -'01	28.35
Avg. Annual Growth Rate, %	5.12
2003 Projected Population	83,818
2006 Projected Population	96,700
2001 Households Estimate	25,115
2003 Projected Households	27,889
2006 Projected Households	32,373

INCOME

% Above/Below National Average	+24
2001 Total Income Estimate	$1,972,060,000
% Cdn. Total	0.30
2001 Average Hhld. Income	$78,500
2001 Per Capita	$26,100
2003 Projected Total Income	$2,338,620,000
2006 Projected Total Income	$3,003,250,000

RETAIL SALES

% Above/Below National Average	+47
2001 Retail Sales Estimate	$995,580,000
% Cdn. Total	0.36
2001 per Household	$39,600
2001 per Capita	$13,200
2001 No. of Establishments	440
2003 Projected Retail Sales	$1,196,660,000
2006 Projected Retail Sales	$1,531,320,000

POPULATION

2001 Estimates:

Total	75,702
Male	37,045
Female	38,657

Age Groups	Male	Female
0-4	2,789	2,568
5-9	3,138	2,897
10-14	3,168	2,976
15-19	2,925	2,840
20-24	2,595	2,647
25-29	2,527	2,646
30-34	2,849	3,136
35-39	3,229	3,577
40-44	3,268	3,518
45-49	2,966	3,071
50-54	2,344	2,350
55-59	1,666	1,618
60-64	1,170	1,174
65-69	852	939
70+	1,559	2,700

DAYTIME POPULATION

2001 Estimates:

Working Population	22,630
At Home Population	32,575
Total	55,205

INCOME

2001 Estimates:

Avg. Household Income	$78,521
Avg. Family Income	$82,088
Per Capita Income	$26,050
Male:	
Avg. Employment Income	$47,093
Avg. Employment Income (Full Time)	$59,474
Female:	
Avg. Employment Income	$28,015
Avg. Employment Income (Full Time)	$40,850

Ontario

DISPOSABLE & DISCRETIONARY INCOME

2001 Estimates:	Per Hhld.
Disposable Income	$63,931
Discretionary Income 1 (minus Food & Shelter)	$47,001
Discretionary Income 2 (minus Food, Shelter, & Other Expenditures)	$36,085

LIQUID ASSETS

1999 Estimates:	Per Hhld.
Equity Investments	$124,561
Interest Bearing Investments	$97,765
Total Liquid Assets	$222,326

CREDIT DATA

July 2000:	
Pool of Credit	$866,109,742
Revolving Credit, No.	139,697
Fixed Loans, No.	39,673
Avg. Credit Limit, per Person	$15,846
Avg. Spent, per Person	$7,002
Satisfactory Ratings, No. per Person	3.18
Avg. No. of Cards, per Person	1.23

LABOUR FORCE

2001 Estimates:	
Male:	
In the Labour Force	23,167
Participation Rate	82.9
Employed	22,637
Unemployed	530
Unemployment Rate	2.3
Not in Labour Force	4,783
Female:	
In the Labour Force	20,696
Participation Rate	68.5
Employed	20,002
Unemployed	694
Unemployment Rate	3.4
Not in Labour Force	9,520

OCCUPATIONS BY MAJOR GROUPS

2001 Estimates:	Male	Female
Management	4,356	1,693
Business, Finance & Admin.	2,607	6,610
Natural & Applied Sciences & Related	2,319	391
Health	206	1,575
Social Sciences, Gov't Services & Religion	505	490
Education	616	1,400
Arts, Culture, Recreation & Sport	387	656
Sales & Service	5,261	6,308
Trades, Transport & Equipment Operators & Related	4,401	337
Primary Industries	488	38
Processing, Mfg. & Utilities	1,688	792

Ontario

Newmarket
(Town)
Toronto CMA
(Cont'd)

LEVEL OF SCHOOLING

2001 Estimates:
Population 15 years + ...58,166
Less than Grade 9 2,561
Grades 9-13 w/o Certif. 12,583
Grade 9-13 with Certif. 8,428
Trade Certif. /Dip. 1,670
Non-Univ. w/o Certif./Dip. 3,942
Non-Univ. with Certif./Dip. 13,336
Univ. w/o Degree 6,355
 Univ. w/o Degree/Certif. 3,136
 Univ. with Certif. 3,219
Univ. with Degree 9,291

AVERAGE HOUSEHOLD EXPENDITURES

2001 Estimates:
Food $7,791
Shelter $11,950
Clothing. $3,018
Transportation. $8,567
Health & Personal Care $2,382
Recr'n, Read'g & Education $5,166
Taxes & Securities $22,156
Other $10,799
Total Expenditures $71,829

PRIVATE HOUSEHOLDS

2001 Estimates:
Private Households, Total 25,115
Pop. in Private Households 74,270
Average no. per Household 3.0

FAMILIES

2001 Estimates:
Families in Private Households 21,456
Husband-Wife Families 18,881
Lone-Parent Families 2,575
Aver. No. Persons per Family 3.3
Aver. No. Sons/Daughters at Home 1.4

HOUSING

2001 Estimates:
Occupied Private Dwellings 25,115
 Owned 19,053
 Rented 6,062
Single-Detached House 16,270
Semi-Detached House 1,748
Row Houses 2,037
Apartment, 5+ Storeys 1,858
 Owned Apartment, 5+ Storeys 465
Apartment, 5 or Fewer Storeys 1,986
Apartment, Detached Duplex 1,171
Other Single-Attached 45

VEHICLES

2001 Estimates:
Model Yrs. '81-'96, No. 30,357
 % Total 74.57
Model Yrs. '97-'98, No. 6,102
 % Total 14.99
'99 Vehicles registered in
 Model Yr. '99, No. 4,251
 % Total 10.44
Total No. '81-'99 40,710

LEGAL MARITAL STATUS

2001 Estimates: (Age 15+)
Single (Never Married). 15,396
Legally Married
 (Not Separated) 34,802
Legally Married (Separated) 2,091
Widowed 2,817
Divorced 3,060

PSYTE CATEGORIES

2001 Estimates	No. of House-holds	% of Total Hhds.	Index
The Affluentials	121	0.48	75
Suburban Executives	2,135	8.50	593
Mortgaged in Suburbia	4,002	15.93	1,146
Technocrafts & Bureaucrats	2,018	8.04	286
Boomers & Teens	3,268	13.01	726
Stable Suburban Families	896	3.57	274
Suburban Nesters	1,025	4.08	255
Satellite Suburbs	4,431	17.64	615
Kindergarten Boom	1,102	4.39	167
High Rise Melting Pot	174	0.69	46
Conservative Homebodies	1,984	7.90	219
High Rise Sunsets	344	1.37	96
Young Urban Mix	516	2.05	97
University Enclaves	521	2.07	102
Young City Singles	562	2.24	98
Town Renters	465	1.85	214
Nesters & Young Homesteaders	887	3.53	151
Struggling Downtowns	458	1.82	58

FINANCIAL P$YTE

2001 Estimates	No. of House-holds	% of Total Hhds.	Index
Platinum Estates	121	0.48	60
Four Star Investors	5,403	21.51	428
Successful Suburbanites	6,916	27.54	415
Canadian Comfort	5,456	21.72	224
Mortgages & Minivans	1,102	4.39	66
Bills & Wills	2,500	9.95	120
Revolving Renters	1,231	4.90	107
Young Urban Struggle	521	2.07	44
Towering Debt	1,659	6.61	85

HOME LANGUAGE

2001 Estimates:		% Total
English	70,011	92.48
French	447	0.59
Arabic	184	0.24
Bulgarian	43	0.06
Chinese	1,111	1.47
Finnish	39	0.05
German	102	0.13
Greek	113	0.15
Gujarati	125	0.17
Hungarian	40	0.05
Italian	213	0.28
Japanese	174	0.23
Khmer (Cambodian)	280	0.37
Korean	185	0.24
Lao	249	0.33
Macedonian	96	0.13
Polish	242	0.32
Spanish	251	0.33
Tagalog (Pilipino)	57	0.08
Vietnamese	265	0.35
Other Languages	289	0.38
Multiple Responses	1,186	1.57
Total	75,702	100.00

BUILDING PERMITS

	1999	1998 $000	1997
Value	82,913	93,447	161,419

HOMES BUILT

	1999	1998	1997
No.	542	555	946

TAXATION

Income Class:	1997	% Total
Under $5,000	5,080	11.58
$5,000-$10,000	4,550	10.37
$10,000-$15,000	4,650	10.60
$15,000-$20,000	3,310	7.55
$20,000-$25,000	2,910	6.63
$25,000-$30,000	3,180	7.25
$30,000-$40,000	5,940	13.54
$40,000-$50,000	4,250	9.69
$50,000 +	9,990	22.77

Total Returns, No. 43,870
Total Income, $000 1,563,008
Total Taxable
 Returns. 33,420
Total Tax, $000 348,009
Average Income, $ 35,628
Average Tax, $ 10,413

VITAL STATISTICS

	1997	1996	1995	1994
Births	922	942	994	902
Deaths	369	386	327	338
Natural Increase	553	556	667	564
Marriages	255	332	404	368

Note: Latest available data.

MEDIA INFO

see Toronto, CMA

North York
(City)
Toronto CMA

In Toronto Metropolitan Municipality. On Jan. 1, 1998, North York, East York, Etobicoke, Scarborough, Toronto and York amalgamated to form the new city of Toronto.

POPULATION

July 1, 2001 Estimate	636,885
% Cdn. Total	2.05
% Change, '96 -'01	4.63
Avg. Annual Growth Rate, %	0.91
2003 Projected Population	647,580
2006 Projected Population	663,217
2001 Households Estimate	232,744
2003 Projected Households	238,539
2006 Projected Households	247,054

INCOME

% Above/Below National Average	+8
2001 Total Income Estimate	$14,522,800,000
% Cdn. Total	2.21
2001 Average Hhld. Income	$62,400
2001 Per Capita	$22,800
2003 Projected Total Income	$15,671,920,000
2006 Projected Total Income	$17,569,690,000

RETAIL SALES

% Above/Below National Average	-7
2001 Retail Sales Estimate	$5,284,590,000
% Cdn. Total	1.90
2001 per Household	$22,700
2001 per Capita	$8,300
2001 No. of Establishments	4,545
2003 Projected Retail Sales	$5,770,840,000
2006 Projected Retail Sales	$6,486,880,000

POPULATION

2001 Estimates:

Total		636,885
Male		304,197
Female		332,688

Age Groups	Male	Female
0-4	20,538	19,443
5-9	20,175	19,029
10-14	19,230	18,211
15-19	19,306	18,163
20-24	20,170	19,513
25-29	21,868	22,591
30-34	24,237	25,559
35-39	24,464	26,202
40-44	22,327	24,918
45-49	20,445	23,494
50-54	17,815	20,860
55-59	15,406	18,389
60-64	14,194	16,879
65-69	13,377	15,962
70+	30,645	43,475

DAYTIME POPULATION

2001 Estimates:

Working Population	333,784
At Home Population	342,383
Total	676,167

INCOME

2001 Estimates:

Avg. Household Income	$62,398
Avg. Family Income	$66,205
Per Capita Income	$22,803
Male:	
Avg. Employment Income	$39,276
Avg. Employment Income (Full Time)	$53,082
Female:	
Avg. Employment Income	$26,550
Avg. Employment Income (Full Time)	$37,210

DISPOSABLE & DISCRETIONARY INCOME

2001 Estimates:	Per Hhld.
Disposable Income	$50,488
Discretionary Income 1 (minus Food & Shelter)	$34,818
Discretionary Income 2 (minus Food, Shelter, & Other Expenditures)	$25,611

LIQUID ASSETS

1999 Estimates:	Per Hhld.
Equity Investments	$115,348
Interest Bearing Investments	$81,882
Total Liquid Assets	$197,230

CREDIT DATA

July 2000:

Pool of Credit	$6,380,661,309
Revolving Credit, No.	1,330,787
Fixed Loans, No.	241,286
Avg. Credit Limit, per Person	$10,423
Avg. Spent, per Person	$4,001
Satisfactory Ratings, No. per Person	2.50
Avg. No. of Cards, per Person	1.12

LABOUR FORCE

2001 Estimates:

Male:	
In the Labour Force	168,666
Participation Rate	69.1
Employed	156,832
Unemployed	11,834
Unemployment Rate	7.0
Not in Labour Force	75,588
Female:	
In the Labour Force	150,817
Participation Rate	54.6
Employed	137,729
Unemployed	13,088
Unemployment Rate	8.7
Not in Labour Force	125,188

OCCUPATIONS BY MAJOR GROUPS

2001 Estimates:	Male	Female
Management	20,245	9,470
Business, Finance & Admin.	24,410	47,993
Natural & Applied Sciences & Related	14,447	3,858
Health	4,574	9,150
Social Sciences, Gov't Services & Religion	4,703	4,827
Education	3,524	7,392
Arts, Culture, Recreation & Sport	4,397	4,852
Sales & Service	36,726	40,972
Trades, Transport & Equipment Operators & Related	29,754	2,314
Primary Industries	1,252	258
Processing, Mfg. & Utilities	17,579	10,833

LEVEL OF SCHOOLING

2001 Estimates:

Population 15 years +	520,259
Less than Grade 9	66,865
Grades 9-13 w/o Certif.	105,781
Grade 9-13 with Certif.	67,921
Trade Certif. /Dip.	13,434
Non-Univ. w/o Certif./Dip.	29,806
Non-Univ. with Certif./Dip.	74,134
Univ. w/o Degree	58,513
Univ. w/o Degree/Certif.	30,187
Univ. with Certif.	28,326
Univ. with Degree	103,805

AVERAGE HOUSEHOLD EXPENDITURES

2001 Estimates:

Food	$6,857
Shelter	$11,218
Clothing	$2,550
Transportation	$7,014
Health & Personal Care	$2,060
Recr'n, Read'g & Education	$3,753
Taxes & Securities	$15,588
Other	$9,039
Total Expenditures	$58,079

PRIVATE HOUSEHOLDS

2001 Estimates:

Private Households, Total	232,744
Pop. in Private Households	627,998
Average no. per Household	2.7

FAMILIES

2001 Estimates:

Families in Private Households	176,089
Husband-Wife Families	143,347
Lone-Parent Families	32,742
Aver. No. Persons per Family	3.0
Aver. No. Sons/Daughters at Home	1.2

HOUSING

2001 Estimates:

Occupied Private Dwellings	232,744
Owned	112,627
Rented	120,117
Single-Detached House	72,869
Semi-Detached House	21,690
Row Houses	13,999
Apartment, 5+ Storeys	93,928
Owned Apartment, 5+ Storeys	17,237
Apartment, 5 or Fewer Storeys	26,119
Apartment, Detached Duplex	3,942
Other Single-Attached	174
Movable Dwellings	23

VEHICLES

2001 Estimates:

Model Yrs. '81-'96, No.	241,442
% Total	75.19
Model Yrs. '97-'98, No.	45,785
% Total	14.26
'99 Vehicles registered in Model Yr. '99, No.	33,900
% Total	10.56
Total No. '81-'99	321,127

LEGAL MARITAL STATUS

2001 Estimates: (Age 15+)

Single (Never Married)	163,514
Legally Married (Not Separated)	272,661
Legally Married (Separated)	17,940
Widowed	37,285
Divorced	28,859

PSYTE CATEGORIES

2001 Estimates	No. of House-holds	% of Total Hhds.	Index
Canadian Establishment	3,451	1.48	891
The Affluentials	7,863	3.38	528
Urban Gentry	18,521	7.96	443
Suburban Executives	1,273	0.55	38
Technocrafts & Bureaucrats	676	0.29	10
Asian Heights	7,845	3.37	532
Boomers & Teens	447	0.19	11
Stable Suburban Families	3,476	1.49	115
Old Bungalow Burbs	803	0.35	21
Suburban Nesters	24,160	10.38	648
Brie & Chablis	15,480	6.65	742
Aging Erudites	776	0.33	22
Satellite Suburbs	652	0.28	10
Kindergarten Boom	585	0.25	10
Europa	42,069	18.08	1,454
Asian Mosaic	2,313	0.99	72
High Rise Melting Pot	36,932	15.87	1,059

Ontario

2001 Estimates	No. of House-holds	% of Total Hhds.	Index
Conservative Homebodies	1,293	0.56	15
High Rise Sunsets	15,656	6.73	470
Young Urban Professionals	3,876	1.67	88
Young Urban Mix	23,337	10.03	473
Young Urban Intelligentsia	2,663	1.14	75
Young City Singles	1,596	0.69	30
Urban Bohemia	589	0.25	22
Old Leafy Towns	70	0.03	1
Town Renters	1,081	0.46	54
Struggling Downtowns	86	0.04	1
Aged Pensioners	2,328	1.00	75
Big City Stress	7,504	3.22	286
Old Grey Towers	3,507	1.51	272

FINANCIAL PSYTE

2001 Estimates	No. of House-holds	% of Total Hhds.	Index
Platinum Estates	11,314	4.86	603
Four Star Investors	20,241	8.70	173
Successful Suburbanites	11,997	5.15	78
Canadian Comfort	24,812	10.66	110
Urban Heights	20,132	8.65	201
Miners & Credit-Liners	803	0.35	11
Mortgages & Minivans	585	0.25	4
Dollars & Sense	44,382	19.07	729
Bills & Wills	24,700	10.61	128
Revolving Renters	15,656	6.73	146
Young Urban Struggle	3,252	1.40	30
Towering Debt	39,695	17.06	219
NSF	7,504	3.22	91
Senior Survivors	5,835	2.51	133

HOME LANGUAGE

2001 Estimates:		% Total
English	392,996	61.71
French	2,763	0.43
Arabic	6,704	1.05
Armenian	2,676	0.42
Bengali	879	0.14
Chinese	41,066	6.45
Croatian	625	0.10
Czech	366	0.06
Estonian	625	0.10
Finnish	417	0.07
German	1,290	0.20
Greek	4,702	0.74
Gujarati	3,050	0.48
Hebrew	1,973	0.31
Hindi	1,306	0.21
Hungarian	2,778	0.44
Italian	32,906	5.17
Japanese	1,165	0.18
Khmer (Cambodian)	895	0.14
Korean	6,640	1.04
Lao	506	0.08
Macedonian	906	0.14
Pashto	397	0.06
Persian (Farsi)	9,167	1.44
Polish	5,732	0.90

Ontario

North York

(City)
Toronto CMA
(Cont'd)

2001 Estimates:		% Total
Portuguese	2,832	0.44
Punjabi	6,123	0.96
Romanian	3,129	0.49
Russian	10,798	1.70
Serbian	1,653	0.26
Serbo-Croatian	542	0.09
Slovak	321	0.05
Spanish	16,829	2.64
Tagalog (Pilipino)	6,695	1.05
Tamil	8,754	1.37
Turkish	994	0.16
Ukrainian	420	0.07
Urdu	3,407	0.53
Vietnamese	6,948	1.09
Yiddish	1,328	0.21
Other Languages	11,102	1.74
Multiple Responses	32,480	5.10
Total	636,885	100.00

BUILDING PERMITS

	1999	1998	1997
			$000
Value	n.a.	n.a.	562,580

HOMES BUILT

	1999	1998	1997
No.	n.a.	n.a.	1,230

TAXATION

Income Class:	1997	% Total
Under $5,000	56,850	16.62
$5,000-$10,000	43,880	12.83
$10,000-$15,000	46,870	13.70
$15,000-$20,000	33,120	9.68
$20,000-$25,000	27,160	7.94
$25,000-$30,000	24,980	7.30
$30,000-$40,000	38,620	11.29
$40,000-$50,000	23,880	6.98
$50,000 +	46,720	13.66
Total Returns, No.	342,080	
Total Income, $000	10,420,278	
Total Taxable Returns	220,900	
Total Tax, $000	2,253,083	
Average Income, $	30,462	
Average Tax, $	10,200	

VITAL STATISTICS

	1997	1996	1995	1994
Births	6,540	6,750	6,994	6,703
Deaths	3,672	3,537	3,641	3,520
Natural Increase	2,868	3,213	3,353	3,183
Marriages	3,078	3,170	3,322	3,496

Note: Latest available data.

MEDIA INFO
see Toronto, CMA

Oakville

(Town)
Toronto CMA

In Halton Regional Municipality.

POPULATION

July 1, 2001 Estimate	147,218
% Cdn. Total	0.47
% Change, '96 -'01	11.27
Avg. Annual Growth Rate, %	2.16
2003 Projected Population	154,387
2006 Projected Population	165,024
2001 Households Estimate	50,761
2003 Projected Households	53,522
2006 Projected Households	57,838

INCOME

% Above/Below National Average	+54
2001 Total Income Estimate	$4,770,650,000
% Cdn. Total	0.73
2001 Average Hhld. Income	$94,000
2001 Per Capita	$32,400
2003 Projected Total Income	$5,310,730,000
2006 Projected Total Income	$6,244,280,000

RETAIL SALES

% Above/Below National Average	-2
2001 Retail Sales Estimate	$1,291,750,000
% Cdn. Total	0.46
2001 per Household	$25,400
2001 per Capita	$8,800
2001 No. of Establishments	963
2003 Projected Retail Sales	$1,466,190,000
2006 Projected Retail Sales	$1,735,800,000

POPULATION

2001 Estimates:		
Total		147,218
Male		72,208
Female		75,010
Age Groups	Male	Female
0-4	4,775	4,511
5-9	5,405	4,989
10-14	5,516	5,161
15-19	5,181	4,898
20-24	4,804	4,701
25-29	4,611	4,718
30-34	5,028	5,402
35-39	5,749	6,249
40-44	5,951	6,495
45-49	5,637	6,086
50-54	4,964	5,193
55-59	4,072	4,107
60-64	3,230	3,294
65-69	2,573	2,757
70+	4,712	6,449

DAYTIME POPULATION

2001 Estimates:	
Working Population	61,509
At Home Population	63,043
Total	124,552

INCOME

2001 Estimates:	
Avg. Household Income	$93,983
Avg. Family Income	$100,208
Per Capita Income	$32,405
Male:	
Avg. Employment Income	$58,499
Avg. Employment Income (Full Time)	$74,257
Female:	
Avg. Employment Income	$29,913
Avg. Employment Income (Full Time)	$43,449

DISPOSABLE & DISCRETIONARY INCOME

2001 Estimates:	Per Hhld.
Disposable Income	$74,668
Discretionary Income 1 (minus Food & Shelter)	$55,676
Discretionary Income 2 (minus Food, Shelter, & Other Expenditures)	$43,597

LIQUID ASSETS

1999 Estimates:	Per Hhld.
Equity Investments	$202,176
Interest Bearing Investments	$129,287
Total Liquid Assets	$331,463

CREDIT DATA

July 2 '00:	
Pool of Credit	$2,053,730,974
Revolving Credit, No.	322,880
Fixed Loans, No.	80,555
Avg. Credit Limit, per Person	$16,666
Avg. Spent, per Person	$7,018
Satisfactory Ratings, No. per Person	3.18
Avg. No. of Cards, per Person	1.29

LABOUR FORCE

2001 Estimates:	
Male:	
In the Labour Force	45,707
Participation Rate	80.9
Employed	44,790
Unemployed	917
Unemployment Rate	2.0
Not in Labour Force	10,805
Female:	
In the Labour Force	40,182
Participation Rate	66.6
Employed	39,006
Unemployed	1,176
Unemployment Rate	2.9
Not in Labour Force	20,167

OCCUPATIONS BY MAJOR GROUPS

2001 Estimates:	Male	Female
Management	10,419	4,229
Business, Finance & Admin.	6,609	12,813
Natural & Applied Sciences & Related	4,362	1,160
Health	734	2,756
Social Sciences, Gov't Services & Religion	1,232	1,515
Education	970	2,565
Arts, Culture, Recreation & Sport	998	1,560
Sales & Service	9,946	11,069
Trades, Transport & Equipment Operators & Related	6,470	354
Primary Industries	580	101
Processing, Mfg. & Utilities	2,962	1,306

LEVEL OF SCHOOLING

2001 Estimates:	
Population 15 years +	116,861
Less than Grade 9	5,949
Grades 9-13 w/o Certif.	19,713
Grade 9-13 with Certif.	14,869
Trade Certif. /Dip.	3,424
Non-Univ. w/o Certif./Dip.	7,194
Non-Univ. with Certif./Dip.	22,178
Univ. w/o Degree	14,466
Univ. w/o Degree/Certif.	7,134
Univ. with Certif.	7,332
Univ. with Degree	29,068

AVERAGE HOUSEHOLD EXPENDITURES

2001 Estimates:	
Food	$8,725
Shelter	$13,803
Clothing	$3,585
Transportation	$9,396
Health & Personal Care	$2,751
Recr'n, Read'g & Education	$5,806
Taxes & Securities	$26,885
Other	$12,431
Total Expenditures	$83,382

PRIVATE HOUSEHOLDS

2001 Estimates:	
Private Households, Total	50,761
Pop. in Private Households	145,332
Average no. per Household	2.9

FAMILIES

2001 Estimates:	
Families in Private Households	42,311
Husband-Wife Families	38,089
Lone-Parent Families	4,222
Aver. No. Persons per Family	3.2
Aver. No. Sons/Daughters at Home	1.3

HOUSING

2001 Estimates:	
Occupied Private Dwellings	50,761
Owned	38,847
Rented	11,914
Single-Detached House	32,695
Semi-Detached House	1,746
Row Houses	6,098
Apartment, 5+ Storeys	7,332
Owned Apartment, 5+ Storeys	1,741
Apartment, 5 or Fewer Storeys	2,300
Apartment, Detached Duplex	548
Other Single-Attached	42

VEHICLES

2001 Estimates:	
Model Yrs. '81-'96, No.	64,139
% Total	69.28
Model Yrs. '97-'98, No.	16,673
% Total	18.01
'99 Vehicles registered in Model Yr. '99, No.	11,771
% Total	12.71
Total No. '81-'99	92,583

LEGAL MARITAL STATUS

2001 Estimates: (Age 15+)	
Single (Never Married)	30,010
Legally Married (Not Separated)	72,519
Legally Married (Separated)	3,092
Widowed	5,433
Divorced	5,807

PSYTE CATEGORIES

2001 Estimates	No. of House-holds	% of Total Hhds.	Index
Canadian Establishment	847	1.67	1,003
The Affluentials	2,099	4.14	647
Urban Gentry	1,164	2.29	128
Suburban Executives	11,095	21.86	1,525
Mortgaged in Suburbia	4,225	8.32	599
Technocrafts & Bureaucrats	6,906	13.60	484
Boomers & Teens	947	1.87	104
Stable Suburban Families	4,333	8.54	655
Old Bungalow Burbs	932	1.84	111
Suburban Nesters	5,229	10.30	643
Brie & Chablis	497	0.98	109
Aging Erudites	445	0.88	58
Satellite Suburbs	881	1.74	60
Kindergarten Boom	415	0.82	31
Blue Collar Winners	656	1.29	51
Europa	54	0.11	9
High Rise Melting Pot	146	0.29	19
Conservative Homebodies	611	1.20	33

Oakville
(Town)
Toronto CMA
(Cont'd)

2001 Estimates	No. of House -holds	% of Total Hhds.	Index
High Rise Sunsets	1,619	3.19	223
Young Urban Mix	2,624	5.17	244
University Enclaves	2,773	5.46	268
Young City Singles	803	1.58	69
Town Renters	126	0.25	29
Struggling Downtowns	465	0.92	29
Old Grey Towers	516	1.02	184

FINANÇIAL P$YTE

2001 Estimates	No. of House -holds	% of Total Hhds.	Index
Platinum Estates	2,946	5.80	720
Four Star Investors	13,206	26.02	518
Successful Suburbanites	15,464	30.46	459
Canadian Comfort	6,766	13.33	137
Urban Heights	942	1.86	43
Miners & Credit-Liners	932	1.84	58
Mortgages & Minivans	415	0.82	12
Dollars & Sense	54	0.11	4
Bills & Wills	3,235	6.37	77
Revolving Renters	1,619	3.19	69
Young Urban Struggle	2,773	5.46	115
Towering Debt	1,540	3.03	39
Senior Survivors	516	1.02	54

HOME LANGUAGE

2001 Estimates:		% Total
English	131,515	89.33
French	1,187	0.81
Arabic	346	0.24
Chinese	1,512	1.03
Croatian	773	0.53
Czech	141	0.10
German	321	0.22
Greek	184	0.12
Gujarati	123	0.08
Hungarian	151	0.10
Italian	1,264	0.86
Japanese	82	0.06
Korean	229	0.16
Lithuanian	105	0.07
Persian (Farsi)	97	0.07
Polish	1,067	0.72
Portuguese	1,787	1.21
Punjabi	838	0.57
Serbian	473	0.32
Spanish	330	0.22
Tagalog (Pilipino)	125	0.08
Ukrainian	285	0.19
Urdu	241	0.16
Vietnamese	211	0.14
Other Languages	1,077	0.73
Multiple Responses	2,754	1.87
Total	147,218	100.00

BUILDING PERMITS

	1999	1998 $000	1997
Value	524,772	396,962	354,261

HOMES BUILT

	1999	1998	1997
No	1,576	776	1,232

TAXATION

Income Class:	1997	% Total
Under $5,000	10,380	11.23
$5,000-$10,000	8,790	9.51
$10,000-$15,000	8,620	9.33
$15,000-$20,000	6,590	7.13
$20,000-$25,000	6,040	6.54
$25,000-$30,000	6,090	6.59
$30,000-$40,000	11,010	11.91
$40,000-$50,000	8,280	8.96
$50,000 +	26,620	28.81
Total Returns, No.	92,410	
Total Income, $000	4,382,613	
Total Taxable Returns	71,790	
Total Tax, $000	1,170,012	
Average Income, $	47,426	
Average Tax, $	16,298	

VITAL STATISTICS

	1997	1996	1995	1994
Births	1,619	1,597	1,624	1,700
Deaths	656	634	674	631
Natural Increase	963	963	950	1,069
Marriages	641	668	687	594

Note: Latest available data.

MEDIA INFO
see Toronto, CMA

Orangeville
(Town)
Toronto CMA

In Dufferin County.

POPULATION

July 1, 2001 Estimate	25,774
% Cdn. Total	0.08
% Change, '96 -'01	16.37
Avg. Annual Growth Rate, %	3.08
2003 Projected Population	27,883
2006 Projected Population	31,150
2001 Households Estimate	8,873
2003 Projected Households	9,635
2006 Projected Households	10,902

INCOME

% Above/Below National Average	+1
2001 Total Income Estimate	$551,550,000
% Cdn. Total	0.08
2001 Average Hhld. Income	$62,200
2001 Per Capita	$21,400
2003 Projected Total Income	$635,780,000
2006 Projected Total Income	$789,000,000

RETAIL SALES

% Above/Below National Average	-22
2001 Retail Sales Estimate	$180,890,000
% Cdn. Total	0.06
2001 per Household	$20,400
2001 per Capita	$7,000
2001 No. of Establishments	190
2003 Projected Retail Sales	$210,040,000
2006 Projected Retail Sales	$255,670,000

POPULATION

2001 Estimates:		
Total		25,774
Male		12,666
Female		13,108
Age Groups	Male	Female
0-4	1,001	955
5-9	1,117	1,080
10-14	1,073	1,017
15-19	944	891
20-24	842	819
25-29	890	906
30-34	1,109	1,156
35-39	1,218	1,248
40-44	1,066	1,098
45-49	874	907
50-54	701	714
55-59	533	538
60-64	399	404
65-69	302	328
70+	597	1,047

DAYTIME POPULATION

2001 Estimates:	
Working Population	7,923
At Home Population	11,313
Total	19,236

INCOME

2001 Estimates:	
Avg. Household Income	$62,161
Avg. Family Income	$66,442
Per Capita Income	$21,400
Male:	
Avg. Employment Income	$39,382
Avg. Employment Income (Full Time)	$48,138
Female:	
Avg. Employment Income	$23,206
Avg. Employment Income (Full Time)	$33,166

Ontario

DISPOSABLE & DISCRETIONARY INCOME

2001 Estimates:	Per Hhld.
Disposable Income	$51,257
Discretionary Income 1 (minus Food & Shelter)	$36,218
Discretionary Income 2 (minus Food, Shelter, & Other Expenditures)	$26,768

LIQUID ASSETS

1999 Estimates:	Per Hhld.
Equity Investments	$81,275
Interest Bearing Investments	$74,836
Total Liquid Assets	$156,111

CREDIT DATA

July 2000:	
Pool of Credit	$301,906,226
Revolving Credit, No.	48,160
Fixed Loans, No.	17,960
Avg. Credit Limit, per Person	$14,185
Avg. Spent, per Person	$7,201
Satisfactory Ratings, No. per Person	3.01
Avg. No. of Cards, per Person	1.08

LABOUR FORCE

2001 Estimates:	
Male:	
In the Labour Force	8,075
Participation Rate	85.2
Employed	7,840
Unemployed	235
Unemployment Rate	2.9
Not in Labour Force	1,400
Female:	
In the Labour Force	6,752
Participation Rate	67.1
Employed	6,472
Unemployed	280
Unemployment Rate	4.1
Not in Labour Force	3,304

OCCUPATIONS BY MAJOR GROUPS

2001 Estimates:	Male	Female
Management	819	289
Business, Finance & Admin.	720	2,139
Natural & Applied Sciences & Related	632	76
Health	22	526
Social Sciences, Gov't Services & Religion	35	157
Education	226	384
Arts, Culture, Recreation & Sport	111	126
Sales & Service	1,739	2,235
Trades, Transport & Equipment Operators & Related	2,246	144
Primary Industries	161	24
Processing, Mfg. & Utilities	1,191	481

Ontario

Orangeville
(Town)
Toronto CMA
(Cont'd)

LEVEL OF SCHOOLING

2001 Estimates:
Population 15 years +	19,531
Less than Grade 9	1,000
Grades 9-13 w/o Certif.	5,058
Grade 9-13 with Certif.	3,621
Trade Certif. /Dip.	732
Non-Univ. w/o Certif./Dip.	1,560
Non-Univ. with Certif./Dip.	4,342
Univ. w/o Degree	1,551
Univ. w/o Degree/Certif.	758
Univ. with Certif.	793
Univ. with Degree	1,667

AVERAGE HOUSEHOLD EXPENDITURES

2001 Estimates:
Food	$6,928
Shelter	$10,400
Clothing	$2,385
Transportation	$7,350
Health & Personal Care	$2,063
Recr'n, Read'g & Education	$4,309
Taxes & Securities	$15,759
Other	$9,482
Total Expenditures	$58,676

PRIVATE HOUSEHOLDS

2001 Estimates:
Private Households, Total	8,873
Pop. in Private Households	25,360
Average no. per Household	2.9

FAMILIES

2001 Estimates:
Families in Private Households	7,229
Husband-Wife Families	6,258
Lone-Parent Families	971
Aver. No. Persons per Family	3.2
Aver. No. Sons/Daughters at Home	1.4

HOUSING

2001 Estimates:
Occupied Private Dwellings	8,873
Owned	6,399
Rented	2,474
Single-Detached House	4,833
Semi-Detached House	1,444
Row Houses	841
Apartment, 5+ Storeys	479
Owned Apartment, 5+ Storeys	100
Apartment, 5 or Fewer Storeys	1,139
Apartment, Detached Duplex	113
Other Single-Attached	24

VEHICLES

2001 Estimates:
Model Yrs. '81-'96, No.	11,064
% Total	70.15
Model Yrs. '97-'98, No.	2,590
% Total	16.42
'99 Vehicles registered in Model Yr. '99, No.	2,119
% Total	13.43
Total No. '81-'99	15,773

LEGAL MARITAL STATUS

2001 Estimates: (Age 15+)
Single (Never Married)	4,891
Legally Married (Not Separated)	11,502
Legally Married (Separated)	784
Widowed	1,111
Divorced	1,243

PSYTE CATEGORIES

2001 Estimates	No. of House -holds	% of Total Hhds.	Index
Mortgaged in Suburbia	873	9.84	708
Technocrafts & Bureaucrats	504	5.68	202
Satellite Suburbs	2,216	24.97	871
Blue Collar Winners	294	3.31	132
Old Towns' New Fringe	2,312	26.06	666
Old Leafy Towns	431	4.86	190
Nesters & Young Homesteaders	1,883	21.22	909
Struggling Downtowns	103	1.16	37
Aged Pensioners	171	1.93	145

FINANCIAL P$YTE

2001 Estimates	No. of House -holds	% of Total Hhds.	Index
Successful Suburbanites	1,377	15.52	234
Canadian Comfort	2,510	28.29	291
Tractors & Tradelines	2,312	26.06	456
Bills & Wills	431	4.86	59
Revolving Renters	1,883	21.22	461
Towering Debt	103	1.16	15
Senior Survivors	171	1.93	102

HOME LANGUAGE

2001 Estimates:		% Total
English	25,426	98.65
French	74	0.29
Chinese	53	0.21
German	22	0.09
Greek	29	0.11
Hindi	13	0.05
Hungarian	23	0.09
Korean	21	0.08
Portuguese	17	0.07
Urdu	18	0.07
Other Languages	22	0.09
Multiple Responses	56	0.22
Total	25,774	100.00

BUILDING PERMITS

	1999	1998 $000	1997
Value	58,091	32,367	43,298

HOMES BUILT

	1999	1998	1997
No	285	236	185

TAXATION

Income Class	1997	% Total
Under $5,000	2,690	12.62
$5,000-$10,000	2,230	10.46
$10,000-$15,000	2,460	11.54
$15,000-$20,000	1,810	8.49
$20,000-$25,000	1,570	7.36
$25,000-$30,000	1,590	7.46
$30,000-$40,000	2,850*	13.37
$40,000-$50,000	2,110	9.90
$50,000 +	4,010	18.81
Total Returns, No.	21,320	
Total Income, $000	676,979	
Total Taxable Returns	16,010	
Total Tax, $000	140,150	
Average Income, $	31,753	
Average Tax, $	8,754	

VITAL STATISTICS

	1997	1996	1995	1994
Births	424	464	480	475
Deaths	165	164	146	156
Natural Increase	259	300	334	319
Marriages	136	166	175	123

Note: Latest available data.

MEDIA INFO
see Toronto, CMA

Pickering
(City)
Toronto CMA

In Durham Regional Municipality.

POPULATION

July 1, 2001 Estimate	93,602
% Cdn. Total	0.30
% Change, '96 -'01	14.96
Avg. Annual Growth Rate, %	2.83
2003 Projected Population	99,494
2006 Projected Population	107,935
2001 Households Estimate	29,355
2003 Projected Households	31,501
2006 Projected Households	34,792

INCOME

% Above/Below National Average	+25
2001 Total Income Estimate	$2,459,880,000
% Cdn. Total	0.37
2001 Average Hhld. Income	$83,800
2001 Per Capita	$26,300
2003 Projected Total Income	$2,782,560,000
2006 Projected Total Income	$3,329,620,000

RETAIL SALES

% Above/Below National Average	-7
2001 Retail Sales Estimate	$779,670,000
% Cdn. Total	0.28
2001 per Household	$26,600
2001 per Capita	$8,300
2001 No. of Establishments	510
2003 Projected Retail Sales	$899,870,000
2006 Projected Retail Sales	$1,084,960,000

POPULATION

2001 Estimates:
Total		93,602
Male		46,328
Female		47,274
Age Groups	Male	Female
0-4	3,217	3,062
5-9	3,682	3,531
10-14	3,910	3,724
15-19	3,692	3,509
20-24	3,220	3,109
25-29	2,935	2,995
30-34	3,382	3,637
35-39	3,948	4,285
40-44	4,097	4,376
45-49	3,905	3,996
50-54	3,225	3,208
55-59	2,360	2,321
60-64	1,678	1,667
65-69	1,230	1,286
70+	1,847	2,568

DAYTIME POPULATION

2001 Estimates:
Working Population	27,450
At Home Population	39,589
Total	67,039

INCOME

2001 Estimates:
Avg. Household Income	$83,798
Avg. Family Income	$82,759
Per Capita Income	$26,280
Male:	
Avg. Employment Income	$47,264
Avg. Employment Income (Full Time)	$59,617
Female:	
Avg. Employment Income	$29,244
Avg. Employment Income (Full Time)	$40,415

DISPOSABLE & DISCRETIONARY INCOME

2001 Estimates:	Per Hhld.
Disposable Income	$68,676
Discretionary Income 1 (minus Food & Shelter)	$51,155
Discretionary Income 2 (minus Food, Shelter, & Other Expenditures)	$39,691

LIQUID ASSETS

1999 Estimates:	Per Hhld.
Equity Investments	$137,943
Interest Bearing Investments	$105,965
Total Liquid Assets	$243,908

CREDIT DATA

July 2000:	
Pool of Credit	$1,173,679,693
Revolving Credit, No.	194,112
Fixed Loans, No.	57,825
Avg. Credit Limit, per Person.	$15,576
Avg. Spent, per Person	$6,864
Satisfactory Ratings, No. per Person	3.22
Avg. No. of Cards, per Person	1.23

LABOUR FORCE

2001 Estimates:	
Male:	
In the Labour Force	29,597
Participation Rate	83.3
Employed	28,776
Unemployed	821
Unemployment Rate	2.8
Not in Labour Force	5,922
Female:	
In the Labour Force	25,804
Participation Rate	69.8
Employed	24,604
Unemployed	1,200
Unemployment Rate	4.7
Not in Labour Force	11,153

OCCUPATIONS BY MAJOR GROUPS

2001 Estimates:	Male	Female
Management	4,835	1,980
Business, Finance & Admin.	3,782	10,031
Natural & Applied Sciences & Related	2,877	714
Health	279	1,824
Social Sciences, Gov't Services & Religion	424	790
Education	807	1,278
Arts, Culture, Recreation & Sport	625	733
Sales & Service	6,505	6,562
Trades, Transport & Equipment Operators & Related	6,134	313
Primary Industries	548	88
Processing, Mfg. & Utilities	2,278	790

LEVEL OF SCHOOLING

2001 Estimates:	
Population 15 years +	72,476
Less than Grade 9	2,829
Grades 9-13 w/o Certif.	14,968
Grade 9-13 with Certif.	11,855
Trade Certif. /Dip.	2,715
Non-Univ. w/o Certif./Dip.	5,602
Non-Univ. with Certif./Dip.	15,608
Univ. w/o Degree	8,173
Univ. w/o Degree/Certif.	4,003
Univ. with Certif.	4,170
Univ. with Degree	10,726

Pickering
(City)
Toronto CMA
(Cont'd)

AVERAGE HOUSEHOLD EXPENDITURES

2001 Estimates:

Food	$8,149
Shelter	$12,369
Clothing	$3,182
Transportation	$9,023
Health & Personal Care	$2,476
Recr'n, Read'g & Education	$5,425
Taxes & Securities	$23,980
Other	$11,275
Total Expenditures	$75,879

PRIVATE HOUSEHOLDS

2001 Estimates:

Private Households, Total	29,355
Pop. in Private Households	92,723
Average no. per Household	3.2

FAMILIES

2001 Estimates:

Families in Private Households	26,752
Husband-Wife Families	23,421
Lone-Parent Families	3,331
Aver. No. Persons per Family	3.3
Aver. No. Sons/Daughters at Home	1.4

HOUSING

2001 Estimates:

Occupied Private Dwellings	29,355
Owned	24,651
Rented	4,704
Single-Detached House	20,790
Semi-Detached House	2,133
Row Houses	2,904
Apartment, 5+ Storeys	1,845
Owned Apartment, 5+ Storeys	854
Apartment, 5 or Fewer Storeys	694
Apartment, Detached Duplex	941
Other Single-Attached	13
Movable Dwellings	35

VEHICLES

2001 Estimates:

Model Yrs. '81-'96, No.	41,410
% Total	76.19
Model Yrs. '97-'98, No.	7,211
% Total	13.27
'99 Vehicles registered in Model Yr. '99, No.	5,732
% Total	10.55
Total No. '81-'99	54,353

LEGAL MARITAL STATUS

2001 Estimates: (Age 15+)

Single (Never Married)	19,512
Legally Married (Not Separated)	43,826
Legally Married (Separated)	2,338
Widowed	2,822
Divorced	3,978

PSYTE CATEGORIES

2001 Estimates	No. of House-holds	% of Total Hhds.	Index
Suburban Executives	1,964	6.69	467
Mortgaged in Suburbia	2,880	9.81	706
Technocrafts & Bureaucrats	5,092	17.35	616
Boomers & Teens	6,035	20.56	1,147
Stable Suburban Families	1,042	3.55	272
Old Bungalow Burbs	2,846	9.70	585
Brie & Chablis	573	1.95	218
Satellite Suburbs	4,550	15.50	540
Kindergarten Boom	1,436	4.89	187
Blue Collar Winners	1,042	3.55	141
Conservative Homebodies	919	3.13	87
Young Urban Mix	475	1.62	76
University Enclaves	251	0.86	42
Young City Singles	155	0.53	23

FINANCIAL PSYTE

FINANCIAL PSYTE

2001 Estimates	No. of House-holds	% of Total Hhds.	Index
Four Star Investors	7,999	27.25	542
Successful Suburbanites	9,014	30.71	463
Canadian Comfort	5,592	19.05	196
Urban Heights	573	1.95	45
Miners & Credit-Liners	2,846	9.70	306
Mortgages & Minivans	1,436	4.89	74
Bills & Wills	1,394	4.75	57
Young Urban Struggle	251	0.86	18
Towering Debt	155	0.53	7

HOME LANGUAGE

2001 Estimates:		% Total
English	87,425	93.40
French	321	0.34
Arabic	298	0.32
Chinese	789	0.84
German	207	0.22
Greek	143	0.15
Gujarati	210	0.22
Hindi	48	0.05
Italian	302	0.32
Korean	170	0.18
Macedonian	140	0.15
Persian (Farsi)	92	0.10
Polish	104	0.11
Portuguese	158	0.17
Punjabi	336	0.36
Slovak	95	0.10
Spanish	306	0.33
Tagalog (Pilipino)	197	0.21
Tamil	62	0.07
Urdu	315	0.34
Vietnamese	63	0.07
Other Languages	402	0.43
Multiple Responses	1,419	1.52
Total	93,602	100.00

BUILDING PERMITS

	1999	1998 $000	1997
Value	159,384	90,784	116,546

HOMES BUILT

	1999	1998	1997
No.	700	523	757

TAXATION

Income Class:	1997	% Total
Under $5,000	6,560	12.12
$5,000-$10,000	5,130	9.48
$10,000-$15,000	5,030	9.29
$15,000-$20,000	3,810	7.04
$20,000-$25,000	3,570	6.60
$25,000-$30,000	3,750	6.93
$30,000-$40,000	7,810	14.43
$40,000-$50,000	5,990	11.07
$50,000 +	12,470	23.04
Total Returns, No.	54,120	
Total Income, $000	1,920,841	
Total Taxable Returns	41,570	
Total Tax, $000	420,813	
Average Income, $	35,492	
Average Tax, $	10,123	

VITAL STATISTICS

	1997	1996	1995	1994
Births	1,111	1,085	1,085	1,120
Deaths	315	319	299	277
Natural Increase	796	766	786	843
Marriages	206	209	195	204

Note: Latest available data.

MEDIA INFO

see Toronto, CMA

Richmond Hill
(Town)
Toronto CMA

In York Regional Municipality.

POPULATION

July 1, 2001 Estimate	136,317
% Cdn. Total	0.44
% Change, '96 -'01	29.80
Avg. Annual Growth Rate, %	5.35
2003 Projected Population	151,719
2006 Projected Population	176,090
2001 Households Estimate	43,525
2003 Projected Households	48,564
2006 Projected Households	56,691

INCOME

% Above/Below National Average	+21
2001 Total Income Estimate	$3,477,980,000
% Cdn. Total	0.53
2001 Average Hhld. Income	$79,900
2001 Per Capita	$25,500
2003 Projected Total Income	$4,121,790,000
2006 Projected Total Income	$5,280,640,000

RETAIL SALES

% Above/Below National Average	-28
2001 Retail Sales Estimate	$874,460,000
% Cdn. Total	0.31
2001 per Household	$20,100
2001 per Capita	$6,400
2001 No. of Establishments	1,082
2003 Projected Retail Sales	$1,053,410,000
2006 Projected Retail Sales	$1,354,400,000

POPULATION

2001 Estimates:

Total	136,317
Male	66,725
Female	69,592

Age Groups	Male	Female
0-4	4,667	4,492
5-9	5,039	4,753
10-14	5,193	4,736
15-19	4,910	4,630
20-24	4,591	4,624
25-29	4,779	5,001
30-34	5,324	5,745
35-39	5,688	6,347
40-44	5,540	6,217
45-49	5,232	5,637
50-54	4,348	4,458
55-59	3,374	3,297
60-64	2,646	2,584
65-69	2,026	2,171
70+	3,368	4,900

DAYTIME POPULATION

2001 Estimates:

Working Population	38,753
At Home Population	63,944
Total	102,697

INCOME

2001 Estimates:

Avg. Household Income	$79,908
Avg. Family Income	$80,367
Per Capita Income	$25,514
Male:	
Avg. Employment Income	$46,103
Avg. Employment Income (Full Time)	$59,262
Female:	
Avg. Employment Income	$30,333
Avg. Employment Income (Full Time)	$42,801

Ontario

DISPOSABLE & DISCRETIONARY INCOME

2001 Estimates:	*Per Hhld.*
Disposable Income	$65,130
Discretionary Income 1 (minus Food & Shelter)	$47,972
Discretionary Income 2 (minus Food, Shelter, & Other Expenditures)	$36,701

LIQUID ASSETS

1999 Estimates:	*Per Hhld.*
Equity Investments	$150,754
Interest Bearing Investments	$105,388
Total Liquid Assets	$256,142

CREDIT DATA

July 2000:

Pool of Credit	$1,655,428,033
Revolving Credit, No.	301,271
Fixed Loans, No.	61,120
Avg. Credit Limit, per Person	$14,162
Avg. Spent, per Person	$5,494
Satisfactory Ratings, No. per Person	3.01
Avg. No. of Cards, per Person	1.31

LABOUR FORCE

2001 Estimates:

Male:	
In the Labour Force	39,190
Participation Rate	75.6
Employed	37,921
Unemployed	1,269
Unemployment Rate	3.2
Not in Labour Force	12,636
Female:	
In the Labour Force	34,876
Participation Rate	62.7
Employed	33,583
Unemployed	1,293
Unemployment Rate	3.7
Not in Labour Force	20,735

OCCUPATIONS BY MAJOR GROUPS

2001 Estimates:	*Male*	*Female*
Management	7,670	3,186
Business, Finance & Admin.	5,317	12,700
Natural & Applied Sciences & Related	4,161	1,219
Health	1,114	2,084
Social Sciences, Gov't Services & Religion	1,195	1,129
Education	739	1,878
Arts, Culture, Recreation & Sport	962	1,018
Sales & Service	8,405	8,921
Trades, Transport & Equipment Operators & Related	6,051	628
Primary Industries	815	167
Processing, Mfg. & Utilities	1,908	862

Ontario

Richmond Hill
(Town)
Toronto CMA
(Cont'd)

LEVEL OF SCHOOLING

2001 Estimates:
Population 15 years +	107,437
Less than Grade 9	9,116
Grades 9-13 w/o Certif.	20,024
Grade 9-13 with Certif.	13,560
Trade Certif. /Dip.	3,280
Non-Univ. w/o Certif./Dip.	6,745
Non-Univ. with Certif./Dip.	18,263
Univ. w/o Degree	12,547
Univ. w/o Degree/Certif.	6,520
Univ. with Certif.	6,027
Univ. with Degree	23,902

AVERAGE HOUSEHOLD EXPENDITURES

2001 Estimates:
Food	$7,906
Shelter	$12,262
Clothing	$3,090
Transportation	$9,016
Health & Personal Care	$2,380
Recr'n, Read'g & Education	$5,200
Taxes & Securities	$22,550
Other	$10,416
Total Expenditures	$72,820

PRIVATE HOUSEHOLDS

2001 Estimates:
Private Households, Total	43,525
Pop. in Private Households	135,124
Average no. per Household	3.1

FAMILIES

2001 Estimates:
Families in Private Households	38,377
Husband-Wife Families	34,456
Lone-Parent Families	3,921
Aver. No. Persons per Family	3.3
Aver. No. Sons/Daughters at Home	1.4

HOUSING

2001 Estimates:
Occupied Private Dwellings	43,525
Owned	33,089
Rented	10,436
Single-Detached House	29,745
Semi-Detached House	985
Row Houses	2,785
Apartment, 5+ Storeys	6,361
Owned Apartment, 5+ Storeys	2,783
Apartment, 5 or Fewer Storeys	2,605
Apartment, Detached Duplex	979
Other Single-Attached	65

VEHICLES

2001 Estimates:
Model Yrs. '81-'96, No.	50,689
% Total	70.47
Model Yrs. '97-'98, No.	12,302
% Total	17.10
'99 Vehicles registered in Model Yr. '99, No.	8,941
% Total	12.43
Total No. '81-'99	71,932

LEGAL MARITAL STATUS

2001 Estimates: (Age 15+)
Single (Never Married)	30,513
Legally Married (Not Separated)	65,112
Legally Married (Separated)	2,403
Widowed	4,816
Divorced	4,593

PSYTE CATEGORIES

2001 Estimates	No. of House-holds	% of Total Hhds.	Index
The Affluentials	732	1.68	263
Suburban Executives	4,517	10.38	724
Mortgaged in Suburbia	3,655	8.40	604
Technocrafts & Bureaucrats	3,928	9.02	321
Asian Heights	6,225	14.30	2,257
Boomers & Teens	6,150	14.13	788
Stable Suburban Families	637	1.46	112
Old Bungalow Burbs	1,258	2.89	174
Suburban Nesters	2,377	5.46	341
Brie & Chablis	2,379	5.47	610
Satellite Suburbs	1,038	2.38	83
Kindergarten Boom	125	0.29	11
Europa	567	1.30	105
Asian Mosaic	758	1.74	127
High Rise Melting Pot	1,101	2.53	169
Conservative Homebodies	2,239	5.14	143
High Rise Sunsets	1,234	2.84	198
Young Urban Mix	3,487	8.01	378
Town Renters	720	1.65	191
Aged Pensioners	181	0.42	31
Old Grey Towers	177	0.41	73

FINANCIAL P$YTE

2001 Estimates	No. of House-holds	% of Total Hhds.	Index
Platinum Estates	732	1.68	209
Four Star Investors	10,667	24.51	488
Successful Suburbanites	14,445	33.19	500
Canadian Comfort	3,415	7.85	81
Urban Heights	2,379	5.47	127
Miners & Credit-Liners	1,258	2.89	91
Mortgages & Minivans	125	0.29	4
Dollars & Sense	1,325	3.04	116
Bills & Wills	5,726	13.16	159
Revolving Renters	1,234	2.84	62
Towering Debt	1,821	4.18	54
Senior Survivors	358	0.82	44

HOME LANGUAGE

2001 Estimates:		% Total
English	97,371	71.43
French	495	0.36
Arabic	675	0.50
Armenian	350	0.26
Bengali	71	0.05
Chinese	21,942	16.10
Finnish	116	0.09
German	321	0.24
Greek	729	0.53
Gujarati	441	0.32
Hebrew	372	0.27
Hindi	187	0.14
Hungarian	295	0.22
Italian	2,958	2.17
Khmer (Cambodian)	137	0.10
Korean	461	0.34
Macedonian	166	0.12
Malay-Bahasa	80	0.06
Persian (Farsi)	1,090	0.80
Polish	224	0.16
Portuguese	204	0.15
Punjabi	240	0.18
Russian	650	0.48
Spanish	535	0.39
Tagalog (Pilipino)	264	0.19
Tamil	93	0.07
Turkish	75	0.06
Urdu	250	0.18
Vietnamese	76	0.06
Other Languages	1,142	0.84
Multiple Responses	4,307	3.16
Total	136,317	100.00

BUILDING PERMITS

	1999	1998 $000	1997
Value	522,490	399,159	474,514

HOMES BUILT

	1999	1998	1997
No.	2,570	2,211	1,132

TAXATION

Income Class:	1997	% Total
Under $5,000	13,530	17.06
$5,000-$10,000	9,480	11.95
$10,000-$15,000	8,470	10.68
$15,000-$20,000	6,200	7.82
$20,000-$25,000	5,310	6.69
$25,000-$30,000	5,270	6.64
$30,000-$40,000	9,410	11.86
$40,000-$50,000	6,580	8.29
$50,000 +	15,100	19.03
Total Returns, No.	79,330	
Total Income, $000	2,627,379	
Total Taxable Returns	54,740	
Total Tax, $000	580,671	
Average Income, $	33,120	
Average Tax, $	10,608	

VITAL STATISTICS

	1997	1996	1995	1994
Births	1,319	1,367	1,414	1,473
Deaths	437	418	409	380
Natural Increase	882	949	1,005	1,093
Marriages	354	341	391	392

Note: Latest available data.

MEDIA INFO
see Toronto, CMA

Scarborough
(City)
Toronto CMA

In Toronto Metropolitan Municipality. On Jan. 1, 1998, Scarborough, East York, Etobicoke, North York, Toronto and York amalgamated to form the new city of Toronto.

POPULATION

July 1, 2001 Estimate	612,581
% Cdn. Total	1.97
% Change, '96 -'01	6.16
Avg. Annual Growth Rate, %	1.20
2003 Projected Population	627,658
2006 Projected Population	649,887
2001 Households Estimate	206,807
2003 Projected Households	213,593
2006 Projected Households	223,719

INCOME

% Above/Below National Average	-8
2001 Total Income Estimate	$11,920,860,000
% Cdn. Total	1.82
2001 Average Hhld. Income	$57,600
2001 Per Capita	$19,500
2003 Projected Total Income	$13,035,910,000
2006 Projected Total Income	$14,904,350,000

RETAIL SALES

% Above/Below National Average	-16
2001 Retail Sales Estimate	$4,587,680,000
% Cdn. Total	1.65
2001 per Household	$22,200
2001 per Capita	$7,500
2001 No. of Establishments	3,423
2003 Projected Retail Sales	$5,083,620,000
2006 Projected Retail Sales	$5,835,950,000

POPULATION

2001 Estimates:

Total		612,581
Male		295,227
Female		317,354

Age Groups	Male	Female
0-4	20,346	19,146
5-9	20,430	19,269
10-14	19,716	18,505
15-19	19,656	18,283
20-24	20,163	19,288
25-29	20,689	21,299
30-34	22,707	24,131
35-39	24,063	25,698
40-44	23,044	25,243
45-49	21,452	24,006
50-54	18,672	20,995
55-59	15,615	17,684
60-64	13,547	15,518
65-69	12,025	14,233
70+	23,102	34,056

DAYTIME POPULATION

2001 Estimates:

Working Population	168,520
At Home Population	320,678
Total	489,198

INCOME

2001 Estimates:

Avg. Household Income	$57,642
Avg. Family Income	$57,749
Per Capita Income	$19,460
Male:	
Avg. Employment Income	$33,380
Avg. Employment Income (Full Time)	$44,168
Female:	
Avg. Employment Income	$25,472
Avg. Employment Income (Full Time)	$35,925

DISPOSABLE & DISCRETIONARY INCOME

2001 Estimates:	Per Hhld.
Disposable Income	$47,974
Discretionary Income 1 (minus Food & Shelter)	$33,624
Discretionary Income 2 (minus Food, Shelter, & Other Expenditures)	$24,702

LIQUID ASSETS

1999 Estimates:	Per Hhld.
Equity Investments	$82,779
Interest Bearing Investments	$71,285
Total Liquid Assets	$154,064

CREDIT DATA

July 2000:	
Pool of Credit	$5,939,830,185
Revolving Credit, No.	1,265,314
Fixed Loans, No.	275,422
Avg. Credit Limit, per Person	$10,415
Avg. Spent, per Person	$4,273
Satisfactory Ratings, No. per Person	2.62
Avg. No. of Cards, per Person	1.11

LABOUR FORCE

2001 Estimates:

Male:	
In the Labour Force	165,823
Participation Rate	70.6
Employed	153,969
Unemployed	11,854
Unemployment Rate	7.1
Not in Labour Force	68,912
Female:	
In the Labour Force	148,441
Participation Rate	57.0
Employed	135,137
Unemployed	13,304
Unemployment Rate	9.0
Not in Labour Force	111,993

OCCUPATIONS BY MAJOR GROUPS

2001 Estimates:	Male	Female
Management	15,963	7,011
Business, Finance & Admin.	25,336	54,883
Natural & Applied Sciences & Related	15,394	3,326
Health	2,295	9,835
Social Sciences, Gov't Services & Religion	2,538	3,587
Education	2,856	5,337
Arts, Culture, Recreation & Sport	3,791	3,610
Sales & Service	38,447	37,261
Trades, Transport & Equipment Operators & Related	31,292	1,853
Primary Industries	1,502	227
Processing, Mfg. & Utilities	18,904	12,492

LEVEL OF SCHOOLING

2001 Estimates:

Population 15 years +	495,169
Less than Grade 9	51,035
Grades 9-13 w/o Certif.	114,459
Grade 9-13 with Certif.	75,269
Trade Certif./Dip.	14,569
Non-Univ. w/o Certif./Dip.	34,871
Non-Univ. with Certif./Dip.	82,451
Univ. w/o Degree	51,761
Univ. w/o Degree/Certif.	25,569
Univ. with Certif.	26,192
Univ. with Degree	70,754

AVERAGE HOUSEHOLD EXPENDITURES

2001 Estimates:

Food	$6,658
Shelter	$10,009
Clothing	$2,336
Transportation	$6,949
Health & Personal Care	$1,972
Recr'n, Read'g & Education	$3,775
Taxes & Securities	$14,961
Other	$8,155
Total Expenditures	$54,815

PRIVATE HOUSEHOLDS

2001 Estimates:

Private Households, Total	206,807
Pop. in Private Households	604,870
Average no. per Household	2.9

FAMILIES

2001 Estimates:

Families in Private Households	171,563
Husband-Wife Families	138,798
Lone-Parent Families	32,765
Aver. No. Persons per Family	3.1
Aver. No. Sons/Daughters at Home	1.3

HOUSING

2001 Estimates:

Occupied Private Dwellings	206,807
Owned	119,899
Rented	86,908
Single-Detached House	90,705
Semi-Detached House	10,944
Row Houses	14,913
Apartment, 5+ Storeys	71,452
Owned Apartment, 5+ Storeys	14,042
Apartment, 5 or Fewer Storeys	9,705
Apartment, Detached Duplex	8,947
Other Single-Attached	141

VEHICLES

2001 Estimates:

Model Yrs. '81-'96, No.	222,349
% Total	78.07
Model Yrs. '97-'98, No.	35,963
% Total	12.63
'99 Vehicles registered in Model Yr. '99, No.	26,492
% Total	9.30
Total No. '81-'99	284,804

LEGAL MARITAL STATUS

2001 Estimates: (Age 15+)

Single (Never Married)	156,840
Legally Married (Not Separated)	262,217
Legally Married (Separated)	17,138
Widowed	31,520
Divorced	27,454

PSYTE CATEGORIES

2001 Estimates	No. of House-holds	% of Total Hhds.	Index
Urban Gentry	2,466	1.19	66
Suburban Executives	1,960	0.95	66
Technocrafts & Bureaucrats	2,750	1.33	47
Asian Heights	22,703	10.98	1,732
Boomers & Teens	3,425	1.66	92
Stable Suburban Families	11,446	5.53	425
Old Bungalow Burbs	6,342	3.07	185
Suburban Nesters	24,839	12.01	749
Brie & Chablis	9,730	4.70	525
Aging Erudites	1,891	0.91	61
Satellite Suburbs	10,067	4.87	170
Kindergarten Boom	4,641	2.24	86
Europa	1,467	0.71	57
Asian Mosaic	13,753	6.65	485
High Rise Melting Pot	28,964	14.01	934

Ontario

2001 Estimates	No. of House-holds	% of Total Hhds.	Index
Conservative			
Homebodies	15,849	7.66	213
High Rise Sunsets	3,245	1.57	110
Young Urban			
Professionals	443	0.21	11
Young Urban Mix	21,492	10.39	490
Young Urban			
Intelligentsia	34	0.02	1
University			
Enclaves	429	0.21	10
Young City Singles	269	0.13	6
Town Renters	3,265	1.58	183
Struggling			
Downtowns	1,108	0.54	17
Aged Pensioners	1,279	0.62	46
Big City Stress	6,278	3.04	269
Old Grey Towers	5,274	2.55	460

FINANCIAL P$YTE

2001 Estimates	No. of House-holds	% of Total Hhds.	Index
Four Star Investors	7,851	3.80	76
Successful Suburbanites	36,899	17.84	269
Canadian Comfort	34,906	16.88	174
Urban Heights	12,064	5.83	136
Miners & Credit-Liners	6,342	3.07	97
Mortgages & Minivans	4,641	2.24	34
Dollars & Sense	15,220	7.36	282
Bills & Wills	37,341	18.06	218
Revolving Renters	3,245	1.57	34
Young Urban Struggle	463	0.22	5
Towering Debt	33,606	16.25	208
NSF	6,278	3.04	86
Senior Survivors	6,553	3.17	168

HOME LANGUAGE

2001 Estimates:		% Total
English	402,812	65.76
French	2,148	0.35
Arabic	3,514	0.57
Armenian	2,105	0.34
Bengali	876	0.14
Chinese	78,511	12.82
Estonian	520	0.08
Finnish	341	0.06
German	1,071	0.17
Greek	7,347	1.20
Gujarati	4,320	0.71
Hindi	1,389	0.23
Hungarian	626	0.10
Italian	6,314	1.03
Japanese	515	0.08
Korean	2,597	0.42
Latvian (Lettish)	332	0.05
Macedonian	4,504	0.74
Malayalam	381	0.06
Pashto	447	0.07
Persian (Farsi)	4,623	0.75
Polish	3,550	0.58
Portuguese	1,356	0.22
Punjabi	3,030	0.49

Ontario

Scarborough

(City)
Toronto CMA
(Cont'd)

2001 Estimates:		% Total
Romanian	470	0.08
Russian	429	0.07
Serbian	510	0.08
Spanish	4,109	0.67
Tagalog (Pilipino)	9,238	1.51
Tamil	23,694	3.87
Turkish	342	0.06
Ukrainian	471	0.08
Urdu	3,982	0.65
Vietnamese	1,332	0.22
Other Languages	8,511	1.39
Multiple Responses	26,264	4.29
Total	612,581	100.00

BUILDING PERMITS

	1999	1998	1997
		$000	
Value	n.a.	n.a.	429,658

HOMES BUILT

	1999	1998	1997
No	n.a.	n.a.	1,939

TAXATION

Income Class:	1997	% Total
Under $5,000	71,150	17.85
$5,000-$10,000	53,530	13.43
$10,000-$15,000	54,130	13.58
$15,000-$20,000	37,580	9.43
$20,000-$25,000	31,780	7.97
$25,000-$30,000	29,890	7.50
$30,000-$40,000	48,810	12.25
$40,000-$50,000	29,090	7.30
$50,000 +	42,540	10.68
Total Returns, No.	398,500	
Total Income, $000	9,562,795	
Total Taxable Returns	252,920	
Total Tax, $000	1,663,039	
Average Income, $	23,997	
Average Tax, $	6,575	

VITAL STATISTICS

	1997	1996	1995	1994
Births	7,454	8,169	8,334	8,328
Deaths	3,451	3,474	3,491	3,300
Natural Increase	4,003	4,695	4,843	5,028
Marriages	3,190	3,352	3,417	3,743

Note: Latest available data.

MEDIA INFO
see Toronto, CMA

Toronto
(City)
Toronto CMA

In Toronto Metropolitan Municipality. On Jan. 1, 1998, Toronto, East York, Etobicoke, North York, Scarborough and York amalgamated to form the new city of Toronto.

POPULATION

July 1, 2001 Estimate	696,006
% Cdn. Total	2.24
% Change, '96 -'01	3.13
Avg. Annual Growth Rate, %	0.62
2003 Projected Population	702,612
2006 Projected Population	712,102
2001 Households Estimate	312,190
2003 Projected Households	317,624
2006 Projected Households	325,548

INCOME

% Above/Below National Average	+31
2001 Total Income Estimate	$19,157,170,000
% Cdn. Total	2.92
2001 Average Hhld. Income	$61,400
2001 Per Capita	$27,500
2003 Projected Total Income	$20,398,590,000
2006 Projected Total Income	$22,422,670,000

RETAIL SALES

% Above/Below National Average	+12
2001 Retail Sales Estimate	$6,952,510,000
% Cdn. Total	2.49
2001 per Household	$22,300
2001 per Capita	$10,000
2001 No. of Establishments	6,597
2003 Projected Retail Sales	$7,545,010,000
2006 Projected Retail Sales	$8,393,930,000

POPULATION

2001 Estimates:		
Total		696,006
Male		340,349
Female		355,657

Age Groups	Male	Female
0-4	23,000	21,622
5-9	19,061	18,007
10-14	16,116	15,361
15-19	15,290	14,437
20-24	18,053	17,900
25-29	25,991	27,109
30-34	34,619	34,545
35-39	36,237	34,934
40-44	31,856	31,738
45-49	27,357	28,248
50-54	22,484	23,423
55-59	17,405	18,351
60-64	14,099	15,086
65-69	12,281	13,742
70+	26,500	41,154

DAYTIME POPULATION

2001 Estimates:	
Working Population	759,939
At Home Population	331,309
Total	1,091,248

INCOME

2001 Estimates:	
Avg. Household Income	$61,364
Avg. Family Income	$75,242
Per Capita Income	$27,524
Male:	
Avg. Employment Income	$43,845
Avg. Employment Income (Full Time)	$58,933
Female:	
Avg. Employment Income	$30,949
Avg. Employment Income (Full Time)	$43,020

DISPOSABLE & DISCRETIONARY INCOME

2001 Estimates:	Per Hhld.
Disposable Income	$49,232
Discretionary Income 1 (minus Food & Shelter)	$34,368
Discretionary Income 2 (minus Food, Shelter, & Other Expenditures)	$25,932

LIQUID ASSETS

1999 Estimates:	Per Hhld.
Equity Investments	$123,313
Interest Bearing Investments	$82,958
Total Liquid Assets	$206,271

CREDIT DATA

July 2000:	
Pool of Credit	$7,761,320,115
Revolving Credit, No.	1,435,355
Fixed Loans, No.	270,644
Avg. Credit Limit, per Person	$11,140
Avg. Spent, per Person	$4,583
Satisfactory Ratings, No. per Person	2.40
Avg. No. of Cards, per Person	1.17

LABOUR FORCE

2001 Estimates:	
Male:	
In the Labour Force	207,582
Participation Rate	73.6
Employed	193,617
Unemployed	13,965
Unemployment Rate	6.7
Not in Labour Force	74,590
Female:	
In the Labour Force	186,197
Participation Rate	61.9
Employed	174,945
Unemployed	11,252
Unemployment Rate	6.0
Not in Labour Force	114,470

OCCUPATIONS BY MAJOR GROUPS

2001 Estimates:	Male	Female
Management	26,045	15,843
Business, Finance & Admin.	30,439	48,846
Natural & Applied Sciences & Related	15,913	4,660
Health	5,252	11,298
Social Sciences, Gov't Services & Religion	10,712	11,372
Education	7,268	10,788
Arts, Culture, Recreation & Sport	16,453	15,918
Sales & Service	47,538	48,481
Trades, Transport & Equipment Operators & Related	25,555	1,830
Primary Industries	1,375	378
Processing, Mfg. & Utilities	12,528	9,391

LEVEL OF SCHOOLING

2001 Estimates:	
Population 15 years +	582,839
Less than Grade 9	72,608
Grades 9-13 w/o Certif.	95,959
Grade 9-13 with Certif.	59,718
Trade Certif. /Dip.	10,593
Non-Univ. w/o Certif./Dip.	30,495
Non-Univ. with Certif./Dip.	71,317
Univ. w/o Degree	71,713
Univ. w/o Degree/Certif.	38,240
Univ. with Certif.	33,473
Univ. with Degree	170,436

AVERAGE HOUSEHOLD EXPENDITURES

2001 Estimates:	
Food	$6,625
Shelter	$10,943
Clothing	$2,564
Transportation	$6,204
Health & Personal Care	$2,073
Recr'n, Read'g & Education	$3,976
Taxes & Securities	$15,844
Other	$9,027
Total Expenditures	$57,256

PRIVATE HOUSEHOLDS

2001 Estimates:	
Private Households, Total	312,190
Pop. in Private Households	670,945
Average no. per Household	2.1

FAMILIES

2001 Estimates:	
Families in Private Households	164,631
Husband-Wife Families	133,422
Lone-Parent Families	31,209
Aver. No. Persons per Family	2.8
Aver. No. Sons/Daughters at Home	1.1

HOUSING

2001 Estimates:	
Occupied Private Dwellings	312,190
Owned	114,574
Rented	197,616
Single-Detached House	51,770
Semi-Detached House	46,265
Row Houses	15,065
Apartment, 5+ Storeys	116,626
Owned Apartment, 5+ Storeys	11,898
Apartment, 5 or Fewer Storeys	67,677
Apartment, Detached Duplex	12,364
Other Single-Attached	2,376
Movable Dwellings	47

VEHICLES

2001 Estimates:	
Model Yrs. '81-'96, No.	205,010
% Total	75.56
Model Yrs. '97-'98, No.	38,819
% Total	14.31
'99 Vehicles registered in Model Yr. '99, No.	27,508
% Total	10.14
Total No. '81-'99	271,337

LEGAL MARITAL STATUS

2001 Estimates: (Age 15+)	
Single (Never Married)	248,854
Legally Married (Not Separated)	231,256
Legally Married (Separated)	23,303
Widowed	35,206
Divorced	44,220

Toronto
(City)
Toronto CMA
(Cont'd)

PSYTE CATEGORIES

2001 Estimates	No. of House-holds	% of Total Hhds.	Index
Canadian			
Establishment	5,546	1.78	1,067
The Affluentials	9,771	3.13	490
Urban Gentry	34,614	11.09	617
Asian Heights	160	0.05	8
Suburban Nesters	9,294	2.98	186
Brie & Chablis	8,308	2.66	297
Aging Erudites	331	0.11	7
Europa	34,326	11.00	884
Asian Mosaic	18,736	6.00	438
High Rise			
Melting Pot	22,743	7.28	486
High Rise Sunsets	2,588	0.83	58
Young Urban			
Professionals	59,429	19.04	1,003
Young Urban Mix	19,280	6.18	291
Young Urban			
Intelligentsia	45,557	14.59	959
University			
Enclaves	3,708	1.19	58
Young City Singles	1,878	0.60	26
Urban Bohemia	10,341	3.31	283
Town Renters	237	0.08	9
Struggling			
Downtowns	2,161	0.69	22
Aged Pensioners	6,421	2.06	155
Big City Stress	8,811	2.82	250
Old Grey Towers	3,636	1.16	210

FINAN¢IAL P$YTE

2001 Estimates	No. of House-holds	% of Total Hhds.	Index
Platinum Estates	15,317	4.91	609
Four Star			
Investors	34,614	11.09	221
Successful			
Suburbanites	160	0.05	1
Canadian Comfort	9,294	2.98	31
Urban Heights	68,068	21.80	507
Dollars & Sense	53,062	17.00	650
Bills & Wills	19,280	6.18	75
Revolving Renters	2,588	0.83	18
Young Urban			
Struggle	59,606	19.09	403
Towering Debt	27,019	8.65	111
NSF	8,811	2.82	80
Senior Survivors	10,057	3.22	171

HOME LANGUAGE

2001 Estimates:		% Total
English	483,664	69.49
French	4,602	0.66
Arabic	1,868	0.27
Bengali	975	0.14
Bulgarian	651	0.09
Chinese	47,616	6.84
Croatian	885	0.13
Czech	579	0.08
Estonian	587	0.08
German	823	0.12
Greek	5,421	0.78
Gujarati	920	0.13
Hindi	595	0.09
Hungarian	1,424	0.20
Italian	10,945	1.57
Japanese	958	0.14
Korean	3,299	0.47
Latvian (Lettish)	582	0.08
Lithuanian	916	0.13
Macedonian	614	0.09
Persian (Farsi)	2,330	0.33
Polish	8,883	1.28
Portuguese	36,380	5.23
Punjabi	1,609	0.23
Romanian	1,434	0.21
Russian	2,365	0.34
Serbian	1,837	0.26
Serbo-Croatian	714	0.10
Spanish	9,403	1.35
Tagalog (Pilipino)	6,150	0.88

2001 Estimates:		% Total
Tamil	5,995	0.86
Turkish	630	0.09
Ukrainian	3,100	0.45
Urdu	1,474	0.21
Vietnamese	11,425	1.64
Other Languages	9,552	1.37
Multiple Responses	24,801	3.56
Total	696,006	100.00

BUILDING PERMITS

	1999	1998	1997
		$000	
Value	2,418,917	2,294,248	790,810

Note: 1999 & 1998 data for amalgamated city.

HOMES BUILT

	1999	1998	1997
No.	7,576	4,382	1,800

Note: 1999 & 1998 data for amalgamated city.

TAXATION

Income Class:	1997	% Total
Under $5,000	108,490	13.68
$5,000-$10,000	105,230	13.27
$10,000-$15,000	118,370	14.92
$15,000-$20,000	75,250	9.49
$20,000-$25,000	61,120	7.71
$25,000-$30,000	54,950	6.93
$30,000-$40,000	87,690	11.06
$40,000-$50,000	56,340	7.10
$50,000 +	125,720	15.85
Total Returns, No.	793,150	
Total Income, $000	27,653,219	
Total Taxable		
Returns	525,830	
Total Tax, $000	6,523,645	
Average Income, $	34,865	
Average Tax, $	12,406	

VITAL STATISTICS

	1997	1996	1995	1994
Births	11,831	12,814	13,310	13,514
Deaths	6,609	7,023	6,895	6,765
Natural				
Increase	5,222	5,791	6,415	6,749
Marriages	6,973	6,980	7,519	7,495

Note: Latest available data.

MEDIA INFO

see Toronto, CMA

Uxbridge
(Township)
Toronto CMA

In Durham Regional Municipality.

POPULATION

July 1, 2001 Estimate	18,472
% Cdn. Total	0.06
% Change, '96 -'01	12.81
Avg. Annual Growth Rate, %.	2.44
2003 Projected Population	19,441
2006 Projected Population	20,812
2001 Households Estimate	6,466
2003 Projected Households	6,872
2006 Projected Households	7,490

INCOME

% Above/Below National Average	+30
2001 Total Income Estimate	$507,290,000
% Cdn. Total	0.08
2001 Average Hhld. Income	$78,500
2001 Per Capita	$27,500
2003 Projected Total Income	$564,550,000
2006 Projected Total Income	$660,130,000

RETAIL SALES

% Above/Below National Average	+33
2001 Retail Sales Estimate	$219,350,000
% Cdn. Total	0.08
2001 per Household	$33,900
2001 per Capita	$11,900
2001 No. of Establishments	133
2003 Projected Retail Sales	$250,430,000
2006 Projected Retail Sales	$296,860,000

POPULATION

2001 Estimates:		
Total		18,472
Male		9,254
Female		9,218
Age Groups	Male	Female
0-4	587	547
5-9	717	656
10-14	754	694
15-19	676	611
20-24	576	522
25-29	515	502
30-34	587	623
35-39	735	778
40-44	780	807
45-49	718	726
50-54	627	611
55-59	515	509
60-64	431	420
65-69	357	354
70+	679	858

DAYTIME POPULATION

2001 Estimates:	
Working Population	4,369
At Home Population	7,893
Total	12,262

INCOME

2001 Estimates:	
Avg. Household Income	$78,455
Avg. Family Income	$84,020
Per Capita Income	$27,463
Male:	
Avg. Employment Income	$43,994
Avg. Employment Income	
(Full Time)	$56,529
Female:	
Avg. Employment Income	$26,670
Avg. Employment Income	
(Full Time)	$40,305

Ontario

DISPOSABLE & DISCRETIONARY INCOME

2001 Estimates:	Per Hhld.
Disposable Income	$63,831
Discretionary Income 1	
(minus Food & Shelter)	$47,266
Discretionary Income 2	
(minus Food, Shelter, & Other	
Expenditures)	$35,833

LIQUID ASSETS

1999 Estimates:	Per Hhld.
Equity Investments	$143,682
Interest Bearing Investments	$100,757
Total Liquid Assets	$244,439

CREDIT DATA

July 2000:	
Pool of Credit	$201,746,910
Revolving Credit, No.	30,727
Fixed Loans, No.	8,366
Avg. Credit Limit, per Person	$14,807
Avg. Spent, per Person	$6,501
Satisfactory Ratings,	
No. per Person	2.80
Avg. No. of Cards, per Person	1.14

LABOUR FORCE

2001 Estimates:	
Male:	
In the Labour Force	5,890
Participation Rate	81.9
Employed	5,748
Unemployed	142
Unemployment Rate	2.4
Not in Labour Force	1,306
Female:	
In the Labour Force	4,914
Participation Rate	67.1
Employed	4,742
Unemployed	172
Unemployment Rate	3.5
Not in Labour Force	2,407

OCCUPATIONS BY MAJOR GROUPS

2001 Estimates:	Male	Female
Management	1,149	382
Business, Finance		
& Admin.	398	1,715
Natural & Applied		
Sciences &		
Related	330	102
Health	35	352
Social Sciences,		
Gov't Services		
& Religion	122	99
Education	172	300
Arts, Culture,		
Recreation &		
Sport	150	185
Sales & Service	1,164	1,188
Trades, Transport		
& Equipment		
Operators &		
Related	1,411	137
Primary Industries	472	182
Processing, Mfg. &		
Utilities	413	198

Ontario

Uxbridge
(Township)
Toronto CMA
(Cont'd)

LEVEL OF SCHOOLING

2001 Estimates:
Population 15 years +	14,517
Less than Grade 9	948
Grades 9-13 w/o Certif.	3,411
Grade 9-13 with Certif.	2,385
Trade Certif./Dip.	602
Non-Univ. w/o Certif./Dip.	1,017
Non-Univ. with Certif./Dip.	3,181
Univ. w/o Degree	1,162
Univ. w/o Degree/Certif.	631
Univ. with Certif.	531
Univ. with Degree	1,811

AVERAGE HOUSEHOLD EXPENDITURES

2001 Estimates:
Food	$7,493
Shelter	$11,758
Clothing	$2,853
Transportation	$9,144
Health & Personal Care	$2,378
Recr'n, Read'g & Education	$4,968
Taxes & Securities	$22,125
Other	$11,074
Total Expenditures	$71,793

PRIVATE HOUSEHOLDS

2001 Estimates:
Private Households, Total	6,466
Pop. in Private Households	18,296
Average no. per Household	2.8

FAMILIES

2001 Estimates:
Families in Private Households	5,366
Husband-Wife Families	4,943
Lone-Parent Families	423
Aver. No. Persons per Family	3.1
Aver. No. Sons/Daughters at Home	1.2

HOUSING

2001 Estimates:
Occupied Private Dwellings	6,466
Owned	5,216
Rented	1,250
Single-Detached House	5,318
Semi-Detached House	79
Row Houses	285
Apartment, 5+ Storeys	111
Apartment, 5 or Fewer Storeys	561
Apartment, Detached Duplex	83
Other Single-Attached	29

VEHICLES

2001 Estimates:
Model Yrs. '81-'96, No.	9,673
% Total	76.52
Model Yrs. '97-'98, No.	1,858
% Total	14.70
'99 Vehicles registered in Model Yr. '99, No.	1,110
% Total	8.78
Total No. '81-'99	12,641

LEGAL MARITAL STATUS

2001 Estimates: (Age 15+)
Single (Never Married)	3,358
Legally Married (Not Separated)	9,161
Legally Married (Separated)	459
Widowed	812
Divorced	727

PSYTE CATEGORIES

2001 Estimates	No. of House-holds	% of Total Hhds.	Index
Mortgaged in Suburbia	532	8.23	592
Boomers & Teens	1,864	28.83	1,608
Small City Elite	1,025	15.85	925
Blue Collar Winners	1,846	28.55	1,134
Old Towns' New Fringe	251	3.88	99
Conservative Homebodies	468	7.24	201
Struggling Downtowns	441	6.82	217

FINANCIAL P$YTE

2001 Estimates	No. of House-holds	% of Total Hhds.	Index
Four Star Investors	1,864	28.83	574
Successful Suburbanites	532	8.23	124
Canadian Comfort	2,871	44.40	457
Tractors & Tradelines	251	3.88	68
Bills & Wills	468	7.24	87
Towering Debt	441	6.82	87

HOME LANGUAGE

2001 Estimates:		% Total
English	18,106	98.02
French	34	0.18
Chinese	42	0.23
Czech	12	0.06
Dutch	11	0.06
Estonian	45	0.24
German	34	0.18
Greek	12	0.06
Hungarian	17	0.09
Italian	18	0.10
Korean	12	0.06
Macedonian	24	0.13
Persian (Farsi)	11	0.06
Serbian	22	0.12
Slovenian	12	0.06
Multiple Responses	60	0.32
Total	18,472	100.00

BUILDING PERMITS

	1999	1998 $000	1997
Value	28,070	27,263	24,759

HOMES BUILT

	1999	1998	1997
No	110	80	129

TAXATION

Income Class:	1997	% Total
Under $5,000	1,190	10.86
$5,000-$10,000	1,150	10.49
$10,000-$15,000	1,260	11.50
$15,000-$20,000	940	8.58
$20,000-$25,000	810	7.39
$25,000-$30,000	850	7.76
$30,000-$40,000	1,350	12.32
$40,000-$50,000	1,050	9.58
$50,000 +	2,350	21.44
Total Returns, No.	10,960	
Total Income, $000	382,793	
Total Taxable Returns	8,420	
Total Tax, $000	82,741	
Average Income, $	34,926	
Average Tax, $	9,827	

VITAL STATISTICS

	1997	1996	1995	1994
Births	220	206	212	227
Deaths	86	121	108	93
Natural Increase	134	85	104	134
Marriages	84	74	107	88

Note: Latest available data.

MEDIA INFO

see Toronto, CMA

Vaughan
(City)
Toronto CMA
In York Regional Municipality.

POPULATION

July 1, 2001 Estimate	167,178
% Cdn. Total	0.54
% Change, '96 -'01	22.16
Avg. Annual Growth Rate, %	4.08
2003 Projected Population	179,829
2006 Projected Population	200,316
2001 Households Estimate	48,708
2003 Projected Households	52,715
2006 Projected Households	59,331

INCOME

% Above/Below National Average	+23
2001 Total Income Estimate	$4,318,970,000
% Cdn. Total	0.66
2001 Average Hhld. Income	$88,700
2001 Per Capita	$25,800
2003 Projected Total Income	$4,974,620,000
2006 Projected Total Income	$6,160,980,000

RETAIL SALES

% Above/Below National Average	+16
2001 Retail Sales Estimate	$1,741,930,000
% Cdn. Total	0.63
2001 per Household	$35,800
2001 per Capita	$10,400
2001 No. of Establishments	1,846
2003 Projected Retail Sales	$2,027,020,000
2006 Projected Retail Sales	$2,500,680,000

POPULATION

2001 Estimates:

Total		167,178
Male		82,951
Female		84,227
Age Groups	Male	Female
0-4	5,650	5,366
5-9	6,174	5,879
10-14	6,566	6,160
15-19	6,445	6,175
20-24	6,216	6,169
25-29	6,234	6,270
30-34	6,321	6,642
35-39	6,429	7,299
40-44	6,391	7,300
45-49	6,281	6,807
50-54	5,419	5,524
55-59	4,484	4,254
60-64	3,617	3,295
65-69	2,732	2,484
70+	3,992	4,603

DAYTIME POPULATION

2001 Estimates:

Working Population	119,333
At Home Population	75,639
Total	194,972

INCOME

2001 Estimates:

Avg. Household Income	$88,671
Avg. Family Income	$85,279
Per Capita Income	$25,835
Male:	
Avg. Employment Income	$45,741
Avg. Employment Income (Full Time)	$58,107
Female:	
Avg. Employment Income	$28,650
Avg. Employment Income (Full Time)	$40,370

DISPOSABLE & DISCRETIONARY INCOME

2001 Estimates:	Per Hhld.
Disposable Income	$72,333
Discretionary Income 1 (minus Food & Shelter)	$51,782
Discretionary Income 2 (minus Food, Shelter, & Other Expenditures)	$38,638

LIQUID ASSETS

1999 Estimates:	Per Hhld.
Equity Investments	$165,893
Interest Bearing Investments	$113,893
Total Liquid Assets	$279,786

CREDIT DATA

July 2000:

Pool of Credit	$2,109,211,797
Revolving Credit, No.	370,166
Fixed Loans, No.	77,457
Avg. Credit Limit, per Person	$14,657
Avg. Spent, per Person	$5,707
Satisfactory Ratings, No. per Person	3.02
Avg. No. of Cards, per Person	1.31

LABOUR FORCE

2001 Estimates:

Male:	
In the Labour Force	51,603
Participation Rate	79.9
Employed	49,646
Unemployed	1,957
Unemployment Rate	3.8
Not in Labour Force	12,958
Female:	
In the Labour Force	43,705
Participation Rate	65.4
Employed	41,864
Unemployed	1,841
Unemployment Rate	4.2
Not in Labour Force	23,117

OCCUPATIONS BY MAJOR GROUPS

2001 Estimates:	Male	Female
Management	9,244	3,633
Business, Finance & Admin.	6,304	15,922
Natural & Applied Sciences & Related	3,955	1,009
Health	1,142	2,202
Social Sciences, Gov't Services & Religion	1,189	1,249
Education	1,141	2,595
Arts, Culture, Recreation & Sport	1,067	1,062
Sales & Service	10,727	11,813
Trades, Transport & Equipment Operators & Related	11,554	801
Primary Industries	968	143
Processing, Mfg. & Utilities	3,309	2,162

LEVEL OF SCHOOLING

2001 Estimates:

Population 15 years +	131,383
Less than Grade 9	20,220
Grades 9-13 w/o Certif.	23,875
Grade 9-13 with Certif.	16,060
Trade Certif./Dip.	4,404
Non-Univ. w/o Certif./Dip.	7,850
Non-Univ. with Certif./Dip.	20,762
Univ. w/o Degree	13,273
Univ. w/o Degree/Certif.	7,735
Univ. with Certif.	5,538
Univ. with Degree	24,939

AVERAGE HOUSEHOLD EXPENDITURES

2001 Estimates:

Food	$9,263
Shelter	$14,274
Clothing	$3,416
Transportation	$10,481
Health & Personal Care	$2,656
Recr'n, Read'g & Education	$5,164
Taxes & Securities	$22,658
Other	$11,869
Total Expenditures	$79,781

PRIVATE HOUSEHOLDS

2001 Estimates:

Private Households, Total	48,708
Pop. in Private Households	165,905
Average no. per Household	3.4

FAMILIES

2001 Estimates:

Families in Private Households	46,867
Husband-Wife Families	43,476
Lone-Parent Families	3,391
Aver. No. Persons per Family	3.4
Aver. No. Sons/Daughters at Home	1.5

HOUSING

2001 Estimates:

Occupied Private Dwellings	48,708
Owned	42,938
Rented	5,770
Single-Detached House	39,033
Semi-Detached House	1,261
Row Houses	2,654
Apartment, 5+ Storeys	4,550
Owned Apartment, 5+ Storeys	3,041
Apartment, 5 or Fewer Storeys	285
Apartment, Detached Duplex	887
Other Single-Attached	38

VEHICLES

2001 Estimates:

Model Yrs. '81-'96, No.	79,615
% Total	71.01
Model Yrs. '97-'98, No.	18,530
% Total	16.53
'99 Vehicles registered in Model Yr. '99, No.	13,966
% Total	12.46
Total No. '81-'99	112,111

LEGAL MARITAL STATUS

2001 Estimates: (Age 15+)

Single (Never Married)	36,376
Legally Married (Not Separated)	84,803
Legally Married (Separated)	2,003
Widowed	4,889
Divorced	3,312

PSYTE CATEGORIES

2001 Estimates	No. of House -holds	% of Total Hhds.	Index
The Affluentials	1,570	3.22	504
Urban Gentry	438	0.90	50
Suburban Executives	5,354	10.99	767
Mortgaged in Suburbia	4,279	8.79	632
Technocrafts & Bureaucrats	4,993	10.25	364
Asian Heights	1,308	2.69	424
Boomers & Teens	4,716	9.68	540
Old Bungalow Burbs	1,012	2.08	125
Brie & Chablis	2,998	6.16	687
Satellite Suburbs	1,508	3.10	108
Blue Collar Winners	485	1.00	40
Europa	18,377	37.73	3,035
High Rise Sunsets	1,357	2.79	195
Young Urban Mix	233	0.48	23
Old Grey Towers	35	0.07	13

Ontario

FINANCIAL P$YTE

2001 Estimates	No. of House -holds	% of Total Hhds.	Index
Platinum Estates	1,570	3.22	400
Four Star Investors	10,508	21.57	429
Successful Suburbanites	10,580	21.72	327
Canadian Comfort	1,993	4.09	42
Urban Heights	2,998	6.16	143
Miners & Credit-Liners	1,012	2.08	66
Dollars & Sense	18,377	37.73	1,443
Bills & Wills	233	0.48	6
Revolving Renters	1,357	2.79	61
Senior Survivors	35	0.07	4

HOME LANGUAGE

2001 Estimates:		% Total
English	122,764	73.43
French	361	0.22
Arabic	216	0.13
Armenian	101	0.06
Chinese	4,992	2.99
Croatian	191	0.11
German	165	0.10
Greek	563	0.34
Gujarati	663	0.40
Hebrew	2,020	1.21
Hindi	308	0.18
Hungarian	373	0.22
Italian	17,510	10.47
Korean	776	0.46
Latvian (Lettish)	121	0.07
Macedonian	164	0.10
Persian (Farsi)	505	0.30
Polish	322	0.19
Portuguese	787	0.47
Punjabi	1,197	0.72
Romanian	149	0.09
Russian	2,001	1.20
Slovenian	163	0.10
Spanish	1,008	0.60
Tagalog (Pilipino)	393	0.24
Urdu	259	0.15
Vietnamese	319	0.19
Yiddish	288	0.17
Other Languages	805	0.48
Multiple Responses	7,694	4.60
Total	167,178	100.00

BUILDING PERMITS

	1999	1998	1997
		$000	
Value	1,043,062	704,619	565,026

HOMES BUILT

	1999	1998	1997
No	4,115	2,144	2,178

Ontario

Vaughan
(City)
Toronto CMA
(Cont'd)

TAXATION

Income Class:	1997	% Total
Under $5,000	7,710	11.58
$5,000-$10,000	7,630	11.46
$10,000-$15,000	7,350	11.04
$15,000-$20,000	5,950	8.93
$20,000-$25,000	5,590	8.39
$25,000-$30,000	5,640	8.47
$30,000-$40,000	9,680	14.53
$40,000-$50,000	6,230	9.35
$50,000 +	10,820	16.25
Total Returns, No.	66,600	
Total Income, $000	2,239,846	
Total Taxable Returns	50,020	
Total Tax, $000	500,229	
Average Income, $	33,631	
Average Tax, $	10,001	

VITAL STATISTICS

	1997	1996	1995	1994
Births	1,108	893	663	733
Deaths	287	296	223	219
Natural Increase	821	597	440	514
Marriages	936	895	888	788

Note: Latest available data.

MEDIA INFO
see Toronto, CMA

Whitchurch-Stouffville
(Town)
Toronto CMA

In York Regional Municipality.

POPULATION

July 1, 2001 Estimate	22,981
% Cdn. Total	0.07
% Change, '96 -'01	12.22
Avg. Annual Growth Rate, %	2.33
2003 Projected Population	23,605
2006 Projected Population	24,738
2001 Households Estimate	7,984
2003 Projected Households	8,225
2006 Projected Households	8,679

INCOME

% Above/Below National Average	+63
2001 Total Income Estimate	$788,200,000
% Cdn. Total	0.12
2001 Average Hhld. Income	$98,700
2001 Per Capita	$34,300
2003 Projected Total Income	$860,940,000
2006 Projected Total Income	$993,970,000

RETAIL SALES

% Above/Below National Average	-28
2001 Retail Sales Estimate	$147,450,000
% Cdn. Total	0.05
2001 per Household	$18,500
2001 per Capita	$6,400
2001 No. of Establishments	203
2003 Projected Retail Sales	$162,430,000
2006 Projected Retail Sales	$187,650,000

POPULATION

2001 Estimates:

Total		22,981
Male		11,409
Female		11,572

Age Groups	Male	Female
0-4	700	659
5-9	805	770
10-14	873	829
15-19	822	776
20-24	725	678
25-29	691	649
30-34	779	784
35-39	913	972
40-44	961	1,011
45-49	924	959
50-54	812	816
55-59	661	634
60-64	532	493
65-69	421	403
70+	790	1,139

DAYTIME POPULATION

2001 Estimates:

Working Population	6,095
At Home Population	9,354
Total	15,449

INCOME

2001 Estimates:

Avg. Household Income	$98,722
Avg. Family Income	$107,813
Per Capita Income	$34,298
Male:	
Avg. Employment Income	$64,721
Avg. Employment Income (Full Time)	$85,270
Female:	
Avg. Employment Income	$28,383
Avg. Employment Income (Full Time)	$40,876

DISPOSABLE & DISCRETIONARY INCOME

2001 Estimates:	Per Hhld.
Disposable Income	$77,338
Discretionary Income 1 (minus Food & Shelter)	$57,453
Discretionary Income 2 (minus Food, Shelter, & Other Expenditures)	$43,940

LIQUID ASSETS

1999 Estimates:	Per Hhld.
Equity Investments	$223,788
Interest Bearing Investments	$135,660
Total Liquid Assets	$359,448

CREDIT DATA

July 2000:	
Pool of Credit	$248,582,731
Revolving Credit, No.	38,850
Fixed Loans, No.	10,296
Avg. Credit Limit, per Person	$15,394
Avg. Spent, per Person	$6,523
Satisfactory Ratings, No. per Person	2.96
Avg. No. of Cards, per Person	1.21

LABOUR FORCE

2001 Estimates:

Male:	
In the Labour Force	7,537
Participation Rate	83.5
Employed	7,438
Unemployed	99
Unemployment Rate	1.3
Not in Labour Force	1,494
Female:	
In the Labour Force	6,189
Participation Rate	66.4
Employed	6,090
Unemployed	99
Unemployment Rate	1.6
Not in Labour Force	3,125

OCCUPATIONS BY MAJOR GROUPS

2001 Estimates:	Male	Female
Management	1,414	561
Business, Finance & Admin.	780	2,313
Natural & Applied Sciences & Related	482	77
Health	80	389
Social Sciences, Gov't Services & Religion	150	218
Education	156	273
Arts, Culture, Recreation & Sport	116	167
Sales & Service	1,625	1,739
Trades, Transport & Equipment Operators & Related	1,879	135
Primary Industries	480	135
Processing, Mfg. & Utilities	300	122

LEVEL OF SCHOOLING

2001 Estimates:

Population 15 years +	18,345
Less than Grade 9	1,162
Grades 9-13 w/o Certif.	4,242
Grade 9-13 with Certif.	2,814
Trade Certif./Dip.	870
Non-Univ. w/o Certif./Dip.	1,099
Non-Univ. with Certif./Dip.	3,599
Univ. w/o Degree	1,892
Univ. w/o Degree/Certif.	844
Univ. with Certif.	1,048
Univ. with Degree	2,667

AVERAGE HOUSEHOLD EXPENDITURES

2001 Estimates:

Food	$8,860
Shelter	$14,250
Clothing	$3,332
Transportation	$10,731
Health & Personal Care	$2,843
Recr'n, Read'g & Education	$5,821
Taxes & Securities	$26,786
Other	$13,245
Total Expenditures	$85,868

PRIVATE HOUSEHOLDS

2001 Estimates:

Private Households, Total	7,984
Pop. in Private Households	22,624
Average no. per Household	2.8

FAMILIES

2001 Estimates:

Families in Private Households	6,508
Husband-Wife Families	6,043
Lone-Parent Families	465
Aver. No. Persons per Family	3.2
Aver. No. Sons/Daughters at Home	1.3

HOUSING

2001 Estimates:

Occupied Private Dwellings	7,984
Owned	6,311
Rented	1,673
Single-Detached House	6,593
Semi-Detached House	98
Row Houses	114
Apartment, 5+ Storeys	144
Apartment, 5 or Fewer Storeys	641
Apartment, Detached Duplex	364
Other Single-Attached	30

VEHICLES

2001 Estimates:

Model Yrs. '81-'96, No.	11,607
% Total	76.70
Model Yrs. '97-'98, No.	2,101
% Total	13.88
'99 Vehicles registered in Model Yr. '99, No.	1,424
% Total	9.41
Total No. '81-'99	15,132

LEGAL MARITAL STATUS

2001 Estimates: (Age 15+)

Single (Never Married)	4,579
Legally Married (Not Separated)	11,153
Legally Married (Separated)	569
Widowed	1,044
Divorced	1,000

PSYTE CATEGORIES

2001 Estimates	No. of House -holds	% of Total Hhds.	Index
Technocrafts & Bureaucrats	346	4.33	154
Boomers & Teens	3,887	48.68	2,716
Suburban Nesters	522	6.54	408
Blue Collar Winners	1,661	20.80	826
Old Towns' New Fringe	185	2.32	59
Conservative Homebodies	893	11.18	310
High Rise Sunsets	274	3.43	240
Young Urban Mix	179	2.24	106

Whitchurch-Stouffville
(Town)
Toronto CMA
(Cont'd)

FINANCIAL P$YTE

2001 Estimates	No. of House-holds	% of Total Hhds.	Index
Four Star Investors	3,887	48.68	969
Successful Suburbanites	346	4.33	65
Canadian Comfort	2,183	27.34	281
Tractors & Tradelines	185	2.32	41
Bills & Wills	1,072	13.43	162
Revolving Renters	274	3.43	75

HOME LANGUAGE

2001 Estimates:		% Total
English	21,942	95.48
French	46	0.20
Armenian	61	0.27
Chinese	101	0.44
Czech	19	0.08
Finnish	43	0.19
German	119	0.52
Greek	41	0.18
Hungarian	35	0.15
Italian	195	0.85
Korean	12	0.05
Persian (Farsi)	32	0.14
Polish	24	0.10
Portuguese	27	0.12
Serbian	12	0.05
Slovenian	37	0.16
Spanish	18	0.08
Multiple Responses	217	0.94
Total	22,981	100.00

BUILDING PERMITS

	1999	1998	1997
		$000	
Value	26,991	27,052	29,906

HOMES BUILT

	1999	1998	1997
No.	137	138	265

TAXATION

Income Class:	1997	% Total
Under $5,000	1,270	10.17
$5,000-$10,000	1,260	10.09
$10,000-$15,000	1,390	11.13
$15,000-$20,000	1,020	8.17
$20,000-$25,000	970	7.77
$25,000-$30,000	980	7.85
$30,000-$40,000	1,620	12.97
$40,000-$50,000	1,150	9.21
$50,000 +	2,820	22.58
Total Returns, No.	12,490	
Total Income, $000	497,025	
Total Taxable Returns	9,630	
Total Tax, $000	115,853	
Average Income, $	39,794	
Average Tax, $	12,030	

VITAL STATISTICS

	1997	1996	1995	1994
Births	211	208	226	231
Deaths	132	108	130	121
Natural Increase	79	100	96	110
Marriages	117	111	100	84

Note: Latest available data.

MEDIA INFO
see Toronto, CMA

York
(City)
Toronto CMA

In Toronto Metropolitan Municipality. On Jan. 1, 1998, York, East York, Etobicoke, Scarborough and Toronto amalgamated to form the new city of Toronto.

POPULATION

July 1, 2001 Estimate	158,425
% Cdn. Total	0.51
% Change, '96 -'01	4.74
Avg. Annual Growth Rate, %	0.93
2003 Projected Population	161,166
2006 Projected Population	165,155
2001 Households Estimate	63,714
2003 Projected Households	65,327
2006 Projected Households	67,708

INCOME

% Above/Below National Average	-10
2001 Total Income Estimate	$2,990,300,000
% Cdn. Total	0.46
2001 Average Hhld. Income	$46,900
2001 Per Capita	$18,900
2003 Projected Total Income	$3,212,650,000
2006 Projected Total Income	$3,577,980,000

RETAIL SALES

% Above/Below National Average	-50
2001 Retail Sales Estimate	$713,790,000
% Cdn. Total	0.26
2001 per Household	$11,200
2001 per Capita	$4,500
2001 No. of Establishments	756
2003 Projected Retail Sales	$785,970,000
2006 Projected Retail Sales	$893,840,000

POPULATION

2001 Estimates:		
Total		158,425
Male		74,945
Female		83,480

Age Groups	Male	Female
0-4	5,625	5,450
5-9	5,396	5,243
10-14	4,761	4,655
15-19	4,408	4,209
20-24	4,474	4,570
25-29	5,214	5,881
30-34	6,488	7,200
35-39	6,911	7,477
40-44	6,266	6,852
45-49	5,290	5,925
50-54	4,302	4,860
55-59	3,543	4,023
60-64	3,123	3,631
65-69	2,851	3,506
70+	6,293	9,998

DAYTIME POPULATION

2001 Estimates:	
Working Population	26,758
At Home Population	85,264
Total	112,022

INCOME

2001 Estimates:	
Avg. Household Income	$46,933
Avg. Family Income	$51,843
Per Capita Income	$18,875
Male:	
Avg. Employment Income	$31,490
Avg. Employment Income (Full Time)	$42,468
Female:	
Avg. Employment Income	$24,071
Avg. Employment Income (Full Time)	$33,587

DISPOSABLE & DISCRETIONARY INCOME

2001 Estimates:	Per Hhld.
Disposable Income	$38,910
Discretionary Income 1 (minus Food & Shelter)	$25,612
Discretionary Income 2 (minus Food, Shelter, & Other Expenditures)	$17,858

LIQUID ASSETS

1999 Estimates:	Per Hhld.
Equity Investments	$64,151
Interest Bearing Investments	$58,109
Total Liquid Assets	$122,260

CREDIT DATA

July 2000:	
Pool of Credit	$1,343,857,949
Revolving Credit, No.	283,466
Fixed Loans, No.	62,866
Avg. Credit Limit, per Person	$9,205
Avg. Spent, per Person	$3,911
Satisfactory Ratings, No. per Person	2.29
Avg. No. of Cards, per Person	1.00

LABOUR FORCE

2001 Estimates:	
Male:	
In the Labour Force	41,288
Participation Rate	69.8
Employed	37,842
Unemployed	3,446
Unemployment Rate	8.3
Not in Labour Force	17,875
Female:	
In the Labour Force	38,144
Participation Rate	56.0
Employed	34,338
Unemployed	3,806
Unemployment Rate	10.0
Not in Labour Force	29,988

OCCUPATIONS BY MAJOR GROUPS

2001 Estimates:	Male	Female
Management	2,979	2,004
Business, Finance & Admin.	5,045	10,355
Natural & Applied Sciences & Related	2,304	613
Health	649	2,069
Social Sciences, Gov't Services & Religion	1,112	1,588
Education	911	1,586
Arts, Culture, Recreation & Sport	1,140	1,198
Sales & Service	9,315	12,184
Trades, Transport & Equipment Operators & Related	10,398	461
Primary Industries	476	98
Processing, Mfg. & Utilities	5,153	3,442

LEVEL OF SCHOOLING

2001 Estimates:	
Population 15 years +	127,295
Less than Grade 9	24,125
Grades 9-13 w/o Certif.	29,226
Grade 9-13 with Certif.	15,636
Trade Certif. /Dip.	3,233
Non-Univ. w/o Certif./Dip.	7,695
Non-Univ. with Certif./Dip.	17,492
Univ. w/o Degree	11,625
Univ. w/o Degree/Certif.	5,658
Univ. with Certif.	5,967
Univ. with Degree	18,263

Ontario

AVERAGE HOUSEHOLD EXPENDITURES

2001 Estimates:	
Food	$5,917
Shelter	$9,194
Clothing	$2,021
Transportation	$5,865
Health & Personal Care	$1,706
Recr'n, Read'g & Education	$2,943
Taxes & Securities	$10,921
Other	$7,223
Total Expenditures	$45,786

PRIVATE HOUSEHOLDS

2001 Estimates:	
Private Households, Total	63,714
Pop. in Private Households	156,650
Average no. per Household	2.5

FAMILIES

2001 Estimates:	
Families in Private Households	41,839
Husband-Wife Families	32,662
Lone-Parent Families	9,177
Aver. No. Persons per Family	3.0
Aver. No. Sons/Daughters at Home	1.2

HOUSING

2001 Estimates:	
Occupied Private Dwellings	63,714
Owned	28,943
Rented	34,771
Single-Detached House	22,162
Semi-Detached House	5,568
Row Houses	518
Apartment, 5+ Storeys	21,535
Owned Apartment, 5+ Storeys	2,959
Apartment, 5 or Fewer Storeys	11,219
Apartment, Detached Duplex	2,438
Other Single-Attached	274

VEHICLES

2001 Estimates:	
Model Yrs. '81-'96, No.	50,046
% Total	83.48
Model Yrs. '97-'98, No.	5,786
% Total	9.65
'99 Vehicles registered in Model Yr. '99, No.	4,117
% Total	6.87
Total No. '81-'99	59,949

LEGAL MARITAL STATUS

2001 Estimates: (Age 15+)	
Single (Never Married)	44,017
Legally Married (Not Separated)	59,589
Legally Married (Separated)	5,915
Widowed	9,223
Divorced	8,551

Ontario

York
(City)
Toronto CMA
(Cont'd)

PSYTE CATEGORIES

2001 Estimates	No. of House -holds	% of Total Hhds.	Index
The Affluentials	848	1.33	208
Urban Gentry	2,480	3.89	217
Suburban Nesters	2,932	4.60	287
Brie & Chablis	2,932	4.60	514
Aging Erudites	427	0.67	44
Europa	17,561	27.56	2,217
Asian Mosaic	168	0.26	19
High Rise Melting Pot	7,562	11.87	792
Conservative Homebodies	4,165	6.54	181
High Rise Sunsets	823	1.29	90
Young Urban Professionals	1,753	2.75	145
Young Urban Mix	6,403	10.05	474
Young Urban Intelligentsia	1,739	2.73	179
University Enclaves	327	0.51	25
Young City Singles	242	0.38	17
Urban Bohemia	1,435	2.25	192
Struggling Downtowns	2,910	4.57	145
Aged Pensioners	1,818	2.85	214
Big City Stress	5,714	8.97	794
Old Grey Towers	1,206	1.89	342

FINANCIAL P$YTE

2001 Estimates	No. of House -holds	% of Total Hhds.	Index
Platinum Estates	848	1.33	165
Four Star Investors	2,480	3.89	77
Canadian Comfort	2,932	4.60	47
Urban Heights	5,112	8.02	187
Dollars & Sense	17,729	27.83	1,064
Bills & Wills	10,568	16.59	200
Revolving Renters	823	1.29	28
Young Urban Struggle	3,501	5.49	116
Towering Debt	10,714	16.82	215
NSF	5,714	8.97	253
Senior Survivors	3,024	4.75	252

HOME LANGUAGE

2001 Estimates:		% Total
English	100,179	63.23
French	338	0.21
Arabic	591	0.37
Armenian	104	0.07
Bengali	221	0.14
Chinese	3,264	2.06
Croatian	460	0.29
Estonian	146	0.09
German	207	0.13
Greek	1,378	0.87
Gujarati	203	0.13
Hungarian	863	0.54
Italian	9,031	5.70
Japanese	127	0.08
Korean	745	0.47
Kurdish	168	0.11
Lao	143	0.09
Lithuanian	153	0.10
Maltese	223	0.14
Pashto	153	0.10
Persian (Farsi)	503	0.32
Polish	2,398	1.51
Portuguese	9,849	6.22
Punjabi	322	0.20
Romanian	227	0.14
Russian	458	0.29
Serbian	421	0.27
Serbo-Croatian	314	0.20
Slovenian	103	0.07
Spanish	6,293	3.97
Tagalog (Pilipino)	1,617	1.02
Tamil	1,150	0.73
Turkish	140	0.09
Ukrainian	984	0.62
Urdu	447	0.28
Vietnamese	2,983	1.88
Other Languages	3,171	2.00
Multiple Responses	8,348	5.27
Total	158,425	100.00

BUILDING PERMITS

	1999	1998	1997
		$000	
Value	n.a.	n.a.	58,718

HOMES BUILT

	1999	1998	1997
No.	n.a.	n.a.	103

TAXATION

Income Class:	1997	% Total
Under $5,000	4,570	11.50
$5,000-$10,000	4,740	11.93
$10,000-$15,000	6,020	15.15
$15,000-$20,000	4,530	11.40
$20,000-$25,000	3,750	9.44
$25,000-$30,000	3,560	8.96
$30,000-$40,000	5,180	13.03
$40,000-$50,000	3,120	7.85
$50,000 +	4,260	10.72
Total Returns, No.	39,740	
Total Income, $000	1,027,942	
Total Taxable Returns	27,810	
Total Tax, $000	179,343	
Average Income, $	25,867	
Average Tax, $	6,449	

VITAL STATISTICS

	1997	1996	1995	1994
Births	843	1,007	1,005	1,173
Deaths	520	510	495	568
Natural Increase	323	497	510	605
Marriages	720	773	815	935

Note: Latest available data.

MEDIA INFO
see Toronto, CMA

West Lincoln
(Township)
In Niagara Regional Municipality.

POPULATION

July 1, 2001 Estimate	12,192
% Cdn. Total	0.04
% Change, '96 -'01	3.00
Avg. Annual Growth Rate, %	0.59
2003 Projected Population	12,323
2006 Projected Population	12,498
2001 Households Estimate	3,895
2003 Projected Households	3,960
2006 Projected Households	4,062

INCOME

% Above/Below National Average	-6
2001 Total Income Estimate	$241,400,000
% Cdn. Total	0.04
2001 Average Hhld. Income	$62,000
2001 Per Capita	$19,800
2003 Projected Total Income	$255,910,000
2006 Projected Total Income	$279,570,000

RETAIL SALES

% Above/Below National Average	+19
2001 Retail Sales Estimate	$129,410,000
% Cdn. Total	0.05
2001 per Household	$33,200
2001 per Capita	$10,600
2001 No. of Establishments	75
2003 Projected Retail Sales	$141,130,000
2006 Projected Retail Sales	$158,700,000

POPULATION

2001 Estimates:		
Total		12,192
Male		6,198
Female		5,994
Age Groups	Male	Female
0-4	386	397
5-9	475	496
10-14	531	523
15-19	518	485
20-24	468	409
25-29	397	350
30-34	425	414
35-39	487	476
40-44	491	476
45-49	468	447
50-54	404	374
55-59	318	295
60-64	254	245
65-69	210	201
70+	366	406

DAYTIME POPULATION

2001 Estimates:	
Working Population	3,764
At Home Population	5,377
Total	9,141

INCOME

2001 Estimates:	
Avg. Household Income	$61,977
Avg. Family Income	$65,674
Per Capita Income	$19,800
Male:	
Avg. Employment Income	$36,148
Avg. Employment Income (Full Time)	$44,250
Female:	
Avg. Employment Income	$20,035
Avg. Employment Income (Full Time)	$29,298

DISPOSABLE & DISCRETIONARY INCOME

2001 Estimates:	Per Hhld.
Disposable Income	$51,054
Discretionary Income 1 (minus Food & Shelter)	$36,564
Discretionary Income 2 (minus Food, Shelter, & Other Expenditures)	$26,072

LIQUID ASSETS

1999 Estimates:	Per Hhld.
Equity Investments	$94,526
Interest Bearing Investments	$77,375
Total Liquid Assets	$171,901

CREDIT DATA

July 2000:	
Pool of Credit	$102,599,735
Revolving Credit, No.	17,360
Fixed Loans, No.	5,605
Avg. Credit Limit, per Person	$11,767
Avg. Spent, per Person	$5,537
Satisfactory Ratings, No. per Person	2.52
Avg. No. of Cards, per Person	0.90

LABOUR FORCE

2001 Estimates:	
Male:	
In the Labour Force	3,968
Participation Rate	82.6
Employed	3,852
Unemployed	116
Unemployment Rate	2.9
Not in Labour Force	838
Female:	
In the Labour Force	2,976
Participation Rate	65.0
Employed	2,880
Unemployed	96
Unemployment Rate	3.2
Not in Labour Force	1,602

OCCUPATIONS BY MAJOR GROUPS

2001 Estimates:	Male	Female
Management	316	195
Business, Finance & Admin.	178	658
Natural & Applied Sciences & Related	196	20
Health	36	217
Social Sciences, Gov't Services & Religion	n.a.	34
Education	82	154
Arts, Culture, Recreation & Sport	27	48
Sales & Service	458	846
Trades, Transport & Equipment Operators & Related	1,505	108
Primary Industries	638	447
Processing, Mfg. & Utilities	473	171

LEVEL OF SCHOOLING

2001 Estimates:	
Population 15 years +	9,384
Less than Grade 9	869
Grades 9-13 w/o Certif.	2,698
Grade 9-13 with Certif.	1,726
Trade Certif. /Dip.	426
Non-Univ. w/o Certif./Dip.	596
Non-Univ. with Certif./Dip.	1,922
Univ. w/o Degree	520
Univ. w/o Degree/Certif.	231
Univ. with Certif.	289
Univ. with Degree	627

West Lincoln
(Township)
(Cont'd)

AVERAGE HOUSEHOLD EXPENDITURES

2001 Estimates:
Food	$6,678
Shelter	$9,926
Clothing	$2,286
Transportation	$8,576
Health & Personal Care	$2,021
Recr'n, Read'g & Education	$4,191
Taxes & Securities	$15,416
Other	$9,511
Total Expenditures	$58,605

PRIVATE HOUSEHOLDS

2001 Estimates:
Private Households, Total	3,895
Pop. in Private Households	12,129
Average no. per Household	3.1

FAMILIES

2001 Estimates:
Families in Private Households	3,336
Husband-Wife Families	3,135
Lone-Parent Families	201
Aver. No. Persons per Family	3.4
Aver. No. Sons/Daughters at Home	1.5

HOUSING

2001 Estimates:
Occupied Private Dwellings	3,895
Owned	3,289
Rented	606
Single-Detached House	3,398
Semi-Detached House	118
Row Houses	168
Apartment, 5 or Fewer Storeys	174
Apartment, Detached Duplex	27
Other Single-Attached	10

VEHICLES

2001 Estimates:
Model Yrs. '81-'96, No.	7,079
% Total	87.18
Model Yrs. '97-'98, No.	633
% Total	7.80
'99 Vehicles registered in Model Yr. '99, No.	408
% Total	5.02
Total No. '81-'99	8,120

LEGAL MARITAL STATUS

2001 Estimates: (Age 15+)
Single (Never Married)	2,417
Legally Married (Not Separated)	5,967
Legally Married (Separated)	234
Widowed	374
Divorced	392

PSYTE CATEGORIES

2001 Estimates	No. of House-holds	% of Total Hhds.	Index
Blue Collar Winners	1,486	38.15	1,515
Old Towns' New Fringe	912	23.41	598
Rustic Prosperity	1,497	38.43	2,130

FINANCIAL PSYTE

2001 Estimates	No. of House-holds	% of Total Hhds.	Index
Canadian Comfort	1,486	38.15	393
Tractors & Tradelines	2,409	61.85	1,082

HOME LANGUAGE

2001 Estimates:		% Total
English	11,822	96.97
Croatian	26	0.21
Dutch	27	0.22
German	10	0.08
Greek	84	0.69
Hungarian	37	0.30
Polish	11	0.09
Portuguese	21	0.17
Slovak	11	0.09
Slovenian	11	0.09
Spanish	25	0.21
Ukrainian	43	0.35
Multiple Responses	64	0.52
Total	12,192	100.00

BUILDING PERMITS

	1999	1998 $000	1997
Value	11,109	16,101	13,374

TAXATION

Income Class:	1997	% Total
Under $5,000	1,150	14.23
$5,000-$10,000	930	11.51
$10,000-$15,000	1,020	12.62
$15,000-$20,000	790	9.78
$20,000-$25,000	670	8.29
$25,000-$30,000	620	7.67
$30,000-$40,000	990	12.25
$40,000-$50,000	730	9.03
$50,000 +	1,190	14.73
Total Returns, No.	8,080	
Total Income, $000	218,507	
Total Taxable Returns	5,740	
Total Tax, $000	38,518	
Average Income, $	27,043	
Average Tax, $	6,710	

VITAL STATISTICS

	1997	1996	1995	1994
Births	158	143	146	159
Deaths	53	53	48	36
Natural Increase	105	90	98	123
Marriages	53	55	46	50

Note: Latest available data.

COMMUNITY NEWSPAPER(S)

	Total Circulation
West Lincoln: Westman Review	15,656

Wilmot
(Township)

In Waterloo Regional Municipality.

POPULATION

July 1, 2001 Estimate	14,695
% Cdn. Total	0.05
% Change, '96 -'01	2.96
Avg. Annual Growth Rate, %	0.59
2003 Projected Population	14,863
2006 Projected Population	14,997
2001 Households Estimate	5,182
2003 Projected Households	5,289
2006 Projected Households	5,422

INCOME

% Above/Below National Average	+14
2001 Total Income Estimate	$353,910,000
% Cdn. Total	0.05
2001 Average Hhld. Income	$68,300
2001 Per Capita	$24,100
2003 Projected Total Income	$379,090,000
2006 Projected Total Income	$416,490,000

RETAIL SALES

% Above/Below National Average	+28
2001 Retail Sales Estimate	$168,870,000
% Cdn. Total	0.06
2001 per Household	$32,600
2001 per Capita	$11,500
2001 No. of Establishments	134
2003 Projected Retail Sales	$185,670,000
2006 Projected Retail Sales	$210,390,000

POPULATION

2001 Estimates:
Total	14,695
Male	7,335
Female	7,360

Age Groups	Male	Female
0-4	440	422
5-9	519	507
10-14	593	551
15-19	615	546
20-24	534	479
25-29	450	425
30-34	469	468
35-39	542	569
40-44	590	611
45-49	556	574
50-54	467	469
55-59	380	373
60-64	324	308
65-69	277	281
70+	579	777

DAYTIME POPULATION

2001 Estimates:
Working Population	12,353
At Home Population	6,501
Total	18,854

INCOME

2001 Estimates:
Avg. Household Income	$68,295
Avg. Family Income	$73,413
Per Capita Income	$24,083
Male:	
Avg. Employment Income	$39,385
Avg. Employment Income (Full Time)	$50,015
Female:	
Avg. Employment Income	$23,437
Avg. Employment Income (Full Time)	$34,563

Ontario

DISPOSABLE & DISCRETIONARY INCOME

2001 Estimates:	Per Hhld.
Disposable Income	$56,004
Discretionary Income 1 (minus Food & Shelter)	$39,848
Discretionary Income 2 (minus Food, Shelter, & Other Expenditures)	$29,187

LIQUID ASSETS

1999 Estimates:	Per Hhld.
Equity Investments	$101,820
Interest Bearing Investments	$83,601
Total Liquid Assets	$185,421

CREDIT DATA

July 2000:	
Pool of Credit	$179,686,775
Revolving Credit, No.	28,684
Fixed Loans, No.	8,385
Avg. Credit Limit, per Person	$13,461
Avg. Spent, per Person	$5,748
Satisfactory Ratings, No. per Person	2.69
Avg. No. of Cards, per Person	1.02

LABOUR FORCE

2001 Estimates:
Male:	
In the Labour Force	4,552
Participation Rate	78.7
Employed	4,470
Unemployed	82
Unemployment Rate	1.8
Not in Labour Force	1,231
Female:	
In the Labour Force	3,825
Participation Rate	65.1
Employed	3,738
Unemployed	87
Unemployment Rate	2.3
Not in Labour Force	2,055

OCCUPATIONS BY MAJOR GROUPS

2001 Estimates:	Male	Female
Management	451	276
Business, Finance & Admin.	303	1,099
Natural & Applied Sciences & Related	301	76
Health	50	287
Social Sciences, Gov't Services & Religion	60	102
Education	124	215
Arts, Culture, Recreation & Sport	67	140
Sales & Service	829	1,190
Trades, Transport & Equipment Operators & Related	1,369	78
Primary Industries	456	137
Processing, Mfg. & Utilities	492	182

Ontario

Wilmot
(Township)
(Cont'd)

LEVEL OF SCHOOLING

2001 Estimates:
Population 15 years + ...11,663
Less than Grade 9 1,427
Grades 9-13 w/o Certif. 2,755
Grade 9-13 with Certif. 1,747
Trade Certif. /Dip. 491
Non-Univ. w/o Certif./Dip. 645
Non-Univ. with Certif./Dip. 2,261
Univ. w/o Degree 1,012
 Univ. w/o Degree/Certif. 581
 Univ. with Certif. 431
Univ. with Degree 1,325

AVERAGE HOUSEHOLD EXPENDITURES

2001 Estimates:
Food $7,084
Shelter $11,352
Clothing. $2,506
Transportation. $8,518
Health & Personal Care $2,168
Recr'n, Read'g & Education $4,278
Taxes & Securities $18,312
Other. $9,704
Total Expenditures $63,922

PRIVATE HOUSEHOLDS

2001 Estimates:
Private Households, Total 5,182
Pop. in Private Households 14,413
Average no. per Household 2.8

FAMILIES

2001 Estimates:
Families in Private Households 4,278
Husband-Wife Families 3,908
Lone-Parent Families 370
Aver. No. Persons per Family 3.2
Aver. No. Sons/Daughters
 at Home 1.3

HOUSING

2001 Estimates:
Occupied Private Dwellings 5,182
 Owned. 4,122
 Rented. 1,060
Single-Detached House 3,981
Semi-Detached House 384
Row Houses 60
Apartment, 5 or Fewer Storeys 576
Apartment, Detached Duplex. 120
Other Single-Attached 33
Movable Dwellings. 28

VEHICLES

2001 Estimates:
Model Yrs. '81-'96, No. 8,341
 % Total 77.12
Model Yrs. '97-'98, No. 1,418
 % Total 13.11
'99 Vehicles registered in
 Model Yr. '99, No. 1,056
 % Total 9.76
Total No. '81-'99. 10,815

LEGAL MARITAL STATUS

2001 Estimates: (Age 15+)
Single (Never Married). 2,872
Legally Married
 (Not Separated) 7,455
Legally Married (Separated) 271
Widowed 619
Divorced. 446

PSYTE CATEGORIES

2001 Estimates	No. of House -holds	% of Total Hhds.	Index
Small City Elite	250	4.82	282
Satellite Suburbs	220	4.25	148
Blue Collar Winners	3,005	57.99	2,303
Old Towns' New Fringe	469	9.05	231
Conservative Homebodies	70	1.35	37
High Rise Sunsets	50	0.96	67
Old Leafy Towns	349	6.73	264
Town Renters	495	9.55	1,105
Struggling Downtowns	222	4.28	136

FINANCIAL P$YTE

2001 Estimates	No. of House -holds	% of Total Hhds.	Index
Canadian Comfort	3,475	67.06	690
Tractors & Tradelines	469	9.05	158
Bills & Wills	419	8.09	98
Revolving Renters	50	0.96	21
Towering Debt	717	13.84	177

HOME LANGUAGE

2001 Estimates:		% Total
English	14,109	96.01
French	48	0.33
Flemish	11	0.07
German	244	1.66
Italian	33	0.22
Polish	11	0.07
Portuguese	43	0.29
Serbo-Croatian	26	0.18
Tagalog (Pilipino)	11	0.07
Other Languages	21	0.14
Multiple Responses	138	0.94
Total	14,695	100.00

BUILDING PERMITS

	1999	1998 $000	1997
Value	27,801	24,455	27,570

TAXATION

Income Class:	1997	% Total
Under $5,000	1,100	10.42
$5,000-$10,000	1,080	10.23
$10,000-$15,000	1,220	11.55
$15,000-$20,000	980	9.28
$20,000-$25,000	920	8.71
$25,000-$30,000	940	8.90
$30,000-$40,000	1,540	14.58
$40,000-$50,000	1,020	9.66
$50,000 +	1,760	16.67
Total Returns, No.	10,560	
Total Income, $000	338,450	
Total Taxable Returns	8,050	
Total Tax, $000	65,181	
Average Income, $	32,050	
Average Tax, $	8,097	

VITAL STATISTICS

	1997	1996	1995	1994
Births	140	157	159	192
Deaths	77	102	88	64
Natural Increase	63	55	71	128
Marriages	103	71	76	83

Note: Latest available data.

COMMUNITY NEWSPAPER(S)

	Total Circulation
New Hamburg:	
New Hamburg Independent	3,006

Windsor
(Census Metropolitan Area)

On Jan. 1, 1998, Maidstone, TP & Belle River, T amalgamated to form Lakeshore Township, TP. On Jan. 1, 1999, Tecumseh, T, Sandwich South, TP, & St. Clair Beach, VL, amalgamated to form Sandwich South-Tecumseh-St. Clair Beach, T.

POPULATION

July 1, 2001 Estimate	308,782
% Cdn. Total	0.99
% Change, '96 -'01	7.43
Avg. Annual Growth Rate, %	1.44
2003 Projected Population	316,679
2006 Projected Population	326,391
2001 Households Estimate	121,084
2003 Projected Households	124,962
2006 Projected Households	130,313

INCOME

% Above/Below National Average	+13
2001 Total Income Estimate	$7,368,250,000
% Cdn. Total	1.12
2001 Average Hhld. Income	$60,900
2001 Per Capita	$23,900
2003 Projected Total Income	$8,046,540,000
2006 Projected Total Income	$9,126,250,000

RETAIL SALES

% Above/Below National Average	+17
2001 Retail Sales Estimate	$3,246,490,000
% Cdn. Total	1.16
2001 per Household	$26,800
2001 per Capita	$10,500
2001 No. of Establishments	2,129
2003 Projected Retail Sales	$3,562,880,000
2006 Projected Retail Sales	$4,009,180,000

POPULATION

2001 Estimates:

Total		308,782
Male		150,612
Female		158,170

Age Groups	Male	Female
0-4	9,996	9,573
5-9	10,285	9,779
10-14	10,316	9,854
15-19	10,226	9,856
20-24	10,616	10,621
25-29	11,225	11,386
30-34	11,849	12,078
35-39	12,252	12,380
40-44	11,775	11,985
45-49	10,889	11,241
50-54	9,457	9,711
55-59	7,767	8,002
60-64	6,484	6,843
65-69	5,663	6,320
70+	11,812	18,541

DAYTIME POPULATION

2001 Estimates:

Working Population	156,482
At Home Population	152,301
Total	308,783

INCOME

2001 Estimates:

Avg. Household Income	$60,852
Avg. Family Income	$70,209
Per Capita Income	$23,862
Male:	
Avg. Employment Income	$42,459
Avg. Employment Income (Full Time)	$54,135
Female:	
Avg. Employment Income	$23,713
Avg. Employment Income (Full Time)	$35,574

DISPOSABLE & DISCRETIONARY INCOME

2001 Estimates:	*Per Hhld.*
Disposable Income	$49,702
Discretionary Income 1 (minus Food & Shelter)	$35,177
Discretionary Income 2 (minus Food, Shelter, & Other Expenditures)	$26,038

LIQUID ASSETS

1999 Estimates:	*Per Hhld.*
Equity Investments	$86,449
Interest Bearing Investments	$73,883
Total Liquid Assets	$160,332

CREDIT DATA

July 2000:

Pool of Credit	$3,454,208,970
Revolving Credit, No.	602,260
Fixed Loans, No.	196,347
Avg. Credit Limit, per Person	$13,198
Avg. Spent, per Person	$6,177
Satisfactory Ratings, No. per Person	2.90
Avg. No. of Cards, per Person	1.03

LABOUR FORCE

2001 Estimates:

Male:

In the Labour Force	89,478
Participation Rate	74.6
Employed	86,023
Unemployed	3,455
Unemployment Rate	3.9
Not in Labour Force	30,537

Female:

In the Labour Force	74,386
Participation Rate	57.7
Employed	70,121
Unemployed	4,265
Unemployment Rate	5.7
Not in Labour Force	54,578

OCCUPATIONS BY MAJOR GROUPS

2001 Estimates:	Male	Female
Management	7,895	3,957
Business, Finance & Admin.	6,590	18,704
Natural & Applied Sciences & Related	4,892	874
Health	1,481	7,386
Social Sciences, Gov't Services & Religion	1,464	1,980
Education	2,330	3,873
Arts, Culture, Recreation & Sport	1,060	1,409
Sales & Service	16,551	25,587
Trades, Transport & Equipment Operators & Related	23,712	1,458
Primary Industries	2,016	507
Processing, Mfg. & Utilities	19,932	5,960

LEVEL OF SCHOOLING

2001 Estimates:

Population 15 years +	248,979
Less than Grade 9	24,500
Grades 9-13 w/o Certif.	58,411
Grade 9-13 with Certif.	40,829
Trade Certif. /Dip.	7,775
Non-Univ. w/o Certif./Dip.	17,101
Non-Univ. with Certif./Dip.	43,322
Univ. w/o Degree	25,692
Univ. w/o Degree/Certif.	14,630
Univ. with Certif.	11,062
Univ. with Degree	31,349

AVERAGE HOUSEHOLD EXPENDITURES

2001 Estimates:

Food	$6,648
Shelter	$10,159
Clothing	$2,340
Transportation	$7,055
Health & Personal Care	$2,042
Recr'n, Read'g & Education	$3,933
Taxes & Securities	$16,006
Other	$9,351
Total Expenditures	$57,534

PRIVATE HOUSEHOLDS

2001 Estimates:

Private Households, Total	121,084
Pop. in Private Households	303,759
Average no. per Household	2.5

Ontario

FAMILIES

2001 Estimates:

Families in Private Households	86,565
Husband-Wife Families	73,080
Lone-Parent Families	13,485
Aver. No. Persons per Family	3.0
Aver. No. Sons/Daughters at Home	1.2

RADIO STATION DATA

Station	Market	Format	Wkly. Reach%*	Aver. Hrs. tuned
All Stations			95	20.7
CBE	Windsor	News, Info.	8	14.6
CBE-FM	Windsor	Multi-format	3	11.3
CBEF	Windsor	Multi-format	1	14.8
CIDR-FM	Windsor	Adult Alternative	10	7.8
CIMX-FM	Windsor	New Rock	15	6.2
CKLW	Windsor	News, Talk, Sports	27	9.0
CKWW	Windsor	Adult Standards, Big Band, Swing	11	12.7

BBM Spring 2000 Radio Reach Survey; area coverage.
*Mon-Sun 5a.m - 1a.m , All Persons 12+

TV STATION DATA

Station	Market	Network Affiliation	Wkly. Reach%*	Aver. Hrs. Tuned
All Stations			96	25.0
A & E	n.a.	Ind.	12	3.4
CBEFT	Windsor	SRC	1	8.6
CBET	Windsor	CBC	36	3.8
CFPL	London	Ind.	37	3.6
CHCH	Toronto/Hamilton	Ind.	13	1.4
CHWI	Windsor	Ind.	n.a.	n.a.
CICO-E	n.a.	n.a.	16	2.7
CIII	n.a.	Global	41	2.5
CITY	Toronto	Ind.	9	1.9
CKCO	Kitchener	CTV	45	3.9
CNN	n.a.	Ind.	6	4.0
OTHERS	n.a.	n.a.	13	2.6
PRIME	n.a.	Ind.	5	2.9
TMN	Toronto	Ind.	8	5.9
TNN	Nashville TN	Ind.	6	2.5
TOON	n.a.	Ind.	5	2.8
TSN	n.a.	Ind.	14	4.1
VCR	n.a.	n.a.	27	3.8
WADL	Mount Clemens MI	FOX	2	3.2
WDIV	Detroit MI	NBC	54	4.7
WDWB	Detroit MI	WB	24	2.6
WJBK	Detroit MI	FOX	40	3.1
WKBD	Detroit MI	UPN	33	3.3
WNWO	Toledo OH	NBC	6	2.0
WTBS	Atlanta GA	Ind.	12	3.5
WTOL	Toledo OH	CBS	6	2.0
WTVS	Detroit MI	PBS	19	2.3
WWJ	Detroit MI	CBS	40	4.0
WXYZ	Detroit MI	ABC	64	5.2
YTV	n.a.	Ind.	10	3.3

BBM Spring 2000 TV Reach Survey; CMA coverage.
*Mon-Sun 6a.m - 2a.m , All Persons 2 +

Ontario

Windsor
(Census Metropolitan Area)
(Cont'd)

HOUSING

2001 Estimates:
Occupied Private Dwellings	121,084
Owned	83,976
Rented	37,108
Single-Detached House	83,420
Semi-Detached House	3,437
Row Houses	5,051
Apartment, 5+ Storeys	13,346
Owned Apartment, 5+ Storeys	1,460
Apartment, 5 or Fewer Storeys	10,919
Apartment, Detached Duplex	4,099
Other Single-Attached	309
Movable Dwellings	503

VEHICLES

2001 Estimates:
Model Yrs. '81-'96, No.	136,111
% Total	72.49
Model Yrs. '97-'98, No.	30,961
% Total	16.49
'99 Vehicles registered in Model Yr. '99, No.	20,698
% Total	11.02
Total No. '81-'99	187,770

LEGAL MARITAL STATUS

2001 Estimates: (Age 15+)
Single (Never Married)	74,280
Legally Married (Not Separated)	132,283
Legally Married (Separated)	6,745
Widowed	17,388
Divorced	18,283

PSYTE CATEGORIES

2001 Estimates	No. of House-holds	% of Total Hhds.	Index
The Affluentials	702	0.58	91
Urban Gentry	1,192	0.98	55
Suburban Executives	1,253	1.03	72
Mortgaged in Suburbia	1,747	1.44	104
Technocrafts & Bureaucrats	1,826	1.51	54
Boomers & Teens	8,126	6.71	374
Stable Suburban Families	2,239	1.85	142
Old Bungalow Burbs	5,462	4.51	272
Suburban Nesters	4,401	3.63	227
Brie & Chablis	620	0.51	57
Aging Erudites	2,762	2.28	151
Satellite Suburbs	3,119	2.58	90
Kindergarten Boom	2,535	2.09	80
Blue Collar Winners	13,858	11.44	455
Old Towns' New Fringe	3,160	2.61	67

2001 Estimates	No. of House-holds	% of Total Hhds.	Index
Rustic Prosperity	684	0.56	31
Europa	801	0.66	53
Conservative Homebodies	23,199	19.16	531
High Rise Sunsets	2,149	1.77	124
Young Urban Professionals	773	0.64	34
Young Urban Mix	407	0.34	16
University Enclaves	6,240	5.15	252
Young City Singles	3,168	2.62	114
Urban Bohemia	407	0.34	29
Old Leafy Towns	680	0.56	22
Town Renters	2,674	2.21	256
Rod & Rifle	146	0.12	5
Struggling Downtowns	18,057	14.91	474
Aged Pensioners	2,848	2.35	177
Big City Stress	3,298	2.72	241
Old Grey Towers	1,511	1.25	225

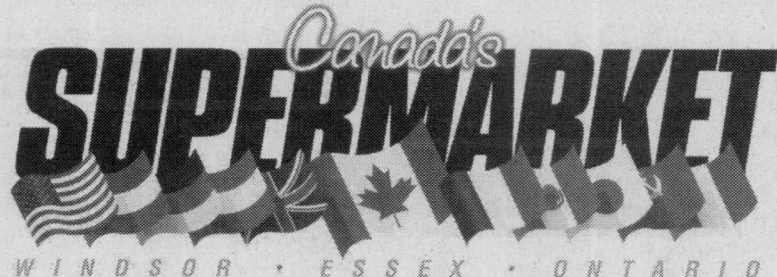

Windsor
(Census Metropolitan Area)
(Cont'd)

FINAN¢IAL P$YTE

2001 Estimates	No. of House -holds	% of Total Hhds.	Index
Platinum Estates	702	0.58	72
Four Star Investors	10,571	8.73	174
Successful Suburbanites	5,812	4.80	72
Canadian Comfort	21,378	17.66	182
Urban Heights	4,155	3.43	80
Miners & Credit-Liners	5,462	4.51	142
Mortgages & Minivans	2,535	2.09	32
Dollars & Sense	801	0.66	25
Tractors & Tradelines	3,844	3.17	56
Bills & Wills	24,286	20.06	242
Revolving Renters	2,149	1.77	39
Young Urban Struggle	6,647	5.49	116
Rural Family Blues	146	0.12	1
Towering Debt	23,899	19.74	253
NSF	3,298	2.72	77
Senior Survivors	4,359	3.60	191

HOME LANGUAGE

2001 Estimates:		% Total
English	266,923	86.44
French	4,329	1.40
Arabic	4,537	1.47
Chinese	3,046	0.99
Croatian	922	0.30
German	709	0.23
Greek	540	0.17
Hindi	160	0.05
Hungarian	491	0.16
Italian	5,512	1.79
Khmer (Cambodian)	184	0.06
Korean	159	0.05
Macedonian	706	0.23
Persian (Farsi)	181	0.06
Polish	2,641	0.86
Portuguese	273	0.09
Punjabi	616	0.20
Romanian	694	0.22
Russian	180	0.06
Serbian	1,432	0.46
Serbo-Croatian	211	0.07
Slovak	261	0.08
Spanish	1,283	0.42
Tagalog (Pilipino)	820	0.27
Turkish	157	0.05
Ukrainian	293	0.09
Urdu	222	0.07
Vietnamese	1,071	0.35
Other Languages	2,473	0.80
Multiple Responses	7,756	2.51
Total	308,782	100.00

BUILDING PERMITS

	1999	1998	1997
		$000	
Value	599,924	483,487	727,683

HOMES BUILT

	1999	1998	1997
No.	2,192	1,810	2,241

TAXATION

Income Class:	1997	% Total
Under $5,000	25,390	12.38
$5,000-$10,000	22,120	10.78
$10,000-$15,000	26,170	12.76
$15,000-$20,000	19,100	9.31
$20,000-$25,000	16,320	7.96
$25,000-$30,000	14,900	7.26
$30,000-$40,000	23,550	11.48
$40,000-$50,000	16,340	7.97
$50,000 +	41,310	20.14
Total Returns, No.	205,110	
Total Income, $000.	6,539,864	
Total Taxable Returns	145,660	
Total Tax, $000	1,330,905	
Average Income, $	31,885	
Average Tax, $	9,137	

Ontario

VITAL STATISTICS

	1997	1996	1995	1994
Births	3,471	3,588	3,842	3,739
Deaths	2,224	2,314	2,293	2,300
Natural Increase	1,247	1,274	1,549	1,439
Marriages	1,807	1,863	1,911	1,826

Note: Latest available data.

DAILY NEWSPAPER(S)

	Circulation Average Paid
The Windsor Star	
Sat	88,035
Mon-Fri	75,351

COMMUNITY NEWSPAPER(S)

	Total Circulation
Belle River: North Essex News	1,997
Essex: Essex Free Press	3,829
Tecumseh, St. Clair Beach: Shoreline Week	12,955
Windsor: Le Rempart	1,001

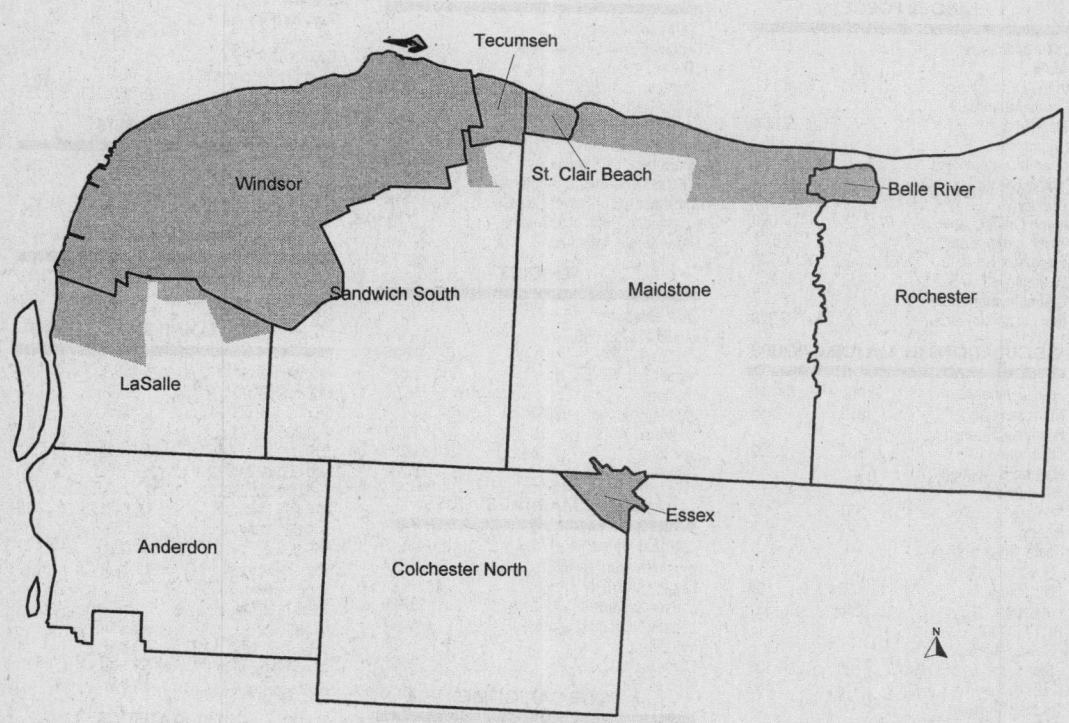

Urban Areas

Ontario

LaSalle
(Town)
Windsor CMA

In Essex County.

POPULATION

July 1, 2001 Estimate	25,930
% Cdn. Total	0.08
% Change, '96 -'01	22.27
Avg. Annual Growth Rate, %	4.10
2003 Projected Population	28,461
2006 Projected Population	32,068
2001 Households Estimate	8,547
2003 Projected Households	9,478
2006 Projected Households	10,859

INCOME

% Above/Below National Average	+38
2001 Total Income Estimate	$752,500,000
% Cdn. Total	0.11
2001 Average Hhld. Income	$88,000
2001 Per Capita	$29,000
2003 Projected Total Income	$884,680,000
2006 Projected Total Income	$1,105,240,000

RETAIL SALES

% Above/Below National Average	-21
2001 Retail Sales Estimate	$183,900,000
% Cdn. Total	0.07
2001 per Household	$21,500
2001 per Capita	$7,100
2001 No. of Establishments	106
2003 Projected Retail Sales	$213,110,000
2006 Projected Retail Sales	$260,150,000

POPULATION

2001 Estimates:

Total		25,930
Male		12,803
Female		13,127

Age Groups	Male	Female
0-4	871	868
5-9	959	954
10-14	1,019	977
15-19	983	977
20-24	915	955
25-29	854	898
30-34	921	1,010
35-39	1,073	1,164
40-44	1,107	1,129
45-49	997	1,033
50-54	840	869
55-59	686	673
60-64	553	503
65-69	421	389
70+	604	728

DAYTIME POPULATION

2001 Estimates:

Working Population	2,737
At Home Population	11,113
Total	13,850

INCOME

2001 Estimates:

Avg. Household Income	$88,043
Avg. Family Income	$91,439
Per Capita Income	$29,020
Male:	
Avg. Employment Income	$52,642
Avg. Employment Income (Full Time)	$63,148
Female:	
Avg. Employment Income	$25,925
Avg. Employment Income (Full Time)	$38,042

DISPOSABLE & DISCRETIONARY INCOME

2001 Estimates:	Per Hhld.
Disposable Income	$70,866
Discretionary Income 1 (minus Food & Shelter)	$52,287
Discretionary Income 2 (minus Food, Shelter, & Other Expenditures)	$39,857

LIQUID ASSETS

1999 Estimates:	Per Hhld.
Equity Investments	$154,785
Interest Bearing Investments	$109,720
Total Liquid Assets	$264,505

CREDIT DATA

July 2000:

Pool of Credit	$321,437,697
Revolving Credit, No.	51,878
Fixed Loans, No.	17,067
Avg. Credit Limit, per Person	$16,763
Avg. Spent, per Person	$7,442
Satisfactory Ratings, No. per Person	3.41
Avg. No. of Cards, per Person	1.17

LABOUR FORCE

2001 Estimates:

Male:	
In the Labour Force	8,117
Participation Rate	81.5
Employed	7,864
Unemployed	253
Unemployment Rate	3.1
Not in Labour Force	1,837

Female:	
In the Labour Force	7,000
Participation Rate	67.8
Employed	6,739
Unemployed	261
Unemployment Rate	3.7
Not in Labour Force	3,328

OCCUPATIONS BY MAJOR GROUPS

2001 Estimates:	Male	Female
Management	819	455
Business, Finance & Admin.	558	2,202
Natural & Applied Sciences & Related	551	76
Health	183	751
Social Sciences, Gov't Services & Religion	59	154
Education	246	337
Arts, Culture, Recreation & Sport	50	136
Sales & Service	1,378	2,169
Trades, Transport & Equipment Operators & Related	2,285	139
Primary Industries	196	14
Processing, Mfg. & Utilities	1,768	420

LEVEL OF SCHOOLING

2001 Estimates:

Population 15 years +	20,282
Less than Grade 9	1,350
Grades 9-13 w/o Certif.	4,609
Grade 9-13 with Certif.	3,440
Trade Certif. /Dip.	713
Non-Univ. w/o Certif./Dip.	1,333
Non-Univ. with Certif./Dip.	4,299
Univ. w/o Degree	1,974
Univ. w/o Degree/Certif.	1,093
Univ. with Certif.	881
Univ. with Degree	2,564

AVERAGE HOUSEHOLD EXPENDITURES

2001 Estimates:

Food	$8,323
Shelter	$13,162
Clothing	$3,112
Transportation	$9,929
Health & Personal Care	$2,561
Recr'n, Read'g & Education	$5,310
Taxes & Securities	$25,111
Other	$11,944
Total Expenditures	$79,452

PRIVATE HOUSEHOLDS

2001 Estimates:

Private Households, Total	8,547
Pop. in Private Households	25,735
Average no. per Household	3.0

FAMILIES

2001 Estimates:

Families in Private Households	7,498
Husband-Wife Families	6,881
Lone-Parent Families	617
Aver. No. Persons per Family	3.3
Aver. No. Sons/Daughters at Home	1.4

HOUSING

2001 Estimates:

Occupied Private Dwellings	8,547
Owned	8,047
Rented	500
Single-Detached House	8,111
Semi-Detached House	107
Row Houses	30
Apartment, 5+ Storeys	78
Owned Apartment, 5+ Storeys	65
Apartment, 5 or Fewer Storeys	118
Apartment, Detached Duplex	82
Other Single-Attached	21

VEHICLES

2001 Estimates:

Model Yrs. '81-'96, No.	11,384
% Total	72.36
Model Yrs. '97-'98, No.	2,621
% Total	16.66
'99 Vehicles registered in Model Yr. '99, No.	1,727
% Total	10.98
Total No. '81-'99	15,732

LEGAL MARITAL STATUS

2001 Estimates: (Age 15+)

Single (Never Married)	5,114
Legally Married (Not Separated)	13,166
Legally Married (Separated)	337
Widowed	795
Divorced	870

PSYTE CATEGORIES

2001 Estimates	No. of House -holds	% of Total Hhds.	Index
Suburban Executives	201	2.35	164
Mortgaged in Suburbia	318	3.72	268
Technocrafts & Bureaucrats	458	5.36	190
Boomers & Teens	1,736	20.31	1,133
Stable Suburban Families	510	5.97	458
Old Bungalow Burbs	697	8.15	492
Satellite Suburbs	487	5.70	199

2001 Estimates	No. of House -holds	% of Total Hhds.	Index
Blue Collar Winners	3,515	41.13	1,633
Old Towns' New Fringe	217	2.54	65
Conservative Homebodies	395	4.62	128

FINANCIAL P$YTE

2001 Estimates	No. of House -holds	% of Total Hhds.	Index
Four Star Investors	1,937	22.66	451
Successful Suburbanites	1,286	15.05	227
Canadian Comfort	4,002	46.82	482
Miners & Credit-Liners	697	8.15	258
Tractors & Tradelines	217	2.54	44
Bills & Wills	395	4.62	56

HOME LANGUAGE

2001 Estimates		% Total
English	23,465	90.49
French	291	1.12
Arabic	194	0.75
Chinese	171	0.66
Croatian	24	0.09
German	52	0.20
Greek	42	0.16
Gujarati	29	0.11
Hungarian	55	0.21
Italian	392	1.51
Korean	35	0.13
Persian (Farsi)	13	0.05
Polish	109	0.42
Portuguese	19	0.07
Punjabi	95	0.37
Serbian	105	0.40
Slovak	31	0.12
Spanish	36	0.14
Tagalog (Pilipino)	40	0.15
Ukrainian	27	0.10
Other Languages	11	0.04
Multiple Responses	694	2.68
Total	25,930	100.00

BUILDING PERMITS

	1999	1998 $000	1997
Value	72,339	50,455	71,207

HOMES BUILT

	1999	1998	1997
No	397	315	375

TAXATION

Income Class:	1997	% Total
Under $5,000	1,280	11.62
$5,000-$10,000	950	8.62
$10,000-$15,000	960	8.71
$15,000-$20,000	830	7.53
$20,000-$25,000	810	7.35
$25,000-$30,000	740	6.72
$30,000-$40,000	1,340	12.16
$40,000-$50,000	1,060	9.62
$50,000 +	3,060	27.77
Total Returns, No.	11,020	
Total Income, $000	408,911	
Total Taxable Returns	8,530	
Total Tax, $000	87,806	
Average Income, $	37,106	
Average Tax, $	10,294	

VITAL STATISTICS

	1997	1996	1995	1994
Births	246	234	245	258
Deaths	78	74	69	48
Natural Increase	168	160	176	210
Marriages	165	179	120	116

Note: Latest available data.

MEDIA INFO
see Windsor, CMA

Maidstone
(Township)
Windsor CMA

In Essex County. On Jan. 1, 1998, Maidstone, TP & Belle River, T, amalgamated to form Lakeshore Township, TP.

POPULATION

July 1, 2001 Estimate	14,278
% Cdn. Total	0.05
% Change, '96 -'01	17.63
Avg. Annual Growth Rate, %	3.30
2003 Projected Population	15,338
2006 Projected Population	16,821
2001 Households Estimate	4,805
2003 Projected Households	5,204
2006 Projected Households	5,792

INCOME

% Above/Below National Average	+42
2001 Total Income Estimate	$428,360,000
% Cdn. Total	0.07
2001 Average Hhld. Income	$89,100
2001 Per Capita	$30,000
2003 Projected Total Income	$489,150,000
2006 Projected Total Income	$589,580,000

RETAIL SALES

% Above/Below National Average	-66
2001 Retail Sales Estimate	$43,280,000
% Cdn. Total	0.02
2001 per Household	$9,000
2001 per Capita	$3,000
2001 No. of Establishments	105
2003 Projected Retail Sales	$50,920,000
2006 Projected Retail Sales	$63,450,000

POPULATION

2001 Estimates:

Total		14,278
Male		7,085
Female		7,193

Age Groups	Male	Female
0-4	456	456
5-9	528	519
10-14	559	546
15-19	550	529
20-24	495	496
25-29	468	470
30-34	497	522
35-39	582	593
40-44	612	596
45-49	566	576
50-54	489	483
55-59	390	363
60-64	295	283
65-69	228	232
70+	370	529

DAYTIME POPULATION

2001 Estimates:

Working Population	947
At Home Population	6,489
Total	7,436

INCOME

2001 Estimates:

Avg. Household Income	$89,148
Avg. Family Income	$95,703
Per Capita Income	$30,001
Male:	
Avg. Employment Income	$58,090
Avg. Employment Income (Full Time)	$73,158
Female:	
Avg. Employment Income	$27,380
Avg. Employment Income (Full Time)	$43,344

DISPOSABLE & DISCRETIONARY INCOME

2001 Estimates:	Per Hhld.
Disposable Income	$70,824
Discretionary Income 1 (minus Food & Shelter)	$52,590
Discretionary Income 2 (minus Food, Shelter, & Other Expenditures)	$40,247

LIQUID ASSETS

1999 Estimates:	Per Hhld.
Equity Investments	$181,702
Interest Bearing Investments	$119,376
Total Liquid Assets	$301,078

CREDIT DATA

July 2000:	
Pool of Credit	$60,145,457
Revolving Credit, No.	8,707
Fixed Loans, No.	3,063
Avg. Credit Limit, per Person	$16,528
Avg. Spent, per Person	$7,364
Satisfactory Ratings, No. per Person	3.09
Avg. No. of Cards, per Person	1.10

LABOUR FORCE

2001 Estimates:

Male:	
In the Labour Force	4,515
Participation Rate	81.5
Employed	4,361
Unemployed	154
Unemployment Rate	3.4
Not in Labour Force	1,027
Female:	
In the Labour Force	3,475
Participation Rate	61.3
Employed	3,295
Unemployed	180
Unemployment Rate	5.2
Not in Labour Force	2,197

OCCUPATIONS BY MAJOR GROUPS

2001 Estimates:	Male	Female
Management	615	227
Business, Finance & Admin.	203	883
Natural & Applied Sciences & Related	264	51
Health	205	342
Social Sciences, Gov't Services & Religion	72	70
Education	92	217
Arts, Culture, Recreation & Sport	38	38
Sales & Service	414	861
Trades, Transport & Equipment Operators & Related	1,275	70
Primary Industries	297	86
Processing, Mfg. & Utilities	983	518

LEVEL OF SCHOOLING

2001 Estimates:

Population 15 years +	11,214
Less than Grade 9	862
Grades 9-13 w/o Certif.	2,489
Grade 9-13 with Certif.	1,912
Trade Certif. /Dip.	365
Non-Univ. w/o Certif./Dip.	755
Non-Univ. with Certif./Dip.	2,122
Univ. w/o Degree	1,187
Univ. w/o Degree/Certif.	673
Univ. with Certif.	514
Univ. with Degree	1,522

AVERAGE HOUSEHOLD EXPENDITURES

2001 Estimates:

Food	$7,981
Shelter	$13,248
Clothing	$3,059
Transportation	$9,932
Health & Personal Care	$2,504
Recr'n, Read'g & Education	$5,438
Taxes & Securities	$25,275
Other	$12,501
Total Expenditures	$79,938

PRIVATE HOUSEHOLDS

2001 Estimates:

Private Households, Total	4,805
Pop. in Private Households	14,099
Average no. per Household	2.9

FAMILIES

2001 Estimates:

Families in Private Households	4,103
Husband-Wife Families	3,785
Lone-Parent Families	318
Aver. No. Persons per Family	3.3
Aver. No. Sons/Daughters at Home	1.3

HOUSING

2001 Estimates:

Occupied Private Dwellings	4,805
Owned	4,440
Rented	365
Single-Detached House	4,514
Semi-Detached House	29
Apartment, 5 or Fewer Storeys	58
Apartment, Detached Duplex	68
Movable Dwellings	136

VEHICLES

2001 Estimates:

Model Yrs. '81-'96, No.	7,274
% Total	69.94
Model Yrs. '97-'98, No.	1,884
% Total	18.12
'99 Vehicles registered in Model Yr. '99, No.	1,242
% Total	11.94
Total No. '81-'99	10,400

LEGAL MARITAL STATUS

2001 Estimates: (Age 15+)

Single (Never Married)	2,772
Legally Married (Not Separated)	7,096
Legally Married (Separated)	233
Widowed	555
Divorced	558

PSYTE CATEGORIES

2001 Estimates	No. of House-holds	% of Total Hhds.	Index
The Affluentials	389	8.10	1,266
Mortgaged in Suburbia	439	9.14	657
Boomers & Teens	1,011	21.04	1,174
Blue Collar Winners	1,809	37.65	1,495
Old Towns' New Fringe	798	16.61	424
Rustic Prosperity	161	3.35	186
Struggling Downtowns	153	3.18	101

FINANCIAL P$YTE

2001 Estimates	No. of House-holds	% of Total Hhds.	Index
Platinum Estates	389	8.10	1,005
Four Star Investors	1,011	21.04	419
Successful Suburbanites	439	9.14	138
Canadian Comfort	1,809	37.65	387
Tractors & Tradelines	959	19.96	349
Towering Debt	153	3.18	41

Ontario

HOME LANGUAGE

2001 Estimates:		% Total
English	13,378	93.70
French	324	2.27
Arabic	29	0.20
Croatian	40	0.28
German	17	0.12
Gujarati	13	0.09
Italian	109	0.76
Macedonian	31	0.22
Polish	53	0.37
Spanish	12	0.08
Turkish	25	0.18
Ukrainian	13	0.09
Other Languages	24	0.17
Multiple Responses	210	1.47
Total	14,278	100.00

BUILDING PERMITS

	1999	1998 $000	1997
Value	n.a.	n.a.	46,881

HOMES BUILT

	1999	1998	1997
No	n.a.	156	139

TAXATION

Income Class:	1997	% Total
Under $5,000	300	11.03
$5,000-$10,000	240	8.82
$10,000-$15,000	310	11.40
$15,000-$20,000	210	7.72
$20,000-$25,000	200	7.35
$25,000-$30,000	210	7.72
$30,000-$40,000	350	12.87
$40,000-$50,000	230	8.46
$50,000 +	680	25.00
Total Returns, No.	2,720	
Total Income, $000	96,316	
Total Taxable Returns	2,080	
Total Tax, $000	20,017	
Average Income, $.	35,410	
Average Tax, $	9,624	

VITAL STATISTICS

	1997	1996	1995	1994
Births	65	66	79	83
Deaths	67	60	43	67
Natural Increase	-2	6	36	16
Marriages	41	41	42	38

Note: Latest available data.

MEDIA INFO
see Windsor, CMA

Ontario

Tecumseh
(Town)
Windsor CMA

In Essex County. On Jan. 1, 1999, Tecumseh, T, Sandwich South, TP, & St. Clair Beach, VL, amalgamated to form Sandwich South-Tecumseh-St. Clair Beach, T.

POPULATION

July 1, 2001 Estimate	15,995
% Cdn. Total	0.05
% Change, '96 -'01	20.88
Avg. Annual Growth Rate, %	3.87
2003 Projected Population	17,450
2006 Projected Population	19,512
2001 Households Estimate	5,353
2003 Projected Households	5,900
2006 Projected Households	6,711

INCOME

% Above/Below National Average	+41
2001 Total Income Estimate	$476,280,000
% Cdn. Total	0.07
2001 Average Hhld. Income	$89,000
2001 Per Capita	$29,800
2003 Projected Total Income	$555,720,000
2006 Projected Total Income	$689,050,000

RETAIL SALES

% Above/Below National Average	-36
2001 Retail Sales Estimate	$92,050,000
% Cdn. Total	0.03
2001 per Household	$17,200
2001 per Capita	$5,800
2001 No. of Establishments	85
2003 Projected Retail Sales	$106,660,000
2006 Projected Retail Sales	$129,750,000

POPULATION

2001 Estimates:

Total		15,995
Male		7,906
Female		8,089

Age Groups	Male	Female
0-4	530	496
5-9	631	577
10-14	698	642
15-19	670	624
20-24	585	574
25-29	507	525
30-34	513	582
35-39	627	708
40-44	699	746
45-49	682	692
50-54	553	532
55-59	385	382
60-64	272	281
65-69	200	213
70+	354	515

DAYTIME POPULATION

2001 Estimates:

Working Population	1,872
At Home Population	6,766
Total	8,638

INCOME

2001 Estimates:

Avg. Household Income	$88,975
Avg. Family Income	$96,040
Per Capita Income	$29,777
Male:	
Avg. Employment Income	$55,416
Avg. Employment Income (Full Time)	$69,317
Female:	
Avg. Employment Income	$30,436
Avg. Employment Income (Full Time)	$44,321

DISPOSABLE & DISCRETIONARY INCOME

2001 Estimates:	Per Hhld.
Disposable Income	$71,341
Discretionary Income 1 (minus Food & Shelter)	$53,168
Discretionary Income 2 (minus Food, Shelter, & Other Expenditures)	$41,198

LIQUID ASSETS

1999 Estimates:	Per Hhld.
Equity Investments	$142,788
Interest Bearing Investments	$110,295
Total Liquid Assets	$253,083

CREDIT DATA

July 2000:

Pool of Credit	$214,441,103
Revolving Credit, No.	33,235
Fixed Loans, No.	12,047
Avg. Credit Limit, per Person	$17,676
Avg. Spent, per Person	$8,086
Satisfactory Ratings, No. per Person	3.54
Avg. No. of Cards, per Person	1.21

LABOUR FORCE

2001 Estimates:

Male:	
In the Labour Force	5,058
Participation Rate	83.6
Employed	4,927
Unemployed	131
Unemployment Rate	2.6
Not in Labour Force	989
Female:	
In the Labour Force	4,372
Participation Rate	68.6
Employed	4,160
Unemployed	212
Unemployment Rate	4.8
Not in Labour Force	2,002

OCCUPATIONS BY MAJOR GROUPS

2001 Estimates:	Male	Female
Management	605	299
Business, Finance & Admin.	477	1,285
Natural & Applied Sciences & Related	312	63
Health	67	545
Social Sciences, Gov't Services & Religion	85	197
Education	265	371
Arts, Culture, Recreation & Sport	46	41
Sales & Service	921	1,061
Trades, Transport & Equipment Operators & Related	1,145	68
Primary Industries	51	33
Processing, Mfg. & Utilities	1,056	244

LEVEL OF SCHOOLING

2001 Estimates:

Population 15 years +	12,421
Less than Grade 9	766
Grades 9-13 w/o Certif.	2,384
Grade 9-13 with Certif.	1,907
Trade Certif. /Dip.	462
Non-Univ. w/o Certif./Dip.	813
Non-Univ. with Certif./Dip.	2,372
Univ. w/o Degree	1,492
Univ. w/o Degree/Certif.	779
Univ. with Certif.	713
Univ. with Degree	2,225

AVERAGE HOUSEHOLD EXPENDITURES

2001 Estimates:

Food	$8,284
Shelter	$12,991
Clothing	$3,334
Transportation	$9,496
Health & Personal Care	$2,590
Recr'n, Read'g & Education	$5,728
Taxes & Securities	$25,702
Other	$11,922
Total Expenditures	$80,047

PRIVATE HOUSEHOLDS

2001 Estimates:

Private Households, Total	5,353
Pop. in Private Households	15,848
Average no. per Household	3.0

FAMILIES

2001 Estimates:

Families in Private Households	4,534
Husband-Wife Families	4,045
Lone-Parent Families	489
Aver. No. Persons per Family	3.3
Aver. No. Sons/Daughters at Home	1.5

HOUSING

2001 Estimates:

Occupied Private Dwellings	5,353
Owned	4,676
Rented	677
Single-Detached House	4,483
Semi-Detached House	203
Row Houses	182
Apartment, 5+ Storeys	377
Apartment, 5 or Fewer Storeys	63
Apartment, Detached Duplex	45

VEHICLES

2001 Estimates:

Model Yrs. '81-'96, No.	6,235
% Total	68.14
Model Yrs. '97-'98, No.	1,771
% Total	19,36
'99 Vehicles registered in Model Yr. '99, No.	1,144
% Total	12.50
Total No. '81-'99	9,150

LEGAL MARITAL STATUS

2001 Estimates: (Age 15+)

Single (Never Married)	3,147
Legally Married (Not Separated)	7,814
Legally Married (Separated)	305
Widowed	527
Divorced	628

PSYTE CATEGORIES

2001 Estimates	No. of House-holds	% of Total Hhds.	Index
Suburban Executives	541	10.11	705
Mortgaged in Suburbia	990	18.49	1,331
Technocrafts & Bureaucrats	594	11.10	394
Boomers & Teens	1,611	30.10	1,679
Old Bungalow Burbs	124	2.32	140
Blue Collar Winners	65	1.21	48
Conservative Homebodies	975	18.21	505
University Enclaves	453	8.46	415

FINANCIAL P$YTE

2001 Estimates	No. of House-holds	% of Total Hhds.	Index
Four Star Investors	2,152	40.20	800
Successful Suburbanites	1,584	29.59	446
Canadian Comfort	65	1.21	12
Miners & Credit-Liners	124	2.32	73
Bills & Wills	975	18.21	220
Young Urban Struggle	453	8.46	179

HOME LANGUAGE

2001 Estimates:		% Total
English	14,800	92.53
French	392	2.45
Arabic	115	0.72
Chinese	24	0.15
Hungarian	12	0.08
Italian	101	0.63
Japanese	35	0.22
Macedonian	18	0.11
Maltese	13	0.08
Romanian	12	0.08
Russian	12	0.08
Serbian	40	0.25
Slovak	33	0.21
Spanish	45	0.28
Tagalog (Pilipino)	26	0.16
Other Languages	25	0.16
Multiple Responses	292	1.83
Total	15,995	100.00

BUILDING PERMITS

	1999	1998	1997
		$000	
Value	45,291	17,840	16,292

Note: 1999 data for new amalgamated area.

HOMES BUILT

	1999	1998	1997
No.	89	124	174

TAXATION

Income Class:	1997	% Total
Under $5,000	1,480	10.87
$5,000-$10,000	1,200	8.81
$10,000-$15,000	1,240	9.10
$15,000-$20,000	1,030	7.56
$20,000-$25,000	910	6.68
$25,000-$30,000	920	6.75
$30,000-$40,000	1,530	11.23
$40,000-$50,000	1,170	8.59
$50,000 +	4,150	30.47
Total Returns, No.	13,620	
Total Income, $000	575,392	
Total Taxable Returns	10,630	
Total Tax, $000	137,475	
Average Income, $.	42,246	
Average Tax, $.	12,933	

VITAL STATISTICS

	1997	1996	1995	1994
Births	195	193	241	232
Deaths	96	105	93	84
Natural Increase	99	88	148	148
Marriages	120	98	96	44

Note: Latest available data.

MEDIA INFO

see Windsor, CMA

Windsor
(City)
Windsor CMA
In census division Essex.

POPULATION

July 1, 2001 Estimate	212,709
% Cdn. Total	0.68
% Change, '96 -'01	4.32
Avg. Annual Growth Rate, %	0.85
2003 Projected Population	214,459
2006 Projected Population	215,649
2001 Households Estimate	88,361
2003 Projected Households	89,879
2006 Projected Households	91,771

INCOME

% Above/Below National Average	+3
2001 Total Income Estimate	$4,640,640,000
% Cdn. Total	0.71
2001 Average Hhld. Income	$52,500
2001 Per Capita	$21,800
2003 Projected Total Income	$4,947,960,000
2006 Projected Total Income	$5,415,380,000

RETAIL SALES

% Above/Below National Average	+33
2001 Retail Sales Estimate	$2,530,940,000
% Cdn. Total	0.91
2001 per Household	$28,600
2001 per Capita	$11,900
2001 No. of Establishments	1,559
2003 Projected Retail Sales	$2,747,120,000
2006 Projected Retail Sales	$3,039,690,000

POPULATION

2001 Estimates:

Total		212,709
Male		102,962
Female		109,747

Age Groups	Male	Female
0-4	6,927	6,602
5-9	6,803	6,478
10-14	6,563	6,294
15-19	6,512	6,298
20-24	7,150	7,213
25-29	8,078	8,213
30-34	8,609	8,587
35-39	8,505	8,385
40-44	7,816	7,919
45-49	7,085	7,355
50-54	6,117	6,401
55-59	5,110	5,447
60-64	4,438	4,892
65-69	4,072	4,740
70+	9,177	14,923

DAYTIME POPULATION

2001 Estimates:

Working Population	129,824
At Home Population	110,256
Total	240,080

INCOME

2001 Estimates:

Avg. Household Income	$52,519
Avg. Family Income	$61,275
Per Capita Income	$21,817
Male:	
Avg. Employment Income	$37,695
Avg. Employment Income (Full Time)	$48,524
Female:	
Avg. Employment Income	$22,181
Avg. Employment Income (Full Time)	$33,174

DISPOSABLE & DISCRETIONARY INCOME

2001 Estimates:	Per Hhld.
Disposable Income	$43,233
Discretionary Income 1 (minus Food & Shelter)	$29,880
Discretionary Income 2 (minus Food, Shelter, & Other Expenditures)	$21,765

LIQUID ASSETS

1999 Estimates:	Per Hhld.
Equity Investments	$65,751
Interest Bearing Investments	$62,762
Total Liquid Assets	$128,513

CREDIT DATA

July 2000:	
Pool of Credit	$2,293,491,062
Revolving Credit, No.	422,510
Fixed Loans, No.	132,355
Avg. Credit Limit, per Person	$12,081
Avg. Spent, per Person	$5,715
Satisfactory Ratings, No. per Person	2.78
Avg. No. of Cards, per Person	0.99

LABOUR FORCE

2001 Estimates:

Male:	
In the Labour Force	59,289
Participation Rate	71.7
Employed	56,627
Unemployed	2,662
Unemployment Rate	4.5
Not in Labour Force	23,380
Female:	
In the Labour Force	49,308
Participation Rate	54.6
Employed	46,013
Unemployed	3,295
Unemployment Rate	6.7
Not in Labour Force	41,065

OCCUPATIONS BY MAJOR GROUPS

2001 Estimates:	Male	Female
Management	4,519	2,353
Business, Finance & Admin.	4,514	11,652
Natural & Applied Sciences & Related	3,037	514
Health	919	4,708
Social Sciences, Gov't Services & Religion	1,019	1,304
Education	1,434	2,359
Arts, Culture, Recreation & Sport	837	1,043
Sales & Service	11,954	18,304
Trades, Transport & Equipment Operators & Related	15,292	908
Primary Industries	851	199
Processing, Mfg. & Utilities	13,597	3,921

LEVEL OF SCHOOLING

2001 Estimates:

Population 15 years +	173,042
Less than Grade 9	18,493
Grades 9-13 w/o Certif.	41,242
Grade 9-13 with Certif.	27,783
Trade Certif. /Dip.	5,089
Non-Univ. w/o Certif./Dip.	12,099
Non-Univ. with Certif./Dip.	28,506
Univ. w/o Degree	18,164
Univ. w/o Degree/Certif.	10,375
Univ. with Certif.	7,789
Univ. with Degree	21,666

AVERAGE HOUSEHOLD EXPENDITURES

2001 Estimates:

Food	$6,196
Shelter	$9,253
Clothing	$2,107
Transportation	$6,137
Health & Personal Care	$1,892
Recr'n, Read'g & Education	$3,486
Taxes & Securities	$13,148
Other	$8,569
Total Expenditures	$50,788

PRIVATE HOUSEHOLDS

2001 Estimates:

Private Households, Total	88,361
Pop. in Private Households	208,707
Average no. per Household	2.4

FAMILIES

2001 Estimates:

Families in Private Households	58,671
Husband-Wife Families	47,727
Lone-Parent Families	10,944
Aver. No. Persons per Family	3.0
Aver. No. Sons/Daughters at Home	1.2

HOUSING

2001 Estimates:

Occupied Private Dwellings	88,361
Owned	54,675
Rented	33,686
Single-Detached House	53,899
Semi-Detached House	2,939
Row Houses	4,576
Apartment, 5+ Storeys	12,830
Owned Apartment, 5+ Storeys	1,395
Apartment, 5 or Fewer Storeys	10,078
Apartment, Detached Duplex	3,744
Other Single-Attached	277
Movable Dwellings	18

VEHICLES

2001 Estimates:

Model Yrs. '81-'96, No.	91,955
% Total	73.52
Model Yrs. '97-'98, No.	19,783
% Total	15.82
'99 Vehicles registered in Model Yr. '99, No.	13,340
% Total	10.67
Total No. '81-'99	125,078

LEGAL MARITAL STATUS

2001 Estimates: (Age 15+)

Single (Never Married)	54,965
Legally Married (Not Separated)	84,508
Legally Married (Separated)	5,243
Widowed	13,795
Divorced	14,531

PSYTE CATEGORIES

2001 Estimates	No. of House-holds	% of Total Hhds.	Index
The Affluentials	313	0.35	55
Urban Gentry	1,146	1.30	72
Suburban Executives	56	0.06	4
Technocrafts & Bureaucrats	774	0.88	31
Boomers & Teens	1,305	1.48	82
Stable Suburban Families	1,729	1.96	150
Old Bungalow Burbs	4,348	4.92	297
Suburban Nesters	4,325	4.89	305
Brie & Chablis	620	0.70	78
Aging Erudites	2,762	3.13	207
Satellite Suburbs	2,632	2.98	104
Kindergarten Boom	2,535	2.87	109
Blue Collar Winners	2,018	2.28	91
Europa	801	0.91	73
Conservative Homebodies	21,829	24.70	685
High Rise Sunsets	2,149	2.43	170
Young Urban Professionals	773	0.87	46

Ontario

2001 Estimates	No. of House -holds	% of Total Hhds.	Index
Young Urban Mix	407	0.46	22
University Enclaves	5,728	6.48	318
Young City Singles	3,070	3.47	152
Urban Bohemia	407	0.46	39
Town Renters	2,587	2.93	339
Struggling Downtowns	17,468	19.77	628
Aged Pensioners	2,848	3.22	242
Big City Stress	3,298	3.73	331
Old Grey Towers	1,511	1.71	309

FINANCIAL P$YTE

2001 Estimates	No. of House -holds	% of Total Hhds.	Index
Platinum Estates	313	0.35	44
Four Star Investors	2,507	2.84	56
Successful Suburbanites	2,503	2.83	43
Canadian Comfort	8,975	10.16	105
Urban Heights	4,155	4.70	109
Miners & Credit-Liners	4,348	4.92	155
Mortgages & Minivans	2,535	2.87	43
Dollars & Sense	801	0.91	35
Bills & Wills	22,236	25.16	304
Revolving Renters	2,149	2.43	53
Young Urban Struggle	6,135	6.94	147
Towering Debt	23,125	26.17	335
NSF	3,298	3.73	105
Senior Survivors	4,359	4.93	262

HOME LANGUAGE

2001 Estimates:		% Total
English	178,242	83.80
French	2,380	1.12
Arabic	4,159	1.96
Chinese	2,851	1.34
Croatian	751	0.35
German	519	0.24
Greek	498	0.23
Hindi	149	0.07
Hungarian	402	0.19
Italian	4,404	2.07
Khmer (Cambodian)	184	0.09
Macedonian	629	0.30
Persian (Farsi)	143	0.07
Polish	2,455	1.15
Portuguese	235	0.11
Punjabi	499	0.23
Romanian	682	0.32
Russian	168	0.08
Serbian	1,160	0.55
Serbo-Croatian	200	0.09
Slovak	185	0.09
Spanish	1,136	0.53
Tagálog (Pilipino)	743	0.35
Turkish	121	0.06
Ukrainian	253	0.12
Urdu	222	0.10
Vietnamese	1,071	0.50
Other Languages	2,347	1.10
Multiple Responses	5,921	2.78
Total	212,709	100.00

Ontario

Windsor
(City)
Windsor CMA
(Cont'd)

BUILDING PERMITS

	1999	1998	1997
		$000	
Value	366,397	295,693	519,282

HOMES BUILT

	1999	1998	1997
No.	1,177	1,012	1,295

TAXATION

Income Class:	1997	% Total
Under $5,000	19,630	12.80
$5,000-$10,000	17,330	11.30
$10,000-$15,000	20,960	13.67
$15,000-$20,000	15,000	9.78
$20,000-$25,000	12,550	8.19
$25,000-$30,000	11,170	7.29
$30,000-$40,000	17,450	11.38
$40,000-$50,000	11,800	7.70
$50,000 +	27,410	17.88
Total Returns, No.	153,300	
Total Income, $000	4,576,112	
Total Taxable Returns	105,830	
Total Tax, $000	891,116	
Average Income, $	29,851	
Average Tax, $	8,420	

VITAL STATISTICS

	1997	1996	1995	1994
Births	2,649	2,738	2,918	2,774
Deaths	1,722	1,810	1,824	1,856
Natural Increase	927	928	1,094	918
Marriages	1,288	1,346	1,453	1,429

Note: Latest available data.

MEDIA INFO
see Windsor, CMA

Woodstock
(Census Agglomeration)

The Census Agglomeration of Woodstock consists solely of Woodstock, C, in Oxford County.

POPULATION

July 1, 2001 Estimate	34,426
% Cdn. Total	0.11
% Change, '96 -'01	4.34
Avg. Annual Growth Rate, %	0.85
2003 Projected Population	34,969
2006 Projected Population	35,565
2001 Households Estimate	13,858
2003 Projected Households	14,181
2006 Projected Households	14,629

INCOME

% Above/Below National Average	-4
2001 Total Income Estimate	$693,650,000
% Cdn. Total	0.11
2001 Average Hhld. Income	$50,100
2001 Per Capita	$20,100
2003 Projected Total Income	$742,770,000
2006 Projected Total Income	$819,450,000

RETAIL SALES

% Above/Below National Average	+15
2001 Retail Sales Estimate	$355,280,000
% Cdn. Total	0.13
2001 per Household	$25,600
2001 per Capita	$10,300
2001 No. of Establishments	259
2003 Projected Retail Sales	$390,710,000
2006 Projected Retail Sales	$439,400,000

POPULATION

2001 Estimates:		
Total		34,426
Male		16,627
Female		17,799
Age Groups	Male	Female
0-4	1,104	1,052
5-9	1,185	1,122
10-14	1,221	1,153
15-19	1,179	1,127
20-24	1,103	1,127
25-29	1,136	1,146
30-34	1,283	1,295
35-39	1,357	1,415
40-44	1,299	1,357
45-49	1,171	1,214
50-54	981	1,003
55-59	793	824
60-64	667	728
65-69	608	723
70+	1,540	2,513

DAYTIME POPULATION

2001 Estimates:	
Working Population	17,013
At Home Population	17,413
Total	34,426

INCOME

2001 Estimates:	
Avg. Household Income	$50,054
Avg. Family Income	$56,349
Per Capita Income	$20,149
Male:	
Avg. Employment Income	$34,842
Avg. Employment Income (Full Time)	$43,853
Female:	
Avg. Employment Income	$20,465
Avg. Employment Income (Full Time)	$30,546

DISPOSABLE & DISCRETIONARY INCOME

2001 Estimates:	Per Hhld.
Disposable Income	$41,316
Discretionary Income 1 (minus Food & Shelter)	$27,898
Discretionary Income 2 (minus Food, Shelter, & Other Expenditures)	$19,879

LIQUID ASSETS

1999 Estimates:	Per Hhld.
Equity Investments	$61,716
Interest Bearing Investments	$60,331
Total Liquid Assets	$122,047

CREDIT DATA

July 2000:	
Pool of Credit	$377,807,830
Revolving Credit, No.	63,233
Fixed Loans, No.	21,986
Avg. Credit Limit, per Person	$12,508
Avg. Spent, per Person	$6,029
Satisfactory Ratings, No. per Person	2.72
Avg. No. of Cards, per Person	0.98

LABOUR FORCE

2001 Estimates:	
Male:	
In the Labour Force	9,736
Participation Rate	74.2
Employed	9,191
Unemployed	545
Unemployment Rate	5.6
Not in Labour Force	3,381
Female:	
In the Labour Force	8,464
Participation Rate	58.5
Employed	7,762
Unemployed	702
Unemployment Rate	8.3
Not in Labour Force	6,008

OCCUPATIONS BY MAJOR GROUPS

2001 Estimates:	Male	Female
Management	861	352
Business, Finance & Admin.	721	2,286
Natural & Applied Sciences & Related	470	110
Health	57	700
Social Sciences, Gov't Services & Religion	90	299
Education	202	349
Arts, Culture, Recreation & Sport	53	202
Sales & Service	1,746	2,958
Trades, Transport & Equipment Operators & Related	2,496	114
Primary Industries	411	53
Processing, Mfg. & Utilities	2,391	693

LEVEL OF SCHOOLING

2001 Estimates:	
Population 15 years +	27,589
Less than Grade 9	2,981
Grades 9-13 w/o Certif.	8,462
Grade 9-13 with Certif.	4,483
Trade Certif. /Dip.	1,007
Non-Univ. w/o Certif./Dip.	1,944
Non-Univ. with Certif./Dip.	5,123
Univ. w/o Degree	1,637
Univ. w/o Degree/Certif.	817
Univ. with Certif.	820
Univ. with Degree	1,952

AVERAGE HOUSEHOLD EXPENDITURES

2001 Estimates:	
Food	$6,033
Shelter	$9,435
Clothing	$1,996
Transportation	$6,125
Health & Personal Care	$1,934
Recr'n, Read'g & Education	$3,406
Taxes & Securities	$11,230
Other	$8,549
Total Expenditures	$48,708

PRIVATE HOUSEHOLDS

2001 Estimates:	
Private Households, Total	13,858
Pop. in Private Households	33,759
Average no. per Household	2.4

FAMILIES

2001 Estimates:	
Families in Private Households	9,827
Husband-Wife Families	8,403
Lone-Parent Families	1,424
Aver. No. Persons per Family	2.9
Aver. No. Sons/Daughters at Home	1.1

HOUSING

2001 Estimates:	
Occupied Private Dwellings	13,858
Owned	8,733
Rented	5,125
Single-Detached House	8,126
Semi-Detached House	1,284
Row Houses	1,468
Apartment, 5+ Storeys	918
Owned Apartment, 5+ Storeys	22
Apartment, 5 or Fewer Storeys	1,731
Apartment, Detached Duplex	259
Other Single-Attached	72

VEHICLES

2001 Estimates:	
Model Yrs. '81-'96, No.	17,759
% Total	80.47
Model Yrs. '97-'98, No.	2,616
% Total	11.85
'99 Vehicles registered in Model Yr. '99, No.	1,695
% Total	7.68
Total No. '81-'99	22,070

LEGAL MARITAL STATUS

2001 Estimates: (Age 15+)	
Single (Never Married)	7,072
Legally Married (Not Separated)	14,970
Legally Married (Separated)	1,194
Widowed	2,232
Divorced	2,121

PSYTE CATEGORIES

2001 Estimates	No. of House-holds	% of Total Hhds.	Index
Mortgaged in Suburbia	33	0.24	17
Small City Elite	507	3.66	213
Old Bungalow Burbs	360	2.60	157
Satellite Suburbs	633	4.57	159
Kindergarten Boom	1,544	11.14	425
Old Towns' New Fringe	1,268	9.15	234
Conservative Homebodies	203	1.46	41
Young City Singles	324	2.34	102
Nesters & Young Homesteaders	8,836	63.76	2,732

Woodstock
(Census Agglomeration)
(Cont'd)

FINANCIAL P$YTE

2001 Estimates	No. of House-holds	% of Total Hhds.	Index
Successful Suburbanites	33	0.24	4
Canadian Comfort	1,140	8.23	85
Miners & Credit-Liners	360	2.60	82
Mortgages & Minivans	1,544	11.14	169
Tractors & Tradelines	1,268	9.15	160
Bills & Wills	203	1.46	18
Revolving Renters	8,836	63.76	1,386
Towering Debt	324	2.34	30

HOME LANGUAGE

2001 Estimates:		% Total
English	32,674	94.91
French	93	0.27
Arabic	59	0.17
Chinese	55	0.16
Dutch	30	0.09
German	60	0.17
Greek	56	0.16
Hungarian	89	0.26
Japanese	82	0.24
Lao	22	0.06
Polish	513	1.49
Portuguese	191	0.55
Serbian	22	0.06
Serbo-Croatian	26	0.08
Ukrainian	33	0.10
Vietnamese	43	0.12
Other Languages	60	0.17
Multiple Responses	318	0.92
Total	34,426	100.00

BUILDING PERMITS

	1999	1998	1997
		$000	
Value	33,420	24,931	29,345

HOMES BUILT

	1999	1998	1997
No	147	100	86

TAXATION

Income Class:	1997	% Total
Under $5,000	3,010	10.91
$5,000-$10,000	3,230	11.71
$10,000-$15,000	3,830	13.88
$15,000-$20,000	2,890	10.47
$20,000-$25,000	2,400	8.70
$25,000-$30,000	2,120	7.68
$30,000-$40,000	3,770	13.66
$40,000-$50,000	2,700	9.79
$50,000 +	3,650	13.23
Total Returns, No.	27,590	
Total Income, $000	763,307	
Total Taxable Returns	19,850	
Total Tax, $000	137,946	
Average Income, $	27,666	
Average Tax, $	6,949	

VITAL STATISTICS

	1997	1996	1995	1994
Births	455	479	489	534
Deaths	358	332	339	336
Natural Increase	97	147	150	198
Marriages	229	255	302	277

Note: Latest available data.

DAILY NEWSPAPER(S)

	Circulation Average Paid
The Sentinel-Review	n.a.

COMMUNITY NEWSPAPER(S)

	Total Circulation
Woodstock: Oxford Shopping News Tue/Sat	28,708

RADIO STATION(S)

	Power
CKDK-FM	52,000w

Ontario

Manitoba

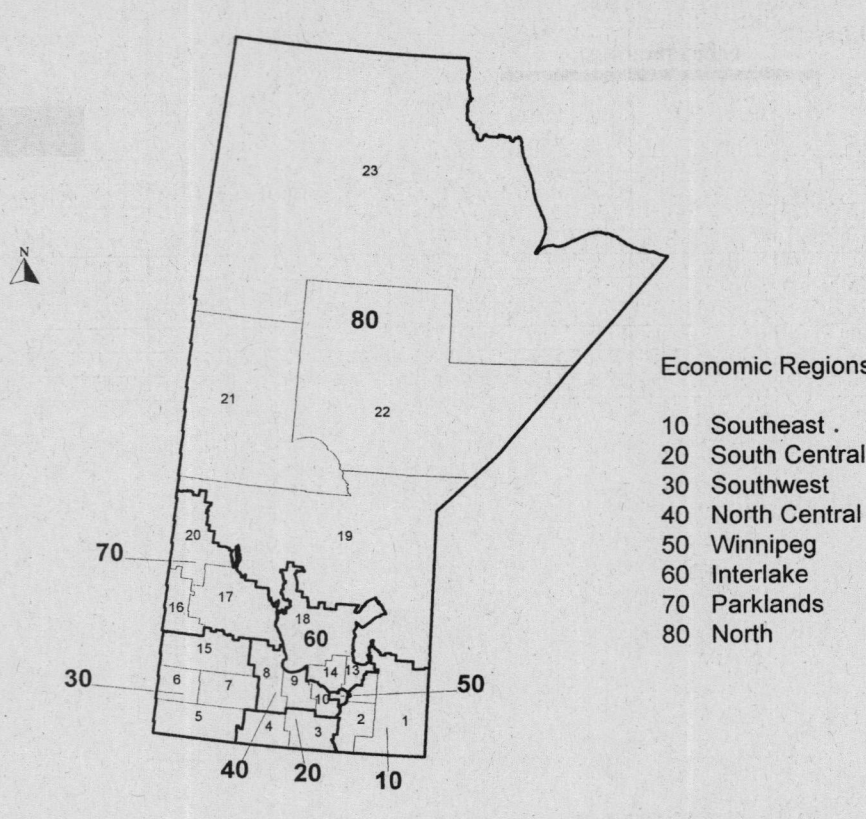

Economic Regions

10 Southeast .
20 South Central
30 Southwest
40 North Central
50 Winnipeg
60 Interlake
70 Parklands
80 North

Region	Population (at July 1)				Households (at July1)		Income				Retail Sales				Taxation Statistics, 1997					
	*1996 Census (000)	2001 Estimate (000)	% of Cdn. Total	% Chg. '96-'01	2001 Estimate (000)	% of Cdn. Total	2001 Estimate $millions	% of Cdn. Total	Per Hhld. $	Income Rating Index	2001 Estimate $millions	% of Cdn. Total	Per Hhld. $	Market Rating Index	Total No. of Returns	Total Income $millions	Total No. Taxable Returns	Total Tax $millions	Avg. Income $	Avg. Tax $
Manitoba	1,134.3	1,155.4	3.71	1.85	445.9	3.69	22,747.3	3.47	51,000	93	9,652.6	3.46	21,600	93	800,990	19,508.6	542,150	3,702.0	24,356	6,828
Southeast (10)	84.5	89.3	0.29	5.75	31.5	0.26	1,644.9	0.25	52,300	87	673.5	0.24	21,400	84	57,270	1,278.0	38,560	219.4	22,316	5,691
Division No. 1	16.5	16.9	0.05	2.49	7.0	0.06	321.2	0.05	45,700	90	116.9	0.04	16,600	77	12,480	272.9	7,800	47.5	21,868	6,088
Division No. 2	49.0	52.4	0.17	6.98	17.1	0.14	895.6	0.14	52,200	81	441.3	0.16	25,700	94	32,110	691.9	21,790	114.1	21,549	5,235
Division No. 12	19.0	20.0	0.06	5.41	7.3	0.06	428.1	0.07	58,800	101	115.3	0.04	15,800	64	12,680	313.2	8,970	57.9	24,699	6,454
South Central (20)	51.8	53.3	0.17	2.9	18.4	0.15	852.0	0.13	46,200	76	416.6	0.15	22,600	87	34,820	740.2	23,280	115.4	21,257	4,955
Division No. 3	41.2	43.0	0.14	4.2	14.8	0.12	697.2	0.11	47,100	77	373.8	0.13	25,300	97	28,370	620.1	19,130	99.0	21,857	5,173
Division No. 4	10.6	10.3	0.03	-2.21	3.7	0.03	154.8	0.02	42,400	71	42.8	0.02	11,700	46	6,450	120.1	4,150	16.4	18,619	3,950
Southwest (30)	106.7	106.6	0.34	-0.1	42.7	0.35	1,885.4	0.29	44,200	84	1,144.1	0.41	26,800	120	75,560	1,658.0	51,250	277.6	21,943	5,416
Division No. 5	15.0	14.6	0.05	-2.49	5.8	0.05	250.6	0.04	43,100	81	151.4	0.05	26,100	116	10,160	211.1	6,860	31.4	20,776	4,572
Division No. 6	10.7	10.7	0.03	0.7	4.0	0.03	153.3	0.02	38,300	68	87.5	0.03	21,800	91	7,590	137.9	4,460	20.0	18,174	4,478
Division No. 7	58.3	58.5	0.19	0.38	23.7	0.20	1,111.1	0.17	46,900	90	749.3	0.27	31,600	143	41,140	990.4	29,610	180.0	24,073	6,077
Division No. 15	22.8	22.8	0.07	-0.13	9.2	0.08	370.4	0.06	40,400	77	155.9	0.06	17,000	77	16,670	318.6	10,320	46.3	19,113	4,486
North Central (40)	47.9	49.0	0.16	2.3	16.5	0.14	776.9	0.12	47,100	75	450.8	0.16	27,300	103	31,030	669.9	20,280	111.6	21,590	5,505
Division No. 8	15.1	15.5	0.05	2.25	5.1	0.04	193.3	0.03	38,200	59	76.0	0.03	15,000	55	9,050	157.3	5,250	21.3	17,379	4,052
Division No. 9	23.7	23.5	0.08	-1.05	8.4	0.07	380.4	0.06	45,100	77	317.8	0.11	37,600	151	16,910	365.2	11,060	60.5	21,598	5,471
Division No. 10	9.1	10.1	0.03	11.14	3.0	0.02	203.2	0.03	67,600	95	57.0	0.02	19,000	63	5,070	147.4	3,970	29.9	29,077	7,520
Winnipeg (50)	631.3	633.0	2.03	0.27	259.0	2.14	13,715.7	2.09	52,900	103	5,422.1	1.95	20,900	96	464,110	12,388.9	333,960	2,493.4	26,694	7,466
Division No. 11	631.3	633.0	2.03	0.27	259.0	2.14	13,715.7	2.09	52,900	103	5,422.1	1.95	20,900	96	464,110	12,388.9	333,960	2,493.4	26,694	7,466
Interlake (60)	80.2	85.9	0.28	7.2	31.0	0.26	1,724.6	0.26	55,600	95	546.4	0.20	17,600	71	52,070	1,201.6	34,670	220.9	23,076	6,371

*Adjusted.

Region	Population (at July 1)				Households (at July1)		Income				Retail Sales				Taxation Statistics, 1997					
	*1996 Census (000)	2001 Estimate (000)	% of Cdn. Total	% Chg. '96-'01	2001 Estimate (000)	% of Cdn. Total	2001 Estimate $millions	% of Cdn. Total	Per Hhld. $	Income Rating Index	2001 Estimate $millions	% of Cdn. Total	Per Hhld. $	Market Rating Index	Total No. of Returns	Total Income $millions	Total No. Taxable Returns	Total Tax $millions	Avg. Income $	Avg. Tax $
Division No. 13	40.1	43.6	0.14	8.74	15.4	0.13	1,006.3	0.15	65,200	109	282.5	0.10	18,300	72	23,140	619.1	16,980	122.3	26,753	7,204
Division No. 14	17.4	18.7	0.06	7.65	6.4	0.05	356.8	0.05	55,400	90	66.5	0.02	10,300	40	11,210	272.7	8,070	50.3	24,328	6,233
Division No. 18	22.6	23.6	0.08	4.11	9.2	0.08	361.5	0.06	39,500	73	197.5	0.07	21,600	94	17,720	309.8	9,620	48.3	17,482	5,016
Parklands (70)	46.8	46.1	0.15	-1.63	18.7	0.15	720.3	0.11	38,500	74	442.1	0.16	23,600	107	34,730	618.8	19,170	89.2	17,818	4,652
Division No. 16	10.9	10.9	0.04	0.74	4.3	0.04	162.0	0.02	38,100	70	105.8	0.04	24,800	108	7,860	129.0	4,010	18.0	16,410	4,500
Division No. 17	24.3	23.6	0.08	-3.12	9.8	0.08	378.0	0.06	38,400	76	199.9	0.07	20,300	95	18,360	330.1	10,160	48.1	17,982	4,730
Division No. 20	11.6	11.6	0.04	-0.72	4.6	0.04	180.2	0.03	39,000	74	136.4	0.05	29,500	132	8,510	159.7	5,000	23.1	18,765	4,616
North (80)	85.2	92.1	0.30	8.14	28.0	0.23	1,427.5	0.22	51,000	74	557.0	0.20	19,900	68	48,940	930.9	20,450	173.3	19,020	8,473
Division No. 19	15.3	17.9	0.06	17.52	5.1	0.04	148.8	0.02	29,000	39	41.1	0.01	8,000	26	7,080	49.1	1,030	4.8	6,939	4,614
Division No. 21	23.6	23.9	0.08	1.15	8.6	0.07	475.6	0.07	55,200	94	209.8	0.08	24,400	98	15,770	390.2	9,290	73.6	24,744	7,921
Division No. 22	36.4	40.1	0.13	10.28	11.4	0.09	629.9	0.10	55,500	74	261.4	0.09	23,000	73	20,910	372.1	7,680	72.8	17,796	9,485
Division No. 23	9.9	10.1	0.03	2.49	2.9	0.02	173.2	0.03	59,100	81	44.8	0.02	15,300	49	5,180	119.4	2,450	22.1	23,049	9,015

*Adjusted.

Manitoba

POPULATION

July 1, 2001 Estimate 1,155,362
% Cdn. Total 3.71
% Change, '96 -'01 . . . . 1.85
Avg. Annual Growth Rate, % 0.37
2003 Projected Population 1,182,230
2006 Projected Population 1,230,462
2001 Households Estimate 445,906
2003 Projected Households 458,307
2006 Projected Households 480,601

INCOME

% Above/Below National Average . . . .-7
2001 Total Income Estimate . . $22,747,280,000
% Cdn. Total 3.47
2001 Average Hhld. Income $51,000
2001 Per Capita $19,700
2003 Projected Total Income . $24,610,970,000
2006 Projected Total Income . $27,921,910,000

RETAIL SALES

% Above/Below National Average . . . .-7
2001 Retail Sales Estimate . . . $9,652,630,000
% Cdn. Total 3.46
2001 per Household $21,600
2001 per Capita $8,400
2001 No. of Establishments 8,153
2003 Projected Retail Sales . . $10,592,790,000
2006 Projected Retail Sales . . $12,065,990,000

POPULATION

2001 Estimates:
Total 1,155,362
Male 568,197
Female 587,165

Age Groups	Male	Female
0-4	40,154	38,143
5-9	41,603	39,690
10-14	41,997	40,039
15-19	41,221	39,368
20-24	40,001	38,423
25-29	38,623	37,888
30-34	40,772	40,611
35-39	43,792	43,786
40-44	43,800	44,107
45-49	40,978	41,444
50-54	35,121	35,413
55-59	28,159	28,614
60-64	23,407	24,298
65-69	20,264	22,434
70+	48,305	72,907

DAYTIME POPULATION

2001 Estimates:
Working Population 566,688
At Home Population 588,668
Total 1,155,356

INCOME

2001 Estimates:
Avg. Household Income $51,014
Avg. Family Income $58,924
Per Capita Income $19,688
Male:
Avg. Employment Income $32,714
Avg. Employment Income
    (Full Time) $42,931
Female:
Avg. Employment Income $20,773
Avg. Employment Income
    (Full Time) $30,784

DISPOSABLE & DISCRETIONARY INCOME

2001 Estimates:	Per Hhld.
Disposable Income	$39,449
Discretionary Income 1 (minus Food & Shelter)	$26,902
Discretionary Income 2 (minus Food, Shelter, & Other Expenditures)	$18,607

LIQUID ASSETS

1999 Estimates:	Per Hhld.
Equity Investments	$62,163
Interest Bearing Investments	$58,322
Total Liquid Assets	$120,485

CREDIT DATA

July 2000:
Pool of Credit $9,516,100,415
Revolving Credit, No. 1,819,714
Fixed Loans, No. 552,790
Avg. Credit Limit, per Person $10,586
Avg. Spent, per Person $4,762
Satisfactory Ratings,
    No. per Person 2.50
Avg. No. of Cards, per Person 0.92

LABOUR FORCE

2001 Estimates:
Male:
In the Labour Force 318,905
Participation Rate 71.8
Employed 300,835
Unemployed 18,070
Unemployment Rate 5.7
Not in Labour Force 125,538
Female:
In the Labour Force 272,220
Participation Rate 58.0
Employed 260,663
Unemployed 11,557
Unemployment Rate 4.2
Not in Labour Force 197,073

AVERAGE WEEKLY EARNINGS

(Including overtime, industrial aggregate)	Manitoba	Canada
Apr 2000	$557.94	$622.92
Apr 1999	$543.53	$608.07
Apr 1998	$532.89	$608.06
Apr 1997	$523.27	$597.26
Apr 1996	$508.29	$575.79

NUMBER OF EMPLOYEES

(Industrial aggregate)
Apr 2000 469,498
Apr 1999 455,589
Apr 1998 431,920
Apr 1997 419,429
Apr 1996 411,904

MANUFACTURING INDUSTRIES

	1997	1992
Plants	1,098	1,047
Employees	59,945	48,263
	$000	
Salaries, Wages	1,856,596	1,433,889
Mfg. Materials, Cost	5,459,826	3,231,240
Mfg. Shipments, Value	9,969,271	6,228,380
Total Value Added	4,659,072	2,945,009

Note: Latest available data.

OCCUPATIONS BY MAJOR GROUPS

2001 Estimates:	Male	Female
Management	30,527	12,994
Business, Finance & Admin.	28,472	74,926
Natural & Applied Sciences & Related	17,624	3,645
Health	6,411	26,334
Social Sciences, Gov't Services & Religion	6,824	8,333
Education	8,707	14,477
Arts, Culture, Recreation & Sport	5,078	6,725
Sales & Service	65,233	93,216
Trades, Transport & Equipment Operators & Related	81,511	4,531
Primary Industries	35,696	9,990
Processing, Mfg. & Utilities	25,466	9,854

LEVEL OF SCHOOLING

2001 Estimates:
Population 15 years + ...913,736
Less than Grade 9 117,286
Grades 9-13 w/o Certif. 265,161
Grade 9-13 with Certif. 101,670
Trade Certif. /Dip. 30,081
Non-Univ. w/o Certif./Dip. 47,149
Non-Univ. with Certif./Dip. 144,181
Univ. w/o Degree 103,554
Univ. w/o Degree/Certif. 54,711
Univ. with Certif. 48,843
Univ. with Degree 104,654

RETAIL SALES

	1999 $000,000	1998 $000,000
Supermarkets & Groceries	2,127	2,102
All Other Food	n.a.	n.a.
Drugs & Patent Medicine	290	281
Shoes	46	50
Men's Clothing	47	45
Women's Clothing	118	109
Other Clothing	201	195
Hhld. Furniture & Appliances	338	324
Hhld. Furnishings	62	51
Motor & Recreation Vehicles	2,595	2,618
Gas Service Stations	682	585
Auto Parts, Accessories & Services	459	448
General Merchandise	1,167	1,117
Other Semi-Durable Goods	228	213
Other Durable Goods	217	208
Other Retail	381	349
Total	9,024	8,772

AVERAGE HOUSEHOLD EXPENDITURES

2001 Estimates:
Food $6,032
Shelter $8,566
Clothing $2,127
Transportation $6,289
Health & Personal Care $1,920
Recr'n, Read'g & Education $3,578
Taxes & Securities $12,703
Other $8,543
Total Expenditures $49,758

PRIVATE HOUSEHOLDS

2001 Estimates:
Private Households, Total 445,906
Pop. in Private Households 1,122,963
Average no. per Household 2.5

FAMILIES

2001 Estimates:
Families in Private Households 311,807
Husband-Wife Families 268,284
Lone-Parent Families 43,523
Aver. No. Persons per Family 3.1
Aver. No. Sons/Daughters
    at Home 1.2

HOUSING

2001 Estimates:
Occupied Private Dwellings 445,906
Owned 295,063
Rented 138,586
Band Housing 12,257
Single-Detached House 308,018
Semi-Detached House 13,382
Row Houses 13,406
Apartment, 5+ Storeys 37,895
    Owned Apartment, 5+ Storeys 3,319
Apartment, 5 or Fewer Storeys 57,433
Apartment, Detached Duplex 6,703
Other Single-Attached 998
Movable Dwellings 8,071

VEHICLES

2001 Estimates:
Model Yrs. '81-'96, No. 517,544
    % Total 81.06
Model Yrs. '97-'98, No. 78,756
    % Total 12.33
'99 Vehicles registered in
    Model Yr. '99, No. 42,184
    % Total 6.61
Total No. '81-'99 638,484

LEGAL MARITAL STATUS

2001 Estimates: (Age 15+)
Single (Never Married) 281,217
Legally Married
    (Not Separated) 487,235
Legally Married (Separated) 25,442
Widowed 65,822
Divorced 54,020

PSYTE CATEGORIES

2001 Estimates	No. of House-holds	% of Total Hhds.	Index
The Affluentials	2,207	0.49	77
Urban Gentry	4,943	1.11	62
Suburban Executives	1,913	0.43	30
Technocrafts & Bureaucrats	21,021	4.71	168
Boomers & Teens	1,446	0.32	18
Stable Suburban Families	7,288	1.63	125
Small City Elite	1,673	0.38	22
Old Bungalow Burbs	13,104	2.94	177
Suburban Nesters	2,436	0.55	34
Brie & Chablis	1,172	0.26	29
Aging Erudites	12,798	2.87	190
Satellite Suburbs	5,989	1.34	47
Kindergarten Boom	21,774	4.88	186
Blue Collar Winners	11,237	2.52	100
Town Boomers	6,764	1.52	150
Old Towns' New Fringe	14,797	3.32	85
Traditional French Cdn. Families	751	0.17	6
Northern Lights	5,356	1.20	243
The New Frontier	9,293	2.08	138
Rustic Prosperity	10,920	2.45	136
Pick-ups & Dirt Bikes	5,820	1.31	156
Quebec's Heartland	722	0.16	16
The Grain Belt	12,505	2.80	473
High Rise Melting Pot	601	0.13	9
Conservative Homebodies	33,231	7.45	207
High Rise Sunsets	9,291	2.08	146
Young Urban Professionals	4,856	1.09	57
Young Urban Mix	1,220	0.27	13
Young Urban Intelligentsia	3,890	0.87	57

2001 Estimates	No. of House -holds	% of Total Hhds.	Index
University Enclaves	15,741	3.53	173
Young City Singles	19,710	4.42	193
Urban Bohemia	1,526	0.34	29
Old Leafy Towns	3,580	0.80	31
Town Renters	4,806	1.08	125
Nesters & Young Homesteaders	915	0.21	9
Young Grey Collar	10,076	2.26	270
Quiet Towns	18,703	4.19	197
Agrarian Blues	6,457	1.45	676
Rod & Rifle	12,297	2.76	119
Down, Down East	185	0.04	6
Big Country Families	20,484	4.59	322
Quebec Rural Blues	628	0.14	6
Old Cdn. Rustics	26,043	5.84	596
Old Quebec Walkups	60	0.01	1
Struggling Downtowns	43,478	9.75	310
Aged Pensioners	12,299	2.76	207
Big City Stress	12,022	2.70	239
Old Grey Towers	3,997	0.90	162

FINANÇIAL P$YTE

2001 Estimates	No. of House -holds	% of Total Hhds.	Index
Platinum Estates	2,207	0.49	61
Four Star Investors	8,302	1.86	37
Successful Suburbanites	33,665	7.55	114
Canadian Comfort	28,099	6.30	65
Urban Heights	18,826	4.22	98
Miners & Credit-Liners	22,397	5.02	159
Mortgages & Minivans	21,774	4.88	74
Tractors & Tradelines	25,717	5.77	101
Bills & Wills	38,031	8.53	103
Country Credit	19,076	4.28	63
Revolving Renters	20,282	4.55	99
Young Urban Struggle	21,157	4.74	100
Rural Family Blues	40,773	9.14	113
Limited Budgets	44,746	10.03	323
Loan Parent Stress	60	0.01	
Towering Debt	68,595	15.38	197
NSF	12,022	2.70	76
Senior Survivors	16,296	3.65	194

HOME LANGUAGE

2001 Estimates:		% Total
English	1,005,824	87.06
French	22,987	1.99
Chinese	7,720	0.67
Cree	20,883	1.81
German	22,816	1.97
Greek	637	0.06
Italian	1,766	0.15
Korean	694	0.06
Lao	834	0.07
Ojibway	6,383	0.55
Polish	4,560	0.39
Portuguese	4,071	0.35
Punjabi	3,730	0.32
Serbo-Croatian	716	0.06
Spanish	2,643	0.23
Tagalog (Pilipino)	9,289	0.80
Ukrainian	4,450	0.39
Vietnamese	1,734	0.15
Other Languages	9,138	0.79
Multiple Responses	24,487	2.12
Total	1,155,362	100.00

BUILDING PERMITS

	1999	1998 $000	1997
Value	879,431	1,031,802	689,564

HOMES BUILT

	1999	1998	1997
No	2,812	2,741	2,943

CAPITAL EXPENDITURES

(Public & Private)	2000	1999 $000,000	1998
Total Expends.	n.a.	n.a.	6,694.0
Capital Expends.	5,099.8	5,148.8	4,990.6
Construction	2,658.8	2,710.1	2,799.0
Machinery & Equip.	2,441.0	2,438.8	2,191.6
Repair Expends.	n.a.	n.a.	1,703.4
Construction	n.a.	n.a.	707.0
Machinery & Equip.	n.a.	n.a.	996.4

TAXATION

Income Class:	1997	% Total
Under $5,000	117,730	14.70
$5,000-$10,000	104,460	13.04
$10,000-$15,000	128,780	16.08
$15,000-$20,000	86,580	10.81
$20,000-$25,000	71,690	8.95
$25,000-$30,000	63,120	7.88
$30,000-$40,000	95,550	11.93
$40,000-$50,000	54,920	6.86
$50,000 +	78,160	9.76
Total Returns, No.	800,990	
Total Income, $000	19,508,616	
Total Taxable Returns	542,150	
Total Tax, $000	3,701,998	
Average Income, $	24,356	
Average Tax, $	6,828	

VITAL STATISTICS

	1997	1996	1995	1994
Births	14,655	15,478	16,113	16,480
Deaths	9,511	9,497	9,658	9,148
Natural Increase	5,144	5,981	6,455	7,332
Marriages	6,620	6,448	6,703	6,585

Note: Latest available data.

TRAVEL STATISTICS

Tourists in Canada	1999	1998
From the U.S. entering by:		
Automobile	562,540	542,609
Bus	17,528	18,907
Air	78,957	74,032
Marine	2	n.a.
Other Methods	3,807	2,332
Total	662,834	637,880
Other Countries:		
Land (via U.S.)	3,814	3,020
Air	14,383	11,763
Total	18,197	14,783
Residents of Canada Returning from the U.S. by:		
Automobile	887,980	887,565
Bus	116,045	121,767
Rail	n.a.	124
Air	105,358	104,685
Marine	n.a.	13
Other Methods	4,900	4,588
Total	1,114,283	1,118,742
From Other Countries:		
Air	41,528	36,612
Total	41,528	36,612

Manitoba

Manitoba

Brandon
(Census Agglomeration)

The Census Agglomeration of Brandon consists of Brandon, C, and Elton, RM, both in census division No. 7.

POPULATION

July 1, 2001 Estimate	41,544
% Cdn. Total	0.13
% Change, '96 -'01	0.51
Avg. Annual Growth Rate, %	0.10
2003 Projected Population	41,761
2006 Projected Population	41,749
2001 Households Estimate	17,520
2003 Projected Households	17,784
2006 Projected Households	18,056

INCOME

% Above/Below National Average	-7
2001 Total Income Estimate	$810,990,000
% Cdn. Total	0.12
2001 Average Hhld. Income	$46,300
2001 Per Capita	$19,500
2003 Projected Total Income	$853,330,000
2006 Projected Total Income	$912,790,000

RETAIL SALES

% Above/Below National Average	+79
2001 Retail Sales Estimate	$666,540,000
% Cdn. Total	0.24
2001 per Household	$38,000
2001 per Capita	$16,000
2001 No. of Establishments	433
2003 Projected Retail Sales	$725,430,000
2006 Projected Retail Sales	$804,430,000

POPULATION

2001 Estimates:

Total		41,544
Male		19,786
Female		21,758
Age Groups	Male	Female
0-4	1,427	1,385
5-9	1,373	1,347
10-14	1,381	1,364
15-19	1,411	1,422
20-24	1,514	1,575
25-29	1,478	1,528
30-34	1,450	1,540
35-39	1,480	1,595
40-44	1,431	1,567
45-49	1,366	1,473
50-54	1,156	1,249
55-59	932	1,006
60-64	769	868
65-69	709	833
70+	1,909	3,006

DAYTIME POPULATION

2001 Estimates:

Working Population	21,010
At Home Population	20,534
Total	41,544

INCOME

2001 Estimates:

Avg. Household Income	$46,290
Avg. Family Income	$55,055
Per Capita Income	$19,521
Male:	
Avg. Employment Income	$31,236
Avg. Employment Income (Full Time)	$40,677
Female:	
Avg. Employment Income	$18,956
Avg. Employment Income (Full Time)	$27,914

DISPOSABLE & DISCRETIONARY INCOME

2001 Estimates:	Per Hhld.
Disposable Income	$36,155
Discretionary Income 1 (minus Food & Shelter)	$24,633
Discretionary Income 2 (minus Food, Shelter, & Other Expenditures)	$17,004

LIQUID ASSETS

1999 Estimates:	Per Hhld.
Equity Investments	$54,070
Interest Bearing Investments	$53,819
Total Liquid Assets	$107,889

CREDIT DATA

July 2000:

Pool of Credit	$377,492,619
Revolving Credit, No.	71,590
Fixed Loans, No.	24,387
Avg. Credit Limit, per Person	$10,937
Avg. Spent, per Person	$5,031
Satisfactory Ratings, No. per Person	2.61
Avg. No. of Cards, per Person	0.95

LABOUR FORCE

2001 Estimates:

Male:	
In the Labour Force	11,231
Participation Rate	72.0
Employed	10,816
Unemployed	415
Unemployment Rate	3.7
Not in Labour Force	4,374
Female:	
In the Labour Force	10,499
Participation Rate	59.4
Employed	10,061
Unemployed	438
Unemployment Rate	4.2
Not in Labour Force	7,163

OCCUPATIONS BY MAJOR GROUPS

2001 Estimates:	Male	Female
Management	1,093	532
Business, Finance & Admin.	909	2,562
Natural & Applied Sciences & Related	446	84
Health	443	1,165
Social Sciences, Gov't Services & Religion	275	386
Education	433	487
Arts, Culture, Recreation & Sport	198	363
Sales & Service	3,319	4,257
Trades, Transport & Equipment Operators & Related	2,936	132
Primary Industries	503	168
Processing, Mfg. & Utilities	530	113

LEVEL OF SCHOOLING

2001 Estimates:

Population 15 years +	33,267
Less than Grade 9	2,784
Grades 9-13 w/o Certif.	9,457
Grade 9-13 with Certif.	3,588
Trade Certif./Dip.	1,230
Non-Univ. w/o Certif./Dip.	1,695
Non-Univ. with Certif./Dip.	5,999
Univ. w/o Degree	4,510
Univ. w/o Degree/Certif.	2,370
Univ. with Certif.	2,140
Univ. with Degree	4,004

AVERAGE HOUSEHOLD EXPENDITURES

2001 Estimates:

Food	$5,757
Shelter	$7,676
Clothing	$2,102
Transportation	$5,157
Health & Personal Care	$2,106
Recr'n, Read'g & Education	$3,488
Taxes & Securities	$11,139
Other	$8,222
Total Expenditures	$45,647

PRIVATE HOUSEHOLDS

2001 Estimates:

Private Households, Total	17,520
Pop. in Private Households	40,426
Average no. per Household	2.3

FAMILIES

2001 Estimates:

Families in Private Households	11,512
Husband-Wife Families	9,741
Lone-Parent Families	1,771
Aver. No. Persons per Family	2.9
Aver. No. Sons/Daughters at Home	1.1

HOUSING

2001 Estimates:

Occupied Private Dwellings	17,520
Owned	10,771
Rented	6,749
Single-Detached House	10,560
Semi-Detached House	669
Row Houses	795
Apartment, 5+ Storeys	751
Apartment, 5 or Fewer Storeys	3,347
Apartment, Detached Duplex	622
Other Single-Attached	107
Movable Dwellings	669

VEHICLES

2001 Estimates:

Model Yrs. '81-'96, No.	19,536
% Total	81.28
Model Yrs. '97-'98, No.	2,971
% Total	12.36
'99 Vehicles registered in Model Yr. '99, No.	1,528
% Total	6.36
Total No. '81-'99	24,035

LEGAL MARITAL STATUS

2001 Estimates: (Age 15+)

Single (Never Married)	10,447
Legally Married (Not Separated)	17,074
Legally Married (Separated)	825
Widowed	2,583
Divorced	2,338

PSYTE CATEGORIES

2001 Estimates	No. of House -holds	% of Total Hhds.	Index
Town Boomers	4,582	26.15	2,580
Rustic Prosperity	211	1.20	67
Pick-ups & Dirt Bikes	284	1.62	194
Nesters & Young Homesteaders	320	1.83	78
Young Grey Collar	10,076	57.51	6,875
Aged Pensioners	1,648	9.41	707
Old Grey Towers	131	0.75	135

FINANCIAL P$YTE

2001 Estimates	No. of House -holds	% of Total Hhds.	Index
Canadian Comfort	4,582	26.15	269
Tractors & Tradelines	211	1.20	21
Country Credit	284	1.62	24
Revolving Renters	10,396	59.34	1,290
Senior Survivors	1,779	10.15	539

HOME LANGUAGE

2001 Estimates:		% Total
English	40,835	98.29
French	51	0.12
Chinese	135	0.32
Cree	62	0.15
German	74	0.18
Punjabi	32	0.08
Ukrainian	42	0.10
Vietnamese	21	0.05
Other Languages	75	0.18
Multiple Responses	217	0.52
Total	41,544	100.00

BUILDING PERMITS

	1999	1998	1997
		$000	
Value	55,079	164,180	38,040

HOMES BUILT

	1999	1998	1997
No.	104	167	122

TAXATION

Income Class:	1997	% Total
Under $5,000	3,760	11.74
$5,000-$10,000	4,300	13.42
$10,000-$15,000	5,170	16.14
$15,000-$20,000	3,750	11.70
$20,000-$25,000	3,040	9.49
$25,000-$30,000	2,660	8.30
$30,000-$40,000	4,090	12.77
$40,000-$50,000	2,320	7.24
$50,000 +	2,950	9.21
Total Returns, No.	32,040	
Total Income, $000	783,474	
Total Taxable Returns	23,040	
Total Tax, $000	145,732	
Average Income, $	24,453	
Average Tax, $	6,325	

VITAL STATISTICS

	1997	1996	1995	1994
Births	498	546	538	567
Deaths	406	405	377	375
Natural Increase	92	141	161	192
Marriages	236	281	285	297

Note: Latest available data.

DAILY NEWSPAPER(S)

	Circulation Average Paid
Brandon Sun	
Sat	22,027
Mon-Fri	16,074

COMMUNITY NEWSPAPER(S)

	Total Circulation
Brandon: Westman Review	n.a.
Brandon: Brandon Wheat City News	n.a.

RADIO STATION(S)

	Power
CBWV-FM	n.a.
CKLQ	10,000w
CKSB-FM	n.a.
CKX	50,000w
CKX-FM	n.a.

TELEVISION STATION(S)

CBWFT-TV
CKX-TV
CKYB-TV

Portage la Prairie
(Census Agglomeration)

The Census Agglomeration of Portage la Prairie consists of Portage la Prairie, C; Portage la Prairie, RM, plus several smaller areas. All are in in census division No. 9.

POPULATION

July 1, 2001 Estimate	20,500
% Cdn. Total	0.07
% Change, '96 -'01	-1.60
Avg. Annual Growth Rate, %	-0.32
2003 Projected Population	20,303
2006 Projected Population	19,859
2001 Households Estimate	7,450
2003 Projected Households	7,440
2006 Projected Households	7,362

INCOME

% Above/Below National Average	-24
2001 Total Income Estimate	$329,890,000
% Cdn. Total	0.05
2001 Average Hhld. Income	$44,300
2001 Per Capita	$16,100
2003 Projected Total Income	$342,780,000
2006 Projected Total Income	$359,400,000

RETAIL SALES

% Above/Below National Average	+67
2001 Retail Sales Estimate	$306,520,000
% Cdn. Total	0.11
2001 per Household	$41,100
2001 per Capita	$15,000
2001 No. of Establishments	189
2003 Projected Retail Sales	$324,830,000
2006 Projected Retail Sales	$346,490,000

POPULATION

2001 Estimates:

Total		20,500
Male		10,029
Female		10,471
Age Groups	Male	Female
0-4	720	666
5-9	771	721
10-14	786	764
15-19	776	754
20-24	701	679
25-29	596	618
30-34	638	668
35-39	759	769
40-44	782	785
45-49	709	715
50-54	607	611
55-59	504	503
60-64	417	427
65-69	359	398
70+	904	1,393

DAYTIME POPULATION

2001 Estimates:

Working Population	9,734
At Home Population	10,766
Total	20,500

INCOME

2001 Estimates:

Avg. Household Income	$44,280
Avg. Family Income	$50,871
Per Capita Income	$16,092
Male:	
Avg. Employment Income	$27,997
Avg. Employment Income (Full Time)	$35,553
Female:	
Avg. Employment Income	$19,160
Avg. Employment Income (Full Time)	$28,342

DISPOSABLE & DISCRETIONARY INCOME

2001 Estimates:	Per Hhld.
Disposable Income	$34,931
Discretionary Income 1 (minus Food & Shelter)	$23,928
Discretionary Income 2 (minus Food, Shelter, & Other Expenditures)	$15,616

LIQUID ASSETS

1999 Estimates:	Per Hhld.
Equity Investments	$43,034
Interest Bearing Investments	$48,941
Total Liquid Assets	$91,975

CREDIT DATA

July 2000:

Pool of Credit	$141,163,997
Revolving Credit, No.	26,235
Fixed Loans, No.	9,048
Avg. Credit Limit, per Person	$9,632
Avg. Spent, per Person	$4,502
Satisfactory Ratings, No. per Person	2.28
Avg. No. of Cards, per Person	0.83

LABOUR FORCE

2001 Estimates:

Male:	
In the Labour Force	5,463
Participation Rate	70.5
Employed	5,246
Unemployed	217
Unemployment Rate	4.0
Not in Labour Force	2,289
Female:	
In the Labour Force	4,565
Participation Rate	54.9
Employed	4,399
Unemployed	166
Unemployment Rate	3.6
Not in Labour Force	3,755

OCCUPATIONS BY MAJOR GROUPS

2001 Estimates:	Male	Female
Management	522	230
Business, Finance & Admin.	349	970
Natural & Applied Sciences & Related	157	44
Health	235	643
Social Sciences, Gov't Services & Religion	149	209
Education	111	215
Arts, Culture, Recreation & Sport	59	84
Sales & Service	1,092	1,626
Trades, Transport & Equipment Operators & Related	1,418	82
Primary Industries	1,049	243
Processing, Mfg. & Utilities	240	101

LEVEL OF SCHOOLING

2001 Estimates:

Population 15 years +	16,072
Less than Grade 9	2,279
Grades 9-13 w/o Certif.	5,432
Grade 9-13 with Certif.	1,670
Trade Certif. /Dip.	506
Non-Univ. w/o Certif./Dip.	863
Non-Univ. with Certif./Dip.	2,958
Univ. w/o Degree	1,364
Univ. w/o Degree/Certif.	564
Univ. with Certif.	800
Univ. with Degree	1,000

AVERAGE HOUSEHOLD EXPENDITURES

2001 Estimates:

Food	$5,483
Shelter	$7,408
Clothing	$1,914
Transportation	$6,452
Health & Personal Care	$1,881
Recr'n, Read'g & Education	$3,213
Taxes & Securities	$10,292
Other	$7,524
Total Expenditures	$44,167

PRIVATE HOUSEHOLDS

2001 Estimates:

Private Households, Total	7,450
Pop. in Private Households	18,739
Average no. per Household	2.5

FAMILIES

2001 Estimates:

Families in Private Households	5,223
Husband-Wife Families	4,370
Lone-Parent Families	853
Aver. No. Persons per Family	3.0
Aver. No. Sons/Daughters at Home	1.2

HOUSING

2001 Estimates:

Occupied Private Dwellings	7,450
Owned	5,023
Rented	2,249
Band Housing	178
Single-Detached House	5,779
Semi-Detached House	170
Row Houses	204
Apartment, 5+ Storeys	163
Apartment, 5 or Fewer Storeys	840
Apartment, Detached Duplex	73
Movable Dwellings	221

VEHICLES

2001 Estimates:

Model Yrs. '81-'96, No.	10,138
% Total	83.52
Model Yrs. '97-'98, No.	1,379
% Total	11.36
'99 Vehicles registered in Model Yr. '99, No.	621
% Total	5.12
Total No. '81-'99	12,138

LEGAL MARITAL STATUS

2001 Estimates: (Age 15+)

Single (Never Married)	5,087
Legally Married (Not Separated)	8,303
Legally Married (Separated)	476
Widowed	1,320
Divorced	886

PSYTE CATEGORIES

2001 Estimates	No. of House-holds	% of Total Hhds.	Index
Town Boomers	447	6.00	592
The New Frontier	1,445	19.40	1,286
Rustic Prosperity	615	8.26	457
Pick-ups & Dirt Bikes	172	2.31	276
The Grain Belt	143	1.92	324
Old Leafy Towns	235	3.15	123
Quiet Towns	3,638	48.83	2,295
Rod & Rifle	338	4.54	196
Big Country Families	223	2.99	210

FINANCIAL PSYTE

2001 Estimates	No. of House-holds	% of Total Hhds.	Index
Canadian Comfort	447	6.00	62
Miners & Credit-Liners	1,445	19.40	613
Tractors & Tradelines	615	8.26	144
Bills & Wills	235	3.15	38
Country Credit	315	4.23	63
Rural Family Blues	561	7.53	93
Limited Budgets	3,638	48.83	1,571

Manitoba

HOME LANGUAGE

2001 Estimates:		% Total
English	19,110	93.22
French	132	0.64
German	890	4.34
Lao	38	0.19
Ojibway	145	0.71
Ukrainian	31	0.15
Other Languages	41	0.20
Multiple Responses	113	0.55
Total	20,500	100.00

BUILDING PERMITS

	1999	1998	1997
		$000	
Value	15,658	22,094	8,388

HOMES BUILT

	1999	1998	1997
No.	14	64	12

TAXATION

Income Class:	1997	% Total
Under $5,000	2,300	15.48
$5,000-$10,000	1,910	12.85
$10,000-$15,000	2,590	17.43
$15,000-$20,000	1,680	11.31
$20,000-$25,000	1,400	9.42
$25,000-$30,000	1,370	9.22
$30,000-$40,000	1,730	11.64
$40,000-$50,000	870	5.85
$50,000 +	1,020	6.86
Total Returns, No.	14,860	
Total Income, $000	324,080	
Total Taxable Returns	9,700	
Total Tax, $000	54,484	
Average Income, $	21,809	
Average Tax, $	5,617	

VITAL STATISTICS

	1997	1996	1995	1994
Births	309	311	318	283
Deaths	208	202	205	197
Natural Increase	101	109	113	86
Marriages	118	114	112	124

Note: Latest available data.

DAILY NEWSPAPER(S)

	Circulation Average Paid
The Daily Graphic	4,028

COMMUNITY NEWSPAPER(S)

	Total Circulation
Portage la Prairie: The Central Manitoba Shopper and News (16/yr)	n.a.
Portage la Prairie: Herald Leader Press	6,333

RADIO STATION(S)

	Power
CFRY	25,000w
CFRY-FM	25,000w

TELEVISION STATION(S)

CHMI-TV

Manitoba

St. Andrews
(Rural Municipality)
In census division No. 13.

POPULATION

July 1, 2001 Estimate	11,364
% Cdn. Total	0.04
% Change, '96 -'01	10.04
Avg. Annual Growth Rate, %	1.93
2003 Projected Population	11,608
2006 Projected Population	12,043
2001 Households Estimate	3,858
2003 Projected Households	3,953
2006 Projected Households	4,130

INCOME

% Above/Below National Average	+12
2001 Total Income Estimate	$268,950,000
% Cdn. Total	0.04
2001 Average Hhld. Income	$69,700
2001 Per Capita	$23,700
2003 Projected Total Income	$287,610,000
2006 Projected Total Income	$320,840,000

RETAIL SALES

% Above/Below National Average	-78
2001 Retail Sales Estimate	$22,320,000
% Cdn. Total	0.01
2001 per Household	$5,800
2001 per Capita	$2,000
2001 No. of Establishments	60
2003 Projected Retail Sales	$24,640,000
2006 Projected Retail Sales	$27,690,000

POPULATION

2001 Estimates:

Total		11,364
Male		5,887
Female		5,477

Age Groups	Male	Female
0-4	325	318
5-9	373	335
10-14	426	372
15-19	440	399
20-24	413	346
25-29	357	279
30-34	350	328
35-39	424	422
40-44	487	490
45-49	499	494
50-54	459	442
55-59	376	358
60-64	313	285
65-69	247	214
70+	398	395

DAYTIME POPULATION

2001 Estimates:

Working Population	1,776
At Home Population	4,840
Total	6,616

INCOME

2001 Estimates:

Avg. Household Income	$69,713
Avg. Family Income	$74,837
Per Capita Income	$23,667
Male:	
Avg. Employment Income	$37,622
Avg. Employment Income (Full Time)	$50,015
Female:	
Avg. Employment Income	$24,397
Avg. Employment Income (Full Time)	$35,235

DISPOSABLE & DISCRETIONARY INCOME

2001 Estimates:	Per Hhld.
Disposable Income	$53,409
Discretionary Income 1 (minus Food & Shelter)	$37,557
Discretionary Income 2 (minus Food, Shelter, & Other Expenditures)	$26,524

LIQUID ASSETS

1999 Estimates:	Per Hhld.
Equity Investments	$107,902
Interest Bearing Investments	$83,157
Total Liquid Assets	$191,059

CREDIT DATA

July 2000:

Pool of Credit	$92,258,489
Revolving Credit, No.	15,123
Fixed Loans, No.	4,616
Avg. Credit Limit, per Person	$13,721
Avg. Spent, per Person	$6,315
Satisfactory Ratings, No. per Person	2.79
Avg. No. of Cards, per Person	1.01

LABOUR FORCE

2001 Estimates:

Male:	
In the Labour Force	3,707
Participation Rate	77.8
Employed	3,591
Unemployed	116
Unemployment Rate	3.1
Not in Labour Force	1,056
Female:	
In the Labour Force	2,886
Participation Rate	64.8
Employed	2,810
Unemployed	76
Unemployment Rate	2.6
Not in Labour Force	1,566

OCCUPATIONS BY MAJOR GROUPS

2001 Estimates:	Male	Female
Management	401	91
Business, Finance & Admin.	303	919
Natural & Applied Sciences & Related	227	70
Health	45	384
Social Sciences, Gov't Services & Religion	63	130
Education	89	91
Arts, Culture, Recreation & Sport	36	34
Sales & Service	618	939
Trades, Transport & Equipment Operators & Related	1,151	39
Primary Industries	362	132
Processing, Mfg. & Utilities	365	35

LEVEL OF SCHOOLING

2001 Estimates:

Population 15 years +	9,215
Less than Grade 9	757
Grades 9-13 w/o Certif.	3,027
Grade 9-13 with Certif.	1,011
Trade Certif. /Dip.	377
Non-Univ. w/o Certif./Dip.	610
Non-Univ. with Certif./Dip.	1,678
Univ. w/o Degree	913
Univ. w/o Degree/Certif.	357
Univ. with Certif.	556
Univ. with Degree	842

AVERAGE HOUSEHOLD EXPENDITURES

2001 Estimates:

Food	$7,121
Shelter	$11,026
Clothing	$2,497
Transportation	$8,889
Health & Personal Care	$2,202
Recr'n, Read'g & Education	$4,401
Taxes & Securities	$18,923
Other	$10,159
Total Expenditures	$65,218

PRIVATE HOUSEHOLDS

2001 Estimates:

Private Households, Total	3,858
Pop. in Private Households	11,188
Average no. per Household	2.9

FAMILIES

2001 Estimates:

Families in Private Households	3,312
Husband-Wife Families	3,121
Lone-Parent Families	191
Aver. No. Persons per Family	3.1
Aver. No. Sons/Daughters at Home	1.1

HOUSING

2001 Estimates:

Occupied Private Dwellings	3,858
Owned	3,696
Rented	162
Single-Detached House	3,685
Apartment, 5 or Fewer Storeys	11
Movable Dwellings	162

VEHICLES

2001 Estimates:

Model Yrs. '81-'96, No.	5,984
% Total	83.92
Model Yrs. '97-'98, No.	786
% Total	11.02
'99 Vehicles registered in Model Yr. '99, No.	361
% Total	5.06
Total No. '81-'99	7,131

LEGAL MARITAL STATUS

2001 Estimates: (Age 15+)

Single (Never Married)	2,352
Legally Married (Not Separated)	5,959
Legally Married (Separated)	166
Widowed	362
Divorced	376

PSYTE CATEGORIES

2001 Estimates	No. of House -holds	% of Total Hhds.	Index
Boomers & Teens	465	12.05	672
Blue Collar Winners	1,692	43.86	1,742
Old Towns' New Fringe	495	12.83	328
Rustic Prosperity	492	12.75	707
Old Leafy Towns	265	6.87	269
Rod & Rifle	449	11.64	503

FINANCIAL P$YTE

2001 Estimates	No. of House -holds	% of Total Hhds.	Index
Four Star Investors	465	12.05	240
Canadian Comfort	1,692	43.86	451
Tractors & Tradelines	987	25.58	447
Bills & Wills	265	6.87	83
Rural Family Blues	449	11.64	144

HOME LANGUAGE

2001 Estimates:		% Total
English	11,140	98.03
French	16	0.14
Cree	11	0.10
German	92	0.81
Hungarian	11	0.10
Portuguese	11	0.10
Ukrainian	11	0.10
Multiple Responses	72	0.63
Total	11,364	100.00

HOMES BUILT

	1999	1998	1997
No	48	47	n.a.

TAXATION

Income Class:	1997	% Total
Under $5,000	710	11.09
$5,000-$10,000	720	11.25
$10,000-$15,000	810	12.66
$15,000-$20,000	610	9.53
$20,000-$25,000	570	8.91
$25,000-$30,000	560	8.75
$30,000-$40,000	910	14.22
$40,000-$50,000	630	9.84
$50,000 +	880	13.75
Total Returns, No.	6,400	
Total Income, $000	183,947	
Total Taxable Returns	4,930	
Total Tax, $000	37,659	
Average Income, $	28,742	
Average Tax, $	7,639	

VITAL STATISTICS

	1997	1996	1995	1994
Births	106	116	104	61
Deaths	58	73	40	29
Natural Increase	48	43	64	32
Marriages	89	78	74	54

Note: Latest available data.

Thompson
(Census Agglomeration)

The Census Agglomeration of Thompson consists solely of Thompson, C in census division No. 22.

POPULATION

July 1, 2001 Estimate	14,195
% Cdn. Total	0.05
% Change, '96-'01	-3.53
Avg. Annual Growth Rate, %	-0.72
2003 Projected Population	13,934
2006 Projected Population	13,474
2001 Households Estimate	5,274
2003 Projected Households	5,356
2006 Projected Households	5,425

INCOME

% Above/Below National Average	+24
2001 Total Income Estimate	$369,870,000
% Cdn. Total	0.06
2001 Average Hhld. Income	$70,100
2001 Per Capita	$26,100
2003 Projected Total Income	$401,360,000
2006 Projected Total Income	$446,210,000

RETAIL SALES

% Above/Below National Average	+25
2001 Retail Sales Estimate	$158,500,000
% Cdn. Total	0.06
2001 per Household	$30,100
2001 per Capita	$11,200
2001 No. of Establishments	.86
2003 Projected Retail Sales	$168,270,000
2006 Projected Retail Sales	$180,490,000

POPULATION

2001 Estimates:

Total		14,195
Male		7,227
Female		6,968

Age Groups	Male	Female
0-4	635	600
5-9	685	645
10-14	657	647
15-19	601	615
20-24	541	565
25-29	536	562
30-34	588	612
35-39	589	598
40-44	537	555
45-49	543	532
50-54	510	424
55-59	375	283
60-64	226	165
65-69	116	81
70+	88	84

DAYTIME POPULATION

2001 Estimates:

Working Population	7,768
At Home Population	6,427
Total	14,195

INCOME

2001 Estimates:

Avg. Household Income	$70,131
Avg. Family Income	$74,533
Per Capita Income	$26,056
Male:	
Avg. Employment Income	$48,781
Avg. Employment Income (Full Time)	$59,969
Female:	
Avg. Employment Income	$25,630
Avg. Employment Income (Full Time)	$37,019

DISPOSABLE & DISCRETIONARY INCOME

2001 Estimates:	Per Hhld.
Disposable Income	$53,468
Discretionary Income 1 (minus Food & Shelter)	$40,006
Discretionary Income 2 (minus Food, Shelter, & Other Expenditures)	$28,990

LIQUID ASSETS

1999 Estimates:	Per Hhld.
Equity Investments	$110,751
Interest Bearing Investments	$87,586
Total Liquid Assets	$198,337

CREDIT DATA

July 2000:

Pool of Credit	$135,072,163
Revolving Credit, No.	18,696
Fixed Loans, No.	7,640
Avg. Credit Limit, per Person	$13,586
Avg. Spent, per Person	$7,220
Satisfactory Ratings, No. per Person	2.51
Avg. No. of Cards, per Person	0.95

LABOUR FORCE

2001 Estimates:

Male:

In the Labour Force	4,457
Participation Rate	84.9
Employed	4,258
Unemployed	199
Unemployment Rate	4.5
Not in Labour Force	793

Female:

In the Labour Force	3,552
Participation Rate	70.0
Employed	3,386
Unemployed	166
Unemployment Rate	4.7
Not in Labour Force	1,524

OCCUPATIONS BY MAJOR GROUPS

2001 Estimates:	Male	Female
Management	321	214
Business, Finance & Admin.	273	924
Natural & Applied Sciences & Related	347	60
Health	66	282
Social Sciences, Gov't Services & Religion	116	173
Education	107	290
Arts, Culture, Recreation & Sport	19	67
Sales & Service	760	1,360
Trades, Transport & Equipment Operators & Related	1,240	46
Primary Industries	766	10
Processing, Mfg. & Utilities	362	10

LEVEL OF SCHOOLING

2001 Estimates:

Population 15 years +	10,326
Less than Grade 9	885
Grades 9-13 w/o Certif.	3,068
Grade 9-13 with Certif.	1,201
Trade Certif./Dip.	538
Non-Univ. w/o Certif./Dip.	576
Non-Univ. with Certif./Dip.	1,968
Univ. w/o Degree	1,065
Univ. w/o Degree/Certif.	575
Univ. with Certif.	490
Univ. with Degree	1,025

AVERAGE HOUSEHOLD EXPENDITURES

2001 Estimates:

Food	$7,014
Shelter	$8,935
Clothing	$2,758
Transportation	$9,048
Health & Personal Care	$2,097
Recr'n, Read'g & Education	$5,329
Taxes & Securities	$18,433
Other	$11,392
Total Expenditures	$65,006

PRIVATE HOUSEHOLDS

2001 Estimates:

Private Households, Total	5,274
Pop. in Private Households	14,090
Average no. per Household	2.7

FAMILIES

2001 Estimates:

Families in Private Households	4,070
Husband-Wife Families	3,262
Lone-Parent Families	808
Aver. No. Persons per Family	3.3
Aver. No. Sons/Daughters at Home	1.5

HOUSING

2001 Estimates:

Occupied Private Dwellings	5,274
Owned	3,008
Rented	2,266
Single-Detached House	2,583
Semi-Detached House	154
Row Houses	388
Apartment, 5+ Storeys	374
Apartment, 5 or Fewer Storeys	1,358
Movable Dwellings	417

VEHICLES

2001 Estimates:

Model Yrs. '81-'96, No.	5,079
% Total	77.25
Model Yrs. '97-'98, No.	1,070
% Total	16.27
'99 Vehicles registered in Model Yr. '99, No.	426
% Total	6.48
Total No. '81-'99	6,575

LEGAL MARITAL STATUS

2001 Estimates: (Age 15+)

Single (Never Married)	3,998
Legally Married (Not Separated)	4,892
Legally Married (Separated)	457
Widowed	226
Divorced	753

PSYTE CATEGORIES

2001 Estimates	No. of House-holds	% of Total Hhds.	Index
Northern Lights	4,809	91.18	18,422
Young City Singles	363	6.88	300
Big Country Families	102	1.93	136

FINANCIAL PSYTE

2001 Estimates	No. of House-holds	% of Total Hhds.	Index
Successful Suburbanites	4,809	91.18	1,374
Rural Family Blues	102	1.93	24
Towering Debt	363	6.88	88

Manitoba

HOME LANGUAGE

2001 Estimates:		% Total
English	13,353	94.07
French	65	0.46
Chinese	40	0.28
Cree	140	0.99
Hindi	25	0.18
Polish	10	0.07
Portuguese	118	0.83
Punjabi	40	0.28
Spanish	38	0.27
Ukrainian	44	0.31
Urdu	15	0.11
Other Languages	10	0.07
Multiple Responses	297	2.09
Total	14,195	100.00

BUILDING PERMITS

	1999	1998	1997
		$000	
Value	1,866	6,850	10,540

HOMES BUILT

	1999	1998	1997
No	n.a.	n.a.	19

TAXATION

Income Class:	1997	% Total
Under $5,000	1,390	14.98
$5,000-$10,000	900	9.70
$10,000-$15,000	950	10.24
$15,000-$20,000	720	7.76
$20,000-$25,000	550	5.93
$25,000-$30,000	520	5.60
$30,000-$40,000	930	10.02
$40,000-$50,000	770	8.30
$50,000+	2,540	27.37
Total Returns, No.	9,280	
Total Income, $000	301,804	
Total Taxable Returns	6,650	
Total Tax, $000	67,552	
Average Income, $	32,522	
Average Tax, $	10,158	

VITAL STATISTICS

	1997	1996	1995	1994
Births	277	307	288	299
Deaths	48	34	32	37
Natural Increase	229	273	256	262
Marriages	54	68	69	56

Note: Latest available data.

COMMUNITY NEWSPAPER(S)

	Total Circulation
Thompson: The Citizen Mon/Wed/Fri.	2,235
Thompson: Thompson Nickel Belt News	6,876

RADIO STATION(S)

	Power
CBWK-FM	9,400w
CHTM	1,000w
CKSB-FM	n.a.

TELEVISION STATION(S)

CBWFT-TV
CKYT-TV

Manitoba

Winnipeg
(Census Metropolitan Area)

POPULATION

July 1, 2001 Estimate	684,512
% Cdn. Total	2.20
% Change, '96 -'01	0.77
Avg. Annual Growth Rate, %	0.15
2003 Projected Population	702,156
2006 Projected Population	737,888
2001 Households Estimate	276,071
2003 Projected Households	284,226
2006 Projected Households	300,051

INCOME

% Above/Below National Average	+3
2001 Total Income Estimate	$14,884,910,000
% Cdn. Total	2.27
2001 Average Hhld. Income	$53,900
2001 Per Capita	$21,700
2003 Projected Total Income	$16,149,170,000
2006 Projected Total Income	$18,470,960,000

RETAIL SALES

% Above/Below National Average	-8
2001 Retail Sales Estimate	$5,625,090,000
% Cdn. Total	2.02
2001 per Household	$20,400
2001 per Capita	$8,200
2001 No. of Establishments	4,227
2003 Projected Retail Sales	$6,197,560,000
2006 Projected Retail Sales	$7,147,060,000

POPULATION

2001 Estimates:

Total	684,512
Male	332,504
Female	352,008

Age Groups	Male	Female
0-4	23,456	22,344
5-9	23,065	22,150
10-14	22,499	21,612
15-19	22,078	21,259
20-24	22,632	22,098
25-29	23,210	23,209
30-34	25,200	25,208
35-39	27,085	27,136
40-44	26,965	27,511
45-49	25,264	26,237
50-54	21,567	22,439
55-59	16,927	17,762
60-64	13,802	14,778
65-69	11,746	13,662
70+	27,008	44,603

DAYTIME POPULATION

2001 Estimates:

Working Population	346,753
At Home Population	337,758
Total	684,511

INCOME

2001 Estimates:

Avg. Household Income	$53,917
Avg. Family Income	$63,394
Per Capita Income	$21,745

Male:

Avg. Employment Income	$35,386
Avg. Employment Income (Full Time)	$46,375

Female:

Avg. Employment Income	$22,486
Avg. Employment Income (Full Time)	$32,578

DISPOSABLE & DISCRETIONARY INCOME

2001 Estimates:	Per Hhld.
Disposable Income	$41,267
Discretionary Income 1 (minus Food & Shelter)	$27,770
Discretionary Income 2 (minus Food, Shelter, & Other Expenditures)	$19,579

LIQUID ASSETS

1999 Estimates:	Per Hhld.
Equity Investments	$67,112
Interest Bearing Investments	$61,991
Total Liquid Assets	$129,103

CREDIT DATA

July 2000:

Pool of Credit	$6,297,773,951
Revolving Credit, No.	1,253,292
Fixed Loans, No.	355,231
Avg. Credit Limit, per Person	$11,182
Avg. Spent, per Person	$4,889
Satisfactory Ratings, No. per Person	2.71
Avg. No. of Cards, per Person	1.00

LABOUR FORCE

2001 Estimates:

Male:

In the Labour Force	191,039
Participation Rate	72.5
Employed	181,020
Unemployed	10,019
Unemployment Rate	5.2
Not in Labour Force	72,445

Female:

In the Labour Force	170,281
Participation Rate	59.6
Employed	163,245
Unemployed	7,036
Unemployment Rate	4.1
Not in Labour Force	115,621

OCCUPATIONS BY MAJOR GROUPS

2001 Estimates:	Male	Female
Management	20,213	8,944
Business, Finance & Admin.	22,306	52,516
Natural & Applied Sciences & Related	13,239	2,887
Health	4,451	16,029
Social Sciences, Gov't Services & Religion	4,558	5,418
Education	5,800	8,689
Arts, Culture, Recreation & Sport	3,956	4,930
Sales & Service	45,329	54,997
Trades, Transport & Equipment Operators & Related	45,682	2,582
Primary Industries	4,499	1,010
Processing, Mfg. & Utilities	16,250	7,719

LEVEL OF SCHOOLING

2001 Estimates:

Population 15 years +	549,386
Less than Grade 9	49,755
Grades 9-13 w/o Certif.	144,555
Grade 9-13 with Certif.	64,201
Trade Certif./Dip.	17,070
Non-Univ. w/o Certif./Dip.	30,145
Non-Univ. with Certif./Dip.	89,983
Univ. w/o Degree	72,799
Univ. w/o Degree/Certif.	40,289
Univ. with Certif.	32,510
Univ. with Degree	80,878

AVERAGE HOUSEHOLD EXPENDITURES

2001 Estimates:

Food	$6,254
Shelter	$9,423
Clothing	$2,211
Transportation	$6,166
Health & Personal Care	$1,926
Recr'n, Read'g & Education	$3,663
Taxes & Securities	$13,921
Other	$8,648
Total Expenditures	$52,212

PRIVATE HOUSEHOLDS

2001 Estimates:

Private Households, Total	276,071
Pop. in Private Households	670,859
Average no. per Household	2.4

FAMILIES

2001 Estimates:

Families in Private Households	186,518
Husband-Wife Families	157,369
Lone-Parent Families	29,149
Aver. No. Persons per Family	3.0
Aver. No. Sons/Daughters at Home	1.2

HOUSING

2001 Estimates:

Occupied Private Dwellings	276,071
Owned	176,861
Rented	99,105
Band Housing	105
Single-Detached House	170,589
Semi-Detached House	10,353
Row Houses	8,740
Apartment, 5+ Storeys	35,559
Owned Apartment, 5+ Storeys	3,308
Apartment, 5 or Fewer Storeys	44,018
Apartment, Detached Duplex	5,199
Other Single-Attached	449
Movable Dwellings	1,164

RADIO STATION DATA

Station	Market	Format	Wkly. Reach%*	Aver. Hrs. Tuned
All Stations			95	22.0
CBW	Winnipeg	News, Info.	13	12.1
CBW-FM	Winnipeg	Multi-format	8	11.3
CFEQ-FM	Winnipeg	Christian Rock/Pop	3	8.2
CFQX-FM	Winnipeg/Selkirk	Country	17	10.6
CFST	Winnipeg	Easy Listening	9	9.9
CFWM-FM	Winnipeg	Adult Contemp.	18	9.6
CHIQ-FM	Winnipeg	Contemp. Hit Radio	30	8.5
CIFX	Winnipeg	News, Talk	n.a.	n.a.
CITI-FM	Winnipeg	Modern Rock	20	8.2
CJKR-FM	Winnipeg	Rock	18	7.7
CJOB	Winnipeg	News, Talk, Info.	31	11.5
CKJS	Winnipeg	Ethnic, Religious	n.a.	n.a.
CKMM-FM	Winnipeg	Contemp. Hit Radio	25	8.3
CKSB	St. Boniface	Multi-format	1	8.3
CKXL	St. Boniface	Multi-format	n.a.	n.a.
CKY	Winnipeg	Oldies, Sports	13	8.1

BBM Spring 2000 Radio Reach Surveys; area coverage.
* Mon-Sun 5a.m.-1a.m., All Persons 12+

TV STATION DATA

Station	Market	Network Affiliation	Wkly. Reach%*	Aver. Hrs. Tuned
All Stations			96	22.6
A & E	n.a.	Ind.	22	3.6
CABLE	n.a.	n.a.	8	2.4
CBWFT	Winnipeg	SRC	1	4.3
CBWT	Winnipeg	CBC	48	3.6
CHMI	Winnipeg	Ind.	47	2.7
CKND	Winnipeg	Global	66	3.8
CKY	Winnipeg	CTV	68	6.1
DSCVRY	n.a.	Ind.	10	1.5
FAMILY	n.a.	Ind.	11	2.3
FOOD	n.a.	Ind.	5	2.3
HISTTV	n.a.	Ind.	6	2.6
KARE	Minneapolis MN	NBC	26	2.2
KGFE	Grand Forks ND	PBS	16	1.7
KNRR	Pembina ND	FOX	2	3.5
NEWSWD	n.a.	CBC	7	2.0
OTHERS	n.a.	n.a.	8	2.6
PRIME	n.a.	Ind.	12	2.5
SPACE	n.a.	Ind.	8	1.9
TLC	n.a.	Ind.	14	2.1
TNN	Nashville TN	Ind.	9	1.7
TOON	n.a.	Ind.	9	2.4
TREE	n.a.	Ind.	7	3.4
TSN	n.a.	Ind.	25	5.1
VCR	n.a.	n.a.	30	4.1
WCCO	Minneapolis MN	CBS	32	2.9
WDAZ	Devils Lake ND	ABC	26	1.8
WTBS	Atlanta GA	Ind.	22	3.0
WUHF	Rochester NY	FOX	23	2.5
YTV	n.a.	Ind.	15	3.2

BBM Spring 2000 TV Reach Surveys; CMA coverage.
*Mon-Sun 6a.m.-2a.m., All Persons 2+

Winnipeg
(Census Metropolitan Area)
(Cont'd)

VEHICLES

2001 Estimates:

Model Yrs. '81-'96, No.	294,708
% Total	79.56
Model Yrs. '97-'98, No.	47,774
% Total	12.90
'99 Vehicles registered in Model Yr. '99, No.	27,948
% Total	7.54
Total No. '81-'99	370,430

LEGAL MARITAL STATUS

2001 Estimates: (Age 15+)

Single (Never Married)	173,029
Legally Married (Not Separated)	282,673
Legally Married (Separated)	17,022
Widowed	38,766
Divorced	37,896

PSYTE CATEGORIES

2001 Estimates	No. of House-holds	% of Total Hhds.	Index
The Affluentials	2,207	0.80	125
Urban Gentry	4,943	1.79	100
Suburban Executives	1,913	0.69	48
Technocrafts & Bureaucrats	21,021	7.61	271
Boomers & Teens	981	0.36	20
Stable Suburban Families	7,288	2.64	203
Small City Elite	365	0.13	8
Old Bungalow Burbs	13,104	4.75	286
Suburban Nesters	2,436	0.88	55
Brie & Chablis	1,172	0.42	47
Aging Erudites	12,405	4.49	298
Satellite Suburbs	5,989	2.17	76
Kindergarten Boom	21,774	7.89	301
Blue Collar Winners	7,898	2.86	114

FINANCIAL P$YTE

2001 Estimates	No. of House-holds	% of Total Hhds.	Index
Platinum Estates	2,207	0.80	99
Four Star Investors	7,837	2.84	57
Successful Suburbanites	28,309	10.25	155
Canadian Comfort	16,688	6.04	62
Urban Heights	18,433	6.68	155
Miners & Credit-Liners	13,104	4.75	150
Mortgages & Minivans	21,774	7.89	120
Tractors & Tradelines	6,541	2.37	41

2001 Estimates	No. of House-holds	% of Total Hhds.	Index
Old Towns' New Fringe	5,313	1.92	49
Rustic Prosperity	1,228	0.44	25
High Rise Melting Pot	601	0.22	15
Conservative Homebodies	32,682	11.84	328
High Rise Sunsets	9,291	3.37	235
Young Urban Professionals	4,856	1.76	93
Young Urban Mix	1,198	0.43	20
Young Urban Intelligentsia	3,890	1.41	93
University Enclaves	15,741	5.70	279
Young City Singles	19,347	7.01	306
Urban Bohemia	1,526	0.55	47
Old Leafy Towns	68	0.02	1
Town Renters	4,806	1.74	201
Nesters & Young Homesteaders	322	0.12	5
Agrarian Blues	151	0.05	26
Rod & Rifle	452	0.16	7
Big Country Families	130	0.05	3
Old Cdn. Rustics	56	0.02	2
Old Quebec Walkups	60	0.02	1
Struggling Downtowns	43,186	15.64	497
Aged Pensioners	9,291	3.37	253
Big City Stress	12,022	4.35	386
Old Grey Towers	3,866	1.40	253

2001 Estimates	No. of House-holds	% of Total Hhds.	Index
Bills & Wills	33,948	12.30	149
Revolving Renters	9,613	3.48	76
Young Urban Struggle	21,157	7.66	162
Rural Family Blues	733	0.27	3
Limited Budgets	56	0.02	1
Loan Parent Stress	60	0.02	..
Towering Debt	67,940	24.61	315
NSF	12,022	4.35	123
Senior Survivors	13,157	4.77	253

HOME LANGUAGE

2001 Estimates:		% Total
English	603,255	88.13
French	13,763	2.01
Arabic	434	0.06
Chinese	7,342	1.07
Cree	578	0.08
German	4,908	0.72
Greek	626	0.09
Italian	1,749	0.26
Korean	694	0.10
Lao	758	0.11
Ojibway	494	0.07
Persian (Farsi)	380	0.06
Polish	4,423	0.65
Portuguese	3,942	0.58
Punjabi	3,645	0.53
Russian	448	0.07
Serbo-Croatian	696	0.10
Spanish	2,475	0.36
Tagalog (Pilipino)	9,289	1.36
Ukrainian	2,547	0.37
Vietnamese	1,695	0.25
Other Languages	5,341	0.78
Multiple Responses	15,030	2.20
Total	684,512	100.00

BUILDING PERMITS

	1999	1998 $000	1997
Value	549,846	532,725	405,822

Manitoba

HOMES BUILT

	1999	1998	1997
No	1,485	1,531	1,750

TAXATION

Income Class:	1997	% Total
Under $5,000	57,680	11.85
$5,000-$10,000	60,610	12.46
$10,000-$15,000	73,230	15.05
$15,000-$20,000	53,230	10.94
$20,000-$25,000	45,480	9.35
$25,000-$30,000	40,800	8.39
$30,000-$40,000	64,090	13.17
$40,000-$50,000	37,720	7.75
$50,000 +	53,770	11.05
Total Returns, No.	486,560	
Total Income, $000	12,994,999	
Total Taxable Returns	350,790	
Total Tax, $000	2,613,406	
Average Income, $	26,708	
Average Tax, $	7,450	

VITAL STATISTICS

	1997	1996	1995	1994
Births	8,147	8,720	9,187	9,484
Deaths	5,388	5,474	5,573	5,212
Natural Increase	2,759	3,246	3,614	4,272
Marriages	3,707	3,833	4,133	4,087

Note: Latest available data.

DAILY NEWSPAPER(S)

	Circulation Average Paid
The Winnipeg Sun	
Sun.	57,519
Mon-Sat.	44,255
Winnipeg Free Press	
Sat.	191,076
Sun.	144,588
Mon-Fri.	128,988

COMMUNITY NEWSPAPER(S)

	Total Circulation
Charleswood, Crestview, Ft. Rouge, Lindenwoods, River Heights, St. James-Assiniboia, Silver Heights, Tuxedo, Westwood: The Metro/The Sunday Metro Thu/Sun.	51,370
East & North Kildonan, East St. Paul, Elmwood, Transcona: The Herald/The Sunday Herald Thu/Sun.	39,530
Fort Garry, Fort Richmond, Island Lakes, Richmond West, River Park South, St. Boniface, St. Norbert, St. Vital, Southdale, Waverley Heights, Windsor Park: The Lance/The Sunday Lance Thu/Sun.	49,040
Garden City, the Maples, the North End, Tyndall Park, the West End, West Kildonan: The Times/The Sunday Times Thu/Sun.	33,625
Winnipeg: The Jewish Post & News	2,779
Winnipeg: Voxair (biwkly)	n.a.

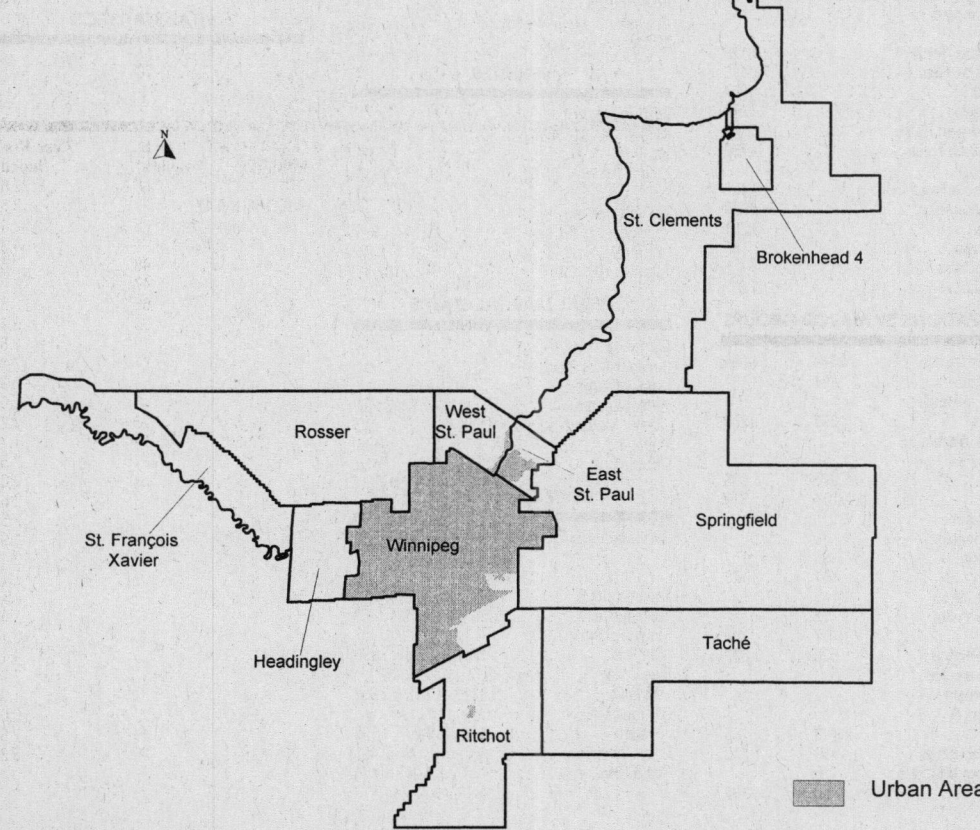

St. Clements

Brokenhead 4

West St. Paul

Rosser

East St. Paul

Springfield

St. François Xavier

Winnipeg

Headingley

Taché

Ritchot

Urban Areas

Manitoba

Springfield
(Rural Municipality)
Winnipeg CMA

In census division No. 12.

POPULATION

July 1, 2001 Estimate	13,161
% Cdn. Total	0.04
% Change, '96 -'01	6.49
Avg. Annual Growth Rate, %	1.27
2003 Projected Population	14,002
2006 Projected Population	15,408
2001 Households Estimate	4,457
2003 Projected Households	4,785
2006 Projected Households	5,348

INCOME

% Above/Below National Average	+9
2001 Total Income Estimate	$303,210,000
% Cdn. Total	0.05
2001 Average Hhld. Income	$68,000
2001 Per Capita	$23,000
2003 Projected Total Income	$342,210,000
2006 Projected Total Income	$413,180,000

RETAIL SALES

% Above/Below National Average	-68
2001 Retail Sales Estimate	$37,400,000
% Cdn. Total	0.01
2001 per Household	$8,400
2001 per Capita	$2,800
2001 No. of Establishments	77
2003 Projected Retail Sales	$41,890,000
2006 Projected Retail Sales	$50,420,000

POPULATION

2001 Estimates:

Total		13,161
Male		6,711
Female		6,450

Age Groups	Male	Female
0-4	423	407
5-9	491	460
10-14	539	510
15-19	532	517
20-24	462	424
25-29	368	342
30-34	397	411
35-39	512	528
40-44	580	602
45-49	571	578
50-54	501	475
55-59	403	349
60-64	299	259
65-69	224	196
70+	409	392

DAYTIME POPULATION

2001 Estimates:

Working Population	1,370
At Home Population	5,572
Total	6,942

INCOME

2001 Estimates:

Avg. Household Income	$68,030
Avg. Family Income	$71,641
Per Capita Income	$23,038
Male:	
Avg. Employment Income	$37,429
Avg. Employment Income (Full Time)	$47,888
Female:	
Avg. Employment Income	$20,925
Avg. Employment Income (Full Time)	$33,860

DISPOSABLE & DISCRETIONARY INCOME

2001 Estimates:	*Per Hhld.*
Disposable Income	$51,521
Discretionary Income 1 (minus Food & Shelter)	$35,892
Discretionary Income 2 (minus Food, Shelter, & Other Expenditures)	$25,197

LIQUID ASSETS

1999 Estimates:	*Per Hhld.*
Equity Investments	$96,701
Interest Bearing Investments	$79,672
Total Liquid Assets	$176,373

CREDIT DATA

July 2000:

Pool of Credit	$103,214,881
Revolving Credit, No.	18,769
Fixed Loans, No.	5,728
Avg. Credit Limit, per Person	$11,389
Avg. Spent, per Person	$5,249
Satisfactory Ratings, No. per Person	2.55
Avg. No. of Cards, per Person	0.93

LABOUR FORCE

2001 Estimates:
Male:

In the Labour Force	4,128
Participation Rate	78.5
Employed	4,054
Unemployed	74
Unemployment Rate	1.8
Not in Labour Force	1,130

Female:

In the Labour Force	3,466
Participation Rate	68.3
Employed	3,381
Unemployed	85
Unemployment Rate	2.5
Not in Labour Force	1,607

OCCUPATIONS BY MAJOR GROUPS

2001 Estimates:	Male	Female
Management	427	181
Business, Finance & Admin.	395	1,269
Natural & Applied Sciences & Related	322	35
Health	44	313
Social Sciences, Gov't Services & Religion	96	57
Education	61	128
Arts, Culture, Recreation & Sport	37	96
Sales & Service	530	1,002
Trades, Transport & Equipment Operators & Related	1,478	66
Primary Industries	458	119
Processing, Mfg. & Utilities	259	102

LEVEL OF SCHOOLING

2001 Estimates:

Population 15 years +	10,331
Less than Grade 9	953
Grades 9-13 w/o Certif.	2,812
Grade 9-13 with Certif.	1,365
Trade Certif./Dip.	459
Non-Univ. w/o Certif./Dip.	455
Non-Univ. with Certif./Dip.	2,119
Univ. w/o Degree	1,108
Univ. w/o Degree/Certif.	661
Univ. with Certif.	447
Univ. with Degree	1,060

AVERAGE HOUSEHOLD EXPENDITURES

2001 Estimates:

Food	$6,909
Shelter	$10,924
Clothing	$2,490
Transportation	$8,654
Health & Personal Care	$2,108
Recr'n, Read'g & Education	$4,195
Taxes & Securities	$18,929
Other	$9,664
Total Expenditures	$63,873

PRIVATE HOUSEHOLDS

2001 Estimates:

Private Households, Total	4,457
Pop. in Private Households	12,812
Average no. per Household	2.9

FAMILIES

2001 Estimates:

Families in Private Households	3,767
Husband-Wife Families	3,571
Lone-Parent Families	196
Aver. No. Persons per Family	3.3
Aver. No. Sons/Daughters at Home	1.3

HOUSING

2001 Estimates:

Occupied Private Dwellings	4,457
Owned	4,186
Rented	271
Single-Detached House	4,273
Semi-Detached House	39
Row Houses	11
Apartment, 5 or Fewer Storeys	28
Movable Dwellings	106

VEHICLES

2001 Estimates:

Model Yrs. '81-'96, No.	7,301
% Total	85.38
Model Yrs. '97-'98, No.	836
% Total	9.78
'99 Vehicles registered in Model Yr. '99, No.	414
% Total	4.84
Total No. '81-'99	8,551

LEGAL MARITAL STATUS

2001 Estimates: (Age 15+)

Single (Never Married)	2,501
Legally Married (Not Separated)	6,797
Legally Married (Separated)	180
Widowed	435
Divorced	418

PSYTE CATEGORIES

2001 Estimates	No. of House-holds	% of Total Hhds.	Index
Technocrafts & Bureaucrats	283	6.35	226
Stable Suburban Families	173	3.88	298
Blue Collar Winners	3,021	67.78	2,692
Old Towns' New Fringe	413	9.27	237
Rustic Prosperity	387	8.68	481
Rod & Rifle	180	4.04	175

FINANCIAL P$YTE

2001 Estimates	No. of House-holds	% of Total Hhds.	Index
Successful Suburbanites	456	10.23	154
Canadian Comfort	3,021	67.78	698
Tractors & Tradelines	800	17.95	314
Rural Family Blues	180	4.04	50

HOME LANGUAGE

2001 Estimates:		% Total
English	12,549	95.35
French	114	0.87
German	449	3.41
Lithuanian	11	0.08
Ukrainian	16	0.12
Multiple Responses	22	0.17
Total	13,161	100.00

BUILDING PERMITS

	1999	1998 $000	1997
Value	18,097	14,276	11,087

HOMES BUILT

	1999	1998	1997
No.	60	53	38

TAXATION

Income Class:	1997	% Total
Under $5,000	920	12.69
$5,000-$10,000	790	10.90
$10,000-$15,000	890	12.28
$15,000-$20,000	730	10.07
$20,000-$25,000	620	8.55
$25,000-$30,000	610	8.41
$30,000-$40,000	1,120	15.45
$40,000-$50,000	670	9.24
$50,000 +	910	12.55
Total Returns, No.	7,250	
Total Income, $000	195,270	
Total Taxable Returns	5,460	
Total Tax, $000	38,242	
Average Income, $	26,934	
Average Tax, $	7,004	

VITAL STATISTICS

	1997	1996	1995	1994
Births	105	133	134	135
Deaths	42	57	50	50
Natural Increase	63	76	84	85
Marriages	43	53	45	53

Note: Latest available data.

MEDIA INFO
see Winnipeg, CMA

Winnipeg
(City)
Winnipeg CMA
In census division No. 11.

POPULATION

July 1, 2001 Estimate	631,373
% Cdn. Total	2.03
% Change, '96 -'01	0.27
Avg. Annual Growth Rate, %	0.05
2003 Projected Population	645,888
2006 Projected Population	676,616
2001 Households Estimate	258,508
2003 Projected Households	265,484
2006 Projected Households	279,368

INCOME

% Above/Below National Average	+3
2001 Total Income Estimate	$13,674,620,000
% Cdn. Total	2.08
2001 Average Hhld. Income	$52,900
2001 Per Capita	$21,700
2003 Projected Total Income	$14,791,220,000
2006 Projected Total Income	$16,853,020,000

RETAIL SALES

% Above/Below National Average	-5
2001 Retail Sales Estimate	$5,368,820,000
% Cdn. Total	1.93
2001 per Household	$20,800
2001 per Capita	$8,500
2001 No. of Establishments	3,871
2003 Projected Retail Sales	$5,908,170,000
2006 Projected Retail Sales	$6,803,200,000

POPULATION

2001 Estimates:

Total		631,373
Male		305,376
Female		325,997

Age Groups	Male	Female
0-4	21,755	20,722
5-9	21,081	20,333
10-14	20,286	19,563
15-19	19,899	19,209
20-24	20,740	20,387
25-29	21,673	21,787
30-34	23,591	23,547
35-39	25,040	25,026
40-44	24,608	25,151
45-49	22,940	23,968
50-54	19,534	20,546
55-59	15,350	16,338
60-64	12,627	13,726
65-69	10,841	12,847
70+	25,411	42,847

DAYTIME POPULATION

2001 Estimates:

Working Population	336,825
At Home Population	315,321
Total	652,146

INCOME

2001 Estimates:

Avg. Household Income	$52,898
Avg. Family Income	$62,586
Per Capita Income	$21,659
Male:	
Avg. Employment Income	$35,152
Avg. Employment Income (Full Time)	$46,197
Female:	
Avg. Employment Income	$22,478
Avg. Employment Income (Full Time)	$32,446

DISPOSABLE & DISCRETIONARY INCOME

2001 Estimates:

	Per Hhld.
Disposable Income	$40,513
Discretionary Income 1 (minus Food & Shelter)	$27,169
Discretionary Income 2 (minus Food, Shelter, & Other Expenditures)	$19,161

LIQUID ASSETS

1999 Estimates:

	Per Hhld.
Equity Investments	$64,755
Interest Bearing Investments	$60,684
Total Liquid Assets	$125,439

CREDIT DATA

July 2000:

Pool of Credit	$5,870,641,432
Revolving Credit, No.	1,177,832
Fixed Loans, No.	332,766
Avg. Credit Limit, per Person	$11,116
Avg. Spent, per Person	$4,856
Satisfactory Ratings, No. per Person	2.71
Avg. No. of Cards, per Person	1.01

LABOUR FORCE

2001 Estimates:

Male:

In the Labour Force	174,148
Participation Rate	71.9
Employed	164,545
Unemployed	9,603
Unemployment Rate	5.5
Not in Labour Force	68,106

Female:

In the Labour Force	156,310
Participation Rate	58.9
Employed	149,569
Unemployed	6,741
Unemployment Rate	4.3
Not in Labour Force	109,069

OCCUPATIONS BY MAJOR GROUPS

2001 Estimates;	Male	Female
Management	18,203	8,192
Business, Finance & Admin.	20,918	47,776
Natural & Applied Sciences & Related	12,296	2,687
Health	4,231	14,726
Social Sciences, Gov't Services & Religion	4,220	5,147
Education	5,466	7,962
Arts, Culture, Recreation & Sport	3,824	4,649
Sales & Service	42,631	50,625
Trades, Transport & Equipment Operators & Related	39,867	2,326
Primary Industries	2,748	467
Processing, Mfg. & Utilities	15,117	7,417

LEVEL OF SCHOOLING

2001 Estimates:

Population 15 years +	507,633
Less than Grade 9	45,975
Grades 9-13 w/o Certif.	132,616
Grade 9-13 with Certif.	58,983
Trade Certif. /Dip.	15,431
Non-Univ. w/o Certif./Dip.	27,966
Non-Univ. with Certif./Dip.	81,604
Univ. w/o Degree	68,396
Univ. w/o Degree/Certif.	37,790
Univ. with Certif.	30,606
Univ. with Degree	76,662

AVERAGE HOUSEHOLD EXPENDITURES

2001 Estimates:

Food	$6,196
Shelter	$9,318
Clothing	$2,192
Transportation	$5,993
Health & Personal Care	$1,908
Recr'n, Read'g & Education	$3,613
Taxes & Securities	$13,607
Other	$8,546
Total Expenditures	$51,373

PRIVATE HOUSEHOLDS

2001 Estimates:

Private Households, Total	258,508
Pop. in Private Households	618,831
Average no. per Household	2.4

FAMILIES

2001 Estimates:

Families in Private Households	171,362
Husband-Wife Families	143,122
Lone-Parent Families	28,240
Aver. No. Persons per Family	3.0
Aver. No. Sons/Daughters at Home	1.2

HOUSING

2001 Estimates:

Occupied Private Dwellings	258,508
Owned	160,509
Rented	97,999
Single-Detached House	153,888
Semi-Detached House	10,292
Row Houses	8,689
Apartment, 5+ Storeys	35,559
Owned Apartment, 5+ Storeys	3,308
Apartment, 5 or Fewer Storeys	43,869
Apartment, Detached Duplex	5,178
Other Single-Attached	398
Movable Dwellings	635

VEHICLES

2001 Estimates:

Model Yrs. '81-'96, No.	265,294
% Total	79.09
Model Yrs. '97-'98, No.	44,000
% Total	13.12
'99 Vehicles registered in Model Yr. '99, No.	26,151
% Total	7.80
Total No. '81-'99	335,445

LEGAL MARITAL STATUS

2001 Estimates: (Age 15+)

Single (Never Married)	162,638
Legally Married (Not Separated)	255,455
Legally Married (Separated)	16,252
Widowed	37,085
Divorced	36,203

Manitoba

PSYTE CATEGORIES

2001 Estimates	No. of House-holds	% of Total Hhds.	Index
The Affluentials	2,207	0.85	134
Urban Gentry	4,943	1.91	106
Suburban Executives	1,913	0.74	52
Technocrafts & Bureaucrats	20,738	8.02	285
Stable Suburban Families	6,761	2.62	201
Old Bungalow Burbs	13,104	5.07	306
Suburban Nesters	2,436	0.94	59
Brie & Chablis	1,172	0.45	51
Aging Erudites	12,405	4.80	318
Satellite Suburbs	5,989	2.32	81
Kindergarten Boom	21,774	8.42	321
Blue Collar Winners	79	0.03	1
Old Towns' New Fringe	286	0.11	3
High Rise Melting Pot	601	0.23	16
Conservative Homebodies	32,334	12.51	347
High Rise Sunsets	9,291	3.59	251
Young Urban Professionals	4,856	1.88	99
Young Urban Mix	1,198	0.46	22
Young Urban Intelligentsia	3,890	1.50	99
University Enclaves	15,741	6.09	298
Young City Singles	19,347	7.48	326
Urban Bohemia	1,526	0.59	50
Town Renters	4,806	1.86	215
Nesters & Young Homesteaders	322	0.12	5
Old Quebec Walkups	60	0.02	1
Struggling Downtowns	43,125	16.68	530
Aged Pensioners	9,291	3.59	270
Big City Stress	12,022	4.65	412
Old Grey Towers	3,866	1.50	270

FINANCIAL P$YTE

2001 Estimates	No. of House-holds	% of Total Hhds.	Index
Platinum Estates	2,207	0.85	106
Four Star Investors	6,856	2.65	53
Successful Suburbanites	27,499	10.64	160
Canadian Comfort	8,504	3.29	34
Urban Heights	18,433	7.13	166
Miners & Credit-Liners	13,104	5.07	160
Mortgages & Minivans	21,774	8.42	128
Tractors & Tradelines	286	0.11	2
Bills & Wills	33,532	12.97	157
Revolving Renters	9,613	3.72	81
Young Urban Struggle	21,157	8.18	173
Loan Parent Stress	60	0.02	—
Towering Debt	67,879	26.26	336
NSF	12,022	4.65	131
Senior Survivors	13,157	5.09	270

Manitoba

Winnipeg
(City)
Winnipeg CMA
(Cont'd)

HOME LANGUAGE

2001 Estimates:		% Total
English	554,249	87.78
French	11,381	1.80
Arabic	412	0.07
Chinese	7,308	1.16
Cree	578	0.09
German	3,863	0.61
Greek	626	0.10
Hungarian	330	0.05
Italian	1,738	0.28
Korean	647	0.10
Lao	758	0.12
Ojibway	482	0.08
Persian (Farsi)	380	0.06
Polish	4,406	0.70
Portuguese	3,853	0.61
Punjabi	3,645	0.58
Russian	448	0.07
Serbo-Croatian	696	0.11
Spanish	2,464	0.39
Tagalog (Pilipino)	9,289	1.47
Ukrainian	2,470	0.39
Vietnamese	1,695	0.27
Other Languages	4,889	0.77
Multiple Responses	14,766	2.34
Total	631,373	100.00

BUILDING PERMITS

	1999	1998	1997
		$000	
Value	484,507	472,865	344,006

HOMES BUILT

	1999	1998	1997
No	1,153	1,138	1,484

TAXATION

Income Class:	1997	% Total
Under $5,000	54,660	11.81
$5,000-$10,000	57,960	12.52
$10,000-$15,000	70,330	15.19
$15,000-$20,000	50,940	11.00
$20,000-$25,000	43,450	9.39
$25,000-$30,000	38,800	8.38
$30,000-$40,000	60,540	13.08
$40,000-$50,000	35,490	7.67
$50,000 +	50,750	10.96
Total Returns, No.	462,930	
Total Income, $000	12,347,885	
Total Taxable Returns	333,030	
Total Tax, $000	2,483,435	
Average Income, $	26,673	
Average Tax, $	7,457	

VITAL STATISTICS

	1997	1996	1995	1994
Births	7,642	8,201	8,665	8,898
Deaths	5,136	5,221	5,342	4,987
Natural Increase	2,506	2,980	3,323	3,911
Marriages	3,495	3,641	3,949	3,919

Note: Latest available data.

MEDIA INFO
see Winnipeg, CMA

Saskatchewan

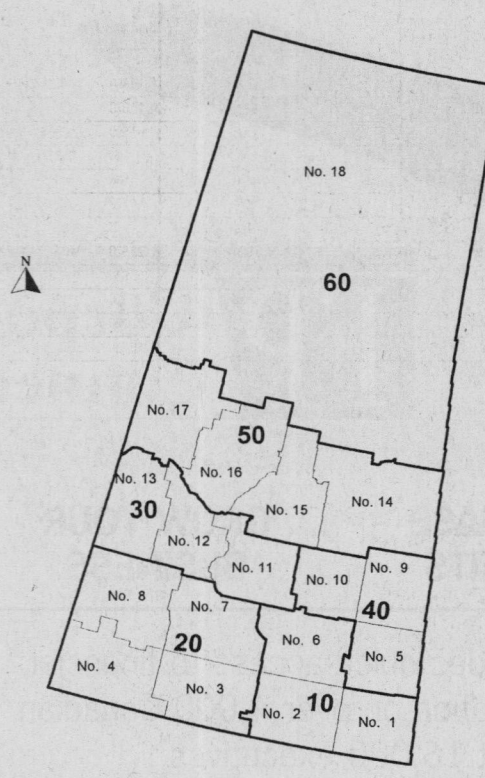

Economic Regions

10 Regina - Moose Mountain
20 Swift Current - Moose Jaw
30 Saskatoon - Biggar
40 Yorkton - Melville
50 Prince Albert
60 Northern

Region	Population (at July 1)				Households (at July1)		Income				Retail Sales				Taxation Statistics, 1997					
	*1996 Census (000)	2001 Estimate (000)	% of Cdn. Total	% Chg. '96-'01	2001 Estimate (000)	% of Cdn. Total	2001 Estimate $millions	% of Cdn. Total	Per Hhld. $	Income Rating Index	2001 Estimate $millions	% of Cdn. Total	Per Hhld. $	Market Rating Index	Total No. of Returns	Total Income $millions	Total No. Taxable Returns	Total Tax $millions	Avg. Income $	Avg. Tax $
Saskatchewan	1,019.4	1,034.3	3.32	1.46	402.7	3.33	19,435.7	2.96	48,300	89	8,157.3	2.93	20,300	88	696,830	17,143.0	475,880	3,242.1	24,601	6,813
Regina - Moose Mountain (10)	284.1	285.5	0.92	0.49	114.0	0.94	6,089.4	0.93	53,400	101	2,429.8	0.87	21,300	95	197,390	5,429.3	144,110	1,111.1	27,506	7,710
Division No. 1	33.2	33.6	0.11	1.23	13.0	0.11	693.6	0.11	53,200	98	231.4	0.08	17,700	77	23,110	663.0	16,890	140.8	28,691	8,335
Division No. 2	23.7	23.1	0.07	-2.74	9.4	0.08	458.2	0.07	49,000	94	130.6	0.05	14,000	63	16,990	426.9	12,480	79.6	25,125	6,376
Division No. 6	227.2	228.8	0.73	0.72	91.6	0.76	4,937.6	0.75	53,900	102	2,067.8	0.74	22,600	101	157,290	4,339.4	114,740	890.8	27,589	7,764
Swift Current - Moose Jaw (20)	112.6	110.0	0.35	-2.28	44.2	0.37	2,098.6	0.32	47,500	90	851.3	0.31	19,300	86	77,400	1,851.1	55,990	327.6	23,915	5,851
Division No. 3	16.9	15.9	0.05	-5.95	6.3	0.05	294.0	0.04	46,600	88	136.0	0.05	21,500	96	11,480	260.7	8,260	43.5	22,707	5,265
Division No. 4	12.6	12.2	0.04	-3.08	4.6	0.04	209.2	0.03	45,000	81	62.1	0.02	13,400	57	7,980	180.1	5,720	29.9	22,566	5,233
Division No. 7	50.6	49.8	0.16	-1.67	20.2	0.17	946.4	0.14	46,900	90	373.8	0.13	18,500	84	34,160	798.7	24,070	143.4	23,382	5,957
Division No. 8	32.5	32.1	0.10	-1.01	13.1	0.11	649.0	0.10	49,700	96	279.5	0.10	21,400	97	23,780	611.6	17,940	110.8	25,719	6,177
Saskatoon - Biggar (30)	289.9	298.6	0.96	3.01	119.2	0.99	5,980.3	0.91	50,200	95	2,343.4	0.84	19,700	88	198,060	5,245.1	141,890	1,041.9	26,482	7,343
Division No. 11	239.3	247.8	0.80	3.57	100.2	0.83	5,060.3	0.77	50,500	97	2,021.7	0.73	20,200	91	164,740	4,447.0	117,930	901.7	26,994	7,646

*Adjusted.

Saskatchewan (continued)

Region	Population (at July 1)				Households (at July 1)		Income				Retail Sales				Taxation Statistics, 1997					
	*1996 Census (000)	2001 Estimate (000)	% of Cdn. Total	% Chg. '96-'01	2001 Estimate (000)	% of Cdn. Total	2001 Estimate $millions	% of Cdn. Total	Per Hhld. $	Income Rating Index	2001 Estimate $millions	% of Cdn. Total	Per Hhld. $	Market Rating Index	Total No. of Returns	Total Income $millions	Total No. Taxable Returns	Total Tax $millions	Avg. Income $	Avg. Tax $
Division No. 12	25.1	25.2	0.08	0.57	9.2	0.08	441.5	0.07	47,700	83	121.5	0.04	13,100	54	15,950	367.0	11,160	63.9	23,010	5,723
Division No. 13	25.6	25.6	0.08	0.1	9.7	0.08	478.5	0.07	49,400	89	200.2	0.07	20,700	87	17,370	431.1	12,800	76.3	24,817	5,964
Yorkton - Melville (40)	96.7	93.5	0.30	-3.3	37.9	0.31	1,456.8	0.22	38,500	74	680.7	0.24	18,000	81	67,560	1,359.4	40,680	214.8	20,121	5,280
Division No. 5	35.9	34.7	0.11	-3.2	13.9	0.12	577.2	0.09	41,500	79	256.9	0.09	18,500	83	25,840	557.6	16,270	93.9	21,579	5,769
Division No. 9	39.5	38.1	0.12	-3.69	15.8	0.13	589.5	0.09	37,300	73	282.8	0.10	17,900	83	27,500	541.8	16,360	84.6	19,700	5,171
Division No. 10	21.3	20.7	0.07	-2.76	8.2	0.07	290.2	0.04	35,400	67	141.0	0.05	17,200	76	14,220	260.0	8,050	36.3	18,287	4,514
Prince Albert (50)	204.0	210.0	0.67	2.97	77.6	0.64	3,392.1	0.52	43,700	77	1,718.4	0.62	22,100	91	138,430	2,962.1	86,230	506.1	21,398	5,870
Division No. 14	41.8	41.1	0.13	-1.78	16.2	0.13	661.5	0.10	40,800	76	301.8	0.11	18,600	82	29,920	618.7	18,830	99.6	20,679	5,287
Division No. 15	82.9	85.1	0.27	2.58	31.5	0.26	1,467.0	0.22	46,600	82	772.0	0.28	24,500	101	55,840	1,236.2	35,680	213.9	22,139	5,996
Division No. 16	38.8	39.5	0.13	1.75	14.8	0.12	602.0	0.09	40,700	72	303.0	0.11	20,500	86	25,310	507.8	15,000	83.6	20,063	5,571
Division No. 17	40.4	44.3	0.14	9.87	15.2	0.13	661.6	0.10	43,500	71	341.7	0.12	22,500	86	27,360	599.3	16,720	109.1	21,905	6,524
Northern (60)	32.2	36.7	0.12	13.89	9.8	0.08	418.6	0.06	42,600	54	133.7	0.05	13,600	41	16,630	272.6	6,250	37.9	16,390	6,065
Division No. 18	32.2	36.7	0.12	13.89	9.8	0.08	418.6	0.06	42,600	54	133.7	0.05	13,600	41	16,630	272.6	6,250	37.9	16,390	6,065

*Adjusted.

Saskatchewan

POPULATION

July 1, 2001 Estimate	1,034,312
% Cdn. Total	3.32
% Change, '96 -'01	1.46
Avg. Annual Growth Rate, %	0.29
2003 Projected Population	1,044,734
2006 Projected Population	1,056,259
2001 Households Estimate	402,717
2003 Projected Households	409,770
2006 Projected Households	420,534

INCOME

% Above/Below National Average	-11
2001 Total Income Estimate	$19,435,740,000
% Cdn. Total	2.96
2001 Average Hhld. Income	$48,300
2001 Per Capita	$18,800
2003 Projected Total Income	$20,757,140,000
2006 Projected Total Income	$22,989,270,000

RETAIL SALES

% Above/Below National Average	-12
2001 Retail Sales Estimate	$8,157,260,000
% Cdn. Total	2.93
2001 per Household	$20,300
2001 per Capita	$7,900
2001 No. of Establishments	8,036
2003 Projected Retail Sales	$8,813,760,000
2006 Projected Retail Sales	$9,732,580,000

POPULATION

2001 Estimates:

Total		1,034,312
Male		509,792
Female		524,520

Age Groups	Male	Female
0-4	34,809	33,227
5-9	37,740	36,124
10-14	40,351	38,687
15-19	40,827	38,883
20-24	37,656	36,179
25-29	33,329	32,884
30-34	33,877	34,658
35-39	36,868	37,983
40-44	38,016	38,371
45-49	35,224	34,826
50-54	29,166	28,821
55-59	23,711	23,825
60-64	20,441	21,292
65-69	18,794	20,422
70+	48,983	68,338

DAYTIME POPULATION

2001 Estimates:

Working Population	495,088
At Home Population	538,661
Total	1,033,749

INCOME

2001 Estimates:

Avg. Household Income	$48,262
Avg. Family Income	$55,745
Per Capita Income	$18,791

Male:

Avg. Employment Income	$30,251
Avg. Employment Income (Full Time)	$39,764

Female:

Avg. Employment Income	$18,846
Avg. Employment Income (Full Time)	$28,414

DISPOSABLE & DISCRETIONARY INCOME

2001 Estimates:	Per Hhld.
Disposable Income	$37,913
Discretionary Income 1 (minus Food & Shelter)	$26,507
Discretionary Income 2 (minus Food, Shelter, & Other Expenditures)	$18,281

LIQUID ASSETS

1999 Estimates:	Per Hhld.
Equity Investments	$66,859
Interest Bearing Investments	$59,236
Total Liquid Assets	$126,095

CREDIT DATA

July 2000:

Pool of Credit	$9,028,821,161
Revolving Credit, No.	1,486,402
Fixed Loans, No.	561,942
Avg. Credit Limit, per Person	$11,634
Avg. Spent, per Person	$5,680
Satisfactory Ratings, No. per Person	2.54
Avg. No. of Cards, per Person	0.84

LABOUR FORCE

2001 Estimates:

Male:

In the Labour Force	281,319
Participation Rate	70.9
Employed	261,307
Unemployed	20,012
Unemployment Rate	7.1
Not in Labour Force	115,573

Female:

In the Labour Force	241,407
Participation Rate	58.0
Employed	225,671
Unemployed	15,736
Unemployment Rate	6.5
Not in Labour Force	175,075

AVERAGE WEEKLY EARNINGS

(Including overtime, industrial aggregate)

	Saskatchewan	Canada
Apr 2000	$550.37	$622.92
Apr 1999	$538.36	$608.07
Apr 1998	$533.46	$608.06
Apr 1997	$529.07	$597.26
Apr 1996	$486.69	$575.79

NUMBER OF EMPLOYEES

(Industrial aggregate)

Apr 2000	353,764
Apr 1999	352,366
Apr 1998	341,667
Apr 1997	329,772
Apr 1996	313,621

MANUFACTURING INDUSTRIES

	1997	1992
Plants	787	750
Employees	26,414	19,588
	$000	
Salaries, Wages	905,113	621,322
Mfg. Materials, Cost	3,636,695	2,128,372
Mfg. Shipments, Value	6,114,491	3,487,557
Total Value Added	2,526,624	1,301,172

Note: Latest available data.

OCCUPATIONS BY MAJOR GROUPS

2001 Estimates:	Male	Female
Management	23,959	11,325
Business, Finance & Admin.	19,449	62,649
Natural & Applied Sciences & Related	12,824	2,616
Health	4,209	23,565
Social Sciences, Gov't Services & Religion	5,738	7,155
Education	7,363	12,672
Arts, Culture, Recreation & Sport	3,812	5,956
Sales & Service	50,455	83,573
Trades, Transport & Equipment Operators & Related	67,792	4,021
Primary Industries	64,728	19,271
Processing, Mfg. & Utilities	15,859	3,247

LEVEL OF SCHOOLING

2001 Estimates:

Population 15 years +	813,374
Less than Grade 9	108,557
Grades 9-13 w/o Certif.	244,291
Grade 9-13 with Certif.	86,464
Trade Certif. /Dip.	24,908
Non-Univ. w/o Certif./Dip.	39,316
Non-Univ. with Certif./Dip.	136,198
Univ. w/o Degree	94,479
Univ. w/o Degree/Certif.	47,780
Univ. with Certif.	46,699
Univ. with Degree	79,161

RETAIL SALES

	1999 $000,000	1998 $000,000
Supermarkets & Groceries	1,847	1,865
All Other Food	n.a.	n.a.
Drugs & Patent Medicine	380	398
Shoes	23	25
Men's Clothing	34	37
Women's Clothing	100	99
Other Clothing	173	163
Hhld. Furniture & Appliances	263	248
Hhld. Furnishings	77	74
Motor & Recreation Vehicles	1,921	1,940
Gas Service Stations	636	557
Auto Parts, Accessories & Services	500	513
General Merchandise	1,060	1,001
Other Semi-Durable Goods	187	188
Other Durable Goods	195	186
Other Retail	276	267
Total	7,735	7,622

AVERAGE HOUSEHOLD EXPENDITURES

2001 Estimates:

Food	$5,722
Shelter	$7,627
Clothing	$2,084
Transportation	$6,198
Health & Personal Care	$1,953
Recr'n, Read'g & Education	$3,466
Taxes & Securities	$11,582
Other	$8,398
Total Expenditures	$47,030

PRIVATE HOUSEHOLDS

2001 Estimates:

Private Households, Total	402,717
Pop. in Private Households	1,002,602
Average no. per Household	2.5

FAMILIES

2001 Estimates:

Families in Private Households	280,736
Husband-Wife Families	243,042
Lone-Parent Families	37,694
Aver. No. Persons per Family	3.1
Aver. No. Sons/Daughters at Home	1.3

HOUSING

2001 Estimates:

Occupied Private Dwellings	402,717
Owned	274,555
Rented	118,251
Band Housing	9,911
Single-Detached House	303,442
Semi-Detached House	10,439
Row Houses	11,483
Apartment, 5+ Storeys	12,044
Owned Apartment, 5+ Storeys	1,251
Apartment, 5 or Fewer Storeys	50,087
Apartment, Detached Duplex	6,740
Other Single-Attached	1,094
Movable Dwellings	7,388

VEHICLES

2001 Estimates:

Model Yrs. '81-'96, No.	548,045
% Total	83.77
Model Yrs. '97-'98, No.	71,511
% Total	10.93
'99 Vehicles registered in Model Yr. '99, No.	34,644
% Total	5.30
Total No. '81-'99	654,200

LEGAL MARITAL STATUS

2001 Estimates: (Age 15+)

Single (Never Married)	247,630
Legally Married (Not Separated)	441,181
Legally Married (Separated)	20,396
Widowed	59,546
Divorced	44,621

PSYTE CATEGORIES

2001 Estimates	No. of House-holds	% of Total Hhds.	Index
Canadian Establishment	23	0.01	3
Urban Gentry	4,797	1.19	66
Suburban Executives	3,284	0.82	57
Mortgaged in Suburbia	672	0.17	12
Technocrafts & Bureaucrats	17,047	4.23	150
Boomers & Teens	877	0.22	12
Stable Suburban Families	4,218	1.05	80
Small City Elite	1,057	0.26	15
Old Bungalow Burbs	9,216	2.29	138
Aging Erudites	10,297	2.56	169
Satellite Suburbs	2,102	0.52	18
Kindergarten Boom	22,271	5.53	211
Blue Collar Winners	2,879	0.71	28
Town Boomers	13,486	3.35	330
Old Towns' New Fringe	6,322	1.57	40
Northern Lights	755	0.19	38
The New Frontier	14,325	3.56	236
Rustic Prosperity	4,303	1.07	59
Pick-ups & Dirt Bikes	14,857	3.69	442
The Grain Belt	32,400	8.05	1,358
Conservative Homebodies	7,775	1.93	54
High Rise Sunsets	5,029	1.25	87
Young Urban Professionals	2,838	0.70	37
Young Urban Mix	1,981	0.49	23
Young Urban Intelligentsia	2,704	0.67	44
University Enclaves	11,578	2.87	141
Young City Singles	15,994	3.97	173

2001 Estimates	No. of House-holds	% of Total Hhds.	Index
Old Leafy Towns	1,785	0.44	17
Town Renters	746	0.19	21
Nesters & Young Homesteaders	418	0.10	4
Young Grey Collar	21,035	5.22	624
Quiet Towns	16,572	4.12	193
Agrarian Blues	316	0.08	37
Rod & Rifle	4,951	1.23	53
Down, Down East	453	0.11	16
Big Country Families	29,448	7.31	513
Old Cdn. Rustics	68,464	17.00	1,733
Struggling Downtowns	24,220	6.01	191
Aged Pensioners	8,179	2.03	153
Big City Stress	5,261	1.31	116
Old Grey Towers	3,042	0.76	136

FINAN¢IAL P$YTE

2001 Estimates	No. of House-holds	% of Total Hhds.	Index
Platinum Estates	23	0.01	1
Four Star Investors	8,958	2.22	44
Successful Suburbanites	22,692	5.63	85
Canadian Comfort	19,524	4.85	50
Urban Heights	13,135	3.26	76
Miners & Credit-Liners	23,541	5.85	185
Mortgages & Minivans	22,271	5.53	84
Tractors & Tradelines	10,625	2.64	46
Bills & Wills	11,541	2.87	35
Country Credit	47,257	11.73	174
Revolving Renters	26,482	6.58	143
Young Urban Struggle	14,282	3.55	75
Rural Family Blues	35,168	8.73	108
Limited Budgets	85,036	21.12	679
Towering Debt	40,960	10.17	130
NSF	5,261	1.31	37
Senior Survivors	11,221	2.79	148

HOME LANGUAGE

2001 Estimates:		% Total
English	968,647	93.65
French	5,407	0.52
Chinese	4,711	0.46
Cree	15,289	1.48
German	7,268	0.70
Greek	561	0.05
Polish	627	0.06
Spanish	1,054	0.10
Tagalog (Pilipino)	883	0.09
Ukrainian	2,865	0.28
Vietnamese	1,216	0.12
Other Languages	11,688	1.13
Multiple Responses	14,096	1.36
Total	1,034,312	100.00

BUILDING PERMITS

	1999	1998 $000	1997
Value	721,627	672,898	626,809

HOMES BUILT

	1999	1998	1997
No	2,722	3,163	2,409

CAPITAL EXPENDITURES

(Public & Private)	2000	1999 $000,000	1998
Total Expends	n.a.	n.a.	8,617.6
Capital Expends	6,759.9	6,777.2	6,603.1
Construction	4,314.5	4,009.9	4,097.9
Machinery & Equip.	2,445.4	2,767.4	2,505.2
Repair Expends	n.a.	n.a.	2,014.5
Construction	n.a.	n.a.	718.7
Machinery & Equip.	n.a.	n.a.	1,295.8

TAXATION

Income Class:	1997	% Total
Under $5,000	93,200	13.37
$5,000-$10,000	95,110	13.65
$10,000-$15,000	117,140	16.81
$15,000-$20,000	74,630	10.71
$20,000-$25,000	60,920	8.74
$25,000-$30,000	55,370	7.95
$30,000-$40,000	80,190	11.51
$40,000-$50,000	50,080	7.19
$50,000 +	70,210	10.08
Total Returns, No.	696,830	
Total Income, $000	17,143,024	
Total Taxable Returns	475,880	
Total Tax, $000	3,242,066	
Average Income, $	24,601	
Average Tax, $	6,813	

VITAL STATISTICS

	1997	1996	1995	1994
Births	12,860	13,300	13,499	14,038
Deaths	8,637	8,765	8,495	8,308
Natural Increase	4,223	4,535	5,004	5,730
Marriages	5,700	5,671	5,799	5,689

Note: Latest available data.

TRAVEL STATISTICS

Tourists in Canada	1999	1998
From the U.S. entering by:		
Automobile	162,417	163,802
Bus	5,465	5,960
Air	31,913	28,094
Other Methods	1,327	798
Total	201,122	198,654
Other Countries:		
Land (via U.S.)	964	965
Air	2,818	2,088
Total	3,782	3,053
Residents of Canada Returning from the U.S. by:		
Automobile	273,137	281,769
Bus	14,771	12,998
Air	37,771	41,921
Other Methods	5,080	4,684
Total	330,759	341,372
From Other Countries:		
Air	13,681	13,101
Total	13,681	13,101

Saskatchewan

Saskatchewan

Estevan
(Census Agglomeration)

The Census Agglomeration of Estevan consists of Estevan, C; Estevan, No. 5, RM, and one smaller area. All are in census division No. 1.

POPULATION

July 1, 2001 Estimate	13,511
% Cdn. Total	0.04
% Change, '96 -'01	3.83
Avg. Annual Growth Rate, %	0.75
2003 Projected Population	13,799
2006 Projected Population	14,125
2001 Households Estimate	5,239
2003 Projected Households	5,373
2006 Projected Households	5,547

INCOME

% Above/Below National Average	+13
2001 Total Income Estimate	$322,990,000
% Cdn. Total	0.05
2001 Average Hhld. Income	$61,700
2001 Per Capita	$23,900
2003 Projected Total Income	$348,020,000
2006 Projected Total Income	$389,120,000

RETAIL SALES

% Above/Below National Average	-6
2001 Retail Sales Estimate	$113,690,000
% Cdn. Total	0.04
2001 per Household	$21,700
2001 per Capita	$8,400
2001 No. of Establishments	111
2003 Projected Retail Sales	$125,170,000
2006 Projected Retail Sales	$141,310,000

POPULATION

2001 Estimates:

Total		13,511
Male		6,800
Female		6,711
Age Groups	Male	Female
0-4	484	451
5-9	520	487
10-14	536	494
15-19	531	502
20-24	524	462
25-29	503	432
30-34	513	484
35-39	553	546
40-44	543	532
45-49	475	439
50-54	372	341
55-59	270	273
60-64	221	245
65-69	207	233
70+	548	790

DAYTIME POPULATION

2001 Estimates:

Working Population	6,963
At Home Population	6,548
Total	13,511

INCOME

2001 Estimates:

Avg. Household Income	$61,650
Avg. Family Income	$72,150
Per Capita Income	$23,905
Male:	
Avg. Employment Income	$42,520
Avg. Employment Income (Full Time)	$53,664
Female:	
Avg. Employment Income	$21,464
Avg. Employment Income (Full Time)	$32,592

DISPOSABLE & DISCRETIONARY INCOME

2001 Estimates:	Per Hhld.
Disposable Income	$47,841
Discretionary Income 1 (minus Food & Shelter)	$34,484
Discretionary Income 2 (minus Food, Shelter, & Other Expenditures)	$23,627

LIQUID ASSETS

1999 Estimates:	Per Hhld.
Equity Investments	$114,461
Interest Bearing Investments	$81,125
Total Liquid Assets	$195,586

CREDIT DATA

July 2000:

Pool of Credit	$113,764,567
Revolving Credit, No.	18,344
Fixed Loans, No.	6,980
Avg. Credit Limit, per Person	$12,058
Avg. Spent, per Person	$5,815
Satisfactory Ratings, No. per Person	2.57
Avg. No. of Cards, per Person	0.94

LABOUR FORCE

2001 Estimates:

Male:	
In the Labour Force	4,029
Participation Rate	76.6
Employed	3,837
Unemployed	192
Unemployment Rate	4.8
Not in Labour Force	1,231
Female:	
In the Labour Force	3,136
Participation Rate	59.4
Employed	3,004
Unemployed	132
Unemployment Rate	4.2
Not in Labour Force	2,143

OCCUPATIONS BY MAJOR GROUPS

2001 Estimates:	Male	Female
Management	410	162
Business, Finance & Admin.	277	997
Natural & Applied Sciences & Related	261	23
Health	22	284
Social Sciences, Gov't Services & Religion	53	33
Education	109	105
Arts, Culture, Recreation & Sport	52	43
Sales & Service	556	1,295
Trades, Transport & Equipment Operators & Related	1,329	50
Primary Industries	622	40
Processing, Mfg. & Utilities	338	11

LEVEL OF SCHOOLING

2001 Estimates:

Population 15 years +	10,539
Less than Grade 9	1,094
Grades 9-13 w/o Certif.	3,603
Grade 9-13 with Certif.	1,278
Trade Certif./Dip.	427
Non-Univ. w/o Certif./Dip.	512
Non-Univ. with Certif./Dip.	1,918
Univ. w/o Degree	1,007
Univ. w/o Degree/Certif.	547
Univ. with Certif.	460
Univ. with Degree	700

AVERAGE HOUSEHOLD EXPENDITURES

2001 Estimates:

Food	$6,862
Shelter	$8,911
Clothing	$2,660
Transportation	$8,345
Health & Personal Care	$2,529
Recr'n, Read'g & Education	$4,565
Taxes & Securities	$14,271
Other	$9,876
Total Expenditures	$58,019

PRIVATE HOUSEHOLDS

2001 Estimates:

Private Households, Total	5,239
Pop. in Private Households	13,268
Average no. per Household	2.5

FAMILIES

2001 Estimates:

Families in Private Households	3,709
Husband-Wife Families	3,295
Lone-Parent Families	414
Aver. No. Persons per Family	3.1
Aver. No. Sons/Daughters at Home	1.3

HOUSING

2001 Estimates:

Occupied Private Dwellings	5,239
Owned	3,783
Rented	1,456
Single-Detached House	3,649
Semi-Detached House	71
Row Houses	121
Apartment, 5+ Storeys	75
Owned Apartment, 5+ Storeys	28
Apartment, 5 or Fewer Storeys	828
Apartment, Detached Duplex	127
Other Single-Attached	32
Movable Dwellings	336

VEHICLES

2001 Estimates:

Model Yrs. '81-'96, No.	7,816
% Total	80.24
Model Yrs. '97-'98, No.	1,381
% Total	14.18
'99 Vehicles registered in Model Yr. '99, No.	544
% Total	5.58
Total No. '81-'99	9,741

LEGAL MARITAL STATUS

2001 Estimates: (Age 15+)

Single (Never Married)	2,951
Legally Married (Not Separated)	6,121
Legally Married (Separated)	209
Widowed	756
Divorced	502

PSYTE CATEGORIES

2001 Estimates	No. of House -holds	% of Total Hhds.	Index
Boomers & Teens	163	3.11	174
Town Boomers	483	9.22	910
The New Frontier	2,569	49.04	3,251
Pick-ups & Dirt Bikes	167	3.19	382
Quiet Towns	1,308	24.97	1,173
Old Cdn. Rustics	507	9.68	987

FINANCIAL P$YTE

2001 Estimates	No. of House -holds	% of Total Hhds.	Index
Four Star Investors	163	3.11	62
Canadian Comfort	483	9.22	95
Miners & Credit-Liners	2,569	49.04	1,549
Country Credit	167	3.19	47
Limited Budgets	1,815	34.64	1,114

HOME LANGUAGE

2001 Estimates:		% Total
English	13,391	99.11
French	11	0.08
Chinese	21	0.16
German	77	0.57
Greek	11	0.08
Total	13,511	100.00

BUILDING PERMITS

	1999	1998	1997
		$000	
Value	12,609	8,547	8,349

HOMES BUILT

	1999	1998	1997
No.	26	34	6

TAXATION

Income Class:	1997	% Total
Under $5,000	1,030	10.71
$5,000-$10,000	1,110	11.54
$10,000-$15,000	1,300	13.51
$15,000-$20,000	910	9.46
$20,000-$25,000	710	7.38
$25,000-$30,000	670	6.96
$30,000-$40,000	1,200	12.47
$40,000-$50,000	830	8.63
$50,000 +	1,880	19.54
Total Returns, No.	9,620	
Total Income, $000	322,782	
Total Taxable Returns	7,410	
Total Tax, $000	77,316	
Average Income, $.	33,553	
Average Tax, $.	10,434	

VITAL STATISTICS

	1997	1996	1995	1994
Births	187	171	191	190
Deaths	109	106	116	101
Natural Increase	78	65	75	89
Marriages	79	82	67	66

Note: Latest available data.

COMMUNITY NEWSPAPER(S)

	Total Circulation
Estevan: Estevan Mercury	3,761
Estevan: Estevan This Week	10,515
Estevan: The Southeast Trader Express	n.a.

RADIO STATION(S)

	Power
CJSL	10,000w

Moose Jaw
(Census Agglomeration)

The Census Agglomeration of Moose Jaw includes: Moose Jaw, C and Moose Jaw No. 161, RM. Both are in census division No. 7.

POPULATION

July 1, 2001 Estimate	35,365
% Cdn. Total	0.11
% Change, '96 -'01	-1.08
Avg. Annual Growth Rate, %	-0.22
2003 Projected Population	35,239
2006 Projected Population	34,791
2001 Households Estimate	14,998
2003 Projected Households	15,039
2006 Projected Households	15,141

INCOME

% Above/Below National Average	-4
2001 Total Income Estimate	$716,790,000
% Cdn. Total	0.11
2001 Average Hhld. Income	$47,800
2001 Per Capita	$20,800
2003 Projected Total Income	$755,490,000
2006 Projected Total Income	$823,910,000

RETAIL SALES

% Above/Below National Average	-1
2001 Retail Sales Estimate	$313,280,000
% Cdn. Total	0.11
2001 per Household	$20,900
2001 per Capita	$8,900
2001 No. of Establishments	270
2003 Projected Retail Sales	$332,360,000
2006 Projected Retail Sales	$355,420,000

POPULATION

2001 Estimates:

Total		35,365
Male		17,187
Female		18,178

Age Groups	Male	Female
0-4	1,120	1,066
5-9	1,189	1,137
10-14	1,285	1,188
15-19	1,293	1,233
20-24	1,185	1,167
25-29	1,065	1,075
30-34	1,148	1,144
35-39	1,319	1,313
40-44	1,339	1,326
45-49	1,196	1,179
50-54	964	946
55-59	762	771
60-64	681	731
65-69	673	776
70+	1,968	3,126

DAYTIME POPULATION

2001 Estimates:

Working Population	15,968
At Home Population	19,397
Total	35,365

INCOME

2001 Estimates:

Avg. Household Income	$47,793
Avg. Family Income	$57,524
Per Capita Income	$20,268

Male:

Avg. Employment Income	$32,680
Avg. Employment Income (Full Time)	$44,257

Female:

Avg. Employment Income	$18,808
Avg. Employment Income (Full Time)	$29,639

DISPOSABLE & DISCRETIONARY INCOME

2001 Estimates:	Per Hhld.
Disposable Income	$37,938
Discretionary Income 1 (minus Food & Shelter)	$26,078
Discretionary Income 2 (minus Food, Shelter, & Other Expenditures)	$18,234

LIQUID ASSETS

1999 Estimates:	Per Hhld.
Equity Investments	$68,654
Interest Bearing Investments	$59,122
Total Liquid Assets	$127,776

CREDIT DATA

July 2000:

Pool of Credit	$333,664,730
Revolving Credit, No.	57,718
Fixed Loans, No.	19,110
Avg. Credit Limit, per Person	$12,056
Avg. Spent, per Person	$6,043
Satisfactory Ratings, No. per Person	2.67
Avg. No. of Cards, per Person	0.93

LABOUR FORCE

2001 Estimates:

Male:

In the Labour Force	8,705
Participation Rate	64.0
Employed	8,236
Unemployed	469
Unemployment Rate	5.4
Not in Labour Force	4,888

Female:

In the Labour Force	7,976
Participation Rate	53.9
Employed	7,421
Unemployed	555
Unemployment Rate	7.0
Not in Labour Force	6,811

OCCUPATIONS BY MAJOR GROUPS

2001 Estimates:	Male	Female
Management	814	305
Business, Finance & Admin.	526	1,653
Natural & Applied Sciences & Related	355	74
Health	261	1,118
Social Sciences, Gov't Services & Religion	155	144
Education	346	408
Arts, Culture, Recreation & Sport	50	218
Sales & Service	2,152	3,421
Trades, Transport & Equipment Operators & Related	2,425	157
Primary Industries	744	136
Processing, Mfg. & Utilities	719	142

LEVEL OF SCHOOLING

2001 Estimates:

Population 15 years +	28,380
Less than Grade 9	2,772
Grades 9-13 w/o Certif.	8,844
Grade 9-13 with Certif.	2,992
Trade Certif. /Dip.	1,343
Non-Univ. w/o Certif./Dip.	1,665
Non-Univ. with Certif./Dip.	5,803
Univ. w/o Degree	2,791
Univ. w/o Degree/Certif.	1,239
Univ. with Certif.	1,552
Univ. with Degree	2,170

AVERAGE HOUSEHOLD EXPENDITURES

2001 Estimates:

Food	$5,955
Shelter	$7,874
Clothing	$2,159
Transportation	$5,210
Health & Personal Care	$2,212
Recr'n, Read'g & Education	$3,602
Taxes & Securities	$11,353
Other	$8,483
Total Expenditures	$46,848

PRIVATE HOUSEHOLDS

2001 Estimates:

Private Households, Total	14,998
Pop. in Private Households	34,041
Average no. per Household	2.3

FAMILIES

2001 Estimates:

Families in Private Households	9,841
Husband-Wife Families	8,341
Lone-Parent Families	1,500
Aver. No. Persons per Family	2.9
Aver. No. Sons/Daughters at Home	1.1

HOUSING

2001 Estimates:

Occupied Private Dwellings	14,998
Owned	9,621
Rented	5,377
Single-Detached House	10,618
Semi-Detached House	326
Row Houses	473
Apartment, 5+ Storeys	701
Owned Apartment, 5+ Storeys	11
Apartment, 5 or Fewer Storeys	2,211
Apartment, Detached Duplex	386
Other Single-Attached	43
Movable Dwellings	240

VEHICLES

2001 Estimates:

Model Yrs. '81-'96, No.	17,558
% Total	85.84
Model Yrs. '97-'98, No.	1,942
% Total	9.49
'99 Vehicles registered in Model Yr. '99, No.	954
% Total	4.66
Total No. '81-'99	20,454

LEGAL MARITAL STATUS

2001 Estimates: (Age 15+)

Single (Never Married)	8,027
Legally Married (Not Separated)	14,713
Legally Married (Separated)	816
Widowed	2,696
Divorced	2,128

PSYTE CATEGORIES

2001 Estimates	No. of House-holds	% of Total Hhds.	Index
Town Boomers	3,227	21.52	2,123
Rustic Prosperity	45	0.30	17
Pick-ups & Dirt Bikes	106	0.71	85
The Grain Belt	55	0.37	62
Young Grey Collar	9,883	65.90	7,877
Aged Pensioners	1,094	7.29	548
Old Grey Towers	218	1.45	262

FINANCIAL P$YTE

2001 Estimates	No. of House-holds	% of Total Hhds.	Index
Canadian Comfort	3,227	21.52	221
Tractors & Tradelines	45	0.30	5
Country Credit	161	1.07	16
Revolving Renters	9,883	65.90	1,432
Senior Survivors	1,312	8.75	464

Saskatchewan

HOME LANGUAGE

2001 Estimates:		% Total
English	34,572	97.76
French	287	0.81
Chinese	201	0.57
Serbo-Croatian	22	0.06
Spanish	21	0.06
Vietnamese	26	0.07
Other Languages	82	0.23
Multiple Responses	154	0.44
Total	35,365	100.00

BUILDING PERMITS

	1999	1998	1997
		$000	
Value	29,524	21,026	15,398

HOMES BUILT

	1999	1998	1997
No.	35	35	80

TAXATION

Income Class:	1997	% Total
Under $5,000	3,060	11.81
$5,000-$10,000	3,230	12.47
$10,000-$15,000	4,380	16.90
$15,000-$20,000	2,910	11.23
$20,000-$25,000	2,420	9.34
$25,000-$30,000	2,320	8.95
$30,000-$40,000	3,150	12.16
$40,000-$50,000	2,100	8.10
$50,000 +	2,360	9.11
Total Returns, No.	25,910	
Total Income, $000	632,504	
Total Taxable Returns	18,530	
Total Tax, $000	117,830	
Average Income, $	24,412	
Average Tax, $	6,359	

VITAL STATISTICS

	1997	1996	1995	1994
Births	421	413	443	444
Deaths	355	396	419	417
Natural Increase	66	17	24	27
Marriages	242	239	233	217

Note: Latest available data.

DAILY NEWSPAPER(S)

	Circulation Average Paid
Times-Herald	9,439

COMMUNITY NEWSPAPER(S)

	Total Circulation
Moose Jaw: Moose Jaw This Week	19,478

RADIO STATION(S)

	Power
CHAB	10,000w

TELEVISION STATION(S)

CBKT-TV
CKMJ-TV

Saskatchewan

North Battleford
(Census Agglomeration)

The Census Agglomeration of North Battleford consists of North Battleford, C, in census division 16, and Battleford, T, in census division No. 12.

POPULATION

July 1, 2001 Estimate	18,351
% Cdn. Total	0.06
% Change, '96 -'01	-0.72
Avg. Annual Growth Rate, %	-0.14
2003 Projected Population	18,225
2006 Projected Population	17,963
2001 Households Estimate	7,461
2003 Projected Households	7,532
2006 Projected Households	7,649

INCOME

% Above/Below National Average	-14
2001 Total Income Estimate	$331,670,000
% Cdn. Total	0.05
2001 Average Hhld. Income	$44,500
2001 Per Capita	$18,100
2003 Projected Total Income	$349,910,000
2006 Projected Total Income	$381,040,000

RETAIL SALES

% Above/Below National Average	-13
2001 Retail Sales Estimate	$143,720,000
% Cdn. Total	0.05
2001 per Household	$19,300
2001 per Capita	$7,800
2001 No. of Establishments	171
2003 Projected Retail Sales	$152,570,000
2006 Projected Retail Sales	$162,520,000

POPULATION

2001 Estimates:

Total		18,351
Male		8,690
Female		9,661

Age Groups	Male	Female
0-4	649	611
5-9	678	646
10-14	705	674
15-19	722	699
20-24	664	660
25-29	545	590
30-34	541	610
35-39	587	660
40-44	600	682
45-49	565	627
50-54	476	507
55-59	386	422
60-64	356	384
65-69	322	377
70+	894	1,512

DAYTIME POPULATION

2001 Estimates:

Working Population	8,235
At Home Population	10,116
Total	18,351

INCOME

2001 Estimates:

Avg. Household Income	$44,454
Avg. Family Income	$52,011
Per Capita Income	$18,074

Male:

Avg. Employment Income	$29,841
Avg. Employment Income (Full Time)	$39,060

Female:

Avg. Employment Income	$18,997
Avg. Employment Income (Full Time)	$29,203

DISPOSABLE & DISCRETIONARY INCOME

2001 Estimates:	Per Hhld.
Disposable Income	$35,347
Discretionary Income 1 (minus Food & Shelter)	$24,441
Discretionary Income 2 (minus Food, Shelter, & Other Expenditures)	$16,524

LIQUID ASSETS

1999 Estimates:	Per Hhld.
Equity Investments	$64,143
Interest Bearing Investments	$55,759
Total Liquid Assets	$119,902

CREDIT DATA

July 2000:

Pool of Credit	$136,320,526
Revolving Credit, No.	23,574
Fixed Loans, No.	8,746
Avg. Credit Limit, per Person	$9,925
Avg. Spent, per Person	$4,795
Satisfactory Ratings, No. per Person	2.21
Avg. No. of Cards, per Person	0.80

LABOUR FORCE

2001 Estimates:

Male:

In the Labour Force	4,536
Participation Rate	68.1
Employed	4,219
Unemployed	317
Unemployment Rate	7.0
Not in Labour Force	2,122

Female:

In the Labour Force	4,226
Participation Rate	54.7
Employed	3,901
Unemployed	325
Unemployment Rate	7.7
Not in Labour Force	3,504

OCCUPATIONS BY MAJOR GROUPS

2001 Estimates:	Male	Female
Management	421	222
Business, Finance & Admin.	340	919
Natural & Applied Sciences & Related	154	10
Health	109	541
Social Sciences, Gov't Services & Religion	117	190
Education	83	203
Arts, Culture, Recreation & Sport	51	79
Sales & Service	1,138	1,649
Trades, Transport & Equipment Operators & Related	1,257	40
Primary Industries	389	92
Processing, Mfg. & Utilities	366	167

LEVEL OF SCHOOLING

2001 Estimates:

Population 15 years +	14,388
Less than Grade 9	1,989
Grades 9-13 w/o Certif.	4,516
Grade 9-13 with Certif.	1,429
Trade Certif. /Dip.	446
Non-Univ. w/o Certif./Dip.	657
Non-Univ. with Certif./Dip.	3,004
Univ. w/o Degree	1,210
Univ. w/o Degree/Certif.	504
Univ. with Certif.	706
Univ. with Degree	1,137

AVERAGE HOUSEHOLD EXPENDITURES

2001 Estimates:

Food	$5,336
Shelter	$7,428
Clothing	$1,929
Transportation	$6,039
Health & Personal Care	$1,848
Recr'n, Read'g & Education	$3,068
Taxes & Securities	$10,371
Other	$7,703
Total Expenditures	$43,722

PRIVATE HOUSEHOLDS

2001 Estimates:

Private Households, Total	7,461
Pop. in Private Households	17,860
Average no. per Household	2.4

FAMILIES

2001 Estimates:

Families in Private Households	5,026
Husband-Wife Families	4,129
Lone-Parent Families	897
Aver. No. Persons per Family	3.0
Aver. No. Sons/Daughters at Home	1.2

HOUSING

2001 Estimates:

Occupied Private Dwellings	7,461
Owned	4,827
Rented	2,634
Single-Detached House	5,534
Semi-Detached House	224
Row Houses	296
Apartment, 5+ Storeys	215
Apartment, 5 or Fewer Storeys	993
Apartment, Detached Duplex	102
Other Single-Attached	21
Movable Dwellings	76

VEHICLES

2001 Estimates:

Model Yrs. '81-'96, No.	8,760
% Total	86.02
Model Yrs. '97-'98, No.	965
% Total	9.48
'99 Vehicles registered in Model Yr. '99, No.	459
% Total	4.51
Total No. '81-'99	10,184

LEGAL MARITAL STATUS

2001 Estimates: (Age 15+)

Single (Never Married)	4,358
Legally Married (Not Separated)	7,312
Legally Married (Separated)	403
Widowed	1,336
Divorced	979

PSYTE CATEGORIES

2001 Estimates	No. of House -holds	% of Total Hhds.	Index
Town Boomers	1,663	22.29	2,199
The New Frontier	401	5.37	356
Pick-ups & Dirt Bikes	298	3.99	478
Young Grey Collar	299	4.01	479
Quiet Towns	3,146	42.17	1,982
Big Country Families	326	4.37	306
Old Cdn. Rustics	862	11.55	1,178
Aged Pensioners	389	5.21	392

FINANCIAL P$YTE

2001 Estimates	No. of House -holds	% of Total Hhds.	Index
Canadian Comfort	1,663	22.29	229
Miners & Credit-Liners	401	5.37	170
Country Credit	298	3.99	59
Revolving Renters	299	4.01	87
Rural Family Blues	326	4.37	54
Limited Budgets	4,008	53.72	1,728
Senior Survivors	389	5.21	277

HOME LANGUAGE

2001 Estimates		% Total
English	17,869	97.37
French	79	0.43
Chinese	21	0.11
Cree	63	0.34
Spanish	36	0.20
Ukrainian	92	0.50
Other Languages	11	0.06
Multiple Responses	180	0.98
Total	18,351	100.00

BUILDING PERMITS

	1999	1998 $000	1997
Value	22,972	9,662	8,162

HOMES BUILT

	1999	1998	1997
No	7	19	10

TAXATION

Income Class:	1997	% Total
Under $5,000	1,730	12.09
$5,000-$10,000	1,910	13.35
$10,000-$15,000	2,590	18.10
$15,000-$20,000	1,650	11.53
$20,000-$25,000	1,370	9.57
$25,000-$30,000	1,230	8.60
$30,000-$40,000	1,660	11.60
$40,000-$50,000	990	6.92
$50,000 +	1,180	8.25
Total Returns, No.	14,310	
Total Income, $000	338,285	
Total Taxable Returns	9,850	
Total Tax, $000	61,944	
Average Income, $.	23,640	
Average Tax, $	6,289	

VITAL STATISTICS

	1997	1996	1995	1994
Births	239	280	273	275
Deaths	203	191	210	182
Natural Increase	36	89	63	93
Marriages	151	154	144	161

Note: Latest available data.

COMMUNITY NEWSPAPER(S)

	Total Circulation
North Battleford: North Battleford Regional Optimist/Advertiser Post	16,000
North Battleford: North Battleford News-Optimist	3,003
North Battleford: The Telegraph	2,587

RADIO STATION(S)

	Power
CBKF-FM	n.a.
CJNB	10,000w

TELEVISION STATION(S)

CFQC-TV
CKBI-TV

Prince Albert
(Census Agglomeration)

The Census Agglomeration of Prince Albert includes: Prince Albert, C; plus several smaller areas. All are in census division No. 15.

POPULATION

July 1, 2001 Estimate	43,922
% Cdn. Total	0.14
% Change, '96 -'01	2.40
Avg. Annual Growth Rate, %	0.48
2003 Projected Population	44,304
2006 Projected Population	44,634
2001 Households Estimate	16,398
2003 Projected Households	16,769
2006 Projected Households	17,232

INCOME

% Above/Below National Average	-10
2001 Total Income Estimate	$834,180,000
% Cdn. Total	0.13
2001 Average Hhld. Income	$50,900
2001 Per Capita	$19,000
2003 Projected Total Income	$901,270,000
2006 Projected Total Income	$1,010,500,000

RETAIL SALES

% Above/Below National Average	+46
2001 Retail Sales Estimate	$574,130,000
% Cdn. Total	0.21
2001 per Household	$35,000
2001 per Capita	$13,100
2001 No. of Establishments	336
2003 Projected Retail Sales	$620,710,000
2006 Projected Retail Sales	$685,440,000

POPULATION

2001 Estimates:

Total		43,922
Male		21,476
Female		22,446

Age Groups	Male	Female
0-4	1,637	1,565
5-9	1,785	1,671
10-14	1,798	1,687
15-19	1,788	1,680
20-24	1,639	1,623
25-29	1,444	1,527
30-34	1,450	1,555
35-39	1,558	1,679
40-44	1,575	1,641
45-49	1,472	1,519
50-54	1,232	1,239
55-59	991	988
60-64	824	843
65-69	702	776
70+	1,581	2,453

DAYTIME POPULATION

2001 Estimates:

Working Population	19,839
At Home Population	24,083
Total	43,922

INCOME

2001 Estimates:

Avg. Household Income	$50,871
Avg. Family Income	$56,984
Per Capita Income	$18,992
Male:	
Avg. Employment Income	$32,401
Avg. Employment Income (Full Time)	$45,326
Female:	
Avg. Employment Income	$19,443
Avg. Employment Income (Full Time)	$30,048

DISPOSABLE & DISCRETIONARY INCOME

2001 Estimates:	Per Hhld.
Disposable Income	$40,396
Discretionary Income 1 (minus Food & Shelter)	$28,097
Discretionary Income 2 (minus Food, Shelter, & Other Expenditures)	$19,835

LIQUID ASSETS

1999 Estimates:	Per Hhld.
Equity Investments	$74,113
Interest Bearing Investments	$62,462
Total Liquid Assets	$136,575

CREDIT DATA

July 2000:

Pool of Credit	$358,115,266
Revolving Credit, No.	60,078
Fixed Loans, No.	30,324
Avg. Credit Limit, per Person	$11,788
Avg. Spent, per Person	$6,100
Satisfactory Ratings, No. per Person	2.79
Avg. No. of Cards, per Person	0.78

LABOUR FORCE

2001 Estimates:

Male:	
In the Labour Force	10,998
Participation Rate	67.7
Employed	9,868
Unemployed	1,130
Unemployment Rate	10.3
Not in Labour Force	5,258
Female:	
In the Labour Force	10,416
Participation Rate	59.4
Employed	9,526
Unemployed	890
Unemployment Rate	8.5
Not in Labour Force	7,107

OCCUPATIONS BY MAJOR GROUPS

2001 Estimates:	Male	Female
Management	881	430
Business, Finance & Admin.	847	2,708
Natural & Applied Sciences & Related	597	64
Health	210	892
Social Sciences, Gov't Services & Religion	392	548
Education	372	641
Arts, Culture, Recreation & Sport	150	225
Sales & Service	2,833	4,090
Trades, Transport & Equipment Operators & Related	2,822	155
Primary Industries	948	293
Processing, Mfg. & Utilities	695	84

LEVEL OF SCHOOLING

2001 Estimates:

Population 15 years +	33,779
Less than Grade 9	4,023
Grades 9-13 w/o Certif.	9,955
Grade 9-13 with Certif.	3,712
Trade Certif. /Dip.	1,309
Non-Univ. w/o Certif./Dip.	1,918
Non-Univ. with Certif./Dip.	6,132
Univ. w/o Degree	3,815
Univ. w/o Degree/Certif.	1,703
Univ. with Certif.	2,112
Univ. with Degree	2,915

AVERAGE HOUSEHOLD EXPENDITURES

2001 Estimates:

Food	$6,197
Shelter	$8,174
Clothing	$2,286
Transportation	$5,623
Health & Personal Care	$2,257
Recr'n, Read'g & Education	$3,792
Taxes & Securities	$12,270
Other	$8,866
Total Expenditures	$49,465

PRIVATE HOUSEHOLDS

2001 Estimates:

Private Households, Total	16,398
Pop. in Private Households	42,424
Average no. per Household	2.6

FAMILIES

2001 Estimates:

Families in Private Households	12,086
Husband-Wife Families	9,679
Lone-Parent Families	2,407
Aver. No. Persons per Family	3.1
Aver. No. Sons/Daughters at Home	1.3

HOUSING

2001 Estimates:

Occupied Private Dwellings	16,398
Owned	10,094
Rented	6,277
Band Housing	27
Single-Detached House	11,377
Semi-Detached House	277
Row Houses	686
Apartment, 5+ Storeys	726
Owned Apartment, 5+ Storeys	34
Apartment, 5 or Fewer Storeys	2,849
Apartment, Detached Duplex	434
Other Single-Attached	11
Movable Dwellings	38

VEHICLES

2001 Estimates:

Model Yrs. '81-'96, No.	20,703
% Total	85.34
Model Yrs. '97-'98, No.	2,375
% Total	9.79
'99 Vehicles registered in Model Yr. '99, No.	1,182
% Total	4.87
Total No. '81-'99	24,260

LEGAL MARITAL STATUS

2001 Estimates: (Age 15+)

Single (Never Married)	11,371
Legally Married (Not Separated)	16,672
Legally Married (Separated)	1,075
Widowed	2,284
Divorced	2,377

PSYTE CATEGORIES

2001 Estimates	No. of House -holds	% of Total Hhds.	Index
Town Boomers	4,549	27.74	2,737
Rustic Prosperity	125	0.76	42
Pick-ups & Dirt Bikes	621	3.79	454
Young Grey Collar	9,662	58.92	7,043
Big Country Families	168	1.02	72
Aged Pensioners	609	3.71	279
Old Grey Towers	335	2.04	369

FINANCIAL P$YTE

2001 Estimates	No. of House -holds	% of Total Hhds.	Index
Canadian Comfort	4,549	27.74	286
Tractors & Tradelines	125	0.76	13
Country Credit	621	3.79	56
Revolving Renters	9,662	58.92	1,281
Rural Family Blues	168	1.02	13
Senior Survivors	944	5.76	306

Saskatchewan

HOME LANGUAGE

2001 Estimates:		% Total
English	42,099	95.85
French	382	0.87
Chinese	41	0.09
Cree	429	0.98
Hungarian	27	0.06
Polish	32	0.07
Spanish	38	0.09
Tagalog (Pilipino)	37	0.08
Ukrainian	110	0.25
Other Languages	110	0.25
Multiple Responses	617	1.40
Total	43,922	100.00

BUILDING PERMITS

	1999	1998 $000	1997
Value	24,183	62,279	21,719

HOMES BUILT

	1999	1998	1997
No.	107	139	55

TAXATION

Income Class:	1997	% Total
Under $5,000	4,220	14.52
$5,000-$10,000	4,130	14.21
$10,000-$15,000	4,890	16.82
$15,000-$20,000	2,940	10.11
$20,000-$25,000	2,480	8.53
$25,000-$30,000	2,110	7.26
$30,000-$40,000	3,160	10.87
$40,000-$50,000	2,080	7.16
$50,000 +	3,080	10.60
Total Returns, No.	29,070	
Total Income, $000	695,668	
Total Taxable Returns	18,920	
Total Tax, $000	130,121	
Average Income, $.	23,931	
Average Tax, $	6,877	

VITAL STATISTICS

	1997	1996	1995	1994
Births	624	631	690	722
Deaths	333	373	346	351
Natural Increase	291	258	344	371
Marriages	247	244	301	297

Note: Latest available data.

DAILY NEWSPAPER(S)

	Circulation Average Paid
Daily Herald	9,016

RADIO STATION(S)

	Power
CBKF-FM	n.a.
CFMM-FM	100,000w
CKBI	10,000w

TELEVISION STATION(S)

CIPA-TV
CKBI-TV

Saskatchewan

Regina
(Census Metropolitan Area)

POPULATION

July 1, 2001 Estimate	200,581
% Cdn. Total	0.64
% Change, '96 -'01	0.57
Avg. Annual Growth Rate, %	0.11
2003 Projected Population	202,989
2006 Projected Population	206,824
2001 Households Estimate	80,840
2003 Projected Households	82,774
2006 Projected Households	85,914

INCOME

% Above/Below National Average	+6
2001 Total Income Estimate	$4,486,080,000
% Cdn. Total	0.68
2001 Average Hhld. Income	$55,500
2001 Per Capita	$22,400
2003 Projected Total Income	$4,830,650,000
2006 Projected Total Income	$5,431,430,000

RETAIL SALES

% Above/Below National Average	+6
2001 Retail Sales Estimate	$1,912,120,000
% Cdn. Total	0.69
2001 per Household	$23,700
2001 per Capita	$9,500
2001 No. of Establishments	1,360
2003 Projected Retail Sales	$2,066,860,000
2006 Projected Retail Sales	$2,292,790,000

POPULATION

2001 Estimates:

Total		200,581
Male		97,276
Female		103,305

Age Groups	Male	Female
0-4	6,982	6,735
5-9	7,108	6,930
10-14	7,318	7,080
15-19	7,364	7,060
20-24	7,221	7,129
25-29	6,868	7,012
30-34	7,175	7,497
35-39	7,761	8,082
40-44	7,786	8,113
45-49	7,109	7,415
50-54	5,799	6,122
55-59	4,591	4,910
60-64	3,787	4,136
65-69	3,263	3,676
70+	7,144	11,408

DAYTIME POPULATION

2001 Estimates:

Working Population	101,685
At Home Population	98,896
Total	200,581

INCOME

2001 Estimates:

Avg. Household Income	$55,493
Avg. Family Income	$64,815
Per Capita Income	$22,365
Male:	
Avg. Employment Income	$35,842
Avg. Employment Income (Full Time)	$47,963
Female:	
Avg. Employment Income	$22,920
Avg. Employment Income (Full Time)	$33,288

DISPOSABLE & DISCRETIONARY INCOME

2001 Estimates:	*Per Hhld.*
Disposable Income	$42,739
Discretionary Income 1 (minus Food & Shelter)	$29,373
Discretionary Income 2 (minus Food, Shelter, & Other Expenditures)	$21,037

LIQUID ASSETS

1999 Estimates:	*Per Hhld.*
Equity Investments	$79,566
Interest Bearing Investments	$68,639
Total Liquid Assets	$148,205

CREDIT DATA

July 2000:

Pool of Credit	$2,123,224,805
Revolving Credit, No.	352,533
Fixed Loans, No.	117,900
Avg. Credit Limit, per Person	$13,287
Avg. Spent, per Person	$6,385
Satisfactory Ratings, No. per Person	2.84
Avg. No. of Cards, per Person	1.00

LABOUR FORCE

2001 Estimates:

Male:	
In the Labour Force	54,950
Participation Rate	72.4
Employed	50,953
Unemployed	3,997
Unemployment Rate	7.3
Not in Labour Force	20,918
Female:	
In the Labour Force	52,210
Participation Rate	63.2
Employed	49,053
Unemployed	3,157
Unemployment Rate	6.0
Not in Labour Force	30,350

OCCUPATIONS BY MAJOR GROUPS

2001 Estimates:	*Male*	*Female*
Management	6,114	2,887
Business, Finance & Admin.	6,742	18,130
Natural & Applied Sciences & Related	4,322	973
Health	1,153	4,779
Social Sciences, Gov't Services & Religion	1,593	1,921
Education	1,489	2,398
Arts, Culture, Recreation & Sport	1,526	1,465
Sales & Service	13,133	16,899
Trades, Transport & Equipment Operators & Related	12,944	647
Primary Industries	2,277	605
Processing, Mfg. & Utilities	2,501	366

LEVEL OF SCHOOLING

2001 Estimates:

Population 15 years +	158,428
Less than Grade 9	12,384
Grades 9-13 w/o Certif.	41,236
Grade 9-13 with Certif.	18,868
Trade Certif./Dip.	4,471
Non-Univ. w/o Certif./Dip.	7,908
Non-Univ. with Certif./Dip.	25,203
Univ. w/o Degree	25,569
Univ. w/o Degree/Certif.	13,844
Univ. with Certif.	11,725
Univ. with Degree	22,789

AVERAGE HOUSEHOLD EXPENDITURES

2001 Estimates:

Food	$6,258
Shelter	$9,287
Clothing	$2,248
Transportation	$6,329
Health & Personal Care	$1,937
Recr'n, Read'g & Education	$3,806
Taxes & Securities	$14,592
Other	$8,614
Total Expenditures	$53,071

PRIVATE HOUSEHOLDS

2001 Estimates:

Private Households, Total	80,840
Pop. in Private Households	197,088
Average no. per Household	2.4

FAMILIES

2001 Estimates:

Families in Private Households	55,318
Husband-Wife Families	46,282
Lone-Parent Families	9,036
Aver. No. Persons per Family	3.1
Aver. No. Sons/Daughters at Home	1.2

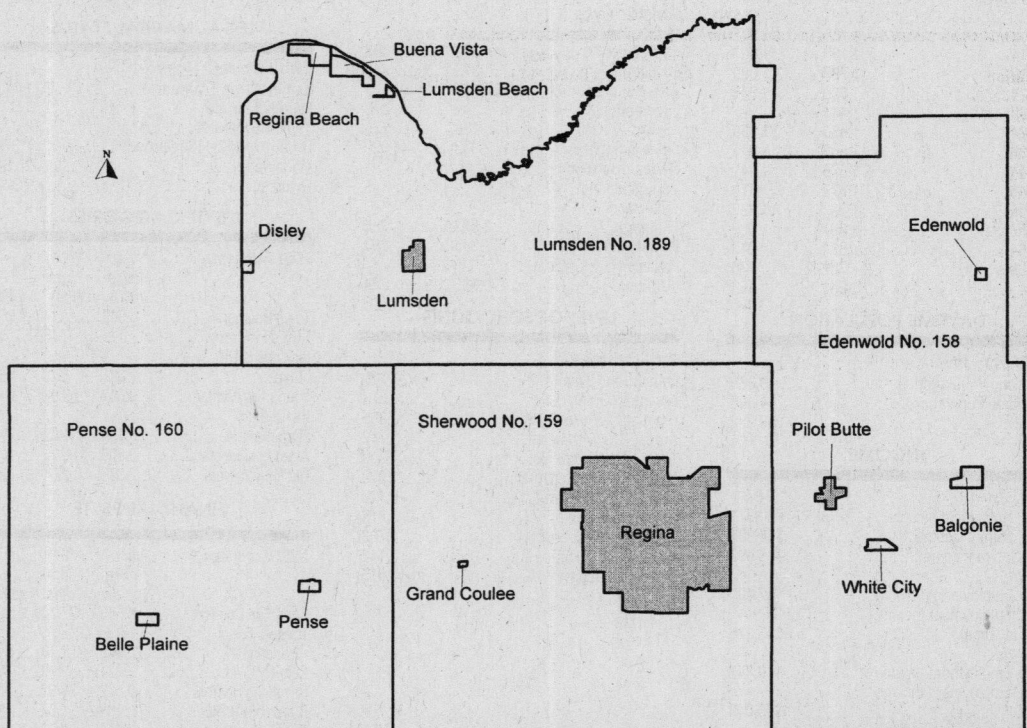

Urban Areas

Regina
(Census Metropolitan Area)
(Cont'd)

HOUSING

2001 Estimates:

Occupied Private Dwellings	80,840
Owned	53,518
Rented	27,322
Single-Detached House	56,021
Semi-Detached House	1,843
Row Houses	3,341
Apartment, 5+ Storeys	4,239
Owned Apartment, 5+ Storeys	537
Apartment, 5 or Fewer Storeys	13,777
Apartment, Detached Duplex	1,139
Other Single-Attached	82
Movable Dwellings	398

VEHICLES

2001 Estimates:

Model Yrs. '81-'96, No.	105,855
% Total	81.39
Model Yrs. '97-'98, No.	15,641
% Total	12.03
'99 Vehicles registered in Model Yr. '99, No.	8,568
% Total	6.59
Total No. '81-'99	130,064

RADIO STATION DATA

Station	Market	Format	Wkly. Reach%*	Aver. Hrs. Tuned
All Stations			96	22.6
CBK	Regina	Multi-format	19	10.5
CBK-FM	Regina	Multi-format	8	9.6
CBKF-FM	Regina	Multi-format	-	1.8
CFWF-FM	Regina	Rock	33	12.4
CHAB	Moose Jaw/Regina	Country	n.a.	n.a.
CHMX-FM	Regina	Country	21	6.2
CIZL-FM	Regina	AOR	41	10.6
CJME	Regina	News, Talk	16	6.7
CKCK	Regina	All Oldies	19	10.8
CKRM	Regina	Country	32	15.3

BBM Spring 2000 Radio Reach Survey; area coverage.
*Mon-Sun 5a.m - 1a.m , All Persons 12+

TV STATION DATA

Station	Market	Network Affiliation	Wkly. Reach%*	Aver. Hrs. Tuned
All Stations			95	22.6
A & E	n.a.	Ind.	34	3.2
CBKFT	Regina	SRC	n.a.	n.a.
CBKT	Regina	CBC	51	3.1
CFRE	Regina	Global	70	4.0
CKCK	Regina	CTV	76	6.8
CNN	n.a.	Ind.	6	2.4
CTV NNT	n.a.	CTV	5	2.0
KCNC	Denver CO	CBS	-	1.0
KRMA	Denver CO	PBS	-	2.3
KTLA	Los Angeles CA	WB	6	2.2
KWGN	Denver CO	WB	-	0.5
MMUSIC	n.a.	Ind.	7	1.8
NEWSWD	n.a.	CBC	10	1.7
OTHERS	n.a.	n.a.	6	2.8
PRIME	n.a.	Ind.	8	2.7
SPACE	n.a.	Ind.	7	1.9
SUPER	n.a.	Ind.	6	4.1
TLC	n.a.	Ind.	10	2.0
TNN	Nashville TN	Ind.	16	1.8
TOON	n.a.	Ind.	7	2.0
TSN	n.a.	Ind.	25	5.0
VCR	n.a.	n.a.	30	3.8
WCCO	Minneapolis MN	CBS	37	2.7
WDIV	Detroit MI	NBC	36	2.5
WPIX	New York NY	WB	5	2.6
WTBS	Atlanta GA	Ind.	18	3.7
WTVS	Detroit MI	PBS	16	1.8
WUHF	Rochester NY	FOX	14	2.6
WXYZ	Detroit MI	ABC	31	2.0
YTV	n.a.	Ind.	16	3.4

BBM Spring 2000 TV Reach Survey; CMA coverage.
*Mon-Sun 6a.m ‹ 2a.m , All Persons 2 +

LEGAL MARITAL STATUS

2001 Estimates: (Age 15+)

Single (Never Married)	50,895
Legally Married (Not Separated)	82,458
Legally Married (Separated)	4,415
Widowed	9,639
Divorced	11,021

PSYTE CATEGORIES

2001 Estimates	No. of House-holds	% of Total Hhds.	Index
Canadian Establishment	23	0.03	17
Urban Gentry	3,647	4.51	251
Suburban Executives	1,615	2.00	139
Mortgaged in Suburbia	672	0.83	60
Technocrafts & Bureaucrats	7,543	9.33	332
Boomers & Teens	571	0.71	39
Stable Suburban Families	3,187	3.94	302
Small City Elite	283	0.35	20
Old Bungalow Burbs	3,432	4.25	256
Aging Erudites	6,110	7.56	501
Satellite Suburbs	2,003	2.48	86
Kindergarten Boom	10,166	12.58	480
Blue Collar Winners	684	0.85	34
Old Towns' New Fringe	1,822	2.25	58
Rustic Prosperity	842	1.04	58

2001 Estimates	No. of House-holds	% of Total Hhds.	Index
The Grain Belt	44	0.05	9
Conservative Homebodies	5,050	6.25	173
High Rise Sunsets	1,332	1.65	115
Young Urban Professionals	424	0.52	28
Young Urban Intelligentsia	768	0.95	62
University Enclaves	3,975	4.92	241
Young City Singles	5,668	7.01	306
Old Leafy Towns	798	0.99	39
Town Renters	326	0.40	47
Big Country Families	22	0.03	2
Struggling Downtowns	13,321	16.48	523
Aged Pensioners	3,554	4.40	330
Big City Stress	2,017	2.50	221
Old Grey Towers	399	0.49	89

FINANCIAL P$YTE

2001 Estimates	No. of House-holds	% of Total Hhds.	Index
Platinum Estates	23	0.03	4
Four Star Investors	5,833	7.22	144
Successful Suburbanites	11,402	14.10	213
Canadian Comfort	2,970	3.67	38
Urban Heights	6,534	8.08	188
Miners & Credit-Liners	3,432	4.25	134
Mortgages & Minivans	10,166	12.58	191
Tractors & Tradelines	2,664	3.30	58
Bills & Wills	5,848	7.23	87
Country Credit	44	0.05	1
Revolving Renters	1,332	1.65	36
Young Urban Struggle	4,743	5.87	124
Rural Family Blues	22	0.03	—
Towering Debt	19,315	23.89	306
NSF	2,017	2.50	71
Senior Survivors	3,953	4.89	260

HOME LANGUAGE

2001 Estimates:		% Total
English	192,100	95.77
French	850	0.42
Chinese	1,805	0.90
German	295	0.15
Greek	333	0.17
Italian	161	0.08
Lao	193	0.10
Polish	108	0.05
Punjabi	209	0.10
Serbo-Croatian	164	0.08
Spanish	433	0.22
Tagalog (Pilipino)	324	0.16
Ukrainian	114	0.06
Vietnamese	602	0.30
Other Languages	1,168	0.58
Multiple Responses	1,722	0.86
Total	200,581	100.00

BUILDING PERMITS

	1999	1998	1997
		$000	
Value	176,667	162,796	186,623

HOMES BUILT

	1999	1998	1997
No.	521	561	383

Saskatchewan

TAXATION

Income Class:	1997	% Total
Under $5,000	14,910	10.75
$5,000-$10,000	16,060	11.58
$10,000-$15,000	19,440	14.01
$15,000-$20,000	13,980	10.08
$20,000-$25,000	12,480	9.00
$25,000-$30,000	12,090	8.72
$30,000-$40,000	18,680	13.47
$40,000-$50,000	12,520	9.03
$50,000 +	18,630	13.43
Total Returns, No.	138,710	
Total Income, $000	3,954,008	
Total Taxable Returns	102,850	
Total Tax, $000	828,443	
Average Income, $	28,506	
Average Tax, $	8,055	

VITAL STATISTICS

	1997	1996	1995	1994
Births	2,411	2,500	2,648	2,755
Deaths	1,437	1,410	1,388	1,259
Natural Increase	974	1,090	1,260	1,496
Marriages	1,135	1,112	1,124	1,215

Note: Latest available data.

DAILY NEWSPAPER(S)

	Circulation Average Paid
The Leader Post	
Fri.	68,395
Sat.	65,208
Mon-Thu	54,516

COMMUNITY NEWSPAPER(S)

	Total Circulation
Lumsden: Waterfront Press	1,560
Regina: L'eau Vive	1,539
Regina: Regina Sun	85,214

Saskatchewan

Regina
(City)
Regina CMA

In census division No. 6.

POPULATION

July 1, 2001 Estimate	186,226
% Cdn. Total	0.60
% Change, '96 -'01	0.23
Avg. Annual Growth Rate, %	0.05
2003 Projected Population	188,092
2006 Projected Population	191,099
2001 Households Estimate	75,919
2003 Projected Households	77,607
2006 Projected Households	80,358

INCOME

% Above/Below National Average	+6
2001 Total Income Estimate	$4,146,960,000
% Cdn. Total	0.63
2001 Average Hhld. Income	$54,600
2001 Per Capita	$22,300
2003 Projected Total Income	$4,451,200,000
2006 Projected Total Income	$4,980,260,000

RETAIL SALES

% Above/Below National Average	+8
2001 Retail Sales Estimate	$1,804,240,000
% Cdn. Total	0.65
2001 per Household	$23,800
2001 per Capita	$9,700
2001 No. of Establishments	1,272
2003 Projected Retail Sales	$1,950,300,000
2006 Projected Retail Sales	$2,161,490,000

POPULATION

2001 Estimates:

Total	186,226
Male	89,920
Female	96,306

Age Groups	Male	Female
0-4	6,536	6,324
5-9	6,575	6,419
10-14	6,667	6,484
15-19	6,677	6,455
20-24	6,685	6,642
25-29	6,491	6,657
30-34	6,778	7,077
35-39	7,214	7,501
40-44	7,133	7,481
45-49	6,494	6,853
50-54	5,292	5,667
55-59	4,210	4,560
60-64	3,482	3,866
65-69	3,015	3,443
70+	6,671	10,877

DAYTIME POPULATION

2001 Estimates:

Working Population	94,456
At Home Population	92,505
Total	186,961

INCOME

2001 Estimates:

Avg. Household Income	$54,623
Avg. Family Income	$64,119
Per Capita Income	$22,268
Male:	
Avg. Employment Income	$35,630
Avg. Employment Income (Full Time)	$47,825
Female:	
Avg. Employment Income	$22,893
Avg. Employment Income (Full Time)	$33,163

DISPOSABLE & DISCRETIONARY INCOME

2001 Estimates:	Per Hhld.
Disposable Income	$42,080
Discretionary Income 1 (minus Food & Shelter)	$28,862
Discretionary Income 2 (minus Food, Shelter, & Other Expenditures)	$20,702

LIQUID ASSETS

1999 Estimates:	Per Hhld.
Equity Investments	$77,139
Interest Bearing Investments	$67,579
Total Liquid Assets	$144,718

CREDIT DATA

July 2000:

Pool of Credit	$1,946,603,489
Revolving Credit, No.	327,928
Fixed Loans, No.	107,936
Avg. Credit Limit, per Person	$13,122
Avg. Spent, per Person	$6,273
Satisfactory Ratings, No. per Person	2.83
Avg. No. of Cards, per Person	1.01

LABOUR FORCE

2001 Estimates:

Male:

In the Labour Force	50,497
Participation Rate	72.0
Employed	46,679
Unemployed	3,818
Unemployment Rate	7.6
Not in Labour Force	19,645

Female:

In the Labour Force	48,528
Participation Rate	63.0
Employed	45,521
Unemployed	3,007
Unemployment Rate	6.2
Not in Labour Force	28,551

OCCUPATIONS BY MAJOR GROUPS

2001 Estimates:	Male	Female
Management	5,625	2,714
Business, Finance & Admin.	6,396	16,877
Natural & Applied Sciences & Related	4,048	946
Health	1,110	4,463
Social Sciences, Gov't Services & Religion	1,483	1,833
Education	1,438	2,261
Arts, Culture, Recreation & Sport	1,433	1,376
Sales & Service	12,522	15,757
Trades, Transport & Equipment Operators & Related	11,610	591
Primary Industries	1,392	256
Processing, Mfg. & Utilities	2,294	347

LEVEL OF SCHOOLING

2001 Estimates:

Population 15 years +	147,221
Less than Grade 9	11,520
Grades 9-13 w/o Certif.	37,839
Grade 9-13 with Certif.	17,671
Trade Certif./Dip.	4,133
Non-Univ. w/o Certif./Dip.	7,375
Non-Univ. with Certif./Dip.	22,945
Univ. w/o Degree	24,006
Univ. w/o Degree/Certif.	13,039
Univ. with Certif.	10,967
Univ. with Degree	21,732

AVERAGE HOUSEHOLD EXPENDITURES

2001 Estimates:

Food	$6,187
Shelter	$9,188
Clothing	$2,232
Transportation	$6,167
Health & Personal Care	$1,915
Recr'n, Read'g & Education	$3,747
Taxes & Securities	$14,406
Other	$8,494
Total Expenditures	$52,336

PRIVATE HOUSEHOLDS

2001 Estimates:

Private Households, Total	75,919
Pop. in Private Households	183,122
Average no. per Household	2.4

FAMILIES

2001 Estimates:

Families in Private Households	51,200
Husband-Wife Families	42,454
Lone-Parent Families	8,746
Aver. No. Persons per Family	3.0
Aver. No. Sons/Daughters at Home	1.2

HOUSING

2001 Estimates:

Occupied Private Dwellings	75,919
Owned	49,092
Rented	26,827
Single-Detached House	51,694
Semi-Detached House	1,819
Row Houses	3,307
Apartment, 5+ Storeys	4,239
Owned Apartment, 5+ Storeys	537
Apartment, 5 or Fewer Storeys	13,661
Apartment, Detached Duplex	1,128
Other Single-Attached	71

VEHICLES

2001 Estimates:

Model Yrs. '81-'96, No.	96,650
% Total	81.42
Model Yrs. '97-'98, No.	14,211
% Total	11.97
'99 Vehicles registered in Model Yr. '99, No.	7,846
% Total	6.61
Total No. '81-'99	118,707

LEGAL MARITAL STATUS

2001 Estimates: (Age 15+)

Single (Never Married)	48,191
Legally Married (Not Separated)	75,160
Legally Married (Separated)	4,178
Widowed	9,220
Divorced	10,472

PSYTE CATEGORIES

2001 Estimates	No. of House-holds	% of Total Hhds.	Index
Urban Gentry	3,647	4.80	267
Suburban Executives	1,615	2.13	148
Mortgaged in Suburbia	672	0.89	64
Technocrafts & Bureaucrats	7,500	9.88	351
Stable Suburban Families	3,187	4.20	322
Old Bungalow Burbs	3,409	4.49	271
Aging Erudites	6,110	8.05	533
Satellite Suburbs	2,003	2.64	92
Kindergarten Boom	10,166	13.39	511
Old Towns' New Fringe	258	0.34	9
Conservative Homebodies	5,050	6.65	184
High Rise Sunsets	1,332	1.75	123
Young Urban Professionals	424	0.56	29
Young Urban Intelligentsia	768	1.01	66
University Enclaves	3,975	5.24	257
Young City Singles	5,668	7.47	326
Town Renters	326	0.43	50
Struggling Downtowns	13,321	17.55	557
Aged Pensioners	3,554	4.68	352
Big City Stress	2,017	2.66	235
Old Grey Towers	399	0.53	95

FINANCIAL P$YTE

2001 Estimates	No. of House-holds	% of Total Hhds.	Index
Four Star Investors	5,262	6.93	138
Successful Suburbanites	11,359	14.96	225
Canadian Comfort	2,003	2.64	27
Urban Heights	6,534	8.61	200
Miners & Credit-Liners	3,409	4.49	142
Mortgages & Minivans	10,166	13.39	203
Tractors & Tradelines	258	0.34	6
Bills & Wills	5,050	6.65	80
Revolving Renters	1,332	1.75	38
Young Urban Struggle	4,743	6.25	132
Towering Debt	19,315	25.44	326
NSF	2,017	2.66	75
Senior Survivors	3,953	5.21	276

HOME LANGUAGE

2001 Estimates:		% Total
English	177,892	95.52
French	839	0.45
Chinese	1,805	0.97
German	213	0.11
Greek	333	0.18
Italian	161	0.09
Lao	193	0.10
Polish	108	0.06
Punjabi	209	0.11
Serbo-Croatian	164	0.09
Spanish	411	0.22
Tagalog (Pilipino)	324	0.17
Ukrainian	114	0.06
Vietnamese	581	0.31
Other Languages	1,157	0.62
Multiple Responses	1,722	0.92
Total	186,226	100.00

BUILDING PERMITS

	1999	1998	1997
		$000	
Value	151,898	137,478	152,331

HOMES BUILT

	1999	1998	1997
No.	398	427	284

Regina
(City)
Regina CMA
(Cont'd)

TAXATION

Income Class:	1997	% Total
Under $5,000	13,880	10.64
$5,000-$10,000	15,170	11.63
$10,000-$15,000	18,400	14.11
$15,000-$20,000	13,240	10.15
$20,000-$25,000	11,770	9.03
$25,000-$30,000	11,390	8.73
$30,000-$40,000	17,490	13.41
$40,000-$50,000	11,660	8.94
$50,000 +	17,420	13.36
Total Returns, No.	130,400	
Total Income, $000	3,712,373	
Total Taxable		
Returns	96,480	
Total Tax, $000	777,563	
Average Income, $	28,469	
Average Tax, $	8,059	

VITAL STATISTICS

	1997	1996	1995	1994
Births	2,269	2,356	2,500	2,609
Deaths	1,385	1,348	1,333	1,207
Natural				
Increase	884	1,008	1,167	1,402
Marriages	1,074	1,058	1,081	1,150

Note: Latest available data.

MEDIA INFO
see Regina, CMA

Saskatoon
(Census Metropolitan Area)

POPULATION

July 1, 2001 Estimate	234,968
% Cdn. Total	0.75
% Change, '96 -'01	4.00
Avg. Annual Growth Rate, %	0.79
2003 Projected Population	238,198
2006 Projected Population	241,491
2001 Households Estimate	94,889
2003 Projected Households	97,224
2006 Projected Households	100,188

INCOME

% Above/Below National Average	-3
2001 Total Income Estimate	$4,823,940,000
% Cdn. Total	0.73
2001 Average Hhld. Income	$50,800
2001 Per Capita	$20,500
2003 Projected Total Income	$5,174,390,000
2006 Projected Total Income	$5,712,710,000

RETAIL SALES

% Above/Below National Average	-9
2001 Retail Sales Estimate	$1,905,260,000
% Cdn. Total	0.68
2001 per Household	$20,100
2001 per Capita	$8,100
2001 No. of Establishments	1,581
2003 Projected Retail Sales	$2,071,160,000
2006 Projected Retail Sales	$2,300,960,000

POPULATION

2001 Estimates:

Total	234,968
Male	114,127
Female	120,841

Age Groups	Male	Female
0-4	8,674	8,292
5-9	8,820	8,374
10-14	8,740	8,345
15-19	8,374	8,272
20-24	8,519	8,902
25-29	8,492	8,949
30-34	8,857	9,163
35-39	9,274	9,751
40-44	9,113	9,592
45-49	8,141	8,482
50-54	6,475	6,709
55-59	4,998	5,231
60-64	4,101	4,418
65-69	3,495	4,009
70+	8,054	12,352

DAYTIME POPULATION

2001 Estimates:

Working Population	116,701
At Home Population	118,264
Total	234,965

INCOME

2001 Estimates:

Avg. Household Income	$50,838
Avg. Family Income	$60,249
Per Capita Income	$20,530
Male:	
Avg. Employment Income	$33,948
Avg. Employment Income	
(Full Time)	$45,212
Female:	
Avg. Employment Income	$19,894
Avg. Employment Income	
(Full Time)	$31,150

DISPOSABLE & DISCRETIONARY INCOME

2001 Estimates:	Per Hhld.
Disposable Income	$39,425
Discretionary Income 1	
(minus Food & Shelter)	$26,675
Discretionary Income 2	
(minus Food, Shelter, & Other	
Expenditures)	$18,964

LIQUID ASSETS

1999 Estimates:	Per Hhld.
Equity Investments	$70,394
Interest Bearing Investments	$62,166
Total Liquid Assets	$132,560

CREDIT DATA

July 2000:	
Pool of Credit	$2,297,072,853
Revolving Credit, No.	388,856
Fixed Loans, No.	131,177
Avg. Credit Limit, per Person	$12,514
Avg. Spent, per Person	$6,008
Satisfactory Ratings,	
No. per Person	2.75
Avg. No. of Cards, per Person	0.96

Saskatchewan

LABOUR FORCE

2001 Estimates:

Male:	
In the Labour Force	64,593
Participation Rate	73.5
Employed	59,969
Unemployed	4,624
Unemployment Rate	7.2
Not in Labour Force	23,300
Female:	
In the Labour Force	58,600
Participation Rate	61.1
Employed	54,590
Unemployed	4,010
Unemployment Rate	6.8
Not in Labour Force	37,230

RADIO STATION DATA

Station	Market	Format	Wkly. Reach%*	Aver. Hrs. Tuned
All Stations			94	20.4
CBK	Regina	Multi-format	18	8.1
CBKS-FM	Saskatoon	Multi-format	9	9.6
CFCR-FM	Saskatoon	Alternative	n.a.	n.a.
CFMC-FM	Saskatoon	Hot Adult Contemp.	53	12.8
CFQC-FM	Saskatoon	Country	15	10.0
CINT	Saskatoon	News, Talk, Sports	14	6.3
CJWW	Saskatoon	Country	23	13.3
CKCK	Regina	All Oldies	n.a.	n.a.
CKOM-FM	Saskatoon	Oldies	27	10.0

BBM Spring 2000 Radio Reach Survey; area coverage.
*Mon-Sun 5a.m - 1a.m , All Persons 12+

TV STATION DATA

Station	Market	Network Affiliation	Wkly. Reach%*	Aver. Hrs. Tuned
All Stations			97	23.0
A & E	n.a.	Ind.	20	3.3
CBKST	Saskatoon	CBC	48	3.0
CFQC	Saskatoon	CTV	77	6.7
CFSK	Saskatoon	Global	64	4.7
DSCVRY	n.a.	Ind.	10	1.6
FAIRTV	n.a.	n.a.	-	32.4
FAMILY	n.a.	Ind.	8	1.6
FOOD	n.a.	Ind.	6	1.9
HISTTV	n.a.	Ind.	7	2.2
MMUSIC	n.a.	Ind.	7	2.0
OTHERS	n.a.	n.a.	10	2.2
PRIME	n.a.	Ind.	11	3.1
SHWCSE	n.a.	Ind.	5	2.1
SNET	n.a.	CTV	9	2.9
SPACE	n.a.	Ind.	9	3.8
SUPER	n.a.	Ind.	6	3.3
TLC	n.a.	Ind.	15	1.7
TNN	Nashville TN	Ind.	9	2.3
TREE	n.a.	Ind.	6	3.5
TSN	n.a.	Ind.	23	5.2
VCR	n.a.	n.a.	35	5.0
WDIV	Detroit MI	NBC	20	2.0
WEATHR	n.a.	Ind.	8	1.6
WTBS	Atlanta GA	Ind.	27	4.3
WTVS	Detroit MI	PBS	10	1.7
WUHF	Rochester NY	FOX	24	2.8
WWJ	Detroit MI	CBS	28	2.3
WXYZ	Detroit MI	ABC	15	2.9
YTV	n.a.	Ind.	12	2.0

BBM Spring 2000 TV Reach Survey; CMA coverage.
*Mon-Sun 6a.m - 2a.m , All Persons 2 +

Saskatchewan

Saskatoon
(Census Metropolitan Area)
(Cont'd)

OCCUPATIONS BY MAJOR GROUPS

2001 Estimates:	Male	Female
Management	6,330	2,997
Business, Finance & Admin.	6,297	15,911
Natural & Applied Sciences & Related	4,596	989
Health	1,328	5,944
Social Sciences, Gov't Services & Religion	1,621	2,002
Education	2,448	2,943
Arts, Culture, Recreation & Sport	1,163	1,999
Sales & Service	14,468	21,155
Trades, Transport & Equipment Operators & Related	16,340	925
Primary Industries	4,275	1,057
Processing, Mfg. & Utilities	4,389	1,298

LEVEL OF SCHOOLING

2001 Estimates:	
Population 15 years +	183,723
Less than Grade 9	15,116
Grades 9-13 w/o Certif.	45,751
Grade 9-13 with Certif.	19,748
Trade Certif. /Dip.	5,086
Non-Univ. w/o Certif./Dip.	9,325
Non-Univ. with Certif./Dip.	33,335
Univ. w/o Degree	26,996
Univ. w/o Degree/Certif.	14,969
Univ. with Certif.	12,027
Univ. with Degree	28,366

AVERAGE HOUSEHOLD EXPENDITURES

2001 Estimates:	
Food	$5,909
Shelter	$8,904
Clothing	$2,130
Transportation	$5,773
Health & Personal Care	$1,830
Recr'n, Read'g & Education	$3,503
Taxes & Securities	$13,125
Other	$8,030
Total Expenditures	$49,204

PRIVATE HOUSEHOLDS

2001 Estimates:	
Private Households, Total	94,889
Pop. in Private Households	230,660
Average no. per Household	2.4

FAMILIES

2001 Estimates:	
Families in Private Households	63,861
Husband-Wife Families	53,790
Lone-Parent Families	10,071
Aver. No. Persons per Family	3.1
Aver. No. Sons/Daughters at Home	1.2

HOUSING

2001 Estimates:	
Occupied Private Dwellings	94,889
Owned	58,186
Rented	36,662
Band Housing	41
Single-Detached House	58,446
Semi-Detached House	3,338
Row Houses	3,099
Apartment, 5+ Storeys	5,515
Owned Apartment, 5+ Storeys	603
Apartment, 5 or Fewer Storeys	20,226
Apartment, Detached Duplex	3,391
Other Single-Attached	112
Movable Dwellings	762

VEHICLES

2001 Estimates:	
Model Yrs. '81-'96, No.	112,897
% Total	83.59
Model Yrs. '97-'98, No.	14,451
% Total	10.70
'99 Vehicles registered in Model Yr. '99, No.	7,705
% Total	5.71
Total No. '81-'99.	135,053

LEGAL MARITAL STATUS

2001 Estimates: (Age 15+)	
Single (Never Married)	59,995
Legally Married (Not Separated)	95,430
Legally Married (Separated)	5,484
Widowed	10,623
Divorced	12,191

PSYTE CATEGORIES

2001 Estimates	No. of House-holds	% of Total Hhds.	Index
Urban Gentry	1,150	1.21	67
Suburban Executives	1,669	1.76	123
Technocrafts & Bureaucrats	9,504	10.02	356
Boomers & Teens	143	0.15	8
Stable Suburban Families	1,031	1.09	83
Small City Elite	467	0.49	29
Old Bungalow Burbs	5,784	6.10	368
Aging Erudites	4,187	4.41	293
Satellite Suburbs	99	0.10	4
Kindergarten Boom	12,105	12.76	487
Blue Collar Winners	1,873	1.97	78
Old Towns' New Fringe	3,608	3.80	97
Rustic Prosperity	1,131	1.19	66
The Grain Belt	109	0.11	19
Conservative Homebodies	2,725	2.87	80
High Rise Sunsets	3,697	3.90	272
Young Urban Professionals	2,414	2.54	134
Young Urban Mix	1,981	2.09	99
Young Urban Intelligentsia	1,936	2.04	134
University Enclaves	7,603	8.01	393
Young City Singles	10,236	10.79	470
Old Leafy Towns	96	0.10	4
Town Renters	420	0.44	51
Nesters & Young Homesteaders	418	0.44	19
Rod & Rifle	1,164	1.23	53
Big Country Families	157	0.17	12
Struggling Downtowns	10,899	11.49	365
Aged Pensioners	2,365	2.49	187
Big City Stress	3,244	3.42	303
Old Grey Towers	1,918	2.02	365

FINANCIAL P$YTE

2001 Estimates	No. of House-holds	% of Total Hhds.	Index
Four Star Investors	2,962	3.12	62
Successful Suburbanites	10,535	11.10	167
Canadian Comfort	2,439	2.57	26
Urban Heights	6,601	6.96	162
Miners & Credit-Liners	5,784	6.10	193
Mortgages & Minivans	12,105	12.76	193
Tractors & Tradelines	4,739	4.99	87
Bills & Wills	4,802	5.06	61
Country Credit	109	0.11	2
Revolving Renters	4,115	4.34	94
Young Urban Struggle	9,539	10.05	212
Rural Family Blues	1,321	1.39	17
Towering Debt	21,555	22.72	291
NSF	3,244	3.42	97
Senior Survivors	4,283	4.51	240

HOME LANGUAGE

2001 Estimates:		% Total
English	222,875	94.85
French	920	0.39
Arabic	314	0.13
Chinese	1,968	0.84
Cree	208	0.09
German	1,137	0.48
Hindi	127	0.05
Lao	132	0.06
Persian (Farsi)	215	0.09
Polish	284	0.12
Serbo-Croatian	217	0.09
Spanish	496	0.21
Tagalog (Pilipino)	509	0.22
Ukrainian	796	0.34
Vietnamese	474	0.20
Other Languages	1,567	0.67
Multiple Responses	2,729	1.16
Total	234,968	100.00

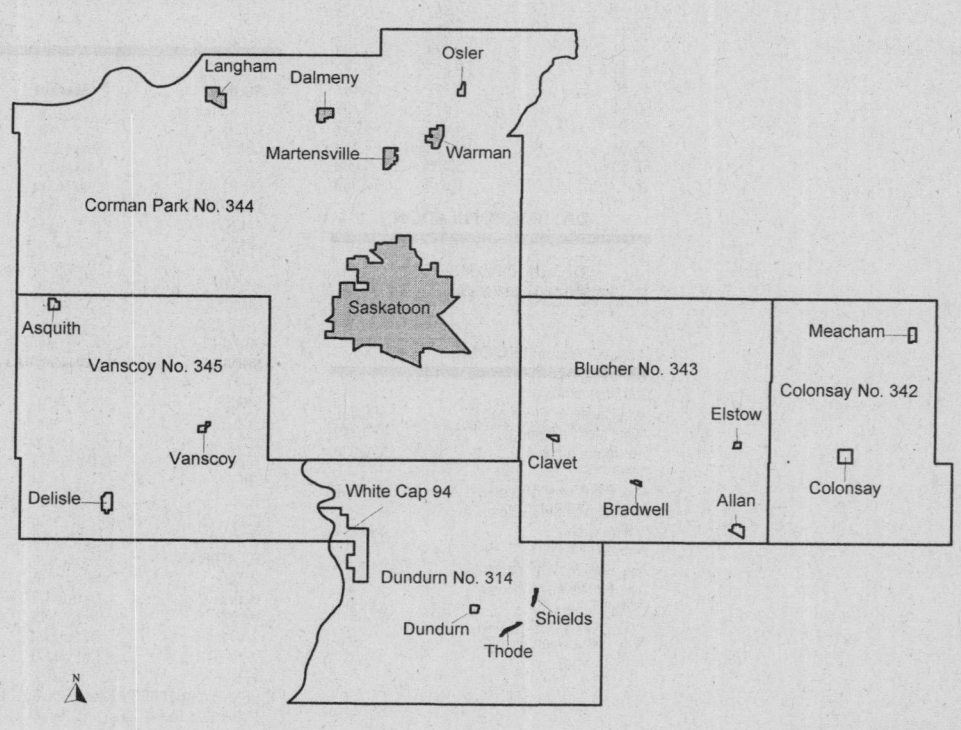

Urban Areas

Saskatoon
(Census Metropolitan Area)
(Cont'd)

BUILDING PERMITS

	1999	1998	1997
		$000	
Value	229,058	218,299	203,218

HOMES BUILT

	1999	1998	1997
No.	981	1,315	1,126

TAXATION

Income Class:	1997	% Total
Under $5,000	18,770	12.08
$5,000-$10,000	20,330	13.09
$10,000-$15,000	22,870	14.72
$15,000-$20,000	16,210	10.43
$20,000-$25,000	13,560	8.73
$25,000-$30,000	12,540	8.07
$30,000-$40,000	19,820	12.76
$40,000-$50,000	12,930	8.32
$50,000 +	18,380	11.83
Total Returns, No.	155,350	
Total Income, $000	4,233,838	
Total Taxable Returns	111,390	
Total Tax, $000	866,991	
Average Income, $	27,254	
Average Tax, $	7,783	

VITAL STATISTICS

	1997	1996	1995	1994
Births	2,981	3,187	3,176	3,398
Deaths	1,543	1,517	1,434	1,379
Natural Increase	1,438	1,670	1,742	2,019
Marriages	1,443	1,516	1,493	1,475

Note: Latest available data.

DAILY NEWSPAPER(S)

	Circulation Average Paid
The Star Phoenix	
Fri	70,128
Sat	66,794
Mon-Thu	57,365

COMMUNITY NEWSPAPER(S)

	Total Circulation
Saskatoon: Saskatoon Sun	97,531

Saskatoon
(City)
Saskatoon CMA

In census division No. 11.

POPULATION

July 1, 2001 Estimate	208,042
% Cdn. Total	0.67
% Change, '96 -'01	4.15
Avg. Annual Growth Rate, %	0.82
2003 Projected Population	211,041
2006 Projected Population	214,167
2001 Households Estimate	85,875
2003 Projected Households	88,048
2006 Projected Households	90,799

INCOME

% Above/Below National Average	-2
2001 Total Income Estimate	$4,309,840,000
% Cdn. Total	0.66
2001 Average Hhld. Income	$50,200
2001 Per Capita	$20,700
2003 Projected Total Income	$4,622,790,000
2006 Projected Total Income	$5,101,650,000

RETAIL SALES

% Above/Below National Average	-1
2001 Retail Sales Estimate	$1,834,840,000
% Cdn. Total	0.66
2001 per Household	$21,400
2001 per Capita	$8,800
2001 No. of Establishments	1,419
2003 Projected Retail Sales	$1,996,720,000
2006 Projected Retail Sales	$2,220,400,000

POPULATION

2001 Estimates:

Total	208,042
Male	100,484
Female	107,558

Age Groups	Male	Female
0-4	7,782	7,444
5-9	7,762	7,357
10-14	7,502	7,152
15-19	7,133	7,102
20-24	7,522	8,003
25-29	7,744	8,213
30-34	8,071	8,305
35-39	8,258	8,635
40-44	7,930	8,411
45-49	7,027	7,459
50-54	5,602	5,903
55-59	4,326	4,605
60-64	3,558	3,909
65-69	3,055	3,592
70+	7,212	11,468

DAYTIME POPULATION

2001 Estimates:

Working Population	108,303
At Home Population	105,873
Total	214,176

INCOME

2001 Estimates:

Avg. Household Income	$50,187
Avg. Family Income	$60,212
Per Capita Income	$20,716
Male:	
Avg. Employment Income	$33,964
Avg. Employment Income (Full Time)	$46,013
Female:	
Avg. Employment Income	$20,066
Avg. Employment Income (Full Time)	$31,543

DISPOSABLE & DISCRETIONARY INCOME

2001 Estimates:	Per Hhld.
Disposable Income	$38,891
Discretionary Income 1 (minus Food & Shelter)	$26,216
Discretionary Income 2 (minus Food, Shelter, & Other Expenditures)	$18,697

LIQUID ASSETS

1999 Estimates:	Per Hhld.
Equity Investments	$69,656
Interest Bearing Investments	$61,706
Total Liquid Assets	$131,362

CREDIT DATA

July 2000:	
Pool of Credit	$1,997,834,134
Revolving Credit, No.	345,173
Fixed Loans, No.	109,849
Avg. Credit Limit, per Person	$12,352
Avg. Spent, per Person	$5,857
Satisfactory Ratings, No. per Person	2.74
Avg. No. of Cards, per Person	0.97

LABOUR FORCE

2001 Estimates:

Male:	
In the Labour Force	56,346
Participation Rate	72.8
Employed	52,086
Unemployed	4,260
Unemployment Rate	7.6
Not in Labour Force	21,092
Female:	
In the Labour Force	51,942
Participation Rate	60.7
Employed	48,299
Unemployed	3,643
Unemployment Rate	7.0
Not in Labour Force	33,663

OCCUPATIONS BY MAJOR GROUPS

2001 Estimates:	Male	Female
Management	5,707	2,665
Business, Finance & Admin.	5,746	14,262
Natural & Applied Sciences & Related	4,311	958
Health	1,233	5,438
Social Sciences, Gov't Services & Religion	1,490	1,818
Education	2,312	2,709
Arts, Culture, Recreation & Sport	1,134	1,855
Sales & Service	13,160	18,820
Trades, Transport & Equipment Operators & Related	13,884	716
Primary Industries	2,408	458
Processing, Mfg. & Utilities	3,709	1,082

LEVEL OF SCHOOLING

2001 Estimates:

Population 15 years +	163,043
Less than Grade 9	12,825
Grades 9-13 w/o Certif.	38,965
Grade 9-13 with Certif.	17,250
Trade Certif. /Dip.	4,340
Non-Univ. w/o Certif./Dip.	8,244
Non-Univ. with Certif./Dip.	29,484
Univ. w/o Degree	25,063
Univ. w/o Degree/Certif.	13,972
Univ. with Certif.	11,091
Univ. with Degree	26,872

Saskatchewan

AVERAGE HOUSEHOLD EXPENDITURES

2001 Estimates:

Food	$5,859
Shelter	$8,880
Clothing	$2,127
Transportation	$5,590
Health & Personal Care	$1,813
Recr'n, Read'g & Education	$3,454
Taxes & Securities	$12,990
Other	$7,927
Total Expenditures	$48,640

PRIVATE HOUSEHOLDS

2001 Estimates:

Private Households, Total	85,875
Pop. in Private Households	204,370
Average no. per Household	2.4

FAMILIES

2001 Estimates:

Families in Private Households	56,177
Husband-Wife Families	46,652
Lone-Parent Families	9,525
Aver. No. Persons per Family	3.0
Aver. No. Sons/Daughters at Home	1.2

HOUSING

2001 Estimates:

Occupied Private Dwellings	85,875
Owned	50,191
Rented	35,684
Single-Detached House	50,190
Semi-Detached House	3,210
Row Houses	2,992
Apartment, 5+ Storeys	5,504
Owned Apartment, 5+ Storeys	603
Apartment, 5 or Fewer Storeys	20,089
Apartment, Detached Duplex	3,362
Other Single-Attached	91
Movable Dwellings	437

VEHICLES

2001 Estimates:

Model Yrs. '81-'96, No.	97,015
% Total	83.08
Model Yrs. '97-'98, No.	12,778
% Total	10.94
'99 Vehicles registered in Model Yr. '99, No.	6,976
% Total	5.97
Total No. '81-'99	116,769

LEGAL MARITAL STATUS

2001 Estimates: (Age 15+)

Single (Never Married)	55,030
Legally Married (Not Separated)	81,692
Legally Married (Separated)	5,113
Widowed	9,852
Divorced	11,356

Saskatchewan

Saskatoon
(City)
Saskatoon CMA
(Cont'd)

PSYTE CATEGORIES

2001 Estimates	No. of House-holds	% of Total Hhds.	Index
Urban Gentry	1,023	1.19	66
Suburban Executives	1,598	1.86	130
Technocrafts & Bureaucrats	9,446	11.00	391
Stable Suburban Families	1,031	1.20	92
Old Bungalow Burbs	5,784	6.74	406
Aging Erudites	4,187	4.88	323
Satellite Suburbs	99	0.12	4
Kindergarten Boom	12,105	14.10	538
Conservative Homebodies	2,725	3.17	88
High Rise Sunsets	3,697	4.31	301
Young Urban Professionals	2,414	2.81	148
Young Urban Mix	1,981	2.31	109
Young Urban Intelligentsia	1,936	2.25	148
University Enclaves	7,603	8.85	434
Young City Singles	10,236	11.92	520
Town Renters	420	0.49	57
Nesters & Young Homesteaders	418	0.49	21
Struggling Downtowns	10,899	12.69	403
Aged Pensioners	2,365	2.75	207
Big City Stress	3,244	3.78	335
Old Grey Towers	1,918	2.23	403

FINANCIAL PSYTE

2001 Estimates	No. of House-holds	% of Total Hhds.	Index
Four Star Investors	2,621	3.05	61
Successful Suburbanites	10,477	12.20	184
Canadian Comfort	99	0.12	1
Urban Heights	6,601	7.69	179
Miners & Credit-Liners	5,784	6.74	213
Mortgages & Minivans	12,105	14.10	214
Bills & Wills	4,706	5.48	66
Revolving Renters	4,115	4.79	104
Young Urban Struggle	9,539	11.11	235
Towering Debt	21,555	25.10	322
NSF	3,244	3.78	107
Senior Survivors	4,283	4.99	265

HOME LANGUAGE

2001 Estimates:		% Total
English	197,088	94.73
French	858	0.41
Arabic	314	0.15
Chinese	1,952	0.94
Cree	208	0.10
German	325	0.16
Greek	114	0.05
Hindi	127	0.06
Lao	132	0.06
Persian (Farsi)	215	0.10
Polish	284	0.14
Serbo-Croatian	217	0.10
Spanish	483	0.23
Tagalog (Pilipino)	509	0.24
Ukrainian	786	0.38
Vietnamese	474	0.23
Other Languages	1,406	0.68
Multiple Responses	2,550	1.23
Total	208,042	100.00

BUILDING PERMITS

	1999	1998 $000	1997
Value	177,252	162,694	153,599

HOMES BUILT

	1999	1998	1997
No	700	1,071	857

TAXATION

Income Class:	1997	% Total
Under $5,000	16,560	11.78
$5,000-$10,000	18,410	13.10
$10,000-$15,000	20,770	14.78
$15,000-$20,000	14,680	10.44
$20,000-$25,000	12,280	8.74
$25,000-$30,000	11,300	8.04
$30,000-$40,000	17,880	12.72
$40,000-$50,000	11,770	8.37
$50,000 +	16,930	12.04
Total Returns, No.	140,570	
Total Income, $000	3,865,800	
Total Taxable Returns	100,810	
Total Tax, $000	796,615	
Average Income, $	27,501	
Average Tax, $	7,902	

VITAL STATISTICS

	1997	1996	1995	1994
Births	2,645	2,862	2,845	3,079
Deaths	1,435	1,404	1,337	1,276
Natural Increase	1,210	1,458	1,508	1,803
Marriages	1,334	1,403	1,389	1,374

Note: Latest available data.

MEDIA INFO
see Saskatoon, CMA

Swift Current
(Census Agglomeration)

The Census Agglomeration of Swift Current consists of Swift Current, C, and Swift Current No. 137, RM. Both are in census division No. 8.

POPULATION

July 1, 2001 Estimate	17,042
% Cdn. Total	0.05
% Change, '96 -'01	1.02
Avg. Annual Growth Rate, %	0.20
2003 Projected Population	17,132
2006 Projected Population	17,114
2001 Households Estimate	7,328
2003 Projected Households	7,435
2006 Projected Households	7,563

INCOME

% Above/Below National Average	-1
2001 Total Income Estimate	$357,090,000
% Cdn. Total	0.05
2001 Average Hhld. Income	$48,700
2001 Per Capita	$21,000
2003 Projected Total Income	$374,990,000
2006 Projected Total Income	$402,150,000

RETAIL SALES

% Above/Below National Average	+13
2001 Retail Sales Estimate	$172,740,000
% Cdn. Total	0.06
2001 per Household	$23,600
2001 per Capita	$10,100
2001 No. of Establishments	176
2003 Projected Retail Sales	$185,170,000
2006 Projected Retail Sales	$201,310,000

POPULATION

2001 Estimates:		
Total		17,042
Male		8,147
Female		8,895

Age Groups	Male	Female
0-4	519	504
5-9	508	507
10-14	566	546
15-19	604	591
20-24	574	570
25-29	508	526
30-34	525	557
35-39	603	619
40-44	630	626
45-49	576	568
50-54	474	471
55-59	393	408
60-64	339	391
65-69	330	414
70+	998	1,597

DAYTIME POPULATION

2001 Estimates:	
Working Population	8,740
At Home Population	8,302
Total	17,042

INCOME

2001 Estimates:	
Avg. Household Income	$48,729
Avg. Family Income	$58,795
Per Capita Income	$20,953
Male:	
Avg. Employment Income	$30,819
Avg. Employment Income (Full Time)	$40,671
Female:	
Avg. Employment Income	$17,609
Avg. Employment Income (Full Time)	$25,672

DISPOSABLE & DISCRETIONARY INCOME

2001 Estimates:	Per Hhld.
Disposable Income	$38,328
Discretionary Income 1 (minus Food & Shelter)	$26,743
Discretionary Income 2 (minus Food, Shelter, & Other Expenditures)	$17,963

LIQUID ASSETS

1999 Estimates:	Per Hhld.
Equity Investments	$73,531
Interest Bearing Investments	$62,294
Total Liquid Assets	$135,825

CREDIT DATA

July 2000:	
Pool of Credit	$158,131,474
Revolving Credit, No.	28,921
Fixed Loans, No.	12,309
Avg. Credit Limit, per Person	$11,403
Avg. Spent, per Person	$5,605
Satisfactory Ratings, No. per Person	2.85
Avg. No. of Cards, per Person	0.85

LABOUR FORCE

2001 Estimates:	
Male:	
In the Labour Force	4,758
Participation Rate	72.6
Employed	4,544
Unemployed	214
Unemployment Rate	4.5
Not in Labour Force	1,796
Female:	
In the Labour Force	4,304
Participation Rate	58.7
Employed	4,077
Unemployed	227
Unemployment Rate	5.3
Not in Labour Force	3,034

OCCUPATIONS BY MAJOR GROUPS

2001 Estimates:	Male	Female
Management	589	233
Business, Finance & Admin.	362	1,154
Natural & Applied Sciences & Related	187	52
Health	67	469
Social Sciences, Gov't Services & Religion	117	82
Education	70	188
Arts, Culture, Recreation & Sport	82	68
Sales & Service	1,054	1,606
Trades, Transport & Equipment Operators & Related	1,255	68
Primary Industries	687	118
Processing, Mfg. & Utilities	273	110

LEVEL OF SCHOOLING

2001 Estimates:	
Population 15 years +	13,892
Less than Grade 9	1,808
Grades 9-13 w/o Certif.	4,351
Grade 9-13 with Certif.	1,552
Trade Certif. /Dip.	525
Non-Univ. w/o Certif./Dip.	859
Non-Univ. with Certif./Dip.	2,475
Univ. w/o Degree	1,415
Univ. w/o Degree/Certif.	571
Univ. with Certif.	844
Univ. with Degree	907

Swift Current
(Census Agglomeration)
(Cont'd)

AVERAGE HOUSEHOLD EXPENDITURES

2001 Estimates:
Food	$5,781
Shelter	$7,846
Clothing	$2,103
Transportation	$6,742
Health & Personal Care	$2,043
Recr'n, Read'g & Education	$3,386
Taxes & Securities	$11,214
Other	$8,084
Total Expenditures	$47,199

PRIVATE HOUSEHOLDS

2001 Estimates:
Private Households, Total	7,328
Pop. in Private Households	16,759
Average no. per Household	2.3

FAMILIES

2001 Estimates:
Families in Private Households	4,969
Husband-Wife Families	4,436
Lone-Parent Families	533
Aver. No. Persons per Family	2.9
Aver. No. Sons/Daughters at Home	1.0

HOUSING

2001 Estimates:
Occupied Private Dwellings	7,328
Owned	4,982
Rented	2,346
Single-Detached House	4,950
Semi-Detached House	280
Row Houses	142
Apartment, 5+ Storeys	121
Apartment, 5 or Fewer Storeys	1,500
Apartment, Detached Duplex	165
Other Single-Attached	11
Movable Dwellings	159

VEHICLES

2001 Estimates:
Model Yrs. '81-'96, No.	9,850
% Total	82.61
Model Yrs. '97-'98, No.	1,426
% Total	11.96
'99 Vehicles registered in Model Yr. '99, No.	647
% Total	5.43
Total No. '81-'99	11,923

LEGAL MARITAL STATUS

2001 Estimates: (Age 15+)
Single (Never Married)	3,449
Legally Married (Not Separated)	8,037
Legally Married (Separated)	342
Widowed	1,300
Divorced	764

PSYTE CATEGORIES

2001 Estimates	No. of House-holds	% of Total Hhds.	Index
Town Boomers	1,148	15.67	1,546
The New Frontier	1,442	19.68	1,305
Pick-ups & Dirt Bikes	317	4.33	518
The Grain Belt	110	1.50	253
Quiet Towns	3,761	51.32	2,412
Down, Down East	47	0.64	91
Old Cdn. Rustics	372	5.08	518
Old Grey Towers	92	1.26	227

FINANCIAL P$YTE

2001 Estimates	No. of House-holds	% of Total Hhds.	Index
Canadian Comfort	1,148	15.67	161
Miners & Credit-Liners	1,442	19.68	622
Country Credit	427	5.83	86
Rural Family Blues	47	0.64	8
Limited Budgets	4,133	56.40	1,814
Senior Survivors	92	1.26	67

HOME LANGUAGE

2001 Estimates		% Total
English	16,552	97.12
French	77	0.45
Chinese	73	0.43
German	222	1.30
Greek	10	0.06
Ukrainian	10	0.06
Urdu	10	0.06
Multiple Responses	88	0.52
Total	17,042	100.00

BUILDING PERMITS

	1999	1998	1997
		$000	
Value	14,435	21,161	16,112

HOMES BUILT

	1999	1998	1997
No	98	126	27

TAXATION

Income Class	1997	% Total
Under $5,000	1,280	9.47
$5,000-$10,000	1,710	12.66
$10,000-$15,000	2,320	17.17
$15,000-$20,000	1,570	11.62
$20,000-$25,000	1,330	9.84
$25,000-$30,000	1,210	8.96
$30,000-$40,000	1,660	12.29
$40,000-$50,000	980	7.25
$50,000 +	1,450	10.73
Total Returns, No.	13,510	
Total Income, $000	353,715	
Total Taxable Returns	10,170	
Total Tax, $000	65,838	
Average Income, $	26,182	
Average Tax, $	6,474	

VITAL STATISTICS

	1997	1996	1995	1994
Births	185	195	186	171
Deaths	181	160	167	193
Natural Increase	4	35	19	-22
Marriages	147	116	148	106

Note: Latest available data.

COMMUNITY NEWSPAPER(S)

	Total Circulation
Swift Current: The Southwest Booster	19,100

RADIO STATION(S)

	Power
CBNO-FM	n.a.
CIMG-FM	100,000w
CKSW	10,000w

TELEVISION STATION(S)

CJFB-TV
CKMC-TV

Yorkton
(Census Agglomeration)

The Census Agglomeration of Yorkton includes: Yorkton, C; Orkney No. 244, RM; plus several smaller areas. All are in census division No. 9.

POPULATION

July 1, 2001 Estimate	17,878
% Cdn. Total	0.06
% Change, '96 -'01	-1.54
Avg. Annual Growth Rate, %	-0.31
2003 Projected Population	17,832
2006 Projected Population	17,655
2001 Households Estimate	7,416
2003 Projected Households	7,421
2006 Projected Households	7,432

INCOME

% Above/Below National Average	-17
2001 Total Income Estimate	$312,940,000
% Cdn. Total	0.05
2001 Average Hhld. Income	$42,200
2001 Per Capita	$17,500
2003 Projected Total Income	$326,460,000
2006 Projected Total Income	$348,210,000

RETAIL SALES

% Above/Below National Average	+18
2001 Retail Sales Estimate	$188,690,000
% Cdn. Total	0.07
2001 per Household	$25,400
2001 per Capita	$10,600
2001 No. of Establishments	206
2003 Projected Retail Sales	$202,840,000
2006 Projected Retail Sales	$220,700,000

POPULATION

2001 Estimates:
Total	17,878
Male	8,363
Female	9,515

Age Groups	Male	Female
0-4	547	532
5-9	572	578
10-14	640	630
15-19	655	647
20-24	582	607
25-29	494	544
30-34	490	583
35-39	545	627
40-44	598	628
45-49	580	591
50-54	476	512
55-59	397	459
60-64	345	444
65-69	319	427
70+	1,123	1,706

DAYTIME POPULATION

2001 Estimates:
Working Population	8,088
At Home Population	9,790
Total	17,878

INCOME

2001 Estimates:
Avg. Household Income	$42,198
Avg. Family Income	$50,799
Per Capita Income	$17,504
Male:	
Avg. Employment Income	$27,935
Avg. Employment Income (Full Time)	$36,770
Female:	
Avg. Employment Income	$17,931
Avg. Employment Income (Full Time)	$26,689

Saskatchewan

DISPOSABLE & DISCRETIONARY INCOME

2001 Estimates	Per Hhld.
Disposable Income	$33,619
Discretionary Income 1 (minus Food & Shelter)	$23,804
Discretionary Income 2 (minus Food, Shelter, & Other Expenditures)	$15,926

LIQUID ASSETS

1999 Estimates	Per Hhld.
Equity Investments	$51,224
Interest Bearing Investments	$50,127
Total Liquid Assets	$101,351

CREDIT DATA

July 2000:
Pool of Credit	$168,683,806
Revolving Credit, No.	29,737
Fixed Loans, No.	10,174
Avg. Credit Limit, per Person.	$11,913
Avg. Spent, per Person	$5,689
Satisfactory Ratings, No. per Person	2.74
Avg. No. of Cards, per Person	0.88

LABOUR FORCE

2001 Estimates:
Male:	
In the Labour Force	4,367
Participation Rate	66.1
Employed	4,010
Unemployed	357
Unemployment Rate	8.2
Not in Labour Force	2,237
Female:	
In the Labour Force	4,279
Participation Rate	55.0
Employed	3,942
Unemployed	337
Unemployment Rate	7.9
Not in Labour Force	3,496

OCCUPATIONS BY MAJOR GROUPS

2001 Estimates	Male	Female
Management	376	255
Business, Finance & Admin.	402	1,075
Natural & Applied Sciences & Related	146	19
Health	117	529
Social Sciences, Gov't Services & Religion	109	129
Education	137	251
Arts, Culture, Recreation & Sport	59	67
Sales & Service	1,081	1,587
Trades, Transport & Equipment Operators & Related	1,071	86
Primary Industries	558	77
Processing, Mfg. & Utilities	210	68

Saskatchewan

Yorkton
(Census Agglomeration)
(Cont'd)

LEVEL OF SCHOOLING

2001 Estimates:
Population 15 years + ...14,379
Less than Grade 9. 2,405
Grades 9-13 w/o Certif. 4,425
Grade 9-13 with Certif. 1,515
Trade Certif. /Dip. 469
Non-Univ. w/o Certif./Dip. 583
Non-Univ. with Certif./Dip. 2,607
Univ. w/o Degree 1,306
  Univ. w/o Degree/Certif. 642
  Univ. with Certif. 664
Univ. with Degree 1,069

AVERAGE HOUSEHOLD EXPENDITURES

2001 Estimates:
Food $4,909
Shelter $6,624
Clothing. $1,832
Transportation. $6,094
Health & Personal Care $1,826
Recr'n, Read'g & Education $2,831
Taxes & Securities $9,869
Other. $7,882
Total Expenditures $41,867

PRIVATE HOUSEHOLDS

2001 Estimates:
Private Households, Total 7,416
Pop. in Private Households 17,491
Average no. per Household 2.4

FAMILIES

2001 Estimates:
Families in Private Households 4,958
Husband-Wife Families 4,330
Lone-Parent Families 628
Aver. No. Persons per Family 3.0
Aver. No. Sons/Daughters
  at Home 1.1

HOUSING

2001 Estimates:
Occupied Private Dwellings 7,416
  Owned. 5,140
  Rented. 2,275
  Band Housing 1
Single-Detached House 5,414
Semi-Detached House 188
Row Houses 268
Apartment, 5 or Fewer Storeys 1,292
Apartment, Detached Duplex 66
Other Single-Attached 10
Movable Dwellings. 178

VEHICLES

2001 Estimates:
Model Yrs. '81-'96, No. 9,415
  % Total 85.90
Model Yrs. '97-'98, No. 1,027
  % Total 9.37
'99 Vehicles registered in
  Model Yr. '99, No. 519
  % Total 4.73
Total No. '81-'99 10,961

LEGAL MARITAL STATUS

2001 Estimates: (Age 15+)
Single (Never Married). 3,786
Legally Married
  (Not Separated) 7,918
Legally Married (Separated) 340
Widowed 1,499
Divorced 836

PSYTE CATEGORIES

2001 Estimates	No. of House -holds	% of Total Hhds.	Index
Town Boomers	1,365	18.41	1,816
Pick-ups & Dirt Bikes	621	8.37	1,003
The Grain Belt. . . .	34	0.46	77
Old Leafy Towns . . .	54	0.73	28
Quiet Towns	2,131	28.74	1,350
Old Cdn. Rustics . . .	3,101	41.81	4,264

FINANCIAL P$YTE

2001 Estimates	No. of House` -holds	% of Total Hhds.	Index
Canadian Comfort . . .	1,365	18.41	189
Bills & Wills	54	0.73	9
Country Credit. . . .	655	8.83	131
Limited Budgets . . .	5,232	70.55	2,270

HOME LANGUAGE

2001 Estimates:		% Total
English	17,326	96.91
Chinese.	20	0.11
German.	20	0.11
Polish	57	0.32
Russian.	15	0.08
Serbo-Croatian	15	0.08
Ukrainian	210	1.17
Vietnamese.	15	0.08
Multiple Responses	200	1.12
Total	17,878	100.00

BUILDING PERMITS

	1999	1998	1997
		$000	
Value	23,348	17,178	18,639

HOMES BUILT

	1999	1998	1997
No	46	44	50

TAXATION

Income Class:	1997	% Total
Under $5,000	1,510	11.06
$5,000-$10,000	1,900	13.92
$10,000-$15,000	2,860	20.95
$15,000-$20,000	1,660	12.16
$20,000-$25,000	1,250	9.16
$25,000-$30,000	1,160	8.50
$30,000-$40,000	1,510	11.06
$40,000-$50,000	920	6.74
$50,000 + ...	910	6.67
Total Returns, No.	13,650	
Total Income, $000	306,216	
Total Taxable Returns	9,240	
Total Tax, $000	52,743	
Average Income, $	22,433	
Average Tax, $	5,708	

VITAL STATISTICS

	1997	1996	1995	1994
Births	205	196	180	201
Deaths	222	241	220	197
Natural Increase	-17	-45	-40	4
Marriages . .	111	127	109	118

Note: Latest available data.

COMMUNITY NEWSPAPER(S)

	Total Circulation
Yorkton: The News	29,600
Yorkton: Yorkton Review	11,207
Yorkton: Yorkton This Week & Enterprise Wed/Sat.	5,752
Yorkton: This Week Marketplace	34,850
Yorkton: Yorkton This Week & Enterprise (suppl.), TV This Week	5,838

RADIO STATION(S)

	Power
CJGX	50,000w

TELEVISION STATION(S)

CICC-TV
CKOS-TV

FINANCIAL POST DATAGROUP

THEN

For 75 years, FP DataGroup has been the premier, unbiased source for corporate and financial information on publicly traded Canadian companies and mutual funds.

FP DataGroup has developed into a solutions provider offering professional investor-oriented products online. Money managers, credit analysts, brokers, and retail investors use FP DataGroup products to make effective investment decisions. With FP DataGroup, you know you're dealing with a brand you can trust.

NOW

Your single source for investment research.

For more information, call 1-800-661-POST
or visit www.financialpost.com

FINANCIAL POST
D A T A G R O U P

CODE ACD01

Economic Regions & Census Divisions

Alberta

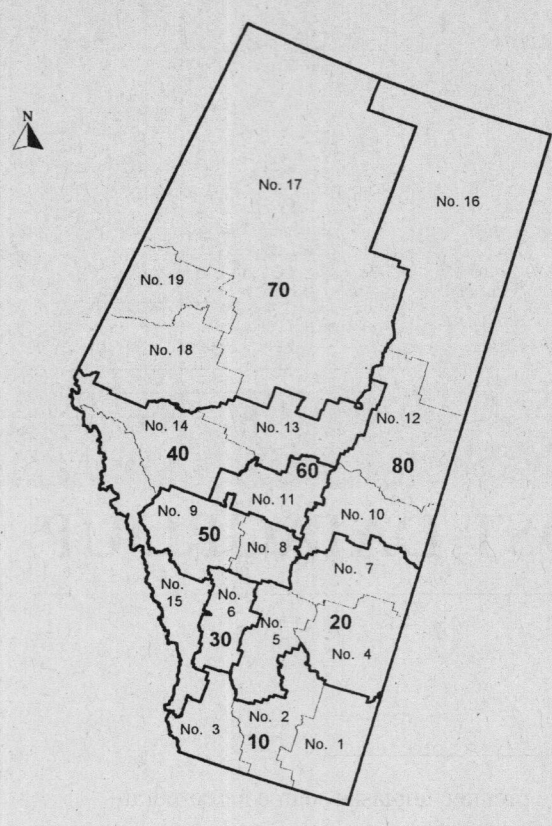

Economic Regions

10 Lethbridge - Medicine Hat
20 Drumheller - Stettler - Wainwright
30 Calgary
40 Athabasca - Jasper - Banff
50 Red Deer - Rocky Mountain House
60 Edmonton
70 Grande Prairie - Peace River
80 Wood Buffalo - Camrose

Region	Population (at July 1)				Households (at July 1)		Income				Retail Sales				Taxation Statistics, 1997					
	*1996 Census (000)	2001 Estimate (000)	% of Cdn. Total	% Chg. '96-'01	2001 Estimate (000)	% of Cdn. Total	2001 Estimate $millions	% of Cdn. Total	Per Hhld. $	Income Rating Index	2001 Estimate $millions	% of Cdn. Total	Per Hhld. $	Market Rating Index	Total No. of Returns	Total Income $millions	Total No. Taxable Returns	Total Tax $millions	Avg. Income $	Avg. Tax $
Alberta	2,780.6	3,065.6	9.85	10.25	1,153.3	9.54	68,436.5	10.43	59,300	106	31,754.6	11.39	27,500	.116	1,986,460	60,305.4	1,424,320	12,024.1	30,358	8,442
Lethbridge - Medicine Hat (10)	231.1	246.7	0.79	6.78	90.1	0.75	4,481.9	0.68	49,800	86	3,457.2	1.24	38,400	157	159,230	4,024.6	109,700	669.0	25,275	6,098
Division No. 1	63.9	69.0	0.22	7.98	26.8	0.22	1,362.5	0.21	50,800	94	876.6	0.31	32,700	142	46,080	1,212.7	33,080	210.6	26,316	6,366
Division No. 2	128.5	137.8	0.44	7.24	50.6	0.42	2,557.2	0.39	50,500	88	2,334.7	0.84	46,100	189	89,340	2,324.0	63,140	393.6	26,013	6,233
Division No. 3	38.6	39.9	0.13	3.23	12.7	0.10	562.2	0.09	44,400	67	245.9	0.09	19,400	69	23,810	488.0	13,480	64.8	20,494	4,808
Drumheller - Stettler - Wainwright (20)	99.1	104.1	0.33	5.1	37.0	0.31	1,866.9	0.28	50,400	85	838.8	0.30	22,700	90	67,040	1,696.9	46,190	278.3	25,312	6,025
Division No. 4	12.3	11.8	0.04	-3.97	4.3	0.04	223.5	0.03	51,400	90	107.9	0.04	24,800	102	7,950	199.5	5,630	31.5	25,094	5,594
Division No. 5	44.6	48.7	0.16	9.13	16.6	0.14	827.4	0.13	49,900	81	338.9	0.12	20,400	78	29,690	723.0	19,750	114.0	24,353	5,773
Division No. 7	42.1	43.6	0.14	3.47	16.1	0.13	816.0	0.12	50,800	89	392.1	0.14	24,400	100	29,400	774.4	20,810	132.8	26,339	6,380
Calgary (30)	906.2	1,049.5	3.37	15.81	401.1	3.32	26,909.3	4.10	67,100	122	10,863.6	3.90	27,100	116	673,310	23,879.9	505,910	5,209.6	35,466	10,297
Division No. 6	906.2	1,049.5	3.37	15.81	401.1	3.32	26,909.3	4.10	67,100	122	10,863.6	3.90	27,100	116	673,310	23,879.9	505,910	5,209.6	35,466	10,297
Athabasca - Jasper - Banff (40)	124.1	133.0	0.43	7.24	49.8	0.41	2,694.6	0.41	54,100	96	1,390.6	0.50	27,900	117	86,530	2,312.5	59,320	434.5	26,725	7,325
Division No. 13	64.1	67.6	0.22	5.51	24.9	0.21	1,250.8	0.19	50,200	88	605.3	0.22	24,300	100	44,100	1,033.6	28,220	173.4	23,438	6,146
Division No. 14	28.2	30.1	0.10	6.74	11.2	0.09	636.8	0.10	57,100	100	304.1	0.11	27,300	113	19,410	566.2	13,660	115.4	29,168	8,447
Division No. 15	31.8	35.4	0.11	11.16	13.7	0.11	807.0	0.12	58,800	108	481.1	0.17	35,000	152	23,020	712.7	17,440	145.7	30,961	8,355
Red Deer - Rocky Mountain House (50)	160.6	177.7	0.57	10.69	65.3	0.54	3,561.3	0.54	54,600	95	2,180.2	0.78	33,400	137	113,260	3,034.8	78,000	548.7	26,795	7,035
Division No. 8	141.9	157.4	0.51	10.89	57.9	0.48	3,189.0	0.49	55,100	96	1,974.5	0.71	34,100	140	101,220	2,727.1	70,140	493.7	26,942	7,039

*Adjusted.

Economic Regions & Census Divisions

Region	Population (at July 1)				Households (at July1)		Income				Retail Sales				Taxation Statistics, 1997					
	*1996 Census (000)	2001 Estimate (000)	% of Cdn. Total	% Chg. '96-'01	2001 Estimate (000)	% of Cdn. Total	2001 Estimate $millions	% of Cdn. Total	Per Hhld. $	Income Rating Index	2001 Estimate $millions	% of Cdn. Total	Per Hhld. $	Market Rating Index	Total No. of Returns	Total Income $millions	Total No. Taxable Returns	Total Tax $millions	Avg. Income $	Avg. Tax $
Division No. 9	18.6	20.3	0.07	9.21	7.4	0.06	372.3	0.06	50,500	87	205.7	0.07	27,900	113	12,040	307.7	7,860	55.0	25,560	6,999
Edmonton (60)	924.5	996.0	3.20	7.74	383.3	3.17	21,808.5	3.32	56,900	104	9,396.8	3.37	24,500	105	659,480	19,095.2	474,120	3,712.9	28,955	7,831
Division No. 11	924.5	996.0	3.20	7.74	383.3	3.17	21,808.5	3.32	56,900	104	9,396.8	3.37	24,500	105	659,480	19,095.2	474,120	3,712.9	28,955	7,831
Grande Prairie - Peace River (70)	154.8	169.0	0.54	9.21	57.8	0.48	3,298.6	0.50	57,100	93	1,639.9	0.59	28,400	108	102,140	2,716.2	67,010	479.3	26,593	7,153
Division No. 17	57.3	63.5	0.20	10.75	20.0	0.17	1,067.2	0.16	53,300	80	476.1	0.17	23,800	84	33,100	766.2	18,730	125.3	23,148	6,692
Division No. 18	15.4	16.2	0.05	5.01	5.6	0.05	331.6	0.05	59,300	97	94.6	0.03	16,900	65	9,590	272.2	6,270	54.9	28,384	8,753
Division No. 19	82.0	89.3	0.29	8.93	32.2	0.27	1,899.8	0.29	59,100	101	1,069.2	0.38	33,200	134	59,450	1,677.8	42,010	299.1	28,222	7,119
Wood Buffalo - Camrose (80)	180.4	189.5	0.61	5.04	69.0	0.57	3,815.6	0.58	55,300	95	1,987.7	0.71	28,800	117	121,880	3,476.6	82,210	684.8	28,525	8,330
Division No. 10	81.8	83.7	0.27	2.3	32.1	0.27	1,520.6	0.23	47,400	86	899.5	0.32	28,000	120	57,090	1,525.5	38,060	283.1	26,721	7,438
Division No. 12	61.1	65.3	0.21	7.01	22.1	0.18	1,108.5	0.17	50,100	80	605.2	0.22	27,300	103	39,710	960.7	25,120	170.2	24,194	6,774
Division No. 16	37.5	40.5	0.13	7.84	14.8	0.12	1,186.4	0.18	80,200	139	483.0	0.17	32,700	133	25,080	990.3	19,030	231.5	39,487	12,167

*Adjusted.

Alberta

POPULATION

July 1, 2001 Estimate 3,065,622
% Cdn. Total 9.85
% Change, '96 -'01 . . . . 10.25
Avg. Annual Growth Rate, % 1.97
2003 Projected Population 3,164,467
2006 Projected Population 3,281,450
2001 Households Estimate 1,153,347
2003 Projected Households 1,201,312
2006 Projected Households 1,267,610

INCOME

% Above/Below National Average . . . . +6
2001 Total Income Estimate . . $68,436,550,000
% Cdn. Total 10.43
2001 Average Hhld. Income $59,300
2001 Per Capita $22,300
2003 Projected Total Income . $74,663,360,000
2006 Projected Total Income . $84,555,820,000

RETAIL SALES

% Above/Below National Average . . . . +16
2001 Retail Sales Estimate . . $31,754,630,000
% Cdn. Total 11.39
2001 per Household $27,500
2001 per Capita $10,400
2001 No. of Establishments 23,202
2003 Projected Retail Sales . . $34,968,930,000
2006 Projected Retail Sales . . $39,583,790,000

POPULATION

2001 Estimates:
Total 3,065,622
Male 1,531,710
Female 1,533,912

Age Groups	Male	Female
0-4	105,470	100,407
5-9	112,159	106,390
10-14	116,421	110,363
15-19	113,140	107,772
20-24	107,508	104,430
25-29	108,200	107,284
30-34	118,827	119,358
35-39	131,456	131,049
40-44	131,746	129,025
45-49	117,454	114,194
50-54	94,053	91,893
55-59	72,189	71,267
60-64	58,070	58,228
65-69	48,442	50,341
70+	96,575	131,911

DAYTIME POPULATION

2001 Estimates:
Working Population 1,633,395
At Home Population 1,433,987
Total 3,067,382

INCOME

2001 Estimates:
Avg. Household Income $59,337
Avg. Family Income $66,046
Per Capita Income $22,324
Male:
Avg. Employment Income $37,726
Avg. Employment Income
(Full Time) $49,601
Female:
Avg. Employment Income $21,552
Avg. Employment Income
(Full Time) $32,465

DISPOSABLE & DISCRETIONARY INCOME

2001 Estimates:	*Per Hhld.*
Disposable Income	$45,280
Discretionary Income 1 (minus Food & Shelter)	$31,501
Discretionary Income 2 (minus Food, Shelter, & Other Expenditures)	$22,330

LIQUID ASSETS

1999 Estimates:	*Per Hhld.*
Equity Investments	$91,955
Interest Bearing Investments	$73,861
Total Liquid Assets	$165,816

CREDIT DATA

July 2000:
Pool of Credit $32,471,165,842
Revolving Credit, No. 5,447,649
Fixed Loans, No. 1,912,337
Avg. Credit Limit, per Person $13,051
Avg. Spent, per Person $6,188
Satisfactory Ratings,
No. per Person 2.82
Avg. No. of Cards, per Person 1.04

LABOUR FORCE

2001 Estimates:
Male:
In the Labour Force 948,535
Participation Rate 79.2
Employed 896,633
Unemployed 51,902
Unemployment Rate 5.5
Not in Labour Force 249,125
Female:
In the Labour Force 788,148
Participation Rate 64.8
Employed 745,712
Unemployed 42,436
Unemployment Rate 5.4
Not in Labour Force 428,604

AVERAGE WEEKLY EARNINGS

(Including overtime, industrial aggregate)

	Alberta	Canada
Apr 2000	$638.97	$622.92
Apr 1999	$622.89	$608.07
Apr 1998	$613.72	$608.06
Apr 1997	$604.88	$597.26
Apr 1996	$550.46	$575.79

NUMBER OF EMPLOYEES

(Industrial aggregate)
Apr 2000 1,258,665
Apr 1999 1,205,116
Apr 1998 1,201,627
Apr 1997 1,133,184
Apr 1996 1,071,745

MANUFACTURING INDUSTRIES

	1997	1992
Plants	2,804	2,512
Employees	120,545	88,330
	$000	
Salaries, Wages	4,590,622	3,060,335
Mfg. Materials, Cost	20,810,030	11,663,532
Mfg. Shipments, Value	34,675,666	19,241,644
Total Value Added	13,710,761	7,106,964

Note: Latest available data.

OCCUPATIONS BY MAJOR GROUPS

2001 Estimates:	Male	Female
Management	101,510	43,630
Business, Finance & Admin.	82,001	241,897
Natural & Applied Sciences & Related	78,411	15,086
Health	14,482	60,756
Social Sciences, Gov't Services & Religion	18,617	23,128
Education	21,849	36,565
Arts, Culture, Recreation & Sport	16,186	20,624
Sales & Service	187,508	269,759
Trades, Transport & Equipment Operators & Related	243,366	15,212
Primary Industries	104,395	30,567
Processing, Mfg. & Utilities	67,374	15,130

LEVEL OF SCHOOLING

2001 Estimates:
Population 15 years + ... 2,414,412
Less than Grade 9 179,124
Grades 9-13 w/o Certif. 629,297
Grade 9-13 with Certif. 285,839
Trade Certif. /Dip. 79,162
Non-Univ. w/o Certif./Dip. 172,894
Non-Univ. with Certif./Dip. 501,462
Univ. w/o Degree 245,247
Univ. w/o Degree/Certif. 124,815
Univ. with Certif. 120,432
Univ. with Degree 321,387

RETAIL SALES

	1999	1998
	$000,000	*$000,000*
Supermarkets & Groceries	6,330	6,102
All Other Food	n.a.	n.a.
Drugs & Patent Medicine	1,296	1,207
Shoes	131	136
Men's Clothing	194	209
Women's Clothing	424	410
Other Clothing	755	790
Hhld. Furniture & Appliances	1,416	1,296
Hhld. Furnishings	290	296
Motor & Recreation Vehicles	7,934	7,653
Gas Service Stations	1,999	1,819
Auto Parts, Accessories & Services	1,626	1,590
General Merchandise	3,399	3,190
Other Semi-Durable Goods	851	800
Other Durable Goods	834	823
Other Retail	1,665	1,541
Total	29,324	28,065

AVERAGE HOUSEHOLD EXPENDITURES

2001 Estimates:
Food $6,565
Shelter $9,534
Clothing $2,436
Transportation $7,035
Health & Personal Care $2,094
Recr'n, Read'g & Education $4,127
Taxes & Securities $15,240
Other $9,167
Total Expenditures $56,198

PRIVATE HOUSEHOLDS

2001 Estimates:
Private Households, Total 1,153,347
Pop. in Private Households 2,991,935
Average no. per Household 2.6

FAMILIES

2001 Estimates:
Families in Private Households 847,655
Husband-Wife Families 741,148
Lone-Parent Families 106,507
Aver. No. Persons per Family 3.1
Aver. No. Sons/Daughters
at Home 1.2

HOUSING

2001 Estimates:
Occupied Private Dwellings 1,153,347
Owned 788,427
Rented 358,737
Band Housing 6,183
Single-Detached House 748,628
Semi-Detached House 48,182
Row Houses 81,619
Apartment, 5+ Storeys 52,328
Owned Apartment, 5+ Storeys 5,927
Apartment, 5 or Fewer Storeys 152,525
Apartment, Detached Duplex 24,874
Other Single-Attached 1,387
Movable Dwellings 43,804

VEHICLES

2001 Estimates:
Model Yrs. '81-'96, No. 1,483,130
% Total 77.82
Model Yrs. '97-'98, No. 262,314
% Total 13.76
'99 Vehicles registered in
Model Yr. '99, No. 160,360
% Total 8.41
Total No. '81-'99 1,905,804

LEGAL MARITAL STATUS

2001 Estimates: (Age 15+)
Single (Never Married) 729,642
Legally Married
(Not Separated) 1,320,280
Legally Married (Separated) 67,731
Widowed 121,695
Divorced 175,064

PSYTE CATEGORIES

2001 Estimates	No. of House -holds	% of Total Hhds.	Index
Canadian Establishment	1,081	0.09	56
The Affluentials	7,708	0.67	105
Urban Gentry	14,146	1.23	68
Suburban Executives	30,942	2.68	187
Mortgaged in Suburbia	40,042	3.47	250
Technocrafts & Bureaucrats	64,582	5.60	199
Asian Heights	440	0.04	6
Boomers & Teens	10,195	0.88	49
Stable Suburban Families	15,020	1.30	100
Small City Elite	14,349	1.24	73
Old Bungalow Burbs	23,205	2.01	121
Suburban Nesters	9,542	0.83	52
Brie & Chablis	1,397	0.12	14
Aging Erudites	24,112	2.09	139
Satellite Suburbs	35,943	3.12	109
Kindergarten Boom	113,866	9.87	377
Blue Collar Winners	26,535	2.30	91
Town Boomers	25,988	2.25	222
Old Towns' New Fringe	50,946	4.42	113
Quebec Melange	168	0.01	1
Northern Lights	16,277	1.41	285
The New Frontier	49,826	4.32	286
Rustic Prosperity	34,356	2.98	165
Pick-ups & Dirt Bikes	38,081	3.30	395
Quebec's Heartland	53	0.00	
The Grain Belt	25,380	2.20	371
High Rise Melting Pot	289	0.03	2
Conservative Homebodies	50,522	4.38	121
High Rise Sunsets	7,267	0.63	44
Young Urban Professionals	16,210	1.41	74

2001 Estimates	No. of House-holds	% of Total Hhds.	Index
Young Urban Mix	18,326	1.59	75
Young Urban Intelligentsia	25,223	2.19	144
University Enclaves	50,138	4.35	213
Young City Singles	72,936	6.32	276
Old Leafy Towns	14,072	1.22	48
Town Renters	20,333	1.76	204
Nesters & Young Homesteaders	23,006	1.99	85
Young Grey Collar	26,221	2.27	272
Quiet Towns	42,412	3.68	173
Agrarian Blues	644	0.06	26
Rod & Rifle	11,370	0.99	43
Down, Down East	609	0.05	8
Big Country Families	20,431	1.77	124
Quebec Rural Blues	382	0.03	1
Old Cdn. Rustics	13,563	1.18	120
Struggling Downtowns	34,840	3.02	96
Aged Pensioners	10,253	0.89	67
Big City Stress	7,394	0.64	57
Old Grey Towers	3,875	0.34	61

FINAN¢IAL P$YTE

2001 Estimates	No. of House-holds	% of Total Hhds.	Index
Platinum Estates	8,789	0.76	95
Four Star Investors	55,283	4.79	95
Successful Suburbanites	136,361	11.82	178
Canadian Comfort	112,357	9.74	100
Urban Heights	41,719	3.62	84
Miners & Credit-Liners	73,031	6.33	200
Mortgages & Minivans	113,866	9.87	150
Tractors & Tradelines	85,302	7.40	129
Bills & Wills	82,920	7.19	87
Country Credit	63,629	5.52	82
Revolving Renters	56,494	4.90	106
Young Urban Struggle	75,361	6.53	138
Rural Family Blues	33,489	2.90	36
Limited Budgets	55,975	4.85	156
Towering Debt	128,398	11.13	143
NSF	7,394	0.64	18
Senior Survivors	14,128	1.22	65

HOME LANGUAGE

2001 Estimates:		% Total
English	2,774,408	90.50
French	17,269	0.56
Arabic	6,565	0.21
Blackfoot	1,986	0.06
Chinese	65,281	2.13
Cree	8,589	0.28
Croatian	1,660	0.05
Dakota/Sioux	2,520	0.08
Dutch	2,847	0.09
German	25,989	0.85
Gujarati	2,840	0.09
Hindi	2,944	0.10
Hungarian	2,006	0.07
Italian	5,214	0.17
Japanese	1,686	0.05
Korean	3,355	0.11
Polish	11,832	0.39
Portuguese	2,817	0.09
Punjabi	14,542	0.47
Russian	2,625	0.09
Serbo-Croatian	1,555	0.05
Spanish	11,777	0.38
Tagalog (Pilipino)	7,656	0.25
Ukrainian	3,964	0.13
Urdu	1,803	0.06
Vietnamese	13,410	0.44
Other Languages	18,929	0.62
Multiple Responses	49,553	1.62
Total	3,065,622	100.00

BUILDING PERMITS

	1999	1998 $000	1997
Value	4,801,885	5,552,208	4,446,316

HOMES BUILT

	1999	1998	1997
No	24,015	25,071	20,259

CAPITAL EXPENDITURES

(Public & Private)	2000	1999	1998
			$000,000
Total Expends	n.a.	n.a.	37,851.6
Capital Expends	34,007.2	31,365.3	32,284.2
Construction	24,114.4	20,803.4	21,598.5
Machinery & Equip.	9,892.7	10,561.9	10,685.9
Repair Expends	n.a.	n.a.	5,567.3
Construction	n.a.	n.a.	2,039.0
Machinery & Equip.	n.a.	n.a.	3,528.3

TAXATION

Income Class:	1997	% Total
Under $5,000	258,910	13.03
$5,000-$10,000	248,220	12.50
$10,000-$15,000	269,780	13.58
$15,000-$20,000	198,910	10.01
$20,000-$25,000	163,080	8.21
$25,000-$30,000	150,270	7.56
$30,000-$40,000	236,310	11.90
$40,000-$50,000	158,710	7.99
$50,000 +	302,270	15.22
Total Returns, No.	1,986,460	
Total Income, $000	60,305,424	
Total Taxable Returns	1,424,320	
Total Tax, $000	12,024,143	
Average Income, $	30,358	
Average Tax, $	8,442	

VITAL STATISTICS

	1997	1996	1995	1994
Births	36,905	37,851	38,914	39,796
Deaths	16,452	16,391	15,895	15,613
Natural Increase	20,453	21,460	23,019	24,183
Marriages	17,860	17,283	18,044	18,096

Note: Latest available data.

TRAVEL STATISTICS

Tourists in Canada	1999	1998
From the U.S. entering by:		
Automobile	344,196	334,905
Bus	13,968	15,195
Air	373,361	364,895
Other Methods	2,942	2,940
Total	734,467	717,935
Other Countries:		
Land (via U.S.)	15,587	15,415
Air	272,197	257,050
Total	287,784	272,465
Residents of Canada Returning from the U.S. by:		
Automobile	397,934	378,261
Bus	19,523	12,087
Air	477,713	470,893
Other Methods	3,143	3,101
Total	898,313	864,342
From Other Countries:		
Land (via U.S.)	6	n.a.
Air	257,959	260,962
Total	257,965	260,962

Alberta

Alberta

Brooks
(Town)

In census division No. 2.

POPULATION

July 1, 2001 Estimate	11,264
% Cdn. Total	0.04
% Change, '96 -'01	8.73
Avg. Annual Growth Rate, %	1.69
2003 Projected Population	11,568
2006 Projected Population	11,780
2001 Households Estimate	4,213
2003 Projected Households	4,373
2006 Projected Households	4,528

INCOME

% Above/Below National Average	+4
2001 Total Income Estimate	$247,110,000
% Cdn. Total	0.04
2001 Average Hhld. Income	$58,700
2001 Per Capita	$21,900
2003 Projected Total Income	$262,610,000
2006 Projected Total Income	$280,460,000

RETAIL SALES

% Above/Below National Average	-65
2001 Retail Sales Estimate	$34,820,000
% Cdn. Total	0.01
2001 per Household	$8,300
2001 per Capita	$3,100
2001 No. of Establishments	58
2003 Projected Retail Sales	$37,500,000
2006 Projected Retail Sales	$41,850,000

POPULATION

2001 Estimates:

Total		11,264
Male		5,883
Female		5,381
Age Groups	Male	Female
0-4	400	387
5-9	425	394
10-14	440	414
15-19	463	413
20-24	534	431
25-29	570	447
30-34	552	454
35-39	524	442
40-44	464	405
45-49	396	353
50-54	297	273
55-59	216	205
60-64	162	162
65-69	123	131
70+	317	470

DAYTIME POPULATION

2001 Estimates:

Working Population	5,001
At Home Population	4,854
Total	9,855

INCOME

2001 Estimates:

Avg. Household Income	$58,655
Avg. Family Income	$63,397
Per Capita Income	$21,938
Male:	
Avg. Employment Income	$38,010
Avg. Employment Income (Full Time)	$48,247
Female:	
Avg. Employment Income	$18,001
Avg. Employment Income (Full Time)	$25,403

DISPOSABLE & DISCRETIONARY INCOME

2001 Estimates:	Per Hhld.
Disposable Income	$44,306
Discretionary Income 1 (minus Food & Shelter)	$31,725
Discretionary Income 2 (minus Food, Shelter, & Other Expenditures)	$20,958

LIQUID ASSETS

1999 Estimates:	Per Hhld.
Equity Investments	$98,568
Interest Bearing Investments	$77,492
Total Liquid Assets	$176,060

CREDIT DATA

July 2000:

Pool of Credit	$104,325,394
Revolving Credit, No.	15,553
Fixed Loans, No.	8,101
Avg. Credit Limit, per Person	$11,524
Avg. Spent, per Person	$6,198
Satisfactory Ratings, No. per Person	2.49
Avg. No. of Cards, per Person	0.83

LABOUR FORCE

2001 Estimates:

Male:	
In the Labour Force	3,896
Participation Rate	84.4
Employed	3,801
Unemployed	95
Unemployment Rate	2.4
Not in Labour Force	722
Female:	
In the Labour Force	2,695
Participation Rate	64.4
Employed	2,571
Unemployed	124
Unemployment Rate	4.6
Not in Labour Force	1,491

OCCUPATIONS BY MAJOR GROUPS

2001 Estimates:	Male	Female
Management	359	53
Business, Finance & Admin.	190	760
Natural & Applied Sciences & Related	151	11
Health	31	200
Social Sciences, Gov't Services & Religion	40	62
Education	61	85
Arts, Culture, Recreation & Sport	11	55
Sales & Service	471	1,195
Trades, Transport & Equipment Operators & Related	1,142	56
Primary Industries	932	72
Processing, Mfg. & Utilities	496	87

LEVEL OF SCHOOLING

2001 Estimates:

Population 15 years +	8,804
Less than Grade 9	745
Grades 9-13 w/o Certif.	2,881
Grade 9-13 with Certif.	1,218
Trade Certif. /Dip.	142
Non-Univ. w/o Certif./Dip.	737
Non-Univ. with Certif./Dip.	1,823
Univ. w/o Degree	804
Univ. w/o Degree/Certif.	511
Univ. with Certif.	293
Univ. with Degree	454

AVERAGE HOUSEHOLD EXPENDITURES

2001 Estimates:

Food	$6,717
Shelter	$8,199
Clothing	$2,658
Transportation	$8,228
Health & Personal Care	$2,541
Recr'n, Read'g & Education	$4,826
Taxes & Securities	$13,197
Other	$9,158
Total Expenditures	$55,524

PRIVATE HOUSEHOLDS

2001 Estimates:

Private Households, Total	4,213
Pop. in Private Households	11,089
Average no. per Household	2.6

FAMILIES

2001 Estimates:

Families in Private Households	2,936
Husband-Wife Families	2,724
Lone-Parent Families	212
Aver. No. Persons per Family	3.2
Aver. No. Sons/Daughters at Home	1.3

HOUSING

2001 Estimates:

Occupied Private Dwellings	4,213
Owned	2,672
Rented	1,541
Single-Detached House	2,384
Semi-Detached House	253
Row Houses	453
Apartment, 5 or Fewer Storeys	693
Apartment, Detached Duplex	99
Other Single-Attached	36
Movable Dwellings	295

VEHICLES

2001 Estimates:

Model Yrs. '81-'96, No.	6,436
% Total	75.06
Model Yrs. '97-'98, No.	1,384
% Total	16.14
'99 Vehicles registered in Model Yr. '99, No.	754
% Total	8.79
Total No. '81-'99	8,574

LEGAL MARITAL STATUS

2001 Estimates: (Age 15+)

Single (Never Married)	2,870
Legally Married (Not Separated)	4,604
Legally Married (Separated)	272
Widowed	464
Divorced	594

PSYTE CATEGORIES

2001 Estimates	No. of House -holds	% of Total Hhds.	Index
The New Frontier	3,368	79.94	5,300
Quiet Towns	845	20.06	943

FINANCIAL P$YTE

2001 Estimates	No. of House -holds	% of Total Hhds.	Index
Miners & Credit-Liners	3,368	79.94	2,525
Limited Budgets	845	20.06	645

HOME LANGUAGE

2001 Estimates:		% Total
English	11,018	97.82
French	12	0.11
Arabic	21	0.19
Dutch	12	0.11
Khmer (Cambodian)	107	0.95
Punjabi	21	0.19
Tagalog (Pilipino)	11	0.10
Multiple Responses	62	0.55
Total	11,264	100.00

BUILDING PERMITS

	1999	1998 $000	1997
Value	16,082	13,294	17,751

HOMES BUILT

	1999	1998	1997
No	70	133	n.a.

TAXATION

Income Class:	1997	% Total
Under $5,000	1,050	10.96
$5,000-$10,000	1,140	11.90
$10,000-$15,000	1,270	13.26
$15,000-$20,000	970	10.13
$20,000-$25,000	810	8.46
$25,000-$30,000	730	7.62
$30,000-$40,000	1,190	12.42
$40,000-$50,000	750	7.83
$50,000 +	1,670	17.43
Total Returns, No.	9,580	
Total Income, $000	293,833	
Total Taxable Returns	7,370	
Total Tax, $000	58,071	
Average Income, $.	30,672	
Average Tax, $.	7,879	

VITAL STATISTICS

	1997	1996	1995	1994
Births	168	164	174	159
Deaths	78	75	78	67
Natural Increase	90	89	96	92
Marriages	94	90	84	79

Note: Latest available data.

COMMUNITY NEWSPAPER(S)

	Total Circulation
Brooks: Brooks Bulletin	5,226
Brooks: Brooks & County Chronicle	9,599

RADIO STATION(S)

	Power
CIBQ	1,000w

Calgary
(Census Metropolitan Area)

POPULATION

July 1, 2001 Estimate	978,032
% Cdn. Total	3.14
% Change, '96 -'01	15.71
Avg. Annual Growth Rate, %	2.96
2003 Projected Population	1,019,230
2006 Projected Population	1,078,507
2001 Households Estimate	375,458
2003 Projected Households	394,034
2006 Projected Households	422,666

INCOME

% Above/Below National Average	+22
2001 Total Income Estimate	$25,120,030,000
% Cdn. Total	3.83
2001 Average Hhld. Income	$66,900
2001 Per Capita	$25,700
2003 Projected Total Income	$27,681,640,000
2006 Projected Total Income	$32,020,830,000

RETAIL SALES

% Above/Below National Average	+18
2001 Retail Sales Estimate	$10,340,650,000
% Cdn. Total	3.71
2001 per Household	$27,500
2001 per Capita	$10,600
2001 No. of Establishments	6,539
2003 Projected Retail Sales	$11,508,390,000
2006 Projected Retail Sales	$13,301,210,000

POPULATION

2001 Estimates:

Total		978,032
Male		487,354
Female		490,678

Age Groups	Male	Female
0-4	34,153	32,507
5-9	34,983	33,269
10-14	35,100	33,287
15-19	33,168	31,588
20-24	32,577	32,044
25-29	35,920	35,785
30-34	41,178	41,379
35-39	45,595	45,512
40-44	45,226	44,317
45-49	39,681	38,536
50-54	30,727	30,029
55-59	22,419	22,431
60-64	17,198	17,866
65-69	13,917	15,137
70+	25,512	36,991

DAYTIME POPULATION

2001 Estimates:

Working Population	543,545
At Home Population	434,485
Total	978,030

INCOME

2001 Estimates:

Avg. Household Income	$66,905
Avg. Family Income	$74,909
Per Capita Income	$25,684
Male:	
Avg. Employment Income	$42,337
Avg. Employment Income (Full Time)	$55,795
Female:	
Avg. Employment Income	$24,749
Avg. Employment Income (Full Time)	$36,513

DISPOSABLE & DISCRETIONARY INCOME

2001 Estimates:	Per Hhld.
Disposable Income	$50,406
Discretionary Income 1 (minus Food & Shelter)	$35,183
Discretionary Income 2 (minus Food, Shelter, & Other Expenditures)	$25,691

LIQUID ASSETS

1999 Estimates:	Per Hhld.
Equity Investments	$112,274
Interest Bearing Investments	$84,322
Total Liquid Assets	$196,596

CREDIT DATA

July 2000:	
Pool of Credit	$11,221,106,101
Revolving Credit, No.	1,925,263
Fixed Loans, No.	567,261
Avg. Credit Limit, per Person	$13,616
Avg. Spent, per Person	$6,150
Satisfactory Ratings, No. per Person	2.89
Avg. No. of Cards, per Person	1.15

LABOUR FORCE

2001 Estimates:

Male:	
In the Labour Force	309,947
Participation Rate	80.9
Employed	295,517
Unemployed	14,430
Unemployment Rate	4.7
Not in Labour Force	73,171
Female:	
In the Labour Force	262,096
Participation Rate	66.9
Employed	249,522
Unemployed	12,574
Unemployment Rate	4.8
Not in Labour Force	129,519

OCCUPATIONS BY MAJOR GROUPS

2001 Estimates:	Male	Female
Management	38,672	15,690
Business, Finance & Admin.	36,758	90,587
Natural & Applied Sciences & Related	38,276	8,082
Health	4,474	19,192
Social Sciences, Gov't Services & Religion	7,054	8,251
Education	6,461	11,678
Arts, Culture, Recreation & Sport	6,297	7,518
Sales & Service	70,140	84,065
Trades, Transport & Equipment Operators & Related	68,975	4,055
Primary Industries	10,474	2,413
Processing, Mfg. & Utilities	18,126	5,922

LEVEL OF SCHOOLING

2001 Estimates:

Population 15 years +	774,733
Less than Grade 9	40,453
Grades 9-13 w/o Certif.	167,622
Grade 9-13 with Certif.	88,871
Trade Certif. /Dip.	22,172
Non-Univ. w/o Certif./Dip.	57,888
Non-Univ. with Certif./Dip.	156,502
Univ. w/o Degree	97,675
Univ. w/o Degree/Certif.	51,242
Univ. with Certif.	46,433
Univ. with Degree	143,550

Alberta

AVERAGE HOUSEHOLD EXPENDITURES

2001 Estimates:

Food	$6,992
Shelter	$10,821
Clothing	$2,699
Transportation	$7,271
Health & Personal Care	$2,182
Recr'n, Read'g & Education	$4,504
Taxes & Securities	$18,180
Other	$9,683
Total Expenditures	$62,332

PRIVATE HOUSEHOLDS

2001 Estimates:

Private Households, Total	375,458
Pop. in Private Households	965,427
Average no. per Household	2.6

FAMILIES

2001 Estimates:

Families in Private Households	271,354
Husband-Wife Families	236,632
Lone-Parent Families	34,722
Aver. No. Persons per Family	3.1
Aver. No. Sons/Daughters at Home	1.2

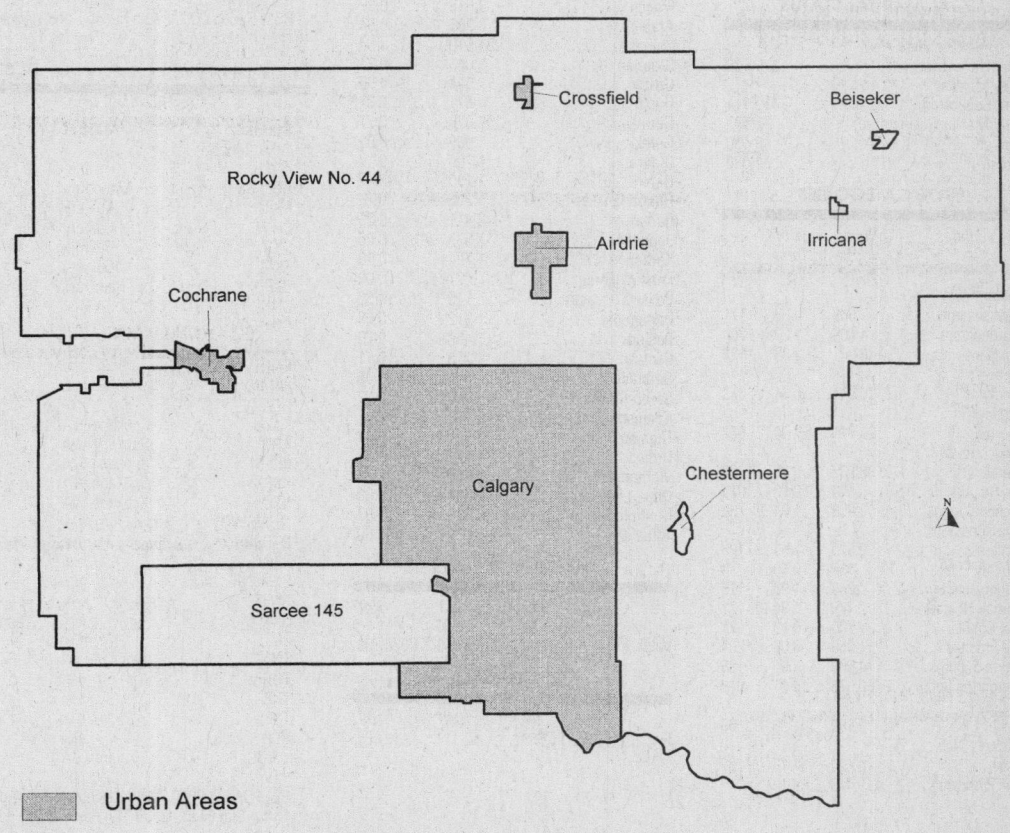

Crossfield · Beiseker · Irricana · Rocky View No. 44 · Airdrie · Cochrane · Chestermere · Calgary · Sarcee 145

Urban Areas

Alberta

Calgary

(Census Metropolitan Area)
(Cont'd)

HOUSING

2001 Estimates:

Occupied Private Dwellings	375,458
Owned	249,705
Rented	125,753
Single-Detached House	227,185
Semi-Detached House	22,704
Row Houses	32,131
Apartment, 5+ Storeys	26,975
Owned Apartment, 5+ Storeys	2,890
Apartment, 5 or Fewer Storeys	50,168
Apartment, Detached Duplex	13,130
Other Single-Attached	156
Movable Dwellings	3,009

VEHICLES

2001 Estimates:

Model Yrs. '81-'96, No.	454,671
% Total	73.86
Model Yrs. '97-'98, No.	98,357
% Total	15.98
'99 Vehicles registered in Model Yr. '99, No.	62,549
% Total	10.16
Total No. '81-'99	615,577

LEGAL MARITAL STATUS

2001 Estimates: (Age 15+)

Single (Never Married)	238,629
Legally Married (Not Separated)	419,111
Legally Married (Separated)	22,533
Widowed	33,430
Divorced	61,030

PSYTE CATEGORIES

2001 Estimates	No. of House-holds	% of Total Hhds.	Index
Canadian Establishment	1,069	0.28	171
The Affluentials	4,886	1.30	204
Urban Gentry	8,941	2.38	133
Suburban Executives	20,044	5.34	372
Mortgaged in Suburbia	27,771	7.40	532
Technocrafts & Bureaucrats	35,232	9.38	333
Asian Heights	440	0.12	18
Boomers & Teens	3,903	1.04	58
Stable Suburban Families	9,570	2.55	196
Small City Elite	382	0.10	6
Old Bungalow Burbs	7,243	1.93	116
Suburban Nesters	7,279	1.94	121
Brie & Chablis	705	0.19	21
Aging Erudites	11,558	3.08	204
Satellite Suburbs	14,683	3.91	136
Kindergarten Boom	60,875	16.21	618
Blue Collar Winners	6,182	1.65	65
Old Towns' New Fringe	4,420	1.18	30
Rustic Prosperity	475	0.13	7

2001 Estimates	No. of House-holds	% of Total Hhds.	Index
Conservative Homebodies	17,777	4.73	131
High Rise Sunsets	2,672	0.71	50
Young Urban Professionals	11,053	2.94	155
Young Urban Mix	11,948	3.18	150
Young Urban Intelligentsia	12,758	3.40	223
University Enclaves	33,908	9.03	442
Young City Singles	35,178	9.37	409
Town Renters	6,071	1.62	187
Nesters & Young Homesteaders	245	0.07	3
Struggling Downtowns	10,127	2.70	86
Aged Pensioners	3,900	1.04	78
Big City Stress	586	0.16	14
Old Grey Towers	1,394	0.37	67

FINANCIAL PSYTE

2001 Estimates	No. of House-holds	% of Total Hhds.	Index
Platinum Estates	5,955	1.59	197
Four Star Investors	32,888	8.76	174
Successful Suburbanites	73,013	19.45	293
Canadian Comfort	28,526	7.60	78
Urban Heights	23,316	6.21	144
Miners & Credit-Liners	7,243	1.93	61
Mortgages & Minivans	60,875	16.21	246
Tractors & Tradelines	4,895	1.30	23
Bills & Wills	29,725	7.92	96
Revolving Renters	2,917	0.78	17
Young Urban Struggle	46,666	12.43	263
Towering Debt	51,376	13.68	175
NSF	586	0.16	4
Senior Survivors	5,294	1.41	75

HOME LANGUAGE

2001 Estimates:		% Total
English	863,557	88.30
French	3,615	0.37
Arabic	3,361	0.34
Chinese	34,610	3.54
Croatian	1,049	0.11
Czech	544	0.06
Dutch	671	0.07
German	2,079	0.21
Greek	809	0.08
Gujarati	1,700	0.17
Hindi	1,133	0.12
Hungarian	1,200	0.12
Italian	2,411	0.25
Japanese	633	0.06
Korean	1,784	0.18
Persian (Farsi)	777	0.08
Polish	5,119	0.52
Portuguese	912	0.09
Punjabi	7,458	0.76
Russian	1,118	0.11
Serbian	494	0.05
Serbo-Croatian	700	0.07
Spanish	5,134	0.52
Tagalog (Pilipino)	3,713	0.38
Urdu	1,121	0.11
Vietnamese	7,358	0.75
Other Languages	6,644	0.68
Multiple Responses	18,328	1.87
Total	978,032	100.00

BUILDING PERMITS

	1999	1998 $000	1997
Value	1,916,798	2,486,053	1,828,192

HOMES BUILT

	1999	1998	1997
No	9,655	12,111	9,185

TAXATION

Income Class:	1997	% Total
Under $5,000	74,300	11.81
$5,000-$10,000	72,050	11.45
$10,000-$15,000	77,140	12.26
$15,000-$20,000	59,970	9.53
$20,000-$25,000	51,660	8.21
$25,000-$30,000	47,790	7.60
$30,000-$40,000	77,990	12.40
$40,000-$50,000	54,290	8.63
$50,000 +	113,860	18.10
Total Returns, No.	629,030	
Total Income, $000	22,483,957	
Total Taxable Returns	474,050	
Total Tax, $000	4,931,754	
Average Income, $	35,744	
Average Tax, $	10,403	

VITAL STATISTICS

	1997	1996	1995	1994
Births	11,241	11,332	11,391	11,645
Deaths	4,265	4,329	4,071	3,823
Natural Increase	6,976	7,003	7,320	7,822
Marriages	4,726	4,796	5,002	5,145

Note: Latest available data.

DAILY NEWSPAPER(S)

	Circulation Average Paid
Calgary Herald	
Fri	154,078
Sat	133,137
Sun	119,355
Mon-Thu	116,521
Calgary Sun	
Sun	100,523
Mon-Sat	70,344

COMMUNITY NEWSPAPER(S)

	Total Circulation
Airdrie: The Airdrie Echo	3,033
Calgary: Calgary Mirror: North & South Zones	151,600
Calgary: Calgary Herald Neighbours, Northwest/Zone 1	n.a.
Calgary: Calgary Herald Neighbours, Northeast/Zone 2	n.a.
Calgary: Calgary Herald Neighbours, West/Zone 3	n.a.
Calgary: Calgary Herald Neighbours, Southwest/Zone 4	n.a.
Calgary: Calgary Herald Neighbours, Southeast/Zone 5	n.a.
Calgary: Le Chinook (mthly)	10,000
Calgary: Community Digest	25,000
Irricana, Rocky View: Irricana Rocky View/ Five Village Weekly	16,045

RADIO STATION DATA

Station	Market	Format	Wkly. Reach%*	Aver. Hrs. Tuned
All Stations			97	22.9
CBR	Calgary	News, Info.	14	12.0
CBR-FM	Calgary	Adult Contemp.	8	8.7
CFAC	Calgary	Country, Western	3	9.4
CFFR	Calgary	All Oldies	12	6.9
CHFM-FM	Calgary	Adult Contemp.	23	11.5
CHQR	Calgary	News, Talk, Sports	18	9.8
CJAY-FM	Calgary	Classic Rock	24	11.0
CJSI-FM	Calgary	Adult Contemp. Christian	n.a.	n.a.
CKIK-FM	Calgary	Top 40	38	11.3
CKIS-FM	Calgary	Adult Contemp.	16	9.9
CKMX	Calgary	Adult Standards	6	8.6
CKRY-FM	Calgary	Contemp. Country	24	15.1
CKUA-FM	Calgary	Multi-Format	n.a.	n.a.

BBM Spring 2000 Radio Reach Survey; area coverage.
*Mon-Sun 5a.m - 1a.m , All Persons 12+

TV STATION DATA

Station	Market	Network Affiliation	Wkly. Reach%*	Aver. Hrs. Tuned
All Stations			96	20.5
A & E	n.a.	Ind.	24	2.8
ACCESS	Edmonton		12	1.6
CBRT	Calgary	CBC	42	2.6
CFCN	Calgary	CTV	69	5.0
CICT	Calgary	Ind.	59	3.7
CKAL	Calgary	Ind.	53	3.6
CKRD	Red Deer	CBC	20	1.7
CNN	n.a.	Ind.	6	2.3
COMEDY	n.a.	Ind.	10	1.3
DSCVRY	n.a.	Ind.	8	1.6
FAIRTV	n.a.	n.a.	-	61.5
FAMILY	n.a.	Ind.	7	1.6
HISTTV	n.a.	Ind.	5	2.4
KAYU	Spokane WA	FOX	24	2.0
KHQ	Spokane WA	NBC	18	1.8
KREM	Spokane WA	CBS	32	2.2
KSPS	Spokane WA	PBS	16	2.5
KXLY	Spokane WA	ABC	26	1.8
NEWSWD	n.a.	CBC	7	1.8
OTHERS	n.a.	n.a.	7	2.5
PRIME	n.a.	Ind.	7	2.1
SHWCSE	n.a.	Ind.	8	1.6
SNET	n.a.	CTV	13	3.6
SPACE	n.a.	Ind.	9	2.5
TLC	n.a.	Ind.	19	2.0
TNN	Nashville TN	Ind.	8	1.7
TOON	n.a.	Ind.	10	1.6
TREE	n.a.	Ind.	7	4.6
TSN	n.a.	Ind.	18	3.5
VCR	n.a.	n.a.	30	3.9
WTBS	Atlanta GA	Ind.	19	3.2
YTV	n.a.	Ind.	17	2.9

BBM Spring 2000 TV Reach Survey; CMA coverage.
*Mon-Sun 6a.m - 2a.m , All Persons 2 +

Airdrie
(City)
Calgary CMA
In census division No. 6.

POPULATION

July 1, 2001 Estimate	21,976
% Cdn. Total	0.07
% Change, '96 -'01	33.94
Avg. Annual Growth Rate, %	6.02
2003 Projected Population	24,772
2006 Projected Population	28,900
2001 Households Estimate	7,153
2003 Projected Households	8,137
2006 Projected Households	9,657

INCOME

% Above/Below National Average	+9
2001 Total Income Estimate	$504,430,000
% Cdn. Total	0.08
2001 Average Hhld. Income	$70,500
2001 Per Capita	$23,000
2003 Projected Total Income	$615,560,000
2006 Projected Total Income	$813,320,000

RETAIL SALES

% Above/Below National Average	-56
2001 Retail Sales Estimate	$87,500,000
% Cdn. Total	0.03
2001 per Household	$12,200
2001 per Capita	$4,000
2001 No. of Establishments	80
2003 Projected Retail Sales	$107,270,000
2006 Projected Retail Sales	$139,240,000

POPULATION

2001 Estimates:

Total		21,976
Male		10,905
Female		11,071

Age Groups	Male	Female
0-4	808	797
5-9	969	917
10-14	1,108	1,038
15-19	1,031	986
20-24	787	779
25-29	678	739
30-34	832	937
35-39	1,024	1,143
40-44	1,078	1,112
45-49	916	862
50-54	615	544
55-59	369	340
60-64	235	242
65-69	166	183
70+	289	452

DAYTIME POPULATION

2001 Estimates:

Working Population	3,339
At Home Population	9,851
Total	13,190

INCOME

2001 Estimates:

Avg. Household Income	$70,520
Avg. Family Income	$72,980
Per Capita Income	$22,954
Male:	
Avg. Employment Income	$44,422
Avg. Employment Income (Full Time)	$53,697
Female:	
Avg. Employment Income	$21,955
Avg. Employment Income (Full Time)	$32,327

DISPOSABLE & DISCRETIONARY INCOME

2001 Estimates: *Per Hhld.*

Disposable Income	$54,113
Discretionary Income 1 (minus Food & Shelter)	$37,715
Discretionary Income 2 (minus Food, Shelter, & Other Expenditures)	$26,892

LIQUID ASSETS

1999 Estimates: *Per Hhld.*

Equity Investments	$102,670
Interest Bearing Investments	$80,518
Total Liquid Assets	$183,188

CREDIT DATA

July 2000:

Pool of Credit	$222,294,603
Revolving Credit, No.	34,796
Fixed Loans, No.	14,528
Avg. Credit Limit, per Person	$15,189
Avg. Spent, per Person	$7,895
Satisfactory Ratings, No. per Person	3.19
Avg. No. of Cards, per Person	1.13

LABOUR FORCE

2001 Estimates:

Male:

In the Labour Force	6,740
Participation Rate	84.0
Employed	6,502
Unemployed	238
Unemployment Rate	3.5
Not in Labour Force	1,280

Female:

In the Labour Force	5,746
Participation Rate	69.1
Employed	5,483
Unemployed	263
Unemployment Rate	4.6
Not in Labour Force	2,573

OCCUPATIONS BY MAJOR GROUPS

2001 Estimates:

	Male	Female
Management	658	250
Business, Finance & Admin.	723	2,142
Natural & Applied Sciences & Related	717	116
Health	46	429
Social Sciences, Gov't Services & Religion	106	105
Education	110	193
Arts, Culture, Recreation & Sport	55	124
Sales & Service	1,391	1,966
Trades, Transport & Equipment Operators & Related	1,976	150
Primary Industries	261	49
Processing, Mfg. & Utilities	619	139

LEVEL OF SCHOOLING

2001 Estimates:

Population 15 years +	16,339
Less than Grade 9	496
Grades 9-13 w/o Certif.	4,293
Grade 9-13 with Certif.	2,200
Trade Certif. /Dip.	667
Non-Univ. w/o Certif./Dip.	1,301
Non-Univ. with Certif./Dip.	4,416
Univ. w/o Degree	1,691
Univ. w/o Degree/Certif.	818
Univ. with Certif.	873
Univ. with Degree	1,275

AVERAGE HOUSEHOLD EXPENDITURES

2001 Estimates:

Food	$7,663
Shelter	$11,251
Clothing	$2,750
Transportation	$8,455
Health & Personal Care	$2,284
Recr'n, Read'g & Education	$4,911
Taxes & Securities	$18,429
Other	$10,209
Total Expenditures	$65,952

PRIVATE HOUSEHOLDS

2001 Estimates:

Private Households, Total	7,153
Pop. in Private Households	21,775
Average no. per Household	3.0

FAMILIES

2001 Estimates:

Families in Private Households	6,141
Husband-Wife Families	5,571
Lone-Parent Families	570
Aver. No. Persons per Family	3.4
Aver. No. Sons/Daughters at Home	1.5

HOUSING

2001 Estimates:

Occupied Private Dwellings	7,153
Owned	5,959
Rented	1,194
Single-Detached House	5,660
Semi-Detached House	486
Row Houses	354
Apartment, 5 or Fewer Storeys	594
Movable Dwellings	59

VEHICLES

2001 Estimates:

Model Yrs. '81-'96, No.	9,356
% Total	79.21
Model Yrs. '97-'98, No.	1,607
% Total	13.61
'99 Vehicles registered in Model Yr. '99, No.	848
% Total	7.18
Total No. '81-'99	11,811

LEGAL MARITAL STATUS

2001 Estimates: (Age 15+)

Single (Never Married)	3,795
Legally Married (Not Separated)	10,502
Legally Married (Separated)	529
Widowed	486
Divorced	1,027

PSYTE CATEGORIES

2001 Estimates

	No. of House-holds	% of Total Hhds.	Index
Mortgaged in Suburbia	318	4.45	320
Technocrafts & Bureaucrats	912	12.75	453
Satellite Suburbs	2,054	28.72	1,001
Kindergarten Boom	1,727	24.14	921
Blue Collar Winners	436	6.10	242
Old Towns' New Fringe	1,653	23.11	590

FINANCIAL PSYTE

2001 Estimates

	No. of House-holds	% of Total Hhds.	Index
Successful Suburbanites	1,230	17.20	259
Canadian Comfort	2,490	34.81	358
Mortgages & Minivans	1,727	24.14	366
Tractors & Tradelines	1,653	23.11	404

Alberta

HOME LANGUAGE

2001 Estimates: *% Total*

English	21,702	98.75
French	65	0.30
Chinese	13	0.06
Dutch	54	0.25
Lao	12	0.05
Polish	27	0.12
Portuguese	14	0.06
Tagalog (Pilipino)	15	0.07
Other Languages	28	0.13
Multiple Responses	46	0.21
Total	21,976	100.00

BUILDING PERMITS

	1999	1998	1997
		$000	
Value	53,052	50,082	43,269

HOMES BUILT

	1999	1998	1997
No.	399	405	206

TAXATION

Income Class:	1997	% Total
Under $5,000	1,660	13.29
$5,000-$10,000	1,310	10.49
$10,000-$15,000	1,220	9.77
$15,000-$20,000	1,070	8.57
$20,000-$25,000	940	7.53
$25,000-$30,000	960	7.69
$30,000-$40,000	1,690	13.53
$40,000-$50,000	1,300	10.41
$50,000 +	2,350	18.82
Total Returns, No.	12,490	
Total Income, $000	407,674	
Total Taxable Returns	9,570	
Total Tax, $000	82,778	
Average Income, $	32,640	
Average Tax, $	8,650	

VITAL STATISTICS

	1997	1996	1995	1994
Births	201	207	235	214
Deaths	62	46	51	46
Natural Increase	139	161	184	168
Marriages	75	60	48	73

Note: Latest available data.

MEDIA INFO
see Calgary, CMA

Alberta

Calgary
(City)
Calgary CMA

In census division No. 6.

POPULATION

July 1, 2001 Estimate	906,673
% Cdn. Total	2.91
* % Change, '96 -'01	14.74
Avg. Annual Growth Rate, %	2.79
2003 Projected Population	939,610
2006 Projected Population	986,705
2001 Households Estimate	352,010
2003 Projected Households	367,637
2006 Projected Households	391,724

INCOME

% Above/Below National Average	+20
2001 Total Income Estimate	$23,002,200,000
% Cdn. Total	3.50
2001 Average Hhld. Income	$65,300
2001 Per Capita	$25,400
2003 Projected Total Income	$25,143,490,000
2006 Projected Total Income	$28,739,290,000

RETAIL SALES

% Above/Below National Average	+23
2001 Retail Sales Estimate	$10,005,930,000
% Cdn. Total	3.59
2001 per Household	$28,400
2001 per Capita	$11,000
2001 No. of Establishments	5,971
2003 Projected Retail Sales	$11,100,790,000
2006 Projected Retail Sales	$12,773,300,000

POPULATION

2001 Estimates:

Total		906,673
Male		451,435
Female		455,238

Age Groups	Male	Female
0-4	31,782	30,206
5-9	32,114	30,552
10-14	31,823	30,233
15-19	29,994	28,673
20-24	30,023	29,651
25-29	33,739	33,586
30-34	38,793	38,802
35-39	42,686	42,309
40-44	41,924	40,904
45-49	36,552	35,480
50-54	28,251	27,718
55-59	20,659	20,827
60-64	15,934	16,712
65-69	12,990	14,311
70+	24,171	35,274

DAYTIME POPULATION

2001 Estimates:

Working Population	528,563
At Home Population	404,567
Total	933,130

INCOME

2001 Estimates:

Avg. Household Income	$65,345
Avg. Family Income	$73,289
Per Capita Income	$25,370
Male:	
Avg. Employment Income	$41,431
Avg. Employment Income (Full Time)	$54,843
Female:	
Avg. Employment Income	$24,607
Avg. Employment Income (Full Time)	$36,263

DISPOSABLE & DISCRETIONARY INCOME

2001 Estimates:	Per Hhld.
Disposable Income	$49,324
Discretionary Income 1 (minus Food & Shelter)	$34,334
Discretionary Income 2 (minus Food, Shelter, & Other Expenditures)	$25,042

LIQUID ASSETS

1999 Estimates:	Per Hhld.
Equity Investments	$106,734
Interest Bearing Investments	$82,087
Total Liquid Assets	$188,821

CREDIT DATA

July 2000:

Pool of Credit	$10,428,295,231
Revolving Credit, No.	1,811,044
Fixed Loans, No.	524,538
Avg. Credit Limit, per Person	$13,461
Avg. Spent, per Person	$6,044
Satisfactory Ratings, No. per Person	2.88
Avg. No. of Cards, per Person	1.15

LABOUR FORCE

2001 Estimates:

Male:	
In the Labour Force	286,494
Participation Rate	80.5
Employed	272,753
Unemployed	13,741
Unemployment Rate	4.8
Not in Labour Force	69,222
Female:	
In the Labour Force	242,954
Participation Rate	66.7
Employed	231,096
Unemployed	11,858
Unemployment Rate	4.9
Not in Labour Force	121,293

OCCUPATIONS BY MAJOR GROUPS

2001 Estimates:	Male	Female
Management	35,463	14,399
Business, Finance & Admin.	34,685	83,818
Natural & Applied Sciences & Related	35,741	7,692
Health	4,150	17,825
Social Sciences, Gov't Services & Religion	6,653	7,908
Education	5,882	10,718
Arts, Culture, Recreation & Sport	5,895	7,015
Sales & Service	65,756	78,365
Trades, Transport & Equipment Operators & Related	63,463	3,599
Primary Industries	7,960	1,569
Processing, Mfg. & Utilities	16,770	5,598

LEVEL OF SCHOOLING

2001 Estimates:

Population 15 years +	719,963
Less than Grade 9	38,628
Grades 9-13 w/o Certif.	154,679
Grade 9-13 with Certif.	82,240
Trade Certif. /Dip.	20,321
Non-Univ. w/o Certif./Dip.	54,026
Non-Univ. with Certif./Dip.	143,375
Univ. w/o Degree	91,486
Univ. w/o Degree/Certif.	48,015
Univ. with Certif.	43,471
Univ. with Degree	135,208

AVERAGE HOUSEHOLD EXPENDITURES

2001 Estimates:

Food	$6,898
Shelter	$10,647
Clothing	$2,659
Transportation	$7,094
Health & Personal Care	$2,154
Recr'n, Read'g & Education	$4,424
Taxes & Securities	$17,709
Other	$9,509
Total Expenditures	$61,094

PRIVATE HOUSEHOLDS

2001 Estimates:

Private Households, Total	352,010
Pop. in Private Households	895,218
Average no. per Household	2.5

FAMILIES

2001 Estimates:

Families in Private Households	250,964
Husband-Wife Families	217,666
Lone-Parent Families	33,298
Aver. No. Persons per Family	3.0
Aver. No. Sons/Daughters at Home	1.2

HOUSING

2001 Estimates:

Occupied Private Dwellings	352,010
Owned	229,725
Rented	122,285
Single-Detached House	207,010
Semi-Detached House	21,733
Row Houses	31,513
Apartment, 5+ Storeys	26,938
Owned Apartment, 5+ Storeys	2,890
Apartment, 5 or Fewer Storeys	49,191
Apartment, Detached Duplex	13,011
Other Single-Attached	129
Movable Dwellings	2,485

VEHICLES

2001 Estimates:

Model Yrs. '81-'96, No.	422,189
% Total	73.55
Model Yrs. '97-'98, No.	92,596
% Total	16.13
'99 Vehicles registered in Model Yr. '99, No.	59,204
% Total	10.31
Total No. '81-'99	573,989

LEGAL MARITAL STATUS

2001 Estimates: (Age 15+)

Single (Never Married)	225,895
Legally Married (Not Separated)	383,002
Legally Married (Separated)	21,335
Widowed	31,792
Divorced	57,939

PSYTE CATEGORIES

2001 Estimates	No. of House-holds	% of Total Hhds.	Index
Canadian Establishment	878	0.25	150
The Affluentials	3,890	1.11	173
Urban Gentry	8,941	2.54	141
Suburban Executives	18,205	5.17	361
Mortgaged in Suburbia	26,063	7.40	533
Technocrafts & Bureaucrats	33,476	9.51	338
Asian Heights	440	0.12	20
Boomers & Teens	1,455	0.41	23
Stable Suburban Families	9,570	2.72	209
Small City Elite	382	0.11	6
Old Bungalow Burbs	7,243	2.06	124.
Suburban Nesters	7,279	2.07	129
Brie & Chablis	705	0.20	22
Aging Erudites	11,558	3.28	218
Satellite Suburbs	12,629	3.59	125
Kindergarten Boom	58,387	16.59	633
Blue Collar Winners	1,023	0.29	12
Old Towns' New Fringe	288	0.08	2
Conservative Homebodies	17,777	5.05	140
High Rise Sunsets	2,672	0.76	53
Young Urban Professionals	11,053	3.14	165
Young Urban Mix	11,948	3.39	160
Young Urban Intelligentsia	12,758	3.62	238
University Enclaves	33,908	9.63	472
Young City Singles	35,071	9.96	434
Town Renters	6,071	1.72	200
Nesters & Young Homesteaders	245	0.07	3
Struggling Downtowns	10,127	2.88	91
Aged Pensioners	3,900	1.11	83
Big City Stress	586	0.17	15
Old Grey Towers	1,394	0.40	72

FINANCIAL P$YTE

2001 Estimates	No. of House-holds	% of Total Hhds.	Index
Platinum Estates	4,768	1.35	168
Four Star Investors	28,601	8.13	162
Successful Suburbanites	69,549	19.76	298
Canadian Comfort	21,313	6.05	62
Urban Heights	23,316	6.62	154
Miners & Credit-Liners	7,243	2.06	65
Mortgages & Minivans	58,387	16.59	251
Tractors & Tradelines	288	0.08	1
Bills & Wills	29,725	8.44	102
Revolving Renters	2,917	0.83	18
Young Urban Struggle	46,666	13.26	280
Towering Debt	51,269	14.56	187
NSF	586	0.17	5
Senior Survivors	5,294	1.50	80

Calgary
(City)
Calgary CMA
(Cont'd)

HOME LANGUAGE

2001 Estimates:		% Total
English	794,073	87.58
French	3,431	0.38
Arabic	3,361	0.37
Chinese	34,463	3.80
Croatian	988	0.11
Czech	510	0.06
Dutch	577	0.06
German	1,558	0.17
Greek	809	0.09
Gujarati	1,657	0.18
Hindi	1,133	0.12
Hungarian	1,200	0.13
Italian	2,351	0.26
Japanese	633	0.07
Korean	1,764	0.19
Lao	454	0.05
Persian (Farsi)	777	0.09
Polish	5,021	0.55
Portuguese	884	0.10
Punjabi	7,263	0.80
Russian	1,118	0.12
Serbian	494	0.05
Serbo-Croatian	700	0.08
Spanish	5,118	0.56
Tagalog (Pilipino)	3,685	0.41
Ukrainian	462	0.05
Urdu	1,121	0.12
Vietnamese	7,358	0.81
Other Languages	5,688	0.63
Multiple Responses	18,022	1.99
Total	906,673	100.00

BUILDING PERMITS

	1999	1998	1997
		$000	
Value	1,628,131	2,200,871	1,575,748

HOMES BUILT

	1999	1998	1997
No	8,130	10,515	7,996

TAXATION

Income Class:	1997	% Total
Under $5,000	70,440	11.77
$5,000-$10,000	68,810	11.50
$10,000-$15,000	73,960	12.36
$15,000-$20,000	57,330	9.58
$20,000-$25,000	49,280	8.23
$25,000-$30,000	45,490	7.60
$30,000-$40,000	74,000	12.36
$40,000-$50,000	51,390	8.59
$50,000 +	107,760	18.01
Total Returns, No.	598,470	
Total Income, $000	21,425,741	
Total Taxable Returns	450,620	
Total Tax, $000	4,708,752	
Average Income, $	35,801	
Average Tax, $	10,449	

VITAL STATISTICS

	1997	1996	1995	1994
Births	10,660	10,706	10,909	11,139
Deaths	4,041	4,108	3,913	3,691
Natural Increase	6,619	6,598	6,996	7,448
Marriages	4,438	4,561	4,814	4,968

Note: Latest available data.

MEDIA INFO
see Calgary, CMA

Rocky View No. 44
(Municipal District)
Calgary CMA

In census division No. 6.

POPULATION

July 1, 2001 Estimate	31,001
% Cdn. Total	0.10
% Change, '96 -'01	29.19
Avg. Annual Growth Rate, %	5.26
2003 Projected Population	34,207
2006 Projected Population	38,925
2001 Households Estimate	10,090
2003 Projected Households	11,230
2006 Projected Households	12,986

INCOME

% Above/Below National Average	+73
2001 Total Income Estimate	$1,133,640,000
% Cdn. Total	0.17
2001 Average Hhld. Income	$112,400
2001 Per Capita	$36,600
2003 Projected Total Income	$1,343,620,000
2006 Projected Total Income	$1,711,750,000

RETAIL SALES

% Above/Below National Average	-57
2001 Retail Sales Estimate	$119,410,000
% Cdn. Total	0.04
2001 per Household	$11,800
2001 per Capita	$3,900
2001 No. of Establishments	354
2003 Projected Retail Sales	$141,950,000
2006 Projected Retail Sales	$177,830,000

POPULATION

2001 Estimates:		
Total		31,001
Male		15,836
Female		15,165

Age Groups	Male	Female
0-4	933	907
5-9	1,138	1,087
10-14	1,335	1,234
15-19	1,345	1,208
20-24	1,126	1,039
25-29	922	905
30-34	905	958
35-39	1,132	1,224
40-44	1,378	1,416
45-49	1,423	1,407
50-54	1,255	1,190
55-59	983	871
60-64	753	637
65-69	561	444
70+	647	638

DAYTIME POPULATION

2001 Estimates:	
Working Population	5,164
At Home Population	12,045
Total	17,209

INCOME

2001 Estimates:	
Avg. Household Income	$112,353
Avg. Family Income	$116,958
Per Capita Income	$36,568
Male:	
Avg. Employment Income	$60,505
Avg. Employment Income (Full Time)	$76,466
Female:	
Avg. Employment Income	$31,374
Avg. Employment Income (Full Time)	$47,007

DISPOSABLE & DISCRETIONARY INCOME

2001 Estimates:	Per Hhld.
Disposable Income	$80,349
Discretionary Income 1 (minus Food & Shelter)	$58,806
Discretionary Income 2 (minus Food, Shelter, & Other Expenditures)	$44,314

LIQUID ASSETS

1999 Estimates:	Per Hhld.
Equity Investments	$298,244
Interest Bearing Investments	$157,764
Total Liquid Assets	$456,008

CREDIT DATA

July 2000:	
Pool of Credit	$230,008,841
Revolving Credit, No.	30,645
Fixed Loans, No.	9,904
Avg. Credit Limit, per Person	$17,616
Avg. Spent, per Person	$8,062
Satisfactory Ratings, No. per Person	2.98
Avg. No. of Cards, per Person	1.18

LABOUR FORCE

2001 Estimates:	
Male:	
In the Labour Force	10,808
Participation Rate	87.0
Employed	10,568
Unemployed	240
Unemployment Rate	2.2
Not in Labour Force	1,622
Female:	
In the Labour Force	8,584
Participation Rate	71.9
Employed	8,310
Unemployed	274
Unemployment Rate	3.2
Not in Labour Force	3,353

OCCUPATIONS BY MAJOR GROUPS

2001 Estimates:	Male	Female
Management	1,781	712
Business, Finance & Admin.	887	3,018
Natural & Applied Sciences & Related	1,139	231
Health	214	588
Social Sciences, Gov't Services & Religion	223	145
Education	327	535
Arts, Culture, Recreation & Sport	266	330
Sales & Service	1,560	1,972
Trades, Transport & Equipment Operators & Related	2,147	176
Primary Industries	1,860	714
Processing, Mfg. & Utilities	389	96

LEVEL OF SCHOOLING

2001 Estimates:	
Population 15 years +	24,367
Less than Grade 9	825
Grades 9-13 w/o Certif.	5,413
Grade 9-13 with Certif.	2,402
Trade Certif. /Dip.	733
Non-Univ. w/o Certif./Dip.	1,601
Non-Univ. with Certif./Dip.	5,231
Univ. w/o Degree	3,063
Univ. w/o Degree/Certif.	1,627
Univ. with Certif.	1,436
Univ. with Degree	5,099

Alberta

AVERAGE HOUSEHOLD EXPENDITURES

2001 Estimates:	
Food	$9,307
Shelter	$16,070
Clothing	$3,892
Transportation	$11,642
Health & Personal Care	$2,991
Recr'n, Read'g & Education	$6,452
Taxes & Securities	$32,437
Other	$14,591
Total Expenditures	$97,382

PRIVATE HOUSEHOLDS

2001 Estimates:	
Private Households, Total	10,090
Pop. in Private Households	30,406
Average no. per Household	3.0

FAMILIES

2001 Estimates:	
Families in Private Households	8,994
Husband-Wife Families	8,628
Lone-Parent Families	366
Aver. No. Persons per Family	3.2
Aver. No. Sons/Daughters at Home	1.3

HOUSING

2001 Estimates:	
Occupied Private Dwellings	10,090
Owned	8,892
Rented	1,198
Single-Detached House	9,671
Semi-Detached House	27
Row Houses	12
Apartment, 5 or Fewer Storeys	14
Apartment, Detached Duplex	26
Other Single-Attached	13
Movable Dwellings	327

VEHICLES

2001 Estimates:	
Model Yrs. '81-'96, No.	14,575
% Total	77.82
Model Yrs. '97-'98, No.	2,590
% Total	13.83
'99 Vehicles registered in Model Yr. '99, No.	1,565
% Total	8.36
Total No. '81-'99	18,730

LEGAL MARITAL STATUS

2001 Estimates: (Age 15+)	
Single (Never Married)	5,743
Legally Married (Not Separated)	16,585
Legally Married (Separated)	334
Widowed	541
Divorced	1,164

Alberta

Rocky View No. 44
(Municipal District)
Calgary CMA
(Cont'd)

PSYTE CATEGORIES

2001 Estimates	No. of House-holds	% of Total Hhds.	Index
Canadian Establishment	191	1.89	1,137
The Affluentials	996	9.87	1,544
Suburban Executives	1,839	18.23	1,272
Boomers & Teens	1,774	17.58	981
Kindergarten Boom	217	2.15	82
Blue Collar Winners	4,555	45.14	1,793
Old Towns' New Fringe	43	0.43	11
Rustic Prosperity	475	4.71	261

FINANÇIAL P$YTE

2001 Estimates	No. of House-holds	% of Total Hhds.	Index
Platinum Estates	1,187	11.76	1,460
Four Star Investors	3,613	35.81	713
Canadian Comfort	4,555	45.14	465
Mortgages & Minivans	217	2.15	33
Tractors & Tradelines	518	5.13	90

HOME LANGUAGE

2001 Estimates:		% Total
English	29,652	95.65
Chinese	102	0.33
Croatian	61	0.20
Czech	34	0.11
Dutch	32	0.10
German	501	1.62
Gujarati	43	0.14
Italian	60	0.19
Korean	20	0.06
Punjabi	195	0.63
Other Languages	51	0.16
Multiple Responses	250	0.81
Total	31,001	100.00

BUILDING PERMITS

	1999	1998 $000	1997
Value	132,419	131,021	123,960

HOMES BUILT

	1999	1998	1997
No	495	590	548

TAXATION

Income Class:	1997	% Total
Under $5,000	310	11.83
$5,000-$10,000	270	10.31
$10,000-$15,000	290	11.07
$15,000-$20,000	230	8.78
$20,000-$25,000	230	8.78
$25,000-$30,000	220	8.40
$30,000-$40,000	370	14.12
$40,000-$50,000	250	9.54
$50,000 +	460	17.56
Total Returns, No.	2,620	
Total Income, $000	83,695	
Total Taxable Returns	2,040	
Total Tax, $000	16,623	
Average Income, $	31,945	
Average Tax, $	8,149	

VITAL STATISTICS

	1997	1996	1995	1994
Births	217	233	110	119
Deaths	70	74	38	29
Natural Increase	147	159	72	90
Marriages	119	113	65	45

Note: Latest available data.

MEDIA INFO
see Calgary, CMA

Camrose
(Census Agglomeration)

The Census Agglomeration of Camrose consists solely of Camrose, C, in census division No. 10.

POPULATION

July 1, 2001 Estimate	14,355
% Cdn. Total	0.05
% Change, '96 -'01	2.27
Avg. Annual Growth Rate, %	0.45
2003 Projected Population	14,470
2006 Projected Population	14,336
2001 Households Estimate	5,942
2003 Projected Households	6,048
2006 Projected Households	6,137

INCOME

% Above/Below National Average	-9
2001 Total Income Estimate	$275,710,000
% Cdn. Total	0.04
2001 Average Hhld. Income	$46,400
2001 Per Capita	$19,200
2003 Projected Total Income	$291,060,000
2006 Projected Total Income	$310,940,000

RETAIL SALES

% Above/Below National Average	+97
2001 Retail Sales Estimate	$253,030,000
% Cdn. Total	0.09
2001 per Household	$42,600
2001 per Capita	$17,600
2001 No. of Establishments	178
2003 Projected Retail Sales	$271,650,000
2006 Projected Retail Sales	$294,070,000

POPULATION

2001 Estimates:		
Total		14,355
Male		6,802
Female		7,553
Age Groups	Male	Female
0-4	416	410
5-9	454	443
10-14	495	488
15-19	504	511
20-24	480	487
25-29	459	463
30-34	455	475
35-39	488	496
40-44	485	503
45-49	440	470
50-54	374	421
55-59	316	367
60-64	282	337
65-69	272	343
70+	882	1,339

DAYTIME POPULATION

2001 Estimates:	
Working Population	6,743
At Home Population	7,612
Total	14,355

INCOME

2001 Estimates:	
Avg. Household Income	$46,400
Avg. Family Income	$55,447
Per Capita Income	$19,206
Male:	
Avg. Employment Income	$29,933
Avg. Employment Income (Full Time)	$40,808
Female:	
Avg. Employment Income	$17,751
Avg. Employment Income (Full Time)	$29,172

DISPOSABLE & DISCRETIONARY INCOME

2001 Estimates:	Per Hhld.
Disposable Income	$35,960
Discretionary Income 1 (minus Food & Shelter)	$24,192
Discretionary Income 2 (minus Food, Shelter, & Other Expenditures)	$15,788

LIQUID ASSETS

1999 Estimates:	Per Hhld.
Equity Investments	$70,524
Interest Bearing Investments	$59,510
Total Liquid Assets	$130,034

CREDIT DATA

July 2000:	
Pool of Credit	$128,155,508
Revolving Credit, No.	24,173
Fixed Loans, No.	7,635
Avg. Credit Limit, per Person	$11,158
Avg. Spent, per Person	$5,106
Satisfactory Ratings, No. per Person	2.66
Avg. No. of Cards, per Person	0.96

LABOUR FORCE

2001 Estimates:	
Male:	
In the Labour Force	3,776
Participation Rate	69.5
Employed	3,587
Unemployed	189
Unemployment Rate	5.0
Not in Labour Force	1,661
Female:	
In the Labour Force	3,441
Participation Rate	55.4
Employed	3,219
Unemployed	222
Unemployment Rate	6.5
Not in Labour Force	2,771

OCCUPATIONS BY MAJOR GROUPS

2001 Estimates:	Male	Female
Management	397	133
Business, Finance & Admin.	242	1,013
Natural & Applied Sciences & Related	170	22
Health	65	456
Social Sciences, Gov't Services & Religion	71	74
Education	143	107
Arts, Culture, Recreation & Sport	64	100
Sales & Service	944	1,328
Trades, Transport & Equipment Operators & Related	915	61
Primary Industries	433	63
Processing, Mfg. & Utilities	301	n.a.

LEVEL OF SCHOOLING

2001 Estimates:	
Population 15 years +	11,649
Less than Grade 9	1,204
Grades 9-13 w/o Certif.	3,604
Grade 9-13 with Certif.	1,320
Trade Certif. /Dip.	436
Non-Univ. w/o Certif./Dip.	622
Non-Univ. with Certif./Dip.	2,450
Univ. w/o Degree	979
Univ. w/o Degree/Certif.	504
Univ. with Certif.	475
Univ. with Degree	1,034

Camrose
(Census Agglomeration)
(Cont'd)

AVERAGE HOUSEHOLD EXPENDITURES

2001 Estimates:
Food	$5,615
Shelter	$8,175
Clothing	$1,913
Transportation	$6,508
Health & Personal Care	$1,926
Recr'n, Read'g & Education	$3,053
Taxes & Securities	$10,825
Other	$7,603
Total Expenditures	$45,618

PRIVATE HOUSEHOLDS

2001 Estimates:
Private Households, Total	5,942
Pop. in Private Households	13,843
Average no. per Household	2.3

FAMILIES

2001 Estimates:
Families in Private Households	3,939
Husband-Wife Families	3,455
Lone-Parent Families	484
Aver. No. Persons per Family	2.9
Aver. No. Sons/Daughters at Home	1.1

HOUSING

2001 Estimates:
Occupied Private Dwellings	5,942
Owned	4,046
Rented	1,896
Single-Detached House	4,160
Semi-Detached House	254
Row Houses	157
Apartment, 5 or Fewer Storeys	991
Apartment, Detached Duplex	248
Movable Dwellings	132

VEHICLES

2001 Estimates:
Model Yrs. '81-'96, No.	7,456
% Total	85.18
Model Yrs. '97-'98, No.	858
% Total	9.80
'99 Vehicles registered in Model Yr. '99, No.	439
% Total	5.02
Total No. '81-'99	8,753

LEGAL MARITAL STATUS

2001 Estimates: (Age 15+)
Single (Never Married)	3,011
Legally Married (Not Separated)	6,383
Legally Married (Separated)	317
Widowed	1,155
Divorced	783

PSYTE CATEGORIES

2001 Estimates
	No. of House -holds	% of Total Hhds.	Index
Town Boomers	913	15.37	1,516
The New Frontier	457	7.69	510
Old Leafy Towns	349	5.87	230
Quiet Towns	4,104	69.07	3,246

FINANCIAL P$YTE

2001 Estimates
	No. of House -holds	% of Total Hhds.	Index
Canadian Comfort	913	15.37	158
Miners & Credit-Liners	457	7.69	243
Bills & Wills	349	5.87	71
Limited Budgets	4,104	69.07	2,222

HOME LANGUAGE

2001 Estimates:
		% Total
English	14,174	98.74
French	11	0.08
Chinese	20	0.14
Khmer (Cambodian)	32	0.22
Polish	10	0.07
Spanish	27	0.19
Ukrainian	23	0.16
Other Languages	21	0.15
Multiple Responses	37	0.26
Total	14,355	100.00

BUILDING PERMITS

	1999	1998	1997
		$000	
Value	20,240	13,567	15,240

HOMES BUILT

	1999	1998	1997
No	118	95	44

TAXATION

Income Class:	1997	% Total
Under $5,000	1,290	10.67
$5,000-$10,000	1,630	13.48
$10,000-$15,000	2,030	16.79
$15,000-$20,000	1,430	11.83
$20,000-$25,000	1,160	9.59
$25,000-$30,000	1,020	8.44
$30,000-$40,000	1,420	11.75
$40,000-$50,000	840	6.95
$50,000 +	1,270	10.50
Total Returns, No.	12,090	
Total Income, $000	306,471	
Total Taxable Returns	8,440	
Total Tax, $000	50,173	
Average Income, $	25,349	
Average Tax, $	5,945	

VITAL STATISTICS

	1997	1996	1995	1994
Births	135	142	142	156
Deaths	181	192	175	181
Natural Increase	-46	-50	-33	-25
Marriages	124	110	107	137

Note: Latest available data.

COMMUNITY NEWSPAPER(S)

	Total Circulation
Camrose: The Booster	12,569
Camrose: Camrose Canadian	13,963

RADIO STATION(S)

	Power
CFCW	n.a.
CKJR	n.a.

Clearwater No. 99
(Municipal District)

In census division No. 9.

POPULATION

July 1, 2001 Estimate	12,001
% Cdn. Total	0.04
% Change, '96 -'01	7.40
Avg. Annual Growth Rate, %	1.44
2003 Projected Population	12,419
2006 Projected Population	12,752
2001 Households Estimate	4,422
2003 Projected Households	4,639
2006 Projected Households	4,892

INCOME

% Above/Below National Average	-14
2001 Total Income Estimate	$217,630,000
% Cdn. Total	0.03
2001 Average Hhld. Income	$49,200
2001 Per Capita	$18,100
2003 Projected Total Income	$238,650,000
2006 Projected Total Income	$268,440,000

RETAIL SALES

% Above/Below National Average	+87
2001 Retail Sales Estimate	$201,010,000
% Cdn. Total	0.07
2001 per Household	$45,500
2001 per Capita	$16,700
2001 No. of Establishments	175
2003 Projected Retail Sales	$222,480,000
2006 Projected Retail Sales	$249,640,000

POPULATION

2001 Estimates:
Total		12,001
Male		6,290
Female		5,711
Age Groups	Male	Female
0-4	389	367
5-9	470	408
10-14	530	444
15-19	524	453
20-24	446	381
25-29	374	348
30-34	397	399
35-39	476	464
40-44	488	461
45-49	447	415
50-54	397	379
55-59	351	326
60-64	313	264
65-69	260	199
70+	428	403

DAYTIME POPULATION

2001 Estimates:
Working Population	4,835
At Home Population	5,062
Total	9,897

INCOME

2001 Estimates:
Avg. Household Income	$49,215
Avg. Family Income	$52,135
Per Capita Income	$18,134
Male:	
Avg. Employment Income	$30,035
Avg. Employment Income (Full Time)	$35,708
Female:	
Avg. Employment Income	$13,703
Avg. Employment Income (Full Time)	$18,933

Alberta

DISPOSABLE & DISCRETIONARY INCOME

2001 Estimates:	*Per Hhld.*
Disposable Income	$38,400
Discretionary Income 1 (minus Food & Shelter)	$27,241
Discretionary Income 2 (minus Food, Shelter, & Other Expenditures)	$18,350

LIQUID ASSETS

1999 Estimates:	*Per Hhld.*
Equity Investments	$65,189
Interest Bearing Investments	$59,379
Total Liquid Assets	$124,568

CREDIT DATA

July 2000:
Pool of Credit	$152,938,343
Revolving Credit, No.	19,528
Fixed Loans, No.	10,742
Avg. Credit Limit, per Person	$12,914
Avg. Spent, per Person	$6,722
Satisfactory Ratings, No. per Person	2.46
Avg. No. of Cards, per Person	0.79

LABOUR FORCE

2001 Estimates:
Male:	
In the Labour Force	4,195
Participation Rate	85.6
Employed	3,879
Unemployed	316
Unemployment Rate	7.5
Not in Labour Force	706
Female:	
In the Labour Force	3,202
Participation Rate	71.3
Employed	3,086
Unemployed	116
Unemployment Rate	3.6
Not in Labour Force	1,290

OCCUPATIONS BY MAJOR GROUPS

2001 Estimates:	Male	Female
Management	210	109
Business, Finance & Admin.	83	878
Natural & Applied Sciences & Related	177	n.a.
Health	25	128
Social Sciences, Gov't Services & Religion	49	66
Education	58	124
Arts, Culture, Recreation & Sport	65	39
Sales & Service	354	949
Trades, Transport & Equipment Operators & Related	1,303	115
Primary Industries	1,483	753
Processing, Mfg. & Utilities	378	17

Alberta

Clearwater No. 99
(Municipal District)
(Cont'd)

LEVEL OF SCHOOLING

2001 Estimates:
Population 15 years +	9,393
Less than Grade 9	972
Grades 9-13 w/o Certif.	3,544
Grade 9-13 with Certif.	1,361
Trade Certif./Dip.	309
Non-Univ. w/o Certif./Dip.	569
Non-Univ. with Certif./Dip.	1,733
Univ. w/o Degree	455
Univ. w/o Degree/Certif.	213
Univ. with Certif.	242
Univ. with Degree	450

AVERAGE HOUSEHOLD EXPENDITURES

2001 Estimates:
Food	$6,377
Shelter	$6,768
Clothing	$2,337
Transportation	$6,909
Health & Personal Care	$1,980
Recr'n, Read'g & Education	$3,340
Taxes & Securities	$10,712
Other	$9,546
Total Expenditures	$47,969

PRIVATE HOUSEHOLDS

2001 Estimates:
Private Households, Total	4,422
Pop. in Private Households	11,787
Average no. per Household	2.7

FAMILIES

2001 Estimates:
Families in Private Households	3,605
Husband-Wife Families	3,367
Lone-Parent Families	238
Aver. No. Persons per Family	3.1
Aver. No. Sons/Daughters at Home	1.2

HOUSING

2001 Estimates:
Occupied Private Dwellings	4,422
Owned	3,898
Rented	524
Single-Detached House	3,231
Semi-Detached House	17
Movable Dwellings	1,174

VEHICLES

2001 Estimates:
Model Yrs. '81-'96, No.	6,785
% Total	81.05
Model Yrs. '97-'98, No.	1,035
% Total	12.36
'99 Vehicles registered in Model Yr. '99, No.	551
% Total	6.58
Total No. '81-'99	8,371

LEGAL MARITAL STATUS

2001 Estimates: (Age 15+)
Single (Never Married)	2,206
Legally Married (Not Separated)	5,984
Legally Married (Separated)	219
Widowed	403
Divorced	581

PSYTE CATEGORIES

2001 Estimates	No. of House-holds	% of Total Hhds.	Index
The New Frontier	197	4.45	295
Rustic Prosperity	95	2.15	119
Pick-ups & Dirt Bikes	2,869	64.88	7,770
The Grain Belt	680	15.38	2,596
Quiet Towns	83	1.88	88
Rod & Rifle	369	8.34	361
Big Country Families	121	2.74	192

FINANCIAL PSYTE

2001 Estimates	No. of House-holds	% of Total Hhds.	Index
Miners & Credit-Liners	197	4.45	141
Tractors & Tradelines	95	2.15	38
Country Credit	3,549	80.26	1,187
Rural Family Blues	490	11.08	137
Limited Budgets	83	1.88	60

HOME LANGUAGE

2001 Estimates:		% Total
English	11,850	98.74
German	75	0.62
Ojibway	53	0.44
Polish	12	0.10
Multiple Responses	11	0.09
Total	12,001	100.00

BUILDING PERMITS

	1999	1998 $000	1997
Value	7,961	9,202	8,397

TAXATION

Income Class:	1997	% Total
Under $5,000	250	16.34
$5,000-$10,000	240	15.69
$10,000-$15,000	260	16.99
$15,000-$20,000	170	11.11
$20,000-$25,000	120	7.84
$25,000-$30,000	90	5.88
$30,000-$40,000	160	10.46
$40,000-$50,000	90	5.88
$50,000 +	160	10.46
Total Returns, No.	1,530	
Total Income, $000	34,640	
Total Taxable Returns	960	
Total Tax, $000	5,682	
Average Income, $	22,641	
Average Tax, $	5,919	

VITAL STATISTICS

	1997	1996	1995	1994
Births	121	123	126	120
Deaths	46	38	30	33
Natural Increase	75	85	96	87
Marriages	59	57	43	46

Note: Latest available data.

Edmonton
(Census Metropolitan Area)

POPULATION

July 1, 2001 Estimate	956,532
% Cdn. Total	3.07
% Change, '96 -'01	7.82
Avg. Annual Growth Rate, %	1.52
2003 Projected Population	978,863
2006 Projected Population	1,005,726
2001 Households Estimate	368,632
2003 Projected Households	381,927
2006 Projected Households	400,188

INCOME

% Above/Below National Average	+4
2001 Total Income Estimate	$21,039,850,000
% Cdn. Total	3.21
2001 Average Hhld. Income	$57,100
2001 Per Capita	$22,000
2003 Projected Total Income	$22,777,800,000
2006 Projected Total Income	$25,527,410,000

RETAIL SALES

% Above/Below National Average	+3
2001 Retail Sales Estimate	$8,837,330,000
% Cdn. Total	3.17
2001 per Household	$24,000
2001 per Capita	$9,200
2001 No. of Establishments	6,734
2003 Projected Retail Sales	$9,659,910,000
2006 Projected Retail Sales	$10,845,360,000

POPULATION

2001 Estimates:		
Total		956,532
Male		473,903
Female		482,629
Age Groups	Male	Female
0-4	32,228	30,840
5-9	33,386	31,864
10-14	34,499	32,747
15-19	34,028	32,391
20-24	33,115	32,431
25-29	33,336	33,611
30-34	36,365	36,852
35-39	40,254	40,484
40-44	40,524	40,618
45-49	36,979	36,936
50-54	30,450	30,429
55-59	23,672	23,796
60-64	18,980	19,437
65-69	15,768	16,814
70+	30,319	43,379

DAYTIME POPULATION

2001 Estimates:	
Working Population	498,814
At Home Population	458,909
Total	957,723

INCOME

2001 Estimates:
Avg. Household Income	$57,075
Avg. Family Income	$64,173
Per Capita Income	$21,996

Male:
Avg. Employment Income	$36,688
Avg. Employment Income (Full Time)	$48,843

Female:
Avg. Employment Income	$21,814
Avg. Employment Income (Full Time)	$32,759

DISPOSABLE & DISCRETIONARY INCOME

2001 Estimates:	Per Hhld.
Disposable Income	$43,823
Discretionary Income 1 (minus Food & Shelter)	$30,097
Discretionary Income 2 (minus Food, Shelter, & Other Expenditures)	$21,460

LIQUID ASSETS

1999 Estimates:	Per Hhld.
Equity Investments	$82,692
Interest Bearing Investments	$70,469
Total Liquid Assets	$153,161

CREDIT DATA

July 2000:	
Pool of Credit	$10,041,263,502
Revolving Credit, No.	1,853,025
Fixed Loans, No.	584,525
Avg. Credit Limit, per Person	$12,731
Avg. Spent, per Person	$5,855
Satisfactory Ratings, No. per Person	2.93
Avg. No. of Cards, per Person	1.07

LABOUR FORCE

2001 Estimates:
Male:
In the Labour Force	290,158
Participation Rate	77.6
Employed	271,825
Unemployed	18,333
Unemployment Rate	6.3
Not in Labour Force	83,632

Female:
In the Labour Force	248,565
Participation Rate	64.2
Employed	233,342
Unemployed	15,223
Unemployment Rate	6.1
Not in Labour Force	138,613

OCCUPATIONS BY MAJOR GROUPS

2001 Estimates:	Male	Female
Management	32,026	13,763
Business, Finance & Admin.	28,750	79,368
Natural & Applied Sciences & Related	24,157	4,676
Health	5,732	20,627
Social Sciences, Gov't Services & Religion	6,891	8,399
Education	7,707	11,783
Arts, Culture, Recreation & Sport	6,117	7,341
Sales & Service	64,210	83,822
Trades, Transport & Equipment Operators & Related	74,958	4,287
Primary Industries	13,749	3,415
Processing, Mfg. & Utilities	20,729	4,825

LEVEL OF SCHOOLING

2001 Estimates:
Population 15 years +	760,968
Less than Grade 9	52,818
Grades 9-13 w/o Certif.	187,503
Grade 9-13 with Certif.	91,758
Trade Certif./Dip.	26,017
Non-Univ. w/o Certif./Dip.	51,952
Non-Univ. with Certif./Dip.	160,593
Univ. w/o Degree	80,928
Univ. w/o Degree/Certif.	41,026
Univ. with Certif.	39,902
Univ. with Degree	109,399

Edmonton
(Census Metropolitan Area)
(Cont'd)

AVERAGE HOUSEHOLD EXPENDITURES

2001 Estimates:

Food	$6,351
Shelter	$9,608
Clothing	$2,320
Transportation	$6,606
Health & Personal Care	$1,966
Recr'n, Read'g & Education	$3,915
Taxes & Securities	$14,996
Other	$8,671
Total Expenditures	$54,433

PRIVATE HOUSEHOLDS

2001 Estimates:

Private Households, Total	368,632
Pop. in Private Households	939,436
Average no. per Household	2.5

FAMILIES

2001 Estimates:

Families in Private Households	266,419
Husband-Wife Families	227,567
Lone-Parent Families	38,852
Aver. No. Persons per Family	3.1
Aver. No. Sons/Daughters at Home	1.2

HOUSING

2001 Estimates:

Occupied Private Dwellings	368,632
Owned	240,204
Rented	127,741
Band Housing	687
Single-Detached House	224,048
Semi-Detached House	11,649
Row Houses	32,410
Apartment, 5+ Storeys	22,690
Owned Apartment, 5+ Storeys	2,867
Apartment, 5 or Fewer Storeys	64,514
Apartment, Detached Duplex	6,813
Other Single-Attached	364
Movable Dwellings	6,144

VEHICLES

2001 Estimates:

Model Yrs. '81-'96, No.	451,444
% Total	79.62
Model Yrs. '97-'98, No.	69,045
% Total	12.18
'99 Vehicles registered in Model Yr. '99, No.	46,543
% Total	8.21
Total No. '81-'99	567,032

LEGAL MARITAL STATUS

2001 Estimates: (Age 15+)

Single (Never Married)	236,901
Legally Married (Not Separated)	405,529
Legally Married (Separated)	22,461
Widowed	38,747
Divorced	57,330

PSYTE CATEGORIES

2001 Estimates	No. of House-holds	% of Total Hhds.	Index
The Affluentials	2,502	0.68	106
Urban Gentry	5,108	1.39	77
Suburban Executives	9,533	2.59	180
Mortgaged in Suburbia	9,413	2.55	184
Technocrafts & Bureaucrats	26,484	7.18	255
Boomers & Teens	3,130	0.85	47
Stable Suburban Families	5,450	1.48	113
Small City Elite	2,950	0.80	47
Old Bungalow Burbs	15,448	4.19	253
Suburban Nesters	2,263	0.61	38
Brie & Chablis	692	0.19	21
Aging Erudites	10,963	2.97	197
Satellite Suburbs	18,279	4.96	173
Kindergarten Boom	46,777	12.69	484
Blue Collar Winners	14,819	4.02	160
Town Boomers	328	0.09	9
Old Towns' New Fringe	16,904	4.59	117
Rustic Prosperity	4,750	1.29	71
Pick-ups & Dirt Bikes	1,841	0.50	60
The Grain Belt	283	0.08	13
High Rise Melting Pot	289	0.08	5
Conservative Homebodies	31,487	8.54	237
High Rise Sunsets	3,525	0.96	67
Young Urban Professionals	4,939	1.34	71
Young Urban Mix	6,272	1.70	80
Young Urban Intelligentsia	12,465	3.38	222
University Enclaves	16,230	4.40	216
Young City Singles	33,335	9.04	394
Old Leafy Towns	1,907	0.52	20
Town Renters	13,409	3.64	421
Nesters & Young Homesteaders	1,891	0.51	22

2001 Estimates	No. of House-holds	% of Total Hhds.	Index
Quiet Towns	2,658	0.72	34
Rod & Rifle	1,249	0.34	15
Big Country Families	1,024	0.28	19
Old Cdn. Rustics	221	0.06	6
Struggling Downtowns	23,757	6.44	205
Aged Pensioners	4,303	1.17	88
Big City Stress	6,808	1.85	164
Old Grey Towers	2,195	0.60	108

FINANCIAL P$YTE

2001 Estimates	No. of House-holds	% of Total Hhds.	Index
Platinum Estates	2,502	0.68	84
Four Star Investors	17,771	4.82	96
Successful Suburbanites	41,347	11.22	169
Canadian Comfort	38,639	10.48	108
Urban Heights	16,594	4.50	105
Miners & Credit-Liners	15,448	4.19	132
Mortgages & Minivans	46,777	12.69	192
Tractors & Tradelines	21,654	5.87	103
Bills & Wills	39,666	10.76	130
Country Credit	2,124	0.58	9
Revolving Renters	5,416	1.47	32
Young Urban Struggle	28,695	7.78	164
Rural Family Blues	2,273	0.62	8
Limited Budgets	2,879	0.78	25
Towering Debt	70,790	19.20	246
NSF	6,808	1.85	52
Senior Survivors	6,498	1.76	94

Alberta

HOME LANGUAGE

2001 Estimates:		% Total
English	850,170	88.88
French	5,867	0.61
Arabic	2,599	0.27
Chinese	27,579	2.88
Dutch	485	0.05
German	2,932	0.31
Greek	505	0.05
Gujarati	1,017	0.11
Hindi	1,640	0.17
Hungarian	487	0.05
Italian	2,547	0.27
Khmer (Cambodian)	587	0.06
Korean	1,169	0.12
Persian (Farsi)	493	0.05
Polish	5,855	0.61
Portuguese	1,840	0.19
Punjabi	6,727	0.70
Russian	980	0.10
Serbo-Croatian	735	0.08
Spanish	4,360	0.46
Tagalog (Pilipino)	3,378	0.35
Ukrainian	2,393	0.25
Urdu	639	0.07
Vietnamese	5,375	0.56
Other Languages	6,316	0.66
Multiple Responses	19,857	2.08
Total	956,532	100.00

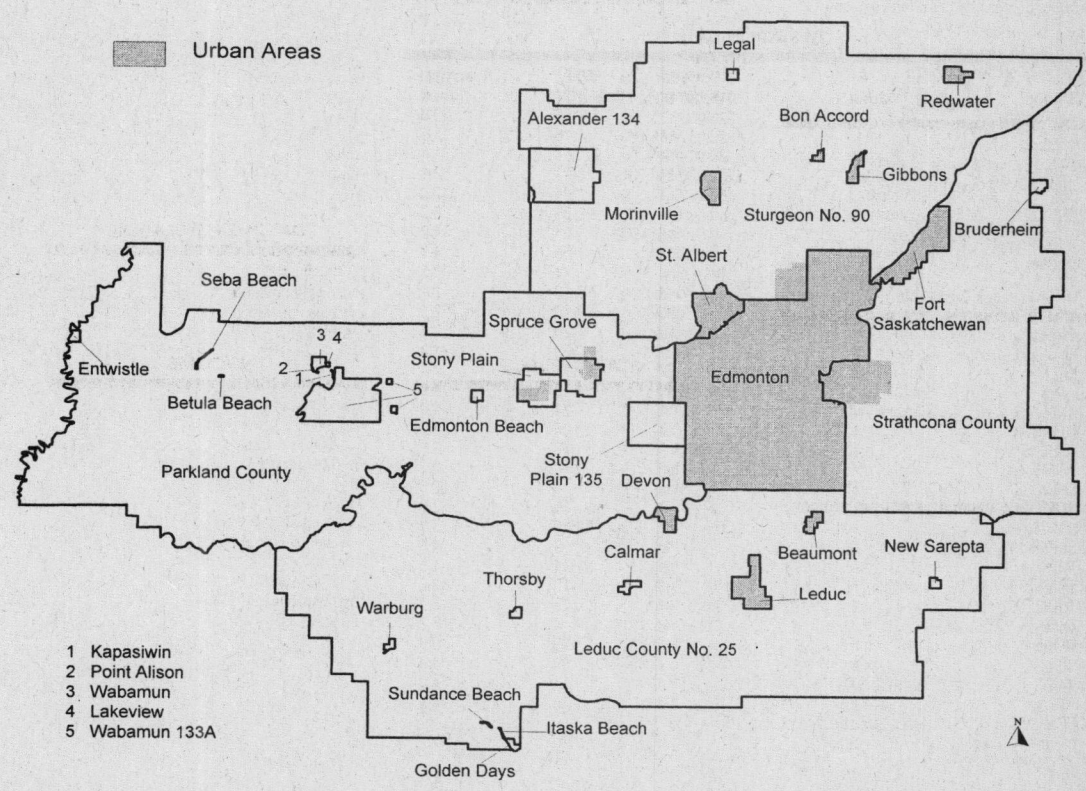

Urban Areas

Legal
Redwater
Alexander 134
Bon Accord
Gibbons
Morinville
Sturgeon No. 90
Bruderheim
St. Albert
Seba Beach
Spruce Grove
Fort Saskatchewan
3 4
Stony Plain
2 1
Edmonton
5
Betula Beach
Entwistle
Edmonton Beach
Strathcona County
Stony Plain 135
Devon
Parkland County
Calmar
Beaumont
New Sarepta
Thorsby
Leduc
Warburg
Leduc County No. 25
Sundance Beach
Itaska Beach
Golden Days

1 Kapasiwin
2 Point Alison
3 Wabamun
4 Lakeview
5 Wabamun 133A

N

Alberta

Edmonton
(Census Metropolitan Area)
(Cont'd)

HOMES BUILT

	1999	1998	1997
No	5,639	5,359	4,143

TAXATION

Income Class:	1997	% Total
Under $5,000	80,900	12.76
$5,000-$10,000	79,760	12.58
$10,000-$15,000	84,410	13.32
$15,000-$20,000	62,970	9.94
$20,000-$25,000	52,830	8.34
$25,000-$30,000	49,270	7.77
$30,000-$40,000	78,400	12.37
$40,000-$50,000	52,730	8.32
$50,000 +	92,590	14.61
Total Returns, No.	633,780	
Total Income, $000	18,427,571	
Total Taxable Returns	457,060	
Total Tax, $000	3,589,939	
Average Income, $	29,076	
Average Tax, $	7,854	

BUILDING PERMITS

	1999	1998	1997
		$000	
Value	1,123,693	1,167,192	878,758

RADIO STATION DATA

Station	Market	Format	Wkly. Reach%*	Aver. Hrs. Tuned
All Stations			95	22.2
CBX	Edmonton	News, Info.	10	11.8
CBX-FM	Edmonton	Multi-format	7	9.8
CFBR-FM	Edmonton	AOR	23	8.7
CFCW	Edmonton/Camrose	Country	8	14.3
CFMG-FM	Edmonton	Adult Contemp.	15	12.5
CFRN	Edmonton	Oldies	8	7.6
CFWE-FM	Edmonton	Country, Aboriginal	n.a.	n.a.
CHED	Edmonton	News, Talk	26	10.2
CHFA	Edmonton	Adult Contemp.	-	16.3
CHQT	Edmonton	Soft Adult Contemp.	11	13.8
CIRK-FM	Edmonton	Rock	16	10.2
CISN-FM	Edmonton	Contemp. Country	18	10.4
CJCA	Edmonton	Contemp. Christian	n.a.	n.a.
CKER-FM	Edmonton	Ethnic, Multiling.	n.a.	n.a.
CKNG-FM	Edmonton	Contemp. Hit Radio	34	9.5
CKRA-FM	Edmonton	Hot Adult Contemp.	20	7.9
CKUA	Edmonton	Multi-format	n.a.	n.a.

BBM Spring 2000 Radio Reach Survey; area coverage.
*Mon-Sun 5a.m - 1a.m , All Persons 12+

TV STATION DATA

Station	Market	Network Affiliation	Wkly. Reach%*	Aver. Hrs. Tuned
All Stations			96	22.3
A & E	n.a.	Ind.	18	3.5
ACCESS	Edmonton	n.a.	14	1.4
CBXFT	Edmonton	SRC	-	2.1
CBXT	Edmonton	CBC	44	3.0
CFRN	Edmonton	CTV	66	5.2
CITV	Edmonton	Ind.	65	4.9
CKEM	Edmonton	Ind.	58	4.1
CNN	n.a.	Ind.	4	3.3
FAMILY	n.a.	Ind.	8	2.1
HISTTV	n.a.	Ind.	6	2.5
KAYU	Spokane WA	FOX	20	2.1
KHQ	Spokane WA	NBC	23	1.9
KREM	Spokane WA	CBS	31	2.4
KSPS	Spokane WA	PBS	13	1.6
KXLY	Spokane WA	ABC	24	2.0
NEWSWD	n.a.	CBC	6	1.9
OTHERS	n.a.	n.a.	8	3.9
PRIME	n.a.	Ind.	10	2.2
SHWCSE	n.a.	Ind.	4	2.8
SNET	n.a.	CTV	11	2.8
SPACE	n.a.	Ind.	6	3.2
SUPER	n.a.	Ind.	3	4.8
TLC	n.a.	Ind.	14	1.9
TNN	Nashville TN	Ind.	10	2.2
TOON	n.a.	Ind.	12	2.3
TREE	n.a.	Ind.	4	3.2
TSN	n.a.	Ind.	15	3.9
VCR	n.a.	n.a.	35	4.0
WTBS	Atlanta GA	Ind.	17	4.0
YTV	n.a.	Ind.	16	3.5

BBM Spring 2000 TV Reach Survey; CMA coverage.
*Mon-Sun 6a.m - 2a.m , All Persons 2 +

VITAL STATISTICS

	1997	1996	1995	1994
Births	10,866	11,490	11,985	12,553
Deaths	4,936	4,938	4,886	4,906
Natural Increase	5,930	6,552	7,099	7,647
Marriages	5,194	5,206	5,496	5,547

Note: Latest available data.

DAILY NEWSPAPER(S)

	Circulation Average Paid
Edmonton Journal	
Fri	161,905
Sun	134,462
Mon-Thu, Sat	137,432
The Edmonton Sun	
Sun	112,133
Mon-Sat	74,367

COMMUNITY NEWSPAPER(S)

	Total Circulation
Beaumont: La Nouvelle de Beaumont	2,255
Calmar: Calmar Community Voice (biwkly)	n.a.
Devon: Devon Dispatch	5,646
Edmonton: Edmonton Examiner	172,066
Edmonton: Le Franco Albertain	3,050
Edmonton: Western Catholic Reporter	37,015
Edmonton: Edmonton Jewish Life (mthly)	n.a.
Fort Saskatchewan: Fort Saskatchewan Record	4,084
Fort Saskatchewan: Fort Saskatchewan This Week	7,822
Leduc: Leduc Representative	12,341
Morinville: Morinville Mirror	6,681
Morinville: The Free Press	9,973
Redwater: Redwater Tribune	5,600
Redwater: The Review	9,104
Spruce Grove: The Examiner	8,570
St. Albert: Saint City News	21,655
St. Albert: St. Albert Gazette	
Wed	23,161
Sat	16,897
Stony Plain: Stony Plain Reporter	9,095
Strathcona County: Strathcona County This Week	22,954
Wabamun: Wabamun Community Voice (biwkly)	n.a.

Edmonton
(City)
Edmonton CMA
In census division No. 11.

POPULATION

July 1, 2001 Estimate	668,093
% Cdn. Total	2.15
% Change, '96 -'01	5.40
Avg. Annual Growth Rate, %	1.06
2003 Projected Population	674,399
2006 Projected Population	679,313
2001 Households Estimate	271,239
2003 Projected Households	277,713
2006 Projected Households	286,018

INCOME

% Above/Below National Average	same
2001 Total Income Estimate	$14,078,960,000
% Cdn. Total	2.14
2001 Average Hhld. Income	$51,900
2001 Per Capita	$21,100
2003 Projected Total Income	$14,959,760,000
2006 Projected Total Income	$16,300,520,000

RETAIL SALES

% Above/Below National Average	+12
2001 Retail Sales Estimate	$6,685,910,000
% Cdn. Total	2.40
2001 per Household	$24,700
2001 per Capita	$10,000
2001 No. of Establishments	5,016
2003 Projected Retail Sales	$7,232,260,000
2006 Projected Retail Sales	$7,991,270,000

POPULATION

2001 Estimates:

Total		668,093
Male		328,824
Female		339,269

Age Groups	Male	Female
0-4	22,740	21,802
5-9	22,406	21,499
10-14	22,022	21,056
15-19	21,424	20,512
20-24	22,363	22,201
25-29	24,324	24,689
30-34	26,909	26,866
35-39	28,869	28,384
40-44	28,102	27,892
45-49	25,068	24,998
50-54	20,214	20,501
55-59	15,748	16,420
60-64	13,209	14,138
65-69	11,638	12,941
70+	23,788	35,370

DAYTIME POPULATION

2001 Estimates:

Working Population	477,235
At Home Population	332,731
Total	809,966

INCOME

2001 Estimates:

Avg. Household Income	$51,906
Avg. Family Income	$59,242
Per Capita Income	$21,073
Male:	
Avg. Employment Income	$33,689
Avg. Employment Income (Full Time)	$45,628
Female:	
Avg. Employment Income	$21,478
Avg. Employment Income (Full Time)	$32,012

DISPOSABLE & DISCRETIONARY INCOME

2001 Estimates:	*Per Hhld.*
Disposable Income	$39,962
Discretionary Income 1 (minus Food & Shelter)	$27,097
Discretionary Income 2 (minus Food, Shelter, & Other Expenditures)	$19,209

LIQUID ASSETS

1999 Estimates:	*Per Hhld.*
Equity Investments	$71,602
Interest Bearing Investments	$64,244
Total Liquid Assets	$135,846

CREDIT DATA

July 2000:

Pool of Credit	$6,979,613,280
Revolving Credit, No.	1,359,424
Fixed Loans, No.	401,124
Avg. Credit Limit, per Person	$11,885
Avg. Spent, per Person	$5,368
Satisfactory Ratings, No. per Person	2.84
Avg. No. of Cards, per Person	1.05

LABOUR FORCE

2001 Estimates:

Male:

In the Labour Force	197,193
Participation Rate:	75.4
Employed	182,969
Unemployed	14,224
Unemployment Rate	7.2
Not in Labour Force	64,463

Female:

In the Labour Force	172,108
Participation Rate	62.6
Employed	160,447
Unemployed	11,661
Unemployment Rate	6.8
Not in Labour Force	102,804

OCCUPATIONS BY MAJOR GROUPS

2001 Estimates:	*Male*	*Female*
Management	19,807	9,761
Business, Finance & Admin.	20,494	52,978
Natural & Applied Sciences & Related	16,433	3,556
Health	4,676	14,364
Social Sciences, Gov't Services & Religion	5,163	6,203
Education	5,378	7,927
Arts, Culture, Recreation & Sport	4,514	5,309
Sales & Service	47,423	59,470
Trades, Transport & Equipment Operators & Related	49,425	2,660
Primary Industries	5,720	888
Processing, Mfg. & Utilities	14,015	3,978

LEVEL OF SCHOOLING

2001 Estimates:

Population 15 years +	536,568
Less than Grade 9	42,128
Grades 9-13 w/o Certif.	129,052
Grade 9-13 with Certif.	60,962
Trade Certif. /Dip.	17,328
Non-Univ. w/o Certif./Dip.	37,949
Non-Univ. with Certif./Dip.	107,102
Univ. w/o Degree	58,204
Univ. w/o Degree/Certif.	29,885
Univ. with Certif.	28,319
Univ. with Degree	83,843

AVERAGE HOUSEHOLD EXPENDITURES

2001 Estimates:

Food	$5,914
Shelter	$9,044
Clothing	$2,160
Transportation	$5,948
Health & Personal Care	$1,850
Recr'n, Read'g & Education	$3,601
Taxes & Securities	$13,519
Other	$8,097
Total Expenditures	$50,133

PRIVATE HOUSEHOLDS

2001 Estimates:

Private Households, Total	271,239
Pop. in Private Households	655,583
Average no. per Household	2.4

FAMILIES

2001 Estimates:

Families in Private Households	182,986
Husband-Wife Families	152,045
Lone-Parent Families	30,941
Aver. No. Persons per Family	3.0
Aver. No. Sons/Daughters at Home	1.2

HOUSING

2001 Estimates:

Occupied Private Dwellings	271,239
Owned	157,487
Rented	113,752
Single-Detached House	142,779
Semi-Detached House	9,312
Row Houses	27,737
Apartment, 5+ Storeys	22,544
Owned Apartment, 5+ Storeys	2,804
Apartment, 5 or Fewer Storeys	59,386
Apartment, Detached Duplex	6,537
Other Single-Attached	294
Movable Dwellings	2,650

VEHICLES

2001 Estimates:

Model Yrs. '81-'96, No.	304,349
% Total	78.87
Model Yrs. '97-'98, No.	47,541
% Total	12.32
'99 Vehicles registered in Model Yr. '99, No.	34,017
% Total	8.81
Total No. '81-'99	385,907

LEGAL MARITAL STATUS

2001 Estimates: (Age 15+)

Single (Never Married)	179,225
Legally Married (Not Separated)	264,805
Legally Married (Separated)	17,376
Widowed	30,776
Divorced	44,386

PSYTE CATEGORIES

2001 Estimates	No. of House -holds	% of Total Hhds.	Index
The Affluentials	2,502	0.92	144
Urban Gentry	5,069	1.87	104
Suburban Executives	6,891	2.54	177
Mortgaged in Suburbia	6,077	2.24	161
Technocrafts & Bureaucrats	10,807	3.98	142
Boomers & Teens	553	0.20	11
Stable Suburban Families	5,044	1.86	143
Old Bungalow Burbs	8,360	3.08	186
Suburban Nesters	1,815	0.67	42
Brie & Chablis	692	0.26	28
Aging Erudites	10,730	3.96	262
Satellite Suburbs	8,786	3.24	113
Kindergarten Boom	44,136	16.27	621
Blue Collar Winners	343	0.13	5
Old Towns' New Fringe	2,217	0.82	21

Alberta

2001 Estimates	No. of House -holds	% of Total Hhds.	Index
Rustic Prosperity	178	0.07	4
High Rise Melting Pot	289	0.11	7
Conservative Homebodies	29,484	10.87	301
High Rise Sunsets	3,348	1.23	86
Young Urban Professionals	4,939	1.82	96
Young Urban Mix	5,655	2.08	98
Young Urban Intelligentsia	12,465	4.60	302
University Enclaves	16,230	5.98	293
Young City Singles	31,942	11.78	514
Town Renters	13,300	4.90	567
Nesters & Young Homesteaders	581	0.21	9
Rod & Rifle	92	0.03	1
Struggling Downtowns	23,155	8.54	271
Aged Pensioners	4,303	1.59	119
Big City Stress	6,808	2.51	222
Old Grey Towers	2,195	0.81	146

FINANCIAL P$YTE

2001 Estimates	No. of House -holds	% of Total Hhds.	Index
Platinum Estates	2,502	0.92	114
Four Star Investors	12,513	4.61	92
Successful Suburbanites	21,928	8.08	122
Canadian Comfort	10,944	4.03	42
Urban Heights	16,361	6.03	140
Miners & Credit-Liners	8,360	3.08	97
Mortgages & Minivans	44,136	16.27	247
Tractors & Tradelines	2,395	0.88	15
Bills & Wills	35,139	12.95	156
Revolving Renters	3,929	1.45	31
Young Urban Struggle	28,695	10.58	224
Rural Family Blues	92	0.03	
Towering Debt	68,686	25.32	324
NSF	6,808	2.51	71
Senior Survivors	6,498	2.40	127

HOME LANGUAGE

2001 Estimates:		% Total
English	568,398	85.08
French	4,150	0.62
Arabic	2,480	0.37
Chinese	27,202	4.07
Croatian	421	0.06
Czech	345	0.05
Dutch	370	0.06
German	2,046	0.31
Greek	467	0.07
Gujarati	972	0.15
Hindi	1,522	0.23
Hungarian	487	0.07
Italian	2,445	0.37
Japanese	342	0.05
Khmer (Cambodian)	587	0.09
Korean	1,151	0.17

Alberta

Edmonton
(City)
Edmonton CMA
(Cont'd)

2001 Estimates:		% Total
Persian (Farsi)	482	0.07
Polish	5,721	0.86
Portuguese	1,795	0.27
Punjabi	6,638	0.99
Russian	969	0.15
Serbo-Croatian	735	0.11
Spanish	4,223	0.63
Tagalog (Pilipino)	3,321	0.50
Ukrainian	2,243	0.34
Urdu	627	0.09
Vietnamese	5,364	0.80
Other Languages	4,650	0.70
Multiple Responses	17,940	2.69
Total	668,093	100.00

BUILDING PERMITS

	1999	1998	1997
		$000	
Value	653,748	684,789	546,399

HOMES BUILT

	1999	1998	1997
No.	3,483	3,084	2,323

TAXATION

Income Class:	1997	% Total
Under $5,000	58,800	12.78
$5,000-$10,000	60,470	13.14
$10,000-$15,000	64,880	14.10
$15,000-$20,000	48,100	10.45
$20,000-$25,000	39,820	8.66
$25,000-$30,000	36,550	7.94
$30,000-$40,000	56,300	12.24
$40,000-$50,000	36,420	7.92
$50,000+	58,740	12.77
Total Returns, No.	460,070	
Total Income, $000	12,891,499	
Total Taxable Returns	326,210	
Total Tax, $000	2,463,876	
Average Income, $	28,021	
Average Tax, $	7,553	

VITAL STATISTICS

	1997	1996	1995	1994
Births	7,944	8,488	8,853	9,261
Deaths	3,863	3,908	3,894	3,974
Natural Increase	4,081	4,580	4,959	5,287
Marriages	3,843	3,883	4,144	4,164

Note: Latest available data.

MEDIA INFO
see Edmonton, CMA

Fort Saskatchewan
(City)
Edmonton CMA
In census division No. 11.

POPULATION

July 1, 2001 Estimate	13,623
% Cdn. Total	0.04
% Change, '96 -'01	6.77
Avg. Annual Growth Rate, %	1.32
2003 Projected Population	13,951
2006 Projected Population	14,344
2001 Households Estimate	4,884
2003 Projected Households	5,075
2006 Projected Households	5,338

INCOME

% Above/Below National Average	+17
2001 Total Income Estimate	$336,030,000
% Cdn. Total	0.05
2001 Average Hhld. Income	$68,800
2001 Per Capita	$24,700
2003 Projected Total Income	$362,160,000
2006 Projected Total Income	$402,940,000

RETAIL SALES

% Above/Below National Average	-23
2001 Retail Sales Estimate	$93,800,000
% Cdn. Total	0.03
2001 per Household	$19,200
2001 per Capita	$6,900
2001 No. of Establishments	88
2003 Projected Retail Sales	$103,530,000
2006 Projected Retail Sales	$118,120,000

POPULATION

2001 Estimates:

Total		13,623
Male		6,805
Female		6,818

Age Groups	Male	Female
0-4	433	413
5-9	489	471
10-14	551	532
15-19	585	542
20-24	525	473
25-29	442	433
30-34	462	455
35-39	529	519
40-44	566	587
45-49	562	574
50-54	492	453
55-59	369	332
60-64	263	250
65-69	181	200
70+	356	584

DAYTIME POPULATION

2001 Estimates:

Working Population	2,396
At Home Population	6,461
Total	8,857

INCOME

2001 Estimates:

Avg. Household Income	$68,802
Avg. Family Income	$74,688
Per Capita Income	$24,666
Male:	
Avg. Employment Income	$45,286
Avg. Employment Income (Full Time)	$60,808
Female:	
Avg. Employment Income	$23,006
Avg. Employment Income (Full Time)	$32,796

DISPOSABLE & DISCRETIONARY INCOME

2001 Estimates:	Per Hhld.
Disposable Income	$52,643
Discretionary Income 1 (minus Food & Shelter)	$36,506
Discretionary Income 2 (minus Food, Shelter, & Other Expenditures)	$25,955

LIQUID ASSETS

1999 Estimates:	Per Hhld.
Equity Investments	$116,600
Interest Bearing Investments	$87,735
Total Liquid Assets	$204,335

CREDIT DATA

July 2000:	
Pool of Credit	$154,641,198
Revolving Credit, No.	25,896
Fixed Loans, No.	10,029
Avg. Credit Limit, per Person	$14,501
Avg. Spent, per Person	$6,928
Satisfactory Ratings, No. per Person	3.16
Avg. No. of Cards, per Person	1.07

LABOUR FORCE

2001 Estimates:

Male:	
In the Labour Force	4,097
Participation Rate	76.8
Employed	3,905
Unemployed	192
Unemployment Rate	4.7
Not in Labour Force	1,235
Female:	
In the Labour Force	3,416
Participation Rate	63.2
Employed	3,253
Unemployed	163
Unemployment Rate	4.8
Not in Labour Force	1,986

OCCUPATIONS BY MAJOR GROUPS

2001 Estimates:	Male	Female
Management	380	116
Business, Finance & Admin.	301	1,138
Natural & Applied Sciences & Related	550	92
Health	51	311
Social Sciences, Gov't Services & Religion	74	99
Education	102	178
Arts, Culture, Recreation & Sport	32	28
Sales & Service	746	1,217
Trades, Transport & Equipment Operators & Related	933	70
Primary Industries	182	72
Processing, Mfg. & Utilities	691	39

LEVEL OF SCHOOLING

2001 Estimates:

Population 15 years +	10,734
Less than Grade 9	382
Grades 9-13 w/o Certif.	2,900
Grade 9-13 with Certif.	1,523
Trade Certif. /Dip.	524
Non-Univ. w/o Certif./Dip.	606
Non-Univ. with Certif./Dip.	2,797
Univ. w/o Degree	991
Univ. w/o Degree/Certif.	418
Univ. with Certif.	573
Univ. with Degree	1,011

AVERAGE HOUSEHOLD EXPENDITURES

2001 Estimates:

Food	$7,395
Shelter	$11,190
Clothing	$2,638
Transportation	$8,329
Health & Personal Care	$2,211
Recr'n, Read'g & Education	$4,501
Taxes & Securities	$18,231
Other	$9,891
Total Expenditures	$64,386

PRIVATE HOUSEHOLDS

2001 Estimates:

Private Households, Total	4,884
Pop. in Private Households	13,285
Average no. per Household	2.7

FAMILIES

2001 Estimates:

Families in Private Households	3,974
Husband-Wife Families	3,528
Lone-Parent Families	446
Aver. No. Persons per Family	3.2
Aver. No. Sons/Daughters at Home	1.3

HOUSING

2001 Estimates:

Occupied Private Dwellings	4,884
Owned	3,793
Rented	1,091
Single-Detached House	3,553
Semi-Detached House	211
Row Houses	474
Apartment, 5 or Fewer Storeys	616
Apartment, Detached Duplex	30

VEHICLES

2001 Estimates:

Model Yrs. '81-'96, No.	7,090
% Total	83.59
Model Yrs. '97-'98, No.	870
% Total	10.26
'99 Vehicles registered in Model Yr. '99, No.	522
% Total	6.15
Total No. '81-'99	8,482

LEGAL MARITAL STATUS

2001 Estimates: (Age 15+)

Single (Never Married)	2,812
Legally Married (Not Separated)	6,427
Legally Married (Separated)	254
Widowed	596
Divorced	645

PSYTE CATEGORIES

2001 Estimates	No. of House-holds	% of Total Hhds.	Index
Mortgaged in Suburbia	368	7.53	542
Technocrafts & Bureaucrats	428	8.76	311
Satellite Suburbs	1,197	24.51	854
Kindergarten Boom	380	7.78	297
Blue Collar Winners	875	17.92	712
Old Leafy Towns	288	5.90	231
Quiet Towns	916	18.76	881
Rod & Rifle	54	1.11	48
Struggling Downtowns	278	5.69	181

Fort Saskatchewan
(City)
Edmonton CMA
(Cont'd)

FINANCIAL PSYTE

2001 Estimates	No. of House-holds	% of Total Hhds.	Index
Successful Suburbanites	796	16.30	246
Canadian Comfort	2,072	42.42	437
Mortgages & Minivans	380	7.78	118
Bills & Wills	288	5.90	71
Rural Family Blues	54	1.11	14
Limited Budgets	916	18.76	603
Towering Debt	278	5.69	73

HOME LANGUAGE

2001 Estimates:		% Total
English	13,378	98.20
French	27	0.20
Croatian	11	0.08
Dutch	16	0.12
German	16	0.12
Spanish	21	0.15
Ukrainian	22	0.16
Other Languages	12	0.09
Multiple Responses	120	0.88
Total	13,623	100.00

BUILDING PERMITS

	1999	1998	1997
		$000	
Value	12,380	109,581	29,548

HOMES BUILT

	1999	1998	1997
No.	74	60	107

TAXATION

Income Class:	1997	% Total
Under $5,000	1,390	12.42
$5,000-$10,000	1,230	10.99
$10,000-$15,000	1,300	11.62
$15,000-$20,000	1,030	9.20
$20,000-$25,000	850	7.60
$25,000-$30,000	820	7.33
$30,000-$40,000	1,320	11.80
$40,000-$50,000	880	7.86
$50,000 +	2,380	21.27
Total Returns, No.	11,190	
Total Income, $000	358,326	
Total Taxable Returns	8,470	
Total Tax, $000	74,514	
Average Income, $	32,022	
Average Tax, $	8,797	

VITAL STATISTICS

	1997	1996	1995	1994
Births	145	131	170	186
Deaths	97	61	69	88
Natural Increase	48	70	101	98
Marriages	77	68	72	71

Note: Latest available data.

MEDIA INFO
see Edmonton, CMA

Leduc
(City)
Edmonton CMA
In census division No. 11.

POPULATION

July 1, 2001 Estimate	15,769
% Cdn. Total	0.05
% Change, '96 -'01	7.19
Avg. Annual Growth Rate, %	1.40
2003 Projected Population	16,097
2006 Projected Population	16,477
2001 Households Estimate	5,655
2003 Projected Households	5,858
2006 Projected Households	6,135

INCOME

% Above/Below National Average	+10
2001 Total Income Estimate	$367,170,000
% Cdn. Total	0.06
2001 Average Hhld. Income	$64,900
2001 Per Capita	$23,300
2003 Projected Total Income	$395,670,000
2006 Projected Total Income	$440,210,000

RETAIL SALES

% Above/Below National Average	+47
2001 Retail Sales Estimate	$208,020,000
% Cdn. Total	0.07
2001 per Household	$36,800
2001 per Capita	$13,200
2001 No. of Establishments	138
2003 Projected Retail Sales	$229,630,000
2006 Projected Retail Sales	$261,760,000

POPULATION

2001 Estimates:		
Total		15,769
Male		7,832
Female		7,937

Age Groups	Male	Female
0-4	515	486
5-9	567	524
10-14	618	573
15-19	638	619
20-24	595	578
25-29	530	506
30-34	541	523
35-39	584	600
40-44	623	647
45-49	641	643
50-54	559	558
55-59	407	414
60-64	286	303
65-69	223	232
70+	505	731

DAYTIME POPULATION

2001 Estimates:	
Working Population	1,952
At Home Population	7,198
Total	9,150

INCOME

2001 Estimates:	
Avg. Household Income	$64,928
Avg. Family Income	$69,682
Per Capita Income	$23,284
Male:	
Avg. Employment Income	$42,089
Avg. Employment Income (Full Time)	$55,842
Female:	
Avg. Employment Income	$19,422
Avg. Employment Income (Full Time)	$29,927

DISPOSABLE & DISCRETIONARY INCOME

2001 Estimates:	Per Hhld.
Disposable Income	$49,721
Discretionary Income 1 (minus Food & Shelter)	$34,297
Discretionary Income 2 (minus Food, Shelter, & Other Expenditures)	$24,202

LIQUID ASSETS

1999 Estimates:	Per Hhld.
Equity Investments	$101,061
Interest Bearing Investments	$79,757
Total Liquid Assets	$180,818

CREDIT DATA

July 2000:	
Pool of Credit	$176,143,911
Revolving Credit, No.	30,016
Fixed Loans, No.	11,377
Avg. Credit Limit, per Person	$14,343
Avg. Spent, per Person	$7,144
Satisfactory Ratings, No. per Person	3.19
Avg. No. of Cards, per Person	1.09

LABOUR FORCE

2001 Estimates:	
Male:	
In the Labour Force	4,998
Participation Rate	81.5
Employed	4,717
Unemployed	281
Unemployment Rate	5.6
Not in Labour Force	1,134
Female:	
In the Labour Force	4,095
Participation Rate	64.4
Employed	3,849
Unemployed	246
Unemployment Rate	6.0
Not in Labour Force	2,259

OCCUPATIONS BY MAJOR GROUPS

2001 Estimates:	Male	Female
Management	504	201
Business, Finance & Admin.	466	1,421
Natural & Applied Sciences & Related	344	34
Health	71	349
Social Sciences, Gov't Services & Religion	36	50
Education	64	121
Arts, Culture, Recreation & Sport	70	67
Sales & Service	876	1,536
Trades, Transport & Equipment Operators & Related	1,577	150
Primary Industries	383	10
Processing, Mfg. & Utilities	548	100

LEVEL OF SCHOOLING

2001 Estimates:	
Population 15 years +	12,486
Less than Grade 9	899
Grades 9-13 w/o Certif.	3,635
Grade 9-13 with Certif.	1,908
Trade Certif. /Dip.	603
Non-Univ. w/o Certif./Dip.	779
Non-Univ. with Certif./Dip.	2,681
Univ. w/o Degree	1,037
Univ. w/o Degree/Certif.	512
Univ. with Certif.	525
Univ. with Degree	944

Alberta

AVERAGE HOUSEHOLD EXPENDITURES

2001 Estimates:	
Food	$7,192
Shelter	$10,675
Clothing	$2,486
Transportation	$7,784
Health & Personal Care	$2,188
Recr'n, Read'g & Education	$4,441
Taxes & Securities	$16,416
Other	$9,896
Total Expenditures	$61,078

PRIVATE HOUSEHOLDS

2001 Estimates:	
Private Households, Total	5,655
Pop. in Private Households	15,467
Average no. per Household	2.7

FAMILIES

2001 Estimates:	
Families in Private Households	4,594
Husband-Wife Families	4,007
Lone-Parent Families	587
Aver. No. Persons per Family	3.1
Aver. No. Sons/Daughters at Home	1.3

HOUSING

2001 Estimates:	
Occupied Private Dwellings	5,655
Owned	4,267
Rented	1,388
Single-Detached House	4,247
Semi-Detached House	151
Row Houses	271
Apartment, 5+ Storeys	74
Owned Apartment, 5+ Storeys	11
Apartment, 5 or Fewer Storeys	721
Apartment, Detached Duplex	34
Other Single-Attached	11
Movable Dwellings	146

VEHICLES

2001 Estimates:	
Model Yrs. '81-'96, No.	8,249
% Total	78.06
Model Yrs. '97-'98, No.	1,431
% Total	13.54
'99 Vehicles registered in Model Yr. '99, No.	887
% Total	8.39
Total No. '81-'99	10,567

LEGAL MARITAL STATUS

2001 Estimates: (Age 15+)	
Single (Never Married)	3,360
Legally Married (Not Separated)	7,317
Legally Married (Separated)	299
Widowed	721
Divorced	789

Alberta

Leduc
(City)
Edmonton CMA
(Cont'd)

PSYTE CATEGORIES

2001 Estimates	No. of House-holds	% of Total Hhds.	Index
Technocrafts & Bureaucrats	525	9.28	330
Boomers & Teens	258	4.56	254
Satellite Suburbs	1,433	25.34	883
Old Towns' New Fringe	2,112	37.35	954
Young City Singles	404	7.14	312
Quiet Towns	882	15.60	733

FINANCIAL PSYTE

2001 Estimates	No. of House-holds	% of Total Hhds.	Index
Four Star Investors	258	4.56	91
Successful Suburbanites	525	9.28	140
Canadian Comfort	1,433	25.34	261
Tractors & Tradelines	2,112	37.35	653
Limited Budgets	882	15.60	502
Towering Debt	404	7.14	92

HOME LANGUAGE

2001 Estimates:		% Total
English	15,489	98.22
French	40	0.25
Dutch	45	0.29
German	22	0.14
Persian (Farsi)	11	0.07
Punjabi	48	0.30
Tagalog (Pilipino)	35	0.22
Multiple Responses	79	0.50
Total	15,769	100.00

BUILDING PERMITS

	1999	1998 $000	1997
Value	14,542	24,003	19,099

HOMES BUILT

	1999	1998	1997
No.	101	108	50

TAXATION

Income Class:	1997	% Total
Under $5,000	1,450	11.72
$5,000-$10,000	1,430	11.56
$10,000-$15,000	1,660	13.42
$15,000-$20,000	1,180	9.54
$20,000-$25,000	1,050	8.49
$25,000-$30,000	900	7.28
$30,000-$40,000	1,520	12.29
$40,000-$50,000	1,070	8.65
$50,000 +	2,110	17.06
Total Returns, No.	12,370	
Total Income, $000	387,309	
Total Taxable Returns	9,240	
Total Tax, $000	77,749	
Average Income, $	31,310	
Average Tax, $	8,414	

VITAL STATISTICS

	1997	1996	1995	1994
Births	143	161	177	211
Deaths	107	138	102	97
Natural Increase	36	23	75	114
Marriages	112	90	95	123

Note: Latest available data.

MEDIA INFO
see Edmonton, CMA

Leduc County No. 25
(County Municipality)
Edmonton CMA

In census division No. 11.

POPULATION

July 1, 2001 Estimate	14,210
% Cdn. Total	0.05
% Change, '96 -'01	11.79
Avg. Annual Growth Rate, %	2.25
2003 Projected Population	14,794
2006 Projected Population	15,569
2001 Households Estimate	4,887
2003 Projected Households	5,162
2006 Projected Households	5,556

INCOME

% Above/Below National Average	same
2001 Total Income Estimate	$298,830,000
% Cdn. Total	0.05
2001 Average Hhld. Income	$61,100
2001 Per Capita	$21,000
2003 Projected Total Income	$331,230,000
2006 Projected Total Income	$383,560,000

RETAIL SALES

% Above/Below National Average	-1
2001 Retail Sales Estimate	$126,510,000
% Cdn. Total	0.05
2001 per Household	$25,900
2001 per Capita	$8,900
2001 No. of Establishments	75
2003 Projected Retail Sales	$142,510,000
2006 Projected Retail Sales	$167,310,000

POPULATION

2001 Estimates:		
Total		14,210
Male		7,411
Female		6,799

Age Groups	Male	Female
0-4	435	426
5-9	526	487
10-14	609	552
15-19	617	573
20-24	513	469
25-29	420	404
30-34	430	440
35-39	544	541
40-44	612	571
45-49	586	533
50-54	512	462
55-59	435	373
60-64	375	306
65-69	309	254
70+	488	408

DAYTIME POPULATION

2001 Estimates:	
Working Population	5,161
At Home Population	6,136
Total	11,297

INCOME

2001 Estimates:	
Avg. Household Income	$61,147
Avg. Family Income	$65,204
Per Capita Income	$21,029
Male:	
Avg. Employment Income	$33,455
Avg. Employment Income (Full Time)	$41,620
Female:	
Avg. Employment Income	$18,749
Avg. Employment Income (Full Time)	$27,335

DISPOSABLE & DISCRETIONARY INCOME

2001 Estimates:	Per Hhld.
Disposable Income	$47,108
Discretionary Income 1 (minus Food & Shelter)	$32,939
Discretionary Income 2 (minus Food, Shelter, & Other Expenditures)	$22,245

LIQUID ASSETS

1999 Estimates:	Per Hhld.
Equity Investments	$91,554
Interest Bearing Investments	$72,620
Total Liquid Assets	$164,174

CREDIT DATA

July 2000:	
Pool of Credit	$108,693,557
Revolving Credit, No.	16,508
Fixed Loans, No.	6,461
Avg. Credit Limit, per Person	$14,500
Avg. Spent, per Person	$7,181
Satisfactory Ratings, No. per Person	2.92
Avg. No. of Cards, per Person	1.00

LABOUR FORCE

2001 Estimates:	
Male:	
In the Labour Force	4,863
Participation Rate	83.3
Employed	4,747
Unemployed	116
Unemployment Rate	2.4
Not in Labour Force	978
Female:	
In the Labour Force	3,570
Participation Rate	66.9
Employed	3,411
Unemployed	159
Unemployment Rate	4.5
Not in Labour Force	1,764

OCCUPATIONS BY MAJOR GROUPS

2001 Estimates:	Male	Female
Management	452	174
Business, Finance & Admin.	188	1,082
Natural & Applied Sciences & Related	180	37
Health	25	163
Social Sciences, Gov't Services & Religion	37	35
Education	94	177
Arts, Culture, Recreation & Sport	65	47
Sales & Service	348	921
Trades, Transport & Equipment Operators & Related	1,455	32
Primary Industries	1,700	765
Processing, Mfg. & Utilities	308	66

LEVEL OF SCHOOLING

2001 Estimates:	
Population 15 years +	11,175
Less than Grade 9	883
Grades 9-13 w/o Certif.	3,717
Grade 9-13 with Certif.	1,537
Trade Certif. /Dip.	577
Non-Univ. w/o Certif./Dip.	575
Non-Univ. with Certif./Dip.	2,393
Univ. w/o Degree	662
Univ. w/o Degree/Certif.	342
Univ. with Certif.	320
Univ. with Degree	831

Leduc County No. 25
(County Municipality)
Edmonton CMA
(Cont'd)

AVERAGE HOUSEHOLD EXPENDITURES

2001 Estimates:
Food	$6,862
Shelter	$9,451
Clothing	$2,374
Transportation	$8,748
Health & Personal Care	$2,091
Recr'n, Read'g & Education	$4,125
Taxes & Securities	$14,674
Other	$9,881
Total Expenditures	$58,206

PRIVATE HOUSEHOLDS

2001 Estimates:
Private Households, Total	4,887
Pop. in Private Households	13,920
Average no. per Household	2.8

FAMILIES

2001 Estimates:
Families in Private Households	4,121
Husband-Wife Families	3,891
Lone-Parent Families	230
Aver. No. Persons per Family	3.2
Aver. No. Sons/Daughters at Home	1.3

HOUSING

2001 Estimates:
Occupied Private Dwellings	4,887
Owned	4,214
Rented	673
Single-Detached House	4,503
Movable Dwellings	384

VEHICLES

2001 Estimates:
Model Yrs. '81-'96, No.	10,915
% Total	76.16
Model Yrs. '97-'98, No.	2,234
% Total	15.59
'99 Vehicles registered in Model Yr. '99, No.	1,182
% Total	8.25
Total No. '81-'99	14,331

LEGAL MARITAL STATUS

2001 Estimates: (Age 15+)
Single (Never Married)	2,732
Legally Married (Not Separated)	7,266
Legally Married (Separated)	210
Widowed	369
Divorced	598

PSYTE CATEGORIES

2001 Estimates	No. of House-holds	% of Total Hhds.	Index
Kindergarten Boom	30	0.61	23
Blue Collar Winners	1,508	30.86	1,226
Rustic Prosperity	2,176	44.53	2,468
Pick-ups & Dirt Bikes	647	13.24	1,586
The Grain Belt	177	3.62	611
Old Leafy Towns	79	1.62	63
Rod & Rifle	237	4.85	210

FINAN¢IAL P$YTE

2001 Estimates	No. of House-holds	% of Total Hhds.	Index
Canadian Comfort	1,508	30.86	318
Mortgages & Minivans	30	0.61	9
Tractors & Tradelines	2,176	44.53	779
Bills & Wills	79	1.62	20
Country Credit	824	16.86	249
Rural Family Blues	237	4.85	60

HOME LANGUAGE

2001 Estimates		% Total
English	13,812	97.20
French	48	0.34
Dutch	33	0.23
German	203	1.43
Polish	11	0.08
Punjabi	41	0.29
Multiple Responses	62	0.44
Total	14,210	100.00

BUILDING PERMITS

	1999	1998	1997
		$000	
Value	78,470	51,341	34,845

HOMES BUILT

	1999	1998	1997
No	57	82	59

TAXATION

Income Class:	1997	% Total
Under $5,000	.80	12.12
$5,000-$10,000	.80	12.12
$10,000-$15,000	.90	13.64
$15,000-$20,000	.70	10.61
$20,000-$25,000	.60	9.09
$25,000-$30,000	.40	6.06
$30,000-$40,000	.90	13.64
$40,000-$50,000	.50	7.58
$50,000 +	.110	16.67
Total Returns, No.	.660	
Total Income, $000	25,386	
Total Taxable Returns	.480	
Total Tax, $000	6,222	
Average Income, $	38,464	
Average Tax, $	12,963	

VITAL STATISTICS

	1997	1996	1995	1994
Births	108	121	117	132
Deaths	54	51	33	39
Natural Increase	54	70	84	93
Marriages	69	68	62	63

Note: Latest available data.

MEDIA INFO
see Edmonton, CMA

Parkland County
(County Municipality)
Edmonton CMA

In census division No. 11.

POPULATION

July 1, 2001 Estimate	29,061
% Cdn. Total	0.09
% Change, '96 -'01	14.09
Avg. Annual Growth Rate, %	2.67
2003 Projected Population	30,559
2006 Projected Population	32,597
2001 Households Estimate	9,756
2003 Projected Households	10,407
2006 Projected Households	11,363

INCOME

% Above/Below National Average	+5
2001 Total Income Estimate	$642,930,000
% Cdn. Total	0.10
2001 Average Hhld. Income	$65,900
2001 Per Capita	$22,100
2003 Projected Total Income	$719,850,000
2006 Projected Total Income	$846,010,000

RETAIL SALES

% Above/Below National Average	-18
2001 Retail Sales Estimate	$213,970,000
% Cdn. Total	0.08
2001 per Household	$21,900
2001 per Capita	$7,400
2001 No. of Establishments	164
2003 Projected Retail Sales	$245,270,000
2006 Projected Retail Sales	$292,810,000

POPULATION

2001 Estimates:
Total	29,061
Male	15,021
Female	14,040

Age Groups	Male	Female
0-4	921	833
5-9	1,113	983
10-14	1,297	1,158
15-19	1,270	1,155
20-24	998	917
25-29	798	767
30-34	872	960
35-39	1,167	1,262
40-44	1,346	1,288
45-49	1,259	1,166
50-54	1,097	1,013
55-59	910	823
60-64	718	615
65-69	540	425
70+	715	675

DAYTIME POPULATION

2001 Estimates:
Working Population	n.a.
At Home Population	12,802
Total	12,802

INCOME

2001 Estimates:
Avg. Household Income	$65,901
Avg. Family Income	$66,858
Per Capita Income	$22,123

Male:
Avg. Employment Income	$38,112
Avg. Employment Income (Full Time)	$46,730

Female:
Avg. Employment Income	$20,729
Avg. Employment Income (Full Time)	$30,763

Alberta

DISPOSABLE & DISCRETIONARY INCOME

2001 Estimates:	Per Hhld.
Disposable Income	$50,681
Discretionary Income 1 (minus Food & Shelter)	$35,647
Discretionary Income 2 (minus Food, Shelter, & Other Expenditures)	$24,987

LIQUID ASSETS

1999 Estimates:	Per Hhld.
Equity Investments	$96,134
Interest Bearing Investments	$78,908
Total Liquid Assets	$175,042

CREDIT DATA

July 2000:
Pool of Credit	$201,929,117
Revolving Credit, No.	30,193
Fixed Loans, No.	12,541
Avg. Credit Limit, per Person	$14,186
Avg. Spent, per Person	$7,097
Satisfactory Ratings, No. per Person	2.84
Avg. No. of Cards, per Person	0.99

LABOUR FORCE

2001 Estimates:
Male:
In the Labour Force	9,672
Participation Rate	82.7
Employed	9,173
Unemployed	499
Unemployment Rate	5.2
Not in Labour Force	2,018

Female:
In the Labour Force	7,373
Participation Rate	66.6
Employed	7,027
Unemployed	346
Unemployment Rate	4.7
Not in Labour Force	3,693

OCCUPATIONS BY MAJOR GROUPS

2001 Estimates:	Male	Female
Management	1,068	350
Business, Finance & Admin.	537	2,644
Natural & Applied Sciences & Related	607	99
Health	89	519
Social Sciences, Gov't Services & Religion	88	192
Education	172	264
Arts, Culture, Recreation & Sport	143	266
Sales & Service	1,313	2,116
Trades, Transport & Equipment Operators & Related	3,441	260
Primary Industries	1,479	501
Processing, Mfg. & Utilities	614	44

Alberta

Parkland County
(County Municipality)
Edmonton CMA
(Cont'd)

LEVEL OF SCHOOLING

2001 Estimates:
Population 15 years +	22,756
Less than Grade 9	1,431
Grades 9-13 w/o Certif.	6,571
Grade 9-13 with Certif.	3,208
Trade Certif./Dip.	998
Non-Univ. w/o Certif./Dip.	1,127
Non-Univ. with Certif./Dip.	5,691
Univ. w/o Degree	1,979
Univ. w/o Degree/Certif.	884
Univ. with Certif.	1,095
Univ. with Degree	1,751

AVERAGE HOUSEHOLD EXPENDITURES

2001 Estimates:
Food	$7,151
Shelter	$10,290
Clothing	$2,530
Transportation	$8,465
Health & Personal Care	$2,216
Recr'n, Read'g & Education	$4,474
Taxes & Securities	$16,793
Other	$10,163
Total Expenditures	$62,082

PRIVATE HOUSEHOLDS

2001 Estimates:
Private Households, Total	9,756
Pop. in Private Households	28,462
Average no. per Household	2.9

FAMILIES

2001 Estimates:
Families in Private Households	8,702
Husband-Wife Families	8,104
Lone-Parent Families	598
Aver. No. Persons per Family	3.2
Aver. No. Sons/Daughters at Home	1.3

HOUSING

2001 Estimates:
Occupied Private Dwellings	9,756
Owned	8,927
Rented	829
Single-Detached House	8,769
Row Houses	36
Apartment, 5 or Fewer Storeys	23
Movable Dwellings	928

VEHICLES

2001 Estimates:
Model Yrs. '81-'96, No.	16,547
% Total	82.25
Model Yrs. '97-'98, No.	2,358
% Total	11.72
'99 Vehicles registered in Model Yr. '99, No.	1,212
% Total	6.02
Total No. '81-'99	20,117

LEGAL MARITAL STATUS

2001 Estimates: (Age 15+)
Single (Never Married)	5,400
Legally Married (Not Separated)	15,010
Legally Married (Separated)	434
Widowed	568
Divorced	1,344

PSYTE CATEGORIES

2001 Estimates	No. of House-holds	% of Total Hhds.	Index
Urban Gentry	39	0.40	22
Technocrafts & Bureaucrats	23	0.24	8
Boomers & Teens	326	3.34	186
Small City Elite	1,348	13.82	806
Satellite Suburbs	81	0.83	29
Kindergarten Boom	28	0.29	11
Blue Collar Winners	2,545	26.09	1,036
Town Boomers	328	3.36	332
Old Towns' New Fringe	2,873	29.45	752
Rustic Prosperity	619	6.34	352
Pick-ups & Dirt Bikes	889	9.11	1,091
The Grain Belt	74	0.76	128
Old Leafy Towns	260	2.67	104
Rod & Rifle	61	0.63	27
Big Country Families	225	2.31	162

FINANCIAL P$YTE

2001 Estimates	No. of House-holds	% of Total Hhds.	Index
Four Star Investors	365	3.74	74
Successful Suburbanites	23	0.24	4
Canadian Comfort	4,302	44.10	454
Mortgages & Minivans	28	0.29	4
Tractors & Tradelines	3,492	35.79	626
Bills & Wills	260	2.67	32
Country Credit	963	9.87	146
Rural Family Blues	286	2.93	36

HOME LANGUAGE

2001 Estimates:		% Total
English	28,758	98.96
French	57	0.20
German	40	0.14
Other Languages	49	0.17
Multiple Responses	157	0.54
Total	29,061	100.00

BUILDING PERMITS

	1999	1998 *$000*	1997
Value	34,006	26,878	25,382

HOMES BUILT

	1999	1998	1997
No	216	171	156

TAXATION

Income Class:	1997	% Total
Under $5,000	740	19.89
$5,000-$10,000	520	13.98
$10,000-$15,000	480	12.90
$15,000-$20,000	330	8.87
$20,000-$25,000	240	6.45
$25,000-$30,000	250	6.72
$30,000-$40,000	380	10.22
$40,000-$50,000	280	7.53
$50,000 +	500	13.44
Total Returns, No.	3,720	
Total Income, $000	90,768	
Total Taxable Returns	2,320	
Total Tax, $000	16,466	
Average Income, $	24,400	
Average Tax, $	7,097	

VITAL STATISTICS

	1997	1996	1995	1994
Births	248	301	280	300
Deaths	87	74	68	50
Natural Increase	161	227	212	250
Marriages	95	109	78	87

Note: Latest available data.

MEDIA INFO
see Edmonton, CMA

Spruce Grove
(City)
Edmonton CMA
In census division No. 11.

POPULATION

July 1, 2001 Estimate	16,820
% Cdn. Total	0.05
% Change, '96 -'01	14.59
Avg. Annual Growth Rate, %	2.76
2003 Projected Population	17,732
2006 Projected Population	18,976
2001 Households Estimate	5,722
2003 Projected Households	6,119
2006 Projected Households	6,699

INCOME

% Above/Below National Average	+9
2001 Total Income Estimate	$387,870,000
% Cdn. Total	0.06
2001 Average Hhld. Income	$67,800
2001 Per Capita	$23,100
2003 Projected Total Income	$436,140,000
2006 Projected Total Income	$515,800,000

RETAIL SALES

% Above/Below National Average	same
2001 Retail Sales Estimate	$151,310,000
% Cdn. Total	0.05
2001 per Household	$26,400
2001 per Capita	$9,000
2001 No. of Establishments	103
2003 Projected Retail Sales	$170,480,000
2006 Projected Retail Sales	$201,140,000

POPULATION
2001 Estimates:

Total		16,820
Male		8,392
Female		8,428

Age Groups	Male	Female
0-4	567	555
5-9	621	618
10-14	695	696
15-19	729	729
20-24	659	639
25-29	588	572
30-34	595	616
35-39	657	703
40-44	706	738
45-49	690	715
50-54	608	592
55-59	464	411
60-64	317	257
65-69	195	174
70+	301	413

DAYTIME POPULATION
2001 Estimates:

Working Population	1,000
At Home Population	7,092
Total	8,092

INCOME
2001 Estimates:

Avg. Household Income	$67,785
Avg. Family Income	$71,335
Per Capita Income	$23,060
Male:	
Avg. Employment Income	$41,468
Avg. Employment Income (Full Time)	$53,024
Female:	
Avg. Employment Income	$21,556
Avg. Employment Income (Full Time)	$32,691

DISPOSABLE & DISCRETIONARY INCOME

2001 Estimates:	Per Hhld.
Disposable Income	$51,937
Discretionary Income 1 (minus Food & Shelter)	$36,236
Discretionary Income 2 (minus Food, Shelter, & Other Expenditures)	$25,847

LIQUID ASSETS

1999 Estimates:	Per Hhld.
Equity Investments	$94,232
Interest Bearing Investments	$80,025
Total Liquid Assets	$174,257

CREDIT DATA
July 2000:

Pool of Credit	$196,896,381
Revolving Credit, No.	31,300
Fixed Loans, No.	12,846
Avg. Credit Limit, per Person	$15,261
Avg. Spent, per Person	$7,731
Satisfactory Ratings, No. per Person	3.21
Avg. No. of Cards, per Person	1.14

LABOUR FORCE
2001 Estimates:

Male:	
In the Labour Force	5,507
Participation Rate	84.6
Employed	5,287
Unemployed	220
Unemployment Rate	4.0
Not in Labour Force	1,002
Female:	
In the Labour Force	4,633
Participation Rate	70.6
Employed	4,387
Unemployed	246
Unemployment Rate	5.3
Not in Labour Force	1,926

OCCUPATIONS BY MAJOR GROUPS

2001 Estimates:	Male	Female
Management	703	225
Business, Finance & Admin.	494	1,577
Natural & Applied Sciences & Related	389	45
Health	72	359
Social Sciences, Gov't Services & Religion	88	81
Education	195	289
Arts, Culture, Recreation & Sport	83	99
Sales & Service	1,157	1,709
Trades, Transport & Equipment Operators & Related	1,747	58
Primary Industries	274	41
Processing, Mfg. & Utilities	281	62

LEVEL OF SCHOOLING
2001 Estimates:

Population 15 years +	13,068
Less than Grade 9	600
Grades 9-13 w/o Certif.	3,622
Grade 9-13 with Certif.	1,629
Trade Certif./Dip.	557
Non-Univ. w/o Certif./Dip.	987
Non-Univ. with Certif./Dip.	3,265
Univ. w/o Degree	1,352
Univ. w/o Degree/Certif.	634
Univ. with Certif.	718
Univ. with Degree	1,056

AVERAGE HOUSEHOLD EXPENDITURES
2001 Estimates:

Food	$7,490
Shelter	$10,835
Clothing	$2,701
Transportation	$8,055
Health & Personal Care	$2,291
Recr'n, Read'g & Education	$4,660
Taxes & Securities	$17,476
Other	$9,981
Total Expenditures	$63,489

PRIVATE HOUSEHOLDS
2001 Estimates:

Private Households, Total	5,722
Pop. in Private Households	16,765
Average no. per Household	2.9

FAMILIES
2001 Estimates:

Families in Private Households	4,895
Husband-Wife Families	4,375
Lone-Parent Families	520
Aver. No. Persons per Family	3.3
Aver. No. Sons/Daughters at Home	1.4

HOUSING
2001 Estimates:

Occupied Private Dwellings	5,722
Owned	4,724
Rented	998
Single-Detached House	4,631
Semi-Detached House	163
Row Houses	251
Apartment, 5 or Fewer Storeys	416
Apartment, Detached Duplex	18
Movable Dwellings	243

VEHICLES
2001 Estimates:

Model Yrs. '81-'96, No.	8,497
% Total	81.61
Model Yrs. '97-'98, No.	1,252
% Total	12.02
'99 Vehicles registered in Model Yr. '99, No.	663
% Total	6.37
Total No. '81-'99	10,412

LEGAL MARITAL STATUS
2001 Estimates: (Age 15+)

Single (Never Married)	3,440
Legally Married (Not Separated)	8,053
Legally Married (Separated)	322
Widowed	394
Divorced	859

PSYTE CATEGORIES

2001 Estimates	No. of House-holds	% of Total Hhds.	Index
Technocrafts & Bureaucrats	1,291	22.56	802
Small City Elite	473	8.27	482
Old Bungalow Burbs	492	8.60	519
Satellite Suburbs	502	8.77	306
Kindergarten Boom	483	8.44	322
Blue Collar Winners	254	4.44	176
Old Towns' New Fringe	1,194	20.87	533
Young Urban Mix	275	4.81	227
Quiet Towns	504	8.81	414
Struggling Downtowns	254	4.44	141

Alberta

FINANCIAL P$YTE

2001 Estimates	No. of House-holds	% of Total Hhds.	Index
Successful Suburbanites	1,291	22.56	340
Canadian Comfort	1,229	21.48	221
Miners & Credit-Liners	492	8.60	272
Mortgages & Minivans	483	8.44	128
Tractors & Tradelines	1,194	20.87	365
Bills & Wills	275	4.81	58
Limited Budgets	504	8.81	283
Towering Debt	254	4.44	57

HOME LANGUAGE
2001 Estimates:

		% Total
English	16,613	98.77
French	43	0.26
Arabic	13	0.08
German	31	0.18
Greek	11	0.07
Serbian	17	0.10
Other Languages	17	0.10
Multiple Responses	75	0.45
Total	16,820	100.00

BUILDING PERMITS

	1999	1998	1997
		$000	
Value	22,985	17,044	14,908

HOMES BUILT

	1999	1998	1997
No.	135	120	163

TAXATION

Income Class:	1997	% Total
Under $5,000	2,440	13.23
$5,000-$10,000	2,190	11.88
$10,000-$15,000	2,080	11.28
$15,000-$20,000	1,600	8.68
$20,000-$25,000	1,340	7.27
$25,000-$30,000	1,360	7.38
$30,000-$40,000	2,330	12.64
$40,000-$50,000	1,720	9.33
$50,000 +	3,380	18.33
Total Returns, No.	18,440	
Total Income, $000	570,965	
Total Taxable Returns	13,600	
Total Tax, $000	113,382	
Average Income, $	30,963	
Average Tax, $	8,337	

VITAL STATISTICS

	1997	1996	1995	1994
Births	237	212	264	223
Deaths	58	42	61	58
Natural Increase	179	170	203	165
Marriages	105	98	118	132

Note: Latest available data.

MEDIA INFO
see Edmonton, CMA

Alberta

St. Albert
(City)
Edmonton CMA
In census division No. 11.

POPULATION

July 1, 2001 Estimate	55,000
% Cdn. Total	0.18
% Change, '96 -'01	14.06
Avg. Annual Growth Rate, %	2.67
2003 Projected Population	58,403
2006 Projected Population	63,112
2001 Households Estimate	18,796
2003 Projected Households	20,242
2006 Projected Households	22,361

INCOME

% Above/Below National Average	+27
2001 Total Income Estimate	$1,468,700,000
% Cdn. Total	0.22
2001 Average Hhld. Income	$78,100
2001 Per Capita	$26,700
2003 Projected Total Income	$1,658,860,000
2006 Projected Total Income	$1,971,500,000

RETAIL SALES

% Above/Below National Average	+20
2001 Retail Sales Estimate	$590,750,000
% Cdn. Total	0.21
2001 per Household	$31,400
2001 per Capita	$10,700
2001 No. of Establishments	337
2003 Projected Retail Sales	$672,540,000
2006 Projected Retail Sales	$797,850,000

POPULATION

2001 Estimates:

Total		55,000
Male		27,212
Female		27,788

Age Groups	Male	Female
0-4	1,751	1,699
5-9	1,979	1,873
10-14	2,283	2,154
15-19	2,379	2,251
20-24	2,144	2,084
25-29	1,806	1,807
30-34	1,780	1,879
35-39	2,083	2,276
40-44	2,304	2,508
45-49	2,322	2,470
50-54	2,057	2,050
55-59	1,554	1,513
60-64	1,075	1,061
65-69	729	745
70+	966	1,418

DAYTIME POPULATION

2001 Estimates:

Working Population	4,239
At Home Population	22,158
Total	26,397

INCOME

2001 Estimates:

Avg. Household Income	$78,139
Avg. Family Income	$82,271
Per Capita Income	$26,704
Male:	
Avg. Employment Income	$45,898
Avg. Employment Income (Full Time)	$58,458
Female:	
Avg. Employment Income	$24,928
Avg. Employment Income (Full Time)	$37,601

DISPOSABLE & DISCRETIONARY INCOME

2001 Estimates:	Per Hhld.
Disposable Income	$59,131
Discretionary Income 1 (minus Food & Shelter)	$42,157
Discretionary Income 2 (minus Food, Shelter, & Other Expenditures)	$31,361

LIQUID ASSETS

1999 Estimates:	Per Hhld.
Equity Investments	$133,132
Interest Bearing Investments	$98,972
Total Liquid Assets	$232,104

CREDIT DATA

July 2000:

Pool of Credit	$703,869,221
Revolving Credit, No.	116,048
Fixed Loans, No.	36,740
Avg. Credit Limit, per Person	$16,541
Avg. Spent, per Person	$7,337
Satisfactory Ratings, No. per Person	3.39
Avg. No. of Cards, per Person	1.27

LABOUR FORCE

2001 Estimates:

Male:	
In the Labour Force	18,035
Participation Rate	85.1
Employed	17,418
Unemployed	617
Unemployment Rate	3.4
Not in Labour Force	3,164
Female:	
In the Labour Force	15,952
Participation Rate	72.3
Employed	15,298
Unemployed	654
Unemployment Rate	4.1
Not in Labour Force	6,110

OCCUPATIONS BY MAJOR GROUPS

2001 Estimates:	Male	Female
Management	3,117	962
Business, Finance & Admin.	2,134	5,619
Natural & Applied Sciences & Related	1,674	262
Health	309	1,405
Social Sciences, Gov't Services & Religion	552	524
Education	732	927
Arts, Culture, Recreation & Sport	415	599
Sales & Service	4,401	4,974
Trades, Transport & Equipment Operators & Related	3,420	216
Primary Industries	335	109
Processing, Mfg. & Utilities	700	106

LEVEL OF SCHOOLING

2001 Estimates:

Population 15 years +	43,261
Less than Grade 9	975
Grades 9-13 w/o Certif.	9,203
Grade 9-13 with Certif.	5,779
Trade Certif. /Dip.	1,243
Non-Univ. w/o Certif./Dip.	2,683
Non-Univ. with Certif./Dip.	10,261
Univ. w/o Degree	5,639
Univ. w/o Degree/Certif.	3,002
Univ. with Certif.	2,637
Univ. with Degree	7,478

AVERAGE HOUSEHOLD EXPENDITURES

2001 Estimates:

Food	$8,035
Shelter	$11,878
Clothing	$3,135
Transportation	$8,394
Health & Personal Care	$2,418
Recr'n, Read'g & Education	$5,259
Taxes & Securities	$21,921
Other	$10,545
Total Expenditures	$71,585

PRIVATE HOUSEHOLDS

2001 Estimates:

Private Households, Total	18,796
Pop. in Private Households	54,270
Average no. per Household	2.9

FAMILIES

2001 Estimates:

Families in Private Households	16,157
Husband-Wife Families	14,308
Lone-Parent Families	1,849
Aver. No. Persons per Family	3.2
Aver. No. Sons/Daughters at Home	1.4

HOUSING

2001 Estimates:

Occupied Private Dwellings	18,796
Owned	16,042
Rented	2,754
Single-Detached House	14,458
Semi-Detached House	638
Row Houses	1,914
Apartment, 5+ Storeys	72
Owned Apartment, 5+ Storeys	52
Apartment, 5 or Fewer Storeys	1,685
Apartment, Detached Duplex	29

VEHICLES

2001 Estimates:

Model Yrs. '81-'96, No.	25,520
% Total	80.73
Model Yrs. '97-'98, No.	3,667
% Total	11.60
'99 Vehicles registered in Model Yr. '99, No.	2,424
% Total	7.67
Total No. '81-'99	31,611

LEGAL MARITAL STATUS

2001 Estimates: (Age 15+)

Single (Never Married)	11,499
Legally Married (Not Separated)	26,834
Legally Married (Separated)	968
Widowed	1,419
Divorced	2,541

PSYTE CATEGORIES

2001 Estimates	No. of House-holds	% of Total Hhds.	Index
Suburban Executives	1,530	8.14	568
Mortgaged in Suburbia	1,813	9.65	694
Technocrafts & Bureaucrats	6,269	33.35	1,185
Boomers & Teens	288	1.53	85
Stable Suburban Families	406	2.16	166

2001 Estimates	No. of House-holds	% of Total Hhds.	Index
Old Bungalow Burbs	2,941	15.65	944
Satellite Suburbs	1,609	8.56	298
Kindergarten Boom	1,443	7.68	293
Conservative Homebodies	796	4.23	117
High Rise Sunsets	177	0.94	66
Young Urban Mix	23	0.12	6
Young City Singles	889	4.73	206
Town Renters	109	0.58	67
Nesters & Young Homesteaders	411	2.19	94

FINANCIAL P$YTE

2001 Estimates	No. of House-holds	% of Total Hhds.	Index
Four Star Investors	1,818	9.67	193
Successful Suburbanites	8,488	45.16	681
Canadian Comfort	1,609	8.56	88
Miners & Credit-Liners	2,941	15.65	494
Mortgages & Minivans	1,443	7.68	116
Bills & Wills	819	4.36	53
Revolving Renters	588	3.13	68
Towering Debt	998	5.31	68

HOME LANGUAGE

2001 Estimates:		% Total
English	53,340	96.98
French	360	0.65
Arabic	84	0.15
Chinese	269	0.49
German	80	0.15
Hindi	87	0.16
Polish	73	0.13
Spanish	40	0.07
Ukrainian	29	0.05
Other Languages	176	0.32
Multiple Responses	462	0.84
Total	55,000	100.00

BUILDING PERMITS

	1999	1998 $000	1997
Value	80,750	68,782	68,746

HOMES BUILT

	1999	1998	1997
No.	521	602	446

TAXATION

Income Class:	1997	% Total
Under $5,000	4,220	11.30
$5,000-$10,000	3,800	10.18
$10,000-$15,000	3,660	9.80
$15,000-$20,000	2,940	7.87
$20,000-$25,000	2,730	7.31
$25,000-$30,000	2,690	7.20
$30,000-$40,000	4,930	13.20
$40,000-$50,000	3,840	10.28
$50,000 +	8,540	22.87
Total Returns, No.	37,340	
Total Income, $000	1,296,410	
Total Taxable Returns	29,330	
Total Tax, $000	272,225	
Average Income, $	34,719	
Average Tax, $	9,281	

VITAL STATISTICS

	1997	1996	1995	1994
Births	546	527	537	591
Deaths	151	164	172	146
Natural Increase	395	363	365	445
Marriages	252	244	272	257

Note: Latest available data.

MEDIA INFO
see Edmonton, CMA

Strathcona County
(Specialized Municipality)
Edmonton CMA

In census division No. 11.

POPULATION

July 1, 2001 Estimate	77,283
% Cdn. Total	0.25
% Change, '96 -'01	17.08
Avg. Annual Growth Rate, %	3.20
2003 Projected Population	82,511
2006 Projected Population	89,784
2001 Households Estimate	25,728
2003 Projected Households	27,853
2006 Projected Households	30,978

INCOME

% Above/Below National Average	+29
2001 Total Income Estimate	$2,102,380,000
% Cdn. Total	0.32
2001 Average Hhld. Income	$81,700
2001 Per Capita	$27,200
2003 Projected Total Income	$2,394,770,000
2006 Projected Total Income	$2,879,710,000

RETAIL SALES

% Above/Below National Average	-41
2001 Retail Sales Estimate	$408,330,000
% Cdn. Total	0.15
2001 per Household	$15,900
2001 per Capita	$5,300
2001 No. of Establishments	389
2003 Projected Retail Sales	$462,340,000
2006 Projected Retail Sales	$547,090,000

POPULATION

2001 Estimates:

Total		77,283
Male		38,805
Female		38,478

Age Groups	Male	Female
0-4	2,526	2,370
5-9	2,885	2,719
10-14	3,230	3,034
15-19	3,312	3,102
20-24	2,889	2,734
25-29	2,418	2,385
30-34	2,473	2,666
35-39	2,991	3,248
40-44	3,295	3,432
45-49	3,254	3,342
50-54	2,925	2,937
55-59	2,323	2,199
60-64	1,642	1,504
65-69	1,089	1,025
70+	1,553	1,781

DAYTIME POPULATION

2001 Estimates:

Working Population	2,302
At Home Population	32,116
Total	34,418

INCOME

2001 Estimates:

Avg. Household Income	$81,716
Avg. Family Income	$84,335
Per Capita Income	$27,204
Male:	
Avg. Employment Income	$47,446
Avg. Employment Income (Full Time)	$60,078
Female:	
Avg. Employment Income	$24,776
Avg. Employment Income (Full Time)	$38,336

DISPOSABLE & DISCRETIONARY INCOME

2001 Estimates: — Per Hhld.

Disposable Income	$61,954
Discretionary Income 1 (minus Food & Shelter)	$44,192
Discretionary Income 2 (minus Food, Shelter, & Other Expenditures)	$32,614

LIQUID ASSETS

1999 Estimates: — Per Hhld.

Equity Investments	$139,670
Interest Bearing Investments	$102,291
Total Liquid Assets	$241,961

CREDIT DATA

July 2000:

Pool of Credit	$793,604,374
Revolving Credit, No.	130,986
Fixed Loans, No.	42,139
Avg. Credit Limit, per Person	$16,194
Avg. Spent, per Person	$7,359
Satisfactory Ratings, No. per Person	3.37
Avg. No. of Cards, per Person	1.22

LABOUR FORCE

2001 Estimates:

Male:	
In the Labour Force	25,421
Participation Rate	84.3
Employed	24,430
Unemployed	991
Unemployment Rate	3.9
Not in Labour Force	4,743
Female:	
In the Labour Force	21,420
Participation Rate	70.6
Employed	20,551
Unemployed	869
Unemployment Rate	4.1
Not in Labour Force	8,935

OCCUPATIONS BY MAJOR GROUPS

2001 Estimates:

	Male	Female
Management	4,021	1,079
Business, Finance & Admin.	2,674	7,763
Natural & Applied Sciences & Related	2,554	340
Health	331	2,107
Social Sciences, Gov't Services & Religion	535	888
Education	614	1,168
Arts, Culture, Recreation & Sport	456	593
Sales & Service	4,336	6,083
Trades, Transport & Equipment Operators & Related	6,320	332
Primary Industries	1,437	518
Processing, Mfg. & Utilities	1,902	286

LEVEL OF SCHOOLING

2001 Estimates:

Population 15 years +	60,519
Less than Grade 9	1,936
Grades 9-13 w/o Certif.	13,556
Grade 9-13 with Certif.	8,325
Trade Certif. /Dip.	2,148
Non-Univ. w/o Certif./Dip.	3,934
Non-Univ. with Certif./Dip.	14,664
Univ. w/o Degree	7,147
Univ. w/o Degree/Certif.	3,595
Univ. with Certif.	3,552
Univ. with Degree	8,809

AVERAGE HOUSEHOLD EXPENDITURES

2001 Estimates:

Food	$8,196
Shelter	$12,482
Clothing	$3,106
Transportation	$9,155
Health & Personal Care	$2,462
Recr'n, Read'g & Education	$5,240
Taxes & Securities	$22,899
Other	$10,982
Total Expenditures	$74,522

PRIVATE HOUSEHOLDS

2001 Estimates:

Private Households, Total	25,728
Pop. in Private Households	76,369
Average no. per Household	3.0

FAMILIES

2001 Estimates:

Families in Private Households	22,681
Husband-Wife Families	20,854
Lone-Parent Families	1,827
Aver. No. Persons per Family	3.3
Aver. No. Sons/Daughters at Home	1.4

HOUSING

2001 Estimates:

Occupied Private Dwellings	25,728
Owned	23,325
Rented	2,403
Single-Detached House	23,018
Semi-Detached House	470
Row Houses	1,132
Apartment, 5 or Fewer Storeys	477
Apartment, Detached Duplex	56
Other Single-Attached	13
Movable Dwellings	562

VEHICLES

2001 Estimates:

Model Yrs. '81-'96, No.	40,237
% Total	81.43
Model Yrs. '97-'98, No.	5,711
% Total	11.56
'99 Vehicles registered in Model Yr. '99, No.	3,466
% Total	7.01
Total No. '81-'99	49,414

LEGAL MARITAL STATUS

2001 Estimates: (Age 15+)

Single (Never Married)	15,104
Legally Married (Not Separated)	39,472
Legally Married (Separated)	1,135
Widowed	1,713
Divorced	3,095

PSYTE CATEGORIES

2001 Estimates	No. of House-holds	% of Total Hhds.	Index
Suburban Executives	1,112	4.32	302
Mortgaged in Suburbia	920	3.58	257
Technocrafts & Bureaucrats	6,300	24.49	870
Boomers & Teens	1,445	5.62	313
Old Bungalow Burbs	3,655	14.21	857
Suburban Nesters	448	1.74	109
Aging Erudites	233	0.91	60
Satellite Suburbs	1,872	7.28	254
Blue Collar Winners	6,642	25.82	1,025
Old Towns' New Fringe	1,189	4.62	118
Rustic Prosperity	458	1.78	99
The Grain Belt	32	0.12	21
Conservative Homebodies	887	3.45	96
Young Urban Mix	319	1.24	59
Old Leafy Towns	41	0.16	6
Struggling Downtowns	70	0.27	9

Alberta

FINAN¢IAL P$YTE

2001 Estimates	No. of House-holds	% of Total Hhds.	Index
Four Star Investors	2,557	9.94	198
Successful Suburbanites	7,220	28.06	423
Canadian Comfort	8,962	34.83	359
Urban Heights	233	0.91	21
Miners & Credit-Liners	3,655	14.21	449
Tractors & Tradelines	1,647	6.40	112
Bills & Wills	1,247	4.85	59
Country Credit	32	0.12	2
Towering Debt	70	0.27	3

HOME LANGUAGE

2001 Estimates:		% Total
English	75,907	98.22
French	211	0.27
Chinese	96	0.12
German	293	0.38
Italian	75	0.10
Spanish	76	0.10
Ukrainian	63	0.08
Other Languages	223	0.29
Multiple Responses	339	0.44
Total	77,283	100.00

BUILDING PERMITS

	1999	1998	1997
		$000	
Value	134,472	119,968	n.a.

HOMES BUILT

	1999	1998	1997
No.	690	763	540

TAXATION

Income Class:	1997	% Total
Under $5,000	5,190	11.28
$5,000-$10,000	4,670	10.15
$10,000-$15,000	4,540	9.87
$15,000-$20,000	3,680	8.00
$20,000-$25,000	3,420	7.43
$25,000-$30,000	3,430	7.46
$30,000-$40,000	6,070	13.20
$40,000-$50,000	4,580	9.96
$50,000 +	10,410	22.63
Total Returns, No.	46,000	
Total Income, $000	1,616,253	
Total Taxable Returns	36,220	
Total Tax, $000	344,500	
Average Income, $	35,136	
Average Tax, $	9,511	

VITAL STATISTICS

	1997	1996	1995	1994
Births	717	774	762	836
Deaths	248	212	222	203
Natural Increase	469	562	540	633
Marriages	330	323	319	358

Note: Latest available data.

MEDIA INFO
see Edmonton, CMA

Alberta

Sturgeon County
(Municipal District)
Edmonton CMA

In census division No. 11. Name changed from Sturgeon No. 90 in 1998.

POPULATION

July 1, 2001 Estimate	17,735
% Cdn. Total	0.06
% Change, '96 -'01	8.14
Avg. Annual Growth Rate, %	1.58
2003 Projected Population	18,129
2006 Projected Population	18,599
2001 Households Estimate	5,731
2003 Projected Households	5,943
2006 Projected Households	6,240

INCOME

% Above/Below National Average	+9
2001 Total Income Estimate	$405,800,000
% Cdn. Total	0.06
2001 Average Hhld. Income	$70,800
2001 Per Capita	$22,900
2003 Projected Total Income	$439,000,000
2006 Projected Total Income	$491,690,000

RETAIL SALES

% Above/Below National Average	-86
2001 Retail Sales Estimate	$22,100,000
% Cdn. Total	0.01
2001 per Household	$3,900
2001 per Capita	$1,200
2001 No. of Establishments	71
2003 Projected Retail Sales	$23,750,000
2006 Projected Retail Sales	$26,400,000

POPULATION

2001 Estimates:

Total		17,735
Male		9,230
Female		8,505
Age Groups	Male	Female
0-4	540	539
5-9	667	653
10-14	841	724
15-19	859	736
20-24	677	600
25-29	498	491
30-34	554	556
35-39	720	711
40-44	784	771
45-49	744	710
50-54	650	595
55-59	514	445
60-64	405	338
65-69	313	248
70+	464	388

DAYTIME POPULATION

2001 Estimates:

Working Population	260
At Home Population	7,460
Total	7,720

INCOME

2001 Estimates:

Avg. Household Income	$70,807
Avg. Family Income	$72,999
Per Capita Income	$22,881
Male:	
Avg. Employment Income	$39,142
Avg. Employment Income (Full Time)	$49,480
Female:	
Avg. Employment Income	$20,417
Avg. Employment Income (Full Time)	$32,314

DISPOSABLE & DISCRETIONARY INCOME

2001 Estimates:	Per Hhld.
Disposable Income	$54,104
Discretionary Income 1 (minus Food & Shelter)	$37,904
Discretionary Income 2 (minus Food, Shelter, & Other Expenditures)	$26,535

LIQUID ASSETS

1999 Estimates:	Per Hhld.
Equity Investments	$115,308
Interest Bearing Investments	$88,321
Total Liquid Assets	$203,629

CREDIT DATA

July 2000:

Pool of Credit	$132,224,785
Revolving Credit, No.	20,124
Fixed Loans, No.	8,652
Avg. Credit Limit, per Person	$14,711
Avg. Spent, per Person	$7,328
Satisfactory Ratings, No. per Person	2.99
Avg. No. of Cards, per Person	1.00

LABOUR FORCE

2001 Estimates:

Male:	
In the Labour Force	6,157
Participation Rate	85.7
Employed	5,872
Unemployed	285
Unemployment Rate	4.6
Not in Labour Force	1,025
Female:	
In the Labour Force	4,499
Participation Rate	68.3
Employed	4,366
Unemployed	133
Unemployment Rate	3.0
Not in Labour Force	2,090

OCCUPATIONS BY MAJOR GROUPS

2001 Estimates:	Male	Female
Management	588	252
Business, Finance & Admin.	333	1,573
Natural & Applied Sciences & Related	332	59
Health	38	313
Social Sciences, Gov't Services & Religion	93	61
Education	124	156
Arts, Culture, Recreation & Sport	83	112
Sales & Service	982	1,315
Trades, Transport & Equipment Operators & Related	1,934	156
Primary Industries	1,121	371
Processing, Mfg. & Utilities	480	32

LEVEL OF SCHOOLING

2001 Estimates:

Population 15 years +	13,771
Less than Grade 9	741
Grades 9-13 w/o Certif.	4,023
Grade 9-13 with Certif.	2,069
Trade Certif. /Dip.	540
Non-Univ. w/o Certif./Dip.	881
Non-Univ. with Certif./Dip.	3,315
Univ. w/o Degree	1,040
Univ. w/o Degree/Certif.	505
Univ. with Certif.	535
Univ. with Degree	1,162

AVERAGE HOUSEHOLD EXPENDITURES

2001 Estimates:

Food	$7,309
Shelter	$11,262
Clothing	$2,567
Transportation	$9,189
Health & Personal Care	$2,244
Recr'n, Read'g & Education	$4,588
Taxes & Securities	$18,379
Other	$10,434
Total Expenditures	$65,972

PRIVATE HOUSEHOLDS

2001 Estimates:

Private Households, Total	5,731
Pop. in Private Households	17,237
Average no. per Household	3.0

FAMILIES

2001 Estimates:

Families in Private Households	5,049
Husband-Wife Families	4,744
Lone-Parent Families	305
Aver. No. Persons per Family	3.3
Aver. No. Sons/Daughters at Home	1.4

HOUSING

2001 Estimates:

Occupied Private Dwellings	5,731
Owned	4,864
Rented	867
Single-Detached House	4,945
Semi-Detached House	145
Apartment, 5 or Fewer Storeys	11
Apartment, Detached Duplex	11
Movable Dwellings	619

VEHICLES

2001 Estimates:

Model Yrs. '81-'96, No.	11,032
% Total	83.37
Model Yrs. '97-'98, No.	1,424
% Total	10.76
'99 Vehicles registered in Model Yr. '99, No.	777
% Total	5.87
Total No. '81-'99	13,233

LEGAL MARITAL STATUS

2001 Estimates: (Age 15+)

Single (Never Married)	3,353
Legally Married (Not Separated)	9,169
Legally Married (Separated)	262
Widowed	308
Divorced	679

PSYTE CATEGORIES

2001 Estimates	No. of House-holds	% of Total Hhds.	Index
Boomers & Teens	260	4.54	253
Small City Elite	133	2.32	135
Blue Collar Winners	2,537	44.27	1,758
Old Towns' New Fringe	1,427	24.90	636
Rustic Prosperity	1,229	21.44	1,188
Young City Singles	100	1.74	76

FINANCIAL P$YTE

2001 Estimates	No. of House-holds	% of Total Hhds.	Index
Four Star Investors	260	4.54	90
Canadian Comfort	2,670	46.59	479
Tractors & Tradelines	2,656	46.34	810
Towering Debt	100	1.74	22

HOME LANGUAGE

2001 Estimates:		% Total
English	17,191	96.93
French	297	1.67
German	139	0.78
Italian	11	0.06
Portuguese	22	0.12
Ukrainian	11	0.06
Multiple Responses	64	0.36
Total	17,735	100.00

BUILDING PERMITS

	1999	1998 $000	1997
Value	n.a.	20,672	16,120

HOMES BUILT

	1999	1998	1997
No.	102	118	67

TAXATION

Income Class:	1997	% Total
Under $5,000	410	18.39
$5,000-$10,000	240	10.76
$10,000-$15,000	200	8.97
$15,000-$20,000	180	8.07
$20,000-$25,000	140	6.28
$25,000-$30,000	180	8.07
$30,000-$40,000	400	17.94
$40,000-$50,000	260	11.66
$50,000 +	210	9.42
Total Returns, No.	2,230	
Total Income, $000	56,830	
Total Taxable Returns	1,610	
Total Tax, $000	9,829	
Average Income, $	25,484	
Average Tax, $	6,105	

VITAL STATISTICS

	1997	1996	1995	1994
Births	174	192	144	180
Deaths	40	40	36	38
Natural Increase	134	152	108	142
Marriages	70	66	61	55

Note: Latest available data.

MEDIA INFO
see Edmonton, CMA

Foothills No. 31
(Municipal District)
In census division No. 6.

POPULATION

July 1, 2001 Estimate	17,628
% Cdn. Total	0.06
% Change, '96 -'01	24.93
Avg. Annual Growth Rate, %	4.55
2003 Projected Population	19,435
2006 Projected Population	22,102
2001 Households Estimate	6,115
2003 Projected Households	6,801
2006 Projected Households	7,855

INCOME

% Above/Below National Average	+67
2001 Total Income Estimate	$620,780,000
% Cdn. Total	0.09
2001 Average Hhld. Income	$101,500
2001 Per Capita	$35,200
2003 Projected Total Income	$730,660,000
2006 Projected Total Income	$921,660,000

RETAIL SALES

% Above/Below National Average	+17
2001 Retail Sales Estimate	$184,850,000
% Cdn. Total	0.07
2001 per Household	$30,200
2001 per Capita	$10,500
2001 No. of Establishments	226
2003 Projected Retail Sales	$219,560,000
2006 Projected Retail Sales	$276,250,000

POPULATION

2001 Estimates:

Total		17,628
Male		9,008
Female		8,620

Age Groups	Male	Female
0-4	520	481
5-9	622	567
10-14	729	653
15-19	715	639
20-24	603	571
25-29	535	519
30-34	536	570
35-39	658	718
40-44	766	784
45-49	754	751
50-54	684	651
55-59	560	522
60-64	460	405
65-69	350	300
70+	516	489

DAYTIME POPULATION

2001 Estimates:

Working Population	8,593
At Home Population	6,776
Total	15,369

INCOME

2001 Estimates:

Avg. Household Income	$101,517
Avg. Family Income	$108,774
Per Capita Income	$35,215
Male:	
Avg. Employment Income	$60,125
Avg. Employment Income (Full Time)	$76,739
Female:	
Avg. Employment Income	$26,081
Avg. Employment Income (Full Time)	$38,689

DISPOSABLE & DISCRETIONARY INCOME

2001 Estimates:	Per Hhld.
Disposable Income	$74,651
Discretionary Income 1 (minus Food & Shelter)	$54,829
Discretionary Income 2 (minus Food, Shelter, & Other Expenditures)	$40,832

LIQUID ASSETS

1999 Estimates:	Per Hhld.
Equity Investments	$257,975
Interest Bearing Investments	$139,676
Total Liquid Assets	$397,651

CREDIT DATA

July 2000:

Pool of Credit	$223,139,165
Revolving Credit, No.	29,840
Fixed Loans, No.	10,183
Avg. Credit Limit, per Person	$16,272
Avg. Spent, per Person	$7,718
Satisfactory Ratings, No. per Person	2.81
Avg. No. of Cards, per Person	1.08

LABOUR FORCE

2001 Estimates:

Male:	
In the Labour Force	6,211
Participation Rate	87.0
Employed	6,097
Unemployed	114
Unemployment Rate	1.8
Not in Labour Force	926
Female:	
In the Labour Force	4,908
Participation Rate	70.9
Employed	4,792
Unemployed	116
Unemployment Rate	2.4
Not in Labour Force	2,011

OCCUPATIONS BY MAJOR GROUPS

2001 Estimates:	Male	Female
Management	1,064	233
Business, Finance & Admin.	263	1,576
Natural & Applied Sciences & Related	477	114
Health	142	372
Social Sciences, Gov't Services & Religion	181	68
Education	93	182
Arts, Culture, Recreation & Sport	127	121
Sales & Service	725	1,092
Trades, Transport & Equipment Operators & Related	1,248	149
Primary Industries	1,709	907
Processing, Mfg. & Utilities	139	70

LEVEL OF SCHOOLING

2001 Estimates:

Population 15 years +	14,056
Less than Grade 9	535
Grades 9-13 w/o Certif.	3,272
Grade 9-13 with Certif.	1,637
Trade Certif. /Dip.	434
Non-Univ. w/o Certif./Dip.	993
Non-Univ. with Certif./Dip.	3,262
Univ. w/o Degree	1,653
Univ. w/o Degree/Certif.	902
Univ. with Certif.	751
Univ. with Degree	2,270

AVERAGE HOUSEHOLD EXPENDITURES

2001 Estimates:

Food	$8,765
Shelter	$14,456
Clothing	$3,439
Transportation	$11,364
Health & Personal Care	$2,818
Recr'n, Read'g & Education	$6,091
Taxes & Securities	$28,919
Other	$13,852
Total Expenditures	$89,704

PRIVATE HOUSEHOLDS

2001 Estimates:

Private Households, Total	6,115
Pop. in Private Households	17,057
Average no. per Household	2.8

FAMILIES

2001 Estimates:

Families in Private Households	5,217
Husband-Wife Families	4,997
Lone-Parent Families	220
Aver. No. Persons per Family	3.1
Aver. No. Sons/Daughters at Home	1.1

HOUSING

2001 Estimates:

Occupied Private Dwellings	6,115
Owned	5,212
Rented	903
Single-Detached House	5,734
Semi-Detached House	149
Apartment, 5 or Fewer Storeys	13
Apartment, Detached Duplex	27
Movable Dwellings	192

VEHICLES

2001 Estimates:

Model Yrs. '81-'96, No.	9,987
% Total	75.52
Model Yrs. '97-'98, No.	2,093
% Total	15.83
'99 Vehicles registered in Model Yr. '99, No.	1,144
% Total	8.65
Total No. '81-'99	13,224

LEGAL MARITAL STATUS

2001 Estimates: (Age 15+)

Single (Never Married)	3,273
Legally Married (Not Separated)	9,202
Legally Married (Separated)	289
Widowed	389
Divorced	903

PSYTE CATEGORIES

2001 Estimates	No. of House-holds	% of Total Hhds.	Index
The Affluentials	320	5.23	818
Suburban Executives	291	4.76	332
Boomers & Teens	2,715	44.40	2,477
Blue Collar Winners	1,539	25.17	1,000
Rustic Prosperity	1,247	20.39	1,130

FINAN¢IAL P$YTE

2001 Estimates	No. of House-holds	% of Total Hhds.	Index
Platinum Estates	320	5.23	649
Four Star Investors	3,006	49.16	979
Canadian Comfort	1,539	25.17	259
Tractors & Tradelines	1,247	20.39	357

Alberta

HOME LANGUAGE

2001 Estimates:		% Total
English	17,037	96.65
French	13	0.07
Dutch	33	0.19
German	296	1.68
Italian	13	0.07
Korean	20	0.11
Punjabi	32	0.18
Other Languages	24	0.14
Multiple Responses	160	0.91
Total	17,628	100.00

BUILDING PERMITS

	1999	1998	1997
		$000	
Value	53,647	71,812	48,487

TAXATION

Income Class:	1997	% Total
Under $5,000	600	10.99
$5,000-$10,000	580	10.62
$10,000-$15,000	520	9.52
$15,000-$20,000	390	7.14
$20,000-$25,000	340	6.23
$25,000-$30,000	350	6.41
$30,000-$40,000	650	11.90
$40,000-$50,000	440	8.06
$50,000 +	1,610	29.49
Total Returns, No.	5,460	
Total Income, $000	296,565	
Total Taxable Returns	4,280	
Total Tax, $000	76,151	
Average Income, $	54,316	
Average Tax, $	17,792	

VITAL STATISTICS

	1997	1996	1995	1994
Births	149	145	142	160
Deaths	39	48	46	31
Natural Increase	110	97	96	129
Marriages	115	136	131	121

Note: Latest available data.

Alberta

Grand Centre
(Census Agglomeration)

The Census Agglomeration of Grand Centre includes: Grand Centre, T; Bonnyville No. 87, MD; Bonnyville, T; Cold Lake, T; Lac La Biche, T; plus several smaller areas. All are in census division No. 12.

POPULATION

July 1, 2001 Estimate	40,682
% Cdn. Total	0.13
% Change, '96 -'01	7.05
Avg. Annual Growth Rate, %	1.37
2003 Projected Population	41,012
2006 Projected Population	40,639
2001 Households Estimate	13,683
2003 Projected Households	13,951
2006 Projected Households	14,218

INCOME

% Above/Below National Average	-13
2001 Total Income Estimate	$742,060,000
% Cdn. Total	0.11
2001 Average Hhld. Income	$54,200
2001 Per Capita	$18,200
2003 Projected Total Income	$791,110,000
2006 Projected Total Income	$859,110,000

RETAIL SALES

% Above/Below National Average	+9
2001 Retail Sales Estimate	$395,770,000
% Cdn. Total	0.14
2001 per Household	$28,900
2001 per Capita	$9,700
2001 No. of Establishments	326
2003 Projected Retail Sales	$428,300,000
2006 Projected Retail Sales	$468,290,000

POPULATION

2001 Estimates:

Total		40,682
Male		21,084
Female		19,598

Age Groups	Male	Female
0-4	1,536	1,463
5-9	1,841	1,702
10-14	1,975	1,774
15-19	1,812	1,583
20-24	1,459	1,282
25-29	1,322	1,277
30-34	1,701	1,634
35-39	1,988	1,842
40-44	1,805	1,627
45-49	1,394	1,273
50-54	1,044	987
55-59	836	771
60-64	721	641
65-69	571	537
70+	1,079	1,205

DAYTIME POPULATION

2001 Estimates:

Working Population	20,797
At Home Population	19,904
Total	40,701

INCOME

2001 Estimates:

Avg. Household Income	$54,232
Avg. Family Income	$57,627
Per Capita Income	$18,241
Male:	
Avg. Employment Income	$35,833
Avg. Employment Income (Full Time)	$44,746
Female:	
Avg. Employment Income	$18,072
Avg. Employment Income (Full Time)	$27,840

DISPOSABLE & DISCRETIONARY INCOME

2001 Estimates:	Per Hhld.
Disposable Income	$41,861
Discretionary Income 1 (minus Food & Shelter)	$29,890
Discretionary Income 2 (minus Food, Shelter, & Other Expenditures)	$20,415

LIQUID ASSETS

1999 Estimates:	Per Hhld.
Equity Investments	$81,448
Interest Bearing Investments	$67,698
Total Liquid Assets	$149,146

CREDIT DATA

July 2000:

Pool of Credit	$347,540,296
Revolving Credit, No.	49,436
Fixed Loans, No.	27,994
Avg. Credit Limit, per Person	$13,071
Avg. Spent, per Person	$6,994
Satisfactory Ratings, No. per Person	2.72
Avg. No. of Cards, per Person	0.83

LABOUR FORCE

2001 Estimates:

Male:	
In the Labour Force	12,973
Participation Rate	82.5
Employed	12,030
Unemployed	943
Unemployment Rate	7.3
Not in Labour Force	2,759
Female:	
In the Labour Force	9,488
Participation Rate	64.7
Employed	8,860
Unemployed	628
Unemployment Rate	6.6
Not in Labour Force	5,171

OCCUPATIONS BY MAJOR GROUPS

2001 Estimates:	Male	Female
Management	1,329	546
Business, Finance & Admin.	326	2,349
Natural & Applied Sciences & Related	735	101
Health	103	689
Social Sciences, Gov't Services & Religion	211	128
Education	314	673
Arts, Culture, Recreation & Sport	76	113
Sales & Service	2,986	3,903
Trades, Transport & Equipment Operators & Related	3,600	215
Primary Industries	2,207	466
Processing, Mfg. & Utilities	924	97

LEVEL OF SCHOOLING

2001 Estimates:

Population 15 years +	30,391
Less than Grade 9	3,234
Grades 9-13 w/o Certif.	8,654
Grade 9-13 with Certif.	4,007
Trade Certif./Dip.	1,408
Non-Univ. w/o Certif./Dip.	2,160
Non-Univ. with Certif./Dip.	6,536
Univ. w/o Degree	2,062
Univ. w/o Degree/Certif.	915
Univ. with Certif.	1,147
Univ. with Degree	2,330

AVERAGE HOUSEHOLD EXPENDITURES

2001 Estimates:

Food	$6,366
Shelter	$7,733
Clothing	$2,443
Transportation	$7,271
Health & Personal Care	$2,164
Recr'n, Read'g & Education	$4,130
Taxes & Securities	$12,625
Other	$9,199
Total Expenditures	$51,931

PRIVATE HOUSEHOLDS

2001 Estimates:

Private Households, Total	13,683
Pop. in Private Households	39,736
Average no. per Household	2.9

FAMILIES

2001 Estimates:

Families in Private Households	10,915
Husband-Wife Families	9,611
Lone-Parent Families	1,304
Aver. No. Persons per Family	3.3
Aver. No. Sons/Daughters at Home	1.4

HOUSING

2001 Estimates:

Occupied Private Dwellings	13,683
Owned	9,303
Rented	4,104
Band Housing	276
Single-Detached House	10,026
Semi-Detached House	1,079
Row Houses	372
Apartment, 5+ Storeys	22
Owned Apartment, 5+ Storeys	11
Apartment, 5 or Fewer Storeys	1,002
Apartment, Detached Duplex	45
Other Single-Attached	37
Movable Dwellings	1,100

VEHICLES

2001 Estimates:

Model Yrs. '81-'96, No.	19,010
% Total	79.52
Model Yrs. '97-'98, No.	3,430
% Total	14.35
'99 Vehicles registered in Model Yr. '99, No.	1,466
% Total	6.13
Total No. '81-'99	23,906

LEGAL MARITAL STATUS

2001 Estimates: (Age 15+)

Single (Never Married)	9,055
Legally Married (Not Separated)	17,319
Legally Married (Separated)	844
Widowed	1,325
Divorced	1,848

PSYTE CATEGORIES

2001 Estimates	No. of House-holds	% of Total Hhds.	Index
Town Boomers	2,129	15.56	1,535
Old Towns' New Fringe	1,203	8.79	225
The New Frontier	4,534	33.14	2,197
Pick-ups & Dirt Bikes	2,641	19.30	2,312

2001 Estimates	No. of House-holds	% of Total Hhds.	Index
The Grain Belt	274	2.00	338
Old Leafy Towns	62	0.45	18
Quiet Towns	648	4.74	223
Rod & Rifle	163	1.19	52
Down, Down East	152	1.11	158
Big Country Families	861	6.29	441
Old Cdn. Rustics	932	6.81	695

FINANCIAL P$YTE

2001 Estimates	No. of House-holds	% of Total Hhds.	Index
Canadian Comfort	2,129	15.56	160
Miners & Credit-Liners	4,534	33.14	1,047
Tractors & Tradelines	1,203	8.79	154
Bills & Wills	62	0.45	5
Country Credit	2,915	21.30	315
Rural Family Blues	1,176	8.59	106
Limited Budgets	1,580	11.55	371

HOME LANGUAGE

2001 Estimates:		% Total
English	37,183	91.40
French	1,620	3.98
Arabic	106	0.26
Chinese	35	0.09
Chipewyan	61	0.15
Cree	274	0.67
Greek	22	0.05
Persian (Farsi)	22	0.05
Polish	28	0.07
Russian	364	0.89
Spanish	41	0.10
Ukrainian	42	0.10
Other Languages	43	0.11
Multiple Responses	841	2.07
Total	40,682	100.00

BUILDING PERMITS

	1999	1998 $000	1997
Value	33,460	32,291	71,425

HOMES BUILT

	1999	1998	1997
No	129	230	220

TAXATION

Income Class:	1997	% Total
Under $5,000	3,830	15.64
$5,000-$10,000	3,220	13.15
$10,000-$15,000	3,420	13.96
$15,000-$20,000	2,240	9.15
$20,000-$25,000	1,720	7.02
$25,000-$30,000	1,530	6.25
$30,000-$40,000	2,920	11.92
$40,000-$50,000	2,500	10.21
$50,000 +	3,140	12.82
Total Returns, No.	24,490	
Total Income, $000	650,527	
Total Taxable Returns	16,710	
Total Tax, $000	123,196	
Average Income, $.	26,563	
Average Tax, $	7,373	

VITAL STATISTICS

	1997	1996	1995	1994
Births	632	604	563	595
Deaths	181	183	172	175
Natural Increase	451	421	391	420
Marriages	171	193	200	193

Note: Latest available data.

COMMUNITY NEWSPAPER(S)

	Total Circulation
Bonnyville: Bonnyville Nouvelle	3,942
Cold Lake: Cold Lake Courier	2,980
Cold Lake: Cold Lake Sun	5,532
Lac la Biche: Lac La Biche Post	2,754

Grande Prairie
(Census Agglomeration)

The Census Agglomeration of Grande Prairie consists solely of Grande Prairie, C, in census division No. 19.

POPULATION

July 1, 2001 Estimate	35,751
% Cdn. Total	0.11
% Change, '96 -'01	11.60
Avg. Annual Growth Rate, %	2.22
2003 Projected Population	37,150
2006 Projected Population	38,559
2001 Households Estimate	13,047
2003 Projected Households	13,785
2006 Projected Households	14,667

INCOME

% Above/Below National Average	+7
2001 Total Income Estimate	$808,640,000
% Cdn. Total	0.12
2001 Average Hhld. Income	$62,000
2001 Per Capita	$22,600
2003 Projected Total Income	$890,010,000
2006 Projected Total Income	$1,002,770,000

RETAIL SALES

% Above/Below National Average	+108
2001 Retail Sales Estimate	$664,260,000
% Cdn. Total	0.24
2001 per Household	$50,900
2001 per Capita	$18,600
2001 No. of Establishments	371
2003 Projected Retail Sales	$746,180,000
2006 Projected Retail Sales	$859,010,000

POPULATION

2001 Estimates:

Total	35,751
Male	18,102
Female	17,649

Age Groups	Male	Female
0-4	1,436	1,365
5-9	1,450	1,360
10-14	1,418	1,350
15-19	1,356	1,307
20-24	1,485	1,420
25-29	1,626	1,554
30-34	1,730	1,677
35-39	1,768	1,678
40-44	1,602	1,475
45-49	1,262	1,162
50-54	880	849
55-59	603	625
60-64	460	484
65-69	359	383
70+	667	960

DAYTIME POPULATION

2001 Estimates:

Working Population	20,582
At Home Population	15,169
Total	35,751

INCOME

2001 Estimates:

Avg. Household Income	$61,979
Avg. Family Income	$65,719
Per Capita Income	$22,619
Male:	
Avg. Employment Income	$39,664
Avg. Employment Income (Full Time)	$50,353
Female:	
Avg. Employment Income	$19,794
Avg. Employment Income (Full Time)	$29,650

DISPOSABLE & DISCRETIONARY INCOME

2001 Estimates:	Per Hhld.
Disposable Income	$47,315
Discretionary Income 1 (minus Food & Shelter)	$33,245
Discretionary Income 2 (minus Food, Shelter, & Other Expenditures)	$23,621

LIQUID ASSETS

1999 Estimates:	Per Hhld.
Equity Investments	$100,291
Interest Bearing Investments	$79,531
Total Liquid Assets	$179,822

CREDIT DATA

July 2000:

Pool of Credit	$409,222,049
Revolving Credit, No.	59,121
Fixed Loans, No.	33,830
Avg. Credit Limit, per Person	$13,879
Avg. Spent, per Person	$7,518
Satisfactory Ratings, No. per Person	2.89
Avg. No. of Cards, per Person	0.94

LABOUR FORCE

2001 Estimates:

Male:	
In the Labour Force	11,898
Participation Rate	86.2
Employed	11,270
Unemployed	628
Unemployment Rate	5.3
Not in Labour Force	1,900
Female:	
In the Labour Force	9,918
Participation Rate	73.1
Employed	9,323
Unemployed	595
Unemployment Rate	6.0
Not in Labour Force	3,656

OCCUPATIONS BY MAJOR GROUPS

2001 Estimates:	Male	Female
Management	1,209	512
Business, Finance & Admin.	784	2,980
Natural & Applied Sciences & Related	724	78
Health	164	760
Social Sciences, Gov't Services & Religion	190	291
Education	248	551
Arts, Culture, Recreation & Sport	149	272
Sales & Service	2,527	3,895
Trades, Transport & Equipment Operators & Related	3,627	219
Primary Industries	1,133	52
Processing, Mfg. & Utilities	1,046	148

LEVEL OF SCHOOLING

2001 Estimates:

Population 15 years +	27,372
Less than Grade 9	1,471
Grades 9-13 w/o Certif.	7,740
Grade 9-13 with Certif.	3,668
Trade Certif. /Dip.	873
Non-Univ. w/o Certif./Dip.	2,206
Non-Univ. with Certif./Dip.	6,666
Univ. w/o Degree	2,194
Univ. w/o Degree/Certif.	1,141
Univ. with Certif.	1,053
Univ. with Degree	2,554

AVERAGE HOUSEHOLD EXPENDITURES

2001 Estimates:

Food	$7,063
Shelter	$9,460
Clothing	$2,692
Transportation	$6,649
Health & Personal Care	$2,586
Recr'n, Read'g & Education	$4,503
Taxes & Securities	$15,357
Other	$10,108
Total Expenditures	$58,418

PRIVATE HOUSEHOLDS

2001 Estimates:

Private Households, Total	13,047
Pop. in Private Households	35,158
Average no. per Household	2.7

FAMILIES

2001 Estimates:

Families in Private Households	9,808
Husband-Wife Families	8,522
Lone-Parent Families	1,286
Aver. No. Persons per Family	3.1
Aver. No. Sons/Daughters at Home	1.3

HOUSING

2001 Estimates:

Occupied Private Dwellings	13,047
Owned	8,230
Rented	4,817
Single-Detached House	8,299
Semi-Detached House	828
Row Houses	593
Apartment, 5+ Storeys	220
Owned Apartment, 5+ Storeys	23
Apartment, 5 or Fewer Storeys	2,711
Apartment, Detached Duplex	180
Other Single-Attached	11
Movable Dwellings	205

VEHICLES

2001 Estimates:

Model Yrs. '81-'96, No.	16,532
% Total	71.04
Model Yrs. '97-'98, No.	4,200
% Total	18.05
'99 Vehicles registered in Model Yr. '99, No.	2,541
% Total	10.92
Total No. '81-'99	23,273

LEGAL MARITAL STATUS

2001 Estimates: (Age 15+)

Single (Never Married)	9,436
Legally Married (Not Separated)	13,923
Legally Married (Separated)	912
Widowed	1,028
Divorced	2,073

PSYTE CATEGORIES

2001 Estimates	No. of House-holds	% of Total Hhds.	Index
Suburban Executives	226	1.73	121
Town Boomers	5,442	41.71	4,115
Young Grey Collar	7,310	56.03	6,697

FINANCIAL PSYTE

2001 Estimates	No. of House-holds	% of Total Hhds.	Index
Four Star Investors	226	1.73	34
Canadian Comfort	5,442	41.71	429
Revolving Renters	7,310	56.03	1,218

Alberta

HOME LANGUAGE

2001 Estimates:		% Total
English	34,281	95.89
French	228	0.64
Arabic	33	0.09
Chinese	220	0.62
Cree	27	0.08
Croatian	18	0.05
German	34	0.10
Hungarian	24	0.07
Polish	88	0.25
Punjabi	109	0.30
Spanish	183	0.51
Other Languages	104	0.29
Multiple Responses	402	1.12
Total	35,751	100.00

BUILDING PERMITS

	1999	1998	1997
		$000	
Value	72,367	89,723	81,425

HOMES BUILT

	1999	1998	1997
No	793	634	440

TAXATION

Income Class:	1997	% Total
Under $5,000	3,190	11.58
$5,000-$10,000	3,030	11.00
$10,000-$15,000	3,370	12.23
$15,000-$20,000	2,620	9.51
$20,000-$25,000	2,190	7.95
$25,000-$30,000	2,030	7.37
$30,000-$40,000	3,480	12.63
$40,000-$50,000	2,570	9.33
$50,000 +	5,080	18.44
Total Returns, No.	27,550	
Total Income, $000	865,959	
Total Taxable Returns	20,760	
Total Tax, $000	167,154	
Average Income, $	31,432	
Average Tax, $	8,052	

VITAL STATISTICS

	1997	1996	1995	1994
Births	531	543	561	529
Deaths	146	154	176	160
Natural Increase	385	389	385	369
Marriages	238	242	263	274

Note: Latest available data.

DAILY NEWSPAPER(S)

	Circulation Average Paid
Daily Herald-Tribune	
Fri	12,507
Mon-Thu	7,950

Alberta

Grande Prairie
(Census Agglomeration)
(Cont'd)

COMMUNITY NEWSPAPER(S)

	Total Circulation
Grande Prairie: Peace Country Extra	17,353
Grande Prairie: Peace Country Farmer	29,047

RADIO STATION(S)

	Power
CBXP-FM	n.a.
CFGP-FM	100,000w
CHFA-FM	n.a.
CJXX	25,000w
CKUA-FM	100,000w

TELEVISION STATION(S)

CBXFT-TV
CBXT-TV
CFRN-TV

Grande Prairie County No. 1
(County Municipality)
In Census division No. 19.

POPULATION

July 1, 2001 Estimate	15,950
% Cdn. Total	0.05
% Change, '96 -'01	12.75
Avg. Annual Growth Rate, %	2.43
2003 Projected Population	16,693
2006 Projected Population	17,490
2001 Households Estimate	5,356
2003 Projected Households	5,704
2006 Projected Households	6,128

INCOME

% Above/Below National Average	+3
2001 Total Income Estimate	$347,040,000
% Cdn. Total	0.05
2001 Average Hhld. Income	$64,800
2001 Per Capita	$21,800
2003 Projected Total Income	$386,900,000
2006 Projected Total Income	$443,410,000

RETAIL SALES

% Above/Below National Average	-65
2001 Retail Sales Estimate	$49,730,000
% Cdn. Total	0.02
2001 per Household	$9,300
2001 per Capita	$3,100
2001 No. of Establishments	49
2003 Projected Retail Sales	$55,010,000
2006 Projected Retail Sales	$62,240,000

POPULATION

2001 Estimates:

Total		15,950
Male		8,296
Female		7,654

Age Groups	Male	Female
0-4	509	497
5-9	593	586
10-14	720	678
15-19	760	683
20-24	643	559
25-29	543	474
30-34	569	557
35-39	658	668
40-44	710	689
45-49	651	577
50-54	529	461
55-59	414	367
60-64	327	283
65-69	251	213
70+	419	362

DAYTIME POPULATION

2001 Estimates:

Working Population	3,314
At Home Population	6,549
Total	9,863

INCOME

2001 Estimates:

Avg. Household Income	$64,794
Avg. Family Income	$67,286
Per Capita Income	$21,758
Male:	
Avg. Employment Income	$36,865
Avg. Employment Income (Full Time)	$48,410
Female:	
Avg. Employment Income	$18,782
Avg. Employment Income (Full Time)	$27,785

DISPOSABLE & DISCRETIONARY INCOME

2001 Estimates:	Per Hhld.
Disposable Income	$49,419
Discretionary Income 1 (minus Food & Shelter)	$35,289
Discretionary Income 2 (minus Food, Shelter, & Other Expenditures)	$24,876

LIQUID ASSETS

1999 Estimates:	Per Hhld.
Equity Investments	$113,327
Interest Bearing Investments	$82,545
Total Liquid Assets	$195,872

CREDIT DATA

July 2000:

Pool of Credit	$119,078,149
Revolving Credit, No.	14,552
Fixed Loans, No.	9,110
Avg. Credit Limit, per Person	$15,545
Avg. Spent, per Person	$8,567
Satisfactory Ratings, No. per Person	2.84
Avg. No. of Cards, per Person	0.88

LABOUR FORCE

2001 Estimates:

Male:	
In the Labour Force	5,527
Participation Rate	85.4
Employed	5,231
Unemployed	296
Unemployment Rate	5.4
Not in Labour Force	947
Female:	
In the Labour Force	4,253
Participation Rate	72.2
Employed	4,111
Unemployed	142
Unemployment Rate	3.3
Not in Labour Force	1,640

OCCUPATIONS BY MAJOR GROUPS

2001 Estimates:	Male	Female
Management	414	129
Business, Finance & Admin.	261	1,432
Natural & Applied Sciences & Related	255	13
Health	24	86
Social Sciences, Gov't Services & Religion	40	60
Education	55	206
Arts, Culture, Recreation & Sport	26	79
Sales & Service	542	1,264
Trades, Transport & Equipment Operators & Related	1,890	203
Primary Industries	1,556	668
Processing, Mfg. & Utilities	451	75

LEVEL OF SCHOOLING

2001 Estimates:

Population 15 years +	12,367
Less than Grade 9	923
Grades 9-13 w/o Certif.	4,260
Grade 9-13 with Certif.	1,512
Trade Certif. /Dip.	453
Non-Univ. w/o Certif./Dip.	849
Non-Univ. with Certif./Dip.	2,842
Univ. w/o Degree	678
Univ. w/o Degree/Certif.	321
Univ. with Certif.	357
Univ. with Degree	850

AVERAGE HOUSEHOLD EXPENDITURES

2001 Estimates:

Food	$7,221
Shelter	$9,395
Clothing	$2,754
Transportation	$7,927
Health & Personal Care	$2,405
Recr'n, Read'g & Education	$4,564
Taxes & Securities	$15,779
Other	$10,591
Total Expenditures	$60,636

PRIVATE HOUSEHOLDS

2001 Estimates:

Private Households, Total	5,356
Pop. in Private Households	15,603
Average no. per Household	2.9

FAMILIES

2001 Estimates:

Families in Private Households	4,681
Husband-Wife Families	4,340
Lone-Parent Families	341
Aver. No. Persons per Family	3.3
Aver. No. Sons/Daughters at Home	1.3

HOUSING

2001 Estimates:

Occupied Private Dwellings	5,356
Owned	4,854
Rented	502
Single-Detached House	4,095
Semi-Detached House	20
Row Houses	13
Movable Dwellings	1,228

VEHICLES

2001 Estimates:

Model Yrs. '81-'96, No.	9,422
% Total	75.48
Model Yrs. '97-'98, No.	2,030
% Total	16.26
'99 Vehicles registered in Model Yr. '99, No.	1,031
% Total	8.26
Total No. '81-'99	12,483

LEGAL MARITAL STATUS

2001 Estimates: (Age 15+)

Single (Never Married)	3,200
Legally Married (Not Separated)	7,935
Legally Married (Separated)	213
Widowed	334
Divorced	685

PSYTE CATEGORIES

2001 Estimates	No. of House -holds	% of Total Hhds.	Index
Boomers & Teens	146	2.73	152
Town Boomers	2,214	41.34	4,078
Old Towns' New Fringe	149	2.78	71
Rustic Prosperity	892	16.65	923
Pick-ups & Dirt Bikes	834	15.57	1,865
The Grain Belt	293	5.47	923
Old Leafy Towns	41	0.77	30
Young Grey Collar	665	12.42	1,484
Big Country Families	104	1.94	136

FINANCIAL P$YTE

2001 Estimates	No. of House -holds	% of Total Hhds.	Index
Four Star Investors	146	2.73	54
Canadian Comfort	2,214	41.34	425
Tractors & Tradelines	1,041	19.44	340
Bills & Wills	41	0.77	9
Country Credit	1,127	21.04	311
Revolving Renters	665	12.42	270
Rural Family Blues	104	1.94	24

Grande Prairie County No. 1
(County Municipality)
(Cont'd)

HOME LANGUAGE

2001 Estimates:		% Total
English	15,702	98.45
French	72	0.45
Cree	16	0.10
Czech	28	0.18
German	103	0.65
Multiple Responses	29	0.18
Total	15,950	100.00

BUILDING PERMITS

	1999	1998	1997
		$000	
Value	37,076	27,918	15,269

TAXATION

Income Class:	1997	% Total
Under $5,000	350	15.49
$5,000-$10,000	280	12.39
$10,000-$15,000	300	13.27
$15,000-$20,000	260	11.50
$20,000-$25,000	180	7.96
$25,000-$30,000	170	7.52
$30,000-$40,000	280	12.39
$40,000-$50,000	160	7.08
$50,000 +	270	11.95
Total Returns, No.	2,260	
Total Income, $000	54,930	
Total Taxable		
Returns	1,520	
Total Tax, $000	8,833	
Average Income, $	24,305	
Average Tax, $	5,811	

VITAL STATISTICS

	1997	1996	1995	1994
Births	177	165	160	150
Deaths	39	52	46	47
Natural				
Increase	138	113	114	103
Marriages	45	42	52	52

Note: Latest available data.

Lacombe County
(County Municipality)
In census division No. 8.

POPULATION

July 1, 2001 Estimate	11,955
% Cdn. Total	0.04
% Change, '96 -'01	11.61
Avg. Annual Growth Rate, %	2.22
2003 Projected Population	12,353
2006 Projected Population	12,722
2001 Households Estimate	3,895
2003 Projected Households	4,068
2006 Projected Households	4,265

INCOME

% Above/Below National Average	-11
2001 Total Income Estimate	$225,000,000
% Cdn. Total	0.03
2001 Average Hhld. Income	$57,800
2001 Per Capita	$18,800
2003 Projected Total Income	$246,710,000
2006 Projected Total Income	$277,730,000

RETAIL SALES

% Above/Below National Average	-80
2001 Retail Sales Estimate	$21,490,000
% Cdn. Total	0.01
2001 per Household	$5,500
2001 per Capita	$1,800
2001 No. of Establishments	20
2003 Projected Retail Sales	$23,300,000
2006 Projected Retail Sales	$26,560,000

POPULATION

2001 Estimates:		
Total		11,955
Male		6,144
Female		5,811
Age Groups	Male	Female
0-4	393	361
5-9	472	443
10-14	528	494
15-19	537	493
20-24	446	414
25-29	369	335
30-34	366	371
35-39	450	481
40-44	523	483
45-49	493	426
50-54	406	373
55-59	321	313
60-64	257	244
65-69	207	183
70+	376	397

DAYTIME POPULATION

2001 Estimates:	
Working Population	3,125
At Home Population	5,164
Total	8,289

INCOME

2001 Estimates:	
Avg. Household Income	$57,765
Avg. Family Income	$61,906
Per Capita Income	$18,820
Male:	
Avg. Employment Income	$32,112
Avg. Employment Income	
(Full Time)	$40,830
Female:	
Avg. Employment Income	$16,976
Avg. Employment Income	
(Full Time)	$23,896

DISPOSABLE & DISCRETIONARY INCOME

2001 Estimates:	Per Hhld.
Disposable Income	$44,630
Discretionary Income 1	
(minus Food & Shelter)	$31,109
Discretionary Income 2	
(minus Food, Shelter, & Other	
Expenditures)	$20,476

LIQUID ASSETS

1999 Estimates:	Per Hhld.
Equity Investments	$88,143
Interest Bearing Investments	$70,388
Total Liquid Assets	$158,531

CREDIT DATA

July 2000:	
Pool of Credit	$27,260,002
Revolving Credit, No.	3,703
Fixed Loans, No.	1,605
Avg. Credit Limit, per Person	$14,469
Avg. Spent, per Person	$7,747
Satisfactory Ratings,	
No. per Person	2.68
Avg. No. of Cards, per Person	0.92

LABOUR FORCE

2001 Estimates:	
Male:	
In the Labour Force	4,005
Participation Rate	84.3
Employed	3,856
Unemployed	149
Unemployment Rate	3.7
Not in Labour Force	746
Female:	
In the Labour Force	3,060
Participation Rate	67.8
Employed	2,918
Unemployed	142
Unemployment Rate	4.6
Not in Labour Force	1,453

OCCUPATIONS BY MAJOR GROUPS

2001 Estimates:	Male	Female
Management	234	61
Business, Finance		
& Admin.	131	781
Natural & Applied		
Sciences &		
Related	147	40
Health	82	260
Social Sciences,		
Gov't Services		
& Religion	24	52
Education	87	147
Arts, Culture,		
Recreation &		
Sport	28	57
Sales & Service	286	561
Trades, Transport		
& Equipment		
Operators &		
Related	1,126	75
Primary Industries	1,615	955
Processing, Mfg. &		
Utilities	219	60

LEVEL OF SCHOOLING

2001 Estimates:	
Population 15 years +	9,264
Less than Grade 9	550
Grades 9-13 w/o Certif.	3,119
Grade 9-13 with Certif.	1,058
Trade Certif. /Dip.	353
Non-Univ. w/o Certif./Dip.	696
Non-Univ. with Certif./Dip.	2,080
Univ. w/o Degree	719
Univ. w/o Degree/Certif.	383
Univ. with Certif.	336
Univ. with Degree	689

Alberta

AVERAGE HOUSEHOLD EXPENDITURES

2001 Estimates:	
Food	$6,694
Shelter	$8,952
Clothing	$2,234
Transportation	$8,786
Health & Personal Care	$2,047
Recr'n, Read'g & Education	$4,242
Taxes & Securities	$12,692
Other	$9,682
Total Expenditures	$55,329

PRIVATE HOUSEHOLDS

2001 Estimates:	
Private Households, Total	3,895
Pop. in Private Households	11,372
Average no. per Household	2.9

FAMILIES

2001 Estimates:	
Families in Private Households	3,285
Husband-Wife Families	3,087
Lone-Parent Families	198
Aver. No. Persons per Family	3.2
Aver. No. Sons/Daughters	
at Home	1.3

HOUSING

2001 Estimates:	
Occupied Private Dwellings	3,895
Owned	3,123
Rented	772
Single-Detached House	3,272
Semi-Detached House	22
Row Houses	26
Apartment, 5 or Fewer Storeys	20
Apartment, Detached Duplex	37
Movable Dwellings	518

VEHICLES

2001 Estimates:	
Model Yrs. '81-'96, No.	6,333
% Total	82.29
Model Yrs. '97-'98, No.	921
% Total	11.97
'99 Vehicles registered in	
Model Yr. '99, No.	442
% Total	5.74
Total No. '81-'99	7,696

LEGAL MARITAL STATUS

2001 Estimates: (Age 15+)	
Single (Never Married)	2,194
Legally Married	
(Not Separated)	6,099
Legally Married (Separated)	170
Widowed	316
Divorced	485

Alberta

Lacombe County
(County Municipality)
(Cont'd)

PSYTE CATEGORIES

2001 Estimates	No. of House -holds	% of Total Hhds.	Index
Small City Elite	87	2.23	130
Blue Collar Winners	281	7.21	287
Old Towns' New Fringe	74	1.90	49
Rustic Prosperity	3,015	77.41	4,290
The Grain Belt	141	3.62	611
Young City Singles	101	2.59	113
Old Leafy Towns	41	1.05	41
Rod & Rifle	133	3.41	148

FINANCIAL PSYTE

2001 Estimates	No. of House -holds	% of Total Hhds.	Index
Canadian Comfort	368	9.45	97
Tractors & Tradelines	3,089	79.31	1,387
Bills & Wills	41	1.05	13
Country Credit	141	3.62	54
Rural Family Blues	133	3.41	42
Towering Debt	101	2.59	33

HOME LANGUAGE

2001 Estimates:		% Total
English	11,452	95.79
Chinese	22	0.18
Dutch	72	0.60
German	386	3.23
Korean	11	0.09
Multiple Responses	12	0.10
Total	11,955	100.00

BUILDING PERMITS

	1999	1998 $000	1997
Value	34,129	50,083	n.a.

TAXATION

Income Class:	1997	% Total
Under $5,000	110	16.92
$5,000-$10,000	110	16.92
$10,000-$15,000	110	16.92
$15,000-$20,000	60	9.23
$20,000-$25,000	60	9.23
$25,000-$30,000	40	6.15
$30,000-$40,000	70	10.77
$40,000-$50,000	40	6.15
$50,000 +	50	7.69
Total Returns, No.	650	
Total Income, $000	13,524	
Total Taxable Returns	370	
Total Tax, $000	1,794	
Average Income, $	20,806	
Average Tax, $	4,849	

VITAL STATISTICS

	1997	1996	1995	1994
Births	133	134	123	143
Deaths	30	25	36	29
Natural Increase	103	109	87	114
Marriages	30	38	34	35

Note: Latest available data.

COMMUNITY NEWSPAPER(S)

	Total Circulation
Lacombe County: Lacombe Globe	3,102

Lethbridge
(Census Agglomeration)

The Census Agglomeration of Lethbridge consists solely of Lethbridge, C, in census division No. 2.

POPULATION

July 1, 2001 Estimate	68,314
% Cdn. Total	0.22
% Change, '96 -'01	5.54
Avg. Annual Growth Rate, %	1.08
2003 Projected Population	69,184
2006 Projected Population	69,051
2001 Households Estimate	27,546
2003 Projected Households	28,185
2006 Projected Households	28,582

INCOME

% Above/Below National Average	-7
2001 Total Income Estimate	$1,341,290,000
% Cdn. Total	0.20
2001 Average Hhld. Income	$48,700
2001 Per Capita	$19,600
2003 Projected Total Income	$1,401,150,000
2006 Projected Total Income	$1,459,250,000

RETAIL SALES

% Above/Below National Average	+196
2001 Retail Sales Estimate	$1,809,290,000
% Cdn. Total	0.65
2001 per Household	$65,700
2001 per Capita	$26,500
2001 No. of Establishments	628
2003 Projected Retail Sales	$1,939,060,000
2006 Projected Retail Sales	$2,097,540,000

POPULATION

2001 Estimates:		
Total		68,314
Male		32,945
Female		35,369

Age Groups	Male	Female
0-4	2,284	2,144
5-9	2,222	2,090
10-14	2,224	2,113
15-19	2,299	2,278
20-24	2,553	2,619
25-29	2,548	2,644
30-34	2,461	2,514
35-39	2,491	2,572
40-44	2,477	2,634
45-49	2,328	2,493
50-54	1,945	2,078
55-59	1,543	1,643
60-64	1,306	1,418
65-69	1,183	1,398
70+	3,081	4,731

DAYTIME POPULATION

2001 Estimates:	
Working Population	34,828
At Home Population	33,486
Total	68,314

INCOME

2001 Estimates:	
Avg. Household Income	$48,693
Avg. Family Income	$56,034
Per Capita Income	$19,634
Male:	
Avg. Employment Income	$31,226
Avg. Employment Income (Full Time)	$43,607
Female:	
Avg. Employment Income	$18,282
Avg. Employment Income (Full Time)	$28,521

DISPOSABLE & DISCRETIONARY INCOME

2001 Estimates:	Per Hhld.
Disposable Income	$37,387
Discretionary Income 1 (minus Food & Shelter)	$24,975
Discretionary Income 2 (minus Food, Shelter, & Other Expenditures)	$17,247

LIQUID ASSETS

1999 Estimates:	Per Hhld.
Equity Investments	$76,119
Interest Bearing Investments	$64,492
Total Liquid Assets	$140,611

CREDIT DATA

July 2000:	
Pool of Credit	$700,608,495
Revolving Credit, No.	132,119
Fixed Loans, No.	41,520
Avg. Credit Limit, per Person	$11,917
Avg. Spent, per Person	$5,623
Satisfactory Ratings, No. per Person	2.82
Avg. No. of Cards, per Person	1.00

LABOUR FORCE

2001 Estimates:	
Male:	
In the Labour Force	19,247
Participation Rate	73.4
Employed	18,407
Unemployed	840
Unemployment Rate	4.4
Not in Labour Force	6,968
Female:	
In the Labour Force	17,543
Participation Rate	60.4
Employed	16,597
Unemployed	946
Unemployment Rate	5.4
Not in Labour Force	11,479

OCCUPATIONS BY MAJOR GROUPS

2001 Estimates:	Male	Female
Management	2,214	852
Business, Finance & Admin.	1,704	5,010
Natural & Applied Sciences & Related	1,128	259
Health	392	1,557
Social Sciences, Gov't Services & Religion	449	499
Education	767	988
Arts, Culture, Recreation & Sport	403	503
Sales & Service	4,633	6,786
Trades, Transport & Equipment Operators & Related	4,993	331
Primary Industries	1,089	177
Processing, Mfg. & Utilities	1,181	269

LEVEL OF SCHOOLING

2001 Estimates:	
Population 15 years +	55,237
Less than Grade 9	3,929
Grades 9-13 w/o Certif.	13,611
Grade 9-13 with Certif.	6,135
Trade Certif. /Dip.	1,476
Non-Univ. w/o Certif./Dip.	4,614
Non-Univ. with Certif./Dip.	11,540
Univ. w/o Degree	6,787
Univ. w/o Degree/Certif.	3,800
Univ. with Certif.	2,987
Univ. with Degree	7,145

Lethbridge
(Census Agglomeration)
(Cont'd)

AVERAGE HOUSEHOLD EXPENDITURES

2001 Estimates:
Food	$5,698
Shelter	$8,721
Clothing	$1,977
Transportation	$5,929
Health & Personal Care	$1,845
Recr'n, Read'g & Education	$3,382
Taxes & Securities	$11,684
Other	$7,974
Total Expenditures	$47,210

PRIVATE HOUSEHOLDS

2001 Estimates:
Private Households, Total	27,546
Pop. in Private Households	66,867
Average no. per Household	2.4

FAMILIES

2001 Estimates:
Families in Private Households	19,332
Husband-Wife Families	16,642
Lone-Parent Families	2,690
Aver. No. Persons per Family	2.9
Aver. No. Sons/Daughters at Home	1.1

HOUSING

2001 Estimates:
Occupied Private Dwellings	27,546
Owned	18,964
Rented	8,582
Single-Detached House	19,029
Semi-Detached House	1,606
Row Houses	1,717
Apartment, 5+ Storeys	908
Owned Apartment, 5+ Storeys	41
Apartment, 5 or Fewer Storeys	2,963
Apartment, Detached Duplex	1,172
Other Single-Attached	72
Movable Dwellings	79

VEHICLES

2001 Estimates:
Model Yrs. '81-'96, No.	33,155
% Total	82.68
Model Yrs. '97-'98, No.	4,277
% Total	10.67
'99 Vehicles registered in Model Yr. '99, No.	2,667
% Total	6.65
Total No. '81-'99	40,099

LEGAL MARITAL STATUS

2001 Estimates: (Age 15+)
Single (Never Married)	16,178
Legally Married (Not Separated)	29,630
Legally Married (Separated)	1,309
Widowed	3,846
Divorced	4,274

PSYTE CATEGORIES

2001 Estimates	No. of House -holds	% of Total Hhds.	Index
Suburban Executives	632	2.29	160
Mortgaged in Suburbia	899	3.26	235
Technocrafts & Bureaucrats	486	1.76	63
Small City Elite	3,182	11.55	674
Aging Erudites	1,536	5.58	370
Satellite Suburbs	371	1.35	47
Kindergarten Boom	2,810	10.20	389
Old Towns' New Fringe	1,670	6.06	155
Rustic Prosperity	74	0.27	15
Conservative Homebodies	819	2.97	82
High Rise Sunsets	231	0.84	59
Young City Singles	900	3.27	142
Town Renters	427	1.55	179
Nesters & Young Homesteaders	11,849	43.02	1,843
Struggling Downtowns	236	0.86	27
Aged Pensioners	959	3.48	262
Old Grey Towers	145	0.53	95

FINANÇIAL P$YTE

2001 Estimates	No. of House -holds	% of Total Hhds.	Index
Four Star Investors	632	2.29	46
Successful Suburbanites	1,385	5.03	76
Canadian Comfort	3,553	12.90	133
Urban Heights	1,536	5.58	130
Mortgages & Minivans	2,810	10.20	155
Tractors & Tradelines	1,744	6.33	111
Bills & Wills	819	2.97	36
Revolving Renters	12,080	43.85	953
Towering Debt	1,563	5.67	73
Senior Survivors	1,104	4.01	213

HOME LANGUAGE

2001 Estimates:		% Total
English	64,443	94.33
French	168	0.25
Blackfoot	64	0.09
Chinese	875	1.28
Dutch	49	0.07
German	89	0.13
Hungarian	158	0.23
Italian	120	0.18
Japanese	133	0.19
Polish	272	0.40
Serbo-Croatian	36	0.05
Spanish	601	0.88
Tagalog (Pilipino)	38	0.06
Vietnamese	223	0.33
Other Languages	299	0.44
Multiple Responses	746	1.09
Total	68,314	100.00

BUILDING PERMITS

	1999	1998	1997
		$000	
Value	142,073	108,303	69,189

HOMES BUILT

	1999	1998	1997
No	499	535	294

TAXATION

Income Class:	1997	% Total
Under $5,000	5,880	11.91
$5,000-$10,000	6,330	12.82
$10,000-$15,000	7,330	14.84
$15,000-$20,000	5,660	11.46
$20,000-$25,000	4,400	8.91
$25,000-$30,000	4,150	8.40
$30,000-$40,000	6,240	12.64
$40,000-$50,000	3,760	7.61
$50,000 +	5,630	11.40
Total Returns, No.	49,380	
Total Income, $000.	1,301,955	
Total Taxable Returns.	35,280	
Total Tax, $000	223,324	
Average Income, $	26,366	
Average Tax, $	6,330	

VITAL STATISTICS

	1997	1996	1995	1994
Births	810	791	837	886
Deaths	538	584	533	540
Natural Increase	272	207	304	346
Marriages	453	463	470	497

Note: Latest available data.

DAILY NEWSPAPER(S)

	Circulation Average Paid
The Lethbridge Herald	
Fri	25,002
Sat	21,665
Sun	19,620
Mon-Thu	20,171

COMMUNITY NEWSPAPER(S)

	Total Circulation
Lethbridge: Lethbridge Shopper	32,500

RADIO STATION(S)

	Power
CBRL-FM	n.a.
CFRV-FM	100,000w
CHFA-FM	n.a.
CHHK-FM	n.a.
CHLB-FM	100,000w
CJOC	10,000w
CKTA	10,000w
CKUA-FM	100,000w

TELEVISION STATION(S)

CBRT-TV
CBXFT-TV
CFCN-TV
CISA-TV
CJIL-TV
CKAL-TV

Alberta

Alberta

Lloydminster
(Census Agglomeration)

The Census Agglomeration of Lloydminster consists solely of Lloydminster, C, divided between census division No. 10 in Alberta and census division No. 17 in Saskatchewan.

POPULATION

July 1, 2001 Estimate	21,403
% Cdn. Total	0.07
% Change, '96 -'01	9.41
Avg. Annual Growth Rate, %	1.81
2003 Projected Population	22,362
2006 Projected Population	23,466
2001 Households Estimate	8,164
2003 Projected Households	8,618
2006 Projected Households	9,267

INCOME

% Above/Below National Average	-4
2001 Total Income Estimate	$433,610,000
% Cdn. Total	0.07
2001 Average Hhld. Income	$53,100
2001 Per Capita	$20,300
2003 Projected Total Income	$477,710,000
2006 Projected Total Income	$545,710,000

RETAIL SALES

% Above/Below National Average	+125
2001 Retail Sales Estimate	$430,340,000
% Cdn. Total	0.15
2001 per Household	$52,700
2001 per Capita	$20,100
2001 No. of Establishments	225
2003 Projected Retail Sales	$483,980,000
2006 Projected Retail Sales	$559,950,000

POPULATION

2001 Estimates:

Total		21,403
Male		10,735
Female		10,668

Age Groups	Male	Female
0-4	891	811
5-9	945	857
10-14	895	853
15-19	854	818
20-24	870	840
25-29	895	858
30-34	929	945
35-39	946	943
40-44	847	822
45-49	685	651
50-54	525	499
55-59	378	378
60-64	304	302
65-69	249	250
70+	522	841

DAYTIME POPULATION

2001 Estimates:

Working Population	11,031
At Home Population	10,372
Total	21,403

INCOME

2001 Estimates:

Avg. Household Income	$53,112
Avg. Family Income	$58,091
Per Capita Income	$20,259
Male:	
Avg. Employment Income	$36,605
Avg. Employment Income (Full Time)	$47,928
Female:	
Avg. Employment Income	$17,966
Avg. Employment Income (Full Time)	$28,171

DISPOSABLE & DISCRETIONARY INCOME

2001 Estimates:	Per Hhld.
Disposable Income	$41,115
Discretionary Income 1 (minus Food & Shelter)	$28,982
Discretionary Income 2 (minus Food, Shelter, & Other Expenditures)	$20,284

LIQUID ASSETS

1999 Estimates:	Per Hhld.
Equity Investments	$85,854
Interest Bearing Investments	$68,428
Total Liquid Assets	$154,282

CREDIT DATA

July 2000:

Pool of Credit	$164,266,884
Revolving Credit, No.	26,996
Fixed Loans, No.	12,598
Avg. Credit Limit, per Person	$11,407
Avg. Spent, per Person	$5,700
Satisfactory Ratings, No. per Person	2.62
Avg. No. of Cards, per Person	0.84

LABOUR FORCE

2001 Estimates:

Male:	
In the Labour Force	6,462
Participation Rate	80.7
Employed	6,128
Unemployed	334
Unemployment Rate	5.2
Not in Labour Force	1,542
Female:	
In the Labour Force	5,202
Participation Rate	63.9
Employed	4,821
Unemployed	381
Unemployment Rate	7.3
Not in Labour Force	2,945

OCCUPATIONS BY MAJOR GROUPS

2001 Estimates:	Male	Female
Management	725	259
Business, Finance & Admin.	367	1,384
Natural & Applied Sciences & Related	322	21
Health	47	301
Social Sciences, Gov't Services & Religion	117	188
Education	115	319
Arts, Culture, Recreation & Sport	137	120
Sales & Service	1,051	2,365
Trades, Transport & Equipment Operators & Related	1,907	88
Primary Industries	1,002	24
Processing, Mfg. & Utilities	552	23

LEVEL OF SCHOOLING

2001 Estimates:

Population 15 years +	16,151
Less than Grade 9	1,380
Grades 9-13 w/o Certif.	5,112
Grade 9-13 with Certif.	1,751
Trade Certif. /Dip.	484
Non-Univ. w/o Certif./Dip.	1,065
Non-Univ. with Certif./Dip.	3,700
Univ. w/o Degree	1,343
Univ. w/o Degree/Certif.	734
Univ. with Certif.	609
Univ. with Degree	1,316

AVERAGE HOUSEHOLD EXPENDITURES

2001 Estimates:

Food	$6,130
Shelter	$8,138
Clothing	$2,373
Transportation	$6,248
Health & Personal Care	$2,226
Recr'n, Read'g & Education	$3,998
Taxes & Securities	$13,206
Other	$8,730
Total Expenditures	$51,049

PRIVATE HOUSEHOLDS

2001 Estimates:

Private Households, Total	8,164
Pop. in Private Households	21,030
Average no. per Household	2.6

FAMILIES

2001 Estimates:

Families in Private Households	5,938
Husband-Wife Families	5,013
Lone-Parent Families	925
Aver. No. Persons per Family	3.1
Aver. No. Sons/Daughters at Home	1.3

HOUSING

2001 Estimates:

Occupied Private Dwellings	8,164
Owned	4,494
Rented	3,670
Single-Detached House	5,076
Semi-Detached House	304
Row Houses	454
Apartment, 5+ Storeys	134
Owned Apartment, 5+ Storeys	34
Apartment, 5 or Fewer Storeys	2,094
Apartment, Detached Duplex	57
Movable Dwellings	45

VEHICLES

2001 Estimates:

Model Yrs. '81-'96, No.	9,698
% Total	76.45
Model Yrs. '97-'98, No.	2,086
% Total	16.44
'99 Vehicles registered in Model Yr. '99, No.	901
% Total	7.10
Total No. '81-'99	12,685

LEGAL MARITAL STATUS

2001 Estimates: (Age 15+)

Single (Never Married)	5,381
Legally Married (Not Separated)	8,361
Legally Married (Separated)	560
Widowed	898
Divorced	951

PSYTE CATEGORIES

2001 Estimates	No. of House-holds	% of Total Hhds.	Index
Town Boomers	3,251	39.82	3,929
The New Frontier	1,305	15.98	1,060
Young Grey Collar	2,939	36.00	4,303
Quiet Towns	368	4.51	212
Aged Pensioners	168	2.06	155

FINANCIAL P$YTE

2001 Estimates	No. of House-holds	% of Total Hhds.	Index
Canadian Comfort	3,251	39.82	410
Miners & Credit-Liners	1,305	15.98	505
Revolving Renters	2,939	36.00	782
Limited Budgets	368	4.51	145
Senior Survivors	168	2.06	109

HOME LANGUAGE

2001 Estimates:		% Total
English	20,975	98.00
French	22	0.10
Chinese	143	0.67
Cree	67	0.31
Croatian	17	0.08
Lao	22	0.10
Spanish	11	0.05
Tagalog (Pilipino)	11	0.05
Vietnamese	17	0.08
Multiple Responses	118	0.55
Total	21,403	100.00

BUILDING PERMITS

	1999	1998 $000	1997
Value	42,718	26,550	30,307

HOMES BUILT

	1999	1998	1997
No.	121	161	123

TAXATION

Income Class:	1997	% Total
Under $5,000	1,910	11.49
$5,000-$10,000	1,930	11.61
$10,000-$15,000	2,280	13.21
$15,000-$20,000	1,760	10.58
$20,000-$25,000	1,310	7.88
$25,000-$30,000	1,240	7.46
$30,000-$40,000	2,010	12.09
$40,000-$50,000	1,420	8.54
$50,000 +	2,760	16.60
Total Returns, No.	16,630	
Total Income, $000	595,576	
Total Taxable Returns	12,600	
Total Tax, $000	142,233	
Average Income, $	35,813	
Average Tax, $	11,288	

VITAL STATISTICS

	1997	1996	1995	1994
Births	346	376	351	316
Deaths	125	140	126	143
Natural Increase	221	236	225	173
Marriages	164	150	165	160

Note: Latest available data.

DAILY NEWSPAPER(S)

	Circulation Average Paid
Daily Times	n.a.

COMMUNITY NEWSPAPER(S)

	Total Circulation
Lloydminster: Lloydminster Meridian Booster	
Wed	14,485
Sun	14,797

RADIO STATION(S)

	Power
CKKY	n.a.
CKSA	50,000w
CKUA-FM	n.a.

TELEVISION STATION(S)

CITL-TV
CKSA-TV

Medicine Hat
(Census Agglomeration)

The Census Agglomeration of Medicine Hat includes: Medicine Hat, C; Cypress No. 1, MD; Redcliff, T: plus one smaller area. All are in census division No. 1.

POPULATION

July 1, 2001 Estimate	62,730
% Cdn. Total	0.20
% Change, '96 -'01	8.11
Avg. Annual Growth Rate, %	1.57
2003 Projected Population	64,622
2006 Projected Population	65,999
2001 Households Estimate	24,870
2003 Projected Households	25,751
2006 Projected Households	26,610

INCOME

% Above/Below National Average	-5
2001 Total Income Estimate	$1,257,460,000
% Cdn. Total	0.19
2001 Average Hhld. Income	$50,600
2001 Per Capita	$20,000
2003 Projected Total Income	$1,350,220,000
2006 Projected Total Income	$1,463,160,000

RETAIL SALES

% Above/Below National Average	+50
2001 Retail Sales Estimate	$843,840,000
% Cdn. Total	0.30
2001 per Household	$33,900
2001 per Capita	$13,500
2001 No. of Establishments	581
2003 Projected Retail Sales	$932,530,000
2006 Projected Retail Sales	$1,048,230,000

POPULATION

2001 Estimates:

Total	62,730
Male	30,876
Female	31,854

Age Groups	Male	Female
0-4	2,050	1,913
5-9	2,184	2,024
10-14	2,347	2,150
15-19	2,342	2,236
20-24	2,188	2,186
25-29	2,105	2,099
30-34	2,239	2,295
35-39	2,508	2,537
40-44	2,600	2,542
45-49	2,270	2,277
50-54	1,744	1,834
55-59	1,349	1,478
60-64	1,207	1,285
65-69	1,113	1,228
70+	2,630	3,770

DAYTIME POPULATION

2001 Estimates:

Working Population	31,766
At Home Population	30,964
Total	62,730

INCOME

2001 Estimates:

Avg. Household Income	$50,561
Avg. Family Income	$56,646
Per Capita Income	$20,046
Male:	
Avg. Employment Income	$34,364
Avg. Employment Income (Full Time)	$44,269
Female:	
Avg. Employment Income	$16,812
Avg. Employment Income (Full Time)	$26,701

DISPOSABLE & DISCRETIONARY INCOME

2001 Estimates:	Per Hhld.
Disposable Income	$39,019
Discretionary Income 1 (minus Food & Shelter)	$26,827
Discretionary Income 2 (minus Food, Shelter, & Other Expenditures)	$18,651

LIQUID ASSETS

1999 Estimates:	Per Hhld.
Equity Investments	$69,679
Interest Bearing Investments	$61,831
Total Liquid Assets	$131,510

CREDIT DATA

July 2000:

Pool of Credit	$663,725,695
Revolving Credit, No.	113,727
Fixed Loans, No.	40,168
Avg. Credit Limit, per Person	$12,530
Avg. Spent, per Person	$5,949
Satisfactory Ratings, No. per Person	2.83
Avg. No. of Cards, per Person	0.96

LABOUR FORCE

2001 Estimates:

Male:	
In the Labour Force	18,240
Participation Rate	75.1
Employed	17,340
Unemployed	900
Unemployment Rate	4.9
Not in Labour Force	6,055
Female:	
In the Labour Force	15,531
Participation Rate	60.3
Employed	14,561
Unemployed	970
Unemployment Rate	6.2
Not in Labour Force	10,236

OCCUPATIONS BY MAJOR GROUPS

2001 Estimates:	Male	Female
Management	1,832	867
Business, Finance & Admin.	1,070	3,521
Natural & Applied Sciences & Related	935	104
Health	246	1,459
Social Sciences, Gov't Services & Religion	217	364
Education	444	550
Arts, Culture, Recreation & Sport	118	302
Sales & Service	3,359	6,728
Trades, Transport & Equipment Operators & Related	5,400	287
Primary Industries	2,504	735
Processing, Mfg. & Utilities	1,875	267

LEVEL OF SCHOOLING

2001 Estimates:

Population 15 years +	50,062
Less than Grade 9	5,460
Grades 9-13 w/o Certif.	15,504
Grade 9-13 with Certif.	5,953
Trade Certif. /Dip.	1,782
Non-Univ. w/o Certif./Dip.	4,029
Non-Univ. with Certif./Dip.	10,176
Univ. w/o Degree	3,562
Univ. w/o Degree/Certif.	1,618
Univ. with Certif.	1,944
Univ. with Degree	3,596

AVERAGE HOUSEHOLD EXPENDITURES

2001 Estimates:

Food	$6,142
Shelter	$8,125
Clothing	$2,250
Transportation	$5,492
Health & Personal Care	$2,277
Recr'n, Read'g & Education	$3,773
Taxes & Securities	$12,141
Other	$8,800
Total Expenditures	$49,000

PRIVATE HOUSEHOLDS

2001 Estimates:

Private Households, Total	24,870
Pop. in Private Households	61,293
Average no. per Household	2.5

FAMILIES

2001 Estimates:

Families in Private Households	18,187
Husband-Wife Families	16,105
Lone-Parent Families	2,082
Aver. No. Persons per Family	3.0
Aver. No. Sons/Daughters at Home	1.1

HOUSING

2001 Estimates:

Occupied Private Dwellings	24,870
Owned	18,301
Rented	6,569
Single-Detached House	18,134
Semi-Detached House	705
Row Houses	1,014
Apartment, 5+ Storeys	234
Apartment, 5 or Fewer Storeys	3,331
Apartment, Detached Duplex	390
Other Single-Attached	22
Movable Dwellings	1,040

VEHICLES

2001 Estimates:

Model Yrs. '81-'96, No.	32,334
% Total	82.05
Model Yrs. '97-'98, No.	4,571
% Total	11.60
'99 Vehicles registered in Model Yr. '99, No.	2,505
% Total	6.36
Total No. '81-'99	39,410

LEGAL MARITAL STATUS

2001 Estimates: (Age 15+)

Single (Never Married)	12,820
Legally Married (Not Separated)	28,874
Legally Married (Separated)	1,288
Widowed	3,423
Divorced	3,657

PSYTE CATEGORIES

2001 Estimates	No. of House -holds	% of Total Hhds.	Index
Town Boomers	6,389	25.69	2,535
Old Towns' New Fringe	106	0.43	11
Rustic Prosperity	126	0.51	28
Pick-ups & Dirt Bikes	467	1.88	225
The Grain Belt	202	0.81	137
High Rise Sunsets	839	3.37	236
Old Leafy Towns	29	0.12	5
Young Grey Collar	16,101	64.74	7,739
Big Country Families	113	0.45	32
Aged Pensioners	352	1.42	106

Alberta

FINANCIAL P$YTE

2001 Estimates	No. of House -holds	% of Total Hhds.	Index
Canadian Comfort	6,389	25.69	264
Tractors & Tradelines	232	0.93	16
Bills & Wills	29	0.12	1
Country Credit	669	2.69	40
Revolving Renters	16,940	68.11	1,481
Rural Family Blues	113	0.45	6
Senior Survivors	352	1.42	75

HOME LANGUAGE

2001 Estimates:		% Total
English	60,827	96.97
French	56	0.09
Chinese	399	0.64
German	437	0.70
Polish	78	0.12
Spanish	329	0.52
Vietnamese	59	0.09
Other Languages	206	0.33
Multiple Responses	339	0.54
Total	62,730	100.00

BUILDING PERMITS

	1999	1998	1997
		$000	
Value	86,886	243,759	82,036

HOMES BUILT

	1999	1998	1997
No.	657	370	475

TAXATION

Income Class:	1997	% Total
Under $5,000	4,950	11.60
$5,000-$10,000	5,690	13.33
$10,000-$15,000	6,730	15.76
$15,000-$20,000	5,100	11.95
$20,000-$25,000	3,770	8.83
$25,000-$30,000	3,220	7.54
$30,000-$40,000	4,920	11.52
$40,000-$50,000	3,110	7.29
$50,000 +	5,230	12.25
Total Returns, No.	42,690	
Total Income, $000	1,130,708	
Total Taxable Returns	30,740	
Total Tax, $000	198,839	
Average Income, $	26,486	
Average Tax, $	6,468	

VITAL STATISTICS

	1997	1996	1995	1994
Births	749	726	783	678
Deaths	449	447	437	401
Natural Increase	300	279	346	277
Marriages	415	402	431	399

Note: Latest available data.

Alberta

Medicine Hat
(Census Agglomeration)
(Cont'd)

DAILY NEWSPAPER(S)

	Circulation Average Paid
News	14,066

COMMUNITY NEWSPAPER(S)

	Total Circulation
Medicine Hat: Medicine Hat Shopper	23,688
Medicine Hat: Prairie Post	31,398

RADIO STATION(S)

	Power
CBRM-FM	n.a.
CFMY-FM	100,000w
CHAT	10,000w
CHFA-FM	n.a.
CKUA-FM	100,000w

TELEVISION STATION(S)

CBXFT-TV
CFCN-TV
CHAT-TV

Mountain View County
(County Municipality)

In census division No. 6. Name changed from Mountain View County No. 17 Jan. 1, 1999.

POPULATION

July 1, 2001 Estimate	13,183
% Cdn. Total	0.04
% Change, '96 -'01	13.61
Avg. Annual Growth Rate, %	2.58
2003 Projected Population	13,803
2006 Projected Population	14,699
2001 Households Estimate	4,700
2003 Projected Households	4,964
2006 Projected Households	5,370

INCOME

% Above/Below National Average	-1
2001 Total Income Estimate	$274,000,000
% Cdn. Total	0.04
2001 Average Hhld. Income	$58,300
2001 Per Capita	$20,820
2003 Projected Total Income	$303,580,000
2006 Projected Total Income	$353,560,000

RETAIL SALES

% Above/Below National Average	-97
2001 Retail Sales Estimate	$3,970,000
% Cdn. Total	0.00
2001 per Household	$800
2001 per Capita	$300
2001 No. of Establishments	19
2003 Projected Retail Sales	$4,330,000
2006 Projected Retail Sales	$5,130,000

POPULATION

2001 Estimates:

Total		13,183
Male		6,796
Female		6,387

Age Groups	Male	Female
0-4	423	409
5-9	502	464
10-14	554	499
15-19	567	507
20-24	474	410
25-29	395	372
30-34	422	455
35-39	508	526
40-44	548	551
45-49	508	486
50-54	442	402
55-59	367	327
60-64	307	284
65-69	260	243
70+	519	452

DAYTIME POPULATION

2001 Estimates:

Working Population	1,448
At Home Population	5,560
Total	7,008

INCOME

2001 Estimates:

Avg. Household Income	$58,298
Avg. Family Income	$62,680
Per Capita Income	$20,784
Male:	
Avg. Employment Income	$30,810
Avg. Employment Income (Full Time)	$36,969
Female:	
Avg. Employment Income	$17,205
Avg. Employment Income (Full Time)	$24,012

DISPOSABLE & DISCRETIONARY INCOME

2001 Estimates:	Per Hhld.
Disposable Income	$45,074
Discretionary Income 1 (minus Food & Shelter)	$31,385
Discretionary Income 2 (minus Food, Shelter, & Other Expenditures)	$20,806

LIQUID ASSETS

1999 Estimates:	Per Hhld.
Equity Investments	$81,362
Interest Bearing Investments	$66,613
Total Liquid Assets	$147,975

CREDIT DATA

July 2000:

Pool of Credit	$35,885,510
Revolving Credit, No.	4,830
Fixed Loans, No.	1,983
Avg. Credit Limit, per Person	$13,619
Avg. Spent, per Person	$6,577
Satisfactory Ratings, No. per Person	2.49
Avg. No. of Cards, per Person	0.95

LABOUR FORCE

2001 Estimates:

Male:

In the Labour Force	4,358
Participation Rate	82.0
Employed	4,261
Unemployed	97
Unemployment Rate	2.2
Not in Labour Force	959

Female:

In the Labour Force	3,445
Participation Rate	68.7
Employed	3,336
Unemployed	109
Unemployment Rate	3.2
Not in Labour Force	1,570

OCCUPATIONS BY MAJOR GROUPS

2001 Estimates:	Male	Female
Management	294	166
Business, Finance & Admin.	168	725
Natural & Applied Sciences & Related	174	24
Health	20	179
Social Sciences, Gov't Services & Religion	31	70
Education	68	152
Arts, Culture, Recreation & Sport	12	107
Sales & Service	315	918
Trades, Transport & Equipment Operators & Related	1,059	128
Primary Industries	1,825	902
Processing, Mfg. & Utilities	392	52

LEVEL OF SCHOOLING

2001 Estimates:

Population 15 years +	10,332
Less than Grade 9	580
Grades 9-13 w/o Certif.	3,488
Grade 9-13 with Certif.	1,262
Trade Certif. /Dip.	378
Non-Univ. w/o Certif./Dip.	703
Non-Univ. with Certif./Dip.	2,401
Univ. w/o Degree	696
Univ. w/o Degree/Certif.	320
Univ. with Certif.	376
Univ. with Degree	824

AVERAGE HOUSEHOLD EXPENDITURES

2001 Estimates:

Food	$6,922
Shelter	$8,954
Clothing	$2,329
Transportation	$8,680
Health & Personal Care	$2,060
Recr'n, Read'g & Education	$4,254
Taxes & Securities	$12,721
Other	$10,096
Total Expenditures	$56,016

PRIVATE HOUSEHOLDS

2001 Estimates:

Private Households, Total	4,700
Pop. in Private Households	13,008
Average no. per Household	2.8

FAMILIES

2001 Estimates:

Families in Private Households	3,858
Husband-Wife Families	3,643
Lone-Parent Families	215
Aver. No. Persons per Family	3.2
Aver. No. Sons/Daughters at Home	1.2

HOUSING

2001 Estimates:

Occupied Private Dwellings	4,700
Owned	3,968
Rented	732
Single-Detached House	3,821
Semi-Detached House	23
Apartment, 5 or Fewer Storeys	35
Apartment, Detached Duplex	11
Movable Dwellings	810

VEHICLES

2001 Estimates:

Model Yrs. '81-'96, No.	9,545
% Total	82.67
Model Yrs. '97-'98, No.	1,301
% Total	11.27
'99 Vehicles registered in Model Yr. '99, No.	700
% Total	6.06
Total No. '81-'99	11,546

LEGAL MARITAL STATUS

2001 Estimates: (Age 15+)

Single (Never Married)	2,331
Legally Married (Not Separated)	6,846
Legally Married (Separated)	179
Widowed	374
Divorced	602

PSYTE CATEGORIES

2001 Estimates	No. of House -holds	% of Total Hhds.	Index
Blue Collar Winners	59	1.26	50
Old Towns' New Fringe	584	12.43	317
Rustic Prosperity	2,946	62.68	3,474
Pick-ups & Dirt Bikes	934	19.87	2,380
Old Leafy Towns	170	3.62	142

FINANCIAL P$YTE

2001 Estimates	No. of House -holds	% of Total Hhds.	Index
Canadian Comfort	59	1.26	13
Tractors & Tradelines	3,530	75.11	1,313
Bills & Wills	170	3.62	44
Country Credit	934	19.87	294

Mountain View County
(County Municipality)
(Cont'd)

HOME LANGUAGE

2001 Estimates:		% Total
English	12,958	98.29
French	23	0.17
Chinese	13	0.10
Dutch	17	0.13
German	137	1.04
Multiple Responses	35	0.27
Total	13,183	100.00

BUILDING PERMITS

	1999	1998	1997
		$000	
Value	n.a.	97,963	20,568

TAXATION

Income Class:	1997	% Total
Under $5,000	80	16.33
$5,000-$10,000	70	14.29
$10,000-$15,000	50	10.20
$15,000-$20,000	40	8.16
$20,000-$25,000	40	8.16
$25,000-$30,000	30	6.12
$30,000-$40,000	60	12.24
$40,000-$50,000	50	10.20
$50,000 +	80	16.33
Total Returns, No.	490	
Total Income, $000	13,713	
Total Taxable Returns	350	
Total Tax, $000	2,496	
Average Income, $	27,986	
Average Tax, $	7,131	

VITAL STATISTICS

	1997	1996	1995	1994
Births	111	127	133	126
Deaths	43	53	46	42
Natural Increase	68	74	87	84
Marriages	65	57	48	44

Note: Latest available data.

Red Deer
(Census Agglomeration)

The Census Agglomeration of Red Deer consists solely of Red Deer, C, in census division No. 8.

POPULATION

July 1, 2001 Estimate	68,368
% Cdn. Total	0.22
% Change, '96 -'01	7.13
Avg. Annual Growth Rate, %	1.39
2003 Projected Population	69,120
2006 Projected Population	68,952
2001 Households Estimate	26,075
2003 Projected Households	26,646
2006 Projected Households	27,067

INCOME

% Above/Below National Average	-3
2001 Total Income Estimate	$1,400,490,000
% Cdn. Total	0.21
2001 Average Hhld. Income	$53,700
2001 Per Capita	$20,500
2003 Projected Total Income	$1,491,860,000
2006 Projected Total Income	$1,609,930,000

RETAIL SALES

% Above/Below National Average	+116
2001 Retail Sales Estimate	$1,320,180,000
% Cdn. Total	0.47
2001 per Household	$50,600
2001 per Capita	$19,300
2001 No. of Establishments	632
2003 Projected Retail Sales	$1,440,750,000
2006 Projected Retail Sales	$1,590,100,000

POPULATION

2001 Estimates:

Total		68,368
Male		33,585
Female		34,783

Age Groups	Male	Female
0-4	2,408	2,385
5-9	2,480	2,413
10-14	2,553	2,408
15-19	2,511	2,432
20-24	2,609	2,599
25-29	2,594	2,636
30-34	2,652	2,719
35-39	2,897	2,928
40-44	2,879	2,933
45-49	2,495	2,533
50-54	1,914	1,967
55-59	1,428	1,475
60-64	1,137	1,192
65-69	953	1,055
70+	2,075	3,108

DAYTIME POPULATION

2001 Estimates:

Working Population	35,892
At Home Population	32,476
Total	68,368

INCOME

2001 Estimates:

Avg. Household Income	$53,710
Avg. Family Income	$60,763
Per Capita Income	$20,485
Male:	
Avg. Employment Income	$35,868
Avg. Employment Income (Full Time)	$48,623
Female:	
Avg. Employment Income	$18,927
Avg. Employment Income (Full Time)	$29,148

DISPOSABLE & DISCRETIONARY INCOME

2001 Estimates:	Per Hhld.
Disposable Income	$41,331
Discretionary Income 1 (minus Food & Shelter)	$27,981
Discretionary Income 2 (minus Food, Shelter, & Other Expenditures)	$19,425

LIQUID ASSETS

1999 Estimates:	Per Hhld.
Equity Investments	$79,273
Interest Bearing Investments	$67,351
Total Liquid Assets	$146,624

CREDIT DATA

July 2000:	
Pool of Credit	$713,076,344
Revolving Credit, No.	122,685
Fixed Loans, No.	47,322
Avg. Credit Limit, per Person	$12,555
Avg. Spent, per Person	$6,224
Satisfactory Ratings, No. per Person	2.86
Avg. No. of Cards, per Person	0.96

LABOUR FORCE

2001 Estimates:	
Male:	
In the Labour Force	20,580
Participation Rate	78.7
Employed	18,867
Unemployed	1,713
Unemployment Rate	8.3
Not in Labour Force	5,564
Female:	
In the Labour Force	18,376
Participation Rate	66.6
Employed	17,138
Unemployed	1,238
Unemployment Rate	6.7
Not in Labour Force	9,201

OCCUPATIONS BY MAJOR GROUPS

2001 Estimates:	Male	Female
Management	2,073	896
Business, Finance & Admin.	1,577	4,879
Natural & Applied Sciences & Related	1,311	163
Health	442	1,792
Social Sciences, Gov't Services & Religion	491	865
Education	637	884
Arts, Culture, Recreation & Sport	463	413
Sales & Service	4,579	7,390
Trades, Transport & Equipment Operators & Related	5,152	323
Primary Industries	2,098	158
Processing, Mfg. & Utilities	1,469	151

LEVEL OF SCHOOLING

2001 Estimates:	
Population 15 years +	53,721
Less than Grade 9	2,891
Grades 9-13 w/o Certif.	16,179
Grade 9-13 with Certif.	6,352
Trade Certif. /Dip.	2,017
Non-Univ. w/o Certif./Dip.	4,942
Non-Univ. with Certif./Dip.	11,757
Univ. w/o Degree	4,428
Univ. w/o Degree/Certif.	2,229
Univ. with Certif.	2,199
Univ. with Degree	5,155

Alberta

AVERAGE HOUSEHOLD EXPENDITURES

2001 Estimates:	
Food	$6,257
Shelter	$9,316
Clothing	$2,215
Transportation	$6,541
Health & Personal Care	$2,018
Recr'n, Read'g & Education	$3,784
Taxes & Securities	$12,835
Other	$8,668
Total Expenditures	$51,634

PRIVATE HOUSEHOLDS

2001 Estimates:	
Private Households, Total	26,075
Pop. in Private Households	66,803
Average no. per Household	2.6

FAMILIES

2001 Estimates:	
Families in Private Households	18,266
Husband-Wife Families	15,172
Lone-Parent Families	3,094
Aver. No. Persons per Family	3.0
Aver. No. Sons/Daughters at Home	1.2

HOUSING

2001 Estimates:	
Occupied Private Dwellings	26,075
Owned	15,516
Rented	10,559
Single-Detached House	13,366
Semi-Detached House	1,999
Row Houses	3,194
Apartment, 5+ Storeys	682
Owned Apartment, 5+ Storeys	11
Apartment, 5 or Fewer Storeys	5,301
Apartment, Detached Duplex	592
Other Single-Attached	11
Movable Dwellings	930

VEHICLES

2001 Estimates:	
Model Yrs. '81-'96, No.	33,148
% Total	79.12
Model Yrs. '97-'98, No.	5,504
% Total	13.14
'99 Vehicles registered in Model Yr. '99, No.	3,243
% Total	7.74
Total No. '81-'99	41,895

LEGAL MARITAL STATUS

2001 Estimates: (Age 15+)	
Single (Never Married)	17,854
Legally Married (Not Separated)	26,500
Legally Married (Separated)	1,812
Widowed	2,708
Divorced	4,847

Alberta

Red Deer
(Census Agglomeration)
(Cont'd)

PSYTE CATEGORIES

2001 Estimates	No. of House -holds	% of Total Hhds.	Index
Technocrafts & Bureaucrats	1,349	5.17	184
Small City Elite	4,984	19.11	1,115
Old Bungalow Burbs	487	1.87	113
Satellite Suburbs	1,416	5.43	189
Kindergarten Boom	2,967	11.38	434
Town Boomers	289	1.11	109
Old Towns' New Fringe	2,123	8.14	208
Young City Singles	2,895	11.10	484
Town Renters	398	1.53	177
Nesters & Young Homesteaders	7,949	30.49	1,306
Aged Pensioners	739	2.83	213
Old Grey Towers	141	0.54	98

FINANCIAL PSYTE

2001 Estimates	No. of House -holds	% of Total Hhds.	Index
Successful Suburbanites	1,349	5.17	78
Canadian Comfort	6,689	25.65	264
Miners & Credit-Liners	487	1.87	59
Mortgages & Minivans	2,967	11.38	172
Tractors & Tradelines	2,123	8.14	142
Revolving Renters	7,949	30.49	663
Towering Debt	3,293	12.63	162
Senior Survivors	880	3.37	179

HOME LANGUAGE

2001 Estimates:		% Total
English	65,987	96.52
French	173	0.25
Arabic	40	0.06
Chinese	377	0.55
Czech	56	0.08
German	40	0.06
Hindi	82	0.12
Hungarian	50	0.07
Khmer (Cambodian)	87	0.13
Lao	63	0.09
Polish	41	0.06
Punjabi	68	0.10
Serbo-Croatian	45	0.07
Spanish	459	0.67
Tagalog (Pilipino)	98	0.14
Vietnamese	188	0.27
Other Languages	127	0.19
Multiple Responses	387	0.57
Total	68,368	100.00

BUILDING PERMITS

	1999	1998 $000	1997
Value	107,043	119,142	84,243

HOMES BUILT

	1999	1998	1997
No	730	563	363

TAXATION

Income Class:	1997	% Total
Under $5,000	5,760	11.90
$5,000-$10,000	6,120	12.65
$10,000-$15,000	6,710	13.87
$15,000-$20,000	4,990	10.31
$20,000-$25,000	4,100	8.47
$25,000-$30,000	4,060	8.39
$30,000-$40,000	5,790	11.97
$40,000-$50,000	3,930	8.12
$50,000 +	6,930	14.32
Total Returns, No.	48,390	
Total Income, $000	1,403,466	
Total Taxable Returns	35,250	
Total Tax, $000	269,213	
Average Income, $	29,003	
Average Tax, $	7,637	

VITAL STATISTICS

	1997	1996	1995	1994
Births	873	890	988	937
Deaths	417	368	345	383
Natural Increase	456	522	643	554
Marriages	433	473	500	530

Note: Latest available data.

DAILY NEWSPAPER(S)

	Circulation Average Paid
Red Deer Advocate	
Fri	22,560
Mon-Thu, Sat	18,789

COMMUNITY NEWSPAPER(S)

	Total Circulation
Red Deer: Central Alberta Adviser	29,126
Red Deer: Red Deer Advocate Central Alberta Life	38,884
Red Deer: Red Deer Life	
Wed	23,225
Sun	27,018
Red Deer: Red Deer Express Sun/Wed	21,858

RADIO STATION(S)

	Power
CBRD-FM	n.a.
CHFA-FM	n.a.
CHIM-FM	n.a.
CHUB-FM	n.a.
CIZZ-FM	100,000w
CKDQ	n.a.
CKGY	50,000w
CKUA-FM	100,000w

TELEVISION STATION(S)

CBXFT-TV
CFRN-TV
CITV-TV
CKEM-TV
CKRD-TV

Red Deer County No. 23
(County Municipality)
In census division No. 8.

POPULATION

July 1, 2001 Estimate	21,187
% Cdn. Total	0.07
% Change, '96 -'01	16.44
Avg. Annual Growth Rate, %	3.09
2003 Projected Population	22,371
2006 Projected Population	23,728
2001 Households Estimate	7,299
2003 Projected Households	7,790
2006 Projected Households	8,414

INCOME

% Above/Below National Average	+8
2001 Total Income Estimate	$481,530,000
% Cdn. Total	0.07
2001 Average Hhld. Income	$66,000
2001 Per Capita	$22,700
2003 Projected Total Income	$541,610,000
2006 Projected Total Income	$631,920,000

RETAIL SALES

% Above/Below National Average	-61
2001 Retail Sales Estimate	$74,770,000
% Cdn. Total	0.03
2001 per Household	$10,200
2001 per Capita	$3,500
2001 No. of Establishments	115
2003 Projected Retail Sales	$83,630,000
2006 Projected Retail Sales	$97,020,000

POPULATION

2001 Estimates:		
Total		21,187
Male		11,167
Female		10,020
Age Groups	Male	Female
0-4	657	629
5-9	762	719
10-14	858	816
15-19	868	776
20-24	750	663
25-29	685	617
30-34	789	727
35-39	949	845
40-44	1,011	858
45-49	917	797
50-54	744	649
55-59	601	532
60-64	502	422
65-69	397	343
70+	677	627

DAYTIME POPULATION

2001 Estimates:	
Working Population	6,864
At Home Population	9,025
Total	15,889

INCOME

2001 Estimates:	
Avg. Household Income	$65,973
Avg. Family Income	$69,881
Per Capita Income	$22,728
Male:	
Avg. Employment Income	$34,190
Avg. Employment Income (Full Time)	$42,273
Female:	
Avg. Employment Income	$21,347
Avg. Employment Income (Full Time)	$28,440

DISPOSABLE & DISCRETIONARY INCOME

2001 Estimates:	Per Hhld.
Disposable Income	$50,548
Discretionary Income 1 (minus Food & Shelter)	$35,414
Discretionary Income 2 (minus Food, Shelter, & Other Expenditures)	$24,255

LIQUID ASSETS

1999 Estimates:	Per Hhld.
Equity Investments	$122,608
Interest Bearing Investments	$84,856
Total Liquid Assets	$207,464

CREDIT DATA

July 2000:	
Pool of Credit	$130,606,312
Revolving Credit, No.	18,996
Fixed Loans, No.	8,595
Avg. Credit Limit, per Person	$13,877
Avg. Spent, per Person	$7,168
Satisfactory Ratings, No. per Person	2.80
Avg. No. of Cards, per Person	0.91

LABOUR FORCE

2001 Estimates:	
Male:	
In the Labour Force	6,895
Participation Rate	77.6
Employed	6,560
Unemployed	335
Unemployment Rate	4.9
Not in Labour Force	1,995
Female:	
In the Labour Force	5,736
Participation Rate	73.0
Employed	5,583
Unemployed	153
Unemployment Rate	2.7
Not in Labour Force	2,120

OCCUPATIONS BY MAJOR GROUPS

2001 Estimates:	Male	Female
Management	542	362
Business, Finance & Admin.	239	1,611
Natural & Applied Sciences & Related	322	16
Health	124	368
Social Sciences, Gov't Services & Religion	93	84
Education	110	329
Arts, Culture, Recreation & Sport	31	136
Sales & Service	657	1,518
Trades, Transport & Equipment Operators & Related	1,845	160
Primary Industries	2,463	1,113
Processing, Mfg. & Utilities	444	15

LEVEL OF SCHOOLING

2001 Estimates:	
Population 15 years +	16,746
Less than Grade 9	947
Grades 9-13 w/o Certif.	5,019
Grade 9-13 with Certif.	2,065
Trade Certif. /Dip.	705
Non-Univ. w/o Certif./Dip.	1,244
Non-Univ. with Certif./Dip.	4,299
Univ. w/o Degree.	1,061
Univ. w/o Degree/Certif.	438
Univ. with Certif.	623
Univ. with Degree	1,406

Red Deer County No. 23
(County Municipality)
(Cont'd)

AVERAGE HOUSEHOLD EXPENDITURES

2001 Estimates:
Food	$7,086
Shelter	$10,338
Clothing	$2,455
Transportation	$9,130
Health & Personal Care	$2,178
Recr'n, Read'g & Education	$4,473
Taxes & Securities	$16,183
Other	$10,184
Total Expenditures	$62,027

PRIVATE HOUSEHOLDS

2001 Estimates:
Private Households, Total	7,299
Pop. in Private Households	19,918
Average no. per Household	2.7

FAMILIES

2001 Estimates:
Families in Private Households	6,088
Husband-Wife Families	5,809
Lone-Parent Families	279
Aver. No. Persons per Family	3.0
Aver. No. Sons/Daughters at Home	1.1

HOUSING

2001 Estimates:
Occupied Private Dwellings	7,299
Owned	6,319
Rented	980
Single-Detached House	5,607
Semi-Detached House	137
Row Houses	11
Apartment, 5 or Fewer Storeys	11
Apartment, Detached Duplex	23
Other Single-Attached	13
Movable Dwellings	1,497

VEHICLES

2001 Estimates:
Model Yrs. '81-'96, No.	12,290
% Total	80.55
Model Yrs. '97-'98, No.	1,926
% Total	12.62
'99 Vehicles registered in Model Yr. '99, No.	1,042
% Total	6.83
Total No. '81-'99	15,258

LEGAL MARITAL STATUS

2001 Estimates: (Age 15+)
Single (Never Married)	3,959
Legally Married (Not Separated)	10,828
Legally Married (Separated)	339
Widowed	553
Divorced	1,067

PSYTE CATEGORIES

2001 Estimates	No. of House -holds	% of Total Hhds.	Index
Urban Gentry	23	0.32	18
Boomers & Teens	240	3.29	183
Small City Elite	55	0.75	44
Aging Erudites	23	0.32	21
Blue Collar Winners	2,013	27.58	1,095
Old Towns' New Fringe	399	5.47	140
Rustic Prosperity	3,487	47.77	2,648
The Grain Belt	246	3.37	569
Young City Singles	241	3.30	144
Old Leafy Towns	247	3.38	132
Big Country Families	61	0.84	59

FINANCIAL P$YTE

2001 Estimates	No. of House -holds	% of Total Hhds.	Index
Four Star Investors	263	3.60	72
Canadian Comfort	2,068	28.33	292
Urban Heights	23	0.32	7
Tractors & Tradelines	3,886	53.24	931
Bills & Wills	247	3.38	41
Country Credit	246	3.37	50
Rural Family Blues	61	0.84	10
Towering Debt	241	3.30	42

HOME LANGUAGE

2001 Estimates:		% Total
English	20,745	97.91
French	24	0.11
Dutch	88	0.42
Finnish	30	0.14
German	233	1.10
Spanish	26	0.12
Multiple Responses	41	0.19
Total	21,187	100.00

BUILDING PERMITS

	1999	1998 $000	1997
Value	29,283	32,897	29,548

TAXATION

Income Class	1997	% Total
Under $5,000	430	12.84
$5,000-$10,000	460	13.73
$10,000-$15,000	430	12.84
$15,000-$20,000	320	9.55
$20,000-$25,000	220	6.57
$25,000-$30,000	240	7.16
$30,000-$40,000	410	12.24
$40,000-$50,000	260	7.76
$50,000 +	590	17.61
Total Returns, No.	3,350	
Total Income, $000	110,543	
Total Taxable Returns	2,390	
Total Tax, $000	22,919	
Average Income, $	32,998	
Average Tax, $	9,590	

VITAL STATISTICS

	1997	1996	1995	1994
Births	181	186	157	177
Deaths	75	53	57	39
Natural Increase	106	133	100	138
Marriages	73	81	82	74

Note: Latest available data.

Wetaskiwin
(Census Agglomeration)

The Census Agglomeration of Wetaskiwin consists solely of Wetaskiwin, C, in census division No. 11.

POPULATION

July 1, 2001 Estimate	11,784
% Cdn. Total	0.04
% Change, '96 -'01	4.55
Avg. Annual Growth Rate, %	0.89
2003 Projected Population	11,834
2006 Projected Population	11,823
2001 Households Estimate	4,727
2003 Projected Households	4,815
2006 Projected Households	4,921

INCOME

% Above/Below National Average	-10
2001 Total Income Estimate	$223,060,000
% Cdn. Total	0.03
2001 Average Hhld. Income	$47,200
2001 Per Capita	$18,900
2003 Projected Total Income	$238,020,000
2006 Projected Total Income	$260,930,000

RETAIL SALES

% Above/Below National Average	+223
2001 Retail Sales Estimate	$340,740,000
% Cdn. Total	0.12
2001 per Household	$72,100
2001 per Capita	$28,900
2001 No. of Establishments	130
2003 Projected Retail Sales	$369,950,000
2006 Projected Retail Sales	$411,310,000

POPULATION

2001 Estimates:
Total	11,784
Male	5,613
Female	6,171

Age Groups	Male	Female
0-4	404	380
5-9	426	402
10-14	438	427
15-19	441	424
20-24	405	391
25-29	380	385
30-34	409	429
35-39	420	448
40-44	395	428
45-49	352	401
50-54	305	334
55-59	253	266
60-64	214	233
65-69	194	232
70+	577	991

DAYTIME POPULATION

2001 Estimates:
Working Population	5,475
At Home Population	6,309
Total	11,784

INCOME

2001 Estimates:
Avg. Household Income	$47,188
Avg. Family Income	$55,563
Per Capita Income	$18,929
Male:	
Avg. Employment Income	$31,733
Avg. Employment Income (Full Time)	$41,650
Female:	
Avg. Employment Income	$18,253
Avg. Employment Income (Full Time)	$27,897

DISPOSABLE & DISCRETIONARY INCOME

2001 Estimates:	Per Hhld.
Disposable Income	$36,716
Discretionary Income 1 (minus Food & Shelter)	$24,400
Discretionary Income 2 (minus Food, Shelter, & Other Expenditures)	$15,877

LIQUID ASSETS

1999 Estimates:	Per Hhld.
Equity Investments	$68,502
Interest Bearing Investments	$57,796
Total Liquid Assets	$126,298

CREDIT DATA

July 2000:
Pool of Credit	$93,206,254
Revolving Credit, No.	16,254
Fixed Loans, No.	7,043
Avg. Credit Limit, per Person	$10,825
Avg. Spent, per Person	$5,381
Satisfactory Ratings, No. per Person	2.58
Avg. No. of Cards, per Person	0.91

LABOUR FORCE

2001 Estimates:
Male:	
In the Labour Force	3,025
Participation Rate	69.6
Employed	2,835
Unemployed	190
Unemployment Rate	6.3
Not in Labour Force	1,320
Female:	
In the Labour Force	2,788
Participation Rate	56.2
Employed	2,686
Unemployed	102
Unemployment Rate	3.7
Not in Labour Force	2,174

OCCUPATIONS BY MAJOR GROUPS

2001 Estimates:	Male	Female
Management	399	136
Business, Finance & Admin.	272	770
Natural & Applied Sciences & Related	66	n.a.
Health	48	203
Social Sciences, Gov't Services & Religion	111	142
Education	99	168
Arts, Culture, Recreation & Sport	35	84
Sales & Service	808	1,194
Trades, Transport & Equipment Operators & Related	730	10
Primary Industries	229	10
Processing, Mfg. & Utilities	186	12

Alberta

Wetaskiwin
(Census Agglomeration)
(Cont'd)

LEVEL OF SCHOOLING

2001 Estimates:
Population 15 years +	9,307
Less than Grade 9	1,199
Grades 9-13 w/o Certif.	2,697
Grade 9-13 with Certif.	1,138
Trade Certif. /Dip.	401
Non-Univ. w/o Certif./Dip.	696
Non-Univ. with Certif./Dip.	1,719
Univ. w/o Degree	669
Univ. w/o Degree/Certif.	309
Univ. with Certif.	360
Univ. with Degree	788

AVERAGE HOUSEHOLD EXPENDITURES

2001 Estimates:
Food	$5,813
Shelter	$8,562
Clothing	$1,822
Transportation	$6,680
Health & Personal Care	$1,900
Recr'n, Read'g & Education	$3,124
Taxes & Securities	$10,947
Other	$7,708
Total Expenditures	$46,556

PRIVATE HOUSEHOLDS

2001 Estimates:
Private Households, Total	4,727
Pop. in Private Households	11,461
Average no. per Household	2.4

FAMILIES

2001 Estimates:
Families in Private Households	3,224
Husband-Wife Families	2,794
Lone-Parent Families	430
Aver. No. Persons per Family	3.0
Aver. No. Sons/Daughters at Home	1.2

HOUSING

2001 Estimates:
Occupied Private Dwellings	4,727
Owned	2,972
Rented	1,755
Single-Detached House	3,029
Semi-Detached House	257
Row Houses	325
Apartment, 5 or Fewer Storeys	902
Apartment, Detached Duplex	51
Movable Dwellings	163

VEHICLES

2001 Estimates:
Model Yrs. '81-'96, No.	5,328
% Total	83.64
Model Yrs. '97-'98, No.	712
% Total	11.18
'99 Vehicles registered in Model Yr. '99, No.	330
% Total	5.18
Total No. '81-'99	6,370

LEGAL MARITAL STATUS

2001 Estimates: (Age 15+)
Single (Never Married)	2,618
Legally Married (Not Separated)	4,755
Legally Married (Separated)	295
Widowed	903
Divorced	736

PSYTE CATEGORIES

2001 Estimates	No. of House-holds	% of Total Hhds.	Index
Small City Elite	199	4.21	246
Old Towns' New Fringe	495	10.47	268
Old Leafy Towns	843	17.83	698
Quiet Towns	3,103	65.64	3,085
Big Country Families	37	0.78	55

FINANCIAL PSYTE

2001 Estimates	No. of House-holds	% of Total Hhds.	Index
Canadian Comfort	199	4.21	43
Tractors & Tradelines	495	10.47	183
Bills & Wills	843	17.83	215
Rural Family Blues	37	0.78	10
Limited Budgets	3,103	65.64	2,112

HOME LANGUAGE

2001 Estimates:		% Total
English	11,370	96.49
French	32	0.27
Chinese	36	0.31
Czech	10	0.08
German	43	0.36
Gujarati	16	0.14
Korean	37	0.31
Spanish	66	0.56
Tagalog (Pilipino)	73	0.62
Multiple Responses	101	0.86
Total	11,784	100.00

BUILDING PERMITS

	1999	1998 $000	1997
Value	17,736	9,670	9,373

HOMES BUILT

	1999	1998	1997
No	27	65	27

TAXATION

Income Class:	1997	% Total
Under $5,000	1,560	15.06
$5,000-$10,000	1,510	14.58
$10,000-$15,000	1,770	17.08
$15,000-$20,000	1,220	11.78
$20,000-$25,000	880	8.49
$25,000-$30,000	740	7.14
$30,000-$40,000	1,110	10.71
$40,000-$50,000	640	6.18
$50,000 +	940	9.07
Total Returns, No.	10,360	
Total Income, $000	241,085	
Total Taxable Returns	6,660	
Total Tax, $000	39,641	
Average Income, $	23,271	
Average Tax, $	5,952	

VITAL STATISTICS

	1997	1996	1995	1994
Births	167	163	167	157
Deaths	120	113	118	104
Natural Increase	47	50	49	53
Marriages	86	86	82	82

Note: Latest available data.

COMMUNITY NEWSPAPER(S)

	Total Circulation
Wetaskiwin: Wetaskiwin Times Advertiser	11,109

RADIO STATION(S)

	Power
CKJR	10,000w

Wetaskiwin County No. 10
(County Municipality)
In census division No. 11.

POPULATION

July 1, 2001 Estimate	11,622
% Cdn. Total	0.04
% Change, '96 -'01	7.97
Avg. Annual Growth Rate, %	1.55
2003 Projected Population	11,863
2006 Projected Population	12,145
2001 Households Estimate	4,151
2003 Projected Households	4,297
2006 Projected Households	4,503

INCOME

% Above/Below National Average	-6
2001 Total Income Estimate	$230,630,000
% Cdn. Total	0.04
2001 Average Hhld. Income	$55,600
2001 Per Capita	$19,800
2003 Projected Total Income	$252,070,000
2006 Projected Total Income	$286,790,000

RETAIL SALES

% Above/Below National Average	-47
2001 Retail Sales Estimate	$55,130,000
% Cdn. Total	0.02
2001 per Household	$13,300
2001 per Capita	$4,700
2001 No. of Establishments	70
2003 Projected Retail Sales	$60,910,000
2006 Projected Retail Sales	$70,320,000

POPULATION

2001 Estimates:

Total		11,622
Male		6,007
Female		5,615

Age Groups	Male	Female
0-4	320	305
5-9	390	391
10-14	486	480
15-19	512	481
20-24	424	361
25-29	334	284
30-34	331	328
35-39	421	406
40-44	471	457
45-49	457	461
50-54	401	411
55-59	356	330
60-64	325	277
65-69	277	225
70+	502	418

DAYTIME POPULATION

2001 Estimates:

Working Population	2,560
At Home Population	4,816
Total	7,376

INCOME

2001 Estimates:

Avg. Household Income	$55,559
Avg. Family Income	$57,833
Per Capita Income	$19,844
Male:	
Avg. Employment Income	$31,303
Avg. Employment Income (Full Time)	$38,258
Female:	
Avg. Employment Income	$17,951
Avg. Employment Income (Full Time)	$24,695

DISPOSABLE & DISCRETIONARY INCOME

2001 Estimates:	Per Hhld.
Disposable Income	$43,198
Discretionary Income 1 (minus Food & Shelter)	$30,059
Discretionary Income 2 (minus Food, Shelter, & Other Expenditures)	$19,878

LIQUID ASSETS

1999 Estimates:	Per Hhld.
Equity Investments	$70,327
Interest Bearing Investments	$63,658
Total Liquid Assets	$133,985

CREDIT DATA

July 2000:

Pool of Credit	$95,820,412
Revolving Credit, No.	12,706
Fixed Loans, No.	6,016
Avg. Credit Limit, per Person	$13,251
Avg. Spent, per Person	$6,664
Satisfactory Ratings, No. per Person	2.47
Avg. No. of Cards, per Person	0.86

LABOUR FORCE

2001 Estimates:

Male:	
In the Labour Force	3,978
Participation Rate	82.7
Employed	3,841
Unemployed	137
Unemployment Rate	3.4
Not in Labour Force	833
Female:	
In the Labour Force	3,139
Participation Rate	70.7
Employed	2,967
Unemployed	172
Unemployment Rate	5.5
Not in Labour Force	1,300

OCCUPATIONS BY MAJOR GROUPS

2001 Estimates:	Male	Female
Management	272	181
Business, Finance & Admin.	144	737
Natural & Applied Sciences & Related	45	27
Health	49	152
Social Sciences, Gov't Services & Religion	38	37
Education	60	106
Arts, Culture, Recreation & Sport	23	89
Sales & Service	397	941
Trades, Transport & Equipment Operators & Related	1,095	36
Primary Industries	1,600	787
Processing, Mfg. & Utilities	227	40

LEVEL OF SCHOOLING

2001 Estimates:

Population 15 years +	9,250
Less than Grade 9	892
Grades 9-13 w/o Certif.	3,128
Grade 9-13 with Certif.	1,176
Trade Certif./Dip.	382
Non-Univ. w/o Certif./Dip.	521
Non-Univ. with Certif./Dip.	1,921
Univ. w/o Degree	617
Univ. w/o Degree/Certif.	310
Univ. with Certif.	307
Univ. with Degree	613

AVERAGE HOUSEHOLD EXPENDITURES

2001 Estimates:

Food	$6,681
Shelter	$8,560
Clothing	$2,211
Transportation	$8,258
Health & Personal Care	$2,040
Recr'n, Read'g & Education	$4,086
Taxes & Securities	$12,194
Other	$9,642
Total Expenditures	$53,672

PRIVATE HOUSEHOLDS

2001 Estimates:

Private Households, Total	4,151
Pop. in Private Households	11,440
Average no. per Household	2.8

FAMILIES

2001 Estimates:

Families in Private Households	3,445
Husband-Wife Families	3,191
Lone-Parent Families	254
Aver. No. Persons per Family	3.1
Aver. No. Sons/Daughters at Home	1.2

HOUSING

2001 Estimates:

Occupied Private Dwellings	4,151
Owned	3,642
Rented	509
Single-Detached House	3,538
Semi-Detached House	22
Row Houses	11
Apartment, 5 or Fewer Storeys	11
Other Single-Attached	11
Movable Dwellings	558

VEHICLES

2001 Estimates:

Model Yrs. '81-'96, No.	8,170
% Total	82.40
Model Yrs. '97-'98, No.	1,147
% Total	11.57
'99 Vehicles registered in Model Yr. '99, No.	598
% Total	6.03
Total No. '81-'99	9,915

LEGAL MARITAL STATUS

2001 Estimates: (Age 15+)

Single (Never Married)	2,203
Legally Married (Not Separated)	5,996
Legally Married (Separated)	186
Widowed	384
Divorced	481

PSYTE CATEGORIES

2001 Estimates	No. of House-holds	% of Total Hhds.	Index
Old Towns' New Fringe	585	14.09	360
Rustic Prosperity	2,288	55.12	3,055
Pick-ups & Dirt Bikes	498	12.00	1,437
The Grain Belt	209	5.03	850
Old Leafy Towns	210	5.06	198
Rod & Rifle	320	7.71	333
Big Country Families	41	0.99	69

FINANCIAL P$YTE

2001 Estimates	No. of House-holds	% of Total Hhds.	Index
Tractors & Tradelines	2,873	69.21	1,210
Bills & Wills	210	5.06	61
Country Credit	707	17.03	252
Rural Family Blues	361	8.70	108

Alberta

HOME LANGUAGE

2001 Estimates:		% Total
English	11,403	98.12
French	24	0.21
Danish	17	0.15
Dutch	12	0.10
German	77	0.66
Tagalog (Pilipino)	15	0.13
Multiple Responses	74	0.64
Total	11,622	100.00

BUILDING PERMITS

	1999	1998	1997
		$000	
Value	9,444	10,501	18,066

TAXATION

Income Class:	1997	% Total
Under $5,000	490	15.12
$5,000-$10,000	580	17.90
$10,000-$15,000	590	18.21
$15,000-$20,000	330	10.19
$20,000-$25,000	260	8.02
$25,000-$30,000	210	6.48
$30,000-$40,000	280	8.64
$40,000-$50,000	190	5.86
$50,000 +	310	9.57
Total Returns, No.	3,240	
Total Income, $000	70,937	
Total Taxable Returns	1,980	
Total Tax, $000	10,966	
Average Income, $.	21,894	
Average Tax, $.	5,538	

VITAL STATISTICS

	1997	1996	1995	1994
Births	103	103	113	113
Deaths	56	51	118	104
Natural Increase	47	52	-5	9
Marriages	58	71	36	59

Note: Latest available data.

Alberta

Wood Buffalo
(Census Agglomeration)

The Census Agglomeration of Wood Buffalo consists of Wood Buffalo, SM, plus many smaller areas. All are in census division No. 16.

POPULATION

July 1, 2001 Estimate	39,941
% Cdn. Total	0.13
% Change, '96 -'01	7.54
Avg. Annual Growth Rate, %	1.46
2003 Projected Population	39,664
2006 Projected Population	38,064
2001 Households Estimate	14,698
2003 Projected Households	14,974
2006 Projected Households	15,076

INCOME

% Above/Below National Average	+40
2001 Total Income Estimate	$1,182,420,000
% Cdn. Total	0.18
2001 Average Hhld. Income	$80,400
2001 Per Capita	$29,600
2003 Projected Total Income	$1,251,100,000
2006 Projected Total Income	$1,323,980,000

RETAIL SALES

% Above/Below National Average	+35
2001 Retail Sales Estimate	$482,960,000
% Cdn. Total	0.17
2001 per Household	$32,900
2001 per Capita	$12,100
2001 No. of Establishments	241
2003 Projected Retail Sales	$510,780,000
2006 Projected Retail Sales	$532,420,000

POPULATION

2001 Estimates:

Total		39,941
Male		20,862
Female		19,079
Age Groups	Male	Female
0-4	1,512	1,414
5-9	1,632	1,568
10-14	1,739	1,683
15-19	1,752	1,668
20-24	1,621	1,481
25-29	1,475	1,405
30-34	1,569	1,581
35-39	1,820	1,815
40-44	2,014	1,845
45-49	1,936	1,665
50-54	1,592	1,249
55-59	1,049	755
60-64	591	409
65-69	298	231
70+	262	310

DAYTIME POPULATION

2001 Estimates:

Working Population	22,116
At Home Population	17,825
Total	39,941

INCOME

2001 Estimates:

Avg. Household Income	$80,448
Avg. Family Income	$84,794
Per Capita Income	$29,604
Male:	
Avg. Employment Income	$56,421
Avg. Employment Income (Full Time)	$74,881
Female:	
Avg. Employment Income	$23,705
Avg. Employment Income (Full Time)	$39,122

DISPOSABLE & DISCRETIONARY INCOME

2001 Estimates:	Per Hhld.
Disposable Income	$59,896
Discretionary Income 1 (minus Food & Shelter)	$44,838
Discretionary Income 2 (minus Food, Shelter, & Other Expenditures)	$32,427

LIQUID ASSETS

1999 Estimates:	Per Hhld.
Equity Investments	$134,680
Interest Bearing Investments	$101,615
Total Liquid Assets	$236,295

CREDIT DATA

July 2000:

Pool of Credit	$535,087,222
Revolving Credit, No.	71,875
Fixed Loans, No.	37,045
Avg. Credit Limit, per Person	$15,781
Avg. Spent, per Person	$8,530
Satisfactory Ratings, No. per Person	3.01
Avg. No. of Cards, per Person	0.99

LABOUR FORCE

2001 Estimates:

Male:
In the Labour Force	13,887
Participation Rate	86.9
Employed	13,053
Unemployed	834
Unemployment Rate	6.0
Not in Labour Force	2,092

Female:
In the Labour Force	9,717
Participation Rate	67.4
Employed	8,896
Unemployed	821
Unemployment Rate	8.4
Not in Labour Force	4,697

OCCUPATIONS BY MAJOR GROUPS

2001 Estimates:	Male	Female
Management	1,076	556
Business, Finance & Admin.	682	2,660
Natural & Applied Sciences & Related	1,337	224
Health	92	437
Social Sciences, Gov't Services & Religion	126	267
Education	314	530
Arts, Culture, Recreation & Sport	78	209
Sales & Service	1,981	3,995
Trades, Transport & Equipment Operators & Related	5,725	348
Primary Industries	821	98
Processing, Mfg. & Utilities	1,557	131

LEVEL OF SCHOOLING

2001 Estimates:

Population 15 years +	30,393
Less than Grade 9	1,809
Grades 9-13 w/o Certif.	7,832
Grade 9-13 with Certif.	3,682
Trade Certif. /Dip.	1,440
Non-Univ. w/o Certif./Dip.	2,365
Non-Univ. with Certif./Dip.	7,760
Univ. w/o Degree	2,848
Univ. w/o Degree/Certif.	1,236
Univ. with Certif.	1,612
Univ. with Degree	2,657

AVERAGE HOUSEHOLD EXPENDITURES

2001 Estimates:

Food	$7,918
Shelter	$9,936
Clothing	$3,105
Transportation	$10,189
Health & Personal Care	$2,363
Recr'n, Read'g & Education	$6,027
Taxes & Securities	$20,688
Other	$12,802
Total Expenditures	$73,028

PRIVATE HOUSEHOLDS

2001 Estimates:

Private Households, Total	14,698
Pop. in Private Households	39,543
Average no. per Household	2.7

FAMILIES

2001 Estimates:

Families in Private Households	11,729
Husband-Wife Families	10,123
Lone-Parent Families	1,606
Aver. No. Persons per Family	3.3
Aver. No. Sons/Daughters at Home	1.4

HOUSING

2001 Estimates:

Occupied Private Dwellings	14,698
Owned	9,413
Rented	4,972
Band Housing	313
Single-Detached House	6,926
Semi-Detached House	957
Row Houses	1,617
Apartment, 5+ Storeys	390
Owned Apartment, 5+ Storeys	11
Apartment, 5 or Fewer Storeys	2,978
Apartment, Detached Duplex	87
Other Single-Attached	25
Movable Dwellings	1,718

VEHICLES

2001 Estimates:

Model Yrs. '81-'96, No.	16,956
% Total	71.71
Model Yrs. '97-'98, No.	4,120
% Total	17.43
'99 Vehicles registered in Model Yr. '99, No.	2,568
% Total	10.86
Total No. '81-'99	23,644

LEGAL MARITAL STATUS

2001 Estimates: (Age 15+)

Single (Never Married)	10,968
Legally Married (Not Separated)	15,577
Legally Married (Separated)	971
Widowed	592
Divorced	2,285

PSYTE CATEGORIES

2001 Estimates	No. of House -holds	% of Total Hhds.	Index
Town Boomers	430	2.93	289
Northern Lights	13,012	88.53	17,886
Pick-ups & Dirt Bikes	128	0.87	104
Young Grey Collar	299	2.03	243
Big Country Families	808	5.50	385

FINANCIAL P$YTE

2001 Estimates	No. of House -holds	% of Total Hhds.	Index
Successful Suburbanites	13,012	88.53	1,334
Canadian Comfort	430	2.93	30
Country Credit	128	0.87	13
Revolving Renters	299	2.03	44
Rural Family Blues	808	5.50	68

HOME LANGUAGE

2001 Estimates:		% Total
English	37,453	93.77
French	392	0.98
Arabic	136	0.34
Chinese	152	0.38
Chipewyan	382	0.96
Cree	197	0.49
Gujarati	53	0.13
Hindi	39	0.10
Hungarian	52	0.13
Persian (Farsi)	29	0.07
Polish	33	0.08
Portuguese	23	0.06
Punjabi	37	0.09
Russian	27	0.07
Spanish	170	0.43
Tagalog (Pilipino)	83	0.21
Urdu	22	0.06
Vietnamese	21	0.05
Other Languages	88	0.22
Multiple Responses	552	1.38
Total	39,941	100.00

BUILDING PERMITS

	1999	1998	1997
		$000	
Value	66,386	59,569	n.a.

HOMES BUILT

	1999	1998	1997
No.	395	341	359

TAXATION

Income Class:	1997	% Total
Under $5,000	3,420	13.64
$5,000-$10,000	2,670	10.65
$10,000-$15,000	2,370	9.45
$15,000-$20,000	1,910	7.62
$20,000-$25,000	1,470	5.86
$25,000-$30,000	1,370	5.46
$30,000-$40,000	2,200	8.77
$40,000-$50,000	1,820	7.26
$50,000 +	7,850	31.30
Total Returns, No.	25,080	
Total Income, $000	990,342	
Total Taxable Returns	19,030	
Total Tax, $000	231,531	
Average Income, $	39,487	
Average Tax, $	12,167	

VITAL STATISTICS

	1997	1996	1995	1994
Births	590	631	708	705
Deaths	98	83	129	93
Natural Increase	492	548	579	612
Marriages	207	153	217	190

Note: Latest available data.

DAILY NEWSPAPER(S)

	Circulation Average Paid
Fort McMurray Today	
Fri.	6,868
Mon-Thu	4,791

RADIO STATION(S)

	Power
CBXN-FM	n.a.
CHFA-FM	n.a.
CJOK-FM	n.a.
CKUA-FM	n.a.
CKYX-FM	n.a.

FP MARKETS –
CANADIAN DEMOGRAPHICS ON CD ROM

FP Markets on CD-ROM offers the fastest, most efficient way to access Canadian demographic data. Advanced queries allow you to cross-reference and sort the data to meet your specifications. Access just the information you require and download the specifics onto your system.

Information includes:
- Population by Age Group
- Average Household Income and Expenditures
- PSYTE Segmentation System
- Retail Sales data
- Vehicle data
- *Much more!*

Explore Canada from coast to coast with our National CD-ROM, or zero in on your market with our Regional CD-ROM. Select one or more of the following regions: British Columbia / Northwest Territories, Prairie Provinces, Ontario, Quebec and the Atlantic Provinces.

FP Markets
Canadian Demographics

National CD-ROM – $695* / all of Canada
Regional CD-ROM – $195* / region

For more information, visit our Web Site:
www.financialpost.com or call 1-800-661-POST
Fax: (416) 350-6501
e-mail: fpdg@fpdata.finpost.com

FINANCIAL POST
DATAGROUP
333 King St. E. Toronto, ON M5A 4N2

Data provided by:

* Plus applicable taxes and shipping

CODE ACD

British Columbia

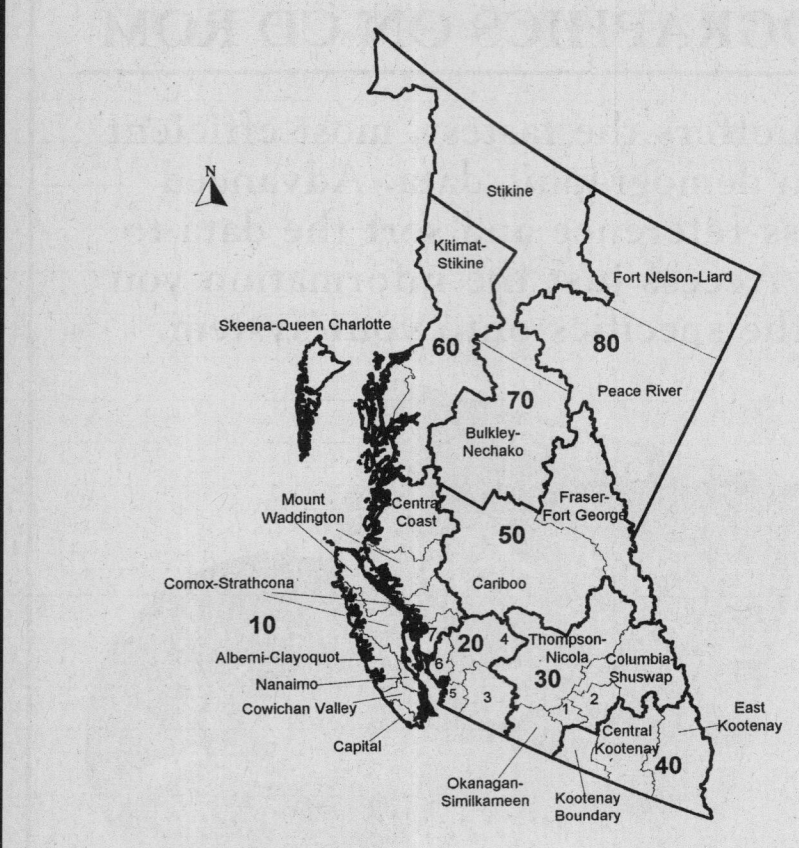

Economic Regions

10 Vancouver Island and Coast
20 Lower Mainland - Southwest
30 Thompson Okanagan
40 Kootenay
50 Cariboo
60 North Coast
70 Nechako
80 Northeast

1 Central Okanagan
2 North Okanagan
3 Fraser Valley
4 Squamish-Lilloet
5 Greater Vancouver
6 Sunshine Coast
7 Powell River

Region	Population (at July 1)				Households (at July 1)		Income				Retail Sales				Taxation Statistics, 1997					
	*1996 Census (000)	2001 Estimate (000)	% of Cdn. Total	% Chg. '96-'01	2001 Estimate (000)	% of Cdn. Total	2001 Estimate $millions	% of Cdn. Total	Per Hhld. $	Income Rating Index	2001 Estimate $millions	% of Cdn. Total	Per Hhld. $	Market Rating Index	Total No. of Returns	Total Income $millions	Total No. Taxable Returns	Total Tax $millions	Avg. Income $	Avg. Tax $
British Columbia	3,882.0	4,137.4	13.29	6.58	1,636.6	13.54	87,782.5	13.37	53,600	101	36,141.4	12.97	22,100	98	2,740,780	77,255.6	1,898,700	15,115.8	28,187	7,961
Vancouver Island and Coast (10)	705.3	726.2	2.33	2.98	306.2	2.53	15,032.8	2.29	49,100	98	5,874.5	2.11	19,200	90	495,920	13,919.8	355,350	2,589.5	28,069	7,287
Capital Regional District	331.0	335.7	1.08	1.42	146.8	1.21	7,522.5	1.15	51,200	106	2,818.6	1.01	19,200	94	240,040	7,167.7	178,600	1,379.9	29,860	7,726
Cowichan Valley Regional District	73.6	77.9	0.25	5.72	30.5	0.25	1,418.2	0.22	46,500	86	488.9	0.18	16,000	70	51,500	1,351.6	35,200	242.3	26,245	6,883
Nanaimo Regional District	126.4	136.1	0.44	7.65	57.1	0.47	2,665.2	0.41	46,700	93	1,057.5	0.38	18,500	87	89,000	2,325.5	62,010	410.1	26,129	6,614
Alberni-Clayoquot Regional District	32.8	31.1	0.10	-5.4	12.7	0.10	568.6	0.09	44,900	87	243.0	0.09	19,200	87	21,390	555.3	14,380	98.2	25,962	6,826
Comox-Strathcona Regional District	101.5	107.1	0.34	5.49	43.4	0.36	2,099.2	0.32	48,400	98	938.2	0.34	21,600	98	68,870	1,842.5	48,320	333.6	26,753	6,903
Powell River Regional District	20.7	20.4	0.07	-1.05	8.7	0.07	394.7	0.06	45,600	92	189.9	0.07	21,900	104	14,130	380.7	9,870	68.6	26,945	6,950
Mount Waddington Regional District	15.1	14.2	0.05	-6.2	5.7	0.05	308.9	0.05	54,600	103	110.8	0.04	19,600	87	8,880	258.6	6,110	51.7	29,119	8,468
Central Coast Regional District	4.1	3.8	0.01	-5.83	1.4	0.01	55.4	0.01	39,800	68	27.5	0.01	19,800	80	2,110	37.8	860	5.2	17,929	6,024
Lower Mainland - Southwest (20)	2,201.7	2,407.9	7.73	9.36	934.5	7.73	53,624.6	8.17	57,400	106	20,127.6	7.22	21,500	93	1,581,290	45,747.5	1,091,310	9,313.8	28,931	8,534

*Adjusted.

British Columbia (continued)

Region	Population (at July 1)				Households (at July1)		Income				Retail Sales				Taxation Statistics, 1997					
	*1996 Census (000)	2001 Estimate (000)	% of Cdn. Total	% Chg. '96-'01	2001 Estimate (000)	% of Cdn. Total	2001 Estimate $millions	% of Cdn. Total	Per Hhld. $	Income Rating Index	2001 Estimate $millions	% of Cdn. Total	Per Hhld. $	Market Rating Index	Total No. of Returns	Total Income $millions	Total No. Taxable Returns	Total Tax $millions	Avg. Income $	Avg. Tax $
Fraser Valley Regional District	231.5	251.0	0.81	8.4	91.0	0.75	4,479.5	0.68	49,200	85	2,199.0	0.79	24,200	98	155,410	3,867.5	104,430	660.3	24,886	6,322
Greater Vancouver Regional District	1,912.1	2,092.7	6.72	9.45	816.8	6.76	47,738.1	7.27	58,400	108	17,323.8	6.22	21,200	92	1,386,450	40,802.3	959,060	8,449.9	29,429	8,811
Sunshine Coast Regional District	25.8	27.9	0.09	8.01	12.0	0.10	559.6	0.09	46,800	95	255.9	0.09	21,400	102	17,820	479.6	12,360	87.5	26,913	7,076
Squamish-Lillooet Regional District	32.2	36.2	0.12	12.45	14.7	0.12	847.5	0.13	57,700	111	348.8	0.13	23,800	108	21,610	598.2	15,460	116.1	27,683	7,512
Thompson - Okanagan (30)	468.2	495.8	1.59	5.9	200.9	1.66	9,184.0	1.40	45,700	88	5,068.0	1.82	25,200	114	332,890	8,482.5	226,600	1,481.2	25,481	6,537
Okanagan-Similkameen Regional District	78.6	81.2	0.26	3.23	35.0	0.29	1,427.3	0.22	40,800	83	690.8	0.25	19,800	95	58,290	1,368.3	38,690	218.4	23,473	5,645
Thompson-Nicola Regional District	123.5	128.2	0.41	3.8	50.8	0.42	2,494.0	0.38	49,100	92	1,296.4	0.47	25,500	113	85,440	2,254.9	57,860	413.4	26,391	7,144
Central Okanagan Regional District	142.0	156.7	0.50	10.37	63.0	0.52	3,029.4	0.46	48,100	92	1,845.9	0.66	29,300	132	102,920	2,726.4	72,520	482.4	26,491	6,652
North Okanagan Regional District	74.3	78.0	0.25	5.01	31.1	0.26	1,334.8	0.20	43,000	81	692.7	0.25	22,300	99	53,020	1,314.3	35,050	227.6	24,789	6,492
Columbia-Shuswap Regional District	49.9	51.8	0.17	3.87	21.1	0.17	898.6	0.14	42,600	82	542.3	0.19	25,700	117	33,220	818.7	22,480	139.5	24,644	6,205
Kootenay (40)	152.8	154.3	0.50	1.02	64.0	0.53	2,823.8	0.43	44,100	87	1,860.7	0.67	29,100	135	104,260	2,716.9	71,320	493.7	26,059	6,923
East Kootenay Regional District	58.5	59.5	0.19	1.72	24.4	0.20	1,181.8	0.18	48,500	94	826.5	0.30	33,900	155	40,090	1,121.0	28,290	211.2	27,962	7,465
Central Kootenay Regional District	60.2	61.5	0.20	2.17	25.6	0.21	1,026.1	0.16	40,100	79	694.8	0.25	27,200	126	40,690	982.9	26,860	172.3	24,155	6,414
Kootenay Boundary Regional District	34.0	33.3	0.11	-2.24	14.1	0.12	615.9	0.09	43,700	88	339.4	0.12	24,100	114	23,480	613.0	16,170	110.3	26,107	6,819
Cariboo (50)	173.1	174.4	0.56	0.78	65.9	0.55	3,588.4	0.55	54,500	98	1,619.0	0.58	24,600	104	113,650	3,193.3	78,610	628.2	28,097	7,992
Cariboo Regional District	70.0	71.0	0.23	1.46	27.1	0.22	1,307.6	0.20	48,200	87	618.9	0.22	22,800	97	45,930	1,188.1	29,930	223.1	25,867	7,455
Fraser-Fort George Regional District	103.1	103.4	0.33	0.31	38.8	0.32	2,280.8	0.35	58,800	105	1,000.1	0.36	25,800	108	67,720	2,005.2	48,680	405.1	29,610	8,322
North Coast (60)	71.2	68.1	0.22	-4.27	24.8	0.21	1,358.8	0.21	54,800	95	501.4	0.18	20,200	82	42,100	1,183.9	27,420	228.8	28,121	8,343
Skeena-Queen Charlotte Regional District	25.8	23.7	0.08	-8.01	8.8	0.07	461.0	0.07	52,500	92	169.0	0.06	19,300	80	14,930	398.5	9,700	71.7	26,694	7,393
Kitimat-Stikine Regional District	45.4	44.4	0.14	-2.16	16.0	0.13	897.8	0.14	56,100	96	332.4	0.12	20,800	84	27,170	785.4	17,720	157.0	28,905	8,863
Nechako (70)	44.8	45.5	0.15	1.57	16.6	0.14	890.8	0.14	53,700	93	402.4	0.14	24,300	99	28,580	773.9	18,930	145.1	27,080	7,666
Bulkley-Nechako Regional District	43.4	44.4	0.14	2.24	16.0	0.13	868.3	0.13	54,200	93	391.5	0.14	24,400	99	27,820	753.5	18,470	141.9	27,084	7,682
Stikine Region	1.4	1.2	0.00	-18.6	.6	0.00	22.5	0.00	40,000	91	10.9	0.00	19,300	103	760	20.4	460	3.2	26,905	7,035
Northeast (80)	65.0	65.0	0.21	0.13	23.8	0.20	1,279.2	0.19	53,800	93	687.8	0.25	28,900	118	42,050	1,237.8	29,160	235.4	29,436	8,073
Peace River Regional District	58.8	58.7	0.19	-0.22	21.6	0.18	1,148.8	0.18	53,100	93	641.7	0.23	29,700	122	38,050	1,105.3	26,170	209.6	29,047	8,010
Fort Nelson-Liard Regional District	6.2	6.4	0.02	3.46	2.2	0.02	130.5	0.02	60,000	97	46.0	0.02	21,200	81	4,000	132.5	2,990	25.8	33,133	8,623

*Adjusted.

British Columbia

POPULATION

July 1, 2001 Estimate 4,137,402
% Cdn. Total 13.29
% Change, '96 -'01 . . . . 6.58
Avg. Annual Growth Rate, % 1.28
2003 Projected Population 4,266,917
2006 Projected Population 4,490,043
2001 Households Estimate 1,636,609
2003 Projected Households 1,697,662
2006 Projected Households 1,802,691

INCOME

% Above/Below National Average . . . . +1
2001 Total Income Estimate . . $87,782,510,000
% Cdn. Total 13.37
2001 Average Hhld. Income $53,600
2001 Per Capita $21,200
2003 Projected Total Income . $96,061,240,000
2006 Projected Total Income $110,768,210,000

RETAIL SALES

% Above/Below National Average . . . . -2
2001 Retail Sales Estimate . . $36,141,380,000
% Cdn. Total 12.97
2001 per Household $22,100
2001 per Capita $8,700
2001 No. of Establishments 31,823
2003 Projected Retail Sales . $39,980,110,000
2006 Projected Retail Sales . $46,125,310,000

POPULATION

2001 Estimates:
Total 4,137,402
Male 2,041,121
Female 2,096,281

Age Groups	Male	Female
0-4	126,938	120,596
5-9	133,491	126,679
10-14	139,476	131,760
15-19	138,926	132,010
20-24	134,979	133,231
25-29	140,753	142,119
30-34	155,811	159,037
35-39	167,480	172,224
40-44	167,986	172,595
45-49	158,937	161,346
50-54	135,379	135,891
55-59	107,750	108,178
60-64	88,250	89,349
65-69	76,094	79,362
70+	168,871	231,904

DAYTIME POPULATION

2001 Estimates:
Working Population 1,948,093
At Home Population 2,199,334
Total 4,147,427

INCOME

2001 Estimates:
Avg. Household Income $53,637
Avg. Family Income $59,666
Per Capita Income $21,217
Male:
Avg. Employment Income $35,371
Avg. Employment Income
  (Full Time) $47,444
Female:
Avg. Employment Income $21,928
Avg. Employment Income
  (Full Time) $33,020

DISPOSABLE & DISCRETIONARY INCOME

2001 Estimates:	Per Hhld.
Disposable Income	$41,345
Discretionary Income 1 (minus Food & Shelter)	$28,465
Discretionary Income 2 (minus Food, Shelter, & Other Expenditures)	$20,183

LIQUID ASSETS

1999 Estimates:	Per Hhld.
Equity Investments	$80,428
Interest Bearing Investments	$69,298
Total Liquid Assets	$149,726

CREDIT DATA

July 2000:
Pool of Credit $41,167,422,296
Revolving Credit, No. 8,113,983
Fixed Loans, No. 1,992,479
Avg. Credit Limit, per Person $11,901
Avg. Spent, per Person $5,131
Satisfactory Ratings,
  No. per Person 2.85
Avg. No. of Cards, per Person 1.07

LABOUR FORCE

2001 Estimates:
Male:
In the Labour Force 1,140,034
Participation Rate 69.5
Employed 1,047,127
Unemployed 92,907
Unemployment Rate 8.1
Not in Labour Force 501,182
Female:
In the Labour Force 996,268
Participation Rate 58.0
Employed 919,478
Unemployed 76,790
Unemployment Rate 7.7
Not in Labour Force 720,978

AVERAGE WEEKLY EARNINGS

(Including overtime, industrial aggregate)

	British Columbia	Canada
Apr 2000	$636.51	$622.92
Apr 1999	$626.65	$608.07
Apr 1998	$614.94	$608.06
Apr 1997	$613.10	$597.26
Apr 1996	$595.76	$575.79

NUMBER OF EMPLOYEES

(Industrial aggregate)
Apr 2000 1,512,381
Apr 1999 1,485,163
Apr 1998 1,468,346
Apr 1997 1,447,858
Apr 1996 1,405,719

MANUFACTURING INDUSTRIES

	1997	1992
Plants	4,228	3,761
Employees	156,422	148,979
	$000	
Salaries, Wages	6,649,942	5,689,490
Mfg. Materials, Cost	19,954,986	13,908,173
Mfg. Shipments, Value	34,582,686	24,853,278
Total Value Added	13,790,265	10,380,292

Note: Latest available data.

OCCUPATIONS BY MAJOR GROUPS

2001 Estimates:	Male	Female
Management	134,580	63,290
Business, Finance & Admin.	101,752	289,746
Natural & Applied Sciences & Related	81,545	15,154
Health	21,183	75,488
Social Sciences, Gov't Services & Religion	23,316	33,079
Education	28,478	47,384
Arts, Culture, Recreation & Sport	26,851	30,531
Sales & Service	239,086	344,741
Trades, Transport & Equipment Operators & Related	297,625	16,522
Primary Industries	73,823	23,949
Processing, Mfg. & Utilities	83,873	25,534

LEVEL OF SCHOOLING

2001 Estimates:
Population 15 years + ... 3,358,462
Less than Grade 9 247,015
Grades 9-13 w/o Certif. 799,119
Grade 9-13 with Certif. 435,444
Trade Certif. /Dip. 115,833
Non-Univ. w/o Certif./Dip. 246,949
Non-Univ. with Certif./Dip. 663,221
Univ. w/o Degree 396,568
  Univ. w/o Degree/Certif. 188,857
  Univ. with Certif. 207,711
Univ. with Degree 454,313

RETAIL SALES

	1999 $000,000	1998 $000,000
Supermarkets & Groceries	7,688	7,628
All Other Food	n.a.	n.a.
Drugs & Patent Medicine	1,792	1,686
Shoes	192	190
Men's Clothing	182	187
Women's Clothing	537	530
Other Clothing	845	784
Hhld. Furniture & Appliances	1,504	1,446
Hhld. Furnishings	431	402
Motor & Recreation Vehicles	7,863	7,837
Gas Service Stations	2,325	2,405
Auto Parts, Accessories & Services	1,731	1,646
General Merchandise	3,976	3,772
Other Semi-Durable Goods	1,133	1,138
Other Durable Goods	1,137	1,125
Other Retail	1,770	1,704
Total	33,672	33,045

AVERAGE HOUSEHOLD EXPENDITURES

2001 Estimates:
Food $6,098
Shelter $9,004
Clothing $2,163
Transportation $6,367
Health & Personal Care $1,931
Recr'n, Read'g & Education $3,692
Taxes & Securities $13,754
Other $8,219
Total Expenditures $51,228

PRIVATE HOUSEHOLDS

2001 Estimates:
Private Households, Total 1,636,609
Pop. in Private Households 4,064,005
Average no. per Household 2.5

FAMILIES

2001 Estimates:
Families in Private Households 1,163,227
Husband-Wife Families 1,005,104
Lone-Parent Families 158,123
Aver. No. Persons per Family 2.9
Aver. No. Sons/Daughters
  at Home 1.1

HOUSING

2001 Estimates:
Occupied Private Dwellings 1,636,609
  Owned 1,070,622
  Rented 561,240
  Band Housing 4,747
Single-Detached House 919,875
Semi-Detached House 44,881
Row Houses 100,689
Apartment, 5+ Storeys 100,079
  Owned Apartment, 5+ Storeys 29,792
Apartment, 5 or Fewer Storeys 323,452
Apartment, Detached Duplex 96,477
Other Single-Attached 3,480
Movable Dwellings 47,676

VEHICLES

2001 Estimates:
Model Yrs. '81-'96, No. 1,772,855
  % Total 82.09
Model Yrs. '97-'98, No. 238,366
  % Total 11.04
'99 Vehicles registered in
  Model Yr. '99, No. 148,479
  % Total 6.87
Total No. '81-'99 2,159,700

LEGAL MARITAL STATUS

2001 Estimates: (Age 15+)
Single (Never Married) 1,018,634
Legally Married
  (Not Separated) 1,765,305
Legally Married (Separated) 113,314
Widowed 198,790
Divorced 262,419

PSYTE CATEGORIES

2001 Estimates	No. of House-holds	% of Total Hhds.	Index
Canadian Establishment	2,683	0.16	99
The Affluentials	20,670	1.26	198
Urban Gentry	35,926	2.20	122
Suburban Executives	12,187	0.74	52
Mortgaged in Suburbia	23,361	1.43	103
Technocrafts & Bureaucrats	18,389	1.12	40
Asian Heights	15,523	0.95	150
Boomers & Teens	56,327	3.44	192
Stable Suburban Families	20,153	1.23	94
Small City Elite	72,228	4.41	258
Old Bungalow Burbs	11,074	0.68	41
Suburban Nesters	21,990	1.34	84
Brie & Chablis	21,893	1.34	149
Aging Erudites	34,563	2.11	140
Satellite Suburbs	78,824	4.82	168
Kindergarten Boom	56,754	3.47	132
Blue Collar Winners	60,393	3.69	147
Town Boomers	33,863	2.07	204
Old Towns' New Fringe	91,853	5.61	143
Northern Lights	7,567	0.46	93
The New Frontier	70,480	4.31	286
Rustic Prosperity	11,443	0.70	39
Pick-ups & Dirt Bikes	18,436	1.13	135
The Grain Belt	806	0.05	8
Asian Mosaic	124,444	7.60	555
Conservative Homebodies	30,402	1.86	52
High Rise Sunsets	41,767	2.55	178
Young Urban Professionals	46,003	2.81	148

2001 Estimates	No. of House -holds	% of Total Hhds.	Index
Young Urban Mix	57,842	3.53	167
Young Urban Intelligentsia	40,185	2.46	161
University Enclaves	49,211	3.01	147
Young City Singles	65,205	3.98	174
Urban Bohemia	14,914	0.91	78
Old Leafy Towns	94,194	5.76	225
Town Renters	15,667	0.96	111
Nesters & Young Homesteaders	77,644	4.74	203
Young Grey Collar	11,875	0.73	87
Quiet Towns	47,098	2.88	135
Rod & Rifle	15,058	0.92	40
Down, Down East	346	0.02	3
Big Country Families	15,796	0.97	68
Old Cdn. Rustics	1,078	0.07	7
Struggling Downtowns	23,236	1.42	45
Aged Pensioners	41,645	2.54	191
Big City Stress	7,239	0.44	39
Old Grey Towers	4,927	0.30	54

FINAN¢IAL P$YTE

2001 Estimates	No. of House -holds	% of Total Hhds.	Index
Platinum Estates	23,353	1.43	177
Four Star Investors	104,440	6.38	127
Successful Suburbanites	84,993	5.19	78
Canadian Comfort	267,298	16.33	168
Urban Heights	102,459	6.26	146
Miners & Credit-Liners	81,554	4.98	157
Mortgages & Minivans	56,754	3.47	53
Dollars & Sense	124,444	7.60	291
Tractors & Tradelines	103,296	6.31	110
Bills & Wills	182,438	11.15	135
Country Credit	19,242	1.18	17
Revolving Renters	131,286	8.02	174
Young Urban Struggle	104,310	6.37	135
Rural Family Blues	31,200	1.91	24
Limited Budgets	48,176	2.94	95
Towering Debt	104,108	6.36	81
NSF	7,239	0.44	13
Senior Survivors	46,572	2.85	151

HOME LANGUAGE

2001 Estimates:		% Total
English	3,532,076	85.37
French	15,195	0.37
Arabic	2,612	0.06
Chinese	235,341	5.69
Croatian	3,062	0.07
Czech	2,274	0.05
Dutch	2,866	0.07
German	15,713	0.38
Greek	2,879	0.07
Gujarati	3,233	0.08
Hindi	10,371	0.25
Hungarian	3,263	0.08
Italian	9,862	0.24
Japanese	10,206	0.25
Korean	15,254	0.37
Persian (Farsi)	10,732	0.26
Polish	9,473	0.23
Portuguese	6,376	0.15
Punjabi	85,747	2.07
Romanian	2,252	0.05
Russian	3,914	0.09
Serbian	2,493	0.06
Spanish	13,074	0.32
Tagalog (Pilipino)	13,727	0.33
Vietnamese	15,218	0.37
Other Languages	25,856	0.62
Multiple Responses	84,333	2.04
Total	4,137,402	100.00

BUILDING PERMITS

	1999	1998	1997
		$000	
Value	4,695,870	4,739,644	5,543,824

HOMES BUILT

	1999	1998	1997
No	18,478	23,458	30,794

CAPITAL EXPENDITURES

(Public & Private)	2000	1999	1998
		$000,000	
Total Expends.	n.a.	n.a.	26,155.1
Capital Expends.	21,784.3	20,687.6	20,055.2
Construction	14,228.6	12,928.0	12,786.5
Machinery & Equip.	7,555.7	7,759.6	7,268.8
Repair Expends.	n.a.	n.a.	6,099.9
Construction	n.a.	n.a.	2,644.0
Machinery & Equip.	n.a.	n.a.	3,456.3

TAXATION

Income Class:	1997	% Total
Under $5,000	369,250	13.47
$5,000-$10,000	356,450	13.01
$10,000-$15,000	385,000	14.05
$15,000-$20,000	256,970	9.38
$20,000-$25,000	213,400	7.79
$25,000-$30,000	197,190	7.19
$30,000-$40,000	338,080	12.34
$40,000-$50,000	229,950	8.39
$50,000 +	394,490	14.39
Total Returns, No.	2,740,780	
Total Income, $000	77,255,615	
Total Taxable Returns	1,898,700	
Total Tax, $000	15,115,784	
Average Income, $	28,187	
Average Tax, $	7,961	

VITAL STATISTICS

	1997	1996	1995	1994
Births	44,577	46,138	46,820	46,998
Deaths	27,412	27,536	26,375	25,939
Natural Increase	17,165	18,602	20,445	21,059
Marriages	23,245	22,834	23,597	23,739

Note: Latest available data.

TRAVEL STATISTICS

Tourists in Canada	1999	1998
From the U.S. entering by:		
Automobile	4,906,632	4,627,153
Bus	179,801	207,210
Rail	39,374	37,599
Air	986,053	954,623
Marine	427,778	395,895
Other Methods	322,042	326,478
Total	6,861,680	6,548,958
Other Countries:		
Land (via U.S.)	256,541	249,064
Air	1,094,604	1,002,527
Marine	56,397	44,069
Total	1,407,542	1,295,660
Residents of Canada Returning from the U.S. by:		
Automobile	7,492,164	8,330,757
Bus	202,767	224,996
Rail	2,975	3,056
Air	924,427	919,285
Marine	59,520	68,529
Other Methods	107,602	104,934
Total	8,789,455	9,651,557
From Other Countries:		
Land (via U.S.)	15	8
Air	798,650	799,711
Marine	n.a.	1
Total	798,665	799,720

British Columbia

British Columbia

Abbotsford
(Census Agglomeration)

The Census Agglomeration of Abbotsford includes: Abbotsford, C; Mission, DM; plus several smaller areas. All are in Fraser Valley Regional District.

POPULATION

July 1, 2001 Estimate	155,040
% Cdn. Total	0.50
% Change, '96 -'01	9.12
Avg. Annual Growth Rate, %	1.76
2003 Projected Population	160,272
2006 Projected Population	167,329
2001 Households Estimate	54,173
2003 Projected Households	56,153
2006 Projected Households	59,252

INCOME

% Above/Below National Average	-13
2001 Total Income Estimate	$2,828,380,000
% Cdn. Total	0.43
2001 Average Hhld. Income	$52,200
2001 Per Capita	$18,200
2003 Projected Total Income	$3,086,900,000
2006 Projected Total Income	$3,521,840,000

RETAIL SALES

% Above/Below National Average	-9
2001 Retail Sales Estimate	$1,262,990,000
% Cdn. Total	0.45
2001 per Household	$23,300
2001 per Capita	$8,100
2001 No. of Establishments	911
2003 Projected Retail Sales	$1,404,330,000
2006 Projected Retail Sales	$1,615,330,000

POPULATION

2001 Estimates:

Total		155,040
Male		76,883
Female		78,157

Age Groups	Male	Female
0-4	5,184	4,960
5-9	5,918	5,570
10-14	6,198	5,729
15-19	5,851	5,483
20-24	5,316	5,237
25-29	5,351	5,395
30-34	5,930	5,959
35-39	6,300	6,251
40-44	6,049	5,902
45-49	5,296	5,194
50-54	4,340	4,290
55-59	3,397	3,517
60-64	2,807	2,968
65-69	2,505	2,772
70+	6,441	8,930

DAYTIME POPULATION

2001 Estimates:

Working Population	69,612
At Home Population	85,428
Total	155,040

INCOME

2001 Estimates:

Avg. Household Income	$52,210
Avg. Family Income	$55,244
Per Capita Income	$18,243
Male:	
Avg. Employment Income	$33,342
Avg. Employment Income (Full Time)	$44,464
Female:	
Avg. Employment Income	$18,890
Avg. Employment Income (Full Time)	$30,032

DISPOSABLE & DISCRETIONARY INCOME

2001 Estimates:	Per Hhld.
Disposable Income	$40,506
Discretionary Income 1 (minus Food & Shelter)	$27,716
Discretionary Income 2 (minus Food, Shelter, & Other Expenditures)	$19,617

LIQUID ASSETS

1999 Estimates:	Per Hhld.
Equity Investments	$74,458
Interest Bearing Investments	$67,587
Total Liquid Assets	$142,045

CREDIT DATA

July 2000:

Pool of Credit	$1,350,328,953
Revolving Credit, No.	273,177
Fixed Loans, No.	71,303
Avg. Credit Limit, per Person	$11,698
Avg. Spent, per Person	$5,264
Satisfactory Ratings, No. per Person	2.88
Avg. No. of Cards, per Person	1.01

LABOUR FORCE

2001 Estimates:

Male:	
In the Labour Force	41,812
Participation Rate	70.2
Employed	38,683
Unemployed	3,129
Unemployment Rate	7.5
Not in Labour Force	17,771
Female:	
In the Labour Force	35,107
Participation Rate	56.7
Employed	31,886
Unemployed	3,221
Unemployment Rate	9.2
Not in Labour Force	26,791

OCCUPATIONS BY MAJOR GROUPS

2001 Estimates:	Male	Female
Management	4,084	1,634
Business, Finance & Admin.	3,118	9,438
Natural & Applied Sciences & Related	1,677	206
Health	552	2,833
Social Sciences, Gov't Services & Religion	753	1,083
Education	866	1,625
Arts, Culture, Recreation & Sport	603	874
Sales & Service	7,866	11,737
Trades, Transport & Equipment Operators & Related	13,212	519
Primary Industries	3,928	2,860
Processing, Mfg. & Utilities	4,399	1,164

LEVEL OF SCHOOLING

2001 Estimates:

Population 15 years +	121,481
Less than Grade 9	11,255
Grades 9-13 w/o Certif.	33,400
Grade 9-13 with Certif.	16,460
Trade Certif./Dip.	4,440
Non-Univ. w/o Certif./Dip.	9,404
Non-Univ. with Certif./Dip.	22,981
Univ. w/o Degree	13,597
Univ. w/o Degree/Certif.	6,801
Univ. with Certif.	6,796
Univ. with Degree	9,944

AVERAGE HOUSEHOLD EXPENDITURES

2001 Estimates:

Food	$5,756
Shelter	$8,941
Clothing	$2,051
Transportation	$6,288
Health & Personal Care	$1,765
Recr'n, Read'g & Education	$3,523
Taxes & Securities	$13,853
Other	$7,963
Total Expenditures	$50,140

PRIVATE HOUSEHOLDS

2001 Estimates:

Private Households, Total	54,173
Pop. in Private Households	151,713
Average no. per Household	2.8

FAMILIES

2001 Estimates:

Families in Private Households	43,246
Husband-Wife Families	37,794
Lone-Parent Families	5,452
Aver. No. Persons per Family	3.1
Aver. No. Sons/Daughters at Home	1.2

HOUSING

2001 Estimates:

Occupied Private Dwellings	54,173
Owned	38,850
Rented	15,279
Band Housing	44
Single-Detached House	31,558
Semi-Detached House	1,021
Row Houses	4,293
Apartment, 5+ Storeys	1,200
Owned Apartment, 5+ Storeys	636
Apartment, 5 or Fewer Storeys	10,767
Apartment, Detached Duplex	4,422
Other Single-Attached	79
Movable Dwellings	833

VEHICLES

2001 Estimates:

Model Yrs. '81-'96, No.	67,848
% Total	85.98
Model Yrs. '97-'98, No.	6,835
% Total	8.66
'99 Vehicles registered in Model Yr. '99, No.	4,228
% Total	5.36
Total No. '81-'99	78,911

LEGAL MARITAL STATUS

2001 Estimates: (Age 15+)

Single (Never Married)	31,442
Legally Married (Not Separated)	71,091
Legally Married (Separated)	3,952
Widowed	6,921
Divorced	8,075

PSYTE CATEGORIES

2001 Estimates	No. of House-holds	% of Total Hhds.	Index
Mortgaged in Suburbia	3,399	6.27	451
Technocrafts & Bureaucrats	1,169	2.16	77
Boomers & Teens	1,648	3.04	170
Stable Suburban Families	74	0.14	10
Aging Erudites	749	1.38	92
Satellite Suburbs	7,933	14.64	510
Kindergarten Boom	4,986	9.20	351
Blue Collar Winners	9,315	17.19	683
Old Towns' New Fringe	5,564	10.27	262
Rustic Prosperity	664	1.23	68
Conservative Homebodies	2,499	4.61	128
High Rise Sunsets	4,447	8.21	574
Young Urban Mix	855	1.58	74
University Enclaves	923	1.70	83
Young City Singles	2,897	5.35	233
Old Leafy Towns	510	0.94	37
Town Renters	1,009	1.86	216
Nesters & Young Homesteaders	1,801	3.32	142
Big Country Families	56	0.10	7
Struggling Downtowns	1,361	2.51	80
Aged Pensioners	1,599	2.95	222
Big City Stress	94	0.17	15

FINANCIAL P$YTE

2001 Estimates	No. of House-holds	% of Total Hhds.	Index
Four Star Investors	1,648	3.04	61
Successful Suburbanites	4,642	8.57	129
Canadian Comfort	17,248	31.84	328
Urban Heights	749	1.38	32
Mortgages & Minivans	4,986	9.20	139
Tractors & Tradelines	6,228	11.50	201
Bills & Wills	3,864	7.13	86
Revolving Renters	6,248	11.53	251
Young Urban Struggle	923	1.70	36
Rural Family Blues	56	0.10	1
Towering Debt	5,267	9.72	125
NSF	94	0.17	5
Senior Survivors	1,599	2.95	157

HOME LANGUAGE

2001 Estimates:		% Total
English	136,896	88.30
French	273	0.18
Chinese	752	0.49
Dutch	209	0.13
German	1,768	1.14
Hindi	96	0.06
Hungarian	136	0.09
Korean	204	0.13
Lao	121	0.08
Polish	229	0.15
Punjabi	10,030	6.47
Spanish	449	0.29
Tagalog (Pilipino)	91	0.06
Vietnamese	342	0.22
Other Languages	583	0.38
Multiple Responses	2,861	1.85
Total	155,040	100.00

BUILDING PERMITS

	1999	1998	1997
		$000	
Value	148,719	168,099	n.a.

HOMES BUILT

	1999	1998	1997
No.	589	744	937

Abbotsford
(Census Agglomeration)
(Cont'd)

TAXATION

Income Class:	1997	% Total
Under $5,000	13,000	13.30
$5,000-$10,000	13,460	13.77
$10,000-$15,000	15,670	16.03
$15,000-$20,000	9,830	10.06
$20,000-$25,000	7,660	7.84
$25,000-$30,000	6,940	7.10
$30,000-$40,000	12,170	12.45
$40,000-$50,000	7,910	8.09
$50,000 +	11,130	11.39
Total Returns, No.	97,760	
Total Income, $000	2,461,957	
Total Taxable Returns	66,090	
Total Tax, $000	427,705	
Average Income, $	25,184	
Average Tax, $	6,472	

VITAL STATISTICS

	1997	1996	1995	1994
Births	2,107	2,135	2,098	2,123
Deaths	1,048	1,059	913	864
Natural Increase	1,059	1,076	1,185	1,259
Marriages	713	718	740	775

Note: Latest available data.

COMMUNITY NEWSPAPER(S)

	Total Circulation
Abbotsford: Abbotsford News	
Thu	30,454
Tue/Sat	42,245
Abbotsford: Abbotsford Times	
Tue/Fri	39,476
Abbotsford, Agassiz, Harrison Hot Springs,Mission: The Valley Express (qtly).	n.a.
Mission: Mission City Record	9,653

RADIO STATION(S)

	Power
CKSR-FM	50,000w

Campbell River
(Census Agglomeration)

The Census Agglomeration of Campbell River includes: Campbell River, DM; Comox-Strathcona, Subd. B, SRD; plus several smaller areas. All are in Comox-Strathcona Regional District.

POPULATION

July 1, 2001 Estimate	36,629
% Cdn. Total	0.12
% Change, '96 -'01	0.17
Avg. Annual Growth Rate, %	0.03
2003 Projected Population	36,703
2006 Projected Population	36,866
2001 Households Estimate	14,383
2003 Projected Households	14,532
2006 Projected Households	14,801

INCOME

% Above/Below National Average	-2
2001 Total Income Estimate	$757,880,000
% Cdn. Total	0.12
2001 Average Hhld. Income	$52,700
2001 Per Capita	20,700
2003 Projected Total Income	$800,530,000
2006 Projected Total Income	$871,770,000

RETAIL SALES

% Above/Below National Average	+12
2001 Retail Sales Estimate	$365,870,000
% Cdn. Total	0.13
2001 per Household	$25,400
2001 per Capita	$10,000
2001 No. of Establishments	336
2003 Projected Retail Sales	$399,750,000
2006 Projected Retail Sales	$448,100,000

POPULATION

2001 Estimates:

Total		36,629
Male		18,541
Female		18,088
Age Groups	Male	Female
0-4	1,118	1,094
5-9	1,302	1,234
10-14	1,462	1,335
15-19	1,449	1,348
20-24	1,274	1,240
25-29	1,186	1,187
30-34	1,289	1,323
35-39	1,507	1,548
40-44	1,617	1,584
45-49	1,578	1,461
50-54	1,326	1,214
55-59	1,019	913
60-64	763	689
65-69	598	562
70+	1,053	1,356

DAYTIME POPULATION

2001 Estimates:

Working Population	17,653
At Home Population	18,977
Total	36,630

INCOME

2001 Estimates:

Avg. Household Income	$52,693
Avg. Family Income	$58,112
Per Capita Income	$20,691
Male:	
Avg. Employment Income	$37,163
Avg. Employment Income (Full Time)	$48,740
Female:	
Avg. Employment Income	$18,088
Avg. Employment Income (Full Time)	$27,530

DISPOSABLE & DISCRETIONARY INCOME

2001 Estimates:	Per Hhld.
Disposable Income	$40,469
Discretionary Income 1 (minus Food & Shelter)	$28,211
Discretionary Income 2 (minus Food, Shelter, & Other Expenditures)	$19,908

LIQUID ASSETS

1999 Estimates:	Per Hhld.
Equity Investments	$76,750
Interest Bearing Investments	$69,821
Total Liquid Assets	$146,571

CREDIT DATA

July 2000:

Pool of Credit	$378,165,362
Revolving Credit, No.	65,374
Fixed Loans, No.	22,867
Avg. Credit Limit, per Person	$12,848
Avg. Spent, per Person	$6,087
Satisfactory Ratings, No. per Person	2.88
Avg. No. of Cards, per Person	1.00

LABOUR FORCE

2001 Estimates:

Male:	
In the Labour Force	10,876
Participation Rate	74.2
Employed	9,891
Unemployed	985
Unemployment Rate	9.1
Not in Labour Force	3,783
Female:	
In the Labour Force	8,752
Participation Rate	60.7
Employed	7,915
Unemployed	837
Unemployment Rate	9.6
Not in Labour Force	5,673

OCCUPATIONS BY MAJOR GROUPS

2001 Estimates:	Male	Female
Management	971	513
Business, Finance & Admin.	504	2,205
Natural & Applied Sciences & Related	699	105
Health	101	526
Social Sciences, Gov't Services & Religion	152	272
Education	178	265
Arts, Culture, Recreation & Sport	22	125
Sales & Service	1,776	3,658
Trades, Transport & Equipment Operators & Related	3,300	226
Primary Industries	1,893	282
Processing, Mfg. & Utilities	1,067	246

LEVEL OF SCHOOLING

2001 Estimates:

Population 15 years +	29,084
Less than Grade 9	1,954
Grades 9-13 w/o Certif.	8,644
Grade 9-13 with Certif.	4,741
Trade Certif. /Dip.	1,226
Non-Univ. w/o Certif./Dip.	2,204
Non-Univ. with Certif./Dip.	5,890
Univ. w/o Degree	2,548
Univ. w/o Degree/Certif.	1,237
Univ. with Certif.	1,311
Univ. with Degree	1,877

AVERAGE HOUSEHOLD EXPENDITURES

2001 Estimates:

Food	$5,948
Shelter	$8,396
Clothing	$2,251
Transportation	$6,218
Health & Personal Care	$2,000
Recr'n, Read'g & Education	$3,733
Taxes & Securities	$13,180
Other	$8,611
Total Expenditures	$50,337

PRIVATE HOUSEHOLDS

2001 Estimates:

Private Households, Total	14,383
Pop. in Private Households	36,260
Average no. per Household	2.5

FAMILIES

2001 Estimates:

Families in Private Households	10,861
Husband-Wife Families	9,314
Lone-Parent Families	1,547
Aver. No. Persons per Family	3.0
Aver. No. Sons/Daughters at Home	1.2

HOUSING

2001 Estimates:

Occupied Private Dwellings	14,383
Owned	10,457
Rented	3,916
Band Housing	10
Single-Detached House	10,243
Semi-Detached House	351
Row Houses	722
Apartment, 5+ Storeys	49
Owned Apartment, 5+ Storeys	33
Apartment, 5 or Fewer Storeys	1,860
Apartment, Detached Duplex	413
Movable Dwellings	745

VEHICLES

2001 Estimates:

Model Yrs. '81-'96, No.	17,420
% Total	85.33
Model Yrs. '97-'98, No.	1,950
% Total	9.55
'99 Vehicles registered in Model Yr. '99, No.	1,044
% Total	5.11
Total No. '81-'99	20,414

British Columbia

Campbell River
(Census Agglomeration)
(Cont'd)

LEGAL MARITAL STATUS

2001 Estimates: (Age 15+)
Single (Never Married)	8,198
Legally Married (Not Separated)	15,697
Legally Married (Separated)	1,151
Widowed	1,341
Divorced	2,697

PSYTE CATEGORIES

2001 Estimates	No. of House -holds	% of Total Hhds.	Index
Small City Elite	307	2.13	125
Blue Collar Winners	292	2.03	81
Town Boomers	7,147	49.69	4,902
Old Towns' New Fringe	1,395	9.70	248
Pick-ups & Dirt Bikes	543	3.78	452
Nesters & Young Homesteaders	2,366	16.45	705
Young Grey Collar	1,728	12.01	1,436
Big Country Families	202	1.40	98
Aged Pensioners	338	2.35	177

FINANCIAL P$YTE

2001 Estimates	No. of House -holds	% of Total Hhds.	Index
Canadian Comfort	7,746	53.86	554
Tractors & Tradelines	1,395	9.70	170
Country Credit	543	3.78	56
Revolving Renters	4,094	28.46	619
Rural Family Blues	202	1.40	17
Senior Survivors	338	2.35	125

HOME LANGUAGE

2001 Estimates:		% Total
English	35,262	96.27
French	162	0.44
Chinese	22	0.06
Finnish	30	0.08
German	81	0.22
Hindi	21	0.06
Italian	52	0.14
Polish	41	0.11
Portuguese	20	0.05
Punjabi	296	0.81
Spanish	30	0.08
Tagalog (Pilipino)	21	0.06
Vietnamese	224	0.61
Other Languages	104	0.28
Multiple Responses	263	0.72
Total	36,629	100.00

BUILDING PERMITS

	1999	1998	1997
		$000	
Value	33,800	26,205	87,760

HOMES BUILT

	1999	1998	1997
No	87	291	313

TAXATION

Income Class:	1997	% Total
Under $5,000	3,210	12.90
$5,000-$10,000	3,080	12.37
$10,000-$15,000	3,380	13.58
$15,000-$20,000	2,240	9.00
$20,000-$25,000	1,900	7.63
$25,000-$30,000	1,690	6.79
$30,000-$40,000	3,230	12.98
$40,000-$50,000	2,160	8.68
$50,000 +	4,000	16.07
Total Returns, No.	24,890	
Total Income, $000	701,980	
Total Taxable Returns	17,640	
Total Tax, $000	132,673	
Average Income, $	28,203	
Average Tax, $	7,521	

VITAL STATISTICS

	1997	1996	1995	1994
Births	422	426	461	419
Deaths	213	216	197	205
Natural Increase	209	210	264	214
Marriages	193	219	207	233

Note: Latest available data.

COMMUNITY NEWSPAPER(S)

	Total Circulation
Campbell River: Campbell River Courier-Islander Tue/Thu.	16,114
Campbell River: Campbell River Mirror Wed/Fri.	14,931
Campbell River: Comox Valley North Islander	40,235

RADIO STATION(S)

	Power
CBCV-FM	n.a.
CBYT-FM	n.a.
CFWB	1,000w
CKLR-FM	n.a.

TELEVISION STATION(S)

CBUT-TV

Capital, Subd. A
(Subdivision of Regional District)

In Capital Regional District.

POPULATION

July 1, 2001 Estimate	14,881
% Cdn. Total	0.05
% Change, '96 -'01	6.62
Avg. Annual Growth Rate, %	1.29
2003 Projected Population	15,029
2006 Projected Population	15,495
2001 Households Estimate	6,814
2003 Projected Households	6,844
2006 Projected Households	7,004

INCOME

% Above/Below National Average	same
2001 Total Income Estimate	$314,560,000
% Cdn. Total	0.05
2001 Average Hhld. Income	$46,200
2001 Per Capita	$21,100
2003 Projected Total Income	$335,360,000
2006 Projected Total Income	$375,890,000

RETAIL SALES

% Above/Below National Average	-29
2001 Retail Sales Estimate	$94,960,000
% Cdn. Total	0.03
2001 per Household	$13,900
2001 per Capita	$6,400
2001 No. of Establishments	147
2003 Projected Retail Sales	$101,440,000
2006 Projected Retail Sales	$113,210,000

POPULATION

2001 Estimates:
Total		14,881
Male		7,151
Female		7,730
Age Groups	Male	Female
0-4	330	314
5-9	376	369
10-14	423	430
15-19	437	429
20-24	383	373
25-29	336	339
30-34	357	369
35-39	418	464
40-44	498	593
45-49	579	650
50-54	577	612
55-59	486	534
60-64	428	482
65-69	432	453
70+	1,091	1,319

DAYTIME POPULATION

2001 Estimates:
Working Population	23
At Home Population	8,248
Total	8,271

INCOME

2001 Estimates:
Avg. Household Income	$46,164
Avg. Family Income	$53,017
Per Capita Income	$21,139
Male:	
Avg. Employment Income	$29,558
Avg. Employment Income (Full Time)	$40,823
Female:	
Avg. Employment Income	$17,971
Avg. Employment Income (Full Time)	$29,357

DISPOSABLE & DISCRETIONARY INCOME

2001 Estimates:	Per Hhld.
Disposable Income	$35,698
Discretionary Income 1 (minus Food & Shelter)	$24,544
Discretionary Income 2 (minus Food, Shelter, & Other Expenditures)	$16,741

LIQUID ASSETS

1999 Estimates:	Per Hhld.
Equity Investments	$63,661
Interest Bearing Investments	$57,372
Total Liquid Assets	$121,033

CREDIT DATA

July 2000:
Pool of Credit	$137,582,566
Revolving Credit, No.	26,158
Fixed Loans, No.	5,060
Avg. Credit Limit, per Person	$11,172
Avg. Spent, per Person	$4,197
Satisfactory Ratings, No. per Person	2.50
Avg. No. of Cards, per Person	1.05

LABOUR FORCE

2001 Estimates:
Male:	
In the Labour Force	3,585
Participation Rate	59.5
Employed	3,357
Unemployed	228
Unemployment Rate	6.4
Not in Labour Force	2,437
Female:	
In the Labour Force	3,443
Participation Rate	52.0
Employed	3,268
Unemployed	175
Unemployment Rate	5.1
Not in Labour Force	3,174

OCCUPATIONS BY MAJOR GROUPS

2001 Estimates:	Male	Female
Management	408	202
Business, Finance & Admin.	230	630
Natural & Applied Sciences & Related	379	39
Health	57	233
Social Sciences, Gov't Services & Religion	107	81
Education	112	141
Arts, Culture, Recreation & Sport	153	232
Sales & Service	762	1,336
Trades, Transport & Equipment Operators & Related	888	152
Primary Industries	333	243
Processing, Mfg. & Utilities	65	45

LEVEL OF SCHOOLING

2001 Estimates:
Population 15 years +	12,639
Less than Grade 9	281
Grades 9-13 w/o Certif.	2,355
Grade 9-13 with Certif.	1,638
Trade Certif. /Dip.	470
Non-Univ. w/o Certif./Dip.	738
Non-Univ. with Certif./Dip.	2,719
Univ. w/o Degree	1,665
Univ. w/o Degree/Certif.	751
Univ. with Certif.	914
Univ. with Degree	2,773

Capital, Subd. A
(Subdivision of Regional District)
(Cont'd)

AVERAGE HOUSEHOLD EXPENDITURES

2001 Estimates:
Food $5,444
Shelter $7,715
Clothing. $1,751
Transportation. $6,255
Health & Personal Care $1,715
Recr'n, Read'g & Education $3,407
Taxes & Securities $11,879
Other $7,093
Total Expenditures $45,259

PRIVATE HOUSEHOLDS

2001 Estimates:
Private Households, Total. 6,814
Pop. in Private Households. 14,626
Average no. per Household 2.1

FAMILIES

2001 Estimates:
Families in Private Households 4,564
Husband-Wife Families 4,013
Lone-Parent Families 551
Aver. No. Persons per Family 2.7
Aver. No. Sons/Daughters
   at Home 0.8

HOUSING

2001 Estimates:
Occupied Private Dwellings 6,814
  Owned. 5,364
  Rented. 1,450
Single-Detached House 6,110
Semi-Detached House 118
Row Houses 113
Apartment, 5 or Fewer Storeys 46
Apartment, Detached Duplex 107
Movable Dwellings. 320

VEHICLES

2001 Estimates:
Model Yrs. '81-'96, No. 7,939
  % Total 91.46
Model Yrs. '97-'98, No. 501
  % Total 5.77
'99 Vehicles registered in
  Model Yr. '99, No. 240
  % Total 2.76
Total No. '81-'99 8,680

LEGAL MARITAL STATUS

2001 Estimates: (Age 15+)
Single (Never Married). 2,874
Legally Married
  (Not Separated) 6,988
Legally Married (Separated). 442
Widowed 946
Divorced 1,389

PSYTE CATEGORIES

2001 Estimates	No. of House-holds	% of Total Hhds.	Index
Technocrafts & Bureaucrats	41	0.60	21
Small City Elite.	2,491	36.56	2,133
Blue Collar Winners	148	2.17	86
Rustic Prosperity	51	0.75	41
Young Urban Professionals	45	0.66	35
Old Leafy Towns	3,886	57.03	2,231
Nesters & Young Homesteaders	149	2.19	94

2001 Estimates	No. of House-holds	% of Total Hhds.	Index
Successful Suburbanites.	41	0.60	9
Canadian Comfort	2,639	38.73	399
Urban Heights.	45	0.66	15
Tractors & Tradelines	51	0.75	13
Bills & Wills	3,886	57.03	689
Revolving Renters.	149	2.19	48

HOME LANGUAGE

2001 Estimates:		% Total
English	14,586	98.02
French	35	0.24
Chinese	30	0.20
Dutch	11	0.07
Estonian	11	0.07
German	55	0.37
Polish	11	0.07
Swedish	12	0.08
Multiple Responses	130	0.87
Total	14,881	100.00

BUILDING PERMITS

	1999	1998	1997
		$000	
Value	74,213	n.a.	n.a.

TAXATION

Income Class:	1997	% Total
Under $5,000	1,150	11.95
$5,000-$10,000	1,410	14.66
$10,000-$15,000	1,560	16.22
$15,000-$20,000	1,080	11.23
$20,000-$25,000	910	9.46
$25,000-$30,000	720	7.48
$30,000-$40,000	1,030	10.71
$40,000-$50,000	670	6.96
$50,000 +	1,100	11.43
Total Returns, No.	9,620	
Total Income, $000	252,273	
Total Taxable Returns	6,630	
Total Tax, $000	45,498	
Average Income, $	26,224	
Average Tax, $	6,862	

VITAL STATISTICS

	1997	1996	1995	1994
Births	106	107	119	92
Deaths	146	122	114	112
Natural Increase	-40	-15	.5	-20
Marriages	138	156	111	118

Note: Latest available data.

Central Kootenay, Subd. B
(Subdivision of Regional District)

In Central Kootenay Regional District.

POPULATION

July 1, 2001 Estimate 16,695
% Cdn. Total. 0.05
% Change, '96 -'01 . . . . .4.88
Avg. Annual Growth Rate, %. 0.96
2003 Projected Population. 17,060
2006 Projected Population. 17,489
2001 Households Estimate 6,884
2003 Projected Households 7,132
2006 Projected Households 7,474

INCOME

% Above/Below National Average . . . . -20
2001 Total Income Estimate $281,110,000
% Cdn. Total. 0.04
2001 Average Hhld. Income. $40,800
2001 Per Capita $16,800
2003 Projected Total Income $298,910,000
2006 Projected Total Income $325,230,000

RETAIL SALES

% Above/Below National Average . . . . -59
2001 Retail Sales Estimate $60,540,000
% Cdn. Total. 0.02
2001 per Household. $8,800
2001 per Capita $3,600
2001 No. of Establishments 70
2003 Projected Retail Sales $66,900,000
2006 Projected Retail Sales $77,610,000

POPULATION

2001 Estimates:

Total		16,695
Male.		8,495
Female		8,200

Age Groups	Male	Female
0-4	441	415
5-9	527	495
10-14	626	603
15-19	646	600
20-24	562	495
25-29	493	434
30-34	504	502
35-39	609	668
40-44	730	761
45-49	776	731
50-54	679	618
55-59	524	476
60-64	403	372
65-69	317	314
70+	658	716

DAYTIME POPULATION

2001 Estimates:
Working Population . . . . .n.a.
At Home Population. 8,881
Total 8,881

INCOME

2001 Estimates:
Avg. Household Income $40,835
Avg. Family Income $46,479
Per Capita Income $16,838
Male:
Avg. Employment Income $26,087
Avg. Employment Income
  (Full Time). $39,708
Female:
Avg. Employment Income $16,741
Avg. Employment Income
  (Full Time). $28,496

British Columbia

DISPOSABLE & DISCRETIONARY INCOME

2001 Estimates:	Per Hhld.
Disposable Income	$31,833
Discretionary Income 1 (minus Food & Shelter)	$21,649
Discretionary Income 2 (minus Food, Shelter, & Other Expenditures)	$14,645

LIQUID ASSETS

1999 Estimates:	Per Hhld.
Equity Investments	$47,640
Interest Bearing Investments	$51,922
Total Liquid Assets	$99,562

CREDIT DATA

July 2000:
Pool of Credit. $74,384,693
Revolving Credit, No. 13,765
Fixed Loans, No. 3,707
Avg. Credit Limit, per Person. $9,413
Avg. Spent, per Person $4,323
Satisfactory Ratings,
  No. per Person. 2.15
Avg. No. of Cards, per Person. 0.85

LABOUR FORCE

2001 Estimates:
Male:
In the Labour Force 4,770
Participation Rate 69.1
Employed 4,252
Unemployed. 518
Unemployment Rate 10.9
Not in Labour Force 2,131
Female:
In the Labour Force 3,906
Participation Rate 58.4
Employed 3,527
Unemployed. 379
Unemployment Rate 9.7
Not in Labour Force 2,781

OCCUPATIONS BY MAJOR GROUPS

2001 Estimates:	Male	Female
Management.	456	280
Business, Finance & Admin.	216	997
Natural & Applied Sciences & Related	372	87
Health	57	269
Social Sciences, Gov't Services & Religion	79	182
Education.	79	175
Arts, Culture, Recreation & Sport	135	156
Sales & Service.	774	1,349
Trades, Transport & Equipment Operators & Related	1,620	72
Primary Industries	562	147
Processing, Mfg. & Utilities	352	50

British Columbia

Central Kootenay, Subd. B

(Subdivision of Regional District)

(cont'd)

LEVEL OF SCHOOLING

2001 Estimates:
Population 15 years +	13,588
Less than Grade 9	1,039
Grades 9-13 w/o Certif.	3,110
Grade 9-13 with Certif.	1,510
Trade Certif. /Dip.	603
Non-Univ. w/o Certif./Dip.	1,019
Non-Univ. with Certif./Dip.	3,215
Univ. w/o Degree	1,673
Univ. w/o Degree/Certif.	725
Univ. with Certif.	948
Univ. with Degree	1,419

AVERAGE HOUSEHOLD EXPENDITURES

2001 Estimates:
Food	$4,965
Shelter	$6,876
Clothing	$1,568
Transportation	$5,507
Health & Personal Care	$1,546
Recr'n, Read'g & Education	$2,920
Taxes & Securities	$10,335
Other	$6,583
Total Expenditures	$40,300

PRIVATE HOUSEHOLDS

2001 Estimates:
Private Households, Total	6,884
Pop. in Private Households	16,534
Average no. per Household	2.4

FAMILIES

2001 Estimates:
Families in Private Households	5,048
Husband-Wife Families	4,417
Lone-Parent Families	631
Aver. No. Persons per Family	2.9
Aver. No. Sons/Daughters at Home	1.1

HOUSING

2001 Estimates:
Occupied Private Dwellings	6,884
Owned	5,587
Rented	1,297
Single-Detached House	6,114
Semi-Detached House	34
Row Houses	31
Apartment, 5+ Storeys	11
Apartment, 5 or Fewer Storeys	33
Apartment, Detached Duplex	102
Other Single-Attached	11
Movable Dwellings	548

VEHICLES

2001 Estimates:
Model Yrs. '81-'96, No.	7,869
% Total	88.16
Model Yrs. '97-'98, No.	704
% Total	7.89
'99 Vehicles registered in Model Yr. '99, No.	353
% Total	3.95
Total No. '81-'99	8,926

LEGAL MARITAL STATUS

2001 Estimates: (Age 15+)
Single (Never Married)	3,828
Legally Married (Not Separated)	7,347
Legally Married (Separated)	552
Widowed	610
Divorced	1,251

PSYTE CATEGORIES

2001 Estimates
	No. of Households	% of Total Hhds.	Index
Small City Elite	422	6.13	358
Town Boomers	626	9.09	897
Old Towns' New Fringe	853	12.39	317
Pick-ups & Dirt Bikes	419	6.09	729
Old Leafy Towns	3,192	46.37	1,814
Quiet Towns	393	5.71	268
Rod & Rifle	940	13.65	590

FINANCIAL PSYTE

2001 Estimates
	No. of Households	% of Total Hhds.	Index
Canadian Comfort	1,048	15.22	157
Tractors & Tradelines	853	12.39	217
Bills & Wills	3,192	46.37	560
Country Credit	419	6.09	90
Rural Family Blues	940	13.65	169
Limited Budgets	393	5.71	184

HOME LANGUAGE

2001 Estimates:
		% Total
English	15,994	95.80
French	108	0.65
German	163	0.98
Hungarian	10	0.06
Russian	217	1.30
Spanish	12	0.07
Other Languages	11	0.07
Multiple Responses	180	1.08
Total	16,695	100.00

BUILDING PERMITS

	1999	1998 $000	1997
Value	31,670	31,440	34,766

TAXATION

Income Class:	1997	% Total
Under $5,000	650	15.59
$5,000-$10,000	670	16.07
$10,000-$15,000	680	16.31
$15,000-$20,000	440	10.55
$20,000-$25,000	300	7.19
$25,000-$30,000	280	6.71
$30,000-$40,000	450	10.79
$40,000-$50,000	300	7.19
$50,000 +	390	9.35
Total Returns, No.	4,170	
Total Income, $000	92,101	
Total Taxable Returns	2,630	
Total Tax, $000	14,799	
Average Income, $	22,087	
Average Tax, $	5,627	

VITAL STATISTICS

	1997	1996	1995	1994
Births	59	65	60	74
Deaths	51	26	40	32
Natural Increase	8	39	20	42
Marriages	45	35	28	26

Note: Latest available data.

Chilliwack

(Census Agglomeration)

The Census Agglomeration of Chilliwack includes: Chilliwack, DM; Fraser Valley, Subd. B, SRD; plus many smaller areas. All are in Fraser Valley Regional District.

POPULATION

July 1, 2001 Estimate	75,535
% Cdn. Total	0.24
% Change, '96 -'01	9.51
Avg. Annual Growth Rate, %	1.83
2003 Projected Population	78,237
2006 Projected Population	81,906
2001 Households Estimate	28,912
2003 Projected Households	30,027
2006 Projected Households	31,757

INCOME

% Above/Below National Average	-17
2001 Total Income Estimate	$1,318,520,000
% Cdn. Total	0.20
2001 Average Hhld. Income	$45,600
2001 Per Capita	$17,500
2003 Projected Total Income	$1,440,350,000
2006 Projected Total Income	$1,644,310,000

RETAIL SALES

% Above/Below National Average	+11
2001 Retail Sales Estimate	$752,230,000
% Cdn. Total	0.27
2001 per Household	$26,000
2001 per Capita	$10,000
2001 No. of Establishments	568
2003 Projected Retail Sales	$842,180,000
2006 Projected Retail Sales	$975,620,000

POPULATION

2001 Estimates:
Total	75,535
Male	36,984
Female	38,551

Age Groups	Male	Female
0-4	2,458	2,359
5-9	2,840	2,682
10-14	2,973	2,750
15-19	2,736	2,590
20-24	2,427	2,397
25-29	2,394	2,461
30-34	2,690	2,811
35-39	2,920	3,025
40-44	2,819	2,866
45-49	2,470	2,508
50-54	1,992	2,079
55-59	1,630	1,759
60-64	1,482	1,659
65-69	1,474	1,672
70+	3,679	4,933

DAYTIME POPULATION

2001 Estimates:
Working Population	32,357
At Home Population	43,179
Total	75,536

INCOME

2001 Estimates:
Avg. Household Income	$45,605
Avg. Family Income	$50,052
Per Capita Income	$17,456
Male:	
Avg. Employment Income	$31,218
Avg. Employment Income (Full Time)	$40,109
Female:	
Avg. Employment Income	$18,419
Avg. Employment Income (Full Time)	$29,414

DISPOSABLE & DISCRETIONARY INCOME

2001 Estimates:	*Per Hhld.*
Disposable Income	$35,610
Discretionary Income 1 (minus Food & Shelter)	$23,909
Discretionary Income 2 (minus Food, Shelter, & Other Expenditures)	$16,367

LIQUID ASSETS

1999 Estimates:	*Per Hhld.*
Equity Investments	$56,185
Interest Bearing Investments	$57,377
Total Liquid Assets	$113,562

CREDIT DATA

July 2000:
Pool of Credit	$618,400,851
Revolving Credit, No.	125,938
Fixed Loans, No.	33,617
Avg. Credit Limit, per Person	$11,047
Avg. Spent, per Person	$5,011
Satisfactory Ratings, No. per Person	2.75
Avg. No. of Cards, per Person	0.98

LABOUR FORCE

2001 Estimates:
Male:	
In the Labour Force	19,538
Participation Rate	68.0
Employed	17,907
Unemployed	1,631
Unemployment Rate	8.3
Not in Labour Force	9,175
Female:	
In the Labour Force	16,318
Participation Rate	53.0
Employed	14,929
Unemployed	1,389
Unemployment Rate	8.5
Not in Labour Force	14,442

OCCUPATIONS BY MAJOR GROUPS

2001 Estimates:	Male	Female
Management	1,819	705
Business, Finance & Admin.	1,183	4,361
Natural & Applied Sciences & Related	929	102
Health	419	1,444
Social Sciences, Gov't Services & Religion	333	373
Education	610	628
Arts, Culture, Recreation & Sport	275	260
Sales & Service	4,357	6,707
Trades, Transport & Equipment Operators & Related	5,732	307
Primary Industries	1,961	733
Processing, Mfg. & Utilities	1,391	208

LEVEL OF SCHOOLING

2001 Estimates:
Population 15 years +	59,473
Less than Grade 9	5,497
Grades 9-13 w/o Certif.	16,091
Grade 9-13 with Certif.	8,543
Trade Certif. /Dip.	2,636
Non-Univ. w/o Certif./Dip.	4,378
Non-Univ. with Certif./Dip.	12,019
Univ. w/o Degree	6,263
Univ. w/o Degree/Certif.	2,648
Univ. with Certif.	3,615
Univ. with Degree	4,046

AVERAGE HOUSEHOLD EXPENDITURES

2001 Estimates:
Food	$5,408
Shelter	$8,128
Clothing	$1,813
Transportation	$5,855
Health & Personal Care	$1,702
Recr'n, Read'g & Education	$3,216
Taxes & Securities	$10,980
Other	$7,609
Total Expenditures	$44,711

Chilliwack
(Census Agglomeration)
(Cont'd)

PRIVATE HOUSEHOLDS

2001 Estimates:
Private Households, Total 28,912
Pop. in Private Households 74,031
Average no. per Household 2.6

FAMILIES

2001 Estimates:
Families in Private Households 21,399
Husband-Wife Families 18,418
Lone-Parent Families 2,981
Aver. No. Persons per Family 3.0
Aver. No. Sons/Daughters at Home 1.1

HOUSING

2001 Estimates:
Occupied Private Dwellings 28,912
 Owned 20,778
 Rented 8,002
 Band Housing .132
Single-Detached House 19,641
Semi-Detached House 809
Row Houses 2,181
Apartment, 5+ Storeys 179
 Owned Apartment, 5+ Storeys 71
Apartment, 5 or Fewer Storeys 4,935
Apartment, Detached Duplex 338
Other Single-Attached 73
Movable Dwellings 756

VEHICLES

2001 Estimates:
Model Yrs. '81-'96, No. 30,982
 % Total 86.12
Model Yrs. '97-'98, No. 3,266
 % Total 9.08
'99 Vehicles registered in
 Model Yr. '99, No. 1,728
 % Total 4.80
Total No. '81-'99 35,976

LEGAL MARITAL STATUS

2001 Estimates: (Age 15+)
Single (Never Married) 14,887
Legally Married
 (Not Separated) 33,708
Legally Married (Separated) 2,418
Widowed 3,996
Divorced 4,464

PSYTE CATEGORIES

2001 Estimates	No. of House -holds	% of Total Hhds.	Index
Mortgaged in Suburbia	184	0.64	46
Technocrafts & Bureaucrats	87	0.30	11
Small City Elite	3,477	12.03	702
Aging Erudites	126	0.44	29
Satellite Suburbs	879	3.04	106
Kindergarten Boom	395	1.37	52
Blue Collar Winners	3,153	10.91	433
Old Towns' New Fringe	6,116	21.15	540
Rustic Prosperity	964	3.33	185
High Rise Sunsets	441	1.53	107
Young City Singles	309	1.07	47
Old Leafy Towns	1,364	4.72	185
Nesters & Young Homesteaders	7,991	27.64	1,184
Young Grey Collar	11	0.04	5
Big Country Families	547	1.89	133
Struggling Downtowns	738	2.55	81
Aged Pensioners	1,875	6.49	487

FINANCIAL PSYTE

2001 Estimates	No. of House -holds	% of Total Hhds.	Index
Successful Suburbanites	271	0.94	14
Canadian Comfort	7,509	25.97	267
Urban Heights	126	0.44	10
Mortgages & Minivans	395	1.37	21

2001 Estimates	No. of House -holds	% of Total Hhds.	Index
Tractors & Tradelines	7,080	24.49	428
Bills & Wills	1,364	4.72	57
Revolving Renters	8,443	29.20	635
Rural Family Blues	547	1.89	23
Towering Debt	1,047	3.62	46
Senior Survivors	1,875	6.49	344

HOME LANGUAGE

2001 Estimates		% Total
English	72,161	95.53
French	499	0.66
Chinese	241	0.32
Dutch	531	0.70
German	533	0.71
Hindi	65	0.09
Hungarian	50	0.07
Korean	121	0.16
Punjabi	163	0.22
Spanish	91	0.12
Ukrainian	40	0.05
Vietnamese	101	0.13
Other Languages	281	0.37
Multiple Responses	658	0.87
Total	75,535	100.00

BUILDING PERMITS

	1999	1998	1997
		$000	
Value	63,697	45,533	72,229

HOMES BUILT

	1999	1998	1997
No	257	501	543

TAXATION

Income Class:	1997	% Total
Under $5,000	5,590	12.14
$5,000-$10,000	6,160	13.37
$10,000-$15,000	7,480	16.24
$15,000-$20,000	4,820	10.46
$20,000-$25,000	3,830	8.32
$25,000-$30,000	3,580	7.77
$30,000-$40,000	5,880	12.77
$40,000-$50,000	3,890	8.45
$50,000 +	4,860	10.55
Total Returns, No.	46,060	
Total Income, $000	1,143,669	
Total Taxable Returns	31,280	
Total Tax, $000	190,305	
Average Income, $	24,830	
Average Tax, $	6,084	

VITAL STATISTICS

	1997	1996	1995	1994
Births	867	922	947	928
Deaths	575	559	544	548
Natural Increase	292	363	403	380
Marriages	391	438	406	387

Note: Latest available data.

COMMUNITY NEWSPAPER(S)

	Total Circulation
Chilliwack: Chilliwack Progress	
Sun	n.a.
Tue/Fri.	27,008
Chilliwack: Chilliwack Times	
Tue/Fri.	26,414

RADIO STATION(S)

	Power
CBUF-FM	100w
CBYF-FM	n.a.
CHWK	n.a.
CHWK-FM	10,000w
CKMA	10,000w
CKSR-FM	n.a.

TELEVISION STATION(S)

CBUFT-TV
CBUT-TV
CHAN-TV

Columbia-Shuswap, Subd. C
(Subdivision of Regional District)

In Columbia-Shuswap Regional District.

POPULATION

July 1, 2001 Estimate 16,014
% Cdn. Total .0.05
% Change, '96 -'01 . . . . .11.50
Avg. Annual Growth Rate, % 2.20
2003 Projected Population 16,947
2006 Projected Population 18,240
2001 Households Estimate 6,637
2003 Projected Households 7,073
2006 Projected Households 7,755

INCOME

% Above/Below National Average . . . .-24
2001 Total Income Estimate $256,380,000
% Cdn. Total 0.04
2001 Average Hhld. Income $38,600
2001 Per Capita $16,000
2003 Projected Total Income $288,700,000
2006 Projected Total Income $344,400,000

RETAIL SALES

% Above/Below National Average . . . .-55
2001 Retail Sales Estimate $63,930,000
% Cdn. Total 0.02
2001 per Household $9,600
2001 per Capita $4,000
2001 No. of Establishments 76
2003 Projected Retail Sales $72,970,000
2006 Projected Retail Sales $86,470,000

POPULATION

2001 Estimates:
Total 16,014
Male 8,144
Female 7,870

Age Groups	Male	Female
0-4	426	385
5-9	515	446
10-14	576	501
15-19	561	488
20-24	454	413
25-29	413	395
30-34	456	487
35-39	546	603
40-44	610	610
45-49	590	555
50-54	519	525
55-59	489	519
60-64	499	516
65-69	507	483
70+	983	944

DAYTIME POPULATION

2001 Estimates:
Working Population 260
At Home Population 9,796
Total 10,056

INCOME

2001 Estimates:
Avg. Household Income $38,629
Avg. Family Income $40,686
Per Capita Income $16,010
Male:
Avg. Employment Income $22,777
Avg. Employment Income
 (Full Time) $34,201
Female:
Avg. Employment Income $13,438
Avg. Employment Income
 (Full Time) $22,898

British Columbia

DISPOSABLE & DISCRETIONARY INCOME

2001 Estimates:	Per Hhld.
Disposable Income	$30,522
Discretionary Income 1 (minus Food & Shelter)	$20,486
Discretionary Income 2 (minus Food, Shelter, & Other Expenditures)	$13,761

LIQUID ASSETS

1999 Estimates:	Per Hhld.
Equity Investments	$43,597
Interest Bearing Investments	$48,382
Total Liquid Assets	$91,979

CREDIT DATA

July 2000:
Pool of Credit $111,434,105
Revolving Credit, No. 20,692
Fixed Loans, No. 5,615
Avg. Credit Limit, per Person $10,995
Avg. Spent, per Person $4,822
Satisfactory Ratings,
 No. per Person 2.49
Avg. No. of Cards, per Person 0.88

LABOUR FORCE

2001 Estimates:
Male:
In the Labour Force 3,958
Participation Rate 59.7
Employed 3,424
Unemployed .534
Unemployment Rate 13.5
Not in Labour Force 2,669
Female:
In the Labour Force 3,040
Participation Rate 46.5
Employed 2,811
Unemployed .229
Unemployment Rate 7.5
Not in Labour Force 3,498

OCCUPATIONS BY MAJOR GROUPS

2001 Estimates:	Male	Female
Management	311	137
Business, Finance & Admin.	193	779
Natural & Applied Sciences & Related	164	27
Health	21	83
Social Sciences, Gov't Services & Religion	23	97
Education	20	129
Arts, Culture, Recreation & Sport	85	121
Sales & Service	528	1,079
Trades, Transport & Equipment Operators & Related	1,417	77
Primary Industries	641	288
Processing, Mfg. & Utilities	436	120

British Columbia

Columbia-Shuswap, Subd. C
(Subdivision of Regional District)
(Cont'd)

LEVEL OF SCHOOLING

2001 Estimates:
Population 15 years +	13,165
Less than Grade 9	991
Grades 9-13 w/o Certif.	4,231
Grade 9-13 with Certif.	1,615
Trade Certif. /Dip.	629
Non-Univ. w/o Certif./Dip.	848
Non-Univ. with Certif./Dip.	3,072
Univ. w/o Degree	1,129
Univ. w/o Degree/Certif.	479
Univ. with Certif.	650
Univ. with Degree	650

AVERAGE HOUSEHOLD EXPENDITURES

2001 Estimates:
Food	$4,791
Shelter	$6,797
Clothing	$1,403
Transportation	$5,363
Health & Personal Care	$1,439
Recr'n, Read'g & Education	$2,839
Taxes & Securities	$9,837
Other	$6,157
Total Expenditures	$38,626

PRIVATE HOUSEHOLDS

2001 Estimates:
Private Households, Total	6,637
Pop. in Private Households	15,743
Average no. per Household	2.4

FAMILIES

2001 Estimates:
Families in Private Households	5,275
Husband-Wife Families	4,807
Lone-Parent Families	468
Aver. No. Persons per Family	2.7
Aver. No. Sons/Daughters at Home	0.8

HOUSING

2001 Estimates:
Occupied Private Dwellings	6,637
Owned	5,582
Rented	1,055
Single-Detached House	5,482
Semi-Detached House	36
Row Houses	42
Apartment, 5 or Fewer Storeys	56
Apartment, Detached Duplex	55
Other Single-Attached	27
Movable Dwellings	939

VEHICLES

2001 Estimates:
Model Yrs. '81-'96, No.	8,496
% Total	86.68
Model Yrs. '97-'98, No.	828
% Total	8.45
'99 Vehicles registered in Model Yr. '99, No.	478
% Total	4.88
Total No. '81-'99	9,802

LEGAL MARITAL STATUS

2001 Estimates: (Age 15+)
Single (Never Married)	2,498
Legally Married (Not Separated)	8,466
Legally Married (Separated)	383
Widowed	661
Divorced	1,157

PSYTE CATEGORIES

2001 Estimates	No. of House-holds	% of Total Hhds.	Index
Old Towns' New Fringe	1,083	16.32	417
Rustic Prosperity	229	3.45	191
Pick-ups & Dirt Bikes	53	0.80	96
Old Leafy Towns	4,341	65.41	2,559
Rod & Rifle	810	12.20	528
Big Country Families	96	1.45	101

FINANCIAL P$YTE

2001 Estimates	No. of House-holds	% of Total Hhds.	Index
Tractors & Tradelines	1,312	19.77	346
Bills & Wills	4,341	65.41	790
Country Credit	53	0.80	12
Rural Family Blues	906	13.65	169

HOME LANGUAGE

2001 Estimates:		% Total
English	15,678	97.90
Czech	59	0.37
Dutch	23	0.14
Finnish	12	0.07
German	142	0.89
Italian	12	0.07
Japanese	12	0.07
Persian (Farsi)	23	0.14
Multiple Responses	53	0.33
Total	16,014	100.00

BUILDING PERMITS

	1999	1998 $000	1997
Value	207	128	748

TAXATION

Income Class:	1997	% Total
Under $5,000	910	13.94
$5,000-$10,000	1,060	16.23
$10,000-$15,000	1,150	17.61
$15,000-$20,000	760	11.64
$20,000-$25,000	540	8.27
$25,000-$30,000	470	7.20
$30,000-$40,000	680	10.41
$40,000-$50,000	440	6.74
$50,000 +	530	8.12
Total Returns, No.	6,530	
Total Income, $000	142,499	
Total Taxable Returns	4,210	
Total Tax, $000	22,266	
Average Income, $	21,822	
Average Tax, $	5,289	

VITAL STATISTICS

	1997	1996	1995	1994
Births	67	83	70	93
Deaths	63	59	71	61
Natural Increase	4	24	-1	32
Marriages	39	65	44	52

Note: Latest available data.

Courtenay
(Census Agglomeration)

The Census Agglomeration of Courtenay includes: Courtenay, C; Comox, T; Comox-Strathcona, Subd. C, SRD; Cumberland, VL; plus two other smaller areas. All are in Comox-Strathcona Regional District.

POPULATION

2001 Estimates	
July 1, 2001 Estimate	63,083
% Cdn. Total	0.20
% Change, '96 -'01	10.52
Avg. Annual Growth Rate, %	2.02
2003 Projected Population	67,166
2006 Projected Population	73,384
2001 Households Estimate	26,086
2003 Projected Households	28,055
2006 Projected Households	31,145

INCOME

% Above/Below National Average	-9
2001 Total Income Estimate	$1,204,580,000
% Cdn. Total	0.18
2001 Average Hhld. Income	$46,200
2001 Per Capita	$19,100
2003 Projected Total Income	$1,361,970,000
2006 Projected Total Income	$1,633,920,000

RETAIL SALES

% Above/Below National Average	-7
2001 Retail Sales Estimate	$525,070,000
% Cdn. Total	0.19
2001 per Household	$20,100
2001 per Capita	$8,300
2001 No. of Establishments	483
2003 Projected Retail Sales	$620,300,000
2006 Projected Retail Sales	$778,260,000

POPULATION

2001 Estimates:
Total	63,083
Male	30,950
Female	32,133

Age Groups	Male	Female
0-4	1,825	1,744
5-9	2,132	2,021
10-14	2,339	2,245
15-19	2,248	2,196
20-24	1,904	1,921
25-29	1,748	1,809
30-34	2,041	2,157
35-39	2,387	2,596
40-44	2,499	2,680
45-49	2,374	2,499
50-54	2,044	2,113
55-59	1,686	1,763
60-64	1,522	1,539
65-69	1,378	1,356
70+	2,823	3,494

DAYTIME POPULATION

2001 Estimates:
Working Population	27,565
At Home Population	35,518
Total	63,083

INCOME

2001 Estimates:
Avg. Household Income	$46,177
Avg. Family Income	$51,195
Per Capita Income	$19,095
Male:	
Avg. Employment Income	$30,698
Avg. Employment Income (Full Time)	$40,743
Female:	
Avg. Employment Income	$18,259
Avg. Employment Income (Full Time)	$28,683

DISPOSABLE & DISCRETIONARY INCOME

2001 Estimates:	Per Hhld.
Disposable Income	$35,843
Discretionary Income 1 (minus Food & Shelter)	$24,070
Discretionary Income 2 (minus Food, Shelter, & Other Expenditures)	$16,526

LIQUID ASSETS

1999 Estimates:	Per Hhld.
Equity Investments	$65,505
Interest Bearing Investments	$60,721
Total Liquid Assets	$126,226

CREDIT DATA

July 2000:	
Pool of Credit	$501,535,791
Revolving Credit, No.	95,261
Fixed Loans, No.	24,658
Avg. Credit Limit, per Person	$11,239
Avg. Spent, per Person	$4,845
Satisfactory Ratings, No. per Person	2.60
Avg. No. of Cards, per Person	0.98

LABOUR FORCE

2001 Estimates:
Male:	
In the Labour Force	16,281
Participation Rate	66.0
Employed	14,692
Unemployed	1,589
Unemployment Rate	9.8
Not in Labour Force	8,373
Female:	
In the Labour Force	14,538
Participation Rate	55.7
Employed	13,058
Unemployed	1,480
Unemployment Rate	10.2
Not in Labour Force	11,585

OCCUPATIONS BY MAJOR GROUPS

2001 Estimates:	Male	Female
Management	1,634	793
Business, Finance & Admin.	937	2,979
Natural & Applied Sciences & Related	1,042	68
Health	219	1,175
Social Sciences, Gov't Services & Religion	201	573
Education	404	841
Arts, Culture, Recreation & Sport	429	431
Sales & Service	3,647	5,838
Trades, Transport & Equipment Operators & Related	4,318	395
Primary Industries	2,211	639
Processing, Mfg. & Utilities	845	217

LEVEL OF SCHOOLING

2001 Estimates:
Population 15 years +	50,777
Less than Grade 9	2,679
Grades 9-13 w/o Certif.	13,956
Grade 9-13 with Certif.	6,892
Trade Certif. /Dip.	2,171
Non-Univ. w/o Certif./Dip.	3,719
Non-Univ. with Certif./Dip.	11,268
Univ. w/o Degree	5,291
Univ. w/o Degree/Certif.	2,295
Univ. with Certif.	2,996
Univ. with Degree	4,801

Courtenay
(Census Agglomeration)
(Cont'd)

AVERAGE HOUSEHOLD EXPENDITURES

2001 Estimates:
Food	$5,480
Shelter	$8,215
Clothing	$1,838
Transportation	$5,819
Health & Personal Care	$1,768
Recr'n, Read'g & Education	$3,274
Taxes & Securities	$10,914
Other	$7,712
Total Expenditures	$45,020

PRIVATE HOUSEHOLDS

2001 Estimates:
Private Households, Total	26,086
Pop. in Private Households	62,382
Average no. per Household	2.4

FAMILIES

2001 Estimates:
Families in Private Households	18,993
Husband-Wife Families	16,423
Lone-Parent Families	2,570
Aver. No. Persons per Family	2.9
Aver. No. Sons/Daughters at Home	1.0

HOUSING

2001 Estimates:
Occupied Private Dwellings	26,086
Owned	18,981
Rented	7,105
Single-Detached House	19,191
Semi-Detached House	1,726
Row Houses	1,062
Apartment, 5 or Fewer Storeys	2,827
Apartment, Detached Duplex	424
Other Single-Attached	79
Movable Dwellings	777

VEHICLES

2001 Estimates:
Model Yrs. '81-'96, No.	28,044
% Total	89.18
Model Yrs. '97-'98, No.	2,169
% Total	6.90
'99 Vehicles registered in Model Yr. '99, No.	1,234
% Total	3.92
Total No. '81-'99	31,447

LEGAL MARITAL STATUS

2001 Estimates: (Age 15+)
Single (Never Married)	12,708
Legally Married (Not Separated)	28,351
Legally Married (Separated)	2,034
Widowed	2,840
Divorced	4,844

PSYTE CATEGORIES

2001 Estimates	No. of House-holds	% of Total Hhds.	Index
Small City Elite	3,316	12.71	742
Satellite Suburbs	422	1.62	56
Kindergarten Boom	552	2.12	81
Blue Collar Winners	98	0.38	15
Town Boomers	2,267	8.69	857
Old Towns' New Fringe	4,858	18.62	476
High Rise Sunsets	63	0.24	17
Young City Singles	459	1.76	77
Old Leafy Towns	3,124	11.98	469
Nesters & Young Homesteaders	10,506	40.27	1,725
Young Grey Collar	312	1.20	143
Quiet Towns	22	0.08	4
Big Country Families	38	0.15	10

FINANCIAL P$YTE

2001 Estimates	No. of House-holds	% of Total Hhds.	Index
Canadian Comfort	6,103	23.40	241
Mortgages & Minivans	552	2.12	32
Tractors & Tradelines	4,858	18.62	326
Bills & Wills	3,124	11.98	145
Revolving Renters	10,881	41.71	907
Rural Family Blues	38	0.15	2
Limited Budgets	22	0.08	3
Towering Debt	459	1.76	23

HOME LANGUAGE

2001 Estimates:		% Total
English	61,351	97.25
French	415	0.66
Chinese	300	0.48
German	139	0.22
Italian	36	0.06
Spanish	38	0.06
Tagalog (Pilipino)	39	0.06
Vietnamese	225	0.36
Other Languages	178	0.28
Multiple Responses	362	0.57
Total	63,083	100.00

BUILDING PERMITS

	1999	1998	1997
		$000	
Value	43,293	52,774	47,878

HOMES BUILT

	1999	1998	1997
No	208	267	591

TAXATION

Income Class:	1997	% Total
Under $5,000	4,810	12.25
$5,000-$10,000	5,200	13.24
$10,000-$15,000	5,810	14.79
$15,000-$20,000	3,890	9.90
$20,000-$25,000	3,240	8.25
$25,000-$30,000	3,030	7.71
$30,000-$40,000	5,190	13.21
$40,000-$50,000	3,630	9.24
$50,000 +	4,500	11.46
Total Returns, No.	39,280	
Total Income, $000	1,011,248	
Total Taxable Returns	27,560	
Total Tax, $000	175,942	
Average Income, $	25,745	
Average Tax, $	6,384	

VITAL STATISTICS

	1997	1996	1995	1994
Births	565	618	607	616
Deaths	425	439	390	363
Natural Increase	140	179	217	253
Marriages	302	332	367	339

Note: Latest available data.

COMMUNITY NEWSPAPER(S)

	Total Circulation
Comox: Comox Totem Times	n.a.
Courtenay: Comox Valley Echo Tue/Fri.	19,884
Courtenay: Comox Valley Record Wed	20,191
Fri	20,236
Courtenay, Campbell River: Courtenay/ Campbell River North Island Weekender	40,298

RADIO STATION(S)

	Power
CBCV-FM	n.a.
CFCP-FM	n.a.
CKLR-FM	4,700w

TELEVISION STATION(S)

CBUT-TV
CHAN-TV

Cowichan Valley, Subd. C
(Subdivision of Regional District)

In Cowichan Valley Regional District.

POPULATION

July 1, 2001 Estimate	16,026
% Cdn. Total	0.05
% Change, '96 -'01	9.26
Avg. Annual Growth Rate, %	1.79
2003 Projected Population	16,666
2006 Projected Population	17,541
2001 Households Estimate	6,161
2003 Projected Households	6,435
2006 Projected Households	6,853

INCOME

% Above/Below National Average	-2
2001 Total Income Estimate	$329,810,000
% Cdn. Total	0.05
2001 Average Hhld. Income	$53,500
2001 Per Capita	$20,600
2003 Projected Total Income	$359,190,000
2006 Projected Total Income	$405,720,000

RETAIL SALES

% Above/Below National Average	-72
2001 Retail Sales Estimate	$39,740,000
% Cdn. Total	0.01
2001 per Household	$6,500
2001 per Capita	$2,500
2001 No. of Establishments	96
2003 Projected Retail Sales	$44,820,000
2006 Projected Retail Sales	$51,810,000

POPULATION

2001 Estimates:
Total	16,026
Male	8,003
Female	8,023

Age Groups	Male	Female
0-4	453	433
5-9	560	528
10-14	612	580
15-19	582	561
20-24	460	448
25-29	381	405
30-34	454	528
35-39	614	679
40-44	694	727
45-49	667	633
50-54	531	508
55-59	425	424
60-64	380	370
65-69	362	362
70+	828	837

DAYTIME POPULATION

2001 Estimates:
Working Population	n.a.
At Home Population	8,682
Total	8,682

INCOME

2001 Estimates:
Avg. Household Income	$53,532
Avg. Family Income	$57,282
Per Capita Income	$20,580
Male:	
Avg. Employment Income	$33,106
Avg. Employment Income (Full Time)	$43,169
Female:	
Avg. Employment Income	$20,422
Avg. Employment Income (Full Time)	$30,000

British Columbia

DISPOSABLE & DISCRETIONARY INCOME

2001 Estimates:	Per Hhld.
Disposable Income	$41,037
Discretionary Income 1 (minus Food & Shelter)	$28,563
Discretionary Income 2 (minus Food, Shelter, & Other Expenditures)	$19,902

LIQUID ASSETS

1999 Estimates:	Per Hhld.
Equity Investments	$83,050
Interest Bearing Investments	$72,288
Total Liquid Assets	$155,338

CREDIT DATA

July 2000:	
Pool of Credit	$192,553,778
Revolving Credit, No.	33,935
Fixed Loans, No.	9,079
Avg. Credit Limit, per Person	$13,265
Avg. Spent, per Person	$5,912
Satisfactory Ratings, No. per Person	2.89
Avg. No. of Cards, per Person	1.00

LABOUR FORCE

2001 Estimates:
Male:	
In the Labour Force	4,189
Participation Rate	65.7
Employed	3,921
Unemployed	268
Unemployment Rate	6.4
Not in Labour Force	2,189
Female:	
In the Labour Force	3,643
Participation Rate	56.2
Employed	3,438
Unemployed	205
Unemployment Rate	5.6
Not in Labour Force	2,839

OCCUPATIONS BY MAJOR GROUPS

2001 Estimates:	Male	Female
Management	453	282
Business, Finance & Admin.	251	1,058
Natural & Applied Sciences & Related	316	35
Health	74	345
Social Sciences, Gov't Services & Religion	88	159
Education	102	211
Arts, Culture, Recreation & Sport	97	122
Sales & Service	764	1,123
Trades, Transport & Equipment Operators & Related	1,349	22
Primary Industries	346	149
Processing, Mfg. & Utilities	248	52

British Columbia

Cowichan Valley, Subd. C

(Subdivision of Regional District)
(Cont'd)

LEVEL OF SCHOOLING

2001 Estimates:
Population 15 years +	12,860
Less than Grade 9	423
Grades 9-13 w/o Certif.	3,251
Grade 9-13 with Certif.	1,748
Trade Certif./Dip.	518
Non-Univ. w/o Certif./Dip.	779
Non-Univ. with Certif./Dip.	3,033
Univ. w/o Degree	1,449
Univ. w/o Degree/Certif.	556
Univ. with Certif.	893
Univ. with Degree	1,659

AVERAGE HOUSEHOLD EXPENDITURES

2001 Estimates:
Food	$5,964
Shelter	$8,634
Clothing	$2,034
Transportation	$6,862
Health & Personal Care	$1,869
Recr'n, Read'g & Education	$3,788
Taxes & Securities	$13,764
Other	$8,061
Total Expenditures	$50,976

PRIVATE HOUSEHOLDS

2001 Estimates:
Private Households, Total	6,161
Pop. in Private Households	15,814
Average no. per Household	2.6

FAMILIES

2001 Estimates:
Families in Private Households	5,020
Husband-Wife Families	4,595
Lone-Parent Families	425
Aver. No. Persons per Family	2.9
Aver. No. Sons/Daughters at Home	1.0

HOUSING

2001 Estimates:
Occupied Private Dwellings	6,161
Owned	5,345
Rented	816
Single-Detached House	5,322
Semi-Detached House	66
Row Houses	11
Apartment, 5 or Fewer Storeys	65
Apartment, Detached Duplex	67
Other Single-Attached	23
Movable Dwellings	607

VEHICLES

2001 Estimates:
Model Yrs. '81-'96, No.	7,617
% Total	87.87
Model Yrs. '97-'98, No.	702
% Total	8.10
'99 Vehicles registered in Model Yr. '99, No.	349
% Total	4.03
Total No. '81-'99	8,668

LEGAL MARITAL STATUS

2001 Estimates: (Age 15+)
Single (Never Married)	2,641
Legally Married (Not Separated)	8,343
Legally Married (Separated)	391
Widowed	526
Divorced	959

PSYTE CATEGORIES

2001 Estimates	No. of House-holds	% of Total Hhds	Index
Technocrafts & Bureaucrats	410	6.65	237
Small City Elite	1,672	27.14	1,584
Aging Erudites	56	0.91	60
Blue Collar Winners	927	15.05	598
Old Towns' New Fringe	1,738	28.21	721
University Enclaves	44	0.71	35
Old Leafy Towns	1,305	21.18	829

FINANCIAL PSYTE

2001 Estimates	No. of House-holds	% of Total Hhds	Index
Successful Suburbanites	410	6.65	100
Canadian Comfort	2,599	42.18	434
Urban Heights	56	0.91	21
Tractors & Tradelines	1,738	28.21	493
Bills & Wills	1,305	21.18	256
Young Urban Struggle	44	0.71	15

HOME LANGUAGE

2001 Estimates:		% Total
English	15,861	98.97
French	23	0.14
Chinese	12	0.07
Dutch	22	0.14
German	11	0.07
Italian	11	0.07
Malay-Bahasa	12	0.07
Persian (Farsi)	11	0.07
Multiple Responses	63	0.39
Total	16,026	100.00

BUILDING PERMITS

	1999	1998 $000	1997
Value	20,537	24,210	33,259

TAXATION

Income Class	1997	% Total
Under $5,000	1,440	11.93
$5,000-$10,000	1,360	11.27
$10,000-$15,000	1,570	13.01
$15,000-$20,000	1,120	9.28
$20,000-$25,000	940	7.79
$25,000-$30,000	900	7.46
$30,000-$40,000	1,690	14.00
$40,000-$50,000	1,180	9.78
$50,000 +	1,880	15.58
Total Returns, No.	12,070	
Total Income, $000	348,366	
Total Taxable Returns	8,950	
Total Tax, $000	65,798	
Average Income, $	28,862	
Average Tax, $	7,352	

VITAL STATISTICS

	1997	1996	1995	1994
Births	144	261	159	168
Deaths	87	101	85	66
Natural Increase	57	160	74	102
Marriages	99	121	123	108

Note: Latest available data.

Cranbrook
(Census Agglomeration)

The Census Agglomeration of Cranbrook consists solely of Cranbrook, C, in East Kootenay Regional District.

POPULATION

July 1, 2001 Estimate	19,424
% Cdn. Total	0.06
% Change, '96 -'01	3.18
Avg. Annual Growth Rate, %	0.63
2003 Projected Population	19,281
2006 Projected Population	18,952
2001 Households Estimate	7,994
2003 Projected Households	8,107
2006 Projected Households	8,225

INCOME

% Above/Below National Average	-12
2001 Total Income Estimate	$361,340,000
% Cdn. Total	0.06
2001 Average Hhld. Income	$45,200
2001 Per Capita	$18,600
2003 Projected Total Income	$382,680,000
2006 Projected Total Income	$412,460,000

RETAIL SALES

% Above/Below National Average	+138
2001 Retail Sales Estimate	$414,230,000
% Cdn. Total	0.15
2001 per Household	$51,800
2001 per Capita	$21,300
2001 No. of Establishments	276
2003 Projected Retail Sales	$440,760,000
2006 Projected Retail Sales	$476,070,000

POPULATION

2001 Estimates:
Total	19,424
Male	9,461
Female	9,963

Age Groups	Male	Female
0-4	601	595
5-9	660	652
10-14	710	690
15-19	731	712
20-24	700	700
25-29	652	681
30-34	673	697
35-39	717	737
40-44	725	753
45-49	692	730
50-54	604	650
55-59	508	522
60-64	421	410
65-69	356	373
70+	711	1,061

DAYTIME POPULATION

2001 Estimates:
Working Population	8,968
At Home Population	10,456
Total	19,424

INCOME

2001 Estimates:
Avg. Household Income	$45,201
Avg. Family Income	$51,706
Per Capita Income	$18,603
Male:	
Avg. Employment Income	$30,915
Avg. Employment Income (Full Time)	$43,756
Female:	
Avg. Employment Income	$17,234
Avg. Employment Income (Full Time)	$28,429

DISPOSABLE & DISCRETIONARY INCOME

2001 Estimates:	Per Hhld.
Disposable Income	$35,063
Discretionary Income 1 (minus Food & Shelter)	$24,315
Discretionary Income 2 (minus Food, Shelter, & Other Expenditures)	$16,542

LIQUID ASSETS

1999 Estimates:	Per Hhld.
Equity Investments	$59,791
Interest Bearing Investments	$59,261
Total Liquid Assets	$119,052

CREDIT DATA

July 2000:
Pool of Credit	$198,585,894
Revolving Credit, No.	36,033
Fixed Loans, No.	12,214
Avg. Credit Limit, per Person	$12,724
Avg. Spent, per Person	$6,229
Satisfactory Ratings, No. per Person	2.93
Avg. No. of Cards, per Person	1.01

LABOUR FORCE

2001 Estimates:
Male:	
In the Labour Force	5,350
Participation Rate	71.4
Employed	4,747
Unemployed	603
Unemployment Rate	11.3
Not in Labour Force	2,140
Female:	
In the Labour Force	4,776
Participation Rate	59.5
Employed	4,379
Unemployed	397
Unemployment Rate	8.3
Not in Labour Force	3,250

OCCUPATIONS BY MAJOR GROUPS

2001 Estimates:	Male	Female
Management	541	227
Business, Finance & Admin.	376	1,346
Natural & Applied Sciences & Related	314	21
Health	53	327
Social Sciences, Gov't Services & Religion	142	219
Education	146	265
Arts, Culture, Recreation & Sport	133	116
Sales & Service	1,220	1,870
Trades, Transport & Equipment Operators & Related	1,513	49
Primary Industries	406	54
Processing, Mfg. & Utilities	376	69

LEVEL OF SCHOOLING

2001 Estimates:
Population 15 years +	15,516
Less than Grade 9	1,161
Grades 9-13 w/o Certif.	4,085
Grade 9-13 with Certif.	2,130
Trade Certif./Dip.	576
Non-Univ. w/o Certif./Dip.	1,273
Non-Univ. with Certif./Dip.	3,561
Univ. w/o Degree	1,476
Univ. w/o Degree/Certif.	520
Univ. with Certif.	956
Univ. with Degree	1,254

Cranbrook
(Census Agglomeration)
(Cont'd)

AVERAGE HOUSEHOLD EXPENDITURES

2001 Estimates:

Food	$5,294
Shelter	$7,340
Clothing	$1,975
Transportation	$5,842
Health & Personal Care	$1,877
Recr'n, Read'g & Education	$3,290
Taxes & Securities	$11,070
Other	$7,389
Total Expenditures	$44,077

PRIVATE HOUSEHOLDS

2001 Estimates:

Private Households, Total	7,994
Pop. in Private Households	19,080
Average no. per Household	2.4

FAMILIES

2001 Estimates:

Families in Private Households	5,735
Husband-Wife Families	4,771
Lone-Parent Families	964
Aver. No. Persons per Family	3.0
Aver. No. Sons/Daughters at Home	1.1

HOUSING

2001 Estimates:

Occupied Private Dwellings	7,994
Owned	5,378
Rented	2,616
Single-Detached House	5,114
Semi-Detached House	335
Row Houses	410
Apartment, 5 or Fewer Storeys	1,502
Apartment, Detached Duplex	186
Other Single-Attached	12
Movable Dwellings	435

VEHICLES

2001 Estimates:

Model Yrs. '81-'96, No.	9,047
% Total	83.15
Model Yrs. '97-'98, No.	1,165
% Total	10.71
'99 Vehicles registered in Model Yr. '99, No.	668
% Total	6.14
Total No. '81-'99	10,880

LEGAL MARITAL STATUS

2001 Estimates: (Age 15+)

Single (Never Married)	4,393
Legally Married (Not Separated)	8,216
Legally Married (Separated)	666
Widowed	1,050
Divorced	1,191

PSYTE CATEGORIES

2001 Estimates	No. of House-holds	% of Total Hhds.	Index
Suburban Executives	116	1.45	101
Town Boomers	1,953	24.43	2,410
The New Frontier	1,464	18.31	1,214
Old Leafy Towns	122	1.53	60
Nesters & Young Homesteaders	507	6.34	272
Young Grey Collar	1,121	14.02	1,676
Quiet Towns	2,660	33.27	1,564

FINANCIAL P$YTE

2001 Estimates	No. of House-holds	% of Total Hhds.	Index
Four Star Investors	116	1.45	29
Canadian Comfort	1,953	24.43	251
Miners & Credit-Liners	1,464	18.31	579
Bills & Wills	122	1.53	18
Revolving Renters	1,628	20.37	443
Limited Budgets	2,660	33.27	1,070

HOME LANGUAGE

2001 Estimates:		% Total
English	19,091	98.29
French	33	0.17
Chinese	11	0.06
German	22	0.11
Italian	80	0.41
Polish	23	0.12
Punjabi	11	0.06
Ukrainian	11	0.06
Other Languages	10	0.05
Multiple Responses	132	0.68
Total	19,424	100.00

BUILDING PERMITS

	1999	1998 $000	1997
Value	34,472	23,841	15,931

HOMES BUILT

	1999	1998	1997
No	78	87	73

TAXATION

Income Class:	1997	% Total
Under $5,000	2,150	12.77
$5,000-$10,000	2,290	13.60
$10,000-$15,000	2,450	14.55
$15,000-$20,000	1,600	9.50
$20,000-$25,000	1,310	7.78
$25,000-$30,000	1,120	6.65
$30,000-$40,000	1,920	11.40
$40,000-$50,000	1,420	8.43
$50,000 +	2,580	15.32
Total Returns, No.	16,840	
Total Income, $000	459,713	
Total Taxable Returns	11,620	
Total Tax, $000	83,887	
Average Income, $	27,299	
Average Tax, $	7,219	

VITAL STATISTICS

	1997	1996	1995	1994
Births	291	258	263	285
Deaths	160	193	145	183
Natural Increase	131	65	118	102
Marriages	135	123	134	119

Note: Latest available data.

DAILY NEWSPAPER(S)

	Circulation Average Paid
Cranbrook Daily Townsman	3,892

COMMUNITY NEWSPAPER(S)

	Total Circulation
Cranbrook: East Kootenay Weekly	n.a.
Cranbrook: The Kootenay Advertiser Mon/Fri.	31,587
Cranbrook: The Kootenay Advertiser (suppl.), 7 Days Magazine	n.a.

RADIO STATION(S)

	Power
CBRR-FM	n.a.
CFEK	n.a.
CKEK	10,000w
CKKR-FM	n.a.

TELEVISION STATION(S)

CATV
CBUT-TV
CISA-TV

Dawson Creek
(Census Agglomeration)

The Census Agglomeration of Dawson Creek consists solely of Dawson Creek, C, in Peace River Regional District.

POPULATION

July 1, 2001 Estimate	11,044
% Cdn. Total	0.04
% Change, '96 -'01	-4.64
Avg. Annual Growth Rate, %	-0.95
2003 Projected Population	10,595
2006 Projected Population	9,849
2001 Households Estimate	4,572
2003 Projected Households	4,479
2006 Projected Households	4,314

INCOME

% Above/Below National Average	-15
2001 Total Income Estimate	$198,320,000
% Cdn. Total	0.03
2001 Average Hhld. Income	$43,400
2001 Per Capita	$18,000
2003 Projected Total Income	$201,710,000
2006 Projected Total Income	$204,140,000

RETAIL SALES

% Above/Below National Average	+65
2001 Retail Sales Estimate	$162,720,000
% Cdn. Total	0.06
2001 per Household	$35,600
2001 per Capita	$14,700
2001 No. of Establishments	108
2003 Projected Retail Sales	$171,150,000
2006 Projected Retail Sales	$178,440,000

POPULATION

2001 Estimates:

Total	11,044
Male	5,379
Female	5,665

Age Groups	Male	Female
0-4	403	368
5-9	436	424
10-14	421	428
15-19	384	395
20-24	373	406
25-29	388	428
30-34	439	446
35-39	459	441
40-44	425	432
45-49	365	382
50-54	289	302
55-59	238	248
60-64	204	227
65-69	187	209
70+	368	529

DAYTIME POPULATION

2001 Estimates:

Working Population	5,316
At Home Population	5,728
Total	11,044

INCOME

2001 Estimates:

Avg. Household Income	$43,378
Avg. Family Income	$49,129
Per Capita Income	$17,958
Male:	
Avg. Employment Income	$31,562
Avg. Employment Income (Full Time)	$42,226
Female:	
Avg. Employment Income	$16,610
Avg. Employment Income (Full Time)	$26,075

British Columbia

DISPOSABLE & DISCRETIONARY INCOME

2001 Estimates:	Per Hhld.
Disposable Income	$33,715
Discretionary Income 1 (minus Food & Shelter)	$23,545
Discretionary Income 2 (minus Food, Shelter, & Other Expenditures)	$15,351

LIQUID ASSETS

1999 Estimates:	Per Hhld.
Equity Investments	$55,463
Interest Bearing Investments	$55,979
Total Liquid Assets	$111,442

CREDIT DATA

July 2000:	
Pool of Credit	$122,144,166
Revolving Credit, No.	18,648
Fixed Loans, No.	10,121
Avg. Credit Limit, per Person	$13,507
Avg. Spent, per Person	$7,053
Satisfactory Ratings, No. per Person	3.02
Avg. No. of Cards, per Person	0.91

LABOUR FORCE

2001 Estimates:	
Male:	
In the Labour Force	3,089
Participation Rate	75.0
Employed	2,786
Unemployed	303
Unemployment Rate	9.8
Not in Labour Force	1,030
Female:	
In the Labour Force	2,836
Participation Rate	63.8
Employed	2,628
Unemployed	208
Unemployment Rate	7.3
Not in Labour Force	1,609

OCCUPATIONS BY MAJOR GROUPS

2001 Estimates:	Male	Female
Management	267	173
Business, Finance & Admin.	145	802
Natural & Applied Sciences & Related	116	28
Health	32	190
Social Sciences, Gov't Services & Religion	98	109
Education	71	108
Arts, Culture, Recreation & Sport	35	59
Sales & Service	777	1,192
Trades, Transport & Equipment Operators & Related	1,009	36
Primary Industries	275	32
Processing, Mfg. & Utilities	209	9

British Columbia

Dawson Creek
(Census Agglomeration)
(Cont'd)

LEVEL OF SCHOOLING

2001 Estimates:
Population 15 years + ... 8,564
Less than Grade 9 753
Grades 9-13 w/o Certif. 2,390
Grade 9-13 with Certif. 1,028
Trade Certif. /Dip. 441
Non-Univ. w/o Certif./Dip. 847
Non-Univ. with Certif./Dip. 1,937
Univ. w/o Degree 695
  Univ. w/o Degree/Certif. 341
  Univ. with Certif. 354
Univ. with Degree 473

AVERAGE HOUSEHOLD EXPENDITURES

2001 Estimates:
Food $5,214
Shelter $6,792
Clothing. $1,957
Transportation. $6,275
Health & Personal Care $1,927
Recr'n, Read'g & Education $3,412
Taxes & Securities $9,929
Other. $7,089
Total Expenditures $42,595

PRIVATE HOUSEHOLDS

2001 Estimates:
Private Households, Total 4,572
Pop. in Private Households. 10,864
Average no. per Household 2.4

FAMILIES

2001 Estimates:
Families in Private Households 3,158
Husband-Wife Families 2,508
Lone-Parent Families 650
Aver. No. Persons per Family 3.0
Aver. No. Sons/Daughters
  at Home 1.2

HOUSING

2001 Estimates:
Occupied Private Dwellings 4,572
  Owned. 2,902
  Rented. 1,670
Single-Detached House 3,253
Semi-Detached House 133
Row Houses 219
Apartment, 5+ Storeys 11
Apartment, 5 or Fewer Storeys 793
Apartment, Detached Duplex 33
Movable Dwellings. 130

VEHICLES

2001 Estimates:
Model Yrs. '81-'96, No. 4,632
  % Total 84.03
Model Yrs. '97-'98, No. 566
  % Total 10.27
'99 Vehicles registered in
  Model Yr. '99, No. 314
  % Total 5.70
Total No. '81-'99 5,512

LEGAL MARITAL STATUS

2001 Estimates: (Age 15+)
Single (Never Married) 2,851
Legally Married
  (Not Separated) 4,019
Legally Married (Separated) 386
Widowed 513
Divorced 795

PSYTE CATEGORIES

2001 Estimates	No. of House -holds	% of Total Hhds.	Index
The New Frontier	2,707	59.21	3,926
High Rise Sunsets	101	2.21	154
Quiet Towns	1,763	38.56	1,812

FINANÇIAL P$YTE

2001 Estimates	No. of House -holds	% of Total Hhds.	Index
Miners & Credit-Liners	2,707	59.21	1,870
Revolving Renters	101	2.21	48
Limited Budgets	1,763	38.56	1,240

HOME LANGUAGE

2001 Estimates:		% Total
English	10,705	96.93
French	129	1.17
Chinese	10	0.09
Cree	10	0.09
German	10	0.09
Polish	55	0.50
Punjabi	15	0.14
Tagalog (Pilipino)	30	0.27
Other Languages	20	0.18
Multiple Responses	60	0.54
Total	11,044	100.00

BUILDING PERMITS

	1999	1998 $000	1997
Value	22,340	11,650	9,512

HOMES BUILT

	1999	1998	1997
No	34	45	28

TAXATION

Income Class:	1997	% Total
Under $5,000	1,310	12.44
$5,000-$10,000	1,580	15.00
$10,000-$15,000	1,580	15.00
$15,000-$20,000	1,000	9.50
$20,000-$25,000	760	7.22
$25,000-$30,000	710	6.74
$30,000-$40,000	1,310	12.44
$40,000-$50,000	880	8.36
$50,000 +	1,390	13.20
Total Returns, No.	10,530	
Total Income, $000	273,371	
Total Taxable Returns	6,950	
Total Tax, $000	45,785	
Average Income, $	25,961	
Average Tax, $	6,588	

VITAL STATISTICS

	1997	1996	1995	1994
Births	221	215	239	224
Deaths	79	86	75	62
Natural Increase	142	129	164	162
Marriages	96	95	95	106

Note: Latest available data.

DAILY NEWSPAPER(S)

	Circulation Average Paid
Peace River Block News	2,132

COMMUNITY NEWSPAPER(S)

	Total Circulation
Dawson Creek: Dawson Creek Mirror	10,000
Dawson Creek: Peace River Block News Regional Weekly	9,633

RADIO STATION(S)

	Power
CBKQ-FM	n.a.
CBUF-FM	100w
CJDC	10,000w

TELEVISION STATION(S)

CATV
CBUFT-TV
CJDC-TV

Duncan
(Census Agglomeration)

The Census Agglomeration of Duncan includes: Duncan, C; Cowichan Valley, Subd. D, SRD; North Cowichan, DM; plus several smaller areas. All are in Cowichan Valley Regional District.

POPULATION

July 1, 2001 Estimate	38,746
% Cdn. Total	0.12
% Change, '96 -'01	4.31
Avg. Annual Growth Rate, %	0.85
2003 Projected Population	39,367
2006 Projected Population	40,090
2001 Households Estimate	15,210
2003 Projected Households	15,501
2006 Projected Households	15,957

INCOME

% Above/Below National Average	-17
2001 Total Income Estimate	$676,520,000
% Cdn. Total	0.10
2001 Average Hhld. Income	$44,500
2001 Per Capita	$17,500
2003 Projected Total Income	$718,340,000
2006 Projected Total Income	$782,890,000

RETAIL SALES

% Above/Below National Average	+7
2001 Retail Sales Estimate	$370,780,000
% Cdn. Total	0.13
2001 per Household	$24,400
2001 per Capita	$9,600
2001 No. of Establishments	398
2003 Projected Retail Sales	$398,540,000
2006 Projected Retail Sales	$437,060,000

POPULATION

2001 Estimates:

Total	38,746
Male	18,924
Female	19,822

Age Groups	Male	Female
0-4	1,146	1,091
5-9	1,332	1,270
10-14	1,466	1,380
15-19	1,441	1,421
20-24	1,246	1,311
25-29	1,129	1,199
30-34	1,220	1,284
35-39	1,413	1,460
40-44	1,449	1,521
45-49	1,403	1,443
50-54	1,227	1,246
55-59	1,009	1,024
60-64	875	878
65-69	779	816
70+	1,789	2,478

DAYTIME POPULATION

2001 Estimates:

Working Population	16,475
At Home Population	22,271
Total	38,746

INCOME

2001 Estimates:

Avg. Household Income	$44,479
Avg. Family Income	$50,248
Per Capita Income	$17,460
Male:	
Avg. Employment Income	$31,865
Avg. Employment Income (Full Time)	$43,889
Female:	
Avg. Employment Income	$17,447
Avg. Employment Income (Full Time)	$26,447

DISPOSABLE & DISCRETIONARY INCOME

2001 Estimates:	Per Hhld.
Disposable Income	$34,418
Discretionary Income 1 (minus Food & Shelter)	$23,342
Discretionary Income 2 (minus Food, Shelter, & Other Expenditures)	$15,981

LIQUID ASSETS

1999 Estimates:	Per Hhld.
Equity Investments	$63,717
Interest Bearing Investments	$59,697
Total Liquid Assets	$123,414

CREDIT DATA

July 2000:	
Pool of Credit	$342,696,361
Revolving Credit, No.	64,530
Fixed Loans, No.	16,959
Avg. Credit Limit, per Person	$11,559
Avg. Spent, per Person	$5,047
Satisfactory Ratings, No. per Person	2.66
Avg. No. of Cards, per Person	0.97

LABOUR FORCE

2001 Estimates:

Male:	
In the Labour Force	9,769
Participation Rate	65.2
Employed	8,837
Unemployed	932
Unemployment Rate	9.5
Not in Labour Force	5,211
Female:	
In the Labour Force	8,613
Participation Rate	53.6
Employed	7,794
Unemployed	819
Unemployment Rate	9.5
Not in Labour Force	7,468

OCCUPATIONS BY MAJOR GROUPS

2001 Estimates:	Male	Female
Management	870	562
Business, Finance & Admin.	533	2,141
Natural & Applied Sciences & Related	647	107
Health	204	602
Social Sciences, Gov't Services & Religion	134	310
Education	217	406
Arts, Culture, Recreation & Sport	197	243
Sales & Service	1,557	3,321
Trades, Transport & Equipment Operators & Related	2,729	70
Primary Industries	1,113	283
Processing, Mfg. & Utilities	1,227	129

LEVEL OF SCHOOLING

2001 Estimates:

Population 15 years +	31,061
Less than Grade 9	2,491
Grades 9-13 w/o Certif.	8,738
Grade 9-13 with Certif.	4,020
Trade Certif./Dip.	1,317
Non-Univ. w/o Certif./Dip.	2,060
Non-Univ. with Certif./Dip.	6,677
Univ. w/o Degree	3,036
Univ. w/o Degree/Certif.	1,424
Univ. with Certif.	1,612
Univ. with Degree	2,722

AVERAGE HOUSEHOLD EXPENDITURES

2001 Estimates:

Food	$5,229
Shelter	$7,681
Clothing	$1,751
Transportation	$5,730
Health & Personal Care	$1,662
Recr'n, Read'g & Education	$3,173
Taxes & Securities	$10,784
Other	$7,252
Total Expenditures	$43,262

PRIVATE HOUSEHOLDS

2001 Estimates:

Private Households, Total	15,210
Pop. in Private Households	37,835
Average no. per Household	2.5

FAMILIES

2001 Estimates:

Families in Private Households	11,167
Husband-Wife Families	9,573
Lone-Parent Families	1,594
Aver. No. Persons per Family	2.9
Aver. No. Sons/Daughters at Home	1.1

HOUSING

2001 Estimates:

Occupied Private Dwellings	15,210
Owned	10,767
Rented	4,355
Band Housing	88
Single-Detached House	10,507
Semi-Detached House	678
Row Houses	809
Apartment, 5 or Fewer Storeys	2,307
Apartment, Detached Duplex	337
Other Single-Attached	11
Movable Dwellings	561

VEHICLES

2001 Estimates:

Model Yrs. '81-'96, No.	16,312
% Total	87.90
Model Yrs. '97-'98, No.	1,399
% Total	7.54
'99 Vehicles registered in Model Yr. '99, No.	847
% Total	4.56
Total No. '81-'99	18,558

LEGAL MARITAL STATUS

2001 Estimates: (Age 15+)	
Single (Never Married)	8,252
Legally Married (Not Separated)	16,863
Legally Married (Separated)	1,028
Widowed	2,098
Divorced	2,820

PSYTE CATEGORIES

2001 Estimates	No. of House-holds	% of Total Hhds.	Index
Boomers & Teens	420	2.76	154
Small City Elite	2,698	17.74	1,035
Kindergarten Boom	292	1.92	73
Blue Collar Winners	594	3.91	155
Old Towns' New Fringe	2,924	19.22	491
Rustic Prosperity	337	2.22	123
High Rise Sunsets	287	1.89	132
Young City Singles	485	3.19	139
Old Leafy Towns	2,258	14.85	581
Nesters & Young Homesteaders	2,714	17.84	764
Quiet Towns	531	3.49	164
Big Country Families	508	3.34	234
Struggling Downtowns	238	1.56	50
Aged Pensioners	700	4.60	346
Big City Stress	160	1.05	93

FINANCIAL P$YTE

2001 Estimates	No. of House -holds	% of Total Hhds.	Index
Four Star Investors	420	2.76	55
Canadian Comfort	3,292	21.64	223
Mortgages & Minivans	292	1.92	29
Tractors & Tradelines	3,261	21.44	375
Bills & Wills	2,258	14.85	179
Revolving Renters	3,001	19.73	429
Rural Family Blues	508	3.34	41
Limited Budgets	531	3.49	112
Towering Debt	723	4.75	61
NSF	160	1.05	30
Senior Survivors	700	4.60	244

HOME LANGUAGE

2001 Estimates:		% Total
English	37,541	96.89
French	36	0.09
Chinese	108	0.28
German	59	0.15
Punjabi	430	1.11
Spanish	21	0.05
Vietnamese	21	0.05
Other Languages	175	0.45
Multiple Responses	355	0.92
Total	38,746	100.00

BUILDING PERMITS

	1999	1998	1997
		$000	
Value	22,876	27,015	29,054

HOMES BUILT

	1999	1998	1997
No	140	199	334

TAXATION

Income Class:	1997	% Total
Under $5,000	3,670	13.84
$5,000-$10,000	3,560	13.43
$10,000-$15,000	4,190	15.81
$15,000-$20,000	2,580	9.73
$20,000-$25,000	2,050	7.73
$25,000-$30,000	1,980	7.47
$30,000-$40,000	3,260	12.30
$40,000-$50,000	2,110	7.96
$50,000 +	3,120	11.77
Total Returns, No.	26,510	
Total Income, $000	670,312	
Total Taxable Returns	17,570	
Total Tax, $000	117,787	
Average Income, $	25,285	
Average Tax, $	6,704	

VITAL STATISTICS

	1997	1996	1995	1994
Births	433	419	440	447
Deaths	359	318	308	302
Natural Increase	74	101	132	145
Marriages	226	245	252	258

Note: Latest available data.

British Columbia

Duncan
(Census Agglomeration)
(Cont'd)

COMMUNITY NEWSPAPER(S)

	Total Circulation
Duncan: Cowichan News Leader	19,662
Duncan: Cowichan Pictorial	22,274
Duncan: Cowichan Valley Citizen Sun/Wed.	22,634

RADIO STATION(S)

	Power
CKAY	10,000w

Fort St. John
(Census Agglomeration)

The Census Agglomeration of Fort St. John consists solely of Fort St. John, C, in Peace River Regional District.

POPULATION

July 1, 2001 Estimate	15,503
% Cdn. Total	0.05
% Change, '96 -'01	-0.88
Avg. Annual Growth Rate, %	-0.18
2003 Projected Population	15,148
2006 Projected Population	14,511
2001 Households Estimate	6,015
2003 Projected Households	6,000
2006 Projected Households	5,961

INCOME

% Above/Below National Average	+5
2001 Total Income Estimate	$344,470,000
% Cdn. Total	0.05
2001 Average Hhld. Income	$57,300
2001 Per Capita	$22,200
2003 Projected Total Income	$358,550,000
2006 Projected Total Income	$377,150,000

RETAIL SALES

% Above/Below National Average	+116
2001 Retail Sales Estimate	$299,230,000
% Cdn. Total	0.11
2001 per Household	$49,700
2001 per Capita	$19,300
2001 No. of Establishments	196
2003 Projected Retail Sales	$317,210,000
2006 Projected Retail Sales	$336,740,000

POPULATION

2001 Estimates:

Total		15,503
Male		7,920
Female		7,583

Age Groups	Male	Female
0-4	594	583
5-9	649	625
10-14	636	599
15-19	585	568
20-24	623	603
25-29	720	666
30-34	771	695
35-39	742	685
40-44	655	615
45-49	528	498
50-54	402	381
55-59	290	279
60-64	220	203
65-69	176	165
70+	329	418

DAYTIME POPULATION

2001 Estimates:

Working Population	7,932
At Home Population	7,571
Total	15,503

INCOME

2001 Estimates:

Avg. Household Income	$57,268
Avg. Family Income	$61,944
Per Capita Income	$22,219
Male:	
Avg. Employment Income	$40,697
Avg. Employment Income (Full Time)	$50,010
Female:	
Avg. Employment Income	$18,776
Avg. Employment Income (Full Time)	$29,584

DISPOSABLE & DISCRETIONARY INCOME

2001 Estimates:	Per Hhld.
Disposable Income	$43,779
Discretionary Income 1 (minus Food & Shelter)	$31,474
Discretionary Income 2 (minus Food, Shelter, & Other Expenditures)	$21,569

LIQUID ASSETS

1999 Estimates:	Per Hhld.
Equity Investments	$97,428
Interest Bearing Investments	$78,737
Total Liquid Assets	$176,165

CREDIT DATA

July 2000:

Pool of Credit	$196,348,489
Revolving Credit, No.	28,286
Fixed Loans, No.	15,174
Avg. Credit Limit, per Person	$13,948
Avg. Spent, per Person	$7,369
Satisfactory Ratings, No. per Person	2.95
Avg. No. of Cards, per Person	0.95

LABOUR FORCE

2001 Estimates:

Male:	
In the Labour Force	5,052
Participation Rate	83.6
Employed	4,522
Unemployed	530
Unemployment Rate	10.5
Not in Labour Force	989

Female:	
In the Labour Force	3,858
Participation Rate	66.8
Employed	3,600
Unemployed	258
Unemployment Rate	6.7
Not in Labour Force	1,918

OCCUPATIONS BY MAJOR GROUPS

2001 Estimates:	Male	Female
Management	557	279
Business, Finance & Admin.	319	1,039
Natural & Applied Sciences & Related	400	45
Health	88	253
Social Sciences, Gov't Services & Religion	45	82
Education	133	189
Arts, Culture, Recreation & Sport	53	116
Sales & Service	703	1,680
Trades, Transport & Equipment Operators & Related	1,770	109
Primary Industries	550	n.a.
Processing, Mfg. & Utilities	349	30

LEVEL OF SCHOOLING

2001 Estimates:

Population 15 years +	11,817
Less than Grade 9	881
Grades 9-13 w/o Certif.	3,534
Grade 9-13 with Certif.	1,830
Trade Certif. /Dip.	393
Non-Univ. w/o Certif./Dip.	959
Non-Univ. with Certif./Dip.	2,359
Univ. w/o Degree	1,060
Univ. w/o Degree/Certif.	448
Univ. with Certif.	612
Univ. with Degree	801

AVERAGE HOUSEHOLD EXPENDITURES

2001 Estimates:

Food	$6,476
Shelter	$8,078
Clothing	$2,571
Transportation	$7,371
Health & Personal Care	$2,426
Recr'n, Read'g & Education	$4,572
Taxes & Securities	$13,383
Other	$9,012
Total Expenditures	$53,889

PRIVATE HOUSEHOLDS

2001 Estimates:

Private Households, Total	6,015
Pop. in Private Households	15,319
Average no. per Household	2.5

FAMILIES

2001 Estimates:

Families in Private Households	4,263
Husband-Wife Families	3,623
Lone-Parent Families	640
Aver. No. Persons per Family	3.2
Aver. No. Sons/Daughters at Home	1.3

HOUSING

2001 Estimates:

Occupied Private Dwellings	6,015
Owned	3,605
Rented	2,410
Single-Detached House	3,473
Semi-Detached House	193
Row Houses	514
Apartment, 5+ Storeys	88
Apartment, 5 or Fewer Storeys	1,288
Apartment, Detached Duplex	133
Other Single-Attached	11
Movable Dwellings	315

VEHICLES

2001 Estimates:

Model Yrs. '81-'96, No.	7,184
% Total	73.32
Model Yrs. '97-'98, No.	1,837
% Total	18.75
'99 Vehicles registered in Model Yr. '99, No.	777
% Total	7.93
Total No. '81-'99	9,798

LEGAL MARITAL STATUS

2001 Estimates: (Age 15+)

Single (Never Married)	4,272
Legally Married (Not Separated)	5,582
Legally Married (Separated)	501
Widowed	519
Divorced	943

PSYTE CATEGORIES

2001 Estimates	No. of House -holds	% of Total Hhds.	Index
Town Boomers	928	15.43	1,522
The New Frontier	3,580	59.52	3,946
Young Grey Collar	1,125	18.70	2,236
Quiet Towns	379	6.30	296

FINANCIAL PSYTE

2001 Estimates	No. of House -holds	% of Total Hhds.	Index
Canadian Comfort	928	15.43	159
Miners & Credit-Liners	3,580	59.52	1,880
Revolving Renters	1,125	18.70	407
Limited Budgets	379	6.30	203

Fort St. John
(Census Agglomeration)
(Cont'd)

HOME LANGUAGE

2001 Estimates:		% Total
English	15,211	98.12
French	30	0.19
Chinese	68	0.44
German	30	0.19
Greek	15	0.10
Hindi	10	0.06
Punjabi	52	0.34
Tagalog (Pilipino)	15	0.10
Multiple Responses	72	0.46
Total	15,503	100.00

BUILDING PERMITS

	1999	1998	1997
		$000	
Value	25,939	26,958	26,488

HOMES BUILT

	1999	1998	1997
No.	175	181	74

TAXATION

Income Class:	1997	% Total
Under $5,000	1,650	11.65
$5,000-$10,000	1,540	10.88
$10,000-$15,000	1,720	12.15
$15,000-$20,000	1,220	8.62
$20,000-$25,000	1,050	7.42
$25,000-$30,000	950	6.71
$30,000-$40,000	1,700	12.01
$40,000-$50,000	1,360	9.60
$50,000 +	2,960	20.90
Total Returns, No.	14,160	
Total Income, $000	455,025	
Total Taxable Returns	10,510	
Total Tax, $000	92,518	
Average Income, $	32,135	
Average Tax, $	8,803	

VITAL STATISTICS

	1997	1996	1995	1994
Births	321	343	335	371
Deaths	78	90	83	91
Natural Increase	243	253	252	280
Marriages	157	130	144	155

Note: Latest available data.

DAILY NEWSPAPER(S)

	Circulation Average Paid
Alaska Highway News	3,518

COMMUNITY NEWSPAPER(S)

	Total Circulation
Fort St. John: North Peace Express	n.a.
Fort St. John: The Northerner	3,500

RADIO STATION(S)

	Power
CBYJ-FM	n.a.
CHRX-FM	n.a.
CKNL	1,000w

TELEVISION STATION(S)

CJDC-TV

Fraser-Fort George, Subd. A
(Subdivision of Regional District)

In Fraser-Fort George Regional District.

POPULATION

July 1, 2001 Estimate	15,234
% Cdn. Total	0.05
% Change, '96 -'01	7.35
Avg. Annual Growth Rate, %	1.43
2003 Projected Population	15,639
2006 Projected Population	16,130
2001 Households Estimate	5,456
2003 Projected Households	5,736
2006 Projected Households	6,138

INCOME

% Above/Below National Average	+8
2001 Total Income Estimate	$346,320,000
% Cdn. Total	0.05
2001 Average Hhld. Income	$63,500
2001 Per Capita	$22,700
2003 Projected Total Income	$382,280,000
2006 Projected Total Income	$437,840,000

RETAIL SALES

% Above/Below National Average	-88
2001 Retail Sales Estimate	$16,740,000
% Cdn. Total	0.01
2001 per Household	$3,100
2001 per Capita	$1,100
2001 No. of Establishments	65
2003 Projected Retail Sales	$18,040,000
2006 Projected Retail Sales	$19,960,000

POPULATION

2001 Estimates:		
Total		15,234
Male		7,927
Female		7,307
Age Groups	Male	Female
0-4	466	440
5-9	557	509
10-14	652	604
15-19	652	624
20-24	526	522
25-29	421	449
30-34	472	554
35-39	610	649
40-44	703	687
45-49	711	639
50-54	638	529
55-59	485	396
60-64	379	282
65-69	287	188
70+	368	235

DAYTIME POPULATION

2001 Estimates:	
Working Population	434
At Home Population	7,436
Total	7,870

INCOME

2001 Estimates:	
Avg. Household Income	$63,476
Avg. Family Income	$66,280
Per Capita Income	$22,734
Male:	
Avg. Employment Income	$39,250
Avg. Employment Income (Full Time)	$49,628
Female:	
Avg. Employment Income	$22,697
Avg. Employment Income (Full Time)	$36,232

DISPOSABLE & DISCRETIONARY INCOME

2001 Estimates:	Per Hhld.
Disposable Income	$48,478
Discretionary Income 1 (minus Food & Shelter)	$33,659
Discretionary Income 2 (minus Food, Shelter, & Other Expenditures)	$23,334

LIQUID ASSETS

1999 Estimates:	Per Hhld.
Equity Investments	$97,469
Interest Bearing Investments	$82,739
Total Liquid Assets	$180,208

CREDIT DATA

July 2000:	
Pool of Credit	$122,519,454
Revolving Credit, No.	18,158
Fixed Loans, No.	8,350
Avg. Credit Limit, per Person	$15,930
Avg. Spent, per Person	$8,512
Satisfactory Ratings, No. per Person	3.29
Avg. No. of Cards, per Person	0.98

LABOUR FORCE

2001 Estimates:	
Male:	
In the Labour Force	4,861
Participation Rate	77.8
Employed	4,263
Unemployed	598
Unemployment Rate	12.3
Not in Labour Force	1,391
Female:	
In the Labour Force	3,722
Participation Rate	64.7
Employed	3,532
Unemployed	190
Unemployment Rate	5.1
Not in Labour Force	2,032

OCCUPATIONS BY MAJOR GROUPS

2001 Estimates:	Male	Female
Management	334	189
Business, Finance & Admin.	187	1,095
Natural & Applied Sciences & Related	253	57
Health	78	266
Social Sciences, Gov't Services & Religion	34	62
Education	54	149
Arts, Culture, Recreation & Sport	57	78
Sales & Service	475	1,319
Trades, Transport & Equipment Operators & Related	2,124	116
Primary Industries	658	260
Processing, Mfg. & Utilities	565	98

LEVEL OF SCHOOLING

2001 Estimates:	
Population 15 years +	12,006
Less than Grade 9	1,092
Grades 9-13 w/o Certif.	3,820
Grade 9-13 with Certif.	1,551
Trade Certif. /Dip.	537
Non-Univ. w/o Certif./Dip.	1,007
Non-Univ. with Certif./Dip.	2,368
Univ. w/o Degree	1,077
Univ. w/o Degree/Certif.	529
Univ. with Certif.	548
Univ. with Degree	554

AVERAGE HOUSEHOLD EXPENDITURES

2001 Estimates:	
Food	$6,964
Shelter	$10,080
Clothing	$2,318
Transportation	$8,105
Health & Personal Care	$2,148
Recr'n, Read'g & Education	$4,313
Taxes & Securities	$15,606
Other	$9,844
Total Expenditures	$59,378

British Columbia

PRIVATE HOUSEHOLDS

2001 Estimates:	
Private Households, Total	5,456
Pop. in Private Households	14,994
Average no. per Household	2.7

FAMILIES

2001 Estimates:	
Families in Private Households	4,653
Husband-Wife Families	4,317
Lone-Parent Families	336
Aver. No. Persons per Family	3.1
Aver. No. Sons/Daughters at Home	1.2

HOUSING

2001 Estimates:	
Occupied Private Dwellings	5,456
Owned	4,894
Rented	562
Single-Detached House	4,787
Semi-Detached House	12
Movable Dwellings	657

VEHICLES

2001 Estimates:	
Model Yrs. '81-'96, No.	6,368
% Total	83.27
Model Yrs. '97-'98, No.	762
% Total	9.96
'99 Vehicles registered in Model Yr. '99, No.	517
% Total	6.76
Total No. '81-'99	7,647

LEGAL MARITAL STATUS

2001 Estimates: (Age 15+)	
Single (Never Married)	3,142
Legally Married (Not Separated)	7,269
Legally Married (Separated)	453
Widowed	329
Divorced	813

PSYTE CATEGORIES

2001 Estimates	No. of House-holds	% of Total Hhds.	Index
Boomers & Teens	132	2.42	135
Small City Elite	157	2.88	168
Blue Collar Winners	1,072	19.65	780
Old Towns' New Fringe	3,123	57.24	1,462
Rustic Prosperity	486	8.91	494
Rod & Rifle	430	7.88	341
Down, Down East	36	0.66	94

British Columbia

Fraser-Fort George, Subd. A
(Subdivision of Regional District)
(Cont'd)

FINANCIAL P$YTE

2001 Estimates	No. of House-holds	% of Total Hhds.	Index
Four Star Investors	132	2.42	48
Canadian Comfort	1,229	22.53	232
Tractors & Tradelines	3,609	66.15	1,157
Rural Family Blues	466	8.54	106

HOME LANGUAGE

2001 Estimates:		% Total
English	14,926	97.98
French	67	0.44
German	83	0.54
Italian	19	0.12
Korean	26	0.17
Spanish	17	0.11
Other Languages	11	0.07
Multiple Responses	85	0.56
Total	15,234	100.00

BUILDING PERMITS

	1999	1998 $000	1997
Value	11,503	12,083	20,115

TAXATION

Income Class:	1997	% Total
Under $5,000	220	20.37
$5,000-$10,000	140	12.96
$10,000-$15,000	170	15.74
$15,000-$20,000	110	10.19
$20,000-$25,000	60	5.56
$25,000-$30,000	60	5.56
$30,000-$40,000	90	8.33
$40,000-$50,000	90	8.33
$50,000 +	150	13.89
Total Returns, No.	1,080	
Total Income, $000	25,215	
Total Taxable Returns	650	
Total Tax, $000	4,581	
Average Income, $	23,347	
Average Tax, $	7,048	

VITAL STATISTICS

	1997	1996	1995	1994
Births	38	44	25	23
Deaths	14	20	23	11
Natural Increase	24	24	2	12
Marriages	7	6	12	7

Note: Latest available data.

Kamloops
(Census Agglomeration)

The Census Agglomeration of Kamloops includes: Kamloops, C; Logan Lake, DM; Thompson-Nicola, Subd. B, SRD; plus several smaller areas. All are in Thompson-Nicola Regional District.

POPULATION

July 1, 2001 Estimate	91,971
% Cdn. Total	0.30
% Change, '96 -'01	4.19
Avg. Annual Growth Rate, %	0.82
2003 Projected Population	92,894
2006 Projected Population	93,586
2001 Households Estimate	36,552
2003 Projected Households	37,364
2006 Projected Households	38,543

INCOME

% Above/Below National Average	-3
2001 Total Income Estimate	$1,884,430,000
% Cdn. Total	0.29
2001 Average Hhld. Income	$51,600
2001 Per Capita	$20,500
2003 Projected Total Income	$2,010,430,000
2006 Projected Total Income	$2,211,170,000

RETAIL SALES

% Above/Below National Average	+23
2001 Retail Sales Estimate	$1,013,580,000
% Cdn. Total	0.36
2001 per Household	$27,700
2001 per Capita	$11,000
2001 No. of Establishments	751
2003 Projected Retail Sales	$1,106,840,000
2006 Projected Retail Sales	$1,233,030,000

POPULATION

2001 Estimates:		
Total		91,971
Male		45,503
Female		46,468

Age Groups	Male	Female
0-4	2,797	2,675
5-9	2,989	2,890
10-14	3,266	3,091
15-19	3,408	3,227
20-24	3,368	3,292
25-29	3,237	3,229
30-34	3,226	3,394
35-39	3,464	3,750
40-44	3,588	3,826
45-49	3,549	3,622
50-54	3,091	3,091
55-59	2,492	2,487
60-64	2,026	2,025
65-69	1,711	1,705
70+	3,291	4,164

DAYTIME POPULATION

2001 Estimates:	
Working Population	43,908
At Home Population	48,063
Total	91,971

INCOME

2001 Estimates:	
Avg. Household Income	$51,555
Avg. Family Income	$57,285
Per Capita Income	$20,489
Male:	
Avg. Employment Income	$34,979
Avg. Employment Income (Full Time)	$47,293
Female:	
Avg. Employment Income	$19,823
Avg. Employment Income (Full Time)	$30,516

DISPOSABLE & DISCRETIONARY INCOME

2001 Estimates:	Per Hhld.
Disposable Income	$39,809
Discretionary Income 1 (minus Food & Shelter)	$27,255
Discretionary Income 2 (minus Food, Shelter, & Other Expenditures)	$19,026

LIQUID ASSETS

1999 Estimates:	Per Hhld.
Equity Investments	$77,128
Interest Bearing Investments	$68,365
Total Liquid Assets	$145,493

CREDIT DATA

July 2000:	
Pool of Credit	$993,632,634
Revolving Credit, No.	180,478
Fixed Loans, No.	57,316
Avg. Credit Limit, per Person	$13,195
Avg. Spent, per Person	$6,216
Satisfactory Ratings, No. per Person	3.01
Avg. No. of Cards, per Person	1.03

LABOUR FORCE

2001 Estimates:	
Male:	
In the Labour Force	26,221
Participation Rate	71.9
Employed	23,598
Unemployed	2,623
Unemployment Rate	10.0
Not in Labour Force	10,230
Female:	
In the Labour Force	22,878
Participation Rate	60.5
Employed	20,804
Unemployed	2,074
Unemployment Rate	9.1
Not in Labour Force	14,934

OCCUPATIONS BY MAJOR GROUPS

2001 Estimates:	Male	Female
Management	2,618	1,230
Business, Finance & Admin.	1,667	6,008
Natural & Applied Sciences & Related	1,442	213
Health	494	2,253
Social Sciences, Gov't Services & Religion	588	791
Education	834	1,089
Arts, Culture, Recreation & Sport	350	493
Sales & Service	5,530	8,728
Trades, Transport & Equipment Operators & Related	8,326	439
Primary Industries	1,713	453
Processing, Mfg. & Utilities	1,660	354

LEVEL OF SCHOOLING

2001 Estimates:	
Population 15 years +	74,263
Less than Grade 9	5,014
Grades 9-13 w/o Certif.	19,317
Grade 9-13 with Certif.	10,220
Trade Certif. /Dip.	3,188
Non-Univ. w/o Certif./Dip.	4,832
Non-Univ. with Certif./Dip.	15,130
Univ. w/o Degree	10,212
Univ. w/o Degree/Certif.	4,899
Univ. with Certif.	5,313
Univ. with Degree	6,350

AVERAGE HOUSEHOLD EXPENDITURES

2001 Estimates:	
Food	$5,869
Shelter	$8,729
Clothing	$2,051
Transportation	$6,365
Health & Personal Care	$1,865
Recr'n, Read'g & Education	$3,577
Taxes & Securities	$12,752
Other	$8,216
Total Expenditures	$49,424

PRIVATE HOUSEHOLDS

2001 Estimates:	
Private Households, Total	36,552
Pop. in Private Households	90,375
Average no. per Household	2.5

FAMILIES

2001 Estimates:	
Families in Private Households	26,930
Husband-Wife Families	22,611
Lone-Parent Families	4,319
Aver. No. Persons per Family	3.0
Aver. No. Sons/Daughters at Home	1.1

HOUSING

2001 Estimates:	
Occupied Private Dwellings	36,552
Owned	26,141
Rented	10,301
Band Housing	110
Single-Detached House	21,906
Semi-Detached House	2,176
Row Houses	2,842
Apartment, 5+ Storeys	643
Owned Apartment, 5+ Storeys	74
Apartment, 5 or Fewer Storeys	5,203
Apartment, Detached Duplex	1,442
Other Single-Attached	50
Movable Dwellings	2,290

VEHICLES

2001 Estimates:	
Model Yrs. '81-'96, No.	43,671
% Total	85.10
Model Yrs. '97-'98, No.	5,022
% Total	9.79
'99 Vehicles registered in Model Yr. '99, No.	2,622
% Total	5.11
Total No. '81-'99	51,315

LEGAL MARITAL STATUS

2001 Estimates: (Age 15+)	
Single (Never Married)	22,250
Legally Married (Not Separated)	38,794
Legally Married (Separated)	2,547
Widowed	3,900
Divorced	6,772

PSYTE CATEGORIES

2001 Estimates	No. of House-holds	% of Total Hhds.	Index
Mortgaged in Suburbia	619	1.69	122
Technocrafts & Bureaucrats	1,209	3.31	118
Boomers & Teens	767	2.10	117
Small City Elite	6,221	17.02	993
Old Bungalow Burbs	507	1.39	84
Aging Erudites	296	0.81	54
Satellite Suburbs	1,222	3.34	117
Kindergarten Boom	665	1.82	69
Blue Collar Winners	2,774	7.59	301
Old Towns' New Fringe	6,415	17.55	448
The New Frontier	37	0.10	7
Rustic Prosperity	296	0.81	45
Conservative Homebodies	2,149	5.88	163
High Rise Sunsets	220	0.60	42

Kamloops
(Census Agglomeration)
(Cont'd)

2001 Estimates	No. of House-holds	% of Total Hhds.	Index
Young City Singles	2,124	5.81	253
Old Leafy Towns	397	1.09	42
Town Renters	412	1.13	130
Nesters & Young Homesteaders	6,751	18.47	791
Quiet Towns	244	0.67	31
Rod & Rifle	466	1.27	55
Big Country Families	211	0.58	40
Struggling Downtowns	752	2.06	65
Aged Pensioners	1,552	4.25	319

FINANCIAL P$YTE

2001 Estimates	No. of House-holds	% of Total Hhds.	Index
Four Star Investors	767	2.10	42
Successful Suburbanites	1,828	5.00	75
Canadian Comfort	10,217	27.95	288
Urban Heights	296	0.81	19
Miners & Credit-Liners	544	1.49	47
Mortgages & Minivans	665	1.82	28
Tractors & Tradelines	6,711	18.36	321
Bills & Wills	2,546	6.97	84
Revolving Renters	6,971	19.07	415
Rural Family Blues	677	1.85	23
Limited Budgets	244	0.67	21
Towering Debt	3,288	9.00	115
Senior Survivors	1,552	4.25	225

HOME LANGUAGE

2001 Estimates:		% Total
English	88,132	95.83
French	180	0.20
Chinese	401	0.44
German	118	0.13
Italian	641	0.70
Japanese	93	0.10
Polish	48	0.05
Punjabi	895	0.97
Spanish	64	0.07
Tagalog (Pilipino)	72	0.08
Ukrainian	54	0.06
Vietnamese	107	0.12
Other Languages	322	0.35
Multiple Responses	844	0.92
Total	91,971	100.00

BUILDING PERMITS

	1999	1998 $000	1997
Value	72,404	80,582	94,241

HOMES BUILT

	1999	1998	1997
No	299	348	622

TAXATION

Income Class:	1997	% Total
Under $5,000	7,640	12.38
$5,000-$10,000	8,110	13.14
$10,000-$15,000	8,840	14.32
$15,000-$20,000	5,850	9.48
$20,000-$25,000	4,670	7.57
$25,000-$30,000	4,340	7.03
$30,000-$40,000	7,450	12.07
$40,000-$50,000	5,330	8.64
$50,000 +	9,500	15.39
Total Returns, No.	61,720	
Total Income, $000	1,707,125	
Total Taxable Returns	43,510	
Total Tax, $000	320,540	
Average Income, $	27,659	
Average Tax, $	7,367	

VITAL STATISTICS

	1997	1996	1995	1994
Births	937	988	1,028	1,023
Deaths	630	563	554	530
Natural Increase	307	425	474	493
Marriages	531	519	529	556

Note: Latest available data.

DAILY NEWSPAPER(S)

	Circulation Average Paid
The Kamloops Daily News	14,891

COMMUNITY NEWSPAPER(S)

	Total Circulation
Kamloops: Kamloops This Week Wed/Fri/Sun.	29,457

RADIO STATION(S)

	Power
CBUF-FM	250w
CBYK-FM	n.a.
CFJC	25,000w
CHNL	25,000w
CIFM-FM	5,000w
CKRV-FM	n.a.

TELEVISION STATION(S)

BCI-TV
CBUFT-TV
CFJC-TV
CHAN-TV
CHKM-TV

Kelowna
(Census Agglomeration)

The Census Agglomeration of Kelowna includes: Kelowna, C; Central Okanagan, Subd. A, SRD; Central Okanagan, Subd. B, SRD; Lake Country, DM; Peachland, DM; Tsinstikeptum 9, R; plus two smaller areas. All are in Central Okanagan Regional District.

POPULATION

July 1, 2001 Estimate	156,701
% Cdn. Total	0.50
% Change, '96 -'01	10.37
Avg. Annual Growth Rate, %	1.99
2003 Projected Population	164,646
2006 Projected Population	176,121
2001 Households Estimate	62,977
2003 Projected Households	66,087
2006 Projected Households	70,964

INCOME

% Above/Below National Average	-8
2001 Total Income Estimate	$3,029,380,000
% Cdn. Total	0.46
2001 Average Hhld. Income	$48,100
2001 Per Capita	$19,300
2003 Projected Total Income	$3,342,630,000
2006 Projected Total Income	$3,880,750,000

RETAIL SALES

% Above/Below National Average	+32
2001 Retail Sales Estimate	$1,845,870,000
% Cdn. Total	0.66
2001 per Household	$29,300
2001 per Capita	$11,800
2001 No. of Establishments	1,289
2003 Projected Retail Sales	$2,059,770,000
2006 Projected Retail Sales	$2,376,190,000

POPULATION

2001 Estimates:		
Total		156,701
Male		76,172
Female		80,529
Age Groups	Male	Female
0-4	4,588	4,386
5-9	5,042	4,712
10-14	5,399	5,038
15-19	5,236	5,002
20-24	4,913	4,968
25-29	5,020	5,131
30-34	5,416	5,708
35-39	5,815	6,233
40-44	5,881	6,223
45-49	5,468	5,713
50-54	4,544	4,812
55-59	3,785	4,113
60-64	3,432	3,741
65-69	3,282	3,665
70+	8,351	11,084

DAYTIME POPULATION

2001 Estimates:	
Working Population	70,538
At Home Population	86,164
Total	156,702

British Columbia

INCOME

2001 Estimates:	
Avg. Household Income	$48,103
Avg. Family Income	$52,961
Per Capita Income	$19,332
Male:	
Avg. Employment Income	$30,842
Avg. Employment Income (Full Time)	$42,479
Female:	
Avg. Employment Income	$18,926
Avg. Employment Income (Full Time)	$29,428

DISPOSABLE & DISCRETIONARY INCOME

2001 Estimates:	Per Hhld.
Disposable Income	$37,339
Discretionary Income 1 (minus Food & Shelter)	$25,343
Discretionary Income 2 (minus Food, Shelter, & Other Expenditures)	$17,642

LIQUID ASSETS

1999 Estimates:	Per Hhld.
Equity Investments	$65,351
Interest Bearing Investments	$61,549
Total Liquid Assets	$126,900

CREDIT DATA

July 2000:	
Pool of Credit	$1,574,892,699
Revolving Credit, No.	318,752
Fixed Loans, No.	79,845
Avg. Credit Limit, per Person	$12,504
Avg. Spent, per Person	$5,528
Satisfactory Ratings, No. per Person	3.04
Avg. No. of Cards, per Person	1.10

LABOUR FORCE

2001 Estimates:	
Male:	
In the Labour Force	41,014
Participation Rate	67.1
Employed	37,788
Unemployed	3,226
Unemployment Rate	7.9
Not in Labour Force	20,129
Female:	
In the Labour Force	37,024
Participation Rate	55.8
Employed	33,946
Unemployed	3,078
Unemployment Rate	8.3
Not in Labour Force	29,369

British Columbia

Kelowna
(Census Agglomeration)
(Cont'd)

OCCUPATIONS BY MAJOR GROUPS

2001 Estimates:	Male	Female
Management	4,972	2,221
Business, Finance & Admin.	3,310	10,224
Natural & Applied Sciences & Related	2,308	259
Health	702	3,043
Social Sciences, Gov't Services & Religion	740	1,166
Education	942	1,365
Arts, Culture, Recreation & Sport	758	926
Sales & Service	9,123	13,947
Trades, Transport & Equipment Operators & Related	11,227	712
Primary Industries	2,696	1,113
Processing, Mfg. & Utilities	3,339	879

LEVEL OF SCHOOLING

2001 Estimates:
Population 15 years +	127,536
Less than Grade 9	9,660
Grades 9-13 w/o Certif.	32,821
Grade 9-13 with Certif.	15,614
Trade Certif. /Dip.	5,388
Non-Univ. w/o Certif./Dip.	8,623
Non-Univ. with Certif./Dip.	28,891
Univ. w/o Degree	15,435
Univ. w/o Degree/Certif.	7,033
Univ. with Certif.	8,402
Univ. with Degree	11,104

AVERAGE HOUSEHOLD EXPENDITURES

2001 Estimates:
Food	$5,541
Shelter	$8,373
Clothing	$1,896
Transportation	$5,948
Health & Personal Care	$1,744
Recr'n, Read'g & Education	$3,318
Taxes & Securities	$12,150
Other	$7,792
Total Expenditures	$46,762

PRIVATE HOUSEHOLDS

2001 Estimates:
Private Households, Total	62,977
Pop. in Private Households	153,722
Average no. per Household	2.4

FAMILIES

2001 Estimates:
Families in Private Households	46,307
Husband-Wife Families	40,321
Lone-Parent Families	5,986
Aver. No. Persons per Family	2.8
Aver. No. Sons/Daughters at Home	1.0

HOUSING

2001 Estimates:
Occupied Private Dwellings	62,977
Owned	45,980
Rented	16,854
Band Housing	143
Single-Detached House	39,500
Semi-Detached House	2,511
Row Houses	3,516
Apartment, 5+ Storeys	525
Owned Apartment, 5+ Storeys	194
Apartment, 5 or Fewer Storeys	10,333
Apartment, Detached Duplex	2,650
Other Single-Attached	149
Movable Dwellings	3,793

VEHICLES

2001 Estimates:
Model Yrs. '81-'96, No.	74,695
% Total	83.20
Model Yrs. '97-'98, No.	9,335
% Total	10.40
'99 Vehicles registered in Model Yr. '99, No.	5,749
% Total	6.40
Total No. '81-'99.	89,779

LEGAL MARITAL STATUS

2001 Estimates: (Age 15+)
Single (Never Married)	32,020
Legally Married (Not Separated)	71,549
Legally Married (Separated)	4,695
Widowed	8,450
Divorced	10,822

PSYTE CATEGORIES

2001 Estimates	No. of House-holds	% of Total Hhds.	Index
Suburban Executives	115	0.18	13
Mortgaged in Suburbia	157	0.25	18
Technocrafts & Bureaucrats	415	0.66	23
Boomers & Teens	2,595	4.12	230
Small City Elite	7,061	11.21	654
Old Bungalow Burbs	547	0.87	52
Suburban Nesters	182	0.29	18
Aging Erudites	817	1.30	86
Satellite Suburbs	1,305	2.07	72
Kindergarten Boom	1,543	2.45	93
Blue Collar Winners	5,996	9.52	378
Old Towns' New Fringe	10,381	16.48	421
Conservative Homebodies	1,557	2.47	69
High Rise Sunsets	2,532	4.02	281
Young Urban Mix	776	1.23	58
University Enclaves	2,840	4.51	221
Young City Singles	2,168	3.44	150
Old Leafy Towns	5,637	8.95	350
Town Renters	364	0.58	67
Nesters & Young Homesteaders	7,519	11.94	512
Quiet Towns	141	0.22	11
Rod & Rifle	609	0.97	42
Big Country Families	305	0.48	34
Struggling Downtowns	4,196	6.66	212
Aged Pensioners	2,754	4.37	329

FINANCIAL P$YTE

2001 Estimates	No. of House-holds	% of Total Hhds.	Index
Four Star Investors	2,710	4.30	86
Successful Suburbanites	572	0.91	14
Canadian Comfort	14,544	23.09	238
Urban Heights	817	1.30	30
Miners & Credit-Liners	547	0.87	27
Mortgages & Minivans	1,543	2.45	37
Tractors & Tradelines	10,381	16.48	288
Bills & Wills	7,970	12.66	153
Revolving Renters	10,051	15.96	347
Young Urban Struggle	2,840	4.51	95
Rural Family Blues	914	1.45	18
Limited Budgets	141	0.22	7
Towering Debt	6,728	10.68	137
Senior Survivors	2,754	4.37	232

HOME LANGUAGE

2001 Estimates:		% Total
English	150,206	95.86
French	730	0.47
Chinese	134	0.09
German	1,446	0.92
Hindi	140	0.09
Hungarian	318	0.20
Italian	206	0.13
Japanese	116	0.07
Persian (Farsi)	111	0.07
Polish	149	0.10
Punjabi	782	0.50
Spanish	202	0.13
Ukrainian	80	0.05
Other Languages	694	0.44
Multiple Responses	1,387	0.89
Total	156,701	100.00

BUILDING PERMITS

	1999	1998	1997
		$000	
Value	176,282	172,001	210,905

HOMES BUILT

	1999	1998	1997
No.	821	1,437	1,537

TAXATION

Income Class:	1997	% Total
Under $5,000	11,280	10.96
$5,000-$10,000	13,240	12.87
$10,000-$15,000	16,640	16.17
$15,000-$20,000	11,500	11.17
$20,000-$25,000	9,300	9.04
$25,000-$30,000	8,040	7.81
$30,000-$40,000	12,980	12.61
$40,000-$50,000	8,070	7.84
$50,000 +	11,910	11.57
Total Returns, No.	102,910	
Total Income, $000.	2,726,433	
Total Taxable Returns	72,520	
Total Tax, $000	482,382	
Average Income, $	26,493	
Average Tax, $	6,652	

VITAL STATISTICS

	1997	1996	1995	1994
Births	1,463	1,467	1,587	1,538
Deaths	1,078	1,067	1,058	1,000
Natural Increase	385	400	529	538
Marriages	842	878	817	803

Note: Latest available data.

DAILY NEWSPAPER(S)

	Circulation Average Paid
Daily Courier	
Sat	18,144
Sun.	16,299
Mon-Fri	17,026

COMMUNITY NEWSPAPER(S)

	Total Circulation
Kelowna: Capital News	
Wed	45,811
Fri	46,883
Sun.	49,557
Kelowna: Capital News, Showcase	
Wed	45,811
Peachland: Peachland Signal	1,231

RADIO STATION(S)

	Power
CBTK-FM	10,000w
CBUF-FM	1,000w
CHSU-FM	n.a.
CILK-FM	11,000w
CKBL	10,000w
CKLZ-FM	36,000w
CKOV	5,000w

TELEVISION STATION(S)

CBUFT-TV
CHAN-TV
CHBC-TV
CHKL-TV

Kitimat
(Census Agglomeration)

The Census Agglomeration of Kitimat consists solely of Kitimat, DM, in Kitimat-Stikine Regional District.

POPULATION

July 1, 2001 Estimate	10,573
% Cdn. Total	0.03
% Change, '96 -'01	-8.83
Avg. Annual Growth Rate, %	-1.83
2003 Projected Population	10,020
2006 Projected Population	9,161
2001 Households Estimate	4,005
2003 Projected Households	3,912
2006 Projected Households	3,738

INCOME

% Above/Below National Average	+18
2001 Total Income Estimate	$262,800,000
% Cdn. Total	0.04
2001 Average Hhld. Income	$65,600
2001 Per Capita	$24,900
2003 Projected Total Income	$269,260,000
2006 Projected Total Income	$275,090,000

RETAIL SALES

% Above/Below National Average	-18
2001 Retail Sales Estimate	$77,690,000
% Cdn. Total	0.03
2001 per Household	$19,400
2001 per Capita	$7,300
2001 No. of Establishments	61
2003 Projected Retail Sales	$78,920,000
2006 Projected Retail Sales	$78,500,000

POPULATION

2001 Estimates:

Total	10,573
Male	5,436
Female	5,137

Age Groups	Male	Female
0-4	328	296
5-9	383	353
10-14	440	431
15-19	471	455
20-24	401	383
25-29	319	322
30-34	327	340
35-39	412	412
40-44	454	465
45-49	470	435
50-54	420	360
55-59	329	275
60-64	244	207
65-69	190	160
70+	248	243

DAYTIME POPULATION

2001 Estimates:

Working Population	5,104
At Home Population	5,469
Total	10,573

INCOME

2001 Estimates:

Avg. Household Income	$65,618
Avg. Family Income	$70,855
Per Capita Income	$24,856

Male:

Avg. Employment Income	$49,871
Avg. Employment Income (Full Time)	$60,784

Female:

Avg. Employment Income	$21,231
Avg. Employment Income (Full Time)	$36,060

DISPOSABLE & DISCRETIONARY INCOME

2001 Estimates:	Per Hhld.
Disposable Income	$49,661
Discretionary Income 1 (minus Food & Shelter)	$36,710
Discretionary Income 2 (minus Food, Shelter, & Other Expenditures)	$25,880

LIQUID ASSETS

1999 Estimates:	Per Hhld.
Equity Investments	$102,001
Interest Bearing Investments	$87,359
Total Liquid Assets	$189,360

CREDIT DATA

July 2000:

Pool of Credit	$116,295,309
Revolving Credit, No.	18,778
Fixed Loans, No.	5,921
Avg. Credit Limit, per Person	$15,105
Avg. Spent, per Person	$7,272
Satisfactory Ratings, No. per Person	3.04
Avg. No. of Cards, per Person	1.09

LABOUR FORCE

2001 Estimates:

Male:

In the Labour Force	3,202
Participation Rate	74.7
Employed	3,039
Unemployed	163
Unemployment Rate	5.1
Not in Labour Force	1,083

Female:

In the Labour Force	2,377
Participation Rate	58.6
Employed	2,085
Unemployed	292
Unemployment Rate	12.3
Not in Labour Force	1,680

OCCUPATIONS BY MAJOR GROUPS

2001 Estimates:	Male	Female
Management	183	169
Business, Finance & Admin.	103	433
Natural & Applied Sciences & Related	247	40
Health	19	162
Social Sciences, Gov't Services & Religion	19	46
Education	53	132
Arts, Culture, Recreation & Sport	47	49
Sales & Service	368	987
Trades, Transport & Equipment Operators & Related	919	66
Primary Industries	90	30
Processing, Mfg. & Utilities	1,097	107

LEVEL OF SCHOOLING

2001 Estimates:

Population 15 years +	8,342
Less than Grade 9	834
Grades 9-13 w/o Certif.	2,481
Grade 9-13 with Certif.	1,407
Trade Certif./Dip.	240
Non-Univ. w/o Certif./Dip.	683
Non-Univ. with Certif./Dip.	1,580
Univ. w/o Degree	620
Univ. w/o Degree/Certif.	288
Univ. with Certif.	332
Univ. with Degree	497

AVERAGE HOUSEHOLD EXPENDITURES

2001 Estimates:

Food	$6,860
Shelter	$8,504
Clothing	$2,745
Transportation	$8,600
Health & Personal Care	$2,307
Recr'n, Read'g & Education	$5,131
Taxes & Securities	$16,234
Other	$10,368
Total Expenditures	$60,749

PRIVATE HOUSEHOLDS

2001 Estimates:

Private Households, Total	4,005
Pop. in Private Households	10,480
Average no. per Household	2.6

FAMILIES

2001 Estimates:

Families in Private Households	3,141
Husband-Wife Families	2,749
Lone-Parent Families	392
Aver. No. Persons per Family	3.2
Aver. No. Sons/Daughters at Home	1.3

HOUSING

2001 Estimates:

Occupied Private Dwellings	4,005
Owned	3,058
Rented	947
Single-Detached House	2,550
Semi-Detached House	426
Row Houses	326
Apartment, 5 or Fewer Storeys	527
Apartment, Detached Duplex	31
Other Single-Attached	58
Movable Dwellings	87

VEHICLES

2001 Estimates:

Model Yrs. '81-'96, No.	4,985
% Total	84.32
Model Yrs. '97-'98, No.	660
% Total	11.16
'99 Vehicles registered in Model Yr. '99, No.	267
% Total	4.52
Total No. '81-'99	5,912

LEGAL MARITAL STATUS

2001 Estimates: (Age 15+)

Single (Never Married)	2,452
Legally Married (Not Separated)	4,826
Legally Married (Separated)	284
Widowed	263
Divorced	517

PSYTE CATEGORIES

2001 Estimates	No. of House -holds	% of Total Hhds.	Index
Town Boomers	277	6.92	682
Northern Lights	1,932	48.24	9,746
The New Frontier	1,592	39.75	2,635
Pick-ups & Dirt Bikes	87	2.17	260
Nesters & Young Homesteaders	117	2.92	125

FINANCIAL PSYTE

2001 Estimates	No. of House -holds	% of Total Hhds.	Index
Successful Suburbanites	1,932	48.24	727
Canadian Comfort	277	6.92	71
Miners & Credit-Liners	1,592	39.75	1,256
Country Credit	87	2.17	32
Revolving Renters	117	2.92	63

HOME LANGUAGE

2001 Estimates:		% Total
English	9,186	86.88
French	128	1.21
Chinese	76	0.72
Czech	24	0.23
Finnish	23	0.22
German	49	0.46
Greek	14	0.13
Hungarian	13	0.12
Italian	57	0.54
Japanese	24	0.23
Persian (Farsi)	14	0.13
Polish	76	0.72
Portuguese	501	4.74
Punjabi	173	1.64
Romanian	15	0.14
Tagalog (Pilipino)	9	0.09
Other Languages	9	0.09
Multiple Responses	182	1.72
Total	10,573	100.00

BUILDING PERMITS

	1999	1998	1997
		$000	
Value	7,827	8,335	26,296

HOMES BUILT

	1999	1998	1997
No.	25	17	8

TAXATION

Income Class:	1997	% Total
Under $5,000	1,120	14.91
$5,000-$10,000	770	10.25
$10,000-$15,000	710	9.45
$15,000-$20,000	480	6.39
$20,000-$25,000	370	4.93
$25,000-$30,000	340	4.53
$30,000-$40,000	630	8.39
$40,000-$50,000	530	7.06
$50,000 +	2,590	34.49
Total Returns, No.	7,510	
Total Income, $000	269,961	
Total Taxable Returns	5,480	
Total Tax, $000	62,454	
Average Income, $	35,947	
Average Tax, $	11,397	

VITAL STATISTICS

	1997	1996	1995	1994
Births	125	150	130	143
Deaths	38	41	44	41
Natural Increase	87	109	86	102
Marriages	38	46	35	45

Note: Latest available data.

British Columbia

Kitimat
(Census Agglomeration)
(Cont'd)

COMMUNITY NEWSPAPER(S)

	Total Circulation
Kitimat: Northern Sentinel	2,249
Kitimat: Northern Sentinel's Weekend Advertiser	n.a.
Kitimat: Northern Sentinel (suppl.), TV & Video Scanner	n.a.

RADIO STATION(S)

	Power
CBUF-FM	100w
CBUK-FM	n.a.
CFNR-FM	50w
CJFW-FM	n.a.
CKTK	1,000w

TELEVISION STATION(S)

CATV
CBUFT-TV
CFTK-TV

Nanaimo
(Census Agglomeration)

The Census Agglomeration of Nanaimo includes: Nanaimo, C; Nanaimo, Subd. A, SRD; plus several smaller areas. All are in Nanaimo Regional District.

POPULATION

July 1, 2001 Estimate	92,927
% Cdn. Total	0.30
% Change, '96 -'01	4.60
Avg. Annual Growth Rate, %	0.90
2003 Projected Population	94,797
2006 Projected Population	96,822
2001 Households Estimate	38,199
2003 Projected Households	38,986
2006 Projected Households	40,086

INCOME

% Above/Below National Average	-9
2001 Total Income Estimate	$1,788,260,000
% Cdn. Total	0.27
2001 Average Hhld. Income	$46,800
2001 Per Capita	$19,200
2003 Projected Total Income	$1,918,420,000
2006 Projected Total Income	$2,128,300,000

RETAIL SALES

% Above/Below National Average	-5
2001 Retail Sales Estimate	$788,910,000
% Cdn. Total	0.28
2001 per Household	$20,700
2001 per Capita	$8,500
2001 No. of Establishments	715
2003 Projected Retail Sales	$873,560,000
2006 Projected Retail Sales	$992,820,000

POPULATION

2001 Estimates:

Total		92,927
Male		45,499
Female		47,428

Age Groups	Male	Female
0-4	2,759	2,643
5-9	2,981	2,889
10-14	3,199	3,169
15-19	3,265	3,167
20-24	3,093	3,042
25-29	2,971	3,053
30-34	3,169	3,308
35-39	3,468	3,645
40-44	3,612	3,816
45-49	3,508	3,641
50-54	2,998	3,084
55-59	2,419	2,437
60-64	2,004	2,022
65-69	1,799	1,896
70+	4,254	5,616

DAYTIME POPULATION

2001 Estimates:

Working Population	41,326
At Home Population	51,600
Total	92,926

INCOME

2001 Estimates:

Avg. Household Income	$46,814
Avg. Family Income	$52,723
Per Capita Income	$19,244
Male:	
Avg. Employment Income	$31,991
Avg. Employment Income (Full Time)	$42,953
Female:	
Avg. Employment Income	$19,715
Avg. Employment Income (Full Time)	$30,018

DISPOSABLE & DISCRETIONARY INCOME

2001 Estimates:	Per Hhld.
Disposable Income	$36,363
Discretionary Income 1 (minus Food & Shelter)	$24,619
Discretionary Income 2 (minus Food, Shelter, & Other Expenditures)	$17,044

LIQUID ASSETS

1999 Estimates:	Per Hhld.
Equity Investments	$60,203
Interest Bearing Investments	$59,358
Total Liquid Assets	$119,561

CREDIT DATA

July 2000:

Pool of Credit	$938,808,947
Revolving Credit, No.	189,254
Fixed Loans, No.	51,997
Avg. Credit Limit, per Person	$12,053
Avg. Spent, per Person	$5,280
Satisfactory Ratings, No. per Person	2.98
Avg. No. of Cards, per Person	0.98

LABOUR FORCE

2001 Estimates:

Male:	
In the Labour Force	24,839
Participation Rate	67.9
Employed	22,188
Unemployed	2,651
Unemployment Rate	10.7
Not in Labour Force	11,721
Female:	
In the Labour Force	21,725
Participation Rate	56.1
Employed	19,534
Unemployed	2,191
Unemployment Rate	10.1
Not in Labour Force	17,002

OCCUPATIONS BY MAJOR GROUPS

2001 Estimates:	Male	Female
Management	2,681	1,194
Business, Finance & Admin.	1,704	6,196
Natural & Applied Sciences & Related	1,859	276
Health	432	1,872
Social Sciences, Gov't Services & Religion	470	660
Education	631	956
Arts, Culture, Recreation & Sport	400	564
Sales & Service	5,280	8,171
Trades, Transport & Equipment Operators & Related	7,227	301
Primary Industries	1,665	291
Processing, Mfg. & Utilities	1,499	209

LEVEL OF SCHOOLING

2001 Estimates:

Population 15 years +	75,287
Less than Grade 9	4,250
Grades 9-13 w/o Certif.	19,752
Grade 9-13 with Certif.	9,225
Trade Certif./Dip.	3,523
Non-Univ. w/o Certif./Dip.	5,301
Non-Univ. with Certif./Dip.	16,861
Univ. w/o Degree	9,113
Univ. w/o Degree/Certif.	4,067
Univ. with Certif.	5,046
Univ. with Degree	7,262

AVERAGE HOUSEHOLD EXPENDITURES

2001 Estimates:

Food	$5,521
Shelter	$8,172
Clothing	$1,896
Transportation	$5,821
Health & Personal Care	$1,750
Recr'n, Read'g & Education	$3,335
Taxes & Securities	$11,490
Other	$7,690
Total Expenditures	$45,675

PRIVATE HOUSEHOLDS

2001 Estimates:

Private Households, Total	38,199
Pop. in Private Households	91,128
Average no. per Household	2.4

FAMILIES

2001 Estimates:

Families in Private Households	27,182
Husband-Wife Families	22,740
Lone-Parent Families	4,442
Aver. No. Persons per Family	2.8
Aver. No. Sons/Daughters at Home	1.0

HOUSING

2001 Estimates:

Occupied Private Dwellings	38,199
Owned	26,601
Rented	11,532
Band Housing	66
Single-Detached House	25,993
Semi-Detached House	1,329
Row Houses	1,610
Apartment, 5+ Storeys	889
Owned Apartment, 5+ Storeys	311
Apartment, 5 or Fewer Storeys	5,621
Apartment, Detached Duplex	1,621
Other Single-Attached	78
Movable Dwellings	1,058

VEHICLES

2001 Estimates:

Model Yrs. '81-'96, No.	43,624
% Total	85.81
Model Yrs. '97-'98, No.	4,297
% Total	8.45
'99 Vehicles registered in Model Yr. '99, No.	2,916
% Total	5.74
Total No. '81-'99	50,837

LEGAL MARITAL STATUS

2001 Estimates: (Age 15+)

Single (Never Married)	21,001
Legally Married (Not Separated)	39,320
Legally Married (Separated)	2,982
Widowed	4,841
Divorced	7,143

PSYTE CATEGORIES

2001 Estimates	No. of House-holds	% of Total Hhds.	Index
Mortgaged in Suburbia	408	1.07	77
Technocrafts & Bureaucrats	808	2.12	75
Boomers & Teens	412	1.08	60
Small City Elite	7,145	18.70	1,091
Aging Erudites	483	1.26	84
Satellite Suburbs	1,197	3.13	109
Blue Collar Winners	756	1.98	79
Old Towns' New Fringe	5,530	14.48	370
Rustic Prosperity	153	0.40	22
Conservative Homebodies	1,537	4.02	112
High Rise Sunsets	712	1.86	130
Young Urban Mix	331	0.87	41
University Enclaves	1,412	3.70	181
Young City Singles	3,185	8.34	364
Old Leafy Towns	4,456	11.67	456
Town Renters	570	1.49	173
Nesters & Young Homesteaders	4,807	12.58	539
Rod & Rifle	55	0.14	6
Big Country Families	168	0.44	31
Struggling Downtowns	2,389	6.25	199
Aged Pensioners	1,426	3.73	281

Nanaimo
(Census Agglomeration)
(Cont'd)

FINANCIAL P$YTE

2001 Estimates	No. of House-holds	% of Total Hhds.	Index
Four Star Investors	412	1.08	21
Successful Suburbanites	1,216	3.18	48
Canadian Comfort	9,098	23.82	245
Urban Heights	483	1.26	29
Tractors & Tradelines	5,683	14.88	260
Bills & Wills	6,324	16.56	200
Revolving Renters	5,519	14.45	314
Young Urban Struggle	1,412	3.70	78
Rural Family Blues	223	0.58	7
Towering Debt	6,144	16.08	206
Senior Survivors	1,426	3.73	198

HOME LANGUAGE

2001 Estimates:		% Total
English	88,559	95.30
French	422	0.45
Chinese	445	0.48
Croatian	71	0.08
Czech	54	0.06
Finnish	56	0.06
German	96	0.10
Hungarian	83	0.09
Italian	101	0.11
Persian (Farsi)	59	0.06
Polish	127	0.14
Punjabi	799	0.86
Spanish	108	0.12
Tagalog (Pilipino)	61	0.07
Vietnamese	875	0.94
Other Languages	369	0.40
Multiple Responses	642	0.69
Total	92,927	100.00

BUILDING PERMITS

	1999	1998	1997
		$000	
Value	133,903	112,271	97,873

HOMES BUILT

	1999	1998	1997
No	414	734	971

TAXATION

Income Class:	1997	% Total
Under $5,000	7,180	11.66
$5,000-$10,000	8,340	13.54
$10,000-$15,000	9,630	15.64
$15,000-$20,000	6,100	9.91
$20,000-$25,000	4,930	8.01
$25,000-$30,000	4,560	7.41
$30,000-$40,000	7,710	12.52
$40,000-$50,000	5,100	8.28
$50,000 +	8,040	13.06
Total Returns, No.	61,580	
Total Income, $000	1,620,199	
Total Taxable Returns	42,640	
Total Tax, $000	287,860	
Average Income, $	26,310	
Average Tax, $	6,751	

VITAL STATISTICS

	1997	1996	1995	1994
Births	869	1,038	936	1,007
Deaths	709	688	653	670
Natural Increase	160	350	283	337
Marriages	457	462	475	529

Note: Latest available data.

DAILY NEWSPAPER(S)

	Circulation Average Paid
Daily News	8,888

COMMUNITY NEWSPAPER(S)

	Total Circulation
Nanaimo: Nanaimo News Bulletin Mon/Thu	31,402
Nanaimo: Harbour City Star	
Tue	34,738
Thu	34,736
Sat	34,741

RADIO STATION(S)

	Power
CKEG	10,000w
CKWV-FM	1,300w

Nanaimo, Subd. B
(Subdivision of Regional District)
In Nanaimo Regional District.

POPULATION

July 1, 2001 Estimate	23,585
% Cdn. Total	0.08
% Change, '96 -'01	14.00
Avg. Annual Growth Rate, %	2.66
2003 Projected Population	25,172
2006 Projected Population	27,357
2001 Households Estimate	9,877
2003 Projected Households	10,551
2006 Projected Households	11,534

INCOME

% Above/Below National Average	-5
2001 Total Income Estimate	$474,020,000
% Cdn. Total	0.07
2001 Average Hhld. Income	$48,000
2001 Per Capita	$20,100
2003 Projected Total Income	$533,420,000
2006 Projected Total Income	$631,570,000

RETAIL SALES

% Above/Below National Average	-57
2001 Retail Sales Estimate	$91,050,000
% Cdn. Total	0.03
2001 per Household	$9,200
2001 per Capita	$3,900
2001 No. of Establishments	140
2003 Projected Retail Sales	$102,960,000
2006 Projected Retail Sales	$121,190,000

POPULATION

2001 Estimates:		
Total		23,585
Male		11,765
Female		11,820
Age Groups	Male	Female
0-4	609	581
5-9	697	672
10-14	790	750
15-19	756	734
20-24	646	635
25-29	602	599
30-34	663	703
35-39	826	874
40-44	913	953
45-49	894	918
50-54	790	819
55-59	704	742
60-64	682	706
65-69	693	660
70+	1,500	1,474

DAYTIME POPULATION

2001 Estimates:	
Working Population	n.a.
At Home Population	13,631
Total	13,631

INCOME

2001 Estimates:	
Avg. Household Income	$47,992
Avg. Family Income	$52,787
Per Capita Income	$20,098
Male:	
Avg. Employment Income	$31,130
Avg. Employment Income (Full Time)	$43,339
Female:	
Avg. Employment Income	$18,766
Avg. Employment Income (Full Time)	$28,911

British Columbia

DISPOSABLE & DISCRETIONARY INCOME

2001 Estimates:	Per Hhld.
Disposable Income	$37,271
Discretionary Income 1 (minus Food & Shelter)	$25,393
Discretionary Income 2 (minus Food, Shelter, & Other Expenditures)	$17,349

LIQUID ASSETS

1999 Estimates:	Per Hhld.
Equity Investments	$65,265
Interest Bearing Investments	$59,294
Total Liquid Assets	$124,559

CREDIT DATA

July 2000:	
Pool of Credit	$206,588,691
Revolving Credit, No.	38,925
Fixed Loans, No.	9,826
Avg. Credit Limit, per Person	$12,657
Avg. Spent, per Person	$5,251
Satisfactory Ratings, No. per Person	2.90
Avg. No. of Cards, per Person	0.99

LABOUR FORCE

2001 Estimates:	
Male:	
In the Labour Force	5,867
Participation Rate	60.7
Employed	5,295
Unemployed	572
Unemployment Rate	9.7
Not in Labour Force	3,802
Female:	
In the Labour Force	5,257
Participation Rate	53.5
Employed	4,668
Unemployed	589
Unemployment Rate	11.2
Not in Labour Force	4,560

OCCUPATIONS BY MAJOR GROUPS

2001 Estimates:	Male	Female
Management	648	302
Business, Finance & Admin.	197	1,352
Natural & Applied Sciences & Related	402	63
Health	102	495
Social Sciences, Gov't Services & Religion	84	119
Education	126	167
Arts, Culture, Recreation & Sport	110	139
Sales & Service	981	1,934
Trades, Transport & Equipment Operators & Related	2,046	198
Primary Industries	752	205
Processing, Mfg. & Utilities	275	65

British Columbia

Nanaimo, Subd. B
(Subdivision of Regional District)
(Cont'd)

LEVEL OF SCHOOLING

2001 Estimates:
Population 15 years +	19,486
Less than Grade 9	839
Grades 9-13 w/o Certif.	5,348
Grade 9-13 with Certif.	2,361
Trade Certif. /Dip.	907
Non-Univ. w/o Certif./Dip.	1,546
Non-Univ. with Certif./Dip.	4,795
Univ. w/o Degree	1,844
Univ. w/o Degree/Certif.	733
Univ. with Certif.	1,111
Univ. with Degree	1,846

AVERAGE HOUSEHOLD EXPENDITURES

2001 Estimates:
Food	$5,666
Shelter	$8,186
Clothing	$1,761
Transportation	$6,400
Health & Personal Care	$1,751
Recr'n, Read'g & Education	$3,487
Taxes & Securities	$12,030
Other	$7,455
Total Expenditures	$46,736

PRIVATE HOUSEHOLDS

2001 Estimates:
Private Households, Total	9,877
Pop. in Private Households	23,197
Average no. per Household	2.3

FAMILIES

2001 Estimates:
Families in Private Households	7,712
Husband-Wife Families	6,923
Lone-Parent Families	789
Aver. No. Persons per Family	2.7
Aver. No. Sons/Daughters at Home	0.8

HOUSING

2001 Estimates:
Occupied Private Dwellings	9,877
Owned	8,194
Rented	1,683
Single-Detached House	8,201
Semi-Detached House	200
Row Houses	124
Apartment, 5 or Fewer Storeys	103
Apartment, Detached Duplex	48
Other Single-Attached	12
Movable Dwellings	1,189

VEHICLES

2001 Estimates:
Model Yrs. '81-'96, No.	12,438
% Total	89.00
Model Yrs. '97-'98, No.	1,037
% Total	7.42
'99 Vehicles registered in Model Yr. '99, No.	501
% Total	3.58
Total No. '81-'99	13,976

LEGAL MARITAL STATUS

2001 Estimates: (Age 15+)
Single (Never Married)	4,010
Legally Married (Not Separated)	12,053
Legally Married (Separated)	679
Widowed	1,020
Divorced	1,724

PSYTE CATEGORIES

2001 Estimates	No. of House-holds	% of Total Hhds.	Index
Small City Elite	1,383	14.00	817
Blue Collar Winners	183	1.85	74
Old Towns' New Fringe	2,571	26.03	665
Old Leafy Towns	5,113	51.77	2,025
Nesters & Young Homesteaders	612	6.20	265

FINANÇIAL P$YTE

2001 Estimates	No. of House-holds	% of Total Hhds.	Index
Canadian Comfort	1,566	15.86	163
Tractors & Tradelines	2,571	26.03	455
Bills & Wills	5,113	51.77	625
Revolving Renters	612	6.20	135

HOME LANGUAGE

2001 Estimates:		% Total
English	23,251	98.58
French	69	0.29
Dutch	30	0.13
German	97	0.41
Slovak	12	0.05
Spanish	29	0.12
Multiple Responses	97	0.41
Total	23,585	100.00

BUILDING PERMITS

	1999	1998	1997
		$000	
Value	45,950	32,860	44,252

TAXATION

Income Class:	1997	% Total
Under $5,000	720	11.18
$5,000-$10,000	870	13.51
$10,000-$15,000	1,050	16.30
$15,000-$20,000	720	11.18
$20,000-$25,000	530	8.23
$25,000-$30,000	500	7.76
$30,000-$40,000	780	12.11
$40,000-$50,000	490	7.61
$50,000 +	800	12.42
Total Returns, No.	6,440	
Total Income, $000	173,884	
Total Taxable Returns	4,550	
Total Tax, $000	32,002	
Average Income, $	27,001	
Average Tax, $	7,033	

VITAL STATISTICS

	1997	1996	1995	1994
Births	140	140	162	155
Deaths	125	145	128	128
Natural Increase	15	-5	34	27
Marriages	82	86	81	77

Note: Latest available data.

Peace River, Subd. B
(Subdivision of Regional District)
In Peace River Regional District.

POPULATION

July 1, 2001 Estimate	11,474
% Cdn. Total	0.04
% Change, '96 -'01	7.11
Avg. Annual Growth Rate, %.	1.38
2003 Projected Population	11,722
2006 Projected Population	12,014
2001 Households Estimate	3,782
2003 Projected Households	3,944
2006 Projected Households	4,183

INCOME

% Above/Below National Average	-6
2001 Total Income Estimate	$226,470,000
% Cdn. Total	0.03
2001 Average Hhld. Income	$59,900
2001 Per Capita	$19,700
2003 Projected Total Income	$247,980,000
2006 Projected Total Income	$281,230,000

RETAIL SALES

% Above/Below National Average	-48
2001 Retail Sales Estimate	$53,750,000
% Cdn. Total	0.02
2001 per Household	$14,200
2001 per Capita	$4,700
2001 No. of Establishments	65
2003 Projected Retail Sales	$59,130,000
2006 Projected Retail Sales	$67,330,000

POPULATION

2001 Estimates:
Total	11,474
Male	5,882
Female	5,592

Age Groups	Male	Female
0-4	376	385
5-9	437	465
10-14	512	508
15-19	540	503
20-24	453	411
25-29	355	347
30-34	372	409
35-39	447	472
40-44	476	473
45-49	458	415
50-54	393	343
55-59	308	276
60-64	255	210
65-69	214	156
70+	286	219

DAYTIME POPULATION

2001 Estimates:
Working Population	2,032
At Home Population	5,721
Total	7,753

INCOME

2001 Estimates:
Avg. Household Income	$59,881
Avg. Family Income	$61,437
Per Capita Income	$19,738
Male:	
Avg. Employment Income	$36,733
Avg. Employment Income (Full Time)	$45,453
Female:	
Avg. Employment Income	$19,435
Avg. Employment Income (Full Time)	$29,251

DISPOSABLE & DISCRETIONARY INCOME

2001 Estimates:	Per Hhld.
Disposable Income	$46,012
Discretionary Income 1 (minus Food & Shelter)	$33,309
Discretionary Income 2 (minus Food, Shelter, & Other Expenditures)	$23,193

LIQUID ASSETS

1999 Estimates:	Per Hhld.
Equity Investments	$98,620
Interest Bearing Investments	$79,585
Total Liquid Assets	$178,205

CREDIT DATA

July 2000:
Pool of Credit	$102,748,151
Revolving Credit, No.	12,480
Fixed Loans, No.	6,800
Avg. Credit Limit, per Person	$15,803
Avg. Spent, per Person	$8,265
Satisfactory Ratings, No. per Person.	2.86
Avg. No. of Cards, per Person	0.90

LABOUR FORCE

2001 Estimates:
Male:	
In the Labour Force	3,745
Participation Rate	82.2
Employed	3,462
Unemployed	283
Unemployment Rate	7.6
Not in Labour Force	812
Female:	
In the Labour Force	2,517
Participation Rate	59.4
Employed	2,355
Unemployed	162
Unemployment Rate	6.4
Not in Labour Force	1,717

OCCUPATIONS BY MAJOR GROUPS

2001 Estimates:	Male	Female
Management	307	108
Business, Finance & Admin.	101	826
Natural & Applied Sciences & Related	147	21
Health	30	108
Social Sciences, Gov't Services & Religion	11	43
Education	42	101
Arts, Culture, Recreation & Sport	45	35
Sales & Service	379	814
Trades, Transport & Equipment Operators & Related	1,227	116
Primary Industries	1,070	333
Processing, Mfg. & Utilities	345	12

LEVEL OF SCHOOLING

2001 Estimates:
Population 15 years +	8,791
Less than Grade 9	1,178
Grades 9-13 w/o Certif.	2,854
Grade 9-13 with Certif.	1,074
Trade Certif. /Dip.	363
Non-Univ. w/o Certif./Dip.	715
Non-Univ. with Certif./Dip.	1,722
Univ. w/o Degree	484
Univ. w/o Degree/Certif.	236
Univ. with Certif.	248
Univ. with Degree	401

Peace River, Subd. B
(Subdivision of Regional District)
(Cont'd)

AVERAGE HOUSEHOLD EXPENDITURES

2001 Estimates:
Food	$6,849
Shelter	$8,189
Clothing	$2,712
Transportation	$7,726
Health & Personal Care	$2,345
Recr'n, Read'g & Education	$4,565
Taxes & Securities	$14,029
Other	$9,809
Total Expenditures	$56,224

PRIVATE HOUSEHOLDS

2001 Estimates:
Private Households, Total	3,782
Pop. in Private Households	11,248
Average no. per Household	3.0

FAMILIES

2001 Estimates:
Families in Private Households	3,226
Husband-Wife Families	3,052
Lone-Parent Families	174
Aver. No. Persons per Family	3.4
Aver. No. Sons/Daughters at Home	1.5

HOUSING

2001 Estimates:
Occupied Private Dwellings	3,782
Owned	3,174
Rented	555
Band Housing	53
Single-Detached House	3,137
Semi-Detached House	10
Row Houses	23
Apartment, 5 or Fewer Storeys	51
Apartment, Detached Duplex	23
Movable Dwellings	538

VEHICLES

2001 Estimates:
Model Yrs. '81-'96, No.	5,611
% Total	73.24
Model Yrs. '97-'98, No.	1,422
% Total	18.56
'99 Vehicles registered in Model Yr. '99, No.	628
% Total	8.20
Total No. '81-'99	7,661

LEGAL MARITAL STATUS

2001 Estimates: (Age 15+)
Single (Never Married)	2,415
Legally Married (Not Separated)	5,472
Legally Married (Separated)	195
Widowed	217
Divorced	492

PSYTE CATEGORIES

2001 Estimates	No. of House -holds	% of Total Hhds.	Index
Mortgaged in Suburbia	20	0.53	38
Town Boomers	1,103	29.16	2,877
The New Frontier	1,242	32.84	2,177
Pick-ups & Dirt Bikes	724	19.14	2,293
The Grain Belt	339	8.96	1,513
Big Country Families	326	8.62	604

FINANCIAL P$YTE

2001 Estimates	No. of House -holds	% of Total Hhds.	Index
Successful Suburbanites	20	0.53	8
Canadian Comfort	1,103	29.16	300
Miners & Credit-Liners	1,242	32.84	1,037
Country Credit	1,063	28.11	416
Rural Family Blues	326	8.62	107

HOME LANGUAGE

2001 Estimates:		% Total
English	10,333	90.06
Dutch	27	0.24
German	1,003	8.74
Norwegian	12	0.10
Russian	55	0.48
Other Languages	33	0.29
Multiple Responses	11	0.10
Total	11,474	100.00

BUILDING PERMITS

	1999	1998 $000	1997
Value	8,568	19,144	9,189

TAXATION

Income Class:	1997	% Total
Under $5,000	.690	19.55
$5,000-$10,000	.500	14.16
$10,000-$15,000	.490	13.88
$15,000-$20,000	.300	8.50
$20,000-$25,000	.250	7.08
$25,000-$30,000	.220	6.23
$30,000-$40,000	.360	10.20
$40,000-$50,000	.220	6.23
$50,000 +	.510	14.45
Total Returns, No.	3,530	
Total Income, $000	89,040	
Total Taxable Returns	2,170	
Total Tax, $000	16,267	
Average Income, $	25,224	
Average Tax, $	7,496	

VITAL STATISTICS

	1997	1996	1995	1994
Births	118	116	105	110
Deaths	24	20	14	22
Natural Increase	94	96	91	88
Marriages	27	43	26	23

Note: Latest available data.

Penticton
(Census Agglomeration)

The Census Agglomeration of Penticton includes: Penticton, C; Okanagan-Similkameen, Subd. A, SRD; plus one smaller area. All are in Okanagan-Similkameen Regional District.

POPULATION

July 1, 2001 Estimate	44,512
% Cdn. Total	0.14
% Change, '96 -'01	4.17
Avg. Annual Growth Rate, %	0.82
2003 Projected Population	45,140
2006 Projected Population	45,730
2001 Households Estimate	19,476
2003 Projected Households	19,751
2006 Projected Households	20,084

INCOME

% Above/Below National Average	-15
2001 Total Income Estimate	$793,570,000
% Cdn. Total	0.12
2001 Average Hhld. Income	$40,700
2001 Per Capita	$17,800
2003 Projected Total Income	$840,870,000
2006 Projected Total Income	$914,320,000

RETAIL SALES

% Above/Below National Average	+21
2001 Retail Sales Estimate	$481,130,000
% Cdn. Total	0.17
2001 per Household	$24,700
2001 per Capita	$10,800
2001 No. of Establishments	444
2003 Projected Retail Sales	$524,460,000
2006 Projected Retail Sales	$581,250,000

POPULATION

2001 Estimates:
Total		44,512
Male		21,331
Female		23,181
Age Groups	Male	Female
0-4	1,180	1,148
5-9	1,317	1,265
10-14	1,429	1,364
15-19	1,409	1,356
20-24	1,285	1,312
25-29	1,213	1,286
30-34	1,306	1,420
35-39	1,516	1,658
40-44	1,617	1,695
45-49	1,491	1,535
50-54	1,253	1,338
55-59	1,072	1,199
60-64	1,020	1,180
65-69	1,072	1,213
70+	3,151	4,212

DAYTIME POPULATION

2001 Estimates:
Working Population	18,025
At Home Population	26,487
Total	44,512

INCOME

2001 Estimates:
Avg. Household Income	$40,746
Avg. Family Income	$46,871
Per Capita Income	$17,828
Male:	
Avg. Employment Income	$27,808
Avg. Employment Income (Full Time)	$38,719
Female:	
Avg. Employment Income	$17,975
Avg. Employment Income (Full Time)	$27,539

DISPOSABLE & DISCRETIONARY INCOME

2001 Estimates:	Per Hhld.
Disposable Income	$31,845
Discretionary Income 1 (minus Food & Shelter)	$21,250
Discretionary Income 2 (minus Food, Shelter, & Other Expenditures)	$14,451

LIQUID ASSETS

1999 Estimates:	Per Hhld.
Equity Investments	$51,258
Interest Bearing Investments	$52,699
Total Liquid Assets	$103,957

CREDIT DATA

July 2000:	
Pool of Credit	$413,126,787
Revolving Credit, No.	87,449
Fixed Loans, No.	22,456
Avg. Credit Limit, per Person	$11,104
Avg. Spent, per Person	$4,619
Satisfactory Ratings, No. per Person	2.86
Avg. No. of Cards, per Person	1.03

LABOUR FORCE

2001 Estimates:	
Male:	
In the Labour Force	10,333
Participation Rate	59.4
Employed	9,392
Unemployed	941
Unemployment Rate	9.1
Not in Labour Force	7,072
Female:	
In the Labour Force	9,711
Participation Rate	50.0
Employed	8,857
Unemployed	854
Unemployment Rate	8.8
Not in Labour Force	9,693

OCCUPATIONS BY MAJOR GROUPS

2001 Estimates:	Male	Female
Management	1,171	605
Business, Finance & Admin.	716	2,413
Natural & Applied Sciences & Related	465	95
Health	213	912
Social Sciences, Gov't Services & Religion	138	317
Education	301	345
Arts, Culture, Recreation & Sport	198	173
Sales & Service	2,388	3,797
Trades, Transport & Equipment Operators & Related	2,604	112
Primary Industries	962	416
Processing, Mfg. & Utilities	994	253

British Columbia

Penticton
(Census Agglomeration)
(Cont'd)

LEVEL OF SCHOOLING

2001 Estimates:
Population 15 years +	36,809
Less than Grade 9	3,236
Grades 9-13 w/o Certif.	10,745
Grade 9-13 with Certif.	4,281
Trade Certif. /Dip.	1,756
Non-Univ. w/o Certif./Dip.	2,421
Non-Univ. with Certif./Dip.	7,903
Univ. w/o Degree	3,697
Univ. w/o Degree/Certif.	1,598
Univ. with Certif.	2,099
Univ. with Degree	2,770

AVERAGE HOUSEHOLD EXPENDITURES

2001 Estimates:
Food	$5,082
Shelter	$7,261
Clothing	$1,732
Transportation	$4,951
Health & Personal Care	$1,748
Recr'n, Read'g & Education	$2,983
Taxes & Securities	$9,446
Other	$7,149
Total Expenditures	$40,352

PRIVATE HOUSEHOLDS

2001 Estimates:
Private Households, Total	19,476
Pop. in Private Households	43,892
Average no. per Household	2.3

FAMILIES

2001 Estimates:
Families in Private Households	13,320
Husband-Wife Families	11,482
Lone-Parent Families	1,838
Aver. No. Persons per Family	2.7
Aver. No. Sons/Daughters at Home	0.9

HOUSING

2001 Estimates:
Occupied Private Dwellings	19,476
Owned	13,120
Rented	6,356
Single-Detached House	11,987
Semi-Detached House	642
Row Houses	1,400
Apartment, 5+ Storeys	372
Owned Apartment, 5+ Storeys	62
Apartment, 5 or Fewer Storeys	4,018
Apartment, Detached Duplex	339
Other Single-Attached	101
Movable Dwellings	617

VEHICLES

2001 Estimates:
Model Yrs. '81-'96, No.	20,322
% Total	85.86
Model Yrs. '97-'98, No.	2,053
% Total	8.67
'99 Vehicles registered in Model Yr. '99, No.	1,293
% Total	5.46
Total No. '81-'99	23,668

LEGAL MARITAL STATUS

2001 Estimates: (Age 15+)
Single (Never Married)	8,413
Legally Married (Not Separated)	20,465
Legally Married (Separated)	1,314
Widowed	3,149
Divorced	3,468

PSYTE CATEGORIES

2001 Estimates
	No. of House-holds	% of Total Hhds.	Index
Small City Elite	2,390	12.27	716
Town Boomers	1,373	7.05	696
Old Towns' New Fringe	28	0.14	4
Rustic Prosperity	453	2.33	129
High Rise Sunsets	216	1.11	78
Old Leafy Towns	1,931	9.91	388
Nesters & Young Homesteaders	5,520	28.34	1,214
Young Grey Collar	5,550	28.50	3,406
Big Country Families	43	0.22	15
Aged Pensioners	1,832	9.41	707

FINANCIAL P$YTE

2001 Estimates
	No. of House-holds	% of Total Hhds.	Index
Canadian Comfort	3,763	19.32	199
Tractors & Tradelines	481	2.47	43
Bills & Wills	1,931	9.91	120
Revolving Renters	11,286	57.95	1,260
Rural Family Blues	43	0.22	3
Senior Survivors	1,832	9.41	499

HOME LANGUAGE

2001 Estimates:
		% Total
English	42,169	94.74
French	104	0.23
Chinese	174	0.39
Danish	27	0.06
German	341	0.77
Hungarian	80	0.18
Italian	66	0.15
Polish	43	0.10
Portuguese	122	0.27
Punjabi	628	1.41
Other Languages	227	0.51
Multiple Responses	531	1.19
Total	44,512	100.00

BUILDING PERMITS

	1999	1998	1997
		$000	
Value	21,672	30,847	33,546

HOMES BUILT

	1999	1998	1997
No	254	168	385

TAXATION

Income Class:	1997	% Total
Under $5,000	3,330	10.47
$5,000-$10,000	4,270	13.42
$10,000-$15,000	5,790	18.20
$15,000-$20,000	3,900	12.26
$20,000-$25,000	2,870	9.02
$25,000-$30,000	2,570	8.08
$30,000-$40,000	3,830	12.04
$40,000-$50,000	2,190	6.88
$50,000 +	3,100	9.74
Total Returns, No.	31,820	
Total Income, $000	791,346	
Total Taxable Returns	21,630	
Total Tax, $000	132,582	
Average Income, $	24,869	
Average Tax, $	6,130	

VITAL STATISTICS

	1997	1996	1995	1994
Births	387	416	440	426
Deaths	476	453	413	459
Natural Increase	-89	-37	27	-33
Marriages	274	261	264	267

Note: Latest available data.

DAILY NEWSPAPER(S)

	Circulation Average Paid
Herald	
Sat	8,599
Mon-Fri.	8,154

COMMUNITY NEWSPAPER(S)

	Total Circulation
Penticton: Western News	
Tue/Sat.	20,082

RADIO STATION(S)

	Power
CBTP-FM	n.a.
CIGV-FM	n.a.
CJMG-FM	1,800w
CKOR	10,000w

TELEVISION STATION(S)

CHAN-TV
CHBC-TV
CHKL-TV

Port Alberni
(Census Agglomeration)

The Census Agglomeration of Port Alberni includes: Port Alberni, C; Alberni-Clayoquot, Subd. A, SRD; plus several smaller areas. All are in Alberni-Clayoquot Regional District.

POPULATION

July 1, 2001 Estimate	26,294
% Cdn. Total	0.08
% Change, '96 -'01	-5.73
Avg. Annual Growth Rate, %	-1.17
2003 Projected Population	25,181
2006 Projected Population	23,417
2001 Households Estimate	10,901
2003 Projected Households	10,668
2006 Projected Households	10,286

INCOME

% Above/Below National Average	-11
2001 Total Income Estimate	$491,500,000
% Cdn. Total	0.07
2001 Average Hhld. Income	$45,100
2001 Per Capita	$18,700
2003 Projected Total Income	$496,440,000
2006 Projected Total Income	$501,860,000

RETAIL SALES

% Above/Below National Average	-16
2001 Retail Sales Estimate	$198,210,000
% Cdn. Total	0.07
2001 per Household	$18,200
2001 per Capita	$7,500
2001 No. of Establishments	237
2003 Projected Retail Sales	$204,350,000
2006 Projected Retail Sales	$208,070,000

POPULATION

2001 Estimates:

Total		26,294
Male		13,252
Female		13,042

Age Groups	Male	Female
0-4	749	688
5-9	832	790
10-14	942	896
15-19	1,015	948
20-24	920	855
25-29	788	743
30-34	775	803
35-39	908	930
40-44	1,013	1,021
45-49	1,050	1,016
50-54	981	906
55-59	817	770
60-64	680	646
65-69	595	554
70+	1,187	1,476

DAYTIME POPULATION

2001 Estimates:

Working Population	11,016
At Home Population	15,281
Total	26,297

INCOME

2001 Estimates:

Avg. Household Income	$45,087
Avg. Family Income	$51,237
Per Capita Income	$18,692

Male:

Avg. Employment Income	$35,500
Avg. Employment Income (Full Time)	$46,412

Female:

Avg. Employment Income	$17,142
Avg. Employment Income (Full Time)	$28,974

DISPOSABLE & DISCRETIONARY INCOME

2001 Estimates: Per Hhld.

Disposable Income	$34,716
Discretionary Income 1 (minus Food & Shelter)	$23,422
Discretionary Income 2 (minus Food, Shelter, & Other Expenditures)	$15,454

LIQUID ASSETS

1999 Estimates: Per Hhld.

Equity Investments	$65,015
Interest Bearing Investments	$60,378
Total Liquid Assets	$125,393

CREDIT DATA

July 2000:

Pool of Credit	$220,196,077
Revolving Credit, No.	45,987
Fixed Loans, No.	14,348
Avg. Credit Limit, per Person	$11,410
Avg. Spent, per Person	$5,080
Satisfactory Ratings, No. per Person	2.92
Avg. No. of Cards, per Person	0.92

LABOUR FORCE

2001 Estimates:

Male:

In the Labour Force	7,130
Participation Rate	66.5
Employed	6,341
Unemployed	789
Unemployment Rate	11.1
Not in Labour Force	3,599

Female:

In the Labour Force	5,354
Participation Rate	50.2
Employed	4,753
Unemployed	601
Unemployment Rate	11.2
Not in Labour Force	5,314

OCCUPATIONS BY MAJOR GROUPS

2001 Estimates:	Male	Female
Management	499	267
Business, Finance & Admin.	285	1,160
Natural & Applied Sciences & Related	391	42
Health	84	487
Social Sciences, Gov't Services & Religion	112	137
Education	137	318
Arts, Culture, Recreation & Sport	112	115
Sales & Service	1,000	2,313
Trades, Transport & Equipment Operators & Related	2,284	90
Primary Industries	814	144
Processing, Mfg. & Utilities	1,263	88

LEVEL OF SCHOOLING

2001 Estimates:

Population 15 years +	21,397
Less than Grade 9	2,270
Grades 9-13 w/o Certif.	7,055
Grade 9-13 with Certif.	2,820
Trade Certif./Dip.	1,011
Non-Univ. w/o Certif./Dip.	1,539
Non-Univ. with Certif./Dip.	4,356
Univ. w/o Degree	1,312
Univ. w/o Degree/Certif.	562
Univ. with Certif.	750
Univ. with Degree	1,034

AVERAGE HOUSEHOLD EXPENDITURES

2001 Estimates:

Food	$5,457
Shelter	$7,732
Clothing	$1,798
Transportation	$6,238
Health & Personal Care	$1,765
Recr'n, Read'g & Education	$3,033
Taxes & Securities	$10,337
Other	$7,480
Total Expenditures	$43,840

PRIVATE HOUSEHOLDS

2001 Estimates:

Private Households, Total	10,901
Pop. in Private Households	25,925
Average no. per Household	2.4

FAMILIES

2001 Estimates:

Families in Private Households	7,928
Husband-Wife Families	6,763
Lone-Parent Families	1,165
Aver. No. Persons per Family	3.0
Aver. No. Sons/Daughters at Home	1.1

HOUSING

2001 Estimates:

Occupied Private Dwellings	10,901
Owned	8,017
Rented	2,839
Band Housing	45
Single-Detached House	8,370
Semi-Detached House	218
Row Houses	310
Apartment, 5+ Storeys	123
Owned Apartment, 5+ Storeys	10
Apartment, 5 or Fewer Storeys	905
Apartment, Detached Duplex	391
Other Single-Attached	35
Movable Dwellings	549

VEHICLES

2001 Estimates:

Model Yrs. '81-'96, No.	12,664
% Total	89.08
Model Yr. '97-'98, No.	1,003
% Total	7.06
'99 Vehicles registered in Model Yr. '99, No.	549
% Total	3.86
Total No. '81-'99	14,216

LEGAL MARITAL STATUS

2001 Estimates: (Age 15+)

Single (Never Married)	5,849
Legally Married (Not Separated)	11,579
Legally Married (Separated)	760
Widowed	1,390
Divorced	1,819

PSYTE CATEGORIES

2001 Estimates	No. of House-holds	% of Total Hhds.	Index
Small City Elite	504	4.62	270
Old Bungalow Burbs	158	1.45	87
Town Boomers	726	6.66	657
Old Towns' New Fringe	957	8.78	224
Rustic Prosperity	1,128	10.35	573
Pick-ups & Dirt Bikes	595	5.46	654
Old Leafy Towns	1,175	10.78	422
Young Grey Collar	199	1.83	218
Quiet Towns	5,008	45.94	2,159
Rod & Rifle	25	0.23	10
Big Country Families	127	1.17	82
Aged Pensioners	281	2.58	194

British Columbia

FINANCIAL P$YTE

2001 Estimates	No. of House-holds	% of Total Hhds.	Index
Canadian Comfort	1,230	11.28	116
Miners & Credit-Liners	158	1.45	46
Tractors & Tradelines	2,085	19.13	334
Bills & Wills	1,175	10.78	130
Country Credit	595	5.46	81
Revolving Renters	199	1.83	40
Rural Family Blues	152	1.39	17
Limited Budgets	5,008	45.94	1,478
Senior Survivors	281	2.58	137

HOME LANGUAGE

2001 Estimates:		% Total
English	24,731	94.06
French	126	0.48
Chinese	118	0.45
Dutch	14	0.05
Finnish	15	0.06
German	30	0.11
Italian	126	0.48
Punjabi	495	1.88
Slovenian	32	0.12
Spanish	19	0.07
Other Languages	88	0.33
Multiple Responses	500	1.90
Total	26,294	100.00

BUILDING PERMITS

	1999	1998	1997
		$000	
Value	51,983	14,377	18,259

HOMES BUILT

	1999	1998	1997
No.	43	97	159

TAXATION

Income Class:	1997	% Total
Under $5,000	2,490	13.63
$5,000-$10,000	2,370	12.97
$10,000-$15,000	2,620	14.34
$15,000-$20,000	1,600	8.76
$20,000-$25,000	1,370	7.50
$25,000-$30,000	1,340	7.33
$30,000-$40,000	1,970	10.78
$40,000-$50,000	1,630	8.92
$50,000 +	2,890	15.82
Total Returns, No.	18,270	
Total Income, $000	485,866	
Total Taxable Returns	12,400	
Total Tax, $000	87,062	
Average Income, $	26,594	
Average Tax, $	7,021	

VITAL STATISTICS

	1997	1996	1995	1994
Births	286	302	326	369
Deaths	226	222	248	211
Natural Increase	60	80	78	158
Marriages	139	171	172	154

Note: Latest available data.

Port Alberni
(Census Agglomeration)
(Cont'd)

DAILY NEWSPAPER(S)

	Circulation Average Paid
Alberni Valley Times	6,128

RADIO STATION(S)

	Power
CBCV-FM	n.a.
CBTQ-FM	n.a.
CBUF-FM	100w
CJAV	1,000w

TELEVISION STATION(S)

CBUT-TV
CHEK-TV

Powell River
(Census Agglomeration)

The Census Agglomeration of Powell River includes: Powell River, DM; Powell River, Subd. A, SRD; plus several smaller areas. All are in Powell River Regional District.

POPULATION

July 1, 2001 Estimate	20,439
% Cdn. Total	0.07
% Change, '96 -'01	-1.05
Avg. Annual Growth Rate, %	-0.21
2003 Projected Population	19,929
2006 Projected Population	19,058
2001 Households Estimate	8,659
2003 Projected Households	8,571
2006 Projected Households	8,448

INCOME

% Above/Below National Average	-8
2001 Total Income Estimate	$394,700,000
% Cdn. Total	0.06
2001 Average Hhld. Income	$45,600
2001 Per Capita	$19,300
2003 Projected Total Income	$406,260,000
2006 Projected Total Income	$424,250,000

RETAIL SALES

% Above/Below National Average	+4
2001 Retail Sales Estimate	$189,940,000
% Cdn. Total	0.07
2001 per Household	$21,900
2001 per Capita	$9,300
2001 No. of Establishments	164
2003 Projected Retail Sales	$197,210,000
2006 Projected Retail Sales	$203,870,000

POPULATION

2001 Estimates:		
Total		20,439
Male		10,306
Female		10,133
Age Groups	Male	Female
0-4	579	504
5-9	677	580
10-14	751	654
15-19	723	664
20-24	606	593
25-29	540	544
30-34	589	649
35-39	694	749
40-44	783	823
45-49	827	809
50-54	776	719
55-59	653	602
60-64	537	507
65-69	489	453
70+	1,082	1,283

DAYTIME POPULATION

2001 Estimates:	
Working Population	8,925
At Home Population	11,514
Total	20,439

INCOME

2001 Estimates:	
Avg. Household Income	$45,583
Avg. Family Income	$52,357
Per Capita Income	$19,311
Male:	
Avg. Employment Income	$34,328
Avg. Employment Income (Full Time)	$46,464
Female:	
Avg. Employment Income	$17,913
Avg. Employment Income (Full Time)	$27,310

DISPOSABLE & DISCRETIONARY INCOME

2001 Estimates:	Per Hhld.
Disposable Income	$35,176
Discretionary Income 1 (minus Food & Shelter)	$23,611
Discretionary Income 2 (minus Food, Shelter, & Other Expenditures)	$15,667

LIQUID ASSETS

1999 Estimates:	Per Hhld.
Equity Investments	$57,101
Interest Bearing Investments	$57,896
Total Liquid Assets	$114,997

CREDIT DATA

July 2000:	
Pool of Credit	$167,278,215
Revolving Credit, No.	31,885
Fixed Loans, No.	7,007
Avg. Credit Limit, per Person	$10,865
Avg. Spent, per Person	$4,537
Satisfactory Ratings, No. per Person	2.43
Avg. No. of Cards, per Person	0.91

LABOUR FORCE

2001 Estimates:	
Male:	
In the Labour Force	5,507
Participation Rate	66.4
Employed	4,998
Unemployed	509
Unemployment Rate	9.2
Not in Labour Force	2,792
Female:	
In the Labour Force	4,347
Participation Rate	51.8
Employed	3,974
Unemployed	373
Unemployment Rate	8.6
Not in Labour Force	4,048

OCCUPATIONS BY MAJOR GROUPS

2001 Estimates:	Male	Female
Management	406	201
Business, Finance & Admin.	183	1,034
Natural & Applied Sciences & Related	305	50
Health	101	372
Social Sciences, Gov't Services & Religion	114	176
Education	96	233
Arts, Culture, Recreation & Sport	99	65
Sales & Service	884	1,761
Trades, Transport & Equipment Operators & Related	1,853	135
Primary Industries	511	117
Processing, Mfg. & Utilities	785	67

LEVEL OF SCHOOLING

2001 Estimates:	
Population 15 years +	16,694
Less than Grade 9	1,303
Grades 9-13 w/o Certif.	4,908
Grade 9-13 with Certif.	2,396
Trade Certif. /Dip.	812
Non-Univ. w/o Certif./Dip.	1,158
Non-Univ. with Certif./Dip.	3,449
Univ. w/o Degree	1,499
Univ. w/o Degree/Certif.	754
Univ. with Certif.	745
Univ. with Degree	1,169

AVERAGE HOUSEHOLD EXPENDITURES

2001 Estimates:	
Food	$5,560
Shelter	$7,899
Clothing	$1,701
Transportation	$6,273
Health & Personal Care	$1,755
Recr'n, Read'g & Education	$3,127
Taxes & Securities	$11,011
Other	$7,223
Total Expenditures	$44,549

PRIVATE HOUSEHOLDS

2001 Estimates:	
Private Households, Total	8,659
Pop. in Private Households	20,118
Average no. per Household	2.3

FAMILIES

2001 Estimates:	
Families in Private Households	6,107
Husband-Wife Families	5,355
Lone-Parent Families	752
Aver. No. Persons per Family	2.9
Aver. No. Sons/Daughters at Home	1.0

HOUSING

2001 Estimates:	
Occupied Private Dwellings	8,659
Owned	6,591
Rented	2,039
Band Housing	29
Single-Detached House	7,334
Semi-Detached House	144
Row Houses	80
Apartment, 5 or Fewer Storeys	699
Apartment, Detached Duplex	161
Other Single-Attached	10
Movable Dwellings	231

VEHICLES

2001 Estimates:	
Model Yrs. '81-'96, No.	9,956
% Total	91.19
Model Yrs. '97-'98, No.	608
% Total	5.57
'99 Vehicles registered in Model Yr. '99, No.	354
% Total	3.24
Total No. '81-'99	10,918

LEGAL MARITAL STATUS

2001 Estimates: (Age 15+)	
Single (Never Married)	4,212
Legally Married (Not Separated)	9,250
Legally Married (Separated)	593
Widowed	1,112
Divorced	1,527

PSYTE CATEGORIES

2001 Estimates	No. of House -holds	% of Total Hhds.	Index
Small City Elite	724	8.36	488
Blue Collar Winners	62	0.72	28
Old Towns' New Fringe	102	1.18	30
Pick-ups & Dirt Bikes	84	0.97	116
Old Leafy Towns	3,876	44.76	1,751
Quiet Towns	2,508	28.96	1,361
Rod & Rifle	954	11.02	476
Big Country Families	244	2.82	198
Old Cdn. Rustics	54	0.62	64

Powell River
(Census Agglomeration)
(Cont'd)

FINAN¢IAL P$YTE

2001 Estimates	No. of House -holds	% of Total Hhds.	Index
Canadian Comfort	786	9.08	93
Tractors & Tradelines	102	1.18	21
Bills & Wills	3,876	44.76	541
Country Credit	84	0.97	14
Rural Family Blues	1,198	13.84	171
Limited Budgets	2,562	29.59	952

HOME LANGUAGE

2001 Estimates:		% Total
English	19,866	97.20
French	179	0.88
Chinese	25	0.12
Dutch	11	0.05
German	42	0.21
Italian	111	0.54
Korean	35	0.17
Punjabi	11	0.05
Other Languages	37	0.18
Multiple Responses	122	0.60
Total	20,439	100.00

BUILDING PERMITS

	1999	1998 $000	1997
Value	11,282	5,387	9,872

HOMES BUILT

	1999	1998	1997
No	46	35	81

TAXATION

Income Class:	1997	% Total
Under $5,000	1,780	12.60
$5,000-$10,000	1,810	12.81
$10,000-$15,000	2,050	14.51
$15,000-$20,000	1,330	9.41
$20,000-$25,000	1,050	7.43
$25,000-$30,000	1,060	7.50
$30,000-$40,000	1,660	11.75
$40,000-$50,000	1,100	7.78
$50,000 +	2,280	16.14
Total Returns, No.	14,130	
Total Income, $000	380,730	
Total Taxable Returns	9,860	
Total Tax, $000	68,595	
Average Income, $	26,945	
Average Tax, $	6,957	

VITAL STATISTICS

	1997	1996	1995	1994
Births	210	195	212	251
Deaths	169	174	162	154
Natural Increase	41	21	50	97
Marriages	105	114	121	101

Note: Latest available data.

COMMUNITY NEWSPAPER(S)

	Total Circulation
Powell River: Powell River Peak Wed/Sat	8,813
Sechelt: The Reporter	12,849
Sechelt: The Slant	13,000

RADIO STATION(S)

	Power
CBCV-FM	n.a.
CBUW-FM	n.a.
CHQB	1,000w
CKLR-FM	n.a.

Prince George
(Census Agglomeration)

The Census Agglomeration of Prince George consists solely of Prince George, C, in Fraser-Fort George Regional District.

POPULATION

July 1, 2001 Estimate	77,703
% Cdn. Total	0.25
% Change, '96 -'01	-0.75
Avg. Annual Growth Rate, %	-0.15
2003 Projected Population	76,478
2006 Projected Population	74,034
2001 Households Estimate	29,493
2003 Projected Households	29,720
2006 Projected Households	29,868

INCOME

% Above/Below National Average	+4
2001 Total Income Estimate	$1,704,480,000
% Cdn. Total	0.26
2001 Average Hhld. Income	$57,800
2001 Per Capita	$21,900
2003 Projected Total Income	$1,802,070,000
2006 Projected Total Income	$1,935,640,000

RETAIL SALES

% Above/Below National Average	+30
2001 Retail Sales Estimate	$907,760,000
% Cdn. Total	0.33
2001 per Household	$30,800
2001 per Capita	$11,700
2001 No. of Establishments	562
2003 Projected Retail Sales	$964,970,000
2006 Projected Retail Sales	$1,032,240,000

POPULATION

2001 Estimates:		
Total		77,703
Male		38,999
Female		38,704

Age Groups	Male	Female
0-4	2,686	2,543
5-9	2,932	2,772
10-14	3,116	2,954
15-19	3,112	2,958
20-24	2,994	2,958
25-29	2,985	3,011
30-34	3,115	3,179
35-39	3,263	3,317
40-44	3,235	3,280
45-49	2,971	3,033
50-54	2,489	2,469
55-59	1,942	1,816
60-64	1,449	1,328
65-69	1,069	1,011
70+	1,641	2,075

DAYTIME POPULATION

2001 Estimates:	
Working Population	38,833
At Home Population	38,870
Total	77,703

INCOME

2001 Estimates:	
Avg. Household Income	$57,793
Avg. Family Income	$62,103
Per Capita Income	$21,936
Male:	
Avg. Employment Income	$37,824
Avg. Employment Income (Full Time)	$49,289
Female:	
Avg. Employment Income	$20,803
Avg. Employment Income (Full Time)	$32,110

DISPOSABLE & DISCRETIONARY INCOME

2001 Estimates:	Per Hhld.
Disposable Income	$44,203
Discretionary Income 1 (minus Food & Shelter)	$30,293
Discretionary Income 2 (minus Food, Shelter, & Other Expenditures)	$21,259

LIQUID ASSETS

1999 Estimates:	Per Hhld.
Equity Investments	$84,821
Interest Bearing Investments	$75,116
Total Liquid Assets	$159,937

CREDIT DATA

July 2000:	
Pool of Credit	$901,256,057
Revolving Credit, No.	150,247
Fixed Loans, No.	56,941
Avg. Credit Limit, per Person	$14,056
Avg. Spent, per Person	$6,992
Satisfactory Ratings, No. per Person	3.09
Avg. No. of Cards, per Person	0.99

LABOUR FORCE

2001 Estimates:	
Male:	
In the Labour Force	23,524
Participation Rate	77.7
Employed	20,937
Unemployed	2,587
Unemployment Rate	11.0
Not in Labour Force	6,741
Female:	
In the Labour Force	20,118
Participation Rate	66.1
Employed	18,439
Unemployed	1,679
Unemployment Rate	8.3
Not in Labour Force	10,317

OCCUPATIONS BY MAJOR GROUPS

2001 Estimates:	Male	Female
Management	2,005	934
Business, Finance & Admin.	1,574	6,187
Natural & Applied Sciences & Related	1,658	308
Health	257	1,289
Social Sciences, Gov't Services & Religion	408	533
Education	645	1,087
Arts, Culture, Recreation & Sport.	267	383
Sales & Service	4,515	7,750
Trades, Transport & Equipment Operators & Related	7,368	333
Primary Industries	1,694	278
Processing, Mfg. & Utilities.	2,631	382

LEVEL OF SCHOOLING

2001 Estimates:	
Population 15 years +	60,700
Less than Grade 9	4,346
Grades 9-13 w/o Certif.	16,737
Grade 9-13 with Certif.	8,304
Trade Certif. /Dip.	2,328
Non-Univ. w/o Certif./Dip.	5,797
Non-Univ. with Certif./Dip.	12,634
Univ. w/o Degree	5,344
Univ. w/o Degree/Certif.	2,647
Univ. with Certif.	2,697
Univ. with Degree	5,210

British Columbia

AVERAGE HOUSEHOLD EXPENDITURES

2001 Estimates:	
Food	$6,498
Shelter	$9,673
Clothing	$2,257
Transportation	$6,961
Health & Personal Care	$2,050
Recr'n, Read'g & Education	$4,025
Taxes & Securities	$14,156
Other	$9,059
Total Expenditures	$54,679

PRIVATE HOUSEHOLDS

2001 Estimates:	
Private Households, Total	29,493
Pop. in Private Households	76,453
Average no. per Household	2.6

FAMILIES

2001 Estimates:	
Families in Private Households	22,306
Husband-Wife Families	18,427
Lone-Parent Families	3,879
Aver. No. Persons per Family	3.1
Aver. No. Sons/Daughters at Home	1.3

HOUSING

2001 Estimates:	
Occupied Private Dwellings	29,493
Owned	20,284
Rented	9,209
Single-Detached House	19,134
Semi-Detached House	1,761
Row Houses	1,330
Apartment, 5+ Storeys	431
Apartment, 5 or Fewer Storeys	3,947
Apartment, Detached Duplex	1,224
Other Single-Attached	76
Movable Dwellings	1,590

VEHICLES

2001 Estimates:	
Model Yrs. '81-'96, No.	37,984
% Total	84.02
Model Yrs. '97-'98, No.	4,759
% Total	10.53
'99 Vehicles registered in Model Yr. '99, No.	2,465
% Total	5.45
Total No. '81-'99	45,208

LEGAL MARITAL STATUS

2001 Estimates: (Age 15+)	
Single (Never Married)	20,429
Legally Married (Not Separated)	30,302
Legally Married (Separated)	2,662
Widowed	2,410
Divorced	4,897

British Columbia

Prince George
(Census Agglomeration)
(Cont'd)

PSYTE CATEGORIES

2001 Estimates	No. of House-holds	% of Total Hhds.	Index
Suburban Executives	358	1.21	85
Mortgaged in Suburbia	599	2.03	146
Technocrats & Bureaucrats	390	1.32	47
Boomers & Teens	1,056	3.58	200
Small City Elite	3,964	13.44	784
Old Bungalow Burbs	567	1.92	116
Aging Erudites	335	1.14	75
Satellite Suburbs	2,624	8.90	310
Kindergarten Boom	1,364	4.62	176
Blue Collar Winners	550	1.86	74
Old Towns' New Fringe	7,545	25.58	654
Conservative Homebodies	215	0.73	20
Young City Singles	857	2.91	127
Old Leafy Towns	83	0.28	11
Town Renters	1,601	5.43	628
Nesters & Young Homesteaders	6,440	21.84	936
Aged Pensioners	797	2.70	203

FINANCIAL PSYTE

2001 Estimates	No. of House-holds	% of Total Hhds.	Index
Four Star Investors	1,414	4.79	95
Successful Suburbanites	989	3.35	51
Canadian Comfort	7,138	24.20	249
Urban Heights	335	1.14	26
Miners & Credit-Liners	567	1.92	61
Mortgages & Minivans	1,364	4.62	70
Tractors & Tradelines	7,545	25.58	447
Bills & Wills	298	1.01	12
Revolving Renters	6,440	21.84	475
Towering Debt	2,458	8.33	107
Senior Survivors	797	2.70	143

HOME LANGUAGE

2001 Estimates:		% Total
English	74,007	95.24
French	291	0.37
Chinese	292	0.38
Croatian	71	0.09
German	156	0.20
Greek	57	0.07
Italian	145	0.19
Korean	52	0.07
Portuguese	84	0.11
Punjabi	1,028	1.32
Spanish	50	0.06
Ukrainian	120	0.15
Other Languages	309	0.40
Multiple Responses	1,041	1.34
Total	77,703	100.00

BUILDING PERMITS

	1999	1998	1997
		$000	
Value	63,828	62,893	111,002

HOMES BUILT

	1999	1998	1997
No	338	284	410

TAXATION

Income Class:	1997	% Total
Under $5,000	7,450	12.41
$5,000-$10,000	7,450	12.41
$10,000-$15,000	7,600	12.66
$15,000-$20,000	5,110	8.51
$20,000-$25,000	4,150	6.91
$25,000-$30,000	4,050	6.75
$30,000-$40,000	7,210	12.01
$40,000-$50,000	5,920	9.86
$50,000 +	11,120	18.52
Total Returns, No.	60,040	
Total Income, $000	1,777,045	
Total Taxable Returns	43,290	
Total Tax, $000	358,053	
Average Income, $	29,598	
Average Tax, $	8,271	

VITAL STATISTICS

	1997	1996	1995	1994
Births	1,175	1,188	1,236	1,289
Deaths	380	424	365	369
Natural Increase	795	764	871	920
Marriages	488	516	572	568

Note: Latest available data.

DAILY NEWSPAPER(S)

	Circulation Average Paid
Citizen	
Fri	17,837
Mon-Thu, Sat	16,203

COMMUNITY NEWSPAPER(S)

	Total Circulation
Prince George: Prince George Free Press Thu/Sun	30,279
Prince George: Prince George This Week Thu/Sun	31,516

RADIO STATION(S)

	Power
CBUF-FM	100w
CBYG-FM	10,000w
CIRX-FM	n.a.
CJCI	10,000w
CKKN-FM	n.a.
CKPG	10,000w

TELEVISION STATION(S)

CBUFT-TV
CHAN-TV
CIFG-TV
CKPG-TV

Prince Rupert
(Census Agglomeration)

The Census Agglomeration of Prince Rupert consists of Prince Rupert, C and Port Edward, DM, both in Skeena-Queen Charlotte Regional District.

POPULATION

July 1, 2001 Estimate	16,373
% Cdn. Total	0.05
% Change, '96 -'01	-9.52
Avg. Annual Growth Rate, %	-1.98
2003 Projected Population	15,609
2006 Projected Population	14,453
2001 Households Estimate	6,059
2003 Projected Households	5,890
2006 Projected Households	5,638

INCOME

% Above/Below National Average	-3
2001 Total Income Estimate	$334,750,000
% Cdn. Total	0.05
2001 Average Hhld. Income	$55,200
2001 Per Capita	$20,400
2003 Projected Total Income	$339,760,000
2006 Projected Total Income	$344,570,000

RETAIL SALES

% Above/Below National Average	-10
2001 Retail Sales Estimate	$131,760,000
% Cdn. Total	0.05
2001 per Household	$21,700
2001 per Capita	$8,000
2001 No. of Establishments	122
2003 Projected Retail Sales	$134,370,000
2006 Projected Retail Sales	$136,750,000

POPULATION

2001 Estimates:		
Total		16,373
Male		8,367
Female		8,006

Age Groups	Male	Female
0-4	598	556
5-9	668	637
10-14	662	656
15-19	627	608
20-24	579	580
25-29	576	578
30-34	641	633
35-39	697	696
40-44	718	679
45-49	671	614
50-54	561	493
55-59	443	360
60-64	329	259
65-69	237	202
70+	360	455

DAYTIME POPULATION

2001 Estimates:	
Working Population	7,593
At Home Population	8,780
Total	16,373

INCOME

2001 Estimates:	
Avg. Household Income	$55,249
Avg. Family Income	$59,401
Per Capita Income	$20,445
Male:	
Avg. Employment Income	$35,298
Avg. Employment Income (Full Time)	$48,238
Female:	
Avg. Employment Income	$20,341
Avg. Employment Income (Full Time)	$32,773

DISPOSABLE & DISCRETIONARY INCOME

2001 Estimates:	Per Hhld.
Disposable Income	$42,231
Discretionary Income 1 (minus Food & Shelter)	$30,817
Discretionary Income 2 (minus Food, Shelter, & Other Expenditures)	$20,958

LIQUID ASSETS

1999 Estimates:	Per Hhld.
Equity Investments	$90,381
Interest Bearing Investments	$75,600
Total Liquid Assets	$165,981

CREDIT DATA

July 2000:	
Pool of Credit	$131,149,774
Revolving Credit, No.	22,190
Fixed Loans, No.	6,569
Avg. Credit Limit, per Person	$11,419
Avg. Spent, per Person	$5,291
Satisfactory Ratings, No. per Person	2.39
Avg. No. of.Cards, per Person	0.96

LABOUR FORCE

2001 Estimates:	
Male:	
In the Labour Force	4,895
Participation Rate	76.0
Employed	4,201
Unemployed	694
Unemployment Rate	14.2
Not in Labour Force	1,544
Female:	
In the Labour Force	4,137
Participation Rate	67.2
Employed	3,493
Unemployed	644
Unemployment Rate	15.6
Not in Labour Force	2,020

OCCUPATIONS BY MAJOR GROUPS

2001 Estimates:	Male	Female
Management	418	173
Business, Finance & Admin.	293	974
Natural & Applied Sciences & Related	292	48
Health	126	259
Social Sciences, Gov't Services & Religion	64	112
Education	73	118
Arts, Culture, Recreation & Sport	47	100
Sales & Service	718	1,523
Trades, Transport & Equipment Operators & Related	1,419	43
Primary Industries	509	83
Processing, Mfg. & Utilities	825	493

LEVEL OF SCHOOLING

2001 Estimates:	
Population 15 years +	12,596
Less than Grade 9	1,167
Grades 9-13 w/o Certif.	3,549
Grade 9-13 with Certif.	1,662
Trade Certif. /Dip.	478
Non-Univ. w/o Certif./Dip.	977
Non-Univ. with Certif./Dip.	2,371
Univ. w/o Degree.	1,330
Univ. w/o Degree/Certif.	618
Univ. with Certif.	712
Univ. with Degree	1,062

Prince Rupert
(Census Agglomeration)
(Cont'd)

AVERAGE HOUSEHOLD EXPENDITURES

2001 Estimates:

Food	$6,133
Shelter	$7,417
Clothing	$2,457
Transportation	$7,656
Health & Personal Care	$2,232
Recr'n, Read'g & Education	$4,572
Taxes & Securities	$13,076
Other	$8,728
Total Expenditures	$52,271

PRIVATE HOUSEHOLDS

2001 Estimates:

Private Households, Total	6,059
Pop. in Private Households	16,160
Average no. per Household	2.7

FAMILIES

2001 Estimates:

Families in Private Households	4,517
Husband-Wife Families	3,753
Lone-Parent Families	764
Aver. No. Persons per Family	3.2
Aver. No. Sons/Daughters at Home	1.4

HOUSING

2001 Estimates:

Occupied Private Dwellings	6,059
Owned	3,661
Rented	2,398
Single-Detached House	3,283
Semi-Detached House	270
Row Houses	486
Apartment, 5+ Storeys	127
Owned Apartment, 5+ Storeys	10
Apartment, 5 or Fewer Storeys	993
Apartment, Detached Duplex	648
Other Single-Attached	20
Movable Dwellings	232

VEHICLES

2001 Estimates:

Model Yrs. '81-'96, No.	6,579
% Total	86.50
Model Yrs. '97-'98, No.	663
% Total	8.72
'99 Vehicles registered in Model Yr. '99, No.	364
% Total	4.79
Total No. '81-'99	7,606

LEGAL MARITAL STATUS

2001 Estimates: (Age 15+)

Single (Never Married)	4,609
Legally Married (Not Separated)	5,984
Legally Married (Separated)	483
Widowed	615
Divorced	905

PSYTE CATEGORIES

2001 Estimates	No. of House-holds	% of Total Hhds.	Index
Northern Lights	1,061	17.51	3,538
The New Frontier	4,477	73.89	4,899
Quiet Towns	516	8.52	400

FINANCIAL P$YTE

2001 Estimates	No. of House-holds	% of Total Hhds.	Index
Successful Suburbanites	1,061	17.51	264
Miners & Credit-Liners	4,477	73.89	2,334
Limited Budgets	516	8.52	274

HOME LANGUAGE

2001 Estimates:		% Total
English	15,090	92.16
French	47	0.29
Chinese	85	0.52
German	9	0.05
Greek	14	0.09
Hindi	10	0.06
Italian	27	0.16
Japanese	9	0.05
Korean	24	0.15
Polish	14	0.09
Portuguese	62	0.38
Punjabi	365	2.23
Spanish	14	0.09
Tagalog (Pilipino)	42	0.26
Ukrainian	19	0.12
Vietnamese	171	1.04
Other Languages	86	0.53
Multiple Responses	285	1.74
Total	16,373	100.00

BUILDING PERMITS

	1999	1998 $000	1997
Value	7,032	7,977	8,283

HOMES BUILT

	1999	1998	1997
No	8	22	57

TAXATION

Income Class:	1997	% Total
Under $5,000	1,370	12.41
$5,000-$10,000	1,470	13.32
$10,000-$15,000	1,450	13.13
$15,000-$20,000	1,000	9.06
$20,000-$25,000	850	7.70
$25,000-$30,000	750	6.79
$30,000-$40,000	1,290	11.68
$40,000-$50,000	1,100	9.96
$50,000 +	1,760	15.94
Total Returns, No.	11,040	
Total Income, $000	305,374	
Total Taxable Returns	7,710	
Total Tax, $000	57,209	
Average Income, $	27,661	
Average Tax, $	7,420	

VITAL STATISTICS

	1997	1996	1995	1994
Births	305	280	310	338
Deaths	86	98	101	93
Natural Increase	219	182	209	245
Marriages	75	82	111	92

Note: Latest available data.

DAILY NEWSPAPER(S)

	Circulation Average Paid
Daily News	n.a.

RADIO STATION(S)

	Power
CFNR-FM	50w
CFPR	10,000w
CHTK	1,000w
CJFW-FM	n.a.

TELEVISION STATION(S)

CATV
CFTK-TV

Quesnel
(Census Agglomeration)

The Census Agglomeration of Quesnel includes: Quesnel, C; Cariboo Subd. A, SRD; plus several smaller areas. All are in Cariboo Regional District.

POPULATION

July 1, 2001 Estimate	26,798
% Cdn. Total	0.09
% Change, '96 -'01	0.71
Avg. Annual Growth Rate, %	0.14
2003 Projected Population	26,546
2006 Projected Population	25,957
2001 Households Estimate	10,264
2003 Projected Households	10,309
2006 Projected Households	10,362

INCOME

% Above/Below National Average	-11
2001 Total Income Estimate	$500,290,000
% Cdn. Total	0.08
2001 Average Hhld. Income	$48,700
2001 Per Capita	$18,700
2003 Projected Total Income	$519,220,000
2006 Projected Total Income	$547,960,000

RETAIL SALES

% Above/Below National Average	-32
2001 Retail Sales Estimate	$163,420,000
% Cdn. Total	0.06
2001 per Household	$15,900
2001 per Capita	$6,100
2001 No. of Establishments	218
2003 Projected Retail Sales	$174,020,000
2006 Projected Retail Sales	$186,090,000

POPULATION

2001 Estimates:

Total	26,798
Male	13,617
Female	13,181

Age Groups	Male	Female
0-4	834	785
5-9	960	912
10-14	1,108	1,023
15-19	1,138	1,045
20-24	989	938
25-29	884	867
30-34	929	954
35-39	1,048	1,067
40-44	1,108	1,102
45-49	1,054	1,043
50-54	905	863
55-59	731	651
60-64	588	519
65-69	487	446
70+	854	966

DAYTIME POPULATION

2001 Estimates:

Working Population	12,132
At Home Population	14,666
Total	26,798

INCOME

2001 Estimates:

Avg. Household Income	$48,743
Avg. Family Income	$53,013
Per Capita Income	$18,669
Male:	
Avg. Employment Income	$35,463
Avg. Employment Income (Full Time)	$46,749
Female:	
Avg. Employment Income	$15,530
Avg. Employment Income (Full Time)	$25,378

British Columbia

DISPOSABLE & DISCRETIONARY INCOME

2001 Estimates:	Per Hhld.
Disposable Income	$37,511
Discretionary Income 1 (minus Food & Shelter)	$26,789
Discretionary Income 2 (minus Food, Shelter, & Other Expenditures)	$18,001

LIQUID ASSETS

1999 Estimates:	Per Hhld.
Equity Investments	$69,967
Interest Bearing Investments	$65,082
Total Liquid Assets	$135,049

CREDIT DATA

July 2000:

Pool of Credit	$247,495,913
Revolving Credit, No.	40,873
Fixed Loans, No.	14,210
Avg. Credit Limit, per Person	$12,542
Avg. Spent, per Person	$6,165
Satisfactory Ratings, No. per Person	2.64
Avg. No. of Cards, per Person	0.83

LABOUR FORCE

2001 Estimates:

Male:	
In the Labour Force	7,899
Participation Rate	73.7
Employed	6,836
Unemployed	1,063
Unemployment Rate	13.5
Not in Labour Force	2,816
Female:	
In the Labour Force	6,077
Participation Rate	58.1
Employed	5,397
Unemployed	680
Unemployment Rate	11.2
Not in Labour Force	4,384

OCCUPATIONS BY MAJOR GROUPS

2001 Estimates:	Male	Female
Management	590	342
Business, Finance & Admin.	238	1,553
Natural & Applied Sciences & Related	302	73
Health	94	358
Social Sciences, Gov't Services & Religion	90	127
Education	136	260
Arts, Culture, Recreation & Sport	64	132
Sales & Service	1,022	2,359
Trades, Transport & Equipment Operators & Related	2,634	210
Primary Industries	1,041	284
Processing, Mfg. & Utilities	1,508	141

British Columbia

Quesnel
(Census Agglomeration)
(Cont'd)

LEVEL OF SCHOOLING

2001 Estimates:
Population 15 years +	21,176
Less than Grade 9	2,177
Grades 9-13 w/o Certif.	7,163
Grade 9-13 with Certif.	3,024
Trade Certif. /Dip.	878
Non-Univ. w/o Certif./Dip.	1,442
Non-Univ. with Certif./Dip.	3,876
Univ. w/o Degree	1,520
Univ. w/o Degree/Certif.	685
Univ. with Certif.	835
Univ. with Degree	1,096

AVERAGE HOUSEHOLD EXPENDITURES

2001 Estimates:
Food	$5,695
Shelter	$6,971
Clothing	$2,202
Transportation	$6,692
Health & Personal Care	$2,060
Recr'n, Read'g & Education	$3,932
Taxes & Securities	$11,335
Other	$7,955
Total Expenditures	$46,842

PRIVATE HOUSEHOLDS

2001 Estimates:
Private Households, Total	10,264
Pop. in Private Households	26,371
Average no. per Household	2.6

FAMILIES

2001 Estimates:
Families in Private Households	7,911
Husband-Wife Families	6,810
Lone-Parent Families	1,101
Aver. No. Persons per Family	3.0
Aver. No. Sons/Daughters at Home	1.2

HOUSING

2001 Estimates:
Occupied Private Dwellings	10,264
Owned	7,646
Rented	2,562
Band Housing	56
Single-Detached House	7,370
Semi-Detached House	246
Row Houses	249
Apartment, 5 or Fewer Storeys	920
Apartment, Detached Duplex	227
Other Single-Attached	22
Movable Dwellings	1,230

VEHICLES

2001 Estimates:
Model Yrs. '81-'96, No.	12,533
% Total	86.94
Model Yrs. '97-'98, No.	1,264
% Total	8.77
'99 Vehicles registered in Model Yr. '99, No.	619
% Total	4.29
Total No. '81-'99	14,416

LEGAL MARITAL STATUS

2001 Estimates: (Age 15+)
Single (Never Married)	6,045
Legally Married (Not Separated)	11,446
Legally Married (Separated)	855
Widowed	1,011
Divorced	1,819

PSYTE CATEGORIES

2001 Estimates	No. of House -holds	% of Total Hhds.	Index
Town Boomers	275	2.68	264
Northern Lights	424	4.13	835
The New Frontier	6,018	58.63	3,887
Pick-ups & Dirt Bikes	648	6.31	756
Old Leafy Towns	170	1.66	65
Young Grey Collar	730	7.11	850
Quiet Towns	1,441	14.04	660
Rod & Rifle	288	2.81	121
Big Country Families	191	1.86	130

FINANCIAL P$YTE

2001 Estimates	No. of House -holds	% of Total Hhds.	Index
Successful Suburbanites	424	4.13	62
Canadian Comfort	275	2.68	28
Miners & Credit-Liners	6,018	58.63	1,852
Bills & Wills	170	1.66	20
Country Credit	648	6.31	93
Revolving Renters	730	7.11	155
Rural Family Blues	479	4.67	58
Limited Budgets	1,441	14.04	452

HOME LANGUAGE

2001 Estimates		% Total
English	25,201	94.04
French	22	0.08
Chinese	46	0.17
German	125	0.47
Greek	15	0.06
Japanese	22	0.08
Punjabi	926	3.46
Serbo-Croatian	15	0.06
Vietnamese	21	0.08
Other Languages	125	0.47
Multiple Responses	280	1.04
Total	26,798	100.00

BUILDING PERMITS

	1999	1998 $000	1997
Value	4,382	9,947	57,824

HOMES BUILT

	1999	1998	1997
No	56	65	236

TAXATION

Income Class:	1997	% Total
Under $5,000	2,690	15.22
$5,000-$10,000	2,490	14.09
$10,000-$15,000	2,560	14.49
$15,000-$20,000	1,440	8.15
$20,000-$25,000	1,090	6.17
$25,000-$30,000	1,070	6.06
$30,000-$40,000	1,770	10.02
$40,000-$50,000	1,710	9.68
$50,000 +	2,840	16.07
Total Returns, No.	17,670	
Total Income, $000	471,849	
Total Taxable Returns	11,660	
Total Tax, $000	91,622	
Average Income, $	26,703	
Average Tax, $	7,858	

VITAL STATISTICS

	1997	1996	1995	1994
Births	332	377	344	335
Deaths	151	157	135	126
Natural Increase	181	220	209	209
Marriages	131	149	182	165

Note: Latest available data.

COMMUNITY NEWSPAPER(S)

	Total Circulation
Quesnel: Cariboo Observer Sun/Wed	4,665

RADIO STATION(S)

	Power
CBYY-FM	n.a.
CFFM-FM	n.a.
CKCQ	10,000w

TELEVISION STATION(S)

CFJC-TV
CHAN-TV
CITM-TV
CKPG-TV

Salmon Arm
(District Municipality)

In Columbia-Shuswap Regional District.

POPULATION

July 1, 2001 Estimate	16,365
% Cdn. Total	0.05
% Change, '96 -'01	7.66
Avg. Annual Growth Rate, %	1.49
2003 Projected Population	16,968
2006 Projected Population	17,763
2001 Households Estimate	6,706
2003 Projected Households	7,000
2006 Projected Households	7,460

INCOME

% Above/Below National Average	-13
2001 Total Income Estimate	$300,350,000
% Cdn. Total	0.05
2001 Average Hhld. Income	$44,800
2001 Per Capita	$18,400
2003 Projected Total Income	$329,880,000
2006 Projected Total Income	$380,090,000

RETAIL SALES

% Above/Below National Average	+49
2001 Retail Sales Estimate	$218,030,000
% Cdn. Total	0.08
2001 per Household	$32,500
2001 per Capita	$13,300
2001 No. of Establishments	186
2003 Projected Retail Sales	$244,790,000
2006 Projected Retail Sales	$283,400,000

POPULATION

2001 Estimates:

Total	16,365
Male	7,866
Female	8,499

Age Groups	Male	Female
0-4	440	428
5-9	514	473
10-14	593	553
15-19	617	601
20-24	531	546
25-29	484	484
30-34	488	521
35-39	534	601
40-44	570	639
45-49	568	612
50-54	484	544
55-59	411	456
60-64	379	412
65-69	349	390
70+	904	1,239

DAYTIME POPULATION

2001 Estimates:

Working Population	4,750
At Home Population	9,022
Total	13,772

INCOME

2001 Estimates:

Avg. Household Income	$44,789
Avg. Family Income	$51,741
Per Capita Income	$18,353
Male:	
Avg. Employment Income	$29,305
Avg. Employment Income (Full Time)	$40,986
Female:	
Avg. Employment Income	$17,100
Avg. Employment Income (Full Time)	$28,066

DISPOSABLE & DISCRETIONARY INCOME

2001 Estimates: *Per Hhld.*

Disposable Income	$34,790
Discretionary Income 1 (minus Food & Shelter)	$23,703
Discretionary Income 2 (minus Food, Shelter, & Other Expenditures)	$16,192

LIQUID ASSETS

1999 Estimates: *Per Hhld.*

Equity Investments	$64,593
Interest Bearing Investments	$59,516
Total Liquid Assets	$124,109

CREDIT DATA

July 2000:

Pool of Credit	$133,733,231
Revolving Credit, No.	25,729
Fixed Loans, No.	6,836
Avg. Credit Limit, per Person	$11,223
Avg. Spent, per Person	$4,989
Satisfactory Ratings, No. per Person	2.63
Avg. No. of Cards, per Person	0.96

LABOUR FORCE

2001 Estimates:

Male:

In the Labour Force	4,260
Participation Rate	67.4
Employed	3,939
Unemployed	321
Unemployment Rate	7.5
Not in Labour Force	2,059

Female:

In the Labour Force	3,782
Participation Rate	53.7
Employed	3,521
Unemployed	261
Unemployment Rate	6.9
Not in Labour Force	3,263

OCCUPATIONS BY MAJOR GROUPS

2001 Estimates:	Male	Female
Management	396	200
Business, Finance & Admin.	264	942
Natural & Applied Sciences & Related	316	45
Health	107	294
Social Sciences, Gov't Services & Religion	78	159
Education	140	251
Arts, Culture, Recreation & Sport	47	83
Sales & Service	846	1,446
Trades, Transport & Equipment Operators & Related	1,221	86
Primary Industries	456	177
Processing, Mfg. & Utilities	335	25

LEVEL OF SCHOOLING

2001 Estimates:

Population 15 years +	13,364
Less than Grade 9	1,107
Grades 9-13 w/o Certif.	3,500
Grade 9-13 with Certif.	1,613
Trade Certif. /Dip.	607
Non-Univ. w/o Certif./Dip.	1,067
Non-Univ. with Certif./Dip.	2,830
Univ. w/o Degree	1,242
Univ. w/o Degree/Certif.	474
Univ. with Certif.	768
Univ. with Degree	1,398

AVERAGE HOUSEHOLD EXPENDITURES

2001 Estimates:

Food	$5,297
Shelter	$7,643
Clothing	$1,736
Transportation	$5,924
Health & Personal Care	$1,680
Recr'n, Read'g & Education	$3,166
Taxes & Securities	$11,117
Other	$7,047
Total Expenditures	$43,610

PRIVATE HOUSEHOLDS

2001 Estimates:

Private Households, Total	6,706
Pop. in Private Households	15,997
Average no. per Household	2.4

FAMILIES

2001 Estimates:

Families in Private Households	4,813
Husband-Wife Families	4,263
Lone-Parent Families	550
Aver. No. Persons per Family	2.9
Aver. No. Sons/Daughters at Home	1.0

HOUSING

2001 Estimates:

Occupied Private Dwellings	6,706
Owned	4,972
Rented	1,734
Single-Detached House	4,564
Semi-Detached House	122
Row Houses	431
Apartment, 5 or Fewer Storeys	648
Apartment, Detached Duplex	296
Other Single-Attached	12
Movable Dwellings	633

VEHICLES

2001 Estimates:

Model Yrs. '81-'96, No.	7,769
% Total	83.93
Model Yrs. '97-'98, No.	967
% Total	10.45
'99 Vehicles registered in Model Yr. '99, No.	521
% Total	5.63
Total No. '81-'99	9,257

LEGAL MARITAL STATUS

2001 Estimates: (Age 15+)

Single (Never Married)	3,074
Legally Married (Not Separated)	7,642
Legally Married (Separated)	464
Widowed	1,134
Divorced	1,050

PSYTE CATEGORIES

2001 Estimates	No. of House-holds	% of Total Hhds.	Index
Small City Elite	496	7.40	432
Town Boomers	1,202	17.92	1,768
Rustic Prosperity	246	3.67	203
Pick-ups & Dirt Bikes	53	0.79	95
Old Leafy Towns	3,073	45.82	1,793
Nesters & Young Homesteaders	297	4.43	190
Quiet Towns	807	12.03	566
Aged Pensioners	454	6.77	509

FINANCIAL P$YTE

2001 Estimates	No. of House-holds	% of Total Hhds.	Index
Canadian Comfort	1,698	25.32	261
Tractors & Tradelines	246	3.67	64
Bills & Wills	3,073	45.82	553
Country Credit	53	0.79	12
Revolving Renters	297	4.43	96
Limited Budgets	807	12.03	387
Senior Survivors	454	6.77	359

British Columbia

HOME LANGUAGE

2001 Estimates:		% Total
English	16,069	98.19
French	34	0.21
Dutch	33	0.20
Finnish	22	0.13
German	125	0.76
Spanish	23	0.14
Multiple Responses	59	0.36
Total	16,365	100.00

BUILDING PERMITS

	1999	1998	1997
		$000	
Value	13,848	34,111	32,222

HOMES BUILT

	1999	1998	1997
No.	57	115	188

TAXATION

Income Class:	1997	% Total
Under $5,000	1,530	12.55
$5,000-$10,000	1,650	13.54
$10,000-$15,000	2,040	16.74
$15,000-$20,000	1,330	10.91
$20,000-$25,000	1,050	8.61
$25,000-$30,000	840	6.89
$30,000-$40,000	1,430	11.73
$40,000-$50,000	970	7.96
$50,000 +	1,350	11.07
Total Returns, No.	12,190	
Total Income, $000	312,585	
Total Taxable Returns	8,180	
Total Tax, $000	54,926	
Average Income, $	25,643	
Average Tax, $	6,715	

VITAL STATISTICS

	1997	1996	1995	1994
Births	153	167	161	160
Deaths	174	146	161	180
Natural Increase	-21	21		-20
Marriages	105	112	119	123

Note: Latest available data.

COMMUNITY NEWSPAPER(S)

	Total Circulation
Salmon Arm: Salmon Arm Observer	3,532
Salmon Arm: The Shuswap Market News	15,024
Salmon Arm: Lakeshore News	15,100

RADIO STATION(S)

	Power
CBUC-FM	n.a.
CKXR	10,000w

TELEVISION STATION(S)

CFSA-TV
CHAN-TV
CHBC-TV

British Columbia

Squamish
(District Municipality)

In Squamish-Lillooet Regional District.

POPULATION

July 1, 2001 Estimate	16,141
% Cdn. Total	0.05
% Change, '96 -'01	5.30
Avg. Annual Growth Rate, %	1.04
2003 Projected Population	16,611
2006 Projected Population	17,263
2001 Households Estimate	6,148
2003 Projected Households	6,170
2006 Projected Households	6,398

INCOME

% Above/Below National Average	+7
2001 Total Income Estimate	$362,760,000
% Cdn. Total	0.06
2001 Average Hhld. Income	$59,000
2001 Per Capita	$22,500
2003 Projected Total Income	$383,510,000
2006 Projected Total Income	$431,310,000

RETAIL SALES

% Above/Below National Average	-26
2001 Retail Sales Estimate	$107,220,000
% Cdn. Total	0.04
2001 per Household	$17,400
2001 per Capita	$6,600
2001 No. of Establishments	137
2003 Projected Retail Sales	$118,460,000
2006 Projected Retail Sales	$135,930,000

POPULATION

2001 Estimates:

Total		16,141
Male		8,200
Female		7,941

Age Groups	Male	Female
0-4	567	540
5-9	645	611
10-14	653	617
15-19	619	589
20-24	548	522
25-29	532	523
30-34	623	635
35-39	718	731
40-44	733	722
45-49	677	633
50-54	539	482
55-59	395	344
60-64	297	276
65-69	236	219
70+	418	497

DAYTIME POPULATION

2001 Estimates:

Working Population	2,034
At Home Population	7,982
Total	10,016

INCOME

2001 Estimates:

Avg. Household Income	$59,005
Avg. Family Income	$62,473
Per Capita Income	$22,475
Male:	
Avg. Employment Income	$38,267
Avg. Employment Income (Full Time)	$50,325
Female:	
Avg. Employment Income	$21,488
Avg. Employment Income (Full Time)	$32,251

DISPOSABLE & DISCRETIONARY INCOME

2001 Estimates: *Per Hhld.*

Disposable Income	$45,278
Discretionary Income 1 (minus Food & Shelter)	$31,601
Discretionary Income 2 (minus Food, Shelter, & Other Expenditures)	$21,986

LIQUID ASSETS

1999 Estimates: *Per Hhld.*

Equity Investments	$88,550
Interest Bearing Investments	$77,848
Total Liquid Assets	$166,398

CREDIT DATA

July 2000:

Pool of Credit	$150,457,929
Revolving Credit, No.	26,911
Fixed Loans, No.	6,245
Avg. Credit Limit, per Person	$11,916
Avg. Spent, per Person	$5,585
Satisfactory Ratings, No. per Person	2.56
Avg. No. of Cards, per Person	0.94

LABOUR FORCE

2001 Estimates:

Male:	
In the Labour Force	4,847
Participation Rate	76.5
Employed	4,549
Unemployed	298
Unemployment Rate	6.1
Not in Labour Force	1,488
Female:	
In the Labour Force	4,014
Participation Rate	65.0
Employed	3,689
Unemployed	325
Unemployment Rate	8.1
Not in Labour Force	2,159

OCCUPATIONS BY MAJOR GROUPS

2001 Estimates:

	Male	Female
Management	526	247
Business, Finance & Admin.	139	896
Natural & Applied Sciences & Related	347	72
Health	78	391
Social Sciences, Gov't Services & Religion	50	89
Education	46	179
Arts, Culture, Recreation & Sport	90	84
Sales & Service	899	1,847
Trades, Transport & Equipment Operators & Related	1,908	76
Primary Industries	271	46
Processing, Mfg. & Utilities	432	12

LEVEL OF SCHOOLING

2001 Estimates:

Population 15 years +	12,508
Less than Grade 9	790
Grades 9-13 w/o Certif.	3,208
Grade 9-13 with Certif.	1,763
Trade Certif. /Dip.	460
Non-Univ. w/o Certif./Dip.	1,142
Non-Univ. with Certif./Dip.	2,903
Univ. w/o Degree	1,138
Univ. w/o Degree/Certif.	535
Univ. with Certif.	603
Univ. with Degree	1,104

AVERAGE HOUSEHOLD EXPENDITURES

2001 Estimates:

Food	$6,375
Shelter	$9,448
Clothing	$2,243
Transportation	$7,533
Health & Personal Care	$2,053
Recr'n, Read'g & Education	$3,994
Taxes & Securities	$14,968
Other	$8,917
Total Expenditures	$55,531

PRIVATE HOUSEHOLDS

2001 Estimates:

Private Households, Total	6,148
Pop. in Private Households	15,996
Average no. per Household	2.6

FAMILIES

2001 Estimates:

Families in Private Households	4,930
Husband-Wife Families	4,249
Lone-Parent Families	681
Aver. No. Persons per Family	3.1
Aver. No. Sons/Daughters at Home	1.2

HOUSING

2001 Estimates:

Occupied Private Dwellings	6,148
Owned	4,501
Rented	1,647
Single-Detached House	3,791
Semi-Detached House	248
Row Houses	547
Apartment, 5+ Storeys	19
Owned Apartment, 5+ Storeys	19
Apartment, 5 or Fewer Storeys	732
Apartment, Detached Duplex	372
Other Single-Attached	90
Movable Dwellings	349

VEHICLES

2001 Estimates:

Model Yrs. '81-'96, No.	7,133
% Total	86.96
Model Yrs. '97-'98, No.	725
% Total	8.84
'99 Vehicles registered in Model Yr. '99, No.	345
% Total	4.21
Total No. '81-'99	8,203

LEGAL MARITAL STATUS

2001 Estimates: (Age 15+)

Single (Never Married)	3,678
Legally Married (Not Separated)	6,865
Legally Married (Separated)	490
Widowed	506
Divorced	969

PSYTE CATEGORIES

2001 Estimates	No. of House -holds	% of Total Hhds.	Index
Mortgaged in Suburbia	100	1.63	117
Boomers & Teens	420	6.83	381
Satellite Suburbs	470	7.64	266
Kindergarten Boom	122	1.98	76
Blue Collar Winners	1,112	18.09	718
Old Towns' New Fringe	1,864	30.32	775
The New Frontier	766	12.46	826
Quiet Towns	1,294	21.05	989

FINANCIAL P$YTE

2001 Estimates	No. of House -holds	% of Total Hhds.	Index
Four Star Investors	420	6.83	136
Successful Suburbanites	100	1.63	25
Canadian Comfort	1,582	25.73	265
Miners & Credit-Liners	766	12.46	394
Mortgages & Minivans	122	1.98	30
Tractors & Tradelines	1,864	30.32	530
Limited Budgets	1,294	21.05	677

HOME LANGUAGE

2001 Estimates: *% Total*

English	14,439	89.46
French	115	0.71
Czech	12	0.07
German	156	0.97
Italian	46	0.28
Polish	35	0.22
Punjabi	1,034	6.41
Slovak	27	0.17
Spanish	12	0.07
Thai	12	0.07
Urdu	28	0.17
Other Languages	23	0.14
Multiple Responses	202	1.25
Total	16,141	100.00

BUILDING PERMITS

	1999	1998 $000	1997
Value	6,253	14,559	19,607

HOMES BUILT

	1999	1998	1997
No	25	62	243

TAXATION

Income Class:*	1997	% Total
Under $5,000	880	12.41
$5,000-$10,000	900	12.69
$10,000-$15,000	880	12.41
$15,000-$20,000	670	9.45
$20,000-$25,000	570	8.04
$25,000-$30,000	540	7.62
$30,000-$40,000	830	11.71
$40,000-$50,000	660	9.31
$50,000 +	1,170	16.50
Total Returns, No.	7,090	
Total Income, $000	195,822	
Total Taxable Returns	5,120	
Total Tax, $000	36,681	
Average Income, $	27,619	
Average Tax, $	7,164	

VITAL STATISTICS

	1997	1996	1995	1994
Births	220	221	236	224
Deaths	75	83	73	85
Natural Increase	145	138	163	139
Marriages	77	71	79	60

Note: Latest available data.

COMMUNITY NEWSPAPER(S)

	Total Circulation
Squamish: Squamish Chief	3,901

RADIO STATION(S)

	Power
CBRU	n.a.
CISQ-FM	20,000w

TELEVISION STATION(S)

CBUT-TV
CHAN-TV

Summerland
(District Municipality)

In Okanagan-Similkameen Regional District.

POPULATION

July 1, 2001 Estimate	11,337
% Cdn. Total	0.04
% Change, '96 -'01	3.44
Avg. Annual Growth Rate, %	0.68
2003 Projected Population	11,450
2006 Projected Population	11,531
2001 Households Estimate	4,634
2003 Projected Households	4,682
2006 Projected Households	4,737

INCOME

% Above/Below National Average	-12
2001 Total Income Estimate	$209,810,000
% Cdn. Total	0.03
2001 Average Hhld. Income	$45,300
2001 Per Capita	$18,500
2003 Projected Total Income	$222,610,000
2006 Projected Total Income	$242,670,000

RETAIL SALES

% Above/Below National Average	-52
2001 Retail Sales Estimate	$49,170,000
% Cdn. Total	0.02
2001 per Household	$10,600
2001 per Capita	$4,300
2001 No. of Establishments	83
2003 Projected Retail Sales	$52,450,000
2006 Projected Retail Sales	$57,940,000

POPULATION

2001 Estimates:

Total		11,337
Male		5,384
Female		5,953

Age Groups	Male	Female
0-4	266	254
5-9	317	302
10-14	378	373
15-19	383	384
20-24	313	309
25-29	267	257
30-34	274	296
35-39	318	390
40-44	362	438
45-49	384	428
50-54	332	363
55-59	286	322
60-64	270	306
65-69	291	329
70+	943	1,202

DAYTIME POPULATION

2001 Estimates:

Working Population	3,145
At Home Population	6,866
Total	10,011

INCOME

2001 Estimates:

Avg. Household Income	$45,276
Avg. Family Income	$50,063
Per Capita Income	$18,507
Male:	
Avg. Employment Income	$27,247
Avg. Employment Income (Full Time)	$40,438
Female:	
Avg. Employment Income	$18,020
Avg. Employment Income (Full Time)	$28,974

DISPOSABLE & DISCRETIONARY INCOME

2001 Estimates:	Per Hhld.
Disposable Income	$35,123
Discretionary Income 1 (minus Food & Shelter)	$23,926
Discretionary Income 2 (minus Food, Shelter, & Other Expenditures)	$16,289

LIQUID ASSETS

1999 Estimates:	Per Hhld.
Equity Investments	$67,984
Interest Bearing Investments	$59,711
Total Liquid Assets	$127,695

CREDIT DATA

July 2000:

Pool of Credit	$109,092,251
Revolving Credit, No.	22,406
Fixed Loans, No.	4,738
Avg. Credit Limit, per Person	$10,639
Avg. Spent, per Person	$4,292
Satisfactory Ratings, No. per Person	2.57
Avg. No. of Cards, per Person	0.97

LABOUR FORCE

2001 Estimates:

Male:

In the Labour Force	2,617
Participation Rate	59.2
Employed	2,362
Unemployed	255
Unemployment Rate	9.7
Not in Labour Force	1,806

Female:

In the Labour Force	2,354
Participation Rate	46.9
Employed	2,180
Unemployed	174
Unemployment Rate	7.4
Not in Labour Force	2,670

OCCUPATIONS BY MAJOR GROUPS

2001 Estimates:	Male	Female
Management	282	73
Business, Finance & Admin.	189	562
Natural & Applied Sciences & Related	157	n.a.
Health	44	311
Social Sciences, Gov't Services & Religion	48	73
Education	152	110
Arts, Culture, Recreation & Sport	22	55
Sales & Service	376	832
Trades, Transport & Equipment Operators & Related	802	46
Primary Industries	252	177
Processing, Mfg. & Utilities	261	62

LEVEL OF SCHOOLING

2001 Estimates:

Population 15 years +	9,447
Less than Grade 9	733
Grades 9-13 w/o Certif.	2,636
Grade 9-13 with Certif.	1,080
Trade Certif. /Dip.	458
Non-Univ. w/o Certif./Dip.	508
Non-Univ. with Certif./Dip.	2,193
Univ. w/o Degree	884
Univ. w/o Degree/Certif.	388
Univ. with Certif.	496
Univ. with Degree.	955

AVERAGE HOUSEHOLD EXPENDITURES

2001 Estimates:

Food	$5,409
Shelter	$7,733
Clothing	$1,705
Transportation	$6,063
Health & Personal Care	$1,688
Recr'n, Read'g & Education	$3,315
Taxes & Securities	$11,309
Other	$7,056
Total Expenditures	$44,278

PRIVATE HOUSEHOLDS

2001 Estimates:

Private Households, Total	4,634
Pop. in Private Households	11,133
Average no. per Household	2.4

FAMILIES

2001 Estimates:

Families in Private Households	3,521
Husband-Wife Families	3,149
Lone-Parent Families	372
Aver. No. Persons per Family	2.7
Aver. No. Sons/Daughters at Home	0.9

HOUSING

2001 Estimates:

Occupied Private Dwellings	4,634
Owned	3,784
Rented	850
Single-Detached House	3,556
Semi-Detached House	152
Row Houses	295
Apartment, 5 or Fewer Storeys	396
Apartment, Detached Duplex	96
Movable Dwellings	139

VEHICLES

2001 Estimates:

Model Yrs. '81-'96, No.	5,083
% Total	87.67
Model Yrs. '97-'98, No.	482
% Total	8.31
'99 Vehicles registered in Model Yr. '99, No.	233
% Total	4.02
Total No. '81-'99	5,798

LEGAL MARITAL STATUS

2001 Estimates: (Age 15+)

Single (Never Married)	1,734
Legally Married (Not Separated)	5,869
Legally Married (Separated)	291
Widowed	880
Divorced	673

PSYTE CATEGORIES

2001 Estimates	No. of House -holds	% of Total Hhds.	Index
Small City Elite	1,008	21.75	1,269
Old Towns' New Fringe	288	6.21	159
High Rise Sunsets	290	6.26	438
Old Leafy Towns	2,455	52.98	2,073
Quiet Towns	325	7.01	330
Big Country Families	268	5.78	405

FINANCIAL PSYTE

2001 Estimates	No. of House -holds	% of Total Hhds.	Index
Canadian Comfort	1,008	21.75	224
Tractors & Tradelines	288	6.21	109
Bills & Wills	2,455	52.98	640
Revolving Renters	290	6.26	136
Rural Family Blues	268	5.78	72
Limited Budgets	325	7.01	226

British Columbia

HOME LANGUAGE

2001 Estimates:		% Total
English	10,858	95.77
French	11	0.10
Chinese	22	0.19
Croatian	11	0.10
Dutch	38	0.34
German	107	0.94
Hungarian	22	0.19
Italian	16	0.14
Persian (Farsi)	11	0.10
Punjabi	99	0.87
Tagalog (Pilipino)	11	0.10
Multiple Responses	131	1.16
Total	11,337	100.00

BUILDING PERMITS

	1999	1998	1997
		$000	
Value	10,440	6,878	11,877

HOMES BUILT

	1999	1998	1997
No.	27	44	n.a.

TAXATION

Income Class:	1997	% Total
Under $5,000	880	10.81
$5,000-$10,000	1,040	12.78
$10,000-$15,000	1,530	18.80
$15,000-$20,000	940	11.55
$20,000-$25,000	700	8.60
$25,000-$30,000	630	7.74
$30,000-$40,000	990	12.16
$40,000-$50,000	580	7.13
$50,000 +	840	10.32

Total Returns, No.	8,140
Total Income, $000	197,548
Total Taxable Returns	5,610
Total Tax, $000	31,520
Average Income, $	24,269
Average Tax, $	5,619

VITAL STATISTICS

	1997	1996	1995	1994
Births	80	91	104	88
Deaths	134	162	140	130
Natural Increase	-54	-71	-36	-42
Marriages	61	73	55	67

Note: Latest available data.

COMMUNITY NEWSPAPER(S)

	Total Circulation
Summerland: Bulletin	3,500
Summerland: Summerland Review	2,321

RADIO STATION(S)

	Power
CHOR	1,000w

British Columbia

Sunshine Coast, Subd. A

(Subdivision of Regional District)

In Sunshine Coast Regional District.

POPULATION

July 1, 2001 Estimate	14,715
% Cdn. Total	0.05
% Change, '96 -'01	8.58
Avg. Annual Growth Rate, %	1.66
2003 Projected Population	15,318
2006 Projected Population	16,048
2001 Households Estimate	6,069
2003 Projected Households	6,299
2006 Projected Households	6,664

INCOME

% Above/Below National Average	-3
2001 Total Income Estimate	$301,510,000
% Cdn. Total	0.05
2001 Average Hhld. Income	$49,700
2001 Per Capita	$20,500
2003 Projected Total Income	$327,460,000
2006 Projected Total Income	$369,950,000

RETAIL SALES

% Above/Below National Average	-80
2001 Retail Sales Estimate	$25,880,000
% Cdn. Total	0.01
2001 per Household	$4,300
2001 per Capita	$1,800
2001 No. of Establishments	130
2003 Projected Retail Sales	$28,300,000
2006 Projected Retail Sales	$33,580,000

POPULATION

2001 Estimates:

Total		14,715
Male		7,390
Female		7,325

Age Groups	Male	Female
0-4	402	393
5-9	485	479
10-14	545	544
15-19	514	499
20-24	379	382
25-29	331	351
30-34	401	446
35-39	517	565
40-44	626	636
45-49	664	622
50-54	577	523
55-59	453	411
60-64	368	358
65-69	343	340
70+	785	776

DAYTIME POPULATION

2001 Estimates:

Working Population	968
At Home Population	8,178
Total	9,146

INCOME

2001 Estimates:

Avg. Household Income	$49,680
Avg. Family Income	$54,258
Per Capita Income	$20,490
Male:	
Avg. Employment Income	$32,162
Avg. Employment Income (Full Time)	$45,703
Female:	
Avg. Employment Income	$18,415
Avg. Employment Income (Full Time)	$29,491

DISPOSABLE & DISCRETIONARY INCOME

2001 Estimates:	Per Hhld.
Disposable Income	$38,139
Discretionary Income 1 (minus Food & Shelter)	$26,059
Discretionary Income 2 (minus Food, Shelter, & Other Expenditures)	$17,856

LIQUID ASSETS

1999 Estimates:	Per Hhld.
Equity Investments	$73,497
Interest Bearing Investments	$64,882
Total Liquid Assets	$138,379

CREDIT DATA

July 2000:

Pool of Credit	$74,535,033
Revolving Credit, No.	12,780
Fixed Loans, No.	3,463
Avg. Credit Limit, per Person	$11,533
Avg. Spent, per Person	$4,954
Satisfactory Ratings, No. per Person	2.47
Avg. No. of Cards, per Person	0.88

LABOUR FORCE

2001 Estimates:

Male:	
In the Labour Force	3,846
Participation Rate	64.6
Employed	3,592
Unemployed	254
Unemployment Rate	6.6
Not in Labour Force	2,112
Female:	
In the Labour Force	3,145
Participation Rate	53.2
Employed	2,956
Unemployed	189
Unemployment Rate	6.0
Not in Labour Force	2,764

OCCUPATIONS BY MAJOR GROUPS

2001 Estimates:	Male	Female
Management	401	205
Business, Finance & Admin.	156	812
Natural & Applied Sciences & Related	297	36
Health	52	214
Social Sciences, Gov't Services & Religion	64	78
Education	118	219
Arts, Culture, Recreation & Sport	112	122
Sales & Service	642	1,144
Trades, Transport & Equipment Operators & Related	1,211	60
Primary Industries	445	56
Processing, Mfg. & Utilities	258	37

LEVEL OF SCHOOLING

2001 Estimates:

Population 15 years +	11,867
Less than Grade 9	485
Grades 9-13 w/o Certif.	2,989
Grade 9-13 with Certif.	1,650
Trade Certif. /Dip.	479
Non-Univ. w/o Certif./Dip.	844
Non-Univ. with Certif./Dip.	2,811
Univ. w/o Degree	1,255
Univ. w/o Degree/Certif.	600
Univ. with Certif.	655
Univ. with Degree	1,354

AVERAGE HOUSEHOLD EXPENDITURES

2001 Estimates:

Food	$5,699
Shelter	$8,336
Clothing	$1,800
Transportation	$6,572
Health & Personal Care	$1,758
Recr'n, Read'g & Education	$3,485
Taxes & Securities	$12,885
Other	$7,442
Total Expenditures	$47,977

PRIVATE HOUSEHOLDS

2001 Estimates:

Private Households, Total	6,069
Pop. in Private Households	14,304
Average no. per Household	2.4

FAMILIES

2001 Estimates:

Families in Private Households	4,488
Husband-Wife Families	4,054
Lone-Parent Families	434
Aver. No. Persons per Family	2.8
Aver. No. Sons/Daughters at Home	1.0

HOUSING

2001 Estimates:

Occupied Private Dwellings	6,069
Owned	4,839
Rented	1,230
Single-Detached House	5,379
Semi-Detached House	91
Row Houses	10
Apartment, 5 or Fewer Storeys	34
Apartment, Detached Duplex	182
Movable Dwellings	373

VEHICLES

2001 Estimates:

Model Yrs. '81-'96, No.	8,339
% Total	89.84
Model Yrs. '97-'98, No.	661
% Total	7.12
'99 Vehicles registered in Model Yr. '99, No.	282
% Total	3.04
Total No. '81-'99	9,282

LEGAL MARITAL STATUS

2001 Estimates: (Age 15+)

Single (Never Married)	2,694
Legally Married (Not Separated)	6,963
Legally Married (Separated)	412
Widowed	582
Divorced	1,216

PSYTE CATEGORIES

2001 Estimates	No. of House-holds	% of Total Hhds.	Index
Urban Gentry	55	0.91	50
Small City Elite	635	10.46	611
Satellite Suburbs	93	1.53	53
Blue Collar Winners	746	12.29	488
Town Boomers	310	5.11	504
Old Towns' New Fringe	428	7.05	180
Old Leafy Towns	3,507	57.79	2,261
Rod & Rifle	143	2.36	102
Old Cdn. Rustics	60	0.99	101

FINANCIAL P$YTE

2001 Estimates	No. of House-holds	% of Total Hhds.	Index
Four Star Investors	55	0.91	18
Canadian Comfort	1,784	29.40	303
Tractors & Tradelines	428	7.05	123
Bills & Wills	3,507	57.79	698
Rural Family Blues	143	2.36	29
Limited Budgets	60	0.99	32

HOME LANGUAGE

2001 Estimates:		% Total
English	14,383	97.74
French	74	0.50
Chinese	34	0.23
Czech	11	0.07
German	78	0.53
Hungarian	17	0.12
Japanese	23	0.16
Polish	11	0.07
Multiple Responses	84	0.57
Total	14,715	100.00

BUILDING PERMITS

	1999	1998 $000	1997
Value	4,077	6,881	n.a.

TAXATION

Income Class:	1997	% Total
Under $5,000	450	11.87
$5,000-$10,000	540	14.25
$10,000-$15,000	620	16.36
$15,000-$20,000	400	10.55
$20,000-$25,000	300	7.92
$25,000-$30,000	290	7.65
$30,000-$40,000	450	11.87
$40,000-$50,000	260	6.86
$50,000 +	500	13.19
Total Returns, No.	3,790	
Total Income, $000	101,240	
Total Taxable Returns	2,650	
Total Tax, $000	18,564	
Average Income, $	26,712	
Average Tax, $	7,005	

VITAL STATISTICS

	1997	1996	1995	1994
Births	52	48	55	54
Deaths	41	42	51	39
Natural Increase	11	6	4	15
Marriages	33	41	38	41

Note: Latest available data.

Terrace
(Census Agglomeration)

The Census Agglomeration of Terrace includes: Terrace, C; Kitimat-Stikine, Subd. C, SRD; plus several smaller areas. All are in Kitimat-Stikine Regional District.

POPULATION

July 1, 2001 Estimate	21,964
% Cdn. Total	0.07
% Change, '96 -'01	0.73
Avg. Annual Growth Rate, %	0.15
2003 Projected Population	21,837
2006 Projected Population	21,583
2001 Households Estimate	8,169
2003 Projected Households	8,367
2006 Projected Households	8,645

INCOME

% Above/Below National Average	+3
2001 Total Income Estimate	$474,980,000
% Cdn. Total	0.07
2001 Average Hhld. Income	$58,100
2001 Per Capita	$21,600
2003 Projected Total Income	$510,490,000
2006 Projected Total Income	$564,410,000

RETAIL SALES

% Above/Below National Average	+10
2001 Retail Sales Estimate	$216,760,000
% Cdn. Total	0.08
2001 per Household	$26,500
2001 per Capita	$9,900
2001 No. of Establishments	178
2003 Projected Retail Sales	$235,230,000
2006 Projected Retail Sales	$258,990,000

POPULATION

2001 Estimates:

Total	21,964
Male	11,196
Female	10,768

Age Groups	Male	Female
0-4	791	751
5-9	914	846
10-14	949	875
15-19	906	846
20-24	838	797
25-29	829	811
30-34	858	876
35-39	888	935
40-44	903	894
45-49	838	795
50-54	722	657
55-59	548	482
60-64	411	358
65-69	315	279
70+	486	566

DAYTIME POPULATION

2001 Estimates:

Working Population	10,793
At Home Population	11,171
Total	21,964

INCOME

2001 Estimates:

Avg. Household Income	$58,144
Avg. Family Income	$62,355
Per Capita Income	$21,625
Male:	
Avg. Employment Income	$38,936
Avg. Employment Income (Full Time)	$51,148
Female:	
Avg. Employment Income	$21,191
Avg. Employment Income (Full Time)	$33,702

DISPOSABLE & DISCRETIONARY INCOME

2001 Estimates:	*Per Hhld.*
Disposable Income	$44,826
Discretionary Income 1 (minus Food & Shelter)	$32,691
Discretionary Income 2 (minus Food, Shelter, & Other Expenditures)	$22,783

LIQUID ASSETS

1999 Estimates:	*Per Hhld.*
Equity Investments	$94,180
Interest Bearing Investments	$78,488
Total Liquid Assets	$172,668

CREDIT DATA

July 2000:

Pool of Credit	$189,706,088
Revolving Credit, No.	32,704
Fixed Loans, No.	12,983
Avg. Credit Limit, per Person	$12,345
Avg. Spent, per Person	$6,163
Satisfactory Ratings, No. per Person	2.80
Avg. No. of Cards, per Person	0.99

LABOUR FORCE

2001 Estimates:

Male:	
In the Labour Force	6,639
Participation Rate	77.7
Employed	5,981
Unemployed	658
Unemployment Rate	9.9
Not in Labour Force	1,903
Female:	
In the Labour Force	5,311
Participation Rate	64.0
Employed	4,958
Unemployed	353
Unemployment Rate	6.6
Not in Labour Force	2,985

OCCUPATIONS BY MAJOR GROUPS

2001 Estimates:	Male	Female
Management	653	263
Business, Finance & Admin.	425	1,441
Natural & Applied Sciences & Related	523	53
Health	71	374
Social Sciences, Gov't Services & Religion	154	228
Education	115	330
Arts, Culture, Recreation & Sport	57	142
Sales & Service	1,027	2,038
Trades, Transport & Equipment Operators & Related	2,235	74
Primary Industries	803	130
Processing, Mfg. & Utilities	444	114

LEVEL OF SCHOOLING

2001 Estimates:

Population 15 years +	16,838
Less than Grade 9	1,473
Grades 9-13 w/o Certif.	4,617
Grade 9-13 with Certif.	2,426
Trade Certif. /Dip.	591
Non-Univ. w/o Certif./Dip.	1,238
Non-Univ. with Certif./Dip.	3,550
Univ. w/o Degree	1,665
Univ. w/o Degree/Certif.	717
Univ. with Certif.	948
Univ. with Degree	1,278

AVERAGE HOUSEHOLD EXPENDITURES

2001 Estimates:

Food	$6,389
Shelter	$7,982
Clothing	$2,538
Transportation	$7,605
Health & Personal Care	$2,273
Recr'n, Read'g & Education	$4,617
Taxes & Securities	$14,095
Other	$9,221
Total Expenditures	$54,720

PRIVATE HOUSEHOLDS

2001 Estimates:

Private Households, Total	8,169
Pop. in Private Households	21,604
Average no. per Household	2.6

FAMILIES

2001 Estimates:

Families in Private Households	6,322
Husband-Wife Families	5,439
Lone-Parent Families	883
Aver. No. Persons per Family	3.2
Aver. No. Sons/Daughters at Home	1.3

HOUSING

2001 Estimates:

Occupied Private Dwellings	8,169
Owned	5,680
Rented	2,402
Band Housing	87
Single-Detached House	5,563
Semi-Detached House	335
Row Houses	401
Apartment, 5 or Fewer Storeys	847
Apartment, Detached Duplex	269
Other Single-Attached	29
Movable Dwellings	725

VEHICLES

2001 Estimates:

Model Yrs. '81-'96, No.	10,015
% Total	81.84
Model Yrs. '97-'98, No.	1,405
% Total	11.48
'99 Vehicles registered in Model Yr. '99, No.	818
% Total	6.68
Total No. '81-'99	12,238

LEGAL MARITAL STATUS

2001 Estimates: (Age 15+)

Single (Never Married)	5,531
Legally Married (Not Separated)	8,658
Legally Married (Separated)	733
Widowed	686
Divorced	1,230

PSYTE CATEGORIES

2001 Estimates	No. of House-holds	% of Total Hhds.	Index
Town Boomers	1,091	13.36	1,318
Northern Lights	1,740	21.30	4,303
The New Frontier	3,927	48.07	3,187
Young Grey Collar	773	9.46	1,131
Quiet Towns	458	5.61	263
Big Country Families	144	1.76	124

FINAN¢IAL P$YTE

2001 Estimates	No. of House-holds	% of Total Hhds.	Index
Successful Suburbanites	1,740	21.30	321
Canadian Comfort	1,091	13.36	137
Miners & Credit-Liners	3,927	48.07	1,519
Revolving Renters	773	9.46	206
Rural Family Blues	144	1.76	22
Limited Budgets	458	5.61	180

HOME LANGUAGE

2001 Estimates:		% Total
English	20,649	94.01
French	157	0.71
Chinese	47	0.21
Czech	11	0.05
Greek	11	0.05
Italian	32	0.15
Portuguese	277	1.26
Punjabi	321	1.46
Serbo-Croatian	31	0.14
Spanish	26	0.12
Tagalog (Pilipino)	31	0.14
Vietnamese	21	0.10
Other Languages	29	0.13
Multiple Responses	321	1.46
Total	21,964	100.00

British Columbia

BUILDING PERMITS

	1999	1998	1997
		$000	
Value	6,620	8,047	21,066

HOMES BUILT

	1999	1998	1997
No.	41	38	142

TAXATION

Income Class:	1997	% Total
Under $5,000	1,880	13.54
$5,000-$10,000	1,600	11.53
$10,000-$15,000	1,660	11.96
$15,000-$20,000	1,270	9.15
$20,000-$25,000	1,000	7.20
$25,000-$30,000	970	6.99
$30,000-$40,000	1,730	12.46
$40,000-$50,000	1,280	9.22
$50,000 +	2,500	18.01
Total Returns, No.	13,880	
Total Income, $000	402,365	
Total Taxable Returns	9,800	
Total Tax, $000	78,214	
Average Income, $.	28,989	
Average Tax, $	7,981	

VITAL STATISTICS

	1997	1996	1995	1994
Births	281	356	328	342
Deaths	99	90	95	89
Natural Increase	182	266	233	253
Marriages	117	140	137	128

Note: Latest available data.

COMMUNITY NEWSPAPER(S)

	Total Circulation
Terrace: Terrace Standard	7,792

RADIO STATION(S)

	Power
CBTH-FM	n.a.
CBUF-FM	100w
CFNR-FM	n.a.
CFTK	1,000w
CJFW-FM	2,500w

TELEVISION STATION(S)

CATV
CBUFT-TV
CFTK-TV

British Columbia

Vancouver
(Census Metropolitan Area)

POPULATION

July 1, 2001 Estimate	2,092,749
% Cdn. Total	6.72
% Change, '96 -'01	9.45
Avg. Annual Growth Rate, %	1.82
2003 Projected Population	2,182,269
2006 Projected Population	2,349,134
2001 Households Estimate	816,803
2003 Projected Households	855,947
2006 Projected Households	925,483

INCOME

% Above/Below National Average	+8
2001 Total Income Estimate	$47,738,050,000
% Cdn. Total	7.27
2001 Average Hhld. Income	$58,400
2001 Per Capita	$22,800
2003 Projected Total Income	$53,038,690,000
2006 Projected Total Income	$62,743,850,000

RETAIL SALES

% Above/Below National Average	-8
2001 Retail Sales Estimate	$17,323,830,000
% Cdn. Total	6.22
2001 per Household	$21,200
2001 per Capita	$8,300
2001 No. of Establishments	14,865
2003 Projected Retail Sales	$19,449,780,000
2006 Projected Retail Sales	$23,039,290,000

POPULATION

2001 Estimates:

Total		2,092,749
Male		1,029,030
Female		1,063,719

Age Groups	Male	Female
0-4	65,666	62,159
5-9	65,148	61,802
10-14	65,427	61,792
15-19	65,630	62,443
20-24	67,473	67,120
25-29	75,319	76,478
30-34	85,033	86,339
35-39	89,516	91,378
40-44	87,153	89,997
45-49	81,604	84,088
50-54	69,439	70,527
55-59	54,634	55,100
60-64	43,605	44,339
65-69	36,246	38,403
70+	77,137	111,754

DAYTIME POPULATION

2001 Estimates:

Working Population	1,011,186
At Home Population	1,081,600
Total	2,092,786

INCOME

2001 Estimates:

Avg. Household Income	$58,445
Avg. Family Income	$65,214
Per Capita Income	$22,811
Male:	
Avg. Employment Income	$37,772
Avg. Employment Income (Full Time)	$50,317
Female:	
Avg. Employment Income	$24,429
Avg. Employment Income (Full Time)	$35,329

DISPOSABLE & DISCRETIONARY INCOME

2001 Estimates:	Per Hhld.
Disposable Income	$44,925
Discretionary Income 1 (minus Food & Shelter)	$30,998
Discretionary Income 2 (minus Food, Shelter, & Other Expenditures)	$22,422

LIQUID ASSETS

1999 Estimates:	Per Hhld.
Equity Investments	$92,868
Interest Bearing Investments	$75,412
Total Liquid Assets	$168,280

CREDIT DATA

July 2000:

Pool of Credit	$21,492,100,378
Revolving Credit, No.	4,459,938
Fixed Loans, No.	912,409
Avg. Credit Limit, per Person	$11,753
Avg. Spent, per Person	$4,789
Satisfactory Ratings, No. per Person	2.90
Avg. No. of Cards, per Person	1.16

LABOUR FORCE

2001 Estimates:

Male:	
In the Labour Force	583,983
Participation Rate	70.1
Employed	543,612
Unemployed	40,371
Unemployment Rate	6.9
Not in Labour Force	248,806
Female:	
In the Labour Force	519,882
Participation Rate	59.2
Employed	483,170
Unemployed	36,712
Unemployment Rate	7.1
Not in Labour Force	358,084

OCCUPATIONS BY MAJOR GROUPS

2001 Estimates:	Male	Female
Management	78,913	34,996
Business, Finance & Admin.	67,439	164,498
Natural & Applied Sciences & Related	46,634	9,159
Health	11,803	38,401
Social Sciences, Gov't Services & Religion	13,170	17,662
Education	15,100	25,005
Arts, Culture, Recreation & Sport	17,247	18,448
Sales & Service	132,401	165,372
Trades, Transport & Equipment Operators & Related	134,938	7,471
Primary Industries	15,831	6,590
Processing, Mfg. & Utilities	35,252	16,200

LEVEL OF SCHOOLING

2001 Estimates:

Population 15 years +	1,710,755
Less than Grade 9	123,945
Grades 9-13 w/o Certif.	355,444
Grade 9-13 with Certif.	220,283
Trade Certif. /Dip.	46,652
Non-Univ. w/o Certif./Dip.	127,786
Non-Univ. with Certif./Dip.	321,065
Univ. w/o Degree	220,687
Univ. w/o Degree/Certif.	107,039
Univ. with Certif.	113,648
Univ. with Degree	294,893

AVERAGE HOUSEHOLD EXPENDITURES

2001 Estimates:

Food	$6,539
Shelter	$9,863
Clothing	$2,348
Transportation	$6,581
Health & Personal Care	$2,032
Recr'n, Read'g & Education	$3,895
Taxes & Securities	$15,437
Other	$8,572
Total Expenditures	$55,267

PRIVATE HOUSEHOLDS

2001 Estimates:

Private Households, Total	816,803
Pop. in Private Households	2,060,382
Average no. per Household	2.5

FAMILIES

2001 Estimates:

Families in Private Households	568,063
Husband-Wife Families	490,081
Lone-Parent Families	77,982
Aver. No. Persons per Family	3.0
Aver. No. Sons/Daughters at Home	1.1

HOUSING

2001 Estimates:

Occupied Private Dwellings	816,803
Owned	488,231
Rented	328,314
Band Housing	258
Single-Detached House	374,133
Semi-Detached House	18,314
Row Houses	59,246
Apartment, 5+ Storeys	87,896
Owned Apartment, 5+ Storeys	26,170
Apartment, 5 or Fewer Storeys	205,626
Apartment, Detached Duplex	65,476
Other Single-Attached	1,332
Movable Dwellings	4,780

VEHICLES

2001 Estimates:

Model Yrs. '81-'96, No.	836,910
% Total	78.47
Model Yrs. '97-'98, No.	137,852
% Total	12.92
'99 Vehicles registered in Model Yr. '99, No.	91,836
% Total	8.61
Total No. '81-'99	1,066,598

LEGAL MARITAL STATUS

2001 Estimates: (Age 15+)

Single (Never Married)	562,273
Legally Married (Not Separated)	873,249
Legally Married (Separated)	53,677
Widowed	97,989
Divorced	123,567

PSYTE CATEGORIES

2001 Estimates	No. of House-holds	% of Total Hhds.	Index
Canadian Establishment	2,441	0.30	180
The Affluentials	20,568	2.52	394
Urban Gentry	26,836	3.29	183
Suburban Executives	11,013	1.35	94
Mortgaged in Suburbia	17,784	2.18	157
Technocrafts & Bureaucrats	13,860	1.70	60
Asian Heights	15,378	1.88	297
Boomers & Teens	43,366	5.31	296
Stable Suburban Families	16,965	2.08	159
Small City Elite	7,060	0.86	50
Old Bungalow Burbs	8,186	1.00	60
Suburban Nesters	20,548	2.52	157
Brie & Chablis	21,458	2.63	293
Aging Erudites	16,806	2.06	136
Satellite Suburbs	60,007	7.35	256
Kindergarten Boom	45,607	5.58	213
Blue Collar Winners	26,695	3.27	130
Old Towns' New Fringe	3,291	0.40	10
The New Frontier	62	0.01	1
Rustic Prosperity	143	0.02	1
Asian Mosaic	123,446	15.11	1,102
Conservative Homebodies	15,679	1.92	53
High Rise Sunsets	24,755	3.03	212
Young Urban Professionals	39,561	4.84	255
Young Urban Mix	51,662	6.32	298
Young Urban Intelligentsia	39,475	4.83	318
University Enclaves	24,938	3.05	150
Young City Singles	42,329	5.18	226
Urban Bohemia	13,908	1.70	145
Old Leafy Towns	1,963	0.24	9
Town Renters	10,789	1.32	153
Nesters & Young Homesteaders	3,421	0.42	18
Rod & Rifle	15	0.00	
Big Country Families	308	0.04	3
Struggling Downtowns	12,031	1.47	47
Aged Pensioners	18,189	2.23	167
Big City Stress	6,095	0.75	66
Old Grey Towers	3,887	0.48	86

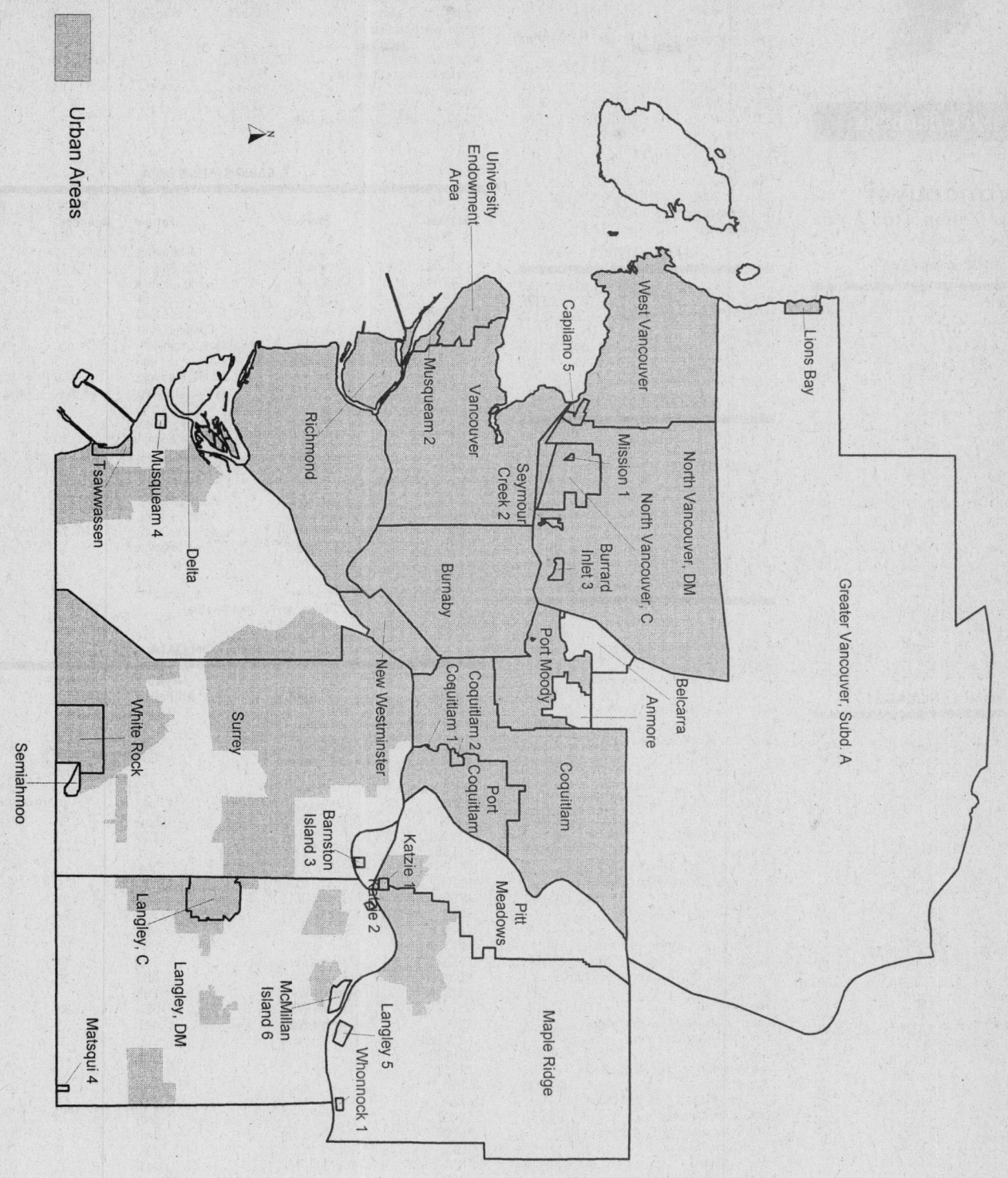

Urban Areas

N

University
Endowment
Area

Musqueam 2

Vancouver

Richmond

Capilano 5

West Vancouver

Mission 1

North Vancouver, DM

North Vancouver, C

Lions Bay

Seymour
Creek 2

Burrard
Inlet 3

Greater Vancouver, Subd. A

Tsawwassen

Musqueam 4

Delta

Burnaby

Port Moody

Belcarra

Anmore

Semiahmoo

White Rock

Surrey

New Westminster

Coquitlam 2

Coquitlam 1

Coquitlam

Port
Coquitlam

Coquitlam

Barnston
Island 3

Katzie

Pitt
Meadows

Langley, C

Pitt
Meadows

Barge 2

Langley, DM

McMillan
Island 6

Langley 5

Maple Ridge

Matsqui 4

Whonnock 1

British Columbia

Vancouver
(Census Metropolitan Area)
(Cont'd)

FINANCIAL P$YTE

2001 Estimates	No. of House-holds	% of Total Hhds.	Index
Platinum Estates	23,009	2.82	350
Four Star Investors	81,215	9.94	198
Successful Suburbanites	63,987	7.83	118
Canadian Comfort	114,310	13.99	144
Urban Heights	77,825	9.53	221
Miners & Credit-Liners	8,248	1.01	32
Mortgages & Minivans	45,607	5.58	85
Dollars & Sense	123,446	15.11	578
Tractors & Tradelines	3,434	0.42	7
Bills & Wills	69,304	8.48	102
Revolving Renters	28,176	3.45	75
Young Urban Struggle	78,321	9.59	203
Rural Family Blues	323	0.04	..
Towering Debt	65,149	7.98	102
NSF	6,095	0.75	21
Senior Survivors	22,076	2.70	143

HOME LANGUAGE

2001 Estimates:		% Total
English	1,587,856	75.87
French	7,605	0.36
Arabic	2,476	0.12
Chinese	226,388	10.82
Croatian	2,499	0.12
Czech	1,728	0.08
Dutch	1,151	0.05
Finnish	1,169	0.06
German	4,998	0.24
Greek	2,484	0.12
Gujarati	3,189	0.15
Hindi	9,939	0.47
Hungarian	2,053	0.10
Italian	7,045	0.34
Japanese	8,929	0.43
Korean	14,319	0.68
Persian (Farsi)	10,013	0.48
Polish	8,090	0.39
Portuguese	3,827	0.18
Punjabi	61,886	2.96
Romanian	2,170	0.10
Russian	2,581	0.12
Serbian	2,431	0.12
Serbo-Croatian	1,709	0.08
Spanish	10,973	0.52
Tagalog (Pilipino)	12,840	0.61
Urdu	1,638	0.08
Vietnamese	12,324	0.59
Other Languages	14,910	0.71
Multiple Responses	63,529	3.04
Total	2,092,749	100.00

BUILDING PERMITS

	1999	1998	1997
		$000	
Value	2,643,536	2,859,755	3,316,213

HOMES BUILT

	1999	1998	1997
No	11,102	13,927	16,041

TAXATION

Income Class:	1997	% Total
Under $5,000	200,270	14.44
$5,000-$10,000	179,790	12.97
$10,000-$15,000	183,770	13.25
$15,000-$20,000	123,410	8.90
$20,000-$25,000	105,570	7.61
$25,000-$30,000	99,490	7.18
$30,000-$40,000	172,520	12.44
$40,000-$50,000	115,090	8.30
$50,000 +	206,630	14.90
Total Returns, No.	1,386,490	
Total Income, $000	40,802,251	
Total Taxable Returns	959,050	
Total Tax, $000	8,449,936	
Average Income, $	29,428	
Average Tax, $	8,811	

VITAL STATISTICS

	1997	1996	1995	1994
Births	22,674	23,299	23,671	23,370
Deaths	12,430	12,650	12,227	12,045
Natural Increase	10,244	10,649	11,444	11,325
Marriages	10,408	10,860	11,482	11,910

Note: Latest available data.

DAILY NEWSPAPER(S)

	Circulation Average Paid
The Province	
Sun	196,012
Mon-Fri	157,325
The Vancouver Sun	
Fri	219,598
Sat	249,470
Mon-Thu	186,448

COMMUNITY NEWSPAPER(S)

	Total Circulation
Bowen Island, West Vancouver: Undercurrent	n.a.
Burnaby: The Burnaby News Leader Sun/Wed	47,165
Burnaby: Burnaby Now Sun/Wed	47,706
Coquitlam, Port Coquitlam, Port Moody: Now Wed/Sat	50,351
Coquitlam, Port Coquitlam, Port Moody: The Tri-City News Wed/Sun	52,686
Delta: Delta Optimist Wed/Sat	16,460
Delta: North Delta Sentinel (biwkly)	n.a.
Delta (South)/Tsawwassen/Ladner: South Delta Leader	15,300
Langley: Langley Advance News Tue/Fri	40,400
Langley: Langley Times Wed/Fri/Sun	38,396
Maple Ridge, Pitt Meadows: The Maple Ridge News Sun/Wed	25,816
Maple Ridge, Pitt Meadows: Maple Ridge-Pitt Meadows Times Tue/Fri	26,081
New Westminster: The News Leader Sun/Wed	14,979
New Westminster: New West Minster Now/Royal City Record	15,982
North Vancouver, West Vancouver: North Shore News Wed/Fri/Sun	64,471
North Vancouver, West Vancouver: The North Shore Outlook	n.a.
Richmond: Richmond News Sun/Wed	43,531
Richmond: Richmond Review Fri	42,673
Wed/Sun	45,085
Surrey: The Peace Arch News Wed/Sat	28,213
Surrey: Surrey/North Delta Now Wed/Sat	106,662

	Total Circulation
Surrey, North Delta: The Leader Wed/Fri/Sun	81,915
Vancouver: The False Creek News	25,000
Vancouver: Westcoast Families (mthly)	50,000
Vancouver: Community Digest	25,000
Vancouver: East Side Revue (biwkly)	4,564
Vancouver: The Georgia Straight	107,995
Vancouver: L'Express du Pacifique (biwkly)	n.a.
Vancouver: The Link	12,450
Vancouver: North Shore News Wed/Fri/Sun	64,471
Vancouver: West Ender	43,681
Vancouver: West Side Revue (biwkly)	7,765

	Total Circulation
Vancouver: Courier East Side Edition Sun/Wed	58,011
Vancouver: Jewish Western Bulletin	2,611
Vancouver: Courier Downtown Edition	23,075
Vancouver: Courier West Side Edition Sun/Wed	59,982
White Rock: The Peace Arch News Wed/Sat	28,213

RADIO STATION DATA

Station	Market	Format	Wkly. Reach%*	Aver. Hrs. Tuned
All Stations			93	20.1
CBU	Vancouver	Multi-format	12	10.7
CBU-FM	Vancouver	Multi-format	11	11.8
CBUF-FM	Vancouver	Multi-format	1	5.4
CFMC	Burnaby	AOR	n.a.	n.a.
CFMI-FM	Vancouver	Classic Rock	17	9.3
CFOX-FM	Vancouver	Contemp. Rock	15	7.2
CFRO-FM	Vancouver	Altern., Community	n.a.	n.a.
CFUN	Vancouver	Talk	5	7.5
CHKG-FM	Vancouver	Ethnic, Multiling.	n.a.	n.a.
CHMB	Vancouver	Ethnic, Multiling.	n.a.	n.a.
CHQM-FM	Vancouver	Adult Contemp.	17	8.5
CISL	Vancouver	Oldies	7	6.9
CJJR-FM	Vancouver	New Country	10	11.4
CJVB	Vancouver	Ethnic, Multiling.	n.a.	n.a.
CKBD	Vancouver	Adult Favourites	6	10.0
CKKQ-FM	Victoria	AOR	3	3.4
CKKS-FM	Vancouver	Adult Contemp.	14	8.0
CKLG	Vancouver	Adult Contemp.	3	4.4
CKNW	Vancouver	News, Talk, Sports	24	11.2
CKSR-FM	Vancouver	Easy Listening	13	5.7
CKST	Vancouver	New, Talk	n.a.	n.a.
CKWX	Vancouver	News	13	4.7
CKZZ-FM	Vancouver	Contemp. Hits	29	7.5

BBM Spring 2000 Radio Reach Survey; area coverage.
*Mon-Sun 5a.m - 1a.m , All Persons 12+

TV STATION DATA

Station	Market	Network Affiliation	Wkly. Reach%*	Aver. Hrs. Tuned
All Stations			94	22.0
A & E	n.a.	Ind.	24	3.1
CBUFT	Vancouver	SRC	1	2.1
CBUT	Vancouver	CBC	45	3.0
CHAN	Vancouver	CTV	64	5.7
CHEK	Victoria	CTV	31	2.3
CIVT	Vancouver	Ind.	49	2.8
CKVU	Vancouver	Global	53	3.2
CTV NNT	n.a.	CTV	6	2.1
DSCVRY	n.a.	Ind.	7	1.6
FAMILY	n.a.	Ind.	6	1.8
HISTTV	n.a.	Ind.	5	2.3
KCPQ	Tacoma WA	FOX	27	2.0
KCTS	Seattle WA	PBS	29	2.6
KING	Seattle WA	NBC	20	1.4
KIRO	Seattle WA	CBS	25	2.1
KNOW	Vancouver	n.a.	14	1.8
KOMO	Seattle WA	ABC	38	1.8
KSPS	Spokane WA	PBS	-	10.8
KSTW	Tacoma WA	UPN	32	2.2
KVOS	Bellingham WA	Ind.	31	1.9
NEWSWD	n.a.	CBC	9	1.7
OTHERS	n.a.	n.a.	9	5.0
PRIME	n.a.	Ind.	7	2.4
SHWCSE	n.a.	Ind.	7	2.1
SNET	n.a.	CTV	18	2.9
SPACE	n.a.	Ind.	7	2.9
SUPER	n.a.	Ind.	3	4.8
TLC	n.a.	Ind.	8	1.6
TNN	Nashville TN	Ind.	6	2.7
TOON	n.a.	Ind.	9	2.8
TSN	n.a.	Ind.	16	3.5
VCR	n.a.	n.a.	39	3.6
WTBS	Atlanta GA	Ind.	17	2.7
WTN	n.a.	Ind.	11	1.2
WTVS	Detroit MI	PBS	7	1.5
YTV	n.a.	Ind.	10	2.1

BBM Spring 2000 TV Reach Survey; CMA coverage.
*Mon-Sun 6a.m - 2a.m , All Persons 2 +

Burnaby
(City)
Vancouver CMA

In Greater Vancouver Regional District.

POPULATION

July 1, 2001 Estimate	201,495
% Cdn. Total	0.65
% Change, '96 -'01	7.70
Avg. Annual Growth Rate, %	1.50
2003 Projected Population	207,988
2006 Projected Population	220,829
2001 Households Estimate	80,555
2003 Projected Households	83,772
2006 Projected Households	89,659

INCOME

% Above/Below National Average	-1
2001 Total Income Estimate	$4,222,840,000
% Cdn. Total	0.64
2001 Average Hhld. Income	$52,400
2001 Per Capita	$21,000
2003 Projected Total Income	$4,634,990,000
2006 Projected Total Income	$5,387,550,000

RETAIL SALES

% Above/Below National Average	-1
2001 Retail Sales Estimate	$1,789,380,000
%·Cdn. Total	0.64
2001 per Household	$22,200
2001 per Capita	$8,900
2001 No. of Establishments	1,395
2003 Projected Retail Sales	$1,991,260,000
2006 Projected Retail Sales	$2,329,100,000

POPULATION

2001 Estimates:

Total		201,495
Male		98,727
Female		102,768

Age Groups	Male	Female
0-4	6,219	5,840
5-9	5,758	5,388
10-14	5,664	5,381
15-19	5,948	5,720
20-24	6,780	6,824
25-29	8,090	8,005
30-34	8,840	8,682
35-39	8,747	8,723
40-44	8,216	8,321
45-49	7,504	7,746
50-54	6,213	6,470
55-59	4,976	5,215
60-64	4,195	4,477
65-69	3,688	4,024
70+	7,889	11,952

DAYTIME POPULATION

2001 Estimates:

Working Population	117,989
At Home Population	109,522
Total	227,511

INCOME

2001 Estimates:

Avg. Household Income	$52,422
Avg. Family Income	$57,845
Per Capita Income	$20,958
Male:	
Avg. Employment Income	$33,711
Avg. Employment Income (Full Time)	$45,415
Female:	
Avg. Employment Income	$23,887
Avg. Employment Income (Full Time)	$34,343

DISPOSABLE & DISCRETIONARY INCOME

2001 Estimates:	Per Hhld.
Disposable Income	$40,767
Discretionary Income 1 (minus Food & Shelter)	$27,404
Discretionary Income 2 (minus Food, Shelter, & Other Expenditures)	$19,316

LIQUID ASSETS

1999 Estimates:	Per Hhld.
Equity Investments	$72,687
Interest Bearing Investments	$65,637
Total Liquid Assets	$138,324

CREDIT DATA

July 2000:

Pool of Credit	$1,944,363,195
Revolving Credit, No.	443,417
Fixed Loans, No.	79,655
Avg. Credit Limit, per Person	$10,403
Avg. Spent, per Person	$3,953
Satisfactory Ratings, No. per Person	2.76
Avg. No. of Cards, per Person	1.11

LABOUR FORCE

2001 Estimates:

Male:	
In the Labour Force	53,757
Participation Rate	66.3
Employed	49,785
Unemployed	3,972
Unemployment Rate	7.4
Not in Labour Force	27,329
Female:	
In the Labour Force	47,650
Participation Rate	55.3
Employed	44,034
Unemployed	3,616
Unemployment Rate	7.6
Not in Labour Force	38,509

OCCUPATIONS BY MAJOR GROUPS

2001 Estimates:	Male	Female
Management	6,783	3,100
Business, Finance & Admin.	6,987	16,865
Natural & Applied Sciences & Related	5,185	933
Health	970	2,949
Social Sciences, Gov't Services & Religion	942	1,544
Education	1,251	2,250
Arts, Culture, Recreation & Sport	1,342	1,261
Sales & Service	12,176	14,599
Trades, Transport & Equipment Operators & Related	12,818	825
Primary Industries	820	281
Processing, Mfg. & Utilities	2,954	1,389

LEVEL OF SCHOOLING

2001 Estimates:

Population 15 years +	167,245
Less than Grade 9	12,857
Grades 9-13 w/o Certif.	34,889
Grade 9-13 with Certif.	21,678
Trade Certif. /Dip.	4,590
Non-Univ. w/o Certif./Dip.	12,806
Non-Univ. with Certif./Dip.	30,984
Univ. w/o Degree	22,094
Univ. w/o Degree/Certif.	10,449
Univ. with Certif.	11,645
Univ. with Degree	27,347

AVERAGE HOUSEHOLD EXPENDITURES

2001 Estimates:

Food	$6,522
Shelter	$9,198
Clothing	$2,197
Transportation	$6,217
Health & Personal Care	$2,005
Recr'n, Read'g & Education	$3,434
Taxes & Securities	$13,101
Other	$7,779
Total Expenditures	$50,453

PRIVATE HOUSEHOLDS

2001 Estimates:

Private Households, Total	80,555
Pop. in Private Households	197,575
Average no. per Household	2.5

FAMILIES

2001 Estimates:

Families in Private Households	54,039
Husband-Wife Families	46,188
Lone-Parent Families	7,851
Aver. No. Persons per Family	2.9
Aver. No. Sons/Daughters at Home	1.1

HOUSING

2001 Estimates:

Occupied Private Dwellings	80,555
Owned	44,021
Rented	36,534
Single-Detached House	30,892
Semi-Detached House	2,156
Row Houses	6,064
Apartment, 5+ Storeys	13,795
Owned Apartment, 5+ Storeys	6,222
Apartment, 5 or Fewer Storeys	21,547
Apartment, Detached Duplex	5,932
Other Single-Attached	121
Movable Dwellings	48

VEHICLES

2001 Estimates:

Model Yrs. '81-'96, No.	85,001
% Total	76.96
Model Yrs. '97-'98, No.	15,476
% Total	14.01
'99 Vehicles registered in Model Yr. '99, No.	9,968
% Total	9.03
Total No. '81-'99	110,445

LEGAL MARITAL STATUS

2001 Estimates: (Age 15+)

Single (Never Married)	58,042
Legally Married (Not Separated)	81,461
Legally Married (Separated)	4,946
Widowed	10,959
Divorced	11,837

PSYTE CATEGORIES

2001 Estimates	No. of House-holds	% of Total Hhds.	Index
The Affluentials	835	1.04	162
Urban Gentry	954	1.18	66
Mortgaged in Suburbia	736	0.91	66
Technocrafts & Bureaucrats	2,773	3.44	122
Asian Heights	980	1.22	192
Boomers & Teens	449	0.56	31
Stable Suburban Families	4,032	5.01	384
Suburban Nesters	7,876	9.78	610
Brie & Chablis	4,776	5.93	662
Aging Erudites	786	0.98	65
Satellite Suburbs	782	0.97	34
Kindergarten Boom	547	0.68	26
Asian Mosaic	22,273	27.65	2,017
Conservative Homebodies	202	0.25	7
High Rise Sunsets	2,134	2.65	185
Young Urban Mix	12,057	14.97	706
Young Urban Intelligentsia	25	0.03	2

British Columbia

2001 Estimates	No. of House-holds	% of Total Hhds.	Index
University Enclaves	3,869	4.80	235
Young City Singles	10,116	12.56	548
Town Renters	484	0.60	70
Struggling Downtowns	79	0.10	3
Aged Pensioners	1,159	1.44	108
Old Grey Towers	1,748	2.17	392

FINANCIAL P$YTE

2001 Estimates	No. of House-holds	% of Total Hhds.	Index
Platinum Estates	835	1.04	129
Four Star Investors	1,403	1.74	35
Successful Suburbanites	8,521	10.58	159
Canadian Comfort	8,658	10.75	111
Urban Heights	5,562	6.90	160
Mortgages & Minivans	547	0.68	10
Dollars & Sense	22,273	27.65	1,058
Bills & Wills	12,259	15.22	184
Revolving Renters	2,134	2.65	58
Young Urban Struggle	3,894	4.83	102
Towering Debt	10,679	13.26	170
Senior Survivors	2,907	3.61	192

HOME LANGUAGE

2001 Estimates:		% Total
English	137,793	68.39
French	760	0.38
Arabic	466	0.23
Bengali	131	0.07
Chinese	30,859	15.32
Croatian	1,002	0.50
Czech	177	0.09
Finnish	147	0.07
German	448	0.22
Greek	118	0.06
Gujarati	763	0.38
Hindi	954	0.47
Hungarian	299	0.15
Italian	1,724	0.86
Japanese	1,185	0.59
Korean	3,398	1.69
Malay-Bahasa	226	0.11
Persian (Farsi)	1,174	0.58
Polish	1,338	0.66
Portuguese	491	0.24
Punjabi	2,952	1.47
Romanian	322	0.16
Russian	324	0.16
Serbian	804	0.40
Serbo-Croatian	547	0.27
Spanish	1,489	0.74
Tagalog (Pilipino)	1,088	0.54
Urdu	194	0.10
Vietnamese	329	0.16
Other Languages	2,156	1.07
Multiple Responses	7,837	3.89
Total	201,495	100.00

British Columbia

Burnaby
(City)
Vancouver CMA
(Cont'd)

BUILDING PERMITS

	1999	1998	1997
		$000	
Value	267,163	328,778	306,468

HOMES BUILT

	1999	1998	1997
No	1,172	1,063	807

TAXATION

Income Class:	1997	% Total
Under $5,000	22,220	16.59
$5,000-$10,000	17,800	13.29
$10,000-$15,000	18,270	13.64
$15,000-$20,000	12,250	9.15
$20,000-$25,000	10,540	7.87
$25,000-$30,000	9,520	7.11
$30,000-$40,000	16,900	12.62
$40,000-$50,000	10,660	7.96
$50,000 +	15,790	11.79
Total Returns, No.	133,930	
Total Income, $000	3,424,080	
Total Taxable Returns	88,940	
Total Tax, $000	639,572	
Average Income, $	25,566	
Average Tax, $	7,191	

VITAL STATISTICS

	1997	1996	1995	1994
Births	2,018	2,103	2,118	2,030
Deaths	1,325	1,412	1,347	1,331
Natural Increase	693	691	771	699
Marriages	910	988	1,014	1,030

Note: Latest available data.

MEDIA INFO
see Vancouver, CMA

Coquitlam
(City)
Vancouver CMA

In Greater Vancouver Regional District.

POPULATION

July 1, 2001 Estimate	122,105
% Cdn. Total	0.39
% Change, '96 -'01	14.88
Avg. Annual Growth Rate, %	2.81
2003 Projected Population	130,605
2006 Projected Population	145,302
2001 Households Estimate	44,492
2003 Projected Households	47,875
2006 Projected Households	53,562

INCOME

% Above/Below National Average	+7
2001 Total Income Estimate	$2,744,970,000
% Cdn. Total	0.42
2001 Average Hhld. Income	$61,700
2001 Per Capita	$22,500
2003 Projected Total Income	$3,147,780,000
2006 Projected Total Income	$3,883,040,000

RETAIL SALES

% Above/Below National Average	-24
2001 Retail Sales Estimate	$825,490,000
% Cdn. Total	0.30
2001 per Household	$18,600
2001 per Capita	$6,800
2001 No. of Establishments	627
2003 Projected Retail Sales	$947,410,000
2006 Projected Retail Sales	$1,154,290,000

POPULATION

2001 Estimates:

Total		122,105
Male		60,536
Female		61,569

Age Groups	Male	Female
0-4	3,940	3,728
5-9	4,178	3,870
10-14	4,320	4,019
15-19	4,232	3,981
20-24	4,112	3,995
25-29	4,363	4,374
30-34	4,867	4,995
35-39	5,305	5,509
40-44	5,319	5,553
45-49	4,969	5,068
50-54	4,130	4,119
55-59	3,163	3,172
60-64	2,449	2,447
65-69	1,897	1,981
70+	3,292	4,758

DAYTIME POPULATION

2001 Estimates:

Working Population	23,014
At Home Population	60,902
Total	83,916

INCOME

2001 Estimates:

Avg. Household Income	$61,696
Avg. Family Income	$65,545
Per Capita Income	$22,480
Male:	
Avg. Employment Income	$38,872
Avg. Employment Income (Full Time)	$50,075
Female:	
Avg. Employment Income	$25,185
Avg. Employment Income (Full Time)	$36,442

DISPOSABLE & DISCRETIONARY INCOME

2001 Estimates:	Per Hhld.
Disposable Income	$47,511
Discretionary Income 1 (minus Food & Shelter)	$33,261
Discretionary Income 2 (minus Food, Shelter, & Other Expenditures)	$24,206

LIQUID ASSETS

1999 Estimates:	Per Hhld.
Equity Investments	$91,957
Interest Bearing Investments	$78,472
Total Liquid Assets	$170,429

CREDIT DATA

July 2000:

Pool of Credit	$1,254,484,779
Revolving Credit, No.	257,670
Fixed Loans, No.	55,332
Avg. Credit Limit, per Person	$12,592
Avg. Spent, per Person	$5,241
Satisfactory Ratings, No. per Person	3.08
Avg. No. of Cards, per Person	1.18

LABOUR FORCE

2001 Estimates:

Male:	
In the Labour Force	34,657
Participation Rate	72.1
Employed	32,857
Unemployed	1,800
Unemployment Rate	5.2
Not in Labour Force	13,441
Female:	
In the Labour Force	30,590
Participation Rate	61.2
Employed	28,710
Unemployed	1,880
Unemployment Rate	6.1
Not in Labour Force	19,362

OCCUPATIONS BY MAJOR GROUPS

2001 Estimates:	Male	Female
Management	5,161	2,194
Business, Finance & Admin.	4,100	11,191
Natural & Applied Sciences & Related	2,857	543
Health	591	2,565
Social Sciences, Gov't Services & Religion	552	895
Education	923	1,415
Arts, Culture, Recreation & Sport	744	828
Sales & Service	7,458	9,144
Trades, Transport & Equipment Operators & Related	9,197	412
Primary Industries	593	56
Processing, Mfg. & Utilities	1,864	641

LEVEL OF SCHOOLING

2001 Estimates:

Population 15 years +	98,050
Less than Grade 9	5,013
Grades 9-13 w/o Certif.	20,475
Grade 9-13 with Certif.	13,926
Trade Certif. /Dip.	2,754
Non-Univ. w/o Certif./Dip.	7,696
Non-Univ. with Certif./Dip.	20,378
Univ. w/o Degree	13,515
Univ. w/o Degree/Certif.	6,569
Univ. with Certif.	6,946
Univ. with Degree	14,293

AVERAGE HOUSEHOLD EXPENDITURES

2001 Estimates:

Food	$6,685
Shelter	$9,955
Clothing	$2,455
Transportation	$7,047
Health & Personal Care	$2,001
Recr'n, Read'g & Education	$4,064
Taxes & Securities	$16,816
Other	$8,967
Total Expenditures	$57,990

PRIVATE HOUSEHOLDS

2001 Estimates:

Private Households, Total	44,492
Pop. in Private Households	119,905
Average no. per Household	2.7

FAMILIES

2001 Estimates:

Families in Private Households	34,524
Husband-Wife Families	30,135
Lone-Parent Families	4,389
Aver. No. Persons per Family	3.1
Aver. No. Sons/Daughters at Home	1.2

HOUSING

2001 Estimates:

Occupied Private Dwellings	44,492
Owned	31,029
Rented	13,463
Single-Detached House	24,925
Semi-Detached House	1,229
Row Houses	3,074
Apartment, 5+ Storeys	1,776
Owned Apartment, 5+ Storeys	1,002
Apartment, 5 or Fewer Storeys	10,346
Apartment, Detached Duplex	2,647
Other Single-Attached	43
Movable Dwellings	452

VEHICLES

2001 Estimates:

Model Yrs. '81-'96, No.	50,852
% Total	81.34
Model Yrs. '97-'98, No.	7,252
% Total	11.60
'99 Vehicles registered in Model Yr. '99, No.	4,415
% Total	7.06
Total No. '81-'99	62,519

LEGAL MARITAL STATUS

2001 Estimates: (Age 15+)

Single (Never Married)	29,702
Legally Married (Not Separated)	54,139
Legally Married (Separated)	3,023
Widowed	4,546
Divorced	6,640

PSYTE CATEGORIES

2001 Estimates	No. of House-holds	% of Total Hhds.	Index
Suburban Executives	411	0.92	64
Mortgaged in Suburbia	1,229	2.76	199
Technocrafts & Bureaucrats	2,534	5.70	202
Asian Heights	3,344	7.52	1,186
Boomers & Teens	3,067	6.89	385
Stable Suburban Families	3,711	8.34	640
Old Bungalow Burbs	3,322	7.47	450
Suburban Nesters	2,565	5.77	360
Brie & Chablis	2,851	6.41	715
Aging Erudites	579	1.30	86
Satellite Suburbs	3,817	8.58	299
Kindergarten Boom	2,188	4.92	188
Blue Collar Winners	551	1.24	49

Coquitlam
(City)
Vancouver CMA
(Cont'd)

2001 Estimates	No. of House-holds	% of Total Hhds.	Index
Asian Mosaic	455	1.02	75
Conservative Homebodies	1,025	2.30	64
Young Urban Mix	5,390	12.11	572
University Enclaves	2,158	4.85	238
Young City Singles	2,041	4.59	200
Town Renters	975	2.19	254
Nesters & Young Homesteaders	343	0.77	33
Struggling Downtowns	772	1.74	55
Aged Pensioners	673	1.51	114

FINANCIAL P$YTE

2001 Estimates	No. of House-holds	% of Total Hhds.	Index
Four Star Investors	3,478	7.82	156
Successful Suburbanites	10,818	24.31	366
Canadian Comfort	6,933	15.58	160
Urban Heights	3,430	7.71	179
Miners & Credit-Liners	3,322	7.47	236
Mortgages & Minivans	2,188	4.92	75
Dollars & Sense	455	1.02	39
Bills & Wills	6,415	14.42	174
Revolving Renters	343	0.77	17
Young Urban Struggle	2,158	4.85	102
Towering Debt	3,788	8.51	109
Senior Survivors	673	1.51	80

HOME LANGUAGE

2001 Estimates:		% Total
English	96,411	78.96
French	620	0.51
Arabic	139	0.11
Bulgarian	80	0.07
Chinese	12,527	10.26
Croatian	194	0.16
Czech	76	0.06
Finnish	104	0.09
German	212	0.17
Gujarati	204	0.17
Hindi	265	0.22
Hungarian	119	0.10
Italian	417	0.34
Japanese	416	0.34
Korean	2,221	1.82
Malay-Bahasa	86	0.07
Persian (Farsi)	748	0.61
Polish	837	0.69
Portuguese	110	0.09
Punjabi	688	0.56
Romanian	399	0.33
Serbian	97	0.08
Slovak	244	0.20
Spanish	506	0.41
Tagalog (Pilipino)	535	0.44
Vietnamese	168	0.14
Other Languages	663	0.54
Multiple Responses	3,019	2.47
Total	122,105	100.00

BUILDING PERMITS

	1999	1998 $000	1997
Value	79,804	124,041	156,610

HOMES BUILT

	1999	1998	1997
No	528	983	885

TAXATION

Income Class:	1997	% Total
Under $5,000	11,860	16.19
$5,000-$10,000	8,480	11.58
$10,000-$15,000	8,530	11.65
$15,000-$20,000	5,960	8.14
$20,000-$25,000	5,290	7.22
$25,000-$30,000	5,160	7.05
$30,000-$40,000	9,710	13.26
$40,000-$50,000	6,790	9.27
$50,000 +	11,470	15.66
Total Returns, No.	73,240	
Total Income, $000	2,058,359	
Total Taxable Returns	51,370	
Total Tax, $000	403,967	
Average Income, $	28,104	
Average Tax, $	7,864	

VITAL STATISTICS

	1997	1996	1995	1994
Births	1,225	1,312	1,309	1,283
Deaths	514	514	495	497
Natural Increase	711	798	814	786
Marriages	311	320	359	423

Note: Latest available data.

MEDIA INFO
see Vancouver, CMA

Delta
(District Municipality)
Vancouver CMA

In Greater Vancouver Regional District.

POPULATION

July 1, 2001 Estimate	102,689
% Cdn. Total	0.33
% Change, '96 -'01	3.10
Avg. Annual Growth Rate, %	0.61
2003 Projected Population	103,586
2006 Projected Population	106,477
2001 Households Estimate	34,999
2003 Projected Households	35,552
2006 Projected Households	36,826

INCOME

% Above/Below National Average	+18
2001 Total Income Estimate	$2,545,090,000
% Cdn. Total	0.39
2001 Average Hhld. Income	$72,700
2001 Per Capita	$24,800
2003 Projected Total Income	$2,737,550,000
2006 Projected Total Income	$3,093,310,000

RETAIL SALES

% Above/Below National Average	-14
2001 Retail Sales Estimate	$793,010,000
% Cdn. Total	0.28
2001 per Household	$22,700
2001 per Capita	$7,700
2001 No. of Establishments	579
2003 Projected Retail Sales	$854,740,000
2006 Projected Retail Sales	$959,610,000

POPULATION

2001 Estimates:		
Total		102,689
Male		50,706
Female		51,983
Age Groups	Male	Female
0-4	3,011	2,880
5-9	3,400	3,304
10-14	3,815	3,622
15-19	3,967	3,702
20-24	3,746	3,510
25-29	3,268	3,169
30-34	3,203	3,324
35-39	3,617	3,900
40-44	3,993	4,328
45-49	4,210	4,502
50-54	3,963	4,045
55-59	3,218	3,116
60-64	2,342	2,293
65-69	1,712	1,766
70+	3,241	4,522

DAYTIME POPULATION

2001 Estimates:	
Working Population	42,495
At Home Population	48,854
Total	91,349

INCOME

2001 Estimates:	
Avg. Household Income	$72,719
Avg. Family Income	$74,948
Per Capita Income	$24,784
Male:	
Avg. Employment Income	$42,270
Avg. Employment Income (Full Time)	$54,085
Female:	
Avg. Employment Income	$24,948
Avg. Employment Income (Full Time)	$37,159

British Columbia

DISPOSABLE & DISCRETIONARY INCOME

2001 Estimates:	Per Hhld.
Disposable Income	$55,745
Discretionary Income 1 (minus Food & Shelter)	$39,965
Discretionary Income 2 (minus Food, Shelter, & Other Expenditures)	$29,570

LIQUID ASSETS

1999 Estimates:	Per Hhld.
Equity Investments	$114,685
Interest Bearing Investments	$92,200
Total Liquid Assets	$206,885

CREDIT DATA

July 2000:	
Pool of Credit	$1,173,827,698
Revolving Credit, No.	220,942
Fixed Loans, No.	53,793
Avg. Credit Limit, per Person	$13,975
Avg. Spent, per Person	$5,833
Satisfactory Ratings, No. per Person	3.22
Avg. No. of Cards, per Person	1.18

LABOUR FORCE

2001 Estimates:	
Male:	
In the Labour Force	30,484
Participation Rate	75.3
Employed	28,932
Unemployed	1,552
Unemployment Rate	5.1
Not in Labour Force	9,996
Female:	
In the Labour Force	27,292
Participation Rate	64.7
Employed	25,471
Unemployed	1,821
Unemployment Rate	6.7
Not in Labour Force	14,885

OCCUPATIONS BY MAJOR GROUPS

2001 Estimates:	Male	Female
Management	4,614	1,819
Business, Finance & Admin.	3,293	8,845
Natural & Applied Sciences & Related	2,412	375
Health	465	2,004
Social Sciences, Gov't Services & Religion	519	827
Education	689	1,539
Arts, Culture, Recreation & Sport	771	689
Sales & Service	6,566	9,050
Trades, Transport & Equipment Operators & Related	7,202	342
Primary Industries	1,237	358
Processing, Mfg. & Utilities	2,144	624

British Columbia

Delta
(District Municipality)
Vancouver CMA
(Cont'd)

LEVEL OF SCHOOLING

2001 Estimates:
Population 15 years +	82,657
Less than Grade 9	3,713
Grades 9-13 w/o Certif.	18,181
Grade 9-13 with Certif.	12,436
Trade Certif. /Dip.	2,575
Non-Univ. w/o Certif./Dip.	6,763
Non-Univ. with Certif./Dip.	17,048
Univ. w/o Degree	10,607
Univ. w/o Degree/Certif.	5,243
Univ. with Certif.	5,364
Univ. with Degree	11,334

AVERAGE HOUSEHOLD EXPENDITURES

2001 Estimates:
Food	$7,254
Shelter	$11,156
Clothing	$2,685
Transportation	$8,133
Health & Personal Care	$2,248
Recr'n, Read'g & Education	$4,655
Taxes & Securities	$20,507
Other	$10,326
Total Expenditures	$66,964

PRIVATE HOUSEHOLDS

2001 Estimates:
Private Households, Total	34,999
Pop. in Private Households	101,537
Average no. per Household	2.9

FAMILIES

2001 Estimates:
Families in Private Households	29,506
Husband-Wife Families	26,462
Lone-Parent Families	3,044
Aver. No. Persons per Family	3.1
Aver. No. Sons/Daughters at Home	1.3

HOUSING

2001 Estimates:
Occupied Private Dwellings	34,999
Owned	27,550
Rented	7,449
Single-Detached House	25,806
Semi-Detached House	927
Row Houses	1,229
Apartment, 5+ Storeys	306
Owned Apartment, 5+ Storeys	198
Apartment, 5 or Fewer Storeys	4,446
Apartment, Detached Duplex	2,047
Other Single-Attached	140
Movable Dwellings	98

VEHICLES

2001 Estimates:
Model Yrs. '81-'96, No.	46,341
% Total	84.81
Model Yrs. '97-'98, No.	4,945
% Total	9.05
'99 Vehicles registered in Model Yr. '99, No.	3,353
% Total	6.14
Total No. '81-'99	54,639

LEGAL MARITAL STATUS

2001 Estimates: (Age 15+)
Single (Never Married)	22,033
Legally Married (Not Separated)	49,603
Legally Married (Separated)	2,184
Widowed	3,969
Divorced	4,868

PSYTE CATEGORIES

2001 Estimates	No. of House-holds	% of Total Hhds.	Index
Suburban Executives	1,907	5.45	380
Mortgaged in Suburbia	174	0.50	36
Technocrafts & Bureaucrats	456	1.30	46
Boomers & Teens	9,278	26.51	1,479
Stable Suburban Families	1,674	4.78	367
Small City Elite	987	2.82	165
Old Bungalow Burbs	837	2.39	144
Suburban Nesters	928	2.65	165
Brie & Chablis	280	0.80	89
Aging Erudites	835	2.39	158
Satellite Suburbs	9,192	26.26	916
Kindergarten Boom	1,346	3.85	147
Blue Collar Winners	1,503	4.29	171
Conservative Homebodies	2,058	5.88	163
High Rise Sunsets	519	1.48	104
Young Urban Mix	912	2.61	123
University Enclaves	189	0.54	26
Young City Singles	355	1.01	44
Old Leafy Towns	159	0.45	18
Town Renters	634	1.81	210
Struggling Downtowns	442	1.26	40
Old Grey Towers	249	0.71	128

FINANCIAL PSYTE

2001 Estimates	No. of House-holds	% of Total Hhds.	Index
Four Star Investors	11,185	31.96	636
Successful Suburbanites	2,304	6.58	99
Canadian Comfort	12,610	36.03	371
Urban Heights	1,115	3.19	74
Miners & Credit-Liners	837	2.39	76
Mortgages & Minivans	1,346	3.85	58
Bills & Wills	3,129	8.94	108
Revolving Renters	519	1.48	32
Young Urban Struggle	189	0.54	11
Towering Debt	1,431	4.09	52
Senior Survivors	249	0.71	38

HOME LANGUAGE

2001 Estimates:		% Total
English	90,936	88.55
French	228	0.22
Arabic	76	0.07
Chinese	2,028	1.97
Croatian	54	0.05
Czech	125	0.12
Dutch	92	0.09
Finnish	77	0.07
German	190	0.19
Greek	129	0.13
Gujarati	57	0.06
Hindi	448	0.44
Italian	126	0.12
Japanese	141	0.14
Korean	172	0.17
Polish	171	0.17
Portuguese	125	0.12
Punjabi	4,197	4.09
Spanish	171	0.17
Tagalog (Pilipino)	315	0.31
Urdu	65	0.06
Other Languages	418	0.41
Multiple Responses	2,348	2.29
Total	102,689	100.00

BUILDING PERMITS

	1999	1998 $000	1997
Value	110,347	84,527	107,465

HOMES BUILT

	1999	1998	1997
No.	146	143	328

TAXATION

Income Class:	1997	% Total
Under $5,000	9,020	12.95
$5,000-$10,000	7,940	11.40
$10,000-$15,000	8,090	11.62
$15,000-$20,000	5,700	8.18
$20,000-$25,000	5,050	7.25
$25,000-$30,000	5,000	7.18
$30,000-$40,000	9,120	13.09
$40,000-$50,000	6,590	9.46
$50,000 +	13,140	18.87
Total Returns, No.	69,650	
Total Income, $000.	2,187,589	
Total Taxable Returns	51,470	
Total Tax, $000.	455,266	
Average Income, $	31,408	
Average Tax, $	8,845	

VITAL STATISTICS

	1997	1996	1995	1994
Births	1,146	1,152	1,203	1,162
Deaths	531	515	522	519
Natural Increase	615	637	681	643
Marriages	335	379	368	449

Note: Latest available data.

MEDIA INFO

see Vancouver, CMA

Langley
(District Municipality)
Vancouver CMA

In Greater Vancouver Regional District.

POPULATION

July 1, 2001 Estimate	96,424
% Cdn. Total	0.31
% Change, '96 -'01	15.20
Avg. Annual Growth Rate, %	2.87
2003 Projected Population	103,185
2006 Projected Population	114,864
2001 Households Estimate	33,159
2003 Projected Households	35,753
2006 Projected Households	40,103

INCOME

% Above/Below National Average	+11
2001 Total Income Estimate	$2,261,150,000
% Cdn. Total	0.34
2001 Average Hhld. Income	$68,200
2001 Per Capita	$23,500
2003 Projected Total Income	$2,599,840,000
2006 Projected Total Income	$3,217,460,000

RETAIL SALES

% Above/Below National Average	-24
2001 Retail Sales Estimate	$654,250,000
% Cdn. Total	0.23
2001 per Household	$19,700
2001 per Capita	$6,800
2001 No. of Establishments	615
2003 Projected Retail Sales	$753,100,000
2006 Projected Retail Sales	$918,830,000

POPULATION

2001 Estimates:

Total	96,424
Male	47,814
Female	48,610

Age Groups	Male	Female
0-4	3,049	2,897
5-9	3,521	3,398
10-14	3,881	3,723
15-19	3,733	3,644
20-24	3,224	3,173
25-29	2,919	2,937
30-34	3,231	3,414
35-39	3,767	4,063
40-44	3,966	4,179
45-49	3,764	3,901
50-54	3,304	3,292
55-59	2,598	2,520
60-64	1,989	1,919
65-69	1,581	1,582
70+	3,287	3,968

DAYTIME POPULATION

2001 Estimates:

Working Population	24,273
At Home Population	45,983
Total	70,256

INCOME

2001 Estimates:

Avg. Household Income	$68,191
Avg. Family Income	$71,055
Per Capita Income	$23,450
Male:	
Avg. Employment Income	$41,570
Avg. Employment Income (Full Time)	$51,460
Female:	
Avg. Employment Income	$24,066
Avg. Employment Income (Full Time)	$35,311

DISPOSABLE & DISCRETIONARY INCOME

2001 Estimates: — Per Hhld.

Disposable Income	$52,535
Discretionary Income 1 (minus Food & Shelter)	$37,423
Discretionary Income 2 (minus Food, Shelter, & Other Expenditures)	$27,435

LIQUID ASSETS

1999 Estimates: — Per Hhld.

Equity Investments	$107,912
Interest Bearing Investments	$86,638
Total Liquid Assets	$194,550

CREDIT DATA

July 2000:

Pool of Credit	$965,587,980
Revolving Credit, No.	182,292
Fixed Loans, No.	45,580
Avg. Credit Limit, per Person	$13,929
Avg. Spent, per Person	$6,268
Satisfactory Ratings, No. per Person	3.23
Avg. No. of Cards, per Person	1.15

LABOUR FORCE

2001 Estimates:

Male:	
In the Labour Force	28,353
Participation Rate	75.9
Employed	27,493
Unemployed	860
Unemployment Rate	3.0
Not in Labour Force	9,010
Female:	
In the Labour Force	24,736
Participation Rate	64.1
Employed	23,383
Unemployed	1,353
Unemployment Rate	5.5
Not in Labour Force	13,856

OCCUPATIONS BY MAJOR GROUPS

2001 Estimates:	Male	Female
Management	3,905	1,432
Business, Finance & Admin.	2,168	8,225
Natural & Applied Sciences & Related	1,763	254
Health	517	1,789
Social Sciences, Gov't Services & Religion	423	802
Education	523	1,210
Arts, Culture, Recreation & Sport	370	683
Sales & Service	5,224	7,777
Trades, Transport & Equipment Operators & Related	9,288	369
Primary Industries	2,031	1,210
Processing, Mfg. & Utilities	1,935	457

LEVEL OF SCHOOLING

2001 Estimates:

Population 15 years +	75,955
Less than Grade 9	3,406
Grades 9-13 w/o Certif.	19,464
Grade 9-13 with Certif.	11,476
Trade Certif./Dip.	2,890
Non-Univ. w/o Certif./Dip.	6,194
Non-Univ. with Certif./Dip.	16,956
Univ. w/o Degree	8,550
Univ. w/o Degree/Certif.	4,096
Univ. with Certif.	4,454
Univ. with Degree	7,019

AVERAGE HOUSEHOLD EXPENDITURES

2001 Estimates:

Food	$6,763
Shelter	$10,678
Clothing	$2,548
Transportation	$7,974
Health & Personal Care	$2,064
Recr'n, Read'g & Education	$4,405
Taxes & Securities	$19,514
Other	$9,523
Total Expenditures	$63,469

PRIVATE HOUSEHOLDS

2001 Estimates:

Private Households, Total	33,159
Pop. in Private Households	95,220
Average no. per Household	2.9

FAMILIES

2001 Estimates:

Families in Private Households	28,083
Husband-Wife Families	25,310
Lone-Parent Families	2,773
Aver. No. Persons per Family	3.1
Aver. No. Sons/Daughters at Home	1.2

HOUSING

2001 Estimates:

Occupied Private Dwellings	33,159
Owned	27,851
Rented	5,308
Single-Detached House	24,785
Semi-Detached House	889
Row Houses	3,699
Apartment, 5+ Storeys	12
Owned Apartment, 5+ Storeys	12
Apartment, 5 or Fewer Storeys	1,349
Apartment, Detached Duplex	1,261
Other Single-Attached	12
Movable Dwellings	1,152

VEHICLES

2001 Estimates:

Model Yrs. '81-'96, No.	47,187
% Total	85.61
Model Yrs. '97-'98, No.	4,673
% Total	8.48
'99 Vehicles registered in Model Yr. '99, No.	3,256
% Total	5.91
Total No. '81-'99	55,116

LEGAL MARITAL STATUS

2001 Estimates: (Age 15+)

Single (Never Married)	18,964
Legally Married (Not Separated)	46,503
Legally Married (Separated)	2,217
Widowed	3,315
Divorced	4,956

PSYTE CATEGORIES

2001 Estimates	No. of House-holds	% of Total Hhds.	Index
Mortgaged in Suburbia	4,170	12.58	905
Technocrafts & Bureaucrats	1,922	5.80	206
Boomers & Teens	5,460	16.47	919
Stable Suburban Families	102	0.31	24
Small City Elite	226	0.68	40
Brie & Chablis	580	1.75	195
Aging Erudites	1,159	3.50	232
Satellite Suburbs	3,797	11.45	399
Kindergarten Boom	445	1.34	51
Blue Collar Winners	9,874	29.78	1,183
Old Towns' New Fringe	1,561	4.71	120
Conservative Homebodies	1,763	5.32	147
High Rise Sunsets	683	2.06	144
Old Leafy Towns	931	2.81	110
Town Renters	345	1.04	120

FINANCIAL P$YTE

2001 Estimates	No. of House-holds	% of Total Hhds.	Index
Four Star Investors	5,460	16.47	328
Successful Suburbanites	6,194	18.68	281
Canadian Comfort	13,897	41.91	431
Urban Heights	1,739	5.24	122
Mortgages & Minivans	445	1.34	20
Tractors & Tradelines	1,561	4.71	82
Bills & Wills	2,694	8.12	98
Revolving Renters	683	2.06	45
Towering Debt	345	1.04	13

British Columbia

HOME LANGUAGE

2001 Estimates:		% Total
English	92,563	96.00
French	168	0.17
Arabic	71	0.07
Chinese	501	0.52
Dutch	174	0.18
German	357	0.37
Italian	136	0.14
Japanese	170	0.18
Korean	409	0.42
Persian (Farsi)	146	0.15
Polish	88	0.09
Punjabi	312	0.32
Serbian	68	0.07
Spanish	123	0.13
Vietnamese	220	0.23
Other Languages	304	0.32
Multiple Responses	614	0.64
Total	96,424	100.00

BUILDING PERMITS

	1999	1998 $000	1997
Value	168,290	161,026	189,447

HOMES BUILT

	1999	1998	1997
No	431	632	845

TAXATION

Income Class:	1997	% Total
Under $5,000	8,590	11.41
$5,000-$10,000	8,700	11.55
$10,000-$15,000	10,060	13.36
$15,000-$20,000	6,850	9.10
$20,000-$25,000	5,860	7.78
$25,000-$30,000	5,830	7.74
$30,000-$40,000	10,000	13.28
$40,000-$50,000	7,060	9.38
$50,000 +	12,350	16.41
Total Returns, No.	75,280	
Total Income, $000	2,242,497	
Total Taxable Returns	55,400	
Total Tax, $000	445,380	
Average Income, $	29,789	
Average Tax, $	8,039	

Note: Data for both Langley, DM & Langley, C.

VITAL STATISTICS

	1997	1996	1995	1994
Births	916	914	818	761
Deaths	458	401	315	282
Natural Increase	458	513	503	479
Marriages	332	367	280	260

Note: Latest available data.

MEDIA INFO
see Vancouver, CMA

British Columbia

Langley
(City)
Vancouver CMA

In Greater Vancouver Regional District.

POPULATION

July 1, 2001 Estimate	25,563
% Cdn. Total	0.08
% Change, '96 -'01	8.74
Avg. Annual Growth Rate, %	1.69
2003 Projected Population	26,506
2006 Projected Population	28,319
2001 Households Estimate	11,010
2003 Projected Households	11,527
2006 Projected Households	12,447

INCOME

% Above/Below National Average	-8
2001 Total Income Estimate	$498,370,000
% Cdn. Total	0.08
2001 Average Hhld. Income	$45,300
2001 Per Capita	$19,500
2003 Projected Total Income	$549,850,000
2006 Projected Total Income	$643,740,000

RETAIL SALES

% Above/Below National Average	+91
2001 Retail Sales Estimate	$437,060,000
% Cdn. Total	0.16
2001 per Household	$39,700
2001 per Capita	$17,100
2001 No. of Establishments	323
2003 Projected Retail Sales	$492,700,000
2006 Projected Retail Sales	$587,390,000

POPULATION

2001 Estimates:

Total		25,563
Male		12,181
Female		13,382

Age Groups	Male	Female
0-4	886	860
5-9	859	860
10-14	828	816
15-19	798	811
20-24	866	905
25-29	967	1,021
30-34	1,042	1,096
35-39	1,041	1,062
40-44	948	990
45-49	851	939
50-54	733	789
55-59	574	583
60-64	426	457
65-69	346	445
70+	1,016	1,748

DAYTIME POPULATION

2001 Estimates:

Working Population	10,145
At Home Population	13,673
Total	23,818

INCOME

2001 Estimates:

Avg. Household Income	$45,266
Avg. Family Income	$52,072
Per Capita Income	$19,496
Male:	
Avg. Employment Income	$32,189
Avg. Employment Income (Full Time)	$41,492
Female:	
Avg. Employment Income	$20,006
Avg. Employment Income (Full Time)	$29,173

DISPOSABLE & DISCRETIONARY INCOME

2001 Estimates: Per Hhld.

Disposable Income	$35,554
Discretionary Income 1 (minus Food & Shelter)	$23,147
Discretionary Income 2 (minus Food, Shelter, & Other Expenditures)	$16,060

LIQUID ASSETS

1999 Estimates: Per Hhld.

Equity Investments	$47,183
Interest Bearing Investments	$53,746
Total Liquid Assets	$100,929

CREDIT DATA

July 2000:

Pool of Credit	$234,874,316
Revolving Credit, No.	49,647
Fixed Loans, No.	12,504
Avg. Credit Limit, per Person	$11,037
Avg. Spent, per Person	$5,164
Satisfactory Ratings, No. per Person	2.87
Avg. No. of Cards, per Person	1.03

LABOUR FORCE

2001 Estimates:

Male:

In the Labour Force	6,801
Participation Rate	70.8
Employed	6,377
Unemployed	424
Unemployment Rate	6.2
Not in Labour Force	2,807

Female:

In the Labour Force	6,223
Participation Rate	57.4
Employed	5,742
Unemployed	481
Unemployment Rate	7.7
Not in Labour Force	4,623

OCCUPATIONS BY MAJOR GROUPS

2001 Estimates:

	Male	Female
Management	751	379
Business, Finance & Admin.	648	1,938
Natural & Applied Sciences & Related	436	52
Health	53	444
Social Sciences, Gov't Services & Religion	78	173
Education	173	226
Arts, Culture, Recreation & Sport	163	131
Sales & Service	1,554	2,352
Trades, Transport & Equipment Operators & Related	2,089	112
Primary Industries	198	63
Processing, Mfg. & Utilities	564	169

LEVEL OF SCHOOLING

2001 Estimates:

Population 15 years +	20,454
Less than Grade 9	1,405
Grades 9-13 w/o Certif.	5,807
Grade 9-13 with Certif.	3,004
Trade Certif. /Dip.	814
Non-Univ. w/o Certif./Dip.	1,623
Non-Univ. with Certif./Dip.	4,305
Univ. w/o Degree	2,027
Univ. w/o Degree/Certif.	1,002
Univ. with Certif.	1,025
Univ. with Degree	1,469

AVERAGE HOUSEHOLD EXPENDITURES

2001 Estimates:

Food	$5,546
Shelter	$8,659
Clothing	$1,905
Transportation	$5,222
Health & Personal Care	$1,698
Recr'n, Read'g & Education	$3,123
Taxes & Securities	$10,916
Other	$7,477
Total Expenditures	$44,546

PRIVATE HOUSEHOLDS

2001 Estimates:

Private Households, Total	11,010
Pop. in Private Households	25,210
Average no. per Household	2.3

FAMILIES

2001 Estimates:

Families in Private Households	7,074
Husband-Wife Families	5,804
Lone-Parent Families	1,270
Aver. No. Persons per Family	2.9
Aver. No. Sons/Daughters at Home	1.1

HOUSING

2001 Estimates:

Occupied Private Dwellings	11,010
Owned	6,448
Rented	4,562
Single-Detached House	3,561
Semi-Detached House	297
Row Houses	1,093
Apartment, 5+ Storeys	52
Owned Apartment, 5+ Storeys	39
Apartment, 5 or Fewer Storeys	5,582
Apartment, Detached Duplex	412
Other Single-Attached	13

VEHICLES

2001 Estimates:

Model Yrs. '81-'96, No.	8,522
% Total	79.14
Model Yrs. '97-'98, No.	1,213
% Total	11.26
'99 Vehicles registered in Model Yr. '99, No.	1,033
% Total	9.59
Total No. '81-'99	10,768

LEGAL MARITAL STATUS

2001 Estimates: (Age 15+)

Single (Never Married)	5,928
Legally Married (Not Separated)	9,937
Legally Married (Separated)	970
Widowed	1,571
Divorced	2,048

PSYTE CATEGORIES

2001 Estimates	No. of House-holds	% of Total Hhds.	Index
Satellite Suburbs	3,352	30.45	1,061
Kindergarten Boom	487	4.42	169
Conservative Homebodies	742	6.74	187
High Rise Sunsets	621	5.64	394
Young Urban Mix	307	2.79	132
University Enclaves	750	6.81	334
Young City Singles	1,465	13.31	580
Town Renters	969	8.80	1,018

2001 Estimates	No. of House-holds	% of Total Hhds.	Index
Nesters & Young Homesteaders	548	4.98	213
Aged Pensioners	1,039	9.44	709
Old Grey Towers	697	6.33	1,143

FINANÇIAL P$YTE

2001 Estimates	No. of House-holds	% of Total Hhds.	Index
Canadian Comfort	3,352	30.45	313
Mortgages & Minivans	487	4.42	67
Bills & Wills	1,049	9.53	115
Revolving Renters	1,169	10.62	231
Young Urban Struggle	750	6.81	144
Towering Debt	2,434	22.11	283
Senior Survivors	1,736	15.77	837

HOME LANGUAGE

2001 Estimates:		% Total
English	24,074	94.18
French	29	0.11
Chinese	424	1.66
Dutch	34	0.13
Finnish	39	0.15
German	58	0.23
Greek	44	0.17
Hungarian	34	0.13
Khmer (Cambodian)	38	0.15
Korean	105	0.41
Lao	17	0.07
Polish	61	0.24
Punjabi	17	0.07
Serbo-Croatian	18	0.07
Spanish	54	0.21
Vietnamese	140	0.55
Other Languages	67	0.26
Multiple Responses	310	1.21
Total	25,563	100.00

BUILDING PERMITS

	1999	1998	1997
		$000	
Value	19,977	10,572	30,786

HOMES BUILT

	1999	1998	1997
No.	20	147	312

TAXATION

Income Class:	1997	% Total
Under $5,000	8,590	11.41
$5,000-$10,000	8,700	11.55
$10,000-$15,000	10,060	13.36
$15,000-$20,000	6,850	9.10
$20,000-$25,000	5,860	7.78
$25,000-$30,000	5,830	7.74
$30,000-$40,000	10,000	13.28
$40,000-$50,000	7,060	9.38
$50,000 +	12,350	16.41
Total Returns, No.	75,280	
Total Income, $000	2,242,497	
Total Taxable Returns	55,400	
Total Tax, $000	445,380	
Average Income, $.	29,789	
Average Tax, $.	8,039	

Note: Data for both Langley, DM & Langley, C.

VITAL STATISTICS

	1997	1996	1995	1994
Births	341	400	516	520
Deaths	245	300	299	305
Natural Increase	96	100	217	215
Marriages	235	253	296	365

Note: Latest available data.

MEDIA INFO

see Vancouver, CMA

Maple Ridge
(District Municipality)
Vancouver CMA

In Greater Vancouver Regional District.

POPULATION

July 1, 2001 Estimate	64,786
% Cdn. Total	0.21
% Change, '96 -'01	10.48
Avg. Annual Growth Rate, %	2.01
2003 Projected Population	67,758
2006 Projected Population	73,227
2001 Households Estimate	23,714
2003 Projected Households	24,958
2006 Projected Households	27,148

INCOME

% Above/Below National Average	-2
2001 Total Income Estimate	$1,340,070,000
% Cdn. Total	0.20
2001 Average Hhld. Income	$56,500
2001 Per Capita	$20,700
2003 Projected Total Income	$1,493,450,000
2006 Projected Total Income	$1,772,160,000

RETAIL SALES

% Above/Below National Average	-19
2001 Retail Sales Estimate	$470,150,000
% Cdn. Total	0.17
2001 per Household	$19,800
2001 per Capita	$7,300
2001 No. of Establishments	352
2003 Projected Retail Sales	$531,220,000
2006 Projected Retail Sales	$635,050,000

POPULATION

2001 Estimates:

Total		64,786
Male		32,430
Female		32,356
Age Groups	Male	Female
0-4	2,130	2,019
5-9	2,514	2,325
10-14	2,657	2,408
15-19	2,476	2,276
20-24	2,067	1,985
25-29	1,921	1,949
30-34	2,315	2,427
35-39	2,862	2,893
40-44	2,922	2,907
45-49	2,653	2,534
50-54	2,089	1,974
55-59	1,531	1,502
60-64	1,208	1,220
65-69	997	1,076
70+	2,088	2,861

DAYTIME POPULATION

2001 Estimates:

Working Population	12,825
At Home Population	33,585
Total	46,410

INCOME

2001 Estimates:

Avg. Household Income	$56,510
Avg. Family Income	$61,133
Per Capita Income	$20,685
Male:	
Avg. Employment Income	$37,690
Avg. Employment Income (Full Time)	$47,059
Female:	
Avg. Employment Income	$22,395
Avg. Employment Income (Full Time)	$32,514

DISPOSABLE & DISCRETIONARY INCOME

2001 Estimates:	*Per Hhld.*
Disposable Income	$43,893
Discretionary Income 1 (minus Food & Shelter)	$30,110
Discretionary Income 2 (minus Food, Shelter, & Other Expenditures)	$21,258

LIQUID ASSETS

1999 Estimates:	*Per Hhld.*
Equity Investments	$71,457
Interest Bearing Investments	$68,522
Total Liquid Assets	$139,979

CREDIT DATA

July 2000:

Pool of Credit	$618,108,043
Revolving Credit, No.	121,144
Fixed Loans, No.	31,302
Avg. Credit Limit, per Person	$12,410
Avg. Spent, per Person	$5,853
Satisfactory Ratings, No. per Person	3.00
Avg. No. of Cards, per Person	1.07

LABOUR FORCE

2001 Estimates:

Male:	
In the Labour Force	18,063
Participation Rate	71.9
Employed	16,925
Unemployed	1,138
Unemployment Rate	6.3
Not in Labour Force	7,066
Female:	
In the Labour Force	15,343
Participation Rate	59.9
Employed	14,488
Unemployed	855
Unemployment Rate	5.6
Not in Labour Force	10,261

OCCUPATIONS BY MAJOR GROUPS

2001 Estimates:	Male	Female
Management	1,929	882
Business, Finance & Admin.	1,187	4,999
Natural & Applied Sciences & Related	1,079	160
Health	318	1,367
Social Sciences, Gov't Services & Religion	197	395
Education	452	601
Arts, Culture, Recreation & Sport	289	366
Sales & Service	3,896	5,312
Trades, Transport & Equipment Operators & Related	6,118	281
Primary Industries	749	342
Processing, Mfg. & Utilities	1,497	280

LEVEL OF SCHOOLING

2001 Estimates:

Population 15 years +	50,733
Less than Grade 9	2,625
Grades 9-13 w/o Certif.	13,133
Grade 9-13 with Certif.	8,232
Trade Certif. /Dip.	2,079
Non-Univ. w/o Certif./Dip.	4,196
Non-Univ. with Certif./Dip.	11,627
Univ. w/o Degree	4,870
Univ. w/o Degree/Certif.	2,081
Univ. with Certif.	2,789
Univ. with Degree	3,971

AVERAGE HOUSEHOLD EXPENDITURES

2001 Estimates:

Food	$6,210
Shelter	$9,564
Clothing	$2,171
Transportation	$6,921
Health & Personal Care	$1,860
Recr'n, Read'g & Education	$3,726
Taxes & Securities	$15,004
Other	$8,498
Total Expenditures	$53,954

PRIVATE HOUSEHOLDS

2001 Estimates:

Private Households, Total	23,714
Pop. in Private Households	63,671
Average no. per Household	2.7

FAMILIES

2001 Estimates:

Families in Private Households	18,391
Husband-Wife Families	16,237
Lone-Parent Families	2,154
Aver. No. Persons per Family	3.1
Aver. No. Sons/Daughters at Home	1.2

HOUSING

2001 Estimates:

Occupied Private Dwellings	23,714
Owned	17,976
Rented	5,738
Single-Detached House	15,827
Semi-Detached House	643
Row Houses	2,844
Apartment, 5+ Storeys	463
Owned Apartment, 5+ Storeys	12
Apartment, 5 or Fewer Storeys	2,623
Apartment, Detached Duplex	966
Other Single-Attached	74
Movable Dwellings	274

VEHICLES

2001 Estimates:

Model Yrs. '81-'96, No.	29,808
% Total	86.77
Model Yrs. '97-'98, No.	2,890
% Total	8.41
'99 Vehicles registered in Model Yr. '99, No.	1,654
% Total	4.81
Total No. '81-'99	34,352

LEGAL MARITAL STATUS

2001 Estimates: (Age 15+)

Single (Never Married)	13,449
Legally Married (Not Separated)	28,861
Legally Married (Separated)	1,804
Widowed	2,675
Divorced	3,944

PSYTE CATEGORIES

2001 Estimates	No. of House-holds	% of Total Hhds.	Index
Mortgaged in Suburbia	137	0.58	42
Boomers & Teens	553	2.33	130
Old Bungalow Burbs	443	1.87	113
Satellite Suburbs	6,298	26.56	926
Kindergarten Boom	3,063	12.92	493
Blue Collar Winners	6,472	27.29	1,084
Old Towns' New Fringe	1,631	6.88	176
Conservative Homebodies	931	3.93	109
High Rise Sunsets	637	2.69	188
Young Urban Mix	249	1.05	50
University Enclaves	121	0.51	25
Young City Singles	350	1.48	64
Struggling Downtowns	955	4.03	128
Aged Pensioners	1,622	6.84	514

British Columbia

FINANCIAL P$YTE

2001 Estimates	No. of House-holds	% of Total Hhds.	Index
Four Star Investors	553	2.33	46
Successful Suburbanites	137	0.58	9
Canadian Comfort	12,770	53.85	554
Miners & Credit-Liners	443	1.87	59
Mortgages & Minivans	3,063	12.92	196
Tractors & Tradelines	1,631	6.88	120
Bills & Wills	1,180	4.98	60
Revolving Renters	637	2.69	58
Young Urban Struggle	121	0.51	11
Towering Debt	1,305	5.50	71
Senior Survivors	1,622	6.84	363

HOME LANGUAGE

2001 Estimates:		% Total
English	61,727	95.28
French	121	0.19
Chinese	529	0.82
Czech	138	0.21
Dutch	140	0.22
German	45	0.07
Gujarati	51	0.08
Hungarian	54	0.08
Italian	53	0.08
Korean	199	0.31
Polish	247	0.38
Punjabi	344	0.53
Romanian	97	0.15
Spanish	104	0.16
Other Languages	346	0.53
Multiple Responses	591	0.91
Total	64,786	100.00

BUILDING PERMITS

	1999	1998	1997
		$000	
Value	84,375	102,907	116,431

HOMES BUILT

	1999	1998	1997
No.	590	605	520

British Columbia

Maple Ridge
(District Municipality)
Vancouver CMA
(Cont'd)

TAXATION

Income Class:	1997	% Total
Under $5,000	4,800	12.12
$5,000-$10,000	4,540	11.47
$10,000-$15,000	5,070	12.81
$15,000-$20,000	3,480	8.79
$20,000-$25,000	3,090	7.81
$25,000-$30,000	2,920	7.38
$30,000-$40,000	5,570	14.07
$40,000-$50,000	4,040	10.20
$50,000 +	6,080	15.36
Total Returns, No.	39,590	
Total Income, $000	1,116,816	
Total Taxable Returns	28,910	
Total Tax, $000	213,536	
Average Income, $	28,210	
Average Tax, $	7,386	

VITAL STATISTICS

	1997	1996	1995	1994
Births	738	797	795	809
Deaths	396	425	347	329
Natural Increase	342	372	448	480
Marriages	296	309	335	304

Note: Latest available data.

MEDIA INFO
see Vancouver, CMA

New Westminster
(City)
Vancouver CMA

In Greater Vancouver Regional District.

POPULATION

July 1, 2001 Estimate	55,686
% Cdn. Total	0.18
% Change, '96 -'01	8.09
Avg. Annual Growth Rate, %	1.57
2003 Projected Population	57,574
2006 Projected Population	61,258
2001 Households Estimate	27,476
2003 Projected Households	28,569
2006 Projected Households	30,556

INCOME

% Above/Below National Average	+8
2001 Total Income Estimate	$1,270,270,000
% Cdn. Total	0.19
2001 Average Hhld. Income	$46,200
2001 Per Capita	$22,800
2003 Projected Total Income	$1,388,670,000
2006 Projected Total Income	$1,603,480,000

RETAIL SALES

% Above/Below National Average	-48
2001 Retail Sales Estimate	$257,940,000
% Cdn. Total	0.09
2001 per Household	$9,400
2001 per Capita	$4,600
2001 No. of Establishments	368
2003 Projected Retail Sales	$286,010,000
2006 Projected Retail Sales	$334,990,000

POPULATION

2001 Estimates:

Total		55,686
Male		27,269
Female		28,417
Age Groups	Male	Female
0-4	1,773	1,665
5-9	1,543	1,451
10-14	1,263	1,219
15-19	1,175	1,180
20-24	1,468	1,574
25-29	2,128	2,194
30-34	2,702	2,578
35-39	2,835	2,602
40-44	2,638	2,317
45-49	2,268	2,073
50-54	1,795	1,767
55-59	1,391	1,418
60-64	1,104	1,181
65-69	935	1,070
70+	2,251	4,128

DAYTIME POPULATION

2001 Estimates:

Working Population	22,846
At Home Population	28,222
Total	51,068

INCOME

2001 Estimates:

Avg. Household Income	$46,232
Avg. Family Income	$57,141
Per Capita Income	$22,811
Male:	
Avg. Employment Income	$32,665
Avg. Employment Income (Full Time)	$43,223
Female:	
Avg. Employment Income	$24,681
Avg. Employment Income (Full Time)	$34,712

DISPOSABLE & DISCRETIONARY INCOME

2001 Estimates:	Per Hhld.
Disposable Income	$35,721
Discretionary Income 1 (minus Food & Shelter)	$23,426
Discretionary Income 2 (minus Food, Shelter, & Other Expenditures)	$16,292

LIQUID ASSETS

1999 Estimates:	Per Hhld.
Equity Investments	$53,827
Interest Bearing Investments	$56,155
Total Liquid Assets	$109,982

CREDIT DATA

July 2000:

Pool of Credit	$546,046,742
Revolving Credit, No.	119,412
Fixed Loans, No.	25,613
Avg. Credit Limit, per Person	$10,744
Avg. Spent, per Person	$4,566
Satisfactory Ratings, No. per Person	2.82
Avg. No. of Cards, per Person	1.11

LABOUR FORCE

2001 Estimates:

Male:	
In the Labour Force	15,944
Participation Rate	70.3
Employed	14,541
Unemployed	1,403
Unemployment Rate	8.8
Not in Labour Force	6,746
Female:	
In the Labour Force	14,369
Participation Rate	59.7
Employed	13,307
Unemployed	1,062
Unemployment Rate	7.4
Not in Labour Force	9,713

OCCUPATIONS BY MAJOR GROUPS

2001 Estimates:	Male	Female
Management	1,698	831
Business, Finance & Admin.	1,980	4,911
Natural & Applied Sciences & Related	1,133	302
Health	304	1,251
Social Sciences, Gov't Services & Religion	399	571
Education	262	658
Arts, Culture, Recreation & Sport	472	508
Sales & Service	3,492	4,135
Trades, Transport & Equipment Operators & Related	4,349	198
Primary Industries	316	121
Processing, Mfg. & Utilities	1,168	420

LEVEL OF SCHOOLING

2001 Estimates:

Population 15 years +	46,772
Less than Grade 9	3,080
Grades 9-13 w/o Certif.	9,956
Grade 9-13 with Certif.	5,709
Trade Certif. /Dip.	1,422
Non-Univ. w/o Certif./Dip.	3,749
Non-Univ. with Certif./Dip.	10,281
Univ. w/o Degree	5,990
Univ. w/o Degree/Certif.	2,407
Univ. with Certif.	3,583
Univ. with Degree	6,585

AVERAGE HOUSEHOLD EXPENDITURES

2001 Estimates:

Food	$5,589
Shelter	$8,726
Clothing	$2,043
Transportation	$5,264
Health & Personal Care	$1,776
Recr'n, Read'g & Education	$3,064
Taxes & Securities	$11,189
Other	$7,587
Total Expenditures	$45,238

PRIVATE HOUSEHOLDS

2001 Estimates:

Private Households, Total	27,476
Pop. in Private Households	54,605
Average no. per Household	2.0

FAMILIES

2001 Estimates:

Families in Private Households	14,279
Husband-Wife Families	11,958
Lone-Parent Families	2,321
Aver. No. Persons per Family	2.7
Aver. No. Sons/Daughters at Home	0.9

HOUSING

2001 Estimates:

Occupied Private Dwellings	27,476
Owned	12,796
Rented	14,680
Single-Detached House	6,945
Semi-Detached House	264
Row Houses	422
Apartment, 5+ Storeys	7,472
Owned Apartment, 5+ Storeys	3,045
Apartment, 5 or Fewer Storeys	10,773
Apartment, Detached Duplex	1,515
Other Single-Attached	46
Movable Dwellings	39

VEHICLES

2001 Estimates:

Model Yrs. '81-'96, No.	22,213
% Total	84.05
Model Yrs. '97-'98, No.	2,682
% Total	10.15
'99 Vehicles registered in Model Yr. '99, No.	1,532
% Total	5.80
Total No. '81-'99	26,427

LEGAL MARITAL STATUS

2001 Estimates: (Age 15+)

Single (Never Married)	16,644
Legally Married (Not Separated)	19,258
Legally Married (Separated)	2,076
Widowed	3,723
Divorced	5,071

PSYTE CATEGORIES

2001 Estimates	No. of House-holds	% of Total Hhds.	Index
Urban Gentry	403	1.47	82
Small City Elite	296	1.08	63
Suburban Nesters	166	0.60	38
Brie & Chablis	3,103	11.29	1,261
Aging Erudites	2,693	9.80	650
Kindergarten Boom	1,092	3.97	152
Asian Mosaic	1,006	3.66	267
Conservative Homebodies	974	3.54	98
High Rise Sunsets	1,664	6.06	424
Young Urban Professionals	407	1.48	78
Young Urban Mix	3,104	11.30	533
Young Urban Intelligentsia	99	0.36	24
University Enclaves	1,226	4.46	219
Young City Singles	7,385	26.88	1,172
Town Renters	405	1.47	171
Struggling Downtowns	377	1.37	44
Aged Pensioners	2,864	10.42	783

New Westminster
(City)
Vancouver CMA
(Cont'd)

FINANCIAL P$YTE

2001 Estimates	No. of House -holds	% of Total Hhds.	Index
Four Star Investors	403	1.47	29
Canadian Comfort	462	1.68	17
Urban Heights	6,203	22.58	525
Mortgages & Minivans	1,092	3.97	60
Dollars & Sense	1,006	3.66	140
Bills & Wills	4,078	14.84	179
Revolving Renters	1,664	6.06	132
Young Urban Struggle	1,325	4.82	102
Towering Debt	8,167	29.72	381
Senior Survivors	2,864	10.42	553

HOME LANGUAGE

2001 Estimates:		% Total
English	47,702	85.66
French	176	0.32
Arabic	112	0.20
Chinese	927	1.66
Dutch	33	0.06
Finnish	37	0.07
German	59	0.11
Greek	69	0.12
Gujarati	105	0.19
Hindi	296	0.53
Hungarian	207	0.37
Italian	117	0.21
Japanese	81	0.15
Korean	448	0.80
Persian (Farsi)	255	0.46
Polish	364	0.65
Portuguese	117	0.21
Punjabi	1,682	3.02
Romanian	179	0.32
Russian	58	0.10
Serbian	157	0.28
Slovak	67	0.12
Spanish	292	0.52
Tagalog (Pilipino)	376	0.68
Ukrainian	58	0.10
Vietnamese	98	0.18
Other Languages	453	0.81
Multiple Responses	1,161	2.08
Total	55,686	100.00

BUILDING PERMITS

	1999	1998 $000	1997
Value	28,699	55,352	73,800

HOMES BUILT

	1999	1998	1997
No	368	482	340

TAXATION

Income Class:	1997	% Total
Under $5,000	4,000	10.40
$5,000-$10,000	4,840	12.59
$10,000-$15,000	5,390	14.02
$15,000-$20,000	3,610	9.39
$20,000-$25,000	3,200	8.32
$25,000-$30,000	3,130	8.14
$30,000-$40,000	5,510	14.33
$40,000-$50,000	3,620	9.41
$50,000 +	5,160	13.42
Total Returns, No.	38,450	
Total Income, $000	1,089,947	
Total Taxable Returns	27,680	
Total Tax, $000	207,859	
Average Income, $	28,347	
Average Tax, $	7,509	

VITAL STATISTICS

	1997	1996	1995	1994
Births	685	674	706	681
Deaths	486	524	476	481
Natural Increase	199	150	230	200
Marriages	383	412	467	450

Note: Latest available data.

MEDIA INFO
see Vancouver, CMA

North Vancouver
(District Municipality)
Vancouver CMA

In Greater Vancouver Regional District.

POPULATION

July 1, 2001 Estimate	86,386
% Cdn. Total	0.28
% Change, '96 -'01	2.91
Avg. Annual Growth Rate, %	0.57
2003 Projected Population	87,059
2006 Projected Population	89,377
2001 Households Estimate	31,013
2003 Projected Households	31,461
2006 Projected Households	32,517

INCOME

% Above/Below National Average	+42
2001 Total Income Estimate	$2,583,660,000
% Cdn. Total	0.39
2001 Average Hhld. Income	$83,300
2001 Per Capita	$29,900
2003 Projected Total Income	$2,762,460,000
2006 Projected Total Income	$3,093,040,000

RETAIL SALES

% Above/Below National Average	-36
2001 Retail Sales Estimate	$498,620,000
% Cdn. Total	0.18
2001 per Household	$16,100
2001 per Capita	$5,800
2001 No. of Establishments	543
2003 Projected Retail Sales	$541,990,000
2006 Projected Retail Sales	$615,510,000

POPULATION

2001 Estimates:		
Total		86,386
Male		42,009
Female		44,377

Age Groups	Male	Female
0-4	2,489	2,383
5-9	2,806	2,699
10-14	3,006	2,925
15-19	2,992	2,928
20-24	2,769	2,686
25-29	2,439	2,444
30-34	2,468	2,750
35-39	3,047	3,497
40-44	3,507	3,958
45-49	3,594	3,928
50-54	3,346	3,482
55-59	2,732	2,734
60-64	2,082	2,112
65-69	1,630	1,715
70+	3,102	4,136

DAYTIME POPULATION

2001 Estimates:	
Working Population	131,278
At Home Population	40,927
Total	172,205

INCOME

2001 Estimates:	
Avg. Household Income	$83,309
Avg. Family Income	$88,798
Per Capita Income	$29,908
Male:	
Avg. Employment Income	$51,642
Avg. Employment Income (Full Time)	$67,818
Female:	
Avg. Employment Income	$28,631
Avg. Employment Income (Full Time)	$41,548

DISPOSABLE & DISCRETIONARY INCOME

2001 Estimates:	Per Hhld.
Disposable Income	$62,625
Discretionary Income 1 (minus Food & Shelter)	$45,704
Discretionary Income 2 (minus Food, Shelter, & Other Expenditures)	$34,658

LIQUID ASSETS

1999 Estimates:	Per Hhld.
Equity Investments	$160,506
Interest Bearing Investments	$112,833
Total Liquid Assets	$273,339

CREDIT DATA

July 2000:	
Pool of Credit	$1,112,980,169
Revolving Credit, No.	202,451
Fixed Loans, No.	34,694
Avg. Credit Limit, per Person	$14,791
Avg. Spent, per Person	$5,714
Satisfactory Ratings, No. per Person	3.13
Avg. No. of Cards, per Person	1.26

LABOUR FORCE

2001 Estimates:	
Male:	
In the Labour Force	25,536
Participation Rate	75.8
Employed	24,625
Unemployed	911
Unemployment Rate	3.6
Not in Labour Force	8,172
Female:	
In the Labour Force	23,467
Participation Rate	64.5
Employed	22,633
Unemployed	834
Unemployment Rate	3.6
Not in Labour Force	12,903

OCCUPATIONS BY MAJOR GROUPS

2001 Estimates:	Male	Female
Management	5,486	2,060
Business, Finance & Admin.	3,138	7,881
Natural & Applied Sciences & Related	2,740	519
Health	384	1,906
Social Sciences, Gov't Services & Religion	972	1,130
Education	761	1,421
Arts, Culture, Recreation & Sport	1,101	1,238
Sales & Service	5,563	6,631
Trades, Transport & Equipment Operators & Related	3,806	180
Primary Industries	551	87
Processing, Mfg. & Utilities	725	117

LEVEL OF SCHOOLING

2001 Estimates:	
Population 15 years +	70,078
Less than Grade 9	1,495
Grades 9-13 w/o Certif.	10,318
Grade 9-13 with Certif.	8,190
Trade Certif. /Dip.	1,745
Non-Univ. w/o Certif./Dip.	4,984
Non-Univ. with Certif./Dip.	14,083
Univ. w/o Degree	11,220
Univ. w/o Degree/Certif.	5,051
Univ. with Certif.	6,169
Univ. with Degree	18,043

British Columbia

AVERAGE HOUSEHOLD EXPENDITURES

2001 Estimates:	
Food	$7,718
Shelter	$12,321
Clothing	$3,067
Transportation	$8,574
Health & Personal Care	$2,541
Recr'n, Read'g & Education	$5,289
Taxes & Securities	$24,320
Other	$11,232
Total Expenditures	$75,062

PRIVATE HOUSEHOLDS

2001 Estimates:	
Private Households, Total	31,013
Pop. in Private Households	85,287
Average no. per Household	2.8

FAMILIES

2001 Estimates:	
Families in Private Households	25,293
Husband-Wife Families	22,426
Lone-Parent Families	2,867
Aver. No. Persons per Family	3.1
Aver. No. Sons/Daughters at Home	1.2

HOUSING

2001 Estimates:	
Occupied Private Dwellings	31,013
Owned	24,157
Rented	6,848
Band Housing	8
Single-Detached House	20,666
Semi-Detached House	551
Row Houses	2,329
Apartment, 5+ Storeys	1,949
Owned Apartment, 5+ Storeys	941
Apartment, 5 or Fewer Storeys	3,150
Apartment, Detached Duplex	2,329
Other Single-Attached	22
Movable Dwellings	17

VEHICLES

2001 Estimates:	
Model Yrs. '81-'96, No.	38,873
% Total	83.41
Model Yrs. '97-'98, No.	4,608
% Total	9.89
'99 Vehicles registered in Model Yr. '99, No.	3,124
% Total	6.70
Total No. '81-'99	46,605

LEGAL MARITAL STATUS

2001 Estimates: (Age 15+)	
Single (Never Married)	19,227
Legally Married (Not Separated)	41,368
Legally Married (Separated)	1,707
Widowed	3,206
Divorced	4,570

British Columbia

North Vancouver
(District Municipality)
Vancouver CMA
(Cont'd)

PSYTE CATEGORIES

2001 Estimates	No. of House-holds	% of Total Hhds.	Index
Canadian Establishment	178	0.57	345
The Affluentials	302	0.97	152
Urban Gentry	5,341	17.22	958
Suburban Executives	3,896	12.56	876
Technocrafts & Bureaucrats	1,715	5.53	197
Boomers & Teens	7,251	23.38	1,304
Stable Suburban Families	2,337	7.54	578
Suburban Nesters	3,002	9.68	604
Brie & Chablis	335	1.08	121
Aging Erudites	3,010	9.71	643
Kindergarten Boom	791	2.55	97
High Rise Sunsets	342	1.10	77
Young Urban Professionals	144	0.46	24
Young Urban Mix	789	2.54	120
Young Urban Intelligentsia	279	0.90	59
University Enclaves	413	1.33	65
Young City Singles	273	0.88	38
Town Renters	278	0.90	104
Old Grey Towers	160	0.52	93

FINANCIAL PSYTE

2001 Estimates	No. of House-holds	% of Total Hhds.	Index
Platinum Estates	480	1.55	192
Four Star Investors	16,488	53.16	1,058
Successful Suburbanites	4,052	13.07	197
Canadian Comfort	3,002	9.68	100
Urban Heights	3,489	11.25	262
Mortgages & Minivans	791	2.55	39
Bills & Wills	789	2.54	31
Revolving Renters	342	1.10	24
Young Urban Struggle	692	2.23	47
Towering Debt	551	1.78	23
Senior Survivors	160	0.52	27

HOME LANGUAGE

2001 Estimates:		% Total
English	76,883	89.00
French	294	0.34
Chinese	2,173	2.52
Croatian	58	0.07
Czech	124	0.14
Finnish	72	0.08
German	373	0.43
Gujarati	235	0.27
Hindi	60	0.07
Italian	102	0.12
Japanese	628	0.73
Korean	654	0.76
Persian (Farsi)	1,710	1.98
Polish	221	0.26
Punjabi	77	0.09
Serbo-Croatian	52	0.06
Slovak	49	0.06
Spanish	200	0.23
Tagalog (Pilipino)	299	0.35
Urdu	48	0.06
Other Languages	532	0.62
Multiple Responses	1,542	1.79
Total	86,386	100.00

BUILDING PERMITS

	1999	1998	1997
		$000	
Value	53,370	67,037	62,957

HOMES BUILT

	1999	1998	1997
No	232	195	345

TAXATION

Income Class:	1997	% Total
Under $5,000	10,500	11.57
$5,000-$10,000	9,690	10.68
$10,000-$15,000	10,180	11.22
$15,000-$20,000	7,530	8.30
$20,000-$25,000	6,720	7.40
$25,000-$30,000	6,590	7.26
$30,000-$40,000	11,920	13.13
$40,000-$50,000	8,690	9.58
$50,000 +	18,940	20.87
Total Returns, No.	90,750	
Total Income, $000	3,149,495	
Total Taxable Returns	68,410	
Total Tax, $000	696,847	
Average Income, $	34,705	
Average Tax, $	10,186	

Note: Data for both Vancouver, DM & Vancouver, C.

VITAL STATISTICS

	1997	1996	1995	1994
Births	934	935	900	946
Deaths	468	428	424	407
Natural Increase	466	507	476	539
Marriages	326	322	349	374

Note: Latest available data.

MEDIA INFO
see Vancouver, CMA

North Vancouver
(City)
Vancouver CMA

In Greater Vancouver Regional District.

POPULATION

July 1, 2001 Estimate	44,878
% Cdn. Total	0.14
% Change, '96 -'01	3.65
Avg. Annual Growth Rate, %.	0.72
2003 Projected Population	45,392
2006 Projected Population	46,849
2001 Households Estimate	21,719
2003 Projected Households	22,108
2006 Projected Households	22,953

INCOME

% Above/Below National Average	+12
2001 Total Income Estimate	$1,057,320,000
% Cdn. Total	0.16
2001 Average Hhld. Income	$48,700
2001 Per Capita	$23,600
2003 Projected Total Income	$1,127,960,000
2006 Projected Total Income	$1,258,110,000

RETAIL SALES

% Above/Below National Average	+39
2001 Retail Sales Estimate	$556,430,000
% Cdn. Total	0.20
2001 per Household	$25,600
2001 per Capita	$12,400
2001 No. of Establishments	457
2003 Projected Retail Sales	$607,770,000
2006 Projected Retail Sales	$694,090,000

POPULATION

2001 Estimates:		
Total		44,878
Male		21,407
Female		23,471
Age Groups	Male	Female
0-4	1,460	1,381
5-9	1,213	1,163
10-14	1,049	1,035
15-19	1,001	1,013
20-24	1,204	1,252
25-29	1,663	1,785
30-34	2,125	2,216
35-39	2,279	2,316
40-44	2,106	2,132
45-49	1,766	1,850
50-54	1,358	1,483
55-59	1,016	1,159
60-64	814	974
65-69	705	879
70+	1,648	2,833

DAYTIME POPULATION

2001 Estimates:	
Working Population	20,761
At Home Population	20,797
Total	41,558

INCOME

2001 Estimates:	
Avg. Household Income	$48,682
Avg. Family Income	$59,000
Per Capita Income	$23,560
Male:	
Avg. Employment Income	$34,336
Avg. Employment Income (Full Time)	$45,881
Female:	
Avg. Employment Income	$25,187
Avg. Employment Income (Full Time)	$34,447

DISPOSABLE & DISCRETIONARY INCOME

2001 Estimates:	Per Hhld.
Disposable Income	$37,592
Discretionary Income 1 (minus Food & Shelter)	$24,877
Discretionary Income 2 (minus Food, Shelter, & Other Expenditures)	$17,666

LIQUID ASSETS

1999 Estimates:	Per Hhld.
Equity Investments	$61,364
Interest Bearing Investments	$60,539
Total Liquid Assets	$121,903

CREDIT DATA

July 2000:	
Pool of Credit	$509,114,228
Revolving Credit, No.	105,663
Fixed Loans, No.	20,490
Avg. Credit Limit, per Person	$11,836
Avg. Spent, per Person	$4,947
Satisfactory Ratings, No. per Person	2.92
Avg. No. of Cards, per Person	1.19

LABOUR FORCE

2001 Estimates:	
Male:	
In the Labour Force	13,057
Participation Rate	73.8
Employed	12,330
Unemployed	727
Unemployment Rate	5.6
Not in Labour Force	4,628
Female:	
In the Labour Force	12,834
Participation Rate	64.5
Employed	12,128
Unemployed	706
Unemployment Rate	5.5
Not in Labour Force	7,058

OCCUPATIONS BY MAJOR GROUPS

2001 Estimates:	Male	Female
Management	1,733	1,079
Business, Finance & Admin.	1,593	4,120
Natural & Applied Sciences & Related	1,227	311
Health	189	933
Social Sciences, Gov't Services & Religion	221	583
Education	159	343
Arts, Culture, Recreation & Sport	530	536
Sales & Service	3,539	4,258
Trades, Transport & Equipment Operators & Related	2,823	92
Primary Industries	268	61
Processing, Mfg. & Utilities	550	192

LEVEL OF SCHOOLING

2001 Estimates:	
Population 15 years +	37,577
Less than Grade 9	1,548
Grades 9-13 w/o Certif.	6,632
Grade 9-13 with Certif.	4,941
Trade Certif. /Dip.	949
Non-Univ. w/o Certif./Dip.	3,617
Non-Univ. with Certif./Dip.	8,277
Univ. w/o Degree	5,312
Univ. w/o Degree/Certif.	2,240
Univ. with Certif.	3,072
Univ. with Degree	6,301

North Vancouver
(City)
Vancouver CMA
(Cont'd)

AVERAGE HOUSEHOLD EXPENDITURES

2001 Estimates:
Food	$5,767
Shelter	$9,016
Clothing	$2,097
Transportation	$5,333
Health & Personal Care	$1,780
Recr'n, Read'g & Education	$3,258
Taxes & Securities	$12,448
Other	$7,729
Total Expenditures	$47,428

PRIVATE HOUSEHOLDS

2001 Estimates:
Private Households, Total	21,719
Pop. in Private Households	44,340
Average no. per Household	2.0

FAMILIES

2001 Estimates:
Families in Private Households	11,704
Husband-Wife Families	9,696
Lone-Parent Families	2,008
Aver. No. Persons per Family	2.7
Aver. No. Sons/Daughters at Home	0.9

HOUSING

2001 Estimates:
Occupied Private Dwellings	21,719
Owned	9,664
Rented	12,014
Band Housing	41
Single-Detached House	4,614
Semi-Detached House	581
Row Houses	1,583
Apartment, 5+ Storeys	2,688
Owned Apartment, 5+ Storeys	808
Apartment, 5 or Fewer Storeys	10,180
Apartment, Detached Duplex	1,977
Other Single-Attached	49
Movable Dwellings	47

VEHICLES

2001 Estimates:
Model Yrs. '81-'96, No.	18,441
% Total	82.06
Model Yrs. '97-'98, No.	2,256
% Total	10.04
'99 Vehicles registered in Model Yr. '99, No.	1,775
% Total	7.90
Total No. '81-'99	22,472

LEGAL MARITAL STATUS

2001 Estimates: (Age 15+)
Single (Never Married)	13,723
Legally Married (Not Separated)	15,624
Legally Married (Separated)	1,621
Widowed	2,527
Divorced	4,082

PSYTE CATEGORIES

2001 Estimates	No. of House-holds	% of Total Hhds.	Index
Suburban Executives	252	1.16	81
Technocrafts & Bureaucrats	446	2.05	73
Suburban Nesters	2,453	11.29	705
Aging Erudites	1,039	4.78	317
Asian Mosaic	491	2.26	165
High Rise Sunsets	630	2.90	203
Young Urban Professionals	790	3.64	192
Young Urban Mix	6,039	27.81	1,312
University Enclaves	6,846	31.52	1,544
Young City Singles	2,344	10.79	471
Town Renters	55	0.25	29
Aged Pensioners	226	1.04	78

FINANCIAL P$YTE

2001 Estimates	No. of House-holds	% of Total Hhds.	Index
Four Star Investors	252	1.16	23
Successful Suburbanites	446	2.05	31
Canadian Comfort	2,453	11.29	116
Urban Heights	1,829	8.42	196
Dollars & Sense	491	2.26	86
Bills & Wills	6,039	27.81	336
Revolving Renters	630	2.90	63
Young Urban Struggle	6,846	31.52	666
Towering Debt	2,399	11.05	142
Senior Survivors	226	1.04	55

HOME LANGUAGE

2001 Estimates		% Total
English	37,883	84.41
French	285	0.64
Arabic	81	0.18
Armenian	28	0.06
Bulgarian	38	0.08
Chinese	745	1.66
Czech	60	0.13
Dutch	44	0.10
German	60	0.13
Greek	65	0.14
Gujarati	50	0.11
Hindi	54	0.12
Hungarian	99	0.22
Italian	120	0.27
Japanese	230	0.51
Korean	151	0.34
Kurdish	65	0.14
Persian (Farsi)	1,527	3.40
Polish	326	0.73
Portuguese	66	0.15
Punjabi	367	0.82
Romanian	104	0.23
Russian	28	0.06
Serbian	80	0.18
Serbo-Croatian	48	0.11
Spanish	291	0.65
Tagalog (Pilipino)	314	0.70
Turkish	98	0.22
Other Languages	344	0.77
Multiple Responses	1,227	2.73
Total	44,878	100.00

BUILDING PERMITS

	1999	1998	1997
		$000	
Value	38,765	39,299	54,377

HOMES BUILT

	1999	1998	1997
No	271	367	521

TAXATION

Income Class:	1997	% Total
Under $5,000	10,500	11.57
$5,000-$10,000	9,690	10.68
$10,000-$15,000	10,180	11.22
$15,000-$20,000	7,530	8.30
$20,000-$25,000	6,720	7.40
$25,000-$30,000	6,590	7.26
$30,000-$40,000	11,920	13.13
$40,000-$50,000	8,690	9.58
$50,000 +	18,940	20.87
Total Returns, No.	90,750	
Total Income, $000	3,149,495	
Total Taxable Returns	68,410	
Total Tax, $000	696,847	
Average Income, $	34,705	
Average Tax, $	10,186	

Note: Data for both Vancouver, DM & Vancouver, C.

VITAL STATISTICS

	1997	1996	1995	1994
Births	467	576	551	510
Deaths	326	333	352	310
Natural Increase	141	243	199	200
Marriages	194	173	203	178

Note: Latest available data.

MEDIA INFO
see Vancouver, CMA

Pitt Meadows
(District Municipality)
Vancouver CMA

In Greater Vancouver Regional District.

POPULATION

July 1, 2001 Estimate	15,934
% Cdn. Total	0.05
% Change, '96 -'01	13.60
Avg. Annual Growth Rate, %	2.58
2003 Projected Population	16,921
2006 Projected Population	18,648
2001 Households Estimate	5,774
2003 Projected Households	6,181
2006 Projected Households	6,873

INCOME

% Above/Below National Average	+3
2001 Total Income Estimate	$347,100,000
% Cdn. Total	0.05
2001 Average Hhld. Income	$60,100
2001 Per Capita	$21,800
2003 Projected Total Income	$396,450,000
2006 Projected Total Income	$486,730,000

RETAIL SALES

% Above/Below National Average	-73
2001 Retail Sales Estimate	$38,580,000
% Cdn. Total	0.01
2001 per Household	$6,700
2001 per Capita	$2,400
2001 No. of Establishments	64
2003 Projected Retail Sales	$43,680,000
2006 Projected Retail Sales	$52,810,000

POPULATION

2001 Estimates:
Total	15,934
Male	7,827
Female	8,107

Age Groups	Male	Female
0-4	531	523
5-9	585	597
10-14	636	631
15-19	590	589
20-24	503	508
25-29	491	521
30-34	564	621
35-39	663	709
40-44	678	713
45-49	607	640
50-54	516	507
55-59	417	387
60-64	312	288
65-69	266	248
70+	468	625

DAYTIME POPULATION

2001 Estimates:
Working Population	1,395
At Home Population	8,087
Total	9,482

INCOME

2001 Estimates:
Avg. Household Income	$60,115
Avg. Family Income	$63,653
Per Capita Income	$21,784

Male:
Avg. Employment Income	$41,270
Avg. Employment Income (Full Time)	$51,384

Female:
Avg. Employment Income	$22,326
Avg. Employment Income (Full Time)	$34,228

British Columbia

DISPOSABLE & DISCRETIONARY INCOME

2001 Estimates:	Per Hhld.
Disposable Income	$46,432
Discretionary Income 1 (minus Food & Shelter)	$31,668
Discretionary Income 2 (minus Food, Shelter, & Other Expenditures)	$22,422

LIQUID ASSETS

1999 Estimates:	Per Hhld.
Equity Investments	$74,765
Interest Bearing Investments	$72,203
Total Liquid Assets	$146,968

CREDIT DATA

July 2000:	
Pool of Credit	$144,802,564
Revolving Credit, No.	29,213
Fixed Loans, No.	7,379
Avg. Credit Limit, per Person	$12,945
Avg. Spent, per Person	$5,997
Satisfactory Ratings, No. per Person	3.20
Avg. No. of Cards, per Person	1.13

LABOUR FORCE

2001 Estimates:
Male:
In the Labour Force	4,531
Participation Rate	74.6
Employed	4,295
Unemployed	236
Unemployment Rate	5.2
Not in Labour Force	1,544

Female:
In the Labour Force	3,859
Participation Rate	60.7
Employed	3,587
Unemployed	272
Unemployment Rate	7.0
Not in Labour Force	2,497

OCCUPATIONS BY MAJOR GROUPS

2001 Estimates:	Male	Female
Management	547	214
Business, Finance & Admin.	458	1,368
Natural & Applied Sciences & Related	283	54
Health	89	339
Social Sciences, Gov't Services & Religion	93	129
Education	74	149
Arts, Culture, Recreation & Sport	68	72
Sales & Service	753	1,272
Trades, Transport & Equipment Operators & Related	1,402	24
Primary Industries	292	139
Processing, Mfg. & Utilities	385	24

British Columbia

Pitt Meadows
(District Municipality)
Vancouver CMA
(Cont'd)

LEVEL OF SCHOOLING

2001 Estimates:
Population 15 years +	12,431
Less than Grade 9	735
Grades 9-13 w/o Certif.	3,268
Grade 9-13 with Certif.	1,843
Trade Certif./Dip.	437
Non-Univ. w/o Certif./Dip.	1,146
Non-Univ. with Certif./Dip.	2,769
Univ. w/o Degree	1,334
Univ. w/o Degree/Certif.	594
Univ. with Certif.	740
Univ. with Degree	899

AVERAGE HOUSEHOLD EXPENDITURES

2001 Estimates:
Food	$6,709
Shelter	$10,208
Clothing	$2,335
Transportation	$7,168
Health & Personal Care	$1,948
Recr'n, Read'g & Education	$4,042
Taxes & Securities	$15,601
Other	$8,953
Total Expenditures	$56,964

PRIVATE HOUSEHOLDS

2001 Estimates:
Private Households, Total	5,774
Pop. in Private Households	15,796
Average no. per Household	2.7

FAMILIES

2001 Estimates:
Families in Private Households	4,586
Husband-Wife Families	3,953
Lone-Parent Families	633
Aver. No. Persons per Family	3.1
Aver. No. Sons/Daughters at Home	1.2

HOUSING

2001 Estimates:
Occupied Private Dwellings	5,774
Owned	4,402
Rented	1,372
Single-Detached House	3,381
Semi-Detached House	48
Row Houses	1,073
Apartment, 5 or Fewer Storeys	917
Apartment, Detached Duplex	266
Movable Dwellings	89

VEHICLES

2001 Estimates:
Model Yrs. '81-'96, No.	5,532
% Total	85.53
Model Yrs. '97-'98, No.	598
% Total	9.25
'99 Vehicles registered in Model Yr. '99, No.	338
% Total	5.23
Total No. '81-'99	6,468

LEGAL MARITAL STATUS

2001 Estimates: (Age 15+)
Single (Never Married)	3,232
Legally Married (Not Separated)	7,193
Legally Married (Separated)	464
Widowed	562
Divorced	980

PSYTE CATEGORIES

2001 Estimates	No. of House-holds	% of Total Hhds.	Index
Satellite Suburbs	2,975	51.52	1,796
Blue Collar Winners	789	13.66	543
Rustic Prosperity	103	1.78	99
Conservative Homebodies	632	10.95	304
Young Urban Mix	674	11.67	551
Young City Singles	427	7.40	322
Town Renters	174	3.01	349

FINANCIAL PSYTE

2001 Estimates	No. of House-holds	% of Total Hhds.	Index
Canadian Comfort	3,764	65.19	671
Tractors & Tradelines	103	1.78	31
Bills & Wills	1,306	22.62	273
Towering Debt	601	10.41	133

HOME LANGUAGE

2001 Estimates:		% Total
English	14,870	93.32
French	97	0.61
Arabic	12	0.08
Chinese	61	0.38
Czech	11	0.07
Dutch	40	0.25
Estonian	12	0.08
German	36	0.23
Greek	12	0.08
Hindi	51	0.32
Hungarian	29	0.18
Persian (Farsi)	49	0.31
Polish	55	0.35
Portuguese	54	0.34
Punjabi	146	0.92
Spanish	51	0.32
Tagalog (Pilipino)	17	0.11
Multiple Responses	331	2.08
Total	15,934	100.00

BUILDING PERMITS

	1999	1998	1997
		$000	
Value	15,018	16,427	19,541

HOMES BUILT

	1999	1998	1997
No.	55	140	122

TAXATION

Income Class:	1997	% Total
Under $5,000	1,100	11.54
$5,000-$10,000	1,000	10.49
$10,000-$15,000	1,180	12.38
$15,000-$20,000	850	8.92
$20,000-$25,000	750	7.87
$25,000-$30,000	730	7.66
$30,000-$40,000	1,370	14.38
$40,000-$50,000	1,050	11.02
$50,000 +	1,500	15.74
Total Returns, No.	9,530	
Total Income, $000	274,742	
Total Taxable Returns	7,150	
Total Tax, $000	52,106	
Average Income, $	28,829	
Average Tax, $	7,288	

VITAL STATISTICS

	1997	1996	1995	1994
Births	186	214	169	184
Deaths	76	75	64	47
Natural Increase	110	139	105	137
Marriages	53	71	65	67

Note: Latest available data.

MEDIA INFO

see Vancouver, CMA

Port Coquitlam
(City)
Vancouver CMA

In Greater Vancouver Regional District.

POPULATION

July 1, 2001 Estimate	58,584
% Cdn. Total	0.19
% Change, '96 -'01	20.22
Avg. Annual Growth Rate, %.	3.75
2003 Projected Population	64,206
2006 Projected Population	73,596
2001 Households Estimate	20,742
2003 Projected Households	22,947
2006 Projected Households	26,564

INCOME

% Above/Below National Average	+5
2001 Total Income Estimate	$1,297,330,000
% Cdn. Total	0.20
2001 Average Hhld. Income	$62,500
2001 Per Capita	$22,100
2003 Projected Total Income	$1,526,710,000
2006 Projected Total Income	$1,943,160,000

RETAIL SALES

% Above/Below National Average	-10
2001 Retail Sales Estimate	$471,950,000
% Cdn. Total	0.17
2001 per Household	$22,800
2001 per Capita	$8,100
2001 No. of Establishments	269
2003 Projected Retail Sales	$563,080,000
2006 Projected Retail Sales	$720,840,000

POPULATION

2001 Estimates:
Total		58,584
Male		29,158
Female		29,426

Age Groups	Male	Female
0-4	2,120	1,977
5-9	2,282	2,087
10-14	2,313	2,131
15-19	2,153	2,016
20-24	1,948	1,911
25-29	2,060	2,107
30-34	2,424	2,587
35-39	2,756	2,910
40-44	2,702	2,767
45-49	2,345	2,326
50-54	1,827	1,787
55-59	1,343	1,321
60-64	979	1,001
65-69	707	766
70+	1,199	1,732

DAYTIME POPULATION

2001 Estimates:
Working Population	12,482
At Home Population	28,234
Total	40,716

INCOME

2001 Estimates:
Avg. Household Income	$62,546
Avg. Family Income	$64,513
Per Capita Income	$22,145
Male:	
Avg. Employment Income	$39,051
Avg. Employment Income (Full Time)	$48,904
Female:	
Avg. Employment Income	$24,628
Avg. Employment Income (Full Time)	$34,711

DISPOSABLE & DISCRETIONARY INCOME

2001 Estimates:	Per Hhld.
Disposable Income	$48,462
Discretionary Income 1 (minus Food & Shelter)	$33,775
Discretionary Income 2 (minus Food, Shelter, & Other Expenditures)	$24,513

LIQUID ASSETS

1999 Estimates:	Per Hhld.
Equity Investments	$84,909
Interest Bearing Investments	$76,574
Total Liquid Assets	$161,483

CREDIT DATA

July 2000:
Pool of Credit	$560,988,205
Revolving Credit, No.	112,696
Fixed Loans, No.	28,567
Avg. Credit Limit, per Person.	$13,161
Avg. Spent, per Person	$5,878
Satisfactory Ratings, No. per Person.	3.25
Avg. No. of Cards, per Person	1.16

LABOUR FORCE

2001 Estimates:
Male:	
In the Labour Force	17,273
Participation Rate	77.0
Employed	16,176
Unemployed	1,097
Unemployment Rate	6.4
Not in Labour Force	5,170
Female:	
In the Labour Force	15,362
Participation Rate	66.1
Employed	14,443
Unemployed	919
Unemployment Rate	6.0
Not in Labour Force	7,869

OCCUPATIONS BY MAJOR GROUPS

2001 Estimates:	Male	Female
Management	2,075	790
Business, Finance & Admin.	1,860	5,301
Natural & Applied Sciences & Related	1,310	226
Health	219	1,288
Social Sciences, Gov't Services & Religion	220	432
Education	341	641
Arts, Culture, Recreation & Sport	353	434
Sales & Service	3,591	5,131
Trades, Transport & Equipment Operators & Related	5,421	341
Primary Industries	301	101
Processing, Mfg. & Utilities	1,289	300

LEVEL OF SCHOOLING

2001 Estimates:
Population 15 years +	45,674
Less than Grade 9	2,041
Grades 9-13 w/o Certif.	10,112
Grade 9-13 with Certif.	7,388
Trade Certif./Dip.	1,495
Non-Univ. w/o Certif./Dip.	4,067
Non-Univ. with Certif./Dip.	11,250
Univ. w/o Degree	4,982
Univ. w/o Degree/Certif.	2,143
Univ. with Certif.	2,839
Univ. with Degree	4,339

Port Coquitlam
(City)
Vancouver CMA
(Cont'd)

AVERAGE HOUSEHOLD EXPENDITURES

2001 Estimates:

Food	$6,817
Shelter	$10,153
Clothing	$2,511
Transportation	$7,158
Health & Personal Care	$2,020
Recr'n, Read'g & Education	$4,289
Taxes & Securities	$16,841
Other	$9,149
Total Expenditures	$58,938

PRIVATE HOUSEHOLDS

2001 Estimates:

Private Households, Total	20,742
Pop. in Private Households	57,760
Average no. per Household	2.8

FAMILIES

2001 Estimates:

Families in Private Households	16,729
Husband-Wife Families	14,294
Lone-Parent Families	2,435
Aver. No. Persons per Family	3.1
Aver. No. Sons/Daughters at Home	1.2

HOUSING

2001 Estimates:

Occupied Private Dwellings	20,742
Owned	15,403
Rented	5,339
Single-Detached House	11,306
Semi-Detached House	600
Row Houses	2,814
Apartment, 5+ Storeys	12
Apartment, 5 or Fewer Storeys	3,871
Apartment, Detached Duplex	2,075
Movable Dwellings	64

VEHICLES

2001 Estimates:

Model Yrs. '81-'96, No.	19,999
% Total	82.37
Model Yrs. '97-'98, No.	2,718
% Total	11.19
'99 Vehicles registered in Model Yr. '99, No.	1,563
% Total	6.44
Total No. '81-'99	24,280

LEGAL MARITAL STATUS

2001 Estimates: (Age 15+)

Single (Never Married)	13,258
Legally Married (Not Separated)	25,454
Legally Married (Separated)	1,625
Widowed	1,868
Divorced	3,469

PSYTE CATEGORIES

2001 Estimates	No. of House-holds	% of Total Hhds.	Index
Mortgaged in Suburbia	2,031	9.79	704
Technocrats & Bureaucrats	1,989	9.59	341
Boomers & Teens	1,418	6.84	381
Old Bungalow Burbs	1,177	5.67	342
Brie & Chablis	277	1.34	149
Satellite Suburbs	5,733	27.64	963
Kindergarten Boom	3,183	15.35	585
Conservative Homebodies	615	2.96	82
High Rise Sunsets	76	0.37	26
Young Urban Mix	1,733	8.36	394
Young City Singles	860	4.15	181
Town Renters	144	0.69	80
Struggling Downtowns	850	4.10	130
Aged Pensioners	555	2.68	201

FINANCIAL P$YTE

2001 Estimates	No. of House-holds	% of Total Hhds.	Index
Four Star Investors	1,418	6.84	136
Successful Suburbanites	4,020	19.38	292
Canadian Comfort	5,733	27.64	284
Urban Heights	277	1.34	31
Miners & Credit-Liners	1,177	5.67	179
Mortgages & Minivans	3,183	15.35	233
Bills & Wills	2,348	11.32	137
Revolving Renters	76	0.37	8
Towering Debt	1,854	8.94	115
Senior Survivors	555	2.68	142

HOME LANGUAGE

2001 Estimates:		% Total
English	51,706	88.26
French	125	0.21
Arabic	113	0.19
Chinese	3,064	5.23
Czech	87	0.15
Greek	95	0.16
Gujarati	38	0.06
Hindi	135	0.23
Hungarian	64	0.11
Italian	121	0.21
Japanese	73	0.12
Korean	206	0.35
Lao	56	0.10
Persian (Farsi)	180	0.31
Polish	253	0.43
Portuguese	51	0.09
Punjabi	588	1.00
Romanian	112	0.19
Slovak	30	0.05
Spanish	119	0.20
Tagalog (Pilipino)	195	0.33
Other Languages	286	0.49
Multiple Responses	887	1.51
Total	58,584	100.00

BUILDING PERMITS

	1999	1998	1997
		$000	
Value	94,748	53,481	48,894

HOMES BUILT

	1999	1998	1997
No	172	242	410

TAXATION

Income Class:	1997	% Total
Under $5,000	4,710	13.38
$5,000-$10,000	3,820	10.86
$10,000-$15,000	3,950	11.22
$15,000-$20,000	2,860	8.13
$20,000-$25,000	2,550	7.25
$25,000-$30,000	2,560	7.27
$30,000-$40,000	5,190	14.75
$40,000-$50,000	3,690	10.49
$50,000 +	5,860	16.65
Total Returns, No.	35,190	
Total Income, $000	1,043,632	
Total Taxable Returns	25,880	
Total Tax, $000	207,174	
Average Income, $	29,657	
Average Tax, $	8,005	

VITAL STATISTICS

	1997	1996	1995	1994
Births	709	723	714	720
Deaths	203	212	208	214
Natural Increase	506	511	506	506
Marriages	211	213	197	172

Note: Latest available data.

MEDIA INFO

see Vancouver, CMA

Port Moody
(City)
Vancouver CMA
In Greater Vancouver Regional District.

POPULATION

2001 Estimates:

July 1, 2001 Estimate	24,306
% Cdn. Total	0.08
% Change, '96 -'01	11.68
Avg. Annual Growth Rate, %	2.23
2003 Projected Population	25,572
2006 Projected Population	27,857
2001 Households Estimate	8,798
2003 Projected Households	9,319
2006 Projected Households	10,224

INCOME

% Above/Below National Average	+24
2001 Total Income Estimate	$635,050,000
% Cdn. Total	0.10
2001 Average Hhld. Income	$72,200
2001 Per Capita	$26,100
2003 Projected Total Income	$719,320,000
2006 Projected Total Income	$874,150,000

RETAIL SALES

% Above/Below National Average	-60
2001 Retail Sales Estimate	$87,950,000
% Cdn. Total	0.03
2001 per Household	$10,000
2001 per Capita	$3,600
2001 No. of Establishments	148
2003 Projected Retail Sales	$100,680,000
2006 Projected Retail Sales	$121,840,000

POPULATION

2001 Estimates:

Total	24,306
Male	12,059
Female	12,247

Age Groups	Male	Female
0-4	852	818
5-9	917	855
10-14	906	858
15-19	816	809
20-24	723	763
25-29	773	816
30-34	957	1,007
35-39	1,111	1,183
40-44	1,124	1,168
45-49	1,029	1,015
50-54	836	823
55-59	649	649
60-64	488	465
65-69	348	319
70+	530	699

DAYTIME POPULATION

2001 Estimates:

Working Population	2,190
At Home Population	10,777
Total	12,967

INCOME

2001 Estimates:

Avg. Household Income	$72,181
Avg. Family Income	$75,843
Per Capita Income	$26,127
Male:	
Avg. Employment Income	$45,366
Avg. Employment Income (Full Time)	$57,559
Female:	
Avg. Employment Income	$25,808
Avg. Employment Income (Full Time)	$36,943

British Columbia

DISPOSABLE & DISCRETIONARY INCOME

2001 Estimates:	Per Hhld.
Disposable Income	$54,939
Discretionary Income 1 (minus Food & Shelter)	$39,213
Discretionary Income 2 (minus Food, Shelter, & Other Expenditures)	$29,094

LIQUID ASSETS

1999 Estimates:	Per Hhld.
Equity Investments	$120,021
Interest Bearing Investments	$92,729
Total Liquid Assets	$212,750

CREDIT DATA

July 2000:	
Pool of Credit	$293,840,414
Revolving Credit, No.	54,871
Fixed Loans, No.	13,506
Avg. Credit Limit, per Person	$14,655
Avg. Spent, per Person	$6,323
Satisfactory Ratings, No. per Person	3.34
Avg. No. of Cards, per Person	1.26

LABOUR FORCE

2001 Estimates:	
Male:	
In the Labour Force	7,478
Participation Rate	79.7
Employed	7,095
Unemployed	383
Unemployment Rate	5.1
Not in Labour Force	1,906
Female:	
In the Labour Force	6,797
Participation Rate	70.0
Employed	6,498
Unemployed	299
Unemployment Rate	4.4
Not in Labour Force	2,919

OCCUPATIONS BY MAJOR GROUPS

2001 Estimates:	Male	Female
Management	1,213	386
Business, Finance & Admin.	990	2,257
Natural & Applied Sciences & Related	720	110
Health	66	546
Social Sciences, Gov't Services & Religion	98	244
Education	312	423
Arts, Culture, Recreation & Sport	138	250
Sales & Service	1,601	2,225
Trades, Transport & Equipment Operators & Related	1,786	43
Primary Industries	94	36
Processing, Mfg. & Utilities	325	133

British Columbia

Port Moody
(City)
Vancouver CMA
(Cont'd)

LEVEL OF SCHOOLING

2001 Estimates:
Population 15 years +	19,100
Less than Grade 9	429
Grades 9-13 w/o Certif.	3,744
Grade 9-13 with Certif.	2,788
Trade Certif. /Dip.	564
Non-Univ. w/o Certif./Dip.	1,499
Non-Univ. with Certif./Dip.	4,375
Univ. w/o Degree	2,659
Univ. w/o Degree/Certif.	1,031
Univ. with Certif.	1,628
Univ. with Degree	3,042

AVERAGE HOUSEHOLD EXPENDITURES

2001 Estimates:
Food	$7,354
Shelter	$10,936
Clothing	$2,813
Transportation	$7,879
Health & Personal Care	$2,225
Recr'n, Read'g & Education	$4,790
Taxes & Securities	$20,438
Other	$10,013
Total Expenditures	$66,448

PRIVATE HOUSEHOLDS

2001 Estimates:
Private Households, Total	8,798
Pop. in Private Households	24,092
Average no. per Household	2.7

FAMILIES

2001 Estimates:
Families in Private Households	7,133
Husband-Wife Families	6,185
Lone-Parent Families	948
Aver. No. Persons per Family	3.0
Aver. No. Sons/Daughters at Home	1.2

HOUSING

2001 Estimates:
Occupied Private Dwellings	8,798
Owned	6,634
Rented	2,164
Single-Detached House	4,315
Semi-Detached House	157
Row Houses	2,086
Apartment, 5+ Storeys	207
Owned Apartment, 5+ Storeys	112
Apartment, 5 or Fewer Storeys	1,349
Apartment, Detached Duplex	642
Movable Dwellings	42

VEHICLES

2001 Estimates:
Model Yrs. '81-'96, No.	9,458
% Total	82.18
Model Yrs. '97-'98, No.	1,238
% Total	10.76
'99 Vehicles registered in Model Yr. '99, No.	813
% Total	7.06
Total No. '81-'99	11,509

LEGAL MARITAL STATUS

2001 Estimates: (Age 15+)
Single (Never Married)	5,404
Legally Married (Not Separated)	10,970
Legally Married (Separated)	631
Widowed	672
Divorced	1,423

PSYTE CATEGORIES

2001 Estimates	No. of House -holds	% of Total Hhds.	Index
Suburban Executives	498	5.66	395
Mortgaged in Suburbia	1,385	15.74	1,133
Technocrafts & Bureaucrats	779	8.85	315
Boomers & Teens	870	9.89	552
Stable Suburban Families	840	9.55	732
Old Bungalow Burbs	644	7.32	442
Satellite Suburbs	1,201	13.65	476
Kindergarten Boom	807	9.17	350
Young Urban Mix	1,302	14.80	698
Town Renters	343	3.90	451
Old Grey Towers	101	1.15	207

FINANÇIAL PȘYTE

2001 Estimates	No. of House -holds	% of Total Hhds.	Index
Four Star Investors	1,368	15.55	310
Successful Suburbanites	3,004	34.14	515
Canadian Comfort	1,201	13.65	140
Miners & Credit-Liners	644	7.32	231
Mortgages & Minivans	807	9.17	139
Bills & Wills	1,302	14.80	179
Towering Debt	343	3.90	50
Senior Survivors	101	1.15	61

HOME LANGUAGE

2001 Estimates:		% Total
English	21,836	89.84
French	105	0.43
Arabic	95	0.39
Chinese	828	3.41
Czech	59	0.24
Finnish	24	0.10
German	38	0.16
Gujarati	30	0.12
Hebrew	16	0.07
Hindi	41	0.17
Korean	68	0.28
Malay-Bahasa	29	0.12
Persian (Farsi)	206	0.85
Polish	180	0.74
Punjabi	34	0.14
Romanian	119	0.49
Russian	49	0.20
Spanish	85	0.35
Tagalog (Pilipino)	24	0.10
Other Languages	91	0.37
Multiple Responses	349	1.44
Total	24,306	100.00

BUILDING PERMITS

	1999	1998	1997
		$000	
Value	19,634	20,165	61,982

HOMES BUILT

	1999	1998	1997
No.	122	385	129

TAXATION

Income Class:	1997	% Total
Under $5,000	1,870	12.17
$5,000-$10,000	1,560	10.16
$10,000-$15,000	1,520	9.90
$15,000-$20,000	1,140	7.42
$20,000-$25,000	1,010	6.58
$25,000-$30,000	1,100	7.16
$30,000-$40,000	2,260	14.71
$40,000-$50,000	1,740	11.33
$50,000 +	3,170	20.64
Total Returns, No.	15,360	
Total Income, $000	506,414	
Total Taxable Returns	11,740	
Total Tax, $000	107,316	
Average Income, $	32,970	
Average Tax, $	9,141	

VITAL STATISTICS

	1997	1996	1995	1994
Births	336	322	320	303
Deaths	74	77	80	73
Natural Increase	262	245	240	230
Marriages	121	87	107	124

Note: Latest available data.

MEDIA INFO
see Vancouver, CMA

Richmond
(City)
Vancouver CMA

In Greater Vancouver Regional District.

POPULATION

July 1, 2001 Estimate	173,778
% Cdn. Total	0.56
% Change, '96 -'01	11.82
Avg. Annual Growth Rate, %	2.26
2003 Projected Population	182,954
2006 Projected Population	199,445
2001 Households Estimate	61,458
2003 Projected Households	65,202
2006 Projected Households	71,667

INCOME

% Above/Below National Average	same
2001 Total Income Estimate	$3,674,980,000
% Cdn. Total	0.56
2001 Average Hhld. Income	$59,800
2001 Per Capita	$21,100
2003 Projected Total Income	$4,155,110,000
2006 Projected Total Income	$5,031,400,000

RETAIL SALES

% Above/Below National Average	+32
2001 Retail Sales Estimate	$2,050,330,000
% Cdn. Total	0.74
2001 per Household	$33,400
2001 per Capita	$11,800
2001 No. of Establishments	1,460
2003 Projected Retail Sales	$2,349,090,000
2006 Projected Retail Sales	$2,847,470,000

POPULATION

2001 Estimates:

Total		173,778
Male		84,489
Female		89,289

Age Groups	Male	Female
0-4	5,214	4,952
5-9	5,298	5,040
10-14	5,754	5,410
15-19	6,217	5,845
20-24	6,165	6,011
25-29	6,135	6,146
30-34	6,317	6,671
35-39	6,579	7,318
40-44	6,871	7,772
45-49	6,982	7,646
50-54	6,038	6,423
55-59	4,628	4,842
60-64	3,633	3,758
65-69	2,897	3,181
70+	5,761	8,274

DAYTIME POPULATION

2001 Estimates:

Working Population	81,806
At Home Population	92,917
Total	174,723

INCOME

2001 Estimates:

Avg. Household Income	$59,797
Avg. Family Income	$61,854
Per Capita Income	$21,148
Male:	
Avg. Employment Income	$35,911
Avg. Employment Income (Full Time)	$47,986
Female:	
Avg. Employment Income	$24,267
Avg. Employment Income (Full Time)	$35,281

DISPOSABLE & DISCRETIONARY INCOME

2001 Estimates:	Per Hhld.
Disposable Income	$46,447
Discretionary Income 1 (minus Food & Shelter)	$31,870
Discretionary Income 2 (minus Food, Shelter, & Other Expenditures)	$22,583

LIQUID ASSETS

1999 Estimates:	Per Hhld.
Equity Investments	$89,773
Interest Bearing Investments	$75,115
Total Liquid Assets	$164,888

CREDIT DATA

July 2000:

Pool of Credit	$1,796,882,864
Revolving Credit, No.	404,874
Fixed Loans, No.	80,173
Avg. Credit Limit, per Person	$11,182
Avg. Spent, per Person	$4,231
Satisfactory Ratings, No. per Person	3.00
Avg. No. of Cards, per Person	1.18

LABOUR FORCE

2001 Estimates:

Male:	
In the Labour Force	46,164
Participation Rate	67.7
Employed	43,141
Unemployed	3,023
Unemployment Rate	6.5
Not in Labour Force	22,059
Female:	
In the Labour Force	41,273
Participation Rate	55.9
Employed	38,740
Unemployed	2,533
Unemployment Rate	6.1
Not in Labour Force	32,614

OCCUPATIONS BY MAJOR GROUPS

2001 Estimates:	Male	Female
Management	7,479	3,125
Business, Finance & Admin.	6,341	14,462
Natural & Applied Sciences & Related	4,146	732
Health	966	2,853
Social Sciences, Gov't Services & Religion	838	762
Education	887	1,734
Arts, Culture, Recreation & Sport	946	1,057
Sales & Service	10,887	13,502
Trades, Transport & Equipment Operators & Related	8,923	510
Primary Industries	1,059	335
Processing, Mfg. & Utilities	2,378	1,111

LEVEL OF SCHOOLING

2001 Estimates:

Population 15 years +	142,110
Less than Grade 9	9,592
Grades 9-13 w/o Certif.	29,432
Grade 9-13 with Certif.	19,640
Trade Certif. /Dip.	3,810
Non-Univ. w/o Certif./Dip.	10,068
Non-Univ. with Certif./Dip.	25,503
Univ. w/o Degree	18,667
Univ. w/o Degree/Certif.	9,277
Univ. with Certif.	9,390
Univ. with Degree	25,398

AVERAGE HOUSEHOLD EXPENDITURES

2001 Estimates:

Food	$7,299
Shelter	$9,932
Clothing	$2,414
Transportation	$7,402
Health & Personal Care	$2,164
Recr'n, Read'g & Education	$4,027
Taxes & Securities	$15,163
Other	$8,270
Total Expenditures	$56,671

PRIVATE HOUSEHOLDS

2001 Estimates:

Private Households, Total	61,458
Pop. in Private Households	172,113
Average no. per Household	2.8

FAMILIES

2001 Estimates:

Families in Private Households	48,782
Husband-Wife Families	42,914
Lone-Parent Families	5,868
Aver. No. Persons per Family	3.1
Aver. No. Sons/Daughters at Home	1.3

HOUSING

2001 Estimates:

Occupied Private Dwellings	61,458
Owned	42,732
Rented	18,726
Single-Detached House	30,596
Semi-Detached House	2,369
Row Houses	9,458
Apartment, 5+ Storeys	2,047
Owned Apartment, 5+ Storeys	1,152
Apartment, 5 or Fewer Storeys	15,166
Apartment, Detached Duplex	1,591
Other Single-Attached	84
Movable Dwellings	147

VEHICLES

2001 Estimates:

Model Yrs. '81-'96, No.	71,242
% Total	56.71
Model Yrs. '97-'98, No.	30,788
% Total	24.51
'99 Vehicles registered in Model Yr. '99, No.	23,591
% Total	18.78
Total No. '81-'99	125,621

LEGAL MARITAL STATUS

2001 Estimates: (Age 15+)

Single (Never Married)	43,023
Legally Married (Not Separated)	79,851
Legally Married (Separated)	3,374
Widowed	7,606
Divorced	8,256

PSYTE CATEGORIES

2001 Estimates	No. of House -holds	% of Total Hhds.	Index
The Affluentials	139	0.23	35
Urban Gentry	710	1.16	64
Suburban Executives	377	0.61	43
Mortgaged in Suburbia	826	1.34	97
Asian Heights	9,577	15.58	2,459
Boomers & Teens	2,526	4.11	229
Stable Suburban Families	4,269	6.95	533
Old Bungalow Burbs	446	0.73	44
Suburban Nesters	1,063	1.73	108
Brie & Chablis	3,285	5.35	597
Aging Erudites	1,424	2.32	154
Satellite Suburbs	578	0.94	33
Kindergarten Boom	1,360	2.21	84
Blue Collar Winners	246	0.40	16
Asian Mosaic	22,280	36.25	2,645
Conservative Homebodies	524	0.85	24
High Rise Sunsets	1,113	1.81	127

British Columbia

2001 Estimates	No. of House -holds	% of Total Hhds.	Index
Young Urban Professionals	152	0.25	13
Young Urban Mix	4,207	6.85	323
University Enclaves	3,185	5.18	254
Young City Singles	616	1.00	44
Town Renters	767	1.25	144
Aged Pensioners	1,567	2.55	192

FINANCIAL P$YTE

2001 Estimates	No. of House -holds	% of Total Hhds.	Index
Platinum Estates	139	0.23	28
Four Star Investors	3,613	5.88	117
Successful Suburbanites	14,672	23.87	360
Canadian Comfort	1,887	3.07	32
Urban Heights	4,861	7.91	184
Miners & Credit-Liners	446	0.73	23
Mortgages & Minivans	1,360	2.21	34
Dollars & Sense	22,280	36.25	1,387
Bills & Wills	4,731	7.70	93
Revolving Renters	1,113	1.81	39
Young Urban Struggle	3,185	5.18	109
Towering Debt	1,383	2.25	29
Senior Survivors	1,567	2.55	135

HOME LANGUAGE

2001 Estimates:		% Total
English	108,527	62.45
French	484	0.28
Arabic	456	0.26
Chinese	45,057	25.93
Croatian	151	0.09
Czech	143	0.08
German	446	0.26
Greek	186	0.11
Gujarati	242	0.14
Hindi	540	0.31
Japanese	1,038	0.60
Korean	437	0.25
Persian (Farsi)	615	0.35
Polish	383	0.22
Punjabi	4,199	2.42
Russian	574	0.33
Serbo-Croatian	94	0.05
Spanish	685	0.39
Tagalog (Pilipino)	1,721	0.99
Thai	98	0.06
Urdu	211	0.12
Vietnamese	363	0.21
Other Languages	1,543	0.89
Multiple Responses	5,585	3.21
Total	173,778	100.00

BUILDING PERMITS

	1999	1998 $000	1997
Value	150,622	239,587	281,822

HOMES BUILT

	1999	1998	1997
No	820	833	2,129

British Columbia

Richmond
(City)
Vancouver CMA
(Cont'd)

TAXATION

Income Class:	1997	% Total
Under $5,000	24,110	20.82
$5,000-$10,000	14,960	12.92
$10,000-$15,000	13,860	11.97
$15,000-$20,000	9,890	8.54
$20,000-$25,000	8,480	7.32
$25,000-$30,000	7,920	6.84
$30,000-$40,000	13,380	11.55
$40,000-$50,000	8,690	7.50
$50,000 +	14,520	12.54
Total Returns, No.	115,810	
Total Income, $000	2,940,718	
Total Taxable Returns	74,750	
Total Tax, $000	569,829	
Average Income, $	25,393	
Average Tax, $	7,623	

VITAL STATISTICS

	1997	1996	1995	1994
Births	1,688	1,723	1,799	1,598
Deaths	782	794	730	723
Natural Increase	906	929	1,069	875
Marriages	957	970	1,081	1,096

Note: Latest available data.

MEDIA INFO
see Vancouver, CMA

Surrey
(City)
Vancouver CMA

In Greater Vancouver Regional District.

POPULATION

July 1, 2001 Estimate	374,118
% Cdn. Total	1.20
% Change, '96 -'01	17.70
Avg. Annual Growth Rate, %	3.31
2003 Projected Population	405,142
2006 Projected Population	457,735
2001 Households Estimate	127,837
2003 Projected Households	139,330
2006 Projected Households	158,419

INCOME

% Above/Below National Average	-2
2001 Total Income Estimate	$7,730,850,000
% Cdn. Total	1.18
2001 Average Hhld. Income	$60,500
2001 Per Capita	$20,700
2003 Projected Total Income	$9,077,110,000
2006 Projected Total Income	$11,546,640,000

RETAIL SALES

% Above/Below National Average	-17
2001 Retail Sales Estimate	$2,767,300,000
% Cdn. Total	0.99
2001 per Household	$21,600
2001 per Capita	$7,400
2001 No. of Establishments	2,087
2003 Projected Retail Sales	$3,245,580,000
2006 Projected Retail Sales	$4,065,250,000

POPULATION

2001 Estimates:

Total		374,118
Male		186,171
Female		187,947

Age Groups	Male	Female
0-4	13,049	12,348
5-9	14,210	13,396
10-14	14,162	13,122
15-19	13,308	12,528
20-24	12,525	12,666
25-29	13,296	13,689
30-34	14,914	15,114
35-39	15,798	15,880
40-44	15,266	15,264
45-49	13,694	13,755
50-54	11,382	11,378
55-59	9,050	8,978
60-64	7,199	7,248
65-69	5,918	6,272
70+	12,400	16,309

DAYTIME POPULATION

2001 Estimates:

Working Population	73,518
At Home Population	199,520
Total	273,038

INCOME

2001 Estimates:

Avg. Household Income	$60,474
Avg. Family Income	$60,903
Per Capita Income	$20,664
Male:	
Avg. Employment Income	$36,763
Avg. Employment Income (Full Time)	$48,764
Female:	
Avg. Employment Income	$22,690
Avg. Employment Income (Full Time)	$33,499

DISPOSABLE & DISCRETIONARY INCOME

2001 Estimates:	Per Hhld.
Disposable Income	$47,062
Discretionary Income 1 (minus Food & Shelter)	$32,870
Discretionary Income 2 (minus Food, Shelter, & Other Expenditures)	$23,673

LIQUID ASSETS

1999 Estimates:	Per Hhld.
Equity Investments	$89,097
Interest Bearing Investments	$75,697
Total Liquid Assets	$164,794

CREDIT DATA

July 2000:

Pool of Credit	$3,418,662,138
Revolving Credit, No.	708,763
Fixed Loans, No.	169,603
Avg. Credit Limit, per Person	$12,085
Avg. Spent, per Person	$5,189
Satisfactory Ratings, No. per Person	3.05
Avg. No. of Cards, per Person	1.11

LABOUR FORCE

2001 Estimates:

Male:	
In the Labour Force	104,691
Participation Rate	72.3
Employed	96,327
Unemployed	8,364
Unemployment Rate	8.0
Not in Labour Force	40,059
Female:	
In the Labour Force	88,658
Participation Rate	59.5
Employed	80,058
Unemployed	8,600
Unemployment Rate	9.7
Not in Labour Force	60,423

OCCUPATIONS BY MAJOR GROUPS

2001 Estimates:	Male	Female
Management	11,853	4,794
Business, Finance & Admin.	9,680	27,896
Natural & Applied Sciences & Related	6,505	968
Health	1,478	6,472
Social Sciences, Gov't Services & Religion	1,245	1,856
Education	1,896	2,995
Arts, Culture, Recreation & Sport	1,590	2,147
Sales & Service	21,691	30,200
Trades, Transport & Equipment Operators & Related	32,435	1,884
Primary Industries	4,171	2,492
Processing, Mfg. & Utilities	9,275	3,231

LEVEL OF SCHOOLING

2001 Estimates:

Population 15 years +	293,831
Less than Grade 9	23,846
Grades 9-13 w/o Certif.	75,554
Grade 9-13 with Certif.	42,182
Trade Certif. /Dip.	10,149
Non-Univ. w/o Certif./Dip.	22,893
Non-Univ. with Certif./Dip.	57,931
Univ. w/o Degree	31,506
Univ. w/o Degree/Certif.	14,766
Univ. with Certif.	16,740
Univ. with Degree	29,770

AVERAGE HOUSEHOLD EXPENDITURES

2001 Estimates:

Food	$6,508
Shelter	$9,916
Clothing	$2,381
Transportation	$7,144
Health & Personal Care	$2,013
Recr'n, Read'g & Education	$4,094
Taxes & Securities	$16,155
Other	$8,920
Total Expenditures	$57,131

PRIVATE HOUSEHOLDS

2001 Estimates:

Private Households, Total	127,837
Pop. in Private Households	370,198
Average no. per Household	2.9

FAMILIES

2001 Estimates:

Families in Private Households	106,718
Husband-Wife Families	92,218
Lone-Parent Families	14,500
Aver. No. Persons per Family	3.1
Aver. No. Sons/Daughters at Home	1.2

HOUSING

2001 Estimates:

Occupied Private Dwellings	127,837
Owned	90,028
Rented	37,809
Single-Detached House	73,901
Semi-Detached House	3,419
Row Houses	11,731
Apartment, 5+ Storeys	3,112
Owned Apartment, 5+ Storeys	1,407
Apartment, 5 or Fewer Storeys	21,850
Apartment, Detached Duplex	11,868
Other Single-Attached	257
Movable Dwellings	1,699

VEHICLES

2001 Estimates:

Model Yrs. '81-'96, No.	141,488
% Total	83.67
Model Yrs. '97-'98, No.	16,770
% Total	9.92
'99 Vehicles registered in Model Yr. '99, No.	10,841
% Total	6.41
Total No. '81-'99	169,099

LEGAL MARITAL STATUS

2001 Estimates: (Age 15+)

Single (Never Married)	79,910
Legally Married (Not Separated)	169,379
Legally Married (Separated)	9,901
Widowed	15,008
Divorced	19,633

PSYTE CATEGORIES

2001 Estimates	No. of House-holds	% of Total Hhds.	Index
The Affluentials	896	0.70	110
Suburban Executives	2,744	2.15	150
Mortgaged in Suburbia	6,231	4.87	351
Technocrafts & Bureaucrats	917	0.72	25
Asian Heights	515	0.40	64
Boomers & Teens	10,920	8.54	476
Small City Elite	3,315	2.59	151
Old Bungalow Burbs	1,317	1.03	62
Suburban Nesters	504	0.39	25
Brie & Chablis	880	0.69	77
Aging Erudites	2,593	2.03	134
Satellite Suburbs	22,282	17.43	608
Kindergarten Boom	30,298	23.70	904
Blue Collar Winners	7,260	5.68	226

Surrey
(City)
Vancouver CMA
(Cont'd)

2001 Estimates	No. of House -holds	% of Total Hhds.	Index
Asian Mosaic	870	0.68	50
Conservative Homebodies	5,807	4.54	126
High Rise Sunsets	3,874	3.03	212
Young Urban Mix	5,684	4.45	210
University Enclaves	1,311	1.03	50
Young City Singles	5,615	4.39	192
Old Leafy Towns	873	0.68	27
Town Renters	4,299	3.36	389
Nesters & Young Homesteaders	2,141	1.67	72
Struggling Downtowns	4,117	3.22	102
Aged Pensioners	1,967	1.54	116
Big City Stress	126	0.10	9

FINANCIAL P$YTE

2001 Estimates	No. of House -holds	% of Total Hhds.	Index
Platinum Estates	896	0.70	87
Four Star Investors	13,664	10.69	213
Successful Suburbanites	7,663	5.99	90
Canadian Comfort	33,361	26.10	269
Urban Heights	3,473	2.72	63
Miners & Credit-Liners	1,317	1.03	33
Mortgages & Minivans	30,298	23.70	359
Dollars & Sense	870	0.68	26
Bills & Wills	12,364	9.67	117
Revolving Renters	6,015	4.71	102
Young Urban Struggle	1,311	1.03	22
Towering Debt	14,031	10.98	141
NSF	126	0.10	3
Senior Survivors	1,967	1.54	82

HOME LANGUAGE

2001 Estimates:		% Total
English	292,236	78.11
French	814	0.22
Arabic	413	0.11
Chinese	9,912	2.65
Croatian	296	0.08
Czech	273	0.07
Dutch	212	0.06
German	682	0.18
Greek	318	0.08
Gujarati	467	0.12
Hindi	4,011	1.07
Hungarian	267	0.07
Italian	408	0.11
Japanese	360	0.10
Korean	2,335	0.62
Lao	375	0.10
Persian (Farsi)	686	0.18
Polish	1,609	0.43
Portuguese	415	0.11
Punjabi	35,442	9.47
Romanian	217	0.06
Serbian	194	0.05
Spanish	1,998	0.53
Tagalog (Pilipino)	1,968	0.53
Urdu	642	0.17
Vietnamese	1,648	0.44
Other Languages	2,337	0.62
Multiple Responses	13,583	3.63
Total	374,118	100.00

BUILDING PERMITS

	1999	1998	1997
		$000	
Value	629,295	614,431	654,446

HOMES BUILT

	1999	1998	1997
No	2,119	2,219	3,085

TAXATION

Income Class:	1997	% Total
Under $5,000	32,200	14.64
$5,000-$10,000	30,450	13.85
$10,000-$15,000	31,130	14.16
$15,000-$20,000	20,230	9.20
$20,000-$25,000	17,050	7.75
$25,000-$30,000	15,850	7.21
$30,000-$40,000	27,090	12.32
$40,000-$50,000	18,000	8.19
$50,000 +	27,880	12.68
Total Returns, No.	219,880	
Total Income, $000	5,764,540	
Total Taxable Returns	149,870	
Total Tax, $000	1,087,619	
Average Income, $	26,217	
Average Tax, $	7,257	

VITAL STATISTICS

	1997	1996	1995	1994
Births	4,949	4,854	4,996	4,800
Deaths	1,698	1,733	1,573	1,476
Natural Increase	3,251	3,121	3,423	3,324
Marriages	1,326	1,365	1,372	1,469

Note: Latest available data.

MEDIA INFO
see Vancouver, CMA

Vancouver
(City)
Vancouver CMA

In Greater Vancouver Regional District.

POPULATION

July 1, 2001 Estimate	560,674
% Cdn. Total	1.80
% Change, '96 -'01	4.49
Avg. Annual Growth Rate, %	0.88
2003 Projected Population	569,525
2006 Projected Population	591,306
2001 Households Estimate	247,102
2003 Projected Households	252,944
2006 Projected Households	264,801

INCOME

% Above/Below National Average	+6
2001 Total Income Estimate	$12,508,670,000
% Cdn. Total	1.91
2001 Average Hhld. Income	$50,600
2001 Per Capita	$22,300
2003 Projected Total Income	$13,430,240,000
2006 Projected Total Income	$15,120,590,000

RETAIL SALES

% Above/Below National Average	same
2001 Retail Sales Estimate	$5,043,840,000
% Cdn. Total	1.81
2001 per Household	$20,400
2001 per Capita	$9,000
2001 No. of Establishments	5,025
2003 Projected Retail Sales	$5,511,430,000
2006 Projected Retail Sales	$6,291,130,000

POPULATION

2001 Estimates:

Total		560,674
Male		276,335
Female		284,339

Age Groups	Male	Female
0-4	16,856	15,850
5-9	13,896	13,234
10-14	12,866	12,266
15-19	13,795	13,076
20-24	16,869	16,871
25-29	22,300	22,739
30-34	26,517	26,084
35-39	26,500	25,813
40-44	24,130	24,374
45-49	22,345	22,643
50-54	18,899	18,805
55-59	14,719	14,668
60-64	12,189	12,149
65-69	10,720	10,905
70+	23,734	34,862

DAYTIME POPULATION

2001 Estimates:

Working Population	404,999
At Home Population	294,372
Total	699,371

INCOME

2001 Estimates:

Avg. Household Income	$50,621
Avg. Family Income	$60,524
Per Capita Income	$22,310

Male:

Avg. Employment Income	$33,384
Avg. Employment Income (Full Time)	$46,225

Female:

Avg. Employment Income	$24,359
Avg. Employment Income (Full Time)	$34,724

British Columbia

DISPOSABLE & DISCRETIONARY INCOME

2001 Estimates:	Per Hhld.
Disposable Income	$38,875
Discretionary Income 1 (minus Food & Shelter)	$26,128
Discretionary Income 2 (minus Food, Shelter, & Other Expenditures)	$18,755

LIQUID ASSETS

1999 Estimates:	Per Hhld.
Equity Investments	$82,129
Interest Bearing Investments	$66,823
Total Liquid Assets	$148,952

CREDIT DATA

July 2000:	
Pool of Credit	$5,777,848,426
Revolving Credit, No.	1,243,822
Fixed Loans, No.	222,435
Avg. Credit Limit, per Person	$10,520
Avg. Spent, per Person	$4,125
Satisfactory Ratings, No. per Person	2.64
Avg. No. of Cards, per Person	1.17

LABOUR FORCE

2001 Estimates:

Male:

In the Labour Force	155,307
Participation Rate	66.7
Employed	141,667
Unemployed	13,640
Unemployment Rate	8.8
Not in Labour Force	77,410

Female:

In the Labour Force	141,005
Participation Rate	58.0
Employed	130,490
Unemployed	10,515
Unemployment Rate	7.5
Not in Labour Force	101,984

OCCUPATIONS BY MAJOR GROUPS

2001 Estimates:	Male	Female
Management	18,714	9,735
Business, Finance & Admin.	20,132	38,438
Natural & Applied Sciences & Related	12,859	3,037
Health	4,357	10,308
Social Sciences, Gov't Services & Religion	5,244	6,180
Education	5,234	7,821
Arts, Culture, Recreation & Sport	7,325	7,062
Sales & Service	40,298	44,179
Trades, Transport & Equipment Operators & Related	24,609	1,613
Primary Industries	2,683	781
Processing, Mfg. & Utilities	7,882	6,919

British Columbia

Vancouver
(City)
Vancouver CMA
(Cont'd)

LEVEL OF SCHOOLING

2001 Estimates:

Population 15 years +	475,706
Less than Grade 9	50,000
Grades 9-13 w/o Certif.	83,240
Grade 9-13 with Certif.	50,232
Trade Certif. /Dip.	8,619
Non-Univ. w/o Certif./Dip.	32,698
Non-Univ. with Certif./Dip.	73,124
Univ. w/o Degree	65,693
Univ. w/o Degree/Certif.	34,117
Univ. with Certif.	31,576
Univ. with Degree	112,100

AVERAGE HOUSEHOLD EXPENDITURES

2001 Estimates:

Food	$6,158
Shelter	$9,160
Clothing	$2,145
Transportation	$5,502
Health & Personal Care	$1,938
Recr'n, Read'g & Education	$3,487
Taxes & Securities	$12,839
Other	$7,513
Total Expenditures	$48,742

PRIVATE HOUSEHOLDS

2001 Estimates:

Private Households, Total	247,102
Pop. in Private Households	549,877
Average no. per Household	2.2

FAMILIES

2001 Estimates:

Families in Private Households	136,810
Husband-Wife Families	114,462
Lone-Parent Families	22,348
Aver. No. Persons per Family	2.8
Aver. No. Sons/Daughters at Home	1.1

HOUSING

2001 Estimates:

Occupied Private Dwellings	247,102
Owned	103,295
Rented	143,807
Single-Detached House	73,621
Semi-Detached House	3,589
Row Houses	7,791
Apartment, 5+ Storeys	47,945
Owned Apartment, 5+ Storeys	9,247
Apartment, 5 or Fewer Storeys	84,988
Apartment, Detached Duplex	28,579
Other Single-Attached	460
Movable Dwellings	129

VEHICLES

2001 Estimates:

Model Yrs. '81-'96, No.	206,832
% Total	78.65
Model Yrs. '97-'98, No.	34,601
% Total	13.16
'99 Vehicles registered in Model Yr. '99, No.	21,557
% Total	8.20
Total No. '81-'99	262,990

LEGAL MARITAL STATUS

2001 Estimates: (Age 15+)

Single (Never Married)	200,523
Legally Married (Not Separated)	194,442
Legally Married (Separated)	15,012
Widowed	29,648
Divorced	36,081

PSYTE CATEGORIES

2001 Estimates	No. of House-holds	% of Total Hhds.	Index
Canadian Establishment	779	0.32	189
The Affluentials	11,547	4.67	731
Urban Gentry	13,322	5.39	300
Mortgaged in Suburbia	725	0.29	21
Technocrafts & Bureaucrats	329	0.13	5
Asian Heights	962	0.39	61
Suburban Nesters	1,667	0.67	42
Brie & Chablis	4,644	1.88	210
Asian Mosaic	76,071	30.79	2,246
High Rise Sunsets	3,859	1.56	109
Young Urban Professionals	37,182	15.05	793
Young Urban Mix	9,004	3.64	172
Young Urban Intelligentsia	36,702	14.85	976
University Enclaves	4,870	1.97	97
Young City Singles	10,482	4.24	185
Urban Bohemia	13,908	5.63	481
Town Renters	917	0.37	43
Rod & Rifle	15	0.01	
Struggling Downtowns	4,386	1.77	56
Aged Pensioners	6,227	2.52	189
Big City Stress	5,969	2.42	214
Old Grey Towers	932	0.38	68

FINANCIAL P$YTE

2001 Estimates	No. of House-holds	% of Total Hhds.	Index
Platinum Estates	12,326	4.99	619
Four Star Investors	13,322	5.39	107
Successful Suburbanites	2,016	0.82	12
Canadian Comfort	1,667	0.67	7
Urban Heights	41,826	16.93	393
Dollars & Sense	76,071	30.79	1,178
Bills & Wills	9,004	3.64	44
Revolving Renters	3,859	1.56	34
Young Urban Struggle	55,480	22.45	474
Rural Family Blues	15	0.01	
Towering Debt	15,785	6.39	82
NSF	5,969	2.42	68
Senior Survivors	7,159	2.90	154

HOME LANGUAGE

2001 Estimates:		% Total
English	357,912	63.84
French	2,908	0.52
Chinese	112,656	20.09
Croatian	662	0.12
Czech	359	0.06
Finnish	358	0.06
German	1,315	0.23
Greek	1,352	0.24
Gujarati	821	0.15
Hindi	3,042	0.54
Hungarian	663	0.12
Italian	3,538	0.63
Japanese	4,025	0.72
Khmer (Cambodian)	438	0.08
Korean	2,869	0.51
Persian (Farsi)	1,490	0.27
Polish	1,835	0.33
Portuguese	2,221	0.40
Punjabi	10,841	1.93
Romanian	523	0.09
Russian	1,227	0.22
Serbian	871	0.16
Serbo-Croatian	862	0.15
Spanish	4,548	0.81
Tagalog (Pilipino)	5,804	1.04
Tamil	481	0.09
Urdu	388	0.07
Vietnamese	9,282	1.66
Other Languages	4,265	0.76
Multiple Responses	23,118	4.12
Total	560,674	100.00

BUILDING PERMITS

	1999	1998	1997
		$000	
Value	803,515	821,490	1,025,186

HOMES BUILT

	1999	1998	1997
No.	3,784	5,168	4,769

TAXATION

Income Class:	1997	% Total
Under $5,000	60,070	14.44
$5,000-$10,000	60,980	14.66
$10,000-$15,000	60,050	14.44
$15,000-$20,000	38,460	9.25
$20,000-$25,000	32,070	7.71
$25,000-$30,000	29,390	7.07
$30,000-$40,000	47,870	11.51
$40,000-$50,000	29,850	7.18
$50,000 +	57,190	13.75
Total Returns, No.	415,940	
Total Income, $000.	12,422,025	
Total Taxable Returns	276,420	
Total Tax, $000	2,677,211	
Average Income, $	29,865	
Average Tax, $	9,685	

VITAL STATISTICS

	1997	1996	1995	1994
Births	5,747	5,959	6,090	6,350
Deaths	3,898	4,086	4,080	4,151
Natural Increase	1,849	1,873	2,010	2,199
Marriages	3,704	3,909	4,242	4,407

Note: Latest available data.

MEDIA INFO
see Vancouver, CMA

West Vancouver
(District Municipality)
Vancouver CMA

In Greater Vancouver Regional District.

POPULATION

July 1, 2001 Estimate	43,369
% Cdn. Total	0.14
% Change, '96 -'01	1.62
Avg. Annual Growth Rate, %	0.32
2003 Projected Population	43,427
2006 Projected Population	44,160
2001 Households Estimate	17,554
2003 Projected Households	17,699
2006 Projected Households	18,127

INCOME

% Above/Below National Average	+102
2001 Total Income Estimate	$1,851,610,000
% Cdn. Total	0.28
2001 Average Hhld. Income	$105,500
2001 Per Capita	$42,700
2003 Projected Total Income	$1,961,180,000
2006 Projected Total Income	$2,165,170,000

RETAIL SALES

% Above/Below National Average	+26
2001 Retail Sales Estimate	$489,920,000
% Cdn. Total	0.18
2001 per Household	$27,900
2001 per Capita	$11,300
2001 No. of Establishments	357
2003 Projected Retail Sales	$527,210,000
2006 Projected Retail Sales	$588,920,000

POPULATION

2001 Estimates:

Total		43,369
Male		20,218
Female		23,151

Age Groups	Male	Female
0-4	912	885
5-9	1,035	1,003
10-14	1,223	1,184
15-19	1,404	1,350
20-24	1,382	1,308
25-29	1,127	1,143
30-34	925	1,071
35-39	960	1,245
40-44	1,206	1,609
45-49	1,570	1,963
50-54	1,721	1,978
55-59	1,561	1,664
60-64	1,313	1,352
65-69	1,128	1,237
70+	2,751	4,159

DAYTIME POPULATION

2001 Estimates:

Working Population	13,675
At Home Population	22,481
Total	36,156

INCOME

2001 Estimates:

Avg. Household Income	$105,481
Avg. Family Income	$126,704
Per Capita Income	$42,694
Male:	
Avg. Employment Income	$73,709
Avg. Employment Income (Full Time)	$97,365
Female:	
Avg. Employment Income	$32,083
Avg. Employment Income (Full Time)	$48,410

DISPOSABLE & DISCRETIONARY INCOME

2001 Estimates:	Per Hhld.
Disposable Income	$74,250
Discretionary Income 1 (minus Food & Shelter)	$54,061
Discretionary Income 2 (minus Food, Shelter, & Other Expenditures)	$42,512

LIQUID ASSETS

1999 Estimates:	Per Hhld.
Equity Investments	$308,368
Interest Bearing Investments	$162,445
Total Liquid Assets	$470,813

CREDIT DATA

July 2000:

Pool of Credit	$655,154,054
Revolving Credit, No.	110,561
Fixed Loans, No.	13,815
Avg. Credit Limit, per Person	$15,492
Avg. Spent, per Person	$5,461
Satisfactory Ratings, No. per Person	2.93
Avg. No. of Cards, per Person	1.29

LABOUR FORCE

2001 Estimates:

Male:	
In the Labour Force	11,443
Participation Rate	67.1
Employed	11,174
Unemployed	269
Unemployment Rate	2.4
Not in Labour Force	5,605
Female:	
In the Labour Force	10,208
Participation Rate	50.8
Employed	9,848
Unemployed	360
Unemployment Rate	3.5
Not in Labour Force	9,871

OCCUPATIONS BY MAJOR GROUPS

2001 Estimates:	Male	Female
Management	3,296	1,314
Business, Finance & Admin.	1,802	3,074
Natural & Applied Sciences & Related	1,114	241
Health	441	619
Social Sciences, Gov't Services & Religion	678	574
Education	248	624
Arts, Culture, Recreation & Sport	557	595
Sales & Service	2,211	2,779
Trades, Transport & Equipment Operators & Related	723	85
Primary Industries	129	51
Processing, Mfg. & Utilities	114	58

LEVEL OF SCHOOLING

2001 Estimates:

Population 15 years +	37,127
Less than Grade 9	669
Grades 9-13 w/o Certif.	5,233
Grade 9-13 with Certif.	3,565
Trade Certif. /Dip.	933
Non-Univ. w/o Certif./Dip.	1,883
Non-Univ. with Certif./Dip.	5,862
Univ. w/o Degree	6,377
Univ. w/o Degree/Certif.	3,119
Univ. with Certif.	3,258
Univ. with Degree	12,605

AVERAGE HOUSEHOLD EXPENDITURES

2001 Estimates:

Food	$8,343
Shelter	$16,147
Clothing	$3,725
Transportation	$8,583
Health & Personal Care	$2,904
Recr'n, Read'g & Education	$6,124
Taxes & Securities	$29,791
Other	$15,975
Total Expenditures	$91,592

PRIVATE HOUSEHOLDS

2001 Estimates:

Private Households, Total	17,554
Pop. in Private Households	42,604
Average no. per Household	2.4

FAMILIES

2001 Estimates:

Families in Private Households	12,749
Husband-Wife Families	11,596
Lone-Parent Families	1,153
Aver. No. Persons per Family	2.9
Aver. No. Sons/Daughters at Home	1.0

HOUSING

2001 Estimates:

Occupied Private Dwellings	17,554
Owned	13,121
Rented	4,433
Single-Detached House	11,208
Semi-Detached House	405
Row Houses	458
Apartment, 5+ Storeys	3,746
Owned Apartment, 5+ Storeys	1,472
Apartment, 5 or Fewer Storeys	1,201
Apartment, Detached Duplex	536

VEHICLES

2001 Estimates:

Model Yrs. '81-'96, No.	19,912
% Total	79.53
Model Yrs. '97-'98, No.	3,306
% Total	13.20
'99 Vehicles registered in Model Yr. '99, No.	1,818
% Total	7.26
Total No. '81-'99	25,036

LEGAL MARITAL STATUS

2001 Estimates: (Age 15+)

Single (Never Married)	9,264
Legally Married (Not Separated)	21,581
Legally Married (Separated)	862
Widowed	2,883
Divorced	2,537

PSYTE CATEGORIES

2001 Estimates	No. of House -holds	% of Total Hhds.	Index
Canadian Establishment	1,484	8.45	5,080
The Affluentials	6,379	36.34	5,684
Urban Gentry	4,293	24.46	1,361
Suburban Nesters	324	1.85	115
Aging Erudites	753	4.29	284
High Rise Sunsets	3,772	21.49	1,503
Young Urban Professionals	343	1.95	103

FINANCIAL P$YTE

2001 Estimates	No. of House -holds	% of Total Hhds.	Index
Platinum Estates	7,863	44.79	5,559
Four Star Investors	4,293	24.46	487
Canadian Comfort	324	1.85	19
Urban Heights	1,096	6.24	145
Revolving Renters	3,772	21.49	467

HOME LANGUAGE

2001 Estimates:		% Total
English	37,219	85.82
French	188	0.43
Arabic	37	0.09
Chinese	2,582	5.95
Czech	31	0.07
Dutch	22	0.05
Finnish	22	0.05
German	438	1.01
Gujarati	54	0.12
Italian	54	0.12
Japanese	371	0.86
Korean	289	0.67
Norwegian	26	0.06
Persian (Farsi)	836	1.93
Polish	50	0.12
Russian	43	0.10
Spanish	163	0.38
Swedish	54	0.12
Tagalog (Pilipino)	49	0.11
Turkish	32	0.07
Other Languages	196	0.45
Multiple Responses	613	1.41
Total	43,369	100.00

BUILDING PERMITS

	1999	1998 $000	1997
Value	56,807	86,879	88,578

HOMES BUILT

	1999	1998	1997
No	104	143	187

TAXATION

Income Class:	1997	% Total
Under $5,000	3,440	11.03
$5,000-$10,000	2,820	9.04
$10,000-$15,000	3,340	10.71
$15,000-$20,000	2,360	7.57
$20,000-$25,000	2,070	6.64
$25,000-$30,000	1,990	6.38
$30,000-$40,000	3,540	11.35
$40,000-$50,000	2,550	8.18
$50,000 +	9,070	29.09
Total Returns, No.	31,180	
Total Income, $000	1,799,300	
Total Taxable Returns	23,660	
Total Tax, $000	520,958	
Average Income, $.	57,707	
Average Tax, $.	22,019	

VITAL STATISTICS

	1997	1996	1995	1994
Births	257	270	282	300
Deaths	469	399	435	431
Natural Increase	-212	-129	-153	-131
Marriages	351	336	348	431

Note: Latest available data.

MEDIA INFO
see Vancouver, CMA

British Columbia

White Rock
(City)
Vancouver CMA

In Greater Vancouver Regional District.

POPULATION

July 1, 2001 Estimate	18,266
% Cdn. Total	0.06
% Change, '96 -'01	1.66
Avg. Annual Growth Rate, %	0.33
2003 Projected Population	18,297
2006 Projected Population	18,621
2001 Households Estimate	9,678
2003 Projected Households	9,757
2006 Projected Households	9,994

INCOME

% Above/Below National Average	+36
2001 Total Income Estimate	$523,080,000
% Cdn. Total	0.08
2001 Average Hhld. Income	$54,000
2001 Per Capita	$28,600
2003 Projected Total Income	$552,520,000
2006 Projected Total Income	$607,560,000

RETAIL SALES

% Above/Below National Average	-66
2001 Retail Sales Estimate	$54,800,000
% Cdn. Total	0.02
2001 per Household	$5,700
2001 per Capita	$3,000
2001 No. of Establishments	120
2003 Projected Retail Sales	$58,290,000
2006 Projected Retail Sales	$64,530,000

POPULATION

2001 Estimates:

Total		18,266
Male		8,104
Female		10,162

Age Groups	Male	Female
0-4	409	379
5-9	356	337
10-14	324	310
15-19	340	320
20-24	394	416
25-29	484	512
30-34	551	586
35-39	582	624
40-44	607	638
45-49	595	690
50-54	559	685
55-59	495	594
60-64	429	528
65-69	390	540
70+	1,589	3,003

DAYTIME POPULATION

2001 Estimates:

Working Population	2,461
At Home Population	10,105
Total	12,566

INCOME

2001 Estimates:

Avg. Household Income	$54,049
Avg. Family Income	$69,727
Per Capita Income	$28,637
Male:	
Avg. Employment Income	$42,838
Avg. Employment Income (Full Time)	$55,811
Female:	
Avg. Employment Income	$28,021
Avg. Employment Income (Full Time)	$37,894

DISPOSABLE & DISCRETIONARY INCOME

2001 Estimates:	Per Hhld.
Disposable Income	$41,273
Discretionary Income 1 (minus Food & Shelter)	$28,070
Discretionary Income 2 (minus Food, Shelter, & Other Expenditures)	$20,058

LIQUID ASSETS

1999 Estimates:	Per Hhld.
Equity Investments	$88,861
Interest Bearing Investments	$71,382
Total Liquid Assets	$160,243

CREDIT DATA

July 2000:

Pool of Credit	$232,999,192
Revolving Credit, No.	48,358
Fixed Loans, No.	9,737
Avg. Credit Limit, per Person	$12,869
Avg. Spent, per Person	$5,183
Satisfactory Ratings, No. per Person	3.18
Avg. No. of Cards, per Person	1.23

LABOUR FORCE

2001 Estimates:

Male:	
In the Labour Force	4,254
Participation Rate	60.6
Employed	4,049
Unemployed	205
Unemployment Rate	4.8
Not in Labour Force	2,761
Female:	
In the Labour Force	4,402
Participation Rate	48.2
Employed	4,166
Unemployed	236
Unemployment Rate	5.4
Not in Labour Force	4,734

OCCUPATIONS BY MAJOR GROUPS

2001 Estimates:	Male	Female
Management	689	422
Business, Finance & Admin.	485	1,272
Natural & Applied Sciences & Related	300	50
Health	90	402
Social Sciences, Gov't Services & Religion	115	154
Education	129	287
Arts, Culture, Recreation & Sport	140	189
Sales & Service	963	1,344
Trades, Transport & Equipment Operators & Related	1,026	75
Primary Industries	131	30
Processing, Mfg. & Utilities	127	51

LEVEL OF SCHOOLING

2001 Estimates:

Population 15 years +	16,151
Less than Grade 9	924
Grades 9-13 w/o Certif.	3,293
Grade 9-13 with Certif.	1,802
Trade Certif./Dip.	526
Non-Univ. w/o Certif./Dip.	1,142
Non-Univ. with Certif./Dip.	3,682
Univ. w/o Degree	2,086
Univ. w/o Degree/Certif.	919
Univ. with Certif.	1,167
Univ. with Degree	2,696

AVERAGE HOUSEHOLD EXPENDITURES

2001 Estimates:

Food	$6,030
Shelter	$9,588
Clothing	$2,105
Transportation	$5,948
Health & Personal Care	$2,067
Recr'n, Read'g & Education	$3,649
Taxes & Securities	$13,804
Other	$8,600
Total Expenditures	$51,791

PRIVATE HOUSEHOLDS

2001 Estimates:

Private Households, Total	9,678
Pop. in Private Households	17,700
Average no. per Household	1.8

FAMILIES

2001 Estimates:

Families in Private Households	5,105
Husband-Wife Families	4,429
Lone-Parent Families	676
Aver. No. Persons per Family	2.5
Aver. No. Sons/Daughters at Home	0.6

HOUSING

2001 Estimates:

Occupied Private Dwellings	9,678
Owned	6,352
Rented	3,326
Single-Detached House	3,719
Semi-Detached House	167
Row Houses	185
Apartment, 5+ Storeys	703
Owned Apartment, 5+ Storeys	385
Apartment, 5 or Fewer Storeys	4,234
Apartment, Detached Duplex	659
Other Single-Attached	11

VEHICLES

2001 Estimates:

Model Yrs. '81-'96, No.	7,250
% Total	84.69
Model Yrs. '97-'98, No.	776
% Total	9.06
'99 Vehicles registered in Model Yr. '99, No.	535
% Total	6.25
Total No. '81-'99	8,561

LEGAL MARITAL STATUS

2001 Estimates: (Age 15+)

Single (Never Married)	3,841
Legally Married (Not Separated)	7,577
Legally Married (Separated)	629
Widowed	2,301
Divorced	1,803

PSYTE CATEGORIES

2001 Estimates	No. of House-holds	% of Total Hhds.	Index
Urban Gentry	778	8.04	447
Small City Elite	1,766	18.25	1,065
Aging Erudites	1,935	19.99	1,325
Conservative Homebodies	406	4.20	116
High Rise Sunsets	3,865	39.94	2,793
Young Urban Professionals	185	1.91	101
Nesters & Young Homemakers	302	3.12	134
Aged Pensioners	290	3.00	225

FINANCIAL P$YTE

2001 Estimates	No. of House-holds	% of Total Hhds.	Index
Four Star Investors	778	8.04	160
Canadian Comfort	1,766	18.25	188
Urban Heights	2,120	21.91	509
Bills & Wills	406	4.20	51
Revolving Renters	4,167	43.06	936
Senior Survivors	290	3.00	159

HOME LANGUAGE

2001 Estimates:		% Total
English	17,470	95.64
French	110	0.60
Chinese	83	0.45
Croatian	11	0.06
Czech	11	0.06
Danish	11	0.06
Dutch	11	0.06
Finnish	11	0.06
German	94	0.51
Gujarati	10	0.05
Hungarian	50	0.27
Italian	28	0.15
Japanese	22	0.12
Korean	34	0.19
Polish	33	0.18
Serbian	11	0.06
Slovenian	11	0.06
Spanish	11	0.06
Ukrainian	11	0.06
Other Languages	39	0.21
Multiple Responses	194	1.06
Total	18,266	100.00

BUILDING PERMITS

	1999	1998 $000	1997
Value	8,631	20,388	19,480

HOMES BUILT

	1999	1998	1997
No.	99	39	46

TAXATION

Income Class:	1997	% Total
Under $5,000	1,380	7.32
$5,000-$10,000	1,820	9.66
$10,000-$15,000	2,770	14.69
$15,000-$20,000	1,960	10.40
$20,000-$25,000	1,570	8.33
$25,000-$30,000	1,530	8.12
$30,000-$40,000	2,660	14.11
$40,000-$50,000	1,710	9.07
$50,000 +	3,440	18.25
Total Returns, No.	18,850	
Total Income, $000	622,218	
Total Taxable Returns	14,390	
Total Tax, $000	126,481	
Average Income, $	33,009	
Average Tax, $	8,790	

VITAL STATISTICS

	1997	1996	1995	1994
Births	145	151	182	190
Deaths	331	303	331	315
Natural Increase	-186	-152	-149	-125
Marriages	121	123	133	130

Note: Latest available data.

MEDIA INFO
see Vancouver, CMA

Vernon
(Census Agglomeration)

The Census Agglomeration of Vernon includes: Vernon, C; Coldstream, DM; North Okanagan, Subd. B, SRD; plus several smaller areas. All are in North Okanagan Regional District.

POPULATION

July 1, 2001 Estimate	59,821
% Cdn. Total	0.19
% Change, '96 -'01	4.22
Avg. Annual Growth Rate, %	0.83
2003 Projected Population	60,804
2006 Projected Population	61,943
2001 Households Estimate	24,116
2003 Projected Households	24,675
2006 Projected Households	25,544

INCOME

% Above/Below National Average	-17
2001 Total Income Estimate	$1,051,140,000
% Cdn. Total	0.16
2001 Average Hhld. Income	$43,600
2001 Per Capita	$17,600
2003 Projected Total Income	$1,111,240,000
2006 Projected Total Income	$1,203,790,000

RETAIL SALES

% Above/Below National Average	+16
2001 Retail Sales Estimate	$622,030,000
% Cdn. Total	0.22
2001 per Household	$25,800
2001 per Capita	$10,400
2001 No. of Establishments	557
2003 Projected Retail Sales	$682,450,000
2006 Projected Retail Sales	$766,500,000

POPULATION

2001 Estimates:

Total		59,821
Male		29,123
Female		30,698

Age Groups	Male	Female
0-4	1,665	1,603
5-9	1,900	1,821
10-14	2,141	2,026
15-19	2,173	2,071
20-24	1,970	1,908
25-29	1,771	1,771
30-34	1,834	1,959
35-39	2,106	2,270
40-44	2,250	2,416
45-49	2,124	2,274
50-54	1,831	1,937
55-59	1,547	1,633
60-64	1,367	1,457
65-69	1,290	1,364
70+	3,154	4,188

DAYTIME POPULATION

2001 Estimates:

Working Population	25,200
At Home Population	34,620
Total	59,820

INCOME

2001 Estimates:

Avg. Household Income	$43,587
Avg. Family Income	$48,695
Per Capita Income	$17,571
Male:	
Avg. Employment Income	$29,897
Avg. Employment Income (Full Time)	$40,230
Female:	
Avg. Employment Income	$17,386
Avg. Employment Income (Full Time)	$28,053

DISPOSABLE & DISCRETIONARY INCOME

2001 Estimates:	Per Hhld.
Disposable Income	$33,987
Discretionary Income 1 (minus Food & Shelter)	$22,792
Discretionary Income 2 (minus Food, Shelter, & Other Expenditures)	$15,548

LIQUID ASSETS

1999 Estimates:	Per Hhld.
Equity Investments	$58,097
Interest Bearing Investments	$57,362
Total Liquid Assets	$115,459

CREDIT DATA

July 2000:

Pool of Credit	$581,655,294
Revolving Credit, No.	113,202
Fixed Loans, No.	30,963
Avg. Credit Limit, per Person	$12,249
Avg. Spent, per Person	$5,413
Satisfactory Ratings, No. per Person	2.92
Avg. No. of Cards, per Person	1.04

LABOUR FORCE

2001 Estimates:

Male:

In the Labour Force	15,135
Participation Rate	64.6
Employed	13,505
Unemployed	1,630
Unemployment Rate	10.8
Not in Labour Force	8,282

Female:

In the Labour Force	13,380
Participation Rate	53.0
Employed	11,942
Unemployed	1,438
Unemployment Rate	10.7
Not in Labour Force	11,868

OCCUPATIONS BY MAJOR GROUPS

2001 Estimates:	Male	Female
Management	1,536	621
Business, Finance & Admin.	906	3,381
Natural & Applied Sciences & Related	714	145
Health	325	1,018
Social Sciences, Gov't Services & Religion	255	307
Education	274	576
Arts, Culture, Recreation & Sport	223	241
Sales & Service	2,950	5,313
Trades, Transport & Equipment Operators & Related	4,327	266
Primary Industries	1,516	561
Processing, Mfg. & Utilities	1,728	390

LEVEL OF SCHOOLING

2001 Estimates:

Population 15 years +	48,665
Less than Grade 9	4,457
Grades 9-13 w/o Certif.	13,838
Grade 9-13 with Certif.	6,502
Trade Certif. /Dip.	2,317
Non-Univ. w/o Certif./Dip.	3,456
Non-Univ. with Certif./Dip.	9,629
Univ. w/o Degree	4,811
Univ. w/o Degree/Certif.	2,100
Univ. with Certif.	2,711
Univ. with Degree	3,655

AVERAGE HOUSEHOLD EXPENDITURES

2001 Estimates:

Food	$5,265
Shelter	$7,775
Clothing	$1,756
Transportation	$5,560
Health & Personal Care	$1,708
Recr'n, Read'g & Education	$3,118
Taxes & Securities	$10,071
Other	$7,430
Total Expenditures	$42,683

PRIVATE HOUSEHOLDS

2001 Estimates:

Private Households, Total	24,116
Pop. in Private Households	58,433
Average no. per Household	2.4

FAMILIES

2001 Estimates:

Families in Private Households	17,632
Husband-Wife Families	15,032
Lone-Parent Families	2,600
Aver. No. Persons per Family	2.9
Aver. No. Sons/Daughters at Home	1.0

HOUSING

2001 Estimates:

Occupied Private Dwellings	24,116
Owned	17,533
Rented	6,549
Band Housing	34
Single-Detached House	15,695
Semi-Detached House	998
Row Houses	1,416
Apartment, 5+ Storeys	182
Owned Apartment, 5+ Storeys	11
Apartment, 5 or Fewer Storeys	3,874
Apartment, Detached Duplex	562
Other Single-Attached	46
Movable Dwellings	1,343

VEHICLES

2001 Estimates:

Model Yrs. '81-'96, No.	27,763
% Total	85.28
Model Yrs. '97-'98, No.	3,076
% Total	9.45
'99 Vehicles registered in Model Yr. '99, No.	1,718
% Total	5.28
Total No. '81-'99	32,557

LEGAL MARITAL STATUS

2001 Estimates: (Age 15+)

Single (Never Married)	12,190
Legally Married (Not Separated)	26,832
Legally Married (Separated)	1,851
Widowed	3,405
Divorced	4,387

PSYTE CATEGORIES

2001 Estimates	No. of House-holds	% of Total Hhds.	Index
Mortgaged in Suburbia	43	0.18	13
Boomers & Teens	28	0.12	6
Small City Elite	4,603	19.09	1,114
Blue Collar Winners	119	0.49	20
Town Boomers	341	1.41	140
Old Towns' New Fringe	5,299	21.97	561
Rustic Prosperity	598	2.48	137
High Rise Sunsets	404	1.68	117
Old Leafy Towns	666	2.76	108
Town Renters	169	0.70	81
Nesters & Young Homesteaders	9,436	39.13	1,676
Rod & Rifle	625	2.59	112
Down, Down East	36	0.15	21
Big Country Families	239	0.99	69
Aged Pensioners	455	1.89	142
Old Grey Towers	812	3.37	608

FINANCIAL PSYTE

2001 Estimates	No. of House-holds	% of Total Hhds.	Index
Four Star Investors	28	0.12	2
Successful Suburbanites	43	0.18	3
Canadian Comfort	5,063	20.99	216
Tractors & Tradelines	5,897	24.45	428
Bills & Wills	666	2.76	33
Revolving Renters	9,840	40.80	887
Rural Family Blues	900	3.73	46
Towering Debt	169	0.70	9
Senior Survivors	1,267	5.25	279

British Columbia

HOME LANGUAGE

2001 Estimates:		% Total
English	57,669	96.40
French	81	0.14
Chinese	142	0.24
Croatian	32	0.05
German	395	0.66
Japanese	54	0.09
Punjabi	529	0.88
Russian	221	0.37
Spanish	54	0.09
Ukrainian	97	0.16
Vietnamese	37	0.06
Other Languages	158	0.26
Multiple Responses	352	0.59
Total	59,821	100.00

BUILDING PERMITS

	1999	1998 $000	1997
Value	58,896	54,877	77,624

HOMES BUILT

	1999	1998	1997
No	223	267	458

TAXATION

Income Class:	1997	% Total
Under $5,000	5,120	12.35
$5,000-$10,000	5,640	13.60
$10,000-$15,000	7,140	17.22
$15,000-$20,000	4,440	10.71
$20,000-$25,000	3,380	8.15
$25,000-$30,000	2,970	7.16
$30,000-$40,000	4,860	11.72
$40,000-$50,000	3,190	7.69
$50,000 +	4,750	11.46
Total Returns, No.	41,460	
Total Income, $000	1,061,950	
Total Taxable Returns	28,000	
Total Tax, $000	188,486	
Average Income, $	25,614	
Average Tax, $	6,732	

VITAL STATISTICS

	1997	1996	1995	1994
Births	541	608	610	603
Deaths	492	484	517	436
Natural Increase	49	124	93	167
Marriages	339	361	387	347

Note: Latest available data.

COMMUNITY NEWSPAPER(S)

	Total Circulation
Lumby: Lumby Valley Times	n.a.
Vernon: The Morning Star Wed/Fri/Sun	30,640
Vernon: Sun Review	30,259

RADIO STATION(S)

	Power
CBYV-FM	n.a.
CICF	n.a.
CJIB	n.a.

TELEVISION STATION(S)

CHAN-TV
CHBC-TV
CHKL-TV

British Columbia

Victoria
(Census Metropolitan Area)

POPULATION

July 1, 2001 Estimate	320,491
% Cdn. Total	1.03
% Change, '96 -'01	1.19
Avg. Annual Growth Rate, %	0.24
2003 Projected Population	331,088
2006 Projected Population	352,367
2001 Households Estimate	139,874
2003 Projected Households	144,438
2006 Projected Households	153,454

INCOME

% Above/Below National Average	+7
2001 Total Income Estimate	$7,206,630,000
% Cdn. Total	1.10
2001 Average Hhld. Income	$51,500
2001 Per Capita	$22,500
2003 Projected Total Income	$7,786,660,000
2006 Projected Total Income	$8,882,480,000

RETAIL SALES

% Above/Below National Average	-5
2001 Retail Sales Estimate	$2,722,280,000
% Cdn. Total	0.98
2001 per Household	$19,500
2001 per Capita	$8,500
2001 No. of Establishments	2,416
2003 Projected Retail Sales	$3,003,050,000
2006 Projected Retail Sales	$3,483,830,000

POPULATION

2001 Estimates:

Total		320,491
Male		153,296
Female		167,195
Age Groups	*Male*	*Female*
0-4	9,026	8,540
5-9	8,967	8,590
10-14	9,229	8,767
15-19	9,252	8,919
20-24	9,657	9,882
25-29	10,617	10,852
30-34	11,544	11,729
35-39	12,128	12,678
40-44	12,349	13,211
45-49	12,192	12,987
50-54	10,505	11,097
55-59	8,178	8,701
60-64	6,581	7,203
65-69	5,788	6,779
70+	17,283	27,260

DAYTIME POPULATION

2001 Estimates:

Working Population	153,564
At Home Population	166,925
Total	320,489

INCOME

2001 Estimates:

Avg. Household Income	$51,522
Avg. Family Income	$61,104
Per Capita Income	$22,486
Male:	
Avg. Employment Income	$32,545
Avg. Employment Income (Full Time)	$43,215
Female:	
Avg. Employment Income	$22,631
Avg. Employment Income (Full Time)	$33,173

DISPOSABLE & DISCRETIONARY INCOME

2001 Estimates:	*Per Hhld.*
Disposable Income	$39,674
Discretionary Income 1 (minus Food & Shelter)	$27,128
Discretionary Income 2 (minus Food, Shelter, & Other Expenditures)	$19,473

LIQUID ASSETS

1999 Estimates:	*Per Hhld.*
Equity Investments	$73,566
Interest Bearing Investments	$66,529
Total Liquid Assets	$140,095

CREDIT DATA

July 2000:

Pool of Credit	$3,426,524,504
Revolving Credit, No.	697,959
Fixed Loans, No.	156,589
Avg. Credit Limit, per Person	$11,979
Avg. Spent, per Person	$5,092
Satisfactory Ratings, No. per Person	2.93
Avg. No. of Cards, per Person	1.08

LABOUR FORCE

2001 Estimates:

Male:	
In the Labour Force	84,849
Participation Rate	67.3
Employed	79,212
Unemployed	5,637
Unemployment Rate	6.6
Not in Labour Force	41,225
Female:	
In the Labour Force	80,632
Participation Rate	57.1
Employed	76,022
Unemployed	4,610
Unemployment Rate	5.7
Not in Labour Force	60,666

OCCUPATIONS BY MAJOR GROUPS

2001 Estimates:	*Male*	*Female*
Management	10,919	5,825
Business, Finance & Admin.	8,653	24,651
Natural & Applied Sciences & Related	7,697	1,678
Health	2,349	7,679
Social Sciences, Gov't Services & Religion	2,625	3,374
Education	2,625	3,846
Arts, Culture, Recreation & Sport	2,347	2,850
Sales & Service	22,412	26,365
Trades, Transport & Equipment Operators & Related	17,499	1,041
Primary Industries	3,273	806
Processing, Mfg. & Utilities	2,601	739

LEVEL OF SCHOOLING

2001 Estimates:

Population 15 years +	267,372
Less than Grade 9	11,600
Grades 9-13 w/o Certif.	56,196
Grade 9-13 with Certif.	32,688

2001 Estimates:

Trade Certif. /Dip.	9,379
Non-Univ. w/o Certif./Dip.	19,570
Non-Univ. with Certif./Dip.	53,054
Univ. w/o Degree	37,436
Univ. w/o Degree/Certif.	18,655
Univ. with Certif.	18,781
Univ. with Degree	47,449

AVERAGE HOUSEHOLD EXPENDITURES

2001 Estimates:

Food	$5,772
Shelter	$8,926
Clothing	$2,062
Transportation	$5,751
Health & Personal Care	$1,857
Recr'n, Read'g & Education	$3,517
Taxes & Securities	$13,408
Other	$8,166
Total Expenditures	$49,459

PRIVATE HOUSEHOLDS

2001 Estimates:

Private Households, Total	139,874
Pop. in Private Households	313,159
Average no. per Household	2.2

FAMILIES

2001 Estimates:

Families in Private Households	89,971
Husband-Wife Families	77,337
Lone-Parent Families	12,634
Aver. No. Persons per Family	2.8
Aver. No. Sons/Daughters at Home	0.9

HOUSING

2001 Estimates:

Occupied Private Dwellings	139,874
Owned	87,350
Rented	52,497
Band Housing	27
Single-Detached House	71,939
Semi-Detached House	5,214
Row Houses	8,306
Apartment, 5+ Storeys	7,140
Owned Apartment, 5+ Storeys	2,143
Apartment, 5 or Fewer Storeys	36,008
Apartment, Detached Duplex	8,929
Other Single-Attached	310
Movable Dwellings	2,028

RADIO STATION DATA

Station	Market	Format	Wkly. Reach%*	Aver. Hrs. Tuned
All Stations			94	21.4
CBCV-FM	Victoria	News, Info.	11	10.8
CBU	Vancouver	Multi-format	11	13.1
CBU-FM	Vancouver	Multi-format	13	14.5
CFAX	Victoria	News, Info.	22	10.7
CFMI-FM	Vancouver	Classic Rock	4	7.7
CFOX-FM	Vancouver	Contemp. Rock	4	4.2
CHQM-FM	Vancouver	Adult Contemp.	3	5.1
CIOC-FM	Victoria	Adult Contemp.	27	10.1
CISL	Vancouver	Oldies	1	20.2
CJJR-FM	Vancouver	New Country	n.a.	n.a.
CJVI	Victoria	Oldies	6	7.8
CKBD	Vancouver	Adult Favourites	5	8.5
CKKQ-FM	Victoria	AOR	30	9.4
CKKS-FM	Vancouver	Adult Contemp.	2	13.9
CKNW	Vancouver	News, Talk, Sports	6	9.6
CKSR-FM	Vancouver	Easy Listening	3	3.6
CKWX	Vancouver	News	3	5.1
CKXM	Victoria	Country	7	13.2
CKZZ-FM	Vancouver	Contemp. Hits	12	5.5

BBM Spring 2000 Radio Reach Survey; area coverage.
*Mon-Sun 5a.m - 1a.m , All Persons 12+

TV STATION DATA

Station	Market	Network Affiliation	Wkly. Reach%*	Aver. Hrs. Tuned
All Stations			97	22.1
A & E	n.a.	Ind.	26	3.5
BRAVO	n.a.	Ind.	13	1.8
CBUT	Vancouver	CBC	47	3.1
CHAN	Vancouver	CTV	60	4.7
CHEK	Victoria	CTV	64	4.8
CIVT	Vancouver	Ind.	44	2.0
CKVU	Vancouver	Global	45	2.9
CNBC	n.a.	NBC	9	2.5
FAMILY	n.a.	Ind.	5	3.5
HISTTV	n.a.	Ind.	6	2.4
KCPQ	Tacoma WA	FOX	21	2.2
KCTS	Seattle WA	PBS	34	1.9
KING	Seattle WA	NBC	22	1.6
KIRO	Seattle WA	CBS	24	1.8
KNOW	Vancouver	n.a.	21	2.1
KOMO	Seattle WA	ABC	24	1.9
KSTW	Tacoma WA	UPN	36	2.0
KVOS	Bellingham WA	Ind.	28	1.8
NEWSWD	n.a.	CBC	14	1.4
PRIME	n.a.	Ind.	7	2.8
SHWCSE	n.a.	Ind.	5	2.4
SNET	n.a.	CTV	17	3.5
SPACE	n.a.	Ind.	6	2.0
SUPER	n.a.	Ind.	2	10.3
TLC	n.a.	Ind.	8	3.1
TNN	Nashville TN	Ind.	10	2.4
TOON	n.a.	Ind.	7	2.6
TSN	n.a.	Ind.	26	2.9
VCR	n.a.	n.a.	41	3.1
WTBS	Atlanta GA	Ind.	8	1.9
WTN	n.a.	Ind.	7	2.3
WTVS	Detroit MI	PBS	14	1.3
YTV	n.a.	Ind.	11	3.5

BBM Spring 2000 TV Reach Survey; CMA coverage.
*Mon-Sun 6a.m - 2a.m , All Persons 2 +

Victoria
(Census Metropolitan Area)
(Cont'd)

VEHICLES

2001 Estimates:
Model Yrs. '81-'96, No.	145,161
% Total	87.74
Model Yrs. '97-'98, No.	12,395
% Total	7.49
'99 Vehicles registered in Model Yr. '99, No.	7,897
% Total	4.77
Total No. '81-'99	165,453

LEGAL MARITAL STATUS

2001 Estimates: (Age 15+)
Single (Never Married)	79,072
Legally Married (Not Separated)	134,626
Legally Married (Separated)	8,688
Widowed	20,599
Divorced	24,387

PSYTE CATEGORIES

2001 Estimates:

	No. of House-holds	% of Total Hhds.	Index
Canadian Establishment	242	0.17	104
The Affluentials	102	0.07	11
Urban Gentry	8,928	6.38	355
Suburban Executives	546	0.39	27
Asian Heights	145	0.10	16
Boomers & Teens	5,483	3.92	219
Stable Suburban Families	3,114	2.23	171
Small City Elite	11,883	8.50	496
Old Bungalow Burbs	1,087	0.78	47
Suburban Nesters	1,260	0.90	56
Brie & Chablis	435	0.31	35
Aging Erudites	14,895	10.65	706
Satellite Suburbs	2,672	1.91	67
Kindergarten Boom	1,228	0.88	33
Blue Collar Winners	4,220	3.02	120
Old Towns' New Fringe	7,475	5.34	137
Asian Mosaic	998	0.71	52
Conservative Homebodies	6,766	4.84	134
High Rise Sunsets	7,041	5.03	352
Young Urban Professionals	6,397	4.57	241
Young Urban Mix	4,218	3.02	142
Young Urban Intelligentsia	710	0.51	33
University Enclaves	18,825	13.46	659
Young City Singles	10,038	7.18	313
Urban Bohemia	1,006	0.72	61
Old Leafy Towns	2,409	1.72	67
Town Renters	753	0.54	62
Nesters & Young Homesteaders	4,720	3.37	145
Rod & Rifle	33	0.02	1
Big Country Families	107	0.08	5
Struggling Downtowns	880	0.63	20
Aged Pensioners	8,596	6.15	462
Big City Stress	890	0.64	56
Old Grey Towers	228	0.16	29

FINANCIAL P$YTE

2001 Estimates:

	No. of House-holds	% of Total Hhds.	Index
Platinum Estates	344	0.25	31
Four Star Investors	14,957	10.69	213
Successful Suburbanites	3,259	2.33	35
Canadian Comfort	20,035	14.32	147
Urban Heights	21,727	15.53	361
Miners & Credit-Liners	1,087	0.78	25
Mortgages & Minivans	1,228	0.88	13
Dollars & Sense	998	0.71	27
Tractors & Tradelines	7,475	5.34	93
Bills & Wills	13,393	9.58	116
Revolving Renters	11,761	8.41	183
Young Urban Struggle	20,541	14.69	310
Rural Family Blues	140	0.10	1
Towering Debt	11,671	8.34	107
NSF	890	0.64	18
Senior Survivors	8,824	6.31	335

HOME LANGUAGE

2001 Estimates:

		% Total
English	302,921	94.52
French	1,388	0.43
Chinese	4,729	1.48
Croatian	264	0.08
Dutch	283	0.09
German	680	0.21
Hungarian	263	0.08
Italian	214	0.07
Japanese	375	0.12
Korean	173	0.05
Persian (Farsi)	253	0.08
Polish	417	0.13
Portuguese	743	0.23
Punjabi	1,662	0.52
Spanish	532	0.17
Tagalog (Pilipino)	208	0.06
Vietnamese	606	0.19
Other Languages	1,647	0.51
Multiple Responses	3,133	0.98
Total	320,491	100.00

BUILDING PERMITS

	1999	1998 $000	1997
Value	411,515	279,886	287,683

HOMES BUILT

	1999	1998	1997
No.	896	1,140	1,245

TAXATION

Income Class:	1997	% Total
Under $5,000	22,240	9.66
$5,000-$10,000	26,650	11.57
$10,000-$15,000	30,940	13.44
$15,000-$20,000	22,450	9.75
$20,000-$25,000	19,390	8.42
$25,000-$30,000	18,200	7.90
$30,000-$40,000	33,990	14.76
$40,000-$50,000	21,730	9.44
$50,000 +	34,680	15.06
Total Returns, No.	230,260	
Total Income, $000	6,912,234	
Total Taxable Returns	171,880	
Total Tax, $000	1,333,898	
Average Income, $	30,019	
Average Tax, $	7,761	

VITAL STATISTICS

	1997	1996	1995	1994
Births	2,953	2,986	3,149	3,313
Deaths	3,126	3,062	2,955	3,024
Natural Increase	-173	-76	194	289
Marriages	1,985	2,058	2,262	2,048

Note: Latest available data.

DAILY NEWSPAPER(S)

	Circulation Average Paid
Times Colonist	
Sun	75,784
Mon-Sat	75,872

British Columbia

COMMUNITY NEWSPAPER(S)

	Total Circulation
Colwood: Colwood Goldstream Gazette	14,445
Esquimalt: Esquimalt News	7,354
Esquimalt: Lookout CFB Esquimalt	5,000
Oak Bay: Oak Bay News	8,755
Saanich: Saanich News	32,563
Sidney: Peninsula News Review	13,738
Sooke: Sooke News Mirror	5,016
Victoria: The Victoria News	
Wed	26,267
Fri	102,449

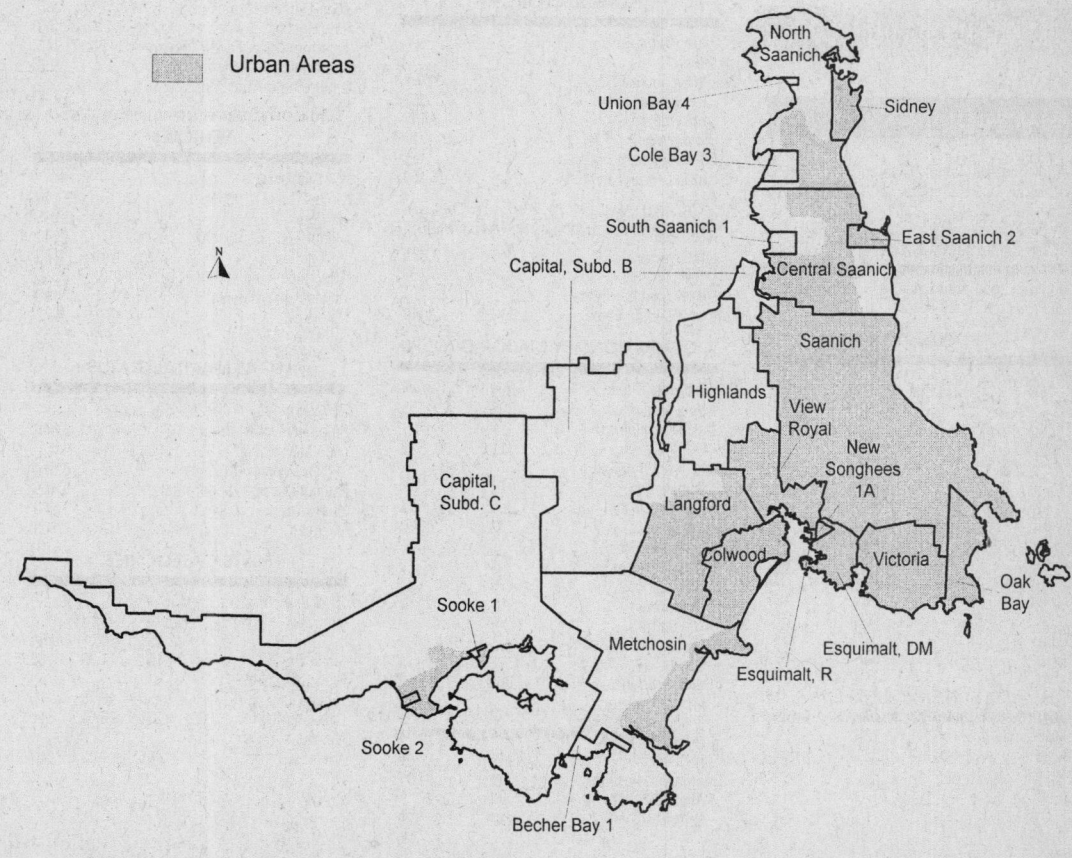

Urban Areas

N

North Saanich · Union Bay 4 · Sidney · Cole Bay 3 · South Saanich 1 · East Saanich 2 · Capital, Subd. B · Central Saanich · Saanich · Highlands · View Royal · New Songhees 1A · Capital, Subd. C · Langford · Colwood · Victoria · Oak Bay · Sooke 1 · Metchosin · Esquimalt, DM · Esquimalt, R · Sooke 2 · Becher Bay 1

British Columbia

Capital, Subd. C

(Subdivision of
Regional District)
Victoria CMA

In Capital Regional District.

POPULATION

July 1, 2001 Estimate	13,386
% Cdn. Total	0.04
% Change, '96 -'01	12.51
Avg. Annual Growth Rate, %	2.38
2003 Projected Population	14,642
2006 Projected Population	16,758
2001 Households Estimate	5,237
2003 Projected Households	5,700
2006 Projected Households	6,477

INCOME

% Above/Below National Average	-10
2001 Total Income Estimate	$254,980,000
% Cdn. Total	0.04
2001 Average Hhld. Income	$48,700
2001 Per Capita	$19,000
2003 Projected Total Income	$295,190,000
2006 Projected Total Income	$368,780,000

RETAIL SALES

% Above/Below National Average	-56
2001 Retail Sales Estimate	$52,240,000
% Cdn. Total	0.02
2001 per Household	$10,000
2001 per Capita	$3,900
2001 No. of Establishments	71
2003 Projected Retail Sales	$60,070,000
2006 Projected Retail Sales	$74,520,000

POPULATION

2001 Estimates:

Total		13,386
Male		6,698
Female		6,688

Age Groups	Male	Female
0-4	435	395
5-9	487	437
10-14	511	489
15-19	469	492
20-24	400	401
25-29	383	384
30-34	455	499
35-39	560	612
40-44	607	639
45-49	567	563
50-54	445	425
55-59	342	316
60-64	273	259
65-69	233	217
70+	531	560

DAYTIME POPULATION

2001 Estimates:

Working Population	2,210
At Home Population	6,848
Total	9,058

INCOME

2001 Estimates:

Avg. Household Income	$48,689
Avg. Family Income	$53,479
Per Capita Income	$19,048
Male:	
Avg. Employment Income	$30,180
Avg. Employment Income (Full Time)	$38,016
Female:	
Avg. Employment Income	$20,535
Avg. Employment Income (Full Time)	$31,182

DISPOSABLE & DISCRETIONARY INCOME

2001 Estimates:	Per Hhld.
Disposable Income	$37,955
Discretionary Income 1 (minus Food & Shelter)	$26,060
Discretionary Income 2 (minus Food, Shelter, & Other Expenditures)	$17,875

LIQUID ASSETS

1999 Estimates:	Per Hhld.
Equity Investments	$60,342
Interest Bearing Investments	$59,790
Total Liquid Assets	$120,132

CREDIT DATA

July 2000:

Pool of Credit	$128,918,544
Revolving Credit, No.	24,609
Fixed Loans, No.	8,130
Avg. Credit Limit, per Person	$11,810
Avg. Spent, per Person	$5,819
Satisfactory Ratings, No. per Person	2.93
Avg. No. of Cards, per Person	0.93

LABOUR FORCE

2001 Estimates:

Male:	
In the Labour Force	3,799
Participation Rate	72.2
Employed	3,488
Unemployed	311
Unemployment Rate	8.2
Not in Labour Force	1,466
Female:	
In the Labour Force	3,255
Participation Rate	60.6
Employed	3,055
Unemployed	200
Unemployment Rate	6.1
Not in Labour Force	2,112

OCCUPATIONS BY MAJOR GROUPS

2001 Estimates:	Male	Female
Management	307	155
Business, Finance & Admin.	221	917
Natural & Applied Sciences & Related	330	63
Health	37	300
Social Sciences, Gov't Services & Religion	73	81
Education	87	113
Arts, Culture, Recreation & Sport	75	113
Sales & Service	989	1,234
Trades, Transport & Equipment Operators & Related	1,023	95
Primary Industries	448	91
Processing, Mfg. & Utilities	130	29

LEVEL OF SCHOOLING

2001 Estimates:

Population 15 years +	10,632
Less than Grade 9	467
Grades 9-13 w/o Certif.	2,614
Grade 9-13 with Certif.	1,365
Trade Certif. /Dip.	495
Non-Univ. w/o Certif./Dip.	719
Non-Univ. with Certif./Dip.	2,721
Univ. w/o Degree	1,185
Univ. w/o Degree/Certif.	463
Univ. with Certif.	722
Univ. with Degree	1,066

AVERAGE HOUSEHOLD EXPENDITURES

2001 Estimates:

Food	$5,737
Shelter	$8,170
Clothing	$1,859
Transportation	$6,412
Health & Personal Care	$1,803
Recr'n, Read'g & Education	$3,605
Taxes & Securities	$11,976
Other	$7,849
Total Expenditures	$47,411

PRIVATE HOUSEHOLDS

2001 Estimates:

Private Households, Total	5,237
Pop. in Private Households	13,310
Average no. per Household	2.5

FAMILIES

2001 Estimates:

Families in Private Households	4,017
Husband-Wife Families	3,486
Lone-Parent Families	531
Aver. No. Persons per Family	2.9
Aver. No. Sons/Daughters at Home	1.0

HOUSING

2001 Estimates:

Occupied Private Dwellings	5,237
Owned	4,234
Rented	1,003
Single-Detached House	4,024
Semi-Detached House	236
Row Houses	58
Apartment, 5 or Fewer Storeys	247
Apartment, Detached Duplex	206
Other Single-Attached	12
Movable Dwellings	454

VEHICLES

2001 Estimates:

Model Yrs. '81-'96, No.	3,148
% Total	88.45
Model Yrs. '97-'98, No.	243
% Total	6.83
'99 Vehicles registered in Model Yr. '99, No.	168
% Total	4.72
Total No. '81-'99	3,559

LEGAL MARITAL STATUS

2001 Estimates: (Age 15+)

Single (Never Married)	2,648
Legally Married (Not Separated)	6,014
Legally Married (Separated)	409
Widowed	578
Divorced	983

PSYTE CATEGORIES

2001 Estimates	No. of House -holds	% of Total Hhds.	Index
Small City Elite	1,151	21.98	1,283
Old Towns' New Fringe	2,450	46.78	1,195
Old Leafy Towns	1,231	23.51	920
Nesters & Young Homesteaders	405	7.73	331

FINANCIAL P$YTE

2001 Estimates	No. of House -holds	% of Total Hhds.	Index
Canadian Comfort	1,151	21.98	226
Tractors & Tradelines	2,450	46.78	818
Bills & Wills	1,231	23.51	284
Revolving Renters	405	7.73	168

HOME LANGUAGE

2001 Estimates:		% Total
English	13,072	97.65
French	63	0.47
Bengali	28	0.21
Chinese	28	0.21
Dutch	12	0.09
German	90	0.67
Lithuanian	11	0.08
Slovak	19	0.14
Other Languages	11	0.08
Multiple Responses	52	0.39
Total	13,386	100.00

BUILDING PERMITS

	1999	1998	1997
		$000	
Value	74,213	78,684	n.a.

HOMES BUILT

	1999	1998	1997
No.	89	151	89

TAXATION

Income Class:	1997	% Total
Under $5,000	1,000	12.47
$5,000-$10,000	980	12.22
$10,000-$15,000	1,120	13.97
$15,000-$20,000	840	10.47
$20,000-$25,000	620	7.73
$25,000-$30,000	620	7.73
$30,000-$40,000	1,170	14.59
$40,000-$50,000	780	9.73
$50,000 +	910	11.35
Total Returns, No.	8,020	
Total Income, $000	204,683	
Total Taxable Returns	5,700	
Total Tax, $000	35,527	
Average Income, $	25,522	
Average Tax, $	6,233	

VITAL STATISTICS

	1997	1996	1995	1994
Births	153	143	153	140
Deaths	74	68	63	77
Natural Increase	79	75	90	63
Marriages	83	99	90	68

Note: Latest available data.

MEDIA INFO

in Victoria, CMA

Central Saanich
(District Municipality)
Victoria CMA
In Capital Regional District.

POPULATION

July 1, 2001 Estimate	15,516
% Cdn. Total	0.05
% Change, '96 -'01	2.01
Avg. Annual Growth Rate, %	0.40
2003 Projected Population	16,057
2006 Projected Population	17,135
2001 Households Estimate	5,953
2003 Projected Households	6,126
2006 Projected Households	6,484

INCOME

% Above/Below National Average	+20
2001 Total Income Estimate	$392,550,000
% Cdn. Total	0.06
2001 Average Hhld. Income	$65,900
2001 Per Capita	$25,300
2003 Projected Total Income	$428,760,000
2006 Projected Total Income	$496,880,000

RETAIL SALES

% Above/Below National Average	-54
2001 Retail Sales Estimate	$64,560,000
% Cdn. Total	0.02
2001 per Household	$10,800
2001 per Capita	$4,200
2001 No. of Establishments	100
2003 Projected Retail Sales	$71,350,000
2006 Projected Retail Sales	$83,910,000

POPULATION

2001 Estimates:

Total		15,516
Male		7,576
Female		7,940
Age Groups	Male	Female
0-4	395	350
5-9	451	412
10-14	509	492
15-19	532	504
20-24	474	445
25-29	389	396
30-34	406	434
35-39	515	554
40-44	606	657
45-49	639	695
50-54	583	600
55-59	452	464
60-64	351	372
65-69	330	349
70+	944	1,216

DAYTIME POPULATION

2001 Estimates:

Working Population	7,360
At Home Population	7,595
Total	14,955

INCOME

2001 Estimates:

Avg. Household Income	$65,942
Avg. Family Income	$71,047
Per Capita Income	$25,300
Male:	
Avg. Employment Income	$39,041
Avg. Employment Income (Full Time)	$49,173
Female:	
Avg. Employment Income	$23,288
Avg. Employment Income (Full Time)	$33,656

DISPOSABLE & DISCRETIONARY INCOME

2001 Estimates:	Per Hhld.
Disposable Income	$50,498
Discretionary Income 1 (minus Food & Shelter)	$36,270
Discretionary Income 2 (minus Food, Shelter, & Other Expenditures)	$26,138

LIQUID ASSETS

1999 Estimates:	Per Hhld.
Equity Investments	$110,702
Interest Bearing Investments	$87,120
Total Liquid Assets	$197,822

CREDIT DATA

July 2000:	
Pool of Credit	$179,520,376
Revolving Credit, No.	34,579
Fixed Loans, No.	8,664
Avg. Credit Limit, per Person	$13,656
Avg. Spent, per Person	$5,681
Satisfactory Ratings, No. per Person	3.21
Avg. No. of Cards, per Person	1.15

LABOUR FORCE

2001 Estimates:

Male:	
In the Labour Force	4,306
Participation Rate	69.2
Employed	4,162
Unemployed	144
Unemployment Rate	3.3
Not in Labour Force	1,915
Female:	
In the Labour Force	3,980
Participation Rate	59.5
Employed	3,816
Unemployed	164
Unemployment Rate	4.1
Not in Labour Force	2,706

OCCUPATIONS BY MAJOR GROUPS

2001 Estimates:	Male	Female
Management	665	261
Business, Finance & Admin.	490	1,455
Natural & Applied Sciences & Related	547	80
Health	130	490
Social Sciences, Gov't Services & Religion	63	82
Education	137	153
Arts, Culture, Recreation & Sport	105	113
Sales & Service	801	1,167
Trades, Transport & Equipment Operators & Related	936	20
Primary Industries	259	77
Processing, Mfg. & Utilities	138	20

LEVEL OF SCHOOLING

2001 Estimates:

Population 15 years +	12,907
Less than Grade 9	328
Grades 9-13 w/o Certif.	2,696
Grade 9-13 with Certif.	1,762
Trade Certif. /Dip.	446
Non-Univ. w/o Certif./Dip.	859
Non-Univ. with Certif./Dip.	2,956
Univ. w/o Degree	1,731
Univ. w/o Degree/Certif.	737
Univ. with Certif.	994
Univ. with Degree	2,129

AVERAGE HOUSEHOLD EXPENDITURES

2001 Estimates:

Food	$6,824
Shelter	$10,090
Clothing	$2,559
Transportation	$7,961
Health & Personal Care	$2,277
Recr'n, Read'g & Education	$4,464
Taxes & Securities	$17,526
Other	$9,728
Total Expenditures	$61,429

PRIVATE HOUSEHOLDS

2001 Estimates:

Private Households, Total	5,953
Pop. in Private Households	15,217
Average no. per Household	2.6

FAMILIES

2001 Estimates:

Families in Private Households	4,746
Husband-Wife Families	4,389
Lone-Parent Families	357
Aver. No. Persons per Family	2.9
Aver. No. Sons/Daughters at Home	1.0

HOUSING

2001 Estimates:

Occupied Private Dwellings	5,953
Owned	4,862
Rented	1,091
Single-Detached House	4,301
Semi-Detached House	127
Row Houses	540
Apartment, 5 or Fewer Storeys	637
Apartment, Detached Duplex	337
Other Single-Attached	11

VEHICLES

2001 Estimates:

Model Yrs. '81-'96, No.	10,726
% Total	90.30
Model Yrs. '97-'98, No.	762
% Total	6.42
'99 Vehicles registered in Model Yr. '99, No.	390
% Total	3.28
Total No. '81-'99	11,878

LEGAL MARITAL STATUS

2001 Estimates: (Age 15+)

Single (Never Married)	2,834
Legally Married (Not Separated)	8,072
Legally Married (Separated)	345
Widowed	821
Divorced	835

PSYTE CATEGORIES

2001 Estimates	No. of House-holds	% of Total Hhds.	Index
Suburban Executives	152	2.55	178
Boomers & Teens	876	14.72	821
Small City Elite	2,985	50.14	2,926
Aging Erudites	238	4.00	265
Blue Collar Winners	716	12.03	478
Conservative Homebodies	281	4.72	131
High Rise Sunsets	394	6.62	463
Young Urban Mix	244	4.10	193

FINANCIAL PSYTE

2001 Estimates	No. of House-holds	% of Total Hhds.	Index
Four Star Investors	1,028	17.27	344
Canadian Comfort	3,701	62.17	640
Urban Heights	238	4.00	93
Bills & Wills	525	8.82	107
Revolving Renters	394	6.62	144

British Columbia

HOME LANGUAGE

2001 Estimates:		% Total
English	15,116	97.42
French	22	0.14
Chinese	21	0.14
Dutch	66	0.43
Finnish	11	0.07
German	11	0.07
Hungarian	16	0.10
Japanese	11	0.07
Portuguese	11	0.07
Punjabi	103	0.66
Swedish	11	0.07
Vietnamese	37	0.24
Multiple Responses	80	0.52
Total	15,516	100.00

BUILDING PERMITS

	1999	1998	1997
		$000	
Value	13,258	17,413	16,356

HOMES BUILT

	1999	1998	1997
No	76	73	100

TAXATION

Income Class:	1997	% Total
Under $5,000	1,140	10.86
$5,000-$10,000	1,130	10.76
$10,000-$15,000	1,290	12.29
$15,000-$20,000	980	9.33
$20,000-$25,000	850	8.10
$25,000-$30,000	840	8.00
$30,000-$40,000	1,570	14.95
$40,000-$50,000	1,000	9.52
$50,000 +	1,700	16.19
Total Returns, No.	10,500	
Total Income, $000	313,690	
Total Taxable Returns	7,810	
Total Tax, $000	59,242	
Average Income, $.	29,875	
Average Tax, $.	7,585	

VITAL STATISTICS

	1997	1996	1995	1994
Births	141	132	177	155
Deaths	127	139	129	133
Natural Increase	14	-7	48	22
Marriages	86	69	93	71

Note: Latest available data.

MEDIA INFO
in Victoria, CMA

British Columbia

Colwood
(City)
Victoria CMA

In Capital Regional District.

POPULATION

July 1, 2001 Estimate	14,260
% Cdn. Total	0.05
% Change, '96 -'01	-1.08
Avg. Annual Growth Rate, %	-0.22
2003 Projected Population	14,516
2006 Projected Population	15,135
2001 Households Estimate	4,909
2003 Projected Households	4,969
2006 Projected Households	5,139

INCOME

% Above/Below National Average	-3
2001 Total Income Estimate	$291,410,000
% Cdn. Total	0.04
2001 Average Hhld. Income	$59,400
2001 Per Capita	$20,400
2003 Projected Total Income	$311,660,000
2006 Projected Total Income	$350,610,000

RETAIL SALES

% Above/Below National Average	-50
2001 Retail Sales Estimate	$63,960,000
% Cdn. Total	0.02
2001 per Household	$13,000
2001 per Capita	$4,500
2001 No. of Establishments	56
2003 Projected Retail Sales	$68,340,000
2006 Projected Retail Sales	$77,090,000

POPULATION

2001 Estimates:

Total		14,260
Male		7,070
Female		7,190
Age Groups	Male	Female
0-4	474	466
5-9	567	575
10-14	603	580
15-19	558	496
20-24	464	399
25-29	428	386
30-34	505	531
35-39	612	656
40-44	612	670
45-49	539	601
50-54	461	481
55-59	359	350
60-64	266	261
65-69	202	221
70+	420	517

DAYTIME POPULATION

2001 Estimates:

Working Population	2,840
At Home Population	7,070
Total	9,910

INCOME

2001 Estimates:

Avg. Household Income	$59,363
Avg. Family Income	$61,954
Per Capita Income	$20,436
Male:	
Avg. Employment Income	$35,292
Avg. Employment Income (Full Time)	$41,954
Female:	
Avg. Employment Income	$21,904
Avg. Employment Income (Full Time)	$32,692

DISPOSABLE & DISCRETIONARY INCOME

2001 Estimates:	*Per Hhld.*
Disposable Income	$45,881
Discretionary Income 1 (minus Food & Shelter)	$32,179
Discretionary Income 2 (minus Food, Shelter, & Other Expenditures)	$22,588

LIQUID ASSETS

1999 Estimates:	*Per Hhld.*
Equity Investments	$76,884
Interest Bearing Investments	$73,522
Total Liquid Assets	$150,406

CREDIT DATA

July 2000:

Pool of Credit	$154,442,282
Revolving Credit, No.	30,106
Fixed Loans, No.	9,088
Avg. Credit Limit, per Person	$13,287
Avg. Spent, per Person	$6,267
Satisfactory Ratings, No. per Person	3.27
Avg. No. of Cards, per Person	1.05

LABOUR FORCE

2001 Estimates:
Male:

In the Labour Force	4,070
Participation Rate	75.0
Employed	3,806
Unemployed	264
Unemployment Rate	6.5
Not in Labour Force	1,356
Female:	
In the Labour Force	3,590
Participation Rate	64.5
Employed	3,410
Unemployed	180
Unemployment Rate	5.0
Not in Labour Force	1,979

OCCUPATIONS BY MAJOR GROUPS

2001 Estimates:	Male	Female
Management	486	188
Business, Finance & Admin.	383	1,350
Natural & Applied Sciences & Related	312	46
Health	84	386
Social Sciences, Gov't Services & Religion	65	67
Education	78	95
Arts, Culture, Recreation & Sport	58	79
Sales & Service	1,228	1,216
Trades, Transport & Equipment Operators & Related	1,084	41
Primary Industries	90	21
Processing, Mfg. & Utilities	117	43

LEVEL OF SCHOOLING

2001 Estimates:

Population 15 years +	10,995
Less than Grade 9	284
Grades 9-13 w/o Certif.	2,732
Grade 9-13 with Certif.	2,092
Trade Certif. /Dip.	648
Non-Univ. w/o Certif./Dip.	835
Non-Univ. with Certif./Dip.	2,419
Univ. w/o Degree	1,203
Univ. w/o Degree/Certif.	528
Univ. with Certif.	675
Univ. with Degree	782

AVERAGE HOUSEHOLD EXPENDITURES

2001 Estimates:

Food	$6,556
Shelter	$9,476
Clothing	$2,311
Transportation	$7,530
Health & Personal Care	$2,085
Recr'n, Read'g & Education	$4,168
Taxes & Securities	$14,917
Other	$9,092
Total Expenditures	$56,135

PRIVATE HOUSEHOLDS

2001 Estimates:

Private Households, Total	4,909
Pop. in Private Households	14,077
Average no. per Household	2.9

FAMILIES

2001 Estimates:

Families in Private Households	4,298
Husband-Wife Families	3,779
Lone-Parent Families	519
Aver. No. Persons per Family	3.1
Aver. No. Sons/Daughters at Home	1.2

HOUSING

2001 Estimates:

Occupied Private Dwellings	4,909
Owned	3,671
Rented	1,238
Single-Detached House	3,543
Semi-Detached House	669
Row Houses	234
Apartment, 5 or Fewer Storeys	261
Apartment, Detached Duplex	202

VEHICLES

2001 Estimates:

Model Yrs. '81-'96, No.	7,352
% Total	90.54
Model Yrs. '97-'98, No.	501
% Total	6.17
'99 Vehicles registered in Model Yr. '99, No.	267
% Total	3.29
Total No. '81-'99	8,120

LEGAL MARITAL STATUS

2001 Estimates: (Age 15+)

Single (Never Married)	2,534
Legally Married (Not Separated)	7,022
Legally Married (Separated)	299
Widowed	417
Divorced	723

PSYTE CATEGORIES

2001 Estimates	No. of House-holds	% of Total Hhds.	Index
Small City Elite	1,660	33.82	1,973
Satellite Suburbs	489	9.96	347
Kindergarten Boom	425	8.66	330
Blue Collar Winners	782	15.93	633
Old Towns' New Fringe	1,172	23.87	610
Nesters & Young Homesteaders	368	7.50	321

FINANCIAL P$YTE

2001 Estimates	No. of House-holds	% of Total Hhds.	Index
Canadian Comfort	2,931	59.71	614
Mortgages & Minivans	425	8.66	131
Tractors & Tradelines	1,172	23.87	418
Revolving Renters	368	7.50	163

HOME LANGUAGE

2001 Estimates:		% Total
English	14,016	98.29
French	25	0.18
Bulgarian	31	0.22
German	76	0.53
Polish	16	0.11
Multiple Responses	96	0.67
Total	14,260	100.00

BUILDING PERMITS

	1999	1998	1997
		$000	
Value	9,819	2,504	10,888

HOMES BUILT

	1999	1998	1997
No.	10	63	12

VITAL STATISTICS

	1997	1996	1995	1994
Births	169	186	178	192
Deaths	111	75	76	89
Natural Increase	58	111	102	103
Marriages	97	78	55	51

Note: Latest available data.

MEDIA INFO
in Victoria, CMA

Esquimalt
(District Municipality)
Victoria CMA
In Capital Regional District.

British Columbia

POPULATION

July 1, 2001 Estimate	16,238
% Cdn. Total	0.05
% Change, '96 -'01	-3.43
Avg. Annual Growth Rate, %	-0.69
2003 Projected Population	16,316
2006 Projected Population	16,704
2001 Households Estimate	7,585
2003 Projected Households	7,585
2006 Projected Households	7,697

INCOME

% Above/Below National Average	-9
2001 Total Income Estimate	$312,050,000
% Cdn. Total	0.05
2001 Average Hhld. Income	$41,100
2001 Per Capita	$19,200
2003 Projected Total Income	$328,550,000
2006 Projected Total Income	$360,750,000

RETAIL SALES

% Above/Below National Average	-46
2001 Retail Sales Estimate	$79,120,000
% Cdn. Total	0.03
2001 per Household	$10,400
2001 per Capita	$4,900
2001 No. of Establishments	66
2003 Projected Retail Sales	$83,740,000
2006 Projected Retail Sales	$92,310,000

POPULATION

2001 Estimates:

Total	16,238
Male	7,913
Female	8,325

Age Groups	Male	Female
0-4	543	493
5-9	511	504
10-14	459	426
15-19	406	370
20-24	438	465
25-29	565	603
30-34	706	704
35-39	770	725
40-44	701	695
45-49	612	609
50-54	487	477
55-59	365	370
60-64	301	332
65-69	276	321
70+	773	1,231

DAYTIME POPULATION

2001 Estimates:

Working Population	4,933
At Home Population	8,636
Total	13,569

INCOME

2001 Estimates:

Avg. Household Income	$41,140
Avg. Family Income	$49,545
Per Capita Income	$19,217
Male:	
Avg. Employment Income	$28,135
Avg. Employment Income (Full Time)	$36,943
Female:	
Avg. Employment Income	$21,252
Avg. Employment Income (Full Time)	$30,727

DISPOSABLE & DISCRETIONARY INCOME

2001 Estimates:	Per Hhld.
Disposable Income	$32,094
Discretionary Income 1 (minus Food & Shelter)	$20,667
Discretionary Income 2 (minus Food, Shelter, & Other Expenditures)	$14,286

LIQUID ASSETS

1999 Estimates:	Per Hhld.
Equity Investments	$45,997
Interest Bearing Investments	$50,751
Total Liquid Assets	$96,748

CREDIT DATA

July 2000:

Pool of Credit	$153,173,686
Revolving Credit, No.	33,587
Fixed Loans, No.	9,102
Avg. Credit Limit, per Person	$10,364
Avg. Spent, per Person	$4,826
Satisfactory Ratings, No. per Person	2.81
Avg. No. of Cards, per Person	0.96

LABOUR FORCE

2001 Estimates:

Male:	
In the Labour Force	4,398
Participation Rate	68.7
Employed	4,071
Unemployed	327
Unemployment Rate	7.4
Not in Labour Force	2,002
Female:	
In the Labour Force	3,842
Participation Rate	55.7
Employed	3,600
Unemployed	242
Unemployment Rate	6.3
Not in Labour Force	3,060

OCCUPATIONS BY MAJOR GROUPS

2001 Estimates:	Male	Female
Management	484	209
Business, Finance & Admin.	379	1,176
Natural & Applied Sciences & Related	308	70
Health	29	314
Social Sciences, Gov't Services & Religion	108	117
Education	68	76
Arts, Culture, Recreation & Sport	75	86
Sales & Service	1,423	1,549
Trades, Transport & Equipment Operators & Related	1,144	92
Primary Industries	135	14
Processing, Mfg. & Utilities	117	43

LEVEL OF SCHOOLING

2001 Estimates:

Population 15 years +	13,302
Less than Grade 9	702
Grades 9-13 w/o Certif.	3,468
Grade 9-13 with Certif.	1,981
Trade Certif. /Dip.	578
Non-Univ. w/o Certif./Dip.	1,079
Non-Univ. with Certif./Dip.	2,758
Univ. w/o Degree	1,404
Univ. w/o Degree/Certif.	637
Univ. with Certif.	767
Univ. with Degree	1,332

AVERAGE HOUSEHOLD EXPENDITURES

2001 Estimates:

Food	$5,121
Shelter	$8,042
Clothing	$1,789
Transportation	$4,668
Health & Personal Care	$1,603
Recr'n, Read'g & Education	$2,801
Taxes & Securities	$9,622
Other	$7,286
Total Expenditures	$40,932

PRIVATE HOUSEHOLDS

2001 Estimates:

Private Households, Total	7,585
Pop. in Private Households	15,693
Average no. per Household	2.1

FAMILIES

2001 Estimates:

Families in Private Households	4,434
Husband-Wife Families	3,534
Lone-Parent Families	900
Aver. No. Persons per Family	2.6
Aver. No. Sons/Daughters at Home	0.9

HOUSING

2001 Estimates:

Occupied Private Dwellings	7,585
Owned	3,562
Rented	4,023
Single-Detached House	2,332
Semi-Detached House	709
Row Houses	447
Apartment, 5+ Storeys	266
Apartment, 5 or Fewer Storeys	3,131
Apartment, Detached Duplex	551
Other Single-Attached	39
Movable Dwellings	110

VEHICLES

2001 Estimates:

Model Yrs. '81-'96, No.	6,542
% Total	90.15
Model Yrs. '97-'98, No.	436
% Total	6.01
'99 Vehicles registered in Model Yr. '99, No.	279
% Total	3.84
Total No. '81-'99	7,257

LEGAL MARITAL STATUS

2001 Estimates: (Age 15+)

Single (Never Married)	4,212
Legally Married (Not Separated)	5,649
Legally Married (Separated)	660
Widowed	1,082
Divorced	1,699

PSYTE CATEGORIES

2001 Estimates	No. of House-holds	% of Total Hhds.	Index
Small City Elite	31	0.41	24
Aging Erudites	390	5.14	341
Conservative Homebodies	1,282	16.90	469
Young Urban Professionals	20	0.26	14
Young Urban Mix	626	8.25	389
University Enclaves	2,185	28.81	1,411
Young City Singles	1,159	15.28	666
Town Renters	88	1.16	134
Nesters & Young Homesteaders	400	5.27	226
Struggling Downtowns	477	6.29	200
Aged Pensioners	856	11.29	848

FINANCIAL P$YTE

2001 Estimates	No. of House-holds	% of Total Hhds.	Index
Canadian Comfort	31	0.41	4
Urban Heights	410	5.41	126
Bills & Wills	1,908	25.15	304
Revolving Renters	400	5.27	115
Young Urban Struggle	2,185	28.81	609
Towering Debt	1,724	22.73	291
Senior Survivors	856	11.29	599

HOME LANGUAGE

2001 Estimates:		% Total
English	15,402	94.85
French	313	1.93
Chinese	93	0.57
Czech	10	0.06
Dutch	10	0.06
Gaelic Languages	10	0.06
German	17	0.10
Greek	25	0.15
Polish	40	0.25
Serbian	15	0.09
Spanish	40	0.25
Tagalog (Pilipino)	10	0.06
Vietnamese	61	0.38
Multiple Responses	192	1.18
Total	16,238	100.00

BUILDING PERMITS

	1999	1998 $000	1997
Value	2,952	3,243	5,338

HOMES BUILT

	1999	1998	1997
No	5	18	43

VITAL STATISTICS

	1997	1996	1995	1994
Births	205	245	199	246
Deaths	148	149	145	131
Natural Increase	57	96	54	115
Marriages	92	140	153	121

Note: Latest available data.

MEDIA INFO
in Victoria, CMA

British Columbia

Langford
(District Municipality)
Victoria CMA

In Capital Regional District.

POPULATION

July 1, 2001 Estimate	19,300
% Cdn. Total	0.06
% Change, '96 –'01	6.05
Avg. Annual Growth Rate, %	1.18
2003 Projected Population	20,408
2006 Projected Population	22,394
2001 Households Estimate	7,228
2003 Projected Households	7,599
2006 Projected Households	8,269

INCOME

% Above/Below National Average	-7
2001 Total Income Estimate	$380,440,000
% Cdn. Total	0.06
2001 Average Hhld. Income	$52,600
2001 Per Capita	$19,700
2003 Projected Total Income	$424,370,000
2006 Projected Total Income	$505,280,000

RETAIL SALES

% Above/Below National Average	-33
2001 Retail Sales Estimate	$115,570,000
% Cdn. Total	0.04
2001 per Household	$16,000
2001 per Capita	$6,000
2001 No. of Establishments	135
2003 Projected Retail Sales	$130,080,000
2006 Projected Retail Sales	$155,880,000

POPULATION

2001 Estimates:

Total	19,300
Male	9,530
Female	9,770

Age Groups	Male	Female
0-4	663	604
5-9	729	690
10-14	732	690
15-19	693	636
20-24	595	563
25-29	570	601
30-34	729	777
35-39	872	918
40-44	849	887
45-49	750	779
50-54	603	623
55-59	458	494
60-64	371	380
65-69	304	301
70+	612	827

DAYTIME POPULATION

2001 Estimates:

Working Population	4,906
At Home Population	9,580
Total	14,486

INCOME

2001 Estimates:

Avg. Household Income	$52,634
Avg. Family Income	$55,649
Per Capita Income	$19,712
Male:	
Avg. Employment Income	$30,129
Avg. Employment Income (Full Time)	$39,615
Female:	
Avg. Employment Income	$22,486
Avg. Employment Income (Full Time)	$31,617

DISPOSABLE & DISCRETIONARY INCOME

2001 Estimates:	*Per Hhld.*
Disposable Income	$40,907
Discretionary Income 1 (minus Food & Shelter)	$28,052
Discretionary Income 2 (minus Food, Shelter, & Other Expenditures)	$19,502

LIQUID ASSETS

1999 Estimates:	*Per Hhld.*
Equity Investments	$64,948
Interest Bearing Investments	$64,909
Total Liquid Assets	$129,857

CREDIT DATA

July 2000:

Pool of Credit	$195,003,686
Revolving Credit, No.	38,228
Fixed Loans, No.	12,464
Avg. Credit Limit, per Person	$12,801
Avg. Spent, per Person	$6,244
Satisfactory Ratings, No. per Person	3.22
Avg. No. of Cards, per Person	1.03

LABOUR FORCE

2001 Estimates:

Male:	
In the Labour Force	5,524
Participation Rate	74.6
Employed	5,116
Unemployed	408
Unemployment Rate	7.4
Not in Labour Force	1,882
Female:	
In the Labour Force	5,028
Participation Rate	64.6
Employed	4,658
Unemployed	370
Unemployment Rate	7.4
Not in Labour Force	2,758

OCCUPATIONS BY MAJOR GROUPS

2001 Estimates:	Male	Female
Management	596	302
Business, Finance & Admin.	462	1,654
Natural & Applied Sciences & Related	340	66
Health	106	471
Social Sciences, Gov't Services & Religion	104	138
Education	76	106
Arts, Culture, Recreation & Sport	40	124
Sales & Service	1,534	1,832
Trades, Transport & Equipment Operators & Related	1,728	55
Primary Industries	190	62
Processing, Mfg. & Utilities	257	44

LEVEL OF SCHOOLING

2001 Estimates:

Population 15 years +	15,192
Less than Grade 9	595
Grades 9-13 w/o Certif.	3,876
Grade 9-13 with Certif.	2,233
Trade Certif. /Dip.	789
Non-Univ. w/o Certif./Dip.	1,279
Non-Univ. with Certif./Dip.	3,844
Univ. w/o Degree	1,420
Univ. w/o Degree/Certif.	688
Univ. with Certif.	732
Univ. with Degree	1,156

AVERAGE HOUSEHOLD EXPENDITURES

2001 Estimates:

Food	$6,098
Shelter	$8,818
Clothing	$2,064
Transportation	$6,588
Health & Personal Care	$1,872
Recr'n, Read'g & Education	$3,818
Taxes & Securities	$12,967
Other	$8,413
Total Expenditures	$50,638

PRIVATE HOUSEHOLDS

2001 Estimates:

Private Households, Total	7,228
Pop. in Private Households	19,122
Average no. per Household	2.6

FAMILIES

2001 Estimates:

Families in Private Households	5,825
Husband-Wife Families	4,823
Lone-Parent Families	1,002
Aver. No. Persons per Family	2.9
Aver. No. Sons/Daughters at Home	1.1

HOUSING

2001 Estimates:

Occupied Private Dwellings	7,228
Owned	5,677
Rented	1,551
Single-Detached House	4,823
Semi-Detached House	517
Row Houses	401
Apartment, 5+ Storeys	11
Apartment, 5 or Fewer Storeys	379
Apartment, Detached Duplex	797
Other Single-Attached	23
Movable Dwellings	277

VEHICLES

2001 Estimates:

Model Yrs. '81-'96, No.	8,154
% Total	90.48
Model Yrs. '97-'98, No.	547
% Total	6.07
'99 Vehicles registered in Model Yr. '99, No.	311
% Total	3.45
Total No. '81-'99	9,012

LEGAL MARITAL STATUS

2001 Estimates: (Age 15+)

Single (Never Married)	4,054
Legally Married (Not Separated)	8,322
Legally Married (Separated)	579
Widowed	737
Divorced	1,500

PSYTE CATEGORIES

2001 Estimates	No. of House-holds	% of Total Hhds.	Index
Small City Elite	1,063	14.71	858
Satellite Suburbs	1,367	18.91	659
Blue Collar Winners	164	2.27	90
Old Towns' New Fringe	3,353	46.39	1,185
Young Urban Mix	265	3.67	173
Town Renters	380	5.26	608
Nesters & Young Homesteaders	461	6.38	273
Struggling Downtowns	145	2.01	64

FINANCIAL PSYTE

2001 Estimates	No. of House-holds	% of Total Hhds.	Index
Canadian Comfort	2,594	35.89	369
Tractors & Tradelines	3,353	46.39	811
Bills & Wills	265	3.67	44
Revolving Renters	461	6.38	139
Towering Debt	525	7.26	93

HOME LANGUAGE

2001 Estimates:		% Total
English	18,878	97.81
French	48	0.25
Czech	11	0.06
German	26	0.13
Polish	23	0.12
Punjabi	92	0.48
Spanish	51	0.26
Vietnamese	12	0.06
Other Languages	12	0.06
Multiple Responses	147	0.76
Total	19,300	100.00

BUILDING PERMITS

	1999	1998 $000	1997
Value	n.a.	n.a.	788

HOMES BUILT

	1999	1998	1997
No.	216	64	88

VITAL STATISTICS

	1997	1996	1995	1994
Births	258	307	285	269
Deaths	111	93	100	97
Natural Increase	147	214	185	172
Marriages	64	91	91	78

Note: Latest available data.

MEDIA INFO
in Victoria, CMA

North Saanich
(District Municipality)
Victoria CMA
In Capital Regional District.

POPULATION

July 1, 2001 Estimate	11,158
% Cdn. Total	0.04
% Change, '96 -'01	2.97
Avg. Annual Growth Rate, %	0.59
2003 Projected Population	11,606
2006 Projected Population	12,465
2001 Households Estimate	4,271
2003 Projected Households	4,421
2006 Projected Households	4,711

INCOME

% Above/Below National Average	+36
2001 Total Income Estimate	$320,230,000
% Cdn. Total	0.05
2001 Average Hhld. Income	$75,000
2001 Per Capita	$28,700
2003 Projected Total Income	$351,220,000
2006 Projected Total Income	$408,860,000

RETAIL SALES

% Above/Below National Average	-77
2001 Retail Sales Estimate	$22,570,000
% Cdn. Total	0.01
2001 per Household	$5,300
2001 per Capita	$2,000
2001 No. of Establishments	63
2003 Projected Retail Sales	$25,710,000
2006 Projected Retail Sales	$30,790,000

POPULATION

2001 Estimates:

Total		11,158
Male		5,500
Female		5,658

Age Groups	Male	Female
0-4	226	231
5-9	295	295
10-14	359	350
15-19	373	361
20-24	322	298
25-29	254	236
30-34	230	244
35-39	284	338
40-44	381	456
45-49	469	518
50-54	473	497
55-59	404	409
60-64	358	345
65-69	317	306
70+	755	774

DAYTIME POPULATION

2001 Estimates:

Working Population	2,602
At Home Population	5,656
Total	8,258

INCOME

2001 Estimates:

Avg. Household Income	$74,977
Avg. Family Income	$79,229
Per Capita Income	$28,699
Male:	
Avg. Employment Income	$43,004
Avg. Employment Income (Full Time)	$53,157
Female:	
Avg. Employment Income	$24,631
Avg. Employment Income (Full Time)	$37,642

DISPOSABLE & DISCRETIONARY INCOME

2001 Estimates:	Per Hhld.
Disposable Income	$57,108
Discretionary Income 1 (minus Food & Shelter)	$41,666
Discretionary Income 2 (minus Food, Shelter, & Other Expenditures)	$30,314

LIQUID ASSETS

1999 Estimates:	Per Hhld.
Equity Investments	$135,659
Interest Bearing Investments	$100,760
Total Liquid Assets	$236,419

CREDIT DATA

July 2000:

Pool of Credit	$144,187,672
Revolving Credit, No.	24,847
Fixed Loans, No.	5,370
Avg. Credit Limit, per Person	$15,251
Avg. Spent, per Person	$5,888
Satisfactory Ratings, No. per Person	3.13
Avg. No. of Cards, per Person	1.20

LABOUR FORCE

2001 Estimates:

Male:	
In the Labour Force	2,975
Participation Rate	64.4
Employed	2,859
Unemployed	116
Unemployment Rate	3.9
Not in Labour Force	1,645
Female:	
In the Labour Force	2,716
Participation Rate	56.8
Employed	2,635
Unemployed	81
Unemployment Rate	3.0
Not in Labour Force	2,066

OCCUPATIONS BY MAJOR GROUPS

2001 Estimates:	Male	Female
Management	538	197
Business, Finance & Admin.	303	908
Natural & Applied Sciences & Related	381	81
Health	71	247
Social Sciences, Gov't Services & Religion	64	80
Education	94	145
Arts, Culture, Recreation & Sport	57	75
Sales & Service	521	838
Trades, Transport & Equipment Operators & Related	632	41
Primary Industries	161	41
Processing, Mfg. & Utilities	128	42

LEVEL OF SCHOOLING

2001 Estimates:

Population 15 years +	9,402
Less than Grade 9	243
Grades 9-13 w/o Certif.	1,578
Grade 9-13 with Certif.	1,277
Trade Certif. /Dip.	433
Non-Univ. w/o Certif./Dip.	609
Non-Univ. with Certif./Dip.	2,025
Univ. w/o Degree	1,403
Univ. w/o Degree/Certif.	566
Univ. with Certif.	837
Univ. with Degree	1,834

AVERAGE HOUSEHOLD EXPENDITURES

2001 Estimates:

Food	$7,629
Shelter	$10,893
Clothing	$2,866
Transportation	$8,932
Health & Personal Care	$2,572
Recr'n, Read'g & Education	$5,218
Taxes & Securities	$19,602
Other	$10,845
Total Expenditures	$68,557

PRIVATE HOUSEHOLDS

2001 Estimates:

Private Households, Total	4,271
Pop. in Private Households	11,086
Average no. per Household	2.6

FAMILIES

2001 Estimates:

Families in Private Households	3,659
Husband-Wife Families	3,464
Lone-Parent Families	195
Aver. No. Persons per Family	2.8
Aver. No. Sons/Daughters at Home	0.9

HOUSING

2001 Estimates:

Occupied Private Dwellings	4,271
Owned	3,785
Rented	486
Single-Detached House	3,968
Semi-Detached House	44
Row Houses	105
Apartment, 5 or Fewer Storeys	22
Apartment, Detached Duplex	94
Other Single-Attached	11
Movable Dwellings	27

VEHICLES

2001 Estimates:

Model Yrs. '81-'96, No.	5,347
% Total	85.73
Model Yrs. '97-'98, No.	545
% Total	8.74
'99 Vehicles registered in Model Yr. '99, No.	345
% Total	5.53
Total No. '81-'99	6,237

LEGAL MARITAL STATUS

2001 Estimates: (Age 15+)

Single (Never Married)	1,775
Legally Married (Not Separated)	6,553
Legally Married (Separated)	176
Widowed	410
Divorced	488

PSYTE CATEGORIES

2001 Estimates	No. of House-holds	% of Total Hhds.	Index
Urban Gentry	383	8.97	499
Boomers & Teens	508	11.89	663
Small City Elite	2,654	62.14	3,626
Aging Erudites	338	7.91	525
Blue Collar Winners	388	9.08	361

FINANCIAL P$YTE

2001 Estimates	No. of House-holds	% of Total Hhds.	Index
Four Star Investors	891	20.86	415
Canadian Comfort	3,042	71.22	733
Urban Heights	338	7.91	184

HOME LANGUAGE

2001 Estimates:		% Total
English	10,935	98.00
French	37	0.33
Chinese	11	0.10
Dutch	16	0.14
German	93	0.83
Portuguese	11	0.10
Swedish	11	0.10
Tagalog (Pilipino)	11	0.10
Ukrainian	11	0.10
Multiple Responses	22	0.20
Total	11,158	100.00

BUILDING PERMITS

	1999	1998	1997
		$000	
Value	8,032	12,286	12,645

HOMES BUILT

	1999	1998	1997
No	34	46	27

VITAL STATISTICS

	1997	1996	1995	1994
Births	62	69	75	55
Deaths	72	73	50	69
Natural Increase	-10	-4	25	-14
Marriages	55	51	71	52

Note: Latest available data.

MEDIA INFO
in Victoria, CMA

British Columbia

Oak Bay
(District Municipality)
Victoria CMA
In Capital Regional District.

POPULATION

July 1, 2001 Estimate 18,035
% Cdn. Total 0.06
% Change, '96 -'01 . . . . -3.01
Avg. Annual Growth Rate, % . . . . -0.61
2003 Projected Population 18,166
2006 Projected Population 18,657
2001 Households Estimate 8,033
2003 Projected Households 8,054
2006 Projected Households 8,199

INCOME

% Above/Below National Average . . . .+46
2001 Total Income Estimate $553,750,000
% Cdn. Total 0.08
2001 Average Hhld. Income $68,900
2001 Per Capita $30,700
2003 Projected Total Income . . . $584,190,000
2006 Projected Total Income . . . $642,790,000

RETAIL SALES

% Above/Below National Average . . . . -70
2001 Retail Sales Estimate $48,230,000
% Cdn. Total 0.02
2001 per Household $6,000
2001 per Capita $2,700
2001 No. of Establishments 110
2003 Projected Retail Sales $51,510,000
2006 Projected Retail Sales $57,370,000

POPULATION

2001 Estimates:
Total 18,035
Male 8,190
Female 9,845

Age Groups	Male	Female
0-4	367	350
5-9	424	401
10-14	516	493
15-19	544	545
20-24	514	537
25-29	443	458
30-34	370	411
35-39	386	483
40-44	519	637
45-49	682	765
50-54	676	709
55-59	529	546
60-64	401	454
65-69	368	465
70+	1,451	2,591

DAYTIME POPULATION

2001 Estimates:
Working Population 5,968
At Home Population 10,253
Total 16,221

INCOME

2001 Estimates:
Avg. Household Income $68,935
Avg. Family Income $86,086
Per Capita Income $30,704
Male:
Avg. Employment Income $44,297
Avg. Employment Income
 (Full Time) $57,970
Female:
Avg. Employment Income $28,543
Avg. Employment Income
 (Full Time) $41,300

DISPOSABLE & DISCRETIONARY INCOME

2001 Estimates: Per Hhld.
Disposable Income $51,294
Discretionary Income 1
 (minus Food & Shelter) $35,940
Discretionary Income 2
 (minus Food, Shelter, & Other
 Expenditures) $26,965

LIQUID ASSETS

1999 Estimates: Per Hhld.
Equity Investments $128,925
Interest Bearing Investments $94,797
Total Liquid Assets $223,722

CREDIT DATA

July 2000:
Pool of Credit $229,090,784
Revolving Credit, No. 44,431
Fixed Loans, No. 6,370
Avg. Credit Limit, per Person $13,264
Avg. Spent, per Person $4,784
Satisfactory Ratings,
 No. per Person 2.91
Avg. No. of Cards, per Person 1.15

LABOUR FORCE

2001 Estimates:
Male:
In the Labour Force 4,268
Participation Rate 62.0
Employed 4,006
Unemployed 262
Unemployment Rate 6.1
Not in Labour Force 2,615
Female:
In the Labour Force 4,050
Participation Rate 47.1
Employed 3,804
Unemployed 246
Unemployment Rate 6.1
Not in Labour Force 4,551

OCCUPATIONS BY MAJOR GROUPS

2001 Estimates:	Male	Female
Management	837	341
Business, Finance & Admin.	496	1,192
Natural & Applied Sciences & Related	470	90
Health	286	367
Social Sciences, Gov't Services & Religion	233	306
Education	404	371
Arts, Culture, Recreation & Sport	197	254
Sales & Service	865	968
Trades, Transport & Equipment Operators & Related	282	45
Primary Industries	96	30
Processing, Mfg. & Utilities	20	n.a.

LEVEL OF SCHOOLING

2001 Estimates:
Population 15 years + ... 15,484
Less than Grade 9 301
Grades 9-13 w/o Certif. 2,435
Grade 9-13 with Certif. 1,358
Trade Certif. /Dip. 388
Non-Univ. w/o Certif./Dip. 756
Non-Univ. with Certif./Dip. 2,105
Univ. w/o Degree 2,730
 Univ. w/o Degree/Certif. 1,566
 Univ. with Certif. 1,164
Univ. with Degree 5,411

AVERAGE HOUSEHOLD EXPENDITURES

2001 Estimates:
Food $6,716
Shelter $11,408
Clothing $2,627
Transportation $6,608
Health & Personal Care $2,331
Recr'n, Read'g & Education $4,680
Taxes & Securities $19,104
Other $9,990
Total Expenditures $63,464

PRIVATE HOUSEHOLDS

2001 Estimates:
Private Households, Total 8,033
Pop. in Private Households 17,651
Average no. per Household 2.2

FAMILIES

2001 Estimates:
Families in Private Households 5,067
Husband-Wife Families 4,613
Lone-Parent Families 454
Aver. No. Persons per Family 2.8
Aver. No. Sons/Daughters
 at Home 0.9

HOUSING

2001 Estimates:
Occupied Private Dwellings 8,033
 Owned 5,847
 Rented 2,186
Single-Detached House 5,462
Semi-Detached House 120
Row Houses 98
Apartment, 5+ Storeys 490
 Owned Apartment, 5+ Storeys 198
Apartment, 5 or Fewer Storeys 1,637
Apartment, Detached Duplex 206
Other Single-Attached 20

VEHICLES

2001 Estimates:
Model Yrs. '81-'96, No. 8,169
 % Total 89.28
Model Yrs. '97-'98, No. 597
 % Total 6.52
'99 Vehicles registered in
 Model Yr. '99, No. 384
 % Total 4.20
Total No. '81-'99 9,150

LEGAL MARITAL STATUS

2001 Estimates: (Age 15+)
Single (Never Married) 3,748
Legally Married
 (Not Separated) 8,497
Legally Married (Separated) 346
Widowed 1,781
Divorced 1,112

PSYTE CATEGORIES

2001 Estimates	No. of House -holds	% of Total Hhds.	Index
Canadian Establishment	242	3.01	1,810
Urban Gentry	4,015	49.98	2,781
Aging Erudites	1,638	20.39	1,352
High Rise Sunsets	1,323	16.47	1,152
Young Urban Intelligentsia	294	3.66	241
Aged Pensioners	381	4.74	357

FINANCIAL P$YTE

2001 Estimates	No. of House -holds	% of Total Hhds.	Index
Platinum Estates	242	3.01	374
Four Star Investors	4,015	49.98	995
Urban Heights	1,638	20.39	474
Revolving Renters	1,323	16.47	358
Young Urban Struggle	294	3.66	77
Senior Survivors	381	4.74	252

HOME LANGUAGE

2001 Estimates:		% Total
English	17,371	96.32
French	41	0.23
Chinese	145	0.80
Croatian	10	0.06
Dutch	10	0.06
Estonian	10	0.06
German	41	0.23
Hungarian	15	0.08
Japanese	67	0.37
Korean	48	0.27
Latvian (Lettish)	10	0.06
Persian (Farsi)	60	0.33
Polish	21	0.12
Punjabi	15	0.08
Russian	20	0.11
Ukrainian	16	0.09
Multiple Responses	135	0.75
Total	18,035	100.00

BUILDING PERMITS

	1999	1998	1997
		$000	
Value	12,192	15,368	9,412

HOMES BUILT

	1999	1998	1997
No	37	12	38

VITAL STATISTICS

	1997	1996	1995	1994
Births	76	104	101	93
Deaths	207	219	223	222
Natural Increase	-131	-115	-122	-129
Marriages	133	163	161	170

Note: Latest available data.

MEDIA INFO
in Victoria, CMA

Saanich
(District Municipality)
Victoria CMA
In Capital Regional District.

POPULATION

July 1, 2001 Estimate	107,091
% Cdn. Total	0.34
% Change, '96 -'01	1.47
Avg. Annual Growth Rate, %	0.29
2003 Projected Population	110,503
2006 Projected Population	117,415
2001 Households Estimate	42,947
2003 Projected Households	44,089
2006 Projected Households	46,460

INCOME

% Above/Below National Average	+11
2001 Total Income Estimate	$2,503,510,000
% Cdn. Total	0.38
2001 Average Hhld. Income	$58,300
2001 Per Capita	$23,400
2003 Projected Total Income	$2,709,460,000
2006 Projected Total Income	$3,096,330,000

RETAIL SALES

% Above/Below National Average	-17
2001 Retail Sales Estimate	$800,210,000
% Cdn. Total	0.29
2001 per Household	$18,600
2001 per Capita	$7,500
2001 No. of Establishments	528
2003 Projected Retail Sales	$882,860,000
2006 Projected Retail Sales	$1,025,910,000

POPULATION

2001 Estimates:

Total		107,091
Male		51,268
Female		55,823

Age Groups	Male	Female
0-4	2,909	2,820
5-9	2,954	2,887
10-14	3,226	3,083
15-19	3,381	3,287
20-24	3,487	3,570
25-29	3,596	3,611
30-34	3,634	3,645
35-39	3,719	4,022
40-44	3,895	4,383
45-49	3,989	4,415
50-54	3,501	3,855
55-59	2,826	3,069
60-64	2,347	2,575
65-69	2,090	2,443
70+	5,714	8,158

DAYTIME POPULATION

2001 Estimates:

Working Population	41,223
At Home Population	54,728
Total	95,951

INCOME

2001 Estimates:

Avg. Household Income	$58,293
Avg. Family Income	$65,099
Per Capita Income	$23,377
Male:	
Avg. Employment Income	$34,121
Avg. Employment Income (Full Time)	$46,177
Female:	
Avg. Employment Income	$22,880
Avg. Employment Income (Full Time)	$33,817

DISPOSABLE & DISCRETIONARY INCOME

2001 Estimates:	Per Hhld.
Disposable Income	$44,699
Discretionary Income 1 (minus Food & Shelter)	$31,327
Discretionary Income 2 (minus Food, Shelter, & Other Expenditures)	$23,004

LIQUID ASSETS

1999 Estimates:	Per Hhld.
Equity Investments	$89,849
Interest Bearing Investments	$76,365
Total Liquid Assets	$166,214

CREDIT DATA

July 2000:

Pool of Credit	$1,169,557,015
Revolving Credit, No.	241,688
Fixed Loans, No.	47,957
Avg. Credit Limit, per Person	$12,418
Avg. Spent, per Person	$4,983
Satisfactory Ratings, No. per Person	3.02
Avg. No. of Cards, per Person	1.12

LABOUR FORCE

2001 Estimates:

Male:	
In the Labour Force	28,250
Participation Rate	67.0
Employed	26,808
Unemployed	1,442
Unemployment Rate	5.1
Not in Labour Force	13,929
Female:	
In the Labour Force	27,416
Participation Rate	58.3
Employed	26,003
Unemployed	1,413
Unemployment Rate	5.2
Not in Labour Force	19,617

OCCUPATIONS BY MAJOR GROUPS

2001 Estimates:	Male	Female
Management	3,980	1,996
Business, Finance & Admin.	2,935	8,570
Natural & Applied Sciences & Related	2,434	454
Health	963	2,551
Social Sciences, Gov't Services & Religion	935	990
Education	1,071	1,695
Arts, Culture, Recreation & Sport	726	1,004
Sales & Service	7,340	8,664
Trades, Transport & Equipment Operators & Related	5,602	380
Primary Industries	1,029	298
Processing, Mfg. & Utilities	760	266

LEVEL OF SCHOOLING

2001 Estimates:

Population 15 years +	89,212
Less than Grade 9	4,391
Grades 9-13 w/o Certif.	17,899
Grade 9-13 with Certif.	11,179
Trade Certif. /Dip.	2,709
Non-Univ. w/o Certif./Dip.	6,422
Non-Univ. with Certif./Dip.	16,582
Univ. w/o Degree	12,779
Univ. w/o Degree/Certif.	6,663
Univ. with Certif.	6,116
Univ. with Degree	17,251

AVERAGE HOUSEHOLD EXPENDITURES

2001 Estimates:

Food	$6,212
Shelter	$9,507
Clothing	$2,215
Transportation	$6,353
Health & Personal Care	$1,986
Recr'n, Read'g & Education	$3,857
Taxes & Securities	$16,084
Other	$8,807
Total Expenditures	$55,021

PRIVATE HOUSEHOLDS

2001 Estimates:

Private Households, Total	42,947
Pop. in Private Households	105,623
Average no. per Household	2.5

FAMILIES

2001 Estimates:

Families in Private Households	31,081
Husband-Wife Families	27,005
Lone-Parent Families	4,076
Aver. No. Persons per Family	2.8
Aver. No. Sons/Daughters at Home	1.0

HOUSING

2001 Estimates:

Occupied Private Dwellings	42,947
Owned	31,329
Rented	11,618
Single-Detached House	27,396
Semi-Detached House	1,117
Row Houses	3,254
Apartment, 5+ Storeys	324
Owned Apartment, 5+ Storeys	216
Apartment, 5 or Fewer Storeys	7,260
Apartment, Detached Duplex	3,482
Other Single-Attached	92
Movable Dwellings	22

VEHICLES

2001 Estimates:

Model Yrs. '81-'96, No.	50,967
% Total	86.78
Model Yrs. '97-'98, No.	4,740
% Total	8.07
'99 Vehicles registered in Model Yr. '99, No.	3,021
% Total	5.14
Total No. '81-'99	58,728

LEGAL MARITAL STATUS

2001 Estimates: (Age 15+)

Single (Never Married)	25,406
Legally Married (Not Separated)	48,889
Legally Married (Separated)	2,373
Widowed	5,896
Divorced	6,648

PSYTE CATEGORIES

2001 Estimates	No. of House -holds	% of Total Hhds.	Index
The Affluentials	102	0.24	37
Urban Gentry	3,529	8.22	457
Suburban Executives	394	0.92	64
Asian Heights	145	0.34	53
Boomers & Teens	3,929	9.15	510
Stable Suburban Families	3,114	7.25	556
Small City Elite	184	0.43	25
Old Bungalow Burbs	1,087	2.53	153
Suburban Nesters	1,260	2.93	183
Brie & Chablis	261	0.61	68
Aging Erudites	9,160	21.33	1,414
Satellite Suburbs	444	1.03	36
Kindergarten Boom	803	1.87	71
Blue Collar Winners	774	1.80	72
Old Towns' New Fringe	112	0.26	7
Asian Mosaic	998	2.32	170
Conservative Homebodies	4,218	9.82	272

British Columbia

2001 Estimates	No. of House -holds	% of Total Hhds.	Index
High Rise Sunsets	1,321	3.08	215
Young Urban Professionals	462	1.08	57
Young Urban Mix	1,604	3.73	176
University Enclaves	7,480	17.42	853
Young City Singles	543	1.26	55
Nesters & Young Homesteaders	772	1.80	77

FINANCIAL P$YTE

2001 Estimates	No. of House -holds	% of Total Hhds.	Index
Platinum Estates	102	0.24	29
Four Star Investors	7,852	18.28	364
Successful Suburbanites	3,259	7.59	114
Canadian Comfort	2,662	6.20	64
Urban Heights	9,883	23.01	535
Miners & Credit-Liners	1,087	2.53	80
Mortgages & Minivans	803	1.87	28
Dollars & Sense	998	2.32	89
Tractors & Tradelines	112	0.26	5
Bills & Wills	5,822	13.56	164
Revolving Renters	2,093	4.87	106
Young Urban Struggle	7,480	17.42	368
Towering Debt	543	1.26	16

HOME LANGUAGE

2001 Estimates:		% Total
English	98,205	91.70
French	322	0.30
Chinese	2,994	2.80
Croatian	143	0.13
Czech	59	0.06
Dutch	103	0.10
German	211	0.20
Hungarian	155	0.14
Italian	157	0.15
Japanese	152	0.14
Korean	104	0.10
Persian (Farsi)	118	0.11
Polish	153	0.14
Portuguese	631	0.59
Punjabi	1,263	1.18
Spanish	120	0.11
Tagalog (Pilipino)	106	0.10
Vietnamese	177	0.17
Other Languages	572	0.53
Multiple Responses	1,346	1.26
Total	107,091	100.00

BUILDING PERMITS

	1999	1998 $000	1997
Value	94,343	64,567	76,477

British Columbia

Saanich
(District Municipality)
Victoria CMA
(Cont'd)

HOMES BUILT

	1999	1998	1997
No.	223	275	326

VITAL STATISTICS

	1997	1996	1995	1994
Births	888	886	1,000	1,110
Deaths	776	741	751	744
Natural Increase	112	145	249	366
Marriages	505	449	551	485

Note: Latest available data.

MEDIA INFO
in Victoria, CMA

Sidney
(Town)
Victoria CMA
In Capital Regional District.

POPULATION

July 1, 2001 Estimate	11,310
% Cdn. Total	0.04
% Change, '96 -'01	1.54
Avg. Annual Growth Rate, %	0.31
2003 Projected Population	11,668
2006 Projected Population	12,408
2001 Households Estimate	5,416
2003 Projected Households	5,570
2006 Projected Households	5,889

INCOME

% Above/Below National Average	+5
2001 Total Income Estimate	$250,870,000
% Cdn. Total	0.04
2001 Average Hhld. Income	$46,300
2001 Per Capita	$22,200
2003 Projected Total Income	$268,920,000
2006 Projected Total Income	$303,240,000

RETAIL SALES

% Above/Below National Average	+31
2001 Retail Sales Estimate	$132,160,000
% Cdn. Total	0.05
2001 per Household	$24,400
2001 per Capita	$11,700
2001 No. of Establishments	116
2003 Projected Retail Sales	$145,440,000
2006 Projected Retail Sales	$169,460,000

POPULATION

2001 Estimates:

Total		11,310
Male		5,227
Female		6,083

Age Groups	Male	Female
0-4	275	255
5-9	295	273
10-14	301	283
15-19	279	279
20-24	250	263
25-29	265	280
30-34	325	326
35-39	364	385
40-44	373	407
45-49	358	389
50-54	317	344
55-59	276	304
60-64	230	284
65-69	224	307
70+	1,095	1,704

DAYTIME POPULATION

2001 Estimates:

Working Population	5,360
At Home Population	6,913
Total	12,273

INCOME

2001 Estimates:

Avg. Household Income	$46,320
Avg. Family Income	$53,630
Per Capita Income	$22,181
Male:	
Avg. Employment Income	$32,222
Avg. Employment Income (Full Time)	$40,309
Female:	
Avg. Employment Income	$21,743
Avg. Employment Income (Full Time)	$31,345

DISPOSABLE & DISCRETIONARY INCOME

2001 Estimates:	*Per Hhld.*
Disposable Income	$35,847
Discretionary Income 1 (minus Food & Shelter)	$23,688
Discretionary Income 2 (minus Food, Shelter, & Other Expenditures)	$16,377

LIQUID ASSETS

1999 Estimates:	*Per Hhld.*
Equity Investments	$60,958
Interest Bearing Investments	$58,602
Total Liquid Assets	$119,560

CREDIT DATA

July 2000:

Pool of Credit	$119,444,372
Revolving Credit, No.	24,868
Fixed Loans, No.	5,684
Avg. Credit Limit, per Person	$11,797
Avg. Spent, per Person	$4,756
Satisfactory Ratings, No. per Person	2.95
Avg. No. of Cards, per Person	1.11

LABOUR FORCE

2001 Estimates:

Male:	
In the Labour Force	2,406
Participation Rate	55.2
Employed	2,225
Unemployed	181
Unemployment Rate	7.5
Not in Labour Force	1,950
Female:	
In the Labour Force	2,370
Participation Rate	45.0
Employed	2,233
Unemployed	137
Unemployment Rate	5.8
Not in Labour Force	2,902

OCCUPATIONS BY MAJOR GROUPS

2001 Estimates:	Male	Female
Management	293	213
Business, Finance & Admin.	182	651
Natural & Applied Sciences & Related	315	70
Health	39	311
Social Sciences, Gov't Services & Religion	n.a.	42
Education	36	26
Arts, Culture, Recreation & Sport	46	106
Sales & Service	591	838
Trades, Transport & Equipment Operators & Related	634	40
Primary Industries	74	10
Processing, Mfg. & Utilities	126	11

LEVEL OF SCHOOLING

2001 Estimates:

Population 15 years +	9,628
Less than Grade 9	513
Grades 9-13 w/o Certif.	2,407
Grade 9-13 with Certif.	1,162
Trade Certif. /Dip.	386
Non-Univ. w/o Certif./Dip.	789
Non-Univ. with Certif./Dip.	2,190
Univ. w/o Degree	1,035
Univ. w/o Degree/Certif.	327
Univ. with Certif.	708
Univ. with Degree	1,146

AVERAGE HOUSEHOLD EXPENDITURES

2001 Estimates:

Food	$5,535
Shelter	$8,674
Clothing	$1,811
Transportation	$5,543
Health & Personal Care	$1,827
Recr'n, Read'g & Education	$3,146
Taxes & Securities	$11,108
Other	$7,744
Total Expenditures	$45,388

PRIVATE HOUSEHOLDS

2001 Estimates:

Private Households, Total	5,416
Pop. in Private Households	11,137
Average no. per Household	2.1

FAMILIES

2001 Estimates:

Families in Private Households	3,445
Husband-Wife Families	3,053
Lone-Parent Families	392
Aver. No. Persons per Family	2.6
Aver. No. Sons/Daughters at Home	0.7

HOUSING

2001 Estimates:

Occupied Private Dwellings	5,416
Owned	3,931
Rented	1,485
Single-Detached House	2,620
Semi-Detached House	324
Row Houses	546
Apartment, 5+ Storeys	110
Owned Apartment, 5+ Storeys	61
Apartment, 5 or Fewer Storeys	1,463
Apartment, Detached Duplex	274
Movable Dwellings	79

VEHICLES

2001 Estimates:

Model Yrs. '81-'96, No.	5,415
% Total	88.83
Model Yrs. '97-'98, No.	423
% Total	6.94
'99 Vehicles registered in Model Yr. '99, No.	258
% Total	4.23
Total No. '81-'99	6,096

LEGAL MARITAL STATUS

2001 Estimates: (Age 15+)

Single (Never Married)	1,798
Legally Married (Not Separated)	5,508
Legally Married (Separated)	270
Widowed	1,283
Divorced	769

PSYTE CATEGORIES

2001 Estimates	No. of House -holds	% of Total Hhds.	Index
Small City Elite	837	15.45	902
Aging Erudites	760	14.03	930
High Rise Sunsets	980	18.09	1,265
Old Leafy Towns	838	15.47	605
Nesters & Young Homesteaders	1,709	31.55	1,352
Aged Pensioners	257	4.75	357

FINANCIAL P$YTE

2001 Estimates	No. of House -holds	% of Total Hhds.	Index
Canadian Comfort	837	15.45	159
Urban Heights	760	14.03	326
Bills & Wills	838	15.47	187
Revolving Renters	2,689	49.65	1,079
Senior Survivors	257	4.75	252

Sidney
(Town)
Victoria CMA
(Cont'd)

HOME LANGUAGE

2001 Estimates:		% Total
English	11,043	97.64
Chinese	75	0.66
Dutch	11	0.10
German	21	0.19
Greek	16	0.14
Polish	21	0.19
Portuguese	37	0.33
Punjabi	11	0.10
Spanish	16	0.14
Vietnamese	16	0.14
Multiple Responses	43	0.38
Total	11,310	100.00

BUILDING PERMITS

	1999	1998	1997
		$000	
Value	14,619	9,548	15,797

HOMES BUILT

	1999	1998	1997
No.	16	56	138

TAXATION

Income Class:	1997	% Total
Under $5,000	1,420	8.96
$5,000-$10,000	1,580	9.97
$10,000-$15,000	2,030	12.82
$15,000-$20,000	1,640	10.35
$20,000-$25,000	1,400	8.84
$25,000-$30,000	1,250	7.89
$30,000-$40,000	2,370	14.96
$40,000-$50,000	1,460	9.22
$50,000 +	2,700	17.05
Total Returns, No.	15,840	
Total Income, $000	512,453	
Total Taxable Returns	12,210	
Total Tax, $000	104,965	
Average Income, $	32,352	
Average Tax, $	8,597	

VITAL STATISTICS

	1997	1996	1995	1994
Births	101	97	110	107
Deaths	160	196	169	178
Natural Increase	-59	-99	-59	-71
Marriages	81	100	88	91

Note: Latest available data.

MEDIA INFO
in Victoria, CMA

Victoria
(City)
Victoria CMA
In Capital Regional District.

POPULATION

July 1, 2001 Estimate	75,919
% Cdn. Total	0.24
% Change, '96 -'01	-0.77
Avg. Annual Growth Rate, %	-0.15
2003 Projected Population	77,398
2006 Projected Population	80,872
2001 Households Estimate	41,178
2003 Projected Households	42,656
2006 Projected Households	45,523

INCOME

% Above/Below National Average	-2
2001 Total Income Estimate	$1,561,340,000
% Cdn. Total	0.24
2001 Average Hhld. Income	$37,900
2001 Per Capita	$20,600
2003 Projected Total Income	$1,644,610,000
2006 Projected Total Income	$1,809,370,000

RETAIL SALES

% Above/Below National Average	+89
2001 Retail Sales Estimate	$1,281,840,000
% Cdn. Total	0.46
2001 per Household	$31,100
2001 per Capita	$16,900
2001 No. of Establishments	1,083
2003 Projected Retail Sales	$1,415,370,000
2006 Projected Retail Sales	$1,634,250,000

POPULATION

2001 Estimates:		
Total		75,919
Male		35,084
Female		40,835

Age Groups	Male	Female
0-4	2,215	2,093
5-9	1,659	1,569
10-14	1,384	1,296
15-19	1,385	1,354
20-24	2,136	2,402
25-29	3,157	3,389
30-34	3,529	3,522
35-39	3,263	3,221
40-44	2,977	2,971
45-49	2,796	2,871
50-54	2,294	2,440
55-59	1,645	1,877
60-64	1,273	1,532
65-69	1,106	1,487
70+	4,265	8,811

DAYTIME POPULATION

2001 Estimates:	
Working Population	69,827
At Home Population	40,161
Total	109,988

INCOME

2001 Estimates:	
Avg. Household Income	$37,917
Avg. Family Income	$49,354
Per Capita Income	$20,566
Male:	
Avg. Employment Income	$26,335
Avg. Employment Income (Full Time)	$36,226
Female:	
Avg. Employment Income	$21,159
Avg. Employment Income (Full Time)	$31,476

DISPOSABLE & DISCRETIONARY INCOME

2001 Estimates:	Per Hhld.
Disposable Income	$29,467
Discretionary Income 1 (minus Food & Shelter)	$18,826
Discretionary Income 2 (minus Food, Shelter, & Other Expenditures)	$13,244

LIQUID ASSETS

1999 Estimates:	Per Hhld.
Equity Investments	$43,241
Interest Bearing Investments	$47,874
Total Liquid Assets	$91,115

CREDIT DATA

July 2000:	
Pool of Credit	$776,028,765
Revolving Credit, No.	166,598
Fixed Credit, No.	34,230
Avg. Credit Limit, per Person	$10,258
Avg. Spent, per Person	$4,541
Satisfactory Ratings, No. per Person	2.61
Avg. No. of Cards, per Person	1.03

LABOUR FORCE

2001 Estimates:	
Male:	
In the Labour Force	20,057
Participation Rate	67.2
Employed	18,179
Unemployed	1,878
Unemployment Rate	9.4
Not in Labour Force	9,769
Female:	
In the Labour Force	19,826
Participation Rate	55.3
Employed	18,486
Unemployed	1,340
Unemployment Rate	6.8
Not in Labour Force	16,051

OCCUPATIONS BY MAJOR GROUPS

2001 Estimates:	Male	Female
Management	2,228	1,573
Business, Finance & Admin.	2,428	5,230
Natural & Applied Sciences & Related	1,906	510
Health	527	1,805
Social Sciences, Gov't Services & Religion	828	1,257
Education	516	937
Arts, Culture, Recreation & Sport	880	790
Sales & Service	5,954	6,715
Trades, Transport & Equipment Operators & Related	3,024	193
Primary Industries	514	74
Processing, Mfg. & Utilities	599	197

LEVEL OF SCHOOLING

2001 Estimates:	
Population 15 years +	65,703
Less than Grade 9	3,184
Grades 9-13 w/o Certif.	12,607
Grade 9-13 with Certif.	6,319
Trade Certif. /Dip.	1,921
Non-Univ. w/o Certif./Dip.	5,059
Non-Univ. with Certif./Dip.	11,934
Univ. w/o Degree	10,989
Univ. w/o Degree/Certif.	5,806
Univ. with Certif.	5,183
Univ. with Degree	13,690

British Columbia

AVERAGE HOUSEHOLD EXPENDITURES

2001 Estimates:	
Food	$4,739
Shelter	$7,668
Clothing	$1,701
Transportation	$3,885
Health & Personal Care	$1,512
Recr'n, Read'g & Education	$2,630
Taxes & Securities	$9,228
Other	$6,709
Total Expenditures	$38,072

PRIVATE HOUSEHOLDS

2001 Estimates:	
Private Households, Total	41,178
Pop. in Private Households	72,682
Average no. per Household	1.8

FAMILIES

2001 Estimates:	
Families in Private Households	18,113
Husband-Wife Families	14,523
Lone-Parent Families	3,590
Aver. No. Persons per Family	2.5
Aver. No. Sons/Daughters at Home	0.7

HOUSING

2001 Estimates:	
Occupied Private Dwellings	41,178
Owned	15,060
Rented	26,118
Single-Detached House	9,047
Semi-Detached House	1,147
Row Houses	2,025
Apartment, 5+ Storeys	5,850
Owned Apartment, 5+ Storeys	1,668
Apartment, 5 or Fewer Storeys	20,660
Apartment, Detached Duplex	2,299
Other Single-Attached	102
Movable Dwellings	48

VEHICLES

2001 Estimates:	
Model Yrs. '81-'96, No.	30,820
% Total	85.78
Model Yrs. '97-'98, No.	2,981
% Total	8.30
'99 Vehicles registered in Model Yr. '99, No.	2,128
% Total	5.92
Total No. '81-'99	35,929

LEGAL MARITAL STATUS

2001 Estimates: (Age 15+)	
Single (Never Married)	25,843
Legally Married (Not Separated)	22,036
Legally Married (Separated)	2,730
Widowed	6,897
Divorced	8,197

British Columbia

Victoria
(City)
Victoria CMA
(Cont'd)

PSYTE CATEGORIES

2001 Estimates	No. of House-holds	% of Total Hhds.	Index
Urban Gentry	1,001	2.43	135
Brie & Chablis	174	0.42	47
Aging Erudites	2,311	5.61	372
High Rise Sunsets	3,023	7.34	513
Young Urban Professionals	5,915	14.36	757
Young Urban Mix	659	1.60	76
Young Urban Intelligentsia	416	1.01	66
University Enclaves	9,073	22.03	1,080
Young City Singles	8,017	19.47	849
Urban Bohemia	1,006	2.44	209
Town Renters	285	0.69	80
Struggling Downtowns	258	0.63	20
Aged Pensioners	7,102	17.25	1,296
Big City Stress	890	2.16	191
Old Grey Towers	228	0.55	100

FINANCIAL PSYTE

2001 Estimates	No. of House-holds	% of Total Hhds.	Index
Four Star Investors	1,001	2.43	48
Urban Heights	8,400	20.40	474
Bills & Wills	659	1.60	19
Revolving Renters	3,023	7.34	160
Young Urban Struggle	10,495	25.49	539
Towering Debt	8,560	20.79	266
NSF	890	2.16	61
Senior Survivors	7,330	17.80	945

HOME LANGUAGE

2001 Estimates:		% Total
English	71,238	93.83
French	378	0.50
Bulgarian	48	0.06
Chinese	1,349	1.78
Croatian	85	0.11
Finnish	106	0.14
German	82	0.11
Hungarian	64	0.08
Italian	57	0.08
Japanese	105	0.14
Persian (Farsi)	64	0.08
Polish	122	0.16
Punjabi	119	0.16
Russian	47	0.06
Serbo-Croatian	57	0.08
Spanish	286	0.38
Tagalog (Pilipino)	65	0.09
Vietnamese	264	0.35
Other Languages	462	0.61
Multiple Responses	921	1.21
Total	75,919	100.00

BUILDING PERMITS

	1999	1998	1997
		$000	
Value	178,247	71,818	80,444

HOMES BUILT

	1999	1998	1997
No.	87	189	218

TAXATION

Income Class:	1997	% Total
Under $5,000	18,570	9.52
$5,000-$10,000	22,880	11.73
$10,000-$15,000	26,400	13.54
$15,000-$20,000	18,920	9.70
$20,000-$25,000	16,450	8.44
$25,000-$30,000	15,420	7.91
$30,000-$40,000	28,790	14.76
$40,000-$50,000	18,400	9.44
$50,000 +	29,170	14.96
Total Returns, No.	194,990	
Total Income, $000	5,849,960	
Total Taxable Returns	145,480	
Total Tax, $000	1,127,498	
Average Income, $	30,001	
Average Tax, $	7,750	

VITAL STATISTICS

	1997	1996	1995	1994
Births	741	694	730	792
Deaths	1,272	1,244	1,188	1,235
Natural Increase	-531	-550	-458	-443
Marriages	736	784	863	821

Note: Latest available data.

MEDIA INFO
in Victoria, CMA

Williams Lake
(Census Agglomeration)

The Census Agglomeration of Williams Lake includes: Williams Lake, C; Cariboo Subd. B, SRD; One Hundred Mile House, DM; plus several smaller areas. All are in Cariboo Regional District.

POPULATION

July 1, 2001 Estimate	41,697
% Cdn. Total	0.13
% Change, '96 -'01	2.73
Avg. Annual Growth Rate, %	0.54
2003 Projected Population	41,868
2006 Projected Population	41,777
2001 Households Estimate	16,005
2003 Projected Households	16,293
2006 Projected Households	16,713

INCOME

% Above/Below National Average	-11
2001 Total Income Estimate	$780,460,000
% Cdn. Total	0.12
2001 Average Hhld. Income	$48,800
2001 Per Capita	$18,700
2003 Projected Total Income	$821,190,000
2006 Projected Total Income	$884,930,000

RETAIL SALES

% Above/Below National Average	+16
2001 Retail Sales Estimate	$432,210,000
% Cdn. Total	0.16
2001 per Household	$27,000
2001 per Capita	$10,400
2001 No. of Establishments	399
2003 Projected Retail Sales	$448,730,000
2006 Projected Retail Sales	$462,060,000

POPULATION

2001 Estimates:		
Total		41,697
Male		21,183
Female		20,514

Age Groups	Male	Female
0-4	1,267	1,193
5-9	1,478	1,360
10-14	1,667	1,566
15-19	1,707	1,612
20-24	1,520	1,469
25-29	1,334	1,334
30-34	1,370	1,401
35-39	1,551	1,613
40-44	1,726	1,740
45-49	1,731	1,706
50-54	1,518	1,451
55-59	1,219	1,112
60-64	991	897
65-69	825	709
70+	1,279	1,351

DAYTIME POPULATION

2001 Estimates:	
Working Population	19,493
At Home Population	22,204
Total	41,697

INCOME

2001 Estimates:	
Avg. Household Income	$48,763
Avg. Family Income	$52,431
Per Capita Income	$18,717
Male:	
Avg. Employment Income	$33,710
Avg. Employment Income (Full Time)	$44,254
Female:	
Avg. Employment Income	$17,034
Avg. Employment Income (Full Time)	$27,572

DISPOSABLE & DISCRETIONARY INCOME

2001 Estimates:	Per Hhld.
Disposable Income	$37,713
Discretionary Income 1 (minus Food & Shelter)	$26,809
Discretionary Income 2 (minus Food, Shelter, & Other Expenditures)	$18,285

LIQUID ASSETS

1999 Estimates:	Per Hhld.
Equity Investments	$75,735
Interest Bearing Investments	$65,736
Total Liquid Assets	$141,471

CREDIT DATA

July 2000:	
Pool of Credit	$388,938,381
Revolving Credit, No.	63,141
Fixed Loans, No.	26,203
Avg. Credit Limit, per Person	$12,563
Avg. Spent, per Person	$6,326
Satisfactory Ratings, No. per Person	2.71
Avg. No. of Cards, per Person	0.89

LABOUR FORCE

2001 Estimates:	
Male:	
In the Labour Force	12,132
Participation Rate	72.3
Employed	10,648
Unemployed	1,484
Unemployment Rate	12.2
Not in Labour Force	4,639
Female:	
In the Labour Force	9,951
Participation Rate	60.7
Employed	8,991
Unemployed	960
Unemployment Rate	9.6
Not in Labour Force	6,444

OCCUPATIONS BY MAJOR GROUPS

2001 Estimates:	Male	Female
Management	1,201	630
Business, Finance & Admin.	506	2,503
Natural & Applied Sciences & Related	638	152
Health	105	531
Social Sciences, Gov't Services & Religion	181	264
Education	270	486
Arts, Culture, Recreation & Sport	167	184
Sales & Service	1,524	4,079
Trades, Transport & Equipment Operators & Related	3,938	248
Primary Industries	1,871	407
Processing, Mfg. & Utilities	1,513	148

LEVEL OF SCHOOLING

2001 Estimates:	
Population 15 years +	33,166
Less than Grade 9	2,481
Grades 9-13 w/o Certif.	11,064
Grade 9-13 with Certif.	4,794
Trade Certif. /Dip.	1,538
Non-Univ. w/o Certif./Dip.	2,406
Non-Univ. with Certif./Dip.	6,228
Univ. w/o Degree.	2,693
Univ. w/o Degree/Certif.	1,285
Univ. with Certif.	1,408
Univ. with Degree	1,962

Williams Lake
(Census Agglomeration)
(Cont'd)

AVERAGE HOUSEHOLD EXPENDITURES

2001 Estimates:
Food	$5,711
Shelter	$7,137
Clothing	$2,181
Transportation	$6,541
Health & Personal Care	$1,967
Recr'n, Read'g & Education	$3,803
Taxes & Securities	$11,617
Other	$7,954
Total Expenditures	$46,911

PRIVATE HOUSEHOLDS

2001 Estimates:
Private Households, Total	16,005
Pop. in Private Households	41,137
Average no. per Household	2.6

FAMILIES

2001 Estimates:
Families in Private Households	12,544
Husband-Wife Families	11,113
Lone-Parent Families	1,431
Aver. No. Persons per Family	3.0
Aver. No. Sons/Daughters at Home	1.1

HOUSING

2001 Estimates:
Occupied Private Dwellings	16,005
Owned	12,084
Rented	3,709
Band Housing	212
Single-Detached House	11,914
Semi-Detached House	238
Row Houses	436
Apartment, 5 or Fewer Storeys	1,079
Apartment, Detached Duplex	267
Other Single-Attached	55
Movable Dwellings	2,016

VEHICLES

2001 Estimates:
Model Yrs. '81-'96, No.	19,095
% Total	82.57
Model Yrs. '97-'98, No.	2,473
% Total	10.69
'99 Vehicles registered in Model Yr. '99, No.	1,557
% Total	6.73
Total No. '81-'99	23,125

LEGAL MARITAL STATUS

2001 Estimates: (Age 15+)
Single (Never Married)	9,425
Legally Married (Not Separated)	18,450
Legally Married (Separated)	1,280
Widowed	1,387
Divorced	2,624

PSYTE CATEGORIES

2001 Estimates	No. of House-holds	% of Total Hhds.	Index
Town Boomers	2,579	16.11	1,590
Old Towns' New Fringe	367	2.29	59
The New Frontier	6,567	41.03	2,720
Pick-ups & Dirt Bikes	2,147	13.41	1,607
Old Leafy Towns	1,668	10.42	408
Young Grey Collar	326	2.04	243
Quiet Towns	1,292	8.07	379
Rod & Rifle	206	1.29	56
Down, Down East	64	0.40	57
Big Country Families	733	4.58	321

FINANCIAL P$YTE

2001 Estimates	No. of House-holds	% of Total Hhds.	Index
Canadian Comfort	2,579	16.11	166
Miners & Credit-Liners	6,567	41.03	1,296
Tractors & Tradelines	367	2.29	40
Bills & Wills	1,668	10.42	126
Country Credit	2,147	13.41	198
Revolving Renters	326	2.04	44
Rural Family Blues	1,003	6.27	78
Limited Budgets	1,292	8.07	260

HOME LANGUAGE

2001 Estimates		% Total
English	39,808	95.47
French	31	0.07
Chinese	40	0.10
German	523	1.25
Punjabi	634	1.52
Russian	46	0.11
Other Languages	124	0.30
Multiple Responses	491	1.18
Total	41,697	100.00

BUILDING PERMITS

	1999	1998	1997
		$000	
Value	42,068	53,335	22,085

HOMES BUILT

	1999	1998	1997
No	144	129	212

TAXATION

Income Class:	1997	% Total
Under $5,000	3,930	14.90
$5,000-$10,000	3,640	13.80
$10,000-$15,000	3,760	14.25
$15,000-$20,000	2,400	9.10
$20,000-$25,000	1,920	7.28
$25,000-$30,000	1,610	6.10
$30,000-$40,000	2,810	10.65
$40,000-$50,000	2,500	9.48
$50,000 +	3,830	14.52
Total Returns, No.	26,380	
Total Income, $000	688,162	
Total Taxable Returns	17,600	
Total Tax, $000	127,922	
Average Income, $	26,087	
Average Tax, $	7,268	

VITAL STATISTICS

	1997	1996	1995	1994
Births	526	481	500	514
Deaths	246	230	196	197
Natural Increase	280	251	304	317
Marriages	203	253	238	233

Note: Latest available data.

COMMUNITY NEWSPAPER(S)

	Total Circulation
100 Mile House: 100 Mile House Free Press	4,571
Williams Lake: The Tribune Tue./Thu.	5,257
Williams Lake: The Weekender	10,349

RADIO STATION(S)

	Power
CBRL	n.a.
CBUS-FM	n.a.
CFFM-FM	100w
CKBX	n.a.
CKWL	n.a.

TELEVISION STATION(S)

CFJC-TV
CHAN-TV
CITM-TV

British Columbia

Northwest Territories

Note: On April 1, 1999, the territory of Nunavut was created from the eastern part of the Northwest Territories.

POPULATION

July 1, 2001 Estimate	42,197
% Cdn. Total	0.14
% Change, '96 -'01	0.88
Avg. Annual Growth Rate, %	0.18
2003 Projected Population	43,560
2006 Projected Population	45,500
2001 Households Estimate	14,352
2003 Projected Households	14,988
2006 Projected Households	16,108

INCOME

% Above/Below National Average	+16
2001 Total Income Estimate	$1,028,990,000
% Cdn. Total	0.16
2001 Average Hhld. Income	$71,700
2001 Per Capita	$24,400
2003 Projected Total Income	$1,132,010,000
2006 Projected Total Income	$1,319,930,000

RETAIL SALES

% Above/Below National Average	-66
2001 Retail Sales Estimate	$128,650,000
% Cdn. Total	0.05
2001 per Household	$9,000
2001 per Capita	$3,000
2001 No. of Establishments	266
2003 Projected Retail Sales	$136,150,000
2006 Projected Retail Sales	$147,240,000

POPULATION

2001 Estimates:

Total	42,197
Male	21,615
Female	20,582

Age Groups	Male	Female
0-4	2,209	2,103
5-9	2,049	2,008
10-14	1,912	1,805
15-19	1,731	1,589
20-24	1,541	1,452
25-29	1,538	1,551
30-34	1,772	1,792
35-39	1,895	1,877
40-44	1,788	1,717
45-49	1,611	1,487
50-54	1,260	1,111
55-59	888	722
60-64	571	476
65-69	359	322
70+	491	570

DAYTIME POPULATION

2001 Estimates:

Working Population	21,744
At Home Population	20,497
Total	42,241

INCOME

2001 Estimates:

Avg. Household Income	$71,697
Avg. Family Income	$74,924
Per Capita Income	$24,385
Male:	
Avg. Employment Income	$42,557
Avg. Employment Income (Full Time)	$59,732
Female:	
Avg. Employment Income	$29,422
Avg. Employment Income (Full Time)	$44,060

DISPOSABLE & DISCRETIONARY INCOME

2001 Estimates:	Per Hhld.
Disposable Income	$53,912
Discretionary Income 1 (minus Food & Shelter)	$39,765
Discretionary Income 2 (minus Food, Shelter, & Other Expenditures)	$28,318

LIQUID ASSETS

1999 Estimates:	Per Hhld.
Equity Investments	$94,202
Interest Bearing Investments	$83,502
Total Liquid Assets	$177,704

CREDIT DATA

July 2000:

Pool of Credit	$369,063,715
Revolving Credit, No.	43,750
Fixed Loans, No.	19,387
Avg. Credit Limit, per Person	$12,856
Avg. Spent, per Person	$6,956
Satisfactory Ratings, No. per Person	2.14
Avg. No. of Cards, per Person	0.85

LABOUR FORCE

2001 Estimates:

Male:	
In the Labour Force	12,522
Participation Rate	81.1
Employed	10,882
Unemployed	1,640
Unemployment Rate	13.1
Not in Labour Force	2,923
Female:	
In the Labour Force	10,648
Participation Rate	72.6
Employed	9,632
Unemployed	1,016
Unemployment Rate	9.5
Not in Labour Force	4,018

AVERAGE WEEKLY EARNINGS

(Including overtime, industrial aggregate)

	Northwest Territories	Canada
Apr 2000	$810.15	$622.92
Apr 1999	$738.60	$608.07
Apr 1998	$732.30	$608.06
Apr 1997	$722.41	$597.26
Apr 1996	$726.67	$575.79

1999 & 2000 data include Nunavut.

NUMBER OF EMPLOYEES

(Industrial aggregate)

Apr 2000	18,230
Apr 1999	17,890
Apr 1998	23,777
Apr 1997	24,491
Apr 1996	23,817

MANUFACTURING INDUSTRIES

	1997	1992
Plants	25	23
Employees	405	275
	$000	
Salaries, Wages	9,975	8,059
Mfg. Materials, Cost	13,688	30,069
Mfg. Shipments, Value	28,863	48,387
Total Value Added	15,045	11,907

Note: Latest available data.

OCCUPATIONS BY MAJOR GROUPS

2001 Estimates:	Male	Female
Management	1,667	820
Business, Finance & Admin.	1,003	3,231
Natural & Applied Sciences & Related	1,132	244
Health	97	754
Social Sciences, Gov't Services & Religion	555	769
Education	336	712
Arts, Culture, Recreation & Sport	258	299
Sales & Service	2,198	3,306
Trades, Transport & Equipment Operators & Related	3,560	146
Primary Industries	1,121	53
Processing, Mfg. & Utilities	302	61

LEVEL OF SCHOOLING

2001 Estimates:

Population 15 years +	30,111
Less than Grade 9	4,332
Grades 9-13 w/o Certif.	6,618
Grade 9-13 with Certif.	2,597
Trade Certif. /Dip.	1,097
Non-Univ. w/o Certif./Dip.	2,276
Non-Univ. with Certif./Dip.	6,633
Univ. w/o Degree	2,809
Univ. w/o Degree/Certif.	1,287
Univ. with Certif.	1,522
Univ. with Degree	3,749

RETAIL SALES

	1999 $000,000	1998 $000,000
Supermarkets & Groceries	82	100
All Other Food	n.a.	n.a.
Drugs & Patent Medicine	n.a.	n.a.
Shoes	n.a.	n.a.
Men's Clothing	n.a.	n.a.
Women's Clothing	n.a.	n.a.
Other Clothing	n.a.	n.a.
Hhld. Furniture & Appliances	n.a.	6
Hhld. Furnishings	n.a.	n.a.
Motor & Recreation Vehicles	74	76
Gas Service Stations	22	20
Auto Parts, Accessories & Services	n.a.	n.a.
General Merchandise	n.a.	n.a.
Other Semi-Durable Goods	n.a.	14
Other Durable Goods	10	10
Other Retail	n.a.	n.a.
Total	371	511

AVERAGE HOUSEHOLD EXPENDITURES

2001 Estimates:

Food	$7,502
Shelter	$9,211
Clothing	$2,907
Transportation	$9,246
Health & Personal Care	$2,241
Recr'n, Read'g & Education	$5,711
Taxes & Securities	$17,908
Other	$11,599
Total Expenditures	$66,325

PRIVATE HOUSEHOLDS

2001 Estimates:

Private Households, Total	14,352
Pop. in Private Households	41,602
Average no. per Household	2.9

FAMILIES

2001 Estimates:

Families in Private Households	10,973
Husband-Wife Families	9,181
Lone-Parent Families	1,792
Aver. No. Persons per Family	3.4
Aver. No. Sons/Daughters at Home	1.5

HOUSING

2001 Estimates:

Occupied Private Dwellings	14,352
Owned	7,099
Rented	7,187
Band Housing	66
Single-Detached House	7,496
Semi-Detached House	715
Row Houses	1,559
Apartment, 5+ Storeys	532
Owned Apartment, 5+ Storeys	70
Apartment, 5 or Fewer Storeys	2,100
Apartment, Detached Duplex	189
Other Single-Attached	87
Movable Dwellings	1,674

VEHICLES

2001 Estimates:

Model Yrs. '81-'96, No.	91
% Total	5.16
Model Yrs. '97-'98, No.	13
% Total	0.74
'99 Vehicles registered in Model Yr. '99, No.	1,661
% Total	94.11
Total No. '81-'99	1,765

LEGAL MARITAL STATUS

2001 Estimates: (Age 15+)

Single (Never Married)	13,777
Legally Married (Not Separated)	12,593
Legally Married (Separated)	1,041
Widowed	827
Divorced	1,873

PSYTE CATEGORIES

2001 Estimates	No. of House-holds	% of Total Hhds.	Index
Town Boomers	104	0.72	71
Northern Lights	9,104	63.43	12,816
The New Frontier	1,860	12.96	859
Big Country Families	3,187	22.21	1,557
Old Cdn. Rustics	22	0.15	16

FINANCIAL PSYTE

2001 Estimates	No. of House-holds	% of Total Hhds.	Index
Successful Suburbanites	9,104	63.43	956
Canadian Comfort	104	0.72	7
Miners & Credit-Liners	1,860	12.96	409
Rural Family Blues	3,187	22.21	275
Limited Budgets	22	0.15	5

HOME LANGUAGE

2001 Estimates:		% Total
English	37,238	88.25
French	386	0.91
Arabic	31	0.07
Chinese	154	0.36
Chipewyan	204	0.48
Cree	46	0.11
Dogrib	1,419	3.36
Inuktitut (Eskimo)	109	0.26
Kutchin-Gwich'in (Loucheux)	51	0.12
Punjabi	33	0.08
South Slave	1,263	2.99
Spanish	22	0.05
Tagalog (Pilipino)	119	0.28
Vietnamese	164	0.39
Other Languages	398	0.94
Multiple Responses	560	1.33
Total	42,197	100.00

BUILDING PERMITS

	1999	1998	1997
		$000	
Value	41,296	80,217	46,868

CAPITAL EXPENDITURES

(Public & Private)	2000	1999	1998
		$000,000	
Total Expends.	n.a.	n.a.	1,138.7
Capital Expends.	632.2	551.8	972.7
Construction	473.6	419.8	795.9
Machinery & Equip.	158.6	132.0	176.8
Repair Expends.	n.a.	n.a.	166.0
Construction	n.a.	n.a.	62.0
Machinery & Equip.	n.a.	n.a.	104.0

TAXATION

Income Class:	1997	% Total
Under $5,000	3,460	14.31
$5,000-$10,000	2,560	10.59
$10,000-$15,000	2,600	10.75
$15,000-$20,000	1,830	7.57
$20,000-$25,000	1,480	6.12
$25,000-$30,000	1,360	5.62
$30,000-$40,000	2,410	9.97
$40,000-$50,000	2,310	9.55
$50,000 +	6,170	25.52
Total Returns, No.	24,180	
Total Income, $000	815,499	
Total Taxable Returns	17,140	
Total Tax, $000	149,676	
Average Income, $	33,726	
Average Tax, $	8,733	

VITAL STATISTICS

	1997	1996	1995	1994
Births	1,468	1,562	1,613	1,580
Deaths	258	272	227	241
Natural Increase	1,215	1,290	1,386	1,339
Marriages	210	206	218	241

Note: Latest available data.

Northwest Territories

Northwest Territories

Yellowknife
(Census Agglomeration)

The Census Agglomeration of Yellowknife consists solely of Yellowknife, C, in Fort Smith Region.

POPULATION

July 1, 2001 Estimate	18,920
% Cdn. Total	0.06
% Change, '96 -'01	3.93
Avg. Annual Growth Rate, %	0.77
2003 Projected Population	19,790
2006 Projected Population	21,034
2001 Households Estimate	6,735
2003 Projected Households	7,122
2006 Projected Households	7,761

INCOME

% Above/Below National Average	+50
2001 Total Income Estimate	$597,510,000
% Cdn. Total	0.09
2001 Average Hhld. Income	$88,700
2001 Per Capita	$31,600
2003 Projected Total Income	$663,010,000
2006 Projected Total Income	$779,810,000

RETAIL SALES

% Above/Below National Average	-59
2001 Retail Sales Estimate	$69,810,000
% Cdn. Total	0.03
2001 per Household	$10,400
2001 per Capita	$3,700
2001 No. of Establishments	113
2003 Projected Retail Sales	$75,160,000
2006 Projected Retail Sales	$82,850,000

POPULATION

2001 Estimates:

Total	18,920
Male	9,661
Female	9,259

Age Groups	Male	Female
0-4	969	924
5-9	834	813
10-14	788	712
15-19	747	657
20-24	681	625
25-29	701	719
30-34	814	877
35-39	910	963
40-44	906	919
45-49	832	787
50-54	633	557
55-59	404	317
60-64	220	168
65-69	108	91
70+	114	130

DAYTIME POPULATION

2001 Estimates:

Working Population	11,484
At Home Population	7,436
Total	18,920

INCOME

2001 Estimates:

Avg. Household Income	$88,718
Avg. Family Income	$92,395
Per Capita Income	$31,581
Male:	
Avg. Employment Income	$50,046
Avg. Employment Income (Full Time)	$63,922
Female:	
Avg. Employment Income	$33,425
Avg. Employment Income (Full Time)	$45,906

DISPOSABLE & DISCRETIONARY INCOME

2001 Estimates:	Per Hhld.
Disposable Income	$65,762
Discretionary Income 1 (minus Food & Shelter)	$49,488
Discretionary Income 2 (minus Food, Shelter, & Other Expenditures)	$35,874

LIQUID ASSETS

1999 Estimates:	Per Hhld.
Equity Investments	$123,366
Interest Bearing Investments	$104,411
Total Liquid Assets	$227,777

CREDIT DATA

July 2000:

Pool of Credit	$202,278,532
Revolving Credit, No.	25,380
Fixed Loans, No.	9,923
Avg. Credit Limit, per Person	$15,306
Avg. Spent, per Person	$7,933
Satisfactory Ratings, No. per Person	2.61
Avg. No. of Cards, per Person	1.11

LABOUR FORCE

2001 Estimates:

Male:	
In the Labour Force	6,282
Participation Rate	88.9
Employed	5,849
Unemployed	433
Unemployment Rate	6.9
Not in Labour Force	788
Female:	
In the Labour Force	5,497
Participation Rate	80.7
Employed	5,163
Unemployed	334
Unemployment Rate	6.1
Not in Labour Force	1,313

OCCUPATIONS BY MAJOR GROUPS

2001 Estimates:	Male	Female
Management	932	452
Business, Finance & Admin.	635	1,924
Natural & Applied Sciences & Related	723	158
Health	64	409
Social Sciences, Gov't Services & Religion	343	413
Education	93	285
Arts, Culture, Recreation & Sport	166	195
Sales & Service	1,108	1,480
Trades, Transport & Equipment Operators & Related	1,452	73
Primary Industries	553	12
Processing, Mfg. & Utilities	148	32

LEVEL OF SCHOOLING

2001 Estimates:

Population 15 years +	13,880
Less than Grade 9	645
Grades 9-13 w/o Certif.	2,778
Grade 9-13 with Certif.	1,487
Trade Certif. /Dip.	425
Non-Univ. w/o Certif./Dip.	969
Non-Univ. with Certif./Dip.	3,224
Univ. w/o Degree	1,829
Univ. w/o Degree/Certif.	863
Univ. with Certif.	966
Univ. with Degree	2,523

AVERAGE HOUSEHOLD EXPENDITURES

2001 Estimates:

Food	$8,566
Shelter	$10,756
Clothing	$3,374
Transportation	$11,259
Health & Personal Care	$2,553
Recr'n, Read'g & Education	$6,590
Taxes & Securities	$22,887
Other	$14,007
Total Expenditures	$79,992

PRIVATE HOUSEHOLDS

2001 Estimates:

Private Households, Total	6,735
Pop. in Private Households	18,733
Average no. per Household	2.8

FAMILIES

2001 Estimates:

Families in Private Households	5,186
Husband-Wife Families	4,474
Lone-Parent Families	712
Aver. No. Persons per Family	3.2
Aver. No. Sons/Daughters at Home	1.3

HOUSING

2001 Estimates:

Occupied Private Dwellings	6,735
Owned	3,398
Rented	3,337
Single-Detached House	2,376
Semi-Detached House	148
Row Houses	782
Apartment, 5+ Storeys	462
Owned Apartment, 5+ Storeys	70
Apartment, 5 or Fewer Storeys	1,479
Apartment, Detached Duplex	142
Other Single-Attached	24
Movable Dwellings	1,322

VEHICLES

2001 Estimates:

Model Yrs. '81-'96, No.	49
% Total	5.90
Model Yrs. '97-'98, No.	10
% Total	1.20
'99 Vehicles registered in Model Yr. '99, No.	772
% Total	92.90
Total No. '81-'99	831

LEGAL MARITAL STATUS

2001 Estimates: (Age 15+)

Single (Never Married)	5,504
Legally Married (Not Separated)	6,666
Legally Married (Separated)	494
Widowed	215
Divorced	1,001

PSYTE CATEGORIES

2001 Estimates	No. of House -holds	% of Total Hhds.	Index
Northern Lights	6,641	98.60	19,921
Big Country Families	76	1.13	79

FINANCIAL P$YTE

2001 Estimates	No. of House -holds	% of Total Hhds.	Index
Successful Suburbanites	6,641	98.60	1,486
Rural Family Blues	76	1.13	14

HOME LANGUAGE

2001 Estimates:		% Total
English	17,663	93.36
French	299	1.58
Arabic	11	0.06
Chinese	143	0.76
Chipewyan	11	0.06
Cree	11	0.06
Dogrib	66	0.35
Hindi	11	0.06
Inuktitut (Eskimo)	33	0.17
Italian	11	0.06
Macedonian	11	0.06
Polish	11	0.06
Punjabi	22	0.12
Spanish	22	0.12
Tagalog (Pilipino)	98	0.52
Vietnamese	164	0.87
Other Languages	49	0.26
Multiple Responses	284	1.50
Total	18,920	100.00

BUILDING PERMITS

	1999	1998	1997
		$000	
Value	19,505	13,480	12,199

HOMES BUILT

	1999	1998	1997
No.	77	5	19

TAXATION

Income Class:	1997	% Total
Under $5,000	1,070	9.48
$5,000-$10,000	850	7.53
$10,000-$15,000	840	7.44
$15,000-$20,000	750	6.64
$20,000-$25,000	650	5.76
$25,000-$30,000	640	5.67
$30,000-$40,000	1,310	11.60
$40,000-$50,000	1,300	11.51
$50,000 +	3,880	34.37
Total Returns, No.	11,290	
Total Income, $000	471,561	
Total Taxable Returns	9,180	
Total Tax, $000	93,665	
Average Income, $	41,768	
Average Tax, $	10,203	

VITAL STATISTICS

	1997	1996	1995	1994
Births	291	334	331	323
Deaths	44	37	27	46
Natural Increase	247	297	304	277
Marriages	77	77	78	90

Note: Latest available data.

COMMUNITY NEWSPAPER(S)

	Total Circulation
NWT, Nunavut: News North	10,899
Yellowknife: L'Aquilon	n.a.
Yellowknife: Yellowknifer Wed/Fri	5,245

RADIO STATION(S)

	Power
CFYK	2,500w
CJCD	300w
CJCD-FM	n.a.
CKLB-FM	130w

TELEVISION STATION(S)

CATV
CFYK-TV

Nunavut

POPULATION

July 1, 2001 Estimate	28,161
% Cdn. Total	0.09
% Change, '96 -'01	9.40
Avg. Annual Growth Rate, %	1.81
2003 Projected Population	29,750
2006 Projected Population	32,220
2001 Households Estimate	7,381
2003 Projected Households	7,873
2006 Projected Households	8,676

INCOME

% Above/Below National Average	-31
2001 Total Income Estimate	$409,340,000
% Cdn. Total	0.06
2001 Average Hhld. Income	$55,500
2001 Per Capita	$14,500
2003 Projected Total Income	$463,710,000
2006 Projected Total Income	$562,800,000

RETAIL SALES

% Above/Below National Average	-83
2001 Retail Sales Estimate	$42,300,000
% Cdn. Total	0.02
2001 per Household	$5,700
2001 per Capita	$1,500
2001 No. of Establishments	.88
2003 Projected Retail Sales	$44,780,000
2006 Projected Retail Sales	$48,750,000

POPULATION

2001 Estimates:

Total		28,161
Male		14,681
Female		13,480

Age Groups	Male	Female
0-4	1,703	1,615
5-9	1,796	1,698
10-14	1,680	1,576
15-19	1,442	1,323
20-24	1,236	1,153
25-29	1,174	1,127
30-34	1,164	1,120
35-39	1,051	971
40-44	889	750
45-49	748	600
50-54	583	475
55-59	440	362
60-64	325	275
65-69	212	188
70+	238	247

DAYTIME POPULATION

2001 Estimates:

Working Population	10,380
At Home Population	17,781
Total	28,161

INCOME

2001 Estimates:

Avg. Household Income	$55,459
Avg. Family Income	$54,362
Per Capita Income	$14,536
Male:	
Avg. Employment Income	$29,856
Avg. Employment Income (Full Time)	$47,957
Female:	
Avg. Employment Income	$22,282
Avg. Employment Income (Full Time)	$40,337

DISPOSABLE & DISCRETIONARY INCOME

2001 Estimates:	Per Hhld.
Disposable Income	$53,466
Discretionary Income 1 (minus Food & Shelter)	$39,773
Discretionary Income 2 (minus Food, Shelter, & Other Expenditures)	$30,715

LIQUID ASSETS

1999 Estimates:	Per Hhld.
Equity Investments	$62,551
Interest Bearing Investments	$61,785
Total Liquid Assets	$124,336

CREDIT DATA

July 2000:

Pool of Credit	$86,362,751
Revolving Credit, No.	11,728
Fixed Loans, No.	4,515
Avg. Credit Limit, per Person	$6,510
Avg. Spent, per Person	$3,342
Satisfactory Ratings, No. per Person	1.19
Avg. No. of Cards, per Person	0.50

LABOUR FORCE

2001 Estimates:

Male:

In the Labour Force	6,667
Participation Rate	70.2
Employed	5,600
Unemployed	1,067
Unemployment Rate	16.0
Not in Labour Force	2,835

Female:

In the Labour Force	5,292
Participation Rate	61.6
Employed	4,501
Unemployed	791
Unemployment Rate	14.9
Not in Labour Force	3,299

NUMBER OF EMPLOYEES

(Industrial aggregate)

Apr 2000	8,343
Apr 1999	7,918

OCCUPATIONS BY MAJOR GROUPS

2001 Estimates:	Male	Female
Management	746	268
Business, Finance & Admin.	424	1,113
Natural & Applied Sciences & Related	327	33
Health	48	178
Social Sciences, Gov't Services & Religion	197	360
Education	299	647
Arts, Culture, Recreation & Sport	475	373
Sales & Service	1,290	1,825
Trades, Transport & Equipment Operators & Related	2,188	73
Primary Industries	286	18
Processing, Mfg. & Utilities	143	102

LEVEL OF SCHOOLING

2001 Estimates:

Population 15 years +	18,093
Less than Grade 9	5,628
Grades 9-13 w/o Certif.	4,006
Grade 9-13 with Certif.	743
Trade Certif./Dip.	823
Non-Univ. w/o Certif./Dip.	1,923
Non-Univ. with Certif./Dip.	2,976
Univ. w/o Degree	742
Univ. w/o Degree/Certif.	266
Univ. with Certif.	476
Univ. with Degree	1,252

RETAIL SALES

	1999 $000,000	1998 $000,000
Supermarkets & Groceries	30	n.a.
All Other Food	n.a.	n.a.
Drugs & Patent Medicine	n.a.	n.a.
Shoes	n.a.	n.a.
Men's Clothing	n.a.	n.a.
Women's Clothing	n.a.	n.a.
Other Clothing	n.a.	n.a.
Hhld. Furniture & Appliances	n.a.	n.a.
Hhld. Furnishings		n.a.
Motor & Recreation Vehicles	n.a.	n.a.
Gas Service Stations	n.a.	n.a.
Auto Parts, Accessories & Services	n.a.	n.a.
General Merchandise	n.a.	n.a.
Other Semi-Durable Goods	n.a.	n.a.
Other Durable Goods	n.a.	n.a.
Other Retail	1	n.a.
Total	174	n.a.

AVERAGE HOUSEHOLD EXPENDITURES

2001 Estimates:

Food	$7,320
Shelter	$8,500
Clothing	$2,548
Transportation	$6,894
Health & Personal Care	$1,768
Recr'n, Read'g & Education	$5,382
Taxes & Securities	$11,820
Other	$9,849
Total Expenditures	$54,081

PRIVATE HOUSEHOLDS

2001 Estimates:

Private Households, Total	7,381
Pop. in Private Households	27,878
Average no. per Household	3.8

FAMILIES

2001 Estimates:

Families in Private Households	6,249
Husband-Wife Families	5,140
Lone-Parent Families	1,109
Aver. No. Persons per Family	4.0
Aver. No. Sons/Daughters at Home	2.2

HOUSING

2001 Estimates:

Occupied Private Dwellings	7,381
Owned	1,361
Rented	6,020
Single-Detached House	4,620
Semi-Detached House	753
Row Houses	1,362
Apartment, 5+ Storeys	99
Apartment, 5 or Fewer Storeys	367
Apartment, Detached Duplex	79
Other Single-Attached	79
Movable Dwellings	22

VEHICLES

2001 Estimates:

Model Yrs. '81-'96, No.	21
% Total	10.82
Model Yrs. '97-'98, No.	3
% Total	1.55
'99 Vehicles registered in Model Yr. '99, No.	170
% Total	87.63
Total No. '81-'99	194

LEGAL MARITAL STATUS

2001 Estimates: (Age 15+)

Single (Never Married)	9,782
Legally Married (Not Separated)	6,607
Legally Married (Separated)	540
Widowed	630
Divorced	534

PSYTE CATEGORIES

2001 Estimates	No. of House-holds	% of Total Hhds.	Index
Northern Lights	979	13.26	2,680
The New Frontier	72	0.98	65
Big Country Families	6,302	85.38	5,985

FINANCIAL P$YTE

2001 Estimates	No. of House-holds	% of Total Hhds.	Index
Successful Suburbanites	979	13.26	200
Miners & Credit-Liners	72	0.98	31
Rural Family Blues	6,302	85.38	1,058

HOME LANGUAGE

2001 Estimates:		% Total
English	9,963	35.38
French	248	0.88
Inuktitut (Eskimo)	16,812	59.70
Other Languages	56	0.20
Multiple Responses	1,082	3.84
Total	28,161	100.00

BUILDING PERMITS

	1999 $000	1998	1997
Value	49,312	n.a.	n.a.

CAPITAL EXPENDITURES

(Public & Private)	2000 $000,000	1999	1998
Total Expends.	n.a.	n.a.	n.a.
Capital Expends.	245.6	203.5	n.a.
Construction	175.1	143.9	n.a.
Machinery & Equip.	70.5	59.6	n.a.
Repair Expends.	n.a.	n.a.	n.a.
Construction	n.a.	n.a.	n.a.
Machinery & Equip.	n.a.	n.a.	n.a.

TAXATION

Income Class:	1997	% Total
Under $5,000	2,800	21.89
$5,000-$10,000	1,740	13.60
$10,000-$15,000	1,580	12.35
$15,000-$20,000	1,130	8.84
$20,000-$25,000	840	6.57
$25,000-$30,000	610	4.77
$30,000-$40,000	880	6.88
$40,000-$50,000	820	6.41
$50,000 +	2,390	18.69
Total Returns, No.	12,790	
Total Income, $000	341,621	
Total Taxable Returns	7,240	
Total Tax, $000	58,212	
Average Income, $	26,710	
Average Tax, $	8,040	

Yukon

POPULATION

July 1, 2001 Estimate 31,370
% Cdn. Total 0.10
% Change, '96 -'01 . . . . -1.78
Avg. Annual Growth Rate, % . . . . . . -0.36
2003 Projected Population 32,277
2006 Projected Population 33,600
2001 Households Estimate 12,382
2003 Projected Households 12,816
2006 Projected Households 13,651

INCOME

% Above/Below National Average . . . . +11
2001 Total Income Estimate $731,240,000
% Cdn. Total 0.11
2001 Average Hhld. Income $59,100
2001 Per Capita $23,300
2003 Projected Total Income . . . $794,120,000
2006 Projected Total Income . . . $915,040,000

RETAIL SALES

% Above/Below National Average . . . . -41
2001 Retail Sales Estimate $166,890,000
% Cdn. Total 0.06
2001 per Household $13,500
2001 per Capita $5,300
2001 No. of Establishments 295
2003 Projected Retail Sales $174,150,000
2006 Projected Retail Sales $184,440,000

POPULATION

2001 Estimates:
Total 31,370
Male 16,154
Female 15,216

Age Groups	Male	Female
0-4	1,153	1,075
5-9	1,240	1,112
10-14	1,309	1,180
15-19	1,206	1,101
20-24	1,073	1,030
25-29	1,068	1,084
30-34	1,210	1,328
35-39	1,398	1,522
40-44	1,533	1,526
45-49	1,457	1,345
50-54	1,187	1,023
55-59	853	676
60-64	581	428
65-69	418	265
70+	468	521

DAYTIME POPULATION

2001 Estimates:
Working Population 14,723
At Home Population 16,688
Total 31,411

INCOME

2001 Estimates:
Avg. Household Income $59,057
Avg. Family Income $65,693
Per Capita Income $23,310
Male:
Avg. Employment Income $34,102
Avg. Employment Income
  (Full Time) $50,142
Female:
Avg. Employment Income $26,758
Avg. Employment Income
  (Full Time) $40,151

DISPOSABLE & DISCRETIONARY INCOME

2001 Estimates: Per Hhld.
Disposable Income $44,941
Discretionary Income 1
  (minus Food & Shelter) $33,014
Discretionary Income 2
  (minus Food, Shelter, & Other
  Expenditures) $23,386

LIQUID ASSETS

1999 Estimates: Per Hhld.
Equity Investments $80,997
Interest Bearing Investments $73,252
Total Liquid Assets $154,249

CREDIT DATA

July 2000:
Pool of Credit $322,760,150
Revolving Credit, No. 43,771
Fixed Loans, No. 20,164
Avg. Credit Limit, per Person $14,121
Avg. Spent, per Person $7,250
Satisfactory Ratings,
  No. per Person 2.65
Avg. No. of Cards, per Person 1.04

LABOUR FORCE

2001 Estimates:
Male:
In the Labour Force 10,303
Participation Rate 82.7
Employed 9,123
Unemployed 1,180
Unemployment Rate 11.5
Not in Labour Force 2,149
Female:
In the Labour Force 9,132
Participation Rate 77.1
Employed 8,240
Unemployed 892
Unemployment Rate 9.8
Not in Labour Force 2,717

AVERAGE WEEKLY EARNINGS

(Including overtime, industrial aggregate)

	Yukon Territory	Canada
Apr 2000	$695.69	$622.92
Apr 1999	$662.53	$608.07
Apr 1998	$686.56	$608.06
Apr 1997	$719.02	$597.26
Apr 1996	$693.54	$575.79

NUMBER OF EMPLOYEES

(Industrial aggregate)
Apr 2000 14,465
Apr 1999 14,430
Apr 1998 13,653
Apr 1997 13,140
Apr 1996 11,763

MANUFACTURING INDUSTRIES

	1997	1992
Plants	20	24
Employees	188	203
	$000	
Salaries, Wages	6,239	5,927
Mfg. Materials, Cost	12,915	7,788
Mfg. Shipments, Value	21,513	19,639
Total Value Added	7,662	12,255

Note: Latest available data.

OCCUPATIONS BY MAJOR GROUPS

2001 Estimates:	Male	Female
Management	1,263	705
Business, Finance & Admin.	647	2,683
Natural & Applied Sciences & Related	908	186
Health	124	426
Social Sciences, Gov't Services & Religion	377	732
Education	277	547
Arts, Culture, Recreation & Sport	238	311
Sales & Service	2,035	2,941
Trades, Transport & Equipment Operators & Related	3,235	267
Primary Industries	678	93
Processing, Mfg. & Utilities	319	70

LEVEL OF SCHOOLING

2001 Estimates:
Population 15 years + ... 24,301
Less than Grade 9 1,279
Grades 9-13 w/o Certif. 5,298
Grade 9-13 with Certif. 2,063
Trade Certif./Dip. 974
Non-Univ. w/o Certif./Dip. 2,108
Non-Univ. with Certif./Dip. 6,099
Univ. w/o Degree 2,908
  Univ. w/o Degree/Certif. 1,276
  Univ. with Certif. 1,632
Univ. with Degree 3,572

RETAIL SALES

	1999 $000,000	1998 $000,000
Supermarkets & Groceries	99	97
All Other Food	n.a.	n.a.
Drugs & Patent Medicine	n.a.	n.a.
Shoes	n.a.	n.a.
Men's Clothing	3	3
Women's Clothing	n.a.	n.a.
Other Clothing	5	n.a.
Hhld. Furniture & Appliances	n.a.	n.a.
Hhld. Furnishings	n.a.	n.a.
Motor & Recreation Vehicles	n.a.	58
Gas Service Stations	n.a.	n.a.
Auto Parts, Accessories & Services	n.a.	n.a.
General Merchandise	n.a.	n.a.
Other Semi-Durable Goods	14	14
Other Durable Goods	n.a.	n.a.
Other Retail	13	n.a.
Total	329	312

AVERAGE HOUSEHOLD EXPENDITURES

2001 Estimates:
Food $6,285
Shelter $7,816
Clothing $2,431
Transportation $7,730
Health & Personal Care $1,925
Recr'n, Read'g & Education $4,712
Taxes & Securities $15,252
Other $9,807
Total Expenditures $55,958

PRIVATE HOUSEHOLDS

2001 Estimates:
Private Households, Total 12,382
Pop. in Private Households 30,050
Average no. per Household 2.4

FAMILIES

2001 Estimates:
Families in Private Households 8,676
Husband-Wife Families 7,317
Lone-Parent Families 1,359
Aver. No. Persons per Family 3.0
Aver. No. Sons/Daughters
  at Home 1.2

HOUSING

2001 Estimates:
Occupied Private Dwellings 12,382
  Owned 7,324
  Rented 4,308
  Band Housing .750
Single-Detached House 8,004
Semi-Detached House 594
Row Houses 602
Apartment, 5 or Fewer Storeys 1,486
Apartment, Detached Duplex 460
Other Single-Attached 75
Movable Dwellings 1,161

VEHICLES

2001 Estimates:
Model Yrs. '81-'96, No. 95
  % Total 45.24
Model Yrs. '97-'98, No. 31
  % Total 14.76
'99 Vehicles registered in
  Model Yr. '99, No. 84
  % Total 40.00
Total No. '81-'99 210

LEGAL MARITAL STATUS

2001 Estimates: (Age 15+)
Single (Never Married) 9,527
Legally Married
  (Not Separated) 10,608
Legally Married (Separated) 1,128
Widowed 730
Divorced 2,308

PSYTE CATEGORIES

2001 Estimates	No. of House-holds	% of Total Hhds.	Index
Town Boomers	156	1.26	124
Northern Lights	8,245	66.59	13,453
The New Frontier	1,133	9.15	607
Young Grey Collar	936	7.56	904
Quiet Towns	188	1.52	71
Big Country Families	1,510	12.20	855

FINANCIAL P$YTE

2001 Estimates	No. of House-holds	% of Total Hhds.	Index
Successful Suburbanites	8,245	66.59	1,003
Canadian Comfort	156	1.26	13
Miners & Credit-Liners	1,133	9.15	289
Revolving Renters	936	7.56	164
Rural Family Blues	1,510	12.20	151
Limited Budgets	188	1.52	49

HOME LANGUAGE

2001 Estimates:		% Total
English	29,829	95.09
French	504	1.61
Chinese	73	0.23
German	134	0.43
Kutchin-Gwich'in (Loucheux)	35	0.11
Persian (Farsi)	40	0.13
Punjabi	50	0.16
Spanish	20	0.06
Vietnamese	159	0.51
Other Languages	193	0.62
Multiple Responses	333	1.06
Total	31,370	100.00

BUILDING PERMITS

	1999	1998	1997
		$000	
Value	48,779	39,943	49,626

CAPITAL EXPENDITURES

(Public & Private)	2000	1999	1998
		$000,000	
Total Expends	n.a.	n.a.	293.1
Capital Expends	272.3	251.7	211.6
Construction	166.9	172.5	140.5
Machinery & Equip.	105.3	79.2	71.1
Repair Expends	n.a.	n.a.	81.5
Construction	n.a.	n.a.	14.7
Machinery & Equip.	n.a.	n.a.	66.7

TAXATION

Income Class:	1997	% Total
Under $5,000	2,600	12.90
$5,000-$10,000	2,040	10.12
$10,000-$15,000	2,100	10.42
$15,000-$20,000	1,710	8.48
$20,000-$25,000	1,550	7.69
$25,000-$30,000	1,430	7.09
$30,000-$40,000	2,610	12.95
$40,000-$50,000	2,160	10.71
$50,000 +	3,970	19.69
Total Returns, No.	20,160	
Total Income, $000	615,307	
Total Taxable Returns	14,460	
Total Tax, $000	100,594	
Average Income, $	30,521	
Average Tax, $	6,957	

VITAL STATISTICS

	1997	1996	1995	1994
Births	474	443	470	442
Deaths	123	120	157	124
Natural Increase	351	323	313	318
Marriages	240	197	207	169

Note: Latest available data.

TRAVEL STATISTICS

Tourists in Canada	1999	1998
From the U.S. entering by:		
Automobile	184,993	180,199
Bus	52,949	44,339
Rail	30,852	26,950
Air	4,442	7,558
Marine	6,127	3,763
Other Methods	2,691	1,555
Total	282,054	264,364
Other Countries:		
Land (via U.S.)	29,238	28,416
Air	3,043	5,624
Marine	268	160
Total	32,549	34,200
Residents of Canada		
Returning from the U.S. by:		
Automobile	59,305	65,422
Bus	5,969	7,362
Rail	119	313
Air	1,356	1,858
Marine	529	275
Other Methods	654	542
Total	67,932	75,772
From Other Countries:		
Air	10	146
Total	10	146

Yukon

Yukon

Whitehorse
(Census Agglomeration)

The Census Agglomeration of Whitehorse consists of Whitehorse, C, plus several smaller areas, in census division Yukon.

POPULATION

July 1, 2001 Estimate	21,792
% Cdn. Total	0.07
% Change, '96 -'01	-3.74
Avg. Annual Growth Rate, %	-0.76
2003 Projected Population	22,143
2006 Projected Population	22,639
2001 Households Estimate	8,610
2003 Projected Households	8,812
2006 Projected Households	9,236

INCOME

% Above/Below National Average	+21
2001 Total Income Estimate	$553,810,000
% Cdn. Total	0.08
2001 Average Hhld. Income	$64,300
2001 Per Capita	$25,400
2003 Projected Total Income	$594,420,000
2006 Projected Total Income	$673,080,000

RETAIL SALES

% Above/Below National Average	-23
2001 Retail Sales Estimate	$150,550,000
% Cdn. Total	0.05
2001 per Household	$17,500
2001 per Capita	$6,900
2001 No. of Establishments	211
2003 Projected Retail Sales	$157,280,000
2006 Projected Retail Sales	$166,220,000

POPULATION

2001 Estimates:

Total		21,792
Male		11,023
Female		10,769

Age Groups	Male	Female
0-4	776	738
5-9	830	771
10-14	900	822
15-19	857	784
20-24	752	726
25-29	727	747
30-34	789	902
35-39	919	1,054
40-44	1,039	1,095
45-49	1,028	1,008
50-54	848	770
55-59	597	496
60-64	390	316
65-69	268	189
70+	303	351

DAYTIME POPULATION

2001 Estimates:

Working Population	10,628
At Home Population	11,165
Total	21,793

INCOME

2001 Estimates:

Avg. Household Income	$64,322
Avg. Family Income	$71,538
Per Capita Income	$25,414
Male:	
Avg. Employment Income	$36,275
Avg. Employment Income (Full Time)	$52,653
Female:	
Avg. Employment Income	$29,538
Avg. Employment Income (Full Time)	$42,668

DISPOSABLE & DISCRETIONARY INCOME

2001 Estimates:	*Per Hhld.*
Disposable Income	$48,702
Discretionary Income 1 (minus Food & Shelter)	$35,990
Discretionary Income 2 (minus Food, Shelter, & Other Expenditures)	$25,736

LIQUID ASSETS

1999 Estimates:	*Per Hhld.*
Equity Investments	$87,888
Interest Bearing Investments	$78,980
Total Liquid Assets	$166,868

CREDIT DATA

July 2000:

Pool of Credit	$244,223,266
Revolving Credit, No.	33,415
Fixed Loans, No.	14,602
Avg. Credit Limit, per Person	$15,191
Avg. Spent, per Person	$7,730
Satisfactory Ratings, No. per Person	2.83
Avg. No. of Cards, per Person	1.13

LABOUR FORCE

2001 Estimates:

Male:	
In the Labour Force	7,143
Participation Rate	83.9
Employed	6,404
Unemployed	739
Unemployment Rate	10.3
Not in Labour Force	1,374
Female:	
In the Labour Force	6,684
Participation Rate	79.2
Employed	6,076
Unemployed	608
Unemployment Rate	9.1
Not in Labour Force	1,754

OCCUPATIONS BY MAJOR GROUPS

2001 Estimates:	*Male*	*Female*
Management	916	524
Business, Finance & Admin.	541	2,195
Natural & Applied Sciences & Related	705	173
Health	106	365
Social Sciences, Gov't Services & Religion	329	555
Education	232	393
Arts, Culture, Recreation & Sport	179	184
Sales & Service	1,561	1,916
Trades, Transport & Equipment Operators & Related	1,957	162
Primary Industries	301	30
Processing, Mfg. & Utilities	175	60

LEVEL OF SCHOOLING

2001 Estimates:

Population 15 years +	16,955
Less than Grade 9	689
Grades 9-13 w/o Certif.	3,815
Grade 9-13 with Certif.	1,408
Trade Certif. /Dip.	540
Non-Univ. w/o Certif./Dip.	1,415
Non-Univ. with Certif./Dip.	3,968
Univ. w/o Degree	2,186
Univ. w/o Degree/Certif.	953
Univ. with Certif.	1,233
Univ. with Degree	2,934

AVERAGE HOUSEHOLD EXPENDITURES

2001 Estimates:

Food	$6,660
Shelter	$8,379
Clothing	$2,573
Transportation	$8,286
Health & Personal Care	$2,020
Recr'n, Read'g & Education	$4,976
Taxes & Securities	$16,757
Other	$10,605
Total Expenditures	$60,256

PRIVATE HOUSEHOLDS

2001 Estimates:

Private Households, Total	8,610
Pop. in Private Households	21,361
Average no. per Household	2.5

FAMILIES

2001 Estimates:

Families in Private Households	6,171
Husband-Wife Families	5,159
Lone-Parent Families	1,012
Aver. No. Persons per Family	3.1
Aver. No. Sons/Daughters at Home	1.2

HOUSING

2001 Estimates:

Occupied Private Dwellings	8,610
Owned	5,575
Rented	2,846
Band Housing	189
Single-Detached House	5,109
Semi-Detached House	478
Row Houses	365
Apartment, 5 or Fewer Storeys	1,275
Apartment, Detached Duplex	438
Other Single-Attached	52
Movable Dwellings	893

VEHICLES

2001 Estimates:

Model Yrs. '81-'96, No.	65
% Total	46.10
Model Yrs. '97-'98, No.	20
% Total	14.18
'99 Vehicles registered in Model Yr. '99, No.	56
% Total	39.72
Total No. '81-'99	141

LEGAL MARITAL STATUS

2001 Estimates: (Age 15+)

Single (Never Married)	6,342
Legally Married (Not Separated)	7,694
Legally Married (Separated)	765
Widowed	470
Divorced	1,684

PSYTE CATEGORIES

2001 Estimates	No. of House -holds	% of Total Hhds.	Index
Town Boomers	156	1.81	179
Northern Lights	6,842	79.47	16,055
Young Grey Collar	868	10.08	1,205
Quiet Towns	188	2.18	103
Big Country Families	522	6.06	425

FINANCIAL PSYTE

2001 Estimates	No. of House -holds	% of Total Hhds.	Index
Successful Suburbanites	6,842	79.47	1,197
Canadian Comfort	156	1.81	19
Revolving Renters	868	10.08	219
Rural Family Blues	522	6.06	75
Limited Budgets	188	2.18	70

HOME LANGUAGE

2001 Estimates:		% Total
English	20,737	95.16
French	411	1.89
Chinese	73	0.33
Czech	11	0.05
German	54	0.25
Persian (Farsi)	40	0.18
Punjabi	50	0.23
Spanish	20	0.09
Vietnamese	159	0.73
Other Languages	80	0.37
Multiple Responses	157	0.72
Total	21,792	100.00

BUILDING PERMITS

	1999	1998 *$000*	1997
Value	19,884	22,874	30,135

TAXATION

Income Class:	1997	% Total
Under $5,000	1,720	11.41
$5,000-$10,000	1,420	9.42
$10,000-$15,000	1,440	9.55
$15,000-$20,000	1,260	8.36
$20,000-$25,000	1,190	7.89
$25,000-$30,000	1,060	7.03
$30,000-$40,000	2,000	13.26
$40,000-$50,000	1,750	11.60
$50,000 +	3,240	21.49
Total Returns, No.	15,080	
Total Income, $000	487,516	
Total Taxable Returns	11,390	
Total Tax, $000	82,415	
Average Income, $	32,329	
Average Tax, $	7,236	

VITAL STATISTICS

	1997	1996	1995	1994
Births	304	297	310	309
Deaths	81	76	97	83
Natural Increase	223	221	213	226
Marriages	111	122	136	112

Note: Latest available data.

DAILY NEWSPAPER(S)

	Circulation Average Paid
The Whitehorse Star	
Fri.	3,923
Mon-Thu	2,234

COMMUNITY NEWSPAPER(S)

	Total Circulation
Whitehorse: L'Aurore Boréale (biwkly)	947
Whitehorse: Yukon News	
Mon	5,575
Wed	6,483
Fri	7,821

RADIO STATION(S)

	Power
CBUF-FM	n.a.
CFWH	5,000w
CHON-FM	n.a.
CKRW	1,000w

TELEVISION STATION(S)

CATV

Glossary of Terms

A & E (TV Station Data) - Stands for Arts & Entertainment.

AOR (Radio Station Data) - Stands for Album Oriented Rock.

ASN (TV Station Data) - Stands for Atlantic Satellite Network.

All Other Food Stores (Retail Sales Table) - Refers to bakery products stores, candy and nut stores, fruit and vegetable stores, meat markets, and other specialty food stores, e.g. health food stores, fish and seafood stores.

All Other Retail (Retail Sales Table) - Refers to liquor stores; wine stores; beer stores; second-hand merchandise stores, opticians' shops; art galleries and artists' supply stores; luggage and leather goods stores; monument and tombstone dealers; pet stores; coin and stamp dealers; mobile home dealers, and other retail stores, which include catalogue sales showrooms, health appliance stores, hearing aids, newspaper and magazine stores, orthopedic aids, picture framing, religious goods, saunas, swimming pools, tobacco stores and stands, water conditioning equipment, and wine making supplies.

Apartment, 5+ storeys (Housing Table) - A dwelling unit in a high-rise building which has five or more storeys.

Apartment, 5 or fewer storeys (Housing Table) - A dwelling unit attached to other dwelling units, commercial units, or other non-residential space in a building that has five or fewer storeys.

Art, Culture, Recreation & Sport Occupations - (Occupations) Occupations in this broad occupational category are primarily concerned with providing artistic and cultural services and providing direct support to the service providers. Occupations include writers and editors, translators, singers, musicians, dancers, actors, artists, graphic artists, interior designers, fashion designers, set decorators, film camera operators, athletes, athletic coaches and audio engineers.

Automotive parts, accessories and services (Retail Sales Table) - Refers to home and auto supply stores, tire, battery, parts and accessories stores, garages (general repairs), paint and body repair shops, muffler replacement shops, motor vehicle glass replacement shops, motor vehicle transmission repair and replacement shops, other motor vehicle repair shops (e.g. air conditioning installation and repair, brake repair, electrical repair, front end alignment, vehicle suspension, vehicle upholstery and radiator repair), car washes, and other motor vehicle services (e.g. van customizing, vehicle diagnosis, rustproofing, surface treating, towing and undercoating).

Average Credit Limit - The amount ($) of authorized credit for all tradelines that have had activity within the past year divided by the number of persons with credit.

Average employment income - For males or females. The aggregate employment income for males or females 15 years of age or over divided by those males or females 15 years of age or over with employment income. Employment income refers to the total income received by persons 15 years of age and over as wages and salaries, and net income from unincorporated non-farm business and/or professional practice and net farm self-employment income. See also "employment income".

Average employment income (full time) - For males or females who work 49-52 weeks a year, mostly full-time. The aggregate employment income for males or females 15 years of age or over divided by those males or females 15 years of age or over with employment income. Employment income refers to the total income received by persons 15 years of age and over as wages and salaries, and net income from unincorporated non-farm business and/or professional practice and net farm self-employment income. See also "employment income".

Average Family Income - The aggregated total income of census families in private households, divided by the total number of census families whether or not they have income.

Average hours tuned in to a radio or a television station - The average number of hours each listener in an area is tuned in to a station during the week, defined to be Monday through Sunday, 5:00 a.m. to 1:00 a.m. for radio stations, and Monday through Sunday, 6:00 a.m. to 2:00 a.m. for television stations.

Average household income - The aggregated total income of households divided by the total number of households whether or not they have income.

Average Income - Average income refers to the weighted mean total income of a group of income units (individuals, families or households) and is calculated from unrounded data by dividing the aggregate income of the group by the number of units in that group. In the case of individuals, average income is calculated only for individuals with income (positive or negative). In all other cases, both with and without income units are included in the calculation.

Average income (Taxation Statistics Table) Total income from all tax returns divided by total returns.

Average number of cards - Average number of national credit cards (e.g., VISA, AMEX) cards per person with credit.

Average number of sons and daughters at home per family (Family Table) - Refers to never-married sons and daughters. See also "never-married sons and/or daughters".

Average Spent - The outstanding balance amount for all tradelines that have had activity within the past year divided by the number of persons with credit.

Average tax (Taxation Statistics Table) - Total tax divided by the total number of taxable returns.

Average weekly earnings (including overtime): represent gross taxable payrolls divided by the number of employees. It is calculated for the total number of employees, for the hourly-rated employees, for the salaried employees and for the other types of employees. Payrolls exclude dollar amounts that are taxable allowances and benefits, certain types of non-wage compensation as well as employer contributions to unemployment insurance, Canada/Quebec pension plans, provincial medical plan, workers compensation and other welfare plans. Annual special payments are excluded while other lump sum special payments are adjusted to coincide with the reference week period. Please note that in 1996 StatsCan expanded its use of administrative data in preparing its estimates. Therefore, for consistency, historical estimates have been revised to reflect this change.

Band housing (Housing Table) - Refers to shelter occupancy on Indian reserves.

Biweekly (Community Newspapers table) - Refers to publications published every other week.

Building permits value - Estimated value of construction for residential, industrial, commercial, institutional and government structures as given on the building permits issued during the years specified.

Business, Finance & Administrative Occupations (Occupations) - Occupations in this broad occupational category are primarily concerned with providing financial and business services, administrative and regulatory services and clerical support services. Occupations include professionals in business and finance (stock brokers, financial analysts), finance and insurance administrators (including clerical), and secretaries (including legal secretaries and clerical supervisors as well as data entry clerks, telephone operators and administrative support personnel). Human Resource personnel are also included in this category.

Buying power indices - Market ratings determined by expressing the income and retail sales on a per capita basis and then relating to the national per capita average to produce income and market rating indices, respectively. An index of 100 indicates the market is on par with the national average for that rating. Each rating has it own usage. Moreover, a comparison of the two will often yield valuable information by indicating the extent to which an area attracts buyers from other areas. If an area has a low income rating but a high market rating it is probable that a large volume of sales is made to residents of surrounding territories. Conversely, a high income rating coupled with a low sales rating suggests that the people who live in the area make extensive purchases elsewhere.

Capital expenditures (Capital Expenditure Table) - The cost of procuring, constructing and installing new durable plant and machinery, whether for replacement of worn or obsolete assets, or as net additions to existing assets. Included are all capitalized costs such as architectural, legal, and engineering fees, as well as the value of work on capital assets undertaken by firms with their own labor forces. No deductions are made for scrap or the trade-in value of old assets. Capital expenditures cover total outlays by Canadian business, institutions and governments, as well as expenditures for housing. Figures for 2000 are stated spending intentions, while 1999 figures are preliminary actual and 1998 are actual. Tables for Canada and the provinces include all sectors, e.g. manufacturing, utilities, trade, etc.

Census Agglomeration (CA) - A census agglomeration (CA) is a large urban area (known as the urban core) together with adjacent urban and rural areas (known as urban and rural fringes) that have a high degree of social and economic integration with the urban core. A CA has an urban core population of at least 10,000, based

on the previous census. However, if the population of the urban core of a CA declines below 10,000, the CA is retired. Once a CA attains an urban core population of at least 100,000, based on the previous census, it is eligible to become a CMA. CAs that have urban cores of at least 50,000, based on the previous census, are subdivided into census tracts. Census tracts are maintained for CAs even if the population of the urban cores subsequently falls below 50,000. A CA may be consolidated with adjacent CAs if they are socially and economically integrated. This new grouping is called a consolidated CA and the component CAs are called primary census agglomerations (PCAs).

Census Division (CD) - Refers to the general term applying to geographic areas established by provincial law, which are intermediate geographic areas between the census subdivision and the province (e.g., counties, regional districts, regional municipalities and other types of provincially legislated areas). In Newfoundland, Manitoba, Saskatchewan and Alberta, provincial law does not provide for these administrative geographic areas. Therefore, census divisions have been created by Statistics Canada in co-operation with these provinces. In the Yukon Territory, the census division is equivalent to the entire territory.

Census Metropolitan Area (CMA) - A census metropolitian area (CMA) is a very large urban area (known as the urban core) together with adjacent urban and rural areas (known as urban and rural fringes) that have a high degree of social and economic integration with the urban core. A CMA has an urban core population of at least 100,000, based on the previous census. Once an area becomes a CMA, it is retained as a CMA even if the population of its urban core declines below 100,00. All CMAs are subdivided into census tracts. A CMA may be consolidated with adjacent census agglomerations (CAs) if they are socially and economiocally integrated. This new grouping is known as a consolidated CMA and the component CMA and CA(s) are known as the primary census metropolitian area (PCMA) and primary census agglomeration(s) (PCA(s)). A CMA may not be consolidated with another CMA.

Census Subdivision (CSD) - The general term applying to municipalities, Indian reserves, Indian settlements and unorganized territories. In Newfoundland, Nova Scotia and British Columbia, the term also describes geostatistical areas that have been created by Statistics Canada in co-operation with the provinces as equivalents for municipalities. The complete set of census subdivision types employed by Statistics Canada is as follows:

BOR	Borough
C	City – Cité
CC	Chartered Community
CM	County (Municipality)
COM	Community
CT	Canton (Municipalité de)
CU	Cantons unis (Municipalité de)
DM	District (Municipality)
HAM	Hamlet
ID	Improvement District
IGD	Indian Government District
LGD	Local Government District
LOT	Township and Royalty
M	Municipalité
MD	Municipal District
NH	Northern Hamlet
NT	Northern Town
NV	Northern Village
P	Paroisse (Municipalité de)
PAR	Parish
R	Indian Reserve – Réserve indienne
RC	Rural Community
RGM	Regional Municipality
RM	Rural Municipality
RV	Resort Village
SA	Special Area
SCM	Subdivision of County Municipality
S-E	Indian Settlement – Établissement Indien
SET	Settlement
SM	Specialized Municipality
SRD	Subdivision of Regional District
SUN	Subdivision of Unorganized
SV	Summer Village
T	Town
TI	Terre inuite
TP	Township
TR	Terres Réservées
UNO	Unorganized – Non organisé
V	Ville
VC	Village Cri
VK	Village Naskapi
VL	Village
VN	Village Nordique

CNN (TV Station Data) - Stands for Cable News Network.

Community Newspapers - Newspapers which do not publish daily editions and which usually circulate in a small area. In this book, unless stated otherwise, community newspapers are published weekly.

Construction (Capital Expenditures Table) - The value of building construction and all types of engineering construction such as roads, dams, transmission lines and pipelines, as well as oil drilling and mine equipment.

Consumer price index - A price index which measures the percentage change through time of a constant quantity and quality of goods and services purchased by a representative Canadian urban family in a specified time period. The index is not a measure of true inflationary or deflationary trends: it only measures percentage changes of a 'basket' of commodities - not all items which contribute to inflation or deflation are included.

Contemp. (Radio Station Data) - Stands for Contemporary.

Daytime Population - The number of people in a particular area during daytime hours.

Discretionary Income - Refers to the household income that is left after federal and provincial taxes and basic necessities have been met. Compusearch has the defined the following "basic necessities" as part of its Discretionary Income product: food, shelter, child care, household operations, health care, transportation, personal care supplies, and telephone. Each of these components can be separated out of the discretionary income measure. For the present purpose, Discretionary Income 1, subtracts food and shelter, whereas Discretionary Income 2 subtracts all eight expenditure categories.

Disposable Income - Refers to the household income that is left after federal and provincial income tax deductions as well as statutory deductions (e.g., CPP/QPP, EI).

Drugs and Patent Medicine Stores (Retail Sales Table) - Includes pharmacies primarily engaged in retail dealing in drugs, pharmaceuticals and patent medicines and drug sundries. Prescribed medicines must be sold but are not necessarily the source of greatest revenue. They may be secondarily engaged in selling other lines such as cosmetics, toiletries, tobacco products, confectionery, stationery, giftware and novelty merchandise. This category also includes patent medicine and toiletries stores which are primarily engaged in retail dealing in patent or proprietary medicines, drug sundries, toiletries and cosmetics. Included are stores primarily engaged in making up and selling herbal medicines. They also may carry a number of secondary lines such as tobacco products, confectionery, stationery, giftware and novelty merchandise.

DSCVRY (TV Station Data) - Stands for The Discovery Channel.

Economic regions (ER) - A grouping of complete census divisions (with one exception in Ontario). Prince Edward Island and the two territories each consist of one economic region. Economic regions are used to analyse regional economic activity.

ECRAN (TV Station Data) - Stands for Super Ecran.

Education Occupations (Occupations) - Occupations in this major group are primarily concerned with teaching. Occupations include both teachers and professors.

Employed - Refers to persons 15 years of age and over (excluding institutional residents) who: a) do any work at all for pay or in self-employment (excluding household activities or volunteer work); or b) are absent from their job or business because of vacation, illness, a labor dispute at their place of work, or are absent for other reasons.

Employee (Number of Employees Table) - All persons drawing pay for services rendered or for paid absences and for whom the employer must complete a Revenue Canada T-4 Supplementary Form constitute employees. The employee concept comprises full-time employees, part-time employees (those who regularly work fewer hours than the standard work week of the establishment). It also comprises working owners, directors, partners and other officers of incorporated businesses.

The employee concept excludes owners or partners of unincorporated businesses and professional practices, the self employed, unpaid family workers, persons working outside Canada, military personnel, and casual workers for whom a T-4 is not required. It also excludes persons who did not receive any pay from the employer for the entire survey reference period (e.g. persons on strike, persons on unpaid holidays, persons receiving remuneration from an insurance, Workmen's compensation or other related fund, etc.); however, employees paid from the employer for a part of the reference period and unemployed or on strike for the rest are counted as employed.

Please note that in 1996, StatsCan expanded its use of administrative data in preparing its estimates. Therefore, for consistency, historical estimates have been revised to reflect this change.

Employment Income - Refers to total income received by persons 15 years of age and over as wages and salaries, net income from unincorporated non-farm business and/or professional practice and net farm self-employment income. Wages and salaries refer to gross wages and salaries before deductions for such items as income tax, pensions, unemployment insurance, etc., and include military pay and allowances, tips, commissions, cash bonuses, as well as all types of casual earnings. Net income from unincorporated non-farm Business and/or Professional Practice refers to net income (gross receipts minus expenses of operation such as wages, rents and depreciation) received from the respondent's non-farm unincorporated business or professional practice. In the

case of a partnership, only the respondent's share was to be reported. Also included is net income from persons babysitting in their own homes, operators of direct distributorships such as those selling and delivering cosmetics, as well as from free-lance activities of artists, writers, music teachers, hairdressers, dressmakers, etc. Net farm self-employment income refers to net income (gross receipts from farm sales minus depreciation and cost of operation) from the operation of a farm, either on own account or in partnership. In the case of partnerships, only the respondent's share of income was reported. Also included are advances, dividends from cooperatives, gross insurance proceeds, and all rebates and farm-support, supplementary or assistance payments to farmers by federal or provincial governments. However, the value of income "in kind", such as agricultural products produced and consumed on the farm, is excluded.

Equity Investments (Liquid Assets) - Include Mutual Funds and Stocks. Mutual funds include all types such as balanced, Canadian and foreign equities, bonds, dividends, money market funds and mortgages. They do not include segregated and pool funds. Stocks include only those directly owned by the household and reflect the market value (not the book value).

Family - Refers to a now-married couple (with or without never-married sons and/or daughters of either or both spouses), a couple living common-law (with or without never-married sons and/or daughters of either or both partners), or a lone parent of any marital status, with at least one never-married son or daughter living in the same dwelling.

FAMILY (TV Station Data) - Stands for the Family Channel.

FAMILE (TV Station Data) - Stands for Canal Family.

FINAN¢IAL P$YTE®

1) **Platinum Estates** - Canada's financial elite. The average household income is approximately $170K. These are older, extremely wealthy families living on expensive, expansive properties. White collar finance, insurance and real-estate tycoons, these people are extremely good credit risks, although they can already afford almost anything without it. Platinum Estates has at least twice as much invested in mutual funds, stocks and demand deposits as Cluster 2, Four Star Investors. Health care costs are high as are their personal taxes and the costs associated with their teenaged children. While you can

often find retail credit cards in their wallets, you will not see them used very often, they prefer VISA, MasterCard and American Express. Cluster 1 households tend to own a wide variety of expensive real estate and material assets including cottages, chalets, condos (in other cities), yachts, sailboats, swimming pools and more.

2) **Four Star Investors** - The average household income for these Four Star Investors is approximately $100K. As the name implies, these people are big on investing: stocks, bonds, and mutual funds. They have been known to carry large balances on their credit cards, but maintain good credit ratings and high limits by never missing monthly payments. These are dual income families paying out high taxes, child care and health care costs. Occupations are typically white collar managerial and administrative, with some teaching and social science professions mixed in. Households in this cluster tend to have over twice the amount of liquid assets as the average Canadian household. They also have about three times the amount tied up in stocks and mutual funds as the average Canadian household.

3) **Successful Suburbanites** - The average household income of these Successful Suburbanites is in the $80-85K range. These people tend to own newer homes in the suburbs. They typically have heavy mortgages but manage them well. Occupations are usually white collar and professional with above average concentrations of natural science jobs. They spend a good portion of their income on the childcare costs associated with having larger families in a high tech world. This cluster has above average concentrations of Cantonese and Mandarin speaking Asians. Cluster 3 households tend to have many credit cards including those from retailers like the Brick and Future Shop. These households do tend to carry a balance but they have very little bad debt. Both their income taxes and liquid assets are usually 50% above the Canadian average. Portfolios in this cluster are apt to be nicely diversified with an equal emphasis on mutual funds, equities, bonds and demand deposits.

4) **Canadian Comfort** - Households in these mid to upscale neighbourhoods in small towns and cities live in Canadian Comfort. The average household income is approximately $70K for these dual income families. Household disposable income has a tendency to be relatively high at around $50K. These households rarely rent, they own, and

their homes are nicer than average. They often have several open lines of credit and they are less risky than the average Canadian. Both their dwelling values and their liquid assets are about 30% greater than average. They tend to be conservative investors and do not typically have a lot of money tied up in residential real estate.

5) **Urban Heights** - City singles, no children. The average household income of this cluster is approximately $63K, although their disposable income is slightly lower than found in cluster 6. They tend to have several lines of credit such as VISA and MasterCard. Dwellings are predominantly high rise condos and rented apartments. Ages are split between young and old, with above average concentrations of 75+. University education predominates and occupations are a mix of white collar and some teaching/social science professions. Female labour force participation is high. The credit limits of the younger set are slowly rising, as are the balances they carry. There are some immigrants from Asia. Despite their younger age these households have relatively large holdings of mutual funds and stocks at approximately 25% greater than the average Canadian household. Dwellings in these upscale urban neighbourhoods are also valued higher than average by about 40%. Apart from residential real estate, the average holdings of non-liquid assets in this cluster is not large.

6) **Miners & Credit-Liners** - These are the successful mining engineers and loggers living in the rural northern areas of the country. The average household income is about $63K and occupations are strongly blue collar. People in this cluster tend to be older (55+) and have generally attended college but not university. Homes are typically owned and single detached and on large properties. Credit limits and balances are high but there is occasional bad debt, particularly on retail credit cards. The female labour force participation is above average, although jobs tend to be clerical or service related. Liquid asset holdings are remarkably high, and approximately 15% more than the national average. Dwelling values are on the low side, owing to the rural settings and much of the value is mortgaged. They typically spend a lot money on transportation, telephone bills, and food. These households tend to own expensive trucks, boats, snowmobiles and ATVs.

7) **Mortgages & Minivans** - Large suburban families with young children. The aver-

age household income is above average but dwelling values are significantly below average. Homes are usually owned and a significant percentage of the home values are mortgaged. There is a high concentration of Francophones. Dual incomes predominate and jobs are a mix of white and grey collar. These people are opening up new lines of credit at a greater than average rate including credit cards, and personal lines of credit. These lines of credit tend to be paid back on time, making these people a low to medium credit risk. When it comes to their retail credit cards, the story is different and there is more bad debt and higher risk. While their demand deposit balances are at about average, these households save money at a less than average rate and have even lower rates of mutual fund and stock holdings. Their income taxes are about 30% above the Canadian average. The tendency towards larger families in Cluster 7 results in significant expenditures on child care, toys and sports equipment.

8) **Dollars & Sense** - Large ethnic urban families with teenagers living at home. There is a concentration of European ethnic people (Italian, Polish, Ukrainian, Greek, and Portuguese). Household incomes are roughly equal to the Canadian average. Their houses tend to be older and are valued almost twice as high as the average. This can be attributed, in part, to the big-city settings and the cultural history of spending heavily on housing. These people have below average credit authorization and are a low to average credit risk as they do not usually carry a balance. They are not inclined to use credit and instead pay for most things in cash. They do use retail cards but default rates are above average. Education levels tend to be low and occupations are usually blue collar. Income taxes are about 20% below average. Their savings accounts and liquid assets are about the same as the Canadian average. Cluster 8 households are conservative investors in terms of large demand deposits and blue chip mutual funds. There is a propensity for larger spending on food and telephone bills.

9) **Tractors & Tradelines** - Self-employed blue-collar farmers and related agricultural occupations dominate this cluster. Household incomes are just below the Canadian average. Middle sized families with younger parents (25-44) and younger children predominate. Dwelling values are relatively low, despite the fact that a significant per-

centage of these values include farm land. These rural farmers are typically higher credit risks. Their credit limits tend to be high, they usually carry an outstanding balance, and there is a tendency to default on retail credit cards. They also carry a balance on personal lines of credit. Below average balances in savings accounts and below average holdings of liquid assets is the norm. More emphasis is placed on savings balances than stocks or mutual funds. These people spend relatively large amounts of money on their children and transportation.

10) **Bills & Wills** - Older, retired, urban empty-nest couples. The average household income is about 8% below the Canadian average. They live either in older single detached homes built before the war or have moved into apartments and condos. Dwellings are valued slightly above the Canadian average. They have a fairly low, often fixed, income. Households in Cluster 10 do not have money to play with - they tend not to invest, do not play the market and often can not make their monthly credit card payments. Cluster 10 households are not great savers nor are they big wealth accumulators. They are likely to have approximately 15% less in liquid assets than the average Canadian household. However, they tend to have above average amounts of money tied up in non-real estate material possessions.

11) **Country Credit** - This rural, blue collar industrial cluster is over 50% French-speaking. Average household incomes are approximately $45K. Income and education levels tend to be low and many people never completed grade 9. There are high concentrations of people in agricultural, mining and quarrying occupations. They usually own their homes and farms but the properties have relatively low value at about $86K. A reasonably large percentage of this amount is mortgaged. These people maintain a fairly low credit risk. They do not tend to invest much and only have small amounts of stocks, bonds and mutual funds. They do have higher than average credit limits and tend to carry a balance. Income taxes paid are about 10% higher than average. They have about 20% smaller liquid asset holdings than average, with more tied up in demand deposits than in investments. They are also below average on non-liquid assets and on net worth generally.

12) **Revolving Renters** - Lower income urban and town apartment dwellers. The average household income in this cluster is approximately $44K. The primary concern for these people is paying the rent that tends to gobble up more than one-third of their income. Ages are split between young (15-24) and old age pensioners; many are singles but there are some couples. Although not everyone in this cluster is a credit risk, there is an above average tendency to be delinquent on payments. There is a greater than average appearance of bankruptcies, foreclosures and bad debt. What these households do manage to save is in the bank and not tied up "in the market". There is not a great deal of value here in material possessions, including real estate. The elderly in this cluster spend a lot on health care and on long distance telephone bills.

13) **Young Urban Struggle** - These young singles do not typically have much money to spend. Their savings account balances are not high and there is very little tendency to invest. What little investments are present are found in very conservative instruments. The average household income is 20% below average at approximately $40K. A large percentage of the income in these neighbourhoods goes towards rent as these central urban locations are generally higher rent areas. Bad debts, unpaid bills, and bankruptcies are relatively common in this cluster. The values of non-liquid assets and net worth are typically low. Despite the presence of some university degrees, the unemployment rate is higher than average and many people are separated or divorced.

14) **Rural Family Blues** - Low educational levels and high unemployment is a theme of this rural cluster, where many Aboriginal and Francophones concentrate. The average household income in these neighbourhoods is approximately $40K. While this average is the same as Cluster 13, there is a larger income range in Cluster 14. The high unemployment rate among these 55+ maintainers is often coupled with the presence of many young mouths to feed. Their dwellings are typically owned, old and need major repairs. Average dwelling values are about half of the Canadian average. Many of these households have either paid off their mortgages or have small monthly payments. Many people work in blue collar occupations including agriculture, logging or mining. They seek new lines of credit and often have trouble making the payments. They are particularly likely to default on their retail card payments but are reasonably good at paying down their personal financing.

These patterns affect credit risk ratings that, overall are slightly higher than average. The balance in most of their savings accounts is typically quite low. Liquid assets, non-liquid assets, and net worth are also low.

15) **Limited Budgets** - The average household income in this cluster is about 30% below the Canadian average. Ages are split in this predominantly rural cluster, with both young (15-24) and old (75+), singles and couples. Homes tend to be older and run-down and are typically worth 40% less than the Canadian average. Occupations are predominantly blue collar. Education levels are often low, grade 9 or high school, and so is income. Many Eastern European immigrants (Polish, Ukrainian) concentrate in this cluster. In general, these people do not carry a lot of credit, outside of personal loans, and do not expect to open up any new tradelines in the future. They tend to carry a balance on the cards they have. Overall, there is only a moderate credit risk. Savings rates are relatively low but so are income tax payments. Liquid assets are usually low, 35% below average, and these people are generally not "in the market". This cluster spends a disproportionate percentage of income on health care.

16) **Loan Parent Stress** - In this urban cluster, lone parents are also loan parents, opening many different lines of credit from personal loans to retail cards. They often have little choice since the household incomes, at approximately 40% below the average household, tends to be insufficient to pay the rent and support their teenaged children. Ages are mixed and education levels are usually low. The same can not be said for the unemployment and divorce rates - both are greater than average. There is a strong concentration of French and Italians in this cluster. Dwellings are usually rented apartments, but if they do own, dwelling values are relatively high as they are located in urban high-rent areas. There is relatively heavy use of retail credit cards but they are reasonably good at making the monthly payments. Their credit limits and balances stay relatively low, making them a low credit risk. The appearance of delinquent payments and bad credit histories in this cluster is no greater than average. These people are not big spenders in any category. Like Cluster 15, saving rates are on average low and they hold few stocks, bonds and mutual funds. Average liquid assets per household are low at about 45% below average and there is also very little accumulation of non-liquid wealth.

17) Towering Debt - These are young singles, including divorced and separated people, living in rented high rises in economically depleted downtown areas. This cluster has bad debt records for most categories: national cards, retail cards, sales financing, and bank loans. Bankruptcies and foreclosures abound. The average household income is 34% below average. Many unemployed single parents, particularly single mothers, are present in this cluster. A relatively large proportion of these households pay more than 30% of their income on housing. Households here are not able to save, invest, or accumulate, and the households do not have assets, liquid or non-liquid to play with or invest. This cluster's towering debt makes many households here a significant risk to potential credit-granting agencies.

18) NSF - The average household income in Cluster 18 is only 65% of the national average. A significant proportion of people here are unemployed and have low educational levels. Welcome to life in the "inner city", where these people live in older pre-war apartment blocks. A large percentage of households pay more than 30% of their income in rent. After basic living expenses are covered, there is almost no discretionary income left at all. There is no money left to save and this cluster has the lowest investment rate. There are very low accumulations of non-liquid assets, even household chattels. Maintainers in this cluster pose an extremely high credit risk.

19) Senior Survivors - The average household income of these Senior Survivors neighbourhoods is the lowest of any cluster at approximately $26K. They tend to be either retired or unemployed and typically live in rented apartments. A very high percentage of households spend more than 30% of their income on housing. Those people who do own their homes have relatively small mortgages. There is a significant concentration of immigrants here, including Eastern Europeans and Asians. They are not apt to have active credit accounts but still tend to have more debt than they can handle. As a result, there is a propensity for bad credit records and a greater than average rate of bankruptcies and foreclosures. They typically haven't invested and typically do not have a lot of savings to fall back on. Although the savings rate is very low, it is not as low as in Cluster 18. Overall, investments are very low and demand deposits are the lowest of any cluster. Despite the years they have had to build up their savings,

Senior Survivors have the third lowest accumulation of non-liquid assets.

The index compares the % of each category in the area with the national %.

Fixed Loan - A tradeline where the outstanding balance amount is being reduced by fixed or predetermined payments over the term of the tradeline. Includes loans with banks as well as with personal and sales finance companies.

Gas Service Stations (Retail Sales Table) - Refers to establishments primarily engaged in retail dealing in gasoline, lubricating oils and greases. Included in this industry are establishments primarily engaged in lubricating motor vehicles.

General Merchandise stores (Retail Sales Table) - There are three types of stores that fall into this category: department stores, general stores, and other general merchandise stores. Department stores are establishments primarily engaged in retail dealing in a general line of merchandise which must include wearing apparel, furniture, appliances and home furnishings but which may also include paint, hardware, toiletries, cosmetics, photographic equipment, jewellery, toys, sporting goods, etc., with no one commodity line representing more than 50% of total revenue. Merchandise lines are normally arranged in separate departments with the accounting on a departmental basis. The departments and functions are integrated under a single management. Such stores usually provide their own charge accounts, deliver merchandise, and maintain open stocks. General stores are engaged in retailing on a non-departmental basis, their most important commodity being food, which can range up to 60% of total revenue, but with no other single commodity line representing more than 50% of total revenue. Other merchandise sold usually includes ready-to-wear apparel, toiletries, cosmetics, hardware, farm supplies, and housewares. Other general merchandise stores engage in retailing on a non-departmental basis, their commodities normally being ready-to-wear apparel, toiletries, cosmetics, hardware and housewares where food and household furniture are not normally commodity lines and where no one commodity line accounts for more than 50% of total revenues. Examples of other general merchandise stores are general merchandise stores, variety stores, and mail order offices of department stores.

HGTV (TV Station Data) - Stands for Home & Garden TV.

HISTTV (TV Station Data) - Stands for History TV.

Health Occupations (Occupations) - Occupations in this broad occupational category are primarily concerned with providing health care services directly to patients and providing support to health care delivery. Occupations in this group are concerned with diagnosing and treating health problems in humans and animals and with providing related services such as pharmacy, nutrition, speech therapy, physiotherapy and occupational therapy. Nurse Supervisors and Registered Nurses are included in this group as are those who provide technical support to medical professional workers.

Homes built (Homes Built Table) - The number of dwelling units completed during the specified year. A dwelling unit is a structurally separate set of living premises with a private entrance either outside the building or from a common hall, lobby or vestibule. Examples of a single dwelling unit are a single house, one half of a double house, one self-contained apartment unit, flat or suite in an apartment building, or one self-contained apartment adjoining a non-residential building. Excluded from the definition of a dwelling unit are seasonal or institutional premises such as summer cottages and school dormitory units.

Home Language - Language most often spoken at home.

Household - Refers to a person or group of persons (other than foreign residents), who occupy the same dwelling and do not have a usual place of residence elsewhere in Canada. It may consist of a family group (census family) with or without other non-family persons, of two or more families sharing a dwelling, of a group of unrelated persons, or of one person living alone. For census purposes, every person is a member of one and only one household. Unless otherwise specified, all household data in this publication are for private households only. (Households are classified into three groups: private households, collective households and households outside Canada).

Household Furniture and Appliance Stores (Retail Sales Table) - Refers to household furniture stores (with appliances and furnishings); household furniture stores (without appliances and furnishings); furniture refinishing and repair shops; appliance, television, radio and stereo stores.

Household Furnishings Stores (Retail Sales Table) - Refers to floor covering stores; drapery stores; other household furnishings stores, which include bedding, blankets, sheets, china, crockery, crystal, cushions, cutlery, decorations, fireplace accessories, flatware, glassware, kitchenware, linen, mattresses, table and floor lamps, table linen, and utensils.

Husband-wife families (Families Table) - Consists of now-married or common-law couples.

In the labour force (Total Labour Force Table) Refers to persons 15 years of age and over, excluding institutional residents, who are either employed or unemployed.

Income class (Taxation Statistics Table) - A specified range of total incomes. The number of all returns which show total income within each specified range are listed in the table.

Income rating indices - Average personal income of residents in each area as measured against the national average personal income. These indices give an indication of purchasing power of each market.

Ind. (TV Station Data) - Stands for Independent.

Industrial aggregate (Average Weekly Earnings table and Number of Employees table) - Represents the sum of the following industries: goods-producing, service-producing, durable and non-durable goods, manufacturing, building construction, industrial and heavy (engineering) construction, educational services and public administration. Excluded are: agriculture, fishing and trapping, religious organizations, private households, and military personnel.

Institutional resident - Residents of "Institutional" collective dwellings (e.g. orphanages, chronic care hospitals, jails - other than staff members).

Interest Bearing Investments (Liquid Assets) - Primarily refer to fixed income instruments, including various types of chequing and savings accounts, guaranteed investment certificates, government bonds, treasury bills, and miscellaneous items such as mortgages and corporate papers.

Labour Force - Refers to the working age population who are employed or unemployed. The remainder of the working age population is classified as not in labour force. Data are given for persons 15 years of age and over, excluding institutional residents.

Level of schooling (Level of Schooling table) - Refers to the highest grade or year of elementary or secondary school attended, or the highest year of university or other non-university completed. University education is considered to be a higher level of schooling than other non-university.

Also, the attainment of a degree, certificate or diploma is considered to be at a higher level than years completed or attended without an educational qualification.

Liquid Assets - Includes Interest Bearing Investments (deposits, bonds, etc.) and Equity Investments (stocks, mutual funds, etc.). Does not include real estate, vehicles, life insurance or other 'non-liquid' assets.

Lone parent (Families Table) - Refers to a mother or a father, with no spouse or common-law partner present, living in a dwelling with one or more never-married sons and/or daughters.

Machinery and equipment (Capital Expenditures Table) - The cost of purchasing all items used in producing goods or providing services. Included are industrial machinery, transportation and equipment, agricultural implements, professional and scientific equipment, office and store furnishings, and other similar capital goods. Excluded are durable goods purchased for personal use. Figures for 2000 are stated spending intentions, while 1999 figures are preliminary actual and 1998 figures are actual.

Management Occupations (Occupations) - Occupations in this broad occupational category are primarily concerned with carrying out the functions of management by planning, organizing, coordinating, directing, controlling, staffing, and formulating, implementing or enforcing policy, either directly or through other levels of management. Supervising is not considered to be a management function. Occupations include Senior Management, Specialist Managers (in specialized fields such as finance or personnel), Managers in Retail Trade, Food and Accommodation Services, and Other Managers not elsewhere classified.

Manufacturing materials, cost (Manufacturing Industries Table) - The laid-down costs of materials, supplies and purchased components used during the year in manufacturing operations. Included are transportation charges by contract carriers, sales taxes, duties, discounts, allowances, return sales, the cost of semi-processed goods received as transfers from another unit, payments for containers and packaging materials, and the amounts paid to others for work done on materials owned by the unit.

Manufacturing shipments, value (Manufacturing Industries Table) - The selling value, net of discounts, returns, allowances, sales taxes, excise duties and taxes, and transportation charges by contract carriers, of shipments and goods produced by the unit or made under contract for it from its mate-

rials. Also included are revenue from repair work and from custom manufacturing done for others using materials owned by others. The value of transfers to other companies or to other units of the same company, the value of shipments of products sold during the given year but shipped during some other year, the value of non-returnable containers and the full installed value of products installed by employees of the unit.

Market for a radio or a television station - The area to which the broadcasts of a station are primarily directed.

Market rating indices - Average retail sales per capita in each area as measured against the national average retail sales per capita. These indices give an indication of the relative retail sales power of each market.

Men's Clothing (Retail Sales Table) - Refers to establishments primarily engaged in retail dealing in men's and boy's clothing (except athletic) and accessories. Men's and boy's clothing includes: Men's and boy's retail apparel, beachwear, clothing, custom tailoring, gloves, haberdashery, hats and caps, hosiery, jackets, neckwear, overcoats, pants and slacks, shirts, sleep and lounge wear, sportswear, suits, sweaters, swimwear, underclothing, uniforms (excluding athletic) and work clothing.

MMUSIC (TV Station Data) - Stands for MuchMusic.

MMM (TV Station Data) - Stands for Much More Music.

Motor vehicle and recreational vehicle dealers - (Retail Sales Table) - Refers to new and used automobile dealers, motor home and travel trailer dealers, boats, outboard motors and boating accessories dealers, motorcycle and snowmobile dealers, and other recreational vehicle dealers, whose retail dealing includes all terrain vehicles (A.T.V.'s), go-carts, and golf carts.

Movable Dwelling (Housing Table) - Single dwelling used as a place of residence, but capable of being moved on short notice, such as a mobile home, tent, recreational vehicle, travel trailer or houseboat.

MUSIQUE (TV Station Data) - Stands for MusiquePlus.

n.a. - Not applicable or not available.

n.e.c. - Not exactly classified.

NEWSWD (TV Station Data) - Stands for CBC Newsworld.

n.i.e. - Stands for not included elsewhere.

Natural & Applied Sciences & Related Occupations (Occupations) - Occupations in this broad occupational category are primarily concerned with conducting theoretical and applied research and providing technical support in natural and applied sciences. Occupations in this group are primarily concerned with conducting experimental and theoretical research into physical and life sciences, applying scientific knowledge in engineering and architectural projects, and designing systems which make use of electronic data processing equipment in industrial and commercial situations.

Never-married sons and/or daughters - Refers to blood, step or adopted sons and daughters who have never married (regardless of age) and are living in the same dwelling as their parent(s). sons and daughters who are currently or were previously married, or who are living common-law, are not considered to be members of their parent(s)' census family even if they are living in the same dwelling. In addition, those never-married sons and daughters who do not live in the same dwelling as their parent(s) are not considered members of their parent(s)' census family.

Non-university education - Refers to the total number of completed years (or less than one year of completed courses) of training at educational institutions which do not grant degrees and are not at the elementary or secondary school level.

Not in the labour force - Refers to those persons aged 15 years of age and over (excluding institutional residents) are neither employed nor unemployed. It includes persons who do not work for pay or in self-employment, and are not looking for paid work, are not on temporary lay-off, and do not have a new job to start in four weeks or less.

Now-married - Persons whose husband or wife is living. Persons living common-law are considered as "now married".

Number of Establishments (Retail Sales) - Refers to the total number of retail establishments in a geographic area.

Number of vehicles in Model Year Period - Vehicles includes cars and trucks recorded with the Ministry of Transportation.

Occupied Private Dwelling - Refers to a private dwelling in which a person or group of persons is permanently residing. Excludes dwellings occupied solely by foreign and/or temporary residents. A private dwelling refers to a separate set of living quarters with private entrance either from outside or from a common hall, lobby, vestibule or stairway inside the building.

Other Category (Average Household Expenditures Table) - Includes: household operation; household furnishings and equipment; tobacco products and alcoholic beverages; gifts and contributions; and miscellaneous.

Other Clothing Stores (Retail Sales Table) - Refers to children's clothing stores; fur goods stores; fabric and yarn stores; and other clothing stores, which includes bathing suits, family clothing and leisure clothing.

Other Durable Goods Stores (Retail Sales Table) - Refers to bicycle shops; musical instrument stores; record, tape and compact disc stores; jewellery stores; watch and jewellery repair shops; camera and photographic supply stores, and sporting goods stores, which include athletic clothing (including uniforms), athletic footwear, fishing tackle, and equipment for archery, baseball, bowling, camping, exercise and fitness, football, golf, hockey, hunting, playground, skiing, soccer, softball, tennis, and track and field.

Other Semi-Durable Goods Stores (Retail Sales Table) - Refers to book and stationery stores; florist shops; lawn and garden centres; hardware stores; paint, glass and wallpaper stores; toy and hobby stores; gift, novelty and souvenir stores.

Other Single Attached House (Housing Table) - A single dwelling that is attached to another building and does not fall into any of the other categories, such as single dwelling attached to a non-residential structure (e.g., store or church) or occasionally to another residential structure (e.g., apartment building).

Owned Apartment 5+ storeys (Housing Table) - An owned dwelling unit in a high-rise apartment building which has five or more storeys.

Participation rate for males or females - Refers to the total labor force expressed as a percentage of the total population 15 years of age and over, excluding institutional residents.

Percent of vehicles in Model Year Period - Vehicles, includes cars and trucks, within certain model year periods, as a percentage of total vehicles currently on the road.

Plant (Manufacturing Table) - The smallest unit which is a separate entity capable of reporting materials and supplies used, goods purchased for resale, fuel and power consumed, number of employees, salaries and wages, man-hours worked and paid, inventories and shipments, and sales. This unit may be either an autonomous operating unit or affiliated with a unit in another place.

Pool of Credit - The total amount ($) of authorized credit for all tradelines that have had activity within the past year.

Primary Industry Occupations (Occupations) - Occupations in this broad occupational category are primarily concerned with operating farms and supervising or doing farm work; operating fishing vessels and doing specialized fishing work; and in doing supervision and production work in oil and gas production and forestry and logging. Occupations can also include landscaping, raising fish, reforestation, mining, drilling for crude oil and natural gas, being in charge of or operating fishing vessels, and hunting and trapping.

Private household - Refers to a person or group of persons (other than foreign residents) who occupy a private dwelling and do not have a usual place of residence elsewhere in Canada.

Processing, Manufacturing & Utilities Industries Occupations (Occupations) - Occupations in this broad occupational category are primarily concerned with supervisory and production work in manufacturing, processing and utilities. Occupations include supervising workers engaged in processing metals, petroleum, chemicals, rubber and plastics, food and beverages, forest products and textiles. They are also concerned with workers engaged in assembly and fabrication of transportation equipment, machinery, electronic equipment, furniture and fixtures, fabric, and other products requiring assembly or fabrication. Occupations can also include operating machines to process metals, petroleum, rubber and plastics, forest products and textiles, manufacturing occupations (including furniture, fabric, and electronic equipment), and machine operator assistants.

PSYTE®

1) **Canadian Establishment** - Canada's most upscale neighbourhood group. Extremely wealthy middle-aged and older established families with teenagers in expensive, large, older dwellings. These are business owners, executives and professionals. Found only in larger cities.

2) **The Affluentials** - Very affluent and educated middle-aged executive and professional families. Expensive, large, lightly mortgaged houses in very stable, older, exclusive sections of large cities. Older children and teenagers.

3) **Suburban Executives** - The most affluent suburban cluster. Well-educated executive and professional middle-aged and older maintainers of large families. Lots of children, especially over age 6. Typically new, large, single-detached dwellings found around larger Canadian cities. 16% immigrant; some Chinese and Jewish.

4) **Urban Gentry** - Affluent, well-educated and cultured older singles, couples and maintainers of relatively small families. Older private homes, condominiums and apartments. Executive occupations or retired. Some university students still at home.

5) **Boomers and Teens** - Middle and late middle-aged, university and college-educated maintainers of larger families with children over age 6, especially teens. Managerial and white collar occupations; commonly two wage earners. Newer, larger, owned single-detached dwellings. 10% Italian mother tongue. Skewed to larger Ontario and B.C. cities.

6) **Mortgaged in Suburbia** - Upscale, predominantly younger (age under 45) large families living in new suburban subdivisions in large, heavily mortgaged houses. Occupations are managerial/ professional and high-status white collar. Most families have two income earners. Education attainment is high. Children are typically under age 10.

7) **Technocrats and Bureaucrats** - Middle-aged maintainers of larger families living in large, new, single-detached dwellings in suburbs of larger and medium-sized Canadian cities. Very well-educated. Public sector and managerial occupations. Most households have two wage earners.

8) **Stable Suburban Families** - Maintainers are strongly concentrated in the 45-65 age range. Small families with late teens and early 20s at home. University and college educated. Managerial and high-status white collar occupations. Owned, single-detached, '60s dwellings in larger cities. 14% "ethnic". Very low mobility.

9) **Asian Heights** - Upscale, very large families with middle-aged, well-educated maintainers. Managerial and white collar occupations. Large proportion of Asian, especially Chinese, households. Large, newer, heavily mortgaged detached homes and townhouses, in expanding suburbs, especially Toronto and Vancouver. Commonly two wage earners.

10) **Suburban Nesters** - Predominantly maintainers over 50. Empty nests or small families. University or college education. Managerial and white collar occupations. Single-detached and other '50s dwellings; 78% owned. Mortgages are small. Skewed to large cities. High female labour force participation rate. 22% "ethnic". Very low mobility.

11) **Northern Lights** - Communities of highly paid bureaucrats, technocrats, technicians, and mining engineers in remote northern towns. The dominant maintainer age is under 45 and children are younger. Many households have two salaries. Dwellings are newer, with a mixture of owned and rented single-detached and other dwellings.

12) **Brie and Chablis** - Upscale singles, couples and small families living in luxury condos and luxury high-rise apartments. Maintainers are very well-educated and tend to have executive, managerial and professional occupations. Dominant age is 50+ years, also a good proportion in the 20-34 year age range. Mostly suburban with some downtown.

13) **Blue Collar Winners** - The most upscale town cluster. Middle-aged and older, high-school and college-educated, blue (and grey) collar maintainers. Upscale towns and ex-urban environs of large cities. Still 10% farming. Some management commuters. Older, owned dwellings with some new subdivisions. Very good income for lower cost of living.

14) **Satellite Suburbs** - Upper middle class, middle-aged maintainers of large families with children of all ages. Typically college-educated with grey collar and managerial occupations. Commonly two wage earners. Largely owned, heavily mortgaged, newer, single-detached and other dwellings. 16% "ethnic".

15) **Small City Elites** - Small, traditional families and older couples headed by middle-aged, well-educated managerial/ executive maintainers. Children are typically over 6. Larger, single-detached post-1971 dwellings. Comfortable neighbourhoods in smaller cities and towns.

16) **Old Bungalow Burbs** - Late middle-aged comfortable suburban households with older teenagers or empty nests. Moderately priced large '60s owned single-detached, and predominantly bungalow-type dwellings. There is a wide range of upscale occupations. Education levels are modest in

relation to income. Typically found around smaller and medium-sized cities.

17) **Aging Erudites** - Older, well-educated singles, couples and small families. Managerial and upscale white collar occupations. Single-detached and other predominantly '50s dwellings; 68% owned; 10% apartments. Mortgages are small. These people soak up culture.

18) **Participaction Quebec** -Younger and middle-aged maintainers of large, French Canadian families. College diplomas are common. Occupations are quite mixed but upscale. Frequently two wage earners. Newer, suburban, single-detached and townhouses, predominantly owned. These people are physically and socially very active.

19) **Town Boomers** - Comfortable, relatively well-off, younger and middle-aged smaller families in towns and small urban areas. Education levels are modest but high for towns. Occupations are grey collar and white collar. Dwellings are typically newer, owned and single-detached. Most households have children.

20) **Young Urban Professionals** - Young singles and some couples, predominantly renting older other dwellings and apartments in in-town areas of big cities. Very well-educated. Occupations are professional, managerial and high-status white collar. High labour force participation rate. About 20% "ethnic". High mobility.

21) **Europa** - (1.52% of Cdn. Hhlds.) Middle-aged and older families of European, particularly, Italian descent. Dwellings are older, single-detached, low-rise row housing. Concentrated in a few Canadian cities, especially Toronto. Occupations are blue and grey collar. Children are common.

22) **The New Frontier** - Similar to Cluster 11, but less northern/remote and older. Maintainers are mainly under 45. College diplomas and high-paying, blue collar or natural resource extraction jobs. Household types are mixed but families are most common. Newer, single-detached, other and mobile homes with 70% owned. Mortgages are small.

23) **Kindergarten Boom** - Younger families in newer (mostly '70s and '80s) suburban, single and semi-detached housing. Many families have three or more children. Typical education levels are college diploma. Occupations are grey collar and white collar. Mortgages are

large. There is a significant "ethnic" presence.

24) **New Quebec Rows** - Middle income, young French Canadian yuppie families in modest, new, semi-detached and row housing outside Quebec towns and cities. About half the dwellings are owned. Maintainers have managerial or medium-to-high-status white collar occupations. Education attainment is typically university degree or college diploma. Children typically under age 6.

25) **Asian Mosaic** - Inner city areas in which Chinese and other Asians are concentrated. In Toronto and Vancouver, these areas are known as "Chinatown". Dwellings are older, a mixture of owned, single-detached, rented semis and low-rises. Many families have children and typically these are teenagers, often at university.

26) **Rustic Prosperity** - Canada's most productive dairy, feedstock, vegetable farms and orchards. Still, many occupations are blue collar/non-farm. Maintainers are middle-aged and older. Families typically have many children. Education levels are high school and college. Most women work outside the house. Unemployment and mobility are low.

27) **Old Towns' New Fringe** - Younger and middle-aged high school and especially college educated, grey collar, blue collar and government workers. Predominantly small families. Towns and fringes of small cities outside of Quebec. Mortgaged, moderately priced, newer, owned single-detached dwellings.

28) **Conservative Homebodies** - A large cluster of predominantly older singles, couples and small families. Middle income derived from middle status blue/grey collar occupations. Mainly lower education attainment. Dwellings are other, single-detached and dominated by '50s and '60s vintage. 12% Eastern European immigrants. Skewed to medium-sized cities.

29) **Young Urban Mix** - A large cluster of predominantly younger singles, couples and small families in large cities. Education levels are mixed but not low. Occupations are middle status white and grey collar. 65% of households rent. Housing is mixed but predominantly '50s and '60s vintage. About 25% "ethnic". High mobility.

30) **Quebec Melange** - A large cluster of middle-class French Canadian neigh-

bourhoods found in a wide range of settlements, especially small cities and towns. Maintainer age is middle to late middle-aged. Mixed household types and not many children. College and high school diplomas. Mixed occupations. Mixed dwellings with 59% ownership.

31) **Old Leafy Towns** - Established stable neighbourhoods of older, single-detached, owned dwellings in the nicer residential areas of towns and townships. Maintainer age has a strong skew to 55+. Education and occupational status are quite mixed. Younger families with children are starting to move in.

32) **Traditional French Canadian Families** - Younger and middle-aged French Canadian small families. Newer, single-detached, owned dwellings in neighbourhoods throughout Quebec. Most concentrations in rural and non-big city environments. Relatively low education levels. Mainly blue collar occupations.

33) **High-rise Sunsets** - Older households, empty nesters and retired, living in high-quality, high-rise apartments on arterial roads in larger urban areas across Canada. A good proportion are singles. These people are well-educated and hold/held executive and managerial positions. There is a significant concentration of Jewish people.

34) **Pick-Ups and Dirt Bikes** - Middle-income, middle-aged and older maintainers of rural families. Largely poorly educated, blue collar natural resource industry workers and farmers. Dwellings are single-detached with some mobile homes. Dwelling payments are very low. Mobility is low. This is truck and huntin' country.

35) **Town Renters** - Young families, couples and lone parent families renting units in low-rise and row housing, built largely in the 1970s and 1980s. Lots of young children. Large towns and small cities. High school and college-educated grey collar workers. Rents are a large percent of incomes.

36) **Young Urban Intelligentsia** - Very well-educated singles and some couples renting mainly newer apartments and other dwellings in central areas of large cities. Very few children. Large percentage of university students. Occupations are white collar and executive/professional. Very high female labour force participation.

37) **Quebec's Heartland** - Poorly educated blue collar workers and farmers doing reasonably well in productive farm

areas of southern Quebec. Epitomized by dairy farming areas. Maintainers are mainly over age 35. Families with children. Dwellings are older, owned and largely paid off. Mobility is low.

38) **The Grain Belt** - Productive prairie grain farming areas. Large families. Predominantly middle-aged and older maintainers. Poorly educated, very high labour force participation, including women. Strong work ethic. Many early immigrants from Eastern and Northern Europe. Large, older, paid-off farm houses. Low mobility.

39) **Nesters and Young Homesteaders** - Old singles and couples, some younger couples and small families. Older neighbourhoods in towns and smaller cities outside of Quebec. Dwellings are mixed row housing and low-rise, single-detached. Mostly rented. High school and college education. Grey collar and service occupations. Relatively low labour force participation.

40) **University Enclaves** - Neighbourhood concentrations of urban university students, artists, musicians, etc. Most residents rent high-rise or low-rise apartments or older, subdivided houses. Education levels are very high. Occupations are white and grey collar. There are some immigrants, including recent immigrants, in these areas.

41) **High-rise Melting Pot** - 47% of the occupants of these big city apartment blocks are immigrants, many from Eastern Europe. Ranks #1 for recent immigrants. Mixed household types but few children. Education levels are mixed but relatively high for the income. Occupations are mixed but predominantly white collar.

42) **Euro Quebec** - Quebec's Cluster 21, but more downscale. Significant percentage of European, especially Italian, immigrants (largely in Montreal). Household types are mixed. Education levels are low. Common occupations are blue/grey collar. Relatively high unemployment. 70% rent in typical other dwellings of '50s and '60s vintage. Rents are a high percentage of income.

43) **Agrarian Blues** - Predominantly older, very poorly educated farm and blue collar workers. Living in less productive agricultural areas. Children are older. Mostly paid-off houses and farmsteads. Labour force participation, especially for women, is relatively low. Unemployment and government

transfers are above average. Mobility is low.

44) Young Grey Collar - A mix of young singles, small families and empty nesters in older neighbourhoods of small cities and towns. Strong prairie representation. College and high school education. Ranks #1 on grey collar occupations. Mixture of rented, other dwellings and older, single-detached.

45) Old Quebec Walkups - Lower-middle-class singles, couples and small families renting low-rise, outside stairway, "walkup" units in larger Quebec cities. The age distribution is bimodal - young and older. Occupations are predominately middle status white collar. Education levels tend to be low or high.

46) Quiet Towns - Old neighbourhoods of small towns with an Atlantic and Western skew. Predominantly older, some younger, singles and couples. Few children. High school and college education. Grey collar and service occupations. Mixture of rented, other dwellings and owned, single-detached. Relatively low monthly payments.

47) Rod and Rifle - Non-agricultural areas of rural Canada with 52% in Atlantic region. Maintainers are predominantly over age 55, with typically older children. Blue collar and natural resource extraction occupations. Unemployment levels are high. Dwellings are older, owned and mostly paid-off. Fishing and hunting are major preoccupations. Low mobility.

48) Struggling Downtowns - A large cluster of younger, some older, poorly educated residents of medium and small city downtowns. Singles, couples and some younger families (especially lone parent). Grey and blue collar occupations. Old, mixed housing with 55% home owners. Housing payments are a significant proportion of income. 16% "ethnic". High mobility.

49) Down Down East - Highly concentrated in the Maritimes and are best epitomized by fishing villages. Maintainer ages are mixed but principally over 45. Most families have children and many families are large. Educational levels are very low. Unemployment levels and government transfer payments are very high. Dwellings are older, owned, single-detached. Mobility is very low.

50) Big Country Families - More remote agricultural and natural resource areas with a western Canada skew. Older, very poorly educated maintainers of large families. Farm, blue collar and white collar government occupations. Lots of children. Significant proportion of native Canadians (25% "ethnic" origin native, and 10% band housing). Significant unemployment. Low mobility.

51) Young City Singles - Very young singles and some couples. Rent predominantly newer, downtown, other dwellings and apartments. Medium/smaller city and western Canada skew. Education levels are mixed and occupations are strongly grey, with some low-status white collar. High labour force participation. Above average unemployment levels. Very high mobility.

52) Quebec Rural Blues - Downscale rural Quebec with 22% in Atlantic provinces. Predominantly older, very poorly educated maintainers. Blue collar or natural resource extraction occupations, or unemployed. Significant government transfers. Families tend to be large with older children. Very low growth. Very low mobility.

53) Quebec Town Elders - Largely older, poorly educated singles, couples and small families, living in rented, older dwellings in Quebec's small cities and towns. 55% rent. Other dwellings and single-detached predominate. High unemployment and government transfers. Low labour force participation rates. Low mobility.

54) Aging Quebec Urbanites - Predominantly older singles with some couples and small families living in other dwellings and apartments, in downtown neighbourhoods of Quebec's larger cities. Educational levels are mixed. Occupations are white and grey collar. Low labour force participation rates. 11% "ethnic".

55) Old Canadian Rustics - Poorly educated, old and retired rural dwellers. Blue/grey collar occupations and subsistence farming. Labour force participation is low and government transfers are high. Few younger families here. Significant out-migration. Dwellings are single-detached and rented low-rise. 75% in Manitoba and Saskatchewan, 12% in Alberta.

56) Urban Bohemia - Well-educated, but low income, young singles and some couples, in older parts of big cities. University students. White and some grey collar occupations but low labour force participation and high unemployment. Rent other dwellings and high-rise apartments. Distinctive French, English and other mother tongue mix. High mobility.

57) Quebec's New Urban Mosaic - Very low income, younger and older singles, couples and smaller families (many lone parent). Rent older, downtown, other dwellings. Very low education levels. Grey collar occupations. Significant unemployment. A significant proportion of relatively new immigrants. High mobility.

58) Aged Pensioners - Largely very old singles, some couples, renting small apartments, flats and other dwellings in in-town areas of small and medium-sized Canadian cities. Very low education levels. High unemployment and government transfer rates. Low-status, grey collar occupations but very low labour force participation. High mobility.

59) Big City Stress - Inner city urban neighbourhoods with second lowest average household income. Probably the most disadvantaged areas of the country. Predominant age skew is young and almost everyone rents. Dwellings are older, low-rise with some newer, high-rise. Household types include singles, couples and lone parent families. A significant but mixed "ethnic" presence. Unemployment levels are very high.

60) Old Grey Towers - 76% of households have maintainers over 65. Average household incomes are the lowest of any cluster. Mostly '70s high-rise with some low-rise buildings. Very low labour force participation. Government transfers are a significant proportion of income. Low mobility.

The index compares the % of each category with the national %.

RDS (TV Station Data) - Stands for Le Reseau des Sports.

Retail Sales Estimates - The retail sales table shows aggregate sales made through retail locations (outlets). Retail sales figures do not include any form of direct selling which bypasses the retail store, for example: direct door-to-door selling; sales made through automatic vending machines; sales of newspapers or magazines sold directly by printers or publishers; and sales made by book and record clubs. The only exception is the mail order and catalogue sales activities of department store businesses, which have been classified to the "general merchandise store" category. Retail trade also excludes: retail sales through ancillary units, for example, warehouses, head offices, etc., sales of contractors whose major activity is not retailing; and retail transactions between individuals.

Revolving Credit - A tradeline where the outstanding balance amount is being reduced at least by a minimum payment each month, e.g. credit cards.

Row house (Housing Table) - One of three or more dwellings joined side by side (or occasionally side to back), such as a town house or garden home, but not having any dwellings either above or below.

Salaries, wages (Manufacturing Industries Table) - Gross earnings of all employees before deductions for such items as income tax and sickness, accident, unemployment insurance and pension benefits. Included are all bonuses, profits shared with employees. Payments for overtime and separation pay are included. Excluded are employer contributions for workmen's compensation and employee welfare and benefit plans and taxable allowances such as free lodging.

Sales & Service Occupations (Occupations) - Occupations in this broad occupational category are primarily concerned with selling goods and services and providing personal, protective, household, tourism and hospitality services. Occupations include sales and service supervisors, insurance and real estate agents, retail salespersons and sales clerks, cashiers, chefs and cooks, food and beverage industry workers, prison guards and security guards, travel agents, porters, childcare workers, and homemakers.

Satisfactory Ratings - Tradelines in which the consumer has met all the required payments in the past 2 years.

Semi-Detached House (Housing Table) - One of two dwellings attached side by side (or back to front) to each other, but not to any other dwelling or structure (except its own garage or shed). A semi-detached dwelling has no dwellings either above it or below it and the two units together have open space on all sides.

Shoe Stores (Retail Sales Table) - Refers to establishments primarily engaged in retail dealing in men's, women's, children's and infant's footwear (except athletic). Included are: felt boots and shoes, moccasins, plastic footwear, rubber footwear, slippers, and work boots.

SHWCSE (TV Station Data) - Stands for Showcase Television.

Single-detached house (Housing Table) - A single dwelling not attached to any other dwelling or structure (except its own garage or shed). A single-detached house has open space on all sides, and has no dwellings either above or below it.

SNET (TV Station Data) - Stands for The Sports Network.

Social Science, Gov't Service & Religious Occupations - (Occupations) Occupations in this broad occupational category are primarily concerned with law, teaching, counseling, conducting social science research, providing religious services, and developing and administering government policies and programs. Occupations include judges, lawyers, psychologists, social workers, clergy, paralegals, and career counselors.

Standard geographical classification - Refers to Statistics Canada's official classification of geographic areas in Canada. The SGC code provides numeric identification for three types of geographic areas:

1) provinces and territories

2) census divisions (CDs)

3) census subdivisions (CSDs)

The three types of areas are hierarchically related. Census subdivisions aggregate to census divisions, which in turn aggregate to provinces or territories. This hierarchical relationship is reflected in the seven-digit standard geographical classification code:

PR	CD	CSD
XX	XX	XXX

                     Census subdivision

         Census division

Province or territory

2 digits 2 digits   3 digits

    (X denotes one digit)

Store Distribution (Shopping Centre Table) - Number of centres within each "store distribution" grouping.

Super (TV Station Data) - Stands for Super Channel.

Supermarkets & Grocery Stores (Retail Sales Table) - Supermarkets are establishments primarily engaged in retailing a balanced line of goods such as: canned, bottled, packaged and frozen foods; fresh meat and poultry; fish; fresh fruits and vegetables; prepared food products; bakery products; dairy products; candy and confectionery; and other food lines. In addition, newspapers, magazines, paper products, soft drinks, tobacco products, health and beauty aids, housewares, flowers, plants and other non-food articles may be sold. Grocery stores exclude supermarkets, and primarily engage in retailing a limited line of goods such as canned, bottled, packaged and frozen foods, dairy products, and candy and confectionery. Gro-

cery stores may also sell other food lines and non-food products similar to supermarkets. Beer and wine may also be sold in grocery stores in some provinces.

Taxation - RevCan bases its tabulations on locality codes. Therefore, the statistics produced may seem inflated in some areas and deflated in others in regard to the population of that area. Also, the provincial taxation results include data for localities which RevCan could not accurately assign to specific areas, but could assign to the province.

Taxes and Securities (Average Household Expenditures Table) - Consists of personal taxes, life insurance premiums, annuity contracts, employment insurance premiums, and retirement and pension fund payments.

TLC (TV Station Data) - Stands for The Learning Channel.

TMN (TV Station Data) - Stands for The Movie Network.

TNN (TV Station Data) - Stands for The Nashville Network.

TOON (TV Station Data) - Stands for Teletoon.

Total Income - Refers to the total money income received from the following sources by persons 15 years of age and over: total wages and salaries; net income from unincorporated non-farm business and/or professional practice; net farm self-employment income; federal child tax credits; old age security pensions and guaranteed income supplements; benefits from Canada or Quebec pension plans; benefits from Unemployment Insurance; other income from government sources; dividends and interest on bonds, deposits, savings certificates and other investment income; retirement pensions, superannuation and annuities; and other money income, e.g. alimony, strike pay.

Total Income (Taxation Statistics Table) - The sum of income from the following sources: wages and salaries, commissions from employment, other employment earnings, such as adult training allowances, net research grants, and tips and gratuities, family allowance, unemployment insurance benefits, old age pensions, Canada Pension Plan, or Quebec Pension Plan Benefits, other pensions or super annuation, net business income, net professional income, net farming income, net fishing income, taxable amount of dividends, bond interest, bank interest, mortgage interest, income from trust, annuity income, other Canadian investment income such as non-dividend income from a personal corporation, foreign investment income, net rental income, net taxable capital gains, and other unspecified miscellaneous income such as alimony or separation allowances received, scholarships, fellowships, and bursaries.

Total returns, number (Taxation Statistics Table) - The number of returns, whether taxable or non-taxable, received from the specified municipality. This number does not include second returns filed in amendment of the original return. In addition, returns received from a specified municipality do not necessarily come from residents of that municipality as a person may file a return from a place of business located there.

Total tax (Taxation Statistics Table) - The total of amounts of federal and provincial tax collected by the federal government. While the figure for total tax is taken after deductions for federal tax credits have been made, it is taken before deductions for provincial tax credits. In addition, in the case of every table for Quebec, the figure does not include provincial tax because the government of the Province of Quebec collects this.

Total value added (Manufacturing Table) - The value of gross output less those purchased inputs which have been embodied in the value of production for all forms of production activity, whether manufacturing or non-manufacturing, engaged in by the unit.

Total vehicle count 1981-1998 - All vehicles (cars and trucks) on the road carrying a model year of 1981 to 1998, plus 1999 new vehicle registrations.

Tradeline - A credit vehicle or debt instrument issued to an individual by a credit grantor. Types of tradelines include Bank Loans, Credit Cards, Retail Cards, Personal Lines of Credit, and Car Loans/Leases.

Trades Certificate/Diploma (Level of Schooling) - Refers to the possession of either a trades certificate or diploma, or an other non-university certificate or diploma, or both, regardless of whether other educational qualifications are held or not. A trades certificate is usually obtained through apprenticeship or journeyman's training over several years, in trade occupations such as welding, plumbing and carpentry. Alternatively, trades certificates may be obtained through in-school (as opposed to on-the-job) training at trade or vocational schools, employment centres or trades divisions of community colleges.

Trades, Transport & Equipment Operators & Related Occupations (Occupations) - Occupations in this broad occupational category are primarily concerned with contracting, supervising and doing trades work; and supervising and operating transportation equipment and heavy equipment. Occupations include trade and transportation supervisors, construction workers (including carpenters, plumbers and roofers), electricians, machine-tool operators, metalworkers, crane operators, and transportation equipment operators (including trucks, buses, subway trains, taxis).

TQS (TV Station Data) - Stands for Télévision Quatre Saisons.

TREE (TV Station Data) - Stands for Treehouse TV.

TSN (TV Station Data) - Stands for The Sports Network.

Unemployed (Labour Force) - Refers to persons 15 years of age and over, excluding institutional residents, who are without paid work are were available for work and either actively looked for work in the past four weeks, were on temporary lay-off and expected to return to their job, or had definite arrangements to start a new job in four weeks or less.

Unemployment rate - Refers to the unemployed labour force expressed as a percentage of the total labour force.

University - This data includes persons with both university and other non-university education, as well as those with university only.

University with certificate - Includes trades certificate, non-university certificate, and university certificate or diploma below the bachelor level.

University with degree - Bachelor's degree or higher.

University without degree - The total of categories "university without degree or certificate" and "university with certificate."

University without degree or certificate (Level of Schooling) - Refers to someone who has attended university but who has not received a university degree (e.g. Bachelors Degree).

Urban area - The general concept of an urban area (UA) is that of an area containing a dense concentration of population. Statistics Canada defines an urban area as an area which has attained a population concentration of at least 1,000, and a population density of at least 400 per square kilometer, at the previous census. All territory lying outside urban areas is considered rural. Taken together, urban and rural areas cover all of Canada.

Urban fringe - An urban area within a CMA or CA, that is not contiguous to the urban core.

Urban core - A large urban area around which a CMA or a CA is delineated. The urban core must have a population (based on the previous census) of at least 100,000 in the case of a CMA, or between 10,000 and 99,999 in the case of a CA.

WEATHR (TV Station Data) - Stands for the Weather Network.

WTN (TV Station Data) - Stands for Women's Television Network.

Weekly reach of a radio or television station The percentage of an area's population that is tuned in to a station for at least 15 minutes during the week, defined to be Monday through Sunday, 5:00 a.m. to 1:00 a.m. for radio stations, and Monday through Sunday 6:00 a.m. to 2:00 a.m. for television stations.

Women's Clothing Stores (Retail Sales Table) - Refers to establishments primarily engaged in retail dealing in women's clothing (except athletic) and accessories. Women's clothing includes: women's retail accessories, apparel, clothing, coats, custom tailoring, dresses, dressing gowns, foundation garments, gloves, headwear, hosiery, lingerie, millinery, neckwear, skirts, slacks and pants, sleepwear, sportswear (excluding athletic), suits, sweaters, undergarments, and uniforms (excluding athletic).

Industrial Development Contacts

NEWFOUNDLAND

Newfoundland
Paul Morris
Director of Trade & Investment Division
Investment Division
P.O. Box 8700
St. John's, NF A1B 4J6
Phone : (709) 729-2781
Fax : (709) 729-3208
Web Site : www.success.nf.net

Canada/Newfoundland Business
Service Centre
90 O'Leary Ave.
P.O. Box 8687
St. John's, NF A1B 3T1
Phone : (709) 772-6022
Phone : 1-800-668-1010
Fax : (709) 772-6030
Email : st.johns@cbsc.ic.gc.ca
Web Site : www.cbsc.org/nf/index.html

Bishop's Falls
Nancy Hanrahan
Manager
Bishop Falls Development
P.O. Box 940
Bishops Falls, NF A0H 1C0
Phone : (709) 258-5821
Fax : (709) 258-5831
Web Site : www.bfdc.nf.ca

Botwood
Edward Evans
Town Manager
P.O. Box 490
Botwood, NF A0H 1E0
Phone : (709) 257-2839
Fax : (709) 257-3330
Web Site : www3.nf.sympatico.ca/botwood

Conception Bay South
Joan Butler
Economic Development Officer
P.O. Box 280
Manuels, NF A1W 1M8
Phone : (709) 834-6518
Fax : (709) 834-8337
Web Site : www.town.cbs.nf.ca

Corner Brook
Patricia M. Pye
Chief Executive Officer
Corner Brook Economic Development Corp.
40 Brook St.
P.O. Box 40, Stn. Main
Corner Brook, NF A2H 6C3
Phone : (709) 637-1588
Fax : (709) 637-1667
Web Site : www.cornerbrook.com

Gander
Libby Staple
Director of Development
Department of Development & Tourism
P.O. Box 280
Gander, NF A1V 1W6
Phone : (709) 651-2930
Fax : (709) 256-2124
Web Site : www.gandercanada.com

Lewisporte
Derek White
Town Manager
P.O. Box 219
Lewisporte, NF A0G 3A0
Phone : (709) 535-2874
Fax : (709) 535-2695
Web Site : www.lewisportecanada.com

Mount Pearl
Bronda Aylward
Director of Economic Development
Economic Development Department
3 Centennial St.
Mount Pearl, NF A1N 1G4
Phone : (709) 748-1096
Fax : (709) 748-1150
Email : baylward@mtpearl.nf.ca
Web Site : www.mtpearl.nf.ca

St. John's
Bruce J. Tilley
General Manager
St. John's Board of Trade
P.O. Box 5127, Stn. C
St. John's, NF A1C 5V5
Phone : (709) 726-2961
Fax : (709) 726-2003
Web Site : www.bot.nf.ca

PRINCE EDWARD ISLAND

Prince Edward Island
Kent Scales
Executive Director
Business Development P.E.I.
P.O. Box 910, Stn. Central
25 University Ave., 3rd floor
Charlottetown, PE C1A 7L9
Phone : (902) 368-5800
Fax : (902) 368-6301
Web Site : www.gov.pe.ca

Canada/Prince Edward Island Business
Service Centre
75 Fitzroy St.
P.O. Box 40
Charlottetown, PE C1A 7K2
Phone : (902) 368-0771
Phone : 1-800-668-1010
Fax : (902) 566-7377
Web Site : www.cbsc.org/pe/index.html

Charlottetown
See Prince Edward Island

Summerside
Michael Thususka
Economic Development Officer
Economic Development Office
45 Summer St.
Summerside, PE C1N 3H7
Phone : (902) 432-1255
Fax : (902) 436-9296
Email : mike@city.summerside.pe.ca
Web Site : www.city.summerside.pe.ca

NOVA SCOTIA

Nova Scotia
Roy Sherwood
Executive Director
Nova Scotia Economic Development
1800 Argyle St., Suite 520
P.O. Box 519
Halifax, NS B3J 2R7
Phone : (902) 424-5659
Fax : (902) 424-5739
Web Site : www.novascotiabusiness.com

Canada/Nova Scotia Business
Service Centre
1575 Brunswick St.
Halifax, NS B3J 2G1
Phone : (902) 426-8604
Phone : 1-800-668-1010
Fax : (902) 426-6530
Email : halifax@cbsc.ic.gc.ca
Web Site : www.cbsc.org/ns/index.html

East Hants
Harold G. Irving
Executive Director
Hants Regional Development Authority
P.O. Box 13
Elmsdale, NS B0N 1M0
Phone : (902) 883-3338
Fax : (902) 883-3024
Email : hantsrda@cnova.net
Web Site : www.hantsrda.ns.ca

Halifax
See Nova Scotia

Kentville
R. Wayne Gibbons
Director of Planning and Development
Town of Kentville
354 Main St.
Kentville, NS B4N 1K6
Phone : (902) 679-2500
Fax : (902) 679-2375
Web Site : www.kentville.ns.ca

Lunenburg
Jim Brown
Business Development Officer
Lunenburg-Queens Regional Development Agency
Town of Lunenberg
P.O. Box 39
220 North St.
Bridgewater, NS B4V 2W6
Phone : (902) 543-0491
Phone : 1-800-303-1541
Fax : (902) 543-1156
Web Site : www.lqrda.ns.ca

New Glasgow
Rob Roy
Chief Executive Officer
Pictou Regional Development Commission
980 East River Rd.
New Glasgow, NS B2H 5E5
Phone : (902) 752-6159
Fax : (902) 755-2722
Web Site : www.prdc.com

Truro

Doug Kirby
Industrial Promotions Officer
P.O. Box 427, Stn. Main
Truro, NS B2N 5C5
Phone : (902) 893-2438
Fax : (902) 893-0501
Web Site : www.town.truro.ns.ca

West Hants

Kenneth Crichton
Executive Director
Hants-Kings Business Development Centre Ltd.
P.O. Box 2788
Windsor, NS B0N 2T0
Phone : (902) 798-5717
Fax : (902) 798-0464

Yarmouth

Arthur McDonald
Town Planner
Town of Yarmouth
Planning Department
400 Main St.
Yarmouth, NS B5A 1G2
Phone : (902) 745-2235
Fax : (902) 749-1474
Web Site : www.munisource.org/yarmouth

NEW BRUNSWICK

New Brunswick

Jim Chandra
Director of Investment
Department of Investment & Exports
P.O. Box 6000, Stn. A
Fredericton, NB E3B 5H1
Phone : (506) 453-3981
Fax : (506) 444-4277
Web Site : www.gnb.ca

Acadian Peninsula Region

Roger Robichaud
General Manager
Economic Expansion Commission
P.O. Box 3666, Stn. Main
Tracadie-Sheila, NB E1X 1G5
Phone : (506) 395-2261
Fax : (506) 395-5672

Bathurst

Bill Levesque
General Manager
Chaleur Regional Development Commission Inc.
275 Main St., Suite 212A
Bathurst, NB E2A 1A9
Phone : (506) 547-7445
Fax : (506) 548-8271

Campbellton

Betty-Ann Levesque
General Manager
Restigouche Regional Economic Development
Commission Inc.
P.O. Box 825, Stn. Main
Campbellton, NB E3N 3H3
Phone : (506) 789-4939
Fax : (506) 789-4933
Web Site : www.restigouchecommission.com

Carleton Region

Gary Melanson
General Manager
Carleton Regional Development Commission Inc.
114 Queen St., Unit 101
Woodstock, NB E7M 2M9
Phone : (506) 325-4488
Fax : (506) 325-4489
Web Site : www.carletonredc.com

Edmundston

Rino Pelletier
General Manager
Northwest Industrial Commission Inc.
121 Church St.
P.O. Box 490, Stn. Main
Edmundston, NB E3V 3L2
Phone : (506) 735-4769
Fax : (506) 739-7486

Fredericton

Jacques Dubé
President
Greater Fredericton Economic
Development Corporation
570 Queen St.
Fredericton, NB E3B 6Z6
Phone : (506) 444-4686
Fax : (506) 444-4649
Web Site : www.greaterfredericton.com

Fundy Region

James Balcomb
General Manager
Fundy Region Development Commission Inc.
49 King St., Unit 1
Saint Andrews, NB E5B 1X6
Phone : (506) 529-5518
Fax : (506) 529-5261
Email : frdc@nbnet.nb.ca

Grand Falls

Ronald Ouellette
President
La Vallée District Planning Commission
65 Broadway, Suite 300
P.O. Box 7301
Grand Falls, NB E3Z 2J6
Phone : (506) 475-2511
Fax : (506) 475-2516
Web Site : www.grandfalls.com

Miramichi Region

Wayne Carpenter
Economic Development Officer
Miramichi Region Development Corp.
158 Wellington St.
Miramichi, NB E1N 1L9
Phone : (506) 622-7890
Fax : (506) 622-2160
Web Site : www.mibc.nb.ca/mrdc

Moncton

Peter Belliveau
General Manager
Moncton Industrial Development Ltd.
910 Main St., Suite 102
Moncton, NB E1C 1G6
Phone : (506) 857-0700
Fax : (506) 859-7206
Web Site : www.mid.nb.ca

Oromocto

See Fredericton

Saint John

Stephen Carson
General Manager
Enterprise Saint John
40 King St.
Saint John, NB E2L 1G3
Phone : (506) 658-2995
Fax : (506) 658-2872
Web Site : www.enterprisesj.nb.ca

South East Region

Don Allain
General Manager
South East Economic Commission
11A Hamilton St.
Shediac, NB E4P 1W1
Phone : (506) 533-3390
Fax : (506) 533-3393

QUÉBEC

Québec

Dominique Bonifacio
V-P of Investment, Promotion & Prospection
Investissements-Québec
393 St-Jacques St., 5 étage
Montréal, QC H2Y 1N9
Phone : (514) 873-4375
Fax : (514) 873-4503
Web Site : www.invest-quebec.com

Abitibi-Ouest

Francine Bessette
Commissaire Industrielle
Centre Local de Développement d'Abitibi-Ouest
260 1ère Rue E.
La Sarre, QC J9Z 2B8
Phone : (819) 333-2214
Fax : (819) 333-3677

Alma

Réjean Couture
Commissaire Industriel et Directeur général
Conseil Économique du Lac-Saint-Jean Est.
625 rue Bergeron O.
Alma, QC G8B 1V3
Phone : (418) 662-6645
Fax : (418) 662-3297
Email : info@cld.lacstjean.qc.ca

Amos

Guy Bourgeois
Directeur du Développement Économique
Ville D'Amos
Développement Économique
182 1ère Rue Est
Amos, QC J9T 2G1
Phone : (819) 732-3254
Fax : (819) 727-9792
Email : guy.bourgeois@ville.amos.qc.ca
Web Site : www.ville.amos.qc.ca

Anjou

Gilles Dault
Directeur
Commissariat Industriel
7701 boul. Louis-H-Lafontaine
Anjou, QC H1K 4B9
Phone : (514) 493-8086
Fax : (514) 493-8089
Email : commissariat.industriel@ville.anjou.qc.ca
Web Site : www.ville.anjou.qc.ca

Asbestos

Michel Lachance
Commissaire Industriel
309 rue Chasse, local 109
Asbestos, QC J1T 2B4
Phone : (819) 879-6643
Fax : (819) 879-5188

Aylmer

See Hull

Baie-Comeau

Ronnie Ouellet
Directeur général
CLD de Manicouagan
1305 boul. Blanche
Baie-Comeau, QC G5C 3J3
Phone : (418) 589-6497
Fax : (418) 589-6407
Email : cldmanic@globetrotter.net

Bécancour

Diane Daviault
Directrice générale
CLD de la MRC de Bécancour
3689 boul. Bécancour, Bureau 1
C.P. 520, Secteur Gentilly
Bécancour, QC G0X 1G0
Phone : (819) 298-2070
Fax : (819) 298-2041

Beloeil

Martin Lévesque
Directeur
Planification et Développement du Territoire
1000 rue Dupré
Boloeil, QC J3G 4A8
Phone : (450) 536-2890
Fax : (450) 536-2896
Email : planification@ville.beloeil.qc.ca
Web Site : www.ville.beloeil.qc.ca

Boucherville

Dianne Dufour
Commissaire du Développement Économique
Département du Développement
Économique de Boucherville
500 rue de la Rivière-aux-Pins
Boucherville, QC J4B 2Z7
Phone : (450) 641-3812
Fax : (450) 449-8208
Email : dufourd@ville.boucherville.qc.ca
Web Site : www.ville.boucherville.qc.ca

Brossard

Marc Laroche
Directeur général
Hôtel de Ville
2001 boul. Rome
Brossard, QC J4W 3K5
Phone : (450) 923-7000
Fax : (450) 923-7032
Web Site : www.ville.brossard.qc.ca

Candiac

Marie Dupont
Economic Development Officer
Ville de Candiac
Economic Development Office
100 boul. Montcalm Nord
Candiac, QC J5R 3L8
Phone : (450) 444-6054
Fax : (450) 444-6009
Web Site : www.ville.candiac.qc.ca

Cap-de-la-Madeleine

See Francheville

Chambly/Richelieu/Carignan

Michel Merleau
Directeur général
Corp. de Développement Économique
et Touristique de Chambly et Région
56 rue Martel
Chambly, QC J3L 1V3
Phone : (450) 658-8788
Fax : (450) 447-4525
Web Site : www.ville.chambly.qc.ca

Chibougamau

Yves Dorval
Agent de Développement
Commission Économique et Touristique
de Chibougamau (CET)
600, 3e Rue
Chibougamau, QC G8P 1P1
Phone : (418) 748-6060
Fax : (418) 748-4020

Chicoutimi

Lucien Turcotte
Commissaire Industriel
Société de Promotion Économique
295 rue Racine E.
C.P. 1023
Chicoutimi, QC G7H 5G4
Phone : (418) 698-3157
Fax : (418) 698-3279
Email : spec@saglac.qc.ca;
         Lucien.Turcotte@spec-chic.qc.ca

Coaticook

Pierre Arcand
Commissaire Industriel & Directeur général
Le centre local de développement de la MRC
de Coaticook
14 rue Adams, Bureau 301
Coaticook, QC J1A 1K3
Phone : (819) 849-7014
Fax : (819) 849-9683
Web Site : www.regioncoaticook.qc.ca/cld

Cowansville

Jean-Guy Masse
Directeur du Développement Économique
Société de Développement Économique
de Cowansville et de la Région Inc.
220 Place Municipale
Cowansville, QC J2K 1T4
Phone : (450) 263-0141
Fax : (450) 263-9357
Web Site : www.ville.cowansville.qc.ca

Deux-Montagnes

Jean-Marc Fauteux
Directeur général
Le centre local de développement de la MRC
de Deux-Montagnes
400 boul. Deux-Montagnes, Bureau 100
Deux-Montagnes, QC J7R 7C2
Phone : (450) 472-1502
Fax : (450) 491-7893
Web Site : www.cld.deux-montagnes.qc.ca

Dolbeau

Guy Grenier
Commissaire Industriel et Directeur général
Le centre local de développement de la MRC
de Maria Chapdelaine
1030 boul. Vezina
Dolbeau-Mistassini, QC G8L 3K9
Phone : (418) 276-0022
Fax : (418) 276-0623
Web Site : www.mrcmaria.qc.ca

Dollard-des-Ormeaux

Byron Coulter
Directeur des services techniques
12001 boul. de Salaberry
Dollard-des-Ormeaux, QC H9B 2A7
Phone : (514) 684-1010
Fax : (514) 684-6899
Email : bcoulter@ddo.qc.ca

Dorval

Germain D'Aoust
Commissaire Industriel
Cité de Dorval
60 av. Martin
Dorval, QC H9S 3R4
Phone : (514) 633-4075
Fax : (514) 633-4078
Web Site : www.city.dorval.qc.ca

Drummondville

Martin Dupont
Directeur général et Commissaire Industriel
Société de Développement
Économique de Drummondville Inc.
1400 rue Michaud
Drummondville, QC J2C 7V3
Phone : (819) 477-5511
Fax : (819) 477-5512
Web Site : www.sded-drummond.qc.ca

Francheville

Roger Béland
Directeur général
Centre Local de Développement (CLD)
de la MRC de Francheville
1075 rue Champflour
Trois-Rivières, QC G9A 2A1
Phone : (819) 374-4061
Fax : (819) 373-6511
Email : rogerbeland@cedic.org
Web Site : www.francheville.org

Gatineau

Mario Lebeau
Directeur
Commissariat au Développement Économique
144 boul. de L'Hôpital, Bureau 510
Gatineau, QC J8T 7S7
Phone : (819) 243-2346
Fax : (819) 243-2363
Email : dev.econ@ville.gatineau.qc.ca
Web Site : www.ville.gatineau.qc.ca

Granby

See Haute-Yamaska

Haute-Yamaska

Guy Champagne
Directeur général
CLD Haute-Yamaska
142 rue Dufferin, Bureau 200
Granby, QC J2G 4X1
Phone : (450) 777-1141
Phone : 1-888-523-1141
Fax : (450) 777-1657
Web Site : www.haute-yamaska.com

Hull

Laurent Thauvette
Commissaire au Développement Économique
Ville de Hull
25 rue Laurier, 2e étage
Hull, QC J8X 4C8
Phone : (819) 595-7298
Fax : (819) 595-7283
Email : Thauvettel@Ville.Hull.qc.ca
Web Site : www.ville.hull.qc.ca

Joliette

Elene Serjerea
Commissaire Industrielle
Corp. de Développement Économique
de la Région de Joliette Inc.
654 rue de Lanaudière
Joliette, QC J6E 3M7
Phone : (450) 752-5566
Fax : (450) 752-5191
Email : cldj@tandore.qc.ca

Kirkland

Guy Filiatrault
Inspecteur de bâtiments
17200 boul. Hymus
Kirkland, QC H9J 3Y8
Phone : (514) 630-2740
Fax : (514) 630-2711
Email : guy_filiatrault@ville.kirkland.qc.ca
Web Site : www.ville.kirkland.qc.ca

La Baie-des-Ha! Ha!

Bruno Minier
Commissaire Industriel et Directeur général
Société de Développement
Économique de Ville de la Baie
1171 7e Ave., 3e étage
La Baie, QC G7B 1S8
Phone : (418) 697-5070
Fax : (418) 697-5068

Lachine

Pierre Dubois
Inspecteur de bâtiments
Service de l'Aménagement
1800 boul. Saint-Joseph
Lachine, QC H8S 2N4
Phone : (514) 634-3471
Fax : (514) 634-8461
Email : duboisp@ville.lachine.qc.ca
Web Site : www.ville.lachine.qc.ca

Lachute

Maurice Gendreau
Directeur général
Centre Local de Développement du
Territoire de la MRC d'Argenteuil
430 rue Grace
Lachute, QC J8H 1M6
Phone : (450) 562-8829
Fax : (450) 562-1635
Web Site : www.argenteuil.qc.ca

LaSalle

Yves Meunier
Commissaire Industriel
Hôtel de Ville
55 av. Dupras
LaSalle, QC H8R 4A8
Phone : (514) 367-6380
Fax : (514) 367-6600
Web Site : www.ville.lasalle.qc.ca

Laval

Gilbert LeBlanc
Commissaire Industriel
Services Développement Économique et Urbain
Laval Technopole
1555 boul. Chomedey, Bureau 100
Laval, QC H7V 3Z1
Phone : (450) 978-5959
Fax : (450) 978-5970
Web Site : www.lavaltechnopole.qc.ca

Lévis

Jean-François Carrier
Directeur général
Centre Local de Développement de la MRC
de Desjardins
13 rue Saint-Louis, Bureau 302
Lévis, QC G6V 4E2
Phone : (418) 837-4781
Fax : (418) 837-4783

Longueuil

Gilles Côté
Commissaire général au Développement
Société d'aide au Développement
Économique de Longueuil
777 rue d'Auvergne
C.P. 5000, Succ. Bureau-Chef
Longueuil, QC J4K 4Y7
Phone : (450) 646-8023
Fax : (450) 646-8297
Web Site : www.ville.longueuil.qc.ca

Magog

Guy Madore
Agent de Liaison et Communication
Ville de Magog
7 rue Principale E.
Magog, QC J1X 1Y4
Phone : (819) 843-2880
Fax : (819) 843-4486

Matane

Guy Dorval
Directeur général
Centre Local de Développement
Région de Matane
235 av. Saint-Jérôme, Bureau 300
Matane, QC G4W 3A7
Phone : (418) 562-1250
Fax : (418) 562-2954
Email : cldmatane@globetrotter.qc.ca

Mirabel

Jean-Luc Riopel
Directeur
Centre Local de Développement
de Mirabel
14026 boul. Curé-Labelle
Mirabel, QC J7J 1A1
Phone : (450) 435-2800
Fax : (450) 435-3177
Web Site : www.cldmirabel.qc.ca

Mont-Royal

Guy Landry
Directeur du Développement Économique
90 av. Roosevelt
Mont-Royal, QC H3R 1Z5
Phone : (514) 734-3011
Fax : (514) 734-3093
Email : guy.landry@ville.mont-royal.qc.ca
Web Site : www.ville.mont-royal.qc.ca

Mont-Saint-Hilaire

Laurent Olivier
Directeur général
Ville de Mont-Saint-Hilaire
100 rue du Centre-Civique
Mont-Saint-Hilaire, QC J3H 3M8
Phone : (450) 467-2854
Fax : (450) 467-6460

Montmagny

Suzanne Lacombe
Commissaire Industrielle
Corp. de Développement Économique de la
Municipalité Régionale du comté de Montmagny
159 rue Saint-Louis
Montmagny, QC G5V 1N5
Phone : (418) 248-4825
Fax : (418) 248-4624
Email : cdemm@montmagny.com
Web Site : www.montmagny.com

Montréal, Ville de

Fabien Cournoyer
Directeur
Services Développement Économique et Urbain (SDEU)
303 rue Notre-Dame Est, 5e étage
Montréal, QC H2Y 3Y8
Phone : (514) 872-4523
Fax : (514) 872-1007
Web Site : www.ville.montreal.qc.ca/econurb

Montréal-Nord

Michel Archambault
Directeur général
Ville de Montréal-Nord
4242 place de l'Hôtel-de-Ville
Montréal-Nord, QC H1H 1S5
Phone : (514) 328-4006
Fax : (514) 328-4282

Pierrefonds

Pierre Rochon
Directeur du service Urbanisme et Développement
13665 boul. Pierrefonds
C.P. 2500, Succ. Bureau-Chef
Pierrefonds, QC H9A 2Z4
Phone : (514) 624-1124
Fax : (514) 624-1333

Pointe-Claire

Tom Buffitt
Directeur général
Ville de Pointe-Claire
451 boul. Saint-Jean
Pointe-Claire, QC H9R 3J3
Phone : (514) 630-1200
Fax : (514) 630-1272
Email : dg@ville.pointe-claire.qc.ca

Portneuf

René Savard
Directeur général
Centre Local de Développement de Portneuf
185 route 138
Cap-Santé, QC G0A 1T0
Phone : (418) 285-4616
Fax : (418) 285-4655
Web Site : www.portneuf.com

Québec, Ville de

Pierre Boulanger
Président et Directeur général
La Société de Promotion Économique
du Québec Métropolitain
1126 Chemin Saint-Louis, Bureau 802
Québec, QC G1S 1E5
Phone : (418) 681-9700
Fax : (418) 681-1535
Email : info@speqm.qc.ca
Web Site : www.speqm.qc.ca

Repentigny/Charlemagne/ Le Gardeur

Thomas Duzyk
Directeur général
Centre Local de Développement (CLD)
de la MRC de L'Assomption
300 B rue Dorval
L'Assomption, QC J5W 3A1
Phone : (450) 589-8888
Fax : (450) 589-5662

Rimouski

Serge Ouellet
Directeur général
CLD Rimouski-Neigette
431 rue des Artisans, Bureau 200
C.P. 710, Succ. Bureau-Chef
Rimouski, QC G5M 1A4
Phone : (418) 722-8766
Fax : (418) 723-5924
Email : cldrn@globetrotter.net

Rivière-du-Loup

Marie-Josée Huot
Directrice générale
Centre Local de Développement (CLD)
de la région de Rivière-du-Loup
299 rue Lafontaine
Rivière-du-Loup, QC G5R 3A9
Phone : (418) 862-1823
Fax : (418) 862-3726
Email : cld@globetrotter.net
Web Site : www.mrc-rdl.qc.ca

Roberval

François Boily
Commissaire Industriel
Centre Local de Développement (CLD)
Domaine-du-Roy
901 boul. Saint-Joseph, Bureau 103
Roberval, QC G8H 2L8
Phone : (418) 275-2755
Fax : (418) 275-5787
Email : sdlsjo@destination.ca

Roussillon

Commissaire Industriel
Société de Développement
Économique de Roussillon
Phone : (450) 444-9529

Rouyn-Noranda, Région de

Danielle Simard
Directrice générale par intérim
Centre Local de Développement
MRC Rouyn-Noranda
100 rue Taschereau E.
C.P. 205
Noranda, QC J9X 5C3
Phone : (819) 797-7142
Fax : (819) 797-7134
Email : cld.dsim@cablevision.qc.ca

Saint-Bruno-de-Montarville

Jean Bergeron
Commissaire Industriel
Ville de Saint-Bruno-de-Montarville
1585 rue Montarville
Saint-Bruno-de-Montarville, QC J3V 3T8
Phone : (450) 441-8367
Fax : (450) 441-8482
Email : planif.dev@ville.stbruno.qc.ca
Web Site : www.ville.stbruno.qc.ca

Saint-Eustache

Denis Trottier
Directeur
La Corporation de Développement Économique
de Saint-Eustache (CODESE)
192 boul. Industriel
Saint-Eustache, QC J7R 5C2
Phone : (450) 974-5005
Fax : (450) 974-5010
Email : dtrottier@codese.com
Web Site : www.codese.com

Saint-Georges-de-Beauce

Claude Morin
Directeur général
Conseil Économique de Beauce Inc.
11515 1ère Av., Bureau 201
Saint-Georges, QC G5Y 2C7
Phone : (418) 228-8123
Fax : (418) 228-5223

Saint-Hubert

Jacques Lamarre
Agent de Développement
Service de Développement du Territoire
de Saint-Hubert
5245 boul. Cousineau, Bureau 2000
Saint-Hubert, QC J3Y 7K8
Phone : (450) 445-7797
Fax : (450) 445-7848

Saint-Hyacinthe

Mario De Tilly
Commissaire Industriel et Directeur général
Centre Local de Développement
de la MRC Les Maskoutains
800 av. Sainte-Anne, Bureau 300
Saint-Hyacinthe, QC J2S 5G7
Phone : (450) 773-4232
Fax : (450) 773-6767
Email : info@cld-lesmaskoutains.qc.ca
Web Site : www.cld-lesmaskoutains.qc.ca

Saint-Jean-sur-Richelieu

Christian Perreault
Directeur général
Conseil Économique du Haut-Richelieu (CLD)
315 rue MacDonald, Bureau 301
Saint-Jean-sur-Richelieu, QC J3B 8J3
Phone : (450) 359-9999
Fax : (450) 359-0994
Web Site : www.haut-richelieu.qc.ca/cld.htm

Saint-Jérôme

Michel Gauthier
Commissaire Industriel
CLD Rivière du Nord
300 boul. Jean-Paul-Hogue
Saint-Antoine, QC J7Z 6Y2
Phone : (450) 431-0707
Fax : (450) 431-7507
Web Site : www.cld-rdn.qc.ca

Saint-Laurent

Réjean Laliberté
Directeur de Développement Économique
710 rue Saint-Germain
Saint-Laurent, QC H4L 3R5
Phone : (514) 855-5750
Fax : (514) 855-5739
Web Site : www.ville.saint-laurent.qc.ca

Saint-Léonard

Pierre Santamaria
Commissaire Industriel et Directeur général
Ville de Saint-Léonard
8400 boul. Lacordaire
Saint-Léonard, QC H1R 3B1
Phone : (514) 328-8400
Fax : (514) 328-8416
Web Site : www.ville.st-leonard.qc.ca

Sainte-Thérèse

Charles Le Borgne
Commissaire Industriel et Directeur général
Société de Développement Économique
de Thérèse-De Blainville
33 rue Blainville O., Bureau 200
Sainte-Thérèse-de-Blainville, QC J7E 1X1
Phone : (450) 430-6666
Fax : (450) 430-9652
Web Site : www.sodet.com

Sept-Îles

Gilles Dechamplain
Commissaire Industriel
Corp. de Promotion Industrielle
et Commerciale de Sept-Îles Inc
546 av. De Quen
Sept-Îles, QC G4R 2R4
Phone : (418) 962-7677
Fax : (418) 968-2084

Shawinigan

Luc Arvisais
Directeur général
Conseil Local de Développement
Centre-de-la-Mauricie
794 5e Rue
C.P. 895
Shawinigan, QC G9N 6W2
Phone : (819) 537-7249
Fax : (819) 537-6260
Web Site : www.directioncm.net

Sherbrooke

Pierre Dagenais
Directeur général et Commissaire au
Développement Économique
Société de Développement Économique
de la Région Sherbrookoise
1308 boul. de Portland
C.P. 1355
Sherbrooke, QC J1H 5L9
Phone : (819) 821-5577
Phone : 1-877-211-5326
Fax : (819) 822-6021
Email : sders@sders.com
Web Site : www.sders.com

Sorel-Tracy & Région

Yves Fortin
Directeur général et Commissaire au
Développement Économique
CLD du Bas-Richelieu
67 rue George
Sorel, QC J3P 1C2
Phone : (450) 742-5933
Fax : (450) 742-0234
Web Site : www.bas-richelieu.com

Terrebonne, Région de
Lise Brouillette
Commissaire Industrielle et Directrice générale
Société Régionale de Développement
Économique des Moulins Inc.
3800 rue Pascal-Gagnon
Terrebonne, QC J6X 4J2
Phone : (450) 477-6464
Fax : (450) 477-9573

Thetford Mines
Michel Routhier
Président
Centre Local de Développement de la MRC
de l'Amiante
690 rue Monfette N.
Thetford Mines, QC G6G 7G9
Phone : (418) 338-2188
Fax : (418) 338-4984
Web Site : www.cldamiante.qc.ca

Trois-Rivières
See Francheville

Val-d'Or
Serge Martel
Directeur général
CLD de la Vallée-de-l'Or
44 place Hammond
Val-d'Or, QC J9P 3A9
Phone : (819) 874-4717
Fax : (819) 874-4771

Valleyfield
Stephen Bellette
Commissaire Industriel
Corp. de Développement Économique
de Valleyfield Inc.
100 Sainte-Cécile, Bureau 100
Salaberry-de-Valleyfield, QC J6T 1M1
Phone : (450) 373-2214
Fax : (450) 373-3386
Email : cldval@rocler.qc.ca
Web Site : www.rocler.qc.ca/cld

Verdun
Raymond Fréchette
Co-ordinateur des services techniques
Ville de Verdun
4555 rue de Verdun
Verdun, QC H4G 1M4
Phone : (514) 765-7001
Fax : (514) 765-7075

Victoriaville
René Thivierge
Commissaire Industriel
Corp. de Développement Économique des Bois-Francs
975 boul. Industriel Est, Bureau 101
C.P. 487, Succ. Bureau-Chef
Victoriaville, QC G6P 6T3
Phone : (819) 758-3172
Fax : (819) 758-1187
Web Site : www.cdebf.qc.ca

ONTARIO

Ontario
Al Paladini
Minister for Economic Development
Ministry of Economic Development & Trade
Hearst Block, 900 Bay St., 9th fl.
Toronto, ON M7A 2E1
Phone : (416) 325-6666
Fax : (416) 325-6918
Web Site : www.ontario-canada.com

Ajax
See Durham Region

Almonte
Stacie Lloyd
Economic Development Officer
3131 Old Perth Rd.
Almonte, ON K0A 1A0
Phone : (613) 256-2064
Fax : (613) 256-4887
Email : slloyd@town.mississippi-mills.on.ca
Web Site : www.mississippimills.com

Ancaster
Patrick Hennessy
Director
Planning and Building Development Department
300 Wilson St. E.
Ancaster, ON L9G 2B9
Phone : (905) 648-4447
Fax : (905) 648-9457
Email : phennessy@town.ancaster.on.ca
Web Site : www.town.ancaster.on.ca

Arnprior
Susan McLean
Chief Administrative Officer
Town Hall
105 Elgin St. W.
P.O. Box 130, Stn. Main
Arnprior, ON K7S 3H4
Phone : (613) 623-4231
Fax : (613) 623-8091
Email : samclean@townarnprior.on.ca
Web Site : www.townarnprior.on.ca

Aurora
Diane Gould
Administrative Assistant to the Mayor
Town of Aurora
100 John West Way
P.O. Box 1000, Stn. Main
Aurora, ON L4G 6J1
Phone : (905) 727-1375
Fax : (905) 727-5025
Web Site : www.town.aurora.on.ca

Barrie
Nancy Tuckett
Director of Economic Development
Economic Development Office
70 Collier St., Suite 208
P.O. Box 400
Barrie, ON L4M 4T5
Phone : (705) 739-4220 ext. 4524
Fax : (705) 739-4246
Web Site : www.city.barrie.on.ca

Belleville
Karen Post
Manager of Economic Development
City of Belleville
City Hall
169 Front St.
Belleville, ON K8N 2Y8
Phone : (613) 967-3273
Fax : (613) 967-3262
Web Site : www.city.belleville.on.ca

Brampton
Dennis Cutajar
Director of Economic Development
Economic Development Office
33 Queen St. W.
Brampton, ON L6Y 1L9
Phone : (905) 874-2650
Fax : (905) 874-2670
Email : edo@city.brampton.on.ca
Web Site :
 www.city.brampton.on.ca/economic-development

Brantford
David Amos
Director of Economic Development
100 Wellington Square
Brantford, ON N3T 2M3
Phone : (519) 759-4150
Fax : (519) 752-6775
Web Site : www.city.brantford.on.ca

Brockville
David C. Paul
Economic Development Officer
1 King St. W.
P.O. Box 5000, Stn. Main
Brockville, ON K6V 7A5
Phone : (613) 342-8772
Fax : (613) 342-8780
Email : dpaul@brockville.com
Web Site : www.brockville.com

Burlington
Gayla McDonald
General Manager
Burlington Economic Development Corp.
1005 Skyview Dr.
Burlington, ON L7P 5B1
Phone : (905)332-9415
Fax : (905) 332-7829
Email : mcdonald@city.burlington.on.ca
Web Site : www.advantageburlington.com

Caledon
Tom Slomke
Manager of Industrial & Commercial Development
Town of Caledon
6311 Old Church Rd.
P.O. Box 1000
Caledon East, ON L0N 1E0
Phone : (905) 584-2272 ext. 2223
Fax : (905) 584-4325
Web Site : www.town.caledon.on.ca

Cambridge
Bozena Densmore
Director of Economic Development
City of Cambridge
73 Water St. N., 2nd Floor
P.O. Box 669, Stn. Galt
Cambridge, ON N1R 5W8
Phone : (519) 740-4536
Fax : (519) 740-4512
Web Site : www.city.cambridge.on.ca

Chatham
Irene Subocz
Director of Economic Development
445 Grand Ave. W.
P.O. Box 1230, Stn. Main
Chatham, ON N7M 5L3
Phone : (519) 351-7700
Fax : (519) 351-7852
Email : irenes@city.chatham-kent.on.ca
Web Site : www.city.chatham-kent.on.ca

Clarington
Jennifer Cooke
Marketing, Tourism & Economic Development Officer
The Municipality of Clarington
40 Temperance St.
Bowmanville, ON L1C 3A6
Phone : (905) 623-3379
Fax : (905) 623-0584
Email : jcooke@municipality.clarington.on.ca
Web Site : www.municipality.clarington.on. ca

Cobourg

Sydney Simmons-Millroy
Economic Development Officer
The Economic Development & Tourism Office
Dressler House
212 King St. W.
Cobourg, ON K9A 2N1
Phone : (905) 372-5481
Fax : (905) 372-1306
Email : econdev@town.cobourg.on.ca
Web Site : www.town.cobourg.on.ca

Collingwood

Catherine Durrant
Director of Economic Development
Town of Collingwood
97 Hurontario St.
P.O. Box 157, Stn. Main
Collingwood, ON L9Y 3Z5
Phone : (705) 445-8441
Fax : (705) 445-4704
Email : cdurrant@town.collingwood.on.ca
Web Site : www.town.collingwood.on.ca

Cornwall

Paul W. Fitzpatrick
Manager of Economic Development
340 Pitt St.
P.O. Box 877, Stn. Main
Cornwall, ON K6H 5T9
Phone : (613) 933-0074
Phone : 1-888-CORNWAL
Fax : (613) 933-0745
Email : fitzpatrick@city.cornwall.ca
Web Site : www.city.cornwall.on.ca

Cumberland

Daniel Champagne
Director of Economic Development
255 Centrum Blvd., Suite 100
Cumberland, ON K1E 3V8
Phone : (613) 830-6205
Fax : (613) 830-6255
Web Site : www.city.cumberland.on.ca

Steve Cunliffe
Commissioner of Planning & Economic Development
255 Centrum Blvd., Suite 100
Cumberland, ON K1E 3V8
Phone : (613) 830-6206
Fax : (613) 830-6255
Web Site : www.city.cumberland.on.ca

Deep River Area

John Walden
Director of Planning & Development
Economic Development Dept.
P.O. Box 400
Deep River Area, ON K0J 1P0
Phone : (613) 584-2000
Fax : (613) 584-3237
Email : jwalden@town.deepriver.on.ca
Web Site : www.town.deepriver.on.ca

Delhi

Frank Gelinas
Chief Administrative Officer
Town of Delhi
183 Main St.
P.O. Box 182
Delhi, ON N4B 2W9
Phone : (519) 582-2100
Phone : 1-800-265-2824
Fax : (519) 582-4571
Web Site : www.kjsgroup.com/delhi

Dryden

James Dayman
Economic Development Manager
30 Van Horne Ave.
Dryden, ON P8N 2A7
Phone : (807) 223-4100
Fax : (807) 223-4102
Web Site : www.cityofdryden.on.ca

Dundas

Lou Spittal
Director of Planning & Development
Town of Dundas
60 Main St.
P.O. Box 8584
Dundas, ON L9H 5E7
Phone : (905) 628-6327
Fax : (905) 628-5995

Dunnville

Ronald T. Sparks
Clerk Administrator
Town of Dunnville
111 Broad St. E.
P.O. Box 187
Dunnville, ON N1A 2X5
Phone : (905) 774-7595
Fax : (905) 774-4294
Web Site : www.dunnvillechamber.on.ca

Durham Region

Patrick Olive
Commissioner of Economic Development
Region of Durham
1615 Dundas St. E., 4th Floor
P.O. Box 623, Stn. Main
Whitby, ON L1N 6A3
Phone : (905) 723-0023
Fax : (905) 436-5359
Email : durecdev@region.durham.on.ca
Web Site : www.region.durham.on.ca

East Gwillimbury

Ruth Coursey
Director
Town of East Gwillimbury
19000 Leslie St.
Sharon, ON L0G 1V0
Phone : (905) 478-4282
Fax : (905) 478-2808
Web Site : www.town.eastgwillimbury.on.ca

East York

See Toronto

Elliot Lake

Merlyn (Lyn) C. Bishop
Chief Administrative Officer
City of Elliot Lake
45 Hillside Drive N.
Elliot Lake, ON P5A 1X5
Phone : (705) 461-7201
Fax : (705) 461-7269
Web Site : www.cityofelliotlake.com

Etobicoke

See Toronto

Fergus

Don Wilson
Chief Administrator & Economic Development Officer
Township of Centre Wellington
1 MacDonald Square,
P.O. Box 10
Elora, ON N0B 1S0
Phone : (519) 846-9691
Fax : (519) 846-2825
Email : DWilson@twp.cwellington.on.ca
Web Site : www.twp.cwellington.on.ca

Fort Erie

Gary Bruno
General Manager
Economic Development Corporation of Fort Erie
660 Garrison Rd., Unit 1
Fort Erie, ON L2A 6E2
Phone : (905) 871-1332
Fax : (905) 871-1077
Email : gbruno@forterie.on.ca
Web Site : www.forterie.on.ca

Fort Frances

Geoff Gillon
Economic Development Co-ordinator
Economic Development Commission
P.O. Box 38, Stn. Main
Fort Frances, ON P9A 3M5
Phone : (807) 274-5323
Fax : (807) 274-8479
Web Site : www.fort-frances.com

Georgina

Stanley Armstrong
Chief Administrative Officer
Civic Centre
RR 2, 26557 Civic Centre Rd.
Keswick, ON L4P 3G1
Phone : (905) 476-4301
Fax : (905) 476-8100
Web Site : www.town.georgina.on.ca

Gloucester

Donald Loguisto
Director of Economic Development
1595 Telesat Court
P.O. Box 8333
Gloucester, ON K1G 3V5
Phone : (613) 748-4194
Fax : (613) 748-4352
Email : Don.Loguisto@city.gloucester.on.ca
Web Site : www.city.gloucester.on.ca

Gravenhurst

Gary King
Chief Administrative Officer
190 Harvie St.
Gravenhurst, ON P1P 1S9
Phone : (705) 687-3412
Fax : (705) 687-7016
Email : GKing@gravenhurst.net
Web Site : www.gravenhurst.net

Grimsby

Keith Vogl
Planning Director
160 Livingston Ave.
P.O. Box 159, Stn. Main
Grimsby, ON L3M 4G3
Phone : (905) 945-9634
Fax : (905) 945-5010
Web Site : www.town.grimsby.on.ca

Guelph

Jim Mairs
Manager of Economic Development Department
Economic Development Department
City Hall
59 Carden St.
Guelph, ON N1H 3A1
Phone : (519) 837-5600
Fax : (519) 837-5636
Email : jmairs@city.guelph.on.ca
Web Site : www.city.guelph.on.ca

Haileybury

Tom Wells
Mayor
P.O. Box 2050
Haileybury, ON P0J 1K0
Phone : (705) 672-3363
Fax : (705) 672-3200
Email : municipality@town.haileybury.on.ca
Web Site : www.town.haileybury.on.ca

Haldimand-Norfolk

Carol Gerrett
Economic Development Officer
Haldimand-Norfolk
70 Town Centre Dr.
Townsend, ON N0A 1S0
Phone : (519) 587-4911
Fax : (519) 587-5554
Email : hnecdev@haldimand-norfolk.on.ca
Web Site : www.haldimand-norfolk.on.ca

Halton Regional Municipality

Elaine Holding
Business Development Officer
Business Development Centre
1151 Bronte Rd.
Oakville, ON L6M 3L1
Phone : (905) 825-6300
Fax : (905) 825-8839
Email : busdev@region.halton.on.ca
Web Site : www.haltonbusiness.com

Hamilton-Wentworth Regional Municipality

Neil Everson
Manager of Business Development
Economic Development Dept.
Regional Municipality of Hamilton-Wentworth
1 James St. S., 8th, fl.
Hamilton, ON L8P 4R5
Phone : (905) 546-4222
Fax : (905) 546-4107
Email : economicdevelopment@hamilton-went.on.ca
Web Site : www.city.hamilton.on.ca

Hanover

Bill Lang
Acting Economic Development Officer
Saugeen Economic Development Corp.
554 7th Ave.
Hanover, ON N4N 2J7
Phone : (519) 364-3694
Fax : (519) 364-6384
Email : edc@hanovercanada.com
Web Site : www.hanovercanada.com

Hawkesbury

Francine Dubé
Managing Director
Hawkesbury Community Economic
Development Corporation
519 Main St. E.
Hawkesbury, ON K6A 1B3
Phone : (613) 636-0697
Fax : (613) 632-7385
Email : sdech@hawk.igs.net
Web Site : www.ville.hawkesbury.on.ca

Huntsville

Terry Sararas
Manager of Planning
37 Main St. E.
Huntsville, ON P1H 1A1
Phone : (705) 789-1751 ext. 2226
Fax : (705) 789-6689
Web Site : www.town.huntsville.on.ca

Ingersoll

Ted Hunt
Director of Economic Development
130 Oxford St.
Ingersoll, ON N5C 2V5
Phone : (519) 485-0120
Fax : (519) 485-3543
Email : thunt@town.ingersoll.on.ca
Web Site : www.town.ingersoll.on.ca

Kanata

Robin MacKay
Manager of Economic Development
580 Terry Fox Dr.
Kanata, ON K2L 4C2
Phone : (613) 592-4291 ext. 283
Fax : (613) 592-8183
Web Site : www.city.kanata.on.ca

Kapuskasing

Yvan Brousseau
Chief Administrative Officer
88 Riverside Dr.
Kapuskasing, ON P5N 1B3
Phone : (705) 335-2341
Fax : (705) 337-1741
Web Site : www.town.kapuskasing.on.ca

Kenora

Rory McMillan
Chief Administrative Officer
Lake of the Woods Business Incentive Corp.
227 1/2 2nd St. South
Kenora, ON P9N 1G1
Phone : (807) 467-4640
Fax : (807) 467-4645
Web Site : www.voyageur.ca/~lowbic

Kingston & Area

Steven Kelly
President and CEO
Kingston Area Economic Development Corp.
181 Wellington St.,Suite 200
Kingston, ON K7L 3E3
Phone : (613) 544-2725 ext. 226
Fax : (613) 546-2882
Email : kelly@kingstoncanada.com
Web Site : www.kingstoncanada.com

Kirkland Lake

Don Studholme
Director of Economic Development
Department of Economic Development and Tourism
Bag 1757, Stn. Main
Kirkland Lake, ON P2N 3P4
Phone : (705) 567-9361
Fax : (705) 567-3535
Email : edkirk@ntl.sympatico.ca
Web Site : www.town.kirklandlake.on.ca

Kitchener

George Borovilos
Director of Economic Development
Economic Development Division
200 King St. W.
P.O. Box 1118, Stn. C
Kitchener, ON N2G 4G7
Phone : (519) 741-2291
Fax : (519) 741-2722
Web Site : www.city.kitchener.on.ca

Leamington

William Marck
Chief Administrative Officer
38 Erie St. N.
Leamington, ON N8H 2Z3
Phone : (519) 326-5761
Fax : (519) 326-2481
Web Site : www.town.leamington.on.ca

Lincoln

Bruce Peever
Acting Chief Administrative Officer
4800 South Service Rd.
Beamsville, ON L0R 1B1
Phone : (905) 563-8205
Fax : (905) 563-6566
Web Site : www.townoflincoln.com

Lindsay

Bryan Brown
Director of Economic Development
County of Victoria Administration Building
26 Francis Street
P.O. Box 9000
Lindsay, ON K9V 5R8
Phone : (705) 324-9411 Ext. 230
Fax : (705) 324-1750
Email : brbrown@countyofvictoria.on.ca
Web Site : www.countyofvictoria.on.ca

London

Cherry Sholltanuk
Economic Development Officer
City of London
P.O. Box 5035
London, ON N6A 4L9
Phone : (519) 661-4546
Fax : (519) 661-5331
Email : csholtan@city.london.on.ca
Web Site : www.city.london.on.ca

Markham

Stephen Chait
Director of Economic Development
101 Town Centre Blvd.
Markham, ON L3R 9W3
Phone : (905) 475-4871
Fax : (905) 479-7764
Email : schait@city.markham.on.ca
Web Site : www.city.markham.on.ca

Midland

Joyce Campbell
General Manager & Economic Development
Commissioner
Chamber of Commerce
Town of Midland
208 King St.
Midland, ON L4R 3L9
Phone : (705) 526-7884
Fax : (705) 526-1744
Web Site : www.southerngeorgianbay.on.ca

Milton

Andrew M. Siltala
Economic Development Officer
Town of Milton
43 Brown St.
Milton, ON L9T 5H2
Phone : (905) 878-7252 ext. 103
Fax : (905) 878-5927
Email : andrew.siltala@town.milton.on.ca
Web Site : www.town.milton.on.ca

Mississauga

Larry Petovello
Director of Economic Development
City of Mississauga
300 City Centre Dr., 3rd Floor
Mississauga, ON L5B 3C1
Phone : (905) 896-5016
Fax : (905) 896-5931
Email : larry.petovello@city.mississauga.on.ca
Web Site : www.city.mississauga.on.ca/edo

Nanticoke

See Haldimand-Norfolk

Napanee

Keith Richmond
Chief Building Official
Town of Greater Napanee
124 John St.
P.O. Box 97
Napanee, ON K7R 3L4
Phone : (613) 354-3351
Fax : (613) 354-6545
Email : krichmond@town.greater.on.ca
Web Site : www.town.greaternapanee.on.ca

Nepean

Michael Murr
Director of Economic Development
City of Nepean
Ben Franklin Place
101 Centrepointe Dr.
Nepean, ON K2G 5K7
Phone : (613) 727-6627
Fax : (613) 727-6694
Email : bizinfo@city.nepean.on.ca
Web Site : www.city.nepean.on.ca

New Tecumseth

Valerie Ryan
Chief Executive Officer
New Tecumseth Economic Development Corp.
169 Dufferin St., Unit 26
P.O. Box 184
Alliston, ON L9R 1V5
Phone : (705) 435-1540
Fax : (705) 435-6907
Email : edc@bconnex.net
Web Site : www.town.newtecumseth.on.ca

54 Queen St. S.
P.O. Box 359
Tottenham, ON L0G 1W0
Phone : (905) 936-5005
Fax : (905) 936-4545

Newcastle

See Durham Region

Newmarket

Tom Taylor
Mayor
Town of Newmarket
395 Mulock Dr.
P.O. Box 328, Stn. Main
Newmarket, ON L3Y 4X7
Phone : (905) 953-5102
Fax : (905) 853-5135
Email : nmayor@town.newmarket.on.ca
Web Site : www.town.newmarket.on.ca

Dennis Perlin
Chief Administrative Officer
Town of Newmarket
395 Mulock Dr.
P.O. Box 328, Stn. Main
Newmarket, ON L3Y 4X7
Phone : (905) 895-5193
Fax : (905) 853-5135
Email : dperlin@town.newmarket.on.ca
Web Site : www.town.newmarket.on.ca

Niagara Falls

Sergio Felicetti
Director of Business Development
Niagara Falls City Hall
4310 Queen St.
P.O. Box 1023
Niagara Falls, ON L2E 6X5
Phone : (905) 356-7521
Fax : (905) 357-9293
Web Site : www.city.niagarafalls.on.ca

Niagara-on-the-Lake

William Walker
Director of Planning and Development
Town of Niagara-on-the-Lake
P.O. Box 100
Virgil, ON L0S 1T0
Phone : (905) 468-3266
Fax : (905) 468-0301
Web Site : www.notl.com

Niagara Region

Allan Teichroeb
Manager of Business Development
Niagara Economic & Tourism Corp.
P.O. Box 1042, Stn. Main
Thorold, ON L2V 4T7
Phone : (905) 685-1308
Fax : (905) 688-5907
Web Site : www.niagaracanada.com

North Bay

Rick Evans
Manager of Economic Development
Economic Development Division
Planning and Development Department
North Bay City Hall
200 McIntyre St. E.
P.O. Box 360, Stn. Main
North Bay, ON P1B 8H8
Phone : (705) 474-0400 ext. 431
Fax : (705) 474-4493
Email : ricke@mbox.city.north-bay.on.ca
Web Site : www.city.north-bay.on.ca

Oakville

David Cash
Chief Executive Officer
Oakville Economic Development Alliance Inc.
1225 Trafalgar Rd.
P.O. Box 6
Oakville, ON L6J 4Z5
Phone : (905) 338-4187
Fax : (905) 815-2011
Email : dcash@oeda.oakville.on.ca
Web Site : www.oeda.oakville.on.ca

Orangeville

Rick Schwarzer
Chief Administrative Officer &
Economic Development Officer
87 Broadway
Orangeville, ON L9W 1K1
Phone : (519) 941-0439
Fax : (519) 941-9033
Email : admin@orangeville.org
Web Site : www.orangeville.org

Orillia

Darrin Mitchell
Development Officer
Economic Development Commission
City of Orillia
50 Andrew St. S.
Orillia, ON L3V 7T5
Phone : (705) 325-4900
Fax : (705) 327-5103
Web Site : www.city.orillia.on.ca

Oro-Medonte

Debbie Brodrick
Economic Development Officer
Community Economic Development Centre
Oro-Medonte Administration Centre
148 Line 7 S.
P.O. Box 100
Oro, ON L0L 2X0
Phone : (705) 487-2171
Fax : (705) 487-0133
Web Site : www.township.oro-medonte.on.ca

Osgoode

Gord Pratt
Economic Development Officer
Economic Development Department
Township of Osgoode
8243 Victoria St.
P.O. Box 130
Metcalfe, ON K0A 2P0
Phone : (613) 821-1107
Phone : 1-800-363-4610
Fax : (613) 821-4359
Web Site : www3.sympatico.ca/twp.osgoode

Oshawa

Judy Dudar & Chris Madej
Managers
City of Oshawa
50 Centre St. S.
Oshawa, ON L1H 3Z7
Phone : (905) 436-5617
Fax : (905) 436-5623
Web Site : www.city.oshawa.on.ca

Owen Sound

Steve Furness
Economic Development Planner
Community Services Dept.
City Hall
808 2nd Ave. E.
Owen Sound, ON N4K 2H4
Phone : (519) 376-1440
Fax : (519) 371-0511
Web Site : www.city.owen-sound.on.ca

Parry Sound and Area

Bill Spinney
Economic Development Officer & General Manager
Parry Sound Area
Community Business & Development Centre
1A Church St.
Parry Sound, ON P2A 1Y2
Phone : (705) 746-4455
Fax : (705) 746-4435
Web Site : www.cbdc.parrysound.on.ca

Pelham

Jack Bernardi
Director of Planning Services
Town of Pelham
20 Pelham Town Square
P.O. Box 400
Fonthill, ON L0S 1E0
Phone : (905) 892-2607
Fax : (905) 892-5055
Web Site : www.niagara.com/~pel-lib1

Pembroke

Susan Ellis
Economic Development Officer
City of Pembroke
1 Pembroke St. E.
P.O. Box 277, Stn. Main
Pembroke, ON K8A 6X3
Phone : (613) 735-6821
Fax : (613) 735-3660
Web Site : www.city.pembroke.on.ca

Perth

Kelly Pender
Clerk Administrator
Town of Perth
80 Gore St. E.
Perth, ON K7H 1H9
Phone : (613) 267-3770
Fax : (613) 267-5635
Web Site : www.perthcanada.com

Peterborough

Susan Cudahy
President & Chief Executive Officer
Greater Peterborough Area Economic
Development Corporation
210 Wolfe St.
Peterborough, ON K9J 2K9
Phone : (705) 743-0777
Fax : (705) 743-3093
Web Site : www.gpaedc.on.ca

Pickering

Lynn Winterstein
Manager of Corporate Promotions
Corporate Promotions & Economic Development
Pickering Civic Complex
1 The Esplanade
Pickering, ON L1V 6K7
Phone : (905) 420-4625
Fax : (905) 420-4610
Web Site : www.cityofpickering.com

Port Colborne

Bill LeFeuvre
Economic Development Officer
City Hall
66 Charlotte St.
Port Colborne, ON L3K 3C8
Phone : (905) 835-2900
Fax : (905) 835-2969

Port Hope

Gaby Mann
Economic Development Officer
Port Hope Industrial
Development Commission
P.O. Box 117, Stn. Main
Port Hope, ON L1A 3V9
Phone : (905) 885-4544
Fax : (905) 885-7698
Web Site : www.town.porthope.on.ca

Prince Edward County

Richard Ellis
Economic Development Officer
332 Main St.
P.O. Box 1550
Picton, ON K0K 2T0
Phone : (613) 476-2148
Fax : (613) 476-8356

Quinte West

Charles Murphy
Director of Planning and Development
City of Quinte West
714 Murray St., RR 1
P.O. Box 490
Trenton, ON K8V 5R6
Phone : (613) 392-4435
Fax : (613) 392-7151
Web Site : www.city.quintewest.on.ca

Rainy River

Geoff Gillon
Economic Development Officer & Community
Investment Manager
Rainy River Future Development Corp.
400 Scott St.
Fort Frances, ON P9A 1H2
Phone : (807) 274-3276
Fax : (807) 274-6989
Web Site : www.rrfdc.on.ca

Rayside-Balfour

Jay Barbeau
Director of Physical & Community Development
Town of Rayside-Balfour
P.O. Box 639
Chelmsford, ON P0M 1L0
Phone : (705) 855-9061
Fax : (705) 855-5737

Renfrew

Norman Anderson
General Manager
Renfrew Industrial Commission
152 Plaunt St. S.
Renfrew, ON K7V 1M8
Phone : (613) 432-5813
Fax : (613) 432-9042
Web Site : www.renfrewontario.com

Richmond Hill

Janet Babcock
Commissioner of Planning and Development
Town of Richmond Hill
225 East Beaver Creek Rd.
P.O. Box 300, Stn. A
Richmond Hill, ON L4C 4Y5
Phone : (905) 771-8910
Fax : (905) 771-2404
Web Site : www.town.richmond-hill.on.ca

Sarnia & Lambton County

George Mallay
General Manager
Sarnia/Lambton Economic Development Office
265 Front St. N., Suite 107
Sarnia, ON N7T 7X1
Phone : (519) 332-1820
Fax : (519) 332-1686
Web Site : www.sarnialambton.on.ca

Sarnia, City

Peter B. Hungerford
Director of Economic Development &
Corporate Planning
City Hall
255 North Christina St.
P.O. Box 3018, Stn. Main
Sarnia, ON N7T 7N2
Phone : (519) 332-0330
Fax : (519) 332-3995
Web Site : www.city.sarnia.on.ca

Sault Ste. Marie

Tom Hernden
Economic Development Officer
Economic Development Corp.
Civic Centre
99 Foster Dr.
P.O. Box 580
Sault Ste. Marie, ON P6A 5X6
Phone : (705) 759-5432
Phone : 1-800-461-6020
Fax : (705) 759-2185
Web Site : www.sault-canada.com

Scarborough

See Toronto

Scugog

See Durham Region

Simcoe

Frances Bell
Chief Administrative Officer
65 Qeensway E.
Simcoe, ON N3Y 4M5
Phone : (519) 429-3334
Fax : (519) 428-2230
Web Site : www.scdc.on.ca

Smiths Falls

Arie Hoogenboom
Economic Development Co-ordinator
Dept. of Economic Development
Town of Smiths Falls
77 Beckwith St. N.
P.O. Box 695, Stn. Main
Smiths Falls, ON K7A 4T6
Phone : (613) 283-4124
Fax : (613) 283-4764
Web Site : www.town.smiths-falls.on.ca

South Bruce

Ron Brown
Chief Administrative Officer
Town of Saugeen Shores
515 Goderich St.
Port Elgin, ON N0H 2C4
Phone : (519) 832-2000
Fax : (519) 832-2140
Web Site : www.town.saugeenshores.on.ca

South Grenville

Andrew Brown
Economic Development Commissioner
Prescott Economic Development
360 Dibble St. W.
Prescott, ON K0E 1T0
Phone : (613) 925-0035
Fax : (613) 925-4381
Web Site : www.town.prescott.on.ca

St. Catharines

Brock Dickinson
Director of Economic Development & Tourism
City Hall
50 Church St.
P.O. Box 3012, Stn. Main
St. Catharines, ON L2R 7C2
Phone : (905) 688-5601 Ext. 1700
Fax : (905) 688-8994
Web Site : www.st.catharines.com

St. Thomas

Robert Wheeler
General Manager
Economic Development Corporation
545 Talbot St.
P.O. Box 520, Stn. Main
St. Thomas, ON N5P 3V7
Phone : (519) 631-1680
Fax : (519) 631-3441
Web Site : www.city.st-thomas.on.ca

Stoney Creek

Dorothy Redfearn
Economic Development Officer
Economic Development Department
City Hall
P.O. Box 9940
Stoney Creek, ON L8G 4N9
Phone : (905) 643-1261
Fax : (905) 643-6161
Email : dredfear@city.hamilton.on.ca
Web Site : www.city.stoney-creek.on.ca

Stratford

Larry Appel
Director of Economic Development and Tourism
City Hall
1 Wellington St.
P.O. Box 818, Stn. Main
Stratford, ON N5A 6W1
Phone : (519) 271-0250
Fax : (519) 273-5041
Web Site : www.city.stratford.on.ca

Strathroy

Chuck Knapp
Town Administrator
Strathroy Town Hall
52 Frank St.
Strathroy, ON N7G 2R4
Phone : (519) 245-1070
Fax : (519) 245-6353
Web Site : www.bam.on.ca/strathroy/index2.html

Sudbury Regional Municipality

Guy Labine
General Manager
Regional Development Corp.
Tom Davies Square, 1st Floor
200 Brady St.
Sudbury, ON P3E 5K3
Phone : (705) 673-4161
Phone : 1-800-708-2505
Fax : (705) 671-6767
Web Site : www.srdc.on.ca

The Diamond Triangle

Cindy Symons-Milroy
Director of Economic Development
Cobourg Economic
Development Commission
212 King St. W.
Cobourg, ON K9A 2N1
Phone : (905) 372-5481
Fax : (905) 372-1306
Web Site : www.developthunderbay.com

Thorold

Bob Castleman
City Administrator
City of Thorold
8 Carleton St. S.
Thorold, ON L2V 4A7
Phone : (905) 227-6613
Fax : (905) 227-5990
Web Site : www.thorold.com

Thunder Bay

Nancy Creighton
Manager
Development Thunder Bay
200 Syndicate Ave. S., Suite 102
Thunder Bay, ON P7E 1C9
Phone : (807) 625-3960
Fax : (807) 623-3962

Tillsonburg

David Morris
Economic Development Commissioner
Town of Tillsonburg
Town Centre Mall, 2nd Floor
200 Broadway St.
Tillsonburg, ON N4G 5A7
Phone : (519) 842-6428
Fax : (519) 842-9431
Web Site : www.town.tillsonburg.on.ca

Timmins

Christy Marinig
Manager
Timmins Economic Development Corp.
54 Spruce St. S.
Timmins, ON P4N 2M5
Phone : (705) 360-8483
Fax : (705) 360-1394
Email : tedc@vianet.on.ca
Web Site : www.city.timmins.on.ca

Toronto, City

Brenda Librecz
Managing Director of Economic Development
City of Toronto
Metro Hall
100 Queen St. W.
8th Fl. East Tower
Toronto, ON M5H 2N2
Phone : (416) 397-4700
Fax : (416) 395-0388
Web Site : www.city.toronto.on.ca/business

Ron Rae
Senior Business Development Officer
Ground Fl., Scarborough Civic Centre
150 Borough Dr.
Scarborough, ON M1P 4N7
Phone : (416) 396-7421
Fax : (416) 396-4241
Web Site : www.city.toronto.on.ca/business

Uxbridge

See Durham Region

Vanier

James Kearns
Directeur de l'Urbanisme et du Développement
Ville de Vanier
Service de l'Urbanisme et du Développement
300 av. des Pères-Blanc
Vanier, ON K1L 7L5
Phone : (613) 747-2515
Fax : (613) 747-2533
Web Site :
    www.intergov.gc.ca/mun/on/vanier/indexf.html

Vaughan

Frank Miele
Commissioner
City of Vaughn Economic and
Technology Development Dept.
2141 Major Mackenzie Dr.
Vaughan, ON L6A 1T1
Phone : (905) 832-8521
Fax : (905) 832-8610
Web Site : www.city.vaughan.on.ca

Walkerton

Pat Lippert
Office Manager
Chamber of Commerce
P.O. Box 1344
Walkerton, ON N0G 2V0
Phone : (519) 881-3413
Fax : (519) 881-4009
Web Site : www.town.walkerton.on.ca

Waterloo

Paul Eichinger
Director of Economic Development
City of Waterloo
Waterloo City Centre
P.O. Box 337, Stn. Waterloo
Waterloo, ON N2J 4A8
Phone : (519) 886-1550
Fax : (519) 747-8760
Web Site : www.city.waterloo.on.ca

Welland

Dan Degazio
Economic Development Officer
Welland Development Commission
City Hall
411 East Main St.
Welland, ON L3B 3X4
Phone : (905) 735-3771
Fax : (905) 714-9614
Web Site : www.callwelland.com

West Carleton

Tim Chadder
Director of Planning and Development
Planning and Development Department
5670 Carp Rd.
Kiburn, ON K0A 2H0
Phone : (613) 832-5644
Fax : (613) 832-3341
Web Site : www.twp.west-carleton.on.ca

Whitby

L. Ravary
Marketing & Economic Development Officer
Marketing & Economic Development Department
575 Rossland Rd. E.
Whitby, ON L1N 2M8
Phone : (905) 430-4303
Fax : (905) 686-7005
Email : ravaryl@town.whitby.on.ca
Web Site : www.town.whitby.on.ca

Whitchurch-Stouffville

Eric Lismanis
Economic Development Manager
Town of Whitchurch-Stouffville
37 Sandiford Dr., 4th Floor
Stouffville, ON L4A 7X5
Phone : (905) 640-1900
Fax : (905) 640-7957
Email : townofws@interlog.com

Windsor-Essex County

Paul Bondy
Development Commissioner
Windsor-Essex County Development Commission
City Centre
333 Riverside Dr. W., Suite 215
Windsor, ON N9A 5K4
Phone : (519) 255-9200
Fax : (519) 255-9987
Email: info@choosewindsor.com
Web Site : www.choosewindsor.com

Woodstock

Paul D. Plant
Development Commissioner
City Hall
500 Dundas St.
P.O. Box 40, Stn. Main
Woodstock, ON N4S 7W5
Phone : (519) 539-1291
Fax : (519) 539-3275
Web Site : www.city.woodstock.on.ca

Woolwich

Kris Fletcher
Chief Administrative Officer
Corporate Services
69 Arthur St. S.
P.O. Box 158
Elmira, ON N3B 2Z6
Phone : (519) 669-1647
Phone : (519) 664-2613
Fax : (519) 669-1820
Email : kfletcher@township.woolwich.on.ca
Web Site : www.township.woolwich.on.ca

York Regional Municipality

Donald G. Eastwood
Director of Economic Development
Region of York
17250 Yonge St.
P.O. Box 147, Stn. Main
Newmarket, ON L3Y 6Z1
Phone : (905) 895-1231
Fax : (905) 895-1238
Web Site : www.region.york.on.ca

York, City

See Toronto

MANITOBA

Brandon

Marlow Kirton
General Manager
Brandon Economic Development Board
1043 Rosser Ave.
Brandon, MB R7A 0L5
Phone : (204) 729-2130
Phone : 1-888-799-1111
Fax : (204) 729-2135
Email : bedb@city.brandon.mb.ca
Web Site : www.bedb.brandon.mb.ca

Dauphin

Terry Arksey
Community Economic Development Manager
City of Dauphin
Community Economic Development Dept.
21 3rd Ave. N.E., Unit C
Dauphin, MB R7N 0Y5
Phone : (204) 638-9747
Phone : 1-877-566-5669
Fax : (204) 638-0879
Email : dauphin_seeds@mb.sympatico.ca
Web Site : www.city.dauphin.mb.ca

Flin Flon

Larry Fancy
City Administrator
City of Flin Flon
20 1st Ave.
Flin Flon, MB R8A 0T7
Phone : (204) 687-9756
Fax : (204) 687-5133
Web Site : www.cityofflinflon.com

Pembina Valley Region

Ilija Dragojevic
General Manager
Pembina Valley Development Corp.
P.O. Box 1180
Altona, MB R0G 0B0
Phone : (204) 324-8641
Fax : (204) 324-1230
Email : pvdcorp@mts.net

Portage la Prairie

Ron N. Roteliuk
General Manager
Central Plains Inc.
Building 136, Room 109
P.O. Box 232
South Port, MB R0H 1N0
Phone : (204) 428-6000
Fax : (204) 428-6006
Web Site : www.centralplains.mb.ca

Selkirk

Peter Mandryk
General Manager
Triple S Business Development Corp.
356 Main St., 2nd Floor
Selkirk, MB R1A 1T6
Phone : (204) 482-2020
Fax : (204) 482-2033
Web Site : www.triplesbdc.mb.ca/triplesbdc

Steinbach

Jack Kehler
Town Manager
City of Steinbach
225 Reimer Ave.
P.O. Box 1090
Steinbach, MB R0A 2A0
Phone : (204) 326-9877
Fax : (204) 326-4171

Thompson

Bill Comaskey .
Mayor/Chairperson
Economic Development Advisory Committee
City Hall
226 Mystery Lake Rd.
Thompson, MB R8N 1S6
Phone : (204) 677-7910
Fax : (204) 677-7981

Lynn Taylor
City Manager
City of Thompson
City Hall
226 Mystery Lake Rd.
Thompson, MB R8N 1S6
Phone : (204) 677-7910
Fax : (204) 677-7981

Winnipeg

Klaus Thiessen
President & Chief Executive Officer
Economic Development Winnipeg
200 Graham Ave., Suite 1100
Winnipeg, MB R3C 4L5
Phone : (204) 944-2000
Fax : (204) 956-2615
Web Site : www.winnipegedw.com

SASKATCHEWAN

Saskatchewan

Janice MacKinnon
Minister
Economic & Co-operative Development
City of Regina
1919 Saskatchewan Dr., 7th Floor
Regina, SK S4P 3V7
Phone : (306) 787-9580
Fax : (306) 787-2159
Web Site : www.gov.sk.ca/econdev

Canada/Saskatchewan Business
Service Centre
122 3rd Ave. N.
Saskatoon, SK S7K 2H6
Phone : (306) 956-2323
Phone : 1-800-677-4374
Fax : (306) 956-2328
Web Site : www.cbsc.org/sask

Estevan

Marcel Hostey
City Manager
City of Estevan
1102 4th St.
Estevan, SK S4A 0W7
Phone : (306) 634-1800
Fax : (306) 634-9790
Web Site : www.cap.estevan.sk.ca

Lloydminster

Scott Kovatch
Economic and Tourism Development Officer
Planning and Development Dept.
City Hall
5011 49th Ave.
Lloydminster, SK S9V 0T8
Phone : (306) 825-6180
Fax : (306) 825-7170
Web Site : www.lloydminsterinfo.com

Melfort

Roger Vogelsang
Director of Planning, Development and Leisure Services
City of Melfort
P.O. Box 2230
Melfort, SK S0E 1A0
Phone : (306) 752-5911
Fax : (306) 752-5556
Web Site : www.nlnet.melfort.sk.ca/city

Melville

Bruno Kossmann
City Manager
City of Melville
P.O. Box 1240
Melville, SK S0A 2P0
Phone : (306) 728-6840
Fax : (306) 728-5911
Web Site : www.spreda.sk.ca

Moose Jaw

D. James Leier
Director of Economic Development
Moose Jaw Regional Economic Development
Authority Inc. (REDA)
88 Saskatchewan St. E.
Moose Jaw, SK S6H 0V4
Phone : (306) 693-7332
Fax : (306) 693-7338
Email : mjreda@sk.sympatico.ca
Web Site : www.citymoosejaw.com

North Battleford

Wayne C. Standbrook
Economic Development Director
City of North Battleford
1291 101st St.
P.O. Box 460, Stn. Main
North Battleford, SK S9A 2Y6
Phone : (306) 445 -1718
Fax : (306) 445-0411
Web Site : www.city.north-battleford.sk.ca

Prince Albert

Denton Yeo
Director of Planning and Economic Development
City of Prince Albert
1084 Central Ave.
Prince Albert, SK S6V 7P3
Phone : (306) 953-4370
Fax : (306) 953-4380
Web Site : www.citypa.com

Regina

Marty Klyne
Regional President & COO
Regina Economic Development Authority
1919 Rose St., Suite 255
Regina, SK S4P 3P1
Phone : (306) 522-0227
Fax : (306) 352-1630
Web Site : www.rreda.com

Saskatoon

Dale Botting
Director
Economic Development Authority
345 3rd Ave. S.
Saskatoon, SK S7K 1M6
Phone : (306) 664-0720
Fax : (306) 244-5033
Email : jhyshka@sreda.com
Web Site : www.sreda.com

Swift Current

Marty Salberg
Director of Business Development
City of Swift Current
P.O. Box 340, Stn. Main
Swift Current, SK S9H 3W1
Phone : (306) 778-2777
Fax : (306) 778-2194
Web Site : www.city.swift-current.sk.ca

Weyburn

Robert Smith
City Commissioner
City of Weyburn
160 3rd St. N.E.
P.O. Box 370, Stn. Main
Weyburn, SK S4H 2K6
Phone : (306) 848-3200
Fax : (306) 842-2001
Web Site : www.city.weyburn.sk.ca

Yorkton

Gord Bulmer
Economic Development Officer
City of Yorkton
37 3rd Ave. N.
P.O. Box 400, Stn. Del. Centre
Yorkton, SK S3N 2W3
Phone : (306) 786-1724
Fax : (306) 786-6880
Web Site : www.city.yorkton.sk.ca

ALBERTA

Alberta

Jon Havelock
Minister
Alberta Economic Development
103 Legislature Bldg.
10800 97th Ave.
Edmonton, AB T5K 2B6
Phone : (780) 427-3162
Fax : (780) 427-6338
Web Site : www.alberta-canada.com

Alberta Economic Development
10155-102 St., 6th Floor
Edmonton, AB T5J 4L6
Phone : (780) 415-1319

Airdrie

Paul Schulz
Director of Economic Development
City of Airdrie
125 Main St.
P.O. Box 5, Stn. Main
Airdrie, AB T4B 2C9
Phone : (403) 948-8800
Phone : 1-888-airdrie
Fax : (403) 948-6567
Web Site : www.airdrie.com

Brooks

Mike Marko
Town Planner
P.O. Bag 880, Stn. Main
Brooks, AB T1R 0Z6
Phone : (403) 362-3333
Fax : (403) 362-4787

Calgary

Don Brownie
President & Chief Executive Officer
Economic Development Authority
City of Calgary
P.O. Box 2100, Stn. M
639 5th Ave. S.W., Suite 300
Calgary, AB T2P 0M9
Phone : (403) 221-7821
Fax : (403) 221-7837
Web Site : www.ceda.calgary.ab.ca

Camrose

Dennis W. Twomey
Economic Development Co-ordinator
City Hall
5204 50th Ave.
Camrose, AB T4V 0S8
Phone : (780) 672-4426
Fax : (780) 672-2469
Web Site : www.camrose.com

Crowsnest Pass

Cliff Reiling
Crowsnest Pass Economic
Development Co-ordinator
P.O. Box 594
Blairmore, AB T0K 0E0
Phone : (403) 562-8857
Fax : (403) 562-7252
Web Site : www.crowsnestpass.com

Edmonton

Jim Edwards
President & Chief Executive Officer
Economic Development Co-ordinator
9797 Jasper Ave. N.W.
Edmonton, AB T5J 1N9
Phone : (780) 424-9191
Fax : (780) 426-0236
Web Site : www.ede.org

Fort Saskatchewan

Terry Stacey
Director of Economic Development
10005 102nd St.
Fort Saskatchewan, AB T8L 2C5
Phone : (780) 992-6200
Fax : (780) 998-4774
Web Site : www.city.fort-saskatchewan.ab.ca

Grande Prairie

Deryl Kloster
City Manager
City Hall
9905 100th St.
P.O. Bag 4000, Stn. Main
Grande Prairie, AB T8V 6V3
Phone : (780) 538-0300
Fax : (780) 539-1056
Web Site : www.city.grande-prairie.ab.ca

Lacombe

Eric Jerrard
Economic Development Officer
Town of Lacombe
5034 52nd St.
Lacombe, AB T4L 1J6
Phone : (403) 782-1263
Fax : (403) 782-5655
Email : ejerrard@town.lacombe.ab.ca
Web Site : www.town.lacombe.ab.ca

Leduc

John Barnard
Executive Director
Leduc-Nisku Economic Development Authority
6422 50th St.
Leduc, AB T9E 7K9
Phone : (780) 986-9538
Fax : (780) 986 -1121
Web Site : www.leduc-nisku.ab.ca

Lethbridge

Darrel D. McKenzie
Economic Development Manager
Economic Development Dept.
City of Lethbridge
910 4th Ave. S., 2nd floor
Lethbridge, AB T1J 0P6
Phone : (403) 320-3910
Phone : 1-800-332-1801
Fax : (403) 320-4259
Email : ecodev@city.lethbridge.ab.ca
Web Site : www.city.lethbridge.ab.ca

Lloydminster

Peter Vana
Director of Planning & Development
City Hall
5011 49th Ave.
Lloydminster, SK S9V 0T8
Phone : (306) 825-6184
Fax : (306) 825-7170
Web Site : www.lloydminsterinfo.com

Medicine Hat
Tim Feduniw
Manager of Economic Development
City Hall
580 1st St. S.E.
Medicine Hat, AB T1A 8E6
Phone : (403) 529-8353
Fax : (403) 502-8055
Web Site : www.city.medicine-hat.ab.ca

Parkland County
Gerry Gabinet
Economic Development Officer
Administration Department
53109A SH 779
Parkland County, AB T7Z 1R1
Phone : (780) 968-8888
Phone : 1-888-880-0858
Fax : (780) 968-8413
Web Site : www.parklandcounty.com

Peace River
Peace River Board of Trade & Commerce
P.O. Box 6599, Stn. Main
Peace River, AB T8S 1S4
Phone : (780) 624-4166
Fax : (780) 624-4663

Red Deer
Alan Scott
Manager, Land and Economic Development
City Hall
P.O. Box 5008
Red Deer, AB T4N 3T4
Phone : (403) 342-8111
Fax : (403) 346-6195
Web Site : www.city.red-deer.ab.ca

Rocky View No.44
Ken Kelly
Director of Planning and Development
Municipal District of Rocky View
Department of Planning and Development
911 32nd Ave NE
Calgary, AB T2E 6X6
Phone : (403) 230-1401
Fax : (403) 277-5977
Email : kkelly@gov.mdrockyview.ab.ca
Web Site : www.mdrockyview.ab.ca

Spruce Grove
Diane Hamel
Director of Economic Development
315 Jespersen Ave.
Spruce Grove, AB T7X 3E8
Phone : (780) 962-2611
Fax : (780) 962-0149
Web Site : www.sprucegrove.org

St. Albert
Larry Horncastle
Economic Development & Tourism Officer
71 St. Albert Rd.
St. Albert, AB T8N 6L5
Phone : (780) 459-1724
Fax : (780) 460-1161
Web Site : www.city.st-albert.ab.ca

Stettler
Rob Stoutenberg
Town Manager
Town of Stettler
P.O. Box 280
Stettler, AB T0C 2L0
Phone : (403) 742-8305
Fax : (403) 742-1404
Web Site : www.stettler.net

Strathcona County
Paul Ross
Manager, Economic Development & Tourism
Economic Development and Tourism Dept.
2001 Sherwood Dr.
Sherwood Park, AB T8A 3W7
Phone : (780) 464-8241
Fax : (780) 464-8444
Web Site : www.strathcona.ab.ca

Wetaskiwin
Greg Stevens
City Manager
4904 51st St.
Wetaskiwin, AB T9A 1L2
Phone : (780) 352-3344
Fax : (780) 352-0930
Web Site : www.city.wetaskiwin.ab.ca

Business Development & Tourism Services
4904 51st St.
Wetaskiwin, AB T9A 1L2
Phone : (780) 361-4401
Phone : 1-800-989-6899
Fax : (780) 352-0930
Web Site : www.city.wetaskiwin.ab.ca

Wood Buffalo
Stephen Clark
Manager, Planning and Development
9909 Franklin Ave.
Fort McMurray, AB T9H 2K4
Phone : (780) 743-7882
Fax : (780) 743-7874
Web Site : www.woodbuffalo.ab.ca

BRITISH COLUMBIA

British Columbia
Gordon Wilson
Minister of Employment and Investment
Ministry of Employment and Investment
Parliament Bldg.
Victoria, BC V8V 1X4
Phone : (250) 356-7020
Fax : (250) 356-5587
Web Site : www.gov.bc.ca/ei/

Ian Waddell
Minister of Small Business, Tourism & Culture
Ministry of Small Business, Tourism & Culture
Parliament Bldg.
Victoria, BC V8V 1X4
Phone : (250) 387-1683
Fax : (250) 387-4348
Web Site : www.sb.gov.bc.ca

Canada/British Columbia Business
Service Centre
601 West Cordova St.
Vancouver, BC V6B 1G1
Phone : (604) 775-5525
Phone : 1-800-667-2272
Fax : (604) 775-5520
Web Site : www.sb.gov.bc.ca

Abbotsford
Richard Danziger
Director of Development Services & Planning
32315 South Fraser Way
Abbotsford, BC V2T 1W7
Phone : (604) 864-5505
Fax : (604) 853-4981
Email : econdev@city.abby.bc.ca
Web Site : www.city.abby.bc.ca

Burnaby
Terry Clark
General Manager and Business Information Officer
Burnaby Board of Trade
201 4555 Kingsway
Burnaby, BC V5H 4T8
Phone : (604) 412-0100
Fax : (604) 412-0102
Email : terry_clark@burnaby.boardoftrade.org
Web Site : www.burnaby.boardoftrade.org

Chilliwack
Dale Wheeldon
Director of Business Development
Chilliwack Economic Partners Corp.
46165 Yale Rd., Suite 104
Chilliwack, BC V2P 2P2
Phone : (604) 792-9311
Phone : 1-800-561-8803
Fax : (604) 792-4511
Email : cepco@chilliwackpartners.com
Web Site : www.chilliwackpartners.com

Comox Valley
Norman D. McLaren
Economic Development Officer
Comox Valley Economic Development Society
2060 Cliffe Ave.
Courtenay, BC V9N 2L3
Phone : (250) 334-2427
Fax : (250) 334-2414
Web Site : www.cveds.com

Coquitlam
Deb Day
General Manager of Planning & Development
3000 Guildford Way
Coquitlam, BC V3B 7N2
Phone : (604) 927-3000
Fax : (604) 927-3405
Web Site : www.city.coquitlam.bc.ca

Courtenay
See Comox Valley

Cranbrook
John Sheehan
Economic Development Officer
Cranbrook Development Authority
P.O. Box 84
Cranbrook, BC V1C 4H6
Phone : (250) 426-5914
Fax : (250) 426-3873
Web Site : www.cranbrookchamber.com

Dawson Creek
Wayne Dahlen
General Manager
Chamber of Commerce
906 102nd Ave.
Dawson Creek, BC V1G 2B7
Phone : (250) 782-4868
Fax : (250) 782-2371
Web Site : www.neonet.bc.ca/dcchamber

District of Delta
John Dumont
Program Development Manager
4500 Clarence Taylor Cres.
Delta, BC V4K 3E2
Phone : (604) 946-4141
Fax : (604) 946-4148
Web Site : www.corp.delta.bc.ca

Fort Nelson-Liard Regional District

Linda Wallace
Director of Regional Development Services
5319 50th Ave. S.
Bag 399
Fort Nelson, BC V0C 1R0
Phone : (250) 774-2541
Fax : (250) 774-6794

Grand Forks

Marten Kruysse
Economic Development Officer
Regional District of Kootenay Boundary
202 843 Rossland Ave.
Trail, BC V1R 4S8
Phone : (250) 368-9148
Fax : (250) 368-3990

Kamloops

M. J. Cousins
Manager
Venture Kamloops
2 510 Lorne St.
Kamloops, BC V2C 1W3
Phone : (250) 828-6818
Phone : 1-888-KAMLOOPS
Fax : (250) 828-7184
Web Site : www.venturekamloops.com

Kelowna

Robert Fine
Executive Director
The Economic Development Commission
City of Kelowna
1450 KLO Rd.
Kelowna, BC V1W 3Z4
Phone : (250) 868-5280
Fax : (250) 868-0512
Web Site : www.edccord.com

Kitimat

Diane Hewlett
Economic Development Officer
District of Kitimat
270 City Centre
Kitimat, BC V8C 2H7
Phone : (250) 632-2161
Fax : (250) 632-4995
Email : dhewlett@city.kitimat.bc.ca
Web Site : www.city.kitimat.bc.ca

Langley

Terry Lyster
Director of Planning & Development
4914 221st St.
Langley, BC V3A 3Z8
Phone : (604) 534-3211
Fax : (604) 533-6110
Web Site : www.tol.bc.ca

Maple Ridge

Brock McDonald
Director of Business Licences, Permits & By-laws
Community Business Development Office
Maple Ridge Municipal Hall
11995 Haney Pl.
Maple Ridge, BC V2X 6A9
Phone : (604) 467-7305
Fax : (604) 467-7330
Web Site : www.mapleridge.org

Mission

Robert Ross
Director of Community Development
District of Mission
8645 Stave Lake St.
P.O. Box 20, Stn. Main
Mission, BC V2V 4L9
Phone : (604) 820-3748
Fax : (604) 826-7951
Email : rross@city.mission.bc.ca
Web Site : www.city.mission.bc.ca

Nanaimo

Les King
Director of Strategic Planning, Engineering
& Economic Development
455 Wallace St.
Nanaimo, BC V9R 5J6
Phone : (250) 754-4251
Fax : (250) 755-4403
Web Site : www.city.nanaimo.bc.ca

New Westminster

Mary Pynenburg
Director of Planning
Planning Department
City of New Westminster
511 Royal Ave.
New Westminster, BC V3L 1H9
Phone : (604) 527-4532
Fax : (604) 527-4511
Web Site : www.city.new-westminster.bc.ca

North Cowichan

Tom Anderson
Manager of Development Services
Cowichan Valley Regional District
137 Evans St.
Duncan, BC V9L 1P5
Phone : (250) 746-2500
Fax : (250) 746-5612
Web Site : www.cvrd.bc.ca

North Vancouver, City

Frances Caouette
Project Manager
City of North Vancouver
141 W. 14th St.
North Vancouver, BC V7M 1H9
Phone : (604) 990-4221
Fax : (604) 985-0586
Web Site : www.cnv.org

Judy Perkins
Executive Director of Economic Development
Economic Development Association of B.C.
3415 Manning Crescent
North Vancouver, BC V7H 2S5
Phone : (604) 924-9250
Fax : (604) 924-9250
Web Site : www.edabc.com

Penticton

Wayne Tebbutt
Economic Development Officer
888 Westminster Ave. W.
Penticton, BC V2A 8R2
Phone : (250) 493-3323
Fax : (250) 493-3481
Web Site : www.penticton.org

Pitt Meadows

Jim Lowrie
Director of Engineering & Development Services
12007 Harris Rd.
Pitt Meadows, BC V3Y 2B5
Phone : (604) 465-2433
Fax : (604) 465-2450
Email : jlowrie@pittmeadows.bc.ca
Web Site : www.pittmeadows.bc.ca

Port Alberni

Bill Ellwyn
Director of Economic Development
Alberni-Clayoquot Regional District
4757 Tebo Ave.
Port Alberni, BC V9Y 8A9
Phone : (250) 723-2188
Fax : (250) 723-1688
Web Site : www.alberni-region.com

Port Coquitlam

Ernie Levesque
Director of Development Services
City Hall
2580 Shaughnessy St.
Port Coquitlam, BC V3C 2A8
Phone : (604) 944-5411
Fax : (604) 944-5404
Web Site : www.city.port-coquitlam.bc.ca

Powell River

Glen MacRae
Economic Development Officer
Corp. of the District of Powell River
6910 Duncan St.
Powell River, BC V8A 1V4
Phone : (604) 485-6291
Fax : (604) 485-2913

Prince George

Dale McMann
Chief Executive Officer
Prince George Region Development Corporation
1399 6th Ave., Suite 201
Prince George, BC V2L 5L6
Phone : (250) 564-0282
Fax : (250) 563-6398
Web Site : www.pgrdc.bc.ca

Prince Rupert

Dave kalinchuk
Economic Development Officer
Prince Rupert Development Commission
P.O. Box 1075
Prince Rupert, BC V8J 4H6
Phone : (250) 627-5138
Fax : (250) 627-5139
Web Site : www.rupert.net/predc.html

Revelstoke

Doug Weir
Economic Development Commissioner
Economic Development Commission
P.O. Box 2398
Revelstoke, BC V0E 2S0
Phone : (250) 837-5345
Fax : (250) 837-4223

Richmond

Marcia Freeman
Manager of Business Liaison & Development
Richmond City Hall
6911 No. 3 Rd.
Richmond, BC V6Y 2C1
Phone : (604) 276-4000
Fax : (604) 276-4162
Web Site : www.city.richmond.bc.ca

Saanich

Alan Hopper
Municipal Planner
District of Saanich
770 Vernon Ave.
Victoria, BC V8X 2W7
Phone : (250) 475-1775
Fax : (250) 475-5450
Web Site : www.gov.saanich.bc.ca

Salmon Arm

Bob McKay
Executive Director & Sr. Vice President
Salmon Arm Economic Development Corporation
371 Hudson Ave. N.E., Suite 101
P.O. Box 130
Salmon Arm, BC V1E 4N2
Phone : (250) 833-0608
Fax : (250) 833-0609
Web Site : www.salmonarmedc.com

Squamish

Brent Leigh
Economic Development Officer
District of Squamish
P.O. Box 310
Squamish, BC V0N 3G0
Phone : (604) 892-5217
Fax : (604) 892-1083
Web Site : www.district.squamish.bc.ca

Surrey

Mary Ann Smith
Senior Economic Development Officer
Economic Development Office
City of Surrey
14245 56th Ave.
Surrey, BC V3X 3A2
Phone : (604) 591-4333
Fax : (604) 594-3055
Web Site : www.city.surrey.bc:ca

Terrace

Ken Veldman
Economic Development Officer
Terrace Economic Development Authority
4621 Lakelse Ave., Suite 102
Terrace, BC V8G 1P9
Phone : (250) 635-4168
Fax : (250) 635-4152
Email : kveldman@kermode.net

Trail

Marten Kruysse
Economic Development Officer
Regional District of Kootenay Boundary
843 Rossland Ave., Suite 202
Trail, BC V1R 4S8
Phone : (250) 368-9148
Fax : (250) 368-3990
Web Site : www.rdkb.com

Vancouver

Hugh Kellas
Administrator of Regional Development
Policy and,Planning
Greater Vancouver Regional District
4330 Kingsway
Burnaby, BC V5H 4G8
Phone : (604) 432-6200
Fax : (604) 436-6970
Web Site : www.gvrd.bc.ca

Vernon

Ken Buchanan
Economic Development Administrator
North Okanagan Economic Development Alliance
City of Vernon
701 Hwy. 97 South
Vernon, BC V1B 3W4
Phone : (250) 549-6776
Fax : (250) 549-3114

Victoria

Donna Atkinson
Economic Development Manager
City of Victoria
City Hall, 1st Floor
1 Centennial Square
Victoria, BC V8W 1P6
Phone : (250) 361-0320
Fax : (250) 361-0348
Web Site : www.city.victoria.bc.ca

Greater Victoria
Economic Development Commission
G7 1001 Douglas St.
Victoria, BC V8W 2C5
Phone: (250) 384-2432
Fax: (250) 384-2590
Email: bizvic@bizvic.com

White Rock

Tom Leathem
City Planner & Economic Development Officer
City of White Rock
15322 Buena Vista Ave.
White Rock, BC V4B 1Y6
Phone : (604) 541-2100
Fax : (604) 541-2168

Williams Lake

Trevor Kier
Economic Development Commissioner
Economic Development Committee
c/o City of Williams Lake
450 Mart St.
Williams Lake, BC V2G 1N3
Phone : (250) 392-2311
Fax : (250) 392-4408
Email : tkier@excite.com
Web Site : www.wlake.com

NORTHWEST TERRITORIES

Northwest Territories

Joseph L. Handley
Deputy Minister of
Resources, Wildlife & Economic Development
P.O. Box 1320, Stn. Main
Yellowknife, NT X1A 2L9
Phone : (867) 669-2344
Fax : (867) 873-0169
Web Site : www.gov.nt.ca

Canada/Northwest Territories Business
Service Centre
Scotia Centre, 8th fl.
P.O. Box 1320
Yellowknife, NT X1A 2L9
Phone : (867) 873-7958
Phone : 1-800-661-0599
Fax : (867) 873-0101
Email : yel@cbsc.ic.gc.ca
Web Site : www.cbsc.org/nwt/index.html

Yellowknife

Peter Neugebauer
Director of Economic Development
City Hall
P.O. Box 580, Stn. Main
Yellowknife, NT X1A 2N4
Phone : (867) 920-5670
Fax : (867) 920-5649
Web Site : www.city.yellowknife.nt.ca

NUNAVUT

Nunavut

Canada/Nunavut Business
Service Centre
1088 Noble House
Entrance E
Iqaluit, NU X0A 0H0
Phone : (867) 979-6813
Phone : 1-877-499-5199
Fax : (867) 979-6823
Email : cnbsc@gov.nu.ca
Web Site : www.cbsc.org/nunavut/index.html

YUKON TERRITORY

Yukon

Maurice Elbert
Deputy Minister of Economic Development
Industry Trade & Investment Yukon
Government
211 Main St., Suite 400
P.O. Box 2703, Stn. Main
Whitehorse, YT Y1A 2C6
Phone : (867) 667-5417
Fax : (867) 667-8601

Canada/Yukon Business
Service Centre
208 Main St., Suite 201
Whitehorse, YT Y1A 2A9
Phone : (867) 633-6257
Phone : 1-800-661-0543
Fax : (867) 667-2001
Email : yukon@cbsc.ic.gc.ca

FINANCIAL POST DATAGROUP

THEN

For 75 years, FP DataGroup has been the premier, unbiased source for corporate and financial information on publicly traded Canadian companies and mutual funds.

FP DataGroup has developed into a solutions provider offering professional investor-oriented products online. Money managers, credit analysts, brokers, and retail investors use FP DataGroup products to make effective investment decisions. With FP DataGroup, you know you're dealing with a brand you can trust.

NOW

Your single source for investment research.

For more information, call 1-800-661-POST
or visit www.financialpost.com

FINANCIAL POST
D A T A G R O U P

CODE ACD01

Index

Place names with area type and province.

Pitt Meadows	DM	BC	589
Pittsburgh	TP	ON	51
Placentia	T	NF	48
Plessisville	V	QC	49
Plympton	TP	ON	51
Pointe-Calumet	VL	QC	49
Pointe-Claire	V	QC	199
Pointe-du-Lac	M	QC	49
Ponoka	T	AB	52
Ponoka County No. 3	CM	AB	52
Pontiac	CD	PQ	128
Port Alberni	C	BC	53
Port Alberni	CA	BC	565
Port Colborne	C	ON	396
Port Coquitlam	C	BC	590
Port Elgin	T	ON	51
Port Hardy	DM	BC	53
Port Hope	CA	ON	382
Port Hope	T	ON	51
Port Moody	C	BC	591
Portage la Prairie	C	MB	52
Portage la Prairie	CA	MB	469
Portage la Prairie	RM	MB	52
Port-Cartier	V	QC	49
Portland	TP	ON	51
Portneuf	CD	PQ	120
Portugal Cove-St. Philips	T	NF	48
Powell River	CA	BC	566
Powell River	DM	BC	53
Powell River Regional District	CD	BC	538
Powell River, Subd. A	SRD	BC	53
Prescott and Russell United Counties	CD	ON	279
Prévost	M	QC	49
Prince Albert	C	SK	52
Prince Albert	CA	SK	485
Prince Albert	ER	SK	479
Prince County	CD	PE	71
Prince Edward County	CD	ON	280
PRINCE EDWARD ISLAND	PR		55, 71, 72
Prince George	C	BC	53
Prince George	CA	BC	567
Prince Rupert	C	BC	53
Prince Rupert	CA	BC	568
Puslinch	TP	ON	51

Q

Qualicum Beach	T	BC	53
QUÉBEC	PR		55, 117, 134
Québec	CMA	QC	231
Québec	ER	PQ	117, 120
Québec	V	QC	241
Queens County	CD	NB	103
Queens County	CD	NS	77
Queens County	CD	PE	71
Queens, Subd. B	SCM	NS	48
Quesnel	C	BC	53
Quesnel	CA	BC	569
Quispamsis	T	NB	48

R

Rainy River District	CD	ON	289
Raleigh	TP	ON	51
Ramara	TP	ON	51
Rayside-Balfour	T	ON	406
Red Deer	C	AB	52
Red Deer	CA	AB	531
Red Deer County No. 23	CM	AB	532
Red Deer - Rocky Mountain House	ER	AB	496
Regina	C	SK	488
Regina	CMA	SK	486
Regina - Moose Mountain	ER	SK	478
Renfrew	T	ON	51
Renfrew County	CD	ON	280
Repentigny	V	QC	200
Restigouche County	CD	NB	103
Revelstoke	C	BC	53
Richmond	C	BC	593
Richmond County	CD	NS	77
Richmond Hill	T	ON	443
Rideau	TP	ON	374
Rigaud	M	QC	49
Rimouski	CA	QC	250
Rimouski	V	QC	49
Rimouski-Neigette	CD	PQ	119
Ritchot	RM	MB	52
Riverview	T	NB	48
Rivière-du-Loup	CA	QC	251
Rivière-du-Loup	CD	PQ	119
Rivière-du-Loup	V	QC	49
Robert-Cliche	CD	PQ	121
Roberval	V	QC	253
Rock Forest	V	QC	266
Rockland	T	ON	51
Rockwood	RM	MB	52
Rocky Mountain House	T	AB	52
Rocky View No. 44	MD	AB	505
Rosemère	V	QC	201
Roussillon	CD	PQ	123
Rouville	CD	PQ	123
Rouyn-Noranda	CA	QC	254
Rouyn-Noranda	CD	PQ	129
Rouyn-Noranda	V	QC	49
Roxboro	V	QC	49
Russell	TP	ON	375

S

Saanich	DM	BC	609
Sackville	T	NB	48
Saguenay - Lac-Saint-Jean	ER	PQ	117, 131
Saint-Amable	M	QC	49
Saint-Antoine	V	QC	202
Saint-Athanase	P	QC	49
Saint-Augustin-de-Desmaures	M	QC	242
Saint-Basile-le-Grand	V	QC	203
Saint-Bruno-de-Montarville	V	QC	204
Saint-Charles-Borromée	M	QC	49
Saint-Charles-de-Drummond	M	QC	49
Saint-Colomban	P	QC	49
Saint-Constant	V	QC	205
Saint-Élie-d'Orford	M	QC	49
Saint-Émile	V	QC	49
Saint-Étienne-de-Lauzon	M	QC	49
Saint-Eustache	V	QC	206
Saint-Félicien	V	QC	49
Saint-Georges	CA	QC	255
Saint-Georges	V	QC	49
Saint-Hippolyte	P	QC	49
Saint-Hubert	V	QC	207
Saint-Hyacinthe	CA	QC	256
Saint-Hyacinthe	V	QC	49
Saint-Jean-Chrysostome	V	QC	243
Saint-Jean-sur-Richelieu	CA	QC	257
Saint-Jean-sur-Richelieu	V	QC	50
Saint-Jérôme	V	QC	209
Saint John	C	NB	115
Saint John	CMA	NB	113
Saint John County	CD	NB	103
Saint John - St. Stephen	ER	NB	103
Saint-Lambert	V	QC	210
Saint-Laurent	V	QC	211
Saint-Lazare	P	QC	212
Saint-Léonard	V	QC	213
Saint-Lin	M	QC	50
Saint-Louis-de-France	V	QC	50
Saint-Luc	V	QC	50
Saint-Nicéphore	M	QC	50
Saint-Nicolas	V	QC	244
Saint-Raymond	V	QC	50
Saint-Rédempteur	V	QC	50
Saint-Rémi	V	QC	50
Saint-Romuald	V	QC	245
Saint-Timothée	V	QC	50
Sainte-Adèle	V	QC	50
Sainte-Agathe-des-Monts	V	QC	50
Sainte-Anne-des-Monts	V	QC	50
Sainte-Anne-des-Plaines	V	QC	215
Sainte-Catherine	V	QC	216
Sainte-Foy	V	QC	246
Sainte-Julie	V	QC	217
Sainte-Julienne	P	QC	50
Sainte-Marie	V	QC	258
Sainte-Marthe-du-Cap	M	QC	50
Sainte-Marthe-sur-le-Lac	V	QC	50
Sainte-Sophie	M	QC	50
Sainte-Thérèse	V	QC	218
Salaberry-de-Valleyfield	CA	QC	259
Salaberry-de-Valleyfield	V	QC	50
Salmon Arm	DM	BC	571
Sandwich South	TP	ON	51
Sarnia	C	ON	51
Sarnia	CA	ON	383
SASKATCHEWAN	PR		55, 478, 480
Saskatchewan CD No. 1	CD	SK	478
Saskatchewan CD No. 2	CD	SK	478
Saskatchewan CD No. 3	CD	SK	478
Saskatchewan CD No. 4	CD	SK	478